Current Law

Legislation Citator

STATUTE CITATOR 2012

STATUTORY INSTRUMENT CITATOR 2012

FOR REFERENCE

ONLY

Current Law

Legislation Citator

STATUTE CITATOR 2012

STATUTORY INSTRUMENT CITATOR 2012

SWEET & MAXWELL

 THOMSON REUTERS

Published in 2013 by Sweet & Maxwell, 100 Avenue Road, London NW3 3PF
Part of Thomson Reuters (Professional) UK Limited
(Registered in England & Wales, Company No 1679046.
Registered Office and address for service:
Aldgate House, 33 Aldgate High Street, London EC3N 1DL)

Typeset by Sweet & Maxwell Ltd, 100 Avenue Road, London, NW3 3PF.

Printed and bound in Great Britain by TJ International, Padstow, Cornwall.

For further information on our products and services, visit:
www.sweetandmaxwell.co.uk

ISBN 978-0-414-02802-9

No forests were destroyed to make this product;
farmed timber was used and then replanted.

A CIP catalogue record for this book is available from The British Library

PREFACE

The Sweet & Maxwell Current Law Service
The Current Law Service began in 1947 and provides a comprehensive guide to developments in case law, primary legislation and secondary legislation in the United Kingdom and mainland Europe. The Current Law service presently consists of the Monthly Digest and the Yearbook, Current Law Statutes Annotated and the Bound Volumes, European Current Law, Current Law Week, the Case Citator and the Legislation Citator.

The Legislation Citator
The Legislation Citator comprises the Statute Citator and the Statutory Instrument Citator and has been published annually in this format since 2005. The Citators list all amendments, modifications, repeals, etc. to primary and secondary legislation made in the years indicated.

Updates to these Citators are available in Current Law Statutes Annotated. This Volume of Legislation Citator contains the Statute Citator 2012 and the Statutory Instrument Citator 2012.

The Statute Citator

The material within the Statute Citator is arranged in chronological order and the following information is provided:

(i) Statutes passed during the specified period;

(ii) Statutes affected during the specified period by Statute or Statutory Instrument;

(iii) Statutes judicially considered during the specified period;

(iv) Statutes repealed and amended during the specified period; and

(v) Statutes under which Statutory Instruments have been made during this period.

The Statutory Instrument Citator

The material within the Statutory Instrument Citator is arranged in chronological order and the following information is provided:

(i) Statutory Instruments amended, repealed, modified, etc. by Statute passed or Statutory Instrument issued during the specified period;

(ii) Statutory Instruments judicially considered during the specified period;

(iii) Statutory Instruments consolidated during the specified period; and

(iv) Statutory Instruments made under the powers of any Statutory Instrument issued during this period.

How To Use The Legislation Citator

The following example entries of the Statute and Statutory Instrument Citators indicate how to determine developments which have occurred to the piece of legislation in which you are interested. Entries to the Citators are arranged chronologically.

Statute Citator	
7. Business Rates Supplement Act 2009	— Chapter number, name of Act and year
Commencement Orders: SI 2009/2892 Art.2	— Commencement orders bringing provisions into force
Royal Assent July 02, 2009	— Date of Royal Assent
s.12, enabling SI 2009/2542	— Statutory Instruments made under the powers of s.1 of the Act
s.2, see *R. v Brown* [2009] Crim.L.R. 43	— Case judicially considering s.2
s.3, amended: 2010 c.3 s.2	— s.3 amended by Act (s.2 of Ch.3 of 2010) and two SIs
s.3, enabling: SI 2009/82; SI 2010/70	
s.4, repealed: 2010 c.3 Sch.4	— s.4 repealed by Sch.4 of Ch.3 of 2010
s.4A added: SI 2009/42	— s.4A added by SI Number 42 of 2009
SI Citator	
3264 Agriculture (Cross compliance) Regulations 2009	— Number, name and year of SI
Reg.2, amended: SI 2010/65 Art.2	— reg.2 amended by art.2 of SI number 65 of 2010
Reg.3, revoked: 2010 c.23 Sch.15	— reg.3 revoked by Sch.15 of Ch.23 of 2010
Reg.4, see *R v. Smith* [2010] C.O.D. 54	— Case judicially considering reg.4

CONTENTS

TABLE OF ABBREVIATIONS

Publishers name follows reports and journals.

(S&M = Sweet & Maxwell; ICLR = Incorporated Council of Law Reporting for England and Wales; LBC = Law Book Company of Australia; OUP = Oxford University Press; Kluwer = Kluwer Law International; Cass = Frank Cass & Co Ltd; CUP = Cambridge University Press; CLP = Central Law Publishing; TSO = The Stationery Office. LLP = Lloyd's of London Press Ltd.) All other names are in full.

A. & B. = Accounting & Business (*Association of Chartered Certified Accountants*)

A. & B.R. = Accounting and Business Research (*The Institute of Chartered Accountants in England & Wales*)

A. & O.P. & E.L.U. = Allen & Overy Pensions & Employment Law Update (*Allen & Overy*)

A. & S.L. = Air & Space Law (*Kluwer*)

A. and ADR Rev. = Arbitration and ADR Review (*First Law*)

A.A. & L. = Art Antiquity and Law (*Institute of Art and Law*)

A.B. = Advising Business (*XPL Publishing*)

A.B.T. Bull. = Association of Banking Teachers Bulletin (*Association of Banking Teachers Bulletin*)

A.C. = Law Reports Appeal Cases (*ICLR*)

A.C.D. = Administrative Court Digest (*S&M*)

A.C.L. Rev. = Asian Commercial Law Review (*S&M*)

A.D.R.L.J. = Arbitration and Dispute Resolution Law Journal (*Informa Publishing Group Ltd*)

A.D.R.L.N. = Arbitration & Dispute Resolution Law Newsletter (*Informa Publishing Group Ltd*)

A.E.L.N. = Alliance Environmental Law News (*Kluwer*)

A.F.I. = Asset Finance International (*Euromoney Institutional Investor Plc*)

A.I. & L. = Artificial Intelligence and Law (*Springer*)

A.I.A.J. = Asian International Arbitration Journal (*Kluwer*)

A.I.B. Review = Allied Irish Banks Review (*Allied Irish Banks Plc*)

A.I.I.J. = Australian Insurance Institute Journal (*Australian Insurance Institute*)

A.I.R. = Asia Insurance Review (*Ins Communications Pte Ltd*)

A.J.I.C.L. = African Journal of International and Comparative Law (*Edinburgh University Press Ltd*)

A.J.I.L. = Journal African De Droit International (*ISAL Publications*)

A.L.E.R. = American Law and Economic Review (*OUP*)

A.L.M. Brief. = Association of Lloyd's Members Briefing (*Association of Lloyd's Members*)

A.L.M. News = Association of Lloyd's Members News (*Association of Lloyd's Members*)

A.L.Q. = Arab Law Quarterly (*Brill Academic Publishers*)

A.P.J.E.L. = Asia Pacific Journal of Environmental Law (*Australian Centre for Environmental Law*)

A.P.J.H.R.L. = Asia-Pacific Journal on Human Rights and the Law (*Martinus Nijhoff Publishers*)

A.P.L.R. = Asia Pacific Law Review (*Butterworth Tolley Publishing*)

A.S.L.R. = Aberdeen Student Law Review (*University of Aberdeen*)

A.W. EC News. = Alsop Wilkinson EC Newsletter (*Alsop Wilkinson*)

AIDA P.I.B. = AIDA Pollution Insurance Bulletin (*Dr Carl Martin Roos*)

ASA Bull. = ASA Bulletin (*Kluwer*)

AVMA M. & L.J. = Action for Victims of Medical Accidents Medical & Legal Journal (*Action for Victims of Medical Accidents Services Ltd*)

Accountancy = Accountancy (*Institute of Chartered Accountants in England and Wales*)

Accountancy Irl. = Accountancy Ireland (*Institute of Chartered Accountants in Ireland*)

Accountant = Accountant (*VRL Financial News*)

Acquisitions M. = Acquisitions Monthly (*Thomson Financial Services*)

Actuary = Actuary (*Institute of Actuaries*)

Ad. & Fos. = Adoption & Fostering (*Sage Publications Ltd*)

Ad. & Mar. L. & P. = Advertising & Marketing Law & Practice (*Cass*)

Ad. & Mar. L.L. = Advertising & Marketing Law Letter (*Informa Publishing Group Ltd*)

Admin. L.R. = Administrative Law Reports (*Butterworth Tolley Publishing*)

Adviser = Adviser (*National Association of Citizens Advice Bureaux*)

Agri. Law = Agricultural Law (*XPL Publishing*)

All E.R. = All England Law Reports (*Butterworth Tolley Publishing*)

All E.R. (EC) = All England Law Reports European Cases (*Butterworth Tolley Publishing*)

All E.R. Rev. = All England Law Reports Annual Review (*Butterworth Tolley Publishing*)

All. E.R. (Comm) = All England Law Reports (Commercial Cases) (*Butterworth Tolley Publishing*)

Amex. B.R. = Amex Bank Review (*American Express Bank Ltd*)

Amicus Curiae = Amicus Curiae (*Institute of Advanced Legal Studies*)

Anglo-Am. L.R. = Anglo-American Law Review (*Vathek Publishing*)

App. C.D. = Appeal Commissioners Decision (*First Law*)

App. Comp. & Comm. L. = Applied Computer & Communications Law (*Informa Publishing Group Ltd*)

Arb. L.M. = Arbitration Law Monthly (*Informa Publishing Group Ltd*)

Arbitration = Arbitration (*Chartered Institute of Arbitrators*)

Arbitration Int. = Arbitration International (*Kluwer*)

Arch. News = Archbold News (*S&M*)

Arch. Rev. = Archbold Review (*S&M*)

Ass. = Assurances (*Assurances Publications Ltd*)

Astin Bull. = Astin Bulletin (*Ceuterick S.A.*)

Aviation I.R. = Aviation Insurance Report (*Informa Publishing Group Ltd*)

Axiom = Axiom (*Hammicks*)

B. & C. Int. = Benefits & Compensation International (*Pension Publications Ltd*)

B. & F.T. = Banking & Financial Training (*Armstrong Information Ltd*)

B. & M.E.B.L. = Baker & McKenzie Employee Benefits Law (*Baker & McKenzie*)

B. & M.E.L. = Baker & McKenzie Employment Law (*Baker & McKenzie*)

B. & M.P.L. = Baker & McKenzie Pensions Law (*Baker & McKenzie*)

B. & M.P.L. & E.B. = Baker & McKenzie Pensions Law & Employee Benefits (*Baker & McKenzie*)

B. & W.A. = Bacon & Woodrow Analysis (*Bacon & Woodrow*)

B. & W.P. = Bacon & Woodrow Primer (*Bacon & Woodrow*)

B. Ire. = Banking Ireland (*Institute of Bankers in Ireland*)

B. News = Business News (*HM Customs and Excise*)

B.A.J. = British Actuarial Journal (*Institute of Actuaries*)

B.B. & F.L.R. = Butterworths Banking & Financial Law Review (*Butterworth Tolley Publishing*)

B.C.C. = British Company Cases (*S&M*)

B.C.L.C. = Butterworths Company Law Cases (*Butterworth Tolley Publishing*)

B.E.Q.B. = Bank of England Quarterly Bulletin (*Bank of England*)

B.F.I.T. = Bulletin For International Taxation (*IBFD Publications BV*)

B.H. Eur. Bus. Brief = Boodle Hatfield European Business Brief (*Boodle Hatfield*)

B.H.R.C. = Butterworths Human Rights Cases (*Butterworth Tolley Publishing*)

B.I.F.D. = Bulletin for International Fiscal Documentation (*IBFD Publications BV*)

B.I.L.A.J. = British Insurance Law Association Journal (*British Insurance Law Association*)

B.J.I.B. & F.L. = Butterworths Journal of International Banking & Financial Law (*Butterworth Tolley Publishing*)

B.L.E. = Business Law Europe (*Financial Times Finance*)

B.L.G.R. = Butterworths Local Government Reports (*Butterworth Tolley Publishing*)

B.L.R. = Building Law Reports (*Informa Publishing Group Ltd*)

B.M. & I.A. = Brokers' Monthly & Insurance Adviser (*LLP*)

B.M.C.R. = Butterworths Merger Control Review (*Butterworth Tolley Publishing*)

B.M.L.R. = Butterworths Medico-Legal Reports (*Butterworth Tolley Publishing*)

B.O.F. = Back Office Focus (*Informa Publishing Group Ltd*)

B.P.I.L.S. = Butterworths Personal Injury Litigation Service (*Butterworth Tolley Publishing*)

B.P.I.R. = Bankruptcy and Personal Insolvency Reports (*Jordan & Sons Ltd*)

B.P.L. = British Pension Lawyer (*Keith Wallace Publishers*)

B.S. = Balance Sheet (*Risk Publications*)

B.S. EU Bull. = Beachcroft Stanleys EU Bulletin (*Beachcroft Stanleys*)

B.S.L.R. = BIO-Science Law Review (*Lawtext Publishing Limited*)

B.T. = Banking Technology (*Banking Technology Ltd*)

B.T.C. = British Tax Cases (*Croner CCH Group Ltd*)

B.T.R. = British Tax Review (*S&M*)

B.V.C. = British Value Added Tax Reporter (*Croner CCH Group Ltd*)

B.W. = Banking World (*Headway, Home and Law Publishing Group Ltd*)

B.Y.B.I.L. = British Year Book of International Law (*OUP*)

BLG E.L.R. = Barlow Lyde & Gilbert Employment Law Review (*Barlow Lyde & Gilbert*)

BLG Ins. Law Q. = Barlow Lyde & Gilbert Insurance Law Quarterly (*Barlow Lyde & Gilbert*)

BLG P. & E.R.D. = Barlow Lyde & Gilbert Pollution & Environmental Risk Digest (*Barlow Lyde & Gilbert*)

Bank. L.R. = Banking Law Reports (*Informa Publishing Group Ltd*)

Bank. Law = Bankers' Law (*Guthrum House Ltd*)

Banker = Banker (*Financial Times Finance*)

Bankers Mag. = Bankers Magazine (*Warren, Gorham & Lamont*)

Bar Review = Bar Review (*S&M/Round Hall*)

Ben. File = Benefits File (*Wyatt Company (UK) Ltd*)

Bests Rev. L./H. = Best's Review Life/Health (*A.M. Best Co Inc*)

Bests Rev. P./C. = Best's Review Property/Casualty (*A.M. Best Co Inc*)

Bileta News. = Bileta Newsletter (*University of Warwick*)

Bracton L.J. = Bracton Law Journal (*Exeter University*)

Brit. J. Criminol. = British Journal of Criminology (*OUP*)

Broker = Broker (*LLP*)

Build. L.M. = Building Law Monthly (*Informa Publishing Group Ltd*)

Building = Building (*UBM*)

Bull. Med. E. = Bulletin of Medical Ethics (*Professional & Scientific Publications*)

Bus. Ins. = Business Insurance (*Crain Communications Inc.*)

Bus. L.B. = Business Law Bulletin (*Sweet & Maxwell/W. Green*)

Bus. L.I. = Business Law International (*International Bar Association*)

Bus. L.R. = Business Law Review (*Kluwer*)

Bus. Risk = Business Risk (*Informa Publishing Group Ltd*)

Bus. T.P. = Business Tax Planning (*S&M*)

Busy P. = Busy Practitioner (*Bloomsbury Publishing Plc*)

Buyer = Buyer (*Richard Lawson*)

C. & C.C. = Consumer & Commercial Contracts (*CLT Publishing*)

C. & E.E.B.L.B. = Central and East European Business Law Bulletin (*Butterworth Tolley Publishing*)

C. & E.L. = Construction & Engineering Law (*XPL Publishing*)

C. & F.L. = Credit and Finance Law (*Informa Publishing Group Ltd*)

C. & F.L.U. = Child & Family Law Update (*SLS Legal Publications (NI)*)

C. Bank. = Central Banking (*Central Banking Publications Ltd*)

C. Mag. = Chambers Magazine (*Chambers & Partners Publishing*)

C. McK. Env. L.B. = CMS Cameron McKenna Environment Law Bulletin (*CMS Cameron McKenna & Co*)

C. Risk = Clinical Risk (*Sage Publications Ltd*)

C.A. = Certified Accountant (*Cork Publishing Ltd*)

C.A. Mag. = Chartered Accountant Magazine (*The Institute of Chartered Accountants of Scotland*)

C.B.Q. = Criminal Bar Quarterly (*Butterworths Tolley Publishing*)

C.B.S.I. Jour. = Chartered Building Societies Institute Journal (*Chartered Building Societies Institute Ltd*)

C.C. = Corporate Cover (*Corporate Cover Publications Ltd*)

C.C. Law = Current Criminal Law (*Sally Ramage*)

C.C.A. = Cargo Claims Analysis (*Turpin Distribution Serv Ltd*)

C.C.B. & E.B. = Clifford Chance Benefits and Employment Bulletin (*Clifford Chance*)

C.C.F. = Child Care Forum (*Child Care Forum Publishing Ltd*)

C.C.L. = Commercial Conflict of Laws (*Informa Publishing Group Ltd*)

C.C.L. Rep. = Community Care Law Reports (*Legal Action Group*)

C.C.L. Rev. = Carbon & Climate Law Review (*Lexxion Verlagsgesellschaft mbH*)

C.C.L.R. = Consumer Credit Law Reports (*S&M - published as part of the Encyclopaedia of Consumer Credit Law*)

C.C.M.L.R. = Clifford Chance Media Law Review (*Clifford Chance*)

C.C.N. = Civil Costs Newsletter (*Butterworth Tolley Publishing*)

C.C.R. = Chambers Client Report (*Chambers & Partners Publishing*)

C.D.F.N. = Clinical Disputes Forum Newsletter (*Clinical Disputes Forum*)

C.E. = Central European (*Euromoney Institutional Investor Plc*)

C.E.C. = European Community Cases (*S&M*)

C.F. = Corporate Finance (*Euromoney Institutional Investor Plc*)

C.F.I.L.R. = Company Financial and Insolvency Law Review (*Informa Publishing Group Ltd*)

C.F.L.Q. = Child and Family Law Quarterly (*Jordan & Sons Ltd*)

C.G. = Corporate Governance (*John Wiley & Sons Ltd*)

C.G.T.B. = Capital Gains Tax Brief (*Tax and Financial Publishing*)

C.H.R.L.D. = Commonwealth Human Rights Law Digest (*Interights*)

C.H.R.L.R. = Cyprus Human Rights Law Review (*Intersentia*)

C.I.C. Reps. = Captive Insurance Company Reports (*Risk Management Publications*)

C.I.C. Rev. = Captive Insurance Company Review (*Risk & Insurance Research Group Ltd*)

C.I.I. Jour. = Chartered Insurance Institute Journal (*Chartered Insurance Institute*)

C.I.L. = Contemporary Issues in Law (*Lawtext Publishing Limited*)

C.I.L.L. = Construction Industry Law Letter (*Informa Publishing Group Ltd*)

C.I.P.A.J. = Chartered Institute of Patent Agents Journal (*The Chartered Institute of Patent Agents*)

C.J. = Contract Journal (*Reed Business Information Ltd*)

C.J.I.C.L. = Cambridge Journal of International and Comparative Law (*University of Cambridge*)

C.J.I.L. = Chinese Journal of International Law (*OUP*)

C.J.Q. = Civil Justice Quarterly (*S&M*)

C.J.R.B. = Commercial Judicial Review Bulletin (*Chancery Law Publishing Ltd*)

C.L. & J. = Criminal Law & Justice Weekly (*Butterworth Tolley Publishing*)

C.L. & P. = Computer Law & Practice (*Butterworth Tolley Publishing*)

C.L. & P.R. = Charity Law and Practice Review (*Key Haven Publications Plc*)

C.L. Int. = Competition Law International (*International Bar Association*)

C.L. Pract. = Commercial Law Practitioner (*S&M/Round Hall*)

C.L.B. = Commonwealth Law Bulletin (*Taylor & Francis Ltd*)

C.L.C. = Commercial Law Cases (*S&M*)

C.L.D. = Company Lawyer (*S&M*)

C.L.E. = Commercial Law of Europe (*S&M*)

C.L.E.A. Newsletter = Commonwealth Legal Education Association Newsletter (*Commonwealth Legal Education Association*)

C.L.I. = Commodity Law International (*Business & Maritime Publications Ltd*)

C.L.J. = Cambridge Law Journal (*CUP*)

C.L.L. = Corporate Legal Letter (*Informa Publishing Group Ltd*)

C.L.L. Rev. = Commercial Liability Law Review (*Informa Publishing Group Ltd*)

C.L.M. = Company Law Monitor (*Informa Publishing Group Ltd*)

C.L.M.D. = Current Law Monthly Digest (*S&M/W. Green*)

C.L.N. = Construction Law Newsletter (*Informa Publishing Group Ltd*)

C.L.O.S. = Criminal Law Online Service (*First Law*)

C.L.P. = Current Legal Problems (*OUP*)

C.L.S. = Current Law Statutes (*S&M/W. Green*)

C.L.S. Rev. = Computer Law & Security Review (*Elsevier*)

C.L.S.R. = Computer Law & Security Report (*Elsevier Advanced Technology*)

C.L.W. = Current Law Week (*S&M*)

C.L.W.R. = Common Law World Review (*Portland Press Ltd*)

C.L.Y. = Current Law Year Book (*S&M*)

C.M. = Compliance Monitor (*Informa Publishing Group Ltd*)

C.M.I.R. = Continuous Mortality Investigation Reports (*The Alden Press*)

C.M.L. Rev. = Common Market Law Review (*Turpin Distribution Serv Ltd*)

C.M.L.J. = Capital Markets Law Journal (*OUP*)

C.M.L.N.U. = Council Mortgage Lenders News Update (*BSA CML Publications*)

C.M.L.R = Common Market Law Reports (*S&M*)

C.M.L.R. (AR) = Common Markets Law Reports (*S&M*)

C.N. = Construction Newsletter (*Bloomsbury Publishing Plc*)

C.O.B. = Compliance Officer Bulletin (*S&M*)

C.O.D. = Crown Office Digest (*S&M*)

C.P. & P. = Civil Practice & Procedure (*First Law*)

C.P. Rep. = Civil Procedure Reports (*S&M*)

C.P. Rev. = Consumer Policy Review (*Consumers' Association Ltd*)

C.P.C.U. Jour. = Chartered Property and Casualty Underwriters Journal (*Society of Chartered Property and Law Casualty Underwriters*)

C.P.L.J. = Conveyancing and Property Law Journal (*S&M/Round Hall*)

C.P.L.R. = Civil Practice Law Reports (*XPL Publishing*)

C.P.N. = Civil Procedure News (*S&M*)

C.R. & I. = Corporate Rescue and Insolvency (*Butterworth Tolley Publishing*)

C.R.N.I. = Competition and Regulation in Network Industries (*Intersentia*)

C.S. = Corporate Solutions (*Financial Times Finance*)

C.S. Bull. = Credit Suisse Bulletin (*Credit Suisse*)

C.S.L.R. = Cambridge Student Law Review (*University of Cambridge*)

C.S.P. = Current Sentencing Practice (*S&M*)

TABLE OF ABBREVIATIONS

C.S.R. = Company Secretary's Review (*Butterworth Tolley Publishing*)

C.S.R. & E.M. = Corporate Social Responsibility and Environmental Management (*John Wiley & Sons Ltd*)

C.S.W. = Chartered Surveyor Weekly (*Builder Group Ltd*)

C.T. & E.P.Q. = Capital Taxes and Estate Planning Quarterly (*S&M/Pearson Prof. Ltd*)

C.T. News & Reps. = Capital Taxes News & Reports (*S&M*)

C.T.L.R. = Computer and Telecommunications Law Review (*S&M/ESC Publishing*)

C.T.P. = Capital Tax Planning (*S&M*)

C.T.R. = Corporate Tax Review (*Key Haven Publications Plc*)

C.W. = Copyright World (*Informa Publishing Group Ltd*)

C.Y.E.L.S. = Cambridge Yearbook of European Legal Studies (*Hart Publishing Ltd*)

CJ Europe = Criminal Justice Europe (*OICJ Europe*)

CPD Papers = Criminal Law Week - CPD Extended Papers (*S&M*)

Cambrian L.R. = Cambrian Law Review (*University College of Wales*)

Can. Ins. = Canadian Insurance (*Stone & Cox Ltd*)

Can. J.L.I. = Canadian Journal of Life Insurance (*Canadian Journal of Life Insurance Publications Ltd*)

Cap. Tax. = Capital Taxes (*S&M*)

Ch. = Law Reports Chancery Division (*ICLR*)

Charities M. = Charities Management (*Mitre House Publishing Ltd*)

Charity F. = Charity Finance (*Civil Society Media Ltd*)

Chart. I. = Charter-Party International (*S&M*)

Childright = Childright (*Children's Legal Centre Ltd*)

Civ. Lit. = Civil Litigation (*XPL Publishing*)

Civ. P.B. = Civil Practice Bulletin (*S&M/W. Green*)

Clarity = Clarity (*Clarity International*)

Co. Acc. = Company Accountant (*Institute of Company Accountants*)

Co. L. Dig. = Company Law Digest (*Butterworth Tolley Publishing*)

Co. L.J. = Commercial Litigation Journal (*Legalease Ltd*)

Co. L.N. = Company Law Newsletter (*S&M*)

Com. Jud. J. = Commonwealth Judicial Journal (*Commonwealth Magistrates & Judges Association*)

Com. L.L. = Commonwealth Law Librarian (*Legal Library Services*)

Com. Lawyer = The Commonwealth Lawyer (*Commonwealth Lawyers' Association*)

Comm. Int. = Communications International (*EMAP Communications*)

Comm. L.J. = Commercial Law Journal (*Legalease Ltd*)

Comm. Law. = Commercial Lawyer (*Chambers and Partners Publishing*)

Comm. Leases = Commercial Leases (*Informa Publishing Group Ltd*)

Comm. Prop. = Commercial Property (*XPL Publishing*)

Comms. L. = Communications Law (*Bloomsbury Publishing Plc*)

Comp. L. Rev. = Competition Law Review (*Competition Law Scholars Forum*)

Comp. L.I. = Competition Law Insight (*Informa Publishing Group Ltd*)

Comp. L.J. = Competition Law Journal (*Jordan & Sons Ltd*)

Comp. L.M. = Competition Law Monitor (*Informa Publishing Group Ltd*)

Comp. Law E.C. = Competition Law in the European Communities (*Fairford Press Ltd*)

Comp. Law. = Company Lawyer (*S&M*)

Comps. & Law = Computers & Law (*Society for Computers and Law*)

Con. L.D. = Construction Law Digest (*John Wiley & Sons Ltd*)

Con. L.R. = Construction Law Reports (*Butterworth Tolley Publishing*)

Cons. & Mar. Law = Consumer and Marketing Law (*Informa Publishing Group Ltd*)

Cons. L. Today = Consumer Law Today (*Richard Lawson*)

Cons. L.I. = Construction Law International (*International Bar Association*)

Cons. Law = Construction Law (*Eclipse/Butterworth Tolley Publishing*)

Const. L.J. = Construction Law Journal (*S&M*)

Const. Ref. = Constitutional Reform (*Constitutional Reform Centre*)

Consum. L.J. = Consumer Law Journal (*CDC Publications*)

Consumer C. = Consumer Credit (*Consumer Credit Trade Association*)

Conv. = Conveyancer and Property Lawyer (*S&M*)

Converg. = Convergence (*International Bar Association*)

Corp. Brief. = Corporate Briefing (*Singlelaw*)

Corp. C. = Corporate Counsel (*Commercial Lawyer*)

Costs L.R. = Costs Law Reports (*XPL Publishing*)

Counsel = Counsel (*Butterworth Tolley Publishing*)

Cov. L.J. = Coventry Law Journal (*Coventry University*)

Cr. App. R. = Criminal Appeal Reports (*S&M*)

Cr. App. R. (S.) = Criminal Appeal Reports (Sentencing) (*S&M*)

Crim. L.B. = Criminal Law Bulletin (*S&M/W. Green*)

Crim. L.F. = Criminal Law Forum (*Springer*)

Crim. L.N. = Criminal Law News (*Sally Ramage*)

Crim. L.R. = Criminal Law Review (*S&M*)

Crim. Law. = Criminal Lawyer (*Bloomsbury Publishing Plc*)

Criminal Law Week = Criminal Law Week (*S&M*)

Criminologist = Criminologist (*Butterworth Tolley Publishing*)

D. & P. = Development & Planning (*Policy Journals*)

D.C.J. = Defense Counsel Journal (*International Association of Defense Counsels*)

D.D. & R.M. = Due Diligence & Risk Management (*XPL Publishing*)

D.E. & E.S.L.R. = Digital Evidence and Electronic Signature Law Review (*Pario Communications Ltd*)

D.E.J. = Digital Evidence Journal (*Pario Communications Ltd*)

D.F.I. = Derivatives & Financial Instruments (*IBFD Publications BV*)

D.H.B. & W. F. & T. News. = Denton Hall Burgin & Warren Film & Television Newsletter (*Denton Hall*)

D.H.E.L. = Denton Hall Energy Law (*Denton Hall*)

D.H.E.N. = Denton Hall Employment Newsletter (*Denton Hall*)

D.H.I.T. News. = Denton Hall Information Technology Newsletter (*Denton Hall*)

D.H.P.N. = Denton Hall Pensions Newsletter (*Denton Hall*)

D.H.T.I. News. = Denton Hall The Interface Newsletter (*Denton Hall*)

D.I. Bank. & F.N. = Denton International Banking & Finance Newsletter (*Denton Hall*)

D.I. Comp. & EC N. = Denton International Competition and EC Newsletter (*Denton Hall*)

D.I. F.T. News. = Denton International Film & Television Newsletter (*Denton International*)

D.I.C.S. = Denton International Creative Spark (*Denton International*)

D.L. = Daily List (*TSO*)

D.L.B. Bus. Brief = Dibb Lupton Broomhead Business Brief (*Dibb Lupton Broomhead*)

D.L.R. = Discrimination Law Reports (*CLT Publishing*)

D.N.Q. = Domain Names Quarterly (*Informa Publishing Group Ltd*)

D.P. & P.P. = Data Protection and Privacy Practice (*Pinsent Masons*)

D.P.I. = Data Protection Ireland (*Privacy & Data Protection*)

D.P.L. & P. = Data Protection Law & Policy (*Cecile Park Publishing Ltd*)

D.P.Q. = Data Protection Quarterly (*Pinsent Masons*)

D.R.I. = Dispute Resolution International (*International Bar Association*)

D.U.L.J. = Dublin University Law Journal (*S&M/Round Hall*)

DLi = DLi University College Galway Law Graduates Association Gazette (*Toevaro Investments Ltd*)

DNV. B.C.U. = DNV Bulk Carrier Update (*Fairplay Publications Ltd*)

Data Base Reps. = Data Base Reports (*Insurance Information Institute*)

De Voil I.T.I. = De Voil Indirect Tax Intelligence (*Butterworth Tolley Publishing*)

Denning L.J. = Denning Law Journal (*University of Buckingham*)

E-Law Review = E-Law Review (*S&M/W. Green*)

E. & L. = Education and the Law (*Taylor & Francis Ltd*)

E. & P. = International Journal of Evidence & Proof (*Vathek Publishing*)

E. & S.L.J. = Entertainment and Sports Law Journal (*Warwick*)

E. St. A.L. = European State Aid Law Quarterly (*Lexxion Verlagsgesellschaft mbH*)

E.A.F. = European Accounting Focus (*Informa Publishing Group Ltd*)

E.B. & F.L.J. = European Banking & Financial Law Journal (*Intersentia NV*)

E.B. Mag. = Environment Business Magazine (*Faversham House Group Ltd*)

E.B.J. = Employee Benefits Journal (*International Foundation of Employee Benefits Plans Inc*)

E.B.L. = Electronic Business Law (*Eclipse/Butterworth Tolley Publishing*)

E.B.L. Rev. = European Business Law Review (*Turpin Distribution Serv Ltd*)

E.B.L.R. = Electronic Business Law Reports (*Butterworth Tolley Publishing*)

E.B.M. = European Business Monitor (*Butterworth Tolley Publishing*)

E.B.O.R. = European Business Organization Law Review (*CUP*)

E.C. Law = European Company Law (*Kluwer*)

E.C.A. = Elderly Client Adviser (*Ark Publishing*)

E.C.C. = European Commercial Cases (*S&M*)

E.C.D.R. = European Copyright and Design Reports (*S&M*)

E.C.F.R. = European Company and Financial Law Review (*Walter de Gruyter GmbH & Co. KG*)

E.C.J. = Environmental Claims Journal (*Executive Enterprises Publications Co Inc*)

E.C.L. = European Corporate Lawyer (*Legalease Ltd*)

E.C.L. & P. = E-Commerce Law & Policy (*Cecile Park Publishing Ltd*)

E.C.L. Rep. = E-Commerce Law Reports (*Cecile Park Publishing Ltd*)

E.C.L. Rev. = Electronic Communications Law Review (*Kluwer*)

E.C.L. Review = European Constitutional Law Review (*CUP*)

E.C.L.R. = European Competition Law Review (*S&M/ESC Publishing*)

E.D.D. & R.M. = Environmental Due Diligence & Risk Management (*XPL Publishing*)

E.E.B.L. = East European Business Law (*Financial Times Finance*)

E.E.E.L.R. = European Energy and Environmental Law Review (*Kluwer*)

E.E.F.N. = Eastern European Forum Newsletter (*International Bar Association*)

E.E.I.R. = East European Insurance Report (*Financial Times Finance*)

E.E.J. = European Energy Journal (*Claeys & Casteels*)

E.E.L.R. = European Environmental Law Review (*Turpin Distribution Serv Ltd*)

E.F.A. Rev. = European Foreign Affairs Review (*Kluwer*)

E.F.F.L.R. = European Food and Feed Law Review (*Lexxion Verlagsgesellschaft mbH*)

E.F.P.L. & P. = E-Finance & Payments Law & Policy (*Cecile Park Publishing Ltd*)

E.F.S.L. = European Financial Services Law (*Kluwer*)

E.F.T.B. = Emmet and Farrand on Title Bulletin (*S&M*)

E.G. = Estates Gazette (*Estates Gazette Ltd*)

E.G.C.S. = Estates Gazette Case Summaries (*Estates Gazette Ltd*)

E.G.L.R. = Estates Gazette Law Reports (*Estates Gazette Ltd*)

E.H.L.R. = Environmental Health Law Reports (*S&M*)

E.H.R.L.R. = European Human Rights Law Review (*S&M*)

E.H.R.R. = European Human Rights Reports (*S&M*)

E.I.B. = Environment Information Bulletin (*Eclipse/Butterworth Tolley Publishing*)

E.I.M. = European Insurance Market (*Informa Publishing Group Ltd*)

E.I.P.R. = European Intellectual Property Review (*S&M/ESC Publishing*)

E.I.R.R. = European Industrial Relations Review (*Reed Business Information Ltd*)

E.I.S. = European Insurance Strategies (*Evandale Publishing Co Ltd*)

E.J.C. = European Journal of Criminology (*Sage Publications Ltd*)

E.J.C.L. = Electronic Journal of Comparative Law (*Electronic Journal of Comparative Law*)

E.J.E.L. & P. = European Journal for Education Law and Policy (*Kluwer*)

E.J.H.L. = European Journal of Health Law (*Martinus Nijhoff Publishers*)

E.J.I.L. = European Journal of International Law (*OUP*)

E.J.L. & E. = European Journal of Law & Economics (*Springer*)

E.J.L.E. = European Journal of Legal Education (*Taylor & Francis Ltd*)

TABLE OF ABBREVIATIONS

E.J.L.R. = European Journal of Law Reform (*Boom Distributiecentrum BV*)

E.J.L.T. = European Journal of Law and Technology (*University of Warwick*)

E.J.M.L. = European Journal of Migration and Law (*Martinus Nijhoff Publishers*)

E.J.R.B. = Environmental Judicial Review Bulletin (*Chancery Law Publishing Ltd*)

E.J.R.R. = European Journal of Risk Regulation (*Lexxion Verlagsgesellschaft mbH*)

E.J.S.L. = European Journal of Social Law (*Ghent University*)

E.J.S.S. = European Journal of Social Security (*Intersentia NV*)

E.L. = Equitable Lawyer (*Gostick Hall Publications*)

E.L. & P.D. = European Life & Pensions Digest (*European Business Digest Ltd*)

E.L. Rev. = European Law Review (*S&M*)

E.L.A. Briefing = Employment Lawyers Association Briefing (*Employment Lawyers Association*)

E.L.B. = Environment Law Brief (*Informa Publishing Group Ltd*)

E.L.F. = Elder Law and Finance (*Jordan & Sons Ltd*)

E.L.G.L.B. = Encyclopedia of Local Government Law Bulletin (*S&M*)

E.L.J. = European Law Journal (*John Wiley & Sons Ltd*)

E.L.L.J. = European Labour Law Journal (*Intersentia NV*)

E.L.L.R. = Environmental Liability Law Review (*Koninklijke Vermande BV*)

E.L.M. = Environmental Law & Management (*Lawtext Publishing Limited*)

E.L.N. = Environmental Law Newsletter (*Butterworth Tolley Publishing*)

E.L.R. = Education Law Reports (*Jordan & Sons Ltd*)

E.L.R.I. = Employment Law Review - Ireland (*First Law*)

E.M. = European Mergers (*Informa Publishing Group Ltd*)

E.M.I. = Emerging Markets Investor (*Chiltern Magazine Services*)

E.M.L.R. = Entertainment and Media Law Reports (*S&M/ESC Publishing*)

E.N.P.R. = European National Patent Reports (*S&M*)

E.O.R. = Equal Opportunities Review (*Michael Rubenstein Publishing*)

E.O.R. Dig. = Equal Opportunities Review and Discrimination Case Law Digest (*Eclipse/Butterworth Tolley Publishing*)

E.P. & L. = Environmental Policy and Law (*IOS Press*)

E.P.E.F. = Economic Policy: A European Forum (*CUP*)

E.P.G. = Environmental Policy and Governance (*John Wiley & Sons Ltd*)

E.P.I.S. = EMIS Personal Injury Service (*XPL Publishing*)

E.P.L. = European Public Law (*Kluwer*)

E.P.L.I. = Education, Public Law and the Individual (*Education Law Association Ltd*)

E.P.L.P.B. = Encyclopedia of Planning Law and Practice Monthly Bulletin (*S&M*)

E.P.O.R. = European Patent Office Reports (*S&M*)

E.P.P.P.L.R. = European Public Private Partnership Law Review (*Lexxion Verlagsgesellschaft mbH*)

E.P.S. = EMIS Property Service (*XPL Publishing*)

E.R.C.L. = European Review of Contract Law (*Walter de Gruyter GmbH & Co. KG*)

E.R.P.L. = European Review of Private Law (*Kluwer*)

E.S.L.J. = E-Signature Law Journal (*Pario Communications Ltd*)

E.T. = Estates Times (*Morgan Grampian Plc*)

E.T.M.R. = European Trade Marks Reports (*S&M*)

E.U. News = European Union News (*S&M*)

E.W.C.B. = European Works Councils Bulletin (*Eclipse/Butterworth Tolley Publishing*)

EC C.P.N. = European Commission Competition Policy Newsletter (*Commission of The European Communities*)

EC E.M. = EC Energy Monthly (*Financial Times Finance*)

EC F.L.M. = EC Food Law Monthly (*Agra Europe (London) Ltd*)

EC P.R. = EC Packaging Report (*Agra Europe (London) Ltd*)

EC T.J. = EC Tax Journal (*Key Haven Publications Plc*)

EC T.R. = EC Tax Review (*Turpin Distribution Serv Ltd*)

EDI L.R. = Electronic Data Interchange Law Review (*Kluwer*)

EMIS E.L.S. = EMIS E-Law Service (*XPL Publishing*)

ENDS = ENDS Report (*Environmental Data Services Ltd*)

EPLC Brief = European Pharma Law Centre Brief (*European Pharma Law Centre Ltd*)

EU Brief. Notes = EU Briefing Notes (*SJ Berwin & Co*)

EU Focus = EU Focus (*S&M*)

Eagle = Eagle (*Stratton Publishing Ltd*)

Ec. Aff. = Economic Affairs (*The Institute of Economic Affairs*)

Ec. Rev. = Economic Review (*Philip Allan Publishers Ltd*)

Ecc. L.J. = Ecclesiastical Law Journal (*CUP*)

Eco M. & A. = Eco-Management & Auditing (*John Wiley & Sons Ltd*)

Ed. C.R. = Education Case Reports (*S&M*)

Ed. L.M. = Education Law Monitor (*Informa Publishing Group Ltd*)

Ed. Law = Education Law Journal (*Jordan & Sons Ltd*)

Edin. L.R. = Edinburgh Law Review (*Edinburgh University Press Ltd*)

Eld. L.J. = Elder Law Journal (*Jordan & Sons Ltd*)

Emp. L. & L. = Employment Law & Litigation (*XPL Publishing*)

Emp. L. & L.U. = Employment Law and Litigation Updates (*XPL Publishing*)

Emp. L. Brief. = Employment Law Briefing (*S&M*)

Emp. L.B. = Employment Law Bulletin (*S&M/W. Green*)

Emp. L.J. = Employment Law Journal (*Legalease Ltd*)

Emp. L.N. = Employment Law Newsletter (*S&M*)

Emp. Law. = Employment Lawyer (*S&M*)

Emp. Lit. = Employment Litigation (*XPL Publishing*)

Employ. L. = Employer's Law (*Reed Business Information Ltd*)

Enc. C.S.P. = Encyclopedia of Current Sentencing Practice (*S&M*)

Enc. F.S.L. = Encyclopedia of Financial Services Law (*S&M*)

Enc. I.T.L. = Encyclopedia of Information Technology Law (*S&M*)

Enc. P.L. & P. = Encyclopedia of Planning Law & Practice (*S&M*)

Ent. L.R. = Entertainment Law Review (*S&M/ESC Publishing*)

Ent. Law = Entertainment Law (*Cass*)

Env. I.B. = Environment In Business (*Butterworth Tolley Publishing*)

Env. L. Rev. = Environmental Law Review (*Vathek Publishing*)

Env. L.B. = Environmental Law Bulletin (*S&M/W. Green*)

Env. L.M. = Environmental Law Monthly (*Informa Publishing Group Ltd*)

Env. L.N. = Environmental Law Newsletter (*SJ Berwin & Co*)

Env. L.R. = Environmental Law Reports (*S&M*)

Env. Law = Environmental Law (*UKELA*)

Env. Liability = Environmental Liability (*Lawtext Publishing Limited*)

Env. Man. = Environmental Manager (*Informa Publishing Group Ltd*)

Env. Risk = Environment Risk (*Euromoney Institutional Investor Plc*)

Eq. L.R. = Equality Law Reports (*Michael Rubenstein Publishing*)

Eu. C.L.R. = European Criminal Law Review (*Hart Publishing Ltd*)

Eu. L.F. = European Legal Forum (*IPR Verlag GmbH*)

Eu. L.R. = European Law Reports (*Hart Publishing Ltd*)

Eur. Access = European Access (*Chadwyck Healey Ltd*)

Eur. Counsel = European Counsel (*Legal & Commercial Publishing*)

Eur. J. Crime Cr. L. Cr. J. = European Journal of Crime, Criminal Law and Criminal Justice (*Martinus Nijhoff Publishers*)

Eurlegal = Eurlegal (*Incorporated Law Society of Ireland*)

Euro. C.J. = European Competition Journal (*Hart Publishing Ltd*)

Euro. C.L. = European Current Law (*S&M*)

Euro. Env. = European Environment (*John Wiley & Sons Ltd*)

Euro. L.B. = European Legal Business (*Legalease Ltd*)

Euro. L.M. = European Law Monitor (*Informa Publishing Group Ltd*)

Euro. Law. = European Lawyer (*Polyview Media Limited*)

Euro. News. = European Newsletter (*S&M*)

Euro T.L. = European Transport Law (*Robert H Wijffels*)

Euro. T.S. = European Tax Service (*BNA International Inc*)

Euro. Tax. = European Taxation (*IBFD Publications BV*)

Euromoney = Euromoney (*Euromoney Institutional Investor Plc*)

Eurosafety = Eurosafety (*Butterworth Tolley Publishing*)

Exp. = Experiodica (*Swiss Reinsurance Company*)

Expert = Expert (*Bristish Academy of Experts*)

F. & C.L. = Finance & Credit Law (*Singlelaw*)

F. & D. = Finance & Development (*Finance & Development*)

F. & D.L.M. = Food & Drink Law Monthly (*Agra Europe*)

F. & D.L.R. = Futures & Derivatives Law Review (*Routledge-Cavendish*)

F.A. = Financial Adviser (*Financial Times Finance*)

F.C.R. = Family Court Reporter (*Butterworth Tolley Publishing*)

F.D. & D.I.B. = Food, Drinks & Drugs Industry Bulletin (*Informa Publishing Group Ltd*)

F.E. & P.I. = Freshfields Employment & Pensions Issues (*Freshfields*)

F.I. = Fraud Intelligence (*Informa Publishing Group Ltd*)

F.I.T.A.R. = Financial Instruments Tax & Accounting Review (*Informa Publishing Group Ltd*)

F.L.N. = Family Law Newsletter (*Butterworth Tolley Publishing*)

F.L.R. = Family Law Reports (*Jordan & Sons Ltd*)

F.L.T. = Family Law Today (*Informa Publishing Group Ltd*)

F.M. = Financial Management (*Chartered Institute Management Accountants*)

F.O.I. = Freedom of Information (*Privacy & Data Protection*)

F.P.B. = Four Pillars Bulletin (*Geneva Association*)

F.R. = Financial Regulator (*Central Banking Publications Ltd*)

F.R. & F.N. = Financial Reinsurance & Futures Newsletter (*Informa Publishing Group Ltd*)

F.R.B.N.Y.Q.R. = Federal Reserve Bank of New York Quarterly Review (*Federal Reserve Bank of New York*)

F.R.I. = Financial Regulation International (*Informa Publishing Group Ltd*)

F.R.N. = Financial Reinsurance Newsletter (*Informa Publishing Group Ltd*)

F.R.R. = Financial Regulation Report (*Informa Publishing Group Ltd*)

F.S. Bulletin = Financial Services Bulletin (*Informa Publishing Group Ltd*)

F.S.B. = Financial Services Brief (*S&M*)

F.S.L.J. = Financial Services Law Journal (*S&M/Round Hall*)

F.S.L.L. = Financial Services Law Letter (*Informa Publishing Group Ltd*)

F.S.R. = Fleet Street Reports (*S&M*)

F.T.I. = Financial Technology Insight (*Elsevier*)

Fairplay = Fairplay (*Fairplay Publications Ltd*)

Fam. = Law Reports Family Division (*ICLR*)

Fam. L.B. = Family Law Bulletin (*S&M/W. Green*)

Fam. L.J. = Family Law Journal (*Legalease Ltd*)

Fam. L.R. = Family Law Reports (Greens) (*S&M/W. Green*)

Fam. Law = Family Law (*Jordan & Sons Ltd*)

Fam. Law B. = Family Law Bulletin (*S&M*)

Fam. M. = Family Matters (*S&M*)

Fam. Med. = Family Mediation (*National Association of Family Mediation & Conciliation Services*)

Farm Law = Farm Law (*Agra Europe*)

Farm T. & F. = Farm Tax & Finance (*Tax and Financial Publishing*)

Farm T.B. = Farm Tax Brief (*Informa Publishing Group Ltd*)

Fem. L.S. = Feminist Legal Studies (*Springer*)

Fin. Con. = Finance Confidential (*Fleet Street Publications Ltd*)

Focus = Focus (*Zurich International (UK) Ltd*)

Food & Drugs I.B. = Food & Drugs Industry Bulletin (*Informa Publishing Group Ltd*)

Food L.M. = Food Law Monthly (*Agra Europe*)

Foresight = Foresight (*Risk & Insurance Research Group Ltd*)

G.A.R. = Global Arbitration Review (*Law Business Research Ltd*)

G.C. = Global Crime (*Taylor & Francis Ltd*)

G.C.L.R. = Global Competition Litigation Review (*S&M/ESC Publishing*)

G.C.R. = Global Competition Review (*Law Business Research Ltd*)

G.I.L.S.I. = Gazette Incorporated Law Society of Ireland (*The Law Society*)

G.L. & B. = Global Law & Business (*Global Law & Business Ltd*)

G.L.J. = Guernsey Law Journal (*Her Majesty's Greffier*)

G.L.S.I. = Gazette of the Law Society Ireland (*The Law Society*)

G.P.R.I.I.P. = Geneva Papers on Risk & Insurance Issues & Practice (*Geneva Association*)

G.P.R.I.T. = Geneva Papers on Risk & Insurance: Theory (*Geneva Association*)

G.R. = Global Reinsurance (*Southern Magazines Ltd*)

G.R.A. = Global Re Analysis (*Southern Magazines Ltd*)

G.T. & C.J. = Global Trade and Customs Journal (*Kluwer*)

G.T.B. = Global Telecoms Business (*Euromoney Institutional Investor Plc*)

G.W.D. = Greens Weekly Digest (*S&M/W. Green*)

Gen. Ins. = General Insurance (*Mitre House Publishing Ltd*)

Global Counsel = Global Counsel (*Legal & Commercial Publishing*)

Go. J.I.L. = Gottingen Journal of International Law (*Universitatsverlag Gottingen*)

Gov. = Governance (*Plaza Publishing*)

Guide = Guide (*S&M*)

H. & S.B. = Health and Safety Bulletin (*Butterworth Tolley Publishing*)

H. & S.L. = Health & Safety Law (*XPL Publishing*)

H. & S.M. = Health & Safety Monitor (*Schofield Publishing*)

H. & S.R. = Health & Safety Review (*IRN Publishing*)

H. & S.W. = Health & Safety at Work (*Butterworth Tolley Publishing*)

H.A.L.L. = Health & Law Letter (*Business & Maritime Publications*)

H.C.L.M. = High Court Litigation Manual (*S&M*)

H.C.W.I.B. = House of Commons Weekly Information Bulletin (*TSO*)

H.J.R.L. = Hague Journal on the Rule of Law (*TMC Asser Press*)

H.K.L.J. = Hong Kong Law Journal (*Hong Kong Law Journal Ltd*)

H.L.J. = Hibernian Law Journal (*Law Society of Ireland*)

H.L.M. = Housing Law Monitor (*Informa Publishing Group Ltd*)

H.L.R. = Housing Law Reports (*S&M*)

H.P.L.R. = Housing & Property Law Review (*Arden Davies Publishing*)

H.R. = Human Rights (*Jordan & Sons Ltd*)

H.R. & I.L.D. = Human Rights & International Legal Discourse (*Intersentia*)

H.R. & UK P. = Human Rights & UK Practice (*XPL Publishing*)

H.R.A. = Human Rights Alerter (*S&M*)

H.R.C.D. = Human Rights Case Digest (*S&M*)

H.R.L. Rev. = Human Rights Law Review (*OUP*)

H.R.L.R. = Human Rights Law Reports (*S&M*)

H.R.U. = Human Rights Updater (*Butterworth Tolley Publishing*)

H.S. = Hazardous Substances (*Informa Publishing Group Ltd*)

H.S. Brief. = Herbert Smith Briefing (*Herbert Smith*)

H.S. at W. = Health & Safety at Work (*Bloomsbury Publishing Plc*)

H.S.I. = Halsbury's Statutory Instruments (*Legal Library Services Ltd*)

H.S.I.B. = Health & Safety Information Bulletin (*Butterworth Tolley Publishing*)

Haldane S.E.L.B. = Haldane Society Employment Law Bulletin (*Haldane Society of Socialist Lawyers*)

Halsbury S. = Halsbury's Statutes (*Legal Library Services Ltd*)

Health Law = Health Law for Healthcare Professionals (*Informa Publishing Group Ltd*)

Hert. L.J. = Hertfordshire Law Journal (*University of Hertfordshire*)

Hold. L.R. = Holdsworth Law Review (*University of Birmingham*)

Hous. L.R. = Greens Housing Law Reports (*S&M/W. Green*)

Howard Journal = Howard Journal of Criminal Justice (*John Wiley & Sons Ltd*)

Hull C.A. = Hull Claims Analysis (*S&M*)

I. & C.T.L. = Information & Communications Technology Law (*Taylor & Francis Ltd*)

I. & N.L. & P. = Immigration & Nationality Law & Practice (*Butterworth Tolley Publishing*)

I. & P.E. = Investment & Pensions Europe (*IPE International Publishers Ltd*)

I. & R.I. = Insolvency and Restructuring International (*International Bar Association*)

I. & R.L.B. = Insurance & Reinsurance Law Briefing (*S&M*)

I. Bull. = Interights Bulletin (*Interights*)

I. Prop. = Intellectual Property (*CLT Publishing*)

I.A. & E.H.R.J. = Inter-American and European Human Rights Journal (*Intersentia*)

I.A.N.L. = Immigration, Asylum and Nationality Law (*Bloomsbury Publishing Plc*)

I.B.F.L. = International Banking and Financial Law (*S&M*)

I.B.L. = International Business Lawyer (*International Bar Association*)

I.B.L.J. = International Business Law Journal (*S&M*)

I.B.L.Q. = Irish Business Law Quarterly (*Clarus Press*)

I.B.N. = International Bar News (*International Bar Association*)

I.B.R. = Irish Banking Review (*Irish Bankers' Federation*)

I.C. = Investors Chronicle (*Investors Chronicle Publications Ltd*)

I.C. Lit. = International Commercial Litigation (*Euromoney Institutional Investor Plc*)

I.C.C.L.J. = International and Comparative Corporate Law Journal (*Institute of Advanced Legal Studies*)

I.C.C.L.R. = International Company and Commercial Law Review (*S&M/ESC Publishing*)

I.C.L. = International Corporate Law (*Euromoney Institutional Investor Plc*)

I.C.L. Rev. = International Construction Law Review (*Informa Publishing Group Ltd*)

I.C.L.B. = International Corporate Law Bulletin (*Kluwer*)

I.C.L.J. = Irish Criminal Law Journal (*S&M/Round Hall*)

I.C.L.M.D. = Irish Current Law Monthly Digest (*S&M/Round Hall*)

I.C.L.Q. = International & Comparative Law Quarterly (*CUP*)

I.C.L.S.A. = Irish Current Law Statutes Annotated (*S&M/Round Hall*)

I.C.R. = Industrial Cases Reports (*ICLR*)

I.D.P.L. = International Data Privacy Law (*OUP*)

I.E.L.J. = Irish Employment Law Journal (*S&M/Round Hall*)

I.E.L.R. = International Energy Law Review (*S&M*)

TABLE OF ABBREVIATIONS

I.E.L.T.R. = International Energy Law & Taxation Review (*S&M*)

I.F.L. = International Family Law (*Jordan & Sons Ltd*)

I.F.L. Rev. = International Financial Law Review (*Euromoney Institutional Investor Plc*)

I.F.O.S.S.L.R. = International Free and Open Source Software Law Review (*Editorial Committee Board*)

I.H.L. = In-House Lawyer (*Legalease Ltd*)

I.H.P. = In-House Perspective (*International Bar Association*)

I.H.R.L.R. = Irish Human Rights Law Review (*Clarus Press*)

I.H.R.R. = International Human Rights Reports (*University of Nottingham, School of Law*)

I.I.E.L. = Immigration and International Employment Law (*Eclipse/Butterworth Tolley Publishing*)

I.I.I. = Insurance Industry International (*Lafferty Publications Ltd*)

I.I.L. Rev. = International Internet Law Review (*Euromoney Institutional Investor Plc*)

I.I.L.R. = Irish Insurance Law Review (*S&M/Round Hall*)

I.I.P.L.Q. = Irish Intellectual Property Law Quarterly (*First Law*)

I.I.P.R. = Irish Intellectual Property Review (*S&M/Round Hall*)

I.I.R. = International Insolvency Review (*John Wiley & Sons Ltd*)

I.I.U. = Insurance Issues Update (*Insurance Information Institute*)

I.J.B.L. = International Journal of Biosciences and the Law (*A B Academic Publishers*)

I.J.C.L. = International Journal of Constitutional Law (*OUP*)

I.J.C.L.E. = International Journal of Clinical Legal Education (*Northumbria Law Press*)

I.J.C.L.P. = International Journal of Communications Law and Policy (*Institute for Information, Telecommunications and Media Law*)

I.J.C.P. = International Journal of Cultural Property (*CUP*)

I.J.D.G. = International Journal of Disclosure and Governance (*Palgrave Macmillan*)

I.J.D.L. = International Journal of Discrimination and the Law (*Sage Publications Ltd*)

I.J.E.C.L. = International Journal of Estuarine and Coastal Law (*Kluwer*)

I.J.E.C.L. & P. = International Journal of Electronic Commerce Law & Practice (*XPL Publishing*)

I.J.E.L. = Irish Journal of European Law (*S&M/Round Hall*)

I.J.F.D.L. = International Journal of Franchising and Distribution Law (*Richmond Law & Tax Ltd*)

I.J.F.L. = Irish Journal of Family Law (*S&M/Round Hall*)

I.J.H.R. = International Journal of Human Rights (*Taylor & Francis Ltd*)

I.J.I.L. = International Journal of Insurance Law (*Informa Publishing Group Ltd*)

I.J.L. & I.T. = International Journal of Law & Information Technology (*OUP*)

I.J.L.B.E. = International Journal of Law in the Built Environment (*Emerald Group Publishing Limited*)

I.J.L.C.J. = International Journal of Law, Crime and Justice (*Elsevier*)

I.J.L.P. = International Journal of the Legal Profession (*Taylor & Francis Ltd*)

I.J.L.S. = Irish Journal of Legal Studies (*University College Cork*)

I.J.M.C.L. = International Journal of Marine & Coastal Law (*Martinus Nijhoff Publishers*)

I.J.N.L. = International Journal of Nuclear Law (*Inderscience Publishers*)

I.J.O.S.L. = International Journal Of Shipping Law (*Informa Publishing Group Ltd*)

I.J.P.L. = International Journal of Private Law (*Inderscience Publishers*)

I.J.P.L. & P. = International Journal of Public Law and Policy (*Inderscience Publishers*)

I.J.R.L. = International Journal of Refugee Law (*OUP*)

I.J.R.L. & P. = International Journal of Regulatory Law & Practice (*Henry Stewart Publications*)

I.J.S.L. = International Journal for the Semiotics of Law (*Springer*)

I.J.T. = Irish Journal of Taxation (*University of Ulster*)

I.J.T.J. = International Journal of Transitional Justice (*OUP*)

I.K. = Inside Knowledge (*Waterlow Legal & Regulatory*)

I.L. & P. = Insolvency Law & Practice (*Butterworth Tolley Publishing*)

I.L. & S. = Islamic Law and Society (*Brill Academic Publishers*)

I.L. Pr. = International Litigation Procedure (*S&M*)

I.L.D. = Immigration Law Digest (*Immigration Advisory Service*)

I.L.F.M. = International Law Firm Management (*Euromoney Institutional Investor Plc*)

I.L.J. = Industrial Law Journal (*OUP*)

I.L.P. = International Legal Practitioner (*International Bar Association*)

I.L.R.M. = Irish Law Reports Monthly (*S&M/Round Hall*)

I.L.T. = Irish Law Times (*S&M/Round Hall*)

I.M. & E. = Insurance: Mathematics & Economics (*Elsevier Science Publishers*)

I.M.L. = International Media Law (*S&M*)

I.N.L. = Internet Newsletter for Lawyers (*Delia Venables*)

I.N.L.R. = Immigration and Nationality Law Reports (*Jordan & Sons Ltd*)

I.O.L.R. = International Organizations Law Review (*Martinus Nijhoff Publishers*)

I.P. = International Peacekeeping (*Kluwer*)

I.P. & I.T. Law = Intellectual Property & Information Technology Law (*XPL Publishing*)

I.P. & I.T.L.U. = Intellectual Property & Information Technology Law Updates (*XPL Publishing*)

I.P. & T. = Intellectual Property and Technology (*Butterworth Tolley Publishing*)

I.P. Business = Intellectual Property Business (*OUP*)

I.P. Law. = Intellectual Property Lawyer (*S&M*)

I.P. News. = Intellectual Property Newsletter (*Informa Publishing Group Ltd*)

I.P.B. Rev. = Intellectual Property in Business Review (*Euromoney Institutional Investor Plc*)

I.P.B. Rev. Brief. = Intellectual Property in Business Briefing (*Euromoney Institutional Investor Plc*)

I.P.D. = Intellectual Property Decisions (*Informa Publishing Group Ltd*)

I.P.E.L.J. = Irish Planning and Environmental Law Journal (*S&M/Round Hall*)

I.P.L. = International Pension Lawyer (*International Association of Pension and Employee Benefits Lawyers*)

I.P.M. = Intellectual Property Magazine (*Informa Publishing Group Ltd*)

I.P.Q. = Intellectual Property Quarterly (*S&M*)

I.R.L.A. = Insurance & Reinsurance Law Alert (*Informa Publishing Group Ltd*)

I.R.L.B. = Industrial Relations Law Bulletin (*Reed Business Information Ltd*)

TABLE OF ABBREVIATIONS

I.R.L.C.T. = International Review of Law Computers & Technology (*Taylor & Francis Ltd*)

I.R.L.I.B. = Industrial Relations Legal Information Bulletin (*Eclipse/Butterworth Tolley Publishing*)

I.R.L.N. = Insurance and Reinsurance Law Newsletter (*Informa Publishing Group Ltd*)

I.R.L.R. = Industrial Relations Law Reports (*Eclipse/Butterworth Tolley Publishing*)

I.R.N. = Industrial Relations News (*IRN Publishing*)

I.R.R.R. = Industrial Relations Review and Report (*Eclipse/Butterworth Tolley Publishing*)

I.R.S.R. = Insurance & Reinsurance Solvency Report (*Informa Publishing Group Ltd*)

I.R.T.B. = Inland Revenue Tax Bulletin (*Inland Revenue*)

I.R.T.L. = Irish Road Traffic Law (*First Law*)

I.R.V. = International Review of Victimology (*Sage Publications Ltd*)

I.S.B. = Insurance Systems Bulletin (*Chiltern Magazine Services*)

I.S.I. = Insurance Systems International (*Informa Publishing Group Ltd*)

I.S.L.J. = International Sports Law Journal (*TMC Asser Press*)

I.S.L.R. = International Sports Law Review (*S&M*)

I.S.L.Rev. = Irish Student Law Review (*The Honourable Society of Kings' Inn*)

I.S.R. = International Securitisation Report (*IFA Publishing Ltd*)

I.T. & C.L.J. = Information Technology & Communications Law Journal (*Legalease Ltd*)

I.T. Rep. = International Tax Report (*Informa Publishing Group Ltd*)

I.T. Rev. = International Tax Review (*Euromoney Institutional Investor Plc*)

I.T.E.L.R. = International Trust and Estate Law Reports (*Bloomsbury Publishing Plc*)

I.T.I. = Information Technology in Insurance (*Informa Publishing Group Ltd*)

I.T.L. Rep. = International Tax Law Reports (*Butterworth Tolley Publishing*)

I.T.L.J. = International Travel Law Journal (*The Travel Law Centre*)

I.T.L.Q. = International Trade Law Quarterly (*Informa Publishing Group Ltd*)

I.T.L.R. = International Technology Law Review (*Euromoney Institutional Investor Plc*)

I.T.P.J. = International Transfer Pricing Journal (*IBFD Publications BV*)

I.V.M. = International VAT Monitor (*IBFD Publications BV*)

I.Y.L.C.T. = International Yearbook of Law, Computers & Technology (*Taylor & Francis Ltd*)

IALS Bull. = Institute of Advanced Legal Studies Bulletin (*Institute of Advanced Legal Studies*)

IBA Global Insight = IBA Global Insight (*International Bar Association*)

IBIS Rep. = International Benefits Information Service Report (*Charles D. Spencer & Associates, Inc.*)

IBIS Review = International Benefits Information Service Review (*Charles D. Spencer & Associates Inc*)

ICSID Rev. = ICSID Review (*OUP*)

IDS Brief = IDS Brief Employment Law & Practice (*S&M/IDS*)

IDS D.W. = IDS Diversity at Work (*S&M/IDS*)

IDS Emp. E. = IDS Employment Europe (*S&M/IDS*)

IDS Emp. L. Brief = IDS Employment Law Brief (*S&M/IDS*)

IDS Euro. R. = IDS European Report (*S&M/IDS*)

IDS HR Study = IDS HR Studies (*S&M/IDS*)

IDS P.B. = IDS Pensions Bulletin (*S&M/IDS*)

IDS P.L.R. = IDS Pensions Law Reports (*S&M/IDS*)

IDS P.S.B. = IDS Pensions Service Bulletin (*S&M/IDS*)

IFA Review = Independent Financial Adviser Review (*Mitre House Publishing Ltd*)

IIB Mag. = Institute of Insurance Brokers Magazine (*MSM International Ltd*)

IIC = International Review of Intellectual Property and Competition Law (*IPR Verlag GmbH*)

INSOL W. = INSOL World (*INSOL International*)

IP Scan = IP Scan (*Register.com, Corporate Services Division*)

IRS Emp. L.B. = IRS Employment Law Bulletin (*Reed Business Information Ltd*)

IRS Emp. Law = IRS Employment Law (*Reed Business Information Ltd*)

IRS Emp. Rev. = IRS Employment Review (*Reed Business Information Ltd*)

IRS Emp. Trends = IRS Employment Trends (*Butterworth Tolley Publishing*)

IRS Euro. Emp. Rev. = IRS European Employment Review (*Reed Business Information Ltd*)

ISBA L. & R.R. = ISBA Legislative & Regulatory Review (*The Incorporated Society of British Advertisers Ltd*)

IT & C.L.R. = IT & Communications Law Reports (*Legalease Ltd*)

IT & Comm. News. = Information Technology & Communications Newsletter (*Legalease Ltd*)

IT L.T. = IT Law Today (*Singlelaw*)

Imm. A.R. = Immigration Appeal Reports (*TSO*)

In Comp. = In Competition (*S&M*)

In-House L. = In-House Lawyer (*Legalease Ltd*)

Ind. L.R. = Independent Law Review (*Clarus Press*)

Ind. Sol. = Independent Solicitor (*British Legal Association*)

Ind. T.R. = Industrial Tribunal Reports (*TSO*)

Info. T.L.R. = Information Technology Law Reports (*Lawtext Publishing Limited*)

Ins. & Reins. Law Int. = Insurance & Reinsurance Law International (*Kluwer*)

Ins. Age = Insurance Age (*Maxwell Business Communications Ltd*)

Ins. Int. = Insurance International (*Mitre House Publishing Ltd*)

Ins. L. & C. = Insurance Law & Claims (*Mitre House Publishing Ltd*)

Ins. L. & P. = Insurance Law & Practice (*Butterworth Tolley Publishing*)

Ins. L.J. = Insurance Law Journal (*Butterworths Pty Ltd*)

Ins. L.M. = Insurance Law Monthly (*Informa Publishing Group Ltd*)

Insolv. B. = Insolvency Bulletin (*Informa Publishing Group Ltd*)

Insolv. Int. = Insolvency Intelligence (*S&M*)

Insolv. L. = Insolvency Lawyer (*S&M*)

Insolv. L. & P. = Insolvency Litigation & Practice (*CLT Publishing*)

Insolv. P. = Insolvency Practitioner (*Association of Business Recovery Professionals*)

Insolvency = Insolvency (*Griffin Multimedia*)

Int. A.L.R. = International Arbitration Law Review (*S&M*)

Int. Acc. = International Accountant (*Association of International Accountants*)

Int. Bank. L. = International Banking Law (*S&M*)

Int. Broker = International Broker (*Risk & Insurance Research Group Ltd*)

Int. C.L. Rev. = International Community Law Review (*Martinus Nijhoff Publishers*)

Int. C.L.R. = International Criminal Law Review (*Martinus Nijhoff Publishers*)

TABLE OF ABBREVIATIONS

Int. C.R. = International Corporate Rescue (*Chase Cambria Co (Publishing) Ltd*)

Int. I.L.R. = International Insurance Law Review (*S&M/ESC Publishing*)

Int. I.R. = International Insurance Report (*Risk & Insurance Research Group Ltd*)

Int. J. Comp. L.L.I.R. = International Journal of Comparative Labour Law and Industrial Relations (*Kluwer*)

Int. J. Law & Fam. = International Journal of Law & the Family (*OUP*)

Int. J. Soc. L. = International Journal of the Sociology of Law (*Elsevier*)

Int. J.F.L. = International Journal of Franchising Law (*Claerhout Publishing Ltd*)

Int. J.I.P.M. = International Journal of Intellectual Property Management (*Inderscience Publishers*)

Int. J.L.C. = International Journal of Law in Context (*CUP*)

Int. J.L.M. = International Journal of Law and Management (*Emerald Group Publishing Limited*)

Int. J.L.P.F. = International Journal of Law, Policy and the Family (*OUP*)

Int. M.L. = International Maritime Law (*Lawtext Publishing Limited*)

Int. Rel. = International Relations (*Sage Publications Ltd*)

Int. Rev. Law & Econ. = International Review of Law & Economics (*Butterworth Tolley Publishing*)

Int. T.L.R. = International Trade Law & Regulation (*S&M/ESC Publishing*)

Intertax = Intertax (*Kluwer*)

Inv. Man. = Investment Management (*Mitre House Publishing Ltd*)

Ir. B.L. = Irish Business Law (*Inns Quay Publishing*)

Ir. L.R. = Irish Law Review (*Clarus Press*)

Ir. T.R. = Irish Tax Review (*Institute of Taxation in Ireland*)

Irish Jurist = Irish Jurist (*S&M/Round Hall*)

J. Civ. Lib. = Journal of Civil Liberties (*Northumbria Law Press*)

J. Com. Mar. St. = Journal of Common Market Studies (*John Wiley & Sons Ltd*)

J. Crim. L. = Journal of Criminal Law (*Vathek Publishing*)

J. En. & Nat. Res. L. = Journal of Energy & Natural Resources Law (*Turpin Distribution Serv Ltd*)

J. Env. L. = Journal of Environmental Law (*OUP*)

J. Int. Arb. = Journal of International Arbitration (*Kluwer*)

J. Int. P. = Journal of International Trust and Corporate Planning (*Jordan & Sons Ltd*)

J. Law & Soc. = Journal of Law and Society (*John Wiley & Sons Ltd*)

J. Leg. Hist. = Journal of Legal History (*Cass*)

J. Priv. Int. L. = Journal of Private International Law (*Hart Publishing Ltd*)

J. Prop. Fin. = Journal of Property Finance (*MCB University Press Ltd*)

J. Soc. Wel. & Fam. L. = Journal of Social Welfare and Family Law (*Taylor & Francis Ltd*)

J. Soc. Wel. L. = Journal of Social Welfare Law (*S&M*)

J.A.C.L. = Journal of Armed Conflict Law (*Nottingham University Press*)

J.A.L. = Journal of African Law (*CUP*)

J.A.M.N. = Journal of ADR, Mediation and Negotiation (*XPL Publishing*)

J.B.L. = Journal of Business Law (*S&M*)

J.B.R. = Journal of Banking Regulation (*Palgrave Macmillan*)

J.C. & S.L. = Journal of Conflict & Security Law (*OUP*)

J.C.C. Law = Journal of Commonwealth Criminal Law (*Association of Commonwealth Criminal Lawyers*)

J.C.C.L. = Journal of Community Care Law (*Arden Davies Publishing*)

J.C.L. = Journal of Child Law (*Butterworth Tolley Publishing*)

J.C.L. & E. = Journal of Competition Law & Economics (*OUP*)

J.C.L.L.E. = Journal of Commonwealth Law and Legal Education (*Taylor & Francis Ltd*)

J.C.L.P. = Journal of Competition Law & Policy (*OECD Publications Service (Databeuro Ltd)*)

J.C.L.S. = Journal of Corporate Law Studies (*Hart Publishing Ltd*)

J.C.P. = Journal of Consumer Policy (*Kluwer*)

J.C.P.P. = Journal of Civil Practice and Procedure (*S&M/Round Hall*)

J.E.C.L. & P. = Journal of Electronic Commerce Law & Practice (*Butterworth Tolley Publishing*)

J.E.C.L. & Pract. = Journal of European Competition Law & Practice (*OUP*)

J.E.E.P.L. = Journal for European Environmental & Planning Law (*Brill Academic Publishers*)

J.E.L.P. = Journal of Employment Law & Practice (*Butterworth Tolley Publishing*)

J.E.L.S. = Journal of Empirical Legal Studies (*John Wiley & Sons Ltd*)

J.E.P.P. = Journal of European Public Policy (*Taylor & Francis Ltd*)

J.E.R.L. = Journal of Energy & Natural Resources Law (*International Bar Association*)

J.F.C. = Journal of Financial Crime (*Emerald Group Publishing Limited*)

J.F.R. & C. = Journal of Financial Regulation and Compliance (*Emerald Group Publishing Limited*)

J.F.S.M. = Journal of Financial Services Marketing (*Henry Stewart Publications*)

J.G.L.R. = Jersey and Guernsey Law Review (*The Jersey and Guernsey Law Review Ltd*)

J.H.L. = Journal of Housing Law (*S&M*)

J.H.R.E. = Journal of Human Rights and the Environment (*Marston Book Services*)

J.I.A. = Journal of the Institute of Actuaries (*Institute of Actuaries*)

J.I.A.N.L. = Journal of Immigration Asylum and Nationality Law (*Bloomsbury Publishing Plc*)

J.I.B. Law = Journal of International Biotechnology Law (*Walter de Gruyter GmbH & Co. KG*)

J.I.B.L. = Journal of International Banking Law (*S&M/ESC Publishing*)

J.I.B.L.R. = Journal of International Banking Law and Regulation (*S&M/ESC Publishing*)

J.I.B.R. = Journal of International Banking Regulation (*Palgrave Macmillan*)

J.I.C.J. = Journal of International Criminal Justice (*OUP*)

J.I.C.L. = Journal of International Commercial Law (*Ashgate Publishing Ltd*)

J.I.C.L.T. = Journal of International Commercial Law and Technology (*International Association of IT Lawyers*)

J.I.C.M. = Journal of the Institute of Credit Management (*Institute of Credit Management*)

J.I.D.S. = Journal of International Dispute Settlement (*OUP*)

J.I.E.L. = Journal of International Economic Law (*OUP*)

J.I.F.D.L. = Journal of International Franchising & Distribution Law (*Butterworth Tolley Publishing*)

J.I.F.M. = Journal of International Financial Markets (*S&M*)

J.I.L. & C. = Journal of Islamic Law and Culture (*Taylor & Francis Ltd*)

J.I.L.T. = Journal of Information, Law & Technology (*CTI Law Technology Centre*)

J.I.M.F. = Journal of International Money and Finance (*Elsevier*)

J.I.M.L. = Journal of International Maritime Law (*Lawtext Publishing Limited*)

J.I.P.L.P. = Journal of Intellectual Property Law & Practice (*OUP*)

J.I.T.L. & P. = Journal of International Trade Law & Policy (*Emerald Group Publishing Limited*)

J.I.T.T.C.P. = Journal of International Tax, Trust and Corporate Planning (*Jordan & Sons Ltd*)

J.J. = Justice Journal (*Justice*)

J.L.A. = Journal of Legal Analysis (*OUP*)

J.L.E. & O. = Journal of Law, Economics & Organization (*OUP*)

J.L.G.L. = Journal of Local Government Law (*S&M*)

J.L.M &. E. = Journal of Law, Medicine & Ethics (*John Wiley & Sons Ltd*)

J.L.S. = Journal of Legislative Studies (*Taylor & Francis Ltd*)

J.L.S.S. = Journal of the Law Society of Scotland (*The Law Society of Scotland*)

J.M.C.B. = Journal of Money, Credit and Banking (*Ohio State University Press*)

J.M.H.L. = Journal of Mental Health Law (*Northumbria Law Press*)

J.M.L. = Journal of Media Law (*Hart Publishing Ltd*)

J.M.L. & P. = Journal of Media Law and Practice (*Butterworth Tolley Publishing*)

J.M.L.C. = Journal of Money Laundering Control (*Emerald Group Publishing Limited*)

J.N.I. = Journal of Network Industries (*Intersentia*)

J.O. & R. = Journal of Obligations & Remedies (*Northumbria Law Press*)

J.P. = Justice of the Peace & Local Government Law (*Butterworth Tolley Publishing*)

J.P.I. Law = Journal of Personal Injury Law (*S&M*)

J.P.I.L. = Journal of Personal Injury Litigation (*S&M*)

J.P.L. = Journal of Planning & Environment Law (*S&M*)

J.P.M. = Journal of Pensions Management (*Henry Stewart Publications*)

J.P.M. & M. = Journal of Pensions Management & Marketing (*Henry Stewart Publications*)

J.P.N. = Justice of the Peace & Local Government Law (*Butterworth Tolley Publishing*)

J.R. = Judicial Review (*Hart Publishing Ltd*)

J.R. & I. = Journal of Risk and Insurance (*American Risk & Insurance Association Inc*)

J.R.L.S. = Jerusalem Review of Legal Studies (*OUP*)

J.R.S. = Journal of Refugee Studies (*OUP*)

J.S.B.J. = Judicial Studies Board Journal (*OUP*)

J.S.F. = Journal of the Society of Fellows (*Chartered Insurance Institute*)

J.S.I.J. = Judicial Studies Instiutute Journal (*Judicial Studies Institute*)

J.S.S.L. = Journal of Social Security Law (*S&M*)

J.T.C.P. = Journal of International Trust & Corporate Planning (*Jordan & Sons Ltd*)

J.W.B.L. = Journal of Welfare Benefits Law (*Arden Davies Publishing*)

J.W.E.L. & B. = Journal of World Energy Law & Business (*OUP*)

J.W.I.P. = Journal of World Intellectual Property (*John Wiley & Sons Ltd*)

J.W.T. = Journal of World Trade (*Turpin Distribution Serv Ltd*)

J.W.T.L. = Journal of World Trade Law (*Werner Publishing Co Ltd*)

Jersey L.R. = Jersey Law Review (*The Jersey and Guernsey Law Review Ltd*)

Jour. G.M. = Journal of General Management (*Braybrooke Press Ltd*)

Jur. Rev. = Juridical Review (*S&M/W. Green*)

Juris. = Jurisprudence (*Hart Publishing Ltd*)

K.B. = Law Reports Kings Bench (*ICLR*)

K.C.L.J. = Kings College Law Journal (*Hart Publishing Ltd*)

K.H.R.P.L.R. = Kurdish Human Rights Project Legal Review (*Kurdish Human Rights Project*)

K.I.R. = Knights Industrial Reports (*Charles Knight Publishing*)

K.L.J. = King's Law Journal (*Hart Publishing Ltd*)

KIM Legal = Knowledge and Information Management (*Waterlow Legal & Regulatory*)

KM Legal = KM Legal (*Ark Publishing*)

Kemp & Kemp = Kemp & Kemp The Quantum of Damages (*S&M*)

Kemp News = Kemp News (*S&M*)

King's Counsel = King's Counsel (*King's College London*)

Kingston L.R. = Kingston Law Review (*Kingston Polytechnic*)

L & T.R. = Landlord and Tenant Reports (*S&M*)

L&P Comp. EC = Linklaters & Paines Competition EC (*Linklaters*)

L&P E. & B.L.N. = Linklaters & Paines Employment & Benefits Law Newsletter (*Linklaters*)

L&P E.C. Law = Linklaters & Paines European Community Law (*Linklaters*)

L&P F.S. News. = Linklaters & Paines Financial Services Newsfile (*Linklaters*)

L&P I.F. News. = Linklaters & Paines Investment Funds Newsfile (*Linklaters*)

L&P I.M. Rep. = Linklaters & Paines Internal Market Report (*Linklaters*)

L&P I.P.N. = Linklaters & Paines Intellectual Property News (*Linklaters*)

L&P P.L.N. = Linklaters & Paines Property Law Now (*Linklaters*)

L. & F.M.R. = Law & Financial Markets Review (*Hart Publishing Ltd*)

L. & H. = Law & Humanities (*Hart Publishing Ltd*)

L. & T. Review = Landlord & Tenant Review (*S&M*)

L. D'I. = Lettre D'Information (*Geneva Association*)

L. Ex. = Legal Executive (*ILEX Publishing & Advertising Services Ltd*)

L.A.L. = Local Authority Law (*S&M*)

L.B.E.B. = Lloyds Bank Economic Bulletin (*Lloyd's Bank Plc*)

L.B.R. = Law Business Review (*Butterworths Tolley Publishing*)

L.C. & A.I. = Law, Computers & Artificial Intelligence (*Taylor & Francis Ltd*)

L.C. News = Law Centres News (*Law Centres Federation*)

L.C.B. = Legal Compliance Bulletin (*Law Society Publishing*)

L.D. = Legal Director (*Legal Week Global Media*)

L.E. = Lawyers' Europe (*The Journal of the Law Society's European Group*)

L.F. = Litigation Funding (*Law Society Publishing*)

L.G. Rev. = Local Government Review (*Butterworth Tolley Publishing*)

L.G. Review = Local Government Review (*First Law*)

L.G. and L. = Local Government and Law (*Informa Publishing Group Ltd*)

L.G.C. = Local Government Chronicle (*Local Government Chronicle Ltd*)

L.G.C. Law & Admin. = Local Government Chronicle Law & Administration (*Local Government Chronicle Ltd*)

L.G.D. = Law, Social Justice & Global Development (*Electronic Law Journals*)

L.G.I. = Law Gazette International (*Law Society Services Ltd*)

L.G.L.R. = Local Government Law Reports (*S&M*)

L.G.R. = Local Government Reports (*Charles Knight Publishing*)

L.G.R. Rep. = Local Government Review Reports (*Barry Rose Law Periodicals*)

L.I.E.I. = Legal Issues of European Integration (*Turpin Distribution Serv Ltd*)

L.I.I. = Life Insurance International (*L.L.P Ltd*)

L.I.M. = Legal Information Management (*CUP*)

L.I.T. = Law, Innovation and Technology (*Hart Publishing Ltd*)

L.J.I.L. = Leiden Journal of International Law (*CUP*)

L.L.I.D. = Lloyd's List Insurance Day (*Informa Publishing Group Ltd*)

L.L.R. = London Law Review (*London Law Review*)

L.M.C.L.Q. = Lloyd's Maritime and Commercial Law Quarterly (*Informa Publishing Group Ltd*)

L.M.E.L.R. = Land Management and Environmental Law Report (*Chancery Law Publishing Ltd*)

L.M.L.N. = Lloyd's Maritime Law Newsletter (*Informa Publishing Group Ltd*)

L.M.N. = London Market Newsletter (*Informa Publishing Group Ltd*)

L.P. & R. = Law, Probability & Risk (*OUP*)

L.P.I.C.T. = Law & Practice of International Courts and Tribunals (*Martinus Nijhoff Publishers*)

L.Q.R. = Law Quarterly Review (*S&M*)

L.R. = Licensing Review (*Benedict Books*)

L.R. & I. = Liability Risk & Insurance (*Informa Publishing Group Ltd*)

L.R.L.R. = Lloyd's Reinsurance Law Reports (*LLP*)

L.S. = Legal Studies (*John Wiley & Sons Ltd*)

L.S. & P. = Law, Science and Policy (*A B Academic Publishers*)

L.S.G. = Law Society's Gazette (*The Law Society's Hall*)

L.T. = Legal Theory (*CUP*)

L.T.J. = Law Technology Journal (*CTI Law Technology Centre*)

L.W.D. EC News. = Lovell White Durrant EC Newsletter (*Lovell White Durrant*)

L.W.D. L.A.P. = Lovell White Durrant Legal Advice on Pensions (*Lovell White Durrant*)

Law = Law (*The Law*)

Law & Crit. = Law and Critique (*Springer*)

Law & Just. = Law & Justice (*Edmund Plowden Trust*)

Law & Phil. = Law & Philosophy (*Springer*)

Law & Pol. = Law & Policy (*John Wiley & Sons Ltd*)

Law & Tax R. = Law & Tax Review (*S&M*)

Law Lib. = Law Librarian (*S&M*)

Law Mag. = Law Magazine (*S&M*)

Law Teach. = Law Teacher (*Taylor & Francis Ltd*)

Law for Bus. = Law for Business (*Wallace Publishing Ltd*)

Law. in Eur. = Lawyers in Europe (*Lawyers in Europe Ltd*)

Lawyer = Lawyer (*Centaur Communications Group*)

Lawyer 2B = Lawyer 2B (*Centaur Communications Group*)

Leg. = Legisprudence (*Hart Publishing Ltd*)

Legal Action = Legal Action (*Legal Action Group*)

Legal Bus. = Legal Business (*Legalease Ltd*)

Legal Ethics = Legal Ethics (*Hart Publishing Ltd*)

Legal I.E.I. = Legal Issues of Economic Integration (*Kluwer*)

Legal IT = Legal IT (*Legal Week Global Media*)

Legal M. = Legal Marketing (*Ark Publishing*)

Legal T.J. = Legal Technology Journal (*Legalease Ltd*)

Legal Times = Legal Times (*Legalease Ltd*)

Legal Week = Legal Week (*Incisive Financial Publishing Ltd*)

Link AWS = Link Association of Women Solicitors (*Association of Women Solicitors*)

Lit. = Litigation (*Butterworth Tolley Publishing*)

Lit. L. = Litigation Letter (*Informa Publishing Group Ltd*)

Litigator = Litigator (*S&M*)

Liverpool L.R. = Liverpool Law Review (*Springer*)

Ll. Ins. Int. = Lloyd's Insurance International (*Lloyd's of London Press Inc*)

Ll. Log = Lloyds Log (*Informa Publishing Group Ltd*)

Ll. News. = Lloyd's of London Newsletter (*Informa Publishing Group Ltd*)

Lloyd's List = Lloyd's List (*Informa Publishing Group Ltd*)

Lloyd's Rep. = Lloyd's Law Reports (*Informa Publishing Group Ltd*)

Lloyd's Rep. Bank. = Lloyd's Law Reports Banking (*Informa Publishing Group Ltd*)

Lloyd's Rep. I.R. = Lloyd's Law Reports Insurance & Reinsurance (*Informa Publishing Group Ltd*)

Lloyd's Rep. Med. = Lloyd's Law Reports Medical (*Informa Publishing Group Ltd*)

Lloyd's Rep. P.N. = Lloyd's Law Reports Professional Negligence (*Informa Publishing Group Ltd*)

M. & A. Ins. Rep. = Marine & Aviation Insurance Report (*Informa Publishing Group Ltd*)

M. Advice = Money Advice (*Money Advice Association*)

M. Advocate = Maritime Advocate (*Merlin Legal Publishing*)

M. Bulletin = Mercer Bulletin European Newsletter (*William M Mercer Ltd*)

M. Direct = Mercer Direct European Communication Newsletter (*William M Mercer Ltd*)

M. EC News. = Mercer European Community Newsletter (*William M Mercer Ltd*)

M. Euro. News = Mercer European News (*William M Mercer Ltd*)

M. Man. = Money Management (*Financial Times Finance*)

M. Prospect = Mercer Prospect Eastern European Newsletter (*William M Mercer Ltd*)

M. Review = Mercer Review (*William M Mercer Ltd*)

M. Transatlantic = Mercer Transatlantic (*William M Mercer Ltd*)

M. Update = Mercer Update (*William M Mercer Ltd*)

M. World = Media World (*Informa Publishing Group Ltd*)

M.A. = Management Accounting (*Chartered Institute Management Accountants*)

M.A.L.Q.R. = Model Arbitration Law Quarterly Reports (*Simmonds & Hill Publishing Ltd*)

M.C.P. = Magistrates' Courts Practice (*XPL Publishing*)

M.D.U. Jour. = Medical Defence Union Journal (*The Medical Defence Union*)

M.E.C.L.R. = Middle East Commercial Law Review (*S&M/ESC Publishing*)

M.F.G. = Mortgage Finance Gazette (*Metropolis International Group Ltd*)

M.F.S. = Managing for Success (*Law Management Section/The Law Society*)

M.I.M. = Motor Insurance Market (*Informa Publishing Group Ltd*)

M.I.P. = Managing Intellectual Property (*Euromoney Institutional Investor Plc*)

M.J. = Municipal Journal (*Hemming Information Services*)

M.J.L.S. = Mountbatten Journal of Legal Studies (*Southampton Institute*)

M.L.B. = Manx Law Bulletin (*Attorney General's Chambers*)

M.L.J.I. = Medico-Legal Journal of Ireland (*S&M/Round Hall*)

M.L.N. = Media Lawyer Newsletter (*The Press Association*)

M.L.R. = Modern Law Review (*John Wiley & Sons Ltd*)

M.M. = Money Marketing (*Centaur Communications Group*)

M.P. = Managing Partner (*Wilmington Publishing and Information Ltd*)

M.R. = Media Review (*SJ Berwin & Co*)

M.R.D.B. = Monthly Report Deutsche Bundesbank (*Deutshe Bundesbank*)

M.R.I. = Maritime Risk International (*Informa Publishing Group Ltd*)

M.T. & F. = Matrimonial Tax & Finance (*Tax and Financial Publishing*)

M.W. = Money Week (*EMAP Communications*)

Maastricht J. = Maastricht Journal of European and Comparative Law (*Intersentia NV*)

Magistrate = Magistrate (*Magistrates Association*)

Man. L. = Managerial Law (*MCB University Press Ltd*)

Marine I.R. = Marine Insurance Report (*Informa Publishing Group Ltd*)

Masons C.L.R. = Masons Computer Law Reports (*Mason's Solicitor*)

McK. E.B.B. = McKenna Employment Benefits Bulletin (*McKenna & Co*)

McK. Env. L.B. = McKenna Environmental Law Bulletin (*Cameron McKenna & Co*)

McK. Euro. R. = McKenna European Review (*McKenna & Co*)

McK. Law Let. = McKenna Law Letter (*McKenna & Co*)

McK. P.B. = McKenna Pension Brief (*McKenna & Co*)

McK. P.L.B. = McKenna Pension Law Bulletin (*McKenna & Co*)

Med. L. Int. = Medical Law International (*Sage Publications Ltd*)

Med. L. Mon. = Medical Law Monitor (*Informa Publishing Group Ltd*)

Med. L. Rev. = Medical Law Review (*OUP*)

Med. L.R. = Medical Law Reports (*Informa Publishing Group Ltd*)

Med. Leg. J. = Medico-Legal Journal (*Sage Publications Ltd*)

Med. Lit. = Medical Litigation (*Medical Litigation Strategies*)

Med. Sci. Law = Medicine, Science & the Law (*The Royal Society of Medicine Press*)

Money L.B. = Money Laundering Bulletin (*Informa Publishing Group Ltd*)

Mortgage M. = Mortgage Monthly (*BSA CML Publication*)

N.E.G.R.I.E. = Newsletter of the European Group of Risk and Insurance Economists (*Geneva Association*)

N.I.C. & L.L.J. = Northern Ireland Conveyancing and Land Law Journal (*SLS Legal Publications (NI)*)

N.I.E.R. = National Institute of Economic Review (*The National Institute of Economic Review*)

N.I.L. Rev. = Netherlands International Law Review (*CUP*)

N.I.L.Q. = Northern Ireland Legal Quarterly (*School of Law*)

N.I.L.R. = Northern Ireland Law Reports (*Butterworth Tolley Publishing*)

N.J.I.L. = Nordic Journal of International Law (*Martinus Nijhoff Publishers*)

N.L.J. = New Law Journal (*Butterworths Tolley Publishing*)

N.L.T. = Northern Law Today (*Northern Law Today*)

N.N. EC News = Nabarro Nathanson EC News (*Nabarro Nathanson*)

N.N.P.D. = Nabarro Nathanson The Pension Dimension (*Nabarro Nathanson*)

N.N.R. = Nabarro Nathanson Resource (*Nabarro Nathanson*)

N.P.C. = New Property Cases (*New Property Cases Ltd*)

N.Q.H.R. = Netherlands Quarterly of Human Rights (*Intersentia NV*)

N.R. EC Init. = Norton Rose M5 Group EC Initiative (*Norton Rose M5 Group*)

N.R. EU Init. = Norton Rose M5 Group EU Initiative (*Norton Rose M5 Group*)

N.R.G.Q. = Netherlands Reinsurance Group Quarterly (*Nederlandse Reassurantie Groep nv*)

N.S.A.I.L. = Non-State Actors and International Law (*Martinus Nijhoff Publishers*)

N.W.B.Q.R. = National Westminster Bank Quarterly Review (*National Westminster Bank Plc*)

Natwest I.T.B. = National Westminster Bank International Trade Bulletin (*National Westminster Bank*)

Nott. L.J. = Nottingham Law Journal (*Nottingham Law School*)

O. & I.T. Rev. = Offshore & International Taxation Review (*Key Haven Publications Plc*)

O.D. and I.L. = Ocean Development and International Law (*Taylor & Francis Ltd*)

O.G.J.F.I. = Open Government: A Journal on Freedom of Information (*Liverpool John Moores University*)

O.G.L.T.R. = Oil & Gas Law & Taxation Review (*S&M/ESC Publishing*)

O.H.R. = Occupational Health Review (*Eclipse/Butterworth Tolley Publishing*)

O.J.L.R. = Oxford Journal of Law and Religion (*OUP*)

O.J.L.S. = Oxford Journal of Legal Studies (*OUP*)

O.L.S. = One Lime Street (*Informa Publishing Group Ltd*)

O.N. = Oftel News (*Oftel Update*)

O.P.L.R. = Occupational Pensions Law Reports (*Eclipse/Butterworth Tolley Publishing*)

O.R. & C. = OpRisk & Compliance (*Incisive Financial Publishing Ltd*)

O.R. & R. = Operational Risk & Regulation (*Incisive Media Plc*)

O.S.S. Bull. = Office for the Supervision of Solicitors Bulletin (*The Law Society's Gazette*)

O.T.P.R. = Offshore Tax Planning Review (*Key Haven Publications Plc*)

O.T.R. = Offshore Tax Planning Review (*Key Haven Publications Plc*)

O.U.C.L.J. = Oxford University Commonwealth Law Journal (*Hart Publishing Ltd*)

Observer = OECD Observer (*Databeuro Ltd*)

Occ. Pen. = Occupational Pensions (*Eclipse/Butterworth Tolley Publishing*)

Offshore Red = Offshore Red (*ClearView Financial Media Ltd*)

P & I Int. = P & I International (*Informa Publishing Group Ltd*)

P. & C.R. = Property, Planning and Compensation Reports (*S&M*)

P. & D.P. = Privacy & Data Protection (*Privacy & Data Protection*)

P. & E.B. = Pensions & Employee Benefits (*Butterworth Tolley Publishing*)

P. & M.I.L.L. = Personal and Medical Injuries Law Letter (*Informa Publishing Group Ltd*)

P. & O.J. = Procurement and Outsourcing Journal (*Legalease Ltd*)

P. & P. = Practice and Procedure (*S&M/Round Hall*)

P. & S. = Punishment & Society (*Sage Publications Ltd*)

P. Injury = Personal Injury (EMIS) (*XPL Publishing*)

P. Int. = Portfolio International (*MSM International*)

P. Treas. = Public Treasurer (*Local Government Chronicle Ltd*)

P. Week = Property Week (*CMP Information Ltd*)

P.A. = Product Adviser (*Financial Times Finance*)

P.A.B.B. = Pay And Benefits Bulletin (*Butterworth Tolley Publishing*)

P.A.D. = Planning Appeal Decisions (*S&M*)

P.B. = Professional Broking (*Timothy Benn Publishing Ltd*)

P.C. & L. = Psychology, Crime & Law (*Taylor & Francis Ltd*)

P.C.A. = Private Client Adviser (*Wilmington Publishing and Information Ltd*)

P.C.B. = Private Client Business (*S&M*)

P.C.L.B. = Practitioners' Child Law Bulletin (*S&M*)

P.C.P. = Private Client Practitioner (*PAM Insight Ltd*)

P.C.R. = Proceeds of Crime Review (*John Edward Law*)

P.E.B.L. = Perspectives on European Business Law (*European Perspectives Publicatons Ltd*)

P.E.L.B. = Planning and Environmental Law Bulletin (*S&M*)

P.F. = Property Finance (*Informa Publishing Group Ltd*)

P.F. & D. = Property Finance & Development (*Informa Publishing Group Ltd*)

P.H.B. = Parliament House Book (*S&M/W. Green*)

P.I. = Personal Injury (Wiley) (*John Wiley & Sons Ltd*)

P.I. Comp. = Personal Injury Compensation (*Informa Publishing Group Ltd*)

P.I.B.U.L.J. = Personal Injury Brief Update Law Journal (*Law Brief Publishing Ltd*)

P.I.C. = Palmer's In Company (*S&M*)

P.I.J. = Planning Inspectorate Journal (*The Planning Inspectorate*)

P.I.L.J. = Personal Injury Law Journal (*Legalease Ltd*)

P.I.L.M.R. = Personal Injury Law and Medical Review (*Butterworth Tolley Publishing*)

P.I.N. = Personal Injury Newsletter (*Butterworth Tolley Publishing*)

P.I.P. = Property in Practice (*Property Section/The Law Society*)

P.I.Q.R. = Personal Injuries and Quantum Reports (*S&M*)

P.L. = Public Law (*S&M*)

P.L. & B.I.N. = Privacy Laws & Business International Newsletter (*Privacy Laws & Business*)

P.L. & B.U.K.N. = Privacy Laws & Business United Kingdom Newsletter (*Privacy Laws & Business*)

P.L. Today = Purchasing Law Today (*Richard Lawson*)

P.L.B. = Property Law Bulletin (S&M) (*S&M*)

P.L.C. = Practical Law Companies (*Practical Law Company Ltd*)

P.L.C.R. = Planning Law Case Reports (*S&M*)

P.L.I. = Product Liability International (*Informa Publishing Group Ltd*)

P.L.J. = Property Law Journal (*Legalease Ltd*)

P.L.N. = Property Law Newsletter (*Butterworth Tolley Publishing*)

P.L.R. = Estates Gazette Planning Law Reports (*Estates Gazette*)

P.L.T. = Professional Liability Today (*Informa Publishing Group Ltd*)

P.L.U. = Pensions Law Update (*Ellison Westhorp Publications*)

P.M. = Pensions Management (*Financial Times Finance*)

P.N. = Professional Negligence (*Bloomsbury Publishing Plc*)

P.N. & L. = Professional Negligence & Liability (*CLT Publishing*)

P.N.L.R. = Professional Negligence and Liability Reports (*S&M*)

P.P. = Professional Pensions (*MSM International Ltd*)

P.P. & D. = Practical Planning & Development (*CLT Publishing*)

P.P.L. = Practical Planning Law (*CLT Publishing*)

P.P.L.R. = Public Procurement Law Review (*S&M*)

P.P.M. = Professional Practice Management (*Informa Publishing Group Ltd*)

P.R. = Property Review (*Eclipse/Butterworth Tolley Publishing*)

P.S. = Pensions Systems (*Mitre House Publishing Ltd*)

P.S.E.L.J. = Public Sector Employment Law Journal (*Legalease Ltd*)

P.S.P. = Police Station Practice (*XPL Publishing*)

P.S.T. = Pension Scheme Trustee (*Informa Publishing Group Ltd*)

P.T. = Pensions Today (*Informa Publishing Group Ltd*)

P.T.P.R. = Personal Tax Planning Review (*Key Haven Publications Plc*)

P.V. = Property Valuer (*Irish Auctioneers & Valuers Institute*)

P.W. = Patent World (*Informa Publishing Group Ltd*)

PS = Private Client Section (*Private Client Section/The Law Society*)

Paisner C.U. = Paisner Company Update (*Paisner & Co*)

Paisner E.B. = Paisner European Bulletin (*Paisner & Co*)

Paisner E.U. = Paisner Environment Update (*Paisner & Co*)

Paisner I.P.B. = Paisner Intellectual Property Briefing (*Paisner & Co*)

Palmer's C.L. = Palmer's Company Law (*S&M*)

Parl. Aff. = Parliamentary Affairs (*OUP*)

Pay Mag. = Pay Magazine (*Wolters Kluwer (UK) Ltd*)

Pen. = Pensions (*Palgrave Macmillan*)

Pen. L.R. = Pensions Law Reports (*Incomes Data Services Ltd*)

Pen. Law. = Pension Lawyer (*Association of Penion Lawyers*)

Pen. Week = Pensions Week (*Financial Times Finance*)

Pen. World = Pensions World (*Butterworth Tolley Publishing*)

Pers. Today = Personnel Today (*Reed Business Information Ltd*)

Pharm. L.I. = Pharmaceutical Law Insight (*Informa Publishing Group Ltd*)

Pl. Sav. = Planned Savings (*EMAP Media Ltd*)

Pol. J. = Police Journal (*Vathek Publishing*)

Policing = Policing (*Police Review Publishing Co Ltd*)

Policing T. = Policing Today (*Police Review Publishing Co Ltd*)

Post Mag. = Post Magazine (*Incisive Media Plc*)

Pract. Today = Practice Today (*S&M*)

Pract. VAT = Practical VAT (*Butterworth Tolley Publishing*)

Press R. = Press Releases (*Centre Office of Information*)

Prison Serv. J. = Prison Service Journal (*Governor, H.M. Prison Leyhill*)

Probat. J. = Probation Journal (*Sage Publications Ltd*)

Prof. L. = Professional Lawyer (*Chancery Law Publishing Ltd*)

Progres = Progres (*Geneva Association*)

Prop. L.B. = Property Law Bulletin (W Green) (*S&M/W. Green*)

Prop. S. = Property Service (*XPL Publishing*)

Prospect = Prospect (*Life Insurance Association*)

Pub. Law Bull. = Public Law Bulletin (*Manchester Metropolitan University*)

Public F. = Public Finance (*FSF Limited*)

Q.A. = Quarterly Account (*Institute of Money Advisers*)

Q.B. = Law Reports Queen's Bench (*ICLR*)

Q.M.J.I.P. = Queen Mary Journal of Intellectual Property (*Marston Book Services*)

Q.R. = Quantum Reports (*S&M*)

Q.R.T.L. = Quarterly Review of Tort Law (*Clarus Press*)

Quantum = Quantum (*S&M*)

R. & B.C.P. = Renton & Brown's Criminal Procedure (*S&M/W. Green*)

R. & B.C.P.L. = Renton & Brown's Criminal Procedure Legislation (*S&M/W. Green*)

R. & B.S.O. = Renton & Brown's Statutory Offences (*S&M/W. Green*)

R.A. = Rating Appeals (*Rating Publishers Ltd*)

R.A.D.I.C. = African Journal of International and Comparative Law (*African Society of International and Comparative Law*)

R.A.L.Q. = Receivers, Administrators and Liquidators Quarterly (*Key Haven Publications Plc*)

R.E.C.I.E.L. = Review of European Community and International Environmental Law (*John Wiley & Sons Ltd*)

R.E.L.P. = Renewable Energy Law and Policy Review (*Lexxion Verlagsgesellschaft mbH*)

R.L.E.J.P. = Research in Law and Economics: A Journal of Policy (*Emerald Group Publishing Limited*)

R.L.R. = Restitution Law Review (*Marenex Productions*)

R.M.B. = Risk Management Bulletin (*Ark Publishing*)

R.M.H.L. = Review of Mental Health Law (*Arden Davies Publishing*)

R.M.R. = Reinsurance Market Report (*Informa Publishing Group Ltd*)

R.P.C. = Reports of Patent, Design and Trade Mark Cases (*S&M*)

R.P.R.M. = Research Programme on Risk Management (*Geneva Association*)

R.Q. = Reinsurance Quarterly (*Evandale Publishing Co Ltd*)

R.R.L.R. = Rent Review & Lease Renewal (*Informa Publishing Group Ltd*)

R.S.I. = Reinsurance Security Insider (*Evandale Publishing Co Ltd*)

R.T.I. = Road Traffic Indicator (*S&M*)

R.T.R. = Road Traffic Reports (*S&M*)

R.V.R. = Rating and Valuation Reporter (*Rating Publishers Ltd*)

R.W.B. = Rights Workers Bulletin (*NACAB*)

R.W.L.R. = Rights of Way Law Review (*Rights of Way Law Review*)

ROW Bulletin = Rights Of Women Bulletin (*Rights Of Women*)

Ratio Juris = Ratio Juris (*John Wiley & Sons Ltd*)

Re Re. = Re Report (*Evandale Publishing Co Ltd*)

Re. L.R. = Reinsurance Law Reports (*Informa Publishing Group Ltd*)

Reactions = Reactions (*Euromoney Institutional Investor Plc*)

Recovery = Recovery (*Association of Business Recovery Professionals*)

Regulator = Regulator & Professional Conduct Quarterly (*Butterworth Tolley Publishing*)

Reins. = Reinsurance (*Incisive Media Plc*)

Rep. B. = Reparation Bulletin (*S&M/W. Green*)

Rep. L.R. = Reparation Law Reports (*S&M/W. Green*)

Res Publica = Res Publica (*Springer*)

Res. B. = Home Office Research Bulletin (*Home Office Research & Statistics Department*)

Resolver = The Resolver (*Chartered Institute of Arbitrators*)

Rev. = The Review (*Resolution*)

Rev. C.E.E. Law = Review of Central and East European Law (*Martinus Nijhoff Publishers*)

Revenue = Revenue (*S&M*)

Review = Review (*Informa Publishing Group Ltd*)

Risk M.R. = Risk Management Reports (*Seawrack Press, Inc.*)

Risk Man. = Risk Management (*Risk Management Society Publishing Inc*)

Risk Update = Risk Update (*Informa Publishing Group Ltd*)

Road L. = Road Law (*Butterworth Tolley Publishing*)

Road L.R. = Road Law Reports (*Butterworth Tolley Publishing*)

Road Law = Road Law and Road Law Reports (*Butterworth Tolley Publishing*)

S. & C.L. = Sports and Character Licensing (*Informa Publishing Group Ltd*)

S. & L.J. = Sport and the Law Journal (*British Association for Sport and Law*)

S. & L.S. = Social & Legal Studies (*Sage Publications Ltd*)

S. & T.I. = Shipping & Transport International (*Guthrum House Ltd*)

S. & T.L.I. = Shipping & Transport Lawyer International (*Guthrum House Ltd*)

S. News = Sentencing News (*S&M*)

TABLE OF ABBREVIATIONS

S.B. = Scottish Banker (*The Chartered Institute of Bankers in Scotland*)
S.B.T. & F. = Small Business Tax & Finance (*Cyan Publishing Services*)
S.C. = Session Cases (*S&M/W. Green*)
S.C.A.L. & P. = Scottish Constitutional and Administrative Law & Practice (*XPL Publishing*)
S.C.C.R. = Scottish Criminal Case Reports (*The Law Society of Scotland*)
S.C.L. = Scottish Criminal Law (*S&M/W. Green*)
S.C.L. Rev. = Scottish Construction Law Review (*S&M/W. Green*)
S.C.L.R. = Scottish Civil Law Reports (*The Law Society of Scotland*)
S.C.L.T. = Social Care Law Today (*Arden Davies Publishing*)
S.C.P. = Supreme Court Practice, The (*S&M*)
S.C.P. News = Supreme Court Practice News (*S&M*)
S.E.G.J. = Law Society Solicitors' European Group Journal (*Butterworth Tolley Publishing*)
S.F.L.L. = Scottish Family Law Legislation (*S&M/W. Green*)
S.H.E. & P.G. = Stephenson Harwood Employment and Pensions Group (*Stephenson Harwood*)
S.H.R.J. = Scottish Human Rights Journal (*S&M/W. Green*)
S.I. = Statutory Instruments (*TSO*)
S.I.R. = Space Insurance Report (*Informa Publishing Group Ltd*)
S.J. = Solicitors Journal (*Waterlow Legal & Regulatory*)
S.J.L.B. = Solicitors Journal LawBrief (*Waterlow Legal & Regulatory*)
S.L. & F. = Sports Law & Finance (*Informa Publishing Group Ltd*)
S.L. Rev. = Student Law Review (*Routledge-Cavendish*)
S.L.A. & P. = Sports Law Administration & Practice (*Ivy House Sports Law Publications Ltd*)
S.L.B. = Sports Law Bulletin (*Anglia Sports Law Research Centre*)
S.L.C.R. = Scottish Land Court Reports (*The Law Society of Scotland*)
S.L.G. = Scottish Law Gazette (*Scottish Law Agents Society*)
S.L.L.P. = Scottish Licensing Law and Practice (*Licensing Services Ltd*)
S.L.P.Q. = Scottish Law & Practice Quarterly (*Butterworth Tolley Publishing*)
S.L.T. = Scots Law Times (*S&M/W. Green*)
S.M.M. = Single Market Monitor (*Butterworth Tolley Publishing*)
S.P.C.L.R. = Scottish Private Client Law Review (*S&M/W. Green*)
S.P.E.L. = Scottish Planning and Environmental Law (*IDOX Information Solutions Ltd*)
S.P.L.P. = Scottish Planning Law & Practice (*IDOX Information Services*)
S.P.L.R. = Scottish Parliament Law Review (*S&M/W. Green*)
S.P.T.L. Reporter = Society of Public Teachers of Law Reporter (*OUP*)
S.S.L.R. = Southampton Student Law Review (*University of Southampton*)
S.T.C. = Simon's Tax Cases (*Butterworth Tolley Publishing*)
S.T.L. = Shipping and Trade Law (*Informa Publishing Group Ltd*)
S.W.T.I. = Simon's Weekly Tax Intelligence (*Butterworth Tolley Publishing*)
SCOLAG = SCOLAG (*Scottish Legal Action Group*)
SCRIPT-ed = SCRIPT-ed (*University of Edinburgh*)

STEP Journal = The STEP Journal (*Barker Brooks Media Ltd*)
Sigma = Sigma (*Swiss Reinsurance Company*)
Soc. L. = Socialist Lawyer (*Haldane Society of Socialist Lawyers*)
Sol. = Solutions (*Dispute Resolution Section/The Law Society*)
Stat. L.R. = Statute Law Review (*OUP*)
Sudebnik = Sudebnik (*Wildy & Sons Ltd*)

T. & E.P. = Trust & Estates Practitioner (*Tru-Est Limited*)
T. & E.T.J. = Trusts and Estates Tax Journal (*Legalease Ltd*)
T. & T. = Trusts & Trustees (*OUP*)
T. Sol. = Today's Solicitor (*S&M*)
T.A.Q. = The Aviation Quarterly (*Informa Publishing Group Ltd*)
T.B. = Technical Bulletin (*Association of Business Recovery Professionals*)
T.B.S.P.I. = Technical Bulletin of the Society of Practitioners of Insolvency (*Association of Business Recovery Professionals*)
T.C. = Tax Cases (*TSO*)
T.C.L.R. = Technology and Construction Law Reports (*S&M*)
T.E.L. & P. = Tolley's Employment Law & Practice (*Butterworth Tolley Publishing*)
T.E.L. & T.J. = Trusts and Estates Law & Tax Journal (*Legalease Ltd*)
T.E.L.J. = Technology and Entertainment Law Journal (*S&M/Round Hall*)
T.E.L.L. = Tolley's Employment Law-Line (*Butterworth Tolley Publishing*)
T.F.A. = Transactions of the Faculty of Actuaries (*Faculty of Actuaries*)
T.I.A. = Troubled Insurer Alert (*Evandale Publishing Co Ltd*)
T.I.J.M.C.L. = The International Journal of Marine & Coastal Law (*Martinus Nijhoff Publishers*)
T.K.B.E.L.I.S. = Turner Kenneth Brown European Legal Information Service (*Turner Kenneth Brown*)
T.L. & P. = Trust Law & Practice (*Cass*)
T.L.J. = Travel Law Journal (*The Travel Law Centre*)
T.L.P. = Transport Law & Policy (*The Waterfront Partnership*)
T.L.T. = Telecoms Law Today (*Informa Publishing Group Ltd*)
T.M.I.F. = Tax Management International Forum (*BNA International Inc*)
T.N.I.B. = Tolley's National Insurance Brief (*Butterworth Tolley Publishing*)
T.O.C. = Transnational Organized Crime (*Cass*)
T.O.T.R. = Tolley's Overseas Tax Reporter (*Butterworth Tolley Publishing*)
T.P.A. & A. = Tolley's Practical Audit & Accounting (*Butterworth Tolley Publishing*)
T.P.H. = Towers Perrin Headlines (*Towers Perrin*)
T.P.I. e-commerce = Tax Planning International e-commerce (*BNA International Inc*)
T.P.I.A.P.F. = Tax Planning International Asia-Pacific Focus (*BNA International Inc*)
T.P.I.E.U.F. = Tax Planning International European Union Focus (*BNA International Inc*)
T.P.I.I.T. = Tax Planning International Indirect Taxes (*BNA International Inc*)
T.P.I.J. = Transfer Pricing International Journal (*BNA International Inc*)
T.P.I.R. = Tax Planning International Review (*BNA International Inc*)
T.P.I.T.P. = Tax Planning International Transfer Pricing (*BNA International Inc*)

TABLE OF ABBREVIATIONS

T.P.I.U. = Towers Perrin International Update (*Towers Perrin*)

T.P.N. = Tolley's Practical NIC (*Butterworth Tolley Publishing*)

T.P.N.N. = Tolley's Practical NIC Newsletter (*Butterworth Tolley Publishing*)

T.P.N.S. = Tolley's Practical NIC Service (*Butterworth Tolley Publishing*)

T.P.T. = Tolley's Practical Tax (*Butterworth Tolley Publishing*)

T.P.T.N. = Tolley's Practical Tax Newsletter (*Butterworth Tolley Publishing*)

T.P.T.S. = Tolley's Practical Tax Service (*Butterworth Tolley Publishing*)

T.P.U. = Towers Perrin Update (*Towers Perrin*)

T.P.V. = Tolley's Practical VAT (*Butterworth Tolley Publishing*)

T.P.V.N. = Tolley's Practical VAT Newsletter (*Butterworth Tolley Publishing*)

T.P.V.S. = Tolley's Practical VAT Service (*Butterworth Tolley Publishing*)

T.Q.R. = Trust Quarterly Review (*Barker Brooks Media Ltd*)

T.T.I. = Tolley's Tax Investigation (*Butterworth Tolley Publishing*)

TW. = Trademark World (*Informa Publishing Group Ltd*)

TACT Review = The Association of Corporate Trustees Review (*The Association of Corporate Trustees*)

Tax & Inv. = Tax and Investment (*Tax & Financial Publishing*)

Tax A. = Tax Adviser (*Butterworth Tolley Publishing*)

Tax B. = Tax Briefing (*Office of the Revenue Commissioners*)

Tax Bus. = Tax Business (*Legalease Ltd*)

Tax C. = Tax Commentary (*Incorporated Law Society of Ireland*)

Tax J. = Tax Journal (*Butterworth Tolley Publishing*)

Tax P.N. = Tax Practice Notes (*Incorporated Law Society of Ireland*)

Tax. = Taxation (*Butterworth Tolley Publishing*)

Tax. Int. = Taxation International (*Butterworth Tolley Publishing*)

Tax. P. = Taxation Practitioner (*The Chartered Institute of Taxation*)

Taxline = Taxline (*ICAEW*)

The Sentence = The Sentence (*Sentencing Guidelines Secretariat*)

Theo. Crim. = Theoretical Criminology (*Sage Publications Ltd*)

Tort & Ins. L.J. = Tort and Insurance Law Journal (*Tort and Insurance Practice Section*)

Tort. L.R. = Tort Law Review (*S&M/ESC Publishing*)

Tr. & Est. = Trusts & Estates (*Informa Publishing Group Ltd*)

Tr. L.R. = Trading Law Reports (*Butterworth Tolley Publishing*)

Tr. Law = Trading Law & Trading Law Reports (*Butterworth Tolley Publishing*)

Trad. L. = Trading Law (*Barry Rose Law Periodicals*)

Trans. L. & P. = Transport Law & Policy (*The Waterfront Partnership*)

Trans. L.T. = Transnational Legal Theory (*Hart Publishing Ltd*)

Trent L.J. = Trent Law Journal (*Nottingham Law School*)

Tribunals = Tribunals (*Judicial Studies Board*)

Tru. & E.L.J. = Trusts & Estates Law Journal (*Legalease Ltd*)

Tru. L.I. = Trust Law International (*Bloomsbury Publishing Plc*)

Trustee = Trustee (*MSM International Ltd*)

U.K. Ins. Broker = UK Insurance Broker (*Institute of Insurance Broker Publication Ltd*)

U.K.C.L.R. = UK Competition Law Reports (*Jordan & Sons Ltd*)

U.K.H.R.R. = United Kingdom Human Rights Reports (*Jordan & Sons Ltd*)

U.L.R. = Utilities Law Review (*Lawtext Publishing Limited*)

UCELNET = Universities and Colleges Education Law Network (*University of Stirling*)

UCL J.L. and J. = UCL Journal of Law and Jurisprudence (*University College London*)

UCL Juris. Rev. = UCL Jurisprudence Review (*University College London*)

UK Prac. Dir. = UK Practice Directions (*TSO*)

UK Pre. Pro. = UK Preaction Protocols (*TSO*)

Uniform L.R. = Uniform Law Review (*UNIDROIT*)

V. & D.R. = Value Added Tax and Duties Tribunals Reports (*TSO*)

V.A.T.T.R. = Value Added Tax Tribunal Reports (*TSO*)

VAT Dig. = VAT Digest (*Bloomsbury Publishing Plc*)

VAT Int. = VAT Intelligence (*Watchfield Publishing Ltd*)

VAT Plan. = VAT Planning (*Butterworth Tolley Publishing*)

W. Comp. = World Competition (*Turpin Distribution Serv Ltd*)

W.B. = Welfare Benefits (*XPL Publishing*)

W.C.R.R. = World Communications Regulation Report (*BNA International Inc*)

W.D.P.R. = World Data Protection Report (*BNA International Inc*)

W.E.C. & I.P.R. = World E-Commerce & IP Report (*BNA International Inc*)

W.F.S.B. = World Fire Statistics Bulletin (*Geneva Association*)

W.I. Rep. = World Insurance Report (*Financial Times Finance*)

W.I.C.R. = World Insurance Corporate Report (*Financial Times Finance*)

W.I.P.O.J. = WIPO Journal (*Sweet and Maxwell*)

W.I.P.R. = World Intellectual Property Report (*BNA International Inc*)

W.L. = Water Law (*Lawtext Publishing Limited*)

W.L.L.R. = World Licensing Law Report (*BNA International Inc*)

W.L.R. = Weekly Law Reports (*ICLR*)

W.L.T.B. = Woodfall Landlord & Tenant Bulletin (*S&M*)

W.M. = Wastes Management (*IWM Business Services Ltd*)

W.O.G.L.R. = World Online Gambling Law Report (*Cecile Park Publishing Ltd*)

W.P.G. = World Policy Guide (*Financial Times Finance*)

W.Q. = Watsons Quarterly (*R. Watson & Sons*)

W.R.T.L.B. = Wilkinson's Road Traffic Law Bulletin (*S&M*)

W.S.L. Rev. = Warwick Student Law Review (*University of Warwick*)

W.S.L.R. = World Sports Law Report (*Cecile Park Publishing Ltd*)

W.T.J. = World Tax Journal (*IBFD Publications BV*)

W.T.L.R. = Wills & Trusts Law Reports (*Legalease Ltd*)

TABLE OF ABBREVIATIONS

W.T.R. = World Tax Report (*Financial Times Finance*)

Watsons E.C. = Watsons Euro Comment (*R. Watson & Sons*)

Watsons I.R. = Watsons Insurance Review (*R. Watson & Sons*)

Watsons P.N. = Watsons Pensions News (*R. Watson & Sons*)

Watsons R.R. = Watsons Remuneration Review (*R. Watson & Sons*)

Watsons W.R. = Watsons Worldwide Review (*R. Watson & Sons*)

Web J.C.L.I. = Web Journal of Current Legal Issues (*Web Journal of Current Legal Issues*)

Wel. & Fam. L. & P. = Welfare and Family: Law & Practice (*XPL Publishing*)

Welf. R. Bull. = Welfare Rights Bulletin (*Child Poverty Action Group Ltd*)

Woodfall = Woodfall: Landlord & Tenant (*S&M*)

World I.L.R. = World Internet Law Report (*BNA International Inc*)

World T.R. = World Trade Review (*CUP*)

Worldlaw Bus. = Worldlaw Business (*Euromoney Institutional Investor Plc*)

Writ = Writ (*Law Society of Northern Ireland*)

Y.C. & M.L. = Yearbook of Copyright & Media Law (*OUP*)

Y.E.L. = Yearbook of European Law (*OUP*)

Y.J. = Youth Justice (*Sage Publications Ltd*)

Y.L.C.T. = Yearbook of Law Computers & Technology (*Taylor & Francis Ltd*)

Y.M.E.L. = Yearbook of Media & Entertainment Law (*OUP*)

YSG Mag. = Young Solicitors Group Magazine (*Young Solicitors Group*)

Yb. Int'l Env. L. = Yearbook of International Environmental Law (*OUP*)

ALPHABETICAL TABLE OF STATUTES

This table lists all the Statutes cited in the Statute Citator

Abolition of Feudal Tenure etc (Scotland) Act 2000 (asp 5)
Abortion Act 1967 (c.87)
Academies Act 2010 (c.32)
Access to Health Records Act 1990 (c.23)
Access to Justice Act 1999 (c.22)
Access to Medical Reports Act 1988 (c.28)
Acquisition of Land (Authorisation Procedure) (Scotland) Act 1947 (c.42)
Acquisition of Land Act 1981 (c.67)
Administration of Estates Act 1925 (c.23)
Administration of Justice (Miscellaneous Provisions) Act 1933 (c.36)
Administration of Justice (Scotland) Act 1972 (c.59)
Administration of Justice Act 1956 (c.46)
Administration of Justice Act 1960 (c.65)
Administration of Justice Act 1970 (c.31)
Administration of Justice Act 1982 (c.53)
Administration of Justice Act 1985 (c.61)
Adoption (Intercountry Aspects) Act 1999 (c.18)
Adoption (Scotland) Act 1978 (c.28)
Adoption and Children (Scotland) Act 2007 (asp 4)
Adoption and Children Act 2002 (c.38)
Adoption of Children Act 1926 (c.29)
Adult Support and Protection (Scotland) Act 2007 (asp 10)
Adults with Incapacity (Scotland) Act 2000 (asp 4)
Age of Legal Capacity (Scotland) Act 1991 (c.50)
Agricultural Credits (Scotland) Act 1929 (c.13)
Agricultural Credits Act 1928 (c.43)
Agricultural Holdings (Amendment) (Scotland) Act 2012 (asp 6)
Agricultural Holdings (Scotland) Act 1991 (c.55)
Agricultural Holdings (Scotland) Act 2003 (asp 11)
Agricultural Holdings Act 1986 (c.5)
Agricultural Marketing Act 1958 (c.47)
Agricultural Produce (Grading and Marking) Act 1928 (c.19)
Agricultural Produce (Grading and Marking) Amendment Act 1931 (c.40)
Agriculture (Miscellaneous Provisions) Act 1972 (c.62)
Agriculture Act 1947 (c.48)
Agriculture Act 1967 (c.22)
Agriculture Act 1970 (c.40)
Agriculture and Horticulture Act 1964 (c.28)
AIDS (Control) Act 1987 (c.33)
Air Force Act 1955 (c.19)
Air Force Constitution Act 1917 (c.71)
Airdrie-Bathgate Railway and Linked Improvements Act 2007 (asp 19)
Airports Act 1986 (c.31)
Alcohol (Minimum Pricing) (Scotland) Act 2012 (asp 4)
Alcohol etc (Scotland) Act 2010 (asp 18)
Alcoholic Liquor Duties Act 1979 (c.4)
Animal Boarding Establishments Act 1963 (c.43)
Animal Health Act 1981 (c.22)
Animal Health and Welfare (Scotland) Act 2006 (asp 11)
Animal Health and Welfare Act 1984 (c.40)
Animal Welfare Act 2006 (c.45)
Animals (Scientific Procedures) Act 1986 (c.14)
Animals Act 1971 (c.22)
Anti-social Behaviour Act 2003 (c.38)

Antisocial Behaviour etc (Scotland) Act 2004 (asp 8)
Anti-terrorism, Crime and Security Act 2001 (c.24)
Apportionment Act 1870 (c.35)
Apprenticeships, Skills, Children and Learning Act 2009 (c.22)
Appropriation (No.2) Act 2009 (c.9)
Appropriation (No.3) Act 2010 (c.30)
Appropriation Act 2009 (c.2)
Appropriation Act 2010 (c.5)
Appropriation Act 2011 (c.2)
Arbitration (Scotland) Act 1894 (c.13)
Arbitration Act 1996 (c.23)
Armed Forces (Pensions and Compensation) Act 2004 (c.32)
Armed Forces Act 1971 (c.33)
Armed Forces Act 1976 (c.52)
Armed Forces Act 1981 (c.55)
Armed Forces Act 1996 (c.46)
Armed Forces Act 2006 (c.52)
Armed Forces Act 2011 (c.18)
Army Act 1881 (c.58)
Army Act 1955 (c.18)
Asylum and Immigration (Treatment of Claimants, etc.) Act 2004 (c.19)
Asylum and Immigration Act 1996 (c.49)
Attachment of Earnings Act 1971 (c.32)
Audit Commission Act 1998 (c.18)
Autism Act 2009 (c.15)
Aviation Security Act 1982 (c.36)
Backing of Warrants (Republic of Ireland) Act 1965 (c.45)
Bail (Amendment) Act 1993 (c.26)
Bail Act 1976 (c.63)
Bank of England Act 1946 (c.27)
Bank of England Act 1998 (c.11)
Bankers Books Evidence Act 1879 (c.11)
Banking (Special Provisions) Act 2008 (c.2)
Banking Act 2009 (c.1)
Banking and Financial Dealings Act 1971 (c.80)
Bankruptcy (Scotland) Act 1913 (c.20)
Bankruptcy (Scotland) Act 1985 (c.66)
Bankruptcy and Diligence etc (Scotland) Act 2007 (asp 3)
Betting and Gaming Act 1960 (c.60)
Betting and Gaming Duties Act 1981 (c.63)
Betting and Lotteries Act 1934 (c.58)
Betting, Gaming and Lotteries Act 1963 (c.2)
Births and Deaths Registration Act 1953 (c.20)
Borders, Citizenship and Immigration Act 2009 (c.11)
Bournemouth Borough Council Act 1985 (c.v)
Breeding of Dogs Act 1973 (c.60)
Bribery Act 2010 (c.23)
British Fishing Boats Act 1983 (c.8)
British Nationality (Hong Kong) Act 1997 (c.20)
British Nationality Act 1981 (c.61)
British Settlements Act 1887 (c.54)
British Settlements Act 1945 (c.7)
British Waterways Act 1971 (c.xviii)
British Waterways Act 1983 (c.ii)
British Waterways Act 1995 (c.i)
Broadcasting Act 1990 (c.42)
Broadcasting Act 1996 (c.55)
Budget (Scotland) Act 2000 (asp 2)
Budget (Scotland) Act 2001 (asp 4)
Budget (Scotland) Act 2002 (asp 7)
Budget (Scotland) Act 2003 (asp 6)

ALPHABETICAL TABLE OF STATUTES

ALPHABETICAL TABLE OF STATUTORY INSTRUMENTS

This table lists all the Statutory Instruments cited in the Statutory Instruments Citator

(A52) Nottingham - West of Grantham Trunk Road (Bingham Bypass) (24-Hour Main Carriageway Clearway) Order 1987 (768)

(A52) Nottingham West of Grantham Trunk Road (Bingham Bypass) (De-Restriction) Order 1987 (767)

A14 Trunk Road (Junction 40 Higham Interchange to Junction 41 Risby Interchange, Suffolk) (Temporary Restriction and Prohibition of Traffic) Order 2012 (509)

A19 Trunk Road (Lindisfarne Roundabout to Silverlink Roundabout) (Temporary Restriction and Prohibition of Traffic) Order 2008 (1388)

A27 Trunk Road (Selmeston Firle) (Temporary Restriction and Prohibition of Traffic) Order 2011 (2771)

A27 Trunk Road and the M27, M275 and A3(M) Motorways (M27 Junction 12 Langstone Interchange) (Temporary Restriction and Prohibition of Traffic) Order 2012 (2779)

A282 Trunk Road (Dartford-Thurrock Crossing Charging Scheme) Order 2008 (1951)

A3 Trunk Road (Hindhead) (Derestriction and Variable Speed Limit) Order 2011 (1534)

A3 Trunk Road (North of Painshill Interchange North of Wisley Interchange) (Temporary 50/40 Miles Per Hour Speed Restriction) Order 2012 (1365)

A303 Trunk Road (Hayes End Roundabout, South Petherton) (40mph Speed Limit and Derestriction) Order 2011 (643)

A31 Trunk Road (Cadnam Interchange West Moors Interchange) (Temporary Prohibition of Traffic) Order 2012 (1080)

A31 Trunk Road (Canford Bottom Roundabout) (40 Miles Per Hour Speed Limit) Order 1999 (924)

A34 Trunk Road and the M3 Motorway (M3 Junction 9) (Temporary Prohibition of Traffic) Order 2012 (607)

A35 Trunk Road (Dorchester Bypass) (Derestriction) Order 2000 (839)

A38 Trunk Road (Chudleigh, Near Newton Abbot) (Temporary Prohibition of Traffic) Order 2011 (2251)

A38 Trunk Road (Dobwalls to Carminow Cross, Bodmin) (40 & 50 Mph Speed Limit) Order 2003 (Variation) and (Twelvewoods Roundabout, Dobwalls) (De-Restriction) Order 2010 (347)

A38 Trunk Road (Drybridge Junction to Marley Head Junction, Near South Brent) (Temporary Prohibition and Restriction of Traffic) (Number 2) Order 2011 (3087)

A38 Trunk Road (Egginton, Derbyshire) (De-;Restriction) Order 1993 (3094)

A38 Trunk Road (Marsh Mills to Forder Valley, Plymouth) (Temporary Restriction and Prohibition of Traffic) Order 2012 (1236)

A38 Trunk Road (Smithaleigh Junction, Plympton Bypass) (Temporary Prohibition of Traffic) Order 2011 (1916)

A40 Trunk Road (Banc-y-felin Junction, Carmarthenshire) (De- Restriction) Order 2004 (1411)

A40 Trunk Road (Meidrim Junction, Carmarthenshire) (De-Restriction) Order 2004 (1215)

A40 Trunk Road (Monmouth, Monmouthshire) (50 MPH Speed Limit) Order 2007 (1333)

A40 Trunk Road (Whitchurch to Ross-on-Wye, Herefordshire) (Temporary Restriction and Prohibition of Traffic) Order 2012 (1318)

A40 Trunk Road (Withybush, Haverfordwest, Pembrokeshire) (40 mph and 50 mph Speed Limits) Order 2006 (1740)

A45 Trunk Road (Ryton on Dunsmore, Warwickshire) (50 Miles Per Hour Speed Limit) Order 2001 (1007)

A45 Trunk Road (Ryton on Dunsmore, Warwickshire) (50 Miles Per Hour Speed Limit) Order 2001 Variation Order 2006 (3016)

A46 and A17 Trunk Roads (Newark Relief Road) (24-Hour Clearway) Order 1991 (1635)

A46 and A17 Trunk Roads (Newark Relief Road) (De-Restriction) Order 1991 (2440)

A470 Trunk Road (Llanrwst, Gwynedd) (De-Restriction) Order 1995 (2692)

A470 Trunk Road (Llanrwst, Gwynedd) (De-Restriction) Order 1995 (Variation) Order 2002 (2585)

A470 Trunk Road (Pontdolgoch, Powys) Order 1999 (3124)

A477 Trunk Road (Milton Village, Pembrokeshire) (40 mph Speed Limit) Order 2002 (2101)

A48 Trunk Road (Porthyrhyd Junction, Carmarthenshire) (De-Restriction) Order 2005 (1118)

A483 Trunk Road (Maesbury Road Junction) (De-restriction) Order 1995 (1096)

A487 Trunk Road (Aberarth, Ceredigion) (30mph and 40 mph Speed limits) Order 2003 (1982)

A487 Trunk Road (Rhydypennau, Ceredigion) (Restricted Road and 40 MPH Speed Limit) Order 2003 (1561)

A487 Trunk Road (Sarnau, Ceredigion) (40 MPH Speed Limit) Order 2003 (2072)

A49 Trunk Road (Redhill, Herefordshire) (Restriction) Order 2004 (1420)

A5 and A55 Trunk Roads (Llanfairpwllgwyngyll to Holyhead, Anglesey) (Deretsriction) Order 2001 (1653)

A5 Trunk Road (Fazeley Two Gates - Wilnecote Bypass, Staffordshire) (Derestriction and 40 Miles Per Hour Speed Limit) Order 1996 (2464)

A5 Trunk Road (Shenstone, Staffordshire) (50 Miles Per Hour Speed Limit) Order 2004 (1212)

A52 Trunk Road (Bingham Bypass, Nottinghamshire) (Derestriction) Order 2000 (3012)

A52 Trunk Road (Bottesford Bypass) (24-Hour Clearway) Order 1990 (174)

A55 Trunk Road (Abergwyngregyn, Gwynedd) (Derestriction) Order 1994 (3087)

A55 Trunk Road (Bodelwyddan - St Asaph, Clwyd) (Derestriction) Order 1993 (2152)

A55 Trunk Road (Glan Conwy - Conwy Morfa, Conwy) (Temporary 70 mph Speed Limit) Order 2010 (808)

A55 Trunk Road (Glan Conwy Conwy Morfa, Conwy County Borough) (Temporary 70 mph Speed Limit) Order 2011 (2330)

A55 Trunk Road (Holyhead, Anglesey) (50 mph Speed Limit &n-Isle of Anglesey (Electoral Arrangements) Order 1992 (2923)

Designation of Nitrate Vulnerable Zones (Scotland) Regulations 2002 (S.S.I. 276)

Designation of Rural Primary Schools (England) Order 2009 (3346)

Designation of Schools Having a Religious Character (Independent Schools) (England) (No.2) Order 2008 (2340)

Designation of Schools Having a Religious Character (Independent Schools) (England) (No.3) Order 2003 (3328)

Designation of Schools Having a Religious Character (Independent Schools) (England) (No.3) Order 2004 (577)

Designation of Schools Having a Religious Character (Independent Schools) (England) (No.4) Order 2004 (1378)

Designation of Schools Having a Religious Character (Independent Schools) (England) (No.4) Order 2010 (3031)

Designation of Schools Having a Religious Character (Independent Schools) (England) (No.5) Order 2004 (2089)

Designation of Schools Having a Religious Character (Independent Schools) (England) (No.6) Order 2004 (2986)

Designation of Schools Having a Religious Character (Independent Schools) (England) Order 2006 (1533)

Detention Centre Rules 2001 (238)

Disability Discrimination Act 1995 (Amendment) Regulations 2003 (1673)

Disabled People's Right to Control (Pilot Scheme) (England) Regulations 2010 (2862)

Disabled Persons (Badges for Motor Vehicles) (England) (Amendment) Regulations 2007 (2531)

Disabled Persons (Badges for Motor Vehicles) (Scotland) Amendment Regulations 2007 (S.S.I. 162)

Disabled Persons (Badges for Motor Vehicles) (Wales) (Amendment) Regulations 2011 (1588)

Disabled Persons (Badges for Motor Vehicles) (Wales) Regulations 2000 (1786)

Discretionary Financial Assistance Regulations 2001 (1167)

Disease Control (England) Order 2003 (1729)

Diseases of Animals (Approved Disinfectants) (England) Order 2007 (448)

Diseases of Animals (Northern Ireland) Order 1981 (1115)

Displaced Persons (Temporary Protection) Regulations 2005 (1379)

Distribution of German Enemy Property (No.1) Order 1950 (1642)

District Court Fees Order 1984 (251)

District Electoral Areas Commissioner (Northern Ireland) Order 1984 (360)

Docking of Working Dogs Tails (England) Regulations 2007 (1120)

Docklands Light Railway (Capacity Enhancement and 2012 Games Preparation) Order 2007 (2297)

Docklands Light Railway (Capacity Enhancement) Order 2005 (3105)

Domiciliary Care Agencies (Wales) Regulations 2004 (219)

Domiciliary Care Agencies Regulations 2002 (3214)

Dormant Bank and Building Society Accounts (Tax) Regulations 2011 (22)

Double Taxation Relief (Bank Levy) (Federal Republic of Germany) Order 2012 (432)

Double Taxation Relief (Taxes on Income) (Barbados) Order 1970 (952)

Double Taxation Relief (Taxes on Income) (Barbados) Order 1973 (2096)

Double Taxation Relief (Taxes on Income) (Singapore) Order 1997 (2988)

Double Taxation Relief (Taxes on Income) (South Africa) Order 2002 (3138)

Double Taxation Relief (Taxes on Income) (Switzerland) Order 1978 (1408)

Double Taxation Relief and International Tax Enforcement (South Africa) Order 2011 (2441)

Drainage Rates (Appeals) Regulations 1970 (1152)

Drivers Hours (Goods Vehicles) (Milk Collection) (Temporary Exemption) Regulations 2007 (2370)

Dumfries and Galloway Council (Garlieston) Harbour Empowerment Order 2008 (S.S.I. 190)

Dumfries and Galloway Council (Isle of Whithorn) Harbour Empowerment Order 2008 (S.S.I. 189)

Dumfries and Galloway Council (Port William) Harbour Empowerment Order 2008 (S.S.I. 188)

Dunham Bridge (Revision of Tolls) Order 2007 (1455)

Duty Stamps Regulations 2006 (202)

Early Years Foundation Stage (Exemptions from Learning and Development Requirements) Regulations 2008 (1743)

Early Years Foundation Stage (Learning and Development Requirements) Order 2007 (1772)

Early Years Foundation Stage (Welfare Requirements) (Amendment) Regulations 2008 (1953)

Early Years Foundation Stage (Welfare Requirements) (Amendment) Regulations 2009 (1549)

Early Years Foundation Stage (Welfare Requirements) Regulations 2007 (1771)

East Cheshire National Health Service Trust (Establishment) Order 1992 (2461)

East Lancashire Hospitals National Health Service Trust (Establishment) and the Blackburn, Hyndburn and Ribble Valley Health Care National Health Service Trust and Burnley Health Care National Health Service Trust (Dissolution) Order 2002 (2073)

Ecclesiastical Judges, Legal Officers and Others (Fees) Order 2011 (1731)

Ecclesiastical Judges, Legal Officers and Others (Fees) Order 2012 (1846)

Ecclesiastical Jurisdiction (Discipline) Rules 1964 (1755)

Ecodesign for Energy-Related Products Regulations 2010 (2617)

Edinburgh City Bypass (Sighthill, Colinton, Burdiehouse, Gilmerton and Millerhill Sections and Connecting Roads) (Speed Limit) Regulations 1989 (2125)

Education (Admissions Appeals Arrangements) (England) (Amendment) Regulations 2007 (3026)

Education (Admissions Appeals Arrangements) (England) Regulations 2002 (2899)

Education (Admissions Appeals Arrangements) (England) (Amendment) Regulations 2008 (3092)

Education (Amount to Follow Permanently Excluded Pupil) Regulations 1999 (495)

Education (Educational Provision for Improving Behaviour) Regulations 2010 (1156)

Education (Fees and Awards) (England) Regulations 2007 (779)

Education (Fees and Awards) (Scotland) Regulations 2007 (S.S.I. 152)

Education (Fees) (Scotland) Regulations 2011 (S.S.I. 389)

Education (Foundation Body) (England) Regulations 2000 (2872)

Education (Governors Allowances) (England) Regulations 2003 (523)

Education (Grammar School Ballots) Regulations 1998 (2876)

Education (Grant) (Financial Support for Students) Regulations 2001 (2894)

Education (Grants etc.) (Dance and Drama) (England) Regulations 2001 (2857)

Education (Head Teachers Qualifications) (Amendment) (England) Regulations 2005 (875)

Education (Head Teachers Qualifications) (England) (Amendment) (No.2) Regulations 2005 (3322)

Education (Head Teachers Qualifications) (England) (Amendment) Regulations 2011 (602)

Education (Head Teachers' Qualifications) (England) Regulations 2003 (3111)

Education (Independent Educational Provision in England) (Provision of Information) Regulations 2010 (2919)

Education (Independent School Standards) (England) Regulations 2010 (1997)

Education (Individual Pupil Information) (Prescribed Persons) (England) Regulations 2009 (1563)

Education (Induction Arrangements for School Teachers) (England) Regulations 2008 (657)

Education (Induction Arrangements for School Teachers) (England) Regulations 2012 (1115)

Education (Induction Arrangements for School Teachers) (Wales) Regulations 2005 (1818)

Education (Infant Class Sizes) (England) (Amendment) Regulations 2006 (3409)

Education (Infant Class Sizes) (England) Regulations 1998 (1973)

Education (Information About Children in Alternative Provision) (England) Regulations 2007 (1065)

Education (Information About Individual Pupils) (England) Regulations 2006 (2601)

Education (Listed Bodies) (Wales) (Amendment) Order 2009 (710)

Education (Listed Bodies) (Wales) Order 2007 (2794)

Education (Mandatory Awards) Regulations 2003 (1994)

Education (Middle Schools) (Amendment) Regulations 1994 (581)

Education (Middle Schools) Regulations 1980 (918)

Education (Miscellaneous Amendments relating to Safeguarding Children) (England) Regulations 2009 (1924)

Education (National Curriculum) (Attainment Targets and Programmes of Study in Information and Communication Technology in respect of the Third and Fourth Key Stages) (England) Order 2008 (1758)

Education (National Curriculum) (Attainment Targets and Programmes of Study in Information and Communication Technology) (England) Order 2000 (1601)

Education (National Curriculum) (Key Stage 1 Assessment Arrangements) (England) Order 2004 (2783)

Education (National Curriculum) (Key Stage 2 Assessment Arrangements) (England) Order 2003 (1038)

Education (National Curriculum) (Key Stage 3 Assessment Arrangements) (England) Order 2003 (1039)

Education (Non-Maintained Special Schools) (England) Regulations 2011 (1627)

Education (Parenting Contracts and Parenting Orders) (England) Regulations 2007 (1869)

Education (Penalty Notices) (England) Regulations 2007 (1867)

Education (Provision of Full-Time Education for Excluded Pupils) (England) Regulations 2007 (1870)

Education (Publication of Draft Proposals and Orders) (Further Education Corporations) (England) Regulations 2001 (782)

Education (Publication of Proposals) (Sixth Form College Corporations) (England) Regulations 2010 (2609)

Education (Pupil Exclusions and Appeals) (Maintained Schools) (England) Regulations 2002 (3178)

Education (Pupil Exclusions and Appeals) (Miscellaneous Amendments) (England) Regulations 2006 (2189)

Education (Pupil Exclusions and Appeals) (Pupil Referral Units) (England) Regulations 2008 (532)

Education (Pupil Exclusions) (Miscellaneous Amendments) (England) Regulations 2004 (402)

Education (Pupil Information) (England) Regulations 2005 (1437)

Education (Pupil Referral Units) (Application of Enactments) (England) Regulations 2007 (2979)

Education (Pupil Referral Units) (Closure) (England) Regulations 2010 (1071)

Education (Pupil Referral Units) (Management Committees etc.) (England) Regulations 2007 (2978)

Education (Pupil Registration) (England) Regulations 2006 (1751)

Education (Recognised Bodies) (Wales) (Amendment) Order 2009 (667)

Education (Recognised Bodies) (Wales) Order 2007 (2795)

Education (Reintegration Interview) (England) Regulations 2007 (1868)

Education (School and Placing Information) (Scotland) Amendment Regulations 1990 (181)

Education (School and Placing Information) (Scotland) Amendment Regulations 2000 (S.S.I. 407)

Education (School and Placing Information) (Scotland) Amendment Regulations 2007 (S.S.I. 487)

Education (School and Placing Information) (Scotland) Amendment, Etc, Regulations 1993 (1604)

Education (School and Placing Information) (Scotland) Regulations 1982 (950)

Education (School Day and School Year) (Wales) Regulations 2003 (3231)

Education (School Government) (Terms of Reference) (England) Regulations 2000 (2122)

Education (School Inspection) (England) Regulations 2005 (2038)

Education (School Performance Information) (England) Regulations 2007 (2324)

Education (School Premises) Regulations 1999 (2)

Education (School Teacher Performance Management) (England) Regulations 2006 (2661)

Education (School Teachers Appraisal) (England) Regulations 2012 (115)

Education (School Teachers Prescribed Qualifications, etc) Order 2003 (1709)

Education (School Teachers Qualifications) (England) Regulations 2003 (1662)

Education (School Teachers Qualifications) (Wales) Regulations 2004 (1729)

Education (Short Stay Schools) (Closure) (England) (Amendment) Regulations 2010 (1920)

Education (Special Educational Needs) (England) (Consolidation) Regulations 2001 (3455)

Fodder Plant Seed (Wales) Regulations 2005 (1207)

Food (Northern Ireland) Order 1989 (846)

Food Additives (England) Regulations 2009 (3238)

Food Additives (Scotland) Regulations 2009 (S.S.I. 436)

Food Additives (Wales) Regulations 2009 (3378)

Food Hygiene (England) Regulations 2006 (14)

Food Hygiene (Scotland) Regulations 2006 (S.S.I. 3)

Food Hygiene (Wales) Regulations 2006 (31)

Food Industry Development Scheme (Specification of Activities) Order 1997 (2674)

Food Labelling Regulations 1996 (1499)

Food Protection (Emergency Prohibitions) (Radioactivity in Sheep) (England) (Partial Revocation) Order 1991 (2776)

Food Protection (Emergency Prohibitions) (Radioactivity in Sheep) (England) (Partial Revocation) Order 1993 (33)

Food Protection (Emergency Prohibitions) (Radioactivity in Sheep) (England) (Partial Revocation) Order 1994 (65)

Food Protection (Emergency Prohibitions) (Radioactivity in Sheep) (England) (Partial Revocation) Order 1995 (39)

Food Protection (Emergency Prohibitions) (Radioactivity in Sheep) (England) (Partial Revocation) Order 1996 (62)

Food Protection (Emergency Prohibitions) (Radioactivity in Sheep) (England) Order 1991 (6)

Food Protection (Emergency Prohibitions) (Radioactivity in Sheep) (Wales) (Partial Revocation) Order 1991 (2780)

Food Protection (Emergency Prohibitions) (Radioactivity in Sheep) (Wales) (Partial Revocation) Order 1994 (63)

Food Protection (Emergency Prohibitions) (Radioactivity in Sheep) (Wales) (Partial Revocation) Order 1995 (46)

Food Protection (Emergency Prohibitions) (Radioactivity in Sheep) (Wales) (Partial Revocation) Order 1998 (72)

Food Protection (Emergency Prohibitions) (Radioactivity in Sheep) (Wales) (Partial Revocation) Order 2011 (2759)

Food Protection (Emergency Prohibitions) (Radioactivity in Sheep) (Wales) Order 1991 (5)

Food Protection (Emergency Prohibitions) (Radioactivity in Sheep) Order 1991 (20)

Food Protection (Emergency Prohibitions) (Radioactivity in Sheep) Partial Revocation (Scotland) Order 2001 (S.S.I. 313)

Food Protection (Emergency Prohibitions) (Radioactivity in Sheep) Partial Revocation (Scotland) Order 2003 (S.S.I. 375)

Food Protection (Emergency Prohibitions) (Radioactivity in Sheep) Partial Revocation (Scotland) Order 2004 (S.S.I. 48)

Food Protection (Emergency Prohibitions) (Radioactivity in Sheep) Partial Revocation (Scotland) Order 2005 (S.S.I. 71)

Food Protection (Emergency Prohibitions) (Radioactivity in Sheep) Partial Revocation (Scotland) Order 2006 (S.S.I. 52)

Food Protection (Emergency Prohibitions) (Radioactivity in Sheep) Partial Revocation (Scotland) Order 2007 (S.S.I. 38)

Food Protection (Emergency Prohibitions) (Radioactivity in Sheep) Partial Revocation (Scotland) Order 2008 (S.S.I. 63)

Food Protection (Emergency Prohibitions) (Radioactivity in Sheep) Partial Revocation Order 1991 (2766)

Food Protection (Emergency Prohibitions) (Radioactivity in Sheep) Partial Revocation Order 1993 (13)

Food Protection (Emergency Prohibitions) (Radioactivity in Sheep) Partial Revocation Order 1994 (50)

Food Protection (Emergency Prohibitions) (Radioactivity in Sheep) Partial Revocation Order 1995 (48)

Food Protection (Emergency Prohibitions) (Radioactivity in Sheep) Partial Revocation Order 1996 (31)

Food Protection (Emergency Prohibitions) (Radioactivity in Sheep) Partial Revocation Order 1997 (62)

Food Protection (Emergency Prohibitions) (Radioactivity in Sheep) Partial Revocation Order 1998 (82)

Food Protection (Emergency Prohibitions) (Radioactivity in Sheep) Partial Revocation Order 1999 (80)

Food Safety (Sampling and Qualifications) Regulations 1990 (2463)

Food Safety (Northern Ireland) Order 1991 (762)

Food Standards Act 1999 (Transitional and Consequential Provisions and Savings) (Scotland) Regulations 2000 (S.S.I. 62)

Foot-and-Mouth Disease (Control of Vaccination) (England) Regulations 2006 (183)

Foot-and-Mouth Disease (England) Order 2006 (182)

Foot-and-Mouth Disease (Scotland) Order 2006 (S.S.I. 44)

Foot-and-Mouth Disease (Slaughter and Vaccination) (Scotland) Regulations 2006 (S.S.I. 45)

Former Yugoslavia (United Nations Sanctions) (Dependent Territories) Order 1994 (2674)

Fostering Services (England) Regulations 2011 (581)

Fostering Services (Wales) Regulations 2003 (237)

Fraserburgh Harbour Revision (Constitution) Order 2001 (S.S.I. 457)

Fraserburgh Harbour Revision Order 1995 (1527)

Fraserburgh Harbour Revision Order 1999 (S.S.I. 40)

Fraserburgh Harbour Revision Order 2011 (S.S.I. 447)

Freedom of Information (Additional Public Authorities) Order 2005 (3593)

Freedom of Information Act 2000 (Commencement No 3) Order 2003 (2603)

Freight Containers (Safety Convention) Regulations 1984 (1890)

Fresh Meat (Import Conditions) Regulations 1996 (3125)

Friendly Societies (Life Assurance Premium Relief) (Change of Rate) Regulations 1980 (1947)

Friendly Societies (Modification of the Corporation Tax Acts) (Amendment) Regulations 2007 (2134)

Friendly Societies (Modification of the Corporation Tax Acts) (Amendment) Regulations 2008 (1937)

Friendly Societies (Modification of the Corporation Tax Acts) Regulations 2005 (2014)

Friendly Societies (Transfers of Other Business) (Modification of the Corporation Tax Acts) Regulations 2008 (1942)

Functions of Primary Care Trusts (Dental Public Health) (England) Regulations 2006 (185)

STATUTE CITATOR 2012

The Statute Citator covers the period 2012 and is up to date to **February 1, 2013**. It covers both public and local Statutes and comprises in a single table:

    (i) Statutes passed during this period;
    (ii) Statutes affected during this period by Statute or Statutory Instrument;
    (iii) Statutes judicially considered during this period;
    (iv) Statutes repealed and amended during this period; and
    (v) Statutes under which Statutory Instruments have been made during this period.

The material is arranged in numerical order under the relevant year.

Definitions of legislative effects:

"added"	: new provisions are inserted by subsequent legislation
"amended"	: text of legislation is modified by subsequent legislation
"applied"	: brought to bear, or exercised by subsequent legislation
"consolidated"	: used where previous Acts in the same subject area are brought together in subsequent legislation, with or without amendments
"disapplied"	: an exception made to the application of an earlier enactment
"enabling"	: giving power for the relevant SI to be made
"referred to"	: direction from other legislation without specific effect or application
"repealed"	: rescinded by subsequent legislation
"restored"	: reinstated by subsequent legislation (where previously repealed/revoked)
"substituted"	: text of provision is completely replaced by subsequent legislation
"varied"	: provisions modified in relation to their application to specified areas or circumstances, however the text itself remains unchanged

ACTS OF THE SCOTTISH PARLIAMENT

2000

asp 1. Public Finance and Accountability (Scotland) Act 2000
s.4, applied: 2012 asp 2 s.4, s.6
s.9, amended: 2012 asp 5 Sch.5 para.37, 2012 c.11 Sch.3 para.32
s.23, applied: 2012 asp 8 s.42
s.23, referred to: 2012 asp 8 s.43
s.23A, applied: 2012 asp 8 s.42
s.24, applied: 2012 asp 8 s.42
Sch.4 para.2, repealed: 2012 asp 3 Sch.3

asp 2. Budget (Scotland) Act 2000
Sch.1, varied: 2012 c.11 s.12
Sch.2 Part 6, varied: 2012 c.11 s.12
Sch.2 Part 7, varied: 2012 c.11 s.12
Sch.2 Part 9, varied: 2012 c.11 s.12

asp 4. Adults with Incapacity (Scotland) Act 2000
applied: SI 2012/2885 Sch.8 para.4, Sch.8 para.12, SI 2012/2886 Sch.1, SI 2012/3145 Sch.1
s.7, enabling: SSI 2012/289
s.47, enabling: SSI 2012/170
s.56, amended: 2012 asp 5 Sch.5 para.38
s.61, amended: 2012 asp 5 Sch.5 para.38

asp 5. Abolition of Feudal Tenure etc (Scotland) Act 2000
s.4, repealed: 2012 asp 5 Sch.5 para.39
s.18A, amended: 2012 asp 5 Sch.5 para.39

2000–cont.

asp 5. Abolition of Feudal Tenure etc (Scotland) Act 2000–*cont.*
s.46, repealed: 2012 asp 5 Sch.5 para.39
s.63, amended: 2012 asp 5 Sch.5 para.39
s.65, repealed: 2012 asp 5 Sch.5 para.39
s.65A, repealed (in part): 2012 asp 5 Sch.5 para.39
s.67, applied: 2012 asp 9 s.71
s.73, amended: 2012 asp 5 Sch.5 para.39
Sch.11, amended: 2012 asp 5 Sch.5 para.39

asp 6. Standards in Scotland's Schools etc Act 2000
s.58, amended: 2012 asp 5 Sch.5 para.40

asp 7. Ethical Standards in Public Life etc (Scotland) Act 2000
Sch.3, amended: 2012 asp 3 Sch.2 para.4, 2012 asp 8 Sch.1 para.14, Sch.7 para.61, Sch.8 Part 1, SI 2012/1659 Sch.3 para.23

asp 8. Education and Training (Scotland) Act 2000
s.1, enabling: SSI 2012/172
s.2, enabling: SSI 2012/172
s.3, enabling: SSI 2012/172

asp 10. National Parks (Scotland) Act 2000
s.6, applied: SSI 2012/88 Reg.3, SSI 2012/162 Sch.1
s.15, amended: 2012 asp 5 Sch.5 para.41
s.15, repealed (in part): 2012 asp 5 Sch.5 para.41

2000–cont.

asp 11. Regulation of Investigatory Powers (Scotland) Act 2000
s.5, amended: 2012 asp 8 Sch.7 para.15
s.8, amended: 2012 asp 8 Sch.7 para.15
s.9, repealed: 2012 asp 8 Sch.8 Part 1
s.10, amended: 2012 asp 8 Sch.7 para.15
s.10, repealed (in part): 2012 asp 8 Sch.8 Part 1
s.10A, repealed: 2012 asp 8 Sch.8 Part 1
s.11, amended: 2012 asp 8 Sch.7 para.15
s.11, repealed (in part): 2012 asp 8 Sch.8 Part 1
s.12, repealed: 2012 asp 8 Sch.8 Part 1
s.12A, repealed: 2012 asp 8 Sch.8 Part 1
s.12ZA, added: 2012 asp 8 Sch.7 para.15
s.14, amended: 2012 asp 8 Sch.7 para.15
s.14, repealed (in part): 2012 asp 8 Sch.8 Part 1
s.15, repealed (in part): 2012 asp 8 Sch.8 Part 1
s.16, amended: 2012 asp 8 Sch.7 para.15
s.16, repealed (in part): 2012 asp 8 Sch.8 Part 1
s.18, amended: 2012 asp 8 Sch.7 para.15
s.18, repealed (in part): 2012 asp 8 Sch.8 Part 1
s.20, amended: 2012 asp 8 Sch.7 para.15
s.20, repealed (in part): 2012 asp 8 Sch.8 Part 1
s.23, amended: 2012 asp 8 Sch.7 para.15
s.24, amended: 2012 asp 8 Sch.7 para.15
s.26, amended: 2012 asp 8 Sch.7 para.15
s.31, amended: 2012 asp 8 Sch.7 para.15, Sch.8 Part 1

2001

asp 2. Transport (Scotland) Act 2001
applied: SI 2012/1128 Art.4
s.5, amended: 2012 asp 8 Sch.7 para.16
s.13, applied: SSI 2012/89 Sch.1
s.15, amended: 2012 asp 8 Sch.7 para.16
s.38, enabling: SSI 2012/33
s.48, amended: 2012 asp 8 Sch.8 Part 1
s.81, enabling: SSI 2012/33
s.82, applied: SSI 2012/89 Sch.1
asp 4. Budget (Scotland) Act 2001
Sch.1, varied: 2012 c.11 s.12
Sch.2 Part 6, varied: 2012 c.11 s.12
Sch.2 Part 7, varied: 2012 c.11 s.12
Sch.2 Part 8, varied: 2012 c.11 s.12
asp 7. Convention Rights (Compliance) (Scotland) Act 2001
s.12, varied: 2012 c.11 s.12
asp 10. Housing (Scotland) Act 2001
s.14, applied: SSI 2012/91 Art.3, SSI 2012/92 Reg.3, SSI 2012/93 Reg.2
s.14, disapplied: SSI 2012/91 Art.3
s.14, enabling: SSI 2012/92, SSI 2012/93
s.14A, applied: SSI 2012/93 Reg.2, SSI 2012/127 Art.2, Art.3, Art.4, Art.5, Art.6, Art.7
s.14A, enabling: SSI 2012/127
s.16, applied: SSI 2012/128, SSI 2012/128 Art.2
s.16, enabling: SSI 2012/128
s.23, amended: 2012 asp 5 Sch.5 para.42
s.24, amended: 2012 asp 5 Sch.5 para.42
s.91, applied: SI 2012/2885 Sch.6 para.21
s.93, applied: SSI 2012/258, SSI 2012/306
s.93, enabling: SSI 2012/258, SSI 2012/306
s.94, repealed (in part): 2012 asp 11 s.4
s.109, applied: SSI 2012/127, SSI 2012/128
s.109, enabling: SSI 2012/92, SSI 2012/128, SSI 2012/258, SSI 2012/306
Sch.2 Part 1 para.1, amended: 2012 asp 8 Sch.8 Part 2

2001–cont.

asp 13. International Criminal Court (Scotland) Act 2001
s.15, amended: 2012 asp 8 Sch.7 para.17
asp 14. Protection from Abuse (Scotland) Act 2001
s.3, amended: 2012 asp 8 Sch.7 para.18
asp 15. Police and Fire Services (Finance) (Scotland) Act 2001
repealed: 2012 asp 8 Sch.8 Part 1

2002

asp 3. Water Industry (Scotland) Act 2002
s.37, enabling: SSI 2012/53
s.42, referred to: 2012 asp 2 Sch.3
asp 5. Community Care and Health (Scotland) Act 2002
s.1, enabling: SSI 2012/109
s.2, enabling: SSI 2012/109
s.13, enabling: SSI 2012/65
s.14, enabling: SSI 2012/65
s.15, applied: SSI 2012/66 Art.3
s.15, enabling: SSI 2012/65
s.23, applied: SSI 2012/109
s.23, enabling: SSI 2012/65, SSI 2012/109
s.24, enabling: SSI 2012/66
asp 7. Budget (Scotland) Act 2002
Sch.1, varied: 2012 c.11 s.12
Sch.2 Part 7, varied: 2012 c.11 s.12
Sch.2 Part 8, varied: 2012 c.11 s.12
asp 11. Scottish Public Services Ombudsman Act 2002
s.3, enabling: SSI 2012/43, SSI 2012/85
s.5, varied: 2012 c.11 s.12
s.7, repealed (in part): 2012 c.7 Sch.7 para.14
s.7, varied: 2012 c.11 s.12
s.19, varied: 2012 c.11 s.12
s.23, varied: 2012 c.11 s.12
s.24, applied: SSI 2012/43, SSI 2012/85
Sch.1 para.2, varied: 2012 c.11 s.12
Sch.2 Part 1 para.2, varied: 2012 c.11 s.12
Sch.2 Part 1 para.13, substituted: 2012 asp 8 Sch.7 para.62
Sch.2 Part 1 para.14, repealed: 2012 asp 8 Sch.8 Part 1
Sch.2 Part 2 para.20B, added: SI 2012/1659 Sch.3 para.24
Sch.2 Part 2 para.21ZZA, added: SSI 2012/43 Art.2
Sch.2 Part 2 para.24, repealed: SSI 2012/85 Art.2
Sch.2 Part 2 para.28A, added: SSI 2012/43 Art.2
Sch.2 Part 2 para.30, amended: 2012 asp 3 Sch.2 para.5
Sch.2 Part 2 para.32A, amended: 2012 asp 8 s.61
Sch.2 Part 2 para.32A, substituted: 2012 asp 8 Sch.7 para.19
Sch.2 Part 2 para.32AA, added: SSI 2012/43 Art.2
Sch.2 Part 2 para.90, repealed: 2012 c.7 Sch.7 para.15
Sch.3 para.4, varied: 2012 c.11 s.12
Sch.4 para.1, amended: 2012 asp 8 s.61, Sch.7 para.19
Sch.4 para.1, repealed (in part): 2012 asp 8 Sch.8 Part 1
Sch.4 para.1, varied: 2012 c.11 s.12
Sch.4 para.6, varied: 2012 c.11 s.12
Sch.4 para.16, repealed: 2012 asp 8 Sch.8 Part 1
asp 13. Freedom of Information (Scotland) Act 2002
applied: SSI 2012/36 Reg.7
s.29, varied: 2012 c.11 s.12

2002–cont.

asp 13. Freedom of Information (Scotland) Act 2002–*cont.*
s.31, varied: 2012 c.11 s.12
s.42, varied: 2012 c.11 s.12
s.52, varied: 2012 c.11 s.12
Sch.1 Part 2 para.6, amended: 2012 asp 8 Sch.7 para.20
Sch.1 Part 2 para.9, substituted: 2012 asp 8 Sch.7 para.63
Sch.1 Part 6 para.50, amended: 2012 asp 8 Sch.7 para.20
Sch.1 Part 6 para.50A, added: 2012 asp 8 Sch.1 para.15
Sch.1 Part 6 para.51, repealed: 2012 asp 8 Sch.8 Part 1
Sch.1 Part 6 para.52, repealed: 2012 asp 8 Sch.8 Part 1
Sch.1 Part 6 para.52A, repealed: 2012 asp 8 Sch.8 Part 1
Sch.1 Part 7 para.61B, added: SI 2012/1659 Sch.3 para.25
Sch.1 Part 7 para.75A, substituted: 2012 asp 8 Sch.7 para.20
Sch.1 Part 7 para.75AA, amended: 2012 asp 8 s.61
Sch.1 Part 7 para.85ZA, added: 2012 asp 8 Sch.7 para.63
Sch.1 Part 7 para.105, amended: 2012 asp 3 Sch.2 para.6

asp 17. Debt Arrangement and Attachment (Scotland) Act 2002
Part 1, applied: SI 2012/1903 Sch.1 para.7
s.10, amended: SSI 2012/301 Sch.1 para.2

2003

asp 1. Local Government in Scotland Act 2003
s.16, amended: 2012 asp 8 s.46, Sch.7 para.64
s.16, applied: 2012 asp 8 s.46
s.16, repealed (in part): 2012 asp 8 s.46
s.20, applied: SSI 2012/303 Reg.5, Sch.4 para.37, Sch.5 para.25, SSI 2012/319 Reg.5
s.22, amended: 2012 asp 8 Sch.8 Part 2
s.22, repealed (in part): 2012 asp 8 Sch.8 Part 2
s.25, repealed: 2012 asp 8 Sch.8 Part 3
s.33, amended: 2012 asp 11 s.2
s.33, repealed (in part): 2012 asp 11 s.2
s.46, amended: 2012 asp 8 Sch.8 Part 1
s.61, amended: 2012 asp 8 Sch.8 Part 1, Sch.8 Part 2
s.61, repealed (in part): 2012 asp 8 Sch.8 Part 1, Sch.8 Part 2

asp 2. Land Reform (Scotland) Act 2003
s.22, applied: 2012 asp 5 s.9, s.73
s.37, applied: 2012 asp 5 s.42
s.40, amended: SSI 2012/38 Sch.1 para.3
s.40, applied: 2012 asp 5 s.42
s.43, applied: 2012 asp 5 s.42
Sch.2 para.15, repealed: SSI 2012/228 Sch.1

asp 4. Public Appointments and Public Bodies etc (Scotland) Act 2003
s.2, applied: SSI 2012/193 Art.2
s.3, enabling: SSI 2012/193
s.18, applied: SSI 2012/193
Sch.2, amended: 2012 asp 8 Sch.1 para.16, Sch.7 para.65, Sch.8 Part 1

asp 6. Budget (Scotland) Act 2003
Sch.1, varied: 2012 c.11 s.12
Sch.2 Part 7, varied: 2012 c.11 s.12
Sch.2 Part 8, varied: 2012 c.11 s.12

2003–cont.

asp 7. Criminal Justice (Scotland) Act 2003
s.21, amended: 2012 c.7 s.213
s.56, amended: 2012 asp 8 Sch.7 para.21
s.68, applied: SSI 2012/88 Reg.23, SSI 2012/89 Reg.26
s.69, applied: SSI 2012/88 Reg.23, SSI 2012/89 Reg.26
s.75, repealed: 2012 asp 8 Sch.8 Part 1
s.76, repealed (in part): 2012 asp 8 Sch.8 Part 1

asp 8. Building (Scotland) Act 2003
s.1, applied: SSI 2012/209
s.1, enabling: SSI 2012/209
s.2, enabling: SSI 2012/209
s.54, enabling: SSI 2012/209

asp 9. Title Conditions (Scotland) Act 2003
s.3, applied: 2012 asp 9 s.11
s.3, disapplied: 2012 asp 9 s.11
s.4, amended: 2012 asp 5 Sch.5 para.43
s.4, referred to: 2012 asp 5 s.48
s.10, applied: 2012 asp 5 s.61
s.12, amended: 2012 asp 9 Sch.1 para.3
s.18, applied: 2012 asp 9 s.35
s.20, amended: 2012 asp 9 Sch.1 para.3
s.38, referred to: SSI 2012/30
s.38, enabling: SSI 2012/30
s.41, amended: 2012 asp 5 Sch.5 para.43
s.51, repealed: 2012 asp 5 Sch.5 para.43
s.58, repealed: 2012 asp 5 Sch.5 para.43
s.60, amended: 2012 asp 5 Sch.5 para.43
s.63, amended: 2012 asp 9 Sch.1 para.3
s.71, amended: 2012 asp 5 Sch.5 para.43
s.73, amended: 2012 asp 5 Sch.5 para.43
s.75, amended: 2012 asp 5 Sch.5 para.43
s.75, applied: 2012 asp 5 s.73, s.90
s.75, referred to: 2012 asp 5 s.48
s.84, amended: 2012 asp 5 Sch.5 para.43
s.105, amended: 2012 asp 9 Sch.1 para.3
s.119, repealed (in part): 2012 asp 5 Sch.5 para.43
s.121, referred to: 2012 asp 5 s.92
s.122, amended: 2012 asp 5 Sch.5 para.43, 2012 asp 9 Sch.1 para.3

asp 10. Homelessness etc (Scotland) Act 2003
Commencement Orders: SSI 2012/330 Art.13
s.1, repealed: SSI 2012/330 Art.13
s.2, applied: SSI 2012/330, SSI 2012/330 Art.2
s.2, enabling: SSI 2012/330
s.3, repealed: SSI 2012/330 Art.13
s.4, amended: SSI 2012/330 Art.14
s.5, repealed: SSI 2012/330 Art.13
s.6, repealed: SSI 2012/330 Art.13

asp 11. Agricultural Holdings (Scotland) Act 2003
s.9, amended: 2012 asp 6 s.2
s.27, amended: SSI 2012/38 Sch.1 para.4

asp 12. Dog Fouling (Scotland) Act 2003
s.3, amended: 2012 asp 8 Sch.7 para.22

asp 13. Mental Health (Care and Treatment) (Scotland) Act 2003
applied: SI 2012/2885 Sch.1 para.5, SI 2012/2886 Sch.1, SI 2012/3144 Reg.24, SI 2012/3145 Sch.1, SSI 2012/303 Reg.5, Reg.15, SSI 2012/319 Reg.5, Reg.15
s.8, amended: 2012 asp 8 Sch.7 para.23
s.17, amended: 2012 asp 8 Sch.7 para.23
s.21, enabling: SSI 2012/132
s.35, amended: 2012 asp 8 Sch.7 para.23
s.286, applied: SSI 2012/211
s.286, enabling: SSI 2012/211
s.292, amended: 2012 asp 8 Sch.7 para.23

2003–cont.

asp 13. Mental Health (Care and Treatment) (Scotland) Act 2003–*cont.*
s.293, amended: 2012 asp 8 Sch.7 para.23
s.326, applied: SSI 2012/211
s.326, enabling: SSI 2012/132
s.328, referred to: SSI 2012/111 Art.2
Sch.1 Part 1 para.7E, varied: 2012 c.11 s.12
Sch.2 Part 1 para.1, varied: 2012 c.11 s.12
Sch.2 Part 3 para.10, enabling: SSI 2012/132

asp 15. Salmon and Freshwater Fisheries (Consolidation) (Scotland) Act 2003
s.37, enabling: SSI 2012/210
s.38, enabling: SSI 2012/6
Sch.1 para.7, enabling: SSI 2012/6
Sch.1 para.10, applied: SSI 2012/6, SSI 2012/210
Sch.1 para.11, applied: SSI 2012/6, SSI 2012/210
Sch.1 para.12, applied: SSI 2012/6
Sch.1 para.14, applied: SSI 2012/210
Sch.1 para.14, enabling: SSI 2012/6

asp 17. Commissioner for Children and Young People (Scotland) Act 2003
Sch.1 para.2, varied: 2012 c.11 s.12

2004

asp 2. Budget (Scotland) Act 2004
Sch.1, varied: 2012 c.11 s.12
Sch.2 Part 7, varied: 2012 c.11 s.12
Sch.2 Part 8, varied: 2012 c.11 s.12

asp 4. Education (Additional Support for Learning) (Scotland) Act 2004
s.17, referred to: SSI 2012/130 Sch.1 para.13
s.18, referred to: SSI 2012/130 Sch.1 para.13
s.19, referred to: SSI 2012/130 Sch.1 para.13
s.20, referred to: SSI 2012/130 Sch.1 para.13
s.21, referred to: SSI 2012/130 Sch.1 para.13
s.22, referred to: SSI 2012/130 Sch.1 para.13
Sch.1 para.3, varied: 2012 c.11 s.12
Sch.2, referred to: SSI 2012/130 Sch.1 para.13
Sch.2 para.2, referred to: SSI 2012/130 Reg.17
Sch.2 para.3, applied: SSI 2012/130 Sch.2 para.1
Sch.2 para.3, referred to: SSI 2012/130 Reg.17
Sch.2 para.4, applied: SSI 2012/130 Sch.2 para.1
Sch.2 para.6, applied: SSI 2012/130 Sch.2 para.1

asp 8. Antisocial Behaviour etc (Scotland) Act 2004
s.1, amended: 2012 asp 8 Sch.7 para.24, Sch.8 Part 1
s.2, amended: 2012 asp 8 Sch.7 para.24, Sch.8 Part 1
s.15, amended: 2012 asp 8 Sch.7 para.24
s.18, amended: 2012 asp 8 Sch.7 para.24
s.20, amended: 2012 asp 8 Sch.8 Part 1
s.31, amended: 2012 asp 8 Sch.7 para.24
s.35, amended: 2012 asp 8 Sch.7 para.24
s.83, applied: SSI 2012/151 Reg.5
s.83, enabling: SSI 2012/151
s.88, enabling: SSI 2012/151
s.119, amended: 2012 asp 8 Sch.7 para.24
s.128, amended: 2012 asp 1 s.3
s.139, amended: 2012 asp 8 Sch.7 para.24
s.141, enabling: SSI 2012/151
Sch.2 Part 2 para.7, repealed: SSI 2012/360 Sch.11 para.3
Sch.4 para.2, repealed: SSI 2012/330 Art.15

asp 9. Local Governance (Scotland) Act 2004
s.3, enabling: SSI 2012/60
s.3A, enabling: SSI 2012/60, SSI 2012/342
s.16, applied: SSI 2012/60, SSI 2012/342
s.16, enabling: SSI 2012/60, SSI 2012/342

2004–cont.

asp 10. Stirling-Alloa-Kincardine Railway and Linked Improvements Act 2004
s.16, amended: 2012 asp 5 Sch.5 para.45

asp 11. Tenements (Scotland) Act 2004
s.1, amended: 2012 asp 5 Sch.5 para.46
s.12, applied: 2012 asp 5 s.61
s.26, applied: 2012 asp 5 s.16
s.29, applied: 2012 asp 5 s.16
Sch.3 para.1, amended: 2012 asp 5 Sch.5 para.46

2005

asp 2. Emergency Workers (Scotland) Act 2005
s.1, amended: 2012 asp 8 Sch.7 para.67
s.7, substituted: 2012 asp 8 Sch.7 para.25

asp 3. Water Services etc (Scotland) Act 2005
Commencement Orders: SSI 2012/192 Art.2
s.14, referred to: 2012 asp 2 Sch.3
s.37, enabling: SSI 2012/192

asp 4. Budget (Scotland) Act 2005
Sch.1, varied: 2012 c.11 s.12
Sch.2 Part 7, varied: 2012 c.11 s.12
Sch.2 Part 8, varied: 2012 c.11 s.12

asp 5. Fire (Scotland) Act 2005
applied: 2012 asp 8 Sch.6 para.3, Sch.6 para.5
Part 1, amended: 2012 asp 8 Sch.7 para.68
s.1, amended: 2012 asp 8 Sch.7 para.68
s.1, applied: 2012 asp 8 s.122, SSI 2012/88 Reg.3
s.1, referred to: SI 2012/2885 Sch.4 para.3, SI 2012/2886 Sch.1, SSI 2012/303 Sch.3 para.9, SSI 2012/319 Sch.2 para.3
s.1, repealed: 2012 asp 8 Sch.8 Part 2
s.1A, added: 2012 asp 8 s.101
s.1A, amended: 2012 asp 8 s.101, Sch.7 para.68
s.1A, applied: 2012 asp 8 s.122
s.2, amended: 2012 asp 8 Sch.7 para.68
s.2, applied: 2012 asp 8 s.122, SI 2012/2885 Sch.4 para.3, SI 2012/2886 Sch.1, SSI 2012/88 Reg.3, SSI 2012/162 Sch.1, SSI 2012/303 Sch.3 para.9
s.2, referred to: SSI 2012/319 Sch.2 para.3
s.2, repealed: 2012 asp 8 Sch.8 Part 2
s.3, amended: 2012 asp 8 Sch.7 para.68
s.3, repealed: 2012 asp 8 Sch.8 Part 2
s.4, amended: 2012 asp 8 Sch.7 para.68
s.4, repealed: 2012 asp 8 Sch.8 Part 2
s.5, amended: 2012 asp 8 Sch.7 para.68
s.5, applied: SSI 2012/88 Reg.3
s.5, repealed: 2012 asp 8 Sch.8 Part 2
s.6, amended: 2012 asp 8 Sch.7 para.68
s.6, applied: SI 2012/632 Reg.3
s.6, repealed: 2012 asp 8 Sch.8 Part 2
s.7, applied: SSI 2012/162 Sch.1
s.7, repealed: 2012 asp 8 Sch.8 Part 2
s.8, amended: 2012 asp 8 s.102
s.9, amended: 2012 asp 8 s.104
s.10, amended: 2012 asp 8 s.105
s.11, amended: 2012 asp 8 s.106
s.12, repealed: 2012 asp 8 Sch.8 Part 2
s.13, amended: 2012 asp 8 s.107
s.14, amended: 2012 asp 8 s.108
s.15, amended: 2012 asp 8 s.109
s.16, amended: 2012 asp 8 s.110
s.16, repealed (in part): 2012 asp 8 Sch.8 Part 2
s.17, amended: 2012 asp 8 Sch.7 para.68
s.18, amended: 2012 asp 8 Sch.7 para.68
s.19, amended: 2012 asp 8 Sch.7 para.68
s.20, amended: 2012 asp 8 Sch.7 para.68
s.21, amended: 2012 asp 8 Sch.7 para.68

2005– cont.

asp 5. Fire (Scotland) Act 2005–*cont.*
s.23, amended: 2012 asp 8 Sch.7 para.68
s.24, amended: 2012 asp 8 Sch.7 para.68
s.25, amended: 2012 asp 8 Sch.7 para.68
s.27, amended: 2012 asp 8 Sch.7 para.68
s.29, amended: 2012 asp 8 Sch.7 para.68
s.30, amended: 2012 asp 8 Sch.7 para.68
s.33, repealed: 2012 asp 8 Sch.8 Part 2
s.34, repealed: 2012 asp 8 Sch.8 Part 2
s.35, amended: 2012 asp 8 s.111
s.36, amended: 2012 asp 8 s.112
s.37, repealed: 2012 asp 8 Sch.8 Part 2
s.39, amended: 2012 asp 8 Sch.7 para.68
s.39A, added: 2012 asp 8 s.113
s.39B, added: 2012 asp 8 s.113
s.39C, added: 2012 asp 8 s.113
s.40, amended: 2012 asp 8 Sch.7 para.68
s.40, applied: SSI 2012/ 146, SSI 2012/ 146 Art.2, SSI 2012/ 253 Art.8
s.40, referred to: SSI 2012/ 146
s.40, enabling: SSI 2012/ 146
s.41, amended: 2012 asp 8 Sch.7 para.68
s.41, referred to: SSI 2012/ 253 Art.8
s.41, repealed (in part): 2012 asp 8 Sch.8 Part 2
s.41A, added: 2012 asp 8 s.114
s.41A, referred to: SSI 2012/ 253 Art.8
s.41A, repealed: 2012 asp 8 Sch.8 Part 2
s.41B, added: 2012 asp 8 s.114
s.41B, repealed: 2012 asp 8 Sch.8 Part 2
s.41C, added: 2012 asp 8 s.114
s.41C, repealed: 2012 asp 8 Sch.8 Part 2
s.41D, added: 2012 asp 8 s.115
s.41D, repealed: 2012 asp 8 Sch.8 Part 2
s.41E, added: 2012 asp 8 s.115
s.41E, repealed: 2012 asp 8 Sch.8 Part 2
s.41F, added: 2012 asp 8 s.115
s.41F, repealed: 2012 asp 8 Sch.8 Part 2
s.41G, added: 2012 asp 8 s.115
s.41G, repealed: 2012 asp 8 Sch.8 Part 2
s.41H, added: 2012 asp 8 s.115
s.41H, repealed: 2012 asp 8 Sch.8 Part 2
s.41J, added: 2012 asp 8 s.115
s 41J, repealed: 2012 asp 8 Sch.8 Part 2
s.41K, added: 2012 asp 8 s.115
s.41K, repealed: 2012 asp 8 Sch.8 Part 2
s.41L, added: 2012 asp 8 s.116
s.41L, repealed: 2012 asp 8 Sch.8 Part 2
s.41M, added: 2012 asp 8 s.117
s.41M, repealed: 2012 asp 8 Sch.8 Part 2
s.42, repealed: 2012 asp 8 Sch.8 Part 2
s.42A, added: 2012 asp 8 s.118
s.42A, repealed: 2012 asp 8 Sch.8 Part 2
s.43, repealed: 2012 asp 8 Sch.8 Part 2
s.43A, added: 2012 asp 8 s.119
s.43A, applied: SI 2012/ 3073 Art.2
s.43A, repealed: 2012 asp 8 Sch.8 Part 2
s.43B, added: 2012 asp 8 s.119
s.43B, amended: 2012 asp 8 s.119
s.43B, applied: SSI 2012/ 333 Sch.2 para.3
s.43B, repealed: 2012 asp 8 Sch.8 Part 2
s.43C, added: 2012 asp 8 s.119
s.43C, amended: 2012 asp 8 s.119
s.43C, applied: SSI 2012/ 333 Sch.2 para.3
s.43C, repealed: 2012 asp 8 Sch.8 Part 2
s.43D, added: 2012 asp 8 s.119
s.43D, repealed: 2012 asp 8 Sch.8 Part 2
s.43E, added: 2012 asp 8 s.119
s.43E, amended: 2012 asp 8 s.119

2005– cont.

asp 5. Fire (Scotland) Act 2005–*cont.*
s.43E, repealed: 2012 asp 8 Sch.8 Part 2
s.43F, added: 2012 asp 8 s.119
s.43F, amended: 2012 asp 8 s.119
s.43F, applied: SSI 2012/ 333 Sch.2 para.3
s.43F, repealed: 2012 asp 8 Sch.8 Part 2
s.43G, added: 2012 asp 8 s.119
s.43G, amended: 2012 asp 8 s.119
s.43G, applied: SSI 2012/ 333 Sch.2 para.3
s.43G, repealed: 2012 asp 8 Sch.8 Part 2
s.44, repealed: 2012 asp 8 Sch.8 Part 2
s.44, added: 2012 asp 8 s.119
s.44, repealed: 2012 asp 8 Sch.8 Part 2
s.45, repealed: 2012 asp 8 Sch.8 Part 2
s.45, substituted: 2012 asp 8 Sch.7 para.68
s.45, repealed: 2012 asp 8 Sch.8 Part 2
s.46, repealed: 2012 asp 8 Sch.8 Part 2
s.46, substituted: 2012 asp 8 Sch.7 para.68
s.46, repealed: 2012 asp 8 Sch.8 Part 2
s.47, substituted: 2012 asp 8 Sch.7 para.68
s.47, amended: 2012 asp 8 Sch.7 para.68
s.47, repealed: 2012 asp 8 Sch.8 Part 2
s.48, repealed: 2012 asp 8 Sch.8 Part 2
s.48, substituted: 2012 asp 8 Sch.7 para.68
s.48, repealed: 2012 asp 8 Sch.8 Part 2
s.49, repealed: 2012 asp 8 Sch.8 Part 2
s.50, repealed: 2012 asp 8 Sch.8 Part 2
s.51, amended: 2012 asp 8 s.120, Sch.7 para.68
s.52, amended: 2012 asp 8 Sch.7 para.68
s.58, enabling: SSI 2012/ 332
s.59, amended: 2012 asp 8 Sch.7 para.68
s.61, amended: 2012 asp 8 s.103
s.61, repealed (in part): 2012 asp 8 Sch.8 Part 2
s.67, amended: 2012 asp 8 s.103
s.67, repealed (in part): 2012 asp 8 Sch.8 Part 2
s.78, amended: SSI 2012/ 332 Reg.2
s.78, enabling: SSI 2012/ 332
s.79, amended: 2012 asp 8 Sch.7 para.68, Sch.8 Part 2
s.80, amended: 2012 asp 8 Sch.7 para.68
s.81, amended: 2012 asp 8 Sch.7 para.68
s.85, amended: 2012 asp 8 Sch.7 para.68
s.86, amended: 2012 asp 8 Sch.7 para.68
s.86A, added: 2012 asp 8 Sch.7 para 68
s.88, applied: SSI 2012/ 332
s.88, repealed (in part): 2012 asp 8 Sch.8 Part 2
s.88, enabling: SSI 2012/ 332
Sch.1 para.1, repealed: 2012 asp 8 Sch.8 Part 2
Sch.1 para.2, repealed: 2012 asp 8 Sch.8 Part 2
Sch.1 para.3, repealed: 2012 asp 8 Sch.8 Part 2
Sch.1A para.1, added: 2012 asp 8 s.101
Sch.1A para.2, added: 2012 asp 8 s.101
Sch.1A para.2, applied: 2012 asp 8 s.122
Sch.1A para.3, added: 2012 asp 8 s.101
Sch.1A para.4, added: 2012 asp 8 s.101
Sch.1A para.5, added: 2012 asp 8 s.101
Sch.1A para.6, added: 2012 asp 8 s.101
Sch.1A para.7, added: 2012 asp 8 s.101
Sch.1A para.8, added: 2012 asp 8 s.101
Sch.1A para.9, added: 2012 asp 8 s.101
Sch.1A para.10, added: 2012 asp 8 s.101
Sch.1A para.11, added: 2012 asp 8 s.101
Sch.1A para.12, added: 2012 asp 8 s.101
Sch.1A para.13, added: 2012 asp 8 s.101
Sch.1A para.14, added: 2012 asp 8 s.101
Sch.1A para.15, added: 2012 asp 8 s.101
Sch.1A para.16, added: 2012 asp 8 s.101
Sch.1A para.17, added: 2012 asp 8 s.101

2006–cont.

asp 10. Police, Public Order and Criminal Justice (Scotland) Act 2006–*cont.*
s.31, repealed: 2012 asp 8 Sch.8 Part 1
s.32, repealed: 2012 asp 8 Sch.8 Part 1
s.33, amended: 2012 asp 8 s.61
s.33, referred to: 2012 asp 8 s.61
s.33, substituted: 2012 asp 8 s.61
s.33A, added: 2012 asp 8 s.62
s.34, amended: 2012 asp 8 Sch.7 para.33
s.34, repealed (in part): 2012 asp 8 Sch.8 Part 1
s.35, amended: 2012 asp 8 Sch.7 para.33
s.36, amended: 2012 asp 8 Sch.7 para.33
s.40A, added: 2012 asp 8 Sch.7 para.33
s.41, amended: 2012 asp 8 Sch.7 para.33
s.41, repealed (in part): 2012 asp 8 Sch.8 Part 1
s.41A, added: 2012 asp 8 s.63
s.41B, added: 2012 asp 8 s.64
s.41C, added: 2012 asp 8 s.65
s.41D, added: 2012 asp 8 s.66
s.41E, added: 2012 asp 8 s.67
s.41F, added: 2012 asp 8 s.68
s.42, repealed: 2012 asp 8 Sch.8 Part 1
s.42A, added: 2012 asp 8 s.69
s.43, amended: 2012 asp 8 Sch.7 para.33
s.44, amended: 2012 asp 8 Sch.7 para.33
s.45, amended: 2012 asp 8 Sch.7 para.33
s.46, amended: 2012 asp 8 Sch.7 para.33
s.46A, added: 2012 asp 8 s.70
s.47, amended: 2012 asp 8 s.61
s.47, substituted: 2012 asp 8 Sch.7 para.33
s.48, repealed: 2012 asp 8 Sch.8 Part 1
s.49, repealed: 2012 asp 8 Sch.8 Part 1
s.50, repealed: 2012 asp 8 Sch.8 Part 1
s.52, amended: 2012 asp 8 Sch.7 para.33
s.52, repealed (in part): 2012 asp 8 Sch.7 para.33
s.57, amended: 2012 asp 8 Sch.7 para.33
s.57, repealed (in part): 2012 asp 8 Sch.7 para.33
s.69, amended: 2012 asp 8 Sch.7 para.33
s.99, amended: 2012 asp 8 Sch.8 Part 1
s.103, amended: 2012 asp 8 Sch.7 para.33
Sch.1 para.1, repealed: 2012 asp 8 Sch.8 Part 1
Sch.1 para.2, repealed: 2012 asp 8 Sch.8 Part 1
Sch.1 para.3, repealed: 2012 asp 8 Sch.8 Part 1
Sch.1 para.4, repealed: 2012 asp 8 Sch.8 Part 1
Sch.1 para.5, repealed: 2012 asp 8 Sch.8 Part 1
Sch.1 para.6, repealed: 2012 asp 8 Sch.8 Part 1
Sch.1 para.7, repealed: 2012 asp 8 Sch.8 Part 1
Sch.1 para.8, repealed: 2012 asp 8 Sch.8 Part 1
Sch.1 para.9, applied: 2012 asp 8 Sch.5 para.11
Sch.1 para.9, repealed: 2012 asp 8 Sch.8 Part 1
Sch.1 para.10, applied: 2012 asp 8 Sch.5 para.7, Sch.5 para.11
Sch.1 para.10, repealed: 2012 asp 8 Sch.8 Part 1
Sch.1 para.11, repealed: 2012 asp 8 Sch.8 Part 1
Sch.1 para.12, repealed: 2012 asp 8 Sch.8 Part 1
Sch.1 para.13, repealed: 2012 asp 8 Sch.8 Part 1
Sch.1 para.14, repealed: 2012 asp 8 Sch.8 Part 1
Sch.1 para.15, repealed: 2012 asp 8 Sch.8 Part 1
Sch.1 para.16, repealed: 2012 asp 8 Sch.8 Part 1
Sch.2 para.1, repealed: 2012 asp 8 Sch.8 Part 1
Sch.2 para.2, repealed: 2012 asp 8 Sch.8 Part 1
Sch.2 para.3, repealed: 2012 asp 8 Sch.8 Part 1
Sch.2 para.4, repealed: 2012 asp 8 Sch.8 Part 1
Sch.2 para.5, repealed: 2012 asp 8 Sch.8 Part 1
Sch.2 para.6, repealed: 2012 asp 8 Sch.8 Part 1
Sch.2 para.7, repealed: 2012 asp 8 Sch.8 Part 1
Sch.2 para.8, repealed: 2012 asp 8 Sch.8 Part 1
Sch.2 para.9, repealed: 2012 asp 8 Sch.8 Part 1

2006–cont.

asp 10. Police, Public Order and Criminal Justice (Scotland) Act 2006–*cont.*
Sch.3 Part 1 para.1, repealed: 2012 asp 8 Sch.8 Part 1
Sch.3 Part 1 para.2, repealed: 2012 asp 8 Sch.8 Part 1
Sch.3 Part 1 para.3, repealed: 2012 asp 8 Sch.8 Part 1
Sch.3 Part 1 para.4, repealed: 2012 asp 8 Sch.8 Part 1
Sch.3 Part 2 para.5, repealed: 2012 asp 8 Sch.8 Part 1
Sch.3 Part 2 para.6, repealed: 2012 asp 8 Sch.8 Part 1
Sch.3 Part 2 para.8, repealed: 2012 asp 8 Sch.8 Part 1
Sch.4 para.1, amended: 2012 asp 8 s.61
Sch.4 para.1, substituted: 2012 asp 8 Sch.7 para.33
Sch.4 para.2, amended: 2012 asp 8 s.61, Sch.7 para.33
Sch.4 para.2, repealed (in part): 2012 asp 8 Sch.8 Part 1
Sch.4 para.2, substituted: 2012 asp 8 Sch.7 para.33
Sch.4 para.3, amended: 2012 asp 8 s.61, Sch.7 para.33
Sch.4 para.3, substituted: 2012 asp 8 Sch.7 para.33
Sch.4 para.4, amended: 2012 asp 8 s.61
Sch.4 para.4, substituted: 2012 asp 8 Sch.7 para.33
Sch.4 para.5, amended: 2012 asp 8 s.61
Sch.4 para.5, substituted: 2012 asp 8 Sch.7 para.33
Sch.4 para.6, amended: 2012 asp 8 s.61
Sch.4 para.6, substituted: 2012 asp 8 Sch.7 para.33
Sch.4 para.7, amended: 2012 asp 8 s.61
Sch.4 para.7, substituted: 2012 asp 8 Sch.7 para.33
Sch.4 para.7A, added: 2012 asp 8 Sch.7 para.33
Sch.4 para.7A, amended: 2012 asp 8 s.61
Sch.4 para.7A, substituted: 2012 asp 8 Sch.7 para.33
Sch.4 para.7B, added: 2012 asp 8 Sch.7 para.33
Sch.4 para.7B, amended: 2012 asp 8 s.61
Sch.4 para.7B, substituted: 2012 asp 8 Sch.7 para.33
Sch.4 para.8, amended: 2012 asp 8 s.61
Sch.4 para.8, substituted: 2012 asp 8 Sch.7 para.33
Sch.4 para.9, amended: 2012 asp 8 s.61
Sch.4 para.9, substituted: 2012 asp 8 Sch.7 para.33
Sch.4 para.10, amended: 2012 asp 8 s.61
Sch.4 para.10, substituted: 2012 asp 8 Sch.7 para.33
Sch.4 para.11, amended: 2012 asp 8 s.61
Sch.4 para.11, substituted: 2012 asp 8 Sch.7 para.33
Sch.6 Part 1 para.1, repealed: 2012 asp 8 Sch.8 Part 1
Sch.6 Part 1 para.7, repealed: 2012 asp 8 Sch.8 Part 1
Sch.6 Part 1 para.10, amended: 2012 asp 8 s.61
Sch.6 Part 1 para.11, amended: 2012 asp 8 s.61
Sch.6 Part 1 para.11, repealed: 2012 asp 8 Sch.8 Part 1
Sch.6 Part 1 para.12, repealed: 2012 asp 8 Sch.8 Part 1

asp 11. Animal Health and Welfare (Scotland) Act 2006
s.20, applied: SSI 2012/40
s.20, enabling: SSI 2012/40
s.49, amended: 2012 asp 8 Sch.7 para.34
s.51, applied: SSI 2012/40

asp 12. Interests of Members of the Scottish Parliament Act 2006
Sch.1 para.2, varied: 2012 c.11 s.12

asp 13. Waverley Railway (Scotland) Act 2006
s.16, amended: 2012 asp 5 Sch.5 para.49

2006– cont.

asp 14. Local Electoral Administration and Registration Services (Scotland) Act 2006
s.5, enabling: SSI 2012/ 61
s.61, applied: SSI 2012/ 61
Sch.2 Part 1 para.2, repealed: SSI 2012/ 31 Art.4
asp 16. Scottish Commission for Human Rights Act 2006
Sch.1 para.3, varied: 2012 c.11 s.12
asp 17. Planning etc (Scotland) Act 2006
s.58, enabling: SSI 2012/ 117

2007

asp 1. Glasgow Airport Rail Link Act 2007
s.15, amended: 2012 asp 5 Sch.5 para.51
asp 3. Bankruptcy and Diligence etc (Scotland) Act 2007
s.83, applied: 2012 asp 5 s.32
s.85, amended: 2012 asp 5 Sch.5 para.52
s.128, amended: 2012 asp 5 Sch.5 para.52
s.215, enabling: SSI 2012/ 136, SSI 2012/ 273
s.216, applied: SSI 2012/ 136 Art.3, Art.6
s.221, amended: SSI 2012/ 301 Sch.1 para.3
asp 4. Adoption and Children (Scotland) Act 2007
applied: SI 2012/ 3144 Reg.8, SI 2012/ 3145 Sch.1
s.71, applied: SI 2012/ 2886 Sch.1, SSI 2012/ 303 Sch.4 para.29
s.81, applied: SSI 2012/ 303 Reg.28, SSI 2012/ 319 Reg.29
s.114, enabling: SSI 2012/ 188
s.116, enabling: SSI 2012/ 99
s.117, enabling: SSI 2012/ 99
asp 5. Legal Profession and Legal Aid (Scotland) Act 2007
Part 1, applied: SSI 2012/ 153 Reg.2
s.2, referred to: SSI 2012/ 153 Reg.2
s.2, varied: SSI 2012/ 153 Reg.2
s.5, applied: SSI 2012/ 154
s.29, disapplied: SSI 2012/ 152 Art.3
s.29, referred to: SSI 2012/ 152 Art.3
s.49, applied: SSI 2012/ 154 Reg.2
s.57A, applied: SSI 2012/ 153 Reg.2
s.57A, referred to: SSI 2012/ 152 Art.3
s.57A, enabling: SSI 2012/ 153
s.57B, referred to: SSI 2012/ 152 Art.3
s.57C, applied: SSI 2012/ 152 Art.3
s.63, applied: SSI 2012/ 154 Reg.5
s.78, amended: SSI 2012/ 212 Reg.4
asp 6. Criminal Proceedings etc (Reform) (Scotland) Act 2007
Commencement Orders: SSI 2012/ 274 Art.2, Sch.1
s.84, enabling: SSI 2012/ 274
asp 9. Budget (Scotland) Act 2007
Sch.2 Part 7, varied: 2012 c.11 s.12
Sch.2 Part 8, varied: 2012 c.11 s.12
asp 10. Adult Support and Protection (Scotland) Act 2007
s.1, varied: SSI 2012/ 66 Art.2
s.2, varied: SSI 2012/ 66 Art.2
s.3, varied: SSI 2012/ 66 Art.2
s.4, varied: SSI 2012/ 66 Art.2
s.5, amended: 2012 asp 8 Sch.7 para.35
s.5, varied: SSI 2012/ 66 Art.2
s.6, varied: SSI 2012/ 66 Art.2
s.7, applied: SSI 2012/ 66 Art.3
s.7, varied: SSI 2012/ 66 Art.2
s.8, applied: SSI 2012/ 66 Art.3
s.8, varied: SSI 2012/ 66 Art.2

2007– cont.

asp 10. Adult Support and Protection (Scotland) Act 2007– *cont.*
s.9, applied: SSI 2012/ 66 Art.3
s.9, varied: SSI 2012/ 66 Art.2
s.10, applied: SSI 2012/ 66 Art.3
s.10, varied: SSI 2012/ 66 Art.2
s.11, applied: SSI 2012/ 66 Art.3
s.11, varied: SSI 2012/ 66 Art.2
s.12, varied: SSI 2012/ 66 Art.2
s.13, varied: SSI 2012/ 66 Art.2
s.14, applied: SSI 2012/ 66 Art.3
s.14, varied: SSI 2012/ 66 Art.2
s.15, varied: SSI 2012/ 66 Art.2
s.16, applied: SSI 2012/ 66 Art.3
s.16, varied: SSI 2012/ 66 Art.2
s.17, varied: SSI 2012/ 66 Art.2
s.18, applied: SSI 2012/ 66 Art.3
s.18, varied: SSI 2012/ 66 Art.2
s.19, varied: SSI 2012/ 66 Art.2
s.20, varied: SSI 2012/ 66 Art.2
s.21, varied: SSI 2012/ 66 Art.2
s.22, varied: SSI 2012/ 66 Art.2
s.23, varied: SSI 2012/ 66 Art.2
s.24, varied: SSI 2012/ 66 Art.2
s.25, varied: SSI 2012/ 66 Art.2
s.26, varied: SSI 2012/ 66 Art.2
s.27, amended: 2012 asp 8 Sch.7 para.35
s.27, varied: SSI 2012/ 66 Art.2
s.28, varied: SSI 2012/ 66 Art.2
s.29, varied: SSI 2012/ 66 Art.2
s.30, varied: SSI 2012/ 66 Art.2
s.30B, varied: SSI 2012/ 66 Art.2
s.31, varied: SSI 2012/ 66 Art.2
s.32, varied: SSI 2012/ 66 Art.2
s.33, varied: SSI 2012/ 66 Art.2
s.34, varied: SSI 2012/ 66 Art.2
s.35, varied: SSI 2012/ 66 Art.2
s.36, varied: SSI 2012/ 66 Art.2
s.37, varied: SSI 2012/ 66 Art.2
s.38, varied: SSI 2012/ 66 Art.2
s.39, varied: SSI 2012/ 66 Art.2
s.40, varied: SSI 2012/ 66 Art.2
s.41, varied: SSI 2012/ 66 Art.2
s.42, amended: 2012 asp 8 Sch.7 para.35
s.42, varied: SSI 2012/ 66 Art.2
s.43, varied: SSI 2012/ 66 Art.2
s.44, varied: SSI 2012/ 66 Art.2
s.45, varied: SSI 2012/ 66 Art.2
s.46, varied: SSI 2012/ 66 Art.2
s.47, varied: SSI 2012/ 66 Art.2
s.48, varied: SSI 2012/ 66 Art.2
s.49, varied: SSI 2012/ 66 Art.2
s.50, varied: SSI 2012/ 66 Art.2
s.51, varied: SSI 2012/ 66 Art.2
s.52, varied: SSI 2012/ 66 Art.2
s.53, varied: SSI 2012/ 66 Art.2
asp 13. Christmas Day and New Year's Day Trading (Scotland) Act 2007
s.7, amended: SI 2012/ 1916 Sch.34 para.45
asp 14. Protection of Vulnerable Groups (Scotland) Act 2007
applied: SSI 2012/ 54 Reg.6
s.1, applied: SI 2012/ 2113 Art.2, Art.3
s.17, amended: 2012 c.7 Sch.15 para.56
s.18, amended: 2012 asp 8 Sch.7 para.36
s.30A, amended: 2012 c.7 Sch.15 para.56, Sch.15 para.58
s.38, amended: 2012 asp 8 Sch.7 para.36

2007– cont.

asp 14. Protection of Vulnerable Groups (Scotland) Act 2007–*cont.*
s.39, amended: SI 2012/3006 Art.34
s.40, amended: SI 2012/3006 Art.34
s.56, varied: 2012 c.11 s.12
s.75, amended: 2012 asp 8 Sch.7 para.36
s.76, amended: 2012 asp 8 Sch.7 para.36
s.97, amended: 2012 asp 8 Sch.7 para.36, SI 2012/3006 Art.34
Sch.4 para.31, varied: 2012 c.11 s.12
Sch.4 para.32, varied: 2012 c.11 s.12
Sch.5, amended: SI 2012/3006 Art.34

asp 16. Edinburgh Airport Rail Link Act 2007
s.9, amended: 2012 asp 5 Sch.5 para.53
s.20, amended: 2012 asp 5 Sch.5 para.53
s.38, amended: 2012 asp 8 Sch.7 para.37

asp 17. Custodial Sentences and Weapons (Scotland) Act 2007
Part 2, referred to: 2012 asp 7 s.2
s.20, amended: 2012 asp 7 s.1
s.20A, added: 2012 asp 7 s.1

asp 19. Airdrie-Bathgate Railway and Linked Improvements Act 2007
s.9, amended: 2012 asp 5 Sch.5 para.54
s.20, amended: 2012 asp 5 Sch.5 para.54

2008

asp 2. Budget (Scotland) Act 2008
Sch.1, amended: 2012 asp 8 s.61
Sch.2 Part 7, varied: 2012 c.11 s.12
Sch.2 Part 9, varied: 2012 c.11 s.12

asp 4. Glasgow Commonwealth Games Act 2008
Commencement Orders: SSI 2012/261 Art.2, Sch.1
s.17, applied: SI 2012/1852 Art.3
s.19, enabling: SSI 2012/323
s.30, amended: 2012 asp 8 Sch.7 para.38
s.37, amended: 2012 asp 8 Sch.7 para.38
s.43, enabling: SSI 2012/323
s.49, enabling: SSI 2012/261

asp 6. Judiciary and Courts (Scotland) Act 2008
s.9, varied: 2012 c.11 s.12
s.17, varied: 2012 c.11 s.12
s.30, varied: 2012 c.11 s.12
Sch.1 para.5, varied: 2012 c.11 s.12
Sch.3 para.4, varied: 2012 c.11 s.12

2009

asp 2. Budget (Scotland) Act 2009
Sch.1, amended: 2012 asp 8 s.61
Sch.2 Part 5, varied: 2012 c.11 s.12
Sch.2 Part 7, varied: 2012 c.11 s.12
Sch.2 Part 9, varied: 2012 c.11 s.12

asp 11. Convention Rights Proceedings (Amendment) (Scotland) Act 2009
repealed: 2012 c.11 s.14
s.1, varied: 2012 c.11 s.12

asp 12. Climate Change (Scotland) Act 2009
s.1, applied: SSI 2012/77
s.2, applied: SSI 2012/77
s.3, applied: SSI 2012/77
s.59, applied: SSI 2012/77
s.59, enabling: SSI 2012/77
s.96, applied: SSI 2012/77
s.96, enabling: SSI 2012/77

2010

asp 3. Tobacco and Primary Medical Services (Scotland) Act 2010
s.10, applied: SSI 2012/29 Reg.3

asp 4. Budget (Scotland) Act 2010
Sch.1, amended: 2012 asp 8 s.61

asp 5. Marine (Scotland) Act 2010
s.25, enabling: SSI 2012/183
s.32, applied: SSI 2012/25
s.32, enabling: SSI 2012/25
s.132, amended: SSI 2012/215 Sch.1 para.2
s.165, enabling: SSI 2012/25, SSI 2012/183
Sch.2 para.12, amended: 2012 asp 8 Sch.7 para.39

asp 8. Public Services Reform (Scotland) Act 2010
Commencement Orders: SSI 2012/218 Art.2
applied: SI 2012/2885 Sch.1 para.25, SI 2012/3144 Sch.1 para.19
s.17, enabling: SSI 2012/102
s.18, referred to: SSI 2012/102
s.25, applied: SSI 2012/102
s.26, applied: SSI 2012/102
s.31, applied: SI 2012/1659 Sch.3 para.26
s.32, applied: SI 2012/1659 Sch.3 para.26
s.58, enabling: SSI 2012/45
s.59, applied: SI 2012/2885 Sch.1 para.25, SI 2012/2886 Sch.1, SI 2012/3144 Sch.1 para.19, SI 2012/3145 Sch.1, SSI 2012/303 Reg.28, SSI 2012/319 Reg.29
s.83, applied: SI 2012/2885 Sch.1 para.25, SI 2012/2886 Sch.1, SI 2012/3144 Sch.1 para.19, SI 2012/3145 Sch.1, SSI 2012/303 Reg.28, SSI 2012/319 Reg.29
s.104, applied: SSI 2012/44
s.104, enabling: SSI 2012/44, SSI 2012/45
s.114, amended: 2012 asp 8 Sch.7 para.40
s.115, amended: 2012 asp 8 Sch.7 para.40
s.134, enabling: SSI 2012/218
Sch.5, amended: 2012 asp 3 Sch.2 para.9, 2012 asp 8 Sch.1 para.17, Sch.7 para.40, Sch.7 para.72, Sch.8 Part 1, SI 2012/1659 Sch.3 para.26
Sch.8, amended: 2012 asp 3 Sch.2 para.9, 2012 asp 8 s.61, Sch.1 para.17, Sch.7 para.40, Sch.7 para.72, Sch.8 Part 1, SI 2012/1659 Sch.3 para.26
Sch.9 para.9, varied: 2012 c.11 s.12
Sch.11 para.10, varied: 2012 c.11 s.12
Sch.12 para.1, referred to: SSI 2012/44 Reg.2
Sch.12 para.1, enabling: SSI 2012/44
Sch.12 para.4, referred to: SSI 2012/44 Reg.3
Sch.12 para.4, enabling: SSI 2012/44
Sch.12 para.13, referred to: SSI 2012/44 Reg.4
Sch.12 para.13, enabling: SSI 2012/44
Sch.16, varied: 2012 c.11 s.12
Sch.18 para.7, varied: 2012 c.11 s.12
Sch.19, amended: 2012 asp 8 Sch.7 para.40, Sch.7 para.72
Sch.20, amended: 2012 asp 8 Sch.7 para.40, Sch.8 Part 2

asp 9. Control of Dogs (Scotland) Act 2010
s.13, amended: 2012 asp 8 Sch.7 para.41

asp 10. Interpretation and Legislative Reform (Scotland) Act 2010
s.28, varied: 2012 c.7 s.304
s.31, varied: 2012 c.7 s.304
s.32, varied: 2012 c.7 s.304
s.50, varied: 2012 c.11 s.12
Sch.1, amended: 2012 asp 8 Sch.8 Part 1
Sch.1, varied: 2012 c.11 s.12

asp 11. Scottish Parliamentary Commissions and Commissioners etc Act 2010
s.4, varied: 2012 c.11 s.12

asp 13. Criminal Justice and Licensing (Scotland) Act 2010
Commencement Orders: SSI 2012/ 160 Art.3, Art.4
s.28, applied: SSI 2012/ 88 Reg.23, SSI 2012/ 89 Reg.26
s.30, applied: SSI 2012/ 88 Reg.23, SSI 2012/ 89 Reg.26
s.31, repealed (in part): 2012 asp 8 Sch.8 Part 1
s.56, repealed: 2012 asp 8 Sch.8 Part 1
s.117, amended: 2012 asp 8 Sch.7 para.42
s.125, applied: 2012 asp 5 s.112
s.164, amended: 2012 asp 8 Sch.7 para.42
s.168, applied: SSI 2012/ 160 Art.4
s.171, applied: SSI 2012/ 160 Art.4
s.171, referred to: SSI 2012/ 160 Art.4
s.179, amended: SSI 2012/ 304 Art.2
s.201, applied: SSI 2012/ 304
s.201, enabling: SSI 2012/ 160
s.204, enabling: SSI 2012/ 304
s.206, enabling: SSI 2012/ 160
Sch.1 para.3, varied: 2012 c.11 s.12
Sch.2 Part 2 para.38, repealed: 2012 c.5 Sch.14 Part 3

asp 14. Crofting Reform (Scotland) Act 2010
Commencement Orders: SSI 2012/ 288 Art.3, Sch.1 Part 1, Sch.2 para.3, para.4, para.6, para.7, para.9, para.10, para.11, para.12, para.2, Art.4, Sch.1 Part 2, Sch.2 para.8, para.5, para.13, para.14, para.15, para.16, para.17, para.18, para.19
s.4, amended: SSI 2012/ 288 Sch.2 para.1
s.4, applied: SSI 2012/ 294 r.6, Sch.1, SSI 2012/ 295 Sch.1, SSI 2012/ 297 Reg.2
s.4, repealed (in part): SSI 2012/ 288 Sch.2 para.1
s.4, enabling: SSI 2012/ 297
s.5, applied: SSI 2012/ 294 r.6, Sch.1, SSI 2012/ 295 Sch.1, SSI 2012/ 297 Reg.2, Reg.3
s.5, enabling: SSI 2012/ 297
s.7, amended: SSI 2012/ 288 Sch.2 para.1
s.7, applied: SSI 2012/ 294 r.9, SSI 2012/ 295 Art.3
s.8, amended: SSI 2012/ 288 Sch.2 para.1
s.9, amended: SSI 2012/ 288 Sch.2 para.1
s.10, amended: SSI 2012/ 288 Sch.2 para.1
s.10, applied: SSI 2012/ 294 r.8
s.12, amended: SSI 2012/ 288 Sch.2 para.1
s.12, applied: SSI 2012/ 296 Art.2
s.12, enabling: SSI 2012/ 296
s.16, applied: SSI 2012/ 294 r.7, Sch.1
s.17, amended: SSI 2012/ 288 Sch.2 para.1
s.19, enabling: SSI 2012/ 294, SSI 2012/ 295, SSI 2012/ 327, SSI 2012/ 328
s.24, amended: SSI 2012/ 288 Sch.2 para.1
s.24, applied: SSI 2012/ 294 r.6, Sch.1, SSI 2012/ 295 Sch.1
s.25, applied: SSI 2012/ 295 Sch.1, SSI 2012/ 297 Reg.3
s.25, enabling: SSI 2012/ 297
s.26, amended: SSI 2012/ 288 Sch.2 para.1
s.26, applied: SSI 2012/ 294 r.6, Sch.1, SSI 2012/ 295 Sch.1
s.32, applied: SSI 2012/ 294 r.6, Sch.1, SSI 2012/ 295 Sch.1
s.53, applied: SSI 2012/ 288
s.53, enabling: SSI 2012/ 288, SSI 2012/ 294, SSI 2012/ 295, SSI 2012/ 296, SSI 2012/ 297, SSI 2012/ 327, SSI 2012/ 328
s.57, enabling: SSI 2012/ 288

asp 16. Legal Services (Scotland) Act 2010
Commencement Orders: SSI 2012/ 152 Art.2, Art.4, Sch.1

asp 16. Legal Services (Scotland) Act 2010–*cont.*
Part 2, applied: SSI 2012/ 155 Reg.2
s.5, applied: SSI 2012/ 153, SSI 2012/ 155, SSI 2012/ 213
s.14, applied: SSI 2012/ 153 Reg.5
s.25, referred to: SSI 2012/ 153 Reg.4
s.26, enabling: SSI 2012/ 153
s.49, applied: SSI 2012/ 213, SSI 2012/ 213 Reg.2
s.49, enabling: SSI 2012/ 213
s.63, applied: SSI 2012/ 154 Reg.5
s.67, applied: SSI 2012/ 154 Reg.3, Reg.4
s.67, enabling: SSI 2012/ 154
s.79, applied: SSI 2012/ 153 Reg.3
s.79, referred to: SSI 2012/ 153 Reg.3
s.79, enabling: SSI 2012/ 153
s.80, applied: SSI 2012/ 152 Art.4
s.81, referred to: SSI 2012/ 152 Art.3
s.146, applied: SSI 2012/ 213
s.146, enabling: SSI 2012/ 154
s.148, applied: SSI 2012/ 212
s.148, enabling: SSI 2012/ 212
s.150, enabling: SSI 2012/ 152
Sch.4 para.2, applied: SSI 2012/ 155 Reg.2
Sch.4 para.2, enabling: SSI 2012/ 155
Sch.4 para.11, applied: SSI 2012/ 155 Reg.3
Sch.4 para.11, enabling: SSI 2012/ 155

asp 17. Housing (Scotland) Act 2010
Commencement Orders: SSI 2012/ 19 Art.2; SSI 2012/ 39 Sch.1, Art.2; SSI 2012/ 91 Art.2, Art.3; SSI 2012/ 283 Art.3, Art.4, Art.2
s.161, enabling: SSI 2012/ 39, SSI 2012/ 91, SSI 2012/ 283
s.163, enabling: SSI 2012/ 38
s.166, enabling: SSI 2012/ 19, SSI 2012/ 39, SSI 2012/ 91, SSI 2012/ 283

asp 18. Alcohol etc (Scotland) Act 2010
s.1, repealed: 2012 asp 4 s.4
s.14, amended: 2012 asp 8 Sch.7 para.43
s.15, amended: 2012 asp 8 Sch.7 para.43
s.15, repealed (in part): 2012 asp 8 Sch.8 Part 1

asp 1. Children's Hearings (Scotland) Act 2011
Commencement Orders: SSI 2012/ 1 Art.2, Sch.1; SSI 2012/ 23 Art.2; SSI 2012/ 246 Sch.1; SSI 2012/ 252 Art.2; SSI 2012/ 246 Art.2
applied: SSI 2012/ 335 Reg.3, Reg.4, SSI 2012/ 336 Reg.3, Reg.7, Reg.8
Part 10, applied: SSI 2012/ 54 Reg.11, SSI 2012/ 336 Reg.3
Part 15, applied: SSI 2012/ 54 Reg.11
s.6, applied: SSI 2012/ 336 Reg.9
s.19, applied: SSI 2012/ 335 Reg.3, Reg.4, Reg.5
s.19, enabling: SSI 2012/ 335
s.30, applied: SSI 2012/ 336 Reg.3
s.31, applied: SSI 2012/ 336 Reg.3, Reg.4, Reg.5
s.32, enabling: SSI 2012/ 54
s.34, enabling: SSI 2012/ 336
s.39, referred to: SSI 2012/ 334 Reg.13
s.55, applied: SSI 2012/ 334 Reg.3, Reg.4, Reg.5, Reg.7, Reg.8, Reg.9
s.55, disapplied: SSI 2012/ 334 Reg.3
s.56, applied: SSI 2012/ 334 Reg.10, Reg.13, Reg.14
s.57, enabling: SSI 2012/ 334
s.61, amended: 2012 asp 8 Sch.7 para.44
s.82, applied: SSI 2012/ 336 Reg.3
s.108, applied: SSI 2012/ 336 Reg.3

2011– cont.

asp 1. Children's Hearings (Scotland) Act 2011– *cont.*
s.114, applied: SSI 2012/336 Reg.3
s.126, applied: SSI 2012/336 Reg.4
s.138, applied: SSI 2012/336 Reg.3
s.154, applied: SSI 2012/336 Reg.3, Reg.6
s.156, applied: SSI 2012/336 Reg.3
s.160, applied: SSI 2012/336 Reg.4
s.160, referred to: SSI 2012/336 Reg.4
s.161, applied: SSI 2012/336 Reg.4
s.162, applied: SSI 2012/336 Reg.4
s.163, applied: SSI 2012/336 Reg.3
s.164, applied: SSI 2012/336 Reg.4
s.165, applied: SSI 2012/336 Reg.4
s.166, applied: SSI 2012/336 Reg.5
s.167, applied: SSI 2012/336 Reg.5
s.193, applied: SSI 2012/337 Reg.2
s.195, enabling: SSI 2012/335, SSI 2012/336, SSI 2012/337
s.206, enabling: SSI 2012/1, SSI 2012/23, SSI 2012/246, SSI 2012/252
Sch.3 para.8, applied: SSI 2012/337 Reg.4
Sch.3 para.8, enabling: SSI 2012/337
Sch.3 para.12, applied: SSI 2012/337 Reg.3, Reg.4
Sch.3 para.12, enabling: SSI 2012/337

asp 4. Budget (Scotland) Act 2011
s.3, amended: SSI 2012/105 Art.2
s.6, repealed: 2012 asp 2 s.8
s.7, applied: SSI 2012/105
s.7, enabling: SSI 2012/105
Sch.1, amended: 2012 asp 8 s.61, SSI 2012/105 Art.3
Sch.1, substituted: SSI 2012/105 Art.3
Sch.2, amended: SSI 2012/105 Art.4
Sch.2, substituted: SSI 2012/105 Art.4
Sch.3, amended: SSI 2012/105 Art.5

asp 5. Patient Rights (Scotland) Act 2011
Commencement Orders: SSI 2012/35 Art.2
s.9, enabling: SSI 2012/110
s.12, applied: SSI 2012/110 Reg.4
s.15, applied: SSI 2012/36 Reg.2, Reg.4
s.15, enabling: SSI 2012/36
s.25, applied: SSI 2012/110
s.25, enabling: SSI 2012/36, SSI 2012/110
s.26, enabling: SSI 2012/35

asp 6. Wildlife and Natural Environment (Scotland) Act 2011
Commencement Orders: SSI 2012/175 Art.2; SSI 2012/116 Art.2; SSI 2012/281 Art.2
s.42, applied: SSI 2012/215
s.42, enabling: SSI 2012/174, SSI 2012/215
s.43, enabling: SSI 2012/116, SSI 2012/175, SSI 2012/281

asp 8. Property Factors (Scotland) Act 2011
Commencement Orders: SSI 2012/149 Art.2, Art.3, Sch.1
s.1, amended: SSI 2012/269 Art.2
s.2, referred to: SSI 2012/181d(property)
s.3, applied: SSI 2012/181 Reg.3, Reg.4, Reg.5
s.3, referred to: SSI 2012/181d(relevant.person)
s.3, enabling: SSI 2012/181
s.5, referred to: SSI 2012/181 Reg.3
s.14, applied: SSI 2012/217
s.14, enabling: SSI 2012/217
s.17, applied: SSI 2012/180 Reg.5, Reg.6, Reg.22
s.18, applied: SSI 2012/180 Reg.8
s.19, applied: SSI 2012/180 Reg.18, Reg.26
s.21, applied: SSI 2012/180 Reg.18, Reg.26
s.22, applied: SSI 2012/180 Reg.26

asp 8. Property Factors (Scotland) Act 2011– *cont.*
s.23, applied: SSI 2012/180 Reg.18, Reg.26
s.25, enabling: SSI 2012/180
s.29, applied: SSI 2012/269
s.29, enabling: SSI 2012/269
s.30, enabling: SSI 2012/149, SSI 2012/180, SSI 2012/181, SSI 2012/269
s.33, enabling: SSI 2012/149

asp 10. Local Electoral Administration (Scotland) Act 2011
s.20, enabling: SSI 2012/31

asp 12. Public Records (Scotland) Act 2011
Commencement Orders: SSI 2012/247 Art.2; SSI 2012/21 Art.2
s.16, enabling: SSI 2012/21, SSI 2012/42, SSI 2012/247
Sch.1, amended: 2012 asp 3 Sch.2 para.10, 2012 asp 8 Sch.1 para.18, Sch.7 para.45, Sch.7 para.73, Sch.8 Part 1, SI 2012/1659 Sch.3 para.27

asp 14. Private Rented Housing (Scotland) Act 2011
Commencement Orders: SSI 2012/2 Art.2, Art.2, Sch.1; SSI 2012/150 Art.2; SSI 2012/267 Art.2; SSI 2012/2 Sch.1
s.41, enabling: SSI 2012/2, SSI 2012/150, SSI 2012/267

2012

asp 1. Offensive Behaviour at Football and Threatening Communications (Scotland) Act 2012
Royal Assent, January 19, 2012
s.12, enabling: SSI 2012/20

asp 2. Budget (Scotland) Act 2012
Royal Assent, March 14, 2012
s.4, amended: SSI 2012/346 Art.2
s.7, applied: SSI 2012/346
s.7, enabling: SSI 2012/346
Sch.1, amended: 2012 asp 8 s.61, SSI 2012/346 Art.3
Sch.2, amended: SSI 2012/346 Art.4

asp 3. National Library of Scotland Act 2012
Royal Assent, June 21, 2012

asp 4. Alcohol (Minimum Pricing) (Scotland) Act 2012
Royal Assent, June 29, 2012

asp 5. Land Registration etc (Scotland) Act 2012
Commencement Orders: SSI 2012/265 Art.2
Royal Assent, July 10, 2012
s.101, applied: 2012 asp 9 s.20, s.23
s.123, enabling: SSI 2012/265

asp 6. Agricultural Holdings (Amendment) (Scotland) Act 2012
Royal Assent, July 12, 2012

asp 7. Criminal Cases (Punishment and Review) (Scotland) Act 2012
Commencement Orders: SSI 2012/249 Art.3
Royal Assent, July 26, 2012
s.1, disapplied: SSI 2012/249 Art.4
s.5, enabling: SSI 2012/249

asp 8. Police and Fire Reform (Scotland) Act 2012
Commencement Orders: SSI 2012/253 Art.3, Art.4, Art.5, Sch.1, Art.2; SSI 2012/333 Art.2, Sch.2 para.3, Art.3, Sch.1
Royal Assent, August 07, 2012
applied: SSI 2012/333 Sch.2 para.3
s.3, amended: SSI 2012/333 Sch.2 para.2
s.34, varied: SSI 2012/253 Art.4
s.35, disapplied: SSI 2012/253 Art.3
s.66, varied: SSI 2012/253 Art.6

2012– cont.

asp **11. Local Government Finance (Unoccupied Properties etc.) (Scotland) Act 2012**– *cont.*
s.71, applied: SI 2012/3073 Art.2, SSI 2012/333 Sch.2 para.3
s.72, applied: SSI 2012/333 Sch.2 para.3
s.73, applied: SSI 2012/333 Sch.2 para.3
s.74, amended: SSI 2012/333 Sch.2 para.2
s.75, amended: SSI 2012/333 Sch.2 para.2
s.76, amended: SSI 2012/333 Sch.2 para.2
s.77, amended: SSI 2012/333 Sch.2 para.2
s.79, amended: SSI 2012/333 Sch.2 para.2
s.80, amended: SSI 2012/333 Sch.2 para.2
s.81, amended: SSI 2012/333 Sch.2 para.2
s.85, amended: SSI 2012/333 Sch.2 para.2
s.114, applied: SSI 2012/253 Art.8
s.119, amended: SSI 2012/333 Sch.2 para.2

2012– cont.

asp **11. Local Government Finance (Unoccupied Properties etc.) (Scotland) Act 2012**– *cont.*
s.129, enabling: SSI 2012/253, SSI 2012/333
Sch.5 para.16, applied: SSI 2012/333 Sch.2 para.3
Sch.6 para.1, enabling: SSI 2012/333
Sch.7 Part 2 para.68, applied: SSI 2012/253 Art.8
Sch.7 Part 2 para.68, referred to: SSI 2012/253 Art.8

asp **9. Long Leases (Scotland) Act 2012**
Royal Assent, August 07, 2012

asp **10. Welfare Reform (Further Provision) (Scotland) Act 2012**
Royal Assent, August 07, 2012

asp **11. Local Government Finance (Unoccupied Properties etc.) (Scotland) Act 2012**
Royal Assent, December 05, 2012

ACTS OF THE PARLIAMENT OF ENGLAND, WALES & THE UNITED KINGDOM

1601

4. Charitable Uses Act 1601
see *Helena Housing Ltd v Revenue and Customs Commissioners* [2012] EWCA Civ 569, [2012] P.T.S.R. 1409 (CA (Civ Div)), Lloyd, L.J.

6 Anne (1706-07)

11. Union with Scotland Act 1706
s.6, see *Imperial Tobacco Ltd, Petitioner* [2012] CSIH 9, 2012 S.C. 297 (IH (1 Div)), Lord President Hamilton

24 Geo. 2 (1750)

44. Constables Protection Act 1750
s.6, see *Fitzpatrick v Commissioner of Police of the Metropolis* [2012] EWHC 12 (Admin), [2012] Lloyd's Rep. F.C. 361 (QBD (Admin)), Globe, J.

1756

10. Poole Harbour Act 1756
repealed: SI 2012/1777 Sch.4 Part 1

33 Geo. 3 (1793)

80. Grand Junction Canal Act 1793
see *Moore v British Waterways Board* [2012] EWHC 182 (Ch), [2012] 1 W.L.R. 3289 (Ch D), Hildyard, J

5 Geo. 4 (1824)

83. Vagrancy Act 1824
s.4, applied: 2012 c.9 s.101

9 Geo. 4 (1828)

14. Statute of Frauds Amendment Act 1828
s.6, see *Roder UK Ltd v West* [2011] EWCA Civ 1126, [2012] Q.B. 752 (CA (Civ Div)), Longmore, L.J.

3 & 4 Will. 4 (1833)

85. Saint Helena Act 1833
s.112, enabling: SI 2012/356, SI 2012/361, SI 2012/362, SI 2012/1389, SI 2012/1755, SI 2012/1756, SI 2012/1757, SI 2012/1758, SI 2012/2596, SI 2012/2748, SI 2012/2749, SI 2012/2750, SI 2012/2751, SI 2012/2753, SI 2012/3064, SI 2012/3065, SI 2012/3066, SI 2012/3067, SI 2012/3068, SI 2012/3069

7 Will. 4 & 1 Vict. (1837)

26. Wills Act 1837
s.9, see *Barrett v Bem* [2012] EWCA Civ 52, [2012] Ch. 573 (CA (Civ Div)), Maurice Kay, L.J.; see *Marley v Rawlings* [2012] EWCA Civ 61, [2012] 4 All E.R. 630 (CA (Civ Div)), Sir John Thomas (President)

1 & 2 Vict. (1837-38)

110. Judgments Act 1838
s.17, applied: 2012 c.7 s.105
s.17, referred to: 2012 c.7 s.143, 2012 c.19 s.57, s.91
s.18, referred to: 2012 c.7 s.138

8 & 9 Vict. (1845)

18. Lands Clauses Consolidation Act 1845
s.63, see *Holliday v Breckland DC* [2012] UKUT 193 (LC), [2012] 49 E.G. 68 (UT (Lands)), George Bartlett Q.C. (President)

19. Lands Clauses Consolidation (Scotland) Act 1845
Sch.A, amended: 2012 asp 5 Sch.5 para.1

20. Railways Clauses Consolidation Act 1845
s.46, amended: SI 2012/2635 Art.3
s.46, applied: SI 2012/2284 Art.3, SI 2012/2635 Art.3, SI 2012/2679 Art.3
s.46, varied: SI 2012/2284 Art.3, SI 2012/2679 Art.3
s.58, applied: SI 2012/2284 Art.3, SI 2012/2635 Art.3, SI 2012/2679 Art.3

8 & 9 Vict. (1845)–cont.

20. Railways Clauses Consolidation Act 1845–*cont.*
s.61, applied: SI 2012/2284 Art.3, SI 2012/2635 Art.3, SI 2012/2679 Art.3
s.68, applied: SI 2012/2284 Art.3, SI 2012/2635 Art.3, SI 2012/2679 Art.3
s.68, disapplied: SI 2012/2679 Art.17
s.71, applied: SI 2012/2284 Art.3, SI 2012/2635 Art.3, SI 2012/2679 Art.3
s.72, applied: SI 2012/2284 Art.3, SI 2012/2635 Art.3, SI 2012/2679 Art.3
s.73, applied: SI 2012/2284 Art.3, SI 2012/2635 Art.3, SI 2012/2679 Art.3
s.75, applied: SI 2012/2679 Art.3
s.77, applied: SI 2012/2284 Art.3, SI 2012/2635 Art.3, SI 2012/2679 Art.3
s.78, applied: SI 2012/2284 Art.3, SI 2012/2635 Art.3, SI 2012/2679 Art.3
s.78A, applied: SI 2012/2284 Art.3, SI 2012/2635 Art.3, SI 2012/2679 Art.3
s.79, applied: SI 2012/2284 Art.3, SI 2012/2635 Art.3, SI 2012/2679 Art.3
s.79A, applied: SI 2012/2284 Art.3, SI 2012/2635 Art.3, SI 2012/2679 Art.3
s.79B, applied: SI 2012/2284 Art.3, SI 2012/2635 Art.3, SI 2012/2679 Art.3
s.80, applied: SI 2012/2284 Art.3, SI 2012/2635 Art.3, SI 2012/2679 Art.3
s.81, applied: SI 2012/2284 Art.3, SI 2012/2635 Art.3, SI 2012/2679 Art.3
s.82, applied: SI 2012/2284 Art.3, SI 2012/2635 Art.3, SI 2012/2679 Art.3
s.83, applied: SI 2012/2284 Art.3, SI 2012/2635 Art.3, SI 2012/2679 Art.3
s.84, applied: SI 2012/2679 Art.3
s.85, applied: SI 2012/2284 Art.3, SI 2012/2635 Art.3, SI 2012/2679 Art.3
s.85A, applied: SI 2012/2284 Art.3, SI 2012/2635 Art.3, SI 2012/2679 Art.3
s.85B, applied: SI 2012/2284 Art.3, SI 2012/2635 Art.3, SI 2012/2679 Art.3
s.85C, applied: SI 2012/2284 Art.3, SI 2012/2635 Art.3, SI 2012/2679 Art.3
s.85D, applied: SI 2012/2284 Art.3, SI 2012/2635 Art.3, SI 2012/2679 Art.3
s.85E, applied: SI 2012/2284 Art.3, SI 2012/2635 Art.3, SI 2012/2679 Art.3
s.103, applied: SI 2012/2679 Art.3
s.105, applied: SI 2012/2284 Art.3, SI 2012/2635 Art.3, SI 2012/2679 Art.3
s.145, applied: SI 2012/2679 Art.3
Sch.1, applied: SI 2012/2284 Art.3, SI 2012/2635 Art.3, SI 2012/2679 Art.3
Sch.2, applied: SI 2012/2635 Art.3, SI 2012/2679 Art.3
Sch.2 para.1, applied: SI 2012/2284 Art.3
Sch.2 para.2, applied: SI 2012/2284 Art.3
Sch.3, applied: SI 2012/2635 Art.3, SI 2012/2679 Art.3

33. Railways Clauses Consolidation (Scotland) Act 1845
s.16, applied: SSI 2012/345 Art.5
s.18, applied: SSI 2012/345 Art.5
s.19, applied: SSI 2012/345 Art.5
s.20, applied: SSI 2012/345 Art.5
s.21, applied: SSI 2012/345 Art.5
s.22, applied: SSI 2012/345 Art.5
s.23, applied: SSI 2012/345 Art.5
s.60, applied: SSI 2012/345 Art.5
s.68, applied: SSI 2012/345 Art.5

8 & 9 Vict. (1845)–cont.

33. Railways Clauses Consolidation (Scotland) Act 1845–*cont.*
s.79, applied: SSI 2012/345 Art.5
118. Inclosure Act 1845
s.147, applied: SI 2012/739 Art.4

10 & 11 Vict. (1847)

16. Commissioners Clauses Act 1847
s.59, amended: 2012 asp 5 Sch.5 para.2
s.75, amended: 2012 asp 5 Sch.5 para.2
27. Harbours, Docks, and Piers Clauses Act 1847
applied: SI 2012/1777 Art.3, SI 2012/1914 Art.3
referred to: SI 2012/1914 Art.3
s.2, applied: SI 2012/1777 Art.3
s.3, amended: SI 2012/1914 Art.2
s.3, applied: SI 2012/1777 Art.3
s.3, referred to: SI 2012/1914 Art.3
s.23, applied: SI 2012/1777 Art.3
s.23, varied: SI 2012/1777 Art.3
s.27, applied: SI 2012/1777 Art.3
s.29, applied: SI 2012/1777 Art.3
s.31, applied: SI 2012/1777 Art.3
s.32, applied: SI 2012/1777 Art.3
s.33, applied: SI 2012/1777 Art.3
s.34, applied: SI 2012/1777 Art.3
s.34, varied: SI 2012/1914 Art.3
s.35, applied: SI 2012/1777 Art.3
s.36, applied: SI 2012/1777 Art.3
s.37, applied: SI 2012/1777 Art.3
s.38, applied: SI 2012/1777 Art.3
s.39, applied: SI 2012/1777 Art.3
s.40, applied: SI 2012/1777 Art.3
s.41, applied: SI 2012/1777 Art.3
s.42, applied: SI 2012/1777 Art.3
s.43, applied: SI 2012/1777 Art.3
s.44, applied: SI 2012/1777 Art.3, Art.36, SI 2012/3080 Art.9
s.45, applied: SI 2012/1777 Art.3
s.46, applied: SI 2012/1777 Art.3
s.52, applied: SI 2012/1777 Art.3
s.53, applied: SI 2012/1777 Art.3
s.53, varied: SI 2012/1777 Art.3
s.55, applied: SI 2012/1777 Art.3
s.56, applied: SI 2012/1777 Art.3
s.57, applied: SI 2012/1777 Art.3
s.58, applied: SI 2012/1777 Art.3
s.58, varied: SI 2012/1777 Art.8
s.59, applied: SI 2012/1777 Art.3
s.61, applied: SI 2012/1777 Art.3
s.62, applied: SI 2012/1777 Art.3
s.63, applied: SI 2012/1777 Art.3
s.63, varied: SI 2012/1777 Art.3, SI 2012/1914 Art.3
s.64, applied: SI 2012/1777 Art.3
s.65, applied: SI 2012/1777 Art.3
s.65, varied: SI 2012/1914 Art.3
s.66, applied: SI 2012/1777 Art.3
s.69, applied: SI 2012/1777 Art.3
s.69, varied: SI 2012/1777 Art.3
s.70, applied: SI 2012/1777 Art.3
s.71, applied: SI 2012/1777 Art.3
s.73, applied: SI 2012/1777 Art.3
s.74, applied: SI 2012/1777 Art.3
s.75, applied: SI 2012/1777 Art.3
s.76, applied: SI 2012/1777 Art.3
s.77, applied: SI 2012/1777 Art.3
s.78, applied: SI 2012/1777 Art.3
s.83, applied: SI 2012/1777 Sch.2 para.36

10 & 11 Vict. (1847)–cont.

89. Town Police Clauses Act 1847

s.37, see *R. (on the application of Shanks (t/a Blue Line Taxis)) v Northumberland CC* [2012] EWHC 1539 (Admin), [2012] R.T.R. 36 (QBD (Admin)), Foskett, J.

s.37, applied: SI 2012/2112 Reg.26

s.45, see *Dudley MBC v Arif* [2011] EWHC 3880 (Admin), [2012] R.T.R. 20 (QBD (Admin)), Beatson, J.

111. Inclosure Act 1847

s.4, referred to: SI 2012/739 Art.4

14 & 15 Vict. (1851)

cxvi. Kensington Improvement Act 1851

see *Herrmann v Withers LLP* [2012] EWHC 1492 (Ch), [2012] 4 Costs L.R. 712 (Ch D), Newey, J.

99. Evidence Act 1851

s.7, applied: SI 2012/1726 r.35.2

18 & 19 Vict. (1855)

117. Ordnance Board Transfer Act 1855

s.5, amended: 2012 asp 5 Sch.5 para.3

20 & 21 Vict. (1857)

26. Registration of Leases (Scotland) Act 1857

applied: 2012 asp 5 s.49

s.1, amended: 2012 asp 5 Sch.2 para.2, Sch.2 para.3

s.2, amended: 2012 asp 5 Sch.2 para.4, Sch.2 para.5

s.3, amended: 2012 asp 5 Sch.2 para.6, Sch.2 para.7

s.3, applied: 2012 asp 9 s.10, s.13

s.10, amended: 2012 asp 5 Sch.2 para.8

s.12, amended: 2012 asp 5 Sch.2 para.9, Sch.2 para.10

s.13, amended: 2012 asp 5 Sch.2 para.11, Sch.2 para.12

s.14, amended: 2012 asp 5 Sch.2 para.13

s.15, substituted: 2012 asp 5 Sch.2 para.14

s.16, amended: 2012 asp 5 Sch.2 para.15

s.20A, added: 2012 asp 5 s.52

s.20B, added: 2012 asp 5 s.52

s.20C, added: 2012 asp 5 Sch.2 para.16

s.20D, added: 2012 asp 5 Sch.2 para.16

s.20E, added: 2012 asp 5 Sch.2 para.16

Sch.A, amended: 2012 asp 5 Sch.2 para.18, Sch.2 para.19

Sch.B, repealed: 2012 asp 5 Sch.2 para.20

Sch.D, repealed: 2012 asp 5 Sch.2 para.21

Sch.G, amended: 2012 asp 5 Sch.2 para.18, Sch.2 para.23

Sch.H, amended: 2012 asp 5 Sch.2 para.18

Sch.ZA, added: 2012 asp 5 Sch.2 para.17

Sch.ZG, added: 2012 asp 5 Sch.2 para.22

31. Inclosure Act 1857

s.4, referred to: SI 2012/739 Art.4

s.5, referred to: SI 2012/739 Art.4

81. Burial Act 1857

s.25, see *R. (on the application of Rudewicz) v Ministry of Justice* [2012] EWCA Civ 499, [2012] 3 W.L.R. 901 (CA (Civ Div)), Lord Neuberger (M.R.)

24 & 25 Vict. (1861)

100. Offences against the Person Act 1861

s.18, see *Attorney General's Reference (No.37 of 2011), Re* [2011] EWCA Crim 1720, [2012] 1 Cr. App. R. (S.) 72 (CA (Crim Div)), Leveson, L.J.; see *R. (on the application of Raeside) v Luton Crown Court* [2012] EWHC 1064 (Admin), [2012] 1 W.L.R. 2777 (DC), Sir John Thomas (President)

s.20, see *R. (on the application of Jones) v First-tier Tribunal (Social Entitlement Chamber)* [2011] EWCA Civ 400, [2012] Q.B. 345 (CA (Civ Div)), Mummery, L.J.; see *R. v Kaeppner (Ben)* [2012] EWCA Crim 158, [2012] 2 Cr. App. R. (S.) 47 (CA (Crim Div)), Hallett, LJ; see *R. v Lawrence (Jerome)* [2011] EWCA Crim 3129, [2012] 2 Cr. App. R. (S.) 42 (CA (Crim Div)), Pitchford, L.J.

s.61, applied: 2012 c.9 s.92

25 & 26 Vict. (1862)

85. Transmission of Moveable Property (Scotland) Act 1862

Sch.A, amended: 2012 asp 5 Sch.5 para.4

Sch.B, amended: 2012 asp 5 Sch.5 para.4

26 & 27 Vict. (1863)

92. Railways Clauses Act 1863

s.5, applied: SI 2012/2284 Art.3, SI 2012/2635 Art.3

s.7, applied: SI 2012/2284 Art.3, SI 2012/2635 Art.3

s.12, applied: SI 2012/2284 Art.3, SI 2012/2635 Art.3, SI 2012/2679 Art.3

28 & 29 Vict. (1865)

18. Criminal Procedure Act 1865

s.2, applied: SI 2012/1726 r.37.3

s.3, applied: SI 2012/1726 r.37.4

s.5, applied: SI 2012/1726 r.62.15, r.50.8

s.6, applied: SI 2012/1726 r.62.15, r.50.8

s.7, applied: SI 2012/1726 r.62.15, r.50.8

29 & 30 Vict. (1866)

109. Naval Discipline Act 1866

s.45, applied: 2012 c.9 s.101

30 & 31 Vict. (1867)

133. Consecration of Churchyards Act 1867

applied: SI 2012/1847 Sch.2 para.1

31 & 32 Vict. (1868)

37. Documentary Evidence Act 1868

varied: SI 2012/2590 Art.5

40. Partition Act 1868

s.4, see *Official Receiver for Northern Ireland v O'Brien* [2012] NICh 12, [2012] B.P.I.R. 826 (Ch D (NI)), Deeny, J.

64. Land Registers (Scotland) Act 1868

s.6, applied: 2012 asp 5 s.38

s.13, repealed: 2012 asp 5 Sch.5 para.5

s.19, repealed: 2012 asp 5 Sch.5 para.5

s.25, repealed: 2012 asp 5 Sch.5 para.5

72. Promissory Oaths Act 1868

s.5A, varied: 2012 c.11 s.12

s.7, varied: 2012 c.11 s.12

31 & 32 Vict. (1868)–cont.

101. Titles to Land Consolidation (Scotland) Act 1868
s.159, substituted: 2012 asp 5 Sch.5 para.6
s.159A, amended: 2012 asp 5 Sch.5 para.6
Sch.BPart 1, amended: 2012 asp 5 Sch.5 para.6

32 & 33 Vict. (1869)

62. Debtors Act 1869
see *Kremen v Agrest* [2011] EWCA Civ 1482, [2012] 1
F.L.R. 894 (CA (Civ Div)), Thorpe, L.J.; see
Young v Young [2012] EWHC 138 (Fam), [2012]
Fam. 198 (Fam Div), Mostyn, J.
s.5, see *Kremen v Agrest* [2011] EWCA Civ 1482,
[2012] 1 F.L.R. 894 (CA (Civ Div)), Thorpe, L.J.
s.6, see *Young v Young* [2012] EWHC 138 (Fam),
[2012] Fam. 198 (Fam Div), Mostyn, J.
115. Metropolitan Public Carriage Act 1869
s.6, applied: SI 2012/2112 Reg.26

33 & 34 Vict. (1870)

35. Apportionment Act 1870
see *Quirkco Investments Ltd v Aspray Transport
Ltd* [2011] EWHC 3060 (Ch), [2012] L. & T.R.
19 (Ch D (Leeds)), Judge Keyser Q.C.

34 & 35 Vict. (1871)

96. Pedlars Act 1871
s.3, see *Jones v Bath and North East Somerset
Council* [2012] EWHC 1361 (Admin), (2012)
176 J.P. 530 (QBD (Admin)), Mitting, J.
s.4, referred to: SI 2012/60 Reg.12

36 & 37 Vict. (1873)

xc. Great Northern Railway (Additional Powers) Act 1873
applied: SI 2012/1993 Sch.1

37 & 38 Vict. (1874)

94. Conveyancing (Scotland) Act 1874
Sch.M, amended: 2012 asp 5 Sch.5 para.7

38 & 39 Vict. (1875)

17. Explosives Act 1875
s.40, applied: SI 2012/1652 Sch.8 Part 3
55. Public Health Act 1875
s.265, varied: 2012 c.7 s.246, s.273

42 & 43 Vict. (1879)

11. Bankers Books Evidence Act 1879
s.7, applied: SI 2012/1726 r.28.1
s.8, applied: SI 2012/1726 r.76.1, r.76.7
s.9, amended: 2012 c.21 Sch.18 para.27

43 & 44 Vict. (1880)

41. Burial Laws Amendment Act 1880
applied: SI 2012/993 Sch.1 para.7
47. Ground Game Act 1880
s.1, applied: 2012 asp 9 s.8

44 & 45 Vict. (1881)

58. Army Act 1881
s.41, applied: 2012 c.9 s.101

45 & 46 Vict. (1882)

42. Civil Imprisonment (Scotland) Act 1882
s.6, see *Duff v Chief Constable of Dumfries and
Galloway* [2012] CSIH 45, 2012 S.L.T. 975 (IH
(Ex Div)), Lord Clarke

46 & 47 Vict. (1883)

38. Trial of Lunatics Act 1883
see *R. v B* [2012] EWCA Crim 770, [2012] 3 All E.R.
1093 (CA (Crim Div)), Aikens, L.J.

48 & 49 Vict. (1885)

69. Criminal Law Amendment Act 1885
s.11, applied: 2012 c.9 s.92

50 & 51 Vict. (1887)

54. British Settlements Act 1887
enabling: SI 2012/356, SI 2012/361, SI 2012/362, SI
2012/1755, SI 2012/1756, SI 2012/1757, SI 2012/
1758, SI 2012/1761, SI 2012/2596, SI 2012/2748,
SI 2012/2749, SI 2012/2750, SI 2012/2751, SI
2012/2753, SI 2012/3064, SI 2012/3065, SI
2012/3066, SI 2012/3067, SI 2012/3068, SI
2012/3069

51 & 52 Vict. (1888)

59. Trustees Act 1888
see *Williams v Central Bank of Nigeria* [2012]
EWCA Civ 415, [2012] 3 W.L.R. 1501 (CA (Civ
Div)), Sir Andrew Morritt (Chancellor)

52 & 53 Vict. (1889)

57. Regulation of Railways Act 1889
s.5, applied: SSI 2012/345 Art.5
69. Public Bodies Corrupt Practices Act 1889
s.1, applied: SSI 2012/88 Reg.23, SSI 2012/89
Reg.26

53 & 54 Vict. (1890)

37. Foreign Jurisdiction Act 1890
applied: SI 2012/798 Sch.1 Part 1
39. Partnership Act 1890
see *Bates van Winkelhof v Clyde & Co LLP* [2012]
EWCA Civ 1207, [2012] I.R.L.R. 992 (CA (Civ
Div)), Lloyd, L.J.; see *Tiffin v Lester Aldridge
LLP* [2012] EWCA Civ 35, [2012] 1 W.L.R. 1887
(CA (Civ Div)), Sir Nicholas Wall (President,
Fam)
s.38, see *Boghani v Nathoo* [2011] EWHC 2101 (Ch),
[2012] Bus. L.R. 429 (Ch D), Sir Andrew Morritt
(Chancellor)
s.39, see *Boghani v Nathoo* [2011] EWHC 2101 (Ch),
[2012] Bus. L.R. 429 (Ch D), Sir Andrew Morritt
(Chancellor)

55 & 56 Vict. (1892)

23. Foreign Marriage Act 1892
applied: SI 2012/798 Art.3, Sch.1 Part 1

55 & 56 Vict. (1892)–cont.

43. Military Lands Act 1892
s.14, enabling: SI 2012/ 1478, SI 2012/ 3088
s.15, enabling: SI 2012/ 1478
s.16, applied: SI 2012/ 1478
s.17, applied: SI 2012/ 1478, SI 2012/ 3088

57 & 58 Vict. (1894)

13. Arbitration (Scotland) Act 1894
applied: SSI 2012/ 345 Art.10
44. Heritable Securities (Scotland) Act 1894
s.5, see *Northern Rock (Asset Management) Plc v Youngson* 2012 Hous. L.R. 100 (Sh Ct (Grampian) (Banff)), Sheriff P Mann
s.5B, see *Northern Rock (Asset Management) Plc v Millar* 2012 S.L.T. (Sh Ct) 58 (Sh Ct (Glasgow)), Sheriff A F Deutsch

58 & 59 Vict. (1895)

14. Courts of Law Fees (Scotland) Act 1895
s.2, enabling: SSI 2012/ 290, SSI 2012/ 291, SSI 2012/ 292, SSI 2012/ 293, SSI 2012/ 322

59 & 60 Vict. (1896)

48. Light Railways Act 1896
applied: SSI 2012/ 345 Art.3
s.2, applied: SSI 2012/ 345
s.7, applied: SSI 2012/ 345
s.7, enabling: SSI 2012/ 345
s.9, applied: SSI 2012/ 345
s.9, enabling: SSI 2012/ 345
s.10, enabling: SSI 2012/ 345
s.11, enabling: SSI 2012/ 345
s.12, enabling: SSI 2012/ 345
s.18, enabling: SSI 2012/ 345

60 & 61 Vict. (1897)

30. Police (Property) Act 1897
s.1, see *Chief Constable of Merseyside v Owens* [2012] EWHC 1515 (Admin), (2012) 176 J.P. 688 (DC), Sir John Thomas (President); see *O'Leary International Ltd v Chief Constable of North Wales* [2012] EWHC 1516 (Admin), (2012) 176 J.P. 514 (DC), Sir John Thomas (President)

61 & 62 Vict. (1898)

35. Vexatious Actions (Scotland) Act 1898
see *Lord Advocate v B* [2012] CSIH 31, 2012 S.L.T. 541 (IH (Ex Div)), Lady Paton
s.1, see *Lord Advocate v B* [2012] CSIH 31, 2012 S.L.T. 541 (IH (Ex Div)), Lady Paton
36. Criminal Evidence Act 1898
s.1, applied: SI 2012/ 1726 r.37.4
s.3, applied: SI 2012/ 1726 r.37.3

6 Edw. 7 (1906)

25. Open Spaces Act 1906
see *Herrmann v Withers LLP* [2012] EWHC 1492 (Ch), [2012] 4 Costs L.R. 712 (Ch D), Newey, J.
34. Prevention of Corruption Act 1906
s.1, see *R. v Majeed (Mazhar)* [2012] EWCA Crim 1186, [2012] 3 All E.R. 737 (CA (Crim Div)), Lord Judge, L.C.J.

6 Edw. 7 (1906)–cont.

34. Prevention of Corruption Act 1906–*cont.*
s.1, applied: SSI 2012/ 88 Reg.23, SSI 2012/ 89 Reg.26
40. Marriage with Foreigners Act 1906
applied: SI 2012/ 798 Art.3
41. Marine Insurance Act 1906
s.17, applied: 2012 c.6 s.2
s.18, see *Sealion Shipping Ltd v Valiant Insurance Co* [2012] EWHC 50 (Comm), [2012] 1 Lloyd's Rep. 252 (QBD (Comm)), Blair, J.
s.18, amended: 2012 c.6 s.11
s.18, applied: 2012 c.6 s.11
s.19, applied: 2012 c.6 s.11
s.19, substituted: 2012 c.6 s.11
s.20, see *Sealion Shipping Ltd v Valiant Insurance Co* [2012] EWHC 50 (Comm), [2012] 1 Lloyd's Rep. 252 (QBD (Comm)), Blair, J.
s.20, amended: 2012 c.6 s.11
s.20, applied: 2012 c.6 s.11
s.57, see *Clothing Management Technology Ltd v Beazley Solutions Ltd (t/a Beazley Marine UK)* [2012] EWHC 727 (QB), [2012] 1 Lloyd's Rep. 571 (QBD (Merc)), Judge Mackie Q.C.; see *Masefield AG v Amlin Corporate Member Ltd* [2011] EWCA Civ 24, [2011] 1 W.L.R. 2012 (CA (Civ Div)), Rix, L.J.
s.60, see *Clothing Management Technology Ltd v Beazley Solutions Ltd (t/a Beazley Marine UK)* [2012] EWHC 727 (QB), [2012] 1 Lloyd's Rep. 571 (QBD (Merc)), Judge Mackie Q.C.
s.78, see *Clothing Management Technology Ltd v Beazley Solutions Ltd (t/a Beazley Marine UK)* [2012] EWHC 727 (QB), [2012] 1 Lloyd's Rep. 571 (QBD (Merc)), Judge Mackie Q.C.; see *Masefield AG v Amlin Corporate Member Ltd* [2011] EWCA Civ 24, [2011] 1 W.L.R. 2012 (CA (Civ Div)), Rix, L.J.
s.84, applied: 2012 c.6 Sch.1 para.17
55. Public Trustee Act 1906
s.13, amended: SI 2012/ 2404 Sch.2 para.1

7 Edw. 7 (1907)

24. Limited Partnerships Act 1907
see *Inversiones Frieira SL v Colyzeo Investors II LP* [2011] EWHC 1762 (Ch), [2012] Bus. L.R. 1136 (Ch D), Norris, J.
51. Sheriff Courts (Scotland) Act 1907
Appendix 1. added: SSI 2012/ 188 Sch.1
Appendix 1. amended: SSI 2012/ 188 r.8, Sch.2, SSI 2012/ 271 r.6
s.40, enabling: SSI 2012/ 7, SSI 2012/ 101, SSI 2012/ 341
s.50, see *Duff v Chief Constable of Dumfries and Galloway* [2012] CSIH 45, 2012 S.L.T. 975 (IH (Ex Div)), Lord Clarke
Sch.1, applied: SI 2012/ 2886 Sch.1, SSI 2012/ 136 Art.3
Sch.1 Pt 3 para.36, see *Syme v East Lothian Council* 2012 Rep. L.R. 66 (Sh Ct (Lothian) (Haddington)), Sheriff P J Braid
Sch.1 Part 5 para.1, amended: SSI 2012/ 188 r.10
Sch.1 Part 6 para.3, repealed: SSI 2012/ 188 r.10
Sch.1 Part 6 para.128, applied: SSI 2012/ 303 Sch.5 para.50
Sch.1 Pt 8 para.1, see *North Lanarkshire Council v Cairns* 2012 S.L.T. (Sh Ct) 128 (Sh Ct (South Strathclyde) (Hamilton)), Sheriff Principal B A Lockhart
Sch.1 Part 12 para.2, substituted: SSI 2012/ 188 r.2

7 Edw. 7 (1907)–cont.

51. Sheriff Courts (Scotland) Act 1907–*cont.*
Sch.1 Part 17 para.2, substituted: SSI 2012/ 188 r.3
Sch.1 Part 17 para.3, substituted: SSI 2012/ 188 r.3
Sch.1 Part 33 para.1, amended: SSI 2012/ 188 r.5
Sch.1 Part 33 para.6A, added: SSI 2012/ 188 r.5
Sch.1 Part 33 para.7, amended: SSI 2012/ 188 r.5, SSI 2012/ 221 r.3
Sch.1 Part 33 para.9, amended: SSI 2012/ 188 r.4
Sch.1 Part 33 para.9, substituted: SSI 2012/ 188 r.4
Sch.1 Part 33A para.9, amended: SSI 2012/ 188 r.4
Sch.1 Part 33A para.9, substituted: SSI 2012/ 188 r.4
Sch.1 Part 33A para.16, amended: SSI 2012/ 188 r.6
Sch.1 Part 33A para.34, amended: SSI 2012/ 188 r.4
Sch.1 Part 33A para.34, substituted: SSI 2012/ 188 r.4
Sch.1 Part 33A para.66, amended: SSI 2012/ 188 r.9
Sch.1 Part 33A para.70, amended: SSI 2012/ 188 r.9
Sch.1 Part 33B para.1, repealed: SSI 2012/ 188 r.7
Sch.1 Part 33B para.2, repealed: SSI 2012/ 188 r.7
Sch.1 Part 33 para.16, amended: SSI 2012/ 188 r.5
Sch.1 Part 33 para.26, amended: SSI 2012/ 188 r.5
Sch.1 Part 33 para.28, amended: SSI 2012/ 188 r.5
Sch.1 Part 33 para.33A, amended: SSI 2012/ 188 r.5
Sch.1 Part 33 para.34, amended: SSI 2012/ 188 r.4, r.5
Sch.1 Part 33 para.34, substituted: SSI 2012/ 188 r.4
Sch.1 Part 33 para.37, amended: SSI 2012/ 188 r.5
Sch.1 Part 36 para.14, applied: SI 2012/ 2886 Sch.1, SSI 2012/ 303 Sch.5 para.50
Sch.1 Part 38 para.1, amended: SSI 2012/ 271 r.6
Sch.1 Part 40 para.11, repealed: SSI 2012/ 188 r.3
Sch.1 Part 43 para.1, amended: SSI 2012/ 271 r.6
Sch.1 Part 43 para.1, substituted: SSI 2012/ 271 r.6
Sch.1 Part 49 para.1, added: SSI 2012/ 188 r.10
Sch.1 Part 49 para.2, added: SSI 2012/ 188 r.10
Sch.1 Part 49 para.3, added: SSI 2012/ 188 r.10
Sch.1 Part 49 para.4, added: SSI 2012/ 188 r.10
Sch.1 Part 49 para.5, added: SSI 2012/ 188 r.10
Sch.1 Part 49 para.6, added: SSI 2012/ 188 r.10
Sch.1 Part 49 para.7, added: SSI 2012/ 188 r.10
Sch.1 Part 49 para.8, added: SSI 2012/ 188 r.10
Sch.1 Part 49 para.9, added: SSI 2012/ 188 r.10
Sch.1 Part 49 para.10, added: SSI 2012/ 188 r.10
Sch.1 Part 49 para.11, added: SSI 2012/ 188 r.10
Sch.1 Part 49 para.12, added: SSI 2012/ 188 r.10
Sch.1 Part 49 para.13, added: SSI 2012/ 188 r.10
Sch.1 Part 50 para.1, added: SSI 2012/ 271 r.2
Sch.1 Part 50 para.2, added: SSI 2012/ 271 r.2
Sch.1 Part 50 para.3, added: SSI 2012/ 271 r.2
Sch.1 Part 50 para.4, added: SSI 2012/ 271 r.2
Sch.1 Part 50 para.5, added: SSI 2012/ 271 r.2
Sch.1 Part 50 para.6, added: SSI 2012/ 271 r.2
Sch.1 Part 50 para.7, added: SSI 2012/ 271 r.2
Sch.1 Part 50 para.8, added: SSI 2012/ 271 r.2
53. Public Health Acts Amendment Act 1907
s.94, amended: SI 2012/ 1659 Sch.3 para.1

8 Edw. 7 (1908)

65. Summary Jurisdiction (Scotlandland) Act 1908
see *Hunter v McPherson* 2012 J.C. 145 (HCJ), Lord Mackay of Drumadoon

1 & 2 Geo. 5 (1911)

46. Copyright Act 1911
varied: SI 2012/ 1753 Art.2

3 & 4 Geo. 5 (1913)

16. Foreign Jurisdiction Act 1913
applied: SI 2012/ 798 Sch.1 Part 1
20. Bankruptcy (Scotland) Act 1913
see *Official Liquidator of Weir Construction (Contracts) Ltd, Noter* [2012] CSOH 51, 2012 S.L.T. 1098 (OH), Lord Hodge

5 & 6 Geo. 5 (1914-15)

90. Indictments Act 1915
s.5, see *R. v Miah (Akmol)* [2011] EWCA Crim 945, [2012] 1 Cr. App. R. (S.) 11 (CA (Crim Div)), Aikens, L.J.; see *R. v Sanghera (Sukwinder Singh)* [2012] EWCA Crim 16, [2012] 2 Cr. App. R. 17 (CA (Crim Div)), Aikens, L.J.; see *R. v Thompson (Frederick George)* [2011] EWCA Crim 102, [2012] 1 W.L.R. 571 (CA (Crim Div)), Thomas, L.J.
s.5, applied: SI 2012/ 1726 r.14.1

7 & 8 Geo. 5 (1917)

71. Air Force Constitution Act 1917
s.41, applied: 2012 c.9 s.101

10 & 11 Geo. 5 (1920)

16. Imperial War Museum Act 1920
Sch.1, amended: SI 2012/ 2590 Sch.1 para.1
33. Maintenance Orders (Facilities for Enforcement) Act 1920
s.3, amended: SI 2012/ 2814 Sch.5 para.1
s.4A, amended: SI 2012/ 2814 Sch.5 para.1
41. Census Act 1920
applied: SI 2012/ 1711 Reg.6
75. Official Secrets Act 1920
s.8, applied: SI 2012/ 1726 r.16.1

11 & 12 Geo. 5 (1921)

58. Trusts (Scotland) Act 1921
Sch.A, amended: 2012 asp 5 Sch.5 para.8
Sch.B, amended: 2012 asp 5 Sch.5 para.8

13 & 14 Geo. 5 (1923)

20. Mines (Working Facilities and Support) Act 1923
s.15, referred to: SI 2012/ 2284 Art.3

14 & 15 Geo. 5 (1924)

27. Conveyancing (Scotland) Act 1924
applied: 2012 asp 5 s.49
s.2, amended: 2012 asp 5 Sch.5 para.9
s.3, amended: 2012 asp 5 Sch.5 para.9
s.4, amended: 2012 asp 5 s.53
s.4A, added: 2012 asp 5 s.53
s.4A, applied: 2012 asp 5 s.24
s.4B, added: 2012 asp 5 s.53
s.44, amended: 2012 asp 5 Sch.5 para.9
s.46A, added: 2012 asp 5 s.54
s.49A, added: 2012 asp 5 s.53
Sch.B, amended: 2012 asp 5 Sch.5 para.9
Sch.B, substituted: 2012 asp 5 Sch.5 para.9
Sch.BA, added: 2012 asp 5 s.53

15 & 16 Geo. 5 (1925)

19. Trustee Act 1925

s.27, see *MCP Pension Trustees Ltd v AON Pension Trustees Ltd* [2010] EWCA Civ 377, [2012] Ch. 1 (CA (Civ Div)), Arden, L.J.

s.31, see *Fine v Fine* [2012] EWHC 1811 (Ch), [2012] W.T.L.R. 1745 (Ch D), David Donaldson Q.C.

s.32, see *Pitt v Holt* [2011] EWCA Civ 197, [2012] Ch. 132 (CA (Civ Div)), Mummery, L.J.; see *Sutton v England* [2011] EWCA Civ 637, [2012] 1 W.L.R. 326 (CA (Civ Div)), Mummery, L.J.

s.57, see *Alexander v Alexander* [2011] EWHC 2721 (Ch), [2012] W.T.L.R. 187 (Ch D), Morgan, J.; see *Sutton v England* [2011] EWCA Civ 637, [2012] 1 W.L.R. 326 (CA (Civ Div)), Mummery, L.J.

s.61, see *Lloyds TSB Bank Plc v Markandan & Uddin (A Firm)* [2012] EWCA Civ 65, [2012] 2 All E.R. 884 (CA (Civ Div)), Mummery, L.J.; see *St Andrew's (Cheam) Lawn Tennis Club Trust, Re* [2012] EWHC 1040 (Ch), [2012] 1 W.L.R. 3487 (Ch D), Arnold, J.

20. Law of Property Act 1925

see *Mexfield Housing Co-operative Ltd v Berrisford* [2012] 1 A.C. 955 (SC), Lord Hope (Deputy President)

s.36, see *Quigley v Masterson* [2011] EWHC 2529 (Ch), [2012] 1 All E.R. 1224 (Ch D), Henderson, J.

s.49, see *Amble Assets LLP (In Administration) v Longbenton Foods Ltd (In Administration)* [2011] EWHC 3774 (Ch), [2012] 1 All E.R. (Comm) 764 (Ch D (Leeds)), Andrew Sutcliffe Q.C.

s.53, see *Drakeford v Cotton* [2012] EWHC 1414 (Ch), [2012] 3 All E.R. 1138 (Ch D), Morgan, J.; see *Hanson v Revenue and Customs Commissioners* [2012] UKFTT 95 (TC), [2012] S.F.T.D. 705 (FTT (Tax)), John Walters Q.C.; see *Hughes v Bourne* [2012] EWHC 2232 (Ch), [2012] W.T.L.R. 1333 (Ch D), Henderson, J.; see *JT Frith Ltd, Re* [2012] EWHC 196 (Ch), [2012] B.C.C. 634 (Ch D (Leeds)), Judge Keyser Q.C.; see *Webster v Ashcroft* [2011] EWHC 3848 (Ch), [2012] 1 W.L.R. 1309 (Ch D), Nicholas Strauss Q.C.

s.64, applied: SI 2012/ 1829 Reg.3

s.84, see *Coldman's Application, Re* [2012] UKUT 6 (LC), [2012] J.P.L. 749 (UT (Lands)), NJ Rose, FRICS; see *Hoyle's Application, Re* [2012] J.P.L. 479 (UT (Lands)), PR Francis FRICS; see *Rasbridge's Application, Re* [2012] UKUT 246 (LC), [2012] J.P.L. 1521 (UT (Lands)), AJ Trott FRICS; see *Stanborough's Application, Re* [2012] UKUT 21 (LC), [2012] J.P.L. 756 (UT (Lands)), AJ Trott FRICS; see *Thames Valley Holdings Ltd v National Trust* [2012] EWCA Civ 1019, [2012] 5 Costs L.O. 630 (CA (Civ Div)), Sir Nicholas Wall (President, Fam); see *Thames Valley Holdings Ltd, Re* [2012] J.P.L. 66 (UT (Lands)), George Bartlett Q.C. (President, LTr); see *Thomas's Application, Re* [2012] J.P.L. 1139 (UT (Lands)), PR Francis FRICS

s.88, see *Swift 1st Ltd v Colin* [2011] EWHC 2410 (Ch), [2012] Ch. 206 (Ch D), Judge Purle Q.C.

s.101, see *Cherry Tree Investments Ltd v Landmain Ltd* [2012] EWCA Civ 736, [2012] 2 P. & C.R. 10 (CA (Civ Div)), Arden, L.J.; see *Swift 1st Ltd v Colin* [2011] EWHC 2410 (Ch), [2012] Ch. 206 (Ch D), Judge Purle Q.C.

s.101, applied: SI 2012/ 2421 Sch.3 para.6

s.104, see *Swift 1st Ltd v Colin* [2011] EWHC 2410 (Ch), [2012] Ch. 206 (Ch D), Judge Purle Q.C.

15 & 16 Geo. 5 (1925)– cont.

20. Law of Property Act 1925– *cont.*

s.120, see *Cherry Tree Investments Ltd v Landmain Ltd* [2012] EWCA Civ 736, [2012] 2 P. & C.R. 10 (CA (Civ Div)), Arden, L.J.

s.136, see *Jones v Link Financial Ltd* [2012] EWHC 2402 (QB), [2012] E.C.C. 23 (QBD (Manchester)), Hamblen, J.; see *McNulty v Revenue and Customs Commissioners* [2012] UKUT 174 (TCC), [2012] S.T.C. 2110 (UT (Tax)), Arnold, J.; see *New Miles Ltd v Revenue and Customs Commissioners* [2012] UKFTT 33 (TC), [2012] S.F.T.D. 695 (FTT (Tax)), Judge Peter Kempster; see *Simpson v Norfolk and Norwich University Hospital NHS Trust* [2011] EWCA Civ 1149, [2012] Q.B. 640 (CA (Civ Div)), Maurice Kay, L.J.

s.146, see *Freeholders of 69 Marina, St Leonards-on-Sea v Oram* [2011] EWCA Civ 1258, [2012] H.L.R. 12 (CA (Civ Div)), Sir Andrew Morritt (Chancellor)

s.147, see *Freeholders of 69 Marina, St Leonards-on-Sea v Oram* [2011] EWCA Civ 1258, [2012] H.L.R. 12 (CA (Civ Div)), Sir Andrew Morritt (Chancellor)

s.149, see *Mexfield Housing Co-operative Ltd v Berrisford* [2012] 1 A.C. 955 (SC), Lord Hope (Deputy President); see *Shuldham, Re* [2012] EWHC 1420 (Ch), [2012] W.T.L.R. 1597 (Ch D), Floyd, J.

s.193, see *ADM Milling Ltd v Tewkesbury Town Council* [2011] EWHC 595 (Ch), [2012] Ch. 99 (Ch D), Lewison, J.

s.194, applied: SI 2012/ 739 Art.4

s.194, referred to: SI 2012/ 739 Art.4

s.196, see *E.ON UK Plc v Gilesports Ltd* [2012] EWHC 2172 (Ch), [2012] 47 E.G. 128 (Ch D), Arnold, J.; see *Quigley v Masterson* [2011] EWHC 2529 (Ch), [2012] 1 All E.R. 1224 (Ch D), Henderson, J.

23. Administration of Estates Act 1925

s.41, see *Hughes v Bourne* [2012] EWHC 2232 (Ch), [2012] W.T.L.R. 1333 (Ch D), Henderson, J.

s.50, see *Erskine 1948 Trust, Re* [2012] EWHC 732 (Ch), [2012] 3 W.L.R. 913 (Ch D), Mark Herbert Q.C.

s.55, applied: SI 2012/ 138 Art.13

73. National Library of Scotland Act 1925

repealed: 2012 asp 3 Sch.3

s.1, applied: 2012 asp 3 s.1, s.2

s.2, applied: 2012 asp 3 Sch.1 para.6

s.3, applied: 2012 asp 3 s.6

s.5, applied: 2012 asp 3 s.5

s.6, applied: 2012 asp 3 s.5

Sch.1 para.1, varied: 2012 c.11 s.12

Sch.1 para.2, varied: 2012 asp 3 Sch.2 para.1

86. Criminal Justice Act 1925

s.33, applied: SI 2012/947 Reg.20, SI 2012/1726 r.2.4, SI 2012/2629 Reg.37

s.41, applied: SI 2012/1726 r.16.1

16 & 17 Geo. 5 (1926)

16. Execution of Diligence (Scotland) Act 1926

s.6, enabling: SSI 2012/ 7, SSI 2012/ 8, SSI 2012/ 340, SSI 2012/ 341

22. Finance Act 1926

see *R. (on the application of William Hill Organization Ltd) v Horserace Betting Levy Board* [2012] EWHC 2039 (Admin), [2012] 1

16 & 17 Geo. 5 (1926)–cont.

22. Finance Act 1926–cont.
see–cont.
W.L.R. 3504 (QBD (Admin)), Stanley Burnton, L.J.

29. Adoption of Children Act 1926
see *Erskine 1948 Trust, Re* [2012] EWHC 732 (Ch), [2012] 3 W.L.R. 913 (Ch D), Mark Herbert Q.C.

36. Parks Regulation (Amendment) Act 1926
s.2, enabling: SI 2012/98, SI 2012/957

50. Burgh Registers (Scotland) Act 1926
repealed: 2012 asp 5 Sch.5 para.10

61. Judicial Proceedings (Regulation of Reports) Act 1926
s.1, applied: SI 2012/1726 r.16.1

17 & 18 Geo. 5 (1927)

36. Landlord and Tenant Act 1927
s.18, see *Teathers Ltd (In Liquidation), Re* [2012] EWHC 2886 (Ch), [2012] 50 E.G. 102 (Ch D), Sir Andrew Morritt (Chancellor)
s.19, see *Crosspite Ltd v Sachdev* [2012] UKUT 321 (LC) (UT (Lands)), Judge Gerald; see *Holding & Management (Solitaire) Ltd v Norton* [2012] UKUT 1 (LC), [2012] L. & T.R. 15 (UT (Lands)), George Bartlett Q.C. (President)
s.23, see *Freetown Ltd v Assethold Ltd* [2012] EWHC 1351 (QB), [2012] 4 All E.R. 194 (QBD), Slade, J.

18 & 19 Geo. 5 (1928)

19. Agricultural Produce (Grading and Marking) Act 1928
disapplied: SI 2012/947 Reg.22, SSI 2012/349 Reg.21

32. Petroleum (Consolidation) Act 1928
s.4, applied: SI 2012/1652 Sch.8 Part 4
s.4, disapplied: SI 2012/1652 Reg.10
s.19, applied: SI 2012/1652 Sch.8 Part 4

43. Agricultural Credits Act 1928
s.5, amended: 2012 c.21 Sch.18 para.28

19 & 20 Geo. 5 (1929)

13. Agricultural Credits (Scotland) Act 1929
s.9, amended: 2012 c.21 Sch.18 para.29

20 & 21 Geo. 5 (1930)

25. Third Parties (Rights against Insurers) Act 1930
see *William McIlroy Swindon Ltd v Quinn Insurance Ltd* [2011] EWCA Civ 825, [2012] 1 All E.R. (Comm) 241 (CA (Civ Div)), Rix, L.J.

28. Finance Act 1930
s.40, applied: 2012 c.14 Sch.14 para.33

21 & 22 Geo. 5 (1931)

28. Finance Act 1931
s.28, amended: 2012 c.11 Sch.3 para.1

40. Agricultural Produce (Grading and Marking) Amendment Act 1931
disapplied: SI 2012/947 Reg.22, SSI 2012/349 Reg.21

22 & 23 Geo. 5 (1931-32)

12. Destructive Imported Animals Act 1932
s.3, applied: SSI 2012/175 Art.3
s.5, repealed (in part): SI 2012/1427 Art.3
s.6, amended: SI 2012/1427 Art.3
s.6, repealed (in part): SI 2012/1427 Art.3
s.8, applied: SSI 2012/175 Art.3
s.10, enabling: SI 2012/1427

23 & 24 Geo. 5 (1932-33)

12. Children and Young Persons Act 1933
Part II, applied: SI 2012/335 Sch.1 para.31, SI 2012/2991 Sch.1 para.30
s.7, see *Wm Morrisons Supermarkets Plc v Reading BC* [2012] EWHC 1358 (Admin), [2012] P.T.S.R. 1643 (DC), Hooper, L.J.
s.34A, applied: SI 2012/1726 r.7.4, r.37.2
s.37, applied: SI 2012/1726 r.16.1
s.39, see *R. (on the application of Y) v Aylesbury Crown Court* [2012] EWHC 1140 (Admin), [2012] E.M.L.R. 26 (QBD (Admin)), Hooper, L.J.
s.39, applied: SI 2012/1726 r.10.5, r.37.2, r.29.19, r.16.1
s.44, see *R. v RLM* [2011] EWCA Crim 2398, [2012] 1 Cr. App. R. (S.) 95 (CA (Crim Div)), Gross, L.J.
s.45, applied: SI 2012/1726 r.37.1
s.45, referred to: SI 2012/1726 r.63.10
s.46, applied: SI 2012/1726 r.37.1, r.37.2
s.47, applied: SI 2012/1726 r.37.2, r.16.1
s.48, applied: SI 2012/1726 r.37.1
s.49, applied: SI 2012/1726 r.37.2, r.16.1
s.59, applied: SI 2012/1726 r.37.1
Sch.1, amended: 2012 c.9 Sch.9 para.136

13. Foreign Judgments (Reciprocal Enforcement) Act 1933
see *New Cap Reinsurance Corp Ltd (In Liquidation) v Grant* [2011] EWCA Civ 971, [2012] Ch. 538 (CA (Civ Div)), Mummery, L.J.; see *Rubin v Eurofinance SA* [2012] UKSC 46, [2012] 3 W.L.R. 1019 (SC), Lord Walker, J.S.C.
s.4, see *New Cap Reinsurance Corp Ltd (In Liquidation) v Grant* [2011] EWCA Civ 971, [2012] Ch. 538 (CA (Civ Div)), Mummery, L.J.
s.6, see *New Cap Reinsurance Corp Ltd (In Liquidation) v Grant* [2011] EWCA Civ 971, [2012] Ch. 538 (CA (Civ Div)), Mummery, L.J.
s.11, see *New Cap Reinsurance Corp Ltd (In Liquidation) v Grant* [2011] EWCA Civ 971, [2012] Ch. 538 (CA (Civ Div)), Mummery, L.J.

36. Administration of Justice (Miscellaneous Provisions) Act 1933
s.2, applied: SI 2012/1726 r.3.11, r.14.1
s.2, referred to: SI 2012/1726 r.14.2

24 & 25 Geo. 5 (1933-34)

41. Law Reform (Miscellaneous Provisions) Act 1934
see *Reynolds v United Kingdom (2694/08)* (2012) 55 E.H.R.R. 35 (ECHR), Judge Garlicki (President)
s.1, applied: SI 2012/3013 Reg.35

58. Betting and Lotteries Act 1934
s.20, see *R. (on the application of William Hill Organization Ltd) v Horserace Betting Levy Board* [2012] EWHC 2039 (Admin), [2012] 1 W.L.R. 3504 (QBD (Admin)), Stanley Burnton, L.J.

26 Geo. 5 & Edw. 8 (1935-36)

17. Voluntary Hospitals (Paying Patients) Act 1936
s.1, amended: 2012 c.7 Sch.5 para.1, Sch.14 para.41
27. Petroleum (Transfer of Licences) Act 1936
s.1, applied: SI 2012/1652 Sch.8 Part 4
49. Public Health Act 1936
s.276, varied: SI 2012/793 Reg.15
s.289, varied: SI 2012/793 Reg.15
s.294, varied: SI 2012/793 Reg.15
s.343, see *Haq v Eastbourne BC* [2012] R.V.R. 18 (UT (Lands)), AJ Trott FRICS

1 Edw. 8 & 1 Geo. 6 (1936-37)

37. Children and Young Persons (Scotland) Act 1937
s.12, see *S v Authority Reporter* 2012 S.L.T. (Sh Ct) 89 (Sh Ct (Lothian) (Edinburgh)), Sheriff Principal M M Stephen
s.101, repealed (in part): 2012 asp 8 Sch.8 Part 1

1 & 2 Geo. 6 (1937-38)

12. Population (Statistics) Act 1938
Sch.1 para.1, amended: SSI 2012/287 Art.2

2 & 3 Geo. 6 (1938-39)

21. Limitation Act 1939
s.19, see *Williams v Central Bank of Nigeria* [2012] EWCA Civ 415, [2012] 3 W.L.R. 1501 (CA (Civ Div)), Sir Andrew Morritt (Chancellor)
82. Personal Injuries (Emergency Provisions) Act 1939
s.1, enabling: SI 2012/670
s.2, enabling: SI 2012/670
89. Trading with the Enemy Act 1939
s.4, enabling: SI 2012/1367
s.15, enabling: SI 2012/1367

3 & 4 Geo. 6 (1939-40)

42. Law Reform (Miscellaneous Provisions) (Scotland) Act 1940
s.3, see *ICL Tech Ltd v Johnston Oils Ltd* [2012] CSOH 62, 2012 S.L.T. 667 (OH), Lord Hodge

7 & 8 Geo. 6 (1943-44)

10. Disabled Persons (Employment) Act 1944
applied: SI 2012/2886 Sch.1, SSI 2012/303 Sch.4 para.50, Sch.5 para.47
s.3, applied: SI 2012/2886 Sch.1

8 & 9 Geo. 6 (1944-45)

7. British Settlements Act 1945
enabling: SI 2012/356, SI 2012/361, SI 2012/362, SI 2012/1755, SI 2012/1756, SI 2012/1757, SI 2012/1758, SI 2012/1761, SI 2012/2596, SI 2012/2748, SI 2012/2749, SI 2012/2750, SI 2012/2751, SI 2012/2753, SI 2012/3064, SI 2012/3065, SI 2012/3066, SI 2012/3067, SI 2012/3068, SI 2012/3069
28. Law Reform (Contributory Negligence) Act 1945
see *Co-operative Group (CWS) Ltd v Pritchard* [2011] EWCA Civ 329, [2012] Q.B. 320 (CA (Civ Div)), Sir Anthony May (President, QB); see *Trebor Bassett Holdings Ltd v ADT Fire &*

8 & 9 Geo. 6 (1944-45)– cont.

28. Law Reform (Contributory Negligence) Act 1945– *cont.*
see– *cont.*
Security Plc [2012] EWCA Civ 1158, [2012] B.L.R. 441 (CA (Civ Div)), Sir Andrew Morritt (Chancellor)

9 & 10 Geo. 6 (1945-46)

27. Bank of England Act 1946
s.4, applied: 2012 c.21 s.61
36. Statutory Instruments Act 1946
s.1, applied: SI 2012/1917 Art.36, Art.64, Sch.5 para.3, Sch.7 para.16
s.6, applied: SI 2012/98
s.6, referred to: SI 2012/957
45. United Nations Act 1946
s.1, enabling: SI 2012/356, SI 2012/362, SI 2012/1756, SI 2012/1757, SI 2012/1758, SI 2012/2559, SI 2012/2592, SI 2012/2748, SI 2012/2749, SI 2012/2750, SI 2012/2751, SI 2012/3064, SI 2012/3065, SI 2012/3066, SI 2012/3067
64. Finance Act 1946
s.52, repealed: 2012 c.14 Sch.39 para.1
s.62, repealed (in part): 2012 c.14 Sch.39 para.54
s.67, repealed: 2012 c.14 Sch.39 para.1

10 & 11 Geo. 6 (1946-47)

33. Foreign Marriage Act 1947
applied: SI 2012/798 Sch.1 Part 1
40. Industrial Organisation and Development Act 1947
s.5, repealed (in part): SI 2012/2654 Sch.1
41. Fire Services Act 1947
applied: SSI 2012/88 Reg.3
s.26, enabling: SI 2012/953, SI 2012/974, SSI 2012/106
s.27A, amended: 2012 c.21 Sch.18 para.30
42. Acquisition of Land (Authorisation Procedure) (Scotland) Act 1947
applied: 2012 asp 8 s.4, SSI 2012/360 Sch.6 para.3
Sch.1 para.15, see *Fox v Scottish Ministers* [2012] CSIH 32, 2012 S.L.T. 1198 (IH (2 Div)), The Lord Justice Clerk (Gill)
44. Crown Proceedings Act 1947
see *C v Advocate General for Scotland* 2012 S.L.T. 103 (OH), Lord Brodie
s.17, applied: SI 2012/1726 r.65.12
s.21, disapplied: SSI 2012/88 Reg.48, SSI 2012/89 Reg.45
s.38, applied: SI 2012/1489 Reg.17, SI 2012/1507 Reg.17, SI 2012/1508 Reg.17, SI 2012/1509 Reg.17, SI 2012/1511 Reg.17, SI 2012/1515 Reg.17, SI 2012/1516 Reg.17, SI 2012/1517 Reg.17
s.38, varied: 2012 c.11 s.12, SI 2012/129 Reg.23, SI 2012/925 Reg.26
s.42, disapplied: SSI 2012/88 Reg.48, SSI 2012/89 Reg.45
48. Agriculture Act 1947
Sch.9 para.13, amended: SI 2012/2404 Sch.2 para.2

11 & 12 Geo. 6 (1947-48)

29. National Assistance Act 1948
enabling: SI 2012/842
s.21, see *DM v Doncaster MBC* [2011] EWHC 3652 (Admin), (2012) 15 C.C.L. Rep. 128 (QBD (Admin)), Langstaff, J.; see *R. (on the*

11 & 12 Geo. 6 (1947-48) – cont.

29. National Assistance Act 1948–*cont.*

s.21–*cont.*

application of NM) v Islington LBC [2012] EWHC 414 (Admin), [2012] P.T.S.R. 1582 (QBD (Admin)), Sales, J.; see *R. (on the application of Bevan & Clarke LLP) v Neath Port Talbot CBC* [2012] EWHC 236 (Admin), [2012] B.L.G.R. 728 (QBD (Admin)), Beatson, J.; see *R. (on the application of de Almeida) v Kensington and Chelsea RLBC* [2012] EWHC 1082 (Admin), (2012) 15 C.C.L. Rep. 318 (QBD (Admin)), Lang, J.; see *R. (on the application of SL) v Westminster City Council* [2011] EWCA Civ 954, [2012] P.T.S.R. 574 (CA (Civ Div)), Laws, L.J.

s.22, see *DM v Doncaster MBC* [2011] EWHC 3652 (Admin), (2012) 15 C.C.L. Rep. 128 (QBD (Admin)), Langstaff, J.

s.22, applied: SI 2012/842 Reg.2, SSI 2012/67 Reg.2

s.22, enabling: SI 2012/663, SI 2012/842, SI 2012/2336, SSI 2012/67, SSI 2012/68

s.24, amended: 2012 c.7 Sch.5 para.3

s.26, see *R. (on the application of Bevan & Clarke LLP) v Neath Port Talbot CBC* [2012] EWHC 236 (Admin), [2012] B.L.G.R. 728 (QBD (Admin)), Beatson, J.

s.26, amended: 2012 c.7 Sch.5 para.4

s.26, applied: SI 2012/2885 Sch.1 para.21, SI 2012/3144 Sch.1 para.15, SI 2012/3145 Sch.1, SSI 2012/303 Sch.4 para.31, SSI 2012/319 Reg.35

s.29, see *R. (on the application of NM) v Islington LBC* [2012] EWHC 414 (Admin), [2012] P.T.S.R. 1582 (QBD (Admin)), Sales, J.; see *R. (on the application of Buckinghamshire CC) v Kingston upon Thames RLBC* [2011] EWCA Civ 457, [2012] P.T.S.R. 854 (CA (Civ Div)), Pill, L.J.

s.29, applied: SI 2012/1917 Sch.2 para.15, SI 2012/2885 Sch.1 para.25, Sch.1 para.26, Sch.2 para.6, Sch.4 para.5, SI 2012/2886 Sch.1, SI 2012/3144 Sch.1 para.19, SI 2012/3145 Sch.1, SSI 2012/303 Reg.28, Sch.1 para.10, SSI 2012/319 Reg.29, Sch.1 para.7, Sch.2 para.5

36. House of Commons Members Fund Act 1948

s.3, enabling: SI 2012/1866

38. Companies Act 1948

s.56, see *First Nationwide v Revenue and Customs Commissioners* [2012] EWCA Civ 278, [2012] S.T.C. 1261 (CA (Civ Div)), Rix, L.J.

57. Public Registers and Records (Scotland) Act 1948

s.1, applied: 2012 asp 5 s.109

s.4, repealed: 2012 asp 5 Sch.5 para.11

58. Criminal Justice Act 1948

s.27, amended: 2012 c.10 Sch.12 para.2, Sch.12 para.3

s.27, applied: SI 2012/2824 Reg.2, SI 2012/2906 Art.7

64. National Service Act 1948

s.47, applied: 2012 c.10 Sch.1 para.8

12, 13 & 14 Geo. 6 (1948-49)

42. Lands Tribunal Act 1949

s.3, see *Wellcome Trust Ltd v 19-22 Onslow Gardens Freehold* [2012] EWCA Civ 1024, [2012] R.V.R. 342 (CA (Civ Div)), Lloyd, L.J.

44. Superannuation Act 1949

s.10, applied: SI 2012/687 Sch.1 para.11

74. Coast Protection Act 1949

Sch.1 Part I para.1, amended: SI 2012/1659 Art.2

12, 13 & 14 Geo. 6 (1948-49) – cont.

76. Marriage Act 1949

see *MA v JA* [2012] EWHC 2219 (Fam), Times, September 25, 2012 (Fam Div), Moylan, J.

applied: SI 2012/1847 Sch.2 para.1

s.4, repealed: 2012 c.9 s.114, Sch.10 Part 11

s.9, applied: SI 2012/993 Sch.1 para.8

s.75, repealed (in part): 2012 c.9 s.114, Sch.10 Part 11

97. National Parks and Access to the Countryside Act 1949

s.15, amended: SI 2012/1927 Reg.26, SSI 2012/228 Reg.7

14 Geo. 6 (1950)

15. Finance Act 1950

s.39, amended: 2012 c.14 Sch.16 para.65

14 & 15 Geo. 6 (1950-51)

35. Pet Animals Act 1951

s.5, applied: SI 2012/2932 Reg.5

65. Reserve and Auxiliary Forces (Protection of Civil Interests) Act 1951

s.57, amended: 2012 c.21 Sch.18 para.31

Sch.2 Part I, amended: 2012 c.7 Sch.5 para.5

15 & 16 Geo. 6 & 1 Eliz. 2 (1951-52)

46. Hypnotism Act 1952

s.4, repealed (in part): 2012 c.9 Sch.2 para.11, Sch.10 Part 2

52. Prison Act 1952

applied: SI 2012/2885 Sch.1 para.5, SI 2012/2886 Sch.1, SI 2012/3144 Reg.24, SI 2012/3145 Sch.1, SSI 2012/303 Reg.5, Reg.15, SSI 2012/319 Reg.5, Reg.15

s.5A, amended: SI 2012/2401 Sch.1 para.2

s.37, enabling: SI 2012/50, SI 2012/681, SI 2012/2990

s.43, amended: 2012 c.10 Sch.12 para.4

s.47, amended: 2012 c.10 s.129

s.47, varied: 2012 c.10 s.129

s.47A, added: 2012 c.10 s.129

s.47A, applied: 2012 c.10 s.129

s.47A, varied: 2012 c.10 s.129

s.49, see *R. (on the application of Woolley) v Ministry of Justice* [2012] EWHC 295 (Admin), [2012] Lloyd's Rep. F.C. 442 (DC), Gross, L.J.

s.49, repealed (in part): 2012 c.10 Sch.10 para.1

s.51, see *Coombs v Dorset NHS Primary Care Trust* [2012] EWHC 521 (QB), [2012] Med. L.R. 438 (QBD), Judge Platts

Sch.A1 para.2, repealed (in part): SI 2012/2401 Sch.1 para.3

Sch.A1 para.4, repealed (in part): SI 2012/2401 Sch.1 para.3

Sch.A1 para.5, repealed (in part): SI 2012/2401 Sch.1 para.3

Sch.A1 para.7, added: SI 2012/2401 Sch.1 para.3

1 & 2 Eliz. 2 (1952-53)

14. Prevention of Crime Act 1953

s.1A, added: 2012 c.10 s.142

s.2, amended: 2012 c.10 Sch.26 para.1

18. Prisons Act (Northern Ireland) 1953

applied: SSI 2012/303 Reg.5, SSI 2012/319 Reg.5

20. Births and Deaths Registration Act 1953

s.9, applied: SI 2012/1203 Reg.9, Reg.12

1 & 2 Eliz. 2 (1952-53)–cont.

20. Births and Deaths Registration Act 1953–*cont.*
s.10A, applied: SI 2012/1203 Reg.12
s.23A, applied: SI 2012/1604 Reg.2

37. Registration Service Act 1953
s.19A, added: 2012 c.5 s.135

2 & 3 Eliz. 2 (1953-54)

46. Protection of Animals (Anaesthetics) Act 1954
s.1, applied: SI 2012/2932 Reg.5

56. Landlord and Tenant Act 1954
see *Brumwell v Powys CC* [2011] EWCA Civ 1613,
[2012] L. & T.R.14 (CA (Civ Div)), Laws, L.J.; see
*Humber Oil Terminals Trustee Ltd v Associated
British Ports* [2012] EWCA Civ 36, [2012]
U.K.C.L.R. 71 (CA (Civ Div)), Mummery, L.J.
Pt II. see *Brumwell v Powys CC* [2011] EWCA Civ
1613, [2012] L. & T.R. 14 (CA (Civ Div)), Laws,
L.J.; see *Humber Oil Terminals Trustee Ltd v
Associated British Ports* [2012] EWCA Civ 596,
[2012] L. & T.R. 27 (CA (Civ Div)), Maurice Kay,
L.J.; see *Whaley v Whaley* [2011] EWCA Civ 617,
[2012] 1 F.L.R. 735 (CA (Civ Div)), Mummery,
L.J.
s.24A, see *Humber Oil Terminals Trustee Ltd v
Associated British Ports* [2012] EWHC 1336
(Ch), [2012] L. & T.R. 28 (Ch D), Sales, J.
s.24D, see *Humber Oil Terminals Trustee Ltd v
Associated British Ports* [2012] EWHC 1336
(Ch), [2012] L. & T.R. 28 (Ch D), Sales, J.
s.25, see *Humber Oil Terminals Trustee Ltd v
Associated British Ports* [2012] EWCA Civ 36,
[2012] U.K.C.L.R. 71 (CA (Civ Div)),
Mummery, L.J.
s.30, see *Frozen Value Ltd v Heron Foods Ltd* [2012]
EWCA Civ 473, [2012] 3 W.L.R. 437 (CA (Civ
Div)), Lloyd, L.J.; see *Humber Oil Terminals
Trustee Ltd v Associated British Ports* [2012]
EWCA Civ 36, [2012] U.K.C.L.R. 71 (CA (Civ
Div)), Mummery, L.J.; see *Humber Oil
Terminals Trustee Ltd v Associated British
Ports* [2012] EWCA Civ 596, [2012] L. & T.R. 27
(CA (Civ Div)), Maurice Kay, L.J.; see *Humber
Oil Terminals Trustee Ltd v Associated British
Ports* [2012] EWHC 1336 (Ch), [2012] L. & T.R.
28 (Ch D), Sales, J.
s.34, see *Humber Oil Terminals Trustee Ltd v
Associated British Ports* [2012] EWCA Civ 36,
[2012] U.K.C.L.R. 71 (CA (Civ Div)),
Mummery, L.J.; see *Humber Oil Terminals
Trustee Ltd v Associated British Ports* [2012]
EWHC 1336 (Ch), [2012] L. & T.R. 28 (Ch D),
Sales, J.
s.44, see *Frozen Value Ltd v Heron Foods Ltd* [2012]
EWCA Civ 473, [2012] 3 W.L.R. 437 (CA (Civ
Div)), Lloyd, L.J.

58. Charitable Trusts (Validation) Act 1954
see *St Andrew's (Cheam) Lawn Tennis Club Trust,
Re* [2012] EWHC 1040 (Ch), [2012] 1 W.L.R.
3487 (Ch D), Arnold, J.

64. Transport Charges &c (Miscellaneous Provisions) Act 1954
s.6, enabling: SI 2012/852

68. Pests Act 1954
s.8, applied: SI 2012/13 Art.2, SI 2012/2941 Art.2
s.8, enabling: SI 2012/13, SI 2012/2941

3 & 4 Eliz. 2 (1954-55)

16. Food and Drugs Act 1955
s.11, amended: SI 2012/1659 Art.2

18. Army Act 1955
applied: SI 2012/3144 Reg.8, SI 2012/3145 Sch.1
s.70, applied: 2012 c.9 s.101

19. Air Force Act 1955
applied: SI 2012/3144 Reg.8, SI 2012/3145 Sch.1
s.70, applied: 2012 c.9 s.101

4 & 5 Eliz. 2 (1955-56)

30. Food and Drugs (Scotland) Act 1956
Part I, amended: SI 2012/1659 Art.2

44. Magistrates Courts (Appeals from Binding Over Orders) Act 1956
s.1, applied: SI 2012/1726 r.63.1

46. Administration of Justice Act 1956
s.47, see *Fish & Fish Ltd v Sea Shepherd UK* 2012
S.L.T. 156 (OH), Lord Emslie

60. Valuation and Rating (Scotland) Act 1956
s.6, see *Assessor for Glasgow v Schuh Ltd* [2012]
CSIH 40, 2012 S.L.T. 904 (LVAC), The Lord
Justice Clerk (Gill); see *Wincanton Plc v
Assessor for Lanarkshire Valuation Joint Board*
[2012] CSIH 36, 2012 S.L.T. 1161 (LVAC), The
Lord Justice Clerk (Gill)
s.6, applied: SSI 2012/28 Reg.3, SSI 2012/353 Reg.3
s.7B, applied: SSI 2012/28 Reg.3, SSI 2012/353
Reg.3

69. Sexual Offences Act 1956
s.12, applied: 2012 c.9 s.92
s.13, applied: 2012 c.9 s.92

5 & 6 Eliz. 2 (1957)

11. Homicide Act 1957
see *R. v Dowds (Stephen Andrew)* [2012] EWCA
Crim 281, [2012] 1 W.L.R. 2576 (CA (Crim
Div)), Hughes, L.J.
s.2, see *R. v Brown (Robert)* [2011] EWCA Crim
2796, [2012] 2 Cr. App. R. (S.) 27 (CA (Crim
Div)), Lord Judge, L.C.J.; see *R. v Dowds
(Stephen Andrew)* [2012] EWCA Crim 281,
[2012] 1 W.L.R. 2576 (CA (Crim Div)),
Hughes, L.J.

31. Occupiers Liability Act 1957
see *Everett v Comojo (UK) Ltd (t/a Metropolitan)*
[2011] EWCA Civ 13, [2012] 1 W.L.R. 150 (CA
(Civ Div)), Rix, L.J.

52. Geneva Conventions Act 1957
referred to: SI 2012/2589 Sch.1 para.1
s.8, enabling: SI 2012/2589
Sch.4, see *Rahmatullah v Secretary of State for
Foreign and Commonwealth Affairs* [2011]
EWCA Civ 1540, [2012] 1 W.L.R. 1462 (CA
(Civ Div)), Lord Neuberger (M.R.)

53. Naval Discipline Act 1957
applied: SI 2012/3144 Reg.8, SI 2012/3145 Sch.1
s.42, applied: 2012 c.9 s.101

6 & 7 Eliz. 2 (1957-58)

24. Land Drainage (Scotland) Act 1958
s.18, amended: 2012 asp 5 Sch.5 para.12

33. Disabled Persons (Employment) Act 1958
applied: SI 2012/2886 Sch.1
s.3, applied: SSI 2012/303 Sch.5 para.48

39. Maintenance Orders Act 1958
s.1, amended: SI 2012/2814 Sch.4 para.1

6 & 7 Eliz. 2 (1957-58) – cont.

39. Maintenance Orders Act 1958–*cont.*
s.2A, applied: SI 2012/2814 Sch.1 para.3

40. Matrimonial Proceedings (Children) Act 1958
applied: SI 2012/3144 Reg.8, SI 2012/3145 Sch.1

47. Agricultural Marketing Act 1958
disapplied: SI 2012/947 Reg.22, SSI 2012/349 Reg.21

51. Public Records Act 1958
varied: SI 2012/147 Art.7
s.2, enabling: SI 2012/1665
s.3, applied: SI 2012/3001 Art.3, SI 2012/3028 Art.2, Art.3
s.5, applied: SI 2012/1726 r.5.4
s.8, applied: SI 2012/1726 r.5.4
Sch.1 Part 1, amended: 2012 c.7 Sch.5 para.6, 2012 c.10 Sch.5 para.1, SI 2012/1831 Art.14
Sch.1 Part 2, amended: 2012 c.5 Sch.13 para.14, 2012 c.7 s.181, Sch.15 para.69

53. Variation of Trusts Act 1958
s.1, see *Alexander v Alexander* [2011] EWHC 2721 (Ch), [2012] W.T.L.R. 187 (Ch D), Morgan, J.

61. Interest on Damages (Scotland) Act 1958
s.1, see *Farstad Supply AS v Enviroco Ltd* 2012 S.L.T. 348 (OH), Lord Hodge

7 & 8 Eliz. 2 (1958-59)

57. Street Offences Act 1959
Sch.1, applied: SI 2012/1726 r.44.1

66. Obscene Publications Act 1959
s.1, see *R. v Smith (Gavin)* [2012] EWCA Crim 398, [2012] 1 W.L.R. 3368 (CA (Crim Div)), Richards, L.J.
s.2, see *R. v Smith (Gavin)* [2012] EWCA Crim 398, [2012] 1 W.L.R. 3368 (CA (Crim Div)), Richards, L.J.

8 & 9 Eliz. 2 (1959-60)

30. Occupiers Liability (Scotland) Act 1960
see *Brown v Lakeland Ltd* [2012] CSOH 105, 2012 Rep. L.R. 140 (OH), Lord Woolman; see *Dawson v Page* [2012] CSOH 33, 2012 Rep. L.R. 56 (OH), Lord Glennie; see *Syme v East Lothian Council* 2012 Rep. L.R. 66 (Sh Ct (Lothian) (Haddington)), Sheriff P J Braid
s.3, see *Kirkham v Link Housing Group Ltd* [2012] CSIH 58, 2012 Hous. L.R. 87 (IH (2 Div)), The Lord Justice Clerk (Gill)

44. Finance Act 1960
s.74, repealed: 2012 c.14 Sch.39 para.2
s.74A, amended: 2012 c.14 Sch.37 para.1
s.74A, applied: SI 2012/3071 Art.4, Art.5
s.74A, repealed (in part): 2012 c.14 Sch.37 para.1
s.74A, enabling: SI 2012/3071

60. Betting and Gaming Act 1960
see *R. (on the application of William Hill Organization Ltd) v Horserace Betting Levy Board* [2012] EWHC 2039 (Admin), [2012] 1 W.L.R. 3504 (QBD (Admin)), Stanley Burnton, L.J.

61. Mental Health (Scotland) Act 1960
s.55, see *Reid (Alexander Lewis Hutchison) v HM Advocate* [2012] HCJAC 18, 2012 S.C.L. 475 (HCJ), Lord Reed

62. Caravan Sites and Control of Development Act 1960
Part I, applied: SI 2012/2421 Sch.1 para.3

8 & 9 Eliz. 2 (1959-60) cont.

62. Caravan Sites and Control of Development Act 1960–*cont.*
s.29, see *Windsor and Maidenhead RBC v Smith* [2012] EWCA Civ 997, [2012] J.P.L. 1494 (CA (Civ Div)), Rix, L.J.
Sch.1 para.1, varied: SI 2012/2421 Sch.1 para.3
Sch.1 para.2, varied: SI 2012/2421 Sch.1 para.3
Sch.1 para.3, varied: SI 2012/2421 Sch.1 para.3
Sch.1 para.4, varied: SI 2012/2421 Sch.1 para.3
Sch.1 para.5, varied: SI 2012/2421 Sch.1 para.3
Sch.1 para.6, varied: SI 2012/2421 Sch.1 para.3
Sch.1 para.7, varied: SI 2012/2421 Sch.1 para.3
Sch.1 para.8, varied: SI 2012/2421 Sch.1 para.3
Sch.1 para.9, see *Bury MBC v Secretary of State for Communities and Local Government* [2011] EWHC 2192 (Admin), [2012] J.P.L. 51 (QBD (Manchester)), Judge Waksman Q.C.
Sch.1 para.9, varied: SI 2012/2421 Sch.1 para.3
Sch.1 para.10, varied: SI 2012/2421 Sch.1 para.3
Sch.1 para.11, varied: SI 2012/2421 Sch.1 para.3
Sch.1 para.11A, varied: SI 2012/2421 Sch.1 para.3
Sch.1 para.12, varied: SI 2012/2421 Sch.1 para.3
Sch.1 para.13, varied: SI 2012/2421 Sch.1 para.3

65. Administration of Justice Act 1960
s.12, see *CVB v MGN Ltd* [2012] EWHC 1148 (QB), [2012] E.M.L.R. 29 (QBD), Tugendhat, J.; see *RB (An Adult), Re* [2011] EWHC 3017 (Fam), [2012] 1 F.L.R. 466 (Fam Div), Munby, L.J.
s.13, see *Director of the Serious Fraud Office v B* [2012] EWCA Crim 901, [2012] 1 W.L.R. 3188 (CA (Crim Div)), Gross, L.J.
s.13, applied: SI 2012/1726 r.68.1, r.74.1

67. Public Bodies (Admission to Meetings) Act 1960
applied: SI 2012/901 Art.7, SI 2012/1273 Art.6
s.2, applied: 2012 c.7 s.181
Sch.1 para.1, amended: 2012 c.7 s.189, Sch.5 para.7, Sch.13 para.2, Sch.14 para.42, Sch.15 para.68, Sch.17 para.1, Sch.19 para.1
Sch.1 para.1, repealed (in part): 2012 c.7 Sch.5 para.7, Sch.15 para.50, Sch.15 para.70
Sch.1 para.2, amended: 2012 c.7 Sch.15 para.68
Sch.1 para.2, repealed (in part): 2012 c.7 Sch.15 para.70

9 & 10 Eliz. 2 (1960-61)

33. Land Compensation Act 1961
see *Harringay Meat Traders Ltd v Secretary of State for Communities and Local Government* [2012] EWHC 1744 (Admin), [2012] J.P.L. 1473 (QBD (Admin)), McCombe, J.
applied: SI 2012/1867 Art.30, SI 2012/1924 Art.8
varied: SI 2012/2679 Art.33
Part I, applied: SI 2012/1867 Art.6, Art.7, Art.27, Art.28, SI 2012/1914 Art.19, Art.20, SI 2012/1924 Art.9, SI 2012/2284 Art.11, Art.14, Art.15, Art.19, Art.23, Art.27, SI 2012/2635 Art.13, Art.15, Art.19, Art.21, Art.25, Art.29, Art.30, Art.31, Art.36, SI 2012/2679 Art.9, Art.10, Art.15, Art.16, Art.17, Art.20, Art.21, Art.28, Art.29, Art.30, Art.35, Art.40
s.4, applied: SI 2012/605 Reg.24
s.5, see *Bishopsgate Parking (No.2) Ltd v Welsh Ministers* [2012] UKUT 22 (LC), [2012] R.V.R. 237 (UT (Lands)), George Bartlett Q.C.; see *Dunbar v Blackburn with Darwen BC* [2012] R.V.R. 40 (UT (Lands)), George Bartlett Q.C. (President); see *Haq v Eastbourne BC* [2012] R.V.R. 18 (UT (Lands)), AJ Trott FRICS

9 & 10 Eliz. 2 (1960-61) – cont.

33. Land Compensation Act 1961– *cont.*
s.10A, see *Dunbar v Blackburn with Darwen BC* [2012] R.V.R. 40 (UT (Lands)), George Bartlett Q.C. (President)
s.14, see *Kingsley v Highways Agency* [2012] R.V.R. 12 (UT (Lands)), George Bartlett Q.C. (President)
s.15, see *Kingsley v Highways Agency* [2012] R.V.R. 12 (UT (Lands)), George Bartlett Q.C. (President)
s.15, varied: SI 2012/628 Art.20
s.16, see *Kaufman v Gateshead BC* [2012] UKUT 8 (LC), [2012] R.V.R. 128 (UT (Lands)), Alice Robinson
s.16, applied: SI 2012/961 Sch.2 para.3
s.17, see *Harringay Meat Traders Ltd v Secretary of State for Communities and Local Government* [2012] EWHC 1744 (Admin), [2012] J.P.L. 1473 (QBD (Admin)), McCombe, J.; see *Kingsley v Highways Agency* [2012] R.V.R. 12 (UT (Lands)), George Bartlett Q.C. (President)
s.17, applied: SI 2012/628 Art.19, SI 2012/634 Art.2, Art.3, Art.5, Art.6, Art.7, SI 2012/843 Art.2, Art.3, Art.4, Art.5, SI 2012/2920 Reg.1, Reg.18
s.18, applied: SI 2012/628 Art.19, SI 2012/634 Art.3, Art.7, SI 2012/843 Art.3
s.20, enabling: SI 2012/634, SI 2012/843
s.29, amended: SI 2012/961 Sch.2 para.1
39. Criminal Justice Act 1961
s.23, amended: 2012 c.10 Sch.10 para.2
s.23, repealed (in part): 2012 c.10 Sch.10 para.2
55. Crown Estate Act 1961
applied: SSI 2012/348
Sch.1 para.1, amended: 2012 c.11 s.18
60. Suicide Act 1961
s.2, see *R. (on the application of Nicklinson) v Ministry of Justice* [2012] EWHC 2381 (Admin), [2012] 3 F.C.R. 233 (DC), Toulson, L.J.

10 & 11 Eliz. 2 (1961-62)

9. Local Government (Financial Provisions etc.) (Scotland) Act 1962
s.4, applied: SSI 2012/28 Reg.3, Reg.5, SSI 2012/29 Reg.4, SSI 2012/48 Reg.7, SSI 2012/353 Reg.3, Reg.5
12. Education Act 1962
s.1, applied: SI 2012/335 Sch.1 para.12, Sch.1 para.13, SI 2012/2991 Sch.1 para.12, Sch.1 para.13, SSI 2012/303 Sch.4 para.22, SSI 2012/319 Sch.3 para.17
s.2, applied: SI 2012/335 Sch.1 para.13, SI 2012/2991 Sch.1 para.13, SSI 2012/303 Reg.20, Sch.4 para.22, Sch.4 para.23, SSI 2012/319 Sch.3 para.17, Sch.3 para.18
46. Transport Act 1962
applied: SI 2012/1659 Art.2
s.1, amended: SI 2012/1659 Sch.2 para.2
s.1, repealed (in part): SI 2012/1659 Sch.2 para.2
s.10, amended: SI 2012/1659 Sch.2 para.3
s.10, repealed (in part): SI 2012/1659 Sch.2 para.3
s.11, amended: SI 2012/1659 Sch.2 para.4
s.12, amended: SI 2012/1659 Sch.2 para.5
s.14, amended: SI 2012/1659 Sch.2 para.6
s.14, repealed (in part): SI 2012/1659 Sch.2 para.6
s.15, amended: SI 2012/1659 Sch.2 para.7
s.15A, amended: SI 2012/1659 Sch.2 para.8
s.17, amended: SI 2012/1659 Sch.2 para.9
s.18, amended: SI 2012/1659 Sch.2 para.10

10 & 11 Eliz. 2 (1961-62) – cont.

46. Transport Act 1962– *cont.*
s.19, amended: SI 2012/1659 Sch.2 para.11
s.19, repealed (in part): SI 2012/1659 Sch.2 para.11
s.20, amended: SI 2012/1659 Sch.2 para.12
s.21, amended: SI 2012/1659 Sch.2 para.13
s.21A, amended: SI 2012/1659 Sch.2 para.14
s.24, amended: SI 2012/1659 Sch.2 para.15
s.24, applied: SI 2012/1659 Sch.4 para.2, Sch.4 para.3, Sch.4 para.4
s.25, amended: SI 2012/1659 Sch.2 para.16
s.27, amended: SI 2012/1659 Sch.2 para.17
s.27, applied: SI 2012/1659 Sch.4 para.2
s.27, repealed (in part): SI 2012/1659 Sch.2 para.17
s.28, amended: SI 2012/1659 Sch.2 para.18
s.41, amended: 2012 c.14 Sch.39 para.1
s.43, amended: SI 2012/1659 Sch.2 para.19
s.50, amended: SI 2012/1659 Sch.2 para.20
s.52, amended: SI 2012/1659 Sch.2 para.21
s.62, amended: SI 2012/1659 Sch.2 para.22
s.63, repealed: SI 2012/1659 Sch.2 para.23
s.73, amended: SI 2012/1659 Sch.2 para.24
s.74, amended: SI 2012/1659 Sch.2 para.25
s.86, amended: SI 2012/1659 Sch.2 para.26
Sch.1 Part I para.6, amended: SI 2012/1659 Sch.2 para.27
Sch.1 Part I para.7, amended: SI 2012/1659 Sch.2 para.27
Sch.1 Part I para.8, amended: SI 2012/1659 Sch.2 para.27
Sch.6 para.1, amended: SI 2012/1659 Sch.2 para.28
Sch.6 para.4, amended: SI 2012/1659 Sch.2 para.28
Sch.9 para.5, amended: SI 2012/1659 Sch.2 para.29
58. Pipe-lines Act 1962
s.37, amended: 2012 asp 8 Sch.7 para.74
s.37, repealed (in part): 2012 asp 8 Sch.8 Part 3

1963

xxiii. Pier and Harbour Order (Bembridge Harbour) Confirmation Act 1963
s.15, see *Mew v Tristmire Ltd* [2011] EWCA Civ 912, [2012] 1 W.L.R. 852 (CA (Civ Div)), Maurice Kay, L.J.
2. Betting, Gaming and Lotteries Act 1963
s.27, see *R. (on the application of William Hill Organization Ltd) v Horserace Betting Levy Board* [2012] EWHC 2039 (Admin), [2012] 1 W.L.R. 3504 (QBD (Admin)), Stanley Burnton, L.J.
s.31, varied: SI 2012/854 Art.3
s.55, see *R. (on the application of William Hill Organization Ltd) v Horserace Betting Levy Board* [2012] EWHC 2039 (Admin), [2012] 1 W.L.R. 3504 (QBD (Admin)), Stanley Burnton, L.J.
37. Children and Young Persons Act 1963
s.18, applied: SI 2012/1726 r.37.1
s.28, applied: SI 2012/1726 r.37.4
43. Animal Boarding Establishments Act 1963
s.3, applied: SI 2012/2932 Reg.5
51. Land Compensation (Scotland) Act 1963
s.9, applied: SSI 2012/360 Sch.6 para.8
s.9, varied: SSI 2012/360 Sch.6 para.8
s.11, applied: SSI 2012/360 Sch.6 para.8
s.11, varied: SSI 2012/360 Sch.6 para.8
s.12, applied: SSI 2012/360 Sch.6 para.6
s.40, applied: SSI 2012/360 Sch.6 para.7

1964

14. Plant Varieties and Seeds Act 1964
s.16, enabling: SI 2012/ 245, SI 2012/ 3035, SSI 2012/ 5
s.24, applied: SI 2012/ 245 Reg.25
s.26, applied: SI 2012/ 245 Reg.24, Reg.25
s.36, enabling: SI 2012/ 245, SI 2012/ 3035, SSI 2012/
5

16. Industrial Training Act 1964
applied: SI 2012/ 717 Sch.1

28. Agriculture and Horticulture Act 1964
disapplied: SI 2012/ 947 Reg.22, SSI 2012/ 349
Reg.21

40. Harbours Act 1964
applied: SI 2012/ 1266, SI 2012/ 1867, SI 2012/ 1867
Art.13
s.14, applied: SI 2012/ 416, SI 2012/ 1154, SI 2012/
1777, SI 2012/ 1984, SI 2012/ 3129, SSI 2012/ 114,
SSI 2012/ 262, SSI 2012/ 302, SSI 2012/ 350
s.14, referred to: SI 2012/ 416, SI 2012/ 1154, SI 2012/
1777, SI 2012/ 3129, SSI 2012/ 350
s.14, enabling: SI 2012/ 416, SI 2012/ 1154, SI 2012/
1777, SI 2012/ 1984, SI 2012/ 3080, SI 2012/ 3129,
SSI 2012/ 114, SSI 2012/ 262, SSI 2012/ 302, SSI
2012/ 350
s.16, applied: SI 2012/ 1914
s.16, referred to: SI 2012/ 1914
s.16, enabling: SI 2012/ 1914
s.26, amended: SI 2012/ 1659 Sch.3 para.2
s.26, applied: SI 2012/ 1777 Art.29, SI 2012/ 3080
Art.4
s.30, amended: SI 2012/ 1659 Sch.3 para.2
s.36, amended: SI 2012/ 1659 Sch.3 para.2
s.42, amended: SI 2012/ 1659 Sch.3 para.2
s.42A, applied: SI 2012/ 1154, SI 2012/ 1914, SI 2012/
3129
s.57, amended: 2012 asp 5 Sch.5 para.13, SI 2012/
1659 Sch.3 para.2
s.57, applied: SSI 2012/ 89 Sch.1, SSI 2012/ 360 Sch.4
para.13
Sch.2, referred to: SSI 2012/ 114, SSI 2012/ 262, SSI
2012/ 302
Sch.2 para.9B, applied: SI 2012/ 1984 Sch.2 para.13
Sch.2 para.9B, referred to: SSI 2012/ 114 Sch.2
para.13
Sch.3 Part I para.4, applied: SI 2012/ 416, SSI 2012/
350
Sch.3 Part I para.5, applied: SSI 2012/ 262
Sch.3 Part I para.6, applied: SSI 2012/ 350
Sch.3 Part I para.8, applied: SSI 2012/ 350
Sch.3 Part I para.9, applied: SSI 2012/ 350
Sch.3 Part I para.10, applied: SSI 2012/ 114, SSI
2012/ 262, SSI 2012/ 302, SSI 2012/ 350
Sch.3 Part I para.15, applied: SI 2012/ 416, SSI 2012/
350
Sch.3 Part I para.17, applied: SSI 2012/ 114, SSI
2012/ 262, SSI 2012/ 302, SSI 2012/ 350
Sch.3 Part I para.19, applied: SSI 2012/ 114, SSI
2012/ 262, SSI 2012/ 302, SSI 2012/ 350

41. Succession (Scotland) Act 1964
s.9, see *Murray, Petitioner* 2012 S.L.T. (Sh Ct) 57 (Sh
Ct (Tayside) (Kirkcaldy)), Sheriff A G
McCulloch
s.21A, amended: 2012 asp 5 Sch.5 para.14

53. Hire-Purchase Act 1964
Part III, applied: SI 2012/ 2886 Sch.1, SSI 2012/ 303
Sch.4 para.34

55. Perpetuities and Accumulations Act 1964
s.9, see *Souglides v Tweedie* [2012] EWHC 561 (Ch),
[2012] 3 W.L.R. 1071 (Ch D), Newey, J

1964– *cont.*

69. Scrap Metal Dealers Act 1964
s.1, amended: 2012 c.10 s.145
s.2, amended: 2012 c.10 s.145, s.146
s.3, amended: 2012 c.10 s.145, s.146
s.3A, added: 2012 c.10 s.146
s.4, amended: 2012 c.10 s.145, s.146
s.5, amended: 2012 c.10 s.145
s.6, amended: 2012 c.10 s.145, s.146

70. Riding Establishments Act 1964
s.4, applied: SI 2012/ 2932 Reg.5

75. Public Libraries and Museums Act 1964
s.1, applied: SI 2012/ 1020 Sch.1
s.7, see *R. (on the application of Bailey) v Brent LBC*
[2011] EWCA Civ 1586, [2012] Eq. L.R. 168 (CA
(Civ Div)), Pill, L.J.; see *R. (on the application of
Green) v Gloucestershire CC* [2011] EWHC 2687
(Admin), [2012] Eq. L.R. 225 (QBD (Admin)),
Judge McKenna

84. Criminal Procedure (Insanity) Act 1964
s.4, applied: SI 2012/ 1726 r.33.1
s.4A, see *R. v B* [2012] EWCA Crim 770, [2012] 3 All
E.R. 1093 (CA (Crim Div)), Aikens, L.J.
s.5, applied: SI 2012/ 1726 r.68.1, r.68.13
s.5A, applied: SI 2012/ 1726 r.68.1
s.8, amended: 2012 c.7 s.38

1965

12. Industrial and Provident Societies Act 1965
applied: SI 2012/ 1128 Art.4, SI 2012/ 1821 Reg.17
s.6, amended: SI 2012/ 961 Sch.1 para.1
s.29D, amended: 2012 asp 5 Sch.5 para.15
s.29G, amended: 2012 asp 5 Sch.5 para.15
Sch.3 Part II, amended: 2012 asp 5 Sch.5 para.15
Sch.4 Part II, amended: 2012 asp 5 Sch.5 para.15

**33. Control of Office and Industrial Development
Act 1965**
Part I, applied: SI 2012/ 1867 Art.32

36. Gas Act 1965
s.17, amended: 2012 asp 8 Sch.7 para.46
s.28, amended: 2012 asp 5 Sch.5 para.16, 2012 asp 8
Sch.8 Part 2

37. Carriage of Goods by Road Act 1965
s.3, referred to: SI 2012/ 1652 Sch.13

**45. Backing of Warrants (Republic of Ireland) Act
1965**
applied: SI 2012/ 1726 r.17.11
s.1, applied: SI 2012/ 1726 r.17.7
s.2, applied: SI 2012/ 1726 r.17.6, r.17.7, r.17.9
s.2A, applied: SI 2012/ 1726 r.17.6, r.17.9, r.17.10
s.3, applied: SI 2012/ 1726 r.17.5
s.4, applied: SI 2012/ 1726 r.17.6
s.5, applied: SI 2012/ 1726 r.17.7
s.7, applied: SI 2012/ 1726 r.17.8

51. National Insurance Act 1965
s.36, amended: SI 2012/ 780 Art.12
s.36, applied: SI 2012/ 2885 Sch.1 para.22, SI 2012/
2886 Sch.1, SI 2012/ 3144 Sch.1 para.16, SI 2012/
3145 Sch.1, SSI 2012/ 319 Reg.38
s.36, referred to: SI 2012/ 2885 Sch.1 para.22, SI
2012/ 3144 Sch.1 para.16, SSI 2012/ 319 Reg.38
s.37, applied: SI 2012/ 2885 Sch.1 para.22, SI 2012/
2886 Sch.1, SI 2012/ 3144 Sch.1 para.16, SSI 2012/
319 Reg.38
s.37, varied: SI 2012/ 780 Art.12

56. Compulsory Purchase Act 1965
applied: SI 2012/ 1924 Sch.1 para.3, SI 2012/ 2284
Art.22, SI 2012/ 2635 Art.24, Sch.9 para.3, SI
2012/ 2679 Art.34

1965–*cont.*

56. Compulsory Purchase Act 1965–*cont.*
disapplied: SI 2012/2635 Art.28
referred to: SI 2012/1924 Art.5, SI 2012/2284 Art.18, Art.20, SI 2012/2679 Sch.10 para.3
varied: SI 2012/1867 Sch.3 para.3, SI 2012/2284 Sch.5 para.3
Part I, applied: SI 2012/1867 Art.22, Art.33, Sch.3 para.3, SI 2012/1924 Art.4, Art.10, Sch.1 para.3, SI 2012/2284 Art.17, Sch.5 para.3, SI 2012/2635 Art.23, Sch.9 para.3, SI 2012/2679 Art.23, Art.36
Part I, referred to: SI 2012/2679 Sch.10 para.3
s.1, varied: SI 2012/1867 Art.22
s.2, varied: SI 2012/1867 Art.22
s.3, varied: SI 2012/1867 Art.22
s.4, varied: SI 2012/1867 Art.22, SI 2012/1924 Art.4, SI 2012/2679 Art.23
s.5, applied: SI 2012/628 Art.20
s.5, varied: SI 2012/1867 Art.22
s.6, varied: SI 2012/1867 Art.22
s.7, see *Holliday v Breckland DC* [2012] UKUT 193 (LC), [2012] 49 E.G. 68 (UT (Lands)), George Bartlett Q.C. (President)
s.7, applied: SI 2012/1867 Sch.3 para.2, SI 2012/2635 Sch.9 para.2
s.7, varied: SI 2012/1867 Art.22, Sch.3 para.4, SI 2012/1924 Sch.1 para.4, SI 2012/2284 Sch.5 para.4, SI 2012/2635 Sch.9 para.4, SI 2012/2679 Sch.10 para.4
s.8, applied: SI 2012/1867 Art.24, Sch.3 para.2, SI 2012/2284 Art.18, SI 2012/2635 Art.24, Sch.9 para.2, SI 2012/2679 Art.25
s.8, disapplied: SI 2012/1867 Art.31, SI 2012/2284 Art.22, SI 2012/2635 Art.28, SI 2012/2679 Art.34
s.8, referred to: SI 2012/1924 Art.6
s.8, varied: SI 2012/1867 Art.22, Sch.3 para.5, SI 2012/1924 Sch.1 para.5, SI 2012/2284 Sch.5 para.5, SI 2012/2635 Sch.9 para.5, SI 2012/2679 Sch.10 para.5
s.9, varied: SI 2012/1867 Art.22, Sch.3 para.6, SI 2012/1924 Sch.1 para.6, SI 2012/2284 Sch.5 para.6, SI 2012/2635 Sch.9 para.6, SI 2012/2679 Sch.10 para.6
s.10, see *Holliday v Breckland DC* [2012] UKUT 193 (LC), [2012] 49 E.G. 68 (UT (Lands)), George Bartlett Q.C. (President)
s.10, applied: SI 2012/1867 Art.27, Art.28, SI 2012/2679 Art.20, Art.29, Art.30
s.10, varied: SI 2012/1867 Art.22
s.11, applied: SI 2012/1867 Art.32, Sch.8 para.4, SI 2012/1924 Art.9, SI 2012/2284 Art.19, Art.23, SI 2012/2635 Art.25, Art.30, SI 2012/2679 Art.29, Art.35, Art.41, Sch.16 para.4
s.11, varied: SI 2012/1867 Art.22, Sch.3 para.7, SI 2012/1924 Sch.1 para.7, SI 2012/2284 Sch.5 para.7, SI 2012/2635 Sch.9 para.7, SI 2012/2679 Sch.10 para.7
s.12, varied: SI 2012/1867 Art.22, SI 2012/1924 Sch.1 para.7, SI 2012/2284 Sch.5 para.7, SI 2012/2635 Sch.9 para.7
s.13, applied: SI 2012/1867 Art.27, Art.28, SI 2012/2284 Art.23, SI 2012/2635 Art.30, Art.31, SI 2012/2679 Art.29, Art.30
s.13, varied: SI 2012/1867 Art.22, SI 2012/1924 Sch.1 para.7, SI 2012/2284 Sch.5 para.7, SI 2012/2635 Sch.9 para.7
s.14, varied: SI 2012/1867 Art.22
s.15, varied: SI 2012/1867 Art.22
s.16, varied: SI 2012/1867 Art.22
s.17, varied: SI 2012/1867 Art.22

1965–*cont.*

56. Compulsory Purchase Act 1965–*cont.*
s.18, varied: SI 2012/1867 Art.22
s.19, varied: SI 2012/1867 Art.22
s.20, varied: SI 2012/1867 Art.22, Sch.3 para.8, SI 2012/1924 Sch.1 para.8, SI 2012/2284 Sch.5 para.8, SI 2012/2635 Sch.9 para.8, SI 2012/2679 Sch.10 para.8
s.21, varied: SI 2012/1867 Art.22
s.22, varied: SI 2012/1867 Art.22, Sch.3 para.9, SI 2012/1924 Sch.1 para.9, SI 2012/2284 Sch.5 para.9, SI 2012/2635 Sch.9 para.9, SI 2012/2679 Sch.10 para.9
s.23, varied: SI 2012/1867 Art.22
s.24, varied: SI 2012/1867 Art.22
s.25, varied: SI 2012/1867 Art.22
s.26, varied: SI 2012/1867 Art.22
s.27, varied: SI 2012/1867 Art.22
s.28, varied: SI 2012/1867 Art.22
s.29, varied: SI 2012/1867 Art.22
s.30, varied: SI 2012/1867 Art.22
s.31, varied: SI 2012/1867 Art.22
s.32, varied: SI 2012/1867 Art.22
Sch.1 para.10, varied: SI 2012/1867 Sch.3 para.6, SI 2012/1924 Sch.1 para.6, SI 2012/2284 Sch.5 para.6, SI 2012/2635 Sch.9 para.6, SI 2012/2679 Sch.10 para.6
Sch.2 para.2, varied: SI 2012/1867 Sch.3 para.6, SI 2012/1924 Sch.1 para.6, SI 2012/2284 Sch.5 para.6, SI 2012/2635 Sch.9 para.6, SI 2012/2679 Sch.10 para.6
Sch.3 para.3, varied: SI 2012/1924 Art.4, SI 2012/2679 Art.23
Sch.4 para.2, varied: SI 2012/1867 Sch.3 para.6, SI 2012/1924 Sch.1 para.6, SI 2012/2284 Sch.5 para.6, SI 2012/2635 Sch.9 para.6, SI 2012/2679 Sch.10 para.6
Sch.4 para.7, varied: SI 2012/1867 Sch.3 para.6, SI 2012/1924 Sch.1 para.6, SI 2012/2284 Sch.5 para.6, SI 2012/2635 Sch.9 para.6, SI 2012/2679 Sch.10 para.6

57. Nuclear Installations Act 1965
s.1, applied: SI 2012/1652 Sch.13, SSI 2012/360 Sch.4 para.13
s.24A, applied: SI 2012/1652 Reg.24

64. Commons Registration Act 1965
see *R. (on the application of Newhaven Port and Properties Ltd) v East Sussex CC* [2012] EWHC 647 (Admin), [2012] 3 W.L.R. 709 (QBD (Admin)), Ouseley, J.
applied: SI 2012/739 Art.4
s.13, see *Betterment Properties (Weymouth) Ltd v Dorset CC* [2012] EWCA Civ 250, [2012] 2 P. & C.R. 3 (CA (Civ Div)), Carnwath, L.J.; see *Paddico (267) Ltd v Kirklees Metropolitan Council* [2012] EWCA Civ 262, [2012] B.L.G.R. 617 (CA (Civ Div)), Carnwath, L.J.
s.14, see *Betterment Properties (Weymouth) Ltd v Dorset CC* [2012] EWCA Civ 250, [2012] 2 P. & C.R. 3 (CA (Civ Div)), Carnwath, L.J.; see *Paddico (267) Ltd v Kirklees Metropolitan Council* [2012] EWCA Civ 262, [2012] B.L.G.R. 617 (CA (Civ Div)), Carnwath, L.J.
s.22, see *Betterment Properties (Weymouth) Ltd v Dorset CC* [2012] EWCA Civ 250, [2012] 2 P. & C.R. 3 (CA (Civ Div)), Carnwath, L.J.; see *Leeds Group Plc v Leeds City Council* [2011] EWCA Civ 1447, [2012] 1 W.L.R. 1561 (CA (Civ Div)), Arden, L.J.; see *Paddico (267) Ltd v Kirklees Metropolitan Council* [2012] EWCA Civ 262,

1965–cont.

64. Commons Registration Act 1965–*cont.*
s.22–*cont.*
[2012] B.L.G.R. 617 (CA (Civ Div)), Carnwath,
L.J.
**69. Criminal Procedure (Attendance of Witnesses)
Act 1965**
s.2, applied: SI 2012/1726 r.28.1, r.61.7
s.2A, applied: SI 2012/1726 r.28.5
s.2B, applied: SI 2012/1726 r.28.7
s.2C, applied: SI 2012/1726 r.28.7, r.76.1, r.76.7
s.2D, applied: SI 2012/1726 r.28.1
s.2E, applied: SI 2012/1726 r.28.7
s.3, referred to: SI 2012/1726 r.62.5
s.4, applied: SI 2012/1726 r.28.3, r.18.2
74. Superannuation Act 1965
Part III, disapplied: SI 2012/687 Sch.1 para.11
Part III, referred to: SI 2012/687 Sch.1 para.11
s.58, applied: SI 2012/687 Sch.1 para.11
s.58, referred to: SI 2012/687 Sch.1 para.11

1966

18. Finance Act 1966
s.45, repealed: 2012 c.14 Sch.39 para.14
28. Docks and Harbours Act 1966
s.37, applied: SI 2012/1984 Art.11
31. Criminal Appeal Act 1966
see *Director of the Serious Fraud Office v B* [2012]
EWCA Crim 901, [2012] 1 W.L.R. 3188 (CA
(Crim Div)), Gross, L.J.
51. Local Government (Scotland) Act 1966
s.24, see *Cosmopolitan Bellshill Ltd v North
Lanarkshire Council* [2012] CSOH 141, 2012
S.L.T. 1063 (OH), Lord Hodge
s.24, amended: 2012 asp 11 s.1
s.24, applied: SSI 2012/28 Reg.3, SSI 2012/353
Reg.3
s.24A, amended: 2012 asp 11 s.1
s.24A, applied: SSI 2012/28 Reg.3, SSI 2012/353
Reg.3
s.24B, amended: 2012 asp 11 s.1
s.25, see *Cosmopolitan Bellshill Ltd v North
Lanarkshire Council* [2012] CSOH 141, 2012
S.L.T. 1063 (OH), Lord Hodge
s.25A, applied: SSI 2012/28 Reg.5, SSI 2012/29
Reg.4, SSI 2012/48 Reg.7, SSI 2012/353 Reg.5
Sch.3, see *Cosmopolitan Bellshill Ltd v North
Lanarkshire Council* [2012] CSOH 141, 2012
S.L.T. 1063 (OH), Lord Hodge

1967

7. Misrepresentation Act 1967
s.2, see *Green v Eadie* [2012] Ch. 363 (Ch D), Mark
Cawson Q.C.
s.3, see *Avrora Fine Arts Investment Ltd v Christie,
Manson & Woods Ltd* [2012] EWHC 2198 (Ch),
[2012] P.N.L.R. 35 (Ch D), Newey, J.
8. Plant Health Act 1967
s.2, enabling: SI 2012/2707, SI 2012/2922, SI 2012/
3033, SSI 2012/266, SSI 2012/326
s.3, enabling: SI 2012/2707, SI 2012/2922, SI 2012/
3033, SSI 2012/266, SSI 2012/326
s.4, enabling: SSI 2012/266, SSI 2012/326
9. General Rate Act 1967
see *Cosmopolitan Bellshill Ltd v North
Lanarkshire Council* [2012] CSOH 141, 2012
S.L.T. 1063 (OH), Lord Hodge

1967–cont.

10. Forestry Act 1967
applied: SI 2012/605 Reg.15
Part II, applied: SI 2012/605 Reg.15
s.1, amended: SSI 2012/77 Art.2
s.5, applied: SI 2012/605 Reg.15
s.7AA, added: SI 2012/2855 Art.2
s.7B, amended: SI 2012/2855 Art.2
s.10, applied: SI 2012/605 Reg.24
s.11, applied: SI 2012/605 Reg.24
13. Parliamentary Commissioner Act 1967
applied: SI 2012/1480 Art.15
varied: SI 2012/147 Art.7
Sch.2, amended: 2012 c.5 Sch.13 para.15, Sch.14 Part
8, 2012 c.7 Sch.7 para.1, Sch.13 para.3, Sch.15
para.50, Sch.17 para.2, Sch.19 para.2, Sch.20
para.1, Sch.20 para.9, 2012 c.9 Sch.9 para.130,
2012 c.10 Sch.5 para.2, SI 2012/246 Sch.1
para.17, SI 2012/964 Sch.1, SI 2012/1923 Sch.1,
SI 2012/2007 Sch.1 para.109, SI 2012/3006
Art.14
Sch.3 para.8, amended: 2012 c.7 Sch.5 para.8
22. Agriculture Act 1967
Sch.5 Part II para.6, amended: SI 2012/2404 Sch.2
para.3
24. Slaughter of Poultry Act 1967
applied: SSI 2012/321 Reg.8, Reg.10
repealed (in part): SSI 2012/321 Sch.5 Part 1
48. Industrial and Provident Societies Act 1967
applied: SI 2012/1128 Art.4
58. Criminal Law Act 1967
s.3, see *Sobczak v DPP* [2012] EWHC 1319 (Admin),
(2012) 176 J.P. 575 (QBD (Admin)), Mitting, J.
77. Police (Scotland) Act 1967
applied: 2012 asp 8 s.98, Sch.5 para.3, SI 2012/1916
Sch.16 Part 3
s.1, applied: SSI 2012/162 Sch.1
s.1, repealed: 2012 asp 8 Sch.8 Part 1
s.2, applied: SSI 2012/88 Reg.3, SSI 2012/162 Sch.1
s.2, repealed: 2012 asp 8 Sch.8 Part 1
s.3, repealed: 2012 asp 8 Sch.8 Part 1
s.3AA, repealed: 2012 asp 8 Sch.8 Part 1
s.4, repealed: 2012 asp 8 Sch.8 Part 1
s.5, repealed: 2012 asp 8 Sch.8 Part 1
s.5A, repealed: 2012 asp 8 Sch.8 Part 1
s.5B, repealed: 2012 asp 8 Sch.8 Part 1
s.5ZA, repealed: 2012 asp 8 Sch.8 Part 1
s.6, repealed: 2012 asp 8 Sch.8 Part 1
s.7, repealed: 2012 asp 8 Sch.8 Part 1
s.8, applied: 2012 asp 8 Sch.5 para.14
s.8, repealed: 2012 asp 8 Sch.8 Part 1
s.9, applied: 2012 asp 8 Sch.5 para.11, Sch.5 para.13,
Sch.5 para.15
s.9, repealed: 2012 asp 8 Sch.8 Part 1
s.9A, repealed: 2012 asp 8 Sch.8 Part 1
s.9B, repealed: 2012 asp 8 Sch.8 Part 1
s.10, repealed: 2012 asp 8 Sch.8 Part 1
s.11, repealed: 2012 asp 8 Sch.8 Part 1
s.12, repealed: 2012 asp 8 Sch.8 Part 1
s.12A, repealed: 2012 asp 8 Sch.8 Part 1
s.13, repealed: 2012 asp 8 Sch.8 Part 1
s.14, repealed: 2012 asp 8 Sch.8 Part 1
s.15, repealed: 2012 asp 8 Sch.8 Part 1
s.16, repealed: 2012 asp 8 Sch.8 Part 1
s.17, see *Paton (John James) v Dunn* [2012] HCJAC
49, 2012 S.C.L. 802 (HCJ), Lord Mackay of
Drumadoon
s.17, repealed: 2012 asp 8 Sch.8 Part 1
s.18, repealed: 2012 asp 8 Sch.8 Part 1

1967– cont.

77. Police (Scotland) Act 1967– *cont.*
s.19, repealed: 2012 asp 8 Sch.8 Part 1
s.19A, repealed: 2012 asp 8 Sch.8 Part 1
s.20, repealed: 2012 asp 8 Sch.8 Part 1
s.21, repealed: 2012 asp 8 Sch.8 Part 1
s.21A, repealed: 2012 asp 8 Sch.8 Part 1
s.21B, applied: SSI 2012/88 Reg.3
s.21B, repealed: 2012 asp 8 Sch.8 Part 1
s.22, repealed: 2012 asp 8 Sch.8 Part 1
s.23, repealed: 2012 asp 8 Sch.8 Part 1
s.24, repealed: 2012 asp 8 Sch.8 Part 1
s.25, repealed: 2012 asp 8 Sch.8 Part 1
s.26, repealed: 2012 asp 8 Sch.8 Part 1
s.26A, repealed: 2012 asp 8 Sch.8 Part 1
s.26B, repealed: 2012 asp 8 Sch.8 Part 1
s.26C, repealed: 2012 asp 8 Sch.8 Part 1
s.27, repealed: 2012 asp 8 Sch.8 Part 1
s.28, repealed: 2012 asp 8 Sch.8 Part 1
s.29, repealed: 2012 asp 8 Sch.8 Part 1
s.30, repealed: 2012 asp 8 Sch.8 Part 1
s.31, repealed: 2012 asp 8 Sch.8 Part 1
s.32, repealed: 2012 asp 8 Sch.8 Part 1
s.32, enabling: SSI 2012/49, SSI 2012/316
s.32A, amended: 2012 asp 8 Sch.7 para.1
s.33, applied: 2012 asp 8 Sch.5 para.16
s.33, repealed: 2012 asp 8 Sch.8 Part 1
s.34, applied: 2012 asp 8 s.76, Sch.5 para.16, SSI 2012/333 Sch.2 para.3
s.34, repealed: 2012 asp 8 Sch.8 Part 1
s.35, repealed: 2012 asp 8 Sch.8 Part 1
s.36, repealed: 2012 asp 8 Sch.8 Part 1
s.37, repealed: 2012 asp 8 Sch.8 Part 1
s.38, repealed: 2012 asp 8 Sch.8 Part 1
s.38A, applied: 2012 asp 8 Sch.5 para.3, Sch.5 para.8
s.38A, repealed: 2012 asp 8 Sch.8 Part 1
s.38B, repealed: 2012 asp 8 Sch.8 Part 1
s.39, applied: 2012 asp 8 Sch.5 para.20
s.39, repealed: 2012 asp 8 Sch.8 Part 1
s.40, repealed: 2012 asp 8 Sch.8 Part 1
s.40A, repealed: 2012 asp 8 Sch.8 Part 1
s.41, see *Coyle v Glasgow City Council* [2012] CSIH 33, 2012 S.L.T. 1018 (IH (Ex Div)), Lord Mackay of Drumadoon
s.41, repealed: 2012 asp 8 Sch.8 Part 1
s.42, amended: 2012 asp 8 Sch.7 para.1
s.43, repealed: 2012 asp 8 Sch.8 Part 1
s.44, repealed: 2012 asp 8 Sch.8 Part 1
s.45, repealed: 2012 asp 8 Sch.8 Part 1
s.46, repealed: 2012 asp 8 Sch.8 Part 1
s.47, repealed: 2012 asp 8 Sch.8 Part 1
s.48, repealed: 2012 asp 8 Sch.8 Part 1
s.49, repealed: 2012 asp 8 Sch.8 Part 1
s.50, repealed: 2012 asp 8 Sch.8 Part 1
s.51, repealed: 2012 asp 8 Sch.8 Part 1
s.52, repealed: 2012 asp 8 Sch.8 Part 1
s.53, repealed: 2012 asp 8 Sch.8 Part 1
Sch.2 para.1, repealed: 2012 asp 8 Sch.8 Part 1
Sch.2 para.2, repealed: 2012 asp 8 Sch.8 Part 1
Sch.2 para.3, repealed: 2012 asp 8 Sch.8 Part 1
Sch.2 para.4, repealed: 2012 asp 8 Sch.8 Part 1
Sch.2 para.5, repealed: 2012 asp 8 Sch.8 Part 1
Sch.2 para.6, repealed: 2012 asp 8 Sch.8 Part 1
Sch.3 para.1, repealed: 2012 asp 8 Sch.8 Part 1
Sch.3 para.2, repealed: 2012 asp 8 Sch.8 Part 1
Sch.3 para.3, repealed: 2012 asp 8 Sch.8 Part 1
Sch.3 para.4, repealed: 2012 asp 8 Sch.8 Part 1
Sch.3 para.5, repealed: 2012 asp 8 Sch.8 Part 1
Sch.3 para.6, repealed: 2012 asp 8 Sch.8 Part 1

1967– cont.

77. Police (Scotland) Act 1967–*cont.*
Sch.3 para.7, repealed: 2012 asp 8 Sch.8 Part 1
Sch.3 para.8, repealed: 2012 asp 8 Sch.8 Part 1
Sch.3 para.9, repealed: 2012 asp 8 Sch.8 Part 1
Sch.3 para.10, repealed: 2012 asp 8 Sch.8 Part 1
Sch.8 para.7, repealed: 2012 asp 8 Sch.8 Part 1
Sch.9 para.2, repealed: 2012 asp 8 Sch.8 Part 1

80. Criminal Justice Act 1967
s.9, see *R. v Ibrahim (Dahir)* [2012] EWCA Crim 837, [2012] 4 All E.R. 225 (CA (Crim Div)), Aikens, L.J.
s.9, applied: SI 2012/1726 r.27.1, r.33.2, r.3.11, r.28.4
s.9, disapplied: SI 2012/1916 Sch.31 para.26
s.10, applied: SI 2012/1726 r.35.2, r.37.6, r.33.2
s.17, see *R. v Sheen (John Henry)* [2011] EWCA Crim 2461, [2012] 2 Cr. App. R. (S.) 3 (CA (Crim Div)), Stanley Burnton, L.J.
s.66, amended: 2012 c.10 s.129
s.89, applied: SI 2012/1726 r.28.4

83. Sea Fisheries (Shellfish) Act 1967
s.1, enabling: SI 2012/1689, SSI 2012/348
s.3, applied: SSI 2012/348, SSI 2012/348 Art.5
s.4, applied: SSI 2012/348
Sch.1, applied: SSI 2012/348
Sch.1 para.1, applied: SI 2012/1689, SSI 2012/348
Sch.1 para.2, applied: SSI 2012/348
Sch.1 para.3, applied: SSI 2012/348
Sch.1 para.6, applied: SSI 2012/348

84. Sea Fish (Conservation) Act 1967
applied: SI 2012/2747 Art.3
s.1, applied: SI 2012/2283 Art.5
s.1, enabling: SI 2012/2283
s.3, enabling: SI 2012/2283
s.4, applied: SI 2012/827 Reg.1
s.4, disapplied: SI 2012/2747 Art.3
s.4A, applied: SI 2012/827 Reg.1
s.4AA, disapplied: SI 2012/2747 Art.3
s.4B, enabling: SI 2012/827
s.5, applied: SSI 2012/63 Art.8
s.5, enabling: SI 2012/2571, SSI 2012/4, SSI 2012/63
s.5A, enabling: SI 2012/2571
s.6, applied: SI 2012/2747 Art.3, SSI 2012/63 Art.8
s.6, disapplied: SI 2012/2747 Art.3
s.6, enabling: SSI 2012/63
s.8, applied: SI 2012/2747 Art.3
s.8, disapplied: SI 2012/2747 Art.3
s.15, enabling: SSI 2012/4, SSI 2012/63
s.20, enabling: SI 2012/2283, SI 2012/2571

87. Abortion Act 1967
s.1, see *British Pregnancy Advisory Service v Secretary of State for Health* [2011] EWHC 235 (Admin), [2012] 1 W.L.R. 580 (QBD (Admin)), Supperstone, J.; see *Doogan v Greater Glasgow and Clyde Health Board* [2012] CSOH 32, 2012 S.L.T. 1041 (OH), Lady Smith
s.1, amended: 2012 c.7 Sch.5 para.9, Sch.14 para.43
s.4, see *British Pregnancy Advisory Service v Secretary of State for Health* [2011] EWHC 235 (Admin), [2012] 1 W.L.R. 580 (QBD (Admin)), Supperstone, J.; see *Doogan v Greater Glasgow and Clyde Health Board* [2012] CSOH 32, 2012 S.L.T. 1041 (OH), Lady Smith

88. Leasehold Reform Act 1967
s.1AA, see *Lovat v Hertsmere BC* [2011] EWCA Civ 1185, [2012] Q.B. 533 (CA (Civ Div)), Longmore, L.J.
s.2, see *Day v Hosebay Ltd* [2012] UKSC 41, [2012] 1 W.L.R. 2884 (SC), Lord Phillips, J.S.C. (President); see *Lovat v Hertsmere BC* [2011]

1967–cont.

88. Leasehold Reform Act 1967–*cont.*

s.2–*cont.*

EWCA Civ 1185, [2012] Q.B. 533 (CA (Civ Div)), Longmore, L.J.

s.8, see *Day v Hosebay Ltd* [2012] UKSC 41, [2012] 1 W.L.R. 2884 (SC), Lord Phillips, J.S.C. (President)

s.9, see *Clarise Properties Ltd, Re* [2012] UKUT 4 (LC), [2012] L. & T.R. 20 (UT (Lands), George Bartlett Q.C. (President, LTr); see *Clarke's Appeal, Re* [2012] UKUT 226 (LC), [2012] 44 E.G. 96 (UT (Lands)), Judge Huskinson

s.10, see *Clarke's Appeal, Re* [2012] UKUT 226 (LC), [2012] 44 E.G. 96 (UT (Lands)), Judge Huskinson

s.15, see *Clarise Properties Ltd, Re* [2012] UKUT 4 (LC), [2012] L. & T.R. 20 (UT (Lands)), George Bartlett Q.C. (President, LTr)

s.27, see *Clarke's Appeal, Re* [2012] UKUT 226 (LC), [2012] 44 E.G. 96 (UT (Lands)), Judge Huskinson

s.28, amended: 2012 c.7 Sch.5 para.10

1968

2. Provisional Collection of Taxes Act 1968

s.1, amended: 2012 c.11 s.26

14. Public Expenditure and Receipts Act 1968

s.5, enabling: SI 2012/760

Sch.3 para.1, enabling: SI 2012/760

Sch.3 para.2, enabling: SI 2012/760

19. Criminal Appeal Act 1968

applied: SI 2012/1726 r.68.3

referred to: SI 2012/1726 r.74.2

Part I, applied: SI 2012/1726 r.68.1, r.68.2, r.71.2, r.71.3, r.71.4, r.71.9, r.74.1

s.1, applied: SI 2012/1726 r.68.1, r.68.3, r.68.4

s.2, see *R. v Blackwood (Romaine)* [2012] EWCA Crim 390, [2012] 2 Cr. App. R. 1 (CA (Crim Div)), Richards, L.J.

s.7, see *R. v F* [2012] EWCA Crim 720, [2012] 1 W.L.R. 3133 (CA (Crim Div)), Jackson, L.J.

s.7, applied: SI 2012/1726 r.68.14

s.8, applied: SI 2012/1726 r.14.1, r.68.14

s.9, applied: SI 2012/1726 r.68.1

s.10, applied: SI 2012/1726 r.68.1

s.11, applied: SI 2012/1726 r.68.3, r.68.4

s.12, applied: SI 2012/1726 r.68.1, r.68.3, r.68.4

s.15, applied: SI 2012/1726 r.68.1, r.68.3, r.68.4

s.16A, applied: SI 2012/1726 r.68.1, r.68.3, r.68.4

s.18, applied: SI 2012/1726 r.68.2, r.65.3

s.18A, applied: SI 2012/1726 r.68.1, r.65.3, r.68.2

s.19, applied: SI 2012/1726 r.68.8

s.21, applied: SI 2012/1726 r.65.11

s.22, applied: SI 2012/1726 r.68.11, r.65.5, r.68.12

s.23, see *R. (on the application of Adams) v Secretary of State for Justice* [2012] 1 A.C. 48 (SC), Lord Phillips (President); see *R. v Beesley (Ricky Liam)* [2011] EWCA Crim 1021, [2012] 1 Cr. App. R. (S.) 15 (CA (Crim Div)), Thomas, L.J.; see *R. v Malook (Sadakat Ali)* [2011] EWCA Crim 254, [2012] 1 W.L.R. 633 (CA (Crim Div)), Thomas, L.J.

s.23, applied: SI 2012/1726 r.68.7

s.31, applied: SI 2012/1726 r.65.1, r.66.6, r.68.3, r.69.3, r.65.5

s.31, referred to: SI 2012/1726 r.71.6, r.71.7, r.71.10

s.31A, applied: SI 2012/1726 r.65.1

s.31B, applied: SI 2012/1726 r.65.1

19. Criminal Appeal Act 1968–*cont.*

s.31C, applied: SI 2012/1726 r.65.1, r.65.5

s.32, applied: SI 2012/1726 r.65.9, r.5.5

s.33, applied: SI 2012/1726 r.74.1, r.74.2

s.34, applied: SI 2012/1726 r.74.2

s.36, applied: SI 2012/1726 r.74.2

s.37, referred to: SI 2012/1726 r.74.3

s.38, applied: SI 2012/1726 r.74.2

s.44, applied: SI 2012/1726 r.65.1, r.65.5

s.50, amended: 2012 c.10 Sch.5 para.3

s.50, applied: SI 2012/1726 r.68.1

s.51, amended: 2012 c.7 s.38

Sch.2 para.2, amended: 2012 c.10 Sch.13 para.6

20. Court Martial Appeals Act 1968

s.31, amended: 2012 c.10 Sch.8 para.2

s.31, enabling: SI 2012/1805

s.31A, added: 2012 c.10 Sch.8 para.3

s.33, amended: 2012 c.10 Sch.8 para.4

s.33A, substituted: 2012 c.10 Sch.8 para.5

s.33B, added: 2012 c.10 Sch.8 para.6

s.33B, enabling: SI 2012/1805

s.33C, added: 2012 c.10 Sch.8 para.7

s.46A, added: 2012 c.10 Sch.8 para.10

s.46B, added: 2012 c.10 Sch.8 para.10

s.47, amended: 2012 c.10 Sch.8 para.11, Sch.8 para.12

s.47A, added: 2012 c.10 Sch.8 para.13

s.47B, added: 2012 c.10 Sch.8 para.14

27. Firearms Act 1968

see *Attorney General's Reference (No.6 of 2011), Re* [2012] EWCA Crim 86, [2012] 2 Cr. App. R. (S.) 67 (CA (Crim Div)), Hallett, L.J.; see *Crozier (Gordon) v HM Advocate* 2012 S.C.L. 37 (HCJ), Lord Eassie; see *McDonald (James Scott) v HM Advocate* 2012 S.C.L. 613 (HCJ), Lord Mackay of Drumadoon

applied: SI 2012/1652 Sch.8 Part 8

s.5, see *Johnstone (Brian) v HM Advocate* 2012 J.C. 79 (HCJ), The Lord Justice Clerk (Gill); see *R. v Brereton (Matthew)* [2012] EWCA Crim 85, [2012] 2 Cr. App. R. (S.) 69 (CA (Crim Div)), Hallett, L.J.

s.16, see *R. v Sheen (John Henry)* [2011] EWCA Crim 2461, [2012] 2 Cr. App. R. (S.) 3 (CA (Crim Div)), Stanley Burnton, L.J.

s.21, amended: 2012 c.10 Sch.10 para.3

s.21, repealed (in part): 2012 c.10 Sch.10 para.3

s.51A, see *R. v Brereton (Matthew)* [2012] EWCA Crim 85, [2012] 2 Cr. App. R. (S.) 69 (CA (Crim Div)), Hallett, L.J.; see *R. v Jones (Sarah Louise)* [2011] EWCA Crim 1448, [2012] 1 Cr. App. R. (S.) 25 (CA (Crim Div)), Laws, L.J.

29. Trade Descriptions Act 1968

applied: SI 2012/1128 Art.4

referred to: 2012 c.19 Sch.6 para.4

s.2, amended: SI 2012/1916 Sch.34 para.37

41. Countryside Act 1968

s.16, amended: SI 2012/1659 Sch.3 para.3

46. Health Services and Public Health Act 1968

s.63, amended: 2012 c.7 Sch.5 para.12

s.63, applied: SI 2012/2886 Sch.1, SI 2012/3145 Sch.1, SSI 2012/303 Reg.54

s.63, repealed (in part): 2012 c.7 Sch.5 para.12

s.64, amended: 2012 c.7 Sch.5 para.13

49. Social Work (Scotland) Act 1968

applied: SI 2012/2886 Sch.1, SI 2012/3144 Reg.8, SI 2012/3145 Sch.1, SSI 2012/303 Reg.20

s.12, applied: SI 2012/2886 Sch.1, SSI 2012/303 Sch.4 para.32, Sch.5 para.22

1968– cont.

49. Social Work (Scotland) Act 1968– *cont.*
s.12B, applied: SI 2012/ 2885 Sch.6 para.29, SI 2012/
2886 Sch.1, SSI 2012/ 303 Sch.4 para.57, Sch.5
para.62, SSI 2012/ 319 Sch.4 para.29
s.78, amended: 2012 c.5 Sch.14 Part 1
s.87, applied: SSI 2012/ 67 Reg.2, SSI 2012/ 68
s.87, enabling: SSI 2012/ 67
s.94, amended: 2012 asp 8 Sch.8 Part 1

52. Caravan Sites Act 1968
s.13, see *Bury MBC v Secretary of State for
Communities and Local Government* [2011]
EWHC 2192 (Admin), [2012] J.P.L. 51 (QBD
(Manchester)), Judge Waksman Q.C.; see
Egan v Basildon BC [2011] EWHC 2416 (QB),
[2012] P.T.S.R. 1117 (QBD), Edwards-Stuart J.

**55. Friendly and Industrial and Provident Societies
Act 1968**
applied: SI 2012/ 1128 Art.4

60. Theft Act 1968
see *Balint v Czech Republic* [2011] EWHC 498
(Admin), [2012] 1 W.L.R. 244 (QBD (Admin)),
Jackson, L.J.
s.6, see *R. v Vinall (George Alfred)* [2011] EWCA
Crim 2652, [2012] 1 Cr. App. R. 29 (CA (Crim
Div)), Pitchford, L.J.
s.9, see *R. v Wiggins (Zaro Pierre)* [2012] EWCA
Crim 885, (2012) 176 J.P. 305 (CA (Crim Div)),
Pitchford, L.J.
s.10, see *R. v Wiggins (Zaro Pierre)* [2012] EWCA
Crim 885, (2012) 176 J.P. 305 (CA (Crim Div)),
Pitchford, L.J.
s.24A, amended: 2012 c.21 Sch.18 para.32
s.31, see *Gray v News Group Newspapers Ltd* [2012]
UKSC 28, [2012] 3 W.L.R. 312 (SC), Lord Hope,
J.S.C. (Deputy President)

64. Civil Evidence Act 1968
s.11, see *British Waterways v Royal & Sun Alliance
Insurance Plc* [2012] EWHC 460 (Comm),
[2012] Lloyd's Rep. I.R. 562 (QBD (Comm)),
Burton, J.

65. Gaming Act 1968
Pt III. see *Rank Group Plc v Revenue and Customs
Commissioners* [2012] UKUT 347 (TCC), [2012]
B.V.C. 1861 (UT (Tax)), Norris, J.
s.14, see *Rank Group Plc v Revenue and Customs
Commissioners* [2012] UKUT 347 (TCC),
[2012] B.V.C. 1861 (UT (Tax)), Norris, J.

67. Medicines Act 1968
applied: SI 2012/ 1916 Sch.32 para.3, Sch.34 para.36
Part II, applied: SI 2012/ 504 Sch.4 para.6, SI 2012/
1916 Sch.34 para.36
Part II, repealed: SI 2012/ 1916 Sch.35
Part IV, applied: SI 2012/ 2113 Art.4
s.1, substituted: SI 2012/ 1916 Sch.34 para.2
s.2A, applied: SI 2012/ 504 Sch.7 para.2, Sch.7
para.4
s.2A, repealed: SI 2012/ 1916 Sch.35
s.3, repealed: SI 2012/ 1916 Sch.35
s.4, applied: SI 2012/ 504 Sch.7 para.2, Sch.7 para.4,
SI 2012/ 1916 Sch.5 para.2
s.4, repealed: SI 2012/ 1916 Sch.35
s.5, repealed: SI 2012/ 1916 Sch.35
s.10, amended: SI 2012/ 1916 Sch.34 para.3
s.10, applied: SI 2012/ 1916 Reg.4, Reg.32, Sch.26
para.11
s.10, referred to: SI 2012/ 1916 Reg.346
s.10, repealed (in part): SI 2012/ 1916 Sch.34 para.3,
Sch.35
s.11, repealed: SI 2012/ 1916 Sch.35
s.12, repealed: SI 2012/ 1916 Sch.35

1968– cont.

67. Medicines Act 1968– *cont.*
s.13, repealed: SI 2012/ 1916 Sch.35
s.14, repealed: SI 2012/ 1916 Sch.35
s.15, amended: SI 2012/ 1916 Sch.34 para.4
s.15, repealed (in part): SI 2012/ 1916 Sch.34 para.4,
Sch.35
s.16, repealed: SI 2012/ 1916 Sch.35
s.17, repealed: SI 2012/ 1916 Sch.35
s.18, repealed: SI 2012/ 1916 Sch.35
s.19, repealed: SI 2012/ 1916 Sch.35
s.20, repealed: SI 2012/ 1916 Sch.35
s.21, applied: SI 2012/ 504 Reg.37
s.21, repealed: SI 2012/ 1916 Sch.35
s.22, applied: SI 2012/ 504 Reg.37
s.22, repealed: SI 2012/ 1916 Sch.35
s.22A, applied: SI 2012/ 1916 Sch.32 para.7
s.22A, repealed: SI 2012/ 1916 Sch.35
s.23, repealed: SI 2012/ 1916 Sch.35
s.24, repealed: SI 2012/ 1916 Sch.35
s.25, repealed: SI 2012/ 1916 Sch.35
s.26, repealed: SI 2012/ 1916 Sch.35
s.27, applied: SI 2012/ 504 Reg.37
s.27, repealed: SI 2012/ 1916 Sch.35
s.28, applied: SI 2012/ 1916 Sch.32 para.3
s.28, repealed: SI 2012/ 1916 Sch.35
s.29, repealed: SI 2012/ 1916 Sch.35
s.30, applied: SI 2012/ 504 Reg.18
s.30, repealed: SI 2012/ 1916 Sch.35
s.31, repealed: SI 2012/ 1916 Sch.35
s.32, repealed: SI 2012/ 1916 Sch.35
s.33, repealed: SI 2012/ 1916 Sch.35
s.34, repealed: SI 2012/ 1916 Sch.35
s.35, repealed: SI 2012/ 1916 Sch.35
s.36, repealed: SI 2012/ 1916 Sch.35
s.37, repealed: SI 2012/ 1916 Sch.35
s.38, repealed: SI 2012/ 1916 Sch.35
s.39, repealed: SI 2012/ 1916 Sch.35
s.40, repealed: SI 2012/ 1916 Sch.35
s.41, repealed: SI 2012/ 1916 Sch.35
s.42, repealed: SI 2012/ 1916 Sch.35
s.43, repealed: SI 2012/ 1916 Sch.35
s.44, applied: SI 2012/ 504 Sch.7 para.4
s.44, repealed: SI 2012/ 1916 Sch.35
s.45, repealed: SI 2012/ 1916 Sch.35
s.46, repealed: SI 2012/ 1916 Sch.35
s.47, repealed: SI 2012/ 1916 Sch.35
s.48, repealed: SI 2012/ 1916 Sch.35
s.49, repealed: SI 2012/ 1916 Sch.35
s.49A, repealed: SI 2012/ 1916 Sch.35
s.49B, repealed: SI 2012/ 1916 Sch.35
s.50, applied: SI 2012/ 504 Reg.14
s.50, repealed: SI 2012/ 1916 Sch.35
s.51, applied: SI 2012/ 504 Reg.5, Sch.2 para.31,
Sch.3 para.7
s.51, repealed: SI 2012/ 1916 Sch.35
s.52, repealed: SI 2012/ 1916 Sch.35
s.53, repealed: SI 2012/ 1916 Sch.35
s.54, repealed: SI 2012/ 1916 Sch.35
s.55, repealed: SI 2012/ 1916 Sch.35
s.56, repealed: SI 2012/ 1916 Sch.35
s.57, repealed: SI 2012/ 1916 Sch.35
s.58, amended: 2012 c.7 s.213, s.220, SI 2012/ 1916
Sch.34 para.5
s.58, repealed (in part): SI 2012/ 1916 Sch.34 para.5,
Sch.35
s.58A, amended: SI 2012/ 1916 Sch.34 para.6
s.58A, repealed (in part): SI 2012/ 1916 Sch.34
para.6

67. Medicines Act 1968–*cont.*

s.59, repealed: SI 2012/ 1916 Sch.35

s.60, applied: SI 2012/ 1916 Sch.32 para.7

s.60, repealed: SI 2012/ 1916 Sch.35

s.61, repealed: SI 2012/ 1916 Sch.35

s.62, amended: SI 2012/ 1916 Sch.34 para.7

s.64, amended: SI 2012/ 1916 Sch.34 para.8

s.65, repealed: SI 2012/ 1916 Sch.35

s.66, repealed: SI 2012/ 1916 Sch.35

s.67, amended: SI 2012/ 1916 Sch.34 para.9

s.67, applied: SI 2012/ 1916 Sch.32 para.7

s.67, repealed (in part): SI 2012/ 1916 Sch.34 para.9, Sch.35

s.68, repealed: SI 2012/ 1916 Sch.35

s.69, applied: SI 2012/ 1909 Sch.2 para.2, SI 2012/ 1916 Sch.17 Part 1, Sch.22

s.72, amended: SI 2012/ 1916 Sch.34 para.10

s.72, applied: SI 2012/ 1909 Reg.74

s.72, referred to: SI 2012/ 1909 Reg.74

s.75, applied: SI 2012/ 1909 Sch.2 para.4

s.82, amended: SI 2012/ 1916 Sch.34 para.11

s.85, repealed: SI 2012/ 1916 Sch.35

s.86, repealed: SI 2012/ 1916 Sch.35

s.87, amended: SI 2012/ 1916 Sch.34 para.12

s.87, enabling: SI 2012/ 1916

s.88, amended: SI 2012/ 1916 Sch.34 para.13

s.88, enabling: SI 2012/ 1916

s.89, repealed: SI 2012/ 1916 Sch.35

s.91, amended: SI 2012/ 1916 Sch.34 para.14

s.91, repealed (in part): SI 2012/ 1916 Sch.34 para.14, Sch.35

s.91, enabling: SI 2012/ 1916

s.92, repealed: SI 2012/ 1916 Sch.35

s.93, repealed: SI 2012/ 1916 Sch.35

s.94, repealed: SI 2012/ 1916 Sch.35

s.95, repealed: SI 2012/ 1916 Sch.35

s.96, repealed: SI 2012/ 1916 Sch.35

s.97, repealed: SI 2012/ 1916 Sch.35

s.98, repealed: SI 2012/ 1916 Sch.35

s.99, repealed: SI 2012/ 1916 Sch.35

s.100, repealed: SI 2012/ 1916 Sch.35

s.101, repealed: SI 2012/ 1916 Sch.35

s.102, repealed: SI 2012/ 1916 Sch.35

s.103, repealed: SI 2012/ 1916 Sch.35

s.104, amended: SI 2012/ 1916 Sch.34 para.15

s.105, amended: SI 2012/ 1916 Sch.34 para.16

s.107, amended: SI 2012/ 1916 Sch.34 para.17

s.108, amended: SI 2012/ 1916 Sch.34 para.18

s.108, repealed (in part): SI 2012/ 1916 Sch.34 para.18, Sch.35

s.109, amended: SI 2012/ 1916 Sch.34 para.19

s.109, repealed (in part): SI 2012/ 1916 Sch.34 para.19, Sch.35

s.110, amended: SI 2012/ 1916 Sch.34 para.20

s.110, repealed (in part): SI 2012/ 1916 Sch.34 para.20, Sch.35

s.111, amended: SI 2012/ 1916 Sch.34 para.21

s.111, repealed (in part): SI 2012/ 1916 Sch.34 para.21, Sch.35

s.112, repealed (in part): SI 2012/ 1916 Sch.35

s.113, amended: SI 2012/ 1916 Sch.34 para.22

s.114, amended: SI 2012/ 1916 Sch.34 para.23

s.115, repealed: SI 2012/ 1916 Sch.35

s.116, repealed: SI 2012/ 1916 Sch.35

s.121, amended: SI 2012/ 1916 Sch.34 para.24

s.122, amended: SI 2012/ 1916 Sch.34 para.25

s.123, amended: SI 2012/ 1916 Sch.34 para.26

s.125, amended: SI 2012/ 1916 Sch.34 para.27

67. Medicines Act 1968–*cont.*

s.126, amended: SI 2012/ 1916 Sch.34 para.28

s.126, repealed (in part): SI 2012/ 1916 Sch.34 para.28, Sch.35

s.128, amended: SI 2012/ 1916 Sch.34 para.29

s.129, amended: SI 2012/ 1916 Sch.34 para.30

s.129, applied: SI 2012/ 504, SI 2012/ 1916, SI 2012/ 2546

s.129, repealed (in part): SI 2012/ 1916 Sch.34 para.30

s.129, enabling: SI 2012/ 1916

s.130, amended: SI 2012/ 1916 Sch.34 para.31

s.130, repealed (in part): SI 2012/ 1916 Sch.34 para.31, Sch.35

s.131, amended: SI 2012/ 1916 Sch.34 para.32

s.132, amended: SI 2012/ 1916 Sch.34 para.33

s.132, repealed (in part): SI 2012/ 1916 Sch.34 para.33, Sch.35

Sch.1 A para.1, repealed: SI 2012/ 1916 Sch.35

Sch.1 A para.2, repealed: SI 2012/ 1916 Sch.35

Sch.1 A para.3, repealed: SI 2012/ 1916 Sch.35

Sch.1 A para.4, repealed: SI 2012/ 1916 Sch.35

Sch.1 A para.5, repealed: SI 2012/ 1916 Sch.35

Sch.1 A para.6, repealed: SI 2012/ 1916 Sch.35

Sch.1 A para.7, applied: SI 2012/ 1916 Sch.32 para.7

Sch.1 A para.7, repealed: SI 2012/ 1916 Sch.35

Sch.1 A para.8, applied: SI 2012/ 1916 Sch.32 para.7

Sch.1 A para.8, repealed: SI 2012/ 1916 Sch.35

Sch.1 A para.9, applied: SI 2012/ 1916 Sch.32 para.7

Sch.1 A para.9, repealed: SI 2012/ 1916 Sch.35

Sch.1 A para.10, applied: SI 2012/ 1916 Sch.32 para.7

Sch.1 A para.10, repealed: SI 2012/ 1916 Sch.35

Sch.1 A para.11, applied: SI 2012/ 1916 Sch.32 para.7

Sch.1 A para.11, repealed: SI 2012/ 1916 Sch.35

Sch.1 A para.12, applied: SI 2012/ 1916 Sch.32 para.7

Sch.1 A para.12, repealed: SI 2012/ 1916 Sch.35

Sch.2 para.1, repealed: SI 2012/ 1916 Sch.35

Sch.2 para.2, repealed: SI 2012/ 1916 Sch.35

Sch.2 para.3, repealed: SI 2012/ 1916 Sch.35

Sch.2 para.4, repealed: SI 2012/ 1916 Sch.35

Sch.2 para.5, applied: SI 2012/ 504 Reg.37

Sch.2 para.5, repealed: SI 2012/ 1916 Sch.35

Sch.2 para.6, repealed: SI 2012/ 1916 Sch.35

Sch.2 para.6, applied: SI 2012/ 504 Reg.37

Sch.2 para.6, repealed: SI 2012/ 1916 Sch.35

Sch.2 para.7, repealed: SI 2012/ 1916 Sch.35

Sch.2 para.8, repealed: SI 2012/ 1916 Sch.35

Sch.2 para.9, repealed: SI 2012/ 1916 Sch.35

Sch.2 para.10, repealed: SI 2012/ 1916 Sch.35

Sch.2 para.11, repealed: SI 2012/ 1916 Sch.35

Sch.2 para.12, repealed: SI 2012/ 1916 Sch.35

Sch.2 para.13, repealed: SI 2012/ 1916 Sch.35

Sch.2 para.14, repealed: SI 2012/ 1916 Sch.35

Sch.2 para.15, repealed: SI 2012/ 1916 Sch.35

Sch.2 para.16, repealed: SI 2012/ 1916 Sch.35

Sch.3 para.5, repealed: SI 2012/ 1916 Sch.34 para.34, Sch.35

Sch.3 para.6, repealed: SI 2012/ 1916 Sch.34 para.34, Sch.35

Sch.3 para.7, repealed: SI 2012/ 1916 Sch.34 para.34, Sch.35

Sch.3 para.8, amended: SI 2012/ 1916 Sch.34 para.34

Sch.3 para.9, amended: SI 2012/ 1916 Sch.34 para.34

Sch.3 para.17, amended: SI 2012/ 1916 Sch.34 para.34

Sch.4 para.1, amended: SI 2012/ 1916 Sch.34 para.35

Sch.4 para.6, amended: SI 2012/ 1916 Sch.34 para.35

Sch.4 para.8, amended: SI 2012/ 1916 Sch.34 para.35

1968– cont.

67. Medicines Act 1968–*cont.*
Sch.4 para.9, amended: SI 2012/ 1916 Sch.34 para.35
Sch.4 para.10, amended: SI 2012/ 1916 Sch.34 para.35

73. Transport Act 1968
applied: SI 2012/ 1659 Art.2
s.43, amended: SI 2012/ 1659 Sch.2 para.31
s.43, repealed (in part): SI 2012/ 1659 Sch.2 para.31
s.43A, added: SI 2012/ 1659 Sch.2 para.32
s.44, amended: SI 2012/ 1659 Sch.2 para.33
s.44, applied: SI 2012/ 1659 Art.5
s.46, amended: SI 2012/ 1659 Sch.2 para.34
s.48, amended: SI 2012/ 1659 Sch.2 para.35
s.49, amended: SI 2012/ 1659 Sch.2 para.36
s.50, amended: SI 2012/ 1659 Sch.2 para.37
s.50, repealed (in part): SI 2012/ 1659 Sch.2 para.37
s.96, enabling: SI 2012/ 1502
s.101, applied: SI 2012/ 1502
s.102, amended: 2012 asp 8 Sch.7 para.47
s.104, amended: SI 2012/ 1659 Sch.2 para.38
s.105, amended: SI 2012/ 1659 Sch.2 para.39
s.106, substituted: SI 2012/ 1659 Sch.2 para.40
s.108, amended: SI 2012/ 1659 Sch.2 para.41
s.109, amended: SI 2012/ 1659 Sch.2 para.42
s.109, repealed (in part): SI 2012/ 1659 Sch.2 para.42
s.110, applied: SI 2012/ 1658 Art.3
s.110, repealed: SI 2012/ 1658 Sch.1
s.110A, repealed: SI 2012/ 1658 Sch.1
s.110B, repealed: SI 2012/ 1658 Sch.1
s.110C, repealed: SI 2012/ 1658 Sch.1
s.111, amended: SI 2012/ 1659 Sch.2 para.43
s.112, amended: SI 2012/ 1659 Sch.2 para.44
s.112, repealed (in part): SI 2012/ 1659 Sch.2 para.44
s.113, amended: SI 2012/ 1659 Sch.2 para.45
s.116, amended: SI 2012/ 1659 Sch.2 para.46
s.116, applied: SI 2012/ 1993 Art.3
s.117, amended: SI 2012/ 1659 Sch.2 para.47
s.117, applied: SI 2012/ 1993 Art.3
s.118, amended: SI 2012/ 1659 Sch.2 para.48
s.118, applied: SI 2012/ 1993 Art.3
s.119, amended: SI 2012/ 1659 Sch.2 para.49
s.121, amended: SI 2012/ 1659 Sch.2 para.50
s.137, amended: SI 2012/ 1659 Sch.2 para.51
s.144, amended: SI 2012/ 1659 Sch.2 para.52
s.160, amended: 2012 c.14 Sch.39 para.1
Sch.13 para.1, amended: SI 2012/ 1659 Sch.2 para.53
Sch.13 para.2, amended: SI 2012/ 1659 Sch.2 para.53
Sch.13 para.3, repealed (in part): SI 2012/ 1658 Sch.1
Sch.13 para.3A, added: SI 2012/ 1659 Sch.2 para.53
Sch.13 para.5, amended: SI 2012/ 1659 Sch.2 para.53

77. Sea Fisheries Act 1968
s.5, applied: SI 2012/ 2747 Art.3
s.5, enabling: SI 2012/ 2729
s.15, applied: SSI 2012/ 348

1969

19. Decimal Currency Act 1969
s.6, applied: 2012 c.14 s.160
s.7, amended: 2012 c.21 Sch.18 para.33

24NI. Industrial and Provident Societies Act (Northern Ireland) 1969
applied: 2012 c.21 s.50

46. Family Law Reform Act 1969
applied: SI 2012/ 3144 Reg.8, SI 2012/ 3145 Sch.1

1969– cont.

46. Family Law Reform Act 1969–*cont.*
s.20, see *Brighton and Hove City Council v PM*
[2011] EWCA Civ 795, [2012] 1 F.L.R. 351 (CA
(Civ Div), Sir Nicholas Wall (President, Fam);
see *LG v DK* [2011] EWHC 2453 (Fam), [2012] 2
All E.R. 115 (CP), Sir Nicholas Wall (President,
Fam)
s.21, see *Brighton and Hove City Council v PM*
[2011] EWCA Civ 795, [2012] 1 F.L.R. 351 (CA
(Civ Div), Sir Nicholas Wall (President, Fam);
see *LG v DK* [2011] EWHC 2453 (Fam), [2012] 2
All E.R. 115 (CP), Sir Nicholas Wall (President,
Fam)
s.23, see *Brighton and Hove City Council v PM*
[2011] EWCA Civ 795, [2012] 1 F.L.R. 351 (CA
(Civ Div)), Sir Nicholas Wall (President, Fam)

51. Development of Tourism Act 1969
Sch.1 para.5, amended: SI 2012/ 2404 Sch.2 para.4

54. Children and Young Persons Act 1969
applied: SI 2012/ 3144 Reg.8, SI 2012/ 3145 Sch.1
s.23, see *R. (on the application of A) v Lewisham
Youth Court* [2011] EWHC 1193 (Admin), [2012]
1 W.L.R. 34 (DC), Toulson, L.J.
s.23, amended: 2012 c.10 Sch.5 para.4, Sch.5 para.5
s.23, applied: 2012 c.10 s.94, s.99, s.107, SI 2012/ 1726
r.18.4, SI 2012/ 2824 Reg.2, SI 2012/ 2906 Art.7
s.23, referred to: SI 2012/ 1726 r.19.2, r.18.4
s.23, repealed: 2012 c.10 Sch.12 para.6
s.23A, repealed: 2012 c.10 Sch.12 para.8
s.23AA, repealed: 2012 c.10 Sch.12 para.7
s.23B, amended: 2012 c.10 Sch.12 para.9
s.32, amended: 2012 c.10 Sch.12 para.10
s.32, repealed (in part): 2012 c.10 Sch.12 para.10
s.34, amended: 2012 c.10 Sch.12 para.11
s.34, repealed (in part): 2012 c.10 Sch.12 para.11
s.69, repealed (in part): 2012 c.10 Sch.12 para.12

57. Employers Liability (Compulsory Insurance) Act 1969
see *AXA General Insurance Ltd, Petitioners* [2012]
1 A.C. 868 (SC), Lord Hope (Deputy President);
see *Durham v BAI (Run Off) Ltd* [2012] UKSC
14, [2012] 1 W.L.R. 867 (SC), Lord Phillips
(President)
s.1, amended: 2012 c.21 Sch.18 para.34
s.3, amended: 2012 c.7 Sch.5 para.14, Sch.14 para.44

1970

9. Taxes Management Act 1970
see *Frank Saul (Fashions) Ltd v Revenue and
Customs Commissioners* [2012] EWHC 1603
(Ch), [2012] B.P.I.R. 985 (Ch D), Vos, J.
applied: SI 2012/ 1868 Reg.3
Part V, applied: 2012 c.14 Sch.38 para.5, Sch.38
para.20, Sch.38 para.31
s.7, amended: 2012 c.14 Sch.1 para.2
s.8, see *Revenue and Customs Commissioners v
Cotter* [2012] EWCA Civ 81, [2012] S.T.C. 745
(CA (Civ Div), Arden, L.J.
s.8, applied: SI 2012/ 1836 Reg.9
s.8A, applied: SI 2012/ 1836 Reg.9
s.8ZA, applied: SI 2012/ 1836 Reg.9
s.9, see *Revenue and Customs Commissioners v
Cotter* [2012] EWCA Civ 81, [2012] S.T.C. 745
(CA (Civ Div)), Arden, L.J.
s.9A, see *Revenue and Customs Commissioners v
Cotter* [2012] EWCA Civ 81, [2012] S.T.C. 745 (CA
(Civ Div)), Arden, L.J.

1970– cont.

9. Taxes Management Act 1970–*cont.*

s.9C, see *Broome v Revenue and Customs Commissioners* [2012] W.T.L.R. 585 (FTT (Tax)), Judge Michael Connell

s.9ZB, see *Revenue and Customs Commissioners v Cotter* [2012] EWCA Civ 81, [2012] S.T.C. 745 (CA (Civ Div)), Arden, L.J.

s.12AA, see *Fitzpatrick & Co Solicitors v Revenue and Customs Commissioners* [2012] UKFTT 238 (TC), [2012] S.F.T.D. 816 (FTT (Tax)), Judge Charles Hellier

s.12AA, applied: SI 2012/ 1836 Reg.9, Reg.12

s.12AB, see *Revenue and Customs Commissioners v Lansdowne Partners LP* [2011] EWCA Civ 1578, [2012] S.T.C. 544 (CA (Civ Div)), Sir Andrew Morritt (Chancellor)

s.17, enabling: SI 2012/ 756

s.18B, enabling: SI 2012/ 756

s.18D, amended: 2012 c.14 s.224

s.20A, repealed: 2012 c.14 Sch.38 para.45

s.20B, repealed: 2012 c.14 Sch.38 para.45

s.20BB, amended: 2012 c.14 Sch.38 para.46

s.20BB, repealed (in part): 2012 c.14 Sch.38 para.46

s.20D, amended: 2012 c.14 Sch.38 para.47

s.20D, repealed (in part): 2012 c.14 Sch.38 para.47

s.28A, see *Trustees of the BT Pension Scheme v Revenue and Customs Commissioners* [2012] S.F.T.D. 107 (FTT (Tax)), Sir Stephen Oliver Q.C.

s.28C, see *Bartram v Revenue and Customs Commissioners* [2012] UKUT 184 (TCC), [2012] S.T.C. 2144 (UT (Tax)), Judge John Clark

s.29, see *Blumenthal v Revenue and Customs Commissioners* [2012] UKFTT 497 (TC), [2012] S.F.T.D. 1264 (FTT (Tax)), Judge Guy Brannan; see *Hankinson v Revenue and Customs Commissioners* [2011] EWCA Civ 1566, [2012] 1 W.L.R. 2322 (CA (Civ Div)), Mummery, L.J.; see *Sanderson v Revenue and Customs Commissioners* [2012] UKFTT 207 (TC), [2012] S.F.T.D. 1033 (FTT (Tax)), Judge John Brooks; see *Shakoor v Revenue and Customs Commissioners* [2012] UKFTT 532 (TC), [2012] S.F.T.D. 1391 (FTT (Tax)), Judge Geraint Jones Q.C.

s.30B, see *Revenue and Customs Commissioners v Lansdowne Partners LP* [2011] EWCA Civ 1578, [2012] S.T.C. 544 (CA (Civ Div)), Sir Andrew Morritt (Chancellor)

s.31, see *Bartram v Revenue and Customs Commissioners* [2012] UKUT 184 (TCC), [2012] S.T.C. 2144 (UT (Tax)), Judge John Clark

s.33, see *Test Claimants in the FII Group Litigation v Revenue and Customs Commissioners* [2012] UKSC 19, [2012] 2 A.C. 337 (SC), Lord Hope

s.42, amended: 2012 c.14 Sch.15 para.11

s.42, disapplied: SI 2012/459 Reg.14

s.42, repealed (in part): 2012 c.14 s.222

s.43, see *Trustees of the BT Pension Scheme v Revenue and Customs Commissioners* [2012] S.F.T.D. 107 (FTT (Tax)), Sir Stephen Oliver Q.C.

s.54, see *Sanderson v Revenue and Customs Commissioners* [2012] UKFTT 207 (TC), [2012] S.F.T.D. 1033 (FTT (Tax)), Judge John Brooks

s.55, repealed (in part): 2012 c.14 Sch.20 para.11

s.59A, enabling: SI 2012/ 822

s.59B, amended: 2012 c.14 Sch.15 para.9

s.59B, enabling: SI 2012/ 822

s.59D, varied: 2012 c.14 Sch.34 para.12

s.59E, amended: 2012 c.14 Sch.20 para.12

1970– cont.

9. Taxes Management Act 1970–*cont.*

s.59F, amended: 2012 c.14 Sch.20 para.13

s.65, see *McNulty v Revenue and Customs Commissioners* [2012] UKUT 174 (TCC), [2012] S.T.C. 2110 (UT (Tax)), Arnold, J.

s.72, repealed: 2012 c.14 s.222

s.73, repealed: 2012 c.14 s.222

s.75, see *Revenue and Customs Commissioners v Ali* [2011] EWHC 880 (Ch), [2012] S.T.C. 42 (Ch D), Warren, J.

s.86, see *Gratton v Revenue and Customs Commissioners* [2012] UKUT 261 (TCC), [2012] S.T.C. 2061 (UT (Tax)), Judge Timothy Herrington

s.93, varied: SI 2012/ 1868 Reg.24

s.93A, varied: SI 2012/ 1868 Reg.24

s.94, varied: SI 2012/ 1868 Reg.24

s.95, varied: SI 2012/ 1868 Reg.24

s.95A, varied: SI 2012/ 1868 Reg.24

s.96, see *McNulty v Revenue and Customs Commissioners* [2012] UKUT 174 (TCC), [2012] S.T.C. 2110 (UT (Tax)), Arnold, J.

s.96, varied: SI 2012/ 1868 Reg.24

s.97, varied: SI 2012/ 1868 Reg.24

s.97A, varied: SI 2012/ 1868 Reg.24

s.97AA, varied: SI 2012/ 1868 Reg.24

s.98, amended: 2012 c.14 s.26, Sch.6 para.23, Sch.8 para.17, Sch.16 para.67, Sch.39 para.5

s.98, varied: SI 2012/ 1868 Reg.24

s.98A, varied: SI 2012/ 1868 Reg.24

s.98A, enabling: SI 2012/ 822

s.98B, varied: SI 2012/ 1868 Reg.24

s.98C, applied: SI 2012/ 1836 Reg.16, SI 2012/ 1868 Reg.3, Reg.22

s.98C, varied: SI 2012/ 1868 Reg.24

s.98C, enabling: SI 2012/ 1836

s.99, repealed: 2012 c.14 Sch.38 para.45

s.99, varied: SI 2012/ 1868 Reg.24

s.99A, varied: SI 2012/ 1868 Reg.24

s.99B, varied: SI 2012/ 1868 Reg.24

s.100, varied: SI 2012/ 1868 Reg.24

s.100A, varied: SI 2012/ 1868 Reg.24

s.100B, see *Hok Ltd v Revenue and Customs Commissioners* [2012] UKUT 363 (TCC), [2012] B.T.C. 1711 (UT (Tax)), Warren, J.

s.100B, varied: SI 2012/ 1868 Reg.24

s.100C, varied: SI 2012/ 1868 Reg.24

s.100D, varied: SI 2012/ 1868 Reg.24

s.101, varied: SI 2012/ 1868 Reg.24

s.102, varied: SI 2012/ 1868 Reg.24

s.103, amended: 2012 c.14 Sch.38 para.48

s.103, repealed (in part): 2012 c.14 Sch.38 para.48

s.103, varied: SI 2012/ 1868 Reg.24

s.103A, varied: SI 2012/ 1868 Reg.24

s.103ZA, amended: 2012 c.14 Sch.38 para.49

s.103ZA, varied: SI 2012/ 1868 Reg.24

s.104, varied: SI 2012/ 1868 Reg.24

s.105, varied: SI 2012/ 1868 Reg.24

s.106, varied: SI 2012/ 1868 Reg.24

s.106A, varied: SI 2012/ 1868 Reg.24

s.107, varied: SI 2012/ 1868 Reg.24

s.108, applied: 2012 c.14 Sch.38 para.36, SI 2012/ 3111 Reg.4

s.113, enabling: SI 2012/ 820, SI 2012/ 822

s.114, see *John Mander Pension Trustees Ltd v Revenue and Customs Commissioners* [2012] S.F.T.D. 322 (FTT (Tax)), Judge Barbara Mosedale

s.114, applied: 2012 c.14 Sch.38 para.36

1970– cont.

9. Taxes Management Act 1970– *cont.*
s.115, applied: 2012 c.14 Sch.38 para.36
s.118, see *Bartram v Revenue and Customs Commissioners* [2012] UKUT 184 (TCC), [2012] S.T.C. 2144 (UT (Tax)), Judge John Clark; see *Cardiff Lift Co v Revenue and Customs Commissioners* [2012] S.F.T.D. 85 (FTT (Tax)), Judge Charles Hellier
s.118, amended: 2012 c.14 s.222, Sch.38 para.50
s.118, applied: SI 2012/ 1868 Reg.3
Sch.1B para.2, see *Revenue and Customs Commissioners v Cotter* [2012] EWCA Civ 81, [2012] S.T.C. 745 (CA (Civ Div)), Arden, L.J.
Sch.3A Pt I para.1, see *Fitzpatrick & Co Solicitors v Revenue and Customs Commissioners* [2012] UKFTT 238 (TC), [2012] S.F.T.D. 816 (FTT (Tax)), Judge Charles Hellier

10. Income and Corporation Taxes Act 1970
s.337, applied: 2012 c.14 s.172

31. Administration of Justice Act 1970
s.28, amended: SI 2012/ 2814 Sch.4 para.2
s.36, see *Zinda v Bank of Scotland Plc* [2011] EWCA Civ 706, [2012] 1 W.L.R. 728 (CA (Civ Div)), Mummery, L.J.
s.41, see *James v RSPCA* [2011] EWHC 1642 (Admin), [2012] 5 Costs L.O. 547 (QBD (Admin)), Keith, J.
s.41, applied: SI 2012/ 1726 r.76.1
Sch.8 para.13C, added: SI 2012/ 2814 Sch.4 para.2

34. Marriage (Registrar General's Licence) Act 1970
s.16, amended: 2012 c.9 s.114

35. Conveyancing and Feudal Reform (Scotland) Act 1970
applied: 2012 asp 5 s.49
Pt II. see *Northern Rock (Asset Management) Plc v Fowlie* 2012 Hous. L.R. 103 (Sh Ct (Grampian) (Banff)), Sheriff P Mann
s.9, amended: 2012 asp 5 Sch.5 para.17, 2012 asp 9 Sch.1 para.1
s.10, amended: 2012 asp 5 Sch.5 para.17
s.11, amended: 2012 asp 5 Sch.5 para.17
s.12, amended: 2012 asp 5 Sch.5 para.17
s.13, amended: 2012 asp 5 Sch.5 para.17
s.14, amended: 2012 asp 5 Sch.5 para.17
s.15, amended: 2012 asp 5 Sch.5 para.17
s.16, amended: 2012 asp 5 Sch.5 para.17
s.17, amended: 2012 asp 5 Sch.5 para.17
s.18, amended: 2012 asp 5 Sch.5 para.17
s.19, see *Bank of Scotland Plc v Stevenson* 2012 S.L.T. (Sh Ct) 155 (Sh Ct (South Strathclyde) (Dumfries)), Sheriff G Jamieson
s.19, amended: 2012 asp 5 Sch.5 para.17
s.20, see *Accord Mortgages Ltd v Edwards* 2012 Hous. L.R. 105 (Sh Ct (Lothian) (Haddington)), Sheriff P J Braid
s.24, see *Accord Mortgages Ltd v Edwards* 2012 Hous. L.R. 105 (Sh Ct (Lothian) (Haddington)), Sheriff P J Braid; see *Bank of Scotland Plc v Stevenson* 2012 S.L.T. (Sh Ct) 155 (Sh Ct (South Strathclyde) (Dumfries)), Sheriff G Jamieson; see *Northern Rock (Asset Management) Plc v Millar* 2012 S.L.T. (Sh Ct) 58 (Sh Ct (Glasgow)), Sheriff A F Deutsch; see *Northern Rock (Asset Management) Plc v Fowlie* 2012 Hous. L.R. 103 (Sh Ct (Grampian) (Banff)), Sheriff P Mann; see *Northern Rock (Asset Management) Plc v Youngson* 2012 Hous. L.R. 100 (Sh Ct (Grampian) (Banff)), Sheriff P Mann

1970– cont.

35. Conveyancing and Feudal Reform (Scotland) Act 1970– *cont.*
s.24A, see *Northern Rock (Asset Management) Plc v Millar* 2012 S.L.T. (Sh Ct) 58 (Sh Ct (Glasgow)), Sheriff A F Deutsch
s.26, amended: 2012 asp 5 Sch.5 para.17
s.27, amended: 2012 asp 5 Sch.5 para.17
s.28, amended: 2012 asp 5 Sch.5 para.17
s.30, amended: 2012 asp 5 Sch.5 para.17
s.53, amended: 2012 asp 5 Sch.5 para.17
Sch.2, amended: 2012 asp 5 Sch.5 para.17
Sch.3, see *Accord Mortgages Ltd v Edwards* 2012 Hous. L.R. 105 (Sh Ct (Lothian) (Haddington)), Sheriff P J Braid; see *Northern Rock (Asset Management) Plc v Fowlie* 2012 Hous. L.R. 103 (Sh Ct (Grampian) (Banff)), Sheriff P Mann
Sch.3 para.12, amended: 2012 asp 5 Sch.5 para.17
Sch.4, amended: 2012 asp 5 Sch.5 para.17
Sch.5, amended: 2012 asp 5 Sch.5 para.17
Sch.6, amended: 2012 asp 5 Sch.5 para.17
Sch.9, amended: 2012 asp 5 Sch.5 para.17

40. Agriculture Act 1970
s.67, applied: SI 2012/ 1916 Sch.17 Part 4

41. Equal Pay Act 1970
see *Abendshine v Sunderland City Council* [2012] I.C.R. 1087 (EAT), Langstaff, J.; see *Andrews v Kings College Hospital NHS Foundation Trust* [2012] Eq. L.R. 1032 (EAT), Wilkie, J.; see *Hosso v European Credit Management Ltd* [2011] EWCA Civ 1589, [2012] I.C.R. 547 (CA (Civ Div)), Mummery, L.J.; see *Simpson v Intralinks Ltd* [2012] I.L.Pr. 34 (EAT), Langstaff, J. (President)
applied: 2012 c.10 Sch.1 para.43, SSI 2012/ 181 Reg.3
s.1, see *Abdulla v Birmingham City Council* [2012] UKSC 47, [2012] I.C.R. 1419 (SC), Lady Hale, J.S.C.; see *Brownbill v St Helens and Knowsley Teaching Hospitals NHS Trust* [2011] EWCA Civ 903, [2012] 1 C.M.L.R. 15 (CA (Civ Div)), Maurice Kay, L.J.; see *Bury MBC v Hamilton* [2012] EWCA Civ 413, [2012] I.C.R. 1216 (CA (Civ Div)), Maurice Kay, L.J.; see *Copple v Littlewoods Plc* [2011] EWCA Civ 1281, [2012] 2 All E.R. 97 (CA (Civ Div)), Mummery, L.J.; see *Edinburgh City Council v Wilkinson* 2012 S.C. 423 (IH (Ex Div)), Lord Eassie; see *Hosso v European Credit Management Ltd* [2011] EWCA Civ 1589, [2012] I.C.R. 547 (CA (Civ Div)), Mummery, L.J.; see *Simpson v Intralinks Ltd* [2012] I.L.Pr. 34 (EAT), Langstaff, J. (President)
s.2, see *Abdulla v Birmingham City Council* [2011] EWCA Civ 1412, [2012] 2 All E.R. 591 (CA (Civ Div)), Mummery, L.J.; see *Abdulla v Birmingham City Council* [2012] UKSC 47, [2012] I.C.R. 1419 (SC), Lady Hale, J.S.C.; see *Foley v NHS Greater Glasgow and Clyde* [2012] Eq. L.R. 1019 (EAT (SC)), Lady Smith; see *Hosso v European Credit Management Ltd* [2011] EWCA Civ 1589, [2012] I.C.R. 547 (CA (Civ Div)), Mummery, L.J.
s.2ZA, see *Abdulla v Birmingham City Council* [2011] EWCA Civ 1412, [2012] 2 All E.R. 591 (CA (Civ Div)), Mummery, L.J.

42. Local Authority Social Services Act 1970
applied: SI 2012/ 1631 Sch.4 para.11
s.7, see *R. (on the application of Bevan & Clarke LLP) v Neath Port Talbot CBC* [2012] EWHC 236 (Admin), [2012] B.L.G.R. 728 (QBD (Admin)), Beatson, J.; see *R. (on the*

1970– cont.

42. Local Authority Social Services Act 1970– *cont.*
s.7– *cont.*
   application of TG) v Lambeth LBC [2011] EWCA
Civ 526, [2012] P.T.S.R. 364 (CA (Civ Div)), Lord
Neuberger (M.R.); see *R. (on the application of
TT) v Merton LBC* [2012] EWHC 2055 (Admin),
[2012] 3 F.C.R. 354 (QBD (Admin)), Edwards-
Stuart, J.
   Sch.1, amended: 2012 c.7 s.43, Sch.5 para.15, 2012
c.10 Sch.12 para.13

**44. Chronically Sick and Disabled Persons Act
1970**
s.2, see *R. (on the application of KM) v
Cambridgeshire CC* [2012] UKSC 23, [2012]
P.T.S.R. 1189 (SC), Lord Phillips, J.S.C.
(President)
   s.17, amended: 2012 c.7 Sch.5 para.16
   s.21, enabling: SI 2012/309

1971

xviii. British Waterways Act 1971
   see *Moore v British Waterways Board* [2012]
EWHC 182 (Ch), [2012] 1 W.L.R. 3289 (Ch D),
Hildyard, J

19. Carriage of Goods by Sea Act 1971
s.1, see *Sideridraulic Systems SpA v BBC
Chartering & Logistics GmbH & Co KG* [2011]
EWHC 3106 (Comm), [2012] 1 Lloyd's Rep.
230 (QBD (Comm)), Andrew Smith, J.

22. Animals Act 1971
   see *Turnbull v Warrener* [2012] EWCA Civ 412,
[2012] P.I.Q.R. P16 (CA (Civ Div)), Maurice
Kay, L.J.
   s.2, see *Bodey v Hall* [2011] EWHC 2162 (QB), [2012]
P.I.Q.R. P1 (QBD), David Pittaway QC; see
Goldsmith v Patchcott [2012] EWCA Civ 183,
[2012] P.I.Q.R. P11 (CA (Civ Div)), Longmore,
L.J.; see *Turnbull v Warrener* [2012] EWCA Civ
412, [2012] P.I.Q.R. P16 (CA (Civ Div)), Maurice
Kay, L.J.
   s.5, see *Bodey v Hall* [2011] EWHC 2162 (QB), [2012]
P.I.Q.R. P1 (QBD), David Pittaway QC; see
Goldsmith v Patchcott [2012] EWCA Civ 183,
[2012] P.I.Q.R. P11 (CA (Civ Div)), Longmore,
L.J.; see *Turnbull v Warrener* [2012] EWCA Civ
412, [2012] P.I.Q.R. P16 (CA (Civ Div)), Maurice
Kay, L.J.

24. Coinage Act 1971
   s.8, enabling: SI 2012/2746

27. Powers of Attorney Act 1971
   applied: SI 2012/2885 Sch.8 para.4, Sch.8 para.12,
SI 2012/2886 Sch.1, SI 2012/3145 Sch.1

29. National Savings Bank Act 1971
   s.4, enabling: SI 2012/795

31. Interest on Damages (Scotland) Act 1971
   see *Farstad Supply AS v Enviroco Ltd* 2012 S.L.T.
348 (OH), Lord Hodge

32. Attachment of Earnings Act 1971
   s.1, amended: 2012 c.10 Sch.5 para.6
   s.2, amended: SI 2012/2814 Sch.4 para.3
   s.3, amended: SI 2012/2814 Sch.4 para.3
   Sch.1 para.14B, added: SI 2012/2814 Sch.4 para.3

33. Armed Forces Act 1971
   Sch.2 para.1, repealed (in part): 2012 c.10 Sch.8
para.8

38. Misuse of Drugs Act 1971
   applied: SI 2012/1909 Sch.4 para.5, Sch.4 para.6,
Sch.4 para.8, Sch.6 para.2
   s.2, applied: SI 2012/1390

1971– cont.

38. Misuse of Drugs Act 1971– *cont.*
   s.2, enabling: SI 2012/1390
   s.2A, applied: SI 2012/980 Art.2
   s.2A, enabling: SI 2012/980
   s.2B, applied: SI 2012/980
   s.4, see *Shetland Islands Council v Hassan* 2012
Hous. L.R. 107 (Sh Ct (Grampian) (Lerwick)),
Sheriff P Mann; see *Sobczak (Poitr) v HM
Advocate* 2012 S.C.L. 178 (HCJ), Lord
Carloway; see *South Lanarkshire Council v
Gillespie* 2012 Hous. L.R. 45 (Sh Ct (South
Strathclyde) (Hamilton)), Sheriff Principal B
A Lockhart
   s.5, see *HM Advocate v Cowie (Yvonne Logan)* 2012
J.C. 203 (HCJ), Lord Clarke
   s.7, applied: SI 2012/384, SI 2012/1310
   s.7, enabling: SI 2012/384, SI 2012/385, SI 2012/973,
SI 2012/1310, SI 2012/1311
   s.7A, enabling: SI 2012/980
   s.10, amended: 2012 c.11 s.19
   s.10, enabling: SI 2012/385, SI 2012/973, SI 2012/
1311, SI 2012/2394
   s.13, amended: 2012 c.11 s.19
   s.14, amended: 2012 c.11 s.19
   s.16, see *South Lanarkshire Council v Gillespie* 2012
Hous. L.R. 45 (Sh Ct (South Strathclyde)
(Hamilton)), Sheriff Principal B A Lockhart
   s.16, amended: 2012 c.11 s.19
   s.22, enabling: SI 2012/385, SI 2012/973, SI 2012/
1311
   s.23, see *HM Advocate v L* [2012] HCJAC 4, 2012
S.L.T. 818 (HCJ), The Lord Justice General
(Hamilton); see *James v DPP* [2012] EWHC
1317 (Admin), (2012) 176 J.P. 346 (QBD
(Admin)), Mitting, J.; see *Young v McLintock*
[2012] HCJAC 104, 2012 S.C.L. 965 (HCJ),
Lord Carloway
   s.30, substituted: 2012 c.11 s.19
   s.31, applied: SI 2012/385, SI 2012/973, SI 2012/2394
   s.31, enabling: SI 2012/385, SI 2012/973, SI 2012/
980, SI 2012/1311, SI 2012/2394
   s.37, see *Sobczak (Poitr) v HM Advocate* 2012 S.C.L.
178 (HCJ), Lord Carloway
   Sch.2 Part II para.1, amended: SI 2012/1390 Art.2
   Sch.2 Part II para.2A, amended: SI 2012/1390
Art.2
   Sch.2 Part III para.1, amended: SI 2012/1390 Art.3
   Sch.3 Part I para.4, amended: 2012 c.11 s.19

48. Criminal Damage Act 1971
   s.2, see *R. v A* [2012] EWCA Crim 1529, [2012] 1
W.L.R. 3378 (CA (Crim Div)), Sir John
Thomas (President)

56. Pensions (Increase) Act 1971
   applied: SI 2012/687 Sch.1 para.3, Sch.1 para.19
   s.1, applied: SI 2012/782 Art.3, Art.4
   s.8, applied: SI 2012/687 Sch.1 para.3, Sch.1 para.19
   s.8, referred to: SI 2012/782 Art.2
   Sch.2 Part I para.34, amended: 2012 c.14 Sch.39
para.54
   Sch.2 Part II, varied: 2012 c.11 s.12
   Sch.2 Part II para.44, amended: 2012 asp 8 Sch.7
para.48

58. Sheriff Courts (Scotland) Act 1971
   s.32, enabling: SSI 2012/136, SSI 2012/144, SSI
2012/188, SSI 2012/221, SSI 2012/271, SSI 2012/
273
   s.34, applied: SSI 2012/136, SSI 2012/144, SSI 2012/
188, SSI 2012/221, SSI 2012/271, SSI 2012/273

1971– cont.

58. Sheriff Courts (Scotland) Act 1971– *cont.*

s.35, see *Homebank Financial Services Ltd v Hain* 2012 S.L.T. (Sh Ct) 196 (Sh Ct (Tayside) (Dundee)), Sheriff G A Way

s.37, see *Midlothian Council, Petitioners* 2012 Fam. L.R. 25 (Sh Ct (Lothian) (Edinburgh)), Sheriff W Holligan

69. Medicines Act 1971

s.1, enabling: SI 2012/504, SI 2012/2546

77. Immigration Act 1971

see *Khaliq (Entry Clearance: Para 321: Pakistan), Re* [2012] Imm. A.R. 1 (UT (IAC)), CMG Ockelton (Vice President); see *R. (on the application of Ahmed) v Secretary of State for the Home Department* [2011] EWHC 2855 (Admin), [2012] Imm. A.R. 185 (QBD (Admin)), Singh, J.; see *R. (on the application of HA (Nigeria)) v Secretary of State for the Home Department* [2012] EWHC 979 (Admin), [2012] Med. L.R. 353 (QBD (Admin)), Singh, J.

s.1, see *R. (on the application of Ahmed) v Secretary of State for the Home Department* [2011] EWHC 2855 (Admin), [2012] Imm. A.R. 185 (QBD (Admin)), Singh, J.

s.3, see *R. (on the application of Abbassi) v Secretary of State for the Home Department* [2012] UKSC 32, [2012] 1 W.L.R. 2192 (SC), Lord Hope, J.S.C. (Deputy President); see *R. (on the application of Ahmed) v Secretary of State for the Home Department* [2011] EWHC 2855 (Admin), [2012] Imm. A.R. 185 (QBD (Admin)), Singh, J.; see *R. (on the application of Alvi) v Secretary of State for the Home Department* [2012] UKSC 33, [2012] 1 W.L.R. 2208 (SC), Lord Hope, J.S.C. (Deputy President); see *R. (on the application of New London College Ltd) v Secretary of State for the Home Department* [2012] EWCA Civ 51, [2012] Imm. A.R. 563 (CA (Civ Div)), Mummery, L.J.

s.3, applied: SI 2012/2886 Sch.1, SI 2012/3098 Reg.31, SI 2012/3144 Reg.26, SI 2012/3145 Sch.1, SSI 2012/303 Reg.16, SSI 2012/319 Reg.16

s.3C, see *Kishver (Limited Leave: Meaning: Pakistan), Re* [2012] Imm. A.R. 128 (UT (IAC)), CMG Ockelton; see *LB (Jamaica) v Secretary of State for the Home Department* [2011] EWCA Civ 1420, [2012] Imm. A.R. 637 (CA (Civ Div)), Maurice Kay, L.J.; see *Qureshi (Tier 4: Effect of Variation: Appendix C: Pakistan), Re* [2012] Imm. A.R. 171 (UT (IAC)), Judge Kekic

s.3D, see *R. (on the application of MK (Tunisia)) v Secretary of State for the Home Department* [2011] EWCA Civ 333, [2012] 1 W.L.R. 700 (CA (Civ Div)), Pill, L.J.

s.5, see *George v Secretary of State for the Home Department* [2012] EWCA Civ 1362, Times, December 17, 2012 (CA (Civ Div)), Maurice Kay, L.J.

s.7, amended: 2012 c.10 Sch.13 para.7

s.8B, enabling: SI 2012/1663, SI 2012/2058, SI 2012/3010

s.11, see *R. (on the application of ST (Eritrea)) v Secretary of State for the Home Department* [2012] UKSC 12, [2012] 2 A.C. 135 (SC), Lord Hope, J.S.C.

1971– cont.

77. Immigration Act 1971– *cont.*

s.24, see *R. (on the application of Arogundade) v Secretary of State for Business, Innovation and Skills* [2012] EWHC 2502 (Admin), [2012] E.L.R. 520 (QBD (Admin)), Robin Purchas Q.C.

s.25, see *R. v Kapoor (Saran Singh)* [2012] EWCA Crim 435, [2012] 1 W.L.R. 3569 (CA (Crim Div)), Hooper, L.J.

s.33, applied: SI 2012/813 Sch.2 para.1

s.36, enabling: SI 2012/2593

Sch.2, applied: 2012 c.10 Sch.1 para.8, Sch.1 para.11

Sch.2 Part I para.21, applied: 2012 c.10 Sch.1 para.26

Sch.2 para.2A, see *Fiaz (Cancellation of Leave to Remain: Fairness), Re* [2012] UKUT 57 (IAC), [2012] Imm. A.R. 497 (UT (IAC)), Blake, J.

Sch.3, see *R. (on the application of Lumba) v Secretary of State for the Home Department* [2012] 1 A.C. 245 (SC), Lord Phillips, J.S.C.

Sch.3, applied: 2012 c.10 Sch.1 para.8, Sch.1 para.25

Sch.3 para.2, applied: 2012 c.10 Sch.1 para.27

Sch.3 para.4, applied: 2012 c.10 Sch.1 para.27

78. Town and Country Planning Act 1971

s.42, see *Eaden Homes Ltd v Dwr Cymru Cyfyngedig (Welsh Water)* [2012] UKUT 153 (LC), [2012] R.V.R. 279 (UT (Lands)), George Bartlett Q.C. (President, LTr)

80. Banking and Financial Dealings Act 1971

applied: SI 2012/323 Reg.18, SI 2012/336 Reg.9, SI 2012/444 Reg.23, SI 2012/827 Reg.4, SI 2012/1017 Reg.4, Reg.37, Reg.45, SI 2012/2031 Reg.4, SI 2012/3012 Reg.53

1972

11. Superannuation Act 1972

see *R. (on the application of Public and Commercial Services Union) v Minister for the Civil Service* [2011] EWHC 2041 (Admin), [2012] 1 All E.R. 985 (QBD (Admin)), McCombe, J.

applied: 2012 c.7 Sch.8 para.8, 2012 c.9 Sch.8 para.5

varied: SI 2012/147 Art.7

s.1, amended: 2012 c.21 Sch.18 para.35

s.1, applied: 2012 c.7 Sch.8 para.8, 2012 c.9 Sch.8 para.5

s.7, applied: SI 2012/534 Art.2, SI 2012/1989, SI 2012/3094 Reg.25, SSI 2012/236, SSI 2012/347

s.7, enabling: SI 2012/1989, SSI 2012/236, SSI 2012/347

s.9, applied: SI 2012/673, SI 2012/2270, SSI 2012/70

s.9, referred to: SI 2012/673, SI 2012/2270

s.9, enabling: SI 2012/673, SI 2012/2270, SSI 2012/70

s.10, applied: SSI 2012/69, SSI 2012/163

s.10, enabling: SI 2012/610, SSI 2012/69, SSI 2012/163

s.12, enabling: SI 2012/610, SI 2012/673, SI 2012/1989, SI 2012/2270, SSI 2012/70, SSI 2012/163, SSI 2012/236, SSI 2012/347

s.24, applied: SI 2012/3094 Reg.25

s.24, enabling: SI 2012/1989, SSI 2012/236, SSI 2012/347

Sch.1, amended: 2012 asp 8 s.61, 2012 c.5 Sch.14 Part 8, 2012 c.7 Sch.7 para.2, Sch.8 para.8, Sch.13 para.4, 2012 c.9 Sch.8 para.5, SI 2012/246 Sch.1 para.18, SI 2012/2654 Sch.1, SI 2012/3006 Art.15

Sch.3, enabling: SI 2012/610, SI 2012/673, SI 2012/2270, SSI 2012/69, SSI 2012/70, SSI 2012/163, SSI 2012/236, SSI 2012/347

Sch.7 para.2, referred to: SI 2012/687 Sch.1 para.11

1972– cont.

18. **Maintenance Orders (Reciprocal Enforcement) Act 1972**
s.3, amended: SI 2012/ 2814 Sch.5 para.2
s.17, amended: SI 2012/ 2814 Sch.5 para.2
s.27A, amended: SI 2012/ 2814 Sch.5 para.2
s.28C, amended: SI 2012/ 2814 Sch.5 para.2
s.35, amended: SI 2012/ 2814 Sch.5 para.2
s.35A, amended: SI 2012/ 2814 Sch.5 para.2
30. **Civil Evidence Act 1972**
s.3, see *2 Travel Group Plc (In Liquidation) v Cardiff City Transport Services Ltd* [2012] Comp. A.R. 121 (CAT), Lord Carlile of Berriew Q.C.
59. **Administration of Justice (Scotland) Act 1972**
s.3, see *Apollo Engineering Ltd v James Scott Ltd* [2012] CSIH 4, 2012 S.C. 282 (IH (Ex Div)), Lady Paton
61. **Land Charges Act 1972**
s.9, enabling: SI 2012/ 2910
s.10, enabling: SI 2012/ 2910
s.16, enabling: SI 2012/ 2884, SI 2012/ 2910
s.17, enabling: SI 2012/ 2884, SI 2012/ 2910
62. **Agriculture (Miscellaneous Provisions) Act 1972**
s.20, enabling: SSI 2012/ 266, SSI 2012/ 326
65. **National Debt Act 1972**
s.3, enabling: SI 2012/ 1877
s.11, enabling: SI 2012/ 1880, SI 2012/ 1882
68. **European Communities Act 1972**
see *B v Home Office* [2012] EWHC 226 (QB), [2012] 4 All E.R. 276 (QBD), Richard Salter QC; see *R. (on the application of GI (Sudan)) v Secretary of State for the Home Department* [2012] EWCA Civ 867, [2012] 4 All E.R. 987 (CA (Civ Div)), Laws, L.J.
applied: SI 2012/ 977, SI 2012/ 1889
s.1, applied: SSI 2012/ 88 Reg.4, SSI 2012/ 89 Reg.4
s.1, referred to: SI 2012/ 357 Art.3, SI 2012/ 358 Art.3, SI 2012/ 797 Art.3
s.1, enabling: SI 2012/ 357, SI 2012/ 358, SI 2012/ 797
s.2, see *Blueshell Mussels Ltd v Foard* 2012 J.C. 62 (HCJ), Lord Eassie; see *ITV Broadcasting Ltd v TV Catchup Ltd* [2011] EWHC 1874 (Pat), [2012] Eu. L.R. 187 (Ch D (Patents Ct)), Floyd, J.
s.2, applied: SI 2012/ 245, SI 2012/ 637, SI 2012/ 1509, SI 2012/ 1741, SI 2012/ 1765, SI 2012/ 2262, SI 2012/ 2267, SI 2012/ 2705, SI 2012/ 2909, SI 2012/ 3032, SI 2012/ 3035, SI 2012/ 3119
s.2, referred to: SI 2012/ 1511, SI 2012/ 1515, SI 2012/ 1516, SI 2012/ 1517, SI 2012/ 2619, SI 2012/ 2707, SSI 2012/ 119, SSI 2012/ 182, SSI 2012/ 184, SSI 2012/ 318
s.2, enabling: SI 2012/ 47, SI 2012/ 56, SI 2012/ 64, SI 2012/ 66, SI 2012/ 114, SI 2012/ 129, SI 2012/ 178, SI 2012/ 190, SI 2012/ 334, SI 2012/ 461, SI 2012/ 501, SI 2012/ 504, SI 2012/ 532, SI 2012/ 632, SI 2012/ 639, SI 2012/ 697, SI 2012/ 745, SI 2012/ 787, SI 2012/ 799, SI 2012/ 809, SI 2012/ 810, SI 2012/ 811, SI 2012/ 916, SI 2012/ 917, SI 2012/ 925, SI 2012/ 947, SI 2012/ 948, SI 2012/ 952, SI 2012/ 975, SI 2012/ 977, SI 2012/ 991, SI 2012/ 1102, SI 2012/ 1139, SI 2012/ 1238, SI 2012/ 1243, SI 2012/ 1301, SI 2012/ 1302, SI 2012/ 1426, SI 2012/ 1489, SI 2012/ 1493, SI 2012/ 1501, SI 2012/ 1502, SI 2012/ 1507, SI 2012/ 1508, SI 2012/ 1509, SI 2012/ 1510, SI 2012/ 1511, SI 2012/ 1515, SI 2012/ 1516, SI 2012/ 1517, SI 2012/ 1538, SI 2012/ 1547, SI 2012/ 1652, SI 2012/ 1657, SI 2012/ 1672, SI 2012/ 1715, SI 2012/ 1741, SI 2012/ 1742, SI 2012/ 1751, SI 2012/ 1759, SI 2012/ 1765, SI 2012/ 1770, SI 2012/ 1791, SI 2012/ 1809, SI 2012/ 1815, SI 2012/ 1844,

1972– cont.

68. **European Communities Act 1972**– *cont.*
s.2, enabling:– *cont.*
SI 2012/ 1848, SI 2012/ 1849, SI 2012/ 1889, SI 2012/ 1906, SI 2012/ 1910, SI 2012/ 1916, SI 2012/ 1927, SI 2012/ 1928, SI 2012/ 1977, SI 2012/ 2015, SI 2012/ 2079, SI 2012/ 2125, SI 2012/ 2262, SI 2012/ 2267, SI 2012/ 2298, SI 2012/ 2301, SI 2012/ 2403, SI 2012/ 2524, SI 2012/ 2546, SI 2012/ 2554, SI 2012/ 2560, SI 2012/ 2567, SI 2012/ 2607, SI 2012/ 2608, SI 2012/ 2609, SI 2012/ 2610, SI 2012/ 2611, SI 2012/ 2629, SI 2012/ 2661, SI 2012/ 2665, SI 2012/ 2711, SI 2012/ 2723, SI 2012/ 2752, SI 2012/ 2786, SI 2012/ 2788, SI 2012/ 2814, SI 2012/ 2862, SI 2012/ 2897, SI 2012/ 2909, SI 2012/ 2977, SI 2012/ 2992, SI 2012/ 3005, SI 2012/ 3027, SI 2012/ 3030, SI 2012/ 3032, SI 2012/ 3038, SI 2012/ 3039, SI 2012/ 3062, SI 2012/ 3082, SI 2012/ 3110, SI 2012/ 3118, SI 2012/ 3122, SI 2012/ 3152, SI 2012/ 3170, SSI 2012/ 3, SSI 2012/ 24, SSI 2012/ 37, SSI 2012/ 75, SSI 2012/ 88, SSI 2012/ 89, SSI 2012/ 108, SSI 2012/ 143, SSI 2012/ 148, SSI 2012/ 166, SSI 2012/ 177, SSI 2012/ 178, SSI 2012/ 179, SSI 2012/ 182, SSI 2012/ 190, SSI 2012/ 198, SSI 2012/ 199, SSI 2012/ 208, SSI 2012/ 228, SSI 2012/ 243, SSI 2012/ 266, SSI 2012/ 284, SSI 2012/ 301, SSI 2012/ 307, SSI 2012/ 315, SSI 2012/ 321, SSI 2012/ 323, SSI 2012/ 349, SSI 2012/ 355
Sch.2, see *Blueshell Mussels Ltd v Foard* 2012 J.C. 62 (HCJ), Lord Eassie
Sch.2 para.1, see *Blueshell Mussels Ltd v Foard* 2012 J.C. 62 (HCJ), Lord Eassie
Sch.2 para.1A, applied: SI 2012/ 1198, SI 2012/ 1501, SI 2012/ 1657, SI 2012/ 2619, SI 2012/ 2705, SI 2012/ 3039
Sch.2 para.1A, referred to: SI 2012/ 2788
Sch.2 para.1A, enabling: SI 2012/ 129, SI 2012/ 178, SI 2012/ 190, SI 2012/ 245, SI 2012/ 639, SI 2012/ 810, SI 2012/ 925, SI 2012/ 947, SI 2012/ 1102, SI 2012/ 1155, SI 2012/ 1243, SI 2012/ 1301, SI 2012/ 1426, SI 2012/ 1489, SI 2012/ 1507, SI 2012/ 1508, SI 2012/ 1509, SI 2012/ 1511, SI 2012/ 1515, SI 2012/ 1516, SI 2012/ 1517, SI 2012/ 1742, SI 2012/ 1751, SI 2012/ 1765, SI 2012/ 1844, SI 2012/ 2524, SI 2012/ 2665, SI 2012/ 2707, SI 2012/ 2909, SI 2012/ 3030, SI 2012/ 3032, SI 2012/ 3035, SI 2012/ 3062, SI 2012/ 3082, SSI 2012/ 37, SSI 2012/ 75, SSI 2012/ 88, SSI 2012/ 89, SSI 2012/ 119, SSI 2012/ 143, SSI 2012/ 166, SSI 2012/ 177, SSI 2012/ 182, SSI 2012/ 184, SSI 2012/ 198, SSI 2012/ 199, SSI 2012/ 266, SSI 2012/ 318, SSI 2012/ 321, SSI 2012/ 349
Sch.2 para.2, applied: SI 2012/ 461, SI 2012/ 952, SI 2012/ 1741, SI 2012/ 1906, SI 2012/ 2079, SI 2012/ 3039, SSI 2012/ 148
Sch.2 para.2, enabling: SI 2012/ 952
Sch.2 para.2A, applied: SI 2012/ 1906
70. **Local Government Act 1972**
applied: SI 2012/ 323 Reg.15, SI 2012/ 444 Reg.20
referred to: SI 2012/ 1917 Art.16
Part VA, applied: SI 2012/ 1020 Reg.5, SI 2012/ 2734 Sch.1 para.1, Sch.1 para.10, Sch.1 para.25
s.3, applied: SI 2012/ 1020 Reg.3
s.5, applied: SI 2012/ 1020 Reg.3
s.54, applied: SI 2012/ 805
s.57, applied: SI 2012/ 2676
s.58, applied: SI 2012/ 805, SI 2012/ 2676
s.58, enabling: SI 2012/ 805, SI 2012/ 2676
s.79, amended: SI 2012/ 1809 Sch.1 Part 1
s.80, amended: SI 2012/ 2404 Sch.2 para.5
s.83, applied: SI 2012/ 336 Reg.10, SI 2012/ 1465 Art.2
s.83, enabling: SI 2012/ 1465

1972– cont.

70. Local Government Act 1972– *cont.*

s.89, applied: SI 2012/ 323 Reg.10, SI 2012/444 Reg.17

s.99, applied: SI 2012/ 2734 Sch.1 para.9, Sch.1 para.24

s.99, varied: SI 2012/ 2734 Reg.6

s.100A, varied: SI 2012/ 2734 Reg.6

s.100B, varied: SI 2012/ 2734 Reg.6

s.100C, varied: SI 2012/ 2734 Reg.6

s.100D, varied: SI 2012/ 2734 Reg.6

s.100E, varied: SI 2012/ 2734 Reg.6

s.100EA, varied: SI 2012/ 2734 Reg.6

s.100F, varied: SI 2012/ 2734 Reg.6

s.100G, varied: SI 2012/ 2734 Reg.6

s.100H, varied: SI 2012/ 2734 Reg.6

s.100I, varied: SI 2012/ 2734 Reg.6

s.100J, varied: SI 2012/ 2734 Reg.6

s.100K, varied: SI 2012/ 2734 Reg.6

s.101, applied: SI 2012/1019 Reg.3, Reg.4, Reg.9, Reg.10, Reg.11, Reg.12, SI 2012/1020 Reg.3, SI 2012/1023 Art.3, SI 2012/2734 Sch.1 para.2, Sch.1 para.11, Sch.1 para.26

s.101, disapplied: SI 2012/1020 Reg.3, SI 2012/3144 Reg.12

s.101, varied: SI 2012/ 2734 Reg.6, Reg.7

s.102, applied: 2012 c.7 s.194, SI 2012/1019 Reg.11, Reg.12, SI 2012/1020 Reg.5, SI 2012/1023 Art.3, SI 2012/2734 Reg.6

s.103, applied: SI 2012/ 2734 Sch.1 para.12, Sch.1 para.27

s.103, varied: SI 2012/ 2734 Reg.6

s.104, applied: SI 2012/ 2734 Sch.1 para.13, Sch.1 para.28

s.104, varied: SI 2012/ 2734 Reg.6

s.111, see *Egan v Basildon BC* [2011] EWHC 2416 (QB), [2012] P.T.S.R. 1117 (QBD), Edwards-Stuart J.; see *R. (on the application of National Secular Society) v Bideford Town Council* [2012] EWHC 175 (Admin), [2012] 2 All E.R. 1175 (QBD (Admin)), Ouseley, J.

s.113, amended: 2012 c.7 Sch.5 para.17, Sch.7 para.3, Sch.14 para.45, Sch.17 para.3

s.120, see *R. (on the application of Barnsley MBC) v Secretary of State for Communities and Local Government* [2012] EWHC 1366 (Admin), [2012] B.L.G.R. 933 (QBD (Admin)), Foskett, J.

s.121, see *R. (on the application of Barnsley MBC) v Secretary of State for Communities and Local Government* [2012] EWHC 1366 (Admin), [2012] B.L.G.R. 933 (QBD (Admin)), Foskett, J.

s.123, see *R. (on the application of Midlands Co-operative Society Ltd) v Birmingham City Council* [2012] EWHC 620 (Admin), [2012] Eu. L.R. 640 (QBD (Admin)), Hickinbottom, J.

s.151, applied: SI 2012/ 335 Sch.1 para.20, SI 2012/ 2991 Sch.1 para.20

s.173, applied: SI 2012/9 Reg.6

s.173, referred to: SI 2012/ 1033 Sch.1 para.6

s.174, applied: SI 2012/9 Reg.6

s.174, referred to: SI 2012/ 1033 Sch.1 para.6

s.222, see *Lamont-Perkins v RSPCA* [2012] EWHC 1002 (Admin), (2012) 176 J.P. 369 (DC), Sir John Thomas (President)

s.223, applied: SI 2012/ 1726 r.2.4

s.224, applied: SI 2012/ 2734 Sch.1 para.14, Sch.1 para.29

s.224, varied: SI 2012/ 2734 Reg.6

s.225, applied: SI 2012/ 2734 Sch.1 para.14, Sch.1 para.29

s.225, varied: SI 2012/ 2734 Reg.6

1972– cont.

70. Local Government Act 1972– *cont.*

s.228, applied: SI 2012/ 2734 Sch.1 para.14, Sch.1 para.29

s.228, varied: SI 2012/ 2734 Reg.6

s.229, applied: SI 2012/ 2734 Sch.1 para.14, Sch.1 para.29

s.229, varied: SI 2012/ 2734 Reg.6

s.230, applied: SI 2012/ 2734 Sch.1 para.14, Sch.1 para.29

s.230, varied: SI 2012/ 2734 Reg.6

s.231, applied: SI 2012/ 2734 Sch.1 para.14, Sch.1 para.29

s.231, varied: SI 2012/ 2734 Reg.6

s.232, applied: SI 2012/ 336 Reg.10, SI 2012/ 2734 Sch.1 para.14, Sch.1 para.29

s.232, varied: SI 2012/ 2734 Reg.6

s.233, applied: SI 2012/ 2734 Sch.1 para.14, Sch.1 para.29

s.233, varied: SI 2012/ 2734 Reg.6

s.234, applied: SI 2012/ 2734 Sch.1 para.14, Sch.1 para.29

s.234, varied: SI 2012/ 2734 Reg.6

s.236, see *Local Government Byelaws (Wales) Bill 2012, Re* [2012] UKSC 53, [2012] 3 W.L.R. 1294 (SC), Lord Neuberger (President)

s.236, applied: SI 2012/472 Art.6, SI 2012/1266 Art.4, SI 2012/1777 Art.28, SI 2012/1867 Art.42

s.236, varied: SI 2012/1777 Art.28, SI 2012/1867 Art.42

s.238, applied: SI 2012/1266 Art.4

s.238, varied: SI 2012/1777 Art.28

s.247, enabling: SI 2012/1760

Sch.12A, applied: SI 2012/ 2734 Sch.1 para.1, Sch.1 para.10, Sch.1 para.25

Sch.12A, referred to: SI 2012/2089 Reg.4, Reg.7

Sch.12 Part VI para.40, applied: SI 2012/ 2734 Sch.1 para.9, Sch.1 para.24

Sch.12 Part VI para.40, varied: SI 2012/ 2734 Reg.6

Sch.12 Part VI para.41, applied: SI 2012/ 2734 Sch.1 para.9, Sch.1 para.24

Sch.12 Part VI para.41, varied: SI 2012/ 2734 Reg.6

Sch.12 Part VI para.42, applied: SI 2012/ 2734 Sch.1 para.9, Sch.1 para.24

Sch.12 Part VI para.42, varied: SI 2012/ 2734 Reg.6

Sch.12 Part VI para.43, applied: SI 2012/ 2734 Sch.1 para.9, Sch.1 para.24

Sch.12 Part VI para.43, varied: SI 2012/ 2734 Reg.6

Sch.12 Part VI para.44, applied: SI 2012/ 2734 Sch.1 para.9, Sch.1 para.24

Sch.12 Part VI para.44, varied: SI 2012/ 2734 Reg.6

Sch.12A Part I, applied: SI 2012/2089 Reg.16

Sch.12A Part I para.1, varied: SI 2012/ 2734 Reg.6

Sch.12A Part I para.2, varied: SI 2012/ 2734 Reg.6

Sch.12A Part I para.2A, varied: SI 2012/ 2734 Reg.6

Sch.12A Part I para.3, applied: SI 2012/2089 Reg.16

Sch.12A Part I para.3, varied: SI 2012/ 2734 Reg.6

Sch.12A Part I para.4, varied: SI 2012/ 2734 Reg.6

Sch.12A Part I para.5, varied: SI 2012/ 2734 Reg.6

Sch.12A Part I para.6, applied: SI 2012/2089 Reg.16

Sch.12A Part I para.6, varied: SI 2012/ 2734 Reg.6

Sch.12A Part I para.6A, varied: SI 2012/ 2734 Reg.6

Sch.12A Part I para.6B, varied: SI 2012/ 2734 Reg.6

Sch.12A Part I para.7, varied: SI 2012/ 2734 Reg.6

Sch.12A Part I para.7A, varied: SI 2012/ 2734 Reg.6

Sch.12A Part I para.7B, varied: SI 2012/ 2734 Reg.6

Sch.12A Part I para.7C, varied: SI 2012/ 2734 Reg.6

Sch.12A Part I para.8, varied: SI 2012/ 2734 Reg.6

Sch.12A Part I para.9, varied: SI 2012/ 2734 Reg.6

Sch.12A Part I para.10, varied: SI 2012/ 2734 Reg.6

1972–cont.

70. Local Government Act 1972–cont.
Sch.12A Part I para.11, varied: SI 2012/2734 Reg.6
Sch.12A Part I para.12, varied: SI 2012/2734 Reg.6
Sch.12A Part I para.13, varied: SI 2012/2734 Reg.6
Sch.12A Part I para.14, varied: SI 2012/2734 Reg.6
Sch.12A Part I para.15, varied: SI 2012/2734 Reg.6
Sch.12A Part II para.1, varied: SI 2012/2734 Reg.6
Sch.12A Part II para.2, varied: SI 2012/2734 Reg.6
Sch.12A Part II para.3, varied: SI 2012/2734 Reg.6
Sch.12A Part II para.4, varied: SI 2012/2734 Reg.6
Sch.12A Part II para.5, varied: SI 2012/2734 Reg.6
Sch.12A Part II para.6, varied: SI 2012/2734 Reg.6
Sch.12A Part II para.6B, varied: SI 2012/2734 Reg.6
Sch.12A Part II para.7, varied: SI 2012/2734 Reg.6
Sch.12A Part II para.8, varied: SI 2012/2734 Reg.6
Sch.12A Part II para.9, varied: SI 2012/2734 Reg.6
Sch.12A Part II para.10, varied: SI 2012/2734 Reg.6
Sch.12A Part III para.1, varied: SI 2012/2734 Reg.6
Sch.12A Part III para.2, varied: SI 2012/2734 Reg.6
Sch.12A Part III para.11, varied: SI 2012/2734 Reg.6
Sch.12A Part IV para.12, varied: SI 2012/2734 Reg.6
Sch.12A Part IV para.13, varied: SI 2012/2734 Reg.6
Sch.12A Part IV para.14, varied: SI 2012/2734 Reg.6
Sch.12A Part IV para.15, varied: SI 2012/2734 Reg.6
Sch.12A Part IV para.16, varied: SI 2012/2734 Reg.6
Sch.12A Part IV para.17, varied: SI 2012/2734 Reg.6
Sch.12A Part IV para.18, varied: SI 2012/2734 Reg.6
Sch.12A Part IV para.18A, varied: SI 2012/2734 Reg.6
Sch.12A Part IV para.18B, varied: SI 2012/2734 Reg.6
Sch.12A Part IV para.18C, varied: SI 2012/2734 Reg.6
Sch.12A Part IV para.19, varied: SI 2012/2734 Reg.6
Sch.12A Part IV para.20, varied: SI 2012/2734 Reg.6
Sch.12A Part IV para.21, varied: SI 2012/2734 Reg.6
Sch.12A Part IV para.22, varied: SI 2012/2734 Reg.6
Sch.12A Part IV para.23, varied: SI 2012/2734 Reg.6
Sch.12A Part IV para.24, varied: SI 2012/2734 Reg.6
Sch.12A Part IV para.25, varied: SI 2012/2734 Reg.6
Sch.12A Part IV para.26, varied: SI 2012/2734 Reg.6
Sch.12A Part IV para.27, varied: SI 2012/2734 Reg.6
Sch.12A Part V para.19, varied: SI 2012/2734 Reg.6
Sch.12A Part V para.20, varied: SI 2012/2734 Reg.6
Sch.12A Part V para.21, varied: SI 2012/2734 Reg.6
Sch.12A Part V para.28, varied: SI 2012/2734 Reg.6
Sch.12A Part V para.29, varied: SI 2012/2734 Reg.6
Sch.12A Part V para.30, varied: SI 2012/2734 Reg.6
Sch.12A Part V para.31, varied: SI 2012/2734 Reg.6
Sch.12A Part V para.32, varied: SI 2012/2734 Reg.6
Sch.12A Part V para.33, varied: SI 2012/2734 Reg.6
Sch.12A Part V para.34, varied: SI 2012/2734 Reg.6
Sch.12A Part VI para.22, varied: SI 2012/2734 Reg.6
Sch.12A Part VI para.35, varied: SI 2012/2734 Reg.6
Sch.16 Part II para.55, amended: SI 2012/961 Sch.2 para.2

1972–cont.

71. Criminal Justice Act 1972
s.36, see *R. v B* [2012] EWCA Crim 414, [2012] 3 All E.R. 205 (CA (Crim Div)), Lord Judge, L.C.J.
s.36, amended: 2012 c.10 Sch.7 para.9
s.36, applied: SI 2012/1726 r.70.1, r.74.1, r.74.2, r.76.1, r.76.4
s.36, repealed (in part): 2012 c.10 Sch.7 para.9

1265. Health and Personal Social Services (Northern Ireland) Order 1972
Art.30, applied: SSI 2012/303 Reg.28

1973

18. Matrimonial Causes Act 1973
see *A v L (Departure from Equality: Needs)* [2011] EWHC 3150 (Fam), [2012] 1 F.L.R. 985 (Fam Div), Moor, J.; see *Dukali v Lamrani* [2012] EWHC 1748 (Fam), [2012] 2 F.L.R. 1099 (Fam Div), Holman, J.; see *Independent Trustee Services Ltd v GP Noble Trustees Ltd* [2012] EWCA Civ 195, [2012] 3 W.L.R. 597 (CA (Civ Div)), Lloyd, L.J.
applied: 2012 c.10 Sch.1 para.33, SI 2012/1969 Art.3, Art.4, SI 2012/3144 Reg.8, SI 2012/3145 Sch.1
s.12, see *A Local Authority v BB* [2011] EWHC 2853 (Fam), [2012] 1 F.L.R. 1080 (Fam Div), Ryder, J.
s.22, substituted: 2012 c.10 s.49
s.22ZA, added: 2012 c.10 s.49
s.22ZB, added: 2012 c.10 s.50
s.24, see *BJ v MJ (Financial Order: Overseas Trust)* [2011] EWHC 2708 (Fam), [2012] 1 F.L.R. 667 (Fam Div), Mostyn, J.; see *Petrodel Resources Ltd v Prest* [2012] EWCA Civ 1395, [2012] 3 F.C.R. 588 (CA (Civ Div)), Thorpe, L.J.
s.24A, amended: 2012 c.10 s.51
s.24B, applied: SI 2012/687 Sch.4 para.2
s.24C, applied: SI 2012/687 Sch.4 para.2
s.24D, applied: SI 2012/687 Sch.4 para.2
s.25, see *AR v AR (Treatment of Inherited Wealth)* [2011] EWHC 2717 (Fam), [2012] 2 F.L.R. 1 (Fam Div), Moylan, J.; see *B v B (Assessment of Assets: Pre-Marital Property)* [2012] EWHC 314 (Fam), [2012] 2 F.L.R. 22 (Fam Div), David Salter; see *BJ v MJ (Financial Order: Overseas Trust)* [2011] EWHC 2708 (Fam), [2012] 1 F.L.R. 667 (Fam Div), Mostyn, J.; see *L v L (Financial Remedies: Deferred Clean Break)* [2011] EWHC 2207 (Fam), [2012] 1 F.L.R. 1283 (Fam Div), King, J.; see *Lawrence v Gallagher* [2012] EWCA Civ 394, [2012] 2 F.L.R. 643 (CA (Civ Div)), Thorpe, L.J.; see *RK v RK (Financial Resources: Trust Assets)* [2011] EWHC 3910 (Fam), [2012] 3 F.C.R. 44 (Fam Div), Moylan, J.; see *V v V (Ancillary Relief: Pre-Nuptial Agreement)* [2011] EWHC 3230 (Fam), [2012] 1 F.L.R. 1315 (Fam Div), Charles, J.; see *Whaley v Whaley* [2011] EWCA Civ 617, [2012] 1 F.L.R. 735 (CA (Civ Div)), Mummery, L.J.; see *X v X (Financial Remedies: Preparation and Presentation)* [2012] EWHC 538 (Fam), [2012] 2 F.L.R. 590 (Fam Div), Charles, J.
s.25A, see *G v G (Financial Remedies: Short Marriage: Trust Assets)* [2012] EWHC 167 (Fam), [2012] 2 F.L.R. 48 (Fam Div), Charles, J.; see *L v L (Financial Remedies: Deferred Clean Break)* [2011] EWHC 2207 (Fam), [2012] 1 F.L.R. 1283 (Fam Div), King, J.
s.25B, applied: SI 2012/687 Sch.4 para.2
s.25C, applied: SI 2012/687 Sch.4 para.2
s.25D, applied: SI 2012/687 Sch.4 para.2

1973– cont.

18. Matrimonial Causes Act 1973– *cont.*
s.31, see *L v L (Financial Remedies: Deferred Clean Break)* [2011] EWHC 2207 (Fam), [2012] 1 F.L.R. 1283 (Fam Div), King, J.; see *NG v SG (Appeal: Non Disclosure)* [2011] EWHC 3270 (Fam), [2012] 1 F.L.R. 1211 (Fam Div), Mostyn, J.

26. Land Compensation Act 1973
see *Thomas v Bridgend CBC* [2011] EWCA Civ 862, [2012] Q.B. 512 (CA (Civ Div)), Mummery, L.J.
s.19, see *Thomas v Bridgend CBC* [2011] EWCA Civ 862, [2012] Q.B. 512 (CA (Civ Div)), Mummery, L.J.
s.20, applied: SI 2012/2284 Art.31
s.20, varied: SI 2012/2635 Art.41
s.20A, applied: SI 2012/2284 Art.31
s.20A, varied: SI 2012/2635 Art.41
s.28, varied: SI 2012/2284 Art.31, SI 2012/2635 Art.41
s.44, varied: SI 2012/1867 Sch.3 para.2, SI 2012/1924 Sch.1 para.2, SI 2012/2284 Sch.5 para.2, SI 2012/2635 Sch.9 para.2, SI 2012/2679 Sch.10 para.2
s.58, varied: SI 2012/1867 Sch.3 para.2, SI 2012/1924 Sch.1 para.2, SI 2012/2284 Sch.5 para.2, SI 2012/2635 Sch.9 para.2, SI 2012/2679 Sch.10 para.2

33. Protection of Wrecks Act 1973
applied: SI 2012/1773 Art.2, SI 2012/1807 Art.2
s.1, applied: SI 2012/1773, SI 2012/1807
s.1, enabling: SI 2012/1773, SI 2012/1807
s.3, enabling: SI 2012/1773

35. Employment Agencies Act 1973
s.9, amended: 2012 c.21 Sch.18 para.36

41. Fair Trading Act 1973
applied: SI 2012/1128 Art.4
referred to: 2012 c.19 Sch.6 para.4
s.93B, repealed: 2012 c.19 Sch.9 para.1

50. Employment and Training Act 1973
s.2, applied: 2012 c.5 s.129, SI 2012/1711 Reg.3, SI 2012/2885 Sch.1 para.8, Sch.2 para.5, SI 2012/2886 Sch.1, SI 2012/3144 Sch.1 para.3, SI 2012/3145 Sch.1, SSI 2012/303 Reg.40, Reg.41, Reg.48, Reg.67, Sch.1 para.8, Sch.1 para.10, Sch.4 para.17, Sch.5 para.39, SSI 2012/319 Reg.48
s.2, referred to: SI 2012/874 Reg.7, SI 2012/2886 Sch.1, SSI 2012/303 Sch.4 para.17
s.2A, added: 2012 c.5 s.144
s.11, amended: 2012 c.5 s.66
s.11, applied: 2012 c.5 s.66

51. Finance Act 1973
s.56, enabling: SI 2012/103, SI 2012/285, SI 2012/504, SI 2012/745, SI 2012/751, SI 2012/1271, SI 2012/1493, SI 2012/2300, SI 2012/2546, SSI 2012/176, SSI 2012/177, SSI 2012/321

52. Prescription and Limitation (Scotland) Act 1973
s.1, amended: 2012 asp 5 Sch.5 para.18
s.1, applied: 2012 asp 5 s.44, s.81
s.2, amended: 2012 asp 5 Sch.5 para.18
s.2, applied: 2012 asp 5 s.81
s.5, amended: 2012 asp 5 Sch.5 para.18
s.6, see *Docherty v Scottish Ministers* 2012 S.C. 150 (IH (1 Div)), The Lord President (Hamilton)
s.11, see *David T Morrison & Co Ltd v ICL Plastics Ltd* [2012] CSOH 44, 2012 S.L.T. 813 (OH), Lord Woolman; see *Prentice v Sandeman* 2012 S.C.L.R. 451 (OH), Lord Stewart
s.15, amended: 2012 asp 5 Sch.5 para.18
s.17, see *Irving v Advocate General for Scotland* [2012] CSOH 103, 2012 Rep. L.R. 122 (OH), Lord Uist

1973– cont.

52. Prescription and Limitation (Scotland) Act 1973– *cont.*
s.19A, see *Irving v Advocate General for Scotland* [2012] CSOH 103, 2012 Rep. L.R. 122 (OH), Lord Uist
Sch.1 para.1, see *Docherty v Scottish Ministers* 2012 S.C. 150 (IH (1 Div)), The Lord President (Hamilton)
Sch.1 para.1, amended: 2012 asp 5 Sch.5 para.18, 2012 asp 9 s.60
Sch.1 para.2, amended: 2012 asp 5 Sch.5 para.18, 2012 asp 9 s.60
Sch.3, amended: 2012 asp 5 Sch.5 para.18

60. Breeding of Dogs Act 1973
s.3, applied: SI 2012/2932 Reg.5

65. Local Government (Scotland) Act 1973
see *Portobello Park Action Group Association v City of Edinburgh Council* [2012] CSIH 69, 2012 S.L.T. 1137 (IH (Ex Div)), Lady Paton
s.29, amended: SI 2012/1809 Sch.1 Part 1
s.56, repealed (in part): 2012 asp 8 Sch.8 Part 1
s.63, repealed: 2012 asp 8 Sch.8 Part 1
s.63A, repealed: 2012 asp 8 Sch.8 Part 2
s.64, repealed (in part): 2012 asp 8 Sch.8 Part 1
s.73, see *Portobello Park Action Group Association v City of Edinburgh Council* [2012] CSIH 69, 2012 S.L.T. 1137 (IH (Ex Div)), Lady Paton; see *Portobello Park Action Group Association v City of Edinburgh Council* [2012] CSOH 38, 2012 S.L.T. 944 (OH), Lady Dorrian
s.75, see *Portobello Park Action Group Association v City of Edinburgh Council* [2012] CSIH 69, 2012 S.L.T. 1137 (IH (Ex Div)), Lady Paton; see *Portobello Park Action Group Association v City of Edinburgh Council* [2012] CSOH 38, 2012 S.L.T. 944 (OH), Lady Dorrian
s.96, referred to: SSI 2012/53 Art.13
s.147, applied: SSI 2012/88 Reg.3
s.210, applied: SSI 2012/360 Sch.8 para.4
s.210, varied: SI 2012/3038 Sch.11 para.13
s.235, applied: SSI 2012/162 Sch.1
s.236, repealed (in part): 2012 asp 8 Sch.8 Part 1

1974

7. Local Government Act 1974
applied: SI 2012/3094 Reg.25, Reg.29, Reg.33
Part III, applied: SI 2012/2734 Sch.1 para.15
s.23, varied: SI 2012/666 Art.5, SI 2012/2734 Reg.6
s.23A, varied: SI 2012/666 Art.5, SI 2012/2734 Reg.6
s.24, varied: SI 2012/666 Art.5, SI 2012/2734 Reg.6
s.24A, varied: SI 2012/666 Art.5, SI 2012/2734 Reg.6
s.25, varied: SI 2012/666 Art.5, SI 2012/2734 Reg.6
s.26, amended: 2012 c.7 Sch.5 para.18
s.26, varied: SI 2012/666 Art.5, SI 2012/2734 Reg.6
s.26A, varied: SI 2012/666 Art.5, SI 2012/2734 Reg.6
s.26B, varied: SI 2012/666 Art.5, SI 2012/2734 Reg.6
s.26C, varied: SI 2012/666 Art.5, SI 2012/2734 Reg.6
s.26D, varied: SI 2012/666 Art.5, SI 2012/2734 Reg.6
s.27, varied: SI 2012/666 Art.5, SI 2012/2734 Reg.6
s.28, varied: SI 2012/666 Art.5, SI 2012/2734 Reg.6
s.29, varied: SI 2012/666 Art.5, SI 2012/2734 Reg.6
s.30, varied: SI 2012/666 Art.5, SI 2012/2734 Reg.6

1974– cont.

7. Local Government Act 1974– *cont.*
s.31, see *R. (on the application of Adams) v Commission for Local Administration in England* [2011] EWHC 2972 (Admin), [2012] P.T.S.R. 1172 (QBD (Admin)), Bean, J.
s.31, varied: SI 2012/666 Art.5, SI 2012/2734 Reg.6
s.31A, varied: SI 2012/666 Art.5, SI 2012/2734 Reg.6
s.31B, varied: SI 2012/666 Art.5, SI 2012/2734 Reg.6
s.32, varied: SI 2012/666 Art.5, SI 2012/2734 Reg.6
s.32A, varied: SI 2012/666 Art.5, SI 2012/2734 Reg.6
s.33, varied: SI 2012/666 Art.5, SI 2012/2734 Reg.6
s.33A, varied: SI 2012/666 Art.5, SI 2012/2734 Reg.6
s.33ZA, varied: SI 2012/666 Art.5, SI 2012/2734 Reg.6
s.33ZB, varied: SI 2012/666 Art.5, SI 2012/2734 Reg.6
s.34, varied: SI 2012/666 Art.5, SI 2012/2734 Reg.6
Sch.5, applied: SI 2012/2734 Sch.1 para.15
Sch.5 para.1, varied: SI 2012/2734 Reg.6
Sch.5 para.2, varied: SI 2012/2734 Reg.6
Sch.5 para.3, varied: SI 2012/2734 Reg.6
Sch.5 para.4, varied: SI 2012/2734 Reg.6
Sch.5 para.5, varied: SI 2012/2734 Reg.6
Sch.5 para.5A, varied: SI 2012/2734 Reg.6
Sch.5 para.5B, varied: SI 2012/2734 Reg.6
Sch.5 para.6, varied: SI 2012/2734 Reg.6
Sch.5 para.7, varied: SI 2012/2734 Reg.6
Sch.5 para.8, varied: SI 2012/2734 Reg.6

23. Juries Act 1974
applied: SI 2012/1726 r.39.2
s.9, applied: SI 2012/1726 r.39.2
s.9A, applied: SI 2012/1726 r.39.2
s.19, enabling: SI 2012/1826
s.20, referred to: SI 2012/1726 r.62.5
Sch.1 Part II para.6, amended: 2012 c.10 Sch.21 para.1, Sch.22 para.11
Sch.1 Part III, varied: 2012 c.11 s.12

24. Prices Act 1974
s.4, applied: SI 2012/1816
s.4, enabling: SI 2012/1816

37. Health and Safety at Work etc Act 1974
applied: SI 2012/335 Sch.1 para.20, Sch.5 para.21, SI 2012/1128 Art.4, SI 2012/1282 Sch.1, SI 2012/1284 Sch.1, SI 2012/1286 Sch.1, SI 2012/1289 Sch.1, SI 2012/1294 Sch.1, SI 2012/1295 Sch.1, SI 2012/1652 Reg.14, Reg.15, Reg.16, Reg.17, SI 2012/1909 Sch.4 para.28, Sch.5 para.18, SI 2012/2991 Sch.1 para.20, Sch.5 para.21
see *Dundee Cold Stores Ltd v HM Advocate* [2012] HCJAC 102, 2012 S.L.T. 1173 (HCJ), Lord Clarke; see *R. v Cotswold Geotechnical Holdings Ltd* [2011] EWCA Crim 1337, [2012] 1 Cr. App. R. (S.) 26 (CA (Crim Div)), Lord Judge, L.C.J.; see *R. v Jonathan (Stephen Thomas)* [2012] EWCA Crim 380, [2012] 2 Cr. App. R. (S.) 74 (CA (Crim Div)), Goldring, L.J.
Part I, applied: 2012 c.19 Sch.6 para.5, SSI 2012/360 Reg.15
s.1, applied: SI 2012/632 Reg.31
s.2, applied: SI 2012/632 Reg.31
s.2, see *Dundee Cold Stores Ltd v HM Advocate* [2012] HCJAC 102, 2012 S.L.T. 1173 (HCJ), Lord Clarke; see *R. v Deeside Metals Ltd* [2011] EWCA Crim 3020, [2012] 2 Cr. App. R. (S.) 29 (CA (Crim Div)), Rafferty, L.J.; see *R. v Tangerine Confectionery Ltd* [2011] EWCA

1974– cont.

37. Health and Safety at Work etc Act 1974– *cont.*
s.2– *cont.*
Crim 2015, (2012) 176 J.P. 349 (CA (Crim Div)), Hughes, L.J. (Vice President); see *Scottish Sea Farms Ltd v HM Advocate* [2012] HCJAC 11, 2012 S.L.T. 299 (HCJ), Lord Mackay of Drumadoon
s.3, applied: SI 2012/632 Reg.31
s.3, see *Dundee Cold Stores Ltd v HM Advocate* [2012] HCJAC 102, 2012 S.L.T. 1173 (HCJ), Lord Clarke; see *R. v Tangerine Confectionery Ltd* [2011] EWCA Crim 2015, (2012) 176 J.P. 349 (CA (Crim Div)), Hughes, L.J. (Vice President)
s.4, applied: SI 2012/632 Reg.31
s.5, applied: SI 2012/632 Reg.31
s.6, applied: SI 2012/632 Reg.31
s.7, applied: SI 2012/632 Reg.31
s.8, applied: SI 2012/632 Reg.31
s.9, applied: SI 2012/632 Reg.31
s.10, applied: SI 2012/632 Reg.31
s.11, applied: SI 2012/1537(b), SI 2012/1652(b), SI 2012/199, SI 2012/632 Reg.31, SI 2012/1652 Reg.8, Sch.7, Sch.13
s.12, applied: SI 2012/632 Reg.31
s.13, applied: SI 2012/632 Reg.31
s.14, applied: SI 2012/632 Reg.31
s.15, applied: SI 2012/632 Reg.31
s.15, enabling: SI 2012/199, SI 2012/632, SI 2012/638, SI 2012/1537
s.16, amended: 2012 c.7 Sch.7 para.5
s.16, applied: SI 2012/632 Reg.31
s.17, applied: SI 2012/632 Reg.31
s.18, applied: SI 2012/632 Reg.31
s.18, enabling: SI 2012/632
s.19, applied: SI 2012/632 Reg.31
s.20, applied: SI 2012/632 Reg.31
s.21, applied: SI 2012/632 Reg.31, SI 2012/1282 Sch.1, SI 2012/1284 Sch.1, SI 2012/1286 Sch.1, SI 2012/1289 Sch.1, SI 2012/1294 Sch.1, SI 2012/1295 Sch.1
s.22, applied: SI 2012/632 Reg.31, SI 2012/1282 Sch.1, SI 2012/1284 Sch.1, SI 2012/1286 Sch.1, SI 2012/1289 Sch.1, SI 2012/1294 Sch.1, SI 2012/1295 Sch.1
s.23, amended: 2012 asp 8 Sch.7 para.49
s.23, applied: SI 2012/632 Reg.31
s.24, applied: SI 2012/632 Reg.31, SI 2012/1652 Reg.17, Reg.24
s.25, applied: SI 2012/632 Reg.31
s.25A, applied: SI 2012/632 Reg.31
s.26, applied: SI 2012/632 Reg.31
s.27, applied: SI 2012/632 Reg.31
s.27A, applied: SI 2012/632 Reg.31
s.28, applied: SI 2012/632 Reg.31
s.29, applied: SI 2012/632 Reg.31
s.30, applied: SI 2012/632 Reg.31
s.31, applied: SI 2012/632 Reg.31
s.32, applied: SI 2012/632 Reg.31
s.33, applied: SI 2012/632 Reg.31
s.33, see *Dundee Cold Stores Ltd v HM Advocate* [2012] HCJAC 102, 2012 S.L.T. 1173 (HCJ), Lord Clarke; see *Scottish Sea Farms Ltd v HM Advocate* [2012] HCJAC 11, 2012 S.L.T. 299 (HCJ), Lord Mackay of Drumadoon
s.34, applied: SI 2012/632 Reg.31
s.35, applied: SI 2012/632 Reg.31
s.36, applied: SI 2012/632 Reg.31
s.37, applied: SI 2012/632 Reg.31
s.38, applied: SI 2012/632 Reg.31
s.39, applied: SI 2012/632 Reg.31

1974– cont.

37. Health and Safety at Work etc Act 1974– *cont.*
s.40, applied: SI 2012/632 Reg.31
s.40, see *R. v Cotswold Geotechnical Holdings Ltd* [2011] EWCA Crim 1337, [2012] 1 Cr. App. R. (S.) 26 (CA (Crim Div)), Lord Judge, L.C.J.
s.41, applied: SI 2012/632 Reg.31
s.42, applied: SI 2012/632 Reg.31
s.43, applied: SI 2012/632 Reg.31
s.43, enabling: SI 2012/1652
s.43A, applied: SI 2012/632 Reg.31
s.44, applied: SI 2012/632 Reg.31
s.45, applied: SI 2012/632 Reg.31
s.46, applied: SI 2012/632 Reg.31
s.47, applied: SI 2012/632 Reg.31
s.48, applied: SI 2012/632 Reg.31, SI 2012/1652 Reg.24
s.49, applied: SI 2012/632 Reg.31
s.49, enabling: SI 2012/1537
s.50, amended: 2012 c.7 Sch.7 para.6
s.50, applied: SI 2012/1537(b), SI 2012/199, SI 2012/632 Reg.31
s.51, applied: SI 2012/632 Reg.31
s.51A, amended: 2012 asp 8 Sch.7 para.2
s.51A, applied: SI 2012/632 Reg.31
s.52, applied: SI 2012/632 Reg.31
s.53, applied: SI 2012/632 Reg.31
s.53, referred to: SI 2012/335 Sch.1 para.20, SI 2012/2991 Sch.1 para.20
s.54, applied: SI 2012/632 Reg.31
s.60, amended: 2012 c.7 Sch.5 para.19
s.80, applied: SI 2012/632 Reg.31
s.80, enabling: SI 2012/632
s.81, applied: SI 2012/632 Reg.31
s.82, applied: SI 2012/632 Reg.31
s.82, enabling: SI 2012/632, SI 2012/638, SI 2012/1652
Sch.2 para.5, amended: SI 2012/2404 Sch.2 para.6
Sch.3 para.1, enabling: SI 2012/632
Sch.3 para.3, enabling: SI 2012/632
Sch.3 para.4, enabling: SI 2012/632
Sch.3 para.6, enabling: SI 2012/632
Sch.3 para.8, enabling: SI 2012/632
Sch.3 para.11, enabling: SI 2012/632
Sch.3 para.13, enabling: SI 2012/632
Sch.3 para.14, enabling: SI 2012/632
Sch.3 para.15, enabling: SI 2012/199, SI 2012/632
Sch.3 para.16, enabling: SI 2012/199, SI 2012/632
Sch.3 para.20, enabling: SI 2012/199, SI 2012/632

38. Land Tenure Reform (Scotland) Act 1974
s.17, applied: 2012 asp 9 s.10

39. Consumer Credit Act 1974
see *American Express Services Europe Ltd v Brandon* [2011] EWCA Civ 1187, [2012] 1 All E.R. (Comm) 415 (CA (Civ Div)), Pill, L.J.; see *Jones v Link Financial Ltd* [2012] EWHC 2402 (QB), [2012] E.C.C. 23 (QBD (Manchester)), Hamblen, J.; see *W v Veolia Environmental Services (UK) Plc* [2011] EWHC 2020 (QB), [2012] 1 All E.R. (Comm) 667 (QBD (Merc) (London)), Judge Mackie Q.C.
applied: 2012 c.21 s.107, SI 2012/1128 Art.4, SI 2012/2886 Sch.1, SSI 2012/303 Sch.4 para.34
referred to: 2012 c.19 Sch.6 para.4
s.9, applied: SI 2012/2079 Reg.1
s.10, applied: SI 2012/2079 Reg.1
s.16, amended: 2012 c.21 Sch.18 para.37
s.20, enabling: SI 2012/1745
s.21, applied: 2012 c.21 s.107, Sch.21 para.7, SI 2012/2079 Reg.25, Sch.1 para.24

1974– cont.

39. Consumer Credit Act 1974– *cont.*
s.25, amended: 2012 c.21 Sch.18 para.37
s.32, amended: 2012 c.21 s.108
s.32, repealed (in part): 2012 c.21 s.108
s.32A, added: 2012 c.21 s.108
s.32B, added: 2012 c.21 s.108
s.33, amended: 2012 c.21 s.108
s.33A, amended: 2012 c.21 s.108
s.34A, amended: 2012 c.21 s.108
s.34ZA, added: 2012 c.21 s.108
s.35, amended: 2012 c.21 Sch.18 para.37
s.37, amended: SI 2012/2404 Sch.2 para.7
s.39, see *R. v Dixon (Sarah Jane)* [2012] EWCA Crim 815, [2012] 2 Cr. App. R. (S.) 100 (CA (Crim Div)), Irwin, J.
s.41, amended: 2012 c.21 s.108
s.47, applied: SI 2012/1745 Reg.6
s.55, enabling: SI 2012/2798
s.60, enabling: SI 2012/2798
s.77A, enabling: SI 2012/2798
s.88, see *American Express Services Europe Ltd v Brandon* [2011] EWCA Civ 1187, [2012] 1 All E.R. (Comm) 415 (CA (Civ Div)), Pill, L.J.
s.95, enabling: SI 2012/2798
s.95B, applied: SI 2012/2798 Reg.3, Reg.4
s.95B, enabling: SI 2012/2798
s.97, enabling: SI 2012/2798
s.140A, see *Harrison v Black Horse Ltd* [2011] EWCA Civ 1128, [2012] E.C.C. 7 (CA (Civ Div)), Lord Neuberger (M.R.)
s.140B, see *Harrison v Black Horse Ltd* [2011] EWCA Civ 1128, [2012] E.C.C. 7 (CA (Civ Div)), Lord Neuberger (M.R.)
s.141, see *Jones v Link Financial Ltd* [2012] EWHC 2402 (QB), [2012] E.C.C. 23 (QBD (Manchester)), Hamblen, J.
s.162, applied: 2012 c.21 s.107
s.163, applied: 2012 c.21 s.107
s.164, applied: 2012 c.21 s.107
s.165, applied: 2012 c.21 s.107
s.167, applied: SI 2012/1745 Reg.6
s.174A, applied: 2012 c.21 s.107
s.182, enabling: SI 2012/1745, SI 2012/2798
s.189, see *Jones v Link Financial Ltd* [2012] EWHC 2402 (QB), [2012] E.C.C. 23 (QBD (Manchester)), Hamblen, J.
s.189, enabling: SI 2012/2798

40. Control of Pollution Act 1974
applied: SI 2012/416 Art.16
s.22, applied: SI 2012/811 Sch.1 para.3
s.60, applied: SI 2012/416 Art.16, SI 2012/1867 Art.52, SI 2012/2284 Art.29, SI 2012/2635 Art.38, SI 2012/2679 Art.38
s.60, referred to: SI 2012/2541 Sch.1, SI 2012/2547 Sch.1, SI 2012/2548 Sch.1, SI 2012/2549 Sch.1, SI 2012/3102 Sch.1, SI 2012/3103 Sch.1, SI 2012/3104 Sch.1, SI 2012/3105 Sch.1, SI 2012/3106 Sch.1, SI 2012/3107 Sch.1
s.61, applied: SI 2012/416 Art.16, SI 2012/1867 Art.52, SI 2012/2284 Art.29, SI 2012/2635 Art.38, SI 2012/2679 Art.38
s.61, disapplied: SI 2012/2679 Art.38
s.62, amended: 2012 asp 8 Sch.7 para.50
s.65, applied: SI 2012/416 Art.16, SI 2012/1867 Art.52, SI 2012/2284 Art.29, SI 2012/2635 Art.38, SI 2012/2679 Art.38
s.65, disapplied: SI 2012/2679 Art.38
s.82, applied: SI 2012/416 Art.16

1974– cont.

46. Friendly Societies Act 1974
applied: SI 2012/ 1128 Art.4

47. Solicitors Act 1974
s.15, amended: SI 2012/ 2404 Sch.2 para.8
s.16, amended: SI 2012/ 2404 Sch.2 para.8
s.20, see *Media Protection Services Ltd v Crawford*
[2012] EWHC 2373 (Admin), [2012] C.P. Rep. 48
(DC), Stanley Burnton, L.J.
s.47, amended: 2012 c.10 Sch.5 para.8
s.49, amended: 2012 c.10 Sch.5 para.9
s.56, applied: SI 2012/ 171
s.56, enabling: SI 2012/ 171
s.70, see *Bari v Rosen (t/a RA Rosen & Co Solicitors)* [2012] EWHC 1782 (QB), [2012] 5 Costs L.R. 851 (QBD), Spencer, J.; see *Tim Martin Interiors Ltd v Akin Gump LLP* [2011] EWCA Civ 1574, [2012] 1 W.L.R. 2946 (CA (Civ Div)), Ward, L.J.
s.71, see *Tim Martin Interiors Ltd v Akin Gump LLP* [2011] EWCA Civ 1574, [2012] 1 W.L.R. 2946 (CA (Civ Div)), Ward, L.J.
s.87, amended: 2012 c.21 Sch.18 para.38

53. Rehabilitation of Offenders Act 1974
applied: 2012 c.10 s.141, SI 2012/ 1726 r.5.8
s.1, amended: 2012 c.9 Sch.9 para.134, 2012 c.10 Sch.25 para.2, Sch.25 para.13
s.2, amended: 2012 c.10 Sch.25 para.3, Sch.25 para.14
s.3, repealed (in part): 2012 c.10 Sch.25 para.4
s.4, amended: 2012 c.10 Sch.25 para.5, Sch.25 para.15
s.4, applied: 2012 c.10 s.141
s.4, enabling: SI 2012/ 1957
s.5, amended: 2012 c.10 s.139, Sch.21 para.2
s.5, applied: SI 2012/ 1726 r.5.8
s.6, amended: 2012 c.10 s.139
s.6, repealed (in part): 2012 c.10 s.139
s.7, amended: 2012 c.10 Sch.25 para.6, Sch.25 para.16
s.7, applied: 2012 c.10 s.141
s.8, repealed (in part): 2012 c.10 Sch.25 para.7
s.8A, amended: 2012 c.10 Sch.24 para.2, Sch.25 para.8
s.8A, repealed (in part): 2012 c.10 Sch.24 para.2
s.8AA, added: 2012 c.10 s.139
s.9, amended: 2012 c.10 Sch.25 para.9, Sch.25 para.17
s.9, repealed (in part): 2012 c.10 Sch.25 para.17
s.9B, amended: 2012 asp 8 Sch.7 para.3
s.10, amended: 2012 c.10 Sch.25 para.10
s.10, applied: SI 2012/ 1957
s.10, enabling: SI 2012/ 1957
Sch.1 para.1, repealed (in part): 2012 c.10 Sch.25 para.11
Sch.1 para.2, repealed (in part): 2012 c.10 Sch.25 para.11
Sch.1 para.3, repealed (in part): 2012 c.10 Sch.25 para.11
Sch.1 para.4, repealed (in part): 2012 c.10 Sch.25 para.11
Sch.1 para.5, repealed (in part): 2012 c.10 Sch.25 para.11
Sch.1 para.6, repealed (in part): 2012 c.10 Sch.25 para.11
Sch.1 para.7, repealed (in part): 2012 c.10 Sch.25 para.11
Sch.2 para.1, amended: 2012 c.10 s.139
Sch.2 para.1, repealed (in part): 2012 c.10 s.139
Sch.2 para.2, amended: 2012 c.10 Sch.24 para.3

1974– cont.

53. Rehabilitation of Offenders Act 1974– *cont.*
Sch.2 para.3, applied: 2012 c.10 s.141
Sch.2 para.3, referred to: 2012 c.10 s.141
Sch.2 para.4, applied: 2012 c.10 s.141
Sch.2 para.4, enabling: SI 2012/ 1957
Sch.2 para.6, applied: 2012 c.10 s.141

1975

14. Social Security Act 1975
s.126A, varied: SI 2012/ 780 Art.4

21. Criminal Procedure (Scotland) Act 1975
s.174, see *Scottish Ministers v Mental Health Tribunal for Scotland* [2012] CSIH 18, 2012 S.C. 471 (IH (Ex Div)), Lord Eassie
s.175, see *Scottish Ministers v Mental Health Tribunal for Scotland* [2012] CSIH 18, 2012 S.C. 471 (IH (Ex Div)), Lord Eassie

22. Oil Taxation Act 1975
Sch.2 para.1, amended: 2012 c.14 Sch.38 para.51

23. Reservoirs Act 1975
s.1, applied: SI 2012/ 1867 Art.9

24. House of Commons Disqualification Act 1975
varied: SI 2012/ 147 Art.7
Sch.1 Part II, amended: 2012 c.5 Sch.13 para.16, 2012 c.7 s.181, Sch.15 para.50, Sch.15 para.54, Sch.15 para.69, Sch.15 para.71, Sch.17 para.4, Sch.19 para.3, Sch.20 para.5, Sch.20 para.9, 2012 c.9 Sch.9 para.131, 2012 c.10 Sch.5 para.10, SI 2012/ 246 Sch.1 para.19, SI 2012/ 700 Sch.1 para.1, SI 2012/ 1916 Sch.34 para.38, SI 2012/ 1923 Sch.1, SI 2012/ 2007 Sch.1 para.109, SI 2012/ 2654 Sch.1
Sch.1 Part III, amended: 2012 c.5 Sch.14 Part 8, 2012 c.7 s.189, Sch.5 para.20, Sch.7 para.7, Sch.13 para.5, Sch.14 para.46, Sch.20 para.2, 2012 c.9 Sch.9 para.1, Sch.9 para.5, Sch.9 para.131, 2012 c.21 Sch.1 para.4, Sch.2 para.6, Sch.18 para.39, SI 2012/ 964 Sch.1, SI 2012/ 1658 Sch.1

25. Northern Ireland Assembly Disqualification Act 1975
Sch.1 Part II, amended: 2012 c.5 Sch.13 para.16, 2012 c.7 s.181, Sch.15 para.50, Sch.15 para.55, Sch.15 para.69, Sch.15 para.71, Sch.17 para.5, Sch.19 para.4, Sch.20 para.5, 2012 c.9 Sch.9 para.132, 2012 c.10 Sch.5 para.11, SI 2012/ 1916 Sch.34 para.39, SI 2012/ 2007 Sch.1 para.109
Sch.1 Part III, amended: 2012 c.7 s.189, Sch.7 para.8, Sch.13 para.6, 2012 c.9 Sch.9 para.2, Sch.9 para.132, 2012 c.21 Sch.1 para.5, Sch.2 para.7, Sch.18 para.40, SI 2012/ 964 Sch.1

26. Ministers of the Crown Act 1975
applied: 2012 c.19 Sch.6 para.4
s.1, enabling: SI 2012/ 2590, SI 2012/ 2747
s.2, enabling: SI 2012/ 2590
s.5A, amended: 2012 c.5 s.126

30. Local Government (Scotland) Act 1975
s.3, see *Assessor for Glasgow v Schuh Ltd* [2012] CSIH 40, 2012 S.L.T. 904 (LVAC), The Lord Justice Clerk (Gill); see *Wincanton Plc v Assessor for Lanarkshire Valuation Joint Board* [2012] CSIH 36, 2012 S.L.T. 1161 (LVAC), The Lord Justice Clerk (Gill)
s.7B, applied: SSI 2012/ 27 Art.2, SSI 2012/ 352 Art.2
s.7B, enabling: SSI 2012/ 27, SSI 2012/ 352
s.37, enabling: SSI 2012/ 27, SSI 2012/ 352

41. Industrial and Provident Societies Act 1975
applied: SI 2012/ 1128 Art.4

51. Salmon and Freshwater Fisheries Act 1975
s.9, disapplied: SI 2012/ 1867 Art.3

1975– cont.

51. Salmon and Freshwater Fisheries Act 1975– cont.

s.40, amended: SI 2012/1659 Sch.3 para.4

52. Safety of Sports Grounds Act 1975

applied: SI 2012/1666

s.1, enabling: SI 2012/1133, SI 2012/1666

s.18, applied: SI 2012/1133, SI 2012/1666

60. Social Security Pensions Act 1975

s.59, applied: SI 2012/687 Sch.1 para.3, Sch.1 para.19, SI 2012/782 Art.6

s.59, enabling: SI 2012/782

s.59A, applied: SI 2012/687 Sch.1 para.3, Sch.1 para.19, SI 2012/782 Art.5

63. Inheritance (Provision for Family and Dependants) Act 1975

see *Ilott v Mitson* [2011] EWCA Civ 346, [2012] 2 F.L.R. 170 (CA (Civ Div)), Sir Nicholas Wall (President, Fam); see *Iqbal v Ahmed* [2011] EWCA Civ 900, [2012] 1 F.L.R. 31 (CA (Civ Div)), Pill, L.J.; see *Lilleyman v Lilleyman (Costs)* [2012] EWHC 1056 (Ch), [2012] 1 W.L.R. 2801 (Ch D), Briggs, J.; see *Lilleyman v Lilleyman* [2012] EWHC 821 (Ch), [2012] 3 W.L.R. 754 (Ch D (Leeds)), Briggs, J.; see *Smith v Smith* [2011] EWHC 2133 (Ch), [2012] 2 F.L.R. 230 (Ch D), Mann, J.

s.3, see *Lilleyman v Lilleyman* [2012] EWHC 821 (Ch), [2012] 3 W.L.R. 754 (Ch D (Leeds)), Briggs, J.

s.5, see *Smith v Smith* [2011] EWHC 2133 (Ch), [2012] 2 F.L.R. 230 (Ch D), Mann, J.

65. Sex Discrimination Act 1975

see *Hosso v European Credit Management Ltd* [2011] EWCA Civ 1589, [2012] I.C.R. 547 (CA (Civ Div)), Mummery, L.J.; see *R. (on the application of Hurley) v Secretary of State for Business, Innovation and Skills* [2012] EWHC 201 (Admin), [2012] H.R.L.R. 13 (DC), Elias, L.J.; see *Simpson v Intralinks Ltd* [2012] I.L.Pr. 34 (EAT), Langstaff, J. (President)

applied: SSI 2012/181 Reg.3

s.1, see *Chief Constable of Hampshire v Haque* [2012] Eq. L.R. 113 (EAT), Langstaff, J.; see *Mather v Devine & Partners Bramhall Park Medical Centre* [2012] Eq. L.R. 1082 (EAT), Judge McMullen Q.C.

s.3, see *Dunn v Institute of Cemetery and Crematorium Management* [2012] I.C.R. 941 (EAT), Judge McMullen Q.C.; see *Hawkins v Atex Group Ltd* [2012] I.C.R. 1315 (EAT), Underhill, J.

s.4A, see *Mather v Devine & Partners Bramhall Park Medical Centre* [2012] Eq. L.R. 1082 (EAT), Judge McMullen Q.C.; see *Warby v Wunda Group Plc* [2012] Eq. L.R. 536 (EAT), Langstaff, J.

s.6, see *Hosso v European Credit Management Ltd* [2011] EWCA Civ 1589, [2012] I.C.R. 547 (CA (Civ Div)), Mummery, L.J.; see *King v Health Professions Council* [2012] Eq. L.R. 852 (EAT), Langstaff, J. (President); see *Simpson v Intralinks Ltd* [2012] I.L.Pr. 34 (EAT), Langstaff, J. (President)

s.8, see *Abdulla v Birmingham City Council* [2012] UKSC 47, [2012] I.C.R. 1419 (SC), Lady Hale, J.S.C.

s.13, see *King v Health Professions Council* [2012] Eq. L.R. 852 (EAT), Langstaff, J. (President)

1975– cont.

65. Sex Discrimination Act 1975– *cont.*

s.63, see *Brennan v Sunderland City Council* [2012] I.C.R. 1183 (EAT), Underhill, J. (President); see *King v Health Professions Council* [2012] Eq. L.R. 852 (EAT), Langstaff, J. (President)

s.63A, see *Dziedziak v Future Electronics Ltd* [2012] Eq. L.R. 543 (EAT), Langstaff, J. (President); see *Hewage v Grampian Health Board* [2012] UKSC 37, [2012] 4 All E.R. 447 (SC), Lord Hope (Deputy President)

s.76, see *Malcolm v Dundee City Council* [2012] CSIH 13, 2012 S.L.T. 457 (IH (Ex Div)), Lady Paton; see *R. (on the application of Staff Side of the Police Negotiating Board) v Secretary of State for Work and Pensions* [2011] EWHC 3175 (Admin), [2012] Eq. L.R. 124 (QBD (Admin)), Elias, L.J.

s.76A, see *R. (on the application of Staff Side of the Police Negotiating Board) v Secretary of State for Work and Pensions* [2011] EWHC 3175 (Admin), [2012] Eq. L.R. 124 (QBD (Admin)), Elias, L.J.

68. Industry Act 1975

Sch.3 Part I para.6, amended: SI 2012/2404 Sch.2 para.9

72. Children Act 1975

applied: SI 2012/3144 Reg.8, SI 2012/3145 Sch.1

s.50, applied: SI 2012/2886 Sch.1, SSI 2012/303 Sch.4 para.29

1976

13. Damages (Scotland) Act 1976

s.1, see *Hamilton v Ferguson Transport (Spean Bridge) Ltd* [2012] CSIH 52, 2012 S.C. 486 (IH (1 Div)), The Lord President (Hamilton); see *MacDonald v Aberdeenshire Council* [2012] CSOH 101, 2012 S.L.T. 863 (OH), Lord Uist; see *Wolff v John Moulds (Kilmarnock) Ltd* 2012 S.L.T. 231 (OH), Lord Doherty

30. Fatal Accidents Act 1976

see *Cox v Ergo Versicherung AG (formerly Victoria)* [2011] EWHC 2806 (QB), [2012] R.T.R. 11 (QB), Sir Christopher Holland; see *Reynolds v United Kingdom (2694/08)* (2012) 55 E.H.R.R. 35 (ECHR), Judge Garlicki (President)

applied: 2012 c.10 Sch.1 para.3

s.1, see *Swift v Secretary of State for Justice* [2012] EWHC 2000 (QB), [2012] P.I.Q.R. P21 (QBD), Eady, J.

35. Police Pensions Act 1976

applied: 2012 asp 8 s.15

referred to: 2012 asp 8 s.12

s.1, applied: SI 2012/640, SI 2012/2811, SI 2012/3057

s.1, enabling: SI 2012/640, SI 2012/2811, SI 2012/3057, SSI 2012/71

s.2, enabling: SI 2012/640

s.3, enabling: SI 2012/640

s.4, enabling: SI 2012/640

s.5, enabling: SI 2012/640

s.6, enabling: SI 2012/640

s.7, amended: SI 2012/2954 Art.2, SI 2012/3006 Art.13

s.7, enabling: SI 2012/640

s.8A, amended: 2012 c.21 Sch.18 para.41

s.11, amended: SI 2012/2954 Art.2, SI 2012/3006 Art.13

s.11A, enabling: SI 2012/2954

1976– cont.

38. Dangerous Wild Animals Act 1976
s.5, amended: SI 2012/ 3039 Reg.27
s.6, applied: SI 2012/ 2932 Reg.5

52. Armed Forces Act 1976
Sch.9 para.21, repealed (in part): 2012 c.10 Sch.25 Part 2

57. Local Government (Miscellaneous Provisions) Act 1976
s.19, see *R. (on the application of Midlands Co-operative Society Ltd) v Birmingham City Council* [2012] EWHC 620 (Admin), [2012] Eu. L.R. 640 (QBD (Admin)), Hickinbottom, J.
s.39, applied: SI 2012/ 2734 Sch.1 para.3, Sch.1 para.16, Sch.1 para.30
s.39, varied: SI 2012/ 2734 Reg.6
s.41, applied: SI 2012/ 2734 Sch.1 para.17, Sch.1 para.31
s.41, varied: SI 2012/ 2734 Reg.6
s.47, see *R. (on the application of Shanks (t/a Blue Line Taxis)) v Northumberland CC* [2012] EWHC 1539 (Admin), [2012] R.T.R. 36 (QBD (Admin)), Foskett, J.
s.48, applied: SI 2012/ 2112 Reg.26

63. Bail Act 1976
referred to: SI 2012/ 1726 r.19.1
s.2, amended: 2012 c.10 Sch.11 para.2
s.3, amended: 2012 c.10 Sch.11 para.3
s.3, applied: 2012 c.10 s.93, SI 2012/ 1726 r.19.7, r.11.4, r.19.12, r.68.8, r.19.17
s.3AA, amended: 2012 c.10 Sch.11 para.4, Sch.12 para.15
s.3AA, referred to: SI 2012/ 1726 r.19.12
s.3AAA, added: 2012 c.10 Sch.11 para.5
s.3AB, amended: 2012 c.10 Sch.11 para.6
s.3AB, referred to: SI 2012/ 1726 r.19.12
s.3AB, repealed (in part): 2012 c.10 Sch.11 para.6
s.3AC, amended: 2012 c.10 Sch.11 para.7
s.3AC, applied: SI 2012/ 1726 r.19.12
s.4, applied: SI 2012/ 1726 r.19.17
s.5, applied: SI 2012/ 1726 r.11.5, r.11.5, r.9.5, r.68.9, r.10.5, r.5.4, r.41.5
s.5, referred to: SI 2012/ 1726 r.19.2, r.19.4
s.5B, applied: SI 2012/ 1726 r.19.6, r.19.7
s.5B, enabling: SI 2012/ 1726
s.6, see *R. v Evans (Scott Lennon)* [2011] EWCA Crim 2842, [2012] 1 W.L.R. 1192 (CA (Crim Div)), Hughes, L.J. VP
s.6, applied: SI 2012/ 1726 r.19.17, r.62.5
s.7, amended: 2012 c.10 Sch.11 para.8, Sch.12 para.16
s.7, applied: SI 2012/ 1726 r.18.2, r.19.17, r.37.11
s.9A, amended: 2012 c.10 Sch.11 para.9
Sch.1, referred to: SI 2012/ 1726 r.19.17
Sch.1 Part I, amended: 2012 c.10 Sch.11 para.11
Sch.1 Part I, applied: SI 2012/ 1726 r.19.17
Sch.1 Part I para.1, amended: 2012 c.10 Sch.11 para.12
Sch.1 Part I para.1A, added: 2012 c.10 Sch.11 para.13
Sch.1 Part I para.2, amended: 2012 c.10 Sch.11 para.14
Sch.1 Part I para.2A, substituted: 2012 c.10 Sch.11 para.16
Sch.1 Part I para.2ZA, added: 2012 c.10 Sch.11 para.15
Sch.1 Part I para.6, substituted: 2012 c.10 Sch.11 para.17
Sch.1 Part I para.6A, amended: 2012 c.10 Sch.11 para.18
Sch.1 Part I para.9, amended: 2012 c.10 Sch.11 para.19

1976– cont.

63. Bail Act 1976–*cont.*
Sch.1 Part I para.9AA, amended: 2012 c.10 Sch.11 para.20
Sch.1 Part I para.9AB, amended: 2012 c.10 Sch.11 para.21
Sch.1 Part IA, amended: 2012 c.10 Sch.11 para.23
Sch.1 Part IA, applied: SI 2012/ 1726 r.19.17
Sch.1 Part IA para.1, amended: 2012 c.10 Sch.11 para.24
Sch.1 Part IA para.1A, added: 2012 c.10 Sch.11 para.25
Sch.1 Part IA para.4, amended: 2012 c.10 Sch.11 para.26
Sch.1 Part II, applied: SI 2012/ 1726 r.19.17
Sch.1 Part II para.2, amended: 2012 c.10 Sch.11 para.28
Sch.1 Part II para.5, amended: 2012 c.10 Sch.11 para.29
Sch.1 Part II para.6, added: 2012 c.10 Sch.11 para.30
Sch.1 Part IIA, applied: SI 2012/ 1726 r.19.7, r.19.17
Sch.1 Part III para.2, amended: 2012 c.10 Sch.11 para.31
Sch.1 Part III para.3, amended: 2012 c.10 Sch.12 para.17

74. Race Relations Act 1976
see *King v Health Professions Council* [2012] Eq. L.R. 852 (EAT), Langstaff, J. (President); see *Moxam v Visible Changes Ltd* [2012] Eq. L.R. 202 (EAT), Judge McMullen Q.C.; see *R. (on the application of Hurley) v Secretary of State for Business, Innovation and Skills* [2012] EWHC 201 (Admin), [2012] H.R.L.R. 13 (DC), Elias, L.J.; see *Redhead v Hounslow LBC* [2012] Eq. L.R. 628 (EAT), Recorder Luba Q.C.; see *Royal Bank of Scotland Plc v Morris* [2012] Eq. L.R. 406 (EAT), Underhill, J.
applied: SSI 2012/ 181 Reg.3
s.1, see *Dziedziak v Future Electronics Ltd* [2012] Eq. L.R. 543 (EAT), Langstaff, J. (President)
s.4, see *Ruhaza v Alexander Hancock Recruitment Ltd* [2012] Eq. L.R. 9 (EAT), Judge Serota Q.C.
s.12, see *Iteshi v General Council of the Bar* [2012] Eq. L.R. 553 (EAT), Lady Smith
s.14, see *Ruhaza v Alexander Hancock Recruitment Ltd* [2012] Eq. L.R. 9 (EAT), Judge Serota Q.C.
s.20, see *Chief Constable of Hampshire v Bullale* [2012] EWHC 1549 (QB), [2012] Eq. L.R. 875 (QBD), Sir Charles Gray
s.29, see *Ruhaza v Alexander Hancock Recruitment Ltd* [2012] Eq. L.R. 9 (EAT), Judge Serota Q.C.
s.54A, see *Bouzir v Country Style Foods Ltd* [2011] EWCA Civ 1519, [2012] Eq. L.R. 163 (CA (Civ Div)), Mummery, L.J.; see *Hewage v Grampian Health Board* [2012] UKSC 37, [2012] 4 All E.R. 447 (SC), Lord Hope (Deputy President)
s.68, see *Bahous v Pizza Express Restaurant Ltd* [2012] Eq. L.R. 4 (EAT), Judge Peter Clark
s.71, see *Medhurst v Secretary of State for Communities and Local Government* [2011] EWHC 3576 (Admin), [2012] J.P.L. 598 (QBD (Admin)), Clive Lewis QC; see *R. (on the application of Essex CC) v Secretary of State for Education* [2012] EWHC 1460 (Admin), [2012] E.L.R. 383 (QBD (Admin)), Mitting, J.; see *R. (on the application of HA (Nigeria)) v Secretary of State for the Home Department* [2012] EWHC 979 (Admin), [2012] Med. L.R. 353 (QBD (Admin)), Singh, J.

1976– cont.

76. Energy Act 1976
s.6, applied: SI 2012/2862 Art.16
s.6, enabling: SI 2012/2862
s.17, enabling: SI 2012/2862
s.21, applied: SI 2012/2106 Art.3

86. Fishery Limits Act 1976
s.2, applied: SI 2012/2747 Art.3

1977

5. Social Security (Miscellaneous Provisions) Act 1977
s.12, enabling: SI 2012/359
s.24, enabling: SI 2012/359

30. Rentcharges Act 1977
s.2, see *Canwell Estate Co Ltd v Smith Brothers Farms Ltd* [2012] EWCA Civ 237, [2012] 1 W.L.R. 2626 (CA (Civ Div)), Mummery, L.J.

36. Finance Act 1977
Sch.7, see *Cameron v Revenue and Customs Commissioners* [2012] EWHC 1174 (Admin), [2012] S.T.C. 1691 (QBD (Admin)), Wyn Williams, J.

37. Patents Act 1977
s.1, see *Halliburton Energy Services Inc's Patent Applications* [2011] EWHC 2508 (Pat), [2012] R.P.C. 12 (Ch D (Patents Ct)), Judge Birss Q.C.; see *Threeway Pressings Ltd's Patent Application, Re* [2012] R.P.C. 20 (PO), Peter Slater
s.2, see *Threeway Pressings Ltd's Patent Application, Re* [2012] R.P.C. 20 (PO), Peter Slater
s.12, see *Innovia Films Ltd v Frito-Lay North America Inc* [2012] EWHC 790 (Pat), [2012] R.P.C. 24 (Ch D (Patents Ct)), Arnold, J.
s.20A, see *Clifford v Comptroller General of Patents, Designs and Trade Marks* [2011] EWHC 1433 (Ch), [2012] Bus. L.R. 475 (Ch D (Patents Ct)), Henry Carr QC
s.60, see *Datacard Corp v Eagle Technologies Ltd* [2011] EWHC 244 (Pat), [2012] Bus. L.R. 160 (Ch D (Patents Ct)), Arnold, J.
s.63, see *Nokia Oyj (Nokia Corp) v IPCom GmbH & Co KG* [2011] EWHC 2719 (Pat), [2012] Bus. L.R. 1311 (Ch D (Patents Ct)), Floyd, J.; see *Nokia Oyj (Nokia Corp) v IPCom GmbH & Co KG* [2011] EWHC 3460 (Pat), [2012] R.P.C. 22 (Ch D (Patents Ct)), Floyd, J.
s.68, see *Schutz (UK) Ltd v Werit UK Ltd* [2011] EWCA Civ 1337, [2012] Bus. L.R. 746 (CA (Civ Div)), Ward, L.J.; see *Schutz (UK) Ltd v Werit UK Ltd* [2011] EWCA Civ 927, [2012] F.S.R. 2 (CA (Civ Div)), Ward, L.J.
s.72, see *Sandvik Intellectual Property AB v Kennametal UK Ltd* [2011] EWHC 3311 (Pat), [2012] R.P.C. 23 (Ch D (Patents Ct)), Arnold, J.
s.82, see *Innovia Films Ltd v Frito-Lay North America Inc* [2012] EWHC 790 (Pat), [2012] R.P.C. 24 (Ch D (Patents Ct)), Arnold, J.
s.89A, see *Clifford v Comptroller General of Patents, Designs and Trade Marks* [2011] EWHC 1433 (Ch), [2012] Bus. L.R. 475 (Ch D (Patents Ct)), Henry Carr QC
s.130, see *Innovia Films Ltd v Frito-Lay North America Inc* [2012] EWHC 790 (Pat), [2012] R.P.C. 24 (Ch D (Patents Ct)), Arnold, J.

42. Rent Act 1977
s.1, applied: SI 2012/3018 Sch.2 para.1

1977– cont.

43. Protection from Eviction Act 1977
s.1, see *R. v Qureshi (Mohammed)* [2011] EWCA Crim 1584, [2012] 1 W.L.R. 694 (CA (Crim Div)), Laws, L.J.

45. Criminal Law Act 1977
s.1, see *R. v Kapoor (Saran Singh)* [2012] EWCA Crim 435, [2012] 1 W.L.R. 3569 (CA (Crim Div)), Hooper, L.J.; see *R. v Majeed (Mazhar)* [2012] EWCA Crim 1186, [2012] 3 All E.R. 737 (CA (Crim Div)), Lord Judge, L.C.J.; see *R. v Nolan (Tracey)* [2012] EWCA Crim 671, [2012] Lloyd's Rep. F.C. 498 (CA (Crim Div)), Rafferty, L.J.
s.2, see *R. v Gnango (Armel)* [2012] 1 A.C. 827 (SC), Lord Phillips (President)
s.5, see *R. v Austin (Alan Brian)* [2011] EWCA Crim 345, [2012] 1 Cr. App. R. 24 (CA (Crim Div)), Thomas, L.J.
s.39, applied: SI 2012/1726 r.4.4
s.48, enabling: SI 2012/1726
s.63, amended: 2012 c.10 Sch.25 Part 2
Sch.12 para.1, amended: 2012 c.10 Sch.25 Part 2
Sch.12 para.2, amended: 2012 c.10 Sch.25 Part 2
Sch.12 para.3, amended: 2012 c.10 Sch.25 Part 2
Sch.12 para.4, amended: 2012 c.10 Sch.25 Part 2
Sch.12 para.6, amended: 2012 c.10 Sch.25 Part 2
Sch.12 para.7, amended: 2012 c.10 Sch.25 Part 2
Sch.12 para.8, amended: 2012 c.10 Sch.25 Part 2
Sch.12 para.9, amended: 2012 c.10 Sch.25 Part 2
Sch.12 para.10, amended: 2012 c.10 Sch.25 Part 2
Sch.12 para.11, amended: 2012 c.10 Sch.25 Part 2
Sch.12 para.12, amended: 2012 c.10 Sch.25 Part 2

49. National Health Service Act 1977
applied: SI 2012/3001 Sch.1
s.16A, applied: SI 2012/2886 Sch.1, SSI 2012/303 Sch.4 para.31, SSI 2012/319 Reg.35
s.16BA, applied: SSI 2012/303 Sch.4 para.31, SSI 2012/319 Reg.35

50. Unfair Contract Terms Act 1977
see *Air Transworld Ltd v Bombardier Inc* [2012] EWHC 243 (Comm), [2012] 2 All E.R. (Comm) 60 (QBD (Comm)), Cooke, J.; see *Avrora Fine Arts Investment Ltd v Christie, Manson & Woods Ltd* [2012] EWHC 2198 (Ch), [2012] P.N.L.R. 35 (Ch D), Newey, J.; see *AXA Sun Life Services Plc v Campbell Martin Ltd* [2011] EWCA Civ 133, [2012] Bus. L.R. 203 (CA (Civ Div)), Rix, L.J.; see *FG Wilson (Engineering) Ltd v John Holt & Co (Liverpool) Ltd* [2012] EWHC 2477 (Comm), [2012] 2 Lloyd's Rep. 479 (QBD (Comm)), Popplewell, J.; see *Robinson v PE Jones (Contractors) Ltd* [2011] EWCA Civ 9, [2012] Q.B. 44 (CA (Civ Div)), Maurice Kay, L.J.; see *United Trust Bank Ltd v Dohil* [2011] EWHC 3302 (QB), [2012] 2 All E.R. (Comm) 765 (QBD), Simon Picken Q.C.
s.2, see *Avrora Fine Arts Investment Ltd v Christie, Manson & Woods Ltd* [2012] EWHC 2198 (Ch), [2012] P.N.L.R. 35 (Ch D), Newey, J.
s.3, see *AXA Sun Life Services Plc v Campbell Martin Ltd* [2011] EWCA Civ 133, [2012] Bus. L.R. 203 (CA (Civ Div)), Rix, L.J.
s.6, see *Air Transworld Ltd v Bombardier Inc* [2012] EWHC 243 (Comm), [2012] 2 All E.R. (Comm) 60 (QBD (Comm)), Cooke, J.
s.12, see *Air Transworld Ltd v Bombardier Inc* [2012] EWHC 243 (Comm), [2012] 2 All E.R. (Comm) 60 (QBD (Comm)), Cooke, J.

1977–cont.

50. Unfair Contract Terms Act 1977–*cont.*
s.13, see *AXA Sun Life Services Plc v Campbell Martin Ltd* [2011] EWCA Civ 133, [2012] Bus. L.R. 203 (CA (Civ Div)), Rix, L.J.
s.26, see *AirTransworld Ltd v Bombardier Inc* [2012] EWHC 243 (Comm), [2012] 2 All E.R. (Comm) 60 (QBD (Comm)), Cooke, J.
Sch.2, see *United Trust Bank Ltd v Dohil* [2011] EWHC 3302 (QB), [2012] 2 All E.R. (Comm) 765 (QBD), Simon Picken Q.C.

1978

19. Oaths Act 1978
s.1, applied: SI 2012/ 1726 r.37.4
s.3, applied: SI 2012/ 1726 r.37.4
s.5, applied: SI 2012/ 1726 r.32.5, r.37.4
s.6, applied: SI 2012/ 1726 r.37.4

22. Domestic Proceedings and Magistrates Courts Act 1978
applied: SI 2012/ 2814 Sch.1 para.7, SI 2012/ 3144 Reg.8, SI 2012/ 3145 Sch.1
s.1, see *Claridge's Trustee in Bankruptcy v Claridge* [2011] EWHC 2047 (Ch), [2012] 1 F.C.R. 388 (Ch D), Sales, J.
s.2, see *Claridge's Trustee in Bankruptcy v Claridge* [2011] EWHC 2047 (Ch), [2012] 1 F.C.R. 388 (Ch D), Sales, J.

28. Adoption (Scotland) Act 1978
s.18, see *O v Aberdeen City Council* 2012 S.C. 60 (IH (2 Div)), The Lord Justice Clerk (Gill)
s.51A, applied: SI 2012/ 2886 Sch.1

29. National Health Service (Scotland) Act 1978
applied: SI 2012/ 1916 Reg.230, Sch.17 Part 1, SI 2012/ 2996 Sch.5 para.5
s.2, applied: SI 2012/ 1631 Sch.5 para.6, SSI 2012/ 162 Sch.1
s.4, applied: SI 2012/ 1631 Sch.5 para.6, SI 2012/ 2996 Sch.5 para.5
s.10, applied: SI 2012/ 1631 Sch.5 para.6, SI 2012/ 2996 Sch.5 para.5
s.10A, applied: SI 2012/ 1631 Sch.5 para.6, SI 2012/ 2996 Sch.5 para.5
s.12A, applied: SI 2012/ 1631 Sch.5 para.6, SI 2012/ 2996 Sch.5 para.5
s.17A, amended: 2012 c.7 Sch.21 para.2
s.17A, repealed (in part): 2012 c.7 Sch.21 para.2
s.17C, amended: 2012 c.7 Sch.21 para.3
s.17C, applied: SI 2012/ 1631 Sch.4 para.15
s.17D, amended: 2012 c.7 Sch.21 para.4
s.17E, enabling: SSI 2012/ 10
s.17N, enabling: SSI 2012/ 9
s.25, applied: SI 2012/ 1631 Sch.4 para.12
s.26, applied: SI 2012/ 1631 Sch.4 para.13
s.27, amended: 2012 c.7 s.213, s.220
s.27, applied: SI 2012/ 1631 Sch.4 para.14
s.27A, applied: SI 2012/ 1631 Sch.4 para.14
s.46, applied: SI 2012/ 2885 Sch.1 para.25, Sch.1 para.26, SI 2012/ 2886 Sch.1, SI 2012/ 3144 Sch.1 para.19, SI 2012/ 3145 Sch.1, SSI 2012/ 303 Reg.28, Sch.1 para.10, SSI 2012/ 319 Reg.29
s.69, enabling: SSI 2012/ 74
s.70, enabling: SSI 2012/ 73
s.73, enabling: SSI 2012/ 73
s.74, enabling: SSI 2012/ 73
s.75A, enabling: SSI 2012/ 171
s.98, enabling: SI 2012/ 87, SSI 2012/ 87

1978–cont.

29. National Health Service (Scotland) Act 1978–*cont.*
s.105, enabling: SI 2012/ 87, SSI 2012/ 9, SSI 2012/ 10, SSI 2012/ 73, SSI 2012/ 74, SSI 2012/ 87, SSI 2012/ 171
s.106, enabling: SSI 2012/ 9
s.108, enabling: SSI 2012/ 9, SSI 2012/ 10, SSI 2012/ 73, SSI 2012/ 74, SSI 2012/ 171
Sch.5A para.9, varied: 2012 c.11 s.12
Sch.11 para.2, enabling: SSI 2012/ 73
Sch.11 para.2A, enabling: SSI 2012/ 73

30. Interpretation Act 1978
applied: SI 2012/ 1159 Art.2
s.6, see *R. v Smith (Gavin)* [2012] EWCA Crim 398, [2012] 1 W.L.R. 3368 (CA (Crim Div)), Richards, L.J.
s.7, see *Calladine-Smith v Saveorder Ltd* [2011] EWHC 2501 (Ch), [2012] L. & T.R. 3 (Ch D), Morgan, J.; see *Freetown Ltd v Assethold Ltd* [2012] EWHC 1351 (QB), [2012] 4 All E.R. 194 (QBD), Slade, J.
s.7, applied: 2012 c.7 s.148, 2012 c.19 s.75, SI 2012/ 938 Reg.11, SI 2012/ 1777 Art.57, SI 2012/ 1867 Art.56, SI 2012/ 1924 Art.13, SI 2012/ 2284 Art.33, SI 2012/ 2629 Reg.27, SI 2012/ 2635 Art.43, SI 2012/ 2679 Art.55, SI 2012/ 3013 Reg.13, SI 2012/ 3030 Reg.20, SI 2012/ 3080 Art.19, SSI 2012/ 139 Reg.16, SSI 2012/ 142 Reg.16, SSI 2012/ 321 Reg.26, SSI 2012/ 360 Reg.8
s.16, see *John Mander Pension Trustees Ltd v Revenue and Customs Commissioners* [2012] S.F.T.D. 322 (FTT (Tax)), Judge Barbara Mosedale
s.17, see *Manchester Ship Canal Co Ltd v United Utilities Water Plc* [2012] EWHC 232 (Ch), [2012] Env. L.R. 31 (Ch D), Newey, J
s.17, disapplied: 2012 c.14 Sch.17 para.36, Sch.19 para.2
s.24, referred to: 2012 c.17 s.20
Sch.1, referred to: SI 2012/ 1726 r.21.1

33. State Immunity Act 1978
s.5, see *Nigeria v Ogbonna* [2012] 1 W.L.R. 139 (EAT), Underhill, J. (President)
s.13, see *SerVaas Inc v Rafidain Bank* [2011] EWCA Civ 1256, [2012] 1 All E.R. (Comm) 527 (CA (Civ Div)), Rix, L.J.; see *SerVaas Inc v Rafidain Bank* [2012] UKSC 40, [2012] 3 W.L.R. 545 (SC), Lord Phillips, J.S.C. (President)

34. Industrial and Provident Societies Act 1978
applied: SI 2012/ 1128 Art.4

35. Import of Live Fish (Scotland) Act 1978
s.1, applied: SSI 2012/ 175 Art.3

37. Protection of Children Act 1978
see *R. (on the application of E) v DPP* [2011] EWHC 1465 (Admin), [2012] 1 Cr. App. R. 6 (DC), Munby, L.J.
s.1, applied: 2012 c.10 Sch.1 para.39

40. Rating (Disabled Persons) Act 1978
applied: SSI 2012/ 28 Reg.3, SSI 2012/ 353 Reg.3

47. Civil Liability (Contribution) Act 1978
see *Brennan v Sunderland City Council* [2012] I.C.R. 1183 (EAT), Underhill, J. (President)
s.1, see *Brennan v Sunderland City Council* [2012] I.C.R. 1183 (EAT), Underhill, J. (President)
s.2, see *Brennan v Sunderland City Council* [2012] I.C.R. 1183 (EAT), Underhill, J. (President)

1979

2. Customs and Excise Management Act 1979
applied: SI 2012/178 Reg.9, SI 2012/810 Art.14, SI 2012/1243 Art.18
s.1, amended: 2012 c.11 s.24, 2012 c.14 Sch.24 para.41
s.50, varied: SI 2012/178 Reg.12, SI 2012/810 Art.14, SI 2012/1243 Art.18
s.52, amended: SI 2012/1809 Sch.1 Part 1
s.68, varied: SI 2012/810 Art.14, SI 2012/1243 Art.18
s.77A, applied: SI 2012/1243 Art.19
s.77A, varied: SI 2012/810 Art.15
s.93, enabling: SI 2012/2786
s.102, amended: 2012 c.14 Sch.24 para.55
s.118A, enabling: SI 2012/3020
s.118BC, substituted: 2012 c.14 Sch.24 para.42
s.118G, amended: 2012 c.14 Sch.24 para.42
s.137, see *Carlsberg UK Ltd v Revenue and Customs Commissioners* [2012] EWCA Civ 82, [2012] S.T.C. 1140 (CA (Civ Div)), Lord Neuberger (M.R.)
s.138, applied: SI 2012/1243 Art.19
s.138, varied: SI 2012/810 Art.15
s.139, see *R. (on the application of Eastenders Cash & Carry Plc) v Revenue and Customs Commissioners* [2012] EWCA Civ 15, [2012] 1 W.L.R. 2067 (CA (Civ Div)), Mummery, L.J.; see *R. (on the application of Eastenders Cash & Carry Plc) v Revenue and Customs Commissioners* [2012] EWCA Civ 689, [2012] 1 W.L.R. 2912 (CA (Civ Div)), Mummery, L.J.
s.139, applied: SI 2012/178 Reg.9
s.144, see *R. (on the application of Eastenders Cash & Carry Plc) v Revenue and Customs Commissioners* [2012] EWCA Civ 15, [2012] 1 W.L.R. 2067 (CA (Civ Div)), Mummery, L.J.; see *R. (on the application of Eastenders Cash & Carry Plc) v Revenue and Customs Commissioners* [2012] EWCA Civ 689, [2012] 1 W.L.R. 2912 (CA (Civ Div)), Mummery, L.J.
s.145, applied: SI 2012/1243 Art.19
s.145, varied: SI 2012/810 Art.15
s.146, applied: SI 2012/1243 Art.19
s.146, varied: SI 2012/810 Art.15
s.146A, applied: SI 2012/1243 Art.19
s.146A, varied: SI 2012/810 Art.15
s.147, applied: SI 2012/1243 Art.19, SI 2012/1726 r.63.1
s.147, varied: SI 2012/810 Art.15
s.148, applied: SI 2012/1243 Art.19
s.148, varied: SI 2012/810 Art.15
s.150, applied: SI 2012/1243 Art.19
s.150, varied: SI 2012/810 Art.15
s.151, applied: SI 2012/1243 Art.19
s.151, varied: SI 2012/810 Art.15
s.152, applied: SI 2012/1243 Art.19
s.152, varied: SI 2012/810 Art.15
s.154, applied: SI 2012/1243 Art.19
s.154, varied: SI 2012/810 Art.15
s.155, applied: SI 2012/1243 Art.19
s.155, varied: SI 2012/810 Art.15
s.170, see *R. v Varma (Aloke)* [2012] UKSC 42, [2012] 3 W.L.R. 776 (SC), Lord Phillips, J.S.C. (President)
s.170, applied: SSI 2012/88 Reg.23, SSI 2012/89 Reg.26
s.170, varied: SI 2012/178 Reg.12, SI 2012/810 Art.14, SI 2012/1243 Art.18
Sch.3 para.5, see *Jones v Revenue and Customs Commissioners* [2011] EWCA Civ 824, [2012] Ch. 414 (CA (Civ Div)), Mummery, L.J.

1979–cont.

4. Alcoholic Liquor Duties Act 1979
see *Carlsberg UK Ltd v Revenue and Customs Commissioners* [2012] EWCA Civ 82, [2012] S.T.C. 1140 (CA (Civ Div)), Lord Neuberger (M.R.)
s.1, amended: 2012 c.14 Sch.39 para.51
s.1, repealed (in part): 2012 c.14 Sch.39 para.52
s.2, see *Carlsberg UK Ltd v Revenue and Customs Commissioners* [2012] EWCA Civ 82, [2012] S.T.C. 1140 (CA (Civ Div)), Lord Neuberger (M.R.)
s.4, amended: 2012 c.14 Sch.39 para.51
s.5, amended: 2012 c.14 s.186
s.6, repealed: 2012 c.14 Sch.39 para.52
s.22, repealed: 2012 c.14 s.187
s.36, amended: 2012 c.14 s.186
s.37, amended: 2012 c.14 s.186
s.41A, enabling: SI 2012/2786
s.55, amended: 2012 c.14 Sch.39 para.51
s.62, amended: 2012 c.14 s.186
Sch.1, amended: 2012 c.14 s.186

5. Hydrocarbon Oil Duties Act 1979
applied: SI 2012/3030 Reg.22
varied: 2012 c.14 s.188
s.6AA, applied: SI 2012/3055 Art.3
s.6AD, applied: SI 2012/3055 Art.3
s.11, applied: SI 2012/3055 Art.4
s.13AA, applied: SI 2012/3055 Art.4
s.13ZA, applied: SI 2012/3055 Art.4
s.14, applied: SI 2012/3055 Art.4
s.14E, amended: 2012 c.14 s.189
s.20AA, enabling: SI 2012/3056

7. Tobacco Products Duty Act 1979
Sch.1, amended: 2012 c.14 s.185

8. Excise Duties (Surcharges or Rebates) Act 1979
s.1, enabling: SI 2012/3055
s.2, enabling: SI 2012/3055

10. Public Lending Right Act 1979
s.3, enabling: SI 2012/63, SI 2012/3123

17. Vaccine Damage Payments Act 1979
applied: 2012 c.10 Sch.1 para.8, Sch.1 para.15
s.4, amended: 2012 c.5 Sch.11 para.2
s.4, applied: 2012 c.5 s.102
s.8, amended: 2012 c.5 Sch.11 para.3

21. Forestry Act 1979
s.1, applied: SI 2012/605 Reg.15, Reg.24

33. Land Registration (Scotland) Act 1979
s.1, repealed: 2012 asp 5 Sch.5 para.19
s.2, repealed: 2012 asp 5 Sch.5 para.19
s.3, repealed: 2012 asp 5 Sch.5 para.19
s.4, applied: 2012 asp 5 Sch.4 para.13, Sch.4 para.25
s.4, repealed: 2012 asp 5 Sch.5 para.19
s.5, repealed: 2012 asp 5 Sch.5 para.19
s.6, repealed: 2012 asp 5 Sch.5 para.19
s.7, repealed: 2012 asp 5 Sch.5 para.19
s.8, repealed: 2012 asp 5 Sch.5 para.19
s.9, applied: 2012 asp 5 Sch.4 para.14, Sch.4 para.17, Sch.4 para.22
s.9, repealed: 2012 asp 5 Sch.5 para.19
s.10, repealed: 2012 asp 5 Sch.5 para.19
s.11, repealed: 2012 asp 5 Sch.5 para.19
s.12, applied: 2012 asp 5 Sch.4 para.15, Sch.4 para.20, Sch.4 para.23
s.12, repealed: 2012 asp 5 Sch.5 para.19
s.13, applied: 2012 asp 5 Sch.4 para.16, Sch.4 para.20
s.13, repealed: 2012 asp 5 Sch.5 para.19
s.14, repealed: 2012 asp 5 Sch.5 para.19
s.15, amended: 2012 asp 5 Sch.5 para.19

1979– cont.

33. Land Registration (Scotland) Act 1979– cont.
s.15, repealed (in part): 2012 asp 5 Sch.5 para.19
s.19, repealed: 2012 asp 5 Sch.5 para.19
s.23, repealed: 2012 asp 5 Sch.5 para.19
s.24, repealed: 2012 asp 5 Sch.5 para.19
s.25, repealed: 2012 asp 5 Sch.5 para.19
s.26, repealed: 2012 asp 5 Sch.5 para.19
s.27, repealed: 2012 asp 5 Sch.5 para.19
s.28, repealed: 2012 asp 5 Sch.5 para.19
s.29, repealed (in part): 2012 asp 5 Sch.5 para.19
s.30, repealed: 2012 asp 5 Sch.5 para.19
Sch.2 para.1, repealed: 2012 asp 5 Sch.5 para.19
Sch.2 para.2, repealed: 2012 asp 5 Sch.5 para.19
Sch.2 para.3, repealed: 2012 asp 5 Sch.5 para.19
Sch.2 para.4, repealed: 2012 asp 5 Sch.5 para.19
Sch.2 para.5, repealed: 2012 asp 5 Sch.5 para.19
Sch.2 para.6, repealed: 2012 asp 5 Sch.5 para.19
Sch.3 para.3, repealed: 2012 asp 5 Sch.5 para.19
Sch.3 para.4, repealed: 2012 asp 5 Sch.5 para.19
Sch.3 para.5, amended: 2012 asp 5 Sch.5 para.19
Sch.3 para.6, amended: 2012 asp 5 Sch.5 para.19
Sch.3 para.6, repealed (in part): 2012 asp 5 Sch.5 para.19
Sch.3 para.7, repealed (in part): 2012 asp 5 Sch.5 para.19
Sch.3 para.8, repealed (in part): 2012 asp 5 Sch.5 para.19
Sch.3 para.10, repealed: 2012 asp 5 Sch.5 para.19
Sch.3 para.11, amended: 2012 asp 5 Sch.5 para.19
Sch.3 para.11, repealed (in part): 2012 asp 5 Sch.5 para.19
Sch.3 para.12, repealed: 2012 asp 5 Sch.5 para.19
Sch.3 para.13, repealed: 2012 asp 5 Sch.5 para.19
Sch.3 para.16, amended: 2012 asp 5 Sch.5 para.19

34. Credit Unions Act 1979
applied: SI 2012/ 1128 Art.4

38. Estate Agents Act 1979
applied: SI 2012/ 1128 Art.4
referred to: 2012 c.19 Sch.6 para.4
s.18, see *Great Estates Group Ltd v Digby* [2011] EWCA Civ 1120, [2012] 2 All E.R. (Comm) 361 (CA (Civ Div)), Rix, L.J.
s.23, amended: SI 2012/ 2404 Sch.2 para.10

41. Pneumoconiosis etc (Workers Compensation) Act 1979
s.1, enabling: SI 2012/ 923
s.2, amended: 2012 c.5 Sch.14 Part 7
s.7, applied: SI 2012/ 923
s.7, enabling: SI 2012/ 923

53. Charging Orders Act 1979
s.3, see *Hughmans Solicitors v Central Stream Services Ltd (In Liquidation)* [2012] EWHC 1222 (Ch), [2012] B.P.I.R. 1013 (Ch D), Briggs, J.; see *National Guild of Removers and Storers Ltd v Jones (t/a ATR Removals)* [2012] EWCA Civ 216, [2012] 1 W.L.R. 2501 (CA (Civ Div)), Lord Neuberger (M.R.)

54. Sale of Goods Act 1979
see *Air Transworld Ltd v Bombardier Inc* [2012] EWHC 243 (Comm), [2012] 2 All E.R. (Comm) 60 (QBD (Comm)), Cooke, J.
s.12, see *Great Elephant Corp v Trafigura Beheer BV* [2012] EWHC 1745 (Comm), [2012] 2 Lloyd's Rep. 503 (QBD (Comm)), Teare, J.
s.13, see *Air Transworld Ltd v Bombardier Inc* [2012] EWHC 243 (Comm), [2012] 2 All E.R. (Comm) 60 (QBD (Comm)), Cooke, J.

1979– cont.

54. Sale of Goods Act 1979– cont.
s.14, see *Activa DPS Europe Sarl v Pressure Seal Solutions Ltd (t/a Welltec System (UK))* [2012] EWCA Civ 943, [2012] T.C.L.R. 7 (CA (Civ Div)), Sir Andrew Morritt (Chancellor); see *Air Transworld Ltd v Bombardier Inc* [2012] EWHC 243 (Comm), [2012] 2 All E.R. (Comm) 60 (QBD (Comm)), Cooke, J.; see *Lowe v W Machell Joinery Ltd* [2011] EWCA Civ 794, [2012] 1 All E.R. (Comm) 153 (CA (Civ Div)), Rix, L.J.; see *MacDonald v Pollock* [2012] CSIH 12, [2012] 1 Lloyd's Rep. 425 (IH (Ex Div)), Lord Eassie
s.49, see *FG Wilson (Engineering) Ltd v John Holt & Co (Liverpool) Ltd* [2012] EWHC 2477 (Comm), [2012] 2 Lloyd's Rep. 479 (QBD (Comm)), Popplewell, J.

58. Isle of Man Act 1979
Sch.1 para.29, repealed: 2012 c.14 s.187

1980

11. Protection of Trading Interests Act 1980
s.5, see *Pace Europe Ltd v Dunham* [2012] EWHC 852 (Ch), [2012] B.P.I.R. 836 (Ch D (Birmingham)), Judge Purle Q.C.

13. Slaughter of Animals (Scotland) Act 1980
applied: SSI 2012/ 321 Reg.8, Reg.10
s.9, repealed: SSI 2012/ 321 Sch.5 Part 1
s.14, repealed (in part): SSI 2012/ 321 Sch.5 Part 1
s.19, amended: SSI 2012/ 321 Sch.4 para.1
s.19, repealed (in part): SSI 2012/ 321 Sch.5 Part 1
s.19A, repealed: SSI 2012/ 321 Sch.5 Part 1
s.20, repealed: SSI 2012/ 321 Sch.5 Part 1
s.21, amended: SSI 2012/ 321 Sch.4 para.1
s.22, amended: 2012 asp 8 Sch.7 para.4

17. National Heritage Act 1980
Sch.1 para.3, amended: SI 2012/ 2404 Sch.2 para.11

21. Competition Act 1980
applied: SI 2012/ 1128 Art.4
referred to: 2012 c.19 Sch.6 para.4

23. Consular Fees Act 1980
s.1, enabling: SI 2012/ 798, SI 2012/ 1752

43. Magistrates Courts Act 1980
applied: SI 2012/ 1726 r.7.2, r.62.16, SI 2012/ 2932 Reg.14
disapplied: 2012 c.10 s.36
referred to: SI 2012/ 1726 r.52.1
Part III, applied: SI 2012/ 1726 r.76.1
Part III, referred to: SI 2012/ 1726 r.52.1
s.1, see *R. (on the application of Desouza) v Croydon Magistrates' Court* [2012] EWHC 1362 (Admin), (2012) 176 J.P. 624 (QBD (Admin)), Mitting, J.
s.1, applied: SI 2012/ 1726 r.2.4, r.18.2, r.7.1, r.37.8
s.2, applied: SI 2012/ 1726 r.37.1
s.4, applied: SI 2012/ 1726 r.10.1
s.5, applied: SI 2012/ 1726 r.3.11
s.5A, applied: SI 2012/ 1726 r.10.2, r.10.5
s.5B, applied: SI 2012/ 1726 r.33.2, r.28.4, r.10.3
s.5C, applied: SI 2012/ 1726 r.10.3
s.5D, applied: SI 2012/ 1726 r.10.3, r.10.5
s.5E, applied: SI 2012/ 1726 r.10.3
s.6, applied: SI 2012/ 1726 r.14.1, r.3.11, r.10.3, r.10.5
s.8, amended: 2012 c.10 Sch.5 para.13
s.8, applied: SI 2012/ 1726 r.10.1, r.16.1, r.10.5
s.8A, amended: 2012 c.10 Sch.5 para.14
s.8A, applied: SI 2012/ 1726 r.33.6, r.36.2, r.3.11
s.8A, referred to: SI 2012/ 1726 r.9.12
s.8B, applied: SI 2012/ 1726 r.35.3, r.34.3, r.35.4

1980–cont.

43. Magistrates Courts Act 1980–*cont.*
s.8C, amended: 2012 c.10 Sch.5 para.15
s.8C, applied: SI 2012/ 1726 r.16.1
s.9, applied: SI 2012/ 1726 r.37.3, r.37.7, r.37.10
s.10, applied: SI 2012/ 1726 r.37.1, r.37.2, r.37.10, r.37.15, r.3.11
s.11, applied: SI 2012/ 1726 r.37.10, r.37.11, r.37.15
s.12, applied: SI 2012/ 1726 r.37.8, r.37.14, r.37.15
s.12A, applied: SI 2012/ 1726 r.37.8
s.13, applied: SI 2012/ 1726 r.37.11
s.14, applied: SI 2012/ 1726 r.37.1, r.37.11
s.15, applied: SI 2012/ 1726 r.37.11
s.16, applied: SI 2012/ 1726 r.37.11
s.17A, applied: SI 2012/ 1726 r.9.1
s.17A, referred to: SI 2012/ 1726 r.9.2, r.9.8, r.9.9, r.9.10
s.17B, applied: SI 2012/ 1726 r.9.1
s.17B, referred to: SI 2012/ 1726 r.9.2
s.17C, applied: SI 2012/ 1726 r.9.1
s.17C, referred to: SI 2012/ 1726 r.9.2
s.17D, applied: SI 2012/ 1726 r.9.1
s.17E, applied: SI 2012/ 1726 r.9.1
s.17E, referred to: SI 2012/ 1726 r.9.1
s.18, applied: SI 2012/ 1726 r.3.11, r.9.1
s.18, referred to: SI 2012/ 1726 r.9.1, r.9.2, r.9.10
s.19, applied: SI 2012/ 1726 r.9.1
s.19, referred to: SI 2012/ 1726 r.9.10
s.20, applied: SI 2012/ 1726 r.5.4, r.9.1
s.20, referred to: SI 2012/ 1726 r.9.11
s.20A, applied: SI 2012/ 1726 r.9.1
s.20A, referred to: SI 2012/ 1726 r.9.5, r.9.11
s.21, applied: SI 2012/ 1726 r.9.1
s.21, referred to: SI 2012/ 1726 r.9.14
s.22, applied: SI 2012/ 1726 r.9.1, r.9.8, r.9.10
s.22, referred to: SI 2012/ 1726 r.9.10
s.22, varied: SI 2012/ 1726 r.9.10
s.23, applied: SI 2012/ 1726 r.5.4, r.9.1
s.23, referred to: SI 2012/ 1726 r.9.2
s.24, see *R. v X* [2012] EWCA Crim 1610, (2012) 176 J.P. 601 (CA (Crim Div)), Sir John Thomas (President)
s.24, applied: SI 2012/ 1726 r.9.1
s.24, referred to: SI 2012/ 1726 r.9.1
s.24A, applied: SI 2012/ 1726 r.9.1
s.24A, referred to: SI 2012/ 1726 r.9.1, r.9.2, r.9.7, r.9.10, r.9.13, r.9.14
s.24B, applied: SI 2012/ 1726 r.9.1
s.24B, referred to: SI 2012/ 1726 r.9.2
s.24C, applied: SI 2012/ 1726 r.9.1
s.24C, referred to: SI 2012/ 1726 r.9.2
s.24D, applied: SI 2012/ 1726 r.9.1
s.24D, referred to: SI 2012/ 1726 r.9.1
s.25, see *R. (on the application of W) v Leeds Crown Court* [2011] EWHC 2326 (Admin), [2012] 1 W.L.R. 2786 (DC), Sir Anthony May (President, QB)
s.25, applied: SI 2012/ 1726 r.9.1, r.9.12
s.25, referred to: SI 2012/ 1726 r.9.12
s.25, varied: SI 2012/ 1726 r.9.12
s.26, applied: SI 2012/ 1726 r.9.1
s.26, referred to: SI 2012/ 1726 r.9.2
s.27, applied: SI 2012/ 1726 r.37.11
s.27A, applied: SI 2012/ 1726 r.37.1, r.37.2
s.27A, referred to: SI 2012/ 1726 r.18.2
s.29, see *R. (on the application of W) v Leeds Crown Court* [2011] EWHC 2326 (Admin), [2012] 1 W.L.R. 2786 (DC), Sir Anthony May (President, QB)
s.29, applied: SI 2012/ 1726 r.37.2

1980–cont.

43. Magistrates Courts Act 1980–*cont.*
s.43, referred to: SI 2012/ 1726 r.19.4
s.43B, applied: SI 2012/ 1726 r.19.6
s.46, applied: SI 2012/ 1726 r.2.4
s.47, applied: SI 2012/ 1726 r.7.4
s.50, see *R. (on the application of Desouza) v Croydon Magistrates' Court* [2012] EWHC 1362 (Admin), (2012) 176 J.P. 624 (QBD (Admin)), Mitting, J.
s.51, applied: SI 2012/ 1726 r.62.16
s.54, applied: SI 2012/ 1726 r.62.16
s.55, applied: SI 2012/ 1726 r.62.16
s.58, applied: SI 2012/ 1726 r.76.1, SI 2012/ 3032 Sch.3 para.5
s.60, amended: SI 2012/ 2814 Sch.4 para.4
s.64, see *R. (on the application of Desouza) v Croydon Magistrates' Court* [2012] EWHC 1362 (Admin), (2012) 176 J.P. 624 (QBD (Admin)), Mitting, J.
s.65, amended: SI 2012/ 1770 Reg.2
s.75, applied: SI 2012/ 1726 r.76.2
s.75, referred to: SI 2012/ 1726 r.52.5
s.76, see *McNulty v Revenue and Customs Commissioners* [2012] UKUT 174 (TCC), [2012] S.T.C. 2110 (UT (Tax)), Arnold, J.; see *R. (on the application of Johnson) v Birmingham Magistrates' Court* [2012] EWHC 596 (Admin), (2012) 176 J.P. 298 (DC), Moses, L.J.
s.76, applied: SI 2012/ 1726 r.18.4, r.18.6, SI 2012/ 2814 Sch.1 para.2, Sch.2 para.3
s.76, referred to: SI 2012/ 1726 r.52.2, SI 2012/ 2814 Sch.2 para.2
s.77, applied: SI 2012/ 1726 r.4.7
s.78, referred to: SI 2012/ 1726 r.52.7
s.79, applied: SI 2012/ 1726 r.52.3
s.79, referred to: SI 2012/ 1726 r.18.6
s.80, applied: SI 2012/ 1726 r.18.4
s.82, see *R. (on the application of Johnson) v Birmingham Magistrates' Court* [2012] EWHC 596 (Admin), (2012) 176 J.P. 298 (DC), Moses, L.J.
s.82, applied: SI 2012/ 1726 r.18.4
s.82, referred to: SI 2012/ 1726 r.18.4
s.83, applied: SI 2012/ 1726 r.18.6
s.85, see *R. v Johnson (John Phillip)* [2012] EWCA Crim 580, [2012] 2 Cr. App. R. (S.) 87 (CA (Crim Div)), Elias, L.J.
s.85, referred to: SI 2012/ 1726 r.52.5
s.85A, referred to: SI 2012/ 1726 r.52.5
s.86, applied: SI 2012/ 1726 r.4.7, r.18.6
s.88, referred to: SI 2012/ 1726 r.52.3
s.92, amended: 2012 c.10 Sch.5 para.16
s.93, applied: SI 2012/ 2814 Sch.1 para.2, Sch.2 para.3, Sch.2 para.10
s.93, referred to: SI 2012/ 2814 Sch.2 para.2
s.95, amended: SI 2012/ 2814 Sch.4 para.4
s.97, applied: SI 2012/ 1726 r.28.1, r.18.2, r.62.4, r.28.3, r.62.5, r.62.16
s.97, referred to: SI 2012/ 1726 r.62.5
s.108, applied: SI 2012/ 1726 r.63.1, r.76.6
s.109, applied: SI 2012/ 1726 r.76.1, r.76.6
s.109, referred to: SI 2012/ 1726 r.63.8
s.111, applied: SI 2012/ 1726 r.64.1, r.64.2
s.114, applied: SI 2012/ 1726 r.64.3
s.119, applied: SI 2012/ 1726 r.41.5
s.119, referred to: SI 2012/ 1726 r.19.14
s.120, referred to: SI 2012/ 1726 r.19.15
s.121, applied: SI 2012/ 1726 r.37.1, r.37.2, r.62.16, r.64.3
s.121, referred to: SI 2012/ 1726 r.16.2

1980–cont.

43. Magistrates Courts Act 1980–*cont.*
s.122, see *R. (on the application of Griffin) v City of Westminster Magistrates' Court* [2011] EWHC 943 (Admin), [2012] 1 W.L.R. 270 (QBD (Admin)), Collins, J.
s.122, applied: SI 2012/ 1726 r.2.4
s.123, applied: SI 2012/ 1726 r.18.4, r.62.16
s.125, applied: SI 2012/ 1726 r.52.3, r.18.5, r.52.8
s.125, referred to: SI 2012/ 1726 r.18.6
s.125A, applied: SI 2012/ 1726 r.52.8, r.18.5
s.125B, applied: SI 2012/ 1726 r.52.8, r.18.5
s.125D, referred to: SI 2012/ 1726 r.52.8, r.18.5
s.125ZA, referred to: SI 2012/ 1726 r.52.7
s.127, see *Lamont-Perkins v RSPCA* [2012] EWHC 1002 (Admin), (2012) 176 J.P. 369 (DC), Sir John Thomas (President)
s.127, applied: SI 2012/ 1726 r.7.2, SI 2012/ 3102 Sch.1, SI 2012/ 3103 Sch.1, SI 2012/ 3104 Sch.1, SI 2012/ 3105 Sch.1, SI 2012/ 3106 Sch.1, SI 2012/ 3107 Sch.1
s.127, disapplied: SI 2012/ 1017 Reg.71, SI 2012/ 1102 Reg.7, SI 2012/ 1726 r.62.16
s.127, referred to: SI 2012/ 2541 Sch.1, SI 2012/ 2547 Sch.1, SI 2012/ 2548 Sch.1, SI 2012/ 2549 Sch.1
s.128, applied: 2012 c.10 s.91, SI 2012/ 1726 r.3.11, r.5.4, r.18.3
s.128, referred to: SI 2012/ 1726 r.19.1
s.129, applied: SI 2012/ 1726 r.3.11, r.10.5
s.130, amended: 2012 c.10 Sch.5 para.17
s.131, repealed (in part): 2012 c.10 Sch.10 para.4
s.136, applied: SI 2012/ 1726 r.18.3, r.18.6
s.142, see *R. (on the application of Williamson) v City of Westminster Magistrates' Court* [2012] EWHC 1444 (Admin), [2012] 2 Cr. App. R. 24 (DC), Gross, L.J.
s.142, referred to: SI 2012/ 1726 r.63.3
s.143, amended: 2012 c.10 s.87
s.144, amended: SI 2012/ 2398 Sch.2 para.1
s.144, applied: SI 2012/ 2018, SI 2012/ 2398 Art.3, SI 2012/ 2563
s.144, repealed (in part): SI 2012/ 2398 Sch.2 para.1
s.144, enabling: SI 2012/ 1275, SI 2012/ 2018, SI 2012/ 2563
s.145, enabling: SI 2012/ 2018, SI 2012/ 2563
s.145A, amended: 2012 c.10 Sch.5 para.18
s.148, applied: SI 2012/ 1726 r.37.1
s.150, applied: SI 2012/ 1726 r.37.1, r.32.9, r.76.1
s.152, applied: SI 2012/ 1726 r.18.3
Sch.3, applied: SI 2012/ 947 Reg.20, SI 2012/ 1726 r.2.4, SI 2012/ 2629 Reg.37
Sch.7 para.134, repealed (in part): 2012 c.10 Sch.25 Part 2

44. Education (Scotland) Act 1980
s.1, see *K v North Ayrshire Council* 2012 S.L.T. 381 (OH), Lord Tyre
s.2, enabling: SSI 2012/ 130
s.16, amended: 2012 asp 5 Sch.5 para.20
s.28A, see *M v City of Edinburgh Council* 2012 S.L.T. (Sh Ct) 38 (Sh Ct (Lothian) (Edinburgh)), Sheriff F R Crowe
s.28A, applied: SSI 2012/ 130 Sch.2 para.1
s.28A, referred to: SSI 2012/ 130 Reg.16, Sch.1 para.13
s.28B, applied: SSI 2012/ 130 Reg.4, Reg.8, Reg.13, Reg.16, Reg.17, Sch.1 para.1, Sch.1 para.13
s.28B, referred to: SSI 2012/ 130 Reg.16, Reg.17
s.28B, enabling: SSI 2012/ 130
s.28C, referred to: SSI 2012/ 130 Sch.1 para.13
s.28D, referred to: SSI 2012/ 130 Sch.1 para.13
s.28E, referred to: SSI 2012/ 130 Sch.1 para.13

1980–cont.

44. Education (Scotland) Act 1980–*cont.*
s.28F, referred to: SSI 2012/ 130 Sch.1 para.13
s.28G, referred to: SSI 2012/ 130 Sch.1 para.13
s.28I, enabling: SSI 2012/ 129
s.49, applied: SI 2012/ 2885 Sch.5 para.18, Sch.5 para.19, SI 2012/ 2886 Sch.1, SSI 2012/ 303 Sch.4 para.15, Sch.4 para.22, Sch.4 para.23, Sch.5 para.55, SSI 2012/ 319 Sch.3 para.17, Sch.3 para.18
s.49, enabling: SSI 2012/ 72
s.50, referred to: SSI 2012/ 130 Sch.1 para.1
s.51, see *K v North Ayrshire Council* 2012 S.L.T. 381 (OH), Lord Tyre
s.51, referred to: SSI 2012/ 130 Sch.1 para.1
s.53, amended: 2012 c.5 Sch.14 Part 1
s.53, repealed (in part): 2012 c.5 Sch.14 Part 1
s.72, amended: SSI 2012/ 102 Art.2
s.73, applied: SI 2012/ 2885 Sch.5 para.18, Sch.5 para.19, SI 2012/ 2886 Sch.1, SI 2012/ 3145 Sch.1, SSI 2012/ 303 Reg.60, Sch.4 para.15, Sch.4 para.22, Sch.4 para.23, Sch.5 para.55, SSI 2012/ 319 Sch.3 para.17, Sch.3 para.18
s.73, referred to: SI 2012/ 2886 Sch.1
s.73, enabling: SI 2012/ 836, SSI 2012/ 22, SSI 2012/ 72
s.73B, enabling: SI 2012/ 836, SSI 2012/ 22
s.73ZA, applied: SI 2012/ 2886 Sch.1, SSI 2012/ 303 Sch.4 para.15, Sch.5 para.55
s.74, enabling: SSI 2012/ 22, SSI 2012/ 72
s.135, applied: SSI 2012/ 162 Sch.1, SSI 2012/ 360 Sch.1 para.3

45. Water (Scotland) Act 1980
s.9A, amended: 2012 asp 8 Sch.7 para.51
s.58, amended: 2012 asp 5 Sch.5 para.21
s.68, amended: 2012 asp 5 Sch.5 para.21
s.109, amended: 2012 asp 8 Sch.8 Part 2
s.109, repealed (in part): 2012 asp 5 Sch.5 para.21
Sch.4 Part I para.1, amended: 2012 asp 8 Sch.8 Part 2
Sch.4 Part V para.19, amended: 2012 asp 8 Sch.7 para.51
Sch.4 Part V para.20, amended: 2012 asp 8 Sch.7 para.51
Sch.4 Part V para.21, amended: 2012 asp 8 Sch.7 para.51
Sch.4 Part V para.21A, amended: 2012 asp 8 Sch.7 para.51

46. Solicitors (Scotland) Act 1980
applied: SI 2012/ 1128 Art.4
Part II, applied: 2012 asp 8 Sch.3 para.1
s.32, see *Homebank Financial Services Ltd v Hain* 2012 S.L.T. (Sh Ct) 196 (Sh Ct (Tayside) (Dundee)), Sheriff G A Way
s.41, applied: SI 2012/ 2885 Sch.1 para.23, SI 2012/ 2886 Sch.1, SI 2012/ 3144 Sch.1 para.17, SI 2012/ 3145 Sch.1, SSI 2012/ 303 Reg.41, Reg.48, SSI 2012/ 319 Reg.39
s.60A, amended: SSI 2012/ 212 Reg.2

48. Finance Act 1980
s.97, repealed: 2012 c.14 Sch.39 para.3

55. Law Reform (Miscellaneous Provisions) (Scotland) Act 1980
Sch.1 Part I, amended: 2012 asp 8 Sch.7 para.5
Sch.1 Part III, varied: 2012 c.11 s.12

58. Limitation Act 1980
see *B v Ministry of Defence* [2012] UKSC 9, [2012] 2 W.L.R. 643 (SC), Lord Phillips, L.C.J.; see *Page v Hewetts Solicitors* [2012] EWCA Civ 805, [2012] C.P. Rep. 40 (CA (Civ Div)), Laws, L.J.

1980–cont.

58. Limitation Act 1980–*cont.*

s.2, see *Arrowhead Capital Finance Ltd (In Liquidation) v KPMG LLP* [2012] EWHC 1801 (Comm), [2012] S.T.C. 2503 (QBD (Comm)), Stephen Males, Q.C.; see *Green v Eadie* [2012] Ch. 363 (Ch D), Mark Cawson Q.C.

s.8, see *Green v Eadie* [2012] Ch. 363 (Ch D), Mark Cawson Q.C.

s.9, see *Bhandal v Revenue and Customs Commissioners* [2011] EWHC 3018 (Admin), [2012] Lloyd's Rep. F.C. 127 (QBD (Admin)), Hickinbottom, J.; see *Green v Eadie* [2012] Ch. 363 (Ch D), Mark Cawson Q.C.

s.11, see *B v Ministry of Defence* [2012] UKSC 9, [2012] 2 W.L.R. 643 (SC), Lord Phillips, L.C.J.

s.14, see *B v Ministry of Defence* [2012] UKSC 9, [2012] 2 W.L.R. 643 (SC), Lord Phillips, L.C.J.; see *Boycott v Perrins Guy Williams* [2011] EWHC 2969 (Ch), [2012] P.N.L.R. 25 (Ch D), Vos, J.

s.14A, see *Boycott v Perrins Guy Williams* [2011] EWHC 2969 (Ch), [2012] P.N.L.R. 25 (Ch D), Vos, J.

s.21, see *Seaton v Seddon* [2012] EWHC 735 (Ch), [2012] 1 W.L.R. 3636 (Ch D), Roth, J.; see *Williams v Central Bank of Nigeria* [2012] EWCA Civ 415, [2012] 3 W.L.R. 1501 (CA (Civ Div)), Sir Andrew Morritt (Chancellor)

s.28, see *Seaton v Seddon* [2012] EWHC 735 (Ch), [2012] 1 W.L.R. 3636 (Ch D), Roth, J.

s.32, see *Alfa Laval Tumba AB v Separator Spares International Ltd* [2012] EWHC 1155 (Ch), [2012] I.L.Pr. 40 (Ch D), Briggs, J.; see *Mortgage Express v Abensons Solicitors* [2012] EWHC 1000 (Ch), [2012] 2 E.G.L.R. 83 (Ch D), Judge David Cooke; see *Seaton v Seddon* [2012] EWHC 735 (Ch), [2012] 1 W.L.R. 3636 (Ch D), Roth, J.; see *Test Claimants in the FII Group Litigation v Revenue and Customs Commissioners* [2012] UKSC 19, [2012] 2 A.C. 337 (SC), Lord Hope

s.33, see *B v Ministry of Defence* [2012] UKSC 9, [2012] 2 W.L.R. 643 (SC), Lord Phillips, L.C.J.; see *Bahous v Pizza Express Restaurant Ltd* [2012] Eq. L.R. 4 (EAT), Judge Peter Clark

s.38, see *Seaton v Seddon* [2012] EWHC 735 (Ch), [2012] 1 W.L.R. 3636 (Ch D), Roth, J.

s.38, amended: 2012 c.5 s.108

62. Criminal Justice (Scotland) Act 1980

s.81, amended: 2012 asp 8 Sch.8 Part 1

65. Local Government, Planning and Land Act 1980

Part X, applied: SI 2012/1659 Art.3

s.2, repealed (in part): 2012 asp 8 Sch.8 Part 2

s.149, enabling: SI 2012/535, SI 2012/2167

s.165B, applied: SI 2012/534, SI 2012/872, SI 2012/3084

s.165B, enabling: SI 2012/534, SI 2012/872, SI 2012/3084

s.166, applied: SI 2012/995

s.166, enabling: SI 2012/995

s.185, amended: SI 2012/1659 Sch.3 para.5

Sch.16 para.18, amended: SI 2012/1659 Sch.3 para.5

Sch.26 para.6, amended: SI 2012/2404 Sch.2 para.12

Sch.29 Part I, referred to: SI 2012/2167 Art.4

Sch.29 Part II, referred to: SI 2012/2167 Art.7

66. Highways Act 1980

see *Kind v Northumberland County Council* [2012] EWHC 603 (Admin), [2012] R.T.R. 30 (DC), Moore-Bick, L.J.

1980–cont.

66. Highways Act 1980–*cont.*

applied: SI 2012/416 Sch.1 para.7, SI 2012/2541 Sch.1, SI 2012/2547 Sch.1, SI 2012/2548 Sch.1, SI 2012/2549 Sch.1, SI 2012/2679 Sch.13 para.3

referred to: SI 2012/1282 Sch.1, SI 2012/1286 Sch.1, SI 2012/1289 Sch.1, SI 2012/1294 Sch.1

Part II, applied: SI 2012/801 Art.19

Part III, applied: SI 2012/801 Art.19

s.1, applied: SI 2012/767 Reg.4

s.10, enabling: SI 2012/48, SI 2012/157, SI 2012/839, SI 2012/1218, SI 2012/1219, SI 2012/1384, SI 2012/2092, SI 2012/2856

s.12, enabling: SI 2012/48, SI 2012/157

s.16, applied: SI 2012/463 Sch.1

s.16, enabling: SI 2012/463, SI 2012/1385

s.17, applied: SI 2012/463 Sch.1

s.17, enabling: SI 2012/463, SI 2012/1385

s.19, enabling: SI 2012/1385

s.28, applied: SI 2012/1914 Art.19

s.28, referred to: SI 2012/1914 Art.19

s.28, varied: SI 2012/1914 Art.19, SI 2012/2679 Art.16

s.31, see *Kotegaonkar v Secretary of State for the Environment, Food and Rural Affairs* [2012] EWHC 1976 (Admin), [2012] A.C.D. 105 (QBD (Admin)), Hickinbottom, J.

s.36, see *Fortune v Wiltshire Council* [2012] EWCA Civ 334, [2012] 3 All E.R. 797 (CA (Civ Div)), Arden, L.J.

s.41, see *AC v Devon CC* [2012] EWHC 796 (QB), [2012] R.T.R. 32 (QBD), Slade, J.

s.41, enabling: SI 2012/839, SI 2012/1219, SI 2012/1384

s.58, see *AC v Devon CC* [2012] EWHC 796 (QB), [2012] R.T.R. 32 (QBD), Slade, J.

s.64, applied: SI 2012/2635 Art.14

s.66, see *Cusack v Harrow LBC* [2011] EWCA Civ 1514, [2012] P.T.S.R. 970 (CA (Civ Div)), Ward, L.J.

s.80, see *Cusack v Harrow LBC* [2011] EWCA Civ 1514, [2012] P.T.S.R. 970 (CA (Civ Div)), Ward, L.J.

s.106, applied: SI 2012/2706 Sch.1, SI 2012/2710 Sch.1

s.106, enabling: SI 2012/870, SI 2012/1219, SI 2012/1384, SI 2012/2706, SI 2012/2710

s.111, amended: SI 2012/1659 Sch.3 para.6

s.116, see *Kind v Northumberland County Council* [2012] EWHC 603 (Admin), [2012] R.T.R. 30 (DC), Moore-Bick, L.J.

s.119, see *Kind v Northumberland County Council* [2012] EWHC 603 (Admin), [2012] R.T.R. 30 (DC), Moore-Bick, L.J.

s.130, see *Ali v Bradford MDC* [2010] EWCA Civ 1282, [2012] 1 W.L.R. 161 (CA (Civ Div)), Longmore, L.J.; see *City of London Corp v Samede* [2012] EWHC 34 (QB), Times, January 27, 2012 (QBD), Lindblom, J.; see *Kind v Northumberland County Council* [2012] EWHC 603 (Admin), [2012] R.T.R. 30 (DC), Moore-Bick, L.J.

s.130A, see *Kind v Northumberland County Council* [2012] EWHC 603 (Admin), [2012] R.T.R. 30 (DC), Moore-Bick, L.J.

s.130B, see *Kind v Northumberland County Council* [2012] EWHC 603 (Admin), [2012] R.T.R. 30 (DC), Moore-Bick, L.J.

s.143, see *City of London Corp v Samede* [2012] EWHC 34 (QB), Times, January 27, 2012 (QBD), Lindblom, J.

1980–cont.

66. Highways Act 1980–*cont.*
s.147, see *Kind v Northumberland County Council* [2012] EWHC 603 (Admin), [2012] R.T.R. 30 (DC), Moore-Bick, L.J.
s.150, see *Ali v Bradford MDC* [2010] EWCA Civ 1282, [2012] 1 W.L.R. 161 (CA (Civ Div)), Longmore, L.J.
s.169, amended: SI 2012/1659 Sch.3 para.6
s.171, applied: SI 2012/2541 Sch.1, SI 2012/2547 Sch.1, SI 2012/2548 Sch.1, SI 2012/2549 Sch.1
s.171, referred to: SI 2012/2541 Sch.1, SI 2012/2547 Sch.1, SI 2012/2548 Sch.1, SI 2012/2549 Sch.1
s.180, applied: SI 2012/1282 Sch.1, SI 2012/1284 Sch.1, SI 2012/1286 Sch.1, SI 2012/1289 Sch.1, SI 2012/1294 Sch.1, SI 2012/1295 Sch.1
s.219, amended: SI 2012/1659 Sch.3 para.6
s.262, amended: SI 2012/961 Sch.2 para.3
s.278, applied: SI 2012/416 Sch.1 para.6, Sch.1 para.9
s.307, varied: SI 2012/1914 Art.19, SI 2012/2679 Art.16
s.329, amended: SI 2012/1659 Sch.3 para.6
Sch.1 Part I para.8, applied: SI 2012/605 Reg.14
Sch.1 Part II para.15, applied: SI 2012/605 Reg.14
Sch.2 para.1, applied: SI 2012/870 Art.4
Sch.4, applied: SI 2012/463 Sch.1
Sch.4, referred to: SI 2012/1385 Art.3
Sch.11 para.4, amended: SI 2012/1659 Sch.3 para.6

1981

7. House of Commons Members Fund and Parliamentary Pensions Act 1981
s.2, enabling: SI 2012/1866

14. Public Passenger Vehicles Act 1981
s.19, amended: SI 2012/2404 Sch.2 para.13
s.52, enabling: SI 2012/306
s.57, amended: SI 2012/2404 Sch.2 para.13
s.60, enabling: SI 2012/306, SSI 2012/32
s.61, applied: SI 2012/306, SSI 2012/32

20. Judicial Pensions Act 1981
s.33A, amended: 2012 c.21 Sch.18 para.42
s.33ZA, applied: SI 2012/516 Reg.3
s.33ZA, enabling: SI 2012/516

22. Animal Health Act 1981
applied: SSI 2012/78 Art.23, SSI 2012/178 Art.3, Art.36, SSI 2012/199 Art.10, Art.22
s.1, enabling: SI 2012/1379, SI 2012/1380, SI 2012/1387, SI 2012/1391, SI 2012/2897, SSI 2012/78, SSI 2012/178, SSI 2012/199
s.7, enabling: SSI 2012/178, SSI 2012/199
s.8, enabling: SI 2012/1391, SI 2012/2897, SSI 2012/78, SSI 2012/178, SSI 2012/199
s.11, enabling: SI 2012/2978, SSI 2012/263
s.15, enabling: SSI 2012/178, SSI 2012/199
s.17, enabling: SSI 2012/178, SSI 2012/199
s.21, see *R. (on the application of Badger Trust) v Secretary of State for the Environment, Food and Rural Affairs* [2012] EWCA Civ 1286, Times, December 14, 2012 (CA (Civ Div)), Laws, L.J.
s.21, applied: SI 2012/1387
s.21, enabling: SI 2012/1387
s.23, enabling: SSI 2012/178, SSI 2012/199
s.25, enabling: SI 2012/1391, SSI 2012/178, SSI 2012/199
s.28, enabling: SSI 2012/178, SSI 2012/199
s.32, applied: SI 2012/1379 Art.3, Art.4, Sch.1 para.4, Sch.1 para.5, SSI 2012/199 Art.21

1981–cont.

22. Animal Health Act 1981–*cont.*
s.32, enabling: SI 2012/1379, SI 2012/1380, SSI 2012/199
s.34, enabling: SI 2012/1380
s.35, enabling: SSI 2012/178, SSI 2012/199
s.72, enabling: SSI 2012/184, SSI 2012/198, SSI 2012/199
s.83, enabling: SSI 2012/78, SSI 2012/178, SSI 2012/199
s.86, enabling: SI 2012/1387
s.87, enabling: SSI 2012/178, SSI 2012/199
s.88, referred to: SSI 2012/78 Art.2
s.88, enabling: SSI 2012/78, SSI 2012/178, SSI 2012/199

28. Licensing (Alcohol Education and Research) Act 1981
repealed: 2012 c.7 s.278

29. Fisheries Act 1981
s.15, enabling: SI 2012/1375, SSI 2012/264
s.17, applied: SSI 2012/264 Art.10
s.30, applied: SI 2012/2747 Art.3
Sch.1 para.5, amended: SI 2012/2404 Sch.2 para.14

35. Finance Act 1981
s.108, repealed: 2012 c.14 Sch.39 para.3
Sch.8 Part II para.16, repealed: 2012 c.14 s.187

37. Zoo Licensing Act 1981
s.3, amended: 2012 asp 8 Sch.7 para.52

49. Contempt of Court Act 1981
s.2, see *Attorney General v Associated Newspapers Ltd* [2012] EWHC 2029 (Admin), [2012] A.C.D. 98 (QBD (Admin)), Sir John Thomas (President); see *Attorney General v MGN Ltd* [2011] EWHC 2074 (Admin), [2012] 1 W.L.R. 2408 (QBD (Admin)), Lord Judge, L.C.J.
s.2, applied: SI 2012/1726 r.16.1
s.4, see *Mobile Phone Voicemail Interception Litigation, Re* [2012] EWHC 397 (Ch), [2012] 1 W.L.R. 2545 (Ch D), Vos, J.
s.4, applied: SI 2012/1726 r.69.1, r.37.2, r.16.1
s.4, referred to: SI 2012/1320 Art.6
s.8, referred to: SI 2012/1726 r.62.5
s.9, applied: SI 2012/1726 r.16.1
s.9, referred to: SI 2012/1726 r.62.5, r.16.10
s.11, see *CVB v MGN Ltd* [2012] EWHC 1148 (QB), [2012] E.M.L.R. 29 (QBD), Tugendhat, J.
s.11, applied: SI 2012/1726 r.37.2, r.69.1, r.16.1
s.12, applied: SI 2012/1726 r.62.4, r.16.1, r.62.5, r.63.1
s.12, referred to: SI 2012/1726 r.62.5
s.14, see *JSC BTA Bank v Ablyazov* [2011] EWCA Civ 1386, [2012] 1 W.L.R. 1988 (CA (Civ Div)), Sir Andrew Morritt (Chancellor); see *W (A Child) (Abduction: Committal), Re* [2011] EWCA Civ 1196, [2012] 1 W.L.R. 1036 (CA (Civ Div)), Hughes, L.J.
s.14, applied: SI 2012/1726 r.62.5, r.62.9
s.14, referred to: SI 2012/1726 r.62.12
Sch.3, referred to: SI 2012/1726 r.62.16

54. Senior Courts Act 1981
s.8, applied: SI 2012/1726 r.6.1, r.63.10
s.15, see *Ryanair Holdings Plc v Office of Fair Trading* [2011] EWCA Civ 1579, [2012] Bus. L.R. 1903 (CA (Civ Div)), Lloyd, L.J.
s.15, applied: SI 2012/1726 r.62.12, r.16.1
s.15, referred to: SI 2012/1726 r.62.3, r.62.4, r.62.5
s.28, amended: 2012 c.10 Sch.5 para.20
s.28, applied: SI 2012/1726 r.64.1
s.28A, applied: SI 2012/1726 r.64.1
s.29, amended: 2012 c.10 Sch.5 para.21

1981– cont.

54. Senior Courts Act 1981–*cont.*

s.31, see *Jooste v General Medical Council* [2012] Eq.
L.R. 1048 (EAT), Judge McMullen Q.C.; see *R. (on the application of 007 Stratford Taxis Ltd) v Stratford on Avon DC* [2011] EWCA Civ 160, [2012] R.T.R. 5 (CA (Civ Div)), Sir Anthony May (President, QB); see *R. (on the application of Berky) v Newport City Council* [2012] EWCA Civ 378, [2012] 2 C.M.L.R. 44 (CA (Civ Div)), Carnwath, L.J.; see *R. (on the application of Garner) v Elmbridge BC* [2010] EWCA Civ 1006, [2012] P.T.S.R. 250 (CA (Civ Div)), Lloyd, L.J.; see *R. (on the application of U & Partners (East Anglia) Ltd) v Broads Authority* [2011] EWHC 1824 (Admin), [2012] Env. L.R. 5 (QBD (Admin)), Collins, J.

s.31A, applied: 2012 c.10 Sch.1 para.19

s.37, see *AES Ust-Kamenogorsk Hydropower Plant LLP v Ust-Kamenogorsk Hydropower Plant JSC* [2011] EWCA Civ 647, [2012] 1 W.L.R. 920 (CA (Civ Div)), Rix, L.J.; see *Blight v Brewster* [2012] EWHC 165 (Ch), [2012] 1 W.L.R. 2841 (Ch D), Gabriel Moss Q.C.; see *Coventry City Council v O* [2011] EWCA Civ 729, [2012] Fam. 210 (CA (Civ Div)), Lord Neuberger of Abbotsbury MR; see *Excalibur Ventures LLC v Texas Keystone Inc* [2011] EWHC 1624 (Comm), [2012] 1 All E.R. (Comm) 933 (QBD (Comm)), Gloster, J.; see *G v A (Financial Remedy: Enforcement) (No.2)* [2011] EWHC 968 (Fam), [2012] 1 F.L.R. 402 (Fam Div), Peter Jackson, J.; see *JSC BTA Bank v Ablyazov* [2012] EWHC 2698 (Comm), [2012] I.L.Pr. 53 (QBD (Comm)), Teare, J.; see *JSC BTA Bank v Solodchenko* [2011] EWHC 2163 (Ch), [2012] 3 W.L.R. 559 (Ch D), Henderson, J.; see *M (A Patient) (Court of Protection: Reporting Restrictions), Re* [2011] EWHC 1197 (Fam), [2012] 1 W.L.R. 287 (CP), Baker, J.; see *Nomihold Securities Inc v Mobile Telesystems Finance SA* [2012] EWHC 130 (Comm), [2012] Bus. L.R. 1289 (QBD (Comm)), Andrew Smith, J.

s.42, applied: SI 2012/ 3098 Reg.42

s.45, applied: SI 2012/ 1726 r.6.13, r.6.22, r.62.12, r.16.1, r.59.6

s.45, referred to: SI 2012/ 1726 r.62.3, r.62.4, r.62.5, r.62.9

s.48, referred to: SI 2012/ 1726 r.63.1

s.50, see *Jones v Ruth* [2011] EWCA Civ 804, [2012] 1 W.L.R. 1495 (CA (Civ Div)), Arden, L.J.

s.51, see *Fisher Meredith LLP v JH* [2012] EWHC 408 (Fam), [2012] 2 F.L.R. 536 (Fam Div), Mostyn, J.; see *Germany v Flatman* [2011] EWHC 2945 (QB), [2012] 2 Costs L.R. 271 (QBD), Eady, J.; see *Hunt v Aziz* [2011] EWCA Civ 1239, [2012] 1 W.L.R. 317 (CA (Civ Div)), Lord Neuberger (M.R.); see *IBM United Kingdom Pensions Trust Ltd v Metcalfe* [2012] EWHC 125 (Ch), [2012] 3 Costs L.O. 420 (Ch D), Warren, J.; see *Sharma v Hunters* [2011] EWHC 2546 (Fam), [2012] 2 Costs L.R. 237 (CP), Henderson, J.

s.52, applied: SI 2012/ 1726 r.76.1, r.61.19, r.76.6

s.52, referred to: SI 2012/ 1726 r.63.8

s.52, enabling: SI 2012/ 1726

s.53, applied: SI 2012/ 1726 r.65.1

s.55, applied: SI 2012/ 1726 r.65.1

s.70, applied: SI 2012/ 1726 r.76.13

1981– cont.

54. Senior Courts Act 1981–*cont.*

s.72, see *Gray v News Group Newspapers Ltd* [2012] EWCA Civ 48, [2012] 2 W.L.R. 848 (CA (Civ Div)), Lord Judge, L.C.J.; see *Gray v News Group Newspapers Ltd* [2012] UKSC 28, [2012] 3 W.L.R. 312 (SC), Lord Hope, J.S.C. (Deputy President)

s.73, referred to: SI 2012/ 1726 r.63.10

s.73, enabling: SI 2012/ 1726

s.74, applied: SI 2012/ 1726 r.6.26

s.74, referred to: SI 2012/ 1726 r.63.10

s.74, enabling: SI 2012/ 1726

s.77, applied: SI 2012/ 1726 r.39.1

s.78, referred to: SI 2012/ 1726 r.18.2

s.79, applied: SI 2012/ 1726 r.18.2

s.79, referred to: SI 2012/ 1726 r.63.1

s.80, applied: SI 2012/ 1726 r.18.2

s.81, applied: SI 2012/ 1726 r.19.8, r.68.3, r.68.4, r.68.8, r.18.2

s.81, referred to: SI 2012/ 1726 r.19.1

s.84, amended: SI 2012/ 2398 Sch.1 para.2

s.84, applied: SI 2012/ 2398 Art.2

s.86, applied: SI 2012/ 2398 Art.2

s.86, repealed: SI 2012/ 2398 Sch.1 para.3

s.86A, amended: SI 2012/ 2398 Sch.1 para.4

s.86B, amended: SI 2012/ 2398 Sch.1 para.5

s.87, applied: SI 2012/ 1726 r.65.8

s.87, enabling: SI 2012/ 1726

s.99, enabling: SI 2012/ 643, SI 2012/ 1954

s.116, see *Ibuna v Arroyo* [2012] EWHC 428 (Ch), [2012] W.T.L.R. 827 (Ch D), Peter Smith, J.; see *Khan v Crossland* [2012] W.T.L.R. 841 (Ch D), Judge Behrens

s.151, amended: SI 2012/ 2398 Sch.1 para.6

Sch.4 para.3, see *Director of the Serious Fraud Office v B* [2012] EWCA Crim 901, [2012] 1 W.L.R. 3188 (CA (Crim Div)), Gross, L.J.

54. Senior Courts Act (formerly known as the Supreme Court Act) 1981

s.51, see *Systemcare (UK) Ltd v Services Design Technology Ltd* [2011] EWCA Civ 546, [2012] 1 B.C.L.C. 14 (CA (Civ Div)), Ward, L.J.

55. Armed Forces Act 1981

Sch.4 para.2, repealed (in part): 2012 c.10 Sch.25 Part 2

56. Transport Act 1981

Sch.2 para.3, amended: SI 2012/ 2404 Sch.2 para.15

Sch.3 para.31, amended: SI 2012/ 1659 Sch.3 para.7

59. Matrimonial Homes (Family Protection) (Scotland) Act 1981

see *Duncan v Duncan* 2012 S.L.T. (Sh Ct) 47 (Sh Ct (Tayside) (Falkirk)), Sheriff T McCartney

s.13, amended: 2012 asp 5 Sch.5 para.22

s.19, see *Duncan v Duncan* 2012 S.L.T. (Sh Ct) 47 (Sh Ct (Tayside) (Falkirk)), Sheriff T McCartney

61. British Nationality Act 1981

see *R. (on the application of GI (Sudan)) v Secretary of State for the Home Department* [2011] EWHC 1875 (Admin), [2012] 1 W.L.R. 2568 (QBD (Admin)), Mitting, J.

applied: SI 2012/ 798 Sch.1 Part 1

s.12, applied: SI 2012/ 813 Sch.2 para.1

s.24, applied: SI 2012/ 813 Sch.2 para.1

s.29, applied: SI 2012/ 813 Sch.2 para.1

s.34, applied: SI 2012/ 813 Sch.2 para.1

s.40, see *Arusha (Deprivation of Citizenship: Delay: Kosovo)* [2012] UKUT 80 (IAC), [2012] Imm. A.R. 645 (UT (IAC)), Judge Latter; see *R. (on the application of GI (Sudan)) v*

1981– *cont.*

61. British Nationality Act 1981– *cont.*
s.40– *cont.*
  Secretary of State for the Home Department
  [2012] EWCA Civ 867, [2012] 4 All E.R. 987
  (CA (Civ Div)), Laws, L.J.
s.40A, see *R. (on the application of GI (Sudan)) v*
  Secretary of State for the Home Department
  [2011] EWHC 1875 (Admin), [2012] 1 W.L.R.
  2568 (QBD (Admin)), Mitting, J.; see *R. (on*
  the application of GI (Sudan)) v Secretary of
  State for the Home Department [2012] EWCA
  Civ 867, [2012] 4 All E.R. 987 (CA (Civ Div)),
  Laws, L.J.
s.40A, applied: 2012 c.10 Sch.1 para.12
s.41, enabling: SI 2012/1588
s.42, applied: SI 2012/813 Sch.2 para.3
s.50, applied: SI 2012/813 Sch.2 para.1, Sch.3 para.2
Sch.3, applied: SI 2012/813 Sch.3 para.2

63. Betting and Gaming Duties Act 1981
applied: SI 2012/1900 Reg.4
s.2, repealed (in part): 2012 c.14 Sch.24 para.43
s.5E, added: 2012 c.14 Sch.25 para.2
s.8ZA, added: 2012 c.14 Sch.25 para.3
s.10A, added: 2012 c.14 Sch.25 para.4
s.21, applied: 2012 c.14 Sch.24 para.59, Sch.24
  para.60, Sch.24 para.62
s.21, repealed: 2012 c.14 Sch.24 para.53
s.21, varied: 2012 c.14 Sch.24 para.62
s.21A, repealed: 2012 c.14 Sch.24 para.53
s.22, repealed: 2012 c.14 Sch.24 para.53
s.23, amended: 2012 c.14 s.192
s.23, applied: 2012 c.14 Sch.24 para.59, Sch.24
  para.60
s.23, repealed: 2012 c.14 Sch.24 para.53
s.24, repealed: 2012 c.14 Sch.24 para.53
s.24A, repealed: 2012 c.14 Sch.24 para.53
s.25, repealed: 2012 c.14 Sch.24 para.53
s.25A, repealed: 2012 c.14 Sch.24 para.53
s.26, repealed: 2012 c.14 Sch.24 para.53
s.26H, amended: 2012 c.14 Sch.24 para.44
s.26H, repealed (in part): 2012 c.14 Sch.24 para.53
s.26IA, added: 2012 c.14 Sch.25 para.5
s.26IB, added: 2012 c.14 Sch.25 para.5
s.26IC, added: 2012 c.14 Sch.25 para.5
s.26IC, enabling: SI 2012/1900
s.26N, repealed (in part): 2012 c.14 Sch.24 para.53
s.27, amended: 2012 c.14 Sch.24 para.54
s.27, applied: 2012 c.14 Sch.24 para.37
s.31, amended: 2012 c.14 Sch.24 para.54
s.31, applied: 2012 c.14 Sch.24 para.38
s.33, amended: 2012 c.14 Sch.24 para.54, Sch.25
  para.6
Sch.A1, applied: SI 2012/1900 Reg.3
Sch.A1 para.1, added: 2012 c.14 Sch.25 para.7
Sch.A1 para.2, added: 2012 c.14 Sch.25 para.7
Sch.A1 para.3, added: 2012 c.14 Sch.25 para.7
Sch.A1 para.4, added: 2012 c.14 Sch.25 para.7
Sch.A1 para.5, added: 2012 c.14 Sch.25 para.7
Sch.A1 para.6, added: 2012 c.14 Sch.25 para.7
Sch.A1 para.7, added: 2012 c.14 Sch.25 para.7
Sch.A1 para.7, amended: 2012 c.14 Sch.24 para.45
Sch.A1 para.8, added: 2012 c.14 Sch.25 para.7
Sch.1 para.2, amended: 2012 c.14 Sch.25 para.8
Sch.1 para.2, enabling: SI 2012/1900
Sch.1 para.2A, amended: 2012 c.14 Sch.25 para.8
Sch.1 para.2A, enabling: SI 2012/1900
Sch.4, applied: 2012 c.14 Sch.24 para.60, Sch.24
  para.62

1981– *cont.*

63. Betting and Gaming Duties Act 1981– *cont.*
Sch.4A, applied: 2012 c.14 Sch.24 para.60, Sch.24
  para.62
Sch.4B, applied: SI 2012/1900 Reg.3
Sch.4 Part I para.1, repealed: 2012 c.14 Sch.24
  para.53
Sch.4 Part I para.2, repealed: 2012 c.14 Sch.24
  para.53
Sch.4 Part I para.3, repealed: 2012 c.14 Sch.24
  para.53
Sch.4 Part I para.4, repealed: 2012 c.14 Sch.24
  para.53
Sch.4 Part II para.5, repealed: 2012 c.14 Sch.24
  para.53
Sch.4 Part II para.6, repealed: 2012 c.14 Sch.24
  para.53
Sch.4 Part II para.7, repealed: 2012 c.14 Sch.24
  para.53
Sch.4 Part II para.7A, applied: 2012 c.14 Sch.24
  para.59
Sch.4 Part II para.7A, repealed: 2012 c.14 Sch.24
  para.53
Sch.4 Part II para.8, repealed: 2012 c.14 Sch.24
  para.53
Sch.4 Part II para.9, repealed: 2012 c.14 Sch.24
  para.53
Sch.4 Part II para.10, repealed: 2012 c.14 Sch.24
  para.53
Sch.4 Part II para.11, repealed: 2012 c.14 Sch.24
  para.53
Sch.4 Part II para.11A, repealed: 2012 c.14 Sch.24
  para.53
Sch.4 Part II para.12, repealed: 2012 c.14 Sch.24
  para.53
Sch.4 Part II para.13, repealed: 2012 c.14 Sch.24
  para.53
Sch.4 Part II para.14, repealed: 2012 c.14 Sch.24
  para.53
Sch.4 Part II para.15, repealed: 2012 c.14 Sch.24
  para.53
Sch.4 Part II para.16, repealed: 2012 c.14 Sch.24
  para.53
Sch.4 Part II para.17, repealed: 2012 c.14 Sch.24
  para.53
Sch.4 Part II para.18, repealed: 2012 c.14 Sch.24
  para.53
Sch.4A para.1, repealed: 2012 c.14 Sch.24 para.53
Sch.4A para.2, repealed: 2012 c.14 Sch.24 para.53
Sch.4A para.3, repealed: 2012 c.14 Sch.24 para.53
Sch.4A para.4, repealed: 2012 c.14 Sch.24 para.53
Sch.4A para.4, varied: 2012 c.14 Sch.24 para.62
Sch.4A para.5, repealed: 2012 c.14 Sch.24 para.53
Sch.4A para.6, repealed: 2012 c.14 Sch.24 para.53
Sch.4A para.7, repealed: 2012 c.14 Sch.24 para.53
Sch.4A para.8, repealed: 2012 c.14 Sch.24 para.53
Sch.4B para.1, added: 2012 c.14 Sch.25 para.9
Sch.4B para.2, added: 2012 c.14 Sch.25 para.9
Sch.4B para.3, added: 2012 c.14 Sch.25 para.9
Sch.4B para.4, added: 2012 c.14 Sch.25 para.9
Sch.4B para.5, added: 2012 c.14 Sch.25 para.9
Sch.4B para.6, added: 2012 c.14 Sch.25 para.9
Sch.4B para.7, added: 2012 c.14 Sch.25 para.9
Sch.4B para.7, amended: 2012 c.14 Sch.24 para.46
Sch.4B para.8, added: 2012 c.14 Sch.25 para.9

64. New Towns Act 1981
Sch.3 para.5, amended: SI 2012/2404 Sch.2 para.16

1981– cont.

66. Compulsory Purchase (Vesting Declarations) Act 1981
applied: SI 2012/ 1867 Art.23, SI 2012/ 1924 Art.5, SI 2012/ 2284 Art.20
varied: SI 2012/ 2284 Art.20, SI 2012/ 2635 Art.26, SI 2012/ 2679 Art.24
s.3, varied: SI 2012/ 1867 Art.23, SI 2012/ 1924 Art.5, SI 2012/ 2284 Art.20, SI 2012/ 2635 Art.26, SI 2012/ 2679 Art.24
s.4, applied: SI 2012/ 1867 Art.33, SI 2012/ 1924 Art.10, SI 2012/ 2284 Art.17, Art.23, SI 2012/ 2635 Art.23, Art.30, SI 2012/ 2679 Art.29, Art.36
s.5, varied: SI 2012/ 1867 Art.23, SI 2012/ 1924 Art.5, SI 2012/ 2284 Art.20, SI 2012/ 2635 Art.26, SI 2012/ 2679 Art.24
s.7, applied: SI 2012/ 628 Art.20
s.7, varied: SI 2012/ 1867 Art.23, SI 2012/ 1924 Art.5, SI 2012/ 2284 Art.20, SI 2012/ 2635 Art.26, SI 2012/ 2679 Art.24
s.8, applied: SI 2012/ 2679 Art.41
s.10, see *Smith v Sandwell MBC* [2012] R.V.R. 38 (UT (Lands)), George Bartlett Q.C. (President, LTr)

67. Acquisition of Land Act 1981
applied: SI 2012/ 961 Sch.2 para.1, Sch.2 para.2, SI 2012/ 1867 Art.22, SI 2012/ 1924 Art.4
referred to: SI 2012/ 2679 Art.23
s.16, amended: 2012 c.7 Sch.5 para.22, Sch.14 para.48
s.16, repealed (in part): 2012 c.7 Sch.5 para.22
s.17, amended: 2012 c.7 Sch.5 para.23, Sch.14 para.49
s.17, repealed (in part): 2012 c.7 Sch.5 para.23
s.19, referred to: SI 2012/ 2679 Art.41
s.23, see *R. (on the application of A) v Secretary of State for Communities and Local Government* [2011] EWCA Civ 1253, [2012] J.P.L. 579 (CA (Civ Div)), Pill, L.J.

69. Wildlife and Countryside Act 1981
Part III, applied: SI 2012/ 801 Art.12
s.11, referred to: SI 2012/ 2941 Sch.1
s.11A, applied: SSI 2012/ 161 Art.2, SSI 2012/ 282 Art.3, Art.4, Art.7
s.14, applied: SSI 2012/ 173 Art.2, Sch.1 Part 1, Sch.1 Part 2, SSI 2012/ 174 Art.2, Sch.1 Part 1, SSI 2012/ 175 Art.3
s.14, referred to: SSI 2012/ 175 Art.3
s.14, enabling: SSI 2012/ 173, SSI 2012/ 174, SSI 2012/ 205, SSI 2012/ 206
s.14B, enabling: SSI 2012/ 174
s.14ZC, applied: SSI 2012/ 174 Art.3, Sch.1 Part 2, SSI 2012/ 175 Art.3
s.14ZC, enabling: SSI 2012/ 174, SSI 2012/ 206
s.16, applied: SI 2012/ 2941 Sch.1, SSI 2012/ 175 Art.3
s.26, applied: SSI 2012/ 124, SSI 2012/ 161, SSI 2012/ 173, SSI 2012/ 174, SSI 2012/ 205, SSI 2012/ 206, SSI 2012/ 282
s.28, applied: SI 2012/ 801 Sch.4
Sch.5, applied: SI 2012/ 13 Sch.1
Sch.6, applied: SI 2012/ 13 Sch.1
Sch.6, referred to: SI 2012/ 2941 Sch.1

1982

10. Industrial Training Act 1982
s.11, applied: SI 2012/ 958, SI 2012/ 959
s.11, enabling: SI 2012/ 958, SI 2012/ 959
s.12, applied: SI 2012/ 958, SI 2012/ 958 Art.15, SI 2012/ 959, SI 2012/ 959 Art.14
s.12, enabling: SI 2012/ 958, SI 2012/ 959

1982– cont.

16. Civil Aviation Act 1982
applied: 2012 c.19 s.112
s.2, amended: 2012 c.19 s.95
s.2, applied: 2012 c.19 Sch.14 para.2, Sch.14 para.3, Sch.14 para.4, Sch.14 para.5
s.2, enabling: SI 2012/ 1017, SI 2012/ 1134
s.4, disapplied: 2012 c.19 s.1, s.61, s.63
s.7, enabling: SI 2012/ 1017, SI 2012/ 1134
s.11, amended: 2012 c.19 s.100, Sch.11 para.2
s.11, applied: 2012 c.19 s.20, SI 2012/ 1017 Reg.33, Reg.39, Reg.47
s.16, amended: 2012 c.19 s.100
s.17, amended: 2012 c.19 s.100
s.20, amended: 2012 c.19 s.101, Sch.11 para.3
s.21, amended: 2012 c.19 s.102
s.23, amended: 2012 c.19 s.105
s.55, amended: 2012 asp 5 Sch.5 para.23
s.60, referred to: 2012 c.19 Sch.6 para.4
s.60, enabling: SI 2012/ 1751
s.61, enabling: SI 2012/ 1751
s.71, amended: 2012 c.19 s.94
s.71, applied: SI 2012/ 1134
s.71, repealed (in part): 2012 c.19 s.94
s.71, enabling: SI 2012/ 1017, SI 2012/ 1134
s.71A, amended: 2012 c.19 s.94
s.71A, enabling: SI 2012/ 1017, SI 2012/ 1134
s.71B, amended: 2012 c.19 s.94
s.71B, applied: SI 2012/ 1017, SI 2012/ 1134
s.76, amended: 2012 c.19 s.106
s.81, repealed: 2012 c.19 s.106
s.86, applied: SI 2012/ 3038 Sch.9 para.8
s.92, amended: 2012 c.19 s.106
s.99, amended: 2012 c.19 s.94, s.107
s.99, repealed (in part): 2012 c.19 s.107
s.101, amended: 2012 c.19 s.106
s.101, enabling: SI 2012/ 1751
s.108, referred to: 2012 c.19 s.112
Sch.1, substituted: 2012 c.19 s.96
Sch.1 para.1, amended: 2012 c.19 s.96
Sch.1 para.2, amended: 2012 c.19 s.96
Sch.1 para.3, amended: 2012 c.19 s.96
Sch.1 para.4, amended: 2012 c.19 s.96
Sch.1 para.5, amended: 2012 c.19 s.96, SI 2012/ 2404 Sch.2 para.17
Sch.1 para.6, amended: 2012 c.19 s.96
Sch.1 para.7, amended: 2012 c.19 s.96
Sch.1 para.7, applied: 2012 c.19 Sch.14 para.6
Sch.1 para.7, repealed (in part): 2012 c.19 s.96
Sch.1 para.8, amended: 2012 c.19 s.96
Sch.1 para.8A, added: 2012 c.19 s.97
Sch.1 para.8A, applied: 2012 c.19 Sch.14 para.2
Sch.1 para.12, amended: 2012 c.19 s.95, s.97
Sch.1 para.13, amended: 2012 c.19 s.97
Sch.1 para.13, applied: 2012 c.19 Sch.14 para.7
Sch.1 para.13, repealed (in part): 2012 c.19 s.96
Sch.1 para.15, enabling: SI 2012/ 1017, SI 2012/ 1134
Sch.1 para.18, substituted: 2012 c.19 s.95
Sch.3 para.2, amended: 2012 c.19 s.97
Sch.13 Part II, enabling: SI 2012/ 1017, SI 2012/ 1134, SI 2012/ 1751
Sch.13 Part III, enabling: SI 2012/ 1751
Sch.13 Part III para.1, enabling: SI 2012/ 1017, SI 2012/ 1134
Sch.13 Part III para.2, enabling: SI 2012/ 1017, SI 2012/ 1134
Sch.13 Part III para.4, amended: 2012 c.19 s.106
Sch.14 para.7, amended: 2012 c.19 s.106

1982– cont.

27. Civil Jurisdiction and Judgments Act 1982
s.1, amended: SI 2012/1770 Reg.4, SI 2012/1809 Sch.1 Part 1
s.5, applied: SI 2012/2814 Sch.1 para.2
s.5, referred to: SI 2012/2814 Sch.2 para.2
s.12, enabling: SI 2012/679, SI 2012/2806
s.18, amended: SI 2012/2814 Sch.4 para.5
s.18, disapplied: SI 2012/2814 Sch.1 para.6, SSI 2012/301 Reg.8
s.24, amended: SI 2012/1809 Sch.1 Part 1
s.27, see *Fish & Fish Ltd v Sea Shepherd UK* 2012 S.L.T. 156 (OH), Lord Emslie
s.32, see *AES Ust-Kamenogorsk Hydropower Plant LLP v Ust-Kamenogorsk Hydropower Plant JSC* [2011] EWCA Civ 647, [2012] 1 W.L.R. 920 (CA (Civ Div)), Rix, L.J.
s.32, amended: SI 2012/2814 Sch.4 para.5
s.33, see *AES Ust-Kamenogorsk Hydropower Plant LLP v Ust-Kamenogorsk Hydropower Plant JSC* [2011] EWCA Civ 647, [2012] 1 W.L.R. 920 (CA (Civ Div)), Rix, L.J.
s.33, amended: SI 2012/2814 Sch.4 para.5
s.34, see *Alliance Bank JSC v Aquanta Corp* [2011] EWIIC 3281 (Comm), [2012] 1 Lloyd's Rep. 181 (QBD (Comm)), Burton, J.
s.48, amended: SI 2012/1770 Reg.5
s.48, varied: SI 2012/1770 Reg.7
s.48, enabling: SI 2012/679, SI 2012/2806
s.50, amended: SI 2012/1770 Reg.6
Sch.4, see *CEF Holdings Ltd v Mundey* [2012] EWHC 1524 (QB), [2012] I.R.L.R. 912 (QBD), Silber, J.
Sch.8, applied: SSI 2012/301 Reg.4

29. Supply of Goods and Services Act 1982
s.4, see *Trebor Bassett Holdings Ltd v ADT Fire & Security Plc* [2012] EWCA Civ 1158, [2012] B.L.R. 441 (CA (Civ Div)), Sir Andrew Morritt (Chancellor)

30. Local Government (Miscellaneous Provisions) Act 1982
s.3, applied: SI 2012/1082 Art.6, SI 2012/1093 Art.5
Sch.3 para.19, see *R. (on the application of Hemming (t/a Simply Pleasure Ltd)) v Westminster City Council* [2012] EWHC 1260 (Admin), [2012] P.T.S.R. 1676 (QBD (Admin)), Keith, J.
Sch.4, applied: SI 2012/1082 Art.6, SI 2012/1093 Art.5
Sch.4 para.1, see *Jones v Bath and North East Somerset Council* [2012] EWHC 1361 (Admin), (2012) 176 J.P. 530 (QBD (Admin)), Mitting, J.
Sch.4 para.10, see *Jones v Bath and North East Somerset Council* [2012] EWHC 1361 (Admin), (2012) 176 J.P. 530 (QBD (Admin)), Mitting, J.

36. Aviation Security Act 1982
applied: 2012 c.19 s.112
Part II, applied: 2012 c.19 s.82, Sch.11 para.18
Part II, amended: 2012 c.19 Sch.11 para.5
Part II, added: 2012 c.19 s.80
Part IIA, applied: SI 2012/837 Art.2
Part III, applied: SI 2012/837 Art.2
s.11, amended: 2012 c.19 Sch.11 para.6
s.11, applied: 2012 c.19 Sch.11 para.18
s.11A, substituted: 2012 c.19 Sch.11 para.7
s.11A, amended: 2012 c.19 Sch.11 para.8
s.12, substituted: 2012 c.19 Sch.11 para.9
s.12, amended: 2012 c.19 Sch.11 para.10
s.13, substituted: 2012 c.19 Sch.11 para.9
s.13A, substituted: 2012 c.19 Sch.11 para.9

1982– cont.

36. Aviation Security Act 1982– *cont.*
s.14, substituted: 2012 c.19 Sch.11 para.9
s.14A, added: 2012 c.19 s.78
s.15, amended: 2012 c.19 Sch.11 para.11
s.16A, added: 2012 c.19 s.78
s.17A, added: 2012 c.19 Sch.11 para.12
s.18A, amended: 2012 c.19 Sch.11 para.13
s.18A, repealed (in part): 2012 c.19 Sch.11 para.13
s.18D, amended: 2012 c.19 Sch.11 para.14
s.20A, amended: 2012 c.19 s.79
s.20B, amended: 2012 c.19 Sch.11 para.15
s.21, amended: 2012 c.19 Sch.11 para.16
s.21G, amended: 2012 c.19 Sch.11 para.17
s.21J, added: 2012 c.19 s.81
s.23A, added: 2012 c.19 s.78
s.24A, amended: 2012 c.19 s.78
s.25AA, enabling: SI 2012/837
s.39, referred to: 2012 c.19 s.112

39. Finance Act 1982
s.129, amended: SI 2012/964 Sch.1

43. Local Government and Planning (Scotland) Act 1982
s.4, enabling: SI 2012/1478
s.15, enabling: SI 2012/1478

45. Civic Government (Scotland) Act 1982
s.8, amended: 2012 asp 8 Sch.7 para.6, Sch.8 Part 2
s.29, amended: SSI 2012/324 Art.2
s.29, applied: SSI 2012/324 Art.1
s.29, enabling: SSI 2012/324
s.52, see *Harris (Douglas Miller) v HM Advocate* [2012] HCJAC 5, 2012 S.C.C.R. 234 (HCJ), Lord Hardie; see *McCluskey (Barry) v HM Advocate* [2012] HCJAC 125, 2012 S.L.T. 1242 (HCJ), Lord Carloway
s.52A, see *Harris (Douglas Miller) v HM Advocate* [2012] HCJAC 5, 2012 S.C.C.R. 234 (HCJ), Lord Hardie
s.54, amended: 2012 asp 8 Sch.7 para.53
s.58, see *Thomson v Richardson* 2012 J.C. 37 (HCJ), Lord Reed
s.61, amended: 2012 asp 8 Sch.7 para.6
s.62, amended: 2012 asp 8 Sch.7 para.6
s.77, amended: 2012 asp 8 Sch.7 para.6
s.77, repealed (in part): 2012 asp 8 Sch.8 Part 1
s.79, amended: 2012 asp 8 Sch.7 para.6
s.85, amended: 2012 asp 8 Sch.7 para.6
s.85, repealed (in part): 2012 asp 8 Sch.8 Part 1
s.86, amended: 2012 asp 8 Sch.7 para.6
s.86D, amended: 2012 asp 8 Sch.7 para.6
s.86F, amended: 2012 asp 8 Sch.7 para.6
s.86F, repealed (in part): 2012 asp 8 Sch.8 Part 1
s.86F, substituted: 2012 asp 8 Sch.7 para.6
s.86J, amended: 2012 asp 8 Sch.7 para.6
s.89, amended: 2012 asp 8 Sch.7 para.53
s.89, repealed (in part): 2012 asp 8 Sch.8 Part 2
s.93, amended: 2012 asp 8 Sch.7 para.53
s.93, repealed (in part): 2012 asp 8 Sch.8 Part 2
s.98, amended: 2012 asp 8 Sch.7 para.53, Sch.8 Part 2
Sch.1 para.2, amended: 2012 asp 8 Sch.7 para.53
Sch.1 para.5, amended: 2012 asp 8 Sch.7 para.53
Sch.1 para.7, amended: 2012 asp 8 Sch.7 para.53
Sch.1 para.9, amended: 2012 asp 8 Sch.7 para.53
Sch.1 para.10, amended: 2012 asp 8 Sch.7 para.53
Sch.1 para.11, amended: 2012 asp 8 Sch.7 para.53
Sch.1 para.12, amended: 2012 asp 8 Sch.7 para.53
Sch.1 para.17, amended: 2012 asp 8 Sch.7 para.53

1982–cont.

45. Civic Government (Scotland) Act 1982–*cont.*
Sch.2 para.3, amended: 2012 asp 8 Sch.7 para.6, Sch.8 Part 2
Sch.2 para.8, amended: 2012 asp 8 Sch.7 para.53
Sch.2 para.10, amended: 2012 asp 8 Sch.7 para.53
Sch.2 para.13, amended: 2012 asp 8 Sch.7 para.53
Sch.2 para.14, amended: 2012 asp 8 Sch.7 para.53
Sch.2 para.15, amended: 2012 asp 8 Sch.7 para.53
Sch.2 para.23, amended: 2012 asp 8 Sch.7 para.53
Sch.2A para.3, amended: 2012 asp 8 Sch.7 para.6
Sch.2A para.8, amended: 2012 asp 8 Sch.7 para.6

48. Criminal Justice Act 1982
s.32, amended: 2012 c.10 Sch.21 para.3, Sch.22 para.13
s.37, amended: 2012 c.10 s.87
s.37, applied: 2012 c.10 s.86
s.37, referred to: 2012 c.10 s.85
Sch.1 Part II, amended: 2012 c.4 Sch.1 para.1
Sch.14 para.37, repealed (in part): 2012 c.10 Sch.25 Part 2

49. Transport Act 1982
s.70, amended: 2012 c.5 Sch.9 para.1
s.70, repealed (in part): 2012 c.5 Sch.14 Part 9

51. Mental Health (Amendment) Act 1982
Sch.3 Part I para.49, repealed: 2012 c.10 Sch.25 Part 2

53. Administration of Justice Act 1982
s.8, see *Wolff v John Moulds (Kilmarnock) Ltd* 2012 S.L.T. 231 (OH), Lord Doherty
s.20, see *Austin v Woodward* [2011] EWHC 2458 (Ch), [2012] W.T.L.R. 559 (Ch D), Daniel Alexander Q.C.; see *Lines v Porter* [2011] EWHC 2310 (Ch), [2012] W.T.L.R. 629 (Ch D), Judge Simon Barker Q.C.; see *Marley v Rawlings* [2012] EWCA Civ 61, [2012] 4 All E.R. 630 (CA (Civ Div)), Sir John Thomas (President)

1983

ii. British Waterways Act 1983
s.8, see *Moore v British Waterways Board* [2012] EWHC 182 (Ch), [2012] 1 W.L.R. 3289 (Ch D), Hildyard, J

2. Representation of the People Act 1983
see *McGeoch v Lord President of the Council* 2012 S.C. 410 (IH (Ex Div)), Lord Reed; see *R. (on the application of Woolas) v Parliamentary Election Court* [2010] EWHC 3169 (Admin), [2012] Q.B. 1 (DC), Thomas, L.J.
applied: SI 2012/323 Reg.15, Sch.3 para.13, Sch.3 para.20, Sch.3 para.36, Sch.5 para.2, Sch.5 para.13, Sch.5 para.22, Sch.5 para.38, SI 2012/444 Reg.20, Sch.3, Sch.5, SI 2012/1917 Art.75, Art.76, Art.77, Art.78, Sch.2 para.8, Sch.9 para.1, SI 2012/2031 Sch.3, Sch.5
referred to: 2012 c.13 Sch.1, SI 2012/323 Sch.3 para.2
Part III, applied: SI 2012/1917 Art.50, Sch.9 para.1
s.7, applied: SI 2012/1917 Sch.2 para.1
s.7A, applied: SI 2012/1917 Sch.2 para.1
s.8, applied: SI 2012/323 Sch.4 para.1, SI 2012/444 Sch.4 para.1, SI 2012/2031 Reg.8, Reg.13
s.13, applied: SI 2012/1917 Art.8, Sch.1 para.1, Sch.1 para.2
s.13A, applied: SI 2012/1917 Art.8, Sch.1 para.1, Sch.1 para.2
s.13B, applied: SI 2012/323 Sch.3 para.17, Sch.3 para.24, Sch.3 para.26, Sch.3 para.27, Sch.3 para.28, Sch.3 para.30, Sch.3 para.32, Sch.3 para.34, Sch.3 para.42, Sch.3 para.43, Sch.3

1983–cont.

2. Representation of the People Act 1983–*cont.*
s.13B, applied:–*cont.*
para.44, Sch.5 para.17, Sch.5 para.26, Sch.5 para.28, Sch.5 para.29, Sch.5 para.30, Sch.5 para.32, Sch.5 para.34, Sch.5 para.36, Sch.5 para.44, Sch.5 para.45, Sch.5 para.46, SI 2012/444 Sch.3, Sch.5, SI 2012/1917 Art.8, Sch.1 para.1, Sch.1 para.2, Sch.3 para.29, Sch.3 para.37, Sch.3 para.39, Sch.3 para.40, Sch.3 para.41, Sch.3 para.42, Sch.3 para.43, Sch.3 para.45, Sch.3 para.47, Sch.3 para.65, Sch.3 para.66, Sch.3 para.67, Sch.3 para.68, SI 2012/2031 Sch.3, Sch.5
s.13B, varied: SI 2012/323 Sch.4 para.1, SI 2012/444 Sch.4 para.1, SI 2012/2031 Sch.4 Part 1
s.13BB, applied: SI 2012/1917 Sch.1 para.1, Sch.1 para.2
s.14, see *R. (on the application of Preston) v Wandsworth LBC* [2011] EWHC 3174 (Admin), [2012] 2 W.L.R. 1134 (QBD (Admin)), Elias, L.J.
s.31, varied: SI 2012/323 Sch.4 para.1, SI 2012/444 Sch.4 para.1, SI 2012/2031 Sch.4 Part 1
s.35, applied: SI 2012/323 Reg.9, SI 2012/444 Reg.15, SI 2012/2031 Reg.9
s.35, varied: SI 2012/323 Sch.4 para.1, SI 2012/444 Sch.4 para.1, SI 2012/2031 Sch.4 Part 1
s.36, varied: SI 2012/323 Sch.4 para.1, SI 2012/444 Sch.4 para.1, SI 2012/2031 Sch.4 Part 1
s.36, enabling: SI 2012/198
s.47, varied: SI 2012/323 Sch.4 para.1, SI 2012/444 Sch.4 para.1, SI 2012/2031 Sch.4 Part 1
s.49, varied: SI 2012/323 Sch.4 para.1, SI 2012/444 Sch.4 para.1, SI 2012/2031 Sch.4 Part 1
s.52, applied: SI 2012/323 Sch.4 para.1, SI 2012/444 Sch.4 para.1, SI 2012/2031 Reg.8, Reg.13
s.53, applied: SI 2012/444 Sch.4 para.1
s.54, applied: SI 2012/323 Sch.4 para.1, SI 2012/2031 Reg.8, Reg.13
s.56, applied: SI 2012/1917 Art.8
s.57, applied: SSI 2012/245 Art.2
s.57, enabling: SSI 2012/245
s.60, applied: SI 2012/1917 Art.75, Art.77
s.60, varied: SI 2012/323 Sch.4 para.1, SI 2012/444 Sch.4 para.1, SI 2012/2031 Sch.4 Part 1
s.61, applied: SI 2012/1917 Art.75, Art.77
s.61, varied: SI 2012/323 Sch.4 para.1, SI 2012/444 Sch.4 para.1, SI 2012/2031 Sch.4 Part 1
s.62A, applied: SI 2012/1917 Art.75, Art.77
s.62A, varied: SI 2012/323 Sch.4 para.1, SI 2012/444 Sch.4 para.1, SI 2012/2031 Sch.4 Part 1
s.62B, applied: SI 2012/1917 Art.75, Art.77
s.63, varied: SI 2012/323 Sch.4 para.1, SI 2012/444 Sch.4 para.1, SI 2012/2031 Sch.4 Part 1
s.65, varied: SI 2012/323 Sch.4 para.1, SI 2012/444 Sch.4 para.1, SI 2012/2031 Sch.4 Part 1
s.66, applied: SI 2012/323 Sch.3 para.19, Sch.5 para.20, Sch.5 para.21, SI 2012/444 Sch.3, Sch.5, SI 2012/2031 Sch.3, Sch.5
s.66, repealed (in part): SSI 2012/31 Art.3
s.66, varied: SI 2012/323 Sch.4 para.1, SI 2012/444 Sch.4 para.1, SI 2012/2031 Sch.4 Part 1
s.66A, varied: SI 2012/323 Sch.4 para.1, SI 2012/444 Sch.4 para.1, SI 2012/2031 Sch.4 Part 1
s.76, amended: SSI 2012/16 Art.2
s.76A, enabling: SSI 2012/16
s.77, referred to: SI 2012/1917 Art.18, Art.34, Art.53
s.92, varied: SI 2012/323 Sch.4 para.1, SI 2012/444 Sch.4 para.1, SI 2012/2031 Sch.4 Part 1
s.94, varied: SI 2012/323 Sch.4 para.1, SI 2012/444 Sch.4 para.1, SI 2012/2031 Sch.4 Part 1

1983–cont.

2. **Representation of the People Act 1983**–*cont.*

s.96, varied: SI 2012/323 Sch.4 para.1, SI 2012/444 Sch.4 para.1, SI 2012/2031 Sch.4 Part 1

s.97, varied: SI 2012/323 Sch.4 para.1, SI 2012/444 Sch.4 para.1, SI 2012/2031 Sch.4 Part 1

s.100, varied: SI 2012/323 Sch.4 para.1, SI 2012/444 Sch.4 para.1, SI 2012/2031 Sch.4 Part 1

s.106, see *R. (on the application of Woolas) v Parliamentary Election Court* [2010] EWHC 3169 (Admin), [2012] Q.B. 1 (DC), Thomas, L.J.

s.109, varied: SI 2012/323 Sch.4 para.1, SI 2012/444 Sch.4 para.1, SI 2012/2031 Sch.4 Part 1

s.110, varied: SI 2012/323 Sch.4 para.1, SI 2012/444 Sch.4 para.1, SI 2012/2031 Sch.4 Part 1

s.110A, varied: SI 2012/444 Sch.4 para.1

s.111, varied: SI 2012/323 Sch.4 para.1, SI 2012/444 Sch.4 para.1, SI 2012/2031 Sch.4 Part 1

s.112, varied: SI 2012/323 Sch.4 para.1, SI 2012/444 Sch.4 para.1, SI 2012/2031 Sch.4 Part 1

s.113, varied: SI 2012/323 Sch.4 para.1, SI 2012/444 Sch.4 para.1, SI 2012/2031 Sch.4 Part 1

s.114, varied: SI 2012/323 Sch.4 para.1, SI 2012/444 Sch.4 para.1, SI 2012/2031 Sch.4 Part 1

s.115, varied: SI 2012/323 Sch.4 para.1, SI 2012/444 Sch.4 para.1, SI 2012/2031 Sch.4 Part 1

s.116, varied: SI 2012/323 Sch.4 para.1, SI 2012/444 Sch.4 para.1, SI 2012/2031 Sch.4 Part 1

s.118, varied: SI 2012/323 Sch.4 para.1, SI 2012/444 Sch.4 para.1, SI 2012/2031 Sch.4 Part 1

s.119, varied: SI 2012/323 Sch.4 para.1, SI 2012/444 Sch.4 para.1, SI 2012/2031 Sch.4 Part 1

s.120, see *R. (on the application of Woolas) v Parliamentary Election Court* [2010] EWHC 3169 (Admin), [2012] Q.B. 1 (DC), Thomas, L.J.

s.127, varied: SI 2012/1917 Sch.9 para.1

s.128, varied: SI 2012/323 Sch.6, SI 2012/444 Sch.6, SI 2012/1917 Sch.9 para.1

s.129, varied: SI 2012/323 Sch.6, SI 2012/444 Sch.6, SI 2012/1917 Sch.9 para.1

s.130, applied: SI 2012/323 Reg.15, SI 2012/444 Reg.20

s.130, varied: SI 2012/323 Sch.6, SI 2012/444 Sch.6, SI 2012/1917 Sch.9 para.1

s.131, varied: SI 2012/323 Sch.6, SI 2012/444 Sch.6, SI 2012/1917 Sch.9 para.1

s.132, varied: SI 2012/323 Sch.6, SI 2012/444 Sch.6, SI 2012/1917 Sch.9 para.1

s.133, varied: SI 2012/323 Sch.6, SI 2012/444 Sch.6, SI 2012/1917 Sch.9 para.1

s.136, varied: SI 2012/323 Sch.6, SI 2012/444 Sch.6, SI 2012/1917 Sch.9 para.1

s.137, applied: SI 2012/1917 Sch.9 para.1

s.137, varied: SI 2012/323 Sch.6, SI 2012/444 Sch.6

s.138, varied: SI 2012/323 Sch.6, SI 2012/444 Sch.6, SI 2012/1917 Sch.9 para.1

s.139, varied: SI 2012/323 Sch.6, SI 2012/444 Sch.6, SI 2012/1917 Sch.9 para.1

s.140, varied: SI 2012/323 Sch.6, SI 2012/444 Sch.6, SI 2012/1917 Sch.9 para.1

s.141, varied: SI 2012/323 Sch.6, SI 2012/444 Sch.6, SI 2012/1917 Sch.9 para.1

s.143, varied: SI 2012/323 Sch.6, SI 2012/444 Sch.6, SI 2012/1917 Sch.9 para.1

s.145, applied: SI 2012/336 Reg.3, Reg.5, SI 2012/1917 Art.75

s.145, varied: SI 2012/323 Sch.6, SI 2012/444 Sch.6, SI 2012/1917 Sch.9 para.1

s.146, see *R. (on the application of Woolas) v Parliamentary Election Court* [2010] EWHC 3169 (Admin), [2012] Q.B. 1 (DC), Thomas, L.J.

1983–cont.

2. **Representation of the People Act 1983**–*cont.*

s.146, varied: SI 2012/323 Sch.6, SI 2012/444 Sch.6, SI 2012/1917 Sch.9 para.1

s.147, varied: SI 2012/323 Sch.6, SI 2012/444 Sch.6, SI 2012/1917 Sch.9 para.1

s.154, applied: SI 2012/1917 Sch.9 para.1

s.154, varied: SI 2012/323 Sch.6, SI 2012/444 Sch.6

s.155, varied: SI 2012/323 Sch.6, SI 2012/444 Sch.6, SI 2012/1917 Sch.9 para.1

s.156, applied: SI 2012/1917 Sch.9 para.1

s.156, varied: SI 2012/323 Sch.6, SI 2012/444 Sch.6

s.157, varied: SI 2012/323 Sch.6, SI 2012/444 Sch.6, SI 2012/1917 Sch.9 para.1

s.158, varied: SI 2012/1917 Sch.9 para.1

s.159, see *R. (on the application of Woolas) v Parliamentary Election Court* [2010] EWHC 3169 (Admin), [2012] Q.B. 1 (DC), Thomas, L.J.

s.159, varied: SI 2012/1917 Sch.9 para.1

s.160, applied: SI 2012/1917 Art.75

s.160, varied: SI 2012/323 Sch.6, SI 2012/444 Sch.6

s.161, applied: SI 2012/1917 Sch.9 para.1

s.161, varied: SI 2012/323 Sch.6, SI 2012/444 Sch.6

s.162, applied: SI 2012/1917 Sch.9 para.1

s.162, varied: SI 2012/323 Sch.6, SI 2012/444 Sch.6

s.163, applied: SI 2012/1917 Sch.9 para.1

s.163, varied: SI 2012/323 Sch.6, SI 2012/444 Sch.6

s.164, applied: SI 2012/323 Reg.15, SI 2012/444 Reg.20

s.164, varied: SI 2012/323 Sch.6, SI 2012/444 Sch.6, SI 2012/1917 Sch.9 para.1

s.165, applied: SI 2012/1917 Art.76

s.166, varied: SI 2012/1917 Sch.9 para.1

s.167, referred to: SI 2012/1917 Art.66

s.167, varied: SI 2012/323 Sch.4 para.1, Sch.6, SI 2012/444 Sch.4 para.1, Sch.6, SI 2012/1917 Sch.9 para.1

s.168, applied: SI 2012/1917 Art.77, Art.78

s.168, varied: SI 2012/323 Sch.4 para.1, SI 2012/444 Sch.4 para.1, SI 2012/1917 Sch.9 para.1, SI 2012/2031 Sch.4 Part 1

s.169, applied: SI 2012/1917 Art.77, Sch.9 para.1

s.169, varied: SI 2012/323 Sch.4 para.1, SI 2012/444 Sch.4 para.1, SI 2012/2031 Sch.4 Part 1

s.170, applied: SI 2012/1917 Sch.9 para.1

s.170, varied: SI 2012/323 Sch.4 para.1, SI 2012/444 Sch.4 para.1, SI 2012/2031 Sch.4 Part 1

s.173, applied: SI 2012/1917 Art.18, Art.34, Art.53, Art.77, Art.78

s.173, varied: SI 2012/323 Sch.4 para.1, SI 2012/444 Sch.4 para.1, SI 2012/2031 Sch.4 Part 1

s.173A, applied: SI 2012/1917 Art.78

s.173A, varied: SI 2012/444 Sch.4 para.1

s.174, applied: SI 2012/1917 Art.75, Art.77, Art.78, Sch.9 para.1

s.174, varied: SI 2012/323 Sch.4 para.1, SI 2012/444 Sch.4 para.1

s.175, varied: SI 2012/323 Sch.4 para.1, SI 2012/444 Sch.4 para.1, SI 2012/1917 Sch.9 para.1, SI 2012/2031 Sch.4 Part 1

s.176, varied: SI 2012/323 Sch.4 para.1, SI 2012/444 Sch.4 para.1, SI 2012/1917 Sch.9 para.1, SI 2012/2031 Sch.4 Part 1

s.177, varied: SI 2012/323 Sch.4 para.1, SI 2012/444 Sch.4 para.1, SI 2012/1917 Sch.9 para.1, SI 2012/2031 Sch.4 Part 1

s.178, varied: SI 2012/323 Sch.4 para.1, SI 2012/444 Sch.4 para.1, SI 2012/1917 Sch.9 para.1, SI 2012/2031 Sch.4 Part 1

1983– cont.

2. Representation of the People Act 1983– *cont.*

s.179, varied: SI 2012/323 Sch.4 para.1, SI 2012/444 Sch.4 para.1, SI 2012/1917 Sch.9 para.1, SI 2012/2031 Sch.4 Part 1

s.180, varied: SI 2012/323 Sch.6, SI 2012/444 Sch.6, SI 2012/1917 Sch.9 para.1

s.180A, varied: SI 2012/1917 Sch.9 para.1

s.181, varied: SI 2012/323 Sch.4 para.1, SI 2012/444 Sch.4 para.1, SI 2012/1917 Sch.9 para.1, SI 2012/2031 Sch.4 Part 1

s.183, varied: SI 2012/323 Sch.6, SI 2012/444 Sch.6, SI 2012/1917 Sch.9 para.1

s.184, varied: SI 2012/323 Sch.6, SI 2012/444 Sch.6, SI 2012/1917 Sch.9 para.1

s.185, varied: SI 2012/323 Sch.4 para.1, Sch.6, SI 2012/444 Sch.4 para.1, Sch.6, SI 2012/1917 Sch.9 para.1, SI 2012/2031 Sch.4 Part 1

s.186, varied: SI 2012/1917 Sch.9 para.1

s.199B, varied: SI 2012/323 Sch.4 para.1, SI 2012/444 Sch.4 para.1, SI 2012/2031 Sch.4 Part 1

s.200, varied: SI 2012/323 Sch.4 para.1, SI 2012/444 Sch.4 para.1, SI 2012/2031 Sch.4 Part 1

s.202, varied: SI 2012/323 Sch.4 para.1, SI 2012/444 Sch.4 para.1, SI 2012/2031 Sch.4 Part 1

s.203, applied: SI 2012/444 Sch.4 para.1, SI 2012/2031 Reg.8, Reg.13

Sch.5, applied: SI 2012/1917 Art.57

8. British Fishing Boats Act 1983

s.1, applied: SI 2012/2747 Art.3

20. Mental Health Act 1983

see *A Local Authority v E* [2012] EWHC 1639 (Fam), [2012] 2 F.C.R. 523 (CP), Peter Jackson, J.; see *A Local Authority v H* [2012] EWHC 49 (Fam), [2012] 1 F.C.R. 590 (CP), Hedley, J.; see *Coombs v Dorset NHS Primary Care Trust* [2012] EWHC 521 (QB), [2012] Med. L.R. 438 (QBD), Judge Platts; see *G v E* [2010] EWCA Civ 822, [2012] Fam. 78 (CA (Civ Div)), Sir Nicholas Wall (President, Fam); see *Rabone v Pennine Care NHS Foundation Trust* [2012] UKSC 2, [2012] 2 A.C. 72 (SC), Lord Walker, J.S.C.; see *Secretary of State for Justice v RB* [2011] EWCA Civ 1608, [2012] 1 W.L.R. 2043 (CA (Civ Div)), Maurice Kay, L.J.

applied: 2012 c.7 s.42, 2012 c.10 Sch.1 para.4, Sch.1 para.5, Sch.1 para.9, SI 2012/1916 Reg.231, SI 2012/2885 Sch.1 para.5, SI 2012/2886 Sch.1, SI 2012/2996 Reg.41, SI 2012/3144 Reg.24, SI 2012/3145 Sch.1, SSI 2012/303 Reg.5, Reg.15, SSI 2012/319 Reg.5, Reg.15

Part III, applied: SI 2012/1726 r.33.1

Pt II. see *R. (on the application of Sessay) v South London and Maudsley NHS Foundation Trust* [2011] EWHC 2617 (QB), [2012] Q.B. 760 (DC), Pitchford, L.J.

s.2, see *Buck v Norfolk and Waveney Mental Health NHS Foundation Trust* [2012] Med. L.R. 266 (CC (Cambridge)), Judge Yelton; see *Coombs v Dorset NHS Primary Care Trust* [2012] EWHC 521 (QB), [2012] Med. L.R. 438 (QBD), Judge Platts; see *DD v Durham CC* [2012] EWHC 1053 (QB), [2012] Med. L.R. 348 (QBD), Eady, J.; see *R. (on the application of GP) v Derby City Council* [2012] EWHC 1451 (Admin), [2012] M.H.L.R. 252 (QBD (Admin)), Judge Pelling Q.C.; see *R. (on the application of Sessay) v South London and Maudsley NHS Foundation Trust* [2011] EWHC 2617 (QB), [2012] Q.B. 760 (DC), Pitchford, L.J.

1983– cont.

20. Mental Health Act 1983– *cont.*

s.3, see *A Local Authority v E* [2012] EWHC 1639 (Fam), [2012] 2 F.C.R. 523 (CP), Peter Jackson, J.; see *Coombs v Dorset NHS Primary Care Trust* [2012] EWHC 521 (QB), [2012] Med. L.R. 438 (QBD), Judge Platts; see *DD v Durham CC* [2012] EWHC 1053 (QB), [2012] Med. L.R. 348 (QBD), Eady, J.; see *DM v Doncaster MBC* [2011] EWHC 3652 (Admin), (2012) 15 C.C.L. Rep. 128 (QBD (Admin)), Langstaff, J.; see *R. (on the application of GP) v Derby City Council* [2012] EWHC 1451 (Admin), [2012] M.H.L.R. 252 (QBD (Admin)), Judge Pelling Q.C.; see *R. (on the application of Modaresi) v Secretary of State for Health* [2011] EWCA Civ 1359, [2012] P.T.S.R. 999 (CA (Civ Div)), Mummery, L.J.; see *Secretary of State for Justice v RB* [2011] EWCA Civ 1608, [2012] 1 W.L.R. 2043 (CA (Civ Div)), Maurice Kay, L.J.

s.4, see *R. (on the application of Sessay) v South London and Maudsley NHS Foundation Trust* [2011] EWHC 2617 (QB), [2012] Q.B. 760 (DC), Pitchford, L.J.

s.5, see *De Toucy v Bonhams 1793 Ltd* [2011] EWHC 3809 (Ch), [2012] B.P.I.R. 793 (Ch D), Vos, J.

s.7, see *C v Blackburn with Darwen BC* [2011] EWHC 3321 (Fam), (2012) 15 C.C.L. Rep. 251 (CP), Peter Jackson, J.

s.8, see *C v Blackburn with Darwen BC* [2011] EWHC 3321 (Fam), (2012) 15 C.C.L. Rep. 251 (CP), Peter Jackson, J.

s.11, see *R. (on the application of GP) v Derby City Council* [2012] EWHC 1451 (Admin), [2012] M.H.L.R. 252 (QBD (Admin)), Judge Pelling Q.C.

s.12ZA, added: 2012 c.7 s.38

s.12ZA, applied: 2012 c.7 Sch.22, Sch.23

s.12ZB, added: 2012 c.7 s.38

s.12ZC, added: 2012 c.7 s.38

s.13, see *DD v Durham CC* [2012] EWHC 1053 (QB), [2012] Med. L.R. 348 (QBD), Eady, J.

s.17, see *Buck v Norfolk and Waveney Mental Health NHS Foundation Trust* [2012] Med. L.R. 266 (CC (Cambridge)), Judge Yelton

s.17B, amended: 2012 c.7 s.299

s.19, amended: 2012 c.7 Sch.5 para.25

s.23, amended: 2012 c.7 Sch.5 para.26

s.23, repealed (in part): 2012 c.7 s.39

s.24, repealed (in part): 2012 c.7 s.39

s.26, see *R. (on the application of GP) v Derby City Council* [2012] EWHC 1451 (Admin), [2012] M.H.L.R. 252 (QBD (Admin)), Judge Pelling Q.C.

s.32, amended: 2012 c.7 Sch.5 para.27

s.34, see *Coombs v Dorset NHS Primary Care Trust* [2012] EWHC 521 (QB), [2012] Med. L.R. 438 (QBD), Judge Platts

s.37, see *Attorney General's Reference (No.54 of 2011), Re* [2011] EWCA Crim 2276, [2012] 1 Cr. App. R. (S.) 106 (CA (Crim Div)), Hughes, L.J. (V-P); see *DC v Nottinghamshire Healthcare NHS Trust* [2012] UKUT 92 (AAC), (2012) 15 C.C.L. Rep. 537 (UT (AAC)), Judge Jacobs; see *R. v S* [2012] EWCA Crim 92, [2012] M.H.L.R. 58 (CA (Crim Div)), Pill, L.J.; see *Secretary of State for Justice v RB* [2011] EWCA Civ 1608, [2012] 1 W.L.R. 2043 (CA (Civ Div)), Maurice Kay, L.J.

s.37, amended: 2012 c.10 Sch.19 para.1, Sch.26 para.2

s.37, applied: SI 2012/1726 r.68.13, r.37.3

s.39, amended: 2012 c.7 Sch.5 para.28

1983–cont.

20. Mental Health Act 1983–cont.

s.41, see *Attorney General's Reference (No.54 of 2011), Re* [2011] EWCA Crim 2276, [2012] 1 Cr. App. R. (S.) 106 (CA (Crim Div)), Hughes, L.J. (V-P); see *DC v Nottinghamshire Healthcare NHS Trust* [2012] UKUT 92 (AAC), (2012) 15 C.C.L. Rep. 537 (UT (AAC)), Judge Jacobs; see *R. v Chiles (Raymond)* [2012] EWCA Crim 196, [2012] M.H.L.R. 60 (CA (Crim Div)), Rafferty, L.J.; see *R. v Parkins (John Robert)* [2012] EWCA Crim 856, [2012] M.H.L.R. 249 (CA (Crim Div)), Davis, L.J.; see *Secretary of State for Justice v RB* [2011] EWCA Civ 1608, [2012] 1 W.L.R. 2043 (CA (Civ Div)), Maurice Kay, L.J.

s.45, applied: SI 2012/1726 r.63.1, r.76.6

s.45A, see *Attorney General's Reference (No.54 of 2011), Re* [2011] EWCA Crim 2276, [2012] 1 Cr. App. R. (S.) 106 (CA (Crim Div)), Hughes, L.J. (V-P); see *R. v S* [2012] EWCA Crim 92, [2012] M.H.L.R. 58 (CA (Crim Div)), Pill, L.J.

s.47, see *Attorney General's Reference (No.54 of 2011), Re* [2011] EWCA Crim 2276, [2012] 1 Cr. App. R. (S.) 106 (CA (Crim Div)), Hughes, L.J. (V-P); see *R. (on the application of W) v Larkin* [2012] EWHC 556 (Admin), [2012] M.H.L.R. 161 (QBD (Admin)), Ouseley, J.

s.47, applied: SI 2012/1726 r.11.3

s.48, see *R. (on the application of Griffin) v City of Westminster Magistrates' Court* [2011] EWHC 943 (Admin), [2012] 1 W.L.R. 270 (QBD (Admin)), Collins, J.; see *R. (on the application of HA (Nigeria)) v Secretary of State for the Home Department* [2012] EWHC 979 (Admin), [2012] Med. L.R. 353 (QBD (Admin)), Singh, J.

s.48, applied: SI 2012/1726 r.11.3

s.50, see *R. (on the application of W) v Larkin* [2012] EWHC 556 (Admin), [2012] M.H.L.R. 161 (QBD (Admin)), Ouseley, J.

s.52, referred to: SI 2012/1726 r.19.4

s.54, amended: 2012 c.7 s.38

s.61, amended: 2012 c.7 s.299

s.62A, amended: 2012 c.7 s.299

s.64C, amended: 2012 c.7 s.299

s.64E, amended: 2012 c.7 s.299

s.64FA, added: 2012 c.7 s.299

s.64H, amended: 2012 c.7 s.299

s.64H, enabling: SI 2012/1118, SI 2012/1265

s.66, see *R. (on the application of Modaresi) v Secretary of State for Health* [2011] EWCA Civ 1359, [2012] P.T.S.R. 999 (CA (Civ Div)), Mummery, L.J.

s.67, see *R. (on the application of Modaresi) v Secretary of State for Health* [2011] EWCA Civ 1359, [2012] P.T.S.R. 999 (CA (Civ Div)), Mummery, L.J.

s.68A, amended: 2012 c.7 s.42

s.68A, repealed (in part): 2012 c.7 s.42

s.71, see *DC v Nottinghamshire Healthcare NHS Trust* [2012] UKUT 92 (AAC), (2012) 15 C.C.L. Rep. 537 (UT (AAC)), Judge Jacobs

s.73, see *DC v Nottinghamshire Healthcare NHS Trust* [2012] UKUT 92 (AAC), (2012) 15 C.C.L. Rep. 537 (UT (AAC)), Judge Jacobs; see *Secretary of State for Justice v RB* [2011] EWCA Civ 1608, [2012] 1 W.L.R. 2043 (CA (Civ Div)), Maurice Kay, L.J.

s.114, amended: 2012 c.7 s.217

s.114A, amended: 2012 c.7 s.217

s.114A, repealed (in part): 2012 c.7 s.217

1983–cont.

20. Mental Health Act 1983–cont.

s.114A, substituted: 2012 c.7 s.217

s.114ZA, added: 2012 c.7 s.217

s.114ZA, applied: SI 2012/1480 Art.14

s.117, see *DM v Doncaster MBC* [2011] EWHC 3652 (Admin), (2012) 15 C.C.L. Rep. 128 (QBD (Admin)), Langstaff, J.

s.117, amended: 2012 c.7 s.40

s.117, applied: SI 2012/2996 Reg.14, Reg.15, SI 2012/3094 Reg.13

s.117, enabling: SI 2012/2996

s.122, amended: 2012 c.7 s.41

s.123, repealed: 2012 c.7 s.42

s.130A, amended: 2012 c.7 s.43

s.130A, applied: SI 2012/2996 Sch.1 para.2

s.130C, amended: 2012 c.7 s.43

s.130C, applied: SI 2012/2996 Sch.1 para.2

s.134, amended: 2012 c.7 s.44, s.185, Sch.5 para.29

s.134, applied: 2012 c.7 s.44

s.135, see *R. (on the application of Sessay) v South London and Maudsley NHS Foundation Trust* [2011] EWHC 2617 (QB), [2012] Q.B. 760 (DC), Pitchford, L.J.

s.136, see *MS v United Kingdom (24527/08)* (2012) 55 E.H.R.R. 23 (ECHR), Judge Garlicki (President); see *R. (on the application of Sessay) v South London and Maudsley NHS Foundation Trust* [2011] EWHC 2617 (QB), [2012] Q.B. 760 (DC), Pitchford, L.J.; see *Seal v United Kingdom (50330/07)* (2012) 54 E.H.R.R. 6 (ECHR), Judge Garlicki (President)

s.138, amended: 2012 c.7 s.42

s.138, referred to: 2012 c.7 s.42

s.139, see *DD v Durham CC* [2012] EWHC 1053 (QB), [2012] Med. L.R. 348 (QBD), Eady, J.; see *Seal v United Kingdom (50330/07)* (2012) 54 E.H.R.R. 6 (ECHR), Judge Garlicki (President)

s.139, amended: 2012 c.7 s.38, Sch.5 para.30, Sch.14 para.50

s.140, amended: 2012 c.7 s.45

s.145, see *DD v Durham CC* [2012] EWHC 1053 (QB), [2012] Med. L.R. 348 (QBD), Eady, J.

s.145, amended: 2012 c.7 s.38, Sch.5 para.31

s.145, applied: SI 2012/1917 Sch.2 para.14, Sch.2 para.15

s.146, amended: 2012 c.7 s.41

Sch.1 Part I para.1, amended: 2012 c.7 s.39

Sch.1 Part II para.1, amended: 2012 c.7 s.39

Sch.4 para.39, repealed: 2012 c.10 Sch.25 Part 2

34. Mobile Homes Act 1983

see *Telchadder v Wickland (Holdings) Ltd* [2012] EWCA Civ 635, [2012] H.L.R. 35 (CA (Civ Div)), Mummery, L.J.

applied: SI 2012/531 Reg.5, Reg.7, Reg.14, Reg.21, Reg.22, Reg.40, Reg.47

referred to: SI 2012/531 Reg.4, Reg.47

s.1, amended: SI 2012/899 Art.3

s.1, applied: SI 2012/531 Sch.1 para.50, Sch.1 para.52, SI 2012/2675 Reg.3

s.1, enabling: SI 2012/2675

s.2, amended: SI 2012/899 Art.3

s.2, applied: SI 2012/531 Reg.47, Sch.1 para.51, Sch.1 para.52

s.2A, amended: SI 2012/899 Art.3

s.4, amended: SI 2012/899 Art.3

s.4, applied: SI 2012/531 Reg.11, Reg.47, Sch.1 para.53

s.4, repealed (in part): SI 2012/899 Art.3

s.5, amended: SI 2012/899 Art.3

1983– cont.

34. Mobile Homes Act 1983–*cont.*
Sch.1 Part I, applied: SI 2012/531 Reg.12, Reg.21, Reg.47, Sch.1 para.54, Sch.1 para.55, Sch.1 para.56, Sch.1 para.57, Sch.1 para.58, Sch.1 para.59, Sch.1 para.60, Sch.1 para.61
Sch.1 Part I para.1, amended: SI 2012/899 Art.3
Sch.1 Part I para.4, amended: SI 2012/899 Art.3
Sch.1 Part I para.5, amended: SI 2012/899 Art.3
Sch.1 Part I para.5A, repealed (in part): SI 2012/899 Art.3
Sch.1 Part I para.6, repealed (in part): SI 2012/899 Art.3
Sch.1 Part I para.8, applied: SI 2012/531 Reg.11
Sch.1 Part I para.8, amended: SI 2012/899 Art.3
Sch.1 Part I para.8, substituted: SI 2012/899 Art.3
Sch.1 Part I para.9, applied: SI 2012/531 Reg.11
Sch.1 Part I para.9, amended: SI 2012/899 Art.3
Sch.1 Part I para.10, amended: SI 2012/899 Art.3
Sch.1 Part I para.16, amended: SI 2012/899 Art.3
Sch.1 Part I para.17, amended: SI 2012/899 Art.3
Sch.1 Part I para.18, amended: SI 2012/899 Art.3
Sch.1 Part I para.19, amended: SI 2012/899 Art.3
Sch.1 Part I para.28, amended: SI 2012/899 Art.3
Sch.1 Part II, applied: SI 2012/531 Reg.47
Sch.1 Part II, referred to: SI 2012/531 Sch.1 para.51
Sch.1 Part II para.1, amended: SI 2012/899 Art.3
Sch.1 Part II para.2, amended: SI 2012/899 Art.3
Sch.1 Part II para.3, amended: SI 2012/899 Art.3
Sch.1 Part II para.4, amended: SI 2012/899 Art.3
Sch.1 Part II para.5, amended: SI 2012/899 Art.3
Sch.1 Part II para.6, amended: SI 2012/899 Art.3
Sch.1 Part II para.7, amended: SI 2012/899 Art.3
Sch.1 Pt I para.4, see *Telchadder v Wickland (Holdings) Ltd* [2012] EWCA Civ 635, [2012] H.L.R. 35 (CA (Civ Div)), Mummery, L.J.

35. Litter Act 1983
s.8, amended: 2012 asp 5 Sch.5 para.24
s.8, repealed (in part): 2012 asp 5 Sch.5 para.24

40. Education (Fees and Awards) Act 1983
s.1, enabling: SI 2012/1653, SSI 2012/72
s.2, enabling: SI 2012/1653, SSI 2012/72

41. Health and Social Services and Social Security Adjudications Act 1983
s.23, amended: 2012 asp 5 Sch.5 para.25

44. National Audit Act 1983
s.6, applied: SI 2012/2421 Reg.15
s.7, applied: SI 2012/2421 Reg.15

47. National Heritage Act 1983
Sch.3 para.3, amended: SI 2012/2404 Sch.2 para.18

54. Medical Act 1983
s.1, see *Zia v General Medical Council* [2011] EWCA Civ 743, [2012] 1 W.L.R. 504 (CA (Civ Div)), Sir Anthony May (V-P, QBD)
s.1, enabling: SI 2012/1654
s.18, applied: SI 2012/2685 Sch.1
s.18A, applied: SI 2012/2685 Sch.1
s.21B, see *R. (on the application of Patel) v General Medical Council* [2012] EWHC 2120 (Admin), (2012) 128 B.M.L.R. 146 (QBD (Admin)), Hickinbottom, J.
s.21C, see *R. (on the application of Patel) v General Medical Council* [2012] EWHC 2120 (Admin), (2012) 128 B.M.L.R. 146 (QBD (Admin)), Hickinbottom, J.
s.27A, applied: SI 2012/2685 Sch.1
s.27B, applied: SI 2012/2685 Sch.1
s.29A, enabling: SI 2012/2685
s.29B, enabling: SI 2012/2685
s.29D, enabling: SI 2012/2685

1983– cont.

54. Medical Act 1983–*cont.*
s.29E, applied: SI 2012/2685 Sch.1
s.29E, enabling: SI 2012/2685
s.29G, applied: SI 2012/2685 Sch.1
s.29H, applied: SI 2012/2685 Sch.1
s.29J, applied: SI 2012/2685
s.29J, enabling: SI 2012/2685
s.30, applied: SI 2012/2685 Sch.1
s.31, applied: SI 2012/2685 Sch.1
s.31A, applied: SI 2012/2685 Sch.1
s.32, applied: SI 2012/2685 Sch.1
s.34D, enabling: SI 2012/344
s.35C, applied: SI 2012/2685 Sch.1
s.35D, applied: SI 2012/2685 Sch.1
s.39, applied: SI 2012/2685 Sch.1
s.40, see *Zia v General Medical Council* [2011] EWCA Civ 743, [2012] 1 W.L.R. 504 (CA (Civ Div)), Sir Anthony May (V-P, QBD)
s.41, applied: SI 2012/2685 Sch.1
s.41, enabling: SI 2012/2685
s.41A, applied: SI 2012/2685 Sch.1
s.41C, applied: SI 2012/2685 Sch.1
s.44, applied: SI 2012/2685 Sch.1
s.44B, applied: SI 2012/2685 Sch.1
Sch.1 Part I para.1A, repealed (in part): 2012 c.7 Sch.20 para.6
Sch.1 Part I para.1B, enabling: SI 2012/1654
Sch.2A para.3, applied: SI 2012/2685 Sch.1
Sch.3A, see *Reddy v General Medical Council* [2012] EWCA Civ 310, [2012] C.P. Rep. 27 (CA (Civ Div)), Mummery, L.J.
Sch.3A para.5, see *Reddy v General Medical Council* [2012] EWCA Civ 310, [2012] C.P. Rep. 27 (CA (Civ Div)), Mummery, L.J.

55. Value Added Tax Act 1983
s.22, see *Revenue and Customs Commissioners v GMAC UK Plc* [2012] UKUT 279 (TCC), [2012] S.T.C. 2349 (UT (Tax)), Warren, J.

1984

12. Telecommunications Act 1984
applied: SI 2012/1128 Art.4
referred to: SI 2012/1705 Art.4
Sch.2, referred to: SI 2012/1082 Art.5, SI 2012/1093 Art.4, SI 2012/1376 Art.4, SI 2012/1571 Art.4, SI 2012/1857 Art.4, SI 2012/2696 Art.4
Sch.2 para.23, applied: SI 2012/2284 Sch.7 para.12, SI 2012/2635 Sch.12 para.13
Sch.4 para.71, repealed (in part): 2012 asp 5 Sch.5 para.26

22. Public Health (Control of Disease) Act 1984
s.13, amended: 2012 c.7 Sch.5 para.32
s.50, repealed: 2012 c.9 Sch.10 Part 2

24. Dentists Act 1984
s.1, enabling: SI 2012/1655
s.26B, see *Rimmer v General Dental Council* [2011] EWHC 3438 (Admin), (2012) 124 B.M.L.R. 40 (QBD (Admin)), Mitting, J.
s.26B, repealed (in part): 2012 c.7 Sch.5 para.34
s.27, see *General Dental Council's Application, Re* [2011] EWHC 3011 (Admin), [2012] Med. L.R. 204 (QBD (Admin)), Sales, J.
s.33B, see *General Dental Council's Application, Re* [2011] EWHC 3011 (Admin), [2012] Med. L.R. 204 (QBD (Admin)), Sales, J.
s.36A, amended: 2012 c.7 Sch.15 para.67
s.36M, repealed (in part): 2012 c.7 Sch.5 para.35
s.40, amended: 2012 c.7 Sch.5 para.36

1984–cont.

24. Dentists Act 1984–*cont.*
s.50D, repealed (in part): 2012 c.7 Sch.5 para.37
s.53, referred to: SI 2012/1917 Sch.2 para.15
Sch.1 Part I para.1A, repealed (in part): 2012 c.7 Sch.20 para.6
Sch.1 Part I para.1B, enabling: SI 2012/1655

27. Road Traffic Regulation Act 1984
applied: SI 2012/1098 Art.4, SI 2012/1282 Sch.1, SI 2012/1284 Sch.1, SI 2012/1286 Sch.1, SI 2012/1289 Sch.1, SI 2012/1294 Sch.1, SI 2012/1295 Sch.1, SI 2012/1802 Art.3, SI 2012/1874 Art.3, SI 2012/1875 Art.3, SI 2012/1884 Art.4, SI 2012/2025 Art.3, SI 2012/2027 Art.5, SI 2012/2028 Art.4, SI 2012/2033 Art.4, SI 2012/2034 Art.7, SI 2012/2284 Art.12, SI 2012/2541 Sch.1, SI 2012/2547 Sch.1, SI 2012/2548 Sch.1, SI 2012/2549 Sch.1, SI 2012/2635 Art.39, SI 2012/2679 Art.37, SI 2012/2735 Art.8, SI 2012/3102 Sch.1, SI 2012/3103 Sch.1, SI 2012/3104 Sch.1, SI 2012/3105 Sch.1, SI 2012/3106 Sch.1, SI 2012/3107 Sch.1, SSI 2012/280
referred to: SI 2012/2635 Art.39
enabling: SI 2012/1934
Part I, applied: SSI 2012/200 Art.3
Part V, applied: SI 2012/496 Art.4
s.1, applied: SSI 2012/82, SSI 2012/83, SSI 2012/133
s.1, enabling: SI 2012/841, SI 2012/1082, SI 2012/1093, SI 2012/1159, SI 2012/1376, SI 2012/1377, SI 2012/1571, SI 2012/1705, SI 2012/1857, SI 2012/2447, SI 2012/2507, SI 2012/2696, SI 2012/2918, SSI 2012/82, SSI 2012/83, SSI 2012/104, SSI 2012/133, SSI 2012/229
s.2, enabling: SI 2012/841, SI 2012/1082, SI 2012/1093, SI 2012/1376, SI 2012/1377, SI 2012/1571, SI 2012/1705, SI 2012/1857, SI 2012/2447, SI 2012/2507, SI 2012/2696, SI 2012/2918, SSI 2012/12, SSI 2012/13, SSI 2012/14, SSI 2012/15, SSI 2012/17, SSI 2012/18, SSI 2012/46, SSI 2012/47, SSI 2012/56, SSI 2012/57, SSI 2012/58, SSI 2012/59, SSI 2012/82, SSI 2012/83, SSI 2012/95, SSI 2012/96, SSI 2012/97, SSI 2012/98, SSI 2012/103, SSI 2012/104, SSI 2012/120, SSI 2012/121, SSI 2012/122, SSI 2012/123, SSI 2012/134, SSI 2012/156, SSI 2012/157, SSI 2012/158, SSI 2012/159, SSI 2012/168, SSI 2012/185, SSI 2012/186, SSI 2012/195, SSI 2012/200, SSI 2012/201, SSI 2012/202, SSI 2012/203, SSI 2012/204, SSI 2012/207, SSI 2012/222, SSI 2012/223, SSI 2012/224, SSI 2012/225, SSI 2012/226, SSI 2012/227, SSI 2012/229, SSI 2012/230, SSI 2012/232, SSI 2012/233, SSI 2012/234, SSI 2012/235, SSI 2012/244, SSI 2012/248, SSI 2012/251, SSI 2012/254, SSI 2012/255, SSI 2012/256, SSI 2012/257, SSI 2012/277, SSI 2012/278, SSI 2012/279, SSI 2012/280, SSI 2012/298, SSI 2012/299, SSI 2012/309, SSI 2012/310, SSI 2012/311, SSI 2012/312, SSI 2012/313, SSI 2012/314, SSI 2012/317, SSI 2012/351, SSI 2012/356, SSI 2012/357, SSI 2012/358, SSI 2012/359
s.3, enabling: SI 2012/1705
s.4, enabling: SI 2012/1082, SI 2012/1093, SI 2012/1705, SI 2012/2447, SSI 2012/12, SSI 2012/13, SSI 2012/14, SSI 2012/15, SSI 2012/17, SSI 2012/18, SSI 2012/46, SSI 2012/47, SSI 2012/56, SSI 2012/57, SSI 2012/58, SSI 2012/59, SSI 2012/95, SSI 2012/96, SSI 2012/97, SSI 2012/98, SSI 2012/103, SSI 2012/120, SSI 2012/121, SSI 2012/122, SSI 2012/123, SSI 2012/134, SSI 2012/156, SSI 2012/157, SSI 2012/158, SSI 2012/159, SSI 2012/168, SSI 2012/185, SSI 2012/186, SSI 2012/195,

1984–cont.

27. Road Traffic Regulation Act 1984–*cont.*
s.4, enabling:–*cont.*
SSI 2012/200, SSI 2012/201, SSI 2012/202, SSI 2012/203, SSI 2012/204, SSI 2012/207, SSI 2012/222, SSI 2012/223, SSI 2012/224, SSI 2012/225, SSI 2012/226, SSI 2012/227, SSI 2012/230, SSI 2012/232, SSI 2012/233, SSI 2012/234, SSI 2012/235, SSI 2012/244, SSI 2012/248, SSI 2012/251, SSI 2012/254, SSI 2012/255, SSI 2012/256, SSI 2012/257, SSI 2012/277, SSI 2012/278, SSI 2012/279, SSI 2012/280, SSI 2012/298, SSI 2012/299, SSI 2012/309, SSI 2012/310, SSI 2012/311, SSI 2012/312, SSI 2012/313, SSI 2012/314, SSI 2012/317, SSI 2012/351, SSI 2012/356, SSI 2012/357, SSI 2012/358, SSI 2012/359
s.9, enabling: SI 2012/80
s.10, enabling: SI 2012/80
s.14, applied: SI 2012/1282 Sch.1, SI 2012/1284 Sch.1, SI 2012/1286 Sch.1, SI 2012/1289 Sch.1, SI 2012/1294 Sch.1, SI 2012/1295 Sch.1, SI 2012/1962, SI 2012/2060, SI 2012/2476, SI 2012/2671, SSI 2012/12, SSI 2012/13, SSI 2012/14, SSI 2012/15, SSI 2012/17, SSI 2012/46, SSI 2012/47, SSI 2012/56, SSI 2012/57, SSI 2012/58, SSI 2012/59, SSI 2012/98, SSI 2012/103, SSI 2012/120, SSI 2012/121, SSI 2012/122, SSI 2012/123, SSI 2012/134, SSI 2012/156, SSI 2012/157, SSI 2012/158, SSI 2012/159, SSI 2012/185, SSI 2012/186, SSI 2012/200, SSI 2012/203, SSI 2012/204, SSI 2012/207, SSI 2012/222, SSI 2012/224, SSI 2012/225, SSI 2012/226, SSI 2012/227, SSI 2012/234, SSI 2012/235, SSI 2012/244, SSI 2012/251, SSI 2012/254, SSI 2012/255, SSI 2012/256, SSI 2012/257, SSI 2012/277, SSI 2012/278, SSI 2012/279, SSI 2012/298, SSI 2012/299, SSI 2012/309, SSI 2012/310, SSI 2012/311, SSI 2012/312, SSI 2012/313, SSI 2012/314
s.14, referred to: SI 2012/1284 Sch.1, SI 2012/2541 Sch.1, SI 2012/2547 Sch.1, SI 2012/2548 Sch.1, SI 2012/2549 Sch.1, SI 2012/3102 Sch.1, SI 2012/3103 Sch.1, SI 2012/3104 Sch.1, SI 2012/3105 Sch.1, SI 2012/3106 Sch.1, SI 2012/3107 Sch.1
s.14, enabling: SI 2012/5, SI 2012/6, SI 2012/7, SI 2012/11, SI 2012/16, SI 2012/19, SI 2012/21, SI 2012/22, SI 2012/23, SI 2012/26, SI 2012/27, SI 2012/28, SI 2012/29, SI 2012/30, SI 2012/31, SI 2012/32, SI 2012/34, SI 2012/35, SI 2012/36, SI 2012/37, SI 2012/38, SI 2012/39, SI 2012/40, SI 2012/41, SI 2012/42, SI 2012/43, SI 2012/44, SI 2012/45, SI 2012/49, SI 2012/53, SI 2012/54, SI 2012/55, SI 2012/69, SI 2012/70, SI 2012/76, SI 2012/77, SI 2012/78, SI 2012/79, SI 2012/81, SI 2012/82, SI 2012/85, SI 2012/86, SI 2012/87, SI 2012/88, SI 2012/89, SI 2012/90, SI 2012/91, SI 2012/92, SI 2012/93, SI 2012/94, SI 2012/99, SI 2012/100, SI 2012/101, SI 2012/102, SI 2012/106, SI 2012/107, SI 2012/108, SI 2012/109, SI 2012/110, SI 2012/111, SI 2012/112, SI 2012/113, SI 2012/117, SI 2012/118, SI 2012/119, SI 2012/124, SI 2012/125, SI 2012/126, SI 2012/127, SI 2012/128, SI 2012/130, SI 2012/131, SI 2012/132, SI 2012/133, SI 2012/135, SI 2012/136, SI 2012/137, SI 2012/139, SI 2012/140, SI 2012/141, SI 2012/142, SI 2012/143, SI 2012/144, SI 2012/162, SI 2012/163, SI 2012/164, SI 2012/165, SI 2012/172, SI 2012/173, SI 2012/174, SI 2012/175, SI 2012/176, SI 2012/177, SI 2012/179, SI 2012/180, SI 2012/181, SI 2012/182, SI 2012/183, SI 2012/184, SI 2012/197, SI 2012/208, SI 2012/209, SI 2012/211, SI 2012/214, SI 2012/217, SI 2012/218, SI

27. Road Traffic Regulation Act 1984– *cont.*
s.14, enabling:– *cont.*

2012/219, SI 2012/220, SI 2012/221, SI 2012/228,
SI 2012/229, SI 2012/231, SI 2012/236, SI 2012/
237, SI 2012/238, SI 2012/239, SI 2012/240, SI
2012/241, SI 2012/242, SI 2012/243, SI 2012/
250, SI 2012/252, SI 2012/253, SI 2012/258, SI
2012/259, SI 2012/260, SI 2012/261, SI 2012/
262, SI 2012/267, SI 2012/268, SI 2012/269, SI
2012/270, SI 2012/271, SI 2012/272, SI 2012/
273, SI 2012/274, SI 2012/275, SI 2012/281, SI
2012/287, SI 2012/288, SI 2012/289, SI 2012/
290, SI 2012/291, SI 2012/294, SI 2012/295, SI
2012/296, SI 2012/297, SI 2012/299, SI 2012/
300, SI 2012/301, SI 2012/302, SI 2012/303, SI
2012/315, SI 2012/316, SI 2012/317, SI 2012/318,
SI 2012/319, SI 2012/337, SI 2012/338, SI 2012/
341, SI 2012/342, SI 2012/343, SI 2012/345, SI
2012/346, SI 2012/347, SI 2012/348, SI 2012/
349, SI 2012/350, SI 2012/351, SI 2012/352, SI
2012/353, SI 2012/354, SI 2012/355, SI 2012/
363, SI 2012/364, SI 2012/365, SI 2012/366, SI
2012/367, SI 2012/368, SI 2012/369, SI 2012/
370, SI 2012/371, SI 2012/372, SI 2012/373, SI
2012/374, SI 2012/375, SI 2012/376, SI 2012/
377, SI 2012/378, SI 2012/379, SI 2012/380, SI
2012/381, SI 2012/382, SI 2012/383, SI 2012/
386, SI 2012/388, SI 2012/389, SI 2012/390, SI
2012/391, SI 2012/392, SI 2012/393, SI 2012/
394, SI 2012/395, SI 2012/396, SI 2012/396
Sch.1, SI 2012/398, SI 2012/399, SI 2012/400, SI
2012/401, SI 2012/402, SI 2012/403, SI 2012/404,
SI 2012/405, SI 2012/406, SI 2012/407, SI 2012/
408, SI 2012/409, SI 2012/410, SI 2012/412, SI
2012/413, SI 2012/414, SI 2012/415, SI 2012/418,
SI 2012/419, SI 2012/420, SI 2012/422, SI 2012/
423, SI 2012/424, SI 2012/426, SI 2012/427, SI
2012/428, SI 2012/429, SI 2012/430, SI 2012/
434, SI 2012/435, SI 2012/436, SI 2012/437, SI
2012/438, SI 2012/439, SI 2012/440, SI 2012/
441, SI 2012/442, SI 2012/445, SI 2012/446, SI
2012/447, SI 2012/449, SI 2012/450, SI 2012/
451, SI 2012/452, SI 2012/453, SI 2012/454, SI
2012/455, SI 2012/456, SI 2012/457, SI 2012/
464, SI 2012/471, SI 2012/473, SI 2012/474, SI
2012/475, SI 2012/477, SI 2012/478, SI 2012/479,
SI 2012/480, SI 2012/481, SI 2012/482, SI 2012/
483, SI 2012/484, SI 2012/485, SI 2012/486, SI
2012/491, SI 2012/493, SI 2012/494, SI 2012/
495, SI 2012/496, SI 2012/497, SI 2012/498, SI
2012/499, SI 2012/506, SI 2012/507, SI 2012/
508, SI 2012/509, SI 2012/510, SI 2012/512, SI
2012/514, SI 2012/526, SI 2012/527, SI 2012/529,
SI 2012/530, SI 2012/540, SI 2012/541, SI 2012/
543, SI 2012/544, SI 2012/545, SI 2012/546, SI
2012/548, SI 2012/549, SI 2012/550, SI 2012/
551, SI 2012/552, SI 2012/553, SI 2012/554, SI
2012/556, SI 2012/557, SI 2012/558, SI 2012/559,
SI 2012/561, SI 2012/562, SI 2012/563, SI 2012/
564, SI 2012/565, SI 2012/566, SI 2012/567, SI
2012/568, SI 2012/569, SI 2012/570, SI 2012/
571, SI 2012/572, SI 2012/575, SI 2012/576, SI
2012/577, SI 2012/578, SI 2012/579, SI 2012/580,
SI 2012/581, SI 2012/582, SI 2012/583, SI 2012/
585, SI 2012/586, SI 2012/587, SI 2012/588, SI
2012/589, SI 2012/590, SI 2012/591, SI 2012/
592, SI 2012/593, SI 2012/595, SI 2012/596, SI
2012/597, SI 2012/598, SI 2012/599, SI 2012/
600, SI 2012/602, SI 2012/603, SI 2012/604, SI
2012/606, SI 2012/607, SI 2012/608, SI 2012/
609, SI 2012/611, SI 2012/612, SI 2012/613, SI
2012/614, SI 2012/615, SI 2012/616, SI 2012/617,

SI 2012/618, SI 2012/620, SI 2012/621, SI 2012/
622, SI 2012/623, SI 2012/625, SI 2012/626, SI
2012/627, SI 2012/633, SI 2012/648, SI 2012/
649, SI 2012/650, SI 2012/651, SI 2012/652, SI
2012/653, SI 2012/654, SI 2012/655, SI 2012/
656, SI 2012/657, SI 2012/658, SI 2012/659, SI
2012/660, SI 2012/661, SI 2012/662, SI 2012/
665, SI 2012/675, SI 2012/676, SI 2012/678, SI
2012/699, SI 2012/703, SI 2012/704, SI 2012/
707, SI 2012/713, SI 2012/714, SI 2012/715, SI
2012/719, SI 2012/720, SI 2012/721, SI 2012/
722, SI 2012/723, SI 2012/726, SI 2012/728, SI
2012/731, SI 2012/732, SI 2012/733, SI 2012/
741, SI 2012/743, SI 2012/744, SI 2012/754, SI
2012/758, SI 2012/759, SI 2012/768, SI 2012/
769, SI 2012/770, SI 2012/772, SI 2012/773, SI
2012/774, SI 2012/775, SI 2012/776, SI 2012/
777, SI 2012/778, SI 2012/781, SI 2012/783, SI
2012/784, SI 2012/830, SI 2012/831, SI 2012/
832, SI 2012/839, SI 2012/840, SI 2012/850, SI
2012/851, SI 2012/855, SI 2012/856, SI 2012/857,
SI 2012/858, SI 2012/859, SI 2012/860, SI 2012/
861, SI 2012/862, SI 2012/864, SI 2012/865, SI
2012/866, SI 2012/876, SI 2012/880, SI 2012/
888, SI 2012/889, SI 2012/890, SI 2012/893, SI
2012/894, SI 2012/900, SI 2012/902, SI 2012/
903, SI 2012/905, SI 2012/912, SI 2012/914, SI
2012/926, SI 2012/927, SI 2012/928, SI 2012/
930, SI 2012/931, SI 2012/932, SI 2012/933, SI
2012/942, SI 2012/944, SI 2012/945, SI 2012/
968, SI 2012/996, SI 2012/997, SI 2012/998, SI
2012/999, SI 2012/1000, SI 2012/1001, SI 2012/
1002, SI 2012/1004, SI 2012/1005, SI 2012/1006,
SI 2012/1007, SI 2012/1009, SI 2012/1010, SI
2012/1011, SI 2012/1012, SI 2012/1015, SI 2012/
1036, SI 2012/1037, SI 2012/1038, SI 2012/1039,
SI 2012/1040, SI 2012/1041, SI 2012/1042, SI
2012/1043, SI 2012/1044, SI 2012/1045, SI 2012/
1047, SI 2012/1048, SI 2012/1049, SI 2012/1050,
SI 2012/1051, SI 2012/1052, SI 2012/1053, SI 2012/
1054, SI 2012/1055, SI 2012/1056, SI 2012/1057, SI
2012/1058, SI 2012/1059, SI 2012/1062, SI 2012/
1063, SI 2012/1064, SI 2012/1065, SI 2012/1066,
SI 2012/1067, SI 2012/1068, SI 2012/1069, SI
2012/1070, SI 2012/1071, SI 2012/1072, SI 2012/
1073, SI 2012/1076, SI 2012/1077, SI 2012/1078,
SI 2012/1079, SI 2012/1080, SI 2012/1081, SI
2012/1083, SI 2012/1084, SI 2012/1086, SI 2012/
1088, SI 2012/1089, SI 2012/1090, SI 2012/1091, SI
2012/1092, SI 2012/1094, SI 2012/1103, SI 2012/
1104, SI 2012/1105, SI 2012/1106, SI 2012/1111, SI
2012/1112, SI 2012/1114, SI 2012/1116, SI 2012/
1117, SI 2012/1119, SI 2012/1120, SI 2012/1122, SI
2012/1130, SI 2012/1131, SI 2012/1132, SI 2012/
1136, SI 2012/1137, SI 2012/1138, SI 2012/1140,
SI 2012/1141, SI 2012/1142, SI 2012/1144, SI
2012/1145, SI 2012/1146, SI 2012/1147, SI 2012/
1148, SI 2012/1149, SI 2012/1152, SI 2012/1160,
SI 2012/1161, SI 2012/1162, SI 2012/1163, SI
2012/1166, SI 2012/1168, SI 2012/1169, SI 2012/
1170, SI 2012/1171, SI 2012/1173, SI 2012/1175, SI
2012/1178, SI 2012/1179, SI 2012/1180, SI 2012/
1181, SI 2012/1182, SI 2012/1183, SI 2012/1184, SI
2012/1185, SI 2012/1190, SI 2012/1191, SI 2012/
1192, SI 2012/1193, SI 2012/1194, SI 2012/1195,
SI 2012/1196, SI 2012/1200, SI 2012/1202, SI
2012/1212, SI 2012/1213, SI 2012/1214, SI 2012/
1216, SI 2012/1217, SI 2012/1220, SI 2012/1222,
SI 2012/1224, SI 2012/1225, SI 2012/1226, SI
2012/1227, SI 2012/1228, SI 2012/1229, SI 2012/
1233, SI 2012/1235, SI 2012/1236, SI 2012/1237, SI
2012/1239, SI 2012/1240, SI 2012/1241, SI 2012/
1242, SI 2012/1245, SI 2012/1247, SI 2012/1249,
SI 2012/1250, SI 2012/1251, SI 2012/1252, SI

1984– cont.
27. Road Traffic Regulation Act 1984– *cont.*
s.14, enabling:– *cont.*
2012/ 1253, SI 2012/ 1254, SI 2012/ 1255, SI 2012/
1268, SI 2012/ 1269, SI 2012/ 1270, SI 2012/ 1272,
SI 2012/ 1276, SI 2012/ 1279, SI 2012/ 1280, SI
2012/ 1281, SI 2012/ 1283, SI 2012/ 1296, SI 2012/
1297, SI 2012/ 1298, SI 2012/ 1299, SI 2012/ 1300,
SI 2012/ 1303, SI 2012/ 1304, SI 2012/ 1306, SI
2012/ 1307, SI 2012/ 1308, SI 2012/ 1314, SI 2012/
1315, SI 2012/ 1316, SI 2012/ 1317, SI 2012/ 1318, SI
2012/ 1321, SI 2012/ 1323, SI 2012/ 1325, SI 2012/
1326, SI 2012/ 1327, SI 2012/ 1355, SI 2012/ 1361,
SI 2012/ 1362, SI 2012/ 1364, SI 2012/ 1365, SI
2012/ 1366, SI 2012/ 1368, SI 2012/ 1369, SI 2012/
1370, SI 2012/ 1371, SI 2012/ 1372, SI 2012/ 1373, SI
2012/ 1374, SI 2012/ 1381, SI 2012/ 1383, SI 2012/
1398, SI 2012/ 1400, SI 2012/ 1405, SI 2012/ 1406,
SI 2012/ 1407, SI 2012/ 1408, SI 2012/ 1409, SI
2012/ 1411, SI 2012/ 1412, SI 2012/ 1413, SI 2012/
1414, SI 2012/ 1415, SI 2012/ 1416, SI 2012/ 1417, SI
2012/ 1419, SI 2012/ 1420, SI 2012/ 1421, SI 2012/
1422, SI 2012/ 1434, SI 2012/ 1435, SI 2012/ 1436,
SI 2012/ 1437, SI 2012/ 1438, SI 2012/ 1441, SI
2012/ 1442, SI 2012/ 1443, SI 2012/ 1444, SI 2012/
1445, SI 2012/ 1446, SI 2012/ 1447, SI 2012/ 1448,
SI 2012/ 1449, SI 2012/ 1450, SI 2012/ 1451, SI
2012/ 1452, SI 2012/ 1453, SI 2012/ 1454, SI 2012/
1455, SI 2012/ 1456, SI 2012/ 1457, SI 2012/ 1458, SI
2012/ 1459, SI 2012/ 1460, SI 2012/ 1461, SI 2012/
1468, SI 2012/ 1469, SI 2012/ 1472, SI 2012/ 1473, SI
2012/ 1474, SI 2012/ 1475, SI 2012/ 1476, SI 2012/
1481, SI 2012/ 1482, SI 2012/ 1484, SI 2012/ 1485,
SI 2012/ 1486, SI 2012/ 1487, SI 2012/ 1488, SI
2012/ 1490, SI 2012/ 1491, SI 2012/ 1492, SI 2012/
1494, SI 2012/ 1495, SI 2012/ 1496, SI 2012/ 1497, SI
2012/ 1498, SI 2012/ 1499, SI 2012/ 1503, SI 2012/
1504, SI 2012/ 1505, SI 2012/ 1520, SI 2012/ 1521, SI
2012/ 1522, SI 2012/ 1524, SI 2012/ 1525, SI 2012/
1526, SI 2012/ 1527, SI 2012/ 1528, SI 2012/ 1529, SI
2012/ 1533, SI 2012/ 1535, SI 2012/ 1539, SI 2012/
1540, SI 2012/ 1541, SI 2012/ 1542, SI 2012/ 1543,
SI 2012/ 1545, SI 2012/ 1546, SI 2012/ 1549, SI
2012/ 1550, SI 2012/ 1551, SI 2012/ 1552, SI 2012/
1556, SI 2012/ 1557, SI 2012/ 1558, SI 2012/ 1560,
SI 2012/ 1561, SI 2012/ 1563, SI 2012/ 1564, SI
2012/ 1565, SI 2012/ 1566, SI 2012/ 1568, SI 2012/
1570, SI 2012/ 1572, SI 2012/ 1575, SI 2012/ 1576, SI
2012/ 1577, SI 2012/ 1578, SI 2012/ 1579, SI 2012/
1580, SI 2012/ 1581, SI 2012/ 1582, SI 2012/ 1583,
SI 2012/ 1584, SI 2012/ 1585, SI 2012/ 1587, SI
2012/ 1589, SI 2012/ 1590, SI 2012/ 1591, SI 2012/
1592, SI 2012/ 1593, SI 2012/ 1594, SI 2012/ 1595,
SI 2012/ 1596, SI 2012/ 1597, SI 2012/ 1599, SI
2012/ 1600, SI 2012/ 1601, SI 2012/ 1602, SI 2012/
1603, SI 2012/ 1605, SI 2012/ 1606, SI 2012/ 1607, SI
2012/ 1608, SI 2012/ 1609, SI 2012/ 1610, SI 2012/
1611, SI 2012/ 1612, SI 2012/ 1614, SI 2012/ 1617, SI
2012/ 1618, SI 2012/ 1619, SI 2012/ 1620, SI 2012/
1621, SI 2012/ 1622, SI 2012/ 1623, SI 2012/ 1624,
SI 2012/ 1625, SI 2012/ 1626, SI 2012/ 1627, SI
2012/ 1628, SI 2012/ 1629, SI 2012/ 1636, SI 2012/
1639, SI 2012/ 1642, SI 2012/ 1648, SI 2012/ 1668, SI
2012/ 1669, SI 2012/ 1670, SI 2012/ 1671, SI 2012/
1676, SI 2012/ 1677, SI 2012/ 1678, SI 2012/ 1679,
SI 2012/ 1680, SI 2012/ 1683, SI 2012/ 1684, SI
2012/ 1685, SI 2012/ 1686, SI 2012/ 1687, SI 2012/
1694, SI 2012/ 1695, SI 2012/ 1700, SI 2012/ 1701,
SI 2012/ 1702, SI 2012/ 1704, SI 2012/ 1706, SI
2012/ 1707, SI 2012/ 1708, SI 2012/ 1716, SI 2012/
1717, SI 2012/ 1718, SI 2012/ 1719, SI 2012/ 1720, SI
2012/ 1721, SI 2012/ 1722, SI 2012/ 1723, SI 2012/
1727, SI 2012/ 1729, SI 2012/ 1730, SI 2012/ 1731,

SI 2012/ 1735, SI 2012/ 1737, SI 2012/ 1738, SI
2012/ 1739, SI 2012/ 1744, SI 2012/ 1746, SI 2012/
1747, SI 2012/ 1774, SI 2012/ 1775, SI 2012/ 1776, SI
2012/ 1778, SI 2012/ 1779, SI 2012/ 1780, SI 2012/
1781, SI 2012/ 1782, SI 2012/ 1784, SI 2012/ 1785,
SI 2012/ 1786, SI 2012/ 1787, SI 2012/ 1788, SI
2012/ 1800, SI 2012/ 1801, SI 2012/ 1822, SI 2012/
1823, SI 2012/ 1827, SI 2012/ 1828, SI 2012/ 1830, SI
2012/ 1834, SI 2012/ 1835, SI 2012/ 1839, SI 2012/
1840, SI 2012/ 1850, SI 2012/ 1853, SI 2012/ 1854,
SI 2012/ 1855, SI 2012/ 1856, SI 2012/ 1858, SI
2012/ 1859, SI 2012/ 1860, SI 2012/ 1861, SI 2012/
1862, SI 2012/ 1873, SI 2012/ 1885, SI 2012/ 1888,
SI 2012/ 1890, SI 2012/ 1892, SI 2012/ 1912, SI
2012/ 1913, SI 2012/ 1920, SI 2012/ 1921, SI 2012/
1922, SI 2012/ 1929, SI 2012/ 1930, SI 2012/ 1931,
SI 2012/ 1932, SI 2012/ 1933, SI 2012/ 1934, SI
2012/ 1935, SI 2012/ 1936, SI 2012/ 1937, SI 2012/
1938, SI 2012/ 1939, SI 2012/ 1941, SI 2012/ 1942,
SI 2012/ 1947, SI 2012/ 1948, SI 2012/ 1949, SI
2012/ 1950, SI 2012/ 1951, SI 2012/ 1952, SI 2012/
1953, SI 2012/ 1962, SI 2012/ 1964, SI 2012/ 1967,
SI 2012/ 1968, SI 2012/ 1973, SI 2012/ 1979, SI
2012/ 1980, SI 2012/ 1981, SI 2012/ 1982, SI 2012/
1983, SI 2012/ 1985, SI 2012/ 1986, SI 2012/ 1987,
SI 2012/ 1988, SI 2012/ 1991, SI 2012/ 1992, SI
2012/ 1994, SI 2012/ 1995, SI 2012/ 1996, SI 2012/
1997, SI 2012/ 1998, SI 2012/ 2001, SI 2012/ 2002,
SI 2012/ 2003, SI 2012/ 2004, SI 2012/ 2005, SI
2012/ 2006, SI 2012/ 2009, SI 2012/ 2010, SI
2012/ 2011, SI 2012/ 2012, SI 2012/ 2013, SI 2012/
2014, SI 2012/ 2016, SI 2012/ 2019, SI 2012/ 2020,
SI 2012/ 2021, SI 2012/ 2022, SI 2012/ 2023, SI
2012/ 2024, SI 2012/ 2026, SI 2012/ 2032, SI
2012/ 2035, SI 2012/ 2036, SI 2012/ 2037, SI 2012/
2038, SI 2012/ 2039, SI 2012/ 2040, SI 2012/ 2041,
SI 2012/ 2042, SI 2012/ 2043, SI 2012/ 2044, SI
2012/ 2045, SI 2012/ 2047, SI 2012/ 2049, SI
2012/ 2050, SI 2012/ 2052, SI 2012/ 2053, SI
2012/ 2054, SI 2012/ 2057, SI 2012/ 2060, SI
2012/ 2061, SI 2012/ 2062, SI 2012/ 2063, SI
2012/ 2064, SI 2012/ 2065, SI 2012/ 2066, SI
2012/ 2068, SI 2012/ 2069, SI 2012/ 2070, SI
2012/ 2071, SI 2012/ 2072, SI 2012/ 2073, SI 2012/
2074, SI 2012/ 2076, SI 2012/ 2077, SI 2012/ 2078,
SI 2012/ 2080, SI 2012/ 2081, SI 2012/ 2082, SI
2012/ 2083, SI 2012/ 2086, SI 2012/ 2093, SI
2012/ 2094, SI 2012/ 2095, SI 2012/ 2096, SI
2012/ 2097, SI 2012/ 2098, SI 2012/ 2099, SI
2012/ 2100, SI 2012/ 2101, SI 2012/ 2102, SI 2012/
2103, SI 2012/ 2104, SI 2012/ 2116, SI 2012/ 2117,
SI 2012/ 2118, SI 2012/ 2119, SI 2012/ 2120, SI
2012/ 2121, SI 2012/ 2122, SI 2012/ 2123, SI 2012/
2124, SI 2012/ 2126, SI 2012/ 2127, SI 2012/ 2128, SI
2012/ 2129, SI 2012/ 2130, SI 2012/ 2131, SI 2012/
2132, SI 2012/ 2133, SI 2012/ 2135, SI 2012/ 2136,
SI 2012/ 2137, SI 2012/ 2139, SI 2012/ 2141, SI
2012/ 2142, SI 2012/ 2143, SI 2012/ 2145, SI 2012/
2146, SI 2012/ 2147, SI 2012/ 2148, SI 2012/ 2149, SI
2012/ 2151, SI 2012/ 2152, SI 2012/ 2153, SI 2012/
2154, SI 2012/ 2155, SI 2012/ 2156, SI 2012/ 2158,
SI 2012/ 2159, SI 2012/ 2161, SI 2012/ 2162, SI
2012/ 2163, SI 2012/ 2164, SI 2012/ 2169, SI 2012/
2170, SI 2012/ 2171, SI 2012/ 2172, SI 2012/ 2173, SI
2012/ 2174, SI 2012/ 2175, SI 2012/ 2176, SI 2012/
2177, SI 2012/ 2178, SI 2012/ 2179, SI 2012/ 2180,
SI 2012/ 2181, SI 2012/ 2182, SI 2012/ 2183, SI
2012/ 2185, SI 2012/ 2188, SI 2012/ 2189, SI 2012/
2190, SI 2012/ 2191, SI 2012/ 2192, SI 2012/ 2193,
SI 2012/ 2194, SI 2012/ 2195, SI 2012/ 2196, SI
2012/ 2198, SI 2012/ 2199, SI 2012/ 2200, SI 2012/
2201, SI 2012/ 2202, SI 2012/ 2203, SI 2012/ 2204,
SI 2012/ 2205, SI 2012/ 2206, SI 2012/ 2207, SI
2012/ 2209, SI 2012/ 2210, SI 2012/ 2211, SI 2012/

1984– cont.

27. Road Traffic Regulation Act 1984– *cont.*
s.14, enabling:– *cont.*

2212, SI 2012/ 2214, SI 2012/ 2215, SI 2012/ 2216, SI
2012/ 2217, SI 2012/ 2218, SI 2012/ 2219, SI 2012/
2220, SI 2012/ 2221, SI 2012/ 2222, SI 2012/
2223, SI 2012/ 2224, SI 2012/ 2225, SI 2012/
2226, SI 2012/ 2227, SI 2012/ 2228, SI 2012/
2229, SI 2012/ 2230, SI 2012/ 2232, SI 2012/
2233, SI 2012/ 2236, SI 2012/ 2237, SI 2012/ 2238,
SI 2012/ 2239, SI 2012/ 2240, SI 2012/ 2241, SI
2012/ 2242, SI 2012/ 2243, SI 2012/ 2244, SI
2012/ 2245, SI 2012/ 2246, SI 2012/ 2247, SI
2012/ 2248, SI 2012/ 2250, SI 2012/ 2251, SI
2012/ 2252, SI 2012/ 2253, SI 2012/ 2254, SI
2012/ 2255, SI 2012/ 2256, SI 2012/ 2258, SI
2012/ 2259, SI 2012/ 2260, SI 2012/ 2266, SI
2012/ 2285, SI 2012/ 2286, SI 2012/ 2287, SI
2012/ 2288, SI 2012/ 2289, SI 2012/ 2291, SI
2012/ 2292, SI 2012/ 2293, SI 2012/ 2294, SI
2012/ 2295, SI 2012/ 2296, SI 2012/ 2297, SI
2012/ 2304, SI 2012/ 2305, SI 2012/ 2308, SI
2012/ 2309, SI 2012/ 2310, SI 2012/ 2311, SI 2012/
2314, SI 2012/ 2315, SI 2012/ 2316, SI 2012/ 2321, SI
2012/ 2322, SI 2012/ 2323, SI 2012/ 2324, SI 2012/
2325, SI 2012/ 2326, SI 2012/ 2327, SI 2012/ 2328,
SI 2012/ 2329, SI 2012/ 2331, SI 2012/ 2332, SI
2012/ 2333, SI 2012/ 2334, SI 2012/ 2338, SI 2012/
2339, SI 2012/ 2340, SI 2012/ 2341, SI 2012/ 2342,
SI 2012/ 2343, SI 2012/ 2344, SI 2012/ 2345, SI
2012/ 2346, SI 2012/ 2347, SI 2012/ 2348, SI
2012/ 2349, SI 2012/ 2350, SI 2012/ 2351, SI 2012/
2352, SI 2012/ 2354, SI 2012/ 2355, SI 2012/ 2356,
SI 2012/ 2357, SI 2012/ 2358, SI 2012/ 2359, SI
2012/ 2360, SI 2012/ 2361, SI 2012/ 2362, SI
2012/ 2363, SI 2012/ 2364, SI 2012/ 2365, SI
2012/ 2366, SI 2012/ 2367, SI 2012/ 2368, SI
2012/ 2369, SI 2012/ 2377, SI 2012/ 2381, SI 2012/
2382, SI 2012/ 2383, SI 2012/ 2384, SI 2012/ 2385,
SI 2012/ 2386, SI 2012/ 2388, SI 2012/ 2389, SI
2012/ 2390, SI 2012/ 2391, SI 2012/ 2392, SI 2012/
2399, SI 2012/ 2402, SI 2012/ 2408, SI 2012/ 2409,
SI 2012/ 2410, SI 2012/ 2415, SI 2012/ 2416, SI
2012/ 2417, SI 2012/ 2418, SI 2012/ 2419, SI 2012/
2422, SI 2012/ 2423, SI 2012/ 2424, SI 2012/
2425, SI 2012/ 2426, SI 2012/ 2427, SI 2012/
2428, SI 2012/ 2429, SI 2012/ 2430, SI 2012/ 2431,
SI 2012/ 2432, SI 2012/ 2433, SI 2012/ 2434, SI
2012/ 2435, SI 2012/ 2436, SI 2012/ 2437, SI 2012/
2438, SI 2012/ 2439, SI 2012/ 2440, SI 2012/ 2441,
SI 2012/ 2442, SI 2012/ 2443, SI 2012/ 2444, SI
2012/ 2445, SI 2012/ 2446, SI 2012/ 2448, SI
2012/ 2449, SI 2012/ 2450, SI 2012/ 2451, SI
2012/ 2452, SI 2012/ 2454, SI 2012/ 2455, SI
2012/ 2456, SI 2012/ 2457, SI 2012/ 2458, SI
2012/ 2459, SI 2012/ 2460, SI 2012/ 2461, SI
2012/ 2462, SI 2012/ 2464, SI 2012/ 2465, SI
2012/ 2467, SI 2012/ 2468, SI 2012/ 2469, SI
2012/ 2470, SI 2012/ 2471, SI 2012/ 2472, SI
2012/ 2473, SI 2012/ 2474, SI 2012/ 2475, SI
2012/ 2476, SI 2012/ 2477, SI 2012/ 2481, SI 2012/
2482, SI 2012/ 2483, SI 2012/ 2484, SI 2012/ 2485,
SI 2012/ 2486, SI 2012/ 2487, SI 2012/ 2489, SI
2012/ 2490, SI 2012/ 2491, SI 2012/ 2492, SI
2012/ 2493, SI 2012/ 2494, SI 2012/ 2495, SI
2012/ 2496, SI 2012/ 2497, SI 2012/ 2498, SI
2012/ 2501, SI 2012/ 2502, SI 2012/ 2503, SI
2012/ 2506, SI 2012/ 2508, SI 2012/ 2509, SI
2012/ 2510, SI 2012/ 2511, SI 2012/ 2512, SI 2012/
2513, SI 2012/ 2514, SI 2012/ 2515, SI 2012/ 2517,
SI 2012/ 2518, SI 2012/ 2519, SI 2012/ 2520, SI
2012/ 2525, SI 2012/ 2526, SI 2012/ 2527, SI 2012/
2528, SI 2012/ 2529, SI 2012/ 2531, SI 2012/ 2534,
SI 2012/ 2535, SI 2012/ 2536, SI 2012/ 2537, SI
2012/ 2538, SI 2012/ 2540, SI 2012/ 2542, SI
2012/ 2543, SI 2012/ 2544, SI 2012/ 2545, SI
2012/ 2556, SI 2012/ 2557, SI 2012/ 2558, SI 2012/
2561, SI 2012/ 2562, SI 2012/ 2564, SI 2012/ 2565,
SI 2012/ 2566, SI 2012/ 2577, SI 2012/ 2578, SI
2012/ 2579, SI 2012/ 2580, SI 2012/ 2581, SI 2012/
2582, SI 2012/ 2583, SI 2012/ 2584, SI 2012/ 2585,
SI 2012/ 2586, SI 2012/ 2600, SI 2012/ 2614, SI
2012/ 2615, SI 2012/ 2616, SI 2012/ 2617, SI 2012/
2618, SI 2012/ 2620, SI 2012/ 2621, SI 2012/ 2622,
SI 2012/ 2623, SI 2012/ 2624, SI 2012/ 2626, SI
2012/ 2627, SI 2012/ 2628, SI 2012/ 2633, SI 2012/
2634, SI 2012/ 2637, SI 2012/ 2638, SI 2012/ 2639,
SI 2012/ 2640, SI 2012/ 2641, SI 2012/ 2642, SI
2012/ 2643, SI 2012/ 2644, SI 2012/ 2645, SI
2012/ 2646, SI 2012/ 2648, SI 2012/ 2649, SI
2012/ 2653, SI 2012/ 2662, SI 2012/ 2663, SI
2012/ 2664, SI 2012/ 2671, SI 2012/ 2673, SI
2012/ 2674, SI 2012/ 2692, SI 2012/ 2693, SI
2012/ 2694, SI 2012/ 2695, SI 2012/ 2697, SI
2012/ 2698, SI 2012/ 2699, SI 2012/ 2701, SI 2012/
2702, SI 2012/ 2703, SI 2012/ 2704, SI 2012/ 2708,
SI 2012/ 2713, SI 2012/ 2714, SI 2012/ 2715, SI
2012/ 2716, SI 2012/ 2717, SI 2012/ 2718, SI 2012/
2719, SI 2012/ 2720, SI 2012/ 2721, SI 2012/ 2722,
SI 2012/ 2724, SI 2012/ 2725, SI 2012/ 2726, SI
2012/ 2727, SI 2012/ 2728, SI 2012/ 2736, SI 2012/
2737, SI 2012/ 2738, SI 2012/ 2739, SI 2012/ 2741, SI
2012/ 2742, SI 2012/ 2744, SI 2012/ 2757, SI 2012/
2758, SI 2012/ 2759, SI 2012/ 2760, SI 2012/ 2762,
SI 2012/ 2763, SI 2012/ 2764, SI 2012/ 2765, SI
2012/ 2766, SI 2012/ 2767, SI 2012/ 2771, SI 2012/
2772, SI 2012/ 2773, SI 2012/ 2774, SI 2012/ 2775,
SI 2012/ 2776, SI 2012/ 2777, SI 2012/ 2778, SI
2012/ 2779, SI 2012/ 2780, SI 2012/ 2781, SI 2012/
2783, SI 2012/ 2784, SI 2012/ 2792, SI 2012/ 2793,
SI 2012/ 2794, SI 2012/ 2795, SI 2012/ 2796, SI
2012/ 2797, SI 2012/ 2799, SI 2012/ 2800, SI
2012/ 2801, SI 2012/ 2802, SI 2012/ 2803, SI
2012/ 2804, SI 2012/ 2805, SI 2012/ 2807, SI
2012/ 2808, SI 2012/ 2809, SI 2012/ 2810, SI 2012/
2815, SI 2012/ 2816, SI 2012/ 2818, SI 2012/ 2819, SI
2012/ 2820, SI 2012/ 2821, SI 2012/ 2823, SI 2012/
2825, SI 2012/ 2826, SI 2012/ 2827, SI 2012/ 2828,
SI 2012/ 2829, SI 2012/ 2830, SI 2012/ 2831, SI
2012/ 2832, SI 2012/ 2833, SI 2012/ 2834, SI
2012/ 2835, SI 2012/ 2836, SI 2012/ 2837, SI 2012/
2838, SI 2012/ 2839, SI 2012/ 2841, SI 2012/ 2842,
SI 2012/ 2843, SI 2012/ 2844, SI 2012/ 2845, SI
2012/ 2846, SI 2012/ 2847, SI 2012/ 2848, SI
2012/ 2849, SI 2012/ 2851, SI 2012/ 2852, SI 2012/
2853, SI 2012/ 2857, SI 2012/ 2858, SI 2012/ 2859,
SI 2012/ 2860, SI 2012/ 2861, SI 2012/ 2863, SI
2012/ 2864, SI 2012/ 2865, SI 2012/ 2866, SI
2012/ 2867, SI 2012/ 2868, SI 2012/ 2869, SI
2012/ 2870, SI 2012/ 2871, SI 2012/ 2872, SI 2012/
2873, SI 2012/ 2874, SI 2012/ 2875, SI 2012/ 2877,
SI 2012/ 2878, SI 2012/ 2880, SI 2012/ 2881, SI
2012/ 2883, SI 2012/ 2887, SI 2012/ 2888, SI 2012/
2889, SI 2012/ 2893, SI 2012/ 2894, SI 2012/ 2895,
SI 2012/ 2896, SI 2012/ 2899, SI 2012/ 2908, SI
2012/ 2912, SI 2012/ 2915, SI 2012/ 2916, SI 2012/
2917, SI 2012/ 2923, SI 2012/ 2924, SI 2012/ 2925,
SI 2012/ 2926, SI 2012/ 2927, SI 2012/ 2928, SI
2012/ 2929, SI 2012/ 2930, SI 2012/ 2931, SI 2012/
2934, SI 2012/ 2936, SI 2012/ 2942, SI 2012/ 2943,
SI 2012/ 2944, SI 2012/ 2945, SI 2012/ 2947, SI
2012/ 2948, SI 2012/ 2949, SI 2012/ 2955, SI
2012/ 2956, SI 2012/ 2957, SI 2012/ 2958, SI
2012/ 2959, SI 2012/ 2960, SI 2012/ 2961, SI
2012/ 2966, SI 2012/ 2967, SI 2012/ 2968, SI
2012/ 2969, SI 2012/ 2971, SI 2012/ 2972, SI
2012/ 2973, SI 2012/ 2979, SI 2012/ 2981, SI 2012/

27. Road Traffic Regulation Act 1984– *cont.*
s.14, enabling:– *cont.*

2982, SI 2012/ 2983, SI 2012/ 2995, SI 2012/ 2997, SI 2012/ 2998, SI 2012/ 3000, SI 2012/ 3031, SI 2012/ 3034, SI 2012/ 3108, SI 2012/ 3114, SI 2012/ 3115, SI 2012/ 3116, SI 2012/ 3117, SI 2012/ 3120, SI 2012/ 3121, SI 2012/ 3126, SI 2012/ 3127, SI 2012/ 3130, SI 2012/ 3131, SI 2012/ 3132, SI 2012/ 3133, SI 2012/ 3137, SI 2012/ 3139, SI 2012/ 3140, SI 2012/ 3141, SI 2012/ 3142, SI 2012/ 3146, SI 2012/ 3147, SI 2012/ 3148, SI 2012/ 3149, SI 2012/ 3151, SI 2012/ 3154, SI 2012/ 3155, SI 2012/ 3156, SI 2012/ 3157, SI 2012/ 3160, SI 2012/ 3161, SI 2012/ 3162, SI 2012/ 3163, SI 2012/ 3164, SI 2012/ 3165, SI 2012/ 3166, SI 2012/ 3167, SI 2012/ 3168, SI 2012/ 3169, SI 2012/ 3175, SI 2012/ 3176, SI 2012/ 3177, SI 2012/ 3178, SI 2012/ 3179, SI 2012/ 3180, SI 2012/ 3181, SI 2012/ 3182, SI 2012/ 3183, SI 2012/ 3184, SI 2012/ 3185, SI 2012/ 3187, SI 2012/ 3188, SI 2012/ 3189, SI 2012/ 3190, SI 2012/ 3191, SI 2012/ 3192, SI 2012/ 3193, SI 2012/ 3194, SI 2012/ 3195, SI 2012/ 3196, SI 2012/ 3197, SI 2012/ 3198, SI 2012/ 3199, SI 2012/ 3200, SI 2012/ 3201, SI 2012/ 3202, SI 2012/ 3203, SI 2012/ 3204, SI 2012/ 3205, SI 2012/ 3206, SI 2012/ 3207, SI 2012/ 3208, SI 2012/ 3209, SI 2012/ 3210, SI 2012/ 3211, SI 2012/ 3212, SI 2012/ 3213, SI 2012/ 3214, SI 2012/ 3215, SI 2012/ 3216, SI 2012/ 3217, SI 2012/ 3218, SI 2012/ 3219, SI 2012/ 3220, SI 2012/ 3221, SI 2012/ 3222, SI 2012/ 3223, SI 2012/ 3224, SI 2012/ 3225, SI 2012/ 3226, SI 2012/ 3227, SI 2012/ 3228, SI 2012/ 3229, SI 2012/ 3230, SI 2012/ 3231, SI 2012/ 3233, SI 2012/ 3234, SI 2012/ 3235, SI 2012/ 3236, SI 2012/ 3237, SI 2012/ 3238, SI 2012/ 3239, SI 2012/ 3240, SI 2012/ 3241, SI 2012/ 3242, SI 2012/ 3243, SI 2012/ 3244, SI 2012/ 3245, SI 2012/ 3246, SI 2012/ 3247, SI 2012/ 3248, SSI 2012/ 12, SSI 2012/ 13, SSI 2012/ 14, SSI 2012/ 15, SSI 2012/ 17, SSI 2012/ 18, SSI 2012/ 46, SSI 2012/ 47, SSI 2012/ 56, SSI 2012/ 57, SSI 2012/ 58, SSI 2012/ 59, SSI 2012/ 95, SSI 2012/ 96, SSI 2012/ 97, SSI 2012/ 98, SSI 2012/ 103, SSI 2012/ 120, SSI 2012/ 121, SSI 2012/ 122, SSI 2012/ 123, SSI 2012/ 134, SSI 2012/ 156, SSI 2012/ 157, SSI 2012/ 158, SSI 2012/ 159, SSI 2012/ 169, SSI 2012/ 185, SSI 2012/ 186, SSI 2012/ 200, SSI 2012/ 201, SSI 2012/ 202, SSI 2012/ 203, SSI 2012/ 204, SSI 2012/ 207, SSI 2012/ 222, SSI 2012/ 224, SSI 2012/ 225, SSI 2012/ 226, SSI 2012/ 227, SSI 2012/ 230, SSI 2012/ 232, SSI 2012/ 233, SSI 2012/ 234, SSI 2012/ 235, SSI 2012/ 244, SSI 2012/ 248, SSI 2012/ 251, SSI 2012/ 254, SSI 2012/ 255, SSI 2012/ 256, SSI 2012/ 257, SSI 2012/ 277, SSI 2012/ 278, SSI 2012/ 279, SSI 2012/ 280, SSI 2012/ 298, SSI 2012/ 309, SSI 2012/ 310, SSI 2012/ 311, SSI 2012/ 312, SSI 2012/ 313, SSI 2012/ 314, SSI 2012/ 356, SSI 2012/ 357, SSI 2012/ 358, SSI 2012/ 359

s.15, applied: SI 2012/ 445 Art.8, SI 2012/ 1282 Sch.1, SI 2012/ 1286 Sch.1, SI 2012/ 1289 Sch.1, SI 2012/ 1294 Sch.1, SI 2012/ 1295 Sch.1

s.15, referred to: SI 2012/ 1284 Sch.1, SI 2012/ 2541 Sch.1, SI 2012/ 2547 Sch.1, SI 2012/ 2548 Sch.1, SI 2012/ 2549 Sch.1, SI 2012/ 3102 Sch.1, SI 2012/ 3103 Sch.1, SI 2012/ 3104 Sch.1, SI 2012/ 3105 Sch.1, SI 2012/ 3106 Sch.1

s.15, enabling: SI 2012/ 1122, SI 2012/ 1579, SI 2012/ 2462, SI 2012/ 2468

s.16, applied: SI 2012/ 1282 Sch.1, SI 2012/ 1284 Sch.1, SI 2012/ 1286 Sch.1, SI 2012/ 1289 Sch.1, SI 2012/ 1294 Sch.1, SI 2012/ 1295 Sch.1

27. Road Traffic Regulation Act 1984– *cont.*

s.16, referred to: SI 2012/ 1284 Sch.1, SI 2012/ 2541 Sch.1, SI 2012/ 2547 Sch.1, SI 2012/ 2548 Sch.1, SI 2012/ 2549 Sch.1, SI 2012/ 3102 Sch.1, SI 2012/ 3103 Sch.1, SI 2012/ 3104 Sch.1, SI 2012/ 3105 Sch.1, SI 2012/ 3106 Sch.1, SI 2012/ 3107 Sch.1

s.16A, applied: SSI 2012/ 168, SSI 2012/ 195, SSI 2012/ 223, SSI 2012/ 317

s.16A, enabling: SI 2012/ 547, SI 2012/ 1165, SI 2012/ 1211, SI 2012/ 1562, SI 2012/ 1613, SI 2012/ 1725, SI 2012/ 1728, SI 2012/ 1732, SI 2012/ 1733, SI 2012/ 1789, SI 2012/ 1790, SI 2012/ 1799, SI 2012/ 1820, SI 2012/ 1891, SI 2012/ 2249, SI 2012/ 2353, SI 2012/ 2650, SI 2012/ 2651, SI 2012/ 2700, SSI 2012/ 168, SSI 2012/ 195, SSI 2012/ 223, SSI 2012/ 299, SSI 2012/ 317, SSI 2012/ 351

s.17, amended: 2012 c.11 s.21

s.17, applied: SSI 2012/ 343, SSI 2012/ 344

s.17, enabling: SI 2012/ 104, SI 2012/ 985, SI 2012/ 1865, SI 2012/ 2134, SSI 2012/ 62, SSI 2012/ 145, SSI 2012/ 147, SSI 2012/ 320, SSI 2012/ 343, SSI 2012/ 344

s.26, applied: SI 2012/ 335 Reg.6, SI 2012/ 2991 Reg.7

s.32, applied: SI 2012/ 2635 Art.39, SI 2012/ 2659 Sch.1

s.46, varied: SSI 2012/ 137 Sch.3 para.1, SSI 2012/ 140 Sch.3 para.1

s.49, applied: SI 2012/ 1282 Sch.1, SI 2012/ 1284 Sch.1, SI 2012/ 1286 Sch.1, SI 2012/ 1289 Sch.1, SI 2012/ 1294 Sch.1, SI 2012/ 1295 Sch.1

s.49, referred to: SI 2012/ 2541 Sch.1, SI 2012/ 2547 Sch.1, SI 2012/ 2548 Sch.1, SI 2012/ 2549 Sch.1, SI 2012/ 3102 Sch.1, SI 2012/ 3103 Sch.1, SI 2012/ 3104 Sch.1, SI 2012/ 3105 Sch.1, SI 2012/ 3106 Sch.1, SI 2012/ 3107 Sch.1

s.55, varied: SSI 2012/ 137 Sch.3 para.2, SSI 2012/ 140 Sch.3 para.2

s.63A, applied: SSI 2012/ 138 Reg.2, SSI 2012/ 141 Reg.2

s.63A, varied: SSI 2012/ 137 Sch.3 para.3, SSI 2012/ 140 Sch.3 para.3

s.63A, enabling: SSI 2012/ 138, SSI 2012/ 141

s.64, amended: 2012 c.11 s.21

s.64, applied: 2012 c.11 s.22, SI 2012/ 41 Art.4, SI 2012/ 54 Art.4, SI 2012/ 95 Art.4, SI 2012/ 120 Art.3, SI 2012/ 123 Art.4, SI 2012/ 128 Art.5, SI 2012/ 175 Art.3, SI 2012/ 243 Art.3, SI 2012/ 255 Art.5, SI 2012/ 262 Art.3, SI 2012/ 271 Art.4, SI 2012/ 294 Art.4, SI 2012/ 300 Art.4, SI 2012/ 301 Art.4, SI 2012/ 302 Art.4, SI 2012/ 341 Art.4, SI 2012/ 355 Art.3, SI 2012/ 383 Art.4, SI 2012/ 406 Art.3, SI 2012/ 407 Art.3, SI 2012/ 413 Art.4, SI 2012/ 420 Art.4, SI 2012/ 436 Art.4, SI 2012/ 437 Art.4, SI 2012/ 440 Art.4, SI 2012/ 447 Art.3, SI 2012/ 454 Art.3, SI 2012/ 512 Art.4, SI 2012/ 529 Art.3, SI 2012/ 543 Art.4, SI 2012/ 600 Art.3, SI 2012/ 604 Art.3, SI 2012/ 611 Art.3, SI 2012/ 721 Art.4, SI 2012/ 722 Art.3, SI 2012/ 723 Art.3, SI 2012/ 733 Art.4, SI 2012/ 859 Art.3, SI 2012/ 876 Art.3, SI 2012/ 997 Art.4, SI 2012/ 1000 Art.3, SI 2012/ 1010 Art.5, SI 2012/ 1041 Art.5, SI 2012/ 1045 Art.4, SI 2012/ 1057 Art.4, SI 2012/ 1119 Art.3, SI 2012/ 1149 Art.3, SI 2012/ 1178 Art.3, SI 2012/ 1214 Art.3, SI 2012/ 1250 Art.3, SI 2012/ 1366 Art.3, SI 2012/ 1371 Art.3, SI 2012/ 1413 Art.4, SI 2012/ 1451 Art.3, SI 2012/ 1452 Art.3, SI 2012/ 1455 Art.4, SI 2012/ 1461 Art.3, SI 2012/ 1527 Art.3, SI 2012/ 1582 Art.3, SI 2012/ 1583 Art.4, SI 2012/ 1612 Art.3, SI 2012/ 1678 Art.3, SI 2012/ 1684 Art.3, SI 2012/ 1707 Art.4, SI 2012/ 1717 Art.4, SI 2012/ 1780 Art.3, SI 2012/

27. Road Traffic Regulation Act 1984–*cont.*
s.64, applied:–*cont.*

1787 Art.4, SI 2012/1854 Art.4, SI 2012/1921
Art.4, SI 2012/1932 Art.3, SI 2012/1949 Art.5,
SI 2012/1951 Art.4, SI 2012/1952 Art.4, SI
2012/2005 Art.3, SI 2012/2014 Art.3, SI 2012/
2020 Art.5, SI 2012/2035 Art.4, SI 2012/2074
Art.3, SI 2012/2078 Art.4, SI 2012/2083 Art.4,
SI 2012/2116 Art.4, SI 2012/2120 Art.4, SI
2012/2133 Art.4, SI 2012/2139 Art.4, SI 2012/
2145 Art.3, SI 2012/2151 Art.4, SI 2012/2180
Art.4, SI 2012/2182 Art.5, SI 2012/2199 Art.4,
SI 2012/2205 Art.3, SI 2012/2207 Art.3, SI
2012/2220 Art.4, SI 2012/2243 Art.4, SI 2012/
2284 Art.12, SI 2012/2286 Art.4, SI 2012/2323
Art.3, SI 2012/2331 Art.3, SI 2012/2342 Art.4,
SI 2012/2344 Art.4, SI 2012/2346 Art.3, SI
2012/2351 Art.3, SI 2012/2363 Art.4, SI 2012/
2426 Art.4, SI 2012/2437 Art.3, SI 2012/2441
Art.3, SI 2012/2442 Art.4, SI 2012/2449 Art.6,
SI 2012/2450 Art.5, SI 2012/2460 Art.3, SI
2012/2472 Art.3, SI 2012/2475 Art.3, SI 2012/
2484 Art.3, SI 2012/2486 Art.3, SI 2012/2496
Art.4, SI 2012/2528 Art.4, SI 2012/2538 Art.3,
SI 2012/2542 Art.5, SI 2012/2580 Art.4, SI
2012/2622 Art.3, SI 2012/2637 Art.3, SI 2012/
2673 Art.5, SI 2012/2744 Art.3, SI 2012/2759
Art.3, SI 2012/2760 Art.3, SI 2012/2780 Art.4,
SI 2012/2783 Art.3, SI 2012/2784 Art.3, SI
2012/2792 Art.3, SI 2012/2803 Art.3, SI 2012/
2816 Art.3, SI 2012/2823 Art.4, SI 2012/2836
Art.4, SI 2012/2848 Art.3, SI 2012/2849 Art.3,
SI 2012/2873 Art.3, SI 2012/2924 Art.4, SI
2012/2927 Art.3, SI 2012/2955 Art.3, SI 2012/
2959 Art.4, SI 2012/2960 Art.4, SI 2012/2961
Art.4, SI 2012/2973 Art.3, SI 2012/2981 Art.4,
SI 2012/2983 Art.5, SI 2012/3114 Art.4, SI
2012/3114 Art.3, SI 2012/3116 Art.3, SI 2012/
3140 Art.3
s.64, referred to: SI 2012/1461 Art.3, SI 2012/2508
Art.3
s.65, applied: SI 2012/2284 Art.12
s.66, applied: SI 2012/1159 Art.5
s.67, applied: SI 2012/1159 Art.5
s.81, applied: SI 2012/1097 Art.4, SI 2012/1098
Art.2, Art.3, SI 2012/1099 Art.2, SI 2012/1113
Art.4, SI 2012/1123 Art.2, SI 2012/1125 Art.2,
SI 2012/1802 Art.2, SI 2012/1874 Art.2, SI
2012/1875 Art.2, SI 2012/1884 Art.3, SI 2012/
2025 Art.2, SI 2012/2027 Art.3, SI 2012/2028
Art.3, SI 2012/2033 Art.3, SI 2012/2034 Art.4,
SI 2012/2138 Art.3, SI 2012/2313 Art.2, SI
2012/2735 Art.5, SI 2012/2974 Art.3, SSI 2012/
268 Art.2
s.81, disapplied: SI 2012/1864 Art.3
s.82, enabling: SI 2012/1097, SI 2012/1098, SI 2012/
1099, SI 2012/1113, SI 2012/1123, SI 2012/1125, SI
2012/1802, SI 2012/1864, SI 2012/1874, SI 2012/
1875, SI 2012/1884, SI 2012/2025, SI 2012/2027,
SI 2012/2028, SI 2012/2033, SI 2012/2034, SI
2012/2138, SI 2012/2313, SI 2012/2735, SI 2012/
2974, SSI 2012/268
s.83, enabling: SI 2012/1097, SI 2012/1098, SI 2012/
1099, SI 2012/1113, SI 2012/1123, SI 2012/1125, SI
2012/1802, SI 2012/1864, SI 2012/1874, SI 2012/
1875, SI 2012/1884, SI 2012/2025, SI 2012/2027,
SI 2012/2028, SI 2012/2033, SI 2012/2034, SI
2012/2138, SI 2012/2313, SI 2012/2735, SI 2012/
2974, SSI 2012/268
s.84, applied: SSI 2012/112, SSI 2012/115, SSI 2012/
231, SSI 2012/268

27. Road Traffic Regulation Act 1984–*cont.*
s.84, enabling: SI 2012/339, SI 2012/1097, SI 2012/
1098, SI 2012/1113, SI 2012/1126, SI 2012/1378, SI
2012/1382, SI 2012/1863, SI 2012/1864, SI 2012/
2034, SI 2012/2138, SI 2012/2144, SI 2012/2150,
SI 2012/2306, SI 2012/2307, SI 2012/2312, SI
2012/2313, SI 2012/2507, SI 2012/2735, SI 2012/
2850, SI 2012/3186, SSI 2012/112, SSI 2012/115,
SSI 2012/231, SSI 2012/268
s.86, amended: 2012 c.11 s.21
s.87, amended: 2012 asp 8 Sch.7 para.54
s.88, amended: 2012 c.11 s.21
s.99, see *Shiva Ltd v Transport for London* [2011]
EWCA Civ 1189, [2012] R.T.R. 13 (CA (Civ
Div)), Lord Neuberger (M.R.)
s.99, amended: 2012 c.9 s.55
s.99, referred to: SSI 2012/138 Reg.2, SSI 2012/141
Reg.2
s.99, enabling: SI 2012/2277
s.101, varied: SSI 2012/137 Sch.3 para.4, SSI 2012/
140 Sch.3 para.4
s.102, amended: 2012 c.9 Sch.9 para.18
s.102, varied: SSI 2012/137 Sch.3 para.5, SSI 2012/
140 Sch.3 para.5
s.122A, enabling: SI 2012/1082, SI 2012/1093, SI
2012/1099, SI 2012/1123
s.124, enabling: SI 2012/339, SI 2012/2507, SSI
2012/112, SSI 2012/115, SSI 2012/169, SSI 2012/
268
s.134, amended: 2012 c.11 s.21
s.134, applied: SI 2012/104, SI 2012/985, SI 2012/
1865, SI 2012/2134, SI 2012/2277, SSI 2012/62,
SSI 2012/138, SSI 2012/141, SSI 2012/145, SSI
2012/147
s.134, varied: SSI 2012/137 Sch.3 para.6, SSI 2012/
140 Sch.3 para.6
s.140, applied: SSI 2012/12 Art.4, SSI 2012/13 Art.4,
SSI 2012/14 Art.4, SSI 2012/15 Art.4, SSI 2012/
47 Art.4, SSI 2012/56 Art.4, SSI 2012/57 Art.4,
SSI 2012/58 Art.4, SSI 2012/59 Art.4, SSI 2012/
203 Art.4, SSI 2012/204 Art.4, SSI 2012/234
Art.4, SSI 2012/235 Art.4, SSI 2012/254 Art.4,
SSI 2012/255 Art.4, SSI 2012/256 Art.4, SSI
2012/257 Art.4
s.142, varied: SSI 2012/137 Sch.3 para.7
s.147, varied: SSI 2012/140 Sch.3 para.7
Sch.9 Part IV para.27, enabling: SI 2012/16, SI 2012/
26, SI 2012/53, SI 2012/110, SI 2012/113, SI 2012/
242, SI 2012/339, SI 2012/1082, SI 2012/1093, SI
2012/1097, SI 2012/1098, SI 2012/1099, SI 2012/
1105, SI 2012/1113, SI 2012/1123, SI 2012/1125, SI
2012/1126, SI 2012/1190, SI 2012/1377, SI 2012/
1378, SI 2012/1382, SI 2012/1459, SI 2012/1571,
SI 2012/1802, SI 2012/1862, SI 2012/1863, SI
2012/1874, SI 2012/1875, SI 2012/1884, SI 2012/
2025, SI 2012/2027, SI 2012/2028, SI 2012/2033,
SI 2012/2034, SI 2012/2138, SI 2012/2144, SI
2012/2150, SI 2012/2313, SI 2012/2350, SI 2012/
2507, SI 2012/2735, SI 2012/2863, SI 2012/3186,
SI 2012/3197, SI 2012/3236, SSI 2012/112, SSI
2012/115, SSI 2012/169, SSI 2012/268
28. County Courts Act 1984
s.2, applied: SI 2012/643 Art.4, SI 2012/1954 Art.3
s.2, enabling: SI 2012/643, SI 2012/1954
s.21, see *Swan Housing Association Ltd v Gill* [2012]
EWHC 3129 (QB), Times, December 13, 2012
(QBD), Eady, J.
s.38, see *Coventry City Council v O* [2011] EWCA
Civ 729, [2012] Fam. 210 (CA (Civ Div)), Lord
Neuberger of Abbotsbury MR

1984–cont.

28. County Courts Act 1984–*cont.*
    s.69, see *Pattni v First Leicester Buses Ltd* [2011] EWCA Civ 1384, [2012] R.T.R. 17 (CA (Civ Div)), Pill, L.J.
    s.71, see *Gittins v Serco Home Affairs* [2012] EWHC 651 (Ch), [2012] 4 All E.R. 1362 (Ch D (Leeds)), Judge Behrens
    s.74, see *Simcoe v Jacuzzi UK Group Plc* [2012] EWCA Civ 137, [2012] 1 W.L.R. 2393 (CA (Civ Div)), Lord Neuberger (M.R.)

30. Food Act 1984
    referred to: SI 2012/629

37. Child Abduction Act 1984
    see *R. v Kayani (Talib Hussein)* [2011] EWCA Crim 2871, [2012] 1 W.L.R. 1927 (CA (Crim Div)), Lord Judge, L.C.J.
    s.1, see *R. (on the application of Nicolaou) v Redbridge Magistrates' Court* [2012] EWHC 1647 (Admin), [2012] 2 Cr. App. R. 23 (DC), Richards, L.J.; see *R. v S* [2012] EWCA Crim 389, [2012] 1 W.L.R. 3081 (CA (Crim Div)), Sir John Thomas (President)
    s.1, amended: 2012 c.10 Sch.12 para.19
    Sch.1 para.2, amended: 2012 c.10 Sch.12 para.20

39. Video Recordings Act 1984
    s.3, amended: 2012 c.7 s.213, s.220
    s.4, applied: SI 2012/1764 Reg.3, SI 2012/1767 Reg.5, Reg.18, Reg.21
    s.7, applied: SI 2012/1767 Reg.9, Reg.11, Reg.12, Reg.19
    s.7, referred to: SI 2012/1767 Reg.9
    s.8, enabling: SI 2012/1767
    s.22A, enabling: SI 2012/1767

40. Animal Health and Welfare Act 1984
    s.6, repealed (in part): SSI 2012/321 Sch.5 Part 1
    s.7, repealed (in part): SSI 2012/321 Sch.5 Part 1
    s.8, repealed (in part): SSI 2012/321 Sch.5 Part 1
    s.9, repealed (in part): SSI 2012/321 Sch.5 Part 1

42. Matrimonial and Family Proceedings Act 1984
    see *Dukali v Lamrani* [2012] EWHC 1748 (Fam), [2012] 2 F.L.R. 1099 (Fam Div), Holman, J.; see *H v S (Recognition of Overseas Divorce)* [2012] 2 F.L.R. 157 (Fam Div), Judge Horowitz Q.C.
    Pt III. see *Dukali v Lamrani* [2012] EWHC 1748 (Fam), [2012] 2 F.L.R. 1099 (Fam Div), Holman, J.; see *Z v A (Financial Remedies: Overseas Divorce)* [2012] EWHC 467 (Fam), [2012] 2 F.L.R. 667 (Fam Div), Coleridge, J.
    s.12, see *Dukali v Lamrani* [2012] EWHC 1748 (Fam), [2012] 2 F.L.R. 1099 (Fam Div), Holman, J.
    s.13, see *H v S (Recognition of Overseas Divorce)* [2012] 2 F.L.R. 157 (Fam Div), Judge Horowitz Q.C.
    s.16, see *Z v A (Financial Remedies: Overseas Divorce)* [2012] EWHC 467 (Fam), [2012] 2 F.L.R. 667 (Fam Div), Coleridge, J.
    s.33, enabling: SI 2012/643, SI 2012/1954
    Sch.1 para.28, repealed (in part): 2012 asp 5 Sch.5 para.27

47. Repatriation of Prisoners Act 1984
    s.1, see *Gilbey (Julian) v HM Advocate* 2012 J.C. 40 (HCJ Appeal), Lord Reed
    s.2, amended: 2012 c.10 Sch.16 para.4
    s.3A, added: 2012 c.10 s.130
    s.6A, added: 2012 c.10 s.131
    s.6B, added: 2012 c.10 s.131
    s.6C, added: 2012 c.10 s.131
    s.6D, added: 2012 c.10 s.131
    s.9, amended: 2012 c.10 s.131

1984–cont.

47. Repatriation of Prisoners Act 1984–*cont.*
    s.9, applied: 2012 c.10 s.153
    Sch.1 Part 1 para.5, applied: 2012 c.10 Sch.1 para.5, Sch.1 para.9

51. Inheritance Tax Act 1984
    Pt V. see *Pawson (Deceased) v Revenue and Customs Commissioners* [2012] UKFTT 51 (TC), [2012] W.T.L.R. 665 (FTT (Tax)), Judge Richard Barlow
    s.3, applied: SI 2012/736 Art.5
    s.6, amended: 2012 c.14 Sch.37 para.2
    s.7, amended: 2012 c.14 Sch.33 para.3
    s.8, amended: 2012 c.14 s.208
    s.25, amended: 2012 c.14 Sch.14 para.27
    s.26A, amended: 2012 c.14 Sch.14 para.28
    s.32, amended: 2012 c.14 Sch.14 para.29
    s.32A, amended: 2012 c.14 Sch.14 para.30
    s.33, amended: 2012 c.14 Sch.14 para.31, Sch.33 para.4
    s.33, applied: 2012 c.14 Sch.14 para.33
    s.34, amended: 2012 c.14 Sch.14 para.32
    s.48, amended: 2012 c.14 s.210
    s.59, amended: 2012 c.14 Sch.16 para.69, 2012 c.21 Sch.18 para.44
    s.60, see *Watkins v Revenue and Customs Commissioners* [2012] W.T.L.R. 677 (FTT (Tax)), Judge Malachy Cornwell-Kelly
    s.74A, added: 2012 c.14 s.210
    s.74B, added: 2012 c.14 s.210
    s.74C, added: 2012 c.14 s.210
    s.78, amended: 2012 c.14 Sch.33 para.5
    s.89, see *Pitt v Holt* [2011] EWCA Civ 197, [2012] Ch. 132 (CA (Civ Div)), Mummery, L.J.
    s.105, see *Pawson (Deceased) v Revenue and Customs Commissioners* [2012] UKFTT 51 (TC), [2012] W.T.L.R. 665 (FTT (Tax)), Judge Richard Barlow
    s.105, amended: SI 2012/2903 Reg.4
    s.105, applied: SI 2012/2903 Reg.6
    s.115, see *Hanson v Revenue and Customs Commissioners* [2012] UKFTT 95 (TC), [2012] S.F.T.D. 705 (FTT (Tax)), John Walters Q.C.
    s.117, see *Atkinson v Revenue and Customs Commissioners* [2012] S.T.C. 289 (UT (Tax)), Warren, J (President)
    s.128, substituted: 2012 c.14 Sch.33 para.6
    s.141A, added: 2012 c.14 Sch.33 para.7
    s.142, amended: 2012 c.14 Sch.33 para.9
    s.155, amended: 2012 c.14 Sch.37 para.3
    s.155, applied: SI 2012/3070 Art.3, SI 2012/3071 Art.4, Art.5
    s.155, enabling: SI 2012/3070, SI 2012/3071
    s.201, amended: 2012 c.14 s.210
    s.216, applied: 2012 c.14 Sch.36 para.22, Sch.36 para.23, SI 2012/1836 Reg.9, Reg.10
    s.217, applied: 2012 c.14 Sch.36 para.22, Sch.36 para.23
    s.224, see *Watkins v Revenue and Customs Commissioners* [2012] W.T.L.R. 677 (FTT (Tax)), Judge Malachy Cornwell-Kelly
    s.234, amended: SI 2012/2903 Reg.5
    s.234, applied: SI 2012/2903 Reg.7
    s.247, repealed (in part): 2012 c.14 Sch.38 para.52
    Sch.1A para.1, added: 2012 c.14 Sch.33 para.1
    Sch.1A para.2, added: 2012 c.14 Sch.33 para.1
    Sch.1A para.3, added: 2012 c.14 Sch.33 para.1
    Sch.1A para.4, added: 2012 c.14 Sch.33 para.1
    Sch.1A para.5, added: 2012 c.14 Sch.33 para.1
    Sch.1A para.6, added: 2012 c.14 Sch.33 para.1

1984– cont.

51. Inheritance Tax Act 1984– *cont.*
Sch.1 A para.7, added: 2012 c.14 Sch.33 para.1
Sch.1 A para.8, added: 2012 c.14 Sch.33 para.1
Sch.1 A para.9, added: 2012 c.14 Sch.33 para.1
Sch.1 A para.10, added: 2012 c.14 Sch.33 para.1
Sch.3, amended: SI 2012/964 Sch.1, SI 2012/2654 Sch.1
Sch.4 Part II para.14, amended: 2012 c.14 Sch.33 para.8
Sch.5, applied: 2012 c.14 Sch.14 para.33

54. Roads (Scotland) Act 1984
s.1, see *MacDonald v Aberdeenshire Council* [2012] CSOH 101, 2012 S.L.T. 863 (OH), Lord Uist
s.5, applied: SSI 2012/239
s.5, enabling: SSI 2012/51, SSI 2012/79, SSI 2012/239, SSI 2012/241
s.12, applied: SSI 2012/80, SSI 2012/240
s.12, enabling: SSI 2012/80, SSI 2012/240, SSI 2012/242
s.20A, applied: SSI 2012/51, SSI 2012/79, SSI 2012/80, SSI 2012/239, SSI 2012/240
s.33, amended: 2012 asp 8 Sch.7 para.7
s.37, amended: 2012 asp 8 Sch.7 para.7
s.55A, applied: SSI 2012/51, SSI 2012/79, SSI 2012/80, SSI 2012/239, SSI 2012/240
s.59, amended: 2012 asp 8 Sch.7 para.7
s.68, applied: SSI 2012/52
s.68, enabling: SSI 2012/52
s.69, applied: SSI 2012/81
s.69, enabling: SSI 2012/81
s.70, enabling: SSI 2012/80, SSI 2012/240
s.71, applied: SSI 2012/81, SSI 2012/240
s.86, amended: 2012 asp 8 Sch.7 para.7
s.98, amended: 2012 asp 8 Sch.7 para.7
s.120A, added: 2012 asp 8 Sch.7 para.7
s.145, enabling: SSI 2012/241, SSI 2012/242
Sch.1 Part I, applied: SSI 2012/51, SSI 2012/79, SSI 2012/80, SSI 2012/239, SSI 2012/240
Sch.1 Part III, applied: SSI 2012/51, SSI 2012/79, SSI 2012/80, SSI 2012/239
Sch.2 para.2, see *Walton v Scottish Ministers* [2012] UKSC 44, 2012 S.L.T. 1211 (SC), Lord Hope, J.S.C. (Deputy President)

55. Building Act 1984
Part II, applied: SI 2012/3118 Reg.32
s.1, enabling: SI 2012/718, SI 2012/3119, SI 2012/3124
s.2A, enabling: SI 2012/3119
s.4, disapplied: SI 2012/3118 Reg.1
s.14, applied: SI 2012/718, SI 2012/3119, SI 2012/3124
s.16, enabling: SI 2012/3119
s.17, enabling: SI 2012/3119
s.34, enabling: SI 2012/3119
s.47, enabling: SI 2012/3119
s.49, enabling: SI 2012/3119
s.50, enabling: SI 2012/3119
s.51, enabling: SI 2012/3119
s.51A, enabling: SI 2012/3119
s.56, enabling: SI 2012/3119
s.91, applied: SI 2012/3118 Reg.32
Sch.1 para.1, enabling: SI 2012/718, SI 2012/3119
Sch.1 para.2, enabling: SI 2012/3119
Sch.1 para.4, enabling: SI 2012/718, SI 2012/3119
Sch.1 para.4A, enabling: SI 2012/718, SI 2012/3119
Sch.1 para.6, enabling: SI 2012/3119
Sch.1 para.7, enabling: SI 2012/718, SI 2012/3119
Sch.1 para.8, enabling: SI 2012/718, SI 2012/3119
Sch.1 para.9, enabling: SI 2012/3119

1984– cont.

55. Building Act 1984– *cont.*
Sch.1 para.10, enabling: SI 2012/718, SI 2012/3119, SI 2012/3124
Sch.1 para.11, enabling: SI 2012/3124

58. Rent (Scotland) Act 1984
Part VIII, applied: SSI 2012/329 Reg.2
s.89A, enabling: SSI 2012/329
Sch.4, applied: SSI 2012/180 Reg.2

60. Police and Criminal Evidence Act 1984
see *James v DPP* [2012] EWHC 1317 (Admin), (2012) 176 J.P. 346 (QBD (Admin)), Mitting, J.; see *R. (on the application of Dulai) v Chelmsford Magistrates' Court* [2012] EWHC 1055 (Admin), [2012] 3 All E.R. 764 (DC), Stanley Burnton, L.J.; see *R. (on the application of Glenn and Co (Essex) Ltd) v Revenue and Customs Commissioners* [2011] EWHC 2998 (Admin), [2012] 1 Cr. App. R. 22 (DC), Laws, L.J.; see *R. v B* [2012] EWCA Crim 414, [2012] 3 All E.R. 205 (CA (Crim Div)), Lord Judge, L.C.J.
applied: SI 2012/178 Reg.9
s.1, see *R. (on the application of Hicks) v Commissioner of Police of the Metropolis* [2012] EWHC 1947 (Admin), [2012] A.C.D. 102 (DC), Richards, L.J.; see *Sobczak v DPP* [2012] EWHC 1319 (Admin), (2012) 176 J.P. 575 (QBD (Admin)), Mitting, J.
s.1, amended: 2012 c.10 Sch.26 para.3
s.2, see *Sobczak v DPP* [2012] EWHC 1319 (Admin), (2012) 176 J.P. 575 (QBD (Admin)), Mitting, J.
s.8, see *Fitzpatrick v Commissioner of Police of the Metropolis* [2012] EWHC 12 (Admin), [2012] Lloyd's Rep. F.C. 361 (QBD (Admin)), Globe, J.; see *R. (on the application of Glenn and Co (Essex) Ltd) v Revenue and Customs Commissioners* [2011] EWHC 2998 (Admin), [2012] 1 Cr. App. R. 22 (DC), Laws, L.J.
s.9, see *R. (on the application of British Sky Broadcasting Ltd) v Central Criminal Court* [2011] EWHC 3451 (Admin), [2012] Q.B. 785 (QBD (Admin)), Moore-Bick, L.J.
s.10, applied: SI 2012/1726 r.6.3, r.6.7, SI 2012/2563 r.4
s.11, applied: SI 2012/1726 r.6.3, r.6.7, SI 2012/2563 r.4
s.12, referred to: 2012 c.14 Sch.38 para.15
s.13, referred to: 2012 c.14 Sch.38 para.15
s.14, applied: SI 2012/1726 r.6.7
s.15, see *R. (on the application of Glenn and Co (Essex) Ltd) v Revenue and Customs Commissioners* [2011] EWHC 2998 (Admin), [2012] 1 Cr. App. R. 22 (DC), Laws, L.J.
s.16, see *R. (on the application of Glenn and Co (Essex) Ltd) v Revenue and Customs Commissioners* [2011] EWHC 2998 (Admin), [2012] 1 Cr. App. R. 22 (DC), Laws, L.J.
s.17, amended: 2012 c.10 s.144, Sch.12 para.21
s.19, see *Chief Constable of Merseyside v Owens* [2012] EWHC 1515 (Admin), (2012) 176 J.P. 688 (DC), Sir John Thomas (President)
s.22, see *Chief Constable of Merseyside v Owens* [2012] EWHC 1515 (Admin), (2012) 176 J.P. 688 (DC), Sir John Thomas (President)
s.24, see *Hayes v Chief Constable of Merseyside* [2011] EWCA Civ 911, [2012] 1 W.L.R. 517 (CA (Civ Div)), Ward, L.J.; see *R. (on the application of Hicks) v Commissioner of Police of the Metropolis* [2012] EWHC 1947 (Admin), [2012] A.C.D. 102 (DC), Richards, L.J.
s.24A, applied: SI 2012/1917 Art.17

1984– cont.

60. Police and Criminal Evidence Act 1984– *cont.*
s.27, amended: 2012 c.9 s.85
s.27, enabling: SI 2012/ 1713
s.34, see *Hayes v Chief Constable of Merseyside* [2011] EWCA Civ 911, [2012] 1 W.L.R. 517 (CA (Civ Div)), Ward, L.J.
s.34, amended: 2012 c.10 Sch.24 para.5
s.37, applied: SI 2012/ 1726 r.7.1
s.37, referred to: SI 2012/ 1726 r.19.6
s.37B, amended: 2012 c.10 Sch.24 para.6
s.37C, referred to: SI 2012/ 1726 r.19.6
s.37CA, referred to: SI 2012/ 1726 r.19.6
s.38, amended: 2012 c.10 Sch.11 para.34
s.38, applied: SI 2012/ 1726 r.7.1
s.46A, referred to: SI 2012/ 1726 r.19.6
s.47, applied: SI 2012/ 1726 r.19.6
s.47, referred to: SI 2012/ 1726 r.19.6
s.61, amended: 2012 c.10 Sch.24 para.7
s.61, repealed (in part): 2012 c.10 Sch.24 para.7
s.63, amended: 2012 c.9 Sch.9 para.3, 2012 c.10 Sch.24 para.8
s.63, repealed (in part): 2012 c.10 Sch.24 para.8
s.63A, applied: 2012 c.9 s.20
s.63AA, added: 2012 c.9 s.23
s.63AB, added: 2012 c.9 s.24
s.63B, enabling: SI 2012/61
s.63D, added: 2012 c.9 s.1
s.63D, applied: 2012 c.9 s.20, s.25
s.63E, added: 2012 c.9 s.2
s.63E, applied: 2012 c.9 s.20, s.25
s.63F, added: 2012 c.9 s.3
s.63F, applied: 2012 c.9 s.20, s.25
s.63G, added: 2012 c.9 s.3
s.63G, applied: 2012 c.9 s.20, s.25
s.63H, added: 2012 c.9 s.4
s.63H, applied: 2012 c.9 s.20, s.25
s.63I, added: 2012 c.9 s.5
s.63I, applied: 2012 c.9 s.20, s.25
s.63J, added: 2012 c.9 s.6
s.63J, applied: 2012 c.9 s.20, s.25
s.63K, added: 2012 c.9 s.7
s.63K, applied: 2012 c.9 s.20, s.25
s.63L, added: 2012 c.9 s.8
s.63L, applied: 2012 c.9 s.20, s.25
s.63M, added: 2012 c.9 s.9
s.63M, applied: 2012 c.9 s.20, s.25
s.63N, added: 2012 c.9 s.10
s.63N, applied: 2012 c.9 s.20, s.25
s.63O, added: 2012 c.9 s.11
s.63O, applied: 2012 c.9 s.20, s.25
s.63P, added: 2012 c.9 s.12
s.63P, applied: 2012 c.9 s.20, s.25
s.63Q, added: 2012 c.9 s.13
s.63Q, applied: 2012 c.9 s.20, s.25
s.63R, added: 2012 c.9 s.14
s.63R, applied: 2012 c.9 s.20, s.25
s.63S, added: 2012 c.9 s.15
s.63S, applied: 2012 c.9 s.20, s.25
s.63T, added: 2012 c.9 s.16
s.63T, applied: 2012 c.9 s.20, s.25
s.63U, added: 2012 c.9 s.17
s.63U, applied: 2012 c.9 s.25
s.64, repealed: 2012 c.9 Sch.9 para.3, Sch.10 Part 1
s.64A, see *R. (on the application of C) v Commissioner of Police of the Metropolis* [2012] EWHC 1681 (Admin), [2012] 1 W.L.R. 3007 (DC), Richards, L.J.
s.64A, amended: 2012 c.10 Sch.23 para.13

1984– cont.

60. Police and Criminal Evidence Act 1984– *cont.*
s.64ZC, amended: 2012 c.10 Sch.24 para.9
s.64ZC, repealed (in part): 2012 c.10 Sch.24 para.9
s.64ZI, repealed (in part): 2012 c.10 Sch.24 para.10
s.65, amended: 2012 c.9 s.18
s.65A, amended: 2012 c.9 s.18, Sch.9 para.137
s.65B, added: 2012 c.9 s.18
s.66, amended: 2012 c.9 Sch.9 para.21
s.66, applied: SI 2012/ 1798(1)
s.66, referred to: SI 2012/ 1798 Art.2
s.67, applied: SI 2012/ 1798(4), SI 2012/ 1798, SI 2012/ 1798(2), SI 2012/ 1798(3)
s.67, enabling: SI 2012/ 1798
s.73, applied: SI 2012/ 1726 r.35.2, r.5.9
s.74, applied: SI 2012/ 1726 r.5.9
s.75, applied: SI 2012/ 1726 r.5.9
s.76, see *R. v Roberts (Neil Daniel)* [2011] EWCA Crim 2974, (2012) 176 J.P. 33 (CA (Crim Div)), Goldring, L.J.
s.78, see *Al-Khawaja v United Kingdom (26766/05)* [2012] 2 Costs L.O. 139 (ECHR (Grand Chamber)), Judge Tulkens (President); see *R. (on the application of Dulai) v Chelmsford Magistrates' Court* [2012] EWHC 1055 (Admin), [2012] 3 All E.R. 764 (DC), Stanley Burnton, L.J.; see *R. v Ibrahim (Dahir)* [2012] EWCA Crim 837, [2012] 4 All E.R. 225 (CA (Crim Div)), Aikens, L.J.; see *R. v Newell (Alan)* [2012] EWCA Crim 650, [2012] 1 W.L.R. 3142 (CA (Crim Div)), Sir John Thomas (President); see *R. v Willett (Tommy)* [2011] EWCA Crim 2710, [2012] 2 Cr. App. R. (S.) 18 (CA (Crim Div)), Richards, L.J.
s.80, see *R. v A* [2012] EWCA Crim 1529, [2012] 1 W.L.R. 3378 (CA (Crim Div)), Sir John Thomas (President)
s.81, applied: SI 2012/ 1726 r.33.4, r.3.5
s.81, enabling: SI 2012/ 1726
s.113, applied: 2012 c.9 s.25
s.113, enabling: SI 2012/ 2505
Sch.1, see *R. (on the application of British Sky Broadcasting Ltd) v Central Criminal Court* [2011] EWHC 3451 (Admin), [2012] Q.B. 785 (QBD (Admin)), Moore-Bick, L.J.
Sch.1 para.2, see *R. (on the application of British Sky Broadcasting Ltd) v Chelmsford Crown Court* [2012] EWHC 1295 (Admin), [2012] 2 Cr. App. R. 33 (DC), Moses, L.J.
Sch.2A Part I para.3, amended: 2012 c.10 Sch.24 para.11
Sch.2A Part III para.11, amended: 2012 c.10 Sch.24 para.11

1985

v. Bournemouth Borough Council Act 1985
s.16, repealed: SI 2012/ 3124 Reg.2
s.18, repealed: SI 2012/ 3124 Reg.2
s.60, repealed: SI 2012/ 3124 Reg.2
s.68, amended: SI 2012/ 3124 Reg.2

4. Milk (Cessation of Production) Act 1985
s.2, repealed (in part): 2012 c.9 Sch.10 Part 2
s.3, repealed (in part): 2012 c.9 Sch.10 Part 2

6. Companies Act 1985
see *Greene King Plc v Revenue and Customs Commissioners* [2012] UKFTT 385 (TC), [2012] S.F.T.D. 1085 (FTT (Tax)), Judge Colin Bishopp; see *Lehman Commercial Mortgage Conduit Ltd v Gatedale Ltd* [2012] EWHC 848 (Ch), Times, June 6, 2012 (Ch D), Vos, J.

1985– cont.

6. Companies Act 1985–*cont.*
applied: SI 2012/ 1128 Art.4
s.155, see *Lehman Commercial Mortgage Conduit Ltd v Gatedale Ltd* [2012] EWHC 848 (Ch), Times, June 6, 2012 (Ch D), Vos, J.
s.158, see *Lehman Commercial Mortgage Conduit Ltd v Gatedale Ltd* [2012] EWHC 848 (Ch), Times, June 6, 2012 (Ch D), Vos, J.
s.256, applied: SI 2012/ 1741 Art.24
s.263, see *Vardy Properties v Revenue and Customs Commissioners* [2012] UKFTT 564 (TC), [2012] S.F.T.D. 1398 (FTT (Tax)), Judge Kevin Poole
s.270, see *Vardy Properties v Revenue and Customs Commissioners* [2012] UKFTT 564 (TC), [2012] S.F.T.D. 1398 (FTT (Tax)), Judge Kevin Poole
s.458, applied: SSI 2012/ 88 Reg.23, SSI 2012/ 89 Reg.26
Sch.15C para.7, substituted: 2012 c.21 Sch.18 para.46
Sch.15D para.28, amended: 2012 c.21 Sch.18 para.47
Sch.15D para.29, amended: 2012 c.21 Sch.18 para.47
Sch.15D para.43, amended: 2012 c.21 Sch.18 para.47

13. Cinemas Act 1985
s.3, amended: 2012 asp 8 Sch.7 para.55
s.8, amended: 2012 asp 8 Sch.7 para.55

16. National Heritage (Scotland) Act 1985
s.18, repealed: 2012 asp 3 Sch.3
s.22, amended: 2012 asp 3 Sch.2 para.2

21. Films Act 1985
Sch.1 para.4, amended: SI 2012/ 1809 Sch.1 Part 1

23. Prosecution of Offences Act 1985
Part II, applied: SI 2012/ 1726 r.76.1
s.3, applied: 2012 c.5 s.128
s.3, enabling: SI 2012/ 1635, SI 2012/ 2067, SI 2012/ 2681
s.5, applied: 2012 c.5 s.128
s.6, see *R. (on the application of Gujra) v Crown Prosecution Service* [2011] EWHC 472 (Admin), [2012] 1 W.L.R. 254 (DC), Richards, L.J.; see *R. (on the application of Gujra) v Crown Prosecution Service* [2012] UKSC 52, [2012] 3 W.L.R. 1227 (SC), Lord Neuberger (President)
s.7, applied: SI 2012/ 1726 r.10.5
s.10, see *R. (on the application of Gujra) v Crown Prosecution Service* [2011] EWHC 472 (Admin), [2012] 1 W.L.R. 254 (DC), Richards, L.J.
s.16, see *R. (on the application of Desouza) v Croydon Magistrates' Court* [2012] EWHC 1362 (Admin), (2012) 176 J.P. 624 (QBD (Admin)), Mitting, J.; see *R. v Patel (Hitendra) (Costs)* [2012] EWCA Crim 1508, [2012] 5 Costs L.R. 873 (CA (Crim Div)), Hooper, L.J.
s.16, amended: 2012 c.10 Sch.7 para.2
s.16, applied: SI 2012/ 1726 r.76.1, r.76.4
s.16, repealed (in part): 2012 c.10 Sch.7 para.2
s.16A, added: 2012 c.10 Sch.7 para.3
s.17, amended: 2012 c.10 Sch.7 para.4
s.17, applied: SI 2012/ 1726 r.76.1, r.8.1, r.76.4
s.17, repealed (in part): 2012 c.10 Sch.7 para.4
s.18, see *R. v Rakib (Mohammed)* [2011] EWCA Crim 870, [2012] 1 Cr. App. R. (S.) 1 (CA (Crim Div)), Elias, L.J.
s.18, applied: SI 2012/ 1726 r.76.1, r.76.5, r.76.6
s.19, amended: 2012 c.10 Sch.5 para.23, Sch.7 para.5
s.19, applied: SI 2012/ 1726 r.3.5, r.76.1, r.76.8

1985– cont.

23. Prosecution of Offences Act 1985–*cont.*
s.19A, applied: SI 2012/ 1726 r.76.1, r.76.9, r.68.1, r.63.1, r.3.5
s.19B, applied: SI 2012/ 1726 r.76.1, r.68.1, r.76.10, r.63.1, r.3.5
s.20, amended: 2012 c.10 Sch.5 para.24, Sch.7 para.6
s.20, enabling: SI 2012/ 1804
s.21, amended: 2012 c.10 Sch.5 para.25, Sch.7 para.7
s.22, see *O'Dowd v United Kingdom (7390/07)* (2012) 54 E.H.R.R. 8 (ECHR), Judge Garlicki (President); see *R. (on the application of Raeside) v Luton Crown Court* [2012] EWHC 1064 (Admin), [2012] 1 W.L.R. 2777 (DC), Sir John Thomas (President)
s.22, amended: 2012 c.10 Sch.12 para.22
s.22, applied: SI 2012/ 1726 r.19.16
s.22, referred to: SI 2012/ 1726 r.19.1, r.19.17
s.22, enabling: SI 2012/ 1344
s.23, applied: SI 2012/ 1726 r.8.1, r.8.2, r.8.3
s.23A, applied: SI 2012/ 1726 r.8.1
s.29, amended: 2012 c.10 Sch.7 para.8
s.29, enabling: SI 2012/ 1344, SI 2012/ 1804
Sch.1 Part II para.8, repealed: 2012 c.10 Sch.7 para.10

29. Enduring Powers of Attorney Act 1985
applied: SI 2012/ 2885 Sch.8 para.4, Sch.8 para.12, SI 2012/ 2886 Sch.1, SI 2012/ 3145 Sch.1

37. Family Law (Scotland) Act 1985
s.8, see *Murdoch v Murdoch* [2012] CSIH 2, 2012 S.C. 271 (IH (Ex Div)), Lord Reed; see *P v P* [2012] CSIH 15, 2012 Fam. L.R. 41 (IH (Ex Div)), Lord Hardie; see *W v W* 2012 S.C.L.R. 591 (Sh Ct (Lothian) (Edinburgh)), Sheriff F R Crowe
s.8, applied: SI 2012/ 687 Sch.4 para.4
s.8A, applied: SI 2012/ 687 Sch.4 para.4
s.9, see *B v B* [2012] CSOH 21, 2012 Fam. L.R. 65 (OH), Lord Tyre; see *Gow v Grant* [2012] UKSC 29, 2012 S.L.T. 829 (SC), Lord Hope, J.S.C. (Deputy President); see *Murdoch v Murdoch* [2012] CSIH 2, 2012 S.C. 271 (IH (Ex Div)), Lord Reed; see *P v P* [2012] CSIH 15, 2012 Fam. L.R. 41 (IH (Ex Div)), Lord Hardie
s.10, see *Hales v Hales* 2012 Fam. L.R. 51 (Sh Ct (Glasgow)), Sheriff W Sheehan; see *Murdoch v Murdoch* [2012] CSIH 2, 2012 S.C. 271 (IH (Ex Div)), Lord Reed; see *P v P* [2012] CSIH 15, 2012 Fam. L.R. 41 (IH (Ex Div)), Lord Hardie
s.11, see *P v P* [2012] CSIH 15, 2012 Fam. L.R. 41 (IH (Ex Div)), Lord Hardie
s.12A, applied: SI 2012/ 687 Sch.4 para.4
s.14, see *Murdoch v Murdoch* [2012] CSIH 2, 2012 S.C. 271 (IH (Ex Div)), Lord Reed

42. Hospital Complaints Procedure Act 1985
applied: SSI 2012/ 36 Reg.9

48. Food and Environment Protection Act 1985
Part I, applied: SSI 2012/ 135 Art.3
s.1, enabling: SI 2012/ 2658, SI 2012/ 2978, SSI 2012/ 135, SSI 2012/ 263
s.24, enabling: SI 2012/ 2658, SI 2012/ 2978, SSI 2012/ 135, SSI 2012/ 263

50. Representation of the People Act 1985
s.1, see *R. (on the application of Preston) v Wandsworth LBC* [2011] EWHC 3174 (Admin), [2012] 2 W.L.R. 1134 (QBD (Admin)), Elias, L.J.
s.15, amended: 2012 c.11 s.2
s.15, applied: SI 2012/ 444 Sch.5, SI 2012/ 1917 Sch.4 para.1

1985—cont.

50. Representation of the People Act 1985—*cont.*
s.15, varied: SI 2012/323 Sch.4 para.1, SI 2012/444 Sch.4 para.1, SI 2012/1917 Sch.4 para.1, SI 2012/2031 Sch.4 Part 1

51. Local Government Act 1985
Part IV, applied: SI 2012/1644 Sch.1, SSI 2012/88 Reg.3
s.10, applied: SI 2012/1644 Sch.1, SSI 2012/88 Reg.3
s.26, applied: SI 2012/1647 Reg.3
s.67, applied: SI 2012/1644 Sch.1, SSI 2012/88 Reg.3
Sch.13 para.2, amended: SI 2012/2404 Sch.2 para.19

54. Finance Act 1985
s.87, amended: 2012 c.14 Sch.39 para.4
s.87, repealed (in part): 2012 c.14 Sch.39 para.4

58. Trustee Savings Banks Act 1985
Sch.1 Part III para.11, amended: 2012 c.21 Sch.18 para.48

60. Child Abduction and Custody Act 1985
see *A, Petitioner* 2012 S.L.T. 370 (OH), Lord Glennie
s.3, applied: 2012 c.10 Sch.1 para.17
s.11, amended: 2012 c.10 Sch.5 para.26
s.14, applied: 2012 c.10 Sch.1 para.17

61. Administration of Justice Act 1985
s.16, amended: SI 2012/2404 Sch.2 para.20
s.18, amended: SI 2012/2404 Sch.2 para.20
s.21, amended: 2012 c.21 Sch.18 para.49
s.40, amended: 2012 c.10 Sch.5 para.28
s.41, amended: 2012 c.10 Sch.5 para.29
s.42, amended: 2012 c.10 Sch.5 para.30
s.43, amended: 2012 c.10 Sch.5 para.31
Sch.2 para.20, amended: 2012 c.10 Sch.5 para.32

65. Insolvency Act 1985
Sch.9 Pt II para.9, see *Official Liquidator of Weir Construction (Contracts) Ltd, Noter* [2012] CSOH 51, 2012 S.L.T. 1098 (OH), Lord Hodge

66. Bankruptcy (Scotland) Act 1985
applied: 2012 asp 8 Sch.1 para.5
s.1B, applied: SSI 2012/118 Reg.4
s.5, amended: 2012 asp 5 Sch.5 para.28
s.5, enabling: SSI 2012/118
s.26A, applied: SSI 2012/118 Reg.5
s.31B, applied: SI 2012/1726 r.60.4
s.40, see *Stewart's Trustee v Stewart* 2012 S.L.T. (Sh Ct) 231 (Sh Ct (Grampian) (Peterhead)), Sheriff P Mann
s.53, applied: SSI 2012/118 Reg.5
s.54, see *Accountant in Bankruptcy v Campbell* 2012 S.L.T. (Sh Ct) 35 (Sh Ct (Lothian) (Edinburgh)), Sheriff W Holligan
s.56A, applied: SI 2012/922 Reg.3, SI 2012/1290 Reg.3, SI 2012/1631 Sch.5 para.5, SI 2012/1640 Sch.2 para.2, SI 2012/2996 Sch.5 para.4, SSI 2012/118 Reg.13
s.56B, applied: SI 2012/922 Reg.3, SI 2012/1290 Reg.3, SI 2012/1631 Sch.5 para.5, SI 2012/1640 Sch.2 para.2, SI 2012/2996 Sch.5 para.4
s.56C, applied: SI 2012/922 Reg.3, SI 2012/1290 Reg.3, SI 2012/1631 Sch.5 para.5, SI 2012/1640 Sch.2 para.2, SI 2012/2996 Sch.5 para.4
s.56D, applied: SI 2012/922 Reg.3, SI 2012/1290 Reg.3, SI 2012/1631 Sch.5 para.5, SI 2012/1640 Sch.2 para.2, SI 2012/2996 Sch.5 para.4
s.56E, applied: SI 2012/922 Reg.3, SI 2012/1290 Reg.3, SI 2012/1631 Sch.5 para.5, SI 2012/1640 Sch.2 para.2, SI 2012/2996 Sch.5 para.4

1985—cont.

66. Bankruptcy (Scotland) Act 1985—*cont.*
s.56F, applied: SI 2012/922 Reg.3, SI 2012/1290 Reg.3, SI 2012/1631 Sch.5 para.5, SI 2012/1640 Sch.2 para.2, SI 2012/2996 Sch.5 para.4
s.56G, applied: SI 2012/922 Reg.3, SI 2012/1290 Reg.3, SI 2012/1631 Sch.5 para.5, SI 2012/1640 Sch.2 para.2, SI 2012/2996 Sch.5 para.4
s.56H, applied: SI 2012/922 Reg.3, SI 2012/1290 Reg.3, SI 2012/1631 Sch.5 para.5, SI 2012/1640 Sch.2 para.2, SI 2012/2996 Sch.5 para.4
s.56J, applied: SI 2012/922 Reg.3, SI 2012/1290 Reg.3, SI 2012/1631 Sch.5 para.5, SI 2012/1640 Sch.2 para.2, SI 2012/2996 Sch.5 para.4
s.56K, applied: SI 2012/922 Reg.3, SI 2012/1290 Reg.3, SI 2012/1631 Sch.5 para.5, SI 2012/1640 Sch.2 para.2, SI 2012/2996 Sch.5 para.4
s.58A, applied: SSI 2012/118 Reg.5
s.69A, enabling: SSI 2012/118
s.72, enabling: SSI 2012/118
s.73, applied: SSI 2012/303 Reg.41, Reg.48, SSI 2012/319 Reg.39
Sch.2 para.9, referred to: SSI 2012/118 Reg.5
Sch.4 para.9, applied: SSI 2012/118 Reg.5
Sch.7 Part I para.15, repealed: 2012 asp 5 Sch.5 para.28

67. Transport Act 1985
s.2, referred to: SI 2012/2387 Sch.3 para.1
s.6, applied: SSI 2012/32 Reg.3
s.6, enabling: SSI 2012/32

68. Housing Act 1985
see *Brumwell v Powys CC* [2011] EWCA Civ 1613, [2012] L. & T.R. 14 (CA (Civ Div)), Laws, L.J.; see *Rooney v Secretary of State for Communities and Local Government* [2011] EWCA Civ 1556, [2012] J.P.L. 684 (CA (Civ Div)), Sir Nicholas Wall (President, Fam)
applied: SI 2012/531 Reg.40
Part IV, applied: SI 2012/887 Art.4, SI 2012/3018 Sch.2 para.1
Part V, applied: SI 2012/734 Art.4
s.17, see *R. (on the application of A) v Secretary of State for Communities and Local Government* [2011] EWCA Civ 1253, [2012] J.P.L. 579 (CA (Civ Div)), Pill, L.J.
s.27, applied: SI 2012/1821 Reg.19
s.27, enabling: SI 2012/1821
s.27AB, enabling: SI 2012/1821
s.81, see *Islington LBC v Boyle* [2011] EWCA Civ 1450, [2012] P.T.S.R. 1093 (CA (Civ Div)), Mummery, L.J.; see *Solihull MBC v Hickin* [2012] UKSC 39, [2012] 1 W.L.R. 2295 (SC), Lord Hope, J.S.C.
s.85A, see *Barking and Dagenham LBC v Bakare* [2012] EWCA Civ 750, [2012] H.L.R. 34 (CA (Civ Div)), Sir Andrew Morritt (Chancellor)
s.87, see *Solihull MBC v Hickin* [2012] UKSC 39, [2012] 1 W.L.R. 2295 (SC), Lord Hope, J.S.C.
s.88, see *Solihull MBC v Hickin* [2012] UKSC 39, [2012] 1 W.L.R. 2295 (SC), Lord Hope, J.S.C.
s.89, see *Solihull MBC v Hickin* [2012] UKSC 39, [2012] 1 W.L.R. 2295 (SC), Lord Hope, J.S.C.
s.89, referred to: SI 2012/628 Art.14, SI 2012/887 Art.4
s.90, referred to: SI 2012/628 Art.14, SI 2012/887 Art.4
s.91, see *Solihull MBC v Hickin* [2012] UKSC 39, [2012] 1 W.L.R. 2295 (SC), Lord Hope, J.S.C.
s.103, see *Rochdale BC v Dixon* [2011] EWCA Civ 1173, [2012] P.T.S.R. 1336 (CA (Civ Div)), Rix, L.J.
s.107B, applied: SI 2012/695 Reg.2

1985–cont.

68. Housing Act 1985–cont.
s.107B, enabling: SI 2012/695
s.107E, enabling: SI 2012/695
s.118, see *Francis v Southwark LBC* [2011] EWCA Civ 1418, [2012] P.T.S.R. 1248 (CA (Civ Div)), Carnwath, L.J.
s.121, amended: SI 2012/2404 Sch.2 para.21
s.122, applied: SI 2012/734 Art.4
s.124, see *Francis v Southwark LBC* [2011] EWCA Civ 1418, [2012] P.T.S.R. 1248 (CA (Civ Div)), Carnwath, L.J.
s.125, applied: SI 2012/734 Art.4
s.125D, applied: SI 2012/734 Art.4
s.125E, applied: SI 2012/734 Art.4
s.126, applied: SI 2012/734 Art.4
s.129, see *Francis v Southwark LBC* [2011] EWCA Civ 1418, [2012] P.T.S.R. 1248 (CA (Civ Div)), Carnwath, L.J.
s.131, applied: SI 2012/734 Art.2, Art.3, Art.4
s.131, enabling: SI 2012/734
s.138, see *Francis v Southwark LBC* [2011] EWCA Civ 1418, [2012] P.T.S.R. 1248 (CA (Civ Div)), Carnwath, L.J.
s.151B, applied: SI 2012/702 Sch.2 para.2
s.170, amended: 2012 c.10 Sch.5 para.33
s.181, see *Francis v Southwark LBC* [2011] EWCA Civ 1418, [2012] P.T.S.R. 1248 (CA (Civ Div)), Carnwath, L.J.
s.265, applied: SI 2012/531 Sch.1 para.45, Sch.1 para.46, Sch.1 para.47, Sch.1 para.48
s.269, applied: SI 2012/531 Reg.46, Sch.1 para.45
s.269A, referred to: SI 2012/531 Sch.1 para.45
s.271, applied: SI 2012/531 Sch.1 para.46
s.272, applied: SI 2012/531 Sch.1 para.46, Sch.1 para.47
s.317, applied: SI 2012/531 Sch.1 para.48
s.318, applied: SI 2012/531 Reg.46, Sch.1 para.49
s.622, amended: 2012 c.21 Sch.18 para.50
Sch.1 para.12, referred to: SI 2012/3018 Sch.2 para.1
Sch.2, applied: SI 2012/887 Art.4
Sch.2 Pt I, see *Barking and Dagenham LBC v Bakare* [2012] EWCA Civ 750, [2012] H.L.R. 34 (CA (Civ Div)), Sir Andrew Morritt (Chancellor)
Sch.2 Part I, referred to: SI 2012/628 Art.14

69. Housing Associations Act 1985
s.1, applied: SSI 2012/303 Sch.5 para.13
s.1, referred to: SI 2012/2886 Sch.1
s.2B, amended: SI 2012/700 Sch.1 para.2, SSI 2012/38 Sch.1 para.1
s.68, amended: 2012 asp 5 Sch.5 para.29

70. Landlord and Tenant Act 1985
see *Redrow Homes (Midlands) Ltd v Hothi* [2012] L. & T.R. 8 (UT (Lands)), Judge Huskinson
s.8, repealed (in part): 2012 c.9 Sch.10 Part 2
s.18, see *Freeholders of 69 Marina, St Leonards-on-Sea v Oram* [2011] EWCA Civ 1258, [2012] H.L.R. 12 (CA (Civ Div)), Sir Andrew Morritt (Chancellor)
s.20, see *Stenau Properties Ltd v Leek* [2012] L. & T.R. 22 (UT (Lands)), Judge Mole Q.C.
s.20B, see *OM Property Management Ltd v Burr* [2012] UKUT 2 (LC), [2012] L. & T.R. 17 (UT (Lands)), Judge Mole Q.C.
s.20C, see *Plantation Wharf Management Co Ltd v Jackson* [2012] L. & T.R. 18 (UT (Lands)), Judge Mole Q.C.

1985–cont.

70. Landlord and Tenant Act 1985–cont.
s.27A, see *Birmingham City Council v Keddie* [2012] UKUT 323 (LC), [2012] 49 E.G. 71 (UT (Lands)), Judge Nigel Gerald

71. Housing (Consequential Provisions) Act 1985
Sch.2 para.43, repealed: 2012 c.14 Sch.39 para.3

72. Weights and Measures Act 1985
applied: SI 2012/1909 Sch.4 para.8, Sch.5 para.7
s.7, see *Unique Pub Properties Ltd v Broad Green Tavern Ltd* [2012] EWHC 2154 (Ch), [2012] 2 P. & C.R. 17 (Ch D), Warren, J.
s.17, see *Unique Pub Properties Ltd v Broad Green Tavern Ltd* [2012] EWHC 2154 (Ch), [2012] 2 P. & C.R. 17 (Ch D), Warren, J.
s.69, applied: SI 2012/3110 Reg.7

73. Law Reform (Miscellaneous Provisions) (Scotland) Act 1985
applied: 2012 asp 5 s.49
s.4, see *Edinburgh Tours Ltd v Singh* 2012 Hous. L.R. 15 (Sh Ct (Lothian) (Edinburgh)), Sheriff Principal M M Stephen; see *Scott v Muir* 2012 S.L.T. (Sh Ct) 179 (Sh Ct (Lothian) (Edinburgh)), Sheriff Principal M M Stephen
s.8, amended: 2012 asp 5 s.55, Sch.5 para.30
s.8, referred to: 2012 asp 5 s.65
s.8A, added: 2012 asp 5 s.55
s.8A, applied: 2012 asp 5 s.67
s.9, amended: 2012 asp 5 s.55
s.9, repealed (in part): 2012 asp 5 s.55

1986

5. Agricultural Holdings Act 1986
see *Shirt v Shirt* [2012] EWCA Civ 1029, [2012] 3 F.C.R. 304 (CA (Civ Div)), Lord Neuberger (M.R.)
Part IV, applied: SI 2012/2421 Sch.3 para.9
s.12, see *Spencer v Secretary of State for Defence* [2012] EWHC 120 (Ch), [2012] 2 All E.R. (Comm) 480 (Ch D), Vos, J.
Sch.6 Part I para.3, applied: SI 2012/2573 Art.2, SI 2012/3022 Art.2
Sch.6 Part I para.4, enabling: SI 2012/2573, SI 2012/3022
Sch.12 para.4, amended: SI 2012/1659 Sch.3 para.8

10. Local Government Act 1986
Part II, applied: SI 2012/2734 Sch.1 para.18, Sch.1 para.32
s.2, varied: SI 2012/2734 Reg.6
s.2A, varied: SI 2012/2734 Reg.6
s.3, varied: SI 2012/2734 Reg.6
s.4, varied: SI 2012/2734 Reg.6
s.5, varied: SI 2012/2734 Reg.6
s.6, varied: SI 2012/2734 Reg.6

14. Animals (Scientific Procedures) Act 1986
applied: SI 2012/3039 Sch.3 para.1, Sch.3 para.7, Sch.3 para.8, Sch.3 para.21
varied: SI 2012/3039 Sch.3 para.12
amended: SI 2012/3039 Reg.26
s.1, amended: SI 2012/3039 Reg.3
s.2, amended: SI 2012/3039 Reg.4
s.2, repealed (in part): SI 2012/3039 Reg.4
s.2A, added: SI 2012/3039 Reg.5
s.2B, added: SI 2012/3039 Reg.6
s.2B, applied: SI 2012/3039 Sch.3 para.11, Sch.3 para.12, Sch.3 para.18
s.2B, referred to: SI 2012/3039 Sch.3 para.3, SI 2012/3050 Art.2, Art.3
s.2C, added: SI 2012/3039 Reg.6

1986– cont.

14. Animals (Scientific Procedures) Act 1986–*cont.*
s.2C, applied: SI 2012/3039 Sch.3 para.3, Sch.3 para.9, Sch.3 para.10, Sch.3 para.11, Sch.3 para.15, SI 2012/3050 Art.2, Art.3
s.2C, referred to: SI 2012/3039 Sch.3 para.9, Sch.3 para.24
s.3, amended: SI 2012/3039 Reg.7
s.4, amended: SI 2012/3039 Reg.8
s.4, applied: SI 2012/3039 Sch.3 para.19
s.5, applied: SI 2012/3039 Sch.3 para.20
s.5, substituted: SI 2012/3039 Reg.9
s.5C, applied: SI 2012/3039 Sch.3 para.26, Sch.3 para.28
s.5E, applied: SI 2012/3039 Sch.3 para.22
s.6, applied: SI 2012/3039 Sch.3 para.2, Sch.3 para.3
s.6, repealed: SI 2012/3039 Reg.26
s.7, applied: SI 2012/3039 Sch.3 para.14, Sch.3 para.18
s.7, repealed: SI 2012/3039 Reg.26
s.8, amended: SI 2012/3039 Reg.26
s.8, enabling: SI 2012/3050
s.8, amended: SI 2012/3039 Reg.26
s.9, amended: SI 2012/3039 Reg.26
s.10, applied: SI 2012/3039 Sch.3 para.4, Sch.3 para.13, Sch.3 para.19, Sch.3 para.24
s.10, substituted: SI 2012/3039 Reg.10
s.11, substituted: SI 2012/3039 Reg.11
s.12, amended: SI 2012/3039 Reg.12
s.12, applied: SI 2012/3039 Sch.3 para.9
s.13, amended: SI 2012/3039 Reg.26
s.13, applied: SI 2012/3039 Sch.3 para.8
s.13A, added: SI 2012/3039 Reg.13
s.14, substituted: SI 2012/3039 Reg.14
s.14, varied: SI 2012/3039 Sch.3 para.30
s.15, amended: SI 2012/3039 Reg.26
s.15A, added: SI 2012/3039 Reg.15
s.15A, applied: SI 2012/3039 Sch.3 para.7, Sch.3 para.8, Sch.3 para.16, Sch.3 para.28
s.15A, varied: SI 2012/3039 Sch.3 para.26
s.17, applied: SI 2012/3039 Sch.3 para.28
s.17, referred to: SI 2012/3039 Sch.3 para.27
s.17, substituted: SI 2012/3039 Reg.17
s.17A, added: SI 2012/3039 Reg.18
s.17A, applied: SI 2012/3039 Sch.3 para.23, Sch.3 para.31
s.18, amended: SI 2012/3039 Reg.19, Reg.26
s.18, applied: SI 2012/3039 Sch.3 para.11, Sch.3 para.21
s.18, referred to: SI 2012/3039 Sch.3 para.15
s.19, amended: SI 2012/2404 Sch.2 para.22
s.19, substituted: SI 2012/3039 Reg.20
s.20, substituted: SI 2012/3039 Reg.20
s.20A, added: SI 2012/3039 Reg.21
s.20B, added: SI 2012/3039 Reg.22
s.21, amended: SI 2012/3039 Reg.26
s.21, applied: SI 2012/3039 Sch.3 para.4, Sch.3 para.18
s.21, repealed (in part): SI 2012/3039 Reg.26
s.21A, added: SI 2012/3039 Reg.23
s.22, amended: SI 2012/3039 Reg.24, Reg.26
s.23, amended: SI 2012/3039 Reg.26
s.25, amended: SI 2012/3039 Reg.25, Reg.26
s.26, amended: SI 2012/3039 Reg.26
s.27, amended: SI 2012/3039 Reg.26
s.29, amended: SI 2012/3039 Reg.26
s.30, amended: SI 2012/3039 Reg.26
Sch.1, applied: SI 2012/3039 Sch.3 para.7, Sch.3 para.16

1986– cont.

14. Animals (Scientific Procedures) Act 1986–*cont.*
Sch.1, amended: SI 2012/3039 Reg.26
Sch.1 para.1, amended: SI 2012/3039 Reg.16, Reg.26
Sch.1 para.2, amended: SI 2012/3039 Reg.26
Sch.1 para.2, repealed: SI 2012/3039 Reg.16
Sch.1 para.3, added: SI 2012/3039 Reg.16
Sch.1 para.3, amended: SI 2012/3039 Reg.26
Sch.2, amended: SI 2012/3039 Reg.26
Sch.2, referred to: SI 2012/3039 Sch.3 para.13
Sch.2, substituted: SI 2012/3039 Reg.26
Sch.2B, applied: SI 2012/3039 Sch.3 para.27
Sch.2A para.1, repealed: SI 2012/3039 Reg.26
Sch.2A para.2, repealed: SI 2012/3039 Reg.26
Sch.2A para.3, repealed: SI 2012/3039 Reg.26
Sch.2A para.4, repealed: SI 2012/3039 Reg.26
Sch.2B para.1, added: SI 2012/3039 Sch.1
Sch.2B para.2, added: SI 2012/3039 Sch.1
Sch.2B para.3, added: SI 2012/3039 Sch.1
Sch.2B para.4, added: SI 2012/3039 Sch.1
Sch.2B para.5, added: SI 2012/3039 Sch.1
Sch.2C Part I para.1, added: SI 2012/3039 Sch.2
Sch.2C Part I para.2, added: SI 2012/3039 Sch.2
Sch.2C Part I para.3, added: SI 2012/3039 Sch.2
Sch.2C Part I para.4, added: SI 2012/3039 Sch.2
Sch.2C Part I para.5, added: SI 2012/3039 Sch.2
Sch.2C Part I para.6, added: SI 2012/3039 Sch.2
Sch.2C Part I para.7, added: SI 2012/3039 Sch.2
Sch.2C Part I para.8, added: SI 2012/3039 Sch.2
Sch.2C Part I para.9, added: SI 2012/3039 Sch.2
Sch.2C Part I para.10, added: SI 2012/3039 Sch.2
Sch.2C Part I para.11, added: SI 2012/3039 Sch.2
Sch.2C Part I para.11, applied: SI 2012/3039 Sch.3 para.5, Sch.3 para.14
Sch.2C Part I para.12, added: SI 2012/3039 Sch.2
Sch.2C Part II para.13, added: SI 2012/3039 Sch.2
Sch.2C Part II para.14, added: SI 2012/3039 Sch.2
Sch.2C Part II para.15, added: SI 2012/3039 Sch.2
Sch.2C Part II para.16, added: SI 2012/3039 Sch.2
Sch.2C Part III para.17, added: SI 2012/3039 Sch.2
Sch.2C Part III para.18, added: SI 2012/3039 Sch.2
Sch.2C Part III para.19, added: SI 2012/3039 Sch.2
Sch.2C Part III para.20, added: SI 2012/3039 Sch.2
Sch.2C Part III para.21, added: SI 2012/3039 Sch.2
Sch.2C Part III para.22, added: SI 2012/3039 Sch.2
Sch.2C Part III para.23, added: SI 2012/3039 Sch.2
Sch.2C Part III para.24, added: SI 2012/3039 Sch.2
Sch.2C Part III para.25, added: SI 2012/3039 Sch.2
Sch.2C Part III para.26, added: SI 2012/3039 Sch.2
Sch.2C Part III para.27, added: SI 2012/3039 Sch.2
Sch.2C Part III para.28, added: SI 2012/3039 Sch.2

20. Horticultural Produce Act 1986
disapplied: SI 2012/947 Reg.22, SSI 2012/349 Reg.21

31. Airports Act 1986
applied: 2012 c.19 Sch.8 para.5, SI 2012/1128 Art.4, SSI 2012/89 Sch.1
referred to: 2012 c.19 Sch.6 para.4, Sch.10 para.6
Part IV, applied: 2012 c.19 Sch.10 para.9
Part V, applied: 2012 c.19 Sch.8 para.5, Sch.10 para.10, Sch.10 para.12
s.36, repealed: 2012 c.19 s.76
s.37, repealed: 2012 c.19 s.76
s.38, applied: 2012 c.19 Sch.10 para.10
s.38, repealed: 2012 c.19 s.76
s.39, repealed: 2012 c.19 s.76
s.40, applied: 2012 c.19 Sch.10 para.4, Sch.10 para.5
s.40, disapplied: 2012 c.19 Sch.10 para.5
s.40, repealed: 2012 c.19 s.76

1986–cont.

31. Airports Act 1986–*cont.*
s.40A, referred to: 2012 c.19 Sch.10 para.5
s.40A, repealed: 2012 c.19 s.76
s.40B, repealed: 2012 c.19 s.76
s.41, repealed: 2012 c.19 s.76
s.42, repealed: 2012 c.19 s.76
s.43, repealed: 2012 c.19 s.76
s.44, repealed: 2012 c.19 s.76
s.44A, repealed: 2012 c.19 s.76
s.44B, repealed: 2012 c.19 s.76
s.45, repealed: 2012 c.19 s.76
s.46, repealed: 2012 c.19 s.76
s.47, repealed: 2012 c.19 s.76
s.48, repealed: 2012 c.19 s.76
s.49, repealed: 2012 c.19 s.76
s.50, repealed: 2012 c.19 s.76
s.51, repealed: 2012 c.19 s.76
s.52, repealed: 2012 c.19 s.76
s.53, repealed: 2012 c.19 s.76
s.54, repealed: 2012 c.19 s.76
s.55, repealed: 2012 c.19 s.76
s.56, repealed: 2012 c.19 s.76
s.57, substituted: 2012 c.19 Sch.8 para.2
s.57A, applied: 2012 c.19 Sch.8 para.5, Sch.10 para.9, Sch.10 para.10
s.57A, referred to: 2012 c.19 Sch.10 para.11
s.66, amended: 2012 c.9 Sch.9 para.19
s.66, repealed (in part): 2012 c.9 Sch.9 para.19, Sch.10 Part 3
s.74, amended: 2012 c.19 Sch.9 para.3
s.74, repealed (in part): 2012 c.19 Sch.9 para.3
s.79, amended: 2012 c.19 Sch.8 para.3
s.82, amended: 2012 c.19 Sch.9 para.4

33. Disabled Persons (Services, Consultation and Representation) Act 1986
s.2, amended: 2012 c.7 Sch.5 para.39, Sch.14 para.51
s.7, amended: 2012 c.7 Sch.5 para.40
s.7, repealed (in part): 2012 c.7 Sch.5 para.40
s.11, amended: 2012 c.7 Sch.5 para.41
s.11, repealed (in part): 2012 c.7 Sch.5 para.41
s.16, amended: 2012 c.7 Sch.5 para.42

35. Protection of Military Remains Act 1986
s.1, applied: SI 2012/1110
s.1, enabling: SI 2012/1110

41. Finance Act 1986
s.76, repealed: 2012 c.14 Sch.39 para.5
s.90, repealed (in part): SI 2012/964 Sch.1
s.93, see *HSBC Holdings Plc v Revenue and Customs Commissioners* [2012] UKFTT 163 (TC), [2012] S.F.T.D. 913 (FTT (Tax)), Judge Barbara Mosedale
s.98, enabling: SI 2012/886
s.102, see *Buzzoni v Revenue and Customs Commissioners* [2012] UKUT 360 (TCC), [2012] B.T.C. 1727 (UT (Tax)), Proudman, J.
s.106, enabling: SI 2012/2903
s.107, enabling: SI 2012/2903

44. Gas Act 1986
applied: SI 2012/1128 Art.4
referred to: 2012 c.19 Sch.6 para.4
Part I, applied: SI 2012/3018 Art.24, SSI 2012/345 Art.9
s.4AA, amended: SI 2012/2400 Art.18
s.5, amended: SI 2012/2400 Art.19
s.5, applied: SI 2012/2400 Art.38
s.6A, amended: SI 2012/2400 Art.20
s.7, applied: SI 2012/801 Art.27
s.7, referred to: SSI 2012/89 Sch.1

1986–cont.

44. Gas Act 1986–*cont.*
s.7AB, added: SI 2012/2400 Art.21
s.7AB, applied: SI 2012/2400 Art.38
s.7B, amended: SI 2012/2400 Art.22
s.8AA, amended: SI 2012/2400 Art.23
s.23B, amended: SI 2012/2400 Art.24
s.33BC, applied: SI 2012/3018
s.33BC, enabling: SI 2012/3018
s.33BD, applied: SI 2012/3018
s.33BD, enabling: SI 2012/3018
s.36, amended: SI 2012/2400 Art.25
s.41C, amended: SI 2012/2400 Art.26
s.41HA, enabling: SI 2012/2400
s.41HB, applied: SI 2012/2400
s.41HC, enabling: SI 2012/2414
s.47, enabling: SI 2012/2400, SI 2012/2414
s.48, amended: SI 2012/2400 Art.27
Sch.4B para.1, amended: SI 2012/2400 Art.28
Sch.4B para.9A, added: SI 2012/2400 Art.28

45. Insolvency Act 1986
see *Jules v Robertson* [2011] EWCA Civ 1322, [2012] B.P.I.R. 126 (CA (Civ Div)), Longmore, L.J.; see *Sanders v Donovan* [2012] B.P.I.R. 219 (Ch D (Bankruptcy Ct)), Chief Registrar Baister; see *Schmitt v Deichmann* [2012] EWHC 62 (Ch), [2012] 3 W.L.R. 681 (Ch D), Proudman, J.; see *Weavering Capital (UK) Ltd (In Liquidation) v Peterson* [2012] EWHC 1480 (Ch), [2012] Lloyd's Rep. F.C. 561 (Ch D), Proudman, J.
applied: 2012 asp 8 Sch.1 para.5, 2012 c.7 s.130, SI 2012/1128 Art.4, SI 2012/1749 Sch.1 para.8
referred to: 2012 c.19 Sch.6 para.4
varied: SI 2012/3013 Sch.1 para.1
Part I, applied: 2012 c.7 s.130, SI 2012/3013 Reg.9
Part II, applied: 2012 c.7 s.130, SI 2012/3013 Reg.9
Part III, applied: 2012 c.7 s.130
Part IV, applied: 2012 c.7 s.130, SI 2012/3013 Reg.9, Reg.14
Part IV c.IX, applied: SI 2012/3013 Reg.34
Part V, applied: 2012 c.7 s.130
Part VI, applied: 2012 c.7 s.130
Part VII, applied: 2012 c.7 s.130
Part VIIA, applied: 2012 c.9 Sch.8 para.2
Part IX, applied: 2012 c.10 Sch.1 para.33
Part XIII, applied: 2012 c.7 s.128
Part XIII, varied: SI 2012/3013 Sch.1 para.1
Pt IX. see *Chadwick v Nash* [2012] B.P.I.R. 70 (Ch D), Registrar Nicholls
Pt VIIA. see *R. (on the application of Payne) v Secretary of State for Work and Pensions* [2012] 2 A.C. 1 (SC), Lady Hale, J.S.C.
s.1, varied: SI 2012/3013 Sch.1 para.1
s.3, applied: SI 2012/3013 Reg.9
s.4A, amended: 2012 c.21 Sch.18 para.52
s.4A, varied: SI 2012/3013 Sch.1 para.1
s.5, varied: SI 2012/3013 Sch.1 para.1
s.6, applied: SI 2012/3013 Reg.9
s.6, varied: SI 2012/3013 Sch.1 para.1
s.7A, varied: SI 2012/3013 Sch.1 para.1
s.30, see *Foster v Davenport Lyons* [2012] EWHC 275 (Ch), [2012] B.P.I.R. 545 (Ch D), Roth, J.
s.30, varied: SI 2012/3013 Sch.1 para.1
s.38, varied: SI 2012/3013 Sch.1 para.1
s.47, varied: SI 2012/3013 Sch.1 para.1
s.72A, varied: SI 2012/3013 Sch.1 para.1
s.72DA, applied: 2012 c.14 Sch.39 para.7
s.72G, amended: SI 2012/700 Sch.1 para.3
s.72G, varied: SI 2012/3013 Sch.1 para.1

1986-cont.

45. Insolvency Act 1986-*cont.*
s.72H, varied: SI 2012/ 3013 Sch.1 para.1
s.73, varied: SI 2012/ 3013 Sch.1 para.1
s.74, varied: SI 2012/ 3013 Sch.1 para.1
s.79, varied: SI 2012/ 3013 Sch.1 para.1
s.81, varied: SI 2012/ 3013 Sch.1 para.1
s.84, applied: SI 2012/ 3013 Reg.14
s.84, varied: SI 2012/ 3013 Sch.1 para.1
s.88, varied: SI 2012/ 3013 Sch.1 para.1
s.95, varied: SI 2012/ 3013 Sch.1 para.1
s.98, varied: SI 2012/ 3013 Sch.1 para.1
s.99, varied: SI 2012/ 3013 Sch.1 para.1
s.101, varied: SI 2012/ 3013 Sch.1 para.1
s.107, varied: SI 2012/ 3013 Sch.1 para.1
s.108, see *Beattie v Smailes* [2011] EWHC 1563 (Ch), [2012] B.C.C. 205 (Ch D), Norris, J.
s.109, varied: SI 2012/ 3013 Sch.1 para.1
s.110, see *Manuplastics Ltd v BPSW19 Ltd* [2011] EWHC 3853 (Ch), [2012] B.C.C. 368 (Ch D), Judge Mackie Q.C.
s.110, varied: SI 2012/ 3013 Sch.1 para.1
s.112, see *MG Rover Dealer Properties Ltd v Hunt* [2012] B.P.I.R. 590 (Ch D (Companies Ct)), Registrar Baister
s.117, varied: SI 2012/ 3013 Sch.1 para.1
s.122, see *Fulham Football Club (1987) Ltd v Richards* [2011] EWCA Civ 855, [2012] Ch. 333 (CA (Civ Div)), Rix, L.J.
s.122, varied: SI 2012/ 3013 Sch.1 para.1
s.123, varied: SI 2012/ 3013 Sch.1 para.1
s.124, varied: SI 2012/ 3013 Sch.1 para.1
s.124A, applied: 2012 c.7 s.130
s.125, see *Integrated Medical Solutions Ltd, Re* [2012] B.C.C. 215 (Ch D (Companies Ct)), Registrar Baister
s.126, varied: SI 2012/ 3013 Sch.1 para.1
s.127, varied: SI 2012/ 3013 Sch.1 para.1
s.128, varied: SI 2012/ 3013 Sch.1 para.1
s.130, varied: SI 2012/ 3013 Sch.1 para.1
s.131, varied: SI 2012/ 3013 Sch.1 para.1
s.133, varied: SI 2012/ 3013 Sch.1 para.1
s.135, varied: SI 2012/ 3013 Sch.1 para.1
s.143, varied: SI 2012/ 3013 Sch.1 para.1
s.144, varied: SI 2012/ 3013 Sch.1 para.1
s.147, varied: SI 2012/ 3013 Sch.1 para.1
s.149, varied: SI 2012/ 3013 Sch.1 para.1
s.152, varied: SI 2012/ 3013 Sch.1 para.1
s.154, varied: SI 2012/ 3013 Sch.1 para.1
s.155, see *MG Rover Dealer Properties Ltd v Hunt* [2012] B.P.I.R. 590 (Ch D (Companies Ct)), Registrar Baister
s.165, varied: SI 2012/ 3013 Sch.1 para.1
s.172, varied: SI 2012/ 3013 Sch.1 para.1
s.173, varied: SI 2012/ 3013 Sch.1 para.1
s.174, varied: SI 2012/ 3013 Sch.1 para.1
s.176A, see *JT Frith Ltd, Re* [2012] EWHC 196 (Ch), [2012] B.C.C. 634 (Ch D (Leeds)), Judge Keyser Q.C.
s.176A, varied: SI 2012/ 3013 Sch.1 para.1
s.177, varied: SI 2012/ 3013 Sch.1 para.1
s.184, varied: SI 2012/ 3013 Sch.1 para.1
s.187, varied: SI 2012/ 3013 Sch.1 para.1
s.189, varied: SI 2012/ 3013 Sch.1 para.1
s.190, varied: SI 2012/ 3013 Sch.1 para.1
s.196, varied: SI 2012/ 3013 Sch.1 para.1
s.197, varied: SI 2012/ 3013 Sch.1 para.1
s.201, varied: SI 2012/ 3013 Sch.1 para.1
s.202, varied: SI 2012/ 3013 Sch.1 para.1

1986-cont.

45. Insolvency Act 1986-*cont.*
s.203, varied: SI 2012/ 3013 Sch.1 para.1
s.205, varied: SI 2012/ 3013 Sch.1 para.1
s.212, see *Idessa (UK) Ltd (In Liquidation), Re* [2011] EWHC 804 (Ch), [2012] B.C.C. 315 (Ch D (Manchester)), Lesley Anderson QC
s.213, see *Bilta (UK) Ltd (In Liquidation) v Nazir* [2012] EWHC 2163 (Ch), [2012] S.T.C. 2424 (Ch D), Sir Andrew Morritt (Chancellor)
s.214, see *Idessa (UK) Ltd (In Liquidation), Re* [2011] EWHC 804 (Ch), [2012] B.C.C. 315 (Ch D (Manchester)), Lesley Anderson QC; see *Kudos Business Solutions Ltd (In Liquidation), Re* [2011] EWHC 1436 (Ch), [2012] 2 B.C.L.C. 65 (Ch D (Companies Ct)), Sarah Asplin QC
s.216, varied: SI 2012/ 3013 Sch.1 para.1
s.217, varied: SI 2012/ 3013 Sch.1 para.1
s.218, varied: SI 2012/ 3013 Sch.1 para.1
s.219, varied: SI 2012/ 3013 Sch.1 para.1
s.220, see *Panter v Rowellian Football Social Club* [2011] EWHC 1301 (Ch), [2012] Ch. 125 (Ch D (Companies Ct)), Judge Behrens
s.221, see *Eurodis Electron Plc (In Administration), Re* [2011] EWHC 1025 (Ch), [2012] B.C.C. 57 (Ch D), Mann, J.
s.233, varied: SI 2012/ 3013 Sch.1 para.1
s.235, varied: SI 2012/ 3013 Sch.1 para.1
s.236, see *Lehman Brothers International (Europe) (In Administration), Re* [2011] EWHC 2022 (Ch), [2012] 1 B.C.L.C. 312 (Ch D (Companies Ct)), Briggs, J.
s.236, varied: SI 2012/ 3013 Sch.1 para.1
s.239, see *F Options Ltd (In Liquidation), Re* [2011] EWHC 3324 (Ch), [2012] B.P.I.R. 107 (Ch D), Charles Hollander Q.C.; see *GHLM Trading Ltd v Maroo* [2012] EWHC 61 (Ch), [2012] 2 B.C.L.C. 369 (Ch D), Newey, J; see *Stealth Construction Ltd, Re* [2011] EWHC 1305 (Ch), [2012] 1 B.C.L.C. 297 (Ch D (Manchester)), David Richards, J.
s.241, see *F Options Ltd (In Liquidation), Re* [2011] EWHC 3324 (Ch), [2012] B.P.I.R. 107 (Ch D), Charles Hollander Q.C.
s.244, see *St George's Property Services (London) Ltd (In Administration), Re* [2011] EWCA Civ 858, [2012] Bus. L.R. 594 (CA (Civ Div)), Mummery, L.J.
s.244, varied: SI 2012/ 3013 Sch.1 para.1
s.245, varied: SI 2012/ 3013 Sch.1 para.1
s.246A, varied: SI 2012/ 3013 Sch.1 para.1
s.246B, varied: SI 2012/ 3013 Sch.1 para.1
s.248, varied: SI 2012/ 3013 Sch.1 para.1
s.249, see *F Options Ltd (In Liquidation), Re* [2011] EWHC 3324 (Ch), [2012] B.P.I.R. 107 (Ch D), Charles Hollander Q.C.
s.251, varied: SI 2012/ 3013 Sch.1 para.1
s.251G, see *Places for People Homes Ltd v Sharples* [2011] EWCA Civ 813, [2012] Ch. 382 (CA (Civ Div)), Mummery, L.J.; see *R. (on the application of Payne) v Secretary of State for Work and Pensions* [2012] 2 A.C. 1 (SC), Lady Hale, J.S.C.
s.260, see *Peterkin v Merton LBC* [2011] EWHC 376 (Ch), [2012] B.P.I.R. 388 (Ch D), Vos, J.
s.262, see *National Westminster Bank Plc v Kapoor* [2011] EWCA Civ 1083, [2012] 1 All E.R. 1201 (CA (Civ Div)), Pill, L.J.; see *National Westminster Bank Plc v Yadgaroff* [2011] EWHC 3711 (Ch), [2012] B.P.I.R. 371 (Ch D), Norris, J.

1986–cont.

45. Insolvency Act 1986–*cont.*

s.263, see *Stericker v Horner* [2012] B.P.I.R. 645 (Ch D), Judge Langan Q.C.

s.267, see *McGuinness v Norwich and Peterborough Building Society* [2011] EWCA Civ 1286, [2012] 2 All E.R. (Comm) 265 (CA (Civ Div)), Ward, L.J.; see *Orrick, Herrington & Sutcliffe (Europe) LLP v Frohlich* [2012] B.P.I.R. 169 (Ch D), Deputy Registrar Schaffer; see *Stericker v Horner* [2012] B.P.I.R. 645 (Ch D), Judge Langan Q.C.

s.268, applied: SSI 2012/88 Reg.23, SSI 2012/89 Reg.26

s.272, see *Gittins v Serco Home Affairs* [2012] EWHC 651 (Ch), [2012] 4 All E.R. 1362 (Ch D (Leeds)), Judge Behrens

s.279, see *Bramston v Haut* [2012] EWHC 1279 (Ch), [2012] B.P.I.R. 672 (Ch D (Bankruptcy Ct)), Arnold, J.; see *Chadwick v Nash* [2012] B.P.I.R. 70 (Ch D), Registrar Nicholls

s.281, see *Hayes v Hayes* [2012] EWHC 1240 (Ch), [2012] B.P.I.R. 739 (Ch D), Judge Pelling Q.C.

s.283, see *Sanders v Donovan* [2012] B.P.I.R. 219 (Ch D (Bankruptcy Ct)), Chief Registrar Baister

s.283A, see *Levy v Ellis-Carr* [2012] EWHC 63 (Ch), [2012] B.P.I.R. 347 (Ch D), Norris, J.

s.284, see *Sanders v Donovan* [2012] B.P.I.R. 219 (Ch D (Bankruptcy Ct)), Chief Registrar Baister

s.285, see *Bank of Scotland Plc (t/a Birmingham Midshires) v Breytenbach* [2012] B.P.I.R. 1 (Ch D), Registrar Baister; see *Places for People Homes Ltd v Sharples* [2011] EWCA Civ 813, [2012] Ch. 382 (CA (Civ Div)), Mummery, L.J.; see *R. (on the application of Payne) v Secretary of State for Work and Pensions* [2012] 2 A.C. 1 (SC), Lady Hale, J.S.C.

s.303, see *Bramston v Haut* [2012] EWHC 1279 (Ch), [2012] B.P.I.R. 672 (Ch D (Bankruptcy Ct)), Arnold, J.; see *Cowey v Insol Funding Ltd* [2012] EWHC 2421 (Ch), [2012] B.P.I.R. 958 (Ch D), Judge Purle Q.C.

s.304, see *Chapper v Jackson* [2012] B.P.I.R. 257 (Ch D (Bankruptcy Ct)), Mark Herbert Q.C.

s.306, see *McNulty v Revenue and Customs Commissioners* [2012] UKUT 174 (TCC), [2012] S.T.C. 2110 (UT (Tax)), Arnold, J.; see *Pick v Chief Land Registrar* [2011] EWHC 206 (Ch), [2012] Ch. 564 (Ch D), Proudman, J.; see *Sanders v Donovan* [2012] B.P.I.R. 219 (Ch D (Bankruptcy Ct)), Chief Registrar Baister

s.306B, applied: SI 2012/1726 r.60.4

s.307, see *Official Receiver v Negus* [2011] EWHC 3719 (Ch), [2012] 1 W.L.R. 1598 (Ch D), Newey, J

s.310, see *Official Receiver v Negus* [2011] EWHC 3719 (Ch), [2012] 1 W.L.R. 1598 (Ch D), Newey, J; see *Raithatha v Williamson* [2012] EWHC 909 (Ch), [2012] 1 W.L.R. 3559 (Ch D), Bernard Livesey Q.C.

s.315, see *Fenland DC v Sheppard* [2011] EWHC 2829 (Ch), [2012] B.P.I.R. 289 (Ch D), Roth, J.

s.320, see *Fenland DC v Sheppard* [2011] EWHC 2829 (Ch), [2012] B.P.I.R. 289 (Ch D), Roth, J.

s.335A, see *Ford v Alexander* [2012] EWHC 266 (Ch), [2012] B.P.I.R. 528 (Ch D), Peter Smith, J.

s.335A, applied: 2012 c.10 Sch.1 para.33

s.336, see *Ruiz (A Bankrupt), Re* [2011] EWCA Civ 1646, [2012] B.P.I.R. 446 (CA (Civ Div)), Thorpe, L.J.

1986–cont.

45. Insolvency Act 1986–*cont.*

s.339, see *Claridge's Trustee in Bankruptcy v Claridge* [2011] EWHC 2047 (Ch), [2012] 1 F.C.R. 388 (Ch D), Sales, J.; see *Garwood v Ambrose* [2012] EWHC 1494 (Ch), [2012] B.P.I.R. 996 (Ch D), Peter Leaver Q.C.; see *Salter v Wetton* [2011] EWHC 3192 (Ch), [2012] B.P.I.R. 63 (Ch D (Bankruptcy Ct)), Briggs, J.

s.341, see *Salter v Wetton* [2011] EWHC 3192 (Ch), [2012] B.P.I.R. 63 (Ch D (Bankruptcy Ct)), Briggs, J.

s.365, see *Williams v Mohammed* [2012] B.P.I.R. 238 (Ch D), Judge Hodge Q.C.

s.375, see *Arif v Zar* [2012] EWCA Civ 986, [2012] B.P.I.R. 948 (CA (Civ Div)), Thorpe, L.J.; see *Ross v Revenue and Customs Commissioners* [2012] EWHC 1054 (Ch), [2012] B.P.I.R. 843 (Ch D), Norris, J.

s.375, applied: SI 2012/1749 Sch.1 para.8

s.381, applied: SSI 2012/303 Reg.41, Reg.48, SSI 2012/319 Reg.39

s.382, see *Bloom v Pensions Regulator* [2011] EWCA Civ 1124, [2012] Bus. L.R. 818 (CA (Civ Div)), Laws, L.J.

s.382, amended: 2012 c.5 s.142

s.387, varied: SI 2012/3013 Sch.1 para.1

s.389A, amended: SI 2012/2404 Sch.2 para.23

s.390, varied: SI 2012/3013 Sch.1 para.1

s.391, applied: 2012 c.19 Sch.6 para.5

s.399, varied: SI 2012/3013 Sch.1 para.1

s.411, applied: 2012 c.7 s.130

s.411, referred to: 2012 c.7 s.130

s.411, varied: SI 2012/3013 Sch.1 para.1

s.412, enabling: SI 2012/469

s.413, applied: SI 2012/469

s.413, varied: SI 2012/3013 Sch.1 para.1

s.413, enabling: SI 2012/469

s.414, varied: SI 2012/3013 Sch.1 para.1

s.415A, varied: SI 2012/3013 Sch.1 para.1

s.415A, enabling: SI 2012/2264

s.416, varied: SI 2012/3013 Sch.1 para.1

s.422, amended: 2012 c.21 Sch.18 para.53

s.423, see *Kaupthing Singer & Friedlander Ltd v Coomber* [2011] EWHC 3589 (Ch), [2012] B.P.I.R. 774 (Ch D (Bankruptcy Ct)), Arnold, J.; see *Revenue and Customs Commissioners v Ben Nevis (Holdings) Ltd* [2012] EWHC 1807 (Ch), [2012] S.T.C. 2157 (Ch D), Judge Pelling Q.C.; see *Rubin v Dweck* [2012] B.P.I.R. 854 (Ch D (Bankruptcy Ct)), Registrar Jones; see *Schmitt v Deichmann* [2012] EWHC 62 (Ch), [2012] 3 W.L.R. 681 (Ch D), Proudman, J.; see *Weavering Capital (UK) Ltd (In Liquidation) v Peterson* [2012] EWHC 1480 (Ch), [2012] Lloyd's Rep. F.C. 561 (Ch D), Proudman, J.

s.423, varied: SI 2012/3013 Sch.1 para.1

s.424, varied: SI 2012/3013 Sch.1 para.1

s.425, see *Kaupthing Singer & Friedlander Ltd v Coomber* [2011] EWHC 3589 (Ch), [2012] B.P.I.R. 774 (Ch D (Bankruptcy Ct)), Arnold, J.

s.426, see *Integrated Medical Solutions Ltd, Re* [2012] B.C.C. 215 (Ch D (Companies Ct)), Registrar Baister; see *New Cap Reinsurance Corp Ltd (In Liquidation) v Grant* [2011] EWCA Civ 971, [2012] Ch. 538 (CA (Civ Div)), Mummery, L.J.; see *Rubin v Eurofinance SA* [2012] UKSC 46, [2012] 3 W.L.R. 1019 (SC), Lord Walker, J.S.C.; see *Schmitt v Deichmann* [2012] EWHC 62 (Ch), [2012] 3 W.L.R. 681 (Ch D), Proudman, J.

1986–cont.

45. Insolvency Act 1986–*cont.*
s.426A, amended: SI 2012/1544 Art.3
s.426B, amended: SI 2012/1544 Art.4
s.427, amended: SI 2012/1544 Art.5
s.429, applied: SI 2012/922 Reg.3, SI 2012/1034 Sch.4 para.11, SI 2012/1290 Reg.3, SI 2012/1631 Sch.5 para.8, SI 2012/1640 Sch.2 para.5, SI 2012/2996 Sch.5 para.8
s.431, varied: SI 2012/3013 Sch.1 para.1
s.432, varied: SI 2012/3013 Sch.1 para.1
s.433, varied: SI 2012/3013 Sch.1 para.1
s.434A, varied: SI 2012/3013 Sch.1 para.1
s.434D, varied: SI 2012/3013 Sch.1 para.1
s.435, see *Salter v Wetton* [2011] EWHC 3192 (Ch), [2012] B.P.I.R. 63 (Ch D (Bankruptcy Ct)), Briggs, J.
s.436, see *Sanders v Donovan* [2012] B.P.I.R. 219 (Ch D (Bankruptcy Ct)), Chief Registrar Baister
s.436, varied: SI 2012/3013 Sch.1 para.1
s.436B, varied: SI 2012/3013 Sch.1 para.1
s.441, amended: SI 2012/1544 Art.6
Sch.A1 Part I para.1, varied: SI 2012/3013 Sch.1 para.1
Sch.A1 Part I para.2, varied: SI 2012/3013 Sch.1 para.1
Sch.A1 Part II para.7, varied: SI 2012/3013 Sch.1 para.1
Sch.A1 Part III para.12, varied: SI 2012/3013 Sch.1 para.1
Sch.A1 Part III para.17, varied: SI 2012/3013 Sch.1 para.1
Sch.A1 Part III para.22, varied: SI 2012/3013 Sch.1 para.1
Sch.A1 Part V para.38, varied: SI 2012/3013 Sch.1 para.1
Sch.A1 Part VI, amended: 2012 c.21 Sch.18 para.54
Sch.A1 Part VI para.40, varied: SI 2012/3013 Sch.1 para.1
Sch.A1 Part VI para.44, amended: 2012 c.21 Sch.18 para.54
Sch.A1 Part VI para.45, varied: SI 2012/3013 Sch.1 para.1
Sch.B1, see *European Directories (DH6) BV, Re* [2010] EWHC 3472 (Ch), [2012] B.C.C. 46 (Ch D), Judge Raynor QC; see *Key2Law (Surrey) LLP v De'Antiquis* [2011] EWCA Civ 1567, [2012] B.C.C. 375 (CA (Civ Div)), Longmore, L.J.; see *Panter v Rowellian Football Social Club* [2011] EWHC 1301 (Ch), [2012] Ch. 125 (Ch D (Companies Ct)), Judge Behrens; see *Wright Hassall LLP v Morris* [2012] EWHC 188 (Ch), [2012] B.C.C. 624 (Ch D (Birmingham)), Judge David Cooke
Sch.B1 Pt 1 para.3, see *European Directories (DH6) BV, Re* [2010] EWHC 3472 (Ch), [2012] B.C.C. 46 (Ch D), Judge Raynor QC; see *Key2Law (Surrey) LLP v De'Antiquis* [2011] EWCA Civ 1567, [2012] B.C.C. 375 (CA (Civ Div)), Longmore, L.J.
Sch.B1 Part 2 para.12, applied: SI 2012/3013 Reg.14
Sch.B1 Pt 2 para.13, see *Bickland Ltd, Re* [2012] EWHC 706 (Ch), [2012] 2 B.C.L.C. 751 (Ch D), Mann, J.; see *M.T.B. Motors Ltd (In Administration), Re* [2010] EWHC 3751 (Ch), [2012] B.C.C. 601 (Ch D (Manchester)), Judge Hodge Q.C.
Sch.B1 Part 3 para.14, applied: SI 2012/3013 Reg.14
Sch.B1 Part 3 para.14, varied: SI 2012/3013 Sch.1 para.1

45. Insolvency Act 1986–*cont.*
Sch.B1 Part 3 para.15, varied: SI 2012/3013 Sch.1 para.1
Sch.B1 Part 4 para.22, applied: SI 2012/3013 Reg.14
Sch.B1 Pt 4 para.22, see *Assured Logistics Solutions Ltd, Re* [2011] EWHC 3029 (Ch), [2012] B.C.C. 541 (Ch D (Birmingham)), Judge Purle Q.C.; see *Business Dream Ltd (In Liquidation), Re* [2011] EWHC 2860 (Ch), [2012] B.C.C. 115 (Ch D (Leeds)), Judge Behrens Q.C.; see *BXL Services, Re* [2012] EWHC 1877 (Ch), [2012] B.C.C. 657 (Ch D (Birmingham)), Judge Purle Q.C.; see *Ceart Risk Services Ltd, Re* [2012] EWHC 1178 (Ch), [2012] B.C.C. 592 (Ch D (Companies Ct)), Arnold, J.; see *MF Global Overseas Ltd (In Administration), Re* [2012] EWHC 1091 (Ch), [2012] B.C.C. 490 (Ch D (Companies Ct)), Mann, J.; see *MK Airlines Ltd, Re* [2012] EWHC 1018 (Ch), [2012] 3 All E.R. 781 (Ch D (Companies Ct)), Sir Andrew Morritt (Chancellor); see *Virtualpurple Professional Services Ltd, Re* [2011] EWHC 3487 (Ch), [2012] B.C.C. 254 (Ch D (Companies Ct)), Norris, J.
Sch.B1 Pt 4 para.26, see *Assured Logistics Solutions Ltd, Re* [2011] EWHC 3029 (Ch), [2012] B.C.C. 541 (Ch D (Birmingham)), Judge Purle Q.C.; see *Bezier Acquisitions Ltd, Re* [2011] EWHC 3299 (Ch), [2012] Bus. L.R. 636 (Ch D (Companies Ct)), Norris, J.; see *BXL Services, Re* [2012] EWHC 1877 (Ch), [2012] B.C.C. 657 (Ch D (Birmingham)), Judge Purle Q.C.; see *MF Global Overseas Ltd (In Administration), Re* [2012] EWHC 1091 (Ch), [2012] B.C.C. 490 (Ch D (Companies Ct)), Mann, J.; see *National Westminster Bank Plc v Msaada Group* [2011] EWHC 3423 (Ch), [2012] B.C.C. 226 (Ch D), Warren, J.; see *Virtualpurple Professional Services Ltd, Re* [2011] EWHC 3487 (Ch), [2012] B.C.C. 254 (Ch D (Companies Ct)), Norris, J.
Sch.B1 Pt 4 para.27, see *Assured Logistics Solutions Ltd, Re* [2011] EWHC 3029 (Ch), [2012] B.C.C. 541 (Ch D (Birmingham)), Judge Purle Q.C.
Sch.B1 Pt 4 para.28, see *Assured Logistics Solutions Ltd, Re* [2011] EWHC 3029 (Ch), [2012] B.C.C. 541 (Ch D (Birmingham)), Judge Purle Q.C.; see *Business Dream Ltd (In Liquidation), Re* [2011] EWHC 2860 (Ch), [2012] B.C.C. 115 (Ch D (Leeds)), Judge Behrens Q.C.; see *National Westminster Bank Plc v Msaada Group* [2011] EWHC 3423 (Ch), [2012] B.C.C. 226 (Ch D), Warren, J.; see *Virtualpurple Professional Services Ltd, Re* [2011] EWHC 3487 (Ch), [2012] B.C.C. 254 (Ch D (Companies Ct)), Norris, J.
Sch.B1 Pt 4 para.29, see *Assured Logistics Solutions Ltd, Re* [2011] EWHC 3029 (Ch), [2012] B.C.C. 541 (Ch D (Birmingham)), Judge Purle Q.C.; see *M.T.B. Motors Ltd (In Administration), Re* [2010] EWHC 3751 (Ch), [2012] B.C.C. 601 (Ch D (Manchester)), Judge Hodge Q.C.
Sch.B1 Pt 4 para.30, see *Assured Logistics Solutions Ltd, Re* [2011] EWHC 3029 (Ch), [2012] B.C.C. 541 (Ch D (Birmingham)), Judge Purle Q.C.
Sch.B1 Part 5 para.39, varied: SI 2012/3013 Sch.1 para.1

1986– cont.

45. Insolvency Act 1986–*cont.*

Sch.B1 Part 6 para.40, amended: 2012 c.21 Sch.18 para.55

Sch.B1 Part 6 para.40, varied: SI 2012/3013 Sch.1 para.1

Sch.B1 Part 6 para.42, amended: 2012 c.21 Sch.18 para.55

Sch.B1 Part 6 para.42, varied: SI 2012/3013 Sch.1 para.1

Sch.B1 Part 6 para.43, varied: SI 2012/3013 Sch.1 para.1

Sch.B1 Part 6 para.44, applied: SI 2012/3013 Reg.9

Sch.B1 Pt 6 para.44, see *Business Dream Ltd (In Liquidation), Re* [2011] EWHC 2860 (Ch), [2012] B.C.C. 115 (Ch D (Leeds)), Judge Behrens Q.C.

Sch.B1 Part 7 para.47, varied: SI 2012/3013 Sch.1 para.1

Sch.B1 Part 7 para.49, varied: SI 2012/3013 Sch.1 para.1

Sch.B1 Part 8 para.73, varied: SI 2012/3013 Sch.1 para.1

Sch.B1 Part 8 para.74, varied: SI 2012/3013 Sch.1 para.1

Sch.B1 Part 9 para.82, amended: 2012 c.21 Sch.18 para.55

Sch.B1 Part 9 para.82, varied: SI 2012/3013 Sch.1 para.1

Sch.B1 Part 9 para.83, varied: SI 2012/3013 Sch.1 para.1

Sch.B1 Part 9 para.84, applied: SI 2012/3013 Reg.34

Sch.B1 Part 9 para.84, varied: SI 2012/3013 Sch.1 para.1

Sch.B1 Part 10 para.96, varied: SI 2012/3013 Sch.1 para.1

Sch.B1 Part 11 para.111, varied: SI 2012/3013 Sch.1 para.1

Sch.B1 para.55, see *Stanleybet UK Investments Ltd, Re* [2011] EWHC 2820 (Ch), [2012] B.C.C. 550 (Ch D), Sales, J.

Sch.B1 para.63, see *Joint Administrators of Rangers Football Club Plc, Noters* [2012] CSOH 55, 2012 S.L.T. 599 (OH), Lord Hodge

Sch.B1 para.69, see *SNR Denton UK LLP v Kirwan* [2012] I.R.L.R. 966 (EAT), Langstaff, J. (President); see *Wright Hassall LLP v Morris* [2012] EWHC 188 (Ch), [2012] B.C.C. 624 (Ch D (Birmingham)), Judge David Cooke

Sch.B1 para.74, see *Joint Administrators of Rangers Football Club Plc, Noters* [2012] CSOH 55, 2012 S.L.T. 599 (OH), Lord Hodge

Sch.B1 para.76, see *Globespan Airways Ltd (In Liquidation), Re* [2012] EWCA Civ 1159, [2012] 4 All E.R. 1124 (CA (Civ Div)), Lord Neuberger (M.R.)

Sch.B1 para.83, see *Globespan Airways Ltd (In Liquidation), Re* [2012] EWCA Civ 1159, [2012] 4 All E.R. 1124 (CA (Civ Div)), Lord Neuberger (M.R.); see *Globespan Airways Ltd (In Liquidation), Re* [2012] EWHC 359 (Ch), [2012] 2 All E.R. 1234 (Ch D (Manchester)), Briggs, J.

Sch.B1 para.88, see *St George's Property Services (London) Ltd (In Administration), Re* [2011] EWCA Civ 858, [2012] Bus. L.R. 594 (CA (Civ Div)), Mummery, L.J.

Sch.B1 para.99, see *MK Airlines Ltd, Re* [2012] EWHC 1018 (Ch), [2012] 3 All E.R. 781 (Ch D (Companies Ct)), Sir Andrew Morritt (Chancellor)

1986– cont.

45. Insolvency Act 1986–*cont.*

Sch.B1 para.104, see *Ceart Risk Services Ltd, Re* [2012] EWHC 1178 (Ch), [2012] B.C.C. 592 (Ch D (Companies Ct)), Arnold, J.

Sch.B1 para.105, see *Baker v London Bar Co Ltd* [2011] EWHC 3398 (Ch), [2012] B.C.C. 69 (Ch D), Henderson, J.

Sch.B1 para.111, see *European Directories (DH6) BV, Re* [2010] EWHC 3472 (Ch), [2012] B.C.C. 46 (Ch D), Judge Raynor QC; see *Panter v Rowellian Football Social Club* [2011] EWHC 1301 (Ch), [2012] Ch. 125 (Ch D (Companies Ct)), Judge Behrens

Sch.1 para.2, varied: SI 2012/3013 Sch.1 para.1

Sch.2A para.10, amended: SI 2012/2400 Art.29

Sch.4A, applied: 2012 c.9 Sch.8 para.2, SI 2012/922 Reg.3, SI 2012/1544, SI 2012/1631 Sch.5 para.5, SI 2012/1640 Sch.2 para.2, SI 2012/2996 Sch.5 para.4

Sch.4ZA, see *Islington LBC v C* [2012] B.P.I.R. 363 (CC (Central London)), District Judge Hart

Sch.4ZB, applied: 2012 c.9 Sch.8 para.2

Sch.4 Part I para.3, varied: SI 2012/3013 Sch.1 para.1

Sch.4 Part I para.3A, varied: SI 2012/3013 Sch.1 para.1

Sch.6 para.14, varied: SI 2012/3013 Sch.1 para.1

Sch.8 para.14, varied: SI 2012/3013 Sch.1 para.1

Sch.8 para.29, varied: SI 2012/3013 Sch.1 para.1

Sch.10, varied: SI 2012/3013 Sch.1 para.1

46. Company Directors Disqualification Act 1986

see *Asegaai Consultants Ltd, Re* [2012] EWHC 1899 (Ch), [2012] Bus. L.R. 1607 (Ch D (Companies Ct)), Newey, J.; see *R. v Randhawa (Jagprit)* [2012] EWCA Crim 1, [2012] S.T.C. 901 (CA (Crim Div)), Hooper, L.J.; see *Secretary of State for Business Innovation and Skills v Chohan* [2011] EWHC 1350 (Ch), [2012] 1 B.C.L.C. 138 (Ch D (Companies Ct)), David Richards, J.

applied: SI 2012/922 Reg.3, SI 2012/1034 Sch.4 para.11, SI 2012/1128 Art.4, SI 2012/1290 Reg.3, SI 2012/1631 Sch.5 para.8, SI 2012/1640 Sch.2 para.5, SI 2012/2996 Sch.5 para.8

s.1, see *Cunningham (David James) v HM Advocate* [2012] HCJAC 90, 2012 S.C.L. 884 (HCJ), Lord Eassie

s.4, see *Asegaai Consultants Ltd, Re* [2012] EWHC 1899 (Ch), [2012] Bus. L.R. 1607 (Ch D (Companies Ct)), Newey, J.

s.6, see *Secretary of State for Business, Innovation and Skills v Khan* [2012] CSOH 85, 2012 S.L.T. 1090 (OH), Lord Hodge

s.7, see *Instant Access Properties Ltd, Re* [2011] EWHC 3022 (Ch), [2012] 1 B.C.L.C. 710 (Ch D (Companies Ct)), Floyd, J.

s.9A, amended: SI 2012/1809 Sch.1 Part 1

s.9E, amended: 2012 c.7 s.74

s.11, amended: SI 2012/2404 Sch.1 para.1

s.13, see *Cunningham (David James) v HM Advocate* [2012] HCJAC 90, 2012 S.C.L. 884 (HCJ), Lord Eassie; see *Hill v Department of Business, Innovation and Skills* [2011] EWHC 3436 (Admin), [2012] B.C.C. 151 (DC), Hooper, L.J.

s.22F, added: SI 2012/3014 Art.2

47. Legal Aid (Scotland) Act 1986

see *M v Scottish Legal Aid Board* 2012 S.L.T. 354 (OH), Lord Malcolm

1986– cont.

47. Legal Aid (Scotland) Act 1986– *cont.*
s.6, see *M v Scottish Legal Aid Board* 2012 S.L.T. 354 (OH), Lord Malcolm
s.8, amended: 2012 c.5 Sch.14 Part 1
s.9, enabling: SSI 2012/84
s.11, amended: 2012 c.5 Sch.14 Part 1
s.21, amended: SI 2012/1809 Sch.1 Part 1
s.31, amended: SSI 2012/212 Reg.3
s.33, enabling: SSI 2012/276, SSI 2012/305
s.36, enabling: SSI 2012/64, SSI 2012/276, SSI 2012/305
s.37, applied: SSI 2012/84
s.41, amended: SSI 2012/212 Reg.3
Sch.1A para.1, amended: SSI 2012/212 Reg.3
Sch.2 Part I para.2, amended: SI 2012/1809 Sch.1 Part 1
50. Social Security Act 1986
s.63, varied: SI 2012/780 Art.4
53. Building Societies Act 1986
applied: SI 2012/1128 Art.4
s.9B, amended: 2012 c.21 s.55
s.42B, amended: 2012 c.21 s.56
s.119, amended: SI 2012/917 Sch.1 para.1
Sch.8A Part II para.9, amended: 2012 c.21 s.56
55. Family Law Act 1986
see *A v B (Jurisdiction)* [2011] EWHC 2752 (Fam), [2012] 1 F.L.R. 768 (Fam Div), Sir Nicholas Wall (President, Fam)
applied: SI 2012/3144 Reg.8, SI 2012/3145 Sch.1
s.1, see *H v H (Jurisdiction to Grant Wardship)* [2011] EWCA Civ 796, [2012] 1 F.L.R. 23 (CA (Civ Div)), Thorpe, L.J.
s.2, see *A v B (Jurisdiction)* [2011] EWHC 2752 (Fam), [2012] 1 F.L.R. 768 (Fam Div), Sir Nicholas Wall (President, Fam); see *H v H (Jurisdiction to Grant Wardship)* [2011] EWCA Civ 796, [2012] 1 F.L.R. 23 (CA (Civ Div)), Thorpe, L.J.
s.3, see *H v H (Jurisdiction to Grant Wardship)* [2011] EWCA Civ 796, [2012] 1 F.L.R. 23 (CA (Civ Div)), Thorpe, L.J.
s.27, applied: 2012 c.10 Sch.1 para.10
s.33, applied: 2012 c.10 Sch.1 para.10, Sch.1 para.13
s.34, applied: 2012 c.10 Sch.1 para.10, Sch.1 para.13
s.37, applied: 2012 c.10 Sch.1 para.10
s.46, see *H v S (Recognition of Overseas Divorce)* [2012] 2 F.L.R. 157 (Fam Div), Judge Horowitz Q.C.
s.55A, see *LG v DK* [2011] EWHC 2453 (Fam), [2012] 2 All E.R. 115 (CP), Sir Nicholas Wall (President, Fam)
64. Public Order Act 1986
s.3, see *R. v Gnango (Armel)* [2012] 1 A.C. 827 (SC), Lord Phillips (President)
s.4, see *Hughes v DPP* [2012] EWHC 606 (Admin), (2012) 176 J.P. 237 (QBD (Admin)), Moses, L.J.; see *Knight v DPP* [2012] EWHC 605 (Admin), (2012) 176 J.P. 177 (DC), Moses, L.J.
s.5, see *Harvey v DPP* [2011] EWHC 3992 (Admin), (2012) 176 J.P. 265 (QBD (Admin)), Bean, J.

1987

4. Ministry of Defence Police Act 1987
s.1, applied: 2012 asp 8 s.16, Sch.1 para.3, Sch.1 para.7
s.3A, enabling: SI 2012/808
s.4, enabling: SI 2012/808

1987– cont.

12. Petroleum Act 1987
s.21, applied: SI 2012/503 Art.2, SI 2012/941 Art.2, SI 2012/1574 Art.2
s.21, referred to: SI 2012/3159 Art.2
s.22, enabling: SI 2012/503, SI 2012/941, SI 2012/1574, SI 2012/3159
s.24, applied: SI 2012/3159(b), SI 2012/503(b), SI 2012/941
Sch.1, referred to: SI 2012/3159 Art.2
14. Recognition of Trusts Act 1987
see *Joint Administrators of Rangers Football Club Plc, Noters* [2012] CSOH 55, 2012 S.L.T. 599 (OH), Lord Hodge
16. Finance Act 1987
s.54, repealed: 2012 c.14 Sch.39 para.3
18. Debtors (Scotland) Act 1987
Part III, applied: SI 2012/2814 Sch.2 para.4
s.15E, see *Fish & Fish Ltd v Sea Shepherd UK* 2012 S.L.T. 156 (OH), Lord Emslie
s.15K, see *Fish & Fish Ltd v Sea Shepherd UK* 2012 S.L.T. 156 (OH), Lord Emslie
s.46, referred to: SI 2012/2814 Sch.2 para.4
s.49, enabling: SSI 2012/308
s.53, amended: SSI 2012/308 Reg.2
s.53, enabling: SSI 2012/308
s.54, amended: SSI 2012/301 Sch.1 para.1
s.55, amended: SSI 2012/301 Sch.1 para.1
s.63, amended: SSI 2012/308 Reg.2
s.63, enabling: SSI 2012/308
s.66, amended: SSI 2012/301 Sch.1 para.1
s.73, amended: SSI 2012/301 Sch.1 para.1
s.73A, amended: SSI 2012/301 Sch.1 para.1
s.73A, repealed (in part): SSI 2012/301 Sch.1 para.1
s.73F, amended: 2012 c.21 Sch.18 para.56
s.75, enabling: SSI 2012/340
s.106, amended: SSI 2012/301 Sch.1 para.1
Sch.2, substituted: SSI 2012/308 Sch.1
26. Housing (Scotland) Act 1987
Part II, applied: SI 2012/1483 Reg.6
s.21, amended: SSI 2012/38 Sch.1 para.2
s.25, repealed: SSI 2012/330 Art.4
s.28, repealed (in part): SSI 2012/330 Art.5
s.29, amended: SSI 2012/330 Art.6
s.30, amended: SSI 2012/330 Art.7
s.30, repealed (in part): SSI 2012/330 Art.7
s.31, amended: SSI 2012/330 Art.8
s.32, amended: SSI 2012/330 Art.9
s.32B, applied: SSI 2012/331, SSI 2012/331 Reg.2
s.32B, enabling: SSI 2012/331
s.33, amended: SSI 2012/330 Art.10
s.40, repealed (in part): SSI 2012/330 Art.11
s.43, amended: SSI 2012/330 Art.12
s.61, amended: 2012 asp 8 Sch.7 para.56
s.82, amended: 2012 asp 8 Sch.8 Part 2
s.191, applied: SSI 2012/113
s.191, repealed: 2012 asp 11 s.4
s.191, enabling: SSI 2012/113
s.192, repealed: 2012 asp 11 s.4
s.192, enabling: SSI 2012/113
s.193, repealed: 2012 asp 11 s.4
s.338, amended: 2012 asp 11 s.4, 2012 c.21 Sch.18 para.57
s.338, referred to: SSI 2012/303 Sch.5 para.13
Sch.15 Part II para.2, repealed (in part): 2012 asp 11 s.4
Sch.15 Part II para.3, applied: SSI 2012/113 Sch.1 para.2

1987–cont.

31. Landlord and Tenant Act 1987
s.47, see *Beitov Properties Ltd v Martin* [2012] UKUT 133 (LC), [2012] L. & T.R. 23 (UT (Lands)), George Bartlett Q.C. (President)
s.48, see *Beitov Properties Ltd v Martin* [2012] UKUT 133 (LC), [2012] L. & T.R. 23 (UT (Lands)), George Bartlett Q.C. (President)

33. AIDS (Control) Act 1987
repealed: 2012 c.7 s.59

38. Criminal Justice Act 1987
applied: SI 2012/1726 r.13.2, r.13.3, r.13.4, r.13.5
s.2, see *JP Morgan Chase Bank National Association v Director of the Serious Fraud Office* [2012] EWHC 1674 (Admin), [2012] Lloyd's Rep. F.C. 655 (QBD (Admin)), Gross, L.J.
s.4, amended: 2012 c.10 Sch.5 para.35
s.4, applied: SI 2012/1726 r.14.1, r.3.11, r.11.5
s.4, referred to: SI 2012/1726 r.11.1, r.11.2
s.5, referred to: SI 2012/1726 r.11.1, r.11.2
s.6, applied: SI 2012/1726 r.13.2, r.13.3, r.13.4
s.6, referred to: SI 2012/1726 r.13.1
s.7, applied: SI 2012/1726 r.15.1, r.3.11
s.8, referred to: SI 2012/1726 r.15.6
s.9, amended: 2012 c.9 Sch.10 Part 10
s.9, applied: SI 2012/1726 r.35.3, r.34.3, r.33.6, r.35.4, r.36.2, r.74.1, r.66.1, r.66.4
s.9, referred to: SI 2012/1726 r.15.1
s.10, applied: SI 2012/1726 r.15.1
s.11, amended: 2012 c.10 Sch.5 para.36
s.11, applied: SI 2012/1726 r.16.1

43. Consumer Protection Act 1987
applied: SI 2012/1128 Art.4
referred to: 2012 c.19 Sch.6 para.4
s.2, see *McGlinchey v General Motors UK Ltd* 2012 Rep. L.R. 20 (OH), Lord Brailsford
s.2, applied: SI 2012/1916 Reg.345
s.3, see *McGlinchey v General Motors UK Ltd* 2012 Rep. L.R. 20 (OH), Lord Brailsford
s.11, see *Imperial Tobacco Ltd, Petitioner* [2012] CSIH 9, 2012 S.C. 297 (IH (1 Div)), Lord President Hamilton; see *Imperial Tobacco Ltd, Petitioner* [2012] UKSC 61 (SC), Lord Hope, J.S.C. (Deputy President)
s.11, applied: SI 2012/1426, SI 2012/1815
s.11, enabling: SI 2012/1426, SI 2012/1815, SI 2012/2263, SI 2012/2963
s.19, varied: SI 2012/1916 Sch.34 para.40

53. Channel Tunnel Act 1987
s.11, enabling: SI 2012/1264

1988

1. Income and Corporation Taxes Act 1988
see *Bartram v Revenue and Customs Commissioners* [2012] UKUT 184 (TCC), [2012] S.T.C. 2144 (UT (Tax)), Judge John Clark; see *John Mander Pension Trustees Ltd v Revenue and Customs Commissioners* [2012] S.F.T.D. 322 (FTT (Tax)), Judge Barbara Mosedale; see *Pope v Revenue and Customs Commissioners* [2012] UKUT 206 (TCC), [2012] S.T.C. 2255 (UT (Tax)), Sir Stephen Oliver Q.C.; see *Samarkand Film Partnership No.3 v Revenue and Customs Commissioners* [2012] S.F.T.D. 1 (FTT (Tax)), Judge Charles Hellier
varied: 2012 c.14 Sch.15 para.17
Part XII c.I, repealed: 2012 c.14 Sch.16 para.44

1988–cont.

1. Income and Corporation Taxes Act 1988–*cont.*
Part XVII c.IV, applied: 2012 c.14 Sch.20 para.50, Sch.20 para.57, Sch.20 para.58
Part XVII c.IV, referred to: 2012 c.14 Sch.20 para.57
s.13, see *Seascope Insurance Services Ltd v Revenue and Customs Commissioners* [2012] S.F.T.D. 524 (FTT (Tax)), Judge John Clark
s.19, see *PA Holdings Ltd v Revenue and Customs Commissioners* [2011] EWCA Civ 1414, [2012] S.T.C. 582 (CA (Civ Div)), Maurice Kay, L.J.
s.20, see *PA Holdings Ltd v Revenue and Customs Commissioners* [2011] EWCA Civ 1414, [2012] S.T.C. 582 (CA (Civ Div)), Maurice Kay, L.J.
s.21, see *Rogge v Revenue and Customs Commissioners* [2012] UKFTT 49 (TC), [2012] W.T.L.R. 537 (FTT (Tax)), Judge John Brooks
s.34, see *John Mander Pension Trustees Ltd v Revenue and Customs Commissioners* [2012] S.F.T.D. 322 (FTT (Tax)), Judge Barbara Mosedale
s.59, see *Pope v Revenue and Customs Commissioners* [2012] UKUT 206 (TCC), [2012] S.T.C. 2255 (UT (Tax)), Sir Stephen Oliver Q.C.
s.73, referred to: 2012 c.14 Sch.17 para.32
s.74, see *Duckmanton v Revenue and Customs Commissioners* [2012] S.F.T.D. 293 (FTT (Tax)), Judge Michael Connell; see *Key IP Ltd v Revenue and Customs Commissioners* [2012] S.F.T.D. 305 (FTT (Tax)), Judge Christopher Staker; see *Revenue and Customs Commissioners v Lansdowne Partners LP* [2011] EWCA Civ 1578, [2012] S.T.C. 544 (CA (Civ Div)), Sir Andrew Morritt (Chancellor)
s.76, applied: 2012 c.14 Sch.17 para.32
s.76, referred to: 2012 c.14 Sch.17 para.23
s.76, repealed: 2012 c.14 Sch.16 para.2
s.76ZA, repealed: 2012 c.14 Sch.16 para.3
s.76ZB, repealed: 2012 c.14 Sch.16 para.4
s.76ZC, repealed: 2012 c.14 Sch.16 para.5
s.76ZD, repealed: 2012 c.14 Sch.16 para.5
s.76ZE, repealed: 2012 c.14 Sch.16 para.5
s.76ZF, repealed: 2012 c.14 Sch.16 para.6
s.76ZG, repealed: 2012 c.14 Sch.16 para.6
s.76ZH, repealed: 2012 c.14 Sch.16 para.6
s.76ZI, repealed: 2012 c.14 Sch.16 para.6
s.76ZJ, repealed: 2012 c.14 Sch.16 para.6
s.76ZK, repealed: 2012 c.14 Sch.16 para.7
s.76ZL, repealed: 2012 c.14 Sch.16 para.8
s.76ZM, repealed: 2012 c.14 Sch.16 para.8
s.76ZN, repealed: 2012 c.14 Sch.16 para.9
s.95ZA, amended: 2012 c.14 Sch.16 para.10
s.114, see *John Mander Pension Trustees Ltd v Revenue and Customs Commissioners* [2012] S.F.T.D. 322 (FTT (Tax)), Judge Barbara Mosedale
s.128, see *Explainaway Ltd v Revenue and Customs Commissioners* [2012] UKUT 362 (TCC), [2012] S.T.C. 2525 (UT (Tax)), Newey, J
s.231, see *Trustees of the BT Pension Scheme v Revenue and Customs Commissioners* [2012] S.F.T.D. 107 (FTT (Tax)), Sir Stephen Oliver Q.C.
s.246A, see *Trustees of the BT Pension Scheme v Revenue and Customs Commissioners* [2012] S.F.T.D. 107 (FTT (Tax)), Sir Stephen Oliver Q.C.
s.246C, see *Trustees of the BT Pension Scheme v Revenue and Customs Commissioners* [2012] S.F.T.D. 107 (FTT (Tax)), Sir Stephen Oliver Q.C.
s.266, amended: 2012 c.21 Sch.18 para.58
s.266, repealed: 2012 c.14 Sch.39 para.28

1988– cont.

1. **Income and Corporation Taxes Act 1988**– *cont.*
s.266A, repealed: 2012 c.14 Sch.39 para.28
s.268, repealed: 2012 c.14 Sch.39 para.31
s.269, repealed: 2012 c.14 Sch.39 para.31
s.270, repealed: 2012 c.14 Sch.39 para.31
s.271, repealed: 2012 c.14 Sch.39 para.31
s.272, repealed: 2012 c.14 Sch.39 para.31
s.274, repealed: 2012 c.14 Sch.39 para.28
s.329, see *Pope v Revenue and Customs Commissioners* [2012] UKUT 206 (TCC), [2012] S.T.C. 2255 (UT (Tax)), Sir Stephen Oliver Q.C.
s.353, see *Eclipse Film Partners No 35 LLP v Revenue and Customs Commissioners* [2012] UKFTT 270 (TC), [2012] S.F.T.D. 823 (FTT (Tax)), Judge Edward Sadler
s.362, see *Eclipse Film Partners No 35 LLP v Revenue and Customs Commissioners* [2012] UKFTT 270 (TC), [2012] S.F.T.D. 823 (FTT (Tax)), Judge Edward Sadler
s.369, applied: SI 2012/ 2885 Sch.5 para.11, SI 2012/ 2886 Sch.1, SSI 2012/ 303 Sch.5 para.26, SSI 2012/ 319 Sch.3 para.10
s.376, amended: 2012 c.21 Sch.18 para.58
s.376A, amended: 2012 c.21 Sch.18 para.58
s.381, see *Samarkand Film Partnership No.3 v Revenue and Customs Commissioners* [2012] S.F.T.D. 1 (FTT (Tax)), Judge Charles Hellier
s.384, see *Samarkand Film Partnership No.3 v Revenue and Customs Commissioners* [2012] S.F.T.D. 1 (FTT (Tax)), Judge Charles Hellier
s.402, see *Felixstowe Dock and Railway Co Ltd v Revenue and Customs Commissioners* [2012] S.F.T.D. 366 (FTT (Tax)), Judge Roger Berner
s.406, see *Felixstowe Dock and Railway Co Ltd v Revenue and Customs Commissioners* [2012] S.F.T.D. 366 (FTT (Tax)), Judge Roger Berner
s.410, see *Felixstowe Dock and Railway Co Ltd v Revenue and Customs Commissioners* [2012] S.F.T.D. 366 (FTT (Tax)), Judge Roger Berner
s.413, see *R. (on the application of Bampton Property Group Ltd) v King* [2012] EWHC 361 (Admin), [2012] S.T.C. 1321 (QBD (Admin)), Blair, J.
s.419, see *Aspect Capital Ltd v Revenue and Customs Commissioners* [2012] UKFTT 430 (TC), [2012] S.F.T.D. 1208 (FTT (Tax)), Judge Barbara Mosedale
s.431, amended: 2012 c.21 Sch.18 para.58
s.431, repealed: 2012 c.14 Sch.16 para.11
s.431A, repealed: 2012 c.14 Sch.16 para.13
s.431B, referred to: 2012 c.14 s.58
s.431B, repealed: 2012 c.14 Sch.16 para.14
s.431BA, repealed: 2012 c.14 Sch.16 para.15
s.431BB, repealed: 2012 c.14 Sch.16 para.16
s.431C, repealed: 2012 c.14 Sch.16 para.17
s.431D, repealed: 2012 c.14 Sch.16 para.18
s.431E, repealed: 2012 c.14 Sch.16 para.18
s.431EA, repealed: 2012 c.14 Sch.16 para.19
s.431F, repealed: 2012 c.14 Sch.16 para.20
s.431G, repealed: 2012 c.14 Sch.16 para.21
s.431H, repealed: 2012 c.14 Sch.16 para.22
s.431ZA, repealed: 2012 c.14 Sch.16 para.12
s.432A, repealed: 2012 c.14 Sch.16 para.25
s.432AA, repealed: 2012 c.14 Sch.16 para.26
s.432AB, repealed: 2012 c.14 Sch.16 para.27
s.432B, repealed: 2012 c.14 Sch.16 para.28
s.432C, applied: SI 2012/ 3009 Reg.14
s.432C, repealed: 2012 c.14 Sch.16 para.28

1988– cont.

1. **Income and Corporation Taxes Act 1988**–*cont.*
s.432CA, applied: SI 2012/ 3009 Reg.13
s.432CA, repealed: 2012 c.14 Sch.16 para.28
s.432CB, repealed: 2012 c.14 Sch.16 para.28
s.432D, repealed: 2012 c.14 Sch.16 para.28
s.432E, repealed: 2012 c.14 Sch.16 para.28
s.432F, repealed: 2012 c.14 Sch.16 para.28
s.432G, repealed: 2012 c.14 Sch.16 para.28
s.432YA, repealed: 2012 c.14 Sch.16 para.23
s.432ZA, repealed: 2012 c.14 Sch.16 para.24
s.434, repealed: 2012 c.14 Sch.16 para.29
s.434A, repealed: 2012 c.14 Sch.16 para.30
s.434AZA, repealed: 2012 c.14 Sch.16 para.31
s.434AZB, repealed: 2012 c.14 Sch.16 para.31
s.434AZC, repealed: 2012 c.14 Sch.16 para.31
s.436A, applied: 2012 c.14 Sch.17 para.29
s.436A, repealed: 2012 c.14 Sch.16 para.32
s.436B, repealed: 2012 c.14 Sch.16 para.33
s.437, repealed: 2012 c.14 Sch.16 para.34
s.437A, repealed: 2012 c.14 Sch.16 para.34
s.438, repealed: 2012 c.14 Sch.16 para.35
s.440, applied: 2012 c.14 Sch.17 para.25
s.440, disapplied: 2012 c.14 Sch.17 para.25
s.440, repealed: 2012 c.14 Sch.16 para.36
s.440A, applied: 2012 c.14 Sch.17 para.26, Sch.17 para.27, Sch.17 para.28
s.440A, referred to: 2012 c.14 Sch.17 para.26
s.440A, repealed: 2012 c.14 Sch.16 para.37
s.440B, repealed: 2012 c.14 Sch.16 para.38
s.440C, repealed: 2012 c.14 Sch.16 para.39
s.440D, repealed: 2012 c.14 Sch.16 para.40
s.442, repealed: 2012 c.14 Sch.16 para.41
s.442A, repealed: 2012 c.14 Sch.16 para.42
s.444A, repealed: 2012 c.14 Sch.16 para.43
s.444AA, repealed: 2012 c.14 Sch.16 para.43
s.444AB, amended: 2012 c.21 Sch.18 para.58
s.444AB, repealed: 2012 c.14 Sch.16 para.43
s.444ABA, repealed: 2012 c.14 Sch.16 para.43
s.444ABAA, repealed: 2012 c.14 Sch.16 para.43
s.444ABB, repealed: 2012 c.14 Sch.16 para.43
s.444ABBA, repealed: 2012 c.14 Sch.16 para.43
s.444ABC, repealed: 2012 c.14 Sch.16 para.43
s.444ABD, repealed: 2012 c.14 Sch.16 para.43
s.444AC, repealed: 2012 c.14 Sch.16 para.43
s.444ACA, repealed: 2012 c.14 Sch.16 para.43
s.444ACZA, repealed: 2012 c.14 Sch.16 para.43
s.444AD, repealed: 2012 c.14 Sch.16 para.43
s.444AE, repealed: 2012 c.14 Sch.16 para.43
s.444AEA, repealed: 2012 c.14 Sch.16 para.43
s.444AEB, repealed: 2012 c.14 Sch.16 para.43
s.444AEC, repealed: 2012 c.14 Sch.16 para.43
s.444AECA, repealed: 2012 c.14 Sch.16 para.43
s.444AECB, repealed: 2012 c.14 Sch.16 para.43
s.444AECC, repealed: 2012 c.14 Sch.16 para.43
s.444AED, repealed: 2012 c.14 Sch.16 para.43
s.444AF, repealed: 2012 c.14 Sch.16 para.44
s.444AH, repealed: 2012 c.14 Sch.16 para.44
s.444AI, repealed: 2012 c.14 Sch.16 para.44
s.444AJ, repealed: 2012 c.14 Sch.16 para.44
s.444AK, repealed: 2012 c.14 Sch.16 para.44
s.444AL, repealed: 2012 c.14 Sch.16 para.44
s.444AZA, repealed: 2012 c.14 Sch.16 para.43
s.444AZB, repealed: 2012 c.14 Sch.16 para.43
s.444BA, applied: 2012 c.14 s.26
s.444BA, referred to: 2012 c.14 s.26
s.444BA, repealed: 2012 c.14 s.26
s.444BB, applied: 2012 c.14 s.26
s.444BB, repealed: 2012 c.14 s.26

1988– cont.

1. Income and Corporation Taxes Act 1988– *cont.*
s.444BC, applied: 2012 c.14 s.26
s.444BC, repealed: 2012 c.14 s.26
s.444BD, repealed: 2012 c.14 s.26
s.459, repealed: 2012 c.14 Sch.18 para.2
s.460, repealed: 2012 c.14 Sch.18 para.3
s.461, referred to: 2012 c.14 Sch.19 para.1
s.461, repealed: 2012 c.14 Sch.18 para.4
s.461A, referred to: 2012 c.14 Sch.19 para.1
s.461A, repealed: 2012 c.14 Sch.18 para.5
s.461B, repealed: 2012 c.14 Sch.18 para.5
s.461C, repealed: 2012 c.14 Sch.18 para.5
s.461D, repealed: 2012 c.14 Sch.18 para.6
s.462, repealed: 2012 c.14 Sch.18 para.7
s.463, repealed: 2012 c.14 Sch.18 para.8
s.464, repealed: 2012 c.14 Sch.18 para.9
s.465, repealed: 2012 c.14 Sch.18 para.10
s.465A, repealed: 2012 c.14 Sch.18 para.11
s.466, repealed: 2012 c.14 Sch.18 para.12
s.508A, amended: 2012 c.14 s.4
s.552, amended: 2012 c.14 s.11
s.590C, referred to: SI 2012/687 Sch.1 para.7
s.591B, see *John Mander Pension Trustees Ltd v Revenue and Customs Commissioners* [2012] S.F.T.D. 322 (FTT (Tax)), Judge Barbara Mosedale
s.591C, see *John Mander Pension Trustees Ltd v Revenue and Customs Commissioners* [2012] S.F.T.D. 322 (FTT (Tax)), Judge Barbara Mosedale
s.591D, see *John Mander Pension Trustees Ltd v Revenue and Customs Commissioners* [2012] S.F.T.D. 322 (FTT (Tax)), Judge Barbara Mosedale
s.647, see *Gratton v Revenue and Customs Commissioners* [2012] UKUT 261 (TCC), [2012] S.T.C. 2061 (UT (Tax)), Judge Timothy Herrington
s.658A, see *John Mander Pension Trustees Ltd v Revenue and Customs Commissioners* [2012] S.F.T.D. 322 (FTT (Tax)), Judge Barbara Mosedale
s.660A, see *Rogge v Revenue and Customs Commissioners* [2012] UKFTT 49 (TC), [2012] W.T.L.R. 537 (FTT (Tax)), Judge John Brooks
s.660D, see *Rogge v Revenue and Customs Commissioners* [2012] UKFTT 49 (TC), [2012] W.T.L.R. 537 (FTT (Tax)), Judge John Brooks
s.713, see *Barnes v Revenue and Customs Commissioners* [2012] UKUT 273 (TCC), [2012] S.T.C. 1904 (UT (Tax)), Roth, J.
s.714, see *Barnes v Revenue and Customs Commissioners* [2012] UKUT 273 (TCC), [2012] S.T.C. 1904 (UT (Tax)), Roth, J.
s.727, see *Barnes v Revenue and Customs Commissioners* [2012] UKUT 273 (TCC), [2012] S.T.C. 1904 (UT (Tax)), Roth, J.
s.730A, see *First Nationwide v Revenue and Customs Commissioners* [2012] EWCA Civ 278, [2012] S.T.C. 1261 (CA (Civ Div)), Rix, L.J.
s.737A, see *First Nationwide v Revenue and Customs Commissioners* [2012] EWCA Civ 278, [2012] S.T.C. 1261 (CA (Civ Div)), Rix, L.J.
s.739, see *Revenue and Customs Commissioners v Anson* [2012] UKUT 59 (TCC), [2012] S.T.C. 1014 (UT (Tax)), Mann, J.
s.741, see *Revenue and Customs Commissioners v Anson* [2012] UKUT 59 (TCC), [2012] S.T.C. 1014 (UT (Tax)), Mann, J.

1988– cont.

1. Income and Corporation Taxes Act 1988– *cont.*
s.743, see *Revenue and Customs Commissioners v Anson* [2012] UKUT 59 (TCC), [2012] S.T.C. 1014 (UT (Tax)), Mann, J.
s.747, disapplied: 2012 c.14 Sch.20 para.58
s.747, repealed: 2012 c.14 Sch.20 para.14
s.747, varied: 2012 c.14 Sch.20 para.58
s.747A, repealed: 2012 c.14 Sch.20 para.14
s.747A, varied: 2012 c.14 Sch.20 para.58
s.748, repealed: 2012 c.14 Sch.20 para.14
s.748, varied: 2012 c.14 Sch.20 para.58
s.748A, repealed: 2012 c.14 Sch.20 para.14
s.748A, varied: 2012 c.14 Sch.20 para.58
s.748ZA, repealed: 2012 c.14 Sch.20 para.14
s.748ZA, varied: 2012 c.14 Sch.20 para.58
s.749, repealed: 2012 c.14 Sch.20 para.14
s.749, varied: 2012 c.14 Sch.20 para.58
s.749A, repealed: 2012 c.14 Sch.20 para.14
s.749A, varied: 2012 c.14 Sch.20 para.58
s.749B, repealed: 2012 c.14 Sch.20 para.14
s.749B, varied: 2012 c.14 Sch.20 para.58
s.750, repealed: 2012 c.14 Sch.20 para.14
s.750, varied: 2012 c.14 Sch.20 para.58
s.750A, repealed: 2012 c.14 Sch.20 para.14
s.750A, varied: 2012 c.14 Sch.20 para.58
s.751, repealed: 2012 c.14 Sch.20 para.14
s.751, varied: 2012 c.14 Sch.20 para.58
s.751A, repealed: 2012 c.14 Sch.20 para.14
s.751A, varied: 2012 c.14 Sch.20 para.58
s.751AA, repealed: 2012 c.14 Sch.20 para.14
s.751AA, varied: 2012 c.14 Sch.20 para.58
s.751AB, repealed: 2012 c.14 Sch.20 para.14
s.751AB, varied: 2012 c.14 Sch.20 para.58
s.751AC, repealed: 2012 c.14 Sch.20 para.14
s.751AC, varied: 2012 c.14 Sch.20 para.58
s.751B, repealed: 2012 c.14 Sch.20 para.14
s.751B, varied: 2012 c.14 Sch.20 para.58
s.752, repealed: 2012 c.14 Sch.20 para.14
s.752, varied: 2012 c.14 Sch.20 para.58
s.752A, repealed: 2012 c.14 Sch.20 para.14
s.752A, varied: 2012 c.14 Sch.20 para.58
s.752B, repealed: 2012 c.14 Sch.20 para.14
s.752B, varied: 2012 c.14 Sch.20 para.58
s.752C, repealed: 2012 c.14 Sch.20 para.14
s.752C, varied: 2012 c.14 Sch.20 para.58
s.753, repealed: 2012 c.14 Sch.20 para.14
s.753, varied: 2012 c.14 Sch.20 para.58
s.754, repealed: 2012 c.14 Sch.20 para.14
s.754, varied: 2012 c.14 Sch.20 para.58
s.754A, repealed: 2012 c.14 Sch.20 para.14
s.754A, varied: 2012 c.14 Sch.20 para.58
s.754AA, repealed: 2012 c.14 Sch.20 para.14
s.754AA, varied: 2012 c.14 Sch.20 para.58
s.754B, repealed: 2012 c.14 Sch.20 para.14
s.754B, varied: 2012 c.14 Sch.20 para.58
s.755, repealed: 2012 c.14 Sch.20 para.14
s.755, varied: 2012 c.14 Sch.20 para.58
s.755A, repealed: 2012 c.14 Sch.20 para.14
s.755A, varied: 2012 c.14 Sch.20 para.58
s.755B, repealed: 2012 c.14 Sch.20 para.14
s.755B, varied: 2012 c.14 Sch.20 para.58
s.755C, repealed: 2012 c.14 Sch.20 para.14
s.755C, varied: 2012 c.14 Sch.20 para.58
s.755D, repealed: 2012 c.14 Sch.20 para.14
s.755D, varied: 2012 c.14 Sch.20 para.58
s.756, repealed: 2012 c.14 Sch.20 para.14
s.756, varied: 2012 c.14 Sch.20 para.58

1988–cont.

1. Income and Corporation Taxes Act 1988–*cont.*

s.788, see *Felixstowe Dock and Railway Co Ltd v Revenue and Customs Commissioners* [2012] S.F.T.D. 366 (FTT (Tax)), Judge Roger Berner

s.790, see *Bayfine UK Products v Revenue and Customs Commissioners* [2011] EWCA Civ 304, [2012] 1 W.L.R. 1630 (CA (Civ Div)), Arden, L.J.

s.795A, see *Bayfine UK Products v Revenue and Customs Commissioners* [2011] EWCA Civ 304, [2012] 1 W.L.R. 1630 (CA (Civ Div)), Arden, L.J.

s.824, repealed (in part): 2012 c.14 Sch.39 para.28, Sch.39 para.31

s.826, see *Teesside Power Holdings Ltd v Electrabel International Holdings BV* [2012] EWHC 33 (Comm), [2012] S.T.C. 774 (QBD (Comm)), Judge Chambers Q.C.

s.831, see *Bartram v Revenue and Customs Commissioners* [2012] UKUT 184 (TCC), [2012] S.T.C. 2144 (UT (Tax)), Judge John Clark

s.832, see *Eclipse Film Partners No 35 LLP v Revenue and Customs Commissioners* [2012] UKFTT 270 (TC), [2012] S.F.T.D. 823 (FTT (Tax)), Judge Edward Sadler

Sch.D, see *Countrywide Estate Agents FS Ltd v Revenue and Customs Commissioners* [2012] S.T.C. 511 (UT (Tax)), Sales, J.; see *Explainaway Ltd v Revenue and Customs Commissioners* [2012] UKUT 362 (TCC), [2012] S.T.C. 2525 (UT (Tax)), Newey, J; see *Scottish Widows Plc v Revenue and Customs Commissioners* [2012] 1 All E.R. 379 (SC), Lord Hope (Deputy President)

Sch.D, applied: SSI 2012/303 Reg.45

Sch.14 Part I para.1, repealed: 2012 c.14 Sch.39 para.28

Sch.14 Part I para.2, repealed: 2012 c.14 Sch.39 para.28

Sch.14 Part I para.3, repealed: 2012 c.14 Sch.39 para.28

Sch.14 Part II para.4, repealed: 2012 c.14 Sch.39 para.28

Sch.14 Part II para.5, repealed: 2012 c.14 Sch.39 para.28

Sch.14 Part II para.6, repealed: 2012 c.14 Sch.39 para.28

Sch.14 Part II para.7, repealed: 2012 c.14 Sch.39 para.28

Sch.14 Part II para.8, repealed: 2012 c.14 Sch.39 para.28

Sch.15, applied: 2012 c.14 s.163

Sch.15 Part I para.3, amended: 2012 c.14 Sch.18 para.13

Sch.15 Part I para.3, referred to: 2012 c.14 s.163

Sch.15 Part I para.4, amended: 2012 c.14 Sch.18 para.13

Sch.15 Part I para.4, referred to: 2012 c.14 s.163

Sch.15 Part I para.5, repealed: 2012 c.14 Sch.18 para.13

Sch.15 Part I para.6, amended: 2012 c.14 Sch.18 para.13

Sch.15 Part I para.6, applied: 2012 c.14 s.159

Sch.15 Part I para.6A, added: 2012 c.14 Sch.18 para.13

Sch.15 Part I para.8, amended: 2012 c.14 Sch.39 para.28

Sch.15 Part III para.24, amended: 2012 c.14 Sch.16 para.45

1988–cont.

1. Income and Corporation Taxes Act 1988–*cont.*

Sch.19ABA Part 1 para.1, repealed: 2012 c.14 Sch.16 para.46

Sch.19ABA Part 2 para.2, repealed: 2012 c.14 Sch.16 para.46

Sch.19ABA Part 2 para.3, repealed: 2012 c.14 Sch.16 para.46

Sch.19ABA Part 2 para.4, repealed: 2012 c.14 Sch.16 para.46

Sch.19ABA Part 2 para.5, repealed: 2012 c.14 Sch.16 para.46

Sch.19ABA Part 2 para.6, repealed: 2012 c.14 Sch.16 para.46

Sch.19ABA Part 2 para.7, repealed: 2012 c.14 Sch.16 para.46

Sch.19ABA Part 2 para.8, repealed: 2012 c.14 Sch.16 para.46

Sch.19ABA Part 2 para.8A, repealed: 2012 c.14 Sch.16 para.46

Sch.19ABA Part 2 para.8B, repealed: 2012 c.14 Sch.16 para.46

Sch.19ABA Part 2 para.8C, repealed: 2012 c.14 Sch.16 para.46

Sch.19ABA Part 2 para.8D, repealed: 2012 c.14 Sch.16 para.46

Sch.19ABA Part 2 para.8E, repealed: 2012 c.14 Sch.16 para.46

Sch.19ABA Part 2 para.8F, repealed: 2012 c.14 Sch.16 para.46

Sch.19ABA Part 2 para.9, repealed: 2012 c.14 Sch.16 para.46

Sch.19ABA Part 2 para.10, repealed: 2012 c.14 Sch.16 para.46

Sch.19ABA Part 2 para.11, repealed: 2012 c.14 Sch.16 para.46

Sch.19ABA Part 3 para.12, repealed: 2012 c.14 Sch.16 para.46

Sch.19ABA Part 3 para.13, repealed: 2012 c.14 Sch.16 para.46

Sch.19ABA Part 3 para.14, repealed: 2012 c.14 Sch.16 para.46

Sch.19ABA Part 3 para.15, repealed: 2012 c.14 Sch.16 para.46

Sch.19ABA Part 3 para.16, repealed: 2012 c.14 Sch.16 para.46

Sch.19ABA Part 3 para.17, repealed: 2012 c.14 Sch.16 para.46

Sch.19ABA Part 3 para.18, repealed: 2012 c.14 Sch.16 para.46

Sch.19ABA Part 3 para.19, repealed: 2012 c.14 Sch.16 para.46

Sch.19ABA Part 3 para.20, repealed: 2012 c.14 Sch.16 para.46

Sch.19ABA Part 3 para.20A, repealed: 2012 c.14 Sch.16 para.46

Sch.19ABA Part 3 para.21, repealed: 2012 c.14 Sch.16 para.46

Sch.19ABA Part 3 para.22, repealed: 2012 c.14 Sch.16 para.46

Sch.19ABA Part 3 para.23, repealed: 2012 c.14 Sch.16 para.46

Sch.19ABA Part 3 para.24, repealed: 2012 c.14 Sch.16 para.46

Sch.19ABA Part 3 para.25, repealed: 2012 c.14 Sch.16 para.46

Sch.19ABA Part 4 para.26, repealed: 2012 c.14 Sch.16 para.46

Sch.19ABA Part 4 para.27, repealed: 2012 c.14 Sch.16 para.46

1. Income and Corporation Taxes Act 1988–*cont.*
Sch.19ABA Part 4 para.28, repealed: 2012 c.14
Sch.16 para.46
Sch.23A, see *Barnes v Revenue and Customs Commissioners* [2012] UKUT 273 (TCC), [2012] S.T.C. 1904 (UT (Tax)), Roth, J.
Sch.23A para.1, see *First Nationwide v Revenue and Customs Commissioners* [2012] EWCA Civ 278, [2012] S.T.C. 1261 (CA (Civ Div)), Rix, L.J.
Sch.23A para.3, see *Barnes v Revenue and Customs Commissioners* [2012] UKUT 273 (TCC), [2012] S.T.C. 1904 (UT (Tax)), Roth, J.
Sch.24 para.4, applied: 2012 c.14 Sch.20 para.57
Sch.25 Part IIIA, applied: 2012 c.14 Sch.20 para.58
Sch.25 Part IIIA para.15F, applied: 2012 c.14 Sch.20 para.58

4. Norfolk and Suffolk Broads Act 1988
Sch.1 para.6, applied: SI 2012/1644 Sch.1

7. Social Security Act 1988
s.13, applied: SI 2012/2886 Sch.1, SSI 2012/303 Sch.4 para.46, Sch.5 para.44

9. Local Government Act 1988
s.17, amended: 2012 c.3 s.2

13. Coroners Act 1988
applied: 2012 c.10 s.10, Sch.1 para.41
s.1, applied: SI 2012/2605 Art.4
s.4, enabling: SI 2012/574
s.4A, enabling: SI 2012/2605
s.11, applied: SI 2012/1604 Reg.2
s.16, amended: 2012 c.4 Sch.1 para.2
s.16, applied: SI 2012/1604 Reg.2
s.17, amended: 2012 c.4 Sch.1 para.2

20. Dartford-Thurrock Crossing Act 1988
s.19, amended: 2012 c.7 Sch.5 para.43

26. Landlord and Tenant Act 1988
s.1, see *Crosspite Ltd v Sachdev* [2012] UKUT 321 (LC) (UT (Lands)), Judge Gerald; see *E. ON UK Plc v Gilesports Ltd* [2012] EWHC 2172 (Ch), [2012] 47 E.G. 128 (Ch D), Arnold, J.

28. Access to Medical Reports Act 1988
s.2, amended: 2012 c.21 Sch.18 para.59

29. Protection of Animals (Amendment) Act 1988
applied: SI 2012/1020 Reg.9

32. Civil Evidence (Scotland) Act 1988
s.8, applied: SSI 2012/111
s.8, disapplied: SSI 2012/111 Art.2
s.8, enabling: SSI 2012/111

33. Criminal Justice Act 1988
see *Al-Khawaja v United Kingdom (26766/05)* [2012] 2 Costs L.O. 139 (ECHR (Grand Chamber)), Judge Tulkens (President); see *McCracken, Re* [2011] EWCA Civ 1620, [2012] Lloyd's Rep. F.C. 148 (CA (Civ Div)), Maurice Kay, L.J.; see *R. (on the application of Horne) v Central Criminal Court* [2012] EWHC 1350 (Admin), [2012] 1 W.L.R. 3152 (QBD (Admin)), Moses, L.J.; see *R. v Bagnall (Darren John)* [2012] EWCA Crim 677, [2012] Lloyd's Rep. F.C. 614 (CA (Crim Div)), Moses, L.J.; see *R. v Castillo (German)* [2011] EWCA Crim 3173, [2012] 2 Cr. App. R. (S.) 36 (CA (Crim Div)), Laws, L.J.
applied: SI 2012/1726 r.29.26
Part VI, applied: SI 2012/1726 r.56.1
s.32, applied: SI 2012/1726 r.29.1, r.29.26, r.37.4
s.32, referred to: SI 2012/1726 r.29.24, r.29.25
s.35, referred to: SI 2012/1726 r.70.1
s.35, enabling: SI 2012/1833

33. Criminal Justice Act 1988–*cont.*
s.36, amended: 2012 c.10 Sch.19 para.2, Sch.26 para.5
s.36, applied: SI 2012/1726 r.65.3, r.70.1, r.74.1, r.74.2
s.40, referred to: SI 2012/1726 r.14.2
s.71, see *R. v Ahmad (Shakeel)* [2012] EWCA Crim 391, [2012] 1 W.L.R. 2335 (CA (Crim Div)), Hooper, L.J.; see *R. v Barnett (Ian Stanley)* [2011] EWCA Crim 2936, [2012] Lloyd's Rep. F.C. 157 (CA (Crim Div)), Pill, L.J.
s.72A, applied: SI 2012/1726 r.56.2
s.72AA, see *R. v Bagnall (Darren John)* [2012] EWCA Crim 677, [2012] Lloyd's Rep. F.C. 614 (CA (Crim Div)), Moses, L.J.
s.73, applied: SI 2012/1726 r.56.1
s.74A, applied: SI 2012/1726 r.56.3
s.74B, applied: SI 2012/1726 r.56.3
s.74C, applied: SI 2012/1726 r.56.3
s.75A, applied: SI 2012/1726 r.56.5
s.80, see *McCracken, Re* [2011] EWCA Civ 1620, [2012] Lloyd's Rep. F.C. 148 (CA (Civ Div)), Maurice Kay, L.J.
s.89, see *Bhandal v Revenue and Customs Commissioners* [2011] EWHC 3018 (Admin), [2012] Lloyd's Rep. F.C. 127 (QBD (Admin)), Hickinbottom, J.
s.93H, applied: SI 2012/1726 r.56.4
s.133, see *R. (on the application of Adams) v Secretary of State for Justice* [2012] 1 A.C. 48 (SC), Lord Phillips (President)
s.139, see *R. v Clancy (Louise)* [2012] EWCA Crim 8, [2012] 1 W.L.R. 2536 (CA (Crim Div)), Moore-Bick, L.J.
s.139AA, added: 2012 c.10 s.142
s.139B, amended: 2012 c.10 Sch.26 para.6
s.148, repealed: 2012 c.9 Sch.10 Part 1
s.152, applied: SI 2012/1726 r.18.3
s.159, applied: SI 2012/1726 r.74.1, r.76.1, r.76.6
s.159, referred to: SI 2012/1726 r.69.1, r.69.8
s.160, see *R. v Leonard (John)* [2012] EWCA Crim 277, [2012] 2 Cr. App. R. 12 (CA (Crim Div)), Lord Judge, L.C.J.
s.172, amended: 2012 c.10 Sch.26 para.7, SI 2012/2404 Sch.2 para.24
Sch.3 para.1, referred to: SI 2012/1726 r.70.2
Sch.3 para.4, applied: SI 2012/1726 r.74.2
Sch.3 para.6, referred to: SI 2012/1726 r.70.7
Sch.3 para.7, referred to: SI 2012/1726 r.70.7
Sch.3 para.8, applied: SI 2012/1726 r.70.7
Sch.3 para.9, applied: SI 2012/1726 r.74.2
Sch.3 para.11, amended: 2012 c.10 Sch.7 para.11
Sch.3 para.11, applied: SI 2012/1726 r.76.1, r.76.4
Sch.3 para.12, amended: 2012 c.10 Sch.7 para.11
Sch.8 Part I para.9, repealed (in part): 2012 c.10 Sch.25 Part 2
Sch.12 para.5, amended: SI 2012/2404 Sch.2 para.24

34. Legal Aid Act 1988
see *Legal Services Commission v Loomba* [2012] EWHC 29 (QB), [2012] 1 W.L.R. 2461 (QBD), Cranston, J.
s.4, see *Legal Services Commission v Loomba* [2012] EWHC 29 (QB), [2012] 1 W.L.R. 2461 (QBD), Cranston, J.
Sch.5 para.13, repealed: 2012 c.10 Sch.5 Part 2

36. Court of Session Act 1988
s.5, enabling: SSI 2012/8, SSI 2012/100, SSI 2012/126, SSI 2012/189, SSI 2012/270, SSI 2012/275, SSI 2012/340

1988– cont.

36. Court of Session Act 1988– *cont.*
s.5A, enabling: SSI 2012/189
s.11, see *Hamilton v Ferguson Transport (Spean Bridge) Ltd* [2012] CSIH 52, 2012 S.C. 486 (IH (1 Div)), The Lord President (Hamilton)
s.32, see *B v G* [2012] UKSC 21, 2012 S.C. (U.K.S.C.) 293 (SC), Lord Hope, J.S.C. (Deputy President)
s.45, applied: 2012 c.19 s.38, s.51, s.86

39. Finance Act 1988
s.29, repealed: 2012 c.14 Sch.39 para.28
s.142, repealed (in part): 2012 c.14 Sch.39 para.3
Sch.3 Part I para.9, repealed: 2012 c.14 Sch.39 para.28

40. Education Reform Act 1988
s.198, applied: SI 2012/1035 Reg.13, Reg.33, Reg.39
s.216, applied: SI 2012/1259 Art.2
s.216, enabling: SI 2012/1259, SI 2012/1260
s.232, enabling: SI 2012/1259
Sch.6, applied: SI 2012/3145 Sch.1, SSI 2012/303 Reg.20
Sch.6, referred to: SI 2012/2886 Sch.1
Sch.10, applied: SI 2012/1035 Reg.13, Reg.33, Reg.39

41. Local Government Finance Act 1988
see *Cosmopolitan Bellshill Ltd v North Lanarkshire Council* [2012] CSOH 141, 2012 S.L.T. 1063 (OH), Lord Hodge
Part III, applied: SI 2012/2730 Reg.4
Part V, applied: SI 2012/2914 Reg.9
s.43, see *Makro Properties Ltd v Nuneaton and Bedworth BC* [2012] EWHC 2250 (Admin), [2012] R.A. 285 (QBD (Admin)), Judge Jarman Q.C.
s.43, applied: SI 2012/57 Art.9, SI 2012/148 Art.1, Art.2, SI 2012/537 Reg.3, Reg.4, Reg.5, SI 2012/811 Reg.4A, Sch.1 para.4, SI 2012/2550 Reg.4, Reg.5
s.43, enabling: SI 2012/148, SI 2012/465
s.44, applied: SI 2012/148 Art.3
s.44, enabling: SI 2012/148, SI 2012/465
s.45, see *Makro Properties Ltd v Nuneaton and Bedworth BC* [2012] EWHC 2250 (Admin), [2012] R.A. 285 (QBD (Admin)), Judge Jarman Q.C.
s.45, applied: SI 2012/537 Reg.3, Reg.4, Reg.5
s.45A, see *Preston City Council v Oyston Angel Charity* [2012] EWHC 2005 (Admin), [2012] R.A. 357 (QBD (Admin)), Hickinbottom, J.
s.47, applied: SI 2012/628 Art.10
s.49A, enabling: SI 2012/537
s.53, enabling: SI 2012/1292
s.59A, added: 2012 c.17 s.1
s.60, amended: 2012 c.17 Sch.3 para.1
s.60, enabling: SI 2012/466, SI 2012/3036
s.62, enabling: SI 2012/466, SI 2012/467
s.64, enabling: SI 2012/1291
s.65, varied: SI 2012/323 Reg.20, SI 2012/444 Reg.25, SI 2012/2031 Reg.15
s.65, enabling: SI 2012/1291
s.66, amended: 2012 c.17 s.6
s.69, applied: SI 2012/628 Art.10
s.74, applied: SI 2012/444 Reg.4, Reg.5, Reg.6
s.74, enabling: SI 2012/213
s.75, applied: SI 2012/444 Reg.4
s.78, amended: 2012 c.17 Sch.2 para.2
s.78A, amended: 2012 c.17 Sch.2 para.3
s.78A, repealed (in part): 2012 c.17 Sch.2 para.3
s.78A, substituted: 2012 c.17 Sch.2 para.3
s.79, amended: 2012 c.17 Sch.2 para.4
s.82, amended: 2012 c.17 Sch.2 para.5

1988– cont.

41. Local Government Finance Act 1988– *cont.*
s.84A, amended: 2012 c.17 Sch.2 para.6
s.84Q, repealed (in part): 2012 c.17 s.3
s.85, repealed: 2012 c.17 s.3
s.86, repealed: 2012 c.17 s.3
s.90, amended: 2012 c.17 Sch.3 para.24
s.97, amended: 2012 c.17 Sch.3 para.25
s.97, repealed (in part): 2012 c.17 Sch.3 para.25
s.98, applied: SI 2012/2914 Reg.3
s.99, amended: 2012 c.17 Sch.3 para.26
s.99, repealed (in part): 2012 c.17 Sch.3 para.26
s.112, applied: SI 2012/2892 Art.4
s.140, amended: 2012 c.17 Sch.3 para.27
s.140, repealed (in part): 2012 c.17 Sch.3 para.27
s.140, enabling: SI 2012/3036
s.141, amended: 2012 c.17 s.3, s.7, Sch.3 para.28
s.143, amended: 2012 c.17 s.1
s.143, enabling: SI 2012/24, SI 2012/148, SI 2012/213, SI 2012/465, SI 2012/466, SI 2012/537, SI 2012/538, SI 2012/664, SI 2012/994, SI 2012/1291, SI 2012/1292, SI 2012/3036
s.144, amended: 2012 c.17 Sch.3 para.29
s.146, enabling: SI 2012/465, SI 2012/466, SI 2012/467, SI 2012/994
Sch.4A, see *Friends Life Co Ltd v Alexander (Valuation Officer)* [2012] R.A. 263 (VT), Graham Zellick Q.C. (President); see *RGM Properties Ltd v Speight (Listing Officer)* [2011] EWHC 2125 (Admin), [2012] R.A. 21 (QBD (Admin)), Langstaff, J.
Sch.5 para.5, see *Cheale Meats Ltd v Ray (Valuation Officer)* [2012] UKUT 61 (LC), [2012] R.A. 145 (UT (Lands)), George Bartlett Q.C. (President)
Sch.6, see *Plymouth City Council v Dearing (Valuation Officer)* [2012] R.A. 58 (VT); see *Read & Partners v Sykes (Valuation Officer)* [2012] R.A. 345 (VT), A Clark FRICS
Sch.6 para.2, see *Wilson v Coll (Listing Officer)* [2011] EWHC 2824 (Admin), [2012] P.T.S.R. 1313 (QBD (Admin)), Singh, J.
Sch.7B Part I para.1, added: 2012 c.17 Sch.1
Sch.7B Part I para.2, added: 2012 c.17 Sch.1
Sch.7B Part I para.3, added: 2012 c.17 Sch.1
Sch.7B Part II para.4, added: 2012 c.17 Sch.1
Sch.7B Part II para.5, added: 2012 c.17 Sch.1
Sch.7B Part III para.6, added: 2012 c.17 Sch.1
Sch.7B Part III para.7, added: 2012 c.17 Sch.1
Sch.7B Part III para.8, added: 2012 c.17 Sch.1
Sch.7B Part IV para.9, added: 2012 c.17 Sch.1
Sch.7B Part IV para.10, added: 2012 c.17 Sch.1
Sch.7B Part IV para.11, added: 2012 c.17 Sch.1
Sch.7B Part V para.12, added: 2012 c.17 Sch.1
Sch.7B Part V para.13, added: 2012 c.17 Sch.1
Sch.7B Part V para.14, added: 2012 c.17 Sch.1
Sch.7B Part V para.15, added: 2012 c.17 Sch.1
Sch.7B Part V para.16, added: 2012 c.17 Sch.1
Sch.7B Part V para.17, added: 2012 c.17 Sch.1
Sch.7B Part V para.18, added: 2012 c.17 Sch.1
Sch.7B Part VI para.19, added: 2012 c.17 Sch.1
Sch.7B Part VI para.20, added: 2012 c.17 Sch.1
Sch.7B Part VI para.21, added: 2012 c.17 Sch.1
Sch.7B Part VII para.22, added: 2012 c.17 Sch.1
Sch.7B Part VII para.23, added: 2012 c.17 Sch.1
Sch.7B Part VII para.24, added: 2012 c.17 Sch.1
Sch.7B Part VII para.25, added: 2012 c.17 Sch.1
Sch.7B Part VII para.26, added: 2012 c.17 Sch.1
Sch.7B Part VII para.27, added: 2012 c.17 Sch.1
Sch.7B Part VII para.28, added: 2012 c.17 Sch.1

1988–cont.

41. Local Government Finance Act 1988–*cont.*
Sch.7B Part VII para.29, added: 2012 c.17 Sch.1
Sch.7B Part VII para.30, added: 2012 c.17 Sch.1
Sch.7B Part VII para.31, added: 2012 c.17 Sch.1
Sch.7B Part VIII para.32, added: 2012 c.17 Sch.1
Sch.7B Part VIII para.33, added: 2012 c.17 Sch.1
Sch.7B Part IX para.34, added: 2012 c.17 Sch.1
Sch.7B Part IX para.35, added: 2012 c.17 Sch.1
Sch.7B Part IX para.36, added: 2012 c.17 Sch.1
Sch.7B Part IX para.37, added: 2012 c.17 Sch.1
Sch.7B Part IX para.38, added: 2012 c.17 Sch.1
Sch.7B Part X para.39, added: 2012 c.17 Sch.1
Sch.7B Part X para.40, added: 2012 c.17 Sch.1
Sch.7B Part X para.41, added: 2012 c.17 Sch.1
Sch.7B Part X para.42, added: 2012 c.17 Sch.1
Sch.7B Part XI para.43, added: 2012 c.17 Sch.1
Sch.7B Part XI para.44, added: 2012 c.17 Sch.1
Sch.7B Part XI para.45, added: 2012 c.17 Sch.1
Sch.8 Part I para.1, amended: 2012 c.17 Sch.3 para.3
Sch.8 Part I para.1, repealed (in part): 2012 c.17 Sch.3 para.3
Sch.8 Part I para.2, amended: 2012 c.17 Sch.3 para.4
Sch.8 Part I para.3, amended: 2012 c.17 Sch.3 para.5
Sch.8 Part II para.3A, added: 2012 c.17 Sch.3 para.6
Sch.8 Part II para.4, amended: 2012 c.17 Sch.3 para.7
Sch.8 Part II para.4, repealed (in part): 2012 c.17 Sch.3 para.7
Sch.8 Part II para.4, enabling: SI 2012/664, SI 2012/3036
Sch.8 Part II para.5, amended: 2012 c.17 Sch.3 para.8
Sch.8 Part II para.6, amended: 2012 c.17 Sch.3 para.9
Sch.8 Part II para.6, repealed (in part): 2012 c.17 Sch.3 para.9
Sch.8 Part II para.6, enabling: SI 2012/466, SI 2012/664, SI 2012/994, SI 2012/3036
Sch.8 Part III para.8, amended: 2012 c.17 Sch.3 para.10
Sch.8 Part III para.8, repealed (in part): 2012 c.17 Sch.3 para.10
Sch.8 Part III para.9, amended: 2012 c.17 Sch.3 para.11
Sch.8 Part III para.9A, amended: 2012 c.17 Sch.3 para.12
Sch.8 Part III para.10, amended: 2012 c.17 Sch.3 para.13
Sch.8 Part III para.11, amended: 2012 c.17 Sch.3 para.14
Sch.8 Part III para.12, amended: 2012 c.17 Sch.3 para.15
Sch.8 Part III para.13, amended: 2012 c.17 Sch.3 para.16
Sch.8 Part III para.14, amended: 2012 c.17 Sch.3 para.17
Sch.8 Part III para.15, amended: 2012 c.17 Sch.3 para.18
Sch.9 para.1, enabling: SI 2012/24, SI 2012/466, SI 2012/467, SI 2012/538, SI 2012/994
Sch.9 para.2, amended: 2012 c.17 s.8
Sch.9 para.2, enabling: SI 2012/24, SI 2012/466, SI 2012/467, SI 2012/538, SI 2012/994
Sch.9 para.3, enabling: SI 2012/24, SI 2012/466, SI 2012/994
Sch.9 para.4, enabling: SI 2012/24, SI 2012/466, SI 2012/994
Sch.11 Part 1 paraA.18A, added: 2012 c.17 Sch.4 para.2

1988–cont.

41. Local Government Finance Act 1988–*cont.*
Sch.11 Part 3 para.8, amended: 2012 c.17 s.17
Sch.11 Part 3 para.10A, amended: 2012 c.17 s.14

43. Housing (Scotland) Act 1988
see *Aberdeenshire Council v Shaw* 2012 S.L.T. (Sh Ct) 144 (Sh Ct (Grampian) (Banff)), Sheriff P Mann
s.32, see *East Lothian Council v Duffy* 2012 S.L.T. (Sh Ct) 113 (Sh Ct (Lothian) (Haddington)), Sheriff P J Braid
s.33, see *Aberdeenshire Council v Shaw* 2012 S.L.T. (Sh Ct) 144 (Sh Ct (Grampian) (Banff)), Sheriff P Mann
s.43, repealed (in part): 2012 asp 8 Sch.8 Part 2
s.45, repealed (in part): 2012 asp 8 Sch.8 Part 2
s.66, applied: SI 2012/2886 Sch.1, SSI 2012/303 Sch.5 para.41
Sch.8 para.4, repealed: 2012 asp 11 s.4
Sch.8 para.5, repealed: 2012 asp 11 s.4

48. Copyright, Designs and Patents Act 1988
Part I, applied: SI 2012/799, SI 2012/799 Art.2, SI 2012/1753, SI 2012/1754
Part I, disapplied: SI 2012/799 Art.5
Part I, enabling: SI 2012/1753, SI 2012/1754
Part II, applied: SI 2012/799 Art.6
Part II, disapplied: SI 2012/799 Art.7
Part II, referred to: SI 2012/799 Art.6
s.1, see *Newspaper Licensing Agency Ltd v Meltwater Holding BV* [2011] EWCA Civ 890, [2012] Bus. L.R. 53 (CA (Civ Div)), Sir Andrew Morritt (Chancellor)
s.3, see *Forensic Telecommunications Services Ltd v Chief Constable of West Yorkshire* [2011] EWHC 2892 (Ch), [2012] F.S.R. 15 (Ch D), Arnold, J.
s.3A, see *Forensic Telecommunications Services Ltd v Chief Constable of West Yorkshire* [2011] EWHC 2892 (Ch), [2012] F.S.R. 15 (Ch D), Arnold, J.
s.4, see *Lucasfilm Ltd v Ainsworth* [2012] 1 A.C. 208 (SC), Lord Phillips (President)
s.16, see *Newspaper Licensing Agency Ltd v Meltwater Holding BV* [2011] EWCA Civ 890, [2012] Bus. L.R. 53 (CA (Civ Div)), Sir Andrew Morritt (Chancellor)
s.17, see *Dramatico Entertainment Ltd v British Sky Broadcasting Ltd* [2012] EWHC 268 (Ch), [2012] 3 C.M.L.R. 14 (Ch D), Arnold, J.
s.18A, disapplied: SI 2012/799 Art.4, Art.5
s.18A, varied: SI 2012/799 Art.4
s.19, disapplied: SI 2012/799 Art.4, Art.5
s.20, see *Dramatico Entertainment Ltd v British Sky Broadcasting Ltd* [2012] EWHC 268 (Ch), [2012] 3 C.M.L.R. 14 (Ch D), Arnold, J.; see *Football Association Premier League Ltd v QC Leisure* [2012] EWHC 108 (Ch), [2012] 2 C.M.L.R. 16 (Ch D), Kitchin, L.J.; see *ITV Broadcasting Ltd v TV Catchup Ltd* [2011] EWHC 1874 (Pat), [2012] Eu. L.R. 187 (Ch D (Patents Ct)), Floyd, J.
s.20, disapplied: SI 2012/799 Art.4, Art.5
s.20, varied: SI 2012/799 Art.4
s.26, disapplied: SI 2012/799 Art.4, Art.5
s.28A, see *ITV Broadcasting Ltd v TV Catchup Ltd* [2011] EWHC 1874 (Pat), [2012] Eu. L.R. 187 (Ch D (Patents Ct)), Floyd, J.; see *ITV Broadcasting Ltd v TV Catchup Ltd* [2011] EWHC 2977 (Pat), [2012] E.C.D.R. 5 (Ch D (Patents Ct)), Floyd, J.; see *Newspaper Licensing Agency Ltd v Meltwater Holding BV* [2011] EWCA Civ 890,

1988–cont.

48. Copyright, Designs and Patents Act 1988–*cont.*
s.28A–*cont.*
[2012] Bus. L.R. 53 (CA (Civ Div)), Sir Andrew Morritt (Chancellor)
s.30, see *BBC, Applicants* [2012] HCJ 2, 2012 S.C.L. 347 (HCJ), Lord Carloway; see *Newspaper Licensing Agency Ltd v Meltwater Holding BV* [2011] EWCA Civ 890, [2012] Bus. L.R. 53 (CA (Civ Div)), Sir Andrew Morritt (Chancellor)
s.45, see *BBC, Petitioners* [2012] HCJ 10, 2012 S.L.T. 476 (HCJ), Lord Woolman
s.48, amended: 2012 c.7 Sch.5 para.44, Sch.14 para.52
s.72, see *Football Association Premier League Ltd v QC Leisure* [2012] EWHC 108 (Ch), [2012] 2 C.M.L.R. 16 (Ch D), Kitchin, L.J.
s.73, see *ITV Broadcasting Ltd v TV Catchup Ltd* [2011] EWHC 1874 (Pat), [2012] Eu. L.R. 187 (Ch D (Patents Ct)), Floyd, J.
s.85, see *Trimingham v Associated Newspapers Ltd* [2012] EWHC 1296 (QB), [2012] 4 All E.R. 717 (QBD), Tugendhat, J.
s.90, see *Crosstown Music Co 1 LLC v Rive Droite Music Ltd* [2010] EWCA Civ 1222, [2012] Ch. 68 (CA (Civ Div)), Mummery, L.J.
s.97A, see *Dramatico Entertainment Ltd v British Sky Broadcasting Ltd* [2012] EWHC 1152 (Ch), [2012] 3 C.M.L.R. 15 (Ch D), Arnold, J.; see *Dramatico Entertainment Ltd v British Sky Broadcasting Ltd* [2012] EWHC 268 (Ch), [2012] 3 C.M.L.R. 14 (Ch D), Arnold, J.; see *Twentieth Century Fox Film Corp v British Telecommunications Plc* [2011] EWHC 1981 (Ch), [2012] Bus. L.R. 1461 (Ch D), Arnold, J.
s.107, disapplied: SI 2012/799 Art.4, Art.5
s.107, varied: SI 2012/799 Art.4
s.154, applied: SI 2012/799 Art.3
s.159, enabling: SI 2012/799, SI 2012/1754
s.170, enabling: SI 2012/1753
s.182C, disapplied: SI 2012/799 Art.7
s.182CA, disapplied: SI 2012/799 Art.7
s.182D, disapplied: SI 2012/799 Art.7
s.183, disapplied: SI 2012/799 Art.7
s.185, disapplied: SI 2012/799 Art.7
s.186, disapplied: SI 2012/799 Art.7
s.187, disapplied: SI 2012/799 Art.7
s.188, disapplied: SI 2012/799 Art.7
s.198, disapplied: SI 2012/799 Art.7
s.208, enabling: SI 2012/799
s.213, see *Ifejika v Ifejika* [2012] F.S.R. 6 (PCC), Judge Birss Q.C.
s.215, see *Ifejika v Ifejika* [2012] F.S.R. 6 (PCC), Judge Birss Q.C.
s.280, see *Atrium Medical Corp v DSB Invest Holding SA* [2011] EWHC 74 (Pat), [2012] Bus. L.R. 133 (Ch D (Patents Ct)), Lewison, J.
s.287, see *Suh v Ryu* [2012] EWPCC 20, [2012] F.S.R. 31 (PCC), Judge Birss Q.C.
s.291, see *Suh v Ryu* [2012] EWPCC 20, [2012] F.S.R. 31 (PCC), Judge Birss Q.C.
s.297, see *Football Association Premier League Ltd v QC Leisure (C-403/08)* [2012] Bus. L.R. 1321 (ECJ (Grand Chamber)), Judge Skouris (President); see *Media Protection Services Ltd v Crawford* [2012] EWHC 2373 (Admin), [2012] C.P. Rep. 48 (DC), Stanley Burnton, L.J.; see *Murphy v Media Protection Services Ltd* [2012] EWHC 466 (Admin), [2012] 3 C.M.L.R. 2 (QBD (Admin)), Stanley Burton, L.J.

1988–cont.

48. Copyright, Designs and Patents Act 1988–*cont.*
s.297A, see *R. (on the application of Vuciterni) v Brent Magistrates' Court* [2012] EWHC 2140 (Admin), (2012) 176 J.P. 705 (DC), Davis, L.J.
Sch.1 para.36, enabling: SI 2012/1753
49. Health and Medicines Act 1988
s.7, amended: 2012 c.7 Sch.5 para.45, Sch.14 para.53
50. Housing Act 1988
see *Mew v Tristmire Ltd* [2011] EWCA Civ 912, [2012] 1 W.L.R. 852 (CA (Civ Div)), Maurice Kay, L.J.
Part I, applied: SI 2012/3018 Sch.2 para.1
Pt I s.19A, see *Corby BC v Scott* [2012] EWCA Civ 276, [2012] H.L.R. 23 (CA (Civ Div)), Lord Neuberger (M.R.)
s.17, see *Amicus Horizon Ltd v Mabbott's Estate* [2012] EWCA Civ 895, [2012] H.L.R. 42 (CA (Civ Div)), Ward, L.J.
s.21, see *Corby BC v Scott* [2012] EWCA Civ 276, [2012] H.L.R. 23 (CA (Civ Div)), Lord Neuberger (M.R.)
s.82, amended: 2012 c.10 Sch.5 para.37
s.129, applied: SI 2012/2886 Sch.1, SSI 2012/303 Sch.5 para.41
Sch.2, see *Byrne v Poplar Housing and Regeneration Community Association Ltd* [2012] EWCA Civ 832, [2012] H.L.R. 33 (CA (Civ Div)), Etherton, L.J.
Sch.2A para.2, see *Saxon Weald Homes Ltd v Chadwick* [2011] EWCA Civ 1202, [2012] H.L.R. 8 (CA (Civ Div)), Mummery, L.J.
Sch.7 para.6, amended: SI 2012/2404 Sch.2 para.25
52. Road Traffic Act 1988
see *Harkin v Brown* [2012] HCJAC 100, 2012 S.L.T. 1071 (HCJ), Lord Carloway; see *Young v Secretary of State for Transport* 2012 S.L.T. (Sh Ct) 212 (Sh Ct (South Strathclyde) (Dumfries)), Sheriff Principal B A Lockhart
s.1, see *HM Advocate v Noche (Pedro)* 2012 S.C.L. 329 (HCJ Appeal), Lord Mackay of Drumadoon; see *McIntyre v Cassidy* [2012] HCJAC 99, 2012 S.C.L. 910 (HCJ), Lord Mackay of Drumadoon
s.1A, added: 2012 c.10 s.143
s.2, see *Elphinstone (Andrew John) v Richardson* [2012] HCJAC 60, 2012 S.C.C.R. 418 (HCJ), Lord Carloway; see *McIntyre v Cassidy* [2012] HCJAC 99, 2012 S.C.L. 910 (HCJ), Lord Mackay of Drumadoon
s.2A, amended: 2012 c.10 s.143
s.3, see *McCourt (Peter Stephen) v HM Advocate* [2012] HCJAC 32, 2012 J.C. 336 (HCJ), The Lord Justice General (Hamilton)
s.3ZB, see *Rai (Jamie) v HM Advocate* 2012 S.C.L. 283 (HCJ), Lord Clarke
s.5, see *Ambrose v Harris* 2012 S.C.C.R. 465 (HCJ), Lord Justice General Hamilton; see *Avery v Crown Prosecution Service* [2011] EWHC 2388 (Admin), [2012] R.T.R. 8 (DC), Sir Anthony May; see *Harkin v Brown* [2012] HCJAC 100, 2012 S.L.T. 1071 (HCJ), Lord Carloway; see *Rai (Jamie) v HM Advocate* 2012 S.C.L. 283 (HCJ), Lord Clarke
s.8, amended: 2012 c.11 s.20
s.11, amended: 2012 c.11 s.20
s.13A, amended: 2012 c.10 Sch.27 para.1
s.22A, see *R. v Meeking (Caroline)* [2012] EWCA Crim 641, [2012] 1 W.L.R. 3349 (CA (Crim Div)), Toulson, L.J.
s.41, enabling: SI 2012/1404

1988– cont.

52. Road Traffic Act 1988–*cont.*
s.45, enabling: SI 2012/307
s.46, enabling: SI 2012/307
s.47, enabling: SI 2012/2652
s.49, see *Vehicle and Operator Services Agency v Kayes* [2012] EWHC 1498 (Admin), (2012) 176 J.P. 654 (QBD (Admin)), Collins, J.
s.49, enabling: SI 2012/305
s.51, enabling: SI 2012/305
s.63A, enabling: SI 2012/305
s.89, enabling: SI 2012/977
s.95, amended: 2012 c.21 Sch.18 para.60
s.97, amended: SI 2012/977 Sch.1 para.2
s.97, repealed (in part): SI 2012/977 Sch.1 para.2
s.97, enabling: SI 2012/977
s.98, repealed (in part): SI 2012/977 Sch.1 para.3
s.98, enabling: SI 2012/977
s.99, amended: SI 2012/977 Sch.1 para.4
s.99, enabling: SI 2012/977
s.99A, enabling: SI 2012/977
s.101, enabling: SI 2012/977
s.103, see *Rai (Jamie) v HM Advocate* 2012 S.C.L. 283 (HCJ), Lord Clarke
s.105, enabling: SI 2012/977
s.108, amended: SI 2012/977 Sch.1 para.5
s.121, see *Young v Secretary of State for Transport* 2012 S.L.T. (Sh Ct) 212 (Sh Ct (South Strathclyde) (Dumfries)), Sheriff Principal B A Lockhart
s.127, applied: SI 2012/1548 Reg.4
s.128, applied: SI 2012/1548 Reg.4
s.129, applied: SI 2012/1548 Reg.4
s.130, applied: SI 2012/1548 Reg.4
s.131A, applied: SI 2012/1356 Art.3, SI 2012/1548 Reg.4, Sch.2 para.14
s.131A, enabling: SI 2012/1548
s.141, enabling: SI 2012/1548
s.143, see *Dudley MBC v Arif* [2011] EWHC 3880 (Admin), [2012] R.T.R. 20 (QBD (Admin)), Beatson, J.; see *Hunter v Brown* [2012] HCJAC 42, 2012 S.L.T. 665 (HCJ), Lord Mackay of Drumadoon
s.144, amended: 2012 c.7 Sch.5 para.46, Sch.14 para.54
s.145, see *British Waterways v Royal & Sun Alliance Insurance Plc* [2012] EWHC 460 (Comm), [2012] Lloyd's Rep. I.R. 562 (QBD (Comm)), Burton, J.
s.151, see *Churchill Insurance Co Ltd v Wilkinson (C-442/10)* [2012] R.T.R. 10 (ECJ (4th Chamber)), Judge Bonichot (President)
s.152, amended: 2012 c.6 s.11
s.155, see *Young v Secretary of State for Transport* 2012 S.L.T. (Sh Ct) 212 (Sh Ct (South Strathclyde) (Dumfries)), Sheriff Principal B A Lockhart
s.172, see *Atkinson v DPP* [2011] EWHC 3363 (Admin), [2012] R.T.R. 14 (DC), Langstaff, J.; see *Elphinstone (Andrew John) v Richardson* [2012] HCJAC 60, 2012 S.C.C.R. 418 (HCJ), Lord Carloway; see *Whiteside v DPP* [2011] EWHC 3471 (Admin), (2012) 176 J.P. 103 (QBD (Admin)), Elias, L.J.
s.195, amended: 2012 c.11 s.20
s.195, applied: SI 2012/307, SI 2012/977, SI 2012/1404

1988– cont.

53. Road Traffic Offenders Act 1988
s.1, see *McIntyre v Cassidy* [2012] HCJAC 99, 2012 S.C.L. 910 (HCJ), Lord Mackay of Drumadoon; see *Richardson v Dalgarno* 2012 J.C. 160 (HCJ), Lord Mackay of Drumadoon
s.2, see *McIntyre v Cassidy* [2012] HCJAC 99, 2012 S.C.L. 910 (HCJ), Lord Mackay of Drumadoon
s.9, referred to: SI 2012/1726 r.55.2
s.20, see *Brotherston v DPP* [2012] EWHC 136 (Admin), (2012) 176 J.P. 153 (DC), Toulson, L.J.
s.23, amended: 2012 c.10 Sch.27 para.3
s.24, amended: 2012 c.10 Sch.27 para.4
s.25, applied: SI 2012/1726 r.37.15, r.4.7, r.55.2
s.26, referred to: SI 2012/1726 r.55.2
s.27, applied: SI 2012/1726 r.55.2
s.30A, referred to: SI 2012/1726 r.55.4
s.34, amended: 2012 c.10 Sch.27 para.5
s.34, applied: SI 2012/1726 r.37.10, r.55.1
s.34, referred to: SI 2012/1726 r.55.2
s.34A, applied: SI 2012/2939 Reg.9
s.34B, applied: SI 2012/2939 Reg.9, Reg.11
s.34B, referred to: SI 2012/2939 Reg.10
s.34B, enabling: SI 2012/2939
s.34BA, applied: SI 2012/2939 Reg.9
s.34BA, enabling: SI 2012/2939
s.34C, applied: SI 2012/2939 Reg.6, Reg.9
s.34C, enabling: SI 2012/2939
s.34D, referred to: SI 2012/1726 r.55.4
s.34E, referred to: SI 2012/1726 r.55.4
s.35, applied: SI 2012/1726 r.37.10, r.55.1
s.35, referred to: SI 2012/1726 r.55.2
s.35A, amended: 2012 c.10 Sch.13 para.8, Sch.14 para.1, Sch.21 para.4
s.35A, repealed (in part): 2012 c.10 Sch.10 para.5, Sch.21 para.4
s.36, amended: 2012 c.10 Sch.27 para.6
s.36, referred to: SI 2012/1726 r.55.2
s.39, applied: SI 2012/1726 r.64.2, r.63.2
s.39, referred to: SI 2012/1726 r.55.2
s.40, applied: SI 2012/1726 r.63.2
s.40, referred to: SI 2012/1726 r.55.2
s.42, applied: SI 2012/1726 r.55.1
s.42, referred to: SI 2012/1726 r.55.2
s.44, applied: SI 2012/1726 r.37.10
s.44, referred to: SI 2012/1726 r.55.2
s.44A, referred to: SI 2012/1726 r.55.2
s.45, amended: 2012 c.10 Sch.27 para.7
s.45A, amended: 2012 c.10 Sch.27 para.8
s.47, applied: SI 2012/1726 r.5.4
s.47, referred to: SI 2012/1726 r.55.2
s.54, referred to: SI 2012/1726 r.55.3
s.55, referred to: SI 2012/1726 r.55.3
s.57, applied: SI 2012/1726 r.5.4
s.57A, applied: SI 2012/1726 r.5.4
s.62, referred to: SI 2012/1726 r.55.3
s.63, referred to: SI 2012/1726 r.55.3
s.64, referred to: SI 2012/1726 r.55.3
s.70, referred to: SI 2012/1726 r.55.3
s.71, applied: SI 2012/1726 r.5.4, r.4.7
s.71, referred to: SI 2012/1726 r.55.3
s.72, referred to: SI 2012/1726 r.55.3
s.73, referred to: SI 2012/1726 r.55.3
s.74, referred to: SI 2012/1726 r.55.3
s.96, referred to: SI 2012/1726 r.55.2
Sch.1 para.4, amended: 2012 c.10 Sch.27 para.9
Sch.2, referred to: SI 2012/1726 r.55.2
Sch.2 Part I, amended: 2012 c.10 s.143

1989

3. Elected Authorities (Northern Ireland) Act 1989
s.10, amended: SI 2012/1809 Sch.1 Part 1

6. Official Secrets Act 1989
s.1, see *R. (on the application of British Sky Broadcasting Ltd) v Central Criminal Court* [2011] EWHC 3451 (Admin), [2012] Q.B. 785 (QBD (Admin)), Moore-Bick, L.J.
s.12, varied: 2012 c.11 s.12
s.12, enabling: SI 2012/2900
s.13, enabling: SI 2012/2900
s.14, applied: SI 2012/2900

15. Water Act 1989
see *Manchester Ship Canal Co Ltd v United Utilities Water Plc* [2012] EWHC 232 (Ch), [2012] Env. L.R. 31 (Ch D), Newey, J
applied: SI 2012/1128 Art.4
s.17, see *Manchester Ship Canal Co Ltd v United Utilities Water Plc* [2012] EWHC 232 (Ch), [2012] Env. L.R. 31 (Ch D), Newey, J
s.174, amended: 2012 c.19 Sch.9 para.5, 2012 c.21 Sch.18 para.61
Sch.2 para.2, see *Manchester Ship Canal Co Ltd v United Utilities Water Plc* [2012] EWHC 232 (Ch), [2012] Env. L.R. 31 (Ch D), Newey, J

26. Finance Act 1989
s.67, amended: 2012 c.14 Sch.16 para.48
s.82, repealed: 2012 c.14 Sch.16 para.49
s.82A, applied: 2012 c.14 Sch.17 para.20
s.82A, repealed: 2012 c.14 Sch.16 para.50
s.82B, applied: 2012 c.14 Sch.17 para.20
s.82B, repealed: 2012 c.14 Sch.16 para.51
s.82C, applied: 2012 c.14 Sch.17 para.20
s.82D, applied: 2012 c.14 Sch.17 para.20
s.82D, repealed: 2012 c.14 Sch.16 para.52
s.82E, applied: 2012 c.14 Sch.17 para.20
s.82E, repealed: 2012 c.14 Sch.16 para.52
s.82F, applied: 2012 c.14 Sch.17 para.20
s.82F, repealed: 2012 c.14 Sch.16 para.52
s.83, see *Scottish Widows Plc v Revenue and Customs Commissioners* [2012] 1 All E.R. 379 (SC), Lord Hope (Deputy President)
s.83, applied: 2012 c.14 Sch.17 para.20
s.83, repealed: 2012 c.14 Sch.16 para.53
s.83A, repealed: 2012 c.14 Sch.16 para.57
s.83B, repealed: 2012 c.14 Sch.16 para.58
s.83XA, applied: 2012 c.14 Sch.17 para.20
s.83XA, disapplied: SI 2012/3009 Reg.4
s.83XA, repealed: 2012 c.14 Sch.16 para.54
s.83YA, applied: 2012 c.14 Sch.17 para.5, Sch.17 para.20
s.83YA, referred to: SI 2012/3009 Reg.4
s.83YA, repealed: 2012 c.14 Sch.16 para.55
s.83YB, applied: 2012 c.14 Sch.17 para.20
s.83YB, repealed: 2012 c.14 Sch.16 para.55
s.83YC, applied: 2012 c.14 Sch.17 para.16, Sch.17 para.20
s.83YC, referred to: 2012 c.14 Sch.17 para.1, SI 2012/3009 Reg.12
s.83YC, repealed: 2012 c.14 Sch.16 para.56
s.83YD, applied: 2012 c.14 Sch.17 para.16, Sch.17 para.20
s.83YD, referred to: 2012 c.14 Sch.17 para.1
s.83YD, repealed: 2012 c.14 Sch.16 para.56
s.83YE, applied: 2012 c.14 Sch.17 para.20
s.83YE, referred to: 2012 c.14 Sch.17 para.1
s.83YE, repealed: 2012 c.14 Sch.16 para.56
s.83YF, applied: 2012 c.14 Sch.17 para.20
s.83YF, referred to: 2012 c.14 Sch.17 para.1
s.83YF, repealed: 2012 c.14 Sch.16 para.56

1989–cont.

26. Finance Act 1989–*cont.*
s.83ZA, applied: 2012 c.14 Sch.17 para.20
s.84, repealed (in part): 2012 c.14 Sch.16 para.247
s.85, repealed: 2012 c.14 Sch.16 para.59
s.85A, applied: 2012 c.14 Sch.17 para.31
s.85A, repealed: 2012 c.14 Sch.16 para.60
s.86, applied: 2012 c.14 Sch.17 para.33
s.86, repealed: 2012 c.14 Sch.16 para.61
s.88, repealed: 2012 c.14 Sch.16 para.62
s.89, applied: 2012 c.14 Sch.17 para.31
s.89, repealed: 2012 c.14 Sch.16 para.63
Sch.8 para.1, repealed: 2012 c.14 Sch.16 para.247
Sch.8 para.2, repealed: 2012 c.14 Sch.16 para.247
Sch.8 para.3, repealed: 2012 c.14 Sch.16 para.247
Sch.8 para.4, repealed: 2012 c.14 Sch.16 para.247
Sch.8 para.5, repealed: 2012 c.14 Sch.16 para.247
Sch.8 para.6, repealed: 2012 c.14 Sch.16 para.247
Sch.8 para.7, repealed: 2012 c.14 Sch.16 para.247

29. Electricity Act 1989
see *R. v Scottish and Southern Energy Plc* [2012] EWCA Crim 539, (2012) 176 J.P. 241 (CA (Crim Div)), Davis, L.J.
applied: SI 2012/1128 Art.4
referred to: 2012 c.19 Sch.6 para.4
Part I, applied: SI 2012/3018 Art.24
s.3A, amended: SI 2012/2400 Art.3
s.4, amended: SI 2012/2400 Art.4
s.4, applied: SI 2012/1646 Art.3, SI 2012/2400 Art.38
s.4, disapplied: SI 2012/2740 Art.3
s.4, referred to: SI 2012/2911 Art.3
s.5, amended: SI 2012/2400 Art.5
s.5, applied: SI 2012/1646, SI 2012/2740, SI 2012/2911
s.5, enabling: SI 2012/1646, SI 2012/2740, SI 2012/2911
s.6, amended: SI 2012/2400 Art.6
s.6, applied: SI 2012/801 Art.27, SI 2012/1646 Art.3, SI 2012/2400 Art.6, Art.36, Art.37, Art.38, SI 2012/2740 Art.4, SSI 2012/89 Sch.1
s.6, referred to: SI 2012/2911 Art.4
s.6A, amended: SI 2012/2400 Art.7
s.7, amended: SI 2012/2400 Art.8
s.7A, amended: SI 2012/2400 Art.9
s.8A, applied: SI 2012/2400 Art.36, Art.37
s.37, see *R. (on the application of Samuel Smith Old Brewery (Tadcaster)) v Secretary of State for Energy and Climate Change* [2012] EWHC 46 (Admin), [2012] 2 All E.R. 849 (QBD (Admin)), Edwards-Stuart J.
s.37, applied: SI 2012/2167 Art.5
s.41A, applied: SI 2012/3018
s.41A, enabling: SI 2012/3018
s.41B, applied: SI 2012/3018
s.41B, enabling: SI 2012/3018
s.43, amended: SI 2012/1809 Sch.1 Part 1
s.47, amended: SI 2012/2400 Art.10
s.56A, amended: SI 2012/2400 Art.11
s.56FA, enabling: SI 2012/2400
s.56FB, applied: SI 2012/2400
s.56FC, enabling: SI 2012/2414
s.58, amended: SI 2012/2400 Art.12
s.60, enabling: SI 2012/2400, SI 2012/2414
s.64, amended: SI 2012/2400 Art.13
s.96, amended: SI 2012/2400 Art.14
s.98, amended: SI 2012/2400 Art.15
Sch.4 para.9, applied: SI 2012/605 Reg.14
Sch.6A para.1, amended: SI 2012/2400 Art.16

1989– cont.

29. Electricity Act 1989– *cont.*
Sch.6A para.9A, added: SI 2012/2400 Art.16
Sch.8, applied: SI 2012/2167 Art.5
Sch.16 para.23, repealed (in part): 2012 asp 5 Sch.5 para.31

30. Dangerous Dogs Act 1989
s.1, see *Hunter v McPherson* 2012 J.C. 145 (HCJ), Lord Mackay of Drumadoon

33. Extradition Act 1989
applied: SI 2012/1726 r.17.3, r.17.4
s.8, applied: SI 2012/1726 r.17.3
s.9, applied: SI 2012/1726 r.17.4
s.10, applied: SI 2012/1726 r.17.1
s.14, applied: SI 2012/1726 r.17.2, r.17.3
s.14A, applied: SI 2012/1726 r.17.4
s.34A, applied: SI 2012/1726 r.17.4
Sch.1A, applied: SI 2012/1726 r.17.4
Sch.1 para.5, applied: SI 2012/1726 r.17.3
Sch.1 para.9, applied: SI 2012/1726 r.17.2, r.17.3

34. Law of Property (Miscellaneous Provisions) Act 1989
s.2, see *Francis v F Berndes Ltd* [2011] EWHC 3377 (Ch), [2012] 1 All E.R. (Comm) 735 (Ch D), Henderson, J.; see *Keay v Morris Homes (West Midlands) Ltd* [2012] EWCA Civ 900, [2012] 1 W.L.R. 2855 (CA (Civ Div)), Laws, L.J.; see *Sharma v Simposh Ltd* [2011] EWCA Civ 1383, [2012] 3 W.L.R. 503 (CA (Civ Div)), Laws, L.J.

37. Football Spectators Act 1989
see *R. v Boggild (Phillip)* [2011] EWCA Crim 1928, [2012] 1 W.L.R. 1298 (CA (Crim Div)), Hughes, L.J. (Vice President)
Part II, applied: SI 2012/340 Art.3
s.11, applied: SI 2012/1470
s.11, enabling: SI 2012/1470
s.14, varied: SI 2012/340 Art.2
s.14, enabling: SI 2012/340
s.14A, see *R. v Boggild (Phillip)* [2011] EWCA Crim 1928, [2012] 1 W.L.R. 1298 (CA (Crim Div)), Hughes, L.J. (Vice President); see *R. v Doyle (Ciaran)* [2012] EWCA Crim 995, (2012) 176 J.P. 337 (CA (Crim Div)), Hughes, L.J.
s.14A, applied: SI 2012/1726 r.50.1, r.68.1, r.63.1, r.74.1, r.68.3, r.68.4
s.14A, referred to: SI 2012/1726 r.50.2
s.14E, repealed (in part): 2012 c.10 Sch.10 para.6
s.14H, applied: SI 2012/1726 r.76.1, r.76.7
s.18, repealed (in part): 2012 c.10 Sch.10 para.6
s.22, applied: SI 2012/1726 r.63.1
s.22A, enabling: SI 2012/340
s.23, see *R. v Boggild (Phillip)* [2011] EWCA Crim 1928, [2012] 1 W.L.R. 1298 (CA (Crim Div)), Hughes, L.J. (Vice President); see *R. v Doyle (Ciaran)* [2012] EWCA Crim 995, (2012) 176 J.P. 337 (CA (Crim Div)), Hughes, L.J.
Sch.1, see *R. v Doyle (Ciaran)* [2012] EWCA Crim 995, (2012) 176 J.P. 337 (CA (Crim Div)), Hughes, L.J.

40. Companies Act 1989
s.82, amended: 2012 c.21 Sch.18 para.63
s.82, repealed (in part): 2012 c.21 Sch.18 para.63
s.87, amended: 2012 c.21 Sch.18 para.64
s.151, repealed: 2012 c.19 Sch.9 para.17
s.157, amended: 2012 c.21 Sch.18 para.65
s.162, amended: 2012 c.21 Sch.18 para.66
s.166, amended: 2012 c.21 s.111
s.167, amended: 2012 c.21 Sch.18 para.67
s.169, amended: 2012 c.21 Sch.18 para.68
s.176, amended: 2012 c.21 Sch.18 para.69

1989– cont.

40. Companies Act 1989– *cont.*
s.190, amended: 2012 c.21 Sch.18 para.70
s.191, amended: 2012 c.21 Sch.18 para.71

41. Children Act 1989
see *AJ (A Minor) (Brussels II Revised), Re* [2011] EWHC 3450 (Fam), [2012] 2 F.L.R. 689 (Fam Div), Baker, J.; see *C (A Child) (Jurisdiction and Enforcement of Orders Relating to Child), Re* [2012] EWHC 907 (Fam), [2012] 2 F.L.R. 1191 (Fam Div (Newcastle)), Moylan, J.; see *Doncaster MBC v Watson* [2011] EWHC 2376 (Fam), [2012] 1 F.L.R. 613 (Fam Div), Sir Nicholas Wall (President, Fam); see *Kremen v Agrest* [2011] EWCA Civ 1482, [2012] 1 F.L.R. 894 (CA (Civ Div)), Thorpe, L.J.; see *L v Angus Council* 2012 S.L.T. 304 (OH), Lord Stewart; see *R. (on the application of CJ) v Cardiff City Council* [2011] EWCA Civ 1590, [2012] P.T.S.R. 1235 (CA (Civ Div)), Laws, L.J.; see *R. (on the application of R) v Children and Family Court Advisory and Support Service* [2011] EWHC 1774 (Admin), [2012] 1 W.L.R. 811 (QBD (Admin)), Munby, L.J.; see *R. (on the application of R) v Croydon LBC* [2011] EWHC 1473 (Admin), [2012] 3 F.C.R. 555 (QBD (Admin)), Kenneth Parker, J.; see *SH v MM (Prohibited Steps Order: Abduction)* [2011] EWHC 3314 (Fam), [2012] 1 F.L.R. 837 (Fam Div), Hedley, J.
applied: SI 2012/335 Sch.1 para.6, SI 2012/1909 Reg.102, SI 2012/2677 Reg.78, SI 2012/2886 Sch.1, SI 2012/2991 Sch.1 para.6, SI 2012/3144 Reg.8, SI 2012/3145 Sch.1, SSI 2012/303 Reg.20
Part II, applied: 2012 c.10 Sch.1 para.13
Part III, applied: SI 2012/2886 Sch.1, SI 2012/3145 Sch.1, SSI 2012/303 Reg.54
Part IV, applied: 2012 c.10 Sch.1 para.1
Part V, applied: 2012 c.10 Sch.1 para.1
Pt IV. see *K (Children with Disabilities: Wardship), Re* [2011] EWHC 4031 (Fam), [2012] 2 F.L.R. 745 (Fam Div), Hedley, J.; see *M (Children) (Child Abuse: Disclosure), Re* [2011] EWCA Civ 1035, [2012] 1 F.L.R. 205 (CA (Civ Div)), Thorpe, L.J.
s.1, see *Doncaster MBC v Watson* [2011] EWHC 2376 (Fam), [2012] 1 F.L.R. 613 (Fam Div), Sir Nicholas Wall (President, Fam); see *H (A Child) (Contact Order: Permissibility of Judge's Actions), Re* [2012] EWCA Civ 714, [2012] 2 F.L.R. 1114 (CA (Civ Div)), Thorpe, L.J.; see *K v K (Children: Permanent Removal from Jurisdiction)* [2011] EWCA Civ 793, [2012] Fam. 134 (CA (Civ Div)), Thorpe, L.J.; see *NHS Trust v Baby X* [2012] EWHC 2188 (Fam), [2012] 127 B.M.L.R. 188 (Fam Div), Hedley, J.; see *R. (on the application of O) v Hammersmith and Fulham LBC* [2011] EWCA Civ 925, [2012] 1 W.L.R. 1057 (CA (Civ Div)), Rix, L.J.; see *S v Z (Leave to Remove)* [2012] EWHC 846 (Fam), [2012] 2 F.L.R. 581 (Fam Div), Holman, J.; see *T (A Child) (One Parent Killed by Other Parent), Re* [2011] EWHC 1185 (Fam), [2012] 1 F.L.R. 472 (Fam Div), Judge Bellamy; see *YC v United Kingdom (4547/10)* [2012] 2 F.L.R. 332 (ECHR), Judge Garlicki (President)
s.3, see *W (Children) (Direct Contact), Re* [2012] EWCA Civ 999, [2012] 3 F.C.R. 277 (CA (Civ Div)), Rix, L.J.
s.4, applied: 2012 c.10 Sch.1 para.13
s.6, applied: 2012 c.10 Sch.1 para.13

1989– cont.

41. Children Act 1989– cont.

s.7, see *S (A Child) (Residence Order: Internal Relocation), Re* [2012] EWCA Civ 1031, [2012] 3 F.C.R. 153 (CA (Civ Div)), Black, L.J.

s.8, see *B (A Child) (Paternal Grandmother: Joinder as Party), Re* [2012] EWCA Civ 737, [2012] 2 F.L.R. 1358 (CA (Civ Div)), Laws, L.J.; see *K (A Child) (Contact: Condition Ousting Parent from Family Home), Re* [2011] EWCA Civ 1075, [2012] 2 F.L.R. 635 (CA (Civ Div)), Ward, L.J.; see *M (Children) (Child Abuse: Disclosure), Re* [2011] EWCA Civ 1035, [2012] 1 F.L.R. 205 (CA (Civ Div)), Thorpe, L.J.; see *O v P (Jurisdiction under Children Act 1989 Sch.1)* [2011] EWHC 2425 (Fam), [2012] 1 F.L.R. 329 (Fam Div), Baker, J.

s.8, applied: SI 2012/3098 Reg.34

s.8, referred to: 2012 c.10 Sch.1 para.10, Sch.1 para.13

s.10, see *B (A Child) (Paternal Grandmother: Joinder as Party), Re* [2012] EWCA Civ 737, [2012] 2 F.L.R. 1358 (CA (Civ Div)), Laws, L.J.; see *T (A Child) (One Parent Killed by Other Parent), Re* [2011] EWHC 1185 (Fam), [2012] 1 F.L.R. 472 (Fam Div), Judge Bellamy

s.11, see *K (A Child) (Contact: Condition Ousting Parent from Family Home), Re* [2011] EWCA Civ 1075, [2012] 2 F.L.R. 635 (CA (Civ Div)), Ward, L.J.

s.11J, see *R (Costs: Contact Enforcement), Re* [2011] EWHC 2777 (Fam), [2012] 1 F.L.R. 445 (Fam Div), Moor, J.

s.13, see *R. (on the application of Nicolaou) v Redbridge Magistrates' Court* [2012] EWHC 1647 (Admin), [2012] 2 Cr. App. R. 23 (DC), Richards, L.J.

s.14F, applied: SI 2012/2886 Sch.1, SSI 2012/303 Sch.4 para.29, Sch.5 para.64

s.15, applied: SI 2012/2814 Sch.1 para.7, SI 2012/2886 Sch.1, SSI 2012/303 Sch.4 para.29

s.17, see *R. (on the application of O) v East Riding of Yorkshire CC* [2011] EWCA Civ 196, [2012] P.T.S.R. 328 (CA (Civ Div)), Rix, L.J.; see *R. (on the application of SA (A Child)) v A Local Authority* [2011] EWCA Civ 1303, [2012] P.T.S.R. 912 (CA (Civ Div)), Ward, L.J.; see *R. (on the application of TG) v Lambeth LBC* [2011] EWCA Civ 526, [2012] P.T.S.R. 364 (CA (Civ Div)), Lord Neuberger (M.R.); see *R. (on the application of VC) v Newcastle City Council* [2011] EWHC 2673 (Admin), [2012] P.T.S.R. 546 (QBD (Admin)), Munby, L.J.

s.17, amended: 2012 c.5 Sch.2 para.1, Sch.14 Part 1

s.17, applied: SI 2012/2886 Sch.1, SSI 2012/303 Sch.4 para.32, Sch.5 para.22

s.17, repealed (in part): 2012 c.5 Sch.14 Part 1

s.17A, amended: 2012 c.5 Sch.2 para.1, Sch.14 Part 1

s.20, see *R. (on the application of O) v East Riding of Yorkshire CC* [2011] EWCA Civ 196, [2012] P.T.S.R. 328 (CA (Civ Div)), Rix, L.J.; see *R. (on the application of O) v Hammersmith and Fulham LBC* [2011] EWCA Civ 925, [2012] 1 W.L.R. 1057 (CA (Civ Div)), Rix, L.J.; see *R. (on the application of SA (A Child)) v A Local Authority* [2011] EWCA Civ 1303, [2012] P.T.S.R. 912 (CA (Civ Div)), Ward, L.J.; see *R. (on the application of TG) v Lambeth LBC* [2011] EWCA Civ 526, [2012] P.T.S.R. 364 (CA (Civ Div)), Lord Neuberger (M.R.)

s.21, amended: 2012 c.7 Sch.5 para.48

s.21, repealed (in part): 2012 c.10 Sch.12 para.24

1989– cont.

41. Children Act 1989– cont.

s.22, see *R. (on the application of SA (A Child)) v A Local Authority* [2011] EWCA Civ 1303, [2012] P.T.S.R. 912 (CA (Civ Div)), Ward, L.J.; see *R. (on the application of TG) v Lambeth LBC* [2011] EWCA Civ 526, [2012] P.T.S.R. 364 (CA (Civ Div)), Lord Neuberger (M.R.)

s.22, applied: 2012 c.9 s.28, 2012 c.10 s.107, SI 2012/10 Sch.1 para.3, SI 2012/2677 Reg.53, SI 2012/2996 Sch.1 para.4

s.22C, applied: SI 2012/2677 Reg.51, Reg.78, SI 2012/2885 Reg.8, Sch.1 para.21, SI 2012/2886 Sch.1, SI 2012/3144 Reg.8, Sch.1 para.15, SI 2012/3145 Sch.1, SSI 2012/303 Reg.11, Sch.4 para.30, SSI 2012/319 Reg.11, Reg.35

s.22C, disapplied: SI 2012/2813 Reg.2

s.22D, disapplied: SI 2012/2813 Reg.2

s.23, see *R. (on the application of SA (A Child)) v A Local Authority* [2011] EWCA Civ 1303, [2012] P.T.S.R. 912 (CA (Civ Div)), Ward, L.J.

s.23, applied: SI 2012/2677 Reg.51, Reg.78, SI 2012/2813 Reg.4, SI 2012/2885 Reg.8, Sch.1 para.21, SI 2012/2886 Sch.1, SI 2012/3144 Reg.8, Sch.1 para.15, SI 2012/3145 Sch.1, SSI 2012/303 Reg.11, Sch.4 para.30, SSI 2012/319 Reg.11, Reg.35

s.23, disapplied: SI 2012/2813 Reg.2

s.23A, applied: SI 2012/2996 Sch.1 para.4

s.23B, applied: SI 2012/2886 Sch.1, SSI 2012/303 Sch.4 para.32, Sch.5 para.22

s.23C, see *R. (on the application of TG) v Lambeth LBC* [2011] EWCA Civ 526, [2012] P.T.S.R. 364 (CA (Civ Div)), Lord Neuberger (M.R.)

s.23C, applied: SI 2012/2886 Sch.1, SSI 2012/303 Sch.4 para.32, Sch.4 para.33, Sch.5 para.22, Sch.5 para.23

s.23CA, applied: SI 2012/1553 Art.3

s.23CA, referred to: SI 2012/1553 Art.3

s.24, amended: 2012 c.7 Sch.5 para.49

s.24, applied: SI 2012/2996 Sch.1 para.4

s.24A, applied: SI 2012/2886 Sch.1, SSI 2012/303 Sch.4 para.32, Sch.5 para.22

s.24C, amended: 2012 c.7 Sch.5 para.50

s.25, amended: 2012 c.10 Sch.5 para.38

s.25, applied: 2012 c.10 Sch.1 para.1

s.25, enabling: SI 2012/3134

s.26, enabling: SI 2012/205

s.27, amended: 2012 c.7 Sch.5 para.51

s.29, amended: 2012 c.5 Sch.2 para.1, Sch.14 Part 1, 2012 c.7 Sch.5 para.52

s.31, see *A Local Authority v K* [2011] EWHC 2581 (Fam), [2012] 1 F.L.R. 765 (Fam Div), Sir Nicholas Wall (President, Fam); see *C (A Child) (Interim Care: Threshold), Re* [2011] EWCA Civ 918, [2012] 2 F.L.R. 251 (CA (Civ Div)), Ward, L.J.; see *D (A Child) (Care Order: Designated Local Authority), Re* [2012] EWCA Civ 627, [2012] 3 W.L.R. 1468 (CA (Civ Div)), Ward, L.J.; see *J (Children) (Care Proceedings: Threshold Criteria), Re* [2012] EWCA Civ 380, [2012] 3 W.L.R. 952 (CA (Civ Div)), Lord Judge, L.C.J.; see *K (Children with Disabilities: Wardship), Re* [2011] EWHC 4031 (Fam), [2012] 2 F.L.R. 745 (Fam Div), Hedley, J.; see *K (Children) (Suspension of Contact), Re* [2011] EWCA Civ 1064, [2012] 1 F.L.R. 195 (CA (Civ Div)), Mummery, L.J.; see *M (Children) (Child Abuse: Disclosure), Re* [2011] EWCA Civ 1035, [2012] 1 F.L.R. 205 (CA (Civ Div)), Thorpe, L.J.; see *WK (Minors), Re* [2012] EWHC 426 (Fam), [2012] 2 F.L.R. 762 (Fam

1989– cont.

41. Children Act 1989– *cont.*
s.31– *cont.*
Div), Baker, J.; see *X (A Child) (Evidence), Re* [2011] EWHC 3401 (Fam), [2012] 2 F.L.R. 456 (Fam Div (Liverpool)), Theis, J.

s.38, see *C (A Child) (Interim Care: Threshold), Re* [2011] EWCA Civ 918, [2012] 2 F.L.R. 251 (CA (Civ Div)), Ward, L.J.; see *TL v Hammersmith and Fulham LBC* [2011] EWCA Civ 812, [2012] 2 F.L.R. 308 (CA (Civ Div)), Sir Nicholas Wall (President, Fam); see *YC v United Kingdom (4547/10)* [2012] 2 F.L.R. 332 (ECHR), Judge Garlicki (President)

s.47, see *I-A (Children) (Allegations of Sexual Abuse), Re* [2012] EWCA Civ 582, [2012] 2 F.L.R. 837 (CA (Civ Div)), Thorpe, L.J.

s.47, amended: 2012 c.7 Sch.5 para.53

s.59, applied: 2012 c.9 s.28, SI 2012/ 2885 Reg.8, Sch.1 para.21, SI 2012/ 2886 Sch.1, SI 2012/ 3144 Reg.8, Sch.1 para.15, SI 2012/ 3145 Sch.1, SSI 2012/ 303 Reg.11, Sch.4 para.30, SSI 2012/ 319 Reg.11, Reg.35

s.80, amended: 2012 c.7 Sch.5 para.54

s.85, amended: 2012 c.7 Sch.5 para.55

s.87, amended: SI 2012/ 976 Sch.1 para.2

s.87B, amended: SI 2012/ 976 Sch.1 para.3

s.87D, enabling: SI 2012/ 511

s.91, see *Doncaster MBC v Haigh* [2011] EWHC 2412 (Fam), [2012] 1 F.L.R. 577 (Fam Div), Sir Nicholas Wall (President, Fam); see *M (A Child) (Section 91(14) Order), Re* [2012] EWCA Civ 446, [2012] 2 F.L.R. 758 (CA (Civ Div)), Thorpe, L.J.; see *T (A Child) (One Parent Killed by Other Parent), Re* [2011] EWHC 1185 (Fam), [2012] 1 F.L.R. 472 (Fam Div), Judge Bellamy

s.92, enabling: SI 2012/ 642, SI 2012/ 1955

s.94, see *A v B (Contact: Alternative Families)* [2012] EWCA Civ 285, [2012] 1 W.L.R. 3456 (CA (Civ Div)), Thorpe, L.J.

s.100, see *A Local Authority v DL* [2012] EWCA Civ 253, [2012] 3 W.L.R. 1439 (CA (Civ Div)), Maurice Kay, L.J.

s.104, enabling: SI 2012/ 205, SI 2012/ 511

s.104A, applied: SI 2012/ 1674

s.104A, enabling: SI 2012/ 205

s.105, see *D (A Child) (Care Order: Designated Local Authority), Re* [2012] EWCA Civ 627, [2012] 3 W.L.R. 1468 (CA (Civ Div)), Ward, L.J.

s.105, amended: 2012 c.5 Sch.14 Part 1, 2012 c.7 Sch.5 para.56

Sch.1, see *DE v AB (Financial Provision for Child)* [2010] EWHC 3792 (Fam), [2012] 2 F.L.R. 1396 (Fam Div), Baron, J.; see *FG v MBW (Financial Remedy for Child)* [2011] EWHC 1729 (Fam), [2012] 1 F.L.R. 152 (Fam Div), Charles, J.; see *G v A (Financial Remedy: Enforcement) (No.1)* [2011] EWHC 2380 (Fam), [2012] 1 F.L.R. 389 (Fam Div), Michael Horowitz Q.C.; see *G v A (Financial Remedy: Enforcement) (No.2)* [2011] EWHC 968 (Fam), [2012] 1 F.L.R. 402 (Fam Div), Peter Jackson, J.; see *G v A (Financial Remedy: Enforcement) (No.3)* [2011] EWHC 2377 (Fam), [2012] 1 F.L.R. 415 (Fam Div), Peter Jackson, J.; see *G v A (Financial Remedy: Enforcement) (No.4)* [2012] 1 F.L.R. 427 (Fam Div), Peter Jackson, J.; see *O v P (Jurisdiction under Children Act 1989 Sch.1)* [2011] EWHC 2425 (Fam), [2012] 1 F.L.R. 329 (Fam Div), Baker, J.

Sch.1, applied: SI 2012/ 2814 Sch.1 para.7

1989– cont.

41. Children Act 1989– *cont.*
Sch.1, see *DE v AB (Financial Provision for Child)* [2010] EWHC 3792 (Fam), [2012] 2 F.L.R. 1396 (Fam Div), Baron, J.; see *FG v MBW (Financial Remedy for Child)* [2011] EWHC 1729 (Fam), [2012] 1 F.L.R. 152 (Fam Div), Charles, J.; see *G v A (Financial Remedy: Enforcement) (No.1)* [2011] EWHC 2380 (Fam), [2012] 1 F.L.R. 389 (Fam Div), Michael Horowitz Q.C.; see *G v A (Financial Remedy: Enforcement) (No.2)* [2011] EWHC 968 (Fam), [2012] 1 F.L.R. 402 (Fam Div), Peter Jackson, J.; see *G v A (Financial Remedy: Enforcement) (No.3)* [2011] EWHC 2377 (Fam), [2012] 1 F.L.R. 415 (Fam Div), Peter Jackson, J.; see *G v A (Financial Remedy: Enforcement) (No.4)* [2012] 1 F.L.R. 427 (Fam Div), Peter Jackson, J.; see *O v P (Jurisdiction under Children Act 1989 Sch.1)* [2011] EWHC 2425 (Fam), [2012] 1 F.L.R. 329 (Fam Div), Baker, J.

Sch.1, substituted: SI 2012/ 2814 Sch.5 para.3

Sch.1 para.15, applied: SI 2012/ 2886 Sch.1, SSI 2012/ 303 Sch.4 para.29

Sch.2 Part I para.6, applied: SI 2012/ 1674, SI 2012/ 1674 Reg.3, Reg.4

Sch.2 Part I para.6, enabling: SI 2012/ 1674

Sch.2 Part II para.19, applied: 2012 c.10 Sch.1 para.1

Sch.2 Part III para.21, amended: 2012 c.5 Sch.2 para.1, Sch.14 Part 1

Sch.2 Part III para.21, disapplied: SI 2012/ 2813 Reg.2, Reg.5

Sch.11 Part I, enabling: SI 2012/ 642, SI 2012/ 1955

Sch.12 para.28, repealed (in part): 2012 c.10 Sch.12 para.25

Sch.14 Part 13 para.36, repealed (in part): 2012 c.10 Sch.25 Part 2

42. Local Government and Housing Act 1989
Part V, applied: SI 2012/ 2087 Reg.3

s.1, disapplied: SI 2012/ 2733 Art.4

s.1, enabling: SI 2012/ 1772

s.2, amended: 2012 c.7 Sch.5 para.57

s.3A, varied: SI 2012/ 1644 Reg.2

s.3A, enabling: SI 2012/ 1644

s.4, applied: SI 2012/ 1020 Reg.10, SI 2012/ 3094 Reg.22

s.5, applied: SI 2012/ 1020 Reg.10

s.15, applied: SI 2012/ 1020 Reg.5

s.18, applied: SI 2012/ 1020 Reg.3

s.21, referred to: SI 2012/ 1644 Sch.1

s.73, referred to: SI 2012/ 2087 Reg.3

s.190, enabling: SI 2012/ 1644, SI 2012/ 1772

Sch.10, see *Sloane Stanley Estate Trustees v Carey-Morgan* [2012] EWCA Civ 1181, [2012] H.L.R. 47 (CA (Civ Div)), Pill, L.J.

44. Opticians Act 1989
referred to: SI 2012/ 1917 Sch.2 para.15

s.11A, enabling: SI 2012/ 2882

s.11B, enabling: SI 2012/ 2882

s.23A, enabling: SI 2012/ 2882

s.31A, enabling: SI 2012/ 2882

s.34, applied: SI 2012/ 2882

Sch.1 para.1A, repealed (in part): 2012 c.7 Sch.20 para.6

45. Prisons (Scotland) Act 1989
applied: SI 2012/ 2885 Sch.1 para.5, SI 2012/ 2886 Sch.1, SI 2012/ 3144 Reg.24, SI 2012/ 3145 Sch.1, SSI 2012/ 303 Reg.5, Reg.15, SSI 2012/ 319 Reg.5, Reg.15

s.8, enabling: SSI 2012/ 26

s.11, enabling: SSI 2012/ 26

1989– cont.

45. Prisons (Scotland) Act 1989– *cont.*
s.12, enabling: SSI 2012/26
s.14, amended: 2012 asp 8 Sch.7 para.8, Sch.8 Part 1
s.14, repealed (in part): 2012 asp 8 Sch.8 Part 1
s.33A, enabling: SSI 2012/26
s.39, enabling: SSI 2012/26

1990

1. Capital Allowances Act 1990
s.24, see *JD Wetherspoon Plc v Revenue and Customs Commissioners* [2012] UKUT 42 (TCC), [2012] S.T.C. 1450 (UT (Tax)), Briggs, J.
s.66, see *JD Wetherspoon Plc v Revenue and Customs Commissioners* [2012] UKUT 42 (TCC), [2012] S.T.C. 1450 (UT (Tax)), Briggs, J.

8. Town and Country Planning Act 1990
see *R. (on the application of Millgate Developments Ltd) v Wokingham BC* [2011] EWCA Civ 1062, [2012] 39 E.G. 120 (CA (Civ Div)), Pill, L.J.
applied: SI 2012/535 Art.4, SI 2012/801 Art.29, SI 2012/2167 Sch.1 para.2, Sch.2 para.3, SI 2012/2635 Art.37
referred to: SI 2012/1914 Art.18, SI 2012/1924 Sch.2 para.2
Part III, applied: SI 2012/605 Reg.14, SI 2012/2167 Art.3, SI 2012/2920 Reg.5, Reg.6
Part VI, applied: SI 2012/628 Art.20, SI 2012/801 Sch.5
Pt VII s.191, see *Haq v Eastbourne BC* [2012] R.V.R. 18 (UT (Lands)), AJ Trott FRICS
s.1, applied: SI 2012/2167 Sch.2 para.1.d(successor.authority), Sch.2 para.2
s.2A, applied: SI 2012/634 Art.4
s.7A, applied: SI 2012/2167 Sch.2 para.2
s.55, see *R. (on the application of Harbige) v Secretary of State for Communities and Local Government* [2012] EWHC 1128 (Admin), [2012] J.P.L. 1245 (QBD (Admin)), Ouseley, J.
s.57, see *R. (on the application of Harbige) v Secretary of State for Communities and Local Government* [2012] EWHC 1128 (Admin), [2012] J.P.L. 1245 (QBD (Admin)), Ouseley, J.
s.59, enabling: SI 2012/634, SI 2012/636, SI 2012/748, SI 2012/801, SI 2012/843, SI 2012/1346, SI 2012/2257, SI 2012/2274, SI 2012/2318, SI 2012/3109
s.60, enabling: SI 2012/748, SI 2012/1346, SI 2012/2257, SI 2012/2318
s.61, enabling: SI 2012/634, SI 2012/748, SI 2012/801, SI 2012/843, SI 2012/1346, SI 2012/2257, SI 2012/2318
s.61A, applied: SI 2012/2167 Sch.1 para.7, Sch.2 para.7
s.61A, enabling: SI 2012/801
s.61B, applied: SI 2012/801 Art.27
s.61E, applied: SI 2012/637 Reg.26, Reg.27
s.61E, enabling: SI 2012/637
s.61F, applied: SI 2012/637 Reg.11, Reg.12, SI 2012/2421 Reg.5
s.61F, referred to: SI 2012/637 Reg.8
s.61F, enabling: SI 2012/637
s.61G, applied: SI 2012/637 Reg.5
s.61G, enabling: SI 2012/637
s.61K, enabling: SI 2012/637
s.61L, enabling: SI 2012/637
s.61M, applied: SI 2012/637 Reg.30
s.61M, enabling: SI 2012/637
s.62, applied: SI 2012/801 Art.8, Art.22

1990– cont.

8. Town and Country Planning Act 1990– *cont.*
s.62, enabling: SI 2012/801, SI 2012/2274, SI 2012/3109
s.65, applied: SI 2012/801 Art.10
s.65, enabling: SI 2012/801
s.69, enabling: SI 2012/636, SI 2012/801
s.70, see *Health and Safety Executive v Wolverhampton City Council* [2012] UKSC 34, [2012] 1 W.L.R. 2264 (SC), Lord Hope, J.S.C. (Deputy President); see *R. (on the application of Godfrey) v Southwark LBC* [2012] EWCA Civ 500, [2012] B.L.G.R. 683 (CA (Civ Div)), Pill, L.J.; see *R. (on the application of Hinds) v Blackpool BC* [2012] EWCA Civ 466, [2012] J.P.L. 1365 (CA (Civ Div)), Hughes, L.J.
s.70, applied: SI 2012/801 Art.21, Art.22, SI 2012/1914 Art.18
s.71, applied: SI 2012/801 Art.21, Art.22
s.71, enabling: SI 2012/801
s.71A, enabling: SI 2012/637
s.72, see *Avon Estates Ltd v Welsh Ministers* [2011] EWCA Civ 553, [2012] P.T.S.R. 958 (CA (Civ Div)), Rix, L.J.
s.73, applied: SI 2012/801 Art.5, SI 2012/1914 Art.18, SI 2012/2920 Sch.1 para.5, Sch.1 para.6
s.73A, applied: SI 2012/801 Art.5, SI 2012/1914 Art.18
s.74, enabling: SI 2012/636, SI 2012/801
s.77, applied: SI 2012/535 Art.4, SI 2012/801 Art.12, Art.13, Art.21, Art.29, SI 2012/3099 Art.4
s.77, enabling: SI 2012/801
s.78, applied: SI 2012/535 Art.4, SI 2012/801 Art.12, Art.21, Art.25, Art.26, Art.29, Sch.5, SI 2012/2167 Sch.1 para.3, Sch.2 para.4, SI 2012/2284 Art.35, SI 2012/2635 Art.7, SI 2012/2920 Reg.9, SI 2012/3099 Art.4
s.78, disapplied: SI 2012/2635 Art.7
s.78, enabling: SI 2012/801
s.79, applied: SI 2012/2284 Art.35, SI 2012/2635 Art.7
s.79, enabling: SI 2012/801
s.83, applied: SI 2012/801 Art.29
s.90, see *R. (on the application of Samuel Smith Old Brewery (Tadcaster)) v Secretary of State for Energy and Climate Change* [2012] EWHC 46 (Admin), [2012] 2 All E.R. 849 (QBD (Admin)), Edwards-Stuart J.
s.90, applied: SI 2012/2679 Art.39
s.96A, applied: SI 2012/2920 Reg.1, Reg.17
s.97, see *Health and Safety Executive v Wolverhampton City Council* [2012] UKSC 34, [2012] 1 W.L.R. 2264 (SC), Lord Hope, J.S.C. (Deputy President)
s.100, applied: SI 2012/535 Art.5, SI 2012/2167 Sch.1 para.4, Sch.2 para.5, SI 2012/3099 Art.5
s.104, applied: SI 2012/535 Art.5, SI 2012/2167 Sch.1 para.4, Sch.2 para.5, SI 2012/3099 Art.5
s.106, see *Bosson v Derbyshire CC* [2011] EWHC 2566 (Admin), [2012] J.P.L. 433 (QBD (Admin)), Kenneth Parker, J.; see *Keay v Morris Homes (West Midlands) Ltd* [2012] EWCA Civ 900, [2012] 1 W.L.R. 2855 (CA (Civ Div)), Laws, L.J.; see *R. (on the application of Midlands Co-operative Society Ltd) v Birmingham City Council* [2012] EWHC 620 (Admin), [2012] Eu. L.R. 640 (QBD (Admin)), Hickinbottom, J.; see *R. (on the application of Millgate Developments Ltd) v Wokingham BC* [2011] EWCA Civ 1062, [2012] 39 E.G. 120 (CA (Civ Div)), Pill, L.J.

8. Town and Country Planning Act 1990–*cont.*

s.106, applied: SI 2012/535 Art.5, SI 2012/2167 Sch.1 para.5, Sch.2 para.6, SI 2012/2421 Sch.3 para.4, SI 2012/3099 Art.5

s.106A, see *R. (on the application of Millgate Developments Ltd) v Wokingham BC* [2011] EWCA Civ 1062, [2012] 39 E.G. 120 (CA (Civ Div)), Pill, L.J.

s.107, see *Health and Safety Executive v Wolverhampton City Council* [2012] UKSC 34, [2012] 1 W.L.R. 2264 (SC), Lord Hope, J.S.C. (Deputy President)

s.107, applied: SI 2012/535 Art.5, SI 2012/2167 Sch.1 para.4, Sch.2 para.5, SI 2012/3099 Art.5

s.108, amended: SI 2012/210 Art.2

s.108, applied: SI 2012/535 Art.5, SI 2012/749 Reg.2, Reg.3, Reg.4, Reg.5, SI 2012/789 Reg.2, Reg.3, Reg.4, Reg.5, SI 2012/2167 Sch.1 para.4, Sch.2 para.5, SI 2012/2319 Reg.2, Reg.3, Reg.4, Reg.5, SI 2012/3099 Art.5

s.108, repealed (in part): SI 2012/210 Art.2

s.108, enabling: SI 2012/749, SI 2012/789, SI 2012/2319

s.115, applied: SI 2012/535 Art.5, SI 2012/2167 Sch.1 para.4, Sch.2 para.5, SI 2012/3099 Art.5

s.118, applied: SI 2012/2167 Sch.2 para.5

s.123, disapplied: SI 2012/628 Art.13

s.124, disapplied: SI 2012/628 Art.13

s.150, see *Harris v Highways Agency* [2012] UKUT 17 (LC), [2012] R.V.R. 152 (UT (Lands)), PR Francis FRICS

s.171B, see *Haq v Eastbourne BC* [2012] R.V.R. 18 (UT (Lands)), AJ Trott FRICS; see *R. (on the application of Harbige) v Secretary of State for Communities and Local Government* [2012] EWHC 1128 (Admin), [2012] J.P.L. 1245 (QBD (Admin)), Ouseley, J.

s.171B, applied: SI 2012/628 Art.13

s.172, see *R. (on the application of Harbige) v Secretary of State for Communities and Local Government* [2012] EWHC 1128 (Admin), [2012] J.P.L. 1245 (QBD (Admin)), Ouseley, J.

s.172, applied: SI 2012/628 Art.13

s.173, referred to: SI 2012/801 Art.30

s.173A, applied: SI 2012/628 Art.13

s.174, see *Kirklees MDC v Angus Heron Ltd* [2011] EWHC 2393 (Admin), [2012] J.P.L. 466 (QBD (Admin)), Langstaff, J.; see *Moore v Secretary of State for Communities and Local Government* [2012] EWCA Civ 1202, [2012] 46 E.G. 122 (CA (Civ Div)), Lord Neuberger (M.R.); see *R. (on the application of Harbige) v Secretary of State for Communities and Local Government* [2012] EWHC 1128 (Admin), [2012] J.P.L. 1245 (QBD (Admin)), Ouseley, J.

s.174, applied: SI 2012/628 Art.13, SI 2012/801 Art.29, SI 2012/2920 Reg.10, Sch.1 para.9

s.174, referred to: SI 2012/2920 Reg.10

s.175, referred to: SI 2012/801 Art.30

s.176, applied: SI 2012/2920 Reg.10

s.176, referred to: SI 2012/2920 Reg.10

s.177, see *Islam v Secretary of State for Communities and Local Government* [2012] EWHC 1314 (Admin), [2012] J.P.L. 1378 (QBD (Admin)), Charles George Q.C.

s.177, applied: SI 2012/2920 Reg.1, Reg.10, Reg.20, Sch.1 para.1, Sch.1 para.9, Sch.1 para.11

s.178, see *Egan v Basildon BC* [2011] EWHC 2416 (QB), [2012] P.T.S.R. 1117 (QBD), Edwards-Stuart J.

8. Town and Country Planning Act 1990–*cont.*

s.185, applied: SI 2012/535 Art.5, SI 2012/2167 Sch.1 para.4, Sch.2 para.5

s.186, applied: SI 2012/535 Art.5, SI 2012/2167 Sch.1 para.4

s.188, referred to: SI 2012/801 Art.30

s.188, enabling: SI 2012/636, SI 2012/801

s.191, applied: SI 2012/801 Art.28, Art.29, SI 2012/2920 Reg.1, Reg.10, Reg.11

s.192, applied: SI 2012/801 Art.28, Art.29, SI 2012/2920 Reg.1, Reg.11

s.193, applied: SI 2012/801 Art.28

s.193, enabling: SI 2012/801

s.195, applied: SI 2012/801 Art.28, SI 2012/2920 Reg.11

s.196, enabling: SI 2012/801

s.198, referred to: SI 2012/605 Reg.13

s.198, enabling: SI 2012/792

s.200, referred to: SI 2012/605 Reg.13

s.201, applied: SI 2012/605 Reg.26

s.202, applied: SI 2012/535 Art.5, SI 2012/2167 Sch.1 para.4, Sch.2 para.5

s.202A, enabling: SI 2012/605

s.202B, enabling: SI 2012/605

s.202C, enabling: SI 2012/605

s.202D, applied: SI 2012/605 Reg.17

s.202D, enabling: SI 2012/605

s.202E, enabling: SI 2012/605

s.202F, enabling: SI 2012/605

s.202G, enabling: SI 2012/605

s.203, see *John Lyon Free Grammar School Keepers and Governors v Westminster City Council* [2012] UKUT 117 (LC), [2012] R.V.R. 283 (UT (Lands)), NJ Rose, FRICS

s.203, applied: SI 2012/535 Art.5, SI 2012/2167 Sch.1 para.4, Sch.2 para.5

s.204, applied: SI 2012/535 Art.5, SI 2012/2167 Sch.1 para.4, Sch.2 para.5

s.206, applied: SI 2012/605 Reg.20, Reg.25

s.206, referred to: SI 2012/605 Reg.20

s.206, enabling: SI 2012/605

s.207, applied: SI 2012/605 Reg.18, Reg.20

s.211, applied: SI 2012/605 Reg.5

s.211, disapplied: SI 2012/605 Reg.15

s.212, enabling: SI 2012/605

s.213, applied: SI 2012/605 Reg.25

s.213, enabling: SI 2012/605

s.220, enabling: SI 2012/791, SI 2012/2372

s.221, enabling: SI 2012/2372

s.222, applied: SI 2012/801 Art.1

s.224, see *Addison Lee Ltd v Westminster City Council* [2012] EWHC 152 (Admin), [2012] J.P.L. 969 (DC), Aikens, L.J.

s.226, see *Manydown Co Ltd v Basingstoke and Deane BC* [2012] EWHC 977 (Admin), [2012] J.P.L. 1188 (QBD (Admin)), Lindblom J.; see *R. (on the application of Barnsley MBC) v Secretary of State for Communities and Local Government* [2012] EWHC 1366 (Admin), [2012] B.L.G.R. 933 (QBD (Admin)), Foskett, J.

s.227, see *Manydown Co Ltd v Basingstoke and Deane BC* [2012] EWHC 977 (Admin), [2012] J.P.L. 1188 (QBD (Admin)), Lindblom J.

s.237, see *Holliday v Breckland DC* [2012] UKUT 193 (LC), [2012] 49 E.G. 68 (UT (Lands)), George Bartlett Q.C. (President); see *R. (on the application of Telford Trustee No.1 Ltd) v Telford and Wrekin Council* [2011] EWCA Civ 896, [2012] P.T.S.R. 935 (CA (Civ Div)), Ward, L.J.

1990–cont.

8. Town and Country Planning Act 1990–*cont.*
s.263, referred to: SI 2012/2421 Sch.1 para.4
s.264, amended: SI 2012/1659 Sch.3 para.9
s.264, applied: SI 2012/416 Art.8, SI 2012/1914 Art.16, SI 2012/2284 Art.28, SI 2012/2635 Art.37, SI 2012/2679 Art.39
s.271, applied: SI 2012/1867 Art.32, Sch.6 para.1, Sch.6 para.3, Sch.8 para.4, SI 2012/1924 Art.9, Sch.2 para.1, Sch.2 para.3, SI 2012/2679 Art.35, Sch.13 para.1
s.271, disapplied: SI 2012/1924 Sch.2 para.5, SI 2012/2679 Sch.16 para.4
s.271, varied: SI 2012/1924 Sch.2 para.2
s.272, applied: SI 2012/1867 Art.32, Sch.6 para.1, Sch.6 para.3, Sch.8 para.4, SI 2012/1924 Art.9, Sch.2 para.1, Sch.2 para.3, SI 2012/2679 Art.35, Sch.13 para.1
s.272, disapplied: SI 2012/1924 Sch.2 para.5, SI 2012/2679 Sch.16 para.4
s.272, varied: SI 2012/1924 Sch.2 para.2
s.273, applied: SI 2012/1867 Sch.6 para.1, Sch.6 para.3, SI 2012/1924 Sch.2 para.1, Sch.2 para.3, SI 2012/2679 Sch.13 para.1
s.273, disapplied: SI 2012/1924 Sch.2 para.5
s.273, varied: SI 2012/1924 Sch.2 para.2
s.274, applied: SI 2012/1867 Sch.6 para.1, SI 2012/1924 Sch.2 para.1, SI 2012/2679 Sch.13 para.1
s.274, disapplied: SI 2012/1924 Sch.2 para.5
s.274, varied: SI 2012/1924 Sch.2 para.2
s.275, applied: SI 2012/1867 Sch.6 para.1, SI 2012/1924 Sch.2 para.1
s.275, disapplied: SI 2012/1924 Sch.2 para.5
s.275, varied: SI 2012/1924 Sch.2 para.2
s.276, applied: SI 2012/1867 Sch.6 para.1, SI 2012/1924 Sch.2 para.1
s.276, disapplied: SI 2012/1924 Sch.2 para.5
s.276, varied: SI 2012/1924 Sch.2 para.2
s.277, applied: SI 2012/1867 Sch.6 para.1, SI 2012/1924 Sch.2 para.1
s.277, disapplied: SI 2012/1924 Sch.2 para.5
s.277, varied: SI 2012/1924 Sch.2 para.2
s.278, applied: SI 2012/801 Art.29, SI 2012/1867 Sch.6 para.1, SI 2012/1924 Sch.2 para.1
s.278, disapplied: SI 2012/1924 Sch.2 para.5
s.278, varied: SI 2012/1924 Sch.2 para.2
s.279, applied: SI 2012/1867 Sch.6 para.1, SI 2012/1924 Sch.2 para.1
s.279, disapplied: SI 2012/1924 Sch.2 para.5
s.279, referred to: SI 2012/2679 Sch.13 para.1
s.279, varied: SI 2012/1924 Sch.2 para.2
s.280, applied: SI 2012/1867 Sch.6 para.1, SI 2012/1924 Sch.2 para.1
s.280, disapplied: SI 2012/1924 Sch.2 para.5
s.280, referred to: SI 2012/2679 Sch.13 para.1
s.280, varied: SI 2012/1924 Sch.2 para.2
s.281, applied: SI 2012/1867 Sch.6 para.1
s.282, applied: SI 2012/1867 Sch.6 para.1, SI 2012/1924 Sch.2 para.1
s.282, disapplied: SI 2012/1924 Sch.2 para.5
s.282, referred to: SI 2012/2679 Sch.13 para.1
s.282, varied: SI 2012/1924 Sch.2 para.2
s.284, see *Islam v Secretary of State for Communities and Local Government* [2012] EWHC 1314 (Admin), [2012] J.P.L. 1378 (QBD (Admin)), Charles George Q.C.
s.284, applied: SI 2012/605 Reg.8
s.287, see *Barker v Hambleton DC* [2012] EWCA Civ 610, [2012] C.P. Rep. 36 (CA (Civ Div)), Maurice Kay, L.J.; see *Hinde v Rugby BC*

1990–cont.

8. Town and Country Planning Act 1990–*cont.*
s.287–*cont.*
[2011] EWHC 3684 (Admin), [2012] J.P.L. 816 (QBD (Admin)), David Elvin Q.C.
s.288, see *Islam v Secretary of State for Communities and Local Government* [2012] EWHC 1314 (Admin), [2012] J.P.L. 1378 (QBD (Admin)), Charles George Q.C.; see *Rooney v Secretary of State for Communities and Local Government* [2011] EWCA Civ 1556, [2012] J.P.L. 684 (CA (Civ Div)), Sir Nicholas Wall (President, Fam)
s.288, applied: SI 2012/535 Art.4, SI 2012/3099 Art.4
s.288, referred to: SI 2012/801 Art.29
s.289, see *Islam v Secretary of State for Communities and Local Government* [2012] EWHC 1314 (Admin), [2012] J.P.L. 1378 (QBD (Admin)), Charles George Q.C.
s.293A, applied: SI 2012/801 Art.12, Art.15, Art.21, Art.29, Sch.4, SI 2012/2920 Reg.1, Reg.12
s.293A, enabling: SI 2012/801
s.303, enabling: SI 2012/2920
s.316, enabling: SI 2012/605
s.320, applied: SI 2012/2920 Reg.10
s.323, enabling: SI 2012/605
s.333, applied: SI 2012/2031
s.333, enabling: SI 2012/605, SI 2012/634, SI 2012/748, SI 2012/791, SI 2012/792, SI 2012/801, SI 2012/843, SI 2012/1346, SI 2012/2257, SI 2012/2318, SI 2012/2372, SI 2012/2920, SI 2012/3109
s.337, enabling: SI 2012/748
Sch.1 para.1, applied: SI 2012/2920 Sch.1 para.8
Sch.1A para.1, enabling: SI 2012/801
Sch.1A para.2, applied: SI 2012/801 Art.16
Sch.1A para.2, enabling: SI 2012/801
Sch.4A, enabling: SI 2012/801
Sch.4A para.1, enabling: SI 2012/636
Sch.4B para.1, enabling: SI 2012/637
Sch.4B para.4, enabling: SI 2012/637
Sch.4B para.5, applied: SI 2012/637 Reg.18, Reg.25
Sch.4B para.6, applied: SI 2012/637 Reg.18, Reg.25
Sch.4B para.7, applied: SI 2012/637 Reg.17, Reg.24, SI 2012/2167 Sch.1 para.9, Sch.2 para.9
Sch.4B para.7, enabling: SI 2012/637
Sch.4B para.8, applied: SI 2012/637 Reg.15, Reg.22, Sch.2 para.1, Sch.3 para.2
Sch.4B para.8, enabling: SI 2012/637
Sch.4B para.10, applied: SI 2012/637 Reg.18, Reg.25
Sch.4B para.10, enabling: SI 2012/637
Sch.4B para.11, enabling: SI 2012/637
Sch.4B para.12, applied: SI 2012/628 Art.12, SI 2012/637 Reg.18, Reg.25, SI 2012/2031 Reg.16
Sch.4B para.12, enabling: SI 2012/637
Sch.4B para.14, applied: SI 2012/2030 Reg.2
Sch.4B para.14, enabling: SI 2012/637
Sch.4B para.15, applied: SI 2012/2030 Reg.2
Sch.4B para.15, enabling: SI 2012/637, SI 2012/2030
Sch.4B para.16, applied: SI 2012/628 Art.12, SI 2012/2031
Sch.4B para.16, enabling: SI 2012/2031
Sch.4C para.3, applied: SI 2012/637 Reg.13
Sch.4C para.3, enabling: SI 2012/637
Sch.4C para.7, referred to: SI 2012/637 Reg.25, Reg.26
Sch.4C para.8, referred to: SI 2012/637 Reg.25, Reg.26
Sch.4C para.9, referred to: SI 2012/637 Reg.25, Reg.26

1990– cont.

8. **Town and Country Planning Act 1990**–*cont.*
Sch.4C para.10, applied: SI 2012/628 Art.12, SI 2012/2031 Reg.16
Sch.4C para.10, referred to: SI 2012/637 Reg.25, Reg.26
Sch.4C para.11, applied: SI 2012/637 Reg.28
Sch.4C para.11, enabling: SI 2012/637
Sch.6, applied: SI 2012/605 Reg.19, SI 2012/2920 Reg.10
Sch.7, applied: SI 2012/801 Art.29
Sch.9, applied: SI 2012/2167 Sch.2 para.5
Sch.9 para.11, applied: SI 2012/535 Art.5, SI 2012/2167 Sch.1 para.4

9. **Planning (Listed Buildings and Conservation Areas) Act 1990**
applied: SI 2012/535 Art.4, SI 2012/2167 Sch.1 para.2, Sch.2 para.3
varied: SI 2012/793 Sch.3
s.2, referred to: SI 2012/793 Reg.17
s.2, enabling: SI 2012/793
s.10, enabling: SI 2012/793, SI 2012/2275
s.11, enabling: SI 2012/793
s.12, applied: SI 2012/793 Reg.9
s.12, referred to: SI 2012/793 Reg.7
s.19, enabling: SI 2012/793
s.20, applied: SI 2012/535 Art.4, SI 2012/793 Reg.7, SI 2012/2167 Sch.1 para.3, Sch.2 para.4
s.20, enabling: SI 2012/793
s.21, applied: SI 2012/793 Reg.7
s.21, enabling: SI 2012/793
s.23, applied: SI 2012/793 Reg.14
s.25, applied: SI 2012/793 Reg.14
s.25, enabling: SI 2012/793
s.28, applied: SI 2012/535 Art.5, SI 2012/793 Reg.13, SI 2012/2167 Sch.1 para.4, Sch.2 para.5
s.28, enabling: SI 2012/793
s.29, applied: SI 2012/535 Art.5, SI 2012/793 Reg.13, SI 2012/2167 Sch.1 para.4, Sch.2 para.5
s.29, enabling: SI 2012/793
s.32, applied: SI 2012/793 Reg.13
s.32, enabling: SI 2012/793
s.42, applied: SI 2012/793 Reg.15
s.42, enabling: SI 2012/793
s.66, see *R. (on the application of Garner) v Elmbridge BC* [2011] EWCA Civ 891, [2012] J.P.L. 119 (CA (Civ Div)), Pill, L.J.
s.74, referred to: SI 2012/793 Reg.16
s.74, enabling: SI 2012/793
s.82, applied: SI 2012/793 Reg.9
s.82, enabling: SI 2012/793
s.82B, applied: SI 2012/793 Reg.7, Reg.8, Reg.11
s.82B, enabling: SI 2012/793
s.82F, enabling: SI 2012/793
s.91, enabling: SI 2012/793
s.93, enabling: SI 2012/793, SI 2012/2275

16. **Food Safety Act 1990**
applied: SI 2012/2619 Reg.27
referred to: SI 2012/2705 Reg.27
s.2, applied: SI 2012/2619 Reg.27, SI 2012/2705 Reg.27
s.2, varied: SSI 2012/318 Reg.27
s.3, varied: SI 2012/2619 Reg.27, SI 2012/2705 Reg.27, SSI 2012/318 Reg.27
s.5, applied: SI 2012/1916 Sch.17 Part 1
s.5, enabling: SI 2012/690, SI 2012/826
s.16, see *Blueshell Mussels Ltd v Foard* 2012 J.C. 62 (HCJ), Lord Eassie

1990– cont.

16. **Food Safety Act 1990**–*cont.*
s.16, enabling: SI 2012/1155, SI 2012/1198, SI 2012/1765, SI 2012/2619, SI 2012/2705, SSI 2012/119, SSI 2012/318, SSI 2012/349
s.17, see *Blueshell Mussels Ltd v Foard* 2012 J.C. 62 (HCJ), Lord Eassie
s.17, enabling: SI 2012/1155, SI 2012/1198, SI 2012/2619, SI 2012/2705, SSI 2012/119, SSI 2012/318, SSI 2012/349
s.26, enabling: SI 2012/2619, SI 2012/2705, SSI 2012/318
s.27, applied: SI 2012/1916 Reg.330, Sch.17 Part 1, Sch.17 Part 4
s.29, applied: SI 2012/2619 Reg.25, SI 2012/2705 Reg.25, SSI 2012/318 Reg.25
s.30, applied: SI 2012/2619 Reg.25, Reg.27, SI 2012/2705 Reg.25, Reg.27, SSI 2012/318 Reg.25
s.30, varied: SSI 2012/318 Reg.27
s.31, enabling: SI 2012/2619, SI 2012/2705, SSI 2012/318
s.32, see *R. (on the application of Dulai) v Chelmsford Magistrates' Court* [2012] EWHC 1055 (Admin), [2012] 3 All E.R. 764 (DC), Stanley Burnton, L.J.
s.32, applied: SI 2012/2619 Reg.27, SI 2012/2705 Reg.27
s.32, varied: SSI 2012/318 Reg.27
s.35, see *Blueshell Mussels Ltd v Foard* 2012 J.C. 62 (HCJ), Lord Eassie
s.44, varied: SI 2012/2619 Reg.27, SI 2012/2705 Reg.27, SSI 2012/318 Reg.27
s.48, applied: SI 2012/1198, SI 2012/1742, SI 2012/2619, SSI 2012/119, SSI 2012/318, SSI 2012/349
s.48, enabling: SI 2012/1155, SI 2012/1198, SI 2012/1742, SI 2012/1765, SI 2012/2619, SI 2012/2705, SSI 2012/119, SSI 2012/318
s.48A, applied: SI 2012/1155, SI 2012/1765, SI 2012/2705

19. **National Health Service and Community Care Act 1990**
s.47, see *R. (on the application of NM) v Islington LBC* [2012] EWHC 414 (Admin), [2012] P.T.S.R. 1582 (QBD (Admin)), Sales, J.; see *R. (on the application of Buckinghamshire CC) v Kingston upon Thames RLBC* [2011] EWCA Civ 457, [2012] P.T.S.R. 854 (CA (Civ Div)), Pill, L.J.
s.47, amended: 2012 c.7 Sch.5 para.59
s.47, applied: SI 2012/2996 Reg.22
s.49, amended: 2012 c.7 Sch.5 para.60
s.60, amended: 2012 c.7 Sch.5 para.61
s.61, repealed (in part): 2012 c.14 s.216
Sch.9 para.24, repealed (in part): 2012 c.7 s.39

23. **Access to Health Records Act 1990**
s.1, amended: 2012 c.7 Sch.5 para.63
s.11, amended: 2012 c.7 Sch.5 para.64, Sch.14 para.55, Sch.19 para.5

27. **Social Security Act 1990**
s.15, enabling: SI 2012/2140, SSI 2012/34

29. **Finance Act 1990**
s.41, repealed: 2012 c.14 Sch.16 para.247
s.42, repealed: 2012 c.14 Sch.16 para.247
s.45, repealed (in part): 2012 c.14 Sch.16 para.247
s.48, repealed: 2012 c.14 Sch.16 para.247
s.49, repealed (in part): 2012 c.14 Sch.18 para.23
s.50, repealed: 2012 c.14 Sch.18 para.23
s.126, repealed: 2012 c.14 Sch.39 para.19
s.128, applied: SI 2012/1271
Sch.6 para.1, repealed: 2012 c.14 Sch.16 para.247

1990– cont.

29. Finance Act 1990–*cont.*
Sch.6 para.4, repealed: 2012 c.14 Sch.16 para.247
Sch.6 para.8, repealed: 2012 c.14 Sch.16 para.247
Sch.6 para.12, applied: 2012 c.14 s.121
Sch.7 para.1, repealed: 2012 c.14 Sch.16 para.247
Sch.7 para.2, repealed: 2012 c.14 Sch.16 para.247
Sch.7 para.3, repealed: 2012 c.14 Sch.16 para.247
Sch.7 para.4, repealed: 2012 c.14 Sch.16 para.247
Sch.7 para.5, repealed: 2012 c.14 Sch.16 para.247
Sch.7 para.6, repealed: 2012 c.14 Sch.16 para.247
Sch.7 para.7, repealed: 2012 c.14 Sch.16 para.247
Sch.7 para.8, repealed: 2012 c.14 Sch.16 para.247
Sch.7 para.9, repealed: 2012 c.14 Sch.16 para.247
Sch.7 para.10, repealed: 2012 c.14 Sch.16 para.247
Sch.9 para.4, repealed: 2012 c.14 Sch.16 para.247
Sch.9 para.6, repealed: 2012 c.14 Sch.18 para.23
Sch.9 para.7, repealed: 2012 c.14 Sch.16 para.247

35. Enterprise and New Towns (Scotland) Act 1990
s.2, applied: SI 2012/2885 Sch.1 para.8, Sch.2 para.5, SI 2012/2886 Sch.1, SI 2012/3144 Sch.1 para.3, SI 2012/3145 Sch.1, SSI 2012/303 Reg.67, Sch.1 para.8, Sch.1 para.10, Sch.4 para.17, Sch.5 para.39, SSI 2012/319 Reg.48, Sch.1 para.6
s.2, referred to: SI 2012/2886 Sch.1, SSI 2012/303 Sch.4 para.17
s.25, referred to: 2012 asp 2 Sch.3
s.26, referred to: 2012 asp 2 Sch.3
s.35, applied: SSI 2012/162 Sch.1

37. Human Fertilisation and Embryology Act 1990
Sch.1 para.4A, amended: SI 2012/2404 Sch.2 para.26

40. Law Reform (Miscellaneous Provisions) (Scotland) Act 1990
applied: SI 2012/1128 Art.4, SSI 2012/213 Sch.1
s.7, applied: SI 2012/922 Reg.3, SI 2012/1290 Reg.3, SI 2012/1631 Sch.5 para.10, SI 2012/1640 Sch.2 para.6, SI 2012/2996 Sch.5 para.10

41. Courts and Legal Services Act 1990
applied: SI 2012/1128 Art.4
s.31B, amended: 2012 c.10 Sch.5 para.39
s.58, amended: 2012 c.10 s.44
s.58A, amended: 2012 c.10 s.44
s.58AA, amended: 2012 c.10 s.45
s.58AA, repealed (in part): 2012 c.10 s.45
s.58C, added: 2012 c.10 s.46
s.120, amended: 2012 c.10 s.44, s.45
Sch.18 para.25, repealed (in part): SI 2012/2398 Sch.2 para.2
Sch.18 para.36, repealed (in part): SI 2012/2398 Sch.1 para.7

42. Broadcasting Act 1990
applied: SI 2012/1128 Art.4
referred to: 2012 c.19 Sch.6 para.4, SI 2012/1917 Art.53
Part I, applied: SI 2012/1917 Art.34, Sch.7 para.8
Part III, applied: SI 2012/1917 Art.34, Sch.7 para.8
s.86, varied: SI 2012/2690 Sch.1 para.2
s.104, varied: SI 2012/2690 Sch.1 para.3
s.104B, disapplied: SI 2012/2690 Sch.1 para.4
s.105, varied: SI 2012/2690 Sch.1 para.5
s.106, varied: SI 2012/2690 Sch.1 para.6
s.106ZA, varied: SI 2012/2690 Sch.1 para.7
s.126, varied: SI 2012/2690 Sch.1 para.8
s.183, amended: 2012 c.11 s.17
s.183, repealed (in part): 2012 c.11 s.17
s.183A, amended: 2012 c.11 s.17
Sch.2, applied: SI 2012/2690 Art.2

1990– cont.

42. Broadcasting Act 1990–*cont.*
Sch.2 Part II para.1, disapplied: SI 2012/2690 Sch.1 para.9
Sch.2 Part II para.1, varied: SI 2012/2690 Art.5
Sch.2 Part II para.2, varied: SI 2012/2690 Art.5
Sch.2 Part II para.3, disapplied: SI 2012/2690 Sch.1 para.9
Sch.2 Part II para.3, varied: SI 2012/2690 Art.5
Sch.2 Part II para.4, varied: SI 2012/2690 Art.5, Sch.1 para.9
Sch.2 Part II para.5, varied: SI 2012/2690 Art.5
Sch.2 Part II para.5A, varied: SI 2012/2690 Art.5
Sch.2 Part II para.6, varied: SI 2012/2690 Art.5
Sch.19 para.12, amended: 2012 c.11 s.17
Sch.19 para.12, repealed (in part): 2012 c.11 s.17

43. Environmental Protection Act 1990
Commencement Orders: SI 2012/898 Art.2
applied: SSI 2012/360 Reg.65
Part II, applied: SI 2012/811 Reg.3, Sch.1 para.2, Sch.1 para.3
s.6, amended: SSI 2012/360 Sch.11 para.1
s.6, applied: SSI 2012/360 Sch.9 para.1, Sch.10 para.8
s.20, applied: SSI 2012/360 Reg.65, Sch.9 para.1
s.21, applied: SSI 2012/360 Reg.65
s.29, amended: SSI 2012/148 Reg.2
s.29, varied: SI 2012/811 Reg.5
s.30, varied: SI 2012/811 Reg.5
s.31, varied: SI 2012/811 Reg.5
s.32, varied: SI 2012/811 Reg.5
s.33, see *Mountpace Ltd v Haringey LBC* [2012] EWHC 698 (Admin), [2012] Env. L.R. 32 (DC), Stanley Burnton, L.J.; see *R. v W* [2010] EWCA Crim 927, [2012] P.T.S.R. 617 (CA (Crim Div)), Hughes, L.J.
s.33, varied: SI 2012/811 Reg.5
s.33A, varied: SI 2012/811 Reg.5
s.33B, varied: SI 2012/811 Reg.5
s.33C, varied: SI 2012/811 Reg.5
s.34, see *Mountpace Ltd v Haringey LBC* [2012] EWHC 698 (Admin), [2012] Env. L.R. 32 (DC), Stanley Burnton, L.J.
s.34, amended: SSI 2012/148 Reg.2, SSI 2012/360 Sch.11 para.1
s.34, applied: SI 2012/811 Reg.3, Sch.1 para.3
s.34, varied: SI 2012/811 Reg.5
s.34A, varied: SI 2012/811 Reg.5
s.34B, varied: SI 2012/811 Reg.5
s.34C, varied: SI 2012/811 Reg.5
s.34D, varied: SI 2012/811 Reg.5
s.35, amended: SSI 2012/360 Sch.11 para.1
s.35, varied: SI 2012/811 Reg.5
s.35A, varied: SI 2012/811 Reg.5
s.36, varied: SI 2012/811 Reg.5
s.36A, varied: SI 2012/811 Reg.5
s.37, varied: SI 2012/811 Reg.5
s.37A, varied: SI 2012/811 Reg.5
s.38, varied: SI 2012/811 Reg.5
s.39, varied: SI 2012/811 Reg.5
s.40, varied: SI 2012/811 Reg.5
s.40A, varied: SI 2012/811 Reg.5
s.41, varied: SI 2012/811 Reg.5
s.42, varied: SI 2012/811 Reg.5
s.43, varied: SI 2012/811 Reg.5
s.44, varied: SI 2012/811 Reg.5
s.44A, varied: SI 2012/811 Reg.5
s.44B, varied: SI 2012/811 Reg.5
s.44ZA, varied: SI 2012/811 Reg.5

1990– cont.

43. Environmental Protection Act 1990–*cont.*
s.44ZB, varied: SI 2012/811 Reg.5
s.44ZC, varied: SI 2012/811 Reg.5
s.44ZD, varied: SI 2012/811 Reg.5
s.45, amended: SSI 2012/148 Reg.2
s.45, applied: SI 2012/811 Reg.4A, Sch.1 para.4
s.45, varied: SI 2012/811 Reg.5
s.45, enabling: SI 2012/811
s.45A, varied: SI 2012/811 Reg.5
s.45B, varied: SI 2012/811 Reg.5
s.45C, added: SSI 2012/148 Reg.2
s.45C, varied: SI 2012/811 Reg.5
s.46, amended: SSI 2012/148 Reg.2
s.46, applied: SI 2012/811 Sch.1 para.4
s.46, varied: SI 2012/811 Reg.5
s.47, varied: SI 2012/811 Reg.5
s.47A, varied: SI 2012/811 Reg.5
s.47ZA, varied: SI 2012/811 Reg.5
s.47ZB, amended: SI 2012/1150 Art.2
s.47ZB, varied: SI 2012/811 Reg.5
s.47ZB, enabling: SI 2012/1150, SI 2012/1151
s.48, varied: SI 2012/811 Reg.5
s.49, varied: SI 2012/811 Reg.5
s.50, varied: SI 2012/811 Reg.5
s.51, varied: SI 2012/811 Reg.5
s.52, applied: SI 2012/811 Sch.1 para.4
s.52, varied: SI 2012/811 Reg.5
s.52A, varied: SI 2012/811 Reg.5
s.53, varied: SI 2012/811 Reg.5
s.54, varied: SI 2012/811 Reg.5
s.55, varied: SI 2012/811 Reg.5
s.56, varied: SI 2012/811 Reg.5
s.57, varied: SI 2012/811 Reg.5
s.58, varied: SI 2012/811 Reg.5
s.59, varied: SI 2012/811 Reg.5
s.59A, varied: SI 2012/811 Reg.5
s.59ZA, varied: SI 2012/811 Reg.5
s.60, varied: SI 2012/811 Reg.5
s.60A, varied: SI 2012/811 Reg.5
s.61, varied: SI 2012/811 Reg.5
s.62, varied: SI 2012/811 Reg.5
s.62A, varied: SI 2012/811 Reg.5
s.63, varied: SI 2012/811 Reg.5
s.63A, varied: SI 2012/811 Reg.5
s.64, varied: SI 2012/811 Reg.5
s.65, varied: SI 2012/811 Reg.5
s.66, varied: SI 2012/811 Reg.5
s.67, varied: SI 2012/811 Reg.5
s.68, varied: SI 2012/811 Reg.5
s.69, varied: SI 2012/811 Reg.5
s.70, varied: SI 2012/811 Reg.5
s.71, varied: SI 2012/811 Reg.5
s.72, varied: SI 2012/811 Reg.5
s.73, varied: SI 2012/811 Reg.5
s.73A, varied: SI 2012/811 Reg.5
s.74, varied: SI 2012/811 Reg.5
s.75, amended: SSI 2012/148 Reg.2
s.75, applied: SI 2012/811 Sch.1 para.4
s.75, referred to: SI 2012/811 Sch.1 para.2
s.75, varied: SI 2012/811 Reg.5
s.75, enabling: SI 2012/811, SI 2012/2320
s.76, varied: SI 2012/811 Reg.5
s.77, varied: SI 2012/811 Reg.5
s.78, varied: SI 2012/811 Reg.5
s.78C, enabling: SI 2012/263, SI 2012/283
s.78G, enabling: SI 2012/263, SI 2012/283
s.78L, enabling: SI 2012/263, SI 2012/283
s.78YB, amended: SSI 2012/360 Sch.11 para.1

1990– cont.

43. Environmental Protection Act 1990–*cont.*
s.79, see *R. (on the application of Fullers Farming Ltd) v Milton Keynes Council* [2011] EWHC 3784 (Admin), [2012] Env. L.R. 17 (QBD (Admin)), Wyn Williams, J.; see *R. (on the application of Khan) v Isleworth Crown Court* [2011] EWHC 3164 (Admin), (2012) 176 J.P. 6 (DC), Laws, L.J.
s.79, applied: SI 2012/416 Art.16, SI 2012/1867 Art.52, SI 2012/2284 Art.29, SI 2012/2635 Art.38, SI 2012/2679 Art.38
s.79, referred to: SI 2012/472 Art.3
s.80, see *R. (on the application of Elvington Park Ltd) v York Crown Court* [2011] EWHC 2213 (Admin), [2012] Env. L.R. 10 (QBD (Admin)), Judge Langan Q.C.; see *R. (on the application of Khan) v Isleworth Crown Court* [2011] EWHC 3164 (Admin), (2012) 176 J.P. 6 (DC), Laws, L.J.
s.82, see *R. (on the application of Desouza) v Croydon Magistrates' Court* [2012] EWHC 1362 (Admin), (2012) 176 J.P. 624 (QBD (Admin)), Mitting, J.
s.82, applied: SI 2012/416 Art.16, SI 2012/472 Art.3, SI 2012/1867 Art.52, SI 2012/2284 Art.29, SI 2012/2635 Art.38, SI 2012/2679 Art.38
s.89, applied: SI 2012/811 Sch.1 para.3, Sch.1 para.4
s.92, applied: SI 2012/811 Sch.1 para.3
s.92C, applied: SI 2012/811 Sch.1 para.3
s.93, applied: SI 2012/811 Sch.1 para.3
s.96, enabling: SI 2012/811
s.140, amended: SI 2012/1923 Sch.1
s.140, repealed (in part): SI 2012/1923 Sch.1
s.142, amended: SI 2012/1916 Sch.34 para.41
s.142, repealed (in part): SI 2012/1923 Sch.1
s.164, enabling: SI 2012/898
Sch.6 para.6, amended: SI 2012/2404 Sch.2 para.27
Sch.12 para.1, repealed: SI 2012/1923 Sch.1
Sch.12 para.2, repealed: SI 2012/1923 Sch.1
Sch.12 para.3, repealed: SI 2012/1923 Sch.1
Sch.12 para.4, repealed: SI 2012/1923 Sch.1
Sch.12 para.5, repealed: SI 2012/1923 Sch.1

1991

22. New Roads and Street Works Act 1991
applied: SI 2012/1284 Sch.1, SI 2012/1286 Sch.1, SI 2012/1289 Sch.1, SI 2012/1294 Sch.1, SI 2012/2541 Sch.1, SI 2012/2547 Sch.1, SI 2012/2548 Sch.1, SI 2012/2549 Sch.1, SI 2012/2635 Art.14, SI 2012/3102 Sch.1, SI 2012/3103 Sch.1, SI 2012/3104 Sch.1, SI 2012/3105 Sch.1, SI 2012/3106 Sch.1, SI 2012/3107 Sch.1
referred to: SI 2012/2541 Sch.1, SI 2012/2547 Sch.1, SI 2012/2548 Sch.1, SI 2012/2549 Sch.1, SI 2012/2679 Art.4, SI 2012/3102 Sch.1, SI 2012/3103 Sch.1, SI 2012/3104 Sch.1, SI 2012/3105 Sch.1, SI 2012/3106 Sch.1, SI 2012/3107 Sch.1
Part III, applied: SI 2012/1867 Art.7, Sch.6 para.5, SI 2012/1924 Sch.2 para.5, SI 2012/2284 Sch.7 para.3, Sch.7 para.14, SI 2012/2635 Art.12, Art.14, Art.33, Art.34, Sch.12 para.3, Sch.12 para.14, SI 2012/2679 Art.4, Sch.13 para.1, Sch.13 para.2, Sch.13 para.3, Sch.14 para.3
s.28, applied: SI 2012/2635 Art.29
s.50, applied: SI 2012/1282 Sch.1, SI 2012/1284 Sch.1, SI 2012/1286 Sch.1, SI 2012/1289 Sch.1, SI 2012/1294 Sch.1, SI 2012/1295 Sch.1, SI 2012/2541 Sch.1, SI 2012/2547 Sch.1, SI 2012/2548 Sch.1, SI 2012/2549 Sch.1, SI 2012/3102 Sch.1, SI

1991–cont.

22. New Roads and Street Works Act 1991–*cont.*
s.50, applied:–*cont.*

2012/3103 Sch.l, SI 2012/3104 Sch.l, SI 2012/3105 Sch.l, SI 2012/3106 Sch.l, SI 2012/3107 Sch.1

s.52, applied: SI 2012/1284 Sch.l, SI 2012/1286 Sch.l, SI 2012/1289 Sch.l, SI 2012/3102 Sch.l, SI 2012/3103 Sch.l, SI 2012/3104 Sch.l, SI 2012/3105 Sch.l, SI 2012/3106 Sch.l, SI 2012/3107 Sch.1

s.52, referred to: SI 2012/1282 Sch.l, SI 2012/1294 Sch.l, SI 2012/1295 Sch.l, SI 2012/2541 Sch.l, SI 2012/2547 Sch.l, SI 2012/2548 Sch.l, SI 2012/2549 Sch.l, SI 2012/3102 Sch.l, SI 2012/3103 Sch.l, SI 2012/3104 Sch.l, SI 2012/3105 Sch.l, SI 2012/3106 Sch.l, SI 2012/3107 Sch.1

s.53, applied: SI 2012/1282 Sch.l, SI 2012/1284 Sch.l, SI 2012/1286 Sch.l, SI 2012/1289 Sch.l, SI 2012/1294 Sch.l, SI 2012/1295 Sch.l, SI 2012/2541 Sch.l, SI 2012/2547 Sch.l, SI 2012/2548 Sch.l, SI 2012/2549 Sch.l, SI 2012/3102 Sch.l, SI 2012/3103 Sch.l, SI 2012/3104 Sch.l, SI 2012/3105 Sch.l, SI 2012/3106 Sch.l, SI 2012/3107 Sch.l

s.53, disapplied: SI 2012/1282 Sch.l, SI 2012/1294 Sch.l, SI 2012/1295 Sch.l, SI 2012/2541 Sch.l, SI 2012/2547 Sch.l, SI 2012/2548 Sch.l, SI 2012/2549 Sch.l, SI 2012/3102 Sch.l, SI 2012/3103 Sch.l, SI 2012/3104 Sch.l, SI 2012/3105 Sch.l, SI 2012/3106 Sch.l, SI 2012/3107 Sch.l

s.53, referred to: SI 2012/1286 Sch.l, SI 2012/1289 Sch.l

s.53A, disapplied: SI 2012/1294 Sch.l

s.54, applied: SI 2012/1282 Sch.l, SI 2012/1284 Sch.l, SI 2012/1286 Sch.l, SI 2012/1294 Sch.l, SI 2012/1295 Sch.l, SI 2012/2284 Art.10, SI 2012/2541 Sch.l, SI 2012/2547 Sch.l, SI 2012/2548 Sch.l, SI 2012/2549 Sch.l, SI 2012/2635 Art.14, SI 2012/2679 Art.4, SI 2012/3102 Sch.l, SI 2012/3103 Sch.l, SI 2012/3104 Sch.l, SI 2012/3105 Sch.l, SI 2012/3106 Sch.l, SI 2012/3107 Sch.1

s.54, disapplied: SI 2012/1282 Sch.l, SI 2012/1294 Sch.l, SI 2012/1295 Sch.l, SI 2012/2541 Sch.l, SI 2012/2547 Sch.l, SI 2012/2549 Sch.l, SI 2012/3102 Sch.l, SI 2012/3103 Sch.l, SI 2012/3104 Sch.l, SI 2012/3105 Sch.l, SI 2012/3106 Sch.l, SI 2012/3107 Sch.l

s.54, referred to: SI 2012/1286 Sch.l, SI 2012/1289 Sch.l, SI 2012/2541 Sch.l, SI 2012/2547 Sch.l, SI 2012/2548 Sch.l, SI 2012/2549 Sch.l, SI 2012/2679 Art.4

s.54, varied: SI 2012/2284 Art.10, SI 2012/2635 Art.14

s.55, applied: SI 2012/1282 Sch.l, SI 2012/1284 Sch.l, SI 2012/1289 Sch.l, SI 2012/1294 Sch.l, SI 2012/1295 Sch.l, SI 2012/2284 Art.10, SI 2012/2635 Art.14, SI 2012/2679 Art.4, SI 2012/3102 Sch.l, SI 2012/3103 Sch.l, SI 2012/3104 Sch.l, SI 2012/3105 Sch.l, SI 2012/3106 Sch.l, SI 2012/3107 Sch.l

s.55, disapplied: SI 2012/1282 Sch.l, SI 2012/1294 Sch.l, SI 2012/1295 Sch.l, SI 2012/2541 Sch.l, SI 2012/2547 Sch.l, SI 2012/2549 Sch.l, SI 2012/3102 Sch.l, SI 2012/3103 Sch.l, SI 2012/3104 Sch.l, SI 2012/3105 Sch.l, SI 2012/3106 Sch.l, SI 2012/3107 Sch.l

s.55, referred to: SI 2012/1286 Sch.l, SI 2012/1289 Sch.l, SI 2012/2541 Sch.l, SI 2012/2547 Sch.l, SI 2012/2548 Sch.l, SI 2012/2549 Sch.l, SI 2012/2679 Art.4

s.55, varied: SI 2012/2284 Art.10, SI 2012/2635 Art.14

1991–cont.

22. New Roads and Street Works Act 1991–*cont.*
s.56, disapplied: SI 2012/1282 Sch.l, SI 2012/1294 Sch.l, SI 2012/1295 Sch.l, SI 2012/2541 Sch.l, SI 2012/2547 Sch.l, SI 2012/2548 Sch.l, SI 2012/2549 Sch.l, SI 2012/3102 Sch.l, SI 2012/3103 Sch.l, SI 2012/3104 Sch.l, SI 2012/3105 Sch.l, SI 2012/3106 Sch.l, SI 2012/3107 Sch.l

s.56, referred to: SI 2012/1284 Sch.l, SI 2012/1286 Sch.l, SI 2012/1289 Sch.l

s.56A, applied: SI 2012/1282 Sch.l, SI 2012/1284 Sch.l, SI 2012/1286 Sch.l, SI 2012/1289 Sch.l, SI 2012/1294 Sch.l, SI 2012/1295 Sch.l, SI 2012/2541 Sch.l, SI 2012/2547 Sch.l, SI 2012/2548 Sch.l, SI 2012/2549 Sch.l, SI 2012/3102 Sch.l

s.56A, disapplied: SI 2012/1294 Sch.l

s.56A, referred to: SI 2012/3103 Sch.l, SI 2012/3104 Sch.l, SI 2012/3105 Sch.l, SI 2012/3106 Sch.l, SI 2012/3107 Sch.l

s.57, applied: SI 2012/1282 Sch.l, SI 2012/1284 Sch.l, SI 2012/1286 Sch.l, SI 2012/1289 Sch.l, SI 2012/1294 Sch.l, SI 2012/1295 Sch.l, SI 2012/2284 Art.10, SI 2012/2635 Art.14, SI 2012/2679 Art.4, SI 2012/3102 Sch.l, SI 2012/3103 Sch.l, SI 2012/3104 Sch.l, SI 2012/3105 Sch.l, SI 2012/3106 Sch.l, SI 2012/3107 Sch.l

s.57, disapplied: SI 2012/1282 Sch.l, SI 2012/1294 Sch.l, SI 2012/1295 Sch.l, SI 2012/2541 Sch.l, SI 2012/2547 Sch.l, SI 2012/2548 Sch.l, SI 2012/2549 Sch.l, SI 2012/3102 Sch.l, SI 2012/3104 Sch.l, SI 2012/3105 Sch.l, SI 2012/3106 Sch.l, SI 2012/3107 Sch.l

s.57, referred to: SI 2012/1289 Sch.l

s.57, varied: SI 2012/2284 Art.10, SI 2012/2679 Art.4

s.58, applied: SI 2012/1282 Sch.l, SI 2012/1284 Sch.l, SI 2012/1289 Sch.l, SI 2012/1294 Sch.l, SI 2012/1295 Sch.l, SI 2012/2541 Sch.l, SI 2012/2547 Sch.l, SI 2012/2548 Sch.l, SI 2012/2549 Sch.l, SI 2012/3102 Sch.l, SI 2012/3103 Sch.l, SI 2012/3104 Sch.l, SI 2012/3105 Sch.l, SI 2012/3106 Sch.l, SI 2012/3107 Sch.l

s.58, referred to: SI 2012/1286 Sch.l, SI 2012/1289 Sch.l, SI 2012/2541 Sch.l, SI 2012/2547 Sch.l, SI 2012/2548 Sch.l, SI 2012/2549 Sch.l

s.58, varied: SI 2012/1282 Sch.l, SI 2012/1294 Sch.l, SI 2012/1295 Sch.l, SI 2012/2541 Sch.l, SI 2012/2547 Sch.l, SI 2012/2548 Sch.l, SI 2012/2549 Sch.l, SI 2012/3102 Sch.l, SI 2012/3103 Sch.l, SI 2012/3104 Sch.l, SI 2012/3105 Sch.l, SI 2012/3106 Sch.l, SI 2012/3107 Sch.l

s.58A, applied: SI 2012/1282 Sch.l, SI 2012/1284 Sch.l, SI 2012/1286 Sch.l, SI 2012/1289 Sch.l, SI 2012/1294 Sch.l, SI 2012/1295 Sch.l, SI 2012/2541 Sch.l, SI 2012/2547 Sch.l, SI 2012/2548 Sch.l, SI 2012/2549 Sch.l, SI 2012/3102 Sch.l, SI 2012/3103 Sch.l, SI 2012/3104 Sch.l, SI 2012/3105 Sch.l, SI 2012/3106 Sch.l, SI 2012/3107 Sch.l

s.58A, referred to: SI 2012/1289 Sch.l, SI 2012/2541 Sch.l, SI 2012/2547 Sch.l, SI 2012/2548 Sch.l, SI 2012/2549 Sch.l

s.58A, varied: SI 2012/1282 Sch.l, SI 2012/1294 Sch.l, SI 2012/1295 Sch.l, SI 2012/2541 Sch.l, SI 2012/2547 Sch.l, SI 2012/2548 Sch.l, SI 2012/2549 Sch.l, SI 2012/3102 Sch.l, SI 2012/3103 Sch.l, SI 2012/3104 Sch.l, SI 2012/3105 Sch.l, SI 2012/3106 Sch.l, SI 2012/3107 Sch.l

s.59, applied: SI 2012/2284 Art.10, SI 2012/2635 Art.14, SI 2012/2679 Art.4, SI 2012/3102 Sch.l, SI 2012/3103 Sch.l, SI 2012/3104 Sch.l, SI 2012/3105 Sch.l, SI 2012/3106 Sch.l, SI 2012/3107 Sch.l

22. New Roads and Street Works Act 1991– *cont.*

s.59, referred to: SI 2012/ 2541 Sch.l, SI 2012/ 2547 Sch.l, SI 2012/ 2548 Sch.l, SI 2012/ 2549 Sch.l, SI 2012/ 3102 Sch.l, SI 2012/ 3103 Sch.l, SI 2012/ 3104 Sch.l, SI 2012/ 3105 Sch.l, SI 2012/ 3106 Sch.l, SI 2012/ 3107 Sch.l

s.60, applied: SI 2012/ 2284 Art.10, SI 2012/ 2541 Sch.l, SI 2012/ 2547 Sch.l, SI 2012/ 2548 Sch.l, SI 2012/ 2549 Sch.l, SI 2012/ 2635 Art.14, SI 2012/ 2679 Art.4, SI 2012/ 3102 Sch.l, SI 2012/ 3103 Sch.l, SI 2012/ 3104 Sch.l, SI 2012/ 3105 Sch.l, SI 2012/ 3106 Sch.l, SI 2012/ 3107 Sch.l

s.61, applied: SI 2012/ 1282 Sch.l, SI 2012/ 1284 Sch.l, SI 2012/ 1286 Sch.l, SI 2012/ 1289 Sch.l, SI 2012/ 1294 Sch.l, SI 2012/ 1295 Sch.l, SI 2012/ 2541 Sch.l, SI 2012/ 2547 Sch.l, SI 2012/ 2548 Sch.l, SI 2012/ 2549 Sch.l

s.61, referred to: SI 2012/ 1282 Sch.l, SI 2012/ 1295 Sch.l, SI 2012/ 3102 Sch.l, SI 2012/ 3103 Sch.l, SI 2012/ 3104 Sch.l, SI 2012/ 3105 Sch.l, SI 2012/ 3106 Sch.l, SI 2012/ 3107 Sch.l

s.62, applied: SI 2012/ 1284 Sch.l, SI 2012/ 1286 Sch.l, SI 2012/ 1289 Sch.l, SI 2012/ 1294 Sch.l, SI 2012/ 2541 Sch.l, SI 2012/ 2547 Sch.l, SI 2012/ 2548 Sch.l, SI 2012/ 2549 Sch.l

s.62, referred to: SI 2012/ 1295 Sch.l, SI 2012/ 3102 Sch.l, SI 2012/ 3103 Sch.l, SI 2012/ 3104 Sch.l, SI 2012/ 3105 Sch.l, SI 2012/ 3106 Sch.l, SI 2012/ 3107 Sch.l

s.63, applied: SI 2012/ 1282 Sch.l, SI 2012/ 1284 Sch.l, SI 2012/ 1286 Sch.l, SI 2012/ 1289 Sch.l, SI 2012/ 1294 Sch.l, SI 2012/ 1295 Sch.l

s.64, applied: SI 2012/ 1282 Sch.l, SI 2012/ 1284 Sch.l, SI 2012/ 1286 Sch.l, SI 2012/ 1289 Sch.l, SI 2012/ 1294 Sch.l, SI 2012/ 1295 Sch.l

s.64, referred to: SI 2012/ 1286 Sch.l

s.64, varied: SI 2012/ 1282 Sch.l, SI 2012/ 1294 Sch.l, SI 2012/ 1295 Sch.l, SI 2012/ 2541 Sch.l, SI 2012/ 2547 Sch.l, SI 2012/ 2548 Sch.l, SI 2012/ 2549 Sch.l, SI 2012/ 3102 Sch.l, SI 2012/ 3103 Sch.l, SI 2012/ 3104 Sch.l, SI 2012/ 3105 Sch.l, SI 2012/ 3106 Sch.l, SI 2012/ 3107 Sch.l

s.65, applied: SI 2012/ 1282 Sch.l, SI 2012/ 1284 Sch.l, SI 2012/ 1286 Sch.l, SI 2012/ 1289 Sch.l, SI 2012/ 1294 Sch.l, SI 2012/ 1295 Sch.l

s.66, applied: SI 2012/ 1282 Sch.l, SI 2012/ 1284 Sch.l, SI 2012/ 1289 Sch.l, SI 2012/ 1294 Sch.l, SI 2012/ 1295 Sch.l, SI 2012/ 3102 Sch.l, SI 2012/ 3103 Sch.l, SI 2012/ 3104 Sch.l, SI 2012/ 3105 Sch.l, SI 2012/ 3106 Sch.l, SI 2012/ 3107 Sch.l

s.66, disapplied: SI 2012/ 1282 Sch.l, SI 2012/ 1294 Sch.l, SI 2012/ 1295 Sch.l, SI 2012/ 2541 Sch.l, SI 2012/ 2547 Sch.l, SI 2012/ 2548 Sch.l, SI 2012/ 2549 Sch.l, SI 2012/ 3102 Sch.l, SI 2012/ 3103 Sch.l, SI 2012/ 3104 Sch.l, SI 2012/ 3105 Sch.l, SI 2012/ 3106 Sch.l

s.66, referred to: SI 2012/ 1284 Sch.l, SI 2012/ 1286 Sch.l, SI 2012/ 1289 Sch.l

s.68, applied: SI 2012/ 2284 Art.10, SI 2012/ 2635 Art.14, SI 2012/ 2679 Art.4

s.69, applied: SI 2012/ 1286 Sch.l, SI 2012/ 1295 Sch.l, SI 2012/ 2284 Art.10, SI 2012/ 2541 Sch.l, SI 2012/ 2547 Sch.l, SI 2012/ 2548 Sch.l, SI 2012/ 2549 Sch.l, SI 2012/ 2635 Art.14, SI 2012/ 2679 Art.4, SI 2012/ 3102 Sch.l, SI 2012/ 3103 Sch.l, SI 2012/ 3104 Sch.l, SI 2012/ 3105 Sch.l, SI 2012/ 3106 Sch.l, SI 2012/ 3107 Sch.l

s.69, referred to: SI 2012/ 1284 Sch.l, SI 2012/ 1286 Sch.l, SI 2012/ 1289 Sch.l

22. New Roads and Street Works Act 1991– *cont.*

s.69, varied: SI 2012/ 1282 Sch.l, SI 2012/ 1294 Sch.l, SI 2012/ 1295 Sch.l, SI 2012/ 2541 Sch.l, SI 2012/ 2547 Sch.l, SI 2012/ 2548 Sch.l, SI 2012/ 2549 Sch.l, SI 2012/ 3102 Sch.l, SI 2012/ 3103 Sch.l, SI 2012/ 3104 Sch.l, SI 2012/ 3105 Sch.l, SI 2012/ 3106 Sch.l, SI 2012/ 3107 Sch.l

s.70, applied: SI 2012/ 1282 Sch.l, SI 2012/ 1284 Sch.l, SI 2012/ 1286 Sch.l, SI 2012/ 1289 Sch.l, SI 2012/ 1294 Sch.l, SI 2012/ 1295 Sch.l, SI 2012/ 2541 Sch.l, SI 2012/ 2547 Sch.l, SI 2012/ 2548 Sch.l, SI 2012/ 2549 Sch.l, SI 2012/ 3102 Sch.l, SI 2012/ 3103 Sch.l, SI 2012/ 3104 Sch.l, SI 2012/ 3105 Sch.l, SI 2012/ 3106 Sch.l, SI 2012/ 3107 Sch.l

s.72, applied: SI 2012/ 1284 Sch.l, SI 2012/ 1286 Sch.l, SI 2012/ 1289 Sch.l, SI 2012/ 1294 Sch.l

s.74, applied: SI 2012/ 1282 Sch.l, SI 2012/ 1284 Sch.l, SI 2012/ 1286 Sch.l, SI 2012/ 1289 Sch.l, SI 2012/ 1294 Sch.l, SI 2012/ 1295 Sch.l, SI 2012/ 2541 Sch.l, SI 2012/ 2547 Sch.l, SI 2012/ 2548 Sch.l, SI 2012/ 2549 Sch.l, SI 2012/ 3102 Sch.l, SI 2012/ 3103 Sch.l, SI 2012/ 3104 Sch.l, SI 2012/ 3105 Sch.l, SI 2012/ 3106 Sch.l, SI 2012/ 3107 Sch.l

s.74, referred to: SI 2012/ 1282 Sch.l, SI 2012/ 1289 Sch.l, SI 2012/ 1295 Sch.l, SI 2012/ 3102 Sch.l, SI 2012/ 3103 Sch.l, SI 2012/ 3104 Sch.l, SI 2012/ 3105 Sch.l, SI 2012/ 3106 Sch.l, SI 2012/ 3107 Sch.l

s.74, varied: SI 2012/ 1282 Sch.l, SI 2012/ 1294 Sch.l, SI 2012/ 1295 Sch.l, SI 2012/ 2541 Sch.l, SI 2012/ 2547 Sch.l, SI 2012/ 2548 Sch.l, SI 2012/ 2549 Sch.l, SI 2012/ 3102 Sch.l, SI 2012/ 3103 Sch.l, SI 2012/ 3104 Sch.l, SI 2012/ 3105 Sch.l, SI 2012/ 3106 Sch.l, SI 2012/ 3107 Sch.l

s.74, enabling: SI 2012/ 2272

s.74A, applied: SI 2012/ 1284 Sch.l, SI 2012/ 1286 Sch.l, SI 2012/ 1289 Sch.l, SI 2012/ 1294 Sch.l, SI 2012/ 2541 Sch.l, SI 2012/ 2547 Sch.l, SI 2012/ 2548 Sch.l, SI 2012/ 2549 Sch.l

s.74A, referred to: SI 2012/ 1282 Sch.l, SI 2012/ 1295 Sch.l, SI 2012/ 3102 Sch.l, SI 2012/ 3103 Sch.l, SI 2012/ 3104 Sch.l, SI 2012/ 3105 Sch.l, SI 2012/ 3106 Sch.l, SI 2012/ 3107 Sch.l

s.74A, enabling: SI 2012/ 425, SI 2012/ 1322

s.76, applied: SI 2012/ 1284 Sch.l, SI 2012/ 1286 Sch.l, SI 2012/ 1289 Sch.l, SI 2012/ 1294 Sch.l, SI 2012/ 2284 Art.10, SI 2012/ 2635 Art.14, SI 2012/ 2679 Art.4

s.76, referred to: SI 2012/ 3102 Sch.l, SI 2012/ 3103 Sch.l, SI 2012/ 3104 Sch.l, SI 2012/ 3105 Sch.l, SI 2012/ 3106 Sch.l, SI 2012/ 3107 Sch.l

s.77, applied: SI 2012/ 2284 Art.10, SI 2012/ 2635 Art.14, SI 2012/ 2679 Art.4

s.80, applied: SI 2012/ 1282 Sch.l, SI 2012/ 1284 Sch.l, SI 2012/ 1286 Sch.l, SI 2012/ 1289 Sch.l, SI 2012/ 1294 Sch.l, SI 2012/ 1295 Sch.l, SI 2012/ 2541 Sch.l, SI 2012/ 2547 Sch.l, SI 2012/ 2548 Sch.l, SI 2012/ 2549 Sch.l, SI 2012/ 3102 Sch.l, SI 2012/ 3103 Sch.l, SI 2012/ 3104 Sch.l, SI 2012/ 3105 Sch.l, SI 2012/ 3106 Sch.l, SI 2012/ 3107 Sch.l

s.81, applied: SI 2012/ 1282 Sch.l, SI 2012/ 1284 Sch.l, SI 2012/ 1286 Sch.l, SI 2012/ 1289 Sch.l, SI 2012/ 1294 Sch.l, SI 2012/ 1295 Sch.l, SI 2012/ 2541 Sch.l, SI 2012/ 2547 Sch.l, SI 2012/ 2548 Sch.l, SI 2012/ 2549 Sch.l, SI 2012/ 3102 Sch.l, SI 2012/ 3103 Sch.l, SI 2012/ 3104 Sch.l, SI 2012/ 3105 Sch.l, SI 2012/ 3106 Sch.l, SI 2012/ 3107 Sch.l

s.81, referred to: SI 2012/ 2541 Sch.l, SI 2012/ 2547 Sch.l, SI 2012/ 2548 Sch.l, SI 2012/ 2549 Sch.l

1991–*cont.*

22. New Roads and Street Works Act 1991–*cont.*

s.84, applied: SI 2012/1284 Sch.1, SI 2012/1286 Sch.1, SI 2012/1289 Sch.1, SI 2012/1294 Sch.1, SI 2012/2541 Sch.1, SI 2012/2547 Sch.1, SI 2012/2548 Sch.1, SI 2012/2549 Sch.1

s.84, referred to: SI 2012/1282 Sch.1, SI 2012/1295 Sch.1, SI 2012/3102 Sch.1, SI 2012/3103 Sch.1, SI 2012/3104 Sch.1, SI 2012/3105 Sch.1, SI 2012/3106 Sch.1, SI 2012/3107 Sch.1

s.85, applied: SI 2012/1282 Sch.1, SI 2012/1284 Sch.1, SI 2012/1286 Sch.1, SI 2012/1289 Sch.1, SI 2012/1294 Sch.1, SI 2012/1295 Sch.1, SI 2012/2541 Sch.1, SI 2012/2547 Sch.1, SI 2012/2548 Sch.1, SI 2012/2549 Sch.1, SI 2012/2635 Art.33, SI 2012/2679 Art.28, Sch.13 para.2, SI 2012/3102 Sch.1, SI 2012/3103 Sch.1, SI 2012/3104 Sch.1, SI 2012/3105 Sch.1, SI 2012/3106 Sch.1, SI 2012/3107 Sch.1

s.86, applied: SI 2012/1282 Sch.1, SI 2012/1284 Sch.1, SI 2012/1286 Sch.1, SI 2012/1289 Sch.1, SI 2012/1295 Sch.1

s.86, referred to: SI 2012/1294 Sch.1, SI 2012/2541 Sch.1, SI 2012/2547 Sch.1, SI 2012/2548 Sch.1, SI 2012/2549 Sch.1, SI 2012/2635 Art.14, SI 2012/2679 Art.4, SI 2012/3102 Sch.1, SI 2012/3103 Sch.1, SI 2012/3104 Sch.1, SI 2012/3105 Sch.1, SI 2012/3106 Sch.1, SI 2012/3107 Sch.1

s.87, applied: SI 2012/1282 Sch.1, SI 2012/1284 Sch.1, SI 2012/1286 Sch.1, SI 2012/1294 Sch.1, SI 2012/1295 Sch.1, SI 2012/2679 Art.4

s.87, referred to: SI 2012/2635 Art.12

s.88, applied: SI 2012/1282 Sch.1, SI 2012/1294 Sch.1, SI 2012/1295 Sch.1

s.88, referred to: SI 2012/1284 Sch.1, SI 2012/1286 Sch.1, SI 2012/1289 Sch.1

s.88, varied: SI 2012/1282 Sch.1, SI 2012/1294 Sch.1, SI 2012/1295 Sch.1, SI 2012/2541 Sch.1, SI 2012/2547 Sch.1, SI 2012/2548 Sch.1, SI 2012/2549 Sch.1, SI 2012/3102 Sch.1, SI 2012/3103 Sch.1, SI 2012/3104 Sch.1, SI 2012/3105 Sch.1, SI 2012/3106 Sch.1, SI 2012/3107 Sch.1

s.89, applied: SI 2012/1282 Sch.1, SI 2012/1294 Sch.1, SI 2012/1295 Sch.1

s.89, referred to: SI 2012/1284 Sch.1, SI 2012/1286 Sch.1, SI 2012/1289 Sch.1

s.89, varied: SI 2012/1282 Sch.1, SI 2012/1294 Sch.1, SI 2012/1295 Sch.1, SI 2012/2541 Sch.1, SI 2012/2547 Sch.1, SI 2012/2548 Sch.1, SI 2012/2549 Sch.1, SI 2012/3102 Sch.1, SI 2012/3103 Sch.1, SI 2012/3104 Sch.1, SI 2012/3105 Sch.1, SI 2012/3106 Sch.1, SI 2012/3107 Sch.1

s.90, applied: SI 2012/1282 Sch.1, SI 2012/1284 Sch.1, SI 2012/1294 Sch.1, SI 2012/1295 Sch.1

s.90, referred to: SI 2012/1286 Sch.1, SI 2012/1289 Sch.1

s.90, varied: SI 2012/1282 Sch.1, SI 2012/1294 Sch.1, SI 2012/1295 Sch.1, SI 2012/2541 Sch.1, SI 2012/2547 Sch.1, SI 2012/2548 Sch.1, SI 2012/2549 Sch.1, SI 2012/3102 Sch.1, SI 2012/3103 Sch.1, SI 2012/3104 Sch.1, SI 2012/3105 Sch.1, SI 2012/3106 Sch.1, SI 2012/3107 Sch.1

s.91, applied: SI 2012/1282 Sch.1, SI 2012/1284 Sch.1, SI 2012/1286 Sch.1, SI 2012/1289 Sch.1, SI 2012/1294 Sch.1, SI 2012/1295 Sch.1

s.93, applied: SI 2012/1282 Sch.1, SI 2012/1284 Sch.1, SI 2012/1286 Sch.1, SI 2012/1289 Sch.1, SI 2012/1294 Sch.1, SI 2012/1295 Sch.1

s.93, referred to: SI 2012/1284 Sch.1, SI 2012/1286 Sch.1, SI 2012/1289 Sch.1, SI 2012/3102 Sch.1, SI 2012/3103 Sch.1, SI 2012/3104 Sch.1, SI 2012/3105 Sch.1, SI 2012/3106 Sch.1, SI 2012/3107 Sch.1

1991–*cont.*

22. New Roads and Street Works Act 1991–*cont.*

s.93, varied: SI 2012/1282 Sch.1, SI 2012/1294 Sch.1, SI 2012/1295 Sch.1, SI 2012/2541 Sch.1, SI 2012/2547 Sch.1, SI 2012/2548 Sch.1, SI 2012/2549 Sch.1

s.96, applied: SI 2012/1284 Sch.1, SI 2012/1286 Sch.1, SI 2012/1289 Sch.1, SI 2012/1294 Sch.1, SI 2012/2541 Sch.1, SI 2012/2547 Sch.1, SI 2012/2548 Sch.1, SI 2012/2549 Sch.1

s.96, referred to: SI 2012/1282 Sch.1, SI 2012/1295 Sch.1, SI 2012/3102 Sch.1, SI 2012/3103 Sch.1, SI 2012/3104 Sch.1, SI 2012/3105 Sch.1, SI 2012/3106 Sch.1, SI 2012/3107 Sch.1

s.98, applied: SI 2012/2541 Sch.1, SI 2012/2547 Sch.1, SI 2012/2548 Sch.1, SI 2012/2549 Sch.1, SI 2012/3102 Sch.1, SI 2012/3103 Sch.1, SI 2012/3104 Sch.1, SI 2012/3105 Sch.1, SI 2012/3106 Sch.1, SI 2012/3107 Sch.1

s.99, applied: SI 2012/1282 Sch.1, SI 2012/1284 Sch.1, SI 2012/1286 Sch.1, SI 2012/1289 Sch.1, SI 2012/1294 Sch.1, SI 2012/1295 Sch.1, SI 2012/2541 Sch.1, SI 2012/2547 Sch.1, SI 2012/2548 Sch.1, SI 2012/2549 Sch.1, SI 2012/3102 Sch.1, SI 2012/3103 Sch.1, SI 2012/3104 Sch.1, SI 2012/3105 Sch.1, SI 2012/3106 Sch.1, SI 2012/3107 Sch.1

s.104, enabling: SI 2012/425, SI 2012/2272

s.112A, applied: SSI 2012/11 Reg.3

s.112A, referred to: SSI 2012/11 Reg.3

s.112A, enabling: SSI 2012/11

s.124, applied: SI 2012/1282 Sch.1, SI 2012/1284 Sch.1, SI 2012/1286 Sch.1, SI 2012/1289 Sch.1, SI 2012/1294 Sch.1, SI 2012/1295 Sch.1

s.132, applied: SI 2012/3103 Sch.1, SI 2012/3104 Sch.1, SI 2012/3105 Sch.1, SI 2012/3106 Sch.1, SI 2012/3107 Sch.1

s.134, enabling: SSI 2012/250

s.140, enabling: SSI 2012/286

s.152, applied: SI 2012/1282 Sch.1, SI 2012/1284 Sch.1, SI 2012/1286 Sch.1, SI 2012/1289 Sch.1, SI 2012/1294 Sch.1, SI 2012/1295 Sch.1

s.163, enabling: SSI 2012/11

s.163A, applied: SSI 2012/11, SSI 2012/250, SSI 2012/286

Sch.4, applied: SI 2012/1282 Sch.1, SI 2012/1284 Sch.1, SI 2012/1286 Sch.1, SI 2012/1289 Sch.1, SI 2012/1294 Sch.1, SI 2012/1295 Sch.1, SI 2012/2541 Sch.1, SI 2012/2547 Sch.1, SI 2012/2548 Sch.1, SI 2012/2549 Sch.1, SI 2012/3102 Sch.1, SI 2012/3103 Sch.1, SI 2012/3104 Sch.1, SI 2012/3105 Sch.1, SI 2012/3106 Sch.1, SI 2012/3107 Sch.1

Sch.4 para.2, applied: SI 2012/3102 Sch.1, SI 2012/3103 Sch.1, SI 2012/3104 Sch.1, SI 2012/3105 Sch.1, SI 2012/3106 Sch.1, SI 2012/3107 Sch.1

Sch.4 para.2, referred to: SI 2012/2541 Sch.1, SI 2012/2547 Sch.1, SI 2012/2548 Sch.1, SI 2012/2549 Sch.1

Sch.8 Part IV para.122, referred to: SI 2012/3102 Sch.1, SI 2012/3103 Sch.1, SI 2012/3104 Sch.1, SI 2012/3105 Sch.1, SI 2012/3106 Sch.1, SI 2012/3107 Sch.1

23. Children and Young Persons (Protection from Tobacco) Act 1991

see *R. (on the application of Sinclair Collis Ltd) v Secretary of State for Health* [2011] EWCA Civ 437, [2012] Q.B. 394 (CA (Civ Div)), Lord Neuberger (M.R.)

s.3A, see *R. (on the application of Sinclair Collis Ltd) v Secretary of State for Health* [2011] EWCA Civ 437, [2012] Q.B. 394 (CA (Civ Div)), Lord Neuberger (M.R.)

1991– cont.

25. Criminal Procedure (Insanity and Unfitness to Plead) Act 1991
s.6, amended: 2012 c.7 s.38

26. Road Traffic (Temporary Restrictions) Act 1991
applied: SI 2012/1286 Sch.1, SI 2012/1294 Sch.1, SI 2012/1295 Sch.1
referred to: SI 2012/1282 Sch.1, SI 2012/1289 Sch.1, SI 2012/2541 Sch.1, SI 2012/2547 Sch.1, SI 2012/2548 Sch.1, SI 2012/2549 Sch.1, SI 2012/3102 Sch.1, SI 2012/3103 Sch.1, SI 2012/3104 Sch.1, SI 2012/3105 Sch.1, SI 2012/3106 Sch.1, SI 2012/3107 Sch.1

29. Property Misdescriptions Act 1991
applied: SI 2012/1128 Art.4
referred to: 2012 c.19 Sch.6 para.4
s.1, amended: 2012 asp 5 Sch.5 para.32

30. Welfare of Animals at Slaughter Act 1991
s.4, repealed (in part): SSI 2012/321 Sch.5 Part 1
s.5, repealed (in part): SSI 2012/321 Sch.5 Part 1

31. Finance Act 1991
s.121, repealed: 2012 c.14 Sch.39 para.20
Sch.7 para.5, repealed: 2012 c.14 Sch.16 para.247
Sch.7 para.12, repealed: 2012 c.14 Sch.16 para.247
Sch.7 para.16, amended: 2012 c.14 Sch.16 para.71
Sch.7 para.16, varied: SI 2012/3008 Reg.3
Sch.9 para.1, repealed: 2012 c.14 Sch.18 para.23
Sch.9 para.2, repealed: 2012 c.14 Sch.18 para.23
Sch.9 para.3, repealed: 2012 c.14 Sch.18 para.23
Sch.15 para.15, repealed: 2012 c.14 Sch.16 para.247

40. Road Traffic Act 1991
s.66, see *Shiva Ltd v Transport for London* [2011] EWCA Civ 1189, [2012] R.T.R. 13 (CA (Civ Div)), Lord Neuberger (M.R.)
s.66, applied: SSI 2012/139 Reg.4, SSI 2012/142 Reg.4
s.66, referred to: SSI 2012/138 Reg.2, SSI 2012/141 Reg.2
s.66, varied: SSI 2012/137 Sch.2 para.1, SSI 2012/140 Sch.2 para.1
s.69, referred to: SSI 2012/138 Reg.2, SSI 2012/141 Reg.2
s.69, varied: SSI 2012/137 Sch.2 para.2, SSI 2012/140 Sch.2 para.2
s.71, applied: SSI 2012/139 Reg.4, SSI 2012/142 Reg.4
s.71, varied: SSI 2012/137 Sch.2 para.3, SSI 2012/140 Sch.2 para.3
s.72, applied: SSI 2012/139 Reg.14, SSI 2012/142 Reg.14
s.72, referred to: SSI 2012/139 Reg.3, SSI 2012/142 Reg.3
s.73, applied: SSI 2012/139 Reg.6, Reg.9, SSI 2012/140 Art.6, SSI 2012/142 Reg.6, Reg.9
s.73, varied: SSI 2012/137 Art.6, Sch.2 para.4, SSI 2012/140 Sch.2 para.4
s.73, enabling: SSI 2012/139, SSI 2012/142
s.74, varied: SSI 2012/137 Sch.2 para.5, SSI 2012/140 Sch.2 para.5
s.82, varied: SSI 2012/137 Sch.2 para.6, SSI 2012/140 Sch.2 para.6
Sch.3 para.1, applied: SSI 2012/137, SSI 2012/140
Sch.3 para.1, enabling: SSI 2012/137, SSI 2012/140
Sch.3 para.2, applied: SSI 2012/137, SSI 2012/140
Sch.3 para.2, enabling: SSI 2012/137, SSI 2012/140
Sch.3 para.3, enabling: SSI 2012/137, SSI 2012/140
Sch.6 para.1, varied: SSI 2012/137 Sch.2 para.7, SSI 2012/140 Sch.2 para.7
Sch.6 para.2, applied: SSI 2012/139 Reg.4, SSI 2012/142 Reg.4

1991– cont.

40. Road Traffic Act 1991–*cont.*
Sch.6 para.2, varied: SSI 2012/137 Sch.2 para.7, SSI 2012/140 Sch.2 para.7
Sch.6 para.3, varied: SSI 2012/137 Sch.2 para.7, SSI 2012/140 Sch.2 para.7
Sch.6 para.4, varied: SSI 2012/137 Sch.2 para.7, SSI 2012/140 Sch.2 para.7
Sch.6 para.5, applied: SSI 2012/139 Reg.14, SSI 2012/142 Reg.14
Sch.6 para.5, referred to: SSI 2012/139 Reg.3, SSI 2012/142 Reg.3
Sch.6 para.5, varied: SSI 2012/137 Sch.2 para.7, SSI 2012/140 Sch.2 para.7
Sch.6 para.6, varied: SSI 2012/137 Sch.2 para.7, SSI 2012/140 Sch.2 para.7
Sch.6 para.7, varied: SSI 2012/137 Sch.2 para.7, SSI 2012/140 Sch.2 para.7
Sch.6 para.8, varied: SSI 2012/137 Sch.2 para.7, SSI 2012/140 Sch.2 para.7
Sch.6 para.9, varied: SSI 2012/137 Sch.2 para.7, SSI 2012/140 Sch.2 para.7
Sch.6 para.10, varied: SSI 2012/137 Sch.2 para.7, SSI 2012/140 Sch.2 para.7

45. Coal Mining Subsidence Act 1991
s.3, see *Newbold v Coal Authority* [2012] UKUT 20 (LC), [2012] R.V.R. 157 (UT (Lands)), George Bartlett Q.C. (President, LTr)

48. Child Support Act 1991
applied: SI 2012/2677 Reg.8, Reg.24, Reg.50, Reg.52, Reg.53, Reg.55, SI 2012/3042 Art.1, Art.5
s.2, amended: SI 2012/2007 Sch.1 para.2
s.3, see *Brough v Law* [2011] EWCA Civ 1183, [2012] 1 W.L.R. 1021 (CA (Civ Div)), Pill, L.J.
s.3, varied: SI 2012/2677 Reg.51, Reg.55
s.3, enabling: SI 2012/2677
s.4, amended: 2012 c.5 s.137, SI 2012/2007 Sch.1 para.3
s.4, applied: SI 2012/2677 Reg.10, Reg.11, Reg.18, Reg.50, SI 2012/3042 Art.3
s.5, enabling: SI 2012/2677
s.7, amended: 2012 c.5 s.137, SI 2012/2007 Sch.1 para.4
s.7, applied: SI 2012/2677 Reg.10, Reg.11, Reg.18, Reg.26, SI 2012/3042 Art.3
s.8, amended: 2012 c.5 Sch.9 para.2, Sch.14 Part 9, SI 2012/2007 Sch.1 para.5
s.9, amended: 2012 c.5 s.136
s.9A, added: 2012 c.5 s.138
s.10, amended: SI 2012/2007 Sch.1 para.6
s.11, amended: SI 2012/2007 Sch.1 para.7
s.11, applied: SI 2012/2677 Reg.12, Reg.13, Reg.24, Reg.25, Reg.26, Reg.35, Sch.1 para.1
s.12, amended: SI 2012/2007 Sch.1 para.8
s.12, applied: SI 2012/2677 Reg.13, Reg.14, Reg.24, Reg.25, Reg.26, Reg.49, Reg.75
s.12, enabling: SI 2012/2677
s.14, amended: SI 2012/2007 Sch.1 para.9
s.14, applied: SI 2012/2677 Reg.18, Reg.22
s.14, enabling: SI 2012/2677, SI 2012/2785, SI 2012/3002
s.15, amended: SI 2012/2007 Sch.1 para.10
s.16, see *Brough v Law* [2011] EWCA Civ 1183, [2012] 1 W.L.R. 1021 (CA (Civ Div)), Pill, L.J.
s.16, amended: SI 2012/2007 Sch.1 para.11
s.16, applied: SI 2012/2677 Reg.14, Reg.61, Reg.75
s.16, enabling: SI 2012/2677
s.17, amended: 2012 c.5 Sch.12 para.2, SI 2012/2007 Sch.1 para.12

1991– *cont.*

48. Child Support Act 1991–*cont.*

s.17, applied: SI 2012/2677 Reg.17, Reg.18, Reg.24, Reg.26, Reg.32, Reg.47, Reg.61, Reg.75

s.17, enabling: SI 2012/712, SI 2012/1267, SI 2012/2677

s.20, amended: 2012 c.5 Sch.11 para.5, Sch.11 para.6, SI 2012/2007 Sch.1 para.13

s.20, applied: 2012 c.5 s.102, SI 2012/2677 Reg.14

s.20, enabling: SI 2012/2677

s.23A, repealed (in part): SI 2012/2007 Sch.1 para.14

s.24, amended: SI 2012/2007 Sch.1 para.15

s.24, repealed (in part): SI 2012/2007 Sch.1 para.15

s.26, amended: SI 2012/2007 Sch.1 para.16

s.27, amended: SI 2012/2007 Sch.1 para.17

s.27A, amended: SI 2012/2007 Sch.1 para.18

s.28, amended: SI 2012/2007 Sch.1 para.19

s.28A, amended: SI 2012/2007 Sch.1 para.23

s.28A, applied: SI 2012/2677 Reg.13

s.28A, referred to: SI 2012/2677 Reg.13

s.28A, enabling: SI 2012/2677

s.28B, amended: SI 2012/2007 Sch.1 para.24

s.28B, applied: SI 2012/2677 Reg.57

s.28B, enabling: SI 2012/2677

s.28C, amended: SI 2012/2007 Sch.1 para.25

s.28C, applied: SI 2012/2677 Reg.62

s.28C, enabling: SI 2012/2677

s.28D, amended: SI 2012/2007 Sch.1 para.26

s.28E, amended: SI 2012/2007 Sch.1 para.27

s.28F, amended: SI 2012/2007 Sch.1 para.28

s.28F, applied: SI 2012/2677 Reg.57, Sch.1 para.1

s.28F, enabling: SI 2012/2677

s.28G, applied: SI 2012/2677 Reg.14, Reg.17

s.28G, enabling: SI 2012/2677

s.28J, amended: SI 2012/2007 Sch.1 para.29

s.28J, applied: SI 2012/2677 Reg.13

s.28ZA, amended: SI 2012/2007 Sch.1 para.20

s.28ZA, applied: SI 2012/2677 Reg.28

s.28ZA, enabling: SI 2012/2677

s.28ZB, amended: SI 2012/2007 Sch.1 para.21

s.28ZB, applied: SI 2012/2677 Reg.29, Reg.30

s.28ZB, referred to: SI 2012/2677 Reg.30

s.28ZB, enabling: SI 2012/2677

s.28ZC, amended: SI 2012/2007 Sch.1 para.22

s.28ZC, applied: SI 2012/2677 Reg.32

s.29, amended: 2012 c.5 s.137, SI 2012/2007 Sch.1 para.30

s.29, enabling: SI 2012/712, SI 2012/2785

s.30, amended: SI 2012/2007 Sch.1 para.31

s.31, amended: SI 2012/2007 Sch.1 para.32

s.32, amended: SI 2012/2007 Sch.1 para.33

s.32A, amended: SI 2012/2007 Sch.1 para.34

s.32B, amended: SI 2012/2007 Sch.1 para.35

s.32C, amended: SI 2012/2007 Sch.1 para.36

s.32E, amended: SI 2012/2007 Sch.1 para.37

s.32F, amended: SI 2012/2007 Sch.1 para.38

s.32H, amended: SI 2012/2007 Sch.1 para.39

s.32I, amended: SI 2012/2007 Sch.1 para.40

s.32J, amended: SI 2012/2007 Sch.1 para.41

s.32L, amended: SI 2012/2007 Sch.1 para.42

s.33, amended: SI 2012/2007 Sch.1 para.43

s.34, amended: SI 2012/2007 Sch.1 para.44

s.35, amended: SI 2012/2007 Sch.1 para.45

s.36, see *Karoonian v Child Maintenance and Enforcement Commission (CMEC)* [2012] EWCA Civ 1379, [2012] 3 F.C.R. 491 (CA (Civ Div)), Ward, L.J.

s.37, amended: SI 2012/2007 Sch.1 para.46

1991– *cont.*

48. Child Support Act 1991–*cont.*

s.38, amended: SI 2012/2007 Sch.1 para.47

s.39A, see *Karoonian v Child Maintenance and Enforcement Commission (CMEC)* [2012] EWCA Civ 1379, [2012] 3 F.C.R. 491 (CA (Civ Div)), Ward, L.J.

s.39A, amended: SI 2012/2007 Sch.1 para.48

s.40B, amended: SI 2012/2007 Sch.1 para.49

s.41, amended: SI 2012/2007 Sch.1 para.50

s.41A, amended: SI 2012/2007 Sch.1 para.51

s.41B, amended: SI 2012/2007 Sch.1 para.52

s.41C, amended: SI 2012/2007 Sch.1 para.53

s.41D, enabling: SI 2012/3002

s.41E, enabling: SI 2012/3002

s.42, enabling: SI 2012/2677

s.43, amended: 2012 c.5 s.139

s.43A, amended: SI 2012/2007 Sch.1 para.54

s.44, amended: SI 2012/2007 Sch.1 para.55

s.44, enabling: SI 2012/2677 Reg.17

s.46A, amended: SI 2012/2007 Sch.1 para.56

s.46B, amended: SI 2012/2007 Sch.1 para.57

s.48, amended: SI 2012/2007 Sch.1 para.58

s.50, amended: SI 2012/2007 Sch.1 para.59

s.50, repealed (in part): SI 2012/2007 Sch.1 para.59

s.50A, repealed: SI 2012/2007 Sch.1 para.60

s.51, enabling: SI 2012/712, SI 2012/2677, SI 2012/2785, SI 2012/3002

s.51A, amended: 2012 c.5 Sch.11 para.7

s.52, amended: 2012 c.5 Sch.11 para.8

s.52, applied: SI 2012/2677, SI 2012/2678, SI 2012/3002

s.52, enabling: SI 2012/712, SI 2012/2677, SI 2012/2678, SI 2012/2785, SI 2012/3002

s.54, amended: 2012 c.5 Sch.14 Part 1, SI 2012/2007 Sch.1 para.61

s.54, enabling: SI 2012/712, SI 2012/1267, SI 2012/2677, SI 2012/2785

s.55, applied: SI 2012/2677 Reg.76

s.55, enabling: SI 2012/2677, SI 2012/2785

Sch.1, applied: SI 2012/2677 Reg.54, Reg.73

Sch.1 Part I, applied: SI 2012/2677 Reg.25, Reg.53, Reg.74, SI 2012/2785 Reg.1

Sch.1 Part I para.2, varied: SI 2012/2678 Reg.2

Sch.1 Part I para.3, enabling: SI 2012/2677

Sch.1 Part I para.4, applied: SI 2012/2677 Reg.44, Reg.45

Sch.1 Part I para.4, referred to: SI 2012/2677 Reg.44, Reg.53, Reg.57, Reg.74

Sch.1 Part I para.4, enabling: SI 2012/2677

Sch.1 Part I para.5, amended: 2012 c.5 Sch.2 para.2, Sch.14 Part 1

Sch.1 Part I para.5, applied: SI 2012/2677 Reg.45

Sch.1 Part I para.5, enabling: SI 2012/2677

Sch.1 Part I para.5A, applied: SI 2012/2677 Reg.18, Reg.25, Reg.48

Sch.1 Part I para.5A, varied: SI 2012/2677 Reg.52, SI 2012/2678 Reg.3

Sch.1 Part I para.5A, enabling: SI 2012/2677

Sch.1 Part I para.6, applied: SI 2012/2677 Reg.49, Reg.53, Reg.74

Sch.1 Part I para.7, amended: SI 2012/2007 Sch.1 para.62

Sch.1 Part I para.7, applied: SI 2012/2677 Reg.46, Reg.53, Reg.74

Sch.1 Part I para.7, varied: SI 2012/2677 Reg.46, Reg.74

Sch.1 Part I para.7, enabling: SI 2012/2677

Sch.1 Part I para.8, applied: SI 2012/2677 Reg.46

Sch.1 Part I para.8, varied: SI 2012/2677 Reg.46

1991– cont.

48. Child Support Act 1991–*cont.*
Sch.1 Part I para.8, enabling: SI 2012/2677
Sch.1 Part I para.9, enabling: SI 2012/2677
Sch.1 Part I para.10, amended: SI 2012/2007 Sch.1 para.62
Sch.1 Part I para.10, enabling: SI 2012/712, SI 2012/2677
Sch.1 Part I para.10A, applied: SI 2012/2677 Reg.53, Reg.57, Reg.74
Sch.1 Part I para.10A, enabling: SI 2012/2678
Sch.1 Part I para.10B, amended: SI 2012/2007 Sch.1 para.62
Sch.1 Part I para.10C, applied: SI 2012/2677 Reg.77
Sch.1 Part I para.10C, enabling: SI 2012/2677
Sch.1 Part II para.11, enabling: SI 2012/2677
Sch.1 Part II para.12, amended: SI 2012/2007 Sch.1 para.62
Sch.1 Part II para.13, amended: SI 2012/2007 Sch.1 para.62
Sch.1 Part II para.15, amended: SI 2012/2007 Sch.1 para.62
Sch.1 Part II para.16, amended: SI 2012/2007 Sch.1 para.62
Sch.1 Part II para.16, applied: SI 2012/2677 Reg.17
Sch.1 para.16, see *Brough v Law* [2011] EWCA Civ 1183, [2012] 1 W.L.R. 1021 (CA (Civ Div)), Pill, L.J.
Sch.4A para.2, enabling: SI 2012/2677
Sch.4A para.4, amended: SI 2012/2007 Sch.1 para.63
Sch.4A para.4, enabling: SI 2012/2677
Sch.4A para.5, enabling: SI 2012/2677
Sch.4B Part I para.2, applied: SI 2012/2677 Reg.63, Reg.64, Reg.65, Reg.66, Reg.67, Reg.68
Sch.4B Part I para.2, enabling: SI 2012/2677
Sch.4B Part I para.4, applied: SI 2012/2677 Reg.69, Reg.70, Reg.71
Sch.4B Part I para.4, enabling: SI 2012/2677
Sch.4B Part II para.5, enabling: SI 2012/2677
Sch.4B Part II para.6, enabling: SI 2012/2677
Sch.4C para.2, amended: 2012 c.5 Sch.12 para.3
50. Age of Legal Capacity (Scotland) Act 1991
Sch.1 para.33, repealed: 2012 c.14 s.222
Sch.1 para.34, repealed: 2012 c.14 s.222
52. Ports Act 1991
s.1, amended: SI 2012/1659 Sch.3 para.10
53. Criminal Justice Act 1991
see *R. (on the application of Elam) v Secretary of State for Justice* [2012] EWCA Civ 29, [2012] 1 W.L.R. 2722 (CA (Civ Div)), Laws, L.J.
applied: SI 2012/1726 r.13.2, r.13.3, r.13.4, r.13.5
Part II, applied: SI 2012/206 Sch.1 para.21
s.20A, applied: SI 2012/1726 r.37.10
s.24, amended: 2012 c.5 s.109
s.37, see *R. (on the application of Elam) v Secretary of State for Justice* [2012] EWCA Civ 29, [2012] 1 W.L.R. 2722 (CA (Civ Div)), Laws, L.J.
s.44, see *R. (on the application of Minter) v Chief Constable of Hampshire* [2011] EWHC 1610 (Admin), [2012] 1 W.L.R. 1157 (DC), Richards, L.J.
s.51, see *R. (on the application of Elam) v Secretary of State for Justice* [2012] EWCA Civ 29, [2012] 1 W.L.R. 2722 (CA (Civ Div)), Laws, L.J.; see *R. (on the application of Minter) v Chief Constable of Hampshire* [2011] EWHC 1610 (Admin), [2012] 1 W.L.R. 1157 (DC), Richards, L.J.
s.53, amended: 2012 c.10 Sch.5 para.40
s.53, applied: SI 2012/1726 r.14.1, r.3.11, r.11.5

1991– cont.

53. Criminal Justice Act 1991–*cont.*
s.53, referred to: SI 2012/1726 r.11.1, r.13.1
s.60, amended: 2012 c.10 Sch.12 para.28
s.60, repealed (in part): 2012 c.10 Sch.12 para.27
s.61, repealed: 2012 c.10 Sch.12 para.29
s.61A, repealed: 2012 c.10 Sch.12 para.30
s.68, repealed (in part): 2012 c.10 Sch.25 Part 2
s.80, applied: 2012 c.10 s.103
s.92, amended: 2012 c.10 Sch.12 para.31
s.92, applied: 2012 c.10 s.103
Sch.3 Part II para.8, repealed (in part): 2012 c.5 s.109
Sch.6, referred to: SI 2012/1726 r.11.1, r.13.1
Sch.6 para.2, referred to: SI 2012/1726 r.11.2
Sch.6 para.5, applied: SI 2012/1726 r.13.2, r.13.3, r.13.4
Sch.6 para.6, applied: SI 2012/1726 r.16.1
Sch.8 para.5, repealed (in part): 2012 c.10 Sch.25 Part 2
Sch.12 para.8, repealed: 2012 c.10 Sch.16 para.5
Sch.12 para.9, repealed: 2012 c.10 Sch.16 para.5
Sch.12 para.10, repealed: 2012 c.10 Sch.16 para.5
Sch.12 para.11, repealed: 2012 c.10 Sch.16 para.5
Sch.12 para.12, repealed: 2012 c.10 Sch.16 para.5
Sch.12 para.13, repealed: 2012 c.10 Sch.16 para.5
Sch.12 para.22, repealed (in part): 2012 c.10 Sch.25 Part 2
55. Agricultural Holdings (Scotland) Act 1991
see *Crewpace Ltd v French* 2012 S.L.T. 126 (OH), Temporary Judge M Wise, QC
s.11, applied: 2012 asp 6 s.4
s.12, applied: 2012 asp 6 s.4
s.13, amended: 2012 asp 6 s.3
s.25, applied: 2012 asp 6 s.4
s.75, amended: 2012 asp 5 Sch.5 para.33
Sch.2 Part III para.1, amended: 2012 asp 6 s.1
56. Water Industry Act 1991
see *Manchester Ship Canal Co Ltd v United Utilities Water Plc* [2012] EWHC 232 (Ch), [2012] Env. L.R. 31 (Ch D), Newey, J
applied: SI 2012/1128 Art.4, SI 2012/1376 Art.4, SI 2012/1571 Art.4, SI 2012/1857 Art.4, SI 2012/2696 Art.4, SSI 2012/89 Sch.1
referred to: 2012 c.13 Sch.1, 2012 c.19 Sch.6 para.4
s.7, see *R. (on the application of Thames Water Utilities Ltd) v Water Services Regulation Authority* [2012] EWCA Civ 218, [2012] P.T.S.R. 1147 (CA (Civ Div)), Laws, L.J.
s.31, amended: SI 2012/1809 Sch.1 Part 1
s.32, applied: SI 2012/1878 Art.1
s.36, see *R. (on the application of Thames Water Utilities Ltd) v Water Services Regulation Authority* [2012] EWCA Civ 218, [2012] P.T.S.R. 1147 (CA (Civ Div)), Laws, L.J.
s.87, amended: 2012 c.7 s.35
s.87, applied: 2012 c.7 s.37
s.87, repealed (in part): 2012 c.7 s.35
s.87, varied: 2012 c.7 s.37
s.87A, amended: 2012 c.7 s.35
s.87A, varied: 2012 c.7 s.37
s.87B, amended: 2012 c.7 s.35
s.87B, repealed (in part): 2012 c.7 s.35
s.87B, varied: 2012 c.7 s.37
s.87C, repealed (in part): 2012 c.7 s.35
s.87C, varied: 2012 c.7 s.37
s.88, varied: 2012 c.7 s.37
s.88A, varied: 2012 c.7 s.37
s.88B, added: 2012 c.7 s.36
s.88B, varied: 2012 c.7 s.37

1991– cont.

56. Water Industry Act 1991– *cont.*
s.88C, added: 2012 c.7 s.36
s.88C, varied: 2012 c.7 s.37
s.88D, added: 2012 c.7 s.36
s.88D, varied: 2012 c.7 s.37
s.88E, added: 2012 c.7 s.36
s.88E, varied: 2012 c.7 s.37
s.88F, added: 2012 c.7 s.36
s.88F, varied: 2012 c.7 s.37
s.88G, added: 2012 c.7 s.36
s.88G, varied: 2012 c.7 s.37
s.88H, added: 2012 c.7 s.36
s.88H, varied: 2012 c.7 s.37
s.88I, added: 2012 c.7 s.36
s.88I, varied: 2012 c.7 s.37
s.88J, added: 2012 c.7 s.36
s.88J, varied: 2012 c.7 s.37
s.88K, added: 2012 c.7 s.36
s.88K, varied: 2012 c.7 s.37
s.88L, added: 2012 c.7 s.36
s.88L, varied: 2012 c.7 s.37
s.88M, added: 2012 c.7 s.36
s.88M, varied: 2012 c.7 s.37
s.88N, added: 2012 c.7 s.36
s.88N, varied: 2012 c.7 s.37
s.88O, added: 2012 c.7 s.36
s.88O, varied: 2012 c.7 s.37
s.89, amended: 2012 c.7 s.35
s.89, repealed (in part): 2012 c.7 s.35
s.89, varied: 2012 c.7 s.37
s.90, varied: 2012 c.7 s.37
s.90A, amended: 2012 c.7 s.35
s.90A, varied: 2012 c.7 s.37
s.91, varied: 2012 c.7 s.37
s.106, applied: SI 2012/1867 Art.13, SI 2012/2284 Art.13, SI 2012/2635 Art.20, SI 2012/2679 Art.19
s.106B, disapplied: SI 2012/2048 Art.3
s.106B, varied: SI 2012/2048 Art.3
s.154A, added: 2012 c.8 s.1
s.154B, added: 2012 c.8 s.2
s.159, see *Manchester Ship Canal Co Ltd v United Utilities Water Plc* [2012] EWHC 232 (Ch), [2012] Env. L.R. 31 (Ch D), Newey, J
s.206, amended: 2012 c.21 Sch.18 para.72
Sch.4A para.16, amended: 2012 c.7 Sch.14 para.56
Sch.15 Part II, amended: 2012 c.19 Sch.9 para.6
57. Water Resources Act 1991
applied: SI 2012/1128 Art.4, SI 2012/2284 Art.13
referred to: 2012 c.19 Sch.6 para.4, SI 2012/1867 Art.13
Part II c.II, applied: SI 2012/2679 Sch.15 para.12
s.24, applied: SI 2012/2782 Art.9
s.25, applied: SI 2012/2782 Art.9
s.65, see *Parkhill v Environment Agency* [2012] UKUT 23 (LC), [2012] R.V.R. 272 (UT (Lands)), Judge Mole Q.C.
s.66, amended: SI 2012/1659 Sch.3 para.11
s.73, applied: SI 2012/3102 Sch.1, SI 2012/3103 Sch.1, SI 2012/3104 Sch.1, SI 2012/3105 Sch.1, SI 2012/3106 Sch.1, SI 2012/3107 Sch.1
s.109, applied: SI 2012/2679 Sch.15 para.12, SI 2012/2782 Art.9
s.109, disapplied: SI 2012/2284 Art.4
s.130, amended: SI 2012/1659 Sch.3 para.11
s.204, amended: 2012 c.21 Sch.18 para.73
Sch.24 Part II, amended: 2012 c.19 Sch.9 para.7
Sch.25 para.5, disapplied: SI 2012/2284 Art.4
Sch.25 para.6, disapplied: SI 2012/2284 Art.4

1991– cont.

57. Water Resources Act 1991– *cont.*
Sch.25 para.6A, disapplied: SI 2012/2284 Art.4
59. Land Drainage Act 1991
applied: SI 2012/879 Art.4
s.3, applied: SI 2012/1024, SI 2012/1025, SI 2012/1026, SI 2012/1027, SI 2012/1028, SI 2012/1029, SI 2012/1030, SI 2012/1031, SI 2012/1032
s.3, referred to: SI 2012/1027
s.3, enabling: SI 2012/1024, SI 2012/1025, SI 2012/1026, SI 2012/1027, SI 2012/1028, SI 2012/1029, SI 2012/1030, SI 2012/1031, SI 2012/1032
s.21, applied: SI 2012/879 Art.4
s.23, applied: SI 2012/879 Art.4
s.23, disapplied: SI 2012/2284 Art.4
s.24, applied: SI 2012/879 Art.4
s.25, applied: SI 2012/879 Art.4
Sch.1, applied: SI 2012/1024 Sch.1, SI 2012/1025 Sch.1, SI 2012/1026 Sch.1, SI 2012/1027 Sch.1, SI 2012/1028 Sch.1, SI 2012/1029 Sch.1, SI 2012/1030 Sch.1, SI 2012/1031 Sch.1, SI 2012/1032 Sch.1
Sch.3 para.2, applied: SI 2012/1024, SI 2012/1025, SI 2012/1026, SI 2012/1027, SI 2012/1028, SI 2012/1029, SI 2012/1030, SI 2012/1031, SI 2012/1032
Sch.3 para.2, referred to: SI 2012/1026, SI 2012/1027, SI 2012/1029, SI 2012/1031, SI 2012/1032
Sch.3 para.4, applied: SI 2012/1026 Sch.1, SI 2012/1027 Sch.1, SI 2012/1029 Sch.1, SI 2012/1031 Sch.1, SI 2012/1032 Sch.1
Sch.3 para.5, applied: SI 2012/1026 Sch.1, SI 2012/1029 Sch.1, SI 2012/1031 Sch.1, SI 2012/1032 Sch.1
60. Water Consolidation (Consequential Provisions) Act 1991
see *Manchester Ship Canal Co Ltd v United Utilities Water Plc* [2012] EWHC 232 (Ch), [2012] Env. L.R. 31 (Ch D), Newey, J; see *Rochdale BC v Dixon* [2011] EWCA Civ 1173, [2012] P.T.S.R. 1336 (CA (Civ Div)), Rix, L.J.
65. Dangerous Dogs Act 1991
s.1, see *R. (on the application of Sandhu) v Isleworth Crown Court* [2012] EWHC 1658 (Admin), (2012) 176 J.P. 537 (DC), Richards, L.J.
s.3, see *Kelleher v DPP* [2012] EWHC 2978 (Admin), (2012) 176 J.P. 729 (QBD (Admin)), Collins, J.
s.4, see *Kelleher v DPP* [2012] EWHC 2978 (Admin), (2012) 176 J.P. 729 (QBD (Admin)), Collins, J.
s.4, applied: SI 2012/1726 r.76.1, r.76.7
s.4A, see *Kelleher v DPP* [2012] EWHC 2978 (Admin), (2012) 176 J.P. 729 (QBD (Admin)), Collins, J.; see *R. (on the application of Sandhu) v Isleworth Crown Court* [2012] EWHC 1658 (Admin), (2012) 176 J.P. 537 (DC), Richards, L.J.

1992

3. Severn Bridges Act 1992
s.9, enabling: SI 2012/3136
4. Social Security Contributions and Benefits Act 1992
see *PA Holdings Ltd v Revenue and Customs Commissioners* [2011] EWCA Civ 1414, [2012] S.T.C. 582 (CA (Civ Div)), Maurice Kay, L.J.; see *Stewart v Secretary of State for Work and Pensions (C-503/09)* [2012] P.T.S.R. 1 (ECJ (2nd Chamber)), Judge Cunha Rodrigues (President)

1992– cont.

4. Social Security Contributions and Benefits Act 1992– *cont.*

applied: SI 2012/360 Art.2, SI 2012/780 Art.6, SI 2012/2677 Reg.44, SI 2012/2885 Sch.1 para.17, Sch.1 para.19, Sch.1 para.22, Sch.1 para.26, Sch.1 para.28, Sch.1 para.29, Sch.1 para.46, SI 2012/2886 Sch.1, SI 2012/3144 Sch.1 para.11, Sch.1 para.13, Sch.1 para.16, SI 2012/3145 Sch.1, SSI 2012/292 Art.3, SSI 2012/303 Reg.28, Reg.31, Reg.35, Reg.37, Reg.41, Sch.6 para.1, SSI 2012/319 Reg.31, Reg.33, Reg.36, Reg.38, Reg.59

Part I, referred to: SI 2012/807

Part II, applied: 2012 c.5 s.96, SI 2012/2885 Sch.1 para.26, SI 2012/2886 Sch.1, SSI 2012/303 Sch.4 para.52

Part III, applied: 2012 c.5 s.96, SI 2012/2885 Sch.1 para.26, SI 2012/2886 Sch.1, SSI 2012/303 Sch.1 para.10, Sch.4 para.52

Part IV, applied: SSI 2012/303 Sch.4 para.52

Part V, applied: SI 2012/2886 Sch.1

Part VII, applied: SI 2012/531 Reg.49, SI 2012/2886 Sch.1

Part VIII, applied: SI 2012/2886 Sch.1, SSI 2012/303 Reg.5, Sch.4 para.36, Sch.5 para.24, SSI 2012/319 Reg.5

Part VIIIA, applied: SSI 2012/303 Sch.5 para.45, SSI 2012/319 Sch.4 para.28

Part X, applied: SI 2012/2886 Sch.1, SSI 2012/303 Sch.4 para.38

Part XIIA, applied: SI 2012/2885 Sch.1 para.25, Sch.1 para.26, Sch.4 para.5, SI 2012/2886 Sch.1, SI 2012/3144 Sch.1 para.19, SI 2012/3145 Sch.1, SSI 2012/303 Reg.20, Reg.28, Sch.1 para.10, Sch.6 para.1, SSI 2012/319 Reg.29, Sch.2 para.5

Part XIIZA, applied: SI 2012/3145 Sch.1

Part XIIZB, applied: SI 2012/3145 Sch.1

s.1, enabling: SI 2012/817

s.2, enabling: SI 2012/816

s.3, see *Forde & McHugh Ltd v Revenue and Customs Commissioners* [2012] EWCA Civ 692, [2012] 3 All E.R. 1256 (CA (Civ Div)), Arden, L.J.

s.3, enabling: SI 2012/817

s.4C, amended: 2012 c.5 Sch.14 Part 1

s.4C, referred to: 2012 c.5 s.127

s.5, enabling: SI 2012/804

s.6, see *Forde & McHugh Ltd v Revenue and Customs Commissioners* [2012] EWCA Civ 692, [2012] 3 All E.R. 1256 (CA (Civ Div)), Arden, L.J.; see *Kuehne & Nagel Drinks Logistics Ltd v Revenue and Customs Commissioners* [2012] EWCA Civ 34, [2012] S.T.C. 840 (CA (Civ Div)), Mummery, L.J.

s.7, enabling: SI 2012/816

s.10, see *Forde & McHugh Ltd v Revenue and Customs Commissioners* [2012] EWCA Civ 692, [2012] 3 All E.R. 1256 (CA (Civ Div)), Arden, L.J.

s.10, enabling: SI 2012/817

s.11, amended: SI 2012/807 Art.2

s.11, applied: SI 2012/2885 Sch.1 para.30, SI 2012/2886 Sch.1, SI 2012/3145 Sch.1, SSI 2012/303 Reg.38, SSI 2012/319 Reg.37

s.11, referred to: SI 2012/2885 Sch.1 para.28, Sch.1 para.30, SSI 2012/319 Reg.37

s.13, amended: SI 2012/807 Art.3

s.13, applied: SSI 2012/319 Sch.2 para.12

s.15, amended: SI 2012/807 Art.4

1992– cont.

4. Social Security Contributions and Benefits Act 1992– *cont.*

s.15, applied: SI 2012/2885 Sch.1 para.30, SI 2012/2886 Sch.1, SSI 2012/303 Reg.38, SSI 2012/319 Reg.37

s.16, amended: 2012 c.14 Sch.38 para.53

s.18, amended: SI 2012/807 Art.4

s.19, enabling: SI 2012/573, SI 2012/817

s.22, amended: 2012 c.5 Sch.3 para.2, Sch.14 Part 1

s.22, enabling: SI 2012/766, SI 2012/913, SI 2012/2680

s.30A, applied: SI 2012/2677 Reg.44, SI 2012/2885 Sch.1 para.25, Sch.4 para.5, SI 2012/2886 Sch.1, SI 2012/3144 Sch.1 para.19, SSI 2012/303 Reg.28, Sch.3 para.12, Sch.4 para.17, SSI 2012/319 Reg.29, Sch.2 para.5

s.30B, amended: 2012 c.5 Sch.9 para.4

s.30B, applied: SI 2012/780 Art.6, SI 2012/2885 Sch.1 para.25, Sch.1 para.26, Sch.4 para.5, SI 2012/2886 Sch.1, SI 2012/3144 Sch.1 para.19, SSI 2012/303 Sch.1 para.10, SSI 2012/319 Sch.2 para.5

s.30B, repealed (in part): 2012 c.5 Sch.14 Part 9

s.30C, applied: SI 2012/2885 Sch.1 para.25, SI 2012/2886 Sch.1, SI 2012/3144 Sch.1 para.19

s.30D, applied: SI 2012/2885 Sch.1 para.25, SI 2012/2886 Sch.1, SI 2012/3144 Sch.1 para.19

s.30DD, applied: SI 2012/2885 Sch.1 para.16, Sch.1 para.25, SI 2012/2886 Sch.1, SI 2012/3144 Sch.1 para.10, Sch.1 para.19, SI 2012/3145 Sch.1, SSI 2012/319 Reg.27

s.30E, applied: SI 2012/2885 Sch.1 para.16, Sch.1 para.25, SI 2012/2886 Sch.1, SI 2012/3144 Sch.1 para.10, Sch.1 para.19, SI 2012/3145 Sch.1, SSI 2012/319 Reg.27

s.35, amended: 2012 c.5 s.63

s.35, applied: 2012 c.5 s.127, SI 2012/2677 Reg.44, SI 2012/2885 Sch.1 para.25, SI 2012/3144 Sch.1 para.19, SI 2012/3145 Sch.1, SSI 2012/303 Reg.28, SSI 2012/319 Reg.29

s.37, applied: SI 2012/2677 Reg.44, SI 2012/2885 Sch.5 para.8, SI 2012/2886 Sch.1, SSI 2012/303 Sch.4 para.20, SSI 2012/319 Sch.3 para.7

s.38, applied: SI 2012/2677 Reg.44

s.39A, applied: SI 2012/2677 Reg.44, SI 2012/2885 Sch.5 para.7, SI 2012/2886 Sch.1, SSI 2012/303 Sch.4 para.20, SSI 2012/319 Sch.3 para.6

s.39B, applied: SI 2012/2677 Reg.44

s.40, applied: SSI 2012/303 Sch.3 para.12, Sch.4 para.17

s.41, applied: SSI 2012/303 Sch.3 para.12, Sch.4 para.17

s.43, applied: SI 2012/2885 Sch.1 para.22, SI 2012/2886 Sch.1, SI 2012/3144 Sch.1 para.16, SI 2012/3145 Sch.1, SSI 2012/319 Reg.38

s.44, amended: SI 2012/780 Art.4

s.44, applied: SI 2012/2677 Reg.44, SI 2012/2885 Sch.1 para.22, SI 2012/2886 Sch.1, SI 2012/3144 Sch.1 para.16, SI 2012/3145 Sch.1, SSI 2012/319 Reg.38

s.44A, amended: 2012 c.5 Sch.14 Part 1

s.44A, applied: SI 2012/2885 Sch.1 para.22, SI 2012/2886 Sch.1, SI 2012/3144 Sch.1 para.16, SI 2012/3145 Sch.1, SSI 2012/319 Reg.38

s.44B, applied: SI 2012/2885 Sch.1 para.22, SI 2012/2886 Sch.1, SI 2012/3144 Sch.1 para.16, SI 2012/3145 Sch.1, SSI 2012/319 Reg.38

s.44C, applied: SI 2012/2885 Sch.1 para.22, SI 2012/2886 Sch.1, SI 2012/3144 Sch.1 para.16, SI 2012/3145 Sch.1, SSI 2012/319 Reg.38

1992– cont.

4. Social Security Contributions and Benefits Act 1992–*cont.*

s.45, applied: SI 2012/ 2885 Sch.1 para.22, SI 2012/ 2886 Sch.1, SI 2012/ 3144 Sch.1 para.16, SI 2012/ 3145 Sch.1, SSI 2012/ 319 Reg.38

s.45A, applied: SI 2012/ 2885 Sch.1 para.22, SI 2012/ 2886 Sch.1, SI 2012/ 3144 Sch.1 para.16, SI 2012/ 3145 Sch.1, SSI 2012/ 319 Reg.38

s.45AA, applied: SI 2012/ 2885 Sch.1 para.22, SI 2012/ 2886 Sch.1, SI 2012/ 3144 Sch.1 para.16, SI 2012/ 3145 Sch.1, SSI 2012/ 319 Reg.38

s.45B, applied: SI 2012/ 2885 Sch.1 para.22, SI 2012/ 2886 Sch.1, SI 2012/ 3144 Sch.1 para.16, SI 2012/ 3145 Sch.1, SSI 2012/ 319 Reg.38

s.46, applied: SI 2012/ 2885 Sch.1 para.22, SI 2012/ 2886 Sch.1, SI 2012/ 3144 Sch.1 para.16, SI 2012/ 3145 Sch.1, SSI 2012/ 319 Reg.38

s.46A, applied: SI 2012/ 2885 Sch.1 para.22, SI 2012/ 2886 Sch.1, SI 2012/ 3144 Sch.1 para.16, SI 2012/ 3145 Sch.1, SSI 2012/ 319 Reg.38

s.47, applied: SI 2012/ 780 Art.6, SI 2012/ 2885 Sch.1 para.22, SI 2012/ 2886 Sch.1, SI 2012/ 3144 Sch.1 para.16, SI 2012/ 3145 Sch.1, SSI 2012/ 319 Reg.38

s.48, applied: SI 2012/ 2885 Sch.1 para.22, SI 2012/ 2886 Sch.1, SI 2012/ 3144 Sch.1 para.16, SI 2012/ 3145 Sch.1, SSI 2012/ 319 Reg.38

s.48A, applied: SI 2012/ 2885 Sch.1 para.22, SI 2012/ 2886 Sch.1, SI 2012/ 3144 Sch.1 para.16, SI 2012/ 3145 Sch.1, SSI 2012/ 319 Reg.38

s.48B, applied: SI 2012/ 2885 Sch.1 para.22, SI 2012/ 2886 Sch.1, SI 2012/ 3144 Sch.1 para.16, SI 2012/ 3145 Sch.1, SSI 2012/ 319 Reg.38

s.48BB, applied: SI 2012/ 2885 Sch.1 para.22, SI 2012/ 2886 Sch.1, SI 2012/ 3144 Sch.1 para.16, SI 2012/ 3145 Sch.1, SSI 2012/ 319 Reg.38

s.48C, applied: SI 2012/ 780 Art.6, SI 2012/ 2677 Reg.44, SI 2012/ 2885 Sch.1 para.22, SI 2012/ 2886 Sch.1, SI 2012/ 3144 Sch.1 para.16, SI 2012/ 3145 Sch.1, SSI 2012/ 319 Reg.38

s.49, applied: SI 2012/ 2885 Sch.1 para.22, SI 2012/ 2886 Sch.1, SI 2012/ 3144 Sch.1 para.16, SI 2012/ 3145 Sch.1, SSI 2012/ 319 Reg.38

s.50, applied: SI 2012/ 2885 Sch.1 para.22, SI 2012/ 2886 Sch.1, SI 2012/ 3144 Sch.1 para.16, SI 2012/ 3145 Sch.1, SSI 2012/ 319 Reg.38

s.51, applied: SI 2012/ 2885 Sch.1 para.22, SI 2012/ 2886 Sch.1, SI 2012/ 3144 Sch.1 para.16, SI 2012/ 3145 Sch.1, SSI 2012/ 319 Reg.38

s.51A, applied: SI 2012/ 2885 Sch.1 para.22, SI 2012/ 2886 Sch.1, SI 2012/ 3144 Sch.1 para.16, SI 2012/ 3145 Sch.1, SSI 2012/ 319 Reg.38

s.52, applied: SI 2012/ 2885 Sch.1 para.22, SI 2012/ 2886 Sch.1, SI 2012/ 3144 Sch.1 para.16, SI 2012/ 3145 Sch.1, SSI 2012/ 319 Reg.38

s.53, applied: SI 2012/ 2885 Sch.1 para.22, SI 2012/ 2886 Sch.1, SI 2012/ 3144 Sch.1 para.16, SI 2012/ 3145 Sch.1, SSI 2012/ 319 Reg.38

s.54, applied: SI 2012/ 2885 Sch.1 para.22, SI 2012/ 2886 Sch.1, SI 2012/ 3144 Sch.1 para.16, SI 2012/ 3145 Sch.1, SSI 2012/ 319 Reg.38

s.55, applied: SI 2012/ 2885 Sch.1 para.22, SI 2012/ 2886 Sch.1, SI 2012/ 3144 Sch.1 para.16, SI 2012/ 3145 Sch.1, SSI 2012/ 319 Reg.38

s.55, referred to: SI 2012/ 2885 Sch.1 para.22, SI 2012/ 3144 Sch.1 para.16, SSI 2012/ 319 Reg.38

s.55A, applied: SI 2012/ 2885 Sch.1 para.22, SI 2012/ 2886 Sch.1, SI 2012/ 3144 Sch.1 para.16, SI 2012/ 3145 Sch.1, SSI 2012/ 319 Reg.38

s.55A, varied: SI 2012/ 780 Art.4, Art.5

s.55C, applied: SI 2012/ 2886 Sch.1, SI 2012/ 3145 Sch.1

1992– cont.

4. Social Security Contributions and Benefits Act 1992– *cont.*

s.55C, referred to: SI 2012/ 2885 Sch.1 para.22, SI 2012/ 3144 Sch.1 para.16, SSI 2012/ 319 Reg.38

s.64, amended: 2012 c.5 Sch.9 para.5

s.64, applied: SI 2012/ 1483 Reg.4, SI 2012/ 2885 Sch.1 para.25, Sch.4 para.5, SI 2012/ 2886 Sch.1, SI 2012/ 3144 Sch.1 para.19, SI 2012/ 3145 Sch.1, SSI 2012/ 303 Reg.28, SSI 2012/ 319 Reg.29

s.64, repealed (in part): 2012 c.5 Sch.14 Part 9

s.65, applied: SI 2012/ 2885 Sch.4 para.5

s.66, applied: SI 2012/ 2885 Sch.4 para.5

s.67, applied: SI 2012/ 2885 Sch.4 para.5

s.68, applied: SI 2012/ 2677 Reg.44, SI 2012/ 2885 Sch.1 para.25, Sch.4 para.5, SI 2012/ 2886 Sch.1, SI 2012/ 3144 Sch.1 para.19, SI 2012/ 3145 Sch.1, SSI 2012/ 303 Reg.28, SSI 2012/ 319 Reg.29, Sch.2 para.5

s.69, applied: SI 2012/ 2885 Sch.4 para.5

s.70, applied: SI 2012/ 2677 Reg.44, SI 2012/ 2885 Sch.4 para.5, SI 2012/ 2886 Sch.1, SSI 2012/ 303 Sch.1 para.11

s.71, applied: SI 2012/ 1483 Reg.4, SI 2012/ 2886 Sch.1, SI 2012/ 3144 Sch.1 para.19, SI 2012/ 3145 Sch.1

s.71, repealed: 2012 c.5 s.90

s.72, applied: SI 2012/ 2885 Sch.2 para.5, Sch.2 para.6, SI 2012/ 2886 Sch.1, SSI 2012/ 303 Sch.1 para.8, Sch.1 para.11, Sch.1 para.12, SSI 2012/ 319 Sch.1 para.6, Sch.1 para.7, Sch.1 para.8

s.72, repealed: 2012 c.5 s.90

s.73, applied: SI 2012/ 1917 Sch.2 para.15, SI 2012/ 2885 Sch.2 para.7

s.73, repealed: 2012 c.5 s.90

s.74, repealed: 2012 c.5 s.90

s.75, repealed: 2012 c.5 s.90

s.76, repealed: 2012 c.5 s.90

s.77, applied: SSI 2012/ 303 Sch.4 para.51

s.78, applied: SI 2012/ 2677 Reg.44

s.79, applied: SI 2012/ 780 Art.3

s.80, amended: SI 2012/ 780 Art.8

s.80, applied: SSI 2012/ 319 Sch.2 para.12

s.90, enabling: SI 2012/ 819

s.94, amended: 2012 c.5 s.64

s.94, applied: SI 2012/ 2677 Reg.44

s.95A, added: 2012 c.5 s.66

s.103, amended: 2012 c.5 s.64

s.104, applied: SI 2012/ 2885 Sch.1 para.25, SI 2012/ 2886 Sch.1, SI 2012/ 3144 Sch.1 para.19, SI 2012/ 3145 Sch.1, SSI 2012/ 303 Reg.28, SSI 2012/ 319 Reg.29

s.106, applied: SSI 2012/ 303 Sch.4 para.52

s.107, applied: SI 2012/ 780 Art.6

s.108, amended: 2012 c.5 s.64

s.108, enabling: SI 2012/ 647, SI 2012/ 1634

s.109, amended: 2012 c.5 s.64

s.111, applied: 2012 c.5 s.64, SI 2012/ 2743 Reg.3

s.111, repealed: 2012 c.5 s.64

s.112, applied: SI 2012/ 2886 Sch.1, SI 2012/ 3145 Sch.1

s.113, applied: SI 2012/ 2885 Sch.1 para.8, Sch.1 para.25, Sch.1 para.26, Sch.2 para.7, SI 2012/ 2886 Sch.1, SI 2012/ 3144 Sch.1 para.3, Sch.1 para.19, SI 2012/ 3145 Sch.1, SSI 2012/ 303 Sch.1 para.10, Sch.1 para.12, SSI 2012/ 319 Sch.1 para.8

s.113, enabling: SI 2012/ 819, SI 2012/ 845

s.116, enabling: SI 2012/ 1656

s.117, enabling: SI 2012/ 867

s.122, amended: 2012 c.5 Sch.14 Part 1

1992–cont.

4. Social Security Contributions and Benefits Act 1992–*cont.*

s.122, enabling: SI 2012/647, SI 2012/766, SI 2012/817, SI 2012/819, SI 2012/913, SI 2012/1634, SI 2012/2680

s.123, repealed: 2012 c.5 Sch.14 Part 1

s.123, enabling: SI 2012/397, SI 2012/757, SI 2012/874, SI 2012/913, SI 2012/919, SI 2012/2575, SI 2012/2587, SI 2012/3040

s.124, amended: 2012 c.5 s.59

s.124, applied: 2012 c.5 s.33, SI 2012/1483 Reg.4

s.124, repealed: 2012 c.5 Sch.14 Part 1

s.124, enabling: SI 2012/757, SI 2012/874, SI 2012/913

s.124A, added: 2012 c.5 s.59

s.124A, repealed: 2012 c.5 Sch.14 Part 1

s.125, repealed: 2012 c.5 Sch.14 Part 1

s.126, amended: SI 2012/780 Art.19

s.126, repealed: 2012 c.5 Sch.14 Part 1

s.127, repealed: 2012 c.5 Sch.14 Part 1

s.128, repealed: 2012 c.5 Sch.14 Part 1

s.129, repealed: 2012 c.5 Sch.14 Part 1

s.130, see *Wychavon DC v EM* [2012] UKUT 12 (AAC), (2012) 15 C.C.L. Rep. 221 (UT (AAC)), Judge Michael Mark

s.130, applied: 2012 c.5 s.33

s.130, repealed: 2012 c.5 Sch.14 Part 1

s.130A, amended: 2012 c.5 s.69

s.130A, repealed: 2012 c.5 Sch.14 Part 1

s.130A, enabling: SI 2012/3040

s.130B, repealed: 2012 c.5 Sch.14 Part 1

s.130C, repealed: 2012 c.5 Sch.14 Part 1

s.130D, repealed: 2012 c.5 Sch.14 Part 1

s.130E, repealed: 2012 c.5 Sch.14 Part 1

s.130F, repealed: 2012 c.5 Sch.14 Part 1

s.130G, repealed: 2012 c.5 Sch.14 Part 1

s.131, applied: 2012 c.5 s.33, SI 2012/1483 Reg.6

s.131, repealed: 2012 c.5 Sch.14 Part 1

s.131, enabling: SI 2012/757, SI 2012/2587

s.132, repealed: 2012 c.5 Sch.14 Part 1

s.133, repealed: 2012 c.5 Sch.14 Part 1

s.134, repealed: 2012 c.5 Sch.14 Part 1

s.135, repealed: 2012 c.5 Sch.14 Part 1

s.135, enabling: SI 2012/913, SI 2012/919, SI 2012/2587

s.136, repealed: 2012 c.5 Sch.14 Part 1

s.136, enabling: SI 2012/397, SI 2012/757, SI 2012/2575

s.136A, repealed: 2012 c.5 Sch.14 Part 1

s.136A, enabling: SI 2012/757

s.137, repealed: 2012 c.5 Sch.14 Part 1

s.137, enabling: SI 2012/397, SI 2012/757, SI 2012/874, SI 2012/913, SI 2012/919, SI 2012/2575, SI 2012/2587, SI 2012/3040

s.138, amended: 2012 c.5 s.71

s.138, referred to: 2012 c.5 s.70

s.138, repealed (in part): 2012 c.5 s.70, Sch.14 Part 8

s.138, enabling: SI 2012/757, SI 2012/1814, SI 2012/2280, SI 2012/2379

s.139, repealed: 2012 c.5 Sch.14 Part 8

s.140, amended: 2012 c.5 s.72

s.140, repealed: 2012 c.5 Sch.14 Part 8

s.142, applied: SI 2012/2886 Sch.1, SI 2012/3145 Sch.1, SSI 2012/303 Reg.20

s.142, referred to: SI 2012/2677 Reg.76

s.142, enabling: SI 2012/818

s.145A, applied: SI 2012/2885 Reg.6, Sch.2 para.7, Sch.2 para.8, SI 2012/2886 Sch.1, SI 2012/3144 Reg.6, SI 2012/3145 Sch.1, SSI 2012/303 Reg.4,

1992–cont.

4. Social Security Contributions and Benefits Act 1992–*cont.*

s.145A, applied:–*cont.*
Sch.1 para.12, Sch.1 para.13, SSI 2012/319 Reg.4, Sch.1 para.8, Sch.1 para.9

s.146, applied: SI 2012/2677 Reg.77

s.146, enabling: SI 2012/2612

s.147, enabling: SI 2012/818

s.150, amended: 2012 c.5 Sch.3 para.3, Sch.9 para.6

s.150, applied: SI 2012/2677 Reg.44

s.150, repealed (in part): 2012 c.5 Sch.14 Part 9

s.157, amended: SI 2012/780 Art.9

s.163, amended: 2012 c.7 Sch.14 para.59

s.164, amended: 2012 c.5 s.63

s.164, applied: 2012 c.5 s.70, SI 2012/2885 Sch.1 para.25, SI 2012/3144 Sch.1 para.19, SI 2012/3145 Sch.1, SSI 2012/303 Reg.28

s.168, applied: 2012 c.5 s.70

s.171, amended: 2012 c.7 Sch.14 para.60

s.171E, applied: SI 2012/2885 Sch.1 para.25, SI 2012/2886 Sch.1, SI 2012/3144 Sch.1 para.19, SI 2012/3145 Sch.1, SSI 2012/303 Reg.20, Reg.28, SSI 2012/319 Reg.29

s.171ZA, amended: 2012 c.5 s.63

s.171ZA, applied: SI 2012/2885 Sch.1 para.25, SI 2012/2886 Sch.1, SI 2012/3144 Sch.1 para.19, SI 2012/3145 Sch.1, SSI 2012/303 Reg.28

s.171ZB, amended: 2012 c.5 s.63

s.171ZB, applied: SI 2012/2885 Sch.1 para.25, SI 2012/2886 Sch.1, SI 2012/3144 Sch.1 para.19, SI 2012/3145 Sch.1, SSI 2012/303 Reg.28

s.171ZEA, amended: 2012 c.5 s.63

s.171ZEA, applied: SI 2012/2885 Sch.1 para.25, SI 2012/2886 Sch.1, SI 2012/3144 Sch.1 para.19, SI 2012/3145 Sch.1, SSI 2012/303 Reg.28

s.171ZEB, amended: 2012 c.5 s.63

s.171ZEB, applied: SI 2012/2885 Sch.1 para.25, SI 2012/2886 Sch.1, SI 2012/3144 Sch.1 para.19, SI 2012/3145 Sch.1

s.171ZJ, amended: 2012 c.7 Sch.14 para.61

s.171ZL, amended: 2012 c.5 s.63

s.171ZL, applied: SI 2012/2885 Sch.1 para.25, SI 2012/2886 Sch.1, SI 2012/3144 Sch.1 para.19, SI 2012/3145 Sch.1, SSI 2012/303 Reg.28

s.171ZS, amended: 2012 c.7 Sch.14 para.62

s.172, applied: SI 2012/647

s.173A, added: 2012 c.5 s.63

s.175, repealed (in part): 2012 c.5 Sch.14 Part 1

s.175, enabling: SI 2012/397, SI 2012/573, SI 2012/647, SI 2012/757, SI 2012/766, SI 2012/804, SI 2012/816, SI 2012/817, SI 2012/819, SI 2012/821, SI 2012/845, SI 2012/867, SI 2012/874, SI 2012/913, SI 2012/1634, SI 2012/1656, SI 2012/1814, SI 2012/2280, SI 2012/2379, SI 2012/2575, SI 2012/2587, SI 2012/2680, SI 2012/3040

s.176, amended: 2012 c.5 s.69

s.176, applied: SI 2012/804, SI 2012/3040

Sch.1, applied: SSI 2012/319 Sch.5 para.3

Sch.1 para.6, enabling: SI 2012/821

Sch.1 para.7B, varied: 2012 c.14 Sch.38 para.54

Sch.2 para.5, amended: 2012 c.14 s.222

Sch.2 para.5, repealed (in part): 2012 c.14 s.222

Sch.3 Part I para.5, amended: 2012 c.5 Sch.14 Part 1

Sch.4, applied: SI 2012/2885 Sch.1 para.25, SI 2012/2886 Sch.1, SI 2012/3144 Sch.1 para.19, SI 2012/3145 Sch.1, SSI 2012/319 Reg.29

Sch.4 Part I, referred to: SI 2012/780 Art.3

Sch.4 Part I, substituted: SI 2012/780 Sch.1

Sch.4 Part II, substituted: SI 2012/780 Sch.1

1992– cont.

4. Social Security Contributions and Benefits Act 1992– *cont.*
Sch.4 Part III, amended: SI 2012/834 Art.2
Sch.4 Part III, referred to: SI 2012/780 Art.3
Sch.4 Part III, substituted: SI 2012/780 Sch.1
Sch.4 Part IV, referred to: SI 2012/780 Art.3
Sch.4 Part IV, substituted: SI 2012/780 Sch.1
Sch.4 Part V, amended: 2012 c.5 s.65
Sch.4 Part V, referred to: SI 2012/780 Art.3
Sch.4 Part V, substituted: SI 2012/780 Sch.1
Sch.4B Part V para.13, amended: SI 2012/189 Art.2
Sch.4B Part V para.13, applied: SI 2012/189 Art.2
Sch.5, applied: SI 2012/2885 Sch.1 para.22, Sch.6 para.28, SI 2012/2886 Sch.1, SI 2012/3144 Sch.1 para.16, SI 2012/3145 Sch.1, SSI 2012/319 Reg.38
Sch.5A, applied: SI 2012/2885 Sch.1 para.22, Sch.6 para.28, SI 2012/2886 Sch.1, SI 2012/3144 Sch.1 para.16, SI 2012/3145 Sch.1, SSI 2012/319 Reg.38
Sch.5 para A.1, varied: SI 2012/780 Art.4
Sch.5 para.1, varied: SI 2012/780 Art.4
Sch.5 para.2, varied: SI 2012/780 Art.4
Sch.5 para.2A, varied: SI 2012/780 Art.4
Sch.5 para.3, varied: SI 2012/780 Art.4
Sch.5 para.3A, varied: SI 2012/780 Art.4
Sch.5 para.3B, varied: SI 2012/780 Art.4
Sch.5 para.3C, varied: SI 2012/780 Art.4
Sch.5 para.4, varied: SI 2012/780 Art.4
Sch.5 para.5, varied: SI 2012/780 Art.4
Sch.5 para.5A, varied: SI 2012/780 Art.4
Sch.5 para.6, varied: SI 2012/780 Art.4
Sch.5 para.6A, varied: SI 2012/780 Art.4
Sch.5 para.7, varied: SI 2012/780 Art.4
Sch.5 para.7A, varied: SI 2012/780 Art.4
Sch.5 para.7B, varied: SI 2012/780 Art.4
Sch.5 para.7C, varied: SI 2012/780 Art.4
Sch.5 para.8, varied: SI 2012/780 Art.4
Sch.5 para.9, varied: SI 2012/780 Art.4
Sch.5A para.2, varied: SI 2012/780 Art.4, Art.5
Sch.7 Part I para.4, amended: SI 2012/823 Art.2
Sch.7 Part I para.4, enabling: SI 2012/823
Sch.7 Part II para.9, applicd: SI 2012/780 Art.6
Sch.7 Part V para.13, applied: SI 2012/780 Art.6
Sch.7 Part V para.13, varied: SI 2012/780 Art.4
Sch.7 Part VI para.14, amended: 2012 c.5 s.67
Sch.8, applied: 2012 c.5 s.64, SI 2012/2743 Reg.2, Reg.3
Sch.8 Part I para.1, repealed: 2012 c.5 s.64
Sch.8 Part I para.2, amended: SI 2012/780 Art.7
Sch.8 Part I para.2, applied: SI 2012/2743 Sch.1
Sch.8 Part I para.2, repealed: 2012 c.5 s.64
Sch.8 Part I para.2, enabling: SI 2012/833
Sch.8 Part I para.3, repealed: 2012 c.5 s.64
Sch.8 Part I para.4, repealed: 2012 c.5 s.64
Sch.8 Part I para.5, repealed: 2012 c.5 s.64
Sch.8 Part I para.6, amended: SI 2012/780 Art.7
Sch.8 Part I para.6, applied: SI 2012/2743 Sch.1
Sch.8 Part I para.6, repealed: 2012 c.5 s.64
Sch.8 Part II para.7, applied: SI 2012/2743 Sch.1
Sch.8 Part II para.7, repealed: 2012 c.5 s.64
Sch.8 Part III para.8, repealed: 2012 c.5 s.64
Sch.9 para.1, enabling: SI 2012/818, SI 2012/833
Sch.11 para.2, amended: 2012 c.5 s.63
Sch.11 para.9, added: 2012 c.5 s.63

5. Social Security Administration Act 1992
applied: 2012 c.5 s.41, SI 2012/188 Art.2, SI 2012/360, SI 2012/360 Art.2, SI 2012/2886 Sch.1
s.1, amended: 2012 c.5 Sch.2 para.4, Sch.9 para.8

1992– cont.

5. Social Security Administration Act 1992– *cont.*
s.1, repealed (in part): 2012 c.5 Sch.9 para.8, Sch.14 Part 1
s.2A, repealed: 2012 c.5 Sch.14 Part 1
s.2A, enabling: SI 2012/874
s.2AA, repealed: 2012 c.5 Sch.14 Part 1
s.2B, repealed: 2012 c.5 Sch.14 Part 1
s.2C, repealed: 2012 c.5 Sch.14 Part 1
s.2D, repealed: 2012 c.5 Sch.14 Part 1
s.2E, repealed: 2012 c.5 Sch.14 Part 1
s.2F, amended: 2012 c.5 s.59
s.2F, repealed: 2012 c.5 Sch.14 Part 1
s.2G, amended: 2012 c.5 s.59
s.2G, repealed: 2012 c.5 Sch.14 Part 1
s.2H, repealed: 2012 c.5 Sch.14 Part 1
s.5, amended: 2012 c.5 s.98, s.99, s.100, s.101, Sch.2 para.5, Sch.4 para.10, Sch.9 para.9, Sch.14 Part 1
s.5, repealed (in part): 2012 c.5 s.99, Sch.14 Part 1
s.5, enabling: SI 2012/757, SI 2012/819, SI 2012/824
s.6, repealed: 2012 c.5 Sch.14 Part 1
s.6, enabling: SI 2012/824
s.7, amended: 2012 c.5 Sch.3 para.5, Sch.14 Part 1
s.7, repealed (in part): 2012 c.5 Sch.14 Part 11, Sch.14 Part 1
s.7A, repealed (in part): 2012 c.5 Sch.14 Part 1
s.12, repealed: 2012 c.5 Sch.14 Part 8
s.13A, added: 2012 c.14 Sch.1 para.3
s.15A, amended: 2012 c.5 Sch.2 para.6, Sch.4 para.11, Sch.14 Part 1, 2012 c.21 Sch.18 para.74
s.15A, repealed (in part): 2012 c.5 Sch.14 Part 1
s.15A, enabling: SI 2012/644
s.22, amended: 2012 c.5 s.99
s.71, amended: 2012 c.5 s.105, s.106, s.107, Sch.9 para.10, Sch.14 Part 11
s.71, repealed (in part): 2012 c.5 Sch.14 Part 1, Sch.14 Part 11
s.71, enabling: SI 2012/645, SI 2012/757, SI 2012/1074
s.71A, repealed: 2012 c.5 Sch.14 Part 1
s.71ZA, amended: 2012 c.5 s.106
s.71ZA, repealed: 2012 c.5 Sch.14 Part 8
s.71ZB, added: 2012 c.5 s.105
s.71ZC, added: 2012 c.5 s.105
s.71ZC, amended: 2012 c.5 s.105
s.71ZD, added: 2012 c.5 s.105
s.71ZE, added: 2012 c.5 s.105
s.71ZF, added: 2012 c.5 s.105
s.71ZG, added: 2012 c.5 s.105
s.71ZH, added: 2012 c.5 s.105
s.71ZH, repealed (in part): 2012 c.5 Sch.14 Part 1, Sch.14 Part 4
s.73, amended: 2012 c.5 Sch.3 para.6, Sch.9 para.11, Sch.14 Part 1
s.74, amended: 2012 c.5 Sch.2 para.7, Sch.14 Part 1
s.74, repealed (in part): 2012 c.5 Sch.14 Part 1
s.74A, amended: 2012 c.5 Sch.2 para.8, Sch.14 Part 1
s.75, see *KW v Lancaster City Council* [2012] 1 F.L.R. 282 (UT (AAC)), Judge Nicholas Wikeley
s.75, amended: 2012 c.5 s.106
s.75, repealed: 2012 c.5 Sch.14 Part 1
s.75, enabling: SI 2012/645
s.76, repealed: 2012 c.5 Sch.14 Part 1
s.76, enabling: SI 2012/645
s.77, repealed: 2012 c.5 Sch.14 Part 1
s.78, amended: 2012 c.5 s.106, Sch.2 para.9, Sch.8 para.2, Sch.14 Part 1
s.78, repealed (in part): 2012 c.5 Sch.14 Part 8

1992– cont.

5. Social Security Administration Act 1992– *cont.*
s.79, amended: 2012 c.5 Sch.8 para.3
s.105, amended: 2012 c.5 Sch.2 para.10, Sch.14 Part 1
s.105, repealed (in part): 2012 c.5 Sch.14 Part 1
s.106, amended: 2012 c.5 Sch.2 para.11, Sch.14 Part 1
s.107, amended: 2012 c.5 Sch.14 Part 1
s.108, amended: 2012 c.5 Sch.2 para.12, Sch.14 Part 1, 2012 c.10 Sch.5 para.41, SI 2012/2814 Sch.4 para.6
s.109, amended: 2012 c.5 Sch.2 para.13, Sch.14 Part 1
s.109A, amended: 2012 c.5 s.122, Sch.14 Part 1
s.109A, repealed (in part): 2012 c.5 Sch.14 Part 1
s.109B, amended: 2012 c.5 s.110, Sch.14 Part 1, 2012 c.21 Sch.18 para.74
s.109BA, amended: 2012 c.5 Sch.14 Part 1
s.109C, amended: 2012 c.5 Sch.14 Part 1
s.110A, repealed: 2012 c.5 Sch.14 Part 1
s.110AA, repealed: 2012 c.5 Sch.14 Part 1
s.110ZA, amended: 2012 c.14 Sch.38 para.56
s.111, amended: 2012 c.5 Sch.14 Part 1
s.112, see *Bennett v Secretary of State for Work and Pensions* [2012] EWHC 371 (Admin), (2012) 176 J.P. 181 (DC), Richards, L.J.
s.115A, amended: 2012 c.5 s.105, s.113, s.114, s.115, Sch.14 Part 1
s.115A, applied: SI 2012/1909 Sch.2 para.3, Sch.4 para.31, Sch.5 para.21
s.115A, repealed (in part): 2012 c.5 Sch.14 Part 1
s.115B, amended: 2012 c.5 s.105, s.115, Sch.14 Part 1
s.115C, added: 2012 c.5 s.116
s.115C, amended: 2012 c.5 Sch.14 Part 1, Sch.14 Part 12
s.115C, applied: SI 2012/1990 Reg.2
s.115C, repealed (in part): 2012 c.5 Sch.14 Part 1
s.115C, enabling: SI 2012/1990
s.115D, added: 2012 c.5 s.116
s.115D, amended: 2012 c.5 Sch.14 Part 1, Sch.14 Part 12
s.115D, applied: SI 2012/1990 Reg.3, Reg.4
s.115D, enabling: SI 2012/1990
s.116, see *Bennett v Secretary of State for Work and Pensions* [2012] EWHC 371 (Admin), (2012) 176 J.P. 181 (DC), Richards, L.J.
s.116, amended: 2012 c.5 s.111, Sch.14 Part 1
s.116, repealed (in part): 2012 c.5 Sch.14 Part 1
s.116A, amended: 2012 c.5 s.112
s.116A, repealed: 2012 c.5 Sch.14 Part 1
s.116ZA, added: 2012 c.5 s.112
s.121C, see *O'Rorke v Revenue and Customs Commissioners* [2012] S.F.T.D. 553 (FTT (Tax)), Judge Stephen Oliver Q.C. (Chairman)
s.121D, see *O'Rorke v Revenue and Customs Commissioners* [2012] S.F.T.D. 553 (FTT (Tax)), Judge Stephen Oliver Q.C. (Chairman)
s.121DA, amended: 2012 c.5 Sch.2 para.14, Sch.9 para.12
s.121DA, repealed (in part): 2012 c.5 Sch.14 Part 1
s.121E, amended: 2012 c.5 Sch.14 Part 13
s.121E, repealed (in part): 2012 c.5 Sch.14 Part 13
s.121F, amended: 2012 c.5 Sch.14 Part 13
s.121F, repealed (in part): 2012 c.5 Sch.14 Part 13
s.122, repealed: 2012 c.5 Sch.14 Part 13
s.122B, amended: 2012 c.5 s.123, Sch.2 para.15, Sch.9 para.13
s.122C, amended: 2012 c.5 Sch.9 para.14
s.122C, repealed: 2012 c.5 Sch.14 Part 1
s.122D, repealed: 2012 c.5 Sch.14 Part 1
s.122E, repealed: 2012 c.5 Sch.14 Part 1

1992– cont.

5. Social Security Administration Act 1992– *cont.*
s.122F, amended: 2012 c.5 Sch.2 para.16, Sch.4 para.12, Sch.14 Part 1
s.122ZA, repealed: 2012 c.5 Sch.14 Part 13
s.123, applied: 2012 c.5 s.132
s.124, amended: 2012 c.5 Sch.2 para.17, Sch.9 para.15
s.124, repealed (in part): 2012 c.5 Sch.14 Part 1
s.125, amended: 2012 c.5 Sch.2 para.18, Sch.9 para.16
s.125, enabling: SI 2012/1604
s.126, amended: 2012 c.5 Sch.2 para.19, Sch.14 Part 1
s.126A, repealed: 2012 c.5 Sch.14 Part 10
s.128A, repealed: 2012 c.5 Sch.14 Part 1
s.130, amended: 2012 c.5 Sch.2 para.20
s.132, amended: 2012 c.5 Sch.2 para.21
s.132A, applied: SI 2012/1868 Reg.20
s.132A, enabling: SI 2012/1868
s.134, repealed: 2012 c.5 Sch.14 Part 1
s.138, repealed: 2012 c.5 Sch.14 Part 1
s.139, repealed: 2012 c.5 Sch.14 Part 1
s.139A, repealed: 2012 c.5 Sch.14 Part 1
s.139B, repealed: 2012 c.5 Sch.14 Part 1
s.139BA, repealed: 2012 c.5 Sch.14 Part 1
s.139C, repealed: 2012 c.5 Sch.14 Part 1
s.139D, repealed: 2012 c.5 Sch.14 Part 1
s.139DA, repealed: 2012 c.5 Sch.14 Part 1
s.139E, repealed: 2012 c.5 Sch.14 Part 1
s.139F, repealed: 2012 c.5 Sch.14 Part 1
s.139G, repealed: 2012 c.5 Sch.14 Part 1
s.139H, repealed: 2012 c.5 Sch.14 Part 1
s.140, repealed: 2012 c.5 Sch.14 Part 1
s.140A, repealed: 2012 c.5 Sch.14 Part 1
s.140B, repealed: 2012 c.5 Sch.14 Part 1
s.140C, repealed: 2012 c.5 Sch.14 Part 1
s.140D, repealed: 2012 c.5 Sch.14 Part 1
s.140E, repealed: 2012 c.5 Sch.14 Part 1
s.140EE, repealed: 2012 c.5 Sch.14 Part 1
s.140F, repealed: 2012 c.5 Sch.14 Part 1
s.140G, repealed: 2012 c.5 Sch.14 Part 1
s.141, applied: SI 2012/807, SI 2012/867
s.141, enabling: SI 2012/807
s.142, enabling: SI 2012/807
s.148, applied: SI 2012/187, SI 2012/528
s.148, enabling: SI 2012/187
s.148A, applied: SI 2012/188
s.148A, enabling: SI 2012/188
s.148AA, applied: SI 2012/189
s.148AA, enabling: SI 2012/189
s.150, see *R. (on the application of Staff Side of the Police Negotiating Board) v Secretary of State for Work and Pensions* [2011] EWHC 3175 (Admin), [2012] Eq. L.R. 124 (QBD (Admin)), Elias, L.J.; see *R. (on the application of Staff Side of the Police Negotiating Board) v Secretary of State for Work and Pensions* [2012] EWCA Civ 332, [2012] 3 All E.R. 301 (CA (Civ Div)), Lord Neuberger (M.R.)
s.150, amended: 2012 c.5 s.97, Sch.2 para.22, Sch.9 para.17, Sch.14 Part 1, Sch.14 Part 9
s.150, applied: SI 2012/782, SI 2012/819, SI 2012/834, SI 2012/835
s.150, referred to: SI 2012/782, SI 2012/834, SI 2012/835
s.150, repealed (in part): 2012 c.5 Sch.14 Part 1, Sch.14 Part 9
s.150, varied: SI 2012/780 Art.4
s.150, enabling: SI 2012/780, SI 2012/834
s.150A, applied: SI 2012/819
s.150A, enabling: SI 2012/780

1992– cont.

5. Social Security Administration Act 1992–*cont.*
s.151, applied: SI 2012/782
s.151, repealed (in part): 2012 c.5 Sch.14 Part 1
s.151, enabling: SI 2012/780
s.155, disapplied: SI 2012/819 Reg.2, SI 2012/845 Reg.2
s.155, enabling: SI 2012/819, SI 2012/845
s.159, amended: 2012 c.5 Sch.9 para.18
s.159, repealed: 2012 c.5 Sch.14 Part 1
s.159A, amended: 2012 c.5 Sch.9 para.19
s.159B, amended: 2012 c.5 Sch.3 para.7, Sch.9 para.20, Sch.14 Part 1
s.159C, amended: 2012 c.5 Sch.9 para.21
s.159D, added: 2012 c.5 Sch.2 para.23
s.159D, amended: 2012 c.5 Sch.3 para.8, Sch.14 Part 1
s.160, amended: 2012 c.5 Sch.9 para.22
s.160, repealed: 2012 c.5 Sch.14 Part 1
s.160A, amended: 2012 c.5 Sch.9 para.23
s.160A, repealed: 2012 c.5 Sch.14 Part 1
s.160B, amended: 2012 c.5 Sch.9 para.24, Sch.14 Part 1
s.160C, added: 2012 c.5 Sch.2 para.24
s.163, repealed (in part): 2012 c.5 Sch.14 Part 1
s.164, repealed (in part): 2012 c.5 Sch.14 Part 7
s.165, amended: 2012 c.5 Sch.2 para.25, Sch.9 para.25
s.166, amended: 2012 c.5 Sch.14 Part 1, Sch.14 Part 7
s.168, repealed: 2012 c.5 Sch.14 Part 8
s.170, amended: 2012 c.5 Sch.2 para.26, Sch.9 para.26
s.170, repealed (in part): 2012 c.5 Sch.14 Part 1
s.172, applied: SI 2012/1634
s.173, applied: SI 2012/397, SI 2012/645, SI 2012/757, SI 2012/853, SI 2012/874, SI 2012/1135, SI 2012/1616, SI 2012/2575, SI 2012/3096
s.176, applied: SI 2012/1990, SI 2012/2994
s.176, repealed (in part): 2012 c.5 Sch.14 Part 1
s.179, amended: 2012 c.5 Sch.2 para.27, Sch.9 para.27
s.179, repealed (in part): 2012 c.5 Sch.14 Part 1
s.179, enabling: SI 2012/360
s.180, amended: 2012 c.5 Sch.2 para.28, Sch.9 para.28
s.182A, repealed (in part): 2012 c.5 Sch.14 Part 1
s.182B, amended: 2012 c.5 Sch.2 para.29, Sch.9 para.29
s.182B, repealed (in part): 2012 c.5 Sch.14 Part 1
s.184, amended: 2012 c.5 Sch.9 para.30
s.185, repealed: 2012 c.5 Sch.14 Part 7
s.187, amended: 2012 c.5 Sch.2 para.30, Sch.9 para.31
s.187, repealed (in part): 2012 c.5 Sch.14 Part 1
s.188, repealed (in part): 2012 c.5 Sch.14 Part 7
s.189, amended: 2012 c.5 s.104, Sch.14 Part 1
s.189, repealed (in part): 2012 c.5 Sch.14 Part 1
s.189, enabling: SI 2012/187, SI 2012/644, SI 2012/645, SI 2012/757, SI 2012/780, SI 2012/819, SI 2012/824, SI 2012/834, SI 2012/845, SI 2012/874, SI 2012/1604, SI 2012/1868, SI 2012/1990
s.190, amended: 2012 c.5 s.114, s.116
s.190, applied: SI 2012/782, SI 2012/807, SI 2012/834, SI 2012/1990
s.190, repealed (in part): 2012 c.5 Sch.14 Part 1
s.190, enabling: SI 2012/845
s.191, amended: 2012 c.5 Sch.2 para.31, Sch.9 para.32, Sch.14 Part 1, Sch.14 Part 7

1992– cont.

5. Social Security Administration Act 1992–*cont.*
s.191, enabling: SI 2012/645, SI 2012/757, SI 2012/819, SI 2012/824, SI 2012/845, SI 2012/874, SI 2012/1990
Sch.2 para.8A, added: 2012 c.5 s.97
Sch.4 Part I, amended: 2012 c.5 Sch.8 para.4, Sch.14 Part 1, Sch.14 Part 8
Sch.4 Part II para.1, amended: 2012 c.5 s.125
Sch.7 Part I para A.1, added: 2012 c.5 Sch.9 para.33
Sch.9 para.1, repealed: 2012 c.5 Sch.14 Part 7
Sch.9 para.1, enabling: SI 2012/833
Sch.9 para.2, repealed: 2012 c.5 Sch.14 Part 7
Sch.9 para.3, repealed: 2012 c.5 Sch.14 Part 7
Sch.9 para.4, repealed: 2012 c.5 Sch.14 Part 7

6. Social Security (Consequential Provisions) Act 1992
Sch.2 para.55, repealed (in part): 2012 c.5 Sch.14 Part 7

7. Social Security Contributions and Benefits (Northern Ireland) Act 1992
s.1, enabling: SI 2012/817
s.2, enabling: SI 2012/816
s.3, enabling: SI 2012/817
s.5, enabling: SI 2012/804
s.7, enabling: SI 2012/816
s.10, enabling: SI 2012/817
s.13, amended: SI 2012/807 Art.3
s.15, amended: SI 2012/807 Art.4
s.18, amended: SI 2012/807 Art.4
s.19, enabling: SI 2012/573, SI 2012/817
s.113, enabling: SI 2012/845
s.116, enabling: SI 2012/1656
s.117, enabling: SI 2012/867
s.121, enabling: SI 2012/817
s.138, enabling: SI 2012/818
s.142, enabling: SI 2012/2612
s.143, enabling: SI 2012/818
s.171, enabling: SI 2012/573, SI 2012/804, SI 2012/816, SI 2012/817, SI 2012/821, SI 2012/845, SI 2012/867, SI 2012/1656
s.172, applied: SI 2012/804
Sch.1 para.6, enabling: SI 2012/821
Sch.1 para.7B, varied: 2012 c.14 Sch.38 para.55
Sch.2, amended: 2012 c.14 s.222
Sch.2, repealed: 2012 c.14 s.222
Sch.4 Part III, amended: SI 2012/835 Art.2
Sch.9 para.1, enabling: SI 2012/818

8. Social Security Administration (Northern Ireland) Act 1992
s.11A, added: 2012 c.14 Sch.1 para.4
s.69, amended: 2012 c.5 s.107
s.69, enabling: SI 2012/1074
s.104ZA, amended: 2012 c.14 Sch.38 para.57
s.129, applied: SI 2012/867
s.129, enabling: SI 2012/807
s.132, enabling: SI 2012/835
s.135, disapplied: SI 2012/845 Reg.2
s.135, enabling: SI 2012/845
s.165, enabling: SI 2012/835, SI 2012/845
s.166, applied: SI 2012/807, SI 2012/835
s.167, enabling: SI 2012/845

12. Taxation of Chargeable Gains Act 1992
see *Schofield v Revenue and Customs Commissioners* [2012] EWCA Civ 927, [2012] S.T.C. 2019 (CA (Civ Div)), Sir Andrew Morritt (Chancellor); see *Stolkin v Revenue and Customs Commissioners* [2012] S.F.T.D. 541 (FTT (Tax)), Judge Howard M Nowlan

12. Taxation of Chargeable Gains Act 1992–*cont.*
applied: 2012 c.14 s.38, s.75, s.99, Sch.17 para.35, SI 2012/1709 Art.5
referred to: 2012 c.14 s.99
Part II c.IV, applied: 2012 c.14 Sch.17 para.27
Part VII, substituted: 2012 c.14 Sch.39 para.49
s.1, see *Schofield v Revenue and Customs Commissioners* [2012] EWCA Civ 927, [2012] S.T.C. 2019 (CA (Civ Div)), Sir Andrew Morritt (Chancellor)
s.2, see *Broome v Revenue and Customs Commissioners* [2012] W.T.L.R. 585 (FTT (Tax)), Judge Michael Connell; see *Explainaway Ltd v Revenue and Customs Commissioners* [2012] UKUT 362 (TCC), [2012] S.T.C. 2525 (UT (Tax)), Newey, J; see *Schofield v Revenue and Customs Commissioners* [2012] EWCA Civ 927, [2012] S.T.C. 2019 (CA (Civ Div)), Sir Andrew Morritt (Chancellor)
s.3, amended: 2012 c.14 s.34, SI 2012/881 Art.2
s.3, disapplied: 2012 c.14 s.34
s.3, enabling: SI 2012/881
s.10B, amended: 2012 c.14 Sch.16 para.73
s.13, repealed (in part): 2012 c.14 s.35
s.24, see *Barker v Revenue and Customs Commissioners* [2012] S.F.T.D. 244 (FTT (Tax)), Judge Malachy Cornwell-Kelly
s.30, see *Land Securities Plc v Revenue and Customs Commissioners* [2012] S.F.T.D. 215 (FTT (Tax)), Judge Howard M Nowlan
s.71, see *McLaughlin v Revenue and Customs Commissioners* [2012] UKFTT 174 (TC), [2012] S.F.T.D. 1003 (FTT (Tax)), Adrian Shipwright
s.99A, amended: 2012 c.14 s.36
s.100, amended: 2012 c.14 Sch.16 para.74, Sch.18 para.15
s.103C, added: 2012 c.14 s.36
s.105, applied: 2012 c.14 Sch.17 para.28
s.105, varied: 2012 c.14 s.121
s.106, see *Land Securities Plc v Revenue and Customs Commissioners* [2012] S.F.T.D. 215 (FTT (Tax)), Judge Howard M Nowlan
s.110, applied: 2012 c.14 Sch.17 para.27
s.116, see *Blumenthal v Revenue and Customs Commissioners* [2012] UKFTT 497 (TC), [2012] S.F.T.D. 1264 (FTT (Tax)), Judge Guy Brannan
s.122, amended: SI 2012/266 Art.17
s.140C, repealed (in part): 2012 c.14 Sch.16 para.75
s.143, see *Explainaway Ltd v Revenue and Customs Commissioners* [2012] UKUT 362 (TCC), [2012] S.T.C. 2525 (UT (Tax)), Newey, J
s.150A, amended: 2012 c.14 Sch.6 para.20, Sch.7 para.27
s.150B, amended: 2012 c.14 Sch.6 para.21
s.150E, added: 2012 c.14 Sch.6 para.3
s.150F, added: 2012 c.14 Sch.6 para.3
s.150G, added: 2012 c.14 Sch.6 para.4
s.151, enabling: SI 2012/705, SI 2012/1871
s.151I, amended: 2012 c.14 Sch.16 para.76
s.152, see *Mertrux Ltd v Revenue and Customs Commissioners* [2012] UKUT 274 (TCC), [2012] S.T.C. 2327 (UT (Tax)), Newey, J
s.155, amended: 2012 c.14 s.37
s.165, see *McLaughlin v Revenue and Customs Commissioners* [2012] UKFTT 174 (TC), [2012] S.F.T.D. 1003 (FTT (Tax)), Adrian Shipwright

12. Taxation of Chargeable Gains Act 1992–*cont.*
s.170, varied: SI 2012/1868 Reg.7
s.171, amended: 2012 c.14 Sch.18 para.16
s.171, applied: 2012 c.14 s.118
s.171A, amended: 2012 c.14 s.181
s.171C, amended: 2012 c.14 Sch.16 para.77
s.171C, repealed (in part): 2012 c.14 Sch.16 para.77
s.173, applied: 2012 c.14 s.118
s.185, amended: 2012 c.14 Sch.16 para.78
s.201, repealed: 2012 c.14 Sch.39 para.45
s.202, amended: 2012 c.14 Sch.39 para.46
s.203, amended: 2012 c.14 Sch.39 para.45, Sch.39 para.47
s.204, amended: 2012 c.14 Sch.16 para.79
s.210A, amended: 2012 c.14 Sch.16 para.80
s.210A, applied: 2012 c.14 s.95
s.210A, repealed (in part): 2012 c.14 Sch.16 para.80
s.210B, amended: 2012 c.14 Sch.16 para.81
s.210B, applied: 2012 c.14 Sch.17 para.28
s.210C, amended: 2012 c.14 Sch.16 para.82
s.211, amended: 2012 c.14 Sch.16 para.83
s.211ZA, amended: 2012 c.14 Sch.16 para.84
s.212, amended: 2012 c.14 Sch.16 para.85
s.212, applied: SI 2012/3044 Reg.2, Reg.6
s.212, repealed (in part): 2012 c.14 Sch.16 para.85
s.212, varied: SI 2012/3044 Reg.2
s.213, amended: 2012 c.14 Sch.16 para.86
s.213A, added: 2012 c.14 Sch.16 para.87
s.213A, enabling: SI 2012/3044
s.219, amended: SI 2012/700 Sch.1 para.4
s.221, repealed: 2012 c.14 Sch.39 para.15
s.222, applied: SI 2012/736 Art.8
s.228, amended: 2012 c.14 s.34
s.249, repealed: 2012 c.14 Sch.39 para.49
s.251, amended: 2012 c.14 s.35
s.252, substituted: 2012 c.14 s.35
s.252A, repealed: 2012 c.14 s.35
s.257, applied: SI 2012/847 Reg.25
s.258, amended: 2012 c.14 Sch.14 para.34
s.259, amended: SI 2012/700 Sch.1 para.4
s.261B, applied: SI 2012/1836 Reg.10
s.263B, see *Barnes v Revenue and Customs Commissioners* [2012] UKUT 273 (TCC), [2012] S.T.C. 1904 (UT (Tax)), Roth, J.
s.271, amended: SI 2012/964 Sch.1
s.272, see *Barker v Revenue and Customs Commissioners* [2012] S.F.T.D. 244 (FTT (Tax)), Judge Malachy Cornwell-Kelly; see *Blumenthal v Revenue and Customs Commissioners* [2012] UKFTT 497 (TC), [2012] S.F.T.D. 1264 (FTT (Tax)), Judge Guy Brannan
s.273, see *Barker v Revenue and Customs Commissioners* [2012] S.F.T.D. 244 (FTT (Tax)), Judge Malachy Cornwell-Kelly
s.276, applied: SI 2012/847 Reg.21
s.282, see *Hamar v Revenue and Customs Commissioners* [2012] W.T.L.R. 469 (FTT (Tax)), Judge John Brooks
s.288, amended: 2012 c.14 Sch.39 para.17
s.288, referred to: SI 2012/1709 Art.5
Sch.A1 para.3, see *Stolkin v Revenue and Customs Commissioners* [2012] S.F.T.D. 541 (FTT (Tax)), Judge Howard M Nowlan
Sch.5B, applied: 2012 c.14 s.39
Sch.5BB para.1, added: 2012 c.14 Sch.6 para.5
Sch.5BB para.2, added: 2012 c.14 Sch.6 para.5
Sch.5BB para.3, added: 2012 c.14 Sch.6 para.5
Sch.5BB para.4, added: 2012 c.14 Sch.6 para.5

12. Taxation of Chargeable Gains Act 1992–*cont.*
Sch.5BB para.5, added: 2012 c.14 Sch.6 para.5
Sch.5BB para.6, added: 2012 c.14 Sch.6 para.5
Sch.5BB para.7, added: 2012 c.14 Sch.6 para.5
Sch.5BB para.8, added: 2012 c.14 Sch.6 para.5
Sch.5B para.1, see *Skye Inns Ltd v Revenue and Customs Commissioners* [2012] S.T.C. 174 (UT (Tax)), Sales, J.
Sch.5B para.1, amended: 2012 c.14 Sch.7 para.29
Sch.5B para.2, amended: 2012 c.14 Sch.6 para.22
Sch.5B para.11A, added: 2012 c.14 Sch.7 para.30
Sch.5B para.13, see *Segesta Ltd v Revenue and Customs Commissioners* [2012] UKUT 176 (TCC), [2012] S.T.C. 1847 (UT (Tax)), Sales, J.
Sch.5B para.16, amended: 2012 c.14 Sch.7 para.31
Sch.5B para.19, amended: 2012 c.14 Sch.7 para.32
Sch.7AC Part I para.6, amended: 2012 c.14 Sch.16 para.88
Sch.7AC Part II para.17, amended: 2012 c.14 Sch.16 para.88
Sch.7AD para.1, amended: 2012 c.14 Sch.16 para.89
Sch.8A para.1, repealed: 2012 c.14 s.35
Sch.8A para.2, repealed: 2012 c.14 s.35
Sch.8A para.3, repealed: 2012 c.14 s.35
Sch.8A para.4, repealed: 2012 c.14 s.35
Sch.9 Part I para.1, enabling: SI 2012/1843
Sch.10 para.14, repealed (in part): 2012 c.14 Sch.16 para.247

13. Further and Higher Education Act 1992
s.16, enabling: SI 2012/1748
s.16A, applied: SI 2012/1748
s.16A, enabling: SI 2012/1157
s.17, enabling: SI 2012/1748
s.20, enabling: SI 2012/1749
s.21, enabling: SI 2012/1749
s.26, applied: SI 2012/631 Art.3
s.26, varied: SI 2012/52 Art.3
s.27, applied: SI 2012/631, SI 2012/924 Art.7
s.27, enabling: SI 2012/52, SI 2012/631, SI 2012/1157
s.27B, enabling: SI 2012/1167
s.33C, applied: SI 2012/1158 Reg.3
s.33C, enabling: SI 2012/1158
s.33N, applied: SI 2012/924 Art.6, SI 2012/1158 Reg.2, Reg.4
s.33N, enabling: SI 2012/1158
s.33P, enabling: SI 2012/1167
s.51, applied: SI 2012/924 Art.7
s.69, enabling: SI 2012/1904
s.85AA, applied: SI 2012/1925 Reg.3
s.85AA, enabling: SI 2012/1925
s.85AC, applied: SI 2012/1925 Reg.3, Reg.4
s.85AC, enabling: SI 2012/1925
s.89, applied: SI 2012/1925
s.89, enabling: SI 2012/1157, SI 2012/1158, SI 2012/1904, SI 2012/1925
s.91, applied: SI 2012/811 Sch.1 para.4, SI 2012/2421 Sch.3 para.14, SI 2012/2576 Reg.3
Sch.4, enabling: SI 2012/1749

14. Local Government Finance Act 1992
applied: SI 2012/444 Reg.21, Reg.22, SI 2012/2885 Sch.1 para.7, Sch.1 para.19, SI 2012/2886 Sch.1, SI 2012/2914 Reg.3, SI 2012/3144 Sch.1 para.2, Sch.1 para.13, SI 2012/3145 Sch.1, SSI 2012/303 Reg.81
Part I c.III, applied: SI 2012/444 Reg.21, Reg.22
Part I c.IVZA, applied: SI 2012/444 Reg.4, Reg.5, Reg.6

14. Local Government Finance Act 1992–*cont.*
s.3, see *Wilson v Coll (Listing Officer)* [2011] EWHC 2824 (Admin), [2012] P.T.S.R. 1313 (QBD (Admin)), Singh, J.
s.4, enabling: SI 2012/2965
s.5, referred to: SI 2012/2914 Reg.5
s.6, see *Macattram v Camden LBC* [2012] EWHC 1033 (Admin), [2012] R.A. 369 (QBD (Admin)), Judge Robinson
s.6, amended: 2012 c.17 s.13
s.6, applied: SI 2012/2885 Reg.9, Sch.1 para.4, SI 2012/2886 Sch.1, SI 2012/3144 Reg.9, SI 2012/3145 Sch.1
s.7, applied: SI 2012/2885 Reg.9, SI 2012/2886 Sch.1, SI 2012/3144 Reg.9, SI 2012/3145 Sch.1
s.9, applied: SI 2012/2885 Sch.1 para.4, Sch.1 para.8, Sch.1 para.9, SI 2012/2886 Sch.1, SI 2012/3144 Sch.1 para.3, SI 2012/3145 Sch.1
s.10, amended: 2012 c.17 Sch.4 para.4
s.11, amended: 2012 c.17 s.12
s.11, applied: SI 2012/2886 Sch.1, SI 2012/3145 Sch.1
s.11A, amended: 2012 c.17 s.11, s.12
s.11A, applied: SI 2012/2886 Sch.1
s.11A, enabling: SI 2012/2964
s.11B, added: 2012 c.17 s.12
s.11B, enabling: SI 2012/2964
s.12, applied: SI 2012/3145 Sch.1
s.13, amended: 2012 c.17 s.12
s.13, applied: SI 2012/2885 Sch.1 para.46, SI 2012/2886 Sch.1, SI 2012/2914 Reg.4, SI 2012/3145 Sch.1, SSI 2012/303 Sch.5 para.40, SSI 2012/319 Sch.4 para.30
s.13A, applied: SI 2012/2885 Sch.1 para.14, Sch.7 para.9, SI 2012/2886 Sch.1, SI 2012/3144, SI 2012/3144 Reg.1, Reg.11, Reg.16, Sch.1 para.8, SI 2012/3145, SI 2012/3145 Sch.1
s.13A, substituted: 2012 c.17 s.10
s.13A, enabling: SI 2012/3144, SI 2012/3145
s.14A, added: 2012 c.17 s.14
s.14B, added: 2012 c.17 s.14
s.14C, added: 2012 c.17 s.14
s.14D, added: 2012 c.17 s.14
s.16, applied: SI 2012/2885 Sch.7 para.8, SI 2012/2886 Sch.1
s.17, see *RGM Properties Ltd v Speight (Listing Officer)* [2011] EWHC 2125 (Admin), [2012] R.A. 21 (QBD (Admin)), Langstaff, J.
s.18, amended: 2012 c.17 s.14
s.22, see *Wilson v Coll (Listing Officer)* [2011] EWHC 2824 (Admin), [2012] P.T.S.R. 1313 (QBD (Admin)), Singh, J.
s.23, see *Wilson v Coll (Listing Officer)* [2011] EWHC 2824 (Admin), [2012] P.T.S.R. 1313 (QBD (Admin)), Singh, J.
s.30, see *Hunt v North Somerset Council* [2012] EWHC 1928 (Admin), [2012] Eq. L.R. 951 (QBD (Admin)), Wyn Williams, J.
s.31, applied: SI 2012/460 Reg.4
s.31, disapplied: SI 2012/460 Reg.4, Reg.6
s.31, enabling: SI 2012/460
s.31A, see *Hunt v North Somerset Council* [2012] EWHC 1928 (Admin), [2012] Eq. L.R. 951 (QBD (Admin)), Wyn Williams, J.
s.31A, applied: SI 2012/444 Reg.7
s.31A, varied: SI 2012/444 Reg.7
s.31B, applied: SI 2012/444 Reg.7, SI 2012/2914 Reg.2, Reg.3, Reg.6, Reg.7, Reg.8, Reg.9, Reg.10
s.31B, referred to: SI 2012/444 Reg.26
s.31B, enabling: SI 2012/2914

14. Local Government Finance Act 1992–*cont.*
s.32, amended: SI 2012/521 Reg.2, Reg.6
s.32, enabling: SI 2012/521
s.33, amended: SI 2012/521 Reg.3
s.33, enabling: SI 2012/521
s.34, amended: 2012 c.17 s.15
s.34, applied: SI 2012/444 Reg.7, SI 2012/2914
    Reg.2, Reg.6, Reg.7, Reg.11
s.34, referred to: SI 2012/444 Reg.26
s.34, enabling: SI 2012/2914
s.35, applied: SI 2012/444 Reg.7
s.36, applied: SI 2012/444 Reg.7
s.36, referred to: SI 2012/444 Reg.26
s.41, applied: SI 2012/444 Reg.7
s.42A, applied: SI 2012/444 Reg.7
s.42B, applied: SI 2012/444 Reg.7, SI 2012/2914
    Reg.2, Reg.7, Reg.8, Reg.10
s.42B, enabling: SI 2012/2914
s.43, amended: SI 2012/521 Reg.4
s.43, enabling: SI 2012/521
s.44, amended: SI 2012/521 Reg.5
s.44, enabling: SI 2012/521
s.45, amended: 2012 c.17 s.15
s.45, applied: SI 2012/444 Reg.7, SI 2012/2914
    Reg.2, Reg.7, Reg.8, Reg.10
s.45, enabling: SI 2012/2914
s.46, applied: SI 2012/444 Reg.7
s.47, applied: SI 2012/444 Reg.7
s.48, applied: SI 2012/2914 Reg.2, Reg.7, Reg.8,
    Reg.10
s.48, enabling: SI 2012/2914
s.52ZB, applied: SI 2012/444 Reg.4, Reg.5, Reg.6,
    Reg.10
s.52ZF, amended: 2012 c.17 s.3
s.52ZF, applied: SI 2012/444 Reg.7, Reg.21, Reg.22
s.52ZF, repealed (in part): 2012 c.17 s.3
s.52ZJ, amended: 2012 c.17 s.3
s.52ZJ, applied: SI 2012/444 Reg.7
s.52ZJ, repealed (in part): 2012 c.17 s.3
s.52ZK, applied: SI 2012/444 Reg.21, Reg.22, SI
    2012/460 Reg.3, Reg.4
s.52ZK, referred to: SI 2012/460 Reg.4
s.52ZK, enabling: SI 2012/460
s.52ZK, varied: SI 2012/460 Reg.4
s.52ZL, applied: SI 2012/444 Reg.8
s.52ZM, applied: SI 2012/444 Reg.21, Reg.22, SI
    2012/460 Reg.5, Reg.6
s.52ZM, enabling: SI 2012/460
s.52ZN, applied: SI 2012/444 Reg.17, SI 2012/460
    Reg.4, Reg.6
s.52ZN, disapplied: SI 2012/460 Reg.4, Reg.6
s.52ZN, enabling: SI 2012/460
s.52ZO, applied: SI 2012/444 Reg.21, Reg.22
s.52ZQ, applied: SI 2012/444, SI 2012/1917 Sch.2
    para.11
s.52ZQ, enabling: SI 2012/444
s.52ZX, applied: SI 2012/444 Reg.8, Reg.27, SI
    2012/2914 Reg.2, Reg.6, Reg.8, Reg.11
s.52ZX, varied: SI 2012/444 Reg.27
s.52ZX, enabling: SI 2012/460, SI 2012/2914
s.52ZX, enabling: SI 2012/2914
s.66, see *Hunt v North Somerset Council* [2012]
    EWHC 1928 (Admin), [2012] Eq. L.R. 951
    (QBD (Admin)), Wyn Williams, J.
s.66, amended: 2012 c.17 s.12, Sch.4 para.5
s.67, amended: 2012 c.17 s.12, Sch.4 para.6
s.69, amended: 2012 c.17 s.3
s.71, amended: 2012 asp 11 s.3

14. Local Government Finance Act 1992–*cont.*
s.72, enabling: SSI 2012/339
s.75, see *Dundee City Council v Dundee Valuation
    Appeal Committee* 2012 S.C. 463 (IH (2 Div)),
    The Lord Justice Clerk (Gill)
s.75, applied: SSI 2012/303 Reg.3, Reg.14, Reg.79,
    SSI 2012/319 Reg.3, Reg.14, Reg.57
s.77, applied: SSI 2012/303 Reg.67, Reg.79, SSI
    2012/319 Reg.48, Reg.56, Reg.57
s.77A, applied: SSI 2012/303 Reg.67, Reg.79, SSI
    2012/319 Reg.48, Reg.56, Reg.57
s.79, applied: SSI 2012/53 Art.9, SSI 2012/303
    Reg.81, SSI 2012/319 Reg.59
s.80, applied: SSI 2012/303 Reg.66, Reg.81, Sch.5
    para.40, SSI 2012/319 Reg.47, Reg.59, Sch.4
    para.30
s.80, enabling: SSI 2012/303, SSI 2012/319
s.80A, applied: SSI 2012/303 Reg.66, SSI 2012/319
    Reg.47
s.81, applied: SSI 2012/53 Art.12
s.82, see *Assessor for Lothian Valuation Joint Board
    v Campbell* 2012 S.L.T. 414 (IH (2 Div)), The Lord
    Justice Clerk (Gill)
s.113, amended: 2012 c.17 s.14
s.113, applied: SI 2012/1917 Sch.2 para.11
s.113, enabling: SI 2012/444, SI 2012/460, SI 2012/
    521, SI 2012/672, SI 2012/2885, SI 2012/2886, SI
    2012/2914, SI 2012/3085, SI 2012/3086, SI 2012/
    3087, SSI 2012/303, SSI 2012/319, SSI 2012/338,
    SSI 2012/339
s.116, enabling: SSI 2012/338
Sch.1, applied: SI 2012/2885 Sch.1 para.4, Sch.1
    para.8, Sch.3 para.3, SI 2012/2886 Sch.1, SI
    2012/3144 Sch.1 para.3, SI 2012/3145 Sch.1, SSI
    2012/303 Reg.14, Reg.67, Reg.79, Sch.2 para.3,
    SSI 2012/319 Reg.14, Reg.48, Reg.57
Sch.1 para.4, applied: SI 2012/3145 Sch.1
Sch.1 para.4, referred to: SI 2012/2885 Sch.1 para.8,
    SI 2012/3144 Sch.1 para.3
Sch.1A para.1, added: 2012 c.17 Sch.4 para.1
Sch.1A para.2, added: 2012 c.17 Sch.4 para.1
Sch.1A para.2, applied: SI 2012/2885 Reg.11,
    Reg.12, Reg.13, Sch.1 para.2, Sch.1 para.3, Sch.1
    para.4
Sch.1A para.3, added: 2012 c.17 Sch.4 para.1
Sch.1A para.4, added: 2012 c.17 Sch.4 para.1
Sch.1A para.5, added: 2012 c.17 Sch.4 para.1
Sch.1A para.6, added: 2012 c.17 Sch.4 para.1
Sch.1A para.7, added: 2012 c.17 Sch.4 para.1
Sch.1A para.8, added: 2012 c.17 Sch.4 para.1
Sch.1A para.9, added: 2012 c.17 Sch.4 para.1
Sch.1B para.1, added: 2012 c.17 Sch.4 para.1
Sch.1B para.2, added: 2012 c.17 Sch.4 para.1
Sch.1B para.3, added: 2012 c.17 Sch.4 para.1
Sch.1B para.3, applied: SI 2012/3144 Reg.19, Reg.25
Sch.1B para.4, added: 2012 c.17 Sch.4 para.1
Sch.1B para.5, added: 2012 c.17 Sch.4 para.1
Sch.1B para.6, added: 2012 c.17 Sch.4 para.1
Sch.1B para.6, applied: SI 2012/3145 Reg.2
Sch.1B para.7, added: 2012 c.17 Sch.4 para.1
Sch.1B para.8, added: 2012 c.17 Sch.4 para.1
Sch.2, amended: 2012 c.17 s.12
Sch.2, substituted: 2012 asp 11 s.3
Sch.2 para.1, enabling: SI 2012/672, SI 2012/3086,
    SI 2012/3087, SSI 2012/303, SSI 2012/319, SSI
    2012/338
Sch.2 para.2, amended: 2012 c.17 s.16
Sch.2 para.2, enabling: SI 2012/672, SI 2012/3086,
    SI 2012/3087, SSI 2012/338

1992– cont.

14. Local Government Finance Act 1992–*cont.*
Sch.2 para.4, amended: 2012 asp 11 s.3, 2012 c.17 s.12
Sch.2 para.4, enabling: SI 2012/3086, SSI 2012/338
Sch.2 para.5, enabling: SI 2012/3086
Sch.2 para.6, enabling: SI 2012/3086
Sch.2 para.8, enabling: SI 2012/3086
Sch.2 para.9, enabling: SI 2012/3086
Sch.2 para.10, enabling: SI 2012/3086
Sch.2 para.11, amended: 2012 c.17 s.17
Sch.2 para.12, amended: 2012 c.17 s.17
Sch.2 para.15A, added: 2012 c.17 s.17
Sch.2 para.15B, added: 2012 c.17 s.17
Sch.2 para.15C, added: 2012 c.17 s.17
Sch.2 para.15D, added: 2012 c.17 s.17
Sch.2 para.16, amended: 2012 c.17 s.17
Sch.2 para.16, enabling: SI 2012/3086
Sch.2 para.21, amended: 2012 c.17 Sch.4 para.7
Sch.3 para.2, amended: 2012 asp 11 s.3
Sch.3 para.3, amended: 2012 c.17 s.14
Sch.3 para.6, amended: 2012 c.17 s.14
Sch.4 para.1, enabling: SI 2012/672
Sch.4 para.2, enabling: SI 2012/672
Sch.4 para.3, enabling: SI 2012/672
Sch.4 para.6, amended: 2012 c.5 Sch.2 para.33, Sch.14 Part 1
Sch.4 para.12, amended: 2012 c.5 Sch.2 para.33, Sch.14 Part 1
Sch.4 para.12, repealed (in part): 2012 c.5 Sch.14 Part 1
Sch.8 para.6, amended: 2012 c.5 Sch.2 para.34, Sch.14 Part 1
Sch.9 para.1, repealed: 2012 c.5 Sch.14 Part 1
Sch.9 para.2, repealed: 2012 c.5 Sch.14 Part 1
Sch.9 para.3, repealed: 2012 c.5 Sch.14 Part 1
Sch.9 para.4, repealed: 2012 c.5 Sch.14 Part 1
Sch.9 para.5, repealed: 2012 c.5 Sch.14 Part 1
Sch.9 para.6, repealed: 2012 c.5 Sch.14 Part 1
Sch.9 para.7, repealed: 2012 c.5 Sch.14 Part 1
Sch.9 para.8, repealed: 2012 c.5 Sch.14 Part 1
Sch.9 para.9, repealed: 2012 c.5 Sch.14 Part 1
Sch.9 para.10, repealed: 2012 c.5 Sch.14 Part 1
Sch.9 para.11, repealed: 2012 c.5 Sch.14 Part 1
Sch.9 para.12, repealed: 2012 c.5 Sch.14 Part 1
Sch.9 para.13, repealed: 2012 c.5 Sch.14 Part 1
Sch.9 para.15, repealed: 2012 c.5 Sch.14 Part 1
Sch.9 para.16, repealed: 2012 c.5 Sch.14 Part 1
Sch.9 para.17, repealed: 2012 c.5 Sch.14 Part 1
Sch.9 para.19, repealed: 2012 c.5 Sch.14 Part 1
Sch.9 para.20, repealed: 2012 c.5 Sch.14 Part 1
Sch.9 para.21, repealed: 2012 c.5 Sch.14 Part 1
Sch.9 para.22, repealed: 2012 c.5 Sch.14 Part 1
Sch.9 para.23, repealed: 2012 c.5 Sch.14 Part 1
Sch.9 para.24, repealed: 2012 c.5 Sch.14 Part 1
Sch.9 para.25, repealed (in part): 2012 c.5 Sch.14 Part 1
Sch.10 Part II para.16, repealed: 2012 c.17 s.3
Sch.12 Part I para.1, enabling: SSI 2012/41, SSI 2012/94
Sch.12 Part I para.2, applied: SSI 2012/41, SSI 2012/94
Sch.12 Part II para.9, applied: SSI 2012/41 Art.3
Sch.12 Part II para.9, enabling: SSI 2012/41
Sch.13 para.78, repealed (in part): 2012 c.17 Sch.3 para.30

34. Sexual Offences (Amendment) Act 1992
s.1, applied: SI 2012/1726 r.37.2, r.16.1

1992– cont.

37. Further and Higher Education (Scotland) Act 1992
Part II, applied: SSI 2012/162 Sch.1
s.3, enabling: SSI 2012/237, SSI 2012/238
s.5, applied: SSI 2012/238
s.12, applied: SI 2012/2886 Sch.1, SSI 2012/303 Sch.4 para.15, Sch.5 para.55
s.25, applied: SSI 2012/237, SSI 2012/238
s.25, enabling: SSI 2012/237, SSI 2012/238
s.36, applied: SSI 2012/162 Sch.1
s.51, applied: SSI 2012/237
s.60, enabling: SSI 2012/237, SSI 2012/238

40. Friendly Societies Act 1992
applied: 2012 c.14 s.158, s.165, s.166, SI 2012/1128 Art.4
s.6, applied: 2012 c.14 s.170
s.91, applied: 2012 c.14 s.166
s.91, referred to: 2012 c.14 s.158

42. Transport and Works Act 1992
s.1, applied: SI 2012/2679
s.1, enabling: SI 2012/472, SI 2012/981, SI 2012/1993, SI 2012/2679, SI 2012/2980
s.2, applied: SI 2012/2679
s.2, enabling: SI 2012/472
s.3, applied: SI 2012/1924, SI 2012/2679
s.3, enabling: SI 2012/1266, SI 2012/1867, SI 2012/1924, SI 2012/2533
s.4, applied: SI 2012/2679
s.5, amended: SI 2012/1659 Sch.3 para.12
s.5, applied: SI 2012/1924, SI 2012/2679
s.5, enabling: SI 2012/472, SI 2012/981, SI 2012/1266, SI 2012/1867, SI 2012/1924, SI 2012/1993, SI 2012/2533, SI 2012/2679, SI 2012/2980
s.11, applied: SI 2012/1924, SI 2012/2679
s.14, applied: SI 2012/1266
s.20, applied: SI 2012/1266
s.20, repealed (in part): SI 2012/1659 Sch.3 para.12
Sch.1, enabling: SI 2012/981
Sch.1 para.1, enabling: SI 2012/472, SI 2012/981, SI 2012/1867, SI 2012/1993, SI 2012/2679, SI 2012/2980
Sch.1 para.2, enabling: SI 2012/981, SI 2012/1867, SI 2012/2679, SI 2012/2980
Sch.1 para.3, enabling: SI 2012/1867, SI 2012/1924, SI 2012/2679
Sch.1 para.4, enabling: SI 2012/981, SI 2012/1867, SI 2012/1924, SI 2012/1993, SI 2012/2679, SI 2012/2980
Sch.1 para.5, enabling: SI 2012/1266, SI 2012/1867, SI 2012/1924, SI 2012/2679
Sch.1 para.7, enabling: SI 2012/1266, SI 2012/1867, SI 2012/1924, SI 2012/2679
Sch.1 para.8, enabling: SI 2012/472, SI 2012/981, SI 2012/1266, SI 2012/1867, SI 2012/1924, SI 2012/1993, SI 2012/2679, SI 2012/2980
Sch.1 para.9, enabling: SI 2012/472, SI 2012/981, SI 2012/2980
Sch.1 para.10, enabling: SI 2012/1867, SI 2012/2679
Sch.1 para.11, enabling: SI 2012/1867, SI 2012/1924, SI 2012/2679
Sch.1 para.12, enabling: SI 2012/472, SI 2012/1266
Sch.1 para.13, enabling: SI 2012/472, SI 2012/981, SI 2012/1266, SI 2012/1867, SI 2012/2980
Sch.1 para.15, enabling: SI 2012/472, SI 2012/981, SI 2012/1266, SI 2012/1867, SI 2012/1993, SI 2012/2533, SI 2012/2679, SI 2012/2980
Sch.1 para.16, enabling: SI 2012/1867, SI 2012/1924, SI 2012/2679
Sch.1 para.17, enabling: SI 2012/1867, SI 2012/2679

1992–cont.

44. Museums and Galleries Act 1992
s.6, applied: 2012 asp 3 s.3
Sch.5 Part I, amended: 2012 asp 3 Sch.2 para.3
Sch.6, amended: 2012 asp 3 Sch.2 para.3

46. Non-Domestic Rating Act 1992
s.4, amended: 2012 c.17 Sch.3 para.20
s.5, amended: 2012 c.17 Sch.3 para.21

50. Carriage of Goods by Sea Act 1992
see *Fortis Bank SA/NV v Indian Overseas Bank*
[2011] EWHC 538 (Comm), [2012] 1 All E.R.
(Comm) 41 (QBD (Comm)), Jonathan Hirst,
Q.C.
s.2, see *Finmoon Ltd v Baltic Reefers Management
Ltd* [2012] EWHC 920 (Comm), [2012] 2 Lloyd's
Rep. 388 (QBD (Comm)), Eder, J.

51. Protection of Badgers Act 1992
s.1, see *R. (on the application of Badger Trust) v
Secretary of State for the Environment, Food
and Rural Affairs* [2012] EWCA Civ 1286,
Times, December 14, 2012 (CA (Civ Div)),
Laws, L.J.
s.10, see *R. (on the application of Badger Trust) v
Secretary of State for the Environment, Food
and Rural Affairs* [2012] EWCA Civ 1286,
Times, December 14, 2012 (CA (Civ Div)),
Laws, L.J.

52. Trade Union and Labour Relations (Consolidation) Act 1992
applied: SI 2012/1464 Sch.1
Part IV c.II, applied: SI 2012/335 Sch.2 para.20, SI
2012/2991 Sch.2 para.28
Pt V. see *Metroline Travel Ltd v Unite the Union*
[2012] EWHC 1778 (QB), [2012] I.R.L.R. 749
(QBD), Supperstone, J.
s.1, applied: SI 2012/1204 Reg.17
s.64, see *Unison v Kelly* [2012] I.R.L.R. 442 (EAT),
Supperstone, J.
s.65, see *Unison v Kelly* [2012] EWCA Civ 1148,
[2012] I.R.L.R. 951 (CA (Civ Div)), Richards,
L.J.; see *Unison v Kelly* [2012] I.R.L.R. 442
(EAT), Supperstone, J.
s.119, applied: SI 2012/1204 Reg.17
s.145E, amended: SI 2012/3007 Sch.1
s.156, amended: SI 2012/3007 Sch.1
s.168, applied: SI 2012/335 Sch.2 para.20, SI 2012/
2991 Sch.2 para.28
s.168A, applied: SI 2012/335 Sch.2 para.20, SI 2012/
2991 Sch.2 para.28
s.170, applied: SI 2012/335 Sch.2 para.20, SI 2012/
2991 Sch.2 para.28
s.176, amended: SI 2012/3007 Sch.1
s.188, see *Phillips v Xtera Communications Ltd*
[2012] I.C.R. 171 (EAT), Recorder Luba Q.C.;
see *University of Stirling v University and
College Union* [2012] I.C.R. 803 (EAT (SC)),
Lady Smith
s.188A, see *Phillips v Xtera Communications Ltd*
[2012] I.C.R. 171 (EAT), Recorder Luba Q.C.
s.195, see *University of Stirling v University and
College Union* [2012] I.C.R. 803 (EAT (SC)),
Lady Smith
s.196, referred to: SI 2012/335 Sch.2 para.20, SI
2012/2991 Sch.2 para.28
s.219, see *Metroline Travel Ltd v Unite the Union*
[2012] EWHC 1778 (QB), [2012] I.R.L.R. 749
(QBD), Supperstone, J.
s.221, see *Balfour Beatty Engineering Services Ltd
v Unite the Union* [2012] EWHC 267 (QB), [2012]
I.C.R. 822 (QBD), Eady, J.; see *Metroline Travel*

1992–cont.

52. Trade Union and Labour Relations (Consolidation) Act 1992–*cont.*
s.221–*cont.*
Ltd v Unite the Union [2012] EWHC 1778 (QB),
[2012] I.R.L.R. 749 (QBD), Supperstone, J.
s.226, see *London Underground Ltd v Associated
Society of Locomotive Engineers and Firemen*
[2011] EWHC 3506 (QB), [2012] I.R.L.R. 196
(QBD), Eder, J.
s.226A, see *Metroline Travel Ltd v Unite the Union*
[2012] EWHC 1778 (QB), [2012] I.R.L.R. 749
(QBD), Supperstone, J.
s.227, see *London Underground Ltd v Associated
Society of Locomotive Engineers and Firemen*
[2011] EWHC 3506 (QB), [2012] I.R.L.R. 196
(QBD), Eder, J.
s.230, see *Balfour Beatty Engineering Services Ltd
v Unite the Union* [2012] EWHC 267 (QB), [2012]
I.C.R. 822 (QBD), Eady, J.
s.231B, see *London Underground Ltd v Associated
Society of Locomotive Engineers and Firemen*
[2011] EWHC 3506 (QB), [2012] I.R.L.R. 196
(QBD), Eder, J.
s.249, amended: SI 2012/2404 Sch.2 para.28
s.261, amended: SI 2012/2404 Sch.2 para.28
s.279, amended: 2012 c.7 Sch.5 para.66

53. Tribunals and Inquiries Act 1992
s.8, applied: SI 2012/1033
s.9, applied: SI 2012/605 Reg.18
s.11, amended: 2012 asp 9 Sch.1 para.2
Sch.1 Part I, applied: SSI 2012/137 Art.6
Sch.1 Part I, varied: SSI 2012/140 Art.6

1993

8. Judicial Pensions and Retirement Act 1993
s.9A, applied: SI 2012/516 Reg.3
s.9A, enabling: SI 2012/516
s.10, amended: 2012 c.21 Sch.18 para.75
s.26, amended: SI 2012/2595 Art.6
s.29, enabling: SI 2012/516
Sch.2 Part I para.1, amended: 2012 c.21 Sch.18
para.75

9. Prisoners and Criminal Proceedings (Scotland) Act 1993
Part I, referred to: 2012 asp 7 s.2
s.1, see *Foye (Robert) v HM Advocate* 2012 J.C. 190
(HCJ), Lord Osborne
s.2, see *Foye (Robert) v HM Advocate* 2012 J.C. 190
(HCJ), Lord Osborne; see *Gilbey (Julian) v HM
Advocate* 2012 J.C. 40 (HCJ Appeal), Lord Reed;
see *S v HM Advocate* 2012 J.C. 69 (HCJ), Lord
Osborne
s.2, amended: 2012 asp 7 s.1
s.2, repealed (in part): 2012 asp 7 s.1
s.2A, added: 2012 asp 7 s.1
s.2B, added: 2012 asp 7 s.1
s.10, see *Gilbey (Julian) v HM Advocate* 2012 J.C. 40
(HCJ Appeal), Lord Reed
s.16, see *Ottaway v Nisbet* [2012] HCJAC 36, 2012
S.L.T. 662 (HCJ), Lady Paton
s.20, enabling: SSI 2012/167, SSI 2012/197
Sch.1 para.2, see *Gilbey (Julian) v HM Advocate*
2012 J.C. 40 (HCJ Appeal), Lord Reed

10. Charities Act 1993
applied: SI 2012/2885 Sch.6 para.33, SI 2012/2886
Sch.1
s.43, referred to: SI 2012/717 Sch.1

1993– cont.

10. Charities Act 1993–*cont.*
s.75F, see *Berry v IBS-STL (UK) Ltd (In Liquidation)* [2012] EWHC 666 (Ch), [2012] P.T.S.R. 1619 (Ch D), David Donaldson Q.C.

11. Clean Air Act 1993
Part III, applied: SI 2012/814 Reg.2, SI 2012/2281 Reg.2
s.20, applied: SI 2012/2282 Art.2
s.20, disapplied: SI 2012/244 Sch.1
s.20, referred to: SI 2012/815 Art.2
s.20, enabling: SI 2012/814, SI 2012/2281
s.21, enabling: SI 2012/244, SI 2012/815, SI 2012/2282
s.30, applied: SI 2012/2567
s.30, enabling: SI 2012/2567
s.31, applied: SI 2012/2567
s.31, enabling: SI 2012/2567
s.32, enabling: SI 2012/2567
s.63, enabling: SI 2012/814, SI 2012/2567

21. Osteopaths Act 1993
s.6, enabling: SI 2012/1101
s.35, applied: SI 2012/1101
s.35, enabling: SI 2012/1101
s.36, applied: SI 2012/1101
s.41, referred to: SI 2012/1917 Sch.2 para.15
Sch.1 Part I para.1A, repealed (in part): 2012 c.7 Sch.20 para.6

26. Bail (Amendment) Act 1993
s.1, amended: 2012 c.10 Sch.11 para.32, Sch.12 para.32
s.1, referred to: SI 2012/1726 r.19.9

28. Leasehold Reform, Housing and Urban Development Act 1993
see *Sloane Stanley Estate Trustees v Carey-Morgan* [2012] EWCA Civ 1181, [2012] H.L.R. 47 (CA (Civ Div)), Pill, L.J.; see *Westbrook Dolphin Square Ltd v Friends Provident Life and Pensions Ltd* [2011] EWHC 2302 (Ch), [2012] L. & T.R. 12 (Ch D), Arnold, J.; see *Westbrook Dolphin Square Ltd v Friends Provident Life and Pensions Ltd* [2012] EWCA Civ 666, [2012] 1 W.L.R. 2752 (CA (Civ Div)), Lord Neuberger (M.R.)
Pt I. see *Howard de Walden Estates Ltd v Broome* [2012] L. & T.R. 16 (CC (Central London)), Judge Dight
s.5, see *Howard de Walden Estates Ltd v Broome* [2012] L. & T.R. 16 (CC (Central London)), Judge Dight; see *Smith v Jafton Properties Ltd* [2011] EWCA Civ 1251, [2012] Ch. 519 (CA (Civ Div)), Lord Neuberger (M.R.)
s.13, see *Smith v Jafton Properties Ltd* [2011] EWCA Civ 1251, [2012] Ch. 519 (CA (Civ Div)), Lord Neuberger (M.R.); see *Westbrook Dolphin Square Ltd v Friends Provident Life and Pensions Ltd* [2011] EWHC 2302 (Ch), [2012] L. & T.R. 12 (Ch D), Arnold, J.; see *Westbrook Dolphin Square Ltd v Friends Provident Life and Pensions Ltd* [2012] EWCA Civ 666, [2012] 1 W.L.R. 2752 (CA (Civ Div)), Lord Neuberger (M.R.)
s.22, see *Westbrook Dolphin Square Ltd v Friends Provident Life and Pensions Ltd* [2012] EWCA Civ 666, [2012] 1 W.L.R. 2752 (CA (Civ Div)), Lord Neuberger (M.R.)
s.29, see *Westbrook Dolphin Square Ltd v Friends Provident Life and Pensions Ltd* [2012] EWCA Civ 666, [2012] 1 W.L.R. 2752 (CA (Civ Div)), Lord Neuberger (M.R.)

1993– cont.

28. Leasehold Reform, Housing and Urban Development Act 1993– *cont.*
s.32, see *Sloane Stanley Estate Trustees v Carey-Morgan* [2012] EWCA Civ 1181, [2012] H.L.R. 47 (CA (Civ Div)), Pill, L.J.
s.39, see *Howard de Walden Estates Ltd v Broome* [2012] L. & T.R. 16 (CC (Central London)), Judge Dight
s.42, see *Calladine-Smith v Saveorder Ltd* [2011] EWHC 2501 (Ch), [2012] L. & T.R. 3 (Ch D), Morgan, J.; see *Howard de Walden Estates Ltd v Broome* [2012] L. & T.R. 16 (CC (Central London)), Judge Dight
s.45, see *Calladine-Smith v Saveorder Ltd* [2011] EWHC 2501 (Ch), [2012] L. & T.R. 3 (Ch D), Morgan, J.
s.48, see *Coolrace Ltd v Midlands Leasehold Valuation Tribunal* [2012] UKUT 69 (LC), [2012] 2 E.G.L.R. 69 (UT (Lands)), PR Francis FRICS
s.101, see *Howard de Walden Estates Ltd v Broome* [2012] L. & T.R. 16 (CC (Central London)), Judge Dight; see *Smith v Jafton Properties Ltd* [2011] EWCA Civ 1251, [2012] Ch. 519 (CA (Civ Div)), Lord Neuberger (M.R.)
s.170, enabling: SI 2012/3099
Sch.6, see *Sloane Stanley Estate Trustees v Carey-Morgan* [2012] EWCA Civ 1181, [2012] H.L.R. 47 (CA (Civ Div)), Pill, L.J.

32. European Communities (Amendment) Act 1993
s.3, amended: SI 2012/1809 Sch.1 Part 1
s.4, amended: SI 2012/1809 Sch.1 Part 1
s.5, amended: SI 2012/1809 Sch.1 Part 1
s.6, amended: SI 2012/1809 Sch.1 Part 1

34. Finance Act 1993
s.86, amended: 2012 c.14 s.37
s.91, repealed (in part): 2012 c.14 Sch.16 para.91
s.103, amended: 2012 c.14 Sch.16 para.247
s.103, repealed (in part): 2012 c.14 Sch.16 para.247

36. Criminal Justice Act 1993
s.52, see *R. v Rollins (Neil)* [2011] EWCA Crim 1825, [2012] 1 Cr. App. R. (S.) 64 (CA (Crim Div)), Lord Judge, L.C.J
s.71, applied: SSI 2012/88 Reg.23, SSI 2012/89 Reg.26
Sch.1 para.5, amended: 2012 c.21 Sch.18 para.76

38. Welsh Language Act 1993
Part II, referred to: SI 2012/3095 Art.2
s.3, applied: SI 2012/1423 Art.2
s.3, referred to: SI 2012/990 Art.3
s.6, enabling: SI 2012/3095
s.22, applied: SI 2012/1726 r.37.13
s.25, enabling: SI 2012/2605, SI 2012/2606
s.26, applied: SI 2012/2553, SI 2012/2768
s.26, enabling: SI 2012/467, SI 2012/1285, SI 2012/1287, SI 2012/1911

39. National Lottery etc Act 1993
s.22, amended: SI 2012/964 Sch.1
Sch.2A para.3, amended: SI 2012/2404 Sch.2 para.29
Sch.4A Part I para.4, amended: SI 2012/2404 Sch.2 para.29

43. Railways Act 1993
applied: SI 2012/1128 Art.4
referred to: 2012 c.19 Sch.6 para.4
Part I, applied: SI 2012/1867 Sch.8 para.18, SI 2012/1993 Art.4, SI 2012/2284 Art.26, SI 2012/2679 Art.42, SSI 2012/345 Art.8
Part I, referred to: SI 2012/2635 Art.35

1993– cont.

43. Railways Act 1993–*cont.*
s.67, amended: SI 2012/1809 Sch.1 Part 1
s.122, applied: SI 2012/2679 Art.38
s.145, amended: 2012 c.19 Sch.9 para.8, 2012 c.21 Sch.18 para.77
s.151, amended: 2012 c.21 Sch.18 para.77

44. Crofters (Scotland) Act 1993
s.4, amended: SSI 2012/288 Sch.2 para.1
s.4A, amended: SSI 2012/288 Sch.2 para.1
s.8, amended: SSI 2012/288 Sch.2 para.1
s.9, amended: SSI 2012/288 Sch.2 para.1
s.19D, amended: SSI 2012/288 Sch.2 para.1
s.20, amended: SSI 2012/288 Sch.2 para.1
s.23, amended: SSI 2012/288 Sch.2 para.1
s.24, amended: SSI 2012/288 Sch.2 para.1
s.25, amended: SSI 2012/288 Sch.2 para.1
s.29A, amended: SSI 2012/288 Sch.2 para.1
s.52, amended: SSI 2012/288 Sch.2 para.1

46. Health Service Commissioners Act 1993
s.2, amended: 2012 c.7 Sch.5 para.68
s.2, applied: SI 2012/3072 Art.2
s.2, repealed (in part): 2012 c.7 Sch.5 para.68, Sch.14 para.63
s.2, enabling: SI 2012/3072
s.2A, amended: 2012 c.7 Sch.5 para.69
s.14, amended: 2012 c.7 s.201, Sch.5 para.70
s.14, repealed (in part): 2012 c.7 Sch.5 para.70

48. Pension Schemes Act 1993
applied: SI 2012/687 Sch.1 para.3, SI 2012/780 Art.6
Part III, applied: SI 2012/187 Art.2, SI 2012/687 Art.10
Part IV c.III, applied: SI 2012/687 Sch.1 para.14, Sch.4 para.13
Part IV c.IV, applied: SI 2012/687 Sch.4 para.5
Part IVA c.I, applied: SI 2012/687 Sch.4 para.5
Part V c.II, applied: SI 2012/687 Sch.4 para.13
Part X, applied: SI 2012/687 Sch.4 para.5
s.12A, referred to: SI 2012/687 Sch.1 para.12, Sch.1 para.13
s.12A, enabling: SI 2012/542, SI 2012/1817
s.12B, applied: SI 2012/687 Sch.1 para.15
s.12C, applied: SI 2012/687 Sch.4 para.13
s.12D, applied: SI 2012/687 Sch.4 para.13
s.13, applied: SI 2012/687 Sch.1 para.4, Sch.4 para.13
s.13, varied: SI 2012/687 Sch.4 para.14
s.14, applied: SI 2012/687 Sch.4 para.13
s.15, applied: SI 2012/687 Sch.4 para.13
s.15, varied: SI 2012/780 Art.5
s.15A, applied: SI 2012/687 Sch.4 para.13
s.16, applied: SI 2012/687 Sch.4 para.13
s.16, enabling: SI 2012/542
s.17, applied: SI 2012/687 Sch.4 para.13
s.18, applied: SI 2012/687 Sch.4 para.13
s.19, applied: SI 2012/687 Sch.4 para.13
s.19, enabling: SI 2012/692
s.20, applied: SI 2012/687 Sch.4 para.13
s.21, applied: SI 2012/687 Sch.4 para.13
s.23, applied: SI 2012/687 Sch.4 para.13
s.24A, applied: SI 2012/687 Sch.4 para.13
s.24B, applied: SI 2012/687 Sch.4 para.13
s.24C, applied: SI 2012/687 Sch.4 para.13
s.24D, applied: SI 2012/687 Sch.4 para.13
s.24E, applied: SI 2012/687 Sch.4 para.13
s.24F, applied: SI 2012/687 Sch.4 para.13
s.24G, applied: SI 2012/687 Sch.2 para.2, Sch.2 para.3, Sch.4 para.13
s.24H, applied: SI 2012/687 Sch.4 para.13

1993– cont.

48. Pension Schemes Act 1993–*cont.*
s.37, applied: SI 2012/687 Sch.4 para.13
s.50, applied: SI 2012/687 Sch.4 para.13
s.51, applied: SI 2012/687 Sch.4 para.13
s.55, referred to: SI 2012/687 Sch.1 para.3
s.73, enabling: SI 2012/692
s.83, applied: SI 2012/687 Sch.1 para.16
s.97, enabling: SI 2012/692
s.101AF, enabling: SI 2012/692
s.101D, enabling: SI 2012/692
s.109, applied: SI 2012/687 Sch.1 para.17, SI 2012/693
s.109, varied: SI 2012/693 Art.2
s.109, enabling: SI 2012/693
s.111A, enabling: SI 2012/215, SI 2012/1257
s.113, applied: SI 2012/687 Sch.4 para.5
s.113, enabling: SI 2012/1811, SI 2012/1817
s.146, see *R. (on the application of Government Actuary's Department) v Pensions Ombudsman* [2012] EWHC 1796 (Admin), [2012] Pens. L.R. 331 (QBD (Admin)), Ouseley, J.
s.149, amended: 2012 c.21 Sch.18 para.78
s.155, applied: SI 2012/687 Sch.4 para.13
s.156, applied: SI 2012/687 Sch.4 para.13
s.158A, amended: 2012 c.21 Sch.18 para.78
s.159, applied: SI 2012/687 Sch.4 para.13
s.171A, amended: 2012 c.5 Sch.14 Part 14
s.171A, repealed (in part): 2012 c.5 Sch.14 Part 14
s.175, enabling: SI 2012/539
s.180A, amended: 2012 c.21 Sch.18 para.78
s.181, enabling: SI 2012/215, SI 2012/539, SI 2012/542, SI 2012/692, SI 2012/1257, SI 2012/1811, SI 2012/1817
s.182, enabling: SI 2012/215, SI 2012/539, SI 2012/542, SI 2012/692, SI 2012/1257, SI 2012/1811
s.185, amended: 2012 c.21 Sch.18 para.78
s.185, applied: SI 2012/215, SI 2012/539, SI 2012/542, SI 2012/692, SI 2012/1817
Sch.2 Part I para.5, enabling: SI 2012/692
Sch.3 para.2, applied: SI 2012/2952 Art.2
Sch.3 para.2, referred to: SI 2012/687 Sch.1 para.16
Sch.3 para.2, enabling: SI 2012/2952

49. Pension Schemes (Northern Ireland) Act 1993
s.177, enabling: SI 2012/692
Sch.1 Part I para.5, enabling: SI 2012/692

51. European Economic Area Act 1993
s.1, referred to: SSI 2012/88 Sch.4, SSI 2012/89 Sch.4

1994

9. Finance Act 1994
s.9, applied: 2012 c.14 Sch.24 para.35
s.12, see *Revenue and Customs Commissioners v Cozens* [2011] EWHC 2782 (Ch), [2012] S.T.C. 420 (Ch D), Floyd, J.
s.12, amended: 2012 c.14 Sch.24 para.47
s.12, applied: 2012 c.14 Sch.24 para.19, Sch.24 para.26
s.13A, amended: 2012 c.14 Sch.25 para.10
s.13A, applied: 2012 c.14 Sch.24 para.27
s.16, see *Gateway Shipping Ltd v Revenue and Customs Commissioners* [2012] UKFTT 328 (TC), [2012] S.F.T.D. 1070 (FTT (Tax)), Judge Theodore Wallace
s.28, amended: 2012 c.14 Sch.23 para.17
s.29, amended: 2012 c.14 Sch.23 para.18
s.29, repealed (in part): 2012 c.14 Sch.23 para.18
s.29A, added: 2012 c.14 Sch.23 para.19

1994– cont.

9. Finance Act 1994– *cont.*
s.30, amended: 2012 c.14 Sch.23 para.1, Sch.23 para.4, Sch.23 para.8, Sch.23 para.20
s.30, repealed (in part): 2012 c.14 Sch.23 para.1, Sch.23 para.8
s.30A, added: 2012 c.14 Sch.23 para.9
s.30A, amended: 2012 c.14 Sch.23 para.21
s.30A, applied: SI 2012/3015 Art.2
s.30A, referred to: 2012 c.14 Sch.23 para.8
s.30A, enabling: SI 2012/3015
s.33, amended: 2012 c.14 Sch.23 para.10
s.33, enabling: SI 2012/3017
s.33A, added: 2012 c.14 Sch.23 para.11
s.33A, enabling: SI 2012/3017
s.34, amended: 2012 c.14 Sch.23 para.12
s.41A, added: 2012 c.14 Sch.23 para.13
s.43, amended: 2012 c.14 Sch.23 para.22
s.43, enabling: SI 2012/3017
s.50, amended: SI 2012/266 Art.2
s.59, amended: SI 2012/266 Art.2
s.69, amended: SI 2012/266 Art.2
s.69A, added: SI 2012/266 Art.2
s.69B, added: SI 2012/266 Art.2
s.69C, added: SI 2012/266 Art.2
s.69D, added: SI 2012/266 Art.2
s.73, amended: SI 2012/266 Art.2
s.197, see *Bartram v Revenue and Customs Commissioners* [2012] UKUT 184 (TCC), [2012] S.T.C. 2144 (UT (Tax)), Judge John Clark
s.225, amended: 2012 c.14 s.25
s.227C, added: 2012 c.14 Sch.20 para.8
Sch.4 Part II para.24, repealed: 2012 c.14 s.187
Sch.5 para.3, repealed (in part): 2012 c.14 s.187, Sch.39 para.52
Sch.6 para.1, enabling: SI 2012/3020
Sch.7 Part VI para.28B, amended: 2012 c.21 Sch.18 para.79
Sch.7A Part I para.3, amended: 2012 c.5 Sch.14 Part 9
Sch.24 para.19, amended: 2012 c.21 Sch.18 para.79

13. Intelligence Services Act 1994
s.6, varied: 2012 c.11 s.12

17. Chiropractors Act 1994
s.43, referred to: SI 2012/1917 Sch.2 para.15
Sch.1 Part I para.1A, repealed (in part): 2012 c.7 Sch.20 para.6

18. Social Security (Incapacity for Work) Act 1994
Sch.1 Part I para.42, repealed: 2012 c.5 Sch.14 Part 7

19. Local Government (Wales) Act 1994
s.57, applied: SI 2012/629
s.58, applied: SI 2012/629
s.58, enabling: SI 2012/629

20. Sunday Trading Act 1994
Sch.1 para.2, applied: 2012 c.12 s.2
Sch.1 para.2, disapplied: 2012 c.12 s.1
Sch.3, applied: 2012 c.12 s.1

21. Coal Industry Act 1994
applied: SI 2012/1128 Art.4, SSI 2012/89 Sch.1
s.19, applied: SI 2012/2886 Sch.1, SI 2012/3145 Sch.1, SSI 2012/303 Reg.41
s.59, amended: 2012 c.21 Sch.18 para.80
Sch.1 Part I para.1, amended: SI 2012/2404 Sch.2 para.30
Sch.9 para.20, repealed (in part): 2012 asp 5 Sch.5 para.34

22. Vehicle Excise and Registration Act 1994
applied: 2012 c.9 Sch.4 para.15, SI 2012/1777 Art.23, SI 2012/3080 Art.24

1994– cont.

22. Vehicle Excise and Registration Act 1994– *cont.*
s.15, see *Vehicle and Operator Services Agency v Kayes* [2012] EWHC 1498 (Admin), (2012) 176 J.P. 654 (QBD (Admin)), Collins, J.
s.27, see *Tanjoukian v Revenue and Customs Commissioners* [2012] UKUT 361 (TCC), [2012] B.V.C. 1905 (UT (Tax)), Henderson, J.
s.57, enabling: SI 2012/304, SI 2012/443
s.61B, enabling: SI 2012/304, SI 2012/443
s.62, see *Vehicle and Operator Services Agency v Kayes* [2012] EWHC 1498 (Admin), (2012) 176 J.P. 654 (QBD (Admin)), Collins, J.
Sch.1 Part I para.1, amended: 2012 c.14 s.195
Sch.1 Part IA para.1B, amended: 2012 c.14 s.195
Sch.1 Part IB para.1J, amended: 2012 c.14 s.195
Sch.1 Part II para.2, amended: 2012 c.14 s.195
Sch.2 para.4, amended: 2012 asp 8 Sch.7 para.58
Sch.2 para.4, referred to: SI 2012/2387 Sch.3 para.1
Sch.2 para.5, amended: 2012 asp 8 Sch.7 para.58
Sch.2 para.5, referred to: SI 2012/2387 Sch.3 para.1
Sch.2 para.6, referred to: SI 2012/2387 Sch.3 para.1
Sch.2 para.7, amended: 2012 c.7 Sch.14 para.64
Sch.2 para.7, referred to: SI 2012/2387 Sch.3 para.1
Sch.2 para.18, referred to: SI 2012/2387 Sch.3 para.1
Sch.2 para.19, referred to: SI 2012/2387 Sch.3 para.1
Sch.2 para.20, referred to: SI 2012/2387 Sch.3 para.1

23. Value Added Tax Act 1994
see *British Disabled Flying Association v Revenue and Customs Commissioners* [2012] S.F.T.D. 313 (FTT (Tax)), Judge Geraint Jones Q.C.; see *Emblaze Mobility Solutions Ltd v Revenue and Customs Commissioners* [2012] B.V.C. 174 (Ch D), Peter Leaver Q.C.; see *Khan (t/a Khan Tandoori II) v Revenue and Customs Commissioners* [2012] UKUT 224 (TCC), [2012] S.T.C. 2281 (UT (Tax)), Judge Greg Sinfield; see *R. (on the application of ToTel Ltd) v First-tier Tribunal (Tax Chamber)* [2012] EWCA Civ 1401, [2012] B.V.C. 333 (CA (Civ Div)), Lord Neuberger (M.R.)
applied: 2012 c.14 s.201, Sch.27 para.2, Sch.27 para.8
referred to: 2012 c.14 Sch.27 para.11
s.3, enabling: SI 2012/1899
s.5, enabling: SI 2012/2953
s.6, enabling: SI 2012/2951
s.7, amended: 2012 c.14 Sch.28 para.3
s.7A, enabling: SI 2012/2787
s.9, see *1st Contact Ltd v Revenue and Customs Commissioners* [2012] UKFTT 84 (TC), [2012] S.F.T.D. 799 (FTT (Tax)), Judge Christopher Staker; see *Matrix Securities Ltd v Revenue and Customs Commissioners* [2012] UKFTT 320 (TC), [2012] S.F.T.D. 1056 (FTT (Tax)), Judge Peter Kempster
s.12, enabling: SI 2012/2951
s.18B, amended: 2012 c.14 Sch.29 para.2
s.18B, enabling: SI 2012/1899
s.18C, amended: 2012 c.14 Sch.29 para.3
s.18C, enabling: SI 2012/1899
s.19, see *Simpson & Marwick v Revenue and Customs Commissioners* [2012] S.T.C. 611 (UT (Tax)), Lord Drummond Young
s.23, substituted: 2012 c.14 Sch.24 para.63
s.25, see *1st Contact Ltd v Revenue and Customs Commissioners* [2012] UKFTT 84 (TC), [2012] S.F.T.D. 799 (FTT (Tax)), Judge Christopher Staker
s.25, enabling: SI 2012/33, SI 2012/1899

1994– cont.

23. **Value Added Tax Act 1994**–*cont.*

s.26, see *1st Contact Ltd v Revenue and Customs Commissioners* [2012] UKFTT 84 (TC), [2012] S.F.T.D. 799 (FTT (Tax)), Judge Christopher Staker

s.26, enabling: SI 2012/ 1899

s.26B, enabling: SI 2012/ 1899

s.30, enabling: SI 2012/ 2907

s.31, see *Paymex Ltd v Revenue and Customs Commissioners* [2012] B.P.I.R. 178 (FTT (Tax)), Judge Roger Berner

s.31, amended: 2012 c.14 s.197

s.31, enabling: SI 2012/ 58

s.33, applied: SI 2012/ 2393 Art.2

s.33, enabling: SI 2012/ 2393

s.33A, enabling: SI 2012/ 2731

s.35, amended: 2012 c.14 Sch.29 para.4

s.35, enabling: SI 2012/ 1899

s.36, see *Simpson & Marwick v Revenue and Customs Commissioners* [2012] S.T.C. 611 (UT (Tax)), Lord Drummond Young

s.36A, enabling: SI 2012/ 2907

s.37, enabling: SI 2012/ 2907, SI 2012/ 3060

s.39, amended: 2012 c.14 Sch.29 para.5

s.39, enabling: SI 2012/ 1899

s.41, amended: 2012 c.7 Sch.14 para.66, 2012 c.14 s.198

s.41, repealed (in part): 2012 c.14 s.198

s.41A, added: 2012 c.14 s.198

s.43, amended: 2012 c.14 s.200

s.43A, applied: 2012 c.14 Sch.27 para.6

s.43AA, applied: 2012 c.14 Sch.27 para.6

s.43B, applied: 2012 c.14 Sch.27 para.6

s.43C, applied: 2012 c.14 Sch.27 para.6

s.43D, applied: 2012 c.14 Sch.27 para.6

s.48, amended: 2012 c.14 Sch.29 para.6

s.48, applied: 2012 c.14 Sch.38 para.34

s.48, enabling: SI 2012/ 1899

s.49, see *Khan (t/a Khan Tandoori II) v Revenue and Customs Commissioners* [2012] UKUT 224 (TCC), [2012] S.T.C. 2281 (UT (Tax)), Judge Greg Sinfield

s.49, enabling: SI 2012/ 1899

s.54, amended: 2012 c.14 Sch.28 para.4, Sch.29 para.7

s.54, enabling: SI 2012/ 1899

s.55, amended: 2012 c.14 Sch.28 para.5

s.55A, amended: 2012 c.14 Sch.28 para.6

s.57, amended: SI 2012/ 882 Art.2

s.57, enabling: SI 2012/ 882

s.69, amended: 2012 c.14 Sch.28 para.7

s.72, applied: SSI 2012/ 88 Reg.23, SSI 2012/ 89 Reg.26

s.73, see *ERF Ltd v Revenue and Customs Commissioners* [2012] UKUT 105 (TCC), [2012] S.T.C. 1738 (UT (Tax)), Mann, J.; see *Matrix Securities Ltd v Revenue and Customs Commissioners* [2012] UKFTT 320 (TC), [2012] S.F.T.D. 1056 (FTT (Tax)), Judge Peter Kempster

s.73, amended: 2012 c.14 Sch.28 para.8

s.74, amended: 2012 c.14 Sch.28 para.9

s.77, amended: 2012 c.14 Sch.28 para.10

s.77A, applied: 2012 c.14 Sch.36 para.11

s.78, see *Grattan Plc v Revenue and Customs Commissioners* [2012] S.F.T.D. 214 (FTT (Tax)), Judge Roger Berner; see *New Miles Ltd v Revenue and Customs Commissioners* [2012]

1994– cont.

23. **Value Added Tax Act 1994**–*cont.*

s.78–*cont.*

UKFTT 33 (TC), [2012] S.F.T.D. 695 (FTT (Tax)), Judge Peter Kempster

s.80, see *Grattan Plc v Revenue and Customs Commissioners* [2012] S.F.T.D. 214 (FTT (Tax)), Judge Roger Berner; see *Investment Trust Companies (In Liquidation) v Revenue and Customs Commissioners* [2012] EWHC 458 (Ch), [2012] S.T.C. 1150 (Ch D), Henderson, J.; see *R. (on the application of Capital Accommodation (London) Ltd (In Liquidation)) v Revenue and Customs Commissioners* [2012] UKUT 276 (TCC), [2012] B.V.C. 1780 (UT (Tax)), Sales, J.

s.81, see *Emblaze Mobility Solutions Ltd v Revenue and Customs Commissioners* [2012] B.V.C. 174 (Ch D), Peter Leaver Q.C.

s.83, see *Benridge Care Homes Ltd v Revenue and Customs Commissioners* [2012] UKUT 132 (TCC), [2012] S.T.C. 1920 (UT (Tax)), Malcolm Gammie Q.C.

s.83, amended: 2012 c.14 s.200

s.83G, see *Data Select Ltd v Revenue and Customs Commissioners* [2012] UKUT 187 (TCC), [2012] S.T.C. 2195 (UT (Tax)), Morgan, J.

s.84, see *R. (on the application of ToTel Ltd) v First-tier Tribunal (Tax Chamber)* [2011] EWHC 652 (Admin), [2012] Q.B. 358 (QBD (Admin)), Simon, J.; see *R. (on the application of ToTel Ltd) v First-tier Tribunal (Tax Chamber)* [2012] EWCA Civ 1401, [2012] B.V.C. 333 (CA (Civ Div)), Lord Neuberger (M.R.)

s.85A, see *Emblaze Mobility Solutions Ltd v Revenue and Customs Commissioners* [2012] B.V.C. 174 (Ch D), Peter Leaver Q.C.

s.96, enabling: SI 2012/ 2907

s.97, amended: 2012 c.14 s.200

Sch.1 para.1, amended: 2012 c.14 Sch.28 para.11, Sch.28 para.13, SI 2012/ 883 Art.3

Sch.1 para.1A, amended: 2012 c.14 Sch.28 para.13

Sch.1 para.2, amended: 2012 c.14 Sch.28 para.13

Sch.1 para.3, amended: 2012 c.14 Sch.28 para.12, Sch.28 para.13

Sch.1 para.4, amended: 2012 c.14 Sch.28 para.13, SI 2012/ 883 Art.3

Sch.1 para.5, amended: 2012 c.14 Sch.28 para.13

Sch.1 para.6, amended: 2012 c.14 Sch.28 para.13

Sch.1 para.7, amended: 2012 c.14 Sch.28 para.13

Sch.1 para.8, amended: 2012 c.14 Sch.28 para.13

Sch.1 para.9, amended: 2012 c.14 Sch.28 para.13

Sch.1 para.10, amended: 2012 c.14 Sch.28 para.13

Sch.1 para.11, amended: 2012 c.14 Sch.28 para.13

Sch.1 para.12, amended: 2012 c.14 Sch.28 para.13

Sch.1 para.13, amended: 2012 c.14 Sch.28 para.13

Sch.1 para.14, amended: 2012 c.14 Sch.28 para.13

Sch.1 para.15, amended: 2012 c.14 Sch.28 para.13

Sch.1 para.15, enabling: SI 2012/ 883

Sch.1 para.16, amended: 2012 c.14 Sch.28 para.13

Sch.1 para.17, amended: 2012 c.14 Sch.28 para.13, Sch.29 para.8

Sch.1 para.17, enabling: SI 2012/ 1899

Sch.1 para.18, amended: 2012 c.14 Sch.28 para.13

Sch.1 para.19, amended: 2012 c.14 Sch.28 para.13

Sch.1A para.1, added: 2012 c.14 Sch.28 para.1

Sch.1A para.2, added: 2012 c.14 Sch.28 para.1

Sch.1A para.3, added: 2012 c.14 Sch.28 para.1

Sch.1A para.4, added: 2012 c.14 Sch.28 para.1

Sch.1A para.5, added: 2012 c.14 Sch.28 para.1

Sch.1A para.6, added: 2012 c.14 Sch.28 para.1

1994– cont.

23. Value Added Tax Act 1994– *cont.*

Sch.1A para.7, added: 2012 c.14 Sch.28 para.1
Sch.1A para.8, added: 2012 c.14 Sch.28 para.1
Sch.1A para.9, added: 2012 c.14 Sch.28 para.1
Sch.1A para.10, added: 2012 c.14 Sch.28 para.1
Sch.1A para.11, added: 2012 c.14 Sch.28 para.1
Sch.1A para.12, added: 2012 c.14 Sch.28 para.1
Sch.1A para.13, added: 2012 c.14 Sch.28 para.1
Sch.1A para.14, added: 2012 c.14 Sch.28 para.1
Sch.1A para.14, enabling: SI 2012/1899
Sch.2 para.1, amended: 2012 c.14 Sch.28 para.14
Sch.2 para.9, amended: 2012 c.14 Sch.29 para.9
Sch.2 para.9, enabling: SI 2012/1899
Sch.3 para.1, amended: 2012 c.14 Sch.28 para.15, SI 2012/883 Art.4
Sch.3 para.2, amended: SI 2012/883 Art.4
Sch.3 para.9, enabling: SI 2012/883
Sch.3 para.10, amended: 2012 c.14 Sch.29 para.10
Sch.3 para.10, enabling: SI 2012/1899
Sch.3A para.1, amended: 2012 c.14 Sch.28 para.16
Sch.3A para.8, amended: 2012 c.14 Sch.29 para.11
Sch.3A para.8, enabling: SI 2012/1899
Sch.3B Part 4 para.18, amended: 2012 c.14 Sch.28 para.17
Sch.4A Part 2 para.9B, added: SI 2012/2787 Art.2
Sch.4A Part 2 para.9C, added: SI 2012/2787 Art.2
Sch.4A Pt 3 para.10, see *Firstpoint (Europe) Ltd v Revenue and Customs Commissioners* [2012] S.F.T.D. 480 (FTT (Tax)), G Pritchard
Sch.5 para.1, see *Tanjoukian v Revenue and Customs Commissioners* [2012] UKUT 361 (TCC), [2012] B.V.C. 1905 (UT (Tax)), Henderson, J.
Sch.5 para.3, see *Matrix Securities Ltd v Revenue and Customs Commissioners* [2012] UKFTT 320 (TC), [2012] S.F.T.D. 1056 (FTT (Tax)), Judge Peter Kempster
Sch.6 para.1, amended: 2012 c.14 s.200
Sch.6 para.8A, added: 2012 c.14 s.200
Sch.7A Part I, amended: 2012 c.14 Sch.26 para.6
Sch.7A Part II, added: 2012 c.14 Sch.26 para.6
Sch.7A Part II, amended: 2012 c.5 Sch.14 Part 9
Sch.7A Pt II Group 1, see *WM Morrison Supermarkets Ltd v Revenue and Customs Commissioners* [2012] UKFTT 366 (TC), [2012] S.F.T.D. 1166 (FTT (Tax)), Jonathan Cannan
Sch.8 Part I, amended: SI 2012/2907 Art.3
Sch.8 Part II, added: SI 2012/2907 Art.3
Sch.8 Part II, amended: 2012 c.5 Sch.14 Part 9, 2012 c.7 Sch.14 para.67, 2012 c.14 Sch.26 para.2, Sch.26 para.3, Sch.26 para.4, SI 2012/700 Sch.1 para.5, SI 2012/1916 Sch.34 para.42
Sch.8 Part II, applied: 2012 c.14 Sch.27 para.3
Sch.8 Part II, repealed (in part): SI 2012/1916 Sch.34 para.42
Sch.8 Part II, varied: SI 2012/1909 Sch.7 para.15
Sch.8 Pt II Group 1, see *GlaxoSmithKline Services Unlimited v Revenue and Customs Commissioners* [2012] UKUT 34 (TCC), Newey, J; see *Sub One Ltd (t/a Subway) v Revenue and Customs Commissioners* [2012] UKUT 34 (TCC), [2012] B.V.C. 1871 (UT (Tax)), Arnold, J.
Sch.8 Pt II Group 3, see *Harrier LLC v Revenue and Customs Commissioners* [2012] S.F.T.D. 348 (FTT (Tax)), Judge Roger Berner

1994– cont.

23. Value Added Tax Act 1994– *cont.*

Sch.8 Group 5, see *Wakefield College v Revenue and Customs Commissioners* [2012] S.T.C. 642 (UT (Tax)), Arnold, J.
Sch.8 Group 8, see *Norwich Airport Ltd v Revenue and Customs Commissioners* [2012] UKFTT 277 (TC), [2012] S.F.T.D. 978 (FTT (Tax)), Barbara Mosedale
Sch.8 Pt II Group 8, see *Davies (t/a Special Occasions/2XL Limos) v Revenue and Customs Commissioners* [2012] UKUT 130 (TCC), [2012] S.T.C. 1978 (UT (Tax)), Judge Howard M Nowlan
Sch.8 Group 12, see *British Disabled Flying Association v Revenue and Customs Commissioners* [2012] S.F.T.D. 313 (FTT (Tax)), Judge Geraint Jones Q.C.; see *Bunning (t/a Stafford Land Rover) v Revenue and Customs Commissioners* [2012] UKFTT 32 (TC), [2012] S.F.T.D. 679 (FTT (Tax)), John Walters Q.C.
Sch.8 Pt II Group 12, see *British Disabled Flying Association v Revenue and Customs Commissioners* [2012] S.F.T.D. 313 (FTT (Tax)), Judge Geraint Jones Q.C.
Sch.8 Group 15, see *British Disabled Flying Association v Revenue and Customs Commissioners* [2012] S.F.T.D. 313 (FTT (Tax)), Judge Geraint Jones Q.C.
Sch.9 Part I, amended: 2012 c.14 s.197, Sch.24 para.64
Sch.9 Part II, added: 2012 c.14 s.197
Sch.9 Part II, amended: 2012 c.7 s.213, s.220, 2012 c.14 Sch.24 para.64, Sch.26 para.5, 2012 c.21 Sch.18 para.81
Sch.9 Part II, repealed (in part): 2012 c.14 Sch.24 para.64
Sch.9 Part II, substituted: SI 2012/58 Art.3
Sch.9 Pt II Group 2, see *Royal Bank of Scotland Group Plc v Revenue and Customs Commissioners* [2012] EWHC 9 (Ch), [2012] S.T.C. 797 (Ch D), Mann, J.
Sch.9 Pt II Group 4, see *Revenue and Customs Commissioners v Rank Group Plc (C-259/10)* [2012] S.T.C. 23 (ECJ (3rd Chamber)), Judge Lenaerts (President)
Sch.9 Pt II Group 5, see *1st Contact Ltd v Revenue and Customs Commissioners* [2012] UKFTT 84 (TC), [2012] S.F.T.D. 799 (FTT (Tax)), Judge Christopher Staker; see *AXA UK Plc v Revenue and Customs Commissioners* [2011] EWCA Civ 1607, [2012] S.T.C. 754 (CA (Civ Div)), Arden, L.J.; see *Paymex Ltd v Revenue and Customs Commissioners* [2012] B.P.I.R. 178 (FTT (Tax)), Judge Roger Berner
Sch.9 Pt II Group 6, see *Marcus Webb Golf Professional v Revenue and Customs Commissioners* [2012] UKUT 378 (TCC), [2012] B.V.C. 1944 (UT (Tax)), Henderson, J.
Sch.9 Group 7, see *British Disabled Flying Association v Revenue and Customs Commissioners* [2012] S.F.T.D. 313 (FTT (Tax)), Judge Geraint Jones Q.C.
Sch.9 Pt II Group 7, see *Moher (t/a Premier Dental Agency) v Revenue and Customs Commissioners* [2012] S.T.C. 1356 (UT (Tax)), Judge Colin Bishopp
Sch.9 Group 9, see *European Tour Operators Association v Revenue and Customs Commissioners* [2012] UKUT 377 (TCC), [2012] B.V.C. 1922 (UT (Tax)), Henderson, J.

1994– cont.

23. Value Added Tax Act 1994– *cont.*

Sch.9 Pt II Group 10, see *Bridport and West Dorset Golf Club Ltd v Revenue and Customs Commissioners* [2012] UKUT 272 (TCC), [2012] S.T.C. 2244 (UT (Tax)), Proudman, J.

Sch.9 Pt II Group 12, see *British Disabled Flying Association v Revenue and Customs Commissioners* [2012] S.F.T.D. 313 (FTT (Tax)), Judge Geraint Jones Q.C.

Sch.10, see *Enterprise Inns Plc v Revenue and Customs Commissioners* [2012] UKUT 240 (TCC), [2012] S.T.C. 2313 (UT (Tax)), Newey, J.

Sch.10 Part 1 para.10, amended: SI 2012/700 Sch.1 para.5

Sch.10A para.2, disapplied: 2012 c.14 s.201

Sch.10A para.3, disapplied: 2012 c.14 s.201

Sch.10A para.4, disapplied: 2012 c.14 s.201

Sch.10A para.6, disapplied: 2012 c.14 s.201

Sch.10A para.7, disapplied: 2012 c.14 s.201

Sch.10A para.7A, added: 2012 c.14 s.201

Sch.10A para.7A, applied: 2012 c.14 s.201

Sch.11, amended: 2012 c.14 Sch.24 para.65

Sch.11 para.2, amended: 2012 c.14 s.202, Sch.29 para.12

Sch.11 para.2, enabling: SI 2012/33, SI 2012/1899

Sch.11 para.2A, applied: 2012 c.14 Sch.27 para.10

Sch.11 para.2A, enabling: SI 2012/1899, SI 2012/2951

Sch.11 para.2B, enabling: SI 2012/2951

Sch.11 para.3, enabling: SI 2012/2951

Sch.11 para.5, see *St. Martin's Medical Services Ltd v Revenue and Customs Commissioners* [2012] UKFTT 485 (TC), [2012] S.F.T.D. 1319 (FTT (Tax)), Judge Howard M Nowlan

Sch.11 para.5, applied: 2012 c.14 Sch.36 para.26, Sch.36 para.27

Sch.11 para.5, referred to: 2012 c.14 Sch.36 para.26

Sch.11 para.6, enabling: SI 2012/2951

Sch.11 para.7, enabling: SI 2012/1899

Sch.11 para.9, amended: 2012 c.14 Sch.24 para.65

26. Trade Marks Act 1994

s.1, see *32 Red Plc v WHG (International) Ltd* [2012] EWCA Civ 19, [2012] E.T.M.R. 14 (CA (Civ Div)), Toulson, L.J.

s.3, see *NMSI Trading Ltd's Trade Mark Application (No.2449033B), Re* [2012] R.P.C. 7 (App Person), Geoffrey Hobbs Q.C.

s.5, see *Advanced Perimeter Systems Ltd v Keycorp Ltd* [2012] R.P.C. 14 (App Person), Daniel Alexander Q.C.; see *Advanced Perimeter Systems Ltd v Keycorp Ltd* [2012] R.P.C. 15 (App Person), Daniel Alexander Q.C.; see *Budejovicky Budvar Narodni Podnik v Anheuser-Busch Inc* [2012] EWCA Civ 880, [2012] 3 All E.R. 1405 (CA (Civ Div)), Ward, L.J.; see *Plentyoffish Media Inc v Plenty More LLP* [2011] EWHC 2568 (Ch), [2012] E.C.C. 15 (Ch D), Judge Birss Q.C.; see *Wella Corp v Alberto-Culver Co* [2011] EWHC 3558 (Ch), [2012] E.T.M.R. 24 (Ch D), Judge Birss Q.C.

s.6, see *Budejovicky Budvar Narodni Podnik v Anheuser-Busch Inc* [2012] EWCA Civ 880, [2012] 3 All E.R. 1405 (CA (Civ Div)), Ward, L.J.

s.10, see *32 Red Plc v WHG (International) Ltd* [2012] EWCA Civ 19, [2012] E.T.M.R. 14 (CA (Civ Div)), Toulson, L.J.; see *Lewis v Client Connection Ltd* [2011] EWHC 1627 (Ch), [2012] E.T.M.R. 6 (Ch D), Norris, J.; see *Weight Watchers (UK) Ltd v Love Bites Ltd* [2012]

1994– cont.

26. Trade Marks Act 1994– *cont.*

s.10– *cont.*

EWPCC 11, [2012] E.T.M.R. 27 (PCC), Judge Birss Q.C.

s.21, see *Samuel Smith Old Brewery (Tadcaster) v Lee (t/a Cropton Brewery)* [2011] EWHC 1879 (Ch), [2012] F.S.R. 7 (Ch D), Arnold, J.

s.41, enabling: SI 2012/1003

s.47, see *Budejovicky Budvar Narodni Podnik v Anheuser-Busch Inc* [2012] EWCA Civ 880, [2012] 3 All E.R. 1405 (CA (Civ Div)), Ward, L.J.

s.76, see *NMSI Trading Ltd's Trade Mark Application (No.2449033B), Re* [2012] R.P.C. 7 (App Person), Geoffrey Hobbs Q.C.; see *Pass J Holdings Ltd v Spencer* [2012] R.P.C. 16 (App Person), Geoffrey Hobbs Q.C.

s.77, amended: SI 2012/2404 Sch.2 para.31

s.78, enabling: SI 2012/1003

s.79, enabling: SI 2012/1003

33. Criminal Justice and Public Order Act 1994

Commencement Orders: 2012 c.10 Sch.12 para.34

s.19, repealed (in part): 2012 c.10 Sch.12 para.34

s.21, repealed: 2012 c.10 Sch.12 para.34

s.23, repealed: 2012 c.10 Sch.12 para.34

s.25, see *O'Dowd v United Kingdom (7390/07)* (2012) 54 E.H.R.R. 8 (ECHR), Judge Garlicki (President)

s.25, amended: 2012 c.10 Sch.11 para.33

s.25, referred to: SI 2012/1726 r.19.17

s.34, see *R. v M* [2011] EWCA Crim 868, [2012] 1 Cr. App. R. 3 (CA (Crim Div)), Stanley Burnton, L.J.

s.35, applied: SI 2012/1726 r.37.3

s.38, see *R. v M* [2011] EWCA Crim 868, [2012] 1 Cr. App. R. 3 (CA (Crim Div)), Stanley Burnton, L.J.

s.57, repealed: 2012 c.9 Sch.10 Part 1

s.60, see *R. (on the application of Hicks) v Commissioner of Police of the Metropolis* [2012] EWHC 1947 (Admin), [2012] A.C.D. 102 (DC), Richards, L.J.; see *R. (on the application of Roberts) v Commissioner of Police of the Metropolis* [2012] EWHC 1977 (Admin), [2012] H.R.L.R. 28 (QBD (Admin)), Moses, L.J.

s.68, see *Nero v DPP* [2012] EWHC 1238 (Admin), (2012) 176 J.P. 450 (QBD (Admin)), Laws, L.J.; see *Peppersharp v DPP* [2012] EWHC 474 (Admin), (2012) 176 J.P. 257 (DC), Gross, L.J.

s.69, see *Nero v DPP* [2012] EWHC 1238 (Admin), (2012) 176 J.P. 450 (QBD (Admin)), Laws, L.J.

s.102, amended: 2012 asp 8 Sch.7 para.9

s.127, amended: 2012 c.10 s.129

s.163, amended: 2012 asp 8 Sch.7 para.9, Sch.8 Part 1

Sch.1 para.1, applied: 2012 c.10 s.103

Sch.9 para.11, repealed (in part): 2012 c.10 Sch.25 Part 2

Sch.9 para.38, repealed: 2012 c.10 Sch.12 para.35

Sch.10 para.30, repealed: 2012 c.10 Sch.25 Part 2

Sch.10 para.53, repealed (in part): 2012 c.10 s.144

37. Drug Trafficking Act 1994

see *Peacock, Re* [2012] UKSC 5, [2012] 1 W.L.R. 550 (SC), Lord Hope (Deputy President)

s.3, applied: SI 2012/1726 r.56.2

s.6, see *Peacock, Re* [2012] UKSC 5, [2012] 1 W.L.R. 550 (SC), Lord Hope (Deputy President)

s.10, applied: SI 2012/1726 r.56.5

s.11, applied: SI 2012/1726 r.56.1

s.13, applied: SI 2012/1726 r.56.3

s.14, applied: SI 2012/1726 r.56.3

1994– cont.

37. Drug Trafficking Act 1994– *cont.*
s.15, applied: SI 2012/ 1726 r.56.3
s.16, see *Peacock, Re* [2012] UKSC 5, [2012] 1 W.L.R. 550 (SC), Lord Hope (Deputy President)
s.22, applied: SI 2012/ 1726 r.56.6
s.49, applied: SSI 2012/ 88 Reg.23, SSI 2012/ 89 Reg.26
s.50, applied: SSI 2012/ 88 Reg.23, SSI 2012/ 89 Reg.26
s.51, applied: SSI 2012/ 88 Reg.23, SSI 2012/ 89 Reg.26
s.55, applied: SI 2012/ 1726 r.56.4

39. Local Government etc (Scotland) Act 1994
applied: SSI 2012/ 88 Reg.3
s.2, applied: SI 2012/ 1916 Reg.323, SI 2012/ 2885 Sch.1 para.8, Sch.1 para.25, Sch.1 para.26, Sch.2 para.6, Sch.4 para.5, SI 2012/ 2886 Sch.1, SI 2012/ 3144 Sch.1 para.19, SI 2012/ 3145 Sch.1, SSI 2012/ 162 Sch.1
s.8, amended: 2012 asp 8 Sch.8 Part 3
s.8, repealed (in part): 2012 asp 8 Sch.8 Part 3
s.43, amended: 2012 asp 8 Sch.7 para.75
s.55, amended: 2012 asp 8 Sch.8 Part 3
s.55, repealed (in part): 2012 asp 8 Sch.8 Part 3
s.150, amended: 2012 asp 8 Sch.7 para.10
s.153, enabling: SSI 2012/ 28, SSI 2012/ 29, SSI 2012/ 48, SSI 2012/ 353

40. Deregulation and Contracting Out Act 1994
s.69, enabling: SI 2012/ 3003
s.70, applied: SI 2012/ 3003
s.70, enabling: SI 2012/ 3003
s.77, applied: SI 2012/ 3003
s.77, enabling: SI 2012/ 3003
Sch.9 para.1, repealed (in part): SSI 2012/ 321 Sch.5 Part 1
Sch.9 para.2, repealed (in part): SSI 2012/ 321 Sch.5 Part 1
Sch.9 para.5, repealed (in part): SSI 2012/ 321 Sch.5 Part 1

1995

i. British Waterways Act 1995
s.17, see *Moore v British Waterways Board* [2012] EWHC 182 (Ch), [2012] 1 W.L.R. 3289 (Ch D), Hildyard, J
s.18, see *Moore v British Waterways Board* [2012] EWHC 182 (Ch), [2012] 1 W.L.R. 3289 (Ch D), Hildyard, J

4. Finance Act 1995
s.51, repealed: 2012 c.14 Sch.16 para.247
Sch.8 Part I para.1, repealed: 2012 c.14 Sch.16 para.247
Sch.8 Part I para.2, repealed: 2012 c.14 Sch.16 para.247
Sch.8 Part I para.3, repealed: 2012 c.14 Sch.16 para.247
Sch.8 Part I para.4, repealed: 2012 c.14 Sch.16 para.247
Sch.8 Part I para.5, repealed: 2012 c.14 Sch.16 para.247
Sch.8 Part I para.6, repealed: 2012 c.14 Sch.16 para.247
Sch.8 Part I para.7, repealed: 2012 c.14 Sch.16 para.247
Sch.8 Part I para.8, repealed: 2012 c.14 Sch.16 para.247
Sch.8 Part I para.9, repealed: 2012 c.14 Sch.16 para.247

1995– cont.

4. Finance Act 1995– *cont.*
Sch.8 Part I para.10, repealed: 2012 c.14 Sch.16 para.247
Sch.8 Part I para.11, repealed: 2012 c.14 Sch.16 para.247
Sch.8 Part I para.12, repealed: 2012 c.14 Sch.16 para.247
Sch.8 Part I para.13, repealed: 2012 c.14 Sch.16 para.247
Sch.8 Part I para.14, repealed: 2012 c.14 Sch.16 para.247
Sch.8 Part I para.15, repealed: 2012 c.14 Sch.16 para.247
Sch.8 Part I para.16, repealed: 2012 c.14 Sch.16 para.247
Sch.8 Part I para.17, repealed: 2012 c.14 Sch.16 para.247
Sch.8 Part I para.18, repealed: 2012 c.14 Sch.16 para.247
Sch.8 Part I para.19, repealed: 2012 c.14 Sch.16 para.247
Sch.8 Part I para.20, repealed: 2012 c.14 Sch.16 para.247
Sch.8 Part I para.21, repealed: 2012 c.14 Sch.16 para.247
Sch.8 Part I para.22, repealed: 2012 c.14 Sch.16 para.247
Sch.8 Part I para.23, repealed: 2012 c.14 Sch.16 para.247
Sch.8 Part I para.24, repealed: 2012 c.14 Sch.16 para.247
Sch.8 Part I para.25, repealed: 2012 c.14 Sch.16 para.247
Sch.8 Part I para.26, repealed: 2012 c.14 Sch.16 para.247
Sch.8 Part I para.27, repealed: 2012 c.14 Sch.16 para.247
Sch.8 Part I para.28, repealed: 2012 c.14 Sch.16 para.247
Sch.8 Part I para.29, repealed: 2012 c.14 Sch.16 para.247
Sch.8 Part I para.30, repealed: 2012 c.14 Sch.16 para.247
Sch.8 Part I para.31, repealed: 2012 c.14 Sch.16 para.247
Sch.8 Part I para.32, repealed: 2012 c.14 Sch.16 para.247
Sch.8 Part I para.33, repealed: 2012 c.14 Sch.16 para.247
Sch.8 Part I para.34, repealed: 2012 c.14 Sch.16 para.247
Sch.8 Part II para.35, repealed: 2012 c.14 Sch.16 para.247
Sch.8 Part II para.36, repealed: 2012 c.14 Sch.16 para.247
Sch.8 Part II para.37, repealed: 2012 c.14 Sch.16 para.247
Sch.8 Part II para.38, repealed: 2012 c.14 Sch.16 para.247
Sch.8 Part II para.39, repealed: 2012 c.14 Sch.16 para.247
Sch.8 Part II para.40, repealed: 2012 c.14 Sch.16 para.247
Sch.8 Part II para.41, repealed: 2012 c.14 Sch.16 para.247
Sch.8 Part II para.42, repealed: 2012 c.14 Sch.16 para.247
Sch.8 Part II para.43, repealed: 2012 c.14 Sch.16 para.247

1995– cont.
4. Finance Act 1995–*cont.*
Sch.8 Part II para.44, repealed: 2012 c.14 Sch.16 para.247
Sch.8 Part II para.45, repealed: 2012 c.14 Sch.16 para.247
Sch.8 Part II para.46, repealed: 2012 c.14 Sch.16 para.247
Sch.8 Part II para.47, repealed: 2012 c.14 Sch.16 para.247
Sch.8 Part II para.48, repealed: 2012 c.14 Sch.16 para.247
Sch.8 Part II para.49, repealed: 2012 c.14 Sch.16 para.247
Sch.8 Part III para.50, repealed: 2012 c.14 Sch.16 para.247
Sch.8 Part III para.51, repealed: 2012 c.14 Sch.16 para.247
Sch.8 Part III para.52, repealed: 2012 c.14 Sch.16 para.247
Sch.8 Part III para.53, repealed: 2012 c.14 Sch.16 para.247
Sch.8 Part III para.54, repealed: 2012 c.14 Sch.16 para.247
Sch.8 Part III para.55, repealed: 2012 c.14 Sch.16 para.247
Sch.8 Part III para.56, repealed: 2012 c.14 Sch.16 para.247
Sch.8 Part III para.57, repealed: 2012 c.14 Sch.16 para.247
Sch.8 Part III para.58, repealed: 2012 c.14 Sch.16 para.247
Sch.9 para.1, repealed: 2012 c.14 Sch.16 para.247
Sch.10 para.1, repealed: 2012 c.14 Sch.18 para.23
Sch.10 para.2, repealed: 2012 c.14 Sch.18 para.23
7. Requirements of Writing (Scotland) Act 1995
s.1, amended: 2012 asp 5 s.96
s.1, substituted: 2012 asp 5 s.96
s.1A, amended: 2012 asp 5 Sch.3 para.2
s.2, amended: 2012 asp 5 Sch.3 para.3, Sch.3 para.4
s.2A, repealed: 2012 asp 5 Sch.3 para.5
s.2B, repealed: 2012 asp 5 Sch.3 para.5
s.2C, repealed: 2012 asp 5 Sch.3 para.5
s.3, amended: 2012 asp 5 Sch.3 para.6
s.3A, repealed: 2012 asp 5 Sch.3 para.7
s.4, amended: 2012 asp 5 Sch.3 para.8
s.5, amended: 2012 asp 5 Sch.3 para.9, Sch.3 para.10
s.5, repealed (in part): 2012 asp 5 Sch.3 para.9
s.6, amended: 2012 asp 5 Sch.3 para.11, Sch.3 para.12
s.6, applied: 2012 asp 5 s.22
s.6A, repealed: 2012 asp 5 Sch.3 para.13
s.7, amended: 2012 asp 5 Sch.3 para.14
s.8, amended: 2012 asp 5 Sch.3 para.15, Sch.3 para.16
s.9, amended: 2012 asp 5 Sch.3 para.17
s.9A, added: 2012 asp 5 s.97
s.9B, added: 2012 asp 5 s.97
s.9C, added: 2012 asp 5 s.97
s.9D, added: 2012 asp 5 s.97
s.9E, added: 2012 asp 5 s.97
s.9F, added: 2012 asp 5 s.97
s.9G, added: 2012 asp 5 s.97
s.9G, applied: 2012 asp 5 s.22
s.10, substituted: 2012 asp 5 Sch.3 para.21
s.11, substituted: 2012 asp 5 Sch.3 para.21
s.11, repealed: 2012 asp 5 Sch.3 para.18
s.12, substituted: 2012 asp 5 Sch.3 para.21
s.12, amended: 2012 asp 5 Sch.3 para.19
s.12, varied: 2012 c.11 s.12

1995– cont.
7. Requirements of Writing (Scotland) Act 1995–*cont.*
s.13, substituted: 2012 asp 5 Sch.3 para.21
s.13, amended: 2012 asp 5 Sch.3 para.20
s.14, substituted: 2012 asp 5 Sch.3 para.21
s.15, substituted: 2012 asp 5 Sch.3 para.21
Sch.1, amended: 2012 asp 5 Sch.3 para.24
Sch.1 para.1, amended: 2012 asp 5 Sch.3 para.23
Sch.1 para.2, amended: 2012 asp 5 Sch.3 para.23
Sch.2 para.1, amended: 2012 asp 5 Sch.3 para.25
Sch.2 para.2, amended: 2012 asp 5 Sch.3 para.25
Sch.2 para.3, amended: 2012 asp 5 Sch.3 para.25
Sch.2 para.3A, amended: 2012 asp 5 Sch.3 para.25
Sch.2 para.4, amended: 2012 asp 5 Sch.3 para.25
Sch.2 para.5, amended: 2012 asp 5 Sch.3 para.25
Sch.2 para.6, amended: 2012 asp 5 Sch.3 para.25
Sch.3 para.2, amended: 2012 asp 5 Sch.3 para.26
Sch.3 para.4, amended: 2012 asp 5 Sch.3 para.26
Sch.3 para.7, amended: 2012 asp 5 Sch.3 para.26
Sch.3 para.9, amended: 2012 asp 5 Sch.3 para.26
Sch.3 para.14, amended: 2012 asp 5 Sch.3 para.26
Sch.4 Part 1 para.1, amended: 2012 asp 5 Sch.3 para.27
14. Land Registers (Scotland) Act 1995
s.1, amended: 2012 asp 5 Sch.5 para.35
s.1, repealed (in part): 2012 asp 5 Sch.5 para.35
16. Prisoners (Return to Custody) Act 1995
s.1, repealed (in part): 2012 c.10 Sch.10 para.7
17. Health Authorities Act 1995
Sch.1 Part III para.107, repealed (in part): 2012 c.7 s.39
Sch.2 para.2, amended: 2012 c.7 Sch.5 para.71
18. Jobseekers Act 1995
see *Secretary of State for Work and Pensions v Elmi* [2011] EWCA Civ 1403, [2012] P.T.S.R. 780 (CA (Civ Div)), Maurice Kay, L.J.
applied: 2012 c.5 s.33, SI 2012/ 2677 Reg.44, SI 2012/ 2885 Sch.1 para.17, Sch.1 para.22, Sch.1 para.46, SI 2012/ 2886 Sch.1, SI 2012/ 3144 Sch.1 para.11, Sch.1 para.16, SI 2012/ 3145 Sch.1, SSI 2012/ 292 Art.3, SSI 2012/ 303 Reg.31, Sch.4 para.8, Sch.5 para.8, SSI 2012/ 319 Reg.2, Reg.31, Reg.38, Reg.59
referred to: SI 2012/ 1616 Reg.2
s.1, amended: 2012 c.5 s.44, s.61
s.1, applied: SI 2012/ 531 Reg.49, SI 2012/ 1483 Reg.4
s.1, repealed (in part): 2012 c.5 s.49, Sch.14 Part 1
s.2, amended: 2012 c.5 Sch.2 para.35, Sch.14 Part 1
s.2, repealed (in part): 2012 c.5 Sch.14 Part 1
s.3, repealed: 2012 c.5 Sch.14 Part 1
s.3A, repealed: 2012 c.5 Sch.14 Part 1
s.3B, repealed: 2012 c.5 Sch.14 Part 1
s.4, amended: 2012 c.5 Sch.5 para.5, Sch.14 Part 1
s.4, repealed (in part): 2012 c.5 Sch.14 Part 1
s.4, enabling: SI 2012/ 913, SI 2012/ 2587
s.4A, repealed: 2012 c.5 Sch.14 Part 1
s.5, amended: 2012 c.5 Sch.14 Part 1
s.6, substituted: 2012 c.5 s.49
s.6, enabling: SI 2012/ 397, SI 2012/ 853, SI 2012/ 874, SI 2012/ 1616
s.6A, substituted: 2012 c.5 s.49
s.6B, substituted: 2012 c.5 s.49
s.6C, substituted: 2012 c.5 s.49
s.6D, substituted: 2012 c.5 s.49
s.6E, substituted: 2012 c.5 s.49
s.6F, substituted: 2012 c.5 s.49
s.6G, substituted: 2012 c.5 s.49
s.6H, substituted: 2012 c.5 s.49

1995– cont.

18. **Jobseekers Act 1995**–*cont.*
s.6I, substituted: 2012 c.5 s.49
s.6J, substituted: 2012 c.5 s.49
s.6K, substituted: 2012 c.5 s.49
s.6L, substituted: 2012 c.5 s.49
s.7, substituted: 2012 c.5 s.49
s.7, enabling: SI 2012/ 397, SI 2012/ 853, SI 2012/ 874, SI 2012/ 1616
s.8, amended: 2012 c.5 s.45, Sch.7 para.2
s.8, repealed (in part): 2012 c.5 Sch.14 Part 3
s.8, substituted: 2012 c.5 s.49
s.8, enabling: SI 2012/ 1616, SI 2012/ 2568
s.9, substituted: 2012 c.5 s.44, s.49
s.9, enabling: SI 2012/ 853
s.10, substituted: 2012 c.5 s.44, s.49
s.12, enabling: SI 2012/ 397, SI 2012/ 757, SI 2012/ 1616, SI 2012/ 2575
s.13, repealed: 2012 c.5 Sch.14 Part 1
s.15, repealed: 2012 c.5 Sch.14 Part 1
s.15A, repealed: 2012 c.5 Sch.14 Part 1
s.15B, repealed: 2012 c.5 Sch.14 Part 1
s.16, amended: 2012 c.5 Sch.7 para.3
s.16, repealed: 2012 c.5 Sch.14 Part 1
s.17, amended: 2012 c.5 Sch.7 para.3
s.17, repealed: 2012 c.5 Sch.14 Part 1
s.17A, amended: 2012 c.5 Sch.7 para.4, Sch.14 Part 1
s.17A, applied: SI 2012/ 2885 Reg.2, SI 2012/ 2886 Sch.1, SI 2012/ 3144 Reg.2, SI 2012/ 3145 Sch.1, SSI 2012/ 319 Reg.2
s.17A, repealed (in part): 2012 c.5 Sch.14 Part 3, Sch.14 Part 4
s.17A, enabling: SI 2012/ 397
s.17B, repealed: 2012 c.5 Sch.14 Part 4
s.17C, repealed: 2012 c.5 s.60
s.18, repealed: 2012 c.5 Sch.14 Part 1
s.19, applied: SI 2012/ 2885 Reg.2, SI 2012/ 3144 Reg.2, SI 2012/ 3145 Sch.1, SSI 2012/ 319 Reg.2
s.19, disapplied: SI 2012/ 3144 Reg.2
s.19, referred to: SI 2012/ 2885 Reg.2, SI 2012/ 2886 Sch.1
s.19, repealed: 2012 c.5 Sch.14 Part 4
s.19, substituted: 2012 c.5 s.46
s.19, enabling: SI 2012/ 1135, SI 2012/ 2568
s.19A, applied: SI 2012/ 2885 Reg.2, SI 2012/ 3144 Reg.2, SI 2012/ 3145 Sch.1, SSI 2012/ 319 Reg.2
s.19A, disapplied: SI 2012/ 3144 Reg.2
s.19A, referred to: SI 2012/ 2885 Reg.2, SI 2012/ 2886 Sch.1
s.19A, repealed: 2012 c.5 Sch.14 Part 4
s.19A, substituted: 2012 c.5 s.46
s.19A, enabling: SI 2012/ 2568
s.19B, applied: SI 2012/ 2885 Reg.2, SI 2012/ 2886 Sch.1, SI 2012/ 3144 Reg.2, SI 2012/ 3145 Sch.1, SSI 2012/ 319 Reg.2
s.19B, repealed: 2012 c.5 Sch.14 Part 4
s.19B, substituted: 2012 c.5 s.46
s.19B, enabling: SI 2012/ 2568
s.19C, added: 2012 c.5 s.46
s.19C, repealed: 2012 c.5 Sch.14 Part 4
s.20, amended: 2012 c.5 Sch.7 para.5
s.20, repealed (in part): 2012 c.5 Sch.14 Part 3, Sch.14 Part 4
s.20, enabling: SI 2012/ 2575
s.20A, repealed: 2012 c.5 Sch.14 Part 3
s.20B, repealed: 2012 c.5 Sch.14 Part 3
s.20B, enabling: SI 2012/ 397
s.20C, repealed: 2012 c.5 Sch.7 para.6

1995– cont.

18. **Jobseekers Act 1995**–*cont.*
s.20D, repealed (in part): 2012 c.5 Sch.7 para.6, 2012 c.10 Sch.24 para.13
s.20E, repealed: 2012 c.5 Sch.14 Part 4
s.22, amended: 2012 c.5 Sch.7 para.7
s.22, repealed (in part): 2012 c.5 Sch.14 Part 4
s.23, repealed: 2012 c.5 Sch.14 Part 1
s.25, repealed: 2012 c.5 Sch.14 Part 1
s.28, repealed: 2012 c.5 Sch.14 Part 1
s.29, amended: 2012 c.5 s.49
s.29, enabling: SI 2012/ 397
s.31, repealed: 2012 c.5 Sch.14 Part 1
s.32, repealed (in part): 2012 c.5 Sch.14 Part 8
s.35, amended: 2012 c.5 s.44, s.49, Sch.7 para.8, Sch.14 Part 1, Sch.14 Part 3, Sch.14 Part 4
s.35, enabling: SI 2012/ 397, SI 2012/ 757, SI 2012/ 853, SI 2012/ 874, SI 2012/ 913, SI 2012/ 1135, SI 2012/ 1616, SI 2012/ 2568, SI 2012/ 2575, SI 2012/ 2587
s.36, amended: 2012 c.5 Sch.7 para.9, Sch.14 Part 6
s.36, repealed (in part): 2012 c.5 Sch.14 Part 4
s.36, enabling: SI 2012/ 397, SI 2012/ 757, SI 2012/ 853, SI 2012/ 874, SI 2012/ 913, SI 2012/ 1135, SI 2012/ 1616, SI 2012/ 2568, SI 2012/ 2575, SI 2012/ 2587
s.37, amended: 2012 c.5 s.46, s.47, s.49, Sch.14 Part 6
s.37, applied: SI 2012/ 397, SI 2012/ 853, SI 2012/ 2568
s.37, repealed (in part): 2012 c.5 Sch.14 Part 4
s.38, amended: 2012 c.5 Sch.14 Part 1
s.38, repealed (in part): 2012 c.5 Sch.14 Part 1
s.40, repealed: 2012 c.5 Sch.14 Part 1
Sch.A1 para.1, repealed: 2012 c.5 s.60
Sch.A1 para.2, repealed: 2012 c.5 s.60
Sch.A1 para.3, repealed: 2012 c.5 s.60
Sch.A1 para.4, repealed: 2012 c.5 s.60
Sch.A1 para.5, repealed: 2012 c.5 s.60
Sch.A1 para.6, repealed: 2012 c.5 s.60
Sch.A1 para.7, repealed: 2012 c.5 s.60
Sch.A1 para.8, repealed: 2012 c.5 s.60
Sch.A1 para.9, repealed: 2012 c.5 s.60
Sch.A1 para.10, repealed: 2012 c.5 s.60
Sch.1, amended: 2012 c.5 s.46
Sch.1 para.4, applied: SI 2012/ 2885 Reg.2, Sch.8 para.5, SI 2012/ 2886 Sch.1, SI 2012/ 3144 Reg.2, SI 2012/ 3145 Sch.1, SSI 2012/ 303 Reg.85, SSI 2012/ 319 Reg.2
Sch.1 para.6, amended: 2012 c.5 Sch.14 Part 1
Sch.1 para.8, amended: 2012 c.5 Sch.7 para.10
Sch.1 para.8, repealed: 2012 c.5 Sch.14 Part 1
Sch.1 para.8A, repealed: 2012 c.5 Sch.14 Part 1
Sch.1 para.8B, repealed: 2012 c.5 Sch.14 Part 4
Sch.1 para.8B, enabling: SI 2012/ 853
Sch.1 para.8ZA, added: 2012 c.5 s.61
Sch.1 para.9, amended: 2012 c.5 s.105
Sch.1 para.9, repealed: 2012 c.5 Sch.14 Part 1
Sch.1 para.9A, repealed: 2012 c.5 Sch.14 Part 1
Sch.1 para.9B, repealed: 2012 c.5 Sch.14 Part 1
Sch.1 para.9C, repealed: 2012 c.5 Sch.14 Part 1
Sch.1 para.9D, repealed: 2012 c.5 Sch.14 Part 1
Sch.1 para.10, amended: 2012 c.5 s.105, Sch.7 para.10
Sch.1 para.10, repealed: 2012 c.5 Sch.14 Part 1
Sch.1 para.11, amended: 2012 c.5 Sch.14 Part 1
Sch.1 para.11, enabling: SI 2012/ 2575
Sch.1 para.14AA, added: 2012 c.5 s.46
Sch.1 para.14AA, enabling: SI 2012/ 2568, SI 2012/ 2575
Sch.1 para.14B, amended: 2012 c.5 s.46
Sch.1 para.16, amended: 2012 c.5 Sch.14 Part 1

1995– cont.

18. Jobseekers Act 1995–*cont.*
Sch.1 para.18, repealed (in part): 2012 c.5 Sch.14 Part 1
Sch.1 para.19, amended: 2012 c.5 Sch.14 Part 6
Sch.2 para.29, repealed: 2012 c.5 Sch.14 Part 1
Sch.2 para.30, repealed: 2012 c.5 Sch.14 Part 1
Sch.2 para.31, repealed: 2012 c.5 Sch.14 Part 1
Sch.2 para.32, repealed: 2012 c.5 Sch.14 Part 1
Sch.2 para.33, repealed: 2012 c.5 Sch.14 Part 1
Sch.2 para.34, repealed: 2012 c.5 Sch.14 Part 1
Sch.2 para.35, repealed: 2012 c.5 Sch.14 Part 1
Sch.2 para.51, repealed: 2012 c.5 Sch.14 Part 8
Sch.2 para.53, repealed (in part): 2012 c.5 Sch.14 Part 1
Sch.2 para.73, repealed (in part): 2012 c.5 Sch.14 Part 1

21. Merchant Shipping Act 1995
Part IX, applied: SI 2012/1777 Art.22, SI 2012/1867 Art.8
Part IXA, referred to: SI 2012/2267 Reg.3
s.30, referred to: SI 2012/1095 Art.6
s.85, enabling: SI 2012/1844, SI 2012/2636
s.86, applied: SI 2012/1844
s.86, referred to: SI 2012/2636
s.86, enabling: SI 2012/1844, SI 2012/2636
s.130, enabling: SI 2012/742
s.135, amended: 2012 asp 8 Sch.7 para.59
s.163, referred to: SI 2012/2267 Reg.3
s.163A, referred to: SI 2012/2267 Reg.3
s.183, see *Dawkins v Carnival Plc (t/a P&O Cruises)* [2011] EWCA Civ 1237, [2012] 1 Lloyd's Rep. 1 (CA (Civ Div)), Pill, L.J.; see *Michael v Musgrove (t/a YNYS Ribs)* [2011] EWHC 1438 (Admlty), [2012] 2 Lloyd's Rep. 37 (QBD (Admlty)), Jervis Kay Q.C. (Admiralty Registrar)
s.183, amended: SI 2012/3152 Reg.14
s.190, see *MIOM 1 Ltd v Sea Echo ENE* [2011] EWHC 2715 (Admlty), [2012] 1 Lloyd's Rep. 140 (QBD (Admlty)), Teare, J.
s.192A, enabling: SI 2012/2267
s.225, applied: SI 2012/1914 Art.8
s.252, applied: SI 2012/1777 Art.19, Art.20
s.253, applied: SI 2012/1777 Art.20
s.256A, applied: 2012 c.9 Sch.2 para.2
s.258, repealed (in part): 2012 c.9 Sch.10 Part 2
s.259, applied: SI 2012/1743 Reg.7, Reg.11, Reg.14
s.267, applied: SI 2012/1743 Reg.3, Reg.11, Reg.14
s.267, enabling: SI 2012/1743
s.284, varied: SI 2012/2267 Reg.9, SI 2012/3152 Reg.9
s.308, applied: SI 2012/1777 Art.20
Sch.6, see *Michael v Musgrove (t/a YNYS Ribs)* [2011] EWHC 1438 (Admlty), [2012] 2 Lloyd's Rep. 37 (QBD (Admlty)), Jervis Kay Q.C. (Admiralty Registrar)
Sch.11ZA, referred to: SI 2012/2267 Reg.3

23. Goods Vehicles (Licensing of Operators) Act 1995
s.26, amended: SI 2012/2404 Sch.2 para.32
s.45, enabling: SI 2012/308
s.57, applied: SI 2012/308
s.57, enabling: SI 2012/308
Sch.3 para.3, amended: 2012 c.10 Sch.10 para.8

25. Environment Act 1995
s.12, applied: SI 2012/2407 Art.2
s.12, disapplied: SI 2012/2407 Art.2
s.13, applied: SI 2012/2406 Art.2
s.13, disapplied: SI 2012/2406 Art.2

1995– cont.

25. Environment Act 1995–*cont.*
s.40, applied: SI 2012/3038 Reg.52, Reg.73, Sch.5 para.3, Sch.5 para.6
s.41, amended: SI 2012/1659 Sch.3 para.13, SI 2012/2788 Reg.4
s.41, repealed (in part): SI 2012/2788 Reg.4
s.41A, amended: SI 2012/2788 Reg.5
s.42, amended: SI 2012/2788 Reg.6
s.48, referred to: 2012 asp 2 Sch.3
s.56, amended: SI 2012/2788 Reg.7
s.56, repealed (in part): SI 2012/2788 Reg.7
s.63, applied: SSI 2012/88 Reg.3
s.93, applied: SI 2012/3082, SI 2012/3082(a), SI 2012/3082(b), SI 2012/3082(c)
s.93, referred to: SI 2012/3082(b)
s.93, enabling: SI 2012/3082
s.94, enabling: SI 2012/3082
s.94A, enabling: SI 2012/3082
s.95, enabling: SI 2012/3082
s.108, amended: 2012 c.9 Sch.2 para.3
s.108, applied: SSI 2012/360 Reg.71
s.108, varied: SI 2012/1715 Reg.6
s.110, varied: SI 2012/1715 Reg.6
s.111, amended: SI 2012/2788 Reg.8
s.113, applied: SSI 2012/360 Reg.66
Sch.1 para.1, amended: SI 2012/2404 Sch.2 para.33
Sch.6 para.7, amended: SI 2012/2404 Sch.2 para.33
Sch.20 para.4, amended: SSI 2012/360 Sch.11 para.2

26. Pensions Act 1995
s.4, amended: SI 2012/2404 Sch.2 para.34
s.29, amended: SI 2012/2404 Sch.2 para.34
s.37, enabling: SI 2012/692
s.47, enabling: SI 2012/692
s.49, amended: 2012 c.21 Sch.18 para.82
s.49, enabling: SI 2012/215, SI 2012/1257
s.50, applied: SI 2012/687 Sch.4 para.6
s.50A, applied: SI 2012/687 Sch.4 para.6
s.50B, applied: SI 2012/687 Sch.4 para.6
s.51, applied: SI 2012/687 Sch.4 para.6
s.51ZA, applied: SI 2012/687 Sch.4 para.6
s.52, applied: SI 2012/687 Sch.4 para.6
s.53, applied: SI 2012/687 Sch.4 para.6
s.54, applied: SI 2012/687 Sch.4 para.6
s.67, see *Danks v Qinetiq Holdings Ltd* [2012] EWHC 570 (Ch), [2012] Pens. L.R. 131 (Ch D), Vos, J.
s.67, applied: SI 2012/687 Sch.2 para.1, Sch.2 para.2
s.67C, enabling: SI 2012/692
s.67D, enabling: SI 2012/1817
s.68, applied: SI 2012/687 Sch.2 para.2, Sch.2 para.3
s.68, enabling: SI 2012/542
s.73, see *Alexander Forbes Trustees Ltd v Doe* [2011] EWHC 3930 (Ch), [2012] Pens. L.R. 231 (Ch D), Judge Purle Q.C.
s.73B, enabling: SI 2012/1817
s.75, see *BESTrustees Plc v Kaupthing Singer & Friedlander Ltd (In Administration)* [2012] EWHC 629 (Ch), [2012] 3 All E.R. 874 (Ch D), Sales, J.; see *Wedgwood Museum Trust Ltd (In Administration), Re* [2011] EWHC 3782 (Ch), [2012] Pens. L.R. 175 (Ch D (Birmingham)), Judge Purle Q.C.
s.75, enabling: SI 2012/692, SI 2012/1817
s.75A, enabling: SI 2012/1817
s.91, see *Bradbury v British Broadcasting Corp* [2012] EWHC 1369 (Ch), [2012] Pens. L.R. 283 (Ch D), Warren, J.
s.91, applied: SI 2012/687 Sch.1 para.16

1995–cont.

26. Pensions Act 1995–*cont.*
s.91, varied: SI 2012/687 Sch.1 para.19
s.92, applied: SI 2012/687 Sch.1 para.5
s.92, varied: SI 2012/687 Sch.1 para.19
s.93, varied: SI 2012/687 Sch.1 para.19
s.94, varied: SI 2012/687 Sch.1 para.19
s.119, enabling: SI 2012/1817
s.120, applied: SI 2012/215, SI 2012/542, SI 2012/692, SI 2012/1817
s.124, enabling: SI 2012/215, SI 2012/542, SI 2012/692, SI 2012/1257, SI 2012/1817
s.172, amended: 2012 c.21 Sch.18 para.82
s.174, enabling: SI 2012/215, SI 2012/542, SI 2012/692, SI 2012/1257

27. Geneva Conventions (Amendment) Act 1995
referred to: SI 2012/2589 Sch.1 para.1

30. Landlord and Tenant (Covenants) Act 1995
s.16, see *K/S Victoria Street v House of Fraser (Stores Management) Ltd* [2011] EWCA Civ 904, [2012] Ch. 497 (CA (Civ Div)), Lord Neuberger (M.R.)
s.17, see *E.ON UK Plc v Gilesports Ltd* [2012] EWHC 2172 (Ch), [2012] 47 E.G. 128 (Ch D), Arnold, J.; see *Greene King Plc v Quisine Restaurants Ltd* [2012] EWCA Civ 698, [2012] 2 E.G.L.R. 64 (CA (Civ Div)), Laws, L.J.
s.24, see *K/S Victoria Street v House of Fraser (Stores Management) Ltd* [2011] EWCA Civ 904, [2012] Ch. 497 (CA (Civ Div)), Lord Neuberger (M.R.)
s.25, see *K/S Victoria Street v House of Fraser (Stores Management) Ltd* [2011] EWCA Civ 904, [2012] Ch. 497 (CA (Civ Div)), Lord Neuberger (M.R.)

35. Criminal Appeal Act 1995
s.9, applied: SI 2012/1726 r.68.1
s.11, applied: SI 2012/1726 r.63.1
s.13, applied: SI 2012/1726 r.68.1
s.13, referred to: SI 2012/1726 r.63.1

36. Children (Scotland) Act 1995
applied: SI 2012/3144 Reg.8, SI 2012/3145 Sch.1
Pt II. see *L v Angus Council* 2012 S.L.T. 304 (OH), Lord Stewart
Pt III. see *L v Angus Council* 2012 S.L.T. 304 (OH), Lord Stewart
s.11, see *B v G* [2012] UKSC 21, 2012 S.C. (U.K.S.C.) 293 (SC), Lord Hope, J.S.C. (Deputy President); see *M v M* 2012 S.L.T. 428 (IH (Ex Div)), Lord Hardie; see *Murtaza v Murtaza* 2012 Fam. L.R. 14 (OH), Lord Stewart; see *S v S* [2012] CSIH 17, 2012 S.C.L.R. 361 (IH (Ex Div)), Lady Paton
s.12, referred to: SSI 2012/111 Art.2
s.13, applied: SI 2012/2886 Sch.1, SSI 2012/303 Sch.5 para.50
s.17, applied: SI 2012/2677 Reg.53
s.22, applied: SI 2012/2886 Sch.1, SSI 2012/303 Sch.4 para.32, Sch.5 para.22
s.22, repealed (in part): 2012 c.5 Sch.14 Part 1
s.26, applied: SI 2012/2677 Reg.78, SI 2012/2885 Sch.1 para.21, SI 2012/2886 Sch.1, SI 2012/3144 Sch.1 para.15, SI 2012/3145 Sch.1
s.29, applied: SI 2012/2886 Sch.1, SSI 2012/303 Sch.4 para.32, Sch.4 para.33, Sch.5 para.22, Sch.5 para.23
s.30, applied: SI 2012/2886 Sch.1, SSI 2012/303 Sch.4 para.32, Sch.5 para.22
s.52, see *B v Authority Reporter for Edinburgh* 2012 S.C. 23 (IH (Ex Div)), Lord Hardie; see *Children's Reporter, Applicant* 2012 S.L.T. (Sh Ct) 217 (Sh Ct (Tayside) (Alloa)), Sheriff K J

1995–cont.

36. Children (Scotland) Act 1995–*cont.*
s.52–*cont.*
McGowan; see *S v Authority Reporter* 2012 S.L.T. (Sh Ct) 89 (Sh Ct (Lothian) (Edinburgh)), Sheriff Principal M M Stephen
s.68, see *Children's Reporter, Applicant* 2012 S.L.T. (Sh Ct) 217 (Sh Ct (Tayside) (Alloa)), Sheriff K J McGowan
s.70, see *Dumfries and Galloway Council, Petitioners* 2012 S.L.T. (Sh Ct) 173 (Sh Ct (South Strathclyde) (Dumfries)), Sheriff K A Ross
s.70, applied: SSI 2012/303 Reg.28, SSI 2012/319 Reg.29
s.73, see *Dumfries and Galloway Council, Petitioners* 2012 S.L.T. (Sh Ct) 173 (Sh Ct (South Strathclyde) (Dumfries)), Sheriff K A Ross
s.78, amended: 2012 asp 8 Sch.7 para.11
s.78, repealed (in part): 2012 asp 8 Sch.7 para.11
s.82, see *Welsh v Richardson* [2012] HCJAC 114, 2012 S.L.T. 1153 (HCJ), Lord Clarke
s.83, see *Welsh v Richardson* [2012] HCJAC 114, 2012 S.L.T. 1153 (HCJ), Lord Clarke
s.93, amended: 2012 asp 8 Sch.7 para.11

38. Civil Evidence Act 1995
applied: SI 2012/1726 r.62.11
referred to: SI 2012/1726 r.50.8
s.1, applied: SI 2012/1726 r.50.1
s.1, referred to: SI 2012/1726 r.62.11
s.2, see *Director of the Serious Fraud Office v B* [2012] EWCA Crim 67, [2012] 1 W.L.R. 3170 (CA (Crim Div)), Gross, L.J.
s.2, applied: SI 2012/1726 r.62.11, r.50.6
s.2, disapplied: SI 2012/1726 r.61.8
s.3, see *Director of the Serious Fraud Office v B* [2012] EWCA Crim 67, [2012] 1 W.L.R. 3170 (CA (Crim Div)), Gross, L.J.
s.3, applied: SI 2012/1726 r.50.7
s.3, referred to: SI 2012/1726 r.62.14
s.4, see *Director of the Serious Fraud Office v B* [2012] EWCA Crim 67, [2012] 1 W.L.R. 3170 (CA (Crim Div)), Gross, L.J.
s.5, applied: SI 2012/1726 r.50.8
s.5, referred to: SI 2012/1726 r.62.15
s.6, referred to: SI 2012/1726 r.62.15
s.13, referred to: SI 2012/1726 r.62.11

39. Criminal Law (Consolidation) (Scotland) Act 1995
s.6, see *Hogan (David) v HM Advocate* [2012] HCJAC 12, 2012 J.C. 307 (HCJ), The Lord Justice General (Hamilton); see *McCluskey (Barry) v HM Advocate* [2012] HCJAC 125, 2012 S.L.T. 1242 (HCJ), Lord Carloway
s.18, enabling: SSI 2012/164
s.47, see *Ashton (Mark) v HM Advocate* 2012 J.C. 213 (HCJ), Lord Clarke
s.49, see *Glancy (Kevin) v HM Advocate* 2012 S.C.L. 275 (HCJ Appeal), Lord Clarke; see *McCourt (Peter Stephen) v HM Advocate* [2012] HCJAC 32, 2012 J.C. 336 (HCJ), The Lord Justice General (Hamilton); see *Robertson (Craig) v HM Advocate* [2012] HCJAC 63, 2012 S.C.L. 871 (HCJ), The Lord Justice Clerk (Gill)
s.50A, see *King v Webster* 2012 S.L.T. 342 (HCJ), Lord Bonomy

40. Criminal Procedure (Consequential Provisions) (Scotland) Act 1995
Sch.2 Part III, amended: 2012 asp 8 Sch.8 Part 1

42. Private International Law (Miscellaneous Provisions) Act 1995

s.9, see *Cox v Ergo Versicherung AG (formerly Victoria)* [2011] EWHC 2806 (QB), [2012] R.T.R. 11 (QBD), Sir Christopher Holland

s.11, see *Cox v Ergo Versicherung AG (formerly Victoria)* [2011] EWHC 2806 (QB), [2012] R.T.R. 11 (QBD), Sir Christopher Holland; see *VTB Capital Plc v Nutritek International Corp* [2012] EWCA Civ 808, [2012] 2 Lloyd's Rep. 313 (CA (Civ Div)), Lloyd, L.J.

s.12, see *VTB Capital Plc v Nutritek International Corp* [2012] EWCA Civ 808, [2012] 2 Lloyd's Rep. 313 (CA (Civ Div)), Lloyd, L.J.

46. Criminal Procedure (Scotland) Act 1995

see *Beggs (William Frederick Ian) v HM Advocate* 2012 J.C. 173 (HCJ), Lord Justice General Hamilton; see *I v Dunn* [2012] HCJAC 108, 2012 S.L.T. 983 (HCJ), Lady Paton; see *Jude (Raymond) v HM Advocate* 2012 S.C. (U.K.S.C.) 222 (SC), Lord Hope (Deputy President)

applied: SI 2012/2885 Sch.1 para.5, SI 2012/2886 Sch.1, SI 2012/3144 Reg.24, SI 2012/3145 Sch.1, SSI 2012/303 Reg.5, Reg.15, SSI 2012/319 Reg.5, Reg.15

Part XIII, substituted: 2012 c.11 s.34

Pt XII s.262, see *A v HM Advocate* [2012] HCJAC 29, 2012 J.C. 343 (HCJ), Lord Bonomy; see *HM Advocate v Malloy (Anthony Francis)* [2012] HCJ 124, 2012 S.L.T. 1167 (HCJ), Lord Bracadale

s.7, see *Hunter v McPherson* 2012 J.C. 145 (HCJ), Lord Mackay of Drumadoon

s.12, amended: 2012 asp 8 Sch.7 para.12

s.12, applied: 2012 asp 8 s.17

s.14, see *Children's Reporter, Applicant* 2012 S.L.T. (Sh Ct) 217 (Sh Ct (Tayside) (Alloa)), Sheriff K J McGowan; see *HM Advocate v Fotheringham (Neil)* 2012 S.L.T. 822 (HCJ), Lady Stacey; see *HM Advocate v L* [2012] HCJAC 4, 2012 S.L.T. 818 (HCJ), The Lord Justice General (Hamilton); see *HM Advocate v Lukstins (Indulis)* 2012 S.L.T. 167 (HCJ), Lady Stacey; see *MacLean v Dunn* [2012] HCJAC 34, 2012 J.C. 293 (HCJ), Lord Hardie

s.18, see *HM Advocate v Cowie (Yvonne Logan)* 2012 J.C. 203 (HCJ), Lord Clarke; see *HM Advocate v Fotheringham (Neil)* 2012 S.L.T. 822 (HCJ), Lady Stacey; see *HM Advocate v Lukstins (Indulis)* 2012 S.L.T. 167 (HCJ), Lady Stacey; see *MacLean v Dunn* [2012] HCJAC 34, 2012 J.C. 293 (HCJ), Lord Hardie

s.18, amended: 2012 asp 8 Sch.7 para.12, 2012 c.9 Sch.1 para.6

s.18A, amended: 2012 asp 8 Sch.7 para.12

s.18C, amended: 2012 asp 8 Sch.7 para.12

s.18F, amended: 2012 asp 8 Sch.7 para.12

s.18G, added: 2012 c.9 Sch.1 para.6

s.18G, applied: 2012 c.9 s.20

s.19, amended: 2012 asp 8 Sch.7 para.12

s.19C, amended: 2012 asp 8 Sch.7 para.12

s.19C, applied: 2012 c.9 s.20

s.23D, see *HM Advocate v K* 2012 J.C. 165 (HCJ), Lord Clarke

s.24, see *Cameron v Cottam* [2012] HCJAC 19, 2012 S.L.T. 173 (HCJ), Lord Eassie

s.51B, referred to: SSI 2012/160 Art.4

s.57A, see *Scottish Ministers v Mental Health Tribunal for Scotland* [2012] CSIH 18, 2012 S.C. 471 (IH (Ex Div)), Lord Eassie; see *Scottish Ministers v Mental Health Tribunal for*

46. Criminal Procedure (Scotland) Act 1995– *cont.*

s.57A – *cont.*

Scotland 2012 S.C. 225 (IH (Ex Div)), Lady Paton

s.58A, see *Application in respect of M* 2012 S.L.T. (Sh Ct) 25 (Sh Ct (Glasgow)), Sheriff J A Baird

s.59, see *Scottish Ministers v Mental Health Tribunal for Scotland* [2012] CSIH 18, 2012 S.C. 471 (IH (Ex Div)), Lord Eassie; see *Scottish Ministers v Mental Health Tribunal for Scotland* 2012 S.C. 225 (IH (Ex Div)), Lady Paton

s.65, see *Nichol (Craig) v HM Advocate* [2012] HCJAC 56, 2012 S.L.T. 915 (HCJ), The Lord Justice Clerk (Gill)

s.67, see *HM Advocate v AB* [2012] HCJAC 13, 2012 J.C. 283 (HCJ), The Lord Justice Clerk (Gill)

s.70A, see *Barclay (John) v HM Advocate* [2012] HCJAC 47, 2012 S.L.T. 855 (HCJ), The Lord Justice General (Hamilton)

s.70A, applied: 2012 asp 5 s.112

s.74, see *HM Advocate v K* [2012] HCJAC 44, 2012 S.L.T. 939 (HCJ), The Lord Justice General (Hamilton)

s.76, see *Foye (Robert) v HM Advocate* 2012 J.C. 190 (HCJ), Lord Osborne

s.94, amended: SSI 2012/272 Art.2

s.99, see *HM Advocate v Paterson (Grant)* [2012] HCJAC 105, 2012 S.L.T. 1182 (HCJ), Lord Carloway

s.106, see *McMillan (David Baillie) v HM Advocate* [2012] HCJAC 3, 2012 S.C.L. 547 (HCJ), Lord Bonomy; see *Shahid (Imran) v HM Advocate* 2012 S.C.L. 5 (HCJ), The Lord Justice General (Hamilton)

s.107, referred to: SSI 2012/187 r.4, SSI 2012/272 Art.3

s.110, see *Jude (Raymond) v HM Advocate* 2012 S.C. (U.K.S.C.) 222 (SC), Lord Hope (Deputy President); see *McMillan (David Baillie) v HM Advocate* [2012] HCJAC 3, 2012 S.C.L. 547 (HCJ), Lord Bonomy

s.112, amended: 2012 c.11 s.36

s.121, amended: 2012 c.11 s.36

s.121A, amended: 2012 c.11 s.36

s.122, amended: 2012 c.11 s.36

s.124, see *Cobanoglu, Petitioner* [2012] HCJAC 35, 2012 S.C.L. 604 (HCJ), The Lord Justice Clerk (Gill)

s.124, amended: 2012 c.11 s.36

s.131, see *HM Advocate v K* [2012] HCJAC 44, 2012 S.L.T. 939 (HCJ), The Lord Justice General (Hamilton)

s.133, see *Hunter v McPherson* 2012 J.C. 145 (HCJ), Lord Mackay of Drumadoon

s.135, applied: 2012 asp 8 s.20

s.136, see *Rodden v Dunn* 2012 J.C. 114 (HCJ), Lord Bonomy

s.136, applied: SI 2012/129 Reg.19, SI 2012/925 Reg.22, SI 2012/1017 Reg.71, SI 2012/1102 Reg.7, SI 2012/1301 Reg.14, SI 2012/1489 Reg.14, SI 2012/1507 Reg.14, SI 2012/1508 Reg.14, SI 2012/1509 Reg.14, SI 2012/1511 Reg.14, SI 2012/1515 Reg.14, SI 2012/1516 Reg.14, SI 2012/1517 Reg.14, SI 2012/1916 Reg.339, SI 2012/3032 Reg.42

s.136, disapplied: SI 2012/1017 Reg.71, SI 2012/1102 Reg.7

s.144, see *Chilcott v McGowan* [2012] HCJAC 7, 2012 S.L.T. 918 (HCJ), Lord Eassie

1995– *cont.*

46. Criminal Procedure (Scotland) Act 1995– *cont.*

s.145A, see *Chilcott v McGowan* [2012] HCJAC 7, 2012 S.L.T. 918 (HCJ), Lord Eassie

s.147, see *HM Advocate v Havrilova* 2012 S.C.C.R. 361 (HCJ), Lord Clarke

s.160, see *Cox v Richardson* 2012 J.C. 22 (HCJ), Lord Eassie

s.174, see *I v Dunn* [2012] HCJAC 108, 2012 S.L.T. 983 (HCJ), Lady Paton

s.177, amended: 2012 c.11 s.36

s.189, see *Gill v Thomson* 2012 J.C. 137 (HCJ), Lord Carloway

s.194B, see *Reid (Alexander Lewis Hutchison) v HM Advocate* [2012] HCJAC 18, 2012 S.C.L. 475 (HCJ), Lord Reed

s.194B, referred to: SSI 2012/187 r.4

s.194C, see *M v HM Advocate* [2012] HCJAC 121, 2012 S.C.L. 1037 (HCJ), The Lord Justice General (Hamilton)

s.194DA, see *M v HM Advocate* [2012] HCJAC 121, 2012 S.C.L. 1037 (HCJ), The Lord Justice General (Hamilton)

s.194I, amended: 2012 asp 8 Sch.7 para.12, Sch.8 Part 1

s.194J, amended: 2012 asp 7 s.3

s.194M, added: 2012 asp 7 s.3

s.194N, added: 2012 asp 7 s.3

s.194O, added: 2012 asp 7 s.3

s.194P, added: 2012 asp 7 s.3

s.194Q, added: 2012 asp 7 s.3

s.194R, added: 2012 asp 7 s.3

s.194S, added: 2012 asp 7 s.3

s.194T, added: 2012 asp 7 s.3

s.196, see *Balgowan (Paul) v HM Advocate* 2012 J.C. 5 (HCJ), Lord Reed; see *Gemmell (James Kelly) v HM Advocate* 2012 J.C. 223 (HCJ), The Lord Justice Clerk (Gill); see *Harkin v Brown* [2012] HCJAC 100, 2012 S.L.T. 1071 (HCJ), Lord Carloway; see *HM Advocate v McNamara (Lee)* [2012] HCJAC 54, 2012 S.L.T. 1037 (HCJ), Lord Carloway; see *Ottaway v Nisbet* [2012] HCJAC 36, 2012 S.L.T. 662 (HCJ), Lady Paton; see *SD Cameron Ltd v Knox* 2012 S.C.L. 434 (HCJ), Lord Mackay of Drumadoon

s.201, see *Gifford (Matilda Rosamond) v HM Advocate* 2012 S.C.L. 267 (HCJ), Lord Reed

s.202, see *Gifford (Matilda Rosamond) v HM Advocate* 2012 S.C.L. 267 (HCJ), Lord Reed

s.210A, see *Gemmell (James Kelly) v HM Advocate* 2012 J.C. 223 (HCJ), The Lord Justice Clerk (Gill)

s.210B, see *Johnstone (Brian) v HM Advocate* 2012 J.C. 79 (HCJ), The Lord Justice Clerk (Gill); see *McMillan (David Baillie) v HM Advocate* [2012] HCJAC 3, 2012 S.C.L. 547 (HCJ), Lord Bonomy

s.210C, see *McMillan (David Baillie) v HM Advocate* [2012] HCJAC 3, 2012 S.C.L. 547 (HCJ), Lord Bonomy

s.210E, see *M v HM Advocate* 2012 S.L.T. 147 (HCJ), Lord Carloway

s.210F, see *Foye (Robert) v HM Advocate* 2012 J.C. 190 (HCJ), Lord Osborne; see *Johnstone (Brian) v HM Advocate* 2012 J.C. 79 (HCJ), The Lord Justice Clerk (Gill); see *McMillan (David Baillie) v HM Advocate* [2012] HCJAC 3, 2012 S.C.L. 547 (HCJ), Lord Bonomy

s.210G, see *Johnstone (Brian) v HM Advocate* 2012 J.C. 79 (HCJ), The Lord Justice Clerk (Gill)

s.227W, see *Kirk v Brown* [2012] HCJAC 96, 2012 S.L.T. 1033 (HCJ), Lord Clarke

1995– *cont.*

46. Criminal Procedure (Scotland) Act 1995– *cont.*

s.256, see *Hunter v Brown* [2012] HCJAC 42, 2012 S.L.T. 665 (HCJ), Lord Mackay of Drumadoon

s.259, see *Brand (Ian Charles) v HM Advocate* 2012 S.L.T. 952 (HCJ), Lord Eassie; see *HM Advocate v Malloy (Anthony Francis)* [2012] HCJ 124, 2012 S.L.T. 1167 (HCJ), Lord Bracadale; see *Murphy (Donna) v HM Advocate* [2012] HCJAC 74, 2012 S.C.L. 855 (HCJ), Lord Carloway

s.260, see *A v HM Advocate* [2012] HCJAC 29, 2012 J.C. 343 (HCJ), Lord Bonomy

s.261, see *Brand (Ian Charles) v HM Advocate* 2012 S.L.T. 952 (HCJ), Lord Eassie

s.261A, see *HM Advocate v Malloy (Anthony Francis)* [2012] HCJ 124, 2012 S.L.T. 1167 (HCJ), Lord Bracadale

s.263, see *A v HM Advocate* [2012] HCJAC 29, 2012 J.C. 343 (HCJ), Lord Bonomy

s.271C, see *I v Dunn* [2012] HCJAC 108, 2012 S.L.T. 983 (HCJ), Lady Paton

s.271D, see *I v Dunn* [2012] HCJAC 108, 2012 S.L.T. 983 (HCJ), Lady Paton

s.280, repealed (in part): 2012 asp 8 Sch.8 Part 1

s.281A, see *Liddle (Jason Thomas) v HM Advocate* [2012] HCJAC 68, 2012 S.C.C.R. 478 (HCJ), Lord Carloway

s.288A, amended: 2012 c.11 s.34

s.288AA, added: 2012 c.11 s.36

s.288B, amended: 2012 c.11 s.36

s.288B, substituted: 2012 c.11 s.36

s.288ZA, added: 2012 c.11 s.34

s.288ZB, added: 2012 c.11 s.35

s.297, see *Ashif v Dunn* 2012 S.L.T. 794 (HCJ), Lord Bonomy

s.300A, see *Gifford (Matilda Rosamond) v HM Advocate* 2012 S.C.L. 267 (HCJ), Lord Reed; see *Murphy (Donna) v HM Advocate* [2012] HCJAC 74, 2012 S.C.L. 855 (HCJ), Lord Carloway

s.302, applied: SI 2012/1909 Sch.2 para.3, Sch.4 para.31, Sch.5 para.21

s.305, enabling: SSI 2012/125, SSI 2012/187, SSI 2012/272, SSI 2012/300

s.307, see *Murphy (Donna) v HM Advocate* [2012] HCJAC 74, 2012 S.C.L. 855 (HCJ), Lord Carloway

s.307, amended: 2012 asp 8 Sch.7 para.12, 2012 c.7 s.213

Sch.1, see *S v Authority Reporter* 2012 S.L.T. (Sh Ct) 89 (Sh Ct (Lothian) (Edinburgh)), Sheriff Principal M M Stephen

Sch.3 para.16, see *Cunningham (David James) v HM Advocate* [2012] HCJAC 90, 2012 S.C.L. 884 (HCJ), Lord Eassie

Sch.5, amended: SSI 2012/215 Sch.1 Part 3

Sch.8, see *HM Advocate v AB* [2012] HCJAC 13, 2012 J.C. 283 (HCJ), The Lord Justice Clerk (Gill)

Sch.8 para.8, see *HM Advocate v AB* [2012] HCJAC 13, 2012 J.C. 283 (HCJ), The Lord Justice Clerk (Gill)

Sch.9, amended: 2012 asp 8 Sch.7 para.12, SSI 2012/215 Sch.1 para.1

Sch.10 para.1, repealed: SSI 2012/215 Sch.1 Part 3

Sch.12 Part II para.46, amended: SI 2012/1809 Sch.1 Part 1

50. Disability Discrimination Act 1995

see *All Saints', Sanderstead, Re* [2012] Fam. 51 (Cons Ct (Southwark)), Chancellor Petchey; see *Barlow v Stone* [2012] I.R.L.R. 898 (EAT),

1995–cont.

50. Disability Discrimination Act 1995–*cont.*
see–*cont.*

Judge David Richardson; see *Barnsley MBC v Norton* [2011] EWCA Civ 834, [2012] P.T.S.R. 56 (CA (Civ Div)), Maurice Kay, L.J.; see *Burnip v Birmingham City Council* [2012] EWCA Civ 629, [2012] H.R.L.R. 20 (CA (Civ Div)), Maurice Kay, L.J.; see *Holmes v Westminster City Council* [2011] EWHC 2857 (QB), [2012] B.L.G.R. 233 (QBD), Eady, J.; see *JP Morgan Europe Ltd v Chweidan* [2011] EWCA Civ 648, [2012] I.C.R. 268 (CA (Civ Div)), Ward, L.J.; see *Lalli v Spirita Housing Ltd* [2012] EWCA Civ 497, [2012] Eq. L.R. 560 (CA (Civ Div)), Ward, L.J.; see *O'Cathail v Transport for London* [2012] I.C.R. 561 (EAT), Judge David Richardson; see *R. (on the application of Hurley) v Secretary of State for Business, Innovation and Skills* [2012] EWHC 201 (Admin), [2012] H.R.L.R. 13 (DC), Elias, L.J.; see *R. (on the application of Maxwell) v Office of the Independent Adjudicator* [2011] EWCA Civ 1236, [2012] P.T.S.R. 884 (CA (Civ Div)), Mummery, L.J.; see *Royal Bank of Scotland Plc v Morris* [2012] Eq. L.R. 406 (EAT), Underhill, J.; see *XX v UKBA* [2012] Eq. L.R. 942 (EAT), Judge McMullen Q.C.

applied: SI 2012/3102 Sch.1, SI 2012/3103 Sch.1, SI 2012/3104 Sch.1, SI 2012/3105 Sch.1, SI 2012/3106 Sch.1, SI 2012/3107 Sch.1, SSI 2012/181 Reg.3

s.1, see *Lalli v Spirita Housing Ltd* [2012] EWCA Civ 497, [2012] Eq. L.R. 560 (CA (Civ Div)), Ward, L.J.

s.3A, see *Cordell v Foreign and Commonwealth Office* [2012] I.C.R. 280 (EAT), Underhill, J. (President)

s.3B, see *Prospects for People with Learning Difficulties v Harris* [2012] Eq. L.R. 781 (EAT), Judge David Richardson

s.4A, see *Cordell v Foreign and Commonwealth Office* [2012] I.C.R. 280 (EAT), Underhill, J. (President)

s.14B, see *Burke v College of Law* [2012] EWCA Civ 37, [2012] Eq. L.R. 279 (CA (Civ Div)), Laws, L.J.

s.17A, see *Barlow v Stone* [2012] I.R.L.R. 898 (EAT), Judge David Richardson

s.18B, see *Cordell v Foreign and Commonwealth Office* [2012] I.C.R. 280 (EAT), Underhill, J. (President)

s.19, see *All Saints', Sanderstead, Re* [2012] Fam. 51 (Cons Ct (Southwark)), Chancellor Petchey; see *Lalli v Spirita Housing Ltd* [2012] EWCA Civ 497, [2012] Eq. L.R. 560 (CA (Civ Div)), Ward, L.J.

s.21E, see *ZH v Commissioner of Police for the Metropolis* [2012] EWHC 604 (QB), [2012] Eq. L.R. 425 (CC (Central London)), Sir Robert Nelson

s.28I, see *ML v Tonbridge Grammar School* [2012] UKUT 283 (AAC), [2012] E.L.R. 508 (UT (AAC)), Judge Rowland

s.49A, see *Barnsley MBC v Norton* [2011] EWCA Civ 834, [2012] P.T.S.R. 56 (CA (Civ Div)), Maurice Kay, L.J.; see *R. (on the application of D) v Manchester City Council* [2012] EWHC 17 (Admin), [2012] Eq. L.R. 251 (QBD (Admin)), Ryder, J.; see *R. (on the application of Essex CC) v Secretary of State for Education* [2012] EWHC 1460 (Admin), [2012] E.L.R. 383 (QBD (Admin)), Mitting, J.; see *R. (on the application of HA (Nigeria)) v Secretary of State for the Home Department* [2012] EWHC 979

1995–cont.

50. Disability Discrimination Act 1995–*cont.*
s.49A–*cont.*

(Admin), [2012] Med. L.R. 353 (QBD (Admin)), Singh, J.; see *R. (on the application of JM) v Isle of Wight Council* [2011] EWHC 2911 (Admin), [2012] Eq. L.R. 34 (QBD (Admin)), Lang, J.; see *R. (on the application of Rajput) v Waltham Forest LBC* [2011] EWCA Civ 1577, [2012] Eq. L.R. 265 (CA (Civ Div)), Carnwath, L.J.

s.49A, applied: SI 2012/3102 Sch.1, SI 2012/3103 Sch.1, SI 2012/3104 Sch.1, SI 2012/3105 Sch.1, SI 2012/3106 Sch.1, SI 2012/3107 Sch.1

s.49A, referred to: SI 2012/3102 Sch.1, SI 2012/3103 Sch.1, SI 2012/3104 Sch.1, SI 2012/3105 Sch.1, SI 2012/3106 Sch.1, SI 2012/3107 Sch.1

s.57, see *Barlow v Stone* [2012] I.R.L.R. 898 (EAT), Judge David Richardson

s.58, see *Barlow v Stone* [2012] I.R.L.R. 898 (EAT), Judge David Richardson

53. Criminal Injuries Compensation Act 1995
see *Rust-Andrews v First-tier Tribunal* [2011] EWCA Civ 1548, [2012] P.I.Q.R. P7 (CA (Civ Div)), Carnwath, L.J.

1996

1. Humber Bridge (Debts) Act 1996
s.1, enabling: SI 2012/716

8. Finance Act 1996
see *Greene King Plc v Revenue and Customs Commissioners* [2012] UKFTT 385 (TC), [2012] S.F.T.D. 1085 (FTT (Tax)), Judge Colin Bishopp

s.30, repealed (in part): 2012 c.14 Sch.29 para.13

s.40, amended: 2012 c.11 s.31

s.42, amended: 2012 c.14 s.205

s.42, applied: SI 2012/940

s.42, enabling: SI 2012/940

s.51, enabling: SI 2012/885

s.53, enabling: SI 2012/885

s.63, enabling: SI 2012/940

s.66, repealed (in part): 2012 c.11 Sch.4 para.2

s.67, repealed (in part): 2012 c.11 Sch.4 para.3

s.70, amended: 2012 c.11 Sch.4 para.4

s.70, repealed (in part): 2012 c.11 Sch.4 para.4

s.81, see *Greene King Plc v Revenue and Customs Commissioners* [2012] UKFTT 385 (TC), [2012] S.F.T.D. 1085 (FTT (Tax)), Judge Colin Bishopp; see *MJP Media Services Ltd v Revenue and Customs Commissioners* [2012] EWCA Civ 1558, [2012] B.T.C. 477 (CA (Civ Div)), Rix, L.J.

s.84, see *Greene King Plc v Revenue and Customs Commissioners* [2012] UKFTT 385 (TC), [2012] S.F.T.D. 1085 (FTT (Tax)), Judge Colin Bishopp; see *Vocalspruce Ltd v Revenue and Customs Commissioners* [2012] UKFTT 36 (TC), [2012] S.F.T.D. 659 (FTT (Tax)), Judge Roger Berner

s.163, repealed: 2012 c.14 Sch.16 para.247

s.166, repealed: 2012 c.14 s.26

s.167, repealed (in part): 2012 c.14 Sch.16 para.247, Sch.39 para.28

s.168, repealed (in part): 2012 c.14 Sch.16 para.247

s.171, repealed: 2012 c.14 Sch.18 para.23

s.197, see *Emblaze Mobility Solutions Ltd v Revenue and Customs Commissioners* [2012] B.V.C. 174 (Ch D), Peter Leaver Q.C.

s.197, applied: 2012 c.14 Sch.24 para.59

1996–cont.

8. Finance Act 1996–*cont.*

Sch.9 para.12, see *Vocalspruce Ltd v Revenue and Customs Commissioners* [2012] UKFTT 36 (TC), [2012] S.F.T.D. 659 (FTT (Tax)), Judge Roger Berner

Sch.9 para.13, see *AH Field (Holdings) Ltd v Revenue and Customs Commissioners* [2012] UKFTT 104 (TC) (FTT (Tax)), Judge Rachel Short

Sch.14 para.23, repealed: 2012 c.14 Sch.16 para.247

Sch.18 para.11, repealed: 2012 c.14 Sch.39 para.28

Sch.20 para.20, repealed: 2012 c.14 Sch.39 para.28

Sch.31 para.1, repealed: 2012 c.14 Sch.16 para.247

Sch.31 para.2, repealed: 2012 c.14 Sch.16 para.247

Sch.31 para.3, repealed: 2012 c.14 Sch.16 para.247

Sch.31 para.4, repealed: 2012 c.14 Sch.16 para.247

Sch.31 para.5, repealed: 2012 c.14 Sch.16 para.247

Sch.31 para.6, repealed: 2012 c.14 Sch.16 para.247

Sch.31 para.7, repealed: 2012 c.14 Sch.16 para.247

Sch.31 para.8, repealed: 2012 c.14 Sch.16 para.247

Sch.31 para.9, repealed: 2012 c.14 Sch.16 para.247

Sch.31 para.10, repealed: 2012 c.14 Sch.16 para.247

Sch.32 para.1, repealed: 2012 c.14 s.26

Sch.32 para.2, repealed: 2012 c.14 s.26

Sch.32 para.27, repealed: 2012 c.14 s.26

Sch.33 para.1, repealed: 2012 c.14 Sch.16 para.247

Sch.33 para.2, repealed: 2012 c.14 Sch.16 para.247

Sch.33 para.3, repealed: 2012 c.14 Sch.16 para.247

Sch.33 para.4, repealed: 2012 c.14 Sch.16 para.247

14. Reserve Forces Act 1996

s.1, referred to: SI 2012/335 Sch.2 para.20, SI 2012/2991 Sch.2 para.28

16. Police Act 1996

applied: SI 2012/1916 Sch.16 Part 3

s.2, applied: SI 2012/2892 Art.5

s.2, applied: 2012 asp 8 s.16, s.90, s.96, Sch.1 para.3, Sch.1 para.7, SI 2012/2632 Reg.2

s.3, applied: SSI 2012/88 Reg.3

s.5B, applied: SSI 2012/88 Reg.3

s.16, applied: SI 2012/2892 Art.4

s.23FA, applied: SI 2012/1690

s.23FA, enabling: SI 2012/1690

s.50, enabling: SI 2012/192, SI 2012/680, SI 2012/1960, SI 2012/1961, SI 2012/2631, SI 2012/2632, SI 2012/2712, SI 2012/3058

s.51, enabling: SI 2012/1961, SI 2012/2631, SI 2012/2632

s.54, applied: SI 2012/2840 Reg.11

s.59, amended: 2012 asp 8 Sch.7 para.13

s.60, amended: 2012 asp 8 Sch.7 para.13

s.60A, repealed (in part): 2012 asp 8 Sch.8 Part 1

s.61, referred to: 2012 asp 8 s.54

s.61, repealed (in part): 2012 asp 8 Sch.8 Part 1

s.62, amended: 2012 asp 8 Sch.7 para.13, Sch.8 Part 1

s.62, applied: SI 2012/2712, SI 2012/3058

s.62, repealed (in part): 2012 asp 8 Sch.8 Part 1

s.63, amended: 2012 asp 8 s.97

s.63, applied: SI 2012/680, SI 2012/1204, SI 2012/1960, SI 2012/2630, SI 2012/2631, SI 2012/2632, SI 2012/2712, SI 2012/2954, SI 2012/3058

s.63, repealed (in part): 2012 asp 8 s.97

s.64, applied: 2012 asp 8 s.51

s.64, repealed (in part): 2012 asp 8 Sch.8 Part 1

s.84, enabling: SI 2012/2631, SI 2012/2632

s.85, applied: SI 2012/2630 r.2

s.85, enabling: SI 2012/2630

s.87, applied: SI 2012/2631 Reg.4, SI 2012/2632 Reg.3

1996–cont.

16. Police Act 1996–*cont.*

s.88, amended: SI 2012/1809 Sch.1 Part 1

s.89, see *Sobczak v DPP* [2012] EWHC 1319 (Admin), (2012) 176 J.P. 575 (QBD (Admin)), Mitting, J.

s.89, amended: SI 2012/1809 Sch.1 Part 1

s.97, amended: SI 2012/2954 Art.3, SI 2012/3006 Art.13

s.97A, enabling: SI 2012/2954

s.99, amended: 2012 asp 8 Sch.7 para.13

Sch.2 para.1, enabling: SI 2012/536

Sch.2 para.6, applied: SI 2012/536

Sch.4A para.2, applied: SI 2012/2840 Reg.10

Sch.4A para.2, repealed (in part): SI 2012/2401 Sch.1 para.5

Sch.4A para.3, enabling: SI 2012/2733

Sch.4A para.4, applied: SI 2012/2840 Reg.11

Sch.4A para.4, repealed (in part): SI 2012/2401 Sch.1 para.5

Sch.4A para.5, applied: SI 2012/2840 Reg.12

Sch.4A para.5, repealed (in part): SI 2012/2401 Sch.1 para.5

Sch.4A para.8, added: SI 2012/2401 Sch.1 para.5

Sch.7 Part II para.37, repealed: 2012 c.9 Sch.10 Part 1

17. Employment Tribunals Act 1996

applied: SI 2012/2885 Sch.1 para.18, SI 2012/3144 Sch.1 para.12, SI 2012/3145 Sch.1, SSI 2012/319 Reg.32

s.4, amended: SI 2012/988 Art.2

s.4, enabling: SI 2012/988

s.7, enabling: SI 2012/468

s.9, amended: SI 2012/149 Art.2

s.9, enabling: SI 2012/149, SI 2012/468

s.13, enabling: SI 2012/468

s.21, see *Francis v Pertemps Recruitment Partnership Ltd* 2012 S.C. 39 (IH (2 Div)), The Lord Justice Clerk (Gill)

s.25, amended: SI 2012/2404 Sch.2 para.35

s.28, see *Francis v Pertemps Recruitment Partnership Ltd* 2012 S.C. 39 (IH (2 Div)), The Lord Justice Clerk (Gill)

s.30, see *Francis v Pertemps Recruitment Partnership Ltd* 2012 S.C. 39 (IH (2 Div)), The Lord Justice Clerk (Gill)

s.33, applied: SI 2012/3098 Reg.42

s.37, see *Francis v Pertemps Recruitment Partnership Ltd* 2012 S.C. 39 (IH (2 Div)), The Lord Justice Clerk (Gill)

s.41, applied: SI 2012/988

s.41, enabling: SI 2012/468

18. Employment Rights Act 1996

see *Edwards v Chesterfield Royal Hospital NHS Foundation Trust* [2012] 2 A.C. 22 (SC), Lord Phillips (President); see *R. (on the application of United Road Transport Union) v Secretary of State for Transport* [2012] EWHC 1909 (Admin), [2012] 3 C.M.L.R. 40 (QBD (Admin)), Hickinbottom, J.

applied: 2012 c.10 Sch.4 para.2, 2012 c.12 s.2, 2012 c.19 Sch.12 para.2, SI 2012/1128 Art.4

Part XI, applied: 2012 c.10 Sch.4 para.2, 2012 c.19 Sch.12 para.2

Pt IVA. see *Commissioner of Police of the Metropolis v Shaw* [2012] I.C.R. 464 (EAT), Underhill, J. (President)

s.1, applied: SI 2012/844 Reg.2

s.7A, applied: SI 2012/844 Reg.2

1996–cont.

18. Employment Rights Act 1996–*cont.*

s.28, applied: SI 2012/2886 Sch.1, SI 2012/3145 Sch.1

s.28, referred to: SSI 2012/303 Sch.3 para.1

s.31, amended: SI 2012/3007 Sch.1

s.34, applied: SI 2012/2886 Sch.1, SI 2012/3145 Sch.1

s.34, referred to: SSI 2012/303 Sch.3 para.1

s.41, applied: 2012 c.12 s.3

s.41, varied: 2012 c.12 s.2

s.42, disapplied: 2012 c.12 s.3

s.42, varied: 2012 c.12 s.2

s.43A, applied: SI 2012/1909 Sch.4 para.28

s.43B, see *Learning Trust v Marshall* [2012] Eq. L.R. 927 (EAT), Judge David Richardson

s.43E, varied: 2012 c.11 s.12

s.43F, enabling: SI 2012/462

s.43K, amended: 2012 c.7 Sch.5 para.73

s.45A, see *Arriva London South Ltd v Nicolaou* [2012] I.C.R. 510 (EAT), Judge Peter Clark

s.47B, see *Fecitt v NHS Manchester* [2011] EWCA Civ 1190, [2012] I.C.R. 372 (CA (Civ Div)), Mummery, L.J.

s.50, amended: 2012 c.7 Sch.5 para.74, Sch.14 para.69, Sch.17 para.6, Sch.19 para.6

s.50, applied: SI 2012/335 Sch.2 para.20, SI 2012/2991 Sch.2 para.28

s.55, applied: SI 2012/335 Sch.2 para.20, SI 2012/2991 Sch.2 para.28

s.64, applied: SI 2012/2886 Sch.1, SI 2012/3145 Sch.1

s.64, referred to: SSI 2012/303 Sch.3 para.1

s.68, applied: SI 2012/2886 Sch.1, SI 2012/3145 Sch.1

s.68, referred to: SSI 2012/303 Sch.3 para.1

s.70, applied: SI 2012/2886 Sch.1, SI 2012/3145 Sch.1

s.70, referred to: SSI 2012/303 Sch.3 para.1

s.71, applied: SI 2012/762 Reg.3

s.73, applied: SI 2012/762 Reg.3

s.75A, applied: SI 2012/762 Reg.3

s.75B, applied: SI 2012/762 Reg.3

s.76, applied: SI 2012/762 Reg.3

s.80A, applied: SI 2012/762 Reg.3

s.80AA, applied: SI 2012/762 Reg.3

s.80B, applied: SI 2012/762 Reg.3

s.80BB, applied: SI 2012/762 Reg.3

s.92, amended: SI 2012/989 Art.2

s.94, see *Ravat v Halliburton Manufacturing & Services Ltd* [2012] UKSC 1, [2012] 2 All E.R. 905 (SC), Lord Hope, J.S.C.; see *Simpson v Intralinks Ltd* [2012] I.L.Pr. 34 (EAT), Langstaff, J. (President)

s.97, see *Hawes & Curtis Ltd v Arfan* [2012] I.C.R. 1244 (EAT), Judge David Richardson

s.98, see *Capita Hartshead Ltd v Byard* [2012] I.C.R. 1256 (EAT), Silber, J.; see *Dziedziak v Future Electronics Ltd* [2012] Eq. L.R. 543 (EAT), Langstaff, J. (President); see *Jobcentre Plus v Graham* [2012] EWCA Civ 903, [2012] I.R.L.R. 759 (CA (Civ Div)), Pill, L.J.; see *Leach v Office of Communications* [2012] EWCA Civ 959, [2012] I.C.R. 1269 (CA (Civ Div)), Mummery, L.J.; see *Meter U Ltd v Ackroyd* [2012] I.C.R. 834 (EAT), Slade, J.; see *SW Global Resourcing Ltd v Docherty* [2012] I.R.L.R. 727 (EAT (SC)), Lady Smith

s.108, amended: SI 2012/989 Art.3

s.112, see *King v Royal Bank of Canada (Europe) Ltd* [2012] I.R.L.R. 280 (EAT), Judge David Richardson

1996–cont.

18. Employment Rights Act 1996–*cont.*

s.112, applied: SI 2012/2886 Sch.1, SI 2012/3145 Sch.1

s.117, applied: SI 2012/2886 Sch.1

s.120, amended: SI 2012/3007 Sch.1

s.124, amended: SI 2012/3007 Sch.1

s.139, see *Packman (t/a Packman Lucas Associates) v Fauchon* [2012] I.C.R. 1362 (EAT), Langstaff, J.

s.164, see *Foster v Bon Groundwork Ltd* [2012] EWCA Civ 252, [2012] I.C.R. 1027 (CA (Civ Div)), Pill, L.J.

s.166, amended: SI 2012/3014 Art.3

s.183, amended: SI 2012/3014 Art.4

s.186, amended: SI 2012/3007 Sch.1

s.209, enabling: SI 2012/989, SI 2012/2733

s.218, amended: 2012 c.7 Sch.5 para.75, Sch.14 para.70, Sch.17 para.6, Sch.19 para.6

s.218, repealed (in part): 2012 c.7 Sch.5 para.75, Sch.7 para.9

s.227, amended: SI 2012/3007 Sch.1

s.230, see *Bates van Winkelhof v Clyde & Co LLP* [2012] EWCA Civ 1207, [2012] I.R.L.R. 992 (CA (Civ Div)), Lloyd, L.J.; see *Bates van Winkelhof v Clyde & Co LLP* [2012] I.R.L.R. 548 (EAT), Judge Peter Clark; see *Hospital Medical Group Ltd v Westwood* [2012] EWCA Civ 1005, [2012] I.R.L.R. 834 (CA (Civ Div)), Maurice Kay, L.J.; see *Moore v President of the Methodist Conference* [2011] EWCA Civ 1581, [2012] Q.B.735 (CA (Civ Div)), Maurice Kay, L.J.

s.236, applied: SI 2012/989

s.236, enabling: SI 2012/989, SI 2012/2733

19. Law Reform (Year and a Day Rule) Act 1996

s.2, amended: 2012 c.4 Sch.1 para.3

23. Arbitration Act 1996

see *Kaye v Nu Skin UK Ltd* [2012] EWHC 958 (QB), [2012] C.T.L.C. 69 (QBD), Judge Denyer Q.C.; see *Parbulk II A/S v Heritage Maritime Ltd SA* [2011] EWHC 2917 (Comm), [2012] 2 All E.R. (Comm) 418 (QBD (Comm)), Eder, J.

s.1, see *AES Ust-Kamenogorsk Hydropower Plant LLP v Ust-Kamenogorsk Hydropower Plant JSC* [2011] EWCA Civ 647, [2012] 1 W.L.R. 920 (CA (Civ Div)), Rix, L.J.; see *Bitumex (HK) Co Ltd v IRPC Public Co Ltd* [2012] EWHC 1065 (Comm), [2012] 2 All E.R. (Comm) 1131 (QBD (Comm)), Judge Mackie, Q.C.

s.9, see *Deutsche Bank AG v Tongkah Harbour Public Co Ltd* [2011] EWHC 2251 (QB), [2012] 1 All E.R. (Comm) 194 (QBD (Comm)), Blair, J.; see *Excalibur Ventures LLC v Texas Keystone Inc* [2011] EWHC 1624 (Comm), [2012] 1 All E.R. (Comm) 933 (QBD (Comm)), Gloster, J.; see *Fulham Football Club (1987) Ltd v Richards* [2011] EWCA Civ 855, [2012] Ch. 333 (CA (Civ Div)), Rix, L.J.; see *Lombard North Central Plc v GATX Corp* [2012] EWHC 1067 (Comm), [2012] 2 All E.R. (Comm) 1119 (QBD (Comm)), Andrew Smith, J.; see *Merit Process Engineering Ltd v Balfour Beatty Engineering Services (HY) Ltd* [2012] EWHC 1376 (TCC), [2012] B.L.R. 364 (QBD (TCC)), Edwards-Stuart, J.; see *Nomihold Securities Inc v Mobile Telesystems Finance SA* [2012] EWHC 130 (Comm), [2012] Bus. L.R. 1289 (QBD (Comm)), Andrew Smith, J.

s.14, see *Finmoon Ltd v Baltic Reefers Management Ltd* [2012] EWHC 920 (Comm), [2012] 2 Lloyd's Rep. 388 (QBD (Comm)), Eder, J.

1996–cont.

23. **Arbitration Act 1996**–cont.

s.15, see *Itochu Corp v Johann MK Blumenthal GmbH & Co KG* [2012] EWCA Civ 996, [2012] 2 Lloyd's Rep. 437 (CA (Civ Div)), Maurice Kay, L.J.

s.18, see *Enercon GmbH v Enercon (India) Ltd* [2012] EWHC 689 (Comm), [2012] 1 Lloyd's Rep. 519 (QBD (Comm)), Eder, J.; see *Itochu Corp v Johann MK Blumenthal GmbH & Co KG* [2012] EWCA Civ 996, [2012] 2 Lloyd's Rep. 437 (CA (Civ Div)), Maurice Kay, L.J.

s.30, see *AES Ust-Kamenogorsk Hydropower Plant LLP v Ust-Kamenogorsk Hydropower Plant JSC* [2011] EWCA Civ 647, [2012] 1 W.L.R. 920 (CA (Civ Div)), Rix, L.J.

s.32, see *Five Oceans Salvage Ltd v Wenzhou Timber Group Co* [2011] EWHC 3282 (Comm), [2012] 1 Lloyd's Rep. 289 (QBD (Comm)), Field, J.

s.33, see *ED&F Man Sugar Ltd v Belmont Shipping Ltd* [2011] EWHC 2992 (Comm), [2012] 1 All E.R. (Comm) 962 (QBD (Comm)), Teare, J.; see *Five Oceans Salvage Ltd v Wenzhou Timber Group Co* [2011] EWHC 3282 (Comm), [2012] 1 Lloyd's Rep. 289 (QBD (Comm)), Field, J.

s.44, see *AES Ust-Kamenogorsk Hydropower Plant LLP v Ust-Kamenogorsk Hydropower Plant JSC* [2011] EWCA Civ 647, [2012] 1 W.L.R. 920 (CA (Civ Div)), Rix, L.J.; see *BNP Paribas SA v Open Joint Stock Company Russian Machines* [2011] EWHC 308 (Comm), [2012] 1 Lloyd's Rep. 61 (QBD (Comm)), Blair, J.; see *Western Bulk Shipowning III A/S v Carbofer Maritime Trading ApS (The Western Moscow)* [2012] EWHC 1224 (Comm), [2012] 2 All E.R. (Comm) 1140 (QBD (Comm)), Christopher Clarke, J.

s.47, see *Rotenberg v Sucafina SA* [2012] EWCA Civ 637, [2012] 2 All E.R. (Comm) 952 (CA (Civ Div)), Sir John Thomas (President)

s.57, see *Navios International Inc v Sangamon Transportation Group* [2012] EWHC 166 (Comm), [2012] 1 Lloyd's Rep. 493 (QBD (Comm)), Hamblen, J.

s.58, see *Rotenberg v Sucafina SA* [2012] EWCA Civ 637, [2012] 2 All E.R. (Comm) 952 (CA (Civ Div)), Sir John Thomas (President)

s.66, see *MobileTelesystems Finance SA v Nomihold Securities Inc* [2011] EWCA Civ 1040, [2012] Bus. L.R. 1166 (CA (Civ Div)), Ward, L.J.; see *Sovarex SA v Romero Alvarez SA* [2011] EWHC 1661 (Comm), [2012] 1 All E.R. (Comm) 207 (QBD (Comm)), Hamblen, J.; see *West Tankers Inc v Allianz SpA (The Front Comor)* [2012] EWCA Civ 27, [2012] Bus. L.R. 1701 (CA (Civ Div)), Carnwath, L.J.

s.67, see *Abuja International Hotels Ltd v Meridien SAS* [2012] EWHC 87 (Comm), [2012] 1 Lloyd's Rep. 461 (QBD (Comm)), Hamblen, J.

s.68, see *Abuja International Hotels Ltd v Meridien SAS* [2012] EWHC 87 (Comm), [2012] 1 Lloyd's Rep. 461 (QBD (Comm)), Hamblen, J.; see *ED&F Man Sugar Ltd v Belmont Shipping Ltd* [2011] EWHC 2992 (Comm), [2012] 1 All E.R. (Comm) 962 (QBD (Comm)), Teare, J.; see *Five Oceans Salvage Ltd v Wenzhou Timber Group Co* [2011] EWHC 3282 (Comm), [2012] 1 Lloyd's Rep. 289 (QBD (Comm)), Field, J.; see *Latvian Shipping Co v Russian People's Insurance Co (ROSNO) Open Ended Joint Stock Co* [2012] EWHC 1412 (Comm), [2012] 2

1996–cont.

23. **Arbitration Act 1996**–cont.

s.68–cont.

Lloyd's Rep. 181 (QBD (Comm)), Field, J.; see *Nestor Maritime SA v Sea Anchor Shipping Co Ltd* [2012] EWHC 996 (Comm), [2012] 2 Lloyd's Rep. 144 (QBD (Comm)), Eder, J.; see *Soeximex SAS v Agrocorp International Pte Ltd* [2011] EWHC 2743 (Comm), [2012] 1 Lloyd's Rep. 52 (QBD (Comm)), Gloster, J.

s.69, see *Eitzen Bulk A/S v TTMI Sarl* [2012] EWHC 202 (Comm), [2012] 2 All E.R. 100 (QBD (Comm)), Eder, J.; see *HMV UK Ltd v Propinvest Friar Ltd Partnership* [2011] EWCA Civ 1708, [2012] 1 Lloyd's Rep. 416 (CA (Civ Div)), Arden, L.J.; see *House of Fraser Ltd v Scottish Widows Plc* [2011] EWHC 2800 (Ch), [2012] 1 E.G.L.R. 9 (Ch D), Peter Smith, J.; see *Latvian Shipping Co v Russian People's Insurance Co (ROSNO) Open Ended Joint Stock Co* [2012] EWHC 1412 (Comm), [2012] 2 Lloyd's Rep. 181 (QBD (Comm)), Field, J.; see *Navios International Inc v Sangamon Transportation Group* [2012] EWHC 166 (Comm), [2012] 1 Lloyd's Rep. 493 (QBD (Comm)), Hamblen, J.; see *Soeximex SAS v Agrocorp International Pte Ltd* [2011] EWHC 2743 (Comm), [2012] 1 Lloyd's Rep. 52 (QBD (Comm)), Gloster, J.

s.70, see *Eitzen Bulk A/S v TTMI Sarl* [2012] EWHC 202 (Comm), [2012] 2 All E.R. 100 (QBD (Comm)), Eder, J.; see *Navios International Inc v Sangamon Transportation Group* [2012] EWHC 166 (Comm), [2012] 1 Lloyd's Rep. 493 (QBD (Comm)), Hamblen, J.

s.73, see *Nestor Maritime SA v Sea Anchor Shipping Co Ltd* [2012] EWHC 996 (Comm), [2012] 2 Lloyd's Rep. 144 (QBD (Comm)), Eder, J.

s.80, see *Nestor Maritime SA v Sea Anchor Shipping Co Ltd* [2012] EWHC 996 (Comm), [2012] 2 Lloyd's Rep. 144 (QBD (Comm)), Eder, J.

s.101, see *Dowans Holding SA v Tanzania Electric Supply Co Ltd* [2011] EWHC 1957 (Comm), [2012] 1 All E.R. (Comm) 820 (QBD (Comm)), Burton, J.

s.103, see *Dowans Holding SA v Tanzania Electric Supply Co Ltd* [2011] EWHC 1957 (Comm), [2012] 1 All E.R. (Comm) 820 (QBD (Comm)), Burton, J.

25. **Criminal Procedure and Investigations Act 1996**

see *R. v Newell (Alan)* [2012] EWCA Crim 650, [2012] 1 W.L.R. 3142 (CA (Crim Div)), Sir John Thomas (President)

applied: SI 2012/ 1726 r.22.1, r.22.5, r.22.9, r.29.19

referred to: SI 2012/ 1726 r.2.3

Part I, applied: SI 2012/ 1726 r.22.1, r.22.9, r.3.11

Part II, applied: SI 2012/ 1726 r.22.1, r.22.9

Part III, applied: SI 2012/ 1726 r.3.11

Part IV, applied: SI 2012/ 1726 r.3.11

s.1, applied: SI 2012/ 1726 r.22.9

s.2, applied: SI 2012/ 1726 r.22.9

s.3, applied: SI 2012/ 1726 r.22.2, r.36.2, r.22.3, r.22.9

s.4, applied: SI 2012/ 1726 r.22.9

s.5, applied: SI 2012/ 1726 r.22.4, r.22.9

s.6, applied: SI 2012/ 1726 r.22.4, r.22.9

s.6A, applied: SI 2012/ 1726 r.22.9

s.6B, applied: SI 2012/ 1726 r.22.9

s.6C, applied: SI 2012/ 1726 r.22.4, r.22.9

s.6D, applied: SI 2012/ 1726 r.22.9

1996– cont.

25. Criminal Procedure and Investigations Act 1996– *cont.*
s.6E, see *R. v Sanghera (Sukwinder Singh)* [2012] EWCA Crim 16, [2012] 2 Cr. App. R. 17 (CA (Crim Div)), Aikens, L.J.
s.6E, applied: SI 2012/ 1726 r.22.9
s.7, applied: SI 2012/ 1726 r.22.3, r.22.9
s.7A, applied: SI 2012/ 1726 r.22.3, r.22.9
s.8, applied: SI 2012/ 1726 r.22.5, r.22.9
s.9, applied: SI 2012/ 1726 r.22.9
s.10, applied: SI 2012/ 1726 r.22.9
s.11, applied: SI 2012/ 1726 r.22.9, r.3.5
s.12, applied: SI 2012/ 1726 r.22.9
s.13, applied: SI 2012/ 1726 r.22.9
s.14, applied: SI 2012/ 1726 r.22.6, r.22.9
s.14A, applied: SI 2012/ 1726 r.22.9
s.15, applied: SI 2012/ 1726 r.22.6, r.22.9
s.16, applied: SI 2012/ 1726 r.22.3, r.22.6, r.22.9
s.17, applied: SI 2012/ 1726 r.22.7, r.22.8, r.22.9, r.62.9, r.62.16
s.17, referred to: SI 2012/ 1726 r.62.9
s.18, applied: SI 2012/ 1726 r.22.8, r.22.9, r.62.9, r.62.16, r.5.8
s.19, applied: SI 2012/ 1726 r.22.3, r.22.6, r.22.7, r.22.8, r.22.9, r.62.16
s.19, enabling: SI 2012/ 1726
s.20, applied: SI 2012/ 1726 r.22.9, r.33.4, r.3.5
s.20, enabling: SI 2012/ 1726
s.21, applied: SI 2012/ 1726 r.22.9
s.21A, applied: SI 2012/ 1726 r.22.9
s.22, applied: SI 2012/ 1726 r.22.9
s.23, applied: SI 2012/ 1726 r.22.9
s.24, applied: SI 2012/ 1726 r.22.9
s.25, applied: SI 2012/ 1726 r.22.9
s.26, applied: SI 2012/ 1726 r.22.9
s.27, applied: SI 2012/ 1726 r.22.9
s.29, applied: SI 2012/ 1726 r.15.1
s.30, referred to: SI 2012/ 1726 r.15.6
s.31, applied: SI 2012/ 1726 r.35.3, r.34.3, r.33.6, r.35.4, r.36.2
s.31, referred to: SI 2012/ 1726 r.15.1
s.34, applied: SI 2012/ 1726 r.15.1
s.35, amended: 2012 c.9 Sch.10 Part 10
s.35, applied: SI 2012/ 1726 r.74.1, r.66.1, r.66.4
s.37, amended: 2012 c.10 Sch.5 para.42
s.37, applied: SI 2012/ 1726 r.16.1
s.40, see *R. v St Regis Paper Co Ltd* [2011] EWCA Crim 2527, [2012] P.T.S.R. 871 (CA (Crim Div)), Moses, L.J.
s.40, applied: SI 2012/ 1726 r.35.3, r.34.3, r.33.6, r.35.4, r.36.2
s.41, applied: SI 2012/ 1726 r.16.1
s.54, applied: SI 2012/ 1726 r.40.1, r.40.4, r.40.5, r.40.6, r.40.7, r.40.8
s.54, referred to: SI 2012/ 1726 r.40.1, r.40.2, r.40.3, r.40.6
s.58, applied: SI 2012/ 1726 r.16.1, r.69.1
Sch.2, applied: SI 2012/ 1726 r.10.4, r.3.11
Sch.2 para.4, enabling: SI 2012/ 1726
Sch.4 para.2, enabling: SI 2012/ 1726

27. Family Law Act 1996
see *Abdullah v Westminster City Council* [2011] EWCA Civ 1171, [2012] H.L.R. 5 (CA (Civ Div)), Mummery, L.J.
applied: SI 2012/ 1969 Sch.4
Part IV, referred to: 2012 c.10 s.10, Sch.1 para.19, Sch.1 para.41
Part IVA, applied: 2012 c.10 Sch.1 para.16
s.8, amended: 2012 c.10 Sch.5 para.44

1996– cont.

27. Family Law Act 1996– *cont.*
s.23, amended: 2012 c.10 Sch.5 para.45
s.23, repealed (in part): 2012 c.10 Sch.5 para.45
s.30, see *Abdullah v Westminster City Council* [2011] EWCA Civ 1171, [2012] H.L.R. 5 (CA (Civ Div)), Mummery, L.J.
s.33, see *Dolan v Corby* [2011] EWCA Civ 1664, [2012] 2 F.L.R. 1031 (CA (Civ Div)), Thorpe, L.J.; see *L (Children), Re* [2012] EWCA Civ 721, [2012] 2 F.L.R. 1417 (CA (Civ Div)), Thorpe, L.J.; see *Ruiz (A Bankrupt), Re* [2011] EWCA Civ 1646, [2012] B.P.I.R. 446 (CA (Civ Div)), Thorpe, L.J.
s.46, applied: SI 2012/ 3098 Reg.33
s.56, applied: SI 2012/ 1969 Sch.3 Part 3
s.63E, applied: SI 2012/ 3098 Reg.33
s.63R, see *A Local Authority v DL* [2012] EWCA Civ 253, [2012] 3 W.L.R. 1439 (CA (Civ Div)), Maurice Kay, L.J.

31. Defamation Act 1996
s.4, see *Thornton v Telegraph Media Group Ltd* [2011] EWHC 1884 (QB), [2012] E.M.L.R. 8 (QBD), Tugendhat, J.
Sch.1 Part II para.11, varied: 2012 c.11 s.12

33. Prisoners Earnings Act 1996
s.4, amended: 2012 c.10 s.129
s.4, repealed (in part): 2012 c.10 s.129
s.5, amended: 2012 c.10 s.129

40. Party Wall etc Act 1996
see *Freetown Ltd v Assethold Ltd* [2012] EWHC 1351 (QB), [2012] 4 All E.R. 194 (QBD), Slade, J.
s.10, see *Freetown Ltd v Assethold Ltd* [2012] EWHC 1351 (QB), [2012] 4 All E.R. 194 (QBD), Slade, J.
s.15, see *Freetown Ltd v Assethold Ltd* [2012] EWHC 1351 (QB), [2012] 4 All E.R. 194 (QBD), Slade, J.

46. Armed Forces Act 1996
s.13, repealed (in part): 2012 c.10 Sch.25 Part 2
Sch.4, repealed (in part): 2012 c.10 Sch.25 Part 2

47. Trusts of Land and Appointment of Trustees Act 1996
see *Designated Officer for Sunderland Magistrates' Court v Krager* [2011] EWHC 3283 (Ch), [2012] 1 W.L.R. 1291 (Ch D (Newcastle)), Briggs, J.; see *G v A (Financial Remedy: Enforcement) (No.1)* [2011] EWHC 2380 (Fam), [2012] 1 F.L.R. 389 (Fam Div), Michael Horowitz Q.C.
applied: 2012 c.10 Sch.1 para.33
s.6, see *Alexander v Alexander* [2011] EWHC 2721 (Ch), [2012] W.T.L.R. 187 (Ch D), Morgan, J.
s.14, see *Jones v Kernott* [2012] 1 A.C. 776 (SC), Lord Walker, J.S.C.
s.14, applied: SI 2012/ 2684 Reg.2

48. Damages Act 1996
s.1, see *Tortolano v Ogilvie Construction Ltd* [2012] CSOH 162, 2012 S.L.T. 1233 (OH), Lord Brodie
s.2, see *Bennett v Stephens* [2012] EWHC 58 (QB), [2012] R.T.R. 27 (QBD), Tugendhat, J.

49. Asylum and Immigration Act 1996
s.13, enabling: SI 2012/ 2593

52. Housing Act 1996
Part I c.I, applied: SI 2012/ 3018 Sch.2 para.1
Part VI, applied: 2012 c.10 Sch.1 para.34, SI 2012/ 1869 Reg.3, SI 2012/ 2588 Reg.3
Part VII, applied: 2012 c.10 Sch.1 para.34, SI 2012/ 1483 Reg.6, SI 2012/ 2588 Reg.3, SI 2012/ 2599 Art.3
Pt VI, see *Bah v United Kingdom (56328/07)* (2012) 54 E.H.R.R. 21 (ECHR), Judge Garlicki (President)

1996–cont.

52. Housing Act 1996–cont.

Pt VII. see *Bah v United Kingdom (56328/07)* (2012) 54 E.H.R.R. 21 (ECHR), Judge Garlicki (President); see *Barnsley MBC v Norton* [2011] EWCA Civ 834, [2012] P.T.S.R. 56 (CA (Civ Div)), Maurice Kay, L.J.; see *Bull v Oxford City Council* [2011] EWCA Civ 609, [2012] 1 W.L.R. 203 (CA (Civ Div)), Pill, L.J.; see *Holmes v Westminster City Council* [2011] EWHC 2857 (QB), [2012] B.L.G.R. 233 (QBD), Eady, J.; see *Konodyba v Kensington and Chelsea RLBC* [2012] EWCA Civ 982, [2012] H.L.R. 45 (CA (Civ Div)), Lord Neuberger (M.R.); see *Maswaku v Westminster City Council* [2012] EWCA Civ 669, [2012] P.T.S.R. 1650 (CA (Civ Div)), Mummery, L.J.

s.2, see *Helena Housing Ltd v Revenue and Customs Commissioners* [2012] EWCA Civ 569, [2012] P.T.S.R. 1409 (CA (Civ Div)), Lloyd, L.J.

s.81, see *Church Commissioners for England v Koyale Enterprises* [2012] L. & T.R. 24 (CC (Central London)), Judge Dight; see *Freeholders of 69 Marina, St Leonards-on-Sea v Oram* [2011] EWCA Civ 1258, [2012] H.L.R. 12 (CA (Civ Div)), Sir Andrew Morritt (Chancellor)

s.122, amended: 2012 c.5 Sch.2 para.36, Sch.4 para.13, Sch.14 Part 1

s.122, repealed (in part): 2012 c.5 Sch.14 Part 1

s.122, enabling: SI 2012/646

s.124, see *Corby BC v Scott* [2012] EWCA Civ 276, [2012] H.L.R. 23 (CA (Civ Div)), Lord Neuberger (M.R.)

s.128, see *Camden LBC v Stafford* [2012] EWCA Civ 839, [2012] 4 All E.R. 180 (CA (Civ Div)), Maurice Kay, L.J.

s.129, see *Camden LBC v Stafford* [2012] EWCA Civ 839, [2012] 4 All E.R. 180 (CA (Civ Div)), Maurice Kay, L.J.

s.130, see *Corby BC v Scott* [2012] EWCA Civ 276, [2012] H.L.R. 23 (CA (Civ Div)), Lord Neuberger (M.R.)

s.153A, applied: 2012 c.10 Sch.1 para.36

s.160ZA, applied: SI 2012/1869 Reg.3

s.160ZA, enabling: SI 2012/1869, SI 2012/2588

s.166A, amended: SI 2012/2989 Reg.2

s.166A, enabling: SI 2012/2989

s.172, applied: SI 2012/2989

s.172, enabling: SI 2012/2588

s.175, see *Bull v Oxford City Council* [2011] EWCA Civ 609, [2012] 1 W.L.R. 203 (CA (Civ Div)), Pill, L.J.

s.176, see *Bull v Oxford City Council* [2011] EWCA Civ 609, [2012] 1 W.L.R. 203 (CA (Civ Div)), Pill, L.J.

s.184, see *Abdullah v Westminster City Council* [2011] EWCA Civ 1171, [2012] H.L.R. 5 (CA (Civ Div)), Mummery, L.J.; see *Bull v Oxford City Council* [2011] EWCA Civ 609, [2012] 1 W.L.R. 203 (CA (Civ Div)), Pill, L.J.; see *Mitu v Camden LBC* [2011] EWCA Civ 1249, [2012] H.L.R. 10 (CA (Civ Div)), Rix, L.J.

s.185, see *Bah v United Kingdom (56328/07)* (2012) 54 E.H.R.R. 21 (ECHR), Judge Garlicki (President); see *Konodyba v Kensington and Chelsea RLBC* [2012] EWCA Civ 982, [2012] H.L.R. 45 (CA (Civ Div)), Lord Neuberger (M.R.)

s.185, enabling: SI 2012/2588

1996–cont.

52. Housing Act 1996–cont.

s.188, see *Bull v Oxford City Council* [2011] EWCA Civ 609, [2012] 1 W.L.R. 203 (CA (Civ Div)), Pill, L.J.; see *R. (on the application of TG) v Lambeth LBC* [2011] EWCA Civ 526, [2012] P.T.S.R. 364 (CA (Civ Div)), Lord Neuberger (M.R.)

s.189, see *Bull v Oxford City Council* [2011] EWCA Civ 609, [2012] 1 W.L.R. 203 (CA (Civ Div)), Pill, L.J.; see *El Goure v Kensington and Chelsea RLBC* [2012] EWCA Civ 670, [2012] P.T.S.R. 1664 (CA (Civ Div)), Mummery, L.J.

s.191, see *Bull v Oxford City Council* [2011] EWCA Civ 609, [2012] 1 W.L.R. 203 (CA (Civ Div)), Pill, L.J.

s.193, see *Bubb v Wandsworth LBC* [2011] EWCA Civ 1285, [2012] P.T.S.R. 1011 (CA (Civ Div)), Lord Neuberger (M.R.); see *Bull v Oxford City Council* [2011] EWCA Civ 609, [2012] 1 W.L.R. 203 (CA (Civ Div)), Pill, L.J.; see *Camden LBC v Stafford* [2012] EWCA Civ 839, [2012] 4 All E.R. 180 (CA (Civ Div)), Maurice Kay, L.J.; see *Holmes v Westminster City Council* [2011] EWHC 2857 (QB), [2012] B.L.G.R. 233 (QBD), Eady, J.; see *Maswaku v Westminster City Council* [2012] EWCA Civ 669, [2012] P.T.S.R. 1650 (CA (Civ Div)), Mummery, L.J.; see *Sheridan v Basildon BC (formerly Basildon DC)* [2012] EWCA Civ 335, [2012] H.L.R. 29 (CA (Civ Div)), Sir Andrew Morritt (Chancellor)

s.193, applied: SI 2012/2601 Art.3

s.199, see *Bull v Oxford City Council* [2011] EWCA Civ 609, [2012] 1 W.L.R. 203 (CA (Civ Div)), Pill, L.J.

s.202, see *Sheridan v Basildon BC (formerly Basildon DC)* [2012] EWCA Civ 335, [2012] H.L.R. 29 (CA (Civ Div)), Sir Andrew Morritt (Chancellor)

s.203, see *Camden LBC v Stafford* [2012] EWCA Civ 839, [2012] 4 All E.R. 180 (CA (Civ Div)), Maurice Kay, L.J.; see *Mitu v Camden LBC* [2011] EWCA Civ 1249, [2012] H.L.R. 10 (CA (Civ Div)), Rix, L.J.

s.204, see *Bubb v Wandsworth LBC* [2011] EWCA Civ 1285, [2012] P.T.S.R. 1011 (CA (Civ Div)), Lord Neuberger (M.R.)

s.210, enabling: SI 2012/2601

s.215, enabling: SI 2012/2588, SI 2012/2601

Sch.1 Part II para.4, amended: SI 2012/2404 Sch.2 para.36

Sch.12 para.1, repealed: 2012 c.5 Sch.14 Part 1

Sch.12 para.2, repealed: 2012 c.5 Sch.14 Part 1

Sch.12 para.3, repealed: 2012 c.5 Sch.14 Part 1

Sch.12 para.4, repealed: 2012 c.5 Sch.14 Part 1

Sch.12 para.5, repealed: 2012 c.5 Sch.14 Part 1

Sch.13 para.3, repealed (in part): 2012 c.5 Sch.14 Part 1

53. Housing Grants, Construction and Regeneration Act 1996

see *Squibb Group Ltd v Vertase FLI Ltd* [2012] EWHC 1958 (TCC), [2012] B.L.R. 408 (QBD (TCC)), Coulson, J.

Part I, applied: 2012 c.10 Sch.1 para.7

s.3, amended: 2012 c.7 Sch.5 para.76

s.30, enabling: SI 2012/397

s.107, see *Sprunt Ltd v Camden LBC* [2011] EWHC 3191 (TCC), [2012] B.L.R. 83 (QBD (TCC)), Akenhead, J.

s.108, see *Sprunt Ltd v Camden LBC* [2011] EWHC 3191 (TCC), [2012] B.L.R. 83 (QBD (TCC)), Akenhead, J.

53. Housing Grants, Construction and Regeneration Act 1996– *cont.*
s.146, enabling: SI 2012/397

55. Broadcasting Act 1996
referred to: 2012 c.19 Sch.6 para.4
Part I, applied: SI 2012/1917 Art.34, Sch.7 para.8
Part I, referred to: SI 2012/292 Art.4
Part II, applied: SI 2012/1917 Art.34, Sch.7 para.8
s.1, varied: SI 2012/292 Sch.1 para.2
s.7, varied: SI 2012/292 Sch.1 para.3, Sch.1 para.4
s.8, varied: SI 2012/292 Sch.1 para.3, Sch.1 para.5
s.9, varied: SI 2012/292 Sch.1 para.3, Sch.1 para.6
s.12, varied: SI 2012/292 Sch.1 para.3, Sch.1 para.7
s.16, varied: SI 2012/292 Sch.1 para.8
s.18, varied: SI 2012/292 Sch.1 para.9
s.19, varied: SI 2012/292 Sch.1 para.10
s.19A, varied: SI 2012/292 Sch.1 para.11
s.19B, varied: SI 2012/292 Sch.1 para.11
s.39, varied: SI 2012/292 Sch.1 para.12

56. Education Act 1996
see *R. (on the application of O) v East Riding of Yorkshire CC* [2011] EWCA Civ 196, [2012] P.T.S.R. 328 (CA (Civ Div)), Rix, L.J.
applied: SI 2012/444 Sch.3, Sch.5
referred to: SI 2012/323 Sch.3 para.11, Sch.5 para.11, SI 2012/2031 Sch.3, Sch.5
Part I, applied: SI 2012/987 Sch.1 para.3
Part IV, applied: 2012 c.10 Sch.1 para.2, Sch.1 para.17, SI 2012/322 Reg.4, Reg.12
Part VI c.II, applied: SI 2012/335 Sch.1 para.11, SI 2012/2991 Sch.1 para.11
Pt IV. see *Essex CC v Williams* [2011] EWCA Civ 1315, [2012] P.T.S.R. 713 (CA (Civ Div)), Maurice Kay, L.J.; see *SC v Learning Trust (SEN)* [2012] UKUT 214 (AAC), [2012] E.L.R. 474 (UT (AAC)), Judge Rowland
s.2, see *Essex CC v Williams* [2011] EWCA Civ 1315, [2012] P.T.S.R. 713 (CA (Civ Div)), Maurice Kay, L.J.
s.4, applied: SI 2012/2421 Sch.3 para.14
s.5, see *Essex CC v Williams* [2011] EWCA Civ 1315, [2012] P.T.S.R. 713 (CA (Civ Div)), Maurice Kay, L.J.
s.5, enabling: SI 2012/1797
s.9, see *R. (on the application of Moyse) v Secretary of State for Education* [2012] EWHC 2758 (Admin), [2012] E.L.R. 551 (QBD (Admin)), Kenneth Parker, J
s.13, applied: SI 2012/2991 Sch.2 para.8
s.15A, applied: SI 2012/335 Sch.1 para.18
s.15B, applied: SI 2012/335 Sch.1 para.18
s.15ZA, applied: SI 2012/335 Sch.1 para.18, SI 2012/2991 Sch.1 para.18
s.15ZC, applied: SI 2012/335 Sch.1 para.18, SI 2012/2991 Sch.1 para.18
s.18, applied: SI 2012/335 Sch.2 para.17, SI 2012/2991 Sch.2 para.7
s.19, applied: SI 2012/335 Sch.2 para.9, SI 2012/2991 Sch.2 para.20
s.19, varied: SI 2012/1107 Art.6
s.19, enabling: SI 2012/1033
s.29, enabling: SI 2012/8, SI 2012/1554
s.32, enabling: SI 2012/1703
s.62, applied: SI 2012/987 Art.4
s.312, see *Essex CC v Williams* [2011] EWCA Civ 1315, [2012] P.T.S.R. 713 (CA (Civ Div)), Maurice Kay, L.J.
s.313, applied: SI 2012/335 Sch.2 para.6

56. Education Act 1996– *cont.*
s.317, see *NC v Leicestershire CC* [2012] UKUT 85 (AAC), [2012] E.L.R. 365 (UT (AAC)), Judge David Pearl
s.318, see *NC v Leicestershire CC* [2012] UKUT 85 (AAC), [2012] E.L.R. 365 (UT (AAC)), Judge David Pearl
s.320, applied: SI 2012/335 Sch.2 para.11, SI 2012/2991 Sch.2 para.21
s.321, applied: SI 2012/335 Sch.1 para.2, SI 2012/2991 Sch.1 para.2
s.321, referred to: SI 2012/322 Reg.23
s.322, amended: 2012 c.7 Sch.5 para.78
s.322, applied: SI 2012/335 Sch.1 para.2, SI 2012/2991 Sch.1 para.2
s.323, see *NC v Leicestershire CC* [2012] UKUT 85 (AAC), [2012] E.L.R. 365 (UT (AAC)), Judge David Pearl
s.323, applied: SI 2012/322 Reg.61, SI 2012/335 Sch.1 para.2, SI 2012/2991 Sch.1 para.2
s.324, see *Dudley BC v S* [2012] EWCA Civ 346, [2012] P.T.S.R. 1393 (CA (Civ Div)), Lord Neuberger (M.R.); see *NC v Leicestershire CC* [2012] UKUT 85 (AAC), [2012] E.L.R. 365 (UT (AAC)), Judge David Pearl; see *SC v Learning Trust (SEN)* [2012] UKUT 214 (AAC), [2012] E.L.R. 474 (UT (AAC)), Judge Rowland
s.324, applied: SI 2012/10 Sch.1 para.2, SI 2012/206 Sch.1 para.11, Sch.1 para.17, Sch.1 para.18, SI 2012/335 Sch.1 para.2, SI 2012/2991 Sch.1 para.2, SI 2012/2996 Sch.1 para.4, Sch.1 para.8
s.325, applied: SI 2012/322 Reg.61, Reg.62, SI 2012/335 Sch.1 para.2, SI 2012/2991 Sch.1 para.2
s.326, see *Dudley BC v S* [2012] EWCA Civ 346, [2012] P.T.S.R. 1393 (CA (Civ Div)), Lord Neuberger (M.R.); see *LB v Kent CC* [2012] E.L.R. 31 (UT (AAC)), Judge CG Ward
s.326, applied: SI 2012/322 Reg.13, Reg.21, SI 2012/335 Sch.1 para.2, SI 2012/2991 Sch.1 para.2
s.326A, applied: SI 2012/322 Reg.62, SI 2012/335 Sch.1 para.2, SI 2012/2991 Sch.1 para.2
s.326A, enabling: SI 2012/322
s.327, amended: SI 2012/976 Sch.1 para.5
s.327, applied: SI 2012/335 Sch.1 para.2, SI 2012/2991 Sch.1 para.2
s.328, applied: SI 2012/322 Reg.13, Reg.62, SI 2012/335 Sch.1 para.2, SI 2012/2991 Sch.1 para.2
s.328A, applied: SI 2012/335 Sch.1 para.2, SI 2012/2991 Sch.1 para.2
s.329, applied: SI 2012/322 Reg.62, SI 2012/335 Sch.1 para.2, SI 2012/2991 Sch.1 para.2
s.329A, applied: SI 2012/322 Reg.61, Reg.62, SI 2012/335 Sch.1 para.2, SI 2012/2991 Sch.1 para.2
s.330, applied: SI 2012/335 Sch.1 para.2, SI 2012/2991 Sch.1 para.2
s.331, applied: SI 2012/335 Sch.1 para.2, SI 2012/2991 Sch.1 para.2
s.332, amended: 2012 c.7 Sch.5 para.79
s.332A, applied: SI 2012/335 Sch.1 para.5, SI 2012/2991 Sch.1 para.5
s.332AA, applied: SI 2012/321 Reg.4
s.332BA, applied: SI 2012/321 Reg.4, SI 2012/322 Reg.12
s.332BB, applied: SI 2012/321 Reg.4
s.332ZA, applied: SI 2012/321 Reg.4
s.332ZB, applied: SI 2012/321 Reg.4
s.332ZC, applied: SI 2012/322 Reg.66, Reg.68
s.332ZC, enabling: SI 2012/322
s.333, applied: SI 2012/322 Reg.11
s.333, enabling: SI 2012/322

1996– cont.

56. Education Act 1996– *cont.*
s.334, enabling: SI 2012/322
s.336, applied: SI 2012/322 Reg.35, Reg.48
s.336, enabling: SI 2012/322, SI 2012/1418
s.336A, applied: SI 2012/322
s.336A, enabling: SI 2012/322
s.347, applied: SI 2012/322 Reg.61, Reg.62
s.348, applied: SI 2012/335 Sch.2 para.11, SI 2012/2991 Sch.2 para.21
s.390, applied: SI 2012/335 Sch.1 para.24, SI 2012/2991 Sch.1 para.24
s.444, applied: SI 2012/1046 Reg.3
s.444B, enabling: SI 2012/1046
s.451, disapplied: SI 2012/962 Reg.2
s.451, enabling: SI 2012/962
s.457, amended: 2012 c.5 Sch.2 para.38, Sch.14 Part 1
s.457, repealed (in part): 2012 c.5 Sch.14 Part 1
s.485, applied: SI 2012/1167 Sch.1 para.11
s.493, applied: SI 2012/335 Sch.2 para.12
s.494, applied: SI 2012/335 Sch.2 para.12
s.494, varied: SI 2012/1107 Art.6
s.494, enabling: SI 2012/1033
s.496, applied: SI 2012/8 Reg.32
s.497, applied: SI 2012/8 Reg.32
s.507A, applied: SI 2012/335 Sch.1 para.19, SI 2012/2991 Sch.1 para.19
s.507B, see *Hunt v North Somerset Council* [2012] EWHC 1928 (Admin), [2012] Eq. L.R. 951 (QBD (Admin)), Wyn Williams, J.
s.507B, applied: SI 2012/335 Sch.1 para.19, SI 2012/2991 Sch.1 para.19
s.508A, applied: SI 2012/335 Sch.1 para.10, SI 2012/2991 Sch.1 para.10
s.508B, applied: SI 2012/206 Sch.1 para.18
s.508E, applied: SI 2012/335 Sch.1 para.10, SI 2012/2991 Sch.1 para.10
s.508F, applied: SI 2012/206 Sch.1 para.18
s.509, applied: SI 2012/335 Sch.1 para.10, SI 2012/2991 Sch.1 para.10
s.509AA, applied: SI 2012/206 Sch.1 para.18
s.510, applied: SI 2012/335 Sch.1 para.10, SI 2012/2991 Sch.1 para.10
s.512, applied: SI 2012/335 Sch.2 para.14
s.512ZA, applied: SI 2012/335 Sch.2 para.14
s.512ZB, amended: 2012 c.5 Sch.2 para.39
s.512ZB, applied: SI 2012/335 Sch.2 para.14
s.512ZB, repealed (in part): 2012 c.5 Sch.14 Part 1
s.513, applied: SI 2012/335 Sch.2 para.14
s.514, applied: SI 2012/335 Sch.1 para.10, SI 2012/2991 Sch.1 para.10
s.518, applied: SI 2012/335 Sch.1 para.10, SI 2012/2886 Sch.1, SI 2012/2991 Sch.1 para.10, SSI 2012/303 Sch.4 para.15, Sch.5 para.55
s.519, amended: SI 2012/976 Sch.1 para.6
s.519, applied: SI 2012/335 Sch.5 para.14, SI 2012/2991 Sch.5 para.14
s.532A, applied: SI 2012/206 Art.2, Sch.1 para.3
s.532B, enabling: SI 2012/206
s.532C, enabling: SI 2012/206
s.537, enabling: SI 2012/1124
s.537A, amended: SI 2012/976 Sch.1 para.7
s.537A, enabling: SI 2012/1274, SI 2012/1919
s.537B, amended: SI 2012/1107 Art.6
s.542, enabling: SI 2012/1943
s.547, amended: SI 2012/976 Sch.1 para.8
s.547, applied: SI 2012/1034 Sch.4 para.14
s.550ZA, applied: SI 2012/619 Reg.2, SI 2012/951 Reg.3

56. Education Act 1996– *cont.*
s.550ZA, enabling: SI 2012/619, SI 2012/951
s.550ZC, applied: SI 2012/951 Reg.3, Reg.4
s.550ZC, enabling: SI 2012/951
s.551, enabling: SI 2012/248
s.554, referred to: SI 2012/1703
s.554, enabling: SI 2012/986, SI 2012/987, SI 2012/1703, SI 2012/2008
s.555, applied: SI 2012/987, SI 2012/1703, SI 2012/2008
s.555, referred to: SI 2012/986
s.556, enabling: SI 2012/986, SI 2012/987, SI 2012/1703, SI 2012/2008
s.568, applied: SI 2012/206
s.569, applied: SI 2012/951
s.569, enabling: SI 2012/248, SI 2012/322, SI 2012/619, SI 2012/1033, SI 2012/1046, SI 2012/1124, SI 2012/1201, SI 2012/1274, SI 2012/1418, SI 2012/1554, SI 2012/1797, SI 2012/1825, SI 2012/1829, SI 2012/1919, SI 2012/1943, SI 2012/3158
s.579, amended: 2012 c.5 Sch.14 Part 1, 2012 c.7 Sch.5 para.80
s.579, referred to: SI 2012/3232 Sch.1 Part 2
Sch.1 para.3, enabling: SI 2012/1201, SI 2012/1825, SI 2012/3158
Sch.1 para.3A, enabling: SI 2012/1825
Sch.1 para.6, enabling: SI 2012/3158
Sch.1 para.15, applied: 2012 c.9 s.28
Sch.1 para.15, enabling: SI 2012/1825, SI 2012/3158
Sch.27, applied: SI 2012/322 Reg.4
Sch.27 para.2, applied: SI 2012/322 Reg.61
Sch.27 para.2A, applied: SI 2012/322 Reg.61
Sch.27 para.2B, applied: SI 2012/322 Reg.61
Sch.27 para.3, see *Dudley BC v S* [2012] EWCA Civ 346, [2012] P.T.S.R. 1393 (CA (Civ Div)), Lord Neuberger (M.R.)
Sch.27 para.4, applied: SI 2012/322 Reg.61, Reg.62
Sch.27 para.6, applied: SI 2012/206 Sch.1 para.3
Sch.27 para.8, applied: SI 2012/322 Reg.13, Reg.21, Reg.62
Sch.27 para.9, see *Essex CC v Williams* [2011] EWCA Civ 1315, [2012] P.T.S.R. 713 (CA (Civ Div)), Maurice Kay, L.J.
Sch.27 para.11, see *Essex CC v Williams* [2011] EWCA Civ 1315, [2012] P.T.S.R. 713 (CA (Civ Div)), Maurice Kay, L.J.
Sch.27 para.11, applied: SI 2012/322 Reg.13, Reg.21
Sch.31, applied: SI 2012/335 Sch.1 para.24, SI 2012/2991 Sch.1 para.24
Sch.36, applied: SI 2012/1703 Art.4
Sch.36, referred to: SI 2012/2008 Art.5

61. Channel Tunnel Rail Link Act 1996
Sch.7 para.5, amended: SI 2012/2590 Sch.1 para.2
Sch.15 Part VI para.1, amended: SI 2012/1659 Sch.3 para.14
Sch.15 Part VI para.2, amended: SI 2012/1659 Sch.3 para.14
Sch.15 Part VI para.3, amended: SI 2012/1659 Sch.3 para.14
Sch.15 Part VI para.4, amended: SI 2012/1659 Sch.3 para.14
Sch.15 Part VI para.5, amended: SI 2012/1659 Sch.3 para.14
Sch.15 Part VI para.6, amended: SI 2012/1659 Sch.3 para.14
Sch.15 Part VI para.7, amended: SI 2012/1659 Sch.3 para.14
Sch.15 Part VI para.8, amended: SI 2012/1659 Sch.3 para.14

1996–cont.

61. Channel Tunnel Rail Link Act 1996–*cont.*
Sch.15 Part VI para.9, amended: SI 2012/1659 Sch.3 para.14
Sch.15 Part VI para.10, amended: SI 2012/1659 Sch.3 para.14
Sch.15 Part VI para.11, amended: SI 2012/1659 Sch.3 para.14

1997

8. Town and Country Planning (Scotland) Act 1997
applied: SSI 2012/360 Reg.18
Pt II. see *Uprichard v Scottish Ministers* 2012 S.C. 172 (IH (2 Div)), The Lord Justice Clerk (Gill)
s.26AA, applied: SSI 2012/260 Reg.2
s.26AA, enabling: SSI 2012/260
s.30, enabling: SSI 2012/131, SSI 2012/165, SSI 2012/285, SSI 2012/325
s.31, enabling: SSI 2012/131, SSI 2012/285
s.31A, enabling: SSI 2012/259
s.32, enabling: SSI 2012/325
s.43, enabling: SSI 2012/165, SSI 2012/325
s.43A, enabling: SSI 2012/325
s.150, applied: SSI 2012/360 Reg.18
s.238, see *Uprichard v Scottish Ministers* 2012 S.C. 172 (IH (2 Div)), The Lord Justice Clerk (Gill)
s.239, see *Bancon Developments Ltd v Scottish Ministers* [2012] J.P.L. 287 (OH), Lord Bannatyne
s.275, enabling: SSI 2012/131, SSI 2012/165, SSI 2012/285, SSI 2012/325
Sch.1 para.7, enabling: SSI 2012/90, SSI 2012/194
Sch.1 para.9, applied: SSI 2012/90
Sch.9, see *G Hamilton (Tullochgribban Mains) Ltd v Highland Council* [2012] UKSC 31, [2012] P.T.S.R. 1495 (SC), Lord Walker, J.S.C.
Sch.9 para.3, see *G Hamilton (Tullochgribban Mains) Ltd v Highland Council* [2012] UKSC 31, [2012] P.T.S.R. 1495 (SC), Lord Walker, J.S.C.
Sch.9 para.9, see *G Hamilton (Tullochgribban Mains) Ltd v Highland Council* [2012] UKSC 31, [2012] P.T.S.R. 1495 (SC), Lord Walker, J.S.C.

12. Civil Procedure Act 1997
s.1, applied: SI 2012/505, SI 2012/2208
s.2, enabling: SI 2012/505, SI 2012/2208

13. United Nations Personnel Act 1997
s.9, enabling: SI 2012/2594

16. Finance Act 1997
s.10, see *Aspinalls Club Ltd v Revenue and Customs Commissioners* [2012] UKUT 242 (TCC), [2012] S.T.C. 2124 (UT (Tax)), Briggs, J.
s.10, amended: 2012 c.14 Sch.24 para.48
s.10, applied: 2012 c.14 Sch.24 para.3
s.10, repealed (in part): 2012 c.14 Sch.24 para.56
s.11, see *Aspinalls Club Ltd v Revenue and Customs Commissioners* [2012] UKUT 242 (TCC), [2012] S.T.C. 2124 (UT (Tax)), Briggs, J.
s.11, amended: 2012 c.14 s.193
s.12, enabling: SI 2012/1897
s.39, see *Revenue and Customs Commissioners v GMAC UK Plc* [2012] UKUT 279 (TCC), [2012] S.T.C. 2349 (UT (Tax)), Warren, J.
s.67, repealed: 2012 c.14 Sch.16 para.247
s.96, amended: 2012 c.21 Sch.18 para.83
s.110, repealed: 2012 c.5 Sch.14 Part 13

20. British Nationality (Hong Kong) Act 1997
applied: SI 2012/813 Sch.2 para.1

27. Social Security (Recovery of Benefits) Act 1997
applied: SI 2012/3098 Reg.32

1997–cont.

27. Social Security (Recovery of Benefits) Act 1997–*cont.*
s.11, amended: 2012 c.5 Sch.11 para.10
s.11, applied: 2012 c.5 s.102
s.29, amended: 2012 c.5 Sch.2 para.41, Sch.9 para.35
s.30, amended: 2012 c.5 Sch.11 para.11
Sch.1 Part I para.5, amended: 2012 c.21 Sch.18 para.84
Sch.2, amended: 2012 c.5 Sch.2 para.42, Sch.9 para.36, Sch.14 Part 1, Sch.14 Part 9

29. Local Government and Rating Act 1997
Sch.2 para.3, applied: SSI 2012/28 Reg.3, SSI 2012/353 Reg.3
Sch.2 para.4, applied: SSI 2012/28 Reg.5, SSI 2012/29 Reg.4, SSI 2012/48 Reg.7, SSI 2012/353 Reg.5

39. Sexual Offences (Protected Material) Act 1997
applied: SI 2012/1726 r.5.8

40. Protection from Harassment Act 1997
see *Jones v Ruth* [2011] EWCA Civ 804, [2012] 1 W.L.R. 1495 (CA (Civ Div)), Arden, L.J.; see *Trimingham v Associated Newspapers Ltd* [2012] EWHC 1296 (QB), [2012] 4 All E.R. 717 (QBD), Tugendhat, J.; see *Vaickuviene v J Sainsbury Plc* [2012] CSOH 69, 2012 S.L.T. 849 (OH), Lady Clark of Calton
s.1, see *Hayes v Willoughby* [2011] EWCA Civ 1541, [2012] 1 W.L.R. 1510 (CA (Civ Div)), Moses, L.J.; see *Jones v Ruth* [2011] EWCA Civ 804, [2012] 1 W.L.R. 1495 (CA (Civ Div)), Arden, L.J.; see *R. v Haque (Mohammed Enamul)* [2011] EWCA Crim 1871, [2012] 1 Cr. App. R. 5 (CA (Crim Div)), Hooper, L.J.; see *Trimingham v Associated Newspapers Ltd* [2012] EWHC 1296 (QB), [2012] 4 All E.R. 717 (QBD), Tugendhat, J.
s.1, amended: 2012 c.9 Sch.9 para.143
s.2A, added: 2012 c.9 s.111
s.2B, added: 2012 c.9 s.112
s.3, see *Jones v Ruth* [2011] EWCA Civ 804, [2012] 1 W.L.R. 1495 (CA (Civ Div)), Arden, L.J.
s.3, applied: 2012 c.10 Sch.1 para.37
s.3A, applied: 2012 c.10 Sch.1 para.37
s.4, see *R. v Haque (Mohammed Enamul)* [2011] EWCA Crim 1871, [2012] 1 Cr. App. R. 5 (CA (Crim Div)), Hooper, L.J.
s.4, amended: 2012 c.9 Sch.9 para.143
s.4A, added: 2012 c.9 s.111
s.5, applied: 2012 c.10 Sch.1 para.6, Sch.1 para.8, Sch.1 para.37, SI 2012/1726 r.50.1
s.5A, see *R. v Brough (Stuart)* [2011] EWCA Crim 2802, [2012] 2 Cr. App. R. (S.) 8 (CA (Crim Div)), Moore-Bick, L.J.; see *R. v K* [2011] EWCA Crim 1843, [2012] 1 Cr. App. R. (S.) 88 (CA (Crim Div)), Leveson, L.J.
s.5A, applied: 2012 c.10 Sch.1 para.6, Sch.1 para.8, Sch.1 para.37, SI 2012/1726 r.50.1
s.7, see *R. v Haque (Mohammed Enamul)* [2011] EWCA Crim 1871, [2012] 1 Cr. App. R. 5 (CA (Crim Div)), Hooper, L.J.
s.8, see *Vaickuviene v J Sainsbury Plc* [2012] CSOH 69, 2012 S.L.T. 849 (OH), Lady Clark of Calton

43. Crime (Sentences) Act 1997
Commencement Orders: SI 2012/2901 Art.2
Part II c.II, applied: 2012 c.10 Sch.15 para.2, SI 2012/206 Sch.1 para.21
s.28, see *R. (on the application of Sturnham) v Parole Board* [2012] EWCA Civ 452, [2012] 3 W.L.R. 476 (CA (Civ Div)), Laws, L.J.; see *R. v Taylor (Ezra)* [2011] EWCA Crim 2236, [2012] 1 W.L.R. 2113 (CA (Crim Div)), Moses, L.J.
s.28, referred to: 2012 c.10 s.128

1997– cont.

43. Crime (Sentences) Act 1997– *cont.*
s.29, see *R. v Gill (Nimal Singh)* [2011] EWCA Crim 2795, [2012] 1 W.L.R. 1441 (CA (Crim Div)), Lord Judge, L.C.J.
s.31A, amended: 2012 c.10 s.117
s.32A, added: 2012 c.10 s.119
s.32B, added: 2012 c.10 s.119
s.34, amended: 2012 c.10 s.117
s.57, enabling: SI 2012/ 2901
Sch.1 Part II para.6, amended: 2012 c.10 Sch.10 para.9
Sch.1 Part II para.8, amended: 2012 c.10 Sch.10 para.9, Sch.14 para.2, Sch.16 para.7
Sch.1 Part II para.8, repealed (in part): 2012 c.10 Sch.10 para.9
Sch.1 Part II para.9, amended: 2012 c.10 Sch.10 para.9, Sch.14 para.2, Sch.16 para.8, Sch.21 para.5
Sch.1 Part II para.9, repealed (in part): 2012 c.10 Sch.10 para.9

44. Education Act 1997
s.32AB, applied: SI 2012/ 1248 Art.3
s.32AB, enabling: SI 2012/ 1248
s.54, applied: SI 2012/ 1248

47. Social Security Administration (Fraud) Act 1997
s.3, repealed: 2012 c.5 Sch.14 Part 1
s.4, repealed (in part): 2012 c.5 Sch.14 Part 1
s.5, repealed: 2012 c.5 Sch.14 Part 1
s.8, repealed: 2012 c.5 Sch.14 Part 1
s.9, repealed: 2012 c.5 Sch.14 Part 1
s.10, repealed: 2012 c.5 Sch.14 Part 1
s.11, repealed: 2012 c.5 Sch.14 Part 10
s.16, repealed: 2012 c.5 Sch.14 Part 1
Sch.1 para.3, repealed: 2012 c.5 Sch.14 Part 1
Sch.1 para.7, repealed: 2012 c.5 Sch.14 Part 1

48. Crime and Punishment (Scotland) Act 1997
s.45, repealed: 2012 asp 8 Sch.8 Part 1
s.46, repealed: 2012 asp 8 Sch.8 Part 1
s.63, repealed (in part): 2012 asp 8 Sch.8 Part 1

50. Police Act 1997
see *R. (on the application of T) v Chief Constable of Greater Manchester* [2012] EWHC 147 (Admin), [2012] 2 Cr. App. R. 3 (QBD (Admin)), Kenneth Parker, J.
Part V, applied: 2012 c.9 s.88, Sch.8 para.8, SI 2012/ 2522 Art.2, SI 2012/ 3006 Art.98, Art.99
s.93, amended: 2012 asp 8 Sch.7 para.14
s.93, repealed (in part): 2012 asp 8 Sch.8 Part 1
s.94, amended: 2012 asp 8 Sch.7 para.14, Sch.8 Part 1
s.94, repealed (in part): 2012 asp 8 Sch.8 Part 1
s.95, amended: 2012 asp 8 Sch.7 para.14
s.105, amended: 2012 asp 8 Sch.7 para.14
s.107, amended: 2012 asp 8 Sch.7 para.14
s.107, repealed (in part): 2012 asp 8 Sch.8 Part 1
s.112, amended: 2012 c.9 s.80, s.84, SI 2012/ 3006 Art.37
s.112, applied: SI 2012/ 1726 r.5.9, SSI 2012/ 181 Reg.4
s.112, enabling: SSI 2012/ 354
s.113A, amended: 2012 c.9 s.80, Sch.9 para.135, SI 2012/ 3006 Art.37, Art.38
s.113A, applied: SI 2012/ 1726 r.5.9, SI 2012/ 2234 Art.5, SI 2012/ 2522 Art.2, SI 2012/ 3094 Reg.42
s.113A, repealed (in part): 2012 c.9 s.79, Sch.9 para.36, Sch.10 Part 5, Sch.10 Part 6
s.113A, enabling: SI 2012/ 2666, SI 2012/ 2667, SI 2012/ 2668, SI 2012/ 2669, SSI 2012/ 354
s.113B, amended: 2012 c.9 s.80, s.82, Sch.10 Part 6, SI 2012/ 3006 Art.37, Art.39

1997– cont.

50. Police Act 1997– *cont.*
s.113B, applied: SI 2012/ 1034 Sch.4 para.15, SI 2012/ 1726 r.5.9, SI 2012/ 2112 Reg.28, SI 2012/ 2234 Art.4, Art.5, SI 2012/ 2522 Art.2
s.113B, repealed (in part): 2012 c.9 s.79, Sch.9 para.37, Sch.10 Part 5, Sch.10 Part 6
s.113B, enabling: SI 2012/ 523, SI 2012/ 2107, SI 2012/ 2108, SI 2012/ 2109, SI 2012/ 2114, SI 2012/ 3016
s.113BA, applied: SI 2012/ 2234 Art.4
s.113BA, repealed (in part): 2012 c.9 Sch.9 para.38, Sch.10 Part 5
s.113BA, enabling: SI 2012/ 523, SI 2012/ 2114
s.113BB, applied: SI 2012/ 2234 Art.4
s.113BB, repealed (in part): 2012 c.9 Sch.9 para.39, Sch.10 Part 5
s.113BB, enabling: SI 2012/ 523, SI 2012/ 2114
s.113BC, amended: 2012 c.9 Sch.9 para.105
s.113E, amended: SI 2012/ 3006 Art.37
s.113E, varied: SI 2012/ 2157 Art.8
s.114, amended: 2012 c.9 s.80, Sch.9 para.106, SI 2012/ 3006 Art.37
s.114, applied: SI 2012/ 2234 Art.5
s.114, varied: 2012 c.11 s.12
s.116, amended: 2012 c.9 s.80, Sch.9 para.107, SI 2012/ 3006 Art.37
s.116, applied: SI 2012/ 2234 Art.5
s.116, varied: 2012 c.11 s.12, SI 2012/ 2157 Art.9
s.116A, added: 2012 c.9 s.83
s.116A, amended: SI 2012/ 3006 Art.37
s.116A, applied: SI 2012/ 2522 Art.2
s.117, amended: 2012 c.9 s.82, Sch.9 para.108, SI 2012/ 3006 Art.37, Art.40
s.117, applied: SI 2012/ 2522 Art.2
s.117A, added: 2012 c.9 s.82
s.117A, amended: SI 2012/ 3006 Art.37
s.118, amended: 2012 c.9 Sch.9 para.109, SI 2012/ 3006 Art.37, Art.41
s.118, applied: SI 2012/ 2522 Art.2
s.119, amended: 2012 c.9 Sch.9 para.40, Sch.9 para.110, Sch.10 Part 5, SI 2012/ 3006 Art.13, Art.37, Art.42, Art.50, Art.52
s.119, applied: SI 2012/ 2522 Art.2
s.119, repealed (in part): 2012 c.9 Sch.9 para.40, Sch.10 Part 5, SI 2012/ 3006 Art.50, Art.52
s.119, substituted: SI 2012/ 3006 Art.42
s.119A, amended: 2012 c.9 Sch.9 para.111, Sch.10 Part 6, SI 2012/ 3006 Art.37
s.119B, repealed (in part): 2012 c.9 Sch.9 para.41, Sch.9 para.111, Sch.10 Part 5, Sch.10 Part 6
s.120, amended: 2012 c.9 s.80, Sch.9 para.112, SI 2012/ 3006 Art.37, Art.43
s.120, applied: SI 2012/ 2522 Art.2, SI 2012/ 3006 Art.110
s.120, repealed (in part): 2012 c.9 Sch.9 para.112, Sch.10 Part 6
s.120A, amended: 2012 asp 8 Sch.7 para.14, 2012 c.9 Sch.9 para.42, Sch.10 Part 5, SI 2012/ 3006 Art.37, Art.44
s.120A, applied: SI 2012/ 2522 Art.2
s.120A, repealed (in part): 2012 c.9 Sch.9 para.42, Sch.10 Part 5
s.120A, substituted: 2012 c.9 Sch.9 para.42
s.120AA, amended: 2012 c.9 s.81, SI 2012/ 3006 Art.37
s.120AA, applied: SI 2012/ 2522 Art.2
s.120AB, amended: SI 2012/ 3006 Art.37, Art.45
s.120AB, applied: SI 2012/ 2522 Art.2, SI 2012/ 3006 Art.105
s.120AC, added: 2012 c.9 s.79

50. Police Act 1997–*cont.*
   s.120AC, amended: SI 2012/3006 Art.37
   s.120AD, added: 2012 c.9 s.79
   s.120AD, amended: SI 2012/3006 Art.37
   s.120ZA, amended: SI 2012/3006 Art.37
   s.120ZA, applied: SI 2012/2522 Art.2, SI 2012/
     3006 Art.110
   s.122, amended: 2012 c.9 Sch.9 para.113, SI 2012/
     3006 Art.37, Art.46
   s.122, applied: SI 2012/2522 Art.2
   s.122, repealed (in part): 2012 c.9 Sch.9 para.114,
     Sch.10 Part 6
   s.122A, repealed (in part): SI 2012/3006 Art.51
   s.124, amended: 2012 c.9 Sch.9 para.115, Sch.10 Part
     6
   s.124, repealed (in part): 2012 c.9 Sch.9 para.115,
     Sch.10 Part 6
   s.124A, amended: 2012 c.9 Sch.9 para.116, Sch.10
     Part 6, SI 2012/3006 Art.37
   s.125, enabling: SI 2012/2107, SI 2012/2108, SI 2012/
     2109, SI 2012/2114, SI 2012/2666, SI 2012/2667, SI
     2012/2668, SI 2012/2669, SI 2012/3016
   s.125B, amended: 2012 c.9 Sch.9 para.117, SI 2012/
     3006 Art.37
   s.125B, applied: SI 2012/2522 Art.2
   s.126, amended: 2012 asp 8 Sch.7 para.14, 2012 c.9
     Sch.9 para.118, SI 2012/3006 Art.47
   s.126A, amended: SI 2012/3006 Art.53
   s.126A, repealed (in part): SI 2012/3006 Art.53
**68. Special Immigration Appeals Commission Act
   1997**
   see *R. (on the application of BB (Algeria)) v Special
     Immigration Appeals Commission* [2011]
     EWHC 336 (Admin), [2012] Q.B. 146 (DC),
     Richards, L.J.
   s.2, applied: SI 2012/813 Sch.1 para.1, SI 2012/971
     Sch.1 para.1
   s.2B, see *R. (on the application of GI (Sudan)) v
     Secretary of State for the Home Department*
     [2011] EWHC 1875 (Admin), [2012] 1 W.L.R.
     2568 (QBD (Admin)), Mitting, J.

1998

1. Education (Student Loans) Act 1998
   s.3, applied: SSI 2012/303 Reg.60
2. Public Processions (Northern Ireland) Act 1998
   Sch.1 para.3, amended: SI 2012/2404 Sch.2 para.37
11. Bank of England Act 1998
   s.1, amended: 2012 c.21 s.1
   s.1, repealed (in part): 2012 c.21 Sch.19
   s.2A, amended: 2012 c.21 s.2
   s.2A, repealed (in part): 2012 c.21 s.2
   s.2B, repealed: 2012 c.21 s.4
   s.2C, repealed: 2012 c.21 s.4
   s.3, substituted: 2012 c.21 s.3
   s.4, amended: 2012 c.21 s.3, Sch.1 para.1, Sch.2
     para.4
   s.9A, added: 2012 c.21 s.4
   s.9B, added: 2012 c.21 s.4
   s.9C, added: 2012 c.21 s.4
   s.9D, added: 2012 c.21 s.4
   s.9E, added: 2012 c.21 s.4
   s.9F, added: 2012 c.21 s.4
   s.9G, added: 2012 c.21 s.4
   s.9H, added: 2012 c.21 s.4
   s.9I, added: 2012 c.21 s.4
   s.9J, added: 2012 c.21 s.4
   s.9K, added: 2012 c.21 s.4

11. Bank of England Act 1998–*cont.*
   s.9L, added: 2012 c.21 s.4
   s.9L, applied: 2012 c.21 Sch.20 para.6
   s.9L, disapplied: 2012 c.21 Sch.20 para.6
   s.9M, added: 2012 c.21 s.4
   s.9N, added: 2012 c.21 s.4
   s.9O, added: 2012 c.21 s.4
   s.9P, added: 2012 c.21 s.4
   s.9Q, added: 2012 c.21 s.4
   s.9R, added: 2012 c.21 s.4
   s.9S, added: 2012 c.21 s.4
   s.9T, added: 2012 c.21 s.4
   s.9U, added: 2012 c.21 s.4
   s.9V, added: 2012 c.21 s.4
   s.9W, added: 2012 c.21 s.4
   s.9X, added: 2012 c.21 s.4
   s.9Y, added: 2012 c.21 s.4
   s.9Z, added: 2012 c.21 s.4
   s.9ZA, added: 2012 c.21 s.4
   s.13, amended: 2012 c.21 s.1
   s.15, amended: 2012 c.21 Sch.1 para.2
   s.16, amended: 2012 c.21 s.3
   s.16, repealed (in part): 2012 c.21 s.3
   s.17, amended: 2012 c.21 Sch.18 para.85
   s.21, repealed: 2012 c.21 Sch.18 para.85
   s.23, repealed (in part): 2012 c.21 Sch.18 para.85
   s.24, repealed: 2012 c.21 Sch.18 para.85
   s.40, amended: 2012 c.21 Sch.1 para.3
   Sch.1 para.1, substituted: 2012 c.21 Sch.2 para.1
   Sch.1 para.2, amended: 2012 c.21 Sch.2 para.1
   Sch.1 para.3, repealed: 2012 c.21 Sch.2 para.1
   Sch.1 para.4, amended: 2012 c.21 Sch.2 para.1
   Sch.1 para.5, amended: 2012 c.21 Sch.2 para.1
   Sch.1 para.6, substituted: 2012 c.21 Sch.2 para.1
   Sch.1 para.7, amended: 2012 c.21 Sch.2 para.1
   Sch.1 para.8, amended: 2012 c.21 Sch.2 para.1, SI
     2012/2404 Sch.2 para.38
   Sch.1 para.11, amended: 2012 c.21 Sch.2 para.1
   Sch.1 para.11, substituted: 2012 c.21 Sch.2 para.1
   Sch.1 para.12A, added: 2012 c.21 Sch.2 para.1
   Sch.1 para.13, amended: 2012 c.21 Sch.2 para.1
   Sch.1 para.14, amended: 2012 c.21 Sch.2 para.1
   Sch.1 para.15, amended: 2012 c.21 Sch.2 para.1
   Sch.2 para.1, amended: 2012 c.21 Sch.18 para.85
   Sch.2A para.1, added: 2012 c.21 Sch.1 Part 1
   Sch.2A para.2, added: 2012 c.21 Sch.1 Part 1
   Sch.2A para.3, added: 2012 c.21 Sch.1 Part 1
   Sch.2A para.4, added: 2012 c.21 Sch.1 Part 1
   Sch.2A para.5, added: 2012 c.21 Sch.1 Part 1
   Sch.2A para.6, added: 2012 c.21 Sch.1 Part 1
   Sch.2A para.7, added: 2012 c.21 Sch.1 Part 1
   Sch.2A para.8, added: 2012 c.21 Sch.1 Part 1
   Sch.2A para.9, added: 2012 c.21 Sch.1 Part 1
   Sch.2A para.10, added: 2012 c.21 Sch.1 Part 1
   Sch.2A para.11, added: 2012 c.21 Sch.1 Part 1
   Sch.2A para.12, added: 2012 c.21 Sch.1 Part 1
   Sch.2A para.13, added: 2012 c.21 Sch.1 Part 1
   Sch.2A para.14, added: 2012 c.21 Sch.1 Part 1
   Sch.3 para.1, amended: 2012 c.21 Sch.2 para.2
   Sch.3 para.2, repealed: 2012 c.21 Sch.2 para.2
   Sch.3 para.2B, added: 2012 c.21 Sch.2 para.2
   Sch.3 para.3, substituted: 2012 c.21 Sch.2 para.2
   Sch.3 para.4, amended: 2012 c.21 Sch.2 para.2
   Sch.3 para.4, repealed (in part): 2012 c.21 Sch.2
     para.2
   Sch.3 para.5A, added: 2012 c.21 Sch.2 para.2
   Sch.3 para.9, amended: 2012 c.21 Sch.2 para.2, SI
     2012/2404 Sch.2 para.38

1998– cont.

11. Bank of England Act 1998– *cont.*
Sch.3 para.9, repealed (in part): 2012 c.21 Sch.2 para.2
Sch.3 para.10, amended: 2012 c.21 Sch.2 para.2
Sch.3 para.11, amended: 2012 c.21 Sch.2 para.2
Sch.3 para.13A, added: 2012 c.21 Sch.2 para.2
Sch.7 para.1, amended: 2012 c.21 Sch.2 para.5
Sch.7 para.3, amended: 2012 c.21 Sch.18 para.85

14. Social Security Act 1998
applied: 2012 c.5 s.41, SI 2012/819 Reg.2
s.2, amended: 2012 c.5 Sch.2 para.44, Sch.9 para.38
s.3, amended: 2012 c.5 s.127, SI 2012/2007 Sch.1 para.64
s.8, amended: 2012 c.5 Sch.2 para.45, Sch.9 para.39, Sch.14 Part 1
s.8, applied: SI 2012/845 Reg.2
s.8, repealed (in part): 2012 c.5 Sch.14 Part 1, Sch.14 Part 8
s.9, amended: 2012 c.5 Sch.14 Part 8
s.9, enabling: SI 2012/824, SI 2012/913, SI 2012/919, SI 2012/2575
s.10, amended: 2012 c.5 Sch.12 para.4, Sch.14 Part 8
s.10, enabling: SI 2012/757, SI 2012/1267, SI 2012/2756
s.11, amended: 2012 c.5 Sch.2 para.46, Sch.9 para.40
s.12, amended: 2012 c.5 s.102, s.105
s.12, applied: 2012 c.5 s.102
s.15A, amended: SI 2012/2007 Sch.1 para.64
s.22, repealed (in part): 2012 c.5 Sch.14 Part 10
s.22, enabling: SI 2012/824
s.27, amended: 2012 c.5 Sch.2 para.47, Sch.9 para.41
s.28, amended: 2012 c.5 Sch.2 para.48, Sch.9 para.42
s.29, repealed (in part): 2012 c.5 s.68
s.30, amended: 2012 c.5 s.68
s.34, repealed: 2012 c.5 Sch.14 Part 1
s.36, repealed: 2012 c.5 Sch.14 Part 8
s.37, repealed: 2012 c.5 Sch.14 Part 8
s.38, repealed: 2012 c.5 Sch.14 Part 8
s.39, amended: 2012 c.5 Sch.2 para.49, Sch.14 Part 1
s.70, repealed (in part): 2012 c.5 Sch.14 Part 8
s.71, repealed: 2012 c.5 Sch.14 Part 8
s.74, repealed: 2012 c.5 Sch.14 Part 10
s.75, repealed: 2012 c.5 Sch.14 Part 8
s.79, amended: 2012 c.5 s.104
s.79, repealed (in part): 2012 c.5 Sch.14 Part 1
s.79, enabling: SI 2012/757, SI 2012/824, SI 2012/913, SI 2012/2575, SI 2012/2756, SI 2012/3040
s.80, amended: 2012 c.5 s.102
s.81, repealed: 2012 c.5 s.143
s.84, enabling: SI 2012/757, SI 2012/824, SI 2012/913, SI 2012/919, SI 2012/1267, SI 2012/2575
Sch.2 para.1, repealed: 2012 c.5 Sch.14 Part 1
Sch.2 para.5A, repealed: 2012 c.5 Sch.14 Part 1
Sch.2 para.6, amended: 2012 c.5 Sch.2 para.50
Sch.2 para.6, repealed (in part): 2012 c.5 Sch.14 Part 1
Sch.2 para.7, repealed: 2012 c.5 Sch.14 Part 1
Sch.2 para.7A, added: 2012 c.5 Sch.2 para.50
Sch.3 Part I, substituted: 2012 c.5 Sch.7 para.11
Sch.3 Part I para.3, amended: 2012 c.5 Sch.9 para.43, Sch.14 Part 6
Sch.3 Part I para.3, repealed (in part): 2012 c.5 s.46, Sch.14 Part 9
Sch.3 Part I para.3A, added: 2012 c.5 Sch.2 para.51
Sch.3 Part I para.5, amended: 2012 c.5 Sch.14 Part 1
Sch.3 Part I para.6A, added: 2012 c.5 s.105
Sch.3 Part I para.6B, added: 2012 c.5 s.105

14. Social Security Act 1998– *cont.*
Sch.3 Part I para.8, amended: 2012 c.5 Sch.7 para.11
Sch.3 Part I para.8, repealed: 2012 c.5 Sch.14 Part 4
Sch.7 para.72, repealed: 2012 c.5 Sch.14 Part 8
Sch.7 para.73, repealed: 2012 c.5 Sch.14 Part 8
Sch.7 para.95, repealed: 2012 c.5 Sch.14 Part 1
Sch.7 para.97, repealed: 2012 c.5 Sch.14 Part 1
Sch.7 para.98, repealed: 2012 c.5 Sch.14 Part 1
Sch.7 para.103, repealed: 2012 c.5 Sch.14 Part 8
Sch.7 para.134, repealed: 2012 c.5 Sch.14 Part 4
Sch.7 para.135, repealed: 2012 c.5 Sch.14 Part 4
Sch.7 para.139, repealed: 2012 c.5 Sch.14 Part 1
Sch.7 para.140, repealed: 2012 c.5 Sch.14 Part 1
Sch.7 para.141, repealed: 2012 c.5 Sch.14 Part 3
Sch.7 para.146, repealed: 2012 c.5 Sch.14 Part 1

17. Petroleum Act 1998
applied: SSI 2012/89 Sch.1
s.5, amended: 2012 asp 5 Sch.5 para.36
s.29, applied: SI 2012/949 Reg.3
s.29, referred to: SI 2012/949 Reg.4
s.34, applied: SI 2012/949 Reg.3
s.34, referred to: SI 2012/949 Reg.4
s.39, applied: SI 2012/949
s.39, enabling: SI 2012/949

18. Audit Commission Act 1998
Part II, applied: SI 2012/666 Art.6
s.2, see *Veolia ES Nottinghamshire Ltd v Nottinghamshire CC* [2010] EWCA Civ 1214, [2012] P.T.S.R. 185 (CA (Civ Div)), Rix, L.J.
s.2, applied: SI 2012/2421 Reg.15
s.5, see *Veolia ES Nottinghamshire Ltd v Nottinghamshire CC* [2010] EWCA Civ 1214, [2012] P.T.S.R. 185 (CA (Civ Div)), Rix, L.J.
s.11, repealed (in part): SI 2012/854 Art.4
s.15, see *Veolia ES Nottinghamshire Ltd v Nottinghamshire CC* [2010] EWCA Civ 1214, [2012] P.T.S.R. 185 (CA (Civ Div)), Rix, L.J.
s.28, amended: 2012 c.17 Sch.3 para.31
s.28, repealed (in part): 2012 c.17 Sch.3 para.31
s.33, repealed (in part): 2012 c.7 Sch.5 para.81, Sch.14 para.72
s.38, repealed: 2012 c.5 Sch.14 Part 1
s.39, repealed: 2012 c.5 Sch.14 Part 1
s.49, see *Veolia ES Nottinghamshire Ltd v Nottinghamshire CC* [2010] EWCA Civ 1214, [2012] P.T.S.R. 185 (CA (Civ Div)), Rix, L.J.
s.50, repealed: 2012 c.5 Sch.14 Part 1
s.53, amended: 2012 c.7 Sch.14 para.73
Sch.1 para.4, amended: SI 2012/2404 Sch.2 para.39
Sch.1 para.8, repealed (in part): 2012 c.5 Sch.14 Part 1
Sch.2, see *Veolia ES Nottinghamshire Ltd v Nottinghamshire CC* [2010] EWCA Civ 1214, [2012] P.T.S.R. 185 (CA (Civ Div)), Rix, L.J.
Sch.2 para.1, repealed (in part): SI 2012/854 Art.4
Sch.2A Part 1 para.1, repealed (in part): SI 2012/2401 Sch.1 para.7
Sch.2A Part 1 para.3, amended: 2012 c.5 Sch.14 Part 1
Sch.2A Part 1 para.3, repealed (in part): 2012 c.5 Sch.14 Part 1
Sch.3 para.23, repealed: 2012 c.5 Sch.14 Part 1

20. Late Payment of Commercial Debts (Interest) Act 1998
see *Smith v Scottish Legal Aid Board* [2012] CSIH 14, 2012 S.L.T. 703 (IH (1 Div)), The Lord President (Hamilton)

22. National Lottery Act 1998
s.16, referred to: SI 2012/964 Art.2

22. National Lottery Act 1998–*cont.*
s.16, repealed: SI 2012/964 Sch.1
s.17, repealed: SI 2012/964 Sch.1
s.18, repealed: SI 2012/964 Sch.1
s.19, repealed: SI 2012/964 Sch.1
s.20, repealed: SI 2012/964 Sch.1
s.21, repealed: SI 2012/964 Sch.1
s.22, repealed: SI 2012/964 Sch.1
s.23, repealed: SI 2012/964 Sch.1
s.24, repealed: SI 2012/964 Sch.1
s.25, repealed: SI 2012/964 Sch.1
Sch.4 para.1, repealed: SI 2012/964 Sch.1
Sch.4 para.2, repealed: SI 2012/964 Sch.1
Sch.4 para.3, repealed: SI 2012/964 Sch.1
Sch.4 para.4, repealed: SI 2012/964 Sch.1
Sch.4 para.5, repealed: SI 2012/964 Sch.1
Sch.4 para.6, repealed: SI 2012/964 Sch.1
Sch.4 para.7, repealed: SI 2012/964 Sch.1
Sch.4 para.8, repealed: SI 2012/964 Sch.1
Sch.4 para.9, repealed: SI 2012/964 Sch.1
Sch.4 para.10, repealed: SI 2012/964 Sch.1
Sch.4 para.11, repealed: SI 2012/964 Sch.1
Sch.4 para.12, repealed: SI 2012/964 Sch.1
Sch.4 para.13, repealed: SI 2012/964 Sch.1

29. Data Protection Act 1998
see *Grinyer v Plymouth Hospitals NHS Trust* (2012)
125 B.M.L.R. 1 (CC (Plymouth)), Judge Cotter
Q.C.; see *Lyons v Chief Constable of Strathclyde*
[2012] CSOH 45, 2012 Rep. L.R. 108 (OH), Lady
Smith; see *R. (on the application of Ali) v
Minister for the Cabinet Office* [2012] EWHC
1943 (Admin), [2012] A.C.D. 89 (QBD
(Admin)), Beatson, J.; see *R. (on the
application of T) v Commissioner of Police of
the Metropolis* [2012] EWHC 1115 (Admin),
[2012] 1 W.L.R. 2978 (QBD (Admin)), Eady, J.;
see *Smeaton v Equifax Plc* [2012] EWHC 2322
(QB), [2012] 4 All E.R. 460 (QBD), Judge
Anthony Thornton Q.C.
applied: 2012 c.9 s.27, SI 2012/129 Sch.1 para.6, SI
2012/925 Sch.1 para.35, SI 2012/1021 Reg.5, SI
2012/1301 Sch.1 para.6, SI 2012/1489 Sch.1
para.6, SI 2012/1507 Sch.1 para.6, SI 2012/1508
Sch.1 para.6, SI 2012/1509 Sch.1 para.6, SI 2012/
1511 Sch.1 para.6, SI 2012/1515 Sch.1 para.6, SI
2012/1516 Sch.1 para.6, SI 2012/1517 Sch.1
para.6, SI 2012/1726 r.5.8, SI 2012/3122 Reg.17
s.1, applied: SI 2012/3118 Sch.1 para.1
s.1, referred to: SI 2012/1017 Reg.52
s.7, see *SM v Sutton LBC* [2011] EWHC 3465
(Admin), [2012] 1 F.L.R. 974 (QBD (Admin)),
Wyn Williams, J.
s.13, see *Grinyer v Plymouth Hospitals NHS Trust*
(2012) 125 B.M.L.R. 1 (CC (Plymouth)), Judge
Cotter Q.C.
s.33, referred to: SI 2012/1917 Sch.2 para.20, Sch.2
para.24
s.35, see *Rugby Football Union v Viagogo Ltd* [2011]
EWCA Civ 1585, [2012] 2 C.M.L.R. 3 (CA (Civ
Div)), Longmore, L.J.; see *SM v Sutton LBC*
[2011] EWHC 3465 (Admin), [2012] 1 F.L.R.
974 (QBD (Admin)), Wyn Williams, J.
s.41C, amended: 2012 c.9 s.106
s.51, amended: 2012 c.9 s.107, Sch.10 Part 8
s.52B, amended: 2012 c.9 s.106
s.55C, amended: 2012 c.9 s.106
s.56, amended: SI 2012/3006 Art.16, Art.73, Art.74
s.67, amended: 2012 c.9 s.107
s.67, applied: SI 2012/1978
s.67, enabling: SI 2012/1978

29. Data Protection Act 1998– *cont.*
s.69, amended: 2012 c.7 s.213, s.220, Sch.5 para.82,
Sch.14 para.74, Sch.17 para.7, Sch.19 para.7
s.69, repealed (in part): 2012 c.7 Sch.5 para.82
s.75, amended: 2012 c.9 s.86, SI 2012/3006 Art.75
Sch.1 Pt II para.7, see *Lyons v Chief Constable of
Strathclyde* [2012] CSOH 45, 2012 Rep. L.R.
108 (OH), Lady Smith
Sch.2, see *R. (on the application of Ali) v Minister
for the Cabinet Office* [2012] EWHC 1943
(Admin), [2012] A.C.D. 89 (QBD (Admin)),
Beatson, J.
Sch.2 para.6, see *South Lanarkshire Council v
Scottish Information Commissioner* [2012]
CSIH 30, 2012 S.L.T. 691 (IH (Ex Div)), Lord
Mackay of Drumadoon
Sch.3, see *R. (on the application of Ali) v Minister
for the Cabinet Office* [2012] EWHC 1943
(Admin), [2012] A.C.D. 89 (QBD (Admin)),
Beatson, J.
Sch.3 para.10, applied: SI 2012/1978 Art.2
Sch.3 para.10, enabling: SI 2012/1978
Sch.5 Part I, amended: 2012 c.9 s.105
Sch.5 Part I para.2, amended: 2012 c.9 s.105
Sch.5 Part I para.2, repealed (in part): 2012 c.9 s.105,
Sch.10 Part 8
Sch.5 Part I para.4, amended: 2012 c.9 s.108
Sch.5 Part I para.4, repealed (in part): 2012 c.9 s.108,
Sch.10 Part 8
Sch.7 para.6, amended: 2012 c.21 Sch.18 para.86

30. Teaching and Higher Education Act 1998
applied: SI 2012/2885 Sch.5 para.19, SI 2012/2886
Sch.1, SI 2012/3145 Sch.1, SSI 2012/303 Reg.20,
Sch.4 para.23, SSI 2012/319 Sch.3 para.18
s.1, enabling: SI 2012/169
s.3, enabling: SI 2012/166
s.4, enabling: SI 2012/166
s.6, enabling: SI 2012/170
s.7, referred to: SI 2012/167
s.7, enabling: SI 2012/167
s.8, enabling: SI 2012/168
s.19, applied: SI 2012/335 Sch.1 para.26, Sch.1
para.27, SI 2012/1115 Sch.1 para.6, SI 2012/2991
Sch.1 para.26
s.19, enabling: SI 2012/724, SI 2012/1675
s.22, applied: SI 2012/335 Sch.1 para.12, SI 2012/
1518 Reg.5, Reg.7, SI 2012/1818 Reg.4, Reg.24,
SI 2012/2885 Sch.5 para.18, SI 2012/2886 Sch.1,
SI 2012/2991 Sch.1 para.12, SI 2012/3145 Sch.1,
SSI 2012/303 Reg.54, Reg.60, Sch.4 para.22,
SSI 2012/319 Sch.3 para.17
s.22, enabling: SI 2012/14, SI 2012/836, SI 2012/
1156, SI 2012/1309, SI 2012/1518, SI 2012/1653,
SI 2012/1818, SI 2012/3059
s.42, applied: SI 2012/166, SI 2012/169
s.42, referred to: SI 2012/170
s.42, enabling: SI 2012/14, SI 2012/166, SI 2012/167,
SI 2012/169, SI 2012/170, SI 2012/724, SI 2012/
836, SI 2012/1156, SI 2012/1309, SI 2012/1518, SI
2012/1653, SI 2012/1675, SI 2012/1818, SI 2012/
3059
s.43, enabling: SI 2012/3059
Sch.1 para.3, enabling: SI 2012/169
Sch.2 para.1, amended: SI 2012/3006 Art.13
Sch.2 para.1, enabling: SI 2012/170

31. School Standards and Framework Act 1998
Part II c.IV, applied: SI 2012/335 Sch.1 para.20, SI
2012/1035 Reg.28, SI 2012/2991 Sch.1 para.20
Part III, applied: SI 2012/8 Reg.19
s.1, enabling: SI 2012/10

1998– cont.

31. School Standards and Framework Act 1998– *cont.*

s.15, referred to: SI 2012/1115 Reg.6

s.16A, applied: SI 2012/1643 Reg.5

s.18A, applied: SI 2012/1643 Reg.5

s.20, applied: SI 2012/1167 Sch.1 para.4

s.30, applied: SI 2012/1035 Reg.40

s.41, applied: SI 2012/1035 Reg.29

s.45A, applied: SI 2012/335 Reg.3, Reg.5, SI 2012/2991 Reg.4, Reg.6

s.45A, enabling: SI 2012/335, SI 2012/2991

s.45AA, enabling: SI 2012/335, SI 2012/2991

s.47, applied: SI 2012/962 Reg.2, SI 2012/2261 Reg.8

s.47, enabling: SI 2012/335, SI 2012/2991

s.47A, applied: SI 2012/335 Sch.2 para.31, SI 2012/2991 Sch.2 para.2

s.47A, enabling: SI 2012/335, SI 2012/2261, SI 2012/2991

s.47ZA, applied: SI 2012/2261 Reg.8

s.47ZA, enabling: SI 2012/335, SI 2012/2991

s.48, applied: SI 2012/335 Reg.26, Sch.1 para.20, SI 2012/1035 Reg.32, Reg.37, Reg.43, Reg.45, SI 2012/2991 Reg.26, Sch.1 para.20

s.48, enabling: SI 2012/335, SI 2012/2991

s.49, applied: SI 2012/335 Sch.5 para.9, SI 2012/1035 Reg.29

s.49, referred to: SI 2012/2991 Sch.5 para.9

s.49, varied: SI 2012/1035 Sch.8 para.1

s.49, enabling: SI 2012/335, SI 2012/2991

s.50, applied: SI 2012/335 Sch.5 para.13, SI 2012/1035 Reg.29, Reg.32, Reg.37, Reg.43, Reg.45

s.50, referred to: SI 2012/2991 Sch.5 para.13

s.50, varied: SI 2012/1035 Sch.8 para.2

s.51, amended: SI 2012/1035 Sch.8 para.3

s.51, applied: SI 2012/1035 Reg.29

s.69, applied: SI 2012/8 Reg.9, Reg.12, SI 2012/1034 Reg.28, Reg.29, Reg.31, Sch.3 para.1, SI 2012/1035 Reg.9, SI 2012/2261 Reg.7

s.69, enabling: SI 2012/967, SI 2012/2265, SI 2012/3174

s.85, enabling: SI 2012/216

s.88, referred to: SI 2012/335 Sch.2 para.13

s.88B, enabling: SI 2012/8

s.88C, applied: SI 2012/8 Reg.7, Reg.12, Reg.13, Reg.14, Reg.15, Reg.17, SI 2012/335 Sch.2 para.13, SI 2012/2991 Sch.2 para.1

s.88C, enabling: SI 2012/8

s.88E, applied: SI 2012/8 Reg.19, Reg.20

s.88E, enabling: SI 2012/8

s.88F, applied: SI 2012/8 Reg.34

s.88F, enabling: SI 2012/8

s.88H, applied: SI 2012/8 Reg.19, Reg.21, Reg.22, Reg.23, Reg.24, Reg.25

s.88H, enabling: SI 2012/8

s.88I, applied: SI 2012/8 Reg.19, Reg.25, Sch.1 para.8

s.88K, enabling: SI 2012/8

s.88M, applied: SI 2012/8 Reg.27, Reg.30

s.88M, enabling: SI 2012/8

s.88N, enabling: SI 2012/8

s.88O, enabling: SI 2012/8

s.88Q, applied: SI 2012/8 Reg.33

s.88Q, enabling: SI 2012/8

s.92, enabling: SI 2012/8, SI 2012/1124

s.94, applied: SI 2012/8 Reg.33, SI 2012/9 Reg.5, Sch.1 para.1, Sch.1 para.2, Sch.1 para.3, SI 2012/10 Sch.1 para.6

s.94, enabling: SI 2012/9

1998– cont.

31. School Standards and Framework Act 1998– *cont.*

s.95, applied: SI 2012/9 Reg.5, Sch.1 para.3

s.95, enabling: SI 2012/9

s.100, applied: SI 2012/8 Reg.5

s.100, enabling: SI 2012/8

s.101, applied: SI 2012/8 Reg.11

s.102, applied: SI 2012/8 Reg.5, Reg.6

s.102, enabling: SI 2012/8

s.103, applied: SI 2012/8 Reg.13

s.104, applied: SI 2012/8 Reg.21

s.104, referred to: SI 2012/8 Reg.8, Reg.13

s.105, applied: SI 2012/8 Reg.21

s.106, applied: SI 2012/8 Reg.21

s.107, applied: SI 2012/8 Reg.21

s.108, applied: SI 2012/8 Reg.13, Reg.21

s.109, applied: SI 2012/8 Reg.13, Reg.21

s.124B, amended: SI 2012/976 Sch.1 para.9

s.124B, applied: SI 2012/967, SI 2012/2265, SI 2012/3174

s.138, enabling: SI 2012/8, SI 2012/9, SI 2012/10, SI 2012/335, SI 2012/2261, SI 2012/2991

s.142, applied: SI 2012/811 Sch.1 para.4

Sch.1A para.17, applied: SI 2012/1643 Reg.5

Sch.1A para.18, referred to: SI 2012/1643 Reg.15

Sch.1A para.19, enabling: SI 2012/1643

Sch.14 para.2A, applied: SI 2012/335 Reg.27, SI 2012/2991 Reg.27

Sch.14 para.2B, enabling: SI 2012/335, SI 2012/2991

Sch.15, applied: SI 2012/1035 Reg.29

Sch.15 para.1, varied: SI 2012/1035 Sch.8 para.4

Sch.15 para.2, varied: SI 2012/1035 Sch.8 para.4

Sch.15 para.4, varied: SI 2012/1035 Sch.8 para.4

Sch.22 Part II para.7, applied: SI 2012/1035 Reg.41

34. Private Hire Vehicles (London) Act 1998

s.7, applied: SI 2012/2112 Reg.26

36. Finance Act 1998

s.32, amended: 2012 c.14 Sch.20 para.16

s.123, repealed (in part): 2012 c.14 Sch.16 para.247

Sch.5 Part III para.39, repealed: 2012 c.14 Sch.16 para.247

Sch.18, see *Marks & Spencer Plc v Revenue and Customs Commissioners* [2011] EWCA Civ 1156, [2012] S.T.C. 231 (CA (Civ Div)), Lloyd, L.J.

Sch.18 Part I para.1, amended: 2012 c.14 Sch.20 para.17

Sch.18 Part II para.3, applied: SI 2012/1836 Reg.9

Sch.18 Part II para.8, amended: 2012 c.14 Sch.20 para.17

Sch.18 Part II para.9, amended: 2012 c.14 Sch.15 para.14

Sch.18 Part II para.14, applied: SI 2012/1836 Reg.12

Sch.18 Part IV para.34, applied: 2012 c.14 Sch.17 para.17

Sch.18 Part VII para.57, amended: 2012 c.14 Sch.15 para.15

Sch.18 Pt VIII para.69, see *Marks & Spencer Plc v Revenue and Customs Commissioners* [2011] EWCA Civ 1156, [2012] S.T.C. 231 (CA (Civ Div)), Lloyd, L.J.

Sch.18 Pt VIII para.74, see *R. (on the application of Bampton Property Group Ltd) v King* [2012] EWHC 361 (Admin), [2012] S.T.C. 1321 (QBD (Admin)), Blair, J.

37. Crime and Disorder Act 1998

Commencement Orders: 2012 c.10 s.118

applied: SI 2012/1726 r.13.2

s.1, see *B v DPP* [2012] EWHC 72 (Admin), [2012] 1 W.L.R. 2357 (DC), Sir John Thomas (President)

1998– cont.

37. Crime and Disorder Act 1998–*cont.*
s.1B, applied: 2012 c.10 Sch.1 para.36
s.1C, see *R. v Brzezinski (Tomaosz Adam)* [2012]
EWCA Crim 198, [2012] 2 Cr. App. R. (S.) 62
(CA (Crim Div)), Davis, L.J.; see *R. v Moore
(Samuel George)* [2011] EWCA Crim 1100,
[2012] 1 Cr. App. R. (S.) 5 (CA (Crim Div)),
Richards, L.J.
s.1C, applied: SI 2012/1726 r.50.1
s.1CA, applied: SI 2012/1726 r.50.1
s.1D, applied: 2012 c.10 Sch.1 para.36, SI 2012/1726
r.50.1
s.1G, applied: 2012 c.10 Sch.1 para.36
s.2, see *R. v Shields (David)* [2011] EWCA Crim
2343, [2012] 1 Cr. App. R. 9 (CA (Crim Div)),
Rix, L.J.
s.2, applied: SI 2012/1726 r.9.2
s.3, applied: SI 2012/1726 r.9.2
s.5, amended: 2012 c.7 Sch.5 para.84
s.5, applied: SI 2012/1020 Sch.1
s.5A, applied: SI 2012/1020 Sch.1
s.6, applied: SI 2012/1020 Sch.1
s.6, enabling: SI 2012/2660
s.8, applied: 2012 c.10 Sch.1 para.1, SI 2012/1726
r.50.1
s.8A, applied: SI 2012/1726 r.50.1
s.8A, referred to: SI 2012/1726 r.50.2
s.9, applied: SI 2012/1726 r.50.1
s.9, referred to: SI 2012/1726 r.50.2
s.10, applied: SI 2012/1726 r.63.1
s.11, applied: 2012 c.10 Sch.1 para.1
s.32, amended: 2012 c.9 Sch.9 para.144
s.38, amended: 2012 c.7 Sch.5 para.85, 2012 c.10
Sch.12 para.37, Sch.24 para.15
s.39, amended: 2012 c.7 Sch.5 para.86, Sch.5 para.87
s.40, applied: SI 2012/1020 Sch.1
s.41, amended: 2012 c.7 Sch.5 para.88
s.41, repealed (in part): 2012 c.10 Sch.12 para.38
s.42, amended: 2012 c.7 Sch.5 para.89
s.47, applied: SI 2012/1726 r.37.1
s.50, amended: 2012 c.10 Sch.5 para.47
s.50, repealed (in part): 2012 c.10 Sch.5 para.47
s.50A, applied: SI 2012/1726 r.9.1
s.50A, referred to: SI 2012/1726 r.9.1, r.9.2
s.51, applied: SI 2012/1320 Art.5, Art.6, SI 2012/
1726 r.14.1, r.8.1, r.9.1, r.3.11, r.13.2
s.51, referred to: SI 2012/1726 r.9.1, r.9.2, r.9.3, r.9.5,
r.9.7, r.9.14, r.13.1
s.51A, amended: 2012 c.10 Sch.21 para.6
s.51A, applied: SI 2012/1726 r.14.1, r.9.1, r.3.11
s.51A, referred to: SI 2012/1726 r.9.1, r.9.2, r.9.7
s.51B, amended: 2012 c.10 Sch.5 para.48
s.51B, applied: SI 2012/1726 r.9.1, r.9.6
s.51B, referred to: SI 2012/1726 r.11.1
s.51C, applied: SI 2012/1726 r.9.1, r.9.6
s.51C, referred to: SI 2012/1726 r.11.1, r.9.6
s.51D, applied: SI 2012/1726 r.14.1, r.9.1
s.51D, referred to: SI 2012/1726 r.9.3, r.9.5
s.51E, applied: SI 2012/1726 r.9.1
s.51E, referred to: SI 2012/1726 r.9.7
s.52, applied: SI 2012/1726 r.9.1
s.52, referred to: SI 2012/1726 r.9.2, r.13.1
s.52A, amended: 2012 c.10 Sch.5 para.49
s.52A, applied: SI 2012/1726 r.9.2, r.16.1
s.57A, amended: 2012 c.10 Sch.12 para.39
s.57A, applied: SI 2012/1726 r.9.2, r.19.2
s.57B, applied: SI 2012/1726 r.9.2, r.19.2
s.57C, applied: SI 2012/1726 r.9.2

1998– cont.

37. Crime and Disorder Act 1998–*cont.*
s.57D, applied: SI 2012/1726 r.9.2, r.37.10
s.57E, applied: SI 2012/1726 r.9.2, r.37.10
s.65, applied: 2012 c.9 s.98, 2012 c.10 s.135
s.65, repealed: 2012 c.10 s.135
s.66, applied: 2012 c.9 s.98, 2012 c.10 s.135
s.66, repealed: 2012 c.10 s.135
s.66A, amended: 2012 c.10 s.137, s.138
s.66A, repealed (in part): 2012 c.10 s.136
s.66B, amended: 2012 c.10 s.138
s.66C, amended: 2012 c.10 s.138
s.66D, amended: 2012 c.10 s.138
s.66G, amended: 2012 c.10 s.138
s.66H, amended: 2012 c.10 Sch.24 para.16
s.66ZA, added: 2012 c.10 s.135
s.66ZA, applied: 2012 c.10 s.135
s.66ZB, added: 2012 c.10 s.135
s.66ZB, applied: 2012 c.10 s.135
s.97, repealed: 2012 c.10 Sch.12 para.40
s.98, applied: 2012 c.10 s.94, s.99, Sch.5 para.5, SI
2012/2824 Reg.2, SI 2012/2906 Art.7
s.98, repealed: 2012 c.10 Sch.12 para.40
s.115, amended: 2012 c.7 Sch.5 para.90
s.115, applied: SI 2012/1726 r.5.9
s.115, repealed (in part): 2012 c.7 Sch.5 para.90
s.121, repealed (in part): 2012 c.10 Sch.24 para.17
Sch.3, referred to: SI 2012/1726 r.13.1
Sch.3 para.1, applied: SI 2012/1320 Art.6, SI 2012/
1726 r.13.2, r.13.3, r.13.4
Sch.3 para.1, referred to: SI 2012/1320 Art.6, SI
2012/1726 r.14.1
Sch.3 para.1, enabling: SI 2012/1345
Sch.3 para.2, applied: SI 2012/1726 r.13.2, r.13.3,
r.13.4
Sch.3 para.3, amended: 2012 c.10 Sch.5 para.50
Sch.3 para.3, applied: SI 2012/1726 r.16.1
Sch.8 para.35, repealed (in part): 2012 c.10 Sch.25
Part 2
Sch.8 para.86, repealed: 2012 c.10 s.118
Sch.8 para.90, repealed: 2012 c.10 s.118
Sch.9 para.5, applied: 2012 c.10 s.135

38. Government of Wales Act 1998
Sch.4 Part I para.13, repealed (in part): SI 2012/990
Art.6

39. National Minimum Wage Act 1998
s.1, enabling: SI 2012/2397
s.2, enabling: SI 2012/2397
s.3, enabling: SI 2012/2397
s.44A, amended: SI 2012/976 Sch.1 para.10
s.45, amended: 2012 c.10 s.129
s.51, applied: SI 2012/2397
s.51, enabling: SI 2012/2397
Sch.1 para.1, amended: SI 2012/2404 Sch.2 para.40

41. Competition Act 1998
see *Barrett Estate Services Ltd v Office of Fair
Trading* [2012] Comp. A.R. 14 (CAT), Lord
Carlile of Berriew Q.C.; see *Crest Nicholson
Plc v Office of Fair Trading (Costs)* [2012]
Comp. A.R. 21 (CAT), Lord Carlile of Berriew
Q.C.; see *Eden Brown Ltd v Office of Fair Trading*
[2012] Comp. A.R. 30 (CAT), Roth, J.; see *GF
Tomlinson Group Ltd v Office of Fair Trading
(Costs)* [2012] Comp. A.R. 47 (CAT), Vivien
Rose (Chairman); see *North Midland
Construction Plc v Office of Fair Trading
(Costs)* [2012] Comp. A.R. 106 (CAT), Barling,
J. (President); see *Tesco Stores Ltd v Office of Fair
Trading* [2012] CAT 6, [2012] Comp. A.R. 188
(CAT), Lord Carlile of Berriew Q.C.

1998– cont.

41. Competition Act 1998–*cont.*
applied: 2012 c.7 s.74, s.80, 2012 c.19 s.46, s.77, SI
    2012/ 1128 Art.4
referred to: 2012 c.19 Sch.6 para.4
Part I, applied: 2012 c.7 s.72
Part I, referred to: 2012 c.19 s.6
Part I c.I, disapplied: SI 2012/ 710, SI 2012/ 710 Art.4
s.1, applied: 2012 c.19 s.62, s.63
s.1, varied: 2012 c.7 s.72
s.2, see *Imperial Tobacco Group Plc v Office of Fair
    Trading* [2012] Comp. A.R. 61 (CAT), Vivien
    Rose (Chairman)
s.2, applied: 2012 c.7 s.72, 2012 c.19 s.62, s.63
s.2, referred to: 2012 c.19 s.62
s.2, varied: 2012 c.7 s.72
s.3, applied: 2012 c.19 s.62, s.63
s.3, varied: 2012 c.7 s.72
s.4, applied: 2012 c.19 s.62, s.63
s.4, varied: 2012 c.7 s.72
s.5, applied: 2012 c.19 s.62, s.63
s.5, varied: 2012 c.7 s.72
s.6, applied: 2012 c.19 s.62, s.63
s.6, varied: 2012 c.7 s.72
s.7, applied: 2012 c.19 s.62, s.63
s.7, varied: 2012 c.7 s.72
s.8, applied: 2012 c.19 s.62, s.63
s.8, varied: 2012 c.7 s.72
s.9, applied: 2012 c.19 s.62, s.63
s.9, varied: 2012 c.7 s.72
s.10, amended: SI 2012/ 1809 Sch.1 Part 1
s.10, applied: 2012 c.19 s.62, s.63
s.10, varied: 2012 c.7 s.72
s.11, amended: SI 2012/ 1809 Sch.1 Part 1
s.11, applied: 2012 c.19 s.62, s.63
s.11, varied: 2012 c.7 s.72
s.12, applied: 2012 c.19 s.62, s.63
s.12, varied: 2012 c.7 s.72
s.13, applied: 2012 c.19 s.62, s.63
s.13, varied: 2012 c.7 s.72
s.14, applied: 2012 c.19 s.62, s.63
s.14, varied: 2012 c.7 s.72
s.15, applied: 2012 c.19 s.62, s.63
s.15, varied: 2012 c.7 s.72
s.16, applied: 2012 c.19 s.62, s.63
s.16, varied: 2012 c.7 s.72
s.17, applied: 2012 c.19 s.62, s.63
s.17, varied: 2012 c.7 s.72
s.18, see *2 Travel Group Plc (In Liquidation) v
    Cardiff City Transport Services Ltd* [2012] CAT
    19, [2012] Comp. A.R. 211 (CAT), Lord Carlile of
    Berriew Q.C.; see *Humber Oil Terminals Trustee
    Ltd v Associated British Ports* [2012] EWCA Civ
    36, [2012] U.K.C.L.R. 71 (CA (Civ Div)),
    Mummery, L.J.
s.18, applied: 2012 c.7 s.72, 2012 c.19 s.62, s.63
s.18, referred to: 2012 c.19 s.6, s.18, s.62
s.18, varied: 2012 c.7 s.72
s.19, applied: 2012 c.19 s.62, s.63
s.19, varied: 2012 c.7 s.72
s.20, applied: 2012 c.19 s.62, s.63
s.20, varied: 2012 c.7 s.72
s.21, applied: 2012 c.19 s.62, s.63
s.21, varied: 2012 c.7 s.72
s.22, applied: 2012 c.19 s.62, s.63
s.22, varied: 2012 c.7 s.72
s.23, applied: 2012 c.19 s.62, s.63
s.23, varied: 2012 c.7 s.72
s.24, applied: 2012 c.19 s.62, s.63

1998– cont.

41. Competition Act 1998–*cont.*
s.24, varied: 2012 c.7 s.72
s.25, amended: SI 2012/ 1809 Sch.1 Part 1
s.25, applied: 2012 c.19 s.62, s.63
s.25, varied: 2012 c.7 s.72
s.26, applied: 2012 c.19 s.62, s.63
s.26, varied: 2012 c.7 s.72
s.27, applied: 2012 c.19 s.62, s.63
s.27, varied: 2012 c.7 s.72
s.28, applied: 2012 c.19 s.62, s.63
s.28, varied: 2012 c.7 s.72
s.28A, applied: 2012 c.19 s.62, s.63
s.28A, varied: 2012 c.7 s.72
s.29, applied: 2012 c.19 s.62, s.63
s.29, varied: 2012 c.7 s.72
s.30, applied: 2012 c.19 s.62, s.63
s.30, varied: 2012 c.7 s.72
s.30A, applied: 2012 c.19 s.62, s.63
s.30A, varied: 2012 c.7 s.72
s.31, amended: SI 2012/ 1809 Sch.1 Part 1
s.31, applied: 2012 c.19 s.62, s.63
s.31, varied: 2012 c.7 s.72
s.31A, applied: 2012 c.19 s.62, s.63
s.31A, varied: 2012 c.7 s.72
s.31B, applied: 2012 c.19 s.62, s.63
s.31B, varied: 2012 c.7 s.72
s.31C, applied: 2012 c.19 s.62, s.63
s.31C, varied: 2012 c.7 s.72
s.31D, applied: 2012 c.19 s.62, s.63
s.31D, disapplied: 2012 c.7 s.72
s.31D, referred to: 2012 c.7 s.72
s.31D, varied: 2012 c.7 s.72
s.31E, applied: 2012 c.19 s.62, s.63
s.31E, varied: 2012 c.7 s.72
s.32, amended: SI 2012/ 1809 Sch.1 Part 1
s.32, applied: 2012 c.19 s.62, s.63
s.32, varied: 2012 c.7 s.72
s.33, amended: SI 2012/ 1809 Sch.1 Part 1
s.33, applied: 2012 c.19 s.62, s.63
s.33, varied: 2012 c.7 s.72
s.34, applied: 2012 c.19 s.62, s.63
s.34, varied: 2012 c.7 s.72
s.35, see *Ryanair Holdings Plc v Office of Fair
    Trading* [2011] EWCA Civ 1579, [2012] Bus.
    L.R. 1903 (CA (Civ Div)), Lloyd, L.J.
s.35, amended: SI 2012/ 1809 Sch.1 Part 1
s.35, applied: 2012 c.19 s.62, s.63
s.35, varied: 2012 c.7 s.72
s.36, amended: SI 2012/ 1809 Sch.1 Part 1
s.36, applied: 2012 c.19 s.62, s.63
s.36, varied: 2012 c.7 s.72
s.37, applied: 2012 c.19 s.62, s.63
s.37, varied: 2012 c.7 s.72
s.38, applied: 2012 c.19 s.62, s.63
s.38, disapplied: 2012 c.7 s.72
s.38, referred to: 2012 c.7 s.72
s.38, varied: 2012 c.7 s.72
s.39, applied: 2012 c.19 s.62, s.63
s.39, varied: 2012 c.7 s.72
s.40, see *2 Travel Group Plc (In Liquidation) v
    Cardiff City Transport Services Ltd* [2012] CAT
    19, [2012] Comp. A.R. 211 (CAT), Lord Carlile of
    Berriew Q.C.
s.40, applied: 2012 c.19 s.62, s.63
s.40, varied: 2012 c.7 s.72
s.41, applied: 2012 c.19 s.62, s.63
s.41, varied: 2012 c.7 s.72
s.42, applied: 2012 c.19 s.62, s.63

41. Competition Act 1998–*cont.*
s.42, varied: 2012 c.7 s.72
s.43, applied: 2012 c.19 s.62, s.63
s.43, varied: 2012 c.7 s.72
s.44, applied: 2012 c.19 s.62, s.63
s.44, varied: 2012 c.7 s.72
s.45, applied: 2012 c.19 s.62, s.63
s.45, varied: 2012 c.7 s.72
s.46, amended: SI 2012/ 1809 Sch.1 Part 1
s.46, applied: 2012 c.19 s.62, s.63
s.46, varied: 2012 c.7 s.72
s.47, applied: 2012 c.19 s.62, s.63
s.47, varied: 2012 c.7 s.72
s.47A, see *2 Travel Group Plc (In Liquidation) v Cardiff City Transport Services Ltd* [2012] CAT 19, [2012] Comp. A.R. 211 (CAT), Lord Carlile of Berriew Q.C.; see *2 Travel Group Plc (In Liquidation) v Cardiff City Transport Services Ltd* [2012] Comp. A.R. 1 (CAT), Lord Carlile of Berriew Q.C.; see *2 Travel Group Plc (In Liquidation) v Cardiff City Transport Services Ltd* [2012] Comp. A.R. 121 (CAT), Lord Carlile of Berriew Q.C.; see *Albion Water Ltd v Dwr Cymru Cyfyngedig* [2012] Comp. A.R. 127 (CAT), Vivien Rose (Chairman); see *BCL Old Co Ltd v BASF SE (formerly BASF AG)* [2012] UKSC 45, [2012] 1 W.L.R. 2922 (SC), Lord Phillips, J.S.C.; see *Deutsche Bahn AG v Morgan Crucible Co Plc* [2012] EWCA Civ 1055, [2012] U.K.C.L.R. 279 (CA (Civ Div)), Mummery, L.J.
s.47A, amended: SI 2012/ 1809 Sch.1 Part 1
s.47A, applied: 2012 c.19 s.62, s.63
s.47A, varied: 2012 c.7 s.72
s.47B, applied: 2012 c.19 s.62, s.63
s.47B, varied: 2012 c.7 s.72
s.48, applied: 2012 c.19 s.62, s.63
s.48, varied: 2012 c.7 s.72
s.49, applied: 2012 c.19 s.62, s.63
s.49, varied: 2012 c.7 s.72
s.50, applied: 2012 c.19 s.62, s.63
s.50, varied: 2012 c.7 s.72
s.51, disapplied: 2012 c.7 s.72
s.51, referred to: 2012 c.7 s.72
s.51, varied: 2012 c.7 s.72
s.52, amended: SI 2012/ 1809 Sch.1 Part 1
s.52, applied: 2012 c.19 s.6, s.62, s.63
s.52, referred to: 2012 c.7 s.72
s.52, varied: 2012 c.7 s.72
s.53, applied: 2012 c.19 s.62, s.63
s.53, varied: 2012 c.7 s.72
s.54, amended: 2012 c.7 s.74
s.54, applied: 2012 c.19 s.62, s.63
s.54, referred to: 2012 c.7 s.72
s.54, varied: 2012 c.7 s.72
s.55, applied: 2012 c.19 s.62, s.63
s.55, varied: 2012 c.7 s.72
s.56, applied: 2012 c.19 s.62, s.63
s.56, varied: 2012 c.7 s.72
s.57, applied: 2012 c.19 s.62, s.63
s.57, varied: 2012 c.7 s.72
s.58, amended: SI 2012/ 1809 Sch.1 Part 1
s.58, applied: 2012 c.19 s.62, s.63
s.58, varied: 2012 c.7 s.72
s.58A, amended: SI 2012/ 1809 Sch.1 Part 1
s.58A, applied: 2012 c.19 s.62, s.63
s.58A, varied: 2012 c.7 s.72
s.59, amended: SI 2012/ 1809 Sch.1 Part 1
s.59, applied: 2012 c.19 s.62, s.63

41. Competition Act 1998–*cont.*
s.59, varied: 2012 c.7 s.72
s.60, applied: 2012 c.19 s.62, s.63
s.60, varied: 2012 c.7 s.72
s.61, amended: SI 2012/ 1809 Sch.1 Part 1
s.62A, amended: SI 2012/ 1809 Sch.1 Part 1
s.65C, amended: SI 2012/ 1809 Sch.1 Part 1
s.65D, amended: SI 2012/ 1809 Sch.1 Part 1
s.73, applied: 2012 c.19 s.77
Sch.2 Part I para.1, repealed: 2012 c.21 Sch.19
Sch.3 para.7, enabling: SI 2012/ 710
Sch.3 para.9, amended: SI 2012/ 1809 Sch.1 Part 1
Sch.7 Part II, applied: 2012 c.7 s.120, 2012 c.19 s.30
Sch.7 Part II para.15, applied: 2012 c.7 Sch.10 para.6
Sch.7 Part II para.19A, amended: 2012 c.21 Sch.19
Sch.7 Part II para.19A, repealed (in part): 2012 c.19 Sch.9 para.9, 2012 c.21 Sch.19
Sch.8 Pt I para.3, see *Imperial Tobacco Group Plc v Office of Fair Trading* [2012] Comp. A.R. 61 (CAT), Vivien Rose (Chairman); see *Tesco Stores Ltd v Office of Fair Trading* [2012] CAT 9, [2012] Comp. A.R. 208 (CAT), Lord Carlile of Berriew Q.C.
Sch.9 para.5, amended: SI 2012/ 1809 Sch.1 Part 1
Sch.12 para.8, repealed: 2012 c.21 Sch.19
Sch.13 Part IV para.26, amended: 2012 c.21 Sch.19
Sch.13 Part IV para.26, repealed (in part): 2012 c.21 Sch.19

42. Human Rights Act 1998
see *A (A Child) (Disclosure of Third Party Information), Re* [2012] UKSC 60, [2012] 3 W.L.R. 1484 (SC), Lord Neuberger, J.S.C.; see *A Local Authority v DL* [2011] EWHC 1022 (Fam), [2012] 1 F.L.R. 1119 (Fam Div), Theis, J.; see *All Saints', Sanderstead, Re* [2012] Fam. 51 (Cons Ct (Southwark)), Chancellor Petchey; see *Beggs (William Frederick Ian) v HM Advocate* 2012 J.C. 173 (HCJ), Lord Justice General Hamilton; see *DD v Durham CC* [2012] EWHC 1053 (QB), [2012] Med. L.R. 348 (QBD), Eady, J.; see *G v A (Financial Remedy: Enforcement) (No.2)* [2011] EWHC 968 (Fam), [2012] 1 F.L.R. 402 (Fam Div), Peter Jackson, J.; see *Gifford (Matilda Rosamond) v HM Advocate* 2012 S.C.L. 267 (HCJ), Lord Reed; see *McCaughey's Application for Judicial Review, Re* [2012] 1 A.C. 725 (SC), Lord Phillips (President); see *MS v United Kingdom (24527/08)* (2012) 55 E.H.R.R. 23 (ECHR), Judge Garlicki (President); see *Nicklinson v Ministry of Justice* [2012] EWHC 304 (QB), [2012] H.R.L.R. 16 (QBD), Charles, J.; see *Official Receiver for Northern Ireland v O'Brien* [2012] NICh 12, [2012] B.P.I.R. 826 (Ch D (NI)), Deeny, J.; see *R. (on the application of Ali) v Minister for the Cabinet Office* [2012] EWHC 1943 (Admin), [2012] A.C.D. 89 (QBD (Admin)), Beatson, J.; see *R. (on the application of DL) v Newham LBC* [2011] EWHC 1890 (Admin), [2012] 1 F.L.R. 1 (QBD (Admin)), Charles, J.; see *R. (on the application of W) v Secretary of State for Education* [2011] EWHC 3256 (Admin), [2012] E.L.R. 172 (QBD (Admin)), Singh, J.; see *Rai v Charity Commission for England and Wales* [2012] EWHC 1111 (Ch), [2012] W.T.L.R. 1053 (Ch D), Norris, J.; see *Reynolds v United Kingdom (2694/08)* (2012) 55 E.H.R.R. 35 (ECHR), Judge Garlicki (President); see *S (A Child), Re* [2010] EWCA Civ 1383, [2012] 2

1998–cont.

42. Human Rights Act 1998–*cont.*
see–*cont.*

F.L.R. 209 (CA (Civ Div)), Sir Nicholas Wall (President, Fam)

applied: 2012 c.10 s.10, s.32, Sch.3 para.2, SI 2012/1726 r.65.12, SI 2012/3098 Reg.54

referred to: SI 2012/1204 Reg.30

s.1, see *Young v Young* [2012] EWHC 138 (Fam), [2012] Fam. 198 (Fam Div), Mostyn, J.

s.2, see *Erskine 1948 Trust, Re* [2012] EWHC 732 (Ch), [2012] 3 W.L.R. 913 (Ch D), Mark Herbert Q.C.; see *Secretary of State for Justice v RB* [2011] EWCA Civ 1608, [2012] 1 W.L.R. 2043 (CA (Civ Div)), Maurice Kay, L.J.

s.3, see *Apollo Engineering Ltd v James Scott Ltd* [2012] CSIH 4, 2012 S.C. 282 (IH (Ex Div)), Lady Paton; see *DM v Doncaster MBC* [2011] EWHC 3652 (Admin), (2012) 15 C.C.L. Rep. 128 (QBD (Admin)), Langstaff, J.; see *Freetown Ltd v Assethold Ltd* [2012] EWHC 1351 (QB), [2012] 4 All E.R. 194 (QBD), Slade, J.; see *I v Dunn* [2012] HCJAC 108, 2012 S.L.T. 983 (HCJ), Lady Paton; see *R. (on the application of Chen) v Secretary of State for the Home Department* [2012] EWHC 2531 (Admin), [2012] H.R.L.R. 33 (QBD (Admin)), Beatson, J.; see *S v L* [2012] UKSC 30, 2012 S.L.T. 961 (SC), Lord Hope, J.S.C.; see *Thomas v Bridgend CBC* [2011] EWCA Civ 862, [2012] Q.B. 512 (CA (Civ Div)), Mummery, L.J.

s.4, see *Eco-Hygiene Ltd v Revenue and Customs Commissioners* [2012] S.F.T.D. 510 (FTT (Tax)), Judge Roger Berner; see *Practice Direction (Sen Cts: Upper Tribunal: Judicial Review Jurisdiction)* [2012] 1 W.L.R. 16 (Sen Cts), Lord Judge, L.C.J.

s.4, applied: SI 2012/1726 r.65.12, SI 2012/1883

s.5, varied: 2012 c.11 s.12

s.6, see *Merchant International Co Ltd v Natsionalna Aktsionerna Kompaniya Naftogaz Ukrayiny* [2012] EWCA Civ 196, [2012] 1 W.L.R. 3036 (CA (Civ Div)), Lord Neuberger (M.R.); see *R. (on the application of HA (Nigeria)) v Secretary of State for the Home Department* [2012] EWHC 979 (Admin), [2012] Med. L.R. 353 (QBD (Admin)), Singh, J.; see *Thour v Royal Free Hampstead NHS Trust* [2012] EWHC 1473 (QB), (2012) 128 B.M.L.R. 137 (QBD), Tugendhat, J.

s.6, applied: 2012 c.10 s.6, 2012 c.21 s.88

s.6, referred to: SI 2012/1033 Sch.1 para.5

s.7, see *Nisbet v Butt* [2012] HCJAC 107, 2012 S.L.T. 1066 (HCJ), Lord Carloway; see *R. (on the application of Broadway Care Centre Ltd) v Caerphilly CBC* [2012] EWHC 37 (Admin), (2012) 15 C.C.L. Rep. 82 (QBD (Admin)), Judge Seys-Llewellyn Q.C.; see *R. (on the application of South West Care Homes Ltd) v Devon CC* [2012] EWHC 1867 (Admin), [2012] A.C.D. 108 (QBD (Admin)), Singh, J.; see *Rabone v Pennine Care NHS Foundation Trust* [2012] UKSC 2, [2012] 2 A.C. 72 (SC), Lord Walker, J.S.C.

s.7, applied: 2012 c.10 Sch.1 para.12

s.8, see *A v Lancashire CC* [2012] EWHC 1689 (Fam), (2012) 15 C.C.L. Rep. 471 (Fam Div), Peter Jackson, J.; see *H (Care Plan: Human Rights), Re* [2011] EWCA Civ 1009, [2012] 1 F.L.R. 191 (CA (Civ Div)), Black, L.J.; see *R. (on the application of Sturnham) v Parole Board* [2012] EWCA Civ 452, [2012] 3 W.L.R.

1998–cont.

42. Human Rights Act 1998–*cont.*
s.8–*cont.*

476 (CA (Civ Div)), Laws, L.J.; see *R. (on the application of Waxman) v Crown Prosecution Service* [2012] EWHC 133 (Admin), (2012) 176 J.P. 121 (QBD (Admin)), Moore-Bick, L.J.

s.10, enabling: SI 2012/1883

s.12, see *CVB v MGN Ltd* [2012] EWHC 1148 (QB), [2012] E.M.L.R. 29 (QBD), Tugendhat, J.; see *Hutcheson v News Group Newspapers Ltd* [2011] EWCA Civ 808, [2012] E.M.L.R. 2 (CA (Civ Div)), Lord Neuberger (M.R.); see *Practice Guidance (HC: Interim Non-Disclosure Orders)* [2012] 1 W.L.R. 1003 (Sen Cts), Lord Neuberger (M.R.); see *RB (An Adult), Re* [2011] EWHC 3017 (Fam), [2012] 1 F.L.R. 466 (Fam Div), Munby, L.J.

s.18, enabling: SI 2012/489

s.21, varied: 2012 c.11 s.12

Sch.2 para.1, enabling: SI 2012/1883

Sch.2 para.2, applied: SI 2012/1883

Sch.2 para.3, applied: SI 2012/1883

Sch.4, enabling: SI 2012/489

45. Regional Development Agencies Act 1998

s.14, applied: SI 2012/1471 Art.2

s.15, applied: SI 2012/1471 Art.2

s.17, applied: SI 2012/1471 Art.2

46. Scotland Act 1998

referred to: SI 2012/700 Art.3

varied: SI 2012/700 Art.3

Part IVA, applied: 2012 asp 2 Sch.1

Part V, amended: 2012 c.11 s.12

s.12, amended: 2012 c.11 s.1

s.12, repealed (in part): 2012 c.11 s.1

s.12A, added: 2012 c.11 s.1

s.19, amended: 2012 c.11 s.4

s.21, amended: 2012 c.11 s.5

s.23, amended: 2012 c.11 s.12

s.29, see *AXA General Insurance Ltd, Petitioners* [2012] 1 A.C. 868 (SC), Lord Hope (Deputy President); see *Cameron v Cottam* [2012] HCJAC 19, 2012 S.L.T 173 (HCJ), Lord Eassie; see *Imperial Tobacco Ltd, Petitioner* [2012] CSIH 9, 2012 S.C. 297 (IH (1 Div)), Lord President Hamilton; see *Imperial Tobacco Ltd, Petitioner* [2012] UKSC 61 (SC), Lord Hope, J.S.C. (Deputy President); see *S v L* 2012 S.C. 8 (IH (1 Div)), The Lord President (Hamilton)

s.29, amended: 2012 c.11 s.9

s.30, amended: 2012 c.11 s.9

s.31, amended: 2012 c.11 s.6

s.34, amended: SI 2012/1809 Sch.1 Part 1

s.39, amended: 2012 c.11 s.7

s.44, see *Kinloch v HM Advocate* [2012] UKSC 62 (SC), Lord Hope, J.S.C. (Deputy President)

s.44, amended: 2012 c.11 s.12

s.45, amended: 2012 c.11 s.12

s.47, amended: 2012 c.11 s.12

s.48, amended: 2012 c.11 s.12

s.49, amended: 2012 c.11 s.12

s.50, amended: 2012 c.11 s.12

s.52, amended: 2012 c.11 s.12

s.55, amended: 2012 c.11 s.12

s.57, see *BBC, Applicants* [2012] HCJ 2, 2012 S.C.L. 347 (HCJ), Lord Carloway; see *Docherty v Scottish Ministers* 2012 S.C. 150 (IH (1 Div)), The Lord President (Hamilton); see *H v Lord*

1998– cont.
46. Scotland Act 1998–*cont.*
s.57–*cont.*
  Advocate [2012] UKSC 24, [2012] 3 W.L.R. 151
  (SC), Lord Hope (Deputy President)
s.57, amended: 2012 c.11 s.12, s.36
s.58, amended: 2012 c.11 s.12
s.59, amended: 2012 c.11 s.12
s.62, amended: 2012 c.11 s.12
s.64, applied: 2012 c.11 s.33
s.65, applied: 2012 asp 2 s.5, s.6
s.66, amended: 2012 c.11 s.12, s.32
s.67, amended: 2012 c.11 s.32
s.67A, added: 2012 c.11 s.32
s.68, amended: 2012 c.11 s.12
s.69, amended: 2012 c.11 s.12
s.70, amended: 2012 c.11 s.12
s.73, repealed: 2012 c.11 s.25
s.74, repealed: 2012 c.11 s.25
s.75, amended: 2012 c.11 s.27
s.75, repealed: 2012 c.11 s.25
s.76, repealed: 2012 c.11 s.25
s.77, repealed: 2012 c.11 s.25
s.78, repealed: 2012 c.11 s.25
s.79, repealed: 2012 c.11 s.25
s.80, repealed: 2012 c.11 s.25
s.80A, added: 2012 c.11 s.23
s.80B, added: 2012 c.11 s.23
s.80C, added: 2012 c.11 s.23, s.25
s.80D, added: 2012 c.11 s.23, s.25
s.80E, added: 2012 c.11 s.23, s.25
s.80F, added: 2012 c.11 s.23, s.25
s.80G, added: 2012 c.11 s.23, s.25
s.80H, added: 2012 c.11 s.23, s.25
s.80I, added: 2012 c.11 s.23, s.28
s.80J, added: 2012 c.11 s.23, s.28
s.80K, added: 2012 c.11 s.23, s.30
s.81, amended: 2012 c.11 s.12
s.84, amended: 2012 c.11 s.12
s.85, amended: 2012 c.11 s.12
s.88, applied: SI 2012/958, SI 2012/959, SI 2012/
  1658, SI 2012/1659, SI 2012/2855
s.90A, added: 2012 c.11 s.16
s.91, amended: 2012 c.11 s.12
s.92, amended: 2012 c.11 s.9, s.12, s.13
s.93, amended: 2012 c.11 s.23
s.97, amended: 2012 c.11 s.12
s.100, see *Docherty v Scottish Ministers* 2012 S.C.
  150 (IH (1 Div), The Lord President
  (Hamilton); see *Jude (Raymond) v HM
  Advocate* 2012 S.C. (U.K.S.C.) 222 (SC), Lord
  Hope (Deputy President)
s.100, amended: 2012 c.11 s.12, s.14
s.100, repealed (in part): 2012 c.11 s.14
s.101, amended: 2012 c.11 s.12
s.102, amended: 2012 c.11 s.12, s.15, s.36
s.104, amended: 2012 c.11 s.12, s.13
s.104, enabling: SI 2012/700, SI 2012/1852, SI 2012/
  2855
s.107, amended: 2012 c.11 s.12
s.108, amended: 2012 c.11 s.12
s.109, amended: 2012 c.11 s.12
s.110, amended: 2012 c.11 Sch.2 para.1
s.112, amended: 2012 c.11 s.12, s.13
s.112, enabling: SI 2012/700, SI 2012/1852, SI 2012/
  2855
s.113, amended: 2012 c.11 s.3, s.39
s.113, varied: 2012 c.11 s.39

1998– cont.
46. Scotland Act 1998–*cont.*
s.113, enabling: SI 2012/700, SI 2012/1852, SI 2012/
  2855
s.114, amended: 2012 c.11 s.32
s.114, enabling: SI 2012/700
s.115, applied: SI 2012/700, SI 2012/2855
s.117, amended: 2012 c.11 s.12
s.118, amended: 2012 c.11 s.12
s.122, amended: 2012 c.11 s.12
s.126, see *Imperial Tobacco Ltd, Petitioner* [2012]
  CSIH 9, 2012 S.C. 297 (IH (1 Div)), Lord
  President Hamilton
s.126, amended: 2012 c.11 s.12
s.126, applied: 2012 c.11 s.33, SI 2012/3073 Art.2, SSI
  2012/88 Reg.50
s.126, enabling: SI 2012/3073
s.127, amended: 2012 c.11 s.12, s.23
Sch.1, repealed: 2012 c.11 Sch.1 para.3
Sch.1 para.1, amended: 2012 c.11 Sch.1 para.8
Sch.1 para.2, amended: 2012 c.11 Sch.1 para.9
Sch.1 para.3, amended: 2012 c.11 Sch.1 para.2
Sch.1 para.4, amended: 2012 c.11 Sch.1 para.2
Sch.1 para.5, amended: 2012 c.11 Sch.1 para.2
Sch.1 para.7, amended: 2012 c.11 Sch.1 para.2, Sch.1
  para.4
Sch.1 para.7, repealed (in part): 2012 c.11 Sch.1
  para.4
Sch.1 para.8, amended: 2012 c.11 Sch.1 para.2, Sch.1
  para.5
Sch.1 para.8, repealed (in part): 2012 c.11 Sch.1
  para.5
Sch.1 para.9, amended: 2012 c.11 Sch.1 para.2
Sch.1 para.10, amended: 2012 c.11 Sch.1 para.2
Sch.1 para.12, amended: 2012 c.11 Sch.1 para.2,
  Sch.1 para.6, Sch.1 para.10
Sch.1 para.12, repealed: 2012 c.11 Sch.1 para.6, Sch.1
  para.10
Sch.1 para.14, amended: 2012 c.11 Sch.1 para.2
Sch.1 para.14, repealed (in part): 2012 c.11 Sch.1
  para.7
Sch.3 para.5, substituted: 2012 c.11 s.4
Sch.4 Pt I para.1, see *Imperial Tobacco Ltd,
  Petitioner* [2012] CSIH 9, 2012 S.C. 297 (IH (1
  Div)), Lord President Hamilton
Sch.4 Part I para.4, amended: 2012 c.11 Sch.2 para.1
Sch.4 Part I para.4A, repealed: 2012 c.11 s.14
Sch.4 Pt I para.2, see *Imperial Tobacco Ltd,
  Petitioner* [2012] CSIH 9, 2012 S.C. 297 (IH (1
  Div)), Lord President Hamilton; see *Imperial
  Tobacco Ltd, Petitioner* [2012] UKSC 61 (SC),
  Lord Hope, J.S.C. (Deputy President)
Sch.4 Part II para.11, amended: 2012 c.11 s.12, s.13
Sch.5 Pt II, see *Imperial Tobacco Ltd, Petitioner*
  [2012] UKSC 61 (SC), Lord Hope, J.S.C.
  (Deputy President)
Sch.5 Part II, disapplied: 2012 c.7 s.307
Sch.5 Part II para.A.1, amended: 2012 c.11 s.23
Sch.5 Part II para.F.1, amended: 2012 c.5 Sch.14 Part
  1
Sch.5 Part II para.B.4, amended: 2012 c.11 s.10
Sch.5 Part II para.L.7, added: 2012 c.11 s.11
Sch.5 para.C7, see *Imperial Tobacco Ltd, Petitioner*
  [2012] CSIH 9, 2012 S.C. 297 (IH (1 Div)), Lord
  President Hamilton; see *Imperial Tobacco Ltd,
  Petitioner* [2012] UKSC 61 (SC), Lord Hope,
  J.S.C. (Deputy President)
Sch.5 para.C8, see *Imperial Tobacco Ltd,
  Petitioner* [2012] CSIH 9, 2012 S.C. 297 (IH (1
  Div)), Lord President Hamilton; see *Imperial*

1998–cont.

46. Scotland Act 1998–*cont.*

Sch.5 para.C8–*cont.*
Tobacco Ltd, Petitioner [2012] UKSC 61 (SC), Lord Hope, J.S.C. (Deputy President)

Sch.6 Pt I para.1, see *H v Lord Advocate* [2012] UKSC 24, [2012] 3 W.L.R. 151 (SC), Lord Hope (Deputy President); see *Kinloch v HM Advocate* [2012] UKSC 62 (SC), Lord Hope, J.S.C. (Deputy President)

Sch.6 Part I para.1, added: 2012 c.11 s.36
Sch.6 Part I para.1, amended: 2012 c.11 s.12
Sch.6 Part II para.13A, added: 2012 c.11 s.37
Sch.6 Part II para.13B, added: 2012 c.11 s.37
Sch.6 Part V para.35, amended: 2012 c.11 s.12
Sch.6 Pt II para.9, see *I v Dunn* [2012] HCJAC 108, 2012 S.L.T. 983 (HCJ), Lady Paton
Sch.6 Pt II para.13, see *H v Lord Advocate* [2012] UKSC 24, [2012] 3 W.L.R. 151 (SC), Lord Hope (Deputy President)
Sch.7 para.1, amended: 2012 c.11 s.3, s.23, s.32, s.39, Sch.2 para.1
Sch.7 para.1, applied: SI 2012/ 700, SI 2012/ 2855
Sch.7 para.2, amended: 2012 c.11 s.3
Sch.7 para.2, applied: SI 2012/ 700, SI 2012/ 2855
Sch.7 para.3, applied: SI 2012/ 700, SI 2012/ 2855
Sch.8 para.7, amended: 2012 c.11 s.12
Sch.8 para.13, amended: 2012 c.11 s.12
Sch.8 para.26, amended: 2012 c.11 s.12
Sch.8 para.31, amended: 2012 c.11 s.12
Sch.8 para.33, amended: 2012 c.11 s.12

47. Northern Ireland Act 1998

referred to: 2012 c.13 Sch.1
s.12, amended: SI 2012/ 1809 Sch.1 Part 1
s.71, see *Northern Ireland Human Rights Commission's Application for Judicial Review, Re* [2012] NIQB 77, [2012] Eq. L.R. 1135 (QBD (NI)), Treacy, J.
s.84, applied: SI 2012/ 3074
s.84, enabling: SI 2012/ 3074
s.86, applied: SI 2012/ 2595
s.86, enabling: SI 2012/ 2595
s.87, enabling: SI 2012/ 2380
Sch.2 para.9C, added: 2012 c.23 s.16

1999

2. Social Security Contributions (Transfer of Functions, etc.) Act 1999

Sch.6 para.2, repealed: 2012 c.5 Sch.14 Part 13
Sch.6 para.10, repealed: 2012 c.5 Sch.14 Part 13

8. Health Act 1999

s.16, amended: 2012 c.7 Sch.14 para.75
s.31, applied: SI 2012/ 335 Sch.1 para.7, SI 2012/ 2991 Sch.1 para.7
s.60, amended: 2012 c.7 s.209, s.210, s.213, Sch.15 para.60, SI 2012/ 1916 Sch.34 para.43
s.60, repealed (in part): 2012 c.7 Sch.15 para.72
s.60A, amended: 2012 c.7 s.209
s.60A, repealed (in part): 2012 c.7 Sch.15 para.72
s.61, amended: 2012 c.7 Sch.5 para.92
Sch.3 para.1A, added: 2012 c.7 s.211
Sch.3 para.1B, added: 2012 c.7 s.211
Sch.3 para.7, amended: 2012 c.7 s.211, Sch.15 para.61
Sch.3 para.8, amended: 2012 c.7 s.211, Sch.15 para.72
Sch.3 para.9, amended: 2012 c.7 s.211
Sch.3 para.10, amended: 2012 c.7 s.211
Sch.3 para.11, amended: 2012 c.7 s.211
Sch.4 para.1, repealed: 2012 c.7 Sch.5 para.93

1999–cont.

8. Health Act 1999–*cont.*

Sch.4 para.3, repealed (in part): 2012 c.7 Sch.5 para.93
Sch.4 para.67, repealed: 2012 c.7 s.42
Sch.4 para.74, repealed: 2012 c.7 Sch.5 para.93
Sch.4 para.82, repealed: 2012 c.7 Sch.5 para.93
Sch.4 para.85, repealed (in part): 2012 c.7 Sch.5 para.93
Sch.4 para.86, repealed: 2012 c.7 Sch.5 para.93

14. Protection of Children Act 1999

s.1, applied: SI 2012/ 1034 Sch.4 para.13, SI 2012/ 2157 Art.7
s.4, applied: 2012 c.10 Sch.1 para.14
s.4A, applied: 2012 c.10 Sch.1 para.14

16. Finance Act 1999

s.81, amended: 2012 c.14 Sch.16 para.93
s.132, applied: SI 2012/ 1836 Reg.17
s.132, enabling: SI 2012/ 33, SI 2012/ 884, SI 2012/ 1836, SI 2012/ 1899
s.133, enabling: SI 2012/ 33, SI 2012/ 822, SI 2012/ 884, SI 2012/ 1899
Sch.5 para.6, varied: 2012 c.11 s.12
Sch.13 Pt III para.16, see *HSBC Holdings Plc v Revenue and Customs Commissioners* [2012] UKFTT 163 (TC), [2012] S.F.T.D. 913 (FTT (Tax)), Judge Barbara Mosedale
Sch.14 para.6, repealed: 2012 c.14 Sch.39 para.3
Sch.14 para.15, repealed: 2012 c.14 Sch.39 para.5

18. Adoption (Intercountry Aspects) Act 1999

s.1, enabling: SI 2012/ 1410

22. Access to Justice Act 1999

see *R. (on the application of Law Society of England and Wales) v Lord Chancellor* [2012] EWHC 794 (Admin), [2012] 3 Costs L.R. 558 (DC), Stanley Burnton, L.J.
Part I, applied: 2012 c.10 s.39
Part I, referred to: 2012 c.10 s.39
s.1, repealed: 2012 c.10 Sch.5 para.51
s.2, repealed: 2012 c.10 Sch.5 para.51
s.3, repealed: 2012 c.10 Sch.5 para.51
s.4, repealed: 2012 c.10 Sch.5 para.51
s.5, repealed: 2012 c.10 Sch.5 para.51
s.6, repealed: 2012 c.10 Sch.5 para.51
s.7, repealed: 2012 c.10 Sch.5 para.51
s.8, repealed: 2012 c.10 Sch.5 para.51
s.8A, repealed: 2012 c.10 Sch.5 para.51
s.9, repealed: 2012 c.10 Sch.5 para.51
s.10, repealed: 2012 c.10 Sch.5 para.51
s.11, see *Leeds City Council v Price* [2012] EWCA Civ 59, [2012] 2 Costs L.O. 242 (CA (Civ Div)), Aikens, L.J.
s.11, applied: SI 2012/ 1726 r.61.22
s.11, repealed: 2012 c.10 Sch.5 para.51
s.11A, repealed: 2012 c.10 Sch.5 para.51
s.12, applied: SI 2012/ 1726 r.62.5
s.12, referred to: SI 2012/ 1726 r.74.3
s.12, repealed: 2012 c.10 Sch.5 para.51
s.13, repealed: 2012 c.10 Sch.5 para.51
s.14, referred to: SI 2012/ 1726 r.74.3
s.14, repealed: 2012 c.10 Sch.5 para.51
s.14, enabling: SI 2012/ 750, SI 2012/ 1343
s.15, repealed: 2012 c.10 Sch.5 para.51
s.16, repealed: 2012 c.10 Sch.5 para.51
s.17, repealed: 2012 c.10 Sch.5 para.51
s.17A, repealed: 2012 c.10 Sch.5 para.51
s.18, repealed: 2012 c.10 Sch.5 para.51
s.18A, repealed: 2012 c.10 Sch.5 para.51
s.19, repealed: 2012 c.10 Sch.5 para.51

22. Access to Justice Act 1999– *cont.*
s.20, applied: SI 2012/ 1726 r.5.8
s.20, repealed: 2012 c.10 Sch.5 para.51
s.21, repealed: 2012 c.10 Sch.5 para.51
s.22, repealed: 2012 c.10 Sch.5 para.51
s.23, repealed: 2012 c.10 Sch.5 para.51
s.24, repealed: 2012 c.10 Sch.5 para.51
s.25, see *R. (on the application of Law Society of England and Wales) v Lord Chancellor* [2012] EWHC 794 (Admin), [2012] 3 Costs L.R. 558 (DC), Stanley Burnton, L.J.
s.25, applied: SI 2012/ 750, SI 2012/ 1343
s.25, referred to: SI 2012/ 1343
s.25, repealed: 2012 c.10 Sch.5 para.51
s.25, enabling: SI 2012/ 750, SI 2012/ 1343
s.26, repealed: 2012 c.10 Sch.5 para.51
s.29, see *Hawksford Trustees Jersey Ltd (Trustee of the Bald Eagle Trust) v Stella Global UK Ltd* [2012] EWCA Civ 987, [2012] 1 W.L.R. 3581 (CA (Civ Div)), Rix, L.J.
s.29, repealed: 2012 c.10 s.46
s.30, repealed: 2012 c.10 s.47
Sch.1 para.1, repealed: 2012 c.10 Sch.5 para.51
Sch.1 para.2, repealed: 2012 c.10 Sch.5 para.51
Sch.1 para.3, repealed: 2012 c.10 Sch.5 para.51
Sch.1 para.4, repealed: 2012 c.10 Sch.5 para.51
Sch.1 para.5, amended: SI 2012/ 2404 Sch.2 para.41
Sch.1 para.5, repealed: 2012 c.10 Sch.5 para.51
Sch.1 para.6, repealed: 2012 c.10 Sch.5 para.51
Sch.1 para.7, repealed: 2012 c.10 Sch.5 para.51
Sch.1 para.8, repealed: 2012 c.10 Sch.5 para.51
Sch.1 para.9, repealed: 2012 c.10 Sch.5 para.51
Sch.1 para.10, repealed: 2012 c.10 Sch.5 para.51
Sch.1 para.11, repealed: 2012 c.10 Sch.5 para.51
Sch.1 para.12, repealed: 2012 c.10 Sch.5 para.51
Sch.1 para.13, repealed: 2012 c.10 Sch.5 para.51
Sch.1 para.14, repealed: 2012 c.10 Sch.5 para.51
Sch.1 para.15, repealed: 2012 c.10 Sch.5 para.51
Sch.1 para.16, repealed: 2012 c.10 Sch.5 para.51
Sch.1 para.17, repealed: 2012 c.10 Sch.5 para.51
Sch.2, repealed: 2012 c.10 Sch.5 para.51
Sch.2 para.1, repealed: 2012 c.10 Sch.5 para.51
Sch.2 para.1A, repealed: 2012 c.10 Sch.5 para.51
Sch.2 para.2, repealed: 2012 c.10 Sch.5 para.51
Sch.2 para.3, repealed: 2012 c.10 Sch.5 para.51
Sch.2 para.4, repealed: 2012 c.10 Sch.5 para.51
Sch.3, referred to: SI 2012/ 1726 r.74.3
Sch.3 para.1, repealed: 2012 c.10 Sch.5 para.51
Sch.3 para.1A, repealed: 2012 c.10 Sch.5 para.51
Sch.3 para.2, repealed: 2012 c.10 Sch.5 para.51
Sch.3 para.2A, repealed: 2012 c.10 Sch.5 para.51
Sch.3 para.3, repealed: 2012 c.10 Sch.5 para.51
Sch.3 para.3A, repealed: 2012 c.10 Sch.5 para.51
Sch.3 para.3B, repealed: 2012 c.10 Sch.5 para.51
Sch.3 para.4, repealed: 2012 c.10 Sch.5 para.51
Sch.3 para.5, repealed: 2012 c.10 Sch.5 para.51
Sch.3 para.6, repealed: 2012 c.10 Sch.5 para.51
Sch.3 para.7, repealed: 2012 c.10 Sch.5 para.51
Sch.3 para.8, repealed: 2012 c.10 Sch.5 para.51
Sch.3A para.1, repealed: 2012 c.10 Sch.5 para.51
Sch.3A para.2, repealed: 2012 c.10 Sch.5 para.51
Sch.3A para.3, repealed: 2012 c.10 Sch.5 para.51
Sch.3A para.4, repealed: 2012 c.10 Sch.5 para.51
Sch.3A para.5, repealed: 2012 c.10 Sch.5 para.51
Sch.3A para.6, repealed: 2012 c.10 Sch.5 para.51
Sch.3A para.7, repealed: 2012 c.10 Sch.5 para.51
Sch.3A para.8, repealed: 2012 c.10 Sch.5 para.51
Sch.4 para.1, repealed: 2012 c.10 Sch.5 Part 2

22. Access to Justice Act 1999– *cont.*
Sch.4 para.4, repealed: 2012 c.10 Sch.12 para.41
Sch.4 para.6, repealed: 2012 c.10 Sch.12 para.41
Sch.4 para.7, repealed: 2012 c.10 Sch.12 para.41
Sch.4 para.8, repealed: 2012 c.10 Sch.5 Part 2
Sch.4 para.10, repealed: 2012 c.10 Sch.5 Part 2
Sch.4 para.11, repealed: 2012 c.10 Sch.5 Part 2
Sch.4 para.12, repealed: 2012 c.10 Sch.5 Part 2
Sch.4 para.15, repealed: 2012 c.10 Sch.5 Part 2
Sch.4 para.16, repealed: 2012 c.10 Sch.5 Part 2
Sch.4 para.17, repealed: 2012 c.10 Sch.5 Part 2
Sch.4 para.18, repealed: 2012 c.10 Sch.5 Part 2
Sch.4 para.19, repealed: 2012 c.10 Sch.5 Part 2
Sch.4 para.29, repealed: 2012 c.10 Sch.5 Part 2
Sch.4 para.30, repealed (in part): 2012 c.10 Sch.5 Part 2
Sch.4 para.33, repealed: 2012 c.10 Sch.5 Part 2
Sch.4 para.35, repealed: 2012 c.10 Sch.5 Part 2
Sch.4 para.38, repealed: 2012 c.10 Sch.5 Part 2
Sch.4 para.39, repealed: 2012 c.10 Sch.5 Part 2
Sch.4 para.40, repealed: 2012 c.10 Sch.5 Part 2
Sch.4 para.45, repealed: 2012 c.10 Sch.5 Part 2
Sch.4 para.47, repealed: 2012 c.10 Sch.5 Part 2
Sch.4 para.48, repealed: 2012 c.5 Sch.14 Part 1
Sch.4 para.49, repealed: 2012 c.10 Sch.5 Part 2
Sch.4 para.51, repealed (in part): 2012 c.10 Sch.5 Part 2
Sch.4 para.52, repealed: 2012 c.10 Sch.5 Part 2
Sch.4 para.55, repealed: 2012 c.10 Sch.5 Part 2
Sch.14 Part II para.2, repealed: 2012 c.10 Sch.5 para.51
Sch.14 Part II para.3, repealed: 2012 c.10 Sch.5 para.51
Sch.14 Part II para.4, repealed: 2012 c.10 Sch.5 para.51
Sch.14 Part II para.5, repealed: 2012 c.10 Sch.5 para.51
Sch.14 Part II para.6, repealed: 2012 c.10 Sch.5 para.51
Sch.14 Part II para.7, repealed: 2012 c.10 Sch.5 para.51
Sch.14 Part II para.8, repealed: 2012 c.10 Sch.5 para.51
Sch.14 Part II para.9, repealed: 2012 c.10 Sch.5 para.51

23. Youth Justice and Criminal Evidence Act 1999
applied: SI 2012/ 1726 r.29.17
s.16, applied: SI 2012/ 1726 r.29.26
s.17, applied: SI 2012/ 1726 r.29.26
s.19, applied: SI 2012/ 1726 r.16.6, r.29.1, r.29.19, r.36.6, r.29.26, r.37.4
s.20, applied: SI 2012/ 1726 r.29.1, r.36.6, r.5.4, r.29.11
s.20, referred to: SI 2012/ 1726 r.29.4, r.29.12
s.21, applied: SI 2012/ 1726 r.29.9, r.29.26
s.21, referred to: SI 2012/ 1726 r.29.13
s.22, applied: SI 2012/ 1726 r.29.9, r.29.26
s.22, referred to: SI 2012/ 1726 r.29.13
s.22A, applied: SI 2012/ 1726 r.29.26
s.23, referred to: SI 2012/ 1726 r.29.1
s.24, applied: SI 2012/ 1726 r.29.26
s.24, referred to: SI 2012/ 1726 r.29.1
s.25, referred to: SI 2012/ 1726 r.29.1
s.26, referred to: SI 2012/ 1726 r.29.1
s.27, referred to: SI 2012/ 1726 r.29.1
s.28, applied: SI 2012/ 1726 r.29.26
s.28, referred to: SI 2012/ 1726 r.29.1
s.29, referred to: SI 2012/ 1726 r.29.1
s.30, referred to: SI 2012/ 1726 r.29.1

1999– cont.

23. Youth Justice and Criminal Evidence Act 1999– cont.

s.33A, applied: SI 2012/ 1726 r.29.1, r.5.4, r.29.26

s.33A, referred to: SI 2012/ 1726 r.29.4, r.29.15, r.29.16

s.33BA, applied: SI 2012/ 1726 r.29.1

s.33BA, referred to: SI 2012/ 1726 r.29.15

s.33BB, applied: SI 2012/ 1726 r.29.1, r.5.4

s.33BB, referred to: SI 2012/ 1726 r.29.4, r.29.16

s.34, applied: SI 2012/ 1726 r.31.1, r.31.2, r.37.4, r.31.3

s.35, applied: SI 2012/ 1726 r.31.1, r.31.2, r.31.3, r.37.4

s.36, applied: SI 2012/ 1726 r.31.1, r.31.2, r.31.3, r.37.4, r.31.4

s.38, applied: SI 2012/ 1726 r.31.2, r.31.3

s.41, see *R. v Ben-Rejab (Anouar)* [2011] EWCA Crim 1136, [2012] 1 W.L.R. 2364 (CA (Crim Div)), Pitchford, L.J.

s.41, applied: SI 2012/ 1726 r.36.1, r.36.3

s.42, see *R. v Ben-Rejab (Anouar)* [2011] EWCA Crim 1136, [2012] 1 W.L.R. 2364 (CA (Crim Div)), Pitchford, L.J.

s.46, applied: SI 2012/ 1726 r.16.1, r.37.2, r.29.19, r.16.4

s.47, applied: SI 2012/ 1726 r.37.2, r.16.1

s.53, applied: SI 2012/ 1726 r.37.4

s.55, applied: SI 2012/ 1726 r.37.4

s.56, applied: SI 2012/ 1726 r.37.4

Sch.1 A para.9A, added: 2012 c.10 Sch.26 para.8

Sch.1 A para.26A, added: 2012 c.10 Sch.26 para.8

Sch.4 para.6, repealed: 2012 c.10 Sch.25 Part 2

24. Pollution Prevention and Control Act 1999

Commencement Orders: 2012 c.14 s.206

s.2, applied: SI 2012/ 630, SSI 2012/ 360

s.2, enabling: SI 2012/ 630, SI 2012/ 3038, SSI 2012/ 360

s.7, enabling: SI 2012/ 630, SI 2012/ 3038

Sch.1, enabling: SI 2012/ 630, SI 2012/ 3038

Sch.1 Part I para.9A, amended: SI 2012/ 2788 Reg.16

26. Employment Relations Act 1999

s.34, enabling: SI 2012/ 3007

s.38, enabling: SI 2012/ 2413

27. Local Government Act 1999

Part I, applied: SI 2012/ 335 Sch.1 para.20, SI 2012/ 2991 Sch.1 para.20

s.13A, repealed (in part): 2012 c.5 Sch.14 Part 1

s.14, repealed: 2012 c.5 Sch.14 Part 1

s.29, repealed (in part): 2012 c.5 Sch.14 Part 1

28. Food Standards Act 1999

Sch.1 para.4, amended: SI 2012/ 2404 Sch.2 para.43

29. Greater London Authority Act 1999

applied: 2012 c.13 Sch.1, SI 2012/ 444 Sch.5, SI 2012/ 472 Art.3, Art.9, SI 2012/ 1008 Art.10, SI 2012/ 2031 Sch.5

referred to: SI 2012/ 323 Sch.5 para.17

varied: SI 2012/ 147 Art.7

Part I, applied: SI 2012/ 323 Reg.10, SI 2012/ 444 Reg.17

s.10, applied: SI 2012/ 323 Reg.10, SI 2012/ 444 Reg.17

s.16, applied: SI 2012/ 323 Reg.10, SI 2012/ 444 Reg.17

s.20, amended: SI 2012/ 1809 Sch.1 Part 1

s.21, amended: SI 2012/ 2404 Sch.2 para.42

s.25, enabling: SI 2012/ 234

s.31, amended: SI 2012/ 1530 Art.2

s.31, enabling: SI 2012/ 1530

s.41, referred to: SI 2012/ 1008 Art.9, Art.10

s.42B, disapplied: SI 2012/ 1008 Art.11

s.73, applied: SI 2012/ 62 Reg.7, Reg.29

1999– cont.

29. Greater London Authority Act 1999– cont.

s.86, amended: 2012 c.17 s.3

s.86, repealed (in part): 2012 c.17 s.3

s.88, applied: SI 2012/ 2914 Reg.2, Reg.7, Reg.8, Reg.10

s.89, applied: SI 2012/ 2914 Reg.2, Reg.7, Reg.8, Reg.10

s.100, amended: 2012 c.17 s.4

s.102, repealed (in part): 2012 c.17 s.3

s.235, amended: 2012 c.19 Sch.9 para.10

s.309E, amended: 2012 c.7 Sch.5 para.94

s.309E, repealed (in part): 2012 c.7 Sch.5 para.94, Sch.14 para.76

s.333F, referred to: SI 2012/ 1008 Art.9

s.351A, referred to: SI 2012/ 1008 Art.10

s.376, amended: SI 2012/ 147 Sch.1

s.420, applied: SI 2012/ 1530

s.420, enabling: SI 2012/ 1530

Sch.6 para.3, amended: SI 2012/ 15 Reg.2, SI 2012/ 3125 Reg.2

Sch.6 para.10, enabling: SI 2012/ 15, SI 2012/ 3125

Sch.11 para.26, referred to: SI 2012/ 472 Art.6

Sch.11 para.26, varied: SI 2012/ 472 Art.6

Sch.17 para.9, applied: SI 2012/ 472 Art.7

30. Welfare Reform and Pensions Act 1999

referred to: SI 2012/ 687 Sch.1 para.12

Part IV, applied: SI 2012/ 687 Sch.4 para.7

s.3, applied: SI 2012/ 2480 Art.3

s.11, see *Raithatha v Williamson* [2012] EWHC 909 (Ch), [2012] 1 W.L.R. 3559 (Ch D), Bernard Livesey Q.C.

s.11, applied: SI 2012/ 687 Sch.4 para.7

s.13, applied: SI 2012/ 687 Sch.4 para.7

s.23, applied: SI 2012/ 687 Sch.4 para.7

s.24, applied: SI 2012/ 687 Sch.4 para.7

s.28, applied: SI 2012/ 687 Sch.1 para.12

s.29, applied: SI 2012/ 687 Sch.3 para.4, Sch.3 para.6

s.57, repealed: 2012 c.5 Sch.14 Part 1

s.58, repealed: 2012 c.5 Sch.14 Part 1

s.67, repealed: 2012 c.5 Sch.14 Part 9

s.72, amended: 2012 c.5 s.134

s.72, repealed (in part): 2012 c.5 s.134, Sch.14 Part 1

Sch.7 para.2, repealed (in part): 2012 c.5 Sch.14 Part 1

Sch.7 para.4, repealed: 2012 c.5 Sch.14 Part 1

Sch.7 para.5, repealed (in part): 2012 c.5 Sch.14 Part 1

Sch.7 para.6, repealed: 2012 c.5 Sch.14 Part 1

Sch.7 para.9, repealed: 2012 c.5 Sch.14 Part 1

Sch.7 para.10, repealed: 2012 c.5 Sch.14 Part 1

Sch.7 para.11, repealed: 2012 c.5 Sch.14 Part 1

Sch.7 para.12, repealed: 2012 c.5 Sch.14 Part 3

Sch.7 para.13, repealed: 2012 c.5 Sch.14 Part 3

Sch.7 para.15, repealed: 2012 c.5 Sch.14 Part 1

Sch.7 para.16, repealed: 2012 c.5 Sch.14 Part 1

Sch.8 Part IV para.28, repealed: 2012 c.5 Sch.14 Part 1

Sch.8 Part V para.29, repealed (in part): 2012 c.5 Sch.14 Part 1, Sch.14 Part 3

Sch.8 Part VIII para.34, repealed (in part): 2012 c.5 Sch.14 Part 10

Sch.12 Part II para.79, repealed: 2012 c.5 Sch.14 Part 1

Sch.12 Part II para.80, repealed: 2012 c.5 Sch.14 Part 1

Sch.12 Part II para.82, repealed: 2012 c.5 Sch.14 Part 1

Sch.12 Part II para.83, repealed: 2012 c.5 Sch.14 Part 1

1999– cont.

30. Welfare Reform and Pensions Act 1999– *cont.*
Sch.12 Part II para.87, repealed: 2012 c.5 Sch.14 Part 1

31. Contracts (Rights of Third Parties) Act 1999
see *Great Eastern Shipping Co Ltd v Far East Chartering Ltd* [2012] EWCA Civ 180, [2012] 2 All E.R. (Comm) 707 (CA (Civ Div)), Longmore, L.J.; see *Petrologic Capital SA v Banque Cantonale de Geneve* [2012] EWHC 453 (Comm), [2012] I.L.Pr. 20 (QBD (Comm)), Stephen Males, Q.C.

33. Immigration and Asylum Act 1999
see *Khaliq (Entry Clearance: Para 321: Pakistan), Re* [2012] Imm. A.R. 1 (UT (IAC)), CMG Ockelton (Vice President)
Pt VIII. see *R. (on the application of Salimi) v Secretary of State for the Home Department* [2011] EWHC 1714 (Admin), [2012] 1 All E.R. 244 (QBD (Admin)), Bean, J.
s.4, see *R. (on the application of K) v Secretary of State for the Home Department* [2011] EWCA Civ 671, [2012] 1 W.L.R. 765 (CA (Civ Div)), Sir Anthony May (President, QB); see *R. (on the application of VC) v Newcastle City Council* [2011] EWHC 2673 (Admin), [2012] P.T.S.R. 546 (QBD (Admin)), Munby, L.J.
s.4, applied: 2012 c.10 Sch.1 para.31
s.10, see *Kabaghe (Appeal from Outside UK: Fairness: Malawi), Re* [2012] Imm. A.R. 312 (UT (IAC)), Blake, J. (President); see *Kishver (Limited Leave: Meaning: Pakistan), Re* [2012] Imm. A.R. 128 (UT (IAC)), CMG Ockelton
s.18, referred to: SI 2012/ 1763 Art.3
s.18, varied: SI 2012/ 1763 Sch.2 para.1
s.41, enabling: SI 2012/116, SI 2012/771
s.53, amended: SI 2012/2595 Art.9
s.58, see *LB (Jamaica) v Secretary of State for the Home Department* [2011] EWCA Civ 1420, [2012] Imm. A.R. 637 (CA (Civ Div)), Maurice Kay, L.J.
s.83, amended: SI 2012/2595 Art.9
s.84, see *RK (Entitlement to Represent: S.84: Bangladesh), Re* [2012] Imm. A.R. 126 (UT (IAC)), Judge Lane
s.86, amended: SI 2012/2595 Art.9
s.95, see *R. (on the application of Chen) v Secretary of State for the Home Department* [2012] EWHC 2531 (Admin), [2012] H.R.L.R. 33 (QBD (Admin)), Beatson, J.; see *R. (on the application of K) v Secretary of State for the Home Department* [2011] EWCA Civ 671, [2012] 1 W.L.R. 765 (CA (Civ Div)), Sir Anthony May (President, QB); see *R. (on the application of VC) v Newcastle City Council* [2011] EWHC 2673 (Admin), [2012] P.T.S.R. 546 (QBD (Admin)), Munby, L.J.
s.95, applied: 2012 c.10 Sch.1 para.31, SI 2012/2886 Sch.1, SI 2012/3145 Sch.1
s.96, see *R. (on the application of K) v Secretary of State for the Home Department* [2011] EWCA Civ 671, [2012] 1 W.L.R. 765 (CA (Civ Div)), Sir Anthony May (President, QB)
s.97, amended: 2012 c.5 Sch.2 para.53
s.97, repealed (in part): 2012 c.5 Sch.14 Part 1
s.98, applied: SI 2012/2886 Sch.1, SI 2012/3145 Sch.1
s.115, amended: 2012 c.5 Sch.2 para.54, Sch.3 para.9, Sch.9 para.44, Sch.14 Part 1
s.115, applied: SI 2012/2885 Reg.12, Sch.8 para.7, SI 2012/2886 Sch.1, SI 2012/3144 Reg.26, SI 2012/3145 Sch.1, SSI 2012/303 Reg.16, Reg.19, SSI 2012/319 Reg.16, Reg.19

1999– cont.

33. Immigration and Asylum Act 1999– *cont.*
s.115, repealed (in part): 2012 c.5 Sch.14 Part 1, Sch.14 Part 9
s.170, enabling: SI 2012/1763, SI 2012/2593
Sch.5 Part I para.4, amended: SI 2012/2595 Art.9
Sch.8 para.3, applied: SI 2012/2886 Sch.1, SI 2012/3145 Sch.1
Sch.9, applied: SI 2012/2886 Sch.1, SI 2012/3145 Sch.1

34. House of Lords Act 1999
s.1, see *Baron Mereworth v Ministry of Justice* [2011] EWHC 1589 (Ch), [2012] Ch. 325 (Ch D), Lewison, J.

2000

1. Northern Ireland Act 2000
referred to: 2012 c.13 Sch.1

2. Representation of the People Act 2000
applied: SI 2012/1917 Sch.2 para.8
s.10, varied: SI 2012/323 Sch.4 para.1, SI 2012/444 Sch.4 para.1, SI 2012/2031 Sch.4 Part 1
s.12, varied: SI 2012/323 Sch.4 para.1, SI 2012/444 Sch.4 para.1, SI 2012/2031 Sch.4 Part 1
Sch.4, applied: SI 2012/323 Reg.11, Reg.12, SI 2012/444 Reg.18
Sch.4 para.1, varied: SI 2012/323 Sch.4 para.1, SI 2012/444 Sch.4 para.1, SI 2012/2031 Sch.4 Part 1
Sch.4 para.2, varied: SI 2012/323 Sch.4 para.1, SI 2012/444 Sch.4 para.1, SI 2012/2031 Sch.4 Part 1
Sch.4 para.3, applied: SI 2012/1917 Sch.2 para.3, Sch.2 para.4, Sch.2 para.8, Sch.2 para.13, Sch.2 para.17
Sch.4 para.3, varied: SI 2012/323 Sch.4 para.1, SI 2012/444 Sch.4 para.1, SI 2012/2031 Sch.4 Part 1
Sch.4 para.4, applied: SI 2012/1917 Sch.2 para.8
Sch.4 para.4, varied: SI 2012/323 Sch.4 para.1, SI 2012/444 Sch.4 para.1, SI 2012/2031 Sch.4 Part 1
Sch.4 para.5, varied: SI 2012/323 Sch.4 para.1, SI 2012/444 Sch.4 para.1, SI 2012/2031 Sch.4 Part 1
Sch.4 para.6, applied: SI 2012/1917 Sch.2 para.4
Sch.4 para.6, varied: SI 2012/323 Sch.4 para.1, SI 2012/444 Sch.4 para.1, SI 2012/2031 Sch.4 Part 1
Sch.4 para.7, applied: SI 2012/1917 Sch.2 para.7, Sch.2 para.8, Sch.2 para.13, Sch.2 para.17
Sch.4 para.7, varied: SI 2012/323 Sch.4 para.1, SI 2012/444 Sch.4 para.1, SI 2012/2031 Sch.4 Part 1
Sch.4 para.7A, varied: SI 2012/323 Sch.4 para.1, SI 2012/2031 Sch.4 Part 1
Sch.4 para.7B, varied: SI 2012/323 Sch.4 para.1, SI 2012/2031 Sch.4 Part 1
Sch.4 para.7C, varied: SI 2012/323 Sch.4 para.1, SI 2012/444 Sch.4 para.1, SI 2012/2031 Sch.4 Part 1
Sch.4 para.7D, varied: SI 2012/323 Sch.4 para.1, SI 2012/444 Sch.4 para.1, SI 2012/2031 Sch.4 Part 1
Sch.4 para.8, varied: SI 2012/323 Sch.4 para.1, SI 2012/2031 Sch.4 Part 1

6. Powers of Criminal Courts (Sentencing) Act 2000
s.1, applied: SI 2012/1726 r.37.10, r.63.2
s.3, see *R. v Ayhan (Murat)* [2011] EWCA Crim 3184, [2012] 1 W.L.R. 1775 (CA (Crim Div)), Lord Judge, L.C.J.
s.3, applied: SI 2012/1726 r.37.10
s.3, referred to: SI 2012/1726 r.9.11
s.3A, amended: 2012 c.10 Sch.21 para.8
s.3A, applied: SI 2012/1726 r.37.10
s.3A, referred to: SI 2012/1726 r.9.11
s.3B, applied: SI 2012/1726 r.37.10
s.3B, referred to: SI 2012/1726 r.9.7

2000–cont.

6. Powers of Criminal Courts (Sentencing) Act 2000– *cont.*

s.3C, amended: 2012 c.10 Sch.21 para.9

s.3C, applied: SI 2012/ 1726 r.37.10

s.3C, referred to: SI 2012/ 1726 r.9.11

s.4, applied: SI 2012/ 1726 r.37.10

s.4, referred to: SI 2012/ 1726 r.9.8

s.4A, applied: SI 2012/ 1726 r.37.10

s.4A, referred to: SI 2012/ 1726 r.9.7

s.6, see *R. v Ayhan (Murat)* [2011] EWCA Crim 3184, [2012] 1 W.L.R. 1775 (CA (Crim Div)), Lord Judge, L.C.J.; see *R. v Morgan (Stuart Anthony)* [2012] EWCA Crim 1939, (2012) 176 J.P. 633 (CA (Crim Div)), Irwin, J.

s.6, applied: SI 2012/ 1726 r.37.10

s.6, referred to: SI 2012/ 1726 r.9.7, r.9.8, r.9.11

s.7, see *R. v Morgan (Stuart Anthony)* [2012] EWCA Crim 1939, (2012) 176 J.P. 633 (CA (Crim Div)), Irwin, J.

s.8, applied: SI 2012/ 1726 r.37.10

s.9, applied: SI 2012/ 1726 r.37.1

s.11, applied: SI 2012/ 1726 r.33.1

s.12, see *R. v Varma (Aloke)* [2012] UKSC 42, [2012] 3 W.L.R. 776 (SC), Lord Phillips, J.S.C. (President)

s.12, amended: 2012 c.10 Sch.19 para.4, Sch.24 para.19, Sch.26 para.10

s.12, applied: SI 2012/ 1696 Sch.1

s.14, applied: 2012 c.9 s.101

s.16, amended: 2012 c.10 s.79

s.16, applied: SI 2012/ 1696 Sch.1

s.17, amended: 2012 c.10 s.79

s.17, repealed (in part): 2012 c.10 s.79

s.41, referred to: SI 2012/ 206 Sch.1 para.21

s.51, referred to: SI 2012/ 206 Sch.1 para.21

s.52, referred to: SI 2012/ 206 Sch.1 para.21

s.76, amended: 2012 c.10 Sch.21 para.10

s.76, applied: SI 2012/ 1696 Sch.1

s.82A, amended: 2012 c.10 Sch.13 para.10, Sch.21 para.11

s.82A, applied: SI 2012/ 1726 r.68.1

s.82A, repealed (in part): 2012 c.10 Sch.21 para.11

s.83, amended: 2012 c.10 Sch.5 para.53

s.85, see *R. (on the application of Minter) v Chief Constable of Hampshire* [2011] EWHC 1610 (Admin), [2012] 1 W.L.R. 1157 (DC), Richards, L.J.

s.86, repealed: 2012 c.10 s.121

s.89, applied: SI 2012/ 1726 r.62.5, r.62.9

s.91, see *R. v M* [2011] EWCA Crim 1833, [2012] 1 Cr. App. R. (S.) 63 (CA (Crim Div)), Leveson, L.J.; see *R. v Q* [2012] EWCA Crim 296, [2012] 2 Cr. App. R. (S.) 54 (CA (Crim Div)), Hooper, L.J.; see *R. v RLM* [2011] EWCA Crim 2398, [2012] 1 Cr. App. R. (S.) 95 (CA (Crim Div)), Gross, L.J.; see *R. v S* [2011] EWCA Crim 1238, [2012] 1 Cr. App. R. (S.) 14 (CA (Crim Div)), Toulson, L.J.

s.99, amended: 2012 c.10 Sch.21 para.12, Sch.22 para.15

s.100, see *R. v Q* [2012] EWCA Crim 296, [2012] 2 Cr. App. R. (S.) 54 (CA (Crim Div)), Hooper, L.J.

s.100, amended: 2012 c.10 Sch.21 para.13, Sch.26 para.11

s.101, amended: 2012 c.10 Sch.12 para.43, Sch.13 para.11

s.103, applied: 2012 c.10 s.80

s.104, amended: 2012 c.10 s.80

s.104, varied: 2012 c.10 s.80

6. Powers of Criminal Courts (Sentencing) Act 2000– *cont.*

s.104A, added: 2012 c.10 s.80

s.104B, added: 2012 c.10 s.80

s.106A, amended: 2012 c.10 Sch.21 para.14, Sch.22 para.16

s.107, applied: 2012 c.10 s.102

s.108, applied: SI 2012/ 1726 r.62.5, r.62.9

s.110, see *R. v Lucas (Kwame)* [2011] EWCA Crim 2806, [2012] 2 Cr. App. R. (S.) 14 (CA (Crim Div)), Jackson, L.J.

s.111, see *R. v Stone (Ben)* [2011] EWCA Crim 2823, [2012] 2 Cr. App. R. (S.) 12 (CA (Crim Div)), Rafferty, L.J.

s.130, amended: 2012 c.10 s.63, Sch.19 para.5, Sch.26 para.12

s.140, applied: SI 2012/ 1726 r.56.5

s.141, applied: SI 2012/ 1726 r.76.2

s.143, see *O'Leary International Ltd v Chief Constable of North Wales* [2012] EWHC 1516 (Admin), (2012) 176 J.P. 514 (DC), Sir John Thomas (President)

s.144, see *O'Leary International Ltd v Chief Constable of North Wales* [2012] EWHC 1516 (Admin), (2012) 176 J.P. 514 (DC), Sir John Thomas (President)

s.146, see *R. v Gilder (Lewis)* [2011] EWCA Crim 1159, [2012] 1 Cr. App. R. (S.) 4 (CA (Crim Div)), Leveson, L.J.

s.146, amended: 2012 c.10 Sch.19 para.6, Sch.26 para.13

s.146, applied: SI 2012/ 1726 r.55.2

s.147, see *R. v Gilder (Lewis)* [2011] EWCA Crim 1159, [2012] 1 Cr. App. R. (S.) 4 (CA (Crim Div)), Leveson, L.J.

s.147, applied: SI 2012/ 1726 r.55.2

s.147A, amended: 2012 c.10 Sch.13 para.12, Sch.14 para.3, Sch.21 para.15

s.147A, repealed (in part): 2012 c.10 Sch.10 para.10, Sch.21 para.15

s.154, see *R. v Hills (Christopher Carl)* [2008] EWCA Crim 1871, [2012] 1 W.L.R. 2121 (CA (Crim Div)), Latham, L.J.; see *R. v Taylor (Ezra)* [2011] EWCA Crim 2236, [2012] 1 W.L.R. 2113 (CA (Crim Div)), Moses, L.J.

s.155, see *R. v Evans (Scott Lennon)* [2011] EWCA Crim 2842, [2012] 1 W.L.R. 1192 (CA (Crim Div)), Hughes, L.J. VP

s.155, amended: 2012 c.10 Sch.5 para.54

s.155, enabling: SI 2012/ 1726

s.161, see *R. v Pinnell (Paul Leslie)* [2010] EWCA Crim 2848, [2012] 1 W.L.R. 17 (CA (Crim Div)), Hughes, L.J.

s.163, amended: 2012 c.10 Sch.9 para.1

s.164, amended: 2012 c.10 Sch.19 para.7, Sch.26 para.14

Sch.3, applied: SI 2012/ 1726 r.44.1

Sch.3 Part III para.10, applied: SI 2012/ 1726 r.63.1

Sch.5, applied: SI 2012/ 1726 r.44.1

Sch.7, applied: SI 2012/ 1726 r.44.1

Sch.8, applied: SI 2012/ 1726 r.44.1

Sch.9 para.48, repealed (in part): 2012 c.10 Sch.25 Part 2

Sch.9 para.93, repealed: 2012 c.10 Sch.12 para.44

Sch.9 para.126, repealed: 2012 c.10 Sch.12 para.44

Sch.9 para.198, repealed: 2012 c.10 Sch.24 para.20

Sch.11 Part III para.13, repealed: 2012 c.10 Sch.25 Part 2

7. Electronic Communications Act 2000

s.7, applied: SI 2012/ 1726 r.5.3

2000–cont.

7. **Electronic Communications Act 2000**–*cont.*
s.8, enabling: SI 2012/25
s.15, applied: SSI 2012/178 Art.2
s.15, referred to: SSI 2012/348 Art.9
8. **Financial Services and Markets Act 2000**
see *Combined Insurance Co of America, Re* [2012] EWHC 632 (Ch), [2012] Lloyd's Rep. I.R. 714 (Ch D (Companies Ct)), Morgan, J.; see *Financial Services Authority v Sinaloa Gold Plc* [2011] EWCA Civ 1158, [2012] Bus. L.R. 753 (CA (Civ Div)), Mummery, L.J.; see *Secretary of State for Business Innovation and Skills v Chohan* [2011] EWHC 1350 (Ch), [2012] 1 B.C.L.C. 138 (Ch D (Companies Ct)), David Richards, J.
applied: 2012 c.6 Sch.2 para.2, 2012 c.7 s.134, s.135, 2012 c.10 s.59, 2012 c.14 s.142, s.221, 2012 c.19 Sch.6 para.5, 2012 c.21 s.73, s.74, s.85, s.107, s.109, s.110, Sch.20 para.7, Sch.21 para.7, SI 2012/1128 Art.4, SI 2012/1538 Reg.10, SI 2012/1906, SI 2012/2554 Reg.5, SI 2012/3122 Reg.13
referred to: 2012 c.10 s.58
Part IV, applied: 2012 c.14 s.65
Part VI, repealed: 2012 c.21 s.16
Part VI, amended: 2012 c.21 s.16
Part VI, added: 2012 c.21 s.19
Part VIIIA, amended: SI 2012/2554 Reg.2
Part IX, applied: SI 2012/3122 Sch.1 para.7
Part XV, substituted: 2012 c.21 Sch.10 para.8
Part XVI, applied: SI 2012/3122 Reg.12
Part XVIII, applied: 2012 c.21 s.85
Part XXI, applied: 2012 c.21 s.54
Part XXII, added: 2012 c.21 Sch.13 para.2
Part XXV, applied: 2012 c.21 s.109
Part XXV, amended: 2012 c.21 Sch.9 para.23
Part XXVI, amended: 2012 c.21 Sch.9 para.34
Part XXVIII, amended: 2012 c.21 Sch.18 para.25
Pt XXIV. see *Ceart Risk Services Ltd, Re* [2012] EWHC 1178 (Ch), [2012] B.C.C. 592 (Ch D (Companies Ct)), Arnold, J.
s.1, substituted: 2012 c.21 s.6
s.1A, applied: 2012 c.21 Sch.20 para.4
s.1E, applied: 2012 c.21 s.73
s.2, substituted: 2012 c.21 s.6
s.2, varied: SI 2012/3122 Reg.14
s.2A, applied: 2012 c.21 Sch.20 para.4
s.2I, applied: 2012 c.21 s.85
s.3, substituted: 2012 c.21 s.6
s.3A, substituted: 2012 c.21 s.6
s.4, substituted: 2012 c.21 s.6
s.5, substituted: 2012 c.21 s.6
s.6, substituted: 2012 c.21 s.6
s.6A, substituted: 2012 c.21 s.6
s.7, substituted: 2012 c.21 s.6
s.8, substituted: 2012 c.21 s.6
s.9, substituted: 2012 c.21 s.6
s.10, substituted: 2012 c.21 s.6
s.11, substituted: 2012 c.21 s.6
s.12, substituted: 2012 c.21 s.6
s.13, substituted: 2012 c.21 s.6
s.14, substituted: 2012 c.21 s.6
s.15, substituted: 2012 c.21 s.6
s.16, substituted: 2012 c.21 s.6
s.17, substituted: 2012 c.21 s.6
s.18, substituted: 2012 c.21 s.6
s.19, see *R. v Napoli (John Francis)* [2012] EWCA Crim 1129, [2012] Lloyd's Rep. F.C. 599 (CA (Crim Div)), Rafferty, L.J.

2000–cont.

8. **Financial Services and Markets Act 2000**–*cont.*
s.20, see *City Index Ltd (t/a FinSpreads) v Balducci* [2011] EWHC 2562 (Ch), [2012] 1 B.C.L.C. 317 (Ch D), Proudman, J.
s.20, amended: 2012 c.21 Sch.9 para.2
s.22, amended: 2012 c.21 s.7
s.22, applied: 2012 c.7 s.145, 2012 c.21 s.107, Sch.21 para.7, SI 2012/1507 Reg.2, SI 2012/1508 Reg.2, SI 2012/1756 Art.2, SI 2012/1757 Art.2, SI 2012/1758 Art.2, SI 2012/2748 Art.3, SI 2012/2751 Art.3, SI 2012/3065 Art.3, SI 2012/3066 Art.3, SI 2012/3067 Art.3, SI 2012/3068 Art.3
s.22, referred to: SI 2012/1507 Reg.2, SI 2012/1508 Reg.2
s.22, substituted: 2012 c.21 s.7
s.22, enabling: SI 2012/1906
s.22A, added: 2012 c.21 s.9
s.22A, applied: 2012 c.21 Sch.20 para.8
s.22B, added: 2012 c.21 s.9
s.23, see *R. v Napoli (John Francis)* [2012] EWCA Crim 1129, [2012] Lloyd's Rep. F.C. 599 (CA (Crim Div)), Rafferty, L.J.
s.23, amended: 2012 c.21 Sch.9 para.3
s.23A, added: 2012 c.21 Sch.9 para.4
s.26A, added: 2012 c.21 Sch.9 para.5
s.27, amended: 2012 c.21 Sch.9 para.6
s.28, amended: 2012 c.21 Sch.9 para.7
s.28A, added: 2012 c.21 Sch.9 para.8
s.28B, added: 2012 c.21 Sch.9 para.8
s.31, amended: 2012 c.21 s.11
s.31, referred to: 2012 c.14 s.221
s.33, amended: 2012 c.21 Sch.18 para.2
s.34, amended: 2012 c.21 Sch.4 para.27
s.35, amended: 2012 c.21 Sch.4 para.28
s.36, amended: 2012 c.21 Sch.18 para.3
s.38, amended: 2012 c.21 Sch.18 para.4
s.38, enabling: SI 2012/763
s.39, amended: 2012 c.21 s.10, Sch.18 para.5, SI 2012/1906 Art.3
s.39, referred to: 2012 c.6 Sch.2 para.2
s.39A, amended: 2012 c.21 Sch.18 para.6
s.40, substituted: 2012 c.21 s.11
s.41, substituted: 2012 c.21 s.11
s.42, substituted: 2012 c.21 s.11
s.43, substituted: 2012 c.21 s.11
s.44, substituted: 2012 c.21 s.11
s.45, amended: SI 2012/1906 Art.3
s.45, substituted: 2012 c.21 s.11
s.46, substituted: 2012 c.21 s.11
s.47, substituted: 2012 c.21 s.11
s.48, substituted: 2012 c.21 s.11
s.49, substituted: 2012 c.21 s.11
s.50, substituted: 2012 c.21 s.11
s.51, substituted: 2012 c.21 s.11
s.52, substituted: 2012 c.21 s.11
s.53, substituted: 2012 c.21 s.11
s.54, substituted: 2012 c.21 s.11
s.54A, added: SI 2012/916 Reg.2
s.54A, substituted: 2012 c.21 s.11
s.54B, added: SI 2012/916 Reg.2
s.54B, substituted: 2012 c.21 s.11
s.55, substituted: 2012 c.21 s.11
s.55B, referred to: 2012 c.21 Sch.20 para.5
s.55C, referred to: 2012 c.21 Sch.20 para.5
s.56, amended: 2012 c.21 s.13
s.56, applied: 2012 c.21 s.109
s.56, repealed (in part): 2012 c.21 s.13
s.57, amended: 2012 c.21 s.13

2000–cont.

8. Financial Services and Markets Act 2000–*cont.*

s.58, amended: 2012 c.21 Sch.5 para.2
s.59, amended: 2012 c.21 s.14, SI 2012/1906 Art.3
s.59, repealed (in part): 2012 c.21 Sch.5 para.3
s.59A, added: 2012 c.21 s.14
s.59B, added: 2012 c.21 s.14
s.60, amended: 2012 c.21 Sch.5 para.4
s.61, amended: 2012 c.21 Sch.5 para.5
s.62, amended: 2012 c.21 Sch.5 para.6
s.63, amended: 2012 c.21 s.14, Sch.5 para.7
s.63A, amended: 2012 c.21 Sch.5 para.8
s.63A, applied: 2012 c.21 s.109
s.63B, amended: 2012 c.21 Sch.5 para.9
s.63C, amended: 2012 c.21 Sch.5 para.10
s.63C, applied: 2012 c.21 s.85
s.63D, amended: 2012 c.21 Sch.5 para.11
s.64, see *R. (on the application of C) v Financial Services Authority* [2012] EWHC 1417 (Admin), [2012] A.C.D. 97 (QBD (Admin)), Silber, J.
s.64, amended: 2012 c.21 s.14, Sch.5 para.12
s.64, applied: 2012 c.21 s.85
s.65, amended: 2012 c.21 Sch.5 para.13
s.66, amended: 2012 c.21 Sch.5 para.14, SI 2012/1906 Art.3
s.66, applied: 2012 c.21 s.109
s.66, varied: SI 2012/3122 Sch.1 para.1
s.67, amended: 2012 c.21 Sch.5 para.15
s.67, varied: SI 2012/3122 Sch.1 para.1
s.68, amended: 2012 c.21 Sch.5 para.16
s.69, amended: 2012 c.21 Sch.5 para.17
s.69, applied: 2012 c.21 s.85
s.69, varied: SI 2012/3122 Sch.1 para.1
s.70, amended: 2012 c.21 Sch.5 para.18
s.73, repealed: 2012 c.21 s.16
s.73A, amended: 2012 c.21 s.16
s.73A, applied: SI 2012/1439 Art.2
s.74, amended: 2012 c.21 s.16
s.75, amended: 2012 c.21 s.16
s.76, amended: 2012 c.21 s.16
s.77, amended: 2012 c.21 s.16
s.78, amended: 2012 c.21 s.16
s.78A, amended: 2012 c.21 s.16, s.17
s.79, amended: 2012 c.21 s.16
s.80, amended: 2012 c.21 s.16
s.81, amended: 2012 c.21 s.16
s.82, amended: 2012 c.21 s.16
s.84, amended: 2012 c.21 s.16
s.84, repealed (in part): SI 2012/1538 Reg.3
s.86, amended: 2012 c.21 s.16, SI 2012/1538 Reg.2, Reg.3
s.87A, amended: 2012 c.21 s.16, SI 2012/1538 Reg.2, Reg.4
s.87B, amended: 2012 c.21 s.16
s.87C, amended: 2012 c.21 s.16
s.87D, amended: 2012 c.21 s.16
s.87E, amended: 2012 c.21 s.16, SI 2012/916 Reg.2
s.87F, amended: 2012 c.21 s.16
s.87G, amended: 2012 c.21 s.16, SI 2012/1538 Reg.5
s.87H, amended: 2012 c.21 s.16, SI 2012/916 Reg.2
s.87I, amended: 2012 c.21 s.16, SI 2012/916 Reg.2, SI 2012/1538 Reg.6
s.87J, amended: 2012 c.21 s.16
s.87K, amended: 2012 c.21 s.16
s.87L, amended: 2012 c.21 s.16
s.87M, amended: 2012 c.21 s.16
s.87M, applied: 2012 c.21 s.109
s.87N, amended: 2012 c.21 s.16

2000–cont.

8. Financial Services and Markets Act 2000–*cont.*

s.87O, amended: 2012 c.21 s.16
s.87P, amended: 2012 c.21 s.16
s.87Q, amended: 2012 c.21 s.16, SI 2012/1538 Reg.5
s.87R, repealed: SI 2012/1538 Reg.3
s.88, amended: 2012 c.21 s.16, s.18
s.88C, applied: 2012 c.21 s.85
s.89, applied: 2012 c.21 s.109
s.89, substituted: 2012 c.21 s.18
s.89A, amended: 2012 c.21 s.16
s.89A, applied: SI 2012/1439 Art.2
s.89B, amended: 2012 c.21 s.16
s.89C, amended: 2012 c.21 s.16
s.89D, amended: 2012 c.21 s.16
s.89E, amended: 2012 c.21 s.16
s.89E, applied: SI 2012/1439 Art.2
s.89F, amended: 2012 c.21 s.16
s.89G, amended: 2012 c.21 s.16
s.89H, amended: 2012 c.21 s.16
s.89I, amended: 2012 c.21 s.16
s.89J, amended: 2012 c.21 s.16
s.89K, amended: 2012 c.21 s.16
s.89K, applied: 2012 c.21 s.109
s.89L, amended: 2012 c.21 s.16
s.89M, amended: 2012 c.21 s.16
s.89N, amended: 2012 c.21 s.16
s.89O, amended: 2012 c.21 s.16
s.89S, applied: 2012 c.21 s.85
s.90, amended: 2012 c.21 s.16, SI 2012/1538 Reg.7
s.90A, amended: 2012 c.21 s.16
s.90B, amended: 2012 c.21 s.16
s.90ZA, amended: 2012 c.21 s.16
s.91, amended: 2012 c.21 s.16, s.20
s.91, applied: 2012 c.21 s.109
s.92, amended: 2012 c.21 s.16
s.93, amended: 2012 c.21 s.16
s.93, applied: 2012 c.21 s.85
s.94, amended: 2012 c.21 s.16
s.95, amended: 2012 c.21 s.16
s.95, repealed: 2012 c.21 s.21
s.96, amended: 2012 c.21 s.16
s.96A, amended: 2012 c.21 s.16, SI 2012/1538 Reg.8
s.96B, amended: 2012 c.21 s.16
s.96C, amended: 2012 c.21 s.16
s.97, amended: 2012 c.21 s.16, Sch.18 para.7
s.99, repealed: 2012 c.21 s.16
s.100, repealed: 2012 c.21 s.16
s.100A, amended: 2012 c.21 s.16, SI 2012/916 Reg.2
s.101, amended: 2012 c.21 s.16
s.101, applied: SI 2012/1439 Art.2
s.101, repealed (in part): 2012 c.21 s.16
s.102, repealed: 2012 c.21 s.16
s.103, amended: 2012 c.21 s.16, SI 2012/1538 Reg.9
s.103, repealed (in part): 2012 c.21 s.16
s.103A, added: 2012 c.21 Sch.6 para.2
s.104, amended: 2012 c.21 s.22
s.105, applied: 2012 c.14 s.143
s.108, see *Combined Insurance Co of America, Re* [2012] EWHC 632 (Ch), [2012] Lloyd's Rep. I.R. 714 (Ch D (Companies Ct)), Morgan, J.
s.109, amended: 2012 c.21 Sch.6 para.3
s.110, substituted: 2012 c.21 Sch.6 para.4
s.112, amended: 2012 c.21 Sch.6 para.5
s.112ZA, added: 2012 c.21 Sch.6 para.6
s.113, amended: 2012 c.21 Sch.6 para.7
s.115, amended: 2012 c.21 Sch.6 para.8
s.119, amended: 2012 c.21 Sch.9 para.9
s.119, applied: 2012 c.21 s.85

2000– cont.

8. Financial Services and Markets Act 2000– *cont.*
s.120, amended: 2012 c.21 Sch.9 para.9
s.121, amended: 2012 c.21 Sch.9 para.9
s.122, amended: 2012 c.21 Sch.9 para.9
s.123, amended: 2012 c.21 Sch.9 para.9
s.123, applied: 2012 c.21 s.109
s.124, amended: 2012 c.21 Sch.9 para.9
s.124, applied: 2012 c.21 s.85
s.125, amended: 2012 c.21 Sch.9 para.9
s.126, amended: 2012 c.21 Sch.9 para.9
s.127, amended: 2012 c.21 Sch.9 para.9
s.128, amended: 2012 c.21 Sch.9 para.9
s.129, amended: 2012 c.21 Sch.9 para.9
s.130, amended: 2012 c.21 Sch.9 para.9
s.130A, amended: 2012 c.21 Sch.9 para.9
s.131A, amended: 2012 c.21 Sch.9 para.9
s.131B, repealed: SI 2012/ 2554 Reg.2
s.131C, repealed: SI 2012/ 2554 Reg.2
s.131D, repealed: SI 2012/ 2554 Reg.2
s.131E, amended: 2012 c.21 s.25, SI 2012/ 2554 Reg.2
s.131E, repealed (in part): SI 2012/ 2554 Reg.2
s.131F, amended: 2012 c.21 s.25, SI 2012/ 2554 Reg.2
s.131F, repealed (in part): SI 2012/ 2554 Reg.2
s.131FA, added: SI 2012/ 2554 Reg.2
s.131FA, amended: 2012 c.21 s.25
s.131FB, added: SI 2012/ 2554 Reg.2
s.131FB, amended: 2012 c.21 s.25
s.131FC, added: SI 2012/ 2554 Reg.2
s.131G, amended: 2012 c.21 s.25, SI 2012/ 2554 Reg.2
s.131G, applied: 2012 c.21 s.109
s.131H, amended: 2012 c.21 s.25
s.131I, amended: 2012 c.21 s.25
s.131J, amended: 2012 c.21 s.25
s.131J, applied: 2012 c.21 s.85
s.131K, amended: 2012 c.21 s.25
s.131L, added: SI 2012/ 2554 Reg.2
s.131L, amended: 2012 c.21 s.25
s.133, amended: 2012 c.21 s.23
s.133A, amended: 2012 c.21 s.23
s.133A, repealed (in part): 2012 c.21 s.23
s.133A, varied: SI 2012/ 3122 Sch.1 para.7
s.133B, amended: 2012 c.21 s.23
s.134, varied: SI 2012/ 3122 Sch.1 para.7
s.135, varied: SI 2012/ 3122 Sch.1 para.7
s.136, amended: 2012 c.21 s.23
s.136, varied: SI 2012/ 3122 Sch.1 para.7
s.138, amended: SI 2012/ 1906 Art.3
s.138, substituted: 2012 c.21 s.24
s.138N, applied: 2012 c.21 s.85
s.139, substituted: 2012 c.21 s.24
s.139A, substituted: 2012 c.21 s.24
s.139B, referred to: 2012 c.21 s.85
s.139B, substituted: 2012 c.21 s.24
s.139C, substituted: 2012 c.21 s.24
s.139D, substituted: 2012 c.21 s.24
s.139E, substituted: 2012 c.21 s.24
s.139F, substituted: 2012 c.21 s.24
s.140, substituted: 2012 c.21 s.24
s.141, substituted: 2012 c.21 s.24
s.142, substituted: 2012 c.21 s.24
s.143, substituted: 2012 c.21 s.24
s.144, substituted: 2012 c.21 s.24
s.145, substituted: 2012 c.21 s.24
s.146, substituted: 2012 c.21 s.24
s.147, substituted: 2012 c.21 s.24
s.148, substituted: 2012 c.21 s.24
s.149, substituted: 2012 c.21 s.24

2000– cont.

8. Financial Services and Markets Act 2000– *cont.*
s.150, see *Camerata Property Inc v Credit Suisse Securities (Europe) Ltd* [2012] EWHC 7 (Comm), [2012] 1 C.L.C. 234 (QBD (Comm)), Flaux, J.; see *City Index Ltd (t/a FinSpreads) v Balducci* [2011] EWHC 2562 (Ch), [2012] 1 B.C.L.C. 317 (Ch D), Proudman, J.
s.150, repealed (in part): SI 2012/ 2554 Reg.2
s.150, substituted: 2012 c.21 s.24
s.151, substituted: 2012 c.21 s.24
s.152, substituted: 2012 c.21 s.24
s.153, substituted: 2012 c.21 s.24
s.154, substituted: 2012 c.21 s.24
s.155, substituted: 2012 c.21 s.24
s.156, substituted: 2012 c.21 s.24
s.157, amended: SI 2012/ 2554 Reg.2
s.157, applied: SI 2012/ 1439 Art.2
s.165, amended: 2012 c.21 Sch.12 para.1
s.165, varied: SI 2012/ 3122 Sch.1 para.2
s.165A, amended: 2012 c.21 Sch.12 para.2
s.165A, varied: SI 2012/ 3122 Sch.1 para.2
s.165B, amended: 2012 c.21 Sch.12 para.3
s.165C, amended: 2012 c.21 Sch.12 para.4
s.166, substituted: 2012 c.21 Sch.12 para.5
s.166, varied: SI 2012/ 3122 Sch.1 para.2
s.166A, added: 2012 c.21 Sch.12 para.6
s.167, amended: 2012 c.21 Sch.12 para.7
s.167, varied: SI 2012/ 3122 Sch.1 para.2
s.168, amended: 2012 c.21 Sch.12 para.8, SI 2012/ 1906 Art.3, SI 2012/ 2554 Reg.2
s.168, repealed (in part): 2012 c.21 Sch.12 para.8
s.168, varied: SI 2012/ 3122 Sch.1 para.2
s.169, amended: 2012 c.21 Sch.12 para.9
s.169, varied: SI 2012/ 3122 Sch.1 para.2
s.169A, amended: 2012 c.21 Sch.12 para.10
s.170, amended: 2012 c.21 Sch.12 para.11
s.170, varied: SI 2012/ 3122 Sch.1 para.2
s.171, varied: SI 2012/ 3122 Sch.1 para.2
s.172, varied: SI 2012/ 3122 Sch.1 para.2
s.173, varied: SI 2012/ 3122 Sch.1 para.2
s.174, amended: 2012 c.21 Sch.12 para.12
s.174, varied: SI 2012/ 3122 Sch.1 para.2
s.175, amended: 2012 c.21 Sch.12 para.13
s.175, varied: SI 2012/ 3122 Sch.1 para.2
s.176, amended: 2012 c.21 Sch.12 para.14
s.176, repealed (in part): 2012 c.21 Sch.12 para.14
s.176, varied: SI 2012/ 3122 Sch.1 para.2
s.176A, added: 2012 c.21 Sch.12 para.15
s.177, amended: 2012 c.21 Sch.18 para.8
s.177, varied: SI 2012/ 3122 Sch.1 para.2
s.178, amended: 2012 c.21 s.26
s.179, amended: 2012 c.21 s.26
s.180, amended: 2012 c.21 s.26
s.185, amended: 2012 c.21 s.26
s.187, amended: 2012 c.21 s.26
s.187A, added: 2012 c.21 s.26
s.187B, added: 2012 c.21 s.26
s.187C, added: 2012 c.21 s.26
s.188, amended: 2012 c.21 s.26
s.189, amended: 2012 c.21 s.26
s.190, amended: 2012 c.21 s.26
s.191, amended: 2012 c.21 s.26
s.191A, amended: 2012 c.21 s.26
s.191B, amended: 2012 c.21 s.26
s.191C, amended: 2012 c.21 s.26
s.191D, amended: 2012 c.21 s.26
s.191E, amended: 2012 c.21 s.26
s.191F, amended: 2012 c.21 s.26

2000–cont.

8. Financial Services and Markets Act 2000–*cont.*
s.191G, amended: 2012 c.21 s.26
s.192A, added: 2012 c.21 s.27
s.192B, added: 2012 c.21 s.27
s.192C, added: 2012 c.21 s.27
s.192D, added: 2012 c.21 s.27
s.192E, added: 2012 c.21 s.27
s.192F, added: 2012 c.21 s.27
s.192G, added: 2012 c.21 s.27
s.192H, added: 2012 c.21 s.27
s.192H, applied: 2012 c.21 s.85
s.192I, added: 2012 c.21 s.27
s.192J, added: 2012 c.21 s.27
s.192K, added: 2012 c.21 s.27
s.192K, applied: 2012 c.21 s.110
s.192L, added: 2012 c.21 s.27
s.192L, applied: 2012 c.21 s.110
s.192M, added: 2012 c.21 s.27
s.192M, applied: 2012 c.21 s.110
s.192N, added: 2012 c.21 s.27
s.192N, applied: 2012 c.21 s.85, s.110
s.193, amended: 2012 c.21 Sch.4 para.30, Sch.4 para.31
s.194, amended: 2012 c.21 Sch.4 para.30, Sch.4 para.32
s.194A, amended: 2012 c.21 Sch.4 para.30, Sch.4 para.33, SI 2012/916 Reg.2
s.195, amended: 2012 c.21 Sch.4 para.30, Sch.4 para.34
s.195, repealed (in part): 2012 c.21 s.16, Sch.4 para.34
s.195A, amended: 2012 c.21 Sch.4 para.30, Sch.4 para.35, SI 2012/916 Reg.2
s.196, amended: 2012 c.21 Sch.4 para.30
s.196, substituted: 2012 c.21 Sch.4 para.36
s.197, amended: 2012 c.21 Sch.4 para.30, Sch.4 para.37
s.198, amended: 2012 c.21 Sch.4 para.30, Sch.4 para.38
s.199, amended: 2012 c.21 Sch.4 para.30, Sch.4 para.39, SI 2012/916 Reg.2, SI 2012/2015 Reg.3
s.199A, amended: 2012 c.21 Sch.4 para.30, Sch.4 para.40
s.200, amended: 2012 c.21 Sch.4 para.30, Sch.4 para.41
s.201, amended: 2012 c.21 Sch.4 para.30
s.201, substituted: 2012 c.21 Sch.4 para.42
s.202, amended: 2012 c.21 Sch.4 para.30, Sch.4 para.43
s.203, amended: 2012 c.21 Sch.4 para.30
s.204, amended: 2012 c.21 Sch.4 para.30
s.204A, added: 2012 c.21 Sch.9 para.10
s.205, amended: 2012 c.21 Sch.9 para.11, SI 2012/1906 Art.3
s.205, applied: 2012 c.21 s.107, s.109
s.206, amended: 2012 c.21 Sch.9 para.12, SI 2012/1906 Art.3
s.206, applied: 2012 c.21 s.107, s.109, SI 2012/3122 Sch.1 para.3
s.206A, amended: 2012 c.21 Sch.9 para.13, SI 2012/1906 Art.3
s.206A, applied: 2012 c.21 s.107, s.109
s.207, amended: 2012 c.21 Sch.9 para.14
s.208, amended: 2012 c.21 Sch.9 para.15
s.209, amended: 2012 c.21 Sch.9 para.16
s.210, amended: 2012 c.21 Sch.9 para.17
s.210, applied: 2012 c.21 s.85, SI 2012/3122 Sch.1 para.3
s.210, varied: SI 2012/3122 Sch.1 para.3
s.211, amended: 2012 c.21 Sch.9 para.18

2000–cont.

8. Financial Services and Markets Act 2000–*cont.*
s.211, applied: SI 2012/3122 Sch.1 para.3
s.212, amended: 2012 c.21 Sch.10 para.2
s.213, amended: 2012 c.21 Sch.10 para.3
s.214, amended: 2012 c.21 Sch.10 para.4
s.214B, amended: 2012 c.21 s.101
s.215, amended: 2012 c.21 Sch.10 para.5
s.217, amended: 2012 c.21 Sch.10 para.6
s.217A, added: 2012 c.21 Sch.10 para.7
s.217B, added: 2012 c.21 Sch.10 para.9
s.218, amended: 2012 c.21 Sch.10 para.10
s.218A, amended: 2012 c.21 Sch.10 para.12
s.218ZA, added: 2012 c.21 Sch.10 para.11
s.221, amended: 2012 c.21 Sch.10 para.13
s.222, amended: 2012 c.21 Sch.10 para.14
s.223B, applied: 2012 c.21 s.58, s.60
s.224, amended: 2012 c.21 Sch.10 para.15
s.224F, amended: 2012 c.21 s.38
s.226, amended: 2012 c.21 Sch.11 para.1
s.226A, amended: 2012 c.21 Sch.11 para.2
s.227, amended: 2012 c.21 Sch.11 para.3
s.228, amended: 2012 c.21 Sch.11 para.4
s.229, amended: 2012 c.21 Sch.11 para.5
s.230, amended: 2012 c.21 Sch.11 para.6
s.230A, added: 2012 c.21 Sch.11 para.7
s.232, amended: 2012 c.21 Sch.11 para.8
s.232A, added: 2012 c.21 Sch.11 para.9
s.234, amended: 2012 c.21 Sch.11 para.10
s.234A, amended: 2012 c.21 Sch.11 para.11
s.234B, added: 2012 c.21 Sch.11 para.12
s.234C, added: 2012 c.21 s.43
s.234D, added: 2012 c.21 s.43
s.234E, added: 2012 c.21 s.43
s.234F, added: 2012 c.21 s.43
s.234G, added: 2012 c.21 s.43
s.234H, added: 2012 c.21 s.43
s.235, see *Secretary of State for Business Innovation and Skills v Chohan* [2011] EWHC 1350 (Ch), [2012] 1 B.C.L.C. 138 (Ch D (Companies Ct)), David Richards, J.
s.237, amended: 2012 c.21 Sch.18 para.9
s.238, amended: 2012 c.21 Sch.18 para.9
s.239, amended: 2012 c.21 Sch.18 para.9
s.242, amended: 2012 c.21 Sch.18 para.9
s.243, amended: 2012 c.21 Sch.18 para.9
s.244, amended: 2012 c.21 Sch.18 para.9
s.245, amended: 2012 c.21 Sch.18 para.9
s.246, amended: 2012 c.21 Sch.18 para.9
s.247, amended: 2012 c.21 Sch.18 para.9
s.248, amended: 2012 c.21 Sch.18 para.9
s.249, amended: 2012 c.21 Sch.18 para.9, Sch.18 para.10
s.249, applied: 2012 c.21 s.109
s.249, referred to: 2012 c.21 s.85
s.249, substituted: 2012 c.21 Sch.18 para.10
s.250, amended: 2012 c.21 Sch.18 para.9, Sch.18 para.11
s.251, amended: 2012 c.21 Sch.18 para.9
s.252, amended: 2012 c.21 Sch.18 para.9
s.252A, amended: 2012 c.21 Sch.18 para.9
s.254, amended: 2012 c.21 Sch.18 para.9
s.255, amended: 2012 c.21 Sch.18 para.9
s.256, amended: 2012 c.21 Sch.18 para.9
s.257, amended: 2012 c.21 Sch.18 para.9, Sch.18 para.12
s.258, amended: 2012 c.21 Sch.18 para.9
s.258A, amended: 2012 c.21 Sch.18 para.9
s.259, amended: 2012 c.21 Sch.18 para.9

2000–cont.

8. Financial Services and Markets Act 2000–*cont.*
s.260, amended: 2012 c.21 Sch.18 para.9
s.261, amended: 2012 c.21 Sch.18 para.9
s.261A, amended: 2012 c.21 Sch.18 para.9
s.261B, amended: 2012 c.21 Sch.18 para.9
s.264, amended: 2012 c.21 Sch.18 para.9, SI 2012/ 2015 Reg.4
s.266, amended: 2012 c.21 Sch.18 para.9
s.267, amended: 2012 c.21 Sch.18 para.13
s.268, amended: 2012 c.21 Sch.18 para.14
s.269, amended: 2012 c.21 Sch.18 para.15
s.270, amended: 2012 c.21 Sch.18 para.16
s.271, amended: 2012 c.21 Sch.18 para.9
s.272, amended: 2012 c.21 Sch.18 para.9
s.273, amended: 2012 c.21 Sch.18 para.9
s.274, amended: 2012 c.21 Sch.18 para.9
s.275, amended: 2012 c.21 Sch.18 para.9
s.276, amended: 2012 c.21 Sch.18 para.9
s.277, amended: 2012 c.21 Sch.18 para.9
s.278, amended: 2012 c.21 Sch.18 para.9
s.279, amended: 2012 c.21 Sch.18 para.9
s.280, amended: 2012 c.21 Sch.18 para.9
s.281, amended: 2012 c.21 Sch.18 para.9
s.282, amended: 2012 c.21 Sch.18 para.9
s.283, amended: 2012 c.21 Sch.18 para.9
s.284, amended: 2012 c.21 Sch.18 para.17
s.285, amended: 2012 c.21 s.28
s.285A, added: 2012 c.21 s.29
s.286, amended: 2012 c.21 s.30, Sch.8 para.2
s.287, amended: 2012 c.21 Sch.8 para.3
s.288, amended: 2012 c.21 Sch.8 para.4
s.289, amended: 2012 c.21 Sch.8 para.5
s.290, amended: 2012 c.21 Sch.8 para.6
s.290, repealed (in part): 2012 c.21 Sch.8 para.6
s.290A, amended: 2012 c.21 Sch.8 para.7
s.292, amended: 2012 c.21 Sch.8 para.8
s.292A, amended: 2012 c.21 Sch.8 para.9
s.293, amended: 2012 c.21 Sch.8 para.10
s.293A, substituted: 2012 c.21 Sch.8 para.11
s.294, amended: 2012 c.21 Sch.8 para.12
s.295, amended: 2012 c.21 Sch.8 para.13
s.295, repealed (in part): 2012 c.21 Sch.8 para.13
s.296, amended: 2012 c.21 Sch.8 para.14
s.296A, added: 2012 c.21 s.31
s.297, amended: 2012 c.21 Sch.8 para.15, SI 2012/916 Reg.2
s.298, amended: 2012 c.21 s.32, Sch.8 para.16
s.298, repealed (in part): 2012 c.21 s.32
s.299, amended: 2012 c.21 Sch.8 para.17
s.300A, amended: 2012 c.21 Sch.8 para.18
s.300B, amended: 2012 c.21 Sch.8 para.19
s.300C, amended: 2012 c.21 Sch.8 para.20
s.300D, amended: 2012 c.21 Sch.8 para.21
s.301, amended: 2012 c.21 Sch.8 para.22
s.301A, amended: 2012 c.21 Sch.8 para.23
s.301B, amended: 2012 c.21 Sch.8 para.24
s.301C, amended: 2012 c.21 Sch.8 para.25
s.301F, amended: 2012 c.21 Sch.8 para.26
s.301G, amended: 2012 c.21 Sch.8 para.27
s.301H, amended: 2012 c.21 Sch.8 para.28
s.301I, amended: 2012 c.21 Sch.8 para.29
s.301J, amended: 2012 c.21 Sch.8 para.30
s.301K, amended: 2012 c.21 Sch.8 para.31
s.301L, amended: 2012 c.21 Sch.8 para.32
s.302, repealed: 2012 c.21 s.34
s.303, repealed: 2012 c.21 s.34
s.304, repealed: 2012 c.21 s.34
s.305, repealed: 2012 c.21 s.34

2000–cont.

8. Financial Services and Markets Act 2000–*cont.*
s.306, repealed: 2012 c.21 s.34
s.307, repealed: 2012 c.21 s.34
s.308, repealed: 2012 c.21 s.34
s.309, repealed: 2012 c.21 s.34
s.310, repealed: 2012 c.21 s.34
s.311, repealed: 2012 c.21 s.34
s.312, repealed: 2012 c.21 s.34
s.312A, amended: 2012 c.21 Sch.8 para.33
s.312B, amended: 2012 c.21 Sch.8 para.34, SI 2012/ 916 Reg.2
s.312C, amended: 2012 c.21 Sch.8 para.35
s.312E, added: 2012 c.21 s.33
s.312E, applied: 2012 c.21 s.110
s.312F, added: 2012 c.21 s.33
s.312F, applied: 2012 c.21 s.110
s.312G, added: 2012 c.21 s.33
s.312H, added: 2012 c.21 s.33
s.312I, added: 2012 c.21 s.33
s.312J, added: 2012 c.21 s.33
s.312J, applied: 2012 c.21 s.85
s.312K, added: 2012 c.21 s.33
s.313, amended: 2012 c.21 Sch.8 para.36
s.313A, amended: 2012 c.21 s.36
s.313B, amended: 2012 c.21 s.36
s.313BA, amended: 2012 c.21 s.36
s.313BB, amended: 2012 c.21 s.36
s.313BC, amended: 2012 c.21 s.36
s.313BD, amended: 2012 c.21 s.36
s.313BE, amended: 2012 c.21 s.36
s.313C, amended: 2012 c.21 s.36, SI 2012/916 Reg.2
s.313D, amended: 2012 c.21 s.36
s.314, amended: 2012 c.21 s.40
s.314A, added: 2012 c.21 s.40
s.315, substituted: 2012 c.21 s.40
s.316, amended: 2012 c.21 s.40
s.316, applied: 2012 c.21 s.85
s.317, amended: 2012 c.21 s.40
s.318, amended: 2012 c.21 s.40
s.318, applied: 2012 c.21 s.85
s.319, amended: 2012 c.21 s.40
s.320, amended: 2012 c.21 s.40
s.321, amended: 2012 c.21 s.40
s.322, amended: 2012 c.21 s.40
s.325, amended: 2012 c.21 Sch.16 para.1
s.328, amended: 2012 c.21 Sch.16 para.2
s.328, applied: 2012 c.21 s.85
s.329, amended: 2012 c.21 Sch.16 para.3
s.330, amended: 2012 c.21 Sch.16 para.4
s.331, amended: 2012 c.21 Sch.16 para.5
s.332, amended: 2012 c.21 Sch.16 para.6
s.334, repealed (in part): 2012 c.21 s.54
s.335, repealed: 2012 c.21 s.54
s.336, repealed: 2012 c.21 s.54
s.337, repealed: 2012 c.21 s.54
s.338, repealed: 2012 c.21 s.54
s.339, repealed: 2012 c.21 s.54
s.340, amended: 2012 c.21 Sch.13 para.3
s.342, amended: 2012 c.21 Sch.13 para.4
s.343, amended: 2012 c.21 Sch.13 para.5
s.344, amended: 2012 c.21 Sch.13 para.6
s.345, applied: 2012 c.21 s.109
s.345, referred to: 2012 c.21 s.85
s.345, substituted: 2012 c.21 Sch.13 para.7
s.345A, referred to: 2012 c.21 s.85
s.345D, applied: 2012 c.21 s.85
s.347, amended: 2012 c.21 Sch.12 para.16
s.347, repealed (in part): 2012 c.21 Sch.12 para.16

2000–*cont.*

8. Financial Services and Markets Act 2000–*cont.*
s.347A, added: 2012 c.21 Sch.12 para.17
s.348, amended: 2012 c.21 Sch.12 para.18
s.348, applied: 2012 c.21 Sch.20 para.9, SI 2012/3122 Reg.17, Sch.1 para.4
s.348, repealed (in part): 2012 c.21 Sch.12 para.18
s.348, varied: SI 2012/3122 Sch.1 para.4
s.349, amended: 2012 c.21 Sch.12 para.19
s.349, applied: SI 2012/3122 Reg.17, Sch.1 para.4
s.349, varied: SI 2012/3122 Sch.1 para.4
s.349, enabling: SI 2012/3019
s.350, amended: 2012 c.21 Sch.12 para.20
s.351, repealed: 2012 c.21 Sch.12 para.21
s.351A, amended: 2012 c.21 Sch.12 para.22
s.352, applied: SI 2012/3122 Reg.17, Sch.1 para.4
s.353, amended: 2012 c.21 Sch.12 para.23
s.353A, added: 2012 c.21 Sch.12 para.24
s.354, substituted: 2012 c.21 Sch.12 para.25
s.355, amended: 2012 c.21 Sch.14 para.2
s.356, amended: 2012 c.21 Sch.14 para.3
s.357, amended: 2012 c.21 Sch.14 para.4
s.358, amended: 2012 c.21 Sch.14 para.5
s.359, amended: 2012 c.21 Sch.14 para.6
s.361, amended: 2012 c.21 Sch.14 para.7
s.362, amended: 2012 c.21 Sch.14 para.8
s.362A, see *Ceart Risk Services Ltd, Re* [2012] EWHC 1178 (Ch), [2012] B.C.C. 592 (Ch D (Companies Ct)), Arnold, J.; see *M.T.B. Motors Ltd (In Administration), Re* [2010] EWHC 3751 (Ch), [2012] B.C.C. 601 (Ch D (Manchester)), Judge Hodge Q.C.
s.362A, amended: 2012 c.21 Sch.14 para.9
s.363, amended: 2012 c.21 Sch.14 para.10
s.364, amended: 2012 c.21 Sch.14 para.11
s.365, amended: 2012 c.21 Sch.14 para.12
s.366, amended: 2012 c.21 Sch.14 para.13
s.367, amended: 2012 c.21 Sch.14 para.14
s.368, amended: 2012 c.21 Sch.14 para.15
s.368, substituted: 2012 c.21 Sch.14 para.15
s.369, amended: 2012 c.21 Sch.14 para.16
s.369A, amended: 2012 c.21 Sch.14 para.17
s.370, substituted: 2012 c.21 Sch.14 para.18
s.371, amended: 2012 c.21 Sch.14 para.19
s.372, amended: 2012 c.21 Sch.14 para.20
s.373, amended: 2012 c.21 Sch.14 para.21
s.374, amended: 2012 c.21 Sch.14 para.22
s.375, amended: 2012 c.21 Sch.14 para.23
s.376, amended: 2012 c.21 Sch.14 para.24
s.380, amended: 2012 c.21 Sch.9 para.19, SI 2012/1906 Art.3, SI 2012/2554 Reg.2
s.380, applied: 2012 c.21 s.110
s.380, repealed (in part): 2012 c.21 Sch.9 para.19
s.381, amended: 2012 c.21 Sch.9 para.20
s.382, amended: 2012 c.21 Sch.9 para.21, SI 2012/1906 Art.3, SI 2012/2554 Reg.2
s.382, applied: 2012 c.21 s.110
s.382, repealed (in part): 2012 c.21 Sch.9 para.21
s.383, amended: 2012 c.21 Sch.9 para.22
s.384, amended: 2012 c.21 Sch.9 para.23, SI 2012/1906 Art.3
s.384, applied: 2012 c.21 s.110
s.384, repealed (in part): 2012 c.21 Sch.9 para.23
s.385, amended: 2012 c.21 Sch.9 para.24
s.386, amended: 2012 c.21 Sch.9 para.25
s.387, amended: 2012 c.21 Sch.9 para.26
s.388, amended: 2012 c.21 Sch.9 para.27
s.388, varied: SI 2012/3122 Sch.1 para.5
s.389, amended: 2012 c.21 Sch.9 para.28

2000–*cont.*

8. Financial Services and Markets Act 2000–*cont.*
s.390, amended: 2012 c.21 Sch.9 para.29
s.390, varied: SI 2012/3122 Sch.1 para.5
s.391, amended: 2012 c.21 s.24, Sch.9 para.30, SI 2012/916 Reg.2
s.391, referred to: 2012 c.21 s.37
s.391, varied: SI 2012/3122 Sch.1 para.5
s.392, amended: 2012 c.21 s.18, Sch.8 para.37, Sch.9 para.31, Sch.13 para.8
s.392, varied: SI 2012/3122 Sch.1 para.5
s.393, amended: 2012 c.21 Sch.9 para.32
s.393, applied: SI 2012/3122 Reg.7
s.394, amended: 2012 c.21 Sch.9 para.33
s.395, amended: 2012 c.21 s.17, s.18, s.19, s.24, Sch.9 para.34
s.395, referred to: 2012 c.21 s.37
s.395, varied: SI 2012/3122 Sch.1 para.5
s.396, amended: 2012 c.21 Sch.9 para.35
s.397, repealed: 2012 c.21 s.95
s.398, amended: 2012 c.21 Sch.9 para.36, SI 2012/2554 Reg.2
s.398, applied: SI 2012/2554 Reg.5
s.400, amended: 2012 c.21 Sch.9 para.37
s.401, amended: 2012 c.21 Sch.9 para.38
s.402, amended: 2012 c.21 Sch.9 para.39
s.403, amended: 2012 c.21 Sch.9 para.40
s.404, amended: 2012 c.21 Sch.18 para.18
s.404A, amended: 2012 c.21 Sch.18 para.19
s.404F, amended: 2012 c.21 Sch.18 para.20
s.405, amended: 2012 c.21 Sch.18 para.21
s.407, amended: 2012 c.21 Sch.18 para.22
s.409, amended: 2012 c.21 Sch.18 para.23
s.409, enabling: SI 2012/2017
s.410, amended: 2012 c.21 s.47
s.410, repealed (in part): 2012 c.21 s.16
s.412A, amended: 2012 c.21 Sch.8 para.38
s.412B, amended: 2012 c.21 Sch.8 para.39
s.413, applied: SI 2012/3122 Sch.1 para.6
s.415, amended: 2012 c.21 Sch.18 para.24
s.415, repealed (in part): 2012 c.21 s.16
s.415A, amended: 2012 c.21 Sch.18 para.25
s.415B, added: 2012 c.21 Sch.9 para.41
s.417, amended: 2012 c.21 s.48, SI 2012/916 Reg.2, SI 2012/1809 Sch.1 Part 1, SI 2012/1906 Art.3, SI 2012/2554 Reg.2
s.417, enabling: SI 2012/3019
s.418, amended: SI 2012/1906 Art.3
s.420, referred to: 2012 c.14 s.221
s.421ZA, added: 2012 c.21 s.48
s.425, amended: SI 2012/1906 Art.3
s.425C, added: 2012 c.21 s.48
s.426, enabling: SI 2012/1906
s.428, enabling: SI 2012/1906, SI 2012/2017
s.429, amended: 2012 c.21 s.49
s.429, repealed (in part): 2012 c.21 s.49
Sch.1 Part I para.1, substituted: 2012 c.21 Sch.3
Sch.1 Part I para.2, substituted: 2012 c.21 Sch.3
Sch.1 Part I para.3, substituted: 2012 c.21 Sch.3
Sch.1 Part I para.4, substituted: 2012 c.21 Sch.3
Sch.1 Part I para.5, substituted: 2012 c.21 Sch.3
Sch.1 Part I para.6, amended: SI 2012/1906 Art.3, SI 2012/2554 Reg.2
Sch.1 Part I para.6, substituted: 2012 c.21 Sch.3
Sch.1 Part I para.7, substituted: 2012 c.21 Sch.3
Sch.1 Part I para.8, substituted: 2012 c.21 Sch.3
Sch.1 Part I para.9, substituted: 2012 c.21 Sch.3
Sch.1 Part I para.10, substituted: 2012 c.21 Sch.3
Sch.1 Part I para.11, substituted: 2012 c.21 Sch.3

2000–cont.

8. Financial Services and Markets Act 2000–*cont.*

Sch.1 Part I para.12, substituted: 2012 c.21 Sch.3
Sch.1 Part II para.13, substituted: 2012 c.21 Sch.3
Sch.1 Part II para.14, substituted: 2012 c.21 Sch.3
Sch.1 Part II para.15, substituted: 2012 c.21 Sch.3
Sch.1 Part III para.16, applied: 2012 c.21 s.109
Sch.1 Part III para.16, substituted: 2012 c.21 Sch.3
Sch.1 Part III para.17, applied: SI 2012/3122 Reg.14
Sch.1 Part III para.17, substituted: 2012 c.21 Sch.3
Sch.1 Part III para.17, varied: SI 2012/3122 Reg.14
Sch.1 Part III para.18, substituted: 2012 c.21 Sch.3
Sch.1 Part IV para.19, applied: SI 2012/3122 Reg.16
Sch.1 Part IV para.19, substituted: 2012 c.21 Sch.3
Sch.1 Part IV para.19A, substituted: 2012 c.21 Sch.3
Sch.1 Part IV para.19B, substituted: 2012 c.21 Sch.3
Sch.1 Part IV para.20, substituted: 2012 c.21 Sch.3
Sch.1 Part IV para.21, substituted: 2012 c.21 Sch.3
Sch.1 Part IV para.25, substituted: 2012 c.21 Sch.3
Sch.1 Part IV para.26, substituted: 2012 c.21 Sch.3
Sch.1 Part IV para.27, substituted: 2012 c.21 Sch.3
Sch.1 Pt IV para.19, see *Financial Services Authority v Sinaloa Gold Plc* [2011] EWCA Civ 1158, [2012] Bus. L.R. 753 (CA (Civ Div)), Mummery, L.J.
Sch.1A Part I para.1, amended: 2012 c.21 Sch.15 para.2, Sch.15 para.16
Sch.1A Part I para.2, amended: 2012 c.21 Sch.15 para.3, Sch.15 para.16
Sch.1A Part I para.3, amended: 2012 c.21 Sch.15 para.4, Sch.15 para.16
Sch.1A Part I para.4, amended: 2012 c.21 Sch.15 para.5, Sch.15 para.16
Sch.1A Part I para.5, amended: 2012 c.21 Sch.15 para.6, Sch.15 para.16
Sch.1A Part I para.6, amended: 2012 c.21 Sch.15 para.16
Sch.1A Part I para.6, substituted: 2012 c.21 Sch.15 para.7
Sch.1A Part I para.6A, amended: 2012 c.21 Sch.15 para.16
Sch.1A Part I para.6B, amended: 2012 c.21 Sch.15 para.16
Sch.1A Part I para.7, amended: 2012 c.21 Sch.15 para.8, Sch.15 para.16
Sch.1A Part I para.8, amended: 2012 c.21 Sch.15 para.9, Sch.15 para.16
Sch.1A Part I para.9, amended: 2012 c.21 Sch.15 para.10, Sch.15 para.16
Sch.1A Part I para.9A, added: 2012 c.21 Sch.15 para.11
Sch.1A Part I para.9A, amended: 2012 c.21 Sch.15 para.16
Sch.1A Part I para.10, amended: 2012 c.21 Sch.15 para.16
Sch.1A Part II para.11, amended: 2012 c.21 Sch.15 para.12, Sch.15 para.16
Sch.1A Part II para.12, amended: 2012 c.21 Sch.15 para.13, Sch.15 para.16
Sch.1A Part II para.13, amended: 2012 c.21 Sch.15 para.14, Sch.15 para.16
Sch.1A Part II para.14, amended: 2012 c.21 Sch.15 para.16
Sch.1A Part III para.15, amended: 2012 c.21 Sch.15 para.15, Sch.15 para.16
Sch.1A Part III para.16, amended: 2012 c.21 Sch.15 para.16
Sch.2, applied: 2012 c.7 s.145, SI 2012/2751 Art.3, SI 2012/3065 Art.3, SI 2012/3066 Art.3, SI 2012/3067 Art.3, SI 2012/3068 Art.3

2000–cont.

8. Financial Services and Markets Act 2000–*cont.*

Sch.2, referred to: SI 2012/1507 Reg.2, SI 2012/1508 Reg.2
Sch.2 Part IIA para.24A, added: 2012 c.21 s.7
Sch.2 Part IIA para.24B, added: 2012 c.21 s.7
Sch.2 Part IIA para.24C, added: 2012 c.21 s.7
Sch.2 Part IIA para.24D, added: 2012 c.21 s.7
Sch.2 Part IIB para.24E, added: 2012 c.21 s.7
Sch.2 Part IIB para.24F, added: 2012 c.21 s.7
Sch.2 Part IIB para.24G, added: 2012 c.21 s.7
Sch.2 Part IIB para.24H, added: 2012 c.21 s.7
Sch.2 Part II para.23, substituted: 2012 c.21 s.7
Sch.2 Part II para.23B, added: 2012 c.21 s.7
Sch.2 Part III para.25, amended: 2012 c.21 s.8
Sch.2 Part III para.25, enabling: SI 2012/1906
Sch.2 Part III para.26, substituted: 2012 c.21 s.8
Sch.3 Part I para.2, amended: SI 2012/917 Sch.1 para.2
Sch.3 Part I para.4D, added: SI 2012/1906 Art.4
Sch.3 Part I para.5, amended: SI 2012/1906 Art.4
Sch.3 Part I para.5, referred to: 2012 c.14 s.65
Sch.3 Part I para.6, amended: SI 2012/1906 Art.4
Sch.3 Part I para.7, amended: SI 2012/1906 Art.4
Sch.3 Part I para.9, amended: SI 2012/1906 Art.4
Sch.3 Part I para.11, amended: SI 2012/1906 Art.4
Sch.3 Part II para.12, amended: SI 2012/1906 Art.4
Sch.3 Part II para.13, amended: 2012 c.21 Sch.4 para.2, SI 2012/1906 Art.4
Sch.3 Part II para.13, repealed (in part): 2012 c.21 Sch.4 para.2
Sch.3 Part II para.14, amended: 2012 c.21 Sch.4 para.3, SI 2012/1906 Art.4
Sch.3 Part II para.14, repealed (in part): 2012 c.21 Sch.4 para.3
Sch.3 Part II para.15, amended: SI 2012/1906 Art.4
Sch.3 Part II para.15, applied: 2012 c.21 s.107, Sch.21 para.7
Sch.3 Part II para.15A, amended: 2012 c.21 Sch.4 para.4
Sch.3 Part II para.15B, amended: 2012 c.21 Sch.4 para.5
Sch.3 Part II para.15C, amended: 2012 c.21 Sch.4 para.6
Sch.3 Part II para.15ZA, added: SI 2012/1906 Art.4
Sch.3 Part II para.17, amended: 2012 c.21 Sch.4 para.7
Sch.3 Part II para.18, amended: 2012 c.21 Sch.4 para.8
Sch.3 Part III, added: 2012 c.21 Sch.4 para.9
Sch.3 Part III para.19, amended: 2012 c.21 Sch.4 para.10, SI 2012/916 Reg.2, SI 2012/1906 Art.4
Sch.3 Part III para.20, amended: 2012 c.21 Sch.4 para.11, SI 2012/1906 Art.4
Sch.3 Part III para.20B, amended: 2012 c.21 Sch.4 para.13
Sch.3 Part III para.20ZA, amended: 2012 c.21 Sch.4 para.12
Sch.3 Part III para.22, amended: 2012 c.21 Sch.4 para.14
Sch.3 Part III para.23, amended: 2012 c.21 Sch.4 para.15
Sch.3 Part III para.24, amended: 2012 c.21 Sch.4 para.16
Sch.3 Part III para.24A, added: 2012 c.21 Sch.4 para.17
Sch.3 Part III para.25, amended: 2012 c.21 Sch.4 para.18
Sch.3 Part III para.26, amended: 2012 c.21 Sch.4 para.19

2000– cont.

8. Financial Services and Markets Act 2000–*cont.*

Sch.3 Part III para.27, amended: 2012 c.21 Sch.4 para.20

Sch.3 Part III para.28, amended: 2012 c.21 Sch.4 para.21

Sch.4, applied: 2012 c.14 s.65

Sch.4 para.3, amended: 2012 c.21 Sch.4 para.23

Sch.4 para.3A, added: 2012 c.21 Sch.4 para.24

Sch.4 para.4, amended: 2012 c.21 Sch.4 para.25

Sch.4 para.5, amended: 2012 c.21 Sch.4 para.26

Sch.6 Part I, referred to: 2012 c.21 Sch.20 para.5

Sch.6 Part II, referred to: 2012 c.21 Sch.20 para.5

Sch.6 Part III para.8, amended: 2012 c.21 Sch.18 para.26

Sch.6 Part III para.9, repealed: 2012 c.21 s.11

Sch.7 para.1, repealed: 2012 c.21 s.16

Sch.7 para.2, repealed: 2012 c.21 s.16

Sch.7 para.3, repealed: 2012 c.21 s.16

Sch.7 para.4, repealed: 2012 c.21 s.16

Sch.7 para.5, repealed: 2012 c.21 s.16

Sch.7 para.6, repealed: 2012 c.21 s.16

Sch.7 para.7, repealed: 2012 c.21 s.16

Sch.7 para.8, repealed: 2012 c.21 s.16

Sch.8 para.1, repealed: 2012 c.21 s.16

Sch.8 para.2, repealed: 2012 c.21 s.16

Sch.8 para.3, repealed: 2012 c.21 s.16

Sch.10 para.1, amended: 2012 c.21 s.16

Sch.10 para.2, amended: 2012 c.21 s.16

Sch.11A Part II para.8, amended: SI 2012/1538 Reg.2

Sch.11A Part II para.9, amended: SI 2012/1538 Reg.2

Sch.12 Part I para.1, amended: 2012 c.21 Sch.6 para.10

Sch.12 Part I para.2, amended: 2012 c.21 Sch.6 para.11

Sch.12 Part I para.3, amended: 2012 c.21 Sch.6 para.12

Sch.12 Part I para.4, amended: 2012 c.21 Sch.6 para.13

Sch.12 Part I para.5, amended: 2012 c.21 Sch.6 para.14

Sch.12 Part I para.5A, amended: 2012 c.21 Sch.6 para.15

Sch.12 Part II para.8, amended: 2012 c.21 Sch.6 para.16

Sch.12 Part II para.9, amended: 2012 c.21 Sch.6 para.17

Sch.12 Part IIA para.9A, amended: 2012 c.21 Sch.6 para.18

Sch.12 Part III para.10, amended: 2012 c.21 Sch.6 para.19

Sch.14 para.1, repealed: 2012 c.21 s.24

Sch.14 para.2, repealed: 2012 c.21 s.24

Sch.14 para.2A, repealed: 2012 c.21 s.24

Sch.14 para.2B, repealed: 2012 c.21 s.24

Sch.14 para.2C, repealed: 2012 c.21 s.24

Sch.14 para.3, repealed: 2012 c.21 s.24

Sch.14 para.4, repealed: 2012 c.21 s.24

Sch.17A, applied: 2012 c.21 s.85, s.110

Sch.17 Part II para.2, substituted: 2012 c.21 Sch.11 para.14

Sch.17 Part II para.3, amended: 2012 c.21 Sch.11 para.15

Sch.17 Part II para.3A, added: 2012 c.21 Sch.11 para.16

Sch.17 Part II para.6, amended: 2012 c.21 Sch.11 para.17

2000– cont.

8. Financial Services and Markets Act 2000– *cont.*

Sch.17 Part II para.7, amended: 2012 c.21 Sch.11 para.18

Sch.17 Part II para.7A, added: 2012 c.21 Sch.11 para.19

Sch.17 Part II para.8, amended: 2012 c.21 Sch.11 para.21

Sch.17 Part II para.8, substituted: 2012 c.21 Sch.11 para.20

Sch.17 Part II para.9, amended: 2012 c.21 Sch.11 para.22

Sch.17 Part II para.9A, added: 2012 c.21 Sch.11 para.23

Sch.17 Part IIIA para.16B, amended: 2012 c.21 Sch.11 para.26

Sch.17 Part IIIA para.16E, amended: 2012 c.21 Sch.11 para.27

Sch.17 Part III para.13, amended: 2012 c.21 Sch.11 para.24

Sch.17 Part III para.14, amended: 2012 c.21 Sch.11 para.25

Sch.17 Part IV para.18, amended: 2012 c.21 Sch.11 para.28

Sch.17 Part IV para.19, amended: 2012 c.21 Sch.11 para.29

Sch.17 Part IV para.20, amended: 2012 c.21 Sch.11 para.30

Sch.17A Part 1 para.1, added: 2012 c.21 Sch.7

Sch.17A Part 1 para.2, added: 2012 c.21 Sch.7

Sch.17A Part 1 para.3, added: 2012 c.21 Sch.7

Sch.17A Part 1 para.4, added: 2012 c.21 Sch.7

Sch.17A Part 1 para.5, added: 2012 c.21 Sch.7

Sch.17A Part 1 para.6, added: 2012 c.21 Sch.7

Sch.17A Part 1 para.7, added: 2012 c.21 Sch.7

Sch.17A Part 1 para.8, added: 2012 c.21 Sch.7

Sch.17A Part 2 para.9, added: 2012 c.21 Sch.7

Sch.17A Part 2 para.10, added: 2012 c.21 Sch.7

Sch.17A Part 2 para.11, added: 2012 c.21 Sch.7

Sch.17A Part 2 para.12, added: 2012 c.21 Sch.7

Sch.17A Part 2 para.13, added: 2012 c.21 Sch.7

Sch.17A Part 2 para.14, added: 2012 c.21 Sch.7

Sch.17A Part 2 para.15, added: 2012 c.21 Sch.7

Sch.17A Part 2 para.16, added: 2012 c.21 Sch.7

Sch.17A Part 2 para.17, added: 2012 c.21 Sch.7

Sch.17A Part 2 para.18, added: 2012 c.21 Sch.7

Sch.17A Part 2 para.19, added: 2012 c.21 Sch.7

Sch.17A Part 2 para.20, added: 2012 c.21 Sch.7

Sch.17A Part 2 para.21, added: 2012 c.21 Sch.7

Sch.17A Part 2 para.22, added: 2012 c.21 Sch.7

Sch.17A Part 2 para.23, added: 2012 c.21 Sch.7

Sch.17A Part 2 para.24, added: 2012 c.21 Sch.7

Sch.17A Part 2 para.25, added: 2012 c.21 Sch.7

Sch.17A Part 2 para.26, added: 2012 c.21 Sch.7

Sch.17A Part 2 para.27, added: 2012 c.21 Sch.7

Sch.17A Part 2 para.28, added: 2012 c.21 Sch.7

Sch.17A Part 2 para.29, added: 2012 c.21 Sch.7

Sch.17A Part 2 para.30, added: 2012 c.21 Sch.7

Sch.17A Part 2 para.31, added: 2012 c.21 Sch.7

Sch.17A Part 2 para.32, added: 2012 c.21 Sch.7

Sch.17A Part 2 para.33, added: 2012 c.21 Sch.7

Sch.17A Part 3 para.34, added: 2012 c.21 Sch.7

Sch.17A Part 3 para.35, added: 2012 c.21 Sch.7

Sch.17A Part 4 para.36, added: 2012 c.21 Sch.7

Sch.17A Part 4 para.37, added: 2012 c.21 Sch.7

10. Crown Prosecution Service Inspectorate Act 2000

Sch.1 para.2, repealed (in part): SI 2012/2401 Sch.1 para.9

10. Crown Prosecution Service Inspectorate Act 2000–*cont.*
Sch.1 para.4, repealed (in part): SI 2012/ 2401 Sch.1 para.9
Sch.1 para.5, repealed (in part): SI 2012/ 2401 Sch.1 para.9
Sch.1 para.9, added: SI 2012/ 2401 Sch.1 para.9

11. Terrorism Act 2000
applied: 2012 c.13 Sch.1, SI 2012/ 1726 r.6.1, r.6.10
Part III, referred to: SI 2012/ 2299 Art.4
Part V, amended: 2012 c.9 Sch.9 para.24
s.1, see *R. v Gul (Mohammed)* [2012] EWCA Crim 280, [2012] 1 W.L.R. 3432 (CA (Crim Div)), Sir John Thomas (President)
s.2, see *R. v Gul (Mohammed)* [2012] EWCA Crim 280, [2012] 1 W.L.R. 3432 (CA (Crim Div)), Sir John Thomas (President)
s.3, enabling: SI 2012/ 1771, SI 2012/ 2937
s.41, applied: SI 2012/ 1792 Art.2
s.43, amended: 2012 c.9 s.60
s.43, repealed (in part): 2012 c.9 Sch.10 Part 4
s.43A, added: 2012 c.9 s.60
s.44, repealed: 2012 c.9 Sch.10 Part 4
s.45, repealed: 2012 c.9 Sch.10 Part 4
s.46, repealed: 2012 c.9 Sch.10 Part 4
s.47, repealed: 2012 c.9 Sch.10 Part 4
s.47A, added: 2012 c.9 s.61
s.47AA, added: 2012 c.9 s.62
s.47AA, applied: SI 2012/ 1794 Art.2, Art.3, SI 2012/ 1794(a), SI 2012/ 1794(b)
s.47AA, referred to: SI 2012/ 1794(a)
s.47AB, added: 2012 c.9 s.62
s.47AB, applied: SI 2012/ 1794, SI 2012/ 1794(c)
s.47AB, enabling: SI 2012/ 1794
s.47AC, added: 2012 c.9 s.62
s.47AD, added: 2012 c.9 s.62
s.47AE, added: 2012 c.9 s.62
s.58, see *R. v Brown (Terence Roy)* [2011] EWCA Crim 2751, [2012] 2 Cr. App. R. (S.) 10 (CA (Crim Div)), Lord Judge, L.C.J.
s.63C, amended: SI 2012/ 1809 Sch.1 Part 1
s.123, amended: 2012 c.9 s.58, Sch.9 para.25
s.123, applied: SI 2012/ 1771, SI 2012/ 1792, SI 2012/ 1794
Sch.2, amended: SI 2012/ 1771 Art.2, SI 2012/ 2937 Art.2
Sch.2, applied: SI 2012/ 1771
Sch.3A, referred to: SI 2012/ 2299 Art.4
Sch.3A Part I para.1, amended: SI 2012/ 1534 Art.2, SI 2012/ 2299 Art.2
Sch.3A Part II para.4, amended: 2012 c.21 Sch.18 para.87
Sch.3A Part III para.5, enabling: SI 2012/ 1534, SI 2012/ 2299
Sch.5 Part I para.4, applied: SI 2012/ 1726 r.6.7
Sch.5 Part I para.5, applied: SI 2012/ 1726 r.6.1, r.6.7, r.6.13
Sch.5 Part I para.6, applied: SI 2012/ 1726 r.6.7
Sch.5 Part I para.7, applied: SI 2012/ 1726 r.6.7
Sch.5 Part I para.8, applied: SI 2012/ 1726 r.6.7
Sch.5 Part I para.9, applied: SI 2012/ 1726 r.6.7
Sch.5 Part I para.10, applied: SI 2012/ 1726 r.6.1, r.6.13
Sch.5 Part I para.10, enabling: SI 2012/ 1726
Sch.5 Part I para.13, applied: SI 2012/ 1726 r.6.1, r.6.8, r.6.13
Sch.5 Part I para.14, applied: SI 2012/ 1726 r.6.13
Sch.6, applied: SI 2012/ 1726 r.6.9
Sch.6A, applied: SI 2012/ 1726 r.6.10

11. Terrorism Act 2000–*cont.*
Sch.6 para.1, applied: SI 2012/ 1726 r.6.1, r.6.13
Sch.6 para.4, applied: SI 2012/ 1726 r.6.1
Sch.6 para.4, enabling: SI 2012/ 1726
Sch.6 para.6, amended: 2012 c.21 Sch.18 para.87
Sch.6 para.7, applied: SI 2012/ 1726 r.6.9
Sch.6A para.2, applied: SI 2012/ 1726 r.6.1, r.6.13
Sch.6A para.4, applied: SI 2012/ 1726 r.6.1
Sch.6A para.5, applied: SI 2012/ 1726 r.6.1
Sch.6A para.5, enabling: SI 2012/ 1726
Sch.6A para.6, applied: SI 2012/ 1726 r.6.13
Sch.6B para.1, added: 2012 c.9 Sch.5
Sch.6B para.2, added: 2012 c.9 Sch.5
Sch.6B para.3, added: 2012 c.9 Sch.5
Sch.6B para.4, added: 2012 c.9 Sch.5
Sch.6B para.5, added: 2012 c.9 Sch.5
Sch.6B para.6, added: 2012 c.9 Sch.5
Sch.6B para.7, added: 2012 c.9 Sch.5
Sch.6B para.8, added: 2012 c.9 Sch.5
Sch.6B para.9, added: 2012 c.9 Sch.5
Sch.6B para.10, added: 2012 c.9 Sch.5
Sch.6B para.11, added: 2012 c.9 Sch.5
Sch.6B para.12, added: 2012 c.9 Sch.5
Sch.6B para.13, added: 2012 c.9 Sch.5
Sch.6B para.14, added: 2012 c.9 Sch.5
Sch.7, see *R. (on the application of CC) v Commissioner of Police of the Metropolis* [2011] EWHC 3316 (Admin), [2012] 1 W.L.R. 1913 (QBD (Admin)), Collins, J.
Sch.7, applied: SI 2012/ 1792 Art.2
Sch.8 Part I para.3, enabling: SI 2012/ 1792
Sch.8 Part I para.4, applied: SI 2012/ 1792(a), SI 2012/ 1792(b)
Sch.8 Part I para.4, enabling: SI 2012/ 1792
Sch.8 Part I para.11, amended: 2012 c.9 Sch.1 para.1
Sch.8 Part I para.14, repealed: 2012 c.9 Sch.1 para.1, Sch.10 Part 1
Sch.8 Part I para.14F, repealed (in part): 2012 c.10 Sch.24 para.22
Sch.8 Part I para.15, amended: 2012 c.9 Sch.1 para.1
Sch.8 Part I para.20, amended: 2012 c.9 Sch.10 Part 1, Sch.1 para.1
Sch.8 Part I para.20, repealed (in part): 2012 c.9 Sch.1 para.1, Sch.10 Part 1
Sch.8 Part I para.20A, added: 2012 c.9 Sch.1 para.1
Sch.8 Part I para.20A, applied: 2012 c.9 s.20
Sch.8 Part I para.20B, added: 2012 c.9 Sch.1 para.1
Sch.8 Part I para.20B, applied: 2012 c.9 s.20
Sch.8 Part I para.20C, added: 2012 c.9 Sch.1 para.1
Sch.8 Part I para.20C, applied: 2012 c.9 s.20
Sch.8 Part I para.20D, added: 2012 c.9 Sch.1 para.1
Sch.8 Part I para.20D, applied: 2012 c.9 s.20
Sch.8 Part I para.20E, added: 2012 c.9 Sch.1 para.1
Sch.8 Part I para.20E, applied: 2012 c.9 s.20
Sch.8 Part I para.20F, added: 2012 c.9 Sch.1 para.1
Sch.8 Part I para.20F, amended: 2012 c.10 Sch.24 para.23
Sch.8 Part I para.20F, applied: 2012 c.9 s.20
Sch.8 Part I para.20G, added: 2012 c.9 Sch.1 para.1
Sch.8 Part I para.20G, applied: 2012 c.9 s.20
Sch.8 Part I para.20H, added: 2012 c.9 Sch.1 para.1
Sch.8 Part I para.20H, applied: 2012 c.9 s.20
Sch.8 Part I para.20I, added: 2012 c.9 Sch.1 para.1
Sch.8 Part I para.20I, applied: 2012 c.9 s.20
Sch.8 Part I para.20J, added: 2012 c.9 Sch.1 para.1
Sch.8 Part I para.20J, applied: 2012 c.9 s.20
Sch.8 Part III para.36, amended: 2012 c.9 s.57, Sch.9 para.26, Sch.10 Part 4

2000–cont.

11. Terrorism Act 2000–*cont.*
Sch.8 Part III para.36, repealed (in part): 2012 c.9 Sch.10 Part 4
Sch.8 Part III para.37, amended: 2012 c.9 Sch.10 Part 4
Sch.8 Part IV para.38, added: 2012 c.9 s.58
Sch.8A para.7, amended: SI 2012/1809 Sch.1 Part 1
Sch.15 para.19, repealed: 2012 c.10 Sch.5 Part 2

12. Limited Liability Partnerships Act 2000
s.1, see *F&C Alternative Investments (Holdings) Ltd v Barthelemy* [2011] EWHC 1731 (Ch), [2012] Ch. 613 (Ch D), Sales, J.
s.3, applied: SI 2012/1907 Sch.1 para.10
s.4, see *Bates van Winkelhof v Clyde & Co LLP* [2012] EWCA Civ 1207, [2012] I.R.L.R. 992 (CA (Civ Div)), Lloyd, L.J.; see *Tiffin v Lester Aldridge LLP* [2012] EWCA Civ 35, [2012] 1 W.L.R. 1887 (CA (Civ Div)), Sir Nicholas Wall (President, Fam)
s.15, enabling: SI 2012/2301
s.17, enabling: SI 2012/2301
s.18, referred to: SI 2012/1017 Reg.5
Sch.1 Part I para.5, applied: SI 2012/1907 Sch.1 para.10

14. Care Standards Act 2000
Part II, applied: SI 2012/1917 Sch.2 para.15
s.11, see *Waghorn v Care Quality Commission* [2012] EWHC 1816 (Admin), (2012) 128 B.M.L.R. 171 (QBD (Admin)), Cox, J.
s.16, enabling: SI 2012/511
s.42, amended: 2012 c.7 Sch.14 para.78
s.54, amended: 2012 c.7 s.212
s.54, repealed (in part): 2012 c.7 s.212
s.55, amended: 2012 c.7 Sch.15 para.2
s.56, amended: 2012 c.7 Sch.15 para.3
s.56, applied: SI 2012/1917 Sch.2 para.15
s.57, amended: 2012 c.7 Sch.15 para.4
s.58, amended: 2012 c.7 Sch.15 para.5
s.58, applied: SI 2012/1480 Art.14
s.58A, amended: 2012 c.7 Sch.15 para.6
s.59, amended: 2012 c.7 Sch.15 para.7
s.60, amended: 2012 c.7 Sch.15 para.8
s.61, amended: 2012 c.7 Sch.15 para.9
s.62, amended: 2012 c.7 Sch.15 para.10
s.62, applied: SI 2012/1480 Art.13
s.63, amended: 2012 c.7 Sch.15 para.11
s.63, applied: SI 2012/1480 Art.14
s.64, amended: 2012 c.7 Sch.15 para.12
s.64, applied: SI 2012/1480 Art.14
s.64, repealed (in part): 2012 c.7 Sch.15 para.12
s.64, substituted: 2012 c.7 Sch.15 para.12
s.65, amended: 2012 c.7 Sch.15 para.13
s.65, applied: SI 2012/1480 Art.14
s.66, amended: 2012 c.7 Sch.15 para.14
s.67, amended: 2012 c.7 s.221, Sch.15 para.15
s.67, applied: 2012 c.7 Sch.22, Sch.23
s.67, repealed (in part): 2012 c.7 Sch.15 para.15
s.68, amended: 2012 c.7 Sch.15 para.16
s.68, applied: SI 2012/1480 Art.12
s.69, amended: 2012 c.7 Sch.15 para.17
s.70, repealed: 2012 c.7 Sch.15 para.18
s.71, amended: 2012 c.7 Sch.15 para.19
s.81, applied: SI 2012/2157 Art.7
s.86, applied: 2012 c.10 Sch.1 para.14
s.87, applied: 2012 c.10 Sch.1 para.14
s.113, repealed (in part): 2012 c.7 Sch.15 para.20
s.114, amended: 2012 c.7 Sch.15 para.21
s.118, amended: 2012 c.7 Sch.15 para.22

14. Care Standards Act 2000–*cont.*
s.118, enabling: SI 2012/511
s.118A, enabling: SI 2012/3023
s.121, amended: 2012 c.7 Sch.5 para.95, Sch.15 para.23
s.122, amended: 2012 c.7 Sch.15 para.24
s.123, repealed (in part): 2012 c.7 Sch.15 para.25
Sch.1 para.1, amended: 2012 c.7 Sch.15 para.43
Sch.1 para.1, repealed: 2012 c.7 Sch.15 para.27
Sch.1 para.2, amended: 2012 c.7 Sch.15 para.28, Sch.15 para.43
Sch.1 para.3, amended: 2012 c.7 Sch.15 para.29, Sch.15 para.43
Sch.1 para.4, amended: 2012 c.7 Sch.15 para.30, Sch.15 para.43
Sch.1 para.5, amended: 2012 c.7 Sch.15 para.31, Sch.15 para.43
Sch.1 para.6, amended: 2012 c.7 Sch.15 para.32, Sch.15 para.43
Sch.1 para.6, enabling: SI 2012/3023
Sch.1 para.7, amended: 2012 c.7 Sch.15 para.33, Sch.15 para.43
Sch.1 para.8, amended: 2012 c.7 Sch.15 para.34, Sch.15 para.43
Sch.1 para.9, amended: 2012 c.7 Sch.15 para.43
Sch.1 para.10, amended: 2012 c.7 Sch.15 para.43
Sch.1 para.11, amended: 2012 c.7 Sch.15 para.43
Sch.1 para.12, amended: 2012 c.7 Sch.15 para.35, Sch.15 para.43
Sch.1 para.13, amended: 2012 c.7 Sch.15 para.36, Sch.15 para.43
Sch.1 para.14, amended: 2012 c.7 Sch.15 para.37, Sch.15 para.43
Sch.1 para.15, amended: 2012 c.7 Sch.15 para.43
Sch.1 para.16, amended: 2012 c.7 Sch.15 para.38, Sch.15 para.43
Sch.1 para.17, amended: 2012 c.7 Sch.15 para.43
Sch.1 para.18, amended: 2012 c.7 Sch.15 para.39, Sch.15 para.43
Sch.1 para.19, amended: 2012 c.7 Sch.15 para.40, Sch.15 para.43
Sch.1 para.20, amended: 2012 c.7 Sch.15 para.41, Sch.15 para.43
Sch.1 para.21, amended: 2012 c.7 Sch.15 para.42, Sch.15 para.43
Sch.1 para.22, amended: 2012 c.7 Sch.15 para.43
Sch.1 para.23, amended: 2012 c.7 Sch.15 para.43
Sch.1 para.24, amended: 2012 c.7 Sch.15 para.43
Sch.1 para.25, amended: 2012 c.7 Sch.15 para.43
Sch.1 para.26, amended: 2012 c.7 Sch.15 para.43
Sch.1 para.27, amended: 2012 c.7 Sch.15 para.43
Sch.2A para.3, amended: 2012 c.7 Sch.14 para.79
Sch.2A para.23, amended: SI 2012/990 Art.7
Sch.2B para.4, amended: 2012 c.7 Sch.14 para.80
Sch.4 para.3, repealed: 2012 c.10 Sch.12 para.45
Sch.4 para.9, repealed (in part): 2012 c.7 s.39
Sch.4 para.17, repealed: 2012 c.10 Sch.12 para.45

17. Finance Act 2000
s.30, enabling: SI 2012/943
s.50, referred to: SI 2012/2999 Reg.3
s.108, repealed: 2012 c.14 Sch.16 para.247
s.109, repealed: 2012 c.14 Sch.16 para.247
s.127, repealed (in part): 2012 c.14 Sch.39 para.5
s.130, repealed: 2012 c.14 Sch.39 para.6
s.131, repealed (in part): 2012 c.14 Sch.39 para.6
Sch.6 Part II para.4, amended: 2012 c.14 Sch.30 para.3, Sch.32 para.2
Sch.6 Part II para.5, amended: 2012 c.14 Sch.30 para.4, Sch.32 para.22

2000– cont.

2000– cont.

17. Finance Act 2000–*cont.*
Sch.6 Part II para.6, amended: 2012 c.14 Sch.30 para.5, Sch.32 para.3
Sch.6 Part II para.14, amended: 2012 c.14 Sch.30 para.6, Sch.32 para.4
Sch.6 Part II para.15, amended: 2012 c.14 Sch.32 para.5
Sch.6 Part II para.15A, added: 2012 c.14 Sch.32 para.6
Sch.6 Part II para.18A, repealed: 2012 c.14 Sch.30 para.7
Sch.6 Part II para.20A, amended: 2012 c.14 Sch.32 para.21
Sch.6 Part II para.20A, repealed: 2012 c.14 Sch.32 para.22
Sch.6 Part II para.20B, repealed: 2012 c.14 Sch.32 para.22
Sch.6 Part II para.22, enabling: SI 2012/943, SI 2012/3049
Sch.6 Part II para.24, amended: 2012 c.14 Sch.32 para.7, Sch.32 para.22
Sch.6 Part III para.26, amended: 2012 c.14 Sch.32 para.8
Sch.6 Part III para.28A, added: 2012 c.14 Sch.32 para.9
Sch.6 Part III para.29, amended: 2012 c.14 Sch.32 para.10
Sch.6 Part III para.34, amended: 2012 c.14 Sch.30 para.8, Sch.32 para.11
Sch.6 Part III para.39, amended: 2012 c.14 Sch.30 para.9, Sch.32 para.12
Sch.6 Part IV para.40, amended: 2012 c.14 Sch.32 para.13
Sch.6 Part IV para.42, amended: 2012 c.14 Sch.30 para.10, Sch.30 para.20
Sch.6 Part IV para.42A, amended: 2012 c.14 Sch.32 para.14, Sch.32 para.20
Sch.6 Part IV para.42A, referred to: 2012 c.14 Sch.32 para.19
Sch.6 Part IV para.42B, added: 2012 c.14 Sch.32 para.15
Sch.6 Part IV para.42C, added: 2012 c.14 Sch.32 para.15
Sch.6 Part IV para.42D, added: 2012 c.14 Sch.32 para.15
Sch.6 Part IV para.43A, added: 2012 c.14 Sch.30 para.11
Sch.6 Part IV para.43A, enabling: SI 2012/943
Sch.6 Part IV para.43B, added: 2012 c.14 Sch.30 para.11
Sch.6 Part IV para.43B, amended: 2012 c.14 Sch.30 para.21
Sch.6 Part IV para.45A, amended: 2012 c.14 Sch.31 para.4
Sch.6 Part IV para.44, amended: 2012 c.14 Sch.31 para.2
Sch.6 Part IV para.45, amended: 2012 c.14 Sch.31 para.3
Sch.6 Part IV para.45A, amended: 2012 c.14 Sch.30 para.1
Sch.6 Part IV para.45A, repealed: 2012 c.14 Sch.30 para.12
Sch.6 Part IV para.45B, amended: 2012 c.14 Sch.31 para.4
Sch.6 Part IV para.46, applied: SSI 2012/360 Sch.4 para.1
Sch.6 Part IV para.47, amended: 2012 c.14 Sch.31 para.5, Sch.31 para.6
Sch.6 Part IV para.48, amended: 2012 c.14 Sch.31 para.7
Sch.6 Part IV para.48, repealed (in part): 2012 c.14 Sch.31 para.7

17. Finance Act 2000–*cont.*
Sch.6 Part IV para.49, amended: 2012 c.14 Sch.31 para.8
Sch.6 Part IV para.49, repealed (in part): 2012 c.14 Sch.31 para.8
Sch.6 Part IV para.50, applied: SI 2012/1976 Reg.10
Sch.6 Part IV para.50, enabling: SI 2012/2999
Sch.6 Part IV para.52A, added: 2012 c.14 Sch.31 para.9
Sch.6 Part IV para.52A, applied: SI 2012/1976 Reg.3
Sch.6 Part IV para.52B, added: 2012 c.14 Sch.31 para.9
Sch.6 Part IV para.52C, added: 2012 c.14 Sch.31 para.9
Sch.6 Part IV para.52D, added: 2012 c.14 Sch.31 para.9
Sch.6 Part IV para.52D, enabling: SI 2012/1976
Sch.6 Part IV para.52E, added: 2012 c.14 Sch.31 para.9
Sch.6 Part IV para.52E, enabling: SI 2012/1976
Sch.6 Part IV para.52F, added: 2012 c.14 Sch.31 para.9
Sch.6 Part IV para.52F, enabling: SI 2012/1976
Sch.6 Part VI para.62, amended: 2012 c.14 Sch.30 para.13, Sch.32 para.16
Sch.6 Part VI para.62, enabling: SI 2012/943
Sch.6 Part VIII para.101, amended: 2012 c.14 Sch.30 para.14
Sch.6 Part XII para.125, enabling: SI 2012/943
Sch.6 Part XII para.137, amended: 2012 c.14 Sch.31 para.10
Sch.6 Part XIII para.146, amended: 2012 c.14 Sch.30 para.15
Sch.6 Part XIII para.146, enabling: SI 2012/943, SI 2012/1976, SI 2012/2999, SI 2012/3049
Sch.6 Part XIV para.147, amended: 2012 c.14 Sch.30 para.16
Sch.6 Part XIV para.149A, repealed: 2012 c.14 Sch.32 para.22
Sch.7 para.3, amended: 2012 c.10 Sch.14 para.4
Sch.22 Part VII para.54, amended: 2012 c.14 Sch.20 para.19
Sch.22 Part VII para.57, amended: 2012 c.14 Sch.20 para.20
Sch.22 Part IX para.79A, added: 2012 c.14 s.24

19. Child Support, Pensions and Social Security Act 2000
see *Brighton and Hove City Council v PM* [2011] EWCA Civ 795, [2012] 1 F.L.R. 351 (CA (Civ Div)), Sir Nicholas Wall (President, Fam)
s.68, repealed: 2012 c.5 Sch.14 Part 1
s.68, enabling: SI 2012/757
s.69, amended: 2012 c.5 Sch.2 para.55, Sch.3 para.11, Sch.4 para.14
s.70, amended: 2012 c.5 Sch.3 para.12
s.70A, added: 2012 c.5 Sch.3 para.13
s.71, repealed: 2012 c.5 Sch.14 Part 1
Sch.6 para.3, repealed: 2012 c.5 Sch.14 Part 1
Sch.7 para.1, repealed: 2012 c.5 Sch.14 Part 1
Sch.7 para.2, repealed: 2012 c.5 Sch.14 Part 1
Sch.7 para.3, repealed: 2012 c.5 Sch.14 Part 1
Sch.7 para.4, amended: 2012 c.5 Sch.12 para.5
Sch.7 para.4, applied: SSI 2012/319 Reg.31
Sch.7 para.4, repealed: 2012 c.5 Sch.14 Part 1
Sch.7 para.4, enabling: SI 2012/757, SI 2012/1267, SI 2012/3040
Sch.7 para.5, repealed: 2012 c.5 Sch.14 Part 1

2000–cont.

19. Child Support, Pensions and Social Security Act 2000–*cont.*

Sch.7 para.6, see *Wirral MBC v Salisbury Independent Living Ltd* [2012] EWCA Civ 84, [2012] P.T.S.R. 1221 (CA (Civ Div)), Maurice Kay, L.J.

Sch.7 para.6, amended: 2012 c.5 Sch.11 para.13
Sch.7 para.6, applied: 2012 c.5 s.102
Sch.7 para.6, repealed: 2012 c.5 Sch.14 Part 1
Sch.7 para.7, repealed: 2012 c.5 Sch.14 Part 1
Sch.7 para.8, repealed: 2012 c.5 Sch.14 Part 1
Sch.7 para.9, repealed: 2012 c.5 Sch.14 Part 1
Sch.7 para.10, repealed: 2012 c.5 Sch.14 Part 1
Sch.7 para.11, repealed: 2012 c.5 Sch.14 Part 1
Sch.7 para.12, repealed: 2012 c.5 Sch.14 Part 1
Sch.7 para.13, repealed: 2012 c.5 Sch.14 Part 1
Sch.7 para.14, repealed: 2012 c.5 Sch.14 Part 1
Sch.7 para.15, repealed: 2012 c.5 Sch.14 Part 1
Sch.7 para.16, repealed: 2012 c.5 Sch.14 Part 1
Sch.7 para.17, repealed: 2012 c.5 Sch.14 Part 1
Sch.7 para.18, repealed: 2012 c.5 Sch.14 Part 1
Sch.7 para.19, repealed: 2012 c.5 Sch.14 Part 1
Sch.7 para.20, amended: 2012 c.5 Sch.11 para.14
Sch.7 para.20, repealed: 2012 c.5 Sch.14 Part 1
Sch.7 para.20, enabling: SI 2012/757, SI 2012/3040
Sch.7 para.21, repealed: 2012 c.5 Sch.14 Part 1
Sch.7 para.22, repealed: 2012 c.5 Sch.14 Part 1
Sch.7 para.23, repealed: 2012 c.5 Sch.14 Part 1
Sch.7 para.23, enabling: SI 2012/1267, SI 2012/3040
Sch.8 para.15, repealed: 2012 c.10 Sch.5 Part 2

20. Government Resources and Accounts Act 2000

s.2, applied: 2012 c.13 s.5
s.4A, applied: SI 2012/717, SI 2012/3135
s.4A, enabling: SI 2012/717, SI 2012/3135
s.10, applied: SI 2012/1803
s.10, enabling: SI 2012/1803
s.14, amended: 2012 c.7 Sch.5 para.96
s.14, applied: SI 2012/1831 Art.11
s.14, repealed (in part): 2012 c.7 Sch.5 para.96
s.14, enabling: SI 2012/2789
s.25, applied: SI 2012/854
s.25, enabling: SI 2012/854

21. Learning and Skills Act 2000

s.110, applied: SI 2012/1157 Sch.1 para.5
s.139A, see *LB v Kent CC* [2012] E.L.R. 31 (UT (AAC)), Judge CG Ward
s.139A, applied: 2012 c.10 Sch.1 para.2, SI 2012/206 Sch.1 para.3, Sch.1 para.11, Sch.1 para.17, Sch.1 para.18
s.139B, referred to: SI 2012/206 Sch.1 para.3
s.140, applied: 2012 c.10 Sch.1 para.2

22. Local Government Act 2000

Commencement Orders: SI 2012/1358 Art.2
see *R. (on the application of Barnsley MBC) v Secretary of State for Communities and Local Government* [2012] EWHC 1366 (Admin), [2012] B.L.G.R. 933 (QBD (Admin)), Foskett, J.; see *R. (on the application of Buck) v Doncaster MBC* [2012] EWHC 2293 (Admin), [2012] B.L.G.R. 663 (QBD (Admin)), Hickinbottom, J.; see *R. (on the application of De Whalley) v Norfolk CC* [2011] EWHC 3739 (Admin), [2012] B.L.G.R. 478 (QBD (Admin)), Nicol, J.
referred to: SI 2012/2913 Art.5
Part I, applied: SI 2012/1008 Art.8
Part 1A, applied: SI 2012/323 Reg.17
Part 1A c.4, applied: SI 2012/57 Art.7
Part II, applied: SI 2012/57 Art.7

2000–cont.

22. Local Government Act 2000–*cont.*

Part III, applied: SI 2012/62 Reg.29, SI 2012/2734 Sch.1 para.33
Part III, referred to: SI 2012/57 Art.8, SI 2012/2913 Art.3
Part III c.III, referred to: SI 2012/2913 Art.6
Part III c.IV, referred to: SI 2012/2913 Art.6
s.2, see *R. (on the application of Barnsley MBC) v Secretary of State for Communities and Local Government* [2012] EWHC 1366 (Admin), [2012] B.L.G.R. 933 (QBD (Admin)), Foskett, J.
s.2, applied: SI 2012/1008 Art.8
s.2, referred to: SI 2012/1008 Art.8
s.4, applied: SI 2012/1020 Sch.1
s.9E, applied: SI 2012/1019 Reg.3, Reg.4, Reg.7
s.9EA, enabling: SI 2012/1019
s.9EB, enabling: SI 2012/1019
s.9F, amended: 2012 c.7 s.190
s.9F, repealed (in part): 2012 c.7 s.190
s.9FC, applied: SI 2012/1020 Reg.6, SI 2012/1022 Art.3
s.9FC, enabling: SI 2012/1022
s.9FE, applied: SI 2012/1021 Reg.8, Reg.9
s.9FF, applied: SI 2012/1021 Reg.3
s.9FG, applied: SI 2012/1021 Reg.7
s.9FI, enabling: SI 2012/1021
s.9G, applied: SI 2012/2089 Reg.12, Reg.13
s.9G, enabling: SI 2012/2089
s.9GA, applied: SI 2012/2089 Reg.5
s.9GA, enabling: SI 2012/1021, SI 2012/2089
s.9H, applied: SI 2012/336 Reg.8, Reg.9
s.9HB, enabling: SI 2012/336
s.9HE, applied: SI 2012/1917 Sch.2 para.11
s.9I, applied: SI 2012/1023 Art.2
s.9IA, applied: SI 2012/1023 Art.2
s.9J, enabling: SI 2012/1020
s.9JA, applied: SI 2012/1020 Reg.4, SI 2012/1023 Art.3
s.9JA, enabling: SI 2012/1020
s.9K, applied: SI 2012/336 Reg.8, Reg.9
s.9KA, applied: SI 2012/336 Reg.8, Reg.9
s.9KC, applied: SI 2012/323 Reg.16
s.9KC, varied: SI 2012/323 Reg.17
s.9MA, applied: SI 2012/323 Reg.4, Reg.14, Reg.17
s.9MB, applied: SI 2012/323 Reg.14
s.9MC, applied: SI 2012/57 Art.7
s.9ME, applied: SI 2012/323 Reg.4, Reg.14
s.9MF, applied: SI 2012/57 Art.7, SI 2012/323 Reg.14
s.9MG, applied: SI 2012/57 Art.7, SI 2012/1917 Sch.2 para.11
s.9MG, referred to: SI 2012/323
s.9MG, enabling: SI 2012/323
s.9N, applied: SI 2012/323 Reg.4, Reg.14, SI 2012/336 Reg.5, Reg.6
s.9N, enabling: SI 2012/324, SI 2012/325, SI 2012/326, SI 2012/327, SI 2012/328, SI 2012/329, SI 2012/330, SI 2012/331, SI 2012/332, SI 2012/333
s.9Q, applied: SI 2012/323 Reg.4, SI 2012/2089 Reg.8
s.21, see *R. (on the application of De Whalley) v Norfolk CC* [2011] EWHC 3739 (Admin), [2012] B.L.G.R. 478 (QBD (Admin)), Nicol, J.
s.21, amended: 2012 c.7 s.190
s.21, repealed (in part): 2012 c.7 s.190
s.21C, amended: 2012 c.7 Sch.5 para.97
s.21C, repealed (in part): 2012 c.7 Sch.5 para.97
s.34, applied: SI 2012/57 Art.7

2000–cont.

22. **Local Government Act 2000**–*cont.*
s.44, applied: SI 2012/323 Sch.5 para.38, SI 2012/444 Sch.5, SI 2012/1917 Sch.2 para.11, SI 2012/2059
s.44, enabling: SI 2012/2059
s.44A, applied: SI 2012/1023 Art.2
s.44B, applied: SI 2012/1023 Art.2
s.44D, applied: SI 2012/1023 Art.2
s.44E, applied: SI 2012/1023 Art.2
s.45, applied: SI 2012/57 Art.7, SI 2012/1917 Sch.2 para.11
s.49, referred to: SI 2012/1463 Art.7, SI 2012/2913 Art.3
s.49, varied: SI 2012/2734 Reg.6
s.50, applied: SI 2012/2913 Art.4
s.50, referred to: SI 2012/2913 Art.6
s.50, varied: SI 2012/2734 Reg.6
s.51, referred to: SI 2012/2913 Art.4, Art.6
s.51, varied: SI 2012/2734 Reg.6
s.52, varied: SI 2012/2734 Reg.6
s.53, varied: SI 2012/2734 Reg.6
s.54, varied: SI 2012/2734 Reg.6
s.54A, varied: SI 2012/2734 Reg.6
s.55, varied: SI 2012/2734 Reg.6
s.56, varied: SI 2012/2734 Reg.6
s.56A, varied: SI 2012/2734 Reg.6
s.57, referred to: SI 2012/57 Art.8
s.57, varied: SI 2012/2734 Reg.6
s.57A, applied: SI 2012/57 Art.8, SI 2012/62 Reg.29
s.57A, varied: SI 2012/2734 Reg.6
s.57B, applied: SI 2012/57 Art.8
s.57B, varied: SI 2012/2734 Reg.6
s.57C, applied: SI 2012/57 Art.8
s.57C, varied: SI 2012/57 Art.8, SI 2012/2734 Reg.6
s.57D, varied: SI 2012/2734 Reg.6
s.58, varied: SI 2012/2734 Reg.6
s.59, varied: SI 2012/2734 Reg.6
s.60, applied: SI 2012/57 Art.8
s.60, referred to: SI 2012/57 Art.8
s.60, varied: SI 2012/2734 Reg.6
s.61, varied: SI 2012/2734 Reg.6
s.62, referred to: SI 2012/57 Art.8
s.62, varied: SI 2012/2734 Reg.6
s.63, referred to: SI 2012/57 Art.8
s.63, varied: SI 2012/2734 Reg.6
s.64, applied: SI 2012/57 Art.8, SI 2012/668 Art.6, SI 2012/1463 Art.7, SI 2012/2913 Art.5
s.64, referred to: SI 2012/57 Art.8
s.64, varied: SI 2012/2734 Reg.6
s.65, applied: SI 2012/57 Art.8, SI 2012/668 Art.6, SI 2012/1463 Art.7, SI 2012/2913 Art.5
s.65, referred to: SI 2012/57 Art.8
s.65, varied: SI 2012/2734 Reg.6
s.65A, varied: SI 2012/2734 Reg.6
s.66, applied: SI 2012/57 Art.8
s.66, referred to: SI 2012/57 Art.8
s.66, varied: SI 2012/2734 Reg.6
s.66A, applied: SI 2012/57 Art.8
s.66A, varied: SI 2012/2734 Reg.6
s.66B, varied: SI 2012/2734 Reg.6
s.66C, varied: SI 2012/2734 Reg.6
s.67, varied: SI 2012/2734 Reg.6
s.67, referred to: SI 2012/57 Art.8
s.67, varied: SI 2012/2734 Reg.6
s.68, varied: SI 2012/2734 Reg.6
s.69, disapplied: SI 2012/2913 Art.6
s.69, varied: SI 2012/2734 Reg.6
s.70, disapplied: SI 2012/2913 Art.6

2000–cont.

22. **Local Government Act 2000**–*cont.*
s.70, varied: SI 2012/2734 Reg.6
s.71, disapplied: SI 2012/2913 Art.6
s.71, varied: SI 2012/2734 Reg.6
s.72, varied: SI 2012/2734 Reg.6
s.73, disapplied: SI 2012/2913 Art.6
s.73, varied: SI 2012/2734 Reg.6
s.74, varied: SI 2012/2734 Reg.6
s.75, varied: SI 2012/2734 Reg.6
s.76, varied: SI 2012/2734 Reg.6
s.77, varied: SI 2012/2734 Reg.6
s.78, applied: SI 2012/57 Art.8
s.78, varied: SI 2012/2734 Reg.6
s.78A, varied: SI 2012/2734 Reg.6
s.78B, varied: SI 2012/2734 Reg.6
s.79, referred to: SI 2012/2913 Art.6
s.79, varied: SI 2012/2734 Reg.6
s.80, varied: SI 2012/2734 Reg.6
s.81, varied: SI 2012/2734 Reg.6
s.82, varied: SI 2012/2734 Reg.6
s.82A, referred to: SI 2012/57 Art.8
s.82A, varied: SI 2012/2734 Reg.6
s.83, referred to: SI 2012/1463 Art.7, SI 2012/2913 Art.3
s.83, varied: SI 2012/2734 Reg.6
s.87, enabling: SI 2012/686
s.93, applied: SI 2012/2885 Sch.6 para.21, SI 2012/2886 Sch.1
s.96, repealed: 2012 c.5 Sch.14 Part 1
s.101, applied: SI 2012/2734 Sch.1 para.4, Sch.1 para.19, Sch.1 para.34
s.101, varied: SI 2012/2734 Reg.6
s.105, applied: SI 2012/323 Sch.5 para.38, SI 2012/324, SI 2012/326, SI 2012/327, SI 2012/328, SI 2012/329, SI 2012/330, SI 2012/331, SI 2012/332, SI 2012/333, SI 2012/444 Sch.5, SI 2012/1917 Sch.2 para.11, SI 2012/2059
s.105, referred to: SI 2012/323
s.105, enabling: SI 2012/323, SI 2012/324, SI 2012/325, SI 2012/326, SI 2012/327, SI 2012/328, SI 2012/329, SI 2012/330, SI 2012/331, SI 2012/332, SI 2012/333, SI 2012/336, SI 2012/686, SI 2012/1019, SI 2012/1020, SI 2012/1021, SI 2012/1022, SI 2012/2059, SI 2012/2089
s.106, enabling: SI 2012/686
s.108, enabling: SI 2012/1358
Sch.A1 para.12, applied: SI 2012/1020 Reg.11
Sch.4 para.4, referred to: SI 2012/57 Art.8
Sch.4 para.11, applied: SI 2012/628 Art.11

23. **Regulation of Investigatory Powers Act 2000**
see *An Informer v Chief Constable* [2012] EWCA Civ 197, [2012] 3 All E.R. 601 (CA (Civ Div)), Pill, L.J.
applied: 2012 c.9, SI 2012/1128 Art.4, SI 2012/1726 r.6.1
Part I, applied: SI 2012/129 Sch.1 para.6, SI 2012/925 Sch.1 para.35, SI 2012/1301 Sch.1 para.6, SI 2012/1489 Sch.1 para.6, SI 2012/1507 Sch.1 para.6, SI 2012/1508 Sch.1 para.6, SI 2012/1509 Sch.1 para.6, SI 2012/1511 Sch.1 para.6, SI 2012/1515 Sch.1 para.6, SI 2012/1516 Sch.1 para.6, SI 2012/1517 Sch.1 para.6
s.1, see *Gray v News Group Newspapers Ltd* [2012] EWCA Civ 48, [2012] 2 W.L.R. 848 (CA (Civ Div)), Lord Judge, L.C.J.
s.4, amended: 2012 c.7 Sch.5 para.98
s.7, varied: 2012 c.11 s.12
s.9, varied: 2012 c.11 s.12
s.10, varied: 2012 c.11 s.12

2000–cont.

23. Regulation of Investigatory Powers Act 2000– cont.

s.17, applied: SI 2012/ 1726 r.22.9
s.21, applied: SI 2012/ 1726 r.6.27
s.22, amended: 2012 c.9 Sch.9 para.7
s.22, applied: SI 2012/ 1726 r.6.27, SI 2012/ 2075 Art.6, SI 2012/ 2563 r.7
s.23, amended: 2012 c.9 Sch.9 para.8
s.23A, added: 2012 c.9 s.37
s.23A, applied: SI 2012/ 1726 r.6.1, r.6.27, r.6.28, SI 2012/ 2563 r.2, r.7, r.8
s.23B, added: 2012 c.9 s.37
s.23B, applied: SI 2012/ 1726 r.6.27, r.6.28, SI 2012/ 2563 r.7
s.26, applied: SI 2012/ 1726 r.6.27
s.28, applied: SI 2012/ 1726 r.6.27, SI 2012/ 2075 Art.6, SI 2012/ 2563 r.7
s.29, applied: SI 2012/ 1726 r.6.27, SI 2012/ 2075 Art.6, SI 2012/ 2563 r.7
s.30, enabling: SI 2012/ 1500
s.32A, added: 2012 c.9 s.38
s.32A, applied: SI 2012/ 1726 r.6.1, r.6.27, r.6.28, SI 2012/ 2563 r.2, r.7, r.8
s.32B, added: 2012 c.9 s.38
s.32B, applied: SI 2012/ 1726 r.6.27, r.6.28, SI 2012/ 2563 r.7
s.43, amended: 2012 c.9 s.38, Sch.9 para.9
s.43, applied: SI 2012/ 1726 r.6.27, SI 2012/ 2563 r.7
s.44, varied: 2012 c.11 s.12
s.57, amended: 2012 c.9 Sch.9 para.10
s.62, amended: 2012 c.9 Sch.9 para.11
s.65, amended: 2012 c.9 Sch.9 para.12
s.67, amended: 2012 c.9 Sch.9 para.13
s.71, amended: 2012 c.9 Sch.9 para.14
s.72, see *Gray v News Group Newspapers Ltd* [2012] EWCA Civ 48, [2012] 2 W.L.R. 848 (CA (Civ Div)), Lord Judge, L.C.J.
s.77A, added: 2012 c.9 Sch.9 para.15
s.77A, enabling: SSI 2012/ 271
s.77B, added: 2012 c.9 Sch.9 para.15
s.78, amended: 2012 c.9 Sch.9 para.16
s.78, enabling: SI 2012/ 1500
s.79, see *Coulson v News Group Newspapers Ltd* [2011] EWHC 3482 (QB), [2012] I.R.L.R. 385 (QBD), Supperstone, J.
s.81, amended: 2012 c.9 Sch.9 para.17
Sch.1 Part I para.19, substituted: 2012 c.21 Sch.18 para.88
Sch.1 Part II para.28A, repealed: SI 2012/ 2007 Sch.1 para.65
Sch.2 para.6, amended: 2012 c.9 Sch.9 para.27

26. Postal Services Act 2000

applied: SI 2012/ 1128 Art.4
referred to: SI 2012/ 1082 Art.5, SI 2012/ 1093 Art.4
s.7, varied: 2012 c.21 Sch.20 para.10
s.111, referred to: SI 2012/ 1095 Art.4
s.112, applied: SI 2012/ 1095 Art.3, Art.4, Art.5, Art.6
s.112, referred to: SI 2012/ 1095 Art.3
s.113, referred to: SI 2012/ 1095 Art.5
s.125, applied: SSI 2012/ 337 Reg.13
s.125, referred to: 2012 asp 9 s.74, 2012 c.7 s.148
Sch.7 para.3, varied: 2012 c.21 Sch.20 para.10

27. Utilities Act 2000

see *R. v Scottish and Southern Energy Plc* [2012] EWCA Crim 539, (2012) 176 J.P. 241 (CA (Crim Div)), Davis, L.J.
applied: SI 2012/ 1128 Art.4
s.5A, amended: SI 2012/ 2400 Art.30

2000–cont.

27. Utilities Act 2000– cont.

s.103, applied: SI 2012/ 3018
s.103, enabling: SI 2012/ 3018
s.103A, applied: SI 2012/ 3018
s.103A, enabling: SI 2012/ 3018
s.105, amended: 2012 c.19 Sch.9 para.11, 2012 c.21 Sch.18 para.89
s.106, amended: SI 2012/ 2400 Art.30

29. Trustee Act 2000

s.8, see *Alexander v Alexander* [2011] EWHC 2721 (Ch), [2012] W.T.L.R. 187 (Ch D), Morgan, J.
s.11, varied: SI 2012/ 3012 Reg.33
s.12, varied: SI 2012/ 3012 Reg.33
s.13, varied: SI 2012/ 3012 Reg.33
s.14, varied: SI 2012/ 3012 Reg.33
s.15, varied: SI 2012/ 3012 Reg.33
s.16, varied: SI 2012/ 3012 Reg.33
s.17, varied: SI 2012/ 3012 Reg.33
s.25, varied: SI 2012/ 3012 Reg.33
s.26, varied: SI 2012/ 3012 Reg.33
s.29, amended: 2012 c.21 Sch.18 para.90
s.31, see *Oakhurst Property Developments (Lowndes Square No.2) Ltd v Blackstar (Isle of Man) Ltd* [2012] EWHC 1131 (Ch), [2012] W.T.L.R. 1255 (Ch D), Morgan, J.
Sch.2 Part II para.40, repealed: 2012 c.7 Sch.20 para.3

35. Children (Leaving Care) Act 2000

s.6, applied: SI 2012/ 2885 Reg.6, SI 2012/ 3144 Reg.6, SI 2012/ 3145 Sch.1, SSI 2012/ 303 Reg.4, SSI 2012/ 319 Reg.4

36. Freedom of Information Act 2000

see *Birkett v Department for the Environment, Food and Rural Affairs* [2011] EWCA Civ 1606, [2012] P.T.S.R. 1299 (CA (Civ Div)), Carnwath, L.J.; see *C v Suffolk CC* [2011] EWCA Civ 870, [2012] E.L.R.105 (CA (Civ Div)), Arden, L.J.; see *Department of Health v Information Commissioner* (2012) 126 B.M.L.R. 110 (FTT (GRC)), Judge John Angel; see *Hardy v United Kingdom (31965/07)* (2012) 55 E.H.R.R. 28 (ECHR), Judge Garlicki (President)
applied: 2012 c.10 s.35, 2012 c.19 s.83, s.84, SI 2012/ 752 Sch.1 para.1, SI 2012/ 1741 Art.19, SI 2012/ 1916 Reg.332, SI 2012/ 2734 Sch.1 para.5, Sch.1 para.20, Sch.1 para.35, SI 2012/ 3094 Reg.25
varied: SI 2012/ 147 Art.7, SI 2012/ 2734 Reg.6
Part VI, applied: SI 2012/ 3029 Art.2
s.1, see *Kennedy v Information Commissioner* [2011] EWCA Civ 367, [2012] 1 W.L.R. 3524 (CA (Civ Div)), Ward, L.J.
s.6, amended: 2012 c.9 s.103, Sch.10 Part 7
s.11, amended: 2012 c.9 s.102
s.11A, added: 2012 c.9 s.102
s.11B, added: 2012 c.9 s.102
s.18, repealed (in part): 2012 c.9 s.105, Sch.10 Part 8
s.19, amended: 2012 c.9 s.102
s.32, see *Kennedy v Information Commissioner* [2011] EWCA Civ 367, [2012] 1 W.L.R. 3524 (CA (Civ Div)), Ward, L.J.; see *Kennedy v Information Commissioner* [2012] EWCA Civ 317, [2012] 1 W.L.R. 3524 (CA (Civ Div)), Ward, L.J.
s.35, see *Department of Health v Information Commissioner* (2012) 126 B.M.L.R. 110 (FTT (GRC)), Judge John Angel
s.40, see *Department of Health v Information Commissioner* (2012) 126 B.M.L.R. 110 (FTT (GRC)), Judge John Angel
s.45, amended: 2012 c.9 s.102

2000–cont.

36. Freedom of Information Act 2000–*cont.*
s.47, amended: 2012 c.9 s.107, Sch.10 Part 8
s.62, applied: SI 2012/3029 Art.3
s.63, see *Kennedy v Information Commissioner* [2011] EWCA Civ 367, [2012] 1 W.L.R. 3524 (CA (Civ Div)), Ward, L.J.
s.80A, repealed: 2012 c.9 s.104, Sch.10 Part 7
s.82, amended: 2012 c.9 s.107
s.84, amended: 2012 c.9 s.102
Sch.1, see *BBC v Sugar* [2012] UKSC 4, [2012] 1 W.L.R. 439 (SC), Lord Phillips (President)
Sch.1 Pt VI, see *BBC v Sugar* [2012] UKSC 4, [2012] 1 W.L.R. 439 (SC), Lord Phillips (President)
Sch.1 Part II para.35E, added: 2012 c.7 s.189
Sch.1 Part III para.36A, repealed: 2012 c.7 Sch.5 para.99
Sch.1 Part III para.37A, added: 2012 c.7 Sch.5 para.99
Sch.1 Part III para.37B, added: 2012 c.7 Sch.5 para.99
Sch.1 Part III para.39, repealed: 2012 c.7 Sch.5 para.99
Sch.1 Part III para.40, amended: 2012 c.7 Sch.14 para.81
Sch.1 Part VI, amended: 2012 c.5 Sch.13 para.17, Sch.14 Part 8, 2012 c.7 Sch.7 para.10, Sch.13 para.7, Sch.15 para.50, Sch.15 para.56, Sch.15 para.69, Sch.15 para.71, Sch.17 para.8, Sch.19 para.8, Sch.20 para.1, Sch.20 para.5, Sch.20 para.9, 2012 c.9 Sch.9 para.133, 2012 c.10 Sch.5 para.55, 2012 c.21 Sch.18 para.91, SI 2012/246 Sch.1 para.20, SI 2012/964 Sch.1, SI 2012/990 Art.8, SI 2012/1206 Sch.1 para.2, SI 2012/1658 Sch.1, SI 2012/1659 Sch.3 para.15, SI 2012/1923 Sch.1, SI 2012/2007 Sch.1 para.109, SI 2012/2398 Sch.1 para.8, Sch.2 para.3, SI 2012/2654 Sch.1, SI 2012/3006 Art.17

37. Countryside and Rights of Way Act 2000
see *R. (on the application of Newhaven Port and Properties Ltd) v East Sussex CC* [2012] EWHC 647 (Admin), [2012] 3 W.L.R. 709 (QBD (Admin)), Ouseley, J.
s.3A, enabling: SI 2012/1559
s.38, enabling: SI 2012/67
s.44, enabling: SI 2012/67
s.45, enabling: SI 2012/67
s.98, see *Leeds Group Plc v Leeds City Council* [2011] EWCA Civ 1447, [2012] 1 W.L.R. 1561 (CA (Civ Div)), Arden, L.J.; see *Paddico (267) Ltd v Kirklees Metropolitan Council* [2012] EWCA Civ 262, [2012] B.L.G.R. 617 (CA (Civ Div)), Carnwath, L.J.
s.103, see *Leeds Group Plc v Leeds City Council* [2011] EWCA Civ 1447, [2012] 1 W.L.R. 1561 (CA (Civ Div)), Arden, L.J.

38. Transport Act 2000
Part I, applied: SI 2012/1128 Art.4
Part I, referred to: 2012 c.19 Sch.6 para.4
s.66, amended: 2012 c.19 s.98
s.66, applied: 2012 c.19 Sch.14 para.8
s.67, amended: 2012 c.19 s.98
s.67, applied: 2012 c.19 Sch.14 para.9
s.73, applied: SI 2012/3038 Sch.9 para.5
s.86, amended: SI 2012/1809 Sch.1 Part 1
s.107, referred to: 2012 c.19 s.112
s.108, applied: SI 2012/767 Reg.10, SI 2012/1020 Sch.1
s.124, applied: SSI 2012/89 Sch.1
s.144, enabling: SI 2012/846, SI 2012/2659
s.167, enabling: SI 2012/2387

2000–cont.

38. Transport Act 2000–*cont.*
s.168, enabling: SI 2012/2387
s.170, applied: SI 2012/2387
s.171, enabling: SI 2012/2387
s.172, enabling: SI 2012/2387
Sch.8 Part III para.10, repealed: 2012 c.19 Sch.9 para.17
Sch.9 para.3, amended: 2012 c.19 Sch.9 para.12, SI 2012/1809 Sch.1 Part 1

39. Insolvency Act 2000
applied: SI 2012/1128 Art.4
s.15, repealed (in part): 2012 c.21 Sch.19

41. Political Parties, Elections and Referendums Act 2000
Part II, applied: SI 2012/1917 Sch.5 para.1
s.6A, applied: SI 2012/323 Sch.3 para.21, Sch.3 para.35, Sch.5 para.23, Sch.5 para.37, SI 2012/444 Sch.3, Sch.5, SI 2012/1917 Art.22, Sch.2 para.26, Sch.3 para.10, Sch.3 para.34, Sch.3 para.48, Sch.3 para.51, Sch.3 para.58, SI 2012/2031 Sch.3, Sch.5
s.6A, referred to: SI 2012/1917 Sch.2 para.31, Sch.2 para.32
s.6A, varied: SI 2012/323 Sch.4 para.1, SI 2012/444 Sch.4 para.1, SI 2012/2031 Sch.4 Part 1
s.6B, applied: SI 2012/323 Sch.3 para.21, Sch.3 para.35, Sch.5 para.23, Sch.5 para.37, SI 2012/444 Sch.3, Sch.5, SI 2012/1917 Art.22, Sch.2 para.26, Sch.3 para.10, Sch.3 para.34, Sch.3 para.48, Sch.3 para.51, Sch.3 para.58, SI 2012/2031 Sch.3, Sch.5
s.6B, referred to: SI 2012/1917 Sch.2 para.31, Sch.2 para.32
s.6B, varied: SI 2012/323 Sch.4 para.1, SI 2012/444 Sch.4 para.1, SI 2012/2031 Sch.4 Part 1
s.6C, applied: SI 2012/323 Sch.3 para.21, Sch.3 para.35, Sch.5 para.23, Sch.5 para.37, SI 2012/444 Sch.3, Sch.5, SI 2012/1917 Art.22, Sch.2 para.26, Sch.3 para.34, Sch.3 para.48, Sch.3 para.51, Sch.3 para.58, SI 2012/2031 Sch.3, Sch.5
s.6C, referred to: SI 2012/1917 Sch.2 para.31, Sch.2 para.32
s.6C, varied: SI 2012/323 Sch.4 para.1, SI 2012/444 Sch.4 para.1, SI 2012/2031 Sch.4 Part 1
s.6D, applied: SI 2012/323 Sch.3 para.21, Sch.3 para.35, Sch.5 para.23, Sch.5 para.37, SI 2012/444 Sch.3, Sch.5, SI 2012/1917 Art.22, Sch.2 para.26, Sch.3 para.34, Sch.3 para.48, Sch.3 para.51, Sch.3 para.58, SI 2012/2031 Sch.3, Sch.5
s.6D, referred to: SI 2012/1917 Sch.2 para.31, Sch.2 para.32
s.6D, varied: SI 2012/323 Sch.4 para.1, SI 2012/444 Sch.4 para.1, SI 2012/2031 Sch.4 Part 1
s.6E, referred to: SI 2012/1917 Sch.2 para.31, Sch.2 para.32
s.6E, varied: SI 2012/323 Sch.4 para.1, SI 2012/444 Sch.4 para.1, SI 2012/2031 Sch.4 Part 1
s.7, amended: 2012 c.11 s.3
s.7, applied: SI 2012/198, SI 2012/1917, SI 2012/1918, SI 2012/2768, SI 2012/3074, SSI 2012/60
s.8, amended: 2012 c.11 s.3
s.10, varied: 2012 c.11 s.12
s.22, amended: SI 2012/1917 Art.24
s.28, applied: SI 2012/1917 Sch.3 para.6
s.28A, applied: SI 2012/1917 Sch.3 para.6, Sch.8 para.5
s.28B, applied: SI 2012/1917 Sch.8 para.5
s.54, applied: SI 2012/1917 Sch.5 para.1, Sch.5 para.6
s.56, applied: SI 2012/1917 Sch.5 para.4, Sch.5 para.7, Sch.5 para.8, Sch.5 para.12

2000–cont.

41. Political Parties, Elections and Referendums Act 2000–*cont.*

s.56, referred to: SI 2012/1917 Sch.5 para.8, Sch.5 para.12

s.56, varied: SI 2012/1917 Sch.5 para.7

s.57, applied: SI 2012/1917 Sch.5 para.7

s.57A, applied: SI 2012/1917 Sch.5 para.7

s.58, applied: SI 2012/1917 Sch.5 para.7

s.59, applied: SI 2012/1917 Sch.5 para.7

s.60, applied: SI 2012/1917 Sch.5 para.7

s.61, applied: SI 2012/1917 Sch.5 para.9

s.67, amended: SI 2012/1917 Art.24

s.162, applied: SI 2012/1917 Sch.5 para.6

Sch.1 para.3, amended: SI 2012/2404 Sch.2 para.44

Sch.6 para.2, applied: SI 2012/1917 Sch.5 para.11

Sch.7 Part I para.1, amended: SI 2012/1917 Art.24

Sch.7 Part V para.15A, amended: SI 2012/1917 Art.24

43. Criminal Justice and Court Services Act 2000

Commencement Orders: 2012 c.10 Sch.12 para.46

referred to: SI 2012/2231 Art.5

s.12, see *R. (on the application of R) v Children and Family Court Advisory and Support Service* [2011] EWHC 1774 (Admin), [2012] 1 W.L.R. 811 (QBD (Admin)), Munby, L.J.; see *R. (on the application of R) v Children and Family Court Advisory and Support Service* [2012] EWCA Civ 853, [2012] 2 F.L.R. 1432 (CA (Civ Div)), Lord Judge, L.C.J.

s.28, see *Attorney General's Reference (No.18 of 2011), Re* [2011] EWCA Crim 1300, [2012] 1 Cr. App. R. (S.) 27 (CA (Crim Div)), Hughes, L.J. (Vice President); see *R. v C* [2011] EWCA Crim 1872, [2012] 1 Cr. App. R. (S.) 89 (CA (Crim Div)), Thomas, L.J.

s.28, applied: 2012 c.10 Sch.1 para.4, SI 2012/1034 Sch.4 para.13

s.29, applied: 2012 c.10 Sch.1 para.4, SI 2012/1034 Sch.4 para.13

s.29A, applied: 2012 c.10 Sch.1 para.4, SI 2012/1034 Sch.4 para.13

s.30, amended: 2012 c.10 Sch.21 para.37, Sch.22 para.39

s.30, repealed (in part): 2012 c.10 Sch.22 para.39

s.31, applied. SI 2012/2231 Art.5

s.32, applied: 2012 c.10 Sch.1 para.14, SI 2012/2231 Art.5

s.33, applied: SI 2012/2231 Art.5

s.56, repealed (in part): 2012 c.10 Sch.24 para.24

s.59, referred to: 2012 c.10 s.129

s.61, referred to: 2012 c.10 s.129, Sch.21 para.36

s.62, amended: 2012 c.10 Sch.21 para.17, Sch.22 para.18

s.64, amended: 2012 c.10 Sch.21 para.18, Sch.22 para.19

Sch.1A para.2, repealed (in part): SI 2012/2401 Sch.1 para.11

Sch.1A para.4, repealed (in part): SI 2012/2401 Sch.1 para.11

Sch.1A para.5, repealed (in part): SI 2012/2401 Sch.1 para.11

Sch.1A para.7, added: SI 2012/2401 Sch.1 para.11

Sch.4 para.3, amended: 2012 c.4 Sch.1 para.4

Sch.7 Part I para.4, amended: 2012 c.10 Sch.12 para.46

Sch.7 Part II para.39, repealed: 2012 c.10 Sch.12 para.46

Sch.7 Part II para.49, repealed: 2012 c.10 Sch.25 Part 2

2001

2. Capital Allowances Act 2001

applied: SI 2012/1709 Art.3, Art.4

Part 2, referred to: 2012 c.14 s.42

Part 2 c.19, amended: 2012 c.14 Sch.16 para.96

Part 2 c.3, amended: 2012 c.14 Sch.39 para.34

Part 4A, disapplied: 2012 c.14 Sch.39 para.36

s.1, repealed (in part): 2012 c.14 Sch.39 para.38

s.2, repealed (in part): 2012 c.14 Sch.39 para.38

s.9, amended: 2012 c.14 Sch.10 para.7

s.15, amended: 2012 c.14 Sch.20 para.9

s.19, amended: 2012 c.14 Sch.16 para.95

s.23, amended: 2012 c.14 Sch.39 para.34

s.27, amended: 2012 c.14 Sch.39 para.34

s.30, repealed: 2012 c.14 Sch.39 para.33

s.31, repealed: 2012 c.14 Sch.39 para.33

s.32, repealed: 2012 c.14 Sch.39 para.33

s.39, amended: 2012 c.14 Sch.11 para.2

s.45A, amended: 2012 c.14 s.45

s.45A, enabling: SI 2012/1832

s.45AA, added: 2012 c.14 s.45

s.45H, enabling: SI 2012/1838, SI 2012/2602

s.45K, added: 2012 c.14 Sch.11 para.3

s.45L, added: 2012 c.14 Sch.11 para.3

s.45M, added: 2012 c.14 Sch.11 para.3

s.45N, added: 2012 c.14 Sch.11 para.3

s.46, amended: 2012 c.14 Sch.11 para.4

s.52, amended: 2012 c.14 Sch.11 para.5

s.52A, amended: 2012 c.14 Sch.11 para.6

s.57, amended: 2012 c.14 Sch.9 para.2, Sch.10 para.8

s.63, applied: SI 2012/847 Reg.25

s.70E, amended: 2012 c.14 s.46

s.104A, amended: 2012 c.14 s.45

s.105, see *Lloyds TSB Equipment Leasing (No.1) Ltd v Revenue and Customs Commissioners* [2012] UKFTT 47 (TC), [2012] S.F.T.D. 572 (FTT (Tax)), Edward Sadler

s.109, see *Lloyds TSB Equipment Leasing (No.1) Ltd v Revenue and Customs Commissioners* [2012] UKFTT 47 (TC), [2012] S.F.T.D. 572 (FTT (Tax)), Edward Sadler

s.110, see *Lloyds TSB Equipment Leasing (No.1) Ltd v Revenue and Customs Commissioners* [2012] UKFTT 47 (TC), [2012] S.F.T.D. 572 (FTT (Tax)), Edward Sadler

s.123, see *Lloyds TSB Equipment Leasing (No.1) Ltd v Revenue and Customs Commissioners* [2012] UKFTT 47 (TC), [2012] S.F.T.D. 572 (FTT (Tax)), Edward Sadler

s.186A, added: 2012 c.14 Sch.10 para.6

s.187A, added: 2012 c.14 Sch.10 para.2

s.187A, applied: 2012 c.14 Sch.10 para.13

s.187B, added: 2012 c.14 Sch.10 para.2

s.198, amended: 2012 c.14 Sch.10 para.3, Sch.10 para.9

s.199, amended: 2012 c.14 Sch.10 para.10

s.201, amended: 2012 c.14 Sch.10 para.4

s.212T, amended: 2012 c.14 Sch.11 para.7

s.212U, added: 2012 c.14 Sch.11 para.7

s.212U, amended: 2012 c.14 Sch.11 para.7

s.214, amended: 2012 c.14 Sch.9 para.3

s.215, substituted: 2012 c.14 Sch.9 para.1

s.216, amended: 2012 c.14 Sch.9 para.4

s.217, disapplied: 2012 c.14 s.41

s.218, amended: 2012 c.14 Sch.9 para.5

s.218ZA, added: 2012 c.14 Sch.9 para.6

s.230, amended: 2012 c.14 s.41, Sch.9 para.7

s.230, repealed (in part): 2012 c.14 Sch.9 para.7

s.254, amended: 2012 c.14 Sch.16 para.97

2001– cont.

2. Capital Allowances Act 2001– *cont.*
s.255, substituted: 2012 c.14 Sch.16 para.98
s.255, varied: SI 2012/3008 Reg.4
s.256, amended: 2012 c.14 Sch.16 para.99
s.256, repealed (in part): 2012 c.14 Sch.16 para.99
s.257, amended: 2012 c.14 Sch.16 para.100
s.261, amended: 2012 c.14 Sch.16 para.101
s.268D, repealed (in part): 2012 c.5 Sch.14 Part 9
s.268E, added: 2012 c.14 Sch.9 para.8
s.360B, enabling: SI 2012/868
s.360C, repealed (in part): 2012 c.14 Sch.39 para.8
s.360D, enabling: SI 2012/868
s.393A, repealed: 2012 c.14 Sch.39 para.37
s.393B, repealed: 2012 c.14 Sch.39 para.37
s.393C, repealed: 2012 c.14 Sch.39 para.37
s.393D, repealed: 2012 c.14 Sch.39 para.37
s.393E, repealed: 2012 c.14 Sch.39 para.37
s.393F, repealed: 2012 c.14 Sch.39 para.37
s.393G, repealed: 2012 c.14 Sch.39 para.37
s.393H, repealed: 2012 c.14 Sch.39 para.37
s.393I, applied: 2012 c.14 Sch.39 para.42
s.393I, repealed: 2012 c.14 Sch.39 para.37
s.393J, applied: 2012 c.14 Sch.39 para.41
s.393J, repealed: 2012 c.14 Sch.39 para.37
s.393K, repealed: 2012 c.14 Sch.39 para.37
s.393L, repealed: 2012 c.14 Sch.39 para.37
s.393M, applied: 2012 c.14 Sch.39 para.42
s.393M, repealed: 2012 c.14 Sch.39 para.37
s.393N, repealed: 2012 c.14 Sch.39 para.37
s.393O, repealed: 2012 c.14 Sch.39 para.37
s.393P, repealed: 2012 c.14 Sch.39 para.37
s.393Q, repealed: 2012 c.14 Sch.39 para.37
s.393R, repealed: 2012 c.14 Sch.39 para.37
s.393S, repealed: 2012 c.14 Sch.39 para.37
s.393T, repealed: 2012 c.14 Sch.39 para.37
s.393U, repealed: 2012 c.14 Sch.39 para.37
s.393V, repealed: 2012 c.14 Sch.39 para.37
s.393W, repealed: 2012 c.14 Sch.39 para.37
s.544, amended: 2012 c.14 Sch.16 para.102, Sch.16 para.103
s.544, repealed (in part): 2012 c.14 Sch.16 para.103
s.545, amended: 2012 c.14 Sch.16 para.102, Sch.16 para.104
s.560, amended: 2012 c.14 Sch.16 para.105
s.563, amended: 2012 c.14 Sch.10 para.5
s.567, amended: 2012 c.14 Sch.39 para.38
s.570, amended: 2012 c.14 Sch.39 para.38
s.570A, amended: 2012 c.14 Sch.39 para.38
s.573, amended: 2012 c.14 Sch.39 para.38
Sch.A1 Part 1 para.7, amended: 2012 c.14 Sch.16 para.106
Sch.A1 Part 1 para.9, amended: 2012 c.14 Sch.16 para.106
Sch.A1 Part 1 para.14, amended: 2012 c.14 Sch.16 para.106
Sch.A1 Part 1 para.16, amended: 2012 c.14 Sch.16 para.106
Sch.A1 Part 1 para.17, amended: 2012 c.5 Sch.3 para.14, Sch.14 Part 1
Sch.A1 Part 2 para.21, amended: 2012 c.14 Sch.16 para.106
Sch.A1 Part 2 para.22, amended: 2012 c.14 Sch.16 para.106
Sch.1 Part 2, amended: 2012 c.14 Sch.16 para.107, Sch.39 para.38
Sch.2 para.72, repealed: 2012 c.14 Sch.39 para.19

2001– cont.

4. Criminal Defence Service (Advice and Assistance) Act 2001
repealed: 2012 c.10 Sch.5 Part 2
9. Finance Act 2001
s.67, repealed: 2012 c.14 Sch.39 para.39
s.92, repealed: 2012 c.14 Sch.39 para.7
s.92A, repealed: 2012 c.14 Sch.39 para.7
s.92B, repealed: 2012 c.14 Sch.39 para.7
Sch.3 Part 2, applied: 2012 c.14 Sch.24 para.59
Sch.3 Part 3, applied: 2012 c.14 Sch.24 para.59
Sch.19 Part 1, repealed: 2012 c.14 Sch.39 para.39
Sch.19 Part 2 para.1, repealed: 2012 c.14 Sch.39 para.39
Sch.19 Part 2 para.2, repealed: 2012 c.14 Sch.39 para.39
Sch.19 Part 2 para.3, repealed: 2012 c.14 Sch.39 para.39
Sch.19 Part 2 para.4, repealed: 2012 c.14 Sch.39 para.39
Sch.19 Part 2 para.5, repealed: 2012 c.14 Sch.39 para.39
Sch.19 Part 2 para.6, repealed: 2012 c.14 Sch.39 para.39
Sch.19 Part 2 para.7, repealed: 2012 c.14 Sch.39 para.39
Sch.19 Part 2 para.8, repealed: 2012 c.14 Sch.39 para.39
11. Social Security Fraud Act 2001
s.1, repealed (in part): 2012 c.5 Sch.14 Part 1
s.2, repealed (in part): 2012 c.5 Sch.14 Part 1
s.6, repealed: 2012 c.5 Sch.14 Part 1
s.6A, amended: 2012 c.5 s.117, Sch.2 para.57, Sch.9 para.46
s.6A, repealed (in part): 2012 c.5 Sch.14 Part 1, Sch.14 Part 9
s.6B, amended: 2012 c.5 s.113, s.118, s.119, s.121, Sch.2 para.58, Sch.3 para.16, Sch.14 Part 1, Sch.14 Part 12
s.6B, applied: SI 2012/2885 Reg.2, Sch.2 para.6, SI 2012/2886 Sch.1, SI 2012/3144 Reg.2, SI 2012/3145 Sch.1, SSI 2012/303 Sch.1 para.11, SSI 2012/319 Reg.2, Sch.1 para.7
s.6B, repealed (in part): 2012 c.5 s.121, Sch.14 Part 1
s.6C, amended: 2012 c.5 s.113, Sch.14 Part 12
s.7, amended: 2012 c.5 s.118, s.119, Sch.2 para.59, Sch.3 para.17, Sch.14 Part 1
s.7, applied: SI 2012/2885 Reg.2, Sch.2 para.6, SI 2012/2886 Sch.1, SI 2012/3144 Reg.2, SI 2012/3145 Sch.1, SSI 2012/303 Sch.1 para.11, SSI 2012/319 Reg.2, Sch.1 para.7
s.7, repealed (in part): 2012 c.5 Sch.14 Part 1
s.8, amended: 2012 c.5 s.113, Sch.2 para.60, Sch.7 para.12, Sch.14 Part 12
s.8, applied: SI 2012/2885 Reg.2, SI 2012/2886 Sch.1, SI 2012/3144 Reg.2, SI 2012/3145 Sch.1, SSI 2012/319 Reg.2
s.8, repealed (in part): 2012 c.5 Sch.7 para.12, Sch.14 Part 1
s.9, amended: 2012 c.5 s.113, Sch.2 para.61, Sch.14 Part 12
s.9, applied: SI 2012/2885 Reg.2, SI 2012/2886 Sch.1, SI 2012/3144 Reg.2, SI 2012/3145 Sch.1, SSI 2012/319 Reg.2
s.9, repealed (in part): 2012 c.5 Sch.14 Part 1
s.10, amended: 2012 c.5 Sch.2 para.62, Sch.9 para.47, Sch.14 Part 1
s.11, amended: 2012 c.5 s.118, s.119, Sch.2 para.63, Sch.3 para.18
s.11, repealed (in part): 2012 c.5 Sch.14 Part 1
s.13, amended: 2012 c.5 Sch.14 Part 1, Sch.14 Part 12

2001–cont.

11. Social Security Fraud Act 2001–*cont.*
s.14, repealed: 2012 c.5 Sch.14 Part 1

12. Private Security Industry Act 2001
s.3, amended: 2012 c.9 Sch.9 para.20
s.3, applied: SI 2012/145 Reg.3
s.3, disapplied: SI 2012/145 Reg.5
s.3, repealed (in part): 2012 c.9 Sch.9 para.20, Sch.10 Part 3
s.4, applied: SI 2012/145 Reg.5, SI 2012/1567
s.4, referred to: SI 2012/145 Reg.5
s.4, enabling: SI 2012/145, SI 2012/1567
s.4A, amended: 2012 c.9 Sch.9 para.20, Sch.10 Part 3
s.4A, repealed (in part): 2012 c.9 Sch.9 para.20, Sch.10 Part 3
s.6, repealed (in part): 2012 c.9 Sch.9 para.20, Sch.10 Part 3
s.19, see *Rodden v Dunn* 2012 J.C. 114 (HCJ), Lord Bonomy
s.22A, repealed (in part): 2012 c.9 Sch.9 para.20, Sch.10 Part 3
s.24, amended: 2012 c.9 Sch.9 para.20, Sch.10 Part 3
s.24, applied: SI 2012/145, SI 2012/1567
s.25, amended: 2012 c.9 Sch.9 para.20, Sch.10 Part 3
Sch.1 para.3, amended: SI 2012/2404 Sch.2 para.45
Sch.2 Part 1 para.3, repealed (in part): 2012 c.9 Sch.9 para.20, Sch.10 Part 3
Sch.2 Part 1 para.3A, repealed (in part): 2012 c.9 Sch.9 para.20, Sch.10 Part 3
Sch.2 Part 2 para.9, repealed (in part): 2012 c.9 Sch.9 para.20, Sch.10 Part 3
Sch.2 Part 2 para.9A, repealed (in part): 2012 c.9 Sch.9 para.20, Sch.10 Part 3

15. Health and Social Care Act 2001
s.57, applied: SI 2012/2885 Sch.6 para.29, SI 2012/2886 Sch.1, SSI 2012/303 Sch.4 para.57, Sch.5 para.62, SSI 2012/319 Sch.4 para.29

16. Criminal Justice and Police Act 2001
s.1, amended: SI 2012/1430 Art.2
s.1, repealed (in part): 2012 c.10 Sch.23 para.2
s.1, enabling: SI 2012/1430
s.2, amended: 2012 c.10 Sch.23 para.3
s.2, repealed (in part): 2012 c.10 Sch.23 para.3
s.2A, added: 2012 c.10 Sch.23 para.4
s.3, amended: 2012 c.10 Sch.23 para.5
s.3, repealed (in part): 2012 c.10 Sch.23 para.5
s.3, enabling: SI 2012/1431
s.4, amended: 2012 c.10 Sch.23 para.6
s.5, amended: 2012 c.10 Sch.23 para.7
s.6, amended: 2012 c.10 Sch.23 para.8
s.8, amended: 2012 c.10 Sch.23 para.9
s.8, referred to: SI 2012/1726 r.52.6
· s.9, referred to: SI 2012/1726 r.52.6
s.10, amended: 2012 c.10 Sch.23 para.10
s.10, referred to: SI 2012/1726 r.52.6
s.10A, added: 2012 c.10 Sch.23 para.11
s.11, amended: 2012 c.10 Sch.23 para.12
s.33, see *R. v Graham (Lesley Elizabeth)* [2011] EWCA Crim 1905, [2012] 1 Cr. App. R. (S.) 57 (CA (Crim Div)), Aikens, L.J.
s.50, see *R. (on the application of Dulai) v Chelmsford Magistrates' Court* [2012] EWHC 1055 (Admin), [2012] 3 All E.R. 764 (DC), Stanley Burnton, L.J.
s.52, see *R. (on the application of Dulai) v Chelmsford Magistrates' Court* [2012] EWHC 1055 (Admin), [2012] 3 All E.R. 764 (DC), Stanley Burnton, L.J.
s.57, amended: 2012 c.21 Sch.18 para.92

2001–cont.

16. Criminal Justice and Police Act 2001–*cont.*
s.59, see *R. (on the application of Dulai) v Chelmsford Magistrates' Court* [2012] EWHC 1055 (Admin), [2012] 3 All E.R. 764 (DC), Stanley Burnton, L.J.
s.82, repealed: 2012 c.9 Sch.10 Part 1
s.84, repealed: 2012 c.9 Sch.10 Part 1
s.130, repealed: 2012 c.10 Sch.12 para.47
s.132, repealed: 2012 c.10 Sch.12 para.47
s.133, repealed (in part): 2012 c.10 Sch.12 para.47
Sch.1 Part 1 para.63A, added: 2012 c.9 Sch.9 para.145
Sch.1 Part 1 para.69A, added: 2012 c.9 Sch.9 para.28
Sch.1 Part 1 para.69B, added: 2012 c.9 Sch.9 para.28
Sch.1 Part 2 para.82A, added: 2012 c.9 Sch.9 para.29

17. International Criminal Court Act 2001
s.6, amended: 2012 c.10 Sch.5 para.56
s.52, see *Nero v DPP* [2012] EWHC 1238 (Admin), (2012) 176 J.P. 450 (QBD (Admin)), Laws, L.J.
Sch.4 para.8, substituted: 2012 c.9 Sch.1 para.2
Sch.7 para.2, amended: 2012 c.10 Sch.13 para.13

24. Anti-terrorism, Crime and Security Act 2001
s.2, repealed (in part): 2012 c.10 Sch.5 Part 2
s.58, enabling: SI 2012/1466
s.73, applied: SI 2012/1466
Sch.1 Part 5 para.16, amended: 2012 c.21 Sch.18 para.93
Sch.4 Part 1 para.47, repealed: 2012 c.10 Sch.5 para.57
Sch.4 Part 1 para.53E, added: 2012 c.10 Sch.5 para.57
Sch.5, amended: SI 2012/1466 Art.2
Sch.5, repealed: SI 2012/1466 Art.2
Sch.7 para.31, repealed: 2012 c.9 Sch.10 Part 4

2002

1. International Development Act 2002
s.11, applied: SI 2012/492, SI 2012/492 Art.3, SI 2012/517, SI 2012/517 Art.3, SI 2012/518, SI 2012/518 Art.3, SI 2012/520, SI 2012/2790
s.11, referred to: SI 2012/492, SI 2012/2790
s.11, enabling: SI 2012/492, SI 2012/517, SI 2012/518, SI 2012/520, SI 2012/2790
Sch.1, amended: 2012 c.7 Sch.5 para.100, Sch.7 para.11, Sch.14 para.82, Sch.17 para.9

9. Land Registration Act 2002
see *Franks v Bedward* [2011] EWCA Civ 772, [2012] 1 W.L.R. 2428 (CA (Civ Div)), Arden, L.J.
applied: SI 2012/1829 Reg.3
s.7, see *E. ON UK Plc v Gilesports Ltd* [2012] EWHC 2172 (Ch), [2012] 47 E.G. 128 (Ch D), Arnold, J.
s.27, applied: SI 2012/1969 Art.4
s.29, see *Hughmans Solicitors v Central Stream Services Ltd (In Liquidation)* [2012] EWHC 1222 (Ch), [2012] B.P.I.R. 1013 (Ch D), Briggs, J.; see *North East Property Buyers Litigation, Re* [2012] EWCA Civ 17, [2012] 1 W.L.R. 1521 (CA (Civ Div)), Lord Neuberger (M.R.); see *R. v Cornelius (Benjamin Jason)* [2012] EWCA Crim 500, [2012] Lloyd's Rep. F.C. 435 (CA (Crim Div)), Sir John Thomas (President)
s.35, see *Silkstone v Tatnall* [2011] EWCA Civ 801, [2012] 1 W.L.R. 400 (CA (Civ Div)), Mummery, L.J.

2002– cont.

9. Land Registration Act 2002–*cont.*

s.36, see *Silkstone v Tatnall* [2011] EWCA Civ 801, [2012] 1 W.L.R. 400 (CA (Civ Div)), Mummery, L.J.

s.41, applied: SI 2012/ 1969 Sch.3 Part 1, Sch.3 Part 4, Sch.4

s.64, applied: SI 2012/ 1969 Sch.3 Part 1

s.73, see *Silkstone v Tatnall* [2011] EWCA Civ 801, [2012] 1 W.L.R. 400 (CA (Civ Div)), Mummery, L.J.

s.86, see *Pick v Chief Land Registrar* [2011] EWHC 206 (Ch), [2012] Ch. 564 (Ch D), Proudman, J.

s.102, enabling: SI 2012/ 1969

s.117, applied: SI 2012/ 1969 Sch.3 Part 1

s.127, applied: SI 2012/ 1969

s.128, enabling: SI 2012/ 1969

Sch.3, see *R. v Cornelius (Benjamin Jason)* [2012] EWCA Crim 500, [2012] Lloyd's Rep. F.C. 435 (CA (Crim Div)), Sir John Thomas (President)

Sch.3 para.2, see *Chaudhary v Yavuz* [2011] EWCA Civ 1314, [2012] 3 W.L.R. 987 (CA (Civ Div)), Ward, L.J.

Sch.4 para.6, see *Paton v Todd* [2012] EWHC 1248 (Ch), [2012] 2 E.G.L.R. 19 (Ch D (Bristol)), Morgan, J.

Sch.6 para.1, see *Swan Housing Association Ltd v Gill* [2012] EWHC 3129 (QB), Times, December 13, 2012 (QBD), Eady, J.

Sch.6 para.5, see *IAM Group Plc v Chowdrey* [2012] EWCA Civ 505, [2012] 2 P. & C.R. 13 (CA (Civ Div)), Thorpe, L.J.; see *Zarb v Parry* [2011] EWCA Civ 1306, [2012] 1 W.L.R. 1240 (CA (Civ Div)), Lord Neuberger (M.R.)

Sch.8, see *Pick v Chief Land Registrar* [2011] EWHC 206 (Ch), [2012] Ch. 564 (Ch D), Proudman, J.

11. Office of Communications Act 2002

Sch.1 para.2, amended: SI 2012/ 2404 Sch.2 para.46

15. Commonhold and Leasehold Reform Act 2002

referred to: SI 2012/ 1969 Sch.3 Part 1

s.9, applied: SI 2012/ 1969 Sch.3 Part 1

s.58, applied: SI 2012/ 1969 Sch.3 Part 1

s.71, see *Gala Unity Ltd v Ariadne Road RTM Co Ltd* [2012] EWCA Civ 1372, [2012] 50 E.G. 105 (CA (Civ Div)), Arden, L.J.

s.72, see *Gala Unity Ltd v Ariadne Road RTM Co Ltd* [2012] 1 E.G.L.R. 99 (UT (Lands)), George Bartlett Q.C. (President); see *Gala Unity Ltd v Ariadne Road RTM Co Ltd* [2012] EWCA Civ 1372, [2012] 50 E.G. 105 (CA (Civ Div)), Arden, L.J.

s.79, see *Gala Unity Ltd v Ariadne Road RTM Co Ltd* [2012] 1 E.G.L.R. 99 (UT (Lands)), George Bartlett Q.C. (President)

s.112, see *Gala Unity Ltd v Ariadne Road RTM Co Ltd* [2012] EWCA Civ 1372, [2012] 50 E.G. 105 (CA (Civ Div)), Arden, L.J.

s.168, see *Beaufort Park Residents Management Ltd v Sabahipour* [2012] 1 E.G.L.R. 53 (UT (Lands)), Judge Walden-Smith; see *Freeholders of 69 Marina, St Leonards-on-Sea v Oram* [2011] EWCA Civ 1258, [2012] H.L.R. 12 (CA (Civ Div)), Sir Andrew Morritt (Chancellor)

s.175, see *Wellcome Trust Ltd v 19-22 Onslow Gardens Freehold* [2012] EWCA Civ 1024, [2012] R.V.R. 342 (CA (Civ Div)), Lloyd, L.J.

2002– cont.

15. Commonhold and Leasehold Reform Act 2002–*cont.*

Sch.11 Pt 1 para.1, see *Holding & Management (Solitaire) Ltd v Norton* [2012] UKUT 1 (LC), [2012] L. & T.R. 15 (UT (Lands)), George Bartlett Q.C. (President)

Sch.11 Pt 1 para.5, see *Crosspite Ltd v Sachdev* [2012] UKUT 321 (LC) (UT (Lands)), Judge Gerald

16. State Pension Credit Act 2002

applied: 2012 c.5 s.96, SI 2012/ 531 Reg.49, SI 2012/ 2885 Sch.1 para.17, Sch.1 para.22, Sch.1 para.46, SI 2012/ 2886 Sch.1, SI 2012/ 3144 Sch.1 para.11, Sch.1 para.16, SI 2012/ 3145 Sch.1, SSI 2012/ 292 Art.3, SSI 2012/ 319 Reg.31, Reg.38, Reg.59

s.1, amended: 2012 c.5 s.75, Sch.4 para.2, Sch.4 para.3

s.1, applied: SI 2012/ 1483 Reg.4

s.1, referred to: 2012 c.5 s.4

s.1, enabling: SI 2012/ 2587

s.2, amended: 2012 c.5 s.74

s.2, enabling: SI 2012/ 913

s.3A, added: 2012 c.5 Sch.4 para.4

s.4, amended: 2012 c.5 Sch.2 para.64

s.6, applied: SI 2012/ 2885 Sch.1 para.14, SI 2012/ 2886 Sch.1, SI 2012/ 3144 Sch.1 para.8, SI 2012/ 3145 Sch.1, SSI 2012/ 319 Reg.25

s.7, amended: 2012 c.5 Sch.4 para.5

s.9, applied: SI 2012/ 2885 Sch.1 para.14, SI 2012/ 2886 Sch.1, SI 2012/ 3144 Sch.1 para.8, SI 2012/ 3145 Sch.1, SSI 2012/ 319 Reg.25

s.12, amended: 2012 c.5 Sch.4 para.6

s.15, repealed (in part): 2012 c.5 Sch.14 Part 1

s.15, enabling: SI 2012/ 757

s.17, amended: 2012 c.5 s.74, Sch.4 para.7, Sch.14 Part 1

s.17, enabling: SI 2012/ 757, SI 2012/ 913, SI 2012/ 2587

s.18A, repealed (in part): 2012 c.5 Sch.14 Part 1

s.19, amended: 2012 c.5 s.75

s.19, enabling: SI 2012/ 757

Sch.2 Part 1 para.2, repealed: 2012 c.5 Sch.14 Part 1

Sch.2 Part 1 para.3, repealed: 2012 c.5 Sch.14 Part 1

Sch.2 Part 1 para.4, repealed: 2012 c.5 Sch.14 Part 1

Sch.2 Part 2 para.9, repealed (in part): 2012 c.5 Sch.4 para.8

Sch.2 Part 3 para.36, repealed: 2012 c.5 Sch.14 Part 1

Sch.2 Part 3 para.37, repealed: 2012 c.5 Sch.14 Part 1

Sch.2 Part 3 para.38, repealed: 2012 c.5 Sch.14 Part 1

Sch.2 Part 3 para.49, repealed: 2012 c.5 Sch.14 Part 12

17. National Health Service Reform and Health Care Professions Act 2002

Part 2, substituted: 2012 c.7 s.222

s.25, amended: 2012 c.7 s.220, s.222, s.223, s.224, Sch.15 para.56, Sch.15 para.62

s.25, applied: SI 2012/ 3094 Reg.34

s.25, substituted: 2012 c.7 s.222

s.25A, added: 2012 c.7 s.224

s.25A, substituted: 2012 c.7 s.222

s.25B, added: 2012 c.7 s.225

s.25B, substituted: 2012 c.7 s.222

s.25C, added: 2012 c.7 s.227

s.25C, substituted: 2012 c.7 s.222

s.25C, varied: SI 2012/ 1319 Art.3

s.25D, added: 2012 c.7 s.228

s.25D, substituted: 2012 c.7 s.222

2002–cont.

17. National Health Service Reform and Health Care Professions Act 2002–*cont.*

s.25E, added: 2012 c.7 s.228
s.25E, substituted: 2012 c.7 s.222
s.25F, added: 2012 c.7 s.228
s.25F, substituted: 2012 c.7 s.222
s.25G, added: 2012 c.7 s.229
s.25G, substituted: 2012 c.7 s.222
s.25H, added: 2012 c.7 s.229
s.25H, substituted: 2012 c.7 s.222
s.25I, added: 2012 c.7 s.229
s.25I, substituted: 2012 c.7 s.222
s.26, amended: 2012 c.7 s.229, Sch.15 para.62, Sch.15 para.63
s.26, repealed (in part): 2012 c.7 Sch.15 para.64
s.26, substituted: 2012 c.7 s.222
s.26A, amended: 2012 c.7 s.223, s.229, Sch.15 para.62, Sch.15 para.65
s.26A, substituted: 2012 c.7 s.222
s.26A, varied: SI 2012/1831 Art.8
s.26B, amended: 2012 c.7 s.223, s.229, Sch.15 para.62
s.26B, substituted: 2012 c.7 s.222
s.27, amended: 2012 c.7 s.223, Sch.15 para.62, Sch.15 para.63
s.27, substituted: 2012 c.7 s.222
s.28, amended: 2012 c.7 s.225, Sch.15 para.62
s.28, substituted: 2012 c.7 s.222
s.29, amended: 2012 c.7 s.213, s.223, Sch.15 para.62, Sch.15 para.63, Sch.15 para.73
s.29, substituted: 2012 c.7 s.222
s.30, substituted: 2012 c.7 s.222
s.31, substituted: 2012 c.7 s.222
s.32, substituted: 2012 c.7 s.222
s.33, substituted: 2012 c.7 s.222
s.34, substituted: 2012 c.7 s.222
s.35, substituted: 2012 c.7 s.222
s.38, amended: 2012 c.7 s.223, s.224, s.225, s.226, s.230
Sch.1 Part 1 para.1, repealed: 2012 c.7 Sch.5 para.102
Sch.1 Part 1 para.2, repealed: 2012 c.7 Sch.5 para.102
Sch.1 Part 1 para.3, repealed: 2012 c.7 Sch.5 para.102
Sch.1 Part 1 para.4, repealed: 2012 c.7 Sch.5 para.102
Sch.1 Part 1 para.5, repealed: 2012 c.7 Sch.5 para.102
Sch.1 Part 1 para.6, repealed: 2012 c.7 Sch.5 para.102
Sch.1 Part 1 para.7, repealed: 2012 c.7 Sch.5 para.102
Sch.1 Part 1 para.8, repealed: 2012 c.7 Sch.5 para.102
Sch.1 Part 1 para.9, repealed: 2012 c.7 Sch.5 para.102
Sch.1 Part 1 para.10, repealed: 2012 c.7 Sch.5 para.102
Sch.1 Part 1 para.11, repealed: 2012 c.7 Sch.5 para.102
Sch.1 Part 1 para.12, repealed: 2012 c.7 Sch.5 para.102
Sch.1 Part 1 para.13, repealed: 2012 c.7 Sch.5 para.102
Sch.1 Part 1 para.14, repealed: 2012 c.7 Sch.5 para.102
Sch.1 Part 1 para.15, repealed: 2012 c.7 Sch.5 para.102
Sch.1 Part 1 para.16, repealed: 2012 c.7 Sch.5 para.102

2002–cont.

17. National Health Service Reform and Health Care Professions Act 2002–*cont.*

Sch.1 Part 1 para.17, repealed: 2012 c.7 Sch.5 para.102
Sch.1 Part 1 para.18, repealed: 2012 c.7 Sch.5 para.102
Sch.1 Part 1 para.19, repealed: 2012 c.7 Sch.5 para.102
Sch.1 Part 1 para.20, repealed: 2012 c.7 Sch.5 para.102
Sch.1 Part 1 para.21, repealed: 2012 c.7 Sch.5 para.102
Sch.1 Part 1 para.22, repealed: 2012 c.7 Sch.5 para.102
Sch.1 Part 1 para.23, repealed: 2012 c.7 Sch.5 para.102
Sch.1 Part 1 para.24, repealed: 2012 c.7 Sch.5 para.102
Sch.1 Part 1 para.25, repealed: 2012 c.7 Sch.5 para.102
Sch.1 Part 1 para.26, repealed: 2012 c.7 Sch.5 para.102
Sch.1 Part 1 para.27, repealed: 2012 c.7 Sch.5 para.102
Sch.1 Part 1 para.28, repealed: 2012 c.7 Sch.5 para.102
Sch.1 Part 1 para.29, repealed: 2012 c.7 Sch.5 para.102
Sch.1 Part 1 para.30, repealed: 2012 c.7 Sch.5 para.102
Sch.1 Part 1 para.31, repealed: 2012 c.7 Sch.5 para.102
Sch.1 Part 1 para.32, repealed: 2012 c.7 Sch.5 para.102
Sch.1 Part 1 para.33, repealed: 2012 c.7 Sch.5 para.102
Sch.1 Part 1 para.34, repealed: 2012 c.7 Sch.5 para.102
Sch.1 Part 1 para.35, repealed: 2012 c.7 Sch.5 para.102
Sch.1 Part 2 para.36, repealed: 2012 c.7 Sch.5 para.102
Sch.1 Part 2 para.37, repealed: 2012 c.7 Sch.5 para.102
Sch.1 Part 2 para.38, repealed: 2012 c.7 Sch.5 para.102
Sch.1 Part 2 para.39, repealed: 2012 c.7 Sch.5 para.102
Sch.1 Part 2 para.40, repealed: 2012 c.7 Sch.5 para.102
Sch.1 Part 2 para.41, repealed: 2012 c.7 Sch.5 para.102
Sch.1 Part 2 para.42, repealed: 2012 c.7 Sch.5 para.102
Sch.1 Part 2 para.43, repealed: 2012 c.7 Sch.5 para.102
Sch.1 Part 2 para.44, repealed: 2012 c.7 Sch.5 para.102
Sch.1 Part 2 para.45, repealed: 2012 c.7 Sch.5 para.102
Sch.1 Part 2 para.46, repealed: 2012 c.7 Sch.5 para.102
Sch.1 Part 2 para.47, repealed: 2012 c.7 Sch.5 para.102
Sch.1 Part 2 para.48, repealed: 2012 c.7 Sch.5 para.102
Sch.1 Part 2 para.49, repealed: 2012 c.7 Sch.5 para.102
Sch.1 Part 2 para.50, repealed: 2012 c.7 Sch.5 para.102

2002– cont.

17. National Health Service Reform and Health Care Professions Act 2002– *cont.*

Sch.1 Part 2 para.51, repealed: 2012 c.7 Sch.5 para.102

Sch.1 Part 2 para.52, repealed: 2012 c.7 Sch.5 para.102

Sch.1 Part 2 para.53, repealed: 2012 c.7 Sch.5 para.102

Sch.1 Part 2 para.54, repealed: 2012 c.7 Sch.5 para.102

Sch.1 Part 2 para.55, repealed: 2012 c.7 Sch.5 para.102

Sch.2 Part 1 para.1, repealed: 2012 c.7 Sch.5 para.103

Sch.2 Part 1 para.2, repealed: 2012 c.7 Sch.5 para.103

Sch.2 Part 1 para.3, repealed: 2012 c.7 Sch.5 para.103

Sch.2 Part 1 para.4, repealed: 2012 c.7 Sch.5 para.103

Sch.2 Part 1 para.5, repealed: 2012 c.7 Sch.5 para.103

Sch.2 Part 1 para.6, repealed: 2012 c.7 Sch.5 para.103

Sch.2 Part 1 para.7, repealed: 2012 c.7 Sch.5 para.103

Sch.2 Part 1 para.8, repealed: 2012 c.7 Sch.5 para.103

Sch.2 Part 1 para.9, repealed: 2012 c.7 Sch.5 para.103

Sch.2 Part 1 para.10, repealed: 2012 c.7 Sch.5 para.103

Sch.2 Part 1 para.11, repealed: 2012 c.7 Sch.5 para.103

Sch.2 Part 1 para.12, repealed: 2012 c.7 Sch.5 para.103

Sch.2 Part 1 para.13, repealed: 2012 c.7 Sch.5 para.103

Sch.2 Part 1 para.14, repealed: 2012 c.7 Sch.5 para.103

Sch.2 Part 1 para.15, repealed: 2012 c.7 Sch.5 para.103

Sch.2 Part 1 para.16, repealed: 2012 c.7 Sch.5 para.103

Sch.2 Part 1 para.17, repealed: 2012 c.7 Sch.5 para.103

Sch.2 Part 1 para.18, repealed: 2012 c.7 Sch.5 para.103

Sch.2 Part 1 para.19, repealed: 2012 c.7 Sch.5 para.103

Sch.2 Part 1 para.20, repealed: 2012 c.7 Sch.5 para.103

Sch.2 Part 1 para.21, repealed: 2012 c.7 Sch.5 para.103

Sch.2 Part 1 para.22, repealed: 2012 c.7 Sch.5 para.103

Sch.2 Part 1 para.23, repealed: 2012 c.7 Sch.5 para.103

Sch.2 Part 1 para.24, repealed: 2012 c.7 Sch.5 para.103

Sch.2 Part 1 para.25, repealed: 2012 c.7 Sch.5 para.103

Sch.2 Part 1 para.26, repealed: 2012 c.7 Sch.5 para.103

Sch.2 Part 1 para.27, repealed: 2012 c.7 Sch.5 para.103

Sch.2 Part 1 para.28, repealed: 2012 c.7 Sch.5 para.103

Sch.2 Part 1 para.29, repealed: 2012 c.7 Sch.5 para.103

2002– cont.

17. National Health Service Reform and Health Care Professions Act 2002– *cont.*

Sch.2 Part 1 para.30, repealed: 2012 c.7 Sch.5 para.103

Sch.2 Part 1 para.31, repealed: 2012 c.7 Sch.5 para.103

Sch.2 Part 1 para.32, repealed: 2012 c.7 Sch.5 para.103

Sch.2 Part 1 para.33, repealed: 2012 c.7 Sch.5 para.103

Sch.2 Part 1 para.34, repealed: 2012 c.7 Sch.5 para.103

Sch.2 Part 1 para.35, repealed: 2012 c.7 Sch.5 para.103

Sch.2 Part 1 para.36, repealed: 2012 c.7 Sch.5 para.103

Sch.2 Part 1 para.37, repealed: 2012 c.7 Sch.5 para.103

Sch.2 Part 2 para.38, repealed: 2012 c.7 Sch.5 para.103

Sch.2 Part 2 para.39, repealed: 2012 c.7 Sch.5 para.103

Sch.2 Part 2 para.40, repealed: 2012 c.7 Sch.5 para.103

Sch.2 Part 2 para.41, repealed: 2012 c.7 Sch.5 para.103

Sch.2 Part 2 para.42, repealed: 2012 c.7 Sch.5 para.103

Sch.2 Part 2 para.43, repealed: 2012 c.7 Sch.5 para.103

Sch.2 Part 2 para.44, repealed: 2012 c.7 Sch.5 para.103

Sch.2 Part 2 para.45, repealed: 2012 c.7 Sch.5 para.103

Sch.2 Part 2 para.46, repealed: 2012 c.7 Sch.5 para.28, Sch.5 para.103

Sch.2 Part 2 para.47, repealed: 2012 c.7 s.40, Sch.5 para.103

Sch.2 Part 2 para.48, repealed (in part): 2012 c.7 s.45, Sch.5 para.103

Sch.2 Part 2 para.49, repealed: 2012 c.7 Sch.5 para.31, Sch.5 para.103

Sch.2 Part 2 para.50, repealed: 2012 c.7 Sch.5 para.103

Sch.2 Part 2 para.51, repealed: 2012 c.7 Sch.5 para.103

Sch.2 Part 2 para.52, repealed: 2012 c.7 Sch.5 para.103

Sch.2 Part 2 para.53, repealed: 2012 c.7 Sch.5 para.103

Sch.2 Part 2 para.54, repealed: 2012 c.7 Sch.5 para.103

Sch.2 Part 2 para.55, repealed: 2012 c.7 Sch.5 para.103

Sch.2 Part 2 para.56, repealed: 2012 c.7 Sch.5 para.103

Sch.2 Part 2 para.57, repealed: 2012 c.7 Sch.5 para.103

Sch.2 Part 2 para.58, repealed: 2012 c.7 Sch.5 para.103

Sch.2 Part 2 para.59, repealed: 2012 c.7 Sch.5 para.103

Sch.2 Part 2 para.60, repealed: 2012 c.7 Sch.5 para.103

Sch.2 Part 2 para.61, repealed: 2012 c.7 Sch.5 para.103

Sch.2 Part 2 para.62, repealed: 2012 c.7 Sch.5 para.103

Sch.2 Part 2 para.63, repealed: 2012 c.7 Sch.5 para.103

2002–cont.

17. National Health Service Reform and Health Care Professions Act 2002–*cont.*

Sch.2 Part 2 para.64, repealed: 2012 c.7 Sch.5 para.103

Sch.2 Part 2 para.65, repealed: 2012 c.7 Sch.5 para.103

Sch.2 Part 2 para.66, repealed: 2012 c.7 Sch.5 para.103

Sch.2 Part 2 para.67, repealed: 2012 c.7 Sch.5 para.103

Sch.2 Part 2 para.68, repealed: 2012 c.7 Sch.5 para.103

Sch.2 Part 2 para.69, repealed: 2012 c.7 Sch.5 para.103

Sch.2 Part 2 para.70, repealed: 2012 c.7 Sch.5 para.103

Sch.2 Part 2 para.71, repealed: 2012 c.7 Sch.5 para.103

Sch.2 Part 2 para.72, repealed: 2012 c.7 Sch.5 para.103

Sch.2 Part 2 para.73, repealed: 2012 c.7 Sch.5 para.103

Sch.2 Part 2 para.74, repealed: 2012 c.7 Sch.5 para.103

Sch.2 Part 2 para.75, repealed: 2012 c.7 Sch.5 para.103

Sch.2 Part 2 para.76, repealed: 2012 c.7 Sch.5 para.103

Sch.2 Part 2 para.77, repealed: 2012 c.7 Sch.5 para.103

Sch.2 Part 2 para.78, repealed: 2012 c.7 Sch.5 para.103

Sch.2 Part 2 para.79, repealed: 2012 c.7 Sch.5 para.103

Sch.2 Part 2 para.80, repealed: 2012 c.7 Sch.5 para.103

Sch.2 Part 2 para.81, repealed: 2012 c.7 Sch.5 para.103

Sch.2 Part 2 para.82, repealed: 2012 c.7 Sch.5 para.103

Sch.3 Part 2 para.12, repealed: 2012 c.7 Sch.21 para.3

Sch.7, amended: 2012 c.7 Sch.15 para.62

Sch.7 para.1, amended: 2012 c.7 Sch.15 para.63, Sch.15 para.65, Sch.15 para.66

Sch.7 para.2, amended: 2012 c.7 Sch.15 para.62, Sch.15 para.66

Sch.7 para.3, amended: 2012 c.7 Sch.15 para.66

Sch.7 para.4, amended: 2012 c.7 s.226, Sch.15 para.63, Sch.15 para.66

Sch.7 para.5, amended: 2012 c.7 Sch.15 para.66

Sch.7 para.6, amended: 2012 c.7 s.226, Sch.15 para.62, Sch.15 para.66

Sch.7 para.7, amended: 2012 c.7 Sch.15 para.62, Sch.15 para.66

Sch.7 para.8, amended: 2012 c.7 Sch.15 para.62, Sch.15 para.66

Sch.7 para.9, amended: 2012 c.7 Sch.15 para.62, Sch.15 para.66

Sch.7 para.10, amended: 2012 c.7 s.226, Sch.15 para.62, Sch.15 para.66

Sch.7 para.11, amended: 2012 c.7 s.226, Sch.15 para.62, Sch.15 para.66

Sch.7 para.12, amended: 2012 c.7 Sch.15 para.62, Sch.15 para.66

Sch.7 para.13, amended: 2012 c.7 Sch.15 para.62, Sch.15 para.66

Sch.7 para.14, amended: 2012 c.7 s.224, Sch.15 para.62, Sch.15 para.66

Sch.7 para.14, repealed (in part): 2012 c.7 s.224

2002–cont.

17. National Health Service Reform and Health Care Professions Act 2002–*cont.*

Sch.7 para.15, amended: 2012 c.7 s.226, Sch.15 para.62, Sch.15 para.66

Sch.7 para.16, amended: 2012 c.7 s.223, s.226, Sch.15 para.62, Sch.15 para.66 ·

Sch.7 para.16, varied: 2012 c.11 s.12

Sch.7 para.17, amended: 2012 c.7 Sch.15 para.62, Sch.15 para.66

Sch.7 para.18, amended: 2012 c.7 Sch.15 para.62, Sch.15 para.66

Sch.7 para.19, amended: 2012 c.7 Sch.15 para.62, Sch.15 para.66

Sch.7 para.20, amended: 2012 c.7 Sch.15 para.66

Sch.7 para.21, amended: 2012 c.7 Sch.15 para.66

Sch.7 para.22, amended: 2012 c.7 Sch.15 para.66

Sch.7 para.23, amended: 2012 c.7 Sch.15 para.66

Sch.7 para.24, amended: 2012 c.7 Sch.15 para.66

20. Industrial and Provident Societies Act 2002

applied: SI 2012/1128 Art.4

21. Tax Credits Act 2002

applied: 2012 c.5 s.33, Sch.6 para.6, SI 2012/2886 Sch.1, SSI 2012/303 Reg.39

Part 1, applied: SI 2012/531 Reg.49

s.1, repealed: 2012 c.5 Sch.14 Part 1

s.2, repealed: 2012 c.5 Sch.14 Part 1

s.3, referred to: SSI 2012/292 Art.3

s.3, repealed: 2012 c.5 Sch.14 Part 1

s.3, enabling: SI 2012/848, SI 2012/2612

s.4, repealed: 2012 c.5 Sch.14 Part 1

s.4, enabling: SI 2012/848

s.5, repealed: 2012 c.5 Sch.14 Part 1

s.6, repealed: 2012 c.5 Sch.14 Part 1

s.6, enabling: SI 2012/848

s.7, repealed: 2012 c.5 Sch.14 Part 1

s.7, enabling: SI 2012/848, SI 2012/849

s.8, repealed: 2012 c.5 Sch.14 Part 1

s.8, enabling: SI 2012/848

s.9, repealed: 2012 c.5 Sch.14 Part 1

s.9, enabling: SI 2012/848, SI 2012/849

s.10, repealed: 2012 c.5 Sch.14 Part 1

s.10, enabling: SI 2012/848

s.11, repealed: 2012 c.5 Sch.14 Part 1

s.11, enabling: SI 2012/848, SI 2012/849

s.12, applied: SI 2012/2885 Sch.1 para.25, SI 2012/2886 Sch.1, SI 2012/3144 Sch.1 para.19, SI 2012/3145 Sch.1, SSI 2012/303 Reg.28, SSI 2012/319 Reg.29

s.12, repealed: 2012 c.5 Sch.14 Part 1

s.12, enabling: SI 2012/848, SI 2012/849

s.13, repealed: 2012 c.5 Sch.14 Part 1

s.13, enabling: SI 2012/849

s.14, repealed: 2012 c.5 Sch.14 Part 1

s.15, repealed: 2012 c.5 Sch.14 Part 1

s.16, repealed: 2012 c.5 Sch.14 Part 1

s.17, repealed: 2012 c.5 Sch.14 Part 1

s.18, repealed: 2012 c.5 Sch.14 Part 1

s.19, repealed: 2012 c.5 Sch.14 Part 1

s.20, repealed: 2012 c.5 Sch.14 Part 1

s.21, repealed: 2012 c.5 Sch.14 Part 1

s.22, repealed: 2012 c.5 Sch.14 Part 1

s.23, repealed: 2012 c.5 Sch.14 Part 1

s.24, repealed: 2012 c.5 Sch.14 Part 1

s.24, enabling: SI 2012/848

s.25, repealed: 2012 c.5 Sch.14 Part 1

s.26, repealed: 2012 c.5 Sch.14 Part 1

s.27, repealed: 2012 c.5 Sch.14 Part 1

s.28, repealed: 2012 c.5 Sch.14 Part 1

2002– cont.

21. Tax Credits Act 2002– *cont.*
s.29, repealed: 2012 c.5 Sch.14 Part 1
s.30, repealed: 2012 c.5 Sch.14 Part 1
s.31, repealed: 2012 c.5 Sch.14 Part 1
s.32, repealed: 2012 c.5 Sch.14 Part 1
s.33, repealed: 2012 c.5 Sch.14 Part 1
s.34, repealed: 2012 c.5 Sch.14 Part 1
s.35, see *R. v Nolan (Tracey)* [2012] EWCA Crim 671, [2012] Lloyd's Rep. F.C. 498 (CA (Crim Div)), Rafferty, L.J.
s.35, amended: 2012 c.5 s.124
s.35, repealed: 2012 c.5 Sch.14 Part 1
s.36, repealed: 2012 c.5 Sch.14 Part 1
s.36A, added: 2012 c.5 s.120
s.36A, amended: 2012 c.5 Sch.14 Part 12
s.36A, repealed (in part): 2012 c.5 s.121, Sch.14 Part 1, Sch.14 Part 12
s.36B, added: 2012 c.5 s.120
s.36B, repealed (in part): 2012 c.5 Sch.14 Part 1, Sch.14 Part 12
s.36C, added: 2012 c.5 s.120
s.36C, repealed: 2012 c.5 Sch.14 Part 1
s.36D, added: 2012 c.5 s.120
s.36D, repealed: 2012 c.5 Sch.14 Part 1
s.37, repealed: 2012 c.5 Sch.14 Part 1
s.38, amended: 2012 c.5 s.120
s.38, repealed: 2012 c.5 Sch.14 Part 1
s.39, repealed: 2012 c.5 Sch.14 Part 1
s.40, repealed: 2012 c.5 Sch.14 Part 1
s.41, repealed: 2012 c.5 Sch.14 Part 1
s.42, repealed: 2012 c.5 Sch.14 Part 1
s.42, enabling: SI 2012/ 848
s.43, repealed: 2012 c.5 Sch.14 Part 1
s.44, repealed: 2012 c.5 Sch.14 Part 1
s.45, repealed: 2012 c.5 Sch.14 Part 1
s.46, repealed: 2012 c.5 Sch.14 Part 1
s.47, repealed: 2012 c.5 Sch.14 Part 1
s.48, repealed: 2012 c.5 Sch.14 Part 1
s.63, amended: SI 2012/ 533 Art.2
s.65, enabling: SI 2012/ 848, SI 2012/ 849
s.66, amended: 2012 c.5 s.120
s.67, amended: 2012 c.5 s.120, Sch.14 Part 12
s.67, enabling: SI 2012/ 848, SI 2012/ 849
Sch.4 para.2, repealed: 2012 c.5 s.107
Sch.4 para.8, repealed: 2012 c.5 s.107
Sch.5 para.4, amended: 2012 c.5 Sch.14 Part 13
Sch.5 para.4, repealed (in part): 2012 c.5 Sch.14 Part 13
Sch.5 para.6, amended: 2012 c.5 Sch.14 Part 13

22. Employment Act 2002
see *Edwards v Chesterfield Royal Hospital NHS Foundation Trust* [2012] 2 A.C. 22 (SC), Lord Phillips (President)
s.13, amended: SI 2012/ 2007 Sch.1 para.66
s.32, see *Aitchison v South Ayrshire Council* 2012 S.C. 444 (IH (Ex Div)), Lady Paton; see *Amery v Perth and Kinross Council* [2012] CSIH 11, 2012 S.L.T. 395 (IH (Ex Div)), Lady Paton; see *Beddoes v Birmingham City Council* [2012] EWCA Civ 585, [2012] Eq. L.R. 695 (CA (Civ Div)), Pill, L.J.; see *Fraser v Southwest London St George's Mental Health Trust* [2012] I.C.R. 403 (EAT), Underhill, J. (President)
s.49, repealed: 2012 c.5 Sch.14 Part 1
Sch.2 Pt 2 para.6, see *Amery v Perth and Kinross Council* [2012] CSIH 11, 2012 S.L.T. 395 (IH (Ex Div)), Lady Paton

2002– cont.

22. Employment Act 2002– *cont.*
Sch.2 Pt 2 para.7, see *Amery v Perth and Kinross Council* [2012] CSIH 11, 2012 S.L.T. 395 (IH (Ex Div)), Lady Paton
Sch.2 Pt 2 para.9, see *Beddoes v Birmingham City Council* [2012] EWCA Civ 585, [2012] Eq. L.R. 695 (CA (Civ Div)), Pill, L.J.
Sch.6 para.2, repealed: 2012 c.5 Sch.14 Part 1
Sch.6 para.3, repealed: 2012 c.5 Sch.14 Part 1
Sch.6 para.5, repealed: 2012 c.5 Sch.14 Part 13
Sch.6 para.6, repealed: 2012 c.5 Sch.14 Part 13
Sch.6 para.11, repealed (in part): 2012 c.5 Sch.14 Part 13
Sch.6 para.13, repealed (in part): 2012 c.5 Sch.14 Part 13
Sch.7 para.9, repealed: 2012 c.5 Sch.14 Part 1
Sch.7 para.10, repealed: 2012 c.5 Sch.14 Part 1
Sch.7 para.12, repealed (in part): 2012 c.5 Sch.14 Part 1
Sch.7 para.15, repealed: 2012 c.5 Sch.14 Part 1
Sch.7 para.50, repealed: 2012 c.5 Sch.14 Part 13
Sch.7 para.51, repealed: 2012 c.5 Sch.14 Part 1

23. Finance Act 2002
s.43, repealed (in part): 2012 c.14 s.37
s.64, referred to: 2012 c.14 s.54
s.64, varied: 2012 c.14 s.54
s.90, repealed: 2012 c.14 Sch.20 para.21
s.110, repealed: 2012 c.14 Sch.39 para.7
s.112, repealed: 2012 c.14 Sch.39 para.5
s.113, repealed: 2012 c.14 Sch.39 para.5
s.123, repealed: 2012 c.14 Sch.32 para.22
s.124, repealed: 2012 c.14 Sch.32 para.22
s.135, applied: SI 2012/ 1836 Reg.17
s.135, enabling: SI 2012/ 33, SI 2012/ 884, SI 2012/ 1836, SI 2012/ 1899
s.136, enabling: SI 2012/ 33, SI 2012/ 820, SI 2012/ 822, SI 2012/ 884, SI 2012/ 1895, SI 2012/ 1899
Sch.35 para.1, repealed: 2012 c.14 Sch.39 para.5
Sch.35 para.2, repealed: 2012 c.14 Sch.39 para.5
Sch.35 para.3, repealed: 2012 c.14 Sch.39 para.5
Sch.35 para.4, repealed: 2012 c.14 Sch.39 para.5
Sch.35 para.5, repealed: 2012 c.14 Sch.39 para.5
Sch.35 para.6, repealed: 2012 c.14 Sch.39 para.5
Sch.35 para.7, repealed: 2012 c.14 Sch.39 para.5
Sch.35 para.8, repealed: 2012 c.14 Sch.39 para.5
Sch.35 para.9, repealed: 2012 c.14 Sch.39 para.5
Sch.35 para.10, repealed: 2012 c.14 Sch.39 para.5
Sch.35 para.11, repealed: 2012 c.14 Sch.39 para.5
Sch.35 para.12, repealed: 2012 c.14 Sch.39 para.5

24. European Parliamentary Elections Act 2002
s.1, applied: SI 2012/ 323 Reg.10, SI 2012/ 444 Reg.17

28. Export Control Act 2002
s.1, enabling: SI 2012/ 810, SI 2012/ 929, SI 2012/ 1243, SI 2012/ 1910, SI 2012/ 2125
s.2, enabling: SI 2012/ 810, SI 2012/ 1243, SI 2012/ 1910, SI 2012/ 2125
s.3, enabling: SI 2012/ 810, SI 2012/ 1243, SI 2012/ 1910, SI 2012/ 2125
s.4, enabling: SI 2012/ 810, SI 2012/ 1243, SI 2012/ 1910, SI 2012/ 2125
s.5, amended: SI 2012/ 1809 Sch.1 Part 1
s.5, enabling: SI 2012/ 810, SI 2012/ 929, SI 2012/ 1243, SI 2012/ 1910, SI 2012/ 2125
s.7, enabling: SI 2012/ 810, SI 2012/ 1243, SI 2012/ 1910, SI 2012/ 2125
s.11, amended: SI 2012/ 1809 Sch.1 Part 1
s.11, applied: SI 2012/ 810 Art.1, SI 2012/ 1243 Art.1
s.16, enabling: SI 2012/ 362

2002– cont.

29. Proceeds of Crime Act 2002

see *Peacock, Re* [2012] UKSC 5, [2012] 1 W.L.R. 550 (SC), Lord Hope (Deputy President); see *R. v Ahmad (Shakeel)* [2012] EWCA Crim 391, [2012] 1 W.L.R. 2335 (CA (Crim Div)), Hooper, L.J.; see *R. v Brown (Terence Roy)* [2011] EWCA Crim 2751, [2012] 2 Cr. App. R. (S.) 10 (CA (Crim Div)), Lord Judge, L.C.J.; see *R. v Thompson (Frederick George)* [2011] EWCA Crim 102, [2012] 1 W.L.R. 571 (CA (Crim Div)), Thomas, L.J.; see *R. v Varma (Aloke)* [2012] UKSC 42, [2012] 3 W.L.R. 776 (SC), Lord Phillips, J.S.C. (President); see *R. v Waya (Terry)* [2012] UKSC 51, [2012] 3 W.L.R. 1188 (SC), Lord Phillips, J.S.C.; see *Serious Organised Crime Agency v Coghlan* [2012] EWHC 429 (QB), [2012] Lloyd's Rep. F.C. 341 (QBD), Simon, J.; see *Serious Organised Crime Agency v Robb* [2012] EWHC 803 (QB), [2012] Lloyd's Rep. F.C. 485 (QBD), Mackay, J.; see *Sumal & Sons (Properties) Ltd v Newham LBC* [2012] EWCA Crim 1840, [2012] Lloyd's Rep. F.C. 692 (CA (Crim Div)), Davis, L.J.

applied: 2012 c.10 Sch.1 para.6, Sch.1 para.8, SI 2012/1726 r.58.1

Part 2, applied: 2012 c.5 s.128, s.129, 2012 c.10 Sch.1 para.40, SI 2012/1726 r.71.1, r.71.2, r.71.4, r.71.5, r.71.8, r.57.2, r.71.9, r.71.10, r.57.3, r.76.1, r.57.8, r.57.9, r.57.14

Part 3, applied: 2012 c.5 s.129

Part 4, applied: 2012 c.5 s.129

Part 5, applied: 2012 c.5 s.128, s.129

Part 7, referred to: SI 2012/2299 Art.4

Part 8, applied: 2012 c.5 s.128, s.129, SI 2012/1726 r.6.1

Pt 3. see *Serious Organised Crime Agency v Perry* [2012] UKSC 35, [2012] 3 W.L.R. 379 (SC), Lord Phillips, J.S.C.

Pt 4. see *Serious Organised Crime Agency v Perry* [2012] UKSC 35, [2012] 3 W.L.R. 379 (SC), Lord Phillips, J.S.C.

Pt 5. see *Hunter v McPherson* 2012 J.C. 145 (HCJ), Lord Mackay of Drumadoon; see *Serious Organised Crime Agency v Perry* [2012] UKSC 35, [2012] 3 W.L.R. 379 (SC), Lord Phillips, J.S.C.

Pt 8. see *R. (on the application of Horne) v Central Criminal Court* [2012] EWHC 1350 (Admin), [2012] 1 W.L.R. 3152 (QBD (Admin)), Moses, L.J.; see *Serious Organised Crime Agency v Perry* [2012] UKSC 35, [2012] 3 W.L.R. 379 (SC), Lord Phillips, J.S.C.

s.4, see *R. v Lambert (Richard)* [2012] EWCA Crim 421, [2012] 2 Cr. App. R. (S.) 90 (CA (Crim Div)), Pill, L.J.

s.6, see *Peacock, Re* [2012] UKSC 5, [2012] 1 W.L.R. 550 (SC), Lord Hope (Deputy President); see *R. v Bajwa (Naripdeep Singh)* [2011] EWCA Crim 1093, [2012] 1 W.L.R. 601 (CA (Crim Div)), Aikens, L.J.; see *R. v Barnett (Ian Stanley)* [2011] EWCA Crim 2936, [2012] Lloyd's Rep. F.C. 157 (CA (Crim Div)), Pill, L.J.; see *R. v Lambert (Richard)* [2012] EWCA Crim 421, [2012] 2 Cr. App. R. (S.) 90 (CA (Crim Div)), Pill, L.J.; see *R. v Varma (Aloke)* [2012] UKSC 42, [2012] 3 W.L.R. 776 (SC), Lord Phillips, J.S.C. (President); see *R. v Walker (Jack)* [2011] EWCA Crim 103, [2012] 1 W.L.R. 173 (CA (Crim Div)), Hooper, L.J.

s.6, applied: SI 2012/1726 r.58.7

2002– cont.

29. Proceeds of Crime Act 2002– *cont.*

s.7, see *R. v Lambert (Richard)* [2012] EWCA Crim 421, [2012] 2 Cr. App. R. (S.) 90 (CA (Crim Div)), Pill, L.J.; see *R. v Walker (Jack)* [2011] EWCA Crim 103, [2012] 1 W.L.R. 173 (CA (Crim Div)), Hooper, L.J.

s.8, see *R. v Barnett (Ian Stanley)* [2011] EWCA Crim 2936, [2012] Lloyd's Rep. F.C. 157 (CA (Crim Div)), Pill, L.J.

s.9, see *R. v Walker (Jack)* [2011] EWCA Crim 103, [2012] 1 W.L.R. 173 (CA (Crim Div)), Hooper, L.J.

s.10, see *R. v Bagnall (Darren John)* [2012] EWCA Crim 677, [2012] Lloyd's Rep. F.C. 614 (CA (Crim Div)), Moses, L.J.; see *R. v Barnett (Ian Stanley)* [2011] EWCA Crim 2936, [2012] Lloyd's Rep. F.C. 157 (CA (Crim Div)), Pill, L.J.; see *R. v Waya (Terry)* [2012] UKSC 51, [2012] 3 W.L.R. 1188 (SC), Lord Phillips, J.S.C.

s.13, see *R. v Varma (Aloke)* [2012] UKSC 42, [2012] 3 W.L.R. 776 (SC), Lord Phillips, J.S.C. (President)

s.14, applied: SI 2012/1726 r.58.2

s.16, applied: SI 2012/1726 r.58.1

s.17, applied: SI 2012/1726 r.58.1

s.18, applied: SI 2012/1726 r.58.1

s.19, applied: SI 2012/1726 r.58.3

s.20, applied: SI 2012/1726 r.58.3

s.21, applied: SI 2012/1726 r.58.3

s.22, applied: SI 2012/1726 r.58.4

s.23, applied: SI 2012/1726 r.58.5

s.24, applied: SI 2012/1726 r.58.6

s.25, applied: SI 2012/1726 r.58.6

s.28, applied: SI 2012/1726 r.58.7, r.58.8, r.58.11

s.29, applied: 2012 c.10 Sch.1 para.40, SI 2012/1726 r.58.7, r.58.11

s.30, applied: SI 2012/1726 r.58.8, r.58.11

s.31, applied: SI 2012/1726 r.72.1, r.71.8, r.72.3, r.57.14

s.35, see *Designated Officer for Sunderland Magistrates' Court v Krager* [2011] EWHC 3283 (Ch), [2012] 1 W.L.R. 1291 (Ch D (Newcastle)), Briggs, J.

s.39, applied: SI 2012/1726 r.58.9

s.41, see *Director of the Serious Fraud Office v B* [2012] EWCA Crim 67, [2012] 1 W.L.R. 3170 (CA (Crim Div)), Gross, L.J.

s.41, applied: 2012 c.10 Sch.1 para.40, SI 2012/1726 r.57.14, r.59.1, r.59.2, r.59.3, r.59.4, r.59.5

s.42, applied: SI 2012/1726 r.59.1, r.57.14, r.61.14, r.59.3, r.59.4, r.59.5

s.43, applied: SI 2012/1726 r.73.1, r.73.2, r.73.3, r.73.4, r.73.5, r.73.6, r.73.7, r.57.14

s.44, applied: SI 2012/1726 r.57.14

s.46, see *Director of the Serious Fraud Office v B* [2012] EWCA Crim 67, [2012] 1 W.L.R. 3170 (CA (Crim Div)), Gross, L.J.

s.47M, applied: 2012 c.10 Sch.1 para.40

s.48, applied: SI 2012/1726 r.60.1, r.60.5, r.57.14, r.60.6, r.60.7, r.60.8

s.49, applied: SI 2012/1726 r.57.14, r.60.2, r.60.6

s.50, applied: SI 2012/1726 r.60.1, r.58.4, r.60.5, r.58.5, r.58.6, r.57.14, r.60.6, r.60.7, r.60.8

s.51, applied: SI 2012/1726 r.57.14, r.60.2

s.54, applied: 2012 c.10 Sch.1 para.40

s.55, applied: SI 2012/1726 r.60.1, r.60.5, r.60.6

s.58, applied: SI 2012/1726 r.57.14, r.61.1

s.59, applied: SI 2012/1726 r.61.1

s.62, applied: 2012 c.10 Sch.1 para.40, SI 2012/1726 r.57.14, r.60.3

s.63, applied: SI 2012/1726 r.57.14, r.60.3

2002-cont.

29. Proceeds of Crime Act 2002-*cont.*
s.65, applied: SI 2012/ 1726 r.73.1, r.73.2, r.73.3, r.73.4, r.73.5, r.73.6, r.73.7, r.57.14
s.66, applied: SI 2012/ 1726 r.57.14
s.67, applied: SI 2012/ 1726 r.58.12
s.67A, applied: 2012 c.10 Sch.1 para.40
s.67D, applied: 2012 c.10 Sch.1 para.40
s.68, applied: SI 2012/ 1726 r.59.1, r.60.1, r.59.4, r.60.2
s.70, see *Sumal & Sons (Properties) Ltd v Newham LBC* [2012] EWCA Crim 1840, [2012] Lloyd's Rep. F.C. 692 (CA (Crim Div)), Davis, L.J.
s.72, applied: 2012 c.10 Sch.1 para.40, SI 2012/ 1726 r.58.10
s.73, applied: 2012 c.10 Sch.1 para.40, SI 2012/ 1726 r.58.11
s.74, see *Serious Organised Crime Agency v Perry* [2012] UKSC 35, [2012] 3 W.L.R. 379 (SC), Lord Phillips, J.S.C.
s.75, see *R. v Bajwa (Naripdeep Singh)* [2011] EWCA Crim 1093, [2012] 1 W.L.R. 601 (CA (Crim Div)), Aikens, L.J.; see *R. v Barnett (Ian Stanley)* [2011] EWCA Crim 2936, [2012] Lloyd's Rep. F.C. 157 (CA (Crim Div)), Pill, L.J.
s.76, see *R. v Bajwa (Naripdeep Singh)* [2011] EWCA Crim 1093, [2012] 1 W.L.R. 601 (CA (Crim Div)), Aikens, L.J.; see *Sumal & Sons (Properties) Ltd v Newham LBC* [2012] EWCA Crim 1840, [2012] Lloyd's Rep. F.C. 692 (CA (Crim Div)), Davis, L.J.
s.79, see *R. v Waya (Terry)* [2012] UKSC 51, [2012] 3 W.L.R. 1188 (SC), Lord Phillips, J.S.C.
s.80, see *R. v Waya (Terry)* [2012] UKSC 51, [2012] 3 W.L.R. 1188 (SC), Lord Phillips, J.S.C.
s.82, see *R. v Walker (Jack)* [2011] EWCA Crim 103, [2012] 1 W.L.R. 173 (CA (Crim Div)), Hooper, L.J.
s.83, see *R. v Walker (Jack)* [2011] EWCA Crim 103, [2012] 1 W.L.R. 173 (CA (Crim Div)), Hooper, L.J.
s.84, see *R. v Walker (Jack)* [2011] EWCA Crim 103, [2012] 1 W.L.R. 173 (CA (Crim Div)), Hooper, L.J.; see *R. v Waya (Terry)* [2012] UKSC 51, [2012] 3 W.L.R. 1188 (SC), Lord Phillips, J.S.C.
s.85, applied: SI 2012/ 1726 r.72.3
s.88, applied: SI 2012/ 1726 r.58.12
s.91, enabling: SI 2012/ 1726
s.240, see *Serious Organised Crime Agency v Robb* [2012] EWHC 803 (QB), [2012] Lloyd's Rep. F.C. 485 (QBD), Mackay, J.
s.241, see *Serious Organised Crime Agency v Hymans* [2011] EWHC 3332 (QB), [2012] Lloyd's Rep. F.C. 199 (QBD), Kenneth Parker, J.; see *Serious Organised Crime Agency v Robb* [2012] EWHC 803 (QB), [2012] Lloyd's Rep. F.C. 485 (QBD), Mackay, J.
s.245A, see *Serious Organised Crime Agency v Perry* [2012] UKSC 35, [2012] 3 W.L.R. 379 (SC), Lord Phillips, J.S.C.
s.245C, amended: 2012 c.10 Sch.5 para.59
s.252, amended: 2012 c.10 Sch.5 para.60
s.282, amended: 2012 c.21 Sch.18 para.94
s.286, see *Serious Organised Crime Agency v Perry* [2012] UKSC 35, [2012] 3 W.L.R. 379 (SC), Lord Phillips, J.S.C.
s.294, see *Scottish Ministers v Devaney* 2012 S.L.T. (Sh Ct) 164 (Sh Ct (Tayside) (Dundee)), Sheriff J K Mundy; see *Secretary of State for the Home Department v Tuncel* [2012] EWHC 402 (Admin), [2012] 1 W.L.R. 3355 (QBD (Admin)), Keith, J.; see *Wiese v UK Border Agency* [2012]

2002-cont.

29. Proceeds of Crime Act 2002-*cont.*
s.294-*cont.*
EWHC 2549 (Admin), [2012] Lloyd's Rep. F.C. 681 (QBD (Admin)), Underhill, J.
s.295, see *Secretary of State for the Home Department v Tuncel* [2012] EWHC 402 (Admin), [2012] 1 W.L.R. 3355 (QBD (Admin)), Keith, J.
s.298, see *Scottish Ministers v Devaney* 2012 S.L.T. (Sh Ct) 164 (Sh Ct (Tayside) (Dundee)), Sheriff J K Mundy; see *Secretary of State for the Home Department v Tuncel* [2012] EWHC 402 (Admin), [2012] 1 W.L.R. 3355 (QBD (Admin)), Keith, J.; see *Wiese v UK Border Agency* [2012] EWHC 2549 (Admin), [2012] Lloyd's Rep. F.C. 681 (QBD (Admin)), Underhill, J.
s.302, applied: SI 2012/ 1726 r.58.10
s.308, see *Serious Organised Crime Agency v Coghlan* [2012] EWHC 429 (QB), [2012] Lloyd's Rep. F.C. 341 (QBD), Simon, J.
s.308, amended: 2012 c.21 Sch.18 para.94
s.316, see *Serious Organised Crime Agency v Perry* [2012] UKSC 35, [2012] 3 W.L.R. 379 (SC), Lord Phillips, J.S.C.
s.316, applied: SI 2012/ 1726 r.6.1
s.327, see *R. v Rollins (Neil)* [2011] EWCA Crim 1825, [2012] 1 Cr. App. R. (S.) 64 (CA (Crim Div)), Lord Judge, L.C.J.
s.328, see *Fitzpatrick v Commissioner of Police of the Metropolis* [2012] EWHC 12 (Admin), [2012] Lloyd's Rep. F.C. 361 (QBD (Admin)), Globe, J.
s.330, see *Fitzpatrick v Commissioner of Police of the Metropolis* [2012] EWHC 12 (Admin), [2012] Lloyd's Rep. F.C. 361 (QBD (Admin)), Globe, J.; see *R. v Swan (Jacqueline)* [2011] EWCA Crim 2275, [2012] 1 Cr. App. R. (S.) 90 (CA (Crim Div)), Moore-Bick, L.J.
s.340, see *DPP of Mauritius v Bholah* [2011] UKPC 44, [2012] 1 W.L.R. 1737 (PC (Mau)), Lord Phillips
s.340, applied: SSI 2012/ 88 Reg.23, SSI 2012/ 89 Reg.26
s.341, see *R. (on the application of Horne) v Central Criminal Court* [2012] EWHC 1350 (Admin), [2012] 1 W.L.R. 3152 (QBD (Admin)), Moses, L.J.
s.341, applied: SI 2012/ 1726 r.6.1
s.342, applied: SI 2012/ 1726 r.6.22
s.343, applied: SI 2012/ 1726 r.6.1
s.345, applied: SI 2012/ 1726 r.6.1, r.6.15, r.6.22
s.346, applied: SI 2012/ 1726 r.6.15
s.347, applied: SI 2012/ 1726 r.6.1, r.6.15, r.6.16
s.348, applied: SI 2012/ 1726 r.6.3, r.6.15, SI 2012/ 2563 r.4
s.349, applied: SI 2012/ 1726 r.6.15
s.350, applied: SI 2012/ 1726 r.6.15
s.351, applied: 2012 c.10 Sch.1 para.40, SI 2012/ 1726 r.6.1, r.6.22
s.351, enabling: SI 2012/ 1726
s.352, see *R. (on the application of Horne) v Central Criminal Court* [2012] EWHC 1350 (Admin), [2012] 1 W.L.R. 3152 (QBD (Admin)), Moses, L.J.
s.357, see *R. (on the application of Horne) v Central Criminal Court* [2012] EWHC 1350 (Admin), [2012] 1 W.L.R. 3152 (QBD (Admin)), Moses, L.J.; see *Serious Organised Crime Agency v Perry* [2012] UKSC 35, [2012] 3 W.L.R. 379 (SC), Lord Phillips, J.S.C.
s.357, applied: SI 2012/ 1726 r.6.1, r.6.17
s.358, applied: SI 2012/ 1726 r.6.17

2002– cont.

29. Proceeds of Crime Act 2002– *cont.*
s.359, applied: SI 2012/ 1726 r.6.22
s.361, applied: SI 2012/ 1726 r.6.3, r.6.17, SI 2012/ 2563 r.4
s.362, applied: 2012 c.10 Sch.1 para.40, SI 2012/ 1726 r.6.1
s.362, enabling: SI 2012/ 1726
s.363, applied: SI 2012/ 1726 r.6.1, r.6.18
s.364, applied: SI 2012/ 1726 r.6.18
s.365, applied: SI 2012/ 1726 r.6.18
s.366, applied: SI 2012/ 1726 r.6.22
s.368, applied: SI 2012/ 1726 r.6.18
s.369, applied: 2012 c.10 Sch.1 para.40, SI 2012/ 1726 r.6.1
s.369, enabling: SI 2012/ 1726
s.370, applied: SI 2012/ 1726 r.6.1, r.6.19, r.6.22
s.371, applied: SI 2012/ 1726 r.6.19
s.374, applied: SI 2012/ 1726 r.6.19
s.375, applied: 2012 c.10 Sch.1 para.40, SI 2012/ 1726 r.6.1, r.6.22
s.375, enabling: SI 2012/ 1726
s.377, applied: SI 2012/ 1726 r.6.14
s.377A, applied: SI 2012/ 1726 r.6.14
s.447, applied: 2012 c.5 s.129
Sch.2 para.4, amended: 2012 c.9 Sch.9 para.138
Sch.9, referred to: SI 2012/ 2299 Art.4
Sch.9 Part 1 para.1, amended: SI 2012/ 1534 Art.3, SI 2012/ 2299 Art.3
Sch.9 Part 2 para.4, amended: 2012 c.21 Sch.18 para.94
Sch.9 Part 3 para.5, enabling: SI 2012/ 1534, SI 2012/ 2299
Sch.11 para.36, repealed: 2012 c.10 Sch.5 Part 2
Sch.11 para.38, repealed: 2012 c.21 Sch.19

30. Police Reform Act 2002
Part 2, applied: 2012 c.22, SI 2012/ 1204 Reg.22, Reg.26, Reg.31, Reg.32, Reg.33, Reg.35, Reg.36
Part 2, disapplied: SI 2012/ 1204 Reg.21, Reg.23
Part 2, referred to: SI 2012/ 1204 Reg.35
s.9, varied: SI 2012/ 1204 Reg.21, Reg.27, Reg.28
s.10, varied: SI 2012/ 62 Reg.3, SI 2012/ 1204 Reg.21, Reg.27, Reg.28
s.11, varied: SI 2012/ 1204 Reg.21, Reg.27, Reg.28
s.12, amended: 2012 c.22 s.2
s.12, varied: SI 2012/ 1204 Reg.21, Reg.27, Reg.28
s.13, varied: SI 2012/ 1204 Reg.21, Reg.27, Reg.28
s.13, enabling: SI 2012/ 1204
s.14, varied: SI 2012/ 1204 Reg.21, Reg.27, Reg.28
s.15, varied: SI 2012/ 1204 Reg.21, Reg.27, Reg.28
s.16, varied: SI 2012/ 1204 Reg.21, Reg.27, Reg.28
s.16A, varied: SI 2012/ 1204 Reg.21, Reg.27, Reg.28
s.17, varied: SI 2012/ 1204 Reg.21, Reg.27, Reg.28
s.18, varied: SI 2012/ 1204 Reg.21, Reg.27, Reg.28
s.19, varied: SI 2012/ 62 Reg.20, SI 2012/ 1204 Reg.21, Reg.27, Reg.28
s.20, applied: SI 2012/ 1204 Reg.12
s.20, referred to: SI 2012/ 1204 Reg.12, Reg.13
s.20, varied: SI 2012/ 1204 Reg.21, Reg.27, Reg.28
s.20, enabling: SI 2012/ 1204
s.21, applied: SI 2012/ 1204 Reg.12, Reg.14, Reg.29
s.21, referred to: SI 2012/ 1204 Reg.12, Reg.13
s.21, varied: SI 2012/ 1204 Reg.21, Reg.27, Reg.28
s.21, enabling: SI 2012/ 1204
s.22, applied: SI 2012/ 1204 Reg.36, SI 2012/ 2631 Reg.4
s.22, varied: SI 2012/ 62 Reg.4, SI 2012/ 1204 Reg.21, Reg.27, Reg.28
s.23, varied: SI 2012/ 1204 Reg.21, Reg.27, Reg.28

2002– cont.

30. Police Reform Act 2002– *cont.*
s.23, enabling: SI 2012/ 1204
s.24, applied: SI 2012/ 1204
s.24, varied: SI 2012/ 1204 Reg.21, Reg.27, Reg.28
s.25, varied: SI 2012/ 1204 Reg.21, Reg.27, Reg.28
s.26, varied: SI 2012/ 1204 Reg.21, Reg.27, Reg.28
s.26A, varied: SI 2012/ 1204 Reg.21, Reg.27, Reg.28
s.26B, varied: SI 2012/ 1204 Reg.21, Reg.27, Reg.28
s.27, applied: SI 2012/ 62 Reg.3
s.27, varied: SI 2012/ 1204 Reg.21, Reg.27, Reg.28
s.28, varied: SI 2012/ 1204 Reg.21, Reg.27, Reg.28
s.28A, added: 2012 c.22 s.2
s.28A, varied: SI 2012/ 1204 Reg.21, Reg.27, Reg.28
s.29, amended: 2012 c.22 s.2
s.29, applied: SI 2012/ 2631 Reg.4, SI 2012/ 2632 Reg.3
s.29, varied: SI 2012/ 1204 Reg.21, Reg.27, Reg.28
s.29, enabling: SI 2012/ 1204
s.36, applied: SI 2012/ 2631 Reg.4
s.39, applied: SI 2012/ 1204, SI 2012/ 1204 Reg.35
s.39, enabling: SI 2012/ 1204
s.43, amended: 2012 c.10 Sch.23 para.14
s.43, enabling: SI 2012/ 2732
s.105, enabling: SI 2012/ 1204, SI 2012/ 2732
s.108, amended: 2012 c.22 s.1
Sch.3, see *R. (on the application of North Yorkshire Police Authority) v Independent Police Complaints Commission* [2010] EWHC 1690 (Admin), [2012] P.T.S.R. 268 (QBD (Admin)), Judge Langan Q.C.
Sch.3, applied: 2012 c.22, SI 2012/ 1204 Reg.3, Reg.5, Reg.7, Reg.11
Sch.3, disapplied: SI 2012/ 1204 Reg.10
Sch.3, referred to: SI 2012/ 2630 r.4, r.5
Sch.3 Part 1 para.2, applied: SI 2012/ 1204 Reg.3, Reg.15
Sch.3 Part 1 para.3, applied: SI 2012/ 1204 Reg.11, Reg.21
Sch.3 Part 1 para.3, enabling: SI 2012/ 1204
Sch.3 Part 1 para.4, applied: SI 2012/ 1204 Reg.4, Reg.21
Sch.3 Part 1 para.4, referred to: SI 2012/ 1204 Reg.30
Sch.3 Part 1 para.4, enabling: SI 2012/ 1204
Sch.3 Part 1 para.5, applied: SI 2012/ 1204 Reg.21
Sch.3 Part 1 para.7, applied: SI 2012/ 1204 Reg.5, Reg.11, Reg.21
Sch.3 Part 1 para.7, enabling: SI 2012/ 1204
Sch.3 Part 1 para.8, applied: SI 2012/ 1204 Reg.3, Reg.7
Sch.3 Part 1 para.8, enabling: SI 2012/ 1204
Sch.3 Part 1 para.8A, applied: SI 2012/ 1204 Reg.6, Reg.11, Reg.21
Sch.3 Part 2, applied: SI 2012/ 1204 Reg.7, Reg.21, Reg.23
Sch.3 Part 2, disapplied: SI 2012/ 1204 Reg.21
Sch.3 Part 2A para.14A, applied: SI 2012/ 1204 Reg.31
Sch.3 Part 2A para.14C, enabling: SI 2012/ 1204
Sch.3 Part 2 para.10, applied: SI 2012/ 1204 Reg.7, Reg.31
Sch.3 Part 2 para.11, applied: SI 2012/ 1204 Reg.7, Reg.31
Sch.3 Part 2 para.11, enabling: SI 2012/ 1204
Sch.3 Part 2 para.13, applied: SI 2012/ 1204 Reg.7
Sch.3 Part 2 para.13, enabling: SI 2012/ 1204

2002–cont.

30. Police Reform Act 2002–*cont.*

Sch.3 Part 3 para.16, applied: SI 2012/1204 Reg.24, SI 2012/2631 Reg.13, Reg.38, Reg.39, Reg.40, SI 2012/2632 Reg.11, Reg.20, Reg.29, Reg.30, Reg.31, Reg.40, Reg.50, Reg.51, Reg.52

Sch.3 Part 3 para.17, applied: SI 2012/1204 Reg.9, Reg.24, SI 2012/2631 Reg.13, Reg.38, Reg.39, Reg.40, SI 2012/2632 Reg.10, Reg.11, Reg.20, Reg.29, Reg.30, Reg.31, Reg.39, Reg.40, Reg.50, Reg.51, Reg.52

Sch.3 Part 3 para.17, enabling: SI 2012/1204

Sch.3 Part 3 para.17A, applied: SI 2012/1204 Reg.24

Sch.3 Part 3 para.18, applied: SI 2012/1204 Reg.24, SI 2012/2631 Reg.13, Reg.38, Reg.39, Reg.40, SI 2012/2632 Reg.10, Reg.11, Reg.20, Reg.29, Reg.30, Reg.31, Reg.39, Reg.40, Reg.50, Reg.51, Reg.52

Sch.3 Part 3 para.19, applied: SI 2012/1204 Reg.10, SI 2012/2631 Reg.13, Reg.38, Reg.39, Reg.40, SI 2012/2632 Reg.10, Reg.11, Reg.20, Reg.29, Reg.30, Reg.31, Reg.39, Reg.40, Reg.50, Reg.51, Reg.52

Sch.3 Part 3 para.19, varied: SI 2012/62 Reg.20

Sch.3 Part 3 para.19B, applied: SI 2012/1204 Reg.16, Reg.18, SI 2012/2630 r.19, r.22, SI 2012/2631 Reg.39, SI 2012/2632 Reg.19, Reg.30, Reg.33, Reg.35, Reg.39, Reg.51, Reg.53, Reg.55

Sch.3 Part 3 para.19B, enabling: SI 2012/1204

Sch.3 Part 3 para.19C, applied: SI 2012/1204 Reg.16, Reg.17, SI 2012/2632 Reg.33, Reg.53

Sch.3 Part 3 para.19C, enabling: SI 2012/1204

Sch.3 Part 3 para.19D, amended: 2012 c.22 s.1

Sch.3 Part 3 para.19D, applied: SI 2012/1204 Reg.19

Sch.3 Part 3 para.19D, enabling: SI 2012/1204

Sch.3 Part 3 para.19F, added: 2012 c.22 s.1

Sch.3 Part 3 para.20, varied: SI 2012/62 Reg.23

Sch.3 Part 3 para.20H, applied: SI 2012/2632 Reg.42, Reg.50, Reg.52

Sch.3 Part 3 para.21, applied: SI 2012/1204 Reg.10, Reg.11, Reg.21, Reg.26

Sch.3 Part 3 para.21, enabling: SI 2012/1204

Sch.3 Part 3 para.22, applied: SI 2012/1204 Reg.10, Reg.12, Reg.20, Reg.36, SI 2012/2631 Reg.4, Reg.12, Reg.31, SI 2012/2632 Reg.19

Sch.3 Part 3 para.22, enabling: SI 2012/1204

Sch.3 Part 3 para.23, applied: SI 2012/1204 Reg.3, Reg.7, Reg.12, Reg.29, Reg.36, SI 2012/2631 Reg.4, Reg.12, SI 2012/2632 Reg.19

Sch.3 Part 3 para.23, disapplied: SI 2012/1204 Reg.29

Sch.3 Part 3 para.23, referred to: SI 2012/1204 Reg.12, Reg.13

Sch.3 Part 3 para.23, enabling: SI 2012/1204

Sch.3 Part 3 para.24, applied: SI 2012/1204 Reg.3, Reg.7, Reg.12, SI 2012/2631 Reg.12, SI 2012/2632 Reg.19

Sch.3 Part 3 para.24, referred to: SI 2012/1204 Reg.12, Reg.13

Sch.3 Part 3 para.24, enabling: SI 2012/1204

Sch.3 Part 3 para.25, applied: SI 2012/1204 Reg.11, Reg.21, Reg.29, Reg.36, SI 2012/2631 Reg.4

Sch.3 Part 3 para.25, disapplied: SI 2012/1204 Reg.29

Sch.3 Part 3 para.25, enabling: SI 2012/1204

Sch.3 Part 3 para.27, applied: SI 2012/1204 Reg.36, SI 2012/2631 Reg.4, Reg.12, Reg.13, Reg.30, Reg.31, Reg.38, Reg.40, SI 2012/2632 Reg.19, Reg.29, Reg.31, Reg.40

Sch.3 Part 3 para.29, enabling: SI 2012/1204

2002–cont.

30. Police Reform Act 2002–*cont.*

Sch.3 Part 3 para.30, applied: SI 2012/1204 Reg.30

Sch.3 Part 3 para.31, applied: SI 2012/1204 Reg.11

Sch.3 Part 3 para.32, applied: SI 2012/1204 Reg.11

Sch.4 Part 1 para.1, amended: 2012 c.10 Sch.23 para.14

Sch.4 Part 1 para.15, amended: 2012 c.9 Sch.9 para.30

Sch.5 para.1, amended: 2012 c.10 Sch.23 para.14

Sch.5A para.1, amended: 2012 c.10 Sch.23 para.14

32. Education Act 2002

applied: SI 2012/1797 Reg.5, Reg.6

Part 1 c.1, applied: SI 2012/1107

s.2, applied: SI 2012/1107

s.2, enabling: SI 2012/1107

s.4, applied: SI 2012/1107

s.12, applied: SI 2012/335 Sch.1 para.20, SI 2012/2991 Sch.1 para.20

s.14, applied: SI 2012/335 Sch.2 para.1, SI 2012/1167 Sch.1 para.12, SI 2012/2886 Sch.1, SSI 2012/303 Sch.4 para.15, Sch.5 para.55

s.19, disapplied: SI 2012/1643 Reg.3

s.19, enabling: SI 2012/421, SI 2012/1034, SI 2012/1035, SI 2012/1643

s.20, enabling: SI 2012/421, SI 2012/1034, SI 2012/1035

s.21, enabling: SI 2012/1845

s.23, disapplied: SI 2012/1643 Reg.3

s.24, applied: SI 2012/335 Reg.22, Sch.3 para.37, SI 2012/1035 Reg.6, SI 2012/2991 Reg.22

s.24, enabling: SI 2012/335, SI 2012/1035, SI 2012/2991

s.25, enabling: SI 2012/1035

s.27, applied: SI 2012/335 Sch.1 para.20, Sch.5 para.25, SI 2012/1034 Sch.1 para.8, SI 2012/1035 Sch.2 para.9, SI 2012/2991 Sch.1 para.20, Sch.5 para.25

s.29A, enabling: SI 2012/2532

s.32, applied: SI 2012/2488 Reg.3

s.34, enabling: SI 2012/1035

s.35, enabling: SI 2012/1035, SI 2012/1740

s.36, enabling: SI 2012/1035, SI 2012/1740

s.44, applied: SI 2012/335 Sch.1 para.20, SI 2012/2991 Sch.1 para.20

s.44, enabling: SI 2012/674

s.51A, applied: SI 2012/1033 Reg.7, Reg.9, Reg.10, Reg.12, Reg.13, Reg.16, Reg.18, Reg.22, Reg.25, Reg.27, Reg.28

s.51A, varied: SI 2012/1033 Reg.21

s.51A, enabling: SI 2012/1033

s.52, applied: SI 2012/335 Reg.23

s.85, amended: SI 2012/2056 Art.2

s.85, repealed (in part): SI 2012/2056 Art.2

s.86, enabling: SI 2012/2056

s.87, applied: SI 2012/335 Sch.1 para.23, SI 2012/838, SI 2012/2991 Sch.1 para.23

s.87, enabling: SI 2012/838

s.91, enabling: SI 2012/1926

s.96, applied: SI 2012/1926

s.101, applied: SI 2012/1797 Reg.8

s.103, applied: SI 2012/724 Reg.3

s.108, enabling: SI 2012/935

s.116A, applied: SI 2012/1797 Reg.7

s.116B, applied: SI 2012/1797 Reg.7

s.116C, applied: SI 2012/1797 Reg.7

s.116D, applied: SI 2012/1797 Reg.7

s.116E, applied: SI 2012/1797 Reg.7

s.116F, applied: SI 2012/1797 Reg.7

s.116G, applied: SI 2012/1797 Reg.7

2002– cont.

32. Education Act 2002–*cont.*
s.116H, applied: SI 2012/ 1797 Reg.7
s.116I, applied: SI 2012/ 1797 Reg.7
s.116J, applied: SI 2012/ 1797 Reg.7
s.116K, applied: SI 2012/ 1797 Reg.7
s.120, applied: SI 2012/ 2051
s.122, applied: SI 2012/ 335 Sch.3 para.19, SI 2012/ 878 Art.3
s.122, enabling: SI 2012/ 694, SI 2012/ 2051
s.123, enabling: SI 2012/ 878, SI 2012/ 2051
s.124, enabling: SI 2012/ 2051
s.125, applied: SI 2012/ 2051
s.126, applied: SI 2012/ 694, SI 2012/ 2051
s.131, applied: SI 2012/ 115, SI 2012/ 431
s.131, enabling: SI 2012/ 115, SI 2012/ 431, SI 2012/ 2055
s.132, applied: SI 2012/ 724 Reg.5, Reg.6, Sch.2 para.11, Sch.2 para.12, Sch.2 para.13
s.132, enabling: SI 2012/ 431, SI 2012/ 724, SI 2012/ 1736
s.133, enabling: SI 2012/ 762, SI 2012/ 1736
s.134, applied: SI 2012/ 724
s.134, enabling: SI 2012/ 762
s.135, enabling: SI 2012/ 18
s.135A, amended: SI 2012/ 976 Sch.1 para.12
s.135A, enabling: SI 2012/ 513, SI 2012/ 1115
s.135B, enabling: SI 2012/ 513, SI 2012/ 1115
s.136, enabling: SI 2012/ 747, SI 2012/ 2165, SI 2012/ 2166
s.141, applied: SI 2012/ 2157 Art.7
s.141A, enabling: SI 2012/ 560
s.141C, applied: SI 2012/ 560 Reg.18, SI 2012/ 1115 Reg.13
s.141C, enabling: SI 2012/ 513, SI 2012/ 1115
s.141D, applied: SI 2012/ 560 Reg.20
s.141D, enabling: SI 2012/ 560
s.141E, applied: SI 2012/ 560 Reg.20
s.141E, enabling: SI 2012/ 560
s.141F, applied: SI 2012/ 1726 r.16.1, r.16.5
s.142, see *R. (on the application of W) v Secretary of State for Education* [2011] EWHC 3256 (Admin), [2012] E.L.R. 172 (QBD (Admin)), Singh, J.
s.142, applied: 2012 c.10 Sch.1 para.4, SI 2012/ 1034 Sch.4 para.13
s.144, applied: 2012 c.10 Sch.1 para.14
s.145, enabling: SI 2012/ 431, SI 2012/ 724, SI 2012/ 747, SI 2012/ 762, SI 2012/ 1736, SI 2012/ 2166
s.156AA, added: SI 2012/ 976 Sch.1 para.13
s.157, enabling: SI 2012/ 2962
s.167C, amended: SI 2012/ 3006 Art.13
s.175, applied: SI 2012/ 335 Sch.1 para.6, SI 2012/ 2991 Sch.1 para.6
s.181, applied: SI 2012/ 2886 Sch.1, SSI 2012/ 303 Sch.4 para.15, Sch.5 para.55
s.186, enabling: SI 2012/ 555
s.207, applied: SI 2012/ 335 Sch.2 para.12
s.210, applied: SI 2012/ 2056
s.210, enabling: SI 2012/ 115, SI 2012/ 431, SI 2012/ 560, SI 2012/ 694, SI 2012/ 724, SI 2012/ 747, SI 2012/ 762, SI 2012/ 838, SI 2012/ 935, SI 2012/ 1033, SI 2012/ 1034, SI 2012/ 1035, SI 2012/ 1107, SI 2012/ 1115, SI 2012/ 1736, SI 2012/ 2055, SI 2012/ 2165, SI 2012/ 2166, SI 2012/ 2532, SI 2012/ 2962
s.214, enabling: SI 2012/ 513, SI 2012/ 1033, SI 2012/ 1115
Sch.1 para.5, see *ML v Tonbridge Grammar School* [2012] UKUT 283 (AAC), [2012] E.L.R. 508 (UT (AAC)), Judge Rowland

2002– cont.

32. Education Act 2002–*cont.*
Sch.11A, enabling: SI 2012/ 560
Sch.11 para.4, amended: SI 2012/ 2404 Sch.2 para.47
Sch.11A para.2, amended: SI 2012/ 3006 Art.13
Sch.11B para.7, amended: SI 2012/ 1809 Sch.1 Part 1
36. Tobacco Advertising and Promotion Act 2002
applied: SI 2012/ 1911 Reg.4
s.2, applied: SI 2012/ 244 Art.2, SI 2012/ 1285 Reg.8, SI 2012/ 1287 Reg.2
s.4, enabling: SI 2012/ 677, SI 2012/ 1285
s.6, enabling: SI 2012/ 677, SI 2012/ 1287
s.7A, applied: SI 2012/ 1285 Reg.3, Reg.4, Reg.5, Reg.6, Reg.7, SI 2012/ 1287 Reg.3
s.7A, enabling: SI 2012/ 1285
s.7B, enabling: SI 2012/ 677, SI 2012/ 1285, SI 2012/ 1287
s.7C, applied: SI 2012/ 1911 Reg.3, Reg.4
s.7C, enabling: SI 2012/ 1911
s.19, applied: SI 2012/ 1911
s.19, enabling: SI 2012/ 677, SI 2012/ 1285, SI 2012/ 1287, SI 2012/ 1911
38. Adoption and Children Act 2002
see *Charity Commission for England and Wales v Catholic Care (Diocese of Leeds)* [2012] W.T.L.R. 1303 (Charity Comm)
applied: SI 2012/ 2885 Reg.8, SI 2012/ 2886 Sch.1, SI 2012/ 3144 Reg.8, SI 2012/ 3145 Sch.1, SSI 2012/ 303 Reg.11, SSI 2012/ 319 Reg.11
Part 1 c.3, applied: 2012 c.10 Sch.1 para.1
s.1, see *Q (A Child) (Adoption: Welfare Requirements), Re* [2011] EWCA Civ 1610, [2012] 1 F.L.R. 1228 (CA (Civ Div)), Munby, L.J.; see *X (Children) (Parental Order: Retrospective Authorisation of Payments), Re* [2011] EWHC 3147 (Fam), [2012] 1 F.L.R. 1347 (Fam Div), Sir Nicholas Wall (President, Fam); see *YC v United Kingdom (4547/10)* [2012] 2 F.L.R. 332 (ECHR), Judge Garlicki (President)
s.2, applied: SI 2012/ 2886 Sch.1, SSI 2012/ 303 Sch.4 para.29, Sch.5 para.63
s.3, applied: SI 2012/ 2886 Sch.1, SSI 2012/ 303 Sch.4 para.29, Sch.5 para.63
s.4, amended: 2012 c.7 Sch.5 para.105
s.4, applied: SI 2012/ 2886 Sch.1, SSI 2012/ 303 Sch.4 para.29, Sch.5 para.63
s.8, amended: 2012 c.7 Sch.5 para.106
s.9, enabling: SI 2012/ 1410, SI 2012/ 1905
s.21, applied: 2012 c.10 Sch.1 para.1
s.24, see *A v Lancashire CC* [2012] EWHC 1689 (Fam), (2012) 15 C.C.L. Rep. 471 (Fam Div), Peter Jackson, J.; see *Coventry City Council v O* [2011] EWCA Civ 729, [2012] Fam. 210 (CA (Civ Div)), Lord Neuberger of Abbotsbury MR
s.26, applied: 2012 c.10 Sch.1 para.1
s.35, see *R. (on the application of DL) v Newham LBC* [2011] EWHC 1890 (Admin), [2012] 1 F.L.R. 1 (QBD (Admin)), Charles, J.
s.36, applied: 2012 c.10 Sch.1 para.1
s.41, applied: 2012 c.10 Sch.1 para.1
s.44, see *Coventry City Council v O* [2011] EWCA Civ 729, [2012] Fam. 210 (CA (Civ Div)), Lord Neuberger of Abbotsbury MR
s.46, applied: 2012 c.10 Sch.1 para.1
s.52, see *Q (A Child) (Adoption: Welfare Requirements), Re* [2011] EWCA Civ 1610, [2012] 1 F.L.R. 1228 (CA (Civ Div)), Munby, L.J.; see *S v L* 2012 S.C. 8 (IH (1 Div)), The Lord President (Hamilton)
s.84, applied: 2012 c.10 Sch.1 para.1

38. Adoption and Children Act 2002– *cont.*
  s.84, enabling: SI 2012/ 1410
  s.102, enabling: SI 2012/ 679
  s.140, enabling: SI 2012/ 1410, SI 2012/ 1905
  s.141, enabling: SI 2012/ 679
  s.142, enabling: SI 2012/ 1410, SI 2012/ 1905
  s.143, applied: SI 2012/ 1726 r.4.3
  Sch.3 para.102, repealed: 2012 c.10 Sch.5 Part 2

40. Enterprise Act 2002
  see *Assured Logistics Solutions Ltd, Re* [2011]
    EWHC 3029 (Ch), [2012] B.C.C. 541 (Ch D
    (Birmingham)), Judge Purle Q.C.
  applied: 2012 c.7 s.80, SI 2012/ 1128 Art.4
  referred to: 2012 c.7 s.133, 2012 c.19 Sch.6 para.4
  Part 3, applied: 2012 c.7 s.79
  Part 3, referred to: 2012 c.7 s.102
  Part 4, applied: 2012 c.7 s.73, s.74, 2012 c.19 s.60
  Part 4, referred to: 2012 c.7 s.102, 2012 c.19 s.6, s.60
  s.15, see *Ryanair Holdings Plc v Office of Fair
    Trading* [2011] EWCA Civ 1579, [2012] Bus.
    L.R. 1903 (CA (Civ Div)), Lloyd, L.J.
  s.15, applied: 2012 c.19 Sch.1 para.2, Sch.4 para.2
  s.16, amended: SI 2012/ 1809 Sch.1 Part 1
  s.22, see *Ryanair Holdings Plc v Office of Fair
    Trading* [2011] EWCA Civ 1579, [2012] Bus.
    L.R. 1903 (CA (Civ Div)), Lloyd, L.J.
  s.22, applied: SI 2012/ 1878 Art.1
  s.24, see *Ryanair Holdings Plc v Office of Fair
    Trading* [2011] EWCA Civ 1579, [2012] Bus.
    L.R. 1903 (CA (Civ Div)), Lloyd, L.J.
  s.25, see *Ryanair Holdings Plc v Office of Fair
    Trading* [2011] EWCA Civ 1579, [2012] Bus.
    L.R. 1903 (CA (Civ Div)), Lloyd, L.J.
  s.30, applied: 2012 c.7 s.79
  s.45, applied: SI 2012/ 1878 Art.1
  s.109, varied: 2012 c.7 Sch.10 para.10
  s.110, varied: 2012 c.7 Sch.10 para.10
  s.111, varied: 2012 c.7 Sch.10 para.10
  s.112, varied: 2012 c.7 Sch.10 para.10
  s.113, varied: 2012 c.7 Sch.10 para.10
  s.114, varied: 2012 c.7 Sch.10 para.10
  s.115, varied: 2012 c.7 Sch.10 para.10
  s.116, varied: 2012 c.7 Sch.10 para.10
  s.117, varied: 2012 c.7 s.73, Sch.10 para.10
  s.120, see *Ryanair Holdings Plc v Office of Fair
    Trading* [2011] EWCA Civ 1579, [2012] Bus.
    L.R. 1903 (CA (Civ Div)), Lloyd, L.J.
  s.121, enabling: SI 2012/ 1878
  s.122, see *Ryanair Holdings Plc v Office of Fair
    Trading* [2011] EWCA Civ 1579, [2012] Bus.
    L.R. 1903 (CA (Civ Div)), Lloyd, L.J.
  s.124, enabling: SI 2012/ 1878
  s.125, varied: 2012 c.7 Sch.10 para.10
  s.131, applied: 2012 c.19 s.61
  s.131, referred to: 2012 c.19 s.60
  s.131, varied: 2012 c.7 s.73
  s.132, applied: 2012 c.19 s.61
  s.132, referred to: 2012 c.19 s.60
  s.132, varied: 2012 c.7 s.73
  s.133, applied: 2012 c.19 s.61
  s.133, referred to: 2012 c.19 s.60
  s.133, varied: 2012 c.7 s.73
  s.134, applied: 2012 c.19 s.61
  s.134, referred to: 2012 c.19 s.60
  s.134, varied: 2012 c.7 s.73
  s.135, applied: 2012 c.19 s.61
  s.135, referred to: 2012 c.19 s.60
  s.135, varied: 2012 c.7 s.73

40. Enterprise Act 2002– *cont.*
  s.136, amended: 2012 c.7 s.74, 2012 c.19 s.61
  s.136, applied: 2012 c.19 s.61
  s.136, referred to: 2012 c.19 s.60
  s.136, varied: 2012 c.7 s.73
  s.137, applied: 2012 c.19 s.61
  s.137, referred to: 2012 c.19 s.60
  s.137, varied: 2012 c.7 s.73
  s.138, applied: 2012 c.19 s.61
  s.138, referred to: 2012 c.19 s.60
  s.138, varied: 2012 c.7 s.73
  s.139, applied: 2012 c.19 s.61
  s.139, referred to: 2012 c.19 s.60
  s.139, varied: 2012 c.7 s.73
  s.140, applied: 2012 c.19 s.61
  s.140, referred to: 2012 c.19 s.60
  s.140, varied: 2012 c.7 s.73
  s.141, applied: 2012 c.19 s.61
  s.141, referred to: 2012 c.19 s.60
  s.141, varied: 2012 c.7 s.73
  s.142, applied: 2012 c.19 s.61
  s.142, referred to: 2012 c.19 s.60
  s.142, varied: 2012 c.7 s.73
  s.143, applied: 2012 c.19 s.61
  s.143, referred to: 2012 c.19 s.60
  s.143, varied: 2012 c.7 s.73
  s.144, applied: 2012 c.19 s.61
  s.144, referred to: 2012 c.19 s.60
  s.144, varied: 2012 c.7 s.73
  s.145, applied: 2012 c.19 s.61
  s.145, referred to: 2012 c.19 s.60
  s.145, varied: 2012 c.7 s.73
  s.146, applied: 2012 c.19 s.61
  s.146, referred to: 2012 c.19 s.60
  s.146, varied: 2012 c.7 s.73
  s.147, applied: 2012 c.19 s.61
  s.147, referred to: 2012 c.19 s.60
  s.147, varied: 2012 c.7 s.73
  s.148, applied: 2012 c.19 s.61
  s.148, referred to: 2012 c.19 s.60
  s.148, varied: 2012 c.7 s.73
  s.149, applied: 2012 c.19 s.61
  s.149, referred to: 2012 c.19 s.60
  s.149, varied: 2012 c.7 s.73
  s.150, applied: 2012 c.19 s.61
  s.150, referred to: 2012 c.19 s.60
  s.150, varied: 2012 c.7 s.73
  s.151, applied: 2012 c.19 s.61
  s.151, referred to: 2012 c.19 s.60
  s.151, varied: 2012 c.7 s.73
  s.152, applied: 2012 c.19 s.61
  s.152, referred to: 2012 c.19 s.60
  s.152, varied: 2012 c.7 s.73
  s.153, applied: 2012 c.19 s.61
  s.153, referred to: 2012 c.19 s.60
  s.153, varied: 2012 c.7 s.73
  s.154, applied: 2012 c.19 s.61
  s.154, referred to: 2012 c.19 s.60
  s.154, varied: 2012 c.7 s.73
  s.155, applied: 2012 c.19 s.61
  s.155, referred to: 2012 c.19 s.60
  s.155, varied: 2012 c.7 s.73
  s.156, applied: 2012 c.19 s.61
  s.156, referred to: 2012 c.19 s.60
  s.156, varied: 2012 c.7 s.73
  s.157, applied: 2012 c.19 s.61
  s.157, referred to: 2012 c.19 s.60
  s.157, varied: 2012 c.7 s.73

2002– cont.

40. Enterprise Act 2002– *cont.*
s.158, applied: 2012 c.19 s.61
s.158, referred to: 2012 c.19 s.60
s.158, varied: 2012 c.7 s.73
s.159, applied: 2012 c.19 s.61
s.159, referred to: 2012 c.19 s.60
s.159, varied: 2012 c.7 s.73
s.160, applied: 2012 c.19 s.61
s.160, referred to: 2012 c.19 s.60
s.160, varied: 2012 c.7 s.73
s.161, applied: 2012 c.19 s.61
s.161, referred to: 2012 c.19 s.60
s.161, varied: 2012 c.7 s.73
s.162, applied: 2012 c.19 s.61
s.162, referred to: 2012 c.19 s.60
s.162, varied: 2012 c.7 s.73
s.163, applied: 2012 c.19 s.61
s.163, referred to: 2012 c.19 s.60
s.163, varied: 2012 c.7 s.73
s.164, applied: 2012 c.19 s.61
s.164, referred to: 2012 c.19 s.60
s.164, varied: 2012 c.7 s.73
s.165, applied: 2012 c.19 s.61
s.165, referred to: 2012 c.19 s.60
s.165, varied: 2012 c.7 s.73
s.166, disapplied: 2012 c.7 s.73
s.166, varied: 2012 c.7 s.73
s.167, applied: 2012 c.19 s.61
s.167, referred to: 2012 c.19 s.60
s.167, varied: 2012 c.7 s.73
s.168, amended: 2012 c.7 s.74, 2012 c.19 Sch.9 para.14, SI 2012/2400 Art.31
s.168, applied: 2012 c.19 s.61
s.168, referred to: 2012 c.19 s.60
s.168, repealed (in part): 2012 c.19 Sch.9 para.14
s.168, varied: 2012 c.7 s.73
s.169, applied: 2012 c.19 s.61
s.169, referred to: 2012 c.19 s.60
s.169, varied: 2012 c.7 s.73
s.170, applied: 2012 c.19 s.61
s.170, referred to: 2012 c.19 s.60
s.170, varied: 2012 c.7 s.73
s.171, applied: 2012 c.19 s.6
s.171, disapplied: 2012 c.7 s.73
s.171, varied: 2012 c.7 s.73
s.172, applied: 2012 c.19 s.61
s.172, referred to: 2012 c.19 s.60
s.172, varied: 2012 c.7 s.73
s.173, applied: 2012 c.19 s.61
s.173, referred to: 2012 c.19 s.60
s.173, varied: 2012 c.7 s.73
s.174, applied: 2012 c.19 s.61
s.174, referred to: 2012 c.19 s.60
s.174, varied: 2012 c.7 s.73
s.175, applied: 2012 c.19 s.61
s.175, referred to: 2012 c.19 s.60
s.175, varied: 2012 c.7 s.73
s.176, applied: 2012 c.19 s.61
s.176, referred to: 2012 c.19 s.60
s.176, varied: 2012 c.7 s.73
s.177, applied: 2012 c.19 s.61
s.177, referred to: 2012 c.19 s.60
s.177, varied: 2012 c.7 s.73
s.178, applied: 2012 c.19 s.61
s.178, referred to: 2012 c.19 s.60
s.178, varied: 2012 c.7 s.73
s.179, applied: 2012 c.19 s.61
s.179, referred to: 2012 c.19 s.60

2002– cont.

40. Enterprise Act 2002– *cont.*
s.179, varied: 2012 c.7 s.73
s.180, applied: 2012 c.7 s.73, 2012 c.19 s.61
s.180, referred to: 2012 c.19 s.60
s.180, varied: 2012 c.7 s.73
s.181, applied: 2012 c.19 s.61
s.181, referred to: 2012 c.19 s.60
s.181, varied: 2012 c.7 s.73
s.182, applied: 2012 c.19 s.61
s.182, referred to: 2012 c.19 s.60
s.182, varied: 2012 c.7 s.73
s.183, applied: 2012 c.19 s.61
s.183, referred to: 2012 c.19 s.60
s.183, varied: 2012 c.7 s.73
s.184, applied: 2012 c.19 s.61
s.184, referred to: 2012 c.19 s.60
s.184, varied: 2012 c.7 s.73
s.209, amended: SI 2012/1809 Sch.1 Part 1
s.213, amended: 2012 c.21 Sch.18 para.95
s.241A, repealed (in part): 2012 c.21 Sch.19
s.243, repealed (in part): 2012 c.21 Sch.19
s.248, referred to: 2012 c.7 s.133
s.254, referred to: 2012 c.7 s.133
s.255, amended: SI 2012/700 Sch.1 para.6
s.255, applied: SSI 2012/88 Reg.23, SSI 2012/89 Reg.26
s.266, applied: SI 2012/1544
s.266, enabling: SI 2012/1544
s.277, referred to: 2012 c.7 s.133
Sch.4 Pt 1 para.1, see *2 Travel Group Plc (In Liquidation) v Cardiff City Transport Services Ltd* [2012] CAT 7, [2012] Comp. A.R. 184 (CAT), Lord Carlile of Berriew Q.C.
Sch.9 Part 1 para.2, repealed (in part): 2012 c.19 Sch.9 para.17
Sch.9 Part 1 para.3, repealed: 2012 c.19 Sch.9 para.17
Sch.9 Part 1 para.11, repealed (in part): 2012 c.19 Sch.9 para.17
Sch.9 Part 1 para.12, repealed: 2012 c.19 Sch.9 para.17
Sch.14, amended: 2012 c.21 Sch.18 para.95
Sch.15, amended: 2012 c.19 Sch.9 para.15
Sch.25 para.5, repealed (in part): 2012 c.19 Sch.9 para.17
Sch.25 para.14, repealed (in part): 2012 c.19 Sch.9 para.17
Sch.25 para.33, repealed (in part): 2012 c.19 Sch.9 para.17
Sch.25 para.40, repealed (in part): 2012 c.21 Sch.19
41. Nationality, Immigration and Asylum Act 2002
Commencement Orders: SI 2012/1263 Art.2; SI 2012/1887 Art.2
see *George v Secretary of State for the Home Department* [2012] EWCA Civ 1362, Times, December 17, 2012 (CA (Civ Div)), Maurice Kay, L.J.; see *Kishver (Limited Leave: Meaning: Pakistan), Re* [2012] Imm. A.R. 128 (UT (IAC)), CMG Ockelton; see *R. (on the application of GI (Sudan)) v Secretary of State for the Home Department* [2011] EWHC 1875 (Admin), [2012] 1 W.L.R. 2568 (QBD (Admin)), Mitting, J.; see *R. (on the application of HA (Nigeria)) v Secretary of State for the Home Department* [2012] EWHC 979 (Admin), [2012] Med. L.R. 353 (QBD (Admin)), Singh, J.
Part 5, applied: 2012 c.10 Sch.1 para.11

2002–cont.

41. Nationality, Immigration and Asylum Act 2002–
cont.

Pt 5. see *Practice Direction (Sen Cts: Upper Tribunal: Judicial Review Jurisdiction)* [2012] 1 W.L.R. 16 (Sen Cts), Lord Judge, L.C.J.

s.17, applied: 2012 c.10 Sch.1 para.31

s.55, amended: SI 2012/961 Sch.1 para.3

s.62, applied: 2012 c.10 Sch.1 para.25, Sch.1 para.26

s.71, applied: 2012 c.10 Sch.1 para.27

s.76, see *George v Secretary of State for the Home Department* [2012] EWCA Civ 1362, Times, December 17, 2012 (CA (Civ Div)), Maurice Kay, L.J.

s.77, see *Kishver (Limited Leave: Meaning: Pakistan), Re* [2012] Imm. A.R. 128 (UT (IAC)), CMG Ockelton

s.78, see *Kishver (Limited Leave: Meaning: Pakistan), Re* [2012] Imm. A.R. 128 (UT (IAC)), CMG Ockelton

s.82, see *Abisoye (Entry Clearance Appeal: Tier 2: Nigeria)* [2012] UKUT 82 (IAC), [2012] Imm. A.R. 712 (UT (IAC)), Judge Kopieczek; see *LB (Jamaica) v Secretary of State for the Home Department* [2011] EWCA Civ 1420, [2012] Imm. A.R. 637 (CA (Civ Div)), Maurice Kay, L.J.; see *R. (on the application of MK (Tunisia)) v Secretary of State for the Home Department* [2011] EWCA Civ 333, [2012] 1 W.L.R. 700 (CA (Civ Div)), Pill, L.J.; see *R. (on the application of S) v First-tier Tribunal (IAC)* [2011] EWCA Civ 1319, [2012] Imm. A.R. 217 (CA (Civ Div)), Maurice Kay, L.J.; see *Sapkota v Secretary of State for the Home Department* [2011] EWCA Civ 1320, [2012] Imm. A.R. 254 (CA (Civ Div)), Arden, L.J.

s.82, applied: SI 2012/813 Sch.1 para.1, SI 2012/971 Sch.1 para.1

s.83, see *R. (on the application of S) v First-tier Tribunal (IAC)* [2011] EWCA Civ 1319, [2012] Imm. A.R. 217 (CA (Civ Div)), Maurice Kay, L.J.

s.84, see *Haque (s.86(2): Adjournment not Required: Bangladesh), Re* [2012] Imm. A.R. 359 (UT (IAC)), King, J.; see *Lamichhane v Secretary of State for the Home Department* [2012] EWCA Civ 260, [2012] 1 W.L.R. 3064 (CA (Civ Div)), Maurice Kay, L.J.; see *Latif (S.120: Revocation of Deportation Order: Pakistan)* [2012] UKUT 78 (IAC), [2012] Imm. A.R. 659 (UT (IAC)), Judge DE Taylor; see *R. (on the application of S) v First-tier Tribunal (IAC)* [2011] EWCA Civ 1319, [2012] Imm. A.R. 217 (CA (Civ Div)), Maurice Kay, L.J.; see *Sapkota v Secretary of State for the Home Department* [2011] EWCA Civ 1320, [2012] Imm. A.R. 254 (CA (Civ Div)), Arden, L.J.

s.85, see *Lamichhane v Secretary of State for the Home Department* [2012] EWCA Civ 260, [2012] 1 W.L.R. 3064 (CA (Civ Div)), Maurice Kay, L.J.; see *Latif (S.120: Revocation of Deportation Order: Pakistan)* [2012] UKUT 78 (IAC), [2012] Imm. A.R. 659 (UT (IAC)), Judge DE Taylor

s.85A, see *Latif (S.120: Revocation of Deportation Order: Pakistan)* [2012] UKUT 78 (IAC), [2012] Imm. A.R. 659 (UT (IAC)), Judge DE Taylor; see *Philipson (ILR : Not PBS : Evidence: India), Re* [2012] UKUT 39 (IAC), [2012] Imm. A.R. 463 (UT (IAC)), Blake, J. (President)

2002–cont.

41. Nationality, Immigration and Asylum Act 2002–
cont.

s.86, see *Haque (s.86(2): Adjournment not Required: Bangladesh), Re* [2012] Imm. A.R. 359 (UT (IAC)), King, J.

s.88A, see *Abisoye (Entry Clearance Appeal: Tier 2: Nigeria)* [2012] UKUT 82 (IAC), [2012] Imm. A.R. 712 (UT (IAC)), Judge Kopieczek; see *Ajakaiye (Visitor Appeals: Right of Appeal: Nigeria), Re* [2012] Imm. A.R. 25 (UT (IAC)), Blake, J. (President)

s.88A, applied: SI 2012/1532 Reg.2

s.88A, referred to: SI 2012/1531 Art.3

s.88A, enabling: SI 2012/1532

s.90, referred to: SI 2012/1531 Art.3

s.92, see *EM (Eritrea) v Secretary of State for the Home Department* [2012] EWCA Civ 1336, Times, December 6, 2012 (CA (Civ Div)), Richards, L.J.; see *R. (on the application of GI (Sudan)) v Secretary of State for the Home Department* [2012] EWCA Civ 867, [2012] 4 All E.R. 987 (CA (Civ Div)), Laws, L.J.; see *R. (on the application of MK (Tunisia)) v Secretary of State for the Home Department* [2011] EWCA Civ 333, [2012] 1 W.L.R. 700 (CA (Civ Div)), Pill, L.J.

s.94, see *Kabaghe (Appeal from Outside UK: Fairness: Malawi), Re* [2012] Imm. A.R. 312 (UT (IAC)), Blake, J. (President)

s.94, applied: 2012 c.10 Sch.1 para.19

s.95, see *Kabaghe (Appeal from Outside UK: Fairness: Malawi), Re* [2012] Imm. A.R. 312 (UT (IAC)), Blake, J. (President)

s.95, applied: SSI 2012/303 Reg.39

s.96, see *HH (Nigeria) v Secretary of State for the Home Department* [2012] CSOH 83, 2012 S.L.T. 1004 (OH), Temporary Judge J Beckett, QC; see *Lamichhane v Secretary of State for the Home Department* [2012] EWCA Civ 260, [2012] 1 W.L.R. 3064 (CA (Civ Div)), Maurice Kay, L.J.

s.96, applied: 2012 c.10 Sch.1 para.19

s.98, applied: SSI 2012/303 Reg.39

s.104, see *LB (Jamaica) v Secretary of State for the Home Department* [2011] EWCA Civ 1420, [2012] Imm. A.R. 637 (CA (Civ Div)), Maurice Kay, L.J.

s.104, applied: SI 2012/1547 Sch.3 para.2, SI 2012/1818 Reg.3

s.106, see *R. (on the application of GI (Sudan)) v Secretary of State for the Home Department* [2011] EWHC 1875 (Admin), [2012] 1 W.L.R. 2568 (QBD (Admin)), Mitting, J.

s.109, enabling: SI 2012/1547, SI 2012/2560

s.112, enabling: SI 2012/1532

s.116, repealed: 2012 c.10 Sch.5 Part 2

s.120, see *Ahmadi (S.47 Decision: Validity: Sapkota: Afghanistan), Re* [2012] UKUT 147 (IAC), [2012] Imm. A.R. 875 (UT (IAC)), Judge Lane; see *Lamichhane v Secretary of State for the Home Department* [2012] EWCA Civ 260, [2012] 1 W.L.R. 3064 (CA (Civ Div)), Maurice Kay, L.J.; see *Latif (S.120: Revocation of Deportation Order: Pakistan)* [2012] UKUT 78 (IAC), [2012] Imm. A.R. 659 (UT (IAC)), Judge DE Taylor; see *Sapkota v Secretary of State for the Home Department* [2011] EWCA Civ 1320, [2012] Imm. A.R. 254 (CA (Civ Div)), Arden, L.J.

s.124, enabling: SI 2012/1894

s.133, amended: 2012 c.7 Sch.5 para.107, Sch.7 para.12, Sch.14 para.83

2002–cont.

41. Nationality, Immigration and Asylum Act 2002– *cont.*

s.133, repealed (in part): 2012 c.7 Sch.5 para.107, Sch.7 para.12

s.135, amended: 2012 c.21 Sch.18 para.96

s.162, enabling: SI 2012/1263, SI 2012/1887

Sch.3, see *EM (Eritrea) v Secretary of State for the Home Department* [2012] EWCA Civ 1336, Times, December 6, 2012 (CA (Civ Div)), Richards, L.J.; see *R. (on the application of VC) v Newcastle City Council* [2011] EWHC 2673 (Admin), [2012] P.T.S.R. 546 (QBD (Admin)), Munby, L.J.

Sch.3 para.1, amended: SI 2012/961 Sch.1 para.4

Sch.8 para.3, applied: SSI 2012/303 Reg.39

Sch.9, applied: SSI 2012/303 Reg.39

2003

1. Income Tax (Earnings and Pensions) Act 2003

Part 2, applied: SI 2012/2677 Reg.36

Part 3 c.10, applied: SI 2012/2677 Reg.38

Part 3 c.11, applied: SI 2012/2677 Reg.38

Part 3 c.2, applied: SI 2012/2677 Reg.38

Part 3 c.3, applied: SI 2012/2677 Reg.38

Part 3 c.4, applied: SI 2012/2677 Reg.38

Part 3 c.5, applied: SI 2012/2677 Reg.38

Part 3 c.6, applied: SI 2012/2677 Reg.38

Part 3 c.7, applied: SI 2012/2677 Reg.38

Part 3 c.8, applied: SI 2012/2677 Reg.38

Part 3 c.9, applied: SI 2012/2677 Reg.38

Part 5, applied: SI 2012/2677 Reg.36

Part 9, applied: SI 2012/2677 Reg.36, Reg.41

Part 10, applied: SI 2012/2677 Reg.36

Part 12, applied: SI 2012/847 Reg.3, Reg.25

Pt 3. see *Reed Employment Plc v Revenue and Customs Commissioners* [2012] UKFTT 28 (TC), [2012] S.F.T.D. 394 (FTT (Tax)), Judge Colin Bishopp

Pt 5. see *Cameron v Revenue and Customs Commissioners* [2012] EWHC 1174 (Admin), [2012] S.T.C. 1691 (QBD (Admin)), Wyn Williams, J.

Pt 6. see *Goldman v Revenue and Customs Commissioners* [2012] UKFTT 313 (TC), [2012] S.F.T.D. 1048 (FTT (Tax)), Judge John Walters Q.C.

Pt 7. see *Sloane Robinson Investment Services Ltd (formerly Sloane Robinson Investment Management Ltd) v Revenue and Customs Commissioners* [2012] UKFTT 451 (TC), [2012] S.F.T.D. 1181 (FTT (Tax)), Judge Malachy Cornwell-Kelly

s.1, amended: 2012 c.14 Sch.1 para.5

s.7, see *Goldman v Revenue and Customs Commissioners* [2012] UKFTT 313 (TC), [2012] S.F.T.D. 1048 (FTT (Tax)), Judge John Walters Q.C.

s.7, referred to: SI 2012/847 Reg.21

s.9, see *Kuehne & Nagel Drinks Logistics Ltd v Revenue and Customs Commissioners* [2012] EWCA Civ 34, [2012] S.T.C. 840 (CA (Civ Div)), Mummery, L.J.

s.10, applied: SI 2012/2677 Reg.38

s.11, see *Goldman v Revenue and Customs Commissioners* [2012] UKFTT 313 (TC), [2012] S.F.T.D. 1048 (FTT (Tax)), Judge John Walters Q.C.

2003–cont.

1. Income Tax (Earnings and Pensions) Act 2003– *cont.*

s.15, see *Goldman v Revenue and Customs Commissioners* [2012] UKFTT 313 (TC), [2012] S.F.T.D. 1048 (FTT (Tax)), Judge John Walters Q.C.

s.18, see *Sloane Robinson Investment Services Ltd (formerly Sloane Robinson Investment Management Ltd) v Revenue and Customs Commissioners* [2012] UKFTT 451 (TC), [2012] S.F.T.D. 1181 (FTT (Tax)), Judge Malachy Cornwell-Kelly

s.62, see *Goldman v Revenue and Customs Commissioners* [2012] UKFTT 313 (TC), [2012] S.F.T.D. 1048 (FTT (Tax)), Judge John Walters Q.C.

s.65, see *Reed Employment Plc v Revenue and Customs Commissioners* [2012] UKFTT 28 (TC), [2012] S.F.T.D. 394 (FTT (Tax)), Judge Colin Bishopp

s.87, repealed (in part): 2012 c.14 Sch.39 para.50

s.89, repealed: 2012 c.14 Sch.39 para.50

s.121, amended: SI 2012/266 Art.3

s.125, amended: 2012 c.14 s.14

s.125A, added: 2012 c.14 s.14

s.139, amended: 2012 c.14 s.17

s.148, amended: SI 2012/266 Art.3

s.148, repealed (in part): SI 2012/266 Art.3

s.150, amended: SI 2012/915 Art.2, SI 2012/3037 Art.2

s.161, amended: SI 2012/3037 Art.3

s.170, enabling: SI 2012/915, SI 2012/3037

s.210, enabling: SI 2012/1808

s.229, see *Cheshire Employer and Skills Development Ltd v Revenue and Customs Commissioners* [2012] S.T.C. 69 (UT (Tax)), Judge Colin Bishopp

s.291, amended: 2012 c.14 s.15

s.297A, amended: 2012 c.14 s.16

s.297B, amended: 2012 c.14 s.16

s.297C, added: 2012 c.14 s.16

s.303, amended: 2012 c.14 Sch.37 para.4

s.303, applied: SI 2012/3070 Art.3, SI 2012/3071 Art.4, Art.5

s.303, enabling: SI 2012/3070, SI 2012/3071

s.343, amended: 2012 c.7 Sch.15 para.51, Sch.15 para.56, SI 2012/3004 Art.2

s.343, enabling: SI 2012/3004

s.357, amended: 2012 c.14 Sch.16 para.111

s.394, amended: 2012 c.14 s.1

s.536, amended: SI 2012/1360 Art.2

s.609, amended: 2012 c.14 Sch.39 para.32

s.655, amended: 2012 c.14 Sch.1 para.5

s.677, amended: 2012 c.5 Sch.9 para.49, Sch.14 Part 9

s.681B, added: 2012 c.14 Sch.1 para.1

s.681B, referred to: 2012 c.14 Sch.1 para.7

s.681C, added: 2012 c.14 Sch.1 para.1

s.681D, added: 2012 c.14 Sch.1 para.1

s.681E, added: 2012 c.14 Sch.1 para.1

s.681F, added: 2012 c.14 Sch.1 para.1

s.681G, added: 2012 c.14 Sch.1 para.1

s.681H, added: 2012 c.14 Sch.1 para.1

s.684, amended: 2012 c.14 s.225, Sch.1 para.5

s.684, enabling: SI 2012/822, SI 2012/1895

s.685, amended: 2012 c.14 Sch.1 para.5

s.686, see *Sloane Robinson Investment Services Ltd (formerly Sloane Robinson Investment Management Ltd) v Revenue and Customs Commissioners* [2012] UKFTT 451 (TC),

2003–cont.

1. Income Tax (Earnings and Pensions) Act 2003– cont.

s.686–cont.
[2012] S.F.T.D. 1181 (FTT (Tax)), Judge Malachy Cornwell-Kelly
s.706, enabling: SI 2012/822
s.707, enabling: SI 2012/822
s.710, enabling: SI 2012/822
s.713, applied: 2012 c.23 Sch.1 para.5
s.717, amended: 2012 c.14 Sch.1 para.5
Sch.1 Part 1, amended: 2012 c.5 Sch.9 para.50
Sch.1 Part 2, amended: 2012 c.14 s.14, Sch.1 para.5
Sch.2 Part 4 para.30, amended: 2012 c.21 Sch.18 para.97
Sch.3 Part 4 para.21, amended: 2012 c.21 Sch.18 para.97
Sch.4 Part 4 para.19, amended: 2012 c.21 Sch.18 para.97
Sch.5 Part 2 para.5, amended: SI 2012/1360 Art.2
Sch.5 Part 2 para.6, amended: SI 2012/1360 Art.2
Sch.5 Part 8 para.54, enabling: SI 2012/1360
Sch.6 Part 1 para.36, repealed: 2012 c.14 Sch.39 para.28
Sch.6 Part 1 para.119, repealed: 2012 c.14 Sch.39 para.28
Sch.6 Part 2 para.179, repealed: 2012 c.5 Sch.14 Part 1
Sch.6 Part 2 para.228, repealed: 2012 c.5 Sch.14 Part 1
Sch.6 Part 2 para.229, repealed: 2012 c.5 Sch.14 Part 1
Sch.6 Part 2 para.230, repealed: 2012 c.5 Sch.14 Part 1
Sch.6 Part 2 para.237, repealed: 2012 c.11 Sch.2 para.2
Sch.7 Part 3 para.18, repealed: 2012 c.14 Sch.39 para.50
Sch.7 Part 4 para.34, repealed: 2012 c.5 Sch.14 Part 1
Sch.7 Part 4 para.35, repealed: 2012 c.5 Sch.14 Part 1
Sch.7 Part 4 para.36, repealed: 2012 c.5 Sch.14 Part 1
Sch.7 Part 4 para.37, repealed: 2012 c.5 Sch.14 Part 1
Sch.7 Part 4 para.38, repealed: 2012 c.5 Sch.14 Part 1

4. Health (Wales) Act 2003
s.2, applied: SI 2012/1631 Sch.5 para.6, SI 2012/2996 Sch.5 para.5
s.4, amended: 2012 c.7 Sch.15 para.56

5. Community Care (Delayed Discharges etc.) Act 2003
s.1, amended: 2012 c.7 Sch.5 para.109, Sch.14 para.84
s.9, amended: 2012 c.7 Sch.5 para.110

6. Police (Northern Ireland) Act 2003
s.30A, amended: SI 2012/2595 Art.11
s.41, amended: SI 2012/2595 Art.11
s.44, amended: SI 2012/2595 Art.11
Sch.2A para.16, amended: 2012 c.9 Sch.9 para.31

14. Finance Act 2003
Part 4, applied: 2012 c.11 s.28
s.43, see Pollen Estate Trustee Co Ltd v Revenue and Customs Commissioners [2012] UKUT 277 (TCC), [2012] S.T.C. 2443 (UT (Tax)), Warren, J.
s.43, applied: SI 2012/736 Art.14
s.44, see Lancer Scott Ltd v Revenue and Customs Commissioners [2012] UKUT 10 (TCC), [2012] S.T.C. 928 (UT (Tax)), Judge Colin Bishopp
s.44, repealed (in part): 2012 c.11 Sch.3 para.3
s.45, see Vardy Properties v Revenue and Customs Commissioners [2012] UKFTT 564 (TC), [2012] S.F.T.D. 1398 (FTT (Tax)), Judge Kevin Poole

2003–cont.

14. Finance Act 2003– cont.
s.45, amended: 2012 c.14 s.212
s.45, applied: SI 2012/2396 Reg.4
s.48, see Pollen Estate Trustee Co Ltd v Revenue and Customs Commissioners [2012] UKUT 277 (TCC), [2012] S.T.C. 2443 (UT (Tax)), Warren, J.
s.48, amended: 2012 c.11 s.29, Sch.3 para.4
s.48, repealed (in part): 2012 c.11 Sch.3 para.4
s.50, enabling: SI 2012/1667
s.54, see Vardy Properties v Revenue and Customs Commissioners [2012] UKFTT 564 (TC), [2012] S.F.T.D. 1398 (FTT (Tax)), Judge Kevin Poole
s.55, amended: 2012 c.11 Sch.3 para.5, 2012 c.14 s.213, Sch.35 para.2
s.55A, added: 2012 c.14 Sch.35 para.3
s.57, repealed: 2012 c.14 Sch.39 para.8
s.57AA, amended: 2012 c.11 Sch.3 para.6
s.60, amended: 2012 c.11 Sch.3 para.7
s.60, repealed (in part): 2012 c.11 Sch.3 para.7
s.61, amended: 2012 c.7 Sch.14 para.86, 2012 c.11 Sch.3 para.8
s.61, repealed (in part): 2012 c.11 Sch.3 para.8
s.63, amended: 2012 c.21 Sch.18 para.98
s.66, amended: 2012 c.7 Sch.14 para.87
s.67A, added: 2012 c.14 s.216
s.67A, varied: 2012 c.14 s.216
s.69, repealed (in part): SI 2012/964 Sch.1
s.71A, repealed (in part): 2012 c.11 Sch.3 para.9
s.72, repealed: 2012 c.11 Sch.3 para.10
s.72A, repealed: 2012 c.11 Sch.3 para.10
s.73, amended: 2012 c.11 Sch.3 para.11
s.73, repealed (in part): 2012 c.11 Sch.3 para.11
s.73AB, amended: 2012 c.11 Sch.3 para.12
s.73B, amended: 2012 c.11 Sch.3 para.13
s.73CA, amended: 2012 c.11 Sch.3 para.14
s.74, amended: 2012 c.14 Sch.35 para.5
s.75, repealed: 2012 c.11 Sch.3 para.15
s.75C, amended: 2012 c.11 Sch.3 para.16
s.76, see Lancer Scott Ltd v Revenue and Customs Commissioners [2012] UKUT 9 (TCC), [2012] S.T.C. 928 (UT (Tax)), Judge Colin Bishopp; see Ryan v Revenue and Customs Commissioners [2012] UKUT 9 (TCC), [2012] S.T.C. 899 (UT (Tax)), Judge Colin Bishopp
s.77, amended: 2012 c.11 Sch.3 para.17
s.79, amended: 2012 c.11 Sch.3 para.18
s.79, repealed (in part): 2012 c.11 Sch.3 para.18
s.81B, repealed (in part): 2012 c.14 s.222
s.93, amended: 2012 c.14 Sch.38 para.58
s.93, repealed (in part): 2012 c.14 Sch.38 para.58
s.96, repealed: 2012 c.14 Sch.38 para.58
s.97, see Ryan v Revenue and Customs Commissioners [2012] UKUT 9 (TCC), [2012] S.T.C. 899 (UT (Tax)), Judge Colin Bishopp
s.103, see Pollen Estate Trustee Co Ltd v Revenue and Customs Commissioners [2012] UKUT 277 (TCC), [2012] S.T.C. 2443 (UT (Tax)), Warren, J.
s.106, repealed (in part): 2012 c.14 s.222
s.107, see Pollen Estate Trustee Co Ltd v Revenue and Customs Commissioners [2012] UKUT 277 (TCC), [2012] S.T.C. 2443 (UT (Tax)), Warren, J.
s.108, amended: 2012 c.11 Sch.3 para.19
s.109, amended: 2012 c.14 Sch.35 para.6
s.112, repealed (in part): 2012 c.14 Sch.39 para.8
s.117, repealed (in part): 2012 c.11 Sch.3 para.20

2003–cont.

14. **Finance Act 2003**–*cont.*
s.119, see *Lancer Scott Ltd v Revenue and Customs Commissioners* [2012] UKUT 10 (TCC), [2012] S.T.C. 928 (UT (Tax)), Judge Colin Bishopp
s.119, amended: 2012 c.11 Sch.3 para.21
s.119, applied: SI 2012/736 Art.14, SI 2012/1709 Art.9
s.121, amended: 2012 c.11 Sch.3 para.22, SI 2012/700 Sch.1 para.7
s.121, repealed (in part): 2012 c.11 Sch.3 para.22
s.122, amended: 2012 c.11 Sch.3 para.23
s.127, repealed: 2012 c.14 Sch.39 para.5
s.128, amended: SI 2012/700 Sch.1 para.7
s.128, repealed: 2012 c.14 Sch.39 para.9
s.129, repealed: 2012 c.14 Sch.39 para.9
s.130, repealed (in part): 2012 c.14 Sch.39 para.9
s.153, amended: 2012 c.14 s.26
s.156, repealed: 2012 c.14 Sch.16 para.109
s.188, repealed: 2012 c.14 Sch.30 para.17
s.193, repealed (in part): 2012 c.14 Sch.32 para.22
s.197, repealed: SI 2012/3062 Sch.1
s.205, enabling: SI 2012/820
Sch.1 para.3, see *Vardy Properties v Revenue and Customs Commissioners* [2012] UKFTT 564 (TC), [2012] S.F.T.D. 1398 (FTT (Tax)), Judge Kevin Poole
Sch.4 para.8, amended: 2012 c.11 Sch.3 para.24
Sch.4 para.10, repealed (in part): 2012 c.11 Sch.3 para.24
Sch.4 para.17, repealed (in part): 2012 c.11 Sch.3 para.24
Sch.4A para.1, added: 2012 c.14 Sch.35 para.4
Sch.4A para.2, added: 2012 c.14 Sch.35 para.4
Sch.4A para.3, added: 2012 c.14 Sch.35 para.4
Sch.4A para.4, added: 2012 c.14 Sch.35 para.4
Sch.4A para.5, added: 2012 c.14 Sch.35 para.4
Sch.4A para.6, added: 2012 c.14 Sch.35 para.4
Sch.4A para.7, added: 2012 c.14 Sch.35 para.4
Sch.4A para.8, added: 2012 c.14 Sch.35 para.4
Sch.4A para.9, added: 2012 c.14 Sch.35 para.4
Sch.5 para.9, amended: 2012 c.14 Sch.35 para.7
Sch.5 para.9A, amended: 2012 c.14 Sch.35 para.7
Sch.6, applied: 2012 c.14 Sch.39 para.13
Sch.6 Part 1 para.1, repealed: 2012 c.14 Sch.39 para.8
Sch.6 Part 1 para.2, repealed: 2012 c.14 Sch.39 para.8
Sch.6 Part 2 para.3, repealed: 2012 c.14 Sch.39 para.8
Sch.6 Part 2 para.4, repealed: 2012 c.14 Sch.39 para.8
Sch.6 Part 2 para.5, repealed: 2012 c.14 Sch.39 para.8
Sch.6 Part 2 para.6, repealed: 2012 c.14 Sch.39 para.8
Sch.6 Part 3 para.7, repealed: 2012 c.14 Sch.39 para.8
Sch.6 Part 3 para.8, repealed: 2012 c.14 Sch.39 para.8
Sch.6 Part 3 para.9, repealed: 2012 c.14 Sch.39 para.8
Sch.6 Part 3 para.10, repealed: 2012 c.14 Sch.39 para.8
Sch.6 Part 4 para.11, repealed: 2012 c.14 Sch.39 para.8
Sch.6 Part 4 para.12, repealed: 2012 c.14 Sch.39 para.8
Sch.6 Part 4 para.13, repealed: 2012 c.14 Sch.39 para.8

14. **Finance Act 2003**–*cont.*
Sch.6B para.2, amended: 2012 c.14 Sch.35 para.8
Sch.8, see *Pollen Estate Trustee Co Ltd v Revenue and Customs Commissioners* [2012] UKUT 277 (TCC), [2012] S.T.C. 2443 (UT (Tax)), Warren, J.
Sch.8 para.1, see *Pollen Estate Trustee Co Ltd v Revenue and Customs Commissioners* [2012] UKUT 277 (TCC), [2012] S.T.C. 2443 (UT (Tax)), Warren, J.
Sch.10 Part 1 para.1, disapplied: 2012 c.11 s.29
Sch.10 Part 1 para.7, repealed (in part): 2012 c.11 Sch.3 para.25
Sch.10 Part 7 para.45, repealed (in part): 2012 c.11 Sch.3 para.25
Sch.13 Part 3 para.14, repealed: 2012 c.14 Sch.38 para.58
Sch.13 Part 3 para.15, repealed: 2012 c.14 Sch.38 para.58
Sch.13 Part 3 para.16, repealed: 2012 c.14 Sch.38 para.58
Sch.13 Part 3 para.17, repealed: 2012 c.14 Sch.38 para.58
Sch.13 Part 3 para.18, repealed: 2012 c.14 Sch.38 para.58
Sch.13 Part 4 para.19, repealed: 2012 c.14 Sch.38 para.58
Sch.13 Part 4 para.20, repealed: 2012 c.14 Sch.38 para.58
Sch.13 Part 4 para.21, repealed: 2012 c.14 Sch.38 para.58
Sch.13 Part 4 para.22, repealed: 2012 c.14 Sch.38 para.58
Sch.13 Part 4 para.23, repealed: 2012 c.14 Sch.38 para.58
Sch.13 Part 4 para.24, repealed: 2012 c.14 Sch.38 para.58
Sch.13 Part 4 para.25, repealed: 2012 c.14 Sch.38 para.58
Sch.13 Part 4 para.26, repealed: 2012 c.14 Sch.38 para.58
Sch.13 Part 4 para.27, repealed: 2012 c.14 Sch.38 para.58
Sch.13 Part 8 para.53, substituted: 2012 c.14 Sch.38 para.58
Sch.15 Part 3 para.11, amended: 2012 c.14 Sch.35 para.9
Sch.15 Part 3 para.12, amended: 2012 c.11 Sch.3 para.26
Sch.15 Part 3 para.17, applied: 2012 c.14 Sch.35 para.10
Sch.15 Part 3 para.17A, applied: 2012 c.14 Sch.35 para.10
Sch.15 Part 3 para.19, amended: 2012 c.14 Sch.35 para.9
Sch.15 Part 3 para.20, amended: 2012 c.11 Sch.3 para.26
Sch.15 Part 3 para.25, amended: 2012 c.14 Sch.39 para.8
Sch.15 Part 3 para.26, repealed: 2012 c.14 Sch.39 para.8
Sch.15 Part 3 para.30, amended: 2012 c.14 Sch.35 para.9
Sch.17A para.1, amended: 2012 c.11 Sch.3 para.27
Sch.17A para.4, amended: 2012 c.11 Sch.3 para.27
Sch.17A para.7, repealed (in part): 2012 c.11 Sch.3 para.27
Sch.17A para.10, amended: 2012 c.11 Sch.3 para.27, SI 2012/1667 Reg.3
Sch.17A para.12A, amended: 2012 c.11 Sch.3 para.27

2003–cont.

14. Finance Act 2003–*cont.*

Sch.17A para.12B, amended: 2012 c.11 Sch.3 para.27

Sch.17A para.13, amended: 2012 c.11 Sch.3 para.27

Sch.17A para.14, amended: 2012 c.11 Sch.3 para.27

Sch.17A para.18A, repealed (in part): 2012 c.14 Sch.39 para.8

Sch.17A para.19, repealed: 2012 c.11 Sch.3 para.27

Sch.19 para.6, repealed (in part): 2012 c.14 Sch.39 para.5

Sch.33 para.1, repealed: 2012 c.14 Sch.16 para.247

Sch.33 para.2, repealed: 2012 c.14 Sch.16 para.247

Sch.33 para.5, repealed: 2012 c.14 Sch.16 para.247

Sch.33 para.8, repealed: 2012 c.14 Sch.16 para.247

Sch.33 para.10, repealed: 2012 c.14 Sch.16 para.247

Sch.33 para.12, repealed: 2012 c.14 Sch.16 para.247

Sch.33 para.20, repealed: 2012 c.14 Sch.16 para.247

Sch.33 para.22, repealed: 2012 c.14 Sch.16 para.247

Sch.33 para.23, repealed: 2012 c.14 Sch.16 para.247

Sch.33 para.24, repealed: 2012 c.14 Sch.16 para.247

Sch.33 para.29, repealed: 2012 c.14 Sch.16 para.247

17. Licensing Act 2003

see *R. (on the application of Raphael) v Highbury Corner Magistrates' Court* [2011] EWCA Civ 462, [2012] P.T.S.R. 427 (CA (Civ Div)), Longmore, L.J.

s.5, amended: 2012 c.7 Sch.5 para.112

s.5, applied: SI 2012/3094 Reg.14

s.7, see *R. (on the application of Raphael) v Highbury Corner Magistrates' Court* [2011] EWCA Civ 462, [2012] P.T.S.R. 427 (CA (Civ Div)), Longmore, L.J.

s.9, enabling: SI 2012/2551

s.10, see *R. (on the application of Raphael) v Highbury Corner Magistrates' Court* [2011] EWCA Civ 462, [2012] P.T.S.R. 427 (CA (Civ Div)), Longmore, L.J.

s.13, amended: 2012 c.7 Sch.5 para.113, SI 2012/1659 Sch.3 para.16

s.13, applied: SI 2012/3094 Reg.14

s.16, amended: 2012 c.7 Sch.14 para.88

s.16, repealed (in part): 2012 c.7 Sch.5 para.114

s.17, enabling: SI 2012/955, SI 2012/2290

s.18, applied: SI 2012/3094 Reg.14

s.27, applied: SI 2012/2730 Reg.7

s.28, applied: SI 2012/2730 Reg.7

s.29, enabling: SI 2012/2290

s.30, enabling: SI 2012/955

s.31, applied: SI 2012/3094 Reg.14

s.34, see *R. (on the application of Albert Court Residents' Association) v Westminster City Council* [2011] EWCA Civ 430, [2012] P.T.S.R. 604 (CA (Civ Div)), Lloyd, L.J.

s.34, applied: SI 2012/2730 Reg.9

s.34, enabling: SI 2012/955, SI 2012/2290

s.35, see *R. (on the application of Albert Court Residents' Association) v Westminster City Council* [2011] EWCA Civ 430, [2012] P.T.S.R. 604 (CA (Civ Div)), Lloyd, L.J.

s.35, applied: SI 2012/3094 Reg.14

s.41A, applied: SI 2012/2730 Reg.9

s.41A, enabling: SI 2012/955, SI 2012/2290

s.41B, applied: SI 2012/3094 Reg.14

s.51, see *R. (on the application of Albert Court Residents' Association) v Westminster City Council* [2011] EWCA Civ 430, [2012] P.T.S.R. 604 (CA (Civ Div)), Lloyd, L.J.; see *R. (on the application of Raphael) v Highbury Corner Magistrates' Court* [2011] EWCA Civ 462,

2003–cont.

17. Licensing Act 2003–*cont.*

s.51–*cont.*

[2012] P.T.S.R. 427 (CA (Civ Div)), Longmore, L.J.

s.51, applied: SI 2012/3094 Reg.14

s.51, enabling: SI 2012/955

s.52, see *R. (on the application of Raphael) v Highbury Corner Magistrates' Court* [2011] EWCA Civ 462, [2012] P.T.S.R. 427 (CA (Civ Div)), Longmore, L.J.

s.52, applied: SI 2012/3094 Reg.14

s.53, applied: SI 2012/3094 Reg.14

s.53A, enabling: SI 2012/955

s.53C, applied: SI 2012/3094 Reg.14

s.54, enabling: SI 2012/955, SI 2012/2290

s.55, applied: SI 2012/2730 Reg.6, Reg.9

s.69, amended: 2012 c.7 Sch.5 para.115, SI 2012/1659 Sch.3 para.16

s.69, applied: SI 2012/3094 Reg.14

s.71, enabling: SI 2012/955, SI 2012/2290

s.72, applied: SI 2012/3094 Reg.14

s.81, applied: SI 2012/2730 Reg.7

s.84, applied: SI 2012/2730 Reg.9

s.84, enabling: SI 2012/955, SI 2012/2290

s.85, applied: SI 2012/3094 Reg.14

s.86A, applied: SI 2012/2730 Reg.9

s.86A, enabling: SI 2012/955, SI 2012/2290

s.86B, applied: SI 2012/3094 Reg.14

s.87, applied: SI 2012/3094 Reg.14

s.87, enabling: SI 2012/955

s.88, applied: SI 2012/3094 Reg.14

s.89, applied: SI 2012/3094 Reg.14

s.91, enabling: SI 2012/955, SI 2012/2290

s.92, applied: SI 2012/2730 Reg.6, Reg.9

s.96, applied: SI 2012/3094 Reg.14

s.100, enabling: SI 2012/960, SI 2012/2290

s.104A, enabling: SI 2012/960

s.106A, enabling: SI 2012/960

s.107, enabling: SI 2012/960

s.133, enabling: SI 2012/946

s.167, applied: SI 2012/3094 Reg.14

s.167, enabling: SI 2012/955

s.169A, applied: SI 2012/963 Reg.3

s.169A, enabling: SI 2012/963

s.172, applied: SI 2012/828

s.172, enabling: SI 2012/828

s.172A, applied: SI 2012/2730 Reg.7

s.172B, amended: 2012 c.7 Sch.5 para.116

s.172B, applied: SI 2012/3094 Reg.14

s.172E, applied: SI 2012/2551 Reg.15

s.177, amended: 2012 c.2 s.1

s.177, repealed (in part): 2012 c.2 s.1

s.177A, added: 2012 c.2 s.1

s.183, enabling: SI 2012/2551

s.193, enabling: SI 2012/946, SI 2012/955, SI 2012/960, SI 2012/2290, SI 2012/2551

s.197, applied: SI 2012/828

s.197, enabling: SI 2012/828

Sch.1 Part 1 para.1, amended: 2012 c.2 s.2

Sch.1 Part 1 para.1, repealed (in part): 2012 c.2 s.2

Sch.1 Part 1 para.3, repealed: 2012 c.2 s.2

Sch.1 Part 1 para.4, substituted: 2012 c.2 s.2

Sch.1 Part 2 para.7, substituted: 2012 c.2 s.2

Sch.1 Part 2 para.8, amended: 2012 c.2 s.2

Sch.1 Part 2 para.9, amended: 2012 c.2 s.2

Sch.1 Part 2 para.10, amended: 2012 c.2 s.2

Sch.1 Part 2 para.11, amended: 2012 c.2 s.2, s.3

Sch.1 Part 2 para.11, repealed (in part): 2012 c.2 s.2

2003–cont.

17. Licensing Act 2003–*cont.*
Sch.1 Part 2 para.11A, repealed (in part): 2012 c.2 s.2
Sch.1 Part 2 para.12, amended: 2012 c.2 s.2
Sch.1 Part 2 para.12A, added: 2012 c.2 s.3
Sch.1 Part 2 para.12B, added: 2012 c.2 s.3
Sch.1 Part 2 para.12C, added: 2012 c.2 s.3

20. Railways and Transport Safety Act 2003
s.33, referred to: SI 2012/472 Art.8
Sch.1 para.2, amended: SI 2012/2404 Sch.2 para.48
Sch.4 Part 1 para.7, amended: SI 2012/2404 Sch.2 para.48
Sch.5 para.4, amended: 2012 c.9 Sch.10 Part 4

21. Communications Act 2003
see *British Telecommunications Plc v Office of Communications* [2011] EWCA Civ 245, [2012] Bus. L.R. 113 (CA (Civ Div)), Sir Andrew Morritt (Chancellor); see *R. (on the application of British Telecommunications Plc) v Secretary of State for Business, Innovation and Skills* [2012] EWCA Civ 232, [2012] Bus. L.R. 1766 (CA (Civ Div)), Arden, L.J.
applied: SI 2012/1128 Art.4, SI 2012/1916 Reg.286
referred to: 2012 c.19 Sch.6 para.4, SI 2012/1726 r.11.1, SI 2012/1916 Reg.314, SI 2012/2447 Art.4, SI 2012/2600 Art.7
Part 3, referred to: SI 2012/292 Art.4
s.1, see *Arqiva Ltd v Everything Everywhere Ltd (formerly T-Mobile (UK) Ltd)* [2011] EWHC 2016 (TCC), [2012] 1 All E.R. 607 (QBD (TCC)), Ramsey, J.
s.4, amended: SI 2012/1809 Sch.1 Part 1
s.5, applied: SI 2012/2817 Reg.9, Reg.115
s.16, applied: SI 2012/1128 Art.3
s.77, amended: SI 2012/1809 Sch.1 Part 1
s.106, applied: SI 2012/801 Art.27
s.119, amended: 2012 c.10 Sch.5 para.61
s.127, see *Iv Dunn* [2012] HCJAC 108, 2012 S.L.T. 983 (HCJ), Lady Paton
s.192, see *British Telecommunications Plc v Office of Communications* [2011] EWCA Civ 245, [2012] Bus. L.R. 113 (CA (Civ Div)), Sir Andrew Morritt (Chancellor)
s.205, applied: SI 2012/1916 Reg.314
s.241, referred to: SI 2012/293 Art.6
s.244, applied: SI 2012/292, SI 2012/1842
s.244, enabling: SI 2012/292, SI 2012/1842
s.245, varied: SI 2012/2690 Sch.1 para.11, Sch.1 para.12
s.246, varied: SI 2012/2690 Sch.1 para.12
s.247, varied: SI 2012/2690 Sch.1 para.12
s.248, varied: SI 2012/2690 Sch.1 para.12
s.249, varied: SI 2012/2690 Sch.1 para.12
s.250, varied: SI 2012/2690 Sch.1 para.12
s.251, varied: SI 2012/2690 Sch.1 para.12
s.252, varied: SI 2012/2690 Sch.1 para.12
s.253, varied: SI 2012/2690 Sch.1 para.12
s.253A, varied: SI 2012/2690 Sch.1 para.12
s.254, varied: SI 2012/2690 Sch.1 para.12
s.255, varied: SI 2012/2690 Sch.1 para.12
s.256, varied: SI 2012/2690 Sch.1 para.12
s.257, varied: SI 2012/2690 Sch.1 para.12
s.258, varied: SI 2012/2690 Sch.1 para.12
s.259, varied: SI 2012/2690 Sch.1 para.12
s.260, varied: SI 2012/2690 Sch.1 para.12
s.261, varied: SI 2012/2690 Sch.1 para.12
s.262, varied: SI 2012/2690 Sch.1 para.12
s.262, enabling: SI 2012/2690
s.277, applied: SI 2012/1842

2003–cont.

21. Communications Act 2003–*cont.*
s.277, enabling: SI 2012/1842
s.309, applied: SI 2012/1842
s.309, varied: SI 2012/292 Sch.1 para.13A
s.309, enabling: SI 2012/1842
s.314, disapplied: SI 2012/2690 Sch.1 para.13
s.319, see *R. (on the application of London Christian Radio Ltd) v Radio Advertising Clearance Centre* [2012] EWHC 1043 (Admin), [2012] H.R.L.R. 19 (QBD (Admin)), Silber, J.
s.321, see *R. (on the application of London Christian Radio Ltd) v Radio Advertising Clearance Centre* [2012] EWHC 1043 (Admin), [2012] H.R.L.R. 19 (QBD (Admin)), Silber, J.
s.325, referred to: SI 2012/1916 Reg.314
s.333, varied: SI 2012/292 Sch.1 para.14
s.355, disapplied: SI 2012/2690 Sch.1 para.13
s.356, disapplied: SI 2012/2690 Sch.1 para.13
s.368R, amended: SI 2012/1916 Sch.34 para.44
s.371, amended: SI 2012/1809 Sch.1 Part 1
s.393, varied: 2012 c.11 s.12
s.402, enabling: SI 2012/292, SI 2012/1842, SI 2012/2688
s.403, applied: SI 2012/936
s.411, enabling: SI 2012/2688
Sch.11 para.6, amended: SI 2012/1809 Sch.1 Part 1
Sch.12 Part 1 para.1, applied: SI 2012/1842
Sch.12 Part 1 para.1, enabling: SI 2012/1842
Sch.12 Part 2 para.7, applied: SI 2012/1842
Sch.12 Part 2 para.7, enabling: SI 2012/1842
Sch.12 Part 2 para.14, referred to: SI 2012/1916 Reg.314
Sch.16 para.5, repealed: 2012 c.21 Sch.19

26. Local Government Act 2003
s.7, enabling: SI 2012/265
s.8, enabling: SI 2012/265
s.9, enabling: SI 2012/265, SI 2012/711, SI 2012/1324, SI 2012/2269
s.11, enabling: SI 2012/711, SI 2012/1324, SI 2012/2269
s.16, enabling: SI 2012/265
s.21, enabling: SI 2012/265
s.46, applied: SI 2012/2550 Reg.4
s.70, repealed (in part): 2012 c.17 Sch.3 para.33
s.76, repealed: 2012 c.17 Sch.4 para.9
s.105, amended: 2012 c.17 Sch.4 para.10
s.123, enabling: SI 2012/711, SI 2012/1324, SI 2012/2269
Sch.4 para.2, amended: SI 2012/2404 Sch.2 para.49
Sch.7 para.17, repealed: 2012 c.17 s.3
Sch.7 para.22, repealed (in part): 2012 c.17 Sch.3 para.34
Sch.7 para.24, repealed (in part): 2012 c.17 s.1
Sch.7 para.26, repealed (in part): 2012 c.17 Sch.3 para.22

28. Legal Deposit Libraries Act 2003
applied: 2012 asp 3 s.8
s.1, applied: 2012 asp 3 s.5
s.5, applied: 2012 asp 3 s.5
s.7, applied: 2012 asp 3 s.3, s.4
s.12, amended: 2012 asp 3 Sch.2 para.7
s.14, amended: 2012 asp 3 Sch.2 para.7
s.14, repealed (in part): 2012 asp 3 Sch.2 para.7
s.15, repealed (in part): 2012 asp 3 Sch.3

32. Crime (International Co-operation) Act 2003
s.3, applied: SI 2012/1726 r.4.4, r.32.1
s.4, applied: SI 2012/1726 r.4.4, r.32.2

2003– cont.

32. Crime (International Co-operation) Act 2003– cont.

s.4A, applied: SI 2012/ 1726 r.4.4
s.4B, applied: SI 2012/ 1726 r.4.4
s.7, applied: SI 2012/ 1726 r.32.3
s.7, enabling: SI 2012/ 146
s.8, applied: SI 2012/ 1726 r.32.3
s.13, see *JP Morgan Chase Bank National Association v Director of the Serious Fraud Office* [2012] EWHC 1674 (Admin), [2012] Lloyd's Rep. F.C. 655 (QBD (Admin)), Gross, L.J.
s.15, see *JP Morgan Chase Bank National Association v Director of the Serious Fraud Office* [2012] EWHC 1674 (Admin), [2012] Lloyd's Rep. F.C. 655 (QBD (Admin)), Gross, L.J.
s.15, applied: SI 2012/ 1726 r.32.4, r.32.5
s.21, applied: SI 2012/ 1726 r.32.10
s.30, applied: SI 2012/ 1726 r.32.6, r.32.7
s.31, applied: SI 2012/ 1726 r.32.6, r.32.8
s.56, applied: SI 2012/ 1726 r.55.5
s.56, disapplied: SI 2012/ 1726 r.55.5
s.57, applied: SI 2012/ 1726 r.55.5
s.57, disapplied: SI 2012/ 1726 r.55.5
s.59, applied: SI 2012/ 1726 r.55.5
s.60, applied: SI 2012/ 1726 r.55.5
s.63, applied: SI 2012/ 1726 r.55.5
s.73, applied: SI 2012/ 1726 r.56.1
Sch.1, applied: SI 2012/ 1726 r.32.4, r.32.5
Sch.1 para.6, applied: SI 2012/ 1726 r.32.5
Sch.2 Part 1, applied: SI 2012/ 1726 r.32.6, r.32.7
Sch.2 Part 2, applied: SI 2012/ 1726 r.32.6, r.32.8
Sch.3 Part 1 para.3, amended: 2012 c.10 Sch.27 para.10
Sch.4, referred to: SI 2012/ 1726 r.56.1

33. Waste and Emissions Trading Act 2003

s.11, enabling: SI 2012/ 65
s.12, enabling: SI 2012/ 65
s.24, enabling: SI 2012/ 65
s.26, enabling: SI 2012/ 65

35. European Union (Accessions) Act 2003

s.2, amended: SI 2012/ 1809 Sch.1 Part 1

37. Water Act 2003

Commencement Orders: SI 2012/ 264 Art.2; SI 2012/ 284 Art.2
applied: SI 2012/ 1128 Art.4
referred to: 2012 c.13 Sch.1, 2012 c.19 Sch.6 para.4
s.105, enabling: SI 2012/ 264, SI 2012/ 284

38. Anti-social Behaviour Act 2003

see *Byrne v Poplar Housing and Regeneration Community Association Ltd* [2012] EWCA Civ 832, [2012] H.L.R. 33 (CA (Civ Div)), Etherton, L.J.
s.87, repealed: 2012 c.10 Sch.23 para.15

39. Courts Act 2003

applied: SI 2012/ 1726 r.2.1, r.6.1
referred to: SI 2012/ 1726 r.52.1
s.2, applied: SI 2012/ 2401 Art.3
s.3, applied: SI 2012/ 1726 r.37.13
s.4, applied: SI 2012/ 1206 Art.2
s.4, repealed: SI 2012/ 1206 Sch.1 para.4
s.5, repealed: SI 2012/ 1206 Sch.1 para.5
s.8, applied: SI 2012/ 1277, SI 2012/ 1555, SI 2012/ 3128
s.8, repealed (in part): SI 2012/ 1206 Sch.1 para.6
s.8, enabling: SI 2012/ 1277, SI 2012/ 1555, SI 2012/ 3128
s.9, referred to: SI 2012/ 1726 r.63.10

2003– cont.

39. Courts Act 2003– cont.

s.20, amended: SI 2012/ 2398 Sch.2 para.5
s.20, repealed (in part): SI 2012/ 2398 Sch.2 para.5
s.28, amended: SI 2012/ 2398 Sch.2 para.6
s.28, referred to: SI 2012/ 1726 r.9.4, r.19.3
s.28, repealed (in part): SI 2012/ 2398 Sch.2 para.6
s.29, referred to: SI 2012/ 1726 r.9.4, r.19.3
s.58, applied: SI 2012/ 2401 Art.2
s.58, repealed: SI 2012/ 2401 Sch.1 para.13
s.59, repealed: SI 2012/ 2401 Sch.1 para.13
s.60, repealed: SI 2012/ 2401 Sch.1 para.13
s.61, repealed: SI 2012/ 2401 Sch.1 para.13
s.61A, repealed: SI 2012/ 2401 Sch.1 para.13
s.66, see *R. (on the application of W) v Leeds Crown Court* [2011] EWHC 2326 (Admin), [2012] 1 W.L.R. 2786 (DC), Sir Anthony May (President, QB)
s.69, applied: SI 2012/ 1726, SI 2012/ 3089
s.69, enabling: SI 2012/ 3089
s.72, applied: SI 2012/ 1726, SI 2012/ 3089
s.75, enabling: SI 2012/ 679, SI 2012/ 1462, SI 2012/ 2046, SI 2012/ 2806, SI 2012/ 3061
s.76, enabling: SI 2012/ 679, SI 2012/ 2046, SI 2012/ 2806, SI 2012/ 3061
s.79, applied: SI 2012/ 679, SI 2012/ 2046, SI 2012/ 3061
s.107, repealed (in part): SI 2012/ 2398 Sch.2 para.7
s.108, enabling: SI 2012/ 1277, SI 2012/ 1555, SI 2012/ 3128
Sch.1 para.1, repealed: SI 2012/ 1206 Sch.1 para.7
Sch.1 para.2, repealed: SI 2012/ 1206 Sch.1 para.7
Sch.1 para.3, repealed: SI 2012/ 1206 Sch.1 para.7
Sch.1 para.4, repealed: SI 2012/ 1206 Sch.1 para.7
Sch.1 para.5, repealed: SI 2012/ 1206 Sch.1 para.7
Sch.1 para.6, repealed: SI 2012/ 1206 Sch.1 para.7
Sch.1 para.7, repealed: SI 2012/ 1206 Sch.1 para.7
Sch.1 para.8, repealed: SI 2012/ 1206 Sch.1 para.7
Sch.1 para.9, repealed: SI 2012/ 1206 Sch.1 para.7
Sch.3A para.1, repealed: SI 2012/ 2401 Sch.1 para.14
Sch.3A para.2, repealed: SI 2012/ 2401 Sch.1 para.14
Sch.3A para.3, repealed: SI 2012/ 2401 Sch.1 para.14
Sch.3A para.4, repealed: SI 2012/ 2401 Sch.1 para.14
Sch.3A para.5, repealed: SI 2012/ 2401 Sch.1 para.14
Sch.3A para.6, repealed: SI 2012/ 2401 Sch.1 para.14
Sch.5, applied: SI 2012/ 1726 r.52.4, r.76.1
Sch.5, referred to: SI 2012/ 1726 r.52.1
Sch.5 Part 3 para.7, amended: 2012 c.10 s.88
Sch.5 Part 4 para.12, applied: SI 2012/ 1726 r.52.4
Sch.5 Part 4 para.12, referred to: SI 2012/ 1726 r.52.2
Sch.5 Pt 4 para.12, see *James v RSPCA* [2011] EWHC 1642 (Admin), [2012] 5 Costs L.O. 547 (QBD (Admin)), Keith, J.
Sch.5 Part 4 para.13, referred to: SI 2012/ 1726 r.52.2
Sch.5 Part 6 para.22, applied: SI 2012/ 1726 r.52.4
Sch.5 Part 6 para.23, referred to: SI 2012/ 1726 r.52.4
Sch.5 Part 8 para.31, applied: SI 2012/ 1726 r.52.4
Sch.5 Part 8 para.32, referred to: SI 2012/ 1726 r.52.4
Sch.5 Part 9 para.37, amended: 2012 c.10 s.88
Sch.5 Part 9 para.37, applied: SI 2012/ 1726 r.52.4
Sch.5 Part 9 para.37, referred to: SI 2012/ 1726 r.52.4
Sch.5 Part 9 para.37A, added: 2012 c.10 s.88
Sch.5 Part 9 para.38, amended: 2012 c.10 s.88
Sch.5 Part 9 para.39, amended: 2012 c.10 s.88

2003– cont.

39. Courts Act 2003–*cont.*

Sch.5 Part 9 para.40, amended: 2012 c.10 s.88

Sch.5 Part 9 para.40A, added: 2012 c.10 s.88

Sch.5 Part 9 para.40B, added: 2012 c.10 s.88

Sch.5 Part 9 para.40C, added: 2012 c.10 s.88

Sch.8 para.135, repealed: 2012 c.10 Sch.12 para.48

Sch.8 para.245, repealed (in part): SI 2012/2398 Sch.2 para.8

Sch.9 para.14, repealed: SI 2012/2401 Sch.1 para.15

41. Extradition Act 2003

see *Assange v Sweden* [2012] UKSC 22, [2012] 2 A.C. 471 (SC), Lord Phillips, J.S.C. (President); see *Pomiechowski v Poland* [2012] UKSC 20, [2012] 1 W.L.R. 1604 (SC), Lord Phillips, J.S.C. (President); see *R. (on the application of HH) v Westminster City Magistrates' Court* [2012] UKSC 25, [2012] 3 W.L.R. 90 (SC), Lord Hope, J.S.C.

s.2, see *Assange v Sweden* [2012] UKSC 22, [2012] 2 A.C. 471 (SC), Lord Phillips, J.S.C. (President); see *Balint v Czech Republic* [2011] EWHC 498 (Admin), [2012] 1 W.L.R. 244 (QBD (Admin)), Jackson, L.J.; see *Kane v Spain* [2011] EWHC 824 (Admin), [2012] 1 W.L.R. 375 (QBD (Admin)), Collins, J.; see *Zakrzewski v Poland* [2012] EWHC 173 (Admin), [2012] 1 W.L.R. 2248 (QBD (Admin)), Lloyd Jones, J.

s.9, see *HM Advocate v Havrilova* 2012 S.C.C.R. 361 (HCJ), Lord Clarke

s.10, see *R. (on the application of Griffin) v City of Westminster Magistrates' Court* [2011] EWHC 943 (Admin), [2012] 1 W.L.R. 270 (QBD (Admin)), Collins, J.

s.14, see *Lord Advocate v K* 2012 S.C.L. 230 (HCJ), The Lord Justice Clerk (Gill); see *Wlodarczyk (Wlodzimierz) v Lord Advocate* [2012] HCJAC 41, 2012 S.C.L. 771 (HCJ), The Lord Justice General (Hamilton)

s.21, see *R. (on the application of HH) v Westminster City Magistrates' Court* [2012] UKSC 25, [2012] 3 W.L.R. 90 (SC), Lord Hope, J.S.C.; see *Wlodarczyk (Wlodzimierz) v Lord Advocate* [2012] HCJAC 41, 2012 S.C.L. 771 (HCJ), The Lord Justice General (Hamilton)

s.25, see *Maziarski (Maciej) v Lord Advocate* [2012] HCJAC 33, 2012 S.L.T. 553 (HCJ), The Lord Justice General (Hamilton); see *R. (on the application of Griffin) v City of Westminster Magistrates' Court* [2011] EWHC 943 (Admin), [2012] 1 W.L.R. 270 (QBD (Admin)), Collins, J.; see *Wlodarczyk (Wlodzimierz) v Lord Advocate* [2012] HCJAC 41, 2012 S.C.L. 771 (HCJ), The Lord Justice General (Hamilton)

s.26, see *Barker v Hambleton DC* [2012] EWCA Civ 610, [2012] C.P. Rep. 36 (CA (Civ Div)), Maurice Kay, L.J.; see *Kane v Spain* [2011] EWHC 824 (Admin), [2012] 1 W.L.R. 375 (QBD (Admin)), Collins, J.; see *Pomiechowski v Poland* [2011] EWHC 2060 (Admin), [2012] 1 W.L.R. 391 (DC), Laws, L.J.; see *Pomiechowski v Poland* [2012] UKSC 20, [2012] 1 W.L.R. 1604 (SC), Lord Phillips, J.S.C. (President)

s.28, see *Lord Advocate v K* 2012 S.C.L. 230 (HCJ), The Lord Justice Clerk (Gill); see *Poland v Walerianczyk* [2010] EWHC 2149 (Admin), [2012] 1 W.L.R. 363 (DC), Stanley Burnton, L.J.; see *Pomiechowski v Poland* [2012] UKSC 20, [2012] 1 W.L.R. 1604 (SC), Lord Phillips, J.S.C. (President)

2003–cont.

41. Extradition Act 2003–*cont.*

s.36, see *Assange v Sweden (Application to Re-Open Appeal)* [2012] 3 W.L.R. 1 (SC), Lord Phillips, J.S.C.

s.45, amended: 2012 c.10 Sch.5 para.63

s.59, amended: 2012 c.10 Sch.10 para.11, Sch.16 para.10

s.59, repealed (in part): 2012 c.10 Sch.16 para.10

s.61, amended: 2012 c.10 Sch.7 para.13

s.62, repealed (in part): 2012 c.10 Sch.7 para.14

s.62A, added: 2012 c.10 Sch.7 para.15

s.62B, added: 2012 c.10 Sch.7 para.15

s.64, see *Balint v Czech Republic* [2011] EWHC 498 (Admin), [2012] 1 W.L.R. 244 (QBD (Admin)), Jackson, L.J.

s.65, see *Sobczak (Poitr) v HM Advocate* 2012 S.C.L. 178 (HCJ), Lord Carloway; see *Zakrzewski v Poland* [2012] EWHC 173 (Admin), [2012] 1 W.L.R. 2248 (QBD (Admin)), Lloyd Jones, J.

s.80, see *Zdinjak v Croatia* [2012] EWHC 1554 (Admin), [2012] A.C.D. 95 (DC), Laws, L.J.

s.81, see *Zdinjak v Croatia* [2012] EWHC 1554 (Admin), [2012] A.C.D. 95 (DC), Laws, L.J.

s.82, see *Zdinjak v Croatia* [2012] EWHC 1554 (Admin), [2012] A.C.D. 95 (DC), Laws, L.J.

s.101, varied: 2012 c.11 s.12

s.103, see *H v Lord Advocate* [2012] UKSC 24, [2012] 3 W.L.R. 151 (SC), Lord Hope (Deputy President); see *Pomiechowski v Poland* [2012] UKSC 20, [2012] 1 W.L.R. 1604 (SC), Lord Phillips, J.S.C. (President)

s.105, see *Pomiechowski v Poland* [2012] UKSC 20, [2012] 1 W.L.R. 1604 (SC), Lord Phillips, J.S.C. (President)

s.108, see *Pomiechowski v Poland* [2012] UKSC 20, [2012] 1 W.L.R. 1604 (SC), Lord Phillips, J.S.C. (President)

s.110, see *Pomiechowski v Poland* [2012] UKSC 20, [2012] 1 W.L.R. 1604 (SC), Lord Phillips, J.S.C. (President)

s.116, see *H v Lord Advocate* [2012] UKSC 24, [2012] 3 W.L.R. 151 (SC), Lord Hope (Deputy President)

s.127, amended: 2012 c.10 Sch.5 para.64

s.132, amended: 2012 c.10 Sch.10 para.11, Sch.16 para.11

s.132, repealed (in part): 2012 c.10 Sch.16 para.11

s.134, amended: 2012 c.10 Sch.7 para.16

s.135, repealed (in part): 2012 c.10 Sch.7 para.17

s.135A, added: 2012 c.10 Sch.7 para.18

s.135B, added: 2012 c.10 Sch.7 para.18

s.138, see *United Arab Emirates v Allen* [2012] EWHC 1712 (Admin), [2012] 1 W.L.R. 3419 (QBD (Admin)), Toulson, L.J.

s.153B, amended: 2012 c.10 Sch.10 para.11, Sch.16 para.12

s.153B, repealed (in part): 2012 c.10 Sch.16 para.12

s.177, applied: 2012 c.10 s.153

s.178, applied: 2012 c.10 s.153

s.182, repealed: 2012 c.10 Sch.5 Part 2

s.191, see *Lord Advocate v K* 2012 S.C.L. 230 (HCJ), The Lord Justice Clerk (Gill)

s.200, repealed (in part): 2012 c.10 Sch.11 para.35

s.201, repealed: 2012 c.10 Sch.12 para.49

s.210, enabling: SSI 2012/125

s.216, repealed (in part): 2012 c.10 Sch.10 para.11

s.222, applied: 2012 c.10 s.153

s.223, amended: 2012 c.10 Sch.7 para.19

2003– cont.

42. Sexual Offences Act 2003
see *R. (on the application of E) v DPP* [2011] EWHC 1465 (Admin), [2012] 1 Cr. App. R. 6 (DC), Munby, L.J.; see *R. v P (Kenneth John)* [2011] EWCA Crim 2496, [2012] 1 Cr. App. R. (S.) 113 (CA (Crim Div)), Lord Judge, L.C.J.; see *R. v Shields (David)* [2011] EWCA Crim 2343, [2012] 1 Cr. App. R. 9 (CA (Crim Div)), Rix, L.J.; see *Young v Brown* [2012] HCJAC 24, 2012 S.L.T. 581 (HCJ), The Lord Justice Clerk (Gill)
applied: 2012 c.10 Sch.1 para.39
Part 1, applied: SI 2012/1909 Reg.33, Reg.86
s.2, see *R. v Nicholson (Gavin)* [2012] EWCA Crim 1568, [2012] 2 Cr. App. R. 31 (CA (Crim Div)), Pitchford, L.J.
s.42, amended: 2012 c.7 Sch.5 para.117
s.42, repealed (in part): 2012 c.7 Sch.5 para.117
s.57, substituted: 2012 c.9 s.109
s.58, substituted: 2012 c.9 s.109
s.59, substituted: 2012 c.9 s.109
s.60, amended: 2012 c.9 s.109
s.60, repealed (in part): 2012 c.9 s.109, Sch.10 Part 9
s.60A, amended: 2012 c.9 Sch.9 para.140
s.60B, amended: 2012 c.9 Sch.9 para.140
s.67, see *R. v B* [2012] EWCA Crim 770, [2012] 3 All E.R. 1093 (CA (Crim Div)), Aikens, L.J.
s.71, applied: 2012 c.9 s.92, s.101
s.75, see *R. v Ciccarelli (Yuri)* [2011] EWCA Crim 2665, [2012] 1 Cr. App. R. 15 (CA (Crim Div)), Lord Judge, L.C.J.
s.82, see *R. (on the application of Minter) v Chief Constable of Hampshire* [2011] EWHC 1610 (Admin), [2012] 1 W.L.R. 1157 (DC), Richards, L.J.; see *R. v B* [2012] EWCA Crim 770, [2012] 3 All E.R. 1093 (CA (Crim Div)), Aikens, L.J.
s.82, referred to: SI 2012/1883
s.83, applied: SI 2012/1876 Reg.10, Reg.11, Reg.12, Reg.14, Reg.15
s.83, enabling: SI 2012/1876
s.84, applied: SI 2012/1876 Reg.11, Reg.13, Reg.15
s.84, enabling: SI 2012/1876
s.85, see *R. (on the application of Minter) v Chief Constable of Hampshire* [2011] EWHC 1610 (Admin), [2012] 1 W.L.R. 1157 (DC), Richards, L.J.
s.85, applied: SI 2012/1876 Reg.9
s.85, enabling: SI 2012/1876
s.86, enabling: SI 2012/1876
s.87, enabling: SSI 2012/50
s.91A, added: SI 2012/1883 Art.3
s.91B, added: SI 2012/1883 Art.3
s.91C, added: SI 2012/1883 Art.3
s.91D, added: SI 2012/1883 Art.3
s.91E, added: SI 2012/1883 Art.3
s.91F, added: SI 2012/1883 Art.3
s.94, amended: SI 2012/2007 Sch.1 para.68
s.94, repealed (in part): SI 2012/2007 Sch.1 para.68
s.95, amended: SI 2012/2007 Sch.1 para.69
s.95, repealed (in part): SI 2012/2007 Sch.1 para.69
s.104, applied: SI 2012/1726 r.50.1
s.113, see *R. v Shields (David)* [2011] EWCA Crim 2343, [2012] 1 Cr. App. R. 9 (CA (Crim Div)), Rix, L.J.
s.123, see *Commissioner of Police of the Metropolis v Ebanks* [2012] EWHC 2368 (Admin), (2012) 176 J.P. 751 (DC), Aikens, L.J.
s.131, amended: 2012 c.10 Sch.21 para.19, Sch.22 para.20
s.133, repealed (in part): 2012 c.10 Sch.24 para.25

2003– cont.

42. Sexual Offences Act 2003– *cont.*
s.138, applied: SI 2012/1876
s.138, enabling: SI 2012/1876
Sch.3, see *R. v B* [2012] EWCA Crim 770, [2012] 3 All E.R. 1093 (CA (Crim Div)), Aikens, L.J.
Sch.3, referred to: SI 2012/2601 Art.3
Sch.3 para.40, see *Thompson v Dunn* [2012] HCJAC 27, 2012 S.L.T. 577 (HCJ), The Lord Justice Clerk (Gill); see *Young v Brown* [2012] HCJAC 24, 2012 S.L.T. 581 (HCJ), The Lord Justice Clerk (Gill)
Sch.3 para.60, see *Akdeniz v Cameron* [2012] HCJAC 26, 2012 S.L.T. 585 (HCJ), The Lord Justice Clerk (Gill); see *Halcrow v Shanks* [2012] HCJAC 23, 2012 S.L.T. 579 (HCJ), The Lord Justice Clerk (Gill); see *Hay (Ian Morris) v HM Advocate* [2012] HCJAC 28, 2012 S.L.T. 569 (HCJ), The Lord Justice Clerk (Gill); see *Heatherall v McGowan* [2012] HCJAC 25, 2012 S.L.T. 583 (HCJ), The Lord Justice Clerk (Gill); see *Thompson v Dunn* [2012] HCJAC 27, 2012 S.L.T. 577 (HCJ), The Lord Justice Clerk (Gill); see *Young v Brown* [2012] HCJAC 24, 2012 S.L.T. 581 (HCJ), The Lord Justice Clerk (Gill)
Sch.5 para.56A, amended: 2012 c.9 Sch.9 para.146
Sch.5 para.57, amended: 2012 c.9 Sch.9 para.146
Sch.5 para.63, amended: 2012 c.9 Sch.9 para.140
Sch.5 para.63A, amended: 2012 c.4 Sch.1 para.5

43. Health and Social Care (Community Health and Standards) Act 2003
s.71, amended: 2012 c.7 Sch.5 para.119
s.71, repealed (in part): 2012 c.7 Sch.5 para.119
s.113, amended: 2012 c.7 Sch.5 para.120
s.115, enabling: SI 2012/3094
s.148, amended: 2012 c.7 Sch.5 para.121, Sch.14 para.90, SI 2012/961 Sch.1 para.6
s.148, repealed (in part): 2012 c.7 Sch.5 para.121, Sch.14 para.90
s.153, enabling: SI 2012/387, SSI 2012/76
s.160, amended: 2012 c.7 Sch.5 para.122, Sch.14 para.91
s.160, repealed (in part): 2012 c.7 Sch.5 para.122
s.162, amended: 2012 c.7 Sch.14 para.92
s.165, amended: 2012 c.7 Sch.5 para.123, Sch.14 para.93
s.165, repealed (in part): 2012 c.7 Sch.5 para.123
s.195, applied: SI 2012/387
s.195, enabling: SI 2012/387, SSI 2012/76
Sch.2 para.5, repealed (in part): 2012 c.7 Sch.13 para.4
Sch.2 para.17, repealed: 2012 c.7 Sch.13 para.3
Sch.2 para.18, repealed: 2012 c.7 Sch.13 para.5
Sch.2 para.19, repealed: 2012 c.7 Sch.13 para.6
Sch.4 para.53, repealed (in part): 2012 c.7 s.39
Sch.4 para.54, repealed: 2012 c.7 s.39
Sch.10 para.4, amended: 2012 c.21 Sch.18 para.99

44. Criminal Justice Act 2003
Commencement Orders: 2012 c.10 s.89, s.118; SI 2012/825 Art.2; SI 2012/1320 Art.2, Art.3, Art.4, Art.5, Art.6; SI 2012/2574 Art.2, Art.3, Art.4, Sch.1; SI 2012/2905 Art.2, Art.3
see *Al-Khawaja v United Kingdom (26766/05)* [2012] 2 Costs L.O. 139 (ECHR (Grand Chamber)), Judge Tulkens (President); see *R. v B* [2012] EWCA Crim 414, [2012] 3 All E.R. 205 (CA (Crim Div)), Lord Judge, L.C.J.; see *R. v Bebbington (Anthony Kynaston)* [2011] EWCA Crim 1206, [2012] 1 Cr. App. R. (S.) 19 (CA (Crim Div)), Moore-Bick, L.J.; see *R. v Beesley (Ricky Liam)* [2011] EWCA Crim 1021,

2003–cont.

44. Criminal Justice Act 2003–*cont.*
see–*cont.*
[2012] 1 Cr. App. R. (S.) 15 (CA (Crim Div)), Thomas, L.J.; see *R. v Brook (Neil)* [2012] EWCA Crim 136, [2012] 2 Cr. App. R. (S.) 76 (CA (Crim Div)), Laws, L.J.; see *R. v Hills (Christopher Carl)* [2008] EWCA Crim 1871, [2012] 1 W.L.R. 2121 (CA (Crim Div)), Latham, L.J.; see *R. v Matthews (Alex Joseph)* [2011] EWCA Crim 3110, [2012] 2 Cr. App. R. (S.) 33 (CA (Crim Div)), Lord Judge, L.C.J.; see *R. v McCloud (Barry Charles)* [2011] EWCA Crim 1516, [2012] 1 Cr. App. R. (S.) 35 (CA (Crim Div)), Pitchford, L.J.; see *R. v Rakib (Mohammed)* [2011] EWCA Crim 870, [2012] 1 Cr. App. R. (S.) 1 (CA (Crim Div)), Elias, L.J.
applied: SI 2012/ 1726 r.9.1, r.22.9, r.41.10, r.29.26
referred to: 2012 c.10 s.77, SI 2012/ 1320 Art.6
Part 9, applied: SI 2012/ 1726 r.74.1
Part 10, applied: SI 2012/ 1726 r.41.11
Part 12, applied: SI 2012/ 1726 r.33.1
Part 12 c.6, applied: SI 2012/ 206 Sch.1 para.21
Pt 10. see *R. v Austin (Alan Brian)* [2011] EWCA Crim 345, [2012] 1 Cr. App. R. 24 (CA (Crim Div)), Thomas, L.J.
Pt 12 s.228, see *R. v X* [2012] EWCA Crim 1610, (2012) 176 J.P. 601 (CA (Crim Div)), Sir John Thomas (President)
s.16, applied: SI 2012/ 1726 r.19.8
s.22, amended: 2012 c.10 s.133, s.134
s.22, applied: SI 2012/ 1726 r.19.8
s.23, amended: 2012 c.10 s.133
s.23A, amended: 2012 c.10 s.133
s.23B, amended: 2012 c.10 s.133
s.25, amended: 2012 c.10 s.133
s.28, applied: SI 2012/ 1726 r.37.14
s.29, applied: SI 2012/ 1726 r.7.1, r.37.8, r.2.4
s.30, applied: SI 2012/ 1726 r.7.1, r.7.2, r.7.4
s.43, repealed: 2012 c.9 Sch.10 Part 10
s.44, applied: SI 2012/ 1726 r.15.1
s.45, amended: 2012 c.9 Sch.9 para.148, Sch.10 Part 10
s.45, referred to: SI 2012/ 1726 r.15.1
s.45, repealed (in part): 2012 c.9 Sch.10 Part 10
s.46, amended: 2012 c.9 Sch.10 Part 10
s.47, applied: SI 2012/ 1726 r.74.1, r.66.1, r.66.4
s.48, amended: 2012 c.9 Sch.10 Part 10
s.49, applied: SI 2012/ 1726 r.65.1, r.66.6
s.51, applied: SI 2012/ 1726 r.29.1, r.37.4, r.29.26
s.51, referred to: SI 2012/ 1726 r.29.4, r.29.24
s.52, applied: SI 2012/ 1726 r.29.1
s.52, referred to: SI 2012/ 1726 r.29.4, r.29.25
s.57, applied: SI 2012/ 1726 r.67.1, r.67.4, r.67.5
s.58, see *R. v Mian (Yousaf)* [2012] EWCA Crim 792, [2012] 3 All E.R. 661 (CA (Crim Div)), Rix, L.J.
s.58, applied: SI 2012/ 1726 r.67.1, r.67.2
s.59, see *R. v Mian (Yousaf)* [2012] EWCA Crim 792, [2012] 3 All E.R. 661 (CA (Crim Div)), Rix, L.J.
s.59, applied: SI 2012/ 1726 r.67.1, r.67.6
s.60, applied: SI 2012/ 1726 r.67.1
s.61, applied: SI 2012/ 1726 r.67.1
s.71, amended: 2012 c.10 Sch.5 para.65
s.71, applied: SI 2012/ 1726 r.16.1
s.73, applied: SI 2012/ 1726 r.67.9
s.76, see *R. v B* [2012] EWCA Crim 414, [2012] 3 All E.R. 205 (CA (Crim Div)), Lord Judge, L.C.J.
s.76, amended: SI 2012/ 1809 Sch.1 Part 1

2003–cont.

44. Criminal Justice Act 2003–*cont.*
s.76, applied: SI 2012/ 1726 r.74.1, r.41.2, r.41.3, r.41.4, r.41.8, r.41.9, r.41.10, r.41.11, r.41.13, r.41.16
s.77, applied: SI 2012/ 1726 r.14.1, r.41.13, r.41.14, r.41.15
s.78, see *R. v B* [2012] EWCA Crim 414, [2012] 3 All E.R. 205 (CA (Crim Div)), Lord Judge, L.C.J.
s.79, see *R. v B* [2012] EWCA Crim 414, [2012] 3 All E.R. 205 (CA (Crim Div)), Lord Judge, L.C.J.
s.80, applied: SI 2012/ 1726 r.41.3, r.41.4, r.41.10, r.41.11
s.82, applied: SI 2012/ 1726 r.41.8, r.16.1, r.41.9
s.88, applied: SI 2012/ 1726 r.41.5
s.89, applied: SI 2012/ 1726 r.41.5, r.41.6
s.90, varied: SI 2012/ 1726 r.41.7
s.98, applied: SI 2012/ 1726 r.35.1
s.100, applied: SI 2012/ 1726 r.35.1
s.101, see *R. v Gillespie (Peter Hugh)* [2011] EWCA Crim 3152, [2012] 2 Cr. App. R. (S.) 24 (CA (Crim Div)), Elias, L.J.; see *R. v L* [2012] EWCA Crim 316, (2012) 176 J.P. 231 (CA (Crim Div)), Hughes, L.J.; see *R. v Phillips (Paul Edward)* [2011] EWCA Crim 2935, [2012] 1 Cr. App. R. 25 (CA (Crim Div)), Pitchford, L.J.; see *R. v Suleman (Omar Mohammed)* [2012] EWCA Crim 1569, [2012] 2 Cr. App. R. 30 (CA (Crim Div)), Pitchford, L.J.
s.101, applied: SI 2012/ 1726 r.35.1
s.102, see *R. v L* [2012] EWCA Crim 316, (2012) 176 J.P. 231 (CA (Crim Div)), Hughes, L.J.
s.102, applied: SI 2012/ 1726 r.35.1
s.103, applied: SI 2012/ 1726 r.35.1
s.104, applied: SI 2012/ 1726 r.35.1
s.105, applied: SI 2012/ 1726 r.35.1
s.106, applied: SI 2012/ 1726 r.35.1
s.107, applied: SI 2012/ 1726 r.35.5
s.110, applied: SI 2012/ 1726 r.35.5
s.111, applied: SI 2012/ 1726 r.35.4
s.114, see *R. (on the application of Bonhoeffer) v General Medical Council* [2011] EWHC 1585 (Admin), [2012] I.R.L.R. 37 (DC), Laws, L.J.; see *R. v Turner (Simon Paul)* [2012] EWCA Crim 1786, (2012) 176 J.P. 640 (CA (Crim Div)), Lord Judge, L.C.J.
s.114, applied: SI 2012/ 1726 r.34.1, r.34.2
s.115, applied: SI 2012/ 1726 r.34.1
s.116, see *R. (on the application of Bonhoeffer) v General Medical Council* [2011] EWHC 1585 (Admin), [2012] I.R.L.R. 37 (DC), Laws, L.J.; see *R. v Ibrahim (Dahir)* [2012] EWCA Crim 837, [2012] 4 All E.R. 225 (CA (Crim Div)), Aikens, L.J.; see *R. v Rowley (William)* [2012] EWCA Crim 1434, (2012) 176 J.P. 505 (CA (Crim Div)), Moore-Bick, L.J.
s.116, applied: SI 2012/ 1726 r.29.19, r.34.2
s.117, applied: SI 2012/ 1726 r.34.2, r.35.2
s.118, applied: SI 2012/ 1726 r.34.1, r.35.2, r.34.2
s.119, applied: SI 2012/ 1726 r.34.2
s.120, see *R. v Chinn (Michael)* [2012] EWCA Crim 501, [2012] 1 W.L.R. 3401 (CA (Crim Div)), Aikens, L.J.
s.120, applied: SI 2012/ 1726 r.34.2
s.121, applied: SI 2012/ 1726 r.34.2
s.125, see *R. v Ibrahim (Dahir)* [2012] EWCA Crim 837, [2012] 4 All E.R. 225 (CA (Crim Div)), Aikens, L.J.
s.127, applied: SI 2012/ 1726 r.34.2, r.33.2
s.132, applied: SI 2012/ 1726 r.34.2, r.34.4, r.3.5
s.132, enabling: SI 2012/ 1726
s.133, applied: SI 2012/ 1726 r.27.4
s.134, applied: SI 2012/ 1726 r.27.4
s.139, applied: SI 2012/ 1726 r.37.4

2003– cont.

44. Criminal Justice Act 2003– *cont.*

s.142, see *R. v Rakib (Mohammed)* [2011] EWCA Crim 870, [2012] 1 Cr. App. R. (S.) 1 (CA (Crim Div)), Elias, L.J.

s.142, amended: 2012 c.10 Sch.19 para.9, Sch.26 para.16

s.142A, amended: 2012 c.10 Sch.26 para.17

s.143, see *R. v Barrass (John Morris)* [2011] EWCA Crim 2629, [2012] 1 Cr. App. R. (S.) 80 (CA (Crim Div)), Rix, L.J.; see *R. v Bebbington (Anthony Kynaston)* [2011] EWCA Crim 1206, [2012] 1 Cr. App. R. (S.) 19 (CA (Crim Div)), Moore-Bick, L.J.; see *R. v Levesconte (Darren James)* [2011] EWCA Crim 2754, [2012] 2 Cr. App. R. (S.) 19 (CA (Crim Div)), Elias, L.J.; see *R. v Mitchell (Billy Richard)* [2011] EWCA Crim 1652, [2012] 1 Cr. App. R. (S.) 68 (CA (Crim Div)), Hooper, L.J.; see *R. v Simpson (Patrick)* [2011] EWCA Crim 1141, [2012] 1 Cr. App. R. (S.) 9 (CA (Crim Div)), Leveson, L.J.

s.143, applied: SI 2012/ 1726 r.37.10

s.144, see *Attorney General's Reference (Nos 41, 42, 43, 44 and 45 of 2011), Re* [2011] EWCA Crim 2174, [2012] 1 Cr. App. R. (S.) 97 (CA (Crim Div)), Pitchford, L.J.

s.144, amended: 2012 c.10 Sch.26 para.18

s.146, amended: 2012 c.10 s.65

s.150, amended: 2012 c.10 Sch.19 para.10, Sch.26 para.19

s.152, amended: 2012 c.10 Sch.19 para.11, Sch.26 para.20

s.153, see *R. v Pinnell (Paul Leslie)* [2010] EWCA Crim 2848, [2012] 1 W.L.R. 17 (CA (Crim Div)), Hughes, L.J.

s.153, amended: 2012 c.10 Sch.19 para.12, Sch.21 para.21, Sch.26 para.21

s.154, applied: 2012 c.5 s.129, s.132, 2012 c.10 Sch.6 para.2, 2012 c.14 Sch.24 para.37, SI 2012/323 Reg.6, SI 2012/810 Art.14, SI 2012/1243 Art.18

s.154, referred to: 2012 c.10 s.33, s.143, SI 2012/444 Reg.12, SI 2012/2031 Reg.6

s.156, amended: 2012 c.10 Sch.19 para.13, Sch.21 para.22

s.156, applied: SI 2012/ 1726 r.37.10

s.157, amended: 2012 c.7 s.38

s.158, applied: SI 2012/ 1726 r.37.10

s.159, applied: SI 2012/ 1726 r.37.10

s.161A, applied: SI 2012/ 1696 Art.3, Art.4, Art.5, Art.6

s.161A, disapplied: SI 2012/ 1696 Art.2

s.161A, enabling: SI 2012/ 1696

s.161B, enabling: SI 2012/ 1696

s.162, applied: SI 2012/ 1726 r.37.10

s.163, amended: 2012 c.10 Sch.19 para.14

s.164, applied: SI 2012/ 1726 r.37.10

s.172, applied: SI 2012/ 1726 r.37.10

s.174, applied: SI 2012/ 1726 r.37.10, r.5.4, SI 2012/ 3089

s.174, substituted: 2012 c.10 s.64

s.174, enabling: SI 2012/ 3089

s.177, amended: 2012 c.10 s.66, s.72, s.76

s.177, applied: SI 2012/ 1696 Sch.1

s.177, referred to: SI 2012/ 206 Sch.1 para.21

s.177, repealed (in part): 2012 c.10 s.70

s.181, repealed: 2012 c.10 s.89

s.181, substituted: 2012 c.10 Sch.9 para.3

s.182, repealed: 2012 c.10 s.89

s.182, substituted: 2012 c.10 Sch.9 para.3

s.183, repealed: 2012 c.10 s.89

s.183, substituted: 2012 c.10 Sch.9 para.3

2003– cont.

44. Criminal Justice Act 2003– *cont.*

s.184, repealed: 2012 c.10 s.89

s.184, substituted: 2012 c.10 Sch.9 para.3

s.185, repealed: 2012 c.10 s.89

s.185, substituted: 2012 c.10 Sch.9 para.3

s.186, repealed: 2012 c.10 s.89

s.186, substituted: 2012 c.10 Sch.9 para.3

s.187, repealed: 2012 c.10 s.89

s.187, substituted: 2012 c.10 Sch.9 para.3

s.188, repealed: 2012 c.10 s.89

s.188, substituted: 2012 c.10 Sch.9 para.3

s.189, amended: 2012 c.10 s.68, Sch.9 para.20

s.189, applied: SI 2012/ 1696 Sch.1

s.189, referred to: SI 2012/ 206 Sch.1 para.21

s.189, substituted: 2012 c.10 Sch.9 para.3

s.190, amended: 2012 c.10 s.72, s.76, Sch.9 para.4

s.190, repealed (in part): 2012 c.10 s.70

s.190, substituted: 2012 c.10 Sch.9 para.3

s.191, amended: 2012 c.10 Sch.9 para.5

s.191, substituted: 2012 c.10 Sch.9 para.3

s.192, substituted: 2012 c.10 Sch.9 para.3

s.193, substituted: 2012 c.10 Sch.9 para.3

s.194, substituted: 2012 c.10 Sch.9 para.3

s.195, amended: 2012 c.10 Sch.9 para.6, Sch.10 para.13

s.195, substituted: 2012 c.10 Sch.9 para.3

s.196, amended: 2012 c.10 Sch.9 para.7, Sch.10 para.14

s.196, repealed (in part): 2012 c.10 Sch.10 para.14

s.197, amended: 2012 c.10 Sch.10 para.15

s.200, amended: 2012 c.10 Sch.9 para.8

s.202, amended: 2012 c.10 s.70, Sch.10 para.16

s.202, repealed (in part): 2012 c.10 s.70

s.204, see *R. v A* [2011] EWCA Crim 2747, (2012) 176 J.P. 1 (CA (Crim Div)), Gross, L.J.

s.204, amended: 2012 c.10 s.71

s.204, repealed (in part): 2012 c.10 Sch.10 para.17

s.206A, added: 2012 c.10 s.72

s.207, amended: 2012 c.7 s.213, 2012 c.10 s.73

s.207, repealed (in part): 2012 c.10 s.73

s.209, referred to: SI 2012/ 206 Sch.1 para.21

s.209, repealed (in part): 2012 c.10 s.74

s.211, amended: 2012 c.10 s.74

s.211, repealed (in part): 2012 c.10 s.74

s.212, referred to: SI 2012/ 206 Sch.1 para.21

s.212, repealed (in part): 2012 c.10 s.75

s.212A, added: 2012 c.10 s.76

s.212A, applied: 2012 c.10 s.77

s.213, amended: 2012 c.10 Sch.9 para.9

s.213, repealed (in part): 2012 c.10 Sch.10 para.18

s.215, amended: 2012 c.10 s.76

s.216, repealed (in part): 2012 c.10 Sch.10 para.19

s.222, applied: 2012 c.10 s.77

s.223, amended: 2012 c.10 s.76

s.223, applied: 2012 c.10 s.77

s.223, repealed (in part): 2012 c.10 s.74, s.75

s.224, amended: 2012 c.10 Sch.19 para.15

s.224, amended: 2012 c.10 Sch.19 para.16

s.224A, added: 2012 c.10 s.122

s.224A, amended: 2012 c.10 Sch.19 para.24

s.225, see *R. v Bond (Dale)* [2011] EWCA Crim 1197, [2012] 1 Cr. App. R. (S.) 29 (CA (Crim Div)), Moore-Bick, L.J.; see *R. v Brook (Neil)* [2012] EWCA Crim 136, [2012] 2 Cr. App. R. (S.) 76 (CA (Crim Div)), Laws, L.J.; see *R. v J* [2012] EWCA Crim 132, [2012] 1 W.L.R. 3055 (CA (Crim Div)), Lord Judge, L.C.J.

s.225, amended: 2012 c.10 Sch.19 para.17

2003–cont.

44. Criminal Justice Act 2003–*cont.*

s.225, applied: SI 2012/1696 Sch.1

s.225, see *R. v Bond (Dale)* [2011] EWCA Crim 1197, [2012] 1 Cr. App. R. (S.) 29 (CA (Crim Div)), Moore-Bick, L.J.; see *R. v Brook (Neil)* [2012] EWCA Crim 136, [2012] 2 Cr. App. R. (S.) 76 (CA (Crim Div)), Laws, L.J.; see *R. v J* [2012] EWCA Crim 132, [2012] 1 W.L.R. 3055 (CA (Crim Div)), Lord Judge, L.C.J.

s.225, amended: 2012 c.10 Sch.21 para.23

s.225, repealed (in part): 2012 c.10 s.123

s.226, amended: 2012 c.10 Sch.19 para.17

s.226, repealed (in part): 2012 c.10 s.123

s.226, amended: 2012 c.10 Sch.21 para.24

s.226A, added: 2012 c.10 s.124

s.226A, amended: 2012 c.10 Sch.21 para.36

s.226A, repealed (in part): 2012 c.10 Sch.21 para.36

s.226B, added: 2012 c.10 s.124

s.226B, amended: 2012 c.10 Sch.21 para.36

s.227, see *R. (on the application of Minter) v Chief Constable of Hampshire* [2011] EWHC 1610 (Admin), [2012] 1 W.L.R. 1157 (DC), Richards, L.J.; see *R. v Pinnell (Paul Leslie)* [2010] EWCA Crim 2848, [2012] 1 W.L.R. 17 (CA (Crim Div)), Hughes, L.J.

s.227, repealed: 2012 c.10 s.123

s.228, repealed: 2012 c.10 s.123

s.229, amended: 2012 c.10 Sch.19 para.18

s.230, amended: 2012 c.10 Sch.19 para.18

s.231, amended: 2012 c.10 Sch.19 para.19

s.231, amended: 2012 c.10 Sch.19 para.20, Sch.21 para.25

s.232, amended: 2012 c.10 Sch.19 para.19

s.232, repealed: 2012 c.10 Sch.21 para.26

s.232A, added: 2012 c.10 Sch.19 para.21

s.233, amended: 2012 c.10 Sch.19 para.19

s.234, amended: 2012 c.10 Sch.19 para.19

s.235, amended: 2012 c.10 Sch.19 para.19

s.235, amended: 2012 c.10 Sch.21 para.27, Sch.21 para.28

s.236, amended: 2012 c.10 Sch.19 para.19

s.237, amended: 2012 c.10 s.110, s.117, Sch.14 para 16, Sch.20 para.2, Sch.22 para.21

s.237, varied: 2012 c.10 s.121

s.238, amended: 2012 c.10 Sch.14 para.16, Sch.20 para.3

s.238, varied: 2012 c.10 s.121

s.239, see *R. (on the application of McGetrick) v Parole Board* [2012] EWHC 882 (Admin), [2012] 1 W.L.R. 2488 (QBD (Admin)), Stanley Burnton, L.J.

s.239, amended: 2012 c.10 Sch.14 para.16

s.239, varied: 2012 c.10 s.121

s.240, amended: 2012 c.10 Sch.14 para.16

s.240, applied: 2012 c.10 Sch.15 para.2

s.240, repealed: 2012 c.10 s.108

s.240, varied: 2012 c.10 s.121

s.240A, amended: 2012 c.10 s.109, Sch.14 para.16, Sch.16 para.14

s.240A, applied: 2012 c.10 Sch.15 para.3

s.240A, repealed (in part): 2012 c.10 s.109

s.240A, varied: 2012 c.10 s.121

s.240ZA, added: 2012 c.10 s.108

s.240ZA, amended: 2012 c.10 Sch.14 para.16, Sch.20 para.4

s.240ZA, referred to: 2012 c.10 Sch.15 para.2

s.240ZA, varied: 2012 c.10 s.121

s.241, amended: 2012 c.10 s.110, Sch.10 para.20, Sch.14 para.16

s.241, repealed (in part): 2012 c.10 Sch.10 para.20

s.241, varied: 2012 c.10 s.121

s.242, amended: 2012 c.10 s.110, Sch.12 para.51, Sch.14 para.16

s.242, repealed (in part): 2012 c.10 Sch.12 para.51

s.242, varied: 2012 c.10 s.121

s.243, amended: 2012 c.10 s.110, Sch.14 para.16

s.243, varied: 2012 c.10 s.121

s.243A, added: 2012 c.10 s.111

s.243A, amended: 2012 c.10 Sch.14 para.16

s.243A, varied: 2012 c.10 s.121

s.244, amended: 2012 c.10 s.114, s.117, s.125, Sch.10 para.21, Sch.14 para.6, Sch.14 para.16, Sch.17 para.2

s.244, repealed (in part): 2012 c.10 Sch.10 para.21

s.244, varied: 2012 c.10 s.121

s.245, amended: 2012 c.10 Sch.14 para.16

s.245, repealed: 2012 c.10 Sch.10 para.22

s.245, varied: 2012 c.10 s.121

s.246, amended: 2012 c.10 s.110, s.112, Sch.10 para.23, Sch.14 para.7, Sch.14 para.16, Sch.20 para.5

s.246, repealed (in part): 2012 c.10 Sch.10 para.23

s.246, varied: 2012 c.10 s.121

s.246A, added: 2012 c.10 s.125

s.246A, amended: 2012 c.10 Sch.14 para.16

s.246A, referred to: 2012 c.10 s.128

s.246A, varied: 2012 c.10 s.121

s.247, amended: 2012 c.10 Sch.14 para.16, Sch.17 para.3

s.247, varied: 2012 c.10 s.121

s.248, amended: 2012 c.10 Sch.14 para.16

s.248, repealed (in part): 2012 c.10 s.116

s.248, varied: 2012 c.10 s.121

s.249, amended: 2012 c.10 Sch.10 para.24, Sch.14 para.8, Sch.14 para.16, Sch.17 para.4

s.249, repealed (in part): 2012 c.10 Sch.10 para.24

s.249, varied: 2012 c.10 s.121

s.250, amended: 2012 c.10 s.117, Sch.10 para.25, Sch.14 para.9, Sch.14 para.16, Sch.20 para.6

s.250, repealed (in part): 2012 c.10 Sch.10 para.25

s.250, varied: 2012 c.10 s.121

s.251, amended: 2012 c.10 Sch.14 para.16

s.251, repealed: 2012 c.10 Sch.10 para.26

s.251, varied: 2012 c.10 s.121

s.252, amended: 2012 c.10 Sch.10 para.27, Sch.14 para.16

s.252, repealed (in part): 2012 c.10 Sch.10 para.27

s.252, varied: 2012 c.10 s.121

s.253, amended: 2012 c.10 s.114, Sch.14 para.10, Sch.14 para.16

s.253, repealed (in part): 2012 c.10 Sch.10 para.28

s.253, varied: 2012 c.10 s.121

s.254, amended: 2012 c.10 s.113, Sch.14 para.16

s.254, applied: 2012 c.10 Sch.15 para.5

s.254, varied: 2012 c.10 s.121

s.255, amended: 2012 c.10 s.113, Sch.14 para.16

s.255, varied: 2012 c.10 s.121

s.255A, amended: 2012 c.10 s.114, Sch.14 para.16

s.255A, varied: 2012 c.10 s.121

s.255A, amended: 2012 c.10 Sch.14 para.16, Sch.20 para.7

s.255A, varied: 2012 c.10 s.121

s.255B, amended: 2012 c.10 s.114, Sch.14 para.16

s.255B, varied: 2012 c.10 s.121

s.255B, amended: 2012 c.10 Sch.14 para.16

s.255B, varied: 2012 c.10 s.121

s.255C, amended: 2012 c.10 s.114, Sch.14 para.16

2003–cont.

44. Criminal Justice Act 2003–cont.

s.255C, varied: 2012 c.10 s.121
s.255C, amended: 2012 c.10 Sch.14 para.16
s.255C, varied: 2012 c.10 s.121
s.255D, amended: 2012 c.10 s.114, Sch.14 para.16
s.255D, varied: 2012 c.10 s.121
s.256, amended: 2012 c.10 Sch.14 para.16
s.256, varied: 2012 c.10 s.121
s.256, amended: 2012 c.10 s.114, s.116, Sch.14 para.16
s.256, varied: 2012 c.10 s.121
s.256A, amended: 2012 c.10 Sch.14 para.16
s.256A, varied: 2012 c.10 s.121
s.256A, amended: 2012 c.10 s.116, Sch.14 para.16
s.256A, varied: 2012 c.10 s.121
s.256B, added: 2012 c.10 s.115
s.256B, amended: 2012 c.10 Sch.14 para.16
s.256B, varied: 2012 c.10 s.121
s.256C, added: 2012 c.10 s.115
s.256C, amended: 2012 c.10 Sch.14 para.16
s.256C, varied: 2012 c.10 s.121
s.257, amended: 2012 c.10 Sch.14 para.16
s.257, varied: 2012 c.10 s.121
s.258, amended: 2012 c.10 s.117, Sch.14 para.16, Sch.17 para.5, Sch.20 para.8
s.258, applied: SI 2012/ 1726 r.62.5, r.62.9
s.258, varied: 2012 c.10 s.121
s.259, amended: 2012 c.10 Sch.14 para.16
s.259, varied: 2012 c.10 s.121
s.259A, amended: 2012 c.10 Sch.14 para.16
s.259A, varied: 2012 c.10 s.121
s.260, amended: 2012 c.10 s.116, Sch.10 para.29, Sch.14 para.11, Sch.14 para.16, Sch.17 para.6, Sch.20 para.9
s.260, varied: 2012 c.10 s.121
s.261, amended: 2012 c.10 s.116, Sch.10 para.30, Sch.14 para.12, Sch.14 para.16, Sch.20 para.10
s.261, varied: 2012 c.10 s.121
s.262, amended: 2012 c.10 Sch.14 para.16
s.262, repealed: 2012 c.10 Sch.16 para.16
s.262, varied: 2012 c.10 s.121
s.263, amended: 2012 c.10 s.116, s.117, Sch.14 para.13, Sch.14 para.16, Sch.17 para.7, Sch.20 para.11
s.263, repealed (in part): 2012 c.10 Sch.10 para.31
s.263, varied: 2012 c.10 s.121
s.264, see *R. (on the application of Elam) v Secretary of State for Justice* [2012] EWCA Civ 29, [2012] 1 W.L.R. 2722 (CA (Civ Div)), Laws, L.J.
s.264, amended: 2012 c.10 s.117, Sch.14 para.14, Sch.14 para.16, Sch.17 para.8, Sch.20 para.12
s.264, repealed (in part): 2012 c.10 Sch.10 para.32, Sch.14 para.14
s.264, varied: 2012 c.10 s.121
s.264A, amended: 2012 c.10 Sch.14 para.16
s.264A, repealed: 2012 c.10 Sch.10 para.33
s.264A, varied: 2012 c.10 s.121
s.265, see *R. v Taylor (Ezra)* [2011] EWCA Crim 2236, [2012] 1 W.L.R. 2113 (CA (Crim Div)), Moses, L.J.
s.265, amended: 2012 c.10 s.117, Sch.14 para.16, Sch.20 para.13
s.265, repealed (in part): 2012 c.10 Sch.10 para.34, Sch.16 para.17
s.265, varied: 2012 c.10 s.121
s.266, amended: 2012 c.10 Sch.14 para.16
s.266, repealed: 2012 c.10 s.118
s.266, varied: 2012 c.10 s.121
s.267, amended: 2012 c.10 Sch.14 para.15, Sch.14 para.16

2003–cont.

44. Criminal Justice Act 2003–cont.

s.267, varied: 2012 c.10 s.121
s.267A, added: 2012 c.10 Sch.16 para.2
s.267A, amended: 2012 c.10 Sch.14 para.16
s.267A, varied: 2012 c.10 s.121
s.267B, added: 2012 c.10 Sch.17 para.9
s.267B, amended: 2012 c.10 Sch.14 para.16
s.267B, varied: 2012 c.10 s.121
s.268, amended: 2012 c.10 Sch.10 para.35, Sch.14 para.16
s.268, varied: 2012 c.10 s.121
s.269, see *R. v Kelly (Marlon)* [2011] EWCA Crim 1462, [2012] 1 W.L.R. 55 (CA (Crim Div)), Lord Judge, L.C.J.; see *R. v Taylor (Ezra)* [2011] EWCA Crim 2236, [2012] 1 W.L.R. 2113 (CA (Crim Div)), Moses, L.J.
s.269, amended: 2012 c.10 s.110
s.269, applied: SI 2012/ 1726 r.68.1
s.270, see *R. v Ahmed (Kafil)* [2012] EWCA Crim 251, [2012] 2 Cr. App. R. (S.) 64 (CA (Crim Div)), Hughes, L.J.
s.270, amended: 2012 c.10 s.64
s.274, applied: SI 2012/ 1726 r.68.1, r.68.2
s.281, referred to: 2012 c.10 s.144
s.302, amended: 2012 c.10 Sch.10 para.36
s.305, see *R. v Pinnell (Paul Leslie)* [2010] EWCA Crim 2848, [2012] 1 W.L.R. 17 (CA (Crim Div)), Hughes, L.J.
s.305, amended: 2012 c.10 s.72, s.76, s.110, Sch.10 para.37, Sch.19 para.22, Sch.19 para.24, Sch.26 para.22
s.321, see *Hanif v United Kingdom (52999/08)* [2012] 3 Costs L.O. 355 (ECHR), Judge Garlicki (President)
s.325, see *R. (on the application of NM) v Islington LBC* [2012] EWHC 414 (Admin), [2012] P.T.S.R. 1582 (QBD (Admin)), Sales, J.
s.325, amended: 2012 c.7 Sch.5 para.124
s.327, amended: 2012 c.10 Sch.21 para.29
s.327B, repealed (in part): 2012 c.10 Sch.24 para.26
s.330, amended: 2012 c.10 s.110, Sch.21 para.30
s.330, repealed (in part): 2012 c.9 Sch.10 Part 10, 2012 c.10 s.110
s.330, enabling: SI 2012/ 1320, SI 2012/ 1696, SI 2012/ 2574
s.336, enabling: SI 2012/ 825, SI 2012/ 1320, SI 2012/ 2574, SI 2012/ 2761, SI 2012/ 2905
s.338, applied: 2012 c.10 s.153
Sch.3, applied: SI 2012/ 1726 r.2.1, r.9.1, r.9.6, r.5.4
Sch.3, referred to: SI 2012/ 1726 r.14.1, r.11.1
Sch.8, applied: SI 2012/ 1726 r.44.1
Sch.8 Part 2 para.9, amended: 2012 c.10 s.66, s.67
Sch.8 Part 2 para.9, applied: SI 2012/ 1726 r.63.1
Sch.8 Part 2 para.10, amended: 2012 c.10 s.66, s.67
Sch.8 Part 2 para.11A, added: 2012 c.10 s.67
Sch.8 Part 3 para.13, applied: SI 2012/ 1726 r.63.1
Sch.8 Part 4 para.19A, added: 2012 c.10 s.66
Sch.8 Pt 5 para.23, see *R. v Brzezinski (Tomaosz Adam)* [2012] EWCA Crim 198, [2012] 2 Cr. App. R. (S.) 62 (CA (Crim Div)), Davis, L.J.
Sch.9 Part 1 para.1, amended: 2012 c.10 s.76
Sch.9 Part 2 para.3, amended: 2012 c.10 s.76
Sch.10 para.1, repealed: 2012 c.10 s.89
Sch.10 para.2, repealed: 2012 c.10 s.89
Sch.10 para.3, repealed: 2012 c.10 s.89
Sch.10 para.4, repealed: 2012 c.10 s.89
Sch.10 para.5, repealed: 2012 c.10 s.89
Sch.10 para.6, repealed: 2012 c.10 s.89
Sch.10 para.7, repealed: 2012 c.10 s.89

2003–cont.

44. Criminal Justice Act 2003–*cont.*

Sch.10 para.8, repealed: 2012 c.10 s.89

Sch.10 para.9, repealed: 2012 c.10 s.89

Sch.11 Part 1 para.1, repealed: 2012 c.10 s.89

Sch.11 Part 2 para.2, repealed: 2012 c.10 s.89

Sch.11 Part 2 para.3, repealed: 2012 c.10 s.89

Sch.11 Part 2 para.4, repealed: 2012 c.10 s.89

Sch.11 Part 2 para.5, repealed: 2012 c.10 s.89

Sch.11 Part 2 para.6, repealed: 2012 c.10 s.89

Sch.11 Part 2 para.7, repealed: 2012 c.10 s.89

Sch.11 Part 2 para.8, repealed: 2012 c.10 s.89

Sch.11 Part 3 para.9, repealed: 2012 c.10 s.89

Sch.11 Part 3 para.10, repealed: 2012 c.10 s.89

Sch.11 Part 3 para.11, repealed: 2012 c.10 s.89

Sch.11 Part 3 para.12, repealed: 2012 c.10 s.89

Sch.11 Part 3 para.13, repealed: 2012 c.10 s.89

Sch.11 Part 4 para.14, repealed: 2012 c.10 s.89

Sch.11 Part 4 para.15, repealed: 2012 c.10 s.89

Sch.11 Part 4 para.16, repealed: 2012 c.10 s.89

Sch.11 Part 4 para.17, repealed: 2012 c.10 s.89

Sch.11 Part 4 para.18, repealed: 2012 c.10 s.89

Sch.11 Part 4 para.19, repealed: 2012 c.10 s.89

Sch.11 Part 4 para.20, repealed: 2012 c.10 s.89

Sch.11 Part 4 para.21, repealed: 2012 c.10 s.89

Sch.11 Part 4 para.22, repealed: 2012 c.10 s.89

Sch.11 Part 5 para.23, repealed: 2012 c.10 s.89

Sch.11 Part 5 para.24, repealed: 2012 c.10 s.89

Sch.12, applied: SI 2012/ 1726 r.44.1

Sch.12 Part 2 para.8, amended: 2012 c.10 s.69, Sch.9 para.10, Sch.10 para.38

Sch.12 Pt 2 para.8, see *R. v Finn (Andrew)* [2012] EWCA Crim 881, [2012] 2 Cr. App. R. (S.) 96 (CA (Crim Div)), Gross, L.J.; see *R. v Morgan (Stuart Anthony)* [2012] EWCA Crim 1939, (2012) 176 J.P. 633 (CA (Crim Div)), Irwin, J.

Sch.12 Part 2 para.9, amended: 2012 c.10 Sch.10 para.38

Sch.12 Part 2 para.9, repealed (in part): 2012 c.10 Sch.10 para.38

Sch.12 Part 2 para.12A, added: 2012 c.10 s.69

Sch.12 Part 3 para.12B, added: 2012 c.10 Sch.9 para.11

Sch.13 Part 1 para.1, amended: 2012 c.10 s.76, Sch.9 para.12

Sch.13 Part 2 para.6, amended: 2012 c.10 s.76, Sch.9 para.12

Sch.15 Part 1 para.57, amended: 2012 c.9 Sch.9 para.147

Sch.15 Part 1 para.63A, amended: 2012 c.4 Sch.1 para.6

Sch.15 Part 2 para.143A, added: 2012 c.9 Sch.9 para.139

Sch.15A Part 1 para.1, repealed: 2012 c.10 Sch.21 para.31

Sch.15A Part 1 para.2, repealed: 2012 c.10 Sch.21 para.31

Sch.15A Part 1 para.3, repealed: 2012 c.10 Sch.21 para.31

Sch.15A Part 1 para.4, repealed: 2012 c.10 Sch.21 para.31

Sch.15A Part 1 para.5, repealed: 2012 c.10 Sch.21 para.31

Sch.15A Part 1 para.6, repealed: 2012 c.10 Sch.21 para.31

Sch.15A Part 1 para.7, repealed: 2012 c.10 Sch.21 para.31

Sch.15A Part 1 para.8, repealed: 2012 c.10 Sch.21 para.31

2003–cont.

44. Criminal Justice Act 2003–*cont.*

Sch.15A Part 1 para.9, repealed: 2012 c.10 Sch.21 para.31

Sch.15A Part 1 para.10, repealed: 2012 c.10 Sch.21 para.31

Sch.15A Part 1 para.11, repealed: 2012 c.10 Sch.21 para.31

Sch.15A Part 1 para.12, repealed: 2012 c.10 Sch.21 para.31

Sch.15A Part 1 para.13, repealed: 2012 c.10 Sch.21 para.31

Sch.15A Part 1 para.14, repealed: 2012 c.10 Sch.21 para.31

Sch.15A Part 1 para.15, repealed: 2012 c.10 Sch.21 para.31

Sch.15A Part 1 para.16, repealed: 2012 c.10 Sch.21 para.31

Sch.15A Part 1 para.17, repealed: 2012 c.10 Sch.21 para.31

Sch.15A Part 1 para.18, repealed: 2012 c.10 Sch.21 para.31

Sch.15A Part 1 para.19, repealed: 2012 c.10 Sch.21 para.31

Sch.15A Part 1 para.20, repealed: 2012 c.10 Sch.21 para.31

Sch.15A Part 1 para.21, repealed: 2012 c.10 Sch.21 para.31

Sch.15A Part 1 para.22, repealed: 2012 c.10 Sch.21 para.31

Sch.15A Part 1 para.23, repealed: 2012 c.10 Sch.21 para.31

Sch.15A Part 2 para.24, repealed: 2012 c.10 Sch.21 para.31

Sch.15A Part 2 para.25, repealed: 2012 c.10 Sch.21 para.31

Sch.15A Part 2 para.26, repealed: 2012 c.10 Sch.21 para.31

Sch.15A Part 2 para.27, repealed: 2012 c.10 Sch.21 para.31

Sch.15A Part 2 para.28, repealed: 2012 c.10 Sch.21 para.31

Sch.15A Part 2 para.29, repealed: 2012 c.10 Sch.21 para.31

Sch.15A Part 2 para.30, repealed: 2012 c.10 Sch.21 para.31

Sch.15A Part 2 para.31, repealed: 2012 c.10 Sch.21 para.31

Sch.15A Part 2 para.32, repealed: 2012 c.10 Sch.21 para.31

Sch.15A Part 2 para.33, repealed: 2012 c.10 Sch.21 para.31

Sch.15A Part 2 para.34, repealed: 2012 c.10 Sch.21 para.31

Sch.15A Part 2 para.35, repealed: 2012 c.10 Sch.21 para.31

Sch.15A Part 3 para.36, repealed: 2012 c.10 Sch.21 para.31

Sch.15A Part 3 para.37, repealed: 2012 c.10 Sch.21 para.31

Sch.15A Part 3 para.38, repealed: 2012 c.10 Sch.21 para.31

Sch.15A Part 3 para.39, repealed: 2012 c.10 Sch.21 para.31

Sch.15A Part 3 para.40, repealed: 2012 c.10 Sch.21 para.31

Sch.15A Part 3 para.41, repealed: 2012 c.10 Sch.21 para.31

Sch.15A Part 3 para.42, repealed: 2012 c.10 Sch.21 para.31

2003–cont.

44. Criminal Justice Act 2003–*cont.*

Sch.15A Part 3 para.43, repealed: 2012 c.10 Sch.21 para.31

Sch.15A Part 3 para.44, repealed: 2012 c.10 Sch.21 para.31

Sch.15A Part 3 para.45, repealed: 2012 c.10 Sch.21 para.31

Sch.15A Part 3 para.46, repealed: 2012 c.10 Sch.21 para.31

Sch.15A Part 3 para.47, repealed: 2012 c.10 Sch.21 para.31

Sch.15A Part 3 para.48, repealed: 2012 c.10 Sch.21 para.31

Sch.15A Part 3 para.49, repealed: 2012 c.10 Sch.21 para.31

Sch.15A Part 3 para.49A, repealed: 2012 c.10 Sch.21 para.31

Sch.15A Part 3 para.49B, repealed: 2012 c.10 Sch.21 para.31

Sch.15A Part 3 para.49C, repealed: 2012 c.10 Sch.21 para.31

Sch.15A Part 3 para.49D, repealed: 2012 c.10 Sch.21 para.31

Sch.15A Part 3 para.49E, repealed: 2012 c.10 Sch.21 para.31

Sch.15A Part 3 para.49F, repealed: 2012 c.10 Sch.21 para.31

Sch.15A Part 3 para.49G, repealed: 2012 c.10 Sch.21 para.31

Sch.15A Part 3 para.49H, repealed: 2012 c.10 Sch.21 para.31

Sch.15A Part 3 para.49I, repealed: 2012 c.10 Sch.21 para.31

Sch.15A Part 3 para.49J, repealed: 2012 c.10 Sch.21 para.31

Sch.15A Part 3 para.49K, repealed: 2012 c.10 Sch.21 para.31

Sch.15A Part 3 para.49L, repealed: 2012 c.10 Sch.21 para.31

Sch.15A Part 3 para.50, repealed: 2012 c.10 Sch.21 para.31

Sch.15A Part 4 para.51, repealed: 2012 c.10 Sch.21 para.31

Sch.15A Part 4 para.52, repealed: 2012 c.10 Sch.21 para.31

Sch.15A Part 5 para.53, repealed: 2012 c.10 Sch.21 para.31

Sch.15B Part 1, added: 2012 c.10 Sch.18

Sch.15B Part 1 para.1, added: 2012 c.10 Sch.18

Sch.15B Part 1 para.2, added: 2012 c.10 Sch.18

Sch.15B Part 1 para.3, added: 2012 c.10 Sch.18

Sch.15B Part 1 para.4, added: 2012 c.10 Sch.18

Sch.15B Part 1 para.5, added: 2012 c.10 Sch.18

Sch.15B Part 1 para.6, added: 2012 c.10 Sch.18

Sch.15B Part 1 para.7, added: 2012 c.10 Sch.18

Sch.15B Part 1 para.8, added: 2012 c.10 Sch.18

Sch.15B Part 1 para.9, added: 2012 c.10 Sch.18

Sch.15B Part 1 para.10, added: 2012 c.10 Sch.18

Sch.15B Part 1 para.11, added: 2012 c.10 Sch.18

Sch.15B Part 1 para.12, added: 2012 c.10 Sch.18

Sch.15B Part 1 para.13, added: 2012 c.10 Sch.18

Sch.15B Part 1 para.14, added: 2012 c.10 Sch.18

Sch.15B Part 1 para.15, added: 2012 c.10 Sch.18

Sch.15B Part 1 para.16, added: 2012 c.10 Sch.18

Sch.15B Part 1 para.17, added: 2012 c.10 Sch.18

Sch.15B Part 1 para.18, added: 2012 c.10 Sch.18

Sch.15B Part 1 para.19, added: 2012 c.10 Sch.18

Sch.15B Part 1 para.20, added: 2012 c.10 Sch.18

Sch.15B Part 1 para.21, added: 2012 c.10 Sch.18

2003–cont.

44. Criminal Justice Act 2003–*cont.*

Sch.15B Part 1 para.22, added: 2012 c.10 Sch.18

Sch.15B Part 1 para.23, added: 2012 c.10 Sch.18

Sch.15B Part 1 para.24, added: 2012 c.10 Sch.18

Sch.15B Part 1 para.25, added: 2012 c.10 Sch.18

Sch.15B Part 1 para.26, added: 2012 c.10 Sch.18

Sch.15B Part 1 para.27, added: 2012 c.10 Sch.18

Sch.15B Part 1 para.28, added: 2012 c.10 Sch.18

Sch.15B Part 1 para.29, added: 2012 c.10 Sch.18

Sch.15B Part 1 para.30, added: 2012 c.10 Sch.18

Sch.15B Part 1 para.31, added: 2012 c.10 Sch.18

Sch.15B Part 1 para.32, added: 2012 c.10 Sch.18

Sch.15B Part 1 para.33, added: 2012 c.10 Sch.18

Sch.15B Part 1 para.34, added: 2012 c.10 Sch.18

Sch.15B Part 1 para.35, added: 2012 c.10 Sch.18

Sch.15B Part 1 para.36, added: 2012 c.10 Sch.18

Sch.15B Part 1 para.37, added: 2012 c.10 Sch.18

Sch.15B Part 1 para.38, added: 2012 c.10 Sch.18

Sch.15B Part 1 para.39, added: 2012 c.10 Sch.18

Sch.15B Part 1 para.40, added: 2012 c.10 Sch.18

Sch.15B Part 1 para.41, added: 2012 c.10 Sch.18

Sch.15B Part 1 para.42, added: 2012 c.10 Sch.18

Sch.15B Part 1 para.43, added: 2012 c.10 Sch.18

Sch.15B Part 1 para.44, added: 2012 c.10 Sch.18

Sch.15B Part 2, added: 2012 c.10 Sch.18

Sch.15B Part 2 para.45, added: 2012 c.10 Sch.18

Sch.15B Part 2 para.46, added: 2012 c.10 Sch.18

Sch.15B Part 3 para.47, added: 2012 c.10 Sch.18

Sch.15B Part 3 para.48, added: 2012 c.10 Sch.18

Sch.15B Part 4 para.49, added: 2012 c.10 Sch.18

Sch.15B Part 5 para.50, added: 2012 c.10 Sch.18

Sch.18 para.4, repealed: 2012 c.10 Sch.21 para.35

Sch.20 para.1, repealed: 2012 c.10 Sch.16 para.16

Sch.20 para.2, repealed: 2012 c.10 Sch.16 para.16

Sch.20 para.3, repealed: 2012 c.10 Sch.16 para.16

Sch.20 para.4, repealed: 2012 c.10 Sch.16 para.16

Sch.20A para.1, added: 2012 c.10 Sch.16 para.3

Sch.20A para.2, added: 2012 c.10 Sch.16 para.3

Sch.20A para.3, added: 2012 c.10 Sch.16 para.3

Sch.20A para.4, added: 2012 c.10 Sch.16 para.3

Sch.20A para.5, added: 2012 c.10 Sch.16 para.3

Sch.20A para.6, added: 2012 c.10 Sch.16 para.3

Sch.20A para.7, added: 2012 c.10 Sch.16 para.3

Sch.20A para.8, added: 2012 c.10 Sch.16 para.3

Sch.20A para.9, added: 2012 c.10 Sch.16 para.3

Sch.20A para.10, added: 2012 c.10 Sch.16 para.3

Sch.20B Part 1 para.1, added: 2012 c.10 Sch.17 para.10

Sch.20B Part 1 para.2, added: 2012 c.10 Sch.17 para.10

Sch.20B Part 2 para.3, added: 2012 c.10 Sch.17 para.10

Sch.20B Part 2 para.4, added: 2012 c.10 Sch.17 para.10

Sch.20B Part 2 para.5, added: 2012 c.10 Sch.17 para.10

Sch.20B Part 2 para.6, added: 2012 c.10 Sch.17 para.10

Sch.20B Part 2 para.6, referred to: 2012 c.10 s.128

Sch.20B Part 2 para.7, added: 2012 c.10 Sch.17 para.10

Sch.20B Part 2 para.8, added: 2012 c.10 Sch.17 para.10

Sch.20B Part 2 para.9, added: 2012 c.10 Sch.17 para.10

Sch.20B Part 2 para.10, added: 2012 c.10 Sch.17 para.10

2003– cont.

44. Criminal Justice Act 2003–*cont.*

Sch.20B Part 2 para.11, added: 2012 c.10 Sch.17 para.10

Sch.20B Part 2 para.12, added: 2012 c.10 Sch.17 para.10

Sch.20B Part 2 para.13, added: 2012 c.10 Sch.17 para.10

Sch.20B Part 2 para.14, added: 2012 c.10 Sch.17 para.10

Sch.20B Part 2 para.15, added: 2012 c.10 Sch.17 para.10

Sch.20B Part 2 para.15, referred to: 2012 c.10 s.128

Sch.20B Part 2 para.16, added: 2012 c.10 Sch.17 para.10

Sch.20B Part 2 para.17, added: 2012 c.10 Sch.17 para.10

Sch.20B Part 2 para.18, added: 2012 c.10 Sch.17 para.10

Sch.20B Part 2 para.19, added: 2012 c.10 Sch.17 para.10

Sch.20B Part 2 para.20, added: 2012 c.10 Sch.17 para.10

Sch.20B Part 2 para.21, added: 2012 c.10 Sch.17 para.10

Sch.20B Part 2 para.22, added: 2012 c.10 Sch.17 para.10

Sch.20B Part 3 para.23, added: 2012 c.10 Sch.17 para.10

Sch.20B Part 3 para.24, added: 2012 c.10 Sch.17 para.10

Sch.20B Part 3 para.25, added: 2012 c.10 Sch.17 para.10

Sch.20B Part 3 para.25, referred to: 2012 c.10 s.128

Sch.20B Part 3 para.26, added: 2012 c.10 Sch.17 para.10

Sch.20B Part 3 para.27, added: 2012 c.10 Sch.17 para.10

Sch.20B Part 3 para.28, added: 2012 c.10 Sch.17 para.10

Sch.20B Part 3 para.28, referred to: 2012 c.10 s.128

Sch.20B Part 3 para.29, added: 2012 c.10 Sch.17 para.10

Sch.20B Part 3 para.30, added: 2012 c.10 Sch.17 para.10

Sch.20B Part 3 para.31, added: 2012 c.10 Sch.17 para.10

Sch.20B Part 3 para.32, added: 2012 c.10 Sch.17 para.10

Sch.20B Part 3 para.33, added: 2012 c.10 Sch.17 para.10

Sch.20B Part 4 para.34, added: 2012 c.10 Sch.17 para.10

Sch.20B Part 4 para.35, added: 2012 c.10 Sch.17 para.10

Sch.20B Part 4 para.36, added: 2012 c.10 Sch.17 para.10

Sch.20B Part 4 para.37, added: 2012 c.10 Sch.17 para.10

Sch.21, see *R. v Dighton (Daniel)* [2011] EWCA Crim 1372, [2012] 1 Cr. App. R. (S.) 30 (CA (Crim Div)), Pill, L.J.; see *R. v Kela (Jarnail Singh)* [2011] EWCA Crim 1277, [2012] 1 Cr. App. R. (S.) 32 (CA (Crim Div)), Pitchford, L.J.; see *R. v Tucker (Michael)* [2011] EWCA Crim 3046, [2012] 2 Cr. App. R. (S.) 30 (CA (Crim Div)), Pill, L.J.

Sch.21 para.3, substituted: 2012 c.10 s.65

Sch.21 para.4, see *R. v Kelly (Marlon)* [2011] EWCA Crim 1462, [2012] 1 W.L.R. 55 (CA (Crim Div)), Lord Judge, L.C.J.; see *R. v Oakes (David)* [2012]

2003– cont.

44. Criminal Justice Act 2003–*cont.*

Sch.21 para.4–*cont.*

EWCA Crim 2435, Times, December 11, 2012 (CA (Crim Div)), Lord Judge, L.C.J.

Sch.21 para.5, see *R. v Kelly (Marlon)* [2011] EWCA Crim 1462, [2012] 1 W.L.R. 55 (CA (Crim Div)), Lord Judge, L.C.J.

Sch.21 para.5, amended: 2012 c.10 s.65

Sch.21 para.5A, see *R. v Challen (Georgina Sarah)* [2011] EWCA Crim 2919, [2012] 2 Cr. App. R. (S.) 20 (CA (Crim Div)), Lord Judge, L.C.J.; see *R. v Kela (Jarnail Singh)* [2011] EWCA Crim 1277, [2012] 1 Cr. App. R. (S.) 32 (CA (Crim Div)), Pitchford, L.J.; see *R. v Kelly (Marlon)* [2011] EWCA Crim 1462, [2012] 1 W.L.R. 55 (CA (Crim Div)), Lord Judge, L.C.J.

Sch.21 para.10, see *R. v Ahmed (Kafil)* [2012] EWCA Crim 251, [2012] 2 Cr. App. R. (S.) 64 (CA (Crim Div)), Hughes, L.J.

Sch.22 para.3, see *R. v Gill (Nimal Singh)* [2011] EWCA Crim 2795, [2012] 1 W.L.R. 1441 (CA (Crim Div)), Lord Judge, L.C.J.

Sch.22 para.6, see *R. v Gill (Nimal Singh)* [2011] EWCA Crim 2795, [2012] 1 W.L.R. 1441 (CA (Crim Div)), Lord Judge, L.C.J.

Sch.22 para.14, applied: SI 2012/ 1726 r.68.1, r.68.2, r.74.1

Sch.26 para.51, repealed: 2012 c.10 Sch.5 Part 2

Sch.27 para.7, varied: 2012 c.11 s.39

Sch.32 Part 1 para.12, repealed (in part): 2012 c.10 Sch.10 para.39

Sch.32 Part 1 para.15, repealed: 2012 c.10 Sch.12 para.52

Sch.32 Part 1 para.18, repealed (in part): 2012 c.10 Sch.25 Part 2

Sch.32 Part 1 para.29, repealed: 2012 c.10 Sch.10 para.39

Sch.32 Part 1 para.57, repealed: 2012 c.10 Sch.10 para.39

Sch.32 Part 1 para.58, repealed: 2012 c.10 Sch.10 para.39

Sch.32 Part 1 para.68, repealed (in part): 2012 c.10 Sch.10 para.39

Sch.33, see *Hanif v United Kingdom (52999/08)* [2012] 3 Costs L.O. 355 (ECHR), Judge Garlicki (President)

2004

5. Planning and Compulsory Purchase Act 2004

Commencement Orders: SI 2012/ 1100 Art.2

see *Heard v Broadland DC* [2012] EWHC 344 (Admin), [2012] Env. L.R. 23 (QBD (Admin)), Ouseley, J.; see *R. (on the application of Millgate Developments Ltd) v Wokingham BC* [2011] EWCA Civ 1062, [2012] 39 E.G. 120 (CA (Civ Div)), Pill, L.J.; see *R. (on the application of Samuel Smith Old Brewery (Tadcaster)) v Secretary of State for Energy and Climate Change* [2012] EWHC 46 (Admin), [2012] 2 All E.R. 849 (QBD (Admin)), Edwards-Stuart J.

Part 2, applied: SI 2012/ 767 Reg.36, SI 2012/ 1020 Sch.1, SI 2012/ 2167 Art.3

Part 3, applied: SI 2012/ 2167 Art.3

s.15, applied: SI 2012/ 767 Reg.7, SI 2012/ 1020 Sch.1

s.16, applied: SI 2012/ 767 Reg.2

s.17, applied: SI 2012/ 767 Reg.5

s.17, enabling: SI 2012/ 767

s.19, applied: SI 2012/ 767 Reg.10, SI 2012/ 2167 Sch.1 para.6

2004– cont.

2004– cont.

5. Planning and Compulsory Purchase Act 2004–
cont.
s.19, referred to: SI 2012/767 Reg.10, Sch.1 para.3
s.19, varied: SI 2012/767 Sch.2 para.2
s.19, enabling: SI 2012/767
s.20, see *Linden Homes Ltd v Bromley LBC* [2011]
EWHC 3430 (Admin), [2012] J.P.L. 703 (QBD
(Admin)), Judge Bidder Q.C.
s.20, applied: SI 2012/57 Art.10, SI 2012/767 Reg.19,
Reg.22, Reg.23, Reg.24, Reg.25, Sch.1 para.3,
Sch.1 para.4, SI 2012/2167 Sch.1 para.6, Sch.1
para.7
s.20, enabling: SI 2012/767
s.21, applied: SI 2012/767 Reg.16, Reg.25, Reg.29,
Reg.30, Sch.1, Sch.1 para.4, Sch.1 para.5, Sch.1
para.6, Sch.1 para.7, Sch.1 para.8
s.22, applied: SI 2012/767 Reg.15, Reg.27
s.23, see *Manydown Co Ltd v Basingstoke and
Deane BC* [2012] EWHC 977 (Admin), [2012]
J.P.L. 1188 (QBD (Admin)), Lindblom J.
s.23, applied: SI 2012/57 Art.10, SI 2012/2167 Sch.1
para.6
s.24, applied: SI 2012/767 Reg.21, Sch.1 para.3
s.24, referred to: SI 2012/767 Reg.20
s.25, applied: SI 2012/767 Reg.15, Reg.28
s.26, applied: SI 2012/2167 Sch.1 para.6
s.27, applied: SI 2012/767 Reg.31, Sch.2, Sch.2
para.1, Sch.2 para.2
s.28, applied: SI 2012/767 Reg.32
s.28, referred to: SI 2012/767 Reg.32
s.28, enabling: SI 2012/767
s.29, applied: SI 2012/767 Reg.33
s.31, applied: SI 2012/767 Reg.33
s.31, enabling: SI 2012/767
s.33A, applied: SI 2012/767 Reg.4, Reg.34
s.33A, enabling: SI 2012/767, SI 2012/2613
s.35, enabling: SI 2012/767
s.36, enabling: SI 2012/767
s.38, see *Harringay Meat Traders Ltd v Secretary of
State for Communities and Local Government*
[2012] EWHC 1744 (Admin), [2012] J.P.L. 1473
(QBD (Admin)), McCombe, J.; see *R. (on the
application of Godfrey) v Southwark LBC*
[2012] EWCA Civ 500, [2012] B.L.G.R. 683 (CA
(Civ Div)), Pill, L.J.; see *R. (on the application of
Samuel Smith Old Brewery (Tadcaster)) v
Secretary of State for Energy and Climate
Change* [2012] EWHC 46 (Admin), [2012] 2 All
E.R. 849 (QBD (Admin)), Edwards-Stuart J.
s.38A, applied: SI 2012/637 Reg.19, Reg.20
s.38A, referred to: SI 2012/637 Reg.17, Reg.18
s.38A, enabling: SI 2012/637, SI 2012/2031
s.38B, referred to: SI 2012/637
s.38C, referred to: SI 2012/637 Reg.30
s.88, enabling: SI 2012/801
s.113, see *Barker v Hambleton DC* [2012] EWCA Civ
610, [2012] C.P. Rep. 36 (CA (Civ Div)), Maurice
Kay, L.J.; see *Heard v Broadland DC* [2012]
EWHC 344 (Admin), [2012] Env. L.R. 23
(QBD (Admin)), Ouseley, J.; see *Hinde v
Rugby BC* [2011] EWHC 3684 (Admin), [2012]
J.P.L. 816 (QBD (Admin)), David Elvin Q.C.;
see *Manydown Co Ltd v Basingstoke and
Deane BC* [2012] EWHC 977 (Admin), [2012]
J.P.L. 1188 (QBD (Admin)), Lindblom J.
s.113, referred to: SI 2012/767 Reg.35
s.121, enabling: SI 2012/1100, SI 2012/1664
s.122, enabling: SI 2012/637, SI 2012/801, SI 2012/
1100, SI 2012/1664, SI 2012/2613
Sch.8, applied: SI 2012/1020 Sch.1

5. Planning and Compulsory Purchase Act 2004–
cont.
Sch.8 para.1, amended: SI 2012/961 Sch.3 para.1
6. Child Trust Funds Act 2004
s.3, enabling: SI 2012/1870
s.13, enabling: SI 2012/886
s.28, enabling: SI 2012/886, SI 2012/1870
7. Gender Recognition Act 2004
s.7, enabling: SI 2012/920
s.24, enabling: SI 2012/920
s.25, amended: 2012 c.7 s.213
8. Higher Education Act 2004
see *R. (on the application of Cardao-Pito) v Office
of the Independent Adjudicator for Higher
Education* [2012] EWHC 203 (Admin), [2012]
E.L.R. 231 (QBD (Admin)), Judge Gilbart Q.C.
s.24, enabling: SI 2012/433, SI 2012/1653
s.26, applied: SI 2012/433
s.28, enabling: SI 2012/1630
s.36, enabling: SI 2012/433
s.47, enabling: SI 2012/433, SI 2012/1630, SI 2012/
1653
12. Finance Act 2004
see *Equity Trust (Singapore) Ltd v Revenue and
Customs Commissioners* [2012] EWCA Civ
192, [2012] S.T.C. 998 (CA (Civ Div)), Lloyd,
L.J.; see *John Mander Pension Trustees Ltd v
Revenue and Customs Commissioners* [2012]
S.F.T.D. 322 (FTT (Tax)), Judge Barbara
Mosedale
applied: SI 2012/687 Sch.1 para.2, Sch.1 para.3,
Sch.1 para.4, Sch.1 para.7, Sch.1 para.8, Sch.1
para.9, Sch.1 para.10, Sch.1 para.14, Sch.1 para.15
Part 7, applied: SI 2012/1868 Reg.3, Reg.22
s.40, repealed: 2012 c.14 Sch.16 para.247
s.41, repealed: 2012 c.14 Sch.16 para.247
s.44, repealed: 2012 c.14 Sch.16 para.247
s.59, amended: 2012 c.7 Sch.14 para.94
s.62, enabling: SI 2012/820
s.66, see *Cardiff Lift Co v Revenue and Customs
Commissioners* [2012] S.F.T.D. 85 (FTT (Tax)),
Judge Charles Hellier
s.67, see *Cardiff Lift Co v Revenue and Customs
Commissioners* [2012] S.F.T.D. 85 (FTT (Tax)),
Judge Charles Hellier
s.71, enabling: SI 2012/820
s.73, enabling: SI 2012/820
s.75, enabling: SI 2012/820
s.150, see *Equity Trust (Singapore) Ltd v Revenue
and Customs Commissioners* [2012] EWCA Civ
192, [2012] S.T.C. 998 (CA (Civ Div)), Lloyd, L.J.
s.150, applied: 2012 c.14 s.160
s.150, varied: 2012 c.11 s.12
s.150, enabling: SI 2012/884, SI 2012/1221
s.152, see *Dalriada Trustees Ltd v Woodward* [2012]
EWHC 21626 (Ch), [2012] W.T.L.R. 1489 (Ch D),
Sir Andrew Morritt (Chancellor)
s.157, applied: 2012 c.14 s.58
s.160, see *Dalriada Trustees Ltd v Faulds* [2011]
EWHC 3391 (Ch), [2012] 2 All E.R. 734 (Ch
D), Bean, J.
s.161, see *Dalriada Trustees Ltd v Faulds* [2011]
EWHC 3391 (Ch), [2012] 2 All E.R. 734 (Ch
D), Bean, J.
s.164, see *Dalriada Trustees Ltd v Faulds* [2011]
EWHC 3391 (Ch), [2012] 2 All E.R. 734 (Ch
D), Bean, J.
s.164, enabling: SI 2012/522, SI 2012/1881
s.169, enabling: SI 2012/884

2004–cont.

12. **Finance Act 2004**–*cont.*
s.173, see *Dalriada Trustees Ltd v Faulds* [2011] EWHC 3391 (Ch), [2012] 2 All E.R. 734 (Ch D), Bean, J.

s.175, see *Dalriada Trustees Ltd v Faulds* [2011] EWHC 3391 (Ch), [2012] 2 All E.R. 734 (Ch D), Bean, J.

s.179, see *Dalriada Trustees Ltd v Faulds* [2011] EWHC 3391 (Ch), [2012] 2 All E.R. 734 (Ch D), Bean, J.

s.180, varied: SI 2012/1258 Reg.2

s.196, amended: 2012 c.14 Sch.16 para.113

s.196, applied: 2012 c.14 Sch.13 para.14, Sch.13 para.31

s.196A, amended: 2012 c.14 Sch.16 para.114

s.196B, added: 2012 c.14 Sch.13 para.1, Sch.13 para.15

s.196B, applied: 2012 c.14 Sch.13 para.3, Sch.13 para.4, Sch.13 para.18, Sch.13 para.20, Sch.13 para.21, Sch.13 para.23, Sch.13 para.29

s.196B, referred to: 2012 c.14 Sch.13 para.3, Sch.13 para.5, Sch.13 para.6, Sch.13 para.9, Sch.13 para.12, Sch.13 para.19

s.196B, repealed: 2012 c.14 Sch.13 para.1

s.196C, added: 2012 c.14 Sch.13 para.1, Sch.13 para.15

s.196C, applied: 2012 c.14 Sch.13 para.3, Sch.13 para.4, Sch.13 para.42

s.196C, referred to: 2012 c.14 Sch.13 para.3, Sch.13 para.5, Sch.13 para.6, Sch.13 para.10, Sch.13 para.12

s.196C, repealed: 2012 c.14 Sch.13 para.1

s.196C, varied: 2012 c.14 Sch.13 para.18

s.196D, added: 2012 c.14 Sch.13 para.1, Sch.13 para.15

s.196D, applied: 2012 c.14 Sch.13 para.3, Sch.13 para.4, Sch.13 para.18, Sch.13 para.20, Sch.13 para.21, Sch.13 para.24, Sch.13 para.29

s.196D, referred to: 2012 c.14 Sch.13 para.3, Sch.13 para.5, Sch.13 para.6, Sch.13 para.11, Sch.13 para.12, Sch.13 para.19, Sch.13 para.24

s.196D, repealed: 2012 c.14 Sch.13 para.1

s.196E, added: 2012 c.14 Sch.13 para.1, Sch.13 para.15

s.196E, applied: 2012 c.14 Sch.13 para.3, Sch.13 para.42

s.196E, repealed: 2012 c.14 Sch.13 para.1

s.196E, varied: 2012 c.14 Sch.13 para.18

s.196F, added: 2012 c.14 Sch.13 para.1, Sch.13 para.15

s.196F, applied: 2012 c.14 Sch.13 para.3, Sch.13 para.18, Sch.13 para.20, Sch.13 para.21, Sch.13 para.25, Sch.13 para.29

s.196F, disapplied: 2012 c.14 Sch.13 para.4

s.196F, referred to: 2012 c.14 Sch.13 para.19

s.196F, repealed: 2012 c.14 Sch.13 para.1

s.196G, added: 2012 c.14 Sch.13 para.1, Sch.13 para.15

s.196G, applied: 2012 c.14 Sch.13 para.3, Sch.13 para.42

s.196G, disapplied: 2012 c.14 Sch.13 para.28

s.196G, referred to: 2012 c.14 Sch.13 para.3

s.196G, repealed: 2012 c.14 Sch.13 para.1

s.196G, varied: 2012 c.14 Sch.13 para.3, Sch.13 para.18

s.196H, added: 2012 c.14 Sch.13 para.1, Sch.13 para.15

s.196H, applied: 2012 c.14 Sch.13 para.3

s.196H, disapplied: 2012 c.14 Sch.13 para.28

s.196H, repealed: 2012 c.14 Sch.13 para.1

s.196I, added: 2012 c.14 Sch.13 para.1, Sch.13 para.15

s.196I, applied: 2012 c.14 Sch.13 para.3

s.196I, repealed: 2012 c.14 Sch.13 para.1

2004– cont.

12. **Finance Act 2004**–*cont.*
s.196I, varied: 2012 c.14 Sch.13 para.17

s.196J, added: 2012 c.14 Sch.13 para.1, Sch.13 para.15

s.196J, applied: 2012 c.14 Sch.13 para.3, Sch.13 para.17, Sch.13 para.42

s.196J, repealed: 2012 c.14 Sch.13 para.1

s.196K, added: 2012 c.14 Sch.13 para.15

s.196L, added: 2012 c.14 Sch.13 para.15

s.196L, amended: 2012 c.14 Sch.16 para.115

s.197, amended: 2012 c.14 Sch.16 para.116

s.199, amended: 2012 c.14 Sch.16 para.117

s.199A, amended: 2012 c.14 Sch.16 para.118

s.200, amended: 2012 c.14 Sch.16 para.119

s.246, amended: 2012 c.14 Sch.16 para.120

s.246A, amended: 2012 c.14 Sch.16 para.121

s.250, enabling: SI 2012/884

s.251, enabling: SI 2012/884

s.267, enabling: SI 2012/886

s.268, enabling: SI 2012/886

s.280, amended: 2012 c.14 Sch.13 para.2, Sch.13 para.16, Sch.16 para.122

s.282, enabling: SI 2012/2940

s.298, repealed (in part): 2012 c.11 Sch.3 para.28, 2012 c.14 Sch.39 para.8

s.306, applied: SI 2012/1868 Reg.5

s.306, enabling: SI 2012/2395

s.306A, applied: SI 2012/1836 Reg.5, Reg.16, SI 2012/1868 Reg.5

s.306A, enabling: SI 2012/1836

s.307, applied: SI 2012/1868 Reg.5

s.307, enabling: SI 2012/1836

s.308, amended: 2012 c.14 s.215

s.308, applied: SI 2012/1836 Reg.4, Reg.5, SI 2012/1868 Reg.5, Reg.8, SI 2012/2396 Reg.5

s.308, varied: SI 2012/2396 Reg.6

s.308, enabling: SI 2012/1836, SI 2012/2396

s.308A, applied: SI 2012/1836 Reg.5, SI 2012/1868 Reg.5

s.308A, enabling: SI 2012/1836

s.309, applied: SI 2012/1836 Reg.4, Reg.5, SI 2012/1868 Reg.5

s.309, enabling: SI 2012/1836

s.310, applied: SI 2012/1836 Reg.4, Reg.5, SI 2012/1868 Reg.5

s.310, enabling: SI 2012/1836

s.311, applied: SI 2012/1836 Reg.6, Reg.11, Reg.13, SI 2012/1868 Reg.5, Reg.8, Reg.15

s.312, applied: SI 2012/1836 Reg.6, Reg.7, Reg.13, SI 2012/1868 Reg.5

s.312, enabling: SI 2012/1836

s.312A, applied: SI 2012/1836 Reg.6, Reg.7, Reg.8, SI 2012/1868 Reg.5

s.312A, enabling: SI 2012/1836

s.313, applied: SI 2012/1836 Reg.9, Reg.10, Reg.11, SI 2012/1868 Reg.5

s.313, enabling: SI 2012/1836

s.313A, applied: SI 2012/1836 Reg.14, SI 2012/1868 Reg.5, Reg.6

s.313A, enabling: SI 2012/1836

s.313B, applied: SI 2012/1836 Reg.14, SI 2012/1868 Reg.5, Reg.6

s.313B, enabling: SI 2012/1836

s.313C, applied: SI 2012/1836 Reg.15, SI 2012/1868 Reg.5

s.313C, enabling: SI 2012/1836

s.313ZA, applied: SI 2012/1836 Reg.13, SI 2012/1868 Reg.5

s.313ZA, enabling: SI 2012/1836

2004–cont.

12. Finance Act 2004–*cont.*
 s.314A, applied: SI 2012/ 1836 Reg.16, SI 2012/ 1868 Reg.5
 s.316, applied: SI 2012/ 1868 Reg.5
 s.317, enabling: SI 2012/ 1836, SI 2012/ 2396
 s.318, enabling: SI 2012/ 1836, SI 2012/ 2395
 s.320, see *Test Claimants in the FII Group Litigation v Revenue and Customs Commissioners* [2012] UKSC 19, [2012] 2 A.C. 337 (SC), Lord Hope
 s.324, amended: SI 2012/ 1809 Sch.1 Part 1
 Sch.6 para.1, repealed: 2012 c.14 Sch.16 para.247
 Sch.6 para.2, repealed: 2012 c.14 Sch.16 para.247
 Sch.6 para.3, repealed: 2012 c.14 Sch.16 para.247
 Sch.6 para.4, repealed: 2012 c.14 Sch.16 para.247
 Sch.6 para.5, repealed: 2012 c.14 Sch.16 para.247
 Sch.6 para.6, repealed: 2012 c.14 Sch.16 para.247
 Sch.6 para.7, repealed: 2012 c.14 Sch.16 para.247
 Sch.6 para.8, repealed: 2012 c.14 Sch.16 para.247
 Sch.6 para.9, repealed: 2012 c.14 Sch.16 para.247
 Sch.7 para.5, repealed: 2012 c.14 Sch.16 para.247
 Sch.7 para.8, repealed: 2012 c.14 Sch.16 para.247
 Sch.7 para.9, repealed (in part): 2012 c.14 Sch.16 para.247
 Sch.11 Part 1 para.4, enabling: SI 2012/ 820
 Sch.11 Part 2 para.8, enabling: SI 2012/ 820
 Sch.11 Part 3 para.12, enabling: SI 2012/ 820
 Sch.28 Part 1 para.14, amended: 2012 c.21 Sch.18 para.100
 Sch.28 Part 1 para.14, enabling: SI 2012/ 2940
 Sch.29, applied: SSI 2012/ 319 Reg.38
 Sch.29 Part 1 para.7, applied: SI 2012/ 2885 Sch.1 para.22, SI 2012/ 3144 Sch.1 para.16, SI 2012/ 3145 Sch.1
 Sch.33 para.5, enabling: SI 2012/ 884
 Sch.34 para.7, enabling: SI 2012/ 1795
 Sch.35 para.9, repealed: 2012 c.14 Sch.39 para.28
 Sch.35 para.10, repealed: 2012 c.14 Sch.39 para.28
 Sch.35 para.11, repealed: 2012 c.14 Sch.39 para.31
 Sch.35 para.20, repealed: 2012 c.14 Sch.16 para.247
 Sch.36, applied: SI 2012/ 687 Sch.1 para.9
 Sch.36 Part 2 para.12, applied: SI 2012/ 687 Sch.1 para.9
 Sch.36 Part 4 para.51, enabling: SI 2012/ 884
13. Scottish Parliament (Constituencies) Act 2004
 s.1, repealed (in part): 2012 c.11 s.8
 Sch.2 para.1, repealed: 2012 c.11 s.8
 Sch.2 para.2, repealed: 2012 c.11 s.8
 Sch.2 para.3, repealed: 2012 c.11 s.8
 Sch.2 para.4, repealed: 2012 c.11 s.8
15. Carers (Equal Opportunities) Act 2004
 s.3, amended: 2012 c.7 Sch.5 para.125
17. Health Protection Agency Act 2004
 s.1, applied: SI 2012/ 1631 Sch.5 para.6, SI 2012/ 2996 Sch.5 para.5
 s.1, repealed: 2012 c.7 s.56
 s.2, repealed: 2012 c.7 s.56
 s.2A, repealed: 2012 c.7 s.56
 s.3, repealed: 2012 c.7 s.56
 s.4, repealed: 2012 c.7 s.56
 s.5, repealed: 2012 c.7 s.56
 s.6, repealed: 2012 c.7 s.56
 s.7, repealed: 2012 c.7 s.56
 s.8, repealed: 2012 c.7 s.56
 s.9, repealed: 2012 c.7 s.56
 s.10, repealed: 2012 c.7 s.56
 s.11, repealed (in part): 2012 c.7 s.56
 s.12, repealed: 2012 c.7 s.56
 s.13, repealed: 2012 c.7 s.56

2004–cont.

17. Health Protection Agency Act 2004–*cont.*
 Sch.1 para.1, repealed: 2012 c.7 s.56
 Sch.1 para.2, repealed: 2012 c.7 s.56
 Sch.1 para.3, repealed: 2012 c.7 s.56
 Sch.1 para.4, repealed: 2012 c.7 s.56
 Sch.1 para.5, repealed: 2012 c.7 s.56
 Sch.1 para.6, repealed: 2012 c.7 s.56
 Sch.1 para.7, repealed: 2012 c.7 s.56
 Sch.1 para.8, repealed: 2012 c.7 s.56
 Sch.1 para.9, repealed: 2012 c.7 s.56
 Sch.1 para.10, repealed: 2012 c.7 s.56
 Sch.1 para.11, repealed: 2012 c.7 s.56
 Sch.1 para.12, repealed: 2012 c.7 s.56
 Sch.1 para.13, repealed: 2012 c.7 s.56
 Sch.1 para.14, repealed: 2012 c.7 s.56
 Sch.1 para.15, repealed: 2012 c.7 s.56
 Sch.1 para.16, repealed: 2012 c.7 s.56
 Sch.1 para.17, repealed: 2012 c.7 s.56
 Sch.1 para.18, repealed: 2012 c.7 s.56
 Sch.1 para.19, repealed: 2012 c.7 s.56
 Sch.1 para.20, repealed: 2012 c.7 s.56
 Sch.1 para.21, repealed: 2012 c.7 s.56
 Sch.1 para.22, repealed: 2012 c.7 s.56
 Sch.1 para.23, repealed: 2012 c.7 s.56
 Sch.1 para.24, repealed: 2012 c.7 s.56
 Sch.1 para.25, repealed: 2012 c.7 s.56
 Sch.1 para.26, repealed: 2012 c.7 s.56
 Sch.1 para.27, repealed: 2012 c.7 s.56
 Sch.1 para.28, repealed: 2012 c.7 s.56
 Sch.1 para.29, repealed: 2012 c.7 s.56
 Sch.1 para.30, repealed: 2012 c.7 s.56
 Sch.2 para.1, repealed: 2012 c.7 s.56
 Sch.2 para.2, repealed: 2012 c.7 s.56
 Sch.2 para.3, repealed: 2012 c.7 s.56
 Sch.2 para.4, repealed: 2012 c.7 s.56
 Sch.2 para.5, repealed: 2012 c.7 s.56
 Sch.2 para.6, repealed: 2012 c.7 s.56
 Sch.3 para.1, repealed: 2012 c.7 s.56
 Sch.3 para.2, repealed: 2012 c.7 s.56
 Sch.3 para.4, repealed: 2012 c.7 s.56
 Sch.3 para.5, repealed: 2012 c.7 s.56
 Sch.3 para.6, repealed: 2012 c.7 s.56
 Sch.3 para.7, repealed: 2012 c.7 s.56
 Sch.3 para.8, repealed: 2012 c.7 s.56
 Sch.3 para.9, repealed: 2012 c.7 s.56
 Sch.3 para.10, repealed: 2012 c.7 s.56
 Sch.3 para.11, repealed: 2012 c.7 s.56
 Sch.3 para.12, repealed: 2012 c.7 s.56
 Sch.3 para.13, repealed: 2012 c.7 s.56
 Sch.3 para.14, repealed: 2012 c.7 s.56
 Sch.3 para.15, repealed: 2012 c.7 s.56
 Sch.3 para.16, repealed: 2012 c.7 s.56
 Sch.3 para.17, repealed: 2012 c.7 s.56
 Sch.3 para.18, repealed: 2012 c.7 s.56
 Sch.3 para.19, repealed: 2012 c.7 s.56
 Sch.3 para.20, repealed: 2012 c.7 s.56
 Sch.4, repealed: 2012 c.7 s.56
18. Traffic Management Act 2004
 applied: SI 2012/ 1282 Sch.1, SI 2012/ 1284 Sch.1, SI 2012/ 1286 Sch.1, SI 2012/ 1289 Sch.1, SI 2012/ 1294 Sch.1, SI 2012/ 1295 Sch.1, SI 2012/ 2541 Sch.1, SI 2012/ 2547 Sch.1, SI 2012/ 2548 Sch.1, SI 2012/ 2549 Sch.1, SI 2012/ 3102 Sch.1, SI 2012/ 3103 Sch.1, SI 2012/ 3104 Sch.1, SI 2012/ 3105 Sch.1, SI 2012/ 3106 Sch.1, SI 2012/ 3107 Sch.1
 referred to: SI 2012/ 2541 Sch.1, SI 2012/ 2547 Sch.1, SI 2012/ 2548 Sch.1, SI 2012/ 2549 Sch.1, SI 2012/ 3102 Sch.1, SI 2012/ 3103 Sch.1, SI 2012/ 3104

2004–cont.

18. Traffic Management Act 2004–*cont.*
referred to: SI 2012/2541 Sch.1–*cont.*
Sch.1, SI 2012/3105 Sch.1, SI 2012/3106 Sch.1, SI 2012/3107 Sch.1
Part 3, applied: SI 2012/1282 Sch.1, SI 2012/1284 Sch.1, SI 2012/1286 Sch.1, SI 2012/1289 Sch.1, SI 2012/1294 Sch.1, SI 2012/1295 Sch.1, SI 2012/3102 Sch.1, SI 2012/3103 Sch.1, SI 2012/3104 Sch.1, SI 2012/3105 Sch.1, SI 2012/3106 Sch.1, SI 2012/3107 Sch.1
s.1, applied: SI 2012/1295 Sch.1
s.16, applied: SI 2012/3102 Sch.1, SI 2012/3103 Sch.1, SI 2012/3104 Sch.1, SI 2012/3105 Sch.1, SI 2012/3106 Sch.1, SI 2012/3107 Sch.1
s.32, applied: SI 2012/3102 Sch.1, SI 2012/3103 Sch.1, SI 2012/3104 Sch.1, SI 2012/3105 Sch.1, SI 2012/3106 Sch.1, SI 2012/3107 Sch.1
s.32, referred to: SI 2012/2541 Sch.1, SI 2012/2547 Sch.1, SI 2012/2548 Sch.1, SI 2012/2549 Sch.1
s.33, applied: SI 2012/2541 Sch.1, SI 2012/2547 Sch.1, SI 2012/2548 Sch.1, SI 2012/2549 Sch.1, SI 2012/3102 Sch.1, SI 2012/3103 Sch.1, SI 2012/3104 Sch.1, SI 2012/3105 Sch.1, SI 2012/3106 Sch.1, SI 2012/3107 Sch.1
s.33, referred to: SI 2012/2541 Sch.1, SI 2012/2547 Sch.1, SI 2012/2548 Sch.1, SI 2012/2549 Sch.1
s.34, applied: SI 2012/1282, SI 2012/1284, SI 2012/1286, SI 2012/1289, SI 2012/1294, SI 2012/1295, SI 2012/2541, SI 2012/2547, SI 2012/2548, SI 2012/2549, SI 2012/3102, SI 2012/3103, SI 2012/3104, SI 2012/3105, SI 2012/3106, SI 2012/3107
s.34, referred to: SI 2012/2541 Sch.1, SI 2012/2547 Sch.1, SI 2012/2548 Sch.1, SI 2012/2549 Sch.1
s.34, enabling: SI 2012/785, SI 2012/1282, SI 2012/1284, SI 2012/1286, SI 2012/1289, SI 2012/1294, SI 2012/1295, SI 2012/2541, SI 2012/2547, SI 2012/2548, SI 2012/2549, SI 2012/3102, SI 2012/3103, SI 2012/3104, SI 2012/3105, SI 2012/3106, SI 2012/3107
s.35, referred to: SI 2012/2541 Sch.1, SI 2012/2547 Sch.1, SI 2012/2548 Sch.1, SI 2012/2549 Sch.1
s.36, referred to: SI 2012/2541 Sch.1, SI 2012/2547 Sch.1, SI 2012/2548 Sch.1, SI 2012/2549 Sch.1
s.37, applied: SI 2012/1282 Sch.1, SI 2012/1295 Sch.1, SI 2012/2541 Sch.1, SI 2012/2547 Sch.1, SI 2012/2548 Sch.1, SI 2012/2549 Sch.1, SI 2012/3102 Sch.1, SI 2012/3103 Sch.1, SI 2012/3104 Sch.1, SI 2012/3105 Sch.1, SI 2012/3106 Sch.1, SI 2012/3107 Sch.1
s.37, referred to: SI 2012/2541 Sch.1, SI 2012/2547 Sch.1, SI 2012/2548 Sch.1, SI 2012/2549 Sch.1
s.38, referred to: SI 2012/2541 Sch.1, SI 2012/2547 Sch.1, SI 2012/2548 Sch.1, SI 2012/2549 Sch.1
s.39, referred to: SI 2012/2541 Sch.1, SI 2012/2547 Sch.1, SI 2012/2548 Sch.1, SI 2012/2549 Sch.1
s.39, enabling: SI 2012/785, SI 2012/1282, SI 2012/1284, SI 2012/1286, SI 2012/1289, SI 2012/1294, SI 2012/1295, SI 2012/2541, SI 2012/2547, SI 2012/2548, SI 2012/2549, SI 2012/3102, SI 2012/3103, SI 2012/3104, SI 2012/3105, SI 2012/3106, SI 2012/3107
s.55, applied: SI 2012/1289 Sch.1
s.72, applied: SI 2012/1295 Sch.1
s.74, enabling: SI 2012/1189
s.84, enabling: SI 2012/1189
s.88, referred to: SI 2012/1289 Sch.1
s.89, referred to: SI 2012/1289 Sch.1
s.89, enabling: SI 2012/846, SI 2012/1189, SI 2012/2659
Sch.7, applied: SI 2012/2635 Art.39

2004–cont.

18. Traffic Management Act 2004–*cont.*
Sch.7 Part 1 para.4, amended: SI 2012/12 Reg.2
Sch.7 Part 1 para.5, enabling: SI 2012/12
Sch.8 Part 2 para.8, applied: SI 2012/846, SI 2012/1189, SI 2012/1520, SI 2012/2659
Sch.8 Part 2 para.8, enabling: SI 2012/846, SI 2012/1189, SI 2012/1520, SI 2012/2659
Sch.10 para.3, applied: SI 2012/846, SI 2012/1189, SI 2012/1520, SI 2012/2659
Sch.10 para.3, enabling: SI 2012/846, SI 2012/1189, SI 2012/1520, SI 2012/2659

19. Asylum and Immigration (Treatment of Claimants, etc.) Act 2004
s.2, see *R. v Kapoor (Saran Singh)* [2012] EWCA Crim 435, [2012] 1 W.L.R. 3569 (CA (Crim Div)), Hooper, L.J.
s.4, amended: 2012 c.9 s.110, Sch.10 Part 9
s.4, see *R. v K* [2011] EWCA Crim 1691, [2012] 3 W.L.R. 933 (CA (Crim Div)), Toulson, L.J.
s.5, amended: 2012 c.9 s.110, Sch.9 para.141, Sch.10 Part 9
s.5, repealed (in part): 2012 c.9 s.110, Sch.9 para.141, Sch.10 Part 9
s.5, substituted: 2012 c.9 s.110
s.8, see *AJ (Pakistan) v Secretary of State for the Home Department* 2012 S.L.T. 162 (IH (Ex Div)), Lord Clarke
s.14, amended: 2012 c.9 Sch.9 para.141
s.42, applied: SI 2012/971

20. Energy Act 2004
s.57, repealed: 2012 c.9 Sch.10 Part 4
s.132, amended: SI 2012/2723 Reg.3, Reg.4, Reg.5
Sch.1 Part 1 para.1, amended: SI 2012/2404 Sch.2 para.50
Sch.8 Pt 4, see *Urenco UK Ltd v Urenco UK Pension Trustee Co Ltd* [2012] EWHC 1495 (Ch), [2012] Pens. L.R. 307 (Ch D), Warren, J.
Sch.10 Part 1 para.2, amended: SI 2012/2404 Sch.2 para.50
Sch.20 Part 4 para.42, amended: 2012 c.21 Sch.18 para.101
Sch.22, applied: 2012 c.7 Sch.12 para.11

21. Fire and Rescue Services Act 2004
s.1, applied: SI 2012/632 Reg.3, SSI 2012/88 Reg.3
s.2, applied: SI 2012/1644 Sch.1, SI 2012/1647 Reg.3, SI 2012/2885 Sch.4 para.3, SI 2012/2886 Sch.1, SSI 2012/88 Reg.3, SSI 2012/303 Sch.3 para.9, SSI 2012/319 Sch.2 para.3
s.4, applied: SI 2012/1647 Reg.3, SI 2012/2879, SI 2012/2885 Sch.4 para.3, SI 2012/2886 Sch.1, SSI 2012/88 Reg.3, SSI 2012/303 Sch.3 para.9
s.4, enabling: SI 2012/2879
s.21, applied: SI 2012/1886
s.21, enabling: SI 2012/934, SI 2012/1886
s.34, amended: 2012 asp 8 Sch.7 para.66
s.34, applied: SI 2012/954, SI 2012/972, SSI 2012/107
s.34, enabling: SI 2012/954, SI 2012/972, SI 2012/2988, SSI 2012/107
s.35, amended: 2012 asp 8 Sch.7 para.66, 2012 c.21 Sch.18 para.102
s.60, enabling: SI 2012/954, SI 2012/972, SI 2012/2988, SSI 2012/107
s.62, enabling: SI 2012/934, SI 2012/972

23. Public Audit (Wales) Act 2004
s.67A, repealed (in part): SI 2012/2401 Sch.1 para.17
Sch.2 para.15, repealed: 2012 c.5 Sch.14 Part 1

2004–cont.

27. Companies (Audit, Investigations and Community Enterprise) Act 2004
s.14, amended: 2012 c.21 Sch.18 para.103
s.14, applied: SI 2012/ 1439 Art.7, SI 2012/ 1439(b)
s.14, referred to: SI 2012/ 1439 Art.2, Art.3
s.14, enabling: SI 2012/ 1439
s.15D, amended: SI 2012/ 1439 Art.6
s.15E, enabling: SI 2012/ 1439
s.16, referred to: SI 2012/ 691 Art.2
s.26, applied: SI 2012/ 1907 Sch.1 para.8
s.34, enabling: SI 2012/ 2335
s.62, applied: SI 2012/ 2335
s.62, enabling: SI 2012/ 2335

28. Domestic Violence, Crime and Victims Act 2004
Commencement Orders: SI 2012/ 1697 Art.2
Part 1, substituted: 2012 c.4 s.1
s.5, see *J (Children) (Care Proceedings: Threshold Criteria), Re* [2012] EWCA Civ 380, [2012] 3 W.L.R. 952 (CA (Civ Div)), Lord Judge, L.C.J.
s.5, amended: 2012 c.4 s.1
s.6, amended: 2012 c.4 Sch.1 para.8
s.6, substituted: 2012 c.4 Sch.1 para.8
s.6A, added: 2012 c.4 s.2
s.8, amended: 2012 c.4 Sch.1 para.9
s.9, amended: 2012 c.7 Sch.5 para.126, Sch.14 para.95
s.17, applied: SI 2012/ 1726 r.15.1
s.18, referred to: SI 2012/ 1726 r.15.1
s.31, repealed: 2012 c.10 Sch.10 para.40
s.37A, amended: 2012 c.7 s.39
s.37A, repealed (in part): 2012 c.7 s.39
s.38A, repealed (in part): 2012 c.7 s.39
s.43A, amended: 2012 c.7 s.39
s.43A, repealed (in part): 2012 c.7 s.39
s.44A, repealed (in part): 2012 c.7 s.39
s.60, enabling: SI 2012/ 1697
s.62, amended: 2012 c.4 Sch.1 para.10
Sch.6 para.1, repealed: 2012 c.10 Sch.10 para.40
Sch.6 para.2, repealed: 2012 c.10 Sch.10 para.40
Sch.6 para.3, repealed: 2012 c.10 Sch.10 para.40
Sch.6 para.4, repealed: 2012 c.10 Sch.10 para.40
Sch.6 para.5, repealed: 2012 c.10 Sch.10 para.40
Sch.6 para.6, repealed: 2012 c.10 Sch.10 para.40
Sch.6 para.7, repealed: 2012 c.10 Sch.10 para.40
Sch.9 para.21, repealed: 2012 c.10 Sch.5 para.66
Sch.10 para.46, repealed: 2012 c.10 Sch.16 para.18
Sch.11, amended: 2012 c.10 Sch.10 para.40

30. Human Tissue Act 2004
s.14, amended: SI 2012/ 1501 Reg.25
s.14, applied: SI 2012/ 1501 Reg.7
s.15, applied: SI 2012/ 1501 Reg.7
s.19, applied: SI 2012/ 1501 Reg.6
s.19, varied: SI 2012/ 1501 Reg.6
s.20, applied: SI 2012/ 1501 Reg.6
s.21, applied: SI 2012/ 1501 Reg.6, Reg.21
s.22, applied: SI 2012/ 1501 Reg.6
s.22, varied: SI 2012/ 1501 Reg.6
s.23, applied: SI 2012/ 1501 Reg.1, Reg.6, Reg.10, Reg.11, Reg.13, Reg.21, Sch.2 para.1, Sch.2 para.2
s.23, varied: SI 2012/ 1501 Reg.6
s.24, applied: SI 2012/ 1501 Reg.6, Reg.10, Reg.13, Reg.21
s.24, varied: SI 2012/ 1501 Reg.6
s.32, amended: SI 2012/ 1501 Reg.25
s.37, applied: SI 2012/ 1501 Reg.6
s.37, varied: SI 2012/ 1501 Reg.6
s.41, amended: SI 2012/ 1501 Reg.25
s.59, amended: SI 2012/ 1501 Reg.25

2004–cont.

30. Human Tissue Act 2004–*cont.*
Sch.2 para.1, amended: SI 2012/ 1501 Reg.25
Sch.2 para.3, amended: SI 2012/ 2404 Sch.2 para.51
Sch.3 para.2, applied: SI 2012/ 1501 Reg.1, Reg.6, Reg.10, Reg.13, Reg.21
Sch.3 para.2, varied: SI 2012/ 1501 Reg.6
Sch.3 para.5, applied: SI 2012/ 1501 Reg.6
Sch.3 para.7, applied: SI 2012/ 1501 Reg.6
Sch.3 para.7, varied: SI 2012/ 1501 Reg.6
Sch.3 para.8, applied: SI 2012/ 1501 Reg.6
Sch.3 para.8, varied: SI 2012/ 1501 Reg.6
Sch.3 para.9, applied: SI 2012/ 1501 Reg.6
Sch.3 para.9, varied: SI 2012/ 1501 Reg.6
Sch.3 para.10, applied: SI 2012/ 1501 Reg.6, Reg.21
Sch.3 para.10, varied: SI 2012/ 1501 Reg.6
Sch.3 para.11, applied: SI 2012/ 1501 Reg.6
Sch.3 para.11, varied: SI 2012/ 1501 Reg.6
Sch.3 para.13, amended: SI 2012/ 1501 Reg.25
Sch.3 para.13, applied: SI 2012/ 1501 Reg.6, Reg.21, Sch.1 para.10

31. Children Act 2004
s.10, amended: 2012 c.7 Sch.5 para.128
s.10, repealed (in part): 2012 c.7 Sch.5 para.128
s.11, see *Castle v Commissioner of Police of the Metropolis* [2011] EWHC 2317 (Admin), [2012] 1 All E.R. 953 (DC), Pitchford, L.J.
s.11, amended: 2012 c.7 Sch.5 para.129
s.11, repealed (in part): 2012 c.7 Sch.5 para.129, Sch.14 para.97
s.12, amended: SI 2012/ 976 Sch.1 para.14
s.12, enabling: SI 2012/ 1278
s.12A, amended: 2012 c.7 Sch.5 para.130
s.13, amended: 2012 c.7 Sch.5 para.131, Sch.14 para.98
s.13, repealed (in part): 2012 c.7 Sch.5 para.131
s.20, repealed (in part): SI 2012/ 2401 Sch.1 para.19
s.28, amended: 2012 c.7 Sch.14 para.99
s.32, enabling: SI 2012/ 1712
s.34, enabling: SI 2012/ 1712
s.66, applied: SI 2012/ 1278
s.66, enabling: SI 2012/ 1278, SI 2012/ 1712

32. Armed Forces (Pensions and Compensation) Act 2004
s.1, applied: SI 2012/ 2677 Reg.44
s.1, enabling: SI 2012/ 1573, SI 2012/ 1796

33. Civil Partnership Act 2004
see *Dunn v Institute of Cemetery and Crematorium Management* [2012] I.C.R. 941 (EAT), Judge McMullen Q.C.
applied: SI 2012/ 687 Sch.1 para.2, SI 2012/ 1969 Art.3, Art.4, SI 2012/ 2655 Sch.1 para.1
Part 2 c.2, applied: 2012 c.10 Sch.1 para.33
Part 2 c.3, applied: 2012 c.10 Sch.1 para.33
s.17, amended: 2012 c.9 s.114, Sch.10 Part 11
s.31, repealed (in part): 2012 c.9 s.114, Sch.10 Part 11
s.34, enabling: SI 2012/ 761
s.112, amended: 2012 asp 5 Sch.5 para.44
s.117, referred to: SSI 2012/ 111 Art.2
s.210, amended: SI 2012/ 3100 Art.2
s.210, enabling: SI 2012/ 3063
s.213, enabling: SI 2012/ 2976
s.240, enabling: SI 2012/ 3063
s.241, enabling: SI 2012/ 3063
s.244, enabling: SI 2012/ 3063
s.258, enabling: SI 2012/ 761
s.259, applied: SSI 2012/ 287
s.259, enabling: SSI 2012/ 287

2004–cont.

33. Civil Partnership Act 2004–*cont.*

Sch.5, see *Lawrence v Gallagher* [2012] EWCA Civ 394, [2012] 2 F.L.R. 643 (CA (Civ Div)), Thorpe, L.J.

Sch.5 Part 3 para.10, amended: 2012 c.10 s.54

Sch.5 Part 8 para.38, amended: 2012 c.10 s.52

Sch.5 Part 8 para.38, substituted: 2012 c.10 s.52

Sch.5 Part 8 para.38A, added: 2012 c.10 s.52

Sch.5 Part 8 para.38A, amended: 2012 c.10 s.52

Sch.5 Part 8 para.38B, added: 2012 c.10 s.53

Sch.5 Part 8 para.38B, amended: 2012 c.10 s.52

Sch.6 Part 6, applied: SI 2012/687 Sch.4 para.9

Sch.15 Part 5, applied: SI 2012/687 Sch.4 para.9

Sch.20, amended: SI 2012/2976 Sch.1 para.2, Sch.1 para.3, Sch.1 para.4, Sch.1 para.5, Sch.1 para.6, Sch.1 para.7, Sch.1 para.8, Sch.1 para.9, Sch.1 para.10, Sch.1 para.11, Sch.1 para.12, Sch.1 para.13, Sch.1 para.14, Sch.1 para.15, Sch.1 para.16, Sch.1 para.17, Sch.1 para.18, Sch.1 para.19

Sch.24 Part 3 para.42, repealed: 2012 c.5 Sch.14 Part 1

Sch.24 Part 3 para.43, repealed: 2012 c.5 Sch.14 Part 1

Sch.24 Part 3 para.44, repealed: 2012 c.5 Sch.14 Part 1

Sch.24 Part 3 para.45, repealed: 2012 c.5 Sch.14 Part 1

Sch.24 Part 3 para.46, repealed: 2012 c.5 Sch.14 Part 1

Sch.24 Part 3 para.53, repealed: 2012 c.5 Sch.14 Part 7

Sch.24 Part 4 para.55, repealed: 2012 c.5 Sch.14 Part 1

Sch.24 Part 4 para.61, repealed: 2012 c.5 Sch.14 Part 8

Sch.24 Part 7 para.118, repealed: 2012 c.5 Sch.14 Part 1

Sch.24 Part 7 para.119, repealed: 2012 c.5 Sch.14 Part 1

Sch.24 Part 7 para.120, repealed: 2012 c.5 Sch.14 Part 1

Sch.24 Part 7 para.121, repealed: 2012 c.5 Sch.14 Part 1

Sch.24 Part 7 para.122, repealed: 2012 c.5 Sch.14 Part 1

Sch.24 Part 14 para.144, repealed: 2012 c.5 Sch.14 Part 1

Sch.24 Part 14 para.145, repealed: 2012 c.5 Sch.14 Part 1

Sch.24 Part 14 para.146, repealed: 2012 c.5 Sch.14 Part 1

Sch.24 Part 14 para.147, repealed: 2012 c.5 Sch.14 Part 1

Sch.27 para.156, repealed: 2012 c.10 Sch.5 Part 2

34. Housing Act 2004

see *Liverpool City Council v Kassim* [2012] UKUT 169 (LC), [2012] J.P.L. 1395 (UT (Lands)), George Bartlett Q.C. (President, LTr)

applied: SI 2012/531 Reg.14, Reg.40

referred to: SI 2012/531 Reg.4

Part 2, applied: SI 2012/531 Sch.1 para.16

s.20, see *Liverpool City Council v Kassim* [2012] UKUT 169 (LC), [2012] J.P.L. 1395 (UT (Lands)), George Bartlett Q.C. (President, LTr)

s.22, applied: SI 2012/531 Reg.45, Sch.1 para.5

s.34, applied: SI 2012/531 Sch.1 para.6

s.41, applied: SI 2012/531 Sch.1 para.9

s.42, referred to: SI 2012/531 Sch.1 para.4, Sch.1 para.11

s.43, applied: SI 2012/531 Sch.1 para.10

2004–cont.

34. Housing Act 2004–*cont.*

s.45, applied: SI 2012/531 Sch.1 para.9, Sch.1 para.10

s.49, applied: SI 2012/531 Reg.45

s.55, applied: SI 2012/2601 Art.3

s.56, applied: SI 2012/2601 Art.3

s.62, applied: SI 2012/531 Reg.45, Sch.1 para.12

s.63, enabling: SI 2012/2111

s.72, applied: SI 2012/531 Sch.1 para.13, SI 2012/628 Art.17

s.73, applied: SI 2012/531 Sch.1 para.13, SI 2012/628 Art.17

s.74, applied: SI 2012/628 Art.17

s.74, referred to: SI 2012/531 Sch.1 para.13

s.77, applied: SI 2012/2421 Sch.1 para.2

s.80, see *Sumal & Sons (Properties) Ltd v Newham LBC* [2012] EWCA Crim 1840, [2012] Lloyd's Rep. F.C. 692 (CA (Crim Div)), Davis, L.J.

s.86, applied: SI 2012/531 Reg.45, Sch.1 para.18

s.87, enabling: SI 2012/2111

s.95, see *Sumal & Sons (Properties) Ltd v Newham LBC* [2012] EWCA Crim 1840, [2012] Lloyd's Rep. F.C. 692 (CA (Crim Div)), Davis, L.J.

s.95, applied: SI 2012/531 Sch.1 para.19

s.96, see *Sumal & Sons (Properties) Ltd v Newham LBC* [2012] EWCA Crim 1840, [2012] Lloyd's Rep. F.C. 692 (CA (Crim Div)), Davis, L.J.

s.96, applied: SI 2012/531 Sch.1 para.19

s.97, referred to: SI 2012/531 Sch.1 para.19

s.102, applied: SI 2012/531 Sch.1 para.22, Sch.1 para.23

s.103, applied: SI 2012/531 Sch.1 para.23

s.104, applied: SI 2012/531 Sch.1 para.22

s.105, applied: SI 2012/531 Sch.1 para.24

s.110, applied: SI 2012/531 Sch.1 para.25

s.110, referred to: SI 2012/531 Sch.1 para.30

s.114, applied: SI 2012/531 Sch.1 para.26

s.120, applied: SI 2012/531 Sch.1 para.27

s.126, applied: SI 2012/531 Reg.45, Sch.1 para.28

s.128, applied: SI 2012/531 Sch.1 para.32

s.130, applied: SI 2012/531 Sch.1 para.29

s.133, applied: SI 2012/531 Sch.1 para.33

s.134, applied: SI 2012/531 Sch.1 para.33, SI 2012/2625 Art.2

s.134, enabling: SI 2012/2625

s.136, applied: SI 2012/531 Sch.1 para.42

s.138, applied: SI 2012/531 Reg.45, Sch.1 para.34, Sch.1 para.42

s.143, applied: SI 2012/531 Sch.1 para.43

s.144, applied: SI 2012/531 Sch.1 para.44

s.213, see *Potts v Densley* [2011] EWHC 1144 (QB), [2012] 1 W.L.R. 1204 (QBD), Sharp, J.; see *Suurpere v Nice* [2011] EWHC 2003 (QB), [2012] 1 W.L.R. 1224 (QBD), Cox, J.; see *Tiensia v Vision Enterprises Ltd (t/a Universal Estates)* [2010] EWCA Civ 1224, [2012] 1 W.L.R. 94 (CA (Civ Div)), Thorpe, L.J.

s.213, applied: SI 2012/628 Art.16

s.214, see *Potts v Densley* [2011] EWHC 1144 (QB), [2012] 1 W.L.R. 1204 (QBD), Sharp, J.; see *Suurpere v Nice* [2011] EWHC 2003 (QB), [2012] 1 W.L.R. 1224 (QBD), Cox, J.; see *Tiensia v Vision Enterprises Ltd (t/a Universal Estates)* [2010] EWCA Civ 1224, [2012] 1 W.L.R. 94 (CA (Civ Div)), Thorpe, L.J.

s.229, enabling: SI 2012/899

s.230, amended: SI 2012/899 Art.4

s.230, applied: SI 2012/531 Reg.23, Reg.25

s.233, applied: SI 2012/531 Sch.1 para.22, SI 2012/2601 Art.3

2004—cont.

34. Housing Act 2004—*cont.*

s.250, applied: SI 2012/899

s.250, enabling: SI 2012/531, SI 2012/899, SI 2012/2111, SI 2012/2625

s.255, applied: SI 2012/531 Sch.1 para.14

s.256, applied: SI 2012/531 Sch.1 para.15

Sch.1 Part 3 para.10, applied: SI 2012/531 Reg.45, Sch.1 para.1, Sch.1 para.2

Sch.1 Part 3 para.11, referred to: SI 2012/531 Sch.1 para.2

Sch.1 Part 3 para.12, referred to: SI 2012/531 Sch.1 para.1, Sch.1 para.2

Sch.1 Part 3 para.13, applied: SI 2012/531 Reg.45, Sch.1 para.3

Sch.2 Part 3 para.7, applied: SI 2012/531 Reg.45, Sch.1 para.7

Sch.2 Part 3 para.8, applied: SI 2012/531 Sch.1 para.7

Sch.2 Part 3 para.9, applied: SI 2012/531 Reg.45, Sch.1 para.8

Sch.3 Part 2 para.4, applied: SI 2012/531 Sch.1 para.4

Sch.3 Part 3 para.9, applied: SI 2012/531 Sch.1 para.11

Sch.3 Part 3 para.11, applied: SI 2012/531 Reg.45, Sch.1 para.4

Sch.3 Part 3 para.11, referred to: SI 2012/531 Sch.1 para.4

Sch.3 Part 3 para.12, applied: SI 2012/531 Sch.1 para.11

Sch.3 Part 3 para.14, applied: SI 2012/531 Sch.1 para.11

Sch.5 Part 1 para.1, applied: SI 2012/531 Sch.1 para.16, Sch.1 para.20

Sch.5 Part 1 para.3, applied: SI 2012/531 Sch.1 para.16, Sch.1 para.20

Sch.5 Part 1 para.5, applied: SI 2012/531 Sch.1 para.16, Sch.1 para.20

Sch.5 Part 1 para.7, applied: SI 2012/531 Sch.1 para.16, Sch.1 para.20

Sch.5 Part 1 para.8, applied: SI 2012/531 Sch.1 para.16, Sch.1 para.20

Sch.5 Part 2 para.14, applied: SI 2012/531 Sch.1 para.17, Sch.1 para.21

Sch.5 Part 2 para.16, applied: SI 2012/531 Sch.1 para.17, Sch.1 para.21

Sch.5 Part 2 para.19, applied: SI 2012/531 Sch.1 para.17, Sch.1 para.21

Sch.5 Part 2 para.21, applied: SI 2012/531 Sch.1 para.17, Sch.1 para.21

Sch.5 Part 2 para.22, applied: SI 2012/531 Sch.1 para.17, Sch.1 para.21

Sch.5 Part 2 para.24, applied: SI 2012/531 Sch.1 para.17, Sch.1 para.21

Sch.5 Part 2 para.26, applied: SI 2012/531 Sch.1 para.17, Sch.1 para.21

Sch.5 Part 2 para.28, applied: SI 2012/531 Sch.1 para.17, Sch.1 para.21

Sch.5 Part 3 para.31, applied: SI 2012/531 Reg.45, Sch.1 para.16, Sch.1 para.20

Sch.5 Part 3 para.32, applied: SI 2012/531 Reg.45, Sch.1 para.17, Sch.1 para.21

Sch.6 Part 1 para.7, applied: SI 2012/531 Sch.1 para.30, Sch.1 para.31

Sch.6 Part 1 para.8, applied: SI 2012/531 Sch.1 para.22, Sch.1 para.23

Sch.6 Part 2 para.9, applied: SI 2012/531 Sch.1 para.31, Sch.1 para.41

Sch.6 Part 2 para.11, applied: SI 2012/531 Sch.1 para.31, Sch.1 para.41

2004—cont.

34. Housing Act 2004—*cont.*

Sch.6 Part 2 para.14, applied: SI 2012/531 Sch.1 para.31, Sch.1 para.41

Sch.6 Part 2 para.16, applied: SI 2012/531 Sch.1 para.31, Sch.1 para.41

Sch.6 Part 2 para.17, applied: SI 2012/531 Sch.1 para.31, Sch.1 para.41

Sch.6 Part 2 para.19, applied: SI 2012/531 Sch.1 para.31, Sch.1 para.41

Sch.6 Part 2 para.20, applied: SI 2012/531 Sch.1 para.31, Sch.1 para.41

Sch.6 Part 2 para.22, applied: SI 2012/531 Sch.1 para.31, Sch.1 para.41

Sch.6 Part 3 para.24, applied: SI 2012/531 Reg.45, Sch.1 para.24, Sch.1 para.26, Sch.1 para.30

Sch.6 Part 3 para.24, referred to: SI 2012/531 Sch.1 para.30

Sch.6 Part 3 para.28, applied: SI 2012/531 Reg.45, Sch.1 para.31

Sch.6 Part 3 para.32, applied: SI 2012/531 Reg.45, Sch.1 para.32

Sch.6 Part 3 para.35, applied: SI 2012/531 Sch.1 para.22, Sch.1 para.23

Sch.7 Part 1 para.1, applied: SI 2012/531 Sch.1 para.35

Sch.7 Part 1 para.2, applied: SI 2012/531 Sch.1 para.36

Sch.7 Part 1 para.5, applied: SI 2012/531 Sch.1 para.37

Sch.7 Part 1 para.5, referred to: SI 2012/531 Sch.1 para.40

Sch.7 Part 2 para.9, applied: SI 2012/531 Sch.1 para.38

Sch.7 Part 2 para.10, applied: SI 2012/531 Sch.1 para.36

Sch.7 Part 2 para.14, applied: SI 2012/531 Sch.1 para.39

Sch.7 Part 3 para.22, applied: SI 2012/531 Sch.1 para.36

Sch.7 Part 4 para.26, applied: SI 2012/531 Reg.45, Sch.1 para.35, Sch.1 para.38, Sch.1 para.40

Sch.7 Part 4 para.26, referred to: SI 2012/531 Sch.1 para.40

Sch.7 Part 4 para.30, applied: SI 2012/531 Reg.45, Sch.1 para.41

Sch.7 Part 4 para.34, applied: SI 2012/531 Reg.45, Sch.1 para.42

Sch.13, enabling: SI 2012/531

Sch.13 para.2, amended: SI 2012/899 Art.4

Sch.13 para.3, amended: SI 2012/899 Art.4

Sch.13 para.8, amended: SI 2012/899 Art.4

Sch.13 para.12, amended: SI 2012/899 Art.4

Sch.13 para.12, applied: SI 2012/531 Reg.35

Sch.14 para.4, applied: SI 2012/249 Reg.2, Sch.1

Sch.14 para.4, enabling: SI 2012/249

35. Pensions Act 2004

see *Bloom v Pensions Regulator* [2011] EWCA Civ 1124, [2012] Bus. L.R. 818 (CA (Civ Div)), Laws, L.J.; see *IBM Pension Plan, Re* [2012] EWHC 2766 (Ch), [2012] Pens. L.R. 469 (Ch D), Warren, J.

s.23, enabling: SI 2012/692

s.86, applied: SI 2012/691

s.86, enabling: SI 2012/691

s.115, amended: 2012 c.21 Sch.18 para.104

s.117, applied: SI 2012/539

s.117, enabling: SI 2012/539

s.121, see *Olympic Airlines SA, Re* [2012] EWHC 1413 (Ch), [2012] I.L.Pr. 35 (Ch D), Sir Andrew Morritt (Chancellor)

2004–cont.

35. Pensions Act 2004–*cont.*

s.127, see *Olympic Airlines SA, Re* [2012] EWHC 1413 (Ch), [2012] I.L.Pr. 35 (Ch D), Sir Andrew Morritt (Chancellor)

s.143, enabling: SI 2012/692, SI 2012/1688, SI 2012/3083

s.143A, enabling: SI 2012/1688, SI 2012/3083

s.151, enabling: SI 2012/1688, SI 2012/3083

s.156, enabling: SI 2012/692, SI 2012/1688, SI 2012/3083

s.177, applied: SI 2012/528 Art.3

s.178, applied: SI 2012/528, SI 2012/528 Art.2

s.178, enabling: SI 2012/528

s.179, enabling: SI 2012/692

s.185, enabling: SI 2012/1688, SI 2012/3083

s.203, enabling: SI 2012/1688, SI 2012/3083

s.207, enabling: SI 2012/1688, SI 2012/3083

s.213, enabling: SI 2012/1688

s.221, see *Olympic Airlines SA, Re* [2012] EWHC 1413 (Ch), [2012] I.L.Pr. 35 (Ch D), Sir Andrew Morritt (Chancellor)

s.227, referred to: SI 2012/688 Sch.1 para.4

s.230, enabling: SI 2012/1817

s.259, enabling: SI 2012/692

s.260, enabling: SI 2012/692

s.292A, enabling: SI 2012/1477

s.307, enabling: SI 2012/1688, SI 2012/3083

s.315, enabling: SI 2012/528, SI 2012/539, SI 2012/692, SI 2012/1477, SI 2012/1688, SI 2012/3083

s.317, applied: SI 2012/539, SI 2012/692, SI 2012/1477, SI 2012/1688, SI 2012/1817

s.318, enabling: SI 2012/539, SI 2012/692, SI 2012/1477, SI 2012/1688, SI 2012/1817, SI 2012/3083

Sch.3, amended: 2012 c.21 Sch.18 para.104, SI 2012/691 Art.2, SI 2012/3006 Art.84

Sch.5 Part 4 para.22, enabling: SI 2012/692

Sch.7 para.26, applied: SI 2012/528 Art.4

Sch.7 para.26, enabling: SI 2012/528

Sch.7 para.27, enabling: SI 2012/528

Sch.8, amended: 2012 c.21 Sch.18 para.104, SI 2012/3006 Art.85

Sch.10 para.3, repealed: 2012 c.5 Sch.14 Part 1

36. Civil Contingencies Act 2004

s.2, enabling: SI 2012/624

s.6, enabling: SI 2012/624

s.14, applied: SI 2012/624

s.14A, applied: SI 2012/624

s.16, applied: SI 2012/624

s.17, enabling: SI 2012/624

Sch.1 Part 1 para.4A, added: 2012 c.7 Sch.5 para.132

Sch.1 Part 1 para.5, amended: 2012 c.7 Sch.14 para.100

Sch.1 Part 1 para.7, repealed: 2012 c.7 Sch.5 para.132

Sch.1 Part 1 para.9, substituted: 2012 c.7 Sch.7 para.16

Sch.1 Part 3 para.26A, added: 2012 c.19 Sch.9 para.16

Sch.1 Part 3 para.29A, repealed: 2012 c.7 Sch.5 para.132

Sch.1 Part 3 para.29ZA, added: 2012 c.7 Sch.5 para.132

Sch.1 Part 4 para.36A, added: 2012 c.19 Sch.9 para.16

2005

2. Prevention of Terrorism Act 2005

see *Secretary of State for the Home Department v BM* [2012] EWHC 714 (Admin), [2012] 1 W.L.R. 2734 (QBD (Admin)), Collins, J.

s.3, see *Secretary of State for the Home Department v CB* [2012] EWCA Civ 418, [2012] 1 W.L.R. 3259 (CA (Civ Div)), Lord Neuberger (M.R.)

4. Constitutional Reform Act 2005

Sch.4 Part 1 para.102, repealed (in part): SI 2012/2398 Sch.2 para.9

Sch.4 Part 1 para.137, repealed: SI 2012/2398 Sch.1 para.9

Sch.4 Part 1 para.310, repealed (in part): SI 2012/1206 Sch.1 para.9

Sch.4 Part 1 para.311, repealed (in part): SI 2012/1206 Sch.1 para.9

Sch.4 Part 1 para.350, repealed (in part): SI 2012/1206 Sch.1 para.9

Sch.7 para.4, amended: 2012 c.21 Sch.19

Sch.9 Part 1 para.68, repealed (in part): 2012 c.10 Sch.5 Part 2

Sch.9 Part 1 para.70, repealed: 2012 c.21 Sch.19

Sch.12 Part 1 para.15, amended: SI 2012/2404 Sch.2 para.52

Sch.13 para.5, amended: SI 2012/2404 Sch.2 para.52

5. Income Tax (Trading and Other Income) Act 2005

see *Donaghy v Revenue and Customs Commissioners* [2012] UKUT 148 (TCC), [2012] S.T.C. 1931 (UT (Tax)), Judge Aleksander (Chairman)

applied: 2012 c.14 Sch.13 para.8, Sch.13 para.22

Part 2, applied: SI 2012/2677 Reg.36, Reg.39

Part 2 c.11, amended: SI 2012/266 Art.4

Part 3, applied: SI 2012/2677 Reg.69

Part 4, applied: SI 2012/2677 Reg.69

Part 4 c.9, disapplied: 2012 c.14 s.61

Part 5, applied: SI 2012/2677 Reg.69

Part 5 c.8, applied: 2012 c.14 Sch.13 para.13, Sch.13 para.30

Part 6 c.3, applied: SI 2012/847 Reg.6, Reg.7

Part 9, applied: 2012 c.14 Sch.13 para.10, Sch.13 para.11, Sch.13 para.24, Sch.13 para.25

Pt 2. see *Donaghy v Revenue and Customs Commissioners* [2012] UKUT 148 (TCC), [2012] S.T.C. 1931 (UT (Tax)), Judge Aleksander (Chairman); see *Samarkand Film Partnership No.3 v Revenue and Customs Commissioners* [2012] S.F.T.D. 1 (FTT (Tax)), Judge Charles Hellier

s.34, see *Duckmanton v Revenue and Customs Commissioners* [2012] S.F.T.D. 293 (FTT (Tax)), Judge Michael Connell

s.48, amended: 2012 c.14 Sch.16 para.126

s.48, repealed (in part): 2012 c.14 Sch.16 para.126

s.71, amended: SI 2012/976 Sch.1 para.15

s.108, applied: SI 2012/847 Reg.25

s.108, repealed (in part): SI 2012/964 Sch.1

s.133, see *Samarkand Film Partnership No.3 v Revenue and Customs Commissioners* [2012] S.F.T.D. 1 (FTT (Tax)), Judge Charles Hellier

s.134, see *Samarkand Film Partnership No.3 v Revenue and Customs Commissioners* [2012] S.F.T.D. 1 (FTT (Tax)), Judge Charles Hellier

s.138, see *Samarkand Film Partnership No.3 v Revenue and Customs Commissioners* [2012] S.F.T.D. 1 (FTT (Tax)), Judge Charles Hellier

s.157, repealed: 2012 c.14 Sch.39 para.43

s.162, repealed: 2012 c.14 Sch.39 para.21

2005– cont.

5. Income Tax (Trading and Other Income) Act 2005– *cont.*

s.168, amended: 2012 c.14 s.53
s.170, amended: SI 2012/266 Art.4
s.172ZA, added: SI 2012/266 Art.4
s.172ZB, added: SI 2012/266 Art.4
s.172ZC, added: SI 2012/266 Art.4
s.172ZD, added: SI 2012/266 Art.4
s.172ZE, added: SI 2012/266 Art.4
s.221, amended: SI 2012/266 Art.7
s.225ZA, added: SI 2012/266 Art.6
s.225ZB, added: SI 2012/266 Art.6
s.225ZC, added: SI 2012/266 Art.6
s.225ZD, added: SI 2012/266 Art.6
s.225ZE, added: SI 2012/266 Art.6
s.225ZF, added: SI 2012/266 Art.6
s.225ZG, added: SI 2012/266 Art.6
s.227, amended: 2012 c.14 s.54
s.319, repealed: 2012 c.14 Sch.39 para.43
s.337, amended: 2012 c.14 Sch.39 para.43
s.339, repealed (in part): 2012 c.14 Sch.39 para.43
s.340, repealed: 2012 c.14 Sch.39 para.43
s.341, repealed: 2012 c.14 Sch.39 para.43
s.342, repealed: 2012 c.14 Sch.39 para.43
s.343, repealed: 2012 c.14 Sch.39 para.43
s.369, amended: 2012 c.14 Sch.39 para.53
s.455, amended: 2012 c.14 Sch.39 para.48
s.473, amended: 2012 c.14 Sch.16 para.127
s.473A, added: 2012 c.14 s.11
s.473A, applied: 2012 c.14 s.11
s.476, amended: 2012 c.14 Sch.16 para.128
s.491, amended: 2012 c.14 s.11
s.504, amended: 2012 c.14 Sch.16 para.129
s.531, amended: 2012 c.14 Sch.16 para.130, Sch.18 para.18
s.609, see *Eclipse Film Partners No 35 LLP v Revenue and Customs Commissioners* [2012] UKFTT 270 (TC), [2012] S.F.T.D. 823 (FTT (Tax)), Judge Edward Sadler
s.620, amended: SI 2012/964 Sch.1
s.620, repealed (in part): SI 2012/964 Sch.1
s.627, amended: 2012 c.14 s.12
s.628, amended: SI 2012/964 Sch.1
s.628, repealed (in part): SI 2012/964 Sch.1
s.640, amended: 2012 c.14 s.1
s.645, amended: 2012 c.14 s.12
s.683, repealed (in part): 2012 c.14 Sch.39 para.21
s.694, enabling: SI 2012/705, SI 2012/1871
s.695, applied: 2012 c.14 s.60
s.695, enabling: SI 2012/1871
s.695A, enabling: SI 2012/1871
s.696, enabling: SI 2012/1871
s.697, enabling: SI 2012/1871
s.698, enabling: SI 2012/1871
s.699, enabling: SI 2012/1871
s.701, enabling: SI 2012/1871
s.717, applied: 2012 c.14 s.83
s.717, varied: 2012 c.14 s.83
s.718, varied: 2012 c.14 s.83
s.724, enabling: SI 2012/2902
s.725, applied: 2012 c.14 s.57
s.732, enabling: SI 2012/1188
s.748, repealed: 2012 c.14 Sch.39 para.21
s.750, repealed: 2012 c.14 Sch.39 para.53
s.806A, enabling: SI 2012/794
s.847, referred to: 2012 c.14 Sch.13 para.8, Sch.13 para.22

2005– cont.

5. Income Tax (Trading and Other Income) Act 2005– *cont.*

s.863, see *Eclipse Film Partners No 35 LLP v Revenue and Customs Commissioners* [2012] UKFTT 270 (TC), [2012] S.F.T.D. 823 (FTT (Tax)), Judge Edward Sadler
s.863, applied: 2012 c.14 Sch.13 para.8, Sch.13 para.22
s.874, applied: SI 2012/847 Reg.21
Sch.1 Part 1 para.123, repealed: 2012 c.14 Sch.39 para.31
Sch.1 Part 1 para.176, repealed: 2012 c.14 Sch.16 para.247
Sch.1 Part 1 para.178, repealed: 2012 c.14 Sch.16 para.247
Sch.1 Part 2 para.416, repealed: 2012 c.14 Sch.39 para.19
Sch.1 Part 2 para.559, repealed: 2012 c.14 Sch.39 para.39
Sch.1 Part 2 para.560, repealed: 2012 c.14 Sch.39 para.39
Sch.2 Part 6 para.118, amended: 2012 c.14 Sch.16 para.131
Sch.4 Part 2, amended: SI 2012/266 Art.8

7. Finance Act 2005

s.96, repealed: 2012 c.14 Sch.39 para.8
Sch.9 para.1, repealed: 2012 c.14 Sch.39 para.8
Sch.9 para.2, repealed: 2012 c.14 Sch.39 para.7
Sch.9 para.3, repealed: 2012 c.14 Sch.39 para.7
Sch.9 para.4, repealed: 2012 c.14 Sch.39 para.8
Sch.9 para.5, repealed: 2012 c.14 Sch.39 para.7

9. Mental Capacity Act 2005

see *A Local Authority v DL* [2011] EWHC 1022 (Fam), [2012] 1 F.L.R. 1119 (Fam Div), Theis, J.; see *A Local Authority v DL* [2012] EWCA Civ 253, [2012] 3 W.L.R. 1439 (CA (Civ Div)), Maurice Kay, L.J.; see *D (Statutory Will), Re* [2010] EWHC 2159 (Ch), [2012] Ch. 57 (CP), Judge Hodge Q.C.; see *D Borough Council v B* [2011] EWHC 101 (Fam), [2012] Fam. 36 (CP), Mostyn, J.; see *D v JC* [2012] W.T.L.R. 1211 (CP), Senior Judge Denzil Lush; see *DM v Doncaster MBC* [2011] EWHC 3652 (Admin), (2012) 15 C.C.L. Rep. 128 (QBD (Admin)), Langstaff, J.; see *G v E* [2010] EWCA Civ 822, [2012] Fam. 78 (CA (Civ Div)), Sir Nicholas Wall (President, Fam); see *JDS, Re* [2012] W.T.L.R. 475 (CP), Senior Judge Denzil Lush; see *K v A Local Authority* [2012] EWCA Civ 79, [2012] 1 F.C.R. 441 (CA (Civ Div)), Thorpe, L.J.; see *RB (An Adult), Re* [2011] EWHC 3017 (Fam), [2012] 1 F.L.R. 466 (Fam Div), Munby, L.J.; see *Seaton v Seddon* [2012] EWHC 735 (Ch), [2012] 1 W.L.R. 3636 (Ch D), Roth, J.; see *XCC v AA* [2012] EWHC 2183 (COP), (2012) 15 C.C.L. Rep. 447 (CP), Parker, J.
applied: 2012 c.9 s.27, 2012 c.10 Sch.1 para.5, SI 2012/2730 Reg.7, SI 2012/2885 Sch.8 para.4, Sch.8 para.12, SI 2012/2886 Sch.1, SI 2012/3094 Reg.23, SI 2012/3145 Sch.1
Pt 1. see *XCC v AA* [2012] EWHC 2183 (COP), (2012) 15 C.C.L. Rep. 447 (CP), Parker, J.
s.1, see *D Borough Council v B* [2011] EWHC 101 (Fam), [2012] Fam. 36 (CP), Mostyn, J.; see *ZH v Commissioner of Police for the Metropolis* [2012] EWHC 604 (QB), [2012] Eq. L.R. 425 (CC (Central London)), Sir Robert Nelson
s.2, see *A Local Authority v E* [2012] EWHC 1639 (Fam), [2012] 2 F.C.R. 523 (CP), Peter Jackson, J.; see *R. v Hopkins (Annette)* [2011] EWCA Crim 1513, (2012) 123 B.M.L.R. 1 (CA (Crim

2005–cont.

9. Mental Capacity Act 2005–*cont.*
s.2–*cont.*
Div)), Pitchford L.J.; see *R. v Nursing (Ligaya)* [2012] EWCA Crim 2521, Times, December 19, 2012 (CA (Crim Div)), Lord Judge, L.C.J.

s.2, applied: SI 2012/2683 Reg.4

s.3, see *A Local Authority v H* [2012] EWHC 49 (Fam), [2012] 1 F.C.R. 590 (CP), Hedley, J.; see *R. v Nursing (Ligaya)* [2012] EWCA Crim 2521, Times, December 19, 2012 (CA (Crim Div)), Lord Judge, L.C.J.

s.4, see *D (Statutory Will), Re* [2010] EWHC 2159 (Ch), [2012] Ch. 57 (CP), Judge Hodge Q.C.; see *D v JC* [2012] W.T.L.R. 1211 (CP), Senior Judge Denzil Lush; see *K v A Local Authority* [2012] EWCA Civ 79, [2012] 1 F.C.R. 441 (CA (Civ Div)), Thorpe, L.J.; see *M (Adult Patient) (Minimally Conscious State: Withdrawal of Treatment), Re* [2011] EWHC 2443 (Fam), [2012] 1 W.L.R. 1653 (CP), Baker, J.; see *Surrey CC v CA* [2011] EWCA Civ 190, [2012] Fam. 170 (CA (Civ Div)), Mummery, L.J.; see *XCC v AA* [2012] EWHC 2183 (COP), (2012) 15 C.C.L. Rep. 447 (CP), Parker, J.

s.5, see *C v Blackburn with Darwen BC* [2011] EWHC 3321 (Fam), (2012) 15 C.C.L. Rep. 251 (CP), Peter Jackson, J.; see *R. (on the application of Sessay) v South London and Maudsley NHS Foundation Trust* [2011] EWHC 2617 (QB), [2012] Q.B. 760 (DC), Pitchford, L.J.; see *ZH v Commissioner of Police for the Metropolis* [2012] EWHC 604 (QB), [2012] Eq. L.R. 425 (CC (Central London)), Sir Robert Nelson

s.6, see *C v Blackburn with Darwen BC* [2011] EWHC 3321 (Fam), (2012) 15 C.C.L. Rep. 251 (CP), Peter Jackson, J.; see *R. (on the application of Sessay) v South London and Maudsley NHS Foundation Trust* [2011] EWHC 2617 (QB), [2012] Q.B. 760 (DC), Pitchford, L.J.; see *ZH v Commissioner of Police for the Metropolis* [2012] EWHC 604 (QB), [2012] Eq. L.R. 425 (CC (Central London)), Sir Robert Nelson

s.7, see *Wychavon DC v EM* [2012] UKUT 12 (AAC), (2012) 15 C.C.L. Rep. 221 (UT (AAC)), Judge Michael Mark

s.10, amended: SI 2012/2404 Sch.2 para.53

s.12, see *RB (An Adult), Re* [2011] EWHC 3017 (Fam), [2012] 1 F.L.R. 466 (Fam Div), Munby, L.J.

s.13, amended: SI 2012/2404 Sch.2 para.53

s.16, see *G v E* [2010] EWCA Civ 822, [2012] Fam. 78 (CA (Civ Div)), Sir Nicholas Wall (President, Fam)

s.18, see *HM (A Child), Re* [2012] Med. L.R. 449 (CP), Judge Hazel Marshall Q.C.

s.21A, see *C v Blackburn with Darwen BC* [2011] EWHC 3321 (Fam), (2012) 15 C.C.L. Rep. 251 (CP), Peter Jackson, J.

s.22, see *Harcourt, Re* [2012] W.T.L.R. 1779 (CP), Senior Judge Denzil Lush

s.24, see *X Primary Care Trust v XB* [2012] EWHC 1390 (Fam), (2012) 127 B.M.L.R. 122 (Fam Div), Theis, J.

s.35, amended: 2012 c.7 Sch.5 para.134

s.42, see *Harcourt, Re* [2012] W.T.L.R. 1779 (CP), Senior Judge Denzil Lush

s.44, see *R. v Hopkins (Annette)* [2011] EWCA Crim 1513, (2012) 123 B.M.L.R. 1 (CA (Crim Div)), Pitchford L.J.; see *R. v Nursing (Ligaya)* [2012]

2005–cont.

9. Mental Capacity Act 2005–*cont.*
s.44–*cont.*
EWCA Crim 2521, Times, December 19, 2012 (CA (Crim Div)), Lord Judge, L.C.J.

s.47, see *M (A Patient) (Court of Protection: Reporting Restrictions), Re* [2011] EWHC 1197 (Fam), [2012] 1 W.L.R. 287 (CP), Baker, J.

s.59, applied: SI 2012/2401 Art.4

s.59, repealed: SI 2012/2401 Sch.2 para.2

s.64, amended: 2012 c.7 Sch.5 para.135, SI 2012/2404 Sch.2 para.53

Sch.A1, see *A Local Authority v H* [2012] EWHC 49 (Fam), [2012] 1 F.C.R. 590 (CP), Hedley, J.

Sch.A1 Pt 2 para.5, see *C v Blackburn with Darwen BC* [2011] EWHC 3321 (Fam), (2012) 15 C.C.L. Rep. 251 (CP), Peter Jackson, J.

Sch.A1 Part 13 para.176, amended: 2012 c.7 Sch.5 para.136

Sch.A1 Part 13 para.180, amended: 2012 c.7 Sch.5 para.136

Sch.A1 Part 13 para.181, amended: 2012 c.7 Sch.5 para.136

Sch.A1 Part 13 para.183, added: 2012 c.7 Sch.5 para.136

Sch.A1 Part 13 para.183, amended: 2012 c.7 Sch.5 para.136

Sch.1 Part 3 para.17, amended: SI 2012/2404 Sch.2 para.53

Sch.4 Part 1 para.2, amended: SI 2012/2404 Sch.2 para.53

Sch.4 Part 5 para.17, amended: SI 2012/2404 Sch.2 para.53

Sch.4 Part 7 para.22, amended: SI 2012/2404 Sch.2 para.53

Sch.6 para.44, repealed: 2012 c.10 Sch.5 Part 2

10. Public Services Ombudsman (Wales) Act 2005
Part 2, applied: SI 2012/2734 Sch.1 para.36
s.2, varied: SI 2012/2734 Reg.6
s.3, varied: SI 2012/2734 Reg.6
s.4, varied: SI 2012/2734 Reg.6
s.5, varied: SI 2012/2734 Reg.6
s.6, varied: SI 2012/2734 Reg.6
s.7, varied: SI 2012/2734 Reg.6
s.8, varied: SI 2012/2734 Reg.6
s.9, varied: SI 2012/2734 Reg.6
s.10, varied: SI 2012/2734 Reg.6
s.11, varied: SI 2012/2734 Reg.6
s.12, varied: SI 2012/2734 Reg.6
s.13, varied: SI 2012/2734 Reg.6
s.14, varied: SI 2012/2734 Reg.6
s.15, varied: SI 2012/2734 Reg.6
s.16, varied: SI 2012/2734 Reg.6
s.17, varied: SI 2012/2734 Reg.6
s.18, varied: SI 2012/2734 Reg.6
s.19, varied: SI 2012/2734 Reg.6
s.20, varied: SI 2012/2734 Reg.6
s.21, varied: SI 2012/2734 Reg.6
s.22, varied: SI 2012/2734 Reg.6
s.23, varied: SI 2012/2734 Reg.6
s.24, varied: SI 2012/2734 Reg.6
s.25, varied: SI 2012/2734 Reg.6
s.25A, varied: SI 2012/2734 Reg.6
s.25B, varied: SI 2012/2734 Reg.6
s.26, varied: SI 2012/2734 Reg.6
s.27, varied: SI 2012/2734 Reg.6
s.28, varied: SI 2012/2734 Reg.6
s.29, varied: SI 2012/2734 Reg.6
s.30, varied: SI 2012/2734 Reg.6
s.31, varied: SI 2012/2734 Reg.6

2005–cont.

10. Public Services Ombudsman (Wales) Act 2005–
cont.
s.32, varied: SI 2012/2734 Reg.6
s.33, varied: SI 2012/2734 Reg.6
s.34, varied: SI 2012/2734 Reg.6
Sch.2, applied: SI 2012/2734 Sch.1 para.36
Sch.2 para.1, varied: SI 2012/2734 Reg.6
Sch.2 para.2, varied: SI 2012/2734 Reg.6
Sch.2 para.3, varied: SI 2012/2734 Reg.6
Sch.2 para.4, varied: SI 2012/2734 Reg.6
Sch.2 para.5, varied: SI 2012/2734 Reg.6
Sch.2 para.6, varied: SI 2012/2734 Reg.6
Sch.2 para.7, varied: SI 2012/2734 Reg.6
Sch.2 para.8, varied: SI 2012/2734 Reg.6
Sch.2 para.9, varied: SI 2012/2734 Reg.6
Sch.2 para.10, varied: SI 2012/2734 Reg.6
Sch.3, amended: SI 2012/990 Art.9

11. Commissioners for Revenue and Customs Act 2005
applied: 2012 c.11 Sch.3 para.35
s.5, amended: 2012 c.5 Sch.3 para.20
s.5, repealed (in part): 2012 c.5 Sch.14 Part 1
s.8, varied: 2012 c.11 s.12
s.18, amended: 2012 c.11 s.24
s.19, amended: 2012 c.11 s.24
s.36, applied: SI 2012/1726 r.8.1
s.44, amended: 2012 c.5 Sch.3 para.21, 2012 c.14 Sch.23 para.14
s.44, repealed (in part): 2012 c.5 Sch.14 Part 1, 2012 c.11 Sch.2 para.3
s.51, amended: 2012 c.11 s.24
s.54, repealed (in part): 2012 c.5 Sch.14 Part 1
Sch.1 para.4, repealed: 2012 c.5 Sch.14 Part 1
Sch.1 para.31, repealed: 2012 c.5 Sch.14 Part 1
Sch.4 para.45, repealed: 2012 c.5 Sch.14 Part 13
Sch.4 para.70, repealed: 2012 c.11 Sch.2 para.3
Sch.4 para.71, repealed: 2012 c.11 Sch.2 para.3
Sch.4 para.72, repealed: 2012 c.11 Sch.2 para.3
Sch.4 para.125, repealed: 2012 c.14 Sch.39 para.9
Sch.4 para.126, repealed: 2012 c.14 Sch.39 para.9
Sch.4 para.127, repealed: 2012 c.14 Sch.39 para.9
Sch.4 para.132, repealed (in part): 2012 c.14 Sch.39 para.43

12. Inquiries Act 2005
s.18, see *Kennedy v Information Commissioner* [2011] EWCA Civ 367, [2012] 1 W.L.R. 3524 (CA (Civ Div)), Ward, L.J.
s.23, amended: 2012 c.21 Sch.18 para.105
s.46, repealed: 2012 c.21 Sch.19

14. Railways Act 2005
referred to: 2012 c.19 Sch.6 para.4

15. Serious Organised Crime and Police Act 2005
s.30, amended: SI 2012/1809 Sch.1 Part 1
s.38, applied: SI 2012/1726 r.8.1
s.57, amended: SI 2012/1809 Sch.1 Part 1
s.71, amended: 2012 c.21 Sch.18 para.106
s.73, see *R. v McGarry (Ian)* [2012] EWCA Crim 255, [2012] 2 Cr. App. R. (S.) 60 (CA (Crim Div)), Hooper, L.J.
s.74, applied: SI 2012/1726 r.74.1, r.68.1
s.75, applied: SI 2012/1726 r.16.1
s.117, repealed (in part): 2012 c.9 Sch.10 Part 1
s.118, repealed (in part): 2012 c.9 Sch.10 Part 1
s.128, enabling: SI 2012/1769, SI 2012/2709
s.132, see *R. (on the application of Gallastegui) v Westminster City Council* [2012] EWHC 1123 (Admin), [2012] 4 All E.R. 401 (DC), Sir John Thomas (President)

2005–cont.

15. Serious Organised Crime and Police Act 2005–
cont.
s.134, see *R. (on the application of Gallastegui) v Westminster City Council* [2012] EWHC 1123 (Admin), [2012] 4 All E.R. 401 (DC), Sir John Thomas (President)
s.138, see *R. (on the application of Gallastegui) v Westminster City Council* [2012] EWHC 1123 (Admin), [2012] 4 All E.R. 401 (DC), Sir John Thomas (President)
s.148, amended: SI 2012/3039 Reg.28
s.148, repealed (in part): SI 2012/3039 Reg.28
s.168, enabling: SI 2012/1762, SI 2012/2561, SI 2012/2591, SI 2012/2598
Sch.1 Part 1 para.4, amended: SI 2012/2404 Sch.2 para.54
Sch.15 para.14, repealed (in part): 2012 c.9 Sch.10 Part 3

16. Clean Neighbourhoods and Environment Act 2005
varied: SI 2012/147 Art.7
Part 6 c.1, applied: SI 2012/1223 Art.2
s.58, enabling: SI 2012/1223
s.87, repealed: SI 2012/147 Sch.1
s.88, repealed: SI 2012/147 Sch.1
s.89, repealed: SI 2012/147 Sch.1
s.90, enabling: SI 2012/147
s.94, repealed (in part): SI 2012/147 Sch.1
s.95, amended: SI 2012/147 Sch.1
s.95, applied: SI 2012/147
s.95, repealed (in part): SI 2012/147 Sch.1
s.95, enabling: SI 2012/147
Sch.2 para.1, repealed: SI 2012/147 Sch.1
Sch.2 para.2, repealed: SI 2012/147 Sch.1
Sch.2 para.3, repealed: SI 2012/147 Sch.1
Sch.2 para.4, repealed: SI 2012/147 Sch.1
Sch.2 para.5, repealed: SI 2012/147 Sch.1
Sch.2 para.6, repealed: SI 2012/147 Sch.1
Sch.2 para.7, repealed: SI 2012/147 Sch.1
Sch.2 para.8, repealed: SI 2012/147 Sch.1
Sch.2 para.9, applied: SI 2012/147 Art.5
Sch.2 para.9, repealed: SI 2012/147 Sch.1
Sch.2 para.10, repealed: SI 2012/147 Sch.1
Sch.2 para.11, repealed: SI 2012/147 Sch.1
Sch.2 para.14, repealed: SI 2012/147 Sch.1
Sch.2 para.15, repealed: SI 2012/147 Sch.1
Sch.3 para.1, repealed: SI 2012/147 Sch.1
Sch.3 para.2, repealed: SI 2012/147 Sch.1
Sch.3 para.3, repealed: SI 2012/147 Sch.1
Sch.3 para.4, repealed: SI 2012/147 Sch.1
Sch.3 para.5, repealed: SI 2012/147 Sch.1
Sch.3 para.6, repealed: SI 2012/147 Sch.1
Sch.3 para.7, repealed: SI 2012/147 Sch.1

18. Education Act 2005
Part 1, applied: SI 2012/2008 Sch.1 para.3
Part 1, referred to: SI 2012/1703 Sch.1 para.2
s.5, applied: SI 2012/1293 Reg.3, Reg.4
s.5, enabling: SI 2012/1293
s.8, applied: SI 2012/1293 Reg.4
s.108, amended: 2012 c.5 Sch.14 Part 1
s.110, amended: 2012 c.5 Sch.14 Part 1
s.110, repealed (in part): 2012 c.5 Sch.14 Part 1
s.120, enabling: SI 2012/1293

19. Gambling Act 2005
applied: SI 2012/3110 Reg.5
s.6, see *Aspinalls Club Ltd v Revenue and Customs Commissioners* [2012] UKUT 242 (TCC), [2012] S.T.C. 2124 (UT (Tax)), Briggs, J.

2005– cont.

19. Gambling Act 2005– *cont.*
s.14, applied: SI 2012/ 2898 Art.5
s.65, applied: SI 2012/ 2500 Sch.1
s.69, enabling: SI 2012/ 829, SI 2012/ 1851
s.73, amended: 2012 c.9 Sch.9 para.119
s.74, applied: SI 2012/ 2550 Reg.4
s.100, enabling: SI 2012/ 829, SI 2012/ 1851
s.103, enabling: SI 2012/ 829
s.104, enabling: SI 2012/ 829, SI 2012/ 1851
s.114, amended: SI 2012/ 2404 Sch.2 para.55
s.128, enabling: SI 2012/ 1851
s.132, enabling: SI 2012/ 1851
s.157, amended: 2012 asp 8 Sch.7 para.69
s.163, applied: SI 2012/ 2550 Reg.4
s.194, amended: SI 2012/ 2404 Sch.2 para.55
s.211, amended: SI 2012/ 1659 Sch.3 para.17
s.231, amended: SI 2012/ 1659 Sch.3 para.17
s.349, applied: SI 2012/ 1020 Sch.1
s.351, enabling: SI 2012/ 1633
s.353, see *Aspinalls Club Ltd v Revenue and Customs Commissioners* [2012] UKUT 242 (TCC), [2012] S.T.C. 2124 (UT (Tax)), Briggs, J.
s.355, applied: SI 2012/ 1633
s.355, enabling: SI 2012/ 829, SI 2012/ 1851
Sch.6 Part 2, amended: 2012 c.21 Sch.18 para.107, SI 2012/ 1633 Art.2
Sch.6 Part 3, amended: SI 2012/ 1633 Art.3
Sch.10 para.15, amended: SI 2012/ 2404 Sch.2 para.55
Sch.14 para.15, amended: SI 2012/ 2404 Sch.2 para.55

22. Finance (No.2) Act 2005
s.17, enabling: SI 2012/ 519, SI 2012/ 1783, SI 2012/ 3043
s.18, amended: 2012 c.14 Sch.16 para.124, 2012 c.21 Sch.18 para.108
s.18, enabling: SI 2012/ 519, SI 2012/ 1783, SI 2012/ 3043
s.47, repealed (in part): 2012 c.11 Sch.3 para.29
s.68, repealed: SI 2012/ 3062 Sch.1
Sch.6 para.2, repealed: 2012 c.14 s.54
Sch.9 para.1, repealed: 2012 c.14 Sch.16 para.247
Sch.9 para.2, repealed: 2012 c.14 Sch.16 para.247
Sch.9 para.3, repealed: 2012 c.14 Sch.16 para.247
Sch.9 para.5, repealed: 2012 c.14 Sch.16 para.247
Sch.9 para.10, repealed: 2012 c.14 Sch.16 para.247
Sch.9 para.12, repealed: 2012 c.14 Sch.16 para.247
Sch.9 para.13, repealed: 2012 c.14 Sch.16 para.247
Sch.9 para.14, repealed: 2012 c.14 Sch.16 para.247
Sch.9 para.15, repealed: 2012 c.14 Sch.16 para.247
Sch.9 para.17, repealed: 2012 c.14 Sch.16 para.247
Sch.9 para.18, repealed: 2012 c.14 Sch.16 para.247

2006

2. European Union (Accessions) Act 2006
s.2, amended: SI 2012/ 1809 Sch.1 Part 1

3. Equality Act 2006
see *R. (on the application of National Secular Society) v Bideford Town Council* [2012] EWHC 175 (Admin), [2012] 2 All E.R. 1175 (QBD (Admin)), Ouseley, J.
s.27, applied: SI 2012/ 322 Reg.12
s.29, amended: 2012 c.10 Sch.5 para.67

9. Criminal Defence Service Act 2006
s.1, repealed: 2012 c.10 Sch.5 Part 2
s.2, repealed: 2012 c.10 Sch.5 Part 2
s.3, repealed: 2012 c.10 Sch.5 Part 2

2006– cont.

9. Criminal Defence Service Act 2006– *cont.*
s.4, repealed (in part): 2012 c.10 Sch.5 Part 2, Sch.12 para.53

11. Terrorism Act 2006
s.2, see *R. v Brown (Terence Roy)* [2011] EWCA Crim 2751, [2012] 2 Cr. App. R. (S.) 10 (CA (Crim Div)), Lord Judge, L.C.J.
s.23, repealed (in part): 2012 c.9 Sch.10 Part 4
s.25, repealed: 2012 c.9 Sch.10 Part 4
s.30, repealed: 2012 c.9 Sch.10 Part 4
s.36, amended: 2012 c.9 s.58, Sch.9 para.32

12. London Olympic Games and Paralympic Games Act 2006
applied: SI 2012/ 1733, SI 2012/ 1790, SI 2012/ 1799
s.1, referred to: SI 2012/ 60 Reg.11
s.14, enabling: SI 2012/ 904, SI 2012/ 1159, SI 2012/ 2070
s.16, enabling: SI 2012/ 1732, SI 2012/ 1733, SI 2012/ 1790, SI 2012/ 1799
s.19, enabling: SI 2012/ 60
s.20, applied: SI 2012/ 60
s.20, enabling: SI 2012/ 60
s.22, applied: SI 2012/ 60 Reg.19
s.22, enabling: SI 2012/ 60
s.25, enabling: SI 2012/ 60
s.26, applied: SI 2012/ 60
s.26, enabling: SI 2012/ 60
s.28, applied: SI 2012/ 60 Reg.19
s.28, enabling: SI 2012/ 60

13. Immigration, Asylum and Nationality Act 2006
see *Kishver (Limited Leave: Meaning: Pakistan), Re* [2012] Imm. A.R. 128 (UT (IAC)), CMG Ockelton
s.4, see *Abisoye (Entry Clearance Appeal: Tier 2: Nigeria)* [2012] UKUT 82 (IAC), [2012] Imm. A.R. 712 (UT (IAC)), Judge Kopieczek
s.31, referred to: SI 2012/ 1763 Art.2
s.31, varied: SI 2012/ 1763 Sch.1
s.32, referred to: SI 2012/ 1763 Art.2
s.32, varied: SI 2012/ 1763 Sch.1
s.34, referred to: SI 2012/ 1763 Art.2
s.34, varied: SI 2012/ 1763 Sch.1
s.39, referred to: SI 2012/ 1763 Art.2
s.39, varied: SI 2012/ 1763 Sch.1
s.47, see *Ahmadi (S.47 Decision: Validity: Sapkota: Afghanistan), Re* [2012] UKUT 147 (IAC), [2012] Imm. A.R. 875 (UT (IAC)), Judge Lane
s.51, enabling: SI 2012/ 813, SI 2012/ 971, SI 2012/ 2276
s.52, enabling: SI 2012/ 813, SI 2012/ 971, SI 2012/ 2276
s.54, see *AH (Algeria) v Secretary of State for the Home Department* [2012] EWCA Civ 395, [2012] 1 W.L.R. 3469 (CA (Civ Div)), Ward, L.J.
s.55, see *MT (Article IF(A): Aiding and Abetting: Zimbabwe), Re* [2012] UKUT 15 (IAC), [2012] Imm. A.R. 509 (UT (IAC)), Judge Storey
s.62, enabling: SI 2012/ 1531
s.63, enabling: SI 2012/ 1763

14. Consumer Credit Act 2006
applied: SI 2012/ 1128 Art.4

15. Identity Cards Act 2006
s.25, see *R. v Unah (Flora)* [2011] EWCA Crim 1837, [2012] 1 W.L.R. 545 (CA (Crim Div)), Elias, L.J.

16. Natural Environment and Rural Communities Act 2006
s.17, applied: SI 2012/ 2654 Art.2
s.17, repealed: SI 2012/ 2654 Sch.1
s.18, repealed: SI 2012/ 2654 Sch.1

2006– cont.

16. Natural Environment and Rural Communities Act 2006–*cont.*
s.19, repealed: SI 2012/2654 Sch.1
s.20, repealed: SI 2012/2654 Sch.1
s.21, repealed: SI 2012/2654 Sch.1
s.22, repealed: SI 2012/2654 Sch.1
s.23, repealed: SI 2012/2654 Sch.1
s.24, repealed: SI 2012/2654 Sch.1
s.25, repealed: SI 2012/2654 Sch.1
s.67, see *Fortune v Wiltshire Council* [2012] EWCA Civ 334, [2012] 3 All E.R. 797 (CA (Civ Div)), Arden, L.J.
s.73, repealed: SI 2012/1658 Sch.1
s.74, repealed: SI 2012/1658 Sch.1
s.75, repealed: SI 2012/1658 Sch.1
s.76, repealed: SI 2012/1658 Sch.1
s.77, repealed: SI 2012/1658 Sch.1
s.108, repealed (in part): SI 2012/1658 Sch.1
Sch.1 para.7, amended: SI 2012/2404 Sch.2 para.56
Sch.2 para.1, repealed: SI 2012/2654 Sch.1
Sch.2 para.2, repealed: SI 2012/2654 Sch.1
Sch.2 para.3, repealed: SI 2012/2654 Sch.1
Sch.2 para.4, repealed: SI 2012/2654 Sch.1
Sch.2 para.5, repealed: SI 2012/2654 Sch.1
Sch.2 para.6, repealed: SI 2012/2654 Sch.1
Sch.2 para.7, amended: SI 2012/2404 Sch.2 para.56
Sch.2 para.7, repealed: SI 2012/2654 Sch.1
Sch.2 para.8, repealed: SI 2012/2654 Sch.1
Sch.2 para.9, repealed: SI 2012/2654 Sch.1
Sch.2 para.10, repealed: SI 2012/2654 Sch.1
Sch.2 para.11, repealed: SI 2012/2654 Sch.1
Sch.2 para.12, repealed: SI 2012/2654 Sch.1
Sch.2 para.13, repealed: SI 2012/2654 Sch.1
Sch.2 para.14, repealed: SI 2012/2654 Sch.1
Sch.2 para.15, repealed: SI 2012/2654 Sch.1
Sch.2 para.16, repealed: SI 2012/2654 Sch.1
Sch.2 para.17, repealed: SI 2012/2654 Sch.1
Sch.2 para.18, repealed: SI 2012/2654 Sch.1
Sch.2 para.19, repealed: SI 2012/2654 Sch.1
Sch.2 para.20, repealed: SI 2012/2654 Sch.1
Sch.2 para.21, repealed: SI 2012/2654 Sch.1
Sch.2 para.22, repealed: SI 2012/2654 Sch.1
Sch.2 para.23, repealed: SI 2012/2654 Sch.1
Sch.2 para.24, repealed: SI 2012/2654 Sch.1
Sch.2 para.25, repealed: SI 2012/2654 Sch.1
Sch.4 para.6, amended: SI 2012/2404 Sch.2 para.56
Sch.7 para.7, amended: SI 2012/1659 Sch.3 para.18
Sch.11 Part 2 para.175, repealed: SI 2012/1658 Sch.1

18. Work and Families Act 2006
Sch.1 para.45, repealed: 2012 c.5 Sch.14 Part 13

21. Childcare Act 2006
Part 1, applied: SI 2012/2885 Sch.1 para.25, SI 2012/3144 Sch.1 para.19, SI 2012/3145 Sch.1, SSI 2012/303 Reg.28
Part 3, applied: SI 2012/938 Reg.4, Reg.5, Reg.6, SI 2012/1034 Sch.4 para.13, SI 2012/2885 Sch.1 para.25, SI 2012/3144 Sch.1 para.19, SI 2012/3145 Sch.1, SSI 2012/303 Reg.28
Part 3 c.2, applied: SI 2012/2885 Sch.1 para.25, SI 2012/2886 Sch.1, SI 2012/3144 Sch.1 para.19, SI 2012/3145 Sch.1, SSI 2012/303 Reg.28, SSI 2012/319 Reg.29
Part 3 c.3, applied: SI 2012/2885 Sch.1 para.25, SI 2012/2886 Sch.1, SI 2012/3144 Sch.1 para.19, SI 2012/3145 Sch.1, SSI 2012/303 Reg.28, SSI 2012/319 Reg.29
s.4, amended: 2012 c.7 Sch.5 para.137
s.4, repealed (in part): 2012 c.7 Sch.5 para.137

2006– cont.

21. Childcare Act 2006–*cont.*
s.7, applied: SI 2012/962 Reg.2, SI 2012/2488 Reg.2, Reg.3, Reg.4
s.7, enabling: SI 2012/2488
s.13, amended: SI 2012/976 Sch.1 para.17
s.13A, amended: 2012 c.5 Sch.14 Part 1
s.13A, repealed (in part): 2012 c.5 Sch.14 Part 1
s.18, applied: SI 2012/2885 Sch.1 para.25, SI 2012/2886 Sch.1, SI 2012/3145 Sch.1, SSI 2012/303 Reg.28
s.18, referred to: SI 2012/2885 Sch.1 para.25, SI 2012/3144 Sch.1 para.19, SSI 2012/319 Reg.29
s.34, applied: SI 2012/2885 Sch.1 para.25, SI 2012/2886 Sch.1, SI 2012/3144 Sch.1 para.19, SI 2012/3145 Sch.1, SSI 2012/303 Reg.28
s.34, referred to: SI 2012/2885 Sch.1 para.25, SI 2012/3144 Sch.1 para.19, SSI 2012/319 Reg.29
s.35, enabling: SI 2012/939
s.36, enabling: SI 2012/939
s.39, applied: SI 2012/938 Reg.3
s.39, enabling: SI 2012/937, SI 2012/938
s.40, applied: SI 2012/938 Reg.3, Reg.10, SI 2012/2488 Reg.2
s.42, applied: SI 2012/937
s.42, enabling: SI 2012/937
s.43, applied: SI 2012/938
s.43, enabling: SI 2012/938
s.44, enabling: SI 2012/937, SI 2012/938
s.45, applied: SI 2012/937
s.46, applied: SI 2012/2488 Reg.2
s.46, enabling: SI 2012/2463
s.49, amended: SI 2012/976 Sch.1 para.18
s.49, enabling: SI 2012/1698
s.50, enabling: SI 2012/1698
s.53, amended: SI 2012/976 Sch.1 para.19
s.53, applied: SI 2012/2885 Sch.1 para.25, SI 2012/2886 Sch.1, SI 2012/3144 Sch.1 para.19, SI 2012/3145 Sch.1, SSI 2012/303 Reg.28
s.53, referred to: SI 2012/2885 Sch.1 para.25, SI 2012/3144 Sch.1 para.19, SSI 2012/319 Reg.29
s.54, enabling: SI 2012/1699
s.55, enabling: SI 2012/1699
s.59, applied: SI 2012/1699
s.59, enabling: SI 2012/1699
s.61, enabling: SI 2012/1698
s.63, amended: SI 2012/976 Sch.1 para.20
s.63, enabling: SI 2012/1699
s.67, applied: SI 2012/1699
s.67, enabling: SI 2012/1699
s.75, amended: 2012 c.10 Sch.24 para.27
s.75, applied: SI 2012/938 Reg.9
s.89, enabling: SI 2012/2168
s.104, enabling: SI 2012/939, SI 2012/1698, SI 2012/1699, SI 2012/2168, SI 2012/2463, SI 2012/2488

22. Electoral Administration Act 2006
s.42, varied: SI 2012/323 Sch.4 para.1, SI 2012/444 Sch.4 para.1, SI 2012/2031 Sch.4 Part 1
s.43, varied: SI 2012/323 Sch.4 para.1, SI 2012/444 Sch.4 para.1, SI 2012/2031 Sch.4 Part 1
s.44, varied: SI 2012/323 Sch.4 para.1, SI 2012/444 Sch.4 para.1, SI 2012/2031 Sch.4 Part 1
s.46, varied: SI 2012/323 Sch.4 para.1, SI 2012/444 Sch.4 para.1, SI 2012/2031 Sch.4 Part 1
s.62, amended: SI 2012/1917 Art.25
s.69, varied: SI 2012/323 Sch.4 para.1, SI 2012/444 Sch.4 para.1, SI 2012/2031 Sch.4 Part 1

25. Finance Act 2006
s.86, repealed: 2012 c.14 Sch.16 para.247

2006–cont.

25. Finance Act 2006–cont.

s.173, see *Revenue and Customs Commissioners v Ben Nevis (Holdings) Ltd* [2012] EWHC 1807 (Ch), [2012] S.T.C. 2157 (Ch D), Judge Pelling Q.C.

s.173, applied: SI 2012/3075, SI 2012/3076, SI 2012/3077, SI 2012/3078, SI 2012/3079

s.173, enabling: SI 2012/3075, SI 2012/3076, SI 2012/3077, SI 2012/3078, SI 2012/3079

Sch.11 para.1, repealed: 2012 c.14 Sch.16 para.247

Sch.11 para.2, repealed: 2012 c.14 Sch.16 para.247

Sch.11 para.3, repealed: 2012 c.14 Sch.16 para.247

Sch.11 para.4, repealed: 2012 c.14 Sch.16 para.247

Sch.11 para.5, repealed: 2012 c.14 Sch.16 para.247

Sch.11 para.6, repealed: 2012 c.14 Sch.16 para.247

Sch.11 para.7, repealed: 2012 c.14 Sch.16 para.247

Sch.11 para.8, repealed: 2012 c.14 Sch.16 para.247

Sch.25 para.5, repealed: 2012 c.11 Sch.3 para.30

26. Commons Act 2006

Commencement Orders: SI 2012/739 Art.2, Art.3, Art.4; SI 2012/806 Art.2

see *R. (on the application of Barnsley MBC) v Secretary of State for Communities and Local Government* [2012] EWHC 1366 (Admin), [2012] B.L.G.R. 933 (QBD (Admin)), Foskett, J.; see *R. (on the application of Newhaven Port and Properties Ltd) v East Sussex CC* [2012] EWHC 647 (Admin), [2012] 3 W.L.R. 709 (QBD (Admin)), Ouseley, J.

s.1, referred to: SI 2012/739 Art.4

s.15, see *Paddico (267) Ltd v Kirklees Metropolitan Council* [2012] EWCA Civ 262, [2012] B.L.G.R. 617 (CA (Civ Div)), Carnwath, L.J.; see *R. (on the application of Newhaven Port and Properties Ltd) v East Sussex CC* [2012] EWHC 647 (Admin), [2012] 3 W.L.R. 709 (QBD (Admin)), Ouseley, J.

s.16, applied: SI 2012/738 Reg.2, Reg.3, Reg.5

s.16, referred to: SI 2012/739 Art.4

s.17, applied: SI 2012/738 Reg.18, Reg.19, SI 2012/739 Art.4, SI 2012/740 Sch.1 Part 2

s.17, referred to: SI 2012/739 Art.4

s.17, enabling: SI 2012/738, SI 2012/740

s.24, enabling: SI 2012/738, SI 2012/740

s.38, applied: SI 2012/737 Reg.2, Reg.21

s.38, disapplied: SI 2012/739 Art.4

s.38, referred to: SI 2012/739 Art.4

s.39, applied: SI 2012/737 Reg.2, Reg.19

s.39, enabling: SI 2012/737

s.40, enabling: SI 2012/737

s.44, referred to: SI 2012/739 Art.4

s.56, enabling: SI 2012/739, SI 2012/806

s.59, enabling: SI 2012/737, SI 2012/738, SI 2012/739, SI 2012/740

28. Health Act 2006

s.6, applied: SI 2012/1536 Reg.3

s.6, referred to: SI 2012/1536 Reg.2

s.6, enabling: SI 2012/1536

s.57, repealed: 2012 c.7 s.279

s.58, repealed: 2012 c.7 s.279

s.59, repealed: 2012 c.7 s.279

s.60, repealed (in part): 2012 c.7 s.279, Sch.15 para.74

s.61, repealed: 2012 c.7 s.279

s.62, repealed: 2012 c.7 s.279

s.63, repealed (in part): 2012 c.7 s.279, Sch.15 para.74

s.64, repealed: 2012 c.7 s.279

s.65, repealed: 2012 c.7 s.279

s.66, repealed: 2012 c.7 s.279

s.67, repealed: 2012 c.7 s.279

2006–cont.

28. Health Act 2006–cont.

s.68, repealed: 2012 c.7 s.279

s.69, repealed: 2012 c.7 s.279

s.70, repealed: 2012 c.7 s.279

s.71, repealed: 2012 c.7 s.279

Sch.4 para.22, applied: 2012 c.7 Sch.20 para.8

Sch.8 para.4, repealed: 2012 c.7 Sch.20 para.5

Sch.8 para.5, repealed: 2012 c.7 Sch.20 para.5

Sch.8 para.45, repealed (in part): 2012 c.7 Sch.20 para.5

29. Compensation Act 2006

see *International Energy Group Ltd v Zurich Insurance Plc UK* [2012] EWHC 69 (Comm), [2012] Lloyd's Rep. I.R. 594 (QBD (Comm)), Cooke, J.

s.3, see *Durham v BAI (Run Off) Ltd* [2012] UKSC 14, [2012] 1 W.L.R. 867 (SC), Lord Phillips (President); see *International Energy Group Ltd v Zurich Insurance Plc UK* [2012] EWHC 69 (Comm), [2012] Lloyd's Rep. I.R. 594 (QBD (Comm)), Cooke, J.

s.3, amended: 2012 c.21 Sch.18 para.109

s.3, repealed (in part): 2012 c.21 Sch.18 para.109

s.5, applied: 2012 c.10 s.59

30. Commissioner for Older People (Wales) Act 2006

Sch.2, amended: SI 2012/990 Art.10

32. Government of Wales Act 2006

Pt 4. see *Local Government Byelaws (Wales) Bill 2012, Re* [2012] UKSC 53, [2012] 3 W.L.R. 1294 (SC), Lord Neuberger (President)

s.59, applied: SI 2012/285

s.60, applied: SSI 2012/303 Reg.5, Sch.4 para.37, Sch.5 para.25, SSI 2012/319 Reg.5

s.63, applied: SI 2012/964, SI 2012/1658, SI 2012/1659

s.72, applied: SI 2012/746, SI 2012/746 Art.3

s.72, enabling: SI 2012/746

s.108, see *Local Government Byelaws (Wales) Bill 2012, Re* [2012] UKSC 53, [2012] 3 W.L.R. 1294 (SC), Lord Neuberger (President)

s.112, see *Local Government Byelaws (Wales) Bill 2012, Re* [2012] UKSC 53, [2012] 3 W.L.R. 1294 (SC), Lord Neuberger (President)

s.113, amended: SI 2012/1809 Sch.1 Part 1

s.133, applied: SI 2012/1261 Reg.5

s.158, referred to: SI 2012/1903 Art.4

Sch.7, see *Local Government Byelaws (Wales) Bill 2012, Re* [2012] UKSC 53, [2012] 3 W.L.R. 1294 (SC), Lord Neuberger (President)

Sch.7 Pt 2, see *Local Government Byelaws (Wales) Bill 2012, Re* [2012] UKSC 53, [2012] 3 W.L.R. 1294 (SC), Lord Neuberger (President)

Sch.7 Pt 3 para.6, see *Local Government Byelaws (Wales) Bill 2012, Re* [2012] UKSC 53, [2012] 3 W.L.R. 1294 (SC), Lord Neuberger (President)

Sch.10 para.40, varied: 2012 c.11 s.12

Sch.11 para.34, applied: SI 2012/899

34. Civil Aviation Act 2006

Sch.2 para.5, repealed: 2012 c.19 Sch.9 para.17

35. Fraud Act 2006

see *Attorney General's Reference (Nos 41, 42, 43, 44 and 45 of 2011), Re* [2011] EWCA Crim 2174, [2012] 1 Cr. App. R. (S.) 97 (CA (Crim Div)), Pitchford, L.J.

s.2, see *United Arab Emirates v Allen* [2012] EWHC 1712 (Admin), [2012] 1 W.L.R. 3419 (QBD (Admin)), Toulson, L.J.

36. Wireless Telegraphy Act 2006
see *Arqiva Ltd v Everything Everywhere Ltd (formerly T-Mobile (UK) Ltd)* [2011] EWHC 2016 (TCC), [2012] 1 All E.R. 607 (QBD (TCC)), Ramsey, J.
s.5, enabling: SI 2012/293
s.6, applied: SI 2012/293
s.8, applied: SI 2012/293 Art.4
s.8, disapplied: 2012 c.20 s.1
s.12, enabling: SI 2012/1075
s.13, enabling: SI 2012/1075
s.14, enabling: SI 2012/2817, SI 2012/2970
s.16, applied: SI 2012/2970
s.29, enabling: SI 2012/3138
s.30, see *Arqiva Ltd v Everything Everywhere Ltd (formerly T-Mobile (UK) Ltd)* [2011] EWHC 2016 (TCC), [2012] 1 All E.R. 607 (QBD (TCC)), Ramsey, J.
s.30, enabling: SI 2012/2187
s.31, applied: SI 2012/2186 Reg.4
s.31, enabling: SI 2012/2186
s.54, applied: SI 2012/1519, SI 2012/1519 Reg.4
s.54, enabling: SI 2012/1519
s.111, varied: 2012 c.11 s.12
s.121, enabling: SI 2012/293
s.122, applied: SI 2012/1075, SI 2012/1519, SI 2012/2186, SI 2012/2187, SI 2012/2817, SI 2012/2970, SI 2012/3138
s.122, disapplied: SI 2012/2970
s.122, enabling: SI 2012/1075, SI 2012/1519, SI 2012/2186, SI 2012/2187, SI 2012/2817, SI 2012/2970
Sch.1 para.6, see *Arqiva Ltd v Everything Everywhere Ltd (formerly T-Mobile (UK) Ltd)* [2011] EWHC 2016 (TCC), [2012] 1 All E.R. 607 (QBD (TCC)), Ramsey, J.
Sch.1 para.7, applied: SI 2012/2187 Reg.8

38. Violent Crime Reduction Act 2006
Commencement Orders: 2012 c.10 Sch.12 para.54
s.6, applied: SI 2012/1726 r.50.1
s.6, referred to: SI 2012/1726 r.50.2
s.10, applied: SI 2012/1726 r.63.1
s.15, enabling: SI 2012/61
s.16, enabling: SI 2012/61
s.17, enabling: SI 2012/61
s.20, applied: SI 2012/61
s.20, enabling: SI 2012/61
s.61, repealed: 2012 c.10 Sch.12 para.54
Sch.1 para.9, repealed (in part): 2012 c.10 s.64

39. Emergency Workers (Obstruction) Act 2006
s.1, amended: 2012 c.7 Sch.5 para.138

40. Education and Inspections Act 2006
Part 2, applied: SI 2012/335 Sch.1 para.10, SI 2012/2991 Sch.1 para.10
Part 4, applied: SI 2012/1034 Reg.18
Part 8 c.4, amended: SI 2012/1879 Art.4
s.7, applied: SI 2012/84 Art.4
s.10, applied: SI 2012/84 Art.4
s.11, applied: SI 2012/84 Art.4
s.15, enabling: SI 2012/1197
s.17, applied: SI 2012/1035 Reg.40
s.18, applied: SI 2012/335 Reg.21, Reg.25, Sch.3 para.15
s.60, applied: SI 2012/335 Sch.1 para.9, SI 2012/2991 Sch.1 para.9
s.60A, applied: SI 2012/335 Sch.1 para.9, SI 2012/2991 Sch.1 para.9
s.62, applied: SI 2012/1115 Reg.6
s.63, applied: SI 2012/335 Sch.1 para.9, SI 2012/2991 Sch.1 para.9

40. Education and Inspections Act 2006–*cont.*
s.64, applied: SI 2012/335 Sch.1 para.9, SI 2012/2991 Sch.1 para.9
s.65, applied: SI 2012/335 Sch.1 para.9, SI 2012/2991 Sch.1 para.9
s.66, applied: SI 2012/335 Sch.1 para.9, SI 2012/2991 Sch.1 para.9
s.68, applied: SI 2012/1035 Reg.40
s.100, enabling: SI 2012/1033
s.102, enabling: SI 2012/1033
s.103, applied: SI 2012/1046 Reg.3
s.104, varied: SI 2012/1107 Art.7
s.104, enabling: SI 2012/1033
s.106, enabling: SI 2012/1046
s.114, enabling: SI 2012/2597
s.120, amended: SI 2012/1879 Art.4
s.124, applied: SI 2012/1115 Reg.6
s.125, applied: SI 2012/2576 Reg.3, Reg.4
s.125, enabling: SI 2012/2576
s.135, amended: SI 2012/961 Sch.1 para.8, SI 2012/1879 Art.4
s.136, amended: SI 2012/1879 Art.4
s.137, amended: SI 2012/1879 Art.4
s.138, amended: SI 2012/1879 Art.4
s.138, repealed (in part): SI 2012/1879 Art.3
s.139, amended: SI 2012/1879 Art.4
s.139, repealed (in part): SI 2012/1879 Art.4
s.140, amended: SI 2012/1879 Art.4
s.140, repealed (in part): SI 2012/1879 Art.4
s.141, amended: SI 2012/1879 Art.4
s.142, amended: SI 2012/1879 Art.4
s.155, enabling: SI 2012/511
s.156, repealed: SI 2012/2401 Sch.1 para.21
s.166, applied: SI 2012/1749 Sch.2 para.4
s.171, amended: SI 2012/3006 Art.13
s.181, enabling: SI 2012/1033, SI 2012/1046
Sch.2, applied: SI 2012/335 Sch.1 para.10, SI 2012/2991 Sch.1 para.10
Sch.2 Part 3, applied: SI 2012/1035 Reg.40
Sch.13 para.1, repealed (in part): SI 2012/2401 Sch.1 para.22
Sch.14 para.77, repealed: SI 2012/2401 Sch.1 para.23
Sch.14 para.78, repealed: SI 2012/2401 Sch.1 para.23
Sch.14 para.79, repealed: SI 2012/2401 Sch.1 para.23
Sch.14 para.80, repealed: SI 2012/2401 Sch.1 para.23
Sch.14 para.81, repealed: SI 2012/2401 Sch.1 para.23
Sch.15 para.4, repealed (in part): SI 2012/2401 Sch.1 para.24
Sch.15 para.9, amended: SI 2012/2401 Sch.1 para.24

41. National Health Service Act 2006
applied: 2012 c.7 s.116, Sch.6 para.8, SI 2012/922 Reg.3, SI 2012/1290 Reg.3, SI 2012/1909 Reg.89, Reg.91, Reg.92, Reg.100, SI 2012/1916 Sch.17 Part 1, SI 2012/2996 Reg.15
referred to: 2012 c.7 s.58
Part 1, substituted: 2012 c.7 Sch.4 para.1
Part 1, substituted: 2012 c.7 s.13
Part 1, substituted: 2012 c.7 s.21
Part 1, substituted: 2012 c.7 Sch.4 para.8
Part 2 c.3, applied: 2012 c.7 s.179
Part 2 c.5, applied: 2012 c.7 s.67, s.104, SI 2012/2657 Art.12
Part 2 c.5, substituted: 2012 c.7 s.180

2006–cont.

41. National Health Service Act 2006–*cont.*
Part 2 c.5, substituted: 2012 c.7 s.172
Part 2 c.5A, applied: 2012 c.7 s.104, s.144
Part 2 c.5A, repealed: 2012 c.7 s.174
Part 2 c.5A, substituted: 2012 c.7 s.177, Sch.14 para.21
Part 2 c.A2, applied: SI 2012/1631 Reg.12
Part 4, substituted: 2012 c.7 Sch.4 para.30
Part 6, applied: SI 2012/2113 Art.4
Part 6, substituted: 2012 c.7 Sch.4 para.54
Part 7 c.1, applied: SI 2012/1909 Reg.62
Part 7 c.6, applied: SI 2012/1909 Reg.11, Reg.76, Sch.7 para.12
Part 9, applied: SI 2012/1909 Reg.95
Part 13, substituted: 2012 c.7 s.46
s.1, substituted: 2012 c.7 s.1
s.1A, added: 2012 c.7 s.2
s.1B, added: 2012 c.7 s.3
s.1C, added: 2012 c.7 s.4
s.1D, added: 2012 c.7 s.5
s.1E, added: 2012 c.7 s.6
s.1F, added: 2012 c.7 s.7
s.1G, added: 2012 c.7 s.8
s.1H, added: 2012 c.7 s.9
s.1H, amended: SI 2012/1831 Art.3
s.1H, applied: SI 2012/1631 Reg.10, Reg.12
s.1I, added: 2012 c.7 s.10
s.2, applied: SI 2012/1831 Art.10
s.2, substituted: 2012 c.7 Sch.4 para.1
s.2A, added: 2012 c.7 s.11
s.2B, added: 2012 c.7 s.12
s.2B, applied: 2012 c.7 s.237
s.3, amended: 2012 c.7 s.13
s.3, applied: SI 2012/2996 Reg.2, Reg.4, Reg.14, Reg.20, Reg.21, Reg.56, Sch.1 para.3, Sch.1 para.4, Sch.1 para.5, Sch.1 para.6, Sch.1 para.7, Sch.1 para.8, SI 2012/3094 Reg.13
s.3, referred to: SI 2012/2996 Reg.4
s.3, repealed (in part): 2012 c.7 s.13
s.3, substituted: 2012 c.7 s.13
s.3, enabling: SI 2012/2996
s.3A, added: 2012 c.7 s.14
s.3A, applied: SI 2012/2996 Reg.4, Reg.21, Reg.56, SI 2012/3094 Reg.13
s.3A, enabling: SI 2012/2996
s.3B, added: 2012 c.7 s.15
s.3B, applied: SI 2012/2996, SI 2012/2996 Reg.2, Reg.21, Reg.56, SI 2012/3094 Reg.13
s.3B, varied: 2012 c.7 Sch.6 para.2
s.3B, enabling: SI 2012/2996
s.4, amended: 2012 c.7 s.16, Sch.14 para.2
s.5, amended: 2012 c.7 s.17
s.6, amended: 2012 c.7 Sch.4 para.2
s.6A, amended: 2012 c.7 Sch.4 para.3
s.6B, amended: 2012 c.7 Sch.4 para.4
s.6C, added: 2012 c.7 s.18
s.6C, applied: 2012 c.7 s.237, SI 2012/3094 Reg.20
s.6D, added: 2012 c.7 s.19
s.6E, added: 2012 c.7 s.20
s.6E, enabling: SI 2012/2996
s.7, amended: 2012 c.7 s.21
s.7, applied: 2012 c.7 s.290
s.7, repealed (in part): 2012 c.7 s.21
s.7, substituted: 2012 c.7 s.21
s.7, varied: 2012 c.7 Sch.6 para.3, Sch.6 para.4, Sch.6 para.5
s.7, enabling: SI 2012/417
s.7A, added: 2012 c.7 s.22

2006–cont.

41. National Health Service Act 2006–*cont.*
s.7A, applied: 2012 c.7 s.237, SI 2012/3094 Reg.20
s.8, amended: 2012 c.7 Sch.4 para.5
s.8, repealed (in part): 2012 c.7 Sch.14 para.3
s.8, enabling: SI 2012/417
s.8, amended: 2012 c.7 Sch.4 para.5
s.8, repealed (in part): 2012 c.7 Sch.4 para.5
s.8, enabling: SI 2012/1909
s.9, amended: 2012 c.7 Sch.4 para.6, Sch.17 para.10, Sch.19 para.9, Sch.21 para.6
s.9, repealed (in part): 2012 c.7 Sch.4 para.6, Sch.7 para.18, Sch.14 para.4
s.10A, added: 2012 c.7 Sch.21 para.7
s.11, amended: 2012 c.7 Sch.4 para.7
s.12, amended: 2012 c.7 Sch.4 para.8
s.12, repealed (in part): 2012 c.7 Sch.4 para.8
s.12A, amended: 2012 c.7 Sch.4 para.10
s.12A, applied: SI 2012/2885 Sch.6 para.29, SI 2012/2886 Sch.1, SI 2012/2996 Reg.57, SSI 2012/303 Sch.4 para.57, Sch.5 para.62, SSI 2012/319 Sch.4 para.29
s.12A, repealed (in part): 2012 c.7 Sch.4 para.10
s.12B, amended: 2012 c.7 Sch.4 para.11
s.12B, applied: SI 2012/2885 Sch.6 para.29, SI 2012/2886 Sch.1, SSI 2012/303 Sch.4 para.57, Sch.5 para.62, SSI 2012/319 Sch.4 para.29
s.12C, applied: SI 2012/2885 Sch.6 para.29, SI 2012/2886 Sch.1, SSI 2012/303 Sch.4 para.57, Sch.5 para.62, SSI 2012/319 Sch.4 para.29
s.12D, amended: 2012 c.7 Sch.4 para.12
s.12D, applied: SI 2012/2886 Sch.1, SSI 2012/303 Sch.5 para.62, SSI 2012/319 Sch.4 para.29
s.12E, added: 2012 c.7 s.147
s.12ZA, added: 2012 c.7 Sch.4 para.9
s.13, disapplied: 2012 c.7 s.33
s.13, repealed: 2012 c.7 s.33
s.13A, added: 2012 c.7 s.23
s.13A, applied: 2012 c.7 s.116
s.13A, referred to: SI 2012/1831 Art.4
s.13A, varied: 2012 c.7 Sch.6 para.2
s.13B, added: 2012 c.7 s.23
s.13C, added: 2012 c.7 s.23
s.13D, added: 2012 c.7 s.23
s.13E, added: 2012 c.7 s.23
s.13E, applied: 2012 c.7 s.66
s.13F, added: 2012 c.7 s.23
s.13G, added: 2012 c.7 s.23
s.13H, added: 2012 c.7 s.23
s.13I, added: 2012 c.7 s.23
s.13J, added: 2012 c.7 s.23
s.13K, added: 2012 c.7 s.23
s.13L, added: 2012 c.7 s.23
s.13M, added: 2012 c.7 s.23
s.13N, added: 2012 c.7 s.23
s.13O, added: 2012 c.7 s.23
s.13P, added: 2012 c.7 s.23
s.13Q, added: 2012 c.7 s.23
s.13R, added: 2012 c.7 s.23
s.13S, added: 2012 c.7 s.23
s.13T, added: 2012 c.7 s.23
s.13U, added: 2012 c.7 s.23
s.13U, referred to: SI 2012/1831 Art.4
s.13V, added: 2012 c.7 s.23
s.13W, added: 2012 c.7 s.23
s.13X, added: 2012 c.7 s.23
s.13Y, added: 2012 c.7 s.23
s.13Z, added: 2012 c.7 s.23
s.13Z1, added: 2012 c.7 s.23

2006–cont.

41. National Health Service Act 2006–*cont.*

s.13Z2, added: 2012 c.7 s.23

s.13Z3, added: 2012 c.7 s.23

s.13Z4, added: 2012 c.7 s.23

s.14, repealed: 2012 c.7 s.33

s.14, enabling: SI 2012/ 502

s.14A, added: 2012 c.7 s.25

s.14A, applied: 2012 c.7 s.94, s.150, SI 2012/ 1631 Reg.2, Reg.10, Reg.12

s.14A, enabling: SI 2012/ 1631

s.14B, added: 2012 c.7 s.25

s.14B, applied: SI 2012/ 1631 Reg.7, Reg.9, Reg.10, SI 2012/ 1831 Art.5

s.14C, added: 2012 c.7 s.25

s.14C, applied: 2012 c.7 Sch.6 para.8, Sch.6 para.9

s.14C, referred to: 2012 c.7 Sch.6 para.8, SI 2012/ 1631 Reg.7, Reg.8, Reg.9, Reg.10

s.14C, enabling: SI 2012/ 1631

s.14D, added: 2012 c.7 s.25

s.14D, applied: 2012 c.7 Sch.6 para.8, SI 2012/ 1631 Reg.8, SI 2012/ 2885 Sch.1 para.21, SI 2012/ 3144 Sch.1 para.15, SI 2012/ 3145 Sch.1

s.14E, added: 2012 c.7 s.25

s.14E, applied: SI 2012/ 1631 Reg.9, Reg.10

s.14E, enabling: SI 2012/ 1631

s.14F, added: 2012 c.7 s.25

s.14G, added: 2012 c.7 s.25

s.14G, applied: SI 2012/ 1631 Reg.7, Reg.10

s.14G, enabling: SI 2012/ 1631

s.14H, added: 2012 c.7 s.25

s.14H, applied: SI 2012/ 1631 Reg.9, Reg.10

s.14H, enabling: SI 2012/ 1631

s.14I, added: 2012 c.7 s.25

s.14J, added: 2012 c.7 s.25

s.14K, added: 2012 c.7 s.25

s.14L, added: 2012 c.7 s.25

s.14L, applied: SI 2012/ 1631 Reg.16

s.14L, enabling: SI 2012/ 1631

s.14M, added: 2012 c.7 s.25

s.14N, added: 2012 c.7 s.25

s.14N, applied: SI 2012/ 1631 Reg.12, Reg.13, Sch.5 para.7

s.14N, enabling: SI 2012/ 1631

s.14O, added: 2012 c.7 s.25

s.14P, added: 2012 c.7 s.26

s.14P, varied: 2012 c.7 Sch.6 para.11

s.14Q, added: 2012 c.7 s.26

s.14Q, varied: 2012 c.7 Sch.6 para.11

s.14R, added: 2012 c.7 s.26

s.14R, varied: 2012 c.7 Sch.6 para.11

s.14S, added: 2012 c.7 s.26

s.14T, added: 2012 c.7 s.26

s.14T, varied: 2012 c.7 Sch.6 para.11

s.14U, added: 2012 c.7 s.26

s.14U, varied: 2012 c.7 Sch.6 para.11

s.14V, added: 2012 c.7 s.26

s.14V, varied: 2012 c.7 Sch.6 para.11

s.14W, added: 2012 c.7 s.26

s.14W, varied: 2012 c.7 Sch.6 para.11

s.14X, added: 2012 c.7 s.26

s.14X, varied: 2012 c.7 Sch.6 para.11

s.14Y, added: 2012 c.7 s.26

s.14Y, varied: 2012 c.7 Sch.6 para.11

s.14Z, added: 2012 c.7 s.26

s.14Z1, added: 2012 c.7 s.26

s.14Z1, varied: 2012 c.7 Sch.6 para.11

s.14Z2, added: 2012 c.7 s.26

s.14Z3, added: 2012 c.7 s.26

2006–cont.

41. National Health Service Act 2006–*cont.*

s.14Z3, applied: SI 2012/ 1631 Sch.1 para.2

s.14Z3, varied: 2012 c.7 Sch.6 para.11

s.14Z4, added: 2012 c.7 s.26

s.14Z4, varied: 2012 c.7 Sch.6 para.11

s.14Z5, added: 2012 c.7 s.26

s.14Z5, varied: 2012 c.7 Sch.6 para.11

s.14Z6, added: 2012 c.7 s.26

s.14Z7, added: 2012 c.7 s.26

s.14Z7, varied: 2012 c.7 Sch.6 para.11

s.14Z8, added: 2012 c.7 s.26

s.14Z8, applied: 2012 c.7 s.241

s.14Z9, added: 2012 c.7 s.26

s.14Z10, added: 2012 c.7 s.26

s.14Z11, added: 2012 c.7 s.26

s.14Z11, applied: SI 2012/ 1831 Art.6

s.14Z11, disapplied: SI 2012/ 1831 Art.6

s.14Z12, added: 2012 c.7 s.26

s.14Z12, disapplied: SI 2012/ 1831 Art.6

s.14Z13, added: 2012 c.7 s.26

s.14Z13, amended: SI 2012/ 1831 Art.6

s.14Z14, added: 2012 c.7 s.26

s.14Z15, added: 2012 c.7 s.26

s.14Z16, added: 2012 c.7 s.26

s.14Z17, added: 2012 c.7 s.26

s.14Z17, varied: 2012 c.7 Sch.6 para.11

s.14Z18, added: 2012 c.7 s.26

s.14Z19, added: 2012 c.7 s.26

s.14Z19, varied: 2012 c.7 Sch.6 para.11

s.14Z20, added: 2012 c.7 s.26

s.14Z21, added: 2012 c.7 s.26

s.14Z21, applied: 2012 c.7 Sch.6 para.8, SI 2012/ 1631 Reg.8

s.14Z21, varied: 2012 c.7 Sch.6 para.11

s.14Z22, added: 2012 c.7 s.26

s.14Z23, added: 2012 c.7 s.26

s.14Z24, added: 2012 c.7 s.26

s.15, repealed: 2012 c.7 s.33

s.16, repealed: 2012 c.7 s.33

s.17, repealed: 2012 c.7 s.33

s.17A, repealed: 2012 c.7 s.33

s.18, applied: SI 2012/ 717 Sch.1, SI 2012/ 767 Reg.4, SI 2012/ 1909 Reg.6, SI 2012/ 2886 Sch.1, SSI 2012/ 303 Sch.4 para.31, SSI 2012/ 319 Reg.35

s.18, disapplied: 2012 c.7 s.34

s.18, repealed: 2012 c.7 s.34

s.19, applied: SI 2012/ 1020 Reg.4, Reg.6, Reg.7, Reg.9

s.19, repealed: 2012 c.7 s.34

s.19, enabling: SI 2012/ 502

s.20, repealed: 2012 c.7 s.34

s.21, repealed: 2012 c.7 s.34

s.22, repealed: 2012 c.7 s.34

s.22, enabling: SI 2012/ 1909

s.23, repealed: 2012 c.7 s.34

s.23A, repealed: 2012 c.7 s.34

s.24, amended: 2012 c.7 s.206

s.24, repealed: 2012 c.7 s.34

s.24A, amended: 2012 c.7 s.206

s.24A, repealed: 2012 c.7 s.34

s.25, applied: 2012 c.7 s.97, s.179, 2012 c.14 s.216, SI 2012/ 717 Sch.1, SI 2012/ 755, SI 2012/ 786, SI 2012/ 788, SI 2012/ 796, SI 2012/ 803, SI 2012/ 1837, SI 2012/ 2317

s.25, referred to: SI 2012/ 796 Art.3

s.25, repealed: 2012 c.7 s.179

2006–cont.

41. National Health Service Act 2006–*cont.*

s.25, enabling: SI 2012/755, SI 2012/786, SI 2012/788, SI 2012/796, SI 2012/803, SI 2012/1514, SI 2012/1837, SI 2012/2317, SI 2012/2570

s.26, repealed: 2012 c.7 s.179

s.27, repealed: 2012 c.7 s.179

s.28, applied: SI 2012/476, SI 2012/901, SI 2012/1273

s.28, repealed (in part): 2012 c.7 Sch.4 para.13

s.28, enabling: SI 2012/476, SI 2012/901, SI 2012/1109, SI 2012/1273, SI 2012/1424, SI 2012/1641

s.28A, added: 2012 c.7 s.48

s.29, amended: 2012 c.7 Sch.4 para.14

s.29, enabling: SI 2012/922, SI 2012/1290

s.30, amended: 2012 c.7 s.159

s.30, applied: SI 2012/717 Sch.1

s.31, repealed (in part): 2012 c.7 Sch.13 para.9, Sch.13 para.9

s.32, repealed: 2012 c.7 Sch.13 para.10

s.33, amended: 2012 c.7 s.151

s.33, applied: 2012 c.7 s.180

s.33, repealed (in part): 2012 c.7 s.159, s.180

s.34, repealed: 2012 c.7 s.160

s.35, amended: 2012 c.7 s.151, s.159

s.35, applied: 2012 c.7 s.180

s.35, repealed (in part): 2012 c.7 s.159, s.160, s.180

s.36, amended: 2012 c.7 s.180

s.36, applied: 2012 c.7 s.88, s.180

s.36, repealed (in part): 2012 c.7 s.160, s.180

s.37, amended: 2012 c.7 s.161

s.37, applied: 2012 c.7 s.161

s.38, repealed: 2012 c.7 s.159

s.39, amended: 2012 c.7 s.151, s.178

s.39, repealed (in part): 2012 c.7 s.111, s.156, s.159

s.39A, added: 2012 c.7 s.162

s.40, amended: 2012 c.7 s.163, Sch.14 para.5

s.41, repealed: 2012 c.7 s.163

s.42, amended: 2012 c.7 s.163, Sch.14 para.6

s.42, repealed (in part): 2012 c.7 s.163

s.42A, added: 2012 c.7 s.163

s.43, amended: 2012 c.7 s.164

s.43, repealed (in part): 2012 c.7 s.164

s.43, substituted: 2012 c.7 s.164

s.44, repealed (in part): 2012 c.7 s.165

s.44, substituted: 2012 c.7 s.165

s.45, repealed: 2012 c.7 s.163

s.46, repealed (in part): 2012 c.7 s.163

s.48, substituted: 2012 c.7 s.166

s.49, repealed: 2012 c.7 s.159

s.50, substituted: 2012 c.7 s.163

s.51, repealed (in part): 2012 c.7 Sch.14 para.7

s.51, enabling: SI 2012/950, SI 2012/2891, SI 2012/2950

s.51A, added: 2012 c.7 s.167

s.52, repealed: 2012 c.7 s.111

s.52C, repealed: 2012 c.7 s.173

s.53, repealed: 2012 c.7 s.173

s.54, repealed: 2012 c.7 s.173

s.55, repealed: 2012 c.7 s.173

s.56, amended: 2012 c.7 s.168, Sch.14 para.8

s.56, repealed (in part): 2012 c.7 s.168

s.56A, added: 2012 c.7 s.169

s.56A, amended: 2012 c.7 Sch.14 para.9

s.56B, added: 2012 c.7 s.170

s.57, amended: 2012 c.7 s.172, s.173, Sch.14 para.10

s.57, repealed (in part): 2012 c.7 s.172, s.173, Sch.14 para.10

s.57, substituted: 2012 c.7 s.172

s.57A, added: 2012 c.7 s.171

2006–cont.

41. National Health Service Act 2006–*cont.*

s.58, repealed: 2012 c.14 s.216

s.59, amended: 2012 c.7 s.151

s.60, amended: 2012 c.7 s.151

s.61, amended: 2012 c.7 s.153

s.64, amended: 2012 c.7 s.158, s.172

s.64, repealed (in part): 2012 c.7 s.173

s.64, enabling: SI 2012/950, SI 2012/2891, SI 2012/2950

s.65, amended: 2012 c.7 Sch.14 para.11

s.65A, amended: 2012 c.7 s.174

s.65A, repealed (in part): 2012 c.7 s.174, Sch.14 para.12

s.65B, applied: SI 2012/1806

s.65B, amended: 2012 c.7 Sch.14 para.13

s.65B, substituted: 2012 c.7 s.174

s.65B, enabling: SI 2012/1806

s.65C, repealed: 2012 c.7 Sch.14 para.14

s.65D, amended: 2012 c.7 s.174

s.65D, applied: 2012 c.7 s.134

s.65D, repealed (in part): 2012 c.7 s.174

s.65D, substituted: 2012 c.7 s.174

s.65DA, added: 2012 c.7 s.175

s.65DA, applied: 2012 c.7 s.175

s.65E, repealed: 2012 c.7 s.173

s.65F, amended: 2012 c.7 s.176, Sch.14 para.15

s.65F, referred to: SI 2012/1824, SI 2012/1824 Art.2

s.65F, repealed (in part): 2012 c.7 s.176, Sch.14 para.15

s.65G, amended: 2012 c.7 s.176, Sch.14 para.16

s.65H, amended: 2012 c.7 s.176, s.189, Sch.14 para.17

s.65H, repealed (in part): 2012 c.7 s.176, Sch.14 para.17

s.65I, amended: 2012 c.7 s.176, Sch.14 para.18

s.65I, repealed (in part): 2012 c.7 Sch.14 para.18

s.65J, amended: 2012 c.7 s.176, Sch.14 para.19

s.65J, applied: SI 2012/1824

s.65J, repealed (in part): 2012 c.7 Sch.14 para.19

s.65J, enabling: SI 2012/1824

s.65K, amended: 2012 c.7 s.177

s.65K, repealed: 2012 c.7 Sch.14 para.20

s.65K, substituted: 2012 c.7 s.177

s.65KA, added: 2012 c.7 s.177

s.65KA, amended: 2012 c.7 Sch.14 para.21

s.65KB, added: 2012 c.7 s.177

s.65KC, added: 2012 c.7 s.177

s.65KD, added: 2012 c.7 s.177

s.65L, amended: 2012 c.7 s.177, Sch.14 para.22

s.65L, repealed (in part): 2012 c.7 s.177, Sch.14 para.22

s.65LA, added: 2012 c.7 s.177

s.65M, amended: 2012 c.7 s.178, Sch.14 para.23

s.65M, repealed (in part): 2012 c.7 Sch.14 para.23

s.65N, amended: 2012 c.7 s.178, Sch.14 para.24

s.65N, repealed (in part): 2012 c.7 Sch.14 para.24

s.65O, amended: 2012 c.7 s.178

s.65P, repealed: 2012 c.7 Sch.4 para.15

s.65Q, repealed: 2012 c.7 Sch.4 para.15

s.65R, repealed: 2012 c.7 Sch.4 para.15

s.65S, repealed: 2012 c.7 Sch.4 para.15

s.65T, repealed: 2012 c.7 Sch.4 para.15

s.65U, repealed: 2012 c.7 Sch.4 para.15

s.65V, repealed: 2012 c.7 Sch.4 para.15

s.65W, repealed: 2012 c.7 Sch.4 para.15

s.65X, repealed: 2012 c.7 Sch.4 para.15

s.65Y, repealed: 2012 c.7 Sch.4 para.15

s.65Z, repealed: 2012 c.7 Sch.4 para.15

s.65Z1, repealed: 2012 c.7 Sch.4 para.15

2006– cont.

41. National Health Service Act 2006– *cont.*
s.65Z2, repealed: 2012 c.7 Sch.4 para.15
s.65Z3, repealed: 2012 c.7 Sch.4 para.15
s.66, amended: 2012 c.7 Sch.21 para.8
s.66, repealed (in part): 2012 c.7 Sch.14 para.25
s.66, varied: 2012 c.7 Sch.21 para.8, SI 2012/1831 Art.13
s.67, amended: 2012 c.7 Sch.4 para.16, Sch.21 para.9
s.68, amended: 2012 c.7 Sch.21 para.10
s.68, repealed (in part): 2012 c.7 Sch.14 para.26
s.68, varied: 2012 c.7 Sch.21 para.10, SI 2012/1831 Art.13
s.70, amended: 2012 c.7 Sch.4 para.17, Sch.14 para.27
s.70, substituted: 2012 c.7 Sch.14 para.27
s.71, amended: 2012 c.7 Sch.4 para.18, Sch.7 para.19, Sch.14 para.28, Sch.17 para.10, Sch.19 para.9
s.71, repealed (in part): 2012 c.7 Sch.4 para.18, Sch.7 para.19, Sch.14 para.28
s.72, amended: 2012 c.7 Sch.19 para.9
s.72, substituted: 2012 c.7 Sch.17 para.10
s.73, repealed (in part): 2012 c.7 Sch.4 para.19
s.73A, added: 2012 c.7 s.30
s.73A, applied: SI 2012/3094 Reg.14
s.73A, enabling: SI 2012/3094
s.73B, added: 2012 c.7 s.31
s.73B, applied: SI 2012/3094 Reg.15
s.73B, enabling: SI 2012/3094
s.73C, added: 2012 c.7 s.32
s.73C, enabling: SI 2012/3094
s.74, amended: 2012 c.7 Sch.4 para.24
s.75, applied: 2012 c.7 s.195, SI 2012/335 Sch.1 para.7, SI 2012/2991 Sch.1 para.7
s.75, enabling: SI 2012/3094
s.76, amended: 2012 c.7 Sch.4 para.25
s.76, applied: SI 2012/3094 Reg.13
s.76, enabling: SI 2012/3094
s.77, amended: 2012 c.7 s.200, Sch.4 para.26, Sch.14 para.29
s.77, applied: 2012 c.7 s.200, SI 2012/3094 Reg.3, Reg.4, Reg.6
s.77, repealed (in part): 2012 c.7 s.200
s.77, enabling: SI 2012/3094
s.78, amended: 2012 c.7 Sch.21 para.11
s.78, repealed (in part): 2012 c.7 Sch.4 para.27, Sch.14 para.30, Sch.21 para.11
s.79, repealed: 2012 c.7 Sch.14 para.30
s.80, amended: 2012 c.7 Sch.4 para.28
s.80, repealed (in part): 2012 c.7 Sch.4 para.28
s.81, amended: 2012 c.7 Sch.4 para.29
s.83, amended: 2012 c.7 Sch.4 para.30
s.83, repealed (in part): 2012 c.7 Sch.4 para.30
s.84, amended: 2012 c.7 Sch.4 para.31
s.85, enabling: SI 2012/970
s.86, amended: 2012 c.7 s.202, Sch.4 para.32
s.87, amended: 2012 c.7 Sch.4 para.33
s.87, applied: SI 2012/1909 Reg.92, Sch.7 para.13
s.89, amended: 2012 c.7 s.28, s.202, Sch.4 para.34
s.89, enabling: SI 2012/970
s.91, amended: 2012 c.7 Sch.4 para.35
s.92, amended: 2012 c.7 Sch.4 para.36
s.92, repealed (in part): 2012 c.7 Sch.4 para.36
s.93, amended: 2012 c.7 s.202, Sch.4 para.37
s.93, repealed (in part): 2012 c.7 Sch.4 para.37
s.94, amended: 2012 c.7 s.28, Sch.4 para.38
s.94, enabling: SI 2012/970
s.95, repealed: 2012 c.7 Sch.4 para.39
s.96, amended: 2012 c.7 Sch.4 para.40
s.97, amended: 2012 c.7 Sch.4 para.41

2006– cont.

41. National Health Service Act 2006– *cont.*
s.97, repealed (in part): 2012 c.7 Sch.4 para.41
s.98A, added: 2012 c.7 s.49
s.99, amended: 2012 c.7 Sch.4 para.42
s.99, repealed (in part): 2012 c.7 Sch.4 para.42
s.99, substituted: 2012 c.7 Sch.4 para.42
s.100, amended: 2012 c.7 Sch.4 para.43
s.102, amended: 2012 c.7 s.203, Sch.4 para.44
s.103, amended: 2012 c.7 Sch.4 para.45
s.104, amended: 2012 c.7 Sch.4 para.46
s.104, enabling: SI 2012/502, SI 2012/2273
s.106, amended: 2012 c.7 Sch.4 para.47
s.107, amended: 2012 c.7 Sch.4 para.48
s.107, applied: 2012 c.7 Sch.4 para.48
s.107, repealed (in part): 2012 c.7 Sch.4 para.48
s.108, amended: 2012 c.7 s.204, Sch.4 para.49
s.108, repealed (in part): 2012 c.7 s.204, Sch.4 para.49
s.109, amended: 2012 c.7 Sch.4 para.50
s.109, enabling: SI 2012/502, SI 2012/2273
s.110, repealed: 2012 c.7 Sch.4 para.51
s.111, amended: 2012 c.7 s.29
s.111, applied: 2012 c.7 s.237
s.111, enabling: SI 2012/3094
s.112, amended: 2012 c.7 Sch.4 para.52
s.113, amended: 2012 c.7 Sch.4 para.53
s.113, repealed (in part): 2012 c.7 Sch.4 para.53
s.114A, added: 2012 c.7 s.49
s.115, amended: 2012 c.7 Sch.4 para.54
s.115, repealed (in part): 2012 c.7 Sch.4 para.54
s.115, enabling: SI 2012/515
s.117, amended: 2012 c.7 Sch.4 para.55
s.118, amended: 2012 c.7 Sch.4 para.56
s.119, amended: 2012 c.7 Sch.4 para.57
s.120, amended: 2012 c.7 Sch.4 para.58
s.121, amended: 2012 c.7 Sch.4 para.59
s.123, amended: 2012 c.7 Sch.4 para.60
s.124, amended: 2012 c.7 Sch.4 para.61
s.125, amended: 2012 c.7 Sch.4 para.62
s.125A, added: 2012 c.7 s.49
s.126, amended: 2012 c.7 s.213, s.220, Sch.4 para.63
s.126, repealed (in part): 2012 c.7 Sch.4 para.63
s.126, enabling: SI 2012/1399, SI 2012/1909, SI 2012/2371
s.127, amended: 2012 c.7 Sch.4 para.64
s.127, referred to: SI 2012/1909 Reg.89
s.128, amended: 2012 c.7 Sch.4 para.65
s.128A, amended: 2012 c.7 s.206
s.128A, applied: SI 2012/1909 Reg.3
s.128A, enabling: SI 2012/1909
s.129, amended: 2012 c.7 s.207, Sch.4 para.66, 2012 c.9 Sch.9 para.121
s.129, applied: SI 2012/1909 Sch.2 para.8
s.129, disapplied: SI 2012/1909 Reg.23, Reg.24, Reg.25, Reg.26, Reg.27, Reg.28, Reg.29
s.129, referred to: SI 2012/1909 Reg.6, Reg.13, Reg.15, Reg.17, Reg.18, Reg.20
s.129, enabling: SI 2012/1399, SI 2012/1909, SI 2012/2371
s.130, amended: 2012 c.7 s.207, Sch.4 para.67
s.130, enabling: SI 2012/1909, SI 2012/2371
s.131, amended: 2012 c.7 Sch.4 para.68
s.131, applied: SI 2012/1909 Sch.7 para.2
s.132, amended: 2012 c.7 Sch.4 para.69, 2012 c.9 Sch.9 para.122
s.132, enabling: SI 2012/1909, SI 2012/2371
s.133, amended: 2012 c.7 Sch.4 para.70
s.134, amended: 2012 c.7 Sch.4 para.71

2006–cont.

41. National Health Service Act 2006–*cont.*
s.134, repealed (in part): 2012 c.7 Sch.4 para.71
s.134, varied: 2012 c.7 Sch.4 para.92
s.135, varied: 2012 c.7 Sch.4 para.92
s.136, amended: 2012 c.7 s.207, Sch.4 para.72
s.136, varied: 2012 c.7 Sch.4 para.92
s.137, amended: 2012 c.7 Sch.4 para.73
s.137, varied: 2012 c.7 Sch.4 para.92
s.138, amended: 2012 c.7 Sch.4 para.74
s.138, varied: 2012 c.7 Sch.4 para.92
s.139, varied: 2012 c.7 Sch.4 para.92
s.140, amended: 2012 c.7 Sch.4 para.75
s.140, varied: 2012 c.7 Sch.4 para.92
s.141, varied: 2012 c.7 Sch.4 para.92
s.142, varied: 2012 c.7 Sch.4 para.92
s.143, varied: 2012 c.7 Sch.4 para.92
s.144, amended: 2012 c.7 Sch.4 para.76
s.144, varied: 2012 c.7 Sch.4 para.93
s.146, repealed: 2012 c.7 s.208
s.147A, added: 2012 c.7 s.208
s.147A, amended: 2012 c.9 Sch.9 para.123
s.147B, added: 2012 c.7 s.208
s.148, amended: 2012 c.7 Sch.4 para.77
s.148, substituted: 2012 c.7 s.208
s.148, enabling: SI 2012/1909
s.149, repealed: 2012 c.7 s.208
s.149, substituted: 2012 c.7 s.208
s.150, repealed: 2012 c.7 s.208
s.150, substituted: 2012 c.7 s.208
s.150A, amended: 2012 c.7 Sch.4 para.78
s.150A, enabling: SI 2012/1909
s.151, amended: 2012 c.7 Sch.4 para.79
s.151, applied: SI 2012/1909 Reg.76, Reg.78, Reg.79, Reg.82, Reg.86, Reg.88
s.151, referred to: SI 2012/1909 Reg.35
s.151, enabling: SI 2012/1909
s.152, amended: 2012 c.7 Sch.4 para.80
s.152, applied: SI 2012/1909 Reg.76, Reg.82, Reg.86, Reg.88
s.154, amended: 2012 c.7 Sch.4 para.81
s.154, applied: SI 2012/1909 Reg.76, Reg.83, Reg.86, Reg.88
s.154, enabling: SI 2012/1909
s.155, amended: 2012 c.7 Sch.4 para.82
s.155, applied: SI 2012/1909 Reg.83, Reg.86, Reg.88
s.157, amended: 2012 c.7 Sch.4 para.83
s.157, applied: SI 2012/1909 Reg.82, Reg.83, Reg.84, Reg.85
s.158, amended: 2012 c.7 Sch.4 para.84
s.158, applied: SI 2012/1909 Reg.82, Reg.84
s.159, amended: 2012 c.7 s.208, Sch.4 para.85
s.159, applied: SI 2012/1290 Reg.3
s.159, repealed (in part): 2012 c.7 s.208
s.159, varied: SI 2012/1909 Reg.87
s.159, enabling: SI 2012/1909
s.160, amended: 2012 c.7 Sch.4 para.86
s.160, enabling: SI 2012/1909
s.161, amended: 2012 c.7 Sch.4 para.87
s.162, amended: 2012 c.7 Sch.4 para.88
s.162, enabling: SI 2012/1909
s.163, enabling: SI 2012/1909
s.164, amended: 2012 c.7 Sch.4 para.89
s.164, applied: SI 2012/1909 Reg.89, Reg.90, Reg.93
s.164, enabling: SI 2012/1909
s.165, applied: SI 2012/1909 Reg.89
s.165A, added: 2012 c.7 s.51
s.166, amended: 2012 c.7 Sch.4 para.90
s.167, amended: 2012 c.7 Sch.4 para.91

2006–cont.

41. National Health Service Act 2006–*cont.*
s.168A, added: 2012 c.7 s.49
s.172, enabling: SI 2012/470, SI 2012/1909
s.175, enabling: SI 2012/1586
s.176, amended: 2012 c.7 Sch.4 para.94
s.176, repealed (in part): 2012 c.7 Sch.4 para.94
s.176, enabling: SI 2012/502
s.177, repealed (in part): 2012 c.7 Sch.4 para.95
s.179, enabling: SI 2012/515
s.180, amended: 2012 c.7 s.205, Sch.4 para.96
s.180, repealed (in part): 2012 c.7 Sch.4 para.96
s.181, amended: 2012 c.7 Sch.4 para.97
s.181, repealed (in part): 2012 c.7 Sch.4 para.97
s.182, enabling: SI 2012/1650, SI 2012/1909
s.183, amended: 2012 c.7 Sch.4 para.98
s.183, enabling: SI 2012/1650
s.184, enabling: SI 2012/1650
s.185, amended: 2012 c.7 Sch.4 para.99, Sch.14 para.31
s.186, amended: 2012 c.7 Sch.4 para.100, Sch.14 para.32
s.186A, added: 2012 c.7 s.50
s.187, amended: 2012 c.7 Sch.4 para.101
s.188, amended: 2012 c.7 Sch.4 para.102
s.195, amended: 2012 c.7 Sch.4 para.103
s.196, amended: 2012 c.7 Sch.4 para.104
s.196, repealed (in part): 2012 c.7 Sch.4 para.104, Sch.14 para.33
s.197, amended: 2012 c.7 Sch.4 para.105
s.201, amended: 2012 c.7 Sch.4 para.106, Sch.15 para.68
s.210, amended: 2012 c.7 Sch.4 para.107
s.211, amended: 2012 c.7 Sch.4 para.108
s.213, amended: 2012 c.7 Sch.4 para.109
s.213, enabling: SI 2012/1512, SI 2012/2755
s.214, amended: 2012 c.7 Sch.4 para.110
s.215, amended: 2012 c.7 Sch.4 para.111
s.215, repealed (in part): 2012 c.7 Sch.4 para.111
s.216, amended: 2012 c.7 Sch.4 para.112
s.217, amended: 2012 c.7 Sch.4 para.113
s.217, repealed (in part): 2012 c.7 Sch.4 para.113, Sch.14 para.34
s.217, enabling: SI 2012/1512, SI 2012/2755
s.218, amended: 2012 c.7 Sch.4 para.114
s.220, amended: 2012 c.7 Sch.4 para.115
s.222, amended: 2012 c.7 Sch.4 para.116
s.223, amended: 2012 c.7 Sch.4 para.117
s.223A, added: 2012 c.7 Sch.4 para.117
s.223B, added: 2012 c.7 s.24
s.223C, added: 2012 c.7 s.24
s.223D, added: 2012 c.7 s.24
s.223E, added: 2012 c.7 s.24
s.223E, enabling: SI 2012/2996
s.223F, added: 2012 c.7 s.24
s.223G, added: 2012 c.7 s.27
s.223G, applied: SI 2012/1631 Reg.10, Sch.3
s.223H, added: 2012 c.7 s.27
s.223I, added: 2012 c.7 s.27
s.223J, added: 2012 c.7 s.27
s.223J, enabling: SI 2012/2996
s.223K, added: 2012 c.7 s.27
s.224, repealed: 2012 c.7 Sch.4 para.118
s.226, amended: 2012 c.7 Sch.4 para.119
s.226, repealed (in part): 2012 c.7 Sch.4 para.119
s.227, amended: 2012 c.7 Sch.4 para.120
s.228, repealed: 2012 c.7 Sch.4 para.121
s.229, repealed: 2012 c.7 Sch.4 para.121
s.230, repealed: 2012 c.7 Sch.4 para.121

2006–cont.

41. National Health Service Act 2006–*cont.*
s.231, repealed: 2012 c.7 Sch.4 para.121
s.234, repealed (in part): 2012 c.7 Sch.4 para.122
s.236, amended: 2012 c.7 Sch.4 para.123
s.242, amended: 2012 c.7 s.206, Sch.14 para.35
s.242, repealed (in part): 2012 c.7 Sch.4 para.126, Sch.14 para.35
s.242A, amended: 2012 c.7 s.206
s.242A, repealed: 2012 c.7 Sch.4 para.127
s.242B, repealed: 2012 c.7 Sch.4 para.127
s.244, amended: 2012 c.7 s.190
s.244, applied: SI 2012/1020 Reg.9, SI 2012/1021 Reg.6
s.244, substituted: 2012 c.7 s.190
s.244, varied: SI 2012/1831 Art.13
s.245, amended: 2012 c.7 s.190, s.191
s.245, applied: SI 2012/1020 Reg.4
s.245, repealed (in part): 2012 c.7 s.191
s.246, amended: 2012 c.7 s.190, s.191
s.247, amended: 2012 c.7 s.190, s.191
s.247A, amended: 2012 c.7 s.190
s.247A, repealed: 2012 c.7 s.191
s.247B, added: 2012 c.7 s.60
s.247C, added: 2012 c.7 s.52
s.247D, added: 2012 c.7 s.53
s.248, repealed: 2012 c.7 s.185
s.249, amended: 2012 c.7 s.29
s.249, varied: SI 2012/1831 Art.13
s.250, repealed: 2012 c.7 s.283
s.250A, repealed: 2012 c.7 s.280
s.250B, repealed: 2012 c.7 s.280
s.250C, repealed: 2012 c.7 s.280
s.250D, applied: 2012 c.7 Sch.20 para.12
s.250D, repealed: 2012 c.7 s.280
s.252, amended: 2012 c.7 s.280
s.252A, added: 2012 c.7 s.46
s.253, amended: 2012 c.7 s.47
s.253, repealed (in part): 2012 c.7 s.47
s.254A, added: 2012 c.7 Sch.4 para.128
s.256, amended: 2012 c.7 Sch.4 para.129
s.256, varied: SI 2012/1831 Art.13
s.257, amended: 2012 c.7 Sch.4 para.130
s.258, amended: 2012 c.7 Sch.4 para.131
s.258, varied: SI 2012/1831 Art.13
s.259, amended: 2012 c.7 Sch.4 para.132
s.262, enabling: SI 2012/2791
s.263, enabling: SI 2012/2791
s.266, enabling: SI 2012/2791
s.268, repealed: 2012 c.7 Sch.4 para.133
s.269, amended: 2012 c.7 s.284
s.269, varied: 2012 c.7 s.284
s.270, amended: 2012 c.7 s.285
s.271, amended: 2012 c.7 s.60, s.172, s.280, Sch.4 para.134
s.271, repealed (in part): 2012 c.7 Sch.20 para.10
s.271A, added: 2012 c.7 Sch.4 para.135
s.272, amended: 2012 c.7 s.13, s.18, s.20, s.21, s.23, s.48, s.50, s.173, s.178, Sch.4 para.136
s.272, repealed (in part): 2012 c.7 s.173, Sch.4 para.136, Sch.14 para.36
s.272, enabling: SI 2012/417, SI 2012/470, SI 2012/476, SI 2012/502, SI 2012/515, SI 2012/779, SI 2012/786, SI 2012/788, SI 2012/796, SI 2012/803, SI 2012/901, SI 2012/922, SI 2012/970, SI 2012/1108, SI 2012/1109, SI 2012/1273, SI 2012/1290, SI 2012/1399, SI 2012/1424, SI 2012/1425, SI 2012/1467, SI 2012/1512, SI 2012/1514, SI 2012/1586, SI 2012/1631, SI 2012/1641, SI 2012/1650, SI

2006–cont.

41. National Health Service Act 2006–*cont.*
s.272, enabling:–*cont.*
2012/1806, SI 2012/1824, SI 2012/1837, SI 2012/1909, SI 2012/2273, SI 2012/2317, SI 2012/2371, SI 2012/2570, SI 2012/2755, SI 2012/2791, SI 2012/2996, SI 2012/3094
s.273, amended: 2012 c.7 s.21, s.47, Sch.4 para.137, SI 2012/1831 Art.12
s.273, enabling: SI 2012/417, SI 2012/476, SI 2012/755, SI 2012/796, SI 2012/803, SI 2012/1109, SI 2012/1424, SI 2012/1425, SI 2012/1514, SI 2012/1641, SI 2012/1837, SI 2012/2317, SI 2012/2570, SI 2012/2891, SI 2012/2950
s.275, amended: 2012 c.7 s.40, s.173, s.178, Sch.4 para.138, Sch.13 para.11, Sch.14 para.37, Sch.17 para.10
s.275, varied: 2012 c.7 Sch.4 para.138, SI 2012/1831 Art.13
s.276, amended: 2012 c.7 s.208, Sch.4 para.139, Sch.13 para.12, Sch.14 para.38
Sch.A1 para.1, added: 2012 c.7 Sch.1
Sch.A1 para.2, added: 2012 c.7 Sch.1
Sch.A1 para.3, added: 2012 c.7 Sch.1
Sch.A1 para.4, added: 2012 c.7 Sch.1
Sch.A1 para.5, added: 2012 c.7 Sch.1
Sch.A1 para.6, added: 2012 c.7 Sch.1
Sch.A1 para.7, added: 2012 c.7 Sch.1
Sch.A1 para.8, added: 2012 c.7 Sch.1
Sch.A1 para.9, added: 2012 c.7 Sch.1
Sch.A1 para.10, added: 2012 c.7 Sch.1
Sch.A1 para.11, added: 2012 c.7 Sch.1
Sch.A1 para.12, added: 2012 c.7 Sch.1
Sch.A1 para.13, added: 2012 c.7 Sch.1
Sch.A1 para.14, added: 2012 c.7 Sch.1
Sch.A1 para.15, added: 2012 c.7 Sch.1
Sch.A1 para.15, amended: SI 2012/1831 Art.3
Sch.A1 para.16, added: 2012 c.7 Sch.1
Sch.A1 para.16, amended: SI 2012/1831 Art.3
Sch.A1 para.17, added: 2012 c.7 Sch.1
Sch.A1 para.18, added: 2012 c.7 Sch.1
Sch.1 para.1, amended: 2012 c.7 s.17
Sch.1 para.1, applied: 2012 c.7 s.237
Sch.1 para.2, amended: 2012 c.7 s.17
Sch.1 para.2, applied: 2012 c.7 s.237
Sch.1 para.2, repealed (in part): 2012 c.7 s.17
Sch.1 para.3, applied: 2012 c.7 s.237
Sch.1 para.4, amended: 2012 c.7 s.17
Sch.1 para.4, applied: 2012 c.7 s.237
Sch.1 para.5, amended: 2012 c.7 s.17
Sch.1 para.5, applied: 2012 c.7 s.237
Sch.1 para.5, repealed (in part): 2012 c.7 s.17
Sch.1 para.6, applied: 2012 c.7 s.237
Sch.1 para.7, applied: 2012 c.7 s.237
Sch.1 para.7A, amended: 2012 c.7 s.17
Sch.1 para.7A, applied: 2012 c.7 s.237
Sch.1 para.7B, amended: 2012 c.7 s.17
Sch.1 para.7B, applied: 2012 c.7 s.237
Sch.1 para.7C, added: 2012 c.7 s.17
Sch.1 para.9, amended: 2012 c.7 s.17
Sch.1 para.9, applied: SI 2012/2885 Sch.1 para.25, Sch.1 para.26, SI 2012/2886 Sch.1, SI 2012/3094 Reg.13, SI 2012/3144 Sch.1 para.19, SI 2012/3145 Sch.1, SSI 2012/303 Reg.28, Sch.1 para.10, SSI 2012/319 Reg.29
Sch.1 para.10, amended: 2012 c.7 s.17
Sch.1 para.10, applied: SI 2012/2885 Sch.1 para.26, SI 2012/3094 Reg.13
Sch.1 para.11, applied: SI 2012/3094 Reg.13
Sch.1 para.12, amended: 2012 c.7 s.17

2006–cont.

41. National Health Service Act 2006–*cont.*
Sch.1 para.12, repealed (in part): 2012 c.7 s.17
Sch.1 para.13, applied: 2012 c.7 s.237, SI 2012/3094 Reg.17
Sch.1 para.13, substituted: 2012 c.7 s.17
Sch.1A Part 1 para.1, added: 2012 c.7 Sch.2
Sch.1A Part 1 para.2, added: 2012 c.7 Sch.2
Sch.1A Part 1 para.2, enabling: SI 2012/1631
Sch.1A Part 1 para.3, added: 2012 c.7 Sch.2
Sch.1A Part 1 para.3, varied: 2012 c.7 Sch.6 para.11
Sch.1A Part 1 para.4, added: 2012 c.7 Sch.2
Sch.1A Part 1 para.5, added: 2012 c.7 Sch.2
Sch.1A Part 1 para.6, added: 2012 c.7 Sch.2
Sch.1A Part 1 para.6, varied: 2012 c.7 Sch.6 para.11
Sch.1A Part 1 para.7, added: 2012 c.7 Sch.2
Sch.1A Part 1 para.8, added: 2012 c.7 Sch.2
Sch.1A Part 1 para.9, added: 2012 c.7 Sch.2
Sch.1A Part 2 para.11, added: 2012 c.7 Sch.2
Sch.1A Part 2 para.11, applied: SI 2012/1631 Reg.16
Sch.1A Part 2 para.12, added: 2012 c.7 Sch.2
Sch.1A Part 2 para.12, varied: 2012 c.7 Sch.6 para.11
Sch.1A Part 2 para.13, added: 2012 c.7 Sch.2
Sch.1A Part 2 para.14, added: 2012 c.7 Sch.2
Sch.1A Part 2 para.15, added: 2012 c.7 Sch.2
Sch.1A Part 2 para.16, added: 2012 c.7 Sch.2
Sch.1A Part 2 para.17, added: 2012 c.7 Sch.2
Sch.1A Part 2 para.17, disapplied: SI 2012/1831 Art.9
Sch.1A Part 2 para.18, added: 2012 c.7 Sch.2
Sch.1A Part 2 para.19, added: 2012 c.7 Sch.2
Sch.1A Part 2 para.20, added: 2012 c.7 Sch.2
Sch.1A Part 2 para.21, added: 2012 c.7 Sch.2
Sch.1A Part 3 para.22, added: 2012 c.7 Sch.2
Sch.1A Part 3 para.23, added: 2012 c.7 Sch.2
Sch.1A Part 3 para.24, added: 2012 c.7 Sch.2
Sch.1A Part 3 para.25, added: 2012 c.7 Sch.2
Sch.1A Part 3 para.26, added: 2012 c.7 Sch.2
Sch.2 para.1, repealed: 2012 c.7 Sch.4 para.20
Sch.2 para.2, repealed: 2012 c.7 Sch.4 para.20
Sch.2 para.3, repealed: 2012 c.7 Sch.4 para.20
Sch.2 para.4, repealed: 2012 c.7 Sch.4 para.20
Sch.2 para.5, repealed: 2012 c.7 Sch.4 para.20
Sch.2 para.6, repealed: 2012 c.7 Sch.4 para.20
Sch.2 para.7, repealed: 2012 c.7 Sch.4 para.20
Sch.2 para.8, repealed: 2012 c.7 Sch.4 para.20
Sch.2 para.9, repealed: 2012 c.7 Sch.4 para.20
Sch.2 para.10, repealed: 2012 c.7 Sch.4 para.20
Sch.2 para.11, repealed: 2012 c.7 Sch.4 para.20
Sch.2 para.12, repealed: 2012 c.7 Sch.4 para.20
Sch.2 para.13, repealed: 2012 c.7 Sch.4 para.20
Sch.2 para.14, repealed: 2012 c.7 Sch.4 para.20
Sch.2 para.15, repealed: 2012 c.7 Sch.4 para.20
Sch.2 para.16, repealed: 2012 c.7 Sch.4 para.20
Sch.2 para.17, repealed: 2012 c.7 Sch.4 para.20
Sch.3 Part 1 para.1, repealed: 2012 c.7 Sch.4 para.21
Sch.3 Part 1 para.2, repealed: 2012 c.7 Sch.4 para.21
Sch.3 Part 1 para.3, repealed: 2012 c.7 Sch.4 para.21
Sch.3 Part 1 para.4, repealed: 2012 c.7 Sch.4 para.21
Sch.3 Part 1 para.5, repealed: 2012 c.7 Sch.4 para.21
Sch.3 Part 1 para.6, repealed: 2012 c.7 Sch.4 para.21
Sch.3 Part 1 para.7, repealed: 2012 c.7 Sch.4 para.21
Sch.3 Part 1 para.8, repealed: 2012 c.7 Sch.4 para.21
Sch.3 Part 1 para.9, repealed: 2012 c.7 Sch.4 para.21
Sch.3 Part 1 para.10, repealed: 2012 c.7 Sch.4 para.21
Sch.3 Part 1 para.11, repealed: 2012 c.7 Sch.4 para.21

2006–cont.

41. National Health Service Act 2006–*cont.*
Sch.3 Part 1 para.12, repealed: 2012 c.7 Sch.4 para.21
Sch.3 Part 2 para.13, repealed: 2012 c.7 Sch.4 para.21
Sch.3 Part 2 para.14, repealed: 2012 c.7 Sch.4 para.21
Sch.3 Part 3 para.15, repealed: 2012 c.7 Sch.4 para.21
Sch.3 Part 3 para.16, repealed: 2012 c.7 Sch.4 para.21
Sch.3 Part 3 para.17, repealed: 2012 c.7 Sch.4 para.21
Sch.3 Part 3 para.18, repealed: 2012 c.7 Sch.4 para.21
Sch.3 Part 3 para.19, repealed: 2012 c.7 Sch.4 para.21
Sch.3 Part 3 para.20, repealed: 2012 c.7 Sch.4 para.21
Sch.3 Part 3 para.21, repealed: 2012 c.7 Sch.4 para.21
Sch.3 Part 3 para.22, repealed: 2012 c.7 Sch.4 para.21
Sch.3 Part 3 para.23, repealed: 2012 c.7 Sch.4 para.21
Sch.3 Part 4 para.24, repealed: 2012 c.7 Sch.4 para.21
Sch.3 Part 4 para.25, repealed: 2012 c.7 Sch.4 para.21
Sch.3 Part 5 para.26, repealed: 2012 c.7 Sch.4 para.21
Sch.3 Part 5 para.27, repealed: 2012 c.7 Sch.4 para.21
Sch.3 Part 5 para.28, repealed: 2012 c.7 Sch.4 para.21
Sch.3 Part 5 para.29, repealed: 2012 c.7 Sch.4 para.21
Sch.4 Part 1 para.5, amended: 2012 c.7 Sch.4 para.22
Sch.4 Part 1 para.5, applied: SI 2012/796 Art.4
Sch.4 Part 1 para.5, enabling: SI 2012/786, SI 2012/788, SI 2012/796
Sch.4 Part 1 para.6, amended: 2012 c.7 Sch.4 para.22
Sch.4 Part 1 para.7, amended: 2012 c.7 Sch.4 para.22
Sch.4 Part 1 para.8, amended: 2012 c.7 Sch.4 para.22
Sch.4 Part 1 para.9, amended: 2012 c.7 Sch.4 para.22
Sch.4 Part 2 para.15, repealed (in part): 2012 c.7 Sch.4 para.22
Sch.4 Part 2 para.18, amended: 2012 c.7 Sch.4 para.22
Sch.4 Part 3 para.28, applied: SI 2012/796, SI 2012/803, SI 2012/2570
Sch.4 Part 3 para.28, referred to: SI 2012/1514
Sch.4 Part 3 para.28, enabling: SI 2012/796, SI 2012/803, SI 2012/1514, SI 2012/2570
Sch.4 Part 3 para.29, amended: 2012 c.7 Sch.4 para.22
Sch.4 Part 3 para.29, varied: SI 2012/1831 Art.13
Sch.4 Part 3 para.30, amended: 2012 c.7 Sch.4 para.22
Sch.5 para.1, applied: SI 2012/779
Sch.5 para.1, enabling: SI 2012/779
Sch.6 para.2, applied: SI 2012/922 Reg.13
Sch.6 para.3, amended: 2012 c.7 Sch.4 para.23
Sch.6 para.5, enabling: SI 2012/922, SI 2012/1108, SI 2012/1290, SI 2012/1425

41. National Health Service Act 2006–*cont.*
Sch.6 para.13, amended: 2012 c.7 Sch.4 para.23
Sch.6 para.13, enabling: SI 2012/922, SI 2012/1108, SI 2012/1290
Sch.7, substituted: 2012 c.7 s.151
Sch.7, amended: 2012 c.7 s.151
Sch.7 para.2, substituted: 2012 c.7 s.164
Sch.7 para.7, amended: 2012 c.7 s.151
Sch.7 para.8, amended: 2012 c.7 s.151, SI 2012/2404 Sch.2 para.57
Sch.7 para.9, amended: 2012 c.7 s.151
Sch.7 para.9, repealed (in part): 2012 c.7 s.151
Sch.7 para.10, amended: 2012 c.7 s.151
Sch.7 para.10A, added: 2012 c.7 s.151
Sch.7 para.10A, amended: 2012 c.7 s.151
Sch.7 para.10B, added: 2012 c.7 s.151
Sch.7 para.10B, amended: 2012 c.7 s.151
Sch.7 para.10C, added: 2012 c.7 s.151
Sch.7 para.10C, amended: 2012 c.7 s.151
Sch.7 para.11, amended: 2012 c.7 s.151
Sch.7 para.12, amended: 2012 c.7 s.151
Sch.7 para.13, amended: 2012 c.7 s.151
Sch.7 para.14, amended: 2012 c.7 s.151
Sch.7 para.17, amended: 2012 c.7 s.151
Sch.7 para.18, amended: 2012 c.7 s.151
Sch.7 para.18A, added: 2012 c.7 s.152
Sch.7 para.18B, added: 2012 c.7 s.152
Sch.7 para.18C, added: 2012 c.7 s.152
Sch.7 para.18D, added: 2012 c.7 s.152
Sch.7 para.18E, added: 2012 c.7 s.152
Sch.7 para.19, applied: 2012 c.7 s.180
Sch.7 para.19, repealed: 2012 c.7 s.180
Sch.7 para.20, amended: 2012 c.7 s.151
Sch.7 para.21, amended: 2012 c.7 s.151
Sch.7 para.22, amended: 2012 c.7 s.178
Sch.7 para.22, repealed (in part): 2012 c.7 s.111, s.156, s.159
Sch.7 para.23, amended: 2012 c.7 s.151
Sch.7 para.24, amended: 2012 c.7 s.154, s.155
Sch.7 para.25, amended: 2012 c.7 s.154, s.155
Sch.7 para.25, applied: 2012 c.7 Sch.8 para.17
Sch.7 para.26, amended: 2012 c.7 s.151, s.156
Sch.7 para.26, varied: 2012 c.7 s.156
Sch.7 para.27, amended: 2012 c.7 s.151, s.156
Sch.7 para.27A, added: 2012 c.7 s.157
Sch.7 para.28, amended: 2012 c.7 s.151
Sch.7 para.28, substituted: 2012 c.7 s.157
Sch.7 para.28A, added: 2012 c.7 s.157
Sch.7 para.30, added: 2012 c.7 s.158
Sch.8 para.1, repealed: 2012 c.7 Sch.13 para.9
Sch.8 para.2, repealed: 2012 c.7 Sch.13 para.9
Sch.8 para.2A, repealed: 2012 c.7 Sch.13 para.9
Sch.8 para.3, repealed: 2012 c.7 Sch.13 para.9
Sch.8 para.4, repealed: 2012 c.7 Sch.13 para.9
Sch.8 para.5, repealed: 2012 c.7 Sch.13 para.9
Sch.8 para.6, repealed: 2012 c.7 Sch.13 para.9
Sch.8 para.7, repealed: 2012 c.7 Sch.13 para.9
Sch.8 para.8, repealed: 2012 c.7 Sch.13 para.9
Sch.8 para.9, repealed: 2012 c.7 Sch.13 para.9
Sch.8 para.10, repealed: 2012 c.7 Sch.13 para.9
Sch.8 para.11, repealed: 2012 c.7 Sch.13 para.9
Sch.8 para.12, repealed: 2012 c.7 Sch.13 para.9
Sch.8 para.13, repealed: 2012 c.7 Sch.13 para.9
Sch.8 para.14, repealed: 2012 c.7 Sch.13 para.9
Sch.8 para.15, repealed: 2012 c.7 Sch.13 para.9
Sch.8 para.16, repealed: 2012 c.7 Sch.13 para.9
Sch.8A para.1, repealed: 2012 c.7 s.173
Sch.8A para.2, repealed: 2012 c.7 s.173

41. National Health Service Act 2006–*cont.*
Sch.8A para.3, repealed: 2012 c.7 s.173
Sch.8A para.4, repealed: 2012 c.7 s.173
Sch.8A para.5, repealed: 2012 c.7 s.173
Sch.8A para.6, repealed: 2012 c.7 s.173
Sch.8A para.7, repealed: 2012 c.7 s.173
Sch.8A para.8, repealed: 2012 c.7 s.173
Sch.8A para.9, repealed: 2012 c.7 s.173
Sch.8A para.10, repealed: 2012 c.7 s.173
Sch.8A para.11, repealed: 2012 c.7 s.173
Sch.8A para.12, repealed: 2012 c.7 s.173
Sch.9 para.1, repealed: 2012 c.7 s.173
Sch.9 para.2, repealed: 2012 c.7 s.173
Sch.9 para.3, repealed: 2012 c.7 s.173
Sch.9 para.4, repealed: 2012 c.7 s.173
Sch.9 para.5, repealed: 2012 c.7 s.173
Sch.9 para.6, repealed: 2012 c.7 s.173
Sch.10 para.4, amended: 2012 c.7 s.151
Sch.10 para.5, amended: 2012 c.7 s.151
Sch.11 para.1, amended: 2012 c.7 Sch.4 para.92
Sch.11 para.2, amended: 2012 c.7 Sch.4 para.92
Sch.11 para.3, amended: 2012 c.7 Sch.4 para.92
Sch.11 para.4, amended: 2012 c.7 Sch.4 para.92
Sch.11 para.5, amended: 2012 c.7 Sch.4 para.92
Sch.11 para.5, repealed (in part): 2012 c.7 Sch.4 para.92
Sch.11 para.7, amended: 2012 c.7 Sch.4 para.92
Sch.12 para.1, amended: 2012 c.7 Sch.4 para.93
Sch.12 para.1, repealed (in part): 2012 c.7 Sch.4 para.93
Sch.12 para.2, amended: 2012 c.7 s.207, Sch.4 para.93
Sch.12 para.3, amended: 2012 c.7 Sch.4 para.93
Sch.12 para.3, enabling: SI 2012/1467
Sch.12A para.1, added: 2012 c.7 Sch.3
Sch.12A para.2, added: 2012 c.7 Sch.3
Sch.12A para.3, added: 2012 c.7 Sch.3
Sch.12A para.4, added: 2012 c.7 Sch.3
Sch.14 para.1, repealed: 2012 c.7 Sch.4 para.124
Sch.14 para.2, repealed: 2012 c.7 Sch.4 para.124
Sch.14 para.3, repealed: 2012 c.7 Sch.4 para.124
Sch.14 para.3A, repealed: 2012 c.7 Sch.4 para.124
Sch.14 para.4, repealed: 2012 c.7 Sch.4 para.124
Sch.15 para.1, applied: SI 2012/2789 Art.1
Sch.15 para.1, repealed (in part): 2012 c.7 Sch.4 para.125, Sch.14 para.39
Sch.15 para.4, repealed (in part): 2012 c.7 Sch.14 para.39
Sch.15 para.5, amended: 2012 c.7 Sch.14 para.39
Sch.15 para.5, repealed (in part): 2012 c.7 Sch.4 para.125
Sch.15 para.6, amended: 2012 c.7 Sch.14 para.39
Sch.15 para.7, applied: SI 2012/1831 Art.11
Sch.15 para.7, disapplied: SI 2012/2789 Art.2
Sch.15 para.7, repealed: 2012 c.7 Sch.4 para.125
Sch.15 para.8, amended: 2012 c.7 Sch.4 para.125
Sch.15 para.8, applied: SI 2012/1831 Art.11
Sch.15 para.9, applied: SI 2012/1831 Art.11
Sch.15 para.9, repealed: 2012 c.7 Sch.4 para.125
Sch.17 Part 1 para.13, amended: 2012 c.7 s.208
Sch.19 para.1, repealed: 2012 c.7 s.283
Sch.19 para.2, repealed: 2012 c.7 s.283
Sch.19 para.3, repealed: 2012 c.7 s.283
Sch.19 para.4, repealed: 2012 c.7 s.283
Sch.19 para.5, repealed: 2012 c.7 s.283
Sch.19 para.5A, repealed: 2012 c.7 s.283
Sch.19 para.6, repealed: 2012 c.7 s.283
Sch.19 para.7, repealed: 2012 c.7 s.283

2006–cont.

41. National Health Service Act 2006–*cont.*
Sch.19 para.8, repealed: 2012 c.7 s.283
Sch.19 para.9, repealed: 2012 c.7 s.283
Sch.19 para.10, repealed: 2012 c.7 s.283

42. National Health Service (Wales) Act 2006
applied: SI 2012/1916 Sch.17 Part 1, SI 2012/3001 Sch.1
Part 6, applied: SI 2012/2113 Art.4
s.2, applied: SI 2012/3094 Reg.13
s.3, applied: SI 2012/3094 Reg.13
s.5, applied: SI 2012/3144 Sch.1 para.19, SI 2012/3145 Sch.1
s.7, amended: 2012 c.7 Sch.17 para.11, Sch.19 para.10, Sch.21 para.13
s.7, repealed (in part): 2012 c.7 Sch.7 para.21, Sch.21 para.13
s.8A, added: 2012 c.7 Sch.21 para.14
s.10, repealed (in part): 2012 c.7 Sch.21 para.15
s.11, applied: SI 2012/1631 Sch.5 para.6, SI 2012/2885 Sch.1 para.21, SI 2012/2996 Sch.5 para.5, SI 2012/3144 Sch.1 para.15, SI 2012/3145 Sch.1, SSI 2012/303 Sch.4 para.31, SSI 2012/319 Reg.35
s.13, amended: 2012 c.7 Sch.21 para.16
s.13, repealed (in part): 2012 c.7 Sch.21 para.16
s.17, amended: 2012 c.7 Sch.21 para.17
s.18, applied: SI 2012/1262
s.18, enabling: SI 2012/1262
s.19, enabling: SI 2012/1261
s.22, repealed (in part): 2012 c.7 Sch.21 para.18
s.26, amended: 2012 c.7 Sch.21 para.19
s.27, amended: 2012 c.7 Sch.21 para.20
s.28, amended: 2012 c.7 Sch.21 para.21
s.30, amended: 2012 c.7 Sch.7 para.22
s.30, repealed (in part): 2012 c.7 Sch.7 para.22
s.34, amended: 2012 c.7 Sch.21 para.22
s.36, repealed (in part): 2012 c.7 Sch.21 para.23
s.38, amended: 2012 c.7 Sch.21 para.24
s.39, amended: 2012 c.7 Sch.21 para.25
s.41, applied: SI 2012/1631 Sch.4 para.15
s.41, repealed (in part): 2012 c.7 Sch.21 para.26
s.51, amended: 2012 c.7 Sch.21 para.27
s.56, repealed (in part): 2012 c.7 Sch.21 para.28
s.57, applied: SI 2012/1631 Sch.4 para.12
s.61, enabling: SI 2012/2572
s.65, amended: 2012 c.7 Sch.21 para.29
s.66, enabling: SI 2012/2572
s.71, applied: SI 2012/1631 Sch.4 para.13
s.72, amended: 2012 c.9 Sch.9 para.125
s.80, amended: 2012 c.7 s.213, s.220
s.80, applied: SI 2012/1631 Sch.4 para.14
s.81, applied: SI 2012/1631 Sch.4 para.14
s.83, amended: 2012 c.9 Sch.9 para.126
s.86, amended: 2012 c.9 Sch.9 para.127
s.92, applied: SI 2012/1631 Sch.4 para.14
s.105, amended: 2012 c.9 Sch.9 para.128
s.106, amended: 2012 c.7 Sch.21 para.30
s.106, repealed (in part): 2012 c.7 Sch.21 para.30
s.115, amended: 2012 c.7 Sch.21 para.31
s.115, repealed (in part): 2012 c.7 Sch.21 para.31
s.125, enabling: SI 2012/1893
s.127, applied: SI 2012/3094 Reg.13
s.128, enabling: SI 2012/684
s.129, enabling: SI 2012/684
s.130, enabling: SI 2012/800
s.131, amended: 2012 c.7 Sch.21 para.32
s.131, enabling: SI 2012/800
s.132, enabling: SI 2012/800
s.144, amended: 2012 c.7 Sch.21 para.33

2006–cont.

42. National Health Service (Wales) Act 2006–*cont.*
s.149, amended: 2012 c.7 Sch.15 para.68
s.161, amended: 2012 c.7 Sch.21 para.34
s.162, amended: 2012 c.7 Sch.21 para.35
s.181, amended: 2012 c.7 Sch.21 para.36
s.184, amended: 2012 c.7 Sch.13 para.13
s.197, amended: 2012 c.7 Sch.21 para.37
s.201, amended: 2012 c.7 s.286
s.203, enabling: SI 2012/684, SI 2012/800, SI 2012/1261, SI 2012/1429, SI 2012/1893, SI 2012/2572
s.204, enabling: SI 2012/1262
s.206, amended: 2012 c.7 s.173, s.178, Sch.14 para.101, Sch.21 para.38
s.206, varied: 2012 c.7 Sch.21 para.38, SI 2012/2657 Art.13
Sch.1, applied: SI 2012/3144 Sch.1 para.19, SI 2012/3145 Sch.1
Sch.1 para.1, applied: SI 2012/3094 Reg.13
Sch.1 para.2, applied: SI 2012/3094 Reg.13
Sch.1 para.3, applied: SI 2012/3094 Reg.13
Sch.1 para.4, applied: SI 2012/3094 Reg.13
Sch.1 para.5, applied: SI 2012/3094 Reg.13
Sch.1 para.6, applied: SI 2012/3094 Reg.13
Sch.1 para.8, applied: SI 2012/3094 Reg.13
Sch.2 Part 1 para.9, amended: 2012 c.7 Sch.21 para.39
Sch.3 Part 1 para.4, enabling: SI 2012/1261
Sch.3 Part 1 para.5, amended: 2012 c.7 Sch.21 para.40
Sch.3 Part 1 para.5, enabling: SI 2012/1262
Sch.3 Part 1 para.6, amended: 2012 c.7 Sch.21 para.40
Sch.3 Part 1 para.7, amended: 2012 c.7 Sch.21 para.40
Sch.3 Part 1 para.8, amended: 2012 c.7 Sch.21 para.40
Sch.3 Part 1 para.9, amended: 2012 c.7 Sch.21 para.40
Sch.3 Part 1 para.9, enabling: SI 2012/1429
Sch.3 Part 2 para.18, amended: 2012 c.7 Sch.21 para.40
Sch.3 Part 3 para.30, amended: 2012 c.7 Sch.21 para.40
Sch.5 para.3, amended: 2012 c.7 Sch.21 para.41
Sch.5 para.13, amended: 2012 c.7 Sch.21 para.41
Sch.7, applied: SI 2012/1631 Sch.4 para.14
Sch.10 para.2, amended: 2012 c.7 Sch.21 para.42
Sch.10 para.3, repealed (in part): 2012 c.7 Sch.21 para.42

43. National Health Service (Consequential Provisions) Act 2006
Sch.1 para.2, repealed (in part): 2012 c.7 Sch.5 para.139
Sch.1 para.30, repealed (in part): 2012 c.7 Sch.5 para.139
Sch.1 para.47, repealed (in part): 2012 c.7 Sch.5 para.139
Sch.1 para.54, repealed (in part): 2012 c.7 Sch.5 para.139
Sch.1 para.70, repealed (in part): 2012 c.7 Sch.5 para.31
Sch.1 para.90, repealed (in part): 2012 c.7 Sch.5 para.139
Sch.1 para.112, repealed (in part): 2012 c.7 Sch.5 para.139
Sch.1 para.125, repealed (in part): 2012 c.7 Sch.5 para.139
Sch.1 para.131, repealed (in part): 2012 c.7 Sch.5 para.139
Sch.1 para.132, repealed: 2012 c.14 s.216

2006–cont.

43. National Health Service (Consequential Provisions) Act 2006–cont.
Sch.1 para.133, repealed: 2012 c.14 s.216
Sch.1 para.141, repealed (in part): 2012 c.7 Sch.5 para.139
Sch.1 para.145, repealed: 2012 c.5 Sch.14 Part 9
Sch.1 para.170, repealed (in part): 2012 c.7 Sch.5 para.139
Sch.1 para.179, repealed (in part): 2012 c.7 Sch.5 para.139
Sch.1 para.180, repealed (in part): 2012 c.7 Sch.5 para.139
Sch.1 para.211, repealed (in part): 2012 c.7 Sch.5 para.139
Sch.1 para.228, repealed (in part): 2012 c.7 Sch.5 para.139
Sch.1 para.233, repealed (in part): 2012 c.7 Sch.5 para.139
Sch.1 para.234, repealed (in part): 2012 c.7 Sch.5 para.139
Sch.1 para.257, repealed: 2012 c.7 Sch.7 para.23
Sch.1 para.258, repealed: 2012 c.7 Sch.7 para.23
Sch.1 para.259, repealed: 2012 c.7 Sch.7 para.23
Sch.1 para.271, repealed (in part): 2012 c.7 Sch.5 para.139
Sch.1 para.284, repealed: 2012 c.7 Sch.20 para.7
Sch.1 para.285, repealed: 2012 c.7 Sch.20 para.7
Sch.1 para.286, repealed: 2012 c.7 Sch.20 para.7
Sch.1 para.294, repealed: 2012 c.7 Sch.5 para.139

44. NHS Redress Act 2006
s.1, amended: 2012 c.7 Sch.5 para.141
s.1, repealed (in part): 2012 c.7 Sch.5 para.141
s.13, repealed (in part): 2012 c.7 s.281
s.18, amended: 2012 c.7 Sch.5 para.142

45. Animal Welfare Act 2006
s.4, see *Lamont-Perkins v RSPCA* [2012] EWHC 1002 (Admin), (2012) 176 J.P. 369 (DC), Sir John Thomas (President)
s.6, applied: SI 2012/61
s.6, enabling: SI 2012/61
s.13, applied: SI 2012/2932, SI 2012/2932 Reg.3
s.18, see *James v RSPCA* [2011] EWHC 1642 (Admin), [2012] 5 Costs L.O. 547 (QBD (Admin)), Keith, J.
s.30, see *Lamont-Perkins v RSPCA* [2012] EWHC 1002 (Admin), (2012) 176 J.P. 369 (DC), Sir John Thomas (President)
s.31, see *Lamont-Perkins v RSPCA* [2012] EWHC 1002 (Admin), (2012) 176 J.P. 369 (DC), Sir John Thomas (President)
s.34, applied: SI 2012/2932 Reg.5
s.58, amended: SI 2012/3039 Reg.29
s.58, repealed (in part): SI 2012/3039 Reg.29
s.61, applied: SI 2012/61, SI 2012/2932

46. Companies Act 2006
applied: 2012 asp 3 Sch.1 para.11, 2012 asp 8 s.4, SI 2012/1439(d), SI 2012/1128 Art.4, SI 2012/1821 Reg.17, SI 2012/2500 Reg.19
referred to: SI 2012/1439 Art.7
Part 7, applied: SI 2012/1907 Sch.1 para.8, Sch.1 para.9
Part 25, applied: SI 2012/1907 Sch.1 para.8, Sch.1 para.10
Part 33 c.1, applied: SI 2012/1907 Sch.1 para.8
Pt 23. see *TXU Europe Group Plc, Re* [2011] EWHC 2072 (Ch), [2012] B.C.C. 363 (Ch D), Newey, J
s.10, applied: SI 2012/1907 Sch.2 para.28
s.14, applied: SI 2012/1907 Sch.1 para.8
s.42, applied: SI 2012/1741 Art.7

2006–cont.

46. Companies Act 2006–cont.
s.45, applied: SI 2012/3012 Reg.23
s.45, referred to: SI 2012/3012 Reg.23
s.45, varied: SI 2012/3012 Reg.23
s.48, amended: 2012 asp 5 Sch.5 para.50
s.49, amended: 2012 asp 5 Sch.5 para.50
s.64, applied: SI 2012/1907 Sch.1 para.8
s.67, applied: SI 2012/1907 Sch.1 para.8, Sch.1 para.10
s.73, applied: SI 2012/1907 Sch.1 para.8, Sch.1 para.10
s.74, applied: SI 2012/1907 Sch.1 para.8, Sch.1 para.10
s.78, applied: SI 2012/1907 Sch.1 para.9
s.80, applied: SI 2012/1907 Sch.1 para.8
s.108, applied: SI 2012/1907 Sch.2 para.28
s.172, see *Bilta (UK) Ltd (In Liquidation) v Nazir* [2012] EWHC 2163 (Ch), [2012] S.T.C. 2424 (Ch D), Sir Andrew Morritt (Chancellor); see *GHLM Trading Ltd v Maroo* [2012] EWHC 61 (Ch), [2012] 2 B.C.L.C. 369 (Ch D), Newey, J
s.242, applied: SI 2012/1907 Sch.3 para.1
s.243, enabling: SI 2012/1907
s.303, see *Smith v Butler* [2012] EWCA Civ 314, [2012] Bus. L.R. 1836 (CA (Civ Div)), Arden, L.J.
s.306, see *Smith v Butler* [2011] EWHC 2301 (Ch), [2012] 1 B.C.L.C. 444 (Ch D (Leeds)), Judge Behrens
s.313, see *Halcrow Holdings Ltd, Re* [2011] EWHC 3662 (Ch), [2012] Pens. L.R. 113 (Ch D), Vos, J.
s.382, referred to: SI 2012/504 Reg.46
s.384, amended: 2012 c.21 Sch.18 para.111
s.394, amended: SI 2012/2301 Reg.8
s.394A, added: SI 2012/2301 Reg.9
s.394B, added: SI 2012/2301 Reg.9
s.394C, added: SI 2012/2301 Reg.9
s.395, amended: SI 2012/2301 Reg.12, Reg.13, Reg.14
s.403, amended: SI 2012/2301 Reg.15, Reg.16, Reg.17
s.441, amended: SI 2012/2301 Reg.10
s.448A, added: SI 2012/2301 Reg.11
s.448B, added: SI 2012/2301 Reg.11
s.448C, added: SI 2012/2301 Reg.11
s.456, applied: SI 2012/1439 Art.4, SI 2012/1439(f)
s.457, enabling: SI 2012/1439
s.461, amended: 2012 c.21 Sch.18 para.112, SI 2012/1439 Art.6, SI 2012/1741 Sch.1 para.2
s.462, enabling: SI 2012/1439
s.464, applied: SI 2012/1741 Art.23, Art.24, SI 2012/2405 Reg.2
s.464, enabling: SI 2012/1741, SI 2012/2405
s.467, amended: 2012 c.21 Sch.18 para.113
s.468, enabling: SI 2012/2301
s.470, amended: 2012 c.21 Sch.18 para.114
s.471, amended: SI 2012/2301 Reg.18
s.473, enabling: SI 2012/2301
s.474, amended: 2012 c.21 Sch.18 para.115
s.475, amended: SI 2012/2301 Reg.6
s.477, amended: SI 2012/2301 Reg.4
s.477, repealed (in part): SI 2012/2301 Reg.4
s.479, amended: SI 2012/2301 Reg.5
s.479, repealed (in part): SI 2012/2301 Reg.5
s.479A, added: SI 2012/2301 Reg.7
s.479B, added: SI 2012/2301 Reg.7
s.479C, added: SI 2012/2301 Reg.7
s.482, amended: SI 2012/1809 Sch.1 Part 1
s.484, enabling: SI 2012/2301
s.504, applied: SI 2012/1741 Art.15

2006–cont.

46. Companies Act 2006–cont.
s.504, enabling: SI 2012/1741
s.522, applied: SI 2012/1741 Art.8
s.523, applied: SI 2012/1741 Art.8
s.525, amended: SI 2012/1741 Sch.1 para.3
s.525, applied: SI 2012/1741 Art.8
s.525, enabling: SI 2012/1741
s.539, amended: 2012 c.21 Sch.18 para.116
s.555, applied: SI 2012/1907 Sch.2 para.28
s.619, applied: SI 2012/1907 Sch.2 para.28
s.621, applied: SI 2012/1907 Sch.2 para.28
s.625, applied: SI 2012/1907 Sch.2 para.28
s.627, applied: SI 2012/1907 Sch.2 para.28
s.644, applied: SI 2012/1907 Sch.1 para.8, Sch.2 para.28
s.645, see *Sportech Plc, Petitioner* [2012] CSOH 58, 2012 S.L.T. 895 (OH), Lord Hodge
s.646, see *Halcrow Holdings Ltd, Re* [2011] EWHC 3662 (Ch), [2012] Pens. L.R. 113 (Ch D), Vos, J.; see *Sportech Plc, Petitioner* [2012] CSOH 58, 2012 S.L.T. 895 (OH), Lord Hodge
s.649, applied: SI 2012/1907 Sch.1 para.8, Sch.2 para.28
s.651, applied: SI 2012/1907 Sch.1 para.8
s.663, applied: SI 2012/1907 Sch.2 para.28
s.665, applied: SI 2012/1907 Sch.1 para.8
s.689, applied: SI 2012/1907 Sch.2 para.28
s.708, applied: SI 2012/1907 Sch.2 para.28
s.730, applied: SI 2012/1907 Sch.2 para.28
s.785, amended: 2012 c.21 s.112
s.832, amended: SI 2012/952 Reg.2
s.832, repealed (in part): SI 2012/952 Reg.2
s.833, amended: SI 2012/952 Reg.2
s.833, repealed (in part): SI 2012/952 Reg.2
s.834, repealed: SI 2012/952 Reg.2
s.835, repealed: SI 2012/952 Reg.2
s.843, amended: 2012 c.21 Sch.18 para.117
s.854, applied: SI 2012/1907 Sch.1 para.8, Sch.1 para.10
s.948, amended: 2012 c.21 Sch.18 para.118
s.950, amended: 2012 c.21 Sch.18 para.119
s.964, repealed (in part): 2012 c.21 Sch.19
s.993, amended: SI 2012/3012 Reg.60, SSI 2012/88 Reg.23, SSI 2012/89 Reg.26
s.994, see *Coroin Ltd, Re* [2012] EWCA Civ 179, [2012] B.C.C. 575 (CA (Civ Div)), Lloyd, L.J.; see *F&C Alternative Investments (Holdings) Ltd v Barthelemy (Costs)* [2011] EWHC 2807 (Ch), [2012] Bus. L.R. 891 (Ch D), Sales, J.; see *Fulham Football Club (1987) Ltd v Richards* [2011] EWCA Civ 855, [2012] Ch. 333 (CA (Civ Div)), Rix, L.J.
s.995, amended: 2012 c.21 Sch.18 para.120
s.996, see *F&C Alternative Investments (Holdings) Ltd v Barthelemy* [2011] EWHC 1731 (Ch), [2012] Ch. 613 (Ch D), Sales, J.; see *Fulham Football Club (1987) Ltd v Richards* [2011] EWCA Civ 855, [2012] Ch. 333 (CA (Civ Div)), Rix, L.J.
s.1003, applied: SI 2012/1907 Sch.1 para.8, Sch.1 para.10
s.1004, applied: SI 2012/3013 Reg.8
s.1004, varied: SI 2012/3013 Reg.8
s.1005, applied: SI 2012/3013 Reg.9
s.1006, applied: SI 2012/3013 Reg.12
s.1006, varied: SI 2012/3013 Reg.12
s.1009, applied: SI 2012/3013 Reg.14
s.1009, varied: SI 2012/3013 Reg.14
s.1022, amended: 2012 asp 5 Sch.5 para.50
s.1024, applied: SI 2012/1907 Sch.1 para.12

46. Companies Act 2006–cont.
s.1033, applied: SI 2012/1907 Sch.1 para.8, Sch.1 para.10
s.1043, enabling: SI 2012/2301
s.1048, applied: SI 2012/1907 Sch.1 para.11
s.1050, applied: SI 2012/1907 Sch.1 para.1
s.1063, enabling: SI 2012/1907, SI 2012/1908
s.1065, applied: SI 2012/1907 Sch.2 para.7, Sch.2 para.11, Sch.2 para.12
s.1078, amended: SI 2012/2301 Reg.19
s.1088, applied: SI 2012/1907 Sch.1 para.12
s.1091, applied: SI 2012/1907 Sch.2 para.7, Sch.2 para.11, Sch.2 para.12, SI 2012/1908 Sch.2 para.3, Sch.2 para.7
s.1096, see *Globespan Airways Ltd (In Liquidation), Re* [2012] EWHC 359 (Ch), [2012] 2 All E.R. 1234 (Ch D (Manchester)), Briggs, J.
s.1099, applied: SI 2012/1907 Sch.2 para.12
s.1104, enabling: SI 2012/2301
s.1105, enabling: SI 2012/2301
s.1108, enabling: SI 2012/2301
s.1121, applied: SI 2012/3012 Reg.23
s.1121, varied: SI 2012/3012 Reg.23
s.1122, applied: SI 2012/3012 Reg.23
s.1122, varied: SI 2012/3012 Reg.23
s.1127, applied: SI 2012/3012 Reg.23, Reg.60
s.1127, varied: SI 2012/3012 Reg.23, Reg.60, SI 2012/3013 Reg.15
s.1128, applied: SI 2012/3012 Reg.23, Reg.60
s.1128, varied: SI 2012/3012 Reg.23, Reg.60, SI 2012/3013 Reg.15
s.1129, applied: SI 2012/3012 Reg.23, Reg.60
s.1129, varied: SI 2012/3012 Reg.23, Reg.60, SI 2012/3013 Reg.15
s.1131, applied: SI 2012/3012 Reg.60
s.1131, varied: SI 2012/3012 Reg.60, SI 2012/3013 Reg.15
s.1132, applied: SI 2012/3012 Reg.23, Reg.60
s.1132, varied: SI 2012/3012 Reg.23, Reg.60, SI 2012/3013 Reg.15
s.1139, applied: SI 2012/1726 r.4.4, SI 2012/3152 Reg.8
s.1157, see *GHLM Trading Ltd v Maroo* [2012] EWHC 61 (Ch), [2012] 2 B.C.L.C. 369 (Ch D), Newey, J; see *Smith v Butler* [2012] EWCA Civ 314, [2012] Bus. L.R. 1836 (CA (Civ Div)), Arden, L.J.
s.1159, applied: SI 2012/2500 Reg.19, SI 2012/3038 Sch.4 para.1, SSI 2012/360 Sch.4 para.1
s.1161, applied: SI 2012/504 Sch.2 para.14
s.1162, applied: SI 2012/504 Sch.2 para.14
s.1164, amended: 2012 c.21 Sch.18 para.121
s.1165, amended: 2012 c.21 Sch.18 para.122
s.1210, amended: SI 2012/1809 Sch.1 Part 1
s.1210, applied: SI 2012/1741 Art.7
s.1214, applied: SI 2012/1741 Art.7
s.1221, applied: SI 2012/1741 Art.7
s.1221, referred to: SI 2012/1741 Art.7
s.1223, applied: SI 2012/1741 Art.12
s.1224, applied: SI 2012/1741 Art.7
s.1225, substituted: SI 2012/1741 Art.4
s.1225D, applied: SI 2012/1741 Art.13
s.1225E, applied: SI 2012/1741 Art.13
s.1228, enabling: SI 2012/1741
s.1229, applied: SI 2012/1741 Art.20
s.1229, referred to: SI 2012/1741, SI 2012/1741 Art.18, Art.20
s.1231, applied: SI 2012/1741 Art.7, Art.19
s.1231, enabling: SI 2012/1741

2006–cont.

46. Companies Act 2006–*cont.*
s.1232, applied: SI 2012/1741 Art.19
s.1237, applied: SI 2012/1741 Art.7
s.1239, applied: SI 2012/1741 Art.7
s.1239, enabling: SI 2012/1741
s.1241, applied: SI 2012/1741 Art.7
s.1243, applied: SI 2012/1741 Art.12
s.1244, applied: SI 2012/1741 Art.7
s.1246, applied: SI 2012/1741 Art.7
s.1252, applied: SI 2012/1741
s.1252, enabling: SI 2012/1741
s.1253, enabling: SI 2012/1741
s.1253A, applied: SI 2012/1741 Art.7
s.1253B, applied: SI 2012/1741 Art.7
s.1253B, referred to: SI 2012/1741 Art.7
s.1253E, referred to: SI 2012/1741 Art.7
s.1254, applied: SI 2012/1741 Art.7
s.1256, varied: SI 2012/1741 Art.14
s.1261, applied: SI 2012/1741 Art.7
s.1263, applied: SI 2012/1741 Art.7
s.1292, applied: SI 2012/1741
s.1292, enabling: SI 2012/1439, SI 2012/1741, SI 2012/1907, SI 2012/1908, SI 2012/2301, SI 2012/2405
Sch.2 Part 1 para.5, substituted: 2012 c.21 Sch.18 para.123
Sch.2 Part 2 para.11, amended: 2012 c.21 Sch.18 para.123
Sch.2 Part 2 para.12, amended: 2012 c.21 Sch.18 para.123
Sch.2 Part 2 para.37, amended: 2012 c.21 Sch.18 para.123
Sch.2 Part 2 para.38, repealed: 2012 c.21 Sch.19
Sch.2 Part 2 para.49, amended: 2012 c.21 Sch.18 para.123
Sch.2 Part 3 para.1, amended: 2012 c.21 Sch.18 para.123
Sch.7, applied: SI 2012/504 Sch.2 para.14
Sch.10 Part 1 para.3, amended: SI 2012/1741 Art.5
Sch.10 Part 2 para.13, amended: SI 2012/1741 Art.5
Sch.10 Part 3 para.23, amended: SI 2012/1741 Art.5
Sch.10 Part 3 para.24, amended: SI 2012/1741 Art.5
Sch.10 Part 3 para.25, amended: SI 2012/1741 Art.5
Sch.11A Part 1 para.5, substituted: 2012 c.21 Sch.18 para.124
Sch.11A Part 2 para.28, amended: 2012 c.21 Sch.18 para.124
Sch.11A Part 2 para.29, amended: 2012 c.21 Sch.18 para.124
Sch.11A Part 2 para.52, amended: 2012 c.21 Sch.18 para.124
Sch.11A Part 2 para.53, repealed: 2012 c.21 Sch.19
Sch.11A Part 2 para.71, amended: 2012 c.21 Sch.18 para.124
Sch.13 para.7, enabling: SI 2012/1741
Sch.13 para.11, enabling: SI 2012/1741
Sch.15 Part 1 para.2, repealed: 2012 c.21 Sch.19
Sch.15 Part 1 para.9, repealed: 2012 c.21 Sch.19

47. Safeguarding Vulnerable Groups Act 2006
Commencement Orders: 2012 c.9 Sch.10 Part 5; SI 2012/2231 Art.2, Art.3, Art.4
see *Attorney General's Reference (No.18 of 2011), Re* [2011] EWCA Crim 1300, [2012] 1 Cr. App. R. (S.) 27 (CA (Crim Div)), Hughes, L.J. (Vice President); see *Independent Safeguarding Authority v SB* [2012] EWCA Civ 977, Times, September 21, 2012 (CA (Civ Div)), Maurice Kay, L.J.; see *R. (on the application of G) v X School Governors* [2012] 1 A.C. 167 (SC), Lord

2006–cont.

47. Safeguarding Vulnerable Groups Act 2006–*cont.*
see–*cont.*
Hope (Deputy President); see *R. v C* [2011] EWCA Crim 1872, [2012] 1 Cr. App. R. (S.) 89 (CA (Crim Div)), Thomas, L.J.; see *R. v Smith (Steven)* [2011] EWCA Crim 1772, [2012] 1 W.L.R. 1316 (CA (Crim Div)), Hughes, L.J.
applied: 2012 c.9 s.88, Sch.8 para.8, SI 2012/3006 Art.98, Art.99, Art.106, Art.109
s.1, repealed: SI 2012/3006 Art.112
s.2, amended: SI 2012/3006 Art.3, Art.4
s.2, applied: SI 2012/2234 Art.8, SI 2012/3006 Art.2
s.2, enabling: SI 2012/2112
s.3, applied: SI 2012/1034 Sch.4 para.13
s.3, referred to: SI 2012/322 Reg.65
s.4, see *Independent Safeguarding Authority v SB* [2012] EWCA Civ 977, Times, September 21, 2012 (CA (Civ Div)), Maurice Kay, L.J.
s.4, amended: 2012 c.9 Sch.9 para.44, SI 2012/3006 Art.3
s.4, applied: 2012 c.10 Sch.1 para.16, SI 2012/2234 Art.10, SI 2012/3006 Art.101
s.4, repealed (in part): 2012 c.9 Sch.9 para.44, Sch.10 Part 5
s.5, amended: 2012 c.9 Sch.9 para.45, Sch.10 Part 5
s.6, amended: 2012 c.7 Sch.5 para.144, 2012 c.9 Sch.9 para.46
s.6, repealed (in part): 2012 c.7 Sch.5 para.144, 2012 c.9 Sch.9 para.46, Sch.10 Part 5
s.7, repealed (in part): 2012 c.9 Sch.9 para.47, Sch.10 Part 5
s.8, repealed: 2012 c.9 Sch.9 para.48, Sch.10 Part 5
s.9, repealed (in part): 2012 c.9 Sch.9 para.49, Sch.10 Part 5
s.10, repealed: 2012 c.9 Sch.9 para.50, Sch.10 Part 5
s.11, repealed: 2012 c.9 Sch.9 para.51, Sch.10 Part 5
s.12, repealed: 2012 c.9 Sch.9 para.52, Sch.10 Part 5
s.13, repealed: 2012 c.9 Sch.9 para.53, Sch.10 Part 5
s.14, repealed: 2012 c.9 Sch.9 para.54, Sch.10 Part 5
s.15, repealed: 2012 c.9 Sch.9 para.55, Sch.10 Part 5
s.16, repealed: 2012 c.9 Sch.9 para.56, Sch.10 Part 5
s.17, amended: 2012 c.7 Sch.5 para.145
s.17, repealed (in part): 2012 c.7 Sch.5 para.145, 2012 c.9 Sch.9 para.57, Sch.10 Part 5
s.18, amended: 2012 c.9 Sch.9 para.58, Sch.10 Part 5
s.19, amended: 2012 c.9 Sch.9 para.59
s.19, repealed (in part): 2012 c.9 Sch.9 para.59, Sch.10 Part 5
s.20, repealed (in part): 2012 c.9 Sch.9 para.60, Sch.10 Part 5
s.21, repealed: 2012 c.9 s.68, Sch.10 Part 5
s.22, repealed (in part): 2012 c.7 Sch.5 para.146, 2012 c.9 s.68, Sch.10 Part 5
s.23, repealed: 2012 c.9 s.68, Sch.10 Part 5
s.23, enabling: SI 2012/2160
s.24, repealed: 2012 c.9 s.69, Sch.10 Part 5
s.24A, repealed: 2012 c.9 s.69, Sch.10 Part 5
s.25, repealed: 2012 c.9 s.69, Sch.10 Part 5
s.26, repealed: 2012 c.9 s.69, Sch.10 Part 5
s.27, repealed: 2012 c.9 s.69, Sch.10 Part 5
s.30, substituted: 2012 c.9 s.72
s.30A, amended: SI 2012/3006 Art.48
s.30A, substituted: 2012 c.9 s.72
s.30B, amended: SI 2012/3006 Art.48
s.30B, substituted: 2012 c.9 s.72
s.31, substituted: 2012 c.9 s.72
s.32, substituted: 2012 c.9 s.72
s.33, amended: 2012 c.9 s.72, SI 2012/3006 Art.48

2006–cont.

47. Safeguarding Vulnerable Groups Act 2006–*cont.*
s.34, amended: 2012 c.9 s.72
s.34ZA, added: 2012 c.9 s.73
s.35, amended: SI 2012/3006 Art.3
s.35, repealed (in part): 2012 c.9 Sch.9 para.61, Sch.10 Part 5
s.35, enabling: SI 2012/2112
s.36, amended: 2012 c.9 Sch.9 para.62, Sch.10 Part 5, SI 2012/3006 Art.3
s.36, enabling: SI 2012/2112
s.37, amended: 2012 c.9 Sch.9 para.63, Sch.10 Part 5, SI 2012/3006 Art.3
s.37, repealed (in part): 2012 c.9 Sch.9 para.63, Sch.10 Part 5
s.37, enabling: SI 2012/2112
s.38, amended: SI 2012/3006 Art.3
s.39, amended: 2012 c.9 s.77, Sch.10 Part 5, SI 2012/3006 Art.3
s.39, enabling: SI 2012/2112
s.40, amended: SI 2012/3006 Art.3
s.41, amended: 2012 c.7 s.213, Sch.15 para.52, 2012 c.9 s.75, Sch.9 para.64, Sch.10 Part 5, SI 2012/3006 Art.3
s.41, enabling: SI 2012/2112
s.42, amended: SI 2012/3006 Art.3
s.42, enabling: SI 2012/2112
s.43, amended: 2012 c.9 s.75, Sch.10 Part 5, SI 2012/3006 Art.3, Art.48, Art.54
s.43, applied: SI 2012/2113 Art.2, Art.3
s.43, enabling: SI 2012/2113
s.44, repealed: 2012 c.9 s.75, Sch.10 Part 5
s.45, amended: 2012 c.9 s.76, Sch.10 Part 5, SI 2012/3006 Art.3
s.45, repealed (in part): 2012 c.9 s.76, Sch.10 Part 5
s.45, enabling: SI 2012/2112
s.46, amended: SI 2012/3006 Art.3
s.46, enabling: SI 2012/2112
s.47, amended: 2012 c.9 s.76, SI 2012/3006 Art.3, Art.48
s.47, repealed (in part): 2012 c.9 s.76, Sch.10 Part 5
s.48, amended: 2012 c.9 s.76, Sch.10 Part 5, SI 2012/3006 Art.48
s.48, applied: SI 2012/2113 Art.2
s.48, repealed (in part): 2012 c.9 s.76, Sch.10 Part 5
s.48, enabling: SI 2012/2113
s.49, amended: 2012 c.9 s.76, Sch.10 Part 5, SI 2012/3006 Art.48
s.49, applied: SI 2012/2113 Art.3
s.49, repealed (in part): 2012 c.9 s.76, Sch.10 Part 5
s.49, enabling: SI 2012/2113
s.50, amended: 2012 c.9 s.76, SI 2012/3006 Art.3, Art.48
s.50A, amended: 2012 c.9 s.77, Sch.9 para.65, SI 2012/3006 Art.3
s.50A, applied: SI 2012/2112 Reg.28
s.50A, enabling: SI 2012/2112
s.51, repealed (in part): 2012 c.9 Sch.9 para.66, Sch.10 Part 5
s.54, repealed (in part): 2012 c.9 Sch.9 para.67, Sch.10 Part 5
s.56, amended: 2012 c.9 Sch.9 para.68, Sch.10 Part 5
s.56, applied: SI 2012/2112, SI 2012/2157, SI 2012/2160
s.56, repealed (in part): 2012 c.9 Sch.9 para.68, Sch.10 Part 5
s.57, amended: 2012 c.9 Sch.9 para.69, Sch.10 Part 5
s.59, amended: 2012 c.7 s.185
s.59, applied: SI 2012/1909 Sch.4 para.28
s.59, repealed (in part): 2012 c.9 s.65, Sch.10 Part 5

2006–cont.

47. Safeguarding Vulnerable Groups Act 2006–*cont.*
s.59, enabling: SI 2012/2157
s.60, amended: 2012 c.9 s.65, Sch.9 para.70, Sch.10 Part 5, SI 2012/3006 Art.5
s.60, repealed (in part): 2012 c.9 Sch.9 para.70, Sch.10 Part 5
s.60, enabling: SI 2012/2112
s.61, amended: 2012 c.9 Sch.9 para.71
s.61, applied: SI 2012/2157, SI 2012/2160
s.61, repealed (in part): 2012 c.9 Sch.9 para.71, Sch.10 Part 5
s.61, enabling: SI 2012/2160
s.64, enabling: SI 2012/2157, SI 2012/2160, SI 2012/2231
s.65, enabling: SI 2012/2231
s.66, enabling: SI 2012/1762, SI 2012/2561, SI 2012/2591, SI 2012/2598
Sch.1 para.1, repealed: SI 2012/3006 Art.112
Sch.1 para.2, amended: SI 2012/2404 Sch.2 para.58
Sch.1 para.2, repealed: SI 2012/3006 Art.112
Sch.1 para.3, repealed: SI 2012/3006 Art.112
Sch.1 para.4, repealed: SI 2012/3006 Art.112
Sch.1 para.5, repealed: SI 2012/3006 Art.112
Sch.1 para.6, repealed: SI 2012/3006 Art.112
Sch.1 para.7, repealed: SI 2012/3006 Art.112
Sch.1 para.8, repealed: SI 2012/3006 Art.112
Sch.1 para.9, applied: SI 2012/3006 Art.108
Sch.1 para.9, repealed: SI 2012/3006 Art.112
Sch.1 para.10, repealed: SI 2012/3006 Art.112
Sch.1 para.11, repealed: SI 2012/3006 Art.112
Sch.1 para.12, applied: SI 2012/3006 Art.108
Sch.1 para.12, repealed: SI 2012/3006 Art.112
Sch.1 para.13, repealed: SI 2012/3006 Art.112
Sch.1 para.14, repealed: SI 2012/3006 Art.112
Sch.1 para.15, repealed: SI 2012/3006 Art.112
Sch.1 para.16, repealed: SI 2012/3006 Art.112
Sch.2 para.1, repealed: SI 2012/3006 Art.112
Sch.2 para.2, repealed: SI 2012/3006 Art.112
Sch.2 para.3, repealed: SI 2012/3006 Art.112
Sch.3, applied: 2012 c.9 Sch.8 para.8
Sch.3 Part 1 para.1, amended: 2012 c.9 s.67, SI 2012/3006 Art.56
Sch.3 Part 1 para.1, applied: SI 2012/2234 Art.12
Sch.3 Part 1 para.1, enabling: SI 2012/2160
Sch.3 Part 1 para.2, amended: 2012 c.9 s.67, SI 2012/3006 Art.3, Art.57
Sch.3 Part 1 para.2, applied: SI 2012/2234 Art.8, Art.12, SI 2012/3006 Art.104
Sch.3 Part 1 para.2, enabling: SI 2012/2160
Sch.3 Part 1 para.3, amended: 2012 c.9 s.67, SI 2012/3006 Art.3
Sch.3 Part 1 para.3, applied: SI 2012/2234 Art.8, Art.12, SI 2012/3006 Art.104
Sch.3 Part 1 para.4, amended: SI 2012/3006 Art.3
Sch.3 Part 1 para.5, amended: 2012 c.9 s.67, SI 2012/3006 Art.3
Sch.3 Part 1 para.5, applied: SI 2012/2234 Art.8, Art.12, SI 2012/3006 Art.104
Sch.3 Part 1 para.5A, added: 2012 c.9 s.74
Sch.3 Part 1 para.5A, amended: SI 2012/3006 Art.3
Sch.3 Part 1 para.6, amended: 2012 c.9 s.74, SI 2012/3006 Art.3
Sch.3 Part 2 para.7, amended: 2012 c.9 s.67, SI 2012/3006 Art.34, Art.58
Sch.3 Part 2 para.7, applied: SI 2012/2234 Art.12
Sch.3 Part 2 para.7, enabling: SI 2012/2160
Sch.3 Part 2 para.8, amended: 2012 c.9 s.67, SI 2012/3006 Art.3, Art.59

2006–cont.

47. Safeguarding Vulnerable Groups Act 2006–*cont.*

Sch.3 Part 2 para.8, applied: SI 2012/2234 Art.8, Art.12, SI 2012/3006 Art.104

Sch.3 Part 2 para.8, enabling: SI 2012/2160

Sch.3 Part 2 para.9, amended: 2012 c.9 s.67, SI 2012/3006 Art.3

Sch.3 Part 2 para.9, applied: SI 2012/2234 Art.8, Art.12, SI 2012/3006 Art.104

Sch.3 Part 2 para.10, amended: SI 2012/3006 Art.3

Sch.3 Part 2 para.11, amended: 2012 c.9 s.67, SI 2012/3006 Art.3

Sch.3 Part 2 para.11, applied: SI 2012/2234 Art.8, Art.12, SI 2012/3006 Art.104

Sch.3 Part 2 para.11A, added: 2012 c.9 s.74

Sch.3 Part 2 para.11A, amended: SI 2012/3006 Art.3

Sch.3 Part 2 para.12, amended: 2012 c.9 s.74, SI 2012/3006 Art.3

Sch.3 Part 3 para.13, amended: SI 2012/3006 Art.3

Sch.3 Part 3 para.14, amended: SI 2012/3006 Art.3

Sch.3 Part 3 para.15, amended: SI 2012/3006 Art.3

Sch.3 Part 3 para.15, enabling: SI 2012/2112

Sch.3 Part 3 para.16, amended: 2012 c.7 Sch.15 para.56, SI 2012/3006 Art.3

Sch.3 Part 3 para.16, applied: SI 2012/3006 Art.104

Sch.3 Part 3 para.17, amended: SI 2012/3006 Art.3

Sch.3 Part 3 para.17, applied: SI 2012/3006 Art.104

Sch.3 Part 3 para.18, amended: SI 2012/3006 Art.3

Sch.3 Part 3 para.18, applied: SI 2012/3006 Art.106

Sch.3 Part 3 para.18A, added: 2012 c.9 s.71

Sch.3 Part 3 para.18A, amended: SI 2012/3006 Art.3

Sch.3 Part 3 para.18A, applied: SI 2012/3006 Art.106

Sch.3 Part 3 para.19, amended: 2012 c.9 s.70, Sch.9 para.129, Sch.10 Part 5, SI 2012/3006 Art.3, Art.48

Sch.3 Part 3 para.19, repealed (in part): 2012 c.9 s.70, Sch.10 Part 5, SI 2012/3006 Art.60

Sch.3 Part 3 para.20, amended: 2012 c.9 s.70, SI 2012/3006 Art.3

Sch.3 Part 3 para.20, repealed (in part): SI 2012/3006 Art.61

Sch.3 Part 3 para.21, amended: SI 2012/3006 Art.3

Sch.3 Part 3 para.22, amended: SI 2012/3006 Art.48

Sch.3 Part 3 para.22A, amended: SI 2012/3006 Art.3

Sch.3 Part 3 para.23, amended: SI 2012/3006 Art.3

Sch.3 Part 3 para.24, repealed (in part): 2012 c.9 Sch.9 para.72, Sch.10 Part 5

Sch.3 Part 3 para.24, enabling: SI 2012/2160

Sch.3 Part 3 para.25, amended: 2012 c.9 Sch.9 para.72, SI 2012/3006 Art.3

Sch.4 Part 1 para.1, amended: 2012 c.9 s.64, Sch.10 Part 5, SI 2012/1879 Art.4

Sch.4 Part 1 para.1, repealed (in part): 2012 c.9 s.64, Sch.10 Part 5

Sch.4 Part 1 para.2, amended: 2012 c.9 s.64

Sch.4 Part 1 para.2, repealed (in part): 2012 c.9 s.64, Sch.10 Part 5

Sch.4 Part 1 para.3, amended: SI 2012/976 Sch.1 para.21

Sch.4 Part 1 para.3, repealed (in part): 2012 c.9 s.64, Sch.10 Part 5

Sch.4 Part 1 para.4, amended: SI 2012/976 Sch.1 para.21

Sch.4 Part 1 para.4, repealed: 2012 c.9 s.64, Sch.10 Part 5

2006–cont.

47. Safeguarding Vulnerable Groups Act 2006–*cont.*

Sch.4 Part 1 para.5A, added: 2012 c.9 s.77

Sch.4 Part 1 para.6, enabling: SI 2012/2157

Sch.4 Part 2 para.7, amended: 2012 c.9 s.66, Sch.10 Part 5

Sch.4 Part 2 para.7, applied: SI 2012/2112 Reg.24, Reg.25, Reg.27, SI 2012/2113 Art.6

Sch.4 Part 2 para.7, referred to: SI 2012/2112 Reg.25, Reg.27, SI 2012/2113 Art.4

Sch.4 Part 2 para.7, repealed (in part): 2012 c.9 s.66, Sch.10 Part 5

Sch.4 Part 2 para.7, enabling: SI 2012/2112

Sch.4 Part 2 para.8, repealed: 2012 c.9 s.66, Sch.10 Part 5

Sch.4 Part 2 para.9, enabling: SI 2012/2113, SI 2012/2157

Sch.4 Part 3 para.10, amended: 2012 c.9 s.64, s.66, Sch.10 Part 5

Sch.5 Part 1 para.1, repealed: 2012 c.9 Sch.9 para.51, Sch.10 Part 5

Sch.5 Part 1 para.2, repealed: 2012 c.9 Sch.9 para.51, Sch.10 Part 5

Sch.5 Part 1 para.3, repealed: 2012 c.9 Sch.9 para.51, Sch.10 Part 5

Sch.5 Part 1 para.4, repealed: 2012 c.9 Sch.9 para.51, Sch.10 Part 5

Sch.5 Part 2 para.5, repealed: 2012 c.9 Sch.9 para.51, Sch.10 Part 5

Sch.5 Part 2 para.6, repealed: 2012 c.9 Sch.9 para.51, Sch.10 Part 5

Sch.5 Part 2 para.7, repealed: 2012 c.9 Sch.9 para.51, Sch.10 Part 5

Sch.5 Part 3 para.8, repealed: 2012 c.9 Sch.9 para.51, Sch.10 Part 5

Sch.5 Part 3 para.9, repealed: 2012 c.9 Sch.9 para.51, Sch.10 Part 5

Sch.5 Part 3 para.10, repealed: 2012 c.9 Sch.9 para.51, Sch.10 Part 5

Sch.5 Part 4 para.11, repealed: 2012 c.9 Sch.9 para.51, Sch.10 Part 5

Sch.5 Part 4 para.12, repealed: 2012 c.9 Sch.9 para.51, Sch.10 Part 5

Sch.5 Part 4 para.12A, repealed: 2012 c.9 Sch.9 para.51, Sch.10 Part 5

Sch.5 Part 4 para.13, repealed: 2012 c.9 Sch.9 para.51, Sch.10 Part 5

Sch.5 Part 4 para.14, repealed: 2012 c.9 Sch.9 para.51, Sch.10 Part 5

Sch.6 para.1, repealed: 2012 c.9 Sch.9 para.52, Sch.10 Part 5

Sch.6 para.2, repealed: 2012 c.9 Sch.9 para.52, Sch.10 Part 5

Sch.6 para.3, repealed: 2012 c.9 Sch.9 para.52, Sch.10 Part 5

Sch.6 para.4, repealed: 2012 c.9 Sch.9 para.52, Sch.10 Part 5

Sch.6 para.5, repealed: 2012 c.9 Sch.9 para.52, Sch.10 Part 5

Sch.6 para.6, repealed: 2012 c.9 Sch.9 para.52, Sch.10 Part 5

Sch.7 para.1, amended: 2012 c.9 s.72, Sch.9 para.73, Sch.10 Part 5, SI 2012/2113 Art.8, SI 2012/3006 Art.3, Art.34

Sch.7 para.1, substituted: 2012 c.9 Sch.9 para.73

Sch.7 para.2, amended: 2012 c.9 s.72

Sch.7 para.2, substituted: 2012 c.9 Sch.9 para.73

Sch.7 para.2, enabling: SI 2012/2113

Sch.7 para.3, amended: SI 2012/2113 Art.9

Sch.7 para.3, repealed (in part): 2012 c.9 s.72, Sch.9 para.73, Sch.10 Part 5

2006–*cont.*

47. Safeguarding Vulnerable Groups Act 2006–*cont.*
Sch.7 para.3, substituted: 2012 c.9 Sch.9 para.73
Sch.7 para.4, substituted: 2012 c.9 Sch.9 para.73
Sch.7 para.5, substituted: 2012 c.9 Sch.9 para.73
Sch.7 para.6, substituted: 2012 c.9 Sch.9 para.73
Sch.8 para.1, amended: SI 2012/3006 Art.3
Sch.8 para.1, applied: SI 2012/3006 Art.109
Sch.8 para.2, amended: SI 2012/3006 Art.3
Sch.8 para.3, amended: SI 2012/3006 Art.3
Sch.8 para.5, repealed: 2012 c.9 Sch.9 para.74, Sch.10 Part 5
Sch.9 Part 2 para.14, repealed (in part): 2012 c.9 Sch.10 Part 5, Sch.10 Part 6
Sch.10, applied: 2012 c.4 Sch.1 para.4, 2012 c.10 Sch.22 para.39
Sch.10, referred to: 2012 c.10 Sch.21 para.37

48. Police and Justice Act 2006
Commencement Orders: 2012 c.10 s.118; SI 2012/2373 Art.2
s.20, applied: SI 2012/1021 Reg.6
s.32, repealed: SI 2012/2401 Sch.1 para.26
s.34, repealed: 2012 c.10 s.118
s.49, amended: SI 2012/2595 Art.13
s.49, enabling: SI 2012/2373
s.53, enabling: SI 2012/2373
Sch.1 Part 1 para.6, amended: SI 2012/2595 Art.14
Sch.1 Part 1 para.6, varied: SI 2012/2595 Art.29
Sch.1 Part 6 para.48, amended: SI 2012/2595 Art.14
Sch.13 Part 2 para.33, repealed: 2012 c.10 Sch.16 para.19

49. Road Safety Act 2006
Commencement Orders: SI 2012/1357 Art.2; SI 2012/2938 Art.2
s.39, amended: SI 2012/977 Sch.2 para.2
s.61, enabling: SI 2012/1357, SI 2012/2938
Sch.3 para.9, amended: SI 2012/977 Sch.2 para.3

50. Charities Act 2006
see *Attorney General v Charity Commission for England and Wales* [2012] W.T.L.R. 977 (UT (Tax)), Warren, J (President)
s.2, see *Attorney General v Charity Commission for England and Wales* [2012] W.T.L.R. 977 (UT (Tax)), Warren, J (President); see *R. (on the application of Independent Schools Council) v Charity Commission for England and Wales* [2012] Ch. 214 (UT (Tax)), Warren, J.
s.3, see *Attorney General v Charity Commission for England and Wales* [2012] W.T.L.R. 977 (UT (Tax)), Warren, J (President); see *R. (on the application of Independent Schools Council) v Charity Commission for England and Wales* [2012] Ch. 214 (UT (Tax)), Warren, J.
s.74, applied: SI 2012/3014
s.74, enabling: SI 2012/3014
s.75, enabling: SI 2012/3014

51. Legislative and Regulatory Reform Act 2006
s.1, enabling: SI 2012/1879, SI 2012/3100
s.3, applied: SI 2012/1879, SI 2012/3100
s.13, applied: SI 2012/1879, SI 2012/3100
s.14, applied: SI 2012/1879, SI 2012/3100
s.15, applied: SI 2012/1879, SI 2012/3100
s.17, applied: SI 2012/1879, SI 2012/3100

52. Armed Forces Act 2006
applied: SI 2012/3144 Reg.8, SI 2012/3145 Sch.1
referred to: 2012 c.10 s.152
s.42, applied: 2012 c.9 s.101
s.51, amended: 2012 c.4 Sch.1 para.11
s.85, enabling: SI 2012/2919
s.86, enabling: SI 2012/2919

2006–*cont.*

52. Armed Forces Act 2006–*cont.*
s.125, applied: SI 2012/669 Art.10, Art.11
s.129, applied: SI 2012/669 Art.10
s.130A, applied: SI 2012/669 Art.9, Art.10, Art.11
s.130A, varied: SI 2012/669 Art.9
s.172, amended: 2012 c.7 s.38
s.175, amended: 2012 c.10 s.63
s.180, amended: 2012 c.10 s.76
s.182, amended: 2012 c.10 s.78
s.187, applied: 2012 c.9 s.101
s.188, amended: 2012 c.10 Sch.22 para.23
s.196, amended: 2012 c.10 Sch.10 para.41
s.196, repealed: 2012 c.10 Sch.10 para.41
s.197, repealed: 2012 c.10 Sch.10 para.41
s.198, repealed: 2012 c.10 Sch.10 para.41
s.199, repealed: 2012 c.10 Sch.10 para.41
s.200, amended: 2012 c.10 Sch.9 para.15
s.200, repealed (in part): 2012 c.10 Sch.9 para.15
s.201, repealed: 2012 c.10 Sch.9 para.16
s.204, amended: 2012 c.10 s.76
s.207, amended: 2012 c.10 Sch.9 para.17, Sch.10 para.41
s.209, amended: 2012 c.10 Sch.22 para.24
s.211, amended: 2012 c.10 Sch.22 para.25
s.213, amended: 2012 c.10 s.80
s.218A, added: 2012 c.10 Sch.22 para.2
s.219, amended: 2012 c.10 Sch.22 para.3, Sch.22 para.4
s.219A, added: 2012 c.10 Sch.22 para.5
s.220, repealed: 2012 c.10 Sch.22 para.6
s.221, amended: 2012 c.10 Sch.22 para.7, Sch.22 para.8, Sch.22 para.26
s.221A, added: 2012 c.10 Sch.22 para.9
s.222, repealed: 2012 c.10 Sch.22 para.10
s.223, amended: 2012 c.10 Sch.22 para.27, Sch.22 para.28
s.224, substituted: 2012 c.10 Sch.22 para.29
s.227A, added: 2012 c.10 Sch.26 para.24
s.228, amended: 2012 c.10 Sch.22 para.30
s.237, amended: 2012 c.10 Sch.22 para.31, Sch.26 para.25
s.239, amended: 2012 c.10 Sch.26 para.26
s.241, amended: 2012 c.10 s.65
s.246, amended: 2012 c.10 Sch.13 para.2, Sch.22 para.32
s.246, applied: 2012 c.10 Sch.15 para.2
s.247, amended: 2012 c.10 Sch.13 para.3
s.252, repealed (in part): 2012 c.10 s.64
s.253, repealed (in part): 2012 c.10 s.64
s.256, amended: 2012 c.10 Sch.22 para.33
s.257, amended: 2012 c.7 Sch.15 para.57
s.258, amended: 2012 c.7 s.38
s.260, amended: 2012 c.10 Sch.22 para.34, Sch.26 para.27
s.261, amended: 2012 c.10 Sch.22 para.35, Sch.26 para.28
s.270A, varied: SI 2012/669 Art.13
s.273, amended: 2012 c.10 Sch.22 para.36, Sch.26 para.29
s.273, applied: SI 2012/1805 Reg.2
s.322, amended: 2012 c.10 s.78
s.323, enabling: SI 2012/2919
s.343B, varied: 2012 c.11 s.12
s.373, amended: 2012 c.10 Sch.13 para.4
s.374, amended: 2012 c.10 Sch.22 para.37
s.380, enabling: SI 2012/2919
s.382, enabling: SI 2012/1750
s.384, amended: SI 2012/2404 Sch.2 para.59

2006–cont.

52. Armed Forces Act 2006–*cont.*
s.384, applied: 2012 c.10 s.153
Sch.2 para.12, amended: 2012 c.10 Sch.26 para.30, Sch.27 para.11
Sch.3A, applied: SI 2012/669 Art.10
Sch.3A Part 3 para.17, applied: SI 2012/669 Art.12
Sch.5 Part 1 para.1, amended: 2012 c.10 s.78
Sch.5 Part 2 para.10, amended: 2012 c.10 s.78
Sch.5 Part 2 para.14A, added: 2012 c.10 s.78
Sch.6 para.5, repealed (in part): 2012 c.10 s.78
Sch.7 Part 1 para.1, amended: 2012 c.10 Sch.9 para.18
Sch.7 Part 1 para.1, substituted: 2012 c.10 Sch.9 para.18
Sch.7 Part 1 para.2, repealed: 2012 c.10 Sch.9 para.18
Sch.7 Part 2 para.6A, added: 2012 c.10 Sch.9 para.18
Sch.7 Part 2 para.9, repealed (in part): 2012 c.10 Sch.10 para.41
Sch.9 para.5, amended: SI 2012/2404 Sch.2 para.59
Sch.16 para.45, see *Director of the Serious Fraud Office v B* [2012] EWCA Crim 901, [2012] 1 W.L.R. 3188 (CA (Crim Div)), Gross, L.J.
Sch.16 para.65, repealed (in part): 2012 c.10 Sch.25 Part 2
Sch.16 para.66, repealed (in part): 2012 c.10 Sch.25 Part 2
Sch.16 para.222, repealed: 2012 c.10 Sch.10 para.41
Sch.16 para.223, repealed: 2012 c.10 Sch.10 para.41
Sch.16 para.228, repealed: 2012 c.10 Sch.13 para.5

2007

3. Income Tax Act 2007
referred to: 2012 c.23 s.21
Part 4, applied: SI 2012/1836 Reg.10
Part 8 c.2, applied: SI 2012/847 Reg.25
Part 8 c.3, applied: SI 2012/847 Reg.25
Part 13 c.5B, referred to: 2012 c.14 s.48
Part 14 c.A1, substituted: 2012 c.14 Sch.12 para.6
Part 14 c.A1, amended: 2012 c.14 Sch.12 para.8
Part 14 c.A1, amended: 2012 c.14 Sch.12 para.9
s.1, amended: 2012 c.14 Sch.1 para.6
s.2, amended: 2012 c.14 Sch.6 para.7
s.6, amended: 2012 c.11 s.26
s.8, amended: 2012 c.14 s.1
s.9, amended: 2012 c.14 s.1
s.10, amended: 2012 c.11 s.26, 2012 c.14 s.2, SI 2012/3047 Art.2
s.12, amended: SI 2012/3047 Art.2
s.16, amended: 2012 c.11 s.26
s.21, disapplied: 2012 c.14 s.2
s.21, enabling: SI 2012/3047
s.26, amended: 2012 c.14 Sch.6 para.8, Sch.39 para.32
s.27, amended: 2012 c.14 Sch.6 para.9, Sch.39 para.32
s.30, amended: 2012 c.14 Sch.1 para.6
s.35, amended: 2012 c.14 s.3, s.4, SI 2012/3047 Art.3
s.35, applied: SI 2012/2885 Sch.1 para.19, Sch.1 para.30, SI 2012/2886 Sch.1, SI 2012/3144 Sch.1 para.13, SI 2012/3145 Sch.1, SSI 2012/303 Reg.35, Reg.38, Reg.41
s.35, referred to: 2012 c.14 s.3
s.36, amended: 2012 c.14 s.4, SI 2012/3047 Art.3
s.36, applied: SI 2012/2885 Sch.1 para.19, Sch.1 para.30, SI 2012/2886 Sch.1, SI 2012/3144 Sch.1 para.13, SI 2012/3145 Sch.1, SSI 2012/319 Reg.33, Reg.37

2007–cont.

3. Income Tax Act 2007–*cont.*
s.37, amended: 2012 c.14 s.4, SI 2012/3047 Art.3
s.37, applied: SI 2012/2885 Sch.1 para.19, Sch.1 para.30, SI 2012/2886 Sch.1, SI 2012/3144 Sch.1 para.13, SI 2012/3145 Sch.1, SSI 2012/319 Reg.33, Reg.37
s.38, amended: SI 2012/3047 Art.3
s.41, repealed (in part): 2012 c.14 s.4
s.43, amended: SI 2012/3047 Art.3
s.45, amended: SI 2012/3047 Art.3
s.46, amended: SI 2012/3047 Art.3
s.57, amended: 2012 c.14 s.4
s.57, disapplied: 2012 c.14 s.3
s.57, repealed (in part): 2012 c.14 s.4
s.57, enabling: SI 2012/3047
s.83, applied: SI 2012/2677 Reg.36
s.96, amended: 2012 c.14 s.9
s.98, applied: 2012 c.14 s.9
s.98A, added: 2012 c.14 s.9
s.117, amended: 2012 c.14 s.10
s.118, applied: SI 2012/2677 Reg.69
s.120, amended: 2012 c.14 s.10
s.125, amended: 2012 c.14 s.9
s.127B, added: 2012 c.14 s.10
s.128, see *Revenue and Customs Commissioners v Cotter* [2012] EWCA Civ 81, [2012] S.T.C.745 (CA (Civ Div)), Arden, L.J.
s.157, repealed (in part): 2012 c.14 Sch.7 para.2
s.158, amended: 2012 c.14 Sch.7 para.3
s.169, amended: 2012 c.14 Sch.6 para.10
s.170, amended: 2012 c.14 Sch.7 para.4
s.170, repealed (in part): 2012 c.14 Sch.7 para.4
s.172, amended: 2012 c.14 Sch.6 para.11, Sch.7 para.5
s.173, amended: 2012 c.14 Sch.7 para.6
s.173A, amended: 2012 c.14 Sch.6 para.12, Sch.7 para.7
s.173A, applied: 2012 c.14 Sch.7 para.22
s.173A, repealed (in part): 2012 c.14 Sch.7 para.7
s.173B, added: 2012 c.14 Sch.6 para.13
s.175, amended: 2012 c.14 Sch.7 para.8
s.178A, added: 2012 c.14 Sch.7 para.9
s.179, amended: 2012 c.14 Sch.7 para.10
s.186, amended: 2012 c.14 Sch.7 para.11
s.186A, amended: 2012 c.14 Sch.7 para.12
s.192, amended: 2012 c.14 Sch.7 para.13
s.192, referred to: 2012 c.14 Sch.7 para.24
s.198A, added: 2012 c.14 Sch.7 para.14
s.198A, amended: 2012 c.14 Sch.7 para.24
s.199, amended: 2012 c.14 Sch.7 para.15
s.200, substituted: 2012 c.14 Sch.7 para.16
s.209, amended: 2012 c.14 Sch.7 para.17
s.239, amended: 2012 c.14 Sch.7 para.18
s.243, amended: 2012 c.14 Sch.7 para.19
s.246, amended: 2012 c.14 Sch.6 para.14
s.251, repealed (in part): 2012 c.14 Sch.7 para.20
s.257, amended: 2012 c.14 Sch.7 para.21
s.257A, added: 2012 c.14 Sch.6 para.1
s.257AA, added: 2012 c.14 Sch.6 para.1
s.257AB, added: 2012 c.14 Sch.6 para.1
s.257AC, added: 2012 c.14 Sch.6 para.1
s.257AD, added: 2012 c.14 Sch.6 para.1
s.257AE, added: 2012 c.14 Sch.6 para.1
s.257B, added: 2012 c.14 Sch.6 para.1
s.257BA, added: 2012 c.14 Sch.6 para.1
s.257BB, added: 2012 c.14 Sch.6 para.1
s.257BC, added: 2012 c.14 Sch.6 para.1
s.257BD, added: 2012 c.14 Sch.6 para.1
s.257BE, added: 2012 c.14 Sch.6 para.1

2007– cont.

3. Income Tax Act 2007–*cont.*

s.257BF, added: 2012 c.14 Sch.6 para.1
s.257C, added: 2012 c.14 Sch.6 para.1
s.257CA, added: 2012 c.14 Sch.6 para.1
s.257CB, added: 2012 c.14 Sch.6 para.1
s.257CC, added: 2012 c.14 Sch.6 para.1
s.257CD, added: 2012 c.14 Sch.6 para.1
s.257CE, added: 2012 c.14 Sch.6 para.1
s.257CF, added: 2012 c.14 Sch.6 para.1
s.257D, added: 2012 c.14 Sch.6 para.1
s.257DA, added: 2012 c.14 Sch.6 para.1
s.257DB, added: 2012 c.14 Sch.6 para.1
s.257DC, added: 2012 c.14 Sch.6 para.1
s.257DD, added: 2012 c.14 Sch.6 para.1
s.257DE, added: 2012 c.14 Sch.6 para.1
s.257DF, added: 2012 c.14 Sch.6 para.1
s.257DG, added: 2012 c.14 Sch.6 para.1
s.257DH, added: 2012 c.14 Sch.6 para.1
s.257DI, added: 2012 c.14 Sch.6 para.1
s.257DJ, added: 2012 c.14 Sch.6 para.1
s.257DK, added: 2012 c.14 Sch.6 para.1
s.257DL, added: 2012 c.14 Sch.6 para.1
s.257DM, added: 2012 c.14 Sch.6 para.1
s.257DN, added: 2012 c.14 Sch.6 para.1
s.257E, added: 2012 c.14 Sch.6 para.1
s.257EA, added: 2012 c.14 Sch.6 para.1
s.257EB, added: 2012 c.14 Sch.6 para.1
s.257EC, added: 2012 c.14 Sch.6 para.1
s.257ED, added: 2012 c.14 Sch.6 para.1
s.257EE, added: 2012 c.14 Sch.6 para.1
s.257EF, added: 2012 c.14 Sch.6 para.1
s.257EG, added: 2012 c.14 Sch.6 para.1
s.257F, added: 2012 c.14 Sch.6 para.1
s.257FA, added: 2012 c.14 Sch.6 para.1
s.257FB, added: 2012 c.14 Sch.6 para.1
s.257FC, added: 2012 c.14 Sch.6 para.1
s.257FD, added: 2012 c.14 Sch.6 para.1
s.257FE, added: 2012 c.14 Sch.6 para.1
s.257FF, added: 2012 c.14 Sch.6 para.1
s.257FG, added: 2012 c.14 Sch.6 para.1
s.257FH, added: 2012 c.14 Sch.6 para.1
s.257FI, added: 2012 c.14 Sch.6 para.1
s.257FJ, added: 2012 c.14 Sch.6 para.1
s.257FK, added: 2012 c.14 Sch.6 para.1
s.257FL, added: 2012 c.14 Sch.6 para.1
s.257FM, added: 2012 c.14 Sch.6 para.1
s.257FN, added: 2012 c.14 Sch.6 para.1
s.257FO, added: 2012 c.14 Sch.6 para.1
s.257FP, added: 2012 c.14 Sch.6 para.1
s.257FQ, added: 2012 c.14 Sch.6 para.1
s.257FR, added: 2012 c.14 Sch.6 para.1
s.257G, added: 2012 c.14 Sch.6 para.1
s.257GA, added: 2012 c.14 Sch.6 para.1
s.257GB, added: 2012 c.14 Sch.6 para.1
s.257GC, added: 2012 c.14 Sch.6 para.1
s.257GD, added: 2012 c.14 Sch.6 para.1
s.257GE, added: 2012 c.14 Sch.6 para.1
s.257GF, added: 2012 c.14 Sch.6 para.1
s.257GG, added: 2012 c.14 Sch.6 para.1
s.257GH, added: 2012 c.14 Sch.6 para.1
s.257GI, added: 2012 c.14 Sch.6 para.1
s.257H, added: 2012 c.14 Sch.6 para.1
s.257HA, added: 2012 c.14 Sch.6 para.1
s.257HB, added: 2012 c.14 Sch.6 para.1
s.257HC, added: 2012 c.14 Sch.6 para.1
s.257HD, added: 2012 c.14 Sch.6 para.1
s.257HE, added: 2012 c.14 Sch.6 para.1
s.257HF, added: 2012 c.14 Sch.6 para.1

2007– cont.

3. Income Tax Act 2007– *cont.*

s.257HG, added: 2012 c.14 Sch.6 para.1
s.257HH, added: 2012 c.14 Sch.6 para.1
s.257HI, added: 2012 c.14 Sch.6 para.1
s.257HJ, added: 2012 c.14 Sch.6 para.1
s.274, amended: 2012 c.14 Sch.8 para.2
s.274, referred to: 2012 c.14 Sch.8 para.18
s.280B, added: 2012 c.14 Sch.8 para.3
s.280B, applied: 2012 c.14 Sch.8 para.18
s.286, amended: 2012 c.14 Sch.6 para.15, Sch.8 para.4
s.287, amended: 2012 c.14 Sch.8 para.5
s.287, repealed (in part): 2012 c.14 Sch.8 para.5
s.292A, amended: 2012 c.14 Sch.6 para.16, Sch.8 para.6
s.292A, repealed (in part): 2012 c.14 Sch.8 para.6
s.292B, added: 2012 c.14 Sch.6 para.17
s.293, amended: 2012 c.14 Sch.8 para.7
s.297, amended: 2012 c.14 Sch.8 para.8
s.297A, amended: 2012 c.14 Sch.8 para.9
s.299A, added: 2012 c.14 Sch.8 para.10
s.303, amended: 2012 c.14 Sch.8 para.11
s.309A, added: 2012 c.14 Sch.8 para.12
s.309A, varied: 2012 c.14 Sch.8 para.12
s.310, amended: 2012 c.14 Sch.8 para.13
s.311, substituted: 2012 c.14 Sch.8 para.14
s.312A, added: 2012 c.14 Sch.8 para.15
s.313, amended: 2012 c.14 Sch.8 para.16
s.413, amended: 2012 c.14 Sch.15 para.8
s.423, amended: 2012 c.14 Sch.39 para.32
s.423, repealed (in part): 2012 c.14 Sch.39 para.32
s.426, repealed (in part): 2012 c.14 s.50
s.429, repealed: 2012 c.14 s.50
s.430, amended: SI 2012/964 Sch.1
s.430, repealed (in part): SI 2012/964 Sch.1
s.446, amended: SI 2012/964 Sch.1
s.446, repealed (in part): SI 2012/964 Sch.1
s.459, repealed: 2012 c.14 Sch.39 para.32
s.460, amended: 2012 c.14 Sch.39 para.32
s.460, repealed (in part): 2012 c.14 Sch.39 para.32
s.538, repealed (in part): 2012 c.14 s.50
s.538A, amended: 2012 c.14 Sch.15 para.1
s.555, varied: SI 2012/700 Sch.1 para.8
s.564B, amended: 2012 c.14 Sch.16 para.133
s.681DP, amended: 2012 c.14 Sch.16 para.134
s.725, amended: 2012 c.14 Sch.20 para.22
s.809BZA, amended: 2012 c.14 Sch.13 para.33
s.809BZF, amended: 2012 c.14 Sch.13 para.34
s.809BZH, amended: 2012 c.14 Sch.13 para.35
s.809BZJ, amended: 2012 c.14 Sch.13 para.36
s.809C, amended: 2012 c.14 Sch.12 para.2
s.809G, amended: 2012 c.14 Sch.39 para.32
s.809H, amended: 2012 c.11 s.26, 2012 c.14 Sch.12 para.3
s.809I, amended: 2012 c.14 Sch.12 para.20
s.809I, applied: 2012 c.14 Sch.12 para.21
s.809M, amended: 2012 c.14 Sch.12 para.13
s.809V, substituted: 2012 c.14 Sch.12 para.4
s.809VA, added: 2012 c.14 Sch.12 para.7
s.809VA, referred to: 2012 c.14 Sch.12 para.17
s.809VB, added: 2012 c.14 Sch.12 para.7
s.809VC, added: 2012 c.14 Sch.12 para.7
s.809VD, added: 2012 c.14 Sch.12 para.7
s.809VE, added: 2012 c.14 Sch.12 para.7
s.809VF, added: 2012 c.14 Sch.12 para.7
s.809VG, added: 2012 c.14 Sch.12 para.7
s.809VH, added: 2012 c.14 Sch.12 para.7
s.809VI, added: 2012 c.14 Sch.12 para.7

2007–cont.

3. Income Tax Act 2007–*cont.*

s.809VJ, added: 2012 c.14 Sch.12 para.7

s.809VJ, referred to: SI 2012/1898 Reg.2

s.809VJ, enabling: SI 2012/1898

s.809VK, added: 2012 c.14 Sch.12 para.7

s.809VL, added: 2012 c.14 Sch.12 para.7

s.809VM, added: 2012 c.14 Sch.12 para.7

s.809VN, added: 2012 c.14 Sch.12 para.7

s.809VO, added: 2012 c.14 Sch.12 para.7

s.809Y, amended: 2012 c.14 Sch.12 para.10

s.809Y, referred to: 2012 c.14 Sch.12 para.17

s.809YA, added: 2012 c.14 Sch.12 para.18

s.809YB, added: 2012 c.14 Sch.12 para.18

s.809YC, added: 2012 c.14 Sch.12 para.18

s.809YD, added: 2012 c.14 Sch.12 para.18

s.809YE, added: 2012 c.14 Sch.14 para.35

s.809Z2, repealed (in part): 2012 c.14 Sch.12 para.11

s.809Z4, amended: 2012 c.14 Sch.12 para.12

s.809Z7, repealed (in part): 2012 c.14 Sch.12 para.14

s.809Z7, substituted: 2012 c.14 Sch.12 para.15

s.809Z8, added: 2012 c.14 Sch.12 para.16

s.809Z9, added: 2012 c.14 Sch.12 para.16

s.809Z10, added: 2012 c.14 Sch.12 para.16

s.811, repealed (in part): 2012 c.14 Sch.39 para.28, Sch.39 para.32

s.833, amended: 2012 c.14 Sch.37 para.5

s.833, applied: SI 2012/3070 Art.3, SI 2012/3071 Art.4, Art.5

s.833, enabling: SI 2012/3070, SI 2012/3071

s.858, applied: SI 2012/847 Reg.9

s.859, applied: SI 2012/847 Reg.9

s.860, applied: SI 2012/847 Reg.9

s.861, applied: SI 2012/847 Reg.9

s.866, amended: 2012 c.14 s.18

s.966, disapplied: 2012 c.14 s.13

s.967, enabling: SI 2012/1359

s.969, enabling: SI 2012/1359

s.970, enabling: SI 2012/1359

s.989, amended: 2012 c.11 s.26, 2012 c.14 Sch.39 para.28

s.993, applied: 2012 c.23 s.5, Sch.1 para.10

s.993, varied: 2012 c.23 s.5

s.1019, applied: SI 2012/847 Reg.6

Sch.1 Part 1 para.232, repealed: 2012 c.14 Sch.39 para.28

Sch.4, amended: 2012 c.14 Sch.6 para.18

5. Welfare Reform Act 2007

applied: SI 2012/2885 Sch.1 para.17, Sch.1 para.22, Sch.1 para.46, SI 2012/2886 Sch.1, SI 2012/3144 Sch.1 para.11, Sch.1 para.16, SI 2012/3145 Sch.1, SSI 2012/292 Art.3, SSI 2012/303 Reg.31, SSI 2012/319 Reg.31, Reg.38, Reg.59

Part 1, applied: 2012 c.5 s.33, SI 2012/360, SI 2012/360 Art.2, SI 2012/531 Reg.49

s.1, amended: 2012 c.5 s.50, s.52, s.53, s.54, s.62, Sch.3 para.23, Sch.14 Part 1

s.1, applied: SI 2012/1483 Reg.4, SI 2012/2885 Sch.4 para.5, SI 2012/2886 Sch.1, SSI 2012/319 Sch.2 para.5

s.1, repealed (in part): 2012 c.5 Sch.14 Part 1

s.1, enabling: SI 2012/757

s.1A, added: 2012 c.5 s.51

s.1A, amended: 2012 c.5 Sch.3 para.26, Sch.14 Part 1

s.1B, added: 2012 c.5 s.52

s.1B, amended: 2012 c.5 Sch.3 para.26

s.1B, repealed (in part): 2012 c.5 Sch.14 Part 1

s.1C, added: 2012 c.5 s.54

s.1C, repealed: 2012 c.5 Sch.14 Part 5

2007–cont.

5. Welfare Reform Act 2007–*cont.*

s.2, amended: 2012 c.5 Sch.3 para.24, Sch.5 para.6, Sch.14 Part 1

s.2, applied: SI 2012/2885 Sch.4 para.5, SI 2012/2886 Sch.1, SSI 2012/319 Sch.2 para.5

s.2, enabling: SI 2012/874, SI 2012/913, SI 2012/919

s.3, amended: 2012 c.5 Sch.3 para.26, Sch.14 Part 1

s.3, applied: SI 2012/2885 Sch.1 para.16, SI 2012/2886 Sch.1, SI 2012/3144 Sch.1 para.10, SI 2012/3145 Sch.1, SSI 2012/319 Reg.27

s.4, repealed: 2012 c.5 Sch.14 Part 1

s.4, enabling: SI 2012/874, SI 2012/913, SI 2012/919, SI 2012/2587

s.5, repealed: 2012 c.5 Sch.14 Part 1

s.6, repealed: 2012 c.5 Sch.14 Part 1

s.8, enabling: SI 2012/3096

s.9, enabling: SI 2012/3096

s.11, substituted: 2012 c.5 s.57

s.11A, substituted: 2012 c.5 s.57

s.11B, substituted: 2012 c.5 s.57

s.11C, substituted: 2012 c.5 s.57

s.11D, substituted: 2012 c.5 s.57

s.11E, substituted: 2012 c.5 s.57

s.11F, substituted: 2012 c.5 s.57

s.11G, substituted: 2012 c.5 s.57

s.11H, substituted: 2012 c.5 s.57

s.11I, substituted: 2012 c.5 s.57

s.11J, substituted: 2012 c.5 s.57

s.11K, substituted: 2012 c.5 s.57

s.12, substituted: 2012 c.5 s.57

s.12, enabling: SI 2012/2756

s.13, amended: 2012 c.5 s.55

s.13, substituted: 2012 c.5 s.57

s.13, enabling: SI 2012/2756

s.14, substituted: 2012 c.5 s.57

s.15, amended: 2012 c.5 s.54

s.15, substituted: 2012 c.5 s.57

s.15A, repealed: 2012 c.5 s.60

s.15A, substituted: 2012 c.5 s.57

s.16, amended: 2012 c.5 s.54, Sch.14 Part 6

s.16, repealed (in part): 2012 c.5 Sch.14 Part 6

s.16, substituted: 2012 c.5 s.57

s.16, enabling: SI 2012/2756

s.16A, added: 2012 c.5 s.56

s.16A, repealed: 2012 c.5 Sch.14 Part 5

s.16A, enabling: SI 2012/2756

s.17, enabling: SI 2012/2575

s.18, amended: 2012 c.5 Sch.3 para.26

s.18, applied: SI 2012/2885 Reg.2, SI 2012/2886 Sch.1, SI 2012/3144 Reg.2, SI 2012/3145 Sch.1, SSI 2012/319 Reg.2

s.18, disapplied: SI 2012/2885 Reg.2, SI 2012/3144 Reg.2

s.19, amended: 2012 c.5 s.57

s.20, amended: 2012 c.5 Sch.3 para.26

s.23, repealed: 2012 c.5 Sch.14 Part 1

s.24, amended: 2012 c.5 s.57, Sch.14 Part 1

s.24, applied: SSI 2012/319 Sch.2 para.5

s.24, referred to: SI 2012/2885 Sch.4 para.5

s.24, repealed (in part): 2012 c.5 Sch.14 Part 5

s.24, enabling: SI 2012/757, SI 2012/874, SI 2012/913, SI 2012/919, SI 2012/2575, SI 2012/2587, SI 2012/3096

s.25, amended: 2012 c.5 s.51, s.57, Sch.14 Part 6

s.25, enabling: SI 2012/757, SI 2012/913, SI 2012/919, SI 2012/2575, SI 2012/2587, SI 2012/2756, SI 2012/3096

s.26, amended: 2012 c.5 s.51, s.57, Sch.14 Part 1

2007–*cont.*

5. Welfare Reform Act 2007–*cont.*

s.26, repealed (in part): 2012 c.5 Sch.14 Part 5, Sch.14 Part 6

s.27, amended: 2012 c.5 Sch.3 para.25

s.27, repealed (in part): 2012 c.5 Sch.14 Part 1

s.28, enabling: SI 2012/913

s.29, repealed: 2012 c.5 Sch.14 Part 1

s.29, enabling: SI 2012/757

s.30, repealed: 2012 c.5 Sch.14 Part 1

s.31, repealed: 2012 c.5 Sch.14 Part 1

s.32, repealed: 2012 c.5 Sch.14 Part 1

s.33, repealed: 2012 c.5 Sch.14 Part 1

s.34, repealed: 2012 c.5 Sch.14 Part 1

s.37, repealed: 2012 c.5 Sch.14 Part 1

s.38, repealed: 2012 c.5 Sch.14 Part 1

s.39, repealed: 2012 c.5 Sch.14 Part 1

s.41, repealed (in part): 2012 c.5 Sch.14 Part 1

s.42, repealed: 2012 c.5 s.133

s.43, repealed: 2012 c.5 s.133

s.46, repealed: 2012 c.5 Sch.14 Part 1

s.47, repealed: 2012 c.5 Sch.14 Part 1

s.48, repealed (in part): 2012 c.5 Sch.14 Part 10, Sch.14 Part 1

s.52, repealed: 2012 c.5 Sch.14 Part 9

s.53, repealed: 2012 c.5 Sch 14 Part 9

s.54, repealed (in part): 2012 c.5 Sch.14 Part 8

s.60, repealed (in part): 2012 c.5 Sch.14 Part 9

s.69, repealed (in part): 2012 c.5 s.133

Sch.1 Part 1 para.1, amended: 2012 c.5 Sch.2 para.65, Sch.3 para.26

Sch.1 Part 1 para.1, repealed (in part): 2012 c.5 Sch.14 Part 1, Sch.14 Part 1

Sch.1 Part 1 para.1, enabling: SI 2012/757

Sch.1 Part 1 para.2, repealed: 2012 c.5 Sch.14 Part 1

Sch.1 Part 1 para.3, amended: 2012 c.5 Sch.3 para.26

Sch.1 Part 1 para.3, repealed: 2012 c.5 Sch.14 Part 1

Sch.1 Part 1 para.4, repealed: 2012 c.5 Sch.14 Part 1

Sch.1 Part 1 para.5, repealed: 2012 c.5 Sch.14 Part 1

Sch.1 Part 2 para.6, repealed: 2012 c.5 Sch.14 Part 1

Sch.1 Part 2 para.6, enabling: SI 2012/757

Sch.1 A para.1, repealed: 2012 c.5 s.60

Sch.1 A para.2, repealed: 2012 c.5 s.60

Sch.1 A para.3, repealed: 2012 c.5 s.60

Sch.1 A para.4, repealed: 2012 c.5 s.60

Sch.1 A para.5, repealed: 2012 c.5 s.60

Sch.1 A para.6, repealed: 2012 c.5 s.60

Sch.1 A para.7, repealed: 2012 c.5 s.60

Sch.1 A para.8, repealed: 2012 c.5 s.60

Sch.1 A para.9, repealed: 2012 c.5 s.60

Sch.1 A para.10, repealed: 2012 c.5 s.60

Sch.2 para.1, enabling: SI 2012/919, SI 2012/3096

Sch.2 para.2, applied: SI 2012/2885 Reg.2, Sch.8 para.5, SI 2012/2886 Sch.1, SI 2012/3144 Reg.2, SI 2012/3145 Sch.1, SSI 2012/303 Reg.85, SSI 2012/319 Reg.2

Sch.2 para.2, enabling: SI 2012/913

Sch.2 para.4, enabling: SI 2012/919

Sch.2 para.4A, added: 2012 c.5 s.54

Sch.2 para.4B, added: 2012 c.5 s.62

Sch.2 para.6, amended: 2012 c.5 Sch.3 para.26, Sch.14 Part 1

Sch.2 para.7, amended: 2012 c.5 Sch.3 para.26, Sch.14 Part 1

Sch.2 para.8, repealed: 2012 c.5 Sch.14 Part 1

Sch.2 para.9, enabling: SI 2012/919, SI 2012/3096

Sch.2 para.10A, amended: 2012 c.5 s.57, Sch.14 Part 6

2007–*cont.*

5. Welfare Reform Act 2007–*cont.*

Sch.2 para.10B, added: 2012 c.5 s.57

Sch.2 para.10ZA, added: 2012 c.5 s.57

Sch.2 para.11, repealed (in part): 2012 c.5 Sch.14 Part 1

Sch.2 para.12, repealed (in part): 2012 c.5 Sch.14 Part 1, Sch.14 Part 6

Sch.2 para.13, amended: 2012 c.5 s.57, Sch.14 Part 6

Sch.3 para.1, repealed: 2012 c.5 Sch.14 Part 1

Sch.3 para.2, repealed: 2012 c.5 Sch.14 Part 1

Sch.3 para.4, repealed: 2012 c.5 Sch.14 Part 1

Sch.3 para.9, repealed (in part): 2012 c.5 Sch.14 Part 1

Sch.3 para.10, repealed (in part): 2012 c.5 Sch.14 Part 13, Sch.14 Part 1

Sch.3 para.12, repealed (in part): 2012 c.5 Sch.14 Part 1

Sch.4 para.1, repealed: 2012 c.5 Sch.14 Part 1

Sch.4 para.1, enabling: SI 2012/757, SI 2012/913, SI 2012/919

Sch.4 para.2, repealed: 2012 c.5 Sch.14 Part 1

Sch.4 para.3, repealed: 2012 c.5 Sch.14 Part 1

Sch.4 para.4, repealed: 2012 c.5 Sch.14 Part 1

Sch.4 para.4, enabling: SI 2012/919

Sch.4 para.5, repealed: 2012 c.5 Sch.14 Part 1

Sch.4 para.6, repealed: 2012 c.5 Sch.14 Part 1

Sch.4 para.7, amended: 2012 c.5 s.51

Sch.4 para.7, repealed: 2012 c.5 Sch.14 Part 1

Sch.4 para.7, enabling: SI 2012/757, SI 2012/913, SI 2012/919

Sch.4 para.8, repealed: 2012 c.5 Sch.14 Part 1

Sch.4 para.8, enabling: SI 2012/919

Sch.4 para.9, repealed: 2012 c.5 Sch.14 Part 1

Sch.4 para.10, repealed: 2012 c.5 Sch.14 Part 1

Sch.4 para.11, repealed: 2012 c.5 Sch.14 Part 1

Sch.5 para.1, repealed: 2012 c.5 Sch.14 Part 1

Sch.5 para.3, repealed: 2012 c.5 Sch.14 Part 1

Sch.5 para.4, repealed: 2012 c.5 Sch.14 Part 1

Sch.5 para.5, repealed: 2012 c.5 Sch.14 Part 1

Sch.5 para.6, repealed: 2012 c.5 Sch.14 Part 1

Sch.5 para.7, repealed: 2012 c.5 Sch.14 Part 1

Sch.5 para.8, repealed: 2012 c.5 Sch.14 Part 1

Sch.5 para.9, repealed: 2012 c.5 Sch.14 Part 1

Sch.5 para.12, repealed: 2012 c.5 Sch.14 Part 1

Sch.5 para.13, repealed: 2012 c.5 Sch.14 Part 1

Sch.7 para.2, repealed (in part): 2012 c.5 Sch.14 Part 8, Sch.14 Part 9

Sch.7 para.3, repealed (in part): 2012 c.5 Sch.14 Part 1, Sch.14 Part 8

Sch.7 para.4, repealed: 2012 c.5 Sch.14 Part 8

6. Justice and Security (Northern Ireland) Act 2007

applied: 2012 c.13 Sch.1

Sch.3, amended: 2012 c.9 Sch.6 para.1

Sch.3 para.4, amended: 2012 c.9 Sch.6 para.1

Sch.3 para.4A, added: 2012 c.9 Sch.6 para.2

Sch.3 para.4B, added: 2012 c.9 Sch.6 para.2

Sch.3 para.4C, added: 2012 c.9 Sch.6 para.2

Sch.3 para.4D, added: 2012 c.9 Sch.6 para.2

Sch.3 para.4E, added: 2012 c.9 Sch.6 para.2

Sch.3 para.4F, added: 2012 c.9 Sch.6 para.2

Sch.3 para.4G, added: 2012 c.9 Sch.6 para.2

Sch.3 para.4H, added: 2012 c.9 Sch.6 para.2

Sch.3 para.4I, added: 2012 c.9 Sch.6 para.2

Sch.3 para.9, amended: 2012 c.9 Sch.6 para.3

11. Finance Act 2007

see *Aspinalls Club Ltd v Revenue and Customs Commissioners* [2012] UKUT 242 (TCC), [2012] S.T.C. 2124 (UT (Tax)), Briggs, J.

2007– cont.

11. Finance Act 2007–*cont.*
referred to: 2012 c.23 s.21
s.16, repealed (in part): SI 2012/2661 Reg.6
s.16, enabling: SI 2012/2661
s.44, repealed: 2012 c.14 Sch.18 para.23
s.107, see *Test Claimants in the FII Group Litigation v Revenue and Customs Commissioners* [2012] UKSC 19, [2012] 2 A.C. 337 (SC), Lord Hope
Sch.7 Part 1 para.3, repealed: 2012 c.14 Sch.16 para.247
Sch.7 Part 1 para.6, repealed: 2012 c.14 Sch.16 para.247
Sch.7 Part 1 para.8, repealed: 2012 c.14 Sch.16 para.247
Sch.7 Part 1 para.9, repealed: 2012 c.14 Sch.16 para.247
Sch.7 Part 1 para.10, repealed: 2012 c.14 Sch.16 para.247
Sch.7 Part 1 para.11, repealed: 2012 c.14 Sch.16 para.247
Sch.7 Part 1 para.12, repealed: 2012 c.14 Sch.16 para.247
Sch.7 Part 1 para.13, repealed: 2012 c.14 Sch.16 para.247
Sch.7 Part 1 para.14, repealed: 2012 c.14 Sch.16 para.247
Sch.7 Part 1 para.16, repealed: 2012 c.14 Sch.16 para.247
Sch.7 Part 1 para.17, repealed: 2012 c.14 Sch.16 para.247
Sch.7 Part 1 para.19, repealed: 2012 c.14 Sch.16 para.247
Sch.7 Part 1 para.21, repealed: 2012 c.14 Sch.16 para.247
Sch.7 Part 1 para.22, repealed: 2012 c.14 Sch.16 para.247
Sch.7 Part 1 para.23, repealed: 2012 c.14 Sch.16 para.247
Sch.7 Part 1 para.25, repealed: 2012 c.14 Sch.16 para.247
Sch.7 Part 1 para.26, repealed: 2012 c.14 Sch.16 para.247
Sch.7 Part 1 para.31, repealed: 2012 c.14 Sch.16 para.247
Sch.7 Part 1 para.32, repealed: 2012 c.14 Sch.16 para.247
Sch.7 Part 1 para.33, repealed: 2012 c.14 Sch.16 para.247
Sch.7 Part 1 para.35, repealed: 2012 c.14 Sch.16 para.247
Sch.7 Part 1 para.36, repealed: 2012 c.14 Sch.16 para.247
Sch.7 Part 1 para.37, repealed: 2012 c.14 Sch.16 para.247
Sch.7 Part 1 para.38, repealed: 2012 c.14 Sch.16 para.247
Sch.7 Part 1 para.40, repealed: 2012 c.14 Sch.18 para.23
Sch.7 Part 1 para.43, repealed: 2012 c.14 Sch.18 para.23
Sch.7 Part 1 para.57, repealed: 2012 c.14 Sch.16 para.247
Sch.7 Part 1 para.58, repealed: 2012 c.14 Sch.16 para.247
Sch.7 Part 1 para.59, repealed: 2012 c.14 Sch.16 para.247
Sch.7 Part 2, applied: 2012 c.14 Sch.17 para.29
Sch.7 Part 2 para.80, repealed: 2012 c.14 Sch.16 para.247

2007– cont.

11. Finance Act 2007–*cont.*
Sch.7 Part 2 para.81, repealed: 2012 c.14 Sch.16 para.247
Sch.7 Part 2 para.82, repealed: 2012 c.14 Sch.16 para.247
Sch.7 Part 2 para.83, repealed: 2012 c.14 Sch.16 para.247
Sch.7 Part 2 para.84, repealed: 2012 c.14 Sch.16 para.247
Sch.8 Part 1 para.2, repealed: 2012 c.14 Sch.16 para.247
Sch.8 Part 1 para.3, repealed: 2012 c.14 Sch.16 para.247
Sch.8 Part 1 para.4, repealed: 2012 c.14 Sch.16 para.247
Sch.8 Part 1 para.5, repealed: 2012 c.14 Sch.16 para.247
Sch.8 Part 1 para.6, repealed: 2012 c.14 Sch.16 para.247
Sch.8 Part 1 para.8, repealed: 2012 c.14 Sch.16 para.247
Sch.8 Part 1 para.9, repealed: 2012 c.14 Sch.16 para.247
Sch.8 Part 1 para.11, repealed: 2012 c.14 Sch.16 para.247
Sch.8 Part 1 para.12, repealed: 2012 c.14 Sch.16 para.247
Sch.8 Part 1 para.13, repealed: 2012 c.14 Sch.16 para.247
Sch.8 Part 1 para.14, repealed: 2012 c.14 Sch.16 para.247
Sch.8 Part 1 para.15, repealed: 2012 c.14 Sch.16 para.247
Sch.8 Part 1 para.16, repealed: 2012 c.14 Sch.16 para.247
Sch.8 Part 2 para.28, repealed: 2012 c.14 Sch.16 para.247
Sch.8 Part 2 para.29, repealed: 2012 c.14 Sch.16 para.247
Sch.9 para.1, repealed (in part): 2012 c.14 Sch.16 para.247
Sch.9 para.3, repealed (in part): 2012 c.14 Sch.16 para.247
Sch.9 para.4, repealed: 2012 c.14 Sch.16 para.247
Sch.9 para.5, repealed: 2012 c.14 Sch.16 para.247
Sch.9 para.6, repealed: 2012 c.14 Sch.16 para.247
Sch.9 para.7, repealed: 2012 c.14 Sch.16 para.247
Sch.9 para.8, repealed: 2012 c.14 Sch.16 para.247
Sch.9 para.10, repealed: 2012 c.14 Sch.16 para.247
Sch.9 para.11, repealed (in part): 2012 c.14 Sch.16 para.247
Sch.9 para.12, repealed: 2012 c.14 Sch.16 para.247
Sch.9 para.15, repealed: 2012 c.14 Sch.16 para.247
Sch.9 para.16, repealed: 2012 c.14 Sch.16 para.247
Sch.10 para.2, repealed (in part): 2012 c.14 Sch.16 para.247
Sch.10 para.4, repealed: 2012 c.14 Sch.16 para.247
Sch.10 para.11, repealed: 2012 c.14 Sch.16 para.247
Sch.10 para.12, repealed: 2012 c.14 Sch.16 para.247
Sch.10 para.13, repealed: 2012 c.14 Sch.16 para.247
Sch.10 para.15, repealed (in part): 2012 c.14 Sch.16 para.247
Sch.11 para.3, amended: 2012 c.14 Sch.20 para.23
Sch.12 para.1, repealed: 2012 c.14 Sch.18 para.23
Sch.12 para.2, repealed: 2012 c.14 Sch.18 para.23
Sch.12 para.3, repealed: 2012 c.14 Sch.18 para.23
Sch.12 para.4, repealed: 2012 c.14 Sch.18 para.23
Sch.12 para.5, repealed: 2012 c.14 Sch.18 para.23
Sch.12 para.6, repealed: 2012 c.14 Sch.18 para.23

2007–cont.

11. Finance Act 2007–*cont.*

Sch.24, see *Hanson v Revenue and Customs Commissioners* [2012] UKFTT 314 (TC), [2012] W.T.L.R. 1769 (FTT (Tax)), Judge Jonathan Cannan

Sch.24, applied: 2012 c.14 Sch.38 para.34

Sch.24 Part 1 para.1, amended: 2012 c.14 Sch.24 para.29

Sch.24 Pt 1 para.1, see *Hanson v Revenue and Customs Commissioners* [2012] UKFTT 314 (TC), [2012] W.T.L.R. 1769 (FTT (Tax)), Judge Jonathan Cannan

Sch.24 Pt 4 para.18, see *Hanson v Revenue and Customs Commissioners* [2012] UKFTT 314 (TC), [2012] W.T.L.R. 1769 (FTT (Tax)), Judge Jonathan Cannan

Sch.24 Part 5 para.21A, amended: 2012 c.14 s.219

12. Mental Health Act 2007

Sch.3 para.10, repealed (in part): 2012 c.7 s.39

Sch.3 para.11, repealed (in part): 2012 c.7 s.39

15. Tribunals, Courts and Enforcement Act 2007

Commencement Orders: SI 2012/1312 Art.2, Art.3 see *C v Suffolk CC* [2011] EWCA Civ 870, [2012] E.L.R. 105 (CA (Civ Div)), Arden, L.J.; see *Practice Note (UT: Immigration and Asylum Chambers: Judicial Titles)* [2012] 1 W.L.R. 14 (UT), Blake, J. (President); see *R. (on the application of Cart) v Upper Tribunal* [2012] 1 A.C. 663 (SC), Lord Phillips (President)

referred to: SI 2012/1726 r.52.1

s.7, enabling: SI 2012/1673

s.11, see *R. (on the application of ToTel Ltd) v First-tier Tribunal (Tax Chamber)* [2012] EWCA Civ 1401, [2012] B.V.C. 333 (CA (Civ Div)), Lord Neuberger (M.R.); see *Wellcome Trust Ltd v 19-22 Onslow Gardens Freehold* [2012] EWCA Civ 1024, [2012] R.V.R. 342 (CA (Civ Div)), Lloyd, L.J.

s.11, applied: 2012 c.10 Sch.1 para.17

s.11, disapplied: 2012 c.14 Sch.38 para.13, Sch.38 para.20

s.12, see *Catana v Revenue and Customs Commissioners* [2012] UKUT 172 (TCC), [2012] S.T.C. 2138 (UT (Tax)), Judge Colin Bishopp

s.13, see *AJ (Pakistan) v Secretary of State for the Home Department* 2012 S.L.T. 162 (IH (Ex Div)), Lord Clarke; see *AL (Albania) v Secretary of State for the Home Department* [2012] EWCA Civ 710, [2012] 1 W.L.R. 2898 (CA (Civ Div)), Maurice Kay, L.J.; see *Eba v Advocate General for Scotland* [2012] 1 A.C. 710 (SC), Lord Phillips (President); see *JD (Congo) v Secretary of State for the Home Department* [2012] EWCA Civ 327, [2012] 1 W.L.R. 3273 (CA (Civ Div)), Lord Neuberger (M.R.); see *LB (Jamaica) v Secretary of State for the Home Department* [2011] EWCA Civ 1420, [2012] Imm. A.R. 637 (CA (Civ Div)), Maurice Kay, L.J.; see *PR (Sri Lanka) v Secretary of State for the Home Department* [2011] EWCA Civ 988, [2012] 1 W.L.R. 73 (CA (Civ Div)), Lord Neuberger (M.R.); see *R. (on the application of Cart) v Upper Tribunal* [2012] 1 A.C. 663 (SC), Lord Phillips (President); see *R. (on the application of Syed) v Secretary of State for the Home Department* [2011] EWCA Civ 1059, [2012] Imm. A.R. 40 (CA (Civ Div)), Sir Anthony May (President, QB); see *Sapkota v Secretary of State for the Home Department* [2011] EWCA Civ 1320, [2012] Imm. A.R. 254 (CA

2007–cont.

15. Tribunals, Courts and Enforcement Act 2007–*cont.*

s.13–*cont.*

(Civ Div)), Arden, L.J.; see *Wellcome Trust Ltd v 19-22 Onslow Gardens Freehold* [2012] EWCA Civ 1024, [2012] R.V.R. 342 (CA (Civ Div)), Lloyd, L.J.

s.13, disapplied: 2012 c.14 Sch.38 para.13, Sch.38 para.20

s.15, see *Practice Direction (Sen Cts: Upper Tribunal: Judicial Review Jurisdiction)* [2012] 1 W.L.R. 16 (Sen Cts), Lord Judge, L.C.J.; see *R. (on the application of Jones) v First-tier Tribunal (Social Entitlement Chamber)* [2011] EWCA Civ 400, [2012] Q.B. 345 (CA (Civ Div)), Mummery, L.J.

s.15, applied: 2012 c.10 Sch.1 para.18

s.18, see *Practice Direction (Sen Cts: Upper Tribunal: Judicial Review Jurisdiction)* [2012] 1 W.L.R. 16 (Sen Cts), Lord Judge, L.C.J.

s.22, applied: SI 2012/605 Reg.24

s.22, enabling: SI 2012/500, SI 2012/1363, SI 2012/2890

s.28, applied: SI 2012/1363

s.29, see *Catana v Revenue and Customs Commissioners* [2012] UKUT 172 (TCC), [2012] S.T.C. 2138 (UT (Tax)), Judge Colin Bishopp; see *G Wilson (Glaziers) Ltd v Revenue and Customs Commissioners* [2012] UKFTT 387 (TC), [2012] S.F.T.D. 1117 (FTT (Tax)), Judge Peter Kempster

s.29, applied: SI 2012/605 Reg.24

s.31, see *Wellcome Trust Ltd v 19-22 Onslow Gardens Freehold* [2012] EWCA Civ 1024, [2012] R.V.R. 342 (CA (Civ Div)), Lloyd, L.J.

s.44, applied: SI 2012/283, SI 2012/1819, SI 2012/1945, SSI 2012/132, SSI 2012/139, SSI 2012/142

s.50, applied: SI 2012/2267 Reg.10, SI 2012/3152 Reg.10

s.62, applied: SI 2012/2814 Sch.2 para.3

s.145, applied: SI 2012/2404

s.145, enabling: SI 2012/2404

s.148, enabling: SI 2012/1312

Sch.1 Pt 4 para.14, see *DDR Distributions Ltd v Revenue and Customs Commissioners* [2012] UKFTT 443 (TC), [2012] S.F.T.D. 1249 (FTT (Tax)), Judge Barbara Mosedale

Sch.2 para.2, enabling: SI 2012/897

Sch.3 para.2, enabling: SI 2012/897

Sch.5, enabling: SI 2012/500, SI 2012/1363, SI 2012/2890

Sch.5 Part 3 para.28, applied: SI 2012/500, SI 2012/2890

Sch.6 Part 3, amended: 2012 c.21 Sch.19

Sch.7 Part 3 para.24, applied: SI 2012/9, SI 2012/283, SI 2012/322, SI 2012/468, SI 2012/531, SI 2012/1003, SI 2012/1017, SI 2012/1134, SI 2012/1418, SI 2012/1819, SI 2012/1945, SI 2012/2630, SSI 2012/53, SSI 2012/132, SSI 2012/139, SSI 2012/142, SSI 2012/180

Sch.12, applied: SI 2012/2814 Sch.2 para.3

Sch.13 para.103, repealed: 2012 c.5 Sch.14 Part 1

17. Consumers, Estate Agents and Redress Act 2007

applied: SI 2012/1128 Art.4

s.20, repealed (in part): 2012 c.21 Sch.19

s.25, amended: SI 2012/2400 Art.32

s.39, repealed: 2012 c.21 Sch.19

Sch.1 Part 1 para.1, repealed (in part): 2012 c.21 Sch.19

2007–cont.

18. Statistics and Registration Service Act 2007
see *R. (on the application of Ali) v Minister for the Cabinet Office* [2012] EWHC 1943 (Admin), [2012] A.C.D. 89 (QBD (Admin)), Beatson, J.
s.4, amended: SI 2012/2404 Sch.2 para.60
s.6, applied: SSI 2012/196
s.6, enabling: SSI 2012/196
s.20, applied: SI 2012/1711 Reg.6, Reg.7
s.39, see *R. (on the application of Ali) v Minister for the Cabinet Office* [2012] EWHC 1943 (Admin), [2012] A.C.D. 89 (QBD (Admin)), Beatson, J.
s.39, applied: SI 2012/1711 Reg.7
s.42, amended: 2012 c.7 s.287
s.47, applied: SI 2012/1711
s.47, enabling: SI 2012/1711
s.65, applied: SI 2012/1711, SSI 2012/196

19. Corporate Manslaughter and Corporate Homicide Act 2007
s.1, see *R. v Cotswold Geotechnical Holdings Ltd* [2011] EWCA Crim 1337, [2012] 1 Cr. App. R. (S.) 26 (CA (Crim Div)), Lord Judge, L.C.J.
s.6, amended: 2012 asp 8 Sch.7 para.71, 2012 c.7 Sch.5 para.147, Sch.14 para.102

20. Forced Marriage (Civil Protection) Act 2007
see *A (Forced Marriage: Special Advocates), Re* [2010] EWHC 2438 (Fam), [2012] Fam. 102 (Fam Div), Sir Nicholas Wall (President, Fam)

21. Offender Management Act 2007
enabling: SI 2012/1215
s.5, applied: SI 2012/717 Sch.1
s.5, enabling: SI 2012/1215
s.13, applied: SI 2012/2886 Sch.1, SI 2012/3144 Reg.24, SI 2012/3145 Sch.1, SSI 2012/303 Reg.5, Reg.15, SSI 2012/319 Reg.5, Reg.15
s.13, referred to: SI 2012/2885 Sch.1 para.5
s.28, amended: 2012 c.10 Sch.21 para.32
Sch.1 para.13, amended: SI 2012/854 Art.4
Sch.1 para.13, repealed (in part): SI 2012/854 Art.4
Sch.1 para.13, enabling: SI 2012/1215

22. Pensions Act 2007
Commencement Orders: SI 2012/911 Art.2
s.30, enabling: SI 2012/911
Sch.1 Part 5 para.25, repealed: 2012 c.5 Sch.14 Part 1
Sch.1 Part 8 para.42, repealed: 2012 c.5 Sch.14 Part 9

23. Sustainable Communities Act 2007
s.5B, applied: SI 2012/1523
s.5B, enabling: SI 2012/1523
s.5D, enabling: SI 2012/1523

24. Greater London Authority Act 2007
varied: SI 2012/147 Art.7

27. Serious Crime Act 2007
Part 2, applied: 2012 c.10 Sch.1 para.39
s.8, applied: SI 2012/1726 r.50.3
s.9, applied: SI 2012/1726 r.68.1
s.19, applied: SI 2012/1726 r.50.1
s.24, applied: SI 2012/1726 r.68.1, r.74.1, r.68.3, r.68.4
s.34, amended: SI 2012/1809 Sch.1 Part 1
s.46, see *R. v Sadique (Omar)* [2011] EWCA Crim 2872, [2012] 1 W.L.R. 1700 (CA (Crim Div)), Hooper, L.J.
s.51, see *R. v Gnango (Armel)* [2012] 1 A.C. 827 (SC), Lord Phillips (President)
Sch.1 Part 1 para.2, amended: 2012 c.9 Sch.9 para.142
Sch.2 para.2, referred to: SI 2012/1726 r.50.3
Sch.2 para.7, referred to: SI 2012/1726 r.50.3
Sch.2 para.13, referred to: SI 2012/1726 r.50.3

2007–cont.

27. Serious Crime Act 2007–*cont.*
Sch.6 Part 1 para.10, repealed: 2012 c.19 Sch.9 para.17
Sch.6 Part 1 para.26, repealed: 2012 c.19 Sch.9 para.17
Sch.8 Part 7 para.159, repealed: 2012 c.10 Sch.5 Part 2

28. Local Government and Public Involvement in Health Act 2007
applied: 2012 c.13 Sch.1
Part 14, substituted: 2012 c.7 s.182
s.8, applied: SI 2012/667
s.10, enabling: SI 2012/667
s.11, enabling: SI 2012/667
s.12, enabling: SI 2012/667
s.13, enabling: SI 2012/667
s.14, enabling: SI 2012/20
s.15, enabling: SI 2012/667
s.31A, applied: SI 2012/57 Art.7
s.32, applied: SI 2012/1020 Reg.3
s.37, applied: SI 2012/57 Art.7, SI 2012/1020 Reg.3
s.39, applied: SI 2012/57 Art.7, SI 2012/1020 Reg.3
s.86, applied: SI 2012/1020 Reg.3
s.92, applied: SI 2012/1013, SI 2012/2854, SI 2012/2993, SI 2012/3150
s.92, enabling: SI 2012/51, SI 2012/1013, SI 2012/2854, SI 2012/2935, SI 2012/2993, SI 2012/3150
s.116, amended: 2012 c.7 s.192
s.116, applied: 2012 c.7 s.196, s.197, SI 2012/1909 Reg.9
s.116A, added: 2012 c.7 s.193
s.116A, applied: 2012 c.7 s.196, s.197
s.116B, added: 2012 c.7 s.193
s.116B, applied: 2012 c.7 s.196
s.123, applied: SI 2012/1020 Reg.4
s.147, repealed (in part): 2012 c.5 Sch.14 Part 1
s.148, repealed (in part): 2012 c.5 Sch.14 Part 1
s.150, repealed: 2012 c.5 Sch.14 Part 1
s.207, applied: SI 2012/1644 Sch.1
s.221, amended: 2012 c.7 s.182
s.221, applied: 2012 c.7 s.188, SI 2012/1640 Reg.10, SI 2012/3094 Reg.38, Reg.40, Reg.41, Reg.44, Reg.47
s.222, amended: 2012 c.7 s.183, Sch.5 para.149
s.222, applied: SI 2012/3094 Reg.35, Reg.36, Reg.37, Reg.38
s.222, repealed (in part): 2012 c.7 Sch.5 para.149, Sch.14 para.104
s.222, enabling: SI 2012/3094
s.222A, added: 2012 c.7 s.183
s.223, amended: 2012 c.7 s.184
s.223, enabling: SI 2012/3094
s.223A, added: 2012 c.7 s.185
s.224, amended: 2012 c.7 s.186, Sch.5 para.150
s.224, applied: SI 2012/3094
s.224, repealed (in part): 2012 c.7 Sch.5 para.150, Sch.14 para.105
s.224, enabling: SI 2012/3094
s.225, amended: 2012 c.7 s.186
s.225, repealed (in part): 2012 c.7 s.186, Sch.5 para.151, Sch.14 para.106
s.226, amended: 2012 c.7 s.186
s.226, applied: SI 2012/3094 Reg.46
s.226, enabling: SI 2012/3094
s.227, amended: 2012 c.7 s.187, Sch.5 para.152
s.227, repealed (in part): 2012 c.7 s.187
s.228, repealed: 2012 c.7 s.188
s.229, enabling: SI 2012/3094

2007– cont.

28. Local Government and Public Involvement in Health Act 2007– *cont.*
s.236, applied: SI 2012/ 1020 Reg.6
s.240, applied: SI 2012/ 667
s.240, enabling: SI 2012/ 20, SI 2012/ 3094
Sch.9 para.1, repealed (in part): SI 2012/ 2401 Sch.1 para.28
Sch.11, repealed: SI 2012/ 2401 Sch.1 para.29

29. Legal Services Act 2007
see *Atrium Medical Corp v DSB Invest Holding SA* [2011] EWHC 74 (Pat), [2012] Bus. L.R. 133 (Ch D (Patents Ct)), Lewison, J.
applied: 2012 c.10 s.59, SI 2012/ 1128 Art.4, SI 2012/ 3098 Reg.24, Reg.40, Reg.41
Part 3, applied: 2012 c.10 s.59
Part 5, applied: 2012 c.10 s.59
s.1, see *Media Protection Services Ltd v Crawford* [2012] EWHC 2373 (Admin), [2012] C.P. Rep. 48 (DC), Stanley Burnton, L.J.
s.12, see *Media Protection Services Ltd v Crawford* [2012] EWHC 2373 (Admin), [2012] C.P. Rep. 48 (DC), Stanley Burnton, L.J.
s.13, applied: SI 2012/ 1726 r.2.4
s.18, see *Atrium Medical Corp v DSB Invest Holding SA* [2011] EWHC 74 (Pat), [2012] Bus. L.R. 133 (Ch D (Patents Ct)), Lewison, J.
s.64, amended: 2012 c.21 Sch.18 para.125
s.69, applied: SI 2012/ 2987
s.69, enabling: SI 2012/ 2987
s.70, applied: SI 2012/ 2987
s.127, see *Media Protection Services Ltd v Crawford* [2012] EWHC 2373 (Admin), [2012] C.P. Rep. 48 (DC), Stanley Burnton, L.J.
s.128, applied: SI 2012/ 3092 Art.2
s.128, enabling: SI 2012/ 3092
s.130, applied: SI 2012/ 3092
s.138, amended: SI 2012/ 3091 Art.2
s.139, applied: SI 2012/ 3091
s.139, enabling: SI 2012/ 3091
s.147, see *Deputy Chief Legal Ombudsman v Young* [2011] EWHC 2923 (Admin), [2012] 1 W.L.R. 3227 (QBD), Lindblom, J.
s.149, see *Deputy Chief Legal Ombudsman v Young* [2011] EWHC 2923 (Admin), [2012] 1 W.L.R. 3227 (QBD), Lindblom, J.
s.169, amended: 2012 c.21 Sch.18 para.125
s.194, amended: 2012 c.10 s.61, Sch.5 para.68
s.195, amended: 2012 c.21 Sch.18 para.125
s.206, applied: SI 2012/ 2987
Sch.1 para.7, amended: SI 2012/ 2404 Sch.2 para.61
Sch.2, see *Media Protection Services Ltd v Crawford* [2012] EWHC 2373 (Admin), [2012] C.P. Rep. 48 (DC), Stanley Burnton, L.J.
Sch.2 para.4, see *Media Protection Services Ltd v Crawford* [2012] EWHC 2373 (Admin), [2012] C.P. Rep. 48 (DC), Stanley Burnton, L.J.
Sch.3, see *Kynaston v Carroll* [2011] EWHC 2179 (QB), [2012] 1 Costs L.O. 5 (QBD), Burnett, J.
Sch.15 para.8, amended: SI 2012/ 2404 Sch.2 para.61
Sch.16 Part 1 para.51, repealed (in part): 2012 c.10 Sch.5 Part 2
Sch.16 Part 2 para.108, repealed (in part): 2012 c.10 Sch.5 Part 2
Sch.21 para.43, repealed: SI 2012/ 2398 Sch.2 para.10
Sch.21 para.46, repealed: SI 2012/ 2398 Sch.1 para.10
Sch.21 para.128, repealed: 2012 c.10 Sch.5 Part 2

2007– cont.

29. Legal Services Act 2007– *cont.*
Sch.21 para.136, repealed: 2012 c.14 Sch.39 para.5

30. UK Borders Act 2007
see *R. (on the application of HA (Nigeria)) v Secretary of State for the Home Department* [2012] EWHC 979 (Admin), [2012] Med. L.R. 353 (QBD (Admin)), Singh, J.
s.5, enabling: SI 2012/ 594
s.6, applied: SI 2012/ 594
s.6, enabling: SI 2012/ 594
s.7, enabling: SI 2012/ 594
s.24, amended: SI 2012/ 2595 Art.16
s.31, repealed: 2012 c.9 Sch.10 Part 9
s.32, see *Mohan v Secretary of State for the Home Department* [2012] EWCA Civ 1363, Times, December 26, 2012 (CA (Civ Div)), Sir Maurice Kay (VP CA Civ); see *RG (Nepal) v Secretary of State for the Home Department* [2012] EWCA Civ 62, [2012] I.N.L.R. 401 (CA (Civ Div)), Rix, L.J.; see *Sanade (British Children: Zambrano: Dereci), Re* [2012] UKUT 48 (IAC), [2012] Imm. A.R. 597 (UT (IAC)), Blake, J.
s.33, see *RG (Nepal) v Secretary of State for the Home Department* [2012] EWCA Civ 62, [2012] I.N.L.R. 401 (CA (Civ Div)), Rix, L.J.; see *Sanade (British Children: Zambrano: Dereci), Re* [2012] UKUT 48 (IAC), [2012] Imm. A.R. 597 (UT (IAC)), Blake, J.
s.36, see *R. (on the application of HA (Nigeria)) v Secretary of State for the Home Department* [2012] EWHC 979 (Admin), [2012] Med. L.R. 353 (QBD (Admin)), Singh, J.
s.36, applied: 2012 c.10 Sch.1 para.25
s.52, applied: SI 2012/ 2876 Art.2, Art.3
s.52, enabling: SI 2012/ 2876
s.55, enabling: SI 2012/ 2876
s.56A, added: 2012 c.10 s.140
s.56A, applied: 2012 c.10 s.141

2008

2. Banking (Special Provisions) Act 2008
s.15, amended: SI 2012/ 917 Sch.1 para.3

4. Criminal Justice and Immigration Act 2008
Commencement Orders: 2012 c.10 s.64
s.1, applied: SI 2012/ 1696 Sch.1
s.13, repealed: 2012 c.10 Sch.21 para.35
s.14, repealed: 2012 c.10 Sch.21 para.35
s.15, repealed: 2012 c.10 Sch.21 para.35
s.16, repealed: 2012 c.10 Sch.21 para.35
s.18, repealed (in part): 2012 c.10 Sch.21 para.35
s.20, repealed (in part): 2012 c.10 Sch.10 para.42, Sch.16 para.20
s.21, repealed (in part): 2012 c.10 s.110
s.22, repealed (in part): 2012 c.10 s.110
s.23, repealed: 2012 c.10 s.110
s.26, repealed: 2012 c.10 Sch.16 para.20
s.27, repealed: 2012 c.10 Sch.16 para.20
s.28, repealed: 2012 c.10 Sch.16 para.20
s.29, repealed (in part): 2012 c.10 s.114
s.32, repealed: 2012 c.10 Sch.16 para.20
s.33, repealed (in part): 2012 c.10 s.118, Sch.16 para.20
s.34, repealed: 2012 c.10 s.118
s.48, repealed (in part): 2012 c.10 Sch.24 para.29
s.56, repealed: 2012 c.10 Sch.5 Part 2
s.57, repealed: 2012 c.10 Sch.5 Part 2
s.58, repealed: 2012 c.10 Sch.5 Part 2

2008– cont.

4. Criminal Justice and Immigration Act 2008– *cont.*

s.63, see *R. v Burns (Robert)* [2012] EWCA Crim 192, [2012] 2 Cr. App. R. (S.) 66 (CA (Crim Div)), Richards, L.J.; see *R. v Oliver (Philip)* [2011] EWCA Crim 3114, [2012] 2 Cr. App. R. (S.) 45 (CA (Crim Div)), Pitchford, L.J.

s.63, applied: SI 2012/951 Reg.4, SI 2012/1925 Reg.4

s.67, see *R. v Oliver (Philip)* [2011] EWCA Crim 3114, [2012] 2 Cr. App. R. (S.) 45 (CA (Crim Div)), Pitchford, L.J.

s.76, amended: 2012 c.10 s.148

s.84, applied: SI 2012/1726 r.52.10

s.85, applied: SI 2012/1726 r.52.10

s.91, referred to: SI 2012/1726 r.52.10

s.92, referred to: SI 2012/1726 r.52.10

s.119, amended: 2012 c.7 Sch.14 para.107

s.119, repealed (in part): 2012 c.7 Sch.5 para.153, Sch.14 para.107

Sch.1 Part 2 para.14, amended: 2012 c.10 s.81

Sch.1 Part 2 para.19, amended: 2012 c.10 Sch.5 para.69

Sch.1 Part 2 para.20, amended: 2012 c.10 s.82

Sch.1 Part 2 para.20, repealed (in part): 2012 c.10 s.82

Sch.1 Part 4 para.32, amended: 2012 c.10 s.83

Sch.2, applied: SI 2012/1726 r.44.1

Sch.2 Part 2 para.6, amended: 2012 c.10 s.83, s.84

Sch.2 Part 2 para.8, amended: 2012 c.10 s.83, s.84

Sch.2 Part 2 para.10, amended: 2012 c.10 s.84

Sch.2 Part 4 para.16, amended: 2012 c.10 s.83

Sch.2 Part 4 para.16A, added: 2012 c.10 s.83

Sch.4 Part 1 para.21, repealed: 2012 c.10 Sch.25 Part 2

Sch.4 Part 1 para.80, repealed: 2012 c.10 s.64

Sch.4 Part 1 para.86, repealed: 2012 c.10 s.70

Sch.5, repealed: 2012 c.10 Sch.21 para.35

Sch.6 para.1, repealed: 2012 c.10 s.110

Sch.6 para.2, repealed: 2012 c.10 s.110

Sch.9 para.2, repealed: 2012 c.10 Sch.24 para.30

Sch.10 para.2, repealed: 2012 c.10 Sch.25 Part 2

Sch.10 para.5, repealed: 2012 c.10 Sch.25 Part 2

Sch.14 para.6, amended: SI 2012/1809 Sch.1 Part 1

Sch.19, referred to: SI 2012/1726 r.52.10

Sch.19 Part 2 para.46, amended: SI 2012/1809 Sch.1 Part 1

Sch.22 Part 2 para.15, amended: 2012 asp 8 s.61

Sch.25 Part 2 para.24, repealed: 2012 c.10 s.64

Sch.26 Part 2 para.5, repealed: 2012 c.10 Sch.12 para.55

Sch.26 Part 2 para.29, repealed (in part): 2012 c.10 Sch.16 para.20

Sch.26 Part 2 para.76, repealed: 2012 c.10 Sch.21 para.35

Sch.27 Part 2 para.8, repealed: 2012 c.10 Sch.16 para.20

Sch.27 Part 2 para.9, repealed: 2012 c.10 Sch.16 para.20

Sch.27 Part 5 para.27, varied: 2012 c.10 s.148

6. Child Maintenance and Other Payments Act 2008

Commencement Orders: SI 2012/1649 Art.2; SI 2012/2523 Art.2; SI 2012/3042 Art.2, Art.3, Art.4, Art.5

Part 4, applied: 2012 c.10 Sch.1 para.8, Sch.1 para.15

s.1, repealed: SI 2012/2007 Sch.1 para.71

s.2, repealed: SI 2012/2007 Sch.1 para.71

s.3, repealed: SI 2012/2007 Sch.1 para.71

s.4, repealed: SI 2012/2007 Sch.1 para.71

s.5, repealed: SI 2012/2007 Sch.1 para.71

2008– cont.

6. Child Maintenance and Other Payments Act 2008– *cont.*

s.6, amended: 2012 c.5 s.140, s.141, SI 2012/2007 Sch.1 para.72

s.7, repealed: SI 2012/2007 Sch.1 para.73

s.8, amended: SI 2012/2007 Sch.1 para.74

s.9, repealed: SI 2012/2007 Sch.1 para.75

s.10, repealed: SI 2012/2007 Sch.1 para.75

s.11, repealed: SI 2012/2007 Sch.1 para.75

s.12, repealed: SI 2012/2007 Sch.1 para.75

s.13, applied: SI 2012/2007 Art.3

s.13, repealed: SI 2012/2007 Sch.1 para.76

s.14, repealed: SI 2012/2007 Sch.1 para.76

s.17, amended: SI 2012/2007 Sch.1 para.77

s.18, amended: SI 2012/2007 Sch.1 para.78

s.25, amended: SI 2012/2007 Sch.1 para.79

s.27, amended: SI 2012/2007 Sch.1 para.80

s.28, amended: SI 2012/2007 Sch.1 para.81

s.29, amended: SI 2012/2007 Sch.1 para.82

s.30, amended: SI 2012/2007 Sch.1 para.83

s.32, amended: SI 2012/2007 Sch.1 para.84

s.33, amended: SI 2012/2007 Sch.1 para.85

s.34, amended: SI 2012/2007 Sch.1 para.86

s.39, amended: SI 2012/2007 Sch.1 para.87

s.40, amended: SI 2012/2007 Sch.1 para.88

s.44, repealed: SI 2012/2007 Sch.1 para.89

s.45, repealed (in part): 2012 c.5 Sch.14 Part 1

s.46, enabling: SI 2012/918

s.49, amended: 2012 c.5 Sch.11 para.16

s.50, amended: 2012 c.5 Sch.11 para.17

s.50, applied: 2012 c.5 s.102

s.53, amended: 2012 c.5 Sch.11 para.18

s.53, applied: SI 2012/918

s.53, enabling: SI 2012/918

s.55, amended: SI 2012/2007 Sch.1 para.90

s.55, repealed (in part): SI 2012/2007 Sch.1 para.90

s.55, enabling: SI 2012/2785

s.56, repealed (in part): SI 2012/2007 Sch.1 para.91

s.57, enabling: SI 2012/2785

s.59, repealed (in part): SI 2012/2007 Sch.1 para.92

s.61, repealed (in part): SI 2012/2007 Sch.1 para.93

s.62, enabling: SI 2012/1649, SI 2012/2523, SI 2012/3042

Sch.1 para.1, repealed: SI 2012/2007 Sch.1 para.71

Sch.1 para.2, repealed: SI 2012/2007 Sch.1 para.71

Sch.1 para.3, repealed: SI 2012/2007 Sch.1 para.71

Sch.1 para.4, repealed: SI 2012/2007 Sch.1 para.71

Sch.1 para.5, repealed: SI 2012/2007 Sch.1 para.71

Sch.1 para.6, repealed: SI 2012/2007 Sch.1 para.71

Sch.1 para.7, repealed: SI 2012/2007 Sch.1 para.71

Sch.1 para.8, repealed: SI 2012/2007 Sch.1 para.71

Sch.1 para.9, repealed: SI 2012/2007 Sch.1 para.71

Sch.1 para.10, repealed: SI 2012/2007 Sch.1 para.71

Sch.1 para.11, repealed: SI 2012/2007 Sch.1 para.71

Sch.1 para.12, repealed: SI 2012/2007 Sch.1 para.71

Sch.1 para.13, repealed: SI 2012/2007 Sch.1 para.71

Sch.1 para.14, repealed: SI 2012/2007 Sch.1 para.71

Sch.1 para.15, repealed: SI 2012/2007 Sch.1 para.71

Sch.1 para.16, repealed: SI 2012/2007 Sch.1 para.71

Sch.1 para.17, repealed: SI 2012/2007 Sch.1 para.71

Sch.1 para.18, repealed: SI 2012/2007 Sch.1 para.71

Sch.1 para.19, repealed: SI 2012/2007 Sch.1 para.71

Sch.1 para.20, repealed: SI 2012/2007 Sch.1 para.71

Sch.1 para.21, repealed: SI 2012/2007 Sch.1 para.71

Sch.1 para.22, repealed: SI 2012/2007 Sch.1 para.71

Sch.1 para.23, repealed: SI 2012/2007 Sch.1 para.71

Sch.1 para.24, repealed: SI 2012/2007 Sch.1 para.71

Sch.1 para.25, repealed: SI 2012/2007 Sch.1 para.71

2008—cont.

6. Child Maintenance and Other Payments Act 2008—*cont.*

Sch.1 para.26, repealed: SI 2012/ 2007 Sch.1 para.71
Sch.1 para.27, repealed: SI 2012/ 2007 Sch.1 para.71
Sch.1 para.28, repealed: SI 2012/ 2007 Sch.1 para.71
Sch.1 para.29, repealed: SI 2012/ 2007 Sch.1 para.71
Sch.1 para.30, repealed: SI 2012/ 2007 Sch.1 para.71
Sch.1 para.31, repealed: SI 2012/ 2007 Sch.1 para.71
Sch.1 para.32, repealed: SI 2012/ 2007 Sch.1 para.71
Sch.2, repealed: SI 2012/ 2007 Sch.1 para.76
Sch.3 Part 1 para.40, repealed (in part): SI 2012/ 2007 Sch.1 para.94
Sch.3 Part 2 para.55, repealed: SI 2012/ 2007 Sch.1 para.94
Sch.4, applied: SI 2012/ 2785 Reg.1
Sch.4 para.8, amended: SI 2012/ 2007 Sch.1 para.95
Sch.4 para.9, amended: SI 2012/ 2007 Sch.1 para.95
Sch.5 para.1, amended: SI 2012/ 2007 Sch.1 para.96
Sch.5 para.2, amended: SI 2012/ 2007 Sch.1 para.96
Sch.5 para.3, amended: 2012 c.5 s.136, SI 2012/ 2007 Sch.1 para.96
Sch.5 para.6, amended: SI 2012/ 2007 Sch.1 para.96
Sch.6 para.1, repealed: SI 2012/ 2007 Sch.1 para.89
Sch.6 para.2, repealed: SI 2012/ 2007 Sch.1 para.89
Sch.6 para.3, repealed: SI 2012/ 2007 Sch.1 para.89
Sch.6 para.4, repealed: SI 2012/ 2007 Sch.1 para.89
Sch.6 para.5, repealed: SI 2012/ 2007 Sch.1 para.89
Sch.6 para.6, repealed: SI 2012/ 2007 Sch.1 para.89
Sch.7 para.1, amended: SI 2012/ 2007 Sch.1 para.97
Sch.7 para.2, repealed (in part): 2012 c.5 Sch.14 Part 13, Sch.14 Part 1
Sch.7 para.3, repealed (in part): 2012 c.5 Sch.14 Part 14

7. European Union (Amendment) Act 2008

s.3, enabling: SI 2012/ 1809

9. Finance Act 2008

s.21, applied: SI 2012/ 1386
s.21, enabling: SI 2012/ 1386
s.31, repealed: 2012 c.14 Sch.7 para.3
s.44, repealed: 2012 c.14 Sch.18 para.23
s.58, see *R. (on the application of Huitson) v Revenue and Customs Commissioners* [2011] EWCA Civ 893, [2012] Q.B. 489 (CA (Civ Div)), Mummery, L.J.
s.95, repealed (in part): 2012 c.14 Sch.39 para.8
s.124, see *R. (on the application of ToTel Ltd) v First-tier Tribunal (Tax Chamber)* [2011] EWHC 652 (Admin), [2012] Q.B. 358 (QBD (Admin)), Simon, J.; see *R. (on the application of ToTel Ltd) v First-tier Tribunal (Tax Chamber)* [2012] EWCA Civ 1401, [2012] B.V.C. 333 (CA (Civ Div)), Lord Neuberger (M.R.)
s.124, enabling: SI 2012/ 533
s.130, see *Emblaze Mobility Solutions Ltd v Revenue and Customs Commissioners* [2012] B.V.C. 174 (Ch D), Peter Leaver Q.C.
s.130, repealed (in part): 2012 c.14 s.50
s.133, see *Emblaze Mobility Solutions Ltd v Revenue and Customs Commissioners* [2012] B.V.C. 174 (Ch D), Peter Leaver Q.C.
s.133, amended: 2012 c.14 s.50
s.136, enabling: SI 2012/ 689
s.160, applied: SI 2012/ 266
s.160, enabling: SI 2012/ 266
Sch.1 Part 2 para.48, repealed: 2012 c.14 Sch.7 para.28
Sch.14 para.2, repealed: 2012 c.14 Sch.16 para.247
Sch.17 para.1, repealed: 2012 c.14 Sch.16 para.247
Sch.17 para.2, repealed: 2012 c.14 Sch.16 para.247

2008—cont.

9. Finance Act 2008—*cont.*

Sch.17 para.4, applied: 2012 c.14 Sch.17 para.16
Sch.17 para.4, repealed: 2012 c.14 Sch.16 para.247
Sch.17 para.5, repealed: 2012 c.14 Sch.16 para.247
Sch.17 para.6, repealed: 2012 c.14 Sch.16 para.247
Sch.17 para.8, repealed: 2012 c.14 Sch.16 para.247
Sch.17 para.9, repealed (in part): 2012 c.14 Sch.16 para.247
Sch.17 para.10, repealed: 2012 c.14 Sch.16 para.247
Sch.17 para.11, repealed: 2012 c.14 Sch.16 para.247
Sch.17 para.17, repealed: 2012 c.14 Sch.16 para.247
Sch.17 para.18, repealed: 2012 c.14 Sch.16 para.247
Sch.17 para.20, repealed: 2012 c.14 Sch.16 para.247
Sch.17 para.21, repealed: 2012 c.14 Sch.16 para.247
Sch.17 para.22, repealed: 2012 c.14 Sch.16 para.247
Sch.17 para.26, repealed: 2012 c.14 Sch.16 para.247
Sch.17 para.28, repealed (in part): 2012 c.14 Sch.16 para.247
Sch.17 para.31, repealed: 2012 c.14 Sch.16 para.247
Sch.17 para.32, repealed: 2012 c.14 Sch.16 para.247
Sch.17 para.33, repealed: 2012 c.14 Sch.16 para.247
Sch.17 para.34, repealed: 2012 c.14 Sch.16 para.247
Sch.17 para.37, repealed: 2012 c.14 Sch.16 para.247
Sch.18 para.1, repealed: 2012 c.14 Sch.18 para.23
Sch.18 para.2, repealed: 2012 c.14 Sch.18 para.23
Sch.18 para.3, repealed: 2012 c.14 Sch.18 para.23
Sch.18 para.4, repealed: 2012 c.14 Sch.18 para.23
Sch.18 para.5, repealed: 2012 c.14 Sch.18 para.23
Sch.30 para.6, repealed: 2012 c.14 Sch.39 para.8
Sch.31 Part 1 para.4, repealed: 2012 c.14 Sch.39 para.8
Sch.31 Part 2 para.9, repealed: 2012 c.14 Sch.39 para.8
Sch.36 Part 1 para.5A, added: 2012 c.14 s.224
Sch.36 Part 1 para.6, amended: 2012 c.14 s.224
Sch.36 Part 4 para.23, applied: 2012 c.14 Sch.38 para.17
Sch.36 Part 5 para.31, amended: 2012 c.14 s.224
Sch.36 Part 9 para.63, amended: SI 2012/ 3062 Reg.6
Sch.39 para.21, repealed: 2012 c.14 Sch.39 para.31
Sch.41, applied: 2012 c.14 Sch.38 para.34
Sch.41 para.1, amended: 2012 c.14 Sch.23 para.15, Sch.24 para.30, Sch.24 para.57, Sch.25 para.11, Sch.28 para.18
Sch.42 para.2, repealed (in part): 2012 c.14 s.187

13. Regulatory Enforcement and Sanctions Act 2008

Part 1, applied: SI 2012/ 246 Art.4
Part 2, applied: SI 2012/ 246 Art.4
Part 3, applied: 2012 c.19 Sch.11 para.18
s.1, repealed (in part): SI 2012/ 246 Sch.1 para.1
s.2, repealed: SI 2012/ 246 Sch.1 para.1
s.5, amended: SI 2012/ 246 Sch.1 para.3
s.6, amended: SI 2012/ 246 Sch.1 para.1, Sch.1 para.4
s.6, repealed (in part): SI 2012/ 246 Sch.1 para.1
s.7, repealed: SI 2012/ 246 Sch.1 para.1
s.8, repealed: SI 2012/ 246 Sch.1 para.1
s.9, repealed: SI 2012/ 246 Sch.1 para.1
s.10, amended: SI 2012/ 246 Sch.1 para.5
s.10, repealed (in part): SI 2012/ 246 Sch.1 para.1
s.11, amended: SI 2012/ 246 Sch.1 para.1, Sch.1 para.6
s.11, applied: SI 2012/ 246 Sch.2 para.1
s.11, repealed (in part): SI 2012/ 246 Sch.1 para.1
s.12, amended: SI 2012/ 246 Sch.1 para.7
s.13, repealed: SI 2012/ 246 Sch.1 para.1
s.14, repealed: SI 2012/ 246 Sch.1 para.1

2008–cont.

13. Regulatory Enforcement and Sanctions Act 2008–*cont.*
s.15, repealed: SI 2012/246 Sch.1 para.1
s.16, amended: SI 2012/246 Sch.1 para.1, Sch.1 para.8
s.16, repealed (in part): SI 2012/246 Sch.1 para.1
s.17, repealed: SI 2012/246 Sch.1 para.1
s.18, applied: SI 2012/246
s.18, enabling: SI 2012/246
s.20, amended: SI 2012/246 Sch.1 para.1
s.20, applied: SI 2012/246
s.20, repealed (in part): SI 2012/246 Sch.1 para.1
s.21, amended: SI 2012/246 Sch.1 para.1
s.25, amended: SI 2012/246 Sch.1 para.10
s.26, amended: SI 2012/246 Sch.1 para.11
s.28, amended: SI 2012/246 Sch.1 para.12
s.30, amended: SI 2012/246 Sch.1 para.13
s.32, repealed: SI 2012/246 Sch.1 para.1
s.33, amended: SI 2012/246 Sch.1 para.1, Sch.1 para.14
s.33, repealed (in part): SI 2012/246 Sch.1 para.1
s.33, substituted: SI 2012/246 Sch.1 para.14
s.35, amended: SI 2012/246 Sch.1 para.1
s.73, amended: 2012 c.19 s.104
Sch.1 para.1, repealed: SI 2012/246 Sch.1 para.1
Sch.1 para.2, repealed: SI 2012/246 Sch.1 para.1
Sch.1 para.3, repealed: SI 2012/246 Sch.1 para.1
Sch.1 para.4, repealed: SI 2012/246 Sch.1 para.1
Sch.1 para.5, repealed: SI 2012/246 Sch.1 para.1
Sch.1 para.6, repealed: SI 2012/246 Sch.1 para.1
Sch.1 para.7, repealed: SI 2012/246 Sch.1 para.1
Sch.1 para.8, repealed: SI 2012/246 Sch.1 para.1
Sch.1 para.9, repealed: SI 2012/246 Sch.1 para.1
Sch.1 para.10, repealed: SI 2012/246 Sch.1 para.1
Sch.1 para.11, amended: SI 2012/246 Sch.1 para.15
Sch.1 para.11, repealed (in part): SI 2012/246 Sch.1 para.1
Sch.1 para.12, repealed: SI 2012/246 Sch.1 para.1
Sch.1 para.13, applied: SI 2012/246 Art.7
Sch.1 para.13, repealed: SI 2012/246 Sch.1 para.1
Sch.1 para.14, repealed: SI 2012/246 Sch.1 para.1
Sch.1 para.15, repealed: SI 2012/246 Sch.1 para.1
Sch.1 para.17, repealed: SI 2012/246 Sch.1 para.1
Sch.1 para.18, repealed: SI 2012/246 Sch.1 para.1
Sch.1 para.19, repealed: SI 2012/246 Sch.1 para.1
Sch.1 para.20, repealed: SI 2012/246 Sch.1 para.1
Sch.2 para.1, repealed: SI 2012/246 Sch.1 para.1
Sch.2 para.2, repealed: SI 2012/246 Sch.1 para.1
Sch.2 para.3, repealed: SI 2012/246 Sch.1 para.1
Sch.2 para.4, repealed: SI 2012/246 Sch.1 para.1
Sch.2 para.5, repealed: SI 2012/246 Sch.1 para.1
Sch.2 para.6, repealed: SI 2012/246 Sch.1 para.1
Sch.4 para.1, amended: SI 2012/246 Sch.1 para.16
Sch.4 para.2, amended: SI 2012/246 Sch.1 para.16
Sch.4 para.3, amended: SI 2012/246 Sch.1 para.16
Sch.4 para.4, amended: SI 2012/246 Sch.1 para.16
Sch.4 para.5, amended: SI 2012/246 Sch.1 para.16
Sch.4 para.6, amended: SI 2012/246 Sch.1 para.16
Sch.4 para.7, amended: SI 2012/246 Sch.1 para.16
Sch.4 para.8, amended: SI 2012/246 Sch.1 para.16
Sch.5, amended: 2012 c.19 s.103, 2012 c.21 Sch.18 para.126
Sch.7, amended: 2012 c.19 s.103

14. Health and Social Care Act 2008
Commencement Orders: 2012 c.7 s.231, 2012 c.7 Sch.15 para.71, para.75
applied: 2012 c.7 s.288
Part 1, referred to: 2012 c.7 s.82

2008–cont.

14. Health and Social Care Act 2008–*cont.*
Part 1 c.2, applied: 2012 c.7 s.82, s.128, s.288
s.1, applied: SI 2012/1631 Sch.5 para.6, SI 2012/2996 Sch.5 para.5
s.4, amended: 2012 c.7 s.189
s.8, enabling: SI 2012/1513
s.10, applied: SI 2012/1916 Reg.231, Reg.232
s.16, enabling: SI 2012/921
s.20, applied: SI 2012/921, SI 2012/1513
s.20, enabling: SI 2012/921, SI 2012/1186, SI 2012/1513
s.20A, added: 2012 c.7 s.280
s.20A, referred to: 2012 c.7 s.280
s.30, amended: 2012 c.7 Sch.5 para.155, Sch.13 para.15
s.30, repealed (in part): 2012 c.7 Sch.5 para.155
s.35, enabling: SI 2012/1513
s.39, amended: 2012 c.7 Sch.5 para.156, Sch.13 para.16
s.39, repealed (in part): 2012 c.7 Sch.5 para.156
s.45, repealed: 2012 c.7 Sch.17 para.12
s.45A, added: 2012 c.7 s.181
s.45A, amended: SI 2012/1831 Art.7
s.45A, applied: SI 2012/1640 Reg.3
s.45B, added: 2012 c.7 s.181
s.45C, added: 2012 c.7 s.181
s.45D, added: 2012 c.7 s.182
s.45D, applied: SI 2012/3094 Reg.43
s.46, amended: 2012 c.7 Sch.5 para.157
s.46, repealed (in part): 2012 c.7 Sch.5 para.157
s.48, amended: 2012 c.7 s.40, s.293, Sch.5 para.158
s.48, repealed (in part): 2012 c.7 Sch.5 para.158
s.49, amended: 2012 c.7 Sch.5 para.159
s.53, amended: 2012 c.7 Sch.17 para.12
s.53, repealed (in part): 2012 c.7 Sch.17 para.12
s.54, amended: 2012 c.7 s.293, Sch.5 para.160
s.54, repealed (in part): 2012 c.7 Sch.5 para.160
s.57, amended: 2012 c.7 s.293
s.59, amended: 2012 c.7 Sch.5 para.161, Sch.13 para.17
s.59, enabling: SI 2012/921
s.64, amended: 2012 c.7 Sch.5 para.162, Sch.19 para.11
s.65, enabling: SI 2012/921
s.70, amended: 2012 c.7 s.289, Sch.5 para.163
s.70, applied: 2012 c.7 s.291
s.72, amended: 2012 c.7 Sch.5 para.164
s.72, repealed (in part): 2012 c.7 Sch.5 para.164
s.80, amended: 2012 c.7 s.280
s.81, amended: 2012 c.7 Sch.5 para.165
s.82, amended: 2012 c.7 s.181, s.294
s.83, amended: 2012 c.7 s.181
s.86, enabling: SI 2012/921
s.87, enabling: SI 2012/921
s.97, amended: 2012 c.7 s.40, Sch.5 para.166, SI 2012/961 Sch.1 para.9
s.97, repealed (in part): 2012 c.7 Sch.5 para.166, Sch.14 para.109
s.98, repealed: 2012 c.7 s.231
s.99, repealed: 2012 c.7 s.231
s.100, repealed: 2012 c.7 s.231
s.101, repealed: 2012 c.7 s.231
s.102, repealed: 2012 c.7 s.231
s.103, repealed: 2012 c.7 s.231
s.104, repealed: 2012 c.7 s.231
s.105, repealed: 2012 c.7 s.231
s.106, repealed: 2012 c.7 s.231
s.107, repealed: 2012 c.7 s.231

2008– cont.

14. Health and Social Care Act 2008–*cont.*
s.108, repealed: 2012 c.7 s.231
s.109, repealed: 2012 c.7 s.231
s.110, repealed: 2012 c.7 s.231
s.118, repealed (in part): 2012 c.7 Sch.15 para.73
s.124, amended: 2012 c.7 Sch.15 para.45
s.125, amended: 2012 c.7 Sch.15 para.46
s.125, repealed (in part): 2012 c.7 Sch.15 para.46
s.126, amended: 2012 c.7 Sch.15 para.47
s.128, amended: 2012 c.7 Sch.15 para.75
s.145, see *R. (on the application of Broadway Care Centre Ltd) v Caerphilly CBC* [2012] EWHC 37 (Admin), (2012) 15 C.C.L. Rep. 82 (QBD (Admin)), Judge Seys-Llewellyn Q.C.
s.153, repealed (in part): 2012 c.7 Sch.5 para.167, Sch.14 para.110
s.157, repealed (in part): 2012 c.7 Sch.20 para.11
s.158, repealed: 2012 c.7 Sch.20 para.11
s.159, repealed (in part): 2012 c.7 Sch.7 para.24
s.161, amended: 2012 c.7 s.294
s.161, enabling: SI 2012/921, SI 2012/1186, SI 2012/1513, SI 2012/1640
s.162, applied: SI 2012/1513
s.162, repealed (in part): 2012 c.7 Sch.15 para.75
s.165, amended: 2012 c.7 s.294
s.167, enabling: SI 2012/1915
s.171, amended: 2012 c.7 Sch.15 para.48
Sch.1 para.3, enabling: SI 2012/1186
Sch.1 para.5, amended: 2012 c.7 s.292
Sch.1 para.6, amended: 2012 c.7 s.181
Sch.1 para.6, applied: 2012 c.7 s.280
Sch.1 para.6, enabling: SI 2012/1640
Sch.4 Part 1 para.1, repealed (in part): SI 2012/2401 Sch.1 para.31
Sch.5 Part 3 para.75, repealed: SI 2012/2401 Sch.1 para.32
Sch.5 Part 3 para.79, repealed: 2012 c.7 Sch.20 para.7
Sch.5 Part 3 para.80, repealed: 2012 c.7 Sch.20 para.7
Sch.5 Part 3 para.84, repealed: 2012 c.7 Sch.14 para.40
Sch.5 Part 3 para.92, repealed: 2012 c.9 Sch.10 Part 5
Sch.5 Part 3 para.93, repealed: 2012 c.9 Sch.10 Part 5
Sch.6 para.1, repealed: 2012 c.7 s.231
Sch.6 para.2, repealed: 2012 c.7 s.231
Sch.6 para.3, repealed: 2012 c.7 s.231
Sch.6 para.4, repealed: 2012 c.7 s.231
Sch.6 para.5, repealed: 2012 c.7 s.231
Sch.6 para.6, repealed: 2012 c.7 s.231
Sch.6 para.7, repealed: 2012 c.7 s.231
Sch.6 para.8, repealed: 2012 c.7 s.231
Sch.6 para.9, repealed: 2012 c.7 s.231
Sch.6 para.10, repealed: 2012 c.7 s.231
Sch.6 para.11, repealed: 2012 c.7 s.231
Sch.6 para.12, repealed: 2012 c.7 s.231
Sch.6 para.13, repealed: 2012 c.7 s.231
Sch.6 para.14, repealed: 2012 c.7 s.231
Sch.6 para.15, repealed: 2012 c.7 s.231
Sch.6 para.16, repealed: 2012 c.7 s.231
Sch.6 para.17, repealed: 2012 c.7 s.231
Sch.6 para.18, repealed: 2012 c.7 s.231
Sch.6 para.19, repealed: 2012 c.7 s.231
Sch.6 para.20, repealed: 2012 c.7 s.231
Sch.6 para.21, repealed: 2012 c.7 s.231
Sch.6 para.22, repealed: 2012 c.7 s.231

2008– cont.

14. Health and Social Care Act 2008–*cont.*
Sch.6 para.23, repealed: 2012 c.7 s.231
Sch.7 Part 1 para.1, repealed: 2012 c.7 s.231
Sch.7 Part 1 para.2, repealed: 2012 c.7 s.231
Sch.7 Part 1 para.3, repealed: 2012 c.7 s.231
Sch.7 Part 1 para.4, repealed: 2012 c.7 s.231
Sch.7 Part 1 para.5, repealed: 2012 c.7 s.231
Sch.7 Part 1 para.6, repealed: 2012 c.7 s.231
Sch.7 Part 1 para.7, repealed: 2012 c.7 s.231
Sch.7 Part 1 para.8, repealed: 2012 c.7 s.231
Sch.7 Part 1 para.9, repealed: 2012 c.7 s.231
Sch.7 Part 1 para.10, repealed: 2012 c.7 s.231
Sch.7 Part 1 para.11, repealed: 2012 c.7 s.231
Sch.7 Part 1 para.12, repealed: 2012 c.7 s.231
Sch.7 Part 1 para.13, repealed: 2012 c.7 s.231
Sch.7 Part 1 para.14, repealed: 2012 c.7 s.231
Sch.7 Part 1 para.15, repealed: 2012 c.7 s.231
Sch.7 Part 1 para.16, repealed: 2012 c.7 s.231
Sch.7 Part 1 para.17, repealed: 2012 c.7 s.231
Sch.7 Part 1 para.18, repealed: 2012 c.7 s.231
Sch.7 Part 1 para.19, repealed: 2012 c.7 s.231
Sch.7 Part 1 para.20, repealed: 2012 c.7 s.231
Sch.7 Part 1 para.21, repealed: 2012 c.7 s.231
Sch.7 Part 1 para.22, repealed: 2012 c.7 s.231
Sch.7 Part 1 para.23, repealed: 2012 c.7 s.231
Sch.7 Part 2 para.24, repealed: 2012 c.7 s.231
Sch.7 Part 2 para.25, repealed: 2012 c.7 s.231
Sch.7 Part 2 para.26, repealed: 2012 c.7 s.231
Sch.7 Part 2 para.27, repealed: 2012 c.7 s.231
Sch.7 Part 2 para.28, repealed: 2012 c.7 s.231
Sch.7 Part 2 para.29, repealed: 2012 c.7 s.231
Sch.7 Part 2 para.30, repealed: 2012 c.7 s.231
Sch.7 Part 2 para.31, repealed: 2012 c.7 s.231
Sch.7 Part 2 para.32, repealed: 2012 c.7 s.231
Sch.7 Part 2 para.33, repealed: 2012 c.7 s.231
Sch.7 Part 2 para.34, repealed: 2012 c.7 s.231
Sch.7 Part 2 para.35, repealed: 2012 c.7 s.231
Sch.7 Part 2 para.36, repealed: 2012 c.7 s.231
Sch.7 Part 2 para.37, repealed: 2012 c.7 s.231
Sch.7 Part 2 para.38, repealed: 2012 c.7 s.231
Sch.7 Part 2 para.39, repealed: 2012 c.7 s.231
Sch.7 Part 2 para.40, repealed: 2012 c.7 s.231
Sch.7 Part 2 para.41, repealed: 2012 c.7 s.231
Sch.7 Part 2 para.42, repealed: 2012 c.7 s.231
Sch.7 Part 2 para.43, repealed: 2012 c.7 s.231
Sch.7 Part 2 para.44, repealed: 2012 c.7 s.231
Sch.7 Part 2 para.45, repealed: 2012 c.7 s.231
Sch.7 Part 2 para.46, repealed: 2012 c.7 s.231
Sch.7 Part 2 para.47, repealed: 2012 c.7 s.231
Sch.7 Part 2 para.48, repealed: 2012 c.7 s.231
Sch.7 Part 2 para.49, repealed: 2012 c.7 s.231
Sch.7 Part 2 para.50, repealed: 2012 c.7 s.231
Sch.7 Part 2 para.51, repealed: 2012 c.7 s.231
Sch.8 para.1, repealed (in part): 2012 c.7 Sch.15 para.72
Sch.9 para.1, amended: 2012 c.7 Sch.15 para.49
Sch.9 para.2, amended: 2012 c.7 Sch.15 para.49
Sch.9 para.3, amended: 2012 c.7 Sch.15 para.49
Sch.9 para.4, amended: 2012 c.7 Sch.15 para.49
Sch.9 para.5, amended: 2012 c.7 Sch.15 para.49
Sch.9 para.6, amended: 2012 c.7 Sch.15 para.49
Sch.9 para.7, amended: 2012 c.7 Sch.15 para.49
Sch.9 para.8, amended: 2012 c.7 Sch.15 para.49
Sch.9 para.9, amended: 2012 c.7 Sch.15 para.49
Sch.9 para.9, repealed: 2012 c.7 Sch.15 para.49
Sch.9 para.10, amended: 2012 c.7 Sch.15 para.49
Sch.10 para.4, repealed (in part): 2012 c.7 Sch.15 para.71

2008–*cont.*

14. Health and Social Care Act 2008–*cont.*
Sch.10 para.5, repealed (in part): 2012 c.7 Sch.15 para.71
Sch.10 para.7, repealed: 2012 c.7 Sch.15 para.75
Sch.10 para.9, repealed: 2012 c.7 Sch.15 para.75
Sch.10 para.13, repealed (in part): 2012 c.7 Sch.15 para.71
Sch.10 para.14, repealed: 2012 c.7 Sch.15 para.75
Sch.10 para.15, repealed: 2012 c.7 Sch.15 para.75
Sch.10 para.18, repealed: 2012 c.7 Sch.15 para.75
Sch.10 para.20, repealed: 2012 c.7 Sch.20 para.7
Sch.10 para.21, repealed: 2012 c.7 Sch.20 para.7
Sch.10 para.22, repealed: 2012 c.7 Sch.15 para.74, Sch.20 para.7
Sch.10 para.23, repealed: 2012 c.7 Sch.20 para.7
Sch.10 para.26, repealed (in part): 2012 c.7 Sch.15 para.69, Sch.15 para.71
Sch.10 para.27, repealed: 2012 c.7 Sch.15 para.71
Sch.11 para.9, repealed: 2012 c.9 Sch.10 Part 2
Sch.14 para.2, repealed: 2012 c.7 Sch.20 para.9
Sch.14 para.3, repealed: 2012 c.7 Sch.20 para.9
Sch.14 para.4, repealed: 2012 c.7 Sch.20 para.9
Sch.14 para.5, repealed: 2012 c.7 Sch.20 para.10

17. Housing and Regeneration Act 2008
s.32, applied: SI 2012/702 Sch.2 para.5
s.180, applied: SI 2012/696 Reg.4
s.180, enabling: SI 2012/696
s.193, applied: SI 2012/628 Art.15
s.194, applied: SI 2012/628 Art.15
s.321, enabling: SI 2012/2552
Sch.4 Part 1 para.8, amended: SI 2012/2590 Sch.1 para.3
Sch.4 Part 2 para.15, amended: SI 2012/2590 Sch.1 para.3
Sch.4 Part 5 para.40, amended: SI 2012/2590 Sch.1 para.3

18. Crossrail Act 2008
applied: SI 2012/3102 Sch.1, SI 2012/3103 Sch.1, SI 2012/3104 Sch.1, SI 2012/3105 Sch.1, SI 2012/3106 Sch.1, SI 2012/3107 Sch.1
s.6, see *Khurana v Transport for London* [2012] R.V.R. 42 (UT (Lands)), PR Francis FRICS
Sch.9 para.5, amended: SI 2012/2590 Sch.1 para.4
Sch.14 para.14, applied: SI 2012/3102 Sch.1, SI 2012/3103 Sch.1, SI 2012/3104 Sch.1, SI 2012/3105 Sch.1, SI 2012/3106 Sch.1, SI 2012/3107 Sch.1
Sch.17 Part 4 para.6, amended: SI 2012/2590 Sch.1 para.4
Sch.17 Part 5 para.1, amended: SI 2012/1659 Sch.3 para.19
Sch.17 Part 5 para.2, amended: SI 2012/1659 Sch.3 para.19
Sch.17 Part 5 para.3, amended: SI 2012/1659 Sch.3 para.19
Sch.17 Part 5 para.4, amended: SI 2012/1659 Sch.3 para.19
Sch.17 Part 5 para.5, amended: SI 2012/1659 Sch.3 para.19
Sch.17 Part 5 para.6, amended: SI 2012/1659 Sch.3 para.19
Sch.17 Part 5 para.7, amended: SI 2012/1659 Sch.3 para.19
Sch.17 Part 5 para.8, amended: SI 2012/1659 Sch.3 para.19
Sch.17 Part 5 para.9, amended: SI 2012/1659 Sch.3 para.19
Sch.17 Part 5 para.10, amended: SI 2012/1659 Sch.3 para.19

2008–*cont.*

18. Crossrail Act 2008–*cont.*
Sch.17 Part 5 para.11, amended: SI 2012/1659 Sch.3 para.19

22. Human Fertilisation and Embryology Act 2008
s.54, see *A v P* [2011] EWHC 1738 (Fam), [2012] Fam. 188 (Fam Div), Theis, J.; see *X (Children) (Parental Order: Retrospective Authorisation of Payments), Re* [2011] EWHC 3147 (Fam), [2012] 1 F.L.R. 1347 (Fam Div), Sir Nicholas Wall (President, Fam)
s.54, applied: SSI 2012/188
Sch.6 Part 1 para.38, repealed: 2012 c.10 Sch.5 Part 2

23. Children and Young Persons Act 2008
Commencement Orders: SI 2012/1553 Art.2
s.8, referred to: SI 2012/2813 Reg.2
s.22, disapplied: SI 2012/1553 Art.3
s.44, enabling: SI 2012/1553
Sch.1 para.8, repealed: 2012 c.10 Sch.12 para.56

24. Employment Act 2008
see *Edwards v Chesterfield Royal Hospital NHS Foundation Trust* [2012] 2 A.C. 22 (SC), Lord Phillips (President)

25. Education and Skills Act 2008
Commencement Orders: SI 2012/2197 Art.2
s.16, amended: 2012 c.7 Sch.5 para.169
s.16, repealed (in part): 2012 c.7 Sch.5 para.169
s.77, amended: 2012 c.7 Sch.5 para.170
s.77, repealed (in part): 2012 c.7 Sch.5 para.170
s.92, applied: 2012 c.9 s.28
s.93A, added: SI 2012/976 Sch.1 para.22
s.93A, varied: SI 2012/976 Art.3
s.130, amended: SI 2012/3006 Art.13
s.141, amended: SI 2012/3006 Art.13
s.147, repealed (in part): 2012 c.9 Sch.10 Part 5
s.173, enabling: SI 2012/2197
Sch.1 Part 1 para.23, amended: SI 2012/3006 Art.13
Sch.1 Part 1 para.41, repealed (in part): 2012 c.9 Sch.10 Part 5
Sch.1 Part 2 para.74, repealed (in part): 2012 c.5 s.134
Sch.1 Part 2 para.89, repealed: 2012 c.9 Sch.10 Part 5

26. Local Transport Act 2008
Sch.4 Part 4 para.54, repealed (in part): 2012 c.19 Sch.8 para.4

27. Climate Change Act 2008
applied: SI 2012/3038 Sch.5 para.3

28. Counter-Terrorism Act 2008
Commencement Orders: SI 2012/1121 Art.2; SI 2012/1724 Art.2; SI 2012/1966 Art.2
see *Bank Mellat v HM Treasury* [2010] EWCA Civ 483, [2012] Q.B. 91 (CA (Civ Div)), Lord Neuberger of Abbotsbury MR
s.1, amended: 2012 c.9 Sch.9 para.33
s.14, repealed (in part): 2012 c.9 Sch.10 Part 1
s.16, repealed: 2012 c.9 Sch.10 Part 1
s.17, repealed: 2012 c.9 Sch.10 Part 1
s.18, applied: 2012 c.9 s.20
s.18, substituted: 2012 c.9 Sch.1 para.4
s.18A, applied: 2012 c.9 s.20
s.18A, repealed (in part): 2012 c.10 Sch.24 para.31
s.18B, applied: 2012 c.9 s.20
s.18C, applied: 2012 c.9 s.20
s.18D, applied: 2012 c.9 s.20
s.18E, applied: 2012 c.9 s.20
s.22, applied: SI 2012/1793 Art.2, SI 2012/1793(a)
s.23, applied: SI 2012/1793 Art.2, SI 2012/1793(a)
s.26, applied: SI 2012/1793, SI 2012/1793(a), SI 2012/1793(b)

2008–cont.

28. Counter-Terrorism Act 2008–*cont.*
s.26, enabling: SI 2012/1793
s.42, applied: SI 2012/1726 r.63.1, r.68.1
s.45, amended: 2012 c.10 Sch.21 para.33
s.63, see *Bank Mellat v HM Treasury* [2011] EWCA Civ 1, [2012] Q.B. 101 (CA (Civ Div)), Maurice Kay, L.J.
s.63, repealed (in part): SI 2012/925 Reg.28
s.97, applied: SI 2012/1793
s.100, enabling: SI 2012/1121, SI 2012/1724, SI 2012/1966
Sch.6 para.5, amended: 2012 c.10 Sch.22 para.38
Sch.7, see *Bank Mellat v HM Treasury* [2010] EWCA Civ 483, [2012] Q.B. 91 (CA (Civ Div)), Lord Neuberger of Abbotsbury MR; see *Bank Mellat v HM Treasury* [2011] EWCA Civ 1, [2012] Q.B. 101 (CA (Civ Div)), Maurice Kay, L.J.
Sch.7, applied: SI 2012/1128 Art.4
Sch.7 Part 1 para.1, enabling: SI 2012/2904
Sch.7 Pt 1 para.1, see *Bank Mellat v HM Treasury* [2011] EWCA Civ 1, [2012] Q.B. 101 (CA (Civ Div)), Maurice Kay, L.J.
Sch.7 Part 2 para.3, enabling: SI 2012/2904
Sch.7 Part 3 para.9, enabling: SI 2012/2904
Sch.7 Pt 3 para.9, see *Bank Mellat v HM Treasury* [2011] EWCA Civ 1, [2012] Q.B. 101 (CA (Civ Div)), Maurice Kay, L.J.
Sch.7 Part 3 para.13, enabling: SI 2012/2904
Sch.7 Part 4 para.14, enabling: SI 2012/2904
Sch.7 Part 5 para.18, amended: 2012 c.21 Sch.18 para.127
Sch.7 Part 5 para.21, amended: 2012 c.21 Sch.18 para.127
Sch.7 Part 6 para.27, amended: 2012 c.21 Sch.18 para.127
Sch.7 Part 6 para.28, amended: 2012 c.21 Sch.18 para.127
Sch.7 Part 7 para.33, amended: 2012 c.21 Sch.18 para.127
Sch.7 Part 8 para.39, amended: 2012 c.21 Sch.18 para.127
Sch.7 Part 8 para.41, amended: 2012 c.21 Sch.18 para.127
Sch.7 Part 8 para.46, amended: 2012 c.21 Sch.18 para.127

29. Planning Act 2008
Commencement Orders: SI 2012/601 Art.2, Sch.1; SI 2012/802 Art.2, Sch.1
Part 5 c.2, referred to: SI 2012/1645 Art.3
Part 6 c.4, applied: SI 2012/2284, SI 2012/2635
s.4, enabling: SI 2012/2732
s.7, enabling: SI 2012/2732
s.14, amended: SI 2012/1645 Art.2
s.14, referred to: SI 2012/2284 Sch.1 Part 1, SI 2012/2635 Sch.1
s.14, enabling: SI 2012/1645
s.25, referred to: SI 2012/2284 Sch.1 Part 1, SI 2012/2635 Sch.1
s.29, amended: SI 2012/1645 Art.2
s.37, applied: SI 2012/2284, SI 2012/2635
s.37, enabling: SI 2012/2732
s.42, enabling: SI 2012/2732
s.48, enabling: SI 2012/2732
s.51, enabling: SI 2012/2732
s.53, see *R. (on the application of Innovia Cellophane Ltd) v Infrastructure Planning Commission* [2011] EWHC 2883 (Admin), [2012] P.T.S.R. 1132 (QBD (Admin)), Cranston, J.
s.56, enabling: SI 2012/2732

2008–cont.

29. Planning Act 2008–*cont.*
s.58, enabling: SI 2012/2732
s.59, enabling: SI 2012/2732
s.83, applied: SI 2012/2284, SI 2012/2635
s.114, enabling: SI 2012/2284, SI 2012/2635
s.115, see *R. (on the application of Innovia Cellophane Ltd) v Infrastructure Planning Commission* [2011] EWHC 2883 (Admin), [2012] P.T.S.R. 1132 (QBD (Admin)), Cranston, J.
s.115, applied: SI 2012/2284 Sch.1 Part 1
s.115, referred to: SI 2012/2635 Sch.1
s.115, enabling: SI 2012/2284, SI 2012/2635
s.120, enabling: SI 2012/2284, SI 2012/2635
s.122, enabling: SI 2012/2284, SI 2012/2635
s.125, applied: SI 2012/2284 Art.23, SI 2012/2635 Art.30, Art.31
s.125, referred to: SI 2012/2284 Art.20, Art.22
s.127, enabling: SI 2012/2732
s.138, applied: SI 2012/2284 Art.19, SI 2012/2635 Art.25
s.152, applied: SI 2012/2284 Art.14, Art.19, Art.23, SI 2012/2635 Art.25, Art.30, Art.31
s.203, applied: SI 2012/210
s.203, enabling: SI 2012/210
s.205, enabling: SI 2012/2975
s.209, enabling: SI 2012/2975
s.211, enabling: SI 2012/2975
s.214, enabling: SI 2012/2975
s.216, enabling: SI 2012/2975
s.217, enabling: SI 2012/2975
s.220, enabling: SI 2012/2975
s.222, applied: SI 2012/2975
s.222, enabling: SI 2012/2975
s.232, applied: SI 2012/1645
s.232, enabling: SI 2012/1645, SI 2012/2732
s.241, enabling: SI 2012/601, SI 2012/802
Sch.5 Part 1 para.1, enabling: SI 2012/2284, SI 2012/2635
Sch.5 Part 1 para.2, enabling: SI 2012/2284, SI 2012/2635
Sch.5 Part 1 para.3, enabling: SI 2012/2284, SI 2012/2635
Sch.5 Part 1 para.10, enabling: SI 2012/2284, SI 2012/2635
Sch.5 Part 1 para.11, enabling: SI 2012/2284, SI 2012/2635
Sch.5 Part 1 para.12, enabling: SI 2012/2284, SI 2012/2635
Sch.5 Part 1 para.13, enabling: SI 2012/2284, SI 2012/2635
Sch.5 Part 1 para.14, enabling: SI 2012/2284, SI 2012/2635
Sch.5 Part 1 para.15, enabling: SI 2012/2284, SI 2012/2635
Sch.5 Part 1 para.16, enabling: SI 2012/2284, SI 2012/2635
Sch.5 Part 1 para.17, enabling: SI 2012/2284, SI 2012/2635
Sch.5 Part 1 para.24, enabling: SI 2012/2284, SI 2012/2635
Sch.5 Part 1 para.26, enabling: SI 2012/2284, SI 2012/2635
Sch.5 Part 1 para.36, enabling: SI 2012/2284, SI 2012/2635
Sch.5 Part 1 para.37, enabling: SI 2012/2284, SI 2012/2635
Sch.6 para.2, enabling: SI 2012/2732
Sch.6 para.4, enabling: SI 2012/2732
Sch.6 para.6, enabling: SI 2012/2732

2008–cont.

30. Pensions Act 2008

Commencement Orders: SI 2012/683 Art.2; SI 2012/1682 Art.2, Sch.1, Sch.2; SI 2012/2480 Art.2

Part 1, applied: SI 2012/1388 Art.3

s.1, varied: SI 2012/1388 Art.2

s.2, enabling: SI 2012/215, SI 2012/1257

s.3, amended: SI 2012/1506 Art.2

s.3, applied: SI 2012/1506 Art.3

s.3, referred to: SI 2012/1506

s.3, enabling: SI 2012/215, SI 2012/1257

s.4, enabling: SI 2012/215

s.5, amended: SI 2012/1506 Art.2

s.5, applied: SI 2012/1388 Art.5, SI 2012/1506 Art.3

s.5, referred to: SI 2012/1506

s.5, enabling: SI 2012/215, SI 2012/1257

s.6, enabling: SI 2012/215, SI 2012/1257

s.7, applied: SI 2012/1388 Art.5

s.7, enabling: SI 2012/215, SI 2012/1257

s.8, enabling: SI 2012/1257

s.9, enabling: SI 2012/1257

s.10, enabling: SI 2012/215, SI 2012/1257

s.11, enabling: SI 2012/215

s.12, enabling: SI 2012/215, SI 2012/1813

s.13, amended: SI 2012/1506 Art.2

s.13, applied: SI 2012/1506 Art.3

s.13, referred to: SI 2012/1506, SI 2012/1506 Art.3

s.14, applied: SI 2012/1506

s.14, enabling: SI 2012/1506

s.15, enabling: SI 2012/215, SI 2012/1257

s.15A, enabling: SI 2012/1506

s.16, enabling: SI 2012/215, SI 2012/1257, SI 2012/2691

s.17, enabling: SI 2012/1257

s.18, enabling: SI 2012/1257

s.22, enabling: SI 2012/215, SI 2012/1257

s.23, enabling: SI 2012/215, SI 2012/1257

s.24, enabling: SI 2012/215, SI 2012/1257

s.25, enabling: SI 2012/1257

s.27, enabling: SI 2012/1257

s.28, enabling: SI 2012/1257

s.29, enabling: SI 2012/215, SI 2012/1813

s.30, enabling: SI 2012/215, SI 2012/1257, SI 2012/1813

s.33, enabling: SI 2012/1257

s.37, enabling: SI 2012/215, SI 2012/1257

s.38, enabling: SI 2012/215

s.40, enabling: SI 2012/215

s.41, enabling: SI 2012/215

s.43, enabling: SI 2012/215

s.52, enabling: SI 2012/215

s.54, enabling: SI 2012/215

s.58, applied: SI 2012/212 Art.2

s.58, enabling: SI 2012/212

s.60, enabling: SI 2012/215, SI 2012/1257

s.96, enabling: SI 2012/1257

s.97, applied: SI 2012/1388

s.97, enabling: SI 2012/1388

s.98, enabling: SI 2012/1257

s.99, enabling: SI 2012/212, SI 2012/215, SI 2012/1257, SI 2012/1813, SI 2012/2691

s.143, applied: SI 2012/1257, SI 2012/1506, SI 2012/2691

s.144, enabling: SI 2012/215, SI 2012/1257, SI 2012/1388, SI 2012/1506, SI 2012/1682, SI 2012/1813, SI 2012/2480, SI 2012/2691

s.145, enabling: SI 2012/709

2008–cont.

30. Pensions Act 2008–*cont.*

s.149, enabling: SI 2012/683, SI 2012/1682, SI 2012/2480

31. Dormant Bank and Building Society Accounts Act 2008

s.7, amended: 2012 c.21 Sch.18 para.128

32. Energy Act 2008

s.19, enabling: SI 2012/461

s.21, enabling: SI 2012/461

s.27, enabling: SI 2012/461

s.41, see *R. (on the application of Homesun Holdings Ltd) v Secretary of State for Energy and Climate Change* [2012] EWCA Civ 28, [2012] Env. L.R. 25 (CA (Civ Div)), Lloyd, L.J.

s.41, enabling: SI 2012/2782

s.43, enabling: SI 2012/671, SI 2012/1393, SI 2012/2268, SI 2012/2782

s.77, amended: 2012 asp 5 Sch.5 para.55

s.88, amended: SI 2012/2400 Art.33

s.100, applied: SI 2012/1999

s.100, enabling: SI 2012/1999

s.104, enabling: SI 2012/461, SI 2012/671, SI 2012/1393, SI 2012/1999, SI 2012/2268, SI 2012/2782

s.105, applied: SI 2012/461, SI 2012/1999

2009

1. Banking Act 2009

Part 1, applied: 2012 c.21 s.58, s.60, s.75

Part 1, substituted: 2012 c.21 s.100

Part 2, applied: 2012 c.21 s.58, s.60, s.75

Part 3, applied: 2012 c.21 s.58, s.60, s.61, s.75

Part 5, applied: 2012 c.21 s.85

s.1, amended: 2012 c.21 s.99, s.100, s.101, s.102, Sch.17 para.2

s.1, referred to: 2012 c.21 s.61

s.2, amended: 2012 c.21 s.101, s.102, Sch.17 para.3

s.3, amended: 2012 c.21 s.96, Sch.17 para.4

s.4, amended: 2012 c.21 s.96, Sch.17 para.5

s.5, amended: 2012 c.21 Sch.17 para.6

s.6, amended: 2012 c.21 Sch.17 para.7

s.6, repealed (in part): 2012 c.21 Sch.17 para.7

s.7, amended: 2012 c.21 Sch.17 para.8

s.8, amended: 2012 c.21 s.96, Sch.17 para.9

s.9, amended: 2012 c.21 Sch.17 para.10

s.10, amended: 2012 c.21 Sch.17 para.11

s.14, amended: SI 2012/917 Sch.1 para.4

s.20, amended: 2012 c.21 s.100

s.24, amended: 2012 c.21 Sch.17 para.12

s.25, amended: 2012 c.21 Sch.17 para.13

s.26, amended: 2012 c.21 Sch.17 para.14

s.26A, added: 2012 c.21 s.97

s.27, amended: 2012 c.21 Sch.17 para.15

s.28, amended: 2012 c.21 Sch.17 para.16

s.29, amended: 2012 c.21 s.97, Sch.17 para.17

s.30, amended: 2012 c.21 Sch.17 para.18

s.31, amended: 2012 c.21 s.97, Sch.17 para.19

s.34, amended: 2012 c.21 s.98

s.36A, added: 2012 c.21 s.100

s.39A, added: 2012 c.21 s.102

s.41, amended: 2012 c.21 Sch.17 para.20

s.42, amended: 2012 c.21 Sch.17 para.21

s.42A, added: 2012 c.21 s.97

s.43, amended: 2012 c.21 Sch.17 para.22

s.44, amended: 2012 c.21 s.97, Sch.17 para.23

s.45, amended: 2012 c.21 s.98, Sch.17 para.24

s.46, amended: 2012 c.21 s.97, s.98, Sch.17 para.25

s.47, amended: 2012 c.21 s.96

2009– cont.

1. **Banking Act 2009**– *cont.*
    s.48A, amended: 2012 c.21 s.97
    s.53, amended: 2012 c.21 s.97
    s.57, amended: 2012 c.21 Sch.17 para.26
    s.75, amended: 2012 c.21 s.101, s.102
    s.79A, added: 2012 c.21 s.99
    s.81A, added: 2012 c.21 s.99
    s.81B, added: 2012 c.21 s.100
    s.81C, added: 2012 c.21 s.100
    s.81D, added: 2012 c.21 s.100
    s.82, amended: 2012 c.21 Sch.17 para.27
    s.83, amended: 2012 c.21 s.97
    s.83A, added: 2012 c.21 Sch.17 para.28
    s.89A, added: 2012 c.21 s.101
    s.89B, added: 2012 c.21 s.102
    s.89C, added: 2012 c.21 s.102
    s.89D, added: 2012 c.21 s.102
    s.89E, added: 2012 c.21 s.102
    s.89F, added: 2012 c.21 s.102
    s.89G, added: 2012 c.21 s.102
    s.91, amended: 2012 c.21 Sch.17 para.30
    s.93, amended: 2012 c.21 Sch.17 para.31
    s.95, amended: 2012 c.21 Sch.17 para.32
    s.96, amended: 2012 c.21 Sch.17 para.33
    s.97, amended: 2012 c.21 Sch.17 para.34
    s.98, amended: 2012 c.21 Sch.17 para.35
    s.100, amended: 2012 c.21 Sch.17 para.36
    s.101, amended: 2012 c.21 Sch.17 para.37
    s.103, amended: 2012 c.21 Sch.17 para.38
    s.108, amended: 2012 c.21 Sch.17 para.39
    s.109, amended: 2012 c.21 Sch.17 para.40
    s.113, amended: 2012 c.21 Sch.17 para.41
    s.115, amended: 2012 c.21 Sch.17 para.42
    s.117, amended: 2012 c.21 Sch.17 para.43
    s.120, amended: 2012 c.21 Sch.17 para.44
    s.129A, added: 2012 c.21 Sch.17 para.45
    s.145A, added: 2012 c.21 s.103
    s.147, amended: 2012 c.21 Sch.17 para.47
    s.153, amended: 2012 c.21 Sch.17 para.48
    s.157, amended: 2012 c.21 Sch.17 para.49
    s.157A, added: 2012 c.21 Sch.17 para.50
    s.159A, added: 2012 c.21 s.101
    s.166, amended: 2012 c.21 Sch.17 para.51
    s.183, amended: 2012 c.21 Sch.17 para.53
    s.186, amended: 2012 c.21 s.104
    s.186A, added: 2012 c.21 s.104
    s.187, amended: 2012 c.21 s.104
    s.188, applied: 2012 c.21 s.85
    s.189, applied: 2012 c.21 s.85
    s.191, substituted: 2012 c.21 s.104
    s.192, amended: 2012 c.21 s.104
    s.197, applied: 2012 c.21 s.110
    s.198, applied: 2012 c.21 s.85, s.110
    s.199, applied: 2012 c.21 s.110
    s.200, applied: 2012 c.21 s.110
    s.202A, added: 2012 c.21 s.104
    s.202A, applied: 2012 c.21 s.110
    s.203A, added: 2012 c.21 s.104
    s.203B, added: 2012 c.21 s.104
    s.204, amended: 2012 c.21 s.104
    s.206A, amended: 2012 c.21 s.104
    s.206B, added: 2012 c.21 s.105
    s.223, amended: 2012 c.21 Sch.17 para.54
    s.232, amended: 2012 c.21 Sch.17 para.55
    s.234, amended: 2012 c.21 Sch.17 para.56
    s.235, amended: 2012 c.21 Sch.17 para.57
    s.244, amended: 2012 c.21 Sch.2 para.3
    s.246, amended: 2012 c.21 Sch.17 para.58

2009– cont.

1. **Banking Act 2009**– *cont.*
    s.249, amended: 2012 c.21 Sch.17 para.59
    s.249, repealed (in part): 2012 c.21 Sch.17 para.59, Sch.19
    s.250, amended: 2012 c.21 Sch.17 para.60
    s.258A, added: 2012 c.21 s.101
    s.259, amended: 2012 c.21 s.100, s.101, s.102, Sch.17 para.61
    s.261, amended: 2012 c.21 s.96, s.97, s.100, s.101, s.102, Sch.17 para.62
2. **Appropriation Act 2009**
    varied: SI 2012/147 Art.7
    Sch.2 Part 2, varied: 2012 c.11 s.12
02. **Local Government (Wales) Measure 2009**
    s.8, applied: SI 2012/2539, SI 2012/2539 Art.2
    s.8, enabling: SI 2012/2539
    s.15, enabling: SI 2012/1143
    s.50, enabling: SI 2012/1143, SI 2012/2539
3. **Northern Ireland Act 2009**
    referred to: 2012 c.13 Sch.1
4. **Corporation Tax Act 2009**
    applied: 2012 c.14 Sch.13 para.8, Sch.13 para.22
    Part 2 c.4, applied: 2012 c.14 s.98, s.101, s.115, s.117, s.120
    Part 3, applied: SI 2012/3009 Reg.4
    Part 3 c.9, amended: SI 2012/266 Art.5
    Part 4 c.3, applied: 2012 c.14 s.74
    Part 5, applied: 2012 c.14 s.126, SI 2012/1709 Art.7, SI 2012/3044 Reg.4
    Part 6, applied: SI 2012/3044 Reg.4
    Part 8, applied: 2012 c.14 s.74, s.88, s.130, Sch.17 para.7, Sch.17 para.24, SI 2012/701 Reg.3, SI 2012/3009 Reg.4
    Part 8, referred to: 2012 c.14 Sch.17 para.24
    Part 9A, applied: 2012 c.14 s.74, s.94, s.111
    Part 10 c.5, applied: 2012 c.14 s.74
    Part 10 c.6, applied: 2012 c.14 s.74
    Part 10 c.7, applied: 2012 c.14 s.74
    Part 10 c.8, applied: 2012 c.14 s.74
    Part 13, applied: SI 2012/286 Art.2
    Part 14 c.4, amended: 2012 c.14 Sch.16 para.200
    Part 16 c.2, applied: 2012 c.14 s.81
    Part 20 c.1, applied: 2012 c.14 s.92
    s.Art.1 sA.1, amended: 2012 c.14 Sch.16 para.136, Sch.18 para.20, Sch.20 para.25
    s.Art.1 sA.1, repealed (in part): 2012 c.14 Sch.16 para.136, Sch.20 para.25
    s.10, applied: 2012 c.14 Sch.13 para.8, Sch.13 para.22
    s.10, referred to: 2012 c.14 s.149, s.179
    s.12, applied: 2012 c.14 Sch.13 para.8, Sch.13 para.22
    s.18A, amended: 2012 c.14 Sch.20 para.3
    s.18CA, added: 2012 c.14 Sch.20 para.4
    s.18CB, added: 2012 c.14 Sch.20 para.4
    s.18F, amended: 2012 c.14 Sch.20 para.5
    s.18G, substituted: 2012 c.14 Sch.20 para.6
    s.18H, substituted: 2012 c.14 Sch.20 para.6
    s.18HA, substituted: 2012 c.14 Sch.20 para.6
    s.18HB, substituted: 2012 c.14 Sch.20 para.6
    s.18HC, substituted: 2012 c.14 Sch.20 para.6
    s.18HD, substituted: 2012 c.14 Sch.20 para.6
    s.18HE, substituted: 2012 c.14 Sch.20 para.6
    s.18I, substituted: 2012 c.14 Sch.20 para.6
    s.18P, amended: 2012 c.14 Sch.20 para.7
    s.18Q, amended: 2012 c.14 Sch.16 para.137
    s.18Q, repealed (in part): 2012 c.14 Sch.16 para.137
    s.24, substituted: 2012 c.14 Sch.16 para.138

2009–cont.

4. Corporation Tax Act 2009–*cont.*

s.35, applied: 2012 c.14 s.55, s.69, s.71, s.116, s.117, s.118, s.119, s.120, s.123, s.125, s.136, Sch.17 para.22, Sch.17 para.35

s.36, amended: 2012 c.14 Sch.16 para.139

s.38, amended: 2012 c.14 Sch.16 para.140

s.39, amended: 2012 c.14 Sch.16 para.141

s.46, repealed (in part): 2012 c.14 Sch.16 para.142

s.47, referred to: 2012 c.14 s.109

s.56, amended: 2012 c.14 Sch.16 para.143

s.56, repealed (in part): 2012 c.14 Sch.16 para.143

s.71, amended: SI 2012/976 Sch.1 para.23

s.75, applied: 2012 c.14 s.81

s.105, amended: SI 2012/964 Sch.1

s.105, applied: SI 2012/847 Reg.25

s.105, repealed (in part): SI 2012/964 Sch.1

s.127A, added: SI 2012/266 Art.10

s.127B, added: SI 2012/266 Art.10

s.127C, added: SI 2012/266 Art.10

s.127D, added: SI 2012/266 Art.10

s.127E, added: SI 2012/266 Art.10

s.127F, added: SI 2012/266 Art.10

s.127G, added: SI 2012/266 Art.10

s.130, amended: 2012 c.14 Sch.16 para.144

s.135, repealed: 2012 c.14 Sch.39 para.44

s.138, repealed: 2012 c.14 Sch.39 para.22

s.145, amended: 2012 c.14 s.53

s.147, amended: SI 2012/266 Art.5

s.149A, added: SI 2012/266 Art.5

s.149B, added: SI 2012/266 Art.5

s.149C, added: SI 2012/266 Art.5

s.149D, added: SI 2012/266 Art.5

s.149E, added: SI 2012/266 Art.5

s.180, amended: 2012 c.14 s.54

s.201, amended: 2012 c.14 Sch.16 para.145

s.203, amended: 2012 c.14 Sch.16 para.146

s.208, applied: 2012 c.14 s.86

s.209, applied: 2012 c.14 s.86

s.258, repealed: 2012 c.14 Sch.39 para.44

s.272, applied: 2012 c.14 s.78

s.272, repealed (in part): 2012 c.14 Sch.39 para.44

s.273, repealed: 2012 c.14 Sch.39 para.44

s.274, repealed: 2012 c.14 Sch.39 para.44

s.275, repealed: 2012 c.14 Sch.39 para.44

s.276, repealed: 2012 c.14 Sch.39 para.44

s.292, varied: 2012 c.14 s.23

s.293, varied: 2012 c.14 s.23

s.294, varied: 2012 c.14 s.23

s.295, varied: 2012 c.14 s.23

s.296, varied: 2012 c.14 s.23

s.297, varied: 2012 c.14 s.23

s.298, amended: 2012 c.14 Sch.16 para.147

s.298, repealed (in part): 2012 c.14 Sch.16 para.147

s.298, varied: 2012 c.14 s.23

s.299, applied: 2012 c.14 Sch.13 para.13, Sch.13 para.30

s.299, varied: 2012 c.14 s.23

s.300, varied: 2012 c.14 s.23

s.301, varied: 2012 c.14 s.23

s.302, varied: 2012 c.14 s.23

s.303, varied: 2012 c.14 s.23

s.304, varied: 2012 c.14 s.23

s.305, varied: 2012 c.14 s.23

s.306, varied: 2012 c.14 s.23

s.307, varied: 2012 c.14 s.23

s.308, varied: 2012 c.14 s.23

s.309, varied: 2012 c.14 s.23

s.310, varied: 2012 c.14 s.23

2009–cont.

4. Corporation Tax Act 2009–*cont.*

s.311, varied: 2012 c.14 s.23

s.312, varied: 2012 c.14 s.23

s.313, varied: 2012 c.14 s.23

s.314, varied: 2012 c.14 s.23

s.315, varied: 2012 c.14 s.23

s.316, varied: 2012 c.14 s.23

s.317, varied: 2012 c.14 s.23

s.318, varied: 2012 c.14 s.23

s.319, varied: 2012 c.14 s.23

s.320, varied: 2012 c.14 s.23

s.321, varied: 2012 c.14 s.23

s.321A, varied: 2012 c.14 s.23

s.322, varied: 2012 c.14 s.23

s.323, varied: 2012 c.14 s.23

s.324, varied: 2012 c.14 s.23

s.325, varied: 2012 c.14 s.23

s.326, varied: 2012 c.14 s.23

s.327, varied: 2012 c.14 s.23

s.328, varied: 2012 c.14 s.23

s.328A, varied: 2012 c.14 s.23

s.328B, varied: 2012 c.14 s.23

s.328C, varied: 2012 c.14 s.23

s.328D, varied: 2012 c.14 s.23

s.328E, varied: 2012 c.14 s.23

s.328F, varied: 2012 c.14 s.23

s.328G, varied: 2012 c.14 s.23

s.328H, varied: 2012 c.14 s.23

s.329, varied: 2012 c.14 s.23

s.330, varied: 2012 c.14 s.23

s.331, varied: 2012 c.14 s.23

s.332, varied: 2012 c.14 s.23

s.333, varied: 2012 c.14 s.23

s.334, varied: 2012 c.14 s.23

s.335, applied: SI 2012/1709 Art.7

s.335, varied: 2012 c.14 s.23

s.336, amended: 2012 c.14 Sch.16 para.148

s.336, varied: 2012 c.14 s.23

s.337, amended: 2012 c.14 Sch.16 para.149

s.337, varied: 2012 c.14 s.23

s.338, varied: 2012 c.14 s.23

s.339, varied: 2012 c.14 s.23

s.340, varied: 2012 c.14 s.23

s.341, varied: 2012 c.14 s.23

s.342, varied: 2012 c.14 s.23

s.343, varied: 2012 c.14 s.23

s.344, varied: 2012 c.14 s.23

s.345, varied: 2012 c.14 s.23

s.346, varied: 2012 c.14 s.23

s.347, varied: 2012 c.14 s.23

s.348, varied: 2012 c.14 s.23

s.349, varied: 2012 c.14 s.23

s.350, varied: 2012 c.14 s.23

s.351, varied: 2012 c.14 s.23

s.352, varied: 2012 c.14 s.23

s.353, varied: 2012 c.14 s.23

s.354, varied: 2012 c.14 s.23

s.355, varied: 2012 c.14 s.23

s.356, varied: 2012 c.14 s.23

s.357, varied: 2012 c.14 s.23

s.358, varied: 2012 c.14 s.23

s.359, varied: 2012 c.14 s.23

s.360, varied: 2012 c.14 s.23

s.361, applied: 2012 c.14 s.23

s.361, referred to: 2012 c.14 s.23

s.361, varied: 2012 c.14 s.23

s.361A, referred to: 2012 c.14 s.23

s.361A, varied: 2012 c.14 s.23

2009–cont.

2009–cont.

4. Corporation Tax Act 2009–*cont.*
s.361B, referred to: 2012 c.14 s.23
s.361B, varied: 2012 c.14 s.23
s.361C, referred to: 2012 c.14 s.23
s.361C, varied: 2012 c.14 s.23
s.362, amended: 2012 c.14 s.23
s.362, disapplied: 2012 c.14 s.23
s.362, referred to: 2012 c.14 s.23
s.362, repealed (in part): 2012 c.14 s.23
s.363, applied: 2012 c.14 s.23
s.363, varied: 2012 c.14 s.23
s.363A, added: 2012 c.14 s.23
s.363A, varied: 2012 c.14 s.23
s.364, varied: 2012 c.14 s.23
s.365, varied: 2012 c.14 s.23
s.366, varied: 2012 c.14 s.23
s.367, varied: 2012 c.14 s.23
s.368, varied: 2012 c.14 s.23
s.369, varied: 2012 c.14 s.23
s.370, varied: 2012 c.14 s.23
s.371, varied: 2012 c.14 s.23
s.372, varied: 2012 c.14 s.23
s.373, varied: 2012 c.14 s.23
s.374, varied: 2012 c.14 s.23
s.375, varied: 2012 c.14 s.23
s.376, varied: 2012 c.14 s.23
s.377, varied: 2012 c.14 s.23
s.378, varied: 2012 c.14 s.23
s.379, varied: 2012 c.14 s.23
s.380, varied: 2012 c.14 s.23
s.381, varied: 2012 c.14 s.23
s.382, varied: 2012 c.14 s.23
s.383, varied: 2012 c.14 s.23
s.384, varied: 2012 c.14 s.23
s.385, varied: 2012 c.14 s.23
s.386, amended: 2012 c.14 Sch.16 para.150
s.386, repealed (in part): 2012 c.14 Sch.16 para.150
s.386, varied: 2012 c.14 s.23
s.387, amended: 2012 c.14 Sch.16 para.151
s.387, varied: 2012 c.14 s.23
s.388, amended: 2012 c.14 Sch.16 para.152
s.388, applied: 2012 c.14 s.73, s.88, s.126
s.388, varied: 2012 c.14 s.23
s.389, amended: 2012 c.14 Sch.16 para.153
s.389, applied: 2012 c.14 s.88
s.389, varied: 2012 c.14 s.23
s.390, amended: 2012 c.14 Sch.16 para.154
s.390, applied: 2012 c.14 s.88
s.390, varied: 2012 c.14 s.23
s.391, amended: 2012 c.14 Sch.16 para.155
s.391, applied: 2012 c.14 s.88
s.391, varied: 2012 c.14 s.23
s.392, varied: 2012 c.14 s.23
s.393, repealed: 2012 c.14 Sch.16 para.156
s.393, varied: 2012 c.14 s.23
s.394, repealed: 2012 c.14 Sch.16 para.156
s.394, varied: 2012 c.14 s.23
s.395, varied: 2012 c.14 s.23
s.396, varied: 2012 c.14 s.23
s.397, varied: 2012 c.14 s.23
s.398, varied: 2012 c.14 s.23
s.399, amended: 2012 c.14 Sch.16 para.157
s.399, varied: 2012 c.14 s.23
s.400, disapplied: 2012 c.14 s.112
s.400, varied: 2012 c.14 s.23
s.400A, disapplied: 2012 c.14 s.112
s.400A, varied: 2012 c.14 s.23

4. Corporation Tax Act 2009–*cont.*
s.400B, disapplied: 2012 c.14 s.112
s.400B, varied: 2012 c.14 s.23
s.400C, disapplied: 2012 c.14 s.112
s.400C, varied: 2012 c.14 s.23
s.401, varied: 2012 c.14 s.23
s.402, varied: 2012 c.14 s.23
s.403, varied: 2012 c.14 s.23
s.404, varied: 2012 c.14 s.23
s.405, varied: 2012 c.14 s.23
s.406, varied: 2012 c.14 s.23
s.407, varied: 2012 c.14 s.23
s.408, varied: 2012 c.14 s.23
s.409, varied: 2012 c.14 s.23
s.410, varied: 2012 c.14 s.23
s.411, varied: 2012 c.14 s.23
s.412, varied: 2012 c.14 s.23
s.413, varied: 2012 c.14 s.23
s.414, varied: 2012 c.14 s.23
s.415, varied: 2012 c.14 s.23
s.416, varied: 2012 c.14 s.23
s.417, varied: 2012 c.14 s.23
s.418, varied: 2012 c.14 s.23
s.418A, varied: 2012 c.14 s.23
s.419, varied: 2012 c.14 s.23
s.420, varied: 2012 c.14 s.23
s.421, varied: 2012 c.14 s.23
s.422, varied: 2012 c.14 s.23
s.423, varied: 2012 c.14 s.23
s.424, varied: 2012 c.14 s.23
s.425, varied: 2012 c.14 s.23
s.426, varied: 2012 c.14 s.23
s.427, varied: 2012 c.14 s.23
s.428, varied: 2012 c.14 s.23
s.429, varied: 2012 c.14 s.23
s.430, varied: 2012 c.14 s.23
s.431, varied: 2012 c.14 s.23
s.432, varied: 2012 c.14 s.23
s.433, varied: 2012 c.14 s.23
s.434, varied: 2012 c.14 s.23
s.435, varied: 2012 c.14 s.23
s.436, varied: 2012 c.14 s.23
s.437, varied: 2012 c.14 s.23
s.438, varied: 2012 c.14 s.23
s.439, varied: 2012 c.14 s.23
s.440, varied: 2012 c.14 s.23
s.441, varied: 2012 c.14 s.23
s.442, varied: 2012 c.14 s.23
s.443, varied: 2012 c.14 s.23
s.444, varied: 2012 c.14 s.23
s.445, varied: 2012 c.14 s.23
s.446, varied: 2012 c.14 s.23
s.447, varied: 2012 c.14 s.23
s.448, varied: 2012 c.14 s.23
s.449, varied: 2012 c.14 s.23
s.450, varied: 2012 c.14 s.23
s.451, varied: 2012 c.14 s.23
s.452, varied: 2012 c.14 s.23
s.453, varied: 2012 c.14 s.23
s.454, varied: 2012 c.14 s.23
s.455, varied: 2012 c.14 s.23
s.455A, varied: 2012 c.14 s.23
s.456, varied: 2012 c.14 s.23
s.457, varied: 2012 c.14 s.23
s.458, varied: 2012 c.14 s.23
s.459, varied: 2012 c.14 s.23
s.460, varied: 2012 c.14 s.23
s.461, varied: 2012 c.14 s.23

2009– cont.

4. Corporation Tax Act 2009– *cont.*
s.462, varied: 2012 c.14 s.23
s.463, varied: 2012 c.14 s.23
s.464, repealed (in part): 2012 c.14 Sch.16 para.158
s.464, varied: 2012 c.14 s.23
s.465, varied: 2012 c.14 s.23
s.465A, varied: 2012 c.14 s.23
s.466, varied: 2012 c.14 s.23
s.467, varied: 2012 c.14 s.23
s.468, varied: 2012 c.14 s.23
s.469, varied: 2012 c.14 s.23
s.470, varied: 2012 c.14 s.23
s.471, amended: 2012 c.14 Sch.16 para.159
s.471, varied: 2012 c.14 s.23
s.472, amended: 2012 c.14 Sch.16 para.160
s.472, varied: 2012 c.14 s.23
s.473, amended: 2012 c.14 Sch.16 para.161
s.473, varied: 2012 c.14 s.23
s.474, varied: 2012 c.14 s.23
s.475, varied: 2012 c.14 s.23
s.476, varied: 2012 c.14 s.23
s.486, amended: 2012 c.14 Sch.16 para.162
s.486D, repealed (in part): 2012 c.14 Sch.20 para.26
s.486E, amended: 2012 c.14 Sch.20 para.27
s.486E, repealed (in part): 2012 c.14 Sch.20 para.27
s.502, amended: 2012 c.14 Sch.16 para.163
s.521E, repealed (in part): 2012 c.14 Sch.20 para.28
s.560, amended: 2012 c.14 Sch.16 para.164
s.561, amended: 2012 c.14 Sch.16 para.165
s.563, amended: 2012 c.14 Sch.16 para.166
s.564, amended: 2012 c.14 Sch.18 para.21
s.574, applied: 2012 c.14 s.88
s.591, amended: 2012 c.14 Sch.16 para.167
s.634, amended: 2012 c.14 Sch.16 para.168
s.635, amended: 2012 c.14 Sch.16 para.169
s.636, repealed: 2012 c.14 Sch.16 para.170
s.699, amended: 2012 c.14 Sch.16 para.171
s.699, repealed (in part): 2012 c.14 Sch.16 para.171
s.710, amended: 2012 c.14 Sch.16 para.172
s.746, amended: 2012 c.14 Sch.16 para.173
s.752, disapplied: 2012 c.14 s.74, s.89
s.780, disapplied: 2012 c.14 Sch.17 para.24
s.800, repealed (in part): 2012 c.14 Sch.16 para.174
s.806, amended: 2012 c.14 Sch.16 para.175
s.810, repealed (in part): 2012 c.14 Sch.16 para.176
s.815, repealed (in part): 2012 c.14 Sch.16 para.177
s.855, amended: 2012 c.14 Sch.16 para.178
s.870, repealed: 2012 c.14 Sch.20 para.29
s.901, substituted: 2012 c.14 Sch.16 para.179
s.902, disapplied: SI 2012/3009 Reg.4
s.902, repealed: 2012 c.14 Sch.16 para.180
s.903, repealed: 2012 c.14 Sch.16 para.180
s.904, repealed: 2012 c.14 Sch.16 para.181
s.906, repealed (in part): 2012 c.14 Sch.16 para.182
s.931CA, added: 2012 c.14 Sch.20 para.30
s.931E, amended: 2012 c.14 Sch.20 para.31
s.931S, amended: 2012 c.14 Sch.16 para.183, Sch.18 para.22
s.931W, repealed (in part): 2012 c.14 Sch.16 para.184
s.976, repealed (in part): 2012 c.14 Sch.39 para.22
s.978, repealed: 2012 c.14 Sch.39 para.22
s.985, amended: 2012 c.14 Sch.16 para.185
s.999, amended: 2012 c.14 Sch.16 para.186
s.1000, amended: 2012 c.14 Sch.16 para.187
s.1000, referred to: 2012 c.14 s.81
s.1000, repealed (in part): 2012 c.14 Sch.16 para.187
s.1013, amended: 2012 c.14 Sch.16 para.188
s.1021, amended: 2012 c.14 Sch.16 para.189

2009– cont.

4. Corporation Tax Act 2009– *cont.*
s.1039, amended: 2012 c.14 Sch.3 para.16
s.1042, amended: 2012 c.14 Sch.3 para.17
s.1043, repealed (in part): 2012 c.14 Sch.3 para.3
s.1044, amended: 2012 c.14 Sch.3 para.2
s.1044, repealed (in part): 2012 c.14 Sch.3 para.3
s.1045, amended: 2012 c.14 Sch.3 para.2, Sch.3 para.3
s.1045, repealed (in part): 2012 c.14 Sch.3 para.3
s.1046, amended: 2012 c.14 Sch.3 para.10, Sch.3 para.18
s.1050, repealed: 2012 c.14 Sch.3 para.3
s.1055, amended: 2012 c.14 Sch.3 para.2
s.1057, amended: 2012 c.14 Sch.3 para.11, Sch.3 para.19
s.1058, amended: 2012 c.14 Sch.3 para.2
s.1058, repealed (in part): 2012 c.14 Sch.3 para.15
s.1059, amended: 2012 c.5 Sch.3 para.28, Sch.14 Part 1
s.1059, repealed (in part): 2012 c.5 Sch.14 Part 1, 2012 c.14 Sch.3 para.15
s.1063, amended: 2012 c.14 Sch.3 para.4
s.1063, repealed (in part): 2012 c.14 Sch.3 para.4
s.1064, repealed: 2012 c.14 Sch.3 para.4
s.1068, amended: 2012 c.14 Sch.3 para.5
s.1068, repealed (in part): 2012 c.14 Sch.3 para.5
s.1069, repealed: 2012 c.14 Sch.3 para.5
s.1074, amended: 2012 c.14 Sch.3 para.6
s.1074, repealed (in part): 2012 c.14 Sch.3 para.6
s.1075, repealed: 2012 c.14 Sch.3 para.6
s.1080, amended: 2012 c.14 Sch.16 para.190
s.1080, repealed (in part): 2012 c.14 Sch.16 para.190
s.1083, repealed (in part): 2012 c.14 Sch.16 para.191
s.1085, amended: 2012 c.14 Sch.3 para.21
s.1085, repealed (in part): 2012 c.14 Sch.3 para.7, Sch.3 para.21
s.1085, substituted: 2012 c.14 Sch.3 para.30
s.1086, substituted: 2012 c.14 Sch.3 para.30
s.1087, amended: 2012 c.14 Sch.3 para.7, Sch.3 para.22
s.1087, repealed (in part): 2012 c.14 Sch.3 para.7, Sch.3 para.22
s.1087, substituted: 2012 c.14 Sch.3 para.30
s.1088, amended: 2012 c.14 Sch.3 para.23
s.1088, substituted: 2012 c.14 Sch.3 para.23, Sch.3 para.30
s.1089, repealed: 2012 c.14 Sch.3 para.24
s.1089, substituted: 2012 c.14 Sch.3 para.30
s.1090, repealed: 2012 c.14 Sch.3 para.24
s.1090, substituted: 2012 c.14 Sch.3 para.30
s.1091, repealed (in part): 2012 c.14 Sch.3 para.25
s.1091, substituted: 2012 c.14 Sch.3 para.25, Sch.3 para.30
s.1092, repealed (in part): 2012 c.14 Sch.3 para.7, Sch.3 para.26
s.1092, substituted: 2012 c.14 Sch.3 para.30
s.1093, repealed: 2012 c.14 Sch.3 para.26
s.1093, substituted: 2012 c.14 Sch.3 para.30
s.1094, amended: 2012 c.14 Sch.3 para.13
s.1094, repealed: 2012 c.14 Sch.3 para.26
s.1094, substituted: 2012 c.14 Sch.3 para.30
s.1095, repealed: 2012 c.14 Sch.3 para.26
s.1095, substituted: 2012 c.14 Sch.3 para.30
s.1096, repealed: 2012 c.14 Sch.3 para.26
s.1096, substituted: 2012 c.14 Sch.3 para.30
s.1097, repealed: 2012 c.14 Sch.3 para.7
s.1097, substituted: 2012 c.14 Sch.3 para.30
s.1098, substituted: 2012 c.14 Sch.3 para.30

2009–cont.

4. Corporation Tax Act 2009–*cont.*
s.1099, repealed: 2012 c.14 Sch.3 para.26
s.1099, substituted: 2012 c.14 Sch.3 para.30
s.1100, amended: 2012 c.14 Sch.3 para.27
s.1100, substituted: 2012 c.14 Sch.3 para.27, Sch.3 para.30
s.1101, substituted: 2012 c.14 Sch.3 para.30
s.1102, substituted: 2012 c.14 Sch.3 para.30
s.1103, repealed: 2012 c.14 Sch.3 para.28
s.1103, substituted: 2012 c.14 Sch.3 para.30
s.1104, repealed: 2012 c.14 Sch.3 para.28
s.1104, substituted: 2012 c.14 Sch.3 para.30
s.1105, repealed: 2012 c.14 Sch.3 para.28
s.1105, substituted: 2012 c.14 Sch.3 para.30
s.1106, amended: 2012 c.14 Sch.3 para.14
s.1106, repealed: 2012 c.14 Sch.3 para.28
s.1106, substituted: 2012 c.14 Sch.3 para.30
s.1107, repealed: 2012 c.14 Sch.3 para.28
s.1107, substituted: 2012 c.14 Sch.3 para.30
s.1108, amended: 2012 c.5 Sch.3 para.29, Sch.14 Part 1
s.1108, repealed (in part): 2012 c.5 Sch.14 Part 1, 2012 c.14 Sch.3 para.28
s.1108, substituted: 2012 c.14 Sch.3 para.30
s.1109, repealed: 2012 c.14 Sch.3 para.28
s.1109, substituted: 2012 c.14 Sch.3 para.30
s.1110, repealed: 2012 c.14 Sch.3 para.28
s.1110, substituted: 2012 c.14 Sch.3 para.30
s.1111, repealed: 2012 c.14 Sch.3 para.28
s.1111, substituted: 2012 c.14 Sch.3 para.30
s.1112, amended: 2012 c.14 Sch.3 para.29
s.1112, repealed (in part): 2012 c.14 Sch.3 para.29
s.1112, substituted: 2012 c.14 Sch.3 para.29, Sch.3 para.30
s.1113, amended: 2012 c.14 Sch.3 para.31
s.1115, amended: 2012 c.14 Sch.3 para.31
s.1128, amended: 2012 c.14 Sch.3 para.34
s.1129, amended: 2012 c.14 Sch.3 para.35
s.1130, amended: 2012 c.14 Sch.3 para.36
s.1131, amended: 2012 c.14 Sch.3 para.37
s.1139, applied: 2012 c.14 Sch.17 para.17
s.1142, enabling: SI 2012/286
s.1143, amended: 2012 c.14 Sch.16 para.192
s.1153, amended: 2012 c.14 Sch.16 para.193
s.1158, amended: 2012 c.14 Sch.16 para.194
s.1159, amended: 2012 c.14 Sch.16 para.195
s.1159, repealed: 2012 c.14 Sch.16 para.196
s.1160, amended: 2012 c.14 Sch.16 para.195, Sch.16 para.197
s.1161, amended: 2012 c.14 Sch.16 para.195, Sch.16 para.198
s.1162, amended: 2012 c.14 Sch.16 para.195, Sch.16 para.199
s.1163, amended: 2012 c.14 Sch.16 para.195
s.1164, amended: 2012 c.14 Sch.16 para.195, Sch.16 para.201
s.1165, amended: 2012 c.14 Sch.16 para.195, Sch.16 para.202
s.1166, amended: 2012 c.14 Sch.16 para.195, Sch.16 para.203
s.1167, amended: 2012 c.14 Sch.16 para.195, Sch.16 para.204
s.1168, amended: 2012 c.14 Sch.16 para.195, Sch.16 para.205
s.1169, amended: 2012 c.14 Sch.16 para.206
s.1219, applied: 2012 c.14 s.81, s.82
s.1220, varied: 2012 c.14 s.81
s.1223A, added: 2012 c.14 Sch.16 para.207

2009–cont.

4. Corporation Tax Act 2009–*cont.*
s.1234, referred to: 2012 c.14 s.81
s.1235, referred to: 2012 c.14 s.81
s.1237, referred to: 2012 c.14 s.81
s.1238, applied: 2012 c.14 s.81
s.1238, referred to: 2012 c.14 s.81
s.1239, referred to: 2012 c.14 s.81
s.1239, varied: 2012 c.14 s.81
s.1240, referred to: 2012 c.14 s.81
s.1241, referred to: 2012 c.14 s.81
s.1242, applied: 2012 c.14 s.81
s.1242, referred to: 2012 c.14 s.81
s.1243, referred to: 2012 c.14 s.81
s.1243, varied: 2012 c.14 s.81
s.1244, applied: 2012 c.14 s.81
s.1244, referred to: 2012 c.14 s.81
s.1249, applied: 2012 c.14 s.82
s.1249, varied: 2012 c.14 s.82
s.1251, amended: 2012 c.14 Sch.16 para.208
s.1251, applied: 2012 c.14 s.82
s.1251, repealed (in part): 2012 c.14 Sch.16 para.208
s.1251, varied: 2012 c.14 s.82
s.1253, applied: 2012 c.14 s.81
s.1257, referred to: 2012 c.14 Sch.13 para.8, Sch.13 para.22
s.1259, applied: 2012 c.14 Sch.13 para.10, Sch.13 para.11, Sch.13 para.24, Sch.13 para.25
s.1260, applied: 2012 c.14 Sch.13 para.10, Sch.13 para.11, Sch.13 para.24, Sch.13 para.25
s.1261, applied: 2012 c.14 Sch.13 para.10, Sch.13 para.11, Sch.13 para.24, Sch.13 para.25
s.1262, applied: 2012 c.14 Sch.13 para.10, Sch.13 para.11, Sch.13 para.24, Sch.13 para.25
s.1263, applied: 2012 c.14 Sch.13 para.10, Sch.13 para.11, Sch.13 para.24, Sch.13 para.25
s.1264, applied: 2012 c.14 Sch.13 para.10, Sch.13 para.11, Sch.13 para.24, Sch.13 para.25
s.1265, applied: 2012 c.14 Sch.13 para.10, Sch.13 para.11, Sch.13 para.24, Sch.13 para.25
s.1273, applied: 2012 c.14 Sch.13 para.8, Sch.13 para.22
s.1283, repealed: 2012 c.14 Sch.39 para.53
s.1288, amended: 2012 c.14 Sch.16 para.209
s.1288, repealed (in part): 2012 c.14 Sch.16 para.209
s.1297, amended: 2012 c.14 Sch.16 para.210
s.1297, substituted: 2012 c.14 Sch.16 para.210
s.1298, amended: 2012 c.14 Sch.16 para.211
s.1304, amended: 2012 c.14 Sch.16 para.212
s.1313, applied: SI 2012/847 Reg.21
Sch.1 Part 1 para.30, repealed: 2012 c.14 Sch.16 para.247
Sch.1 Part 1 para.31, repealed: 2012 c.14 Sch.16 para.247
Sch.1 Part 1 para.32, repealed: 2012 c.14 Sch.16 para.247
Sch.1 Part 1 para.33, repealed: 2012 c.14 Sch.16 para.247
Sch.1 Part 1 para.34, repealed: 2012 c.14 Sch.16 para.247
Sch.1 Part 1 para.35, repealed: 2012 c.14 Sch.16 para.247
Sch.1 Part 1 para.36, repealed: 2012 c.14 Sch.16 para.247
Sch.1 Part 1 para.37, repealed: 2012 c.14 Sch.16 para.247
Sch.1 Part 1 para.38, repealed: 2012 c.14 Sch.16 para.247
Sch.1 Part 1 para.39, repealed: 2012 c.14 Sch.16 para.247

4. Corporation Tax Act 2009–*cont.*

Sch.1 Part 1 para.40, repealed: 2012 c.14 Sch.16 para.247

Sch.1 Part 1 para.41, repealed: 2012 c.14 Sch.16 para.247

Sch.1 Part 1 para.42, repealed: 2012 c.14 Sch.16 para.247

Sch.1 Part 1 para.43, repealed: 2012 c.14 Sch.16 para.247

Sch.1 Part 1 para.44, repealed: 2012 c.14 Sch.16 para.247

Sch.1 Part 1 para.126, repealed: 2012 c.14 Sch.16 para.247

Sch.1 Part 1 para.127, repealed: 2012 c.14 Sch.16 para.247

Sch.1 Part 1 para.128, repealed: 2012 c.14 Sch.16 para.247

Sch.1 Part 1 para.129, repealed: 2012 c.14 Sch.16 para.247

Sch.1 Part 1 para.130, repealed: 2012 c.14 Sch.16 para.247

Sch.1 Part 1 para.131, repealed: 2012 c.14 Sch.16 para.247

Sch.1 Part 1 para.132, repealed: 2012 c.14 Sch.16 para.247

Sch.1 Part 1 para.133, repealed: 2012 c.14 Sch.16 para.247

Sch.1 Part 1 para.134, repealed: 2012 c.14 Sch.16 para.247

Sch.1 Part 1 para.135, repealed: 2012 c.14 Sch.16 para.247

Sch.1 Part 1 para.136, repealed: 2012 c.14 Sch.16 para.247

Sch.1 Part 1 para.137, repealed: 2012 c.14 Sch.16 para.247

Sch.1 Part 1 para.138, repealed: 2012 c.14 Sch.16 para.247

Sch.1 Part 1 para.139, repealed: 2012 c.14 Sch.16 para.247

Sch.1 Part 1 para.140, repealed: 2012 c.14 Sch.16 para.247

Sch.1 Part 1 para.141, repealed: 2012 c.14 Sch.16 para.247

Sch.1 Part 1 para.142, repealed: 2012 c.14 Sch.16 para.247

Sch.1 Part 1 para.143, repealed: 2012 c.14 Sch.16 para.247

Sch.1 Part 1 para.144, repealed: 2012 c.14 Sch.16 para.247

Sch.1 Part 1 para.145, repealed: 2012 c.14 Sch.16 para.247

Sch.1 Part 1 para.146, repealed: 2012 c.14 Sch.16 para.247

Sch.1 Part 1 para.147, repealed: 2012 c.14 Sch.16 para.247

Sch.1 Part 1 para.148, repealed: 2012 c.14 Sch.16 para.247

Sch.1 Part 1 para.149, repealed: 2012 c.14 Sch.16 para.247

Sch.1 Part 1 para.150, repealed: 2012 c.14 Sch.16 para.247

Sch.1 Part 1 para.151, repealed: 2012 c.14 Sch.16 para.247

Sch.1 Part 1 para.152, repealed: 2012 c.14 Sch.16 para.247

Sch.1 Part 1 para.153, repealed: 2012 c.14 Sch.16 para.247

Sch.1 Part 1 para.154, repealed: 2012 c.14 Sch.16 para.247

Sch.1 Part 1 para.155, repealed: 2012 c.14 s.26

4. Corporation Tax Act 2009–*cont.*

Sch.1 Part 1 para.156, repealed: 2012 c.14 s.26

Sch.1 Part 1 para.282, repealed: 2012 c.14 Sch.16 para.247

Sch.1 Part 2 para.307, repealed (in part): 2012 c.14 Sch.16 para.247

Sch.1 Part 2 para.341, repealed: 2012 c.14 Sch.16 para.247

Sch.1 Part 2 para.342, repealed: 2012 c.14 Sch.16 para.247

Sch.1 Part 2 para.343, repealed: 2012 c.14 Sch.16 para.247

Sch.1 Part 2 para.344, repealed: 2012 c.14 Sch.16 para.247

Sch.1 Part 2 para.345, repealed: 2012 c.14 Sch.16 para.247

Sch.1 Part 2 para.346, repealed: 2012 c.14 Sch.16 para.247

Sch.1 Part 2 para.347, repealed: 2012 c.14 Sch.16 para.247

Sch.1 Part 2 para.348, repealed: 2012 c.14 Sch.16 para.247

Sch.1 Part 2 para.349, repealed: 2012 c.14 Sch.16 para.247

Sch.1 Part 2 para.350, repealed: 2012 c.14 Sch.16 para.247

Sch.1 Part 2 para.351, repealed: 2012 c.14 Sch.16 para.247

Sch.1 Part 2 para.505, repealed: 2012 c.14 Sch.39 para.39

Sch.1 Part 2 para.506, repealed: 2012 c.14 Sch.39 para.39

Sch.1 Part 2 para.507, repealed: 2012 c.14 Sch.39 para.39

Sch.2 Part 21 para.139, amended: 2012 c.14 Sch.16 para.213

Sch.2 Part 21 para.140, amended: 2012 c.14 Sch.16 para.213

Sch.4, amended: 2012 c.14 Sch.3 para.8, Sch.3 para.32, Sch.16 para.214, SI 2012/266 Art.11, SI 2012/735 Art.7

05. Education (Wales) Measure 2009

Commencement Orders: SI 2012/320 Art.2, Art.3, Art.4

s.17, applied: SI 2012/321 Reg.3, SI 2012/322 Reg.5

s.17, enabling: SI 2012/321

s.24, enabling: SI 2012/320

s.26, enabling: SI 2012/320

6. Geneva Conventions and United Nations Personnel (Protocols) Act 2009

referred to: SI 2012/2589 Sch.1 para.1

s.1, varied: SI 2012/2589 Sch.1 para.2, Sch.1 para.3

s.2, applied: SI 2012/2594 Art.3

s.3, applied: SI 2012/2594

7. Business Rate Supplements Act 2009

s.21, enabling: SI 2012/994

s.29, enabling: SI 2012/994

9. Appropriation (No.2) Act 2009

varied: SI 2012/147 Art.7

10. Finance Act 2009

applied: SI 2012/687 Sch.1 para.4

s.46, repealed: 2012 c.14 Sch.16 para.247

s.47, applied: 2012 c.14 s.30

s.47, repealed: 2012 c.14 s.30

s.77, repealed (in part): 2012 c.14 Sch.29 para.13

s.94, applied: 2012 c.14 Sch.38 para.28

s.101, applied: 2012 c.14 Sch.24 para.28

s.102, applied: 2012 c.14 Sch.24 para.28

s.103, applied: 2012 c.14 Sch.24 para.28

2009–cont.

10. Finance Act 2009–*cont.*
s.104, applied: 2012 c.14 Sch.24 para.28
Sch.1 para.3, repealed: 2012 c.14 Sch.39 para.28
Sch.1 para.4, repealed: 2012 c.14 Sch.39 para.28
Sch.1 para.5, repealed: 2012 c.14 Sch.39 para.28
Sch.7 Part 2 para.24, repealed: 2012 c.14 Sch.16 para.247
Sch.11 Part 2 para.60, repealed: 2012 c.14 Sch.16 para.247
Sch.16 Part 2, amended: 2012 c.14 Sch.20 para.36
Sch.16 Part 2 para.12, amended: 2012 c.14 Sch.20 para.33
Sch.16 Part 2 para.12, repealed (in part): 2012 c.14 Sch.20 para.33
Sch.16 Part 2 para.15, repealed: 2012 c.14 Sch.20 para.34
Sch.16 Part 2 para.16, amended: 2012 c.14 Sch.20 para.35
Sch.16 Part 2 para.16, repealed (in part): 2012 c.14 Sch.20 para.35
Sch.22 Part 2 para.11, repealed (in part): SI 2012/952 Reg.4
Sch.23 para.1, repealed: 2012 c.14 Sch.16 para.247
Sch.23 para.2, repealed: 2012 c.14 Sch.16 para.247
Sch.23 para.3, repealed: 2012 c.14 Sch.16 para.247
Sch.23 para.4, repealed: 2012 c.14 Sch.16 para.247
Sch.23 para.5, repealed: 2012 c.14 Sch.16 para.247
Sch.23 para.6, repealed: 2012 c.14 Sch.16 para.247
Sch.23 para.7, repealed: 2012 c.14 Sch.16 para.247
Sch.54 Part 2 para.9D, repealed: 2012 c.14 Sch.39 para.28
Sch.55, applied: 2012 c.14 Sch.38 para.34
Sch.55 para.1, amended: 2012 c.14 Sch.24 para.31
Sch.55 para.2, amended: 2012 c.14 Sch.24 para.32
Sch.55 para.13A, amended: 2012 c.14 Sch.24 para.32
Sch.55 para.13F, amended: 2012 c.14 Sch.24 para.32
Sch.56, see *Algarve Granite Ltd v Revenue and Customs Commissioners* [2012] UKFTT 463 (TC), [2012] S.F.T.D. 1354 (FTT (Tax)), Judge Guy Brannan; see *Core Technology Systems (UK) Ltd v Revenue and Customs Commissioners* [2012] UKFTT 629 (TC), Times, December 05, 2012 (FTT (Tax)), Judge Radford
Sch.56 para.1, amended: 2012 c.14 Sch.24 para.33, Sch.24 para.34
Sch.56 para.2, amended: 2012 c.14 Sch.24 para.34
Sch.56 para.3, amended: 2012 c.14 Sch.24 para.34
Sch.56 para.8A, amended: 2012 c.14 Sch.24 para.34
Sch.56 para.8F, amended: 2012 c.14 Sch.24 para.34
Sch.56 para.9, see *Algarve Granite Ltd v Revenue and Customs Commissioners* [2012] UKFTT 463 (TC), [2012] S.F.T.D. 1354 (FTT (Tax)), Judge Guy Brannan
Sch.56 para.11, see *Algarve Granite Ltd v Revenue and Customs Commissioners* [2012] UKFTT 463 (TC), [2012] S.F.T.D. 1354 (FTT (Tax)), Judge Guy Brannan
Sch.56 para.16, see *Algarve Granite Ltd v Revenue and Customs Commissioners* [2012] UKFTT 463 (TC), [2012] S.F.T.D. 1354 (FTT (Tax)), Judge Guy Brannan
Sch.61 Part 1 para.1, amended: 2012 c.11 Sch.3 para.31
Sch.61 Part 3 para.5, amended: 2012 c.11 Sch.3 para.31
Sch.61 Part 3 para.5, repealed (in part): 2012 c.11 Sch.3 para.31

2009–cont.

10. Finance Act 2009–*cont.*
Sch.61 Part 3 para.6, amended: 2012 c.11 Sch.3 para.31
Sch.61 Part 3 para.7, amended: 2012 c.11 Sch.3 para.31
Sch.61 Part 3 para.9, amended: 2012 c.11 Sch.3 para.31
Sch.61 Part 3 para.11, amended: 2012 c.11 Sch.3 para.31
Sch.61 Part 3 para.12, amended: 2012 c.11 Sch.3 para.31
Sch.61 Part 3 para.18, amended: 2012 c.11 Sch.3 para.31
Sch.61 Part 3 para.19, amended: 2012 c.11 Sch.3 para.31
Sch.61 Part 3 para.19, repealed (in part): 2012 c.11 Sch.3 para.31

11. Borders, Citizenship and Immigration Act 2009
s.7, amended: 2012 c.14 Sch.24 para.49
s.7, repealed (in part): 2012 c.14 Sch.24 para.58
s.29, enabling: SI 2012/2840
s.37, enabling: SI 2012/2840
s.55, see *AJ (India) v Secretary of State for the Home Department* [2011] EWCA Civ 1191, [2012] Imm. A.R. 10 (CA (Civ Div)), Pill, L.J.; see *HH (Nigeria) v Secretary of State for the Home Department* [2012] CSOH 83, 2012 S.L.T. 1004 (OH), Temporary Judge J Beckett, QC; see *RM (Iran) v Secretary of State for the Home Department* [2012] CSOH 53, 2012 S.L.T. 1203 (OH), Lord Glennie; see *T (s.55 BCIA 2009: Entry Clearance: Jamaica), Re* [2012] Imm. A.R. 346 (UT (IAC)), Blake, J. (President)

12. Political Parties and Elections Act 2009
s.35, applied: SI 2012/1944, SI 2012/1944 Art.4, SI 2012/3232
s.35, referred to: SI 2012/3232 Art.4
s.35, enabling: SI 2012/1944, SI 2012/3232
s.36, applied: SI 2012/1944, SI 2012/1944 Art.5, SI 2012/3232
s.36, referred to: SI 2012/3232 Art.5
s.36, enabling: SI 2012/1944, SI 2012/3232

15. Autism Act 2009
s.4, amended: 2012 c.7 Sch.5 para.171
s.4, repealed (in part): 2012 c.7 Sch.5 para.171, Sch.14 para.111

16. Holocaust (Return of Cultural Objects) Act 2009
s.1, amended: 2012 asp 3 Sch.2 para.8
s.2, amended: 2012 asp 3 Sch.2 para.8
s.2, applied: 2012 asp 3 s.3

17. Driving Instruction (Suspension and Exemption Powers) Act 2009
Commencement Orders: SI 2012/1356 Art.3, Art.4
s.7, enabling: SI 2012/1356

20. Local Democracy, Economic Development and Construction Act 2009
applied: 2012 c.13 Sch.1
s.57, applied: SI 2012/1020 Reg.3
s.58, applied: SI 2012/1, SI 2012/2, SI 2012/3, SI 2012/4, SI 2012/159, SI 2012/160, SI 2012/161, SI 2012/875, SI 2012/877, SI 2012/1394, SI 2012/1395, SI 2012/1396, SI 2012/1812, SI 2012/1872, SI 2012/2769, SI 2012/2984, SI 2012/2985, SI 2012/2986, SI 2012/3113
s.58, enabling: SI 2012/2769
s.59, enabling: SI 2012/1, SI 2012/2, SI 2012/3, SI 2012/4, SI 2012/159, SI 2012/160, SI 2012/161, SI 2012/875, SI 2012/877, SI 2012/1394, SI 2012/1395, SI 2012/1396, SI 2012/1812, SI 2012/1872,

20. Local Democracy, Economic Development and Construction Act 2009– *cont.*
s.59, enabling:– *cont.*
SI 2012/2769, SI 2012/2984, SI 2012/2985, SI 2012/2986, SI 2012/3113
s.123, amended: 2012 c.7 Sch.5 para.172
s.123, repealed (in part): 2012 c.7 Sch.5 para.172

21. Health Act 2009
Commencement Orders: SI 2012/1288 Art.2; SI 2012/1902 Art.2; SI 2012/2647 Art.2
s.1, amended: 2012 c.7 Sch.5 para.174
s.2, amended: 2012 c.7 Sch.5 para.174, Sch.5 para.175, Sch.13 para.18, Sch.17 para.13, Sch.19 para.12
s.2, repealed (in part): 2012 c.7 Sch.5 para.175, Sch.14 para.113
s.3, amended: 2012 c.7 Sch.5 para.174
s.3, repealed (in part): 2012 c.7 Sch.5 para.176
s.4, amended: 2012 c.7 Sch.5 para.174
s.5, amended: 2012 c.7 Sch.5 para.174
s.6, amended: 2012 c.7 Sch.5 para.174
s.7, amended: 2012 c.7 Sch.5 para.174
s.8, amended: 2012 c.7 Sch.5 para.174, Sch.5 para.177
s.8, repealed (in part): 2012 c.7 Sch.5 para.177, Sch.14 para.114
s.8, enabling: SI 2012/3081
s.9, amended: 2012 c.7 Sch.5 para.174, Sch.5 para.178
s.9, enabling: SI 2012/3081
s.10, amended: 2012 c.7 Sch.5 para.174
s.10, enabling: SI 2012/3081
s.11, amended: 2012 c.7 Sch.5 para.174
s.12, amended: 2012 c.7 Sch.5 para.174
s.13, amended: 2012 c.7 Sch.5 para.174
s.14, amended: 2012 c.7 Sch.5 para.174
s.15, repealed: 2012 c.7 s.173
s.18, repealed (in part): 2012 c.7 s.173
s.22, see *R. (on the application of Sinclair Collis Ltd) v Secretary of State for Health* [2011] EWCA Civ 437, [2012] Q.B. 394 (CA (Civ Div)), Lord Neuberger (M.R.)
s.29, repealed (in part): 2012 c.7 Sch.4 para.76, Sch.4 para.93
s.33, repealed: 2012 c.7 s.165
s.36, amended: 2012 c.7 Sch.5 para.179
s.37, enabling: SI 2012/1909
s.40, enabling: SI 2012/1288, SI 2012/1902, SI 2012/2647
Sch.1 para.14, repealed: 2012 c.9 Sch.10 Part 5
Sch.1 para.15, repealed: 2012 c.9 Sch.10 Part 5
Sch.3 Part 1 para.2, repealed: 2012 c.7 Sch.20 para.3
Sch.3 Part 1 para.8, repealed: 2012 c.7 Sch.20 para.7
Sch.3 Part 1 para.12, repealed: 2012 c.7 Sch.13 para.9
Sch.3 Part 1 para.13, repealed: 2012 c.7 s.283

22. Apprenticeships, Skills, Children and Learning Act 2009
s.1, enabling: SI 2012/1199
s.32, applied: SI 2012/844 Reg.2, Reg.4
s.32, enabling: SI 2012/844
s.36, applied: SI 2012/844 Reg.3, Reg.4
s.36, enabling: SI 2012/844
s.151B, applied: SI 2012/1768 Art.4
s.151B, enabling: SI 2012/1768
s.207, applied: SI 2012/1087 Art.6
s.262, applied: SI 2012/1768
s.262, enabling: SI 2012/844, SI 2012/1199
s.265, enabling: SI 2012/3112
Sch.9 para.3, applied: SI 2012/924 Art.4, Art.5

22. Apprenticeships, Skills, Children and Learning Act 2009– *cont.*
Sch.9 para.3A, applied: SI 2012/924 Art.4
Sch.9 para.6, applied: SI 2012/924 Art.5
Sch.12 para.43, repealed: 2012 c.9 Sch.10 Part 5

23. Marine and Coastal Access Act 2009
s.67, enabling: SSI 2012/183
s.74, applied: SSI 2012/25
s.74, enabling: SSI 2012/25
s.316, enabling: SI 2012/67, SSI 2012/25, SSI 2012/183
s.320, enabling: SI 2012/698
Sch.9 Part 4 para.9, varied: SI 2012/698 Art.2
Sch.20 para.4, enabling: SI 2012/67

24. Welfare Reform Act 2009
Commencement Orders: 2012 c.5 Sch.14 Part 2; SI 2012/68 Art.2; SI 2012/1256 Art.2; SI 2012/2523 Art.2
s.1, repealed (in part): 2012 c.5 Sch.14 Part 3, Sch.14 Part 4
s.2, repealed: 2012 c.5 Sch.14 Part 1
s.3, amended: 2012 c.5 s.58
s.3, repealed (in part): 2012 c.5 Sch.14 Part 1, Sch.14 Part 5
s.4, repealed (in part): 2012 c.5 Sch.14 Part 1, Sch.14 Part 2
s.5, repealed: 2012 c.5 Sch.14 Part 1
s.8, amended: 2012 c.5 s.58
s.8, repealed (in part): 2012 c.5 Sch.14 Part 1, Sch.14 Part 2, Sch.14 Part 5
s.9, repealed: 2012 c.5 Sch.14 Part 1
s.10, repealed: 2012 c.5 Sch.14 Part 5
s.11, repealed: 2012 c.5 s.60
s.14, repealed: 2012 c.5 Sch.14 Part 9
s.16, repealed: 2012 c.5 s.73
s.17, repealed: 2012 c.5 s.73
s.18, repealed: 2012 c.5 s.73
s.19, repealed: 2012 c.5 s.73
s.20, repealed: 2012 c.5 s.73
s.21, repealed: 2012 c.5 s.73
s.22, repealed: 2012 c.5 s.101
s.25, repealed: 2012 c.5 Sch.14 Part 3
s.29, amended: 2012 c.5 Sch.7 para.14
s.29, repealed: 2012 c.5 Sch.14 Part 4
s.31, amended: 2012 c.5 s.54, Sch.7 para.15
s.32, amended: 2012 c.5 Sch.7 para.16, Sch.14 Part 2, Sch.14 Part 6
s.32, repealed (in part): 2012 c.5 Sch.14 Part 2, Sch.14 Part 3, Sch.14 Part 4, Sch.14 Part 6
s.33, repealed: 2012 c.5 Sch.14 Part 3
s.34, repealed (in part): 2012 c.5 Sch.14 Part 1
s.35, repealed: 2012 c.5 Sch.14 Part 1
s.36, repealed: 2012 c.5 Sch.14 Part 1
s.37, repealed (in part): 2012 c.5 Sch.14 Part 1
s.41, enabling: SI 2012/3048
s.44, applied: SI 2012/3048
s.44, enabling: SI 2012/3048
s.45, enabling: SI 2012/3048
s.46, enabling: SSI 2012/3048
s.47, applied: SI 2012/3048
s.49, applied: SI 2012/3048
s.50, enabling: SI 2012/3048
s.51, amended: SI 2012/2007 Sch.1 para.99
s.57, enabling: SI 2012/1203
s.61, enabling: SI 2012/68, SI 2012/1256, SI 2012/2523
Sch.1 Part 1 para.1, repealed: 2012 c.5 Sch.14 Part 2
Sch.1 Part 1 para.2, repealed: 2012 c.5 Sch.14 Part 2

2009–cont.

24. Welfare Reform Act 2009–*cont.*

Sch.1 Part 1 para.3, repealed: 2012 c.5 Sch.14 Part 2
Sch.1 Part 1 para.4, repealed: 2012 c.5 Sch.14 Part 2
Sch.1 Part 1 para.5, repealed: 2012 c.5 Sch.14 Part 2
Sch.1 Part 1 para.6, repealed: 2012 c.5 Sch.14 Part 2
Sch.1 Part 1 para.7, repealed: 2012 c.5 Sch.14 Part 2
Sch.1 Part 1 para.8, repealed: 2012 c.5 Sch.14 Part 2
Sch.1 Part 1 para.9, repealed: 2012 c.5 Sch.14 Part 2
Sch.1 Part 1 para.10, repealed: 2012 c.5 Sch.14 Part 2
Sch.1 Part 1 para.11, repealed: 2012 c.5 Sch.14 Part 2
Sch.1 Part 1 para.12, repealed: 2012 c.5 Sch.14 Part 2
Sch.1 Part 1 para.13, repealed: 2012 c.5 Sch.14 Part 2
Sch.1 Part 1 para.14, repealed: 2012 c.5 Sch.14 Part 2
Sch.1 Part 1 para.15, repealed: 2012 c.5 Sch.14 Part 2
Sch.1 Part 1 para.16, repealed: 2012 c.5 Sch.14 Part 2
Sch.1 Part 1 para.17, repealed: 2012 c.5 Sch.14 Part 2
Sch.1 Part 1 para.18, repealed: 2012 c.5 Sch.14 Part 2
Sch.1 Part 1 para.19, repealed: 2012 c.5 Sch.14 Part 2
Sch.1 Part 1 para.20, repealed: 2012 c.5 Sch.14 Part 2
Sch.1 Part 1 para.21, repealed: 2012 c.5 Sch.14 Part 2
Sch.1 Part 1 para.22, repealed: 2012 c.5 Sch.14 Part 2
Sch.1 Part 1 para.23, repealed: 2012 c.5 Sch.14 Part 2
Sch.1 Part 2 para.24, repealed: 2012 c.5 Sch.14 Part 2
Sch.1 Part 2 para.25, repealed: 2012 c.5 Sch.14 Part 2
Sch.1 Part 2 para.26, repealed: 2012 c.5 Sch.14 Part 2
Sch.2 para.1, repealed: 2012 c.5 Sch.14 Part 1
Sch.2 para.2, repealed: 2012 c.5 Sch.14 Part 1
Sch.2 para.3, repealed: 2012 c.5 Sch.14 Part 1
Sch.2 para.4, repealed: 2012 c.5 Sch.14 Part 1
Sch.2 para.5, repealed: 2012 c.5 Sch.14 Part 1
Sch.2 para.6, repealed: 2012 c.5 Sch.14 Part 1
Sch.2 para.7, repealed: 2012 c.5 Sch.14 Part 1
Sch.2 para.8, repealed: 2012 c.5 Sch.14 Part 1
Sch.2 para.9, repealed: 2012 c.5 Sch.14 Part 1
Sch.2 para.10, repealed: 2012 c.5 Sch.14 Part 1
Sch.2 para.11, repealed: 2012 c.5 Sch.14 Part 1
Sch.2 para.12, repealed: 2012 c.5 Sch.14 Part 1
Sch.2 para.13, repealed: 2012 c.5 Sch.14 Part 1
Sch.2 para.14, repealed: 2012 c.5 Sch.14 Part 1
Sch.2 para.15, repealed: 2012 c.5 Sch.14 Part 1
Sch.2 para.16, repealed: 2012 c.5 Sch.14 Part 1
Sch.2 para.17, repealed: 2012 c.5 Sch.14 Part 1
Sch.3 Part 1 para.1, repealed: 2012 c.5 s.60
Sch.3 Part 1 para.2, repealed: 2012 c.5 s.60
Sch.3 Part 1 para.3, repealed: 2012 c.5 s.60
Sch.3 Part 1 para.4, repealed: 2012 c.5 s.60
Sch.3 Part 1 para.5, repealed: 2012 c.5 s.60
Sch.3 Part 2 para.6, repealed: 2012 c.5 s.60
Sch.3 Part 2 para.7, repealed: 2012 c.5 s.60
Sch.3 Part 2 para.8, repealed: 2012 c.5 s.60
Sch.3 Part 2 para.9, repealed: 2012 c.5 s.60
Sch.4 Part 1 para.3, repealed: 2012 c.5 Sch.14 Part 1
Sch.5 para.3, amended: SI 2012/2007 Sch.1 para.100
Sch.5 para.5, amended: SI 2012/2007 Sch.1 para.100
Sch.5 para.6, amended: SI 2012/2007 Sch.1 para.100
Sch.7 Part 1, repealed: 2012 c.5 Sch.14 Part 1
Sch.7 Part 3, amended: 2012 c.5 Sch.14 Part 1, Sch.14 Part 2, Sch.14 Part 3, Sch.14 Part 6

2009–cont.

25. Coroners and Justice Act 2009

Commencement Orders: SI 2012/1810 Art.2; SI 2012/2374 Art.2, Art.3; SI 2012/2401 Sch.1 para.34, para.35
see *R. v Dowds (Stephen Andrew)* [2012] EWCA Crim 281, [2012] 1 W.L.R. 2576 (CA (Crim Div)), Hughes, L.J.
applied: SI 2012/1726 r.6.1
Part 7, applied: SI 2012/1726 r.6.1
s.19, amended: 2012 c.7 s.54
s.20, amended: 2012 c.7 s.54
s.39, repealed: SI 2012/2401 Sch.1 para.34
s.51, repealed: 2012 c.10 Sch.5 Part 2
s.52, see *R. v Brown (Robert)* [2011] EWCA Crim 2796, [2012] 2 Cr. App. R. (S.) 27 (CA (Crim Div)), Lord Judge, L.C.J.
s.54, see *R. v Clinton (Jon-Jacques)* [2012] EWCA Crim 2, [2012] 3 W.L.R. 515 (CA (Crim Div)), Lord Judge, L.C.J.
s.55, see *Attorney General's Reference (No.23 of 2011), Re* [2011] EWCA Crim 1496, [2012] 1 Cr. App. R. (S.) 45 (CA (Crim Div)), Lord Judge, L.C.J.; see *R. v Clinton (Jon-Jacques)* [2012] EWCA Crim 2, [2012] 3 W.L.R. 515 (CA (Crim Div)), Lord Judge, L.C.J.
s.62, applied: SI 2012/951 Reg.4, SI 2012/1925 Reg.4
s.76, applied: SI 2012/1726 r.6.1
s.77, applied: SI 2012/1726 r.6.24
s.78, applied: SI 2012/1726 r.6.24
s.79, applied: SI 2012/1726 r.6.1, r.6.26
s.80, applied: SI 2012/1726 r.6.1, r.6.25, r.6.26
s.86, applied: SI 2012/1726 r.16.6, r.29.1, r.29.26
s.88, see *R. v Willett (Tommy)* [2011] EWCA Crim 2710, [2012] 2 Cr. App. R. (S.) 18 (CA (Crim Div)), Richards, L.J.
s.88, applied: SI 2012/1726 r.29.19, r.29.22
s.88, referred to: SI 2012/1726 r.29.26
s.89, applied: SI 2012/1726 r.29.22
s.89, referred to: SI 2012/1726 r.29.26
s.91, applied: SI 2012/1726 r.29.1, r.29.21
s.92, applied: SI 2012/1726 r.29.1, r.29.21
s.93, applied: SI 2012/1726 r.29.1, r.29.21
s.115, see *R. (on the application of A) v Lewisham Youth Court* [2011] EWHC 1193 (Admin), [2012] 1 W.L.R. 34 (DC), Toulson, L.J.
s.115, referred to: SI 2012/1726 r.19.1, r.19.10
s.120, applied: SI 2012/1726 r.37.10
s.122, applied: SI 2012/1726 r.9.10
s.122, varied: SI 2012/1726 r.9.10
s.125, see *R. v Blackshaw (Jordan Philip)* [2011] EWCA Crim 2312, [2012] 1 W.L.R. 1126 (CA (Crim Div)), Lord Judge, L.C.J.
s.125, amended: 2012 c.10 Sch.19 para.23, Sch.26 para.31
s.126, amended: 2012 c.10 Sch.21 para.34
s.126, repealed (in part): 2012 c.10 Sch.21 para.34
s.145, repealed: 2012 c.10 Sch.16 para.21
s.149, repealed: 2012 c.10 Sch.5 Part 2
s.150, repealed: 2012 c.10 Sch.5 Part 2
s.151, repealed: 2012 c.10 Sch.5 Part 2
s.152, repealed: 2012 c.10 Sch.5 Part 2
s.153, repealed: 2012 c.10 Sch.5 Part 2
s.176, enabling: SI 2012/2374
s.182, enabling: SI 2012/1810, SI 2012/2374
Sch.1 Part 1 para.1, amended: 2012 c.4 Sch.1 para.12
Sch.12 para.7, amended: SI 2012/1809 Sch.1 Part 1
Sch.13 para.6, amended: SI 2012/1809 Sch.1 Part 1
Sch.17 para.12, repealed (in part): 2012 c.10 s.79
Sch.18, repealed: 2012 c.10 Sch.5 Part 2

2009– cont.

25. Coroners and Justice Act 2009– *cont.*
  Sch.21 Part 1 para.46, repealed: SI 2012/ 2401 Sch.1 para.35
  Sch.21 Part 8 para.84, repealed: 2012 c.10 s.64
  Sch.22 Part 5 para.43, repealed: 2012 c.10 Sch.16 para.21
  Sch.23, applied: 2012 c.4 Sch.1 para.2
26. Policing and Crime Act 2009
  Commencement Orders: 2012 c.9 Sch.10 Part 5, 6; SI 2012/ 2235 Art.2
  Part 4, applied: 2012 c.10 Sch.1 para.38
  s.18, repealed (in part): 2012 c.10 Sch.25 Part 2
  s.57, amended: SI 2012/ 2595 Art.18
  s.71, repealed (in part): 2012 c.10 Sch.10 para.43
  s.81, amended: 2012 c.9 Sch.10 Part 5
  s.81, applied: SI 2012/ 3006 Art.34, Art.35
  s.81, repealed (in part): 2012 c.9 Sch.10 Part 5
  s.82, repealed (in part): 2012 c.9 Sch.10 Part 5
  s.83, repealed (in part): 2012 c.9 Sch.10 Part 5
  s.84, repealed (in part): 2012 c.9 Sch.10 Part 5
  s.85, repealed (in part): 2012 c.9 Sch.10 Part 5
  s.86, repealed (in part): 2012 c.9 Sch.10 Part 5
  s.87, repealed (in part): 2012 c.9 s.77, Sch.10 Part 5
  s.88, amended: SI 2012/ 3006 Art.34
  s.89, repealed (in part): 2012 c.9 s.77, Sch.10 Part 5
  s.90, repealed (in part): 2012 c.9 Sch.7 para.14, Sch.10 Part 5
  s.91, amended: SI 2012/ 3006 Art.34
  s.92, repealed (in part): 2012 c.9 Sch.10 Part 5
  s.93, repealed (in part): 2012 c.9 s.79, Sch.10 Part 6
  s.116, amended: SI 2012/ 2595 Art.18
  s.116, enabling: SI 2012/ 2235
  Sch.5A Part 3 para.14, amended: 2012 c.10 Sch.12 para.58
  Sch.7 Part 6 para.65, repealed: 2012 c.10 Sch.5 Part 2
  Sch.7 Part 7 para.98, repealed: 2012 c.10 Sch.5 Part 2
  Sch.8 Part 8, amended: 2012 c.9 Sch.10 Part 5

2010

01. Children and Families (Wales) Measure 2010
  Commencement Orders: SI 2012/ 191 Art.2, Art.3, Art.4, Art.5, Sch.1 para.1, para.2, para.3, para.4, Sch.2; SI 2012/ 2453 Art.2
  Part 2, applied: SI 2012/ 1034 Sch.4 para.13, SI 2012/ 2885 Sch.1 para.25, SI 2012/ 3144 Sch.1 para.19, SI 2012/ 3145 Sch.1, SSI 2012/ 303 Reg.28, SSI 2012/ 319 Reg.29
  Part 3, applied: SI 2012/ 204 Reg.2, Sch.1
  s.7, enabling: SI 2012/ 205
  s.11, enabling: SI 2012/ 2555
  s.58, enabling: SI 2012/ 204
  s.60, enabling: SI 2012/ 202
  s.62, referred to: SI 2012/ 202 Reg.4
  s.62, enabling: SI 2012/ 202
  s.63, enabling: SI 2012/ 205
  s.65, applied: SI 2012/ 202 Reg.3
  s.74, enabling: SI 2012/ 191, SI 2012/ 205
  s.75, enabling: SI 2012/ 191, SI 2012/ 2453
03. Red Meat Industry (Wales) Measure 2010
  s.4, enabling: SI 2012/ 247
  s.17, enabling: SI 2012/ 247
4. Corporation Tax Act 2010
  applied: 2012 c.14 Sch.22 para.22
  referred to: 2012 c.23 s.21
  Part 3, applied: 2012 c.14 s.7, s.102
  Part 4 c.2, applied: 2012 c.14 s.127
  Part 4 c.4, applied: 2012 c.14 s.127

2010– cont.

4. Corporation Tax Act 2010– *cont.*
  Part 4 c.4, disapplied: 2012 c.14 s.87
  Part 5, applied: 2012 c.14 s.125, s.126, s.127
  Part 6, applied: SI 2012/ 847 Reg.25
  Part 8, referred to: 2012 c.14 s.6, s.7
  Part 8A, applied: 2012 c.14 Sch.2 para.7
  Part 10, applied: SI 2012/ 701 Reg.3
  Part 16 c.2, referred to: 2012 c.14 s.48
  s.9A, applied: 2012 c.14 Sch.20 para.57
  s.17, amended: 2012 c.14 Sch.16 para.216
  s.17, repealed (in part): 2012 c.14 Sch.16 para.216
  s.37, applied: 2012 c.14 s.123, s.124, s.126, s.127, Sch.17 para.34
  s.40, amended: 2012 c.14 Sch.21 para.5
  s.45, applied: 2012 c.14 Sch.17 para.29, Sch.17 para.30
  s.54, amended: 2012 c.14 Sch.16 para.217
  s.67B, added: 2012 c.14 Sch.16 para.218
  s.99, applied: 2012 c.14 s.125
  s.105, applied: 2012 c.14 s.125
  s.137, applied: 2012 c.14 s.124
  s.154, amended: SI 2012/ 266 Art.13
  s.155, amended: SI 2012/ 266 Art.13
  s.155A, added: SI 2012/ 266 Art.13
  s.155B, added: SI 2012/ 266 Art.13
  s.156, amended: SI 2012/ 266 Art.13
  s.161, amended: 2012 c.21 Sch.18 para.129
  s.162, amended: 2012 c.14 s.32
  s.164, amended: 2012 c.14 s.32
  s.173, amended: SI 2012/ 266 Art.14
  s.174A, added: SI 2012/ 266 Art.14
  s.174B, added: SI 2012/ 266 Art.14
  s.194, repealed (in part): 2012 c.14 s.33
  s.202, amended: SI 2012/ 964 Sch.1
  s.202, repealed (in part): SI 2012/ 964 Sch.1
  s.217, amended: SI 2012/ 964 Sch.1
  s.217, repealed (in part): SI 2012/ 964 Sch.1
  s.270, amended: 2012 c.14 Sch.22 para.18
  s.330, amended: 2012 c.14 s.182, Sch.21 para.2, Sch.22 para.18
  s.330A, added: 2012 c.14 Sch.21 para.3
  s.330B, added: 2012 c.14 Sch.21 para.3
  s.330C, added: 2012 c.14 Sch.21 para.3
  s.333, substituted: 2012 c.14 Sch.22 para.17
  s.334, amended: 2012 c.14 Sch.22 para.2
  s.334, substituted: 2012 c.14 Sch.22 para.17
  s.335, substituted: 2012 c.14 Sch.22 para.17
  s.336, substituted: 2012 c.14 Sch.22 para.17
  s.337, amended: 2012 c.14 Sch.22 para.3
  s.337, substituted: 2012 c.14 Sch.22 para.3, Sch.22 para.17
  s.338, amended: 2012 c.14 Sch.22 para.4
  s.338, substituted: 2012 c.14 Sch.22 para.17
  s.339, amended: 2012 c.14 Sch.22 para.5
  s.339, substituted: 2012 c.14 Sch.22 para.17
  s.340, amended: 2012 c.14 Sch.22 para.6
  s.340, substituted: 2012 c.14 Sch.22 para.17
  s.341, amended: 2012 c.14 Sch.22 para.7
  s.341, substituted: 2012 c.14 Sch.22 para.17
  s.342, amended: 2012 c.14 Sch.22 para.8
  s.342, substituted: 2012 c.14 Sch.22 para.17
  s.343, amended: 2012 c.14 Sch.22 para.9
  s.343, substituted: 2012 c.14 Sch.22 para.17
  s.344, amended: 2012 c.14 Sch.22 para.10
  s.344, substituted: 2012 c.14 Sch.22 para.17
  s.345, amended: 2012 c.14 Sch.22 para.11
  s.345, substituted: 2012 c.14 Sch.22 para.17
  s.346, amended: 2012 c.14 Sch.22 para.12

2010– cont.

4. **Corporation Tax Act 2010**–*cont.*
s.346, substituted: 2012 c.14 Sch.22 para.17
s.347, amended: 2012 c.14 Sch.22 para.13
s.347, substituted: 2012 c.14 Sch.22 para.17
s.348, substituted: 2012 c.14 Sch.22 para.17
s.349, amended: 2012 c.14 Sch.22 para.14
s.349, substituted: 2012 c.14 Sch.22 para.17
s.349, enabling: SI 2012/ 3153
s.349A, added: 2012 c.14 Sch.22 para.15
s.349A, substituted: 2012 c.14 Sch.22 para.17
s.350, substituted: 2012 c.14 Sch.22 para.17
s.351, substituted: 2012 c.14 Sch.22 para.17
s.352, amended: SI 2012/3153 Art.3
s.352, substituted: 2012 c.14 Sch.22 para.17
s.353, amended: SI 2012/ 3153 Art.4
s.353, substituted: 2012 c.14 Sch.22 para.17
s.354, substituted: 2012 c.14 Sch.22 para.17
s.355, substituted: 2012 c.14 Sch.22 para.17
s.355A, added: SI 2012/ 3153 Art.5
s.355A, substituted: 2012 c.14 Sch.22 para.17
s.355B, added: SI 2012/ 3153 Art.5
s.355B, substituted: 2012 c.14 Sch.22 para.17
s.355C, added: SI 2012/ 3153 Art.5
s.355C, substituted: 2012 c.14 Sch.22 para.17
s.356, amended: SI 2012/ 3153 Art.6
s.356, substituted: 2012 c.14 Sch.22 para.17
s.357, amended: 2012 c.14 Sch.22 para.16
s.357, substituted: 2012 c.14 Sch.22 para.17
s.357A, added: 2012 c.14 Sch.2 para.1
s.357A, applied: 2012 c.14 Sch.2 para.7
s.357A, varied: 2012 c.14 Sch.2 para.8
s.357B, added: 2012 c.14 Sch.2 para.1
s.357BA, added: 2012 c.14 Sch.2 para.1
s.357BB, added: 2012 c.14 Sch.2 para.1
s.357BC, added: 2012 c.14 Sch.2 para.1
s.357BD, added: 2012 c.14 Sch.2 para.1
s.357BE, added: 2012 c.14 Sch.2 para.1
s.357C, added: 2012 c.14 Sch.2 para.1
s.357CA, added: 2012 c.14 Sch.2 para.1
s.357CB, added: 2012 c.14 Sch.2 para.1
s.357CC, added: 2012 c.14 Sch.2 para.1
s.357CD, added: 2012 c.14 Sch.2 para.1
s.357CE, added: 2012 c.14 Sch.2 para.1
s.357CF, added: 2012 c.14 Sch.2 para.1
s.357CG, added: 2012 c.14 Sch.2 para.1
s.357CH, added: 2012 c.14 Sch.2 para.1
s.357CI, added: 2012 c.14 Sch.2 para.1
s.357CJ, added: 2012 c.14 Sch.2 para.1
s.357CK, added: 2012 c.14 Sch.2 para.1
s.357CL, added: 2012 c.14 Sch.2 para.1
s.357CM, added: 2012 c.14 Sch.2 para.1
s.357CN, added: 2012 c.14 Sch.2 para.1
s.357CO, added: 2012 c.14 Sch.2 para.1
s.357CP, added: 2012 c.14 Sch.2 para.1
s.357CQ, added: 2012 c.14 Sch.2 para.1
s.357D, added: 2012 c.14 Sch.2 para.1
s.357DA, added: 2012 c.14 Sch.2 para.1
s.357DB, added: 2012 c.14 Sch.2 para.1
s.357DC, added: 2012 c.14 Sch.2 para.1
s.357E, added: 2012 c.14 Sch.2 para.1
s.357EA, added: 2012 c.14 Sch.2 para.1
s.357EA, referred to: 2012 c.14 Sch.2 para.8
s.357EB, added: 2012 c.14 Sch.2 para.1
s.357EB, applied: 2012 c.14 Sch.2 para.8
s.357EB, referred to: 2012 c.14 Sch.2 para.8
s.357EC, added: 2012 c.14 Sch.2 para.1
s.357EC, applied: 2012 c.14 Sch.2 para.8
s.357ED, added: 2012 c.14 Sch.2 para.1

2010– cont.

4. **Corporation Tax Act 2010**–*cont.*
s.357EE, added: 2012 c.14 Sch.2 para.1
s.357EF, added: 2012 c.14 Sch.2 para.1
s.357F, added: 2012 c.14 Sch.2 para.1
s.357FA, added: 2012 c.14 Sch.2 para.1
s.357FB, added: 2012 c.14 Sch.2 para.1
s.357G, added: 2012 c.14 Sch.2 para.1
s.357GA, added: 2012 c.14 Sch.2 para.1
s.357GB, added: 2012 c.14 Sch.2 para.1
s.357GC, added: 2012 c.14 Sch.2 para.1
s.357GD, added: 2012 c.14 Sch.2 para.1
s.357GE, added: 2012 c.14 Sch.2 para.1
s.385, amended: 2012 c.14 s.24
s.385, substituted: 2012 c.14 s.24
s.392, amended: 2012 c.14 s.24
s.394A, substituted: 2012 c.14 s.24
s.394ZA, added: 2012 c.14 s.24
s.398D, amended: 2012 c.14 Sch.20 para.38
s.427, amended: 2012 c.14 s.24
s.427, substituted: 2012 c.14 s.24
s.468, amended: SI 2012/ 964 Sch.1
s.468, repealed (in part): SI 2012/ 964 Sch.1
s.472, repealed (in part): 2012 c.14 s.50
s.475, repealed (in part): 2012 c.14 s.50
s.477A, amended: 2012 c.14 Sch.15 para.3
s.491A, added: 2012 c.14 Sch.15 para.4
s.508, varied: SI 2012/ 700 Sch.1 para.4
s.523, applied: 2012 c.14 Sch.4 para.13, Sch.4 para.21, Sch.4 para.36
s.524, applied: 2012 c.14 Sch.4 para.13, Sch.4 para.21
s.525, amended: 2012 c.14 Sch.4 para.2
s.525, repealed (in part): 2012 c.14 Sch.4 para.2
s.527, amended: 2012 c.14 Sch.4 para.3, Sch.4 para.14
s.528, amended: 2012 c.14 Sch.4 para.4, Sch.4 para.15
s.528A, added: 2012 c.14 Sch.4 para.16
s.528B, added: 2012 c.14 Sch.4 para.16
s.530, amended: 2012 c.14 Sch.4 para.22
s.530A, added: 2012 c.14 Sch.4 para.23
s.531, amended: 2012 c.14 Sch.4 para.27
s.531, referred to: 2012 c.14 Sch.4 para.32
s.538, repealed: 2012 c.14 Sch.4 para.33
s.539, repealed: 2012 c.14 Sch.4 para.33
s.540, repealed: 2012 c.14 Sch.4 para.33
s.543, amended: 2012 c.14 Sch.4 para.40
s.544, amended: 2012 c.14 Sch.4 para.41
s.545, amended: 2012 c.14 Sch.4 para.34
s.545, applied: 2012 c.14 Sch.4 para.34
s.547, repealed (in part): 2012 c.14 Sch.4 para.28
s.548, applied: 2012 c.14 s.74
s.556, amended: 2012 c.14 Sch.4 para.43
s.556, repealed (in part): 2012 c.14 Sch.4 para.35
s.558, amended: 2012 c.14 Sch.4 para.5, Sch.4 para.36
s.559, amended: 2012 c.14 Sch.4 para.6, Sch.4 para.37
s.561, amended: 2012 c.14 Sch.4 para.7, Sch.4 para.17
s.562, amended: 2012 c.14 Sch.4 para.8
s.562, applied: 2012 c.14 Sch.4 para.13
s.562, repealed (in part): 2012 c.14 Sch.4 para.8
s.562A, added: 2012 c.14 Sch.4 para.9
s.562B, added: 2012 c.14 Sch.4 para.18
s.562C, added: 2012 c.14 Sch.4 para.18
s.564, repealed (in part): 2012 c.14 Sch.4 para.24
s.565, amended: 2012 c.14 Sch.4 para.25
s.566, amended: 2012 c.14 Sch.4 para.29
s.566, repealed (in part): 2012 c.14 Sch.4 para.29

2010– cont.

4. **Corporation Tax Act 2010**–*cont.*
s.567, repealed: 2012 c.14 Sch.4 para.30
s.568, amended: 2012 c.14 Sch.4 para.31
s.572, amended: 2012 c.14 Sch.4 para.10, Sch.4 para.19
s.573A, added: 2012 c.14 Sch.4 para.11
s.573B, added: 2012 c.14 Sch.4 para.20
s.577, amended: 2012 c.14 Sch.4 para.12
s.583, repealed (in part): 2012 c.14 Sch.4 para.38
s.595, repealed: 2012 c.14 Sch.4 para.39
s.596, repealed: 2012 c.14 Sch.4 para.39
s.597, repealed: 2012 c.14 Sch.4 para.39
s.606, amended: 2012 c.14 Sch.16 para.219
s.620, amended: SI 2012/2595 Art.21
s.635, amended: 2012 c.21 Sch.18 para.129
s.658, amended: 2012 c.14 s.52
s.658, applied: SI 2012/2550 Reg.4
s.661D, added: 2012 c.14 Sch.15 para.6
s.665A, added: 2012 c.14 Sch.15 para.7
s.758, amended: 2012 c.14 Sch.13 para.38
s.763, amended: 2012 c.14 Sch.13 para.39
s.765, amended: 2012 c.14 Sch.13 para.40
s.767, amended: 2012 c.14 Sch.13 para.41
s.776, applied: 2012 c.14 Sch.13 para.6, Sch.13 para.7, Sch.13 para.21
s.783, amended: 2012 c.14 Sch.16 para.220
s.785, amended: 2012 c.14 Sch.16 para.221
s.791, amended: 2012 c.14 Sch.16 para.222
s.793, amended: 2012 c.14 s.22
s.799, amended: 2012 c.14 Sch.16 para.223
s.812, amended: 2012 c.14 s.22
s.835, amended: 2012 c.14 Sch.16 para.224
s.836, amended: 2012 c.14 Sch.16 para.225
s.839, amended: 2012 c.14 Sch.16 para.226
s.840, amended: 2012 c.14 Sch.16 para.227
s.860, amended: 2012 c.14 Sch.16 para.228
s.886, amended: 2012 c.14 Sch.16 para.229
s.938M, amended: 2012 c.14 Sch.20 para.39
s.950, amended: 2012 c.14 s.24
s.967, amended: 2012 c.14 Sch.15 para.10
s.986, amended: 2012 c.7 Sch.14 para.115
s.991, repealed: 2012 c.14 Sch.39 para.16
s.992, repealed: 2012 c.14 Sch.39 para.16
s.993, repealed: 2012 c.14 Sch.39 para.16
s.994, repealed: 2012 c.14 Sch.39 para.16
s.995, repealed: 2012 c.14 Sch.39 para.16
s.998, amended: 2012 c.14 s.33
s.1001, amended: 2012 c.14 s.33
s.1002, repealed: 2012 c.14 s.33
s.1020, amended: 2012 c.14 s.33
s.1021, repealed: 2012 c.14 s.33
s.1029, amended: SI 2012/266 Art.16
s.1030A, added: SI 2012/266 Art.16
s.1030B, added: SI 2012/266 Art.16
s.1120, amended: 2012 c.21 Sch.18 para.129
s.1122, applied: SI 2012/2500 Sch.1
s.1139, amended: 2012 c.14 Sch.20 para.40
s.1139, varied: 2012 c.14 s.132
s.1171, amended: 2012 c.14 Sch.16 para.230
s.1172, applied: 2012 c.14 s.77
s.1173, amended: 2012 c.14 Sch.16 para.231
s.1173, applied: 2012 c.14 s.74, s.89
Sch.1 Part 1 para.9, repealed: 2012 c.14 Sch.16 para.247
Sch.1 Part 1 para.10, repealed: 2012 c.14 Sch.16 para.247
Sch.1 Part 1 para.42, repealed: 2012 c.14 Sch.16 para.247

2010– cont.

4. **Corporation Tax Act 2010**–*cont.*
Sch.1 Part 1 para.43, repealed: 2012 c.14 Sch.16 para.247
Sch.1 Part 1 para.44, repealed: 2012 c.14 Sch.16 para.247
Sch.1 Part 1 para.45, repealed: 2012 c.14 Sch.16 para.247
Sch.1 Part 1 para.46, repealed: 2012 c.14 Sch.16 para.247
Sch.1 Part 1 para.47, repealed: 2012 c.14 Sch.16 para.247
Sch.1 Part 1 para.48, repealed: 2012 c.14 Sch.16 para.247
Sch.1 Part 1 para.49, repealed: 2012 c.14 Sch.16 para.247
Sch.1 Part 1 para.50, repealed: 2012 c.14 Sch.16 para.247
Sch.1 Part 1 para.51, repealed: 2012 c.14 Sch.16 para.247
Sch.1 Part 2 para.196, repealed: 2012 c.14 Sch.39 para.5
Sch.1 Part 2 para.213, repealed: 2012 c.14 Sch.16 para.247
Sch.1 Part 2 para.214, repealed: 2012 c.14 Sch.16 para.247
Sch.1 Part 2 para.251, repealed: 2012 c.14 Sch.39 para.17
Sch.1 Part 2 para.366, repealed: 2012 c.14 Sch.39 para.7
Sch.1 Part 2 para.372, repealed: 2012 c.14 Sch.39 para.5
Sch.1 Part 2 para.376, repealed: 2012 c.14 Sch.39 para.5
Sch.1 Part 2 para.489, repealed: SI 2012/952 Reg.4
Sch.1 Part 2 para.672, repealed: 2012 c.14 Sch.3 para.32
Sch.1 Part 2 para.673, repealed: 2012 c.14 Sch.3 para.32
Sch.1 Part 2 para.674, repealed: 2012 c.14 Sch.3 para.32
Sch.4, amended: 2012 c.14 Sch.2 para.1, Sch.22 para.19

5. **Appropriation Act 2010**
varied: SI 2012/147 Art.7

05. **Carers Strategies (Wales) Measure 2010**
s.5, enabling: SI 2012/282
s.10, enabling: SI 2012/282

07. **Mental Health (Wales) Measure 2010**
Commencement Orders: SI 2012/1397 Art.2; SI 2012/2411 Art.2
Part 1, applied: SI 2012/1244 Reg.3
Part 2, applied: SI 2012/1428 Art.3
Part 3, applied: SI 2012/1244 Reg.4, SI 2012/1428 Art.3
Part 3, disapplied: SI 2012/1244 Reg.4
Part 5, applied: SI 2012/1244 Reg.3, Reg.4
s.7, applied: SI 2012/1305 Reg.3
s.7, enabling: SI 2012/1305
s.8, applied: SI 2012/1305 Reg.3
s.22, applied: SI 2012/1428 Art.4
s.23, applied: SI 2012/1428 Art.4
s.43, referred to: SI 2012/1244 Reg.4
s.44, applied: SI 2012/1305 Reg.4
s.45, disapplied: SI 2012/1244 Reg.3
s.45, enabling: SI 2012/1244
s.46, enabling: SI 2012/1244
s.47, enabling: SI 2012/1305
s.49, enabling: SI 2012/1428

2010– cont.

07. Mental Health (Wales) Measure 2010–*cont.*
s.52, applied: SI 2012/ 1244, SI 2012/ 1305, SI 2012/ 1428
s.52, enabling: SI 2012/ 1244, SI 2012/ 1305, SI 2012/ 1397, SI 2012/ 1428, SI 2012/ 2411
s.55, enabling: SI 2012/ 1397, SI 2012/ 2411

8. Taxation (International and Other Provisions) Act 2010
Part 3, applied: 2012 c.14 Sch.36 para.16, Sch.36 para.17
Part 4, disapplied: 2012 c.14 s.129
Part 9A, applied: 2012 c.14 Sch.20 para.49, Sch.20 para.50, Sch.20 para.57, Sch.20 para.58
Part 9A c.10, applied: 2012 c.14 Sch.20 para.58
Part 9A c.11, applied: SI 2012/ 3024 Reg.3, Reg.4, Reg.5
Part 9A c.19, added: 2012 c.14 Sch.20 para.1
s.2, enabling: SI 2012/ 3075, SI 2012/ 3076, SI 2012/ 3077, SI 2012/ 3078, SI 2012/ 3079
s.5, applied: SI 2012/ 3075, SI 2012/ 3076, SI 2012/ 3077, SI 2012/ 3078, SI 2012/ 3079
s.43, amended: 2012 c.14 Sch.16 para.233
s.72, repealed (in part): 2012 c.14 Sch.16 para.234
s.96, amended: 2012 c.14 Sch.16 para.235
s.97, substituted: 2012 c.14 Sch.16 para.236
s.98, repealed: 2012 c.14 Sch.16 para.237
s.99, amended: 2012 c.14 Sch.16 para.238
s.102, repealed: 2012 c.14 Sch.16 para.239
s.103, amended: 2012 c.14 Sch.16 para.240
s.104, amended: 2012 c.14 Sch.16 para.241
s.136, disapplied: 2012 c.14 Sch.36 para.19
s.138, applied: 2012 c.14 Sch.36 para.18
s.140, applied: 2012 c.14 Sch.36 para.18
s.143, applied: 2012 c.14 Sch.36 para.16
s.166, amended: 2012 c.14 Sch.2 para.3
s.167A, added: 2012 c.14 Sch.2 para.4
s.170, amended: 2012 c.14 Sch.2 para.5
s.171, amended: 2012 c.14 Sch.2 para.6
s.179, amended: 2012 c.14 Sch.20 para.42
s.262, amended: 2012 c.14 Sch.5 para.2
s.269, amended: 2012 c.14 Sch.16 para.242
s.276, amended: 2012 c.14 Sch.5 para.3
s.280, amended: 2012 c.14 Sch.5 para.4
s.288, amended: 2012 c.14 Sch.5 para.5
s.292, amended: 2012 c.14 Sch.5 para.6, SI 2012/ 3045 Reg.3
s.293, substituted: SI 2012/ 3045 Reg.4
s.296, amended: 2012 c.14 Sch.5 para.7, SI 2012/ 3045 Reg.5
s.298, amended: SI 2012/ 3045 Reg.6
s.298A, added: 2012 c.14 Sch.20 para.43
s.298A, enabling: SI 2012/ 3045
s.305A, added: 2012 c.14 Sch.5 para.8
s.310, amended: 2012 c.14 Sch.16 para.243
s.310, repealed (in part): 2012 c.14 Sch.16 para.243
s.313, amended: 2012 c.14 Sch.5 para.9
s.314, amended: 2012 c.14 Sch.5 para.10, Sch.20 para.44
s.314A, added: 2012 c.14 Sch.20 para.45
s.314A, amended: SI 2012/ 3045 Reg.7
s.316, repealed (in part): 2012 c.14 Sch.5 para.11
s.329, amended: 2012 c.14 Sch.5 para.12
s.330, amended: 2012 c.14 Sch.5 para.13
s.331ZA, added: 2012 c.14 Sch.5 para.14
s.332D, added: SI 2012/ 3111 Reg.2
s.332E, added: SI 2012/ 3111 Reg.2
s.336A, enabling: SI 2012/ 3111
s.337, substituted: 2012 c.14 Sch.5 para.15

2010– cont.

8. Taxation (International and Other Provisions) Act 2010–*cont.*
s.339, amended: 2012 c.14 Sch.5 para.16
s.348, amended: 2012 c.14 Sch.5 para.17
s.348A, added: 2012 c.14 Sch.5 para.18
s.351, amended: 2012 c.14 Sch.5 para.19
s.353, amended: 2012 c.14 Sch.5 para.20
s.353AA, added: 2012 c.14 Sch.5 para.21
s.371AA, added: 2012 c.14 Sch.20 para.1
s.371BA, added: 2012 c.14 Sch.20 para.1
s.371BB, added: 2012 c.14 Sch.20 para.1
s.371BC, added: 2012 c.14 Sch.20 para.1
s.371BD, added: 2012 c.14 Sch.20 para.1
s.371BE, added: 2012 c.14 Sch.20 para.1
s.371BF, added: 2012 c.14 Sch.20 para.1
s.371BG, added: 2012 c.14 Sch.20 para.1
s.371BH, added: 2012 c.14 Sch.20 para.1
s.371BH, varied: SI 2012/ 3044 Reg.5
s.371CA, added: 2012 c.14 Sch.20 para.1
s.371CB, added: 2012 c.14 Sch.20 para.1
s.371CC, added: 2012 c.14 Sch.20 para.1
s.371CD, added: 2012 c.14 Sch.20 para.1
s.371CE, added: 2012 c.14 Sch.20 para.1
s.371CF, added: 2012 c.14 Sch.20 para.1
s.371CG, added: 2012 c.14 Sch.20 para.1
s.371DA, added: 2012 c.14 Sch.20 para.1
s.371DB, added: 2012 c.14 Sch.20 para.1
s.371DC, added: 2012 c.14 Sch.20 para.1
s.371DD, added: 2012 c.14 Sch.20 para.1
s.371DE, added: 2012 c.14 Sch.20 para.1
s.371DF, added: 2012 c.14 Sch.20 para.1
s.371DG, added: 2012 c.14 Sch.20 para.1
s.371DH, added: 2012 c.14 Sch.20 para.1
s.371DI, added: 2012 c.14 Sch.20 para.1
s.371DJ, added: 2012 c.14 Sch.20 para.1
s.371DK, added: 2012 c.14 Sch.20 para.1
s.371DL, added: 2012 c.14 Sch.20 para.1
s.371EA, added: 2012 c.14 Sch.20 para.1
s.371EB, added: 2012 c.14 Sch.20 para.1
s.371EC, added: 2012 c.14 Sch.20 para.1
s.371ED, added: 2012 c.14 Sch.20 para.1
s.371EE, added: 2012 c.14 Sch.20 para.1
s.371FA, added: 2012 c.14 Sch.20 para.1
s.371FA, disapplied: SI 2012/ 3041 Reg.3
s.371FB, added: 2012 c.14 Sch.20 para.1
s.371FC, added: 2012 c.14 Sch.20 para.1
s.371FD, added: 2012 c.14 Sch.20 para.1
s.371FD, enabling: SI 2012/ 3041
s.371FE, added: 2012 c.14 Sch.20 para.1
s.371GA, added: 2012 c.14 Sch.20 para.1
s.371HA, added: 2012 c.14 Sch.20 para.1
s.371IA, added: 2012 c.14 Sch.20 para.1
s.371IB, added: 2012 c.14 Sch.20 para.1
s.371IC, added: 2012 c.14 Sch.20 para.1
s.371ID, added: 2012 c.14 Sch.20 para.1
s.371IE, added: 2012 c.14 Sch.20 para.1
s.371IF, added: 2012 c.14 Sch.20 para.1
s.371IG, added: 2012 c.14 Sch.20 para.1
s.371IH, added: 2012 c.14 Sch.20 para.1
s.371II, added: 2012 c.14 Sch.20 para.1
s.371IJ, added: 2012 c.14 Sch.20 para.1
s.371JA, added: 2012 c.14 Sch.20 para.1
s.371JB, added: 2012 c.14 Sch.20 para.1
s.371JB, varied: 2012 c.14 Sch.20 para.58
s.371JC, added: 2012 c.14 Sch.20 para.1
s.371JD, added: 2012 c.14 Sch.20 para.1
s.371JD, disapplied: 2012 c.14 Sch.20 para.58
s.371JE, added: 2012 c.14 Sch.20 para.1

2010– cont.

8. Taxation (International and Other Provisions) Act 2010– *cont.*

s.371 JE, referred to: 2012 c.14 Sch.20 para.58
s.371 JE, varied: 2012 c.14 Sch.20 para.58
s.371 JF, added: 2012 c.14 Sch.20 para.1
. s.371 JF, disapplied: 2012 c.14 Sch.20 para.58
s.371 JG, added: 2012 c.14 Sch.20 para.1
s.371 KA, added: 2012 c.14 Sch.20 para.1
s.371 KB, added: 2012 c.14 Sch.20 para.1
s.371 KB, applied: SI 2012/3024 Reg.4
s.371 KB, enabling: SI 2012/3024
s.371 KC, added: 2012 c.14 Sch.20 para.1
s.371 KC, varied: SI 2012/3024 Reg.4
s.371 KD, added: 2012 c.14 Sch.20 para.1
s.371 KE, added: 2012 c.14 Sch.20 para.1
s.371 KF, added: 2012 c.14 Sch.20 para.1
s.371 KG, added: 2012 c.14 Sch.20 para.1
s.371 KH, added: 2012 c.14 Sch.20 para.1
s.371 KI, added: 2012 c.14 Sch.20 para.1
s.371 KJ, added: 2012 c.14 Sch.20 para.1
s.371 LA, added: 2012 c.14 Sch.20 para.1
s.371 LB, added: 2012 c.14 Sch.20 para.1
s.371 LC, added: 2012 c.14 Sch.20 para.1
s.371 MA, added: 2012 c.14 Sch.20 para.1
s.371 MB, added: 2012 c.14 Sch.20 para.1
s.371 MC, added: 2012 c.14 Sch.20 para.1
s.371 NA, added: 2012 c.14 Sch.20 para.1
s.371 NB, added: 2012 c.14 Sch.20 para.1
s.371 NC, added: 2012 c.14 Sch.20 para.1
s.371 ND, added: 2012 c.14 Sch.20 para.1
s.371 ND, applied: 2012 c.14 Sch.20 para.59
s.371 NE, added: 2012 c.14 Sch.20 para.1
s.371 OA, added: 2012 c.14 Sch.20 para.1
s.371 OB, added: 2012 c.14 Sch.20 para.1
s.371 OC, added: 2012 c.14 Sch.20 para.1
s.371 OD, added: 2012 c.14 Sch.20 para.1
s.371 OE, added: 2012 c.14 Sch.20 para.1
s.371 PA, added: 2012 c.14 Sch.20 para.1
s.371 QA, added: 2012 c.14 Sch.20 para.1
s.371 QB, added: 2012 c.14 Sch.20 para.1
s.371 QC, added: 2012 c.14 Sch.20 para.1
s.371 QD, added: 2012 c.14 Sch.20 para.1
s.371 QE, added: 2012 c.14 Sch.20 para.1
s.371 QF, added: 2012 c.14 Sch.20 para.1
s.371 QG, added: 2012 c.14 Sch.20 para.1
s.371 RA, added: 2012 c.14 Sch.20 para.1
s.371 RB, added: 2012 c.14 Sch.20 para.1
s.371 RC, added: 2012 c.14 Sch.20 para.1
s.371 RD, added: 2012 c.14 Sch.20 para.1
s.371 RE, added: 2012 c.14 Sch.20 para.1
s.371 RE, applied: SI 2012/3044 Reg.3
s.371 RF, added: 2012 c.14 Sch.20 para.1
s.371 SA, added: 2012 c.14 Sch.20 para.1
s.371 SB, added: 2012 c.14 Sch.20 para.1
s.371 SC, added: 2012 c.14 Sch.20 para.1
s.371 SD, added: 2012 c.14 Sch.20 para.1
s.371 SD, applied: 2012 c.14 Sch.20 para.56
s.371 SE, added: 2012 c.14 Sch.20 para.1
s.371 SF, added: 2012 c.14 Sch.20 para.1
s.371 SH, added: 2012 c.14 Sch.20 para.1
s.371 SH, applied: 2012 c.14 Sch.20 para.57
s.371 SI, added: 2012 c.14 Sch.20 para.1
s.371 SJ, added: 2012 c.14 Sch.20 para.1
s.371 SK, added: 2012 c.14 Sch.20 para.1
s.371 SK, applied: 2012 c.14 Sch.20 para.56
s.371 SL, added: 2012 c.14 Sch.20 para.1
s.371 SM, added: 2012 c.14 Sch.20 para.1
s.371 SM, applied: 2012 c.14 Sch.20 para.56

2010– cont.

8. Taxation (International and Other Provisions) Act 2010– *cont.*

s.371 SN, added: 2012 c.14 Sch.20 para.1
s.371 SO, added: 2012 c.14 Sch.20 para.1
s.371 SP, added: 2012 c.14 Sch.20 para.1
s.371 SQ, added: 2012 c.14 Sch.20 para.1
s.371 SR, added: 2012 c.14 Sch.20 para.1
s.371 TA, added: 2012 c.14 Sch.20 para.1
s.371 TA, applied: SI 2012/3024 Reg.4
s.371 TB, added: 2012 c.14 Sch.20 para.1
s.371 TC, added: 2012 c.14 Sch.20 para.1
s.371 UA, added: 2012 c.14 Sch.20 para.1
s.371 UB, added: 2012 c.14 Sch.20 para.1
s.371 UC, added: 2012 c.14 Sch.20 para.1
s.371 UD, added: 2012 c.14 Sch.20 para.1
s.371 UE, added: 2012 c.14 Sch.20 para.1
s.371 UF, added: 2012 c.14 Sch.20 para.1
s.371 VA, added: 2012 c.14 Sch.20 para.1
s.371 VB, added: 2012 c.14 Sch.20 para.1
s.371 VC, added: 2012 c.14 Sch.20 para.1
s.371 VD, added: 2012 c.14 Sch.20 para.1
s.371 VE, added: 2012 c.14 Sch.20 para.1
s.371 VF, added: 2012 c.14 Sch.20 para.1
s.371 VG, added: 2012 c.14 Sch.20 para.1
s.371 VH, added: 2012 c.14 Sch.20 para.1
s.371 VI, added: 2012 c.14 Sch.20 para.1
s.371 VJ, added: 2012 c.14 Sch.20 para.1
Sch.8 Part 1 para.9, repealed: 2012 c.14 s.26
Sch.8 Part 1 para.34, repealed: 2012 c.14 Sch.16 para.247
Sch.11 Part 1, amended: 2012 c.14 Sch.16 para.244

9. Child Poverty Act 2010

see *Humphreys v Revenue and Customs Commissioners* [2012] UKSC 18, [2012] 1 W.L.R. 1545 (SC), Lord Walker, J.S.C.
referred to: 2012 c.5
Part 1, amended: 2012 c.5 Sch.13 para.8
s.6, repealed (in part): 2012 c.5 Sch.13 para.5
s.8, substituted: 2012 c.5 Sch.13 para.2
s.9, amended: 2012 c.5 s.146
s.10, repealed (in part): 2012 c.5 Sch.13 para.6
s.10, substituted: 2012 c.5 Sch.13 para.6
s.13, repealed (in part): 2012 c.5 Sch.13 para.7
s.13, substituted: 2012 c.5 Sch.13 para.7
s.14, repealed: 2012 c.5 Sch.13 para.8
s.15, amended: 2012 c.5 Sch.13 para.9
s.16, amended: 2012 c.5 Sch.13 para.10
s.18, amended: 2012 c.5 Sch.13 para.11
s.20, amended: 2012 c.7 Sch.5 para.183
s.20, repealed (in part): 2012 c.7 Sch.5 para.183
s.28, amended: 2012 c.5 Sch.13 para.12
Sch.1 para.1, substituted: 2012 c.5 Sch.13 para.3
Sch.1 para.2, substituted: 2012 c.5 Sch.13 para.3
Sch.1 para.3, substituted: 2012 c.5 Sch.13 para.3
Sch.1 para.4, substituted: 2012 c.5 Sch.13 para.3
Sch.1 para.5, substituted: 2012 c.5 Sch.13 para.3
Sch.1 para.6, substituted: 2012 c.5 Sch.13 para.3
Sch.1 para.7, substituted: 2012 c.5 Sch.13 para.3
Sch.1 para.8, substituted: 2012 c.5 Sch.13 para.3
Sch.1 para.9, substituted: 2012 c.5 Sch.13 para.3
Sch.1 para.10, substituted: 2012 c.5 Sch.13 para.3
Sch.1 para.11, substituted: 2012 c.5 Sch.13 para.3
Sch.1 para.12, substituted: 2012 c.5 Sch.13 para.3
Sch.1 para.13, substituted: 2012 c.5 Sch.13 para.3
Sch.1 para.14, substituted: 2012 c.5 Sch.13 para.3
Sch.1 para.15, substituted: 2012 c.5 Sch.13 para.3
Sch.1 para.16, substituted: 2012 c.5 Sch.13 para.3
Sch.1 para.17, substituted: 2012 c.5 Sch.13 para.3

2010–cont.

9. Child Poverty Act 2010–*cont.*
Sch.1 para.18, substituted: 2012 c.5 Sch.13 para.3
Sch.1 para.19, substituted: 2012 c.5 Sch.13 para.3
Sch.1 para.20, substituted: 2012 c.5 Sch.13 para.3
Sch.1 para.21, substituted: 2012 c.5 Sch.13 para.3
Sch.2 para.1, amended: 2012 c.5 Sch.13 para.13
Sch.2 para.3, amended: 2012 c.5 Sch.13 para.13
Sch.2 para.6, repealed (in part): 2012 c.5 Sch.13 para.13
Sch.2 para.7, repealed (in part): 2012 c.5 Sch.13 para.13

13. Finance Act 2010
s.47, applied: SI 2012/3009 Reg.13
s.47, repealed: 2012 c.14 Sch.16 para.247
Sch.1 Part 3 para.45, amended: 2012 c.21 Sch.18 para.130
Sch.6 Part 1, applied: SI 2012/735
Sch.6 Part 1 para.1, varied: SI 2012/735 Art.5, Art.6
Sch.6 Part 2 para.29, enabling: SI 2012/735
Sch.6 Part 3 para.31, repealed: 2012 c.14 s.52
Sch.6 Part 4 para.33, applied: SI 2012/735 Art.5, Art.6
Sch.6 Part 4 para.34, enabling: SI 2012/736
Sch.8 para.3, repealed (in part): 2012 c.14 s.50
Sch.8 para.4, repealed (in part): 2012 c.14 Sch.15 para.12
Sch.8 para.6, repealed: 2012 c.14 Sch.15 para.16

15. Equality Act 2010
Commencement Orders: SI 2012/1569 Art.2, Art.3; SI 2012/2184 Art.2
see *All Saints', Sanderstead, Re* [2012] Fam. 51 (Cons Ct (Southwark)), Chancellor Petchey; see *Barnsley MBC v Norton* [2011] EWCA Civ 834, [2012] P.T.S.R. 56 (CA (Civ Div)), Maurice Kay, L.J.; see *Conway v Community Options Ltd* [2012] Eq. L.R. 871 (EAT), Judge Peter Clark; see *Dunn v Institute of Cemetery and Crematorium Management* [2012] I.C.R. 941 (EAT), Judge McMullen Q.C.; see *R. (on the application of Bailey) v Brent LBC* [2011] EWCA Civ 1586, [2012] Eq. L.R. 168 (CA (Civ Div)), Pill, L.J.; see *R. (on the application of Essex CC) v Secretary of State for Education* [2012] EWHC 1460 (Admin), [2012] E.L.R. 383 (QBD (Admin)), Mitting, J.; see *Timbo v Greenwich Council for Racial Equality* [2012] Eq. L.R. 1010 (EAT), Judge David Richardson
applied: 2012 c.10 Sch.1 para.12, Sch.1 para.17, Sch.1 para.20, Sch.1 para.43, SI 2012/335 Sch.1 para.20, SI 2012/1033 Reg.6, Reg.24, Sch.1 para.2, SI 2012/1909 Sch.5 para.18, SI 2012/2991 Sch.1 para.20, SSI 2012/181 Reg.3
referred to: SI 2012/1033 Sch.1 para.5, SI 2012/1909 Sch.4 para.28, SI 2012/2541 Sch.1, SI 2012/2547 Sch.1, SI 2012/2548 Sch.1, SI 2012/2549 Sch.1
Part 2 c.1, applied: SI 2012/1909 Reg.9
Part 5 c.2, applied: SI 2012/687 Sch.4 para.10
Part 6 c.1, applied: SI 2012/322 Reg.4
Part 11, applied: SI 2012/2734 Sch.1 para.6, Sch.1 para.21, Sch.1 para.37
s.1, repealed (in part): 2012 c.7 Sch.5 para.181
s.6, see *Sussex Partnership NHS Foundation Trust v Norris* [2012] Eq. L.R. 1068 (EAT), Slade, J. DBE
s.9, referred to: SSI 2012/162 Reg.8
s.29, see *All Saints', Sanderstead, Re* [2012] Fam. 51 (Cons Ct (Southwark)), Chancellor Petchey
s.31, see *All Saints', Sanderstead, Re* [2012] Fam. 51 (Cons Ct (Southwark)), Chancellor Petchey
s.53, see *Jooste v General Medical Council* [2012] Eq. L.R. 1048 (EAT), Judge McMullen Q.C.

2010–cont.

15. Equality Act 2010–*cont.*
s.85, amended: SI 2012/976 Sch.1 para.25
s.87, amended: SI 2012/976 Sch.1 para.26
s.120, see *Jooste v General Medical Council* [2012] Eq. L.R. 1048 (EAT), Judge McMullen Q.C.
s.128, see *Abdulla v Birmingham City Council* [2012] UKSC 47, [2012] I.C.R. 1419 (SC), Lady Hale, J.S.C.
s.147, amended: SI 2012/334 Art.2
s.149, see *Hunt v North Somerset Council* [2012] EWHC 1928 (Admin), [2012] Eq. L.R. 951 (QBD (Admin)), Wyn Williams, J.; see *R. (on the application of Bailey) v Brent LBC* [2011] EWCA Civ 1586, [2012] Eq. L.R. 168 (CA (Civ Div)), Pill, L.J.; see *R. (on the application of Barrett) v Lambeth LBC* [2012] EWHC 4557 (Admin), [2012] B.L.G.R. 299 (QBD (Admin)), Ouseley, J.; see *R. (on the application of D) v Manchester City Council* [2012] EWHC 17 (Admin), [2012] Eq. L.R. 251 (QBD (Admin)), Ryder, J.; see *R. (on the application of Greenwich Community Law Centre) v Greenwich LBC* [2012] EWCA Civ 496, [2012] Eq. L.R. 572 (CA (Civ Div)), Ward, L.J.; see *R. (on the application of Siwak) v Newham LBC* [2012] EWHC 1520 (Admin), [2012] Eq. L.R. 670 (QBD (Admin)), Cranston, J.; see *R. (on the application of Williams) v Surrey CC* [2012] EWHC 867 (QB), [2012] Eq. L.R. 656 (QBD (Admin)), Wilkie, J.
s.149, referred to: SSI 2012/162 Reg.4, Reg.5
s.149, varied: SI 2012/2734 Reg.6
s.150, varied: SI 2012/2734 Reg.6
s.151, varied: SI 2012/2734 Reg.6
s.151, enabling: SSI 2012/55
s.152, applied: SSI 2012/55
s.152, varied: SI 2012/2734 Reg.6
s.153, applied: SSI 2012/162
s.153, varied: SI 2012/2734 Reg.6
s.153, enabling: SSI 2012/162
s.154, varied: SI 2012/2734 Reg.6
s.155, varied: SI 2012/2734 Reg.6
s.155, enabling: SSI 2012/162
s.156, varied: SI 2012/2734 Reg.6
s.157, varied: SI 2012/2734 Reg.6
s.158, varied: SI 2012/2734 Reg.6
s.159, varied: SI 2012/2734 Reg.6
s.183, enabling: SI 2012/105
s.184, applied: SI 2012/105
s.193, see *Catholic Care (Diocese of Leeds) v Charity Commission for England and Wales* [2012] UKUT 395 (TCC), [2012] Eq. L.R. 1119 (UT (Tax)), Sales, J.
s.195, amended: SI 2012/2466 Art.9
s.197, enabling: SI 2012/2466
s.207, enabling: SI 2012/105, SI 2012/322, SI 2012/2466, SSI 2012/162
s.208, applied: SI 2012/2466
s.210, enabling: SSI 2012/55, SSI 2012/162
s.216, enabling: SI 2012/1569, SI 2012/2184
Sch.1 Pt 1 para.2, see *Sussex Partnership NHS Foundation Trust v Norris* [2012] Eq. L.R. 1068 (EAT), Slade, J. DBE
Sch.1 Pt 1 para.5, see *Sussex Partnership NHS Foundation Trust v Norris* [2012] Eq. L.R. 1068 (EAT), Slade, J. DBE
Sch.3 Part 1 para.2, varied: 2012 c.11 s.12
Sch.3 Part 4 para.15A, added: SI 2012/2466 Art.2
Sch.3 Part 5 para.20, substituted: SI 2012/2466 Art.3

2010– *cont.*

15. Equality Act 2010– *cont.*
Sch.3 Part 5 para.20A, added: SI 2012/2466 Art.3
Sch.3 Part 5 para.20A, substituted: SI 2012/2466 Art.3
Sch.3 Part 5 para.21, substituted: SI 2012/2466 Art.3
Sch.3 Part 5 para.22, repealed: SI 2012/2992 Reg.2
Sch.3 Part 5 para.22, substituted: SI 2012/2466 Art.3
Sch.3 Part 5 para.23, substituted: SI 2012/2466 Art.3
Sch.3 Part 7 para.26, amended: SI 2012/2466 Art.4
Sch.3 Part 7 para.27, amended: SI 2012/2466 Art.4
Sch.3 Part 7 para.28, amended: SI 2012/2466 Art.4
Sch.3 Part 7 para.29, amended: SI 2012/2466 Art.4
Sch.3 Part 7 para.30, amended: SI 2012/2466 Art.4
Sch.3 Part 7 para.30A, added: SI 2012/2466 Art.4
Sch.3 Part 7 para.30A, amended: SI 2012/2466 Art.4
Sch.3 Part 7 para.30B, added: SI 2012/2466 Art.5
Sch.3 Part 7 para.30B, amended: SI 2012/2466 Art.4
Sch.3 Part 7 para.30C, added: SI 2012/2466 Art.6
Sch.3 Part 7 para.30C, amended: SI 2012/2466 Art.4
Sch.3 Part 7 para.30D, added: SI 2012/2466 Art.7
Sch.3 Part 7 para.30D, amended: SI 2012/2466 Art.4
Sch.6 para.2, varied: 2012 c.11 s.12
Sch.10 para.6, amended: SI 2012/976 Sch.1 para.27
Sch.11 Part 2 para.5, amended: SI 2012/976 Sch.1 para.28
Sch.16 para.1A, added: SI 2012/2466 Art.8
Sch.17, see *ML v Tonbridge Grammar School* [2012] UKUT 283 (AAC), [2012] E.L.R. 508 (UT (AAC)), Judge Rowland
Sch.17 Part 2 para.3A, applied: SI 2012/321 Reg.4
Sch.17 Part 2 para.4, applied: SI 2012/322 Reg.12, Reg.16, Reg.57
Sch.17 Part 2 para.6, applied: SI 2012/322 Reg.35, Reg.48
Sch.17 Part 2 para.6, enabling: SI 2012/322
Sch.17 Part 2 para.6A, enabling: SI 2012/322
Sch.17 Part 2 para.6B, applied: SI 2012/321 Reg.4
Sch.17 Part 2 para.6C, applied: SI 2012/321 Reg.4, SI 2012/322 Reg.12
Sch.17 Part 2 para.6D, applied: SI 2012/321 Reg.4
Sch.19 Part 1, amended: 2012 c.7 Sch.5 para.182, Sch.13 para.19, Sch.14 para.116, Sch.17 para.14, Sch.19 para.13, 2012 c.10 Sch.5 para.70, 2012 c.21 Sch.18 para.131, SI 2012/2007 Sch.1 para.109
Sch.19 Part 2, amended: SI 2012/990 Art.11
Sch.19 Part 3, added: SSI 2012/55 Art.2
Sch.19 Part 3, amended: 2012 asp 8 s.61
Sch.22 para.1, applied: SI 2012/687 Sch.4 para.10
Sch.22 para.1, varied: 2012 c.11 s.12
Sch.22 para.2, applied: SI 2012/687 Sch.4 para.10
Sch.23 para.1, applied: SI 2012/687 Sch.4 para.10
Sch.24, applied: SI 2012/687 Sch.4 para.10
Sch.25 para.7, amended: SI 2012/1809 Sch.1 Part 1

17. Crime and Security Act 2010
Commencement Orders: 2012 c.9 Sch.10 Part 3; SI 2012/584 Art.2; SI 2012/1615 Art.2, Art.3
s.13, amended: SI 2012/2595 Art.22
s.14, repealed: 2012 c.9 Sch.9 para.4, Sch.10 Part 1
s.16, repealed: 2012 c.9 Sch.9 para.4, Sch.10 Part 1
s.17, repealed: 2012 c.9 Sch.9 para.4, Sch.10 Part 1
s.18, repealed: 2012 c.9 Sch.9 para.4, Sch.10 Part 1
s.19, repealed: 2012 c.9 Sch.9 para.4, Sch.10 Part 1

2010– *cont.*

17. Crime and Security Act 2010– *cont.*
s.21, repealed: 2012 c.9 Sch.9 para.4, Sch.10 Part 1
s.22, repealed (in part): 2012 c.9 Sch.9 para.4, Sch.10 Part 1
s.23, repealed: 2012 c.9 Sch.9 para.4, Sch.10 Part 1
s.42, amended: SI 2012/2595 Art.22
s.42, repealed (in part): 2012 c.9 Sch.10 Part 3
s.44, amended: SI 2012/2595 Art.22
s.44, repealed (in part): 2012 c.9 Sch.10 Part 3
s.55, amended: SI 2012/1659 Sch.3 para.21
s.58, repealed (in part): 2012 c.9 Sch.9 para.4, Sch.10 Part 1
s.59, amended: SI 2012/2595 Art.22
s.59, enabling: SI 2012/584, SI 2012/1615
Sch.1 para.3, repealed (in part): 2012 c.9 Sch.10 Part 3
Sch.1 para.7, repealed (in part): 2012 c.9 Sch.10 Part 3

23. Bribery Act 2010
s.1, applied: SI 2012/2414 Sch.5 para.1, SSI 2012/88 Reg.23, SSI 2012/89 Reg.26
s.2, applied: SI 2012/2414 Sch.5 para.1
s.6, applied: SI 2012/2414 Sch.5 para.1, SSI 2012/88 Reg.23, SSI 2012/89 Reg.26
s.9, amended: SI 2012/2595 Art.19
s.17, amended: SI 2012/2595 Art.19

24. Digital Economy Act 2010
Commencement Orders: SI 2012/1164 Art.2; SI 2012/1766 Art.2
see *R. (on the application of British Telecommunications Plc) v Secretary of State for Business, Innovation and Skills* [2012] EWCA Civ 232, [2012] Bus. L.R. 1766 (CA (Civ Div)), Arden, L.J.
s.44, enabling: SI 2012/1764
s.47, enabling: SI 2012/1164, SI 2012/1766

25. Constitutional Reform and Governance Act 2010
Commencement Orders: SI 2012/3001 Art.2, Art.3, Sch.1; SI 2012/3028 Art.2, Art.3; SI 2012/3029 Art.2, Art.3
s.1, repealed (in part): SI 2012/2595 Art.20
s.5, varied: 2012 c.11 s.12
s.15, varied: 2012 c.11 s.12
s.16, varied: 2012 c.11 s.12
s.23, amended: 2012 c.14 s.218
s.45, disapplied: SI 2012/3028 Art.2
s.45, enabling: SI 2012/3028
s.46, applied: 2012 c.9 s.104
s.46, enabling: SI 2012/3029
s.52, enabling: SI 2012/3001
Sch.7 para.4, disapplied: SI 2012/3029 Art.2
Sch.7 para.4, referred to: 2012 c.9 s.104
Sch.7 para.6, repealed: 2012 c.9 Sch.10 Part 7

27. Energy Act 2010
Commencement Orders: SI 2012/1841 Art.2
s.38, enabling: SI 2012/1841

28. Financial Services Act 2010
s.1, repealed: 2012 c.21 Sch.19
s.2, repealed (in part): 2012 c.21 Sch.19
s.3, repealed (in part): 2012 c.21 Sch.19
s.6, repealed: 2012 c.21 Sch.19
s.7, repealed: 2012 c.21 Sch.19
Sch.2 Part 1 para.2, repealed: 2012 c.21 Sch.19
Sch.2 Part 1 para.3, repealed: 2012 c.21 Sch.19
Sch.2 Part 1 para.4, repealed: 2012 c.21 Sch.19
Sch.2 Part 1 para.5, repealed: 2012 c.21 Sch.19
Sch.2 Part 1 para.6, repealed: 2012 c.21 Sch.19

2010– cont.

28. Financial Services Act 2010– *cont.*
Sch.2 Part 1 para.11, repealed: 2012 c.21 Sch.19
Sch.2 Part 1 para.12, repealed: 2012 c.21 Sch.19
Sch.2 Part 1 para.13, repealed: 2012 c.21 Sch.19
Sch.2 Part 1 para.14, repealed: 2012 c.21 Sch.19
Sch.2 Part 1 para.27, repealed: 2012 c.21 Sch.19
Sch.2 Part 1 para.34, repealed: 2012 c.21 Sch.19

29. Flood and Water Management Act 2010
Commencement Orders: SI 2012/ 879 Art.3, Art.4; SI 2012/ 2000 Art.2; SI 2012/ 2048 Art.2, Art.3
s.30, enabling: SI 2012/ 1692, SI 2012/ 1693, SI 2012/ 1819, SI 2012/ 1945
s.42, applied: SI 2012/ 2048(b)
s.48, enabling: SI 2012/ 879, SI 2012/ 1692, SI 2012/ 1693, SI 2012/ 1819, SI 2012/ 1945, SI 2012/ 2048
s.49, enabling: SI 2012/ 879, SI 2012/ 2000, SI 2012/ 2048
Sch.1 para.6, applied: SI 2012/ 1692 Reg.2, SI 2012/ 1693 Reg.2
Sch.1 para.8, applied: SI 2012/ 1819 Reg.3, SI 2012/ 1945 Reg.3
Sch.1 para.15, applied: SI 2012/ 1819, SI 2012/ 1945
Sch.1 para.15, enabling: SI 2012/ 1819, SI 2012/ 1945
Sch.1 para.16, enabling: SI 2012/ 1692, SI 2012/ 1693
Sch.2 para.32, disapplied: SI 2012/ 879 Art.4
Sch.2 para.33, disapplied: SI 2012/ 879 Art.4
Sch.2 para.34, disapplied: SI 2012/ 879 Art.4
Sch.3 para.11, amended: SI 2012/ 1659 Sch.3 para.20

30. Appropriation (No.3) Act 2010
varied: SI 2012/ 147 Art.7

31. Finance (No.2) Act 2010
s.9, repealed: 2012 c.14 Sch.16 para.247

32. Academies Act 2010
see *ML v Tonbridge Grammar School* [2012] UKUT 283 (AAC), [2012] E.L.R. 508 (UT (AAC)), Judge Rowland
s.1, see *R. (on the application of Moyse) v Secretary of State for Education* [2012] EWHC 2758 (Admin), [2012] E.L.R. 551 (QBD (Admin)), Kenneth Parker, J
s.1, applied: SI 2012/ 717 Sch.1, SI 2012/ 811 Sch.1 para.4, SI 2012/ 1167 Sch.1 para.6, SI 2012/ 2421 Sch.3 para.14
s.1A, applied: SI 2012/ 1293 Reg.3
s.1D, enabling: SI 2012/ 1201
s.3, applied: SI 2012/ 1035 Reg.46
s.3, enabling: SI 2012/ 1035
s.4, see *R. (on the application of Moyse) v Secretary of State for Education* [2012] EWHC 2758 (Admin), [2012] E.L.R. 551 (QBD (Admin)), Kenneth Parker, J
s.5, see *R. (on the application of Moyse) v Secretary of State for Education* [2012] EWHC 2758 (Admin), [2012] E.L.R. 551 (QBD (Admin)), Kenneth Parker, J
s.6, see *ML v Tonbridge Grammar School* [2012] UKUT 283 (AAC), [2012] E.L.R. 508 (UT (AAC)), Judge Rowland
s.6, applied: SI 2012/ 1035 Reg.40, Reg.44, SI 2012/ 1107 Art.4
s.7, applied: SI 2012/ 1107 Art.4
s.9, see *R. (on the application of Moyse) v Secretary of State for Education* [2012] EWHC 2758 (Admin), [2012] E.L.R. 551 (QBD (Admin)), Kenneth Parker, J
s.9, varied: SI 2012/ 1107 Art.8
Sch.1 Part 2 para.13, applied: SI 2012/ 1035 Reg.41
Sch.1 Part 4 para.21, enabling: SI 2012/ 1829

2010– cont.

33. Finance (No.3) Act 2010
s.15, repealed: 2012 c.14 Sch.16 para.247
Sch.3 para.1, repealed (in part): 2012 c.14 s.33

37. Superannuation Act 2010
see *R. (on the application of Public and Commercial Services Union) v Minister for the Civil Service* [2011] EWHC 2041 (Admin), [2012] 1 All E.R. 985 (QBD (Admin)), McCombe, J.

38. Terrorist Asset-Freezing etc Act 2010
s.23, amended: 2012 c.10 Sch.5 para.71, 2012 c.21 Sch.18 para.132
s.41, amended: 2012 c.21 Sch.18 para.132

41. Loans to Ireland Act 2010
applied: 2012 c.13 Sch.1

2011

01. Welsh Language (Wales) Measure 2011
Commencement Orders: SI 2012/46 Art.2; SI 2012/ 223 Art.2; SI 2012/969 Art.2; SI 2012/ 1096 Art.2; SI 2012/ 1423 Art.2
Part 8 c.1, applied: SI 2012/ 753 Reg.2
s.23, enabling: SI 2012/ 59
s.138, enabling: SI 2012/ 753
s.146, enabling: SI 2012/ 752
s.150, enabling: SI 2012/46, SI 2012/ 752, SI 2012/ 969, SI 2012/990, SI 2012/ 1096, SI 2012/ 1423
s.154, enabling: SI 2012/990
s.156, enabling: SI 2012/46, SI 2012/ 223, SI 2012/ 969, SI 2012/ 1096, SI 2012/ 1423
Sch.4 Part 1 para.5, enabling: SI 2012/ 59
Sch.6, amended: 2012 c.21 Sch.18 para.144
Sch.12 para.1, enabling: SI 2012/ 752
Sch.12 para.2, enabling: SI 2012/ 752

2. Appropriation Act 2011
varied: SI 2012/ 147 Art.7

4. Budget Responsibility and National Audit Act 2011
s.25, applied: SI 2012/ 727 Art.2
s.25, enabling: SI 2012/ 727
s.28, enabling: SI 2012/ 725
Sch.4 para.1, applied: SI 2012/ 727 Art.2
Sch.4 para.1, enabling: SI 2012/ 727
Sch.4 para.5, applied: SI 2012/ 727 Art.2
Sch.4 para.5, enabling: SI 2012/ 727

04. Local Government (Wales) Measure 2011
Commencement Orders: SI 2012/ 1187 Art.2
s.1, applied: SI 2012/ 685 Reg.3, Reg.4
s.1, enabling: SI 2012/ 685
s.2, applied: SI 2012/ 685 Reg.5
s.2, enabling: SI 2012/ 685
s.175, applied: SI 2012/ 685
s.178, enabling: SI 2012/ 1187

05. Housing (Wales) Measure 2011
Commencement Orders: SI 2012/ 2091 Art.2
s.34, enabling: SI 2012/ 2090
s.89, enabling: SI 2012/ 2090
s.90, enabling: SI 2012/ 2091

5. Postal Services Act 2011
Commencement Orders: SI 2012/ 1095 Art.3
referred to: 2012 c.19 Sch.6 para.4
Part 2, applied: SI 2012/ 687 Sch.1 para.3
Part 3, applied: SI 2012/ 1917 Sch.2 para.40
s.15, applied: SI 2012/ 1095 Art.4, Art.5, Art.6
s.17, applied: SI 2012/ 687 Sch.1 para.1
s.17, enabling: SI 2012/ 687
s.18, enabling: SI 2012/ 687

2011– cont.

5. Postal Services Act 2011–*cont.*
s.19, enabling: SI 2012/687
s.20, applied: SI 2012/687
s.20, enabling: SI 2012/687
s.21, enabling: SI 2012/688
s.22, applied: SI 2012/688
s.22, enabling: SI 2012/688
s.23, enabling: SI 2012/764
s.25, applied: SI 2012/687, SI 2012/687 Art.1, SI 2012/688
s.25, enabling: SI 2012/687, SI 2012/688, SI 2012/932, SI 2012/966
s.26, enabling: SI 2012/687, SI 2012/688
s.30, enabling: SI 2012/936
s.56, applied: SI 2012/1128, SI 2012/1128 Art.3, Art.4, Art.5
s.56, enabling: SI 2012/1128
s.89, applied: SI 2012/1127, SI 2012/1128
s.89, enabling: SI 2012/687, SI 2012/688, SI 2012/764
s.93, enabling: SI 2012/1095
Sch.7 para.7, applied: SI 2012/1127, SI 2012/1127 Art.2, Sch.1
Sch.7 para.7, enabling: SI 2012/1127
Sch.10 Part 3 para.41, amended: 2012 c.21 Sch.18 para.133

07. Education (Wales) Measure 2011
Commencement Orders: SI 2012/2656 Art.2
s.6, enabling: SI 2012/2655
s.32, enabling: SI 2012/2655, SI 2012/2656

10. Supply and Appropriation (Main Estimates) Act 2011
varied: 2012 c.1 s.3
Sch.1, varied: 2012 c.11 s.12

11. Finance Act 2011
s.5, amended: 2012 c.14 s.5
s.7, amended: 2012 c.14 Sch.21 para.4
s.43, repealed (in part): 2012 c.14 Sch.3 para.32
s.56, repealed: 2012 c.14 Sch.16 para.247
s.63, repealed (in part): 2012 c.14 Sch.22 para.20
s.70, enabling: SI 2012/1258
s.79, amended: 2012 c.14 Sch.30 para.18, Sch.30 para.22
s.80, repealed: 2012 c.14 Sch.30 para.18
Sch.3 Part 5 para.27, applied: SI 2012/700 Sch.1 para.8, Sch.1 para.9
Sch.19 Part 2 para.4, applied: SI 2012/458 Reg.9, SI 2012/459 Reg.7
Sch.19 Part 2 para.6, amended: 2012 c.14 Sch.34 para.2, Sch.34 para.5
Sch.19 Part 2 para.7, amended: 2012 c.14 Sch.34 para.3, Sch.34 para.6
Sch.19 Part 4 para.26, applied: SI 2012/458 Reg.6
Sch.19 Part 4 para.37, amended: 2012 c.21 Sch.18 para.134
Sch.19 Part 4 para.38, amended: 2012 c.21 Sch.18 para.134
Sch.19 Part 5 para.43, amended: 2012 c.14 Sch.34 para.8
Sch.19 Part 5 para.44, amended: 2012 c.14 Sch.34 para.9
Sch.19 Part 6 para.50, referred to: SI 2012/458 Reg.8, SI 2012/459 Reg.6
Sch.19 Part 6 para.51, referred to: SI 2012/458 Reg.8, SI 2012/459 Reg.6
Sch.19 Part 7 para.66, amended: 2012 c.14 Sch.34 para.11
Sch.19 Part 7 para.66, applied: SI 2012/458 Reg.12, SI 2012/459 Reg.10

2011– cont.

11. Finance Act 2011–*cont.*
Sch.19 Part 7 para.66, enabling: SI 2012/432, SI 2012/459
Sch.19 Part 7 para.67, applied: SI 2012/458 Reg.12, SI 2012/459 Reg.10
Sch.19 Part 7 para.67, enabling: SI 2012/458
Sch.19 Part 7 para.67A, added: 2012 c.14 Sch.34 para.11
Sch.19 Part 7 para.67A, enabling: SI 2012/2933
Sch.19 Part 7 para.68, repealed: 2012 c.14 Sch.34 para.11
Sch.19 Part 8 para.73, amended: 2012 c.14 Sch.16 para.246
Sch.20 para.7, repealed: 2012 c.14 Sch.32 para.17
Sch.20 para.8, amended: 2012 c.14 Sch.32 para.18
Sch.20 para.8, repealed (in part): 2012 c.14 Sch.32 para.18
Sch.20 para.9, referred to: 2012 c.14 Sch.32 para.19
Sch.20 para.9, varied: 2012 c.14 Sch.32 para.19
Sch.22 para.4, repealed: 2012 c.14 Sch.39 para.8
Sch.23 Part 1 para.1, enabling: SI 2012/847
Sch.23 Part 2 para.9, applied: SI 2012/847 Reg.3
Sch.23 Part 2 para.9, referred to: SI 2012/847 Reg.3
Sch.23 Part 2 para.11, referred to: SI 2012/847 Reg.4
Sch.23 Part 2 para.12, applied: SI 2012/847 Reg.7
Sch.23 Part 2 para.12, disapplied: SI 2012/847 Reg.6, Reg.7
Sch.23 Part 2 para.12, referred to: SI 2012/847 Reg.5, Reg.7
Sch.23 Part 2 para.13, referred to: SI 2012/847 Reg.11
Sch.23 Part 2 para.14, referred to: SI 2012/847 Reg.12
Sch.23 Part 2 para.15, referred to: SI 2012/847 Reg.13
Sch.23 Part 2 para.16, referred to: SI 2012/847 Reg.14
Sch.23 Part 2 para.17, referred to: SI 2012/847 Reg.15
Sch.23 Part 2 para.18, referred to: SI 2012/847 Reg.16
Sch.23 Part 2 para.19, referred to: SI 2012/847 Reg.17
Sch.23 Part 2 para.20, referred to: SI 2012/847 Reg.18
Sch.23 Part 2 para.21, referred to: SI 2012/847 Reg.19
Sch.23 Part 2 para.22, referred to: SI 2012/847 Reg.20
Sch.23 Part 2 para.23, referred to: SI 2012/847 Reg.21
Sch.23 Part 2 para.24, applied: SI 2012/847 Reg.22
Sch.23 Part 2 para.24, referred to: SI 2012/847 Reg.22
Sch.23 Part 2 para.25, referred to: SI 2012/847 Reg.23
Sch.23 Part 2 para.26, referred to: SI 2012/847 Reg.24
Sch.23 Part 2 para.27, referred to: SI 2012/847 Reg.25
Sch.23 Part 5 para.44, applied: SI 2012/847
Sch.23 Part 5 para.45, amended: SI 2012/3062 Reg.6

12. European Union Act 2011
s.3, applied: 2012 c.15 s.1
s.4, disapplied: 2012 c.15 s.1
s.16, enabling: SSI 2012/42

2011– cont.

13. Police Reform and Social Responsibility Act 2011
Commencement Orders: SI 2012/75 Art.2; SI 2012/896 Art.2; SI 2012/1129 Art.2; SI 2012/2670 Art.2; SI 2012/2892 Art.2, Art.4, Art.5, Art.6
applied: SI 2012/1918 Reg.3
Part 1 c.6, applied: SI 2012/1917 Art.76
Pt 3. see *R. (on the application of Gallastegui) v Westminster City Council* [2012] EWHC 1123 (Admin), [2012] 4 All E.R. 401 (DC), Sir John Thomas (President)
s.1, applied: SI 2012/2595 Art.29, SI 2012/2606 Art.2, SI 2012/2892 Art.4
s.2, applied: SI 2012/2393 Art.2, SI 2012/2606 Art.3
s.4, applied: SI 2012/2393 Art.2
s.11, enabling: SI 2012/2479
s.13, applied: SI 2012/62 Reg.28
s.29, applied: SI 2012/62 Reg.28
s.29, disapplied: SI 2012/2892 Art.5
s.31, enabling: SI 2012/62
s.33, applied: SI 2012/62 Reg.28
s.50, applied: SI 2012/323 Reg.10, SI 2012/444 Reg.17, SI 2012/1917 Art.79
s.51, applied: SI 2012/323 Reg.10, SI 2012/444 Reg.17, SI 2012/1917 Art.80
s.51, referred to: SI 2012/1917 Art.79
s.54, applied: SI 2012/1917 Art.84, SI 2012/1965 Art.2, SI 2012/2085 Art.3
s.54, enabling: SI 2012/1918, SI 2012/1965, SI 2012/2085
s.55, applied: SI 2012/2088 Reg.7
s.55, enabling: SI 2012/2088, SI 2012/2378
s.57, applied: SI 2012/1917 Sch.3 para.62
s.58, applied: SI 2012/1918 Reg.3
s.58, enabling: SI 2012/1917, SI 2012/2768
s.59, applied: SI 2012/1917 Art.80
s.62, disapplied: SI 2012/2892 Art.5
s.65, applied: SI 2012/2087 Reg.2
s.65, referred to: SI 2012/2087 Reg.2
s.65, enabling: SI 2012/2087
s.66, applied: SI 2012/2087 Reg.3
s.66, enabling: SI 2012/2087
s.70, enabling: SI 2012/2553
s.75, applied: SI 2012/1963 Art.2, SI 2012/2084 Art.3
s.75, enabling: SI 2012/1963, SI 2012/2084
s.102, varied: SI 2012/2892 Art.5
s.119, amended: SI 2012/1659 Sch.3 para.22
s.125, applied: SI 2012/2730 Reg.9
s.126, enabling: SI 2012/2730
s.128, enabling: SI 2012/2730
s.129, enabling: SI 2012/2730
s.130, applied: SI 2012/2550 Reg.3
s.130, enabling: SI 2012/2550
s.131, applied: SI 2012/2550 Reg.3
s.131, enabling: SI 2012/2730
s.134, enabling: SI 2012/2730
s.135, applied: SI 2012/2550 Reg.4, Reg.5
s.135, enabling: SI 2012/2550
s.136, applied: SI 2012/2730
s.136, enabling: SI 2012/2550, SI 2012/2730
s.143, see *R. (on the application of Gallastegui) v Westminster City Council* [2012] EWHC 1123 (Admin), [2012] 4 All E.R. 401 (DC), Sir John Thomas (President)
s.154, applied: SI 2012/62, SI 2012/1917, SI 2012/2504, SI 2012/2730, SI 2012/2768

2011– cont.

13. Police Reform and Social Responsibility Act 2011– *cont.*
s.154, enabling: SI 2012/62, SI 2012/75, SI 2012/1917, SI 2012/1918, SI 2012/2087, SI 2012/2088, SI 2012/2378, SI 2012/2553, SI 2012/2768, SI 2012/2892
s.157, enabling: SI 2012/75, SI 2012/896, SI 2012/1129, SI 2012/2670, SI 2012/2892
Sch.1 para.6, applied: SI 2012/62 Reg.7, SI 2012/2892 Art.4
Sch.2 para.3, applied: SI 2012/2606 Art.3
Sch.2 para.4, applied: SI 2012/2892 Art.5
Sch.2 para.5, applied: SI 2012/2892 Art.5
Sch.3 para.2, applied: SI 2012/62 Reg.7
Sch.5 para.2, applied: SI 2012/2271 Reg.3
Sch.5 para.3, applied: SI 2012/2271 Reg.4, Reg.5, Reg.8
Sch.5 para.4, applied: SI 2012/2271 Reg.4, Reg.5
Sch.5 para.6, applied: SI 2012/2271 Reg.5
Sch.5 para.7, enabling: SI 2012/2271
Sch.5 para.8, enabling: SI 2012/2271
Sch.6 Part 2 para.3, varied: SI 2012/2504 Reg.2
Sch.6 Part 4 para.36, enabling: SI 2012/2734
Sch.6 Part 4 para.37, enabling: SI 2012/1433
Sch.6 Part 4 para.38, enabling: SI 2012/1433
Sch.6 Part 4 para.39, enabling: SI 2012/1433
Sch.6 Part 4 para.40, enabling: SI 2012/2504
Sch.7, enabling: SI 2012/62
Sch.8 Part 1 para.4, disapplied: SI 2012/2271 Reg.10
Sch.8 Part 1 para.5, applied: SI 2012/2271 Reg.9
Sch.8 Part 1 para.6, applied: SI 2012/2271 Reg.10
Sch.8 Part 1 para.9, enabling: SI 2012/2271
Sch.8 Part 1 para.10, enabling: SI 2012/2271
Sch.9, applied: SI 2012/1917 Sch.3 para.62
Sch.9 para.3, applied: SI 2012/1917 Sch.3 para.59
Sch.9 para.4, applied: SI 2012/1917 Sch.3 para.59, Sch.3 para.60, Sch.3 para.61
Sch.14 para.4, varied: SI 2012/2892 Art.6
Sch.15 Part 2 para.7, applied: SI 2012/2733 Art.4, SI 2012/2892 Art.5
Sch.15 Part 4 para.24, enabling: SI 2012/2733
Sch.16 Part 3 para.360, applied: SI 2012/2892 Art.7
Sch.16 Part 3 para.360, varied: SI 2012/2892 Art.7

16. Energy Act 2011
Commencement Orders: SI 2012/873 Art.4; SSI 2012/191 Art.2; SI 2012/873 Art.2, Art.3
Part 1 c.1, applied: SI 2012/2079 Reg.4, Reg.6, SSI 2012/329 Reg.2
s.1, applied: SI 2012/2105 Art.3
s.1, enabling: SI 2012/2105
s.2, applied: SI 2012/2106 Art.3, Art.4
s.2, referred to: SI 2012/3118 Sch.1 para.1
s.2, enabling: SI 2012/2079, SI 2012/2106
s.3, applied: SI 2012/2079 Reg.7
s.3, enabling: SI 2012/2079
s.4, referred to: SI 2012/2079 Reg.26
s.4, enabling: SI 2012/2079
s.5, applied: SI 2012/2079 Reg.38, Reg.39
s.5, referred to: SI 2012/2079 Reg.26
s.5, enabling: SI 2012/2079
s.6, enabling: SI 2012/2079
s.7, applied: SI 2012/2079 Reg.26, Reg.41
s.8, applied: SI 2012/2079 Reg.24, Reg.26, Reg.41, Reg.42, Reg.44, Reg.46, Reg.50
s.8, enabling: SI 2012/2079, SI 2012/3021
s.11, amended: SI 2012/3170 Reg.2

2011– cont.

16. Energy Act 2011–*cont.*
s.12, applied: SI 2012/ 1660 Reg.3, Reg.4, Reg.5, Reg.6, SI 2012/ 2079 Reg.62
s.12, disapplied: SI 2012/ 2079 Reg.45, Reg.49
s.12, enabling: SI 2012/ 1660
s.13, enabling: SI 2012/ 2079
s.14, applied: SI 2012/ 1661 Reg.5
s.14, enabling: SI 2012/ 1661, SSI 2012/ 214
s.15, enabling: SI 2012/ 1661, SI 2012/ 2079, SSI 2012/ 214
s.16, enabling: SI 2012/ 2079
s.34, enabling: SI 2012/ 2079
s.35, enabling: SI 2012/ 2079
s.38, applied: SI 2012/ 2079
s.40, applied: SI 2012/ 1660, SI 2012/ 1661, SI 2012/ 2079, SI 2012/ 2105, SI 2012/ 2106, SI 2012/ 3021
s.40, enabling: SI 2012/ 1660, SI 2012/ 1661, SI 2012/ 2079, SI 2012/ 3021, SSI 2012/ 214
s.74, enabling: SI 2012/ 809, SI 2012/ 3118
s.75, enabling: SSI 2012/ 315
s.121, enabling: SI 2012/ 873, SSI 2012/ 191

18. Armed Forces Act 2011
Commencement Orders: SI 2012/ 669 Art.3, Art.4; SI 2012/ 2921 Art.3
s.2, varied: 2012 c.11 s.12
s.32, enabling: SI 2012/ 669, SI 2012/ 2921

19. Pensions Act 2011
Commencement Orders: SI 2012/ 682 Art.2; SI 2012/ 1681 Art.2, Art.3
s.38, enabling: SI 2012/ 682, SI 2012/ 1681
Sch.4 para.1, applied: SI 2012/ 1688
Sch.4 para.2, applied: SI 2012/ 1688
Sch.4 para.3, applied: SI 2012/ 1688
Sch.4 para.4, applied: SI 2012/ 1688
Sch.4 para.5, applied: SI 2012/ 1688
Sch.4 para.6, applied: SI 2012/ 1688
Sch.4 para.7, applied: SI 2012/ 1688
Sch.4 para.8, applied: SI 2012/ 1688
Sch.4 para.9, applied: SI 2012/ 1688
Sch.4 para.10, applied: SI 2012/ 1688
Sch.4 para.11, applied: SI 2012/ 1688
Sch.4 para.12, applied: SI 2012/ 1688
Sch.4 para.13, applied: SI 2012/ 1688
Sch.4 para.14, applied: SI 2012/ 1688
Sch.4 para.15, applied: SI 2012/ 1688
Sch.4 para.16, applied: SI 2012/ 1688

20. Localism Act 2011
Commencement Orders: SI 2012/ 57 Art.2, Art.3, Art.4, Art.5, Art.6, Art.7, Art.9, Art.10, Art.11; SI 2012/ 193 Art.2; SI 2012/ 411 Art.2; SI 2012/ 628 Art.3, Art.4, Art.5, Art.6, Art.7, Art.8, Art.9, Art.10, Art.11, Art.12, Art.13, Art.14, Art.15, Art.16, Art.17, Art.18, Art.19, Art.20; SI 2012/ 887 Art.2, Art.3, Art.4; SI 2012/ 1008 Art.2, Art.3, Art.4, Art.5, Art.6; SI 2012/ 1463 Art.2, Art.3, Art.4, Art.5, Art.7; SI 2012/ 2029 Art.3, Art.5; SI 2012/ 2420 Art.2; SI 2012/ 2599 Art.2; SI 2012/ 2913 Art.2, Art.3, Art.4, Art.5, Art.6
Part 1, applied: 2012 c.5 s.133
Part 1 c.1, applied: 2012 c.5 s.133
Part 1 c.7, applied: SI 2012/ 1464 Reg.2, SI 2012/ 2734 Sch.1 para.8, Sch.1 para.23, SI 2012/ 2913 Art.4
s.1, applied: SSI 2012/ 303 Reg.5, Sch.4 para.37, Sch.5 para.25, SSI 2012/ 319 Reg.5
s.8, applied: SI 2012/ 965 Art.2, SSI 2012/ 303 Sch.4 para.37, Sch.5 para.25, SSI 2012/ 319 Reg.5
s.8, enabling: SI 2012/ 965

2011– cont.

20. Localism Act 2011–*cont.*
s.23, enabling: SI 2012/ 1023
s.25, applied: SI 2012/ 2734 Sch.1 para.7, Sch.1 para.22
s.25, varied: SI 2012/ 2734 Reg.6
s.26, referred to: SI 2012/ 2913 Art.5
s.26, varied: SI 2012/ 2734 Reg.6
s.27, varied: SI 2012/ 2734 Reg.6
s.28, varied: SI 2012/ 2734 Reg.6, SI 2012/ 2913 Art.4
s.29, varied: SI 2012/ 2734 Reg.6
s.30, varied: SI 2012/ 2734 Reg.6
s.30, enabling: SI 2012/ 1464
s.31, varied: SI 2012/ 2734 Reg.6
s.32, varied: SI 2012/ 2734 Reg.6
s.33, varied: SI 2012/ 2734 Reg.6
s.34, varied: SI 2012/ 2734 Reg.6
s.35, varied: SI 2012/ 2734 Reg.6
s.36, varied: SI 2012/ 2734 Reg.6
s.37, varied: SI 2012/ 2734 Reg.6
s.37, enabling: SI 2012/ 57
s.52, varied: 2012 c.11 s.12
s.81, applied: SI 2012/ 1313 Reg.3, Reg.4, SI 2012/ 1647 Reg.3, Sch.1 para.1
s.81, referred to: SI 2012/ 1313 Sch.1 para.6, SI 2012/ 1647 Sch.1 para.1
s.81, enabling: SI 2012/ 1313, SI 2012/ 1647
s.83, applied: SI 2012/ 1647 Reg.4
s.83, enabling: SI 2012/ 1647
s.87, enabling: SI 2012/ 2421
s.88, enabling: SI 2012/ 2421
s.89, applied: SI 2012/ 2421 Reg.4, Reg.5
s.89, enabling: SI 2012/ 2421
s.91, applied: SI 2012/ 2421 Reg.9, Sch.2 para.1
s.91, enabling: SI 2012/ 2421
s.92, enabling: SI 2012/ 2421
s.95, applied: SI 2012/ 2421 Reg.2, Reg.12, Reg.13, Reg.14, Reg.21, Sch.3 para.15
s.95, disapplied: SI 2012/ 2421 Reg.13
s.95, referred to: SI 2012/ 2421 Sch.3 para.11
s.95, enabling: SI 2012/ 2421
s.99, enabling: SI 2012/ 2421
s.101, enabling: SI 2012/ 2421
s.109, enabling: SI 2012/ 3046
s.150, applied: SI 2012/ 1008 Art.12
s.151, varied: SI 2012/ 57 Art.11
s.153, varied: SI 2012/ 57 Art.11
s.158, disapplied: SI 2012/ 696 Reg.3
s.158, enabling: SI 2012/ 696
s.194, enabling: SI 2012/ 666, SI 2012/ 702
s.197, applied: SI 2012/ 310
s.198, enabling: SI 2012/ 310, SI 2012/ 2167
s.202, applied: SI 2012/ 2167
s.235, applied: SI 2012/ 961, SI 2012/ 965, SI 2012/ 1647
s.235, enabling: SI 2012/ 965, SI 2012/ 1313, SI 2012/ 1464, SI 2012/ 1647, SI 2012/ 2167
s.236, enabling: SI 2012/ 635, SI 2012/ 641, SI 2012/ 666, SI 2012/ 961
s.237, referred to: SI 2012/ 2913 Art.5
s.240, enabling: SI 2012/ 57, SI 2012/ 193, SI 2012/ 411, SI 2012/ 628, SI 2012/ 887, SI 2012/ 1008, SI 2012/ 1463, SI 2012/ 1714, SI 2012/ 2029, SI 2012/ 2420, SI 2012/ 2599, SI 2012/ 2913
Sch.3 para.58, disapplied: SI 2012/ 1023 Art.2
Sch.3 para.59, disapplied: SI 2012/ 1023 Art.2
Sch.3 para.61, disapplied: SI 2012/ 1023 Art.2
Sch.3 para.62, disapplied: SI 2012/ 1023 Art.2
Sch.3 para.75, repealed (in part): 2012 c.7 s.191

2011– cont.

20. Localism Act 2011– cont.
Sch.3 para.76, repealed: 2012 c.7 s.191
Sch.3 para.77, repealed (in part): 2012 c.7 s.191
Sch.3 para.78, repealed: 2012 c.7 s.191
Sch.4, referred to: SI 2012/ 2913 Art.5
Sch.4 Part 2 para.57, applied: SI 2012/ 57 Art.8
Sch.4 Part 2 para.57, enabling: SI 2012/668
Sch.4 Part 2 para.58, applied: SI 2012/ 57 Art.8
Sch.24 Part 3, enabling: SI 2012/ 701
Sch.25 Part 5, referred to: SI 2012/ 2913 Art.5

21. Education Act 2011
Commencement Orders: SI 2012/ 84 Art.2, Art.3, Art.4; SI 2012/924 Art.2, Art.3; SI 2012/ 1087 Art.2, Art.3, Art.4; SI 2012/2213 Art.2, Art.3, Art.4, Art.5
s.11, enabling: SI 2012/ 765, SI 2012/ 1153
s.16, enabling: SI 2012/ 765
s.26, enabling: SI 2012/ 765
s.49, disapplied: SI 2012/924 Art.7
s.49, referred to: SI 2012/924 Art.6
s.50, applied: SI 2012/ 1033 Reg.16
s.54, enabling: SI 2012/976, SI 2012/979
s.67, enabling: SI 2012/956
s.76, varied: SI 2012/ 1309 Reg.15
s.76, enabling: SI 2012/ 1309
s.77, enabling: SI 2012/ 433
s.78, applied: SI 2012/976
s.78, enabling: SI 2012/433, SI 2012/765, SI 2012/ 956, SI 2012/976, SI 2012/979, SI 2012/1153, SI 2012/ 1309
s.82, applied: SI 2012/924, SI 2012/2213
s.82, enabling: SI 2012/84, SI 2012/924, SI 2012/ 1087, SI 2012/2213
Sch.12 para.7, referred to: SI 2012/924 Art.7
Sch.12 para.20, referred to: SI 2012/924 Art.6
Sch.12 para.23, disapplied: SI 2012/924 Art.7
Sch.14 para.1, varied: SI 2012/ 84 Art.5
Sch.14 para.2, varied: SI 2012/ 84 Art.5
Sch.14 para.3, varied: SI 2012/ 84 Art.5
Sch.14 para.4, varied: SI 2012/ 84 Art.5
Sch.14 para.5, varied: SI 2012/ 84 Art.5
Sch.14 para.6, varied: SI 2012/ 84 Art.5
Sch.14 para.7, varied: SI 2012/ 84 Art.5
Sch.14 para.8, varied: SI 2012/ 84 Art.5
Sch.14 para.9, varied: SI 2012/ 84 Art.5
Sch.14 para.10, varied: SI 2012/ 84 Art.5
Sch.14 para.11, varied: SI 2012/ 84 Art.5
Sch.14 para.12, varied: SI 2012/ 84 Art.5
Sch.14 para.13, varied: SI 2012/ 84 Art.5
Sch.14 para.14, varied: SI 2012/ 84 Art.5
Sch.14 para.15, varied: SI 2012/ 84 Art.5
Sch.14 para.16, varied: SI 2012/ 84 Art.5
Sch.14 para.17, varied: SI 2012/ 84 Art.5
Sch.14 para.18, varied: SI 2012/ 84 Art.5
Sch.14 para.19, varied: SI 2012/ 84 Art.5
Sch.14 para.20, varied: SI 2012/ 84 Art.5

23. Terrorism Prevention and Investigation Measures Act 2011
see *Secretary of State for the Home Department v BM* [2012] EWHC 714 (Admin), [2012] 1 W.L.R. 2734 (QBD (Admin)), Collins, J.
s.9, see *Secretary of State for the Home Department v BM* [2012] EWHC 714 (Admin), [2012] 1 W.L.R. 2734 (QBD (Admin)), Collins, J.
Sch.1 Pt 1 para.1, see *Secretary of State for the Home Department v BM* [2012] EWHC 714 (Admin), [2012] 1 W.L.R. 2734 (QBD (Admin)), Collins, J.

2011– cont.

23. Terrorism Prevention and Investigation Measures Act 2011– cont.
Sch.1 Part 1 para.5, amended: 2012 c.21 Sch.18 para.135
Sch.6 para.5, applied: 2012 c.9 s.20
Sch.6 para.6, applied: 2012 c.9 s.20
Sch.6 para.7, applied: 2012 c.9 s.20
Sch.6 para.8, applied: 2012 c.9 s.20
Sch.6 para.9, applied: 2012 c.9 s.20
Sch.6 para.10, amended: 2012 c.9 Sch.1 para.5, 2012 c.10 Sch.24 para.32
Sch.6 para.10, applied: 2012 c.9 s.20
Sch.6 para.10, repealed (in part): 2012 c.10 Sch.24 para.32
Sch.6 para.11, applied: 2012 c.9 s.20
Sch.6 para.12, applied: 2012 c.9 s.20
Sch.6 para.13, applied: 2012 c.9 s.20
Sch.6 para.14, applied: 2012 c.9 s.20
Sch.8 para.3, see *Secretary of State for the Home Department v BM* [2012] EWHC 714 (Admin), [2012] 1 W.L.R. 2734 (QBD (Admin)), Collins, J.

24. Public Bodies Act 2011
Commencement Orders: SI 2012/ 1662 Art.2
s.1, enabling: SI 2012/964, SI 2012/1206, SI 2012/ 1658, SI 2012/ 1923, SI 2012/ 2007, SI 2012/ 2398, SI 2012/ 2401, SI 2012/ 2406, SI 2012/ 2407, SI 2012/ 2654
s.5, enabling: SI 2012/ 1659
s.6, applied: SI 2012/ 1659
s.6, enabling: SI 2012/964, SI 2012/ 1206, SI 2012/ 1658, SI 2012/ 1659, SI 2012/ 1923, SI 2012/ 2007, SI 2012/ 2398, SI 2012/ 2401, SI 2012/ 2406, SI 2012/ 2407, SI 2012/ 2654
s.8, applied: SI 2012/ 1206, SI 2012/ 1658, SI 2012/ 1659, SI 2012/ 2007, SI 2012/ 2401, SI 2012/ 2406, SI 2012/ 2654
s.8, referred to: SI 2012/964, SI 2012/ 1658, SI 2012/ 2007, SI 2012/ 2401, SI 2012/ 2654
s.9, applied: SI 2012/964, SI 2012/ 1658, SI 2012/ 1659, SI 2012/ 2401
s.10, applied: SI 2012/964, SI 2012/ 1658, SI 2012/ 1659, SI 2012/ 2007, SI 2012/ 2401, SI 2012/ 2406, SI 2012/ 2654
s.11, applied: SI 2012/ 1206, SI 2012/ 1658, SI 2012/ 1659, SI 2012/ 2007, SI 2012/ 2401, SI 2012/ 2406, SI 2012/ 2654
s.11, referred to: SI 2012/964, SI 2012/ 1658, SI 2012/ 1659, SI 2012/ 2007, SI 2012/ 2406, SI 2012/ 2654
s.13, enabling: SI 2012/ 1903
s.15, enabling: SI 2012/ 1903
s.16, applied: SI 2012/ 1903
s.18, applied: SI 2012/ 1903
s.19, applied: SI 2012/ 1903
s.21, applied: SI 2012/ 1659
s.23, enabling: SI 2012/ 2007
s.25, enabling: SI 2012/ 1709
s.30, enabling: SI 2012/ 1471
s.35, enabling: SI 2012/964, SI 2012/ 1206, SI 2012/ 1658, SI 2012/ 1659, SI 2012/ 1923, SI 2012/ 2007, SI 2012/ 2398, SI 2012/ 2401, SI 2012/ 2406, SI 2012/ 2407, SI 2012/ 2654
s.38, enabling: SI 2012/ 1662
Sch.1, amended: SI 2012/964 Art.3, SI 2012/ 1206 Art.3, SI 2012/ 1923 Sch.1, SI 2012/ 2007 Sch.1 para.109, SI 2012/ 2398 Art.2, Art.3, SI 2012/ 2401 Sch.1 para.37, Sch.2 para.4, SI 2012/ 2407 Art.3, SI 2012/ 2654 Sch.1
Sch.1, repealed (in part): SI 2012/ 2406 Art.3

2011– cont.

25. Charities Act 2011
applied: SSI 2012/ 319 Sch.4 para.34
referred to: SI 2012/ 3012 Reg.31
Part 8, referred to: SI 2012/ 3013 Reg.41
Part 11, applied: SI 2012/ 3094 Reg.35
Part 16, applied: SI 2012/ 3012 Reg.61
s.1, varied: SI 2012/ 735 Art.5, Art.6
s.29, varied: SI 2012/ 3012 Reg.6
s.30, disapplied: SI 2012/ 3012 Reg.6
s.30, enabling: SI 2012/ 1734, SI 2012/ 3012
s.31, disapplied: SI 2012/ 3012 Reg.6
s.32, disapplied: SI 2012/ 3012 Reg.6
s.33, disapplied: SI 2012/ 3012 Reg.6
s.34, disapplied: SI 2012/ 3012 Reg.6
s.35, disapplied: SI 2012/ 3012 Reg.6
s.35, varied: SI 2012/ 3012 Reg.6
s.36, varied: SI 2012/ 3012 Reg.6
s.38, varied: SI 2012/ 3012 Reg.6
s.42, applied: SI 2012/ 3013 Reg.37
s.42, enabling: SI 2012/ 3012
s.43, applied: SI 2012/ 3013 Reg.37
s.44, applied: SI 2012/ 3013 Reg.37
s.52, applied: SI 2012/ 3012 Reg.26, Reg.27
s.80, amended: SI 2012/ 2404 Sch.2 para.62
s.88, applied: SI 2012/ 3013 Reg.25
s.105, applied: SI 2012/ 3012 Reg.36
s.109, amended: 2012 c.21 Sch.18 para.136
s.111, applied: SI 2012/ 3012 Reg.27
s.115, see *Rai v Charity Commission for England and Wales* [2012] EWHC 1111 (Ch), [2012] W.T.L.R. 1053 (Ch D), Norris, J.
s.131, applied: SI 2012/ 3012 Reg.10, SI 2012/ 3013 Reg.39
s.132, varied: SI 2012/ 3013 Reg.41
s.133, applied: SI 2012/ 3012 Reg.62
s.134, applied: SI 2012/ 3013 Reg.39
s.134, varied: SI 2012/ 3013 Reg.41
s.138, varied: SI 2012/ 3013 Reg.41
s.140, varied: SI 2012/ 3013 Reg.41
s.146, varied: SI 2012/ 3013 Reg.41
s.149, amended: 2012 c.7 Sch.5 para.184
s.149, repealed (in part): 2012 c.7 Sch.5 para.184, Sch.14 para.118
s.150, amended: 2012 c.7 Sch.14 para.119
s.153, varied: SI 2012/ 3013 Reg.41
s.162, varied: SI 2012/ 3013 Reg.41
s.163, varied: SI 2012/ 3013 Reg.41
s.164, varied: SI 2012/ 3013 Reg.41
s.169, varied: SI 2012/ 3013 Reg.41
s.173, varied: SI 2012/ 3013 Reg.41
s.178, amended: SI 2012/ 2404 Sch.2 para.62
s.178, referred to: SI 2012/ 3012 Reg.31
s.180, amended: SI 2012/ 2404 Sch.2 para.62, SI 2012/ 3014 Art.5
s.181, amended: SI 2012/ 3014 Art.6
s.183, amended: SI 2012/ 2404 Sch.2 para.62, SI 2012/ 3014 Art.7
s.183, referred to: SI 2012/ 3012 Reg.32
s.184, referred to: SI 2012/ 3012 Reg.32
s.206, applied: SI 2012/ 3012 Reg.13
s.206, enabling: SI 2012/ 3012
s.207, applied: SI 2012/ 3012 Reg.7
s.207, enabling: SI 2012/ 3012
s.208, referred to: SI 2012/ 3013 Reg.37
s.216, referred to: SI 2012/ 3012 Reg.14
s.223, enabling: SI 2012/ 3012
s.224, applied: SI 2012/ 3012 Reg.16, Reg.35
s.224, referred to: SI 2012/ 3012 Reg.15

2011– cont.

25. Charities Act 2011– *cont.*
s.225, referred to: SI 2012/ 3012 Reg.15
s.226, referred to: SI 2012/ 3012 Reg.15
s.227, referred to: SI 2012/ 3012 Reg.15, Reg.17
s.228, disapplied: SI 2012/ 3011 Art.2
s.229, disapplied: SI 2012/ 3011 Art.2
s.230, disapplied: SI 2012/ 3011 Art.2
s.231, disapplied: SI 2012/ 3011 Art.2
s.232, disapplied: SI 2012/ 3011 Art.2
s.233, disapplied: SI 2012/ 3011 Art.2
s.234, disapplied: SI 2012/ 3011 Art.2
s.235, applied: SI 2012/ 3012 Reg.35
s.240, applied: SI 2012/ 3012 Reg.35
s.245, enabling: SI 2012/ 3013
s.246, enabling: SI 2012/ 3012
s.310, applied: SI 2012/ 3012 Reg.61
s.310, varied: SI 2012/ 3012 Reg.61
s.311, see *Berry v IBS-STL (UK) Ltd (In Liquidation)* [2012] EWHC 666 (Ch), [2012] P.T.S.R. 1619 (Ch D), David Donaldson Q.C.
s.312, applied: SI 2012/ 3012 Reg.61
s.312, varied: SI 2012/ 3012 Reg.61
s.324, enabling: SI 2012/ 3014
s.335, applied: SI 2012/ 3012 Reg.26
s.336, applied: SI 2012/ 3012 Reg.26, Reg.27
s.337, applied: SI 2012/ 3012 Reg.26, Reg.27
s.347, enabling: SI 2012/ 3012, SI 2012/ 3013, SI 2012/ 3014
s.348, applied: SI 2012/ 3012, SI 2012/ 3013
s.349, applied: SI 2012/ 3014
Sch.6, amended: SI 2012/ 3014 Art.8
Sch.7 Part 1 para.3, varied: SI 2012/ 3012 Reg.61
Sch.8 Part 1 para.3, enabling: SI 2012/ 3014
Sch.9 para.29, enabling: SI 2012/ 3011

2012

1. Supply and Appropriation (Anticipation and Adjustments) Act 2012
Royal Assent, March 08, 2012
s.1, applied: 2012 c.13 s.3, s.4
Sch.1, varied: 2012 c.11 s.12

2. Live Music Act 2012
Royal Assent, March 08, 2012
s.4, enabling: SI 2012/ 2115

3. Public Services (Social Value) Act 2012
Commencement Orders: SI 2012/ 3173 Art.2
Royal Assent, March 08, 2012
s.4, enabling: SI 2012/ 3173

4. Domestic Violence, Crime and Victims (Amendment) Act 2012
Royal Assent, March 08, 2012
s.4, enabling: SI 2012/ 1432

5. Welfare Reform Act 2012
Commencement Orders: SI 2012/ 863 Art.2; SI 2012/ 1246 Art.2; SI 2012/ 1651 Art.2, Art.3; SI 2012/ 2530 Art.2; SI 2012/ 2946 Art.2; SI 2012/ 3090 Art.2, Art.3
Royal Assent, March 08, 2012
applied: 2012 asp 10 s.3
referred to: 2012 asp 10 s.4
Part 1, applied: 2012 asp 10 s.1
Part 4, applied: 2012 asp 10 s.2, SI 2012/ 2885 Sch.2 para.5, Sch.2 para.6, Sch.3 para.2, SI 2012/ 2886 Sch.1, SI 2012/ 3144 Sch.1 para.19, SI 2012/ 3145 Sch.1
s.24, applied: SI 2012/ 2886 Sch.1, SSI 2012/ 303 Sch.1 para.18

2012– cont.

5. **Welfare Reform Act 2012**– *cont.*
s.41, applied: 2012 asp 10 s.1
s.45, applied: SI 2012/ 2568
s.46, applied: SI 2012/ 2568
s.51, referred to: SI 2012/ 913
s.52, referred to: SI 2012/ 913
s.64, applied: SI 2012/ 2743 Reg.2
s.64, enabling: SI 2012/ 2743, SI 2012/ 2812
s.69, applied: SI 2012/ 3040
s.78, applied: SI 2012/ 2885 Sch.2 para.7, SI 2012/ 2886 Sch.1
s.86, applied: SI 2012/ 2885 Sch.1 para.8, Sch.1 para.25, Sch.1 para.26, Sch.2 para.7, SI 2012/ 2886 Sch.1, SI 2012/ 3144 Sch.1 para.3, Sch.1 para.19, SI 2012/ 3145 Sch.1, SSI 2012/ 303 Sch.1 para.10, Sch.1 para.12, SSI 2012/ 319 Sch.1 para.8
s.86, disapplied: SI 2012/ 2885 Sch.2 para.6
s.96, applied: SI 2012/ 2994
s.96, enabling: SI 2012/ 2994
s.97, applied: SI 2012/ 2994
s.97, enabling: SI 2012/ 2994
s.103, enabling: SI 2012/ 1267
s.116, applied: SI 2012/ 1990
s.122, applied: SI 2012/ 1246 Art.2
s.123, applied: SI 2012/ 1246 Art.2
s.125, applied: SI 2012/ 1246 Art.2
s.127, amended: SI 2012/ 2007 Sch.1 para.102
s.128, amended: SI 2012/ 2007 Sch.1 para.103
s.129, amended: SI 2012/ 2007 Sch.1 para.104
s.130, applied: SI 2012/ 1483 Reg.3, Reg.4
s.130, enabling: SI 2012/ 1483
s.131, applied: SI 2012/ 1483 Reg.5, Reg.6, Reg.7, Reg.8, Reg.9, Reg.10
s.131, enabling: SI 2012/ 1483
s.132, applied: SI 2012/ 1483 Reg.10
s.132, enabling: SI 2012/ 1483
s.133, enabling: SI 2012/ 1483
s.136, amended: SI 2012/ 2007 Sch.1 para.105
s.137, amended: SI 2012/ 2007 Sch.1 para.106
s.138, amended: SI 2012/ 2007 Sch.1 para.107
s.150, enabling: SI 2012/ 863, SI 2012/ 1246, SI 2012/ 1440, SI 2012/ 1651, SI 2012/ 2530, SI 2012/ 2946, SI 2012/ 3090
Sch.7, applied: SI 2012/ 2568
Sch.11 para.5, amended: SI 2012/ 2007 Sch.1 para.108
Sch.11 para.6, amended: SI 2012/ 2007 Sch.1 para.108

6. **Consumer Insurance (Disclosure and Representations) Act 2012**
Royal Assent, March 08, 2012

7. **Health and Social Care Act 2012**
Commencement Orders: SI 2012/ 1319 Art.2; SI 2012/ 1831 Art.2, Art.10, Art.11; SI 2012/ 2657 Art.2
Royal Assent, March 27, 2012
applied: 2012 c.14 s.216
Part 7, referred to: SI 2012/ 1480 Art.3
s.29, applied: SI 2012/ 3094 Reg.18
s.33, referred to: SI 2012/ 1831 Art.12
s.34, applied: SI 2012/ 1831 Art.10
s.64, amended: SI 2012/ 2657 Art.3
s.67, amended: SI 2012/ 2657 Art.4
s.71, amended: SI 2012/ 2657 Art.5
s.75, enabling: SI 2012/ 2996
s.78, amended: SI 2012/ 2657 Art.6
s.95, amended: SI 2012/ 2657 Art.7
s.98, amended: SI 2012/ 2657 Art.8

2012– cont.

7. **Health and Social Care Act 2012**– *cont.*
s.101, amended: SI 2012/ 2657 Art.9
s.104, amended: SI 2012/ 2657 Art.9
s.145, amended: 2012 c.21 Sch.18 para.137
s.194, referred to: SI 2012/ 1831 Art.6
s.213, disapplied: SI 2012/ 1480 Art.16
s.214, referred to: SI 2012/ 1480 Art.2
s.230, enabling: SI 2012/ 1480
s.300, applied: SI 2012/ 2996 Sch.1 para.6, Sch.1 para.7
s.303, applied: SI 2012/ 1479
s.303, enabling: SI 2012/ 1479, SI 2012/ 1641, SI 2012/ 2672
s.304, enabling: SI 2012/ 1319, SI 2012/ 1480, SI 2012/ 1631, SI 2012/ 1831, SI 2012/ 2657
s.306, enabling: SI 2012/ 1319, SI 2012/ 1831, SI 2012/ 2657
s.307, applied: SI 2012/ 1319, SI 2012/ 2657
Sch.2, referred to: SI 2012/ 1831 Art.9
Sch.4 Part 1 para.1, referred to: SI 2012/ 1831 Art.10
Sch.4 Part 10 para.125, disapplied: SI 2012/ 1831 Art.11
Sch.4 Part 10 para.125, referred to: SI 2012/ 1831 Art.11
Sch.5 para.96, disapplied: SI 2012/ 1831 Art.11
Sch.5 para.96, referred to: SI 2012/ 1831 Art.11
Sch.6 para.8, enabling: SI 2012/ 1631
Sch.8 para.13, amended: SI 2012/ 2657 Art.11
Sch.8 para.13, repealed (in part): SI 2012/ 2657 Art.11
Sch.15 Part 1 para.16, disapplied: SI 2012/ 1480 Art.12

8. **Water Industry (Financial Assistance) Act 2012**
Royal Assent, May 01, 2012

9. **Protection of Freedoms Act 2012**
Commencement Orders: SI 2012/ 1205 Art.2, Art.3, Art.4; SI 2012/ 2075 Art.2, Art.3, Art.4, Art.5, Art.6; SI 2012/ 2157; SI 2012/ 2234 Art.2, Art.3, Art.4, Art.5, Art.8, Art.9, Art.10; SI 2012/ 2499 Art.2; SI 2012/ 2521 Art.2, Art.3
Royal Assent, May 01, 2012
s.64, referred to: SI 2012/ 2114 Reg.1
s.65, referred to: SI 2012/ 2114 Reg.1
s.66, referred to: SI 2012/ 2112 Reg.1, SI 2012/ 2114 Reg.1
s.67, amended: SI 2012/ 3006 Art.34
s.70, amended: SI 2012/ 3006 Art.34
s.71, amended: SI 2012/ 3006 Art.34
s.72, applied: SI 2012/ 2157 Art.6
s.72, referred to: SI 2012/ 2234 Art.15
s.75, amended: SI 2012/ 3006 Art.34
s.76, amended: SI 2012/ 3006 Art.34
s.77, amended: SI 2012/ 3006 Art.34
s.79, referred to: SI 2012/ 1762 Art.4, SI 2012/ 2591 Art.4, SI 2012/ 2598 Art.4
s.79, varied: SI 2012/ 1762 Sch.1 para.1, SI 2012/ 2591 Sch.1 para.1, Sch.1 para.4, SI 2012/ 2598 Sch.1 para.1
s.80, referred to: SI 2012/ 1762 Art.4, SI 2012/ 2591 Art.4, SI 2012/ 2598 Art.4
s.80, varied: SI 2012/ 1762 Sch.1 para.2, SI 2012/ 2591 Sch.1 para.2, Sch.1 para.4, SI 2012/ 2598 Sch.1 para.2
s.81, varied: SI 2012/ 2591 Sch.1 para.4
s.82, referred to: SI 2012/ 1762 Art.4, SI 2012/ 2591 Art.4, SI 2012/ 2598 Art.4
s.82, varied: SI 2012/ 1762 Sch.1 para.3, SI 2012/ 2591 Sch.1 para.3, Sch.1 para.4, SI 2012/ 2598 Sch.1 para.3

2012– cont.

9. Protection of Freedoms Act 2012–*cont.*

s.83, referred to: SI 2012/ 1762 Art.4, SI 2012/ 2591 Art.4, SI 2012/ 2598 Art.4

s.83, varied: SI 2012/ 2591 Sch.1 para.4

s.84, referred to: SI 2012/ 1762 Art.4, SI 2012/ 2591 Art.4, SI 2012/ 2598 Art.4

s.84, varied: SI 2012/ 2591 Sch.1 para.4

s.84A, varied: SI 2012/ 1762 Sch.1 para.4, SI 2012/ 2591 Sch.1 para.4, SI 2012/ 2598 Sch.1 para.4

s.85, varied: SI 2012/ 2591 Sch.1 para.4

s.86, varied: SI 2012/ 2591 Sch.1 para.4

s.87, referred to: SI 2012/ 1762 Art.4, SI 2012/ 2591 Art.4, SI 2012/ 2598 Art.4

s.87, varied: SI 2012/ 1762 Sch.1 para.5, SI 2012/ 2591 Sch.1 para.5, SI 2012/ 2598 Sch.1 para.5

s.88, referred to: SI 2012/ 1762 Art.4, SI 2012/ 2591 Art.4, SI 2012/ 2598 Art.4

s.88, varied: SI 2012/ 1762 Sch.1 para.6, SI 2012/ 2591 Sch.1 para.6, SI 2012/ 2598 Sch.1 para.6

s.88, enabling: SI 2012/ 3006

s.89, applied: SI 2012/ 3006

s.89, referred to: SI 2012/ 1762 Art.4, SI 2012/ 2591 Art.4, SI 2012/ 2598 Art.4

s.89, varied: SI 2012/ 1762 Sch.1 para.7, SI 2012/ 2591 Sch.1 para.7, SI 2012/ 2598 Sch.1 para.7

s.89, enabling: SI 2012/ 3006

s.90, amended: SI 2012/ 3006 Art.34

s.92, applied: SI 2012/ 2279 Art.2

s.95, applied: SI 2012/ 2279 Art.2, Art.4

s.95, enabling: SI 2012/ 2279

s.115, enabling: SI 2012/ 2278

s.116, enabling: SI 2012/ 2075, SI 2012/ 2234

s.118, enabling: SI 2012/ 1762, SI 2012/ 2561, SI 2012/ 2591, SI 2012/ 2598

s.120, enabling: SI 2012/ 1205, SI 2012/ 2075, SI 2012/ 2234, SI 2012/ 2499, SI 2012/ 2521

Sch.7 para.4, amended: SI 2012/ 3006 Art.34

Sch.7 para.7, amended: SI 2012/ 3006 Art.34

Sch.7 para.8, amended: SI 2012/ 3006 Art.34

Sch.7 para.12, amended: SI 2012/ 3006 Art.34

Sch.7 para.13, amended: SI 2012/ 3006 Art.34

Sch.7 para.14, amended: SI 2012/ 3006 Art.34

Sch.8, applied: SI 2012/ 2522 Art.2

Sch.8 para.8, enabling: SI 2012/ 2522

Sch.9 Part 6, referred to: SI 2012/ 1762 Art.4, SI 2012/ 2591 Art.4, SI 2012/ 2598 Art.4

Sch.9 Part 6 para.36, varied: SI 2012/ 1762 Sch.2 para.1, SI 2012/ 2591 Sch.2 para.1, SI 2012/ 2598 Sch.2 para.1

Sch.9 Part 6 para.37, varied: SI 2012/ 1762 Sch.2 para.1, SI 2012/ 2591 Sch.2 para.1, SI 2012/ 2598 Sch.2 para.1

Sch.9 Part 6 para.40, varied: SI 2012/ 1762 Sch.2 para.2, SI 2012/ 2591 Sch.2 para.2, SI 2012/ 2598 Sch.2 para.2

Sch.9 Part 6 para.41, varied: SI 2012/ 1762 Sch.2 para.2, SI 2012/ 2591 Sch.2 para.2, SI 2012/ 2598 Sch.2 para.2

Sch.9 Part 6 para.42, varied: SI 2012/ 1762 Sch.2 para.2, SI 2012/ 2591 Sch.2 para.2, SI 2012/ 2598 Sch.2 para.2

Sch.9 Part 6 para.43, varied: SI 2012/ 1762 Sch.2 para.3, SI 2012/ 2591 Sch.2 para.3, SI 2012/ 2598 Sch.2 para.3

Sch.9 Part 6 para.44, varied: SI 2012/ 1762 Sch.2 para.3, SI 2012/ 2591 Sch.2 para.3, SI 2012/ 2598 Sch.2 para.3

2012– cont.

9. Protection of Freedoms Act 2012–*cont.*

Sch.9 Part 6 para.45, varied: SI 2012/ 1762 Sch.2 para.3, SI 2012/ 2591 Sch.2 para.3, SI 2012/ 2598 Sch.2 para.3

Sch.9 Part 6 para.46, varied: SI 2012/ 1762 Sch.2 para.3, SI 2012/ 2591 Sch.2 para.3, SI 2012/ 2598 Sch.2 para.3

Sch.9 Part 6 para.47, varied: SI 2012/ 1762 Sch.2 para.3, SI 2012/ 2591 Sch.2 para.3, SI 2012/ 2598 Sch.2 para.3

Sch.9 Part 6 para.48, varied: SI 2012/ 1762 Sch.2 para.3, SI 2012/ 2591 Sch.2 para.3, SI 2012/ 2598 Sch.2 para.3

Sch.9 Part 6 para.49, varied: SI 2012/ 1762 Sch.2 para.3, SI 2012/ 2591 Sch.2 para.3, SI 2012/ 2598 Sch.2 para.3

Sch.9 Part 6 para.50, varied: SI 2012/ 1762 Sch.2 para.3, SI 2012/ 2591 Sch.2 para.3, SI 2012/ 2598 Sch.2 para.3

Sch.9 Part 6 para.51, varied: SI 2012/ 1762 Sch.2 para.3, SI 2012/ 2591 Sch.2 para.3, SI 2012/ 2598 Sch.2 para.3

Sch.9 Part 6 para.52, varied: SI 2012/ 1762 Sch.2 para.3, SI 2012/ 2591 Sch.2 para.3, SI 2012/ 2598 Sch.2 para.3

Sch.9 Part 6 para.53, varied: SI 2012/ 1762 Sch.2 para.3, SI 2012/ 2591 Sch.2 para.3, SI 2012/ 2598 Sch.2 para.3

Sch.9 Part 6 para.54, varied: SI 2012/ 1762 Sch.2 para.3, SI 2012/ 2591 Sch.2 para.3, SI 2012/ 2598 Sch.2 para.3

Sch.9 Part 6 para.55, varied: SI 2012/ 1762 Sch.2 para.3, SI 2012/ 2591 Sch.2 para.3, SI 2012/ 2598 Sch.2 para.3

Sch.9 Part 6 para.56, varied: SI 2012/ 1762 Sch.2 para.3, SI 2012/ 2591 Sch.2 para.3, SI 2012/ 2598 Sch.2 para.3

Sch.9 Part 6 para.57, varied: SI 2012/ 1762 Sch.2 para.3, SI 2012/ 2591 Sch.2 para.3, SI 2012/ 2598 Sch.2 para.3

Sch.9 Part 6 para.58, varied: SI 2012/ 1762 Sch.2 para.3, SI 2012/ 2591 Sch.2 para.3, SI 2012/ 2598 Sch.2 para.3

Sch.9 Part 6 para.59, varied: SI 2012/ 1762 Sch.2 para.3, SI 2012/ 2591 Sch.2 para.3, SI 2012/ 2598 Sch.2 para.3

Sch.9 Part 6 para.60, varied: SI 2012/ 1762 Sch.2 para.3, SI 2012/ 2591 Sch.2 para.3, SI 2012/ 2598 Sch.2 para.3

Sch.9 Part 6 para.61, varied: SI 2012/ 1762 Sch.2 para.3, SI 2012/ 2591 Sch.2 para.3, SI 2012/ 2598 Sch.2 para.3

Sch.9 Part 6 para.62, varied: SI 2012/ 1762 Sch.2 para.3, SI 2012/ 2591 Sch.2 para.3, SI 2012/ 2598 Sch.2 para.3

Sch.9 Part 6 para.63, varied: SI 2012/ 1762 Sch.2 para.3, SI 2012/ 2591 Sch.2 para.3, SI 2012/ 2598 Sch.2 para.3

Sch.9 Part 6 para.64, varied: SI 2012/ 1762 Sch.2 para.3, SI 2012/ 2591 Sch.2 para.3, SI 2012/ 2598 Sch.2 para.3

Sch.9 Part 6 para.65, varied: SI 2012/ 1762 Sch.2 para.3, SI 2012/ 2591 Sch.2 para.3, SI 2012/ 2598 Sch.2 para.3

Sch.9 Part 6 para.66, varied: SI 2012/ 1762 Sch.2 para.3, SI 2012/ 2591 Sch.2 para.3, SI 2012/ 2598 Sch.2 para.3

Sch.9 Part 6 para.67, varied: SI 2012/ 1762 Sch.2 para.3, SI 2012/ 2591 Sch.2 para.3, SI 2012/ 2598 Sch.2 para.3

2012– cont.

9. Protection of Freedoms Act 2012–*cont.*

Sch.9 Part 6 para.68, varied: SI 2012/1762 Sch.2 para.3, SI 2012/2591 Sch.2 para.3, SI 2012/2598 Sch.2 para.3

Sch.9 Part 6 para.69, varied: SI 2012/1762 Sch.2 para.3, SI 2012/2591 Sch.2 para.3, SI 2012/2598 Sch.2 para.3

Sch.9 Part 6 para.70, varied: SI 2012/1762 Sch.2 para.3, SI 2012/2591 Sch.2 para.3, SI 2012/2598 Sch.2 para.3

Sch.9 Part 6 para.71, varied: SI 2012/1762 Sch.2 para.3, SI 2012/2591 Sch.2 para.3, SI 2012/2598 Sch.2 para.3

Sch.9 Part 6 para.72, varied: SI 2012/1762 Sch.2 para.3, SI 2012/2591 Sch.2 para.3, SI 2012/2598 Sch.2 para.3

Sch.9 Part 6 para.73, varied: SI 2012/1762 Sch.2 para.3, SI 2012/2591 Sch.2 para.3, SI 2012/2598 Sch.2 para.3

Sch.9 Part 6 para.74, varied: SI 2012/1762 Sch.2 para.3, SI 2012/2591 Sch.2 para.3, SI 2012/2598 Sch.2 para.3

Sch.9 Part 6 para.75, varied: SI 2012/1762 Sch.2 para.3, SI 2012/2591 Sch.2 para.3, SI 2012/2598 Sch.2 para.3

Sch.9 Part 6 para.76, varied: SI 2012/1762 Sch.2 para.3, SI 2012/2591 Sch.2 para.3, SI 2012/2598 Sch.2 para.3

Sch.9 Part 6 para.77, varied: SI 2012/1762 Sch.2 para.3, SI 2012/2591 Sch.2 para.3, SI 2012/2598 Sch.2 para.3

Sch.9 Part 6 para.78, varied: SI 2012/1762 Sch.2 para.3, SI 2012/2591 Sch.2 para.3, SI 2012/2598 Sch.2 para.3

Sch.9 Part 6 para.79, varied: SI 2012/1762 Sch.2 para.3, SI 2012/2591 Sch.2 para.3, SI 2012/2598 Sch.2 para.3

Sch.9 Part 6 para.80, varied: SI 2012/1762 Sch.2 para.3, SI 2012/2591 Sch.2 para.3, SI 2012/2598 Sch.2 para.3

Sch.9 Part 6 para.81, varied: SI 2012/1762 Sch.2 para.3, SI 2012/2591 Sch.2 para.3, SI 2012/2598 Sch.2 para.3

Sch.9 Part 6 para.82, varied: SI 2012/1762 Sch.2 para.3, SI 2012/2591 Sch.2 para.3, SI 2012/2598 Sch.2 para.3

Sch.9 Part 6 para.83, varied: SI 2012/1762 Sch.2 para.3, SI 2012/2591 Sch.2 para.3, SI 2012/2598 Sch.2 para.3

Sch.9 Part 6 para.84, varied: SI 2012/1762 Sch.2 para.3, SI 2012/2591 Sch.2 para.3, SI 2012/2598 Sch.2 para.3

Sch.9 Part 6 para.85, varied: SI 2012/1762 Sch.2 para.3, SI 2012/2591 Sch.2 para.3, SI 2012/2598 Sch.2 para.3

Sch.9 Part 6 para.86, varied: SI 2012/1762 Sch.2 para.3, SI 2012/2591 Sch.2 para.3, SI 2012/2598 Sch.2 para.3

Sch.9 Part 6 para.87, varied: SI 2012/1762 Sch.2 para.3, SI 2012/2591 Sch.2 para.3, SI 2012/2598 Sch.2 para.3

Sch.9 Part 6 para.88, varied: SI 2012/1762 Sch.2 para.3, SI 2012/2591 Sch.2 para.3, SI 2012/2598 Sch.2 para.3

Sch.9 Part 6 para.89, varied: SI 2012/1762 Sch.2 para.3, SI 2012/2591 Sch.2 para.3, SI 2012/2598 Sch.2 para.3

Sch.9 Part 6 para.90, varied: SI 2012/1762 Sch.2 para.3, SI 2012/2591 Sch.2 para.3, SI 2012/2598 Sch.2 para.3

2012– cont.

9. Protection of Freedoms Act 2012–*cont.*

Sch.9 Part 6 para.91, varied: SI 2012/1762 Sch.2 para.3, SI 2012/2591 Sch.2 para.3, SI 2012/2598 Sch.2 para.3

Sch.9 Part 6 para.92, varied: SI 2012/1762 Sch.2 para.3, SI 2012/2591 Sch.2 para.3, SI 2012/2598 Sch.2 para.3

Sch.9 Part 6 para.93, varied: SI 2012/1762 Sch.2 para.3, SI 2012/2591 Sch.2 para.3, SI 2012/2598 Sch.2 para.3

Sch.9 Part 6 para.94, varied: SI 2012/1762 Sch.2 para.3, SI 2012/2591 Sch.2 para.3, SI 2012/2598 Sch.2 para.3

Sch.9 Part 6 para.95, varied: SI 2012/1762 Sch.2 para.3, SI 2012/2591 Sch.2 para.3, SI 2012/2598 Sch.2 para.3

Sch.9 Part 6 para.96, varied: SI 2012/1762 Sch.2 para.3, SI 2012/2591 Sch.2 para.3, SI 2012/2598 Sch.2 para.3

Sch.9 Part 6 para.97, varied: SI 2012/1762 Sch.2 para.3, SI 2012/2591 Sch.2 para.3, SI 2012/2598 Sch.2 para.3

Sch.9 Part 6 para.98, varied: SI 2012/1762 Sch.2 para.3, SI 2012/2591 Sch.2 para.3, SI 2012/2598 Sch.2 para.3

Sch.9 Part 6 para.99, varied: SI 2012/1762 Sch.2 para.3, SI 2012/2591 Sch.2 para.3, SI 2012/2598 Sch.2 para.3

Sch.9 Part 6 para.100, varied: SI 2012/1762 Sch.2 para.3, SI 2012/2591 Sch.2 para.3, SI 2012/2598 Sch.2 para.3

Sch.9 Part 6 para.101, varied: SI 2012/1762 Sch.2 para.3, SI 2012/2591 Sch.2 para.3, SI 2012/2598 Sch.2 para.3

Sch.9 Part 6 para.102, varied: SI 2012/1762 Sch.2 para.3, SI 2012/2591 Sch.2 para.3, SI 2012/2598 Sch.2 para.3

Sch.9 Part 6 para.103, varied: SI 2012/1762 Sch.2 para.3, SI 2012/2591 Sch.2 para.3, SI 2012/2598 Sch.2 para.3

Sch.9 Part 7, referred to: SI 2012/1762 Art.4, SI 2012/2591 Art.4, SI 2012/2598 Art.4

Sch.9 Part 7 para.107, varied: SI 2012/2591 Sch.3 para.1

Sch.9 Part 7 para.109, varied: SI 2012/1762 Sch.3 para.1, SI 2012/2591 Sch.3 para.2, SI 2012/2598 Sch.3 para.1

Sch.9 Part 7 para.110, varied: SI 2012/1762 Sch.3 para.2, SI 2012/2591 Sch.3 para.3, SI 2012/2598 Sch.3 para.2

Sch.9 Part 7 para.112, varied: SI 2012/1762 Sch.3 para.3, SI 2012/2591 Sch.3 para.4, SI 2012/2598 Sch.3 para.3

Sch.9 Part 7 para.113, varied: SI 2012/1762 Sch.3 para.4, SI 2012/2591 Sch.3 para.5, SI 2012/2598 Sch.3 para.4

Sch.9 Part 7 para.114, varied: SI 2012/1762 Sch.3 para.4, SI 2012/2591 Sch.3 para.5, SI 2012/2598 Sch.3 para.4

Sch.9 Part 7 para.117, varied: SI 2012/1762 Sch.3 para.5

Sch.9 Part 7 para.119, varied: SI 2012/1762 Sch.3 para.6, SI 2012/2591 Sch.3 para.6, SI 2012/2598 Sch.3 para.5

Sch.9 Part 7 para.120, varied: SI 2012/1762 Sch.3 para.6, SI 2012/2591 Sch.3 para.6, SI 2012/2598 Sch.3 para.5

Sch.9 Part 7 para.121, varied: SI 2012/1762 Sch.3 para.6, SI 2012/2591 Sch.3 para.6, SI 2012/2598 Sch.3 para.5

2012– cont.

9. Protection of Freedoms Act 2012–*cont.*

Sch.9 Part 7 para.122, varied: SI 2012/1762 Sch.3 para.6, SI 2012/2591 Sch.3 para.6, SI 2012/2598 Sch.3 para.5

Sch.9 Part 7 para.123, varied: SI 2012/1762 Sch.3 para.6, SI 2012/2591 Sch.3 para.6, SI 2012/2598 Sch.3 para.5

Sch.9 Part 7 para.124, varied: SI 2012/1762 Sch.3 para.6, SI 2012/2591 Sch.3 para.6, SI 2012/2598 Sch.3 para.5

Sch.9 Part 7 para.125, varied: SI 2012/1762 Sch.3 para.6, SI 2012/2591 Sch.3 para.6, SI 2012/2598 Sch.3 para.5

Sch.9 Part 7 para.126, varied: SI 2012/1762 Sch.3 para.6, SI 2012/2591 Sch.3 para.6, SI 2012/2598 Sch.3 para.5

Sch.9 Part 7 para.127, varied: SI 2012/1762 Sch.3 para.6, SI 2012/2591 Sch.3 para.6, SI 2012/2598 Sch.3 para.5

Sch.9 Part 7 para.128, varied: SI 2012/1762 Sch.3 para.6, SI 2012/2591 Sch.3 para.6, SI 2012/2598 Sch.3 para.5

Sch.9 Part 7 para.129, varied: SI 2012/1762 Sch.3 para.6, SI 2012/2591 Sch.3 para.6, SI 2012/2598 Sch.3 para.5

Sch.10 Part 5, referred to: SI 2012/1762 Art.4, SI 2012/2591 Art.4, SI 2012/2598 Art.4

Sch.10 Part 5, varied: SI 2012/1762 Sch.4, SI 2012/2591 Sch.4, SI 2012/2598 Sch.4

Sch.10 Part 6, referred to: SI 2012/1762 Art.4, SI 2012/2591 Art.4, SI 2012/2598 Art.4

Sch.10 Part 6, varied: SI 2012/1762 Sch.5, SI 2012/2591 Sch.5, SI 2012/2598 Sch.5

10. Legal Aid, Sentencing and Punishment of Offenders Act 2012

Commencement Orders: SI 2012/1956 Art.2; SI 2012/2412 Art.2; SI 2012/2770 Art.2; SI 2012/2906 Art.2, Art.3, Art.4, Art.5, Art.6, Art.7

Royal Assent, May 01, 2012

applied: SI 2012/3144 Reg.8, SI 2012/3145 Sch.1

Part 1, applied: SI 2012/3098 Reg.13

Part 3 c.3, referred to: SI 2012/2906 Art.7

s.2, applied: SI 2012/3098 Reg.17, Reg.22, Reg.23, Reg.24, Reg.31, Reg.41, Reg.58, Reg.62, Reg.67

s.5, enabling: SI 2012/3098

s.9, applied: SI 2012/3098 Reg.16, Reg.21, Reg.29, Reg.39, Reg.50, Reg.60

s.10, applied: SI 2012/3098 Reg.47, Reg.66, Reg.67, Reg.68, Reg.69

s.11, applied: SI 2012/3098 Reg.26, Reg.32, Reg.42, Reg.54, Reg.58

s.12, enabling: SI 2012/3098

s.21, applied: SI 2012/3098 Reg.26, Reg.42, Reg.45, Reg.52, Reg.58, Reg.64

s.23, applied: SI 2012/3098 Reg.36

s.28, enabling: SI 2012/3098

s.32, referred to: SI 2012/3098 Reg.31

s.41, enabling: SI 2012/2683, SI 2012/3098

s.57, amended: 2012 c.21 Sch.18 para.138

s.58, amended: 2012 c.21 Sch.18 para.138

s.59, amended: 2012 c.21 Sch.18 para.138

s.65, referred to: SI 2012/2906 Art.3

s.66, referred to: SI 2012/2906 Art.5

s.67, referred to: SI 2012/2906 Art.4

s.69, referred to: SI 2012/2906 Art.4

s.71, referred to: SI 2012/2906 Art.3

s.72, referred to: SI 2012/2906 Art.3

s.81, referred to: SI 2012/2906 Art.3

s.83, referred to: SI 2012/2906 Art.5

2012– cont.

10. Legal Aid, Sentencing and Punishment of Offenders Act 2012–*cont.*

s.84, referred to: SI 2012/2906 Art.4

s.91, applied: SI 2012/2813 Reg.5, SI 2012/2822 Reg.2

s.102, applied: SI 2012/1726 r.18.4, SI 2012/2822 Reg.2

s.102, referred to: SI 2012/1726 r.18.4

s.103, enabling: SI 2012/2822

s.104, enabling: SI 2012/2813

s.105, disapplied: SI 2012/2906 Art.7

s.106, enabling: SI 2012/2813

s.123, referred to: SI 2012/2906 Art.6

s.141, applied: SI 2012/2412 Art.3

s.141, enabling: SI 2012/2412

s.149, enabling: SI 2012/2824

s.151, enabling: SI 2012/1956, SI 2012/2412, SI 2012/2770, SI 2012/2906

Sch.1 Part 1, applied: SI 2012/3098 Reg.43, Reg.44, Reg.58

Sch.1 Part 1, referred to: SI 2012/3098 Reg.25, Reg.45

Sch.1 Part 1 para.12, applied: SI 2012/2684 Reg.2, SI 2012/3098 Reg.23, Reg.33, Reg.42

Sch.1 Part 1 para.12, enabling: SI 2012/2684

Sch.1 Part 1 para.13, applied: SI 2012/3098 Reg.23, Reg.34, Reg.42

Sch.1 Part 1 para.14, applied: SI 2012/2684 Reg.2

Sch.1 Part 1 para.14, enabling: SI 2012/2684

Sch.1 Part 1 para.30, referred to: SI 2012/2683 Reg.3, Reg.4

Sch.1 Part 1 para.30, enabling: SI 2012/2683

Sch.1 Part 1 para.32, applied: SI 2012/3098 Reg.31

Sch.1 Part 1 para.32, referred to: SI 2012/3098 Reg.31

Sch.1 Part 1 para.42, applied: SI 2012/2687 Reg.2

Sch.1 Part 1 para.42, enabling: SI 2012/2687

Sch.3 para.3, applied: SI 2012/3098 Reg.15

Sch.3 para.3, enabling: SI 2012/3098

Sch.12 para.6, referred to: SI 2012/2906 Art.7

Sch.12 para.7, referred to: SI 2012/2906 Art.7

Sch.12 para.8, referred to: SI 2012/2906 Art.7

Sch.12 para.10, referred to: SI 2012/2906 Art.7

Sch.12 para.11, referred to: SI 2012/2906 Art.7

Sch.12 para.12, referred to: SI 2012/2906 Art.7

Sch.12 para.17, referred to: SI 2012/2906 Art.7

Sch.12 para.20, referred to: SI 2012/2906 Art.7

Sch.12 para.21, referred to: SI 2012/2906 Art.7

Sch.12 para.23, referred to: SI 2012/2906 Art.7

Sch.12 para.24, referred to: SI 2012/2906 Art.7

Sch.12 para.25, referred to: SI 2012/2906 Art.7

Sch.12 para.28, referred to: SI 2012/2906 Art.7

Sch.12 para.29, referred to: SI 2012/2906 Art.7

Sch.12 para.31, referred to: SI 2012/2906 Art.7

Sch.12 para.33, referred to: SI 2012/2906 Art.7

Sch.12 para.34, referred to: SI 2012/2906 Art.7

Sch.12 para.35, referred to: SI 2012/2906 Art.7

Sch.12 para.36, referred to: SI 2012/2906 Art.7

Sch.12 para.37, referred to: SI 2012/2906 Art.7

Sch.12 para.38, referred to: SI 2012/2906 Art.7

Sch.12 para.39, referred to: SI 2012/2906 Art.7

Sch.12 para.40, referred to: SI 2012/2906 Art.7

Sch.12 para.41, referred to: SI 2012/2906 Art.7

Sch.12 para.42, referred to: SI 2012/2906 Art.7

Sch.12 para.43, referred to: SI 2012/2906 Art.7

Sch.12 para.44, referred to: SI 2012/2906 Art.7

Sch.12 para.45, referred to: SI 2012/2906 Art.7

Sch.12 para.46, referred to: SI 2012/2906 Art.7

2012– cont.

23. Small Charitable Donations Act 2012–*cont.*
Sch.12 para.47, referred to: SI 2012/ 2906 Art.7
Sch.12 para.48, referred to: SI 2012/ 2906 Art.7
Sch.12 para.49, referred to: SI 2012/ 2906 Art.7
Sch.12 para.50, referred to: SI 2012/ 2906 Art.7
Sch.12 para.51, referred to: SI 2012/ 2906 Art.7
Sch.12 para.52, referred to: SI 2012/ 2906 Art.7
Sch.12 para.53, referred to: SI 2012/ 2906 Art.7
Sch.12 para.54, referred to: SI 2012/ 2906 Art.7
Sch.12 para.55, referred to: SI 2012/ 2906 Art.7
Sch.12 para.56, referred to: SI 2012/ 2906 Art.7
Sch.12 para.57, referred to: SI 2012/ 2906 Art.7
Sch.12 para.58, referred to: SI 2012/ 2906 Art.7
Sch.22 Part 1 para.3, referred to: SI 2012/ 2906 Art.6
Sch.22 Part 1 para.4, referred to: SI 2012/ 2906 Art.6
Sch.22 Part 1 para.6, referred to: SI 2012/ 2906 Art.6
Sch.22 Part 1 para.7, referred to: SI 2012/ 2906 Art.6
Sch.22 Part 1 para.8, referred to: SI 2012/ 2906 Art.6
Sch.22 Part 1 para.10, referred to: SI 2012/ 2906 Art.6

11. Scotland Act 2012
Commencement Orders: SI 2012/ 1710 Art.2, Art.3; SI 2012/ 2516 Art.2, Art.3
Royal Assent, May 01, 2012
s.44, enabling: SI 2012/ 1710, SI 2012/ 2516

12. Sunday Trading (London Olympic Games and Paralympic Games) Act 2012
Royal Assent, May 01, 2012

13. Supply and Appropriation (Main Estimates) Act 2012
Royal Assent, July 17, 2012

14. Finance Act 2012
Royal Assent, July 17, 2012
Part 2, referred to: SI 2012/ 3009 Reg.4
s.57, varied: SI 2012/ 3008 Reg.5
s.57A, varied: SI 2012/ 3008 Reg.6
s.63, varied: SI 2012/ 3008 Reg.7
s.66, varied: SI 2012/ 3008 Reg.8
s.67, applied: SI 2012/ 3009 Reg.2, Reg.15
s.67, varied: SI 2012/ 3008 Reg.9
s.97, varied: SI 2012/ 3008 Reg.10
s.98, varied: SI 2012/ 3008 Reg.11
s.114, varied: SI 2012/ 3008 Reg.12
s.115, varied: SI 2012/ 3008 Reg.13
s.151, enabling: SI 2012/ 3008
s.158, applied: SI 2012/ 3008 Reg.2
s.158, enabling: SI 2012/ 3008
s.166, applied: SI 2012/ 3008 Reg.2
s.166, enabling: SI 2012/ 3008
s.167, applied: SI 2012/ 3008 Reg.2
s.167, enabling: SI 2012/ 3008
s.172, varied: SI 2012/ 3008 Reg.14

2012– cont.

14. Finance Act 2012–*cont.*
s.174, varied: SI 2012/ 3008 Reg.15
Sch.7 Part 1 para.23, enabling: SI 2012/ 1896
Sch.7 Part 2 para.33, enabling: SI 2012/ 1896
Sch.8 para.20, enabling: SI 2012/ 1901
Sch.17, referred to: SI 2012/ 3009 Reg.15
Sch.17 Part 1 para.3, applied: SI 2012/ 3009 Reg.10
Sch.17 Part 1 para.4, applied: SI 2012/ 3009 Reg.10
Sch.17 Part 1 para.6, enabling: SI 2012/ 3009
Sch.17 Part 1 para.7, applied: SI 2012/ 3009 Reg.7
Sch.17 Part 1 para.7, enabling: SI 2012/ 3009
Sch.17 Part 1 para.8, referred to: SI 2012/ 3009 Reg.9, Reg.12, Reg.13, Reg.14
Sch.17 Part 1 para.8, enabling: SI 2012/ 3009
Sch.17 Part 1 para.9, referred to: SI 2012/ 3009 Reg.15
Sch.17 Part 1 para.10, applied: SI 2012/ 3009 Reg.15
Sch.17 Part 1 para.14, applied: SI 2012/ 3009 Reg.15
Sch.17 Part 1 para.16, applied: SI 2012/ 3009 Reg.12
Sch.17 Part 1 para.20, amended: SI 2012/ 3009 Reg.16
Sch.17 Part 3 para.37, enabling: SI 2012/ 3009
Sch.24 Part 1 para.7, applied: SI 2012/ 2898 Art.6
Sch.24 Part 1 para.8, enabling: SI 2012/ 2898
Sch.24 Part 1 para.10, applied: SI 2012/ 2500 Sch.2
Sch.24 Part 1 para.18, applied: SI 2012/ 2500 Reg.12
Sch.24 Part 1 para.18, enabling: SI 2012/ 2500
Sch.24 Part 1 para.19, enabling: SI 2012/ 2500
Sch.24 Part 1 para.22, applied: SI 2012/ 2500 Sch.1
Sch.24 Part 1 para.23, applied: SI 2012/ 2500 Reg.10
Sch.24 Part 1 para.24, enabling: SI 2012/ 2500
Sch.24 Part 1 para.39, enabling: SI 2012/ 2500, SI 2012/ 2898
Sch.24 Part 1 para.40, applied: SI 2012/ 2500 Reg.7
Sch.27 Part 3 para.10, enabling: SI 2012/ 1899

15. European Union (Approval of Treaty Amendment Decision) Act 2012
Royal Assent, October 31, 2012

16. Infrastructure (Financial Assistance) Act 2012
Royal Assent, October 31, 2012

17. Local Government Finance Act 2012
Royal Assent, October 31, 2012

18. Mental Health (Approval Functions) Act 2012
Royal Assent, October 31, 2012

19. Civil Aviation Act 2012
Royal Assent, December 19, 2012

20. Prisons (Interference with Wireless Telegraphy) Act 2012
Royal Assent, December 19, 2012

21. Financial Services Act 2012
Royal Assent, December 19, 2012

22. Police (Complaints and Conduct) Act 2012
Royal Assent, December 19, 2012

23. Small Charitable Donations Act 2012
Royal Assent, December 19, 2012

STATUTORY INSTRUMENT
CITATOR 2012

The Statutory Instrument Citator covers the period 2012 and is up to date to **February 1, 2013**. It comprises in a single table:

  (i) Statutory Instruments amended, repealed, modified, etc. by Statute passed or Statutory Instrument issued during this period;
 (ii) Statutory Instruments judicially considered during this period;
(iii) Statutory Intruments consolidated during this period; and
 (iv) Statutory Instruments made under the powers of any Statutory Instrument issued during this period.

The material is arranged in numerical order under the relevant year.

Definitions of legislative effects:

"added"	: new provisions are inserted by subsequent legislation
"amended"	: text of legislation is modified by subsequent legislation
"applied"	: brought to bear, or exercised by subsequent legislation
"consolidated"	: used where previous legislation in the same subject area is brought together in subsequent legislation, with or without amendments
"disapplied"	: an exception made to the application of an earlier enactment
"enabling"	: giving power for the relevant SI to be made
"referred to"	: direction from other legislation without specific effect or application
"repealed"	: rescinded by subsequent legislation
"restored"	: reinstated by subsequent legislation (where previously repealed/revoked)
"substituted"	: text of provision is completely replaced by subsequent legislation
"varied"	: provisions modified in relation to their application to specified areas or circumstances, however the text itself remains unchanged

STATUTORY INSTRUMENTS ISSUED BY THE SCOTTISH PARLIAMENT

1999

40. Fraserburgh Harbour Revision Order 1999
referred to: SSI 2012/262 Art.1

127. West of Scotland Water Authority (Lochran-za-Allt Easan Biorach) Water Order 1999
Art.2, varied: 2012 c.11 s.12

128. West of Scotland Water Authority (Kilberry, Allt Dail A'Chairn) Water Order 1999
Art.2, varied: 2012 c.11 s.12

187. Hill Livestock (Compensatory Allowances) (Scotland) Regulations 1999
Reg.2, varied: 2012 c.11 s.12

194. Shetland Islands Regulated Fishery (Scotland) Order 1999
Art.2, varied: 2012 c.11 s.12

199. National Trust for Scotland (Canna) Harbour Revision Order 1999
Art.2, varied: 2012 c.11 s.12

201. Highland Council (Eigg) Harbour Empowerment Order 1999
Art.2, varied: 2012 c.11 s.12

1999– cont.

201. Highland Council (Eigg) Harbour Empowerment Order 1999– cont.
Art.3, varied: 2012 c.11 s.12
Art.25, varied: 2012 c.11 s.12

202. Scottish Natural Heritage (Rum) Harbour Empowerment Order 1999
Art.2, varied: 2012 c.11 s.12

203. Highland Council (Muck) Harbour Empowerment Order 1999
Art.2, varied: 2012 c.11 s.12
Art.3, varied: 2012 c.11 s.12
Art.26, varied: 2012 c.11 s.12

2000

32. Scrabster (Inner Harbour Development) Harbour Revision Order 2000
Art.2, varied: 2012 c.11 s.12

2000–cont.

62. Food Standards Act 1999 (Transitional and Consequential Provisions and Savings) (Scotland) Regulations 2000
Reg.10, revoked (in part): SSI 2012/321 Sch.5 Part 2
Sch.8 Part III para.1, revoked: SSI 2012/321 Sch.5 Part 2
Sch.8 Part III para.2, revoked: SSI 2012/321 Sch.5 Part 2
Sch.8 Part III para.3, revoked: SSI 2012/321 Sch.5 Part 2
Sch.8 Part III para.4, revoked: SSI 2012/321 Sch.5 Part 2

96. Designation of Nitrate Vulnerable Zones (Scotland) Regulations 2000
Reg.2, varied: 2012 c.11 s.12

110. Repayment of Student Loans (Scotland) Regulations 2000
Reg.2, amended: SSI 2012/22 Reg.3
Reg.9, amended: SSI 2012/22 Reg.4
Reg.13A, amended: SSI 2012/22 Reg.5
Reg.13B, amended: SSI 2012/22 Reg.6

173. Loch Moidart, North Channel, Scallop Several Fishery (Scotland) Order 2000
Art.2, varied: 2012 c.11 s.12

174. A737 Trunk Road (Kilwinning) (Restricted Roads) Order 2000
revoked: SSI 2012/268 Art.5

178. Contaminated Land (Scotland) Regulations 2000
Reg.2, amended: SSI 2012/360 Sch.11 para.10

236. West of Scotland Water Authority (Dalmally, River Strae) Water Order 2000
Art.2, varied: 2012 c.11 s.12

237. West of Scotland Water Authority (Eredine, Allt Garbh) Water Order 2000
Art.2, varied: 2012 c.11 s.12

289. Associated British Ports (Troon) Harbour Revision Order 2000
Art.2, varied: 2012 c.11 s.12

294. West of Scotland Water Authority (Craighouse, Abhainn a Mhinisteir) Water Order 2000
Art.2, varied: 2012 c.11 s.12

307. Budget (Scotland) Act 2000 (Amendment) Order 2000
Art.2, varied: 2012 c.11 s.12

310. West of Scotland Water Authority (Lochnaw) Ordinary Drought Order 2000
Art.2, varied: 2012 c.11 s.12

315. Act of Adjournal (Criminal Procedure Rules Amendment No 2) (Human Rights Act 1998) 2000
r.2, varied: 2012 c.11 s.12

316. Act of Sederunt (Rules of the Court of Session Amendment No 6) (Human Rights Act 1998) 2000
r.2, varied: 2012 c.11 s.12

323. Pollution Prevention and Control (Scotland) Regulations 2000
applied: SI 2012/1715 Reg.6, SSI 2012/360 Sch.10 para.3, Sch.10 para.14
referred to: SSI 2012/360 Sch.10 para.14
revoked: SSI 2012/360 Sch.12
Reg.2, amended: SSI 2012/148 Reg.3
Reg.7, amended: SSI 2012/148 Reg.3
Reg.9, applied: SSI 2012/360 Sch.10 para.6
Reg.9A, added: SSI 2012/148 Reg.3
Reg.9B, added: SSI 2012/148 Reg.3
Reg.9F, revoked (in part): SSI 2012/148 Reg.3

2000–cont.

323. Pollution Prevention and Control (Scotland) Regulations 2000–cont.
Reg.10, amended: SSI 2012/148 Reg.3
Reg.10A, amended: SSI 2012/148 Reg.3
Reg.13, amended: SSI 2012/148 Reg.3
Reg.22, amended: SSI 2012/148 Reg.3
Reg.23, applied: SSI 2012/360 Sch.10 para.6
Sch.1 Part I, applied: SSI 2012/360 Sch.10 para.2
Sch.3 Part 5 para.25, amended: SSI 2012/148 Reg.3
Sch.4 Part 1 para.1B, amended: SSI 2012/148 Reg.3
Sch.4 Part 1 para.8, amended: SSI 2012/148 Reg.3

400. Mink Keeping (Scotland) Order 2000
revoked: SSI 2012/174 Sch.2

407. Education (School and Placing Information) (Scotland) Amendment Regulations 2000
revoked: SSI 2012/130 Sch.3

448. Agricultural Business Development Scheme (Scotland) Regulations 2000
Reg.2, varied: 2012 c.11 s.12

2001

7. Budget (Scotland) Act 2000 (Amendment) Order 2001
Art.2, varied: 2012 c.11 s.12
Sch.1 para.2, varied: 2012 c.11 s.12

68. Budget (Scotland) Act 2000 (Amendment) (No.2) Order 2001
Sch.1 para.2, varied: 2012 c.11 s.12

137. NHS 24 (Scotland) Order 2001
Sch.Part III, amended: SI 2012/1479 Sch.1 para.22

219. Public Service Vehicles (Registration of Local Services) (Scotland) Regulations 2001
Reg.2, amended: SSI 2012/32 Reg.2
Reg.5, substituted: SSI 2012/32 Reg.2
Reg.7, amended: SSI 2012/32 Reg.2
Reg.7, referred to: SSI 2012/32 Reg.3
Reg.8, amended: SSI 2012/32 Reg.2
Reg.8, referred to: SSI 2012/32 Reg.3
Reg.13, amended: SSI 2012/32 Reg.2
Reg.14, substituted: SSI 2012/32 Reg.2
Sch.1 para.1, substituted: SSI 2012/32 Sch.1
Sch.1 Part 1 para.1, substituted: SSI 2012/32 Sch.1
Sch.1 Part 1 para.2, substituted: SSI 2012/32 Sch.1
Sch.1 Part 1 para.3, substituted: SSI 2012/32 Sch.1
Sch.1 Part 1 para.4, substituted: SSI 2012/32 Sch.1
Sch.1 Part 1 para.5, substituted: SSI 2012/32 Sch.1
Sch.1 para.2, substituted: SSI 2012/32 Sch.1
Sch.1 Part 2 para.1, substituted: SSI 2012/32 Sch.1
Sch.1 Part 2 para.2, substituted: SSI 2012/32 Sch.1
Sch.1 Part 2 para.3, substituted: SSI 2012/32 Sch.1
Sch.1 Part 2 para.4, substituted: SSI 2012/32 Sch.1
Sch.1 Part 2 para.5, substituted: SSI 2012/32 Sch.1
Sch.1 Part 2 para.6, substituted: SSI 2012/32 Sch.1
Sch.1 para.3, substituted: SSI 2012/32 Sch.1
Sch.1 Part 3 para.1, substituted: SSI 2012/32 Sch.1
Sch.1 Part 3 para.2, substituted: SSI 2012/32 Sch.1
Sch.1 Part 3 para.3, substituted: SSI 2012/32 Sch.1
Sch.1 Part 3 para.4, substituted: SSI 2012/32 Sch.1
Sch.1 Part 3 para.5, substituted: SSI 2012/32 Sch.1
Sch.1 Part 3 para.6, substituted: SSI 2012/32 Sch.1
Sch.1 para.4, substituted: SSI 2012/32 Sch.1
Sch.1 para.5, substituted: SSI 2012/32 Sch.1
Sch.1 para.6, substituted: SSI 2012/32 Sch.1
Sch.1 para.7, substituted: SSI 2012/32 Sch.1
Sch.1 para.8, substituted: SSI 2012/32 Sch.1
Sch.1 para.9, substituted: SSI 2012/32 Sch.1
Sch.1 para.10, substituted: SSI 2012/32 Sch.1

2001– cont.

219. **Public Service Vehicles (Registration of Local Services) (Scotland) Regulations 2001**– *cont.*
Sch.1 para.11, substituted: SSI 2012/ 32 Sch.1
Sch.1 para.12, substituted: SSI 2012/ 32 Sch.1

232. **Lerwick Harbour Revision Order 2001**
Art.2, varied: 2012 c.11 s.12

257. **Products of Animal Origin (Import and Export) Amendment (Scotland) Regulations 2001**
revoked: SSI 2012/ 177 Reg.38

262. **Comhairle nan Eilean Siar (Aird Mhor, Barra) Harbour Empowerment Order 2001**
Art.2, varied: 2012 c.11 s.12

265. **Consumer Protection Act 1987 (Product Liability) (Modification) (Scotland) Order 2001**
varied: 2012 c.11 s.12

303. **Scottish Social Services Council (Appointments, Procedure and Access to the Register) Regulations 2001**
Reg.4, amended: SI 2012/ 1479 Sch.1 para.23

313. **Food Protection (Emergency Prohibitions) (Radioactivity in Sheep) Partial Revocation (Scotland) Order 2001**
revoked: SSI 2012/ 263 Sch.1

315. **Parole Board (Scotland) Rules 2001**
Part I r.2, amended: SSI 2012/ 167 r.3, SSI 2012/ 197 r.2
Part II r.5, amended: SSI 2012/ 167 r.4
Part II r.11, amended: SSI 2012/ 167 r.5
Part II r.12A, amended: SSI 2012/ 167 r.6
Part III r.14, amended: SSI 2012/ 167 r.7
Part III r.14, substituted: SSI 2012/ 197 r.2
Part III r.15, revoked (in part): SSI 2012/ 167 r.8
Part III r.15A, amended: SSI 2012/ 167 r.9
Part III r.15B, amended: SSI 2012/ 167 r.10
Part III r.15E, amended: SSI 2012/ 167 r.11
Part III r.15H, amended: SSI 2012/ 167 r.12, SSI 2012/ 197 r.2
Part III r.16, substituted: SSI 2012/ 167 r.13, SSI 2012/ 197 r.2
Part IV r.18, amended: SSI 2012/ 167 r.14
Part IV r.19, amended: SSI 2012/ 167 r.15
Part IV r.21, amended: SSI 2012/ 167 r.16
Part IV r.28, amended: SSI 2012/ 167 r.17
Sch.1 para.5, substituted: SSI 2012/ 167 r.18

332. **Fishing Vessels (Decommissioning) (Scotland) Scheme 2001**
Art.2, amended: SI 2012/ 1809 Sch.1 Part 3
Art.5, amended: SI 2012/ 1809 Sch.1 Part 3
Art.6, amended: SI 2012/ 1809 Sch.1 Part 3

369. **North of Scotland Water Authority (River Lochy Abstraction Scheme) Water Order 2001**
Art.2, varied: 2012 c.11 s.12

424. **Scottish Social Services Council (Consultation on Codes of Practice) Order 2001**
Art.2, amended: SI 2012/ 1479 Sch.1 para.24

457. **Fraserburgh Harbour Revision (Constitution) Order 2001**
applied: SSI 2012/ 262 Art.3, Art.6
referred to: SSI 2012/ 262 Art.1
Art.3, revoked: SSI 2012/ 262 Sch.1
Art.4, revoked: SSI 2012/ 262 Sch.1
Art.5, revoked: SSI 2012/ 262 Sch.1
Art.6, revoked: SSI 2012/ 262 Sch.1
Art.7, revoked: SSI 2012/ 262 Sch.1
Art.8, revoked: SSI 2012/ 262 Sch.1
Art.12, amended: SSI 2012/ 262 Art.8
Art.16, revoked (in part): SSI 2012/ 262 Sch.1

2001– cont.

457. **Fraserburgh Harbour Revision (Constitution) Order 2001**– *cont.*
Sch.2 para.10, amended: SSI 2012/ 262 Art.7
Sch.2 para.10, applied: SSI 2012/ 262 Art.3

476. **Panels of Persons to Safeguard the Interests of Children (Scotland) Regulations 2001**
applied: SSI 2012/ 54 Reg.4

480. **Budget (Scotland) Act 2001 (Amendment) Order 2001**
Art.2, varied: 2012 c.11 s.12
Sch.2, varied: 2012 c.11 s.12

2002

103. **NHS Education for Scotland Order 2002**
Sch.1 Part III, amended: SI 2012/ 1479 Sch.1 para.25

121. **Clydeport (Closure of Yorkhill Basin) Harbour Revision Order 2002**
Art.2, varied: 2012 c.11 s.12

132. **Act of Sederunt (Summary Cause Rules) 2002**
Sch.1 Appendix, amended: SSI 2012/ 144 r.2, Sch.1, SSI 2012/ 188 Sch.3
Sch.1 Appendix, substituted: SSI 2012/ 188 r.11
Sch.1 Part 14 para.14.1, amended: SSI 2012/ 144 r.2
Sch.1 Part 20 para.20.1, amended: SSI 2012/ 271 r.7
Sch.1 Part 34 para.34.1, substituted: SSI 2012/ 144 r.2
Sch.1 Part 34 para.34.2, substituted: SSI 2012/ 144 r.2
Sch.1 Part 34 para.34.3, substituted: SSI 2012/ 144 r.2
Sch.1 Part 34 para.34.4, substituted: SSI 2012/ 144 r.2
Sch.1 Part 34 para.34.5, substituted: SSI 2012/ 144 r.2
Sch.1 Part 34 para.34.6, substituted: SSI 2012/ 144 r.2
Sch.1 Part 34 para.34.7, substituted: SSI 2012/ 144 r.2
Sch.1 Part 34 para.34.8, substituted: SSI 2012/ 144 r.2
Sch.1 Part 34 para.34.9, substituted: SSI 2012/ 144 r.2
Sch.1 Part 34 para.34.10, substituted: SSI 2012/ 144 r.2
Sch.1 Part 34 para.34.11, substituted: SSI 2012/ 144 r.2
Sch.1 Part 34 para.34.12, substituted: SSI 2012/ 144 r.2
Sch.1 Part 34 para.34.13, substituted: SSI 2012/ 144 r.2
Sch.1 Part 34 para.34.14, referred to: SSI 2012/ 144 r.3
Sch.1 Part 34 para.34.14, substituted: SSI 2012/ 144 r.2

133. **Act of Sederunt (Small Claim Rules) 2002**
Sch.1 Part 18 para.18.1, amended: SSI 2012/ 271 r.8

134. **Budget (Scotland) Act 2001 (Amendment) Order 2002**
Art.2, varied: 2012 c.11 s.12
Sch.2 para.2, varied: 2012 c.11 s.12
Sch.3, varied: 2012 c.11 s.12

190. **Adults with Incapacity (Ethics Committee) (Scotland) Regulations 2002**
Reg.3, amended: SI 2012/ 1479 Sch.1 para.26

2002–cont.

201. Loch Lomond and The Trossachs National Park Designation, Transitional and Consequential Provisions (Scotland) Order 2002
Art.7, amended: SSI 2012/ 117 Art.2
Art.7, revoked (in part): SSI 2012/ 117 Art.2

276. Designation of Nitrate Vulnerable Zones (Scotland) Regulations 2002
Reg.4, varied: 2012 c.11 s.12
Reg.6, varied: 2012 c.11 s.12

289. Bus Service Operators Grant (Scotland) Regulations 2002
Reg.2, amended: SSI 2012/ 33 Reg.2
Reg.3, amended: SSI 2012/ 33 Reg.2

303. Community Care (Personal Care and Nursing Care) (Scotland) Regulations 2002
Reg.2, amended: SSI 2012/ 109 Reg.2

305. National Waiting Times Centre Board (Scotland) Order 2002
Sch.1 Part III, amended: SI 2012/ 1479 Sch.1 para.27

312. Scottish Secure Tenants (Compensation for Improvements) Regulations 2002
Reg.4, amended: SSI 2012/ 38 Sch.1 para.5

320. Scottish Secure Tenancies (Proceedings for Possession) Regulations 2002
revoked: SSI 2012/92 Reg.1

410. Comhairle nan Eilean Siar (Various Harbours) Harbour Revision Order 2002
Art.2, varied: 2012 c.11 s.12
Art.52, varied: 2012 c.11 s.12

493. Large Combustion Plants (Scotland) Regulations 2002
revoked: SSI 2012/ 360 Sch.12

494. Civil Legal Aid (Scotland) Regulations 2002
Reg.40, amended: SSI 2012/ 64 Reg.2
Reg.46, amended: SSI 2012/ 301 Sch.1 para.4

523. Kava-kava in Food (Scotland) Regulations 2002
Reg.2, amended: SI 2012/ 1809 Sch.1 Part 3

533. Community Care (Joint Working etc.) (Scotland) Regulations 2002
Reg.1, amended: SSI 2012/ 65 Reg.2
Reg.2, revoked (in part): SSI 2012/ 65 Reg.2
Reg.3, revoked (in part): SSI 2012/ 65 Reg.2
Reg.4, amended: SSI 2012/ 65 Reg.2
Reg.5, amended: SSI 2012/ 65 Reg.2
Reg.9A, added: SSI 2012/ 65 Reg.2
Reg.10, amended: SSI 2012/ 65 Reg.2
Reg.10, revoked (in part): SSI 2012/ 65 Reg.2
Reg.11, amended: SSI 2012/ 65 Reg.2
Sch.2 para.1, amended: SSI 2012/ 65 Reg.2
Sch.2 para.2, amended: SSI 2012/ 65 Reg.2
Sch.3, amended: SSI 2012/65 Reg.2
Sch.5 para.1, added: SSI 2012/ 65 Sch.1
Sch.5 para.2, added: SSI 2012/ 65 Sch.1
Sch.5 para.3, added: SSI 2012/ 65 Sch.1
Sch.6 para.1, added: SSI 2012/ 65 Sch.1
Sch.6 para.2, added: SSI 2012/ 65 Sch.1
Sch.6 para.3, added: SSI 2012/ 65 Sch.1

546. Designation of Nitrate Vulnerable Zones (Scotland) (No.2) Regulations 2002
Reg.4, varied: 2012 c.11 s.12

557. Inverness Harbour Revision (Constitution) Order 2002
Art.2A, added: SSI 2012/ 302 Art.3
Art.3, amended: SSI 2012/ 302 Art.4
Art.4, revoked: SSI 2012/ 302 Art.4
Art.11, amended: SSI 2012/ 302 Art.4
Sch.2 para.9, amended: SSI 2012/ 302 Art.4

2002–cont.

566. Act of Sederunt (Fees of Messengers-at-Arms) (No.2) 2002
Sch.1 para.15, substituted: SSI 2012/ 340 Sch.1

567. Act of Sederunt (Fees of Sheriff Officers) (No.2) 2002
Sch.1 para.17, substituted: SSI 2012/ 341 Sch.1

2003

1. Cairngorms National Park Designation, Transitional and Consequential Provisions (Scotland) Order 2003
Art.7, amended: SSI 2012/ 117 Art.3
Art.7, revoked (in part): SSI 2012/ 117 Art.3

87. Fishing Vessels (Decommissioning) (Scotland) Scheme 2003
Art.2, amended: SI 2012/ 1809 Sch.1 Part 3
Art.5, amended: SI 2012/ 1809 Sch.1 Part 3
Art.6, amended: SI 2012/ 1809 Sch.1 Part 3

146. Pollution Prevention and Control (Scotland) Amendment Regulations 2003
revoked: SSI 2012/ 360 Sch.12

154. Health Education Board for Scotland Amendment Order 2003
Art.5, varied: 2012 c.11 s.12

158. National Health Service (Dental Charges) (Scotland) Regulations 2003
Reg.1, varied: 2012 c.11 s.12

170. Waste Incineration (Scotland) Regulations 2003
revoked: SSI 2012/ 360 Sch.12

179. Advice and Assistance (Assistance by Way of Representation) (Scotland) Regulations 2003
Reg.3, amended: SSI 2012/ 84 Reg.2

209. SFGS Farmland Premium Scheme 2003
Art.2, varied: 2012 c.11 s.12

221. Pollution Prevention and Control (Scotland) Amendment (No.2) Regulations 2003
revoked: SSI 2012/ 360 Sch.12

231. Rehabilitation of Offenders Act 1974 (Exclusions and Exceptions) (Scotland) Order 2003
Sch.3 para.11, amended: SSI 2012/ 88 Sch.7 Part B, SSI 2012/ 89 Sch.5 Part B
Sch.4 Part 1 para.10, amended: SI 2012/ 1479 Sch.1 para.34

235. Landfill (Scotland) Regulations 2003
applied: SSI 2012/ 360 Reg.8, Reg.60, Reg.61, Reg.63, Reg.71, Sch.1 Part 1, Sch.9 para.1
Reg.2, amended: SSI 2012/ 360 Sch.11 para.11
Reg.6, applied: SSI 2012/ 360 Reg.18, Sch.4 para.2
Reg.8, revoked: SSI 2012/ 360 Sch.12
Reg.10, amended: SSI 2012/ 360 Sch.11 para.11
Reg.10, applied: SSI 2012/ 360 Reg.13, Reg.46, Reg.58
Reg.11, amended: SSI 2012/ 148 Reg.4
Reg.13, amended: SSI 2012/ 360 Sch.11 para.11
Reg.17, amended: SSI 2012/ 360 Sch.11 para.11
Reg.17, applied: SSI 2012/ 360 Reg.58, Sch.9 para.1
Reg.18, applied: SSI 2012/ 360 Reg.58, Reg.67, Sch.8 para.2
Reg.19, applied: SSI 2012/ 360 Sch.9 para.1
Sch.5 para.1, applied: SSI 2012/ 360 Reg.58, Sch.9 para.1
Sch.5 para.1, revoked: SSI 2012/ 360 Sch.12
Sch.5 para.2, revoked (in part): SSI 2012/ 360 Sch.12
Sch.5 para.3, revoked (in part): SSI 2012/ 360 Sch.12
Sch.5 para.4, revoked: SSI 2012/ 360 Sch.12
Sch.5 para.5, applied: SSI 2012/ 360 Sch.9 para.1
Sch.6 para.3, revoked: SSI 2012/ 360 Sch.12

2003–cont.

375. **Food Protection (Emergency Prohibitions) (Radioactivity in Sheep) Partial Revocation (Scotland) Order 2003**
revoked: SSI 2012/263 Sch.1

415. **Road Works (Inspection Fees) (Scotland) Regulations 2003**
Reg.3, amended: SSI 2012/250 Reg.2

435. **Stornoway Harbour Revision (Constitution) Order 2003**
Art.17, varied: 2012 c.11 s.12

453. **Title Conditions (Scotland) Act 2003 (Conservation Bodies) Order 2003**
Sch.1 Part II, amended: SSI 2012/30 Art.2

460. **National Health Service (Travelling Expenses and Remission of Charges) (Scotland) (No.2) Regulations 2003**
Reg.3, applied: SI 2012/2886 Sch.1, SSI 2012/303 Sch.4 para.45, Sch.5 para.43
Reg.5, applied: SI 2012/2886 Sch.1, SSI 2012/303 Sch.4 para.45, Sch.5 para.43
Reg.11, applied: SI 2012/2886 Sch.1, SSI 2012/303 Sch.4 para.45, Sch.5 para.43
Sch.1 Part I para.2, amended: SSI 2012/171 Reg.2

528. **Mink Keeping (Scotland) Order 2003**
revoked: SSI 2012/174 Sch.2

560. **Prohibition of Keeping or Release of Live Fish (Specified Species) (Scotland) Order 2003**
revoked: SSI 2012/174 Sch.2

2004

1. **Shetland Islands Regulated Fishery (Scotland) Variation Order 2004**
Art.2, varied: 2012 c.11 s.12

6. **Meat Products (Scotland) Regulations 2004**
Reg.2, amended: SI 2012/1809 Sch.1 Part 3

26. **Solvent Emissions (Scotland) Regulations 2004**
revoked: SSI 2012/360 Sch.12

48. **Food Protection (Emergency Prohibitions) (Radioactivity in Sheep) Partial Revocation (Scotland) Order 2004**
revoked: SSI 2012/263 Sch.1

110. **Pollution Prevention and Control (Scotland) Amendment Regulations 2004**
revoked: SSI 2012/360 Sch.12

111. **Potatoes Originating in Egypt (Scotland) Regulations 2004**
Reg.2, amended: SSI 2012/37 Reg.2
Reg.3, substituted: SSI 2012/37 Reg.2
Reg.4, amended: SSI 2012/37 Reg.2
Reg.5, amended: SSI 2012/37 Reg.2
Reg.6, amended: SSI 2012/37 Reg.2
Reg.7, substituted: SSI 2012/37 Reg.2
Reg.7A, added: SSI 2012/37 Reg.2

112. **Special Waste Amendment (Scotland) Regulations 2004**
Reg.3, revoked: SSI 2012/360 Sch.12

115. **National Health Service (General Medical Services Contracts) (Scotland) Regulations 2004**
Reg.2, amended: SI 2012/1479 Sch.1 para.40, SI 2012/1916 Sch.34 para.83
Sch.5 Part 3 para.41, amended: SI 2012/1916 Sch.34 para.83
Sch.5 Part 3 para.45, referred to: SI 2012/1916 Reg.253
Sch.5 Part 4 para.61, varied: 2012 c.11 s.12
Sch.5 Part 5 para.72, amended: SI 2012/1479 Sch.1 para.40

2004–cont.

115. **National Health Service (General Medical Services Contracts) (Scotland) Regulations 2004**–cont.
Sch.5 Part 6 para.82, substituted: SSI 2012/36 Sch.1 para.1
Sch.5 Part 6 para.83, revoked: SSI 2012/36 Sch.1 para.1
Sch.5 Part 6 para.84, revoked: SSI 2012/36 Sch.1 para.1
Sch.5 Part 6 para.85, revoked: SSI 2012/36 Sch.1 para.1
Sch.5 Part 6 para.86, revoked: SSI 2012/36 Sch.1 para.1
Sch.5 Part 6 para.87, amended: SSI 2012/36 Sch.1 para.1
Sch.5 Part 6 para.88, revoked: SSI 2012/36 Sch.1 para.1
Sch.5 Part 8 para.94, amended: SSI 2012/36 Sch.1 para.1
Sch.5 Part 8 para.99A, substituted: SSI 2012/9 Reg.2
Sch.5 Part 8 para.101, amended: SSI 2012/9 Reg.2
Sch.5 Part 8 para.101A, amended: SSI 2012/9 Reg.2

116. **National Health Service (Primary Medical Services Section 17C Agreements) (Scotland) Regulations 2004**
Reg.2, amended: SI 2012/1479 Sch.1 para.41, SI 2012/1916 Sch.34 para.84
Sch.1 Part 3 para.13, amended: SI 2012/1916 Sch.34 para.84
Sch.1 Part 4 para.31, varied: 2012 c.11 s.12
Sch.1 Part 5 para.38, amended: SI 2012/1479 Sch.1 para.41
Sch.1 Part 6 para.47, substituted: SSI 2012/36 Sch.1 para.2
Sch.1 Part 6 para.48, revoked: SSI 2012/36 Sch.1 para.2
Sch.1 Part 6 para.49, revoked: SSI 2012/36 Sch.1 para.2
Sch.1 Part 6 para.50, revoked: SSI 2012/36 Sch.1 para.2
Sch.1 Part 6 para.51, revoked: SSI 2012/36 Sch.1 para.2
Sch.1 Part 6 para.52, amended: SSI 2012/36 Sch.1 para.2
Sch.1 Part 6 para.53, revoked: SSI 2012/36 Sch.1 para.2
Sch.1 Part 8 para.59, amended: SSI 2012/36 Sch.1 para.2
Sch.1 Part 8 para.66, amended: SSI 2012/10 Reg.2
Sch.1 Part 8 para.66A, amended: SSI 2012/10 Reg.2

117. **Housing (Scotland) Act 2001 (Assistance to Registered Social Landlords and Other Persons) (Grants) Regulations 2004**
Reg.2, amended: SSI 2012/38 Sch.1 para.6, SSI 2012/258 Reg.2
Reg.3, amended: SSI 2012/258 Reg.2
Reg.4, amended: SSI 2012/258 Reg.2
Sch.1 Part 1 para.1, amended: SSI 2012/258 Reg.2
Sch.1 Part 3 para.4, amended: SSI 2012/258 Reg.2
Sch.1 Part 4 para.13, substituted: SSI 2012/258 Reg.2
Sch.2 Part 1 para.1, substituted: SSI 2012/258 Sch.1
Sch.2 Part 1 para.2, substituted: SSI 2012/258 Sch.1
Sch.2 Part 2 para.3, substituted: SSI 2012/258 Sch.1
Sch.2 Part 3 para.4, substituted: SSI 2012/258 Sch.1
Sch.2 Part 4 para.5, substituted: SSI 2012/258 Sch.1
Sch.2 Part 4 para.6, substituted: SSI 2012/258 Sch.1
Sch.2 Part 4 para.7, substituted: SSI 2012/258 Sch.1

2004–cont.

117. **Housing (Scotland) Act 2001 (Assistance to Registered Social Landlords and Other Persons) (Grants) Regulations 2004**–*cont.*
Sch.2 Part 4 para.8, substituted: SSI 2012/ 258 Sch.1
Sch.2 Part 4 para.9, substituted: SSI 2012/ 258 Sch.1
Sch.5 Part 1 para.1, added: SSI 2012/ 258 Sch.2
Sch.5 Part 1 para.2, added: SSI 2012/ 258 Sch.2
Sch.5 Part 2 para.3, added: SSI 2012/ 258 Sch.2
Sch.5 Part 3 para.4, added: SSI 2012/ 258 Sch.2
Sch.5 Part 4 para.5, added: SSI 2012/ 258 Sch.2
Sch.5 Part 4 para.6, added: SSI 2012/ 258 Sch.2
Sch.5 Part 4 para.7, added: SSI 2012/ 258 Sch.2
Sch.5 Part 4 para.8, added: SSI 2012/ 258 Sch.2
Sch.5 Part 4 para.9, added: SSI 2012/ 258 Sch.2

133. **Jam and Similar Products (Scotland) Regulations 2004**
Reg.2, amended: SI 2012/ 1809 Sch.1 Part 3

142. **General Medical Services (Transitional and Other Ancillary Provisions) (Scotland) Order 2004**
Art.13, varied: 2012 c.11 s.12

163. **General Medical Services and Section 17C Agreements (Transitional and other Ancillary Provisions) (Scotland) Order 2004**
Art.21, varied: 2012 c.11 s.12

171. **Highland Council (Inverie) Harbour Empowerment Order 2004**
Art.2, varied: 2012 c.11 s.12
Art.3, varied: 2012 c.11 s.12
Art.25, varied: 2012 c.11 s.12

180. **Scottish Water (River Isla) Ordinary Drought Order 2004**
Art.2, varied: 2012 c.11 s.12

207. **Clydeport (Closure of Govan Basin) Harbour Revision Order 2004**
Art.2, varied: 2012 c.11 s.12

248. **Plant Health (Export Certification) (Scotland) Order 2004**
Sch.1, varied: 2012 c.11 s.12

260. **Assynt Coigach Area Protection Order 2004**
Art.2, varied: 2012 c.11 s.12

358. **Environmental Protection (Restriction on Use of Lead Shot) (Scotland) (No.2) Regulations 2004**
revoked: SI 2012/ 1923 Sch.1

406. **Building (Scotland) Regulations 2004**
Reg.17, amended: SSI 2012/ 209 Reg.2
Sch.5 Part 6 para.6.9, amended: SSI 2012/ 209 Reg.2

475. **Conservation (Natural Habitats, &c.) Amendment (Scotland) Regulations 2004**
Reg.5, revoked: SSI 2012/ 228 Sch.1

485. **Mallaig Harbour Revision Order 2004**
Art.2, varied: 2012 c.11 s.12

512. **Control of Volatile Organic Compounds (Petrol Vapour Recovery) (Scotland) Regulations 2004**
Reg.4, revoked: SSI 2012/ 360 Sch.12

2005

71. **Food Protection (Emergency Prohibitions) (Radioactivity in Sheep) Partial Revocation (Scotland) Order 2005**
revoked: SSI 2012/ 263 Sch.1

101. **Pollution Prevention and Control (Scotland) Amendment Regulations 2005**
revoked: SSI 2012/ 360 Sch.12

2005–cont.

125. **Gender Recognition (Disclosure of Information) (Scotland) Order 2005**
Art.5, amended: SI 2012/ 1479 Sch.1 para.47

164. **Budget (Scotland) Act 2004 Amendment Order 2005**
Art.2, varied: 2012 c.11 s.12

305. **Nitrate (Public Participation etc.) (Scotland) Regulations 2005**
Reg.3, varied: 2012 c.11 s.12

318. **Regulation of Care (Social Service Workers) (Scotland) Order 2005**
Art.3, revoked (in part): SI 2012/ 1479 Sch.1 para.76

329. **Fodder Plant Seed (Scotland) Regulations 2005**
Reg.2, amended: SSI 2012/ 5 Reg.3
Reg.8A, added: SSI 2012/ 5 Reg.4
Reg.15, amended: SSI 2012/ 5 Reg.5
Reg.16, amended: SSI 2012/ 5 Reg.6
Reg.17, amended: SSI 2012/ 5 Reg.7
Reg.24, amended: SSI 2012/ 5 Reg.8
Sch.3 para.1, substituted: SSI 2012/ 5 Reg.9
Sch.3 para.2, substituted: SSI 2012/ 5 Reg.9
Sch.3 para.3, added: SSI 2012/ 5 Reg.9
Sch.3 para.3, substituted: SSI 2012/ 5 Reg.9
Sch.4B Part I para.1, added: SSI 2012/ 5 Sch.1
Sch.4B Part I para.2, added: SSI 2012/ 5 Sch.1
Sch.4B Part I para.3, added: SSI 2012/ 5 Sch.1
Sch.4B Part I para.4, added: SSI 2012/ 5 Sch.1
Sch.4B Part I para.5, added: SSI 2012/ 5 Sch.1
Sch.4B Part II para.1, added: SSI 2012/ 5 Sch.1
Sch.4B Part II para.2, added: SSI 2012/ 5 Sch.1
Sch.4B Part III para.1, added: SSI 2012/ 5 Sch.1
Sch.6 Part II para.8A, added: SSI 2012/ 5 Reg.11

340. **Pollution Prevention and Control (Scotland) Amendment (No.2) Regulations 2005**
revoked: SSI 2012/ 360 Sch.12

359. **Caledonian MacBrayne (Oban Quay) Harbour Revision Order 2005**
Art.2, varied: 2012 c.11 s.12

393. **Teachers Superannuation (Scotland) Regulations 2005**
Part C regC.3, amended: SSI 2012/ 70 Reg.3

432. **Regulation of Care (Prescribed Registers) (Scotland) Order 2005**
Art.2, amended: SI 2012/ 1479 Sch.1 para.77

453. **Fire and Rescue Services (Framework) (Scotland) Order 2005**
revoked: SSI 2012/ 146 Art.3
Art.2, varied: 2012 c.11 s.12

464. **Mental Health (Safety and Security) (Scotland) Regulations 2005**
Reg.2, amended: SSI 2012/ 211 Reg.2

491. **Peterhead Port Authority Harbour (Constitution) Revision Order 2005**
Art.5, varied: 2012 c.11 s.12

494. **Civil Contingencies Act 2004 (Contingency Planning) (Scotland) Regulations 2005**
Reg.40, varied: 2012 c.11 s.12
Reg.45, varied: 2012 c.11 s.12
Reg.46, varied: 2012 c.11 s.12

508. **Scottish Water (Allt Beithe) Water Order 2005**
Art.2, varied: 2012 c.11 s.12

509. **Scottish Water (Loch a'Bhaid Luachraich) Water Order 2005**
Art.2, varied: 2012 c.11 s.12

510. **Pollution Prevention and Control (Public Participation etc.) (Scotland) Regulations 2005**
revoked: SSI 2012/ 360 Sch.12

2005–cont.

513. Scottish Water (Abhainn Chro Bheinn) Water Order 2005
Art.2, varied: 2012 c.11 s.12

519. Mental Health Tribunal for Scotland (Practice and Procedure) (No.2) Rules 2005
Part VII r.58, substituted: SSI 2012/ 132 r.2

558. Private Landlord Registration (Information and Fees) (Scotland) Regulations 2005
Reg.1, amended: SSI 2012/ 151 Reg.2
Reg.5, added: SSI 2012/ 151 Reg.3
Sch.1 para.3, amended: SSI 2012/ 151 Reg.4
Sch.1 para.10, amended: SSI 2012/ 151 Reg.4
Sch.2 para.6, amended: SSI 2012/ 38 Sch.1 para.7

576. Scottish Water (Allt nan Corp) Water Order 2005
Art.2, varied: 2012 c.11 s.12

577. Scottish Water (Allt Ach Na Braighe) Water Order 2005
Art.2, varied: 2012 c.11 s.12

578. Scottish Water (Loch Bealach na Gaoithe) Water Order 2005
Art.2, varied: 2012 c.11 s.12

613. Plant Health (Scotland) Order 2005
Art.2, amended: SSI 2012/ 266 Art.3, SSI 2012/ 326 Art.3
Art.8, amended: SSI 2012/ 326 Art.4
Art.22, amended: SSI 2012/ 326 Art.5
Art.39, amended: SSI 2012/ 266 Art.4
Art.40, substituted: SSI 2012/ 266 Art.5
Art.44A, added: SSI 2012/ 266 Art.6
Art.45, amended: SSI 2012/ 266 Art.6
Art.46, substituted: SSI 2012/ 266 Art.6
Sch.1 Part B, amended: SSI 2012/ 266 Art.7, SSI 2012/ 326 Art.6
Sch.2 Part B, amended: SSI 2012/ 326 Art.7
Sch.3, amended: SSI 2012/ 266 Art.8
Sch.4 Part A, amended: SSI 2012/ 266 Art.9, SSI 2012/ 326 Art.8
Sch.4 Part B, amended: SSI 2012/ 266 Art.9, SSI 2012/ 326 Art.8
Sch.5 Part A para.1, amended: SSI 2012/ 326 Art.9
Sch.5 Part A para.2, amended: SSI 2012/ 326 Art.9
Sch.6 Part A para.3b, added: SSI 2012/ 266 Art.10
Sch.6 Part A para.8, substituted: SSI 2012/ 266 Art.10
Sch.6 Part A para.9, added: SSI 2012/ 326 Art.10
Sch.7 Part A para.3b, added: SSI 2012/ 266 Art.11
Sch.7 Part A para.8, substituted: SSI 2012/ 266 Art.11
Sch.7 Part A para.9, added: SSI 2012/ 326 Art.11
Sch.8 Part A para.1, substituted: SSI 2012/ 266 Art.12
Sch.8 Part A para.5, amended: SSI 2012/ 266 Art.12
Sch.8 Part B para.1, substituted: SSI 2012/ 266 Art.12
Sch.8 Part B para.5, amended: SSI 2012/ 266 Art.12
Sch.15 para.7, amended: SSI 2012/ 266 Art.13

649. Scottish Water (Mill Loch) Order 2005
Art.2, varied: 2012 c.11 s.12

2006

1. Public Contracts (Scotland) Regulations 2006
applied: SSI 2012/ 88 Reg.52
revoked: SSI 2012/ 88 Sch.7 Part A
varied: SI 2012/ 147 Art.7

2. Utilities Contracts (Scotland) Regulations 2006
applied: SSI 2012/ 89 Reg.49
revoked: SSI 2012/ 89 Sch.5 Part A

2006–cont.

3. Food Hygiene (Scotland) Regulations 2006
applied: SSI 2012/ 177 Reg.27
Reg.2, amended: SSI 2012/ 75 Reg.2
Reg.9, amended: SSI 2012/ 75 Reg.2
Reg.22, amended: SSI 2012/ 75 Reg.2
Reg.32A, added: SSI 2012/ 75 Reg.2
Sch.1, substituted: SSI 2012/ 75 Sch.1
Sch.6A para.1, added: SSI 2012/ 75 Sch.2
Sch.6A para.2, added: SSI 2012/ 75 Sch.2

17. Highland Council (Raasay) Harbour Revision Order 2006
Art.2, varied: 2012 c.11 s.12
Art.30, varied: 2012 c.11 s.12
Sch.1, varied: 2012 c.11 s.12

44. Foot-and-Mouth Disease (Scotland) Order 2006
Art.2, amended: SSI 2012/ 321 Sch.4 para.2
Art.2, varied: 2012 c.11 s.12

45. Foot-and-Mouth Disease (Slaughter and Vaccination) (Scotland) Regulations 2006
Reg.2, amended: SSI 2012/ 321 Sch.4 para.3

52. Food Protection (Emergency Prohibitions) (Radioactivity in Sheep) Partial Revocation (Scotland) Order 2006
revoked: SSI 2012/ 263 Sch.1

133. Water Environment (Oil Storage) (Scotland) Regulations 2006
Reg.6, amended: SSI 2012/ 360 Sch.11 para.13

135. National Health Service (General Ophthalmic Services) (Scotland) Regulations 2006
Reg.2, amended: SSI 2012/ 36 Sch.1 para.3
Sch.1 para.2, amended: SSI 2012/ 36 Sch.1 para.3
Sch.1 para.11, substituted: SSI 2012/ 36 Sch.1 para.3
Sch.1 para.12, amended: SSI 2012/ 36 Sch.1 para.3

152. Scottish Water (Allt an Lagain) Water Order 2006
Art.2, varied: 2012 c.11 s.12

153. Scottish Water (Unapool Burn) Water Order 2006
Art.2, varied: 2012 c.11 s.12

218. Charities Accounts (Scotland) Regulations 2006
Reg.1, amended: SSI 2012/ 38 Sch.1 para.8

230. Ceramic Articles in Contact with Food (Scotland) Regulations 2006
revoked: SSI 2012/ 318 Sch.2

267. A737 Trunk Road (Kilwinning) (30 mph Speed Limit) Variation and Kilwinning Academy and Abbey Primary School (Part-time 20 mph Speed Limit) Order 2006
revoked: SSI 2012/ 268 Art.5

296. Scottish Water (Loch Braigh Horrisdale) Water Order 2006
Art.2, varied: 2012 c.11 s.12

330. National Health Service (Discipline Committees) (Scotland) Regulations 2006
Reg.2, amended: SSI 2012/ 36 Sch.1 para.4
Reg.2, revoked (in part): SSI 2012/ 36 Sch.1 para.4
Reg.4, revoked (in part): SSI 2012/ 36 Sch.1 para.4
Reg.6, amended: SSI 2012/ 36 Sch.1 para.4
Reg.6, revoked (in part): SSI 2012/ 36 Sch.1 para.4
Sch.2 para.6, amended: SSI 2012/ 36 Sch.1 para.4

333. Education (Student Loans for Tuition Fees) (Scotland) Regulations 2006
Reg.2, amended: SSI 2012/ 72 Reg.3
Reg.2, revoked (in part): SSI 2012/ 72 Reg.3
Reg.3, amended: SSI 2012/ 72 Reg.4
Reg.4, amended: SSI 2012/ 72 Reg.5
Sch.1 para.2, amended: SSI 2012/ 72 Reg.6
Sch.1 para.4, amended: SSI 2012/ 72 Reg.6

2006–cont.

333. Education (Student Loans for Tuition Fees) (Scotland) Regulations 2006–cont.
Sch.1 para.8, substituted: SSI 2012/72 Reg.6
Sch.1 para.11, added: SSI 2012/72 Reg.6
Sch.2 para.8, added: SSI 2012/72 Reg.7
Sch.2 para.9, added: SSI 2012/72 Reg.7

336. Avian Influenza and Influenza of Avian Origin in Mammals (Scotland) Order 2006
Art.70, amended: SI 2012/3039 Reg.37

344. Human Tissue (Scotland) Act 2006 (Maintenance of Records and Supply of Information Regarding the Removal and Use of Body Parts) Regulations 2006
Sch.2 Part 3 para.5, amended: SI 2012/1809 Sch.1 Part 3

360. Scottish Water (Abhainn Dhubh) Water Order 2006
Art.2, varied: 2012 c.11 s.12

361. Scottish Water (Tomich Boreholes) Water Order 2006
Art.2, varied: 2012 c.11 s.12

390. Human Organ and Tissue Live Transplants (Scotland) Regulations 2006
Reg.2, amended: SI 2012/1501 Reg.29
Reg.3, amended: SI 2012/1501 Reg.29
Reg.5, amended: SI 2012/1501 Reg.29

450. Animals and Animal Products (Import and Export) (Scotland) Amendment (No.2) Regulations 2006
revoked: SSI 2012/177 Reg.38

455. Teaching Council (Scotland) (Legal Assessor) Rules 2006
revoked: SSI 2012/86 r.3

456. Fire Safety (Scotland) Regulations 2006
Reg.8, revoked (in part): SSI 2012/332 Reg.3
Reg.10, revoked (in part): SSI 2012/332 Reg.3
Reg.17, amended: SSI 2012/332 Reg.3
Reg.19, revoked (in part): SSI 2012/332 Reg.3

474. Plant Health (Scotland) Amendment Order 2006
Art.2, revoked (in part): SSI 2012/266 Art.14

536. Animal Health and Welfare (Scotland) Act 2006 (Consequential Provisions) Order 2006
Sch.2 para.1, revoked: SSI 2012/321 Sch.5 Part 2

588. Personal Injuries (NHS Charges) (Amounts) (Scotland) Regulations 2006
Reg.2D, amended: SSI 2012/76 Reg.2
Reg.2E, added: SSI 2012/76 Reg.2
Reg.3, amended: SSI 2012/76 Reg.2
Reg.6, amended: SSI 2012/76 Reg.2

607. Police, Public Order and Criminal Justice (Scotland) Act 2006 (Commencement No 2) Order 2006
amended: 2012 asp 8 s.61
Sch.1, amended: 2012 asp 8 s.61

2007

1. Products of Animal Origin (Third Country Imports) (Scotland) Regulations 2007
revoked: SSI 2012/177 Reg.38

19. Tweed Regulation Order 2007
Art.13, varied: 2012 c.11 s.12

38. Food Protection (Emergency Prohibitions) (Radioactivity in Sheep) Partial Revocation (Scotland) Order 2007
revoked: SSI 2012/263 Sch.1

2007–cont.

61. Avian Influenza (H5N1 in Wild Birds) (Scotland) Order 2007
Sch.1 Part 4 para.13, amended: SSI 2012/179 Reg.3

62. Avian Influenza (H5N1 in Poultry) (Scotland) Order 2007
Art.14, amended: SSI 2012/179 Reg.4

80. Conservation (Natural Habitats, &c.) Amendment (Scotland) Regulations 2007
Reg.6, revoked: SSI 2012/228 Sch.1
Sch.2, varied: 2012 c.11 s.12

92. Management of Offenders etc (Scotland) Act 2005 (Specification of Persons) Order 2007
Sch.1, amended: SSI 2012/38 Sch.1 para.9

94. Potatoes Originating in Egypt (Scotland) Amendment Regulations 2007
Reg.2, revoked (in part): SSI 2012/37 Reg.3

105. Adults with Incapacity (Requirements for Signing Medical Treatment Certificates) (Scotland) Regulations 2007
Reg.2, substituted: SSI 2012/170 Reg.2

123. Town and Country Planning (Prescribed Date) (Scotland) Regulations 2007
revoked: SSI 2012/260 Reg.3

149. Education Authority Bursaries (Scotland) Regulations 2007
applied: SI 2012/3145 Sch.1
Reg.2, amended: SSI 2012/72 Reg.9
Sch.1 para.2, amended: SSI 2012/72 Reg.10
Sch.1 para.4, amended: SSI 2012/72 Reg.10
Sch.1 para.8, substituted: SSI 2012/72 Reg.10
Sch.1 para.9, substituted: SSI 2012/72 Reg.10
Sch.1 para.12, amended: SSI 2012/72 Reg.10
Sch.2 para.1, amended: SSI 2012/72 Reg.11
Sch.2 para.2, amended: SSI 2012/72 Reg.11
Sch.2 para.2, revoked (in part): SSI 2012/72 Reg.11
Sch.2 para.3, amended: SSI 2012/72 Reg.11
Sch.2 para.3, revoked (in part): SSI 2012/72 Reg.11

151. Nursing and Midwifery Student Allowances (Scotland) Regulations 2007
Reg.2, amended: SSI 2012/72 Reg.13
Reg.4, amended: SSI 2012/72 Reg.14
Reg.5, amended: SSI 2012/72 Reg.15
Sch.1 para.1, amended: SSI 2012/72 Reg.16
Sch.1 para.2, amended: SSI 2012/72 Reg.16
Sch.1 para.4, amended: SSI 2012/72 Reg.16
Sch.1 para.8, substituted: SSI 2012/72 Reg.16
Sch.1 para.9, substituted: SSI 2012/72 Reg.16
Sch.1 para.11, amended: SSI 2012/72 Reg.16
Sch.1 para.12, added: SSI 2012/72 Reg.16
Sch.2 para.1, amended: SSI 2012/72 Reg.17
Sch.2 para.2, amended: SSI 2012/72 Reg.17
Sch.2 para.2, revoked (in part): SSI 2012/72 Reg.17
Sch.2 para.3, amended: SSI 2012/72 Reg.17
Sch.2 para.3, revoked (in part): SSI 2012/72 Reg.17

152. Education (Fees and Awards) (Scotland) Regulations 2007
Reg.2, amended: SSI 2012/72 Reg.19
Reg.7A, added: SSI 2012/72 Reg.20
Reg.8, revoked: SSI 2012/72 Reg.21
Reg.9, revoked: SSI 2012/72 Reg.21
Reg.10, revoked: SSI 2012/72 Reg.21
Sch.1 para.2, amended: SSI 2012/72 Reg.22
Sch.1 para.4, amended: SSI 2012/72 Reg.22
Sch.1 para.8, substituted: SSI 2012/72 Reg.22
Sch.1 para.9, substituted: SSI 2012/72 Reg.22
Sch.1 para.11, revoked: SSI 2012/72 Reg.22
Sch.1 para.12, revoked: SSI 2012/72 Reg.22
Sch.1 para.14A, amended: SSI 2012/72 Reg.22

152. Education (Fees and Awards) (Scotland) Regulations 2007–*cont.*

Sch.1 para.14B, added: SSI 2012/72 Reg.22
Sch.1A para.1, added: SSI 2012/72 Reg.23
Sch.1A para.2, added: SSI 2012/72 Reg.23
Sch.1A para.3, added: SSI 2012/72 Reg.23
Sch.2 para.1, revoked: SSI 2012/72 Reg.21
Sch.2 para.2, revoked: SSI 2012/72 Reg.21
Sch.2 para.3, revoked: SSI 2012/72 Reg.21
Sch.2 para.4, revoked: SSI 2012/72 Reg.21
Sch.2 para.5, revoked: SSI 2012/72 Reg.21
Sch.2 para.6, revoked: SSI 2012/72 Reg.21
Sch.2 para.6A, revoked: SSI 2012/72 Reg.21
Sch.2 para.7, revoked: SSI 2012/72 Reg.21
Sch.2 para.8, revoked: SSI 2012/72 Reg.21
Sch.2 para.9, revoked: SSI 2012/72 Reg.21
Sch.2 para.10, revoked: SSI 2012/72 Reg.21
Sch.2 para.10A, revoked: SSI 2012/72 Reg.21
Sch.2 para.11, revoked: SSI 2012/72 Reg.21
Sch.3 para.1, revoked: SSI 2012/72 Reg.21
Sch.3 para.2, revoked: SSI 2012/72 Reg.21
Sch.3 para.3, revoked: SSI 2012/72 Reg.21
Sch.3 para.4, revoked: SSI 2012/72 Reg.21
Sch.3 para.5, revoked: SSI 2012/72 Reg.21
Sch.3 para.6, revoked: SSI 2012/72 Reg.21
Sch.3 para.7, revoked: SSI 2012/72 Reg.21

153. Students Allowances (Scotland) Regulations 2007

Reg.2, amended: SSI 2012/72 Reg.25
Reg.3, amended: SSI 2012/72 Reg.26
Reg.4, amended: SSI 2012/72 Reg.27
Reg.4, applied: SI 2012/3145 Sch.1, SSI 2012/303 Reg.20
Reg.5, amended: SSI 2012/72 Reg.28
Sch.1 para.2, amended: SSI 2012/72 Reg.29
Sch.1 para.4, amended: SSI 2012/72 Reg.29
Sch.1 para.8, substituted: SSI 2012/72 Reg.29
Sch.1 para.9, substituted: SSI 2012/72 Reg.29
Sch.1 para.11, amended: SSI 2012/72 Reg.29
Sch.1 para.12, added: SSI 2012/72 Reg.29
Sch.2 para.1, amended: SSI 2012/72 Reg.30
Sch.2 para.2, amended: SSI 2012/72 Reg.30
Sch.2 para.2, revoked (in part): SSI 2012/72 Reg.30
Sch.2 para.3, amended: SSI 2012/72 Reg.30
Sch.2 para.3, revoked (in part): SSI 2012/72 Reg.30

154. Education (Student Loans) (Scotland) Regulations 2007

Reg.2, amended: SSI 2012/72 Reg.32
Reg.2, revoked (in part): SSI 2012/72 Reg.32
Reg.3, amended: SSI 2012/72 Reg.33
Reg.4, amended: SSI 2012/72 Reg.34
Sch.1 para.2, amended: SSI 2012/72 Reg.35
Sch.1 para.4, amended: SSI 2012/72 Reg.35
Sch.1 para.8, substituted: SSI 2012/72 Reg.35
Sch.1 para.8A, added: SSI 2012/72 Reg.35
Sch.1 para.11, added: SSI 2012/72 Reg.35
Sch.2 para.8, added: SSI 2012/72 Reg.36
Sch.2 para.9, added: SSI 2012/72 Reg.36

156. Education Maintenance Allowances (Scotland) Regulations 2007

Reg.2, amended: SSI 2012/72 Reg.38
Sch.1 para.2, amended: SSI 2012/72 Reg.39
Sch.1 para.4, amended: SSI 2012/72 Reg.39
Sch.1 para.8, substituted: SSI 2012/72 Reg.39
Sch.1 para.11, amended: SSI 2012/72 Reg.39
Sch.2 para.1, amended: SSI 2012/72 Reg.40
Sch.2 para.2, amended: SSI 2012/72 Reg.40
Sch.2 para.2, revoked (in part): SSI 2012/72 Reg.40

162. Disabled Persons (Badges for Motor Vehicles) (Scotland) Amendment Regulations 2007

Reg.5, varied: 2012 c.11 s.12

170. Representation of the People (Absent Voting at Local Government Elections) (Scotland) Regulations 2007

Reg.8, amended: SI 2012/1479 Sch.1 para.52

174. Cattle Identification (Scotland) Regulations 2007

applied: SSI 2012/78 Art.7, Art.12, Art.13, Art.15, Art.16

175. Town and Country Planning (Marine Fish Farming) (Scotland) Regulations 2007

Reg.1, amended: SSI 2012/259 Reg.2
Reg.2, amended: SSI 2012/259 Reg.2
Reg.3, amended: SSI 2012/259 Reg.2

194. Animals and Animal Products (Import and Export) (Scotland) Regulations 2007

revoked: SSI 2012/177 Reg.38
Sch.4 Part III para.16, varied: 2012 c.11 s.12
Sch.5 Part II para.1, varied: 2012 c.11 s.12
Sch.8 Part II para.4, varied: 2012 c.11 s.12
Sch.8 Part II para.5, varied: 2012 c.11 s.12

199. Firefighters Pension Scheme (Scotland) Order 2007

Sch.1, added: SSI 2012/107 Art.4
Sch.1, amended: SSI 2012/107 Art.3

201. Police Pensions (Scotland) Regulations 2007

Reg.7, substituted: SSI 2012/71 Reg.3

204. Charities Reorganisation (Scotland) Regulations 2007

Reg.1, amended: SSI 2012/220 Reg.4
Reg.2, amended: SSI 2012/220 Reg.5
Reg.2, applied: SSI 2012/220 Reg.1
Reg.3, amended: SSI 2012/220 Reg.6
Reg.4, amended: SSI 2012/220 Reg.7
Reg.5, substituted: SSI 2012/220 Reg.8
Reg.6, amended: SSI 2012/220 Reg.9
Reg.7, added: SSI 2012/220 Reg.10
Sch.1, added: SSI 2012/220 Reg.11

220. Bankruptcy Fees (Scotland) Amendment Regulations 2007

revoked: SSI 2012/118 Sch.2

243. Mental Health (Safety and Security) (Scotland) Amendment Regulations 2007

revoked: SSI 2012/211 Reg.3

251. National Waste Management Plan for Scotland Regulations 2007

Reg.2, varied: 2012 c.11 s.12

263. Representation of the People (Postal Voting for Local Government Elections) (Scotland) Regulations 2007

Reg.5, amended: SSI 2012/31 Art.6
Reg.6, amended: SSI 2012/31 Art.7
Reg.31, amended: SSI 2012/31 Art.8

264. Representation of the People (Post-Local Government Elections Supply and Inspection of Documents) (Scotland) Regulations 2007

Reg.6, amended: SSI 2012/61 Reg.2

268. Town and Country Planning (Marine Fish Farming) (Scotland) Order 2007

Sch.1 Part 2, amended: SSI 2012/117 Art.4

284. Lerwick Harbour Revision Order 2007

Art.2, varied: 2012 c.11 s.12

304. Products of Animal Origin (Third Country Imports) (Scotland) Amendment Regulations 2007

revoked: SSI 2012/177 Reg.38

2007– cont.

307. European Fisheries Fund (Grants) (Scotland) Regulations 2007
Reg.2, amended: SSI 2012/166 Reg.3
Reg.2A, added: SSI 2012/166 Reg.4
Reg.2B, added: SSI 2012/166 Reg.4
Reg.2C, added: SSI 2012/166 Reg.4
Reg.2D, added: SSI 2012/166 Reg.4
Reg.3, amended: SSI 2012/166 Reg.5
Reg.4, amended: SSI 2012/166 Reg.6
Reg.5, amended: SSI 2012/166 Reg.7
Reg.6, amended: SSI 2012/166 Reg.8
Reg.7, amended: SSI 2012/166 Reg.9
Reg.8, amended: SSI 2012/166 Reg.10
Reg.9, amended: SSI 2012/166 Reg.11
Reg.10, amended: SSI 2012/166 Reg.12
Reg.14, amended: SSI 2012/166 Reg.13
Reg.15, amended: SSI 2012/166 Reg.14
Reg.15A, added: SSI 2012/166 Reg.15

308. Port of Cairnryan Harbour Empowerment Order 2007
applied: SSI 2012/350 Art.1
Art.2, amended: SSI 2012/350 Art.2
Art.2, varied: 2012 c.11 s.12
Art.4, amended: SSI 2012/350 Art.2
Art.4, revoked (in part): SSI 2012/350 Art.2
Art.5, amended: SSI 2012/350 Art.2
Art.7, amended: SSI 2012/350 Art.2
Art.16, amended: SSI 2012/350 Art.2
Art.18, amended: SSI 2012/350 Art.2
Sch.1 Part 1, substituted: SSI 2012/350 Sch.1
Sch.1 Part 2, substituted: SSI 2012/350 Sch.1
Sch.1 Part 2 para.1, substituted: SSI 2012/350 Sch.1
Sch.1 Part 2 para.2, substituted: SSI 2012/350 Sch.1
Sch.1 Part 2 para.3, substituted: SSI 2012/350 Sch.1
Sch.1 Part 2 para.4, substituted: SSI 2012/350 Sch.1
Sch.1 Part 3, substituted: SSI 2012/350 Sch.1
Sch.1 Part 4, substituted: SSI 2012/350 Sch.1
Sch.1 Part 5, substituted: SSI 2012/350 Sch.1
Sch.1 Part 6 para.1, substituted: SSI 2012/350 Sch.1
Sch.1 Part 6 para.2, substituted: SSI 2012/350 Sch.1
Sch.1 Part 6 para.3, substituted: SSI 2012/350 Sch.1
Sch.1 Part 7, substituted: SSI 2012/350 Sch.1
Sch.1 Part 8, substituted: SSI 2012/350 Sch.1
Sch.1 Part 9, substituted: SSI 2012/350 Sch.1
Sch.1 Part 10, substituted: SSI 2012/350 Sch.1
Sch.1 Part 11, substituted: SSI 2012/350 Sch.1

347. Renfrewshire Council (Cart Navigation) Harbour Revision Order 2007
Art.2, varied: 2012 c.11 s.12

375. Animals and Animal Products (Import and Export) (Scotland) Amendment Regulations 2007
revoked: SSI 2012/177 Reg.38
Sch.1, varied: 2012 c.11 s.12

482. Perth Harbour Revision Order 2007
Art.3, varied: 2012 c.11 s.12

487. Education (School and Placing Information) (Scotland) Amendment Regulations 2007
revoked: SSI 2012/130 Sch.3

537. Fishery Products (Official Controls Charges) (Scotland) Regulations 2007
Reg.2, amended: SSI 2012/177 Sch.4 para.4

551. Budget (Scotland) Act 2007 Amendment Order 2007
Art.3, varied: 2012 c.11 s.12
Art.4, varied: 2012 c.11 s.12

2007– cont.

565. Public Contracts and Utilities Contracts (Scotland) Amendment Regulations 2007
revoked (in part): SSI 2012/88 Sch.7 Part A, SSI 2012/89 Sch.5 Part A

570. Transport and Works (Scotland) Act 2007 (Applications and Objections Procedure) Rules 2007
Sch.3, amended: SI 2012/1658 Sch.1

2008

5. Bankruptcy Fees (Scotland) Amendment Regulations 2008
revoked: SSI 2012/118 Sch.2
Sch.1, varied: 2012 c.11 s.12

11. Bluetongue (Scotland) Order 2008
revoked: SSI 2012/199 Art.34
Art.6, amended: SSI 2012/177 Sch.4 para.1
Art.8, substituted: SSI 2012/184 Art.2
Art.18A, added: SSI 2012/177 Sch.4 para.1, SSI 2012/198 Art.3

16. Scottish Road Works Register (Prescribed Fees and Amounts) Regulations 2008
Reg.3, applied: SSI 2012/11 Reg.3

52. Adults with Incapacity (Public Guardian's Fees) (Scotland) Regulations 2008
Sch.1, substituted: SSI 2012/289 Sch.1, Sch.2, Sch.3

63. Food Protection (Emergency Prohibitions) (Radioactivity in Sheep) Partial Revocation (Scotland) Order 2008
revoked: SSI 2012/263 Sch.1

66. Leader Grants (Scotland) Regulations 2008
Reg.2, amended: SSI 2012/182 Reg.2
Reg.2A, added: SSI 2012/182 Reg.2
Reg.2B, added: SSI 2012/182 Reg.2
Reg.2C, added: SSI 2012/182 Reg.2
Reg.2D, added: SSI 2012/182 Reg.2
Reg.12, amended: SSI 2012/182 Reg.2

78. Community Care (Personal Care and Nursing Care) (Scotland) Amendment Regulations 2008
revoked: SSI 2012/109 Reg.3

79. Bankruptcy Fees (Scotland) Amendment (No.2) Regulations 2008
revoked: SSI 2012/118 Sch.2

88. Road Works (Scottish Road Works Register, Notices, Directions and Designations) (Scotland) Regulations 2008
Reg.2, varied: 2012 c.11 s.12

94. Public Contracts and Utilities Contracts (Scotland) Amendment Regulations 2008
revoked (in part): SSI 2012/88 Sch.7 Part A, SSI 2012/89 Sch.5 Part A

100. Rural Development Contracts (Rural Priorities) (Scotland) Regulations 2008
Sch.1, amended: SSI 2012/215 Sch.1 para.6
Sch.1, varied: 2012 c.11 s.12
Sch.2 Part 1, amended: SSI 2012/307 Reg.3, Reg.4
Sch.4 Part 2, amended: SSI 2012/360 Sch.11 para.18

128. Sexual Offences Act 2003 (Prescribed Police Stations) (Scotland) Regulations 2008
Sch.1, amended: SSI 2012/50 Reg.2

131. Official Statistics (Scotland) Order 2008
Art.2, substituted: SSI 2012/196 Art.2
Sch.1, amended: SSI 2012/196 Sch.1

143. Protected Trust Deeds (Scotland) Regulations 2008
Reg.10, applied: SSI 2012/118 Reg.8
Reg.19, applied: SSI 2012/118 Reg.12

2008–cont.

148. Specified Products from China (Restriction on First Placing on the Market) (Scotland) Regulations 2008
Reg.2, amended: SSI 2012/3 Reg.2
Reg.3, amended: SSI 2012/3 Reg.2
Reg.3, substituted: SSI 2012/3 Reg.2
Reg.4, revoked: SSI 2012/3 Reg.2
Reg.5, amended: SSI 2012/3 Reg.2
Reg.6, amended: SSI 2012/3 Reg.2
Reg.7, amended: SSI 2012/3 Reg.2
Reg.8, added: SSI 2012/3 Reg.2

155. Animals and Animal Products (Import and Export) (Scotland) Amendment Regulations 2008
revoked: SSI 2012/177 Reg.38

159. Rural Development Contracts (Land Managers Options) (Scotland) Regulations 2008
Sch.3 Part 2, amended: SSI 2012/360 Sch.11 para.19

170. Bathing Waters (Scotland) Regulations 2008
Reg.2, amended: SSI 2012/88 Sch.7 Part B, SSI 2012/243 Reg.2
Reg.8, amended: SSI 2012/243 Reg.2
Reg.11, amended: SSI 2012/243 Reg.2
Reg.12, substituted: SSI 2012/243 Reg.2

182. Caledonian Maritime Assets Limited (Largs) Harbour Revision Order 2008
Art.2, varied: 2012 c.11 s.12

188. Dumfries and Galloway Council (Port William) Harbour Empowerment Order 2008
Art.2, varied: 2012 c.11 s.12
Art.48, varied: 2012 c.11 s.12

189. Dumfries and Galloway Council (Isle of Whithorn) Harbour Empowerment Order 2008
Art.2, varied: 2012 c.11 s.12
Art.48, varied: 2012 c.11 s.12

190. Dumfries and Galloway Council (Garlieston) Harbour Empowerment Order 2008
Art.2, varied: 2012 c.11 s.12
Art.48, varied: 2012 c.11 s.12

216. Spreadable Fats, Milk and Milk Products (Scotland) Regulations 2008
Reg.3, amended: SI 2012/1809 Sch.1 Part 3

224. National Health Service Pension Scheme (Scotland) Regulations 2008
Reg.1, amended: SSI 2012/163 Reg.13
Reg.1, amended: SSI 2012/163 Reg.14
Reg.1, amended: SSI 2012/163 Reg.19
Reg.1, amended: SSI 2012/163 Reg.22
Reg.2, amended: SSI 2012/69 Reg.6
Reg.2, revoked (in part): SSI 2012/69 Reg.6
Reg.2, amended: SSI 2012/69 Reg.9, SSI 2012/163 Reg.21
Reg.2, revoked (in part): SSI 2012/163 Reg.21
Reg.3, amended: SSI 2012/163 Reg.12
Reg.3, amended: SSI 2012/69 Reg.7
Reg.4, amended: SSI 2012/69 Reg.8
Reg.4, amended: SSI 2012/163 Reg.18
Reg.5, amended: SSI 2012/163 Reg.15
Reg.5, amended: SSI 2012/163 Reg.23
Reg.7, amended: SSI 2012/163 Reg.20
Reg.8, amended: SSI 2012/163 Reg.16
Reg.8, amended: SSI 2012/163 Reg.24
Reg.10, amended: SSI 2012/163 Reg.17
Reg.10, amended: SSI 2012/163 Reg.25

228. Local Government Pension Scheme (Administration) (Scotland) Regulations 2008
Reg.5, amended: SSI 2012/347 Reg.18
Reg.5, revoked (in part): SSI 2012/347 Reg.18

2008–cont.

228. Local Government Pension Scheme (Administration) (Scotland) Regulations 2008–*cont.*
Reg.6, substituted: SSI 2012/347 Reg.19
Reg.9, amended: SSI 2012/347 Reg.20
Reg.10, substituted: SSI 2012/347 Reg.21
Reg.11, amended: SSI 2012/347 Reg.22
Reg.13, amended: SSI 2012/347 Reg.23
Reg.15, amended: SSI 2012/347 Reg.24
Reg.16, amended: SSI 2012/347 Reg.25
Reg.17, amended: SSI 2012/347 Reg.26
Reg.18, amended: SSI 2012/347 Reg.27
Reg.29, amended: SSI 2012/347 Reg.28
Reg.34, amended: SSI 2012/347 Reg.29
Reg.34, revoked (in part): SSI 2012/347 Reg.29
Reg.62A, added: SSI 2012/347 Reg.30
Sch.1, amended: SSI 2012/347 Reg.31
Sch.2, amended: SSI 2012/236 Reg.3
Sch.3 para.1, amended: SSI 2012/347 Reg.32
Sch.3 para.2, amended: SSI 2012/347 Reg.32
Sch.3 para.2A, added: SSI 2012/347 Reg.32
Sch.3 para.2A, amended: SSI 2012/347 Reg.32
Sch.3 para.3, amended: SSI 2012/347 Reg.32
Sch.3 para.4, amended: SSI 2012/347 Reg.32
Sch.3 para.5, amended: SSI 2012/347 Reg.32
Sch.3 para.6, amended: SSI 2012/347 Reg.32
Sch.3 para.7, amended: SSI 2012/347 Reg.32
Sch.3 para.8, amended: SSI 2012/347 Reg.32
Sch.3 para.9, amended: SSI 2012/347 Reg.32
Sch.3 para.10, amended: SSI 2012/347 Reg.32
Sch.3 para.11, amended: SSI 2012/347 Reg.32
Sch.3 para.12, amended: SSI 2012/347 Reg.32
Sch.4 Part I para.2A, added: SSI 2012/347 Reg.33
Sch.4 Part I para.2B, added: SSI 2012/347 Reg.33
Sch.4 Part I para.3, amended: SSI 2012/347 Reg.33
Sch.4 Part I para.5, substituted: SSI 2012/347 Reg.33
Sch.4 Part II, amended: SSI 2012/236 Reg.3

229. Local Government Pension Scheme (Transitional Provisions) (Scotland) Regulations 2008
Reg.3, amended: SSI 2012/347 Reg.14
Reg.4, amended: SSI 2012/347 Reg.15
Sch.2 para.3, amended: SSI 2012/347 Reg.16

230. Local Government Pension Scheme (Benefits, Membership and Contributions) (Scotland) Regulations 2008
Reg.2, amended: SSI 2012/347 Reg.3
Reg.3, amended: SSI 2012/347 Reg.4
Reg.9, amended: SSI 2012/347 Reg.5
Reg.14A, amended: SSI 2012/347 Reg.6
Reg.18, amended: SSI 2012/347 Reg.7
Reg.26, amended: SSI 2012/347 Reg.8
Reg.28, amended: SSI 2012/347 Reg.9
Reg.30, amended: SSI 2012/347 Reg.10
Reg.33, amended: SSI 2012/347 Reg.11
Reg.39, amended: SSI 2012/347 Reg.12

234. Bluetongue (Scotland) Amendment Order 2008
revoked: SSI 2012/199 Art.34

261. Plastic Materials and Articles in Contact with Food (Scotland) Amendment Regulations 2008
revoked: SSI 2012/318 Sch.2

291. Public Contracts and Utilities Contracts (Common Procurement Vocabulary Codes) Amendment (Scotland) Regulations 2008
revoked (in part): SSI 2012/88 Sch.7 Part A, SSI 2012/89 Sch.5 Part A

2008–cont.

298. Action Programme for Nitrate Vulnerable Zones (Scotland) Regulations 2008
Reg.8, amended: SSI 2012/360 Sch.11 para.20

306. Adult Support and Protection (Scotland) Act 2007 (Restriction on the Authorisation of Council Officers) Order 2008
varied: SSI 2012/66 Art.3
Art.3, amended: SI 2012/1479 Sch.1 para.58

309. Energy Performance of Buildings (Scotland) Regulations 2008
Reg.2, amended: SSI 2012/190 Reg.3, SSI 2012/208 Reg.3, SSI 2012/315 Reg.3
Reg.3, amended: SSI 2012/208 Reg.4
Reg.5, amended: SSI 2012/190 Reg.4
Reg.5, substituted: SSI 2012/208 Reg.5
Reg.5A, added: SSI 2012/208 Reg.6
Reg.6, amended: SSI 2012/190 Reg.5, SSI 2012/208 Reg.7
Reg.6A, added: SSI 2012/190 Reg.6, SSI 2012/208 Reg.8
Reg.7, amended: SSI 2012/208 Reg.9
Reg.7, substituted: SSI 2012/315 Reg.4
Reg.8, amended: SSI 2012/208 Reg.10
Reg.9, substituted: SSI 2012/208 Reg.11
Reg.10, amended: SSI 2012/190 Reg.7
Reg.10, substituted: SSI 2012/190 Reg.7
Reg.10A, added: SSI 2012/208 Reg.12
Reg.11, substituted: SSI 2012/190 Reg.8
Reg.12, substituted: SSI 2012/190 Reg.9, SSI 2012/315 Reg.5
Reg.13, amended: SSI 2012/190 Reg.10
Reg.13, substituted: SSI 2012/315 Reg.6
Reg.14, amended: SSI 2012/190 Reg.11, SSI 2012/208 Reg.13
Reg.14, substituted: SSI 2012/315 Reg.7
Reg.16, amended: SSI 2012/208 Reg.14
Reg.17, amended: SSI 2012/208 Reg.15
Reg.17A, added: SSI 2012/208 Reg.16
Reg.17B, added: SSI 2012/208 Reg.16
Reg.18, amended: SSI 2012/208 Reg.17
Reg.18A, added: SSI 2012/208 Reg.18
Sch.1 Part 1, added: SSI 2012/315 Sch.1
Sch.1 Part 2, added: SSI 2012/315 Sch.1
Sch.1 Part 3, added: SSI 2012/315 Sch.1

326. Fish Farming Businesses (Record Keeping) (Scotland) Order 2008
Sch.1 para.5, varied: 2012 c.11 s.12

327. Bluetongue (Scotland) Amendment (No.2) Order 2008
revoked: SSI 2012/199 Art.34

328. Justice of the Peace Court (Sheriffdom of Glasgow and Strathkelvin) Order 2008
Sch.2, varied: 2012 c.11 s.12

331. Peterhead Port Authority Harbour Revision Order 2008
Art.2, varied: 2012 c.11 s.12

334. Bankruptcy (Scotland) Amendment Regulations 2008
Sch.1, amended: SSI 2012/118 Reg.14

350. Plant Health (Scotland) Amendment (No.2) Order 2008
Art.6, revoked (in part): SSI 2012/266 Art.14
Art.7, revoked: SSI 2012/266 Art.14

363. Justice of the Peace Courts (Sheriffdom of Tayside, Central and Fife) Order 2008
Sch.4, varied: 2012 c.11 s.12

366. Act of Sederunt (Fees of Messengers-at-Arms) (EC Service Regulation) 2008
revoked: SSI 2012/340 Art.3

2008–cont.

374. Justice of the Peace Court (Sheriffdom of Glasgow and Strathkelvin) Amendment Order 2008
Art.2, varied: 2012 c.11 s.12

376. Public Contracts and Utilities Contracts (Postal Services and Common Procurement Vocabulary Codes) Amendment (Scotland) Regulations 2008
revoked (in part): SSI 2012/88 Sch.7 Part A, SSI 2012/89 Sch.5 Part A

410. Pollution Prevention and Control (Scotland) Amendment Regulations 2008
revoked: SSI 2012/360 Sch.12

427. Planning etc (Scotland) Act 2006 (Development Planning) (Saving, Transitional and Consequential Provisions) Order 2008
Art.4, applied: SSI 2012/228 Reg.5
Art.5, applied: SSI 2012/228 Reg.5

432. Town and Country Planning (Development Management Procedure) (Scotland) Regulations 2008
Reg.3, amended: SSI 2012/165 Reg.2
Reg.11, amended: SSI 2012/325 Reg.2
Reg.11, revoked (in part): SSI 2012/325 Reg.2
Reg.26, amended: SSI 2012/325 Reg.2
Sch.5 para.5, amended: SSI 2012/165 Reg.2

433. Town and Country Planning (Schemes of Delegation and Local Review Procedure) (Scotland) Regulations 2008
Reg.2, amended: SSI 2012/325 Reg.3

2009

1. Rural Development Contracts (Rural Priorities) (Scotland) Amendment Regulations 2009
Reg.3, varied: 2012 c.11 s.12

20. Justice of the Peace Courts (Sheriffdom of Tayside, Central and Fife) Amendment Order 2009
Art.2, varied: 2012 c.11 s.12

30. Plastic Materials and Articles in Contact with Food (Scotland) Regulations 2009
revoked: SSI 2012/318 Sch.2

44. International Organisations (Immunities and Privileges) (Scotland) Order 2009
varied: 2012 c.11 s.12

45. Specified Animal Pathogens (Scotland) Order 2009
applied: SSI 2012/178 Art.4, SSI 2012/199 Art.8
Art.5, amended: SI 2012/1916 Sch.34 para.98
Art.5, revoked (in part): SI 2012/1916 Sch.34 para.98

48. Home Energy Assistance Scheme (Scotland) Regulations 2009
Reg.2, amended: SSI 2012/34 Reg.4, SSI 2012/38 Sch.1 para.10
Reg.6, amended: SSI 2012/34 Reg.5
Reg.8, amended: SSI 2012/34 Reg.6

85. Aquatic Animal Health (Scotland) Regulations 2009
Reg.19, amended: SSI 2012/177 Sch.4 para.6

97. Bankruptcy Fees (Scotland) Amendment Regulations 2009
revoked: SSI 2012/118 Sch.2
Sch.1, varied: 2012 c.11 s.12

120. Budget (Scotland) Acts 2007 and 2008 Amendment Order 2009
Art.7, varied: 2012 c.11 s.12

2009– cont.

138. **Community Care (Personal Care and Nursing Care) (Scotland) Amendment Regulations 2009**
revoked: SSI 2012/109 Reg.3

140. **Renewables Obligation (Scotland) Order 2009**
Sch.2, referred to: SSI 2012/48 Sch.1 Part 2

154. **Adoption Agencies (Scotland) Regulations 2009**
applied: SI 2012/2885 Reg.8, SI 2012/2886 Sch.1, SI 2012/3144 Reg.8, SSI 2012/303 Reg.11, SSI 2012/319 Reg.11

173. **Swine Vesicular Disease (Scotland) Order 2009**
Art.3, amended: SSI 2012/177 Sch.4 para.5

182. **Adoptions with a Foreign Element (Scotland) Regulations 2009**
Reg.2, varied: 2012 c.11 s.12

183. **National Health Service (Pharmaceutical Services) (Scotland) Regulations 2009**
Reg.2, amended: SI 2012/1479 Sch.1 para.62, SI 2012/1916 Sch.34 para.99
Sch.1 para.3, amended: SSI 2012/36 Sch.1 para.5
Sch.1 para.4, amended: SI 2012/1916 Sch.34 para.99
Sch.1 para.10, amended: SI 2012/1916 Sch.34 para.99
Sch.1 para.12, substituted: SSI 2012/36 Sch.1 para.5
Sch.1 para.13, amended: SSI 2012/36 Sch.1 para.5

210. **Looked After Children (Scotland) Regulations 2009**
applied: SI 2012/2885 Sch.1 para.21, Sch.1 para.25, SI 2012/2886 Sch.1, SI 2012/3144 Sch.1 para.15, Sch.1 para.19, SI 2012/3145 Sch.1, SSI 2012/303 Reg.28, SSI 2012/319 Reg.29
Reg.33, applied: SI 2012/2886 Sch.1, SSI 2012/303 Sch.4 para.30, SSI 2012/319 Reg.35
Reg.51, applied: SI 2012/2886 Sch.1, SSI 2012/303 Sch.4 para.30, SSI 2012/319 Reg.35

227. **Animals and Animal Products (Import and Export) (Scotland) Amendment Regulations 2009**
revoked: SSI 2012/177 Reg.38

228. **Products of Animal Origin (Third Country Imports) (Scotland) Amendment Regulations 2009**
revoked: SSI 2012/177 Reg.38

247. **Waste Batteries (Scotland) Regulations 2009**
Reg.6, revoked: SSI 2012/360 Sch.12

262. **Meat (Official Controls Charges) (Scotland) Regulations 2009**
Reg.2, amended: SSI 2012/321 Sch.4 para.4

267. **Adoption and Children (Scotland) Act 2007 (Commencement No 4, Transitional and Savings Provisions) Order 2009**
Art.16, amended: SSI 2012/99 Art.2
Art.18, amended: SSI 2012/99 Art.2
Art.18, substituted: SSI 2012/99 Art.2
Art.21, amended: SSI 2012/99 Art.2

283. **Act of Sederunt (Rules of the Court of Session Amendment No.7) (Adoption and Children (Scotland) Act 2007) 2009**
r.2, varied: 2012 c.11 s.12

284. **Act of Sederunt (Sheriff Court Rules Amendment) (Adoption and Children (Scotland) Act 2007) 2009**
Sch.1, added: SSI 2012/271 r.5
Sch.1, varied: 2012 c.11 s.12

331. **Justice of the Peace Courts (Sheriffdom of North Strathclyde) etc Order 2009**
Sch.4, varied: 2012 c.11 s.12

2009– cont.

332. **Justice of the Peace Courts (Sheriffdom of South Strathclyde, Dumfries and Galloway) etc Order 2009**
Sch.3, varied: 2012 c.11 s.12

336. **Pollution Prevention and Control (Scotland) Amendment Regulations 2009**
revoked: SSI 2012/360 Sch.12

376. **Rural Payments (Appeals) (Scotland) Regulations 2009**
Reg.2, amended: SSI 2012/143 Reg.3
Reg.3, substituted: SSI 2012/143 Reg.4
Reg.5, amended: SSI 2012/143 Reg.5
Sch.1 para.1, revoked: SSI 2012/143 Reg.6
Sch.1 para.2, revoked: SSI 2012/143 Reg.6
Sch.1 para.3, substituted: SSI 2012/143 Reg.6
Sch.1 para.4, substituted: SSI 2012/143 Reg.6
Sch.1 para.5, substituted: SSI 2012/143 Reg.6
Sch.1 para.6, substituted: SSI 2012/143 Reg.6
Sch.1 para.7, substituted: SSI 2012/143 Reg.6
Sch.1 para.8, substituted: SSI 2012/143 Reg.6
Sch.1 para.10, substituted: SSI 2012/143 Reg.6

409. **Justice of the Peace Courts (Sheriffdom of North Strathclyde) etc Amendment Order 2009**
Art.2, varied: 2012 c.11 s.12

428. **Public Contracts and Utilities Contracts (Scotland) Amendment Regulations 2009**
revoked (in part): SSI 2012/88 Sch.7 Part A, SSI 2012/89 Sch.5 Part A

434. **Budget (Scotland) Act 2009 Amendment Order 2009**
Art.4, varied: 2012 c.11 s.12

436. **Food Additives (Scotland) Regulations 2009**
Reg.2, amended: SSI 2012/119 Reg.2
Reg.14, amended: SSI 2012/119 Reg.2
Reg.14, revoked (in part): SSI 2012/119 Reg.2
Reg.18, amended: SSI 2012/119 Reg.2
Sch.1, amended: SSI 2012/119 Reg.2

439. **Public Contracts and Utilities Contracts (Scotland) Amendment (Amendment) Regulations 2009**
revoked (in part): SSI 2012/88 Sch.7 Part A, SSI 2012/89 Sch.5 Part A

440. **INSPIRE (Scotland) Regulations 2009**
Reg.2, amended: SSI 2012/284 Reg.3
Reg.7, amended: SSI 2012/284 Reg.4
Reg.7A, added: SSI 2012/284 Reg.5
Reg.8, amended: SSI 2012/284 Reg.6
Reg.8, revoked (in part): SSI 2012/284 Reg.6
Reg.9, amended: SSI 2012/284 Reg.7
Reg.13, amended: SSI 2012/284 Reg.8
Reg.15, amended: SSI 2012/284 Reg.9

446. **Official Feed and Food Controls (Scotland) Regulations 2009**
Sch.3, amended: SSI 2012/177 Sch.4 para.3

448. **Scottish Criminal Cases Review Commission (Permitted Disclosure of Information) Order 2009**
revoked: 2012 asp 7 s.4

2010

7. **Act of Sederunt (Registration Appeal Court) 2010**
revoked: SSI 2012/245 Art.2

8. **Snares (Scotland) Order 2010**
revoked: SSI 2012/215 Sch.1 Part 4

2010–cont.

9. Sea Fish (Prohibited Methods of Fishing) (Firth of Clyde) Order 2010
revoked: SSI 2012/4 Art.5

10. Water Services Charges (Billing and Collection) (Scotland) Order 2010
Art.3, applied: SSI 2012/53 Art.3
Art.5, applied: SSI 2012/53 Art.3

15. Justice of the Peace Courts (Sheriffdom of South Strathclyde, Dumfries and Galloway) etc Amendment Order 2010
Art.2, varied: 2012 c.11 s.12

61. Town and Country Planning (Prescribed Date) (Scotland) Amendment Regulations 2010
revoked: SSI 2012/260 Reg.3

64. Police Grant (Scotland) Order 2010
Art.2, amended: SSI 2012/49 Art.5
Art.3, amended: SSI 2012/49 Art.5

76. Bankruptcy Fees (Scotland) Amendment Regulations 2010
revoked: SSI 2012/118 Sch.2

117. Community Care (Personal Care and Nursing Care) (Scotland) Amendment Regulations 2010
revoked: SSI 2012/109 Reg.3

118. Budget (Scotland) Act 2009 Amendment Order 2010
Art.4, varied: 2012 c.11 s.12

168. Police Act 1997 (Criminal Records) (Scotland) Regulations 2010
Reg.5, amended: SSI 2012/354 Reg.2

186. International Organisations (Immunities and Privileges) (Scotland) Amendment Order 2010
varied: 2012 c.11 s.12

199. Sports Grounds and Sporting Events (Designation) (Scotland) Order 2010
Sch.1 Part 1, amended: SSI 2012/164 Art.2
Sch.2 Part I para.7, added: SSI 2012/164 Art.2

208. National Health Service (General Dental Services) (Scotland) Regulations 2010
Sch.1 Part I para.2, amended: SSI 2012/36 Sch.1 para.6
Sch.1 Part IV para.36, substituted: SSI 2012/36 Sch.1 para.6
Sch.1 Part IV para.37, amended: SSI 2012/36 Sch.1 para.6
Sch.1 Part IV para.38, revoked: SSI 2012/36 Sch.1 para.6

225. Products of Animal Origin (Third Country Imports) (Scotland) Amendment Regulations 2010
revoked: SSI 2012/177 Reg.38

236. Solvent Emissions (Scotland) Regulations 2010
revoked: SSI 2012/360 Sch.12

273. Less Favoured Area Support Scheme (Scotland) Regulations 2010
Reg.2, amended: SSI 2012/24 Reg.3
Reg.9, amended: SSI 2012/24 Reg.4

292. M8/A8 and A737/A738 Trunk Roads (White Cart Viaduct) (Temporary Prohibition of Traffic, Temporary Prohibition of Overtaking and Temporary Speed Restriction) Order 2010
revoked: SSI 2012/169 Art.2

327. Materials and Articles in Contact with Food (Scotland) Regulations 2010
revoked: SSI 2012/318 Sch.2

2010–cont.

342. Plant Health (Scotland) Amendment (No.2) Order 2010
Art.4, revoked: SSI 2012/266 Art.14
Art.5, revoked: SSI 2012/266 Art.14

343. Animals and Animal Products (Import and Export) (Scotland) Amendment Regulations 2010
revoked: SSI 2012/177 Reg.38

387. Prohibited Procedures on Protected Animals (Exemptions) (Scotland) Regulations 2010
Sch.1, amended: SSI 2012/40 Reg.2
Sch.2, amended: SSI 2012/40 Reg.2
Sch.4, amended: SSI 2012/40 Reg.2
Sch.5, amended: SSI 2012/40 Reg.2
Sch.7, amended: SSI 2012/40 Reg.2

390. Cleaner Road Transport Vehicles (Scotland) Regulations 2010
Reg.2, amended: SSI 2012/88 Sch.7 Part B, SSI 2012/89 Sch.5 Part B
Reg.6, amended: SSI 2012/88 Sch.7 Part B, SSI 2012/89 Sch.5 Part B

440. Non-Domestic Rates (Levying) (Scotland) (No.2) Regulations 2010
Reg.2, revoked: SSI 2012/28 Reg.6
Reg.3, revoked: SSI 2012/28 Reg.6
Reg.4, revoked: SSI 2012/28 Reg.6
Reg.6, revoked: SSI 2012/28 Reg.6
Reg.7, revoked: SSI 2012/28 Reg.6

446. Protection of Vulnerable Groups (Scotland) Act 2007 (Miscellaneous Provisions) Order 2010
Art.7, amended: SI 2012/3006 Art.34
Art.8, amended: SI 2012/3006 Art.34
Art.15, amended: SI 2012/3006 Art.34

2011

43. Scottish Road Works Register (Prescribed Fees) Regulations 2011
revoked: SSI 2012/11 Reg.4

55. National Health Service (Free Prescriptions and Charges for Drugs and Appliances) (Scotland) Regulations 2011
Reg.3, amended: SSI 2012/74 Reg.2

57. Marine Licensing (Exempted Activities) (Scottish Offshore Region) Order 2011
Art.3, amended: SSI 2012/25 Art.8
Art.4, amended: SSI 2012/25 Art.9
Art.6, amended: SSI 2012/25 Art.10
Art.13, amended: SSI 2012/25 Art.11
Art.15, amended: SSI 2012/25 Art.12
Art.16A, added: SSI 2012/25 Art.13
Art.16B, added: SSI 2012/25 Art.13

63. Muntjac Keeping (Scotland) Regulations 2011
revoked: SSI 2012/174 Sch.2

78. Marine Licensing (Fees) (Scotland) Regulations 2011
Reg.2, amended: SSI 2012/183 Reg.3
Reg.3, amended: SSI 2012/183 Reg.4
Reg.3A, added: SSI 2012/183 Reg.5
Reg.5, amended: SSI 2012/183 Reg.6
Reg.6, amended: SSI 2012/183 Reg.7

100. Plastic Materials and Articles in Contact with Food (Scotland) Amendment Regulations 2011
revoked: SSI 2012/318 Sch.2

2011– cont.

106. Rural Development Contracts (Rural Priorities) (Scotland) Amendment Regulations 2011
Reg.12, varied: 2012 c.11 s.12

107. Individual Learning Account (Scotland) Regulations 2011
Reg.3, amended: SSI 2012/172 Reg.2
Reg.4, amended: SSI 2012/172 Reg.2
Reg.10, revoked (in part): SSI 2012/172 Reg.2
Reg.12, amended: SSI 2012/172 Reg.2

109. Local Government Finance (Scotland) Order 2011
Art.2, revoked: SSI 2012/41 Art.5
Sch.1, amended: SSI 2012/41 Art.5

117. National Health Service Superannuation Scheme (Scotland) Regulations 2011
Part N regN.4, amended: SSI 2012/163 Reg.4
Part r regR.7, amended: SSI 2012/163 Reg.5
Part T regT.3, amended: SSI 2012/163 Reg.7
Part T regT.8, amended: SSI 2012/163 Reg.8
Part U regU.2, amended: SSI 2012/163 Reg.9
Part D regD.1, amended: SSI 2012/69 Reg.3
Part D regD.1, revoked (in part): SSI 2012/69 Reg.3
Part D regD.2, amended: SSI 2012/163 Reg.3
s.1, amended: SSI 2012/163 Reg.6
Sch.1 Part II para.5, amended: SSI 2012/163 Reg.10
Sch.1 Part IV para.14, amended: SSI 2012/69 Reg.4, SSI 2012/163 Reg.10
Sch.1 Part IV para.14, revoked (in part): SSI 2012/163 Reg.10

123. National Assistance (Sums for Personal Requirements) (Scotland) Regulations 2011
revoked: SSI 2012/67 Reg.3

124. National Assistance (Assessment of Resources) Amendment (Scotland) Regulations 2011
Reg.2, revoked: SSI 2012/68 Reg.4
Reg.3, revoked: SSI 2012/68 Reg.4

142. Bankruptcy Fees (Scotland) Amendment Regulations 2011
revoked: SSI 2012/118 Sch.2

145. Town and Country Planning (Marine Fish Farming) (Scotland) Amendment Regulations 2011
Reg.2, revoked (in part): SSI 2012/259 Reg.3

171. Animal By-Products (Enforcement) (Scotland) Regulations 2011
Reg.4, amended: SSI 2012/179 Reg.2
Reg.6, amended: SSI 2012/179 Reg.2
Sch.1, amended: SSI 2012/179 Reg.2
Sch.2 para.13, revoked: SSI 2012/360 Sch.12
Sch.2 para.14, revoked: SSI 2012/360 Sch.12

172. Muntjac Keeping (Scotland) Order 2011
revoked: SSI 2012/174 Sch.2

182. Healthcare Improvement Scotland (Requirements as to Independent Health Care Services) Regulations 2011
Reg.1, amended: SI 2012/1479 Sch.1 para.67

185. Public Services Reform (Social Services Inspections) (Scotland) Regulations 2011
Reg.3A, added: SSI 2012/45 Reg.2

204. Marine Licensing (Exempted Activities) (Scottish Inshore Region) Order 2011
Art.2, amended: SSI 2012/25 Art.3
Art.5, amended: SSI 2012/25 Art.4
Art.15, amended: SSI 2012/25 Art.5
Art.18A, added: SSI 2012/25 Art.6
Art.18B, added: SSI 2012/25 Art.6

2011– cont.

209. Water Environment (Controlled Activities) (Scotland) Regulations 2011
applied: SI 2012/2782 Art.9
Sch.10 Part 2 para.18, amended: SSI 2012/360 Sch.11 para.25

210. Social Care and Social Work Improvement Scotland (Requirements for Care Services) Regulations 2011
Reg.4, amended: SI 2012/1479 Sch.1 para.68

215. Public Services Reform (General Teaching Council for Scotland) Order 2011
Art.18, applied: SSI 2012/86 r.2
Sch.4 para.1, applied: SSI 2012/86 r.2
Sch.4 para.2, applied: SSI 2012/86 r.2
Sch.4 para.3, enabled: SSI 2012/86

226. Waste (Scotland) Regulations 2011
Reg.7, revoked: SSI 2012/360 Sch.12
Sch.1 Part 2 para.5, revoked: SSI 2012/360 Sch.12
Sch.1 Part 2 para.6, revoked: SSI 2012/360 Sch.12
Sch.1 Part 2 para.7, revoked: SSI 2012/360 Sch.12
Sch.1 Part 2 para.8, revoked: SSI 2012/360 Sch.12
Sch.1 Part 2 para.9, revoked: SSI 2012/360 Sch.12

228. Waste Management Licensing (Scotland) Regulations 2011
Reg.2, amended: SSI 2012/360 Sch.11 para.24
Reg.3, amended: SSI 2012/360 Sch.11 para.24
Reg.13A, added: SSI 2012/148 Reg.5
Reg.16, amended: SSI 2012/360 Sch.11 para.24
Reg.17, amended: SSI 2012/148 Reg.5
Reg.19, amended: SSI 2012/148 Reg.5
Reg.21, amended: SSI 2012/360 Sch.11 para.24
Reg.30, amended: SSI 2012/360 Sch.11 para.24
Sch.1 para.1, amended: SSI 2012/360 Sch.11 para.24
Sch.1 para.2, amended: SSI 2012/360 Sch.11 para.24
Sch.1 para.3, amended: SSI 2012/360 Sch.11 para.24
Sch.1 para.5, amended: SSI 2012/360 Sch.11 para.24
Sch.1 para.7, amended: SSI 2012/148 Reg.5
Sch.1 para.9, amended: SSI 2012/360 Sch.11 para.24
Sch.1 para.12, amended: SSI 2012/148 Reg.5
Sch.1 para.19, amended: SSI 2012/148 Reg.5
Sch.1 para.23, amended: SSI 2012/148 Reg.5
Sch.1 para.24, amended: SSI 2012/360 Sch.11 para.24
Sch.1 para.29, amended: SSI 2012/360 Sch.11 para.24
Sch.1 para.44, amended: SSI 2012/360 Sch.11 para.24
Sch.1 para.45, amended: SSI 2012/360 Sch.11 para.24
Sch.4 Part 1 para.1, amended: SSI 2012/360 Sch.11 para.24
Sch.4 Part 1 para.5, amended: SSI 2012/148 Reg.5, SSI 2012/360 Sch.11 para.24
Sch.4 Part 1 para.7, amended: SSI 2012/360 Sch.11 para.24

230. Community Care (Personal Care and Nursing Care) (Scotland) Amendment Regulations 2011
revoked: SSI 2012/109 Reg.3

233. Equality Act 2010 (Specification of Public Authorities) (Scotland) Order 2011
Art.2, amended: 2012 asp 8 s.61

2011– cont.

268. Damages (Scotland) Act 2011 (Commencement, Transitional Provisions and Savings) Order 2011
Art.4, applied: SSI 2012/144 r.3
284. Scrabster (Deep Inner Berth) Harbour Revision Order 2011
Art.2, varied: 2012 c.11 s.12
285. Pollution Prevention and Control (Scotland) Amendment Regulations 2011
revoked: SSI 2012/360 Sch.12
325. Bananas (Enforcement of Quality Standards) (Scotland) Regulations 2011
revoked: SSI 2012/349 Reg.22
331. Prisons and Young Offenders Institutions (Scotland) Rules 2011
Part 1 r.2, amended: SSI 2012/26 r.2
Part 1 r.6, amended: SSI 2012/26 r.2
Part 2 r.12, substituted: SSI 2012/26 r.2
Part 3 r.18, amended: SSI 2012/26 r.2
Part 3 r.19, amended: SSI 2012/26 r.2
Part 3 r.19, revoked (in part): SSI 2012/26 r.2
Part 4 r.32, amended: SSI 2012/26 r.2
Part 4 r.32, revoked (in part): SSI 2012/26 r.2
Part 8 r.55, amended: SSI 2012/26 r.2
Part 8 r.55, revoked (in part): SSI 2012/26 r.2
Part 9 r.82, amended: SSI 2012/26 r.2
Part 9 r.85, revoked (in part): SSI 2012/26 r.2
Part 9 r.86, substituted: SSI 2012/26 r.2
Part 10 r.100, amended: SSI 2012/26 r.2
Part 10 r.105, amended: SSI 2012/26 r.2
Part 15 r.135, amended: SSI 2012/26 r.2
Part 15 r.138, amended: SSI 2012/26 r.2
Sch.2, amended: SSI 2012/26 r.2
362. M9/A90/M90 Trunk Road (Kirkliston to Scotstoun) and M9/A9 Trunk Road (Newbridge to Winchburgh) Temporary Prohibition of Traffic Order 2011
revoked: SSI 2012/134 Art.9
389. Education (Fees) (Scotland) Regulations 2011
Reg.2, amended: SSI 2012/72 Reg.42
Sch.1 para.1, amended: SSI 2012/72 Reg.43
Sch.1 para.3, amended: SSI 2012/72 Reg.43
Sch.2 para.2, amended: SSI 2012/72 Reg.44
399. Scottish Local Government Elections Order 2011
Art.5, amended: SSI 2012/60 Art.2
Sch.1, added: SSI 2012/60 Art.2, SSI 2012/342 Art.4, Art.5
Sch.1, amended: SSI 2012/60 Art.2
Sch.1, applied: SSI 2012/342 Art.6
Sch.1, referred to: SSI 2012/342 Art.6
Sch.1, revoked: SSI 2012/60 Art.2
Sch.1, varied: SSI 2012/342 Art.6
418. Control of Volatile Organic Compounds (Petrol Vapour Recovery) (Scotland) Regulations 2011
Reg.4, revoked: SSI 2012/360 Sch.12
431. Act of Sederunt (Fees of Messengers-at-Arms) (No.2) 2011
Art.2, amended: SSI 2012/8 Art.2
432. Act of Sederunt (Fees of Sheriff Officers) (No.2) 2011
Art.2, amended: SSI 2012/7 Art.2
433. Wildlife and Natural Environment (Scotland) Act 2011 (Commencement No 2) Order 2011
Art.2, amended: SSI 2012/281 Art.2
447. Fraserburgh Harbour Revision Order 2011
referred to: SSI 2012/262 Art.1
Art.22, revoked: SSI 2012/262 Sch.1

2011– cont.

447. Fraserburgh Harbour Revision Order 2011– cont.
Art.23, revoked: SSI 2012/262 Sch.1
Art.24, revoked: SSI 2012/262 Sch.1
Art.25, revoked: SSI 2012/262 Sch.1
Sch.1, referred to: SSI 2012/262 Art.4

2012

21. Public Records (Scotland) Act 2011 (Commencement No 1) Order 2012
Art.2, amended: SSI 2012/42 Art.2
28. Non-Domestic Rates (Levying) (Scotland) Regulations 2012
revoked: SSI 2012/353 Reg.6
39. Housing (Scotland) Act 2010 (Commencement No 6, Transitional and Savings Provisions) Order 2012
Sch.2 para.18, amended: SSI 2012/91 Art.4
41. Local Government Finance (Scotland) Order 2012
Sch.1, substituted: SSI 2012/94 Sch.1
43. Scottish Public Services Ombudsman Act 2002 Amendment Order 2012
Art.2, amended: 2012 asp 8 s.61
49. Police Grant and Variation (Scotland) Order 2012
Art.2, amended: SSI 2012/316 Art.2
Art.3, amended: SSI 2012/316 Art.2
88. Public Contracts (Scotland) Regulations 2012
applied: SSI 2012/89 Reg.5, Reg.21
Sch.1, amended: SSI 2012/108 Reg.2
89. Utilities Contracts (Scotland) Regulations 2012
Reg.3, applied: SSI 2012/88 Reg.6, Reg.33, Reg.36
Reg.9, applied: SSI 2012/88 Reg.6
Sch.1, referred to: SSI 2012/88 Reg.6
Sch.5 Part A, amended: SSI 2012/108 Reg.3
Sch.5 Part B, amended: SSI 2012/108 Reg.3
124. Snares (Training) (Scotland) Order 2012
revoked: SSI 2012/161 Art.4
136. Act of Sederunt (Actions for removing from heritable property) 2012
Art.3, amended: SSI 2012/273 Art.2
Sch.1, amended: SSI 2012/273 Sch.1
140. Road Traffic (Permitted Parking Area and Special Parking Area) (South Ayrshire Council) Designation Order 2012
applied: SSI 2012/142 Reg.2
referred to: SSI 2012/139 Reg.2
144. Act of Sederunt (Summary Cause Rules Amendment) (Personal Injuries Actions) 2012
Sch.1, amended: SSI 2012/188 r.14
148. Waste (Scotland) Regulations 2012
Reg.3, revoked: SSI 2012/360 Sch.12
167. Parole Board (Scotland) Amendment Rules 2012
r.7, revoked: SSI 2012/197 r.3
r.12, revoked (in part): SSI 2012/197 r.3
r.13, revoked: SSI 2012/197 r.3
173. Wildlife and Countryside Act 1981 (Exceptions to section 14) (Scotland) Order 2012
Art.2, amended: SSI 2012/205 Art.2
Sch.1 Part 2, substituted: SSI 2012/205 Sch.1
174. Wildlife and Countryside Act 1981 (Keeping and Release and Notification Requirements) (Scotland) Order 2012
Art.2, amended: SSI 2012/206 Art.2
Art.3, amended: SSI 2012/206 Art.2
Sch.1 Part 1, substituted: SSI 2012/206 Sch.1

2012– cont.

321. Welfare of Animals at the Time of Killing (Scotland) Regulations 2012– *cont.*
Sch.1 Part 2, substituted: SSI 2012/206 Sch.1
Sch.2, referred to: SSI 2012/175 Art.3

175. Wildlife and Natural Environment (Scotland) Act 2011 (Commencement No 4, Savings and Transitional Provisions) Order 2012
Art.3, applied: SSI 2012/174 Art.5

177. Trade in Animals and Related Products (Scotland) Regulations 2012
Reg.11, applied: SSI 2012/178 Art.4
Reg.23, amended: SSI 2012/198 Art.2
Reg.33, amended: SSI 2012/198 Art.2
Sch.2 Part 1 para.5, amended: SSI 2012/198 Art.2
Sch.4 para.1, revoked (in part): SSI 2012/198 Art.2, SSI 2012/199 Art.34

184. Bluetongue (Scotland) Amendment Order 2012
revoked: SSI 2012/199 Art.34

188. Act of Sederunt (Sheriff Court Rules) (Miscellaneous Amendments) 2012
r.4, amended: SSI 2012/221 r.2

190. Energy Performance of Buildings (Scotland) Amendment Regulations 2012
Reg.4, revoked: SSI 2012/208 Reg.20
Reg.5, revoked: SSI 2012/208 Reg.20
Reg.6, revoked: SSI 2012/208 Reg.20
Reg.7, amended: SSI 2012/208 Reg.20
Reg.9, revoked: SSI 2012/315 Reg.9
Reg.10, revoked: SSI 2012/315 Reg.9
Reg.11, revoked: SSI 2012/315 Reg.9

198. Trade in Animals and Related Products (Scotland) Amendment Order 2012
Art.3, revoked: SSI 2012/199 Art.34

208. Energy Performance of Buildings (Scotland) Amendment (No.2) Regulations 2012
Reg.9, revoked: SSI 2012/315 Reg.10
Reg.13, revoked: SSI 2012/315 Reg.10

258. Housing (Scotland) Act 2001 (Assistance to Registered Social Landlords and Other Persons) (Grants) Amendment Regulations 2012
revoked: SSI 2012/306 Reg.2

2012– cont.

290. Court of Session etc Fees Amendment Order 2012
Art.1, amended: SSI 2012/322 Art.3
Sch.1, amended: SSI 2012/322 Art.4
Sch.2, amended: SSI 2012/322 Art.5

291. High Court of Justiciary Fees Amendment Order 2012
Art.1, amended: SSI 2012/322 Art.6

293. Sheriff Court Fees Amendment Order 2012
Art.1, amended: SSI 2012/322 Art.7

294. Crofting Register (Scotland) Rules 2012
r.6, amended: SSI 2012/327 r.2
Sch.1, amended: SSI 2012/327 r.2

295. Crofting Register (Fees) (Scotland) Order 2012
Sch.1, amended: SSI 2012/328 Art.2

303. Council Tax Reduction (Scotland) Regulations 2012
applied: SSI 2012/319 Sch.4 para.22
Reg.20, applied: SSI 2012/319 Reg.5, Reg.47, Sch.5 para.1
Reg.39, applied: SSI 2012/319 Reg.48, Sch.5 para.2
Reg.68, applied: SSI 2012/319 Reg.54
Reg.70, applied: SSI 2012/319 Reg.54
Reg.73, applied: SSI 2012/319 Reg.54
Reg.75, applied: SSI 2012/319 Reg.54
Sch.1 Part 3 para.10, applied: SSI 2012/319 Reg.29
Sch.4 para.27, applied: SSI 2012/319 Reg.48
Sch.4 para.39, applied: SSI 2012/319 Sch.5 para.2
Sch.4 para.41, applied: SSI 2012/319 Reg.48, Sch.5 para.2

321. Welfare of Animals at the Time of Killing (Scotland) Regulations 2012
Reg.30, amended: SSI 2012/355 Reg.2
Sch.1, amended: SSI 2012/355 Reg.2
Sch.1 para.9, amended: SSI 2012/355 Reg.2
Sch.1 para.10, amended: SSI 2012/355 Reg.2
Sch.1 para.11, amended: SSI 2012/355 Reg.2
Sch.5 Part 1, amended: SSI 2012/355 Reg.2

STATUTORY RULES ISSUED BY THE UK PARLIAMENT

1906

679. Locomotives and Wagons (Used in Lines and Sidings) Regulations 1906
revoked: SI 2012/1537 Reg.2

1927

343. Coroners (Orders as to Districts) Rules 1927
applied: SI 2012/574

1933

106. Musk Rats (Prohibition of Importation and Keeping) Order 1933
revoked (in part): SSI 2012/174 Sch.2

1937

478. Grey Squirrels (Prohibition of Importation and Keeping) Order 1937
revoked (in part): SSI 2012/174 Sch.2

1945

347. Trading with the Enemy (Transfer of Negotiable Instruments, etc.) (France and Monaco) Order 1945
revoked: SI 2012/1367 Sch.1

859. Trading with the Enemy (Transfer of Negotiable Instruments, etc.) (Belgium and Luxembourg) Order 1945
revoked: SI 2012/1367 Sch.1

1945–cont.

961. Trading with the Enemy (Transfer of Negotiable Instruments, etc.) (Denmark) Order 1945
revoked: SI 2012/1367 Sch.1

1031. Trading with the Enemy (Transfer of Negotiable Instruments, etc.) (Finland) Order 1945
revoked: SI 2012/1367 Sch.1

1078. Trading with the Enemy (Transfer of Negotiable Instruments, etc.) (Greece) Order 1945
revoked: SI 2012/1367 Sch.1

1099. Trading with the Enemy (Transfer of Negotiable Instruments, etc.) (Italy) Order 1945
revoked: SI 2012/1367 Sch.1

1118. Trading with the Enemy (Transfer of Negotiable Instruments, etc.) (Netherlands) Order 1945
revoked: SI 2012/1367 Sch.1

1358. Trading with the Enemy (Transfer of Negotiable Instruments, etc.) (Czechoslovakia) Order 1945
revoked: SI 2012/1367 Sch.1

1495. Trading with the Enemy (Transfer of Negotiable Instruments, etc.) (Yugoslavia) Order 1945
revoked: SI 2012/1367 Sch.1

1946

293. Trading with the Enemy (Transfer of Negotiable Instruments, etc.) (Siam) Order 1946
revoked: SI 2012/1367 Sch.1

441. Trading with the Enemy (Transfer of Negotiable Instruments, etc.) Order 1946
revoked: SI 2012/1367 Sch.1

1043. Trading with the Enemy (Transfer of Negotiable Instruments, etc.) (No.2) Order 1946
revoked: SI 2012/1367 Sch.1

1060. Trading with the Enemy (Transfer of Negotiable Instruments, etc.) (Poland) Order 1946
revoked: SI 2012/1367 Sch.1

1433. Trading with the Enemy (Transfer of Negotiable Instruments, etc.) (Hungary) Order 1946
revoked: SI 2012/1367 Sch.1

1947

665. Trading with the Enemy (Transfer of Negotiable Instruments, etc.) (Roumania) Order 1947
revoked: SI 2012/1367 Sch.1

2088. Trading with the Enemy (Transfer of Negotiable Instruments, etc.) (General) Order 1947
revoked: SI 2012/1367 Sch.1

2204. Trading with the Enemy (Transfer of Negotiable Instruments, etc.) (Austria) Order 1947
revoked: SI 2012/1367 Sch.1

1949

606. Trading with the Enemy (Transfer of Negotiable Instruments, etc.) (Germany) Order 1949
revoked: SI 2012/1367 Sch.1

1950

29. Trading with the Enemy (Transfer of Negotiable Instruments, etc.) (Japan) Order 1950
revoked: SI 2012/1367 Sch.1

65. Pottery (Health and Welfare) Special Regulations 1950
revoked: SI 2012/1537 Reg.2

1642. Distribution of German Enemy Property (No.1) Order 1950
Art.22, revoked: 2012 c.9 Sch.2 para.10, Sch.10 Part 2

1952

5. Trading with the Enemy (Transfer of Negotiable Instruments, etc.) (Germany) Order 1952
revoked: SI 2012/1367 Sch.1

1954

927. Non-Indigenous Rabbits (Prohibition of Importation and Keeping) Order 1954
revoked (in part): SSI 2012/174 Sch.2

1958

1263. Family Allowances, National Insurance and Industrial Injuries (Yugoslavia) Order 1958
Sch.1, varied: SI 2012/360 Sch.2

1959

364. Schools Regulations 1959
Sch.2, applied: SI 2012/762 Reg.4

1960

543. Election Petition Rules 1960
applied: SI 2012/323 Reg.15, SI 2012/444 Reg.20, SI 2012/1917 Sch.9 para.2
r.2, varied: SI 2012/323 Sch.7, SI 2012/444 Sch.7, SI 2012/1917 Sch.9 para.2
r.4, varied: SI 2012/323 Sch.7, SI 2012/444 Sch.7, SI 2012/1917 Sch.9 para.2
r.6, varied: SI 2012/1917 Sch.9 para.2
r.9, varied: SI 2012/1917 Sch.9 para.2
r.10, varied: SI 2012/323 Sch.7, SI 2012/444 Sch.7
r.12, varied: SI 2012/323 Sch.7, SI 2012/444 Sch.7, SI 2012/1917 Sch.9 para.2
r.14, varied: SI 2012/323 Sch.7, SI 2012/444 Sch.7, SI 2012/1917 Sch.9 para.2
r.16, varied: SI 2012/323 Sch.7, SI 2012/444 Sch.7, SI 2012/1917 Sch.9 para.2
r.18, varied: SI 2012/323 Sch.7, SI 2012/444 Sch.7
r.19, varied: SI 2012/1917 Sch.9 para.2
Sch.1, varied: SI 2012/323 Sch.7, SI 2012/444 Sch.7, SI 2012/1917 Sch.9 para.2

581. Visiting Forces and Allied Headquarters (Stamp Duties) (Designation) Order 1960
revoked: SI 2012/3071 Sch.1

1961

580. Visiting Forces and Allied Headquarters (Income Tax and Death Duties) (Designation) Order 1961
revoked: SI 2012/3071 Sch.1

584. National Insurance and Industrial Injuries (Turkey) Order 1961
varied: SI 2012/360 Sch.2

1962

1667. Non-ferrous Metals (Melting and Founding) Regulations 1962
revoked: SI 2012/1537 Reg.2

1963

1172. Various Trunk Roads (Prohibition of Waiting)(Clearways) Order 1963
Sch.1, revoked: SI 2012/1082 Art.7
Sch.1, substituted: SI 2012/1571 Art.6

1964

925. Visiting Forces (Stamp Duties) (Designation) Order 1964
revoked: 2012 c.14 Sch.39 para.2
939. National Assistance (Professions Supplementary to Medicine) Regulations 1964
Reg.2, amended: SI 2012/1479 Sch.1 para.1
1755. Ecclesiastical Jurisdiction (Discipline) Rules 1964
r.49, applied: SI 2012/1847 Sch.2 para.4

1965

536. Special Constables Regulations 1965
Reg.1, amended: SI 2012/1961 Reg.3
Reg.1A, amended: SI 2012/1961 Reg.5
Reg.1B, added: SI 2012/1961 Reg.6
Reg.1C, added: SI 2012/1961 Reg.6
Reg.1ZA, added: SI 2012/1961 Reg.4
Reg.1ZB, added: SI 2012/1961 Reg.4
Reg.1ZC, added: SI 2012/1961 Reg.4
Reg.1ZD, added: SI 2012/1961 Reg.4
Reg.1ZE, added: SI 2012/1961 Reg.4
1056. Charities (Exception from Registration and Accounts) Regulations 1965
Reg.2, amended: SI 2012/3012 Sch.4 para.1
1776. Rules of the Supreme Court (Revision) 1965
Ord.52, see *Attorney General v Dallas* [2012] EWHC 156 (Admin), [2012] 1 W.L.R. 991 (DC), Lord Judge, L.C.J.

1966

965. Charities (Exception of Universities from Registration) Regulations 1966
Reg.2, amended: SI 2012/3012 Sch.4 para.2

1967

1353. Trunk Roads (40 m.p.h Speed Limit) (No.1) (Wales) Order 1967
varied: SI 2012/2633 Art.7

1968

989. Commons Registration (Objections and Maps) Regulations 1968
Reg.9, varied: SI 2012/740 Reg.4
1202. Mallaig Harbour Revision Order 1968
Sch.1, revoked: SSI 2012/114 Sch.3
Sch.2, revoked: SSI 2012/114 Sch.3
1822. Transport Act 1968 (Commencement No 1) Order 1968
Sch.2 paraC., amended: SI 2012/1659 Art.2
2049. Registration of Births, Deaths and Marriages Regulations 1968
Reg.5, amended: SI 2012/2404 Sch.3 para.1

1969

690. Asbestos Regulations 1969
Reg.13, applied: SI 2012/632 Reg.28
1421. Bath Cheltenham Evesham Coventry Leicester Lincoln Trunk Road (Prohibition of Waiting) (Clearways) Order 1969
revoked: SI 2012/1082 Art.8

1970

952. Double Taxation Relief (Taxes on Income) (Barbados) Order 1970
revoked: SI 2012/3076 Sch.1
1151. Transport Act 1968 (Commencement No 8) Order 1970
Sch.1, amended: SI 2012/1659 Art.2
1152. Drainage Rates (Appeals) Regulations 1970
Reg.5, amended: SI 2012/1659 Sch.3 para.28
1691. Trunk Roads (40 m.p.h Speed Limit) (No.26) Order 1970
revoked: SI 2012/2313 Art.3
1958. Functions of Traffic Wardens Order 1970
Art.3, amended: SI 2012/2278 Art.3
Sch.1 para.4, amended: SI 2012/2278 Art.4

1971

1267. Medicines (Surgical Materials) Order 1971
applied: SI 2012/504 Sch.4 para.6
1326. Medicines (Importation of Medicinal Products for Re-exportation) Order 1971
revoked: SI 2012/1916 Sch.35
1410. Medicines (Exemption from Licences) (Foods and Cosmetics) Order 1971
revoked: SI 2012/1916 Sch.35
1450. Medicines (Exemption from Licences) (Special and Transitional Cases) Order 1971
revoked: SI 2012/1916 Sch.35
Art.2, applied: SI 2012/504 Reg.24, Sch.2 para.30
2084. Indictments (Procedure) Rules 1971
r.6, referred to: SI 2012/1726 r.14.1
r.7, referred to: SI 2012/1726 r.14.1
r.8, referred to: SI 2012/1726 r.14.1
r.9, referred to: SI 2012/1726 r.14.1
r.10, referred to: SI 2012/1726 r.14.1

1972

853. Local Authorities (Goods and Services) (Public Bodies) Order 1972
Sch.1 Part I, amended: SI 2012/2552 Art.2
1200. Medicines (Exemption from Licences) (Special Cases and Miscellaneous Provisions) Order 1972
revoked: SI 2012/1916 Sch.35
1265. Health and Personal Social Services (Northern Ireland) Order 1972
applied: SI 2012/1631 Sch.5 para.6, SI 2012/1916 Sch.17 Part 1, SI 2012/2996 Sch.5 para.5
Art.2, amended: SI 2012/1916 Sch.34 para.46
Art.15, applied: SI 2012/2885 Sch.6 para.29, SI 2012/2886 Sch.1
Art.30, applied: SI 2012/2885 Sch.1 para.25, SI 2012/2886 Sch.1, SI 2012/3144 Sch.1 para.19, SI 2012/3145 Sch.1, SSI 2012/303 Sch.1 para.10, SSI 2012/319 Reg.29
Art.57D, amended: SI 2012/1916 Sch.34 para.46
1298. Pensions Increase (Annual Review) Order 1972
applied: SI 2012/782 Art.3, Art.4

1972– cont.

1957. Cooking Utensils (Safety) Regulations 1972
revoked: SI 2012/1815 Sch.1

2076. Medicines (Data Sheet) Regulations 1972
revoked: SI 2012/1916 Sch.35

1973

36. Employment Medical Advisory Service (Factories Act Orders etc Amendment) Order 1973
revoked: SI 2012/1537 Reg.2

367. Medicines (Extension to Antimicrobial Substances) Order 1973
revoked: SI 2012/1916 Sch.35

798. Misuse of Drugs (Safe Custody) Regulations 1973
varied: SI 2012/980 Art.3

1370. Pensions Increase (Annual Review) Order 1973
applied: SI 2012/782 Art.3, Art.4

1642. Dairy Herd Conversion Premium Regulations 1973
Reg.2, amended: 2012 c.9 Sch.2 para.4, Sch.10 Part 2
Reg.5, revoked (in part): 2012 c.9 Sch.2 para.4, Sch.10 Part 2
Reg.7, revoked (in part): 2012 c.9 Sch.2 para.4, Sch.10 Part 2

2079. Medicines (Exemption from Licences) (Foods and Cosmetics) Amendment Order 1973
revoked: SI 2012/1916 Sch.35

2096. Double Taxation Relief (Taxes on Income) (Barbados) Order 1973
revoked: SI 2012/3076 Sch.1

2143. Motor Vehicles (Compulsory Insurance) (No.2) Regulations 1973
Reg.6, amended: SI 2012/1809 Sch.1 Part 2

1974

316. Medicines (Exemption from Licences) (Emergency Importation) Order 1974
revoked: SI 2012/1916 Sch.35

494. National Health Service (Professions Supplementary to Medicine) Regulations 1974
Reg.2, amended: SI 2012/1479 Sch.1 para.2

495. National Health Service (Speech Therapists) Regulations 1974
Reg.3, amended: SI 2012/1479 Sch.1 para.3

502. Motorways Traffic (Speed Limit) Regulations 1974
Reg.3, disapplied: SI 2012/5 Art.10

539. Land Compensation Development Order 1974
revoked (in part): SI 2012/634 Art.7, SI 2012/843 Art.6
Art.4, applied: SI 2012/634 Art.7

549. National Health Service (Professions Supplementary to Medicine) (Scotland) Regulations 1974
Reg.2, amended: SI 2012/1479 Sch.1 para.4

1150. Medicines (Exemption from Licences) (Ingredients) Order 1974
revoked: SI 2012/1916 Sch.35

1286. Land Charges Rules 1974
r.2, amended: SI 2012/2884 Sch.1 para.1
r.3, amended: SI 2012/2884 Sch.1 para.2
r.4, amended: SI 2012/2884 Sch.1 para.3
r.5, amended: SI 2012/2884 Sch.1 para.3
r.6, revoked: SI 2012/2884 Sch.1 para.4

1974– cont.

1286. Land Charges Rules 1974– *cont.*
r.8, amended: SI 2012/2884 Sch.1 para.5
r.10, amended: SI 2012/2884 Sch.1 para.6
r.11, amended: SI 2012/2884 Sch.1 para.6
r.12, amended: SI 2012/2884 Sch.1 para.6
r.13, revoked (in part): SI 2012/2884 Sch.1 para.7
r.14, amended: SI 2012/2884 Sch.1 para.8
r.16, substituted: SI 2012/2884 Sch.1 para.9
r.17, amended: SI 2012/2884 Sch.1 para.10
r.18, revoked: SI 2012/2884 Sch.1 para.11
r.19, substituted: SI 2012/2884 Sch.1 para.12
r.19A, amended: SI 2012/2884 Sch.1 para.13
r.20, substituted: SI 2012/2884 Sch.1 para.14
r.21, amended: SI 2012/2884 Sch.1 para.15
r.23, amended: SI 2012/2884 Sch.1 para.16
r.24, amended: SI 2012/2884 Sch.1 para.17
Sch.1, amended: SI 2012/2884 Sch.1 para.18, Sch.1 para.19
Sch.2, amended: SI 2012/2884 r.4, Sch.2
Sch.3, substituted: SI 2012/2884 Sch.3
Sch.3 Part I, substituted: SI 2012/2884 Sch.3
Sch.3 Part II, substituted: SI 2012/2884 Sch.3

1373. Pensions Increase (Annual Review) Order 1974
applied: SI 2012/782 Art.3, Art.4

2034. Agriculture (Tractor Cabs) Regulations 1974
applied: SI 2012/1652 Reg.3

2211. Rabies (Importation of Dogs, Cats and Other Mammals) Order 1974
Art.4, amended: SSI 2012/177 Sch.4 para.7
Sch.1, referred to: SSI 2012/177 Sch.3 para.6

1975

193. Local Authorities (Goods and Services) (Public Bodies) Order 1975
Sch.1, amended: SI 2012/979 Sch.1 para.1

423. Recovery Abroad of Maintenance (Convention Countries) Order 1975
Sch.1, amended: SI 2012/2814 Sch.4 para.7, Sch.5 para.4

434. Industrial Training (Transfer of the Activities of Establishments) Order 1975
referred to: SI 2012/958 Sch.1

493. Social Security (Benefit) (Members of the Forces) Regulations 1975
Reg.1, amended: SI 2012/1656 Reg.2
Reg.2, amended: SI 2012/1656 Reg.2
Reg.2, revoked (in part): SI 2012/1656 Reg.2

529. Social Security (Mariners Benefits) Regulations 1975
applied: SI 2012/2886 Sch.1, SI 2012/3145 Sch.1, SSI 2012/303 Reg.37

555. Social Security (Hospital In-Patients) Regulations 1975
applied: SI 2012/2885 Sch.1 para.16, SI 2012/2886 Sch.1

556. Social Security (Credits) Regulations 1975
Reg.8A, amended: SI 2012/2568 Reg.9
Reg.8B, amended: SI 2012/913 Reg.2
Reg.8B, applied: SI 2012/2885 Sch.1 para.25, Sch.4 para.6, SI 2012/2886 Sch.1, SI 2012/3144 Sch.1 para.19, SI 2012/3145 Sch.1, SSI 2012/303 Reg.28, Sch.3 para.12, SSI 2012/319 Reg.29, Sch.2 para.6
Reg.9C, amended: SI 2012/766 Reg.2
Reg.9C, substituted: SI 2012/766 Reg.2
Reg.9F, amended: SI 2012/2680 Reg.2

1975–cont.

563. Social Security Benefit (Persons Abroad) Regulations 1975
Reg.5, applied: SI 2012/819 Reg.3, SI 2012/845 Reg.3

762. Medicines (Exemption from Licences) (Wholesale Dealing in Confectionery) Order 1975
revoked: SI 2012/1916 Sch.35

1023. Rehabilitation of Offenders Act 1974 (Exceptions) Order 1975
see *R. (on the application of T) v Chief Constable of Greater Manchester* [2012] EWHC 147 (Admin), [2012] 2 Cr. App. R. 3 (QBD (Admin)), Kenneth Parker, J.
Art.2, amended: SI 2012/1957 Art.4, Art.7
Art.3, amended: SI 2012/1957 Art.5, Art.8, SI 2012/3006 Art.19, Art.70
Art.3A, amended: SI 2012/1957 Art.9
Art.4, amended: SI 2012/1957 Art.5, Art.8
Art.4A, added: SI 2012/1957 Art.3
Sch.1 Part I para.1, substituted: SI 2012/1957 Art.6
Sch.1 Part I para.4, revoked (in part): SI 2012/1957 Art.6
Sch.1 Part I para.6, revoked (in part): SI 2012/1957 Art.6
Sch.1 Part I para.7, revoked (in part): SI 2012/1957 Art.6
Sch.1 Part I para.8, revoked (in part): SI 2012/1957 Art.6
Sch.1 Part I para.8A, revoked (in part): SI 2012/1957 Art.6
Sch.1 Part I para.10, amended: SI 2012/1479 Sch.1 para.5
Sch.1 Part I para.10, revoked (in part): SI 2012/1957 Art.6
Sch.1 Part I para.11, revoked (in part): SI 2012/1957 Art.6
Sch.1 Part I para.12, revoked (in part): SI 2012/1957 Art.6
Sch.1 Part II para.12A, amended: SI 2012/1957 Art.10
Sch.1 Part II para.14, amended: SI 2012/979 Sch.1 para.2
Sch.1 Part II para.14A, amended: SI 2012/1957 Art.10
Sch.1 Part II para.34, amended: SI 2012/1957 Art.10
Sch.1 Part II para.37, revoked (in part): SI 2012/1957 Art.10
Sch.1 Part II para.38, amended: SI 2012/3006 Art.20
Sch.1 Part II para.44, revoked: SI 2012/3006 Art.20, Art.71
Sch.1 Part IV, amended: SI 2012/1957 Art.6, Art.11
Sch.1 Part IV, substituted: SI 2012/1957 Art.6

1157. Industrial Training (Transfer of the Activities of Establishments) (No.2) Order 1975
referred to: SI 2012/958 Sch.1

1326. Medicines (Advertising of Medicinal Products) (No.2) Regulations 1975
applied: SI 2012/1916 Sch.32 para.3

1384. Pensions Increase (Annual Review) Order 1975
applied: SI 2012/782 Art.3, Art.4

2187. Reciprocal Enforcement of Maintenance Orders (Designation of Reciprocating Countries) Order 1975
Sch.1, amended: SI 2012/2814 Sch.5 para.5

2223. Mink (Keeping) Regulations 1975
revoked (in part): SSI 2012/174 Sch.2

1976

2. Children's Clothing (Hood Cords) Regulations 1976
revoked: SI 2012/1815 Sch.1

246. Local Government Area Changes Regulations 1976
applied: SI 2012/805 Art.1

396. Industrial Training (Transfer of the Activities of Establishments) Order 1976
referred to: SI 2012/958 Sch.1

897. European Communities (Designation) Order 1976
referred to: SI 2012/1815

968. Medicines (Specified Articles and Substances) Order 1976
revoked: SI 2012/1916 Sch.35

1042. Sex Discrimination (Northern Ireland) Order 1976
Art.63A, see *Pace Telecom Ltd v McAuley* [2012] Eq. L.R. 148 (CA (NI)), Coghlin, L.J.

1186. Trunk Roads (40 mph &amp 50 mph Speed Limit) (No.1) Order 1976
revoked: SI 2012/2735 Art.6

1213. Pharmacy (Northern Ireland) Order 1976
Art.2, amended: SI 2012/1916 Sch.34 para.47

1214. Poisons (Northern Ireland) Order 1976
Art.2, amended: SI 2012/1916 Sch.34 para.48

1356. Pensions Increase (Annual Review) Order 1976
applied: SI 2012/782 Art.3, Art.4

1572. Immigration (Variation of Leave) Order 1976
see *Kishver (Limited Leave: Meaning: Pakistan), Re* [2012] Imm. A.R. 128 (UT (IAC)), CMG Ockelton

1635. Industrial Training (Transfer of the Activities of Establishments) (No.2) Order 1976
referred to: SI 2012/958 Sch.1

1726. Medicines (Labelling) Regulations 1976
applied: SI 2012/1916 Sch.32 para.2, Sch.32 para.3

2012. National Savings Stock Register Regulations 1976
Reg.2, amended: SI 2012/1877 Reg.3
Reg.5, amended: SI 2012/1877 Reg.4
Reg.8, amended: SI 2012/1877 Reg.5
Reg.9, amended: SI 2012/1877 Reg.6
Reg.9A, added: SI 2012/1877 Reg.7
Reg.10, amended: SI 2012/1877 Reg.8
Reg.12, revoked: SI 2012/1877 Reg.9
Reg.13, amended: SI 2012/1877 Reg.10
Reg.14, amended: SI 2012/1877 Reg.4
Reg.15, amended: SI 2012/1877 Reg.4
Reg.21, amended: SI 2012/1877 Reg.11
Reg.21A, added: SI 2012/1877 Reg.12
Reg.21B, added: SI 2012/1877 Reg.12
Reg.22, amended: SI 2012/1877 Reg.13
Reg.25, amended: SI 2012/1877 Reg.14
Reg.26, amended: SI 2012/1877 Reg.15
Reg.27, amended: SI 2012/1877 Reg.16
Reg.28, amended: SI 2012/1877 Reg.17
Reg.31, amended: SI 2012/1877 Reg.18
Reg.38, amended: SI 2012/1877 Reg.19
Reg.41, amended: SI 2012/1877 Reg.20
Reg.42, amended: SI 2012/1877 Reg.21
Reg.45, amended: SI 2012/1877 Reg.4
Reg.46, amended: SI 2012/1877 Reg.22
Reg.48, amended: SI 2012/1877 Reg.23
Reg.49, revoked: SI 2012/1877 Reg.24
Reg.53, amended: SI 2012/1877 Reg.25
Reg.55, substituted: SI 2012/1877 Reg.26

1976–cont.

2012. National Savings Stock Register Regulations 1976–*cont.*
Reg.57, amended: SI 2012/1877 Reg.27

2110. Industrial Training (Transfer of the Activities of Establishments) (No.3) Order 1976
referred to: SI 2012/958 Sch.1

2162. Petroleum Stocks Order 1976
revoked: SI 2012/2862 Art.18

1977

343. Social Security Benefit (Dependency) Regulations 1977
Sch.2 Part I para.2B, amended: SI 2012/819 Reg.4

500. Safety Representatives and Safety Committees Regulations 1977
applied: SI 2012/335 Sch.2 para.20, SI 2012/2991 Sch.2 para.28
Reg.6, amended: SI 2012/199 Reg.6

626. British Shipbuilders Regulations 1977
Reg.4, amended: SI 2012/2404 Sch.3 para.2

640. Medicines (Importation of Medicinal Products for Re-exportation) Amendment Order 1977
revoked: SI 2012/1916 Sch.35

670. Medicines (Bal Jivan Chamcho Prohibition) (No.2) Order 1977
Art.2, amended: SI 2012/1809 Sch.1 Part 2

1038. Medicines (Manufacturer's Undertakings for Imported Products) Regulations 1977
revoked: SI 2012/1916 Sch.35

1055. Medicines (Leaflets) Regulations 1977
applied: SI 2012/1916 Sch.32 para.2, Sch.32 para.3
revoked: SI 2012/1916 Sch.35

1210. National Savings Bank (Investment Deposits) (Limits) Order 1977
Art.3B, amended: SI 2012/795 Art.2

1387. Pensions Increase (Annual Review) Order 1977
applied: SI 2012/782 Art.3, Art.4

1951. Industrial Training (Transfer of the Activities of Establishments) Order 1977
referred to: SI 2012/958 Sch.1

2042. Import Duties (End-Use Goods) Regulations 1977
Reg.2, amended: SI 2012/1809 Sch.1 Part 2

2122. Mink (Keeping) (Amendment) Regulations 1977
revoked (in part): SSI 2012/174 Sch.2

2126. Medicines (Pharmacy and General Sale) (Appointed Day) Order 1977
revoked: SI 2012/1916 Sch.35

2168. Medicines (Labelling) Amendment (No.2) Regulations 1977
revoked: SI 2012/1916 Sch.35

1978

40. Medicines (Fluted Bottles) Regulations 1978
revoked: SI 2012/1916 Sch.35

41. Medicines (Labelling and Advertising to the Public) Regulations 1978
applied: SI 2012/1916 Sch.32 para.3
revoked: SI 2012/1916 Sch.35
Reg.5, amended: SI 2012/1479 Sch.1 para.6

393. Social Security (Graduated Retirement Benefit) (No.2) Regulations 1978
Sch.2 para.1, varied: SI 2012/780 Art.12
Sch.2 para.2, varied: SI 2012/780 Art.12
Sch.2 para.3, varied: SI 2012/780 Art.12

1978–cont.

393. Social Security (Graduated Retirement Benefit) (No.2) Regulations 1978–*cont.*
Sch.2 para.4, varied: SI 2012/780 Art.12

448. Industrial Training (Transfer of the Activities of Establishments) Order 1978
referred to: SI 2012/958 Sch.1

1006. Medicines (Administration of Radioactive Substances) Regulations 1978
applied: SI 2012/1916 Reg.240, Sch.32 para.7
Reg.2, applied: SI 2012/1916 Reg.173
Reg.3, applied: SI 2012/1916 Sch.32 para.7
Reg.7, applied: SI 2012/1916 Sch.32 para.7
Reg.8, amended: SI 2012/1916 Sch.34 para.65
Reg.8, applied: SI 2012/1916 Sch.32 para.7

1039. Health and Safety at Work (Northern Ireland) Order 1978
applied: SI 2012/1128 Art.4
Part 1, applied: SI 2012/1128 Art.4
Part I, applied: SI 2012/1128 Art.4
Part II, applied: SI 2012/1128 Art.4
Part III, applied: SI 2012/1128 Art.4
Part IV, applied: SI 2012/1128 Art.4
Art, applied: SI 2012/1128 Art.4
Art.1, applied: SI 2012/1128 Art.4
Art.2, applied: SI 2012/1128 Art.4
Art.3, applied: SI 2012/1128 Art.4
Art.4, applied: SI 2012/1128 Art.4
Art.(5), applied: SI 2012/1128 Art.4
Art.5, applied: SI 2012/1128 Art.4
Art.6, applied: SI 2012/1128 Art.4
Art.6(b), applied: SI 2012/1128 Art.4
Art.6, applied: SI 2012/1128 Art.4
Art.7, applied: SI 2012/1128 Art.4
Art.8, applied: SI 2012/1128 Art.4
Art.9, applied: SI 2012/1128 Art.4
Art.12, applied: SI 2012/1128 Art.4
Art.13, applied: SI 2012/1128 Art.4
Art.15, applied: SI 2012/1128 Art.4
Art.16, applied: SI 2012/1128 Art.4
Art.17, applied: SI 2012/1128 Art.4
Art.17(4), applied: SI 2012/1128 Art.4
Art.17(5), applied: SI 2012/1128 Art.4
Art.17(6), applied: SI 2012/1128 Art.4
Art.18, applied: SI 2012/1128 Art.4
Art.20, applied: SI 2012/1128 Art.4
Art.21, applied: SI 2012/1128 Art.4
Art.22, applied: SI 2012/1128 Art.4
Art.23, applied: SI 2012/1128 Art.4
Art.24, applied: SI 2012/1128 Art.4
Art.25, applied: SI 2012/1128 Art.4
Art.26, applied: SI 2012/1128 Art.4
Art.27, applied: SI 2012/1128 Art.4
Art.28, applied: SI 2012/1128 Art.4
Art.29, applied: SI 2012/1128 Art.4
Art.29A, applied: SI 2012/1128 Art.4
Art.30, applied: SI 2012/1128 Art.4
Art.31, applied: SI 2012/1128 Art.4
Art.32, applied: SI 2012/1128 Art.4
Art.33, applied: SI 2012/1128 Art.4
Art.34, applied: SI 2012/1128 Art.4
Art.34A, applied: SI 2012/1128 Art.4
Art.35, applied: SI 2012/1128 Art.4
Art.36, applied: SI 2012/1128 Art.4
Art.37, applied: SI 2012/1128 Art.4
Art.38, applied: SI 2012/1128 Art.4
Art.39, applied: SI 2012/1128 Art.4
Art.40, applied: SI 2012/1128 Art.4
Art.40(2), applied: SI 2012/1128 Art.4

1978– cont.

1039. Health and Safety at Work (Northern Ireland) Order 1978– *cont.*
Art.40(4), applied: SI 2012/ 1128 Art.4
Art.43, applied: SI 2012/ 1128 Art.4
Art.44, applied: SI 2012/ 1128 Art.4
Art.45, applied: SI 2012/ 1128 Art.4
Art.46, applied: SI 2012/ 1128 Art.4
Art.46(1), applied: SI 2012/ 1128 Art.4
Art.47A, applied: SI 2012/ 1128 Art.4
Art.48, applied: SI 2012/ 1128 Art.4
Art.49, applied: SI 2012/ 1128 Art.4
Art.51, applied: SI 2012/ 1128 Art.4
Art.53, applied: SI 2012/ 1128 Art.4
Art.(54, applied: SI 2012/ 1128 Art.4
Art.54, applied: SI 2012/ 1128 Art.4
Art.54(5), applied: SI 2012/ 1128 Art.4
Art.(55, applied: SI 2012/ 1128 Art.4
Art.55, applied: SI 2012/ 1128 Art.4
Art.55(2), applied: SI 2012/ 1128 Art.4
Art.56, applied: SI 2012/ 1128 Art.4
Art.71, applied: SI 2012/ 1128 Art.4
Art.105, applied: SI 2012/ 1128 Art.4
para, applied: SI 2012/ 1128 Art.4
para(.13), applied: SI 2012/ 1128 Art.4
para(.15), applied: SI 2012/ 1128 Art.4
para(.2), applied: SI 2012/ 1128 Art.4
para(.6), applied: SI 2012/ 1128 Art.4
para.1(1), applied: SI 2012/ 1128 Art.4
r.5, applied: SI 2012/ 1128 Art.4
Reg.3, applied: SI 2012/ 1128 Art.4
Reg.35, applied: SI 2012/ 1128 Art.4
Reg.36, applied: SI 2012/ 1128 Art.4
Reg.37, applied: SI 2012/ 1128 Art.4
s.1, applied: SI 2012/ 1128 Art.4
s.2, applied: SI 2012/ 1128 Art.4
s.5, applied: SI 2012/ 1128 Art.4
s.27, applied: SI 2012/ 1128 Art.4
s.46, applied: SI 2012/ 1128 Art.4
s.55, applied: SI 2012/ 1128 Art.4
Sch.1, applied: SI 2012/ 1128 Art.4
Sch.2, applied: SI 2012/ 1128 Art.4
Sch.3, applied: SI 2012/ 1128 Art.4
Sch.3A, applied: SI 2012/ 1128 Art.4
Sch.4, applied: SI 2012/ 1128 Art.4
Sch.5, applied: SI 2012/ 1128 Art.4
Sch.6, applied: SI 2012/ 1128 Art.4
Sch.7, applied: SI 2012/ 1128 Art.4

1045. Matrimonial Causes (Northern Ireland) Order 1978
Art.23A, applied: SI 2012/ 687 Sch.4 para.3
Art.27B, applied: SI 2012/ 687 Sch.4 para.3
Art.27C, applied: SI 2012/ 687 Sch.4 para.3
Art.27D, applied: SI 2012/ 687 Sch.4 para.3

1138. Medicines (Intra-Uterine Contraceptive Devices) (Appointed Day) Order 1978
revoked: SI 2012/ 1916 Sch.35

1140. Medicines (Licensing of Intra-Uterine Contraceptive Devices) (Miscellaneous Amendments) Regulations 1978
revoked: SI 2012/ 1916 Sch.35

1211. Pensions Increase (Annual Review) Order 1978
applied: SI 2012/ 782 Art.3, Art.4

1225. Industrial Training (Transfer of the Activities of Establishments) (No.2) Order 1978
referred to: SI 2012/ 958 Sch.1

1978– cont.

1408. Double Taxation Relief (Taxes on Income) (Switzerland) Order 1978
Sch.1, referred to: SI 2012/ 3079 Art.2

1579. Jurors Allowances Regulations 1978
Reg.7A, added: SI 2012/ 1826 Reg.3

1643. Industrial Training (Transfer of the Activities of Establishments) (No.3) Order 1978
referred to: SI 2012/ 958 Sch.1

1689. Social Security (Categorisation of Earners) Regulations 1978
Reg.1, amended: SI 2012/ 816 Reg.3
Sch.1, see *ITV Services Ltd v Revenue and Customs Commissioners* [2012] UKUT 47 (TCC), [2012] S.T.C. 1213 (UT (Tax)), Sales, J.
Sch.1 Part I, amended: SI 2012/ 816 Reg.4
Sch.3, see *ITV Services Ltd v Revenue and Customs Commissioners* [2012] UKUT 47 (TCC), [2012] S.T.C. 1213 (UT (Tax)), Sales, J.
Sch.3, amended: SI 2012/ 816 Reg.5

1716. Indication of Prices (Beds) Order 1978
revoked: SI 2012/ 1816 Art.2

1723. Compressed Acetylene (Importation) Regulations 1978
applied: SI 2012/ 1652 Sch.8 Part 3

1908. Rehabilitation of Offenders (Northern Ireland) Order 1978
Art.6, amended: 2012 c.10 Sch.22 para.12

1979

597. Social Security (Overlapping Benefits) Regulations 1979
applied: SI 2012/ 2885 Sch.1 para.16, Sch.2 para.5, SI 2012/ 2886 Sch.1, SI 2012/ 3144 Sch.1 para.10, SI 2012/ 3145 Sch.1, SSI 2012/ 303 Sch.1 para.8, SSI 2012/ 319 Reg.27, Sch.1 para.6
Reg.2, amended: SI 2012/ 956 Art.2

793. Industrial Training (Transfer of the Activities of Establishments) Order 1979
referred to: SI 2012/ 958 Sch.1

1047. Pensions Increase (Review) Order 1979
applied: SI 2012/ 782 Art.3, Art.4

1114. Medicines (Exemption from Licences) (Assembly) Order 1979
revoked: SI 2012/ 1916 Sch.35

1573. Statutory Rules (Northern Ireland) Order 1979
applied: 2012 c.10 Sch.6 para.4, 2012 c.17 s.18

1669. Mink (Keeping) (Amendment) Regulations 1979
revoked (in part): SSI 2012/ 174 Sch.2

1745. Medicines (Contract Lens Fluids and Other Substances) (Exemption from Licences) Amendment Order 1979
revoked: SI 2012/ 1916 Sch.35

1759. Medicines (Contact Lens Fluids and Other Substances) (Labelling) Regulations 1979
revoked: SI 2012/ 1916 Sch.35

1980

14. Importation of Animal Products and Poultry Products Order 1980
Art.1A, added: SSI 2012/ 177 Sch.4 para.2
Sch.1, amended: SI 2012/ 1916 Sch.34 para.66

39. Otmoor Range Byelaws 1980
revoked: SI 2012/ 1478 Reg.10

397. County Courts (Northern Ireland) Order 1980
applied: SI 2012/ 1017 Reg.67

1980-cont.

918. Education (Middle Schools) Regulations 1980
revoked (in part): SI 2012/1797 Reg.2

1017. Trunk Road (Britannia Bridge, Gwynedd) (50 mph Speed Limit) Order 1980
disapplied: SI 2012/1195 Art.5

1302. Pensions Increase (Review) Order 1980
applied: SI 2012/782 Art.3, Art.4

1467. Medicines (Intra-Uterine Contraceptive Devices) (Termination of Transitional Exemptions) Order 1980
revoked: SI 2012/1916 Sch.35

1697. Rent Act 1977 (Forms etc.) Regulations 1980
Sch.1, amended: SI 2012/641 Art.2, SI 2012/702 Sch.1 para.5

1753. Industrial Training (Transfer of the Activities of Establishments) (No.2) Order 1980
referred to: SI 2012/958 Sch.1

1923. Medicines (Sale or Supply) (Miscellaneous Provisions) Regulations 1980
Reg.1, amended: SI 2012/1479 Sch.1 para.7

1924. Medicines (Pharmacy and General Sale Exemption) Order 1980
revoked: SI 2012/1916 Sch.35
Art.1, amended: SI 2012/1479 Sch.1 para.8

1947. Friendly Societies (Life Assurance Premium Relief) (Change of Rate) Regulations 1980
Reg.5, substituted: 2012 c.14 Sch.39 para.26
Reg.8, substituted: 2012 c.14 Sch.39 para.26

1948. Industrial Assurance (Life Assurance Premium Relief) (Change of Rate) Regulations 1980
Reg.5, substituted: 2012 c.14 Sch.39 para.27
Reg.8, substituted: 2012 c.14 Sch.39 para.27

1981

15. Public Bodies Land (Appropriate Ministers) Order 1981
Art.2, amended: SI 2012/641 Art.2

154. Road Traffic (Northern Ireland) Order 1981
Art.98A, amended: 2012 c.6 s.11

226. Judgments Enforcement (Northern Ireland) Order 1981
applied: SI 2012/2862 Art.7

228. Legal Aid, Advice and Assistance (Northern Ireland) Order 1981
applied: 2012 c.10 Sch.6 para.1
Art.14, amended: SI 2012/2595 Art.5

597. National Health Service (Standing Advisory Committees) Order 1981
applied: 2012 c.7 s.283

917. Health and Safety (First-Aid) Regulations 1981
Reg.3, applied: SI 2012/1652 Reg.18, Reg.20

1041. Industrial Training (Transfer of the Activities of Establishments) Order 1981
referred to: SI 2012/958 Sch.1

1115. Diseases of Animals (Northern Ireland) Order 1981
Art.38, amended: SI 2012/1916 Sch.34 para.49

1217. Pensions Increase (Review) Order 1981
applied: SI 2012/782 Art.3, Art.4

1324. Licensing (Alcohol Education and Research) Act 1981 (Commencement) Order 1981
revoked: 2012 c.7 s.278

1332. Health and Safety (Foundries etc.) (Metrication) Regulations 1981
revoked: SI 2012/1537 Reg.2

1981-cont.

1499. Building (Procedure) (Scotland) Regulations 1981
Reg.3, varied: 2012 c.11 s.12

1633. Medicines (Data Sheet) Amendment Regulations 1981
revoked: SI 2012/1916 Sch.35

1675. Magistrates Courts (Northern Ireland) Order 1981
Art.19, disapplied: SI 2012/1017 Reg.71, SI 2012/1102 Reg.7
Art.62, applied: SI 2012/3032 Sch.3 para.5

1690. Medicines (Contact Lens Fluids and Other Substances) (Termination of Transitional Exemptions) Order 1981
revoked: SI 2012/1916 Sch.35

1694. Motor Vehicles (Tests) Regulations 1981
Reg.6, amended: SI 2012/2652 Reg.3
Reg.9, amended: SI 2012/2404 Sch.3 para.3
Reg.20, amended: SI 2012/307 Reg.3

1791. Medicines (Labelling) Amendment Regulations 1981
revoked: SI 2012/1916 Sch.35

1794. Transfer of Undertakings (Protection of Employment) Regulations 1981
see *Foley v NHS Greater Glasgow and Clyde* [2012] Eq. L.R. 1019 (EAT (SC)), Lady Smith

1982

9. Secretary of State for Transport (Harbour Authorities) Charging Scheme 1982
Sch.1, amended: SI 2012/1659 Sch.3 para.29

27. Medicines (Pharmacy and General Sale-Exemption) Amendment Order 1982
revoked: SI 2012/1916 Sch.35

106. Education (Teachers) Regulations 1982
Sch.6 para.5, applied: SI 2012/762 Reg.4

719. Public Lending Right Scheme 1982 (Commencement) Order 1982
Part V para.46, amended: SI 2012/63 Art.2, SI 2012/3123 Art.2
Appendix 1, applied: SI 2012/2885 Sch.1 para.17, SSI 2012/303 Reg.36, SSI 2012/319 Reg.31
Appendix 1, referred to: SSI 2012/319 Reg.31

877. Pottery (Health etc.) (Metrication) Regulations 1982
revoked: SI 2012/1537 Reg.2

950. Education (School and Placing Information) (Scotland) Regulations 1982
revoked: SSI 2012/130 Sch.3

968. Petroleum Stocks (Amendment) Order 1982
revoked: SI 2012/2862 Art.18

1070. British Protectorates, Protected States and Protected Persons Order 1982
Art.11, applied: SI 2012/813 Sch.2 para.1

1163. Motorways Traffic (England and Wales) Regulations 1982
Reg.3, applied: SI 2012/1789 Art.7, SI 2012/1822 Art.7, SI 2012/2013 Art.3, SI 2012/2289 Art.4, SI 2012/2291 Art.4, SI 2012/2455 Art.6, SI 2012/2815 Art.8
Reg.3, referred to: SI 2012/2618 Art.7
Reg.3, varied: SI 2012/985 Reg.3, SI 2012/1865 Reg.3
Reg.4, varied: SI 2012/985 Reg.3, SI 2012/1865 Reg.3
Reg.5, applied: SI 2012/135 Art.7

1982–cont.

1163. Motorways Traffic (England and Wales) Regulations 1982–*cont.*

Reg.5, disapplied: SI 2012/31 Art.3, SI 2012/32 Art.7, SI 2012/91 Art.8, SI 2012/94 Art.5, SI 2012/112 Art.7, SI 2012/117 Art.7, SI 2012/132 Art.9, SI 2012/186 Art.7, SI 2012/211 Art.8, SI 2012/224 Art.9, SI 2012/226 Art.7, SI 2012/240 Art.6, SI 2012/250 Art.7, SI 2012/253 Art.10, SI 2012/268 Art.4, SI 2012/298 Art.3, SI 2012/369 Art.7, SI 2012/375 Art.7, SI 2012/424 Art.6, SI 2012/438 Art.5, SI 2012/449 Art.7, SI 2012/473 Art.5, SI 2012/530 Art.7, SI 2012/553 Art.4, SI 2012/554 Art.5, SI 2012/596 Art.7, SI 2012/650 Art.6, SI 2012/968 Art.4, SI 2012/1050 Art.6, SI 2012/1144 Art.5, SI 2012/1200 Art.7, SI 2012/1240 Art.5, SI 2012/1279 Art.5, SI 2012/1434 Art.7, SI 2012/1600 Art.8, SI 2012/1738 Art.8, SI 2012/1778 Art.6, SI 2012/1786 Art.5, SI 2012/2060 Art.6, SI 2012/2076 Art.7, SI 2012/2077 Art.7, SI 2012/2129 Art.5, SI 2012/2135 Art.5, SI 2012/2141 Art.7, SI 2012/2155 Art.4, SI 2012/2181 Art.7, SI 2012/2225 Art.5, SI 2012/2259 Art.5, SI 2012/2288 Art.7, SI 2012/2310 Art.5, SI 2012/2417 Art.6, SI 2012/2428 Art.9, SI 2012/2433 Art.4, SI 2012/2435 Art.8, SI 2012/2454 Art.7, SI 2012/2455 Art.6, SI 2012/2462 Art.9, SI 2012/2464 Art.5, SI 2012/2468 Art.9, SI 2012/2491 Art.4, SI 2012/2501 Art.7, SI 2012/2511 Art.7, SI 2012/2527 Art.5, SI 2012/2564 Art.5, SI 2012/2581 Art.8, SI 2012/2585 Art.7, SI 2012/2618 Art.7, SI 2012/2645 Art.3, SI 2012/2653 Art.9, SI 2012/2671 Art.6, SI 2012/2693 Art.7, SI 2012/2695 Art.6, SI 2012/2717 Art.7, SI 2012/2764 Art.4, SI 2012/2779 Art.7, SI 2012/2815 Art.8, SI 2012/2839 Art.7, SI 2012/2861 Art.5, SI 2012/2868 Art.5, SI 2012/2872 Art.6, SI 2012/2958 Art.7, SI 2012/3108 Art.9, SI 2012/3164 Art.10, SI 2012/3190 Art.5, SI 2012/3215 Art.7

Reg.5, varied: SI 2012/201 Art.5, SI 2012/270 Art.7, SI 2012/280 Art.5, SI 2012/372 Art.8, SI 2012/495 Art.7, SI 2012/566 Art.4, SI 2012/567 Art.3, SI 2012/575 Art 7, SI 2012/576 Art.10, SI 2012/661 Art.7, SI 2012/719 Art.7, SI 2012/758 Art.5, SI 2012/776 Art.7, SI 2012/778 Art.7, SI 2012/850, SI 2012/850 Art.5, SI 2012/851 Art.4, SI 2012/855 Art.7, SI 2012/902 Art.7, SI 2012/926 Art.6, SI 2012/928 Art.6, SI 2012/1001 Art.6, SI 2012/1040 Art.5, SI 2012/1048 Art.3, SI 2012/1068 Art.7, SI 2012/1071 Art.4, SI 2012/1078 Art.5, SI 2012/1091 Art.5, SI 2012/1094 Art.8, SI 2012/1152 Art.5, SI 2012/1162 Art.3, SI 2012/1163 Art.4, SI 2012/1179 Art.4, SI 2012/1213 Art.4, SI 2012/1237 Art.5, SI 2012/1239 Art.5, SI 2012/1242 Art.6, SI 2012/1247 Art.7, SI 2012/1306 Art.5, SI 2012/1308 Art.7, SI 2012/1364 Art.7, SI 2012/1370 Art.6, SI 2012/1409 Art.7, SI 2012/1437 Art.6, SI 2012/1445 Art.4, SI 2012/1448 Art.11, SI 2012/1473 Art.5, SI 2012/1481 Art.3, SI 2012/1541 Art.7, SI 2012/1543 Art.7, SI 2012/1558 Art.5, SI 2012/1593 Art.6, SI 2012/1601 Art.5, SI 2012/1611 Art.7, SI 2012/1677 Art.6, SI 2012/1722 Art.7, SI 2012/1789 Art.7, SI 2012/1822 Art.7, SI 2012/1830 Art.3, SI 2012/1855 Art.8, SI 2012/1934 Art.7, SI 2012/1937 Art.6, SI 2012/1962 Art.6, SI 2012/1973 Art.3, SI 2012/1996 Art.7, SI 2012/1998 Art.7, SI 2012/2013 Art.6, SI 2012/2019 Art.5, SI 2012/2021 Art.3, SI 2012/2036 Art.7, SI 2012/2038 Art.7, SI 2012/2098 Art.7, SI 2012/2128 Art.9, SI 2012/2176 Art.7, SI 2012/2177 Art.8, SI 2012/2185 Art.7, SI 2012/2193

1982–cont.

1163. Motorways Traffic (England and Wales) Regulations 1982–*cont.*

Reg.5, varied:–*cont.*

Art.9, SI 2012/2194 Art.7, SI 2012/2211 Art.7, SI 2012/2223 Art.3, SI 2012/2232 Art.8, SI 2012/2246 Art.3, SI 2012/2248 Art.3, SI 2012/2250 Art.3, SI 2012/2253 Art.3, SI 2012/2289 Art.4, SI 2012/2291 Art.4, SI 2012/2339 Art.13, SI 2012/2352 Art.7, SI 2012/2355 Art.7, SI 2012/2430 Art.3, SI 2012/2452 Art.4, SI 2012/2490 Art.8, SI 2012/2493 Art.6, SI 2012/2641 Art.7, SI 2012/2642 Art.5, SI 2012/2643 Art.4, SI 2012/2928 Art.6, SI 2012/2936 Art.7

Reg.5A, disapplied: SI 2012/2839 Art.7

Reg.5A, varied: SI 2012/985 Reg.3, SI 2012/1865 Reg.3

Reg.6, disapplied: SI 2012/5 Art.9, SI 2012/2141 Art.7, SI 2012/2462 Art.9, SI 2012/2468 Art.9, SI 2012/2653 Art.9, SI 2012/2839 Art.7

Reg.6, varied: SI 2012/1855 Art.8, SI 2012/2177 Art.8

Reg.7, disapplied: SI 2012/2839 Art.7

Reg.7, varied: SI 2012/985 Reg.3, SI 2012/1865 Reg.3

Reg.8, disapplied: SI 2012/2839 Art.7

Reg.9, applied: SI 2012/135 Art.7

Reg.9, disapplied: SI 2012/31 Art.3, SI 2012/32 Art.7, SI 2012/91 Art.8, SI 2012/94 Art.5, SI 2012/112 Art.7, SI 2012/117 Art.7, SI 2012/132 Art.9, SI 2012/186 Art.7, SI 2012/211 Art.8, SI 2012/224 Art.9, SI 2012/226 Art.7, SI 2012/240 Art.6, SI 2012/250 Art.7, SI 2012/253 Art.10, SI 2012/268 Art.4, SI 2012/298 Art.3, SI 2012/369 Art.7, SI 2012/375 Art.7, SI 2012/424 Art.6, SI 2012/438 Art.5, SI 2012/449 Art.7, SI 2012/473 Art.5, SI 2012/530 Art.7, SI 2012/553 Art.4, SI 2012/554 Art.5, SI 2012/596 Art.7, SI 2012/650 Art.6, SI 2012/968 Art.4, SI 2012/1050 Art.6, SI 2012/1144 Art.5, SI 2012/1200 Art.7, SI 2012/1240 Art.5, SI 2012/1279 Art.5, SI 2012/1434 Art.7, SI 2012/1600 Art.8, SI 2012/1738 Art.8, SI 2012/1778 Art.6, SI 2012/1786 Art.5, SI 2012/2060 Art.6, SI 2012/2076 Art.7, SI 2012/2077 Art.7, SI 2012/2129 Art.5, SI 2012/2135 Art.5, SI 2012/2141 Art.7, SI 2012/2155 Art.4, SI 2012/2181 Art.7, SI 2012/2225 Art.5, SI 2012/2259 Art.5, SI 2012/2288 Art.7, SI 2012/2310 Art.5, SI 2012/2417 Art.6, SI 2012/2428 Art.9, SI 2012/2433 Art.4, SI 2012/2435 Art.8, SI 2012/2454 Art.7, SI 2012/2455 Art.6, SI 2012/2462 Art.9, SI 2012/2464 Art.5, SI 2012/2468 Art.9, SI 2012/2491 Art.4, SI 2012/2501 Art.7, SI 2012/2511 Art.7, SI 2012/2527 Art.5, SI 2012/2564 Art.5, SI 2012/2581 Art.8, SI 2012/2585 Art.7, SI 2012/2618 Art.7, SI 2012/2645 Art.3, SI 2012/2653 Art.9, SI 2012/2671 Art.6, SI 2012/2693 Art.7, SI 2012/2695 Art.6, SI 2012/2717 Art.7, SI 2012/2764 Art.4, SI 2012/2779 Art.7, SI 2012/2815 Art.8, SI 2012/2839 Art.7, SI 2012/2861 Art.5, SI 2012/2868 Art.5, SI 2012/2872 Art.6, SI 2012/2958 Art.7, SI 2012/3108 Art.9, SI 2012/3164 Art.10, SI 2012/3190 Art.5, SI 2012/3215 Art.7

Reg.9, varied: SI 2012/201 Art.5, SI 2012/270 Art.7, SI 2012/280 Art.5, SI 2012/372 Art.8, SI 2012/495 Art.7, SI 2012/566 Art.4, SI 2012/567 Art.3, SI 2012/575 Art.7, SI 2012/576 Art.10, SI 2012/661 Art.7, SI 2012/719 Art.7, SI 2012/758 Art.5, SI 2012/776 Art.7, SI 2012/778 Art.7, SI 2012/850, SI 2012/850 Art.5, SI 2012/851 Art.4, SI 2012/855 Art.7, SI 2012/902 Art.7, SI 2012/926 Art.6, SI 2012/928 Art.6, SI 2012/985 Reg.3, SI

1982–cont.

1163. Motorways Traffic (England and Wales) Regulations 1982–*cont.*

Reg.9, varied:–*cont.*

2012/1001 Art.6, SI 2012/1040 Art.5, SI 2012/1048 Art.3, SI 2012/1068 Art.7, SI 2012/1071 Art.4, SI 2012/1078 Art.5, SI 2012/1091 Art.5, SI 2012/1094 Art.8, SI 2012/1152 Art.5, SI 2012/1162 Art.3, SI 2012/1163 Art.4, SI 2012/1179 Art.4, SI 2012/1213 Art.4, SI 2012/1237 Art.5, SI 2012/1239 Art.5, SI 2012/1242 Art.6, SI 2012/1247 Art.7, SI 2012/1306 Art.5, SI 2012/1308 Art.7, SI 2012/1364 Art.7, SI 2012/1370 Art.6, SI 2012/1409 Art.7, SI 2012/1437 Art.6, SI 2012/1445 Art.4, SI 2012/1448 Art.11, SI 2012/1473 Art.5, SI 2012/1481 Art.3, SI 2012/1541 Art.7, SI 2012/1543 Art.7, SI 2012/1558 Art.5, SI 2012/1593 Art.6, SI 2012/1601 Art.5, SI 2012/1611 Art.7, SI 2012/1677 Art.6, SI 2012/1722 Art.7, SI 2012/1789 Art.7, SI 2012/1822 Art.7, SI 2012/1830 Art.3, SI 2012/1855 Art.8, SI 2012/1865 Reg.3, SI 2012/1934 Art.7, SI 2012/1937 Art.6, SI 2012/1962 Art.6, SI 2012/1973 Art.3, SI 2012/1996 Art.7, SI 2012/1998 Art.7, SI 2012/2013 Art.6, SI 2012/2019 Art.5, SI 2012/2021 Art.3, SI 2012/2036 Art.7, SI 2012/2038 Art.7, SI 2012/2098 Art.7, SI 2012/2128 Art.9, SI 2012/2176 Art.7, SI 2012/2177 Art.8, SI 2012/2185 Art.7, SI 2012/2193 Art.9, SI 2012/2194 Art.7, SI 2012/2211 Art.7, SI 2012/2223 Art.3, SI 2012/2232 Art.8, SI 2012/2246 Art.3, SI 2012/2248 Art.3, SI 2012/2250 Art.3, SI 2012/2253 Art.3, SI 2012/2289 Art.4, SI 2012/2291 Art.4, SI 2012/2339 Art.13, SI 2012/2352 Art.7, SI 2012/2355 Art.7, SI 2012/2430 Art.3, SI 2012/2452 Art.4, SI 2012/2490 Art.8, SI 2012/2493 Art.6, SI 2012/2641 Art.7, SI 2012/2642 Art.5, SI 2012/2643 Art.4, SI 2012/2928 Art.6, SI 2012/2936 Art.7

Reg.12, varied: SI 2012/985 Reg.3, SI 2012/1865 Reg.3

Reg.14, varied: SI 2012/985 Reg.3, SI 2012/1865 Reg.3

Reg.16, enabled: SI 2012/2019, SI 2012/2060, SI 2012/2128, SI 2012/2135, SI 2012/2153, SI 2012/2155, SI 2012/2181, SI 2012/2185, SI 2012/2193, SI 2012/2194, SI 2012/2223, SI 2012/2246, SI 2012/2248, SI 2012/2250, SI 2012/2253, SI 2012/2259, SI 2012/2289, SI 2012/2291, SI 2012/2428, SI 2012/2430, SI 2012/2433, SI 2012/2435, SI 2012/2452, SI 2012/2454, SI 2012/2490, SI 2012/2491, SI 2012/2564, SI 2012/2618, SI 2012/2641, SI 2012/2642, SI 2012/2643, SI 2012/2645, SI 2012/2693, SI 2012/2695, SI 2012/2713, SI 2012/2717, SI 2012/2764, SI 2012/2815, SI 2012/2839, SI 2012/2868, SI 2012/2872, SI 2012/2928, SI 2012/2936, SI 2012/2958, SI 2012/3108, SI 2012/3164, SI 2012/3190, SI 2012/3215

1178. Pensions Increase (Review) Order 1982

applied: SI 2012/782 Art.3, Art.4

1489. Workmen's Compensation (Supplementation) Scheme 1982

Art.5, amended: SI 2012/833 Art.2

Sch.1 Part I, substituted: SI 2012/833 Art.3

Sch.1 Part II, substituted: SI 2012/833 Art.3

1883. Mink (Keeping) (Amendment) Regulations 1982

revoked (in part): SSI 2012/174 Sch.2

1983

497. Licensing Compensation Funds Repayment Scheme 1983

revoked: 2012 c.7 s.278

686. Personal Injuries (Civilians) Scheme 1983

Art.23, applied: SSI 2012/303 Sch.4 para.55

Art.25A, applied: SI 2012/2885 Sch.4 para.5, Sch.5 para.3, SI 2012/2886 Sch.1, SSI 2012/303 Sch.4 para.12, SSI 2012/319 Sch.2 para.5, Sch.3 para.2

Art.27, applied: SI 2012/2885 Sch.5 para.5, SI 2012/2886 Sch.1, SSI 2012/303 Sch.4 para.54, SSI 2012/319 Sch.3 para.4

Sch.3, substituted: SI 2012/670 Sch.1

Sch.4, applied: SSI 2012/319 Sch.3 para.4

Sch.4, referred to: SI 2012/2885 Sch.5 para.5, SI 2012/2886 Sch.1

Sch.4, substituted: SI 2012/670 Sch.2

713. Civil Courts Order 1983

Sch.1, amended: SI 2012/643 Art.6, SI 2012/1954 Art.5

Sch.3, amended: SI 2012/643 Art.6, SI 2012/1954 Art.5

909. Petroleum Stocks (Amendment) Order 1983

revoked: SI 2012/2862 Art.18

1264. Pensions Increase (Review) Order 1983

applied: SI 2012/782 Art.3, Art.4

1553. Consumer Credit (Agreements) Regulations 1983

Sch.1, amended: SI 2012/2798 Sch.1 para.1

Sch.8 Part I, amended: SI 2012/2798 Sch.1 para.1

1564. Consumer Credit (Settlement Information) Regulations 1983

Sch.1 para.3A, amended: SI 2012/2798 Sch.1 para.2

1649. Asbestos (Licensing) Regulations 1983

Reg.7, applied: SI 2012/632 Reg.32

1724. Medicines (Medicines Act 1968 Amendment) Regulations 1983

revoked: SI 2012/1916 Sch.35

1729. Medicines (Labelling) Amendment Regulations 1983

revoked: SI 2012/1916 Sch.35

1772. Trunk Road (A5) (Llanfairpwllgwyngyll, Gwynedd) (50 mph Speed Limit) Order 1983

disapplied: SI 2012/1195 Art.6, SI 2012/1268 Art.5

varied: SI 2012/1485 Art.11

1984

251. District Court Fees Order 1984

revoked: SSI 2012/292 Art.4

252. High Court of Justiciary Fees Order 1984

Art.2, substituted: SSI 2012/291 Art.3

Sch.1 Part 001, substituted: SSI 2012/291 Sch.1, Sch.2, Sch.3

360. District Electoral Areas Commissioner (Northern Ireland) Order 1984

Art.2, amended: SI 2012/3074 Art.2

Art.2, applied: SI 2012/3074 Art.3

Art.2, referred to: SI 2012/3074 Art.3

Art.3, amended: SI 2012/3074 Art.2

Sch.2 para.6A, added: SI 2012/3074 Art.2

552. Coroners Rules 1984

r.20, see *Allman v HM Coroner for West Sussex* [2012] EWHC 534 (Admin), (2012) 176 J.P. 285 (QBD (Admin)), Judge Anthony Thornton Q.C.

673. Medicines (Exemption from Licences) (Importation) Order 1984

revoked: SI 2012/1916 Sch.35

1984–cont.

719. Customs Duty (Community Reliefs) Order 1984
Art.2, amended: SI 2012/1809 Sch.1 Part 2

746. Value Added Tax (Imported Goods) Relief Order 1984
Sch.2 Part 8, substituted: 2012 c.14 s.199

1307. Pensions Increase (Review) Order 1984
applied: SI 2012/782 Art.3, Art.4

1719. Special Road (A55) (Llanddulas to Colwyn Bay) Regulations 1984
disapplied: SI 2012/2032 Art.8
varied: SI 2012/945 Art.13, SI 2012/1086 Art.8

1802. Gas Catalytic Heaters (Safety) Regulations 1984
revoked: SI 2012/1815 Sch.1

1817. Social Security (United States of America) Order 1984
Sch.1, varied: SI 2012/360 Sch.2

1890. Freight Containers (Safety Convention) Regulations 1984
applied: SI 2012/1652 Reg.4

1985

805. Companies (Tables A to F) Regulations 1985
see *Smith v Butler* [2012] EWCA Civ 314, [2012] Bus. L.R. 1836 (CA (Civ Div)), Arden, L.J.

824. Special Road Order (Colwyn Bay to Glan Conwy) Regulations 1985
disapplied: SI 2012/6 Art.10, SI 2012/275 Art.10
varied: SI 2012/945 Art.12, SI 2012/1086 Art.9

967. Social Security (Industrial Injuries) (Prescribed Diseases) Regulations 1985
Sch.1 Part I, amended: SI 2012/647 Reg.2, SI 2012/1634 Reg.2

1205. Credit Unions (Northern Ireland) Order 1985
applied: 2012 c.21 s.50

1540. Medicines (Products Other Than Veterinary Drugs) (General Sale List) Amendment Order 1985
revoked: SI 2012/1916 Sch.35

1558. Medicines (Labelling) Amendment Regulations 1985
revoked: SI 2012/1916 Sch.35

1575. Pensions Increase (Review) Order 1985
applied: SI 2012/782 Art.3, Art.4

1662. Industrial Training (Transfer of the Activities of Establishments) Order 1985
referred to: SI 2012/958 Sch.1

2008. Medicines (Labelling) and (Leaflets for Veterinary Drugs) (Amendment) Regulations 1985
revoked: SI 2012/1916 Sch.35

1986

17. Trunk Road (A55/A494) (Ewloe Interchange, Clwyd) (De-restriction) Order 1986
varied: SI 2012/945 Art.16

26. Textile Products (Indications of Fibre Content) Regulations 1986
revoked: SI 2012/1102 Sch.1

183. Removal and Disposal of Vehicles Regulations 1986
Reg.3, amended: SI 2012/2277 Reg.3, Reg.4
Reg.4, amended: SI 2012/2277 Reg.5
Reg.5, amended: SI 2012/2277 Reg.6
Reg.5A, see *Shiva Ltd v Transport for London* [2011] EWCA Civ 1189, [2012] R.T.R. 13 (CA (Civ Div)), Lord Neuberger (M.R.)

1986–cont.

590. Value Added Tax Tribunals Rules 1986
see *Atlantic Electronics Ltd v Revenue and Customs Commissioners* [2012] UKUT 45 (TCC), [2012] S.T.C. 931 (UT (Tax)), Warren, J.
r.13, see *New Miles Ltd v Revenue and Customs Commissioners* [2012] UKFTT 33 (TC), [2012] S.F.T.D. 695 (FTT (Tax)), Judge Peter Kempster
r.29, see *Atlantic Electronics Ltd v Revenue and Customs Commissioners* [2012] UKUT 45 (TCC), [2012] S.T.C. 931 (UT (Tax)), Warren, J.

594. Education and Libraries (Northern Ireland) Order 1986
Art.50, applied: SI 2012/3145 Sch.1

595. Mental Health (Northern Ireland) Order 1986
applied: SSI 2012/303 Reg.5, SSI 2012/319 Reg.5
Art.4, applied: SI 2012/2885 Sch.1 para.5, SI 2012/2886 Sch.1, SI 2012/3144 Reg.24, SI 2012/3145 Sch.1
Art.12, applied: SI 2012/2885 Sch.1 para.5, SI 2012/2886 Sch.1, SI 2012/3144 Reg.24, SI 2012/3145 Sch.1

599. Air Navigation (Aircraft and Aircraft Engine Emissions) Order 1986
applied: 2012 c.19 Sch.6 para.4

603. Trunk Road (A5) (At its Junction with M42 Moturway) (De-Restriction) Order 1986
revoked: SI 2012/1125 Art.3

939. Value Added Tax (Small Non-Commercial Consignments) Relief Order 1986
Art.3, amended: SI 2012/3060 Art.2

952. Insolvency Practitioners Tribunal (Conduct of Investigations) Rules 1986
applied: SI 2012/3013 Sch.1 para.2

975. National Health Service (General Ophthalmic Services) Regulations 1986
Reg.7D, varied: 2012 c.11 s.12
Reg.9D, varied: 2012 c.11 s.12

1024. Trunk Roads (A38) (Branston Interchange) (De-Restriction) Order 1986
revoked: SI 2012/2034 Art.5

1032. Companies (Northern Ireland) Order 1986
Art.264, applied: SI 2012/1741 Art.24

1078. Road Vehicles (Construction and Use) Regulations 1986
Sch.7B Part I para.7, amended: SI 2012/1404 Reg.4

1116. Pensions Increase (Review) Order 1986
applied: SI 2012/782 Art.3, Art.4

1335. Costs in Criminal Cases (General) Regulations 1986
applied: SI 2012/1726 r.10.5
see *R. v Henrys Solicitors* [2012] EWCA Crim 1480, [2012] 6 Costs L.O. 858 (CA (Crim Div)), Pitchford, L.J.
Part II, applied: SI 2012/1726 r.76.1
Part IIA, applied: SI 2012/1726 r.76.1
Part IIB, applied: SI 2012/1726 r.76.1
Reg.3, applied: SI 2012/1726 r.76.1, r.76.8
Reg.3B, applied: SI 2012/1726 r.68.1, r.63.1
Reg.3C, applied: SI 2012/1726 r.63.1, r.68.1
Reg.3D, applied: SI 2012/1726 r.76.1
Reg.3F, applied: SI 2012/1726 r.76.1, r.68.1, r.76.10, r.63.1
Reg.3H, applied: SI 2012/1726 r.63.1, r.68.1
Reg.3I, applied: SI 2012/1726 r.76.1
Reg.4, applied: SI 2012/1726 r.76.4
Reg.4A, added: SI 2012/1804 Reg.5
Reg.4A, applied: SI 2012/1726 r.76.4
Reg.5, applied: SI 2012/1726 r.76.4
Reg.6, applied: SI 2012/1726 r.76.4

1986– cont.

1335. Costs in Criminal Cases (General) Regulations 1986– cont.
Reg.7, applied: SI 2012/1726 r.76.4
Reg.7, substituted: SI 2012/1804 Reg.6
Reg.7, see *Watson v HM Courts and Tribunals Service National Taxing Team* [2012] EWHC 2865 (Admin), [2012] 6 Costs L.R. 1129 (DC), Laws, L.J.
Reg.8, applied: SI 2012/1726 r.76.4
Reg.9, applied: SI 2012/1726 r.76.4
Reg.10, applied: SI 2012/1726 r.76.4
Reg.11, applied: SI 2012/1726 r.76.4
Reg.12, applied: SI 2012/1726 r.76.4
Reg.14, applied: SI 2012/1726 r.76.4, r.76.5
Reg.20, amended: SI 2012/1804 Reg.7

1654. Trunk Road (A5 Watling Street, Brownhills) (40 MPH Speed Limit) Order 1986
revoked: SI 2012/2735 Art.7

1700. Medicines Act 1968 (Hearings by Persons Appointed) (Scotland) Rules 1986
r.2, amended: SI 2012/1916 Sch.34 para.67
r.2, revoked (in part): SI 2012/1916 Sch.34 para.67

1711. Stamp Duty Reserve Tax Regulations 1986
Sch.1 Part I, amended: SI 2012/886 Reg.4
Sch.1 Part II, amended: SI 2012/886 Reg.4
Sch.1 Part II, revoked: SI 2012/886 Reg.4

1761. Medicines Act 1968 (Hearings by Persons Appointed) Rules 1986
r.2, amended: SI 2012/1916 Sch.34 para.68
r.2, revoked (in part): SI 2012/1916 Sch.34 para.68

1764. Insolvency Practitioners (Recognised Professional Bodies) Order 1986
applied: SI 2012/3013 Sch.1 para.2

1911. Animals (Scientific Procedures) (Procedure for Representations) Rules 1986
r.3, amended: SI 2012/3039 Reg.30

1915. Insolvency (Scotland) Rules 1986
Part I r.1.6, amended: SI 2012/2404 Sch.3 para.4
Part 2 r.2.36H, amended: SI 2012/2404 Sch.3 para.4
Part 2 r.2.36J, amended: SI 2012/2404 Sch.3 para.4
Part 4 r.4.48, amended: SI 2012/2404 Sch.3 para.4
Part 4 r.4.50, amended: SI 2012/2404 Sch.3 para.4

1925. Insolvency Rules 1986
applied: SI 2012/3013 Sch.1 para.2
see *Assured Logistics Solutions Ltd, Re* [2011] EWHC 3029 (Ch), [2012] B.C.C. 541 (Ch D (Birmingham)), Judge Purle Q.C.; see *Hayes v Hayes* [2012] EWHC 1240 (Ch), [2012] B.P.I.R. 739 (Ch D), Judge Pelling Q.C.; see *Orrick, Herrington & Sutcliffe (Europe) LLP v Frohlich* [2012] B.P.I.R. 169 (Ch D), Deputy Registrar Schaffer; see *Virtualpurple Professional Services Ltd, Re* [2011] EWHC 3487 (Ch), [2012] B.C.C. 254 (Ch D (Companies Ct)), Norris, J.
Part 2 r.2.55, amended: SI 2012/2404 Sch.3 para.5
Part 2 r.2.57, amended: SI 2012/2404 Sch.3 para.5
Part 3 r.3.21, amended: SI 2012/2404 Sch.3 para.5
Part 3 r.3.23, amended: SI 2012/2404 Sch.3 para.5
Part 4 r.4.159, amended: SI 2012/2404 Sch.3 para.5
Part 4 r.4.161, amended: SI 2012/2404 Sch.3 para.5
Part 5A r.5A.2, amended: SI 2012/469 r.3
Part 6 r.6.156, amended: SI 2012/2404 Sch.3 para.5
Part 6 r.6.158, amended: SI 2012/2404 Sch.3 para.5
Part 6 r.6.223, amended: SI 2012/469 r.3
Part 12 r.12.3, amended: SI 2012/469 r.3
Part 13 r.13.7, referred to: SI 2012/2421 Sch.3 para.7

1986– cont.

1925. Insolvency Rules 1986– cont.
Pt 2, see *Assured Logistics Solutions Ltd, Re* [2011] EWHC 3029 (Ch), [2012] B.C.C. 541 (Ch D (Birmingham)), Judge Purle Q.C.; see *Bezier Acquisitions Ltd, Re* [2011] EWHC 3299 (Ch), [2012] Bus. L.R. 636 (Ch D (Companies Ct)), Norris, J.; see *MF Global Overseas Ltd (In Administration), Re* [2012] EWHC 1091 (Ch), [2012] B.C.C. 490 (Ch D (Companies Ct)), Mann, J.; see *National Westminster Bank Plc v Msaada Group* [2011] EWHC 3423 (Ch), [2012] B.C.C. 226 (Ch D), Warren, J.
Pt 4, see *MK Airlines Ltd, Re* [2012] EWHC 1018 (Ch), [2012] 3 All E.R. 781 (Ch D (Companies Ct)), Sir Andrew Morritt (Chancellor)
Pt 5 r.5.22, see *National Westminster Bank Plc v Yadgaroff* [2011] EWHC 3711 (Ch), [2012] B.P.I.R. 371 (Ch D), Norris, J.
Pt 5 r.5.23, see *National Westminster Bank Plc v Kapoor* [2011] EWCA Civ 1083, [2012] 1 All E.R. 1201 (CA (Civ Div)), Pill, L.J.
Pt 7, see *De Toucy v Bonhams 1793 Ltd* [2011] EWHC 3809 (Ch), [2012] B.P.I.R. 793 (Ch D), Vos, J.
r.2.67, see *Bickland Ltd, Re* [2012] EWHC 706 (Ch), [2012] 2 B.C.L.C. 751 (Ch D), Mann, J.
r.4.79, see *MG Rover Dealer Properties Ltd v Hunt* [2012] B.P.I.R. 590 (Ch D (Companies Ct)), Registrar Baister
r.4.96, see *JT Frith Ltd, Re* [2012] EWHC 196 (Ch), [2012] B.C.C. 634 (Ch D (Leeds)), Judge Keyser Q.C.
r.4.218, see *Bickland Ltd, Re* [2012] EWHC 706 (Ch), [2012] 2 B.C.L.C. 751 (Ch D), Mann, J.
r.6.5, see *Davies v Barnes Webster & Sons Ltd* [2011] EWHC 2560 (Ch), [2012] B.P.I.R. 97 (Ch D), Mann, J.; see *Inbakumar v United Trust Bank Ltd* [2012] EWHC 845 (Ch), [2012] B.P.I.R. 758 (Ch D), Vos, J.; see *Mahon v FBN Bank (UK) Ltd* [2011] EWHC 1432 (Ch), [2012] 2 B.C.L.C. 83 (Ch D (Birmingham)), Judge Simon Barker Q.C.
r.7.6A, see *Arif v Zar* [2012] EWCA Civ 986, [2012] B.P.I.R. 948 (CA (Civ Div)), Thorpe, L.J.
r.7.15, see *Arif v Zar* [2012] EWCA Civ 986, [2012] B.P.I.R. 948 (CA (Civ Div)), Thorpe, L.J.
r.7.44, see *De Toucy v Bonhams 1793 Ltd* [2011] EWHC 3809 (Ch), [2012] B.P.I.R. 793 (Ch D), Vos, J.
r.7.51A, see *Arif v Zar* [2012] EWCA Civ 986, [2012] B.P.I.R. 948 (CA (Civ Div)), Thorpe, L.J.
r.7.55, see *Assured Logistics Solutions Ltd, Re* [2011] EWHC 3029 (Ch), [2012] B.C.C. 541 (Ch D (Birmingham)), Judge Purle Q.C.
r.8.1, see *Horler v Rubin* [2012] EWCA Civ 4, [2012] B.P.I.R. 749 (CA (Civ Div)), Mummery, L.J.
r.8.3, see *Horler v Rubin* [2012] EWCA Civ 4, [2012] B.P.I.R. 749 (CA (Civ Div)), Mummery, L.J.
r.12A.5, see *Bezier Acquisitions Ltd, Re* [2011] EWHC 3299 (Ch), [2012] Bus. L.R. 636 (Ch D (Companies Ct)), Norris, J.
r.12.3, see *Hayes v Hayes* [2012] EWHC 1240 (Ch), [2012] B.P.I.R. 739 (Ch D), Judge Pelling Q.C.
r.12.7, see *Assured Logistics Solutions Ltd, Re* [2011] EWHC 3029 (Ch), [2012] B.C.C. 541 (Ch D (Birmingham)), Judge Purle Q.C.
r.12.17, see *Assured Logistics Solutions Ltd, Re* [2011] EWHC 3029 (Ch), [2012] B.C.C. 541 (Ch D (Birmingham)), Judge Purle Q.C.

1986– cont.

1925. Insolvency Rules 1986– *cont.*
r.13.4, see *Bezier Acquisitions Ltd, Re* [2011] EWHC 3299 (Ch), [2012] Bus. L.R. 636 (Ch D (Companies Ct)), Norris, J.
r.13.12, see *Bloom v Pensions Regulator* [2011] EWCA Civ 1124, [2012] Bus. L.R. 818 (CA (Civ Div)), Laws, L.J.
Sch.4, see *Assured Logistics Solutions Ltd, Re* [2011] EWHC 3029 (Ch), [2012] B.C.C. 541 (Ch D (Birmingham)), Judge Purle Q.C.

1953. Air Navigation (Investigation of Air Accidents involving Civil and Military Aircraft or Installations) Regulations 1986
applied: 2012 c.19 Sch.6 para.4

1960. Statutory Maternity Pay (General) Regulations 1986
Reg.6, amended: SI 2012/ 780 Art.10

1996. Insolvency Proceedings (Monetary Limits) Order 1986
applied: SI 2012/ 3013 Sch.1 para.2

2092. Local Government Reorganisation (Preservation of Right to Buy) Order 1986
Sch.1 Part I para.42, amended: SI 2012/ 1659 Sch.3 para.30

2128. Passenger and Goods Vehicles (Recording Equipment) (Approval of fitters and workshops) (Fees) Regulations 1986
Reg.2, amended: SI 2012/ 1502 Reg.5

2148. Inward Processing Relief Arrangements (Customs Duties and Agricultural Levies) Regulations 1986
Reg.2, amended: SI 2012/ 1809 Sch.1 Part 2

2194. Housing (Right to Buy) (Prescribed Forms) Regulations 1986
Sch.1, amended: SI 2012/ 702 Sch.1 para.3

1987

37. Dangerous Substances in Harbour Areas Regulations 1987
Part IX, applied: SI 2012/ 1652 Reg.11

130. Pensions Increase (Review) Order 1987
applied: SI 2012/ 782 Art.3, Art.4

133. Authorised Officers (Meat Inspection) Regulations 1987
revoked (in part): SI 2012/ 690 Reg.2, SI 2012/ 826 Reg.2

250. Social Security (Notification of Deaths) Regulations 1987
revoked: SI 2012/ 1604 Reg.6

257. Police Pensions Regulations 1987
Reg.1, amended: SI 2012/ 2811 Reg.4
Reg.2, substituted: SI 2012/ 640 Reg.2, SSI 2012/ 71 Reg.2
Reg.3, amended: SI 2012/ 2811 Reg.4
Reg.5A, added: SI 2012/ 3057 Reg.2
Reg.19, amended: SI 2012/ 2811 Reg.3
Sch.A, amended: SI 2012/ 2954 Art.4
Sch.C Part I para.1, amended: SI 2012/ 2811 Reg.4
Sch.D Part I para.1, amended: SI 2012/ 2811 Reg.4
Sch.D Part I para.3, amended: SI 2012/ 2811 Reg.4
Sch.J Part I para.2, substituted: SI 2012/ 2811 Reg.4
Sch.J Part VII para.5, amended: SI 2012/ 2811 Reg.4
Sch.J Part IV para.8, amended: SI 2012/ 2811 Reg.4

299. Prosecution of Offences (Custody Time Limits) Regulations 1987
applied: SI 2012/ 1726 r.3.11
referred to: SI 2012/ 1726 r.19.1

1987– cont.

299. Prosecution of Offences (Custody Time Limits) Regulations 1987– *cont.*
see *O'Dowd v United Kingdom (7390/07)* (2012) 54 E.H.R.R. 8 (ECHR), Judge Garlicki (President)
Reg.4, applied: SI 2012/ 1726 r.19.16
Reg.5, amended: SI 2012/ 1344 Reg.2
Reg.5, applied: SI 2012/ 1726 r.19.16
Reg.7, referred to: SI 2012/ 1726 r.19.16

460. Audit (Northern Ireland) Order 1987
applied: SI 2012/ 1128 Art.4

516. Stamp Duty (Exempt Instruments) Regulations 1987
revoked: 2012 c.14 Sch.39 para.4

530. Income Tax (Entertainers and Sportsmen) Regulations 1987
Reg.2, amended: SI 2012/ 1359 Reg.2
Reg.4, amended: SI 2012/ 1359 Reg.2

764. Town and Country Planning (Use Classes) Order 1987
see *Hertfordshire CC v Secretary of State for Communities and Local Government* [2012] EWHC 277 (Admin), [2012] J.P.L. 836 (QBD (Admin)), Ouseley, J.; see *R. (on the application of Harbige) v Secretary of State for Communities and Local Government* [2012] EWHC 1128 (Admin), [2012] J.P.L. 1245 (QBD (Admin)), Ouseley, J.
Sch.1, referred to: SI 2012/ 2920 Reg.6
Sch.1 Pt 3 para.3, see *Moore v Secretary of State for Communities and Local Government* [2012] EWCA Civ 1202, [2012] 46 E.G. 122 (CA (Civ Div)), Lord Neuberger (M.R.)

767. (A52) Nottingham West of Grantham Trunk Road (Bingham Bypass) (De-Restriction) Order 1987
revoked: SI 2012/ 1099 Art.3

768. (A52) Nottingham &mdash West of Grantham Trunk Road (Bingham Bypass) (24-Hour Main Carriageway Clearway) Order 1987
revoked: SI 2012/ 1093 Art.7

773. Patronage (Benefices) Rules 1987
applied: SI 2012/ 1846 Sch.1 Part TABLEf

1110. Personal Pension Schemes (Disclosure of Information) Regulations 1987
Reg.1, amended: SI 2012/ 1817 Sch.1 para.1

1337. Bunk Beds (Entrapment Hazards) (Safety) Regulations 1987
revoked: SI 2012/ 1815 Sch.1

1832. AIDS (Control) (Northern Ireland) Order 1987
revoked: 2012 c.7 s.59

1967. Income Support (General) Regulations 1987
Reg.2, amended: SI 2012/ 757 Reg.3, SI 2012/ 956 Art.3, SI 2012/ 2575 Reg.2
Reg.2, applied: SI 2012/ 2886 Sch.1, SI 2012/ 3145 Sch.1
Reg.4ZA, applied: SI 2012/ 2885 Sch.1 para.25, SI 2012/ 2886 Sch.1, SI 2012/ 3144 Sch.1 para.19, SSI 2012/ 303 Reg.28, SSI 2012/ 319 Reg.29
Reg.6, applied: SI 2012/ 2886 Sch.1, SI 2012/ 3145 Sch.1, SSI 2012/ 303 Reg.68
Reg.13, amended: SI 2012/ 757 Reg.14, SI 2012/ 913 Reg.3
Reg.15, varied: SI 2012/ 780 Art.18
Reg.17, referred to: SI 2012/ 780 Art.17
Reg.18, referred to: SI 2012/ 780 Art.17
Reg.21, referred to: SI 2012/ 780 Art.17
Reg.21AA, amended: SI 2012/ 2587 Reg.2

1987– cont.

1967. Income Support (General) Regulations 1987– *cont.*

Reg.21AA, see *Secretary of State for Work and Pensions v Elmi* [2011] EWCA Civ 1403, [2012] P.T.S.R. 780 (CA (Civ Div)), Maurice Kay, L.J.

Reg.22A, referred to: SI 2012/ 780 Sch.4

Reg.29, amended: SI 2012/ 2575 Reg.2

Reg.51, applied: SI 2012/ 2886 Sch.1, SI 2012/ 3145 Sch.1, SSI 2012/ 303 Reg.49

Reg.61, amended: SI 2012/ 956 Art.3

Sch.1 B, substituted: SI 2012/ 757 Reg.11

Sch.1 B para.1, applied: SI 2012/ 874 Sch.1 para.1

Sch.1 B para.1, substituted: SI 2012/ 874 Reg.2

Sch.1 B para.2, disapplied: SI 2012/ 874 Sch.1 para.1

Sch.1 B para.2A, disapplied: SI 2012/ 874 Sch.1 para.1

Sch.1 B para.3, disapplied: SI 2012/ 874 Sch.1 para.1

Sch.1 B para.4, disapplied: SI 2012/ 874 Sch.1 para.1

Sch.1 B para.5, disapplied: SI 2012/ 874 Sch.1 para.1

Sch.1 B para.6, disapplied: SI 2012/ 874 Sch.1 para.1

Sch.1 B para.7, applied: SI 2012/ 2885 Sch.1 para.25, SI 2012/ 2886 Sch.1, SI 2012/ 3144 Sch.1 para.19, SI 2012/ 3145 Sch.1, SSI 2012/ 303 Reg.28, SSI 2012/ 319 Reg.29

Sch.1 B para.7, disapplied: SI 2012/ 874 Sch.1 para.1

Sch.1 B para.8, disapplied: SI 2012/ 874 Sch.1 para.1

Sch.1 B para.9, disapplied: SI 2012/ 874 Sch.1 para.1

Sch.1 B para.9A, disapplied: SI 2012/ 874 Sch.1 para.1

Sch.1 B para.10, disapplied: SI 2012/ 874 Sch.1 para.1

Sch.1 B para.11, disapplied: SI 2012/ 874 Sch.1 para.1

Sch.1 B para.12, disapplied: SI 2012/ 874 Sch.1 para.1

Sch.1 B para.13, disapplied: SI 2012/ 874 Sch.1 para.1

Sch.1 B para.14, applied: SI 2012/ 2885 Sch.1 para.25, SI 2012/ 2886 Sch.1, SI 2012/ 3144 Sch.1 para.19, SI 2012/ 3145 Sch.1, SSI 2012/ 303 Reg.28, SSI 2012/ 319 Reg.29

Sch.1 B para.14, disapplied: SI 2012/ 874 Sch.1 para.1

Sch.1 B para.14A, disapplied: SI 2012/ 874 Sch.1 para.1

Sch.1 B para.14B, amended: SI 2012/ 757 Reg.3

Sch.1 B para.14B, disapplied: SI 2012/ 874 Sch.1 para.1

Sch.1 B para.15, disapplied: SI 2012/ 874 Sch.1 para.1

Sch.1 B para.15A, amended: SI 2012/ 757 Reg.11

Sch.1 B para.15A, disapplied: SI 2012/ 874 Sch.1 para.1

Sch.1 B para.15A, revoked (in part): SI 2012/ 757 Reg.11

Sch.1 B para.16, disapplied: SI 2012/ 874 Sch.1 para.1

Sch.1 B para.16A, disapplied: SI 2012/ 874 Sch.1 para.1

Sch.1 B para.17, disapplied: SI 2012/ 874 Sch.1 para.1

Sch.1 B para.18, disapplied: SI 2012/ 874 Sch.1 para.1

Sch.1 B para.18A, disapplied: SI 2012/ 874 Sch.1 para.1

Sch.1 B para.19, disapplied: SI 2012/ 874 Sch.1 para.1

Sch.1 B para.20, disapplied: SI 2012/ 874 Sch.1 para.1

Sch.1 B para.21, disapplied: SI 2012/ 874 Sch.1 para.1

1987– cont.

1967. Income Support (General) Regulations 1987– *cont.*

Sch.1 B para.22, disapplied: SI 2012/ 874 Sch.1 para.1

Sch.1 B para.23, disapplied: SI 2012/ 874 Sch.1 para.1

Sch.1 B para.24, disapplied: SI 2012/ 874 Sch.1 para.1

Sch.1 B para.25, disapplied: SI 2012/ 874 Sch.1 para.1

Sch.1 B para.26, disapplied: SI 2012/ 874 Sch.1 para.1

Sch.1 B para.27, disapplied: SI 2012/ 874 Sch.1 para.1

Sch.1 B para.28, disapplied: SI 2012/ 874 Sch.1 para.1

Sch.1 B para.28, amended: SI 2012/ 956 Art.3

Sch.1 B para.28, disapplied: SI 2012/ 874 Sch.1 para.1

Sch.2 Part I para.1, substituted: SI 2012/ 780 Sch.2

Sch.2 Part I para.2, substituted: SI 2012/ 780 Sch.2

Sch.2 Part III para.13A, referred to: SI 2012/ 780 Art.17

Sch.2 Part III para.14, referred to: SI 2012/ 780 Art.17

Sch.2 Part IV para.15, substituted: SI 2012/ 780 Sch.3

Sch.3 para.1, amended: SI 2012/ 913 Reg.3

Sch.3 para.3, referred to: SI 2012/ 780 Art.17

Sch.3 para.4, see *Ahmed v Secretary of State for Work and Pensions* [2011] EWCA Civ 1186, [2012] H.L.R. 7 (CA (Civ Div)), Longmore, L.J.

Sch.3 para.5, referred to: SI 2012/ 780 Sch.4

Sch.3 para.6, referred to: SI 2012/ 780 Sch.4

Sch.3 para.7, referred to: SI 2012/ 780 Sch.4

Sch.3 para.8, referred to: SI 2012/ 780 Sch.4

Sch.3 para.10, referred to: SI 2012/ 780 Sch.4

Sch.3 para.11, referred to: SI 2012/ 780 Sch.4

Sch.3 para.12, referred to: SI 2012/ 780 Sch.4

Sch.3 para.18, amended: SI 2012/ 780 Art.17

Sch.7, referred to: SI 2012/ 780 Sch.4

Sch.8 para.15A, substituted: SI 2012/ 2575 Reg.2

Sch.9 para.4A, amended: SI 2012/ 757 Reg.3

Sch.10 para.7, applied: SI 2012/ 2885 Sch.6 para.22, SI 2012/ 2886 Sch.1, SSI 2012/ 319 Sch.4 para.22

Sch.10 para.44, see *HM (A Child), Re* [2012] Med. L.R. 449 (CP), Judge Hazel Marshall Q.C.

1968. Social Security (Claims and Payments) Regulations 1987

applied: SI 2012/ 2885 Sch.8 para.6, SI 2012/ 2886 Sch.1, SSI 2012/ 319 Reg.62

Reg.21, amended: SI 2012/ 757 Reg.15

Reg.21, revoked (in part): SI 2012/ 757 Reg.15

Reg.32, amended: SI 2012/ 824 Reg.2

Reg.32, revoked (in part): SI 2012/ 824 Reg.2

Reg.33, applied: SI 2012/ 2885 Sch.8 para.4, SI 2012/ 2886 Sch.1, SI 2012/ 3145 Sch.1

Reg.38, amended: SI 2012/ 757 Reg.15

Sch.9 para.1, amended: SI 2012/ 700 Sch.1 para.10, SI 2012/ 757 Reg.15

Sch.9 para.4, amended: SI 2012/ 819 Reg.5

Sch.9 para.8, amended: SI 2012/ 757 Reg.15

Sch.9A para.7, amended: SI 2012/ 644 Reg.2

Sch.9A para.8, amended: SI 2012/ 702 Sch.1 para.6

Sch.9A para.8, revoked (in part): SI 2012/ 641 Art.2

1979. Asbestos Products (Safety) (Amendment) Regulations 1987

Reg.2, revoked: SI 2012/ 1815 Sch.1

1987– cont.

2004. Local Authorities (Publicity Account) (Exemption) Order 1987
applied: SI 2012/2734 Sch.1 para.18, Sch.1 para.32
varied: SI 2012/2734 Reg.6

2023. Insolvent Companies (Disqualification of Unfit Directors) Proceedings Rules 1987
r.3, see *Secretary of State for Business Innovation and Skills v Chohan* [2011] EWHC 1350 (Ch), [2012] 1 B.C.L.C. 138 (Ch D (Companies Ct)), David Richards, J.

2024. Non-Contentious Probate Rules 1987
r.20, see *Ibuna v Arroyo* [2012] EWHC 428 (Ch), [2012] W.T.L.R. 827 (Ch D), Peter Smith, J.; see *Khan v Crossland* [2012] W.T.L.R. 841 (Ch D), Judge Behrens
r.28, see *Ibuna v Arroyo* [2012] EWHC 428 (Ch), [2012] W.T.L.R. 827 (Ch D), Peter Smith, J.
r.30, see *Ibuna v Arroyo* [2012] EWHC 428 (Ch), [2012] W.T.L.R. 827 (Ch D), Peter Smith, J.

2049. Consumer Protection(Northern Ireland) Order 1987
referred to: 2012 c.19 Sch.6 para.4
Art.5, applied: SI 2012/1916 Reg.345

2088. Registration of Births and Deaths Regulations 1987
Reg.2, amended: SI 2012/1203 Reg.2
Reg.3, amended: SI 2012/1203 Reg.3
Reg.5, amended: SI 2012/1203 Reg.4
Reg.9, amended: SI 2012/1203 Reg.5
Reg.9, substituted: SI 2012/1203 Reg.5
Reg.11, revoked: SI 2012/1203 Reg.6
Reg.12, amended: SI 2012/1203 Reg.7
Reg.12, revoked (in part): SI 2012/1203 Reg.7
Reg.12, substituted: SI 2012/1203 Reg.7
Reg.13, amended: SI 2012/1203 Reg.8
Reg.15, substituted: SI 2012/1203 Reg.10
Reg.17, amended: SI 2012/1203 Reg.11
Reg.17, revoked (in part): SI 2012/1203 Reg.11
Reg.33A, added: SI 2012/1203 Reg.13
Reg.34, amended: SI 2012/1203 Reg.14
Reg.35, amended: SI 2012/1203 Reg.15
Reg.35, revoked (in part): SI 2012/1203 Reg.15
Reg.36, amended: SI 2012/1203 Reg.16
Reg.42A, applied: SI 2012/1604 Reg.2
Reg.69, amended: SI 2012/1203 Reg.17

2089. Registration of Births and Deaths (Welsh Language) Regulations 1987
Reg.4, amended: SI 2012/1203 Reg.18

2195. Coypus (Prohibition on Keeping) Order 1987
revoked (in part): SSI 2012/174 Sch.2

2197. Civil Jurisdiction (Offshore Activities) Order 1987
Art.1, applied: SI 2012/1652 Reg.17

2203. Adoption (Northern Ireland) Order 1987
applied: SI 2012/2885 Reg.8, SI 2012/2886 Sch.1, SI 2012/3144 Reg.8, SI 2012/3145 Sch.1
Art.14, see *Northern Ireland Human Rights Commission's Application for Judicial Review, Re* [2012] NIQB 77, [2012] Eq. L.R. 1135 (QBD (NI)), Treacy, J.
Art.15, see *Northern Ireland Human Rights Commission's Application for Judicial Review, Re* [2012] NIQB 77, [2012] Eq. L.R. 1135 (QBD (NI)), Treacy, J.

2215. Police Pensions (Purchase of Increased Benefits) Regulations 1987
Reg.5, amended: SI 2012/640 Reg.4, SSI 2012/71 Reg.4

1987– cont.

2215. Police Pensions (Purchase of Increased Benefits) Regulations 1987– *cont.*
Sch.1 Part I para.4, revoked (in part): SI 2012/640 Reg.4, SSI 2012/71 Reg.4

2225. Mink (Keeping) (Amendment) Regulations 1987
revoked (in part): SSI 2012/174 Sch.2

1988

34. Social Fund (Application for Review) Regulations 1988
referred to: SI 2012/3090 Art.3
Reg.2, referred to: SI 2012/3090 Art.3

217. Pensions Increase (Review) Order 1988
applied: SI 2012/782 Art.3, Art.4

538. European Communities (Iron and Steel Employees Re-adaptation Benefits Scheme) (No.2) Regulations 1988
revoked: SI 2012/2262 Reg.2
Sch.1, applied: SI 2012/2885 Sch.1 para.18

643. Department of Transport (Fees) Order 1988
applied: SI 2012/1271

664. Social Security (Payments on account, Overpayments and Recovery) Regulations 1988
Reg.11, amended: SI 2012/757 Reg.16
Reg.13, amended: SI 2012/645 Reg.2
Reg.16, amended: SI 2012/645 Reg.3

668. Pneumoconiosis etc (Workers Compensation) (Payment of Claims) Regulations 1988
Reg.5, amended: SI 2012/923 Reg.2
Reg.6, amended: SI 2012/923 Reg.2
Reg.8, amended: SI 2012/923 Reg.2
Sch.1 Part 1, substituted: SI 2012/923 Sch.1
Sch.1 Part 2, substituted: SI 2012/923 Sch.1

1001. Cereals Co-responsibility Levy Regulations 1988
Reg.8, revoked (in part): 2012 c.9 Sch.2 para.6, Sch.10 Part 2
Reg.9, amended: 2012 c.9 Sch.2 para.6, Sch.10 Part 2
Reg.11, amended: 2012 c.9 Sch.2 para.6

1047. AIDS (Control) (Contents of Reports) (No.2) Order 1988
revoked: 2012 c.7 s.59

1155. Trunk Road (Great Yarmouth Western Bypass) (Prohibition of Right Turns) Order 1988
disapplied: SI 2012/2775 Art.5
varied: SI 2012/1296 Art.5

1350. Textile Products (Indications of Fibre Content) (Amendment) Regulations 1988
revoked: SI 2012/1102 Sch.1

1478. Goods Vehicles (Plating and Testing) Regulations 1988
Reg.12, amended: SI 2012/305 Reg.3
Reg.16, amended: SI 2012/305 Reg.4
Reg.25, amended: SI 2012/305 Reg.5
Reg.34, amended: SI 2012/305 Reg.5, Reg.6
Reg.37B, amended: SI 2012/305 Reg.5

1691. Criminal Justice Act 1987 (Notice of Transfer) Regulations 1988
applied: SI 2012/1726 r.3.11
referred to: SI 2012/1726 r.11.1

1724. Social Fund Cold Weather Payments (General) Regulations 1988
Sch.1, amended: SI 2012/2379 Reg.2
Sch.1, substituted: SI 2012/2280 Sch.1
Sch.2, substituted: SI 2012/2280 Sch.2

1988–cont.

1994. Air Navigation (Aeroplane and Aeroplane Engine Emission of Unburned Hydrocarbons) Order 1988
applied: 2012 c.19 Sch.6 para.4

1989

149. Gas Cooking Appliances (Safety) Regulations 1989
revoked: SI 2012/1815 Sch.1

193. Town and Country Planning (Fees for Applications and Deemed Applications) Regulations 1989
revoked (in part): SI 2012/2920 Sch.3
Reg.7, applied: SI 2012/2920 Reg.20
Reg.8, applied: SI 2012/2920 Reg.20
Reg.10A, applied: SI 2012/2920 Reg.20
Reg.11, applied: SI 2012/2920 Reg.20

306. National Health Service (Charges to Overseas Visitors) Regulations 1989
Reg.1, amended: SI 2012/1809 Sch.1 Part 2
Reg.4, amended: SI 2012/1809 Sch.1 Part 2

339. Civil Legal Aid (General) Regulations 1989
see *Legal Services Commission v Loomba* [2012] EWHC 29 (QB), [2012] 1 W.L.R. 2461 (QBD), Cranston, J.
Reg.100, see *Legal Services Commission v Henthorn* [2011] EWCA Civ 1415, [2012] 1 W.L.R. 1173 (CA (Civ Div)), Lord Neuberger (M.R.)
Reg.112, see *Legal Services Commission v Henthorn* [2011] EWCA Civ 1415, [2012] 1 W.L.R. 1173 (CA (Civ Div)), Lord Neuberger (M.R.)

364. National Health Service (Charges to Overseas Visitors) (Scotland) Regulations 1989
Reg.5, amended: SSI 2012/87 Reg.2

433. Grant-aided Colleges (Scotland) Grant Regulations 1989
applied: SSI 2012/237 Art.4, SSI 2012/238 Art.4

477. Pensions Increase (Review) Order 1989
applied: SI 2012/782 Art.3, Art.4

582. Evidence in Divorce Actions (Scotland) Order 1989
Art.2, amended: SSI 2012/111 Art.3

635. Electricity at Work Regulations 1989
see *Berry v Ashtead Plant Hire Co Ltd* [2011] EWCA Civ 1304, [2012] P.I.Q.R. P6 (CA (Civ Div)), Longmore, L.J.

638. European Economic Interest Grouping Regulations 1989
Reg.9, applied: SI 2012/1908 Sch.1 para.5
Reg.11, applied: SI 2012/1908 Sch.1 para.5
Reg.12, applied: SI 2012/1908 Sch.1 para.5
Sch.4 Part 1 para.26, applied: SI 2012/1908 Sch.1 para.5

684. Medicines (Fixing of Fees Relating to Medicinal Products for Human Use) Order 1989
Art.1, amended: SI 2012/1916 Sch.34 para.69
Sch.1 para.1, amended: SI 2012/1916 Sch.34 para.69
Sch.1 para.1A, added: SI 2012/1916 Sch.34 para.69
Sch.1 para.2, amended: SI 2012/1916 Sch.34 para.69
Sch.1 para.3, substituted: SI 2012/1916 Sch.34 para.69
Sch.1 para.4, substituted: SI 2012/1916 Sch.34 para.69
Sch.1 para.8, substituted: SI 2012/1916 Sch.34 para.69

1989–cont.

684. Medicines (Fixing of Fees Relating to Medicinal Products for Human Use) Order 1989–*cont.*
Sch.1 para.9A, revoked: SI 2012/1916 Sch.34 para.69
Sch.1 para.9C, revoked: SI 2012/1916 Sch.34 para.69
Sch.1 para.9D, revoked: SI 2012/1916 Sch.34 para.69
Sch.1 para.10, amended: SI 2012/1916 Sch.34 para.69
Sch.1 para.11, amended: SI 2012/1916 Sch.34 para.69

846. Food (Northern Ireland) Order 1989
Art.38, applied: SI 2012/1916 Sch.17 Part 1

869. Consumer Credit (Exempt Agreements) Order 1989
Sch.1 Part II, amended: SI 2012/702 Sch.1 para.1

971. Offshore Installations (Safety Representatives and Safety Committees) Regulations 1989
Reg.17, amended: SI 2012/199 Reg.7

1058. Non-Domestic Rating (Collection and Enforcement) (Local Lists) Regulations 1989
applied: SI 2012/466 Reg.8, Reg.9
Reg.2, amended: SI 2012/25 Art.2
Reg.4, amended: SI 2012/24 Reg.2
Reg.7, amended: SI 2012/24 Reg.2
Reg.7, revoked (in part): SI 2012/24 Reg.2
Reg.7C, substituted: SI 2012/466 Reg.3
Reg.7D, added: SI 2012/994 Reg.2
Reg.8, amended: SI 2012/24 Reg.2
Reg.15, see *Shamlou v Blackpool and Fleetwood Magistrates' Court* [2011] EWHC 2874 (Admin), [2012] R.V.R. 90 (QBD (Admin)), Judge Stephen Davies
Sch.1H, added: SI 2012/994 Sch.2
Sch.1D para.1, amended: SI 2012/466 Reg.4
Sch.1D para.2, amended: SI 2012/466 Reg.4
Sch.1D para.3, amended: SI 2012/466 Reg.4
Sch.1D para.4, amended: SI 2012/466 Reg.4
Sch.1D para.5, amended: SI 2012/466 Reg.4
Sch.1D para.6, amended: SI 2012/466 Reg.4
Sch.1D para.7, amended: SI 2012/466 Reg.4
Sch.1D para.8, amended: SI 2012/466 Reg.4
Sch.1D para.9, amended: SI 2012/466 Reg.4
Sch.1D para.10, amended: SI 2012/466 Reg.4
Sch.1D para.11, amended: SI 2012/466 Reg.4
Sch.1D para.12, amended: SI 2012/466 Reg.4
Sch.1D para.13, amended: SI 2012/466 Reg.4
Sch.1D para.14, amended: SI 2012/466 Reg.4
Sch.1G para.1, added: SI 2012/994 Sch.1
Sch.1G para.1, revoked (in part): SI 2012/24 Reg.2
Sch.1G para.2, added: SI 2012/994 Sch.1
Sch.1G para.2, revoked (in part): SI 2012/24 Reg.2
Sch.1G para.3, added: SI 2012/994 Sch.1
Sch.1G para.3, revoked (in part): SI 2012/24 Reg.2
Sch.1G para.4, added: SI 2012/994 Sch.1
Sch.1G para.4, revoked (in part): SI 2012/24 Reg.2
Sch.1G para.5, added: SI 2012/994 Sch.1
Sch.1G para.5, revoked (in part): SI 2012/24 Reg.2
Sch.1G para.6, added: SI 2012/994 Sch.1
Sch.1G para.6, revoked (in part): SI 2012/24 Reg.2
Sch.1G para.7, added: SI 2012/994 Sch.1
Sch.1G para.7, revoked (in part): SI 2012/24 Reg.2
Sch.1G para.8, added: SI 2012/994 Sch.1
Sch.1G para.8, revoked (in part): SI 2012/24 Reg.2
Sch.1G para.9, added: SI 2012/994 Sch.1
Sch.1G para.9, revoked (in part): SI 2012/24 Reg.2

1989– cont.

1058. Non-Domestic Rating (Collection and Enforcement) (Local Lists) Regulations 1989– cont.
Sch.1 G para.10, added: SI 2012/994 Sch.1
Sch.1 G para.10, revoked (in part): SI 2012/24 Reg.2
Sch.1 G para.11, added: SI 2012/994 Sch.1
Sch.1 G para.11, revoked (in part): SI 2012/24 Reg.2
Sch.1 G para.12, added: SI 2012/994 Sch.1
Sch.1 G para.12, revoked (in part): SI 2012/24 Reg.2
Sch.1 G para.13, added: SI 2012/994 Sch.1
Sch.1 G para.13, revoked (in part): SI 2012/24 Reg.2
Sch.1 G para.14, added: SI 2012/994 Sch.1
Sch.1 G para.14, revoked (in part): SI 2012/24 Reg.2
Sch.1 G para.15, added: SI 2012/994 Sch.1
Sch.1 G para.15, revoked (in part): SI 2012/24 Reg.2
Sch.1 G para.16, added: SI 2012/994 Sch.1
Sch.1 G para.16, revoked (in part): SI 2012/24 Reg.2

1183. Medicines (Data Sheet and Labelling) Amendment Regulations 1989
revoked: SI 2012/1916 Sch.35

1184. Medicines (Exemption from Licences) (Special and Transitional Cases) Amendment Order 1989
revoked: SI 2012/1916 Sch.35

1263. Sludge (Use in Agriculture) Regulations 1989
applied: SI 2012/811 Reg.3

1339. Limitation (Northern Ireland) Order 1989
Art.21, see *Official Receiver for Northern Ireland v O'Brien* [2012] NICh 12, [2012] B.P.I.R. 826 (Ch D (NI)), Deeny, J.

1341. Police and Criminal Evidence (Northern Ireland) Order 1989
applied: 2012 c.9 Sch.1 para.7, SI 2012/178 Reg.9
Art.61, disapplied: 2012 c.9 Sch.1 para.7
Art.64, applied: 2012 c.9 Sch.1 para.7
Art.64, disapplied: 2012 c.9 Sch.1 para.7
Art.64ZC, amended: 2012 c.10 Sch.24 para.12
Art.64ZC, revoked (in part): 2012 c.10 Sch.24 para.12
Art.65, substituted: 2012 c.9 Sch.9 para.22

1355. Cider and Perry Regulations 1989
see *Bramston v Revenue and Customs Commissioners* [2012] UKUT 44 (TCC), [2012] S.T.C. 695 (UT (Tax)), Roth, J.
Reg.7, see *Bramston v Revenue and Customs Commissioners* [2012] UKUT 44 (TCC), [2012] S.T.C. 695 (UT (Tax)), Roth, J.
Reg.13, see *Bramston v Revenue and Customs Commissioners* [2012] UKUT 44 (TCC), [2012] S.T.C. 695 (UT (Tax)), Roth, J.

1356. Wine and Made-wine Regulations 1989
see *Bramston v Revenue and Customs Commissioners* [2012] UKUT 44 (TCC), [2012] S.T.C. 695 (UT (Tax)), Roth, J.
Reg.12, see *Bramston v Revenue and Customs Commissioners* [2012] UKUT 44 (TCC), [2012] S.T.C. 695 (UT (Tax)), Roth, J.
Reg.13, see *Bramston v Revenue and Customs Commissioners* [2012] UKUT 44 (TCC), [2012] S.T.C. 695 (UT (Tax)), Roth, J.

1490. Civil Legal Aid (Scotland) (Fees) Regulations 1989
Reg.3, see *Smith v Scottish Legal Aid Board* [2012] CSIH 14, 2012 S.L.T. 703 (IH (1 Div)), The Lord President (Hamilton)
Reg.11, see *Smith v Scottish Legal Aid Board* [2012] CSIH 14, 2012 S.L.T. 703 (IH (1 Div)), The Lord President (Hamilton)

1989– cont.

1491. Criminal Legal Aid (Scotland) (Fees) Regulations 1989
Reg.2, amended: SSI 2012/276 Reg.4
Reg.3A, added: SSI 2012/276 Reg.12
Reg.3A, amended: SSI 2012/305 Reg.2
Sch.2 Part 001, amended: SSI 2012/276 Reg.5, Reg.6, Reg.8, Reg.11
Sch.2 para.3, amended: SSI 2012/276 Reg.13
Sch.2 para.13, amended: SSI 2012/276 Reg.7
Sch.2 para.14, amended: SSI 2012/276 Reg.7
Sch.2 para.15, amended: SSI 2012/276 Reg.7
Sch.2 para.15, revoked (in part): SSI 2012/276 Reg.7
Sch.2 para.15A, added: SSI 2012/276 Reg.6
Sch.2 para.15B, added: SSI 2012/276 Reg.6
Sch.2 para.16, amended: SSI 2012/276 Reg.10
Sch.2 para.16A, added: SSI 2012/276 Reg.8
Sch.2 para.17, amended: SSI 2012/276 Reg.5, Reg.8, Reg.10
Sch.2 para.19, amended: SSI 2012/276 Reg.9
Sch.2 para.20, substituted: SSI 2012/276 Reg.14
Sch.2 para.21, substituted: SSI 2012/276 Reg.14
Sch.2 para.22, amended: SSI 2012/276 Reg.4

1671. Offshore Installations and Pipeline Works (First-Aid) Regulations 1989
Reg.5, applied: SI 2012/1652 Reg.19

1834. Trunk Road (A38) (Exeter-Leeds) (De-Restriction) Order 1989
revoked: SI 2012/2034 Art.6

1958. A55 Trunk Road (Penmaenmawr, Gwynedd) (Derestriction) Order 1989
disapplied: SI 2012/141 Art.14, SI 2012/163 Art.14
restored: SI 2012/423 Art.13
revoked (in part): SI 2012/423 Art.13
varied: SI 2012/945 Art.10

2125. Edinburgh City Bypass (Sighthill, Colinton, Burdiehouse, Gilmerton and Millerhill Sections and Connecting Roads) (Speed Limit) Regulations 1989
revoked: SSI 2012/62 Reg.6

2158. Trunk Road (A55) (Llanfairfechan, Gwynedd) (Derestriction) Order 1989
restored: SI 2012/423 Art.12
revoked (in part): SI 2012/423 Art.12
varied: SI 2012/945 Art.6

2260. Non-Domestic Rating (Collection and Enforcement) (Central Lists) Regulations 1989
applied: SI 2012/466 Reg.8, Reg.9
Reg.4, amended: SI 2012/24 Reg.3
Reg.7B, substituted: SI 2012/466 Reg.6
Reg.7C, added: SI 2012/994 Reg.3
Sch.1 B para.1, amended: SI 2012/466 Reg.7
Sch.1 B para.2, amended: SI 2012/466 Reg.7
Sch.1 B para.3, amended: SI 2012/466 Reg.7
Sch.1 B para.4, amended: SI 2012/466 Reg.7
Sch.1 B para.5, amended: SI 2012/466 Reg.7
Sch.1 B para.6, amended: SI 2012/466 Reg.7
Sch.1 B para.7, amended: SI 2012/466 Reg.7
Sch.1 B para.8, amended: SI 2012/466 Reg.7
Sch.1 B para.9, amended: SI 2012/466 Reg.7
Sch.1 B para.10, amended: SI 2012/466 Reg.7
Sch.1 B para.11, amended: SI 2012/466 Reg.7
Sch.1 B para.11, revoked (in part): SI 2012/466 Reg.7
Sch.1 B para.12, amended: SI 2012/466 Reg.7
Sch.1 B para.13, amended: SI 2012/466 Reg.7
Sch.1 B para.14, amended: SI 2012/466 Reg.7
Sch.1 B para.14, revoked (in part): SI 2012/466 Reg.7
Sch.1 C para.1, added: SI 2012/994 Sch.3

1989–cont.

2260. Non-Domestic Rating (Collection and Enforcement) (Central Lists) Regulations 1989–
cont.
Sch.1C para.2, added: SI 2012/994 Sch.3
Sch.1C para.3, added: SI 2012/994 Sch.3
Sch.1C para.4, added: SI 2012/994 Sch.3
Sch.1C para.5, added: SI 2012/994 Sch.3
Sch.1C para.6, added: SI 2012/994 Sch.3
Sch.1C para.7, added: SI 2012/994 Sch.3
Sch.1C para.8, added: SI 2012/994 Sch.3
Sch.1C para.9, added: SI 2012/994 Sch.3
Sch.1C para.10, added: SI 2012/994 Sch.3
Sch.1C para.11, added: SI 2012/994 Sch.3
Sch.1C para.12, added: SI 2012/994 Sch.3
Sch.1C para.13, added: SI 2012/994 Sch.3
Sch.1C para.14, added: SI 2012/994 Sch.3
Sch.1C para.15, added: SI 2012/994 Sch.3
Sch.1C para.16, added: SI 2012/994 Sch.3

2288. All-Terrain Motor Vehicles (Safety) Regulations 1989
revoked: SI 2012/1815 Sch.1

2323. Medicines (Exemption from Licences) (Special and Transitional Cases) (Amendment) Order 1989
revoked: SI 2012/1916 Sch.35

2404. Companies (Northern Ireland) Order 1989
Part II, applied: SI 2012/1640 Sch.2 para.5

2405. Insolvency (Northern Ireland) Order 1989
applied: SI 2012/1128 Art.4, SI 2012/1290 Reg.3
referred to: 2012 c.19 Sch.6 para.4
see *Irish Bank Resolution Corp Ltd v Quinn* [2012] NICh 1, [2012] B.C.C. 608 (Ch D (NI)), Deeny, J.
Part VIIA, applied: 2012 c.9 Sch.8 para.2
Art.242, applied: SSI 2012/88 Reg.23, SSI 2012/89 Reg.26
Art.279BA, applied: SI 2012/1726 r.60.4
Art.350, applied: 2012 c.19 Sch.6 para.5
Sch.B1 para.5, applied: 2012 c.9 Sch.8 para.2
Sch.2A, applied: SI 2012/1290 Reg.3, SI 2012/1544, SI 2012/1631 Sch.5 para.5, SI 2012/1640 Sch.2 para.2, SI 2012/2996 Sch.5 para.4

2493. Caernarfon Harbour Revision Order 1989
applied: SI 2012/1984 Sch.2 para.22
Art.3, revoked (in part): SI 2012/1984 Art.12
Art.4, revoked: SI 2012/1984 Art.12
Art.5, revoked: SI 2012/1984 Art.12
Art.6, revoked: SI 2012/1984 Art.12
Art.7, revoked: SI 2012/1984 Art.12
Art.8, revoked: SI 2012/1984 Art.12
Art.9, revoked (in part): SI 2012/1984 Art.12
Art.12, applied: SI 2012/1984 Sch.2 para.19
Art.13, revoked: SI 2012/1984 Art.12
Art.14, revoked: SI 2012/1984 Art.12

1990

174. A52 Trunk Road (Bottesford Bypass) (24-Hour Clearway) Order 1990
revoked: SI 2012/1093 Art.8

181. Education (School and Placing Information) (Scotland) Amendment Regulations 1990
revoked: SSI 2012/130 Sch.3

200. Official Secrets Act 1989 (Prescription) Order 1990
Sch.1, amended: SI 2012/725 Art.2
Sch.2, amended: SI 2012/725 Art.2, SI 2012/2900 Art.2

1990–cont.

247. Health and Personal Social Services(Special Agencies)(Northern Ireland) Order 1990
applied: SI 2012/1631 Sch.5 para.6, SI 2012/2996 Sch.5 para.5

327. Land Charges Fees Rules 1990
r.1, amended: SI 2012/2910 r.3
r.3, substituted: SI 2012/2910 r.4
r.4, amended: SI 2012/2910 r.5
Sch.1, substituted: SI 2012/2910 Sch.1
Sch.2 para.5, substituted: SI 2012/2910 r.7

328. Trunk Road (A55) (Penmaenbach-Dwygyfylchi, Gwynedd) (One-Way Traffic) Order 1990
disapplied: SI 2012/141 Art.10, SI 2012/163 Art.10

483. Pensions Increase (Review) Order 1990
applied: SI 2012/782 Art.3, Art.4

566. Medicines (Exemption from Licences) (Wholesale Dealing) Order 1990
revoked: SI 2012/1916 Sch.35

851. Local Government Officers (Political Restrictions) Regulations 1990
Reg.2, amended: SI 2012/1772 Reg.2
Reg.3, amended: SI 2012/1772 Reg.2

928. Industrial Training (Transfer of the Activities of Establishment) Order 1990
referred to: SI 2012/958 Sch.1

1095. Trunk Road (A55) (Travellers Inn, Clwyd) (Derestriction) Order 1990
varied: SI 2012/945 Art.15

1129. Medicines (Products Other Than Veterinary Drugs) (General Sale List) Amendment Order 1990
revoked: SI 2012/1916 Sch.35

1137. Trunk Road (A48) (Foelgastell, Dyfed) (DeRestriction) Order 1990
disapplied: SI 2012/11 Art.6

1147. Town and Country Planning (Listed Buildings in Wales and Buildings in Conservation Areas in Wales) (Welsh Forms) Regulations 1990
revoked: SI 2012/793 Sch.5

1159. Insurance Companies (Legal Expenses Insurance) Regulations 1990
Reg.6, see *Brown-Quinn v Equity Syndicate Management Ltd* [2011] EWHC 2661 (Comm), [2012] 1 All E.R. 778 (QBD (Comm)), Burton, J.

1514. Air Navigation (Noise Certification) Order 1990
applied: 2012 c.19 Sch.6 para.4

1519. Planning (Listed Buildings and Conservation Areas) Regulations 1990
revoked (in part): SI 2012/793 Sch.5
Reg.3, amended: SI 2012/2275 Reg.2
Sch.4 Part 1, amended: SI 2012/2590 Sch.1 para.5
Sch.4 Part 2, amended: SI 2012/2590 Sch.1 para.5

1586. Special Road (Glan Conwy to Conwy Morfa) Regulations 1990
disapplied: SI 2012/6 Art.9, SI 2012/141 Art.13, SI 2012/163 Art.13, SI 2012/275 Art.9
varied: SI 2012/945 Art.11

1715. EEC Merger Control (Distinct Market Investigations) Regulations 1990
applied: SI 2012/1128 Art.4

2024. National Health Service Trusts (Membership and Procedure) Regulations 1990
Reg.1, amended: SI 2012/1641 Sch.3 para.1, Sch.4 para.1

1990–cont.

2024. **National Health Service Trusts (Membership and Procedure) Regulations 1990**–cont.
Reg.11, amended: SI 2012/1109 Sch.1 para.1, SI 2012/1641 Sch.3 para.1, Sch.4 para.1, SI 2012/2404 Sch.3 para.6
Reg.11, revoked (in part): SI 2012/1641 Sch.2 para.1

2360. **Public Lending Right Scheme 1982 (Commencement of Variations) Order 1990**
Part V para.46, varied: SI 2012/63 Art.2, SI 2012/3123 Art.2

2463. **Food Safety (Sampling and Qualifications) Regulations 1990**
Sch.1, amended: SI 2012/2619 Reg.28, SI 2012/2705 Reg.28, SSI 2012/318 Reg.28

2473. **Town and Country Planning (Fees for Applications and Deemed Applications) (Amendment) Regulations 1990**
revoked (in part): SI 2012/2920 Sch.3

2639. **Health Education Board for Scotland Order 1990**
Art.4, varied: 2012 c.11 s.12
Sch.1 Part III, amended: SI 2012/1479 Sch.1 para.9

1991

5. **Food Protection (Emergency Prohibitions) (Radioactivity in Sheep) (Wales) Order 1991**
referred to: SI 2012/2978
revoked: SI 2012/2978 Sch.1

6. **Food Protection (Emergency Prohibitions) (Radioactivity in Sheep) (England) Order 1991**
referred to: SI 2012/2658
revoked: SI 2012/2658 Sch.1

20. **Food Protection (Emergency Prohibitions) (Radioactivity in Sheep) Order 1991**
revoked (in part): SSI 2012/263 Sch.1

58. **Export of Sheep (Prohibition) Order 1991**
revoked (in part): SI 2012/2978 Sch.1, SSI 2012/263 Sch.1

167. **Occupational Pension Schemes (Preservation of Benefit) Regulations 1991**
Reg.12, amended: SI 2012/692 Reg.3

194. **Health and Personal Social Services (Northern Ireland) Order 1991**
applied: SI 2012/1631 Sch.5 para.6, SI 2012/2996 Sch.5 para.5
Art.8, amended: 2012 c.7 Sch.21 para.43
Art.8, revoked (in part): 2012 c.7 Sch.7 para.25, Sch.21 para.43

472. **Environmental Protection (Prescribed Processes and Substances) Regulations 1991**
Reg.3A, substituted: SSI 2012/360 Sch.11 para.4

684. **Pensions Increase (Review) Order 1991**
applied: SI 2012/782 Art.3, Art.4

762. **Food Safety(Northern Ireland) Order 1991**
Art.27, applied: SI 2012/1916 Reg.330, Sch.17 Part 1, Sch.17 Part 4

859. **Estate Agents (Provision of Information) Regulations 1991**
see *Great Estates Group Ltd v Digby* [2011] EWCA Civ 1120, [2012] 2 All E.R. (Comm) 361 (CA (Civ Div)), Rix, L.J.
Reg.5, see *Great Estates Group Ltd v Digby* [2011] EWCA Civ 1120, [2012] 2 All E.R. (Comm) 361 (CA (Civ Div)), Rix, L.J.

1031. **Savings Certificates Regulations 1991**
Reg.2, amended: SI 2012/1882 Reg.3
Reg.3, amended: SI 2012/1882 Reg.4

1991–cont.

1031. **Savings Certificates Regulations 1991**–cont.
Reg.4, substituted: SI 2012/1882 Reg.5
Reg.5, amended: SI 2012/1882 Reg.6
Reg.5A, added: SI 2012/1882 Reg.7
Reg.6, amended: SI 2012/1882 Reg.8
Reg.6A, added: SI 2012/1882 Reg.9
Reg.6B, added: SI 2012/1882 Reg.9
Reg.7, amended: SI 2012/1882 Reg.10
Reg.7, revoked (in part): SI 2012/1882 Reg.10
Reg.8, substituted: SI 2012/1882 Reg.11
Reg.9, amended: SI 2012/1882 Reg.12
Reg.10, amended: SI 2012/1882 Reg.13
Reg.13, amended: SI 2012/1882 Reg.14
Reg.15, amended: SI 2012/1882 Reg.15
Reg.21, amended: SI 2012/1882 Reg.16
Reg.21A, added: SI 2012/1882 Reg.17
Reg.23, amended: SI 2012/1882 Reg.18
Reg.24, revoked: SI 2012/1882 Reg.19
Reg.27, amended: SI 2012/1882 Reg.20
Reg.29, substituted: SI 2012/1882 Reg.21
Reg.36, revoked (in part): SI 2012/1882 Reg.22
Sch.2 para.6, amended: SI 2012/1882 Reg.23

1184. **County Courts (Interest on Judgment Debts) Order 1991**
see *Simcoe v Jacuzzi UK Group Plc* [2012] EWCA Civ 137, [2012] 1 W.L.R. 2393 (CA (Civ Div), Lord Neuberger (M.R.)
Art.2, see *Simcoe v Jacuzzi UK Group Plc* [2012] EWCA Civ 137, [2012] 1 W.L.R. 2393 (CA (Civ Div)), Lord Neuberger (M.R.)

1220. **Planning(Northern Ireland) Order 1991**
Art.3, see *Central Craigavon Ltd's Application for Judicial Review, Re* [2012] N.I. 60 (CA (NI)), Higgins, L.J.
Art.111, applied: SI 2012/3038 Sch.12 para.3
Art.127, varied: SI 2012/3038 Sch.12 para.4

1222. **County Court Remedies Regulations 1991**
see *Suh v Ryu* [2012] EWPCC 20, [2012] F.S.R. 31 (PCC), Judge Birss Q.C.
Reg.2, see *Suh v Ryu* [2012] EWPCC 20, [2012] F.S.R. 31 (PCC), Judge Birss Q.C.
Reg.3, see *Suh v Ryu* [2012] EWPCC 20, [2012] F.S.R. 31 (PCC), Judge Birss Q.C.

1247. **Family Proceedings Rules 1991**
see *BJ v MJ (Financial Order: Overseas Trust)* [2011] EWHC 2708 (Fam), [2012] 1 F.L.R. 667 (Fam Div), Mostyn, J.
r.1.4, see *Fisher Meredith LLP v JH* [2012] EWHC 408 (Fam), [2012] 2 F.L.R. 536 (Fam Div), Mostyn, J.

1407. **Savings Certificates (Children's Bonus Bonds) Regulations 1991**
Reg.2, amended: SI 2012/1880 Reg.3
Reg.3, amended: SI 2012/1880 Reg.4
Reg.4, amended: SI 2012/1880 Reg.5
Reg.5, substituted: SI 2012/1880 Reg.6
Reg.5A, added: SI 2012/1880 Reg.7
Reg.5B, added: SI 2012/1880 Reg.7
Reg.6, amended: SI 2012/1880 Reg.8
Reg.7, amended: SI 2012/1880 Reg.9
Reg.7, revoked (in part): SI 2012/1880 Reg.9
Reg.7A, added: SI 2012/1880 Reg.10
Reg.10A, added: SI 2012/1880 Reg.11
Reg.17, amended: SI 2012/1880 Reg.12
Reg.18, amended: SI 2012/1880 Reg.13
Reg.18A, added: SI 2012/1880 Reg.14
Reg.20, amended: SI 2012/1880 Reg.15
Reg.21, revoked: SI 2012/1880 Reg.16
Reg.24, amended: SI 2012/1880 Reg.17

1991–cont.

1407. Savings Certificates (Children's Bonus Bonds) Regulations 1991–cont.
Reg.26, substituted: SI 2012/1880 Reg.18
Reg.28, amended: SI 2012/1880 Reg.19
Reg.32, revoked (in part): SI 2012/1880 Reg.20

1408. Broadcasting (Independent Productions) Order 1991
Art.3, amended: SI 2012/1842 Art.6, Art.7, Art.8

1487. Advisory Committee on Hazardous Substances Order 1991
revoked: SI 2012/1923 Sch.1

1488. Advisory Committee on Hazardous Substances (Terms of Office) Regulations 1991
revoked: SI 2012/1923 Sch.1

1505. Children (Secure Accommodation) Regulations 1991
Reg.5A, added: SI 2012/2813 Reg.6
Reg.6, amended: SI 2012/2824 Reg.2, SI 2012/3134 Reg.2
Reg.6, revoked (in part): SI 2012/3134 Reg.2
Reg.13, amended: SI 2012/2824 Reg.2

1531. Control of Explosives Regulations 1991
applied: SI 2012/1652 Reg.9
Reg.4, applied: SI 2012/1652 Reg.9, Sch.8 Part 8

1624. Controlled Waste (Registration of Carriers and Seizure of Vehicles) Regulations 1991
Sch.1, amended: SSI 2012/360 Sch.11 para.5

1635. A46 and A17 Trunk Roads (Newark Relief Road) (24-Hour Clearway) Order 1991
amended: SI 2012/1082 Art.9

1744. Dangerous Dogs Compensation and Exemption Schemes Order 1991
Art.4, see *R. (on the application of Sandhu) v Isleworth Crown Court* [2012] EWHC 1658 (Admin), (2012) 176 J.P. 537 (DC), Richards, L.J.

2398. Scarborough and North East Yorkshire Health Care National Health Service Trust (Establishment) Order 1991
revoked: SI 2012/1514 Art.2

2440. A46 and A17 Trunk Roads (Newark Relief Road) (De-Restriction) Order 1991
Sch.1, revoked: SI 2012/1123 Art.3

2509. Coal Mining Subsidence (Notices and Claims) Regulations 1991
Sch.1, see *Newbold v Coal Authority* [2012] UKUT 20 (LC), [2012] R.V.R.157 (UT (Lands)), George Bartlett Q.C. (President, LTr)

2693. Heating Appliances (Fireguards) (Safety) Regulations 1991
revoked: SI 2012/1815 Sch.1

2735. Town and Country Planning (Fees for Applications and Deemed Applications) (Amendment) Regulations 1991
revoked (in part): SI 2012/2920 Sch.3

2766. Food Protection (Emergency Prohibitions) (Radioactivity in Sheep) Partial Revocation Order 1991
revoked (in part): SSI 2012/263 Sch.1

2776. Food Protection (Emergency Prohibitions) (Radioactivity in Sheep) (England) (Partial Revocation) Order 1991
revoked: SI 2012/2658 Sch.1

2780. Food Protection (Emergency Prohibitions) (Radioactivity in Sheep) (Wales) (Partial Revocation) Order 1991
revoked: SI 2012/2978 Sch.1

2804. Town and Country Planning (Enforcement Notices and Appeals) Regulations 1991
Reg.10, revoked (in part): SI 2012/793 Sch.5

1991–cont.

2839. Environmental Protection (Duty of Care) Regulations 1991
Reg.2, amended: SSI 2012/360 Sch.11 para.6

2890. Social Security (Disability Living Allowance) Regulations 1991
Reg.4, amended: SI 2012/780 Art.13
Reg.8, see *Secretary of State for Work and Pensions v Slavin* [2011] EWCA Civ 1515, [2012] P.T.S.R. 692 (CA (Civ Div)), Pill, L.J.
Reg.12A, see *Secretary of State for Work and Pensions v Slavin* [2011] EWCA Civ 1515, [2012] P.T.S.R. 692 (CA (Civ Div)), Pill, L.J.

1992

15. Income Tax (Interest Payments) (Information Powers) Regulations 1992
revoked: SI 2012/756 Reg.3

42. Taxes (Relief for Gifts) (Designated Educational Establishments) Regulations 1992
Reg.2, amended: SI 2012/979 Sch.1 para.3
Sch.1 Part I para.4, substituted: SI 2012/979 Sch.1 para.3
Sch.1 Part I para.5A, added: SI 2012/979 Sch.1 para.3

129. Firemen's Pension Scheme Order 1992
Part AI para.1, added: SI 2012/953 Art.4, SI 2012/974 Art.4
Part AI para.1, amended: SI 2012/953 Art.4
Part AI para.1, substituted: SI 2012/974 Art.4, SSI 2012/106 Art.4
Part AI para.2, added: SI 2012/953 Art.4, SI 2012/974 Art.4
Part AI para.2, amended: SI 2012/953 Art.4
Part AI para.2, substituted: SI 2012/974 Art.4, SSI 2012/106 Art.4
Part AI para.3, added: SI 2012/953 Art.4, SI 2012/974 Art.4
Part AI para.3, amended: SI 2012/953 Art.4
Part AI para.3, substituted: SI 2012/974 Art.4, SSI 2012/106 Art.4
Part I para.1, amended: SI 2012/953 Art.4
Part I para.1, substituted: SI 2012/974 Art.4, SSI 2012/106 Art.4
Part I para.2, amended: SI 2012/953 Art.4
Part I para.2, substituted: SI 2012/974 Art.4, SSI 2012/106 Art.4
Part I para.3, amended: SI 2012/953 Art.4
Part I para.3, substituted: SI 2012/974 Art.4, SSI 2012/106 Art.4
Part I para.4, amended: SI 2012/953 Art.4
Part I para.4, substituted: SI 2012/974 Art.4, SSI 2012/106 Art.4
Part I para.5, amended: SI 2012/953 Art.4
Part I para.5, substituted: SI 2012/974 Art.4, SSI 2012/106 Art.4
Part 1A para.1, added: SSI 2012/106 Art.4
Part 1A para.1, amended: SI 2012/953 Art.4
Part 1A para.1, substituted: SI 2012/974 Art.4, SSI 2012/106 Art.4
Part 1A para.2, added: SSI 2012/106 Art.4
Part 1A para.2, amended: SI 2012/953 Art.4
Part 1A para.2, substituted: SI 2012/974 Art.4, SSI 2012/106 Art.4
Part 1A para.3, added: SSI 2012/106 Art.4
Part 1A para.3, amended: SI 2012/953 Art.4
Part 1A para.3, substituted: SI 2012/974 Art.4, SSI 2012/106 Art.4
Part II para.1, amended: SI 2012/953 Art.4

1992–cont.

129. Firemen's Pension Scheme Order 1992–*cont.*
Part II para.1, substituted: SI 2012/974 Art.4, SSI 2012/106 Art.4
Part II para.2, amended: SI 2012/953 Art.4
Part II para.2, substituted: SI 2012/974 Art.4, SSI 2012/106 Art.4
Part II para.3, amended: SI 2012/953 Art.4
Part II para.3, substituted: SI 2012/974 Art.4, SSI 2012/106 Art.4
Part III para.1, amended: SI 2012/953 Art.4
Part III para.1, substituted: SI 2012/974 Art.4, SSI 2012/106 Art.4
Part III para.2, amended: SI 2012/953 Art.4
Part III para.2, substituted: SI 2012/974 Art.4, SSI 2012/106 Art.4
Part III para.3, amended: SI 2012/953 Art.4
Part III para.3, substituted: SI 2012/974 Art.4, SSI 2012/106 Art.4
Part III para.4, amended: SI 2012/953 Art.4
Part III para.4, substituted: SI 2012/974 Art.4, SSI 2012/106 Art.4
Part III para.5, amended: SI 2012/953 Art.4
Part III para.5, substituted: SI 2012/974 Art.4, SSI 2012/106 Art.4
Sch.2 Part G, amended: SI 2012/953 Art.3, SI 2012/974 Art.3, SSI 2012/106 Art.3
Sch.2 Part G, revoked (in part): SI 2012/953 Art.3, SI 2012/974 Art.3, SSI 2012/106 Art.3

198. Pensions Increase (Review) Order 1992
applied: SI 2012/782 Art.3, Art.4

223. Town and Country Planning (General Permitted Development) (Scotland) Order 1992
Sch.1 Part 6A, added: SSI 2012/131 Art.2
Sch.1 Part 6A, amended: SSI 2012/285 Art.2
Sch.1 Part 6A para.21A, added: SSI 2012/131 Art.2
Sch.1 Part 6A para.21A, amended: SSI 2012/285 Art.2
Sch.1 Part 6A para.21B, added: SSI 2012/131 Art.2
Sch.1 Part 6A para.21B, amended: SSI 2012/285 Art.2
Sch.1 Part 6A para.21C, added: SSI 2012/131 Art.2
Sch.1 Part 6A para.21C, amended: SSI 2012/285 Art.2
Sch.1 Part 6A para.21D, added: SSI 2012/131 Art.2
Sch.1 Part 6A para.21D, amended: SSI 2012/285 Art.2
Sch.1 Part 6A para.21E, added: SSI 2012/131 Art.2
Sch.1 Part 6A para.21E, amended: SSI 2012/285 Art.2
Sch.1 Part 6A para.21F, added: SSI 2012/131 Art.2

231. Electricity (Northern Ireland) Order 1992
applied: SI 2012/1128 Art.4
Art.10, applied: SSI 2012/89 Sch.1

364. British Transport Police Force Scheme 1963 (Amendment) Order 1992
Sch.2, amended: SI 2012/1659 Art.2

548. Council Tax (Discount Disregards) Order 1992
Sch.1 Part IV para.8, amended: SI 2012/956 Art.4

549. Council Tax (Chargeable Dwellings) Order 1992
Art.2, amended: SI 2012/1915 Art.2
Art.3A, amended: SI 2012/1915 Art.2

550. Council Tax (Situation and Valuation of Dwellings) Regulations 1992
Reg.6, see *Wilson v Coll (Listing Officer)* [2011] EWHC 2824 (Admin), [2012] P.T.S.R. 1313 (QBD (Admin)), Singh, J.

1992–cont.

551. Council Tax (Liability for Owners) Regulations 1992
Reg.2, amended: SI 2012/1915 Art.3

554. Council Tax (Reductions for Disabilities) Regulations 1992
applied: SI 2012/2914 Reg.5

558. Council Tax (Exempt Dwellings) Order 1992
see *Edem v Basingstoke & Deane BC* [2012] EWHC 2433 (Admin), [2012] R.V.R. 339 (QBD (Admin)), Judge Seys-Llewellyn Q.C.
Art.2, revoked (in part): SI 2012/2965 Art.2
Art.3, amended: SI 2012/2965 Art.2
Art.3, see *Appeal against Harrow LBC, Re* [2012] R.A. 36 (VT), Graham Zellick; see *Harrow LBC v Ayiku* [2012] EWHC 1200 (Admin), [2012] R.A. 270 (QBD (Admin)), Sales, J.; see *Hutchings v Cardiff City Council* [2011] EWCA Civ 1670, [2012] R.V.R. 123 (CA (Civ Div)), Pitchford, L.J.; see *Stowe School Ltd v Aylesbury Vale DC* [2012] R.A. 111 (VT), Graham Zellick

588. Controlled Waste Regulations 1992
revoked (in part): SI 2012/811 Reg.7

605. Medicines Act 1968 (Application to Radiopharmaceutical-associated Products) Regulations 1992
revoked: SI 2012/1916 Sch.35

612. Local Authorities (Calculation of Council Tax Base) Regulations 1992
revoked (in part): SI 2012/2914 Sch.1
Reg.2, amended: SI 2012/460 Sch.1 para.1
Reg.3, amended: SI 2012/460 Sch.1 para.2
Reg.6, amended: SI 2012/460 Sch.1 para.3
Reg.7, amended: SI 2012/460 Sch.1 para.4
Reg.8, amended: SI 2012/460 Sch.1 para.5
Reg.9, amended: SI 2012/460 Sch.1 para.6
Reg.10, amended: SI 2012/460 Sch.1 para.7
Reg.10A, added: SI 2012/460 Sch.1 para.8

613. Council Tax (Administration and Enforcement) Regulations 1992
Reg.1, amended: SI 2012/3086 Reg.2
Reg.2, amended: SI 2012/3086 Reg.2
Reg.4, amended: SI 2012/3086 Reg.2
Reg.9, amended: SI 2012/3086 Reg.2
Reg.10, amended: SI 2012/3086 Reg.2
Reg.11, amended: SI 2012/3086 Reg.2
Reg.13, amended: SI 2012/3086 Reg.2
Reg.14, amended: SI 2012/3086 Reg.2
Reg.15, amended: SI 2012/3086 Reg.2
Reg.16, amended: SI 2012/3086 Reg.2
Reg.20, amended: SI 2012/3086 Reg.2
Reg.20, applied: SI 2012/3145 Sch.1
Reg.20, referred to: SI 2012/2885 Sch.8 para.14, SI 2012/2886 Sch.1
Reg.21, amended: SI 2012/3086 Reg.2
Reg.21A, added: SI 2012/672 Reg.2
Reg.21B, added: SI 2012/672 Reg.2
Sch.1 Part I para.2, amended: SI 2012/3086 Reg.2
Sch.1 Part III para.10, amended: SI 2012/3086 Reg.2

662. National Health Service (Pharmaceutical Services) Regulations 1992
applied: SI 2012/1909 Sch.5 para.15, Sch.5 para.16
referred to: SI 2012/1909 Sch.4 para.25, Sch.4 para.26
Reg.2, amended: SI 2012/1479 Sch.1 para.10
Sch.2 Part II para.4, applied: SI 2012/1909 Sch.5 para.15
Sch.4, referred to: SI 2012/1909 Sch.4 para.26

1992–cont.

664. National Health Service (Service Committees and Tribunal) Regulations 1992
applied: SI 2012/1909 Sch.7 para.12, Sch.7 para.13, Sch.7 para.14
revoked (in part): SI 2012/1909 Sch.8 para.1

666. Town and Country Planning (Control of Advertisements) Regulations 1992
applied: SI 2012/323 Reg.19, SI 2012/444 Reg.24, SI 2012/1917 Art.83
Reg.3, referred to: SI 2012/60 Reg.9
Reg.5, referred to: SI 2012/60 Reg.9
Reg.6, referred to: SI 2012/60 Reg.9
Reg.9, substituted: SI 2012/791 Reg.2
Sch.2, referred to: SI 2012/60 Reg.9
Sch.3, referred to: SI 2012/60 Reg.9
Sch.3 Part I, referred to: SI 2012/60 Reg.9
Sch.3 Part I para.2, referred to: SI 2012/60 Reg.9
Sch.3 Part I para.11, referred to: SI 2012/60 Reg.9
Sch.3 Part II, applied: SI 2012/60 Reg.9

695. Oilseeds Producers (Support System) Regulations 1992
Reg.2, amended: 2012 c.9 Sch.2 para.7, Sch.10 Part 2
Reg.5, revoked (in part): 2012 c.9 Sch.2 para.7, Sch.10 Part 2
Reg.6, revoked (in part): 2012 c.9 Sch.2 para.7, Sch.10 Part 2
Reg.9, revoked (in part): 2012 c.9 Sch.2 para.7, Sch.10 Part 2
Reg.10, revoked (in part): 2012 c.9 Sch.2 para.7, Sch.10 Part 2

812. Social Security (Barbados) Order 1992
Sch.1, varied: SI 2012/360 Sch.2

1209. Road Traffic Offenders (Prescribed Devices) Order 1992
see *Brotherston v DPP* [2012] EWHC 136 (Admin), (2012) 176 J.P. 153 (DC), Toulson, L.J.

1303. Serbia and Montenegro (United Nations Sanctions) (Dependent Territories) Order 1992
revoked: SI 2012/362 Sch.4

1305. Serbia and Montenegro (United Nations Prohibition of Flights) (Dependent Territories) Order 1992
revoked: SI 2012/2592 Sch.2

1315. Transfer of Functions (Financial Services) Order 1992
revoked: SI 2012/1759 Sch.1

1332. Council Tax (Administration and Enforcement) (Scotland) Regulations 1992
Reg.1, amended: SSI 2012/303 Sch.7 para.1
Reg.2A, added: SSI 2012/338 Reg.3
Reg.9, amended: SSI 2012/338 Reg.4
Reg.11, amended: SSI 2012/338 Reg.5
Reg.12, amended: SSI 2012/338 Reg.5, Reg.6
Reg.13, amended: SSI 2012/338 Reg.5, Reg.7
Reg.14, amended: SSI 2012/338 Reg.5, Reg.8
Reg.15, amended: SSI 2012/338 Reg.5, Reg.9
Reg.17, applied: SSI 2012/53 Art.8
Reg.20, amended: SSI 2012/338 Reg.10
Reg.20, applied: SSI 2012/53 Art.10
Reg.21, applied: SSI 2012/53 Art.10
Reg.22, applied: SSI 2012/53 Art.10
Reg.23, applied: SSI 2012/53 Art.10
Reg.24, applied: SSI 2012/53 Art.10
Reg.25, applied: SSI 2012/53 Art.10
Reg.27, applied: SSI 2012/53 Art.10
Reg.28, amended: SSI 2012/338 Reg.11
Reg.28A, revoked (in part): SSI 2012/303 Sch.7 para.1
Sch.1, applied: SSI 2012/53 Art.10

1992–cont.

1332. Council Tax (Administration and Enforcement) (Scotland) Regulations 1992–cont.
Sch.1 Part II para.6, amended: SSI 2012/338 Reg.12
Sch.2 Part I para.5, amended: SSI 2012/303 Sch.7 para.1, SSI 2012/338 Reg.13
Sch.2 Part I para.8, amended: SSI 2012/303 Sch.7 para.1, SSI 2012/338 Reg.14
Sch.2 Part II para.9, amended: SSI 2012/338 Reg.15

1335. Council Tax (Reductions for Disabilities) (Scotland) Regulations 1992
Reg.4, amended: SSI 2012/303 Sch.7 para.2

1492. Town and Country Planning General Regulations 1992
Reg.9AA, varied: SI 2012/2167 Art.6

1670. Criminal Justice Act 1991 (Notice of Transfer) Regulations 1992
applied: SI 2012/1726 r.3.11
referred to: SI 2012/1726 r.11.1

1673. Road Works (Maintenance) (Scotland) Regulations 1992
Reg.4, amended: SSI 2012/286 Reg.2

1689. Street Works (Reinstatement) Regulations 1992
Reg.3, applied: SI 2012/3102 Sch.1, SI 2012/3103 Sch.1, SI 2012/3104 Sch.1, SI 2012/3105 Sch.1, SI 2012/3106 Sch.1, SI 2012/3107 Sch.1

1703. Housing (Right to Buy) (Prescribed Persons) Order 1992
Sch.1, amended: SI 2012/1659 Sch.3 para.31

1708. Housing (Service Charge Loans) Regulations 1992
Reg.1, amended: SI 2012/702 Sch.1 para.4
Reg.2, amended: SI 2012/702 Sch.1 para.4

1742. Local Authorities (Calculation of Council Tax Base) (Amendment) Regulations 1992
revoked (in part): SI 2012/2914 Sch.1

1813. Child Support (Maintenance Assessment Procedure) Regulations 1992
revoked (in part): SI 2012/2785 Reg.10
Reg.20, amended: SI 2012/1267 Reg.2
Reg.23, amended: SI 2012/712 Reg.4, SI 2012/1267 Reg.2
Sch.1 para.1, substituted: SI 2012/2785 Reg.2
Sch.1 para.1A, revoked: SI 2012/2785 Reg.2
Sch.1 para.2, amended: SI 2012/2785 Reg.2
Sch.1 para.3, amended: SI 2012/2785 Reg.2
Sch.1 para.4, amended: SI 2012/2785 Reg.2
Sch.1 para.6, substituted: SI 2012/2785 Reg.2
Sch.1 para.7, added: SI 2012/2785 Reg.2

1814. Council Tax Benefit (General) Regulations 1992
applied: SSI 2012/303 Sch.1 para.4, Sch.1 para.10
Sch.1 Part II para.3, applied: SSI 2012/303 Sch.1 para.4
Sch.1 Part III para.12, applied: SSI 2012/303 Sch.1 para.4
Sch.1 Part III para.13, applied: SSI 2012/303 Sch.6 para.1, Sch.6 para.2

1815. Child Support (Maintenance Assessments and Special Cases) Regulations 1992
revoked (in part): SI 2012/2785 Reg.10
Sch.1 Part I para.5B, added: SI 2012/712 Reg.5
Sch.1 Part I para.5B, amended: SI 2012/2007 Sch.1 para.110

1817. Town and Country Planning (Fees for Applications and Deemed Applications) (Amendment) Regulations 1992
revoked (in part): SI 2012/2920 Sch.3

312

1992– cont.

1878. Act of Sederunt (Fees of Witnesses and Short-hand Writers in the Sheriff Court) 1992
Sch.2 para.1, amended: SSI 2012/101 Art.2
Sch.2 para.4, amended: SSI 2012/101 Art.2
Sch.2 para.5, amended: SSI 2012/101 Art.2

1901. Charities (Misleading Names) Regulations 1992
Sch.1, amended: SI 2012/3012 Sch.4 para.3

1989. Child Support (Collection and Enforcement) Regulations 1992
applied: SI 2012/2785 Reg.12
see *KW v Lancaster City Council* [2012] 1 F.L.R. 282 (UT (AAC)), Judge Nicholas Wikeley
Reg.4, substituted: SI 2012/2785 Reg.4
Reg.5, amended: SI 2012/712 Reg.2
Reg.8, amended: SI 2012/2785 Reg.4
Reg.8, applied: SI 2012/2785 Reg.11
Reg.10, applied: SI 2012/2785 Reg.11
Reg.10, substituted: SI 2012/2785 Reg.4
Reg.11, applied: SI 2012/2785 Reg.11
Reg.11, substituted: SI 2012/2785 Reg.4
Reg.20, amended: SI 2012/2785 Reg.4
Reg.20, applied: SI 2012/2785 Reg.11
Reg.25A, amended: SI 2012/2007 Sch.1 para.111
Reg.25AA, amended: SI 2012/2007 Sch.1 para.111
Reg.25AB, amended: SI 2012/2007 Sch.1 para.111
Reg.25AC, amended: SI 2012/2007 Sch.1 para.111
Reg.25AD, amended: SI 2012/2007 Sch.1 para.111
Reg.25C, amended: SI 2012/2785 Reg.4
Reg.25E, amended: SI 2012/2007 Sch.1 para.111
Reg.25F, amended: SI 2012/2007 Sch.1 para.111
Reg.25G, amended: SI 2012/2007 Sch.1 para.111, SI 2012/2785 Reg.4
Reg.25I, amended: SI 2012/2007 Sch.1 para.111
Reg.25J, amended: SI 2012/2007 Sch.1 para.111
Reg.25K, amended: SI 2012/2007 Sch.1 para.111
Reg.25L, amended: SI 2012/2007 Sch.1 para.111
Reg.25M, amended: SI 2012/2007 Sch.1 para.111
Reg.25N, amended: SI 2012/2007 Sch.1 para.111
Reg.25O, amended: SI 2012/2007 Sch.1 para.111
Reg.25R, amended: SI 2012/2007 Sch.1 para.111
Reg.25T, amended: SI 2012/2007 Sch.1 para.111
Reg.25U, amended: SI 2012/2007 Sch.1 para.111
Reg.25V, amended: SI 2012/2007 Sch.1 para.111
Reg.25X, amended: SI 2012/2007 Sch.1 para.111
Reg.25Z, amended: SI 2012/2007 Sch.1 para.111
Reg.28, see *KW v Lancaster City Council* [2012] 1 F.L.R. 282 (UT (AAC)), Judge Nicholas Wikeley
s.art IIIA Reg.25S, amended: SI 2012/2007 Sch.1 para.111

2370. Zootechnical Standards Regulations 1992
revoked (in part): SI 2012/2665 Reg.14

2461. East Cheshire National Health Service Trust (Establishment) Order 1992
referred to: SI 2012/1512 Sch.1

2574. Oxfordshire Learning Disability National Health Service Trust (Establishment) Order 1992
revoked: SI 2012/2570 Art.2

2620. Child Resistant Packaging and Tactile Danger Warnings (Safety) (Revocation) Regulations 1992
applied: SI 2012/1815
revoked: SI 2012/1815 Sch.1

2645. Child Support (Maintenance Arrangements and Jurisdiction) Regulations 1992
Reg.1, amended: SI 2012/2785 Reg.5

1992– cont.

2645. Child Support (Maintenance Arrangements and Jurisdiction) Regulations 1992– *cont.*
Reg.5, amended: SI 2012/2785 Reg.5
Reg.8A, amended: SI 2012/2785 Reg.5

2789. Transport Levying Bodies Regulations 1992
Reg.2, amended: SI 2012/213 Reg.3
Reg.3, amended: SI 2012/213 Reg.4
Reg.4, amended: SI 2012/213 Reg.5
Reg.7, amended: SI 2012/213 Reg.6, SI 2012/2914 Reg.12
Reg.12, amended: SI 2012/460 Sch.1 para.9
Reg.13, amended: SI 2012/460 Sch.1 para.10

2790. Statistics of Trade (Customs and Excise) Regulations 1992
Reg.4, substituted: SI 2012/532 Reg.3
Reg.6, amended: SI 2012/532 Reg.4
Reg.8, amended: SI 2012/532 Reg.5
Sch.1, revoked: SI 2012/532 Reg.6

2844. Medicines (Exemption from Licensing) (Radiopharmaceuticals) Order 1992
revoked: SI 2012/1916 Sch.35

2845. Medicines (Manufacturer's Undertakings for Imported Products) Amendment Regulations 1992
revoked: SI 2012/1916 Sch.35

2870. European Communities (Designation) (No.4) Order 1992
referred to: SI 2012/916 Sch.1

2903. Levying Bodies (General) Regulations 1992
Reg.6, amended: SI 2012/2914 Reg.12
Reg.11, amended: SI 2012/460 Sch.1 para.11

2904. Local Authorities (Calculation of Council Tax Base) (Supply of Information) Regulations 1992
Reg.3, amended: SI 2012/2914 Reg.12

2923. Borough of Ynys Mn-Isle of Anglesey (Electoral Arrangements) Order 1992
revoked: SI 2012/2676 Art.3

2943. Local Authorities (Calculation of Council Tax Base) (Amendment) (No.2) Regulations 1992
revoked (in part): SI 2012/2914 Sch.1

2966. Personal Protective Equipment at Work Regulations 1992
Reg.3, amended: SI 2012/632 Sch.3

2977. National Assistance (Assessment of Resources) Regulations 1992
Reg.20, amended: SSI 2012/68 Reg.2
Reg.20A, amended: SI 2012/842 Reg.4
Reg.28, amended: SSI 2012/68 Reg.3
Sch.3 Part I para.11, amended: SI 2012/2336 Reg.2
Sch.3 Part I para.11 A, added: SI 2012/2336 Reg.2
Sch.3 Part I para.11 B, added: SI 2012/2336 Reg.2
Sch.3 Part II para.31, amended: SI 2012/2336 Reg.2

3004. Workplace (Health, Safety and Welfare) Regulations 1992
Reg.12, see *Clark v Quantum Claims Compensation Specialists Ltd* [2012] CSOH 54, 2012 S.L.T. 979 (OH), Lord Glennie

3013. Road Traffic (Courses for Drink-Drive Offenders) Regulations 1992
revoked: SI 2012/2939 Reg.13

3052. Town and Country Planning (Fees for Applications and Deemed Applications) (Amendment) (No.2) Regulations 1992
revoked (in part): SI 2012/2920 Sch.3

3067. Asbestos (Prohibitions) Regulations 1992
Reg.8, applied: SI 2012/632 Reg.32

1992– cont.

3082. Non-Domestic Rating Contributions (England) Regulations 1992
Reg.6, varied: SI 2012/994 Reg.5
Sch.1 Part 1 para.3, amended: SI 2012/664 Reg.3

3111. Value Added Tax (Removal of Goods) Order 1992
Art.4, amended: SI 2012/2953 Art.2
Art.4, revoked (in part): SI 2012/2953 Art.2
Art.5, amended: SI 2012/2953 Art.2

3121. Value Added Tax (Place of Supply of Services) Order 1992
Art.16, see *Matrix Securities Ltd v Revenue and Customs Commissioners* [2012] UKFTT 320 (TC), [2012] S.F.T.D. 1056 (FTT (Tax)), Judge Peter Kempster

3122. Value Added Tax (Cars) Order 1992
see *Revenue and Customs Commissioners v GMAC UK Plc* [2012] UKUT 279 (TCC), [2012] S.T.C. 2349 (UT (Tax)), Warren, J.
Art.8, see *Pendragon Plc v Revenue and Customs Commissioners* [2012] UKUT 90 (TCC), [2012] S.T.C. 1638 (UT (Tax)), Morgan, J.

3134. Tobacco for Oral Use (Safety) Regulations 1992
see *Imperial Tobacco Ltd, Petitioner* [2012] CSIH 9, 2012 S.C. 297 (IH (1 Div)), Lord President Hamilton

3159. Specified Diseases (Notification and Slaughter) Order 1992
Art.2, amended: SI 2012/2629 Reg.40, SSI 2012/178 Art.39

3230. Transport and Works (Descriptions of Works Interfering with Navigation) Order 1992
Art.2, enabled: SI 2012/1867

3238. Non-Domestic Rating Contributions (Wales) Regulations 1992
Reg.6, varied: SI 2012/466 Reg.8
Sch.4, substituted: SI 2012/3036 Sch.1

3273. Medicines (Labelling) Amendment Regulations 1992
revoked: SI 2012/1916 Sch.35

3274. Medicines (Leaflets) Amendment Regulations 1992
revoked: SI 2012/1916 Sch.35

3288. Package Travel, Package Holidays and Package Tours Regulations 1992
Reg.2, see *Titshall v Qwerty Travel Ltd* [2011] EWCA Civ 1569, [2012] 2 All E.R. 627 (CA (Civ Div)), Longmore, L.J.

1993

13. Food Protection (Emergency Prohibitions) (Radioactivity in Sheep) Partial Revocation Order 1993
revoked (in part): SSI 2012/263 Sch.1

33. Food Protection (Emergency Prohibitions) (Radioactivity in Sheep) (England) (Partial Revocation) Order 1993
revoked: SI 2012/2658 Sch.1

231. Air Navigation (Third Amendment) Order 1993
applied: 2012 c.19 Sch.6 para.4

252. Non-Domestic Rating (Demand Notices) (Wales) Regulations 1993
Reg.2, varied: SI 2012/466 Reg.9
Sch.2 Part I para.1, amended: SI 2012/467 Reg.2

355. Council Tax (Alteration of Lists and Appeals) (Scotland) Regulations 1993
Part IV, applied: SSI 2012/53 Art.12

1993– cont.

355. Council Tax (Alteration of Lists and Appeals) (Scotland) Regulations 1993– *cont.*
Pt II, see *Assessor for Lothian Valuation Joint Board v Campbell* 2012 S.L.T. 414 (IH (2 Div)), The Lord Justice Clerk (Gill)
Reg.4, see *Assessor for Lothian Valuation Joint Board v Campbell* 2012 S.L.T. 414 (IH (2 Div)), The Lord Justice Clerk (Gill)
Reg.19, see *Assessor for Lothian Valuation Joint Board v Campbell* 2012 S.L.T. 414 (IH (2 Div)), The Lord Justice Clerk (Gill)
Reg.21, revoked (in part): SSI 2012/303 Sch.7 para.3
Reg.37, see *Assessor for Lothian Valuation Joint Board v Campbell* 2012 S.L.T. 414 (IH (2 Div)), The Lord Justice Clerk (Gill)

486. Bankruptcy Fees (Scotland) Regulations 1993
revoked: SSI 2012/118 Sch.2

543. Education (Teachers) Regulations 1993
Sch.2 Part I para.3, applied: SI 2012/724 Sch.2 para.9

584. Child Support (Northern Ireland Reciprocal Arrangements) Regulations 1993
Reg.2, amended: SI 2012/2380 Reg.2
Sch.1C, added: SI 2012/2380 Sch.1

593. Reciprocal Enforcement of Maintenance Orders (Hague Convention Countries) Order 1993
Sch.1, amended: SI 2012/2814 Sch.4 para.8

607. Air Navigation (Fourth Amendment) Order 1993
applied: 2012 c.19 Sch.6 para.4

779. Pensions Increase (Review) Order 1993
applied: SI 2012/782 Art.3, Art.4

811. Walsgrave Hospitals National Health Service Trust (Establishment) Order 1993
referred to: SI 2012/1512 Sch.1

834. Medicines Act 1968 (Amendment) Regulations 1993
revoked: SI 2012/1916 Sch.35

920. Act of Sederunt (Child Support Rules) 1993
applied: SSI 2012/271 r.11
Art.1, amended: SSI 2012/271 r.9
Art.2, amended: SSI 2012/271 r.9
Art.5, amended: SSI 2012/271 r.9
Art.5AA, amended: SSI 2012/271 r.9
Art.5AB, amended: SSI 2012/271 r.9
Art.5AC, amended: SSI 2012/271 r.9
Sch.1, amended: SSI 2012/271 r.9

925. Child Support (Maintenance Assessments and Special Cases) Amendment Regulations 1993
revoked: SI 2012/2785 Reg.10

1119. Transport and Works Applications (Inland Waterways Procedure) Rules 1993
Reg.3, amended: SI 2012/1659 Sch.3 para.32
Sch.1 para.1, revoked: SI 2012/1659 Sch.3 para.32
Sch.1 para.3, amended: SI 2012/1658 Sch.1, SI 2012/1659 Sch.3 para.32
Sch.1 para.3, revoked (in part): SI 2012/1658 Sch.1
Sch.2 para.2, amended: SI 2012/1659 Sch.3 para.32

1195. Serbia and Montenegro (United Nations Sanctions) (Dependent Territories) Order 1993
revoked: SI 2012/2592 Sch.2

1200. Export of Goods (Control) (Bosnia-Herzegovina) (ECSC) (Revocation) Order 1993
revoked: SI 2012/2125 Art.2

1993– cont.

1228. Beer Regulations 1993
see *Carlsberg UK Ltd v Revenue and Customs Commissioners* [2012] EWCA Civ 82, [2012] S.T.C. 1140 (CA (Civ Div)), Lord Neuberger (M.R.)
Reg.15, see *Carlsberg UK Ltd v Revenue and Customs Commissioners* [2012] EWCA Civ 82, [2012] S.T.C. 1140 (CA (Civ Div)), Lord Neuberger (M.R.)
Reg.16, see *Carlsberg UK Ltd v Revenue and Customs Commissioners* [2012] EWCA Civ 82, [2012] S.T.C. 1140 (CA (Civ Div)), Lord Neuberger (M.R.)

1572. House of Commons Disqualification Order 1993
Sch.1 Part 1 para.1, amended: SI 2012/1923 Sch.1

1604. Education (School and Placing Information) (Scotland) Amendment, Etc, Regulations 1993
Reg.2, revoked: SSI 2012/130 Sch.3
Reg.3, revoked: SSI 2012/130 Sch.3
Reg.4, revoked: SSI 2012/130 Sch.3
Reg.5, revoked: SSI 2012/130 Sch.3
Reg.6, revoked: SSI 2012/130 Sch.3
Reg.8, revoked: SSI 2012/130 Sch.3
Sch.1 para.1, revoked: SSI 2012/130 Sch.3
Sch.1 para.2, revoked: SSI 2012/130 Sch.3
Sch.1 para.3, revoked: SSI 2012/130 Sch.3
Sch.1 para.4, revoked: SSI 2012/130 Sch.3
Sch.1 para.5, revoked: SSI 2012/130 Sch.3
Sch.1 para.6, revoked: SSI 2012/130 Sch.3

1658. Extraction Solvents in Food Regulations 1993
Sch.1 Part I, amended: SI 2012/1155 Reg.3, SI 2012/1198 Reg.3

1698. Road Traffic Offenders (Prescribed Devices) Order 1993
see *Brotherston v DPP* [2012] EWHC 136 (Admin), (2012) 176 J.P. 153 (DC), Toulson, L.J.

1797. Immigration (Jersey) Order 1993
Sch.1 Part I para.5, amended: SI 2012/2593 Art.2

1813. Channel Tunnel (International Arrangements) Order 1993
Art.2, amended: SI 2012/1264 Art.3
Art.4, amended: SI 2012/1264 Art.4
Sch.1, amended: SI 2012/1264 Art.5
Sch.3 Part I para.2, amended: SI 2012/1264 Art.6
Sch.3 Part I para.3, amended: SI 2012/1264 Art.6
Sch.4 Part I para.5, amended: SI 2012/1547 Sch.2 para.1

1956. Act of Sederunt (Sheriff Court Ordinary Cause Rules) 1993
applied: SI 2012/2886 Sch.1
see *Bank of Scotland Plc v Stevenson* 2012 S.L.T. (Sh Ct) 155 (Sh Ct (South Strathclyde) (Dumfries)), Sheriff G Jamieson; see *Murtaza v Murtaza* 2012 Fam. L.R. 14 (OH), Lord Stewart
Sch.1, applied: SI 2012/2885 Sch.6 para.17, SI 2012/2886 Sch.1, SSI 2012/319 Sch.4 para.17
Sch.1, see *Murtaza v Murtaza* 2012 Fam. L.R. 14 (OH), Lord Stewart; see *Simpson v Downie* [2012] CSIH 74, 2012 Fam. L.R. 121 (IH (Ex Div)), Lord Emslie

2004. Income Tax (Manufactured Overseas Dividends) Regulations 1993
Reg.4, see *First Nationwide v Revenue and Customs Commissioners* [2012] EWCA Civ 278, [2012] S.T.C. 1261 (CA (Civ Div)), Rix, L.J.

2102. Animals (Scientific Procedures) Act (Amendment) Regulations 1993
revoked: SI 2012/3039 Reg.31

1993– cont.

2103. Animals (Scientific Procedures) Act (Amendment) Order 1993
Art.3, revoked: SI 2012/3039 Reg.32

2152. A55 Trunk Road (Bodelwyddan &mdash St Asaph, Clwyd) (Derestriction) Order 1993
varied: SI 2012/945 Art.14

2232. Export of Goods (Control) (Haiti) (Revocation) Order 1993
revoked: SI 2012/2125 Art.2

2240. Housing (Extension of Right to Buy) Order 1993
Sch.1 para.3, amended: SI 2012/2090 Sch.1 para.2
Sch.1 para.5, added: SI 2012/2090 Sch.1 para.2
Sch.1 para.5, amended: SI 2012/2090 Sch.1 para.2

2241. Housing (Preservation of Right to Buy) Regulations 1993
Sch.1 Part I para.1, amended: SI 2012/2090 Sch.1 para.1
Sch.1 Part I para.2, amended: SI 2012/2090 Sch.1 para.1
Sch.1 Part I para.5, amended: SI 2012/2090 Sch.1 para.1
Sch.2, added: SI 2012/2090 Sch.1 para.1
Sch.2, amended: SI 2012/2090 Sch.1 para.1

2574. Royal Wolverhampton Hospitals National Health Service Trust (Establishment) Order 1993
Art.1, amended: SI 2012/1837 Art.2, Art.3
Art.2, amended: SI 2012/1837 Art.3
Art.6, revoked: SI 2012/1837 Art.4
Art.7, revoked: SI 2012/1837 Art.4

2661. European Communities (Designation) (No.3) Order 1993
referred to: SI 2012/916 Sch.1
revoked: SI 2012/1759 Sch.1

2670. Air Navigation (Fifth Amendment) Order 1993
applied: 2012 c.19 Sch.6 para.4

2808. Libya (United Nations Sanctions) (Dependent Territories) Order 1993
revoked: SI 2012/362 Sch.4

2838. Velindre National Health Service Trust (Establishment) Order 1993
Art.1, amended: SI 2012/1262 Art.2
Art.3, amended: SI 2012/1262 Art.3

2854. Employment Appeal Tribunal Rules 1993
r.3, see *Francis v Pertemps Recruitment Partnership Ltd* 2012 S.C. 39 (IH (2 Div)), The Lord Justice Clerk (Gill); see *Jooste v General Medical Council* [2012] Eq. L.R. 1048 (EAT), Judge McMullen Q.C.

2923. Imitation Dummies (Safety) Regulations 1993
revoked: SI 2012/1815 Sch.1

3053. Commercial Agents (Council Directive) Regulations 1993
see *Rossetti Marketing Ltd v Diamond Sofa Co Ltd* [2011] EWHC 2482 (QB), [2012] Bus. L.R. 571 (QBD), Cranston, J.; see *Rossetti Marketing Ltd v Diamond Sofa Co Ltd* [2012] EWCA Civ 1021, [2012] C.P. Rep. 45 (CA (Civ Div)), Lord Neuberger (M.R.)
Reg.18, see *Rossetti Marketing Ltd v Diamond Sofa Co Ltd* [2012] EWCA Civ 1021, [2012] C.P. Rep. 45 (CA (Civ Div)), Lord Neuberger (M.R.)

3094. A38 Trunk Road (Egginton, Derbyshire) (DeRestriction) Order 1993
revoked: SI 2012/2027 Art.4

1993– cont.

3138. Merchant Shipping (Registration of Ships) Regulations 1993
Reg.1, amended: SI 2012/1809 Sch.1 Part 2

3170. Town and Country Planning (Fees for Applications and Deemed Applications) (Amendment) Regulations 1993
revoked (in part): SI 2012/2920 Sch.3

3228. Public Services Contracts Regulations 1993
Reg.32, see *Sita UK Ltd v Greater Manchester Waste Disposal Authority* [2011] EWCA Civ 156, [2012] P.T.S.R. 645 (CA (Civ Div)), Arden, L.J.

1994

50. Food Protection (Emergency Prohibitions) (Radioactivity in Sheep) Partial Revocation Order 1994
revoked (in part): SSI 2012/263 Sch.1

63. Food Protection (Emergency Prohibitions) (Radioactivity in Sheep) (Wales) (Partial Revocation) Order 1994
revoked: SI 2012/2978 Sch.1

65. Food Protection (Emergency Prohibitions) (Radioactivity in Sheep) (England) (Partial Revocation) Order 1994
revoked: SI 2012/2658 Sch.1

104. Medicines (Labelling and Leaflets) Amendment Regulations 1994
revoked: SI 2012/1916 Sch.35

105. Medicines (Homoeopathic Medicinal Products for Human Use) Regulations 1994
applied: SI 2012/504 Reg.40
revoked: SI 2012/1916 Sch.35
Reg.1, amended: SI 2012/504 Reg.56
Reg.1, revoked (in part): SI 2012/504 Reg.58
Reg.4, applied: SI 2012/504 Reg.41
Reg.12, revoked: SI 2012/504 Reg.58
Reg.13, revoked: SI 2012/504 Reg.58
Reg.14, revoked: SI 2012/504 Reg.58
Reg.15, revoked: SI 2012/504 Reg.58
Reg.15A, revoked: SI 2012/504 Reg.58
Reg.16, revoked: SI 2012/504 Reg.58
Reg.17, revoked: SI 2012/504 Reg.58
Reg.18, revoked: SI 2012/504 Reg.58
Sch.2 para.1, revoked: SI 2012/504 Reg.58
Sch.2 para.2, revoked: SI 2012/504 Reg.58
Sch.2 para.3, revoked: SI 2012/504 Reg.58
Sch.2A para.1, revoked: SI 2012/504 Reg.58
Sch.2A para.2, revoked: SI 2012/504 Reg.58
Sch.3 para.1, revoked: SI 2012/504 Reg.58
Sch.3 para.2, revoked: SI 2012/504 Reg.58
Sch.5 Part 3 para.12, applied: SI 2012/504 Reg.37

141. European Communities (Iron and Steel Employees Re-adaptation Benefits Scheme) (No.2) (Scheme Termination) Regulations 1994
revoked: SI 2012/2262 Reg.2

180. Trafford Healthcare National Health Service Trust (Establishment) Order 1994
revoked: SI 2012/803 Art.2

192. Trunk Road (A55) (Pen-y-clip Section, Gwynedd) (One Way Traffic) Order 1994
restored: SI 2012/423 Art.9
revoked (in part): SI 2012/423 Art.9

1994– cont.

307. Royal Hospital of St Bartholomew, the Royal London Hospital and London Chest Hospital National Health Service Trust (Establishment) Order 1994
applied: SI 2012/796 Art.6
revoked (in part): SI 2012/796 Art.6

308. Newham Healthcare National Health Service Trust (Establishment) Order 1994
applied: SI 2012/796 Art.6
revoked (in part): SI 2012/796 Art.6

351. Self-Governing Schools (Application and Amendment of Regulations) (Scotland) Regulations 1994
Reg.9, revoked: SSI 2012/130 Sch.3

426. Airports (Northern Ireland) Order 1994
applied: 2012 c.19 Sch.8 para.11, Sch.10 para.6, Sch.10 para.16, SSI 2012/89 Sch.1
referred to: 2012 c.19 Sch.6 para.4
Part II, added: 2012 c.19 Sch.8 para.8
Part II, applied: 2012 c.19 Sch.10 para.17
Part IV, applied: 2012 c.19 Sch.10 para.15, SI 2012/1128 Art.4
Art.2, amended: 2012 c.19 Sch.8 para.7
Art.2A, applied: 2012 c.19 Sch.8 para.11, Sch.10 para.15, Sch.10 para.16
Art.19, amended: SI 2012/2595 Art.7
Art.25, applied: 2012 c.19 Sch.10 para.17
Art.26, applied: 2012 c.19 Sch.10 para.17
Art.27, revoked: 2012 c.19 s.76
Art.28, revoked: 2012 c.19 s.76
Art.29, applied: 2012 c.19 Sch.10 para.16
Art.29, revoked: 2012 c.19 s.76
Art.30, revoked: 2012 c.19 s.76
Art.31, applied: 2012 c.19 Sch.10 para.4, Sch.10 para.5
Art.31, disapplied: 2012 c.19 Sch.10 para.5
Art.31, revoked: 2012 c.19 s.76
Art.31A, referred to: 2012 c.19 Sch.10 para.5
Art.31A, revoked: 2012 c.19 s.76
Art.31B, revoked: 2012 c.19 s.76
Art.32, revoked: 2012 c.19 s.76
Art.33, revoked: 2012 c.19 s.76
Art.34, revoked: 2012 c.19 s.76
Art.35, revoked: 2012 c.19 s.76
Art.35A, revoked: 2012 c.19 s.76
Art.35B, revoked: 2012 c.19 s.76
Art.36, revoked: 2012 c.19 s.76
Art.37, revoked: 2012 c.19 s.76
Art.38, revoked: 2012 c.19 s.76
Art.39, revoked: 2012 c.19 s.76
Art.40, revoked: 2012 c.19 s.76
Art.41, revoked: 2012 c.19 s.76
Art.42, revoked: 2012 c.19 s.76
Art.43, revoked: 2012 c.19 s.76
Art.44, revoked: 2012 c.19 s.76
Art.45, revoked: 2012 c.19 s.76
Art.46, revoked: 2012 c.19 s.76
Art.47, revoked: 2012 c.19 s.76
Art.48, revoked: 2012 c.19 s.76
Art.49, revoked: 2012 c.19 s.76
Art.70, amended: 2012 c.19 Sch.8 para.9
Sch.9 para.10, revoked: 2012 c.19 Sch.9 para.17

450. Textile Products (Indications of Fibre Content) (Amendment) Regulations 1994
revoked: SI 2012/1102 Sch.1

581. Education (Middle Schools) (Amendment) Regulations 1994
revoked (in part): SI 2012/1797 Reg.2

1994– cont.

757. European Communities (Designation) Order 1994
referred to: SI 2012/ 916 Sch.1

776. Pensions Increase (Review) Order 1994
applied: SI 2012/ 782 Art.3, Art.4

790. A55 Trunk Road (Pen-y-clip Section, Gwynedd) (Derestriction) Order 1994
restored: SI 2012/423 Art.10
revoked (in part): SI 2012/423 Art.10
varied: SI 2012/945 Art.8

899. Medicines (Homoeopathic Medicinal Products for Human Use) Amendment Regulations 1994
revoked: SI 2012/ 1916 Sch.35

1324. Haiti (United Nations Sanctions) (Dependent Territories) Order 1994
revoked: SI 2012/ 362 Sch.4

1381. Ancient Monuments (Class Consents) Order 1994
Sch.1 Part 3, amended: SI 2012/1659 Art.2

1404. Marketing Development Scheme (Specification of Activities) Order 1994
Art.2, amended: SSI 2012/ 215 Sch.1 para.3

1443. Act of Sederunt (Rules of the Court of Session 1994) 1994
Appendix 1, amended: SSI 2012/ 126 r.4, r.5, SSI 2012/ 189 Sch.1, SSI 2012/ 275 r.7
Sch.2, see *Clark v Shirra* [2012] CSOH 30, 2012 Rep. L.R. 76 (OH), Lord Stewart; see *L v Angus Council* 2012 S.L.T. 304 (OH), Lord Stewart; see *MacDonald v Aberdeenshire Council* [2012] CSOH 101, 2012 S.L.T. 863 (OH), Lord Uist
Sch.2 para.2.1, see *MacReath, Petitioner* [2012] CSOH 81, 2012 S.L.T. 1195 (OH), Lord Brodie
Sch.2 Part 2 para.12B.1, added: SSI 2012/ 189 r.2
Sch.2 Part 2 para.12B.2, added: SSI 2012/ 189 r.2
Sch.2 Part 2 para.12B.3, added: SSI 2012/ 189 r.2
Sch.2 Part 3, added: SSI 2012/ 275 r.6
Sch.2 Part 3 para.14.10, added: SSI 2012/ 126 r.2
Sch.2 Pt 3 para.23.4, see *MacReath, Petitioner* [2012] CSOH 81, 2012 S.L.T. 1195 (OH), Lord Brodie
Sch.2 Part 3 para.41.46, revoked: SSI 2012/ 189 r.3
Sch.2 Part 3 para.41.46A, revoked: SSI 2012/ 189 r.3
Sch.2 Part 3 para.41.47, revoked: SSI 2012/ 189 r.3
Sch.2 Part 3 para.41.48, revoked: SSI 2012/ 189 r.3
Sch.2 Part 3 para.41.49, revoked: SSI 2012/ 189 r.3
Sch.2 Part 3 para.41.50, revoked: SSI 2012/ 189 r.3
Sch.2 Part 3 para.41.51, revoked: SSI 2012/ 189 r.3
Sch.2 Part 3 para.41.52, revoked: SSI 2012/ 189 r.3
Sch.2 Part 3 para.41.52A, revoked: SSI 2012/ 189 r.3
Sch.2 Part 3 para.41.52B, revoked: SSI 2012/ 189 r.3
Sch.2 Part 3 para.41.52C, revoked: SSI 2012/ 189 r.3
Sch.2 Part 3 para.41.53, revoked: SSI 2012/ 189 r.3
Sch.2 Part 3 para.41.54, revoked: SSI 2012/ 189 r.3
Sch.2 Part 3 para.41.55, revoked: SSI 2012/ 189 r.3
Sch.2 Part 3 para.41.57, revoked: SSI 2012/ 189 r.3
Sch.2 Part 3 para.41.59, revoked: SSI 2012/ 189 r.3
Sch.2 Part 3 para.42.16, amended: SSI 2012/ 100 r.2, SSI 2012/ 270 r.3
Sch.2 Part 4 para.43.1A, amended: SSI 2012/ 126 r.3
Sch.2 Pt 4 para.43.5, see *MacDonald v Aberdeenshire Council* [2012] CSOH 101, 2012 S.L.T. 863 (OH), Lord Uist
Sch.2 Pt 4 para.43.13, see *Lasseter v Highway Insurance Co Ltd* 2012 Rep. L.R. 24 (OH), Temporary Judge J Beckett, QC
Sch.2 Part 4 para.47.3, amended: SSI 2012/ 275 r.2

1994– cont.

1443. Act of Sederunt (Rules of the Court of Session 1994) 1994– *cont.*
Sch.2 Part 4 para.47.4, amended: SSI 2012/ 275 r.2
Sch.2 Part 4 para.47.6, amended: SSI 2012/ 275 r.2
Sch.2 Part 4 para.47.7, amended: SSI 2012/ 275 r.2
Sch.2 Pt 4 para.47.7, see *Whyte and Mackay Ltd v Blyth & Blyth Consulting Engineers Ltd* [2012] CSOH 89, 2012 S.L.T. 1073 (OH), Lord Malcolm
Sch.2 Part 4 para.47.10, amended: SSI 2012/ 275 r.2
Sch.2 Part 4 para.47.11, amended: SSI 2012/ 275 r.2
Sch.2 Part 4 para.47.12, substituted: SSI 2012/ 275 r.2
Sch.2 Part 4 para.47.13A, added: SSI 2012/ 275 r.2
Sch.2 Part 4 para.47.14, amended: SSI 2012/ 275 r.2
Sch.2 Part 4 para.55.1, amended: SSI 2012/ 275 r.3
Sch.2 Part 4 para.55.3, substituted: SSI 2012/ 275 r.3
Sch.2 Part 4 para.55.4, amended: SSI 2012/ 275 r.3
Sch.2 Part 4 para.55.5B, added: SSI 2012/ 275 r.3
Sch.2 Part 4 para.55.5C, added: SSI 2012/ 275 r.3
Sch.2 Part 4 para.55.6, amended: SSI 2012/ 275 r.3
Sch.2 Part 4 para.55.12, amended: SSI 2012/ 275 r.3
Sch.2 Part 4 para.55.13, amended: SSI 2012/ 275 r.3
Sch.2 Part 4 para.58.7, amended: SSI 2012/ 275 r.4
Sch.2 Part 4 para.58.8, amended: SSI 2012/ 275 r.4
Sch.2 Part 4 para.58.12, added: SSI 2012/ 275 r.4
Sch.2 Part 5, amended: SSI 2012/ 275 r.7
Sch.2 Part 5 para.62.18, amended: SSI 2012/ 275 r.7
Sch.2 Part 5 para.65.1, amended: SSI 2012/ 275 r.7
Sch.2 Part 5 para.67.24, varied: 2012 c.11 s.12
Sch.2 Part 5 para.76.37, amended: SSI 2012/ 275 r.5
Sch.2 Part 5 para.82.3, varied: 2012 c.11 s.12
Sch.2 Part 5 para.87.1, amended: SSI 2012/ 275 r.7
Sch.2 para.7.7, see *Official Liquidator of Weir Construction (Contracts) Ltd, Noter* [2012] CSOH 51, 2012 S.L.T. 1098 (OH), Lord Hodge
Sch.2 para.19.2, see *Royal Bank of Scotland Plc v Matheson* 2012 S.C.L.R. 76 (OH), Lord Glennie
Sch.2 para.25.1, see *Whyte and Mackay Ltd v Blyth & Blyth Consulting Engineers Ltd* [2012] CSOH 89, 2012 S.L.T. 1073 (OH), Lord Malcolm
Sch.2 para.38.15, see *Percy v Govan Initiative Ltd* [2012] CSIH 22, 2012 S.C.L.R. 476 (IH (Ex Div)), Lady Paton
Sch.2 para.38.16, see *Percy v Govan Initiative Ltd* [2012] CSIH 22, 2012 S.C.L.R. 476 (IH (Ex Div)), Lady Paton
Sch.2 para.38.18, see *Percy v Govan Initiative Ltd* [2012] CSIH 22, 2012 S.C.L.R. 476 (IH (Ex Div)), Lady Paton
Sch.2 para.41.2, see *Francis v Pertemps Recruitment Partnership Ltd* 2012 S.C. 39 (IH (2 Div)), The Lord Justice Clerk (Gill)
Sch.2 para.41.20, see *Francis v Pertemps Recruitment Partnership Ltd* 2012 S.C. 39 (IH (2 Div)), The Lord Justice Clerk (Gill)
Sch.2 para.42.5, see *Lasseter v Highway Insurance Co Ltd* 2012 Rep. L.R. 24 (OH), Temporary Judge J Beckett, QC
Sch.2 para.58.8, see *AXA General Insurance Ltd, Petitioners* [2012] 1 A.C. 868 (SC), Lord Hope (Deputy President); see *MacReath, Petitioner* [2012] CSOH 81, 2012 S.L.T. 1195 (OH), Lord Brodie

1516. Insurance Companies Regulations 1994
Reg.45, see *Scottish Widows Plc v Revenue and Customs Commissioners* [2012] 1 All E.R. 379 (SC), Lord Hope (Deputy President)

1994– cont.

1737. Aircraft Operators (Accounts and Records) Regulations 1994
Sch.1, amended: SI 2012/3020 Reg.3, Reg.4

1738. Air Passenger Duty Regulations 1994
Reg.2, amended: SI 2012/3017 Reg.3
Reg.3, amended: SI 2012/3017 Reg.4
Reg.7, amended: SI 2012/2404 Sch.3 para.7
Reg.12, amended: SI 2012/3017 Reg.5
Sch.1, amended: SI 2012/3017 Reg.6

1821. Air Passenger Duty (Connected Flights) Order 1994
Art.3, amended: 2012 c.14 Sch.23 para.2, Sch.23 para.5

1901. Reciprocal Enforcement of Foreign Judgments (Australia) Order 1994
Art.4, see *New Cap Reinsurance Corp Ltd (In Liquidation) v Grant* [2011] EWCA Civ 971, [2012] Ch. 538 (CA (Civ Div)), Mummery, L.J.

1932. Medicines (Advertising) Regulations 1994
revoked: SI 2012/1916 Sch.35

1933. Medicines (Monitoring of Advertising) Regulations 1994
revoked: SI 2012/1916 Sch.35

1986. Race Relations (Prescribed Public Bodies) (No.2) Regulations 1994
Sch.1, varied: SI 2012/725 Art.2

2409. Medicines (Pharmacy and General Sale-Exemption) Amendment Order 1994
revoked: SI 2012/1916 Sch.35

2507. Insolvency Regulations 1994
applied: SI 2012/3013 Sch.1 para.2

2674. Former Yugoslavia (United Nations Sanctions) (Dependent Territories) Order 1994
revoked: SI 2012/2592 Sch.2

2716. Conservation (Natural Habitats, &c.) Regulations 1994
Reg.2, amended: SSI 2012/228 Reg.3
Reg.3, substituted: SSI 2012/228 Reg.4
Reg.4, applied: SSI 2012/360 Sch.4 para.13
Reg.6, revoked (in part): SSI 2012/228 Reg.3
Reg.10, applied: SSI 2012/360 Sch.4 para.13
Reg.37, amended: SSI 2012/228 Reg.5
Reg.37, revoked (in part): SSI 2012/228 Reg.5
Reg.84A, amended: SSI 2012/360 Sch.11 para.7
Reg.101A, amended: SSI 2012/215 Sch.1 para.4
Reg.111, added: SSI 2012/228 Reg.6
Sch.2A, varied: 2012 c.11 s.12

2716. Conservation (Natural Habitats, &c.) Regulations 1994
see *Cornwall Waste Forum St Dennis Branch v Secretary of State for Communities and Local Government* [2011] EWHC 2761 (Admin), [2012] Env. L.R. 13 (QBD (Admin)), Collins, J.

2802. Social Security (Jersey and Guernsey) Order 1994
Sch.1, varied: SI 2012/360 Sch.2

2813. Sea Fishing (Licences and Notices) Regulations 1994
revoked (in part): SI 2012/827 Reg.7

2826. Local Government Changes for England (Calculation of Council Tax Base) Regulations 1994
Reg.3, amended: SI 2012/2914 Reg.12
Reg.4, amended: SI 2012/2914 Reg.12

2946. Social Security (Incapacity Benefit) Regulations 1994
Reg.10, amended: SI 2012/780 Art.14

1994– cont.

3047. Court of Protection (Enduring Powers of Attorney) Rules 1994
varied: SI 2012/945 Art.5

3087. A55 Trunk Road (Abergwyngregyn, Gwynedd) (Derestriction) Order 1994
restored: SI 2012/423 Art.14
revoked (in part): SI 2012/423 Art.14

3088. A55 Trunk Road (Penmaenbach Tunnel, Gwynedd) (Closure of Central Reservation Crossings) Order 1994
disapplied: SI 2012/141 Art.11, SI 2012/163 Art.11

3140. Construction (Design and Management) Regulations 1994
applied: SI 2012/1284 Sch.1, SI 2012/1286 Sch.1, SI 2012/1289 Sch.1

3144. Medicines for Human Use (Marketing Authorisations Etc.) Regulations 1994
applied: SI 2012/504 Reg.47
revoked: SI 2012/1916 Sch.35
Reg.1, amended: SI 2012/1479 Sch.1 para.11
Reg.4, applied: SI 2012/504 Reg.18
Sch.2 Part 1 para.5, applied: SI 2012/504 Sch.7 para.2
Sch.2 Part 2 para.11, applied: SI 2012/504 Reg.37
Sch.2 Part 3 para.16, applied: SI 2012/504 Reg.37
Sch.6 para.1, applied: SI 2012/1916 Sch.32 para.2

3170. Council Tax (Reduction of Liability) (Scotland) Regulations 1994
Reg.4, amended: SSI 2012/303 Sch.7 para.4

3200. Non-Domestic Rating (Unoccupied Property) (Scotland) Regulations 1994
see *Cosmopolitan Bellshill Ltd v North Lanarkshire Council* [2012] CSOH 141, 2012 S.L.T. 1063 (OH), Lord Hodge

3260. Electrical Equipment (Safety) Regulations 1994
Reg.5, applied: SI 2012/2601 Art.3
Reg.7, applied: SI 2012/2601 Art.3

1995

39. Food Protection (Emergency Prohibitions) (Radioactivity in Sheep) (England) (Partial Revocation) Order 1995
revoked: SI 2012/2658 Sch.1

46. Food Protection (Emergency Prohibitions) (Radioactivity in Sheep) (Wales) (Partial Revocation) Order 1995
revoked: SI 2012/2978 Sch.1

48. Food Protection (Emergency Prohibitions) (Radioactivity in Sheep) Partial Revocation Order 1995
revoked (in part): SSI 2012/263 Sch.1

288. Waste Management Licensing (Amendment etc.) Regulations 1995
revoked (in part): SI 2012/811 Reg.7

300. National Health Service Pension Scheme Regulations 1995
Reg.1, amended: SI 2012/610 Reg.4
Reg.1, revoked (in part): SI 2012/610 Reg.4
Reg.2, amended: SI 2012/610 Reg.3
Reg.2A, amended: SI 2012/610 Reg.7
Reg.8, amended: SI 2012/610 Reg.5
s.art S Reg.1, amended: SI 2012/610 Reg.6
Sch.2 para.10, amended: SI 2012/610 Reg.8

310. Social Security (Incapacity Benefit) (Transitional) Regulations 1995
Reg.18, amended: SI 2012/780 Art.15

1995–cont.

311. Social Security (Incapacity for Work) (General) Regulations 1995
Reg.13A, applied: SI 2012/2885 Sch.1 para.26, SI 2012/2886 Sch.1, SSI 2012/303 Sch.1 para.10

418. Town and Country Planning (General Permitted Development) Order 1995
applied: SI 2012/605 Reg.14, SI 2012/1914 Art.17, SI 2012/2920 Reg.1
Art.3, applied: SI 2012/416 Art.8, SI 2012/1914 Art.16, Art.17, Art.18, Art.36, Art.39
Art.3, disapplied: SI 2012/1914 Art.17, SI 2012/2920 Reg.5
Art.4, applied: SI 2012/749 Reg.3, SI 2012/789 Reg.3, SI 2012/2319 Reg.3, SI 2012/2920 Reg.5
Art.5, applied: SI 2012/749 Reg.3, Reg.6, SI 2012/789 Reg.3, Reg.4, Reg.6, SI 2012/2319 Reg.3, Reg.4
Art.5, referred to: SI 2012/749 Reg.4
Art.6, applied: SI 2012/749 Reg.3, Reg.6, SI 2012/789 Reg.3, Reg.6, SI 2012/2319 Reg.3, Reg.4
Sch.2, referred to: SI 2012/2920 Reg.5
Sch.2 Part 1, applied: SI 2012/789 Reg.2, SI 2012/2319 Reg.2
Sch.2 Part 1, referred to: SI 2012/749 Reg.2
Sch.2 Part 1 paraA.1, amended: SI 2012/1346 Art.2
Sch.2 Part 1 paraC.1, amended: SI 2012/1346 Art.2
Sch.2 Part 2, referred to: SI 2012/749 Reg.2
Sch.2 Part 3 paraF, amended: SI 2012/2257 Art.2
Sch.2 Part 3, amended: SI 2012/2257 Art.2
Sch.2 Part 3, referred to: SI 2012/749 Reg.2
Sch.2 Part 3 paraF.1, amended: SI 2012/2257 Art.2
Sch.2 Pt 5, see *Bury MBC v Secretary of State for Communities and Local Government* [2011] EWHC 2192 (Admin), [2012] J.P.L. 51 (QBD (Manchester)), Judge Waksman Q.C.
Sch.2 Pt 6 para.A, see *Murrell v Secretary of State for Communities and Local Government* [2010] EWCA Civ 1367, [2012] 1 P. & C.R. 6 (CA (Civ Div)), Rix, L.J.
Sch.2 Part 6 paraA.1, amended: SI 2012/748 Art.2, SI 2012/2318 Art.2
Sch.2 Part 6 paraB.1, amended: SI 2012/748 Art.2, SI 2012/2318 Art.2
Sch.2 Part 6 paraA.2, amended: SI 2012/748 Art.2, SI 2012/2318 Art.2
Sch.2 Pt 6 para.A2, see *Murrell v Secretary of State for Communities and Local Government* [2010] EWCA Civ 1367, [2012] 1 P. & C.R. 6 (CA (Civ Div)), Rix, L.J.
Sch.2 Part 6 paraB.5, amended: SI 2012/748 Art.2, SI 2012/2318 Art.2
Sch.2 Part 6 paraD.8, added: SI 2012/748 Art.2, SI 2012/2318 Art.2
Sch.2 Part 6 paraD.9, added: SI 2012/748 Art.2, SI 2012/2318 Art.2
Sch.2 Part 7 paraA.1, amended: SI 2012/748 Art.3, SI 2012/2318 Art.3
Sch.2 Part 7 paraA.3, added: SI 2012/748 Art.3
Sch.2 Part 7 paraA.4, added: SI 2012/2318 Art.3
Sch.2 Part 8, applied: SI 2012/789 Reg.2, SI 2012/2319 Reg.2
Sch.2 Part 8, referred to: SI 2012/749 Reg.2
Sch.2 Pt 8 para.B, see *Hertfordshire CC v Secretary of State for Communities and Local Government* [2012] EWHC 277 (Admin), [2012] J.P.L. 836 (QBD (Admin)), Ouseley, J.
Sch.2 Part 11, applied: SI 2012/1914 Art.17, Art.18, Art.36, Art.39
Sch.2 Part 17, applied: SI 2012/472 Art.4, SI 2012/1914 Art.17, Art.18, Art.36, Art.39

1995–cont.

418. Town and Country Planning (General Permitted Development) Order 1995–*cont.*
Sch.2 Part 17 paraA, varied: SI 2012/472 Art.4
Sch.2 Part 17, disapplied: SI 2012/1914 Art.17
Sch.2 Part 17, applied: SI 2012/1914 Art.17
Sch.2 Part 17 paraA.1, varied: SI 2012/472 Art.4
Sch.2 Part 17 paraA.2, varied: SI 2012/472 Art.4
Sch.2 Part 24, applied: SI 2012/801 Art.23
Sch.2 Part 32, applied: SI 2012/789 Reg.2, SI 2012/2319 Reg.2
Sch.2 Part 32, referred to: SI 2012/749 Reg.2
Sch.2 Part 40, applied: SI 2012/789 Reg.2, SI 2012/2319 Reg.2
Sch.2 Part 40, referred to: SI 2012/749 Reg.2
Sch.2 Part 40 paraA, substituted: SI 2012/1346 Art.2
Sch.2 Part 40 paraB, substituted: SI 2012/1346 Art.2
Sch.2 Part 40 paraC, substituted: SI 2012/1346 Art.2
Sch.2 Part 40 paraD, substituted: SI 2012/1346 Art.2
Sch.2 Part 40 paraE, substituted: SI 2012/1346 Art.2
Sch.2 Part 40 paraF, substituted: SI 2012/1346 Art.2
Sch.2 Part 40, substituted: SI 2012/1346 Art.2
Sch.2 Part 40 paraH, substituted: SI 2012/1346 Art.2
Sch.2 Part 40 paraI, substituted: SI 2012/1346 Art.2
Sch.2 Part 40 paraJ, amended: SI 2012/748 Art.4
Sch.2 Part 40 paraJ, substituted: SI 2012/1346 Art.2
Sch.2 Part 40 paraA.1, substituted: SI 2012/1346 Art.2
Sch.2 Part 40 paraB.1, substituted: SI 2012/1346 Art.2
Sch.2 Part 40 paraE.1, substituted: SI 2012/1346 Art.2
Sch.2 Part 40 paraF.1, substituted: SI 2012/1346 Art.2
Sch.2 Part 40 paraH.1, substituted: SI 2012/1346 Art.2
Sch.2 Part 40 paraI.1, substituted: SI 2012/1346 Art.2
Sch.2 Part 40 paraA.2, substituted: SI 2012/1346 Art.2
Sch.2 Part 40 paraB.2, substituted: SI 2012/1346 Art.2
Sch.2 Part 40 paraH.2, substituted: SI 2012/1346 Art.2
Sch.2 Part 40 paraI.2, substituted: SI 2012/1346 Art.2
Sch.2 Part 40 paraH.3, substituted: SI 2012/1346 Art.2
Sch.2 Part 40 paraI.3, substituted: SI 2012/1346 Art.2
Sch.2 Part 41, referred to: SI 2012/749 Reg.2
Sch.2 Part 42, referred to: SI 2012/749 Reg.2
Sch.2 Part 43, applied: SI 2012/2319 Reg.2
Sch.2 Part 43, referred to: SI 2012/749 Reg.2
Sch.2 Part 43 paraA, added: SI 2012/748 Sch.1, SI 2012/2318 Sch.1
Sch.2 Part 43 paraB, added: SI 2012/748 Sch.1, SI 2012/2318 Sch.1
Sch.2 Part 43 paraC, added: SI 2012/748 Sch.1, SI 2012/2318 Sch.1

1995– cont.

1995– cont.

418. Town and Country Planning (General Permitted Development) Order 1995– *cont.*
Sch.2 Part 43 paraD, added: SI 2012/748 Sch.1, SI 2012/2318 Sch.1
Sch.2 Part 43 paraE, added: SI 2012/748 Sch.1, SI 2012/2318 Sch.1
Sch.2 Part 43 paraF, added: SI 2012/748 Sch.1, SI 2012/2318 Sch.1
Sch.2 Part 43, added: SI 2012/748 Sch.1, SI 2012/2318 Sch.1
Sch.2 Part 43 paraA.1, added: SI 2012/748 Sch.1, SI 2012/2318 Sch.1
Sch.2 Part 43 paraB.1, added: SI 2012/748 Sch.1, SI 2012/2318 Sch.1
Sch.2 Part 43 paraC.1, added: SI 2012/748 Sch.1, SI 2012/2318 Sch.1
Sch.2 Part 43 paraD.1, added: SI 2012/748 Sch.1, SI 2012/2318 Sch.1
Sch.2 Part 43 paraE.1, added: SI 2012/748 Sch.1, SI 2012/2318 Sch.1
Sch.2 Part 43 paraF.1, added: SI 2012/748 Sch.1, SI 2012/2318 Sch.1
Sch.2 Part 43 paraA.2, added: SI 2012/748 Sch.1, SI 2012/2318 Sch.1
Sch.2 Part 43 paraB.2, added: SI 2012/748 Sch.1, SI 2012/2318 Sch.1
Sch.2 Part 43 paraC.2, added: SI 2012/748 Sch.1, SI 2012/2318 Sch.1

419. Town and Country Planning (General Development Procedure) Order 1995
applied: SI 2012/801 Art.33
revoked: SI 2012/801 Sch.8
Art.8, applied: SI 2012/801 Art.33
Art.22, see *R. (on the application of Telford Trustee No.1 Ltd) v Telford and Wrekin Council* [2011] EWCA Civ 896, [2012] P.T.S.R. 935 (CA (Civ Div)), Ward, L.J.

449. Medical Devices (Consultation Requirements) (Fees) Regulations 1995
Reg.1, amended: SI 2012/1916 Sch.34 para.70

572. Valuation Appeal Committee (Procedure in Appeals under the Valuation Acts) (Scotland) Regulations 1995
Reg.5, see *JD Wetherspoon v Lothian Valuation Joint Board Assessor* [2012] R.V.R. 124 (Lands Tr (Scot)), J N Wright, Q.C.
Reg.19, see *Assessor for Lanarkshire Valuation Joint Board v Jane Norman Ltd* [2012] CSIH 50, [2012] R.A. 387 (LVAC), The Lord Justice Clerk (Gill)

574. State Hospitals Board for Scotland Order 1995
Sch.1 Part III, amended: SI 2012/1479 Sch.1 para.12

639. Judicial Pensions (Additional Voluntary Contributions) Regulations 1995
Reg.2.15, amended: SI 2012/516 Reg.6

708. Pensions Increase (Review) Order 1995
applied: SI 2012/782 Art.3, Art.4

731. Welfare of Animals (Slaughter or Killing) Regulations 1995
applied: SSI 2012/321 Reg.8, Reg.10
Reg.4, revoked (in part): SSI 2012/321 Reg.30
Reg.6, revoked (in part): SSI 2012/321 Reg.30
Reg.7, revoked (in part): SSI 2012/321 Reg.30
Reg.8, revoked (in part): SSI 2012/321 Reg.30
Reg.9, revoked (in part): SSI 2012/321 Reg.30
Reg.10, revoked (in part): SSI 2012/321 Reg.30
Reg.11, revoked (in part): SSI 2012/321 Reg.30
Reg.12, revoked (in part): SSI 2012/321 Reg.30
Reg.15, amended: SI 2012/501 Reg.3

731. Welfare of Animals (Slaughter or Killing) Regulations 1995– *cont.*
Reg.22, revoked (in part): SSI 2012/321 Reg.30
Reg.26A, added: SI 2012/501 Reg.4
Reg.29, added: SI 2012/501 Reg.5
Sch.1 para.1, revoked (in part): SSI 2012/321 Reg.30
Sch.1 para.2, revoked (in part): SSI 2012/321 Reg.30
Sch.1 para.3, revoked (in part): SSI 2012/321 Reg.30
Sch.1 para.4, revoked (in part): SSI 2012/321 Reg.30
Sch.1 para.5, revoked (in part): SSI 2012/321 Reg.30
Sch.1 para.6, revoked (in part): SSI 2012/321 Reg.30
Sch.1 para.7, revoked (in part): SSI 2012/321 Reg.30
Sch.1 para.8, revoked (in part): SSI 2012/321 Reg.30
Sch.1 para.9, revoked (in part): SSI 2012/321 Reg.30
Sch.1 para.10, revoked (in part): SSI 2012/321 Reg.30
Sch.1 para.11, revoked (in part): SSI 2012/321 Reg.30
Sch.1 para.12, revoked (in part): SSI 2012/321 Reg.30
Sch.2 Part I para.1, revoked (in part): SSI 2012/321 Reg.30
Sch.2 Part II para.2, revoked (in part): SSI 2012/321 Reg.30
Sch.2 Part II para.3, revoked (in part): SSI 2012/321 Reg.30
Sch.2 Part II para.4, revoked (in part): SSI 2012/321 Reg.30
Sch.2 Part III para.5, revoked (in part): SSI 2012/321 Reg.30
Sch.3 Part I para.1, revoked (in part): SSI 2012/321 Reg.30
Sch.3 Part II para.2, revoked (in part): SSI 2012/321 Reg.30
Sch.3 Part II para.3, revoked (in part): SSI 2012/321 Reg.30
Sch.3 Part II para.4, revoked (in part): SSI 2012/321 Reg.30
Sch.3 Part II para.5, revoked (in part): SSI 2012/321 Reg.30
Sch.3 Part III para.6, revoked (in part): SSI 2012/321 Reg.30
Sch.3 Part III para.7, revoked (in part): SSI 2012/321 Reg.30
Sch.3 Part III para.8, revoked (in part): SSI 2012/321 Reg.30
Sch.3 Part III para.9, revoked (in part): SSI 2012/321 Reg.30
Sch.3 Part III para.10, revoked (in part): SSI 2012/321 Reg.30
Sch.3 Part III para.11, revoked (in part): SSI 2012/321 Reg.30
Sch.3 Part III para.12, revoked (in part): SSI 2012/321 Reg.30
Sch.3 Part III para.13, revoked (in part): SSI 2012/321 Reg.30
Sch.3 Part IV para.14, revoked (in part): SSI 2012/321 Reg.30
Sch.3 Part IV para.15, revoked (in part): SSI 2012/321 Reg.30
Sch.3 Part V para.16, revoked (in part): SSI 2012/321 Reg.30
Sch.4 para.1, revoked (in part): SSI 2012/321 Reg.30
Sch.4 para.2, revoked (in part): SSI 2012/321 Reg.30
Sch.4 para.3, revoked (in part): SSI 2012/321 Reg.30
Sch.4 para.4, revoked (in part): SSI 2012/321 Reg.30

731. Welfare of Animals (Slaughter or Killing) Regulations 1995–*cont.*
Sch.4 para.5, revoked (in part): SSI 2012/321 Reg.30
Sch.4 para.6, revoked (in part): SSI 2012/321 Reg.30
Sch.4 para.7, revoked (in part): SSI 2012/321 Reg.30
Sch.4 para.8, revoked (in part): SSI 2012/321 Reg.30
Sch.4 para.9, revoked (in part): SSI 2012/321 Reg.30
Sch.5 Part I para.1, revoked (in part): SSI 2012/321 Reg.30
Sch.5 Part I para.2, revoked (in part): SSI 2012/321 Reg.30
Sch.5 Part II para.3, revoked (in part): SSI 2012/321 Reg.30
Sch.5 Part II para.4, revoked (in part): SSI 2012/321 Reg.30
Sch.5 Part II para.5, revoked (in part): SSI 2012/321 Reg.30
Sch.5 Part II para.6, revoked (in part): SSI 2012/321 Reg.30
Sch.5 Part II para.7, revoked (in part): SSI 2012/321 Reg.30
Sch.5 Part II para.8, revoked (in part): SSI 2012/321 Reg.30
Sch.5 Part II para.9, revoked (in part): SSI 2012/321 Reg.30
Sch.5 Part II para.10, revoked (in part): SSI 2012/321 Reg.30
Sch.5 Part II para.11, revoked (in part): SSI 2012/321 Reg.30
Sch.5 Part II para.12, revoked (in part): SSI 2012/321 Reg.30
Sch.5 Part III para.13, amended: SI 2012/501 Reg.6
Sch.5 Part III para.13, revoked (in part): SSI 2012/321 Reg.30
Sch.5 Part III para.14, revoked (in part): SSI 2012/321 Reg.30
Sch.6 para.1, revoked (in part): SSI 2012/321 Reg.30
Sch.6 para.2, revoked (in part): SSI 2012/321 Reg.30
Sch.6 para.3, revoked (in part): SSI 2012/321 Reg.30
Sch.6 para.4, revoked (in part): SSI 2012/321 Reg.30
Sch.6 para.5, revoked (in part): SSI 2012/321 Reg.30
Sch.7 Part I para.1, revoked (in part): SSI 2012/321 Reg.30
Sch.7 Part I para.2, revoked (in part): SSI 2012/321 Reg.30
Sch.7 Part II para.3, revoked (in part): SSI 2012/321 Reg.30
Sch.7 Part II para.4, revoked (in part): SSI 2012/321 Reg.30
Sch.7 Part II para.5, revoked (in part): SSI 2012/321 Reg.30
Sch.7 Part II para.6, revoked (in part): SSI 2012/321 Reg.30
Sch.7 Part III para.7, amended: SI 2012/501 Reg.7
Sch.7 Part III para.7, revoked (in part): SSI 2012/321 Reg.30
Sch.7 Part III para.8, amended: SI 2012/501 Reg.7
Sch.7 Part III para.8, revoked (in part): SSI 2012/321 Reg.30
Sch.7 Part III para.9, amended: SI 2012/501 Reg.7
Sch.7 Part III para.9, revoked (in part): SSI 2012/321 Reg.30

731. Welfare of Animals (Slaughter or Killing) Regulations 1995–*cont.*
Sch.7 Part III para.10, amended: SI 2012/501 Reg.7
Sch.7 Part III para.10, revoked (in part): SSI 2012/321 Reg.30
Sch.7A Part I para.1, amended: SI 2012/501 Reg.8
Sch.7A Part II para.2, amended: SI 2012/501 Reg.8
Sch.7A Part II para.2, substituted: SI 2012/501 Reg.8
Sch.7A Part III para.3, amended: SI 2012/501 Reg.8
Sch.7A Part III para.3, revoked (in part): SI 2012/501 Reg.8
Sch.7A Part IV para.4, amended: SI 2012/501 Reg.8
Sch.7A Part IV para.5, amended: SI 2012/501 Reg.8
Sch.7A Part IV para.6, amended: SI 2012/501 Reg.8
Sch.7A Part V para.7, amended: SI 2012/501 Reg.8
Sch.8 para.1, revoked (in part): SSI 2012/321 Reg.30
Sch.8 para.2, revoked (in part): SSI 2012/321 Reg.30
Sch.8 para.3, revoked (in part): SSI 2012/321 Reg.30
Sch.9 para.2, amended: SSI 2012/321 Reg.30
Sch.12 Part II para.8, revoked (in part): SSI 2012/321 Reg.30

755. Children (Northern Ireland) Order 1995
Art.2, referred to: SI 2012/2886 Sch.1, SSI 2012/303 Sch.4 para.29
Art.15, applied: SI 2012/2886 Sch.1, SSI 2012/303 Sch.4 para.29
Sch.1 para.17, applied: SI 2012/2886 Sch.1, SSI 2012/303 Sch.4 para.29

866. National Health Service (Injury Benefits) Regulations 1995
see *Newcastle upon Tyne Hospitals NHS Foundation Trust v Bagley* [2012] Eq. L.R. 634 (EAT), Judge Birtles
Reg.4, amended: SI 2012/610 Reg.21

1032. United Nations Arms Embargoes (Dependent Territories) Order 1995
revoked: SI 2012/362 Sch.4

1038. Air Navigation Order 1995
applied: 2012 c.19 Sch.6 para.4

1054. Civil Aviation (Air Travel Organisers Licensing) Regulations 1995
revoked: SI 2012/1017 Sch.1

1096. A483 Trunk Road (Maesbury Road Junction) (Derestriction) Order 1995
revoked: SI 2012/3186 Art.3

1210. Merchant Shipping (Survey and Certification) Regulations 1995
Reg.1, amended: SI 2012/2636 Reg.2
Reg.27, added: SI 2012/2636 Reg.2

1268. Value Added Tax (Special Provisions) Order 1995
Art.5, see *Pendragon Plc v Revenue and Customs Commissioners* [2012] UKUT 90 (TCC), [2012] S.T.C. 1638 (UT (Tax)), Morgan, J.; see *Royal Bank of Scotland Group Plc v Revenue and Customs Commissioners* [2012] EWHC 9 (Ch), [2012] S.T.C. 797 (Ch D), Mann, J.

1296. Air Navigation (Isle of Man) (Revocation) Order 1995
applied: 2012 c.19 Sch.6 para.4

1527. Fraserburgh Harbour Revision Order 1995
referred to: SSI 2012/262 Art.1

1629. Gas Appliances (Safety) Regulations 1995
Reg.1, revoked (in part): SI 2012/1815 Sch.1
Reg.4, revoked (in part): SI 2012/1815 Sch.1

1995–cont.

1629. Gas Appliances (Safety) Regulations 1995–
cont.
Reg.24, revoked (in part): 2012 c.9 Sch.2 para.13,
Sch.10 Part 2
1739. Education Authority Bursaries (Scotland)
Regulations 1995
Reg.4, applied: SI 2012/2886 Sch.1
1970. Air Navigation (No.2) Order 1995
applied: 2012 c.19 Sch.6 para.4
2038. Borehole Sites and Operations Regulations
1995
Reg.6, applied: SI 2012/1652 Sch.17
2321. Medicines Act 1968 (Amendment) Regulations
1995
revoked: SI 2012/1916 Sch.35
2427. Spring Traps Approval Order 1995
revoked: SI 2012/13 Art.3
2478. Bovine Embryo (Collection, Production and
Transfer) Regulations 1995
applied: SI 2012/2665 Reg.10
2507. Motorways Traffic (Scotland) Regulations
1995
Reg.2, varied: SSI 2012/147 Reg.4, SSI 2012/343
Reg.5, SSI 2012/344 Reg.5
Reg.6, varied: SSI 2012/147 Reg.4, SSI 2012/343
Reg.5, SSI 2012/344 Reg.5
Reg.8, varied: SSI 2012/147 Reg.4, SSI 2012/343
Reg.5, SSI 2012/344 Reg.5
Reg.12, varied: SSI 2012/147 Reg.4, SSI 2012/343
Reg.5, SSI 2012/344 Reg.5
2518. Value Added Tax Regulations 1995
Reg.2, amended: SI 2012/1899 Reg.4
Reg.4A, added: SI 2012/1899 Reg.5
Reg.4B, added: SI 2012/1899 Reg.5
Reg.5, amended: SI 2012/1899 Reg.6
Reg.5, revoked (in part): SI 2012/1899 Reg.6
Reg.6, amended: SI 2012/1899 Reg.7
Reg.10, amended: SI 2012/1899 Reg.8
Reg.13, amended: SI 2012/2951 Reg.2
Reg.13A, amended: SI 2012/2951 Reg.2
Reg.13ZA, revoked: SI 2012/2951 Reg.2
Reg.14, amended: SI 2012/2951 Reg.2
Reg.15B, added: SI 2012/1899 Reg.9
Reg.16A, added: SI 2012/2951 Reg.2
Reg.22, amended: SI 2012/1899 Reg.10
Reg.22A, amended: SI 2012/1899 Reg.11
Reg.22C, amended: SI 2012/1899 Reg.12
Reg.25, amended: SI 2012/1899 Reg.13
Reg.25A, amended: SI 2012/33 Reg.4, Reg.6,
Reg.8, Reg.9, Reg.10, Reg.11, Reg.12, Reg.13, SI
2012/1899 Reg.14
Reg.25A, revoked (in part): SI 2012/33 Reg.5,
Reg.7, Reg.14
Reg.29, see *Best Buys Supplies Ltd v Revenue and*
Customs Commissioners [2012] S.T.C. 885 (UT
(Tax)), Judge Theodore Wallace
Reg.34, amended: SI 2012/1899 Reg.15
Reg.35, see *R. (on the application of Capital*
Accommodation (London) Ltd (In
Liquidation)) v Revenue and Customs
Commissioners [2012] UKUT 276 (TCC),
[2012] B.V.C. 1780 (UT (Tax)), Sales, J.
Reg.38, see *Revenue and Customs Commissioners*
v GMAC UK Plc [2012] UKUT 279 (TCC), [2012]
S.T.C. 2349 (UT (Tax)), Warren, J.
Reg.86, revoked (in part): SI 2012/2951 Reg.2
Reg.87, revoked: SI 2012/2951 Reg.2

1995–cont.

2518. Value Added Tax Regulations 1995–cont.
Reg.90, see *Royal Bank of Scotland Group Plc v*
Revenue and Customs Commissioners [2012]
EWHC 9 (Ch), [2012] S.T.C. 797 (Ch D),
Mann, J.
Reg.99, amended: SI 2012/1899 Reg.16
Reg.102, see *London Clubs Management Ltd v*
Revenue and Customs Commissioners [2011]
EWCA Civ 1323, [2012] S.T.C. 388 (CA (Civ
Div)), Ward, L.J.
Reg.113A, added: SI 2012/1899 Reg.17
Reg.145B, amended: SI 2012/1899 Reg.18
Reg.145C, amended: SI 2012/1899 Reg.19
Reg.191, amended: SI 2012/1899 Reg.20
Reg.201A, substituted: SI 2012/1899 Reg.21
Reg.203, amended: SI 2012/1899 Reg.22
Reg.204, amended: SI 2012/1899 Reg.23
Reg.205, amended: SI 2012/1899 Reg.24
Reg.206, amended: SI 2012/1899 Reg.25
Reg.208, amended: SI 2012/1899 Reg.26
Sch.1, revoked: SI 2012/1899 Reg.27
2631. Amusement Machine Licence Duty Regula-
tions 1995
revoked: 2012 c.14 Sch.24 para.53
2692. A470 Trunk Road (Llanrwst, Gwynedd) (De-
Restriction) Order 1995
revoked: SI 2012/339 Art.3
2705. Jobseekers (Northern Ireland) Order 1995
Art.2, enabled: SI 2012/2569
Art.24, enabled: SI 2012/2569
Art.36, enabled: SI 2012/2569
2709. Reciprocal Enforcement of Maintenance
Orders (United States of America) Order
1995
Sch.2 para.16, amended: SI 2012/2814 Sch.5 para.6
Sch.3, amended: SI 2012/2814 Sch.5 para.6
2716. Other Fuel Substitutes (Rates of Excise Duty
etc) Order 1995
applied: SI 2012/3055 Art.5
2800. National Health Service Litigation Authority
(Establishment and Constitution) Order 1995
Art.1, amended: SI 2012/1641 Sch.3 para.3
2801. National Health Service Litigation Authority
Regulations 1995
Reg.1, amended: SI 2012/1641 Sch.3 para.2, Sch.4
para.2
Reg.7, amended: SI 2012/1641 Sch.3 para.2, Sch.4
para.2, SI 2012/2404 Sch.3 para.8
2803. National Park Authorities (Wales) Order
1995
Art.18, revoked: SI 2012/801 Sch.8
Sch.5 para.21, revoked: SI 2012/801 Sch.8
2869. Goods Vehicles (Licensing of Operators)
Regulations 1995
Reg.31, amended: SI 2012/2404 Sch.3 para.9
2880. Sale of Registration Marks Regulations 1995
see *Tanjoukian v Revenue and Customs*
Commissioners [2012] UKUT 361 (TCC),
[2012] B.V.C. 1905 (UT (Tax)), Henderson, J.
2909. Public Service Vehicles (Operators Licences)
(Fees) Regulations 1995
Sch.1, amended: SI 2012/306 Reg.2
3000. Goods Vehicles (Licensing of Operators)
(Fees) Regulations 1995
Sch.1 Part I, amended: SI 2012/308 Reg.2
3091. National Health Service (Service Committees
and Tribunal) Amendment Regulations 1995
revoked (in part): SI 2012/1909 Sch.8 para.1

1995–cont.

3163. Reporting of Injuries, Diseases and Dangerous Occurrences Regulations 1995
Reg.3, amended: SI 2012/199 Reg.2
Reg.7, amended: SI 2012/199 Reg.3
Reg.10, amended: SI 2012/199 Reg.4
Sch.4 Part III para.1, added: SI 2012/199 Reg.5
Sch.4 Part III para.2, added: SI 2012/199 Reg.5
Sch.4 Part III para.3, added: SI 2012/199 Reg.5
Sch.4 Part III para.4, added: SI 2012/199 Reg.5

3336. Town and Country Planning (General Development Procedure) (Welsh Forms) Order 1995
revoked: SI 2012/801 Sch.8

1996

26. Plant Health (Licence Fees) (England and Wales) Regulations 1996
revoked (in part): SI 2012/745 Reg.7, SI 2012/1493 Reg.7

31. Food Protection (Emergency Prohibitions) (Radioactivity in Sheep) Partial Revocation Order 1996
revoked (in part): SSI 2012/263 Sch.1

62. Food Protection (Emergency Prohibitions) (Radioactivity in Sheep) (England) (Partial Revocation) Order 1996
revoked: SI 2012/2658 Sch.1

180. Charities (Exception from Registration) Regulations 1996
Reg.4, amended: SI 2012/1734 Reg.2, SI 2012/3012 Sch.4 para.4
Reg.5, amended: SI 2012/3012 Sch.4 para.4

192. Equipment and Protective Systems Intended for Use in Potentially Explosive Atmospheres Regulations 1996
Sch.5, amended: SI 2012/1809 Sch.1 Part 2

207. Jobseeker's Allowance Regulations 1996
Reg.1, amended: SI 2012/757 Reg.4, SI 2012/956 Art.5, SI 2012/1616 Reg.2
Reg.1, applied: SI 2012/2885 Sch.1 para.35, SI 2012/3145 Sch.1, SSI 2012/303 Reg.49, SSI 2012/319 Reg.45
Reg.4, amended: SI 2012/2568 Reg.5
Reg.11, amended: SI 2012/956 Art.5
Reg.14, amended: SI 2012/397 Reg.2, SI 2012/1616 Reg.2
Reg.14A, added: SI 2012/853 Reg.2
Reg.14A, amended: SI 2012/1479 Sch.1 para.70
Reg.17A, amended: SI 2012/2568 Reg.5
Reg.17A, referred to: SI 2012/2886 Sch.1, SI 2012/3145 Sch.1
Reg.17B, added: SI 2012/874 Reg.3
Reg.19, amended: SI 2012/853 Reg.2, SI 2012/1616 Reg.2
Reg.19, applied: SI 2012/2886 Sch.1, SI 2012/3145 Sch.1, SSI 2012/303 Reg.41
Reg.21B, added: SI 2012/874 Reg.3
Reg.23, amended: SI 2012/2568 Reg.5
Reg.23A, amended: SI 2012/2568 Reg.5
Reg.24, amended: SI 2012/824 Reg.3, SI 2012/2568 Reg.5
Reg.27, amended: SI 2012/2568 Reg.5
Reg.27A, revoked: SI 2012/2568 Reg.5
Reg.27B, revoked: SI 2012/2568 Reg.5
Reg.28, revoked: SI 2012/2568 Reg.5
Reg.29, revoked: SI 2012/2568 Reg.5
Reg.30, amended: SI 2012/1616 Reg.2
Reg.30, revoked: SI 2012/2568 Reg.5

1996–cont.

207. Jobseeker's Allowance Regulations 1996–*cont.*
Reg.34, amended: SI 2012/853 Reg.2
Reg.47, amended: SI 2012/2568 Reg.5
Reg.50, amended: SI 2012/2575 Reg.3
Reg.52, amended: SI 2012/2568 Reg.5
Reg.55, amended: SI 2012/2568 Reg.5
Reg.55A, amended: SI 2012/2568 Reg.5
Reg.57, amended: SI 2012/956 Art.5
Reg.61, amended: SI 2012/2568 Reg.5
Reg.63, amended: SI 2012/2568 Reg.5
Reg.64, amended: SI 2012/2568 Reg.5
Reg.65, amended: SI 2012/2568 Reg.5
Reg.66, amended: SI 2012/2568 Reg.5
Reg.67, amended: SI 2012/2568 Reg.5
Reg.68, amended: SI 2012/2568 Reg.5
Reg.69, substituted: SI 2012/2568 Reg.2
Reg.70, substituted: SI 2012/2568 Reg.2
Reg.70A, added: SI 2012/2568 Reg.2
Reg.70B, added: SI 2012/2568 Reg.2
Reg.70C, added: SI 2012/2568 Reg.2
Reg.72, amended: SI 2012/1135 Reg.2, SI 2012/2575 Reg.3
Reg.72, substituted: SI 2012/2568 Reg.2
Reg.73, revoked: SI 2012/2568 Reg.2
Reg.73A, revoked: SI 2012/2568 Reg.2
Reg.74, amended: SI 2012/2568 Reg.2
Reg.74A, revoked: SI 2012/2575 Reg.3
Reg.74B, revoked: SI 2012/2568 Reg.2
Reg.75, amended: SI 2012/956 Art.5, SI 2012/2568 Reg.2
Reg.75, applied: SI 2012/3145 Sch.1
Reg.75, referred to: SI 2012/2886 Sch.1, SI 2012/3145 Sch.1
Reg.75, revoked (in part): SI 2012/2568 Reg.2
Reg.79, amended: SI 2012/780 Art.24
Reg.83, referred to: SI 2012/780 Art.25
Reg.84, referred to: SI 2012/780 Art.25
Reg.85, referred to: SI 2012/780 Art.25
Reg.85A, amended: SI 2012/2587 Reg.3
Reg.87, amended: SI 2012/2568 Reg.5
Reg.94, amended: SI 2012/1616 Reg.2, SI 2012/2575 Reg.3
Reg.113, applied: SI 2012/2885 Sch.1 para.35, SI 2012/2886 Sch.1, SI 2012/3145 Sch.1, SSI 2012/303 Reg.49, SSI 2012/319 Reg.45
Reg.113, referred to: SI 2012/2885 Sch.1 para.35
Reg.115, applied: SI 2012/2886 Sch.1
Reg.130, amended: SI 2012/956 Art.5
Reg.140, amended: SI 2012/2568 Reg.3
Reg.140, revoked (in part): SI 2012/2568 Reg.3
Reg.140A, revoked: SI 2012/2568 Reg.3
Reg.141, amended: SI 2012/2568 Reg.3
Reg.142, amended: SI 2012/2568 Reg.3
Reg.145, referred to: SI 2012/780 Sch.16
Reg.146A, amended: SI 2012/2568 Reg.4
Reg.146A, revoked (in part): SI 2012/2568 Reg.4
Reg.146B, revoked: SI 2012/2568 Reg.4
Reg.146C, amended: SI 2012/2568 Reg.4
Reg.146D, amended: SI 2012/2568 Reg.4
Reg.146G, referred to: SI 2012/780 Sch.16
Reg.152, amended: SI 2012/2568 Reg.5
Reg.161, amended: SI 2012/2568 Reg.5
Reg.170, amended: SI 2012/956 Art.5
Reg.172, amended: SI 2012/780 Art.26
Sch.A1 para.16, amended: SI 2012/956 Art.5
Sch.1 Part I para.1, substituted: SI 2012/780 Sch.13
Sch.1 Part I para.2, substituted: SI 2012/780 Sch.13
Sch.1 Part II para.4, referred to: SI 2012/780 Art.25

1996–cont.

207. Jobseeker's Allowance Regulations 1996–*cont.*
Sch.1 Part III para.15A, referred to: SI 2012/780 Art.25
Sch.1 Part III para.16, referred to: SI 2012/780 Art.25
Sch.1 Part IV, substituted: SI 2012/780 Sch.14
Sch.1 Part IVB para.20M, substituted: SI 2012/780 Sch.15
Sch.2 para.1, amended: SI 2012/913 Reg.4
Sch.2 para.5, referred to: SI 2012/780 Sch.16
Sch.2 para.6, referred to: SI 2012/780 Sch.16
Sch.2 para.7, referred to: SI 2012/780 Sch.16
Sch.2 para.9, referred to: SI 2012/780 Sch.16
Sch.2 para.10, referred to: SI 2012/780 Sch.16
Sch.2 para.11, referred to: SI 2012/780 Sch.16
Sch.2 para.17, amended: SI 2012/780 Art.25
Sch.5 para.4, referred to: SI 2012/780 Sch.16
Sch.5 para.14, referred to: SI 2012/780 Sch.16
Sch.5A para.3, referred to: SI 2012/780 Sch.16
Sch.6 para.19, substituted: SI 2012/1616 Reg.2
Sch.6A para.5, revoked: SI 2012/1616 Reg.2
Sch.7 para.4, amended: SI 2012/757 Reg.4
Sch.7 para.5, amended: SI 2012/757 Reg.4
Sch.8 para.12, applied: SI 2012/2885 Sch.6 para.22, SI 2012/2886 Sch.1, SSI 2012/319 Sch.4 para.22

251. National Health Service (Clinical Negligence Scheme) Regulations 1996
Reg.3, amended: SI 2012/1641 Sch.3 para.4

263. Charter Trustees Regulations 1996
Reg.13, amended: SI 2012/460 Sch.1 para.13

275. Gas (Northern Ireland) Order 1996
applied: SI 2012/1128 Art.4
referred to: 2012 c.19 Sch.6 para.4
Art.8, applied: SSI 2012/89 Sch.1

428. Noise Insulation (Railways and Other Guided Transport Systems) Regulations 1996
applied: SI 2012/2284 Sch.1 para.10

430. Council Tax (Administration and Enforcement) (Scotland) Amendment Regulations 1996
Reg.18, revoked: SSI 2012/303 Sch.7 para.5

482. Medicines (Homoeopathic Medicinal Products for Human Use) Amendment Regulations 1996
revoked: SI 2012/1916 Sch.35

513. Act of Adjournal (Criminal Procedure Rules) 1996
Sch.2 Part III para.8.1, amended: SSI 2012/125 r.2
Sch.2 Part III para.9.6, amended: SSI 2012/125 r.3
Sch.2 Part III para.15.1, amended: SSI 2012/187 r.2
Sch.2 Part III para.15.5A, amended: SSI 2012/300 r.2
Sch.2 Part III para.15.16, amended: SSI 2012/187 r.2
Sch.2 Part IV para.17.1, amended: SSI 2012/125 r.4
Sch.2 Part IV para.19B.1, amended: SSI 2012/187 r.3
Sch.2 Part IV para.19.1, amended: SSI 2012/125 r.5
Sch.2 Part IV para.19.14, amended: SSI 2012/187 r.2
Sch.2 Part IV para.19.19, amended: SSI 2012/187 r.2
Sch.2 Part VII para.34.2A, added: SSI 2012/125 r.6
Sch.2 Part VII para.41.3, varied: 2012 c.11 s.12

525. Local Government Reorganisation (Wales) (Consequential Amendments) Order 1996
Art.3, revoked: SI 2012/801 Sch.8
Sch.1 Part III para.20, revoked: SI 2012/801 Sch.8

551. Gas Safety (Management) Regulations 1996
applied: SI 2012/1652 Reg.15, Sch.12
Reg.11, applied: SI 2012/1652 Sch.12

661. Coroners Districts (Wales) Order 1996
Sch.1, amended: SI 2012/2605 Art.5

1996–cont.

662. Coroners Districts (Designation of Relevant Councils) (Wales) Order 1996
Sch.1, amended: SI 2012/2605 Art.6

686. National Health Service (Existing Liabilities Scheme) Regulations 1996
Reg.3, amended: SI 2012/1641 Sch.3 para.5

703. National Health Service (Service Committees and Tribunal) Amendment Regulations 1996
revoked (in part): SI 2012/1909 Sch.8 para.1

707. Health Authorities (Membership and Procedure) Regulations 1996
Reg.1, amended: SI 2012/1641 Sch.4 para.3, SI 2012/1909 Sch.8 para.1
Reg.10, amended: SI 2012/1641 Sch.4 para.3, SI 2012/2404 Sch.3 para.10
Reg.14, amended: SI 2012/1909 Sch.8 para.1

716. United Nations (International Tribunal) (Former Yugoslavia) Order 1996
Sch.1, amended: SI 2012/2559 Sch.1

800. Pensions Increase (Review) Order 1996
applied: SI 2012/782 Art.3, Art.4

825. Pipelines Safety Regulations 1996
applied: SI 2012/1652 Reg.15
Reg.13A, applied: SI 2012/1282 Sch.1, SI 2012/1284 Sch.1, SI 2012/1286 Sch.1, SI 2012/1289 Sch.1, SI 2012/1294 Sch.1, SI 2012/1295 Sch.1

972. Special Waste Regulations 1996
Reg.15, amended: SSI 2012/360 Sch.11 para.8
Reg.17, amended: SSI 2012/360 Sch.11 para.8

1022. Lands Tribunal Rules 1996
r.10, see *Smith v Sandwell MBC* [2012] R.V.R. 38 (UT (Lands)), George Bartlett Q.C. (President, LTr)

1130. A82 Trunk Road (Crianlarich Western Bypass) Order 1996
revoked: SSI 2012/241 Art.2

1131. A82 Trunk Road (Crianlarich Western Bypass) (Side Roads) Order 1996
revoked: SSI 2012/242 Art.2

1172. Occupational Pension Schemes (Contracting-out) Regulations 1996
Part VII, applied: SI 2012/687 Sch.4 para.15
Reg.1, amended: SI 2012/1817 Sch.1 para.2
Reg.19, applied: SI 2012/687 Sch.4 para.15
Reg.20, applied: SI 2012/687 Sch.4 para.15
Reg.20A, applied: SI 2012/687 Sch.4 para.15
Reg.21, applied: SI 2012/687 Sch.4 para.15
Reg.23, amended: SI 2012/1817 Sch.1 para.2
Reg.42, applied: SI 2012/687 Sch.4 para.15
Reg.44, applied: SI 2012/687 Sch.4 para.15
Reg.45, applied: SI 2012/687 Sch.4 para.15
Reg.62, amended: SI 2012/542 Reg.2
Sch.3 para.4, amended: SI 2012/542 Reg.2

1296. United Nations (International Tribunal) (Rwanda) Order 1996
Sch.1, amended: SI 2012/2559 Sch.2

1301. Air Navigation (Amendment) Order 1996
applied: 2012 c.19 Sch.6 para.4

1362. A77 Trunk Road (Cairnryan) (30mph Speed Limit) Order 1996
revoked: SSI 2012/115 Art.4

1390. Civil Aviation (Air Travel Organisers Licensing) (Amendment) Regulations 1996
revoked: SI 2012/1017 Sch.1

1423. Amusement Machine Licence Duty (Special Licences) Regulations 1996
revoked: 2012 c.14 Sch.24 para.53

1996-cont.

1462. Contracting-out (Transfer and Transfer Payment) Regulations 1996
applied: SI 2012/687 Sch.4 para.15

1499. Food Labelling Regulations 1996
Reg.2, see *Torfaen CBC v Douglas Willis Ltd* [2012] EWHC 296 (Admin), [2012] P.T.S.R. 1482 (DC), Aikens, L.J.
Reg.2, amended: SI 2012/2619 Reg.29, SI 2012/2705 Reg.29, SSI 2012/318 Reg.29
Reg.3, amended: SI 2012/1809 Sch.1 Part 2
Reg.4, see *Torfaen CBC v Douglas Willis Ltd* [2012] EWHC 296 (Admin), [2012] P.T.S.R. 1482 (DC), Aikens, L.J.
Reg.5, see *Torfaen CBC v Douglas Willis Ltd* [2012] EWHC 296 (Admin), [2012] P.T.S.R. 1482 (DC), Aikens, L.J.
Reg.44, see *Torfaen CBC v Douglas Willis Ltd* [2012] EWHC 296 (Admin), [2012] P.T.S.R. 1482 (DC), Aikens, L.J.

1513. Health and Safety (Consultation with Employees) Regulations 1996
applied: SI 2012/335 Sch.2 para.20, SI 2012/2991 Sch.2 para.28

1527. Landfill Tax Regulations 1996
Reg.31, amended: SI 2012/885 Reg.2
Reg.33, amended: SSI 2012/360 Sch.11 para.9

1564. Protection of Water Against Agricultural Nitrate Pollution (Scotland) Regulations 1996
Reg.2, varied: 2012 c.11 s.12

1655. Occupational Pension Schemes (Disclosure of Information) Regulations 1996
Reg.1, amended: SI 2012/1811 Reg.2, SI 2012/1817 Sch.1 para.5
Reg.4, amended: SI 2012/1811 Reg.2
Sch.1 para.2, substituted: SI 2012/1811 Reg.2

1656. Work in Compressed Air Regulations 1996
applied: SI 2012/1652 Sch.5

1715. Occupational Pension Schemes (Scheme Administration) Regulations 1996
Reg.4, amended: SI 2012/692 Reg.4
Reg.16, amended: SI 2012/215 Reg.40

1817. Town and Country Planning (General Development Procedure) (Amendment) Order 1996
revoked: SI 2012/801 Sch.8

1847. Occupational Pension Schemes (Transfer Values) Regulations 1996
Reg.1, amended: SI 2012/692 Reg.5
Reg.7, applied: SI 2012/687 Sch.2 para.17
Reg.7A, applied: SI 2012/687 Sch.2 para.17
Reg.7B, applied: SI 2012/687 Sch.2 para.17, Sch.4 para.5
Reg.7C, applied: SI 2012/687 Sch.2 para.17
Reg.7E, applied: SI 2012/687 Sch.2 para.17

1898. Welsh Language Schemes (Public Bodies) Order 1996
Sch.1, amended: SI 2012/1659 Art.2

1919. Employment Rights (Northern Ireland) Order 1996
Art.130, see *Pace Telecom Ltd v McAuley* [2012] Eq. L.R. 148 (CA (NI)), Coghlin, L.J.

1975. Occupational Pension Schemes (Requirement to obtain Audited Accounts and a Statement from the Auditor) Regulations 1996
Sch.1 para.8, amended: SI 2012/1741 Sch.1 para.4

2085. Road Vehicles (Construction And Use) (Amendment) (No.4) Regulations 1996
Reg.4, revoked: SI 2012/1404 Sch.1

1996-cont.

2195. Medicines (Exemptions from Licences) (Revocation) Order 1996
revoked: SI 2012/1916 Sch.35

2235. Deregulation (Slaughterhouses Act 1974 and Slaughter of Animals (Scotland) Act 1980) Order 1996
Art.9, revoked (in part): SSI 2012/321 Sch.5 Part 2

2420. Medicines (Data Sheet) Amendment Regulations 1996
revoked: SI 2012/1916 Sch.35

2464. A5 Trunk Road (Fazeley Two Gates — Wilnecote Bypass, Staffordshire) (Derestriction and 40 Miles Per Hour Speed Limit) Order 1996
Sch.1, amended: SI 2012/1125 Art.4

2475. Personal and Occupational Pension Schemes (Pensions Ombudsman) Regulations 1996
see *R. (on the application of Government Actuary's Department) v Pensions Ombudsman* [2012] EWHC 1796 (Admin), [2012] Pens. L.R. 331 (QBD (Admin)), Ouseley, J.
Reg.1, see *R. (on the application of Government Actuary's Department) v Pensions Ombudsman* [2012] EWHC 1796 (Admin), [2012] Pens. L.R. 331 (QBD (Admin)), Ouseley, J.

2489. Local Authorities Traffic Orders (Procedure) (England and Wales) Regulations 1996
Reg.18, see *R. (on the application of Herron) v Parking Adjudicator* [2011] EWCA Civ 905, [2012] P.T.S.R. 1257 (CA (Civ Div)), Stanley Burnton, L.J.

2552. British Waterways Board (Sheffield and Tinsley Canal) (Reclassification) Order 1996
varied: SI 2012/1659 Art.2
Art.1, varied: SI 2012/1659 Art.2

2628. Specified Diseases (Notification) Order 1996
Sch.1 Part I, amended: SI 2012/2629 Reg.40
Sch.1 Part I, revoked (in part): SSI 2012/178 Art.39

2714. Greater Manchester (Light Rapid Transit System) (Eccles Extension) Order 1996
Art.55, applied: SI 2012/981 Art.6
Art.55, varied: SI 2012/2980 Art.6

2745. Social Security Benefit (Computation of Earnings) Regulations 1996
Reg.7, applied: SI 2012/780 Art.6

2756. Stands for Carry-cots (Safety) (Revocation) Regulations 1996
revoked: SI 2012/1815 Sch.1

2794. National Park Authorities (Levies) (England) Regulations 1996
Reg.9, amended: SI 2012/460 Sch.1 para.12

2798. Civil Aviation (Investigation of Air Accidents and Incidents) Regulations 1996
applied: 2012 c.19 Sch.6 para.4

2890. Housing Renewal Grants Regulations 1996
Reg.41, amended: SI 2012/956 Art.6

2907. Child Support Departure Direction and Consequential Amendments Regulations 1996
revoked: SI 2012/2785 Reg.10
Reg.1, amended: SI 2012/2007 Sch.1 para.112
Reg.24, amended: SI 2012/2007 Sch.1 para.112
Reg.32E, amended: SI 2012/1267 Reg.3

2918. Bedfordshire Fire Services (Combination Scheme) Order 1996
Sch.1 Part II para.4, amended: SI 2012/2879 Art.2

2991. Insurance Companies (Reserves) (Tax) Regulations 1996
Reg.8A, amended: 2012 c.14 Sch.20 para.47
Reg.8B, amended: 2012 c.14 Sch.20 para.48

1996–cont.

2991. Insurance Companies (Reserves) (Tax) Regulations 1996–*cont.*
Reg.10, applied: 2012 c.14 s.28

3090. Animals (Scientific Procedures) Act 1986 (Fees) (No.1) Order 1996
Art.2, amended: SI 2012/3039 Reg.33

3124. Products of Animal Origin (Import and Export) Regulations 1996
revoked: SSI 2012/177 Reg.38

3125. Fresh Meat (Import Conditions) Regulations 1996
revoked (in part): SSI 2012/177 Reg.38

3126. Occupational Pension Schemes (Winding Up) Regulations 1996
Reg.1, amended: SI 2012/1817 Sch.1 para.3
Reg.4, amended: SI 2012/1817 Sch.1 para.3
Reg.13, see *Alexander Forbes Trustees Ltd v Doe* [2011] EWHC 3930 (Ch), [2012] Pens. L.R. 231 (Ch D), Judge Purle Q.C.

3128. Occupational Pension Schemes (Deficiency on Winding Up etc.) Regulations 1996
Reg.2, amended: SI 2012/692 Reg.6, SI 2012/1817 Sch.1 para.4
Sch.1, amended: SI 2012/692 Reg.6, SI 2012/1817 Sch.1 para.4

3159. Registration of Clubs (Northern Ireland) Order 1996
Art.51, amended: SI 2012/2595 Art.8

3182. European Communities (Iron and Steel Employees Re-adaptation Benefits Scheme) (No.2) (Amendment) Regulations 1996
revoked: SI 2012/2262 Reg.2
Sch.1, applied: SSI 2012/319 Reg.32

1997

37. Town and Country Planning (Fees for Applications and Deemed Applications) (Amendment) Regulations 1997
revoked (in part): SI 2012/2920 Sch.3

62. Food Protection (Emergency Prohibitions) (Radioactivity in Sheep) Partial Revocation Order 1997
revoked (in part): SSI 2012/263 Sch.1

189. Plant Protection Products (Basic Conditions) Regulations 1997
applied: SI 2012/1657 Reg.31
revoked: SI 2012/1657 Reg.32

264. London Underground (East London Line Extension) Order 1997
Art.2, amended: SI 2012/1659 Art.2

276. Road Traffic Regulation (Northern Ireland) Order 1997
Art.4, enabled: SI 2012/1829

287. Air Navigation (Second Amendment) Order 1997
applied: 2012 c.19 Sch.6 para.4

291. Act of Sederunt (Child Care and Maintenance Rules) 1997
Part 1 r.1.6, added: SSI 2012/271 r.4
Sch.1, amended: SSI 2012/188 r.13
Sch.3, amended: SSI 2012/271 r.4

619. Housing (Right to Acquire) Regulations 1997
Sch.1 para.1, amended: SI 2012/2090 Sch.1 para.3
Sch.1 para.2, amended: SI 2012/2090 Sch.1 para.3
Sch.1 para.4, amended: SI 2012/2090 Sch.1 para.3
Sch.2, added: SI 2012/2090 Sch.1 para.3
Sch.2, amended: SI 2012/2090 Sch.1 para.3

1997–cont.

634. Pensions Increase (Review) Order 1997
applied: SI 2012/782 Art.3, Art.4

687. Sheriff Court Fees Order 1997
Art.2, amended: SSI 2012/293 Art.2
Art.3A, added: SSI 2012/293 Art.2
Art.4, amended: SSI 2012/293 Art.2
Art.5, amended: SSI 2012/293 Art.2
Art.7, amended: SSI 2012/293 Art.2
Art.9, amended: SSI 2012/293 Art.2
Art.10, amended: SSI 2012/293 Art.2
Sch.1, amended: SSI 2012/293 Sch.1, Sch.2, Sch.3

688. Court of Session etc Fees Order 1997
Art.3, amended: SSI 2012/290 Art.3
Art.5A, amended: SSI 2012/290 Art.4
Art.5B, amended: SSI 2012/290 Art.4, Art.5
Sch.1, substituted: SSI 2012/290 Sch.1, Sch.2, Sch.3

728. Council Tax (Exempt Dwellings) (Scotland) Order 1997
Sch.1 para.4, amended: SSI 2012/339 Art.2

784. Occupational Pension Schemes (Discharge of Liability) Regulations 1997
Reg.1, amended: SI 2012/692 Reg.7

818. National Health Service (Optical Charges and Payments) Regulations 1997
Reg.19, amended: SI 2012/515 Reg.2, SI 2012/684 Reg.2
Sch.1, amended: SI 2012/515 Reg.2, SI 2012/684 Reg.3
Sch.2 para.1, amended: SI 2012/515 Reg.2, SI 2012/684 Reg.3
Sch.2 para.2, amended: SI 2012/515 Reg.2, SI 2012/684 Reg.3
Sch.3, amended: SI 2012/515 Reg.2
Sch.3, substituted: SI 2012/684 Sch.1

858. Town and Country Planning (General Development Procedure) (Amendment) Order 1997
revoked: SI 2012/801 Sch.8

859. Amusement Machine Licence Duty (Amendment) Regulations 1997
revoked: 2012 c.14 Sch.24 para.53

871. Social Security (Jamaica) Order 1997
Sch.1, varied: SI 2012/360 Sch.2
Sch.2, varied: SI 2012/360 Sch.2

932. Jobseeker's Allowance (Members of the Forces) (Northern Ireland) Regulations 1997
Reg.1, amended: SI 2012/2569 Reg.2
Reg.3, revoked: SI 2012/2569 Reg.2
Reg.7, amended: SI 2012/2569 Reg.2
Reg.7, revoked (in part): SI 2012/2569 Reg.2

980. National Health Service (Indicative Amounts) Regulations 1997
Reg.1, amended: SI 2012/1909 Sch.8 para.2

1001. Misuse of Drugs (Supply to Addicts) Regulations 1997
Reg.3, amended: SI 2012/2394 Reg.3

1033. Criminal Procedure and Investigations Act 1996 (Code of Practice) (No.2) Order 1997
applied: SI 2012/1726 r.22.9

1160. Hedgerows Regulations 1997
applied: SI 2012/1914 Sch.1 para.24

1350. Medicines (Pharmacy and General Sale-Exemption) (Amendment) Order 1997
revoked: SI 2012/1916 Sch.35

1544. Road Vehicles (Construction and Use) (Amendment) (No.5) Regulations 1997
Reg.4, revoked: SI 2012/1404 Sch.1

1603. Finance Act 1997, Section 110, (Appointed Day) Order 1997
revoked: 2012 c.5 Sch.14 Part 13

1997–cont.

1639. Royal Parks and Other Open Spaces Regulations 1997
Reg.3A, added: SI 2012/957 Reg.2
Reg.3B, added: SI 2012/957 Reg.2
Reg.3C, added: SI 2012/957 Reg.2
Sch.1 para.1, substituted: SI 2012/98 Reg.2
Sch.1 para.3A, added: SI 2012/98 Reg.2

1729. Animals and Animal Products (Examination for Residues and Maximum Residue Limits) Regulations 1997
Reg.9, applied: SSI 2012/177 Reg.30
Reg.23, amended: SI 2012/2897 Art.2

1753. United Nations (International Tribunals) (Former Yugoslavia and Rwanda) (Dependent Territories) Order 1997
referred to: SI 2012/2559 Art.1
Art.2, amended: SI 2012/2559 Art.4

1830. Prescription Only Medicines (Human Use) Order 1997
Art.1, amended: SI 2012/1479 Sch.1 para.13, SI 2012/1916 Sch.34 para.71
Art.1, revoked (in part): SI 2012/1916 Sch.34 para.71, Sch.35
Art.2, revoked: SI 2012/1916 Sch.35
Art.3, revoked: SI 2012/1916 Sch.35
Art.3A, revoked: SI 2012/1916 Sch.35
Art.3B, revoked: SI 2012/1916 Sch.35
Art.3C, revoked: SI 2012/1916 Sch.35
Art.4, revoked: SI 2012/1916 Sch.35
Art.5, amended: SI 2012/1916 Sch.34 para.71
Art.5, applied: SI 2012/1916 Sch.1 para.1
Art.5A, revoked: SI 2012/1916 Sch.35
Art.5B, revoked: SI 2012/1916 Sch.35
Art.6, revoked: SI 2012/1916 Sch.35
Art.7, revoked: SI 2012/1916 Sch.35
Art.7A, revoked: SI 2012/1916 Sch.35
Art.7B, revoked: SI 2012/1916 Sch.35
Art.8, revoked: SI 2012/1916 Sch.35
Art.9, revoked: SI 2012/1916 Sch.35
Art.10, amended: SI 2012/1916 Sch.34 para.71
Art.10, applied: SI 2012/1916 Sch.1 para.1
Art.11, revoked: SI 2012/1916 Sch.35
Art.12, revoked: SI 2012/1916 Sch.35
Art.12A, revoked: SI 2012/1916 Sch.35
Art.12B, revoked: SI 2012/1916 Sch.35
Art.12C, revoked: SI 2012/1916 Sch.35
Art.12D, revoked: SI 2012/1916 Sch.35
Art.12E, revoked: SI 2012/1916 Sch.35
Art.12F, revoked: SI 2012/1916 Sch.35
Art.13, revoked: SI 2012/1916 Sch.35
Art.13A, amended: SI 2012/1479 Sch.1 para.13
Art.13A, revoked: SI 2012/1916 Sch.35
Art.14, revoked: SI 2012/1916 Sch.35
Art.15, revoked: SI 2012/1916 Sch.35
Art.16, revoked: SI 2012/1916 Sch.35
Sch.1, applied: SI 2012/1916 Sch.1 para.1
Sch.2, applied: SI 2012/1916 Sch.1 para.1
Sch.3, revoked: SI 2012/1916 Sch.35
Sch.3A, revoked: SI 2012/1916 Sch.35
Sch.3B, revoked: SI 2012/1916 Sch.35
Sch.4, revoked: SI 2012/1916 Sch.35
Sch.5 Part I, revoked: SI 2012/1916 Sch.35
Sch.5 Part II, revoked: SI 2012/1916 Sch.35
Sch.5 Part III, revoked: SI 2012/1916 Sch.35
Sch.6, revoked: SI 2012/1916 Sch.35
Sch.7 Part I, revoked: SI 2012/1916 Sch.35
Sch.7 Part II, revoked: SI 2012/1916 Sch.35
Sch.7 Part IIA, revoked: SI 2012/1916 Sch.35

1997–cont.

1830. Prescription Only Medicines (Human Use) Order 1997–cont.
Sch.7 Part III, revoked: SI 2012/1916 Sch.35

1984. Rent Officers (Housing Benefit Functions) Order 1997
Art.2, amended: SI 2012/646 Art.2
Art.4B, amended: SI 2012/646 Art.2
Sch.3B para.1, amended: SI 2012/646 Art.2
Sch.3B para.2, amended: SI 2012/646 Art.2
Sch.3B para.2, revoked (in part): SI 2012/646 Art.2

1995. Rent Officers (Housing Benefit Functions) (Scotland) Order 1997
Art.2, amended: SI 2012/646 Art.3
Art.4B, amended: SI 2012/646 Art.3
Sch.3B para.1, amended: SI 2012/646 Art.3
Sch.3B para.2, amended: SI 2012/646 Art.3
Sch.3B para.2, revoked (in part): SI 2012/646 Art.3

2196. Gaming Duty Regulations 1997
Reg.5, amended: SI 2012/1897 Reg.4

2674. Food Industry Development Scheme (Specification of Activities) Order 1997
Art.2, amended: SSI 2012/215 Sch.1 para.5

2750. Mink (Keeping) (Amendment) Regulations 1997
revoked (in part): SSI 2012/174 Sch.2

2751. Coypus (Special Licence) (Fees) Regulations 1997
revoked (in part): SSI 2012/174 Sch.2

2778. Waste and Contaminated Land (Northern Ireland) Order 1997
Art.33, amended: SI 2012/1916 Sch.34 para.50

2779. Shops (Sunday Trading &c.) (Northern Ireland) Order 1997
Art.4, amended: SI 2012/1916 Sch.34 para.51

2862. Local Authorities (Contracts) Regulations 1997
Reg.5, revoked (in part): SI 2012/666 Sch.2

2866. Wheeled Child Conveyances (Safety) Regulations 1997
revoked: SI 2012/1815 Sch.1

2912. Civil Aviation (Air Travel Organisers Licensing) (Second Amendment) Regulations 1997
revoked: SI 2012/1017 Sch.1

2988. Double Taxation Relief (Taxes on Income) (Singapore) Order 1997
Sch.1, applied: SI 2012/3078 Art.2
Sch.1 Part I, amended: SI 2012/3078 Sch.1
Sch.1 Part I, revoked: SI 2012/3078 Sch.1
Sch.1 Part I, substituted: SI 2012/3078 Sch.1

3001. Teachers Pensions Regulations 1997
see *Owens v Dudley MBC* [2011] EWCA Civ 359, [2012] P.T.S.R. 280 (CA (Civ Div)), Ward, L.J.
Reg.33, see *Department for Education v Molyneux* [2012] EWCA Civ 193, [2012] E.L.R. 357 (CA (Civ Div)), Sir John Thomas (President)

3023. Products of Animal Origin (Import and Export) (Amendment) Regulations 1997
revoked: SSI 2012/177 Reg.38

3032. Copyright and Rights in Databases Regulations 1997
Reg.12, see *Beechwood House Publishing Ltd (t/a Binley's) v Guardian Products Ltd* [2012] E.C.C. 14 (PCC), Judge Birss Q.C.
Reg.16, see *Beechwood House Publishing Ltd (t/a Binley's) v Guardian Products Ltd* [2012] E.C.C. 14 (PCC), Judge Birss Q.C.

3055. Conservation (Natural Habitats, &c.) (Amendment) Regulations 1997
revoked (in part): SSI 2012/228 Sch.1

1998

72. Food Protection (Emergency Prohibitions) (Radioactivity in Sheep) (Wales) (Partial Revocation) Order 1998
revoked: SI 2012/2978 Sch.1

82. Food Protection (Emergency Prohibitions) (Radioactivity in Sheep) Partial Revocation Order 1998
revoked (in part): SSI 2012/263 Sch.1

107. Medicines (Pharmacy and General Sale-Exemption) Amendment Order 1998
revoked: SI 2012/1916 Sch.35

141. Bread and Flour Regulations 1998
Reg.3, amended: SI 2012/1809 Sch.1 Part 2

209. Merchant Shipping (Compulsory Insurance Ships Receiving Trans-shipped Fish) Regulations 1998
referred to: SI 2012/2267 Reg.3

366. Local Government Pension Scheme (Scotland) Regulations 1998
Reg.4, see *City of Edinburgh Council v Scottish Council for Research in Education* 2012 S.L.T. 587 (OH), Lord Menzies
Reg.74, see *City of Edinburgh Council v Scottish Council for Research in Education* 2012 S.L.T. 587 (OH), Lord Menzies
Reg.76, see *City of Edinburgh Council v Scottish Council for Research in Education* 2012 S.L.T. 587 (OH), Lord Menzies
Reg.77, see *City of Edinburgh Council v Scottish Council for Research in Education* 2012 S.L.T. 587 (OH), Lord Menzies
Reg.78, see *City of Edinburgh Council v Scottish Council for Research in Education* 2012 S.L.T. 587 (OH), Lord Menzies

494. Health and Safety (Enforcing Authority) Regulations 1998
Sch.2 para.4A, amended: SI 2012/632 Sch.3

503. Pensions Increase (Review) Order 1998
applied: SI 2012/782 Art.3, Art.4

642. National Health Service (Optical Charges and Payments) (Scotland) Regulations 1998
Reg.12, applied: SSI 2012/73 Reg.3
Reg.17, applied: SSI 2012/73 Reg.3
Reg.19, amended: SSI 2012/73 Reg.2
Sch.1, amended: SSI 2012/73 Reg.2
Sch.2, substituted: SSI 2012/73 Sch.1
Sch.3 para.1, amended: SSI 2012/73 Reg.2
Sch.3 para.2, amended: SSI 2012/73 Reg.2

649. Scheme for Construction Contracts (England and Wales) Regulations 1998
Sch.1 Pt I para.2, see *Sprunt Ltd v Camden LBC* [2011] EWHC 3191 (TCC), [2012] B.L.R. 83 (QBD (TCC)), Akenhead, J.

674. National Health Service (Service Committees and Tribunal) Amendment Regulations 1998
revoked (in part): SI 2012/1909 Sch.8 para.1

687. Scheme for Construction Contracts (Scotland) Regulations 1998
Sch.1 para.23, see *Carillion Utility Services Ltd v SP Power Systems Ltd* 2012 S.L.T. 119 (OH), Lord Hodge

753. Air Navigation (Third Amendment) Order 1998
applied: 2012 c.19 Sch.6 para.4

1064. Federal Republic of Yugoslavia (United Nations Sanctions) (Dependent Territories) Order 1998
revoked: SI 2012/2592 Sch.2

1998– cont.

1070. Asylum and Immigration Act 1996 (Jersey) Order 1998
Sch.1 para.6A, added: SI 2012/2593 Art.3

1130. Cash Ratio Deposits (Eligible Liabilities) Order 1998
Art.2, amended: SI 2012/917 Sch.2 para.1

1169. Textile Products (Indications of Fibre Content) (Amendment) Regulations 1998
revoked: SI 2012/1102 Sch.1

1235. A720 Trunk Road (Calder Junction to Hermiston Gait Area) (50mph Speed Limit) Order 1998
revoked: SSI 2012/112 Art.5

1272. Yorkshire Ouse (Pilotage Powers) Order 1998
amended: SI 2012/1659 Art.2
Art.2, amended: SI 2012/1659 Art.2

1397. Occupational Pension Schemes (Contracting-out) (Amount Required for Restoring State Scheme Rights and Miscellaneous Amendment) Regulations 1998
Reg.4, amended: SI 2012/692 Reg.8

1451. National Health Service Superannuation Scheme (Scotland) (Additional Voluntary Contributions) Regulations 1998
Reg.10, amended: SSI 2012/163 Reg.26
Reg.10, revoked (in part): SSI 2012/163 Reg.26

1503. Civil Aviation (Investigation of Air Accidents and Incidents) (Guernsey) Order 1998
applied: 2012 c.19 Sch.6 para.4

1506. Social Security (Northern Ireland) Order 1998
Art.9, applied: SI 2012/845 Reg.2

1513. Visiting Forces and Allied Headquarters (Income Tax and Capital Gains Tax) (Designation) Order 1998
revoked: SI 2012/3071 Sch.1

1514. Visiting Forces (Income Tax and Capital Gains Tax) (Designation) Order 1998
revoked: SI 2012/3071 Sch.1

1515. Visiting Forces and Allied Headquarters (Inheritance Tax) (Designation) Order 1998
revoked: SI 2012/3071 Sch.1

1516. Visiting Forces (Inheritance Tax) (Designation) Order 1998
revoked: SI 2012/3071 Sch.1

1517. Visiting Forces and Allied Headquarters (Stamp Duties) (Designation) Order 1998
revoked: SI 2012/3071 Sch.1

1518. Visiting Forces (Stamp Duties) (Designation) Order 1998
revoked: SI 2012/3071 Sch.1

1563. Road Vehicles (Construction and Use) (Amendment) (No.5) Regulations 1998
Reg.4, revoked: SI 2012/1404 Sch.1

1594. National Health Service (Scotland) (Injury Benefits) Regulations 1998
Reg.2, amended: SSI 2012/163 Reg.28
Reg.4, amended: SSI 2012/163 Reg.29

1713. Faculty Jurisdiction (Appeals) Rules 1998
referred to: SI 2012/1846 Sch.1 Part TABLEa
Part II r.4, applied: SI 2012/1846 Sch.1 Part TABLEa
Part II r.5, applied: SI 2012/1846 Sch.1 Part TABLEa
Part II r.6, applied: SI 2012/1846 Sch.1 Part TABLEa
Part IV r.17, applied: SI 2012/1846 Sch.1 Part TABLEa
Part V r.19, applied: SI 2012/1846 Sch.1 Part TABLEa

1998– cont.

1760. Education (Student Support) (Northern Ireland) Order 1998
Art.3, applied: SI 2012/2886 Sch.1, SI 2012/3145 Sch.1

1764. Trial of the Pyx Order 1998
Art.2, amended: SI 2012/2746 Art.2
Art.3, amended: SI 2012/2746 Art.2
Art.3, revoked (in part): SI 2012/2746 Art.2
Art.7, amended: SI 2012/2746 Art.2
Art.9, amended: SI 2012/2746 Art.2
Art.9A, added: SI 2012/2746 Art.2
Art.10, revoked (in part): SI 2012/2746 Art.2
Art.11, amended: SI 2012/2746 Art.2
Art.12, amended: SI 2012/2746 Art.2
Art.14, amended: SI 2012/2746 Art.2

1797. Humber Bridge (Debts) Order 1998
Sch.1 para.3, referred to: SI 2012/716 Art.2

1833. Working Time Regulations 1998
see *Arriva London South Ltd v Nicolaou* [2012] I.C.R. 510 (EAT), Judge Peter Clark; see *Hughes v Corps of Commissionaires Management Ltd* [2011] EWCA Civ 1061, [2012] 1 C.M.L.R. 25 (CA (Civ Div)), Sir Anthony May (President, QB); see *NHS Leeds v Larner* [2012] EWCA Civ 1034, [2012] 4 All E.R. 1006 (CA (Civ Div)), Mummery, L.J.; see *R. (on the application of United Road Transport Union) v Secretary of State for Transport* [2012] EWHC 1909 (Admin), [2012] 3 C.M.L.R. 40 (QBD (Admin)), Hickinbottom, J.; see *Wray v JW Lees & Co (Brewers) Ltd* [2012] I.C.R. 43 (EAT), Underhill, J. (President)
Reg.4, see *Arriva London South Ltd v Nicolaou* [2012] I.C.R. 510 (EAT), Judge Peter Clark
Reg.10, see *Associated British Ports v Bridgeman* [2012] 2 C.M.L.R. 47 (EAT), Supperstone, J.
Reg.12, see *Associated British Ports v Bridgeman* [2012] 2 C.M.L.R. 47 (EAT), Supperstone, J.; see *Hughes v Corps of Commissionaires Management Ltd* [2011] EWCA Civ 1061, [2012] 1 C.M.L.R. 25 (CA (Civ Div)), Sir Anthony May (President, QB)
Reg.13, see *Russell v Transocean International Resources Ltd* [2012] 2 All E.R. 166 (SC), Lord Hope (Deputy President)
Reg.13A, see *NHS Leeds v Larner* [2012] EWCA Civ 1034, [2012] 4 All E.R. 1006 (CA (Civ Div)), Mummery, L.J.
Reg.15, see *Fraser v Southwest London St George's Mental Health Trust* [2012] I.C.R. 403 (EAT), Underhill, J. (President); see *NHS Leeds v Larner* [2012] EWCA Civ 1034, [2012] 4 All E.R. 1006 (CA (Civ Div)), Mummery, L.J.; see *Russell v Transocean International Resources Ltd* [2012] 2 All E.R. 166 (SC), Lord Hope (Deputy President)
Reg.16, see *Fraser v Southwest London St George's Mental Health Trust* [2012] I.C.R. 403 (EAT), Underhill, J. (President)
Reg.21, see *Associated British Ports v Bridgeman* [2012] 2 C.M.L.R. 47 (EAT), Supperstone, J.; see *Hughes v Corps of Commissionaires Management Ltd* [2011] EWCA Civ 1061, [2012] 1 C.M.L.R. 25 (CA (Civ Div)), Sir Anthony May (President, QB)
Reg.24, see *Associated British Ports v Bridgeman* [2012] 2 C.M.L.R. 47 (EAT), Supperstone, J.; see *Hughes v Corps of Commissionaires Management Ltd* [2011] EWCA Civ 1061, [2012] 1 C.M.L.R. 25 (CA (Civ Div)), Sir Anthony May (President, QB)

1998– cont.

1839. Amusement Machine Licence Duty (Monetary Amounts) Order 1998
revoked: 2012 c.14 Sch.24 para.53

1870. Individual Savings Account Regulations 1998
Reg.2, amended: SI 2012/1871 Reg.5, Reg.6
Reg.2A, amended: SI 2012/1871 Reg.7
Reg.2D, amended: SI 2012/1871 Reg.8
Reg.2F, added: SI 2012/1871 Reg.9
Reg.4ZA, amended: SI 2012/705 Reg.2
Reg.5B, revoked: SI 2012/1871 Reg.10
Reg.5D, added: SI 2012/1871 Reg.11
Reg.5DA, added: SI 2012/1871 Reg.11
Reg.5DB, added: SI 2012/1871 Reg.11
Reg.5DC, added: SI 2012/1871 Reg.11
Reg.5DD, added: SI 2012/1871 Reg.11
Reg.5DE, added: SI 2012/1871 Reg.11
Reg.5DF, added: SI 2012/1871 Reg.11
Reg.5DG, added: SI 2012/1871 Reg.11
Reg.5DH, added: SI 2012/1871 Reg.11
Reg.5DI, added: SI 2012/1871 Reg.11
Reg.5DJ, added: SI 2012/1871 Reg.11
Reg.5DK, added: SI 2012/1871 Reg.11
Reg.5DL, added: SI 2012/1871 Reg.11
Reg.5DM, added: SI 2012/1871 Reg.11
Reg.7, amended: SI 2012/1871 Reg.12
Reg.8, amended: SI 2012/1871 Reg.13
Reg.12, amended: SI 2012/1871 Reg.14
Reg.19, substituted: SI 2012/1871 Reg.15
Reg.20, amended: SI 2012/2404 Sch.3 para.11
Reg.21, amended: SI 2012/1871 Reg.16
Reg.21A, amended: SI 2012/1871 Reg.17
Reg.21B, amended: SI 2012/1871 Reg.18
Reg.29, substituted: SI 2012/1871 Reg.19
Reg.31, amended: SI 2012/1871 Reg.20

1936. Greater Manchester (Light Rapid Transit System) (Ashton-under-Lyne Extension) Order 1998
Art.43, amended: SI 2012/1659 Art.2

1973. Education (Infant Class Sizes) (England) Regulations 1998
revoked: SI 2012/10 Reg.3

1974. Animals (Scientific Procedures) Act 1986 (Amendment) Regulations 1998
Sch.1 para.3, revoked: SI 2012/3039 Reg.34
Sch.1 para.4, revoked: SI 2012/3039 Reg.34
Sch.1 para.5, revoked: SI 2012/3039 Reg.34
Sch.1 para.6, revoked: SI 2012/3039 Reg.34

2207. Amusement Machine Licence Duty (Small-prize Machines) Order 1998
revoked: 2012 c.14 Sch.24 para.53

2306. Provision and Use of Work Equipment Regulations 1998
see *British Waterways v Royal & Sun Alliance Insurance Plc* [2012] EWHC 460 (Comm), [2012] Lloyd's Rep. I.R. 562 (QBD (Comm)), Burton, J.
Reg.12, amended: SI 2012/632 Sch.3
Reg.12, see *Whitehead v Trustees of the Chatsworth Settlement* [2012] EWCA Civ 263, [2012] I.C.R. 1154 (CA (Civ Div)), Sir Andrew Morritt (Chancellor)

2307. Lifting Operations and Lifting Equipment Regulations 1998
Reg.9, applied: SI 2012/1652 Sch.16

2368. Medicines (Pharmacy and General Sale-Exemption) Amendment (No.2) Order 1998
revoked: SI 2012/1916 Sch.35

1998– cont.

2406. Pencils and Graphic Instruments (Safety) Regulations 1998
revoked: SI 2012/ 2963 Reg.3

2451. Gas Safety (Installation and Use) Regulations 1998
see *R. v Jonathan (Stephen Thomas)* [2012] EWCA Crim 380, [2012] 2 Cr. App. R. (S.) 74 (CA (Crim Div)), Goldring, L.J.
Reg.16, applied: SI 2012/ 1282 Sch.1, SI 2012/ 1284 Sch.1, SI 2012/ 1286 Sch.1, SI 2012/ 1289 Sch.1, SI 2012/ 1294 Sch.1, SI 2012/ 1295 Sch.1
Reg.36, applied: SI 2012/ 2601 Art.3

2573. Employers Liability (Compulsory Insurance) Regulations 1998
Sch.2 para.8, revoked: SI 2012/ 765 Art.2
Sch.2 para.22, substituted: SI 2012/ 725 Art.2

2768. Judicial Pensions (European Court of Human Rights) Order 1998
Art.6, amended: SI 2012/489 Art.3

2876. Education (Grammar School Ballots) Regulations 1998
Reg.2, amended: SI 2012/979 Sch.1 para.4
Reg.4, amended: SI 2012/979 Sch.1 para.4
Reg.20, amended: SI 2012/979 Sch.1 para.4
Reg.21, amended: SI 2012/979 Sch.1 para.4

2911. General Teaching Council for Wales Order 1998
Art.3, amended: SI 2012/ 168 Art.2

2997. Housing (Right to Buy) (Limits on Discount) Order 1998
revoked (in part): SI 2012/ 734 Art.5

3081. Controlled Foreign Companies (Excluded Countries) Regulations 1998
revoked: 2012 c.14 Sch.20 para.14

3105. Medicines for Human Use (Marketing Authorisations Etc.) Amendment Regulations 1998
revoked: SI 2012/ 1916 Sch.35

3132. Civil Procedure Rules 1998
applied: SI 2012/322 Reg.35, Reg.71
see *Chapman v Dwr Cymru Welsh Water* [2012] UKUT 89 (LC), [2012] R.V.R. 148 (UT (Lands)), PR Francis FRICS; see *Dockerill v Tullett* [2012] EWCA Civ 184, [2012] 1 W.L.R. 2092 (CA (Civ Div)), Arden, L.J.; see *Hinde v Rugby BC* [2011] EWHC 3684 (Admin), [2012] J.P.L. 816 (QBD (Admin)), David Elvin Q.C.; see *Northern Rock (Asset Management) Plc v Chancellors Associates Ltd* [2011] EWHC 3229 (TCC), [2012] 2 All E.R. 501 (QBD (TCC)), Akenhead, J.; see *Page v Hewetts Solicitors* [2012] EWCA Civ 805, [2012] C.P. Rep. 40 (CA (Civ Div)), Laws, L.J.; see *Pomiechowski v Poland* [2011] EWHC 2060 (Admin), [2012] 1 W.L.R. 391 (DC), Laws, L.J.; see *R. (on the application of A) v Secretary of State for Communities and Local Government* [2011] EWCA Civ 1253, [2012] J.P.L. 579 (CA (Civ Div)), Pill, L.J.; see *Seaton v Seddon* [2012] EWHC 735 (Ch), [2012] 1 W.L.R. 3636 (Ch D), Roth, J.; see *Solomon v Cromwell Group Plc* [2011] EWCA Civ 1584, [2012] 1 W.L.R. 1048 (CA (Civ Div)), Pill, L.J.; see *Summers v Fairclough Homes Ltd* [2012] UKSC 26, [2012] 1 W.L.R. 2004 (SC), Lord Hope (Deputy President)
Part 5, referred to: SI 2012/ 1234 Reg.5
Part 21 r.21.2, applied: SI 2012/ 3098 Reg.22, Reg.30

1998– cont.

3132. Civil Procedure Rules 1998– *cont.*
Part 21 r.21.11, applied: SI 2012/ 2885 Sch.6 para.17, SI 2012/ 2886 Sch.1, SSI 2012/ 303 Sch.5 para.51, SSI 2012/ 319 Sch.4 para.17
Part 26 r.26.3, amended: SI 2012/ 2208 r.3
Part 27 r.27.5, amended: SI 2012/ 2208 r.4
Part 27 r.27.14, amended: SI 2012/ 2208 r.4
Part 30 r.30.8, amended: SI 2012/ 1809 Sch.1 Part 2
Part 31 r.31.1, varied: SI 2012/ 1726 r.61.9
Part 31 r.31.2, varied: SI 2012/ 1726 r.61.9
Part 31 r.31.3, varied: SI 2012/ 1726 r.61.9
Part 31 r.31.4, varied: SI 2012/ 1726 r.61.9
Part 31 r.31.5, varied: SI 2012/ 1726 r.61.9
Part 31 r.31.6, varied: SI 2012/ 1726 r.61.9
Part 31 r.31.7, varied: SI 2012/ 1726 r.61.9
Part 31 r.31.8, varied: SI 2012/ 1726 r.61.9
Part 31 r.31.9, varied: SI 2012/ 1726 r.61.9
Part 31 r.31.10, varied: SI 2012/ 1726 r.61.9
Part 31 r.31.11, varied: SI 2012/ 1726 r.61.9
Part 31 r.31.12, varied: SI 2012/ 1726 r.61.9
Part 31 r.31.13, varied: SI 2012/ 1726 r.61.9
Part 31 r.31.14, varied: SI 2012/ 1726 r.61.9
Part 31 r.31.15, varied: SI 2012/ 1726 r.61.9
Part 31 r.31.16, varied: SI 2012/ 1726 r.61.9
Part 31 r.31.17, varied: SI 2012/ 1726 r.61.9
Part 31 r.31.18, varied: SI 2012/ 1726 r.61.9
Part 31 r.31.19, varied: SI 2012/ 1726 r.61.9
Part 31 r.31.20, varied: SI 2012/ 1726 r.61.9
Part 31 r.31.21, varied: SI 2012/ 1726 r.61.9
Part 31 r.31.22, varied: SI 2012/ 1726 r.61.9
Part 31 r.31.23, amended: SI 2012/ 2208 r.5
Part 31 r.31.23, revoked (in part): SI 2012/ 2208 r.5
Part 31 r.31.23, varied: SI 2012/ 1726 r.61.9
Part 32 r.32.14, amended: SI 2012/ 2208 r.6
Part 32 r.32.14, revoked (in part): SI 2012/ 2208 r.6
Part 40 r.40.2, amended: SI 2012/ 2208 r.7
Part 52, applied: SI 2012/ 1726 r.64.3, r.76.13
Part 52, referred to: SI 2012/ 1805 Reg.9
Part 52 r.52.2, amended: SI 2012/ 2208 r.8
Part 52 r.52.3, amended: SI 2012/ 2208 r.8
Part 52 r.52.15, amended: SI 2012/ 2208 r.8
Part 54 r.54.1A, added: SI 2012/ 2208 r.9
Part 54 r.54.7A, added: SI 2012/ 2208 r.9
Part 63 r.63.1, amended: SI 2012/ 2208 r.10
Part 63 r.63.27, added: SI 2012/ 2208 r.10
Part 63 r.63.28, added: SI 2012/ 2208 r.10
Part 65 r.65.6, amended: SI 2012/ 2208 r.11
Part 65 r.65.47, amended: SI 2012/ 2208 r.11
Part 71 r.71.2, amended: SI 2012/ 505 r.3, SI 2012/ 2208 r.12
Part 71 r.71.8, amended: SI 2012/ 2208 r.12
Part 72 r.72.3, amended: SI 2012/ 505 r.4
Part 73 r.73.3, amended: SI 2012/ 505 r.5
Part 76 r.76.12, amended: SI 2012/ 2208 r.13
Part 76 r.76.16, amended: SI 2012/ 2208 r.13
Part 79 r.79.14B, amended: SI 2012/ 2208 r.14
Part 80 r.80.8, amended: SI 2012/ 2208 r.15
Part 80 r.80.12, amended: SI 2012/ 2208 r.15
Part 81, applied: SI 2012/ 2208 r.20
Part 81 r.81.1, added: SI 2012/ 2208 Sch.1
Part 81 r.81.2, added: SI 2012/ 2208 Sch.1
Part 81 r.81.3, added: SI 2012/ 2208 Sch.1
Part 81 r.81.4, added: SI 2012/ 2208 Sch.1
Part 81 r.81.5, added: SI 2012/ 2208 Sch.1
Part 81 r.81.6, added: SI 2012/ 2208 Sch.1
Part 81 r.81.7, added: SI 2012/ 2208 Sch.1
Part 81 r.81.8, added: SI 2012/ 2208 Sch.1
Part 81 r.81.9, added: SI 2012/ 2208 Sch.1

1998– cont.

3132. Civil Procedure Rules 1998– *cont.*

Part 81 r.81.10, added: SI 2012/ 2208 Sch.1
Part 81 r.81.11, added: SI 2012/ 2208 Sch.1
Part 81 r.81.12, added: SI 2012/ 2208 Sch.1
Part 81 r.81.13, added: SI 2012/ 2208 Sch.1
Part 81 r.81.14, added: SI 2012/ 2208 Sch.1
Part 81 r.81.15, added: SI 2012/ 2208 Sch.1
Part 81 r.81.16, added: SI 2012/ 2208 Sch.1
Part 81 r.81.17, added: SI 2012/ 2208 Sch.1
Part 81 r.81.18, added: SI 2012/ 2208 Sch.1
Part 81 r.81.19, added: SI 2012/ 2208 Sch.1
Part 81 r.81.20, added: SI 2012/ 2208 Sch.1
Part 81 r.81.21, added: SI 2012/ 2208 Sch.1
Part 81 r.81.22, added: SI 2012/ 2208 Sch.1
Part 81 r.81.23, added: SI 2012/ 2208 Sch.1
Part 81 r.81.24, added: SI 2012/ 2208 Sch.1
Part 81 r.81.25, added: SI 2012/ 2208 Sch.1
Part 81 r.81.26, added: SI 2012/ 2208 Sch.1
Part 81 r.81.27, added: SI 2012/ 2208 Sch.1
Part 81 r.81.28, added: SI 2012/ 2208 Sch.1
Part 81 r.81.29, added: SI 2012/ 2208 Sch.1
Part 81 r.81.30, added: SI 2012/ 2208 Sch.1
Part 81 r.81.31, added: SI 2012/ 2208 Sch.1
Part 81 r.81.32, added: SI 2012/ 2208 Sch.1
Part 81 r.81.33, added: SI 2012/ 2208 Sch.1
Part 81 r.81.34, added: SI 2012/ 2208 Sch.1
Part 81 r.81.35, added: SI 2012/ 2208 Sch.1
Part 81 r.81.36, added: SI 2012/ 2208 Sch.1
Part 81 r.81.37, added: SI 2012/ 2208 Sch.1
Part 81 r.81.38, added: SI 2012/ 2208 Sch.1

Pt 1, see *2 Travel Group Plc (In Liquidation) v Cardiff City Transport Services Ltd* [2012] CAT 7, [2012] Comp. A.R. 184 (CAT), Lord Carlile of Berriew Q.C.; see *Mengi v Hermitage* [2012] EWHC 2045 (QB), [2012] 5 Costs L.O. 641 (QBD), Tugendhat, J.

Pt 16, see *CVB v MGN Ltd* [2012] EWHC 1148 (QB), [2012] E.M.L.R. 29 (QBD), Tugendhat, J.

Pt 18, see *Beller v Valentine* [2011] EWHC 2397 (Ch), [2012] B.P.I.R. 15 (Ch D), Richard Snowden QC; see *National Grid Electricity Transmission Plc v ABB Ltd* [2012] EWHC 869 (Ch), [2012] U.K.C.L.R. 220 (Ch D), Roth, J.

Pt 20, see *Inhakumar v United Trust Bank Ltd* [2012] EWHC 845 (Ch), [2012] B.P.I.R. 758 (Ch D), Vos, J.

Pt 21, see *De Toucy v Bonhams 1793 Ltd* [2011] EWHC 3809 (Ch), [2012] B.P.I.R. 793 (Ch D), Vos, J.; see *Dunhill v Burgin* [2012] EWCA Civ 397, [2012] C.P. Rep. 29 (CA (Civ Div)), Ward, L.J.; see *Dunhill v Burgin* [2012] EWHC 3163 (QB), [2012] 1 W.L.R. 3739 (QBD (Manchester)), Bean, J.; see *Levy v Ellis-Carr* [2012] EWHC 63 (Ch), [2012] B.P.I.R. 347 (Ch D), Norris, J.

Pt 23, see *R. (on the application of Simmons) v Bolton MBC* [2011] EWHC 2729 (Admin), [2012] Env. L.R. 20 (QBD (Admin)), Judge Pelling Q.C.

Pt 25, see *CVB v MGN Ltd* [2012] EWHC 1148 (QB), [2012] E.M.L.R. 29 (QBD), Tugendhat, J.

Pt 26, see *Sullivan v Bristol Film Studios Ltd* [2012] EWCA Civ 570, [2012] C.P. Rep. 34 (CA (Civ Div)), Ward, L.J.

Pt 36, see *Brit Inns Ltd (In Liquidation) v BDW Trading Ltd (Costs)* [2012] EWHC 2489 (TCC), [2012] B.L.R. 531 (QBD (TCC)), Coulson, J.; see *C v D* [2011] EWCA Civ 646, [2012] 1 W.L.R. 1962 (CA (Civ Div)), Rix, L.J.; see *Epsom College v Pierse Constructing*

1998– cont.

3132. Civil Procedure Rules 1998– *cont.*

Pt 36– *cont.*
Southern Ltd (In Liquidation) (formerly Biseley Construction Ltd) (Costs) [2011] EWCA Civ 1449, [2012] T.C.L.R. 2 (CA (Civ Div)), Rix, L.J.; see *F&C Alternative Investments (Holdings) Ltd v Barthelemy (Costs)* [2011] EWHC 2807 (Ch), [2012] Bus. L.R. 891 (Ch D), Sales, J.; see *F&C Alternative Investments (Holdings) Ltd v Barthelemy (Costs)* [2012] EWCA Civ 843, [2012] 4 All E.R. 1096 (CA (Civ Div)), Arden, L.J.; see *Fortune v Roe* [2011] EWHC 2953 (QB), [2012] 2 Costs L.R. 288 (QBD), Sir Robert Nelson; see *French v Groupama Insurance Co Ltd* [2011] EWCA Civ 1119, [2012] C.P. Rep. 2 (CA (Civ Div)), Rix, L.J.; see *Lilleyman v Lilleyman (Costs)* [2012] EWHC 1056 (Ch), [2012] 1 W.L.R. 2801 (Ch D), Briggs, J.; see *MIOM 1 Ltd v Sea Echo ENE* [2011] EWHC 2715 (Admlty), [2012] 1 Lloyd's Rep. 140 (QBD (Admlty)), Teare, J.; see *PGF II SA v OMFS Co* [2012] EWHC 83 (TCC), [2012] 3 Costs L.O. 404 (QBD (TCC)), Recorder Furst Q.C.; see *SG (A Child) v Hewitt (Costs)* [2012] EWCA Civ 1053, [2012] 5 Costs L.R. 937 (CA (Civ Div)), Pill, L.J.; see *Shovelar v Lane* [2011] EWCA Civ 802, [2012] 1 W.L.R. 637 (CA (Civ Div)), Ward, L.J.; see *Summers v Fairclough Homes Ltd* [2012] UKSC 26, [2012] 1 W.L.R. 2004 (SC), Lord Hope (Deputy President); see *Wharton v Bancroft* [2012] EWHC 91 (Ch), [2012] W.T.L.R. 727 (Ch D), Norris, J.

Pt 43, see *Raggett v John Lewis Plc* [2012] 6 Costs L.R. 1053 (EAT), Slade, J.

Pt 44, see *AL (Albania) v Secretary of State for the Home Department* [2012] EWCA Civ 710, [2012] 1 W.L.R. 2898 (CA (Civ Div)), Maurice Kay, L.J.; see *Brit Inns Ltd (In Liquidation) v BDW Trading Ltd (Costs)* [2012] EWHC 2489 (TCC), [2012] B.L.R. 531 (QBD (TCC)), Coulson, J.; see *Epsom College v Pierse Constructing Southern Ltd (In Liquidation) (formerly Biseley Construction Ltd) (Costs)* [2011] EWCA Civ 1449, [2012] T.C.L.R. 2 (CA (Civ Div)), Rix, L.J.; see *Letts v Royal Sun Alliance Plc* [2012] EWHC 875 (QB), [2012] 3 Costs L.R. 591 (Sen Cts Costs Office), Mackay, J.; see *Shovelar v Lane* [2011] EWCA Civ 802, [2012] 1 W.L.R. 637 (CA (Civ Div)), Ward, L.J.

Pt 45, see *BOS GmbH & Co KG v Cobra UK Automotive Products Division Ltd (In Administration) (Costs)* [2012] EWPCC 44, [2012] 6 Costs L.R. 1083 (PCC), Judge Birss Q.C.; see *Letts v Royal Sun Alliance Plc* [2012] EWHC 875 (QB), [2012] 3 Costs L.R. 591 (Sen Cts Costs Office), Mackay, J.

Pt 48, see *Brown-Quinn v Equity Syndicate Management Ltd* [2011] EWHC 2661 (Comm), [2012] 1 All E.R. 778 (QBD (Comm)), Burton, J.

Pt 54, see *R. (on the application of Simmons) v Bolton MBC* [2011] EWHC 2729 (Admin), [2012] Env. L.R. 20 (QBD (Admin)), Judge Pelling Q.C.

Pt 55, see *Holmes v Westminster City Council* [2011] EWHC 2857 (QB), [2012] B.L.G.R. 233 (QBD), Eady, J.; see *Sun Street Property Ltd v Persons Unknown* [2011] EWHC 3432 (Ch), Times, January 16, 2012 (Ch D), Roth, J.

Pt 63, see *DKH Retail Ltd v Republic (Retail) Ltd* [2012] EWHC 877 (Ch), [2012] Bus. L.R. 1363 (Ch D), Judge Birss Q.C.; see *Sullivan v Bristol Film Studios Ltd* [2012] EWCA Civ 570, [2012] C.P. Rep. 34 (CA (Civ Div)), Ward, L.J.

1998–cont.

3132. Civil Procedure Rules 1998–*cont.*

Pt 7, see *Bamford v Harvey* [2012] EWHC 2858 (Ch), Times, December 07, 2012 (Ch D), Roth, J.; see *Deputy Chief Legal Ombudsman v Young* [2011] EWHC 2923 (Admin), [2012] 1 W.L.R. 3227 (QBD), Lindblom, J.; see *F&C Alternative Investments (Holdings) Ltd v Barthelemy (Costs)* [2011] EWHC 2807 (Ch), [2012] Bus. L.R. 891 (Ch D), Sales, J.; see *IBM United Kingdom Pensions Trust Ltd v Metcalfe* [2012] EWHC 125 (Ch), [2012] 3 Costs L.O. 420 (Ch D), Warren, J.; see *Solomon v Cromwell Group Plc* [2011] EWCA Civ 1584, [2012] 1 W.L.R. 1048 (CA (Civ Div)), Pill, L.J.

Pt 73, see *National Guild of Removers and Storers Ltd v Jones (t/a ATR Removals)* [2012] EWCA Civ 216, [2012] 1 W.L.R. 2501 (CA (Civ Div)), Lord Neuberger (M.R.)

Pt 76, see *Secretary of State for the Home Department v CB* [2012] EWCA Civ 418, [2012] 1 W.L.R. 3259 (CA (Civ Div)), Lord Neuberger (M.R.)

Pt 79, see *Bank Mellat v HM Treasury* [2010] EWCA Civ 483, [2012] Q.B. 91 (CA (Civ Div)), Lord Neuberger of Abbotsbury MR

Pt 8, see *Deputy Chief Legal Ombudsman v Young* [2011] EWHC 2923 (Admin), [2012] 1 W.L.R. 3227 (QBD), Lindblom, J.; see *Spurling v Broadhurst* [2012] EWHC 2883 (Ch), [2012] W.T.L.R. 1813 (Ch D), Hildyard, J; see *West Country Renovations Ltd v McDowell* [2012] EWHC 307 (TCC), [2012] 3 All E.R. 106 (QBD (TCC)), Akenhead, J.

r.1.1, see *Community Care North East (A Partnership) v Durham CC* [2010] EWHC 959 (QB), [2012] 1 W.L.R. 338 (QBD), Ramsey, J.; see *Dhillon v Asiedu* [2012] EWCA Civ 1020, [2012] C.P. Rep. 44 (CA (Civ Div)), Arden, L.J.

r.1.2, see *Northern Rock (Asset Management) Plc v Chancellors Associates Ltd* [2011] EWHC 3229 (TCC), [2012] 2 All E.R. 501 (QBD (TCC)), Akenhead, J.

r.1.4, see *Community Care North East (A Partnership) v Durham CC* [2010] EWHC 959 (QB), [2012] 1 W.L.R. 338 (QBD), Ramsey, J.

r.2.3, see *Mobile Phone Voicemail Interception Litigation, Re* [2012] EWHC 397 (Ch), [2012] 1 W.L.R. 2545 (Ch D), Vos, J.

r.2.8, see *Hinde v Rugby BC* [2011] EWHC 3684 (Admin), [2012] J.P.L. 816 (QBD (Admin)), David Elvin Q.C.

r.3.1, see *Arif v Zar* [2012] EWCA Civ 986, [2012] B.P.I.R. 948 (CA (Civ Div)), Thorpe, L.J.; see *Bhandal v Revenue and Customs Commissioners* [2011] EWHC 3018 (Admin), [2012] Lloyd's Rep. F.C. 127 (QBD (Admin)), Hickinbottom, J.; see *Community Care North East (A Partnership) v Durham CC* [2010] EWHC 959 (QB), [2012] 1 W.L.R. 338 (QBD), Ramsey, J.; see *Ferrexpo AG v Gilson Investments Ltd* [2012] EWHC 721 (Comm), [2012] 1 Lloyd's Rep. 588 (QBD (Comm)), Andrew Smith, J.; see *Kojima v HSBC Bank Ltd* [2011] EWCA Civ 1709, [2012] 1 All E.R. 1392 (CA (Civ Div)), Lord Neuberger (M.R.); see *Latvian Shipping Co v Russian People's Insurance Co (ROSNO) Open Ended Joint Stock Co* [2012] EWHC 1412 (Comm), [2012] 2 Lloyd's Rep. 181 (QBD (Comm)), Field, J.; see *Northern Rock (Asset Management) Plc v Chancellors Associates Ltd* [2011] EWHC 3229 (TCC), [2012] 2 All E.R. 501 (QBD (TCC)),

1998–cont.

3132. Civil Procedure Rules 1998–*cont.*

r.3.1–*cont.*

Akenhead, J.; see *Reddy v General Medical Council* [2012] EWCA Civ 310, [2012] C.P. Rep. 27 (CA (Civ Div)), Mummery, L.J.; see *Serious Organised Crime Agency v Namli* [2011] EWCA Civ 1411, [2012] C.P. Rep. 10 (CA (Civ Div)), Carnwath, L.J.; see *Tibbles v SIG Plc (t/a Asphaltic Roofing Supplies)* [2012] EWCA Civ 518, [2012] 1 W.L.R. 2591 (CA (Civ Div)), Rix, L.J.

r.3.3, see *National Guild of Removers and Storers Ltd v Jones (t/a ATR Removals)* [2012] EWCA Civ 216, [2012] 1 W.L.R. 2501 (CA (Civ Div)), Lord Neuberger (M.R.)

r.3.4, see *Humber Oil Terminals Trustee Ltd v Associated British Ports* [2012] EWCA Civ 36, [2012] U.K.C.L.R. 71 (CA (Civ Div)), Mummery, L.J.; see *Summers v Fairclough Homes Ltd* [2012] UKSC 26, [2012] 1 W.L.R. 2004 (SC), Lord Hope (Deputy President)

r.3.9, see *Bhandal v Revenue and Customs Commissioners* [2011] EWHC 3018 (Admin), [2012] Lloyd's Rep. F.C. 127 (QBD (Admin)), Hickinbottom, J.; see *Byrne v Poplar Housing and Regeneration Community Association Ltd* [2012] EWCA Civ 832, [2012] H.L.R. 33 (CA (Civ Div)), Etherton, L.J.; see *Data Select Ltd v Revenue and Customs Commissioners* [2012] UKUT 187 (TCC), [2012] S.T.C. 2195 (UT (Tax)), Morgan, J.; see *Eden v Rubin* [2011] EWHC 3090 (QB), [2012] 1 Costs L.O. 66 (QBD), Coulson, J.; see *Fred Perry (Holdings) Ltd v Brands Plaza Trading Ltd (t/a Brands Plaza)* [2012] EWCA Civ 224, [2012] 6 Costs L.R. 1007 (CA (Civ Div)), Maurice Kay, L.J.; see *Manning v King's College Hospital NHS Trust* [2011] EWHC 2954 (QB), [2012] 1 Costs L.R. 105 (QBD), Spencer, J.; see *Purushothaman v Malik* [2011] EWCA Civ 1734, [2012] R.T.R. 21 (CA (Civ Div)), Aikens, L.J.; see *R. (on the application of Simmons) v Bolton MBC* [2011] EWHC 2729 (Admin), [2012] Env. L.R. 20 (QBD (Admin)), Judge Pelling Q.C.

r.3.10, see *Poland v Walerianczyk* [2010] EWHC 2149 (Admin), [2012] 1 W.L.R. 363 (DC), Stanley Burnton, L.J.; see *Pomiechowski v Poland* [2011] EWHC 2060 (Admin), [2012] 1 W.L.R. 391 (DC), Laws, L.J.

r.5.4C, see *ABC Ltd v Y* [2010] EWHC 3176 (Ch), [2012] 1 W.L.R. 532 (Ch D), Lewison, J.; see *CVB v MGN Ltd* [2012] EWHC 1148 (QB), [2012] E.M.L.R. 29 (QBD), Tugendhat, J.; see *Mobile Phone Voicemail Interception Litigation, Re* [2012] EWHC 397 (Ch), [2012] 1 W.L.R. 2545 (Ch D), Vos, J.

r.6.2, see *Joyce v West Bus Coach Services Ltd* [2012] EWHC 404 (QB), [2012] 3 Costs L.R. 540 (QBD), Kenneth Parker, J.

r.6.5, see *SSL International Plc v TTK LIG Ltd* [2011] EWCA Civ 1170, [2012] 1 W.L.R. 1842 (CA (Civ Div)), Mummery, L.J.

r.6.15, see *Abela v Baadarani* [2011] EWCA Civ 1571, [2012] C.P. Rep. 11 (CA (Civ Div)), Arden, L.J.; see *Bacon v Automattic Inc* [2011] EWHC 1072 (QB), [2012] 1 W.L.R. 753 (QBD), Tugendhat, J.; see *Bitumex (HK) Co Ltd v IRPC Public Co Ltd* [2012] EWHC 1065 (Comm), [2012] 2 All E.R. (Comm) 1131 (QBD (Comm)), Judge Mackie, Q.C.; see *BNP Paribas SA v Open Joint Stock Company Russian Machines* [2011] EWHC 308

1998–cont.

3132. Civil Procedure Rules 1998–*cont.*

r.6.15–*cont.*

(Comm), [2012] 1 Lloyd's Rep. 61 (QBD (Comm)), Blair, J.; see *Joint Stock Asset Management Co Ingosstrakh-Investments v BNP Paribas SA* [2012] EWCA Civ 644, [2012] 1 Lloyd's Rep. 649 (CA (Civ Div)), Lloyd, L.J.

r.6.21, see *Global 5000 Ltd v Wadhawan* [2012] EWCA Civ 13, [2012] 2 All E.R. (Comm) 18 (CA (Civ Div)), Rix, L.J.

r.6.36, see *BNP Paribas SA v Open Joint Stock Company Russian Machines* [2011] EWHC 308 (Comm), [2012] 1 Lloyd's Rep. 61 (QBD (Comm)), Blair, J.; see *Parbulk II AS v PT Humpuss Intermoda Transportasi TBK (The Mahakam)* [2011] EWHC 3143 (Comm), [2012] 2 All E.R. (Comm) 513 (QBD (Comm)), Gloster, J.

r.6.37, see *Abela v Baadarani* [2011] EWCA Civ 1571, [2012] C.P. Rep. 11 (CA (Civ Div)), Arden, L.J.; see *Bacon v Automattic Inc* [2011] EWHC 1072 (QB), [2012] 1 W.L.R. 753 (QBD), Tugendhat, J.; see *Global 5000 Ltd v Wadhawan* [2012] EWCA Civ 13, [2012] 2 All E.R. (Comm) 18 (CA (Civ Div)), Rix, L.J.

r.6.40, see *Bacon v Automattic Inc* [2011] EWHC 1072 (QB), [2012] 1 W.L.R. 753 (QBD), Tugendhat, J.; see *BNP Paribas SA v Open Joint Stock Company Russian Machines* [2011] EWHC 308 (Comm), [2012] 1 Lloyd's Rep. 61 (QBD (Comm)), Blair, J.

r.8.2, see *R. (on the application of A) v Secretary of State for Communities and Local Government* [2011] EWCA Civ 1253, [2012] J.P.L. 579 (CA (Civ Div)), Pill, L.J.

r.8.2A, see *Alexander Forbes Trustees Ltd v Doe* [2011] EWHC 3930 (Ch), [2012] Pens. L.R. 231 (Ch D), Judge Purle Q.C.

r.13.3, see *Merchant International Co Ltd v Natsionalna Aktsionerna Kompaniya Naftogaz Ukrayiny* [2012] EWCA Civ 196, [2012] 1 W.L.R. 3036 (CA (Civ Div)), Lord Neuberger (M.R.)

r.14.1, see *Kojima v HSBC Bank Ltd* [2011] EWCA Civ 1709, [2012] 1 All E.R. 1392 (CA (Civ Div)), Lord Neuberger (M.R.)

r.16.4, see *Seaton v Seddon* [2012] EWHC 735 (Ch), [2012] 1 W.L.R. 3636 (Ch D), Roth, J.; see *Whessoe Oil and Gas Ltd v Dale* [2012] EWHC 1788 (TCC), [2012] P.N.L.R. 33 (QBD (TCC)), Akenhead, J.

r.19.2, see *Fisher Meredith LLP v JH* [2012] EWHC 408 (Fam), [2012] 2 F.L.R. 536 (Fam Div), Mostyn, J.; see *Starlight Shipping Co v Allianz Marine & Aviation Versicherungs AG* [2011] EWHC 3381 (Comm), [2012] 2 All E.R. (Comm) 608 (QBD (Comm)), Burton, J.

r.19.7, see *IBM United Kingdom Pensions Trust Ltd v Metcalfe* [2012] EWHC 125 (Ch), [2012] 3 Costs L.O. 420 (Ch D), Warren, J.

r.19.8, see *Millburn-Snell v Evans* [2011] EWCA Civ 577, [2012] 1 W.L.R. 41 (CA (Civ Div)), Lord Neuberger of Abbotsbury MR

r.21.3, see *De Toucy v Bonhams 1793 Ltd* [2011] EWHC 3809 (Ch), [2012] B.P.I.R. 793 (Ch D), Vos, J.; see *Dunhill v Burgin* [2012] EWCA Civ 397, [2012] C.P. Rep. 29 (CA (Civ Div)), Ward, L.J.; see *Levy v Ellis-Carr* [2012] EWHC 63 (Ch), [2012] B.P.I.R. 347 (Ch D), Norris, J.

r.21.10, see *Dockerill v Tullett* [2012] EWCA Civ 184, [2012] 1 W.L.R. 2092 (CA (Civ Div)), Arden, L.J.; see *Dunhill v Burgin* [2012] EWHC 3163

3132. Civil Procedure Rules 1998–*cont.*

r.21.10–*cont.*

(QB), [2012] 1 W.L.R. 3739 (QBD (Manchester)), Bean, J.

r.23.3, see *R. (on the application of Simmons) v Bolton MBC* [2011] EWHC 2729 (Admin), [2012] Env. L.R. 20 (QBD (Admin)), Judge Pelling Q.C.

r.23.8, see *Church v MGN Ltd* [2012] EWHC 693 (QB), [2012] E.M.L.R. 28 (QBD), Tugendhat, J.

r.23.9, see *CVB v MGN Ltd* [2012] EWHC 1148 (QB), [2012] E.M.L.R. 29 (QBD), Tugendhat, J.

r.25.3, see *Practice Guidance (HC: Interim Non-Disclosure Orders)* [2012] 1 W.L.R. 1003 (Sen Cts), Lord Neuberger (M.R.)

r.25.7, see *Berry v Ashtead Plant Hire Co Ltd* [2011] EWCA Civ 1304, [2012] P.I.Q.R. P6 (CA (Civ Div)), Longmore, L.J.; see *Fred Perry (Holdings) Ltd v Brands Plaza Trading Ltd (t/a Brands Plaza)* [2012] EWCA Civ 224, [2012] 6 Costs L.R. 1007 (CA (Civ Div)), Maurice Kay, L.J.; see *Revenue and Customs Commissioners v GKN Group* [2012] EWCA Civ 57, [2012] 1 W.L.R. 2375 (CA (Civ Div)), Ward, L.J.

r.25.13, see *Ackerman v Ackerman* [2011] EWHC 2183 (Ch), [2012] 3 Costs L.O. 303 (Ch D), Roth, J.; see *Mengi v Hermitage* [2012] EWHC 2045 (QB), [2012] 5 Costs L.O. 641 (QBD), Tugendhat, J.

r.25.14, see *Chilab v King's College London* [2012] EWCA Civ 1178, Times, November 8, 2012 (CA (Civ Div)), Hughes, L.J.

r.26.6, see *Dockerill v Tullett* [2012] EWCA Civ 184, [2012] 1 W.L.R. 2092 (CA (Civ Div)), Arden, L.J.

r.30.3, see *SM v Sutton LBC* [2011] EWHC 3465 (Admin), [2012] 1 F.L.R. 974 (QBD (Admin)), Wyn Williams, J.

r.30.5, see *Arif v Zar* [2012] EWCA Civ 986, [2012] B.P.I.R. 948 (CA (Civ Div)), Thorpe, L.J.; see *DKH Retail Ltd v Republic (Retail) Ltd* [2012] EWHC 877 (Ch), [2012] Bus. L.R. 1363 (Ch D), Judge Birss Q.C.

r.31.3, see *Danisco A/S v Novozymes A/S* [2012] EWHC 389 (Pat), [2012] F.S.R. 22 (Ch D), Morgan, J.

r.31.5, see *Serious Organised Crime Agency v Namli* [2011] EWCA Civ 1411, [2012] C.P. Rep. 10 (CA (Civ Div)), Carnwath, L.J.

r.31.6, see *Serious Organised Crime Agency v Namli* [2011] EWCA Civ 1411, [2012] C.P. Rep. 10 (CA (Civ Div)), Carnwath, L.J.; see *Shah v HSBC Private Bank (UK) Ltd* [2011] EWCA Civ 1154, [2012] Lloyd's Rep. F.C. 105 (CA (Civ Div)), Pill, L.J.

r.31.8, see *North Shore Ventures Ltd v Anstead Holdings Inc* [2012] EWCA Civ 11, [2012] W.T.L.R. 1241 (CA (Civ Div)), Pill, L.J.

r.31.14, see *Danisco A/S v Novozymes A/S* [2012] EWHC 389 (Pat), [2012] F.S.R. 22 (Ch D), Morgan, J.

r.31.19, see *Danisco A/S v Novozymes A/S* [2012] EWHC 389 (Pat), [2012] F.S.R. 22 (Ch D), Morgan, J.; see *Serious Organised Crime Agency v Namli* [2011] EWCA Civ 1411, [2012] C.P. Rep. 10 (CA (Civ Div)), Carnwath, L.J.

r.31.22, see *National Grid Electricity Transmission Plc v ABB Ltd* [2011] EWHC 1717 (Ch), [2012] E.C.C. 1 (Ch D), Roth, J.; see *Shlaimoun v Mining Technologies International Inc* [2011] EWHC 3278 (QB), [2012] 1 W.L.R. 1276 (QBD), Coulson, J.; see *Shuldham, Re* [2012]

1998–cont.

3132. Civil Procedure Rules 1998–*cont.*

r.31.22–*cont.*

EWHC 1420 (Ch), [2012] W.T.L.R. 1597 (Ch D), Floyd, J.

r.32.5, see *Williams v Hinton* [2011] EWCA Civ 1123, [2012] C.P. Rep. 3 (CA (Civ Div)), Moore-Bick, L.J.

r.32.9, see *Tesco Stores Ltd v Office of Fair Trading* [2012] CAT 13, [2012] Comp. A.R. 434 (CAT), Lord Carlile of Berriew Q.C.

r.32.14, see *Ali v Esure Services Ltd* [2011] EWCA Civ 1582, [2012] 1 W.L.R. 1868 (CA (Civ Div)), Mummery, L.J.

r.34.12, see *British Sky Broadcasting Group Plc v Digital Satellite Warranty Cover Ltd* [2011] EWHC 3062 (Ch), [2012] 1 W.L.R. 219 (Ch D), Robin Knowles Q.C.

r.35.4, see *Odedra v Ball* [2012] EWHC 1790 (TCC), [2012] B.L.R. 434 (QBD (TCC)), Coulson, J.

r.36.2, see *Carillion JM Ltd v PHI Group Ltd* [2012] EWCA Civ 588, [2012] C.P. Rep. 37 (CA (Civ Div)), Rix, L.J.; see *Hutchinson v Neale* [2012] EWCA Civ 345, [2012] 5 Costs L.O. 588 (CA (Civ Div)), Patten, L.J.; see *Thewlis v Groupama Insurance Co Ltd* [2012] EWHC 3 (TCC), [2012] B.L.R. 259 (QBD (TCC)), Judge Behrens

r.36.10, see *PGF II SA v OMFS Co* [2012] EWHC 83 (TCC), [2012] 3 Costs L.O. 404 (QBD (TCC)), Recorder Furst Q.C.; see *SG (A Child) v Hewitt (Costs)* [2012] EWCA Civ 1053, [2012] 5 Costs L.R. 937 (CA (Civ Div)), Pill, L.J.; see *Solomon v Cromwell Group Plc* [2011] EWCA Civ 1584, [2012] 1 W.L.R. 1048 (CA (Civ Div)), Pill, L.J.

r.36.11, see *Thewlis v Groupama Insurance Co Ltd* [2012] EWHC 3 (TCC), [2012] B.L.R. 259 (QBD (TCC)), Judge Behrens

r.36.13, see *Beasley v Alexander* [2012] EWHC 2715 (QB), [2012] 6 Costs L.R. 1137 (QBD), Sir Raymond Jack; see *Ted Baker Plc v AXA Insurance UK Plc* [2012] EWHC 1779 (Comm), [2012] 6 Costs L.R. 1023 (QBD (Comm)), Eder, J.

r.36.14, see *Bent v Highways and Utilities Construction (Costs)* [2011] EWCA Civ 1539, [2012] 2 Costs L.O. 127 (CA (Civ Div)), Pill, L.J.; see *Carillion JM Ltd v PHI Group Ltd* [2012] EWCA Civ 588, [2012] C.P. Rep. 37 (CA (Civ Div)), Rix, L.J.; see *Epsom College v Pierse Constructing Southern Ltd (In Liquidation) (formerly Biseley Construction Ltd) (Costs)* [2011] EWCA Civ 1449, [2012] T.C.L.R. 2 (CA (Civ Div)), Rix, L.J.; see *F&C Alternative Investments (Holdings) Ltd v Barthelemy (Costs)* [2012] EWCA Civ 843, [2012] 4 All E.R. 1096 (CA (Civ Div)), Arden, L.J.; see *Lilleyman v Lilleyman (Costs)* [2012] EWHC 1056 (Ch), [2012] 1 W.L.R. 2801 (Ch D), Briggs, J.; see *PGF II SA v OMFS Co* [2012] EWHC 83 (TCC), [2012] 3 Costs L.O. 404 (QBD (TCC)), Recorder Furst Q.C.

r.38.6, see *Fresenius Kabi Deutschland GmbH v Carefusion 303 Inc* [2011] EWCA Civ 1288, [2012] Bus. L.R. 1276 (CA (Civ Div)), Lord Neuberger (M.R.)

r.38.7, see *Spicer v Tuli* [2012] EWCA Civ 845, [2012] 1 W.L.R. 3088 (CA (Civ Div)), Lord Neuberger (M.R.); see *Westbrook Dolphin Square Ltd v Friends Provident Life and Pensions Ltd* [2011] EWHC 2302 (Ch), [2012] L. & T.R. 12 (Ch D), Arnold, J.; see *Westbrook Dolphin Square Ltd v*

1998–cont.

3132. Civil Procedure Rules 1998–*cont.*

r.38.7–*cont.*

Friends Provident Life and Pensions Ltd [2012] EWCA Civ 666, [2012] 1 W.L.R. 2752 (CA (Civ Div)), Lord Neuberger (M.R.)

r.39.2, see *2 Travel Group Plc (In Liquidation) v Cardiff City Transport Services Ltd* [2012] CAT 7, [2012] Comp. A.R. 184 (CAT), Lord Carlile of Berriew Q.C.; see *CVB v MGN Ltd* [2012] EWHC 1148 (QB), [2012] E.M.L.R. 29 (QBD), Tugendhat, J.; see *Shuldham, Re* [2012] EWHC 1420 (Ch), [2012] W.T.L.R. 1597 (Ch D), Floyd, J.

r.39.3, see *Williams v Hinton* [2011] EWCA Civ 1123, [2012] C.P. Rep. 3 (CA (Civ Div)), Moore-Bick, L.J.

r.40.7, see *M.T.B. Motors Ltd (In Administration), Re* [2010] EWHC 3751 (Ch), [2012] B.C.C. 601 (Ch D (Manchester)), Judge Hodge Q.C.

r.40.8, see *Simcoe v Jacuzzi UK Group Plc* [2012] EWCA Civ 137, [2012] 1 W.L.R. 2393 (CA (Civ Div)), Lord Neuberger (M.R.)

r.43.2, see *Manning v King's College Hospital NHS Trust* [2011] EWHC 2954 (QB), [2012] 1 Costs L.R. 105 (QBD), Spencer, J.

r.44.3, see *Abbott v Long* [2011] EWCA Civ 874, [2012] R.T.R. 1 (CA (Civ Div)), Arden, L.J.; see *AL (Albania) v Secretary of State for the Home Department* [2012] EWCA Civ 710, [2012] 1 W.L.R. 2898 (CA (Civ Div)), Maurice Kay, L.J.; see *Ali v Stagecoach* [2011] EWCA Civ 1494, [2012] 2 Costs L.O. 89 (CA (Civ Div)), Longmore, L.J.; see *Brit Inns Ltd (In Liquidation) v BDW Trading Ltd (Costs)* [2012] EWHC 2489 (TCC), [2012] B.L.R. 531 (QBD (TCC)), Coulson, J.; see *Cheshire West and Chester Council v P (Costs)* [2011] EWCA Civ 1333, [2012] 1 Costs L.R. 150 (CA (Civ Div)), Pill, L.J.; see *F&C Alternative Investments (Holdings) Ltd v Barthelemy (Costs)* [2012] EWCA Civ 843, [2012] 4 All E.R. 1096 (CA (Civ Div)), Arden, L.J.; see *Frank Saul (Fashions) Ltd v Revenue and Customs Commissioners* [2012] EWHC 1603 (Ch), [2012] B.P.I.R. 985 (Ch D), Vos, J.; see *French v Groupama Insurance Co Ltd* [2011] EWCA Civ 1119, [2012] C.P. Rep. 2 (CA (Civ Div)), Rix, L.J.; see *Hutchinson v Neale* [2012] EWCA Civ 345, [2012] 5 Costs L.O. 588 (CA (Civ Div)), Patten, L.J.; see *M v Croydon LBC* [2012] EWCA Civ 595, [2012] 1 W.L.R. 2607 (CA (Civ Div)), Lord Neuberger (M.R.); see *Manning v King's College Hospital NHS Trust (Costs)* [2011] EWHC 3054 (QB), [2012] 1 Costs L.R. 154 (QBD), Spencer, J.; see *R (Costs: Contact Enforcement), Re* [2011] EWHC 2777 (Fam), [2012] 1 F.L.R. 445 (Fam Div), Moor, J.; see *R. (on the application of Royal Brompton and Harefield NHS Foundation Trust) v Joint Committee of Primary Care Trusts (Costs)* [2011] EWHC 3364 (Admin), [2012] 3 Costs L.R. 478 (QBD (Admin)), Owen, J.; see *Ted Baker Plc v AXA Insurance UK Plc* [2012] EWHC 1779 (Comm), [2012] 6 Costs L.R. 1023 (QBD (Comm)), Eder, J.; see *Thomas Brown Estates Ltd v Hunters Partners Ltd (formerly Countywide Franchising Ltd)* [2012] EWHC 30 (QB), [2012] 4 Costs L.R. 623 (QBD), Eder, J.

r.44.3B, see *Manning v King's College Hospital NHS Trust* [2011] EWHC 2954 (QB), [2012] 1 Costs L.R. 105 (QBD), Spencer, J.

1998–cont.

3132. Civil Procedure Rules 1998–*cont.*

r.44.4, see *QBE Management Services (UK) Ltd v Dymoke* [2012] EWHC 116 (QB), [2012] I.R.L.R. 458 (QBD), Haddon-Cave, J.

r.44.5, see *Dockerill v Tullett* [2012] EWCA Civ 184, [2012] 1 W.L.R. 2092 (CA (Civ Div), Arden, L.J.; see *KMT (A Child) v Kent CC* [2012] EWHC 2088 (QB), [2012] 6 Costs L.R. 1039 (QBD), Eady, J.

r.44.11, see *Tibbles v SIG Plc (t/a Asphaltic Roofing Supplies)* [2012] EWCA Civ 518, [2012] 1 W.L.R. 2591 (CA (Civ Div)), Rix, L.J.

r.44.12, see *Letts v Royal Sun Alliance Plc* [2012] EWHC 875 (QB), [2012] 3 Costs L.R. 591 (Sen Cts Costs Office), Mackay, J.; see *Solomon v Cromwell Group Plc* [2011] EWCA Civ 1584, [2012] 1 W.L.R. 1048 (CA (Civ Div)), Pill, L.J.

r.44.12A, see *Citation Plc v Ellis Whittam Ltd* [2012] EWHC 764 (QB), [2012] 5 Costs L.R. 826 (QBD), Tugendhat, J.; see *Solomon v Cromwell Group Plc* [2011] EWCA Civ 1584, [2012] 1 W.L.R. 1048 (CA (Civ Div)), Pill, L.J.

r.44.15, see *Manning v King's College Hospital NHS Trust* [2011] EWHC 2954 (QB), [2012] 1 Costs L.R. 105 (QBD), Spencer, J.

r.44.18, see *Comic Enterprises Ltd v Twentieth Century Fox Film Corp* [2012] EWPCC 13, [2012] F.S.R. 30 (Ch D), Judge Birss Q.C.

r.45.7, see *Dockerill v Tullett* [2012] EWCA Civ 184, [2012] 1 W.L.R. 2092 (CA (Civ Div)), Arden, L.J.; see *Solomon v Cromwell Group Plc* [2011] EWCA Civ 1584, [2012] 1 W.L.R. 1048 (CA (Civ Div)), Pill, L.J.

r.45.8, see *Solomon v Cromwell Group Plc* [2011] EWCA Civ 1584, [2012] 1 W.L.R. 1048 (CA (Civ Div)), Pill, L.J.

r.45.9, see *Dockerill v Tullett* [2012] EWCA Civ 184, [2012] 1 W.L.R. 2092 (CA (Civ Div)), Arden, L.J.

r.45.10, see *Dockerill v Tullett* [2012] EWCA Civ 184, [2012] 1 W.L.R. 2092 (CA (Civ Div)), Arden, L.J.

r.45.42, see *BOS GmbH & Co KG v Cobra UK Automotive Products Division Ltd (In Administration) (Costs)* [2012] EWPCC 44, [2012] 6 Costs L.R. 1083 (PCC), Judge Birss Q.C.; see *Gimex International Groupe Import Export v Chill Bag Co Ltd* [2012] EWPCC 34, [2012] 6 Costs L.R. 1069 (PCC), Judge Birss Q.C.; see *Liversidge v Owen Mumford Ltd* [2012] EWPCC 40, [2012] 6 Costs L.R. 1076 (PCC), Judge Birss Q.C.

r.47.15, see *Beattie v Smailes* [2011] EWHC 3865 (Ch), [2012] 3 Costs L.R. 445 (Ch D), Norris, J.

r.47.18, see *Manning v King's College Hospital NHS Trust (Costs)* [2011] EWHC 3054 (QB), [2012] 1 Costs L.R. 154 (QBD), Spencer, J.

r.48.3, see *Brown-Quinn v Equity Syndicate Management Ltd* [2011] EWHC 2661 (Comm), [2012] 1 All E.R. 778 (QBD (Comm)), Burton, J.

r.48.8, see *Tim Martin Interiors Ltd v Akin Gump LLP* [2011] EWCA Civ 1574, [2012] 1 W.L.R. 2946 (CA (Civ Div)), Ward, L.J.

r.52.2, see *Poland v Walerianczyk* [2010] EWHC 2149 (Admin), [2012] 1 W.L.R. 363 (DC), Stanley Burnton, L.J.

r.52.3, see *Masri v Consolidated Contractors International Co SAL* [2011] EWCA Civ 898, [2012] 1 W.L.R. 223 (CA (Civ Div)), Maurice Kay, L.J.

r.52.9, see *Unison v Kelly* [2012] EWCA Civ 1148, [2012] I.R.L.R. 951 (CA (Civ Div)), Richards, L.J.

1998–cont.

3132. Civil Procedure Rules 1998–*cont.*

r.52.10, see *Kennedy v Information Commissioner* [2011] EWCA Civ 367, [2012] 1 W.L.R. 3524 (CA (Civ Div)), Ward, L.J.; see *Ryanair Holdings Plc v Office of Fair Trading* [2011] EWCA Civ 1579, [2012] Bus. L.R. 1903 (CA (Civ Div)), Lloyd, L.J.

r.52.11, see *KMT (A Child) v Kent CC* [2012] EWHC 2088 (QB), [2012] 6 Costs L.R. 1039 (QBD), Eady, J.; see *St Andrew's Catholic Primary School Governing Body v Blundell* [2011] EWCA Civ 427, [2012] I.C.R. 295 (CA (Civ Div)), Lord Neuberger of Abbotsbury MR

r.52.15, see *R. (on the application of MD (Afghanistan)) v Secretary of State for the Home Department* [2012] EWCA Civ 194, [2012] 1 W.L.R. 2422 (CA (Civ Div)), Hooper, L.J.

r.54.5, see *Allman v HM Coroner for West Sussex* [2012] EWHC 534 (Admin), (2012) 176 J.P. 285 (QBD (Admin)), Judge Anthony Thornton Q.C.; see *R. (on the application of Berky) v Newport City Council* [2012] EWCA Civ 378, [2012] 2 C.M.L.R. 44 (CA (Civ Div)), Carnwath, L.J.; see *R. (on the application of Kilroy) v Parrs Wood High School Governing Body* [2011] EWHC 3489 (Admin), [2012] E.L.R. 146 (QBD (Admin)), Judge Pelling Q.C.; see *R. (on the application of Macrae) v Herefordshire DC* [2011] EWHC 2810 (Admin), [2012] 1 C.M.L.R. 28 (QBD (Admin)), David Elvin Q.C.; see *R. (on the application of Macrae) v Herefordshire DC* [2012] EWCA Civ 457, [2012] J.P.L. 1356 (CA (Civ Div)), Pill, L.J.; see *R. (on the application of U & Partners (East Anglia) Ltd) v Broads Authority* [2011] EWHC 1824 (Admin), [2012] Env. L.R. 5 (QBD (Admin)), Collins, J.; see *Shamlou v Blackpool and Fleetwood Magistrates' Court* [2011] EWHC 2874 (Admin), [2012] R.V.R. 90 (QBD (Admin)), Judge Stephen Davies

r.54.12, see *R. (on the application of MD (Afghanistan)) v Secretary of State for the Home Department* [2012] EWCA Civ 194, [2012] 1 W.L.R. 2422 (CA (Civ Div)), Hooper, L.J.

r.55.6, see *Sun Street Property Ltd v Persons Unknown* [2011] EWHC 3432 (Ch), Times, January 16, 2012 (Ch D), Roth, J.

r.57.7, see *Wharton v Bancroft* [2012] EWHC 91 (Ch), [2012] W.T.L.R. 727 (Ch D), Norris, J.

r.58.7, see *Parbulk II AS v PT Humpuss Intermoda Transportasi TBK (The Mahakam)* [2011] EWHC 3143 (Comm), [2012] 2 All E.R. (Comm) 513 (QBD (Comm)), Gloster, J.

r.61.4, see *MIOM 1 Ltd v Sea Echo ENE* [2011] EWHC 2715 (Admlty), [2012] 1 Lloyd's Rep. 140 (QBD (Admlty)), Teare, J.

r.62.3, see *Merit Process Engineering Ltd v Balfour Beatty Engineering Services (HY) Ltd* [2012] EWHC 1376 (TCC), [2012] B.L.R. 364 (QBD (TCC)), Edwards-Stuart, J.

r.62.5, see *AES Ust-Kamenogorsk Hydropower Plant LLP v Ust-Kamenogorsk Hydropower Plant JSC* [2011] EWCA Civ 647, [2012] 1 W.L.R. 920 (CA (Civ Div)), Rix, L.J.; see *BNP Paribas SA v Open Joint Stock Company Russian Machines* [2011] EWHC 308 (Comm), [2012] 1 Lloyd's Rep. 61 (QBD (Comm)), Blair, J.; see *Enercon GmbH v Enercon (India) Ltd* [2012] EWHC 689 (Comm), [2012] 1 Lloyd's Rep. 519 (QBD (Comm)), Eder, J.; see *Western Bulk*

1998–cont.

3132. Civil Procedure Rules 1998–*cont.*

r.62.5–*cont.*

Shipowning III A/S v Carbofer Maritime Trading ApS (The Western Moscow) [2012] EWHC 1224 (Comm), [2012] 2 All E.R. (Comm) 1140 (QBD (Comm)), Christopher Clarke, J.

r.62.7, see *Sovarex SA v Romero Alvarez SA* [2011] EWHC 1661 (Comm), [2012] 1 All E.R. (Comm) 207 (QBD (Comm)), Hamblen, J.

r.62.9, see *Nestor Maritime SA v Sea Anchor Shipping Co Ltd* [2012] EWHC 996 (Comm), [2012] 2 Lloyd's Rep. 144 (QBD (Comm)), Eder, J.

r.62.18, see *BNP Paribas SA v Open Joint Stock Company Russian Machines* [2011] EWHC 308 (Comm), [2012] 1 Lloyd's Rep. 61 (QBD (Comm)), Blair, J.

r.63.2, see *DKH Retail Ltd v Republic (Retail) Ltd* [2012] EWHC 877 (Ch), [2012] Bus. L.R. 1363 (Ch D), Judge Birss Q.C.

r.63.3, see *DKH Retail Ltd v Republic (Retail) Ltd* [2012] EWHC 877 (Ch), [2012] Bus. L.R. 1363 (Ch D), Judge Birss Q.C.

r.63.13, see *DKH Retail Ltd v Republic (Retail) Ltd* [2012] EWHC 877 (Ch), [2012] Bus. L.R. 1363 (Ch D), Judge Birss Q.C.

r.69.10, see *McCracken, Re* [2011] EWCA Civ 1620, [2012] Lloyd's Rep. F.C. 148 (CA (Civ Div)), Maurice Kay, L.J.

r.71.2, see *North Shore Ventures Ltd v Anstead Holdings Inc* [2012] EWCA Civ 11, [2012] W.T.L.R. 1241 (CA (Civ Div)), Pill, L.J.

r.73.8, see *National Guild of Removers and Storers Ltd v Jones (t/a ATR Removals)* [2012] EWCA Civ 216, [2012] 1 W.L.R. 2501 (CA (Civ Div)), Lord Neuberger (M.R.)

r.73.10, see *National Guild of Removers and Storers Ltd v Jones (t/a ATR Removals)* [2012] EWCA Civ 216, [2012] 1 W.L.R. 2501 (CA (Civ Div)), Lord Neuberger (M.R.)

r.76.2, see *R. v Fitzgerald (Costs)* [2012] 3 Costs L.R. 437 (Central Crim Ct), Judge Gordon

r.76.21, see *Secretary of State for the Home Department v CB* [2012] EWCA Civ 418, [2012] 1 W.L.R. 3259 (CA (Civ Div)), Lord Neuberger (M.R.)

r.76.29, see *Secretary of State for the Home Department v BM* [2012] EWHC 714 (Admin), [2012] 1 W.L.R. 2734 (QBD (Admin)), Collins, J.

r.76.31, see *Secretary of State for the Home Department v CB* [2012] EWCA Civ 418, [2012] 1 W.L.R. 3259 (CA (Civ Div)), Lord Neuberger (M.R.)

r.80.25, see *Secretary of State for the Home Department v BM* [2012] EWHC 714 (Admin), [2012] 1 W.L.R. 2734 (QBD (Admin)), Collins, J.

Sch.1, referred to: SI 2012/1726 r.19.8, r.19.9

Sch.1 Part 45 para.3, amended: SI 2012/2208 r.18

Sch.1 Part 45 para.4, amended: SI 2012/2208 r.18

Sch.1 Part 45 para.5, revoked: SI 2012/2208 r.18

Sch.1 Part 45 para.6, revoked: SI 2012/2208 r.18

Sch.1 Part 45 para.7, revoked: SI 2012/2208 r.18

Sch.1 Part 45 para.12, revoked (in part): SI 2012/2208 r.18

Sch.1 Part 46 para.5, substituted: SI 2012/2208 r.18

Sch.1 Ord.52, see *NLW v ARC* [2012] EWHC 55 (Fam), [2012] 2 F.L.R. 129 (Fam Div), Mostyn, J.

Sch.1 Part 52 para.1, revoked: SI 2012/2208 r.18

Sch.1 Ord.52 r.1, see *Ali v Esure Services Ltd* [2011] EWCA Civ 1582, [2012] 1 W.L.R. 1868 (CA (Civ Div)), Mummery, L.J.; see *Deputy Chief Legal*

1998–cont.

3132. Civil Procedure Rules 1998–*cont.*

Sch.1 Ord.52 r.1–*cont.*

Ombudsman v Young [2011] EWHC 2923 (Admin), [2012] 1 W.L.R. 3227 (QBD), Lindblom, J.

Sch.1 Part 52 para.2, revoked: SI 2012/2208 r.18

Sch.1 Part 52 para.3, revoked: SI 2012/2208 r.18

Sch.1 Part 52 para.4, revoked: SI 2012/2208 r.18

Sch.1 Part 52 para.5, revoked: SI 2012/2208 r.18

Sch.1 Part 52 para.6, revoked: SI 2012/2208 r.18

Sch.1 Ord.52 r.6, see *Doncaster MBC v Watson* [2011] EWHC 2376 (Fam), [2012] 1 F.L.R. 613 (Fam Div), Sir Nicholas Wall (President, Fam)

Sch.1 Part 52 para.7, revoked: SI 2012/2208 r.18

Sch.1 Part 52 para.7A, revoked: SI 2012/2208 r.18

Sch.1 Part 52 para.8, revoked: SI 2012/2208 r.18

Sch.1 Part 52 para.9, revoked: SI 2012/2208 r.18

Sch.1 Part 64 para.4, revoked: SI 2012/2208 r.18

Sch.2 Part 27 para.3, amended: SI 2012/505 r.6

Sch.2 Part 29 para.1, revoked: SI 2012/2208 r.19

Sch.2 Part 29 para.1A, revoked: SI 2012/2208 r.19

Sch.2 Part 29 para.2, revoked: SI 2012/2208 r.19

Sch.2 Part 29 para.3, revoked: SI 2012/2208 r.19

Sch.2 Part 34 para.1, revoked: SI 2012/2208 r.19

Sch.2 Part 34 para.1A, revoked: SI 2012/2208 r.19

Sch.2 Part 34 para.2, revoked: SI 2012/2208 r.19

Sch.2 Part 34 para.3, revoked: SI 2012/2208 r.19

Sch.2 Part 34 para.4, revoked: SI 2012/2208 r.19

3162. Fair Employment and Treatment (Northern Ireland) Order 1998

see *Northern Ireland Fire and Rescue Service v McNally* [2012] Eq. L.R. 821 (CA (NI)), Higgins, L.J.

3175. Corporation Tax (Instalment Payments) Regulations 1998

Reg.6, varied: 2012 c.14 Sch.34 para.12

Reg.7, varied: 2012 c.14 Sch.34 para.12

Reg.8, varied: 2012 c.14 Sch.34 para.12

Reg.9, varied: 2012 c.14 Sch.34 para.12

Reg.10, varied: 2012 c.14 Sch.34 para.12

Reg.11, varied: 2012 c.14 Sch.34 para.12

Reg.13, varied: 2012 c.14 Sch.34 para.12

3178. Scotland Act 1998 (Commencement) Order 1998

Sch.3, varied: 2012 c.11 s.12

1999

2. Education (School Premises) Regulations 1999

Reg.1A, added: SI 2012/1943 Reg.3

40. Health and Safety at Work etc Act 1974 (Application to Environmentally Hazardous Substances) (Amendment) Regulations 1999

applied: SI 2012/1286 Sch.1

71. Allocation of Housing and Homelessness (Review Procedures) Regulations 1999

see *Mitu v Camden LBC* [2011] EWCA Civ 1249, [2012] H.L.R. 10 (CA (Civ Div)), Rix, L.J.

Reg.6, see *El Goure v Kensington and Chelsea RLBC* [2012] EWCA Civ 670, [2012] P.T.S.R. 1664 (CA (Civ Div)), Mummery, L.J.; see *Maswaku v Westminster City Council* [2012] EWCA Civ 669, [2012] P.T.S.R. 1650 (CA (Civ Div)), Mummery, L.J.

Reg.8, see *Maswaku v Westminster City Council* [2012] EWCA Civ 669, [2012] P.T.S.R. 1650 (CA (Civ Div)), Mummery, L.J.; see *Mitu v Camden LBC* [2011] EWCA Civ 1249, [2012] H.L.R. 10 (CA (Civ Div)), Rix, L.J.

1999–cont.

80. Food Protection (Emergency Prohibitions) (Radioactivity in Sheep) Partial Revocation Order 1999
revoked (in part): SSI 2012/263 Sch.1

157. Miscellaneous Products of Animal Origin (Import Conditions) Regulations 1999
revoked: SSI 2012/177 Reg.38

220. National Institute for Clinical Excellence (Establishment and Constitution) Order 1999
Art.1, amended: SI 2012/476 Art.3
Art.7, added: SI 2012/476 Art.4
Art.8, added: SI 2012/476 Art.4

260. National Institute for Clinical Excellence Regulations 1999
Reg.1, amended: SI 2012/1641 Sch.4 para.4
Reg.5, amended: SI 2012/2404 Sch.3 para.12

267. Medicines (Advertising and Monitoring of Advertising) Amendment Regulations 1999
revoked: SI 2012/1916 Sch.35

281. Federal Republic of Yugoslavia (United Nations Sanctions) (Dependent Territories) (Amendment) Order 1999
revoked: SI 2012/2592 Sch.2

293. Town and Country Planning (Environmental Impact Assessment) (England and Wales) Regulations 1999
see *R. (on the application of Burridge) v Breckland DC* [2012] EWHC 1102 (Admin), [2012] Env. L.R. 36 (QBD (Admin)), Judge Waksman Q.C.; see *R. (on the application of Loader) v Secretary of State for Communities and Local Government* [2011] EWHC 2010 (Admin), [2012] Env. L.R. 8 (QBD (Admin)), Lloyd Jones, J.; see *R. (on the application of Loader) v Secretary of State for Communities and Local Government* [2012] EWCA Civ 869, [2012] 3 C.M.L.R. 29 (CA (Civ Div)), Pill, L.J.; see *R. (on the application of Mageean) v Secretary of State for Communities and Local Government* [2011] EWCA Civ 863, [2012] Env. L.R. 3 (CA (Civ Div)), Mummery, L.J.; see *R. (on the application of U & Partners (East Anglia) Ltd) v Broads Authority* [2011] EWHC 1824 (Admin), [2012] Env. L.R. 5 (QBD (Admin)), Collins, J.
Reg.2, see *R. (on the application of Loader) v Secretary of State for Communities and Local Government* [2012] EWCA Civ 869, [2012] 3 C.M.L.R. 29 (CA (Civ Div)), Pill, L.J.
Reg.7, see *R. (on the application of Burridge) v Breckland DC* [2012] EWHC 1102 (Admin), [2012] Env. L.R. 36 (QBD (Admin)), Judge Waksman Q.C.
Sch.2, applied: SI 2012/801 Art.18
Sch.2, see *R. (on the application of Burridge) v Breckland DC* [2012] EWHC 1102 (Admin), [2012] Env. L.R. 36 (QBD (Admin)), Judge Waksman Q.C.; see *R. (on the application of Loader) v Secretary of State for Communities and Local Government* [2011] EWHC 2010 (Admin), [2012] Env. L.R. 8 (QBD (Admin)), Lloyd Jones, J.; see *R. (on the application of Warley) v Wealden DC* [2011] EWHC 2083 (Admin), [2012] Env. L.R. 4 (QBD (Admin)), Rabinder Singh Q.C.
Sch.2 para.2, see *R. (on the application of Warley) v Wealden DC* [2011] EWHC 2083 (Admin), [2012] Env. L.R. 4 (QBD (Admin)), Rabinder Singh Q.C.

1999–cont.

293. Town and Country Planning (Environmental Impact Assessment) (England and Wales) Regulations 1999–*cont.*
Sch.2 para.3, see *R. (on the application of Burridge) v Breckland DC* [2012] EWHC 1102 (Admin), [2012] Env. L.R. 36 (QBD (Admin)), Judge Waksman Q.C.
Sch.3, see *R. (on the application of Loader) v Secretary of State for Communities and Local Government* [2011] EWHC 2010 (Admin), [2012] Env. L.R. 8 (QBD (Admin)), Lloyd Jones, J.
Sch.4 Pt I para.4, see *Bowen-West v Secretary of State for Communities and Local Government* [2012] EWCA Civ 321, [2012] Env. L.R. 22 (CA (Civ Div)), Laws, L.J.

400. Welfare of Animals (Slaughter or Killing) (Amendment) Regulations 1999
Reg.2, revoked (in part): SSI 2012/321 Sch.5 Part 2

421. Local Authorities (Goods and Services) (Public Bodies) (No.1) Order 1999
Art.2, amended: SI 2012/765 Art.3

441. Scotland Act 1998 (Transitory and Transitional Provisions) (Finance) Order 1999
Art.4, varied: 2012 c.11 s.12
Art.5, varied: 2012 c.11 s.12
Art.9, varied: 2012 c.11 s.12

491. Criminal Legal Aid (Fixed Payments) (Scotland) Regulations 1999
see *McGowan v Marshall* 2012 S.L.T. (Sh Ct) 109 (Sh Ct (Lothian) (Edinburgh)), Sheriff N M P Morrison, QC
Reg.2, amended: SI 2012/1809 Sch.1 Part 3

495. Education (Amount to Follow Permanently Excluded Pupil) Regulations 1999
varied: SI 2012/1107 Art.9
Reg.2, substituted: SI 2012/1033 Sch.2 para.1
Reg.3, amended: SI 2012/1033 Sch.2 para.1
Reg.4, amended: SI 2012/1033 Sch.2 para.1

522. Pensions Increase (Review) Order 1999
applied: SI 2012/782 Art.3, Art.4

584. National Minimum Wage Regulations 1999
see *Wray v JW Lees & Co (Brewers) Ltd* [2012] I.C.R. 43 (EAT), Underhill, J. (President)
Reg.2, amended: SI 2012/956 Art.7
Reg.2, see *Jose v Julio* [2012] I.C.R. 487 (EAT), Supperstone, J.; see *Nambalat v Taher* [2012] EWCA Civ 1249, [2012] I.R.L.R. 1004 (CA (Civ Div)), Pill, L.J.
Reg.11, amended: SI 2012/2397 Reg.2
Reg.12, amended: SI 2012/2397 Reg.2
Reg.13, amended: SI 2012/2397 Reg.2
Reg.13A, added: SI 2012/3112 Art.2
Reg.16, see *Wray v JW Lees & Co (Brewers) Ltd* [2012] I.C.R. 43 (EAT), Underhill, J. (President)
Reg.31, amended: SI 2012/700 Sch.1 para.11, SI 2012/979 Sch.1 para.5
Reg.33, amended: SI 2012/2397 Reg.2
Reg.35, amended: SI 2012/2397 Reg.2
Reg.36, amended: SI 2012/2397 Reg.2

662. Water (Northern Ireland) Order 1999
applied: SI 2012/1128 Art.4

672. National Assembly for Wales (Transfer of Functions) Order 1999
Art.2, see *Local Government Byelaws (Wales) Bill 2012, Re* [2012] UKSC 53, [2012] 3 W.L.R. 1294 (SC), Lord Neuberger (President)
Sch.1, amended: 2012 c.17 Sch.3 para.22

1999– cont.

672. National Assembly for Wales (Transfer of Functions) Order 1999– *cont.*
Sch.1, see *Local Government Byelaws (Wales) Bill 2012, Re* [2012] UKSC 53, [2012] 3 W.L.R. 1294 (SC), Lord Neuberger (President)

681. Magistrates Courts (Hearsay Evidence in Civil Proceedings) Rules 1999
r.3, applied: SI 2012/ 1726 r.50.6
r.3, referred to: SI 2012/ 1726 r.50.6
r.4, applied: SI 2012/ 1726 r.50.6
r.5, applied: SI 2012/ 1726 r.50.6

686. Scottish Ambulance Service Board Order 1999
Sch.1 Part III, amended: SI 2012/ 1479 Sch.1 para.15

728. Prison Rules 1999
r.45, see *R. (on the application of King) v Secretary of State for Justice* [2012] EWCA Civ 376, [2012] 1 W.L.R. 3602 (CA (Civ Div)), Maurice Kay, L.J.
r.53, see *R. (on the application of Garland) v Secretary of State for Justice* [2011] EWCA Civ 1335, [2012] 1 W.L.R. 1879 (CA (Civ Div)), Hughes, L.J.

732. Police (Efficiency) Regulations 1999
Reg.3, varied: SI 2012/ 2631 Reg.3
Reg.4, varied: SI 2012/ 2631 Reg.3
Reg.8, varied: SI 2012/ 2631 Reg.3

743. Control of Major Accident Hazards Regulations 1999
applied: SI 2012/ 1652 Reg.22, Reg.24
Reg.5, applied: SSI 2012/ 360 Sch.4 para.13
Reg.7, applied: SSI 2012/ 360 Sch.4 para.1, Sch.4 para.13, Sch.4 para.18

752. Bankruptcy Fees (Scotland) Amendment Regulations 1999
revoked: SSI 2012/ 118 Sch.2

784. Medicines (Monitoring of Advertising) Amendment Regulations 1999
revoked: SI 2012/ 1916 Sch.35

787. Scottish Parliament (Elections etc.) Order 1999
varied: 2012 c.11 s.3

818. Police Appeals Tribunals Rules 1999
varied: SI 2012/ 2630 r.2
r.3, varied: SI 2012/ 2630 r.2
r.4, varied: SI 2012/ 2630 r.2

873. National Health Service (Liabilities to Third Parties Scheme) Regulations 1999
Reg.3, amended: SI 2012/ 1641 Sch.3 para.6

874. National Health Service (Property Expenses Scheme) Regulations 1999
Reg.3, amended: SI 2012/ 1641 Sch.3 para.7

901. Scotland Act 1998 (General Transitory, Transitional and Savings Provisions) Order 1999
Art.2, varied: 2012 c.11 s.12
Art.4, varied: 2012 c.11 s.12

904. Prosecution of Offences Act 1985 (Specified Proceedings) Order 1999
Art.3, amended: SI 2012/ 1635 Art.2, SI 2012/ 2067 Art.2, SI 2012/ 2681 Art.3
Sch.1 para.1, substituted: SI 2012/ 2681 Art.4
Sch.1 Part 1 para.3, substituted: SI 2012/ 2681 Art.5
Sch.1 Part 1 para.6, added: SI 2012/ 2681 Art.6
Sch.1 Part 1 para.7, added: SI 2012/ 2681 Art.6
Sch.1 Part 1 para.8, added: SI 2012/ 2681 Art.6
Sch.1 Part 1 para.9, added: SI 2012/ 2681 Art.6
Sch.1 Part 1 para.10, added: SI 2012/ 2681 Art.6
Sch.1 Part 1 para.11, added: SI 2012/ 2681 Art.6
Sch.1 Part 1 para.12, added: SI 2012/ 2681 Art.6
Sch.1 Part 1 para.13, added: SI 2012/ 2681 Art.6
Sch.1 Part 1 para.14, added: SI 2012/ 2681 Art.6

1999– cont.

904. Prosecution of Offences Act 1985 (Specified Proceedings) Order 1999– *cont.*
Sch.1 Part 1 para.15, added: SI 2012/ 2681 Art.6
Sch.1 Part 1 para.16, added: SI 2012/ 2681 Art.6
Sch.1 para.2, substituted: SI 2012/ 2681 Art.4
Sch.1 Part 2 para.17, added: SI 2012/ 2681 Art.6
Sch.1 para.3, substituted: SI 2012/ 2681 Art.4
Sch.1 para.4, substituted: SI 2012/ 2681 Art.4
Sch.1 para.5, substituted: SI 2012/ 2681 Art.4

913. North West London Hospitals National Health Service Trust (Establishment) Order 1999
referred to: SI 2012/ 1512 Sch.1

924. A31 Trunk Road (Canford Bottom Roundabout) (40 Miles Per Hour Speed Limit) Order 1999
revoked: SI 2012/ 1382 Art.3

929. Act of Sederunt (Summary Applications, Statutory Applications and Appeals etc Rules) 1999
Part 2 r.2.42, added: SSI 2012/ 271 r.3
Part 3, substituted: SSI 2012/ 188 r.12
Part 3, added: SSI 2012/ 271 r.10
Part 3 r.3.41.1, amended: SSI 2012/ 188 r.12
Part 3 r.3.41.1, substituted: SSI 2012/ 188 r.12
r.2.31, see *Duff v Chief Constable of Dumfries and Galloway* [2012] CSIH 45, 2012 S.L.T. 975 (IH (Ex Div)), Lord Clarke
r.3.4.3, see *Northern Rock (Asset Management) Plc v Youngson* 2012 Hous. L.R. 100 (Sh Ct (Grampian) (Banff)), Sheriff P Mann
Sch.1, added: SSI 2012/ 271 Sch.1

991. Social Security and Child Support (Decisions and Appeals) Regulations 1999
Reg.1, amended: SI 2012/ 2007 Sch.1 para.113, SI 2012/ 2785 Reg.6
Reg.3, amended: SI 2012/ 824 Reg.4, SI 2012/ 913 Reg.5, SI 2012/ 919 Reg.2, SI 2012/ 2568 Reg.6, SI 2012/ 2575 Reg.4
Reg.3A, amended: SI 2012/ 2007 Sch.1 para.113
Reg.3A, revoked: SI 2012/ 2785 Reg.6
Reg.4, amended: SI 2012/ 2785 Reg.6
Reg.5A, revoked: SI 2012/ 2785 Reg.6
Reg.6, amended: SI 2012/ 1267 Reg.4, SI 2012/ 2568 Reg.6
Reg.6A, amended: SI 2012/ 1267 Reg.4, SI 2012/ 2007 Sch.1 para.113
Reg.6A, revoked: SI 2012/ 2785 Reg.6
Reg.6B, amended: SI 2012/ 1267 Reg.4, SI 2012/ 2007 Sch.1 para.113
Reg.6B, revoked: SI 2012/ 2785 Reg.6
Reg.7, amended: SI 2012/ 757 Reg.17, SI 2012/ 1267 Reg.4, SI 2012/ 2568 Reg.6, SI 2012/ 2756 Reg.8
Reg.7, revoked (in part): SI 2012/ 2568 Reg.6, SI 2012/ 2756 Reg.8
Reg.7B, revoked: SI 2012/ 2785 Reg.6
Reg.7C, amended: SI 2012/ 2007 Sch.1 para.113
Reg.7C, revoked: SI 2012/ 2785 Reg.6
Reg.15A, amended: SI 2012/ 2007 Sch.1 para.113
Reg.15A, revoked: SI 2012/ 2785 Reg.6
Reg.15B, amended: SI 2012/ 2007 Sch.1 para.113
Reg.15B, revoked: SI 2012/ 2785 Reg.6
Reg.15C, amended: SI 2012/ 2007 Sch.1 para.113
Reg.15C, revoked: SI 2012/ 2785 Reg.6
Reg.17, amended: SI 2012/ 824 Reg.4
Reg.23, amended: SI 2012/ 2007 Sch.1 para.113
Reg.23, revoked: SI 2012/ 2785 Reg.6
Reg.24, amended: SI 2012/ 2007 Sch.1 para.113
Reg.24, revoked: SI 2012/ 2785 Reg.6

1999– cont.

991. Social Security and Child Support (Decisions and Appeals) Regulations 1999– *cont.*

Reg.30, amended: SI 2012/ 2007 Sch.1 para.113, SI 2012/ 2785 Reg.6

Reg.32, amended: SI 2012/ 2007 Sch.1 para.113

Reg.33, amended: SI 2012/ 2007 Sch.1 para.113

Reg.33, revoked (in part): SI 2012/ 2785 Reg.6

Sch.3D para.1, revoked: SI 2012/ 2785 Reg.6

Sch.3D para.2, revoked: SI 2012/ 2785 Reg.6

Sch.3D para.3, revoked: SI 2012/ 2785 Reg.6

Sch.3D para.3A, revoked: SI 2012/ 2785 Reg.6

Sch.3D para.4, revoked: SI 2012/ 2785 Reg.6

Sch.3D para.5, revoked: SI 2012/ 2785 Reg.6

Sch.3D para.6, revoked: SI 2012/ 2785 Reg.6

Sch.3D para.7, revoked: SI 2012/ 2785 Reg.6

Sch.3D para.8, revoked: SI 2012/ 2785 Reg.6

Sch.3D para.9, amended: SI 2012/ 2007 Sch.1 para.113

Sch.3D para.9, revoked: SI 2012/ 2785 Reg.6

Sch.3D para.10, amended: SI 2012/ 2007 Sch.1 para.113

Sch.3D para.10, revoked: SI 2012/ 2785 Reg.6

Sch.3D para.11, amended: SI 2012/ 1267 Reg.4, SI 2012/ 2007 Sch.1 para.113

Sch.3D para.11, revoked: SI 2012/ 2785 Reg.6

Sch.3D para.12, revoked: SI 2012/ 2785 Reg.6

1042. Scotland Act 1998 (Consequential Modifications) (No.1) Order 1999

Sch.1 Part I para.2, varied: 2012 c.11 s.12

Sch.1 Part I para.5, varied: 2012 c.11 s.12

Sch.1 Part II para.23, varied: 2012 c.11 s.12

1081. Scotland Act 1998 (Transitory and Transitional Provisions) (Grants to Members and Officeholders) Order 1999

Art.6, varied: 2012 c.11 s.12

1082. Scotland Act 1998 (Transitory and Transitional Provisions) (Scottish Parliamentary Pension Scheme) Order 1999

Art.2, varied: 2012 c.11 s.12

1095. Scotland Act 1998 (Transitory and Transitional Provisions) (Standing Orders and Parliamentary Publications) Order 1999

Sch.1 Part 2 para.4, varied: 2012 c.11 s.12

Sch.1 Part 2 para.9, varied: 2012 c.11 s.12

Sch.1 Part 4 para.1, varied: 2012 c.11 s.12

Sch.1 Part 4 para.2, varied: 2012 c.11 s.12

Sch.1 Part 4 para.3, varied: 2012 c.11 s.12

Sch.1 Part 4 para.4, varied: 2012 c.11 s.12

Sch.1 Part 4 para.5, varied: 2012 c.11 s.12

Sch.1 Part 4 para.6, varied: 2012 c.11 s.12

Sch.1 Part 5, varied: 2012 c.11 s.12

Sch.1 Part 5 para.1, varied: 2012 c.11 s.12

Sch.1 Part 6 para.1, varied: 2012 c.11 s.12

Sch.1 Part 6 para.2, varied: 2012 c.11 s.12

Sch.1 Part 7 para.1, varied: 2012 c.11 s.12

Sch.1 Part 8 para.1, varied: 2012 c.11 s.12

Sch.1 Part 9 para.1, varied: 2012 c.11 s.12

Sch.1 Part 9 para.2, varied: 2012 c.11 s.12

Sch.1 Part 9 para.3, varied: 2012 c.11 s.12

Sch.1 Part 9 para.4, varied: 2012 c.11 s.12

Sch.1 Part 9 para.6, varied: 2012 c.11 s.12

Sch.1 Part 9 para.7, varied: 2012 c.11 s.12

Sch.1 Part 9 para.13, varied: 2012 c.11 s.12

Sch.1 Part 10, varied: 2012 c.11 s.12

Sch.1 Part 10 para.2, varied: 2012 c.11 s.12

Sch.1 Part 10 para.3, varied: 2012 c.11 s.12

Sch.1 Part 10 para.4, varied: 2012 c.11 s.12

Sch.1 Part 10 para.5, varied: 2012 c.11 s.12

1999– cont.

1095. Scotland Act 1998 (Transitory and Transitional Provisions) (Standing Orders and Parliamentary Publications) Order 1999– *cont.*

Sch.1 Part 12 para.3, varied: 2012 c.11 s.12

Sch.1 Part 13, varied: 2012 c.11 s.12

Sch.1 Part 13 para.1, varied: 2012 c.11 s.12

Sch.1 Part 13 para.2, varied: 2012 c.11 s.12

Sch.1 Part 13 para.3, varied: 2012 c.11 s.12

Sch.1 Part 14 para.4, varied: 2012 c.11 s.12

Sch.1 Part 17 para.2, varied: 2012 c.11 s.12

1097. Scotland Act 1998 (Transitory and Transitional Provisions) (Salaries and Allowances) Order 1999

Art.3, varied: 2012 c.11 s.12

Art.6, varied: 2012 c.11 s.12

Sch.1, varied: 2012 c.11 s.12

1123. Air Navigation (Fourth Amendment) Order 1999

applied: 2012 c.19 Sch.6 para.4

1127. Scottish Administration (Offices) Order 1999

Sch.1, amended: SI 2012/ 3073 Art.3

1131. Students Allowances (Scotland) Regulations 1999

Reg.4, applied: SI 2012/ 2886 Sch.1

1319. Scotland Act 1998 (Cross-Border Public Authorities) (Specification) Order 1999

Sch.1, amended: SI 2012/ 1658 Sch.1, SI 2012/ 1659 Sch.3 para.33, SI 2012/ 1923 Sch.1

1334. Scotland Act 1998 (General Transitory, Transitional and Savings Provisions) Amendment Order 1999

Art.2, varied: 2012 c.11 s.12

1379. Scotland Act 1998 (Transitory and Transitional Provisions) (Publication and Interpretation etc of Acts of the Scottish Parliament) Order 1999

Sch.1 para.15, see *Johnstone (Brian) v HM Advocate* 2012 J.C. 79 (HCJ), The Lord Justice Clerk (Gill)

1408. Non-resident Companies (General Insurance Business) Regulations 1999

revoked: 2012 c.14 Sch.20 para.14

1436. Unfair Dismissal and Statement of Reasons for Dismissal (Variation of Qualifying Period) Order 1999

revoked: SI 2012/ 989 Art.5

1521. Road Vehicles (Construction and Use) (Amendment) Regulations 1999

revoked: SI 2012/ 1404 Sch.1

1549. Public Interest Disclosure (Prescribed Persons) Order 1999

Sch.1, amended: SI 2012/ 462 Sch.1, SI 2012/ 725 Art.2, SI 2012/ 1479 Sch.1 para.71, SI 2012/ 1641 Sch.4 para.5, SI 2012/ 2400 Art.34

1619. General Teaching Council for Wales (Constitution) Regulations 1999

Reg.5, amended: SI 2012/ 169 Reg.2

Reg.10, amended: SI 2012/ 169 Reg.2

1726. General Teaching Council for England (Constitution) Regulations 1999

revoked: SI 2012/ 1153 Sch.1

1745. Scottish Parliament (Assistance for Registered Political Parties) Order 1999

Art.3, varied: 2012 c.11 s.12

Art.5, varied: 2012 c.11 s.12

1999– cont.

1750. Scotland Act 1998 (Transfer of Functions to the Scottish Ministers etc.) Order 1999
Sch.1, amended: 2012 c.11 s.17, 2012 c.19 Sch.9 para.17
Sch.2, amended: 2012 c.11 s.17
Sch.3, amended: 2012 c.11 s.22
Sch.5 para.9, varied: 2012 c.11 s.12
Sch.5 para.10, revoked (in part): 2012 c.11 s.17
Sch.5 para.14, varied: 2012 c.11 s.12

1820. Scotland Act 1998 (Consequential Modifications) (No.2) Order 1999
Sch.2 Part I para.13, varied: 2012 c.11 s.12
Sch.2 Part I para.40, revoked (in part): SSI 2012/ 321 Sch.5 Part 2
Sch.2 Part I para.62, revoked (in part): SSI 2012/321 Sch.5 Part 2
Sch.2 Part II para.158, revoked (in part): SSI 2012/ 321 Sch.5 Part 2
Sch.2 Part III para.173, varied: 2012 c.11 s.12

1892. Town and Country Planning (Trees) Regulations 1999
Reg.1, revoked (in part): SI 2012/ 605 Reg.26
Reg.2, revoked (in part): SI 2012/ 605 Reg.26
Reg.3, revoked (in part): SI 2012/ 605 Reg.26
Reg.4, revoked (in part): SI 2012/ 605 Reg.26
Reg.5, revoked (in part): SI 2012/ 605 Reg.26
Reg.6, revoked (in part): SI 2012/ 605 Reg.26
Reg.7, revoked (in part): SI 2012/ 605 Reg.26
Reg.8, revoked (in part): SI 2012/ 605 Reg.26
Reg.9, revoked (in part): SI 2012/ 605 Reg.26
Reg.9A, revoked (in part): SI 2012/ 605 Reg.26
Reg.9B, added: SI 2012/ 792 Reg.2
Reg.9B, revoked (in part): SI 2012/ 605 Reg.26
Reg.10, revoked (in part): SI 2012/ 605 Reg.26
Reg.11, revoked (in part): SI 2012/ 605 Reg.26
Reg.12, revoked (in part): SI 2012/ 605 Reg.26
Reg.13, revoked (in part): SI 2012/ 605 Reg.26
Reg.14, revoked (in part): SI 2012/ 605 Reg.26
Reg.15, revoked (in part): SI 2012/ 605 Reg.26
Reg.16, revoked (in part): SI 2012/ 605 Reg.26
Reg.17, revoked (in part): SI 2012/ 605 Reg.26
Reg.18, revoked (in part): SI 2012/ 605 Reg.26
Sch.1, amended: SI 2012/ 792 Reg.2
Sch.1, revoked (in part): SI 2012/ 605 Reg.26

1959. Road Vehicles (Construction and Use) (Amendment No 2) Regulations 1999
revoked: SI 2012/ 1404 Sch.1

2001. Pressure Equipment Regulations 1999
Sch.1 para.7, amended: SI 2012/ 1809 Sch.1 Part 2

2019. General Teaching Council for England (Constitution) (Amendment) Regulations 1999
revoked: SI 2012/ 1153 Sch.1

2059. Air Navigation (Fifth Amendment) Order 1999
applied: 2012 c.19 Sch.6 para.4

2083. Unfair Terms in Consumer Contracts Regulations 1999
applied: SI 2012/ 1128 Art.4
see *Rochdale BC v Dixon* [2011] EWCA Civ 1173, [2012] P.T.S.R. 1336 (CA (Civ Div)), Rix, L.J.; see *Spreadex Ltd v Cochrane* [2012] EWHC 1290 (Comm), Times, August 24, 2012 (QBD (Comm)), David Donaldson Q.C.

2166. Education (Teachers Qualifications and Health Standards) (England) Regulations 1999
Sch.2 Part 1 para.3, applied: SI 2012/ 724 Sch.2 para.9

1999– cont.

2170. Environmental Protection (Restriction on Use of Lead Shot) (England) Regulations 1999
revoked: SI 2012/ 1923 Sch.1

2277. Redundancy Payments (Continuity of Employment in Local Government, etc.) (Modification) Order 1999
Sch.1 para.2, substituted: SI 2012/ 2733 Art.2
Sch.1 para.9A, added: SI 2012/ 666 Sch.1 para.2
Sch.1 para.13, revoked (in part): SI 2012/ 641 Art.2
Sch.1 para.41A, revoked: SI 2012/ 666 Sch.1 para.2
Sch.2 Part II para.2A, added: SI 2012/ 666 Sch.1 para.2

2337. Primary Care Trusts (Consultation on Establishment, Dissolution and Transfer of Staff) Regulations 1999
Reg.1, amended: SI 2012/ 1479 Sch.1 para.16

2535. Medicines (Products Other Than Veterinary Drugs) (General Sale List) Amendment (No.2) Order 1999
revoked: SI 2012/ 1916 Sch.35

2539. Stamp Duty (Exempt Instruments) (Amendment) Regulations 1999
revoked: 2012 c.14 Sch.39 para.4

2720. Neath to Abergavenny Trunk Road (A465) (Abergavenny to Hirwaun Dualling and Slip Roads) and East of Abercynon to East of Dowlais Road (A4060), Cardiff to Glan Conwy Trunk Road (A470) (Connecting Roads) Order 1999
Art.6, amended: SI 2012/ 2092 Art.2
Sch.2 para.7, substituted: SI 2012/ 2092 Art.3
Sch.2 para.8, substituted: SI 2012/ 2092 Art.3
Sch.2 para.9, substituted: SI 2012/ 2092 Art.3
Sch.2 para.10, substituted: SI 2012/ 2092 Art.3
Sch.2 para.11, substituted: SI 2012/ 2092 Art.3
Sch.2 para.12, substituted: SI 2012/ 2092 Art.3
Sch.4, substituted: SI 2012/ 2092 Art.4

2734. Housing Benefit (General) Amendment (No.3) Regulations 1999
applied: SI 2012/ 2885 Sch.5 para.24
Reg.13, applied: SI 2012/ 2886 Sch.1, SSI 2012/ 303 Sch.4 para.9, SSI 2012/ 319 Sch.3 para.23

2817. Education (Teachers Qualifications and Health Standards) (Wales) Regulations 1999
Reg.11, amended: SI 2012/ 724 Reg.9
Reg.11, applied: SI 2012/ 724 Reg.5
Reg.12, amended: SI 2012/ 724 Reg.9
Reg.12, applied: SI 2012/ 724 Reg.5
Reg.13, amended: SI 2012/ 724 Reg.9
Reg.13, applied: SI 2012/ 724 Reg.5
Reg.14, applied: SI 2012/ 724 Reg.5
Sch.2 Part 1 para.3, applied: SI 2012/ 724 Sch.2 para.9

2864. Motor Vehicles (Driving Licences) Regulations 1999
Reg.3, amended: SI 2012/ 977 Sch.3 para.2
Reg.4, substituted: SI 2012/ 977 Sch.3 para.3
Reg.5, amended: SI 2012/ 977 Sch.3 para.4
Reg.6, amended: SI 2012/ 977 Sch.3 para.5
Reg.7, amended: SI 2012/ 977 Sch.3 para.6
Reg.8, amended: SI 2012/ 977 Sch.3 para.7
Reg.9, amended: SI 2012/ 977 Sch.3 para.8
Reg.9, revoked (in part): SI 2012/ 977 Sch.3 para.8
Reg.15A, added: SI 2012/ 977 Sch.3 para.9
Reg.16, amended: SI 2012/ 977 Sch.3 para.10
Reg.17, amended: SI 2012/ 977 Sch.3 para.11
Reg.19, amended: SI 2012/ 977 Sch.3 para.12, Sch.3 para.13
Reg.19, revoked (in part): SI 2012/ 977 Sch.3 para.13

1999–cont.

2864. Motor Vehicles (Driving Licences) Regulations 1999–cont.

Reg.22, amended: SI 2012/977 Sch.3 para.14
Reg.23A, amended: SI 2012/977 Sch.3 para.15
Reg.27, amended: SI 2012/977 Sch.3 para.16
Reg.30, amended: SI 2012/977 Sch.3 para.17
Reg.32, amended: SI 2012/977 Sch.3 para.18
Reg.35, amended: SI 2012/977 Sch.3 para.19
Reg.35, revoked (in part): SI 2012/977 Sch.3 para.19
Reg.37, amended: SI 2012/977 Sch.3 para.20
Reg.37, revoked (in part): SI 2012/977 Sch.3 para.20
Reg.38, amended: SI 2012/977 Sch.3 para.21
Reg.39, amended: SI 2012/977 Sch.3 para.22
Reg.40, amended: SI 2012/977 Sch.3 para.23
Reg.40A, amended: SI 2012/977 Sch.3 para.24
Reg.40C, amended: SI 2012/977 Sch.3 para.25
Reg.42, amended: SI 2012/977 Sch.3 para.26
Reg.43, amended: SI 2012/977 Sch.3 para.27
Reg.43, revoked (in part): SI 2012/977 Sch.3 para.27
Reg.44, revoked: SI 2012/977 Sch.3 para.28
Reg.44A, amended: SI 2012/977 Sch.3 para.29, Sch.3 para.30
Reg.45, amended: SI 2012/977 Sch.3 para.31
Reg.46, amended: SI 2012/977 Sch.3 para.32
Reg.47, amended: SI 2012/977 Sch.3 para.33
Reg.60, amended: SI 2012/977 Sch.3 para.34
Reg.61, amended: SI 2012/977 Sch.3 para.35
Reg.64, amended: SI 2012/977 Sch.3 para.36, Sch.3 para.37
Reg.65, amended: SI 2012/977 Sch.3 para.38
Reg.68, amended: SI 2012/977 Sch.3 para.39
Reg.68, revoked (in part): SI 2012/977 Sch.3 para.39
Reg.68A, added: SI 2012/977 Sch.3 para.40
Reg.69, amended: SI 2012/977 Sch.3 para.41
Reg.70, amended: SI 2012/977 Sch.3 para.42
Reg.76, amended: SI 2012/977 Sch.3 para.43
Reg.79, amended: SI 2012/977 Sch.3 para.44
Reg.79A, added: SI 2012/977 Sch.3 para.45
Sch.2 Part 1, amended: SI 2012/977 Sch.3 para.46
Sch.2 Part 4, added: SI 2012/977 Sch.3 para.46
Sch.2 Part 5, added: SI 2012/977 Sch.3 para.46
Sch.2 Part 6, added: SI 2012/977 Sch.3 para.46
Sch.3 Part 1, amended: SI 2012/977 Sch.3 para.47
Sch.5, amended: SI 2012/977 Sch.3 para.48
Sch.5 Part 1, amended: SI 2012/977 Sch.3 para.48
Sch.5 Part 2, amended: SI 2012/977 Sch.3 para.48
Sch.5A Part 1, amended: SI 2012/977 Sch.3 para.49
Sch.5A Part 1, revoked: SI 2012/977 Sch.3 para.49
Sch.5A Part 2, amended: SI 2012/977 Sch.3 para.49
Sch.7 Part 1, amended: SI 2012/977 Sch.3 para.50
Sch.7 Part 1 paraA, amended: SI 2012/977 Sch.3 para.50
Sch.7 Part 1 paraB, amended: SI 2012/977 Sch.3 para.50
Sch.7 Part 1 paraC, amended: SI 2012/977 Sch.3 para.50
Sch.7 Part 1 paraD, amended: SI 2012/977 Sch.3 para.50
Sch.7 Part 1 paraE, amended: SI 2012/977 Sch.3 para.50
Sch.7 Part 1 paraF, amended: SI 2012/977 Sch.3 para.50
Sch.7 Part 1, amended: SI 2012/977 Sch.3 para.50
Sch.8A, amended: SI 2012/977 Sch.3 para.52
Sch.8 Part 2, amended: SI 2012/977 Sch.3 para.51

1999–cont.

2864. Motor Vehicles (Driving Licences) Regulations 1999–cont.

Sch.10D Part 1, amended: SI 2012/977 Sch.3 para.53

3107. Motor Fuel (Composition and Content) Regulations 1999

Reg.2, amended: SI 2012/2567 Reg.3
Reg.5B, amended: SI 2012/2567 Reg.4

3110. Tax Credit (New Category of Child Care Provider) Regulations 1999

applied: SI 2012/2885 Sch.1 para.25, SI 2012/2886 Sch.1, SI 2012/3144 Sch.1 para.19, SI 2012/3145 Sch.1, SSI 2012/303 Reg.28, SSI 2012/319 Reg.29

3121. Value Added Tax (Input Tax) (Specified Supplies) Order 1999

Art.3, see *1st Contact Ltd v Revenue and Customs Commissioners* [2012] UKFTT 84 (TC), [2012] S.F.T.D. 799 (FTT (Tax)), Judge Christopher Staker

3123. Local Authorities (Calculation of Council Tax Base) (Amendment) (England) Regulations 1999

revoked: SI 2012/2914 Sch.1

3124. A470 Trunk Road (Pontdolgoch, Powys) Order 1999

varied: SI 2012/777 Art.8

3147. Welfare Reform and Pensions (Northern Ireland) Order 1999

Part IV, applied: SI 2012/687 Sch.4 para.8
Part V, applied: SI 2012/687 Sch.4 para.8
Art.12, applied: SI 2012/687 Sch.4 para.8

3232. Ionising Radiations Regulations 1999

applied: SI 2012/1652 Reg.8, Sch.5
Reg.6, applied: SI 2012/1652 Sch.7
Reg.21, applied: SI 2012/1652 Reg.8, Sch.7
Reg.35, applied: SI 2012/1652 Sch.7
Sch.1 para.1, applied: SI 2012/1652 Reg.8, Sch.7

3242. Management of Health and Safety at Work Regulations 1999

applied: SI 2012/632 Reg.15, SI 2012/1282 Sch.1, SI 2012/1284 Sch.1, SI 2012/1289 Sch.1, SI 2012/1294 Sch.1, SI 2012/1295 Sch.1
referred to: SI 2012/1284 Sch.1, SI 2012/1286 Sch.1
Reg.3, see *R. v Deeside Metals Ltd* [2011] EWCA Crim 3020, [2012] 2 Cr. App. R. (S.) 29 (CA (Crim Div)), Rafferty, L.J.
Reg.21, referred to: SI 2012/632 Reg.34

3267. General Optical Council (Rules relating to Injury or Disease of the Eye) Order of Council 1999

Sch.1, amended: SI 2012/1916 Sch.34 para.72

3312. Maternity and Parental Leave etc Regulations 1999

Reg.7, applied: SI 2012/1115 Reg.8

3437. Local Authorities (Calculation of Council Tax Base) (Amendment-Greater London Authority) Regulations 1999

revoked: SI 2012/2914 Sch.1

2000

10. Children (Performances) Amendment Regulations 2000

varied: 2012 c.11 s.12

52. Adoption (Intercountry Aspects) Act 1999 (Commencement No 1) Order 2000

varied: 2012 c.11 s.12

2000–cont.

89. Primary Care Trusts (Membership, Procedure and Administration Arrangements) Regulations 2000
Reg.1, amended: SI 2012/ 1641 Sch.4 para.6
Reg.5, amended: SI 2012/ 1479 Sch.1 para.17, SI 2012/ 1641 Sch.4 para.6, SI 2012/ 2404 Sch.3 para.13
Sch.1, amended: SI 2012/ 1109 Sch.1 para.2, SI 2012/ 1641 Sch.2 para.2

108. Superannuation (Admission to Schedule 1 to the Superannuation Act 1972) Order 2000
varied: SI 2012/ 147 Art.7

427. Greater London Authority Elections (No.2) Rules 2000
applied: SI 2012/444 Sch.5
referred to: SI 2012/ 323 Sch.5 para.17

432. Greater London Authority (Disqualification) Order 2000
Sch.1 Part II para.13, revoked: SI 2012/ 725 Art.2
Sch.1 Part II para.20, substituted: SI 2012/ 725 Art.2

441. Community Legal Service (Costs) Regulations 2000
Reg.4, applied: SI 2012/ 1726 r.61.16
Reg.10, see *Leeds City Council v Price* [2012] EWCA Civ 59, [2012] 2 Costs L.O. 242 (CA (Civ Div)), Aikens, L.J.

480. Animals (Scientific Procedures) Act 1986 (Fees) Order 2000
revoked: SI 2012/ 3050 Art.4

617. NHS Bodies and Local Authorities Partnership Arrangements Regulations 2000
applied: SI 2012/ 1313 Sch.2 para.2
Reg.2, amended: SI 2012/ 3094 Reg.12
Reg.3, amended: SI 2012/ 3094 Reg.12
Reg.3, revoked (in part): SI 2012/ 3094 Reg.12
Reg.4, amended: SI 2012/ 3094 Reg.12
Reg.4, revoked (in part): SI 2012/ 3094 Reg.12
Reg.5, amended: SI 2012/ 3094 Reg.12
Reg.5, referred to: SI 2012/ 3094 Reg.3
Reg.6, amended: SI 2012/ 3094 Reg.12
Reg.6, referred to: SI 2012/ 3094 Reg.3
Reg.6, revoked (in part): SI 2012/ 3094 Reg.12
Reg.7, amended: SI 2012/ 3094 Reg.12
Reg.8, amended: SI 2012/ 3094 Reg.12
Reg.9, amended: SI 2012/ 3094 Reg.12

618. National Health Service (Payments by Local Authorities to NHS Bodies) (Prescribed Functions) Regulations 2000
revoked: SI 2012/ 3094 Reg.13
Reg.2, amended: SI 2012/ 1909 Sch.8 para.3

620. National Health Service (Charges for Drugs and Appliances) Regulations 2000
applied: SI 2012/ 1909 Reg.96
Reg.2, amended: SI 2012/ 1479 Sch.1 para.18, SI 2012/ 1909 Sch.8 para.4
Reg.3, amended: SI 2012/ 470 Reg.2
Reg.3, referred to: SI 2012/ 1909 Sch.4 para.7, Sch.5 para.6
Reg.4, amended: SI 2012/ 470 Reg.2
Reg.4, referred to: SI 2012/ 1909 Sch.6 para.4
Reg.4A, amended: SI 2012/470 Reg.2
Reg.5, amended: SI 2012/470 Reg.2, SI 2012/ 1916 Sch.34 para.73
Reg.6, amended: SI 2012/470 Reg.2
Reg.6A, amended: SI 2012/ 470 Reg.2, SI 2012/ 1916 Sch.34 para.73
Reg.7, applied: SI 2012/ 1909 Sch.4 para.7, Sch.5 para.6, Sch.6 para.4

2000–cont.

620. National Health Service (Charges for Drugs and Appliances) Regulations 2000–*cont.*
Reg.7, referred to: SI 2012/ 1909 Sch.4 para.7, Sch.6 para.4
Reg.7C, amended: SI 2012/ 1909 Sch.8 para.4
Reg.10, applied: SI 2012/ 1909 Reg.96
Sch.1, amended: SI 2012/470 Reg.2

672. Pensions Increase (Review) Order 2000
applied: SI 2012/ 782 Art.3, Art.4

704. Asylum Support Regulations 2000
Reg.2, see *R. (on the application of Chen) v Secretary of State for the Home Department* [2012] EWHC 2531 (Admin), [2012] H.R.L.R. 33 (QBD (Admin)), Beatson, J.

729. Social Fund Winter Fuel Payment Regulations 2000
Reg.3, amended: SI 2012/ 757 Reg.18
Reg.4, amended: SI 2012/ 757 Reg.18

824. Community Legal Service (Cost Protection) Regulations 2000
Reg.5, see *Leeds City Council v Price* [2012] EWCA Civ 59, [2012] 2 Costs L.O. 242 (CA (Civ Div)), Aikens, L.J.

839. A35 Trunk Road (Dorchester Bypass) (Derestriction) Order 2000
Art.3, added: SI 2012/ 2150 Art.2
Sch.1, amended: SI 2012/ 2150 Art.2

1032. Greater London Authority (Limitation of Salaries) Order 2000
Art.2, amended: SI 2012/ 234 Art.2

1038. General Osteopathic Council (Application for Registration and Fees) Rules Order of Council 2000
Sch.1, amended: SI 2012/ 1101 Sch.1

1054. Pension Sharing (Pension Credit Benefit) Regulations 2000
Reg.10, amended: SI 2012/692 Reg.10

1059. Ionising Radiation (Medical Exposure) Regulations 2000
Reg.4, referred to: SI 2012/ 1916 Reg.240

1071. Access to Justice Act 1999 (Destination of Appeals) Order 2000
Art.5, see *Reddy v General Medical Council* [2012] EWCA Civ 310, [2012] C.P. Rep. 27 (CA (Civ Div)), Mummery, L.J.

1104. Air Navigation (Cosmic Radiation) Order 2000
applied: 2012 c.19 Sch.6 para.4

1106. United Nations (Sanctions) (Amendment) Order 2000
Sch.1, amended: SI 2012/ 362 Sch.2

1139. National Police Records (Recordable Offences) Regulations 2000
Sch.1 para.41A, added: SI 2012/ 1713 Reg.2
Sch.1 para.41B, added: SI 2012/ 1713 Reg.2

1161. Immigration (Leave to Enter and Remain) Order 2000
see *Khaliq (Entry Clearance: Para 321: Pakistan), Re* [2012] Imm. A.R. 1 (UT (IAC)), CMG Ockelton (Vice President)
Art.4, see *Khaliq (Entry Clearance: Para 321: Pakistan), Re* [2012] Imm. A.R. 1 (UT (IAC)), CMG Ockelton (Vice President)
Art.13, see *Fiaz (Cancellation of Leave to Remain: Fairness), Re* [2012] UKUT 57 (IAC), [2012] Imm. A.R. 497 (UT (IAC)), Blake, J.; see *R. (on the application of MK (Tunisia)) v Secretary of State for the Home Department* [2011] EWCA Civ 333, [2012] 1 W.L.R. 700 (CA (Civ Div)), Pill, L.J.

2000–cont.

1345. Civil Aviation (Investigation of Air Accidents and Incidents) (Jersey) Order 2000
applied: 2012 c.19 Sch.6 para.4

1346. Air Navigation (Jersey) Order 2000
applied: 2012 c.19 Sch.6 para.4

1403. Stakeholder Pension Schemes Regulations 2000
Reg.1, amended: SI 2012/1817 Sch.1 para.6

1414. Whipps Cross Hospital National Health Service Trust (Establishment) Order 2000
applied: SI 2012/796 Art.6
revoked: SI 2012/796 Art.6

1434. Road Vehicles (Construction and Use) (Amendment) Regulations 2000
Reg.3, revoked: SI 2012/1404 Sch.1

1447. General Teaching Council for England (Constitution) (Amendment) Regulations 2000
revoked: SI 2012/1153 Sch.1

1551. Part-time Workers (Prevention of Less Favourable Treatment) Regulations 2000
see *O'Brien v Ministry of Justice (C-393/10)* [2012] All E.R. (EC) 757 (ECJ (2nd Chamber)), Judge Cunha Rodrigues (President)
Reg.17, see *O'Brien v Ministry of Justice (C-393/10)* [2012] All E.R. (EC) 757 (ECJ (2nd Chamber)), Judge Cunha Rodrigues (President)

1557. Eritrea and Ethiopia (United Nations Sanctions) (Overseas Territories) Order 2000
revoked: SI 2012/2592 Sch.2

1562. Air Navigation Order 2000
applied: 2012 c.19 Sch.6 para.4

1563. Scotland Act 1998 (Transfer of Functions to the Scottish Ministers etc.) Order 2000
Sch.1, amended: 2012 c.11 s.22

1601. Education (National Curriculum) (Attainment Targets and Programmes of Study in Information and Communication Technology) (England) Order 2000
referred to: SI 2012/1926 Reg.2

1625. Town and Country Planning Appeals (Determination by Inspectors) (Inquiries Procedure) (England) Rules 2000
r.16, see *Medhurst v Secretary of State for Communities and Local Government* [2011] EWHC 3576 (Admin), [2012] J.P.L. 598 (QBD (Admin)), Clive Lewis QC

1786. Disabled Persons (Badges for Motor Vehicles) (Wales) Regulations 2000
Reg.2, amended: SI 2012/309 Reg.2
Reg.4, amended: SI 2012/309 Reg.2
Reg.6, substituted: SI 2012/309 Reg.2
Reg.7, amended: SI 2012/309 Reg.2
Reg.8, amended: SI 2012/309 Reg.2
Reg.9, amended: SI 2012/309 Reg.2
Reg.11, substituted: SI 2012/309 Reg.2
Sch.1 Part I, amended: SI 2012/309 Reg.2
Sch.1 Part IA, added: SI 2012/309 Sch.1
Sch.1 Part II, amended: SI 2012/309 Reg.2
Sch.1 Part IIA, added: SI 2012/309 Sch.2
Sch.1 Part III, amended: SI 2012/309 Reg.2
Sch.1 Part IIIA para.1, added: SI 2012/309 Sch.3
Sch.1 Part IIIA para.2, added: SI 2012/309 Sch.3
Sch.1 Part IIIA para.3, added: SI 2012/309 Sch.3

1787. Northern Ireland Act 1998 (Designation of Public Authorities) Order 2000
Sch.1, amended: SI 2012/2595 Art.10

2000–cont.

1821. Eritrea and Ethiopia (United Nations Sanctions) (Overseas Territories) (Amendment) Order 2000
revoked: SI 2012/2592 Sch.2

1919. Medicines (Pharmacy and General Sale Exemption) Amendment Order 2000
revoked: SI 2012/1916 Sch.35

1926. Social Security (Work-focused Interviews for Lone Parents) and Miscellaneous Amendments Regulations 2000
Reg.2ZA, amended: SI 2012/874 Reg.4

1941. General Teaching Council for Wales (Additional Functions) Order 2000
Sch.1 Part II para.22B, added: SI 2012/167 Art.2
Sch.1 Part II para.23A, amended: SI 2012/167 Art.2
Sch.1 Part II para.23B, amended: SI 2012/167 Art.2

1973. Pollution Prevention and Control (England and Wales) Regulations 2000
Reg.32, see *R. v St Regis Paper Co Ltd* [2011] EWCA Crim 2527, [2012] P.T.S.R. 871 (CA (Crim Div)), Moses, L.J.

1979. General Teaching Council for Wales (Functions) Regulations 2000
Reg.3, amended: SI 2012/166 Reg.2
Sch.1 para.21A, added: SI 2012/166 Reg.2
Sch.1 para.22A, amended: SI 2012/166 Reg.2
Sch.1 para.22B, amended: SI 2012/166 Reg.2
Sch.2 para.12B, added: SI 2012/166 Reg.2
Sch.2 para.13A, amended: SI 2012/166 Reg.2
Sch.2 para.13B, amended: SI 2012/166 Reg.2

2040. Scotland Act 1998 (Consequential Modifications) Order 2000
Sch.1 Part I para.19, varied: 2012 c.11 s.12

2047. Faculty Jurisdiction Rules 2000
applied: SI 2012/1846 Sch.1 Part TABLE
Part II r.4, applied: SI 2012/1846 Sch.1 Part TABLE
Part III r.7, applied: SI 2012/1846 Sch.1 Part TABLE
Part III r.8, applied: SI 2012/1846 Sch.1 Part TABLE
Part III r.10, applied: SI 2012/1846 Sch.1 Part TABLE
Part IV r.19, applied: SI 2012/1846 Sch.1 Part TABLE
Part IV r.26, applied: SI 2012/1846 Sch.1 Part TABLE

2048. Faculty Jurisdiction (Care of Places of Worship) Rules 2000
applied: SI 2012/1846 Sch.1 Part TABLE

2122. Education (School Government) (Terms of Reference) (England) Regulations 2000
Reg.8, revoked: SI 2012/1845 Reg.2

2175. General Teaching Council for England (Additional Functions) Order 2000
revoked: SI 2012/1153 Sch.1

2176. General Teaching Council for England (Registration of Teachers) Regulations 2000
revoked: SI 2012/1153 Sch.1

2334. Consumer Protection (Distance Selling) Regulations 2000
applied: SI 2012/1128 Art.4

2384. Children (Performances) (Amendment) (No.2) Regulations 2000
varied: 2012 c.11 s.12

2526. Medicines (Products Other Than Veterinary Drugs) (General Sale List) Amendment (No.2) Order 2000
revoked: SI 2012/1916 Sch.35

2000–cont.

2687. Merchant Shipping (Passenger Ships on Domestic Voyages) Regulations 2000
Reg.2, amended: SI 2012/2636 Reg.3
Reg.4, amended: SI 2012/2636 Reg.3
Reg.4, revoked (in part): SI 2012/2636 Reg.3
Reg.6, amended: SI 2012/2636 Reg.3
Reg.7, amended: SI 2012/2636 Reg.3
Reg.11, added: SI 2012/2636 Reg.3

2692. Personal Pension Schemes (Payments by Employers) Regulations 2000
Reg.5, amended: SI 2012/215 Reg.41

2724. Immigration (Designation of Travel Bans) Order 2000
Sch.1 Part 1, substituted: SI 2012/1663 Sch.1
Sch.1 Part 2, amended: SI 2012/2058 Art.2, SI 2012/3010 Art.2
Sch.1 Part 2, substituted: SI 2012/1663 Sch.1

2831. Genetically Modified Organisms (Contained Use) Regulations 2000
applied: SI 2012/1652 Reg.13, Reg.24
Reg.9, applied: SI 2012/1652 Sch.10
Reg.10, applied: SI 2012/1652 Sch.10
Reg.11, applied: SI 2012/1652 Sch.10
Reg.12, applied: SI 2012/1652 Sch.10
Reg.14, applied: SI 2012/1652 Reg.13
Reg.15, applied: SI 2012/1652 Reg.13, Sch.10
Reg.18, applied: SI 2012/1652 Sch.10

2851. Local Authorities (Arrangements for the Discharge of Functions) (England) Regulations 2000
revoked: SI 2012/1019 Reg.13

2853. Local Authorities (Functions and Responsibilities) (England) Regulations 2000
see *R. (on the application of Buck) v Doncaster MBC* [2012] EWHC 2293 (Admin), [2012] B.L.G.R. 663 (QBD (Admin)), Hickinbottom, J.
Reg.2, see *R. (on the application of 007 Stratford Taxis Ltd) v Stratford on Avon DC* [2011] EWCA Civ 160, [2012] R.T.R. 5 (CA (Civ Div)), Sir Anthony May (President, QB)
Reg.5, see *R. (on the application of 007 Stratford Taxis Ltd) v Stratford on Avon DC* [2011] EWCA Civ 160, [2012] R.T.R. 5 (CA (Civ Div)), Sir Anthony May (President, QB)
Sch.1, see *R. (on the application of 007 Stratford Taxis Ltd) v Stratford on Avon DC* [2011] EWCA Civ 160, [2012] R.T.R. 5 (CA (Civ Div)), Sir Anthony May (President, QB)
Sch.4, see *R. (on the application of 007 Stratford Taxis Ltd) v Stratford on Avon DC* [2011] EWCA Civ 160, [2012] R.T.R. 5 (CA (Civ Div)), Sir Anthony May (President, QB)

2872. Education (Foundation Body) (England) Regulations 2000
Sch.4 para.2, amended: SI 2012/2404 Sch.3 para.14

3012. A52 Trunk Road (Bingham Bypass, Nottinghamshire) (Derestriction) Order 2000
revoked: SI 2012/1099 Art.4

3057. European Communities (Designation) (No.4) Order 2000
revoked: SI 2012/1759 Sch.1

3158. Controlled Foreign Companies (Designer Rate Tax Provisions) Regulations 2000
referred to: 2012 c.14 Sch.20 para.59
revoked: 2012 c.14 Sch.20 para.14
varied: 2012 c.14 Sch.20 para.59

3177. Child Support (Voluntary Payments) Regulations 2000
Reg.1, amended: SI 2012/2785 Reg.7

2000–cont.

3177. Child Support (Voluntary Payments) Regulations 2000–*cont.*
Reg.2, amended: SI 2012/2785 Reg.7

3241. Iraq (United Nations Sanctions) Order 2000
revoked: SI 2012/1489 Sch.2
Art.5, applied: SI 2012/1489 Reg.19
Sch.1, amended: SI 2012/362 Sch.2

3242. Iraq (United Nations Sanctions) (Overseas Territories) Order 2000
revoked: SI 2012/2748 Sch.6
Sch.1, amended: SI 2012/362 Sch.2

3244. Iraq (United Nations Sanctions) (Channel Islands) Order 2000
Sch.1, amended: SI 2012/362 Sch.2

3245. Iraq (United Nations Sanctions) (Isle of Man) Order 2000
Sch.1, amended: SI 2012/362 Sch.2

3246. Air Navigation (Jersey) (Amendment) Order 2000
applied: 2012 c.19 Sch.6 para.4

3251. Scotland Act 1998 (Cross-Border Public Authorities) (Adaptation of Functions etc.) (No.2) Order 2000
Sch.3 Part I para.1, revoked: SI 2012/1658 Sch.1
Sch.3 Part II para.2, revoked: SI 2012/1658 Sch.1

3253. Scotland Act 1998 (Transfer of Functions to the Scottish Ministers etc.) (No.2) Order 2000
Sch.3 Part I para.2, varied: 2012 c.11 s.12
Sch.3 Part II para.4, varied: 2012 c.11 s.12
Sch.3 Part II para.5, varied: 2012 c.11 s.12
Sch.3 Part II para.6, varied: 2012 c.11 s.12
Sch.3 Part II para.8, varied: 2012 c.11 s.12

3272. Local Authorities (Executive Arrangements) (Access to Information) (England) Regulations 2000
revoked: SI 2012/2089 Reg.23

3357. Whole of Government Accounts (Designation of Bodies) Order 2000
varied: SI 2012/147 Art.7

3363. Borough of Rugby (Electoral Changes) (No.2) Order 2000
revoked: SI 2012/4 Art.9

3371. Young Offender Institution Rules 2000
see *R. (on the application of King) v Secretary of State for Justice* [2012] EWCA Civ 376, [2012] 1 W.L.R. 3602 (CA (Civ Div)), Maurice Kay, L.J.

2001

23. General Teaching Council for England (Registration of Teachers) (Amendment) Regulations 2001
revoked: SI 2012/1153 Sch.1

155. Child Support (Maintenance Calculations and Special Cases) Regulations 2001
revoked: SI 2012/2785 Reg.10
Reg.1, amended: SI 2012/712 Reg.6
Sch.Part II para.5, amended: SI 2012/712 Reg.6
Sch.Part II para.6A, added: SI 2012/712 Reg.6
Sch.Part II para.6A, amended: SI 2012/2007 Sch.1 para.114
Sch.Part III para.9A, added: SI 2012/712 Reg.6
Sch.Part III para.9A, amended: SI 2012/2007 Sch.1 para.114

156. Child Support (Variations) Regulations (2000) 2001
revoked: SI 2012/2785 Reg.10
Reg.1, amended: SI 2012/2007 Sch.1 para.115

2001– cont.

156. Child Support (Variations) Regulations (2000) 2001– *cont.*
Reg.19, amended: SI 2012/2007 Sch.1 para.115

157. Child Support (Maintenance Calculation Procedure) Regulations 2001
revoked (in part): SI 2012/2785 Reg.10
Sch.1 para.1, substituted: SI 2012/2785 Reg.3
Sch.1 para.1A, revoked: SI 2012/2785 Reg.3
Sch.1 para.2, amended: SI 2012/2785 Reg.3
Sch.1 para.3, amended: SI 2012/2785 Reg.3
Sch.1 para.4, amended: SI 2012/2785 Reg.3
Sch.1 para.6, substituted: SI 2012/2785 Reg.3
Sch.1 para.7, added: SI 2012/2785 Reg.3

211. Solihull Primary Care Trust (Establishment) Order 2001
referred to: SI 2012/1512 Sch.1

237. Employment Tribunals (Increase of Maximum Deposit) Order 2001
revoked: SI 2012/149 Art.1

238. Detention Centre Rules 2001
r.35, see *R. (on the application of HA (Nigeria)) v Secretary of State for the Home Department* [2012] EWHC 979 (Admin), [2012] Med. L.R. 353 (QBD (Admin)), Singh, J.

328. Barnet Primary Care Trust (Establishment) Order 2001
referred to: SI 2012/1512 Sch.1

341. Representation of the People (England and Wales) Regulations 2001
applied: SI 2012/1917 Sch.2 para.11
Part V, applied: SI 2012/323 Reg.13
Reg.3, varied: SI 2012/323 Sch.4 para.1, SI 2012/444 Sch.4 para.1, SI 2012/2031 Sch.4 Part 1
Reg.4, varied: SI 2012/323 Sch.4 para.1, SI 2012/444 Sch.4 para.1, SI 2012/2031 Sch.4 Part 1
Reg.5, varied: SI 2012/323 Sch.4 para.1, SI 2012/444 Sch.4 para.1, SI 2012/2031 Sch.4 Part 1
Reg.6, varied: SI 2012/323 Sch.4 para.1, SI 2012/444 Sch.4 para.1, SI 2012/2031 Sch.4 Part 1
Reg.7, varied: SI 2012/323 Sch.4 para.1, SI 2012/444 Sch.4 para.1, SI 2012/2031 Sch.4 Part 1
Reg.8, varied: SI 2012/323 Sch.4 para.1, SI 2012/444 Sch.4 para.1, SI 2012/2031 Sch.4 Part 1
Reg.11, varied: SI 2012/323 Sch.4 para.1, SI 2012/444 Sch.4 para.1, SI 2012/2031 Sch.4 Part 1
Reg.35, applied: SI 2012/1917 Sch.2 para.27
Reg.43, applied: SI 2012/1917 Sch.10 para.2, Sch.10 para.3
Reg.50, varied: SI 2012/323 Sch.4 para.1, SI 2012/444 Sch.4 para.1, SI 2012/2031 Sch.4 Part 1
Reg.51, varied: SI 2012/323 Sch.4 para.1, SI 2012/444 Sch.4 para.1, SI 2012/2031 Sch.4 Part 1
Reg.51A, varied: SI 2012/323 Sch.4 para.1, SI 2012/444 Sch.4 para.1, SI 2012/2031 Sch.4 Part 1
Reg.51AA, varied: SI 2012/323 Sch.4 para.1, SI 2012/444 Sch.4 para.1, SI 2012/2031 Sch.4 Part 1
Reg.51B, varied: SI 2012/323 Sch.4 para.1, SI 2012/444 Sch.4 para.1, SI 2012/2031 Sch.4 Part 1
Reg.52, varied: SI 2012/323 Sch.4 para.1, SI 2012/444 Sch.4 para.1, SI 2012/2031 Sch.4 Part 1
Reg.53, amended: SI 2012/1479 Sch.1 para.19
Reg.55, varied: SI 2012/323 Sch.4 para.1, SI 2012/444 Sch.4 para.1, SI 2012/2031 Sch.4 Part 1
Reg.56, varied: SI 2012/323 Sch.4 para.1, SI 2012/444 Sch.4 para.1, SI 2012/2031 Sch.4 Part 1
Reg.57, varied: SI 2012/323 Sch.4 para.1, SI 2012/444 Sch.4 para.1, SI 2012/2031 Sch.4 Part 1
Reg.58, varied: SI 2012/323 Sch.4 para.1, SI 2012/444 Sch.4 para.1, SI 2012/2031 Sch.4 Part 1

2001– cont.

341. Representation of the People (England and Wales) Regulations 2001– *cont.*
Reg.59, varied: SI 2012/323 Sch.4 para.1, SI 2012/444 Sch.4 para.1, SI 2012/2031 Sch.4 Part 1
Reg.61B, varied: SI 2012/323 Sch.4 para.1, SI 2012/444 Sch.4 para.1, SI 2012/2031 Sch.4 Part 1
Reg.62, varied: SI 2012/323 Sch.4 para.1, SI 2012/444 Sch.4 para.1, SI 2012/2031 Sch.4 Part 1
Reg.64, varied: SI 2012/323 Sch.4 para.1, SI 2012/444 Sch.4 para.1, SI 2012/2031 Sch.4 Part 1
Reg.65, applied: SI 2012/323 Reg.13, Sch.5 para.38, SI 2012/444 Sch.5
Reg.65, varied: SI 2012/323 Sch.4 para.1, SI 2012/444 Sch.4 para.1, SI 2012/2031 Sch.4 Part 1
Reg.66, varied: SI 2012/323 Sch.4 para.1, SI 2012/444 Sch.4 para.1, SI 2012/2031 Sch.4 Part 1
Reg.67, varied: SI 2012/323 Sch.4 para.1, SI 2012/444 Sch.4 para.1
Reg.68, varied: SI 2012/323 Sch.4 para.1, SI 2012/444 Sch.4 para.1, SI 2012/2031 Sch.4 Part 1
Reg.69, varied: SI 2012/323 Sch.4 para.1, SI 2012/444 Sch.4 para.1, SI 2012/2031 Sch.4 Part 1
Reg.70, varied: SI 2012/323 Sch.4 para.1, SI 2012/444 Sch.4 para.1, SI 2012/2031 Sch.4 Part 1
Reg.71, varied: SI 2012/323 Sch.4 para.1, SI 2012/444 Sch.4 para.1, SI 2012/2031 Sch.4 Part 1
Reg.72, varied: SI 2012/323 Sch.4 para.1, SI 2012/444 Sch.4 para.1, SI 2012/2031 Sch.4 Part 1
Reg.73, varied: SI 2012/323 Sch.4 para.1, SI 2012/444 Sch.4 para.1, SI 2012/2031 Sch.4 Part 1
Reg.74, varied: SI 2012/323 Sch.4 para.1, SI 2012/444 Sch.4 para.1, SI 2012/2031 Sch.4 Part 1
Reg.75, varied: SI 2012/323 Sch.4 para.1, SI 2012/444 Sch.4 para.1, SI 2012/2031 Sch.4 Part 1
Reg.76, varied: SI 2012/323 Sch.4 para.1, SI 2012/444 Sch.4 para.1, SI 2012/2031 Sch.4 Part 1
Reg.77, varied: SI 2012/323 Sch.4 para.1, SI 2012/444 Sch.4 para.1, SI 2012/2031 Sch.4 Part 1
Reg.78, varied: SI 2012/323 Sch.4 para.1, SI 2012/444 Sch.4 para.1, SI 2012/2031 Sch.4 Part 1
Reg.79, varied: SI 2012/323 Sch.4 para.1, SI 2012/444 Sch.4 para.1, SI 2012/2031 Sch.4 Part 1
Reg.80, varied: SI 2012/323 Sch.4 para.1, SI 2012/444 Sch.4 para.1, SI 2012/2031 Sch.4 Part 1
Reg.81, varied: SI 2012/323 Sch.4 para.1, SI 2012/444 Sch.4 para.1, SI 2012/2031 Sch.4 Part 1
Reg.82, varied: SI 2012/323 Sch.4 para.1, SI 2012/444 Sch.4 para.1
Reg.83, varied: SI 2012/323 Sch.4 para.1, SI 2012/444 Sch.4 para.1, SI 2012/2031 Sch.4 Part 1
Reg.84, varied: SI 2012/323 Sch.4 para.1, SI 2012/444 Sch.4 para.1
Reg.84A, varied: SI 2012/323 Sch.4 para.1, SI 2012/444 Sch.4 para.1
Reg.85, varied: SI 2012/323 Sch.4 para.1, SI 2012/444 Sch.4 para.1, SI 2012/2031 Sch.4 Part 1
Reg.85A, varied: SI 2012/323 Sch.4 para.1, SI 2012/444 Sch.4 para.1, SI 2012/2031 Sch.4 Part 1
Reg.85B, varied: SI 2012/323 Sch.4 para.1, SI 2012/444 Sch.4 para.1, SI 2012/2031 Sch.4 Part 1
Reg.86, varied: SI 2012/323 Sch.4 para.1, SI 2012/444 Sch.4 para.1
Reg.86A, varied: SI 2012/323 Sch.4 para.1, SI 2012/444 Sch.4 para.1, SI 2012/2031 Sch.4 Part 1
Reg.87, varied: SI 2012/323 Sch.4 para.1, SI 2012/444 Sch.4 para.1
Reg.88, varied: SI 2012/323 Sch.4 para.1, SI 2012/444 Sch.4 para.1
Reg.89, varied: SI 2012/323 Sch.4 para.1, SI 2012/444 Sch.4 para.1

2001– cont.

341. Representation of the People (England and Wales) Regulations 2001– *cont.*
Reg.91, varied: SI 2012/323 Sch.4 para.1, SI 2012/444 Sch.4 para.1, SI 2012/2031 Sch.4 Part 1
Reg.92, varied: SI 2012/444 Sch.4 para.1
Reg.93, applied: SI 2012/1917 Sch.1 para.1, Sch.1 para.3, Sch.1 para.4, Sch.1 para.5
Reg.98, varied: SI 2012/444 Sch.4 para.1, SI 2012/2031 Sch.4 Part 1
Reg.100, applied: SI 2012/1917 Sch.10 para.2
Reg.105, applied: SI 2012/1917 Sch.2 para.20, Sch.10 para.2
Reg.106, applied: SI 2012/1917 Sch.2 para.20, Sch.10 para.2
Reg.109, applied: SI 2012/1917 Sch.10 para.2, Sch.10 para.3, Sch.10 para.5
Reg.113, applied: SI 2012/1917 Sch.10 para.2
Reg.115, varied: SI 2012/444 Sch.4 para.1
Reg.116, varied: SI 2012/323 Sch.4 para.1
Reg.118, varied: SI 2012/323 Sch.4 para.1, SI 2012/444 Sch.4 para.1
Reg.119, varied: SI 2012/323 Sch.4 para.1, SI 2012/444 Sch.4 para.1
Sch.3, varied: SI 2012/323 Sch.4 para.1, SI 2012/444 Sch.4 para.1, SI 2012/2031 Sch.4 Part 1

395. Iraq (United Nations Sanctions) (Overseas Territories) (Amendment) Order 2001
revoked: SI 2012/2748 Sch.6

397. Air Navigation (Amendment) Order 2001
applied: 2012 c.19 Sch.6 para.4

405. Income Tax (Interest Payments) (Information Powers) (Amendment) Regulations 2001
revoked: SI 2012/756 Reg.3

476. Hill Farm Allowance Regulations 2001
revoked: SI 2012/114 Reg.9

478. Parent Governor Representatives (England) Regulations 2001
Reg.2, applied: SI 2012/1020 Reg.14
Reg.3, applied: SI 2012/1020 Reg.14
Reg.4, applied: SI 2012/1020 Reg.14
Reg.5, applied: SI 2012/1020 Reg.14
Reg.6, applied: SI 2012/1020 Reg.14
Reg.7, applied: SI 2012/1020 Reg.14
Reg.8, applied: SI 2012/1020 Reg.14
Reg.9, applied: SI 2012/1020 Reg.14
Reg.10, applied: SI 2012/1020 Reg.14

497. Representation of the People (Scotland) Regulations 2001
Reg.53, amended: SI 2012/1479 Sch.1 para.20

544. Financial Services and Markets Act 2000 (Regulated Activities) Order 2001
Part II, added: SI 2012/1906 Art.2
Art.3, see *Digital Satellite Warranty Cover Ltd, Re* [2011] EWCA Civ 1413, [2012] Bus. L.R. 990 (CA (Civ Div)), Maurice Kay, L.J.
Art.3, amended: SI 2012/1906 Art.2
Art.82A, added: SI 2012/1906 Art.2
Sch.1 Part II para I, applied: 2012 c.14 s.56
Sch.1 Part II para I, referred to: 2012 c.14 s.154
Sch.1 Part II para II, applied: 2012 c.14 s.56
Sch.1 Part II para II, referred to: 2012 c.14 s.154
Sch.1 Part II para III, applied: 2012 c.14 s.56
Sch.1 Part II para III, referred to: 2012 c.14 s.154
Sch.1 Part II para VII, applied: 2012 c.14 s.56
Sch.1 para.16, see *Digital Satellite Warranty Cover Ltd, Re* [2011] EWCA Civ 1413, [2012] Bus. L.R. 990 (CA (Civ Div)), Maurice Kay, L.J.

2001– cont.

600. Special Educational Needs Tribunal Regulations 2001
revoked (in part): SI 2012/322 Reg.4
Reg.39A, applied: SI 2012/322 Reg.58

662. Climate Change Agreements (Eligible Facilities) Regulations 2001
revoked: SI 2012/2999 Reg.9

664. Pensions Increase (Review) Order 2001
applied: SI 2012/782 Art.3, Art.4

715. National Treatment Agency Regulations 2001
Reg.1, amended: SI 2012/1641 Sch.4 para.7
Reg.3, amended: SI 2012/1641 Sch.4 para.7, SI 2012/2404 Sch.3 para.15

782. Education (Publication of Draft Proposals and Orders) (Further Education Corporations) (England) Regulations 2001
applied: SI 2012/924 Art.7

838. Climate Change Levy (General) Regulations 2001
Reg.2, amended: SI 2012/943 Reg.3
Reg.8, amended: SI 2012/943 Reg.4
Reg.11, amended: SI 2012/943 Reg.5
Reg.12, amended: SI 2012/943 Reg.6
Reg.33, amended: SI 2012/943 Reg.7
Reg.34, amended: SI 2012/943 Reg.8, Reg.9
Reg.35, amended: SI 2012/943 Reg.8, Reg.10
Reg.36, amended: SI 2012/943 Reg.8
Reg.37, amended: SI 2012/943 Reg.8
Reg.38, amended: SI 2012/943 Reg.8
Reg.39, amended: SI 2012/943 Reg.8
Reg.40, amended: SI 2012/943 Reg.8
Reg.41, amended: SI 2012/943 Reg.8
Reg.42, amended: SI 2012/943 Reg.8
Reg.43, amended: SI 2012/943 Reg.8
Reg.44, amended: SI 2012/943 Reg.8
Reg.45, amended: SI 2012/943 Reg.8
Reg.51A, amended: SI 2012/3049 Reg.3
Sch.1 para.1, amended: SI 2012/943 Reg.11
Sch.1 para.2, amended: SI 2012/943 Reg.11
Sch.1 para.2A, amended: SI 2012/943 Reg.11
Sch.1 para.3, amended: SI 2012/943 Reg.11
Sch.1 para.4, amended: SI 2012/943 Reg.11
Sch.1 para.5, amended: SI 2012/943 Reg.11
Sch.1 para.6, amended: SI 2012/943 Reg.11
Sch.1 para.7, amended: SI 2012/943 Reg.11
Sch.1 para.8, amended: SI 2012/943 Reg.11
Sch.1 para.9, amended: SI 2012/943 Reg.11
Sch.1 para.9A, amended: SI 2012/943 Reg.11
Sch.1 para.9B, amended: SI 2012/943 Reg.11
Sch.1 para.9C, amended: SI 2012/943 Reg.11
Sch.1 para.10, amended: SI 2012/943 Reg.11
Sch.1 para.11, amended: SI 2012/943 Reg.11
Sch.1 para.12, amended: SI 2012/943 Reg.11
Sch.1 para.13, amended: SI 2012/943 Reg.11
Sch.1 para.14, amended: SI 2012/943 Reg.11
Sch.1 para.15, amended: SI 2012/943 Reg.11
Sch.1 para.16, amended: SI 2012/943 Reg.11
Sch.2 para.1, amended: SI 2012/3049 Reg.4
Sch.2 para.11, amended: SI 2012/3049 Reg.4

880. Biocidal Products Regulations 2001
applied: SI 2012/1652 Reg.24
amended: SI 2012/1916 Sch.34 para.74

894. Road Traffic (Permitted Parking Area and Special Parking Area) (City of Salford) Order 2001
revoked: SI 2012/2659 Art.2

2001– cont.

1002. Housing Benefit and Council Tax Benefit (Decisions and Appeals) Regulations 2001

Reg.1, amended: SI 2012/757 Reg.19

Reg.1, referred to: SI 2012/2886 Sch.1

Reg.3, see *Wirral MBC v Salisbury Independent Living Ltd* [2012] EWCA Civ 84, [2012] P.T.S.R. 1221 (CA (Civ Div)), Maurice Kay, L.J.

Reg.4, amended: SI 2012/2994 Reg.3

Reg.7, amended: SI 2012/1267 Reg.5, SI 2012/2994 Reg.3

Reg.8, see *KW v Lancaster City Council* [2012] 1 F.L.R. 282 (UT (AAC)), Judge Nicholas Wikeley

Reg.8, amended: SI 2012/1267 Reg.5, SI 2012/2994 Reg.3, SI 2012/3040 Reg.2

Reg.11, applied: SSI 2012/303 Reg.92

1004. Social Security (Contributions) Regulations 2001

Reg.1, amended: SI 2012/817 Reg.3

Reg.1, revoked (in part): SI 2012/817 Reg.3

Reg.6, amended: SI 2012/817 Reg.4

Reg.10, amended: SI 2012/804 Reg.3

Reg.11, amended: SI 2012/804 Reg.4

Reg.21, amended: SI 2012/573 Reg.2

Reg.22A, see *Cheshire Employer and Skills Development Ltd v Revenue and Customs Commissioners* [2012] S.T.C. 69 (UT (Tax)), Judge Colin Bishopp

Reg.40, revoked (in part): SI 2012/817 Reg.7

Reg.52A, amended: SI 2012/817 Reg.8

Reg.67, amended: SI 2012/821 Reg.3

Reg.80, amended: SI 2012/821 Reg.19

Reg.83A, added: SI 2012/821 Reg.17

Reg.90H, amended: SI 2012/821 Reg.4

Reg.100, amended: SI 2012/573 Reg.2

Reg.123, revoked: SI 2012/817 Reg.7

Reg.125, amended: SI 2012/867 Reg.2

Reg.145, amended: SI 2012/817 Reg.7

Reg.145, revoked (in part): SI 2012/817 Reg.7

Sch.2 para.13, see *Forde & McHugh Ltd v Revenue and Customs Commissioners* [2012] EWCA Civ 692, [2012] 3 All E.R. 1256 (CA (Civ Div)), Arden, L.J.

Sch.3 Part V, applied: SI 2012/2886 Sch.1, SI 2012/3145 Sch.1, SSI 2012/319 Reg.32

Sch.3 Part VI para.2, amended: SI 2012/817 Reg.6

Sch.3 Part VI para.10, amended: SI 2012/817 Reg.6

Sch.3 Part VIII para.2, revoked (in part): SI 2012/817 Reg.7

Sch.3 Part VIII para.12A, substituted: SI 2012/817 Reg.9

Sch.3 Part VIII para.12B, substituted: SI 2012/817 Reg.9

Sch.3 Part VIII para.12C, added: SI 2012/817 Reg.9

Sch.4 Part I para.1, amended: SI 2012/821 Reg.5, Reg.20

Sch.4 Part II para.7, amended: SI 2012/817 Reg.5, SI 2012/821 Reg.21

Sch.4 Part II para.9, amended: SI 2012/821 Reg.22

Sch.4 Part IIIB para.29M, added: SI 2012/821 Reg.18

Sch.4 Part IIIB para.29N, added: SI 2012/821 Reg.18

Sch.4 Part IIIB para.29O, added: SI 2012/821 Reg.18

Sch.4 Part IIIB para.29P, added: SI 2012/821 Reg.18

Sch.4 Part IIIB para.29Q, added: SI 2012/821 Reg.18

2001– cont.

1004. Social Security (Contributions) Regulations 2001– *cont.*

Sch.4 Part IIIB para.29R, added: SI 2012/821 Reg.18

Sch.4 Part IIIB para.29S, added: SI 2012/821 Reg.18

Sch.4 Part IIIB para.29T, added: SI 2012/821 Reg.18

Sch.4 Part IIIB para.29U, added: SI 2012/821 Reg.18

Sch.4 Part IIIB para.29V, added: SI 2012/821 Reg.18

Sch.4 Part IIIB para.29W, added: SI 2012/821 Reg.18

Sch.4 Part IIIB para.29X, added: SI 2012/821 Reg.18

Sch.4 Part III para.10, amended: SI 2012/821 Reg.6, Reg.23

Sch.4 Part III para.11, amended: SI 2012/821 Reg.7, Reg.24, Reg.25

Sch.4 Part III para.11ZA, added: SI 2012/821 Reg.8

Sch.4 Part III para.14, amended: SI 2012/821 Reg.9

Sch.4 Part III para.15, amended: SI 2012/821 Reg.10, Reg.26

Sch.4 Part III para.16, amended: SI 2012/821 Reg.26

Sch.4 Part III para.21A, added: SI 2012/821 Reg.11

Sch.4 Part III para.21A, applied: SI 2012/821 Reg.16

Sch.4 Part III para.21B, added: SI 2012/821 Reg.11

Sch.4 Part III para.21B, applied: SI 2012/821 Reg.16

Sch.4 Part III para.21C, added: SI 2012/821 Reg.11

Sch.4 Part III para.21C, applied: SI 2012/821 Reg.16

Sch.4 Part III para.21D, added: SI 2012/821 Reg.11

Sch.4 Part III para.21D, applied: SI 2012/821 Reg.16

Sch.4 Part III para.21E, added: SI 2012/821 Reg.11

Sch.4 Part III para.21F, added: SI 2012/821 Reg.11

Sch.4 Part III para.22, amended: SI 2012/821 Reg.12, Reg.27, Reg.28

Sch.4 Part III para.22, revoked (in part): SI 2012/821 Reg.27

Sch.4 Part III para.24, amended: SI 2012/821 Reg.29

Sch.4 Part III para.24, revoked (in part): SI 2012/821 Reg.29

Sch.4 Part III para.25, amended: SI 2012/821 Reg.13, Reg.30

Sch.4A para.1, added: SI 2012/821 Sch.1

Sch.4A para.2, added: SI 2012/821 Sch.1

Sch.4A para.3, added: SI 2012/821 Sch.1

Sch.4A para.4, added: SI 2012/821 Sch.1

Sch.4A para.5, added: SI 2012/821 Sch.1

Sch.4A para.6, added: SI 2012/821 Sch.1

Sch.4A para.7, added: SI 2012/821 Sch.1

Sch.4A para.8, added: SI 2012/821 Sch.1

Sch.4A para.9, added: SI 2012/821 Sch.1

Sch.4A para.10, added: SI 2012/821 Sch.1

Sch.4A para.11, added: SI 2012/821 Sch.1

Sch.4A para.12, added: SI 2012/821 Sch.1

Sch.4A para.13, added: SI 2012/821 Sch.1

Sch.4A para.14, added: SI 2012/821 Sch.1

Sch.4A para.15, added: SI 2012/821 Sch.1

Sch.4A para.16, added: SI 2012/821 Sch.1

Sch.4A para.17, added: SI 2012/821 Sch.1

Sch.4A para.18, added: SI 2012/821 Sch.1

Sch.4B para.1, added: SI 2012/821 Sch.1

2001–cont.

1004. Social Security (Contributions) Regulations 2001–cont.
Sch.4B para.2, added: SI 2012/821 Sch.1
Sch.4B para.3, added: SI 2012/821 Sch.1
Sch.4B para.4, added: SI 2012/821 Sch.1
Sch.4B para.5, added: SI 2012/821 Sch.1
Sch.4B para.6, added: SI 2012/821 Sch.1
Sch.4B para.7, added: SI 2012/821 Sch.1
Sch.6 Part 1, applied: SI 2012/2885 Sch.4 para.3, SI 2012/2886 Sch.1, SSI 2012/319 Sch.2 para.3
Sch.6 Part 1, referred to: SSI 2012/303 Sch.3 para.9
Sch.7 Part II, amended: SI 2012/821 Reg.26, Reg.31

1007. A45 Trunk Road (Ryton on Dunsmore, Warwickshire) (50 Miles Per Hour Speed Limit) Order 2001
revoked: SI 2012/2144 Art.3

1054. British Waterways Board (Limit for Borrowing) Order 2001
varied: SI 2012/1659 Art.2
Art.1, varied: SI 2012/1659 Art.2

1091. Offshore Combustion Installations (Prevention and Control of Pollution) Regulations 2001
Reg.13, applied: SI 2012/3038 Reg.17
Reg.13, referred to: SI 2012/3038 Reg.17
Reg.18, applied: SI 2012/3038 Reg.17

1161. Prison Service (Pay Review Body) Regulations 2001
Sch.para.1, amended: SI 2012/2404 Sch.3 para.16

1167. Discretionary Financial Assistance Regulations 2001
applied: SSI 2012/303 Sch.5 para.11
Reg.2, applied: SI 2012/2886 Sch.1, SSI 2012/303 Sch.4 para.62

1177. Financial Services and Markets Act 2000 (Carrying on Regulated Activities by Way of Business) Order 2001
Art.2, see *R. v Napoli (John Francis)* [2012] EWCA Crim 1129, [2012] Lloyd's Rep. F.C. 599 (CA (Crim Div)), Rafferty, L.J.

1201. Financial Services and Markets Act 2000 (Exemption) Order 2001
Sch.Part III para.34C, added: SI 2012/763 Art.2
Sch.Part IV para.48, amended: SI 2012/700 Sch.1 para.12
Sch.Part IV para.48, revoked (in part): SI 2012/641 Art.2

1217. Financial Services and Markets Act 2000 (Appointed Representatives) Regulations 2001
Reg.2, amended: SI 2012/1906 Art.5

1227. Financial Services and Markets Act 2000 (Professions) (Non-Exempt Activities) Order 2001
Art.4, amended: SI 2012/1906 Art.6

1267. General Teaching Council for England (Registration of Teachers) (Amendment No 2) Regulations 2001
revoked: SI 2012/1153 Sch.1

1268. General Teaching Council for England (Disciplinary Functions) Regulations 2001
revoked: SI 2012/1153 Sch.1

1270. General Teaching Council for England (Additional Functions) (Amendment) Order 2001
revoked: SI 2012/1153 Sch.1

2001–cont.

1281. Street Works (Charges for Unreasonably Prolonged Occupation of the Highway) (England) Regulations 2001
applied: SI 2012/3102 Sch.1, SI 2012/3103 Sch.1, SI 2012/3104 Sch.1, SI 2012/3105 Sch.1, SI 2012/3106 Sch.1, SI 2012/3107 Sch.1

1299. Local Authorities (Alternative Arrangements) (England) Regulations 2001
revoked: SI 2012/1020 Reg.15

1348. Leeds Supertram (Land Acquisition and Road Works) Order 2001
Sch.6 para.1, amended: SI 2012/1659 Art.2
Sch.6 para.3, substituted: SI 2012/1659 Art.2

1368. Greater Manchester (Light Rapid Transit System) (Mumps Surface Crossing) Order 2001
Art.3, amended: SI 2012/981 Art.7

1399. Scottish Parliament (Elections etc.) (Amendment) Order 2001
varied: 2012 c.11 s.3

1403. Immigration and Asylum Act 1999 (Part V Exemption Educational Institutions and Health Sector Bodies) Order 2001
Sch.2 para.1, amended: SI 2012/979 Sch.1 para.6

1420. Financial Services and Markets Act 2000 (Service of Notices) Regulations 2001
applied: SI 2012/3122 Sch.1 para.8

1424. General Teaching Council for Wales (Disciplinary Functions) Regulations 2001
Reg.2, amended: SI 2012/170 Reg.2
Reg.9, amended: SI 2012/170 Reg.2, SI 2012/3006 Art.22
Reg.25, substituted: SI 2012/170 Reg.2

1437. Criminal Defence Service (General) (No.2) Regulations 2001
referred to: SI 2012/1726 r.74.3
Reg.16, see *R. (on the application of Clive Rees Associates) v Swansea Magistrates' Court* [2011] EWHC 3155 (Admin), (2012) 176 J.P. 39 (QBD (Admin)), Beatson, J.

1633. A55 Trunk Road (Holyhead, Anglesey) (50 mph Speed Limit &amp Prohibition of Pedestrians) Order 2001
disapplied: SI 2012/1268 Art.7

1653. A5 and A55 Trunk Roads (Llanfairpwllgwyngyll to Holyhead, Anglesey) (Deretsriction) Order 2001
disapplied: SI 2012/1268 Art.6

1712. Tobacco Products Regulations 2001
Reg.13, see *R. v Bajwa (Naripdeep Singh)* [2011] EWCA Crim 1093, [2012] 1 W.L.R. 601 (CA (Crim Div)), Aikens, L.J.

1742. National Patient Safety Agency Regulations 2001
Reg.1, amended: SI 2012/1425 Reg.2
Reg.2, amended: SI 2012/1425 Reg.2
Reg.3, amended: SI 2012/1425 Reg.2, SI 2012/2404 Sch.3 para.17
Reg.4, revoked: SI 2012/1425 Reg.2
Reg.5, amended: SI 2012/1425 Reg.2
Reg.5, revoked (in part): SI 2012/1425 Reg.2
Reg.5A, revoked: SI 2012/1425 Reg.2
Reg.5B, revoked: SI 2012/1425 Reg.2
Reg.6, revoked: SI 2012/1425 Reg.2
Reg.6A, revoked: SI 2012/1425 Reg.2
Reg.7, amended: SI 2012/1425 Reg.2
Reg.9, substituted: SI 2012/1425 Reg.2
Reg.10, amended: SI 2012/1425 Reg.2
Reg.10, revoked (in part): SI 2012/1425 Reg.2

2001– cont.

1742. National Patient Safety Agency Regulations 2001– cont.
Sch.para.1, revoked: SI 2012/ 1425 Reg.2
Sch.para.2, revoked: SI 2012/ 1425 Reg.2
Sch.para.3, revoked: SI 2012/ 1425 Reg.2
Sch.para.4, revoked: SI 2012/ 1425 Reg.2
Sch.para.5, revoked: SI 2012/ 1425 Reg.2
Sch.para.6, revoked: SI 2012/ 1425 Reg.2

1743. National Patient Safety Agency (Establishment and Constitution) Order 2001
revoked: 2012 c.7 s.281
Art.1, amended: SI 2012/ 1424 Art.2
Art.3, amended: SI 2012/ 1424 Art.2
Art.3, revoked (in part): SI 2012/476 Art.2
Art.4, substituted: SI 2012/ 1424 Art.2
Art.5, revoked: SI 2012/ 1424 Art.2
Art.6, revoked: SI 2012/ 1424 Art.2
Art.7, revoked: SI 2012/ 1424 Art.2
Art.8, revoked: SI 2012/ 1424 Art.2
Art.9, revoked: SI 2012/ 1424 Art.2

1744. General Social Care Council (Appointments and Procedure) Regulations 2001
Reg.4, amended: SI 2012/ 2404 Sch.3 para.18
Reg.6, amended: SI 2012/ 2404 Sch.3 para.18

1748. Scottish Parliament (Elections etc.) (Amendment) (No.2) Order 2001
varied: 2012 c.11 s.3

1750. Scottish Parliament (Elections etc.) (Amendment) (No.3) Order 2001
varied: 2012 c.11 s.3

1825. Road Vehicles (Construction and Use) (Amendment) (No.3) Regulations 2001
Reg.5, revoked: SI 2012/ 1404 Sch.1

1841. Medicines (Aristolochia and Mu Tong etc.) (Prohibition) Order 2001
Art.1, amended: SI 2012/ 1809 Sch.1 Part 2
Art.4, amended: SI 2012/ 1916 Sch.34 para.75

2127. Health and Safety at Work etc Act 1974 (Application outside Great Britain) Order 2001
applied: SI 2012/ 632 Reg.31

2136. Care Council for Wales (Appointment, Membership and Procedure) Regulations 2001
Reg.1, amended: SI 2012/ 3023 Reg.2
Reg.2, revoked (in part): SI 2012/ 3023 Reg.2
Reg.5, amended: SI 2012/ 2404 Sch.3 para.19, SI 2012/ 3023 Reg.2
Reg.6, amended: SI 2012/ 3023 Reg.2

2183. Cowes Harbour (Constitution) Revision Order 2001
applied: SI 2012/ 3080 Art.9, Art.14, Art.18, Art.25
Art.14, revoked: SI 2012/ 3080 Art.26
Art.16, amended: SI 2012/ 3080 Art.26

2188. Financial Services and Markets Act 2000 (Disclosure of Confidential Information) Regulations 2001
Reg.2, amended: SI 2012/916 Reg.3, SI 2012/917 Sch.2 para.2, SI 2012/ 2554 Reg.3
Reg.2, varied: SI 2012/ 3122 Sch.1 para.9
Reg.3, amended: SI 2012/916 Reg.3
Reg.5, amended: SI 2012/916 Reg.3
Reg.5, varied: SI 2012/ 3122 Sch.1 para.9
Reg.8, amended: SI 2012/916 Reg.3
Reg.8, varied: SI 2012/ 3122 Sch.1 para.9
Reg.9, amended: SI 2012/916 Reg.3
Reg.9, varied: SI 2012/ 3122 Sch.1 para.9
Reg.10, amended: SI 2012/916 Reg.3
Reg.11, amended: SI 2012/916 Reg.3

2001– cont.

2188. Financial Services and Markets Act 2000 (Disclosure of Confidential Information) Regulations 2001– cont.
Reg.11, varied: SI 2012/ 3122 Sch.1 para.9
Reg.12, amended: SI 2012/916 Reg.3, SI 2012/ 2554 Reg.3
Reg.12A, amended: SI 2012/ 725 Art.2, SI 2012/ 916 Reg.3
Reg.12B, amended: SI 2012/916 Reg.3
Reg.12BI, amended: SI 2012/916 Reg.3
Reg.12C, amended: SI 2012/916 Reg.3
Reg.14, amended: SI 2012/916 Reg.3
Reg.15, amended: SI 2012/916 Reg.3
Sch.1 Part 1, amended: SI 2012/916 Reg.3
Sch.1 Part 1, varied: SI 2012/ 3122 Sch.1 para.9
Sch.1 Part 2, amended: SI 2012/916 Reg.3
Sch.1 Part 3, amended: SI 2012/916 Reg.3
Sch.1 Part 4, amended: SI 2012/916 Reg.3
Sch.1 Part 5, amended: SI 2012/916 Reg.3
Sch.1 Part 5, varied: SI 2012/ 3122 Sch.1 para.9
Sch.2, amended: SI 2012/916 Reg.3, SI 2012/ 3019 Reg.2

2256. Financial Services and Markets Act 2000 (Rights of Action) Regulations 2001
see *Camerata Property Inc v Credit Suisse Securities (Europe) Ltd* [2012] EWHC 7 (Comm), [2012] 1 C.L.C. 234 (QBD (Comm)), Flaux, J.

2276. Conduct of Members (Principles) (Wales) Order 2001
applied: SI 2012/ 2734 Sch.1 para.33
varied: SI 2012/ 2734 Reg.6

2279. Standards Committees (Grant of Dispensations) (Wales) Regulations 2001
applied: SI 2012/ 2734 Sch.1 para.33
varied: SI 2012/ 2734 Reg.6

2281. Local Government Investigations (Functions of Monitoring Officers and Standards Committees)(Wales) Regulations 2001
varied: SI 2012/ 2734 Reg.6

2288. Adjudications by Case Tribunals and Interim Case Tribunals (Wales) Regulations 2001
applied: SI 2012/ 2734 Sch.1 para.33
varied: SI 2012/ 2734 Reg.6

2541. Capital Allowances (Energy-saving Plant and Machinery) Order 2001
Art.2, amended: SI 2012/ 1832 Art.3

2544. Local Authorities (Elected Mayors) (Elections, Terms of Office and Casual Vacancies) (England) Regulations 2001
revoked: SI 2012/ 336 Reg.13

2561. Central Council for Education and Training in Social Work (Transfer Scheme) Order 2001
revoked: 2012 c.7 Sch.15 para.18
Art.5, applied: SI 2012/ 1480 Art.14

2645. Police and Criminal Evidence Act 1984 (Drug Testing of Persons in Police Detention) (Prescribed Persons) Regulations 2001
Reg.2, amended: SI 2012/ 61 Reg.2

2719. Town and Country Planning (Fees for Applications and Deemed Applications) (Amendment) (England) Regulations 2001
revoked: SI 2012/ 2920 Sch.3

2793. Road User Charging And Workplace Parking Levy (Classes Of Motor Vehicles) (England) Regulations 2001
referred to: SI 2012/ 2387 Art.4

2820. Poole Harbour Revision Order 2001
Art.3, amended: SI 2012/ 1777 Sch.3 para.1

2001–cont.

2820. Poole Harbour Revision Order 2001–*cont.*
Art.3, revoked (in part): SI 2012/1777 Sch.3 para.1
Art.4, amended: SI 2012/1777 Sch.3 para.2
Art.6, revoked (in part): SI 2012/1777 Sch.4 Part 2
Art.7, amended: SI 2012/1777 Sch.3 para.3, Sch.3 para.4, Sch.4 Part 2
Art.7, revoked (in part): SI 2012/1777 Sch.4 Part 2
Art.10, amended: SI 2012/1777 Sch.3 para.5
Sch.1, amended: SI 2012/1777 Sch.3 para.6
Sch.2 para A.1, added: SI 2012/1777 Sch.3 para.7
Sch.2 para.9, amended: SI 2012/1777 Sch.3 para.8, Sch.3 para.9
Sch.2 para.9A, added: SI 2012/1777 Sch.3 para.10
Sch.2 para.10, substituted: SI 2012/1777 Sch.3 para.11

2857. Education (Grants etc.) (Dance and Drama) (England) Regulations 2001
Reg.12, amended: SI 2012/956 Art.8

2879. Value Added Tax (Refund of Tax to Museums and Galleries) Order 2001
Sch.1, amended: SI 2012/2731 Sch.1

2891. Higher Education Funding Council for England (Supplementary Functions) Order 2001
Art.2, amended: SI 2012/979 Sch.1 para.7

2894. Education (Grant) (Financial Support for Students) Regulations 2001
Reg.2, amended: SI 2012/979 Sch.1 para.8

2960. Tyne Tunnel (Revision of Tolls and Traffic Classification) Order 2001
Sch.1, substituted: SI 2012/3053 Sch.1

2975. Radiation (Emergency Preparedness and Public Information) Regulations 2001
Reg.14, applied: SI 2012/1652 Reg.8, Sch.7

2993. Competition Act 1998 (Section 11 Exemption) Regulations 2001
Reg.2, amended: SI 2012/1809 Sch.1 Part 2
Reg.3, amended: SI 2012/1809 Sch.1 Part 2

3084. Financial Services and Markets Act 2000 (Gibraltar) Order 2001
Art.2, amended: SI 2012/2017 Art.2
Art.3A, added: SI 2012/2017 Art.2
Art.4, amended: SI 2012/2017 Art.2

3363. Terrorism (United Nations Measures) (Channel Islands) Order 2001
Sch.1, amended: SI 2012/362 Sch.1

3384. Local Authorities (Standing Orders) (England) Regulations 2001
Sch.2 Part I para.8, amended: SI 2012/460 Sch.1 para.14
Sch.2 Part I para.14, revoked: SI 2012/460 Sch.1 para.14
Sch.2 Part II para.6, amended: SI 2012/460 Sch.1 para.14
Sch.2 Part II para.10, revoked: SI 2012/460 Sch.1 para.14

3455. Education (Special Educational Needs) (England) (Consolidation) Regulations 2001
Reg.7, see *NM v Lambeth LBC* [2012] E.L.R. 224 (UT (AAC)), Judge Michael Mark
Sch.1 Part A, amended: SI 2012/979 Sch.1 para.9

3495. European Communities (Designation) (No.3) Order 2001
referred to: SI 2012/916 Sch.1

3510. Seeds (National Lists of Varieties) Regulations 2001
applied: SI 2012/245 Reg.3
Reg.22, substituted: SI 2012/2897 Art.3

2001–cont.

3625. Financial Services and Markets Act 2000 (Control of Business Transfers) (Requirements on Applicants) Regulations 2001
Reg.3, see *Combined Insurance Co of America, Re* [2012] EWHC 632 (Ch), [2012] Lloyd's Rep. I.R. 714 (Ch D (Companies Ct)), Morgan, J.

3649. Financial Services and Markets Act 2000 (Consequential Amendments and Repeals) Order 2001
Art.599, revoked: SI 2012/1489 Sch.2

3739. National Health Service (General Ophthalmic Services) Amendment (No.2) Regulations 2001
Reg.4, varied: 2012 c.11 s.12
Reg.6, varied: 2012 c.11 s.12

3744. Abolition of the NHS Tribunal (Consequential Provisions) Regulations 2001
Reg.6, applied: SI 2012/922 Reg.3, SI 2012/1290 Reg.3

3747. Stamp Duty (Disadvantaged Areas) Regulations 2001
revoked: 2012 c.14 Sch.39 para.7
Sch.3, varied: 2012 c.11 s.12

3755. Uncertificated Securities Regulations 2001
Sch.1 para.28, amended: SI 2012/917 Sch.2 para.3
Sch.2 para.1, amended: SI 2012/917 Sch.2 para.3

3763. M25 Motorway (Junctions 10 to 16) (Variable Speed Limits) Regulations 2001
revoked: SI 2012/2134 Reg.4

3788. Care Trusts (Applications and Consultation) Regulations 2001
revoked: SI 2012/3094 Reg.11

3941. Local Elections (Declaration of Acceptance of Office) Order 2001
revoked: SI 2012/1465 Art.3

3961. Local Authorities (Arrangements for the Discharge of Functions) (England) (Amendment) Regulations 2001
revoked: SI 2012/1019 Reg.13

3965. Care Homes Regulations 2001
see *R. v Hopkins (Annette)* [2011] EWCA Crim 1513, (2012) 123 B.M.L.R. 1 (CA (Crim Div)), Pitchford L.J.

3967. Children's Homes Regulations 2001
Reg.3, amended: SI 2012/979 Sch.1 para.10
Reg.6, amended: SI 2012/2404 Sch.3 para.20
Reg.18, amended: SI 2012/979 Sch.1 para.10

3982. Special Educational Needs Tribunal (Time Limits) (Wales) Regulations 2001
revoked: SI 2012/322 Reg.4

3993. General Teaching Council for England (Deduction of Fees) Regulations 2001
revoked: SI 2012/1153 Sch.1

3997. Misuse of Drugs (Designation) Order 2001
Sch.1 Part I para.1, amended: SI 2012/1310 Art.2

3998. Misuse of Drugs Regulations 2001
referred to: SI 2012/1916 Reg.253
varied: SI 2012/980 Art.3
Reg.2, amended: SI 2012/973 Reg.3, SI 2012/1479 Sch.1 para.21, SI 2012/1916 Sch.34 para.76
Reg.4, amended: SI 2012/973 Reg.4
Reg.5, applied: SI 2012/1916 Sch.17 Part 2, Sch.17 Part 5
Reg.6, amended: SI 2012/973 Reg.5
Reg.6A, amended: SI 2012/973 Reg.6
Reg.6B, substituted: SI 2012/973 Reg.7
Reg.7, amended: SI 2012/973 Reg.8
Reg.8, amended: SI 2012/973 Reg.9
Reg.8, applied: SI 2012/1916 Sch.17 Part 3

2001–cont.

3998. Misuse of Drugs Regulations 2001–*cont.*
Reg.9, amended: SI 2012/973 Reg.10
Reg.9, applied: SI 2012/1916 Sch.17 Part 3
Reg.10, amended: SI 2012/973 Reg.11
Reg.14, amended: SI 2012/973 Reg.12
Reg.18, amended: SI 2012/973 Reg.13
Reg.26, amended: SI 2012/973 Reg.14
Sch.1 para.1, amended: SI 2012/1311 Reg.3
Sch.3 para.1, amended: SI 2012/1311 Reg.4
Sch.3 para.2, substituted: SI 2012/1311 Reg.5
Sch.3 para.3, substituted: SI 2012/1311 Reg.5
Sch.3 para.4, substituted: SI 2012/1311 Reg.5
Sch.4, applied: SI 2012/1916 Reg.225
Sch.4, referred to: SI 2012/1909 Sch.4 para.5, Sch.4 para.6, Sch.4 para.8, Sch.6 para.2
Sch.4 Part II para.1, substituted: SI 2012/973 Reg.15
Sch.4 Part II para.2, substituted: SI 2012/973 Reg.15
Sch.4 Part II para.3, substituted: SI 2012/973 Reg.15
Sch.4 Part II para.4, substituted: SI 2012/973 Reg.15
Sch.4 Part II para.5, substituted: SI 2012/973 Reg.15
Sch.4 Part II para.6, substituted: SI 2012/973 Reg.15
Sch.4 Part II para.7, substituted: SI 2012/973 Reg.15
Sch.5, applied: SI 2012/1916 Reg.225
Sch.5, referred to: SI 2012/1909 Sch.4 para.5, Sch.4 para.6, Sch.4 para.8, Sch.6 para.2
Sch.8 para.1, amended: SI 2012/973 Reg.16

4028. Amusement Machine Licence Duty (Medium-prize Machines) Order 2001
revoked: 2012 c.14 Sch.24 para.53

4060. Street Works (Charges for Occupation of the Highway) (England) Regulations 2001
revoked: SI 2012/425 Reg.8

4111. Medicines (Products Other Than Veterinary Drugs) (General Sale List) Amendment (No.2) Order 2001
revoked: SI 2012/1916 Sch.35

2002

111. Al-Qa'ida and Taliban (United Nations Measures) Order 2002
Sch.1, amended: SI 2012/362 Sch.2

112. Al-Qa'ida and Taliban (United Nations Measures) (Overseas Territories) Order 2002
revoked: SI 2012/1757 Art.30
Art.7, applied: SI 2012/1757 Art.31
Art.7, referred to: SI 2012/1758 Art.30
Sch.1, amended: SI 2012/362 Sch.2

205. Income Tax (Exemption of Minor Benefits) Regulations 2002
Reg.2, amended: SI 2012/1808 Reg.2
Reg.3, revoked: SI 2012/1808 Reg.2

233. Police Act 1997 (Criminal Records) Regulations 2002
Reg.2, amended: SI 2012/523 Reg.2
Reg.5A, amended: SI 2012/523 Reg.3, SI 2012/979 Sch.1 para.11, SI 2012/2114 Reg.3, Reg.5, Reg.6, Reg.8, Reg.9, Reg.10, SI 2012/3016 Reg.4
Reg.5A, revoked (in part): SI 2012/2114 Reg.4, Reg.7, SI 2012/3006 Art.77
Reg.9, amended: SI 2012/2669 Reg.2
Reg.10, revoked: SI 2012/2114 Reg.11
Reg.11, amended: SI 2012/3006 Art.78
Reg.12, amended: SI 2012/979 Sch.1 para.11

2002–cont.

236. Medicines (Codification Amendments Etc.) Regulations 2002
revoked: SI 2012/1916 Sch.35

253. Nursing and Midwifery Order (2001) 2002
Art.3, enabled: SI 2012/2745
Art.5, applied: SI 2012/1305 Sch.1 para.1
Art.7, applied: SI 2012/3026
Art.7, enabled: SI 2012/2754, SI 2012/3026
Art.12, enabled: SI 2012/2754
Art.21, applied: SI 2012/3025 Sch.1
Art.26, enabled: SI 2012/17
Art.30, enabled: SI 2012/17
Art.31, see *Perry v Nursing and Midwifery Council* [2012] EWHC 2275 (Admin), [2012] Med. L.R. 723 (QBD (Admin)), Thirlwall, J.
Art.32, enabled: SI 2012/17, SI 2012/2754
Art.33, enabled: SI 2012/3026
Art.42, enabled: SI 2012/3025
Art.43, applied: SI 2012/3025 Sch.1
Art.43, enabled: SI 2012/3025
Art.47, applied: SI 2012/17, SI 2012/17 Sch.1, SI 2012/2754, SI 2012/3025, SI 2012/3026
Art.47, enabled: SI 2012/17, SI 2012/2754, SI 2012/3025, SI 2012/3026
Art.48, applied: SI 2012/17, SI 2012/2754, SI 2012/3025, SI 2012/3026
Sch.1 Part I para.1A, enabled: SI 2012/2745
Sch.1 Part I para.1B, enabled: SI 2012/2745

254. Health and Social Work Professions Order 2002
amended: 2012 c.7 s.213
applied: SI 2012/1480 Art.14, Art.16
referred to: SI 2012/1480 Art.4, SI 2012/1917 Sch.2 para.15
Art.1, amended: 2012 c.7 s.213
Art.3, amended: 2012 c.7 s.214, s.215, s.218, SI 2012/2672 Art.2
Art.3, substituted: 2012 c.7 s.214
Art.5, applied: SI 2012/1305 Sch.1 para.1, SI 2012/1480 Art.14
Art.6, amended: 2012 c.7 s.215
Art.7, amended: 2012 c.7 s.215
Art.9, amended: 2012 c.7 s.215
Art.10, amended: 2012 c.7 s.215
Art.12, amended: 2012 c.7 s.215
Art.12, applied: SI 2012/1480 Art.14
Art.13, amended: SI 2012/1479 Art.2
Art.13A, substituted: 2012 c.7 s.215
Art.13B, added: 2012 c.7 s.215
Art.14, amended: 2012 c.7 s.218
Art.15A, added: 2012 c.7 s.218
Art.15B, added: 2012 c.7 s.218
Art.16, amended: 2012 c.7 s.218
Art.17, amended: 2012 c.7 s.218
Art.18, amended: 2012 c.7 s.218
Art.19, amended: 2012 c.7 s.215
Art.19, applied: SI 2012/1480 Art.14
Art.20, amended: 2012 c.7 s.215
Art.21, amended: 2012 c.7 s.218
Art.33, applied: SI 2012/1480 Art.8
Art.33, varied: SI 2012/1480 Art.11
Art.37, amended: 2012 c.7 s.215, s.216
Art.38, amended: 2012 c.7 s.216
Art.39, amended: 2012 c.7 s.215
Art.44A, added: 2012 c.7 s.219
Art.45, amended: 2012 c.7 s.218
Sch.1 Part I para.1A, amended: 2012 c.7 s.213

2002–cont.

254. **Health and Social Work Professions Order 2002**–*cont.*
Sch.3 para.1, amended: 2012 c.7 s.213, s.214, s.215, s.219

258. **Al-Qa'ida and Taliban (United Nations Measures) (Channel Islands) Order 2002**
Sch.1, substituted: SI 2012/362 Sch.1

264. **Air Navigation (Amendment) Order 2002**
applied: 2012 c.19 Sch.6 para.4

266. **Al-Qa'ida and Taliban (United Nations Measures) (Overseas Territories) (Amendment) Order 2002**
revoked: SI 2012/1757 Art.30

271. **Hill Farm Allowance Regulations 2002**
revoked: SI 2012/114 Reg.9

308. **Pennine Acute Hospitals National Health Service Trust (Establishment) and the Bury Health Care National Health Service Trust, the Rochdale Healthcare National Health Service Trust, the Oldham National Health Service Trust and the North Manchester 2002**
referred to: SI 2012/1512 Sch.1

315. **Export of Goods (Federal Republic of Yugoslavia) (Control) (Revocation) Order 2002**
revoked: SI 2012/2125 Art.2

324. **Care Homes (Wales) Regulations 2002**
Reg.7, amended: SI 2012/2404 Sch.3 para.21

327. **Children's Homes (Wales) Regulations 2002**
Reg.6, amended: SI 2012/2404 Sch.3 para.22

378. **School Budget Shares (Prescribed Purposes) (England) Regulations 2002**
applied: SI 2012/335 Sch.3 para.27

419. **European Union Extradition Regulations 2002**
Sch.2, varied: 2012 c.11 s.12
Sch.6, varied: 2012 c.11 s.12

454. **Whole of Government Accounts (Designation of Bodies) Order 2002**
varied: SI 2012/147 Art.7

522. **Local Authorities (Goods and Services) (Public Bodies) (England) Order 2002**
Art.2, amended: SI 2012/961 Sch.1 para.5

618. **Medical Devices Regulations 2002**
Reg.2, amended: SI 2012/1426 Reg.2

699. **Pensions Increase (Review) Order 2002**
applied: SI 2012/782 Art.3, Art.4

716. **Local Authorities (Executive Arrangements) (Access to Information) (England) Amendment Regulations 2002**
revoked: SI 2012/2089 Reg.23

768. **Town and Country Planning (Fees for Applications and Deemed Applications) (Amendment) (England) Regulations 2002**
revoked: SI 2012/2920 Sch.3

797. **Abolition of the Central Council for Education and Training in Social Work Order 2002**
revoked: 2012 c.7 Sch.15 para.18

798. **Air Navigation (Environmental Standards) Order 2002**
applied: 2012 c.19 Sch.6 para.4

888. **National Health Service (Local Pharmaceutical Services and Pharmaceutical Services) Regulations 2002**
Reg.1, amended: SI 2012/1909 Sch.8 para.5
Reg.3, amended: SI 2012/1909 Sch.8 para.5

894. **Walsall Primary Care Trust (Establishment) Order 2002**
referred to: SI 2012/1512 Sch.1

2002–cont.

912. **Companies (Particulars of Usual Residential Address) (Confidentiality Orders) Regulations 2002**
Sch.1, varied: 2012 c.11 s.12

919. **Registration of Social Care and Independent Health Care (Wales) Regulations 2002**
Sch.1 Part I para.3, amended: SI 2012/2404 Sch.3 para.23

1077. **Overseas Territories (Zimbabwe) (Restrictive Measures) Order 2002**
revoked: SI 2012/2753 Sch.7
Sch.1, amended: SI 2012/362 Sch.2

1078. **Air Navigation (Jersey) (Amendment No 2) Order 2002**
applied: 2012 c.19 Sch.6 para.4

1144. **Personal Protective Equipment Regulations 2002**
applied: SI 2012/632 Reg.11
Reg.16, amended: SI 2012/1848 Reg.7
Reg.20, amended: SI 2012/1848 Reg.7

1394. **School Teacher Appraisal (Wales) Regulations 2002**
applied: SI 2012/1115 Sch.1 para.24

1474. **Road Vehicles (Construction and Use) (Amendment) (No.2) Regulations 2002**
Reg.4, revoked: SI 2012/1404 Sch.1

1628. **Air Navigation (Amendment) (No.2) Order 2002**
applied: 2012 c.19 Sch.6 para.4

1663. **Further Education Teachers Qualifications (Wales) Regulations 2002**
Reg.2, amended: SI 2012/724 Reg.11
Reg.3, amended: SI 2012/724 Reg.11
Reg.3, revoked (in part): SI 2012/724 Reg.11

1703. **Social Security (Jobcentre Plus Interviews) Regulations 2002**
Reg.4A, amended: SI 2012/874 Reg.5

1730. **Environmental Protection (Restriction on Use of Lead Shot) (Wales) Regulations 2002**
revoked: SI 2012/1923 Sch.1

1775. **Electronic Commerce Directive (Financial Services and Markets) Regulations 2002**
Reg.2, amended: SI 2012/1809 Sch.1 Part 2

1792. **State Pension Credit Regulations 2002**
Reg.1, amended: SI 2012/757 Reg.5
Reg.1, applied: SI 2012/2885 Sch.1 para.35, SSI 2012/319 Reg.45
Reg.2, amended: SI 2012/1809 Sch.1 Part 2, SI 2012/2587 Reg.4
Reg.6, amended: SI 2012/780 Art.27
Reg.6, referred to: SI 2012/780 Sch.17
Reg.7, amended: SI 2012/780 Art.27
Reg.7, referred to: SI 2012/780 Art.27, Sch.17
Reg.13, applied: SI 2012/3145 Sch.1, SSI 2012/319 Reg.2
Reg.13, disapplied: SI 2012/2885 Reg.2, SI 2012/3144 Reg.2
Reg.15, amended: SI 2012/757 Reg.5
Reg.17A, amended: SI 2012/757 Reg.5
Reg.21, applied: SI 2012/2886 Sch.1, SI 2012/3145 Sch.1, SSI 2012/319 Reg.45
Reg.21, referred to: SI 2012/2885 Sch.1 para.35
Sch.2, applied: SI 2012/2885 Sch.5 para.12, SI 2012/2886 Sch.1
Sch.2, referred to: SSI 2012/319 Sch.3 para.11
Sch.2 para.1, amended: SI 2012/913 Reg.6
Sch.2 para.6, referred to: SI 2012/780 Sch.17
Sch.2 para.7, referred to: SI 2012/780 Sch.17
Sch.2 para.8, referred to: SI 2012/780 Sch.17

2002–cont.

1792. State Pension Credit Regulations 2002–cont.
Sch.2 para.9, referred to: SI 2012/780 Sch.17
Sch.2 para.14, amended: SI 2012/780 Art.27
Sch.3 para.1, amended: SI 2012/780 Art.27
Sch.3 para.2, referred to: SI 2012/780 Sch.17
Sch.5 Part I para.20A, applied: SI 2012/2885 Sch.6 para.22, SI 2012/2886 Sch.1, SSI 2012/319 Sch.4 para.22

1822. Anti-terrorism (Financial and Other Measures) (Overseas Territories) Order 2002
Art.2, amended: SI 2012/362 Sch.1

1837. Penalties for Disorderly Behaviour (Amount of Penalty) Order 2002
Sch.1 Part II, amended: SI 2012/1431 Art.2

1868. Wiltshire County Council (Semington Aqueduct) Scheme 2000 Confirmation Instrument 2002
Sch.1 Part 1 para.4, amended: SI 2012/1659 Art.2

1877. Town and Country Planning (General Development Procedure) (Amendment) (Wales) Order 2002
revoked: SI 2012/801 Sch.8

1883. National Health Service (General Ophthalmic Services) (Amendment) (Wales) Regulations 2002
Reg.4, varied: 2012 c.11 s.12
Reg.6, varied: 2012 c.11 s.12

1889. Companies (Disclosure of Information) (Designated Authorities) (No.2) Order 2002
Art.2, amended: SI 2012/725 Art.2
Art.3, amended: SI 2012/725 Art.2

1920. Abolition of the NHS Tribunal (Consequential Provisions) Regulations 2002
Reg.6, applied: SI 2012/922 Reg.3, SI 2012/1290 Reg.3

1963. Controlled Foreign Companies (Excluded Countries) (Amendment) Regulations 2002
revoked: 2012 c.14 Sch.20 para.14

1985. Special Educational Needs and Disability Tribunal (General Provisions and Disability Claims Procedure) Regulations 2002
revoked (in part): SI 2012/322 Reg.4
Reg.39A, applied: SI 2012/322 Reg.58

2005. Working Tax Credit (Entitlement and Maximum Rate) Regulations 2002
Reg.2, amended: SI 2012/848 Rcg.2
Reg.2, varied: 2012 c.11 s.12
Reg.3, amended: SI 2012/848 Reg.2
Reg.3, revoked (in part): SI 2012/848 Reg.2
Reg.4, amended: SI 2012/848 Reg.2
Reg.4, revoked (in part): SI 2012/848 Reg.2
Reg.5, amended: SI 2012/848 Reg.2
Reg.5A, amended: SI 2012/848 Reg.2
Reg.6, amended: SI 2012/848 Reg.2
Reg.7A, amended: SI 2012/848 Reg.2
Reg.7B, amended: SI 2012/848 Reg.2
Reg.7D, amended: SI 2012/848 Reg.2
Reg.9, amended: SI 2012/848 Reg.2
Reg.10, revoked (in part): SI 2012/848 Reg.2
Reg.11, amended: SI 2012/848 Reg.2
Reg.11, revoked (in part): SI 2012/848 Reg.2
Reg.13, amended: SI 2012/848 Reg.2
Reg.16, amended: SI 2012/848 Reg.2
Reg.18, referred to: SI 2012/2886 Sch.1
Reg.18, revoked: SI 2012/848 Reg.2
Reg.20, amended: SI 2012/848 Reg.2
Reg.20, applied: SI 2012/2885 Sch.4 para.10, SI 2012/2886 Sch.1, SSI 2012/303 Sch.1 para.10, Sch.3 para.18, SSI 2012/319 Sch.2 para.10

2005. Working Tax Credit (Entitlement and Maximum Rate) Regulations 2002–cont.
Reg.20, referred to: SI 2012/2885 Sch.1 para.26, SI 2012/2886 Sch.1
Reg.20, revoked (in part): SI 2012/848 Reg.2
Sch.2, amended: SI 2012/849 Reg.3
Sch.2, applied: SI 2012/2885 Sch.4 para.5, SI 2012/2886 Sch.1, SSI 2012/319 Sch.2 para.5

2006. Tax Credits (Definition and Calculation of Income) Regulations 2002
Reg.4, amended: SI 2012/848 Reg.3
Reg.8, amended: SI 2012/848 Reg.3

2007. Child Tax Credit Regulations 2002
Reg.2, amended: SI 2012/848 Reg.4
Reg.3, amended: SI 2012/848 Reg.4
Reg.3, see *Humphreys v Revenue and Customs Commissioners* [2012] UKSC 18, [2012] 1 W.L.R. 1545 (SC), Lord Walker, J.S.C.
Reg.4, amended: SI 2012/848 Reg.4
Reg.7, amended: SI 2012/849 Reg.2

2008. Tax Credits (Income Thresholds and Determination of Rates) Regulations 2002
Reg.5, amended: SI 2012/849 Reg.4
Reg.5, substituted: SI 2012/849 Reg.4
Reg.7, amended: 2012 c.5 s.76, SI 2012/849 Reg.4
Reg.8, amended: SI 2012/849 Reg.4

2013. Electronic Commerce (EC Directive) Regulations 2002
see *Dramatico Entertainment Ltd v British Sky Broadcasting Ltd* [2012] EWHC 1152 (Ch), [2012] 3 C.M.L.R. 15 (Ch D), Arnold, J.
Reg.2, amended: SI 2012/1809 Sch.1 Part 2
Reg.19, see *Davison v Habeeb* [2011] EWHC 3031 (QB), [2012] 3 C.M.L.R. 6 (QBD), Judge Parkes Q.C.; see *Tamiz v Google Inc* [2012] EWHC 449 (QB), [2012] E.M.L.R. 24 (QBD), Eady, J.

2014. Tax Credits (Claims and Notifications) Regulations 2002
Reg.7, amended: SI 2012/848 Reg.5
Reg.8, amended: SI 2012/848 Reg.5
Reg.21, amended: SI 2012/848 Reg.5
Reg.21, revoked (in part): SI 2012/848 Reg.5
Reg.25, amended: SI 2012/848 Reg.5
Reg.26, amended: SI 2012/848 Reg.5
Reg.26A, amended: SI 2012/848 Reg.5

2016. National Health Service (Local Pharmaceutical Services and Pharmaceutical Services) (No.2) Regulations 2002
applied: SI 2012/1909 Sch.7 para.2
Reg.1, amended: SI 2012/1909 Sch.8 para.6
Reg.4, amended: SI 2012/1909 Sch.8 para.6
Reg.4, applied: SI 2012/1909 Reg.28

2034. Fixed-term Employees (Prevention of Less Favourable Treatment) Regulations 2002
Reg.8, see *Hudson v Department for Work and Pensions* [2012] I.R.L.R. 900 (EAT), Recorder Luba Q.C.
Reg.9, see *Hudson v Department for Work and Pensions* [2012] I.R.L.R. 900 (EAT), Recorder Luba Q.C.
Reg.18, see *Hudson v Department for Work and Pensions* [2012] I.R.L.R. 900 (EAT), Recorder Luba Q.C.
Reg.19, see *Hudson v Department for Work and Pensions* [2012] I.R.L.R. 900 (EAT), Recorder Luba Q.C.
Reg.20, see *Hudson v Department for Work and Pensions* [2012] I.R.L.R. 900 (EAT), Recorder Luba Q.C.

2002– cont.

2034. Fixed-term Employees (Prevention of Less Favourable Treatment) Regulations 2002– *cont.*
Reg.20, amended: SI 2012/3112 Art.3

2073. East Lancashire Hospitals National Health Service Trust (Establishment) and the Blackburn, Hyndburn and Ribble Valley Health Care National Health Service Trust and Burnley Health Care National Health Service Trust (Dissolution) Order 2002
referred to: SI 2012/1512 Sch.1

2086. Education (Teacher Student Loans) (Repayment etc.) Regulations 2002
revoked: SI 2012/555 Reg.2
Reg.4, amended: SI 2012/979 Sch.1 para.12
Reg.11, applied: SI 2012/2886 Sch.1

2101. A477 Trunk Road (Milton Village, Pembrokeshire) (40 mph Speed Limit) Order 2002
disapplied: SI 2012/3034 Art.6

2102. Environmental Protection (Restriction on Use of Lead Shot) (England) (Amendment) Regulations 2002
revoked: SI 2012/1923 Sch.1

2173. Tax Credits (Payments by the Commissioners) Regulations 2002
Reg.11, amended: SI 2012/848 Reg.6

2375. National Health Service (Functions of Strategic Health Authorities and Primary Care Trusts and Administration Arrangements) (England) Regulations 2002
Reg.3, applied: SI 2012/2996 Sch.1 para.6, Sch.1 para.7
Sch.5, substituted: SI 2012/417 Reg.2

2406. Controlled Foreign Companies (Excluded Countries) (Amendment No 2) Regulations 2002
revoked: 2012 c.14 Sch.20 para.14

2469. National Health Service Reform and Health Care Professions Act 2002 (Supplementary, Consequential etc Provisions) Regulations 2002
Sch.1 Part 2 para.58, revoked: SI 2012/1909 Sch.8 para.1
Sch.12 Part 2 para.6, revoked: SI 2012/1909 Sch.8 para.1
Sch.12 Part 2 para.7, revoked: SI 2012/1909 Sch.8 para.1
Sch.12 Part 2 para.8, revoked: SI 2012/1909 Sch.8 para.1
Sch.12 Part 2 para.9, revoked: SI 2012/1909 Sch.8 para.1
Sch.12 Part 2 para.10, revoked: SI 2012/1909 Sch.8 para.1
Sch.12 Part 2 para.11, revoked: SI 2012/1909 Sch.8 para.1
Sch.12 Part 2 para.12, revoked: SI 2012/1909 Sch.8 para.1
Sch.12 Part 2 para.13, revoked: SI 2012/1909 Sch.8 para.1
Sch.12 Part 2 para.14, revoked: SI 2012/1909 Sch.8 para.1
Sch.12 Part 2 para.15, revoked: SI 2012/1909 Sch.8 para.1
Sch.12 Part 2 para.16, revoked: SI 2012/1909 Sch.8 para.1
Sch.12 Part 2 para.17, revoked: SI 2012/1909 Sch.8 para.1
Sch.12 Part 2 para.18, revoked: SI 2012/1909 Sch.8 para.1

2002– cont.

2469. National Health Service Reform and Health Care Professions Act 2002 (Supplementary, Consequential etc Provisions) Regulations 2002– *cont.*
Sch.12 Part 2 para.19, revoked: SI 2012/1909 Sch.8 para.1
Sch.12 Part 2 para.20, revoked: SI 2012/1909 Sch.8 para.1
Sch.12 Part 2 para.21, revoked: SI 2012/1909 Sch.8 para.1
Sch.12 Part 2 para.22, revoked: SI 2012/1909 Sch.8 para.1
Sch.12 Part 2 para.23, revoked: SI 2012/1909 Sch.8 para.1
Sch.12 Part 2 para.24, revoked: SI 2012/1909 Sch.8 para.1
Sch.12 Part 2 para.25, revoked: SI 2012/1909 Sch.8 para.1
Sch.12 Part 2 para.26, revoked: SI 2012/1909 Sch.8 para.1
Sch.12 Part 2 para.27, revoked: SI 2012/1909 Sch.8 para.1
Sch.12 Part 2 para.28, revoked: SI 2012/1909 Sch.8 para.1
Sch.12 Part 2 para.29, revoked: SI 2012/1909 Sch.8 para.1

2585. A470 Trunk Road (Llanrwst, Gwynedd) (De-Restriction) Order 1995 (Variation) Order 2002
revoked: SI 2012/339 Art.4

2627. Overseas Territories (Zimbabwe) (Restrictive Measures) (Amendment) Order 2002
revoked: SI 2012/2753 Sch.7

2628. Somalia (United Nations Sanctions) Order 2002
Sch.1, amended: SI 2012/362 Sch.1

2629. Somalia (United Nations Sanctions) (Channel Islands) Order 2002
Sch.1, amended: SI 2012/362 Sch.1

2630. Somalia (United Nations Sanctions) (Isle of Man) Order 2002
Sch.1, amended: SI 2012/362 Sch.1

2631. Somalia (United Nations Sanctions) (Overseas Territories) Order 2002
revoked: SI 2012/3065 Art.1
Sch.1, amended: SI 2012/362 Sch.1

2665. Electricity Safety, Quality and Continuity Regulations 2002
Reg.1, amended: SI 2012/2400 Art.35
Reg.4, amended: SI 2012/2400 Art.35

2675. Control of Asbestos at Work Regulations 2002
Reg.25, applied: SI 2012/632 Reg.32
Reg.27, referred to: SI 2012/632 Reg.33

2676. Control of Lead at Work Regulations 2002
applied: SI 2012/1652 Reg.7

2677. Control of Substances Hazardous to Health Regulations 2002
applied: SI 2012/1652 Sch.5
Reg.5, amended: SI 2012/632 Sch.3
Sch.3 Part I para.3, referred to: SI 2012/1652 Reg.24

2742. Road Vehicles (Registration and Licensing) Regulations 2002
Sch.2 para.1, amended: SI 2012/443 Reg.3
Sch.2 para.3A, substituted: SI 2012/443 Reg.4
Sch.2 para.4C, added: SI 2012/443 Reg.5
Sch.2 para.4D, added: SI 2012/443 Reg.5
Sch.2 para.5, amended: SI 2012/443 Reg.6
Sch.2 para.7, amended: SI 2012/443 Reg.7

2002– cont.

2742. Road Vehicles (Registration and Licensing) Regulations 2002– *cont.*
Sch.2 para.13, amended: SI 2012/304 Reg.3

2779. Scottish Parliament (Elections etc.) Order 2002
varied: 2012 c.11 s.3

2786. Air Navigation (Dangerous Goods) Regulations 2002
Reg.3, amended: SI 2012/3054 Reg.2

2787. Special Educational Needs Tribunal (Amendment) Regulations 2002
revoked (in part): SI 2012/322 Reg.4

2818. Statutory Paternity Pay and Statutory Adoption Pay (Weekly Rates) Regulations 2002
Reg.2, amended: SI 2012/780 Art.11
Reg.3, amended: SI 2012/780 Art.11

2840. European Communities (Designation) (No.4) Order 2002
referred to: SI 2012/916 Sch.1
revoked: SI 2012/1759 Sch.1

2899. Education (Admissions Appeals Arrangements) (England) Regulations 2002
revoked: SI 2012/9 Reg.4

2978. School Companies Regulations 2002
Reg.5, amended: SI 2012/979 Sch.1 para.13
Sch.1 para.1, amended: SI 2012/2404 Sch.3 para.24

2998. Magistrates Courts (Detention and Forfeiture of Cash) Rules 2002
r.9, amended: SI 2012/1275 r.2

3041. Tobacco Products (Manufacture, Presentation and Sale) (Safety) Regulations 2002
see *Imperial Tobacco Ltd, Petitioner* [2012] CSIH 9, 2012 S.C. 297 (IH (1 Div)), Lord President Hamilton

3045. Sale and Supply of Goods to Consumers Regulations 2002
applied: SI 2012/1128 Art.4

3048. Local Authority (Overview and Scrutiny Committees Health Scrutiny Functions) Regulations 2002
Reg.1, amended: SI 2012/1641 Sch.4 para.8
Reg.4A, amended. SI 2012/1641 Sch.4 para.8

3113. Traffic Signs Regulations and General Directions 2002
applied: SSI 2012/12 Art.3, Art.4, Art.5, SSI 2012/13 Art.3, Art.4, Art.5, SSI 2012/14 Art.3, Art.4, Art.5, SSI 2012/15 Art.3, Art.4, Art.5, SSI 2012/17 Art.2, SSI 2012/18 Art.2, SSI 2012/47 Art.2, Art.3, Art.4, Art.5, SSI 2012/58 Art.3, Art.4, Art.5, SSI 2012/59 Art.3, Art.4, Art.5, SSI 2012/277 Art.3, Art.4, Art.5, SSI 2012/278 Art.3, Art.4, Art.5, SSI 2012/279 Art.3, Art.4, Art.5, SSI 2012/280 Art.3, Art.4, Art.5
referred to: SSI 2012/56 Art.3, Art.4, Art.5, SSI 2012/57 Art.3, Art.4, Art.5, SSI 2012/207 Art.2, SSI 2012/230 Art.2
Part I, applied: SSI 2012/203 Art.3, Art.4, Art.5, SSI 2012/204 Art.3, Art.4, Art.5, SSI 2012/268 Art.3
Part I, referred to: SSI 2012/98 Art.3, Art.4, Art.5, SSI 2012/120, SSI 2012/120 Art.3, Art.4, Art.5, SSI 2012/121 Art.3, Art.4, Art.5, SSI 2012/122 Art.3, Art.4, Art.5, SSI 2012/123 Art.3, Art.4, Art.5, SSI 2012/156 Art.3, Art.4, Art.5, SSI 2012/157 Art.3, Art.4, Art.5, SSI 2012/158 Art.3, Art.4, Art.5, SSI 2012/159 Art.3, Art.4, Art.5, SSI 2012/168 Art.2, SSI 2012/185 Art.2
Part II, referred to: SSI 2012/254 Art.4, Art.5, SSI 2012/255 Art.4, Art.5, SSI 2012/256 Art.4, Art.5

2002– cont.

3113. Traffic Signs Regulations and General Directions 2002– *cont.*
Part II, referred to: SSI 2012/234 Art.3, SSI 2012/235 Art.3, Art.5, SSI 2012/251 Art.2, SSI 2012/254 Art.3, SSI 2012/255 Art.3, Art.5, SSI 2012/256 Art.3, Art.5, SSI 2012/257 Art.3, Art.5
Pt I, see *R. (on the application of Herron) v Parking Adjudicator* [2011] EWCA Civ 905, [2012] P.T.S.R. 1257 (CA (Civ Div)), Stanley Burnton, L.J.
Reg.7, referred to: SSI 2012/248 Art.2
Reg.002, applied: SSI 2012/97 Art.4, Art.5, SSI 2012/134 Art.4, Art.6, SSI 2012/222 Art.2, SSI 2012/224 Art.4, Art.5, SSI 2012/225 Art.4, Art.5, SSI 2012/226 Art.4, Art.5, SSI 2012/227 Art.4, Art.5, SSI 2012/298 Art.3, Art.4, Art.5
Reg.002, referred to: SSI 2012/103 Art.2, SSI 2012/186 Art.2, SSI 2012/234 Art.4, Art.5, SSI 2012/235 Art.4, Art.5, SSI 2012/244 Art.2, SSI 2012/257 Art.4, Art.5, SSI 2012/309 Art.4, Art.5, SSI 2012/310 Art.4, Art.5, SSI 2012/311 Art.4, Art.5, SSI 2012/312 Art.4, Art.5, SSI 2012/313 Art.2, SSI 2012/314 Art.4, Art.6
Reg.006, applied: SI 2012/2145
Reg.023, applied: SSI 2012/97 Art.3, Art.5, SSI 2012/134 Art.2, SSI 2012/223 Art.2, SSI 2012/224 Art.3, Art.5, SSI 2012/225 Art.3, Art.5, SSI 2012/226 Art.3, Art.5, SSI 2012/227 Art.3, Art.5, SSI 2012/298 Art.2, Art.5, SSI 2012/299 Art.2
Reg.023, referred to: SSI 2012/195 Art.2, SSI 2012/309 Art.3, Art.5, SSI 2012/310 Art.3, Art.5, SSI 2012/311 Art.3, Art.5, SSI 2012/312 Art.3, Art.5, SSI 2012/314 Art.2, Art.6, SSI 2012/317 Art.2
Reg.024, applied: SSI 2012/97 Art.3, SSI 2012/134 Art.2, SSI 2012/223 Art.2, SSI 2012/224 Art.3, SSI 2012/225 Art.3, SSI 2012/226 Art.3, SSI 2012/227 Art.3, SSI 2012/299 Art.2
Reg.024, referred to: SSI 2012/195 Art.2, SSI 2012/309 Art.3, SSI 2012/310 Art.3, SSI 2012/311 Art.3, SSI 2012/312 Art.3, SSI 2012/314 Art.2, SSI 2012/317 Art.2
Reg.025, applied: SSI 2012/134 Art.2, Art.3
Reg.025, referred to: SSI 2012/314 Art.3
Reg.027, referred to: SSI 2012/234 Art.5
Reg.040, varied: 2012 c.11 s.12

3133. Proceeds of Crime Act 2002 (Enforcement in different parts of the United Kingdom) Order 2002
Art.6, applied: SI 2012/1726 r.57.4, r.57.5, r.57.6

3138. Double Taxation Relief (Taxes on Income) (South Africa) Order 2002
see *Revenue and Customs Commissioners v Ben Nevis (Holdings) Ltd* [2012] EWHC 1807 (Ch), [2012] S.T.C. 2157 (Ch D), Judge Pelling Q.C.

3150. Company Directors Disqualification (Northern Ireland) Order 2002
applied: SI 2012/922 Reg.3, SI 2012/1034 Sch.4 para.11, SI 2012/1290 Reg.3, SI 2012/1631 Sch.5 para.8, SI 2012/1640 Sch.2 para.5, SI 2012/2996 Sch.5 para.8

3153. Environment (Northern Ireland) Order 2002
Sch.1 Part I para.9A, revoked: SI 2012/2788 Reg.10
Sch.1 Part I para.9B, amended: SI 2012/2788 Reg.10
Sch.1 Part II para.24, amended: SI 2012/2788 Reg.11
Sch.1 Part II para.24A, amended: SI 2012/2788 Reg.11
Sch.1 Part II para.26, amended: SI 2012/2788 Reg.12

2002– cont.

3169. Kava-kava in Food (England) Regulations 2002
Reg.2, amended: SI 2012/ 1809 Sch.1 Part 2

3170. Medicines for Human Use (Kava-kava) (Prohibition) Order 2002
Art.1, amended: SI 2012/ 1809 Sch.1 Part 2
Art.3, amended: SI 2012/ 1916 Sch.34 para.77

3177. School Companies (Private Finance Initiative Companies) Regulations 2002
Reg.5, amended: SI 2012/979 Sch.1 para.14
Sch.1 para.1, amended: SI 2012/ 2404 Sch.3 para.25

3178. Education (Pupil Exclusions and Appeals) (Maintained Schools) (England) Regulations 2002
revoked: SI 2012/ 1033 Sch.3

3213. Residential Family Centres Regulations 2002
Reg.5, amended: SI 2012/ 2404 Sch.3 para.26

3214. Domiciliary Care Agencies Regulations 2002
applied: SI 2012/ 3144 Sch.1 para.19

2003

82. Proceeds of Crime Act 2002 (Appeals under Part 2) Order 2003
applied: SI 2012/ 1726 r.71.5, r.71.8
referred to: SI 2012/ 1726 r.71.1
Art.6, applied: SI 2012/ 1726 r.72.1, r.71.2
Art.7, applied: SI 2012/ 1726 r.71.2, r.71.3
Art.8, referred to: SI 2012/ 1726 r.71.6, r.71.7
Art.12, applied: SI 2012/ 1726 r.71.10
Art.15, referred to: SI 2012/ 1726 r.71.10

235. National Endowment for Science, Technology and the Arts (Increase of Endowment) Order 2003
revoked: SI 2012/964 Sch.1

237. Fostering Services (Wales) Regulations 2003
applied: SI 2012/ 2885 Sch.1 para.25, SI 2012/ 2886 Sch.1, SI 2012/ 3144 Sch.1 para.19, SI 2012/ 3145 Sch.1, SSI 2012/ 303 Reg.28, SSI 2012/ 319 Reg.29
Reg.5, amended: SI 2012/ 2404 Sch.3 para.27

289. Hill Farm Allowance Regulations 2003
revoked: SI 2012/ 114 Reg.9

333. Proceeds of Crime Act 2002 (Commencement No 5, Transitional Provisions, Savings and Amendment) Order 2003
see *Peacock, Re* [2012] UKSC 5, [2012] 1 W.L.R. 550 (SC), Lord Hope (Deputy President)
Art.3, see *Peacock, Re* [2012] UKSC 5, [2012] 1 W.L.R. 550 (SC), Lord Hope (Deputy President)
Art.10, see *Peacock, Re* [2012] UKSC 5, [2012] 1 W.L.R. 550 (SC), Lord Hope (Deputy President)

373. Consistent Financial Reporting (England) Regulations 2003
revoked: SI 2012/674 Reg.6

419. Energy (Northern Ireland) Order 2003
applied: SI 2012/ 1128 Art.4

431. Health and Personal Social Services (Quality, Improvement and Regulation) (Northern Ireland) Order 2003
applied: SI 2012/ 1631 Sch.5 para.6, SI 2012/ 2996 Sch.5 para.5

435. Access to Justice (Northern Ireland) Order 2003
applied: 2012 c.10 Sch.6 para.1

489. Whole of Government Accounts (Designation of Bodies) Order 2003
varied: SI 2012/ 147 Art.7

492. Child Benefit and Guardian's Allowance (Administration) Regulations 2003
Reg.42A, added: SI 2012/ 1074 Reg.3

2003– cont.

518. Immigration Appeals (Family Visitor) Regulations 2003
referred to: SI 2012/ 1531 Art.3
Reg.2, see *Ajakaiye (Visitor Appeals: Right of Appeal: Nigeria), Re* [2012] Imm. A.R. 25 (UT (IAC)), Blake, J. (President)

523. Education (Governors Allowances) (England) Regulations 2003
Reg.5, amended: SI 2012/979 Sch.1 para.15

527. Police Regulations 2003
Reg.3, amended: SI 2012/ 192 Reg.3, SI 2012/ 680 Reg.2
Reg.5, amended: SI 2012/ 2712 Reg.3
Reg.7, substituted: SI 2012/ 1960 Reg.3
Reg.8, substituted: SI 2012/ 1960 Reg.3
Reg.9, substituted: SI 2012/ 1960 Reg.3
Reg.10, amended: SI 2012/ 680 Reg.2
Reg.10A, added: SI 2012/ 1960 Reg.4
Reg.11, amended: SI 2012/ 2712 Reg.4
Reg.14A, added: SI 2012/ 3058 Reg.2
Reg.18, amended: SI 2012/ 1960 Reg.5
Reg.19, amended: SI 2012/ 680 Reg.2, SI 2012/ 1960 Reg.6
Reg.19A, amended: SI 2012/ 680 Reg.2
Reg.24, amended: SI 2012/ 192 Reg.4
Reg.26, amended: SI 2012/ 2712 Reg.5
Reg.33, applied: SI 2012/ 2631 Reg.11, SI 2012/ 2632 Reg.3
Reg.41A, amended: SI 2012/ 192 Reg.5
Reg.44A, added: SI 2012/ 192 Reg.6
Sch.3 para.1, amended: SI 2012/ 192 Reg.7
Sch.3 para.7, amended: SI 2012/ 2712 Reg.6
Sch.3 para.9, added: SI 2012/ 192 Reg.7

548. British Nationality (General) Regulations 2003
Reg.4, amended: SI 2012/ 1588 Reg.2
Reg.9, amended: SI 2012/ 1588 Reg.2

628. National Assistance (Sums for Personal Requirements) (England) Regulations 2003
Reg.2, amended: SI 2012/ 663 Reg.2

653. Tax Credits (Immigration) Regulations 2003
Reg.3, amended: SI 2012/ 848 Reg.7

654. Tax Credits (Residence) Regulations 2003
Reg.3, amended: SI 2012/ 848 Reg.8, SI 2012/ 2612 Reg.6

658. Immigration (Notices) Regulations 2003
see *R. (on the application of E (Russia)) v Secretary of State for the Home Department* [2012] EWCA Civ 357, [2012] 1 W.L.R. 3198 (CA (Civ Div)), Pill, L.J.
Reg.2, amended: SI 2012/ 1547 Sch.2 para.2

681. Pensions Increase (Review) Order 2003
applied: SI 2012/ 782 Art.3, Art.4

697. Medicines (Pharmacy and General Sale-Exemption) Amendment Order 2003
revoked: SI 2012/ 1916 Sch.35

714. Financial Assistance for Environmental Purposes (England) Order 2003
varied: SI 2012/ 147 Art.7

742. Tax Credits (Polygamous Marriages) Regulations 2003
Reg.29, substituted: SI 2012/ 848 Reg.9

777. Air Navigation (Amendment) Order 2003
applied: 2012 c.19 Sch.6 para.4

781. Residential Family Centres (Wales) Regulations 2003
Reg.5, amended: SI 2012/ 2404 Sch.3 para.28

2003– cont.

931. National Assistance (Residential Accommodation)(Additional Payments, Relevant Contributions and Assessment of Resources)(Wales) Regulations 2003
Reg.2, amended: SI 2012/842 Reg.5
Reg.4, amended: SI 2012/842 Reg.5
Reg.5, revoked (in part): SI 2012/842 Reg.5

985. General Teaching Council for England (Deduction of Fees) (Amendment) Regulations 2003
revoked: SI 2012/1153 Sch.1

1021. Local Authorities (Members Allowances) (England) Regulations 2003
Reg.34, amended: SI 2012/1033 Sch.2 para.2

1034. Special Immigration Appeals Commission (Procedure) Rules 2003
r.8, see *R. (on the application of MK (Tunisia)) v Secretary of State for the Home Department* [2011] EWCA Civ 333, [2012] 1 W.L.R. 700 (CA (Civ Div)), Pill, L.J.
r.39, see *W (Algeria) v Secretary of State for the Home Department* [2012] UKSC 8, [2012] 2 A.C. 115 (SC), Lord Phillips (President)

1038. Education (National Curriculum) (Key Stage 2 Assessment Arrangements) (England) Order 2003
Art.4, amended: SI 2012/838 Art.3
Art.4, revoked (in part): SI 2012/838 Art.3
Art.5, amended: SI 2012/838 Art.4
Art.6, amended: SI 2012/838 Art.5
Art.7, amended: SI 2012/838 Art.5
Art.10, revoked: SI 2012/765 Art.4

1039. Education (National Curriculum) (Key Stage 3 Assessment Arrangements) (England) Order 2003
referred to: SI 2012/1926 Reg.2
Art.11, revoked: SI 2012/765 Art.5

1056. Stamp Duty (Disadvantaged Areas) (Application of Exemptions) Regulations 2003
revoked: 2012 c.14 Sch.39 para.7

1075. Network Rail (West Coast Main Line) Order 2003
Art.18, amended: SI 2012/1659 Art.2
Art.19, amended: SI 2012/1659 Art.2
Art.20, amended: SI 2012/1659 Art.2
Sch.13 Part V para.41, amended: SI 2012/1659 Art.2
Sch.13 Part V para.42, amended: SI 2012/1659 Art.2
Sch.13 Part V para.43, amended: SI 2012/1659 Art.2
Sch.13 Part V para.44, amended: SI 2012/1659 Art.2
Sch.13 Part V para.45, amended: SI 2012/1659 Art.2
Sch.13 Part V para.46, amended: SI 2012/1659 Art.2
Sch.13 Part V para.47, amended: SI 2012/1659 Art.2
Sch.13 Part V para.48, amended: SI 2012/1659 Art.2
Sch.13 Part V para.49, amended: SI 2012/1659 Art.2
Sch.13 Part V para.50, amended: SI 2012/1659 Art.2
Sch.13 Part V para.51, amended: SI 2012/1659 Art.2
Sch.13 Part V para.52, amended: SI 2012/1659 Art.2
Sch.13 Part V para.53, amended: SI 2012/1659 Art.2
Sch.13 Part V para.54, amended: SI 2012/1659 Art.2

1076. Medicines and Healthcare Products Regulatory Agency Trading Fund Order 2003
Art.1, amended: SI 2012/1916 Sch.34 para.78

1185. Immigration (Passenger Transit Visa) Order 2003
Sch.1, amended: SI 2012/116 Art.2, SI 2012/771 Art.2

1186. General Teaching Council for England (Disciplinary Functions) (Amendment) Regulations 2003
revoked: SI 2012/1153 Sch.1

2003– cont.

1252. Immigration and Asylum Act 1999 (Jersey) Order 2003
Sch.1, amended: SI 2012/2593 Art.4

1326. Government Resources and Accounts Act 2000 (Audit of Public Bodies) Order 2003
Art.3, amended: SI 2012/854 Art.6
Sch.1, amended: SI 2012/854 Art.6

1370. Enterprise Act 2002 (Merger Fees and Determination of Turnover) Order 2003
Art.5, amended: SI 2012/1878 Art.2
Sch.1 para.1, amended: SI 2012/1809 Sch.1 Part 2

1372. Competition Appeal Tribunal Rules 2003
see *British Telecommunications Plc v Office of Communications* [2011] EWCA Civ 245, [2012] Bus. L.R. 113 (CA (Civ Div)), Sir Andrew Morritt (Chancellor)
Part V r.60, amended: SI 2012/1809 Sch.1 Part 2
r.19, see *2 Travel Group Plc (In Liquidation) v Cardiff City Transport Services Ltd* [2012] CAT 4, [2012] Comp. A.R. 179 (CAT), Lord Carlile of Berriew Q.C.; see *Ryanair Holdings Plc v Office of Fair Trading* [2011] EWCA Civ 1579, [2012] Bus. L.R. 1903 (CA (Civ Div)), Lloyd, L.J.
r.31, see *BCL Old Co Ltd v BASF SE (formerly BASF AG)* [2012] UKSC 45, [2012] 1 W.L.R. 2922 (SC), Lord Phillips, J.S.C.
r.40, see *Deutsche Bahn AG v Morgan Crucible Co Plc* [2012] EWCA Civ 1055, [2012] U.K.C.L.R. 279 (CA (Civ Div)), Mummery, L.J.
r.45, see *2 Travel Group Plc (In Liquidation) v Cardiff City Transport Services Ltd* [2012] Comp. A.R. 1 (CAT), Lord Carlile of Berriew Q.C.
r.50, see *2 Travel Group Plc (In Liquidation) v Cardiff City Transport Services Ltd* [2012] CAT 7, [2012] Comp. A.R. 184 (CAT), Lord Carlile of Berriew Q.C.
r.55, see *Barrett Estate Services Ltd v Office of Fair Trading* [2012] Comp. A.R. 14 (CAT), Lord Carlile of Berriew Q.C.; see *GF Tomlinson Group Ltd v Office of Fair Trading (Costs)* [2012] Comp. A.R. 47 (CAT), Vivien Rose (Chairman); see *Kier Group Plc v Office of Fair Trading* [2012] Comp. A.R. 94 (CAT), Barling, J. (President); see *North Midland Construction Plc v Office of Fair Trading (Costs)* [2012] Comp. A.R. 106 (CAT), Barling, J. (President); see *Quarmby Construction Co Ltd v Office of Fair Trading* [2012] Comp. A.R. 113 (CAT), Lord Carlile of Berriew Q.C.
r.61, see *Ryanair Holdings Plc v Office of Fair Trading* [2011] EWCA Civ 1579, [2012] Bus. L.R. 1903 (CA (Civ Div)), Lloyd, L.J.

1374. Enterprise Act 2002 (Part 8 Community Infringements Specified UK Laws) Order 2003
Sch.1, amended: SI 2012/1916 Sch.34 para.79

1376. Enterprise Act 2002 (Part 8 Notice to OFT of Intended Prosecution Specified Enactments, Revocation and Transitional Provision) Order 2003
Sch.1, amended: SI 2012/1916 Sch.34 para.80

1377. School Governance (Procedures) (England) Regulations 2003
Reg.3, varied: SI 2012/1035 Sch.6 para.1
Reg.5, amended: SI 2012/1035 Sch.6 para.3
Reg.5, varied: SI 2012/1035 Sch.6 para.2
Reg.6, amended: SI 2012/1035 Sch.6 para.3, Sch.6 para.4

2003– cont.

1377. School Governance (Procedures) (England) Regulations 2003– *cont.*
Reg.8, amended: SI 2012/ 1035 Sch.6 para.3, Sch.6 para.5, Sch.6 para.6
Reg.10, amended: SI 2012/ 1035 Sch.6 para.7
Reg.11, see *R. (on the application of Kilroy) v Parrs Wood High School Governing Body* [2011] EWHC 3489 (Admin), [2012] E.L.R. 146 (QBD (Admin)), Judge Pelling Q.C.
Reg.11, amended: SI 2012/ 1035 Sch.6 para.3, Sch.6 para.4, Sch.6 para.5
Reg.11, applied: SI 2012/ 1035 Reg.7, Reg.30
Reg.12, amended: SI 2012/ 1035 Sch.6 para.4
Reg.12A, amended: SI 2012/ 1035 Sch.6 para.3
Reg.13, amended: SI 2012/ 1035 Sch.6 para.3, Sch.6 para.4
Reg.14, amended: SI 2012/ 1035 Sch.6 para.3, Sch.6 para.5
Reg.15, see *R. (on the application of Kilroy) v Parrs Wood High School Governing Body* [2011] EWHC 3489 (Admin), [2012] E.L.R. 146 (QBD (Admin)), Judge Pelling Q.C.
Reg.15, amended: SI 2012/ 1035 Sch.6 para.3, Sch.6 para.8
Reg.16, amended: SI 2012/ 1035 Sch.6 para.5
Reg.17, amended: SI 2012/ 1033 Sch.2 para.3, SI 2012/ 1035 Sch.6 para.4
Reg.18, amended: SI 2012/ 1035 Sch.6 para.5
Reg.19, amended: SI 2012/ 1035 Sch.6 para.9
Reg.21, amended: SI 2012/ 1035 Sch.6 para.5, Sch.6 para.7
Reg.23, amended: SI 2012/ 1035 Sch.6 para.7
Reg.24, amended: SI 2012/ 1035 Sch.6 para.3, Sch.6 para.4, Sch.6 para.5
Sch.1 para.1, amended: SI 2012/ 1035 Sch.6 para.3
Sch.1 para.3, amended: SI 2012/ 1035 Sch.6 para.3, Sch.6 para.5

1417. Land Registration Rules 2003
Part 4 r.21, applied: SI 2012/ 2421 Reg.19
Part 4 r.27A, added: SI 2012/ 2421 Sch.4 para.2
Part 6 r.54, applied: SI 2012/ 1969 Sch.3 Part 1
Part 8 r.93, amended: SI 2012/ 2421 Sch.4 para.3
Part 8 r.94, amended: SI 2012/ 2421 Sch.4 para.4
Part 9 r.108, applied: SI 2012/ 1969 Sch.3 Part 1
Part 9 r.109, applied: SI 2012/ 1969 Sch.3 Part 1
Part 10 r.118, applied: SI 2012/ 1969 Sch.3 Part 1
Part 15 r.204, applied: SI 2012/ 1969 Sch.3 Part 4
Part 15 r.217, amended: SI 2012/ 2421 Sch.4 para.5
Sch.4, added: SI 2012/ 2421 Sch.4 para.6
Sch.4, applied: SI 2012/ 1969 Sch.3 Part 1, Sch.4

1434. Income Tax (Exemption of Minor Benefits) (Amendment) Regulations 2003
Reg.3, revoked: SI 2012/ 1808 Reg.3

1516. Iraq (United Nations Sanctions) (Overseas Territories) Order 2003
Art.3, revoked: SI 2012/ 2748 Sch.6
Art.4, amended: SI 2012/ 2748 Sch.7
Art.9, revoked: SI 2012/ 2748 Sch.6
Art.10, revoked: SI 2012/ 2748 Sch.6
Sch.1, amended: SI 2012/ 362 Sch.1
Sch.3 para.1, revoked: SI 2012/ 2748 Sch.6
Sch.3 para.2, revoked: SI 2012/ 2748 Sch.6
Sch.3 para.3, revoked: SI 2012/ 2748 Sch.6
Sch.3 para.4, revoked: SI 2012/ 2748 Sch.6
Sch.3 para.5, revoked: SI 2012/ 2748 Sch.6
Sch.3 para.6, revoked: SI 2012/ 2748 Sch.6
Sch.3 para.7, revoked: SI 2012/ 2748 Sch.6
Sch.3 para.8, revoked: SI 2012/ 2748 Sch.6

2003– cont.

1519. Iraq (United Nations Sanctions) Order 2003
see *R. v D* [2011] EWCA Crim 2082, [2012] 1 All E.R. 1108 (CA (Crim Div)), Thomas, L.J.
Art.3, revoked: SI 2012/ 1489 Sch.2
Art.4, amended: SI 2012/ 1489 Sch.2
Art.5, see *R. v D* [2011] EWCA Crim 2082, [2012] 1 All E.R. 1108 (CA (Crim Div)), Thomas, L.J.
Art.9, revoked: SI 2012/ 1489 Sch.2
Art.10, revoked: SI 2012/ 1489 Sch.2
Sch.1 para.1, revoked: SI 2012/ 1489 Sch.2
Sch.1 para.2, revoked: SI 2012/ 1489 Sch.2
Sch.1 para.3, revoked: SI 2012/ 1489 Sch.2
Sch.1 para.4, revoked: SI 2012/ 1489 Sch.2
Sch.1 para.5, revoked: SI 2012/ 1489 Sch.2
Sch.1 para.6, revoked: SI 2012/ 1489 Sch.2
Sch.1 para.7, revoked: SI 2012/ 1489 Sch.2
Sch.1 para.8, revoked: SI 2012/ 1489 Sch.2
Sch.2, amended: SI 2012/ 362 Sch.1

1521. Iraq (United Nations Sanctions) (Channel Islands) Order 2003
Sch.2, amended: SI 2012/ 362 Sch.1

1522. Iraq (United Nations Sanctions) (Isle of Man) Order 2003
Sch.2, amended: SI 2012/ 362 Sch.1

1545. Regulatory Reform (British Waterways Board) Order 2003
revoked: SI 2012/ 1659 Art.7

1561. A487 Trunk Road (Rhydypennau, Ceredigion) (Restricted Road and 40 MPH Speed Limit) Order 2003
varied: SI 2012/ 1398 Art.8

1571. Health Professions (Parts of and Entries in the Register) Order of Council 2003
Art.1, amended: SI 2012/ 1479 Art.3
Art.6, amended: SI 2012/ 1916 Sch.34 para.81
Art.7, applied: SI 2012/ 1480 Art.4
Art.7, referred to: SI 2012/ 1480 Art.4
Sch.1, amended: SI 2012/ 1479 Art.3

1572. Health Professions Council (Registration and Fees) Rules Order of Council 2003
Sch.1, added: SI 2012/ 1479 Art.4
Sch.1, amended: SI 2012/ 1479 Art.4

1573. Health Professions Council (Screeners) Rules Order of Council 2003
Sch.1, amended: SI 2012/ 1479 Art.5

1574. Health Professions Council (Investigating Committee) Procedure Rules Order of Council 2003
Sch.1, amended: SI 2012/ 1479 Art.6

1575. Health Professions Council (Conduct and Competence Committee) (Procedure) Rules Order of Council 2003
Sch.1, amended: SI 2012/ 1479 Art.7

1576. Health Professions Council (Health Committee) (Procedure) Rules Order of Council 2003
Sch.1, amended: SI 2012/ 1479 Art.8

1577. Health Professions Council (Functions of Assessors) Rules Order of Council 2003
Sch.1, amended: SI 2012/ 1479 Sch.1 para.29

1578. Health and Social Work Professions Order 2001 (Legal Assessors) Order of Council 2003
amended: SI 2012/ 1479 Sch.1 para.30
Art.1, amended: SI 2012/ 1479 Sch.1 para.30

1579. Health Professions Council (Registration Appeals) Rules Order of Council 2003
Sch.1, amended: SI 2012/ 1479 Art.9

2003– cont.

1618. Medicines for Human Use (Marketing Author-isations Etc.) Amendment Regulations 2003
revoked: SI 2012/1916 Sch.35

1626. Race Relations Act 1976 (Amendment) Regulations 2003
Reg.51, varied: 2012 c.11 s.12

1660. Employment Equality (Religion or Belief) Regulations 2003
applied: SSI 2012/181 Reg.3
Reg.3, see *Pasab Ltd (t/a Jhoots Pharmacy) v Woods* [2012] Eq. L.R. 392 (EAT), Judge Peter Clark; see *Unison v Kelly* [2012] I.R.L.R. 442 (EAT), Supperstone, J.
Reg.5, see *Unison v Kelly* [2012] I.R.L.R. 442 (EAT), Supperstone, J.

1661. Employment Equality (Sexual Orientation) Regulations 2003
applied: SSI 2012/181 Reg.3
Reg.6, see *Bivonas LLP v Bennett* [2012] Eq. L.R. 216 (EAT), Judge Birtles
Reg.29, see *Bivonas LLP v Bennett* [2012] Eq. L.R. 216 (EAT), Judge Birtles

1662. Education (School Teachers Qualifications) (England) Regulations 2003
Reg.3, amended: SI 2012/431 Reg.3
Reg.5, applied: SI 2012/1115 Sch.1 para.19, Sch.1 para.22, Sch.1 para.23
Reg.5, substituted: SI 2012/431 Reg.4
Reg.10, revoked: SI 2012/431 Reg.5
Reg.11, substituted: SI 2012/431 Reg.6
Sch.1 Part 2 para.4A, added: SI 2012/431 Reg.7
Sch.2 Part 1 para.1, amended: SI 2012/431 Reg.8
Sch.2 Part 1 para.7, amended: SI 2012/1736 Reg.2
Sch.2 Part 1 para.9, amended: SI 2012/431 Reg.8
Sch.2 Part 1 para.9, applied: SI 2012/762 Sch.1 para.4
Sch.2 Part 1 para.10, amended: SI 2012/431 Reg.8, SI 2012/1736 Reg.2
Sch.2 Part 1 para.10, applied: SI 2012/762 Sch.1 para.4
Sch.2 Part 1 para.10, revoked (in part): SI 2012/431 Reg.8
Sch.2 Part 1 para.11, amended: SI 2012/431 Reg.8
Sch.2 Part 1 para.13, applied: SI 2012/1115 Sch.1 para.17, Sch.1 para.19
Sch.2 Part 1 para.13A, added: SI 2012/431 Reg.8
Sch.2 Part 1 para.13A, applied: SI 2012/1115 Sch.1 para.22
Sch.2 Part 1 para.13B, added: SI 2012/431 Reg.8
Sch.2 Part 1 para.13B, applied: SI 2012/115 Reg.6, SI 2012/1115 Sch.1 para.23

1663. Education (Specified Work and Registration) (England) Regulations 2003
revoked: SI 2012/762 Reg.6
Sch.2 para.4, applied: SI 2012/724 Sch.2 para.9
Sch.2 para.10, applied: SI 2012/9 Sch.1 para.4

1673. Disability Discrimination Act 1995 (Amendment) Regulations 2003
Reg.5, varied: 2012 c.11 s.12

1680. Unlicensed Medicinal Products for Human Use (Transmissible Spongiform Encephalopathies) (Safety) Regulations 2003
Reg.1, amended: SI 2012/1916 Sch.34 para.82
Reg.1, revoked (in part): SI 2012/1916 Sch.34 para.82

1690. Road Vehicles (Construction and Use) (Amendment) (No.2) Regulations 2003
Reg.6, revoked: SI 2012/1404 Sch.1

2003– cont.

1709. Education (School Teachers Prescribed Qualifications, etc) Order 2003
Art.3, amended: SI 2012/694 Art.3
Art.7, amended: SI 2012/694 Art.4, Art.5

1712. Immigration (Leave to Remain) (Prescribed Forms and Procedures) Regulations 2003
Reg.11, see *Kishver (Limited Leave: Meaning: Pakistan), Re* [2012] Imm. A.R. 128 (UT (IAC)), CMG Ockelton
Reg.12, see *Kishver (Limited Leave: Meaning: Pakistan), Re* [2012] Imm. A.R. 128 (UT (IAC)), CMG Ockelton

1724. Transport of Animals (Cleansing and Disinfection) (England) (No.3) Order 2003
Art.10, amended: SI 2012/2897 Art.4

1729. Disease Control (England) Order 2003
Art.18, substituted: SI 2012/2897 Art.5
Art.22, amended: SI 2012/2897 Art.5

1741. Civil Aviation (Air Travel Organisers Licensing)(Amendment) Regulations 2003
revoked: SI 2012/1017 Sch.1

1887. Secretary of State for Constitutional Affairs Order 2003
Sch.2 para.12, amended: 2012 c.9 Sch.10 Part 8

1888. European Communities (Designation) (No.3) Order 2003
referred to: SI 2012/916 Sch.1

1907. Greater London Authority Elections (Election Addresses) Order 2003
Art.9, amended: SI 2012/666 Sch.2

1917. Education (Teacher Student Loans) (Repayment etc.) Regulations 2003
Reg.2, amended: SI 2012/956 Art.9
Reg.4, amended: SI 2012/956 Art.9, SI 2012/979 Sch.1 para.16
Reg.5, amended: SI 2012/956 Art.9
Reg.10, amended: SI 2012/555 Reg.3
Reg.11, applied: SSI 2012/303 Sch.4 para.16

1937. National Health Service Reform and Health Care Professions Act 2002 (Supplementary, Consequential etc Provisions) Regulations 2003
Sch.1 Part 2 para.3, revoked (in part): SI 2012/1909 Sch.8 para.1
Sch.1 Part 2 para.4, revoked (in part): SI 2012/1909 Sch.8 para.1

1982. A487 Trunk Road (Aberarth, Ceredigion) (30mph and 40 mph Speed limits) Order 2003
disapplied: SI 2012/1270 Art.8

1987. Service Charges (Consultation Requirements) (England) Regulations 2003
Reg.3, amended: SI 2012/961 Sch.1 para.7

1994. Education (Mandatory Awards) Regulations 2003
Sch.2 Part 2 para.7, applied: SI 2012/2886 Sch.1
Sch.2 Part 2 para.7, referred to: SI 2012/3145 Sch.1, SSI 2012/303 Reg.55
Sch.2 Part 2 para.9, applied: SI 2012/2886 Sch.1, SI 2012/3145 Sch.1, SSI 2012/303 Reg.20
Sch.2 Part 3, applied: SI 2012/2886 Sch.1, SI 2012/3145 Sch.1, SSI 2012/303 Reg.54

2039. Education Act 2002 (School Teachers) (Consequential Amendments, etc) (England) Regulations 2003
Reg.3, revoked: SI 2012/1153 Sch.1

2072. A487 Trunk Road (Sarnau, Ceredigion) (40 MPH Speed Limit) Order 2003
varied: SI 2012/1522 Art.8

2003– cont.

2075. Meat Products (England) Regulations 2003
Reg.3, amended: SI 2012/1809 Sch.1 Part 2

2076. Capital Allowances (Environmentally Beneficial Plant and Machinery) Order 2003
Art.2, amended: SI 2012/1838 Art.3, SI 2012/2602 Art.3

2085. Social Security (Contributions) (Amendment No 5) Regulations 2003
Reg.6, revoked (in part): SI 2012/817 Reg.10

2097. Insolvency Act 1986 (Prescribed Part) Order 2003
applied: SI 2012/3013 Sch.1 para.2

2099. Leasehold Valuation Tribunals (Procedure) (England) Regulations 2003
see *Havering LBC v MacDonald* [2012] UKUT 154 (LC), [2012] 36 E.G. 100 (UT (Lands)), Judge Walden-Smith
Reg.18, see *Clarise Properties Ltd, Re* [2012] UKUT 4 (LC), [2012] L. & T.R. 20 (UT (Lands)), George Bartlett Q.C. (President, LTr)

2171. Adjudicator to Her Majesty's Land Registry (Practice and Procedure) Rules 2003
see *Silkstone v Tatnall* [2011] EWCA Civ 801, [2012] 1 W.L.R. 400 (CA (Civ Div)), Mummery, L.J.

2314. Religious Character of Schools (Designation Procedure) (Independent Schools) (England) Regulations 2003
referred to: SI 2012/967, SI 2012/2265

2317. Medicines (Child Safety) Regulations 2003
revoked: SI 2012/1916 Sch.35
Reg.1, amended: SI 2012/1479 Sch.1 para.31

2382. National Health Service (Travel Expenses and Remission of Charges) Regulations 2003
Reg.5, applied: SI 2012/1909 Sch.4 para.7, Sch.5 para.6, Sch.6 para.4, SI 2012/2886 Sch.1, SSI 2012/303 Sch.4 para.45, Sch.5 para.43
Reg.5, referred to: SI 2012/1909 Sch.5 para.6
Reg.6, applied: SI 2012/2886 Sch.1, SSI 2012/303 Sch.4 para.45, Sch.5 para.43
Reg.12, applied: SI 2012/2886 Sch.1, SSI 2012/303 Sch.4 para.45, Sch.5 para.43
Sch.1, amended: SI 2012/1650 Reg.2

2461. Registered Health Care Profession (Designation) Order 2003
Art.2, amended: SI 2012/1479 Sch.1 para.32

2462. Registered Health Care Profession (Designation No 2) Order 2003
Art.2, amended: SI 2012/1479 Sch.1 para.33

2512. Environmental Protection (Restriction on Use of Lead Shot) (England) (Amendment) Regulations 2003
revoked: SI 2012/1923 Sch.1

2527. Nurses Agencies (Wales) Regulations 2003
Reg.7, amended: SI 2012/2404 Sch.3 para.29

2563. Pipelines Safety (Amendment) Regulations 2003
applied: SI 2012/1294 Sch.1
referred to: SI 2012/1282 Sch.1, SI 2012/1284 Sch.1, SI 2012/1286 Sch.1, SI 2012/1289 Sch.1

2577. Olive Oil (Marketing Standards) Regulations 2003
Reg.3, amended: SI 2012/2897 Art.6

2603. Freedom of Information Act 2000 (Commencement No 3) Order 2003
varied: SI 2012/147 Art.7

2613. Council Tax and Non-Domestic Rating (Demand Notices) (England) Regulations 2003
Reg.1, amended: SI 2012/2914 Reg.12

2003– cont.

2613. Council Tax and Non-Domestic Rating (Demand Notices) (England) Regulations 2003– cont.
Reg.1, varied: SI 2012/994 Reg.4
Reg.3, amended: SI 2012/538 Reg.3
Sch.2 Part 1 para.7, amended: SI 2012/538 Reg.4
Sch.2 Part 3 para.3, amended: SI 2012/538 Reg.5

2614. Democratic Republic of the Congo (United Nations Sanctions) (Isle of Man) Order 2003
Sch.1, amended: SI 2012/362 Sch.1

2616. Democratic Republic of the Congo (United Nations Sanctions) (Channel Islands) Order 2003
Sch.1, amended: SI 2012/362 Sch.1

2627. Democratic Republic of the Congo (Restrictive Measures) (Overseas Territories) Order 2003
Art.2, amended: SI 2012/2750 Art.3
Art.3, amended: SI 2012/2750 Art.4
Art.4, amended: SI 2012/2750 Art.5
Art.5, amended: SI 2012/2750 Art.6
Art.5A, added: SI 2012/2750 Art.7
Art.5B, added: SI 2012/2750 Art.7
Art.6, amended: SI 2012/2750 Art.8
Art.9, amended: SI 2012/2750 Art.9
Art.15, amended: SI 2012/2750 Art.10
Sch.1, amended: SI 2012/362 Sch.1
Sch.2 para.4, amended: SI 2012/2750 Art.11

2682. Income Tax (Pay As You Earn) Regulations 2003
referred to: SI 2012/822 Reg.57
Part 4, amended: SI 2012/822 Reg.27
Part 10, amended: SI 2012/822 Reg.48
Part 10, added: SI 2012/822 Reg.49
Reg.2, amended: SI 2012/822 Reg.3, Reg.60
Reg.2A, added: SI 2012/822 Reg.4
Reg.2B, added: SI 2012/822 Reg.4
Reg.11, amended: SI 2012/822 Reg.5
Reg.18, see *Prince v Revenue and Customs Commissioners* [2012] UKFTT 157 (TC), [2012] S.F.T.D. 786 (FTT (Tax)), Judge Colin Bishopp
Reg.19, see *Prince v Revenue and Customs Commissioners* [2012] UKFTT 157 (TC), [2012] S.F.T.D. 786 (FTT (Tax)), Judge Colin Bishopp
Reg.34, amended: SI 2012/822 Reg.64
Reg.36, amended: SI 2012/822 Reg.6
Reg.37, amended: SI 2012/822 Reg.65
Reg.37, revoked (in part): SI 2012/822 Reg.65
Reg.38, amended: SI 2012/822 Reg.7
Reg.39, amended: SI 2012/822 Reg.8
Reg.40, amended: SI 2012/822 Reg.9
Reg.40A, added: SI 2012/822 Reg.10
Reg.42, amended: SI 2012/822 Reg.11
Reg.45A, added: SI 2012/822 Reg.12
Reg.46, amended: SI 2012/822 Reg.13, Reg.66
Reg.46, revoked (in part): SI 2012/822 Reg.61
Reg.47, amended: SI 2012/822 Reg.67
Reg.47, revoked (in part): SI 2012/822 Reg.62
Reg.48, revoked (in part): SI 2012/822 Reg.62
Reg.49A, added: SI 2012/822 Reg.14
Reg.49B, added: SI 2012/822 Reg.14
Reg.49C, added: SI 2012/822 Reg.14
Reg.49D, added: SI 2012/822 Reg.14
Reg.49E, added: SI 2012/822 Reg.14
Reg.50, amended: SI 2012/822 Reg.16
Reg.50, substituted: SI 2012/822 Reg.15
Reg.50A, amended: SI 2012/822 Reg.17

2003– cont.

2682. Income Tax (Pay As You Earn) Regulations 2003– *cont.*
Reg.51, amended: SI 2012/822 Reg.18
Reg.52, amended: SI 2012/822 Reg.19
Reg.53, amended: SI 2012/822 Reg.21
Reg.53, substituted: SI 2012/822 Reg.20
Reg.54B, amended: SI 2012/822 Reg.24
Reg.54B, substituted: SI 2012/822 Reg.23
Reg.54ZA, added: SI 2012/822 Reg.22
Reg.58, substituted: SI 2012/822 Reg.25
Reg.59, amended: SI 2012/822 Reg.26
Reg.67B, applied: SI 2012/822 Reg.54, Reg.55, Reg.56
Reg.67CA, added: SI 2012/1895 Reg.2
Reg.67D, applied: SI 2012/822 Reg.54, Reg.55, Reg.56
Reg.68, amended: SI 2012/822 Reg.29
Reg.68, substituted: SI 2012/822 Reg.28
Reg.69, amended: SI 2012/822 Reg.30
Reg.70, amended: SI 2012/822 Reg.31, Reg.63
Reg.71, amended: SI 2012/822 Reg.32, Reg.33
Reg.72H, added: SI 2012/822 Reg.34
Reg.73, applied: SI 2012/1836 Reg.12
Reg.75A, added: SI 2012/822 Reg.35
Reg.75B, added: SI 2012/822 Reg.35
Reg.77, amended: SI 2012/822 Reg.36
Reg.78, amended: SI 2012/822 Reg.37
Reg.80, amended: SI 2012/822 Reg.38
Reg.81, applied: 2012 c.14 Sch.36 para.11
Reg.82, amended: SI 2012/822 Reg.39
Reg.84, amended: SI 2012/822 Reg.40
Reg.97, amended: SI 2012/822 Reg.41
Reg.97B, amended: SI 2012/822 Reg.42
Reg.97D, amended: SI 2012/822 Reg.43
Reg.97M, added: SI 2012/822 Reg.58
Reg.97N, added: SI 2012/822 Reg.58
Reg.97O, added: SI 2012/822 Reg.58
Reg.97P, added: SI 2012/822 Reg.58
Reg.97Q, added: SI 2012/822 Reg.58
Reg.97R, added: SI 2012/822 Reg.58
Reg.97T, added: SI 2012/822 Reg.58
Reg.97U, added: SI 2012/822 Reg.58
Reg.97V, added: SI 2012/822 Reg.58
Reg.97W, added: SI 2012/822 Reg.58
Reg.97X, added: SI 2012/822 Reg.58
Reg.104, amended: SI 2012/822 Reg.44
Reg.107, amended: SI 2012/822 Reg.45
Reg.198A, amended: SI 2012/822 Reg.46
Reg.199, amended: SI 2012/822 Reg.47
Reg.211, amended: SI 2012/822 Reg.68
Reg.213, amended: SI 2012/822 Reg.59
Reg.218, amended: SI 2012/822 Reg.50
Reg.219, amended: SI 2012/822 Reg.51
s.Art.4A Reg.97S, added: SI 2012/822 Reg.58
Sch.A1 para.1, added: SI 2012/822 Sch.1
Sch.A1 para.2, added: SI 2012/822 Sch.1
Sch.A1 para.2, referred to: SI 2012/822 Reg.53, Reg.54
Sch.A1 para.3, added: SI 2012/822 Sch.1
Sch.A1 para.3, referred to: SI 2012/822 Reg.53, Reg.54
Sch.A1 para.4, added: SI 2012/822 Sch.1
Sch.A1 para.4, referred to: SI 2012/822 Reg.53, Reg.54
Sch.A1 para.5, added: SI 2012/822 Sch.1
Sch.A1 para.6, added: SI 2012/822 Sch.1
Sch.A1 para.7, added: SI 2012/822 Sch.1
Sch.A1 para.8, added: SI 2012/822 Sch.1

2003– cont.

2682. Income Tax (Pay As You Earn) Regulations 2003– *cont.*
Sch.A1 para.8, referred to: SI 2012/822 Reg.54
Sch.A1 para.9, added: SI 2012/822 Sch.1
Sch.A1 para.9, referred to: SI 2012/822 Reg.54
Sch.A1 para.10, added: SI 2012/822 Sch.1
Sch.A1 para.10, referred to: SI 2012/822 Reg.54
Sch.A1 para.11, added: SI 2012/822 Sch.1
Sch.A1 para.11, referred to: SI 2012/822 Reg.54
Sch.A1 para.12, added: SI 2012/822 Sch.1
Sch.A1 para.12, referred to: SI 2012/822 Reg.54
Sch.A1 para.13, added: SI 2012/822 Sch.1
Sch.A1 para.13, referred to: SI 2012/822 Reg.54
Sch.A1 para.14, added: SI 2012/822 Sch.1
Sch.A1 para.15, added: SI 2012/822 Sch.1
Sch.A1 para.15, referred to: SI 2012/822 Reg.54
Sch.A1 para.16, added: SI 2012/822 Sch.1
Sch.A1 para.16, referred to: SI 2012/822 Reg.54
Sch.A1 para.17, added: SI 2012/822 Sch.1
Sch.A1 para.17, referred to: SI 2012/822 Reg.54
Sch.A1 para.18, added: SI 2012/822 Sch.1
Sch.A1 para.19, added: SI 2012/822 Sch.1
Sch.A1 para.20, added: SI 2012/822 Sch.1
Sch.A1 para.21, added: SI 2012/822 Sch.1
Sch.A1 para.22, added: SI 2012/822 Sch.1
Sch.A1 para.23, added: SI 2012/822 Sch.1
Sch.A1 para.24, added: SI 2012/822 Sch.1
Sch.A1 para.25, added: SI 2012/822 Sch.1
Sch.A1 para.26, added: SI 2012/822 Sch.1
Sch.A1 para.27, added: SI 2012/822 Sch.1
Sch.A1 para.28, added: SI 2012/822 Sch.1
Sch.A1 para.29, added: SI 2012/822 Sch.1
Sch.A1 para.30, added: SI 2012/822 Sch.1
Sch.A1 para.31, added: SI 2012/822 Sch.1
Sch.A1 para.32, added: SI 2012/822 Sch.1
Sch.A1 para.33, added: SI 2012/822 Sch.1
Sch.A1 para.34, added: SI 2012/822 Sch.1
Sch.A1 para.35, added: SI 2012/822 Sch.1
Sch.A1 para.36, added: SI 2012/822 Sch.1
Sch.A1 para.37, added: SI 2012/822 Sch.1
Sch.A1 para.38, added: SI 2012/822 Sch.1
Sch.A1 para.39, added: SI 2012/822 Sch.1
Sch.A1 para.40, added: SI 2012/822 Sch.1
Sch.A1 para.41, added: SI 2012/822 Sch.1
Sch.A1 para.42, added: SI 2012/822 Sch.1
Sch.A1 para.43, added: SI 2012/822 Sch.1
Sch.A1 para.44, added: SI 2012/822 Sch.1
Sch.A1 para.45, added: SI 2012/822 Sch.1
Sch.A1 para.45, referred to: SI 2012/822 Reg.54
Sch.A1 para.46, added: SI 2012/822 Sch.1

2753. Lincolnshire (Coroners&apos Districts) Order 2003
revoked: SI 2012/574 Art.5

2764. Export of Goods, Transfer of Technology and Provision of Technical Assistance (Control) Order 2003
Art.3, see *R. v D* [2011] EWCA Crim 2082, [2012] 1 All E.R. 1108 (CA (Crim Div)), Thomas, L.J.

2765. Trade in Goods (Control) Order 2003
Art.3, see *R. v D* [2011] EWCA Crim 2082, [2012] 1 All E.R. 1108 (CA (Crim Div)), Thomas, L.J.

2818. Nationality, Immigration and Asylum Act 2002 (Juxtaposed Controls) Order 2003
Sch.2 para.5, amended: SI 2012/1547 Sch.2 para.3

2905. Air Navigation (Amendment) (No.2) Order 2003
applied: 2012 c.19 Sch.6 para.4

2003– cont.

3011. Council Tax (Prescribed Classes of Dwellings) (England) Regulations 2003
Reg.2, substituted: SI 2012/2964 Reg.2
Reg.3, amended: SI 2012/2964 Reg.2
Reg.8, added: SI 2012/2964 Reg.2
Reg.9, added: SI 2012/2964 Reg.2
Reg.10, added: SI 2012/2964 Reg.2

3012. Local Authorities (Calculation of Council Tax Base) (Amendment) (England) Regulations 2003
revoked: SI 2012/2914 Sch.1

3100. Registration of Establishments (Laying Hens) (England) Regulations 2003
Reg.10, substituted: SI 2012/2897 Art.7

3111. Education (Head Teachers&apos Qualifications) (England) Regulations 2003
revoked: SI 2012/18 Sch.1

3120. Jam and Similar Products (England) Regulations 2003
Reg.2, amended: SI 2012/1809 Sch.1 Part 2

3146. Local Authorities (Capital Finance and Accounting) (England) Regulations 2003
Reg.1, amended: SI 2012/265 Reg.3, SI 2012/711 Reg.4, SI 2012/1324 Reg.3
Reg.2A, added: SI 2012/265 Reg.4
Reg.3, amended: SI 2012/265 Reg.4
Reg.6, substituted: SI 2012/265 Reg.4
Reg.7, amended: SI 2012/265 Reg.5
Reg.7A, substituted: SI 2012/265 Reg.5
Reg.9A, revoked: SI 2012/711 Reg.5
Reg.9B, added: SI 2012/265 Reg.6
Reg.10, amended: SI 2012/711 Reg.6
Reg.10, revoked (in part): SI 2012/711 Reg.6
Reg.12, substituted: SI 2012/711 Reg.7
Reg.13, substituted: SI 2012/711 Reg.7
Reg.14, revoked (in part): SI 2012/2269 Reg.3
Reg.14, substituted: SI 2012/711 Reg.7
Reg.15, amended: SI 2012/2269 Reg.4
Reg.15, applied: SI 2012/711 Reg.3
Reg.15, substituted: SI 2012/711 Reg.7
Reg.16, substituted: SI 2012/711 Reg.7
Reg.16A, applied: SI 2012/711 Reg.3
Reg.16A, substituted: SI 2012/711 Reg.7
Reg.16B, substituted: SI 2012/711 Reg.7
Reg.17, substituted: SI 2012/711 Reg.7
Reg.18, substituted: SI 2012/711 Reg.7
Reg.19, applied: SI 2012/711 Reg.3
Reg.19, substituted: SI 2012/711 Reg.7
Reg.20, substituted: SI 2012/711 Reg.7
Reg.20A, substituted: SI 2012/711 Reg.7
Reg.21, substituted: SI 2012/711 Reg.7
Reg.23, amended: SI 2012/2269 Reg.5
Reg.23, revoked (in part): SI 2012/711 Reg.8
Reg.25, amended: SI 2012/265 Reg.7
Reg.25, revoked (in part): SI 2012/265 Reg.7
Reg.31, amended: SI 2012/265 Reg.8
Sch.1, amended: SI 2012/711 Sch.1, SI 2012/1324 Sch.1, SI 2012/2269 Reg.6
Sch.1 para.1, amended: SI 2012/711 Sch.1
Sch.1 para.2, amended: SI 2012/711 Sch.1
Sch.1 para.3, amended: SI 2012/711 Sch.1, SI 2012/2269 Reg.6
Sch.1 para.3, amended: SI 2012/711 Sch.1
Sch.1 para.4, amended: SI 2012/711 Sch.1, SI 2012/2269 Reg.6
Sch.1 para.4, amended: SI 2012/711 Sch.1
Sch.1 para.5, amended: SI 2012/711 Sch.1
Sch.1 para.6, amended: SI 2012/711 Sch.1

2003– cont.

3146. Local Authorities (Capital Finance and Accounting) (England) Regulations 2003– cont.
Sch.1 para.6, substituted: SI 2012/2269 Reg.6
Sch.1 para.6, amended: SI 2012/711 Sch.1
Sch.1 para.7, amended: SI 2012/711 Sch.1
Sch.1 para.8, amended: SI 2012/711 Sch.1
Sch.1 para.9, amended: SI 2012/711 Sch.1
Sch.1 para.10, amended: SI 2012/711 Sch.1
Sch.1 para.11, amended: SI 2012/711 Sch.1
Sch.1 para.12, amended: SI 2012/711 Sch.1

3181. Local Authorities (Calculation of Council Tax Base) (Amendment) (England) (No.2) Regulations 2003
revoked: SI 2012/2914 Sch.1

3195. Communications (Bailiwick of Guernsey) Order 2003
Sch.2 para.50, substituted: SI 2012/2688 Art.2
Sch.2 para.87, substituted: SI 2012/2688 Art.3

3230. Independent Schools (Provision of Information) (Wales) Regulations 2003
Sch.1 Part 2 para.3, amended: SI 2012/3006 Art.80, Art.82
Sch.1 Part 3 para.7, amended: SI 2012/3006 Art.81, Art.83
Sch.1 Part 4 para.10, amended: SI 2012/3006 Art.81, Art.83

3231. Education (School Day and School Year) (Wales) Regulations 2003
Reg.5, amended: SI 2012/248 Reg.3

3297. Reporting of Savings Income Information Regulations 2003
Reg.10, amended: SI 2012/756 Reg.2
Reg.12, amended: SI 2012/756 Reg.2
Reg.15, amended: SI 2012/756 Reg.2

3328. Designation of Schools Having a Religious Character (Independent Schools) (England) (No.3) Order 2003
Sch.1, amended: SI 2012/3174 Sch.2

2004

1. Medicines (Pharmacy and General Sale Exemption) Amendment Order 2004
revoked: SI 2012/1916 Sch.35

12. Scallop Fishing Order 2004
revoked (in part): SI 2012/2283 Art.6

118. Crime and Disorder Strategies (Prescribed Descriptions) (England) Order 2004
Art.2, amended: SI 2012/979 Sch.1 para.17

145. Hill Farm Allowance Regulations 2004
revoked: SI 2012/114 Reg.9

219. Domiciliary Care Agencies (Wales) Regulations 2004
applied: SI 2012/3145 Sch.1, SSI 2012/303 Reg.28, SSI 2012/319 Reg.29
Reg.8, amended: SI 2012/2404 Sch.3 para.30

291. National Health Service (General Medical Services Contracts) Regulations 2004
applied: SI 2012/1909 Sch.7 para.10
Reg.2, amended: SI 2012/970 Reg.2, SI 2012/1479 Sch.1 para.35, SI 2012/1909 Sch.8 para.7, SI 2012/1916 Sch.34 para.85
Reg.5, amended: SI 2012/2404 Sch.3 para.31
Reg.18, amended: SI 2012/970 Reg.3
Reg.18, revoked (in part): SI 2012/970 Reg.3
Reg.26A, added: SI 2012/970 Reg.4
Sch.2 para.4, substituted: SI 2012/970 Reg.5
Sch.2 para.5, amended: SI 2012/970 Reg.5

2004–cont.

291. National Health Service (General Medical Services Contracts) Regulations 2004–cont.

Sch.5 para.l, amended: SI 2012/1909 Sch.8 para.7
Sch.6 Part 2 para.17, amended: SI 2012/970 Reg.6
Sch.6 Part 2 para.29, revoked: SI 2012/970 Reg.6
Sch.6 Part 2 para.29A, added: SI 2012/970 Reg.6
Sch.6 Part 2 para.29B, added: SI 2012/970 Reg.6
Sch.6 Part 2 para.29C, added: SI 2012/970 Reg.6
Sch.6 Part 2 para.29D, added: SI 2012/970 Reg.6
Sch.6 Part 2 para.29E, added: SI 2012/970 Reg.6
Sch.6 Part 2 para.30, revoked: SI 2012/970 Reg.6
Sch.6 Part 2 para.31, revoked: SI 2012/970 Reg.6
Sch.6 Part 2 para.35, amended: SI 2012/970 Reg.6
Sch.6 Part 3, applied: SI 2012/1909 Sch.7 para.10
Sch.6 Part 3 para.39, applied: SI 2012/1909 Sch.6 para.3
Sch.6 Part 3 para.39A, applied: SI 2012/1909 Sch.6 para.3
Sch.6 Part 3 para.40, amended: SI 2012/1909 Sch.8 para.7
Sch.6 Part 3 para.40, revoked (in part): SI 2012/1909 Sch.8 para.7
Sch.6 Part 3 para.42, applied: SI 2012/1909 Sch.6 para.3
Sch.6 Part 3 para.43, amended: SI 2012/1916 Sch.34 para.85
Sch.6 Part 3 para.47, revoked: SI 2012/1909 Sch.8 para.7
Sch.6 Part 3 para.48, revoked: SI 2012/1909 Sch.8 para.7
Sch.6 Part 3 para.48A, revoked: SI 2012/1909 Sch.8 para.7
Sch.6 Part 3 para.48B, applied: SI 2012/1909 Sch.7 para.10
Sch.6 Part 3 para.48B, revoked: SI 2012/1909 Sch.8 para.7
Sch.6 Part 3 para.48C, revoked: SI 2012/1909 Sch.8 para.7
Sch.6 Part 3 para.48D, revoked: SI 2012/1909 Sch.8 para.7
Sch.6 Part 3 para.48E, revoked: SI 2012/1909 Sch.8 para.7
Sch.6 Part 3 para.49, revoked: SI 2012/1909 Sch.8 para.7
Sch.6 Part 3 para.49A, revoked: SI 2012/1909 Sch.8 para.7
Sch.6 Part 3 para.50, revoked: SI 2012/1909 Sch.8 para.7
Sch.6 Part 3 para.51, applied: SI 2012/1909 Sch.7 para.10
Sch.6 Part 3 para.51, revoked: SI 2012/1909 Sch.8 para.7
Sch.6 Part 5 para.73, amended: SI 2012/970 Reg.6
Sch.6 Part 5 para.76A, added: SI 2012/970 Reg.6
Sch.6 Part 5 para.80, amended: SI 2012/1479 Sch.1 para.35
Sch.6 Part 8 para.113, amended: SI 2012/2404 Sch.3 para.31
Sch.8, revoked: SI 2012/970 Reg.7
Sch.10 para.7, substituted: SI 2012/970 Reg.8

293. European Parliamentary Elections Regulations 2004

applied: SI 2012/2031 Sch.4 para.8
Reg.2, varied: SI 2012/444 Sch.4 para.1, SI 2012/2031 Sch.4 para.10
Reg.11, varied: SI 2012/444 Sch.4 para.1, SI 2012/2031 Sch.4 para.11
Sch.1 Part 3 para.23, varied: SI 2012/444 Sch.4 para.1, SI 2012/2031 Sch.4 para.12

293. European Parliamentary Elections Regulations 2004–cont.

Sch.2 Part 1 para.3, applied: SI 2012/1917 Sch.2 para.3, Sch.2 para.4, Sch.2 para.8, Sch.2 para.13, Sch.2 para.17
Sch.2 Part 1 para.4, applied: SI 2012/1917 Sch.2 para.8
Sch.2 Part 1 para.6, applied: SI 2012/1917 Sch.2 para.4
Sch.2 Part 1 para.7, applied: SI 2012/1917 Sch.2 para.7, Sch.2 para.8, Sch.2 para.13, Sch.2 para.17
Sch.2 Part 2 para.17, varied: SI 2012/444 Sch.4 para.1, SI 2012/2031 Sch.4 para.13
Sch.2 Part 2 para.23, amended: SI 2012/1479 Sch.1 para.36
Sch.2 Part 4, varied: SI 2012/444 Sch.4 para.1
Sch.2 Part 4 para.40, amended: SI 2012/1917 Sch.4 para.2
Sch.2 Part 4 para.40, varied: SI 2012/444 Sch.4 para.1, SI 2012/2031 Sch.4 para.13
Sch.2 Part 4 para.41, varied: SI 2012/2031 Sch.4 para.13
Sch.3 Part 1 para.2, amended: SI 2012/1917 Sch.4 para.2
Sch.3 Part 1 para.2, varied: SI 2012/444 Sch.4 para.1, SI 2012/2031 Sch.4 para 14

294. Representation of the People (Combination of Polls) (England and Wales) Regulations 2004

Reg.2, amended: SI 2012/1917 Sch.4 para.4
Reg.2, varied: SI 2012/444 Sch.4 para.1, SI 2012/2031 Sch.4 para.2
Reg.4, amended: SI 2012/1917 Sch.4 para.5
Reg.4, varied: SI 2012/444 Sch.4 para.1, SI 2012/2031 Sch.4 para.3
Reg.5, amended: SI 2012/1917 Sch.4 para.6
Reg.5, applied: SI 2012/2031 Sch.5
Reg.5, referred to: SI 2012/1918 Sch.4
Reg.5, varied: SI 2012/444 Sch.4 para.1, SI 2012/2031 Sch.4 para.4
Reg.6, amended: SI 2012/1917 Sch.4 para.7
Reg.6, varied: SI 2012/444 Sch.4 para.1, SI 2012/2031 Sch.4 para.5
Reg.8, amended: SI 2012/1917 Sch.4 para.8
Reg.8, varied: SI 2012/444 Sch.4 para.1, SI 2012/2031 Sch.4 para.6
Sch.2 para.2, amended: SI 2012/1917 Sch.4 para.9
Sch.2 para.2, varied: SI 2012/444 Sch.4 para.1, SI 2012/2031 Sch.4 para.7
Sch.2 para.3, varied: SI 2012/444 Sch.4 para.1, SI 2012/2031 Sch.4 para.7
Sch.2 para.22, varied: SI 2012/444 Sch.4 para.1, SI 2012/2031 Sch.4 para.7

302. Merchant Shipping (High Speed Craft) Regulations 2004

Reg.2, amended: SI 2012/2636 Reg.4
Reg.3, amended: SI 2012/2636 Reg.4
Reg.3, revoked (in part): SI 2012/2636 Reg.4
Reg.7A, amended: SI 2012/2636 Reg.4
Reg.10, amended: SI 2012/2636 Reg.4
Reg.13, added: SI 2012/2636 Reg.4

305. Liberia (United Nations Sanctions) (Isle of Man) Order 2004

Sch.1, amended: SI 2012/362 Sch.1

306. Liberia (United Nations Sanctions)(Channel Islands) Order 2004

Sch.1, amended: SI 2012/362 Sch.1

347. Liberia (Restrictive Measures) (Overseas Territories) Order 2004

Art.2, amended: SI 2012/2749 Art.2

347. **Liberia (Restrictive Measures) (Overseas Territories) Order 2004**–*cont.*
Art.3, amended: SI 2012/2749 Art.3
Art.4, amended: SI 2012/2749 Art.4
Art.5, amended: SI 2012/2749 Art.5
Art.5A, added: SI 2012/2749 Art.6
Art.5B, added: SI 2012/2749 Art.6
Art.8, amended: SI 2012/2749 Art.7
Art.11, amended: SI 2012/2749 Art.8
Art.17, amended: SI 2012/2749 Art.9
Sch.1, amended: SI 2012/362 Sch.1
Sch.2 para.4, amended: SI 2012/2749 Art.10

348. **Liberia (United Nations Sanctions) Order 2004**
Sch.1, amended: SI 2012/362 Sch.1

349. **Sudan (Restrictive Measures) (Overseas Territories) Order 2004**
revoked: SI 2012/361 Art.1
Sch.1, amended: SI 2012/362 Sch.1

352. **Petroleum Licensing (Exploration and Production) (Seaward and Landward Areas) Regulations 2004**
Sch.1 para.23, varied: 2012 c.11 s.12
Sch.2 para.41, varied: 2012 c.11 s.12
Sch.3 para.42, varied: 2012 c.11 s.12
Sch.4 para.40, varied: 2012 c.11 s.12

389. **Network Rail (West Coast Main Line) Order 2004**
Art.18, amended: SI 2012/1659 Art.2
Sch.13 Part V para.41, amended: SI 2012/1659 Art.2
Sch.13 Part V para.42, amended: SI 2012/1659 Art.2
Sch.13 Part V para.43, amended: SI 2012/1659 Art.2
Sch.13 Part V para.44, amended: SI 2012/1659 Art.2
Sch.13 Part V para.45, amended: SI 2012/1659 Art.2
Sch.13 Part V para.46, amended: SI 2012/1659 Art.2
Sch.13 Part V para.47, amended: SI 2012/1659 Art.2
Sch.13 Part V para.48, amended: SI 2012/1659 Art.2
Sch.13 Part V para.49, amended: SI 2012/1659 Art.2
Sch.13 Part V para.50, amended: SI 2012/1659 Art.2
Sch.13 Part V para.51, amended: SI 2012/1659 Art.2
Sch.13 Part V para.52, amended: SI 2012/1659 Art.2
Sch.13 Part V para.53, amended: SI 2012/1659 Art.2
Sch.13 Part V para.54, amended: SI 2012/1659 Art.2

393. **Consistent Financial Reporting (England) (Amendment) Regulations 2004**
revoked: SI 2012/674 Reg.6

402. **Education (Pupil Exclusions) (Miscellaneous Amendments) (England) Regulations 2004**
Reg.4, revoked: SI 2012/1033 Sch.3
Reg.6, revoked: SI 2012/1033 Sch.3
Reg.7, revoked: SI 2012/1033 Sch.3
Reg.8, revoked: SI 2012/1033 Sch.3
Reg.9, revoked: SI 2012/1033 Sch.3

478. **National Health Service (General Medical Services Contracts) (Wales) Regulations 2004**
Reg.2, amended: SI 2012/1479 Sch.1 para.37, SI 2012/1916 Sch.34 para.86
Reg.5, amended: SI 2012/2404 Sch.3 para.32
Sch.6 Part 3 para.43, amended: SI 2012/1916 Sch.34 para.86
Sch.6 Part 5 para.78, amended: SI 2012/1479 Sch.1 para.37
Sch.6 Part 8 para.111, amended: SI 2012/2404 Sch.3 para.32

553. **Jam and Similar Products (Wales) Regulations 2004**
Reg.2, amended: SI 2012/1809 Sch.1 Part 4

572. **Street Works (Inspection Fees) (England) (Amendment) Regulations 2004**
applied: SI 2012/2541 Sch.1, SI 2012/2547 Sch.1, SI 2012/2548 Sch.1, SI 2012/2549 Sch.1

577. **Designation of Schools Having a Religious Character (Independent Schools) (England) (No.3) Order 2004**
Sch.1, amended: SI 2012/3174 Sch.2

585. **National Health Service (Performers Lists) Regulations 2004**
Reg.2, amended: SI 2012/476 Sch.1 para.2
Reg.4, amended: SI 2012/476 Sch.1 para.2
Reg.10, referred to: SI 2012/922 Reg.3, SI 2012/1290 Reg.3
Reg.11, amended: SI 2012/476 Sch.1 para.2
Reg.16, amended: SI 2012/476 Sch.1 para.2
Reg.16, varied: 2012 c.11 s.12
Reg.20, amended: SI 2012/476 Sch.1 para.2
Reg.20, varied: 2012 c.11 s.12

593. **Insolvency Proceedings (Fees) Order 2004**
applied: SI 2012/3013 Sch.1 para.2

627. **National Health Service (Personal Medical Services Agreements) Regulations 2004**
applied: SI 2012/1909 Sch.7 para.10
Reg.2, amended: SI 2012/970 Reg.9, SI 2012/1479 Sch.1 para.38, SI 2012/1909 Sch.8 para.8, SI 2012/1916 Sch.34 para.87
Reg.5, amended: SI 2012/2404 Sch.3 para.33
Reg.11, amended: SI 2012/970 Reg.10
Reg.11, revoked (in part): SI 2012/970 Reg.10
Reg.18A, added: SI 2012/970 Reg.11
Sch.3, amended: SI 2012/1909 Sch.8 para.8
Sch.5 Part 2 para.16, amended: SI 2012/970 Reg.12
Sch.5 Part 2 para.28, revoked: SI 2012/970 Reg.12
Sch.5 Part 2 para.28A, added: SI 2012/970 Reg.12
Sch.5 Part 2 para.28B, added: SI 2012/970 Reg.12
Sch.5 Part 2 para.28C, added: SI 2012/970 Reg.12
Sch.5 Part 2 para.28D, added: SI 2012/970 Reg.12
Sch.5 Part 2 para.28E, added: SI 2012/970 Reg.12
Sch.5 Part 2 para.29, revoked: SI 2012/970 Reg.12
Sch.5 Part 2 para.30, revoked: SI 2012/970 Reg.12
Sch.5 Part 2 para.34, amended: SI 2012/970 Reg.12
Sch.5 Part 3, applied: SI 2012/1909 Sch.7 para.10
Sch.5 Part 3 para.39, amended: SI 2012/1909 Sch.8 para.8
Sch.5 Part 3 para.39, revoked (in part): SI 2012/1909 Sch.8 para.8
Sch.5 Part 3 para.42, amended: SI 2012/1916 Sch.34 para.87
Sch.5 Part 3 para.45, revoked: SI 2012/1909 Sch.8 para.8
Sch.5 Part 3 para.46, revoked: SI 2012/1909 Sch.8 para.8
Sch.5 Part 3 para.47, revoked: SI 2012/1909 Sch.8 para.8
Sch.5 Part 3 para.47A, revoked: SI 2012/1909 Sch.8 para.8
Sch.5 Part 3 para.47B, applied: SI 2012/1909 Sch.7 para.10
Sch.5 Part 3 para.47B, revoked: SI 2012/1909 Sch.8 para.8
Sch.5 Part 3 para.47C, revoked: SI 2012/1909 Sch.8 para.8
Sch.5 Part 3 para.47D, revoked: SI 2012/1909 Sch.8 para.8
Sch.5 Part 3 para.47E, revoked: SI 2012/1909 Sch.8 para.8
Sch.5 Part 3 para.48, revoked: SI 2012/1909 Sch.8 para.8

2004–cont.

627. National Health Service (Personal Medical Services Agreements) Regulations 2004–cont.
Sch.5 Part 3 para.48A, revoked: SI 2012/1909 Sch.8 para.8
Sch.5 Part 3 para.49, revoked: SI 2012/1909 Sch.8 para.8
Sch.5 Part 3 para.49A, revoked: SI 2012/1909 Sch.8 para.8
Sch.5 Part 3 para.50, revoked: SI 2012/1909 Sch.8 para.8
Sch.5 Part 3 para.51, applied: SI 2012/1909 Sch.7 para.10
Sch.5 Part 3 para.51, revoked: SI 2012/1909 Sch.8 para.8
Sch.5 Part 5 para.70, amended: SI 2012/970 Reg.12
Sch.5 Part 5 para.72A, added: SI 2012/970 Reg.12
Sch.5 Part 5 para.76, amended: SI 2012/1479 Sch.1 para.38
Sch.5 Part 8 para.105, amended: SI 2012/2404 Sch.3 para.33
Sch.8, revoked: SI 2012/970 Reg.13
Sch.10 para.6, substituted: SI 2012/970 Reg.14

629. National Health Service (General Medical Services Contracts) (Prescription of Drugs etc.) Regulations 2004
Sch.1, applied: SI 2012/3094 Reg.13
Sch.2, applied: SI 2012/1909 Sch.4 para.8
Sch.2, referred to: SI 2012/1909 Sch.4 para.5, Sch.6 para.2, Sch.6 para.3, Sch.6 para.5, SI 2012/3094 Reg.13

643. Police (Complaints and Misconduct) Regulations 2004
revoked: SI 2012/1204 Reg.2
varied: SI 2012/1204 Reg.2
Reg.1, varied: SI 2012/1204 Reg.2
Reg.4, applied: SI 2012/62 Reg.28
Reg.4, varied: SI 2012/62 Reg.28
Reg.7, applied: SI 2012/1204 Reg.3, Reg.7
Reg.15, applied: SI 2012/1204 Reg.3, Reg.7
Reg.15, referred to: SI 2012/1204 Reg.7
Reg.27, varied: SI 2012/62 Reg.37

645. Police (Conduct) Regulations 2004
applied: SI 2012/2632 Reg.19
varied: SI 2012/2632 Reg.2
Reg.3, varied: SI 2012/2632 Sch.1 para.11
Reg.5, varied: SI 2012/2632 Sch.1 para.12
Reg.19, varied: SI 2012/2632 Sch.1 para.13

692. Communications (Television Licensing) Regulations 2004
Sch.4 Part 2 para.7, amended: SI 2012/700 Sch.1 para.13

693. Enterprise Act 2002 (Part 9 Restrictions on Disclosure of Information) (Specification) Order 2004
Sch.1, amended: SI 2012/3032 Reg.47

705. Air Navigation (Amendment) Order 2004
applied: 2012 c.19 Sch.6 para.4

752. Employment Act 2002 (Dispute Resolution) Regulations 2004
Reg.9, see *Aitchison v South Ayrshire Council* 2012 S.C.444 (IH (Ex Div)), Lady Paton; see *Beddoes v Birmingham City Council* [2012] EWCA Civ 585, [2012] Eq. L.R. 695 (CA (Civ Div)), Pill, L.J.
Reg.11, see *Allen v Hounga* [2012] EWCA Civ 609, [2012] I.R.L.R. 685 (CA (Civ Div)), Longmore, L.J.

2004–cont.

756. Civil Aviation (Working Time) Regulations 2004
Reg.4, see *British Airways Plc v Williams* [2012] UKSC 43, [2012] I.C.R. 1375 (SC), Lord Hope, J.S.C. (Deputy President)
Reg.7, see *British Airways Plc v Williams* [2012] UKSC 43, [2012] I.C.R. 1375 (SC), Lord Hope, J.S.C. (Deputy President)

758. Pensions Increase (Review) Order 2004
applied: SI 2012/782 Art.3, Art.4

765. Tobacco Advertising and Promotion (Point of Sale) Regulations 2004
revoked (in part): SI 2012/1285 Reg.9

865. General Medical Services and Personal Medical Services Transitional and Consequential Provisions Order 2004
Art.94, revoked: SI 2012/1909 Sch.8 para.1
Art.95, revoked: SI 2012/1909 Sch.8 para.1
Art.96, revoked: SI 2012/1909 Sch.8 para.1
Art.97, revoked: SI 2012/1909 Sch.8 para.1
Art.98, revoked: SI 2012/1909 Sch.8 para.1
Art.99, revoked: SI 2012/1909 Sch.8 para.1
Art.100, revoked: SI 2012/1909 Sch.8 para.1
Art.101, revoked: SI 2012/1909 Sch.8 para.1
Art.102, revoked: SI 2012/1909 Sch.8 para.1
Art.103, revoked: SI 2012/1909 Sch.8 para.1
Art.104, revoked: SI 2012/1909 Sch.8 para.1
Sch.1 para.10, revoked (in part): SI 2012/1909 Sch.8 para.1

915. Railway Safety Accreditation Scheme Regulations 2004
Reg.4, amended: SI 2012/2732 Reg.2

932. Milton Keynes (Urban Area and Planning Functions) Order 2004
revoked: SI 2012/3099 Art.2

1020. National Health Service (Performers Lists) (Wales) Regulations 2004
Reg.16, varied: 2012 c.11 s.12
Reg.20, varied: 2012 c.11 s.12

1022. National Health Service (General Medical Services Contracts) (Prescription of Drugs Etc.) (Wales) Regulations 2004
Sch.2, amended: SI 2012/1916 Sch.34 para.88

1031. Medicines for Human Use (Clinical Trials) Regulations 2004
applied: SI 2012/504 Sch.2 para.32, SI 2012/1916 Reg.187
Reg.2, amended: SI 2012/1479 Sch.1 para.39, SI 2012/1641 Sch.3 para.8, SI 2012/1916 Sch.34 para.53
Reg.4, amended: SI 2012/1916 Sch.34 para.54
Reg.13, referred to: SI 2012/1916 Reg.46
Reg.17, amended: SI 2012/504 Reg.55
Reg.18, applied: SI 2012/504 Reg.34
Reg.19, amended: SI 2012/1916 Sch.34 para.55
Reg.19, applied: SI 2012/504 Reg.34
Reg.20, applied: SI 2012/504 Reg.34
Reg.24, amended: SI 2012/504 Reg.55
Reg.24, applied: SI 2012/504 Reg.19
Reg.36, applied: SI 2012/1916 Reg.167
Reg.38, amended: SI 2012/504 Reg.55
Reg.44, amended: SI 2012/504 Reg.55
Reg.44, applied: SI 2012/504 Reg.18
Reg.46, amended: SI 2012/1916 Sch.34 para.56
Reg.47, amended: SI 2012/1916 Sch.34 para.57
Reg.48, amended: SI 2012/1916 Sch.34 para.58
Reg.49, amended: SI 2012/1916 Sch.34 para.59
Reg.53, amended: SI 2012/1916 Sch.34 para.60
Sch.2 para.3, amended: SI 2012/1641 Sch.3 para.8

1031. Medicines for Human Use (Clinical Trials) Regulations 2004–*cont.*

Sch.2 para.6, amended: SI 2012/ 1641 Sch.3 para.8

Sch.3 Part 2 para.11, applied: SI 2012/504 Reg.19, Sch.7 para.10

Sch.5 para.3, applied: SI 2012/ 504 Reg.37

Sch.5 para.4, amended: SI 2012/ 1916 Sch.34 para.61

Sch.7 Part 2 para.5, amended: SI 2012/ 1916 Sch.34 para.62

Sch.7 Part 2 para.9, amended: SI 2012/ 1916 Sch.34 para.62

Sch.7 Part 2 para.13, amended: SI 2012/ 1916 Sch.34 para.62

Sch.7 Part 3 para.6, amended: SI 2012/ 1916 Sch.34 para.62

Sch.7 Part 3 para.8, amended: SI 2012/ 1916 Sch.34 para.62

Sch.8 para.4, applied: SI 2012/ 504 Reg.37

Sch.8 para.5, amended: SI 2012/ 1916 Sch.34 para.63

Sch.9 para.1, substituted: SI 2012/ 1916 Sch.34 para.64

Sch.9 para.2, substituted: SI 2012/ 1916 Sch.34 para.64

Sch.9 para.3, substituted: SI 2012/ 1916 Sch.34 para.64

Sch.9 para.4, substituted: SI 2012/ 1916 Sch.34 para.64

Sch.9 para.5, substituted: SI 2012/ 1916 Sch.34 para.64

Sch.9 para.6, substituted: SI 2012/ 1916 Sch.34 para.64

Sch.9 para.7, substituted: SI 2012/ 1916 Sch.34 para.64

Sch.9 para.8, substituted: SI 2012/ 1916 Sch.34 para.64

Sch.9 para.9, substituted: SI 2012/ 1916 Sch.34 para.64

Sch.9 para.10, substituted: SI 2012/ 1916 Sch.34 para.64

Sch.9 para.11, substituted: SI 2012/ 1916 Sch.34 para.64

Sch.9 para.12, substituted: SI 2012/ 1916 Sch.34 para.64

Sch.9 para.13, substituted: SI 2012/ 1916 Sch.34 para.64

Sch.9 para.14, substituted: SI 2012/ 1916 Sch.34 para.64

Sch.9 para.15, substituted: SI 2012/ 1916 Sch.34 para.64

Sch.9 para.16, substituted: SI 2012/ 1916 Sch.34 para.64

Sch.9 para.17, substituted: SI 2012/ 1916 Sch.34 para.64

Sch.9 para.18, substituted: SI 2012/ 1916 Sch.34 para.64

Sch.9 para.19, substituted: SI 2012/ 1916 Sch.34 para.64

Sch.9 para.20, substituted: SI 2012/ 1916 Sch.34 para.64

1034. Crime (International Co-operation) Act 2003 (Designation of Prosecuting Authorities) Order 2004

Art.2, amended: SI 2012/ 146 Art.2

1045. Credit Institutions (Reorganisation and Winding up) Regulations 2004

see *Rawlinson and Hunter Trustees SA v Kaupthing Bank HF* [2011] EWHC 566 (Comm), [2012] B.C.C. 441 (QBD (Comm)), Burton, J.

1045. Credit Institutions (Reorganisation and Winding up) Regulations 2004–*cont.*

Reg.5, see *Joint Administrators of Heritable Bank Plc v Winding Up Board of Landsbanki Islands HF* 2012 S.C. 209 (IH (1 Div)), The Lord President (Hamilton)

Reg.22, see *Joint Administrators of Heritable Bank Plc v Winding Up Board of Landsbanki Islands HF* 2012 S.C. 209 (IH (1 Div)), The Lord President (Hamilton)

1051. Magistrates Courts (Foreign Travel Orders) Rules 2004

r.3, amended: SI 2012/ 2018 r.2

r.3, revoked (in part): SI 2012/ 2018 r.2

Sch.2, revoked: SI 2012/ 2018 r.2

Sch.3, revoked: SI 2012/ 2018 r.2

1052. Magistrates Courts (Notification Orders) Rules 2004

r.3, amended: SI 2012/ 2018 r.3

r.3, revoked (in part): SI 2012/ 2018 r.3

Sch.2, revoked: SI 2012/ 2018 r.3

Sch.3, revoked: SI 2012/ 2018 r.3

Sch.4, revoked: SI 2012/ 2018 r.3

1053. Magistrates Courts (Risk of Sexual Harm Orders) Rules 2004

r.3, amended: SI 2012/ 2018 r.4

r.3, revoked (in part): SI 2012/ 2018 r.4

Sch.2, revoked: SI 2012/ 2018 r.4

Sch.3, revoked: SI 2012/ 2018 r.4

Sch.4, revoked: SI 2012/ 2018 r.4

1054. Magistrates Courts (Sexual Offences Prevention Orders) Rules 2004

r.4, revoked (in part): SI 2012/ 2018 r.5

Sch.2, revoked: SI 2012/ 2018 r.5

1077. Competition Act 1998 (Concurrency) Regulations 2004

applied: SI 2012/ 1128 Art.4

Reg.2, amended: SI 2012/ 1809 Sch.1 Part 2

Reg.3, amended: SI 2012/ 1809 Sch.1 Part 2

1111. Overseas Territories (Zimbabwe) (Restrictive Measures) (Amendment) Order 2004

revoked: SI 2012/ 2753 Sch.7

1165. Potatoes Originating in Egypt (England) Regulations 2004

Reg.2, amended: SI 2012/ 697 Reg.2

Reg.3, amended: SI 2012/ 697 Reg.2

Reg.6, amended: SI 2012/ 697 Reg.2

Reg.6, revoked (in part): SI 2012/ 745 Reg.7

1190. Medicines (Pharmacy and General Sale Exemption) Amendment (No.2) Order 2004

revoked: SI 2012/ 1916 Sch.35

1192. Courts Boards Areas Order 2004

revoked: SI 2012/ 1206 Sch.1 para.10

1193. Courts Boards (Appointments and Procedure) Regulations 2004

revoked: SI 2012/ 1206 Sch.1 para.11

1212. A5 Trunk Road (Shenstone, Staffordshire) (50 Miles Per Hour Speed Limit) Order 2004

revoked: SI 2012/ 1097 Art.5

1215. A40 Trunk Road (Meidrim Junction, Carmarthenshire) (De-Restriction) Order 2004

disapplied: SI 2012/ 11 Art.6

1220. Sexual Offences Act 2003 (Travel Notification Requirements) Regulations 2004

Reg.5, amended: SI 2012/ 1876 Reg.5

Reg.5, varied: SI 2012/ 1876 Reg.3

Reg.6, substituted: SI 2012/ 1876 Reg.6

Reg.7, amended: SI 2012/ 1876 Reg.7

2004–cont.

1220. Sexual Offences Act 2003 (Travel Notification Requirements) Regulations 2004–cont.
Reg.8, amended: SI 2012/1876 Reg.8
1261. Competition Act 1998 and Other Enactments (Amendment) Regulations 2004
Reg.2, amended: SI 2012/1809 Sch.1 Part 2
1264. Liberia (Freezing of Funds and Economic Resources) Regulations 2004
revoked: SI 2012/1516 Reg.18
1267. European Parliamentary Elections (Northern Ireland) Regulations 2004
Reg.2, amended: SI 2012/1809 Sch.1 Part 2
1277. Tobacco Advertising and Promotion (Specialist Tobacconists) Regulations 2004
revoked (in part): SI 2012/1287 Reg.4
1283. European Communities (Designation) (No.3) Order 2004
revoked: SI 2012/1759 Sch.1
1378. Designation of Schools Having a Religious Character (Independent Schools) (England) (No.4) Order 2004
Sch.1, amended: SI 2012/3174 Sch.2
1396. Meat Products (Wales) Regulations 2004
Reg.3, amended: SI 2012/1809 Sch.1 Part 4
1411. A40 Trunk Road (Banc-y-felin Junction, Carmarthenshire) (De&ndash Restriction) Order 2004
disapplied: SI 2012/11 Art.6
1420. A49 Trunk Road (Redhill, Herefordshire) (Restriction) Order 2004
revoked: SI 2012/1098 Art.5
1434. Town and Country Planning (General Development Procedure) (Amendment) (Wales) Order 2004
revoked: SI 2012/801 Sch.8
1450. Child Trust Funds Regulations 2004
Reg.12, amended: SI 2012/1870 Reg.2
Reg.20, amended: SI 2012/2404 Sch.3 para.34
Reg.29, revoked (in part): SI 2012/886 Reg.2
1480. Medicines (Advertising) Amendment Regulations 2004
revoked: SI 2012/1916 Sch.35
1483. Consumer Credit (Early Settlement) Regulations 2004
Reg.1, amended: SI 2012/2798 Sch.1 para.3
Reg.4A, amended: SI 2012/2798 Sch.1 para.3
Reg.6, substituted: SI 2012/2798 Sch.1 para.3
1490. Landfill Allowances Scheme (Wales) Regulations 2004
Reg.2, amended: SI 2012/65 Reg.5, Reg.6
Reg.6, amended: SI 2012/65 Reg.7, Reg.8
Reg.8, substituted: SI 2012/65 Reg.9
Reg.9, amended: SI 2012/65 Reg.8
Reg.10, amended: SI 2012/65 Reg.8
Reg.11, amended: SI 2012/65 Reg.6
Reg.13, amended: SI 2012/65 Reg.8
Reg.14, amended: SI 2012/65 Reg.7, Reg.8
Reg.15, amended: SI 2012/65 Reg.6
Reg.16, amended: SI 2012/65 Reg.6, Reg.8
1498. Iraq (United Nations Sanctions)(Amendment) Order 2004
revoked: SI 2012/1489 Sch.2
1573. British Transport Police (Transitional and Consequential Provisions) Order 2004
Art.12, revoked (in part): 2012 c.9 Sch.10 Part 4
1654. Nursing and Midwifery Council (Fees) Rules Order of Council 2004
Sch.1, amended: SI 2012/3026 Sch.1

2004–cont.

1660. Iraq (United Nations Sanctions) Order 2000 (Amendment) Regulations 2004
revoked: SI 2012/1489 Sch.2
1706. Road Vehicles (Construction and Use) (Amendment) Regulations 2004
revoked: SI 2012/1404 Sch.1
1729. Education (School Teachers Qualifications) (Wales) Regulations 2004
revoked: SI 2012/724 Reg.4
Reg.5, applied: SI 2012/724 Sch.2 para.14
Reg.7, varied: SI 2012/724 Sch.1 para.1
1744. Education (Specified Work and Registration) (Wales) Regulations 2004
Sch.2 para.3, applied: SI 2012/724 Sch.2 para.9
1756. Adult Placement Schemes (Wales) Regulations 2004
Reg.8, amended: SI 2012/2404 Sch.3 para.35
1761. Nursing and Midwifery Council (Fitness to Practise) Rules Order of Council 2004
Sch.1, added: SI 2012/17 Sch.1
Sch.1, amended: SI 2012/17 Sch.1
Sch.1, revoked: SI 2012/17 Sch.1
Sch.1, substituted: SI 2012/17 Sch.1
1764. Nursing and Midwifery Council (Midwives) Rules Order of Council 2004
revoked: SI 2012/3025 Sch.1
1767. Nursing and Midwifery Council (Education, Registration and Registration Appeals) Rules Order of Council 2004
Sch.1, added: SI 2012/2754 Sch.1
Sch.1, amended: SI 2012/2754 Sch.1
Sch.1, substituted: SI 2012/2754 Sch.1
1771. Health Act 1999 (Consequential Amendments) (Nursing and Midwifery) Order 2004
Sch.1 Part 2 para.44, revoked (in part): SI 2012/1909 Sch.8 para.1
1779. Iraq (United Nations Sanctions) Order 2000 (Amendment No.2) Regulations 2004
revoked: SI 2012/1489 Sch.2
1861. Employment Tribunals (Constitution and Rules of Procedure) Regulations 2004
Appendix 1, amended: SI 2012/725 Art.2, SI 2012/1479 Sch.1 para.73, SI 2012/1641 Sch.4 para.9
Reg.4, amended: SI 2012/2404 Sch.3 para.36
Reg.16, applied: SI 2012/1652 Reg.17, Reg.24
Sch.1, applied: SI 2012/1652 Reg.17, Reg.24
Sch.1 para.10, see *Brennan v Sunderland City Council* [2012] I.C.R. 1183 (EAT), Underhill, J. (President); see *F v G* [2012] I.C.R. 246 (EAT), Underhill, J. (President)
Sch.1 para.18, see *Conway v Community Options Ltd* [2012] Eq. L.R. 871 (EAT), Judge Peter Clark; see *Timbo v Greenwich Council for Racial Equality* [2012] Eq. L.R. 1010 (EAT), Judge David Richardson
Sch.1 para.20, amended: SI 2012/468 Reg.2
Sch.1 para.27, see *O'Cathail v Transport for London* [2012] I.C.R. 561 (EAT), Judge David Richardson
Sch.1 para.27, amended: SI 2012/468 Reg.2
Sch.1 para.30, see *Chief Constable of Hampshire v Haque* [2012] Eq. L.R. 113 (EAT), Langstaff, J.
Sch.1 para.38, amended: SI 2012/468 Reg.2
Sch.1 para.40, see *AQ Ltd v Holden* [2012] I.R.L.R. 648 (EAT), Judge David Richardson; see *Arrowsmith v Nottingham Trent University* [2011] EWCA Civ 797, [2012] I.C.R. 159 (CA (Civ Div)), Laws, L.J.; see *Yerrakalva v Barnsley MBC* [2011] EWCA Civ 1255, [2012] 2 All E.R. 215 (CA (Civ Div)), Mummery, L.J.

2004– cont.

1861. Employment Tribunals (Constitution and Rules of Procedure) Regulations 2004– *cont.*
Sch.1 para.40, amended: SI 2012/468 Reg.2
Sch.1 para.41, amended: SI 2012/468 Reg.2
Sch.1 para.45, amended: SI 2012/468 Reg.2
Sch.1 para.49, see *F v G* [2012] I.C.R. 246 (EAT), Underhill, J. (President)
Sch.1 para.50, see *F v G* [2012] I.C.R. 246 (EAT), Underhill, J. (President)
Sch.1 para.54, see *Tariq v Home Office* [2012] 1 A.C. 452 (SC), Lord Phillips (President)
Sch.1 para.58, amended: SI 2012/1809 Sch.1 Part 2
Sch.1 para.61, amended: SI 2012/468 Reg.2
Sch.4, applied: SI 2012/1652 Reg.17, Reg.24

1862. Financial Conglomerates and Other Financial Groups Regulations 2004
Reg.1, amended: SI 2012/916 Reg.4, SI 2012/917 Sch.2 para.4
Reg.2, amended: SI 2012/916 Reg.4
Reg.8, amended: SI 2012/916 Reg.4

1864. Tax Avoidance Schemes (Information) Regulations 2004
revoked: SI 2012/1836 Sch.1

1865. Tax Avoidance Schemes (Promoters and Prescribed Circumstances) Regulations 2004
referred to: SI 2012/1868 Reg.7
Reg.1, varied: SI 2012/1868 Reg.27
Reg.4, varied: SI 2012/1868 Reg.27
Reg.6, amended: SI 2012/1836 Reg.18
Reg.6, applied: SI 2012/1836 Reg.5
Reg.6, varied: SI 2012/1868 Reg.27

1886. General Teaching Council for England (Additional Functions) Order 2004
revoked: SI 2012/1153 Sch.1

1932. Student Fees (Amounts) (England) Regulations 2004
Reg.4, amended: SI 2012/433 Reg.3
Reg.5, amended: SI 2012/433 Reg.3
Reg.6, amended: SI 2012/433 Reg.3
Reg.6, substituted: SI 2012/433 Reg.3

1935. General Teaching Council for England (Constitution) (Amendment) Regulations 2004
revoked: SI 2012/1153 Sch.1

1964. Fur Farming (Compensation Scheme) (England) Order 2004
Sch.6 Part 6 para.14, amended: SI 2012/632 Sch.3

1975. Contracting Out (Functions relating to Broadcast Advertising) and Specification of Relevant Functions Order 2004
Art.2, amended: SI 2012/1916 Sch.34 para.89
Art.7, amended: SI 2012/1916 Sch.34 para.89
Art.8, amended: SI 2012/1916 Sch.34 para.89
Art.11, amended: SI 2012/1916 Sch.34 para.89

1983. Iraq (United Nations Sanctions) (Overseas Territories) (Amendment) Order 2004
Art.3, revoked: SI 2012/2748 Sch.6

1993. Dangerous Wild Animals (Northern Ireland) Order 2004
Art.7, amended: SI 2012/3039 Reg.35

2035. Courts Act 2003 (Consequential Amendments) Order 2004
applied: SI 2012/1726 r.2.1

2066. Courts Act 2003 (Commencement No 6 and Savings) Order 2004
applied: SI 2012/1726 r.2.1

2004– cont.

2089. Designation of Schools Having a Religious Character (Independent Schools) (England) (No.5) Order 2004
Sch.1, amended: SI 2012/3174 Sch.2

2095. Financial Services (Distance Marketing) Regulations 2004
applied: SI 2012/1128 Art.4
Reg.2, amended: SI 2012/1809 Sch.1 Part 2

2204. Town and Country Planning (Local Development) (England) Regulations 2004
revoked: SI 2012/767 Reg.37
Reg.15, varied: 2012 c.11 s.12

2245. Potatoes Originating in Egypt (Wales) Regulations 2004
Reg.6, revoked: SI 2012/1493 Reg.7

2467. Fishing Boats (Satellite-Tracking Devices) (England) Scheme 2004
revoked: SI 2012/1375 Art.16

2473. Student Fees (Approved Plans) (England) Regulations 2004
Reg.8, amended: SI 2012/433 Reg.2
Reg.9, amended: SI 2012/765 Art.6

2526. Employment Appeal Tribunal (Amendment) Rules 2004
r.3, see *Malcolm v Dundee City Council* [2012] CSIH 13, 2012 S.L.T. 457 (IH (Ex Div)), Lady Paton

2574. Liberia (Freezing of Funds and Economic Resources) (Amendment No 2) Regulations 2004
revoked: SI 2012/1516 Reg.18

2608. General Medical Council (Fitness to Practise) Rules Order of Council 2004
see *Lawrence v General Medical Council* [2012] EWHC 464 (Admin), [2012] Med. L.R. 608 (QBD (Admin)), Stadlen, J.
Sch.1, see *Zia v General Medical Council* [2011] EWCA Civ 743, [2012] 1 W.L.R. 504 (CA (Civ Div)), Sir Anthony May (V-P, QBD)

2613. Tax Avoidance Schemes (Promoters, Prescribed Circumstances and Information) (Amendment) Regulations 2004
Reg.3, revoked: SI 2012/1836 Sch.1

2642. European Communities (Designation) (No.5) Order 2004
referred to: SI 2012/916 Sch.1
revoked: SI 2012/1759 Sch.1

2671. Iraq (United Nations Sanctions) (Overseas Territories) (Amendment) (No.2) Order 2004
Art.5, revoked: SI 2012/2748 Sch.6
Art.6, revoked: SI 2012/2748 Sch.6
Sch.1 para.1, revoked: SI 2012/2748 Sch.6
Sch.1 para.2, revoked: SI 2012/2748 Sch.6
Sch.1 para.3, revoked: SI 2012/2748 Sch.6
Sch.1 para.4, revoked: SI 2012/2748 Sch.6
Sch.1 para.5, revoked: SI 2012/2748 Sch.6
Sch.1 para.6, revoked: SI 2012/2748 Sch.6
Sch.1 para.7, revoked: SI 2012/2748 Sch.6
Sch.1 para.8, revoked: SI 2012/2748 Sch.6
Sch.1 para.9, revoked: SI 2012/2748 Sch.6

2751. Competition Act 1998 (Office of Fair Trading's Rules) Order 2004
Sch.1 para.1, amended: SI 2012/1809 Sch.1 Part 2
Sch.1 para.2, amended: SI 2012/1809 Sch.1 Part 2
Sch.1 para.4, amended: SI 2012/1809 Sch.1 Part 2
Sch.1 para.7, amended: SI 2012/1809 Sch.1 Part 2
Sch.1 para.10, amended: SI 2012/1809 Sch.1 Part 2

2004–cont.

2783. Education (National Curriculum) (Key Stage 1 Assessment Arrangements) (England) Order 2004
Art.8, revoked: SI 2012/ 765 Art.7

2876. A55 Trunk Road (Penmaenmawr &mdash Conwy Morfa, Conwy) (Derestriction) Order 2004
disapplied: SI 2012/ 141 Art.12, SI 2012/ 163 Art.12
restored: SI 2012/ 423 Art.11
revoked (in part): SI 2012/ 423 Art.11
varied: SI 2012/ 945 Art.9

2881. Oil and Fibre Plant Seed (Wales) Regulations 2004
revoked: SI 2012/ 245 Reg.34

2986. Designation of Schools Having a Religious Character (Independent Schools) (England) (No.6) Order 2004
Sch.1, amended: SI 2012/ 3174 Sch.2

3082. Local Authorities (Indemnities for Members and Officers) Order 2004
applied: SI 2012/ 2734 Sch.1 para.4, Sch.1 para.19
varied: SI 2012/ 2734 Reg.6

3101. Export of Goods, Transfer of Technology and Provision of Technical Assistance (Control) (Overseas Territories) Order 2004
Sch.1, amended: SI 2012/ 362 Sch.1

3102. Trade in Goods (Control) (Overseas Territories) Order 2004
Sch.1, amended: SI 2012/ 362 Sch.1

3103. Trade in Controlled Goods (Embargoed Destinations) (Overseas Territories) Order 2004
Sch.1, amended: SI 2012/ 362 Sch.1

3130. Financing of Maintained Schools (England) Regulations 2004
revoked: SI 2012/ 2991 Reg.2

3154. Wireless Telegraphy (Spectrum Trading) Regulations 2004
revoked: SI 2012/ 2187 Sch.1

3155. Wireless Telegraphy (Register) Regulations 2004
revoked: SI 2012/ 2186 Sch.1

3156. Town and Country Planning (Electronic Communications) (Wales) (No.1) Order 2004
Art.11, revoked: SI 2012/ 801 Sch.8
Sch.1 para.1, revoked: SI 2012/ 801 Sch.8
Sch.1 para.2, revoked: SI 2012/ 801 Sch.8
Sch.1 para.3, revoked: SI 2012/ 801 Sch.8
Sch.1 para.4, revoked: SI 2012/ 801 Sch.8
Sch.1 para.5, revoked: SI 2012/ 801 Sch.8
Sch.1 para.6, revoked: SI 2012/ 801 Sch.8
Sch.1 para.7, revoked: SI 2012/ 801 Sch.8
Sch.1 para.8, revoked: SI 2012/ 801 Sch.8
Sch.1 para.9, revoked: SI 2012/ 801 Sch.8

3206. Water Mergers (Determination of Turnover) Regulations 2004
Sch.1 para.1, amended: SI 2012/ 1809 Sch.1 Part 2

3279. General Food Regulations 2004
Reg.4, see *Blueshell Mussels Ltd v Foard* 2012 J.C. 62 (HCJ), Lord Eassie
Reg.5, see *Blueshell Mussels Ltd v Foard* 2012 J.C. 62 (HCJ), Lord Eassie
Reg.8, see *Blueshell Mussels Ltd v Foard* 2012 J.C. 62 (HCJ), Lord Eassie
Reg.16, see *Blueshell Mussels Ltd v Foard* 2012 J.C. 62 (HCJ), Lord Eassie

3315. Non-Domestic Rating (Small Business Rate Relief) (England) Order 2004
revoked: SI 2012/ 148 Art.5

2004–cont.

3328. European Communities (Designation) (No.7) Order 2004
referred to: SI 2012/ 916 Sch.1
revoked: SI 2012/ 1759 Sch.1

3391. Environmental Information Regulations 2004
see *Birkett v Department for the Environment, Food and Rural Affairs* [2011] EWCA Civ 1606, [2012] P.T.S.R. 1299 (CA (Civ Div)), Carnwath, L.J.; see *Hardy v United Kingdom (31965/07)* (2012) 55 E.H.R.R. 28 (ECHR), Judge Garlicki (President)
Reg.12, see *Birkett v Department for the Environment, Food and Rural Affairs* [2011] EWCA Civ 1606, [2012] P.T.S.R. 1299 (CA (Civ Div)), Carnwath, L.J.

3410. Postgraduate Medical Education and Training Board (Members Removal from Office) Rules Order 2004
Sch.1, amended: SI 2012/ 2404 Sch.3 para.37

2005

41. Licensing Act 2003 (Personal licences) Regulations 2005
Sch.1, amended: SI 2012/ 946 Sch.1
Sch.2, amended: SI 2012/ 946 Sch.2
Sch.3, amended: SI 2012/ 946 Sch.3

42. Licensing Act 2003 (Premises licences and club premises certificates) Regulations 2005
Part 4, substituted: SI 2012/ 955 Reg.5
Reg.2, amended: SI 2012/ 955 Reg.3
Reg.22, amended: SI 2012/ 955 Reg.4
Reg.26, amended: SI 2012/ 955 Reg.6
Reg.26A, amended: SI 2012/ 955 Reg.7
Reg.26B, added: SI 2012/ 955 Reg.8
Reg.26C, added: SI 2012/ 955 Reg.8
Reg.37, amended: SI 2012/ 955 Reg.9
Reg.39, amended: SI 2012/ 955 Reg.9
Sch.2, amended: SI 2012/ 2290 Sch.1
Sch.3, amended: SI 2012/ 2290 Sch.2
Sch.4, amended: SI 2012/ 2290 Sch.3
Sch.4B, amended: SI 2012/ 2290 Sch.4
Sch.6, substituted: SI 2012/ 955 Sch.1
Sch.8, substituted: SI 2012/ 955 Sch.2
Sch.9, amended: SI 2012/ 2290 Sch.5
Sch.10, amended: SI 2012/ 2290 Sch.6

44. Licensing Act 2003 (Hearings) Regulations 2005
Reg.5, substituted: SI 2012/ 2551 Reg.7
Reg.26, amended: SI 2012/ 2551 Reg.8
Reg.28, amended: SI 2012/ 2551 Reg.9
Sch.1, amended: SI 2012/ 2551 Reg.10
Sch.2, amended: SI 2012/ 2551 Reg.11
Sch.3, amended: SI 2012/ 2551 Reg.12
Sch.4 para.15A, added: SI 2012/ 2551 Reg.13

52. Education (Student Support) Regulations 2005
Reg.13, applied: SI 2012/ 2886 Sch.1, SI 2012/ 3145 Sch.1

67. Trunk Road (A48/A40) (Carmarthen, Dyfed) (De-restriction) Order 1983 (Variation) Order 2005
disapplied: SI 2012/ 11 Art.6

120. Merseytram (Liverpool City Centre to Kirkby) Order 2005
Art.20, amended: SI 2012/ 1659 Art.2
Art.70, amended: SI 2012/ 1659 Art.2
Sch.13 para.1, amended: SI 2012/ 1659 Art.2
Sch.13 para.2, amended: SI 2012/ 1659 Art.2
Sch.13 para.3, amended: SI 2012/ 1659 Art.2
Sch.13 para.4, amended: SI 2012/ 1659 Art.2

2005–cont.

120. Merseytram (Liverpool City Centre to Kirkby) Order 2005– *cont.*
Sch.13 para.5, amended: SI 2012/1659 Art.2
Sch.13 para.6, amended: SI 2012/1659 Art.2
Sch.13 para.7, amended: SI 2012/1659 Art.2
Sch.13 para.8, amended: SI 2012/1659 Art.2
Sch.13 para.9, amended: SI 2012/1659 Art.2
Sch.13 para.10, amended: SI 2012/1659 Art.2
Sch.13 para.11, amended: SI 2012/1659 Art.2
Sch.13 para.12, amended: SI 2012/1659 Art.2
Sch.13 para.13, amended: SI 2012/1659 Art.2
Sch.13 para.14, amended: SI 2012/1659 Art.2
Sch.13 para.15, amended: SI 2012/1659 Art.2
Sch.13 para.16, amended: SI 2012/1659 Art.2
Sch.13 para.17, amended: SI 2012/1659 Art.2
Sch.13 para.18, amended: SI 2012/1659 Art.2
Sch.13 para.19, amended: SI 2012/1659 Art.2

154. Hill Farm Allowance Regulations 2005
revoked: SI 2012/114 Reg.9

185. Controlled Foreign Companies (Excluded Countries) (Amendment) Regulations 2005
revoked: 2012 c.14 Sch.20 para.14

186. Controlled Foreign Companies (Excluded Countries) (Amendment No 2) Regulations 2005
revoked: 2012 c.14 Sch.20 para.14

224. Private Security Industry Act 2001 (Amendments to Schedule 2) Order 2005
revoked: 2012 c.9 Sch.10 Part 3

228. Anthrax Prevention Order 1971 etc (Revocation) Regulations 2005
revoked: SI 2012/1537 Reg.2

230. Asylum and Immigration Tribunal (Procedure) Rules 2005
r.4, see *TN (Evidence by Electronic Means: Zimbabwe), Re* [2012] Imm. A.R. 207 (UT (IAC)), CMG Ockelton (Vice President)
r.45, see *TN (Evidence by Electronic Means: Zimbabwe), Re* [2012] Imm. A.R. 207 (UT (IAC)), CMG Ockelton (Vice President)
r.48, see *RK (Entitlement to Represent: S.84: Bangladesh), Re* [2012] Imm. A.R. 126 (UT (IAC)), Judge Lane
r.51, see *Butt (Para 245AA(B): Specified Documents: Judicial Verification: Pakistan), Re* [2012] Imm. A.R. 88 (UT (IAC)), CMG Ockelton

242. Ivory Coast (Restrictive Measures) (Overseas Territories) Order 2005
revoked: SI 2012/3067 Art.1
Sch.1, amended: SI 2012/362 Sch.1

384. Criminal Procedure Rules 2005
applied: SI 2012/1726 r.2.1
r.67.2, see *R. v Mian (Yousaf)* [2012] EWCA Crim 792, [2012] 3 All E.R. 661 (CA (Crim Div)), Rix, L.J.

389. Adoption Agencies Regulations 2005
see *O v Coventry City Council* [2012] 1 F.L.R. 302 (CC (Coventry)), Judge Clifford Bellamy
Reg.2, amended: SI 2012/1410 Reg.3, SI 2012/1479 Sch.1 para.74
Reg.12, amended: SI 2012/1410 Reg.4
Reg.17, amended: SI 2012/1410 Reg.5
Reg.19, amended: SI 2012/1410 Reg.6
Reg.37, amended: SI 2012/1479 Sch.1 para.74

392. Adoptions with a Foreign Element Regulations 2005
Reg.10, amended: SI 2012/1410 Reg.9
Reg.38, amended: SI 2012/1410 Reg.10

2005–cont.

392. Adoptions with a Foreign Element Regulations 2005– *cont.*
Reg.48, amended: SI 2012/1410 Reg.11

408. Health Protection Agency Regulations 2005
Reg.1, amended: SI 2012/1641 Sch.4 para.10
Reg.1, varied: 2012 c.11 s.12
Reg.3, amended: SI 2012/2404 Sch.3 para.38

433. Children and Family Court Advisory and Support Service (Membership, Committee and Procedure) Regulations 2005
Reg.6, amended: SI 2012/2404 Sch.3 para.39

439. Armed Forces and Reserve Forces (Compensation Scheme) Order 2005
Art.31, applied: SI 2012/2886 Sch.1

441. Pension Protection Fund (Multi-employer Schemes) (Modification) Regulations 2005
Reg.6, amended: SI 2012/1688 Reg.2, SI 2012/3083 Reg.2
Reg.8, amended: SI 2012/1688 Reg.2, SI 2012/3083 Reg.2
Reg.10, amended: SI 2012/1688 Reg.2, SI 2012/3083 Reg.2
Reg.11, amended: SI 2012/1688 Reg.2, SI 2012/3083 Reg.2
Reg.23, amended: SI 2012/1688 Reg.2, SI 2012/3083 Reg.2
Reg.25, amended: SI 2012/1688 Reg.2, SI 2012/3083 Reg.2
Reg.28, amended: SI 2012/1688 Reg.2, SI 2012/3083 Reg.2
Reg.37A, added: SI 2012/1688 Reg.2, SI 2012/3083 Reg.2
Reg.38, amended: SI 2012/1688 Reg.2, SI 2012/3083 Reg.2
Reg.40, amended: SI 2012/1688 Reg.2, SI 2012/3083 Reg.2
Reg.41, amended: SI 2012/1688 Reg.2, SI 2012/3083 Reg.2
Reg.42, amended: SI 2012/1688 Reg.2, SI 2012/3083 Reg.2
Reg.45, amended: SI 2012/1688 Reg.2, SI 2012/3083 Reg.2
Reg.53A, added: SI 2012/1688 Reg.2, SI 2012/3083 Reg.2
Reg.54, amended: SI 2012/1688 Reg.2, SI 2012/3083 Reg.2
Reg.56, amended: SI 2012/1688 Reg.2, SI 2012/3083 Reg.2
Reg.57, amended: SI 2012/1688 Reg.2, SI 2012/3083 Reg.2
Reg.58, amended: SI 2012/1688 Reg.2, SI 2012/3083 Reg.2
Reg.68, amended: SI 2012/1688 Reg.2, SI 2012/3083 Reg.2

448. Gangmasters (Licensing Authority) Regulations 2005
Reg.5, amended: SI 2012/2404 Sch.3 para.40

454. Social Security (Graduated Retirement Benefit) Regulations 2005
Sch.1, applied: SI 2012/2885 Sch.1 para.22, Sch.6 para.28, SI 2012/2886 Sch.1, SI 2012/3144 Sch.1 para.16, SI 2012/3145 Sch.1, SSI 2012/319 Reg.38
Sch.1 Part 1 para.1, varied: SI 2012/780 Art.12
Sch.1 Part 1 para.2, varied: SI 2012/780 Art.12
Sch.1 Part 1 para.3, varied: SI 2012/780 Art.12
Sch.1 Part 1 para.4, varied: SI 2012/780 Art.12
Sch.1 Part 1 para.5, varied: SI 2012/780 Art.12
Sch.1 Part 1 para.6, varied: SI 2012/780 Art.12
Sch.1 Part 1 para.7, varied: SI 2012/780 Art.12

2005–cont.

454. Social Security (Graduated Retirement Benefit) Regulations 2005–*cont.*
Sch.1 Part 1 para.8, varied: SI 2012/780 Art.12
Sch.1 Part 1 para.9, varied: SI 2012/780 Art.12
Sch.1 Part 1 para.10, varied: SI 2012/780 Art.12
Sch.1 Part 2A para.20A, varied: SI 2012/780 Art.12
Sch.1 Part 2A para.20B, varied: SI 2012/780 Art.12
Sch.1 Part 2A para.20C, varied: SI 2012/780 Art.12
Sch.1 Part 2A para.20D, varied: SI 2012/780 Art.12
Sch.1 Part 2 para.11, varied: SI 2012/780 Art.12
Sch.1 Part 2 para.12, varied: SI 2012/780 Art.12
Sch.1 Part 2 para.13, varied: SI 2012/780 Art.12
Sch.1 Part 2 para.14, varied: SI 2012/780 Art.12
Sch.1 Part 2 para.15, varied: SI 2012/780 Art.12
Sch.1 Part 2 para.16, varied: SI 2012/780 Art.12
Sch.1 Part 2 para.17, varied: SI 2012/780 Art.12
Sch.1 Part 2 para.18, varied: SI 2012/780 Art.12
Sch.1 Part 2 para.19, varied: SI 2012/780 Art.12
Sch.1 Part 2 para.20, varied: SI 2012/780 Art.12
Sch.1 Part 2 para.20ZA, varied: SI 2012/780 Art.12
Sch.1 Part 2 para.20ZB, varied: SI 2012/780 Art.12
Sch.1 Part 3 para.21, varied: SI 2012/780 Art.12

471. Public Record Office (Fees) Regulations 2005
revoked: SI 2012/1665 Reg.3

477. Water Industry (Determination of Turnover for Penalties) Order 2005
Art.2, amended: SI 2012/1809 Sch.1 Part 2

486. Whole of Government Accounts (Designation of Bodies) Order 2005
varied: SI 2012/147 Art.7

500. Health and Social Care Information Centre Regulations 2005
Reg.3, amended: SI 2012/1641 Sch.4 para.11, SI 2012/2404 Sch.3 para.41

524. Insolvency Practitioners Regulations 2005
applied: SI 2012/3013 Sch.1 para.2

551. Central Rating List (England) Regulations 2005
Sch.1 Part 12, amended: SI 2012/1292 Reg.2

553. Justices of the Peace (Size and Chairmanship of Bench) Rules 2005
applied: SI 2012/1726 r.37.1
referred to: SI 2012/1277 Sch.1 para.1

554. Local Justice Areas Order 2005
Sch.1, amended: SI 2012/1277 Art.4, SI 2012/1555 Art.4, SI 2012/3128 Art.4

560. Asylum and Immigration Tribunal (Fast Track Procedure) Rules 2005
Sch.2, referred to: SI 2012/2683 Reg.4

590. Pension Protection Fund (Entry Rules) Regulations 2005
Reg.1, amended: SI 2012/917 Sch.2 para.5
Reg.24, amended: SI 2012/1688 Reg.3, SI 2012/3083 Reg.3
Sch.1 para.8, amended: SI 2012/1741 Sch.1 para.5

626. Occupational and Personal Pension Schemes (General Levy) Regulations 2005
Reg.6, amended: SI 2012/539 Reg.2
Reg.7, amended: SI 2012/539 Reg.2

639. Road Transport (Working Time) Regulations 2005
see *R. (on the application of United Road Transport Union) v Secretary of State for Transport* [2012] EWHC 1909 (Admin), [2012] 3 C.M.L.R. 40 (QBD (Admin)), Hickinbottom, J.
Reg.2, amended: SI 2012/991 Reg.3
Reg.3, amended: SI 2012/991 Reg.4
Reg.3, revoked (in part): SI 2012/991 Reg.4
Reg.3A, added: SI 2012/991 Reg.5

2005–cont.

639. Road Transport (Working Time) Regulations 2005–*cont.*
Reg.4, amended: SI 2012/991 Reg.6
Reg.6, amended: SI 2012/991 Reg.7
Reg.7, amended: SI 2012/991 Reg.8
Reg.7, see *R. (on the application of United Road Transport Union) v Secretary of State for Transport* [2012] EWHC 1909 (Admin), [2012] 3 C.M.L.R. 40 (QBD (Admin)), Hickinbottom, J.
Reg.8, amended: SI 2012/991 Reg.9
Reg.8, see *R. (on the application of United Road Transport Union) v Secretary of State for Transport* [2012] EWHC 1909 (Admin), [2012] 3 C.M.L.R. 40 (QBD (Admin)), Hickinbottom, J.
Reg.9, amended: SI 2012/991 Reg.10
Reg.11A, added: SI 2012/991 Reg.11
Reg.13, amended: SI 2012/991 Reg.12

641. National Health Service (Pharmaceutical Services) Regulations 2005
applied: SI 2012/1909 Reg.2, Reg.6, Reg.36, Reg.40, Reg.50, Reg.65, Reg.66, Reg.100, Sch.5 para.13, Sch.5 para.15, Sch.5 para.16, Sch.7 para.1, Sch.7 para.2, Sch.7 para.3, Sch.7 para.5, Sch.7 para.6, Sch.7 para.7, Sch.7 para.8, Sch.7 para.12, Sch.7 para.13
referred to: SI 2012/1909 Reg.48, Sch.4 para.25, Sch.4 para.26, Sch.7 para.9
revoked: SI 2012/1909 Sch.8 para.9
varied: SI 2012/1909 Sch.7 para.11
Part 5, applied: SI 2012/1909 Sch.7 para.3
Reg.2, amended: SI 2012/1479 Sch.1 para.44
Reg.3F, applied: SI 2012/1909 Sch.7 para.1
Reg.5, applied: SI 2012/1909 Sch.7 para.2, Sch.7 para.12
Reg.6, applied: SI 2012/1909 Sch.7 para.2
Reg.6, referred to: SI 2012/1909 Reg.24
Reg.7, applied: SI 2012/1909 Sch.7 para.2
Reg.7, referred to: SI 2012/1909 Reg.24
Reg.7A, applied: SI 2012/1909 Sch.7 para.2
Reg.8, applied: SI 2012/1909 Sch.7 para.2
Reg.9, applied: SI 2012/1909 Sch.7 para.2
Reg.10, applied: SI 2012/1909 Sch.7 para.2
Reg.12, applied: SI 2012/1909 Sch.7 para.2, Sch.7 para.6
Reg.13, applied: SI 2012/1909 Reg.64, Reg.65, Reg.66, Sch.7 para.2, Sch.7 para.4, Sch.7 para.6
Reg.13, referred to: SI 2012/1909 Reg.24
Reg.14, applied: SI 2012/1909 Reg.66
Reg.15, applied: SI 2012/1909 Sch.7 para.4
Reg.16, applied: SI 2012/1909 Reg.24
Reg.18, applied: SI 2012/1909 Reg.51
Reg.18ZA, applied: SI 2012/1909 Reg.41
Reg.18ZA, referred to: SI 2012/1909 Reg.41
Reg.20, applied: SI 2012/1909 Reg.47, Reg.60, Sch.7 para.7, Sch.7 para.8
Reg.22, applied: SI 2012/1909 Reg.40
Reg.23, applied: SI 2012/1909 Sch.7 para.2
Reg.28, varied: 2012 c.11 s.12
Reg.31, applied: SI 2012/1909 Sch.7 para.5
Reg.33, applied: SI 2012/1909 Sch.7 para.2
Reg.33, referred to: SI 2012/1909 Sch.7 para.2
Reg.35, applied: SI 2012/1909 Reg.42, Sch.7 para.6, Sch.7 para.7
Reg.38, referred to: SI 2012/1909 Sch.7 para.3
Reg.40, applied: SI 2012/1909 Sch.7 para.2, Sch.7 para.12
Reg.41, applied: SI 2012/1909 Sch.7 para.2

2005–cont.

641. National Health Service (Pharmaceutical Services) Regulations 2005–*cont.*
Reg.54, applied: SI 2012/1909 Sch.7 para.2, Sch.7 para.12
Reg.58, applied: SI 2012/1909 Sch.7 para.12
Reg.60, applied: SI 2012/1909 Sch.7 para.3
Reg.65, applied: SI 2012/1909 Reg.55
Sch.1, applied: SI 2012/1909 Sch.7 para.12
Sch.1 Part 2 para.8, amended: SI 2012/1399 Reg.2
Sch.1 Part 2 para.8, revoked (in part): SI 2012/1399 Reg.2
Sch.1 Part 5, applied: SI 2012/1909 Sch.7 para.13
Sch.3, applied: SI 2012/1909 Sch.7 para.12
Sch.3 para.13AA, amended: SI 2012/1399 Reg.2

643. Criminal Justice Act 2003 (Sentencing) (Transitory Provisions) Order 2005
Art.2, revoked (in part): 2012 c.10 Sch.9 para.13, Sch.10 para.44
Art.3, revoked (in part): 2012 c.10 s.117, Sch.9 para.13, SI 2012/2824 Reg.3

657. House of Commons Members Fund Resolution 2005
r.1, amended: SI 2012/1866 r.001

669. Pension Protection Fund (Review and Reconsideration of Reviewable Matters) Regulations 2005
Reg.3, amended: SI 2012/1688 Reg.4, SI 2012/3083 Reg.4
Reg.15, amended: SI 2012/1688 Reg.4, SI 2012/3083 Reg.4
Sch.1, amended: SI 2012/1688 Reg.4, SI 2012/3083 Reg.4

672. Pension Protection Fund (Valuation) Regulations 2005
Reg.1, amended: SI 2012/1688 Reg.5, SI 2012/3083 Reg.5
Reg.2A, added: SI 2012/1688 Reg.5, SI 2012/3083 Reg.5
Reg.3, amended: SI 2012/1688 Reg.5, SI 2012/3083 Reg.5
Reg.4, amended: SI 2012/1688 Reg.5, SI 2012/3083 Reg.5
Reg.6, amended: SI 2012/1688 Reg.5, SI 2012/3083 Reg.5
Reg.7, amended: SI 2012/1688 Reg.5, SI 2012/3083 Reg.5
Reg.7A, added: SI 2012/1688 Reg.5, SI 2012/3083 Reg.5
Reg.9A, added: SI 2012/1688 Reg.5, SI 2012/3083 Reg.5
Reg.10, amended: SI 2012/692 Reg.11
Sch.1 para.8, amended: SI 2012/1741 Sch.1 para.6

674. Pension Protection Fund (Provision of Information) Regulations 2005
Sch.2 para.1, amended: SI 2012/1688 Reg.6, SI 2012/3083 Reg.6

678. Occupational Pension Schemes (Employer Debt) Regulations 2005
Reg.2, amended: SI 2012/1817 Sch.1 para.7
Reg.5, see *BESTrustees Plc v Kaupthing Singer & Friedlander Ltd (In Administration)* [2012] EWHC 629 (Ch), [2012] 3 All E.R. 874 (Ch D), Sales, J.
Reg.5, amended: SI 2012/1817 Sch.1 para.7
Reg.6, amended: SI 2012/1817 Sch.1 para.7
Sch.1, amended: SI 2012/1817 Sch.1 para.7
Sch.1D, amended: SI 2012/1817 Sch.1 para.7

2005–cont.

686. Pensions Regulator (Freezing Orders and Consequential Amendments) Regulations 2005
Reg.2, amended: SI 2012/692 Reg.12

715. Supervision of Accounts and Reports (Prescribed Body) Order 2005
applied: SI 2012/1439 Art.7

735. Work at Height Regulations 2005
Reg.4, see *Winn-Pope v ES Access Platforms Ltd* [2012] CSOH 87, 2012 S.L.T. 929 (OH), Lord Brodie
Reg.5, see *Winn-Pope v ES Access Platforms Ltd* [2012] CSOH 87, 2012 S.L.T. 929 (OH), Lord Brodie
Reg.6, see *Winn-Pope v ES Access Platforms Ltd* [2012] CSOH 87, 2012 S.L.T. 929 (OH), Lord Brodie
Reg.7, see *Winn-Pope v ES Access Platforms Ltd* [2012] CSOH 87, 2012 S.L.T. 929 (OH), Lord Brodie
Reg.9, see *Winn-Pope v ES Access Platforms Ltd* [2012] CSOH 87, 2012 S.L.T. 929 (OH), Lord Brodie
Reg.11, see *Winn-Pope v ES Access Platforms Ltd* [2012] CSOH 87, 2012 S.L.T. 929 (OH), Lord Brodie
Reg.14, see *Winn-Pope v ES Access Platforms Ltd* [2012] CSOH 87, 2012 S.L.T. 929 (OH), Lord Brodie

758. Non-Domestic Rating (Alteration of Lists and Appeals) (Wales) Regulations 2005
Reg.14, see *Goulborn v Cowell (Valuation Officer)* [2012] R.A. 303 (UT (Lands)), AJ Trott FRICS

765. Medicines for Human Use (Prescribing) Order 2005
revoked: SI 2012/1916 Sch.35
Art.1, amended: SI 2012/1479 Sch.1 para.45

766. Medicines (Pharmacy and General Sale Exemption) Amendment Order 2005
revoked: SI 2012/1916 Sch.35

768. Medicines for Human Use (Marketing Authorisations Etc.) Amendment Regulations 2005
revoked: SI 2012/1916 Sch.35

842. Occupational Pension Schemes (Levies) Regulations 2005
Reg.6, amended: SI 2012/539 Reg.3

848. Opticians Act 1989 (Amendment) Order 2005
Sch.1 Part 3 para.24, revoked (in part): SI 2012/1909 Sch.8 para.1

858. Pensions Increase (Review) Order 2005
applied: SI 2012/782 Art.3, Art.4

875. Education (Head Teachers Qualifications) (Amendment) (England) Regulations 2005
revoked: SI 2012/18 Sch.1

881. Merchant Shipping (Accident Reporting and Investigation) Regulations 2005
revoked: SI 2012/1743 Reg.1

894. Hazardous Waste (England and Wales) Regulations 2005
Reg.8, varied: 2012 c.11 s.12
Reg.9, varied: 2012 c.11 s.12
Reg.11, varied: 2012 c.11 s.12

902. Crime and Disorder Act 1998 (Service of Prosecution Evidence) Regulations 2005
applied: SI 2012/1726 r.3.11
referred to: SI 2012/1726 r.14.1, r.9.15
Reg.2, amended: SI 2012/1345 Reg.2
Reg.2, referred to: SI 2012/1726 r.9.15
Reg.3, amended: SI 2012/1345 Reg.2

2005– cont.

916. Gender Recognition (Disclosure of Information) (England, Wales and Northern Ireland) (No.2) Order 2005
Art.5, amended: SI 2012/ 1479 Sch.1 para.46
925. Greenhouse Gas Emissions Trading Scheme Regulations 2005
applied: SI 2012/ 3038 Reg.86, SSI 2012/ 360 Reg.17
revoked: SI 2012/ 3038 Reg.85
Part 1, applied: SI 2012/ 3038 Reg.86
Part 4, applied: SI 2012/ 3038 Reg.86
Part 5, applied: SI 2012/ 3038 Reg.86
Part 8, applied: SI 2012/ 3038 Reg.86
Part 9, applied: SI 2012/ 3038 Reg.86
Part 10, applied: SI 2012/ 3038 Reg.86
Reg.2, referred to: SI 2012/ 3038 Reg.86
Reg.8, amended: SSI 2012/ 360 Sch.11 para.12
Reg.8, applied: SI 2012/ 3038 Reg.88
Reg.9, applied: SI 2012/ 3038 Reg.88
Reg.10, applied: SI 2012/ 3038 Reg.53, SSI 2012/ 360 Reg.17
Reg.10, disapplied: SI 2012/ 3038 Reg.53
Reg.11, applied: SSI 2012/ 360 Reg.17
Reg.14, applied: SI 2012/ 3038 Reg.88
Reg.15, applied: SI 2012/ 3038 Reg.88
Reg.16, applied: SI 2012/ 3038 Reg.86
Reg.17, applied: SI 2012/ 3038 Reg.86
Reg.18, applied: SI 2012/ 3038 Reg.86
Reg.22, applied: SI 2012/ 3038 Reg.86
Reg.22, disapplied: SI 2012/ 3038 Reg.86
Reg.22, varied: SI 2012/ 3038 Reg.86
Reg.26, applied: SI 2012/ 3038 Reg.86
Reg.26, varied: SI 2012/ 3038 Reg.86
Reg.27A, applied: SI 2012/ 3038 Reg.86
Reg.32, referred to: SI 2012/ 3038 Reg.86
Reg.32, varied: SI 2012/ 3038 Reg.86
Reg.35, applied: SI 2012/ 3038 Reg.86
Reg.36, applied: SI 2012/ 3038 Reg.86
Reg.37, applied: SI 2012/ 3038 Reg.86
Reg.38, applied: SI 2012/ 3038 Reg.86
Reg.39, applied: SI 2012/ 3038 Reg.86
Reg.40, applied: SI 2012/ 3038 Reg.86
Reg.41, applied: SI 2012/ 3038 Reg.86
Sch.1, applied: SI 2012/ 3038 Reg.86
Sch.2, applied: SI 2012/ 3038 Reg.86
Sch.3, applied: SI 2012/ 3038 Reg.86
Sch.4, applied: SI 2012/ 3038 Reg.86
Sch.6 para.1, revoked (in part): SI 2012/ 2788 Reg.17
927. Midland Metro (Wednesbury to Brierley Hill and Miscellaneous Amendments) Order 2005
Art.58, amended: SI 2012/ 1659 Art.2
Sch.11 Part 1 para.1, amended: SI 2012/ 1659 Art.2
Sch.11 Part 1 para.2, amended: SI 2012/ 1659 Art.2
Sch.11 Part 1 para.3, amended: SI 2012/ 1659 Art.2
Sch.11 Part 1 para.4, amended: SI 2012/ 1659 Art.2
Sch.11 Part 1 para.5, amended: SI 2012/ 1659 Art.2
Sch.11 Part 1 para.6, amended: SI 2012/ 1659 Art.2
Sch.11 Part 1 para.7, amended: SI 2012/ 1659 Art.2
Sch.11 Part 1 para.8, amended: SI 2012/ 1659 Art.2
Sch.11 Part 1 para.9, amended: SI 2012/ 1659 Art.2
Sch.11 Part 1 para.10, amended: SI 2012/ 1659 Art.2
Sch.11 Part 1 para.11, amended: SI 2012/ 1659 Art.2
Sch.11 Part 1 para.12, amended: SI 2012/ 1659 Art.2
Sch.11 Part 1 para.13, amended: SI 2012/ 1659 Art.2
Sch.11 Part 1 para.14, amended: SI 2012/ 1659 Art.2
Sch.11 Part 1 para.15, amended: SI 2012/ 1659 Art.2
Sch.11 Part 1 para.16, amended: SI 2012/ 1659 Art.2
Sch.11 Part 1 para.17, amended: SI 2012/ 1659 Art.2
Sch.11 Part 1 para.18, amended: SI 2012/ 1659 Art.2

2005– cont.

927. Midland Metro (Wednesbury to Brierley Hill and Miscellaneous Amendments) Order 2005– cont.
Sch.11 Part 1 para.19, amended: SI 2012/ 1659 Art.2
Sch.11 Part 1 para.20, amended: SI 2012/ 1659 Art.2
950. Criminal Justice Act 2003 (Commencement No.8 and Transitional and Saving Provisions) Order 2005
Sch.2 Part 001 para.5, amended: SI 2012/ 2905 Art.4
Sch.2 Part 003 para.14, revoked: 2012 c.10 Sch.14 para.17
Sch.2 Part 003 para.15, revoked: 2012 c.10 s.121
Sch.2 Part 003 para.16, revoked: 2012 c.10 s.121
Sch.2 Part 003 para.17, revoked: 2012 c.10 s.121
Sch.2 Part 003 para.18, revoked: 2012 c.10 s.121
Sch.2 Part 003 para.19, revoked (in part): 2012 c.10 s.121
Sch.2 Part 003 para.20, revoked: 2012 c.10 s.121
Sch.2 Part 003 para.22, revoked: 2012 c.10 s.121
Sch.2 Part 003 para.23, revoked: 2012 c.10 s.121
Sch.2 Part 003 para.24, revoked: 2012 c.10 s.121
Sch.2 Part 003 para.25, revoked: 2012 c.10 s.121
Sch.2 Part 003 para.26, revoked: 2012 c.10 s.121
Sch.2 Part 003 para.27, revoked: 2012 c.10 s.121
Sch.2 Part 003 para.28, revoked: 2012 c.10 s.121
Sch.2 Part 003 para.29, revoked: SI 2012/ 2905 Art.4
Sch.2 Part 003 para.30, revoked: 2012 c.10 s.121
Sch.2 Part 003 para.31, revoked: 2012 c.10 s.121
Sch.2 Part 003 para.32, revoked: 2012 c.10 s.121
Sch.2 Part 003 para.33, revoked: 2012 c.10 s.121
Sch.2 Part 003 para.34, revoked: 2012 c.10 s.121
Sch.2 Pt 003 para.19, see *R. (on the application of Elam) v Secretary of State for Justice* [2012] EWCA Civ 29, [2012] 1 W.L.R. 2722 (CA (Civ Div)), Laws, L.J.
985. Criminal Procedure and Investigations Act 1996 (Code of Practice) Order 2005
applied: SI 2012/ 1726 r.22.9
1015. National Health Service (Pharmaceutical Services) Amendment Regulations 2005
Reg.2, revoked: SI 2012/ 1909 Sch.8 para.9
1082. Manufacture and Storage of Explosives Regulations 2005
Reg.2, applied: SI 2012/ 1652 Sch.8 Part 1
Reg.9, applied: SI 2012/ 1652 Sch.8 Part 1
Reg.10, applied: SI 2012/ 1652 Sch.8 Part 1, Sch.8 Part 2
Reg.11, applied: SI 2012/ 1652 Sch.8 Part 2
Reg.16, applied: SI 2012/ 1652 Sch.8 Part 1, Sch.8 Part 2
Reg.20, applied: SI 2012/ 1652 Sch.8 Part 1, Sch.8 Part 2
Sch.1 para.1, applied: SI 2012/ 1652 Reg.9
Sch.1 para.2, applied: SI 2012/ 1652 Reg.9
1094. Medicines (Advisory Bodies) Regulations 2005
Reg.1, revoked: SI 2012/ 1916 Sch.35
Reg.2, revoked: SI 2012/ 1916 Sch.35
Reg.3, revoked: SI 2012/ 1916 Sch.35
Reg.4, revoked: SI 2012/ 1916 Sch.35
Reg.5, revoked: SI 2012/ 1916 Sch.35
Reg.6, revoked: SI 2012/ 1916 Sch.35
Reg.7, revoked: SI 2012/ 1916 Sch.35
Reg.8, revoked: SI 2012/ 1916 Sch.35
Reg.9, revoked: SI 2012/ 1916 Sch.35
Reg.10, revoked: SI 2012/ 1916 Sch.35
Reg.11, revoked: SI 2012/ 1916 Sch.35
Reg.12, revoked: SI 2012/ 1916 Sch.35

2005–cont.

1094. Medicines (Advisory Bodies) Regulations 2005–*cont.*
Sch.1 para.1, revoked: SI 2012/1916 Sch.35
Sch.1 para.2, revoked: SI 2012/1916 Sch.35
Sch.1 para.3, revoked: SI 2012/1916 Sch.35
Sch.1 para.4, revoked: SI 2012/1916 Sch.35
Sch.1 para.5, revoked: SI 2012/1916 Sch.35
Sch.1 para.6, revoked: SI 2012/1916 Sch.35
Sch.1 para.7, revoked: SI 2012/1916 Sch.35
Sch.1 para.8, revoked: SI 2012/1916 Sch.35
Sch.1 para.9, revoked: SI 2012/1916 Sch.35
Sch.1 para.10, revoked: SI 2012/1916 Sch.35
Sch.1 para.11, revoked: SI 2012/1916 Sch.35
Sch.1 para.12, revoked (in part): SI 2012/1916 Sch.35
Sch.1 para.13, revoked: SI 2012/1916 Sch.35
Sch.1 para.14, revoked: SI 2012/1916 Sch.35
Sch.1 para.15, revoked: SI 2012/1916 Sch.35
Sch.2 para.1, revoked: SI 2012/1916 Sch.35
Sch.2 para.2, revoked: SI 2012/1916 Sch.35
Sch.2 para.3, revoked: SI 2012/1916 Sch.35
Sch.2 para.4, revoked: SI 2012/1916 Sch.35
Sch.3 para.1, revoked: SI 2012/1916 Sch.35
Sch.3 para.2, revoked: SI 2012/1916 Sch.35

1118. A48 Trunk Road (Porthyrhyd Junction, Carmarthenshire) (De-Restriction) Order 2005
disapplied: SI 2012/11 Art.6

1207. Fodder Plant Seed (Wales) Regulations 2005
revoked: SI 2012/245 Reg.34

1258. Sudan (United Nations Measures) (Overseas Territories) Order 2005
Sch.1, amended: SI 2012/362 Sch.1

1313. Adoption Agencies (Wales) Regulations 2005
Reg.2, amended: SI 2012/1479 Sch.1 para.75, SI 2012/1905 Reg.3
Reg.7, amended: SI 2012/1905 Reg.4
Reg.8A, added: SI 2012/1905 Reg.5
Reg.17, amended: SI 2012/1905 Reg.6
Reg.17, applied: SI 2012/1905 Reg.9
Reg.18, applied: SI 2012/1905 Reg.9
Reg.19, amended: SI 2012/1905 Reg.7
Reg.19, applied: SI 2012/1905 Reg.9

1379. Displaced Persons (Temporary Protection) Regulations 2005
Reg.2, amended: SI 2012/700 Sch.1 para.14

1401. Textile Products (Indications of Fibre Content) (Amendment) Regulations 2005
revoked: SI 2012/1102 Sch.1

1437. Education (Pupil Information) (England) Regulations 2005
Reg.2, amended: SI 2012/765 Art.8, SI 2012/979 Sch.1 para.18
Reg.5, amended: SI 2012/979 Sch.1 para.18
Sch.2 para.6, amended: SI 2012/765 Art.8

1446. NHS Institute for Innovation and Improvement (Establishment and Constitution) Order 2005
revoked: 2012 c.7 s.282

1447. NHS Institute for Innovation and Improvement Regulations 2005
Reg.3, amended: SI 2012/1641 Sch.4 para.12, SI 2012/2404 Sch.3 para.42

1461. Democratic Republic of the Congo (United Nations Sanctions) (Overseas Territories) Order 2005
Sch.1, amended: SI 2012/362 Sch.1

1462. Sudan (United Nations Measures) (Channel Islands) Order 2005
Sch.1 Part 1, amended: SI 2012/362 Sch.1

2005–cont.

1463. Sudan (United Nations Measures) (Isle of Man) Order 2005
Sch.1 Part 1, amended: SI 2012/362 Sch.1

1467. Scottish Administration (Offices) Order 2005
revoked: SI 2012/3073 Art.4

1468. Democratic Republic of the Congo (United Nations Sanctions) (Channel Islands) Order 2005
Sch.1 Part 1, amended: SI 2012/362 Sch.1

1469. Democratic Republic of the Congo (United Nations Sanctions) (Isle of Man) Order 2005
Sch.1 Part 1, amended: SI 2012/362 Sch.1

1473. General Optical Council (Continuing Education and Training Rules) Order of Council 2005
Sch.1, added: SI 2012/2882 Sch.1
Sch.1, amended: SI 2012/2882 Sch.1
Sch.1, revoked: SI 2012/2882 Sch.1
Sch.1, substituted: SI 2012/2882 Sch.1

1474. General Optical Council (Committee Constitution Rules) Order of Council 2005
Sch.1, amended: SI 2012/3006 Art.13

1478. General Optical Council (Registration Rules) Order of Council 2005
Sch.1, amended: SI 2012/1916 Sch.34 para.90

1501. National Health Service (Pharmaceutical Services) (Amendment No 2) Regulations 2005
revoked: SI 2012/1909 Sch.8 para.9

1517. Democratic Republic of the Congo (United Nations Measures) Order 2005
revoked: SI 2012/1511 Reg.18

1520. Medicines (Sale or Supply) (Miscellaneous Amendments) Regulations 2005
revoked: SI 2012/1916 Sch.35

1527. International Criminal Tribunal for the Former Yugoslavia (Financial Sanctions Against Indictees) Regulations 2005
revoked: SI 2012/1510 Reg.2

1530. Home Energy Efficiency Scheme (England) Regulations 2005
Reg.2, amended: SI 2012/2140 Reg.3
Reg.3, amended: SI 2012/2140 Reg.3
Reg.4, amended: SI 2012/2140 Reg.3
Reg.9, amended: SI 2012/2140 Reg.3

1541. Regulatory Reform (Fire Safety) Order 2005
see *R. v Draper (Joseph)* [2011] EWCA Crim 2786, [2012] 1 Cr. App. R. (S.) 112 (CA (Crim Div)), Richards, L.J.; see *R. v O'Rourke (John Patrick)* [2011] EWCA Crim 3263, [2012] 1 Cr. App. R. (S.) 93 (CA (Crim Div)), Pitchford, L.J.
Art.8, see *R. v Draper (Joseph)* [2011] EWCA Crim 2786, [2012] 1 Cr. App. R. (S.) 112 (CA (Crim Div)), Richards, L.J.
Art.9, see *R. v O'Rourke (John Patrick)* [2011] EWCA Crim 3263, [2012] 1 Cr. App. R. (S.) 93 (CA (Crim Div)), Pitchford, L.J.
Art.17, applied: SI 2012/3124 Reg.4
Art.24, enabled: SI 2012/1085
Art.32, see *R. v O'Rourke (John Patrick)* [2011] EWCA Crim 3263, [2012] 1 Cr. App. R. (S.) 93 (CA (Crim Div)), Pitchford, L.J.

1641. Road Vehicles (Construction and Use) (Amendment) Regulations 2005
revoked: SI 2012/1404 Sch.1

1710. Medicines (Provision of False or Misleading Information and Miscellaneous Amendments) Regulations 2005
revoked: SI 2012/1916 Sch.35

2005–cont.

1788. Community Interest Company Regulations 2005
Reg.29, amended: SI 2012/ 2335 Reg.2
Reg.29A, added: SI 2012/ 2335 Reg.2
1794. Midland Metro (Birmingham City Centre Extension, etc.) Order 2005
Art.54, amended: SI 2012/ 1659 Art.2
Sch.8 Part 2 para.1, amended: SI 2012/ 1659 Art.2
Sch.8 Part 2 para.2, amended: SI 2012/ 1659 Art.2
Sch.8 Part 2 para.3, amended: SI 2012/ 1659 Art.2
Sch.8 Part 2 para.4, amended: SI 2012/ 1659 Art.2
Sch.8 Part 2 para.5, amended: SI 2012/ 1659 Art.2
Sch.8 Part 2 para.6, amended: SI 2012/ 1659 Art.2
Sch.8 Part 2 para.7, amended: SI 2012/ 1659 Art.2
Sch.8 Part 2 para.8, amended: SI 2012/ 1659 Art.2
Sch.8 Part 2 para.9, amended: SI 2012/ 1659 Art.2
Sch.8 Part 2 para.10, amended: SI 2012/ 1659 Art.2
Sch.8 Part 2 para.11, amended: SI 2012/ 1659 Art.2
Sch.8 Part 2 para.12, amended: SI 2012/ 1659 Art.2
Sch.8 Part 2 para.13, amended: SI 2012/ 1659 Art.2
Sch.8 Part 2 para.14, amended: SI 2012/ 1659 Art.2
Sch.8 Part 2 para.15, amended: SI 2012/ 1659 Art.2
Sch.8 Part 2 para.16, amended: SI 2012/ 1659 Art.2
Sch.8 Part 2 para.17, amended: SI 2012/ 1659 Art.2
Sch.8 Part 2 para.18, amended: SI 2012/ 1659 Art.2
Sch.8 Part 2 para.19, amended: SI 2012/ 1659 Art.2
Sch.8 Part 2 para.20, amended: SI 2012/ 1659 Art.2
1803. General Product Safety Regulations 2005
Reg.15, amended: SI 2012/ 1848 Reg.6
Reg.15, applied: SI 2012/ 3032 Sch.3 para.4
Reg.15, varied: SI 2012/ 3032 Sch.3 para.4
1806. Hazardous Waste (Wales) Regulations 2005
Reg.8, varied: 2012 c.11 s.12
Reg.9, varied: 2012 c.11 s.12
Reg.11, varied: 2012 c.11 s.12
1818. Education (Induction Arrangements for School Teachers) (Wales) Regulations 2005
Reg.3, amended: SI 2012/ 1675 Reg.3, Reg.4
Reg.5, amended: SI 2012/ 1675 Reg.4
Reg.7, amended: SI 2012/ 1675 Reg.4
Reg.8, substituted: SI 2012/ 1675 Reg.5
Reg.9, substituted: SI 2012/ 1675 Reg.6
Reg.12, substituted: SI 2012/ 1675 Reg.7
Reg.13, amended: SI 2012/ 1675 Reg.4
Reg.14, applied: SI 2012/ 1115 Reg.12, Sch.1 para.2
Reg.14, substituted: SI 2012/ 1675 Reg.8
Reg.16, amended: SI 2012/ 1675 Reg.4
Reg.18, revoked (in part): SI 2012/ 1675 Reg.9
Reg.20, amended: SI 2012/ 1675 Reg.4
Sch.1 para.2, substituted: SI 2012/ 1675 Reg.10
Sch.1 para.4, revoked: SI 2012/ 1675 Reg.10
Sch.1 para.5, revoked: SI 2012/ 1675 Reg.10
Sch.1 para.6, revoked: SI 2012/ 1675 Reg.10
Sch.1 para.22, amended: SI 2012/ 724 Reg.10, SI 2012/ 1675 Reg.10
Sch.1 para.23, amended: SI 2012/ 724 Reg.10
Sch.2 para.2, applied: SI 2012/ 1115 Reg.12
1868. Stamp Duty Land Tax Avoidance Schemes (Prescribed Descriptions of Arrangements) Regulations 2005
Reg.1, amended: SI 2012/ 2395 Reg.3, Reg.4
Reg.2, substituted: SI 2012/ 2395 Reg.5
Sch.1, amended: SI 2012/ 2395 Reg.6
1869. Tax Avoidance Schemes (Information) (Amendment) Regulations 2005
referred to: SI 2012/ 1836 Reg.4
revoked: SI 2012/ 1836 Sch.1

2005–cont.

1970. Air Navigation Order 2005
applied: 2012 c.19 Sch.6 para.4
1973. Children Act 2004 (Joint Area Reviews) Regulations 2005
Sch.1 para.9, revoked: SI 2012/ 2401 Sch.1 para.39
1996. Registration of Civil Partnerships (Fees) Order 2005
Sch.1, amended: SI 2012/ 761 Art.2
2014. Friendly Societies (Modification of the Corporation Tax Acts) Regulations 2005
revoked: SI 2012/ 3008 Sch.1
2017. Partnerships (Restrictions on Contributions to a Trade) Regulations 2005
see *Samarkand Film Partnership No.3 v Revenue and Customs Commissioners* [2012] S.F.T.D. 1 (FTT (Tax)), Judge Charles Hellier
Reg.5, see *Samarkand Film Partnership No.3 v Revenue and Customs Commissioners* [2012] S.F.T.D. 1 (FTT (Tax)), Judge Charles Hellier
2024. Pension Protection Fund (Reference of Reviewable Matters to the PPF Ombudsman) Regulations 2005
Reg.3, amended: SI 2012/ 1688 Reg.7
2038. Education (School Inspection) (England) Regulations 2005
Reg.4, amended: SI 2012/ 956 Art.10
2042. Civil Contingencies Act 2004 (Contingency Planning) Regulations 2005
Reg.3, amended: SI 2012/ 624 Reg.3
Reg.4, substituted: SI 2012/ 624 Reg.4
Reg.7, amended: SI 2012/ 624 Reg.5
Reg.16, amended: SI 2012/ 624 Reg.6
Reg.44A, added: SI 2012/ 624 Reg.7
Reg.47, amended: SI 2012/ 624 Reg.8
Reg.59, added: SI 2012/ 624 Reg.9
2045. Income Tax (Construction Industry Scheme) Regulations 2005
Reg.2, amended: SI 2012/ 820 Reg.3
Reg.8, amended: SI 2012/ 820 Reg.4
Reg.32, amended: SI 2012/ 820 Reg.5
Reg.45, amended: SI 2012/ 820 Reg.6
Reg.56, amended: SI 2012/ 820 Reg.7
2078. Mental Health (Care and Treatment) (Scotland) Act 2003 (Consequential Provisions) Order 2005
Art.5, amended: SI 2012/ 2595 Art.12
Art.6, amended: SI 2012/ 2595 Art.12
Art.7, amended: SI 2012/ 2595 Art.12
2184. Occupational Pension Schemes (Fraud Compensation Payments and Miscellaneous Amendments) Regulations 2005
Reg.1, amended: SI 2012/ 1688 Reg.8, SI 2012/ 3083 Reg.7
2222. River Tyne (Tunnels) Order 2005
applied: SI 2012/ 3053 Art.2
Sch.14, enabled: SI 2012/ 3053
2415. NHS Business Services Authority (Awdurdod Gwasanaethau Busnes y GIG) Regulations 2005
Reg.1, amended: SI 2012/ 1641 Sch.3 para.10
Reg.3, amended: SI 2012/ 1641 Sch.3 para.10, Sch.4 para.13, SI 2012/ 2404 Sch.3 para.43
2467. Employment Equality (Sex Discrimination) Regulations 2005
Reg.13, varied: 2012 c.11 s.12
Reg.35, varied: 2012 c.11 s.12
2517. Plant Health (Forestry) Order 2005
Art.2, amended: SI 2012/ 2707 Art.2
Art.8, amended: SI 2012/ 2707 Art.2

2005–cont.

2517. Plant Health (Forestry) Order 2005–*cont.*
Art.21, amended: SI 2012/2707 Art.2
Art.38, substituted: SI 2012/2707 Art.2
Art.39, amended: SI 2012/2707 Art.2
Sch.1 para.1a, added: SI 2012/2707 Art.2
Sch.2 Part A, amended: SI 2012/2707 Art.2
Sch.4 Part A, amended: SI 2012/2707 Art.2
Sch.4 Part B, amended: SI 2012/2707 Art.2
Sch.5 Part A para.1b, added: SI 2012/2707 Art.2
Sch.5 Part A para.1c, added: SI 2012/2707 Art.2
Sch.6 Part A para.6, added: SI 2012/2707 Art.2
Sch.7 Part A para.6, added: SI 2012/2707 Art.2

2530. Plant Health (England) Order 2005
Art.2, amended: SI 2012/2922 Art.2
Art.8, amended: SI 2012/2922 Art.2
Art.12, applied: SI 2012/745 Reg.2
Art.19, amended: SI 2012/3033 Art.2
Art.22, amended: SI 2012/2922 Art.2
Art.40, applied: SI 2012/745 Reg.4
Art.40, substituted: SI 2012/2922 Art.2
Art.41, amended: SI 2012/2922 Art.2
Art.41, applied: SI 2012/745 Reg.4
Art.44A, added: SI 2012/697 Reg.3
Art.45, amended: SI 2012/697 Reg.3
Art.46, substituted: SI 2012/697 Reg.3
Sch.1 Part B, amended: SI 2012/2922 Art.2
Sch.2 Part B, amended: SI 2012/2922 Art.2
Sch.4 Part A, amended: SI 2012/2922 Art.2
Sch.4 Part B, amended: SI 2012/2922 Art.2, SI 2012/3033 Art.2
Sch.5 Part A para.1, amended: SI 2012/2922 Art.2
Sch.5 Part A para.2, amended: SI 2012/2922 Art.2
Sch.6 Part A para.9, added: SI 2012/2922 Art.2
Sch.7 Part A para.9, added: SI 2012/2922 Art.2
Sch.8 Part A para.1, substituted: SI 2012/697 Reg.4
Sch.8 Part A para.5, amended: SI 2012/697 Reg.4
Sch.8 Part B para.1, substituted: SI 2012/697 Reg.4
Sch.8 Part B para.5, amended: SI 2012/697 Reg.4

2531. NHS Blood and Transplant (Gwaed a Thrawsblaniadau'r GIG) Regulations 2005
Reg.1, amended: SI 2012/1641 Sch.3 para.9
Reg.3, amended: SI 2012/1641 Sch.3 para.9, Sch.4 para.14, SI 2012/2404 Sch.3 para.44

2572. Thurrock Development Corporation (Planning Functions) Order 2005
revoked: SI 2012/535 Art.2

2681. Housing (Right to Buy) (Information to Secure Tenants) (Wales) Order 2005
Sch.1 para.1, amended: SI 2012/2090 Sch.1 para.4

2693. Civil Aviation (Investigation of Military Air Accidents at Civil Aerodromes) Regulations 2005
applied: 2012 c.19 Sch.6 para.4

2720. Adoption Support Agencies (England) and Adoption Agencies (Miscellaneous Amendments) Regulations 2005
Reg.7, amended: SI 2012/2404 Sch.3 para.45

2721. London Thames Gateway Development Corporation (Planning Functions) Order 2005
revoked: SI 2012/2167 Art.8

2722. Planning and Compulsory Purchase Act 2004 (Commencement No 4 and Consequential, Transitional and Savings Provisions) (Wales) Order 2005
Art.6, revoked: SI 2012/1664 Art.3
Sch.1, amended: SI 2012/1664 Art.2

2005–cont.

2750. Medicines (Traditional Herbal Medicinal Products for Human Use) Regulations 2005
Reg.1, revoked: SI 2012/1916 Sch.35
Reg.2, revoked: SI 2012/1916 Sch.35
Reg.3, revoked: SI 2012/1916 Sch.35
Reg.4, revoked: SI 2012/1916 Sch.35
Reg.5, applied: SI 2012/504 Reg.47
Reg.5, revoked: SI 2012/1916 Sch.35
Reg.6, applied: SI 2012/504 Reg.18
Reg.6, revoked: SI 2012/1916 Sch.35
Reg.7, revoked: SI 2012/1916 Sch.35
Reg.8, applied: SI 2012/504 Sch.7 para.3
Reg.8, revoked: SI 2012/1916 Sch.35
Reg.9, revoked: SI 2012/1916 Sch.35
Reg.10, revoked: SI 2012/1916 Sch.35
Reg.11, revoked: SI 2012/1916 Sch.35
Reg.12, revoked: SI 2012/1916 Sch.35
Sch.1 para.1, amended: SI 2012/1479 Sch.1 para.48
Sch.1 para.1, revoked: SI 2012/1916 Sch.35
Sch.1 para.2, revoked: SI 2012/1916 Sch.35
Sch.1 para.3, revoked: SI 2012/1916 Sch.35
Sch.1 para.4, revoked: SI 2012/1916 Sch.35
Sch.1 para.5, revoked: SI 2012/1916 Sch.35
Sch.1 para.6, revoked: SI 2012/1916 Sch.35
Sch.1 para.7, revoked: SI 2012/1916 Sch.35
Sch.2 Part 1, revoked: SI 2012/1916 Sch.35
Sch.2 Part 2, revoked: SI 2012/1916 Sch.35
Sch.2 Part 2 para.12, applied: SI 2012/504 Reg.37
Sch.2 Part 3 para.15, revoked: SI 2012/1916 Sch.35
Sch.2 Part 3 para.16, revoked: SI 2012/1916 Sch.35
Sch.2 Part 3 para.17, applied: SI 2012/504 Reg.37
Sch.2 Part 3 para.17, revoked: SI 2012/1916 Sch.35
Sch.2 Part 4 para.18, revoked: SI 2012/1916 Sch.35
Sch.2 Part 4 para.19, revoked: SI 2012/1916 Sch.35
Sch.2 Part 4 para.20, applied: SI 2012/504 Reg.37
Sch.2 Part 4 para.20, revoked: SI 2012/1916 Sch.35
Sch.2 Part 5 para.21, revoked: SI 2012/1916 Sch.35
Sch.3 para.1, revoked: SI 2012/1916 Sch.35
Sch.3 para.2, revoked: SI 2012/1916 Sch.35
Sch.3 para.3, revoked: SI 2012/1916 Sch.35
Sch.3 para.4, revoked: SI 2012/1916 Sch.35
Sch.3 para.5, revoked: SI 2012/1916 Sch.35
Sch.3 para.6, revoked: SI 2012/1916 Sch.35
Sch.3 para.7, revoked: SI 2012/1916 Sch.35
Sch.3 para.8, revoked: SI 2012/1916 Sch.35
Sch.3 para.9, revoked: SI 2012/1916 Sch.35
Sch.3 para.10, revoked: SI 2012/1916 Sch.35
Sch.3 para.11, revoked: SI 2012/1916 Sch.35
Sch.3 para.12, revoked: SI 2012/1916 Sch.35
Sch.3 para.13, revoked: SI 2012/1916 Sch.35
Sch.3 para.14, revoked: SI 2012/1916 Sch.35
Sch.3 para.15, revoked: SI 2012/1916 Sch.35
Sch.3 para.16, revoked: SI 2012/1916 Sch.35
Sch.3 para.17, revoked: SI 2012/1916 Sch.35
Sch.3 para.18, revoked: SI 2012/1916 Sch.35
Sch.3 para.19, revoked: SI 2012/1916 Sch.35
Sch.3 para.20, revoked: SI 2012/1916 Sch.35
Sch.3 para.21, revoked: SI 2012/1916 Sch.35
Sch.3 para.22, revoked: SI 2012/1916 Sch.35
Sch.3 para.23, revoked: SI 2012/1916 Sch.35
Sch.3 para.24, revoked: SI 2012/1916 Sch.35
Sch.3 para.25, revoked: SI 2012/1916 Sch.35
Sch.7 para.8, revoked (in part): SI 2012/1916 Sch.35

2754. Medicines (Advisory Bodies) (No.2) Regulations 2005
Reg.1, revoked: SI 2012/1916 Sch.35
Reg.2, revoked: SI 2012/1916 Sch.35
Reg.3, revoked: SI 2012/1916 Sch.35

2005– cont.

2754. Medicines (Advisory Bodies) (No.2) Regulations 2005– *cont.*
Reg.4, revoked (in part): SI 2012/ 1916 Sch.35
Reg.5, revoked (in part): SI 2012/ 1916 Sch.35
Reg.6, revoked: SI 2012/ 1916 Sch.35
Sch.1 para.1, revoked: SI 2012/ 1916 Sch.35
Sch.1 para.2, revoked: SI 2012/ 1916 Sch.35
Sch.1 para.3, revoked: SI 2012/ 1916 Sch.35
Sch.1 para.4, revoked: SI 2012/ 1916 Sch.35
Sch.2 para.1, revoked: SI 2012/ 1916 Sch.35
Sch.4 para.1, revoked: SI 2012/ 1916 Sch.35
Sch.4 para.2, revoked: SI 2012/ 1916 Sch.35
Sch.4 para.4, revoked: SI 2012/ 1916 Sch.35
Sch.4 para.5, revoked: SI 2012/ 1916 Sch.35
Sch.4 para.6, revoked: SI 2012/ 1916 Sch.35
Sch.4 para.7, revoked (in part): SI 2012/ 1916 Sch.35
Sch.5 Part 1 para.1, revoked: SI 2012/ 1916 Sch.35
Sch.5 Part 1 para.2, revoked: SI 2012/ 1916 Sch.35
Sch.5 Part 1 para.3, revoked: SI 2012/ 1916 Sch.35
Sch.5 Part 1 para.4, revoked: SI 2012/ 1916 Sch.35
Sch.5 Part 1 para.5, revoked: SI 2012/ 1916 Sch.35
Sch.5 Part 1 para.6, revoked: SI 2012/ 1916 Sch.35
Sch.5 Part 1 para.7, revoked: SI 2012/ 1916 Sch.35
Sch.5 Part 1 para.8, revoked: SI 2012/ 1916 Sch.35
Sch.5 Part 1 para.9, revoked: SI 2012/ 1916 Sch.35
Sch.5 Part 1 para.10, revoked: SI 2012/ 1916 Sch.35
Sch.5 Part 1 para.11, revoked: SI 2012/ 1916 Sch.35
Sch.5 Part 1 para.12, revoked: SI 2012/ 1916 Sch.35
Sch.5 Part 1 para.13, revoked: SI 2012/ 1916 Sch.35
Sch.5 Part 1 para.14, revoked: SI 2012/ 1916 Sch.35
Sch.5 Part 1 para.15, revoked: SI 2012/ 1916 Sch.35
Sch.5 Part 1 para.16, revoked: SI 2012/ 1916 Sch.35
Sch.5 Part 1 para.17, revoked: SI 2012/ 1916 Sch.35
Sch.5 Part 1 para.18, revoked: SI 2012/ 1916 Sch.35
Sch.5 Part 1 para.19, revoked: SI 2012/ 1916 Sch.35
Sch.5 Part 1 para.20, revoked: SI 2012/ 1916 Sch.35
Sch.5 Part 1 para.21, revoked: SI 2012/ 1916 Sch.35
Sch.5 Part 1 para.22, revoked: SI 2012/ 1916 Sch.35
Sch.5 Part 2 para.1, revoked: SI 2012/ 1916 Sch.35
Sch.5 Part 2 para.2, revoked: SI 2012/ 1916 Sch.35
Sch.5 Part 2 para.3, revoked: SI 2012/ 1916 Sch.35
Sch.5 Part 3 para.1, revoked: SI 2012/ 1916 Sch.35
Sch.5 Part 3 para.2, revoked: SI 2012/ 1916 Sch.35
Sch.5 Part 3 para.3, revoked: SI 2012/ 1916 Sch.35
Sch.5 Part 3 para.4, revoked: SI 2012/ 1916 Sch.35
Sch.5 Part 3 para.5, revoked: SI 2012/ 1916 Sch.35
Sch.5 Part 3 para.6, revoked: SI 2012/ 1916 Sch.35
Sch.5 Part 3 para.7, revoked: SI 2012/ 1916 Sch.35
Sch.5 Part 3 para.8, revoked: SI 2012/ 1916 Sch.35
Sch.5 Part 3 para.9, revoked: SI 2012/ 1916 Sch.35
Sch.5 Part 3 para.10, revoked: SI 2012/ 1916 Sch.35
Sch.5 Part 3 para.11, revoked: SI 2012/ 1916 Sch.35
Sch.5 Part 3 para.12, revoked: SI 2012/ 1916 Sch.35
Sch.5 Part 3 para.13, revoked: SI 2012/ 1916 Sch.35
Sch.5 Part 3 para.14, revoked: SI 2012/ 1916 Sch.35
Sch.5 Part 3 para.15, revoked: SI 2012/ 1916 Sch.35
Sch.5 Part 3 para.16, revoked: SI 2012/ 1916 Sch.35
Sch.5 Part 3 para.17, revoked: SI 2012/ 1916 Sch.35
Sch.5 Part 3 para.18, revoked: SI 2012/ 1916 Sch.35
Sch.5 Part 3 para.19, revoked: SI 2012/ 1916 Sch.35
Sch.5 Part 3 para.20, revoked: SI 2012/ 1916 Sch.35
Sch.5 Part 3 para.21, revoked: SI 2012/ 1916 Sch.35
Sch.5 Part 4 para.1, revoked: SI 2012/ 1916 Sch.35
Sch.5 Part 4 para.2, revoked: SI 2012/ 1916 Sch.35
Sch.5 Part 4 para.3, revoked: SI 2012/ 1916 Sch.35
Sch.5 Part 4 para.4, revoked: SI 2012/ 1916 Sch.35
Sch.5 Part 4 para.5, revoked: SI 2012/ 1916 Sch.35
Sch.5 Part 4 para.6, revoked: SI 2012/ 1916 Sch.35

2005– cont.

2755. Bus Lane Contraventions (Approved Local Authorities) (England) Order 2005
Sch.2, amended: SI 2012/ 846 Art.5, SI 2012/ 2659 Art.4
2761. Civil Partnership (Registration Abroad and Certificates) Order 2005
applied: SI 2012/ 798 Sch.1 Part 1
Art.2, amended: SI 2012/ 3063 Art.3
Art.3, amended: SI 2012/ 3063 Art.4
Art.4, amended: SI 2012/ 3063 Art.4
Art.5, amended: SI 2012/ 3063 Art.4
Art.6, amended: SI 2012/ 3063 Art.4
Art.7, amended: SI 2012/ 3063 Art.4
Art.8, amended: SI 2012/ 3063 Art.4
Art.10, amended: SI 2012/ 3063 Art.4
Art.11, amended: SI 2012/ 3063 Art.4
Art.12, amended: SI 2012/ 3063 Art.4
Art.13, amended: SI 2012/ 3063 Art.4
Art.14, amended: SI 2012/ 3063 Art.4
Art.15, amended: SI 2012/ 3063 Art.4
Art.16, amended: SI 2012/ 3063 Art.4
Art.17, amended: SI 2012/ 3063 Art.4
Sch.1, amended: SI 2012/ 3063 Art.4
2773. Volatile Organic Compounds in Paints, Varnishes and Vehicle Refinishing Products Regulations 2005
revoked: SI 2012/ 1715 Reg.10
2786. Leicestershire County Council (Ashby de la Zouch Canal Extension) Order 2005
Art.2, amended: SI 2012/ 1659 Art.2
Sch.9 para.1, amended: SI 2012/ 1659 Art.2
Sch.9 para.2, amended: SI 2012/ 1659 Art.2
2787. Medicines (Advertising Amendments) Regulations 2005
revoked: SI 2012/ 1916 Sch.35
2789. Medicines for Human Use (Manufacturing, Wholesale Dealing and Miscellaneous Amendments) Regulations 2005
revoked: SI 2012/ 1916 Sch.35
2791. Herbal Medicines Advisory Committee Order 2005
revoked: SI 2012/ 1916 Sch.35
2798. Criminal Justice Act 2003 (Mandatory Life Sentences Appeals in Transitional Cases) Order 2005
applied: SI 2012/ 1726 r.65.1, r.68.11, r 68.12, r.65.5
Art.12, applied: SI 2012/ 1726 r.74.1, r.74.2
Art.13, applied: SI 2012/ 1726 r.74.2
Art.15, applied: SI 2012/ 1726 r.74.2
2900. Waste (Household Waste Duty of Care) (England and Wales) Regulations 2005
Reg.4, revoked: SI 2012/ 811 Sch.2 para.1
2903. Greenhouse Gas Emissions Trading Scheme (Amendment) and National Emissions Inventory Regulations 2005
Reg.4, revoked: SI 2012/ 3038 Reg.85
2914. Government of Maintained Schools (Wales) Regulations 2005
varied: SI 2012/ 1643 Reg.4
Reg.2, varied: SI 2012/ 1643 Reg.4
Reg.3, varied: SI 2012/ 1643 Reg.4
Reg.4, applied: SI 2012/ 1643 Reg.6
Reg.4, varied: SI 2012/ 1643 Reg.4
Reg.5, applied: SI 2012/ 1643 Reg.6
Reg.5, varied: SI 2012/ 1643 Reg.4
Reg.6, applied: SI 2012/ 1643 Reg.6
Reg.6, varied: SI 2012/ 1643 Reg.4
Reg.7, applied: SI 2012/ 1643 Reg.6
Reg.7, varied: SI 2012/ 1643 Reg.4

2005–cont.

2914. Government of Maintained Schools (Wales) Regulations 2005–*cont.*

Reg.8, applied: SI 2012/1643 Reg.6
Reg.8, varied: SI 2012/1643 Reg.4
Reg.9, applied: SI 2012/1643 Reg.6
Reg.9, varied: SI 2012/1643 Reg.4
Reg.10, applied: SI 2012/1643 Reg.6
Reg.10, varied: SI 2012/1643 Reg.4
Reg.11, applied: SI 2012/1643 Reg.6
Reg.11, varied: SI 2012/1643 Reg.4
Reg.12, applied: SI 2012/1643 Reg.6
Reg.12, varied: SI 2012/1643 Reg.4
Reg.12A, applied: SI 2012/1643 Reg.6
Reg.12A, varied: SI 2012/1643 Reg.4
Reg.13, applied: SI 2012/1643 Reg.7
Reg.13, varied: SI 2012/1643 Reg.4
Reg.14, applied: SI 2012/1643 Reg.7
Reg.14, varied: SI 2012/1643 Reg.4
Reg.15, applied: SI 2012/1643 Reg.7
Reg.15, varied: SI 2012/1643 Reg.4
Reg.16, applied: SI 2012/1643 Reg.7
Reg.16, varied: SI 2012/1643 Reg.4
Reg.17, applied: SI 2012/1643 Reg.7
Reg.17, varied: SI 2012/1643 Reg.4
Reg.18, applied: SI 2012/1643 Reg.7
Reg.18, varied: SI 2012/1643 Reg.4
Reg.19, applied: SI 2012/1643 Reg.7
Reg.19, varied: SI 2012/1643 Reg.4
Reg.20, applied: SI 2012/1643 Reg.7
Reg.20, varied: SI 2012/1643 Reg.4
Reg.20A, varied: SI 2012/1643 Reg.4
Reg.21, varied: SI 2012/1643 Reg.4
Reg.22, varied: SI 2012/1643 Reg.4
Reg.23, varied: SI 2012/1643 Reg.4
Reg.24, applied: SI 2012/1643 Reg.8, SI 2012/2655 Reg.7
Reg.24, varied: SI 2012/1643 Reg.4
Reg.25, varied: SI 2012/1643 Reg.4
Reg.26, applied: SI 2012/1643 Reg.8
Reg.26, varied: SI 2012/1643 Reg.4
Reg.27, applied: SI 2012/1643 Reg.8
Reg.27, varied: SI 2012/1643 Reg.4
Reg.28, applied: SI 2012/1643 Reg.8
Reg.28, varied: SI 2012/1643 Reg.4
Reg.29, applied: SI 2012/1643 Reg.8
Reg.29, varied: SI 2012/1643 Reg.4
Reg.30, applied: SI 2012/1643 Reg.8
Reg.30, varied: SI 2012/1643 Reg.4
Reg.33, varied: SI 2012/1643 Reg.4
Reg.34, varied: SI 2012/1643 Reg.4
Reg.35, varied: SI 2012/1643 Reg.4
Reg.36, varied: SI 2012/1643 Reg.4
Reg.38, varied: SI 2012/1643 Reg.4
Reg.39, applied: SI 2012/1643 Reg.15
Reg.39, varied: SI 2012/1643 Reg.4
Reg.40, varied: SI 2012/1643 Reg.4
Reg.41, varied: SI 2012/1643 Reg.4
Reg.42, applied: SI 2012/1643 Reg.15
Reg.42, varied: SI 2012/1643 Reg.4
Reg.43, varied: SI 2012/1643 Reg.4
Reg.44, varied: SI 2012/1643 Reg.4
Reg.44A, varied: SI 2012/1643 Reg.4
Reg.45, varied: SI 2012/1643 Reg.4
Reg.46, varied: SI 2012/1643 Reg.4
Reg.47, varied: SI 2012/1643 Reg.4
Reg.48, varied: SI 2012/1643 Reg.4
Reg.49, applied: SI 2012/2655 Reg.8
Reg.49, varied: SI 2012/1643 Reg.4

2005–cont.

2914. Government of Maintained Schools (Wales) Regulations 2005–*cont.*

Reg.50, applied: SI 2012/2655 Reg.4
Reg.50, varied: SI 2012/1643 Reg.4
Reg.51, applied: SI 2012/2655 Reg.4
Reg.51, varied: SI 2012/1643 Reg.4
Reg.52, applied: SI 2012/2655 Reg.4
Reg.52, varied: SI 2012/1643 Reg.4
Reg.54, varied: SI 2012/1643 Reg.4
Reg.55, varied: SI 2012/1643 Reg.4
Reg.56, varied: SI 2012/1643 Reg.4
Reg.57, varied: SI 2012/1643 Reg.4
Reg.58, varied: SI 2012/1643 Reg.4
Reg.59, varied: SI 2012/1643 Reg.4
Reg.60, varied: SI 2012/1643 Reg.4
Reg.61, varied: SI 2012/1643 Reg.4
Reg.63, varied: SI 2012/1643 Reg.4
Sch.1 para.1, varied: SI 2012/1643 Reg.4
Sch.1 para.2, varied: SI 2012/1643 Reg.4
Sch.1 para.3, varied: SI 2012/1643 Reg.4
Sch.1 para.4, varied: SI 2012/1643 Reg.4
Sch.1 para.5, varied: SI 2012/1643 Reg.4
Sch.1 para.6, varied: SI 2012/1643 Reg.4
Sch.1 para.7, varied: SI 2012/1643 Reg.4
Sch.1 para.8, varied: SI 2012/1643 Reg.4
Sch.1 para.9, varied: SI 2012/1643 Reg.4
Sch.1 para.10, varied: SI 2012/1643 Reg.4
Sch.1 para.11, varied: SI 2012/1643 Reg.4
Sch.1 para.12, varied: SI 2012/1643 Reg.4
Sch.2 para.1, varied: SI 2012/1643 Reg.4
Sch.2 para.2, varied: SI 2012/1643 Reg.4
Sch.2 para.3, varied: SI 2012/1643 Reg.4
Sch.2 para.4, varied: SI 2012/1643 Reg.4
Sch.2 para.5, varied: SI 2012/1643 Reg.4
Sch.2 para.6, varied: SI 2012/1643 Reg.4
Sch.3 para.1, varied: SI 2012/1643 Reg.4
Sch.3 para.2, varied: SI 2012/1643 Reg.4
Sch.3 para.3, varied: SI 2012/1643 Reg.4
Sch.3 para.4, varied: SI 2012/1643 Reg.4
Sch.3 para.5, varied: SI 2012/1643 Reg.4
Sch.3 para.6, varied: SI 2012/1643 Reg.4
Sch.3 para.7, varied: SI 2012/1643 Reg.4
Sch.4 para.1, varied: SI 2012/1643 Reg.4
Sch.4 para.2, applied: SI 2012/2655 Sch.1 para.2
Sch.4 para.2, varied: SI 2012/1643 Reg.4
Sch.4 para.3, varied: SI 2012/1643 Reg.4
Sch.5, applied: SI 2012/1643 Reg.8
Sch.5, varied: SI 2012/1643 Reg.4
Sch.5 para.1, varied: SI 2012/1643 Reg.4
Sch.5 para.2, applied: SI 2012/2655 Reg.7
Sch.5 para.2, varied: SI 2012/1643 Reg.4
Sch.5 para.3, applied: SI 2012/2655 Reg.7
Sch.5 para.3, varied: SI 2012/1643 Reg.4
Sch.5 para.4, applied: SI 2012/2655 Reg.7
Sch.5 para.4, varied: SI 2012/1643 Reg.4
Sch.5 para.5, applied: SI 2012/2655 Reg.7
Sch.5 para.5, varied: SI 2012/1643 Reg.4
Sch.5 para.6, applied: SI 2012/2655 Reg.7
Sch.5 para.6, varied: SI 2012/1643 Reg.4
Sch.5 para.7, applied: SI 2012/2655 Reg.7
Sch.5 para.7, varied: SI 2012/1643 Reg.4
Sch.5 para.8, applied: SI 2012/2655 Reg.7
Sch.5 para.8, varied: SI 2012/1643 Reg.4
Sch.5 para.9, applied: SI 2012/2655 Reg.7
Sch.5 para.9, varied: SI 2012/1643 Reg.4
Sch.5 para.10, applied: SI 2012/2655 Reg.7
Sch.5 para.10, varied: SI 2012/1643 Reg.4
Sch.5 para.11, applied: SI 2012/2655 Reg.7

2005–cont.

2914. Government of Maintained Schools (Wales) Regulations 2005–*cont.*
Sch.5 para.11, varied: SI 2012/ 1643 Reg.4
Sch.5 para.12, applied: SI 2012/ 2655 Reg.7
Sch.5 para.12, varied: SI 2012/ 1643 Reg.4
Sch.5 para.13, varied: SI 2012/ 1643 Reg.4
Sch.6 para.1, varied: SI 2012/ 1643 Reg.4
Sch.6 para.2, varied: SI 2012/ 1643 Reg.4
Sch.6 para.3, varied: SI 2012/ 1643 Reg.4
Sch.6 para.4, varied: SI 2012/ 1643 Reg.4
Sch.6 para.5, varied: SI 2012/ 1643 Reg.4
Sch.6 para.6, varied: SI 2012/ 1643 Reg.4
Sch.7 para.1, varied: SI 2012/ 1643 Reg.4
Sch.7 para.2, varied: SI 2012/ 1643 Reg.4
Sch.7 para.3, varied: SI 2012/ 1643 Reg.4
Sch.7 para.4, varied: SI 2012/ 1643 Reg.4
Sch.7 para.5, varied: SI 2012/ 1643 Reg.4

2918. Licensing Act 2003 (Permitted Temporary Activities) (Notices) Regulations 2005
Reg.2, substituted: SI 2012/ 960 Reg.3
Reg.4, revoked: SI 2012/ 960 Reg.5
Reg.4, substituted: SI 2012/ 960 Reg.6
Reg.5, revoked: SI 2012/ 960 Reg.5
Reg.5, substituted: SI 2012/ 960 Reg.6
Reg.6, revoked: SI 2012/ 960 Reg.5
Reg.6, substituted: SI 2012/ 960 Reg.6
Reg.7, substituted: SI 2012/ 960 Reg.6
Sch.1, amended: SI 2012/ 960 Sch.1, SI 2012/ 2290 Sch.7
Sch.2, amended: SI 2012/ 960 Sch.2
Sch.2, revoked: SI 2012/ 960 Reg.5
Sch.3, added: SI 2012/ 960 Sch.3
Sch.4, added: SI 2012/ 960 Sch.4

3035. Vegetable Seed (Wales) Regulations 2005
revoked: SI 2012/ 245 Reg.34

3036. Cereal Seed (Wales) Regulations 2005
revoked: SI 2012/ 245 Reg.34

3037. Beet Seed (Wales) Regulations 2005
revoked: SI 2012/ 245 Reg.34

3038. Seed (Registration, Licensing and Enforcement) (Wales) Regulations 2005
applied: SI 2012/ 245 Reg.33
revoked: SI 2012/ 245 Reg.34

3050. Railway (Licensing of Railway Undertakings) Regulations 2005
Sch.2 para.2, amended: SI 2012/ 2404 Sch.3 para.46

3061. Social Fund Maternity and Funeral Expenses (General) Regulations 2005
Reg.5A, substituted: SI 2012/ 1814 Reg.2

3105. Docklands Light Railway (Capacity Enhancement) Order 2005
Art.2, amended: SI 2012/ 1659 Art.2
Art.44, amended: SI 2012/ 1659 Art.2
Sch.14 para.1, amended: SI 2012/ 1659 Art.2
Sch.14 para.2, amended: SI 2012/ 1659 Art.2
Sch.14 para.3, amended: SI 2012/ 1659 Art.2
Sch.14 para.4, amended: SI 2012/ 1659 Art.2
Sch.14 para.5, amended: SI 2012/ 1659 Art.2
Sch.14 para.6, amended: SI 2012/ 1659 Art.2
Sch.14 para.7, amended: SI 2012/ 1659 Art.2
Sch.14 para.8, amended: SI 2012/ 1659 Art.2
Sch.14 para.9, amended: SI 2012/ 1659 Art.2
Sch.14 para.10, amended: SI 2012/ 1659 Art.2
Sch.14 para.11, amended: SI 2012/ 1659 Art.2
Sch.14 para.12, amended: SI 2012/ 1659 Art.2
Sch.14 para.13, amended: SI 2012/ 1659 Art.2
Sch.14 para.14, amended: SI 2012/ 1659 Art.2

2005–cont.

3105. Docklands Light Railway (Capacity Enhancement) Order 2005–*cont.*
Sch.14 para.15, amended: SI 2012/ 1659 Art.2
Sch.14 para.16, amended: SI 2012/ 1659 Art.2
Sch.14 para.17, amended: SI 2012/ 1659 Art.2
Sch.14 para.18, amended: SI 2012/ 1659 Art.2
Sch.14 para.19, amended: SI 2012/ 1659 Art.2
Sch.14 para.20, amended: SI 2012/ 1659 Art.2
Sch.14 para.21, amended: SI 2012/ 1659 Art.2
Sch.14 para.22, amended: SI 2012/ 1659 Art.2
Sch.14 para.23, amended: SI 2012/ 1659 Art.2
Sch.14 para.24, amended: SI 2012/ 1659 Art.2

3117. Offshore Installations (Safety Case) Regulations 2005
applied: SI 2012/ 1652 Reg.14, Sch.11
Reg.2, applied: SI 2012/ 1652 Reg.17
Reg.6, applied: SI 2012/ 1652 Sch.11
Reg.9, applied: SI 2012/ 1652 Sch.11
Reg.23, applied: SI 2012/ 1652 Sch.11

3167. Registration of Civil Partnerships (Fees) (No.2) Order 2005
Sch.1, amended: SI 2012/ 761 Art.3

3172. Water Services etc (Scotland) Act 2005 (Consequential Provisions and Modifications) Order 2005
applied: SI 2012/ 1128 Art.4

3181. Proceeds of Crime Act 2002 (External Requests and Orders) Order 2005
applied: SI 2012/ 1726 r.57.14
Art.5, enabled: SI 2012/ 138
Art.8, see *Stanford, Re* [2012] Lloyd's Rep. F.C. 255 (Central Crim Ct), Gloster, J.
Art.8, applied: SI 2012/ 1726 r.57.14
Art.9, applied: SI 2012/ 1726 r.57.14
Art.10, applied: SI 2012/ 138 Art.3, Art.4, Art.5, Art.6, Art.7, Art.8, Art.12, SI 2012/ 1726 r.57.14
Art.11, applied: SI 2012/ 138 Art.14, Art.15, Art.16, SI 2012/ 1726 r.57.14
Art.15, applied: SI 2012/ 1726 r.57.14
Art.16, applied: SI 2012/ 1726 r.57.14
Art.17, applied: SI 2012/ 1726 r.57.14
Art.23, applied: SI 2012/ 138 Art.3, Art.4, Art.5, Art.6, Art.7, Art.8, Art.12, SI 2012/ 1726 r.57.14
Art.24, applied: SI 2012/ 138 Art.14, Art.15, Art.16
Art.27, applied: SI 2012/ 1726 r.57.14
Art.28, applied: SI 2012/ 1726 r.57.14
Art.41, applied: SI 2012/ 1726 r.57.14
Art.42, applied: SI 2012/ 1726 r.57.14
Art.44, applied: SI 2012/ 138 Art.3, Art.4, Art.5, Art.6, Art.7, Art.8, Art.12, SI 2012/ 1726 r.57.14
Art.45, applied: SI 2012/ 138 Art.14, Art.15, Art.16, SI 2012/ 1726 r.57.14
Art.46, see *Stanford, Re* [2012] Lloyd's Rep. F.C. 255 (Central Crim Ct), Gloster, J.
Art.47, enabled: SI 2012/ 138
Art.48, enabled: SI 2012/ 138
Pt 2, see *Serious Organised Crime Agency v Perry* [2012] UKSC 35, [2012] 3 W.L.R. 379 (SC), Lord Phillips, J.S.C.

3183. Overseas Territories (Zimbabwe) (Restrictive Measures) (Amendment) Order 2005
revoked: SI 2012/ 2753 Sch.7

3208. Housing Health and Safety Rating System (England) Regulations 2005
see *Liverpool City Council v Kassim* [2012] UKUT 169 (LC), [2012] J.P.L. 1395 (UT (Lands)), George Bartlett Q.C. (President, LTr)

2005–cont.

3222. Electronic Commerce Directive (Adoption and Children Act 2002) Regulations 2005
Reg.2, amended: SI 2012/1809 Sch.1 Part 2

3227. Offshore Installations (Safety Zones) (No.3) Order 2005
Sch.1, amended: SI 2012/3159 Art.3

3315. National Health Service (Primary Medical Services) (Miscellaneous Amendments) (No.2) Regulations 2005
Reg.14, revoked: SI 2012/1909 Sch.8 para.9

3322. Education (Head Teachers Qualifications) (England) (Amendment) (No.2) Regulations 2005
revoked: SI 2012/18 Sch.1

3360. Social Security (Hospital In-Patients) Regulations 2005
applied: SI 2012/3144 Sch.1 para.10, SI 2012/3145 Sch.1, SSI 2012/319 Reg.27
Reg.2, applied: SI 2012/2885 Sch.1 para.25, SI 2012/2886 Sch.1, SI 2012/3144 Sch.1 para.19, SI 2012/3145 Sch.1, SSI 2012/303 Reg.28

3361. National Health Service (General Dental Services Contracts) Regulations 2005
Reg.2, amended: SI 2012/502 Reg.2
Reg.4, amended: SI 2012/2404 Sch.3 para.47
Reg.14, amended: SI 2012/502 Reg.2
Sch.2 Part 1 para.2, amended: SI 2012/2273 Reg.2
Sch.3 Part 9 para.65, amended: SI 2012/502 Reg.2
Sch.3 Part 9 para.71, amended: SI 2012/2404 Sch.3 para.47

3373. National Health Service (Personal Dental Services Agreements) Regulations 2005
Reg.4, amended: SI 2012/2404 Sch.3 para.48
Sch.2 Part 1 para.2, amended: SI 2012/2273 Reg.3
Sch.3 Part 9 para.63, amended: SI 2012/502 Reg.3
Sch.3 Part 9 para.69, amended: SI 2012/2404 Sch.3 para.48

3377. Occupational Pension Schemes (Scheme Funding) Regulations 2005
Reg.2, amended: SI 2012/1817 Sch.1 para.8
Reg.15, amended: SI 2012/1817 Sch.1 para.8

3430. Parliamentary Commissioner (No.2) Order 2005
varied: SI 2012/147 Art.7

3432. Lebanon and Syria (United Nations Measures) Order 2005
revoked: SI 2012/1517 Reg.18

3434. Individual Ascertainment of Value (England) Order 2005
revoked: SI 2012/1380 Art.5

3439. Clean Neighbourhoods and Environment Act 2005 (Commencement No 3) Order 2005
varied: SI 2012/147 Art.7

3452. Registered Pension Schemes (Discharge of Liabilities under Sections 267 and 268 of the Finance Act 2004) Regulations 2005
Reg.4, revoked: SI 2012/886 Reg.3

3477. National Health Service (Dental Charges) Regulations 2005
Reg.4, amended: SI 2012/502 Reg.4

3491. National Health Service (Performers Lists) Amendment Regulations 2005
Reg.12, revoked (in part): SI 2012/1909 Sch.8 para.9

3522. Older Cattle (Disposal) (England) Regulations 2005
Reg.5, revoked: 2012 c.9 Sch.2 para.8, Sch.10 Part 2

3558. Enterprise Act 2002 (Merger Fees) (Amendment) Order 2005
revoked: SI 2012/1878 Art.3

2005–cont.

3593. Freedom of Information (Additional Public Authorities) Order 2005
Sch.1, amended: SI 2012/1206 Sch.1 para.13

2006

5. Public Contracts Regulations 2006
applied: 2012 c.7 s.76
varied: SI 2012/147 Art.7
see *Alstom Transport v Eurostar International Ltd* [2012] EWHC 28 (Ch), [2012] 3 All E.R. 263 (Ch D), Roth, J.; see *McLaughlin & Harvey Ltd v Department of Finance and Personnel* [2012] B.L.R. 26 (CA (NI)), Morgan, L.C.J.; see *Mears Ltd v Leeds City Council* [2011] EWHC 2694 (TCC), [2012] 4 Costs L.O. 456 (QBD (TCC)), Ramsey, J.; see *R. (on the application of Midlands Co-operative Society Ltd) v Birmingham City Council* [2012] EWHC 620 (Admin), [2012] Eu. L.R. 640 (QBD (Admin)), Hickinbottom, J.; see *Turning Point Ltd v Norfolk CC* [2012] EWHC 2121 (TCC), [2012] Eu. L.R. 800 (QBD (TCC)), Akenhead, J.
Reg.2, see *Henry Brothers (Magherafelt) Ltd v Department of Education for Northern Ireland* [2012] B.L.R. 36 (CA (NI)), Morgan, L.C.J.
Reg.4, see *Community Care North East (A Partnership) v Durham CC* [2010] EWHC 959 (QB), [2012] 1 W.L.R. 338 (QBD), Ramsey, J.; see *McLaughlin & Harvey Ltd v Department of Finance and Personnel* [2012] B.L.R. 26 (CA (NI)), Morgan, L.C.J.
Reg.8, applied: SI 2012/2261 Reg.9
Reg.19, see *Henry Brothers (Magherafelt) Ltd v Department of Education for Northern Ireland* [2012] B.L.R. 36 (CA (NI)), Morgan, L.C.J.
Reg.30, see *Henry Brothers (Magherafelt) Ltd v Department of Education for Northern Ireland* [2012] B.L.R. 36 (CA (NI)), Morgan, L.C.J.; see *J Varney & Sons Waste Management Ltd v Hertfordshire CC* [2011] EWCA Civ 708, [2012] P.T.S.R. 670 (CA (Civ Div)), Rix, L.J.
Reg.32, see *Community Care North East (A Partnership) v Durham CC* [2010] EWHC 959 (QB), [2012] 1 W.L.R. 338 (QBD), Ramsey, J.
Reg.47, see *Henry Brothers (Magherafelt) Ltd v Department of Education for Northern Ireland* [2012] B.L.R. 36 (CA (NI)), Morgan, L.C.J.; see *J Varney & Sons Waste Management Ltd v Hertfordshire CC* [2011] EWCA Civ 708, [2012] P.T.S.R. 670 (CA (Civ Div)), Rix, L.J.; see *McLaughlin & Harvey Ltd v Department of Finance and Personnel* [2012] B.L.R. 26 (CA (NI)), Morgan, L.C.J.
Reg.47D, see *Turning Point Ltd v Norfolk CC* [2012] EWHC 2121 (TCC), [2012] Eu. L.R. 800 (QBD (TCC)), Akenhead, J.
Sch.1, varied: SI 2012/725 Art.2
Sch.2, see *Community Care North East (A Partnership) v Durham CC* [2010] EWHC 959 (QB), [2012] 1 W.L.R. 338 (QBD), Ramsey, J.

6. Utilities Contracts Regulations 2006
see *Alstom Transport v Eurostar International Ltd* [2012] EWHC 28 (Ch), [2012] 3 All E.R. 263 (Ch D), Roth, J.
Sch.1, amended: SI 2012/1659 Sch.3 para.34

14. Food Hygiene (England) Regulations 2006
applied: SI 2012/1742 Reg.3
Reg.2, amended: SI 2012/1742 Reg.2
Reg.32A, added: SI 2012/1742 Reg.2
Sch.1, substituted: SI 2012/1742 Sch.1

2006–cont.

14. Food Hygiene (England) Regulations 2006–*cont.*
Sch.6A para.l, added: SI 2012/1742 Sch.2
Sch.6A para.2, added: SI 2012/1742 Sch.2

31. Food Hygiene (Wales) Regulations 2006
Reg.2, amended: SI 2012/1765 Reg.2
Reg.9, amended: SI 2012/975 Reg.2
Reg.22, amended: SI 2012/975 Reg.2
Reg.32A, added: SI 2012/1765 Reg.2
Sch.l, substituted: SI 2012/1765 Sch.1
Sch.6A para.l, added: SI 2012/1765 Sch.2
Sch.6A para.2, added: SI 2012/1765 Sch.2

33. Occupational Pension Schemes (Early Leavers Cash Transfer Sums and Contribution Refunds) Regulations 2006
Reg.l, amended: SI 2012/692 Reg.13

60. Climate Change Agreements (Eligible Facilities) Regulations 2006
revoked: SI 2012/2999 Reg.9

69. Local Authorities (Executive Arrangements) (Access to Information) (Amendment) (England) Regulations 2006
revoked: SI 2012/2089 Reg.23

123. Waste (Household Waste Duty of Care) (Wales) Regulations 2006
Reg.2, revoked (in part): SI 2012/811 Sch.2 para.2

129. Registered Pension Schemes (Relevant Annuities) Regulations 2006
Reg.3, amended: SI 2012/2940 Reg.2
Reg.3, referred to: SI 2012/2940 Reg.1

168. Cattle Compensation (England) Order 2006
revoked: SI 2012/1379 Art.6

169. Common Agricultural Policy Single Payment and Support Schemes (Reductions from Payments) (England) Regulations 2006
revoked: SI 2012/3027 Reg.3

181. National Health Service (General Ophthalmic Services Supplementary List) and (General Ophthalmic Services) (Amendment and Consequential Amendment) (Wales) Regulations 2006
Reg.16, varied: 2012 c.ll s.12
Reg.20, varied: 2012 c.ll s.12

182. Foot-and-Mouth Disease (England) Order 2006
Art.59, amended: SI 2012/2897 Art.8

183. Foot-and-Mouth Disease (Control of Vaccination) (England) Regulations 2006
Reg.43, amended: SI 2012/2897 Art.9

185. Functions of Primary Care Trusts (Dental Public Health) (England) Regulations 2006
applied: SI 2012/3094 Reg.18
revoked: SI 2012/3094 Reg.18

202. Duty Stamps Regulations 2006
Reg.10, amended: SI 2012/2404 Sch.3 para.49

206. Pension Schemes (Categories of Country and Requirements for Overseas Pension Schemes and Recognised Overseas Pension Schemes) Regulations 2006
see *Equity Trust (Singapore) Ltd v Revenue and Customs Commissioners* [2012] EWCA Civ 192, [2012] S.T.C. 998 (CA (Civ Div)), Lloyd, L.J.
Reg.2, amended: SI 2012/884 Reg.3
Reg.2, see *Equity Trust (Singapore) Ltd v Revenue and Customs Commissioners* [2012] EWCA Civ 192, [2012] S.T.C. 998 (CA (Civ Div)), Lloyd, L.J.
Reg.3, amended: SI 2012/884 Reg.4, SI 2012/1221 Reg.2
Sch.1, substituted: SI 2012/884 Reg.5
Sch.2, added: SI 2012/884 Reg.6

2006–cont.

207. Pensions Schemes (Application of UK Provisions to Relevant Non-UK Schemes) Regulations 2006
Reg.6, substituted: SI 2012/1795 Reg.3
Reg.7, substituted: SI 2012/1795 Reg.4
Reg.14, amended: SI 2012/1795 Reg.5
Reg.15, amended: SI 2012/1795 Reg.6

208. Pension Schemes (Information Requirements Qualifying Overseas Pension Schemes, Qualifying Recognised Overseas Pensions Schemes and Corresponding Relief) Regulations 2006
Reg.3, amended: SI 2012/884 Reg.8
Reg.3A, added: SI 2012/884 Reg.9
Reg.3B, added: SI 2012/884 Reg.9
Reg.3C, added: SI 2012/884 Reg.9
Reg.4, amended: SI 2012/884 Reg.10

213. Housing Benefit Regulations 2006
see *Basey v Oxford City Council* [2012] EWCA Civ 115, [2012] P.T.S.R. 1324 (CA (Civ Div)), Mummery, L.J.; see *Burnip v Birmingham City Council* [2012] EWCA Civ 629, [2012] H.R.L.R. 20 (CA (Civ Div)), Maurice Kay, L.J.
Part 3 regA.13, added: SI 2012/3040 Reg.5
Part 3 regB.13, added: SI 2012/3040 Reg.5
Reg.2, amended: SI 2012/700 Sch.1 para.15, SI 2012/757 Reg.7, SI 2012/956 Art.11, SI 2012/2994 Reg.2, SI 2012/3040 Reg.5
Reg.10, amended: SI 2012/1809 Sch.1 Part 2, SI 2012/2587 Reg.5
Reg.11, amended: SI 2012/3040 Reg.5
Reg.12B, amended: SI 2012/3040 Reg.5
Reg.12BA, added: SI 2012/3040 Reg.5
Reg.12D, amended: SI 2012/3040 Reg.5
Reg.13C, amended: SI 2012/700 Sch.1 para.15, SI 2012/3040 Reg.3
Reg.13C, applied: SI 2012/1483 Reg.7
Reg.13C, revoked (in part): SI 2012/3040 Reg.3
Reg.13D, see *Burnip v Birmingham City Council* [2012] EWCA Civ 629, [2012] H.R.L.R. 20 (CA (Civ Div)), Maurice Kay, L.J.
Reg.27, referred to: SI 2012/780 Art.20
Reg.28, amended: SI 2012/757 Reg.7
Reg.35, amended: SI 2012/757 Reg.7
Reg.36, amended: SI 2012/757 Reg.7
Reg.49, applied: SI 2012/2886 Sch.1, SI 2012/3145 Sch.1, SSI 2012/303 Reg.49
Reg.53, amended: SI 2012/956 Art.11
Reg.56, amended: SI 2012/757 Reg.12
Reg.72E, added: SI 2012/2994 Reg.2
Reg.73E, added: SI 2012/2994 Reg.2
Reg.74, amended: SI 2012/780 Art.20
Reg.75A, added: SI 2012/2994 Reg.2
Reg.75B, added: SI 2012/2994 Reg.2
Reg.75C, added: SI 2012/2994 Reg.2
Reg.75D, added: SI 2012/2994 Reg.2
Reg.75E, added: SI 2012/2994 Reg.2
Reg.75F, added: SI 2012/2994 Reg.2
Reg.75G, added: SI 2012/2994 Reg.2
Reg.79, see *KW v Lancaster City Council* [2012] 1 F.L.R. 282 (UT (AAC)), Judge Nicholas Wikeley
Reg.81, applied: SSI 2012/303 Sch.1 para.4
Reg.81, referred to: SI 2012/2886 Sch.1, SSI 2012/303 Sch.1 para.4
Reg.96, applied: SI 2012/1483 Reg.7
Reg.98, amended: SI 2012/824 Reg.5

2006–cont.

213. Housing Benefit Regulations 2006–*cont.*
Reg.100, see *KW v Lancaster City Council* [2012] 1 F.L.R. 282 (UT (AAC)), Judge Nicholas Wikeley
Reg.102, amended: SI 2012/645 Reg.3
Reg.104, amended: SI 2012/645 Reg.2
Sch.1 Part 1 para.2, amended: SI 2012/780 Art.20
Sch.1 Part 2 para.6, amended: SI 2012/780 Art.20
Sch.2 para.3, amended: SI 2012/3040 Reg.5
Sch.2 para.3, revoked (in part): SI 2012/3040 Reg.5
Sch.3 Part 1 para.1, amended: SI 2012/780 Sch.5
Sch.3 Part 1 para.1A, amended: SI 2012/913 Reg.7
Sch.3 Part 1 para.2, amended: SI 2012/780 Sch.5
Sch.3 Part 2 para.3, applied: SI 2012/2886 Sch.1, SSI 2012/303 Sch.1 para.4
Sch.3 Part 2 para.3, referred to: SI 2012/780 Art.20
Sch.3 Part 4, amended: SI 2012/780 Sch.6
Sch.3 Part 5 para.21A, amended: SI 2012/913 Reg.7
Sch.3 Part 6 para.25, amended: SI 2012/780 Art.20
Sch.3 Part 6 para.26, amended: SI 2012/780 Art.20
Sch.3 Part 7 para.27, amended: SI 2012/913 Reg.7
Sch.3 Part 7 para.28, amended: SI 2012/919 Reg.3
Sch.3 Part 7 para.28, revoked (in part): SI 2012/919 Reg.3
Sch.3 Part 7 para.29, amended: SI 2012/919 Reg.3
Sch.4 para.17, referred to: SI 2012/780 Art.20
Sch.5 para.56, referred to: SI 2012/780 Art.20
Sch.10 Part 2 para.4, substituted: SI 2012/3040 Reg.5

214. Housing Benefit (Persons who have attained the qualifying age for state pension credit) Regulations 2006
Reg.2, amended: SI 2012/700 Sch.1 para.16, SI 2012/757 Reg.8, SI 2012/956 Art.12, SI 2012/3040 Reg.6
Reg.2, applied: SI 2012/2885 Sch.1 para.35
Reg.10, amended: SI 2012/1809 Sch.1 Part 2, SI 2012/2587 Reg.6
Reg.13C, amended: SI 2012/700 Sch.1 para.16, SI 2012/3040 Reg.4
Reg.13C, applied: SI 2012/1483 Reg.7
Reg.13C, revoked (in part): SI 2012/3040 Reg.4
Reg.29, amended: SI 2012/757 Reg.8
Reg.30, referred to: SI 2012/780 Art.21
Reg.31, amended: SI 2012/757 Reg.8
Reg.35, amended: SI 2012/757 Reg.8
Reg.36, amended: SI 2012/757 Reg.8
Reg.47, applied: SI 2012/2885 Sch.1 para.35, SI 2012/2886 Sch.1, SI 2012/3145 Sch.1, SSI 2012/319 Reg.45
Reg.47, referred to: SI 2012/2885 Sch.1 para.35
Reg.55, amended: SI 2012/780 Art.21
Reg.77, applied: SI 2012/1483 Reg.7
Reg.79, amended: SI 2012/824 Reg.5
Reg.83, amended: SI 2012/645 Reg.3
Reg.85, amended: SI 2012/645 Reg.2
Sch.1 Pt 1 para.1, see *Basey v Oxford City Council* [2012] EWCA Civ 115, [2012] P.T.S.R. 1324 (CA (Civ Div)), Mummery, L.J.
Sch.1 Part 1 para.2, amended: SI 2012/780 Art.21
Sch.1 Part 2 para.6, amended: SI 2012/780 Art.21
Sch.3 Part 1 para.1, substituted: SI 2012/780 Sch.7
Sch.3 Part 1 para.2, amended: SI 2012/780 Sch.7
Sch.3 Part 2 para.3, referred to: SI 2012/780 Art.21
Sch.3 Part 4, substituted: SI 2012/780 Sch.8
Sch.4 para.9, referred to: SI 2012/780 Art.21
Sch.5 para.21, referred to: SI 2012/780 Art.21

215. Council Tax Benefit Regulations 2006
applied: SSI 2012/303 Sch.1 para.4, Sch.1 para.10

2006–cont.

215. Council Tax Benefit Regulations 2006–*cont.*
Reg.2, amended: SI 2012/757 Reg.9, SI 2012/956 Art.13
Reg.7, amended: SI 2012/1809 Sch.1 Part 2, SI 2012/2587 Reg.7
Reg.17, referred to: SI 2012/780 Art.22
Reg.18, amended: SI 2012/757 Reg.9
Reg.25, amended: SI 2012/757 Reg.9
Reg.26, amended: SI 2012/757 Reg.9
Reg.43, amended: SI 2012/956 Art.13
Reg.45, amended: SI 2012/757 Reg.13
Reg.58, amended: SI 2012/780 Art.22
Reg.81, amended: SI 2012/824 Reg.5
Reg.86, amended: SI 2012/645 Reg.4
Reg.89, amended: SI 2012/645 Reg.2
Sch.1 Part 1 para.1, substituted: SI 2012/780 Sch.9
Sch.1 Part 1 para.1A, amended: SI 2012/913 Reg.8
Sch.1 Part 1 para.2, amended: SI 2012/780 Sch.9
Sch.1 Part 2 para.3, applied: SSI 2012/303 Sch.1 para.4
Sch.1 Part 2 para.3, referred to: SI 2012/780 Art.22
Sch.1 Part 3 para.12, applied: SSI 2012/303 Sch.1 para.4
Sch.1 Part 4, substituted: SI 2012/780 Sch.10
Sch.1 Part 5 para.21A, amended: SI 2012/913 Reg.8
Sch.1 Part 5 para.23, applied: SSI 2012/303 Sch.1 para.4
Sch.1 Part 5 para.24, applied: SSI 2012/303 Sch.1 para.4
Sch.1 Part 6 para.25, amended: SI 2012/780 Art.22
Sch.1 Part 6 para.26, amended: SI 2012/780 Art.22
Sch.1 Part 7 para.27, amended: SI 2012/913 Reg.8
Sch.1 Part 7 para.28, amended: SI 2012/919 Reg.4
Sch.1 Part 7 para.28, revoked (in part): SI 2012/919 Reg.4
Sch.1 Part 7 para.29, amended: SI 2012/919 Reg.4
Sch.2 para.1, amended: SI 2012/780 Art.22
Sch.3 para.16, referred to: SI 2012/780 Art.22
Sch.4 para.56, referred to: SI 2012/780 Art.22
Sch.5 para.9, applied: SI 2012/2885 Sch.6 para.22, SI 2012/2886 Sch.1

216. Council Tax Benefit (Persons who have attained the qualifying age for state pension credit) Regulations 2006
Reg.2, amended: SI 2012/757 Reg.10, SI 2012/956 Art.14
Reg.7, amended: SI 2012/1809 Sch.1 Part 2, SI 2012/2587 Reg.8
Reg.19, amended: SI 2012/757 Reg.10
Reg.20, referred to: SI 2012/780 Art.23
Reg.21, amended: SI 2012/757 Reg.10
Reg.25, amended: SI 2012/757 Reg.10
Reg.26, amended: SI 2012/757 Reg.10
Reg.42, amended: SI 2012/780 Art.23
Reg.66, amended: SI 2012/824 Reg.5
Reg.71, amended: SI 2012/645 Reg.4
Reg.74, amended: SI 2012/645 Reg.2
Sch.1 Part 1 para.1, substituted: SI 2012/780 Sch.11
Sch.1 Part 1 para.2, substituted: SI 2012/780 Sch.11
Sch.1 Part 2 para.3, referred to: SI 2012/780 Art.23
Sch.1 Part 4, substituted: SI 2012/780 Sch.12
Sch.2 para.9, referred to: SI 2012/780 Art.23
Sch.3 para.21, referred to: SI 2012/780 Art.23
Sch.6 para.1, amended: SI 2012/780 Art.23

223. Child Benefit (General) Regulations 2006
Reg.1, amended: SI 2012/818 Reg.3, Reg.4, Reg.5, Reg.6
Reg.1, revoked (in part): SI 2012/818 Reg.6

2006–cont.

223. Child Benefit (General) Regulations 2006–*cont.*
Reg.1, varied: 2012 c.11 s.12
Reg.5, amended: SI 2012/ 818 Reg.7
Reg.16, amended: SI 2012/ 818 Reg.8, Reg.9, Reg.10
Reg.23, amended: SI 2012/ 2612 Reg.3
Reg.27, amended: SI 2012/ 2612 Reg.4
Reg.36, amended: SI 2012/ 818 Reg.11

246. Transfer of Undertakings (Protection of Employment) Regulations 2006
applied: 2012 c.21 s.51, Sch.21 para.5, Sch.21 para.10, SI 2012/534 Art.3, SI 2012/872 Art.3, SI 2012/ 2413 Reg.2
referred to: 2012 c.7 s.188
varied: SI 2012/ 246 Art.6
see *Abellio London Ltd (formerly Travel London Ltd) v Musse* [2012] I.R.L.R. 360 (EAT), Langstaff, J. (President); see *F&G Cleaners Ltd v Saddington* [2012] I.R.L.R. 892 (EAT), Judge Burke Q.C.; see *Kuehne & Nagel Drinks Logistics Ltd v Revenue and Customs Commissioners* [2012] EWCA Civ 34, [2012] S.T.C. 840 (CA (Civ Div)), Mummery, L.J.; see *Procter & Gamble Co v Svenska Cellulosa Aktiebolaget SCA* [2012] EWHC 1257 (Ch), [2012] I.R.L.R. 733 (Ch D), Hildyard, J; see *Turning Point Ltd v Norfolk CC* [2012] EWHC 2121 (TCC), [2012] Eu. L.R. 800 (QBD (TCC)), Akenhead, J.
Reg.3, see *Eddie Stobart Ltd v Moreman* [2012] I.C.R. 919 (EAT), Underhill, J. (President); see *Enterprise Management Services Ltd v Connect-up Ltd* [2012] I.R.L.R. 190 (EAT), Judge Peter Clark; see *Hunter v McCarrick* [2012] I.C.R. 533 (EAT), Slade, J.; see *Pannu v Geo W King Ltd (In Liquidation)* [2012] I.R.L.R. 193 (EAT), Judge Peter Clark; see *Seawell Ltd v Ceva Freight (UK) Ltd* [2012] I.R.L.R. 802 (EAT (SC)), Lady Smith; see *SNR Denton UK LLP v Kirwan* [2012] I.R.L.R. 966 (EAT), Langstaff, J. (President)
Reg.4, applied: SI 2012/ 2413 Reg.2
Reg.4, see *Abellio London Ltd (formerly Travel London Ltd) v Musse* [2012] I.R.L.R. 360 (EAT), Langstaff, J. (President); see *Eddie Stobart Ltd v Moreman* [2012] I.C.R. 919 (EAT), Underhill, J. (President); see *Enterprise Management Services Ltd v Connect-up Ltd* [2012] I.R.L.R. 190 (EAT), Judge Peter Clark; see *F&G Cleaners Ltd v Saddington* [2012] I.R.L.R. 892 (EAT), Judge Burke Q.C.; see *Key2Law (Surrey) LLP v De'Antiquis* [2011] EWCA Civ 1567, [2012] B.C.C. 375 (CA (Civ Div)), Longmore, L.J.; see *Procter & Gamble Co v Svenska Cellulosa Aktiebolaget SCA* [2012] EWHC 1257 (Ch), [2012] I.R.L.R. 733 (Ch D), Hildyard, J
Reg.7, see *Key2Law (Surrey) LLP v De'Antiquis* [2011] EWCA Civ 1567, [2012] B.C.C. 375 (CA (Civ Div)), Longmore, L.J.; see *Meter U Ltd v Ackroyd* [2012] I.C.R. 834 (EAT), Slade, J.; see *Spaceright Europe Ltd v Baillavoine* [2011] EWCA Civ 1565, [2012] 2 All E.R. 812 (CA (Civ Div)), Mummery, L.J.
Reg.8, see *Key2Law (Surrey) LLP v De'Antiquis* [2011] EWCA Civ 1567, [2012] B.C.C. 375 (CA (Civ Div)), Longmore, L.J.
Reg.10, see *Procter & Gamble Co v Svenska Cellulosa Aktiebolaget SCA* [2012] EWHC 1257 (Ch), [2012] I.R.L.R. 733 (Ch D), Hildyard, J

2006–cont.

246. Transfer of Undertakings (Protection of Employment) Regulations 2006–*cont.*
Reg.13, applied: SI 2012/ 335 Sch.2 para.20, SI 2012/ 2991 Sch.2 para.28
Reg.13, see *Seawell Ltd v Ceva Freight (UK) Ltd* [2012] I.R.L.R. 802 (EAT (SC)), Lady Smith
Reg.15, see *Seawell Ltd v Ceva Freight (UK) Ltd* [2012] I.R.L.R. 802 (EAT (SC)), Lady Smith

249. Local Authorities (Indemnities for Members and Officers) (Wales) Order 2006
applied: SI 2012/ 2734 Sch.1 para.34
varied: SI 2012/ 2734 Reg.6

264. Community Benefit Societies (Restriction on Use of Assets) Regulations 2006
Reg.2, amended: SI 2012/ 700 Sch.1 para.17

311. Lebanon and Syria (United Nations Measures) (Overseas Territories) Order 2006
Sch.1, amended: SI 2012/ 362 Sch.1

339. Wireless Telegraphy (Spectrum Trading) (Amendment) Regulations 2006
revoked: SI 2012/ 2187 Sch.1

340. Wireless Telegraphy (Register) (Amendment) Regulations 2006
revoked: SI 2012/ 2186 Sch.1

349. Occupational and Personal Pension Schemes (Consultation by Employers and Miscellaneous Amendment) Regulations 2006
Reg.6, amended: SI 2012/ 692 Reg.2
Reg.8, amended: SI 2012/ 692 Reg.2

364. Registered Pension Schemes (Modification of the Rules of Existing Schemes) Regulations 2006
Reg.3, varied: SI 2012/ 687 Sch.1 para.3

367. Housing (Empty Dwelling Management Orders) (Prescribed Exceptions and Requirements) (England) Order 2006
Art.4, amended: SI 2012/ 2625 Art.3

373. Licensing and Management of Houses in Multiple Occupation and Other Houses (Miscellaneous Provisions) (England) Regulations 2006
Reg.7, amended: SI 2012/ 2111 Reg.2
Sch.2 para.5, added: SI 2012/ 2111 Reg.2

395. Medicines (Traditional Herbal Medicinal Products for Human Use) (Consequential Amendment) Regulations 2006
revoked: SI 2012/ 1916 Sch.35

396. National Endowment for Science, Technology and the Arts (Increase of Endowment) Order 2006
revoked: SI 2012/ 964 Sch.1

437. Consistent Financial Reporting (England) (Amendment) Regulations 2006
revoked: SI 2012/ 674 Reg.6

489. National Health Service (Personal Dental Services Agreements) (Wales) Regulations 2006
Reg.4, amended: SI 2012/ 2404 Sch.3 para.50
Sch.2 Part 1 para.2, amended: SI 2012/ 2572 Reg.3
Sch.3 Part 9 para.69, amended: SI 2012/ 2404 Sch.3 para.50

490. National Health Service (General Dental Services Contracts) (Wales) Regulations 2006
Reg.4, amended: SI 2012/ 2404 Sch.3 para.51
Sch.2 Part 1 para.2, amended: SI 2012/ 2572 Reg.2
Sch.3 Part 9 para.71, amended: SI 2012/ 2404 Sch.3 para.51

2006–cont.

491. National Health Service (Dental Charges) (Wales) Regulations 2006
Reg.4, amended: SI 2012/1893 Reg.2

501. Fines Collection Regulations 2006
referred to: SI 2012/1726 r.52.1

552. National Health Service (Local Pharmaceutical Services etc.) Regulations 2006
applied: SI 2012/1909 Sch.7 para.2
Reg.2, amended: SI 2012/1479 Sch.1 para.49, SI 2012/1909 Sch.8 para.10
Reg.4, applied: SI 2012/1909 Reg.32
Reg.7, amended: SI 2012/2404 Sch.3 para.52
Reg.15, amended: SI 2012/1909 Sch.8 para.10
Reg.15, applied: SI 2012/1909 Reg.28
Reg.17, revoked: SI 2012/1909 Sch.8 para.10
Sch.2 para.6, amended: SI 2012/1467 Reg.2
Sch.2 para.6, revoked (in part): SI 2012/1467 Reg.2
Sch.2 para.29, amended: SI 2012/2404 Sch.3 para.52
Sch.3 Part 1 para.1, revoked: SI 2012/1909 Sch.8 para.9, Sch.8 para.10
Sch.3 Part 1 para.2, revoked: SI 2012/1909 Sch.8 para.9, Sch.8 para.10
Sch.3 Part 1 para.3, revoked: SI 2012/1909 Sch.8 para.9, Sch.8 para.10
Sch.3 Part 1 para.4, revoked: SI 2012/1909 Sch.8 para.9, Sch.8 para.10
Sch.3 Part 1 para.5, revoked: SI 2012/1909 Sch.8 para.9, Sch.8 para.10
Sch.3 Part 1 para.6, revoked: SI 2012/1909 Sch.8 para.9, Sch.8 para.10
Sch.3 Part 1 para.7, revoked: SI 2012/1909 Sch.8 para.9, Sch.8 para.10
Sch.3 Part 1 para.8, revoked: SI 2012/1909 Sch.8 para.9, Sch.8 para.10
Sch.3 Part 1 para.9, revoked: SI 2012/1909 Sch.8 para.9, Sch.8 para.10
Sch.3 Part 1 para.10, revoked: SI 2012/1909 Sch.8 para.9, Sch.8 para.10
Sch.3 Part 1 para.11, revoked: SI 2012/1909 Sch.8 para.9, Sch.8 para.10
Sch.3 Part 1 para.12, revoked: SI 2012/1909 Sch.8 para.9, Sch.8 para.10
Sch.3 Part 1 para.13, revoked: SI 2012/1909 Sch.8 para.9, Sch.8 para.10
Sch.3 Part 1 para.14, revoked: SI 2012/1909 Sch.8 para.9, Sch.8 para.10
Sch.3 Part 1 para.15, revoked: SI 2012/1909 Sch.8 para.9, Sch.8 para.10
Sch.3 Part 1 para.16, revoked: SI 2012/1909 Sch.8 para.9, Sch.8 para.10
Sch.3 Part 1 para.17, revoked: SI 2012/1909 Sch.8 para.9, Sch.8 para.10
Sch.3 Part 1 para.18, revoked: SI 2012/1909 Sch.8 para.9, Sch.8 para.10

557. Health and Safety (Enforcing Authority for Railways and Other Guided Transport Systems) Regulations 2006
Reg.4, amended: SI 2012/632 Sch.3

562. General Dental Services, Personal Dental Services and Abolition of the Dental Practice Board Transitional and Consequential Provisions Order 2006
Sch.1 para.3, revoked: SI 2012/1909 Sch.8 para.1
Sch.1 para.23, revoked: SI 2012/1909 Sch.8 para.9

567. Registered Pension Schemes (Provision of Information) Regulations 2006
Reg.3, amended: SI 2012/884 Reg.12
Reg.11BA, added: SI 2012/884 Reg.13

2006–cont.

567. Registered Pension Schemes (Provision of Information) Regulations 2006–cont.
Reg.11C, amended: SI 2012/884 Reg.14

569. Registered Pension Schemes (Splitting of Schemes) Regulations 2006
Sch.2, amended: SI 2012/2879 Art.3

570. Registered Pension Schemes and Overseas Pension Schemes (Electronic Communication of Returns and Information) Regulations 2006
Sch.1, amended: SI 2012/884 Reg.15
Sch.2, amended: SI 2012/884 Reg.15

596. Functions of Primary Care Trusts and Strategic Health Authorities and the NHS Business Services Authority (Awdurdod Gwasanaethau Busnes y GIG) (Primary Dental Services) (England) Regulations 2006
Sch.1, amended: SI 2012/502 Reg.5

597. Pension Protection Fund (Valuation of the Assets and Liabilities of the Pension Protection Fund) Regulations 2006
Reg.6, amended: SI 2012/692 Reg.14

599. Railways and Other Guided Transport Systems (Safety) Regulations 2006
applied: SSI 2012/345 Art.3

606. Naval, Military and Air Forces Etc (Disablement and Death) Service Pensions Order 2006
applied: SI 2012/2885 Sch.5 para.4
Part II, applied: SI 2012/2885 Sch.5 para.13, SI 2012/2886 Sch.1, SSI 2012/303 Sch.4 para.52, SSI 2012/319 Sch.3 para.12
Part III, applied: SI 2012/2885 Sch.5 para.13, SI 2012/2886 Sch.1, SSI 2012/303 Sch.4 para.52, SSI 2012/319 Sch.3 para.12
Art.12, amended: SI 2012/359 Art.3
Art.20, applied: SI 2012/2885 Sch.4 para.5, Sch.5 para.3, SI 2012/2886 Sch.1, SSI 2012/303 Sch.4 para.12, SSI 2012/319 Sch.2 para.5, Sch.3 para.2
Art.23, applied: SI 2012/2885 Sch.5 para.4, SI 2012/2886 Sch.1, SSI 2012/303 Sch.4 para.53, SSI 2012/319 Sch.3 para.3, Sch.3 para.5
Art.23, referred to: SI 2012/2885 Sch.5 para.6
Art.36, amended: SI 2012/359 Art.4
Sch.1 Part II, amended: SI 2012/359 Sch.1
Sch.1 Part III, amended: SI 2012/359 Sch.2
Sch.1 Part IV, amended: SI 2012/359 Sch.3
Sch.2 Part II, amended: SI 2012/359 Sch.4
Sch.2 Part III, amended: SI 2012/359 Sch.5
Sch.6 Part II, amended: SI 2012/359 Art.7

610. Ivory Coast (Restrictive Measures) (Overseas Territories) (Amendment) Order 2006
revoked: SI 2012/3067 Art.1

616. West Northamptonshire Development Corporation (Planning Functions) Order 2006
revoked: SI 2012/535 Art.2

679. Permitted Persons (Designation) Order 2006
Art.2, amended: SI 2012/1479 Sch.1 para.79

737. Greenhouse Gas Emissions Trading Scheme (Amendment) Regulations 2006
revoked: SI 2012/3038 Reg.85

741. Pensions Increase (Review) Order 2006
applied: SI 2012/782 Art.3, Art.4

750. Police Act 1997 (Criminal Records) (Registration) Regulations 2006
Reg.2, amended: SI 2012/3006 Art.87, Art.88
Reg.3, amended: SI 2012/3006 Art.88
Reg.4, amended: SI 2012/3006 Art.88
Reg.7, amended: SI 2012/3006 Art.88

2006-cont.

750. Police Act 1997 (Criminal Records) (Registration) Regulations 2006-*cont.*
Reg.8, amended: SI 2012/3006 Art.88
Reg.9, amended: SI 2012/3006 Art.88
Reg.10, amended: SI 2012/3006 Art.88

758. Gender Recognition (Application Fees) Order 2006
Art.2, amended: SI 2012/920 Art.2
Art.3, amended: SI 2012/920 Art.2
Art.5, amended: SI 2012/920 Art.2

759. Occupational Pension Schemes (Modification of Schemes) Regulations 2006
Reg.1, amended: SI 2012/1817 Sch.1 para.9
Reg.4, amended: SI 2012/692 Reg.15
Reg.5, amended: SI 2012/1817 Sch.1 para.9
Reg.7A, added: SI 2012/542 Reg.3

802. Occupational Pension Schemes (Payments to Employer) Regulations 2006
Reg.6, amended: SI 2012/692 Reg.16

913. National Health Service (Miscellaneous Amendments Relating to Independent Prescribing) Regulations 2006
Reg.3, revoked: SI 2012/1909 Sch.8 para.9

937. Waste Management (England and Wales) Regulations 2006
Reg.5, revoked: SI 2012/811 Sch.2 para.3

949. Public Services Ombudsman for Wales (Standards Investigations) Order 2006
applied: SI 2012/2734 Sch.1 para.33
varied: SI 2012/2734 Reg.6

964. Authorised Investment Funds (Tax) Regulations 2006
Reg.13, amended: SI 2012/519 Reg.3
Reg.22, amended: SI 2012/519 Reg.4
Reg.31, applied: SI 2012/847 Reg.10
Reg.48, amended: SI 2012/519 Reg.5, SI 2012/3043 Reg.2
Reg.49, amended: SI 2012/519 Reg.6
Reg.49, revoked (in part): SI 2012/519 Reg.6
Reg.69C, amended: SI 2012/1783 Reg.3
Reg.69Z24E, added: SI 2012/1783 Reg.4
Reg.69Z24F, added: SI 2012/1783 Reg.4
Reg.69Z24G, added: SI 2012/1783 Reg.4
Reg.69Z24H, added: SI 2012/1783 Reg.4
Reg.93, amended: SI 2012/519 Reg.7
Reg.96A, added: SI 2012/519 Reg.8
Sch.1 Part 1, amended: SI 2012/3043 Reg.2
Sch.1 Part 2, amended: SI 2012/1783 Reg.5

965. Child Benefit (Rates) Regulations 2006
Reg.2, referred to: SI 2012/834 Art.3

994. Town and Country Planning (Fees for Applications and Deemed Applications) (Amendment) (England) Regulations 2006
revoked: SI 2012/2920 Sch.3

1003. Immigration (European Economic Area) Regulations 2006
applied: SI 2012/1547 Sch.3 para.2
see *B v Home Office* [2012] EWHC 226 (QB), [2012] 4 All E.R. 276 (QBD), Richard Salter QC; see *de Brito v Secretary of State for the Home Department* [2012] EWCA Civ 709, [2012] 3 C.M.L.R. 24 (CA (Civ Div)), Mummery, L.J.; see *Flaneur's Application for Judicial Review, Re* [2012] N.I. 176 (CA (NI)), Morgan, L.C.J.; see *JYZ (China) v Secretary of State for the Home Department* [2012] CSOH 78, 2012 S.L.T. 1130 (OH), Lord Turnbull
Reg.2, amended: SI 2012/1547 Sch.1 para.1, SI 2012/2560 Sch.1 para.7

2006-cont.

1003. Immigration (European Economic Area) Regulations 2006-*cont.*
Reg.4, amended: SI 2012/1547 Sch.1 para.2, SI 2012/1809 Sch.1 Part 2, SI 2012/2560 Sch.1 para.7
Reg.4, see *Bassey v Secretary of State for the Home Department* [2012] N.I. 218 (CA (NI)), Girvan, L.J.
Reg.5, amended: SI 2012/2560 Sch.1 para.7
Reg.5, see *de Brito v Secretary of State for the Home Department* [2012] EWCA Civ 709, [2012] 3 C.M.L.R. 24 (CA (Civ Div)), Mummery, L.J.
Reg.6, applied: SI 2012/2885 Reg.12, SI 2012/2886 Sch.1, SI 2012/3144 Reg.26, SI 2012/3145 Sch.1, SSI 2012/303 Reg.16, SSI 2012/319 Reg.16
Reg.6, see *Begum (EEA: Worker: Jobseeker: Pakistan), Re* [2012] 2 C.M.L.R. 13 (UT (IAC)), CMG Ockelton; see *de Brito v Secretary of State for the Home Department* [2012] EWCA Civ 709, [2012] 3 C.M.L.R. 24 (CA (Civ Div)), Mummery, L.J.; see *Konodyba v Kensington and Chelsea RLBC* [2012] EWCA Civ 982, [2012] H.L.R. 45 (CA (Civ Div)), Lord Neuberger (M.R.)
Reg.7, applied: SI 2012/2885 Reg.12, SI 2012/2886 Sch.1, SI 2012/3144 Reg.26, SI 2012/3145 Sch.1, SSI 2012/303 Reg.16, SSI 2012/319 Reg.16
Reg.8, amended: SI 2012/2560 Sch.1 para.1
Reg.9, amended: SI 2012/2560 Sch.1 para.7
Reg.10, amended: SI 2012/1547 Sch.1 para.3
Reg.10, applied: 2012 c.10 Sch.1 para.29
Reg.11, amended: SI 2012/1547 Sch.1 para.4, SI 2012/2560 Sch.1 para.2
Reg.12, amended: SI 2012/1547 Sch.1 para.5
Reg.12, applied: SI 2012/1547 Sch.3 para.2
Reg.12, see *B v Home Office* [2012] EWHC 226 (QB), [2012] 4 All E.R. 276 (QBD), Richard Salter QC
Reg.13, amended: SI 2012/1547 Sch.1 para.6
Reg.13, applied: SI 2012/2885 Reg.12, SI 2012/2886 Sch.1, SI 2012/3144 Reg.26, SI 2012/3145 Sch.1, SSI 2012/303 Reg.16, SSI 2012/319 Reg.16
Reg.14, amended: SI 2012/1547 Sch.1 para.7
Reg.14, see *MDB (Italy) v Secretary of State for the Home Department* [2012] EWCA Civ 1015, [2012] 3 C.M.L.R. 43 (CA (Civ Div)), Maurice Kay, L.J. (VP, CA Crim)
Reg.15, amended: SI 2012/1547 Sch.1 para.8
Reg.15, applied: SI 2012/1547 Sch.3 para.2, SI 2012/2885 Reg.12, SI 2012/2886 Sch.1, SI 2012/3144 Reg.26, SI 2012/3145 Sch.1, SSI 2012/303 Reg.16, SSI 2012/319 Reg.16
Reg.15, see *Barnett (EEA Regulations: Rights and Documentation: Jamaica), Re* [2012] UKUT 142 (IAC), [2012] Imm. A.R. 828 (UT (IAC)), Judge Lane; see *de Brito v Secretary of State for the Home Department* [2012] EWCA Civ 709, [2012] 3 C.M.L.R. 24 (CA (Civ Div)), Mummery, L.J.; see *Jarusevicius (EEA Reg.21: Effect of Imprisonment: Lithuania)* [2012] UKUT 120 (IAC), [2012] Imm. A.R. 760 (UT (IAC)), Blake, J. (President); see *MDB (Italy) v Secretary of State for the Home Department* [2012] EWCA Civ 1015, [2012] 3 C.M.L.R. 43 (CA (Civ Div)), Maurice Kay, L.J. (VP, CA Crim)
Reg.15A, added: SI 2012/1547 Sch.1 para.9
Reg.15A, amended: SI 2012/2560 Sch.1 para.3
Reg.15A, applied: SI 2012/2885 Reg.12, SI 2012/2886 Sch.1, SI 2012/3144 Reg.26, SI 2012/3145 Sch.1

2006-cont.

1003. Immigration (European Economic Area) Regulations 2006-*cont.*

Reg.15A, referred to: SI 2012/ 2886 Sch.l, SI 2012/ 3144 Reg.26

Reg.15B, added: SI 2012/ 1547 Sch.l para.l0

Reg.17, see *B v Home Office* [2012] EWHC 226 (QB), [2012] 4 All E.R. 276 (QBD), Richard Salter QC; see *Barnett (EEA Regulations: Rights and Documentation: Jamaica), Re* [2012] UKUT 142 (IAC), [2012] Imm. A.R. 828 (UT (IAC)), Judge Lane

Reg.18, see *Barnett (EEA Regulations: Rights and Documentation: Jamaica), Re* [2012] UKUT 142 (IAC), [2012] Imm. A.R. 828 (UT (IAC)), Judge Lane

Reg.18A, added: SI 2012/ 1547 Sch.l para.ll

Reg.20, amended: SI 2012/ 1547 Sch.l para.12

Reg.20A, added: SI 2012/ 1547 Sch.l para.13

Reg.21, see *Jarusevicius (EEA Reg.21: Effect of Imprisonment: Lithuania)* [2012] UKUT 120 (IAC), [2012] Imm. A.R. 760 (UT (IAC)), Blake, J. (President); see *R. (on the application of Essa) v Upper Tribunal (Immigration and Asylum Chamber)* [2012] EWHC 1533 (QB), [2012] 3 C.M.L.R. 26 (QBD (Admin)), Lang, J.; see *Secretary of State for the Home Department v FV (Italy)* [2012] EWCA Civ 1199, [2012] 3 C.M.L.R. 56 (CA (Civ Div)), Pill, L.J.

Reg.21A, added: SI 2012/ 1547 Sch.l para.14

Reg.21A, amended: SI 2012/ 2560 Sch.l para.4

Reg.22, amended: SI 2012/ 1547 Sch.l para.15

Reg.23, amended: SI 2012/ 1547 Sch.l para.16

Reg.24, amended: SI 2012/ 1547 Sch.l para.17

Reg.24A, amended: SI 2012/ 1547 Sch.l para.18

Reg.25, amended: SI 2012/ 1547 Sch.l para.19

Reg.26, amended: SI 2012/ 1547 Sch.l para.20, SI 2012/ 2560 Sch.l para.5

Reg.26, applied: 2012 c.l0 Sch.l para.12

Reg.27, amended: SI 2012/ 1547 Sch.l para.21

Reg.29A, added: SI 2012/ 2560 Sch.l para.6

Sch.2 para.2, amended: SI 2012/ 1547 Sch.l para.22

Sch.2 para.3, amended: SI 2012/ 1547 Sch.l para.23

Sch.2 para.4, amended: SI 2012/ 1547 Sch.l para.24

Sch.4 para.6, substituted: SI 2012/ 1547 Sch.l para.25

1016. Lord Chancellor (Transfer of Functions and Supplementary Provisions) (No.2) Order 2006

Sch.l para.36, revoked: SI 2012/ 2401 Sch.2 para.6

Sch.2 para.4, revoked (in part): SI 2012/ 1206 Sch.l para.15

Sch.2 para.5, revoked (in part): SI 2012/ 1206 Sch.l para.15

Sch.2 para.6, revoked (in part): SI 2012/ 1206 Sch.l para.15

Sch.2 para.7, revoked (in part): SI 2012/ 1206 Sch.l para.15

1030. Cross-Border Insolvency Regulations 2006

see *Rubin v Eurofinance SA* [2012] UKSC 46, [2012] 3 W.L.R. 1019 (SC), Lord Walker, J.S.C.; see *Schmitt v Deichmann* [2012] EWHC 62 (Ch), [2012] 3 W.L.R. 681 (Ch D), Proudman, J.

Sch.l, see *Larsen v Navios International Inc* [2011] EWHC 878 (Ch), [2012] Bus. L.R. 1124 (Ch D), Norris, J.; see *New Paragon Investments Ltd, Re* [2012] B.C.C. 371 (Ch D (Companies Ct)), Registrar Nicholls

1031. Employment Equality (Age) Regulations 2006

see *King v Health Professions Council* [2012] Eq. L.R. 852 (EAT), Langstaff, J. (President)

2006-cont.

1031. Employment Equality (Age) Regulations 2006-*cont.*

Reg.3, see *Homer v Chief Constable of West Yorkshire* [2012] UKSC 15, [2012] 3 All E.R. 1287 (SC), Lord Hope (Deputy President); see *Seldon v Clarkson Wright & Jakes* [2012] UKSC 16, [2012] 3 All E.R. 1301 (SC), Lord Hope (Deputy President); see *Woodcock v Cumbria Primary Care Trust* [2012] EWCA Civ 330, [2012] I.C.R. 1126 (CA (Civ Div)), Arden, L.J.

Sch.6, see *Bailey v R&R Plant (Peterborough) Ltd* [2012] EWCA Civ 410, [2012] I.R.L.R. 503 (CA (Civ Div)), Ward, L.J.

Sch.6 para.2, see *Bailey v R&R Plant (Peterborough) Ltd* [2012] EWCA Civ 410, [2012] I.R.L.R. 503 (CA (Civ Div)), Ward, L.J.

Sch.6 para.5, see *Bailey v R&R Plant (Peterborough) Ltd* [2012] EWCA Civ 410, [2012] I.R.L.R. 503 (CA (Civ Div)), Ward, L.J.

1056. Smoking, Health and Social Care (Scotland) Act 2005 (Consequential Modifications) (England, Wales and Northern Ireland) Order 2006

Sch.l Part 2 para.12, revoked: SI 2012/ 1909 Sch.8 para.9

1116. Criminal Justice Act 1988 (Reviews of Sentencing) Order 2006

referred to: SI 2012/ 1726 r.70.1

Sch.l para.1A, added: SI 2012/ 1833 Art.2

Sch.l para.2, amended: SI 2012/ 1833 Art.2

Sch.l para.4, substituted: SI 2012/ 1833 Art.2

1160. Seed Potatoes (Fees) (England) Regulations 2006

revoked: SI 2012/ 745 Reg.7

1179. Ceramic Articles in Contact with Food (England) Regulations 2006

revoked: SI 2012/ 2619 Reg.31

1254. Fire and Rescue Services (Northern Ireland) Order 2006

Sch.l para.3, amended: SI 2012/ 2404 Sch.3 para.53

1260. Human Tissue Act 2004 (Ethical Approval, Exceptions from Licensing and Supply of Information about Transplants) Regulations 2006

Reg.3, amended: SI 2012/ 1501 Reg.27

Sch.2 para.10, amended: SI 2012/ 1809 Sch.l Part 2

1294. Allocation of Housing and Homelessness (Eligibility) (England) Regulations 2006

Reg.4, amended: SI 2012/ 1809 Sch.l Part 2, SI 2012/ 2588 Reg.2

Reg.6, amended: SI 2012/ 2588 Reg.2

1380. Contaminated Land (England) Regulations 2006

Reg.3, amended: SI 2012/ 263 Reg.2

Reg.11, amended: SI 2012/ 263 Reg.2

Sch.2 para.6, amended: SI 2012/ 263 Reg.2

1386. Town and Country Planning (Miscellaneous Amendments and Modifications relating to Crown Land) (Wales) Order 2006

Art.4, revoked: SI 2012/ 801 Sch.8

1388. Planning (Listed Buildings, Conservation Areas and Hazardous Substances) (Amendments relating to Crown Land) (Wales) Regulations 2006

Reg.2, revoked: SI 2012/ 793 Sch.5

1406. Police (Complaints and Misconduct) (Amendment) Regulations 2006

revoked: SI 2012/ 1204 Reg.2

2006–cont.

1445. Road Traffic (Permitted Parking Area and Special Parking Area) (City of Derby) Order 2006
revoked: SI 2012/846 Art.2

1454. Sudan (United Nations Measures) Order 2006
revoked: SI 2012/1507 Reg.18

1466. Transport and Works (Applications and Objections Procedure) (England and Wales) Rules 2006
applied: SI 2012/472, SI 2012/1266, SI 2012/1867, SI 2012/1924, SI 2012/1993, SI 2012/2533, SI 2012/2679, SI 2012/2980
varied: SI 2012/147 Art.7
Sch.5, amended: SI 2012/1658 Sch.1, SI 2012/1659 Art.2, SI 2012/2590 Sch.1 para.6
Sch.6, amended: SI 2012/147 Sch.1

1501. National Health Service (Primary Medical Services and Pharmaceutical Services) (Miscellaneous Amendments) Regulations 2006
Reg.6, revoked: SI 2012/1909 Sch.8 para.9
Reg.7, revoked: SI 2012/1909 Sch.8 para.9

1533. Designation of Schools Having a Religious Character (Independent Schools) (England) Order 2006
Sch.1, amended: SI 2012/3174 Sch.2

1543. Tax Avoidance Schemes (Prescribed Descriptions of Arrangements) Regulations 2006
referred to: SI 2012/1836 Reg.4, SI 2012/1868 Reg.6, Reg.17
Reg.1, varied: SI 2012/1868 Reg.25
Reg.5, varied: SI 2012/1868 Reg.25
Reg.6, varied: SI 2012/1868 Reg.25
Reg.7, varied: SI 2012/1868 Reg.25
Reg.8, varied: SI 2012/1868 Reg.25
Reg.9, varied: SI 2012/1868 Reg.25
Reg.10, varied: SI 2012/1868 Reg.25
Reg.11, varied: SI 2012/1868 Reg.25
Reg.12, varied: SI 2012/1868 Reg.25
Reg.13, varied: SI 2012/1868 Reg.25
Reg.14, varied: SI 2012/1868 Reg.25
Reg.15, varied: SI 2012/1868 Reg.25
Reg.16, varied: SI 2012/1868 Reg.25
Reg.17, varied: SI 2012/1868 Reg.25
Reg.17A, varied: SI 2012/1868 Reg.25

1544. Tax Avoidance Schemes (Information) (Amendment) Regulations 2006
revoked: SI 2012/1836 Sch.1

1641. Residential Property Tribunal Procedure (Wales) Regulations 2006
revoked: SI 2012/531 Reg.51

1642. Residential Property Tribunal (Fees) (Wales) Regulations 2006
revoked: SI 2012/531 Reg.51

1643. Plant Health (Wales) Order 2006
Art.12, applied: SI 2012/1493 Reg.2
Art.40, referred to: SI 2012/1493 Reg.4
Art.41, referred to: SI 2012/1493 Reg.4

1659. Human Tissue Act 2004 (Persons who Lack Capacity to Consent and Transplants) Regulations 2006
Reg.2, amended: SI 2012/1501 Reg.26
Reg.11, amended: SI 2012/1501 Reg.26

1699. Proceeds of Crime Act 2002 (Recovery of Cash in Summary Proceedings Minimum Amount) Order 2006
see *Scottish Ministers v Devaney* 2012 S.L.T. (Sh Ct) 164 (Sh Ct (Tayside) (Dundee)), Sheriff J K Mundy

2006–cont.

1704. Ceramic Articles in Contact with Food (Wales) Regulations 2006
revoked: SI 2012/2705 Reg.30

1705. Local Safeguarding Children Boards (Wales) Regulations 2006
Reg.2, amended: SI 2012/1712 Reg.2
Reg.3, amended: SI 2012/1712 Reg.2
Reg.4, substituted: SI 2012/1712 Reg.3

1740. A40 Trunk Road (Withybush, Haverfordwest, Pembrokeshire) (40 mph and 50 mph Speed Limits) Order 2006
varied: SI 2012/2444 Art.6

1751. Education (Pupil Registration) (England) Regulations 2006
Reg.8, amended: SI 2012/1033 Sch.2 para.4
Reg.8, varied: SI 2012/1107 Art.10
Reg.12, amended: SI 2012/1107 Art.10

1756. Road Vehicles (Construction and Use) (Amendment) Regulations 2006
revoked: SI 2012/1404 Sch.1

1807. Wireless Telegraphy (Spectrum Trading) (Amendment) (No.2) Regulations 2006
revoked: SI 2012/2187 Sch.1

1808. Wireless Telegraphy (Register) (Amendment) (No.2) Regulations 2006
revoked: SI 2012/2186 Sch.1

1831. Private Security Industry Act 2001 (Amendments to Schedule 2) Order 2006
Art.3, revoked (in part): 2012 c.9 Sch.10 Part 3
Art.4, revoked (in part): 2012 c.9 Sch.10 Part 3

1851. Kava-kava in Food (Wales) Regulations 2006
Reg.2, amended: SI 2012/1809 Sch.1 Part 4

1931. Climate Change Agreements (Eligible Facilities) (Amendment) Regulations 2006
revoked: SI 2012/2999 Reg.9

1952. Medicines for Human Use (National Rules for Homoeopathic Products) Regulations 2006
revoked: SI 2012/1916 Sch.35

2072. Primary Care Trusts (Establishment and Dissolution) (England) Order 2006
referred to: SI 2012/1512 Sch.1

2135. Serious Organised Crime and Police Act 2005 (Appeals under Section 74) Order 2006
applied: SI 2012/1726 r.65.1, r.68.11, r.68.12, r.65.5
Art.15, applied: SI 2012/1726 r.74.1, r.74.2
Art.16, applied: SI 2012/1726 r.74.2
Art.18, applied: SI 2012/1726 r.74.2
Art.19, referred to: SI 2012/1726 r.74.3
Art.20, applied: SI 2012/1726 r.74.2

2185. Olympic Delivery Authority (Planning Functions) Order 2006
revoked: SI 2012/2167 Art.8

2186. London Thames Gateway Development Corporation (Planning Functions) (Amendment) Order 2006
revoked: SI 2012/2167 Art.8

2189. Education (Pupil Exclusions and Appeals) (Miscellaneous Amendments) (England) Regulations 2006
Reg.2, revoked: SI 2012/1033 Sch.3
Reg.3, revoked: SI 2012/1033 Sch.3
Reg.5, revoked: SI 2012/1033 Sch.3
Reg.6, revoked (in part): SI 2012/1033 Sch.3

2316. Air Navigation (Amendment) Order 2006
applied: 2012 c.19 Sch.6 para.4

2323. International Development Association (Multilateral Debt Relief Initiative) Order 2006
Art.3, amended: SI 2012/520 Art.2

2006–cont.

2380. Appointments Commission Regulations 2006
Reg.5, amended: SI 2012/2404 Sch.3 para.54

2407. Veterinary Medicines Regulations 2006
Sch.9 Part 1 para.6, revoked: SI 2012/3039 Reg.36

2601. Education (Information About Individual Pupils) (England) Regulations 2006
Reg.3A, amended: SI 2012/1919 Reg.2
Reg.4A, added: SI 2012/1919 Reg.2
Reg.5, amended: SI 2012/1919 Reg.2
Sch.1 Part 2 para.1, amended: SI 2012/1033 Sch.2 para.5
Sch.2A para.1, added: SI 2012/1919 Reg.2

2661. Education (School Teacher Performance Management) (England) Regulations 2006
applied: SI 2012/1115 Sch.1 para.24
revoked: SI 2012/115 Reg.9

2701. Avian Influenza (Preventive Measures) (England) Regulations 2006
Reg.22, amended: SI 2012/2897 Art.10

2702. Avian Influenza and Influenza of Avian Origin in Mammals (England) (No.2) Order 2006
Art.71, amended: SI 2012/3039 Reg.38
Art.85, amended: SI 2012/2897 Art.11

2703. Avian Influenza (Vaccination) (England) Regulations 2006
Reg.23, amended: SI 2012/2897 Art.12

2739. Control of Asbestos Regulations 2006
revoked: SI 2012/632 Reg.33
Reg.8, applied: SI 2012/632 Reg.32
Reg.32, applied: SI 2012/632 Reg.32
Reg.33, applied: SI 2012/632 Reg.32
Reg.36, referred to: SI 2012/632 Reg.33

2821. Salmonella in Turkey Flocks and Slaughter Pigs (Survey Powers) (England) Regulations 2006
revoked: SI 2012/2897 Art.13
Reg.6, revoked: 2012 c.9 Sch.2 para.9, Sch.10 Part 2

2914. Local Government (Early Termination of Employment) (Discretionary Compensation) (England and Wales) Regulations 2006
Reg.2, amended: SI 2012/1989 Reg.3

2927. Avian Influenza and Influenza of Avian Origin in Mammals (Wales) (No 2) Order 2006
Art.71, amended: SI 2012/3039 Reg.39

2929. Seed Potatoes (Wales) Regulations 2006
Reg.8, applied: SI 2012/1493 Reg.3
Reg.9, applied: SI 2012/1493 Reg.3

2961. Seed Potatoes (Fees) (Wales) (No 2) Regulations 2006
revoked: SI 2012/1493 Reg.7

2989. Contaminated Land (Wales) Regulations 2006
Reg.3, amended: SI 2012/283 Reg.2
Reg.11, amended: SI 2012/283 Reg.2
Sch.2 para.5, amended: SI 2012/283 Reg.2
Sch.2 para.6, amended: SI 2012/283 Reg.2

3016. A45 Trunk Road (Ryton on Dunsmore, Warwickshire) (50 Miles Per Hour Speed Limit) Order 2001 Variation Order 2006
revoked: SI 2012/2144 Art.3

3105. Occupational Pension Schemes (Levy Ceiling Earnings Percentage Increase) Order 2006
revoked: SI 2012/528 Sch.1

3199. Further Education (Providers of Education) (England) Regulations 2006
Reg.9, amended: SI 2012/979 Sch.1 para.19
Reg.19, amended: SI 2012/979 Sch.1 para.19

3221. Capital Requirements Regulations 2006
Reg.1, amended: SI 2012/917 Reg.3
Reg.3, amended: SI 2012/917 Reg.4

2006–cont.

3221. Capital Requirements Regulations 2006–*cont.*
Reg.10A, amended: SI 2012/917 Reg.5
Reg.10B, amended: SI 2012/917 Reg.6
Reg.11, amended: SI 2012/917 Reg.7
Reg.12A, amended: SI 2012/917 Reg.8
Reg.14, amended: SI 2012/917 Reg.9
Reg.16A, amended: SI 2012/917 Reg.10
Reg.16E, amended: SI 2012/917 Reg.11
Reg.16F, amended: SI 2012/917 Reg.12
Reg.16G, added: SI 2012/917 Reg.13
Reg.26, amended: SI 2012/917 Reg.14

3223. Merchant Shipping (Inland Waterway and Limited Coastal Operations) (Boatmasters Qualifications and Hours of Work) Regulations 2006
Sch.2 Part 1, amended: SI 2012/1659 Sch.3 para.35

3247. Avian Influenza (H5N1 in Poultry) (England) Order 2006
Art.24, amended: SI 2012/2897 Art.14

3249. Avian Influenza (H5N1 in Wild Birds) (England) Order 2006
Art.25, amended: SI 2012/2897 Art.15

3250. Cereal Seed (Wales) and Fodder Plant Seed (Wales) (Amendment) Regulations 2006
revoked: SI 2012/245 Reg.34

3260. Welfare of Animals (Transport) (England) Order 2006
Art.29, amended: SI 2012/2897 Art.16

3271. Overseas Life Insurance Companies Regulations 2006
Reg.24, referred to: 2012 c.14 Sch.17 para.20

3284. Gambling (Operating Licence and Single-Machine Permit Fees) Regulations 2006
Reg.2, amended: SI 2012/829 Reg.3
Reg.3, amended: SI 2012/829 Reg.4
Reg.6, amended: SI 2012/829 Reg.5
Reg.7, amended: SI 2012/829 Reg.6
Reg.8, amended: SI 2012/829 Reg.7
Reg.8A, amended: SI 2012/829 Reg.8
Reg.9, amended: SI 2012/829 Reg.9
Reg.10, amended: SI 2012/829 Reg.10
Reg.11, amended: SI 2012/829 Reg.11
Reg.12, amended: SI 2012/829 Reg.12
Reg.13, amended: SI 2012/829 Reg.13
Reg.13A, added: SI 2012/829 Reg.14
Reg.13A, amended: SI 2012/1851 Reg.4
Reg.14, amended: SI 2012/829 Reg.15
Reg.14, revoked (in part): SI 2012/829 Reg.15
Reg.14A, amended: SI 2012/829 Reg.16
Reg.15, amended: SI 2012/829 Reg.17, SI 2012/1851 Reg.5
Reg.16, amended: SI 2012/829 Reg.18
Reg.16A, amended: SI 2012/829 Reg.19
Reg.17, amended: SI 2012/829 Reg.20
Reg.17A, amended: SI 2012/829 Reg.21
Reg.18, amended: SI 2012/829 Reg.22
Reg.19, amended: SI 2012/829 Reg.23
Reg.20, amended: SI 2012/829 Reg.24
Reg.20A, added: SI 2012/829 Reg.25
Reg.20A, amended: SI 2012/1851 Reg.6
Reg.21, amended: SI 2012/829 Reg.26
Reg.21A, added: SI 2012/829 Reg.27
Reg.23, amended: SI 2012/829 Reg.28, Reg.29
Reg.23A, amended: SI 2012/829 Reg.30
Reg.23B, amended: SI 2012/829 Reg.31
Reg.24, amended: SI 2012/829 Reg.32, SI 2012/1851 Reg.7
Reg.24A, added: SI 2012/829 Reg.33

2006–cont.

3284. Gambling (Operating Licence and Single-Machine Permit Fees) Regulations 2006–*cont.*

Reg.26, substituted: SI 2012/829 Reg.34

Sch.1, amended: SI 2012/829 Sch.1, SI 2012/1851 Reg.8

Sch.2, amended: SI 2012/829 Sch.2

Sch.3, amended: SI 2012/829 Sch.3

Sch.4, amended: SI 2012/829 Sch.4, SI 2012/1851 Reg.9

Sch.5, amended: SI 2012/829 Sch.5

Sch.6, amended: SI 2012/829 Sch.6

3285. Gambling (Personal Licence Fees) Regulations 2006

Reg.4, amended: SI 2012/1851 Reg.3

3289. Waste Electrical and Electronic Equipment Regulations 2006

Reg.2, amended: SSI 2012/360 Sch.11 para.14

3304. Local Elections (Principal Areas) (England and Wales) Rules 2006

applied: SI 2012/2031 Sch.4 para.8

r.2, amended: SI 2012/1917 Sch.4 para.10

r.2, varied: SI 2012/444 Sch.4 para.1, SI 2012/2031 Sch.4 para.16

Sch.3, applied: SI 2012/1918 Reg.4

Sch.3, varied: SI 2012/444 Sch.4 para.1, SI 2012/2031 Sch.4 para.17

3305. Local Elections (Parishes and Communities) (England and Wales) Rules 2006

applied: SI 2012/2031 Sch.4 para.8

r.2, amended: SI 2012/1917 Sch.4 para.11

r.2, varied: SI 2012/444 Sch.4 para.1, SI 2012/2031 Sch.4 para.19

r.5, varied: SI 2012/4 Art.10, SI 2012/160 Art.9

Sch.3, applied: SI 2012/1918 Reg.4

Sch.3, varied: SI 2012/444 Sch.4 para.1, SI 2012/2031 Sch.4 para.20

3317. Accession (Immigration and Worker Authorisation) Regulations 2006

Reg.1, amended: SI 2012/1809 Sch.1 Part 2

Reg.5, amended: SI 2012/1809 Sch.1 Part 2

3327. North Korea (United Nations Measures) (Overseas Territories) Order 2006

revoked: SI 2012/3066 Art.1

Sch.1, amended: SI 2012/362 Sch.1

3336. Water and Sewerage Services (Northern Ireland) Order 2006

applied: SI 2012/1128 Art.4

referred to: 2012 c.19 Sch.6 para.4

3373. National Health Service (Pharmaceutical Services) (Amendment) Regulations 2006

Reg.8, revoked: SI 2012/1909 Sch.8 para.9

Reg.9, revoked: SI 2012/1909 Sch.8 para.9

Reg.10, revoked: SI 2012/1909 Sch.8 para.9

Reg.11, revoked: SI 2012/1909 Sch.8 para.9

Reg.12, revoked: SI 2012/1909 Sch.8 para.9

Reg.13, revoked: SI 2012/1909 Sch.8 para.9

Reg.14, revoked: SI 2012/1909 Sch.8 para.9

Reg.15, revoked: SI 2012/1909 Sch.8 para.9

Reg.16, revoked: SI 2012/1909 Sch.8 para.9

Reg.17, revoked: SI 2012/1909 Sch.8 para.9

Reg.18, revoked: SI 2012/1909 Sch.8 para.9

Reg.19, revoked: SI 2012/1909 Sch.8 para.9

Reg.20, revoked: SI 2012/1909 Sch.8 para.9

Reg.21, revoked: SI 2012/1909 Sch.8 para.9

Reg.22, revoked: SI 2012/1909 Sch.8 para.9

Reg.23, revoked: SI 2012/1909 Sch.8 para.9

Reg.24, revoked: SI 2012/1909 Sch.8 para.9

Reg.25, revoked: SI 2012/1909 Sch.8 para.9

2006–cont.

3373. National Health Service (Pharmaceutical Services) (Amendment) Regulations 2006–*cont.*

Reg.26, revoked: SI 2012/1909 Sch.8 para.9

Reg.27, revoked: SI 2012/1909 Sch.8 para.9

Reg.28, revoked: SI 2012/1909 Sch.8 para.9

Reg.29, revoked: SI 2012/1909 Sch.8 para.9

Reg.30, revoked: SI 2012/1909 Sch.8 para.9

Reg.31, revoked: SI 2012/1909 Sch.8 para.9

Reg.32, revoked: SI 2012/1909 Sch.8 para.9

Reg.33, revoked: SI 2012/1909 Sch.8 para.9

Reg.34, revoked: SI 2012/1909 Sch.8 para.9

Reg.35, revoked: SI 2012/1909 Sch.8 para.9

Reg.36, revoked: SI 2012/1909 Sch.8 para.9

Reg.37, revoked: SI 2012/1909 Sch.8 para.9

Reg.38, revoked: SI 2012/1909 Sch.8 para.9

Reg.39, revoked: SI 2012/1909 Sch.8 para.9

Reg.40, revoked: SI 2012/1909 Sch.8 para.9

Reg.41, revoked: SI 2012/1909 Sch.8 para.9

Reg.42, revoked: SI 2012/1909 Sch.8 para.9

Reg.43, revoked: SI 2012/1909 Sch.8 para.9

3390. Town and Country Planning (General Development Procedure) (Amendment) (Wales) Order 2006

revoked: SI 2012/801 Sch.8

3409. Education (Infant Class Sizes) (England) (Amendment) Regulations 2006

revoked: SI 2012/10 Reg.3

3415. Police Pensions Regulations 2006

Reg.6, amended: SI 2012/3057 Reg.4

Reg.6, revoked (in part): SI 2012/3057 Reg.4

Reg.7, substituted: SI 2012/640 Reg.3

Reg.8, amended: SI 2012/3057 Reg.5

Reg.9, amended: SI 2012/3057 Reg.6

Reg.9, revoked (in part): SI 2012/3057 Reg.6

Reg.20, amended: SI 2012/2811 Reg.3

Sch.2 para.9, amended: SI 2012/3057 Reg.7

3418. Electromagnetic Compatibility Regulations 2006

Reg.43, amended: SI 2012/1848 Reg.8

Reg.44, amended: SI 2012/1848 Reg.8

Reg.46, amended: SI 2012/1848 Reg.8

3432. Firefighters Pension Scheme (England) Order 2006

Sch.1, amended: SI 2012/954 Art.3, Art.4, SI 2012/2988 Sch.1 para.1, Sch.1 para.2, Sch.1 para.3

2007

75. Rural Development (Enforcement) (England) Regulations 2007

Reg.2, amended: SI 2012/666 Sch.2

115. Personal Injuries (NHS Charges) (Amounts) Regulations 2007

Reg.2, amended: SI 2012/387 Reg.2

119. Seed (Wales) (Amendments for Tests and Trials etc.) Regulations 2007

revoked: SI 2012/245 Reg.34

121. National Health Service (Free Prescriptions and Charges for Drugs and Appliances) (Wales) Regulations 2007

Reg.2, amended: SI 2012/1479 Sch.1 para.50, SI 2012/1916 Sch.34 para.91

Reg.7, amended: SI 2012/1916 Sch.34 para.91

Reg.7A, amended: SI 2012/1916 Sch.34 para.91

126. Financial Services and Markets Act 2000 (Markets in Financial Instruments) Regulations 2007

Reg.4C, amended: SI 2012/917 Sch.2 para.6

2007–cont.

175. **Environmental Offences (Fixed Penalties) (Miscellaneous Provisions) Regulations 2007**
Reg.2, amended: SI 2012/1151 Reg.2
Reg.3, amended: SI 2012/1151 Reg.2

236. **National Assembly for Wales (Representation of the People) Order 2007**
Art.2, amended: SI 2012/1809 Sch.1 Part 2
Art.23, enabled: SI 2012/2478
Sch.1 para.4, amended: SI 2012/1479 Sch.1 para.51

274. **Air Navigation (Amendment) Order 2007**
applied: 2012 c.19 Sch.6 para.4

282. **Iran (United Nations and European Union Measures) (Overseas Territories) Order 2007**
applied: SI 2012/1756 Art.54
revoked: SI 2012/1756 Art.53

283. **Lebanon (United Nations Sanctions) (Overseas Territories) Order 2007**
Sch.1, amended: SI 2012/362 Sch.1

307. **Review of Children's Cases (Wales) Regulations 2007**
applied: SI 2012/205 Reg.2
Reg.3, amended: SI 2012/1479 Sch.1 para.80

320. **Construction (Design and Management) Regulations 2007**
applied: SI 2012/1282 Sch.1, SI 2012/1286 Sch.1, SI 2012/1289 Sch.1, SI 2012/1294 Sch.1, SI 2012/1295 Sch.1
referred to: SI 2012/1284 Sch.1
Reg.17, amended: SI 2012/632 Sch.3

380. **Wireless Telegraphy (Spectrum Trading) (Amendment) Regulations 2007**
revoked: SI 2012/2187 Sch.1

381. **Wireless Telegraphy (Register) (Amendment) Regulations 2007**
revoked: SI 2012/2186 Sch.1

448. **Diseases of Animals (Approved Disinfectants) (England) Order 2007**
Art.12, amended: SI 2012/2897 Art.17

463. **Childcare Act 2006 (Childcare Assessments) Regulations 2007**
Reg.2, amended: SI 2012/979 Sch.1 para.20

465. **Greenhouse Gas Emissions Trading Scheme (Amendment) Regulations 2007**
revoked: SI 2012/3038 Reg.85

529. **Cattle Identification Regulations 2007**
applied: SI 2012/1379 Art.4
Reg.2, amended: SI 2012/2897 Art.18
Reg.10, amended: SI 2012/2897 Art.18
Reg.12, amended: SI 2012/2897 Art.18
Reg.16, amended: SI 2012/2897 Art.18
Sch.2, applied: SI 2012/114 Sch.1 para.10

599. **Consistent Financial Reporting (England) (Amendment) Regulations 2007**
revoked: SI 2012/674 Reg.6

603. **Education and Inspections Act 2006 (Consequential Amendments) Regulations 2007**
Reg.15, revoked (in part): SI 2012/2401 Sch.1 para.41

674. **National Health Service (Pharmaceutical Services) (Remuneration for Persons providing Pharmaceutical Services) (Amendment) Regulations 2007**
Reg.2, amended: SI 2012/1909 Sch.8 para.9
Reg.3, revoked: SI 2012/1909 Sch.8 para.9
Reg.4, revoked: SI 2012/1909 Sch.8 para.9
Reg.5, revoked: SI 2012/1909 Sch.8 para.9
Reg.6, revoked: SI 2012/1909 Sch.8 para.9
Reg.7, revoked: SI 2012/1909 Sch.8 para.9

2007–cont.

694. **Her Majesty's Chief Inspector of Education, Children's Services and Skills (Fees and Frequency of Inspections) (Children's Homes etc.) Regulations 2007**
Reg.14, amended: SI 2012/511 Reg.2
Reg.15, amended: SI 2012/511 Reg.2
Reg.17, amended: SI 2012/511 Reg.3
Reg.18, amended: SI 2012/511 Reg.4

720. **Plant Health (Plant Passport Fees) (England) Regulations 2007**
revoked (in part): SI 2012/745 Reg.7

740. **Tuberculosis (England) Order 2007**
Art.1, amended: SI 2012/1391 Art.2
Art.3, amended: SI 2012/1391 Art.2
Art.8, applied: SI 2012/1379 Sch.1 para.4
Art.9, revoked (in part): SI 2012/1391 Art.2
Art.20, amended: SI 2012/1391 Art.2
Art.23, amended: SI 2012/2897 Art.19
Art.25, added: SI 2012/1391 Art.2
Sch.1 para.3, substituted: SI 2012/1391 Art.2
Sch.1 para.5, added: SI 2012/1391 Art.2

778. **Student Fees (Qualifying Courses and Persons) (England) Regulations 2007**
Reg.2, amended: SI 2012/1653 Reg.5
Sch.1 para.1, amended: SI 2012/1653 Reg.6
Sch.1 para.9, amended: SI 2012/1653 Reg.7

779. **Education (Fees and Awards) (England) Regulations 2007**
Reg.2, amended: SI 2012/1653 Reg.8
Reg.4, amended: SI 2012/765 Art.9
Reg.7, amended: SI 2012/765 Art.9
Reg.9, amended: SI 2012/956 Art.15

783. **Town and Country Planning (Control of Advertisements) (England) Regulations 2007**
applied: SI 2012/1917 Art.83, SI 2012/2031 Reg.14
Reg.6, referred to: SI 2012/2920 Reg.13
Reg.7, applied: SI 2012/2920 Reg.13
Reg.9, applied: SI 2012/2920 Reg.13
Sch.1, amended: SI 2012/2372 Reg.2
Sch.3, see *Addison Lee Ltd v Westminster City Council* [2012] EWHC 152 (Admin), [2012] J.P.L. 969 (DC), Aikens, L.J.
Sch.3 Part 1, added: SI 2012/2372 Reg.2
Sch.3 Part 1, amended: SI 2012/2372 Reg.2
Sch.3 Part 1, substituted: SI 2012/2372 Reg.2

785. **National Insurance Contributions (Application of Part 7 of the Finance Act 2004) Regulations 2007**
revoked: SI 2012/1868 Reg.29

801. **Pensions Increase (Review) Order 2007**
applied: SI 2012/782 Art.3, Art.4

865. **Pension Protection Fund (Closed Schemes) Regulations 2007**
Reg.3, amended: SI 2012/1688 Reg.9, SI 2012/3083 Reg.8
Reg.5, amended: SI 2012/692 Reg.17
Sch.1 Part 2 para.8, amended: SI 2012/1741 Sch.1 para.7

871. **Producer Responsibility Obligations (Packaging Waste) Regulations 2007**
Reg.2, amended: SSI 2012/360 Sch.11 para.17
Reg.42, added: SI 2012/3082 Reg.3
Sch.2 para.1, amended: SI 2012/3082 Reg.4
Sch.2 para.3, amended: SI 2012/3082 Reg.4
Sch.2 para.5, substituted: SI 2012/3082 Reg.4
Sch.2 para.6, amended: SI 2012/3082 Reg.4
Sch.2 para.6A, added: SI 2012/3082 Reg.4
Sch.2 para.8, substituted: SI 2012/3082 Reg.4
Sch.2 para.11, added: SI 2012/3082 Reg.4

2007–cont.

912. Policing (Miscellaneous Provisions) (Northern Ireland) Order 2007
Art.1, amended: SI 2012/2595 Art.15
Art.1, revoked (in part): SI 2012/2595 Art.15

923. Smoke-free (Signs) Regulations 2007
revoked: SI 2012/1536 Reg.4

930. Serious Organised Crime and Police Act 2005 (Designated Sites under Section 128) Order 2007
Art.2, amended: SI 2012/1769 Art.2, SI 2012/2709 Art.2
Sch.11, added: SI 2012/1769 Art.2

937. Scottish Parliament (Elections etc.) Order 2007
varied: 2012 c.11 s.3

945. Business Premises Renovation Allowances Regulations 2007
Reg.2A, added: SI 2012/868 Reg.3
Reg.4, amended: SI 2012/868 Reg.4
Reg.5, added: SI 2012/868 Reg.5

957. School Governance (Constitution) (England) Regulations 2007
revoked: SI 2012/1034 Reg.4
see *R. (on the application of Parent Governors of the Cardinal Vaughan Memorial School) v Roman Catholic Archbishop of Westminster* [2011] EWCA Civ 433, [2012] P.T.S.R. 291 (CA (Civ Div)), Rix, L.J.
Reg.1, applied: SI 2012/1035 Reg.4
Reg.2, applied: SI 2012/1035 Reg.4
Reg.3, applied: SI 2012/1035 Reg.4
Reg.5, amended: SI 2012/421 Reg.2
Reg.8, amended: SI 2012/421 Reg.2
Reg.9, amended: SI 2012/421 Reg.2
Reg.13, applied: SI 2012/1035 Reg.4
Reg.14, applied: SI 2012/1035 Reg.4
Reg.15, applied: SI 2012/1035 Reg.4
Reg.16, amended: SI 2012/421 Reg.2
Reg.16, applied: SI 2012/1035 Reg.4
Reg.17, applied: SI 2012/1035 Reg.4
Reg.18, amended: SI 2012/421 Reg.2
Reg.18, applied: SI 2012/1035 Reg.4
Reg.19, applied: SI 2012/1035 Reg.4
Reg.20, applied: SI 2012/1035 Reg.4
Reg.21, applied: SI 2012/1035 Reg.4
Reg.22, amended: SI 2012/421 Reg.2
Reg.22, applied: SI 2012/1035 Reg.4
Reg.23, applied: SI 2012/1035 Reg.4
Reg.24, applied: SI 2012/1035 Reg.4
Reg.25, applied: SI 2012/1035 Reg.4
Reg.26, applied: SI 2012/1035 Reg.4
Reg.27, applied: SI 2012/1035 Reg.4
Reg.28, amended: SI 2012/421 Reg.2
Reg.28, applied: SI 2012/1035 Reg.4
Reg.29, applied: SI 2012/1035 Reg.4
Reg.30, applied: SI 2012/1035 Reg.4
Reg.32, applied: SI 2012/1034 Reg.2, SI 2012/1035 Reg.2, Reg.4
Sch.1 para.10, see *R. (on the application of Parent Governors of the Cardinal Vaughan Memorial School) v Roman Catholic Archbishop of Westminster* [2011] EWCA Civ 433, [2012] P.T.S.R. 291 (CA (Civ Div)), Rix, L.J.
Sch.6 para.4, revoked: SI 2012/421 Reg.2
Sch.6 para.6, amended: SI 2012/421 Reg.2

958. School Governance (New Schools) (England) Regulations 2007
Part 3, applied: SI 2012/1035 Reg.31, Reg.35, Reg.41
Part 4, applied: SI 2012/1035 Reg.31, Reg.35, Reg.41

2007–cont.

958. School Governance (New Schools) (England) Regulations 2007–*cont.*
Reg.3, amended: SI 2012/1034 Reg.32
Reg.48, amended: SI 2012/1033 Sch.2 para.6
Reg.52, amended: SI 2012/1034 Reg.32
Reg.54, amended: SI 2012/1034 Reg.32
Sch.2 para.5, amended: SI 2012/2404 Sch.3 para.55

960. School Governance (Federations) (England) Regulations 2007
revoked: SI 2012/1035 Reg.3
Reg.14, amended: SI 2012/421 Reg.3
Reg.17, amended: SI 2012/421 Reg.3
Reg.18, amended: SI 2012/421 Reg.3

991. Energy Performance of Buildings (Certificates and Inspections) (England and Wales) Regulations 2007
applied: SI 2012/2601 Art.3
revoked: SI 2012/3118 Sch.3
Reg.2, amended: SI 2012/809 Reg.3
Reg.6, amended: SI 2012/809 Reg.4
Reg.7, amended: SI 2012/809 Reg.5
Reg.11, amended: SI 2012/809 Reg.6
Reg.11, revoked (in part): SI 2012/809 Reg.6
Reg.14, revoked: SI 2012/809 Reg.7
Reg.30, revoked: SI 2012/809 Reg.7
Reg.31, amended: SI 2012/809 Reg.8
Reg.32, substituted: SI 2012/809 Reg.9
Reg.33, substituted: SI 2012/809 Reg.9
Reg.34, substituted: SI 2012/809 Reg.9
Reg.34A, substituted: SI 2012/809 Reg.9
Reg.35, substituted: SI 2012/809 Reg.9
Reg.35A, substituted: SI 2012/809 Reg.9
Reg.35B, substituted: SI 2012/809 Reg.9
Reg.36, substituted: SI 2012/809 Reg.9
Reg.36A, substituted: SI 2012/809 Reg.9
Reg.37, substituted: SI 2012/809 Reg.9
Sch.2 para.1, added: SI 2012/809 Sch.1
Sch.2 Part 1, added: SI 2012/809 Sch.1
Sch.2 para.2, added: SI 2012/809 Sch.1
Sch.2 Part 2, added: SI 2012/809 Sch.1
Sch.3 Part 1 para.1, added: SI 2012/809 Sch.1
Sch.3 Part 1 para.2, added: SI 2012/809 Sch.1
Sch.3 Part 2 para.3, added: SI 2012/809 Sch.1
Sch.3 Part 3 para.4, added: SI 2012/809 Sch.1

1022. Courts Boards Areas (Amendment) Order 2007
revoked: SI 2012/1206 Sch.1 para.16

1024. Local Authorities (Mayoral Elections) (England and Wales) Regulations 2007
applied: SI 2012/2031 Sch.4 para.8
Appendix 1, added: SI 2012/2059 Sch.3
Reg.2, amended: SI 2012/1917 Sch.4 para.12
Reg.2, varied: SI 2012/444 Sch.4 para.1, SI 2012/2031 Sch.4 para.22
Reg.3, amended: SI 2012/2059 Reg.2
Reg.4, amended: SI 2012/2059 Reg.2
Reg.4, substituted: SI 2012/2059 Reg.2
Sch.1, amended: SI 2012/2059 Reg.2, Sch.1
Sch.2A, added: SI 2012/2059 Sch.2
Sch.3, amended: SI 2012/1917 Sch.4 para.12, SI 2012/2059 Reg.2
Sch.3, applied: SI 2012/1918 Reg.4
Sch.3, varied: SI 2012/444 Sch.4 para.1, SI 2012/2031 Sch.4 para.23
Sch.3A para.1, added: SI 2012/2059 Sch.3
Sch.3A para.2, added: SI 2012/2059 Sch.3
Sch.3A para.3, added: SI 2012/2059 Sch.3
Sch.3A para.4, added: SI 2012/2059 Sch.3

2007–cont.

1065. Education (Information About Children in Alternative Provision) (England) Regulations 2007
Reg.2, varied: SI 2012/1107 Art.11
Reg.3, amended: SI 2012/979 Sch.1 para.21
Reg.3, varied: SI 2012/1107 Art.11
Reg.6, amended: SI 2012/979 Sch.1 para.21
Reg.8, revoked (in part): SI 2012/765 Art.10, SI 2012/956 Art.16
Reg.8, varied: 2012 c.11 s.12

1072. Firefighters Pension Scheme (Wales) Order 2007
Sch.1, added: SI 2012/972 Art.4
Sch.1, amended: SI 2012/972 Art.3

1079. Criminal Justice Act 2003 (Surcharge)(No 2) Order 2007
revoked: SI 2012/1696 Art.7

1086. Local Authorities (Allowances for Members) (Wales) Regulations 2007
Reg.9, revoked: SI 2012/1905 Reg.8

1096. Greenhouse Gas Emissions Trading Scheme (Miscellaneous Provisions) Regulations 2007
revoked: SI 2012/3038 Reg.85

1098. Police, Public Order and Criminal Justice (Scotland) Act 2006 (Consequential Provisions and Modifications) Order 2007
amended: 2012 asp 8 s.61
Art.2, amended: 2012 asp 8 s.61

1104. National Health Service (Travelling Expenses and Remission of Charges) (Wales) Regulations 2007
Reg.5, applied: SI 2012/2886 Sch.1, SSI 2012/303 Sch.4 para.45, Sch.5 para.43
Reg.6, applied: SI 2012/2886 Sch.1, SSI 2012/303 Sch.4 para.45, Sch.5 para.43
Reg.11, applied: SI 2012/2886 Sch.1, SSI 2012/303 Sch.4 para.45, Sch.5 para.43
Sch.1, amended: SI 2012/800 Reg.3

1115. Air Navigation (Isle of Man) Order 2007
applied: 2012 c.19 Sch.6 para.4

1120. Docking of Working Dogs Tails (England) Regulations 2007
Reg.2, amended: SI 2012/61 Reg.3
Reg.3, amended: SI 2012/61 Reg.3

1166. Local Government Pension Scheme (Benefits, Membership and Contributions) Regulations 2007
Reg.1, amended: SI 2012/1989 Reg.5
Reg.2, amended: SI 2012/1989 Reg.6
Reg.2, revoked (in part): SI 2012/1989 Reg.6
Reg.8, amended: SI 2012/1989 Reg.7
Reg.14A, amended: SI 2012/1989 Reg.8
Reg.18, amended: SI 2012/1989 Reg.9
Reg.26, amended: SI 2012/1989 Reg.10
Reg.28, amended: SI 2012/1989 Reg.11
Reg.30, amended: SI 2012/1989 Reg.12
Reg.30A, amended: SI 2012/1989 Reg.13
Reg.31, substituted: SI 2012/1989 Reg.14
Reg.33, amended: SI 2012/1989 Reg.15
Reg.34, amended: SI 2012/1989 Reg.16
Reg.39, amended: SI 2012/1989 Reg.17

1167. Consumer Credit (Information Requirements and Duration of Licences and Charges) Regulations 2007
Reg.2, amended: SI 2012/2798 Sch.1 para.4
Reg.4, amended: SI 2012/2798 Sch.1 para.4
Sch.1 Part 2A para.4A, added: SI 2012/2798 Sch.1 para.4

2007–cont.

1170. Her Majesty's Inspectors of Constabulary (Specified Organisations) Order 2007
Art.2, revoked (in part): SI 2012/2733 Art.3

1174. Criminal Defence Service (Funding) Order 2007
see *Lord Chancellor v Ian Henery Solicitors Ltd* [2011] EWHC 3246 (QB), [2012] 1 Costs L.R. 205 (QBD), Spencer, J.; see *Lord Chancellor v McCarthy* [2012] EWHC 2325 (QB), [2012] 5 Costs L.R. 965 (QBD), Sweeney, J.; see *R. v Qu (Costs)* [2012] 3 Costs L.R. 599 (Sen Cts Costs Office), Costs Judge Campbell; see *R. v Richards (Costs)* [2012] 5 Costs L.R. 998 (Sen Cts Costs Office), Costs Judge Campbell
Art.3, amended: SI 2012/750 Art.3
Art.6, amended: SI 2012/750 Art.4, SI 2012/1343 Art.3
Art.6, see *R v Dumbaya (Costs)* [2012] 5 Costs L.R. 976 (Sen Cts Costs Office), Costs Judge Campbell; see *R v Grigoropolou (Costs)* [2012] 5 Costs L.R. 982 (Sen Cts Costs Office), Costs Judge Campbell
Art.12, amended: SI 2012/1343 Art.4
Art.12, substituted: SI 2012/1343 Art.4
Art.14, amended: SI 2012/750 Art.4, SI 2012/1343 Art.5
Art.14, see *R. v Ward (Costs)* [2012] 3 Costs L.R. 605 (Sen Cts Costs Office), Costs Judge Gordon-Saker
Art.26, see *R. v Richards (Costs)* [2012] 5 Costs L.R. 998 (Sen Cts Costs Office), Costs Judge Campbell
Art.27, applied: SI 2012/1726 r.76.9
Art.32, see *R v Grigoropolou (Costs)* [2012] 5 Costs L.R. 982 (Sen Cts Costs Office), Costs Judge Campbell
Sch.1, see *R. v O'Donnell (Costs)* [2012] 2 Costs L.R. 431 (Sen Cts Costs Office), Costs Judge Campbell
Sch.1 Part 1 para.1, amended: SI 2012/750 Art.5, Art.6
Sch.1 Part 1 para.2, amended: SI 2012/1343 Art.6
Sch.1 Part 1 para.2, revoked (in part): SI 2012/750 Art.7
Sch.1 Part 3 para.5A, amended: SI 2012/1343 Art.7
Sch.1 Part 3A para.7A, amended: SI 2012/1343 Art.8
Sch.1 Part 4 para.14, amended: SI 2012/750 Art.8
Sch.1 Part 4 para.18, amended: SI 2012/1343 Art.9
Sch.1 Part 4 para.19, amended: SI 2012/750 Art.9
Sch.1 Part 5 para.25, amended: SI 2012/750 Art.10
Sch.1 Part 5 para.29, amended: SI 2012/750 Art.11
Sch.2, see *Lord Chancellor v McLarty and Co Solicitors* [2011] EWHC 3182 (QB), [2012] 1 Costs L.R. 190 (QBD), Burnett, J.
Sch.2 Part 1 para.1, amended: SI 2012/750 Art.12
Sch.2 Pt 1 para.1, see *Lord Chancellor v McLarty and Co Solicitors* [2011] EWHC 3182 (QB), [2012] 1 Costs L.R. 190 (QBD), Burnett, J.; see *R. v Ward (Costs)* [2012] 3 Costs L.R. 605 (Sen Cts Costs Office), Costs Judge Gordon-Saker
Sch.2 Part 1 para.2, amended: SI 2012/1343 Art.10
Sch.2 Part 2 para.3A, amended: SI 2012/1343 Art.11
Sch.2 Part 2A para.8A, amended: SI 2012/1343 Art.12
Sch.2 Part 2B para.10, amended: SI 2012/750 Art.13
Sch.2 Pt 2 para.10, see *R. v Richards (Costs)* [2012] 5 Costs L.R. 998 (Sen Cts Costs Office), Costs Judge Campbell

2007– cont.

1174. Criminal Defence Service (Funding) Order 2007– *cont.*
Sch.2 Part 3 para.15, amended: SI 2012/750 Art.14, SI 2012/1343 Art.13
Sch.2 Pt 3 para.15, see *Lord Chancellor v McLarty and Co Solicitors* [2011] EWHC 3182 (QB), [2012] 1 Costs L.R. 190 (QBD), Burnett, J.
Sch.2 Part 3 para.16, amended: SI 2012/1343 Art.14
Sch.2 Pt 4 para.21, see *Lord Chancellor v McLarty and Co Solicitors* [2011] EWHC 3182 (QB), [2012] 1 Costs L.R. 190 (QBD), Burnett, J.
Sch.2 Pt 4 para.22, see *Lord Chancellor v McLarty and Co Solicitors* [2011] EWHC 3182 (QB), [2012] 1 Costs L.R. 190 (QBD), Burnett, J.
Sch.2 Pt 4 para.24, see *Lord Chancellor v McLarty and Co Solicitors* [2011] EWHC 3182 (QB), [2012] 1 Costs L.R. 190 (QBD), Burnett, J.
Sch.4 para.14, see *R. v Fitzgerald (Costs)* [2012] 3 Costs L.R. 437 (Central Crim Ct), Judge Gordon
Sch.5 para.1, amended: SI 2012/750 Art.15, Art.16

1176. Her Majesty's Inspectorate of Court Administration (Specified Organisations) Order 2007
revoked: SI 2012/2401 Sch.1 para.42

1183. Licensing Act 2003 (Persistent Selling of Alcohol to Children) (Prescribed Form of Closure Notice) Regulations 2007
revoked: SI 2012/963 Reg.2

1253. Lasting Powers of Attorney, Enduring Powers of Attorney and Public Guardian Regulations 2007
Reg.8, amended: SI 2012/1479 Sch.1 para.81

1263. Equality Act (Sexual Orientation) Regulations 2007
see *Black v Wilkinson* [2012] Eq. L.R. 1090 (CC (Slough)), Recorder Moulder; see *Hall v Bull* [2012] EWCA Civ 83, [2012] 1 W.L.R. 2514 (CA (Civ Div)), Sir Andrew Morritt (Chancellor)
Reg.3, see *Black v Wilkinson* [2012] Eq. L.R. 1090 (CC (Slough)), Recorder Moulder; see *Hall v Bull* [2012] EWCA Civ 83, [2012] 1 W.L.R. 2514 (CA (Civ Div)), Sir Andrew Morritt (Chancellor)
Reg.4, see *Black v Wilkinson* [2012] Eq. L.R. 1090 (CC (Slough)), Recorder Moulder; see *Hall v Bull* [2012] EWCA Civ 83, [2012] 1 W.L.R. 2514 (CA (Civ Div)), Sir Andrew Morritt (Chancellor)
Reg.6, see *Black v Wilkinson* [2012] Eq. L.R. 1090 (CC (Slough)), Recorder Moulder
Reg.18, see *Charity Commission for England and Wales v Catholic Care (Diocese of Leeds)* [2012] W.T.L.R. 1303 (Charity Comm)

1288. School Organisation (Establishment and Discontinuance of Schools) (England) Regulations 2007
Reg.5, revoked (in part): SI 2012/956 Art.17
Reg.10, revoked (in part): SI 2012/956 Art.17
Reg.13, revoked (in part): SI 2012/956 Art.17
Reg.15, revoked (in part): SI 2012/956 Art.17
Reg.25, revoked (in part): SI 2012/956 Art.17
Sch.2 Part 1 para.25, amended: SI 2012/956 Art.17
Sch.2 Part 2 para.54, amended: SI 2012/956 Art.17
Sch.3 Part 1 para.26, amended: SI 2012/956 Art.17
Sch.3 Part 2 para.62, amended: SI 2012/956 Art.17

1289. School Organisation (Prescribed Alterations to Maintained Schools) (England) Regulations 2007
Sch.1 Part 2 para.5, amended: SI 2012/956 Art.18
Sch.1 Part 2 para.17, amended: SI 2012/956 Art.18

2007– cont.

1289. School Organisation (Prescribed Alterations to Maintained Schools) (England) Regulations 2007– *cont.*
Sch.1 Part 2 para.21, amended: SI 2012/956 Art.18
Sch.3 Part 1 para.13, amended: SI 2012/956 Art.18
Sch.3 Part 2 para.27, amended: SI 2012/956 Art.18
Sch.3 Part 2 para.33, amended: SI 2012/956 Art.18
Sch.3 Part 2 para.34, revoked (in part): SI 2012/956 Art.18
Sch.3 Part 2 para.41, amended: SI 2012/956 Art.18
Sch.3 Part 2 para.41, revoked (in part): SI 2012/956 Art.18
Sch.5 Part 1 para.13, amended: SI 2012/956 Art.18
Sch.5 Part 2 para.33, amended: SI 2012/956 Art.18
Sch.5 Part 2 para.34, revoked (in part): SI 2012/956 Art.18
Sch.5 Part 2 para.41, amended: SI 2012/956 Art.18

1319. Bovine Semen (England) Regulations 2007
applied: SI 2012/2665 Reg.10

1333. A40 Trunk Road (Monmouth, Monmouthshire) (50 MPH Speed Limit) Order 2007
applied: SI 2012/2446 Art.4
disapplied: SI 2012/427 Art.8

1334. Export Control (North Korea) Order 2007
Art.1, amended: SI 2012/1809 Sch.1 Part 2
Art.5, amended: SI 2012/1809 Sch.1 Part 2

1351. Safeguarding Vulnerable Groups (Northern Ireland) Order 2007
applied: 2012 c.9 s.88, Sch.8 para.8, SI 2012/3006 Art.98, Art.99, Art.106, Art.109
Art.2, amended: 2012 c.9 Sch.7 para.2, Sch.9 para.76, Sch.10 Part 5, SI 2012/3006 Art.6
Art.2, revoked (in part): 2012 c.9 Sch.9 para.76, Sch.10 Part 5
Art.3, revoked: 2012 c.9 Sch.7 para.2, Sch.10 Part 5
Art.5, substituted: SI 2012/3006 Art.7
Art.6, amended: SI 2012/3006 Art.6, Art.8
Art.6, applied: SI 2012/2113 Art.2, Art.3, SI 2012/2234 Art.8, SI 2012/3006 Art.2
Art.8, amended: 2012 c.9 Sch.9 para.77, SI 2012/3006 Art.6
Art.8, applied: SI 2012/2234 Art.10, SI 2012/3006 Art.101
Art.8, revoked (in part): 2012 c.9 Sch.9 para.77, Sch.10 Part 5
Art.9, revoked (in part): 2012 c.9 Sch.9 para.78, Sch.10 Part 5
Art.10, amended: 2012 c.9 Sch.7 para.14, Sch.9 para.79
Art.10, revoked (in part): 2012 c.9 Sch.9 para.79, Sch.10 Part 5
Art.11, revoked (in part): 2012 c.9 Sch.9 para.80, Sch.10 Part 5
Art.12, revoked: 2012 c.9 Sch.9 para.81, Sch.10 Part 5
Art.13, revoked (in part): 2012 c.9 Sch.9 para.82, Sch.10 Part 5
Art.14, revoked: 2012 c.9 Sch.9 para.83, Sch.10 Part 5
Art.15, revoked: 2012 c.9 Sch.9 para.84, Sch.10 Part 5
Art.16, revoked: 2012 c.9 Sch.9 para.85, Sch.10 Part 5
Art.17, revoked: 2012 c.9 Sch.9 para.86, Sch.10 Part 5
Art.18, revoked: 2012 c.9 Sch.9 para.87, Sch.10 Part 5
Art.19, revoked: 2012 c.9 Sch.9 para.88, Sch.10 Part 5
Art.20, revoked: 2012 c.9 Sch.9 para.89, Sch.10 Part 5
Art.21, revoked: 2012 c.9 Sch.9 para.90, Sch.10 Part 5

2007–cont.

1351. Safeguarding Vulnerable Groups (Northern Ireland) Order 2007– *cont.*

Art.22, amended: 2012 c.9 Sch.9 para.91, Sch.10 Part 5

Art.23, amended: 2012 c.9 Sch.9 para.92

Art.23, revoked (in part): 2012 c.9 Sch.9 para.92, Sch.10 Part 5

Art.24, revoked (in part): 2012 c.9 Sch.9 para.93, Sch.10 Part 5

Art.25, revoked: 2012 c.9 Sch.7 para.5, Sch.10 Part 5

Art.26, revoked: 2012 c.9 Sch.7 para.5, Sch.10 Part 5

Art.27, revoked: 2012 c.9 Sch.7 para.5, Sch.10 Part 5

Art.28, revoked: 2012 c.9 Sch.7 para.6, Sch.10 Part 5

Art.28A, revoked: 2012 c.9 Sch.7 para.6, Sch.10 Part 5

Art.29, revoked: 2012 c.9 Sch.7 para.6, Sch.10 Part 5

Art.30, revoked: 2012 c.9 Sch.7 para.6, Sch.10 Part 5

Art.31, revoked: 2012 c.9 Sch.7 para.6, Sch.10 Part 5

Art.32, substituted: 2012 c.9 Sch.7 para.9

Art.32A, amended: SI 2012/3006 Art.49

Art.32B, amended: SI 2012/3006 Art.49

Art.33, substituted: 2012 c.9 Sch.7 para.9

Art.34, substituted: 2012 c.9 Sch.7 para.9

Art.35, amended: 2012 c.9 Sch.7 para.9, SI 2012/3006 Art.49

Art.36, amended: 2012 c.9 Sch.7 para.9

Art.36ZA, added: 2012 c.9 Sch.7 para.10

Art.37, amended: SI 2012/3006 Art.6

Art.37, revoked (in part): 2012 c.9 Sch.9 para.94, Sch.10 Part 5

Art.38, amended: 2012 c.9 Sch.9 para.95, Sch.10 Part 5, SI 2012/3006 Art.6

Art.39, amended: 2012 c.9 Sch.9 para.96, Sch.10 Part 5, SI 2012/3006 Art.6

Art.39, revoked (in part): 2012 c.9 Sch.9 para.96, Sch.10 Part 5

Art.40, amended: SI 2012/3006 Art.6

Art.41, amended: 2012 c.9 Sch.7 para.14, Sch.10 Part 5, SI 2012/3006 Art.6

Art.42, amended: SI 2012/3006 Art.6

Art.43, amended: 2012 c.9 Sch.7 para.12, Sch.10 Part 5, SI 2012/1479 Sch.1 para.53, SI 2012/3006 Art.6

Art.43, revoked (in part): 2012 c.9 Sch.7 para.12, Sch.10 Part 5

Art.44, amended: SI 2012/3006 Art.6

Art.45, amended: 2012 c.9 Sch.7 para.12, SI 2012/3006 Art.6, Art.34, Art.49, Art.62

Art.46, revoked: 2012 c.9 Sch.7 para.12, Sch.10 Part 5

Art.47, amended: 2012 c.9 Sch.7 para.13, Sch.10 Part 5, SI 2012/3006 Art.6

Art.47, revoked (in part): 2012 c.9 Sch.7 para.13, Sch.10 Part 5

Art.48, amended: SI 2012/3006 Art.6

Art.49, amended: 2012 c.9 Sch.7 para.13, SI 2012/3006 Art.6, Art.49

Art.49, revoked (in part): 2012 c.9 Sch.7 para.13, Sch.10 Part 5

Art.50, amended: 2012 c.9 Sch.7 para.13, Sch.10 Part 5, SI 2012/3006 Art.49

Art.50, revoked (in part): 2012 c.9 Sch.7 para.13, Sch.10 Part 5

Art.51, amended: 2012 c.9 Sch.7 para.13, Sch.10 Part 5, SI 2012/3006 Art.49

Art.51, revoked (in part): 2012 c.9 Sch.7 para.13, Sch.10 Part 5

Art.52, amended: 2012 c.9 Sch.7 para.13, SI 2012/3006 Art.6, Art.49

2007–cont.

1351. Safeguarding Vulnerable Groups (Northern Ireland) Order 2007– *cont.*

Art.52A, amended: 2012 c.9 Sch.7 para.14, Sch.9 para.97, SI 2012/3006 Art.6

Art.53, revoked (in part): 2012 c.9 Sch.9 para.98, Sch.10 Part 5

Art.56, revoked (in part): 2012 c.9 Sch.9 para.99, Sch.10 Part 5

Art.57, amended: 2012 c.9 Sch.9 para.100, Sch.10 Part 5

Sch.1, applied: 2012 c.9 Sch.8 para.8

Sch.1 Part I para.1, amended: 2012 c.9 Sch.7 para.4, SI 2012/3006 Art.64

Sch.1 Part I para.1, applied: SI 2012/2234 Art.14

Sch.1 Part I para.2, amended: 2012 c.9 Sch.7 para.4, SI 2012/3006 Art.6, Art.65

Sch.1 Part I para.2, applied: SI 2012/2234 Art.8, Art.14, SI 2012/3006 Art.104

Sch.1 Part I para.3, amended: 2012 c.9 Sch.7 para.4, SI 2012/3006 Art.6

Sch.1 Part I para.3, applied: SI 2012/2234 Art.8, Art.14, SI 2012/3006 Art.104

Sch.1 Part I para.4, amended: SI 2012/3006 Art.6

Sch.1 Part I para.5, amended: 2012 c.9 Sch.7 para.4, SI 2012/3006 Art.6

Sch.1 Part I para.5, applied: SI 2012/2234 Art.8, Art.14, SI 2012/3006 Art.104

Sch.1 Part I para.5A, added: 2012 c.9 Sch.7 para.11

Sch.1 Part I para.5A, amended: SI 2012/3006 Art.6

Sch.1 Part I para.6, amended: 2012 c.9 Sch.7 para.11, SI 2012/3006 Art.6

Sch.1 Part II para.7, amended: 2012 c.9 Sch.7 para.4, SI 2012/3006 Art.66

Sch.1 Part II para.7, applied: SI 2012/2234 Art.14

Sch.1 Part II para.8, amended: 2012 c.9 Sch.7 para.4, SI 2012/3006 Art.6, Art.67

Sch.1 Part II para.8, applied: SI 2012/2234 Art.8, Art.14, SI 2012/3006 Art.104

Sch.1 Part II para.9, amended: 2012 c.9 Sch.7 para.4, SI 2012/3006 Art.6

Sch.1 Part II para.9, applied: SI 2012/2234 Art.8, Art.14, SI 2012/3006 Art.104

Sch.1 Part II para.10, amended: SI 2012/3006 Art.6

Sch.1 Part II para.11, amended: 2012 c.9 Sch.7 para.4, SI 2012/3006 Art.6

Sch.1 Part II para.11, applied: SI 2012/2234 Art.8, Art.14, SI 2012/3006 Art.104

Sch.1 Part II para.11A, added: 2012 c.9 Sch.7 para.11

Sch.1 Part II para.11A, amended: SI 2012/3006 Art.6

Sch.1 Part II para.12, amended: 2012 c.9 Sch.7 para.11, SI 2012/3006 Art.6

Sch.1 Part III para.13, amended: SI 2012/3006 Art.6

Sch.1 Part III para.14, amended: SI 2012/3006 Art.6

Sch.1 Part III para.15, amended: SI 2012/3006 Art.6

Sch.1 Part III para.16, amended: SI 2012/3006 Art.6

Sch.1 Part III para.16, applied: SI 2012/3006 Art.104

Sch.1 Part III para.17, amended: SI 2012/3006 Art.6

Sch.1 Part III para.17, applied: SI 2012/3006 Art.104

Sch.1 Part III para.18, amended: SI 2012/3006 Art.6

Sch.1 Part III para.18, applied: SI 2012/3006 Art.106

2007– cont.

1351. Safeguarding Vulnerable Groups (Northern Ireland) Order 2007– *cont.*

Sch.1 Part III para.18A, added: 2012 c.9 Sch.7 para.8

Sch.1 Part III para.18A, amended: SI 2012/3006 Art.6

Sch.1 Part III para.18A, applied: SI 2012/3006 Art.106

Sch.1 Part III para.19, amended: 2012 c.9 Sch.7 para.7, Sch.10 Part 5, SI 2012/3006 Art.6

Sch.1 Part III para.19, revoked (in part): 2012 c.9 Sch.7 para.7, Sch.10 Part 5

Sch.1 Part III para.20, amended: 2012 c.9 Sch.7 para.7, SI 2012/3006 Art.6

Sch.1 Part III para.20, revoked (in part): SI 2012/3006 Art.68

Sch.1 Part III para.21, amended: SI 2012/3006 Art.6

Sch.1 Part III para.22, amended: SI 2012/3006 Art.49

Sch.1 Part III para.22A, amended: SI 2012/3006 Art.6

Sch.1 Part III para.23, amended: SI 2012/3006 Art.6

Sch.1 Part III para.24, revoked (in part): 2012 c.9 Sch.9 para.101, Sch.10 Part 5

Sch.1 Part III para.25, amended: 2012 c.9 Sch.9 para.101, SI 2012/3006 Art.6

Sch.2 Part I para.1, amended: 2012 c.9 Sch.7 para.1

Sch.2 Part I para.1, revoked (in part): 2012 c.9 Sch.7 para.1, Sch.10 Part 5

Sch.2 Part I para.2, amended: 2012 c.9 Sch.7 para.1

Sch.2 Part I para.2, revoked (in part): 2012 c.9 Sch.7 para.1, Sch.10 Part 5

Sch.2 Part I para.4, revoked: 2012 c.9 Sch.7 para.1, Sch.10 Part 5

Sch.2 Part I para.5A, added: 2012 c.9 Sch.7 para.14

Sch.2 Part II para.7, amended: 2012 c.9 Sch.7 para.3, Sch.10 Part 5

Sch.2 Part II para.7, revoked (in part): 2012 c.9 Sch.7 para.3, Sch.10 Part 5

Sch.2 Part II para.8, revoked: 2012 c.9 Sch.7 para.3, Sch.10 Part 5

Sch.2 Part III para.10, amended: 2012 c.9 Sch.7 para.1, Sch.7 para.3, Sch.10 Part 5

Sch.2 Part III para.10, revoked (in part): 2012 c.9 Sch.10 Part 5

Sch.3 Part I para.1, revoked: 2012 c.9 Sch.9 para.84, Sch.10 Part 5

Sch.3 Part I para.2, revoked: 2012 c.9 Sch.9 para.84, Sch.10 Part 5

Sch.3 Part I para.3, revoked: 2012 c.9 Sch.9 para.84, Sch.10 Part 5

Sch.3 Part I para.4, revoked: 2012 c.9 Sch.9 para.84, Sch.10 Part 5

Sch.3 Part II para.5, revoked: 2012 c.9 Sch.9 para.84, Sch.10 Part 5

Sch.3 Part II para.6, revoked: 2012 c.9 Sch.9 para.84, Sch.10 Part 5

Sch.3 Part II para.7, revoked: 2012 c.9 Sch.9 para.84, Sch.10 Part 5

Sch.3 Part III para.8, revoked: 2012 c.9 Sch.9 para.84, Sch.10 Part 5

Sch.3 Part III para.9, revoked: 2012 c.9 Sch.9 para.84, Sch.10 Part 5

Sch.3 Part III para.10, revoked: 2012 c.9 Sch.9 para.84, Sch.10 Part 5

Sch.3 Part IV para.11, revoked: 2012 c.9 Sch.9 para.84, Sch.10 Part 5

2007– cont.

1351. Safeguarding Vulnerable Groups (Northern Ireland) Order 2007– *cont.*

Sch.3 Part IV para.12, revoked: 2012 c.9 Sch.9 para.84, Sch.10 Part 5

Sch.3 Part IV para.13, revoked: 2012 c.9 Sch.9 para.84, Sch.10 Part 5

Sch.3 Part IV para.14, revoked: 2012 c.9 Sch.9 para.84, Sch.10 Part 5

Sch.4 para.1, revoked: 2012 c.9 Sch.9 para.85, Sch.10 Part 5

Sch.4 para.2, revoked: 2012 c.9 Sch.9 para.85, Sch.10 Part 5

Sch.4 para.3, revoked: 2012 c.9 Sch.9 para.85, Sch.10 Part 5

Sch.4 para.4, revoked: 2012 c.9 Sch.9 para.85, Sch.10 Part 5

Sch.4 para.5, revoked: 2012 c.9 Sch.9 para.85, Sch.10 Part 5

Sch.4 para.6, revoked: 2012 c.9 Sch.9 para.85, Sch.10 Part 5

Sch.5 para.1, amended: 2012 c.9 Sch.7 para.9, Sch.9 para.102, Sch.10 Part 5

Sch.5 para.2, amended: 2012 c.9 Sch.7 para.9, Sch.9 para.102

Sch.5 para.3, amended: 2012 c.9 Sch.9 para.102

Sch.5 para.3, revoked (in part): 2012 c.9 Sch.7 para.9, Sch.9 para.102, Sch.10 Part 5

Sch.5 para.4, amended: 2012 c.9 Sch.9 para.102

Sch.5 para.5, amended: 2012 c.9 Sch.9 para.102

Sch.5 para.6, amended: 2012 c.9 Sch.9 para.102

Sch.6 para.1, amended: SI 2012/3006 Art.6

Sch.6 para.1, applied: SI 2012/3006 Art.109

Sch.6 para.2, amended: SI 2012/3006 Art.6

Sch.6 para.3, amended: SI 2012/3006 Art.6

Sch.6 para.5, revoked: 2012 c.9 Sch.9 para.103, Sch.10 Part 5

1355. School Organisation (Transitional Provisions) (England) Regulations 2007

Reg.17, revoked (in part): SI 2012/956 Art.19

Reg.18, revoked (in part): SI 2012/956 Art.19

Reg.28, revoked (in part): SI 2012/956 Art.19

Reg.29, amended: SI 2012/956 Art.19

Reg.36, amended: SI 2012/956 Art.19

1357. Local Authority Adoption Service (Wales) Regulations 2007

Reg.16, amended: SI 2012/3006 Art.90, Art.92

Sch.4 para.5, amended: SI 2012/3006 Art.91, Art.93

1455. Dunham Bridge (Revision of Tolls) Order 2007

revoked: SI 2012/852 Art.4

1492. Whole of Government Accounts (Designation of Bodies) Order 2007

varied: SI 2012/147 Art.7

1523. Human Tissue (Quality and Safety for Human Application) Regulations 2007

Reg.2, amended: SI 2012/1916 Sch.34 para.92

Reg.2, revoked (in part): SI 2012/1916 Sch.34 para.92

Reg.9, amended: SI 2012/1501 Reg.28

Reg.20, applied: SI 2012/1501 Reg.16

1550. Electronic Commerce Directive (Terrorism Act 2006) Regulations 2007

Reg.2, amended: SI 2012/1809 Sch.1 Part 2

1609. Justices of the Peace (Training and Development Committee) Rules 2007

referred to: SI 2012/1277 Sch.1 para.1

r.2, amended: SI 2012/1206 Sch.1 para.18

r.42, amended: SI 2012/1206 Sch.1 para.19

2007–cont.

1609. Justices of the Peace (Training and Development Committee) Rules 2007–cont.
Sch.3, added: SI 2012/1206 Sch.1 para.20

1610. Family Proceedings Courts (Constitution of Committees and Right to Preside) Rules 2007
referred to: SI 2012/1277 Sch.1 para.1

1611. Youth Courts (Constitution of Committees and Right to Preside) Rules 2007
applied: SI 2012/1555 Sch.1 para.1, SI 2012/1726 r.37.1
referred to: SI 2012/1277 Sch.1 para.1

1624. Health Protection Agency (Amendment) Regulations 2007
Reg.2, varied: 2012 c.11 s.12

1669. Energy Performance of Buildings (Certificates and Inspections) (England and Wales) (Amendment) Regulations 2007
revoked: SI 2012/3118 Sch.3

1711. Transfrontier Shipment of Waste Regulations 2007
Reg.5, see *R. v V* [2011] EWCA Crim 2342, [2012] Eu. L.R. 302 (CA (Crim Div)), Hughes, L.J.
Reg.23, see *R. v Ideal Waste Paper Co Ltd* [2011] EWCA Crim 3237, [2012] Env. L.R. 19 (CA (Crim Div)), Pill, L.J.; see *R. v V* [2011] EWCA Crim 2342, [2012] Eu. L.R. 302 (CA (Crim Div)), Hughes, L.J.

1744. Court of Protection Rules 2007
r.82, see *M (A Patient) (Court of Protection: Reporting Restrictions), Re* [2011] EWHC 1197 (Fam), [2012] 1 W.L.R. 287 (CP), Baker, J.
r.90, see *M (A Patient) (Court of Protection: Reporting Restrictions), Re* [2011] EWHC 1197 (Fam), [2012] 1 W.L.R. 287 (CP), Baker, J.
r.92, see *M (A Patient) (Court of Protection: Reporting Restrictions), Re* [2011] EWHC 1197 (Fam), [2012] 1 W.L.R. 287 (CP), Baker, J.
r.157, see *Cheshire West and Chester Council v P (Costs)* [2011] EWCA Civ 1333, [2012] 1 Costs L.R. 150 (CA (Civ Div)), Pill, L.J.

1765. Plant Health (Plant Passport Fees) (Wales) Regulations 2007
revoked: SI 2012/1493 Reg.7

1766. NHS Foundation Trusts (Trust Funds Appointment of Trustees) Order 2007
Art.1, amended: SI 2012/2891 Art.2, SI 2012/2950 Art.2
Art.2, amended: SI 2012/2891 Art.2, SI 2012/2950 Art.2
Art.3, amended: SI 2012/2891 Art.2, SI 2012/2950 Art.2
Art.3A, amended: SI 2012/2891 Art.2, SI 2012/2950 Art.2
Art.4, amended: SI 2012/2891 Art.2, SI 2012/2950 Art.2

1770. Public Guardian Board Regulations 2007
revoked: SI 2012/2401 Sch.2 para.7

1771. Early Years Foundation Stage (Welfare Requirements) Regulations 2007
revoked: SI 2012/938 Reg.13

1772. Early Years Foundation Stage (Learning and Development Requirements) Order 2007
Art.2, amended: SI 2012/937 Art.3
Art.3, amended: SI 2012/937 Art.4, Art.5
Art.4, amended: SI 2012/937 Art.6
Art.5, amended: SI 2012/937 Art.5
Art.6, amended: SI 2012/937 Art.4, Art.5
Art.7, amended: SI 2012/937 Art.4, Art.5

2007–cont.

1817. Road Vehicles (Construction and Use) (Amendment) Regulations 2007
revoked: SI 2012/1404 Sch.1

1819. Community Drivers Hours and Recording Equipment Regulations 2007
applied: SI 2012/1502 Reg.6
Sch.1 Part 1 para.1, amended: SI 2012/1659 Sch.3 para.36

1830. Crime and Disorder (Formulation and Implementation of Strategy) Regulations 2007
Reg.9A, added: SI 2012/2660 Reg.2
Reg.13A, added: SI 2012/2660 Reg.2
Reg.14A, added: SI 2012/2660 Reg.2

1842. Offshore Marine Conservation (Natural Habitats, &c.) Regulations 2007
referred to: SI 2012/637 Sch.2 para.1
Reg.6, amended: SI 2012/1928 Reg.3
Reg.14, amended: SI 2012/1928 Reg.4
Reg.14A, amended: SI 2012/1928 Reg.5
Reg.15, amended: SI 2012/1928 Reg.6
Reg.16, amended: SI 2012/1928 Reg.7
Reg.19, amended: SI 2012/1928 Reg.8
Reg.23, amended: SI 2012/1928 Reg.9
Reg.32, amended: SI 2012/1809 Sch.1 Part 2, SI 2012/1928 Reg.10
Reg.34, amended: SI 2012/1809 Sch.1 Part 2
Reg.39, amended: SI 2012/1809 Sch.1 Part 2
Reg.40, amended: SI 2012/1809 Sch.1 Part 2
Reg.43, amended: SI 2012/1809 Sch.1 Part 2
Reg.45, amended: SI 2012/1928 Reg.11
Reg.47, amended: SI 2012/1928 Reg.12
Reg.67, amended: SI 2012/1928 Reg.13
Reg.73, amended: SI 2012/1928 Reg.14
Reg.76, added: SI 2012/1928 Reg.15

1843. Conservation (Natural Habitats, &c.) (Amendment) Regulations 2007
Reg.5, amended: SSI 2012/228 Sch.1

1867. Education (Penalty Notices) (England) Regulations 2007
Reg.4, amended: SI 2012/1046 Reg.2

1868. Education (Reintegration Interview) (England) Regulations 2007
revoked: SI 2012/1033 Sch.3

1869. Education (Parenting Contracts and Parenting Orders) (England) Regulations 2007
Reg.4, amended: SI 2012/1033 Sch.2 para.7

1870. Education (Provision of Full-Time Education for Excluded Pupils) (England) Regulations 2007
Reg.2, amended: SI 2012/1033 Sch.2 para.8
Reg.4, amended: SI 2012/1033 Sch.2 para.8
Reg.4, varied: SI 2012/1107 Art.12
Reg.6, substituted: SI 2012/1033 Sch.2 para.8
Reg.7, substituted: SI 2012/1033 Sch.2 para.8
Reg.8, amended: SI 2012/1033 Sch.2 para.8
Reg.10, revoked: SI 2012/1033 Sch.2 para.8

1883. General Teaching Council for England (Registration of Teachers) (Amendment) Regulations 2007
revoked: SI 2012/1153 Sch.1

1895. Civil Aviation (Access to Air Travel for Disabled Persons and Persons with Reduced Mobility) Regulations 2007
Reg.3, see *Hook v British Airways Plc* [2012] EWCA Civ 66, [2012] 2 All E.R. (Comm) 1265 (CA (Civ Div)), Maurice Kay, L.J.
Reg.4, see *Hook v British Airways Plc* [2012] EWCA Civ 66, [2012] 2 All E.R. (Comm) 1265 (CA (Civ Div)), Maurice Kay, L.J.

2007–cont.

1895. Civil Aviation (Access to Air Travel for Disabled Persons and Persons with Reduced Mobility) Regulations 2007–*cont.*
Reg.9, see *Hook v British Airways Plc* [2012] EWCA Civ 66, [2012] 2 All E.R. (Comm) 1265 (CA (Civ Div)), Maurice Kay, L.J.

1933. Mobile Roaming (European Communities) Regulations 2007
Reg.6, amended: SI 2012/1809 Sch.1 Part 2

1951. Street Works (Registers, Notices, Directions and Designations) (England) Regulations 2007
applied: SI 2012/2541 Sch.1, SI 2012/2547 Sch.1, SI 2012/2548 Sch.1, SI 2012/2549 Sch.1, SI 2012/3102 Sch.1, SI 2012/3103 Sch.1, SI 2012/3104 Sch.1, SI 2012/3105 Sch.1, SI 2012/3106 Sch.1, SI 2012/3107 Sch.1

1952. Street Works (Fixed Penalty) (England) Regulations 2007
Reg.5, applied: SI 2012/1282 Sch.1, SI 2012/1286 Sch.1, SI 2012/1289 Sch.1, SI 2012/1295 Sch.1, SI 2012/3102 Sch.1, SI 2012/3103 Sch.1, SI 2012/3104 Sch.1, SI 2012/3105 Sch.1, SI 2012/3106 Sch.1, SI 2012/3107 Sch.1
Reg.5, referred to: SI 2012/1284 Sch.1, SI 2012/1294 Sch.1

2005. Reciprocal Enforcement of Maintenance Orders (United States of America) Order 2007
Sch.1 para.15, amended: SI 2012/2814 Sch.5 para.7
Sch.2, amended: SI 2012/2814 Sch.5 para.7

2078. Welfare of Farmed Animals (England) Regulations 2007
Reg.8, amended: SI 2012/2897 Art.20

2089. Local Authorities (Conduct of Referendums) (England) Regulations 2007
revoked: SI 2012/323 Reg.21

2116. Further Education Teachers Continuing Professional Development and Registration (England) Regulations 2007
revoked: SI 2012/2165 Reg.2
Reg.2, amended: SI 2012/747 Reg.3
Reg.4, amended: SI 2012/747 Reg.3
Reg.5, amended: SI 2012/747 Reg.3
Reg.5, revoked (in part): SI 2012/747 Reg.3

2117. Education (Specified Work and Registration) (England) (Amendment) Regulations 2007
revoked: SI 2012/762 Reg.6

2132. Iran (United Nations Measures) (Overseas Territories) (Amendment) Order 2007
revoked: SI 2012/1756 Art.53

2134. Friendly Societies (Modification of the Corporation Tax Acts) (Amendment) Regulations 2007
revoked: SI 2012/3008 Sch.1

2145. Insurance Companies (Tax Exempt Business) Regulations 2007
revoked: SI 2012/3008 Sch.1

2153. Tax Avoidance Schemes (Information) (Amendment) Regulations 2007
revoked: SI 2012/1836 Sch.1

2157. Money Laundering Regulations 2007
applied: SI 2012/1128 Art.4, SI 2012/2298 Reg.18, SSI 2012/88 Reg.23, SSI 2012/89 Reg.26
Reg.3, amended: SI 2012/1906 Art.7, SI 2012/2298 Reg.3
Reg.4, amended: SI 2012/2298 Reg.4
Reg.17, amended: SI 2012/2298 Reg.5
Reg.18, revoked: SI 2012/2298 Reg.6
Reg.22, amended: SI 2012/2298 Reg.7

2007–cont.

2157. Money Laundering Regulations 2007–*cont.*
Reg.23, amended: SI 2012/2298 Reg.8
Reg.24A, added: SI 2012/2298 Reg.9
Reg.28, amended: SI 2012/2298 Reg.10
Reg.28, revoked (in part): SI 2012/2298 Reg.10
Reg.30, amended: SI 2012/1791 Reg.2, SI 2012/2298 Reg.11
Reg.34, amended: SI 2012/2298 Reg.12
Reg.37, amended: SI 2012/2298 Reg.13
Reg.42, amended: SI 2012/2298 Reg.14
Reg.43, amended: SI 2012/2298 Reg.15
Reg.45, amended: SI 2012/2298 Reg.16
Sch.2 para.2, amended: SI 2012/1809 Sch.1 Part 2
Sch.3 para.1, substituted: SI 2012/2298 Sch.1
Sch.3 Part 1 para.1, substituted: SI 2012/2298 Sch.1
Sch.3 Part 1 para.2, substituted: SI 2012/2298 Sch.1
Sch.3 Part 1 para.3, substituted: SI 2012/2298 Sch.1
Sch.3 Part 1 para.4, substituted: SI 2012/2298 Sch.1
Sch.3 Part 1 para.5, substituted: SI 2012/2298 Sch.1
Sch.3 Part 1 para.6, substituted: SI 2012/2298 Sch.1
Sch.3 Part 1 para.7, substituted: SI 2012/2298 Sch.1
Sch.3 Part 1 para.8, substituted: SI 2012/2298 Sch.1
Sch.3 Part 1 para.9, substituted: SI 2012/2298 Sch.1
Sch.3 Part 1 para.10, substituted: SI 2012/2298 Sch.1
Sch.3 Part 1 para.11, substituted: SI 2012/2298 Sch.1
Sch.3 para.2, substituted: SI 2012/2298 Sch.1
Sch.3 Part 2 para.12, substituted: SI 2012/2298 Sch.1
Sch.3 Part 2 para.13, substituted: SI 2012/2298 Sch.1
Sch.3 Part 2 para.14, substituted: SI 2012/2298 Sch.1
Sch.3 Part 2 para.15, substituted: SI 2012/2298 Sch.1
Sch.3 Part 2 para.16, substituted: SI 2012/2298 Sch.1
Sch.3 Part 2 para.17, substituted: SI 2012/2298 Sch.1
Sch.3 Part 2 para.18, substituted: SI 2012/2298 Sch.1
Sch.3 Part 2 para.19, substituted: SI 2012/2298 Sch.1
Sch.3 Part 2 para.20, substituted: SI 2012/2298 Sch.1
Sch.3 Part 2 para.21, substituted: SI 2012/2298 Sch.1
Sch.3 Part 2 para.22, substituted: SI 2012/2298 Sch.1
Sch.3 para.3, substituted: SI 2012/2298 Sch.1
Sch.3 para.4, substituted: SI 2012/2298 Sch.1
Sch.3 para.5, substituted: SI 2012/2298 Sch.1
Sch.3 para.6, substituted: SI 2012/2298 Sch.1
Sch.3 para.7, substituted: SI 2012/2298 Sch.1
Sch.3 para.8, substituted: SI 2012/2298 Sch.1
Sch.3 para.9, substituted: SI 2012/2298 Sch.1
Sch.3 para.10, substituted: SI 2012/2298 Sch.1
Sch.3 para.11, substituted: SI 2012/2298 Sch.1
Sch.3 para.12, substituted: SI 2012/2298 Sch.1
Sch.3 para.13, substituted: SI 2012/2298 Sch.1
Sch.3 para.14, substituted: SI 2012/2298 Sch.1
Sch.3 para.15, substituted: SI 2012/2298 Sch.1
Sch.3 para.16, substituted: SI 2012/2298 Sch.1
Sch.3 para.17, substituted: SI 2012/2298 Sch.1
Sch.3 para.18, substituted: SI 2012/2298 Sch.1
Sch.3 para.19, substituted: SI 2012/2298 Sch.1
Sch.3 para.20, substituted: SI 2012/2298 Sch.1

2007–cont.

2157. Money Laundering Regulations 2007–cont.
Sch.3 para.21, substituted: SI 2012/2298 Sch.1
Sch.3 para.22, substituted: SI 2012/2298 Sch.1
2181. Terrorism Act 2006 (Disapplication of Section 25) Order 2007
revoked: 2012 c.9 Sch.10 Part 4
2182. Children Act 2004 Information Database (England) Regulations 2007
revoked: SI 2012/1278 Reg.2
2201. Private Security Industry Act 2001 (Amendments to Schedule 2) Order 2007
Art.3, revoked (in part): 2012 c.9 Sch.10 Part 3
Art.4, revoked (in part): 2012 c.9 Sch.10 Part 3
2260. Education (Supply of Information about the School Workforce) (No.2) (England) Regulations 2007
Reg.8, revoked (in part): SI 2012/765 Art.11, SI 2012/956 Art.20
Reg.9, revoked (in part): SI 2012/765 Art.11
2264. Further Education Teachers Qualifications (England) Regulations 2007
Reg.2, amended: SI 2012/747 Reg.2, SI 2012/2166 Reg.3
Reg.5, substituted: SI 2012/2166 Reg.4
Reg.6, substituted: SI 2012/2166 Reg.4
2297. Docklands Light Railway (Capacity Enhancement and 2012 Games Preparation) Order 2007
Art.2, amended: SI 2012/1659 Art.2
Art.38, amended: SI 2012/1659 Art.2
Sch.13 para.1, amended: SI 2012/1659 Art.2
Sch.13 para.2, amended: SI 2012/1659 Art.2
Sch.13 para.3, amended: SI 2012/1659 Art.2
Sch.13 para.4, amended: SI 2012/1659 Art.2
Sch.13 para.5, amended: SI 2012/1659 Art.2
Sch.13 para.6, amended: SI 2012/1659 Art.2
Sch.13 para.7, amended: SI 2012/1659 Art.2
Sch.13 para.8, amended: SI 2012/1659 Art.2
Sch.13 para.9, amended: SI 2012/1659 Art.2
Sch.13 para.10, amended: SI 2012/1659 Art.2
Sch.13 para.11, amended: SI 2012/1659 Art.2
Sch.13 para.12, amended: SI 2012/1659 Art.2
Sch.13 para.13, amended: SI 2012/1659 Art.2
Sch.13 para.14, amended: SI 2012/1659 Art.2
Sch.13 para.15, amended: SI 2012/1659 Art.2
Sch.13 para.16, amended: SI 2012/1659 Art.2
Sch.13 para.17, amended: SI 2012/1659 Art.2
Sch.13 para.18, amended: SI 2012/1659 Art.2
Sch.13 para.19, amended: SI 2012/1659 Art.2
Sch.13 para.20, amended: SI 2012/1659 Art.2
Sch.13 para.21, amended: SI 2012/1659 Art.2
Sch.13 para.22, amended: SI 2012/1659 Art.2
Sch.13 para.23, amended: SI 2012/1659 Art.2
Sch.13 para.24, amended: SI 2012/1659 Art.2
2316. Children and Young People's Plan (Wales) Regulations 2007
Reg.7, amended: SI 2012/990 Art.13
2324. Education (School Performance Information) (England) Regulations 2007
Reg.2, amended: SI 2012/765 Art.12, SI 2012/1274 Reg.2
Reg.5, amended: SI 2012/1274 Reg.2
Reg.12A, added: SI 2012/1274 Reg.2
Reg.14, amended: SI 2012/765 Art.12
Sch.1 para.2, added: SI 2012/1274 Reg.2
Sch.8 Part A1 para.1, added: SI 2012/1274 Reg.2

2007–cont.

2325. Large Combustion Plants (National Emission Reduction Plan) Regulations 2007
Reg.3, amended: SSI 2012/360 Sch.11 para.15
Sch.1 Part 1 para.1, amended: SSI 2012/360 Sch.11 para.15
Sch.2 para.2, revoked (in part): SSI 2012/360 Sch.12
2370. Drivers Hours (Goods Vehicles) (Milk Collection) (Temporary Exemption) Regulations 2007
revoked: SI 2012/1502 Reg.4
2399. Zoonoses (Monitoring) (England) Regulations 2007
Reg.8, amended: SI 2012/2897 Art.21
2441. Community Legal Service (Funding) Order 2007
Sch.5, see *A Local Authority v DS* [2012] EWHC 1442 (Fam), [2012] 1 W.L.R. 3098 (Fam Div), Sir Nicholas Wall (President, Fam)
Sch.6 Pt 002 para.2, see *A Local Authority v DS* [2012] EWHC 1442 (Fam), [2012] 1 W.L.R. 3098 (Fam Div), Sir Nicholas Wall (President, Fam)
2531. Disabled Persons (Badges for Motor Vehicles) (England) (Amendment) Regulations 2007
Reg.5, varied: 2012 c.11 s.12
2535. Road Traffic (Permitted Parking Area and Special Parking Area) (Metropolitan Borough of Solihull) Order 2007
revoked: SI 2012/846 Art.2
2583. Supervision of Accounts and Reports (Prescribed Body) Order 2007
revoked: SI 2012/1439 Art.7
2602. Equality Act 2006 (Dissolution of Commissions and Consequential and Transitional Provisions) Order 2007
Sch.1 para.2, revoked (in part): SI 2012/1153 Sch.1
2655. Charities (Exception from Registration) (Amendment) Regulations 2007
Reg.2, revoked (in part): SI 2012/1734 Reg.3
2708. Spring Traps Approval (Variation) (England) Order 2007
revoked: SI 2012/13 Art.3
2755. Imperial College Healthcare National Health Service Trust (Establishment) and the Hammersmith Hospitals National Health Service Trust and the St Mary's National Health Service Trust... 2007
Art.3, substituted: SI 2012/755 Art.2
2781. European Communities (Recognition of Professional Qualifications) Regulations 2007
Part 2, applied: SI 2012/724 Sch.2 para.4, SI 2012/1115 Sch.1 para.10
Part 3, applied: SI 2012/724 Sch.2 para.4, SI 2012/1115 Sch.1 para.10
Sch.1 Part 1, amended: SI 2012/765 Art.13, SI 2012/1479 Sch.1 para.82
2794. Education (Listed Bodies) (Wales) Order 2007
revoked: SI 2012/1259 Art.3
2795. Education (Recognised Bodies) (Wales) Order 2007
revoked: SI 2012/1260 Art.3
2951. Administrative Justice and Tribunals Council (Listed Tribunals) Order 2007
Art.2, amended: 2012 c.7 Sch.15 para.71, SI 2012/1909 Sch.8 para.1

2007– cont.

2974. Companies (Cross-Border Mergers) Regulations 2007
see *Itau BBA International Ltd, Re* [2012] EWHC 1783 (Ch), Times, September 11, 2012 (Ch D), Henderson, J
Reg.3, see *Itau BBA International Ltd, Re* [2012] EWHC 1783 (Ch), Times, September 11, 2012 (Ch D), Henderson, J
Reg.16, see *Wood DIY Ltd, Re* [2011] EWHC 3089 (Ch), [2012] B.C.C. 67 (Ch D), Roth, J.

2978. Education (Pupil Referral Units) (Management Committees etc.) (England) Regulations 2007
Reg.2, amended: SI 2012/ 1825 Reg.2
Reg.3, amended: SI 2012/ 1825 Reg.2
Reg.4, amended: SI 2012/ 1825 Reg.2
Reg.12, amended: SI 2012/ 1825 Reg.2
Reg.22, amended: SI 2012/ 3158 Reg.2
Reg.22, revoked (in part): SI 2012/ 3158 Reg.2
Reg.23, revoked: SI 2012/ 3158 Reg.2
Reg.24, added: SI 2012/ 1825 Reg.2
Sch.1 para.15, added: SI 2012/ 1825 Reg.2
Sch.2 para.2A, added: SI 2012/ 1825 Reg.2
Sch.2 para.5, amended: SI 2012/ 2404 Sch.3 para.56
Sch.3 para.2, amended: SI 2012/ 3158 Reg.2
Sch.3 para.5, revoked (in part): SI 2012/ 3158 Reg.2
Sch.3 para.11, amended: SI 2012/ 3158 Reg.2
Sch.3 para.14, amended: SI 2012/ 3158 Reg.2
Sch.4 para.1, added: SI 2012/ 1825 Reg.2
Sch.4 para.2, added: SI 2012/ 1825 Reg.2
Sch.4 para.3, added: SI 2012/ 1825 Reg.2
Sch.4 para.4, added: SI 2012/ 1825 Reg.2
Sch.4 para.5, added: SI 2012/ 1825 Reg.2
Sch.4 para.6, added: SI 2012/ 1825 Reg.2
Sch.4 para.7, added: SI 2012/ 1825 Reg.2
Sch.4 para.8, added: SI 2012/ 1825 Reg.2
Sch.4 para.9, added: SI 2012/ 1825 Reg.2
Sch.4 para.10, added: SI 2012/ 1825 Reg.2
Sch.4 para.11, added: SI 2012/ 1825 Reg.2
Sch.4 para.12, added: SI 2012/ 1825 Reg.2
Sch.4 para.13, added: SI 2012/ 1825 Reg.2
Sch.4 para.14, added: SI 2012/ 1825 Reg.2
Sch.4 para.15, added: SI 2012/ 1825 Reg.2
Sch.4 para.16, added: SI 2012/ 1825 Reg.2

2979. Education (Pupil Referral Units) (Application of Enactments) (England) Regulations 2007
Sch.1 Part 1 para.17A, added: SI 2012/ 3158 Reg.3
Sch.1 Part 1 para.17B, added: SI 2012/ 3158 Reg.3
Sch.1 Part 1 para.19A, added: SI 2012/ 3158 Reg.3
Sch.1 Part 1 para.20, substituted: SI 2012/ 3158 Reg.3
Sch.1 Part 1 para.20A, added: SI 2012/ 3158 Reg.3
Sch.1 Part 1 para.20B, added: SI 2012/ 1201 Reg.3
Sch.1 Part 1 para.22, revoked: SI 2012/ 3158 Reg.3
Sch.1 Part 1 para.23, amended: SI 2012/ 1825 Reg.3
Sch.1 Part 1 para.23B, added: SI 2012/ 1201 Reg.4
Sch.1 Part 1 para.23C, added: SI 2012/ 1201 Reg.4
Sch.1 Part 1 para.23D, added: SI 2012/ 1201 Reg.4
Sch.1 Part 1 para.23E, added: SI 2012/ 1201 Reg.4
Sch.1 Part 1 para.23EA, added: SI 2012/ 1201 Reg.4, SI 2012/ 3158 Reg.3
Sch.1 Part 1 para.23F, added: SI 2012/ 1201 Reg.4
Sch.1 Part 2 para.26, revoked: SI 2012/ 3158 Reg.3
Sch.1 Part 2 para.28, substituted: SI 2012/ 3158 Reg.3
Sch.1 Part 2 para.29, substituted: SI 2012/ 3158 Reg.3

2007– cont.

2999. Civil Aviation (Contributions to the Air Travel Trust) Regulations 2007
Reg.2, amended: SI 2012/ 1017 Reg.72
Reg.7, applied: SI 2012/ 1017 Reg.32
Reg.8, amended: SI 2012/ 1017 Reg.72
Reg.8, applied: SI 2012/ 1017 Reg.32
Reg.9, applied: SI 2012/ 1017 Reg.32
Reg.19, revoked: SI 2012/ 1017 Sch.1

3026. Education (Admissions Appeals Arrangements) (England) (Amendment) Regulations 2007
revoked: SI 2012/ 9 Reg.4

3072. Renewable Transport Fuel Obligations Order 2007
applied: SI 2012/ 3030 Reg.6, Reg.13
Sch.1 para.3, applied: SI 2012/ 3030 Reg.5

3101. European Qualifications (Health and Social Care Professions) Regulations 2007
Reg.195, revoked (in part): SI 2012/ 1909 Sch.8 para.1

3103. Tax Avoidance Schemes (Information) (Amendment) (No.2) Regulations 2007
revoked: SI 2012/ 1836 Sch.1

3104. Tax Avoidance Schemes (Penalty) Regulations 2007
referred to: SI 2012/ 1868 Reg.22
varied: SI 2012/ 1868 Reg.28

3106. Persistent Organic Pollutants Regulations 2007
Reg.4, amended: SSI 2012/ 360 Sch.11 para.16

3164. Mobile Homes (Written Statement) (Wales) Regulations 2007
revoked: SI 2012/ 2675 Reg.4

3167. Zootechnical Standards (Amendment) (England) Regulations 2007
revoked: SI 2012/ 2665 Reg.14

3224. Secretaries of State for Children, Schools and Families, for Innovation, Universities and Skills and for Business, Enterprise and Regulatory Reform Order 2007
Sch.1 Part 2 para.30, revoked (in part): SI 2012/ 1153 Sch.1

3290. Immigration (Restrictions on Employment) Order 2007
Sch.1 Part LIST.B para.4, amended: SI 2012/ 1547 Sch.2 para.4
Sch.1 Part LIST.B para.5A, added: SI 2012/ 1547 Sch.2 para.4

3302. Energy Performance of Buildings (Certificates and Inspections) (England and Wales) (Amendment No 2) Regulations 2007
revoked: SI 2012/ 3118 Sch.3

3372. Traffic Management Permit Scheme (England) Regulations 2007
applied: SI 2012/ 2541 Sch.1, SI 2012/ 2547 Sch.1, SI 2012/ 2548 Sch.1, SI 2012/ 2549 Sch.1, SI 2012/ 3102 Sch.1, SI 2012/ 3103 Sch.1, SI 2012/ 3104 Sch.1, SI 2012/ 3105 Sch.1, SI 2012/ 3106 Sch.1, SI 2012/ 3107 Sch.1
referred to: SI 2012/ 1284 Sch.1, SI 2012/ 1286 Sch.1, SI 2012/ 1294 Sch.1, SI 2012/ 2541 Sch.1, SI 2012/ 2547 Sch.1, SI 2012/ 2548 Sch.1, SI 2012/ 2549 Sch.1
Part 5, applied: SI 2012/ 1282 Sch.1, SI 2012/ 1284 Sch.1, SI 2012/ 1286 Sch.1, SI 2012/ 1289 Sch.1, SI 2012/ 1294 Sch.1, SI 2012/ 1295 Sch.1
Part 7, applied: SI 2012/ 2541 Sch.1, SI 2012/ 2547 Sch.1, SI 2012/ 2548 Sch.1, SI 2012/ 2549 Sch.1, SI 2012/ 3102 Sch.1, SI 2012/ 3103 Sch.1, SI 2012/ 3104 Sch.1, SI 2012/ 3105 Sch.1, SI 2012/ 3106 Sch.1, SI 2012/ 3107 Sch.1

2007–cont.

3372. Traffic Management Permit Scheme (England) Regulations 2007–*cont.*

Part 8, applied: SI 2012/785 Art.4, SI 2012/1282 Art.4, Sch.1, SI 2012/1284 Art.4, Sch.1, SI 2012/1286 Art.4, Sch.1, SI 2012/1289 Sch.1, SI 2012/1294 Art.4, Sch.1, SI 2012/1295 Art.4, Sch.1, SI 2012/2541 Art.4, SI 2012/2547 Art.4, SI 2012/2548 Art.4, SI 2012/2549 Art.4, SI 2012/3102 Art.4, SI 2012/3103 Art.4, SI 2012/3104 Art.4, SI 2012/3105 Art.4, SI 2012/3106 Art.4 SI 2012/3107 Art.4

Part 9, applied: SI 2012/1282 Sch.1

Reg.3, applied: SI 2012/1282 Sch.1, SI 2012/1284 Sch.1, SI 2012/1286 Sch.1, SI 2012/1289 Sch.1, SI 2012/1294 Sch.1, SI 2012/1295 Sch.1, SI 2012/2541 Sch.1, SI 2012/2547 Sch.1, SI 2012/2548 Sch.1, SI 2012/2549 Sch.1, SI 2012/3102 Sch.1, SI 2012/3103 Sch.1, SI 2012/3104 Sch.1, SI 2012/3105 Sch.1, SI 2012/3106 Sch.1, SI 2012/3107 Sch.1

Reg.3, referred to: SI 2012/2541 Sch.1, SI 2012/2547 Sch.1, SI 2012/2548 Sch.1, SI 2012/2549 Sch.1

Reg.4, applied: SI 2012/1282 Sch.1, SI 2012/1284 Sch.1, SI 2012/1286 Sch.1, SI 2012/1289 Sch.1, SI 2012/1294 Sch.1, SI 2012/1295 Sch.1

Reg.5, applied: SI 2012/2541 Sch.1, SI 2012/2547 Sch.1, SI 2012/2548 Sch.1, SI 2012/2549 Sch.1, SI 2012/3102 Sch.1, SI 2012/3103 Sch.1, SI 2012/3104 Sch.1, SI 2012/3105 Sch.1, SI 2012/3106 Sch.1, SI 2012/3107 Sch.1

Reg.9, applied: SI 2012/1282 Sch.1, SI 2012/1284 Sch.1, SI 2012/1286 Sch.1, SI 2012/1289 Sch.1, SI 2012/1294 Sch.1, SI 2012/1295 Sch.1, SI 2012/3102 Sch.1, SI 2012/3103 Sch.1, SI 2012/3104 Sch.1, SI 2012/3105 Sch.1, SI 2012/3106 Sch.1, SI 2012/3107 Sch.1

Reg.9, referred to: SI 2012/2541 Sch.1, SI 2012/2547 Sch.1, SI 2012/2548 Sch.1, SI 2012/2549 Sch.1

Reg.10, applied: SI 2012/1282 Sch.1, SI 2012/1284 Sch.1, SI 2012/1286 Sch.1, SI 2012/1289 Sch.1, SI 2012/1294 Sch.1, SI 2012/1295 Sch.1, SI 2012/2541 Sch.1, SI 2012/2547 Sch.1, SI 2012/2548 Sch.1, SI 2012/2549 Sch.1, SI 2012/3102 Sch.1, SI 2012/3103 Sch.1, SI 2012/3104 Sch.1, SI 2012/3105 Sch.1, SI 2012/3106 Sch.1, SI 2012/3107 Sch.1

Reg.10, referred to: SI 2012/1294 Sch.1

Reg.11, applied: SI 2012/2541 Sch.1, SI 2012/2547 Sch.1, SI 2012/2548 Sch.1, SI 2012/2549 Sch.1, SI 2012/3102 Sch.1, SI 2012/3103 Sch.1, SI 2012/3104 Sch.1, SI 2012/3105 Sch.1, SI 2012/3106 Sch.1, SI 2012/3107 Sch.1

Reg.11, referred to: SI 2012/2541 Sch.1, SI 2012/2547 Sch.1, SI 2012/2548 Sch.1, SI 2012/2549 Sch.1

Reg.12, applied: SI 2012/2541 Sch.1, SI 2012/2547 Sch.1, SI 2012/2548 Sch.1, SI 2012/2549 Sch.1, SI 2012/3102 Sch.1, SI 2012/3103 Sch.1, SI 2012/3104 Sch.1, SI 2012/3105 Sch.1, SI 2012/3106 Sch.1, SI 2012/3107 Sch.1

Reg.13, applied: SI 2012/2541 Sch.1, SI 2012/2547 Sch.1, SI 2012/2548 Sch.1, SI 2012/2549 Sch.1, SI 2012/3102 Sch.1, SI 2012/3103 Sch.1, SI 2012/3104 Sch.1, SI 2012/3105 Sch.1, SI 2012/3106 Sch.1, SI 2012/3107 Sch.1

Reg.15, applied: SI 2012/2541 Sch.1, SI 2012/2547 Sch.1, SI 2012/2548 Sch.1, SI 2012/2549 Sch.1, SI 2012/3102 Sch.1, SI 2012/3103 Sch.1, SI 2012/3104 Sch.1, SI 2012/3105 Sch.1, SI 2012/3106 Sch.1, SI 2012/3107 Sch.1

Reg.16, applied: SI 2012/3102 Sch.1, SI 2012/3103 Sch.1, SI 2012/3104 Sch.1, SI 2012/3105 Sch.1, SI 2012/3106 Sch.1, SI 2012/3107 Sch.1

2007–cont.

3372. Traffic Management Permit Scheme (England) Regulations 2007–*cont.*

Reg.17, referred to: SI 2012/2541 Sch.1, SI 2012/2547 Sch.1, SI 2012/2548 Sch.1, SI 2012/2549 Sch.1

Reg.18, applied: SI 2012/1282 Sch.1, SI 2012/1284 Sch.1, SI 2012/1286 Sch.1, SI 2012/1289 Sch.1, SI 2012/1294 Sch.1, SI 2012/1295 Sch.1, SI 2012/2541 Sch.1, SI 2012/2547 Sch.1, SI 2012/2548 Sch.1, SI 2012/2549 Sch.1, SI 2012/3102 Sch.1, SI 2012/3103 Sch.1, SI 2012/3104 Sch.1, SI 2012/3105 Sch.1, SI 2012/3106 Sch.1, SI 2012/3107 Sch.1

Reg.18, referred to: SI 2012/2541 Sch.1, SI 2012/2547 Sch.1, SI 2012/2548 Sch.1, SI 2012/2549 Sch.1, SI 2012/3102 Sch.1, SI 2012/3103 Sch.1, SI 2012/3104 Sch.1, SI 2012/3105 Sch.1, SI 2012/3106 Sch.1, SI 2012/3107 Sch.1

Reg.19, applied: SI 2012/1282 Sch.1, SI 2012/1284 Sch.1, SI 2012/1286 Sch.1, SI 2012/1289 Sch.1, SI 2012/1294 Sch.1, SI 2012/1295 Sch.1, SI 2012/2541 Sch.1, SI 2012/2547 Sch.1, SI 2012/2548 Sch.1, SI 2012/2549 Sch.1, SI 2012/3102 Sch.1, SI 2012/3103 Sch.1, SI 2012/3104 Sch.1, SI 2012/3105 Sch.1, SI 2012/3106 Sch.1, SI 2012/3107 Sch.1

Reg.20, applied: SI 2012/1282 Sch.1, SI 2012/1284 Sch.1, SI 2012/1286 Sch.1, SI 2012/1289 Sch.1, SI 2012/1294 Sch.1, SI 2012/1295 Sch.1, SI 2012/2541 Sch.1, SI 2012/2547 Sch.1, SI 2012/2548 Sch.1, SI 2012/2549 Sch.1, SI 2012/3102 Sch.1, SI 2012/3103 Sch.1, SI 2012/3104 Sch.1, SI 2012/3105 Sch.1, SI 2012/3106 Sch.1, SI 2012/3107 Sch.1

Reg.21, applied: SI 2012/2541 Sch.1, SI 2012/2547 Sch.1, SI 2012/2548 Sch.1, SI 2012/2549 Sch.1

Reg.22, applied: SI 2012/2541 Sch.1, SI 2012/2547 Sch.1, SI 2012/2548 Sch.1, SI 2012/2549 Sch.1

Reg.23, applied: SI 2012/2541 Sch.1, SI 2012/2547 Sch.1, SI 2012/2548 Sch.1, SI 2012/2549 Sch.1

Reg.23, referred to: SI 2012/2541 Sch.1, SI 2012/2547 Sch.1, SI 2012/2548 Sch.1, SI 2012/2549 Sch.1

Reg.24, applied: SI 2012/2541 Sch.1, SI 2012/2547 Sch.1, SI 2012/2548 Sch.1, SI 2012/2549 Sch.1

Reg.25, applied: SI 2012/2541 Sch.1, SI 2012/2547 Sch.1, SI 2012/2548 Sch.1, SI 2012/2549 Sch.1

Reg.26, applied: SI 2012/2541 Sch.1, SI 2012/2547 Sch.1, SI 2012/2548 Sch.1, SI 2012/2549 Sch.1

Reg.27, applied: SI 2012/2541 Sch.1, SI 2012/2547 Sch.1, SI 2012/2548 Sch.1, SI 2012/2549 Sch.1, SI 2012/3102 Sch.1, SI 2012/3103 Sch.1, SI 2012/3104 Sch.1, SI 2012/3105 Sch.1, SI 2012/3106 Sch.1, SI 2012/3107 Sch.1

Reg.28, applied: SI 2012/2541 Sch.1, SI 2012/2547 Sch.1, SI 2012/2548 Sch.1, SI 2012/2549 Sch.1, SI 2012/3102 Sch.1, SI 2012/3103 Sch.1, SI 2012/3104 Sch.1, SI 2012/3105 Sch.1, SI 2012/3106 Sch.1, SI 2012/3107 Sch.1

Reg.29, applied: SI 2012/3102 Sch.1, SI 2012/3103 Sch.1, SI 2012/3104 Sch.1, SI 2012/3105 Sch.1, SI 2012/3106 Sch.1, SI 2012/3107 Sch.1

Reg.29, referred to: SI 2012/2541 Sch.1, SI 2012/2547 Sch.1, SI 2012/2548 Sch.1

Reg.30, applied: SI 2012/1282 Sch.1, SI 2012/1284 Sch.1, SI 2012/1286 Sch.1, SI 2012/1289 Sch.1, SI 2012/1294 Sch.1, SI 2012/1295 Sch.1, SI 2012/2541 Sch.1, SI 2012/2547 Sch.1, SI 2012/2548 Sch.1, SI 2012/2549 Sch.1, SI 2012/3102 Sch.1, SI 2012/3103 Sch.1, SI 2012/3104 Sch.1, SI 2012/3105 Sch.1, SI 2012/3106 Sch.1, SI 2012/3107 Sch.1

Reg.31, referred to: SI 2012/2541 Sch.1, SI 2012/2547 Sch.1, SI 2012/2548 Sch.1, SI 2012/2549 Sch.1

2007– cont.

3372. Traffic Management Permit Scheme (England) Regulations 2007– cont.

Reg.37, applied: SI 2012/3102 Sch.1, SI 2012/3103 Sch.1, SI 2012/3104 Sch.1, SI 2012/3105 Sch.1, SI 2012/3106 Sch.1, SI 2012/3107 Sch.1

Reg.39, applied: SI 2012/1282 Sch.1, SI 2012/3102 Sch.1, SI 2012/3103 Sch.1, SI 2012/3104 Sch.1, SI 2012/3105 Sch.1, SI 2012/3106 Sch.1, SI 2012/3107 Sch.1

Reg.40, applied: SI 2012/2541 Sch.1, SI 2012/2547 Sch.1, SI 2012/2548 Sch.1, SI 2012/2549 Sch.1, SI 2012/3102 Sch.1, SI 2012/3103 Sch.1, SI 2012/3104 Sch.1, SI 2012/3105 Sch.1, SI 2012/3106 Sch.1, SI 2012/3107 Sch.1

Sch.1, applied: SI 2012/2541 Sch.1, SI 2012/2547 Sch.1, SI 2012/2548 Sch.1, SI 2012/2549 Sch.1, SI 2012/3102 Sch.1, SI 2012/3103 Sch.1, SI 2012/3104 Sch.1, SI 2012/3105 Sch.1, SI 2012/3106 Sch.1, SI 2012/3107 Sch.1

Sch.2, applied: SI 2012/2541 Sch.1, SI 2012/2547 Sch.1, SI 2012/2548 Sch.1, SI 2012/2549 Sch.1

Sch.2, referred to: SI 2012/3102 Sch.1, SI 2012/3103 Sch.1, SI 2012/3104 Sch.1, SI 2012/3105 Sch.1, SI 2012/3106 Sch.1, SI 2012/3107 Sch.1

3387. Wireless Telegraphy (Spectrum Trading) (Amendment) (No.2) Regulations 2007

revoked: SI 2012/2187 Sch.1

3389. Wireless Telegraphy (Register) (Amendment) (No.2) Regulations 2007

revoked: SI 2012/2186 Sch.1

3433. Greenhouse Gas Emissions Trading Scheme (Amendment No 2) Regulations 2007

revoked: SI 2012/3038 Reg.85

3467. Air Navigation (Amendment) (No.2) Order 2007

applied: 2012 c.19 Sch.6 para.4

3470. Parliamentary Commissioner Order 2007

varied: SI 2012/147 Art.7

3475. School Organisation (Removal of Foundation, Reduction in Number of Foundation Governors and Ability of Foundation to Pay Debts) (England) Regulations 2007

Reg.7, amended: SI 2012/956 Art.21

3482. Civil Enforcement of Parking Contraventions (England) Representations and Appeals Regulations 2007

applied: SI 2012/1234 Reg.3

Reg.6, applied: SI 2012/1234 Reg.5

Reg.7, applied: SI 2012/1234 Reg.3, Reg.5

3494. Statutory Auditors and Third Country Auditors Regulations 2007

Reg.29, amended: SI 2012/1741 Sch.1 para.1

3534. Independent Supervisor Appointment Order 2007

revoked: SI 2012/1741 Art.17

3538. Environmental Permitting (England and Wales) Regulations 2007

Sch.21 Part 2 para.33, revoked: SI 2012/811 Sch.2 para.4

Sch.21 Part 2 para.36, revoked: SI 2012/811 Sch.2 para.4

3541. Greater London Authority Elections Rules 2007

applied: SI 2012/2031 Sch.4 para.8

r.2, varied: SI 2012/444 Sch.4 para.1, SI 2012/2031 Sch.4 para.25

r.5, varied: SI 2012/444 Sch.4 para.1, SI 2012/2031 Sch.4 para.26

r.6, amended: SI 2012/198 r.2

Sch.1 Part 4 para.17, amended: SI 2012/198 r.3

2007– cont.

3541. Greater London Authority Elections Rules 2007– cont.

Sch.1 Part 5 para.54, amended: SI 2012/198 r.3

Sch.2 Part 1 para.2, varied: SI 2012/2031 Sch.4 para.27

Sch.2 Part 4 para.56, amended: SI 2012/198 r.4

Sch.2 Part 5 para.57, amended: SI 2012/198 r.4

Sch.3 Part 3 para.7, amended: SI 2012/198 r.5

Sch.3 Part 3 para.10, amended: SI 2012/198 r.5

Sch.3 Part 4 para.17, amended: SI 2012/198 r.5

Sch.3 Part 4 para.53, amended: SI 2012/198 r.6

Sch.5 Part 1 para.2, varied: SI 2012/444 Sch.4 para.1

Sch.5 Part 4 para.17, amended: SI 2012/198 r.3

Sch.5 Part 5 para.54, amended: SI 2012/198 r.3

Sch.6 Part 1 para.2, varied: SI 2012/444 Sch.4 para.1, SI 2012/2031 Sch.4 para.28

Sch.6 Part 4 para.50, varied: SI 2012/444 Sch.4 para.1, SI 2012/2031 Sch.4 para.28

Sch.6 Part 5 para.57, amended: SI 2012/198 r.4

Sch.7 Part 1 para.2, varied: SI 2012/444 Sch.4 para.1, SI 2012/2031 Sch.4 para.29

Sch.7 Part 3 para.7, amended: SI 2012/198 r.5

Sch.7 Part 3 para.10, amended: SI 2012/198 r.5

Sch.7 Part 4 para.17, amended: SI 2012/198 r.5

Sch.7 Part 4 para.49, varied: SI 2012/444 Sch.4 para.1, SI 2012/2031 Sch.4 para.29

Sch.8 para.2, varied: SI 2012/444 Sch.4 para.1, SI 2012/2031 Sch.4 para.30

Sch.10 para.2, amended: SI 2012/198 Sch.1, Sch.2, Sch.3

3544. Legislative and Regulatory Reform (Regulatory Functions) Order 2007

Sch.1 Part 1, amended: SI 2012/641 Art.2, SI 2012/3006 Art.94

Sch.1 Part 1A, amended: SI 2012/1479 Sch.1 para.83

Sch.1 Part 2, amended: SI 2012/1916 Sch.34 para.93, SI 2012/3032 Reg.47

Sch.1 Part 3, amended: SI 2012/1916 Sch.34 para.93

Sch.1 Part 6, amended: SI 2012/1916 Sch.34 para.93

Sch.1 Part 8, amended: SI 2012/1916 Sch.34 para.93

Sch.1 Part 13, amended: SI 2012/1916 Sch.34 para.93

3552. Criminal Defence Service (Funding) (Amendment) Order 2007

see *R. v Richards (Costs)* [2012] 5 Costs L.R. 998 (Sen Cts Costs Office), Costs Judge Campbell

3574. Control of Salmonella in Poultry Order 2007

Art.2, amended: SI 2012/2897 Art.22

Art.3, amended: SI 2012/2897 Art.22

Art.13, amended: SI 2012/2897 Art.22

Sch.1 para.8, amended: SI 2012/2897 Art.22

Sch.1 para.12, amended: SI 2012/2897 Art.22

2008

4. Information as to Provision of Education (England) Regulations 2008

Reg.3, amended: SI 2012/1554 Reg.2

Reg.4, amended: SI 2012/1554 Reg.2

Sch.1 para.1, amended: SI 2012/1554 Reg.2

Sch.1 para.2, amended: SI 2012/1554 Reg.2

Sch.1 para.3, amended: SI 2012/1554 Reg.2

Sch.1 para.3, substituted: SI 2012/1554 Reg.2

Sch.1 para.4, amended: SI 2012/1554 Reg.2

Sch.1 para.5, amended: SI 2012/1554 Reg.2

Sch.1 para.6, amended: SI 2012/1554 Reg.2

Sch.1 para.6A, added: SI 2012/1554 Reg.2

4. Information as to Provision of Education (England) Regulations 2008– *cont.*
Sch.1 para.6A, amended: SI 2012/ 1554 Reg.2
Sch.1 para.7, amended: SI 2012/ 1554 Reg.2
Sch.1 para.7, substituted: SI 2012/ 1554 Reg.2
Sch.1 para.7A, added: SI 2012/ 1554 Reg.2
Sch.1 para.7A, amended: SI 2012/ 1554 Reg.2
Sch.1 para.8, amended: SI 2012/ 1554 Reg.2
Sch.1 para.9, amended: SI 2012/ 1554 Reg.2
Sch.1 para.10, added: SI 2012/ 1554 Reg.2
Sch.1 para.10, amended: SI 2012/ 1554 Reg.2

6. Textile Products (Indications of Fibre Content) (Amendment) Regulations 2008
revoked: SI 2012/ 1102 Sch.1

15. Textile Products (Determination of Composition) Regulations 2008
revoked: SI 2012/ 1102 Sch.1

16. Safeguarding Vulnerable Groups Act 2006 (Barred List Prescribed Information) Regulations 2008
amended: SI 2012/ 3006 Art.13
Reg.1, amended: SI 2012/ 2112 Reg.3, Reg.4, SI 2012/ 3006 Art.13
Reg.2, amended: SI 2012/ 3006 Art.13
Reg.3, amended: SI 2012/ 2112 Reg.6, SI 2012/ 3006 Art.13
Reg.3, revoked (in part): SI 2012/ 2112 Reg.5
Reg.4, amended: SI 2012/ 2112 Reg.7, SI 2012/ 3006 Art.13

37. Restriction of the Use of Certain Hazardous Substances in Electrical and Electronic Equipment Regulations 2008
applied: SI 2012/ 3032 Reg.7
revoked: SI 2012/ 3032 Reg.7

46. Consistent Financial Reporting (England) (Amendment) Regulations 2008
revoked: SI 2012/ 674 Reg.6

168. Collaboration Between Maintained Schools (Wales) Regulations 2008
revoked: SI 2012/ 2655 Reg.2

188. Electricity and Gas (Carbon Emissions Reduction) Order 2008
applied: SI 2012/ 3018 Art.21

217. Occupational Pension Schemes (Levy Ceiling Earnings Percentage Increase) Order 2008
revoked: SI 2012/ 528 Sch.1

228. School Finance (England) Regulations 2008
revoked: SI 2012/ 335 Reg.2

230. Port of Weston Harbour Revision Order 2008
amended: SI 2012/ 1659 Art.2
Art.2, amended: SI 2012/ 1659 Art.2

238. Local Government Pension Scheme (Transitional Provisions) Regulations 2008
Reg.3, amended: SI 2012/ 1989 Reg.19
Reg.10, amended: SI 2012/ 1989 Reg.20
Sch.1, amended: SI 2012/ 1989 Reg.21
Sch.2 para.1, substituted: SI 2012/ 1989 Reg.22
Sch.2 para.3, amended: SI 2012/ 1989 Reg.22

239. Local Government Pension Scheme (Administration) Regulations 2008
applied: SI 2012/ 1989 Reg.46
Reg.6, amended: SI 2012/ 1989 Reg.24
Reg.6, revoked (in part): SI 2012/ 1989 Reg.24
Reg.7, substituted: SI 2012/ 1989 Reg.25
Reg.8B, added: SI 2012/ 1989 Reg.26
Reg.9, amended: SI 2012/ 1989 Reg.27
Reg.12, amended: SI 2012/ 1989 Reg.28
Reg.13, substituted: SI 2012/ 1989 Reg.29
Reg.18, amended: SI 2012/ 1989 Reg.30

239. Local Government Pension Scheme (Administration) Regulations 2008– *cont.*
Reg.19, amended: SI 2012/ 1989 Reg.31
Reg.20, amended: SI 2012/ 1989 Reg.32
Reg.21, amended: SI 2012/ 1989 Reg.33
Reg.32, amended: SI 2012/ 1989 Reg.34
Reg.38, amended: SI 2012/ 1989 Reg.35
Reg.38, revoked (in part): SI 2012/ 1989 Reg.35
Reg.56, amended: SI 2012/ 1989 Reg.36
Reg.66, amended: SI 2012/ 1989 Reg.37
Reg.68, amended: SI 2012/ 1989 Reg.38
Reg.68A, added: SI 2012/ 1989 Reg.39
Reg.83, amended: SI 2012/ 1989 Reg.40
Reg.86, amended: SI 2012/ 1989 Reg.41
Sch.1, amended: SI 2012/ 1989 Reg.42
Sch.2 Part 1 para.6, substituted: SI 2012/ 1989 Reg.43
Sch.2 Part 1 para.19, revoked: SI 2012/ 1989 Reg.43
Sch.2 Part 1 para.20, revoked: SI 2012/ 1989 Reg.43
Sch.2 Part 1 para.22, amended: SI 2012/ 961 Sch.1 para.10
Sch.2 Part 1 para.25, revoked: SI 2012/ 1989 Reg.43
Sch.2 Part 1 para.27, added: SI 2012/ 1989 Reg.43
Sch.2 Part 1 para.28, added: SI 2012/ 1989 Reg.43
Sch.2 Part 2 para.9, revoked: SI 2012/ 1989 Reg.43
Sch.2 Part 2 para.10, revoked: SI 2012/ 1989 Reg.43
Sch.3 para.1, amended: SI 2012/ 1989 Reg.44
Sch.3 para.2, amended: SI 2012/ 1989 Reg.44
Sch.3 para.2A, added: SI 2012/ 1989 Reg.44
Sch.3 para.2A, amended: SI 2012/ 1989 Reg.44
Sch.3 para.3, amended: SI 2012/ 1989 Reg.44
Sch.3 para.4, amended: SI 2012/ 1989 Reg.44
Sch.3 para.5, amended: SI 2012/ 1989 Reg.44
Sch.3 para.6, amended: SI 2012/ 1989 Reg.44
Sch.3 para.7, amended: SI 2012/ 1989 Reg.44
Sch.3 para.8, amended: SI 2012/ 1989 Reg.44
Sch.3 para.9, amended: SI 2012/ 1989 Reg.44
Sch.3 para.10, amended: SI 2012/ 1989 Reg.44
Sch.3 para.11, amended: SI 2012/ 1989 Reg.44
Sch.3 para.12, amended: SI 2012/ 1989 Reg.44
Sch.4 Part 1 para.2, substituted: SI 2012/ 1989 Reg.45
Sch.4 Part 1 para.6, substituted: SI 2012/ 1989 Reg.45
Sch.4 Part 1 para.7, amended: SI 2012/ 1989 Reg.45

310. Immigration, Asylum and Nationality Act 2006 (Commencement No 8 and Transitional and Saving Provisions) Order 2008
see *Abisoye (Entry Clearance Appeal: Tier 2: Nigeria)* [2012] UKUT 82 (IAC), [2012] Imm. A.R. 712 (UT (IAC)), Judge Kopieczek
Art.4, amended: SI 2012/ 1531 Art.2
Art.4, see *Abisoye (Entry Clearance Appeal: Tier 2: Nigeria)* [2012] UKUT 82 (IAC), [2012] Imm. A.R. 712 (UT (IAC)), Judge Kopieczek

314. Site Waste Management Plans Regulations 2008
applied: SI 2012/ 2284 Sch.1 para.8, SI 2012/ 2635 Sch.2 para.8
Reg.3, amended: SI 2012/ 630 Reg.17
Reg.8, amended: SI 2012/ 630 Reg.17

346. Regulated Covered Bonds Regulations 2008
Reg.1, amended: SI 2012/ 917 Sch.2 para.7
Reg.2, amended: SI 2012/ 700 Sch.1 para.18

2008–cont.

386. Non-Domestic Rating (Unoccupied Property) (England) Regulations 2008
see *Makro Properties Ltd v Nuneaton and Bedworth BC* [2012] EWHC 2250 (Admin), [2012] R.A. 285 (QBD (Admin)), Judge Jarman Q.C.

465. Products of Animal Origin (Disease Control) (England) Regulations 2008
Reg.24, substituted: SI 2012/2897 Art.23

473. Safeguarding Vulnerable Groups Act 2006 (Transitional Provisions) Order 2008
applied: SI 2012/3006 Art.101, Art.104
Art.2, amended: SI 2012/3006 Art.11, Art.12
Art.3, amended: SI 2012/3006 Art.11, Art.12
Art.4, amended: SI 2012/3006 Art.11, Art.12

474. Safeguarding Vulnerable Groups Act 2006 (Barring Procedure) Regulations 2008
Reg.2, amended: SI 2012/2112 Reg.9, SI 2012/3006 Art.13
Reg.3, amended: SI 2012/3006 Art.13
Reg.4, amended: SI 2012/3006 Art.13
Reg.5, amended: SI 2012/3006 Art.13
Reg.6, amended: SI 2012/3006 Art.13
Reg.7, amended: SI 2012/3006 Art.13
Reg.8, amended: SI 2012/3006 Art.13
Reg.9, amended: SI 2012/3006 Art.13
Reg.10, amended: SI 2012/3006 Art.13
Reg.11, amended: SI 2012/3006 Art.13

496. Statutory Auditors (Delegation of Functions etc) Order 2008
referred to: SI 2012/1741
revoked: SI 2012/1741 Art.6

514. Smoke Control Areas (Authorised Fuels) (England) Regulations 2008
revoked: SI 2012/814 Sch.2

528. Local Involvement Networks Regulations 2008
revoked: SI 2012/3094 Reg.47
Reg.5, applied: SI 2012/3094 Reg.47
Reg.5, varied: SI 2012/3094 Reg.47
Reg.6, applied: SI 2012/3094 Reg.47
Reg.6, varied: SI 2012/3094 Reg.47

532. Education (Pupil Exclusions and Appeals) (Pupil Referral Units) (England) Regulations 2008
revoked: SI 2012/1033 Sch.3

548. Medicines for Human Use (Prohibition) (Senecio and Miscellaneous Amendments) Order 2008
Art.1, amended: SI 2012/1809 Sch.1 Part 2
Art.3, amended: SI 2012/1916 Sch.34 para.94

562. Income Tax (Purchased Life Annuities) Regulations 2008
Reg.7, amended: SI 2012/2902 Reg.2
Reg.7, referred to: SI 2012/2902 Reg.2

570. Supply of Information (Register of Deaths) (England and Wales) Order 2008
Sch.1 para.6, varied: 2012 c.11 s.12

580. Town and Country Planning (Mayor of London) Order 2008
Art.4, applied: SI 2012/634 Art.4

623. Companies (Defective Accounts and Directors Reports) (Authorised Person) and Supervision of Accounts and Reports (Prescribed Body) Order 2008
revoked: SI 2012/1439 Art.7

626. Local Government Finance (New Parishes) (England) Regulations 2008
Reg.3, amended: SI 2012/460 Sch.1 para.15

2008–cont.

629. Charities (Accounts and Reports) Regulations 2008
Reg.16, amended: SI 2012/1741 Sch.1 para.9
Reg.40, applied: SI 2012/3012 Sch.1 para.9
Reg.41, applied: SI 2012/3012 Sch.1 para.9

630. Police Authority Regulations 2008
Reg.19A, amended: SI 2012/536 Reg.2
Reg.41, amended: SI 2012/536 Reg.2
Reg.41, revoked (in part): SI 2012/536 Reg.2

647. Energy Performance of Buildings (Certificates and Inspections) (England and Wales) (Amendment) Regulations 2008
revoked: SI 2012/3118 Sch.3

651. Accounting Standards (Prescribed Body) Regulations 2008
revoked: SI 2012/1741 Art.22
Reg.4, applied: SI 2012/1741 Art.24

653. National Health Service Pension Scheme Regulations 2008
Reg.1, amended: SI 2012/610 Reg.11
Reg.1, amended: SI 2012/610 Reg.15
Reg.1, amended: SI 2012/610 Reg.17
Reg.1, amended: SI 2012/610 Reg.19
Reg.2, amended: SI 2012/610 Reg.12
Reg.2, revoked (in part): SI 2012/610 Reg.12
Reg.2, amended: SI 2012/610 Reg.18
Reg.3, amended: SI 2012/610 Reg.10
Reg.3, amended: SI 2012/610 Reg.13
Reg.4, amended: SI 2012/610 Reg.14
Reg.8, amended: SI 2012/610 Reg.16
Reg.8, amended: SI 2012/610 Reg.20
Reg.14, revoked (in part): SI 2012/1909 Sch.8 para.1

657. Education (Induction Arrangements for School Teachers) (England) Regulations 2008
applied: SI 2012/115 Reg.1
revoked: SI 2012/1115 Reg.2
Reg.3, amended: SI 2012/513 Reg.3
Reg.6, amended: SI 2012/513 Reg.4
Reg.7, amended: SI 2012/513 Reg.5
Reg.8, amended: SI 2012/513 Reg.6
Reg.9, amended: SI 2012/513 Reg.7
Reg.10, amended: SI 2012/513 Reg.8
Reg.16, amended: SI 2012/513 Reg.9
Reg.17, amended: SI 2012/513 Reg.10
Reg.18, amended: SI 2012/513 Reg.11
Reg.18A, added: SI 2012/513 Reg.12
Reg.19, amended: SI 2012/513 Reg.13
Reg.21, amended: SI 2012/513 Reg.14
Sch.2 para.14, amended: SI 2012/513 Reg.15
Sch.2 para.18, amended: SI 2012/513 Reg.15
Sch.2 para.22, added: SI 2012/513 Reg.15
Sch.2 para.23, added: SI 2012/513 Reg.15
Sch.3 para.3, amended: SI 2012/513 Reg.16
Sch.3 para.5, amended: SI 2012/513 Reg.16
Sch.4 para.1, amended: SI 2012/513 Reg.17
Sch.4 para.2, amended: SI 2012/513 Reg.17
Sch.4 para.3, amended: SI 2012/513 Reg.17
Sch.4 para.4, amended: SI 2012/513 Reg.17
Sch.4 para.5, amended: SI 2012/513 Reg.17
Sch.4 para.6, amended: SI 2012/513 Reg.17
Sch.4 para.7, amended: SI 2012/513 Reg.17
Sch.4 para.8, amended: SI 2012/513 Reg.17
Sch.4 para.9, amended: SI 2012/513 Reg.17
Sch.4 para.10, amended: SI 2012/513 Reg.17
Sch.4 para.11, amended: SI 2012/513 Reg.17
Sch.4 para.12A, added: SI 2012/513 Reg.17
Sch.4 para.13, amended: SI 2012/513 Reg.17
Sch.4 para.15, amended: SI 2012/513 Reg.17

2008– cont.

657. Education (Induction Arrangements for School Teachers) (England) Regulations 2008– cont.
Sch.4 para.16, amended: SI 2012/513 Reg.17
Sch.4 para.17, amended: SI 2012/513 Reg.17
Sch.4 para.18, amended: SI 2012/513 Reg.17

677. Copyright and Performances (Application to Other Countries) Order 2008
revoked: SI 2012/799 Art.1

683. National Health Service (Pharmaceutical Services) (Amendment) Regulations 2008
revoked: SI 2012/1909 Sch.8 para.9

688. Wireless Telegraphy (Spectrum Trading) (Amendment) Regulations 2008
revoked: SI 2012/2187 Sch.1

689. Wireless Telegraphy (Register) (Amendment) Regulations 2008
revoked: SI 2012/2186 Sch.1

700. Supply of Information (Register of Deaths) (Northern Ireland) Order 2008
Sch.1 para.7, varied: 2012 c.11 s.12

711. Pensions Increase (Review) Order 2008
applied: SI 2012/782 Art.3, Art.4

788. Local Authorities (Model Code of Conduct) (Wales) Order 2008
applied: SI 2012/2734 Sch.1 para.33
varied: SI 2012/2734 Reg.6

794. Employment and Support Allowance Regulations 2008
applied: SI 2012/2885 Sch.1 para.25, SI 2012/2886 Sch.1, SI 2012/3144 Sch.1 para.10, Sch.1 para.19, SI 2012/3145 Sch.1, SSI 2012/303 Reg.20
Part 5, applied: SI 2012/3096 Reg.2
Part 6, applied: SI 2012/3096 Reg.2
Reg.2, amended: SI 2012/757 Reg.6, SI 2012/919 Reg.5, SI 2012/956 Art.22, SI 2012/2756 Reg.2
Reg.2, applied: SI 2012/2885 Sch.1 para.35, SI 2012/3145 Sch.1, SSI 2012/303 Reg.49, SSI 2012/319 Reg.45
Reg.5, amended: SI 2012/919 Reg.5
Reg.7, amended: SI 2012/874 Reg.6, SI 2012/913 Reg.9, SI 2012/919 Reg.5
Reg.7, applied: SI 2012/2885 Sch.4 para.5, SI 2012/2886 Sch.1, SSI 2012/303 Sch.1 para.18
Reg.8, amended: SI 2012/757 Reg.20
Reg.8, revoked (in part): SI 2012/757 Reg.20
Reg.14, amended: SI 2012/757 Reg.20, SI 2012/956 Art.22
Reg.19, amended: SI 2012/3096 Reg.3
Reg.19, applied: SI 2012/3096 Reg.2
Reg.20, amended: SI 2012/3096 Reg.3
Reg.25, substituted: SI 2012/3096 Reg.3
Reg.26, amended: SI 2012/3096 Reg.3
Reg.29, amended: SI 2012/3096 Reg.3
Reg.30, applied: SI 2012/2886 Sch.1, SSI 2012/303 Sch.1 para.25, Sch.1 para.28
Reg.34, amended: SI 2012/3096 Reg.4
Reg.34, applied: SI 2012/3096 Reg.2
Reg.35, amended: SI 2012/3096 Reg.4
Reg.35A, added: SI 2012/919 Reg.5
Reg.61, revoked (in part): SI 2012/2756 Reg.3
Reg.63, amended: SI 2012/2756 Reg.4
Reg.63, applied: SI 2012/2886 Sch.1, SI 2012/3145 Sch.1, SSI 2012/303 Reg.39
Reg.64, revoked (in part): SI 2012/2756 Reg.5
Reg.64A, added: SI 2012/2756 Reg.6
Reg.64B, added: SI 2012/2756 Reg.6
Reg.64C, added: SI 2012/2756 Reg.6
Reg.64D, added: SI 2012/2756 Reg.6

2008– cont.

794. Employment and Support Allowance Regulations 2008– cont.
Reg.70, amended: SI 2012/1809 Sch.1 Part 2, SI 2012/2587 Reg.9
Reg.91, amended: SI 2012/2575 Reg.5
Reg.115, applied: SI 2012/2885 Sch.1 para.35, SI 2012/2886 Sch.1, SI 2012/3145 Sch.1, SSI 2012/303 Reg.49, SSI 2012/319 Reg.45
Reg.115, referred to: SI 2012/2885 Sch.1 para.35
Reg.131, amended: SI 2012/956 Art.22
Reg.144, amended: SI 2012/913 Reg.9
Reg.145, applied: SI 2012/2886 Sch.1, SSI 2012/303 Sch.1 para.26, Sch.1 para.27
Reg.145, revoked (in part): SI 2012/919 Reg.5
Reg.148, revoked: SI 2012/919 Reg.5
Reg.149, revoked: SI 2012/919 Reg.5
Reg.150, revoked: SI 2012/919 Reg.5
Sch.2, applied: SI 2012/3096 Reg.2
Sch.2 Part 1, amended: SI 2012/3096 Reg.5
Sch.2 Part 2, substituted: SI 2012/3096 Reg.5
Sch.3, amended: SI 2012/3096 Reg.6
Sch.3, applied: SI 2012/3096 Reg.2
Sch.4 Part 1 para.1, amended: SI 2012/780 Sch.18
Sch.4 Part 3 para.11, amended: SI 2012/780 Sch.19
Sch.4 Part 4 para.12, amended: SI 2012/780 Art.28
Sch.4 Part 4 para.13, amended: SI 2012/780 Art.28
Sch.6 para.1, amended: SI 2012/913 Reg.9, SI 2012/919 Reg.5
Sch.6 para.7, referred to: SI 2012/780 Sch.20
Sch.6 para.8, referred to: SI 2012/780 Sch.20
Sch.6 para.11, referred to: SI 2012/780 Sch.20
Sch.6 para.12, referred to: SI 2012/780 Sch.20
Sch.6 para.13, referred to: SI 2012/780 Sch.20
Sch.6 para.19, amended: SI 2012/780 Art.28
Sch.7 para.11A, added: SI 2012/2575 Reg.5
Sch.9 para.11, applied: SI 2012/2885 Sch.6 para.22, SI 2012/2886 Sch.1, SSI 2012/319 Sch.4 para.22

912. Offender Management Act 2007 (Consequential Amendments) Order 2008
Sch.1 Part 1 para.13, revoked (in part): 2012 c.10 Sch.12 para.57
Sch.1 Part 1 para.21, revoked: 2012 c.9 Sch.10 Part 5
Sch.1 Part 2 para.26, revoked (in part): SI 2012/2401 Sch.1 para.44
Sch.1 Part 2 para.27, revoked (in part): SI 2012/2401 Sch.1 para.44
Sch.2 para.15, revoked: SI 2012/1278 Reg.3

915. Local Involvement Networks (Duty of Services-Providers to Allow Entry) Regulations 2008
Reg.3, applied: SI 2012/1909 Reg.11
Reg.3, referred to: SI 2012/1909 Reg.47

944. Specified Animal Pathogens Order 2008
applied: SI 2012/2629 Reg.4
Art.5, amended: SI 2012/1916 Sch.34 para.95
Art.5, revoked (in part): SI 2012/1916 Sch.34 para.95
Art.11, substituted: SI 2012/2897 Art.24

948. Companies Act 2006 (Consequential Amendments etc) Order 2008
Sch.1 Part 2 para.219, revoked: SI 2012/700 Sch.1 para.19

958. Town and Country Planning (Fees for Applications and Deemed Applications) (Amendment) (England) Regulations 2008
revoked: SI 2012/2920 Sch.3

962. Bluetongue Regulations 2008
Reg.2, amended: SI 2012/1977 Reg.2
Reg.3, substituted: SI 2012/1977 Reg.2
Reg.13, amended: SI 2012/1977 Reg.2

2008–cont.

962. Bluetongue Regulations 2008–*cont.*
Reg.17, substituted: SI 2012/1977 Reg.2
Reg.18, substituted: SI 2012/1977 Reg.2
Reg.19, substituted: SI 2012/1977 Reg.2
Reg.27, amended: SI 2012/2897 Art.25
Reg.30, added: SI 2012/1977 Reg.2
Reg.30, amended: SI 2012/2897 Art.25

974. Childcare (Early Years Register) Regulations 2008
Sch.1 Part 1 para.3A, added: SI 2012/939 Reg.2
Sch.2 Part 1 para.8, substituted: SI 2012/939 Reg.2
Sch.2 Part 2 para.18, revoked: SI 2012/939 Reg.2
Sch.2 Part 2 para.19, revoked: SI 2012/939 Reg.2
Sch.2 Part 2 para.20, revoked: SI 2012/939 Reg.2
Sch.2 Part 2 para.21, revoked: SI 2012/939 Reg.2
Sch.2 Part 2 para.22, revoked: SI 2012/939 Reg.2
Sch.2 Part 2 para.23, revoked: SI 2012/939 Reg.2

975. Childcare (General Childcare Register) Regulations 2008
Reg.2, amended: SI 2012/1699 Reg.3
Sch.1 Part 1 para.4A, added: SI 2012/1699 Reg.4
Sch.2 Part 1 para.5, substituted: SI 2012/1699 Reg.5
Sch.2 Part 2 para.15, revoked: SI 2012/1699 Reg.5
Sch.2 Part 2 para.16, revoked: SI 2012/1699 Reg.5
Sch.3 para.2, amended: SI 2012/1699 Reg.6
Sch.3 para.8, amended: SI 2012/1699 Reg.6
Sch.3 para.10, revoked: SI 2012/1699 Reg.6
Sch.3 para.26, amended: SI 2012/1699 Reg.6
Sch.5 Part 1 para.5, substituted: SI 2012/1699 Reg.7
Sch.5 Part 2 para.15, revoked: SI 2012/1699 Reg.7
Sch.5 Part 2 para.16, revoked: SI 2012/1699 Reg.7
Sch.6 para.3, substituted: SI 2012/1699 Reg.8
Sch.6 para.3A, substituted: SI 2012/1699 Reg.8
Sch.6 para.10, amended: SI 2012/1699 Reg.8

1053. Civil Proceedings Fees Order 2008
applied: SI 2012/3013 Sch.1 para.2

1062. Safeguarding Vulnerable Groups Act 2006 (Prescribed Criteria) (Transitional Provisions) Regulations 2008
Reg.2, amended: SI 2012/3006 Art.13
Reg.3, amended: SI 2012/3006 Art.13

1079. Specified Products from China (Restriction on First Placing on the Market) (England) Regulations 2008
applied: SI 2012/47 Reg.3
Reg.2, amended: SI 2012/47 Reg.2
Reg.3, amended: SI 2012/47 Reg.2
Reg.3, substituted: SI 2012/47 Reg.2
Reg.4, revoked: SI 2012/47 Reg.2
Reg.5, amended: SI 2012/47 Reg.2
Reg.6, amended: SI 2012/47 Reg.2
Reg.7, added: SI 2012/47 Reg.2
Reg.8, added: SI 2012/47 Reg.2

1080. Specified Products from China (Restriction on First Placing on the Market) (Wales) Regulations 2008
Reg.2, amended: SI 2012/64 Reg.2
Reg.3, amended: SI 2012/64 Reg.2
Reg.4, revoked: SI 2012/64 Reg.2
Reg.5, amended: SI 2012/64 Reg.2
Reg.6, amended: SI 2012/64 Reg.2
Reg.7, added: SI 2012/64 Reg.2
Reg.8, added: SI 2012/64 Reg.2

1085. Standards Committee (England) Regulations 2008
Reg.17, applied: SI 2012/1463 Art.7, SI 2012/2913 Art.5

2008–cont.

1085. Standards Committee (England) Regulations 2008–*cont.*
Reg.21, applied: SI 2012/1463 Art.7, SI 2012/2913 Art.5

1090. Bluetongue (Wales) Regulations 2008
Reg.2, amended: SI 2012/2403 Reg.2
Reg.3, substituted: SI 2012/2403 Reg.2
Reg.13, amended: SI 2012/2403 Reg.2
Reg.17, substituted: SI 2012/2403 Reg.2
Reg.18, substituted: SI 2012/2403 Reg.2
Reg.19, substituted: SI 2012/2403 Reg.2

1098. Export Control (Burma) Order 2008
Art.1, amended: SI 2012/2125 Art.4
Art.1, applied: SI 2012/2125 Art.4
Art.2, added: SI 2012/2125 Art.4
Art.2, revoked: SI 2012/2125 Art.4
Art.4, added: SI 2012/2125 Art.4
Art.4, revoked: SI 2012/2125 Art.4
Art.6, amended: SI 2012/2125 Art.4
Art.6, revoked (in part): SI 2012/2125 Art.4
Art.7, added: SI 2012/2125 Art.4
Art.7, revoked (in part): SI 2012/2125 Art.4
Art.8, added: SI 2012/2125 Art.4
Art.8, revoked: SI 2012/2125 Art.4
Art.9, added: SI 2012/2125 Art.4
Art.9, revoked (in part): SI 2012/2125 Art.4
Art.10, added: SI 2012/2125 Art.4
Art.10, revoked (in part): SI 2012/2125 Art.4
Art.11, amended: SI 2012/2125 Art.4
Art.11, revoked (in part): SI 2012/2125 Art.4
Art.13, added: SI 2012/2125 Art.4

1183. Immigration (Biometric Registration) (Pilot) Regulations 2008
applied: SI 2012/813 Sch.1 para.8
Reg.3, applied: SI 2012/813 Sch.1 para.9
Reg.5, applied: SI 2012/813 Sch.1 para.9
Reg.8, applied: SI 2012/813 Sch.1 para.9

1184. Mental Health (Hospital, Guardianship and Treatment) (England) Regulations 2008
Reg.28, amended: SI 2012/1118 Reg.2
Sch.1, amended: SI 2012/1118 Reg.2

1206. Mental Health (Approved Mental Health Professionals) (Approval) (England) Regulations 2008
Reg.2, amended: SI 2012/1479 Sch.1 para.84
Reg.3, amended: SI 2012/1479 Sch.1 para.84
Sch.1, amended: SI 2012/1479 Sch.1 para.54, Sch.1 para.84
Sch.1, revoked: SI 2012/1479 Sch.1 para.84

1270. Specified Animal Pathogens (Wales) Order 2008
Art.5, amended: SI 2012/1916 Sch.34 para.96
Art.5, revoked (in part): SI 2012/1916 Sch.34 para.96

1276. Business Protection from Misleading Marketing Regulations 2008
applied: SI 2012/1128 Art.4

1277. Consumer Protection from Unfair Trading Regulations 2008
applied: SI 2012/1128 Art.4
see *Purely Creative Ltd v Office of Fair Trading* [2011] EWCA Civ 920, [2012] 1 C.M.L.R. 21 (CA (Civ Div)), Sir Andrew Morritt (Chancellor); see *R. v Scottish and Southern Energy Plc* [2012] EWCA Crim 539, (2012) 176 J.P. 241 (CA (Crim Div)), Davis, L.J.
Reg.9, see *Price v Cheshire East BC* [2012] EWHC 2927 (Admin), (2012) 176 J.P. 697 (QBD (Admin)), Collins, J.; see *R. v Scottish and*

2008– cont.

1277. Consumer Protection from Unfair Trading Regulations 2008– *cont.*

Reg.9– *cont.*

Southern Energy Plc [2012] EWCA Crim 539, (2012) 176 J.P. 241 (CA (Crim Div)), Davis, L.J.; see *R. v UK Parking Control Ltd* [2012] EWCA Crim 1560, (2012) 176 J.P. 648 (CA (Crim Div)), Moses, L.J.

Reg.11, see *Price v Cheshire East BC* [2012] EWHC 2927 (Admin), (2012) 176 J.P. 697 (QBD (Admin)), Collins, J.

Reg.21, see *R. (on the application of Vuciterni) v Brent Magistrates' Court* [2012] EWHC 2140 (Admin), (2012) 176 J.P. 705 (DC), Davis, L.J.

Reg.22, see *R. (on the application of Vuciterni) v Brent Magistrates' Court* [2012] EWHC 2140 (Admin), (2012) 176 J.P. 705 (DC), Davis, L.J.

Sch.1 para.9, see *R. (on the application of Vuciterni) v Brent Magistrates' Court* [2012] EWHC 2140 (Admin), (2012) 176 J.P. 705 (DC), Davis, L.J.

Sch.1 para.31, see *Purely Creative Ltd v Office of Fair Trading* [2011] EWCA Civ 920, [2012] 1 C.M.L.R. 21 (CA (Civ Div)), Sir Andrew Morritt (Chancellor)

1284. Cosmetic Products (Safety) Regulations 2008

Sch.2 para.69, added: SI 2012/ 2263 Reg.2

Sch.4 Part 1, amended: SI 2012/ 2263 Sch.1

1341. Spreadable Fats (Marketing Standards) and the Milk and Milk Products (Protection of Designations) (Wales) Regulations 2008

Reg.3, amended: SI 2012/ 1809 Sch.1 Part 4

1342. European Regional Development Fund (London Operational Programme) (Implementation) Regulations 2008

Reg.2, amended: SI 2012/ 666 Sch.1 para.1

1371. Town and Country Planning (Local Development) (England) (Amendment) Regulations 2008

revoked: SI 2012/ 767 Reg.37

1388. A19 Trunk Road (Lindisfarne Roundabout to Silverlink Roundabout) (Temporary Restriction and Prohibition of Traffic) Order 2008

revoked: SI 2012/ 1122 Art.2

1430. Local Authorities (Alcohol Disorder Zones) Regulations 2008

Reg.15, amended: SI 2012/ 61 Reg.4

Reg.21, amended: SI 2012/ 61 Reg.4

1466. Criminal Justice and Immigration Act 2008 (Commencement No.1 and Transitional Provisions) Order 2008

Art.3, revoked: 2012 c.10 Sch.16 para.22

1487. Air Navigation (Isle of Man) (Amendment) Order 2008

applied: 2012 c.19 Sch.6 para.4

1514. Local Involvement Networks (Miscellaneous Amendments) Regulations 2008

Reg.5, revoked: SI 2012/ 1909 Sch.8 para.9

1586. Criminal Justice and Immigration Act 2008 (Commencement No 2 and Transitional and Saving Provisions) Order 2008

Sch.2 para.2, amended: 2012 c.10 Sch.16 para.15

1587. Criminal Justice and Immigration Act 2008 (Transitory Provisions) Order 2008

Art.2, revoked (in part): SI 2012/ 2824 Reg.4

1660. Cross-border Railway Services (Working Time) Regulations 2008

Sch.2 para.2, revoked (in part): 2012 c.9 Sch.2 para.14, Sch.10 Part 2

2008– cont.

1692. Medicines for Human Use (Prescribing by EEA Practitioners) Regulations 2008

revoked: SI 2012/ 1916 Sch.35

1700. Primary Ophthalmic Services Amendment, Transitional and Consequential Provisions Regulations 2008

Reg.10, revoked: SI 2012/ 1909 Sch.8 para.1

Reg.11, revoked: SI 2012/ 1909 Sch.8 para.1

Reg.12, revoked: SI 2012/ 1909 Sch.8 para.1

Reg.13, revoked: SI 2012/ 1909 Sch.8 para.1

Reg.14, revoked: SI 2012/ 1909 Sch.8 para.1

Reg.15, revoked: SI 2012/ 1909 Sch.8 para.1

Reg.16, revoked: SI 2012/ 1909 Sch.8 para.1

Sch.1 para.3, revoked: SI 2012/ 1909 Sch.8 para.1

1702. Road Vehicles (Construction and Use) (Amendment) Regulations 2008

revoked: SI 2012/ 1404 Sch.1

1724. Local Authority (Duty to Secure Early Years Provision Free of Charge) Regulations 2008

revoked: SI 2012/ 2488 Reg.5

1729. Childcare (Inspections) Regulations 2008

Reg.2, amended: SI 2012/ 1698 Reg.2

Reg.3, revoked: SI 2012/ 1698 Reg.2

Reg.4, revoked: SI 2012/ 1698 Reg.2

Reg.5, amended: SI 2012/ 979 Sch.1 para.22

Reg.5, revoked: SI 2012/ 1698 Reg.2

Reg.6, revoked: SI 2012/ 1698 Reg.2

Reg.7, revoked: SI 2012/ 1698 Reg.2

Reg.8, revoked: SI 2012/ 1698 Reg.2

Reg.9, revoked: SI 2012/ 1698 Reg.2

Reg.10, revoked: SI 2012/ 1698 Reg.2

Reg.11, revoked: SI 2012/ 1698 Reg.2

Reg.14, revoked: SI 2012/ 1698 Reg.2

Reg.15, revoked (in part): SI 2012/ 1698 Reg.2

Reg.16, revoked (in part): SI 2012/ 1698 Reg.2

Reg.17, revoked: SI 2012/ 1698 Reg.2

1743. Early Years Foundation Stage (Exemptions from Learning and Development Requirements) Regulations 2008

Reg.1, amended: SI 2012/ 2463 Reg.3

Reg.2, substituted: SI 2012/ 2463 Reg.4

Reg.3, amended: SI 2012/ 2463 Reg.5

Reg.4, substituted: SI 2012/ 2463 Reg.6

Reg.4A, added: SI 2012/ 2463 Reg.7

Reg.4B, added: SI 2012/ 2463 Reg.7

Reg.4C, added: SI 2012/ 2463 Reg.7

Reg.5, revoked: SI 2012/ 2463 Reg.8

Reg.6, revoked: SI 2012/ 2463 Reg.8

1745. Terrorism Act 2006 (Disapplication of Section 25) Order 2008

revoked: 2012 c.9 Sch.10 Part 4

1758. Education (National Curriculum) (Attainment Targets and Programmes of Study in Information and Communication Technology in respect of the Third and Fourth Key Stages) (England) Order 2008

referred to: SI 2012/ 1926 Reg.2

1782. Air Navigation (Amendment) Order 2008

applied: 2012 c.19 Sch.6 para.4

1797. Trade Marks Rules 2008

see *Pass J Holdings Ltd v Spencer* [2012] R.P.C. 16 (App Person), Geoffrey Hobbs Q.C.

r.14, amended: SI 2012/ 1003 r.2

r.14, revoked (in part): SI 2012/ 1003 r.2

r.27, amended: SI 2012/ 1003 r.2

r.27, revoked (in part): SI 2012/ 1003 r.2

r.74, see *Pass J Holdings Ltd v Spencer* [2012] R.P.C. 16 (App Person), Geoffrey Hobbs Q.C.

2008–cont.

1804. Childcare (Fees) Regulations 2008
Reg.10, amended: SI 2012/2168 Reg.2

1816. Cancellation of Contracts made in a Consumer's Home or Place of Work etc Regulations 2008
see *W v Veolia Environmental Services (UK) Plc* [2011] EWHC 2020 (QB), [2012] 1 All E.R. (Comm) 667 (QBD (Merc) (London)), Judge Mackie Q.C.
Reg.7, see *W v Veolia Environmental Services (UK) Plc* [2011] EWHC 2020 (QB), [2012] 1 All E.R. (Comm) 667 (QBD (Merc) (London)), Judge Mackie Q.C.

1825. Community Emissions Trading Scheme (Allocation of Allowances for Payment) Regulations 2008
revoked: SI 2012/2661 Reg.6

1858. Mental Capacity (Deprivation of Liberty Standard Authorisations, Assessments and Ordinary Residence) Regulations 2008
Reg.2, amended: SI 2012/1479 Sch.1 para.85
Reg.5, amended: SI 2012/1479 Sch.1 para.55, Sch.1 para.85
Reg.5, revoked (in part): SI 2012/1479 Sch.1 para.85

1863. Serious Crime Act 2007 (Appeals under Section 24) Order 2008
applied: SI 2012/1726 r.65.1, r.65.5
Part 3, applied: SI 2012/1726 r.76.1
Art.14, applied: SI 2012/1726 r.76.1, r.76.4
Art.15, applied: SI 2012/1726 r.76.1, r.76.6
Art.16, applied: SI 2012/1726 r.76.1, r.76.8
Art.17, applied: SI 2012/1726 r.76.1, r.76.9
Art.18, applied: SI 2012/1726 r.76.1, r.76.10
Art.21, applied: SI 2012/1726 r.76.4
Art.22, applied: SI 2012/1726 r.76.4
Art.23, applied: SI 2012/1726 r.76.4
Art.24, applied: SI 2012/1726 r.76.4
Art.25, applied: SI 2012/1726 r.76.4
Art.26, applied: SI 2012/1726 r.76.4
Art.27, applied: SI 2012/1726 r.76.4
Art.28, applied: SI 2012/1726 r.76.4
Art.31, applied: SI 2012/1726 r.76.1

1883. Education (Specified Work and Registration) (England) (Amendment) Regulations 2008
revoked: SI 2012/762 Reg.6

1884. General Teaching Council for England (Eligibility for Provisional Registration) Regulations 2008
revoked: SI 2012/1153 Sch.1

1891. Superannuation (Admission to Schedule 1 to the Superannuation Act 1972) Order 2008
Art.2, amended: 2012 asp 8 s.61
para.2, amended: 2012 asp 8 s.61

1907. Whole of Government Accounts (Designation of Bodies) (No.2) Order 2008
varied: SI 2012/147 Art.7

1911. Limited Liability Partnerships (Accounts and Audit) (Application of Companies Act 2006) Regulations 2008
applied: SI 2012/1439 Art.8
Reg.9, amended: SI 2012/2301 Reg.20
Reg.10, amended: SI 2012/2301 Reg.20
Reg.17, amended: SI 2012/2301 Reg.20
Reg.19A, added: SI 2012/2301 Reg.20
Reg.23, amended: SI 2012/1439 Art.8
Reg.23, applied: SI 2012/1439 Art.8
Reg.24, amended: SI 2012/1439 Art.8
Reg.24, applied: SI 2012/1439 Art.8
Reg.25, substituted: SI 2012/1741 Sch.1 para.8

2008–cont.

1911. Limited Liability Partnerships (Accounts and Audit) (Application of Companies Act 2006) Regulations 2008–cont.
Reg.29, amended: SI 2012/2301 Reg.20
Reg.32, amended: SI 2012/1439 Art.8
Reg.32, applied: SI 2012/1439 Art.8
Reg.33, amended: SI 2012/2301 Reg.20
Reg.34, amended: SI 2012/2301 Reg.20
Reg.34A, added: SI 2012/2301 Reg.20
Reg.46, amended: SI 2012/1439 Art.8
Reg.46, applied: SI 2012/1439 Art.8

1926. Financing-Arrangement-Funded Transfers to Shareholders Regulations 2008
applied: SI 2012/3009 Reg.12

1937. Friendly Societies (Modification of the Corporation Tax Acts) (Amendment) Regulations 2008
revoked: SI 2012/3008 Sch.1

1942. Friendly Societies (Transfers of Other Business) (Modification of the Corporation Tax Acts) Regulations 2008
revoked: SI 2012/3008 Sch.1

1947. Tax Avoidance Schemes (Information) (Amendment) Regulations 2008
revoked: SI 2012/1836 Sch.1

1951. A282 Trunk Road (Dartford-Thurrock Crossing Charging Scheme) Order 2008
revoked: SI 2012/2387 Art.7

1953. Early Years Foundation Stage (Welfare Requirements) (Amendment) Regulations 2008
revoked: SI 2012/938 Reg.13

1958. Trade Marks (Fees) Rules 2008
Sch.1, amended: SI 2012/1003 r.3

1963. Mesothelioma Lump Sum Payments (Conditions and Amounts) Regulations 2008
Sch.1, amended: SI 2012/918 Reg.2

1976. Private Dentistry (Wales) Regulations 2008
applied: SI 2012/1916 Reg.232

2104. Wireless Telegraphy (Register) (Amendment) (No.2) Regulations 2008
revoked: SI 2012/2186 Sch.1

2105. Wireless Telegraphy (Spectrum Trading) (Amendment) (No.2) Regulations 2008
revoked: SI 2012/2187 Sch.1

2252. Care Quality Commission (Membership) Regulations 2008
Reg.1, amended: SI 2012/1641 Sch.4 para.15
Reg.2, amended: SI 2012/1186 Reg.3
Sch.1 para.27, revoked: SI 2012/1186 Reg.3

2260. Town and Country Planning (Trees) (Amendment) (England) Regulations 2008
revoked: SI 2012/605 Reg.26

2265. Social Fund (Applications and Miscellaneous Provisions) Regulations 2008
referred to: SI 2012/3090 Art.3

2336. Town and Country Planning (General Development Procedure) (Amendment) (Wales) Order 2008
revoked: SI 2012/801 Sch.8

2340. Designation of Schools Having a Religious Character (Independent Schools) (England) (No.2) Order 2008
Sch.1, amended: SI 2012/3174 Sch.2

2342. Smoke Control Areas (Authorised Fuels) (England) (Amendment) Regulations 2008
revoked: SI 2012/814 Sch.2

2349. Nitrate Pollution Prevention Regulations 2008
Reg.6, amended: SI 2012/1849 Reg.2

2008–cont.

2349. Nitrate Pollution Prevention Regulations 2008–*cont.*
Reg.8, revoked: SI 2012/ 1849 Reg.2
Reg.9, revoked: SI 2012/ 1849 Reg.2
Reg.10, revoked: SI 2012/ 1849 Reg.2
Reg.11 A, added: SI 2012/ 1849 Reg.2
Reg.11 B, added: SI 2012/ 1849 Reg.2
Reg.11 C, added: SI 2012/ 1849 Reg.2
Reg.11 D, added: SI 2012/ 1849 Reg.2
Reg.11 E, added: SI 2012/ 1849 Reg.2
Reg.47 A, added: SI 2012/ 1849 Reg.2

2361. Housing (Right to Manage) (England) Regulations 2008
applied: SI 2012/ 1821 Reg.22, Reg.25
revoked: SI 2012/ 1821 Reg.2
Reg.9, applied: SI 2012/ 1821 Reg.23, Reg.24, Reg.25
Reg.11, applied: SI 2012/ 1821 Reg.23
Reg.11, referred to: SI 2012/ 1821 Reg.23
Reg.12, applied: SI 2012/ 1821 Reg.24
Reg.12, referred to: SI 2012/ 1821 Reg.24
Reg.13, applied: SI 2012/ 1821 Reg.25
Reg.14, applied: SI 2012/ 1821 Reg.25
Reg.15, applied: SI 2012/ 1821 Reg.25
Reg.16, applied: SI 2012/ 1821 Reg.25
Reg.17, applied: SI 2012/ 1821 Reg.25
Reg.18, applied: SI 2012/ 1821 Reg.25
Reg.19, applied: SI 2012/ 1821 Reg.25
Reg.20, applied: SI 2012/ 1821 Reg.25

2363. Energy Performance of Buildings (Certificates and Inspections) (England and Wales) (Amendment No.2) Regulations 2008
revoked: SI 2012/ 3118 Sch.3

2367. Removal and Disposal of Vehicles (Traffic Officers) (England) Regulations 2008
Reg.8, amended: SI 2012/ 2278 Art.6

2428. Employment and Support Allowance (Miscellaneous Amendments) Regulations 2008
applied: SI 2012/ 3144 Sch.1 para.10

2436. Mental Health (Approval of Persons to be Approved Mental Health Professionals) (Wales) Regulations 2008
Sch.1 para.1, amended: SI 2012/ 1479 Sch.1 para.57

2439. Mental Health (Hospital, Guardianship, Community Treatment and Consent to Treatment) (Wales) Regulations 2008
Reg.40, amended: SI 2012/ 1265 Reg.2
Sch.1, amended: SI 2012/ 1265 Reg.2

2551. Child Support Information Regulations 2008
Reg.2, amended: SI 2012/ 2785 Reg.8
Reg.2, revoked (in part): SI 2012/ 2785 Reg.8
Reg.3, amended: SI 2012/ 2007 Sch.1 para.116
Reg.4, amended: SI 2012/ 2007 Sch.1 para.116
Reg.5, amended: SI 2012/ 2007 Sch.1 para.116
Reg.6, amended: SI 2012/ 2007 Sch.1 para.116
Reg.7, revoked (in part): SI 2012/ 2785 Reg.8
Reg.8, amended: SI 2012/ 2007 Sch.1 para.116
Reg.9, amended: SI 2012/ 2007 Sch.1 para.116
Reg.9A, added: SI 2012/ 2785 Reg.8
Reg.10, amended: SI 2012/ 2007 Sch.1 para.116
Reg.12, amended: SI 2012/ 2007 Sch.1 para.116
Reg.13, amended: SI 2012/ 2007 Sch.1 para.116, SI 2012/ 2785 Reg.8, SI 2012/ 3002 Reg.3
Reg.14, amended: SI 2012/ 725 Art.2
Reg.16, revoked: SI 2012/ 2007 Sch.1 para.116

2553. Nursing and Midwifery Council (Constitution) Order 2008
Art.2, amended: SI 2012/ 2745 Art.2

2008–cont.

2553. Nursing and Midwifery Council (Constitution) Order 2008–*cont.*
Art.3, amended: SI 2012/ 2745 Art.2
Art.5, amended: SI 2012/ 3006 Art.13
Art.10, amended: SI 2012/ 2745 Art.2

2554. General Medical Council (Constitution) Order 2008
Art.2, amended: SI 2012/ 1654 Art.2
Art.5, amended: SI 2012/ 3006 Art.13
Art.8, substituted: SI 2012/ 1654 Art.2
Art.11, amended: SI 2012/ 1654 Art.2

2558. National Information Governance Board Regulations 2008
Reg.1, amended: SI 2012/ 1641 Sch.4 para.16

2562. Air Navigation (Jersey) Order 2008
applied: 2012 c.19 Sch.6 para.4

2643. Non-resident Companies (General Insurance Business) (Amendment) Regulations 2008
revoked: 2012 c.14 Sch.20 para.14

2678. National Insurance Contributions (Application of Part 7 of the Finance Act 2004) (Amendment) Regulations 2008
revoked: SI 2012/ 1868 Reg.29

2682. Income Tax (Deposit-takers and Building Societies) (Interest Payments) Regulations 2008
Reg.4, applied: SI 2012/ 847 Reg.8

2683. Tribunals, Courts and Enforcement Act 2007 (Transitional and Consequential Provisions) Order 2008
Sch.1 para.51, revoked (in part): SI 2012/ 1909 Sch.8 para.1
Sch.1 para.52, revoked (in part): SI 2012/ 1909 Sch.8 para.1
Sch.1 para.53, revoked (in part): SI 2012/ 1909 Sch.8 para.1
Sch.1 para.54, revoked (in part): SI 2012/ 1909 Sch.8 para.1
Sch.1 para.55, revoked (in part): SI 2012/ 1909 Sch.8 para.1
Sch.1 para.203, revoked (in part): SI 2012/ 1033 Sch.3

2685. Tribunal Procedure (First-tier Tribunal) (Social Entitlement Chamber) Rules 2008
applied: SI 2012/ 2677 Reg.14, Sch.1 para.2, Sch.1 para.3
referred to: SI 2012/ 2677 Sch.1 para.2
Part 2 r.19, amended: SI 2012/ 2007 Sch.1 para.117
Part 3 r.23, amended: SI 2012/ 500 r.4
Sch.1, amended: SI 2012/ 2785 Reg.9

2688. Income Tax (Interest Payments) (Information Powers) (Amendment) Regulations 2008
revoked: SI 2012/ 756 Reg.3

2692. Qualifications for Appointment of Members to the First-tier Tribunal and Upper Tribunal Order 2008
Art.2, amended: SI 2012/ 897 Art.3

2698. Tribunal Procedure (Upper Tribunal) Rules 2008
Part 1 r.1, amended: SI 2012/ 1363 r.5
Part 2 r.19, amended: SI 2012/ 2007 Sch.1 para.118
Part 2 r.20A, amended: SI 2012/ 1363 r.6
Part 3 r.23, amended: SI 2012/ 1363 r.7
Part 3 r.24, amended: SI 2012/ 1363 r.8
Part 3 r.26A, amended: SI 2012/ 500 r.5
Part 7 r.44, amended: SI 2012/ 2890 r.3
r.10, see *Revenue and Customs Commissioners v Anson* [2012] UKUT 59 (TCC), [2012] S.T.C. 1014 (UT (Tax)), Mann, J.

2008–cont.

2698. Tribunal Procedure (Upper Tribunal) Rules 2008–*cont.*
r.45, see *Wychavon DC v EM* [2012] UKUT 12 (AAC), (2012) 15 C.C.L. Rep. 221 (UT (AAC)), Judge Michael Mark
Sch.1 para.1, amended: SI 2012/1363 r.9
Sch.1 para.2, amended: SI 2012/1363 r.9
Sch.1 para.3, amended: SI 2012/1363 r.9
Sch.1 para.4, amended: SI 2012/1363 r.9
Sch.1 para.5, amended: SI 2012/1363 r.9
Sch.1 para.6, amended: SI 2012/1363 r.9
Sch.1 para.7, amended: SI 2012/1363 r.9
Sch.1 para.8, amended: SI 2012/1363 r.9
Sch.1 para.9, amended: SI 2012/1363 r.9
Sch.1 para.10, amended: SI 2012/1363 r.9
Sch.1 para.11, amended: SI 2012/1363 r.9

2699. Tribunal Procedure (First-tier Tribunal) (Health, Education and Social Care Chamber) Rules 2008
applied: SI 2012/1909 Reg.35, Reg.79, Reg.82, Reg.84
Part 3 r.21, amended: SI 2012/1363 r.3
Part 4 r.32, amended: SI 2012/500 r.3
Part 4 r.35, amended: SI 2012/500 r.3
r.8, see *SC v Learning Trust (SEN)* [2012] UKUT 214 (AAC), [2012] E.L.R. 474 (UT (AAC)), Judge Rowland

2770. Non-Domestic Rating (Small Business Relief) (Wales) Order 2008
Art.7, amended: SI 2012/465 Art.2
Art.11, amended: SI 2012/465 Art.2
Art.11A, amended: SI 2012/465 Art.2

2775. Protection of Wrecks (Designation) (England) Order 2008
revoked: SI 2012/1773 Art.3

2834. Appeals from the Upper Tribunal to the Court of Appeal Order 2008
see *JD (Congo) v Secretary of State for the Home Department* [2012] EWCA Civ 327, [2012] 1 W.L.R. 3273 (CA (Civ Div)), Lord Neuberger (M.R.)

2836. Allocation and Transfer of Proceedings Order 2008
Art.15, see *Guidance Note to Family Proceedings Courts* [2012] 1 F.L.R. 432 (Fam Div)
Sch.1, amended: SI 2012/642 Art.3, SI 2012/1955 Art.3

2852. REACH Enforcement Regulations 2008
Sch.3 Part 3 para.2, amended: SI 2012/632 Sch.3

2862. Police (Performance) Regulations 2008
applied: SI 2012/2630 r.2
revoked: SI 2012/2631 Reg.3
Reg.4, varied: SI 2012/2631 Reg.3

2863. Police Appeals Tribunals Rules 2008
revoked: SI 2012/2630 r.2
varied: SI 2012/2630 r.2
r.2, applied: SI 2012/2630 r.2
r.3, varied: SI 2012/2630 r.2
r.8, varied: SI 2012/2630 r.2
r.19, varied: SI 2012/2630 r.2
r.22, varied: SI 2012/2630 r.2

2864. Police (Conduct) Regulations 2008
applied: SI 2012/2630 r.2
revoked: SI 2012/2632 Reg.2
varied: SI 2012/2632 Reg.2
Reg.2, applied: SI 2012/2632 Reg.2
Reg.3, varied: SI 2012/2632 Sch.1 para.3
Reg.7, applied: SI 2012/1204 Reg.16
Reg.22, applied: SI 2012/1204 Reg.16

2008–cont.

2864. Police (Conduct) Regulations 2008–*cont.*
Reg.25, varied: SI 2012/2632 Sch.1 para.4
Reg.26, varied: SI 2012/2632 Sch.1 para.5
Reg.26A, applied: SI 2012/2632 Reg.2
Reg.26A, varied: SI 2012/2632 Sch.1 para.6, Sch.1 para.7
Reg.27, varied: SI 2012/2632 Sch.1 para.5
Reg.34, applied: SI 2012/2632 Reg.2
Reg.34, varied: SI 2012/2632 Sch.1 para.6
Reg.34A, varied: SI 2012/2632 Sch.1 para.6
Reg.35, applied: SI 2012/2632 Reg.2
Reg.35, varied: SI 2012/2632 Sch.1 para.6
Reg.36, varied: SI 2012/2632 Sch.1 para.6
Reg.47, varied: SI 2012/2632 Sch.1 para.5
Reg.47A, applied: SI 2012/2632 Reg.2
Reg.47A, varied: SI 2012/2632 Sch.1 para.6, Sch.1 para.8
Reg.48, varied: SI 2012/2632 Sch.1 para.5
Reg.54, applied: SI 2012/2632 Reg.2
Reg.54, varied: SI 2012/2632 Sch.1 para.6
Reg.54A, varied: SI 2012/2632 Sch.1 para.6
Reg.55, applied: SI 2012/2632 Reg.2
Reg.55, varied: SI 2012/2632 Sch.1 para.6
Reg.56, varied: SI 2012/2632 Sch.1 para.6
Reg.58, varied: SI 2012/2632 Sch.1 para.9

2866. Police (Complaints and Misconduct) (Amendment) Regulations 2008
revoked: SI 2012/1204 Reg.2

2927. Council for Healthcare Regulatory Excellence (Appointment, Procedure etc.) Regulations 2008
Reg.1, amended: SI 2012/2672 Art.4
Reg.2, amended: SI 2012/1479 Sch.1 para.56, SI 2012/3006 Art.13
Reg.2, applied: SI 2012/1480 Art.16

2975. Rail Vehicle Accessibility Exemption Orders (Parliamentary Procedures) Regulations 2008
Reg.5, applied: SI 2012/105

2998. Pre-release Access to Official Statistics Order 2008
Sch.1 Part 1 para.3, varied: 2012 c.11 s.12
Sch.1 Part 2 para.15, varied: 2012 c.11 s.12

3022. Local Government (Structural Changes) (Finance) Regulations 2008
Part 4, applied: SI 2012/444 Reg.26
Reg.3, amended: SI 2012/20 Reg.3
Reg.4, amended: SI 2012/20 Reg.4
Reg.12, amended: SI 2012/20 Reg.5, SI 2012/2914 Reg.12
Reg.15, amended: SI 2012/20 Reg.6
Reg.15A, added: SI 2012/20 Reg.7
Reg.16, amended: SI 2012/20 Reg.8
Sch.1 para.1, revoked (in part): SI 2012/20 Reg.9
Sch.1 para.2, amended: SI 2012/20 Reg.9
Sch.2 para.1, amended: SI 2012/20 Sch.1
Sch.2 para.2, amended: SI 2012/20 Sch.1
Sch.2 para.2, referred to: SI 2012/444 Reg.26
Sch.2 para.3, amended: SI 2012/20 Sch.1
Sch.2 para.3, referred to: SI 2012/444 Reg.26
Sch.2 para.4, amended: SI 2012/20 Sch.1
Sch.2 para.4, referred to: SI 2012/444 Reg.26
Sch.2 para.5, amended: SI 2012/20 Sch.1
Sch.2 para.6, amended: SI 2012/20 Sch.1
Sch.2 para.7, amended: SI 2012/20 Sch.1
Sch.2 para.8, amended: SI 2012/20 Sch.1
Sch.2 para.8, amended: SI 2012/20 Sch.1, SI 2012/2914 Reg.12
Sch.2 para.9, amended: SI 2012/20 Sch.1

2008–cont.

3022. Local Government (Structural Changes) (Finance) Regulations 2008–*cont.*
Sch.2 para.9, amended: SI 2012/20 Sch.1, SI 2012/2914 Reg.12
Sch.2 para.10, amended: SI 2012/20 Sch.1
Sch.2 para.10, amended: SI 2012/20 Sch.1, SI 2012/2914 Reg.12
Sch.2 para.11, amended: SI 2012/20 Sch.1
Sch.2 para.12, amended: SI 2012/20 Sch.1
Sch.2 para.13, amended: SI 2012/20 Sch.1
Sch.2 para.14, amended: SI 2012/20 Sch.1
Sch.3 Part 1 para.1, added: SI 2012/20 Sch.2
Sch.3 Part 1 para.2, added: SI 2012/20 Sch.2
Sch.3 Part 1 para.3, added: SI 2012/20 Sch.2
Sch.3 Part 1 para.4, added: SI 2012/20 Sch.2
Sch.3 Part 1 para.5, added: SI 2012/20 Sch.2
Sch.3 Part 1 para.6, added: SI 2012/20 Sch.2
Sch.3 Part 1 para.7, added: SI 2012/20 Sch.2
Sch.3 Part 1 para.8, added: SI 2012/20 Sch.2
Sch.3 Part 2 para.9, added: SI 2012/20 Sch.2
Sch.3 Part 2 para.10, added: SI 2012/20 Sch.2
Sch.3 Part 2 para.11, added: SI 2012/20 Sch.2
Sch.3 Part 2 para.12, added: SI 2012/20 Sch.2
Sch.3 Part 2 para.13, added: SI 2012/20 Sch.2
Sch.3 Part 2 para.14, added: SI 2012/20 Sch.2
Sch.3 Part 2 para.15, added: SI 2012/20 Sch.2
Sch.3 Part 2 para.16, added: SI 2012/20 Sch.2
Sch.3 Part 3 para.17, added: SI 2012/20 Sch.2

3047. General Chiropractic Council (Constitution) Order 2008
Art.5, amended: SI 2012/3006 Art.13

3048. Immigration (Biometric Registration) Regulations 2008
Reg.2, substituted: SI 2012/594 Reg.3
Reg.3, substituted: SI 2012/594 Reg.4
Reg.4, revoked: SI 2012/594 Reg.5
Reg.8, amended: SI 2012/594 Reg.6
Reg.13, amended: SI 2012/594 Reg.7
Reg.21, amended: SI 2012/594 Reg.8
Reg.22, amended: SI 2012/594 Reg.9
Reg.23, substituted: SI 2012/594 Reg.10

3080. National Child Measurement Programme Regulations 2008
Reg.2, amended: SI 2012/979 Sch.1 para.23

3082. Collaboration Arrangements (Maintained Schools and Further Education Bodies) (Wales) Regulations 2008
revoked: SI 2012/2655 Reg.2

3089. School Admissions (Admission Arrangements) (England) Regulations 2008
revoked: SI 2012/8 Reg.3

3090. School Admissions (Co-ordination of Admission Arrangements) (England) Regulations 2008
applied: SI 2012/8 Reg.31
revoked: SI 2012/8 Reg.3

3091. School Admissions (Local Authority Reports and Admission Forums) (England) Regulations 2008
revoked: SI 2012/8 Reg.3

3092. Education (Admissions Appeals Arrangements)(England)(Amendment) Regulations 2008
revoked: SI 2012/9 Reg.4

3093. School Information (England) Regulations 2008
Reg.2, amended: SI 2012/1124 Reg.2
Reg.5, amended: SI 2012/979 Sch.1 para.24
Reg.6, amended: SI 2012/979 Sch.1 para.24
Reg.9, amended: SI 2012/979 Sch.1 para.24

2008–cont.

3093. School Information (England) Regulations 2008–*cont.*
Reg.10, substituted: SI 2012/1124 Reg.2
Reg.11, amended: SI 2012/1124 Reg.2
Sch.2 Part 1 para.2, amended: SI 2012/8 Reg.4
Sch.2 Part 2 para.15, revoked (in part): SI 2012/8 Reg.4
Sch.3 Part 2 para.13, amended: SI 2012/979 Sch.1 para.24
Sch.3 Part 2 para.15, amended: SI 2012/979 Sch.1 para.24
Sch.4 para.1, added: SI 2012/1124 Reg.2
Sch.4 para.2, added: SI 2012/1124 Reg.2
Sch.4 para.3, added: SI 2012/1124 Reg.2
Sch.4 para.4, added: SI 2012/1124 Reg.2
Sch.4 para.5, added: SI 2012/1124 Reg.2
Sch.4 para.6, added: SI 2012/1124 Reg.2
Sch.4 para.7, added: SI 2012/1124 Reg.2
Sch.4 para.8, added: SI 2012/1124 Reg.2
Sch.4 para.9, added: SI 2012/1124 Reg.2
Sch.4 para.10, added: SI 2012/1124 Reg.2
Sch.4 para.11, added: SI 2012/1124 Reg.2
Sch.4 para.12, added: SI 2012/1124 Reg.2

3095. Parish Councils (Power to Promote Well-being) (Prescribed Conditions) Order 2008
Art.4, applied: SI 2012/1008 Art.8

3097. Medicines for Human Use (Marketing Authorisations Etc.) Amendment Regulations 2008
revoked: SI 2012/1916 Sch.35

3115. Parliamentary Commissioner Order 2008
varied: SI 2012/147 Art.7

3121. Air Navigation (Guernsey) (Revocation) Order 2008
applied: 2012 c.19 Sch.6 para.4

3131. Medical Profession (Miscellaneous Amendments) Order 2008
Art.1, enabled: SI 2012/2686

3133. Air Navigation (Environmental Standards For Non-EASA Aircraft) Order 2008
applied: 2012 c.19 Sch.6 para.4

3143. Nitrate Pollution Prevention (Wales) Regulations 2008
Reg.2, substituted: SI 2012/1238 Reg.2
Reg.7, substituted: SI 2012/1238 Reg.3
Reg.8, substituted: SI 2012/1238 Reg.3
Reg.9, substituted: SI 2012/1238 Reg.3
Reg.10, substituted: SI 2012/1238 Reg.3

3148. Nursing and Midwifery Council (Midwifery and Practice Committees) (Constitution) Rules Order of Council 2008
Sch.1, amended: SI 2012/3006 Art.13

3159. Authorised Investment Funds (Tax) (Amendment No 3) Regulations 2008
Reg.1, amended: SI 2012/519 Reg.9
Reg.17, amended: SI 2012/519 Reg.9
Reg.30, revoked: SI 2012/519 Reg.9

3192. Wireless Telegraphy (Spectrum Trading) (Amendment) (No.3) Regulations 2008
revoked: SI 2012/2187 Sch.1

3193. Wireless Telegraphy (Register) (Amendment) (No.3) Regulations 2008
revoked: SI 2012/2186 Sch.1

3202. Town and Country Planning (Trees) (Amendment No 2) (England) Regulations 2008
revoked: SI 2012/605 Reg.26

3206. Spirit Drinks Regulations 2008
Sch.2 Part 2, amended: SI 2012/1809 Sch.1 Part 2

2008–cont.

3231. Export Control Order 2008
Art.2, amended: SI 2012/1910 Sch.1 para.1
Art.2A, added: SI 2012/1910 Sch.1 para.2
Art.4A, added: SI 2012/929 Art.3
Art.4A, amended: SI 2012/1910 Sch.1 para.3
Art.14A, added: SI 2012/1910 Sch.1 para.4
Art.17, amended: SI 2012/929 Art.3, SI 2012/1910 Sch.1 para.5
Art.28, amended: SI 2012/1910 Sch.1 para.6
Art.28A, added: SI 2012/1910 Sch.1 para.7
Art.29, amended: SI 2012/1910 Sch.1 para.8
Art.30, amended: SI 2012/1910 Sch.1 para.9
Art.33A, added: SI 2012/1910 Sch.1 para.10
Art.37, amended: SI 2012/1910 Sch.1 para.11
Art.38, amended: SI 2012/1910 Sch.1 para.12
Art.41, amended: SI 2012/929 Art.3
Art.46, added: SI 2012/1910 Sch.1 para.13
Sch.1 Part 2 para.10, amended: SI 2012/1910 Sch.1 para.14
Sch.1 Part 2 para.12, amended: SI 2012/1910 Sch.1 para.14
Sch.1 Part 2 para.14, amended: SI 2012/1910 Sch.1 para.14
Sch.2 Part 1, amended: SI 2012/1910 Sch.1 para.15
Sch.3, amended: SI 2012/1910 Sch.1 para.16

3256. General Teaching Council for England (Disciplinary Functions) (Amendment) Regulations 2008
revoked: SI 2012/1153 Sch.1

3258. Health Service Branded Medicines (Control of Prices and Supply of Information) (No.2) Regulations 2008
Reg.1, amended: SI 2012/1916 Sch.34 para.97
Reg.2, amended: SI 2012/2791 Reg.2

3261. Overview and Scrutiny (Reference by Councillors) (Excluded Matters) (England) Order 2008
revoked: SI 2012/1022 Art.5

3265. Safeguarding Vulnerable Groups Act 2006 (Prescribed Information) Regulations 2008
referred to: SI 2012/2112 Reg.10
Reg.2, amended: SI 2012/2112 Reg.11, SI 2012/3006 Art.13
Reg.3, amended: SI 2012/2112 Reg.12
Reg.4, amended: SI 2012/2112 Reg.13, Reg.14
Reg.5, amended: SI 2012/2112 Reg.15
Reg.6, amended: SI 2012/3006 Art.13
Reg.6, revoked: SI 2012/2112 Reg.16
Reg.8, revoked: SI 2012/2112 Reg.16
Reg.10, revoked: SI 2012/2112 Reg.16
Reg.13, amended: SI 2012/3006 Art.13
Sch.1 para.1, amended: SI 2012/2112 Reg.17
Sch.1 para.1, revoked (in part): SI 2012/2112 Reg.17
Sch.1 para.2, amended: SI 2012/2112 Reg.18
Sch.1 para.4, amended: SI 2012/2112 Reg.19
Sch.1 para.5, amended: SI 2012/3006 Art.13
Sch.1 para.6, amended: SI 2012/2112 Reg.20, SI 2012/3006 Art.13
Sch.1 para.9, amended: SI 2012/2112 Reg.21
Sch.1 para.10, amended: SI 2012/3006 Art.13

3268. Charities Act 1993 (Exception from Registration) Regulations 2008
Reg.2, amended: SI 2012/3012 Sch.4 para.5

2009

5. Local Government (Structural Changes) (Further Financial Provisions and Amendment) Regulations 2009
Reg.3, amended: SI 2012/460 Sch.1 para.16
Reg.6, amended: SI 2012/460 Sch.1 para.17

14. Wireless Telegraphy (Register) (Amendment) Regulations 2009
revoked: SI 2012/2186 Sch.1

26. General Chiropractic Council (Constitution of the Statutory Committees) Rules Order of Council 2009
Sch.1, amended: SI 2012/3006 Art.13

37. Safeguarding Vulnerable Groups Act 2006 (Prescribed Criteria and Miscellaneous Provisions) Regulations 2009
Sch.1 para.1, amended: SI 2012/2160 Reg.3
Sch.1 para.2, amended: SI 2012/2160 Reg.3
Sch.1 para.3, amended: SI 2012/2160 Reg.3
Sch.1 para.4, amended: SI 2012/2160 Reg.3

56. Transfer of Tribunal Functions and Revenue and Customs Appeals Order 2009
see *Atlantic Electronics Ltd v Revenue and Customs Commissioners* [2012] UKUT 45 (TCC), [2012] S.T.C. 931 (UT (Tax)), Warren, J.; see *R. (on the application of ToTel Ltd) v First-tier Tribunal (Tax Chamber)* [2011] EWHC 652 (Admin), [2012] Q.B. 358 (QBD (Admin)), Simon, J.
Sch.1 para.221, see *R. (on the application of ToTel Ltd) v First-tier Tribunal (Tax Chamber)* [2012] EWCA Civ 1401, [2012] B.V.C. 333 (CA (Civ Div)), Lord Neuberger (M.R.)
Sch.3 para.7, see *Atlantic Electronics Ltd v Revenue and Customs Commissioners* [2012] UKUT 45 (TCC), [2012] S.T.C. 931 (UT (Tax)), Warren, J.

119. Local Government (Structural Changes) (Areas and Membership of Public Bodies in Bedfordshire and Cheshire) Order 2009
Art.2, amended: SI 2012/2879 Art.3
Art.8, amended: SI 2012/2879 Art.3
Sch.1 para.1, amended: SI 2012/2879 Art.3

153. Environmental Damage (Prevention and Remediation) Regulations 2009
Reg.10, amended: SI 2012/630 Reg.18
Reg.12, amended: SI 2012/2897 Art.26

154. Adoption Agencies (Scotland) Regulations 2009
applied: SI 2012/3145 Sch.1

200. Occupational Pension Schemes (Levy Ceiling Earnings Percentage Increase) Order 2009
revoked: SI 2012/528 Sch.1

203. Police Act 1997 (Criminal Records) (Electronic Communications) Order 2009
Art.12, revoked: 2012 c.9 Sch.10 Part 5
Art.13, revoked: 2012 c.9 Sch.10 Part 5
Art.14, revoked: 2012 c.9 Sch.10 Part 5
Art.15, revoked: 2012 c.9 Sch.10 Part 5

205. Plastic Materials and Articles in Contact with Food (England) Regulations 2009
revoked: SI 2012/2619 Reg.31

208. National Insurance Contributions (Application of Part 7 of the Finance Act 2004) (Amendment) Regulations 2009
revoked: SI 2012/1868 Reg.29

209. Payment Services Regulations 2009
applied: SI 2012/1128 Art.4
Reg.2, amended: SI 2012/1809 Sch.1 Part 2
Reg.13, amended: SI 2012/1791 Reg.3
Reg.14, amended: SI 2012/1791 Reg.3
Reg.29, amended: SI 2012/1791 Reg.3

2009–cont.

209. Payment Services Regulations 2009–*cont.*
Reg.83, revoked: 2012 c.9 Sch.2 para.15, Sch.10 Part 2
Reg.125A, added: SI 2012/ 1791 Reg.3
Sch.3 Part 2 para.19, amended: SI 2012/ 1741 Sch.1 para.11, SI 2012/ 1791 Reg.3

214. Companies (Disclosure of Address) Regulations 2009
Reg.2, applied: SI 2012/ 1907 Sch.3 para.1
Reg.3, applied: SI 2012/ 1907 Sch.3 para.1
Sch.1, amended: SI 2012/ 700 Sch.1 para.20

216. Ozone-Depleting Substances (Qualifications) Regulations 2009
Reg.7, amended: SI 2012/ 2897 Art.27

260. Control of Salmonella in Broiler Flocks Order 2009
Art.2, amended: SI 2012/ 2897 Art.28
Art.3, amended: SI 2012/ 2897 Art.28
Art.5, amended: SI 2012/ 2897 Art.28
Art.8, amended: SI 2012/ 2897 Art.28
Art.14, amended: SI 2012/ 2897 Art.28

261. Fluorinated Greenhouse Gases Regulations 2009
Reg.56, amended: SI 2012/ 2897 Art.29

263. General Osteopathic Council (Constitution) Order 2009
Art.5, amended: SI 2012/ 3006 Art.13

273. Tribunal Procedure (First-tier Tribunal) (Tax Chamber) Rules 2009
see *Atlantic Electronics Ltd v Revenue and Customs Commissioners* [2012] UKUT 45 (TCC), [2012] S.T.C. 931 (UT (Tax)), Warren, J.; see *Foulser v Revenue and Customs Commissioners* [2012] S.F.T.D. 94 (FTT (Tax)), Judge Roger Berner
r.1, see *G Wilson (Glaziers) Ltd v Revenue and Customs Commissioners* [2012] UKFTT 387 (TC), [2012] S.F.T.D. 1117 (FTT (Tax)), Judge Peter Kempster
r.2, see *Data Select Ltd v Revenue and Customs Commissioners* [2012] UKUT 187 (TCC), [2012] S.T.C. 2195 (UT (Tax)), Morgan, J.; see *Foulser v Revenue and Customs Commissioners* [2012] S.F.T.D. 94 (FTT (Tax)), Judge Roger Berner
r.5, see *DDR Distributions Ltd v Revenue and Customs Commissioners* [2012] UKFTT 443 (TC), [2012] S.F.T.D. 1249 (FTT (Tax)), Judge Barbara Mosedale; see *Foulser v Revenue and Customs Commissioners* [2012] S.F.T.D. 94 (FTT (Tax)), Judge Roger Berner
r.6, see *DDR Distributions Ltd v Revenue and Customs Commissioners* [2012] UKFTT 443 (TC), [2012] S.F.T.D. 1249 (FTT (Tax)), Judge Barbara Mosedale
r.8, see *Foulser v Revenue and Customs Commissioners* [2012] S.F.T.D. 94 (FTT (Tax)), Judge Roger Berner
r.9, see *New Miles Ltd v Revenue and Customs Commissioners* [2012] UKFTT 33 (TC), [2012] S.F.T.D. 695 (FTT (Tax)), Judge Peter Kempster
r.10, see *Atlantic Electronics Ltd v Revenue and Customs Commissioners* [2012] UKUT 45 (TCC), [2012] S.T.C. 931 (UT (Tax)), Warren, J.; see *Catana v Revenue and Customs Commissioners* [2012] UKUT 172 (TCC), [2012] S.T.C. 2138 (UT (Tax)), Judge Colin Bishopp; see *G Wilson (Glaziers) Ltd v Revenue and Customs Commissioners* [2012]

2009–cont.

273. Tribunal Procedure (First-tier Tribunal) (Tax Chamber) Rules 2009–*cont.*
r.10–*cont.*
UKFTT 387 (TC), [2012] S.F.T.D. 1117 (FTT (Tax)), Judge Peter Kempster
r.20, see *G Wilson (Glaziers) Ltd v Revenue and Customs Commissioners* [2012] UKFTT 387 (TC), [2012] S.F.T.D. 1117 (FTT (Tax)), Judge Peter Kempster
r.23, see *G Wilson (Glaziers) Ltd v Revenue and Customs Commissioners* [2012] UKFTT 387 (TC), [2012] S.F.T.D. 1117 (FTT (Tax)), Judge Peter Kempster
r.32, see *A v Revenue and Customs Commissioners* [2012] UKFTT 541 (TC), [2012] S.F.T.D. 1257 (FTT (Tax)), Judge Colin Bishopp

303. Street Works (Charges for Unreasonably Prolonged Occupation of the Highway) (England) Regulations 2009
applied: SI 2012/ 2541 Sch.1, SI 2012/ 2547 Sch.1, SI 2012/ 2548 Sch.1, SI 2012/ 2549 Sch.1
disapplied: SI 2012/ 425 Reg.5
Reg.3, amended: SI 2012/ 2272 Reg.3
Reg.6, applied: SI 2012/ 425 Reg.5
Reg.9, substituted: SI 2012/ 2272 Reg.4

309. Local Authority Social Services and National Health Service Complaints (England) Regulations 2009
applied: SI 2012/ 1909 Sch.4 para.34, Sch.5 para.24
Reg.2, amended: SI 2012/ 1909 Sch.8 para.11
Sch.1 para.1, revoked: SI 2012/ 1909 Sch.8 para.9

395. Independent Review of Determinations (Adoption and Fostering) Regulations 2009
Reg.2, amended: SI 2012/ 1479 Sch.1 para.86

401. Town and Country Planning (Local Development) (England) (Amendment) Regulations 2009
revoked: SI 2012/ 767 Reg.37

442. General Optical Council (Constitution) Order 2009
Art.5, amended: SI 2012/ 3006 Art.13

462. Health and Social Care Act 2008 (Commencement No.9, Consequential Amendments and Transitory, Transitional and Saving Provisions) Order 2009
Sch.3 para.8, amended: SI 2012/ 1641 Sch.4 para.17

468. General Osteopathic Council (Constitution of the Statutory Committees) Rules Order of Council 2009
Sch.1, amended: SI 2012/ 3006 Art.13

470. Education (Student Loans) (Repayment) Regulations 2009
Part 3, applied: SI 2012/ 1309 Reg.1
Part 4, applied: SI 2012/ 1309 Reg.1
Reg.2, amended: SI 2012/ 836 Reg.3
Reg.3, amended: SI 2012/ 1309 Reg.3
Reg.3, substituted: SI 2012/ 1309 Reg.3
Reg.9, amended: SI 2012/ 1309 Reg.4
Reg.15, amended: SI 2012/ 1309 Reg.5
Reg.18A, added: SI 2012/ 1309 Reg.6
Reg.19, amended: SI 2012/ 1309 Reg.7
Reg.20, amended: SI 2012/ 1309 Reg.8
Reg.21, amended: SI 2012/ 1309 Reg.9
Reg.21A, added: SI 2012/ 1309 Reg.10
Reg.29, amended: SI 2012/ 1309 Reg.11
Reg.33, amended: SI 2012/ 836 Reg.4
Reg.38, substituted: SI 2012/ 836 Reg.5
Reg.41, amended: SI 2012/ 836 Reg.6
Reg.41A, added: SI 2012/ 836 Reg.7

2009– cont.

470. Education (Student Loans) (Repayment) Regulations 2009– *cont.*
Reg.43, substituted: SI 2012/836 Reg.8
Reg.43A, added: SI 2012/836 Reg.9
Reg.50, amended: SI 2012/836 Reg.10
Reg.54, amended: SI 2012/836 Reg.11
Reg.54, revoked (in part): SI 2012/836 Reg.11
Reg.54A, added: SI 2012/836 Reg.12
Reg.55, amended: SI 2012/836 Reg.13
Reg.56, amended: SI 2012/836 Reg.14
Reg.59, amended: SI 2012/836 Reg.15
Reg.59A, added: SI 2012/836 Reg.16
Reg.59B, added: SI 2012/836 Reg.16
Reg.59C, added: SI 2012/836 Reg.16
Reg.59D, added: SI 2012/836 Reg.16
Reg.59E, added: SI 2012/836 Reg.16
Reg.59F, added: SI 2012/836 Reg.16
Reg.67, amended: SI 2012/836 Reg.17
Reg.71, amended: SI 2012/1309 Reg.12
Reg.75, amended: SI 2012/1309 Reg.13
Reg.76, amended: SI 2012/1309 Reg.14
Reg.76, revoked (in part): SI 2012/1309 Reg.14
Sch.1, amended: SI 2012/836 Reg.18
Sch.2 para.1, added: SI 2012/836 Reg.19
Sch.2 para.2, added: SI 2012/836 Reg.19
Sch.2 para.3, added: SI 2012/836 Reg.19
Sch.2 para.4, added: SI 2012/836 Reg.19
Sch.2 para.5, added: SI 2012/836 Reg.19

476. Government Resources and Accounts Act 2000 (Audit of Non-profit-making Companies) Order 2009
Art.5, amended: SI 2012/1809 Sch.1 Part 2
Sch.1, amended: SI 2012/854 Art.5, Art.7

481. Plastic Materials and Articles in Contact with Food (Wales) Regulations 2009
revoked: SI 2012/2705 Reg.30

537. Scotland Act 1998 (Designation of Receipts) Order 2009
Art.2, varied: 2012 c.11 s.12

549. Industrial Training Levy (Construction Industry Training Board) Order 2009
see *Construction Industry Training Board v Beacon Roofing Ltd* [2011] EWCA Civ 1203, [2012] I.C.R. 672 (CA (Civ Div)), Longmore, L.J.
Art.2, see *Construction Industry Training Board v Beacon Roofing Ltd* [2011] EWCA Civ 1203, [2012] I.C.R. 672 (CA (Civ Div)), Longmore, L.J.
Art.8, see *Construction Industry Training Board v Beacon Roofing Ltd* [2011] EWCA Civ 1203, [2012] I.C.R. 672 (CA (Civ Div)), Longmore, L.J.

581. Restriction of the Use of Certain Hazardous Substances in Electrical and Electronic Equipment (Amendment) Regulations 2009
revoked: SI 2012/3032 Reg.7

599. National Health Service (Pharmaceutical Services and Local Pharmaceutical Services) Amendment Regulations 2009
Reg.2, revoked: SI 2012/1909 Sch.8 para.9

611. Tax Avoidance Schemes (Information) (Amendment) Regulations 2009
revoked: SI 2012/1836 Sch.1

612. National Insurance Contributions (Application of Part 7 of the Finance Act 2004) (Amendment) (No.2) Regulations 2009
revoked: SI 2012/1868 Reg.29

667. Education (Recognised Bodies) (Wales) (Amendment) Order 2009
revoked: SI 2012/1260 Art.3

2009– cont.

669. Co-ordination of Regulatory Enforcement (Regulatory Functions in Scotland and Northern Ireland) Order 2009
Sch.1 Part 1, amended: SI 2012/1916 Sch.34 para.100
Sch.1 Part 2, amended: SI 2012/1916 Sch.34 para.100
Sch.1 Part 4, amended: SI 2012/1916 Sch.34 para.100
Sch.2 Part 2, amended: SI 2012/1916 Sch.34 para.100

692. Pensions Increase (Review) Order 2009
applied: SI 2012/782 Art.3, Art.4

710. Education (Listed Bodies) (Wales) (Amendment) Order 2009
revoked: SI 2012/1259 Art.3

711. Department for Transport (Fees) Order 2009
applied: SI 2012/306, SI 2012/308
Sch.1 Part 3 para.21, referred to: SI 2012/307
Sch.1 Part 3 para.22, referred to: SI 2012/307
Sch.1 Part 3 para.23, referred to: SI 2012/307
Sch.1 Part 3 para.24, referred to: SI 2012/307
Sch.1 Part 3 para.25, referred to: SI 2012/307
Sch.1 Part 3 para.26, referred to: SI 2012/307
Sch.1 Part 3 para.27, referred to: SI 2012/307
Sch.1 Part 3 para.28, referred to: SI 2012/305
Sch.1 Part 3 para.29, referred to: SI 2012/305
Sch.1 Part 3 para.30, referred to: SI 2012/305
Sch.1 Part 3 para.31, referred to: SI 2012/305
Sch.1 Part 3 para.32, referred to: SI 2012/305
Sch.1 Part 3 para.33, referred to: SI 2012/305
Sch.1 Part 3 para.34, referred to: SI 2012/305
Sch.1 Part 3 para.35, referred to: SI 2012/305
Sch.1 Part 4 para.42, referred to: SI 2012/304
Sch.1 Part 4 para.43, referred to: SI 2012/304
Sch.2, referred to: SI 2012/304, SI 2012/307

716. Chemicals (Hazard Information and Packaging for Supply) Regulations 2009
applied: SI 2012/632 Sch.2 para.1, SI 2012/1652 Reg.24

718. Road Vehicles (Individual Approval) (Fees) Regulations 2009
Reg.3A, added: SI 2012/1271 Reg.2

779. Local Health Boards (Constitution, Membership and Procedures) (Wales) Regulations 2009
Reg.2, amended: SI 2012/1641 Sch.3 para.14
Sch.2 Part 1 para.1, amended: SI 2012/1641 Sch.3 para.14

783. Mental Capacity (Deprivation of Liberty Assessments, Standard Authorisations and Disputes about Residence) (Wales) Regulations 2009
Reg.5, amended: SI 2012/1479 Sch.1 para.59

845. Land Registration Fee Order 2009
revoked: SI 2012/1969 Art.15

886. Iran (United Nations Sanctions) Order 2009
Sch.1, amended: SI 2012/362 Sch.1

888. Judicial Proceedings in Specified Overseas Territories (Restrictive Measures) Order 2009
Art.1, amended: SI 2012/362 Sch.1
Art.2, amended: SI 2012/362 Sch.1
Art.4, amended: SI 2012/362 Sch.1

890. Waste Batteries and Accumulators Regulations 2009
Sch.4 Part 2 para.12, amended: SSI 2012/360 Sch.11 para.21

2009–cont.

995. Environmental Damage (Prevention and Remediation) (Wales) Regulations 2009
Reg.10, amended: SI 2012/630 Reg.19
Reg.11, amended: SI 2012/630 Reg.19
Sch.3 para.1, amended: SI 2012/630 Reg.19
Sch.3 para.1, revoked (in part): SI 2012/630 Reg.19

1024. Town and Country Planning (General Development Procedure) (Amendment) (Wales) Order 2009
revoked: SI 2012/801 Sch.8

1026. Planning (Listed Buildings and Conservation Areas) (Amendment) (Wales) Regulations 2009
revoked: SI 2012/793 Sch.5

1034. Textile Products (Indications of Fibre Content) (Amendment) (No.2) Regulations 2009
revoked: SI 2012/1102 Sch.1

1059. Armed Forces Act 2006 (Transitional Provisions etc) Order 2009
Sch.2 para.2, revoked (in part): 2012 c.10 Sch.9 para.19
Sch.2 para.9A, added: SI 2012/2824 Reg.5
Sch.2 para.13, revoked: SI 2012/2824 Reg.5
Sch.2 para.16, amended: SI 2012/2824 Reg.5

1109. Armed Forces (Forfeitures and Deductions) Regulations 2009
Reg.2, amended: SI 2012/2814 Sch.4 para.9
Reg.8, amended: SI 2012/2814 Sch.4 para.9
Reg.9, amended: SI 2012/2814 Sch.4 para.9

1164. Medicines for Human Use (Miscellaneous Amendments) Regulations 2009
Reg.1, revoked: SI 2012/1916 Sch.35
Reg.2, revoked: SI 2012/1916 Sch.35
Reg.4, revoked: SI 2012/1916 Sch.35

1171. Registered Pension Schemes (Authorised Payments) Regulations 2009
Reg.1, amended: SI 2012/1881 Reg.3
Reg.5A, added: SI 2012/1881 Reg.4
Reg.11A, added: SI 2012/522 Reg.2
Reg.20, added: SI 2012/1881 Reg.5

1174. Export Control (Uzbekistan) (Amendment) Order 2009
revoked: SI 2012/810 Sch.1

1182. Health Care and Associated Professions (Miscellaneous Amendments and Practitioner Psychologists) Order 2009
Art.1, revoked (in part): 2012 c.9 Sch.10 Part 5
Sch.5 Part 1 para.9, revoked (in part): 2012 c.9 s.75, Sch.10 Part 5
Sch.5 Part 3 para.13, revoked (in part): 2012 c.9 Sch.10 Part 5

1299. Swine Vesicular Disease Regulations 2009
Reg.45, amended: SI 2012/2897 Art.30

1300. Nottingham Express Transit System Order 2009
Art.20, amended: SI 2012/1659 Art.2
Art.73, amended: SI 2012/1659 Art.2
Sch.13 para.1, amended: SI 2012/1659 Art.2
Sch.13 para.2, amended: SI 2012/1659 Art.2
Sch.13 para.3, amended: SI 2012/1659 Art.2
Sch.13 para.4, amended: SI 2012/1659 Art.2
Sch.13 para.5, amended: SI 2012/1659 Art.2
Sch.13 para.6, amended: SI 2012/1659 Art.2
Sch.13 para.7, amended: SI 2012/1659 Art.2
Sch.13 para.8, amended: SI 2012/1659 Art.2
Sch.13 para.9, amended: SI 2012/1659 Art.2
Sch.13 para.10, amended: SI 2012/1659 Art.2
Sch.13 para.11, amended: SI 2012/1659 Art.2

2009–cont.

1300. Nottingham Express Transit System Order 2009–cont.
Sch.13 para.12, amended: SI 2012/1659 Art.2
Sch.13 para.13, amended: SI 2012/1659 Art.2
Sch.13 para.14, amended: SI 2012/1659 Art.2
Sch.13 para.15, amended: SI 2012/1659 Art.2
Sch.13 para.16, amended: SI 2012/1659 Art.2
Sch.13 para.17, amended: SI 2012/1659 Art.2
Sch.13 para.18, amended: SI 2012/1659 Art.2
Sch.13 para.19, amended: SI 2012/1659 Art.2
Sch.13 para.20, amended: SI 2012/1659 Art.2
Sch.13 para.21, amended: SI 2012/1659 Art.2
Sch.13 para.22, amended: SI 2012/1659 Art.2
Sch.13 para.23, amended: SI 2012/1659 Art.2
Sch.13 para.24, amended: SI 2012/1659 Art.2
Sch.13 para.25, amended: SI 2012/1659 Art.2

1302. Infrastructure Planning (National Policy Statement Consultation) Regulations 2009
varied: SI 2012/147 Art.7
Reg.2, amended: SI 2012/2732 Reg.3
Reg.3, amended: SI 2012/1659 Art.2, SI 2012/2654 Sch.1, SI 2012/2732 Reg.3
Reg.3, varied: 2012 c.11 s.12

1343. Research and Development (Qualifying Bodies) (Tax) Order 2009
revoked: SI 2012/286 Art.3

1345. Health Professions Council (Constitution) Order 2009
Art.1, amended: SI 2012/1479 Sch.1 para.60
Art.5, amended: SI 2012/3006 Art.13

1347. Magnetic Toys (Safety) (Revocation) Regulations 2009
revoked: SI 2012/1815 Sch.1

1348. Carriage of Dangerous Goods and Use of Transportable Pressure Equipment Regulations 2009
applied: SI 2012/632 Reg.24, Sch.2 para.1

1350. Education (Supply of Information) (Wales) Regulations 2009
Reg.1, amended: SI 2012/3006 Art.25

1355. Health Professions Council (Practice Committees and Miscellaneous Amendments) Rules Order of Council 2009
Sch.1, added: SI 2012/1479 Art.10
Sch.1, amended: SI 2012/1479 Art.10, SI 2012/3006 Art.13

1356. Seed (Conservation Varieties Amendments) (Wales) Regulations 2009
revoked: SI 2012/245 Reg.34

1360. Audit Commission for Local Authorities and the National Health Service in England (Specified Organisations) (England) Order 2009
Art.2, revoked (in part): SI 2012/666 Sch.2

1380. Scotland Act 1998 (Modification of Schedule 4) Order 2009
revoked: 2012 c.11 s.14
Art.2, varied: 2012 c.11 s.12

1385. Public Health Wales National Health Service Trust (Membership and Procedure) Regulations 2009
Reg.1, amended: SI 2012/1641 Sch.3 para.12, Sch.4 para.18
Reg.15, amended: SI 2012/1641 Sch.3 para.12, Sch.4 para.18

1495. Burma/Myanmar (Financial Restrictions) Regulations 2009
Part 3, disapplied: SI 2012/1302 Reg.2
Part 5, disapplied: SI 2012/1302 Reg.2

2009–cont.

1508. **Childcare (Inspections) (Amendment) Regulations 2009**
revoked: SI 2012/1698 Reg.3

1548. **Safeguarding Vulnerable Groups Act 2006 (Miscellaneous Provisions) Regulations 2009**
Reg.2, revoked: SI 2012/2112 Reg.23
Reg.4, revoked: SI 2012/2112 Reg.23

1549. **Early Years Foundation Stage (Welfare Requirements) (Amendment) Regulations 2009**
revoked: SI 2012/938 Reg.13

1554. **Childcare (Provision of Information About Young Children) (England) Regulations 2009**
Reg.7, revoked (in part): SI 2012/765 Art.14

1555. **Education (Student Support) Regulations 2009**
see *R. (on the application of Arogundade) v Secretary of State for Business, Innovation and Skills* [2012] EWHC 2502 (Admin), [2012] E.L.R. 520 (QBD (Admin)), Robin Purchas Q.C.
Sch.1 Pt 2 para.5, see *R (on the application of Arogundade) v Secretary of State for Business, Innovation and Skills* [2012] EWHC 2502 (Admin), [2012] E.L.R. 520 (QBD (Admin)), Robin Purchas Q.C.

1563. **Education (Individual Pupil Information) (Prescribed Persons) (England) Regulations 2009**
Reg.2, amended: SI 2012/979 Sch.1 para.25
Reg.3, amended: SI 2012/979 Sch.1 para.25
Reg.3, revoked (in part): SI 2012/765 Art.15, SI 2012/956 Art.23

1603. **Supreme Court Rules 2009**
Part 6 r.42, amended: SI 2012/1809 Sch.1 Part 2

1735. **Air Navigation (Single European Sky) (Penalties) Order 2009**
applied: 2012 c.19 Sch.6 para.4

1742. **Air Navigation (Amendment) Order 2009**
applied: 2012 c.19 Sch.6 para.4

1749. **North Korea (United Nations Sanctions) Order 2009**
Sch.1, amended: SI 2012/362 Sch.1

1797. **Safeguarding Vulnerable Groups Act 2006 (Miscellaneous Provisions) Order 2009**
Art.2, revoked: SI 2012/2157 Art.3
Art.3, amended: SI 2012/2157 Art.4
Art.3, revoked (in part): SI 2012/2157 Art.4
Art.4, revoked: SI 2012/2157 Art.3

1801. **Overseas Companies Regulations 2009**
referred to: SI 2012/1907 Sch.3 para.3
Part 2, applied: SI 2012/1907 Sch.1 para.4, Sch.1 para.11
Part 3, applied: SI 2012/1907 Sch.1 para.11
Part 5, applied: SI 2012/1907 Sch.1 para.11
Part 6, applied: SI 2012/1907 Sch.1 para.11
Reg.21, applied: SI 2012/1907 Sch.3 para.1
Reg.23, applied: SI 2012/1907 Sch.3 para.1
Reg.24, applied: SI 2012/1907 Sch.3 para.1
Sch.1, amended: SI 2012/700 Sch.1 para.21

1803. **Registrar of Companies and Applications for Striking Off Regulations 2009**
Reg.6, amended: SI 2012/2301 Reg.21
Reg.7, amended: SI 2012/2301 Reg.21
Reg.8, amended: SI 2012/2301 Reg.21

1804. **Limited Liability Partnerships (Application of Companies Act 2006) Regulations 2009**
Reg.9, applied: SI 2012/1907 Sch.1 para.10
Reg.11, applied: SI 2012/1907 Sch.1 para.10
Reg.19, applied: SI 2012/1907 Sch.3 para.1
Reg.30, applied: SI 2012/1907 Sch.1 para.10

2009–cont.

1804. **Limited Liability Partnerships (Application of Companies Act 2006) Regulations 2009**–*cont.*
Reg.51, applied: SI 2012/1907 Sch.1 para.10
Reg.56, applied: SI 2012/1907 Sch.1 para.12
Reg.58, applied: SI 2012/1907 Sch.1 para.10
Reg.61, applied: SI 2012/1907 Sch.2 para.7, Sch.2 para.11, Sch.2 para.12
Reg.63, amended: SI 2012/2301 Reg.22
Reg.66, applied: SI 2012/1907 Sch.1 para.12, Sch.2 para.7, Sch.2 para.11, Sch.2 para.12
Reg.68, amended: SI 2012/2301 Reg.22

1806. **Road Vehicles (Construction and Use) (Amendment) (No.2) Regulations 2009**
revoked: SI 2012/1404 Sch.1

1808. **General Dental Council (Constitution) Order 2009**
Art.2, amended: SI 2012/1655 Art.2
Art.5, amended: SI 2012/3006 Art.13
Art.8, substituted: SI 2012/1655 Art.2
Art.11, amended: SI 2012/1655 Art.2

1813. **General Dental Council (Constitution of Committees) Rules Order of Council 2009**
Sch.1, amended: SI 2012/3006 Art.13

1843. **Criminal Defence Service (Funding) (Amendment) Order 2009**
see *R. v Richards (Costs)* [2012] 5 Costs L.R. 998 (Sen Cts Costs Office), Costs Judge Campbell

1882. **Police Act 1997 (Criminal Records) (No.2) Regulations 2009**
Reg.5, amended: SI 2012/523 Reg.4
Reg.5, substituted: SI 2012/2114 Reg.12
Reg.6, amended: SI 2012/523 Reg.5
Reg.6, substituted: SI 2012/2114 Reg.13

1883. **Terrorism Act 2006 (Disapplication of Section 25) Order 2009**
revoked: 2012 c.9 Sch.10 Part 4

1887. **Community Care, Services for Carers and Children's Services (Direct Payments) (England) Regulations 2009**
see *R. (on the application of KM) v Cambridgeshire CC* [2012] UKSC 23, [2012] P.T.S.R. 1189 (SC), Lord Phillips, J.S.C. (President)

1900. **Energy Performance of Buildings (Certificates and Inspections) (England and Wales) (Amendment) Regulations 2009**
revoked: SI 2012/3118 Sch.3

1905. **Electricity and Gas (Community Energy Saving Programme) Order 2009**
applied: SI 2012/3018 Art.21

1914. **Heavy Goods Vehicles (Charging for the Use of Certain Infrastructure on the Trans-European Road Network) Regulations 2009**
Reg.14, amended: SI 2012/1809 Sch.1 Part 2

1919. **Local Authorities (Overview and Scrutiny Committees) (England) Regulations 2009**
revoked: SI 2012/1021 Reg.10

1922. **Police and Criminal Evidence Act 1984 (Armed Forces) Order 2009**
Art.15, amended: SI 2012/2505 Art.2
Sch.2 para.17, amended: SI 2012/2505 Art.2

1924. **Education (Miscellaneous Amendments relating to Safeguarding Children) (England) Regulations 2009**
Reg.3, revoked: SI 2012/1153 Sch.1

1931. **Solicitors (Non-Contentious Business) Remuneration Order 2009**
applied: SI 2012/1846 Sch.1 Part TABLEf, SI 2012/1847 Sch.1 Part TABLEa, Sch.2 para.1, Sch.2 para.4

2009–cont.

1931. Solicitors (Non-Contentious Business) Remuneration Order 2009–*cont.*
Art.2, amended: SI 2012/171 Art.2

1941. Companies Act 2006 (Consequential Amendments, Transitional Provisions and Savings) Order 2009
Sch.1 para.191, revoked (in part): SI 2012/700 Sch.1 para.22
Sch.1 para.261, amended: 2012 asp 8 s.61

1973. Whole of Government Accounts (Designation of Bodies) Order 2009
varied: SI 2012/147 Art.7

1974. School Teachers Incentive Payments (England) Order 2009
Art.2, amended: SI 2012/765 Art.16

1976. Tribunal Procedure (First-tier Tribunal) (General Regulatory Chamber) Rules 2009
Part 2 r.9, amended: SI 2012/500 r.2
Part 3 r.22, amended: SI 2012/500 r.2

1978. Scottish Parliament (Elections etc.) (Amendment) Order 2009
varied: 2012 c.11 s.3

2037. Corporation Tax (Land Remediation Relief) Order 2009
Art.4, amended: SSI 2012/360 Sch.11 para.22

2039. Lloyd's Underwriters (Equalisation Reserves) (Tax) Regulations 2009
revoked: 2012 c.14 s.30

2048. Port Security Regulations 2009
applied: SI 2012/2607 Art.3, Art.4, Sch.2 para.3, SI 2012/2608 Art.3, Art.4, Sch.2 para.3, SI 2012/2609 Art.3, Art.4, Sch.2 para.3, SI 2012/2610 Art.3, Art.4, Sch.2 para.3, SI 2012/2611 Art.3, Art.4, Sch.2 para.3
Reg.3, applied: SI 2012/2607 Art.2, SI 2012/2608 Art.2, SI 2012/2609 Art.2, SI 2012/2610 Art.2, SI 2012/2611 Art.2

2056. Armed Forces (Powers of Stop and Search, Search, Seizure and Retention) Order 2009
Art.2, amended: SI 2012/2919 Art.3
Art.6, substituted: SI 2012/2919 Art.8
Art.8, amended: SI 2012/2919 Art.4
Art.8, revoked (in part): SI 2012/2919 Art.4
Art.9, amended: SI 2012/2919 Art.5
Art.10, amended: SI 2012/2919 Art.6
Art.18, amended: SI 2012/2919 Art.10
Sch.1 para.1, amended: SI 2012/2919 Art.9
Sch.1 para.2, amended: SI 2012/2919 Art.7, Art.9
Sch.1 para.3, amended: SI 2012/2919 Art.7, Art.9
Sch.1 para.4, amended: SI 2012/2919 Art.9
Sch.1 para.4A, added: SI 2012/2919 Art.9
Sch.1 para.4A, amended: SI 2012/2919 Art.9
Sch.1 para.5, amended: SI 2012/2919 Art.9
Sch.1 para.6, amended: SI 2012/2919 Art.9
Sch.1 para.7, amended: SI 2012/2919 Art.9
Sch.1 para.8, amended: SI 2012/2919 Art.9
Sch.1 para.9, amended: SI 2012/2919 Art.9
Sch.1 para.10, amended: SI 2012/2919 Art.9
Sch.1 para.11, amended: SI 2012/2919 Art.9
Sch.1 para.11A, added: SI 2012/2919 Art.9
Sch.1 para.11A, amended: SI 2012/2919 Art.9
Sch.1 para.12, amended: SI 2012/2919 Art.7, Art.9
Sch.1 para.12A, added: SI 2012/2919 Art.7
Sch.1 para.12A, amended: SI 2012/2919 Art.9
Sch.1 para.13, amended: SI 2012/2919 Art.9
Sch.1 para.14, amended: SI 2012/2919 Art.9

2091. Huntingdonshire (Parishes) Order 2009
applied: SI 2012/51 Sch.1

2009–cont.

2101. Registrar of Companies (Fees) (Companies, Overseas Companies and Limited Liability Partnerships) Regulations 2009
revoked: SI 2012/1907 Reg.8

2129. Church Representation Rules (Amendment) Resolution 2009
applied: SI 2012/1847 Sch.2 para.1

2154. Non-Domestic Rating (Deferred Payments) (Wales) Regulations 2009
Reg.4, revoked: SI 2012/466 Reg.10
Reg.5, revoked: SI 2012/466 Reg.10

2163. Eggs and Chicks (England) Regulations 2009
Reg.17, amended: SI 2012/2897 Art.31

2166. Spring Traps Approval (Variation) (England) Order 2009
revoked: SI 2012/13 Art.3

2191. Smoke Control Areas (Authorised Fuels) (England) (Amendment) Regulations 2009
revoked: SI 2012/814 Sch.2

2205. National Health Service (Miscellaneous Amendments Relating to Community Pharmaceutical Services and Optometrist Prescribing) Regulations 2009
Reg.2, revoked: SI 2012/1909 Sch.8 para.9
Reg.3, revoked: SI 2012/1909 Sch.8 para.9
Reg.4, revoked: SI 2012/1909 Sch.8 para.9
Reg.5, revoked: SI 2012/1909 Sch.8 para.9
Reg.6, revoked: SI 2012/1909 Sch.8 para.9
Reg.7, revoked: SI 2012/1909 Sch.8 para.9
Reg.8, revoked: SI 2012/1909 Sch.8 para.9
Reg.9, revoked: SI 2012/1909 Sch.8 para.9
Reg.10, revoked: SI 2012/1909 Sch.8 para.9
Reg.11, revoked: SI 2012/1909 Sch.8 para.9
Reg.12, revoked: SI 2012/1909 Sch.8 para.9
Reg.13, revoked: SI 2012/1909 Sch.8 para.9
Reg.14, revoked: SI 2012/1909 Sch.8 para.9
Reg.15, revoked: SI 2012/1909 Sch.8 para.9
Reg.16, revoked: SI 2012/1909 Sch.8 para.9
Reg.17, revoked: SI 2012/1909 Sch.8 para.9
Reg.18, revoked: SI 2012/1909 Sch.8 para.9
Reg.19, revoked: SI 2012/1909 Sch.8 para.9
Reg.20, revoked: SI 2012/1909 Sch.8 para.9
Reg.21, revoked: SI 2012/1909 Sch.8 para.9
Reg.22, revoked: SI 2012/1909 Sch.8 para.9
Reg.23, revoked: SI 2012/1909 Sch.8 para.9
Reg.24, revoked: SI 2012/1909 Sch.8 para.9
Reg.25, revoked: SI 2012/1909 Sch.8 para.9
Reg.26, revoked: SI 2012/1909 Sch.8 para.9
Reg.27, revoked: SI 2012/1909 Sch.8 para.9
Reg.28, revoked: SI 2012/1909 Sch.8 para.9

2263. Infrastructure Planning (Environmental Impact Assessment) Regulations 2009
referred to: SI 2012/1645 Art.3
Reg.2, amended: SI 2012/635 Reg.2
Reg.3, amended: SI 2012/635 Reg.2, SI 2012/787 Reg.3
Reg.4, amended: SI 2012/635 Reg.2
Reg.5, amended: SI 2012/635 Reg.2, SI 2012/787 Reg.4
Reg.6, amended: SI 2012/635 Reg.2, SI 2012/787 Reg.5
Reg.7, amended: SI 2012/635 Reg.2
Reg.8, amended: SI 2012/635 Reg.2, SI 2012/787 Reg.6
Reg.9, amended: SI 2012/635 Reg.2
Reg.12, amended: SI 2012/635 Reg.2
Reg.13, amended: SI 2012/635 Reg.2
Reg.14, amended: SI 2012/635 Reg.2

2009–cont.

2263. Infrastructure Planning (Environmental Impact Assessment) Regulations 2009 *cont.*
Reg.14, revoked (in part): SI 2012/787 Reg.7
Reg.15, amended: SI 2012/635 Reg.2
Reg.16, amended: SI 2012/635 Reg.2, SI 2012/787 Reg.8
Reg.16, revoked (in part): SI 2012/635 Reg.2, SI 2012/787 Reg.8
Reg.17, amended: SI 2012/635 Reg.2, SI 2012/787 Reg.9
Reg.17, revoked (in part): SI 2012/787 Reg.9
Reg.18, amended: SI 2012/787 Reg.10
Reg.18, revoked (in part): SI 2012/787 Reg.10
Reg.18A, substituted: SI 2012/787 Reg.11
Reg.19, substituted: SI 2012/787 Reg.11
Reg.20, substituted: SI 2012/787 Reg.12
Reg.22, amended: SI 2012/635 Reg.2
Reg.22, revoked (in part): SI 2012/635 Reg.2
Reg.23, amended: SI 2012/635 Reg.2
Reg.23, revoked (in part): SI 2012/635 Reg.2
Reg.24, amended: SI 2012/635 Reg.2
Sch.5, amended: SI 2012/635 Reg.2, SI 2012/787 Reg.13

2264. Infrastructure Planning (Applications Prescribed Forms and Procedure) Regulations 2009
applied: SI 2012/2284, SI 2012/2635
referred to: SI 2012/1645 Art.3
varied: SI 2012/147 Art.7
Reg.2, amended: SI 2012/635 Reg.3, SI 2012/2732 Reg.4
Reg.4, amended: SI 2012/635 Reg.3
Reg.5, amended: SI 2012/635 Reg.3
Reg.8, amended: SI 2012/635 Reg.3
Reg.9, amended: SI 2012/635 Reg.3
Reg.10, amended: SI 2012/635 Reg.3
Reg.11, amended: SI 2012/635 Reg.3
Reg.11, revoked (in part): SI 2012/635 Reg.3
Sch.1, amended: SI 2012/1659 Art.2, SI 2012/2654 Sch.1, SI 2012/2732 Reg.4
Sch.2, amended: SI 2012/635 Reg.3
Sch.3, amended: SI 2012/635 Reg.3

2268. Non-Domestic Rating (Alteration of Lists and Appeals) (England) Regulations 2009
Part 2, applied: SI 2012/537 Reg.6
Reg.6, see *Imperial Tobacco Group Ltd v Alexander (Valuation Officer)* [2012] R.V.R. 218 (VT), Graham Zellick Q.C. (President)
Reg.8, see *Imperial Tobacco Group Ltd v Alexander (Valuation Officer)* [2012] R.V.R. 218 (VT), Graham Zellick Q.C. (President)
Reg.13, see *Imperial Tobacco Group Ltd v Alexander (Valuation Officer)* [2012] R.V.R. 218 (VT), Graham Zellick Q.C. (President)
Reg.14, applied: SI 2012/537 Reg.6

2269. Valuation Tribunal for England (Council Tax and Rating Appeals) (Procedure) Regulations 2009
Reg.8, see *Mayday Optical Co Ltd v Kendrick (Valuation Officer)* [2012] R.V.R. 235 (VT), Graham Zellick Q.C. (President)
Reg.38, see *Friends Life Co Ltd v Alexander (Valuation Officer)* [2012] R.A. 263 (VT), Graham Zellick Q.C. (President)
Reg.40, see *Mayday Optical Co Ltd v Kendrick (Valuation Officer)* [2012] R.V.R. 235 (VT), Graham Zellick Q.C. (President)

2009–cont.

2343. Social Security (Miscellaneous Amendments) (No.3) Regulations 2009
applied: SI 2012/3144 Sch.1 para.10

2403. Registrar of Companies (Fees) (European Economic Interest Grouping and European Public Limited-Liability Company) Regulations 2009
applied: SI 2012/1908 Reg.5
revoked: SI 2012/1908 Reg.6

2436. Unregistered Companies Regulations 2009
Sch.1 para.10, amended: SI 2012/1741 Sch.1 para.10
Sch.1 para.19, amended: SI 2012/2301 Reg.23

2439. Registrar of Companies (Fees) (Amendment) Regulations 2009
revoked: SI 2012/1907 Reg.8

2458. Climate Change Agreements (Eligible Facilities) (Amendment) Regulations 2009
revoked: SI 2012/2999 Reg.9

2492. European Economic Interest Grouping and European Public Limited-Liability Company (Fees) Revocation Regulations 2009
revoked: SI 2012/2300 Reg.2

2610. Safeguarding Vulnerable Groups Act 2006 (Regulated Activity, Miscellaneous and Transitional Provisions and Commencement No 5) Order 2009
Art.1, amended: SI 2012/2157 Art.5
Art.4, revoked: SI 2012/2157 Art.5
Art.5, revoked: SI 2012/2157 Art.5
Art.6, revoked: SI 2012/2157 Art.5
Art.7, revoked: SI 2012/2157 Art.5
Art.8, revoked: SI 2012/2157 Art.5
Art.9, revoked: SI 2012/2157 Art.5
Art.10, revoked: SI 2012/2157 Art.5
Art.11, revoked: SI 2012/2157 Art.5
Art.12, revoked: SI 2012/2157 Art.5
Art.13, revoked: SI 2012/2157 Art.5
Art.14, revoked: SI 2012/2157 Art.5
Art.15, revoked: SI 2012/2157 Art.5
Art.16, revoked: SI 2012/2157 Art.5
Art.17, revoked: SI 2012/2157 Art.5
Art.18, revoked: SI 2012/2157 Art.5
Art.19, revoked: SI 2012/2157 Art.5
Art.20, revoked: SI 2012/2157 Art.5
Art.21, amended: SI 2012/1153 Art.2
Art.21, revoked: SI 2012/2157 Art.5
Art.22, revoked: SI 2012/2157 Art.5
Art.26, revoked: 2012 c.9 Sch.10 Part 5
Art.27, revoked: 2012 c.9 Sch.10 Part 5
Art.28, revoked: 2012 c.9 Sch.10 Part 5
Art.29, revoked: 2012 c.9 Sch.10 Part 5
Art.30, revoked (in part): 2012 c.9 Sch.10 Part 5

2611. Safeguarding Vulnerable Groups Act 2006 (Commencement No 6, Transitional Provisions and Savings) Order 2009
see *R. v C* [2011] EWCA Crim 1872, [2012] 1 Cr. App. R. (S.) 89 (CA (Crim Div)), Thomas, L.J.
Art.3, amended: SI 2012/3006 Art.13
Art.3, see *Attorney General's Reference (No.18 of 2011), Re* [2011] EWCA Crim 1300, [2012] 1 Cr. App. R. (S.) 27 (CA (Crim Div)), Hughes, L.J. (Vice President)
Art.5, amended: SI 2012/3006 Art.13
Art.6, amended: SI 2012/3006 Art.13
Art.7, amended: SI 2012/3006 Art.13

2615. Company, Limited Liability Partnership and Business Names (Sensitive Words and Expressions) Regulations 2009
Sch.2 Part 1, amended: SI 2012/2007 Sch.1 para.119

2009– cont.

2615. Company, Limited Liability Partnership and Business Names (Sensitive Words and Expressions) Regulations 2009– *cont.*
Sch.2 Part 1, varied: 2012 c.11 s.12
Sch.2 Part 2, amended: SI 2012/ 2595 Art.17

2680. School Staffing (England) Regulations 2009
Reg.3, varied: SI 2012/ 1035 Sch.7 para.1
Reg.4, amended: SI 2012/ 1035 Sch.7 para.2, SI 2012/ 1740 Reg.2
Reg.6, amended: SI 2012/ 1035 Sch.7 para.3
Reg.7, amended: SI 2012/ 1035 Sch.7 para.2
Reg.8, amended: SI 2012/ 1035 Sch.7 para.2
Reg.8A, added: SI 2012/ 1740 Reg.2
Reg.11, amended: SI 2012/ 1035 Sch.7 para.4
Reg.12, amended: SI 2012/ 979 Sch.1 para.26, SI 2012/ 1035 Sch.7 para.5
Reg.13, amended: SI 2012/ 1035 Sch.7 para.6
Reg.18, amended: SI 2012/ 979 Sch.1 para.26, SI 2012/ 1035 Sch.7 para.2, Sch.7 para.5
Reg.19, amended: SI 2012/ 1035 Sch.7 para.8
Reg.19, varied: SI 2012/ 1035 Sch.7 para.7
Reg.20, amended: SI 2012/ 1035 Sch.7 para.2
Reg.21, amended: SI 2012/ 1035 Sch.7 para.2, Sch.7 para.5
Reg.23, amended: SI 2012/ 1035 Sch.7 para.9
Reg.24, amended: SI 2012/ 979 Sch.1 para.26, SI 2012/ 1035 Sch.7 para.5
Reg.27, varied: SI 2012/ 1035 Sch.7 para.10
Reg.30, amended: SI 2012/ 979 Sch.1 para.26, SI 2012/ 1035 Sch.7 para.2, Sch.7 para.5
Reg.31, amended: SI 2012/ 1035 Sch.7 para.2
Reg.34, amended: SI 2012/ 1035 Sch.7 para.11
Reg.35, amended: SI 2012/ 1035 Sch.7 para.12
Reg.36, varied: SI 2012/ 1035 Sch.7 para.13
Reg.37, varied: SI 2012/ 1035 Sch.7 para.13
Reg.38, varied: SI 2012/ 1035 Sch.7 para.13
Reg.40, amended: SI 2012/ 1035 Sch.7 para.14
Sch.2 para.5, amended: SI 2012/ 1035 Sch.7 para.2
Sch.2 para.6, amended: SI 2012/ 1035 Sch.7 para.2

2725. Financial Restrictions (Iran) Order 2009
see *Bank Mellat v HM Treasury* [2010] EWCA Civ 483, [2012] Q.B. 91 (CA (Civ Div)), Lord Neuberger of Abbotsbury MR; see *Bank Mellat v HM Treasury* [2011] EWCA Civ 1, [2012] Q.B. 101 (CA (Civ Div)), Maurice Kay, L.J.

2739. General Medical Council (Licence to Practise) Regulations Order of Council 2009
referred to: SI 2012/ 2685 Sch.1
Sch.1, revoked: SI 2012/ 2685 Sch.1

2745. Copyright and Performances (Application to Other Countries) (Amendment) Order 2009
revoked: SI 2012/ 799 Art.1

2818. Pre-release Access to Official Statistics (Wales) Order 2009
Sch.1 para.1, varied: 2012 c.11 s.12

2982. Company, Limited Liability Partnership and Business Names (Public Authorities) Regulations 2009
Sch.1, amended: SI 2012/ 2007 Sch.1 para.120

2999. Provision of Services Regulations 2009
Reg.2, amended: SI 2012/ 1809 Sch.1 Part 2
Reg.4, amended: SI 2012/ 1809 Sch.1 Part 2
Reg.5, amended: SI 2012/ 1809 Sch.1 Part 2
Reg.18, see *R. (on the application of Hemming (t/a Simply Pleasure Ltd)) v Westminster City Council* [2012] EWHC 1260 (Admin), [2012] P.T.S.R. 1676 (QBD (Admin)), Keith, J.

3001. Offshore Funds (Tax) Regulations 2009
Reg.18, disapplied: 2012 c.14 s.89

2009– cont.

3008. Burma (Restrictive Measures) (Overseas Territories) Order 2009
Art.2, amended: SI 2012/ 2596 Art.3
Art.4, disapplied: SI 2012/ 2596 Art.4
Art.5, disapplied: SI 2012/ 2596 Art.4
Art.6, disapplied: SI 2012/ 2596 Art.4
Art.7, disapplied: SI 2012/ 2596 Art.4
Art.8, disapplied: SI 2012/ 2596 Art.4
Art.9, disapplied: SI 2012/ 2596 Art.4
Art.10, disapplied: SI 2012/ 2596 Art.4
Art.11, disapplied: SI 2012/ 2596 Art.4
Art.12, disapplied: SI 2012/ 2596 Art.4
Art.13, disapplied: SI 2012/ 2596 Art.4
Art.14, disapplied: SI 2012/ 2596 Art.4
Art.15, disapplied: SI 2012/ 2596 Art.4
Art.16, disapplied: SI 2012/ 2596 Art.4
Art.17, disapplied: SI 2012/ 2596 Art.4
Art.18, disapplied: SI 2012/ 2596 Art.4
Art.19, disapplied: SI 2012/ 2596 Art.4

3015. Air Navigation Order 2009
applied: 2012 c.19 Sch.6 para.4
Part 3, referred to: SI 2012/ 1751 Art.3
Part 3A, referred to: SI 2012/ 1751 Art.3
Part 6, referred to: SI 2012/ 1751 Art.3
Part 7, referred to: SI 2012/ 1751 Art.3
Part 8, referred to: SI 2012/ 1751 Art.3
Part 24, referred to: SI 2012/ 1751 Art.3
Part 25A, referred to: SI 2012/ 1751 Art.3
Art.3, amended: SI 2012/ 1751 Art.5
Art.18, amended: SI 2012/ 1751 Art.55
Art.25, amended: SI 2012/ 1751 Art.56
Art.29, amended: SI 2012/ 1751 Art.6
Art.31, amended: SI 2012/ 1751 Art.7
Art.36A, added: SI 2012/ 1751 Art.57
Art.36B, added: SI 2012/ 1751 Art.57
Art.36C, added: SI 2012/ 1751 Art.57
Art.36D, added: SI 2012/ 1751 Art.57
Art.36E, added: SI 2012/ 1751 Art.57
Art.36F, added: SI 2012/ 1751 Art.57
Art.36G, added: SI 2012/ 1751 Art.57
Art.36H, added: SI 2012/ 1751 Art.57
Art.36I, added: SI 2012/ 1751 Art.57
Art.36J, added: SI 2012/ 1751 Art.57
Art.36K, added: SI 2012/ 1751 Art.57
Art.36L, added: SI 2012/ 1751 Art.57
Art.36M, added: SI 2012/ 1751 Art.57
Art.36N, added: SI 2012/ 1751 Art.57
Art.36O, added: SI 2012/ 1751 Art.57
Art.50, substituted: SI 2012/ 1751 Art.8
Art.52, amended: SI 2012/ 1751 Art.9
Art.53, amended: SI 2012/ 1751 Art.10
Art.54, amended: SI 2012/ 1751 Art.11
Art.55, amended: SI 2012/ 1751 Art.12, Art.63
Art.56, amended: SI 2012/ 1751 Art.13, Art.63
Art.60, amended: SI 2012/ 1751 Art.14
Art.61, substituted: SI 2012/ 1751 Art.15
Art.62, substituted: SI 2012/ 1751 Art.16
Art.63, amended: SI 2012/ 1751 Art.17
Art.64, amended: SI 2012/ 1751 Art.18
Art.65, amended: SI 2012/ 1751 Art.19
Art.66, amended: SI 2012/ 1751 Art.20
Art.67, amended: SI 2012/ 1751 Art.21
Art.68, amended: SI 2012/ 1751 Art.22
Art.69, substituted: SI 2012/ 1751 Art.23
Art.71, amended: SI 2012/ 1751 Art.24
Art.72, substituted: SI 2012/ 1751 Art.25
Art.72A, substituted: SI 2012/ 1751 Art.25
Art.72B, substituted: SI 2012/ 1751 Art.25

418

2009–cont.

3015. Air Navigation Order 2009–*cont.*
Art.73, substituted: SI 2012/1751 Art.25
Art.74, amended: SI 2012/1751 Art.26
Art.75, amended: SI 2012/1751 Art.27
Art.78, substituted: SI 2012/1751 Art.28
Art.79, amended: SI 2012/1751 Art.29
Art.80, amended: SI 2012/1751 Art.30
Art.81, substituted: SI 2012/1751 Art.31
Art.82, substituted: SI 2012/1751 Art.32
Art.82A, added: SI 2012/1751 Art.33
Art.106, amended: SI 2012/1751 Art.63
Art.131, applied: SI 2012/1657 Sch.2 para.7
Art.132, enabled: SI 2012/3054
Art.156, amended: SI 2012/1751 Art.34
Art.158, amended: SI 2012/1751 Art.35
Art.161, enabled: SI 2012/71, SI 2012/72, SI 2012/73,
SI 2012/74, SI 2012/83, SI 2012/150, SI 2012/151,
SI 2012/152, SI 2012/153, SI 2012/154, SI 2012/
155, SI 2012/156, SI 2012/194, SI 2012/195, SI
2012/196, SI 2012/487, SI 2012/488, SI 2012/
490, SI 2012/524, SI 2012/525, SI 2012/706, SI
2012/708, SI 2012/729, SI 2012/730, SI 2012/
790, SI 2012/812, SI 2012/869, SI 2012/871, SI
2012/891, SI 2012/892, SI 2012/895, SI 2012/
906, SI 2012/907, SI 2012/908, SI 2012/909, SI
2012/910, SI 2012/978, SI 2012/982, SI 2012/
983, SI 2012/984, SI 2012/1014, SI 2012/1016, SI
2012/1018, SI 2012/1060, SI 2012/1061, SI 2012/
1172, SI 2012/1174, SI 2012/1176, SI 2012/1177, SI
2012/1207, SI 2012/1208, SI 2012/1209, SI 2012/
1210, SI 2012/1230, SI 2012/1231, SI 2012/1232, SI
2012/1328, SI 2012/1329, SI 2012/1330, SI 2012/
1331, SI 2012/1332, SI 2012/1333, SI 2012/1334, SI
2012/1335, SI 2012/1336, SI 2012/1337, SI 2012/
1338, SI 2012/1339, SI 2012/1340, SI 2012/1341,
SI 2012/1342, SI 2012/1347, SI 2012/1348, SI
2012/1349, SI 2012/1350, SI 2012/1351, SI 2012/
1352, SI 2012/1353, SI 2012/1354, SI 2012/1401,
SI 2012/1402, SI 2012/1403, SI 2012/1598, SI
2012/1632, SI 2012/1637, SI 2012/1638, SI 2012/
1691, SI 2012/1940, SI 2012/1946, SI 2012/1958,
SI 2012/1959, SI 2012/1970, SI 2012/1971, SI
2012/1972, SI 2012/1974, SI 2012/1975, SI 2012/
2110, SI 2012/2302, SI 2012/2303, SI 2012/2330,
SI 2012/2337, SI 2012/2370, SI 2012/2375, SI
2012/2376, SI 2012/2603, SI 2012/2604, SI
2012/2682, SI 2012/2689, SI 2012/3051, SI 2012/
3052
Art.169, amended: SI 2012/1751 Art.60
Art.171, amended: SI 2012/1751 Art.60
Art.177, substituted: SI 2012/1751 Art.61
Art.178, revoked: SI 2012/1751 Art.61
Art.179, revoked: SI 2012/1751 Art.61
Art.180, revoked: SI 2012/1751 Art.61
Art.181, revoked: SI 2012/1751 Art.61
Art.182, revoked: SI 2012/1751 Art.61
Art.183, revoked: SI 2012/1751 Art.61
Art.184, revoked: SI 2012/1751 Art.61
Art.185, substituted: SI 2012/1751 Art.61
Art.186, revoked: SI 2012/1751 Art.61
Art.187, revoked: SI 2012/1751 Art.61
Art.188, revoked: SI 2012/1751 Art.61
Art.189, revoked: SI 2012/1751 Art.61
Art.190, revoked: SI 2012/1751 Art.61
Art.191, enabled: SI 2012/1353
Art.191, revoked: SI 2012/1751 Art.61
Art.192, revoked: SI 2012/1751 Art.61
Art.193, amended: SI 2012/1751 Art.61
Art.194, substituted: SI 2012/1751 Art.61
Art.196, substituted: SI 2012/1751 Art.61

2009–cont.

3015. Air Navigation Order 2009–*cont.*
Art.198, substituted: SI 2012/1751 Art.61
Art.199, amended: SI 2012/1751 Art.61
Art.200, revoked: SI 2012/1751 Art.61
Art.201, substituted: SI 2012/1751 Art.61
Art.204, amended: SI 2012/1751 Art.60
Art.204A, added: SI 2012/1751 Art.62
Art.204B, added: SI 2012/1751 Art.62
Art.204C, added: SI 2012/1751 Art.62
Art.229, amended: SI 2012/1751 Art.36
Art.231, amended: SI 2012/1751 Art.37
Art.238, revoked (in part): SI 2012/1751 Art.61
Art.241, amended: SI 2012/1751 Art.38
Art.246, amended: SI 2012/1751 Art.39
Art.246, revoked (in part): SI 2012/1751 Art.39
Art.255, amended: SI 2012/1751 Art.40, Art.58,
Art.60, Art.61
Art.264, amended: SI 2012/1751 Art.63
Sch.7 Part A, amended: SI 2012/1751 Art.41,
Art.42, Art.43, Art.44, Art.46
Sch.7 Part A, revoked: SI 2012/1751 Art.45
Sch.7 Part B, substituted: SI 2012/1751 Art.47
Sch.7 Part B, substituted: SI 2012/1751 Art.48
Sch.7 Part B, added: SI 2012/1751 Art.49
Sch.7 Part B para.1, amended: SI 2012/1751 Art.47
Sch.7 Part B para.1, amended: SI 2012/1751 Art.48
Sch.7 Part B para.4, amended: SI 2012/1751 Art.47
Sch.7 Part C, amended: SI 2012/1751 Art.52
Sch.7 Part C para.1, amended: SI 2012/1751 Art.50
Sch.7 Part C para.2, amended: SI 2012/1751 Art.50
Sch.7 Part C para.4, amended: SI 2012/1751 Art.50
Sch.7 Part C para.5, amended: SI 2012/1751 Art.50
Sch.7 Part C para.6, amended: SI 2012/1751 Art.50
Sch.7 Part C para.7, amended: SI 2012/1751 Art.50
Sch.7 Part C para.9, amended: SI 2012/1751 Art.50
Sch.7 Part C para.9A, added: SI 2012/1751 Art.50
Sch.7 Part C para.9B, added: SI 2012/1751 Art.50
Sch.7 Part C para.10, amended: SI 2012/1751 Art.51
Sch.7 Part C para.10, revoked (in part): SI 2012/1751
Art.51
Sch.7 Part C para.11, amended: SI 2012/1751 Art.52
Sch.7 Part C para.13, added: SI 2012/1751 Art.53
Sch.10 Part A para.1, revoked: SI 2012/1751 Art.61
Sch.10 Part A para.2, revoked: SI 2012/1751 Art.61
Sch.10 Part B para.1, revoked: SI 2012/1751 Art.61
Sch.10 Part B para.2, revoked: SI 2012/1751 Art.61
Sch.10 Part B para.3, revoked: SI 2012/1751 Art.61
Sch.10 Part B para.4, revoked: SI 2012/1751 Art.61
Sch.13 Part A, added: SI 2012/1751 Art.54
Sch.13 Part A, amended: SI 2012/1751 Art.61,
Art.62
Sch.13 Part B, amended: SI 2012/1751 Art.59
Sch.13 Part C, added: SI 2012/1751 Art.61
Sch.13 Part C, amended: SI 2012/1751 Art.54,
Art.61

**3043. Private Security Industry Act 2001 (Amend-
ments to Schedule 2) Order 2009**
Art.3, revoked (in part): 2012 c.9 Sch.10 Part 3
Art.4, revoked (in part): 2012 c.9 Sch.10 Part 3

**3062. Medicines (Exemptions and Miscellaneous
Amendments) Order 2009**
revoked: SI 2012/1916 Sch.35
Art.1, amended: SI 2012/1479 Sch.1 para.61

**3069. Ministry of Defence Police (Conduct) Regula-
tions 2009**
Reg.3, amended: SI 2012/808 Reg.42
Reg.12, amended: SI 2012/808 Reg.42
Reg.19, amended: SI 2012/808 Reg.42

2009–cont.

3069. Ministry of Defence Police (Conduct) Regulations 2009–cont.
Reg.20, amended: SI 2012/808 Reg.42

3070. Ministry of Defence Police Appeals Tribunals Regulations 2009
applied: SI 2012/808 Reg.37
Reg.3, amended: SI 2012/808 Reg.43
Reg.4A, added: SI 2012/808 Reg.43
Reg.9, amended: SI 2012/808 Reg.43

3073. Taxes, etc (Fees for Payment by Telephone) Regulations 2009
revoked: SI 2012/689 Reg.3

3097. Welsh Health Specialised Services Committee (Wales) Regulations 2009
Reg.2, amended: SI 2012/1641 Sch.3 para.13
Sch.2 Part 1 para.1, amended: SI 2012/1641 Sch.3 para.13

3112. Care Quality Commission (Registration) Regulations 2009
Reg.16, amended: SI 2012/921 Reg.3, SI 2012/1186 Reg.2, SI 2012/1641 Sch.3 para.11
Reg.17, amended: SI 2012/921 Reg.4
Reg.17, revoked (in part): SI 2012/921 Reg.4
Reg.18, amended: SI 2012/921 Reg.5, SI 2012/1186 Reg.2, SI 2012/1641 Sch.3 para.11
Reg.18, revoked (in part): SI 2012/921 Reg.5
Reg.22A, added: SI 2012/921 Reg.6
Reg.26, revoked: SI 2012/921 Reg.7
Reg.27, added: SI 2012/921 Reg.8
Sch.3 para.3, substituted: SI 2012/921 Reg.9

3130. Greenhouse Gas Emissions Data and National Implementation Measures Regulations 2009
revoked: SI 2012/3038 Reg.85

3145. Volatile Organic Compounds in Paints, Varnishes and Vehicle Refinishing Products (Amendment) (England) Regulations 2009
revoked: SI 2012/1715 Reg.10

3151. Child Support (Management of Payments and Arrears) Regulations 2009
Reg.2, amended: SI 2012/3002 Reg.2
Reg.3, amended: SI 2012/712 Reg.3, SI 2012/2007 Sch.1 para.121
Reg.4, amended: SI 2012/2007 Sch.1 para.121
Reg.5, amended: SI 2012/2007 Sch.1 para.121
Reg.6, amended: SI 2012/2007 Sch.1 para.121
Reg.7, amended: SI 2012/2007 Sch.1 para.121
Reg.8, amended: SI 2012/2007 Sch.1 para.121
Reg.9, amended: SI 2012/2007 Sch.1 para.121
Reg.10, amended: SI 2012/2007 Sch.1 para.121
Reg.11, amended: SI 2012/2007 Sch.1 para.121
Reg.12, amended: SI 2012/2007 Sch.1 para.121
Reg.13, amended: SI 2012/2007 Sch.1 para.121
Reg.13A, added: SI 2012/3002 Reg.2
Reg.13B, added: SI 2012/3002 Reg.2
Reg.13C, added: SI 2012/3002 Reg.2
Reg.13D, added: SI 2012/3002 Reg.2
Reg.13E, added: SI 2012/3002 Reg.2
Reg.13F, added: SI 2012/3002 Reg.2
Reg.13G, added: SI 2012/3002 Reg.2
Reg.13H, added: SI 2012/3002 Reg.2
Reg.13I, added: SI 2012/3002 Reg.2
Reg.13J, added: SI 2012/3002 Reg.2

3157. INSPIRE Regulations 2009
Reg.2, amended: SI 2012/1672 Reg.3
Reg.6, amended: SI 2012/1672 Reg.4
Reg.6A, added: SI 2012/1672 Reg.5
Reg.7, amended: SI 2012/1672 Reg.6
Reg.7, revoked (in part): SI 2012/1672 Reg.6

2009–cont.

3157. INSPIRE Regulations 2009–cont.
Reg.8, amended: SI 2012/1672 Reg.7
Reg.11, amended: SI 2012/1672 Reg.8
Reg.11, revoked (in part): SI 2012/1672 Reg.8
Reg.12, amended: SI 2012/1672 Reg.9
Reg.14, amended: SI 2012/1672 Reg.10
Reg.15, added: SI 2012/1672 Reg.11

3184. Courts Boards Areas (Amendment) Order 2009
revoked: SI 2012/1206 Sch.1 para.21

3193. Council Tax (Demand Notices) (England) Regulations 2009
Reg.2, amended: SI 2012/2914 Reg.12

3200. General Teaching Council (Registration of Temporary Teachers from Relevant European States) (England and Wales) Regulations 2009
revoked (in part): SI 2012/1153 Sch.1

3215. Police Act 1997 (Criminal Records) (Guernsey) Order 2009
Art.1, amended: SI 2012/1762 Art.3
Art.2, revoked (in part): SI 2012/1762 Art.3
Art.6, revoked: SI 2012/1762 Art.3
Art.7, revoked: SI 2012/1762 Art.3
Art.8, revoked: SI 2012/1762 Art.3
Sch.1 para.15, amended: SI 2012/1762 Art.3
Sch.3 Part 1 para.1, revoked: SI 2012/1762 Art.3
Sch.3 Part 1 para.2, revoked: SI 2012/1762 Art.3
Sch.3 Part 2 para.3, revoked: SI 2012/1762 Art.3
Sch.3 Part 3 para.4, revoked: SI 2012/1762 Art.3

3219. Sheep and Goats (Records, Identification and Movement) (England) Order 2009
Art.21, applied: SI 2012/114 Sch.1 para.13
Art.22, applied: SI 2012/114 Sch.1 para.13
Art.24, applied: SI 2012/114 Sch.1 para.13
Art.41, amended: SI 2012/2897 Art.32

3238. Food Additives (England) Regulations 2009
applied: SI 2012/1155 Reg.4
Reg.2, amended: SI 2012/1155 Reg.2
Reg.14, amended: SI 2012/1155 Reg.2
Reg.14, revoked (in part): SI 2012/1155 Reg.2
Sch.1, amended: SI 2012/1155 Reg.2

3263. Common Agricultural Policy Single Payment and Support Schemes (Integrated Administration and Control System) Regulations 2009
Reg.12, revoked (in part): SI 2012/66 Reg.3

3271. Control of Salmonella in Turkey Flocks Order 2009
Art.2, revoked (in part): SI 2012/2897 Art.33
Art.3, revoked (in part): SI 2012/2897 Art.33
Art.13, amended: SI 2012/2897 Art.33

3297. Police Act 1997 (Criminal Records and Registration) (Guernsey) Regulations 2009
Reg.9, amended: SI 2012/2666 Reg.2
Reg.10, revoked: SI 2012/2107 Reg.2

3340. National Health Service (Pharmaceutical Services) (Appliances) (Amendment) Regulations 2009
revoked: SI 2012/1909 Sch.8 para.9

3346. Designation of Rural Primary Schools (England) Order 2009
revoked: SI 2012/1197 Art.3

3350. London Penzance Trunk Road (A38) (Dobwalls to Trerulefoot Roundabout) (Prohibition of Waiting) (Clearways) Order 1978 (Variation) Order 2009
revoked: SI 2012/1377 Art.2

2009–cont.

3365. Agriculture (Cross compliance) (No.2) Regulations 2009
Reg.5, amended: SI 2012/66 Reg.2, SI 2012/2897 Art.34
Reg.5, revoked (in part): SI 2012/66 Reg.2
Sch.1 para.3, amended: SI 2012/2897 Art.34
Sch.1 para.3, substituted: SI 2012/66 Reg.2
Sch.1 para.5, amended: SI 2012/66 Reg.2, SI 2012/2897 Art.34
Sch.1 para.6, amended: SI 2012/2897 Art.34
Sch.1 para.6, substituted: SI 2012/66 Reg.2

3378. Food Additives (Wales) Regulations 2009
Reg.2, amended: SI 2012/1198 Reg.2
Reg.14, amended: SI 2012/1198 Reg.2
Reg.14, revoked (in part): SI 2012/1198 Reg.2
Sch.1, amended: SI 2012/1198 Reg.2

3380. Protection of Military Remains Act 1986 (Designation of Vessels and Controlled Sites) Order 2009
revoked: SI 2012/1110 Art.4

2010

1. Occupational Pension Schemes (Levy Ceiling Earnings Percentage Increase) Order 2010
revoked: SI 2012/528 Sch.1

4. Employers Duties (Implementation) Regulations 2010
Reg.1, amended: SI 2012/215 Reg.3, SI 2012/1813 Reg.2
Reg.2, amended: SI 2012/215 Reg.4, SI 2012/1813 Reg.2
Reg.3, amended: SI 2012/215 Reg.5, SI 2012/1813 Reg.2
Reg.3, revoked (in part): SI 2012/215 Reg.5
Reg.4, amended: SI 2012/1813 Reg.2
Reg.4A, added: SI 2012/1813 Reg.2
Reg.5, amended: SI 2012/215 Reg.6, SI 2012/1813 Reg.2
Reg.6, amended: SI 2012/215 Reg.7, SI 2012/1813 Reg.2

5. Employers Duties (Registration and Compliance) Regulations 2010
Reg.1, amended: SI 2012/215 Reg.9
Reg.2, amended: SI 2012/215 Reg.10
Reg.3, amended: SI 2012/215 Reg.11
Reg.4, amended: SI 2012/215 Reg.12
Reg.6, amended: SI 2012/215 Reg.13
Reg.7, amended: SI 2012/215 Reg.14
Reg.13, amended: SI 2012/215 Reg.15
Reg.14, amended: SI 2012/215 Reg.16

22. Transfer of Tribunal Functions Order 2010
Sch.3 para.77, revoked (in part): SI 2012/1909 Sch.8 para.9
Sch.3 para.78, revoked (in part): SI 2012/1909 Sch.8 para.9
Sch.3 para.79, revoked (in part): SI 2012/1909 Sch.8 para.9
Sch.3 para.80, revoked (in part): SI 2012/1909 Sch.8 para.9
Sch.3 para.81, revoked (in part): SI 2012/1909 Sch.8 para.9
Sch.3 para.82, revoked (in part): SI 2012/1909 Sch.8 para.9
Sch.3 para.83, revoked (in part): SI 2012/1909 Sch.8 para.9
Sch.3 para.84, revoked (in part): SI 2012/1909 Sch.8 para.9

2010–cont.

22. Transfer of Tribunal Functions Order 2010– cont.
Sch.3 para.85, revoked (in part): SI 2012/1909 Sch.8 para.9
Sch.3 para.86, revoked (in part): SI 2012/1909 Sch.8 para.9
Sch.3 para.87, revoked (in part): SI 2012/1909 Sch.8 para.9
Sch.3 para.88, revoked (in part): SI 2012/1909 Sch.8 para.9
Sch.3 para.89, revoked (in part): SI 2012/1909 Sch.8 para.9

49. Care Quality Commission (Registration) Amendment Regulations 2010
revoked: SI 2012/921 Reg.12

60. Criminal Procedure Rules 2010
see *R. (on the application of Guardian News and Media Ltd) v City of Westminster Magistrates' Court* [2012] EWCA Civ 420, [2012] 3 W.L.R. 1343 (CA (Civ Div)), Lord Neuberger (M.R.);
see *R. v Brough (Stuart)* [2011] EWCA Crim 2802, [2012] 2 Cr. App. R. (S.) 8 (CA (Crim Div)), Moore-Bick, L.J.
Pt 50, see *R. v K* [2011] EWCA Crim 1843, [2012] 1 Cr. App. R. (S.) 88 (CA (Crim Div)), Leveson, L.J.
r.14.2, see *R. v Hartley (John)* [2011] EWCA Crim 1299, [2012] 1 Cr. App. R. 7 (CA (Crim Div)), Hughes, L.J. (Vice President)
r.50.9, see *R. v K* [2011] EWCA Crim 1843, [2012] 1 Cr. App. R. (S.) 88 (CA (Crim Div)), Leveson, L.J.

89. Cross-Border Payments in Euro Regulations 2010
revoked: SI 2012/3122 Reg.22

93. Agency Workers Regulations 2010
Reg.11, amended: SI 2012/2397 Reg.3

102. Infrastructure Planning (Interested Parties) Regulations 2010
varied: SI 2012/147 Art.7
Reg.2, amended: SI 2012/635 Reg.4, SI 2012/2732 Reg.5
Reg.3, amended: SI 2012/635 Reg.4
Sch.1, amended: SI 2012/635 Reg.4, SI 2012/1659 Art.2, SI 2012/2654 Sch.1, SI 2012/2732 Reg.5
Sch.1, varied: 2012 c.11 s.12

103. Infrastructure Planning (Examination Procedure) Rules 2010
applied: SI 2012/2284, SI 2012/2635
r.1, amended: SI 2012/635 Reg.5
r.2, amended: SI 2012/635 Reg.5
r.3, amended: SI 2012/635 Reg.5
r.4, amended: SI 2012/635 Reg.5
r.8, amended: SI 2012/635 Reg.5
r.10, amended: SI 2012/635 Reg.5
r.14, amended: SI 2012/635 Reg.5
r.16, amended: SI 2012/635 Reg.5
r.17, amended: SI 2012/635 Reg.5
r.19, amended: SI 2012/635 Reg.5
r.20, revoked (in part): SI 2012/635 Reg.5
r.21, amended: SI 2012/635 Reg.5
r.23, amended: SI 2012/635 Reg.5
Sch.1 Part 1 para.1, amended: SI 2012/635 Reg.5
Sch.1 Part 2 para.4, amended: SI 2012/635 Reg.5
Sch.1 Part 2 para.4, revoked (in part): SI 2012/635 Reg.5

104. Infrastructure Planning (Compulsory Acquisition) Regulations 2010
varied: SI 2012/147 Art.7

2010–cont.

104. Infrastructure Planning (Compulsory Acquisition) Regulations 2010– *cont.*
Reg.2, amended: SI 2012/635 Reg.6, SI 2012/2732 Reg.6
Reg.5, amended: SI 2012/635 Reg.6
Reg.6, amended: SI 2012/635 Reg.6
Reg.7, amended: SI 2012/635 Reg.6
Reg.8, amended: SI 2012/635 Reg.6
Reg.9, amended: SI 2012/635 Reg.6
Reg.10, amended: SI 2012/635 Reg.6
Reg.15, amended: SI 2012/635 Reg.6
Reg.16, amended: SI 2012/635 Reg.6
Reg.17, amended: SI 2012/635 Reg.6
Reg.19, amended: SI 2012/635 Reg.6
Reg.20, amended: SI 2012/635 Reg.6
Sch.1, amended: SI 2012/635 Reg.6
Sch.2, amended: SI 2012/1659 Art.2, SI 2012/2654 Sch.1
Sch.2, varied: 2012 c.11 s.12
Sch.3, amended: SI 2012/635 Reg.6
Sch.4, amended: SI 2012/635 Reg.6

105. Infrastructure Planning (Miscellaneous Prescribed Provisions) Regulations 2010
Sch.1 Part 1 para.7, revoked (in part): SI 2012/630 Reg.20
Sch.1 Part 1 para.8, revoked (in part): SI 2012/630 Reg.20
Sch.1 Part 1 para.26, substituted: SI 2012/630 Reg.20
Sch.1 Part 1 para.28, amended: SI 2012/630 Reg.20
Sch.1 Part 1 para.39, revoked (in part): SI 2012/630 Reg.20
Sch.1 Part 2 para.23, substituted: SI 2012/630 Reg.20

106. Infrastructure Planning (Fees) Regulations 2010
Reg.2, amended: SI 2012/635 Reg.7
Reg.3, amended: SI 2012/635 Reg.7
Reg.4, amended: SI 2012/635 Reg.7
Reg.5, amended: SI 2012/635 Reg.7
Reg.6, amended: SI 2012/635 Reg.7
Reg.7, amended: SI 2012/635 Reg.7
Reg.8, amended: SI 2012/635 Reg.7
Reg.9, amended: SI 2012/635 Reg.7
Reg.10, amended: SI 2012/635 Reg.7
Reg.11, revoked: SI 2012/635 Reg.7

108. Poultry Compartments (England) Order 2010
Art.4, amended: SI 2012/2897 Art.35

115. Video Recordings (Labelling) Regulations 2010
revoked: SI 2012/1767 Reg.24

167. Hill Farm Allowance Regulations 2010
applied: SI 2012/114 Reg.4, Reg.5

195. Offender Management Act 2007 (Establishment of Probation Trusts) Order 2010
Art.3A, added: SI 2012/1215 Art.2

197. Criminal Justice Act 2003 (Mandatory Life Sentence Determination of Minimum Term) Order 2010
see *R. v Kela (Jarnail Singh)* [2011] EWCA Crim 1277, [2012] 1 Cr. App. R. (S.) 32 (CA (Crim Div)), Pitchford, L.J.

210. School Finance (England) (Amendment) Regulations 2010
revoked: SI 2012/335 Reg.2

231. Pharmacy Order 2010
Part 4, applied: SI 2012/3171, SI 2012/3171 Sch.1
Part 5, applied: SI 2012/3171, SI 2012/3171 Sch.1
Part 6, applied: SI 2012/3171, SI 2012/3171 Sch.1
Part 7, applied: SI 2012/3171, SI 2012/3171 Sch.1

2010–cont.

231. Pharmacy Order 2010– *cont.*
Art.3, referred to: SI 2012/1917 Sch.2 para.15
Art.18, applied: SI 2012/3171 Sch.1
Art.18, enabled: SI 2012/3171
Art.23, applied: SI 2012/3171 Sch.1
Art.23, enabled: SI 2012/3171
Art.51, amended: SI 2012/3006 Art.13
Art.61, applied: SI 2012/3171 Sch.1
Art.61, enabled: SI 2012/3171
Art.63, applied: SI 2012/3171 Sch.1
Art.63, enabled: SI 2012/3171
Art.66, amended: SI 2012/2672 Art.2
Art.66, applied: SI 2012/3171, SI 2012/3171 Sch.1
Art.66, enabled: SI 2012/3171
Sch.1 para.5, enabled: SI 2012/3171
Sch.4 Part 1 para.10, amended: SI 2012/2672 Art.2
Sch.4 Part 2 para.25, revoked (in part): SI 2012/1909 Sch.8 para.1
Sch.4 Part 2 para.47, revoked: SI 2012/1909 Sch.8 para.9
Sch.6 Part 2 para.6, revoked: SI 2012/1909 Sch.8 para.9

234. General and Specialist Medical Practice (Education, Training and Qualifications) Order 2010
see *Reddy v General Medical Council* [2012] EWCA Civ 310, [2012] C.P. Rep. 27 (CA (Civ Div)), Mummery, L.J.

239. Parliamentary Commissioner Order 2010
varied: SI 2012/147 Art.7

244. Pitcairn Constitution Order 2010
Sch.2, applied: SI 2012/1761 Art.3

265. Mercury Export and Data (Enforcement) Regulations 2010
Reg.5, amended: SI 2012/630 Reg.21, SSI 2012/360 Sch.11 para.23

279. National Health Service (Quality Accounts) Regulations 2010
Reg.1, amended: SI 2012/3081 Reg.2
Reg.2, amended: SI 2012/3081 Reg.3
Reg.2, revoked (in part): SI 2012/3081 Reg.3
Reg.3, amended: SI 2012/3081 Reg.4
Reg.4, amended: SI 2012/3081 Reg.5
Reg.5, amended: SI 2012/3081 Reg.6
Reg.5, revoked (in part): SI 2012/3081 Reg.6
Reg.7, amended: SI 2012/3081 Reg.7
Reg.8, substituted: SI 2012/3081 Reg.8
Reg.9, substituted: SI 2012/3081 Reg.8
Reg.12, added: SI 2012/3081 Reg.9
Sch.1, amended: SI 2012/3081 Reg.10

300. General Pharmaceutical Council (Constitution) Order 2010
Art.5, amended: SI 2012/3006 Art.13

301. Local Authority (Duty to Secure Early Years Provision Free of Charge) (Amendment) Regulations 2010
revoked: SI 2012/2488 Reg.5

305. Infrastructure Planning (Decisions) Regulations 2010
Reg.3, amended: SI 2012/635 Reg.8
Reg.3A, amended: SI 2012/635 Reg.8
Reg.6, amended: SI 2012/635 Reg.8
Reg.7, amended: SI 2012/635 Reg.8

330. Merchant Shipping and Fishing Vessels (Health and Safety at Work) (Chemical Agents) Regulations 2010
Reg.2, amended: SI 2012/1844 Reg.2
Reg.24, added: SI 2012/1844 Reg.3

2010–cont.

333. Notification of Conventional Tower Cranes Regulations 2010
applied: SI 2012/1652 Reg.21
Reg.4, applied: SI 2012/1652 Sch.16

344. Schools Forums (England) Regulations 2010
revoked: SI 2012/2261 Reg.2

347. A38 Trunk Road (Dobwalls to Carminow Cross, Bodmin) (40 &amp 50 Mph Speed Limit) Order 2003 (Variation) and (Twelve-woods Roundabout, Dobwalls) (De-Restriction) Order 2010
revoked: SI 2012/1863 Art.2

404. Building (Local Authority Charges) Regulations 2010
Reg.2, amended: SI 2012/3119 Reg.33

410. Tax Avoidance Schemes (Information) (Amendment) Regulations 2010
revoked: SI 2012/1836 Sch.1

441. Registration of Births, Deaths and Marriages (Fees) Order 2010
Art.1, amended: SI 2012/760 Art.2
Art.1, revoked (in part): SI 2012/760 Art.2
Art.2, substituted: SI 2012/760 Art.3
Sch.1, substituted: SI 2012/760 Art.4

445. Tobacco Advertising and Promotion (Display) (England) Regulations 2010
Reg.4, amended: SI 2012/677 Reg.2
Reg.6, substituted: SI 2012/677 Reg.2
Reg.10, added: SI 2012/677 Reg.2

446. Tobacco Advertising and Promotion (Specialist Tobacconists) (England) Regulations 2010
Reg.2, amended: SI 2012/677 Reg.3
Reg.5, added: SI 2012/677 Reg.3

447. Education (Student Support) (European University Institute) Regulations 2010
Reg.3, amended: SI 2012/3059 Reg.3
Reg.8, amended: SI 2012/3059 Reg.4
Reg.9, amended: SI 2012/3059 Reg.5
Reg.10, amended: SI 2012/3059 Reg.6
Reg.11, amended: SI 2012/3059 Reg.7
Sch.1 Part 1 para.1, amended: SI 2012/3059 Reg.8

460. Animal Gatherings Order 2010
Art.13, amended: SI 2012/2897 Art.36

472. Town and Country Planning (Fees for Applications and Deemed Applications) (Amendment) (England) Regulations 2010
revoked: SI 2012/2920 Sch.3

473. Postgraduate Medical Education and Training Order of Council 2010
Sch.1, substituted: SI 2012/344 Art.2
Sch.1 Part 1, substituted: SI 2012/344 Art.2
Sch.1 Part 2, substituted: SI 2012/344 Art.2
Sch.1 Part 3, substituted: SI 2012/344 Art.2
Sch.1 Part 4, substituted: SI 2012/344 Art.2

480. Regulation of Investigatory Powers (Communications Data) Order 2010
applied: SI 2012/1726 r.6.27
Sch.2 Part 2, amended: SI 2012/2007 Sch.1 para.122

481. Fire and Rescue Authorities (Improvement Plans) (Wales) Order 2010
revoked: SI 2012/1143 Art.3

482. Local Government (Performance Indicators and Standards) (Wales) Order 2010
revoked: SI 2012/2539 Art.3

490. Conservation of Habitats and Species Regulations 2010
applied: SI 2012/637 Reg.24
referred to: SI 2012/637 Sch.2 para.1

2010–cont.

490. Conservation of Habitats and Species Regulations 2010–*cont.*
see *Cornwall Waste Forum St Dennis Branch v Secretary of State for Communities and Local Government* [2011] EWHC 2761 (Admin), [2012] Env. L.R. 13 (QBD (Admin)), Collins, J.; see *Cornwall Waste Forum St Dennis Branch v Secretary of State for Communities and Local Government* [2012] EWCA Civ 379, [2012] Env. L.R. 34 (CA (Civ Div)), Arden, L.J.; see *Hargreaves v Secretary of State for Communities and Local Government* [2011] EWHC 1999 (Admin), [2012] Env. L.R. 9 (QBD (Admin)), Judge Pelling
Reg.2, amended: SI 2012/1927 Reg.3
Reg.2, revoked (in part): SI 2012/1927 Reg.3
Reg.3, amended: SI 2012/1927 Reg.4
Reg.5, amended: SI 2012/1927 Reg.5
Reg.7, amended: SI 2012/1927 Reg.6
Reg.8, amended: SI 2012/1927 Reg.7
Reg.9, substituted: SI 2012/1927 Reg.8
Reg.12A, amended: SI 2012/1927 Reg.9
Reg.18, amended. SI 2012/1927 Reg.10
Reg.19, amended: SI 2012/1927 Reg.11
Reg.19, revoked (in part): SI 2012/1927 Reg.11
Reg.20, revoked: SI 2012/1927 Reg.12
Reg.21, amended: SI 2012/1927 Reg.13
Reg.22, revoked: SI 2012/1927 Reg.14
Reg.23, substituted: SI 2012/1927 Reg.15
Reg.36, amended: SI 2012/1927 Reg.16
Reg.38, revoked (in part): SI 2012/1927 Reg.17
Reg.58, amended: SI 2012/1927 Reg.18
Reg.60, amended: SI 2012/1927 Reg.19
Reg.61, amended: SI 2012/1927 Reg.20
Reg.61, applied: SI 2012/1914 Art.36
Reg.61, see *Cornwall Waste Forum St Dennis Branch v Secretary of State for Communities and Local Government* [2011] EWHC 2761 (Admin), [2012] Env. L.R. 13 (QBD (Admin)), Collins, J.; see *Cornwall Waste Forum St Dennis Branch v Secretary of State for Communities and Local Government* [2012] EWCA Civ 379, [2012] Env. L.R. 34 (CA (Civ Div)), Arden, L.J.
Reg.62, see *Hargreaves v Secretary of State for Communities and Local Government* [2011] EWHC 1999 (Admin), [2012] Env. L.R. 9 (QBD (Admin)), Judge Pelling
Reg.64, see *Cornwall Waste Forum St Dennis Branch v Secretary of State for Communities and Local Government* [2011] EWHC 2761 (Admin), [2012] Env. L.R. 13 (QBD (Admin)), Collins, J.
Reg.65, see *Cornwall Waste Forum St Dennis Branch v Secretary of State for Communities and Local Government* [2011] EWHC 2761 (Admin), [2012] Env. L.R. 13 (QBD (Admin)), Collins, J.; see *Cornwall Waste Forum St Dennis Branch v Secretary of State for Communities and Local Government* [2012] EWCA Civ 379, [2012] Env. L.R. 34 (CA (Civ Div)), Arden, L.J.
Reg.67, amended: SI 2012/1927 Reg.21
Reg.73, disapplied: SI 2012/1914 Art.36
Reg.78A, added: SI 2012/637 Sch.2 para.3
Reg.82, revoked (in part): SI 2012/635 Reg.9
Reg.83, amended: SI 2012/635 Reg.9
Reg.98, amended: SI 2012/630 Reg.22
Reg.102A, added: SI 2012/637 Sch.2 para.4
Reg.107, amended: SI 2012/637 Sch.2 para.5

2010–cont.

490. Conservation of Habitats and Species Regulations 2010–*cont.*
Reg.129A, added: SI 2012/1927 Reg.22
Reg.135, added: SI 2012/1927 Reg.23
Sch.6 Part 2 para.6, revoked: SI 2012/1927 Reg.24

501. Charities Act 2006 (Principal Regulators of Exempt Charities) Regulations 2010
Reg.1, amended: SI 2012/2590 Sch.1 para.7

502. Charities (Exception from Registration) Regulations 2010
Reg.2, amended: SI 2012/3012 Sch.4 para.6
Reg.3, amended: SI 2012/3012 Sch.4 para.6
Reg.4, added: SI 2012/3012 Sch.4 para.6

521. Regulation of Investigatory Powers (Directed Surveillance and Covert Human Intelligence Sources) Order 2010
applied: SI 2012/1726 r.6.27
Art.3, amended: SI 2012/1500 Art.2
Art.4, amended: SI 2012/1500 Art.2
Art.7A, added: SI 2012/1500 Art.2
Sch.1 Part 2, amended: SI 2012/2007 Sch.1 para.123

540. Common Agricultural Policy Single Payment and Support Schemes Regulations 2010
Reg.8, substituted: SI 2012/3027 Reg.2
Sch.1, amended: SI 2012/3027 Reg.2

551. Medicines (Products for Human Use) (Fees) Regulations 2010
referred to: SI 2012/504 Reg.57
revoked: SI 2012/504 Reg.57
varied: SI 2012/504 Reg.57

575. Policing of Aerodromes (Belfast International Airport) Order 2010
revoked: SI 2012/837 Art.3

576. Smoke Control Areas (Authorised Fuels) (England) (Amendment) Regulations 2010
revoked: SI 2012/814 Sch.2

579. Health and Safety (Fees) Regulations 2010
revoked: SI 2012/1652 Reg.27

593. Excise Goods (Holding, Movement and Duty Point) Regulations 2010
Reg.62, amended: SI 2012/2786 Reg.3

601. Town and Country Planning (Regional Strategy) (England) Regulations 2010
Reg.2, amended: SI 2012/2654 Sch.1

602. Local Democracy, Economic Development and Construction Act 2009 (Consequential Amendments) (England) Order 2010
Art.4, revoked: SI 2012/767 Reg.37

610. Field Allowance for New Oil Fields Order 2010
revoked: SI 2012/3153 Art.7

630. Marine and Coastal Access Act 2009 (Commencement No 1, Consequential, Transitional and Savings Provisions) (England and Wales) Order 2010
Sch.4, amended: SI 2012/2571 Art.4

638. Federation of Maintained Schools and Miscellaneous Amendments (Wales) Regulations 2010
Reg.32, applied: SI 2012/2655 Reg.7
Reg.58, applied: SI 2012/2655 Reg.8
Reg.59, applied: SI 2012/2655 Reg.4
Reg.60, applied: SI 2012/2655 Reg.4
Reg.61, applied: SI 2012/2655 Reg.4
Sch.5 para.2, applied: SI 2012/2655 Sch.1 para.2
Sch.7 para.2, applied: SI 2012/2655 Reg.7
Sch.7 para.3, applied: SI 2012/2655 Reg.7
Sch.7 para.4, applied: SI 2012/2655 Reg.7
Sch.7 para.5, applied: SI 2012/2655 Reg.7

2010–cont.

638. Federation of Maintained Schools and Miscellaneous Amendments (Wales) Regulations 2010–*cont.*
Sch.7 para.6, applied: SI 2012/2655 Reg.7
Sch.7 para.7, applied: SI 2012/2655 Reg.7
Sch.7 para.8, applied: SI 2012/2655 Reg.7
Sch.7 para.9, applied: SI 2012/2655 Reg.7
Sch.7 para.10, applied: SI 2012/2655 Reg.7
Sch.7 para.11, applied: SI 2012/2655 Reg.7
Sch.7 para.12, applied: SI 2012/2655 Reg.7

675. Environmental Permitting (England and Wales) Regulations 2010
Reg.2, amended: SI 2012/630 Reg.3, SI 2012/811 Sch.2 para.5
Reg.12, applied: SI 2012/1867 Art.13, SI 2012/2284 Art.13, SI 2012/2635 Art.20, SI 2012/2679 Art.19
Reg.17, amended: SI 2012/630 Reg.4
Reg.19, amended: SI 2012/630 Reg.5
Reg.20, amended: SI 2012/630 Reg.6
Reg.21, amended: SI 2012/630 Reg.7
Reg.60, amended: SI 2012/630 Reg.8
Reg.67A, added: SI 2012/630 Reg.9
Reg.109, revoked (in part): SI 2012/630 Reg.10
Reg.110, added: SI 2012/630 Reg.11
Sch.1 Part 2, referred to: SI 2012/2999 Sch.1 para.23
Sch.1 Part 2, referred to: SI 2012/2999 Sch.1 para.36
Sch.1 Part 2, amended: SI 2012/630 Reg.12
Sch.1 Part 2 para.1, substituted: SI 2012/630 Reg.12
Sch.1 Part 2 para.1, referred to: SI 2012/2999 Sch.1 para.36
Sch.1 Part 2 para.1, amended: SI 2012/630 Reg.12
Sch.1 Part 2 para.2, referred to: SI 2012/2999 Sch.1 para.36
Sch.1 Part 2 para.2, substituted: SI 2012/630 Reg.12
Sch.1 Part 2 para.3, substituted: SI 2012/630 Reg.12
Sch.1 Part 2 para.5, substituted: SI 2012/630 Reg.12
Sch.1 Part 2 para.6, added: SI 2012/630 Reg.12
Sch.3 Part 1, amended: SI 2012/630 Reg.13
Sch.3 Part 1 para.1, amended: SI 2012/630 Reg.13
Sch.3 Part 1 para.5, amended: SI 2012/630 Reg.13
Sch.3 Part 1 para.6, amended: SI 2012/630 Reg.13
Sch.3 Part 1 para.8, amended: SI 2012/630 Reg.13
Sch.3 Part 1 para.10, amended: SI 2012/630 Reg.13
Sch.3 Part 1 para.11, amended: SI 2012/630 Reg.13
Sch.3 Part 1 para.11, varied: 2012 c.11 s.12
Sch.3 Part 1 para.16, amended: SI 2012/630 Reg.13
Sch.3 Part 1 para.16, substituted: SI 2012/630 Reg.13
Sch.3 Part 1 para.19, amended: SI 2012/630 Reg.13
Sch.3 Part 1 para.19, substituted: SI 2012/630 Reg.13
Sch.3 Part 1 para.23, amended: SI 2012/630 Reg.13
Sch.3 Part 1 para.24, amended: SI 2012/630 Reg.13
Sch.3 Part 1 para.25, amended: SI 2012/630 Reg.13
Sch.3 Part 1 para.27, amended: SI 2012/630 Reg.13
Sch.3 Part 1 para.27, substituted: SI 2012/630 Reg.13
Sch.3 Part 1 para.30, amended: SI 2012/630 Reg.13
Sch.5 Part 1 para.1, amended: SI 2012/630 Reg.14
Sch.5 Part 1 para.2, amended: SI 2012/630 Reg.14
Sch.10 para.2, amended: SI 2012/630 Reg.15
Sch.23 Part 2 para.2, amended: SI 2012/630 Reg.16
Sch.23 Part 3 para.3, amended: SI 2012/630 Reg.16
Sch.23 Part 7 para.10, amended: SI 2012/630 Reg.16
Sch.23 Part 7 para.25, amended: SI 2012/630 Reg.16

2010– cont.

675. Environmental Permitting (England and Wales) Regulations 2010– *cont.*
Sch.25 Pt 2 para.1, see *Ardley Against Incineration v Secretary of State for Communities and Local Government* [2011] EWHC 2230 (Admin), [2012] J.P.L. 268 (QBD (Admin)), John Howell Q.C.
Sch.25 Pt 2 para.4, see *Ardley Against Incineration v Secretary of State for Communities and Local Government* [2011] EWHC 2230 (Admin), [2012] J.P.L. 268 (QBD (Admin)), John Howell Q.C.

677. Apprenticeships, Skills, Children and Learning Act 2009, Parts 7 and 8 (Consequential Amendments) Order 2010
Art.3, revoked: SI 2012/ 765 Art.18
Art.8, revoked (in part): SI 2012/ 765 Art.18
Art.9, revoked (in part): SI 2012/ 765 Art.18
Art.10, revoked (in part): SI 2012/ 765 Art.18
Art.12, revoked (in part): SI 2012/ 765 Art.18
Art.17, revoked (in part): SI 2012/ 765 Art.18
Art.19, revoked: SI 2012/ 765 Art.18
Art.20, revoked (in part): SI 2012/ 765 Art.18
Art.22, revoked: SI 2012/ 765 Art.18

678. Feed-in Tariffs (Specified Maximum Capacity and Functions) Order 2010
applied: SI 2012/ 2782 Art.40
revoked: SI 2012/ 2782 Sch.3
Art.2, amended: SI 2012/ 1393 Art.2
Art.5A, amended: SI 2012/ 671 Art.2, SI 2012/ 2268 Art.2
Art.8, applied: SI 2012/ 2782 Art.40
Art.10, amended: SI 2012/ 1393 Art.3
Art.13, applied: SI 2012/ 2782 Art.40
Art.13, substituted: SI 2012/ 1393 Art.4
Art.13A, added: SI 2012/ 1393 Art.5
Art.14, applied: SI 2012/ 2782 Art.40
Art.28, applied: SI 2012/ 2782 Art.40

699. Environment Agency (Inland Waterways) Order 2010
Art.10, amended: SI 2012/ 1659 Art.2

743. National Health Service Trusts (Consultation on Establishment and Dissolution) Regulations 2010
Reg.2, amended: SI 2012/ 3094 Reg.11

746. Independent Review of Determinations (Adoption and Fostering) (Wales) Regulations 2010
Reg.2, amended: SI 2012/ 1479 Sch.1 para.87

764. Police Act 1997 (Criminal Records) (Isle of Man) Order 2010
Art.1, amended: SI 2012/ 2598 Art.3
Art.2, amended: SI 2012/ 2598 Art.3
Art.6, revoked: SI 2012/ 2598 Art.3
Art.7, revoked: SI 2012/ 2598 Art.3
Art.8, revoked: SI 2012/ 2598 Art.3
Art.9, applied: SI 2012/ 2109
Sch.3 Part 1 para.1, revoked: SI 2012/ 2598 Art.3
Sch.3 Part 1 para.2, revoked: SI 2012/ 2598 Art.3
Sch.3 Part 2 para.3, revoked: SI 2012/ 2598 Art.3
Sch.3 Part 3 para.4, revoked: SI 2012/ 2598 Art.3

765. Police Act 1997 (Criminal Records) (Jersey) Order 2010
Art.1, amended: SI 2012/ 2591 Art.3
Art.2, amended: SI 2012/ 2591 Art.3
Art.6, revoked: SI 2012/ 2591 Art.3
Art.7, revoked: SI 2012/ 2591 Art.3
Art.8, revoked: SI 2012/ 2591 Art.3
Sch.1 para.17, amended: SI 2012/ 2591 Art.3
Sch.3 Part 1 para.1, revoked: SI 2012/ 2591 Art.3
Sch.3 Part 1 para.2, revoked: SI 2012/ 2591 Art.3
Sch.3 Part 2 para.3, revoked: SI 2012/ 2591 Art.3

2010– cont.

765. Police Act 1997 (Criminal Records) (Jersey) Order 2010– *cont.*
Sch.3 Part 3 para.4, revoked: SI 2012/ 2591 Art.3

770. Air Navigation (Amendment) Order 2010
applied: 2012 c.19 Sch.6 para.4

772. Occupational and Personal Pension Schemes (Automatic Enrolment) Regulations 2010
referred to: SI 2012/ 1257 Reg.1
Reg.1, amended: SI 2012/ 215 Reg.43, SI 2012/ 1257 Reg.3
Reg.2, substituted: SI 2012/ 215 Reg.18
Reg.4, amended: SI 2012/ 215 Reg.19
Reg.4, revoked (in part): SI 2012/ 215 Reg.19
Reg.5, substituted: SI 2012/ 215 Reg.20
Reg.5A, added: SI 2012/ 1477 Reg.2
Reg.9, amended: SI 2012/ 215 Reg.43
Reg.12, amended: SI 2012/ 215 Reg.21
Reg.12, revoked (in part): SI 2012/ 215 Reg.21
Reg.14, substituted: SI 2012/ 215 Reg.22
Reg.17, amended: SI 2012/ 215 Reg.23
Reg.17, revoked (in part): SI 2012/ 215 Reg.23
Reg.21, amended: SI 2012/ 215 Reg.24
Reg.21, revoked (in part): SI 2012/ 215 Reg.24
Reg.24, amended: SI 2012/ 215 Reg.25
Reg.24, substituted: SI 2012/ 215 Reg.26
Reg.25, amended: SI 2012/ 215 Reg.25
Reg.25, revoked: SI 2012/ 215 Reg.27
Reg.26, amended: SI 2012/ 215 Reg.25
Reg.26, revoked: SI 2012/ 215 Reg.27
Reg.27, substituted: SI 2012/ 215 Reg.28
Reg.29, amended: SI 2012/ 215 Reg.29
Reg.32A, added: SI 2012/ 1257 Reg.4
Reg.32B, added: SI 2012/ 1257 Reg.4
Reg.32C, added: SI 2012/ 1257 Reg.4
Reg.32D, added: SI 2012/ 1257 Reg.4
Reg.32E, added: SI 2012/ 1257 Reg.4
Reg.32F, added: SI 2012/ 1257 Reg.4
Reg.32G, added: SI 2012/ 1257 Reg.4
Reg.32H, added: SI 2012/ 1257 Reg.4
Reg.32I, added: SI 2012/ 1257 Reg.4
Reg.32J, added: SI 2012/ 1257 Reg.4
Reg.32K, added: SI 2012/ 1257 Reg.4
Reg.33, substituted: SI 2012/ 215 Reg.30
Reg.34, revoked: SI 2012/ 215 Reg.31
Reg.35, substituted: SI 2012/ 1257 Reg.5
Reg.36, amended: SI 2012/ 1257 Reg.6, SI 2012/ 2691 Reg.2
Reg.37, amended: SI 2012/ 215 Reg.32
Reg.38, amended: SI 2012/ 215 Reg.33
Reg.39, amended: SI 2012/ 215 Reg.34
Reg.39A, added: SI 2012/ 215 Reg.35
Reg.41, revoked: SI 2012/ 215 Reg.36
Reg.42, revoked: SI 2012/ 215 Reg.36
Reg.43, amended: SI 2012/ 215 Reg.37
Reg.47, amended: SI 2012/ 215 Reg.38
Reg.47A, added: SI 2012/ 215 Reg.39
Reg.50, amended: SI 2012/ 215 Reg.42
Reg.51, added: SI 2012/ 1257 Reg.7
Reg.52, added: SI 2012/ 1257 Reg.7
Reg.53, added: SI 2012/ 1257 Reg.8
Sch.1, amended: SI 2012/ 215 Reg.43
Sch.2 para.1, added: SI 2012/ 215 Sch.1
Sch.2 para.2, added: SI 2012/ 215 Sch.1
Sch.2 para.3, added: SI 2012/ 215 Sch.1
Sch.2 para.4, added: SI 2012/ 215 Sch.1
Sch.2 para.5, added: SI 2012/ 215 Sch.1
Sch.2 para.6, added: SI 2012/ 215 Sch.1
Sch.2 para.7, added: SI 2012/ 215 Sch.1

2010– cont.

772. **Occupational and Personal Pension Schemes (Automatic Enrolment) Regulations 2010–** *cont.*
Sch.2 para.8, added: SI 2012/ 215 Sch.1
Sch.2 para.9, added: SI 2012/ 215 Sch.1
Sch.2 para.10, added: SI 2012/ 215 Sch.1
Sch.2 para.11, added: SI 2012/ 215 Sch.1
Sch.2 para.12, added: SI 2012/ 215 Sch.1
Sch.2 para.13, added: SI 2012/ 215 Sch.1
Sch.2 para.14, added: SI 2012/ 215 Sch.1
Sch.2 para.15, added: SI 2012/ 215 Sch.1
Sch.2 para.16, added: SI 2012/ 215 Sch.1
Sch.2 para.17, added: SI 2012/ 215 Sch.1
Sch.2 para.18, added: SI 2012/ 215 Sch.1
Sch.2 para.19, added: SI 2012/ 215 Sch.1
Sch.2 para.20, added: SI 2012/ 215 Sch.1
Sch.2 para.21, added: SI 2012/ 215 Sch.1
Sch.2 para.22, added: SI 2012/ 215 Sch.1
Sch.2 para.23, added: SI 2012/ 215 Sch.1
Sch.2 para.24, added: SI 2012/ 215 Sch.1
Sch.2 para.25, added: SI 2012/ 215 Sch.1

781. **Health and Social Care Act 2008 (Regulated Activities) Regulations 2010**
applied: SI 2012/ 2886 Sch.1, SSI 2012/ 303 Reg.28, SSI 2012/ 319 Reg.29
Reg.2, amended: SI 2012/ 1479 Sch.1 para.64
Reg.4, amended: SI 2012/ 1513 Reg.3
Reg.12, amended: SI 2012/ 1513 Reg.4
Reg.18, substituted: SI 2012/ 1513 Reg.5
Reg.21, amended: SI 2012/ 1479 Sch.1 para.88
Reg.27, amended: SI 2012/ 1513 Reg.6
Reg.30, added: SI 2012/ 1513 Reg.7
Sch.1 para.1, amended: SI 2012/ 1513 Reg.8
Sch.1 para.1, applied: SI 2012/ 2885 Sch.1 para.25
Sch.1 para.2, amended: SI 2012/ 979 Sch.1 para.27
Sch.1 para.5, amended: SI 2012/ 1479 Sch.1 para.88
Sch.1 para.6, amended: SI 2012/ 1513 Reg.8
Sch.1 para.7, amended: SI 2012/ 1513 Reg.8
Sch.1 para.8, amended: SI 2012/ 1513 Reg.8
Sch.1 para.9, amended: SI 2012/ 1513 Reg.8
Sch.1 para.10, amended: SI 2012/ 1513 Reg.8
Sch.2 para.4, substituted: SI 2012/ 1513 Reg.9
Sch.2 para.5, amended: SI 2012/ 1513 Reg.9
Sch.2 para.5, revoked (in part): SI 2012/ 1513 Reg.9
Sch.2 para.8, amended: SI 2012/ 1513 Reg.9
Sch.2 para.10, amended: SI 2012/ 1513 Reg.9
Sch.2 para.18, added: SI 2012/ 1513 Reg.9
Sch.4, amended: SI 2012/ 921 Reg.11

782. **UK Border Agency (Complaints and Misconduct) Regulations 2010**
Reg.3, see *R. (on the application of Salimi) v Secretary of State for the Home Department* [2011] EWHC 1714 (Admin), [2012] 1 All E.R. 244 (QBD (Admin)), Bean, J.

783. **Volatile Organic Compounds in Paints, Varnishes and Vehicle Refinishing Products (Amendment) Regulations 2010**
revoked: SI 2012/ 1715 Reg.10

801. **Transmissible Spongiform Encephalopathies (England) Regulations 2010**
Reg.20, amended: SI 2012/ 2897 Art.37

808. **A55 Trunk Road (Glan Conwy &ndash Conwy Morfa, Conwy) (Temporary 70 mph Speed Limit) Order 2010**
varied: SI 2012/ 945 Art.7

813. **Health and Social Care Act 2008 (Consequential Amendments No.2) Order 2010**
Art.19, revoked (in part): 2012 c.9 Sch.10 Part 5

2010– cont.

825. **Right to Manage (Prescribed Particulars and Forms) (England) Regulations 2010**
see *Gala Unity Ltd v Ariadne Road RTM Co Ltd* [2012] 1 E.G.L.R. 99 (UT (Lands)), George Bartlett Q.C. (President)
Sch.2, see *Gala Unity Ltd v Ariadne Road RTM Co Ltd* [2012] 1 E.G.L.R. 99 (UT (Lands)), George Bartlett Q.C. (President)

864. **Protection from Tobacco (Sales from Vending Machines) (England) Regulations 2010**
see *R. (on the application of Sinclair Collis Ltd) v Secretary of State for Health* [2011] EWCA Civ 437, [2012] Q.B. 394 (CA (Civ Div)), Lord Neuberger (M.R.)

912. **Management of Offenders etc (Scotland) Act 2005 (Disclosure of Information) Order 2010**
Art.2, amended: SI 2012/ 2007 Sch.1 para.124
Art.3, amended: SI 2012/ 2007 Sch.1 para.124
Art.3, revoked (in part): SI 2012/ 2007 Sch.1 para.124
Art.4, amended: SI 2012/ 2007 Sch.1 para.124
Art.4, revoked (in part): SI 2012/ 2007 Sch.1 para.124

914. **National Health Service (Pharmaceutical Services and Local Pharmaceutical Services) (Amendment) Regulations 2010**
Reg.2, revoked: SI 2012/ 1909 Sch.8 para.9
Reg.3, revoked: SI 2012/ 1909 Sch.8 para.9
Reg.4, revoked: SI 2012/ 1909 Sch.8 para.9
Reg.5, revoked: SI 2012/ 1909 Sch.8 para.9
Reg.6, revoked: SI 2012/ 1909 Sch.8 para.9
Reg.7, revoked: SI 2012/ 1909 Sch.8 para.9
Reg.8, revoked: SI 2012/ 1909 Sch.8 para.9
Reg.9, revoked: SI 2012/ 1909 Sch.8 para.9
Reg.10, revoked: SI 2012/ 1909 Sch.8 para.9

948. **Community Infrastructure Levy Regulations 2010**
Reg.5, amended: SI 2012/ 2975 Reg.3
Reg.5, applied: SI 2012/ 2975 Reg.10
Reg.9, amended: SI 2012/ 2975 Reg.3
Reg.11, revoked (in part): SI 2012/ 635 Reg.10
Reg.15, revoked (in part): SI 2012/ 2975 Reg.4
Reg.19, amended: SI 2012/ 2975 Reg.4
Reg.25, amended: SI 2012/ 2975 Reg.4
Reg.40, amended: SI 2012/ 2975 Reg.5
Reg.50, amended: SI 2012/ 2975 Reg.6
Reg.50, revoked (in part): SI 2012/ 2975 Reg.6
Reg.53, amended: SI 2012/ 702 Sch.1 para.2
Reg.59, amended: SI 2012/ 2975 Reg.7
Reg.60, amended: SI 2012/ 666 Sch.2
Reg.62, applied: SI 2012/ 767 Reg.34
Reg.64, applied: SI 2012/ 2975 Reg.10
Reg.64A, applied: SI 2012/ 2975 Reg.10
Reg.67, amended: SI 2012/ 2975 Reg.8
Reg.70, amended: SI 2012/ 2975 Reg.8
Reg.74A, added: SI 2012/ 2975 Reg.8
Reg.75, amended: SI 2012/ 2975 Reg.8
Reg.76, amended: SI 2012/ 2975 Reg.8
Reg.78, amended: SI 2012/ 635 Reg.10
Reg.78, revoked (in part): SI 2012/ 635 Reg.10
Reg.128A, added: SI 2012/ 2975 Reg.9
Reg.128B, added: SI 2012/ 2975 Reg.9

959. **Care Planning, Placement and Case Review (England) Regulations 2010**
applied: SI 2012/ 2813 Reg.3
Reg.46, amended: SI 2012/ 1479 Sch.1 para.89

976. **Northern Ireland Act 1998 (Devolution of Policing and Justice Functions) Order 2010**
applied: SI 2012/ 2595 Art.3

2010–cont.

976. Northern Ireland Act 1998 (Devolution of Policing and Justice Functions) Order 2010–cont.
Art.22, revoked: SI 2012/2595 Art.3

983. Beef and Veal Labelling Regulations 2010
Reg.3, amended: SI 2012/2897 Art.38

985. Human Fertilisation and Embryology (Parental Orders) Regulations 2010
see *X (Children) (Parental Order: Retrospective Authorisation of Payments), Re* [2011] EWHC 3147 (Fam), [2012] 1 F.L.R. 1347 (Fam Div), Sir Nicholas Wall (President, Fam)
Reg.4, applied: SSI 2012/188
Sch.3, applied: SSI 2012/188

988. Crossrail (Devolution of Functions) Order 2010
Art.3, amended: SI 2012/1659 Art.2
Art.11, amended: SI 2012/1659 Art.2

990. Teachers Pensions Regulations 2010
Reg.6, amended: SI 2012/2270 Reg.3
Reg.7, amended: SI 2012/2270 Reg.4
Reg.8, amended: SI 2012/2270 Reg.5
Reg.9, amended: SI 2012/2270 Reg.6
Reg.10, amended: SI 2012/2270 Reg.7
Reg.11, amended: SI 2012/2270 Reg.8
Reg.16, amended: SI 2012/673 Reg.3
Reg.64, amended: SI 2012/673 Reg.4
Reg.105, revoked (in part): SI 2012/673 Reg.5
Reg.116, amended: SI 2012/673 Reg.6
Reg.118, amended: SI 2012/673 Reg.7
Reg.119, revoked (in part): SI 2012/673 Reg.8
Sch.1, amended: SI 2012/673 Reg.9, SI 2012/2270 Reg.9
Sch.2 Part 1 para.2, amended: SI 2012/673 Reg.10, SI 2012/979 Sch.1 para.28
Sch.3 para.1, amended: SI 2012/673 Reg.11
Sch.3 para.2, amended: SI 2012/673 Reg.11
Sch.4 para.3, amended: SI 2012/673 Reg.12
Sch.7 para.4, amended: SI 2012/673 Reg.13

1000. National Health Service (Direct Payments) Regulations 2010
Reg.14, amended: SI 2012/2672 Art.2

1004. Identification and Traceability of Explosives Regulations 2010
Reg.1, amended: SI 2012/638 Reg.3
Reg.7A, added: SI 2012/638 Reg.3

1011. Consumer Credit (Total Charge for Credit) Regulations 2010
Reg.2, amended: SI 2012/1745 Reg.3
Reg.6, substituted: SI 2012/1745 Reg.4
Sch.1 para.3, amended: SI 2012/1745 Reg.5

1013. Consumer Credit (Disclosure of Information) Regulations 2010
Sch.1 para.4, amended: SI 2012/2798 Sch.1 para.5

1014. Consumer Credit (Agreements) Regulations 2010
Sch.1, amended: SI 2012/2798 Sch.1 para.6

1051. Whole of Government Accounts (Designation of Bodies) Order 2010
varied: SI 2012/147 Art.7

1060. Additional Statutory Paternity Pay (Weekly Rates) Regulations 2010
Reg.2, amended: SI 2012/780 Art.11

1071. Education (Pupil Referral Units) (Closure) (England) Regulations 2010
amended: SI 2012/1825 Reg.4
Reg.1, amended: SI 2012/1825 Reg.4
Reg.7, amended: SI 2012/1825 Reg.4

2010–cont.

1087. Police Act 1997 (Criminal Records and Registration) (Jersey) Regulations 2010
Reg.8, amended: SI 2012/2668 Reg.2
Reg.9, revoked: SI 2012/2108 Reg.2

1101. Safeguarding Vulnerable Groups Act 2006 (Commencement No 6, Transitional Provisions and Savings (Amendment)) and (Commencement No 7) Order 2010
Art.2, amended: SI 2012/3006 Art.13
Art.5, amended: SI 2012/3006 Art.13
Art.8, amended: SI 2012/3006 Art.34
Art.9, amended: SI 2012/3006 Art.34
Art.10, amended: SI 2012/3006 Art.34

1146. Safeguarding Vulnerable Groups Act 2006 (Controlled Activity and Miscellaneous Provisions) Regulations 2010
Reg.2, revoked: SI 2012/2160 Reg.2
Reg.3, revoked: SI 2012/2160 Reg.2
Reg.4, revoked (in part): 2012 c.9 Sch.10 Part 5, SI 2012/2160 Reg.2
Reg.5, revoked: SI 2012/2160 Reg.2
Reg.6, revoked: SI 2012/2160 Reg.2
Reg.7, revoked: SI 2012/2160 Reg.2
Reg.8, revoked: 2012 c.9 Sch.10 Part 5, SI 2012/2160 Reg.2

1154. Safeguarding Vulnerable Groups Act 2006 (Regulated Activity, Devolution and Miscellaneous Provisions) Order 2010
Art.3, revoked (in part): 2012 c.9 Sch.10 Part 5
Art.5, revoked: 2012 c.9 Sch.10 Part 5
Art.7, revoked (in part): 2012 c.9 Sch.10 Part 5
Art.8, revoked: 2012 c.9 Sch.10 Part 5
Art.11, revoked: 2012 c.9 Sch.10 Part 5

1156. Education (Educational Provision for Improving Behaviour) Regulations 2010
Reg.3, revoked (in part): SI 2012/2532 Reg.3
Reg.4, amended: SI 2012/2532 Reg.4
Reg.4A, added: SI 2012/2532 Reg.5
Reg.6, amended: SI 2012/2532 Reg.6
Reg.7, revoked: SI 2012/2532 Reg.7

1158. Local Education Authorities and Children's Services Authorities (Integration of Functions) Order 2010
Sch.2 Part 2 para.62, revoked: 2012 c.9 Sch.10 Part 5

1172. Local Education Authorities and Children's Services Authorities (Integration of Functions) (Local and Subordinate Legislation) Order 2010
Sch.3 para.76, revoked: SI 2012/1278 Reg.4

1213. Children Act 2004 Information Database (England) (Amendment) Regulations 2010
revoked: SI 2012/1278 Reg.2

1222. Jobseeker's Allowance (Work for Your Benefit Pilot Scheme) Regulations 2010
revoked: SI 2012/397 Reg.4

1228. Merchant Shipping (Ship-to-Ship Transfers) Regulations 2010
Reg.1, amended: SI 2012/742 Reg.2, Reg.3
Reg.1A, added: SI 2012/742 Reg.2
Reg.2, amended: SI 2012/742 Reg.3
Reg.3, amended: SI 2012/742 Reg.3
Reg.5A, added: SI 2012/742 Reg.3
Reg.8, amended: SI 2012/742 Reg.3
Sch.3 para.1, added: SI 2012/742 Sch.1
Sch.3 para.2, added: SI 2012/742 Sch.1
Sch.3 para.3, added: SI 2012/742 Sch.1
Sch.3 para.4, added: SI 2012/742 Sch.1
Sch.3 para.5, added: SI 2012/742 Sch.1
Sch.3 para.6, added: SI 2012/742 Sch.1

2010–cont.

1228. Merchant Shipping (Ship-to-Ship Transfers) Regulations 2010–*cont.*
Sch.3 para.7, added: SI 2012/742 Sch.1
Sch.3 para.8, added: SI 2012/742 Sch.1

1456. Energy Performance of Buildings (Certificates and Inspections) (England and Wales) (Amendment) Regulations 2010
revoked: SI 2012/3118 Sch.3

1513. Energy Act 2008 (Consequential Modifications) (Offshore Environmental Protection) Order 2010
Art.8, revoked: SI 2012/3038 Reg.85

1554. Pyrotechnic Articles (Safety) Regulations 2010
Reg.2, amended: SI 2012/1848 Reg.9
Reg.15, substituted: SI 2012/2963 Reg.2
Reg.33, amended: SI 2012/1848 Reg.9
Reg.37, amended: SI 2012/1848 Reg.9
Reg.46, amended: SI 2012/1848 Reg.9
Reg.46, revoked (in part): SI 2012/1848 Reg.9
Reg.47, amended: SI 2012/1848 Reg.9
Reg.47, revoked (in part): SI 2012/1848 Reg.9

1600. Fishing Boats (Electronic Transmission of Fishing Activities Data) (England) Scheme 2010
revoked: SI 2012/1375 Art.16

1614. General Pharmaceutical Council (Appeals Committee Rules) Order of Council 2010
Sch.1, amended: SI 2012/3006 Art.13

1615. General Pharmaceutical Council (Fitness to Practise and Disqualification etc Rules) Order of Council 2010
Sch.1, added: SI 2012/3171 Sch.1
Sch.1, amended: SI 2012/3006 Art.13, SI 2012/3171 Sch.1
Sch.1, revoked: SI 2012/3171 Sch.1
Sch.1, substituted: SI 2012/3171 Sch.1

1616. General Pharmaceutical Council (Statutory Committees and their Advisers Rules) Order of Council 2010
Sch.1, added: SI 2012/3171 Sch.1
Sch.1, amended: SI 2012/2672 Art.3, SI 2012/3171 Sch.1
Sch.1, revoked: SI 2012/3171 Sch.1
Sch.1, substituted: SI 2012/3171 Sch.1

1617. General Pharmaceutical Council (Registration Rules) Order of Council 2010
Sch.1, added: SI 2012/3171 Sch.1
Sch.1, amended: SI 2012/3171 Sch.1
Sch.1, substituted: SI 2012/3171 Sch.1

1677. Gaming Duty (Amendment) Regulations 2010
revoked: SI 2012/1897 Reg.3

1690. Integrated Family Support Teams (Composition of Teams and Board Functions) (Wales) Regulations 2010
revoked: SI 2012/202 Reg.5

1700. Integrated Family Support Teams (Review of Cases) (Wales) Regulations 2010
Reg.1, revoked: SI 2012/205 Reg.9
Reg.2, revoked: SI 2012/205 Reg.9
Reg.3, revoked: SI 2012/205 Reg.9
Reg.4, revoked: SI 2012/205 Reg.9
Reg.5, revoked: SI 2012/205 Reg.9
Reg.6, revoked: SI 2012/205 Reg.9
Reg.7, revoked: SI 2012/205 Reg.9
Reg.8, revoked: SI 2012/205 Reg.9
Reg.9, varied: SI 2012/205 Reg.9

2010–cont.

1701. Integrated Family Support Teams (Family Support Functions) (Wales) Regulations 2010
revoked: SI 2012/204 Reg.3

1704. Cancellation of Student Loans for Living Costs Liability (Wales) Regulations 2010
applied: SI 2012/1518 Reg.5

1721. Network Rail (Nuneaton North Chord) Order 2010
Art.13, amended: SI 2012/1659 Art.2

1808. Seed (Miscellaneous Amendments) (Wales) Regulations 2010
revoked: SI 2012/245 Reg.34

1836. Secretary of State for Education Order 2010
Sch.1 Part 2 para.8, revoked: SI 2012/1278 Reg.5
Sch.1 Part 2 para.11, revoked (in part): SI 2012/1153 Sch.1

1882. Medicines for Human Use (Advanced Therapy Medicinal Products and Miscellaneous Amendments) Regulations 2010
revoked: SI 2012/1916 Sch.35
Reg.9, applied: SI 2012/1916 Sch.32 para.6

1907. Employment and Support Allowance (Transitional Provisions, Housing Benefit and Council Tax Benefit) (Existing Awards) (No.2) Regulations 2010
applied: SI 2012/360 Sch.1, SI 2012/2886 Sch.1
referred to: SSI 2012/303 Sch.1 para.25, Sch.1 para.28
Reg.4, applied: SI 2012/3096 Reg.2
Reg.5, applied: SSI 2012/303 Sch.1 para.25
Reg.5, referred to: SI 2012/2886 Sch.1, SSI 2012/303 Sch.1 para.28
Reg.7, amended: SI 2012/913 Reg.10
Reg.16, amended: SI 2012/757 Reg.21
Reg.21, amended: SI 2012/913 Reg.10, SI 2012/919 Reg.6
Sch.2 Part 1 para.2A, added: SI 2012/913 Reg.10

1909. Terrorism Act 2006 (Disapplication of Section 25) Order 2010
revoked: 2012 c.9 Sch.10 Part 4

1920. Education (Short Stay Schools) (Closure) (England) (Amendment) Regulations 2010
revoked: SI 2012/1825 Reg.5

1924. Parochial Fees Order 2010
revoked: SI 2012/993 Art.4

1941. Apprenticeships, Skills, Children and Learning Act 2009 (Consequential Amendments to Subordinate Legislation) (England) Order 2010
Art.8, revoked: SI 2012/956 Art.24
Art.13, revoked: SI 2012/956 Art.24
Art.20, revoked: SI 2012/956 Art.24
Art.21, revoked (in part): SI 2012/956 Art.24
Art.23, revoked: SI 2012/956 Art.24
Art.24, revoked: SI 2012/956 Art.24
Art.25, revoked: SI 2012/956 Art.24

1996. Aviation Greenhouse Gas Emissions Trading Scheme Regulations 2010
applied: SI 2012/3038 Reg.87
referred to: SI 2012/3038 Reg.87
revoked: SI 2012/3038 Reg.85
Part 8, applied: SI 2012/3038 Reg.87
Part 11, applied: SI 2012/3038 Reg.87
Part 12, applied: SI 2012/3038 Reg.87
Reg.18, applied: SI 2012/3038 Reg.89
Reg.18, referred to: SI 2012/3038 Reg.87
Reg.21, applied: SI 2012/3038 Reg.87
Reg.22, applied: SI 2012/3038 Reg.87
Reg.26, applied: SI 2012/3038 Reg.87

2010–cont.

1996. Aviation Greenhouse Gas Emissions Trading Scheme Regulations 2010–*cont.*
Reg.27, applied: SI 2012/3038 Reg.87
Reg.28, applied: SI 2012/3038 Reg.87
Reg.29, applied: SI 2012/3038 Reg.87
Reg.49, applied: SI 2012/3038 Reg.87
Reg.55, applied: SI 2012/3038 Reg.87
Reg.56, applied: SI 2012/3038 Reg.87
Reg.57, applied: SI 2012/3038 Reg.87
Reg.58, applied: SI 2012/3038 Reg.87
Reg.59, applied: SI 2012/3038 Reg.87
Reg.60, applied: SI 2012/3038 Reg.87
Sch.3, applied: SI 2012/3038 Reg.87
Sch.4, applied: SI 2012/3038 Reg.87
Sch.5, applied: SI 2012/3038 Reg.87
Sch.6, applied: SI 2012/3038 Reg.87

1997. Education (Independent School Standards) (England) Regulations 2010
Reg.2, amended: SI 2012/979 Sch.1 para.29, SI 2012/2962 Reg.2
Reg.3, amended. SI 2012/979 Sch.1 para.29
Sch.1 Part 1 para.2, amended: SI 2012/2962 Reg.2
Sch.1 Part 2 para.5, substituted: SI 2012/2962 Reg.2
Sch.1 Part 3 para.10, amended: SI 2012/2962 Reg.2
Sch.1 Part 3 para.11, substituted: SI 2012/2962 Reg.2
Sch.1 Part 3 para.12, revoked: SI 2012/2962 Reg.2
Sch.1 Part 4 para.19, amended: SI 2012/2962 Reg.2
Sch.1 Part 4 para.20, amended: SI 2012/979 Sch.1 para.29, SI 2012/2962 Reg.2
Sch.1 Part 4 para.21, amended: SI 2012/979 Sch.1 para.29
Sch.1 Part 5 para.23, substituted: SI 2012/2962 Reg.2
Sch.1 Part 6 para.24, amended: SI 2012/2962 Reg.2
Sch.1 Part 7 para.25, amended: SI 2012/2962 Reg.2
Sch.1 Part 7 para.25, revoked (in part): SI 2012/2962 Reg.2

2060. Road Vehicles (Construction and Use) (Amendment) (No.3) Regulations 2010
Reg.2, revoked (in part): SI 2012/1404 Sch.1

2126. Social Security (Miscellaneous Amendments) (No.4) Regulations 2010
applied: SI 2012/3144 Sch.1 para.10

2134. Town and Country Planning (General Permitted Development) (Amendment) (No.2) (England) Order 2010
see *R. (on the application of Milton Keynes Council) v Secretary of State for Communities and Local Government* [2011] EWCA Civ 1575, [2012] J.P.L. 728 (CA (Civ Div)), Pill, L.J.

2135. Town and Country Planning (Compensation) (No.3) (England) Regulations 2010
see *R. (on the application of Milton Keynes Council) v Secretary of State for Communities and Local Government* [2011] EWCA Civ 1575, [2012] J.P.L. 728 (CA (Civ Div)), Pill, L.J.

2184. Town and Country Planning (Development Management Procedure) (England) Order 2010
Art.4, revoked (in part): SI 2012/3109 Art.3
Art.6, amended: SI 2012/3109 Art.3
Art.10, amended: SI 2012/3109 Art.4
Art.10, applied: SI 2012/2920 Sch.1 para.8
Art.18, amended: SI 2012/2274 Art.2
Art.18, applied: SI 2012/2975 Reg.10
Art.18, referred to: SI 2012/2920 Sch.1 para.7
Art.29, amended: SI 2012/3109 Art.4
Art.29, applied: SI 2012/2920 Reg.9

2010–cont.

2184. Town and Country Planning (Development Management Procedure) (England) Order 2010–*cont.*
Art.30, applied: SI 2012/2920 Reg.9
Art.31, amended: SI 2012/2274 Art.2
Art.34, applied: SI 2012/2167 Sch.1 para.7, Sch.2 para.7
Art.34, referred to: SI 2012/749 Reg.5
Art.34, revoked (in part): SI 2012/636 Art.3
Art.35, applied: SI 2012/2920 Reg.11
Art.37A, added: SI 2012/636 Art.4
Art.38, substituted: SI 2012/636 Art.5
Sch.2, applied: SI 2012/2920 Reg.14
Sch.5, amended: SI 2012/636 Art.3, SI 2012/1659 Art.2
Sch.5 para.1, revoked (in part): SI 2012/636 Art.3

2214. Building Regulations 2010
applied: SI 2012/2048 Art.3
Reg.2, amended: SI 2012/718 Reg.3, SI 2012/3119 Reg.3
Reg.8, amended: SI 2012/3119 Reg.4
Reg.9, amended: SI 2012/3119 Reg.5
Reg.12, amended: SI 2012/3119 Reg.6
Reg.14, revoked (in part): SI 2012/3119 Reg.7
Reg.15, amended: SI 2012/3119 Reg.8
Reg.16, amended: SI 2012/3119 Reg.9
Reg.17, amended: SI 2012/3119 Reg.10
Reg.17A, added: SI 2012/3119 Reg.11
Reg.19, amended: SI 2012/3119 Reg.12
Reg.20, amended: SI 2012/3119 Reg.13
Reg.21, amended: SI 2012/3119 Reg.14
Reg.23, substituted: SI 2012/3119 Reg.15
Reg.24, applied: SI 2012/3118 Reg.9, Reg.15, Reg.27
Reg.25, amended: SI 2012/3119 Reg.16
Reg.25A, added: SI 2012/3119 Reg.17
Reg.25B, added: SI 2012/3119 Reg.17
Reg.29, amended: SI 2012/809 Reg.11, SI 2012/3119 Reg.18
Reg.29, applied: SI 2012/3118 Reg.10, Reg.34, Reg.35, Reg.36, Reg.38
Reg.29, revoked (in part): SI 2012/809 Reg.11, SI 2012/3119 Reg.18
Reg.29A, added: SI 2012/3119 Reg.19
Reg.30, amended: SI 2012/809 Reg.11, SI 2012/3119 Reg.20
Reg.33, amended: SI 2012/3119 Reg.21
Reg.34, referred to: SI 2012/3118 Reg.34, Reg.35, Reg.36, Reg.38
Reg.34, substituted: SI 2012/3119 Reg.22
Reg.35, amended: SI 2012/3119 Reg.23
Reg.43, amended: SI 2012/3119 Reg.24
Reg.47, substituted: SI 2012/3119 Reg.25
Reg.48, amended: SI 2012/3119 Reg.26
Sch.1, revoked: SI 2012/3119 Reg.27
Sch.1, substituted: SI 2012/3119 Sch.2
Sch.2 Part CLASSf, amended: SI 2012/3119 Reg.28
Sch.3, amended: SI 2012/718 Reg.3, SI 2012/3119 Reg.29, Reg.30, Reg.31
Sch.4 para.1, revoked (in part): SI 2012/3119 Reg.32
Sch.4 para.2, revoked: SI 2012/3119 Reg.32
Sch.4 para.3, revoked: SI 2012/3119 Reg.32
Sch.4 para.3A, added: SI 2012/3119 Reg.32
Sch.4 para.4, amended: SI 2012/3119 Reg.32
Sch.5, amended: SI 2012/3118 Sch.3
Sch.6 para.2, revoked: SI 2012/3118 Sch.3

2215. Building (Approved Inspectors etc.) Regulations 2010
Reg.5A, added: SI 2012/3119 Reg.35

2010– cont.

2215. Building (Approved Inspectors etc.) Regulations 2010– cont.
Reg.7, amended: SI 2012/3119 Reg.36
Reg.8, amended: SI 2012/3119 Reg.37
Reg.16, amended: SI 2012/3119 Reg.38
Reg.20, amended: SI 2012/3119 Reg.39
Reg.30, revoked (in part): SI 2012/3119 Reg.40
Sch.1, amended: SI 2012/3119 Reg.41
Sch.2 para.5, revoked: SI 2012/3119 Reg.42
Sch.2 para.6, substituted: SI 2012/3119 Reg.42
Sch.3 para.6, substituted: SI 2012/3119 Reg.43
Sch.4 para.5, substituted: SI 2012/3119 Reg.44

2221. Storage of Carbon Dioxide (Licensing etc.) Regulations 2010
Reg.1, amended: SI 2012/461 Reg.3
Reg.16, added: SI 2012/461 Reg.4
Reg.17, added: SI 2012/461 Reg.4
Reg.18, added: SI 2012/461 Reg.4
Reg.19, added: SI 2012/461 Reg.4
Reg.20, added: SI 2012/461 Reg.4
Sch.2 para.7, amended: SI 2012/461 Reg.5
Sch.3 para.1, added: SI 2012/461 Sch.1 para.1
Sch.3 para.2, added: SI 2012/461 Sch.1 para.1
Sch.3 para.3, added: SI 2012/461 Sch.1 para.1

2225. Materials and Articles in Contact with Food (England) Regulations 2010
revoked: SI 2012/2619 Reg.31

2260. M1 and M6 Motorways (M1 Junctions 19 to 20) (Temporary Restriction and Prohibition of Traffic) Order 2010
revoked: SI 2012/253 Art.11

2288. Materials and Articles in Contact with Food (Wales) Regulations 2010
revoked: SI 2012/2705 Reg.30

2447. Spring Traps Approval (Wales) Order 2010
revoked: SI 2012/2941 Art.3

2462. Central London Community Healthcare National Health Service Trust (Establishment) Order 2010
referred to: SI 2012/1512 Sch.1

2476. Scottish Parliament (Disqualification) Order 2010
varied: SI 2012/147 Art.7
Sch.1 Part I, amended: 2012 asp 8 s.61, SI 2012/725 Art.2, SI 2012/1479 Sch.1 para.90, SI 2012/2672 Art.2

2571. Care Leavers (England) Regulations 2010
Reg.5, amended: SI 2012/979 Sch.1 para.30

2574. Child Minding and Day Care (Wales) Regulations 2010
Reg.2, amended: SI 2012/3006 Art.34
Reg.11, applied: SI 2012/3145 Sch.1
Reg.11, referred to: SI 2012/2886 Sch.1, SI 2012/3144 Sch.1 para.19
Reg.12, applied: SI 2012/3145 Sch.1
Reg.12, referred to: SI 2012/2886 Sch.1, SI 2012/3144 Sch.1 para.19
Reg.14, applied: SI 2012/3145 Sch.1
Reg.14, referred to: SI 2012/2886 Sch.1, SI 2012/3144 Sch.1 para.19
Reg.20, amended: SI 2012/3006 Art.34
Sch.1 Part 1 para.7, amended: SI 2012/3006 Art.34
Sch.1 Part 1 para.12, amended: SI 2012/3006 Art.34
Sch.1 Part 1 para.13, amended: SI 2012/3006 Art.34
Sch.1 Part 2 para.20, amended: SI 2012/3006 Art.34
Sch.1 Part 2 para.25, amended: SI 2012/3006 Art.34

2010– cont.

2574. Child Minding and Day Care (Wales) Regulations 2010– cont.
Sch.1 Part 2 para.31, amended: SI 2012/3006 Art.34
Sch.1 Part 2 para.36, amended: SI 2012/3006 Art.34
Sch.1 Part 2 para.37, amended: SI 2012/3006 Art.34
Sch.2 Part 1 para.19, amended: SI 2012/3006 Art.34
Sch.2 Part 2 para.42, amended: SI 2012/3006 Art.34

2600. Tribunal Procedure (Upper Tribunal) (Lands Chamber) Rules 2010
Part 4 r.24, amended: SI 2012/500 r.6
Part 5 r.28, amended: SI 2012/500 r.6
r.8, see *Thames Valley Holdings Ltd, Re* [2012] J.P.L. 66 (UT (Lands)), George Bartlett Q.C. (President, LTr)

2609. Education (Publication of Proposals) (Sixth Form College Corporations) (England) Regulations 2010
revoked: SI 2012/1158 Reg.2

2616. Houses in Multiple Occupation (Specified Educational Establishments) (England) (No.2) Regulations 2010
revoked: SI 2012/249 Reg.3

2617. Ecodesign for Energy-Related Products Regulations 2010
Sch.1 para.4, amended: SI 2012/3005 Reg.2

2655. First-tier Tribunal and Upper Tribunal (Chambers) Order 2010
Art.10, amended: SI 2012/1673 Art.3

2660. Protection of Vulnerable Groups (Scotland) Act 2007 (Consequential Provisions) Order 2010
Art.2, amended: SI 2012/3006 Art.28
Art.11, amended: SI 2012/3006 Art.29, Art.34
Art.18, amended: SI 2012/3006 Art.29
Art.19, amended: SI 2012/3006 Art.29
Art.20, amended: SI 2012/3006 Art.29

2693. Plant Health (Import Inspection Fees) (England) Regulations 2010
revoked: SI 2012/745 Reg.7
Sch.2, substituted: SI 2012/103 Reg.2

2710. Education (Specified Work and Registration) (Wales) Regulations 2010
Sch.2 para.3, applied: SI 2012/724 Sch.2 para.9

2818. Rate of Bereavement Benefits Regulations 2010
Reg.2, amended: SI 2012/780 Art.16
Reg.3, amended: SI 2012/780 Art.16

2839. Child Minding and Day Care Exceptions (Wales) Order 2010
Art.11, applied: SI 2012/2885 Sch.1 para.25, SSI 2012/303 Reg.28, SSI 2012/319 Reg.29
Art.12, applied: SI 2012/2885 Sch.1 para.25, SSI 2012/303 Reg.28, SSI 2012/319 Reg.29
Art.14, applied: SI 2012/2885 Sch.1 para.25, SSI 2012/303 Reg.28, SSI 2012/319 Reg.29

2841. Medical Profession (Responsible Officers) Regulations 2010
applied: SI 2012/2685 Sch.1
Reg.9, amended: SI 2012/1641 Sch.4 para.19
Reg.18, amended: SI 2012/476 Sch.1 para.1

2849. Producer Responsibility Obligations (Packaging Waste) (Amendment) Regulations 2010
Reg.17, revoked (in part): SI 2012/3082 Reg.5

2010– cont.

2862. Disabled People's Right to Control (Pilot Scheme) (England) Regulations 2010
Reg.1, amended: SI 2012/3048 Reg.2
Reg.3, revoked (in part): SI 2012/3048 Reg.2

2880. Single Use Carrier Bags Charge (Wales) Regulations 2010
Sch.1 para.1, amended: SI 2012/1916 Sch.34 para.101

2882. Spring Traps Approval (Variation) (England) Order 2010
revoked: SI 2012/13 Art.3

2893. Official Statistics Order 2010
varied: SI 2012/147 Art.7
Sch.1, amended: SI 2012/765 Art.17

2917. Plant Health (Import Inspection Fees) (Wales) Regulations 2010
revoked: SI 2012/1493 Reg.7
Sch.2, substituted: SI 2012/285 Reg.2

2919. Education (Independent Educational Provision in England) (Provision of Information) Regulations 2010
Reg.1, amended: SI 2012/979 Sch.1 para.31
Reg.2, amended: SI 2012/979 Sch.1 para.31
Reg.3, amended: SI 2012/979 Sch.1 para.31
Sch.1 Part 2 para.3, amended: SI 2012/979 Sch.1 para.31

2927. National Insurance Contributions (Application of Part 7 of the Finance Act 2004) (Amendment) Regulations 2010
revoked: SI 2012/1868 Reg.29

2928. Tax Avoidance Schemes (Information) (Amendment) (No.2) Regulations 2010
revoked: SI 2012/1836 Sch.1

2937. Iran (European Union Financial Sanctions) Regulations 2010
revoked: SI 2012/925 Reg.28
Reg.3, amended: SI 2012/190 Reg.3
Reg.4, amended: SI 2012/190 Reg.3
Reg.5, amended: SI 2012/190 Reg.3
Reg.6, amended: SI 2012/190 Reg.4
Reg.7, amended: SI 2012/190 Reg.4
Reg.8A, added: SI 2012/190 Reg.5
Reg.8B, added: SI 2012/190 Reg.5

2955. Family Procedure Rules 2010
see *R v A Local Authority* [2011] EWCA Civ 1451, [2012] 1 F.L.R.1302 (CA (Civ Div)), Sir Nicholas Wall (President, Fam)
Part 1 r.1.4, amended: SI 2012/3061 r.3
Part 2 r.2.3, amended: SI 2012/679 r.3, SI 2012/2007 Sch.1 para.125, SI 2012/2046 r.3, SI 2012/2806 r.4, SI 2012/3006 Art.30
Part 4 r.4.1, amended: SI 2012/679 r.4
Part 5 r.5.1, amended: SI 2012/679 r.5, SI 2012/2806 r.5
Part 5 r.5.3, amended: SI 2012/2806 r.6
Part 6 r.6.15, amended: SI 2012/679 r.6
Part 7 r.7.6, substituted: SI 2012/679 r.7
Part 7 r.7.10, amended: SI 2012/679 r.8
Part 7 r.7.12, amended: SI 2012/679 r.9
Part 7 r.7.19, amended: SI 2012/679 r.10
Part 7 r.7.20, amended: SI 2012/679 r.11
Part 7 r.7.27, amended: SI 2012/679 r.12
Part 7 r.7.32, amended: SI 2012/679 r.13
Part 7 r.7.36, amended: SI 2012/679 r.14
Part 8 r.8.20, amended: SI 2012/679 r.15
Part 8 r.8.38, amended: SI 2012/2007 Sch.1 para.125
Part 9 r.9.3, amended: SI 2012/2806 r.7
Part 9 r.9.12, amended: SI 2012/2806 r.8

2010– cont.

2955. Family Procedure Rules 2010– *cont.*
Part 9 r.9.14, amended: SI 2012/679 r.16, SI 2012/2806 r.9
Part 9 r.9.18, amended: SI 2012/2806 r.10
Part 9 r.9.19, amended: SI 2012/679 r.17, SI 2012/2806 r.11
Part 9 r.9.26A, amended: SI 2012/2806 r.12
Part 9 r.9.26AA, added: SI 2012/2806 r.13
Part 9 r.9.26B, added: SI 2012/679 r.18
Part 9 r.9.36, amended: SI 2012/679 r.19
Part 11 r.11.4, amended: SI 2012/679 r.20
Part 11 r.11.9, amended: SI 2012/679 r.21
Part 12, amended: SI 2012/3061 r.5
Part 12 r.12.1, amended: SI 2012/3061 r.5
Part 12 r.12.2, amended: SI 2012/3061 r.5
Part 12 r.12.3, amended: SI 2012/3061 r.5
Part 12 r.12.4, amended: SI 2012/3061 r.5
Part 12 r.12.5, amended: SI 2012/3061 r.5
Part 12 r.12.6, amended: SI 2012/3061 r.5
Part 12 r.12.7, amended: SI 2012/3061 r.5
Part 12 r.12.8, amended: SI 2012/3061 r.5
Part 12 r.12.9, amended: SI 2012/3061 r.5
Part 12 r.12.10, amended: SI 2012/3061 r.5
Part 12 r.12.11, amended: SI 2012/3061 r.5
Part 12 r.12.12, amended: SI 2012/3061 r.5
Part 12 r.12.13, amended: SI 2012/3061 r.5
Part 12 r.12.14, amended: SI 2012/3061 r.5
Part 12 r.12.15, amended: SI 2012/3061 r.5
Part 12 r.12.16, amended: SI 2012/3061 r.5
Part 12 r.12.17, amended: SI 2012/3061 r.5
Part 12 r.12.18, amended: SI 2012/3061 r.5
Part 12 r.12.19, amended: SI 2012/3061 r.5
Part 12 r.12.20, amended: SI 2012/3061 r.5
Part 12 r.12.20, revoked: SI 2012/3061 r.4
Part 12 r.12.21, amended: SI 2012/3061 r.5
Part 12 r.12.22, amended: SI 2012/3061 r.5
Part 12 r.12.23, amended: SI 2012/3061 r.5
Part 12 r.12.24, amended: SI 2012/3061 r.5
Part 12 r.12.25, amended: SI 2012/3061 r.5
Part 12 r.12.26, amended: SI 2012/3061 r.5
Part 12 r.12.27, amended: SI 2012/3061 r.5
Part 12 r.12.28, amended: SI 2012/3061 r.5
Part 12 r.12.29, amended: SI 2012/3061 r.5
Part 12 r.12.30, amended: SI 2012/3061 r.5
Part 12 r.12.31, amended: SI 2012/3061 r.5
Part 12 r.12.32, amended: SI 2012/3061 r.5
Part 12 r.12.33, amended: SI 2012/3061 r.5
Part 12 r.12.34, amended: SI 2012/3061 r.5
Part 12 r.12.35, amended: SI 2012/3061 r.5
Part 12 r.12.36, amended: SI 2012/3061 r.5
Part 12 r.12.37, amended: SI 2012/3061 r.5
Part 12 r.12.38, amended: SI 2012/3061 r.5
Part 12 r.12.39, amended: SI 2012/3061 r.5
Part 12 r.12.40, amended: SI 2012/3061 r.5
Part 12 r.12.41, amended: SI 2012/3061 r.5
Part 12 r.12.42, amended: SI 2012/3061 r.5
Part 12 r.12.43, amended: SI 2012/3061 r.5
Part 12 r.12.44, amended: SI 2012/3061 r.5
Part 12 r.12.45, amended: SI 2012/3061 r.5
Part 12 r.12.46, amended: SI 2012/3061 r.5
Part 12 r.12.47, amended: SI 2012/3061 r.5
Part 12 r.12.48, amended: SI 2012/3061 r.5
Part 12 r.12.49, amended: SI 2012/3061 r.5
Part 12 r.12.50, amended: SI 2012/3061 r.5
Part 12 r.12.51, amended: SI 2012/3061 r.5
Part 12 r.12.52, amended: SI 2012/3061 r.5
Part 12 r.12.53, amended: SI 2012/3061 r.5
Part 12 r.12.54, amended: SI 2012/3061 r.5

2010–cont.

2955. Family Procedure Rules 2010–*cont.*
Part 12 r.12.55, amended: SI 2012/3061 r.5
Part 12 r.12.56, amended: SI 2012/3061 r.5
Part 12 r.12.57, amended: SI 2012/3061 r.5
Part 12 r.12.58, amended: SI 2012/2046 r.4, SI 2012/3061 r.5
Part 12 r.12.59, amended: SI 2012/2046 r.5, SI 2012/3061 r.5
Part 12 r.12.60, amended: SI 2012/2046 r.5, SI 2012/3061 r.5
Part 12 r.12.61, amended: SI 2012/3061 r.5
Part 12 r.12.62, amended: SI 2012/3061 r.5
Part 12 r.12.63, amended: SI 2012/2046 r.5, SI 2012/3061 r.5
Part 12 r.12.64, amended: SI 2012/3061 r.5
Part 12 r.12.65, amended: SI 2012/3061 r.5
Part 12 r.12.66, amended: SI 2012/3061 r.5
Part 12 r.12.67, amended: SI 2012/2046 r.5, SI 2012/3061 r.5
Part 12 r.12.68, amended: SI 2012/3061 r.5
Part 12 r.12.69, amended: SI 2012/2046 r.5, SI 2012/3061 r.5
Part 12 r.12.70, amended: SI 2012/2046 r.5, SI 2012/3061 r.5
Part 12 r.12.71, amended: SI 2012/3061 r.5
Part 12 r.12.72, amended: SI 2012/679 r.22, SI 2012/3061 r.5
Part 12 r.12.73, amended: SI 2012/3061 r.5
Part 12 r.12.74, amended: SI 2012/3061 r.5
Part 12 r.12.74, revoked: SI 2012/3061 r.4
Part 12 r.12.75, amended: SI 2012/3061 r.5
Part 16 r.16.2, applied: 2012 c.10 Sch.1 para.15
Part 16 r.16.6, applied: 2012 c.10 Sch.1 para.15, SI 2012/3098 Reg.22, Reg.30
Part 16 r.16.36, amended: SI 2012/679 r.23
Part 17 r.17.1, amended: SI 2012/2806 r.14
Part 17 r.17.2, amended: SI 2012/2806 r.15
Part 20 r.20.7, amended: SI 2012/679 r.24, SI 2012/2806 r.16
Part 22 r.22.7, amended: SI 2012/2806 r.17
Part 25 r.25.1, substituted: SI 2012/3061 Sch.1
Part 25 r.25.2, substituted: SI 2012/3061 Sch.1
Part 25 r.25.3, substituted: SI 2012/3061 Sch.1
Part 25 r.25.4, substituted: SI 2012/3061 Sch.1
Part 25 r.25.5, substituted: SI 2012/3061 Sch.1
Part 25 r.25.6, substituted: SI 2012/3061 Sch.1
Part 25 r.25.7, substituted: SI 2012/3061 Sch.1
Part 25 r.25.8, substituted: SI 2012/3061 Sch.1
Part 25 r.25.9, substituted: SI 2012/3061 Sch.1
Part 25 r.25.10, substituted: SI 2012/3061 Sch.1
Part 25 r.25.11, substituted: SI 2012/3061 Sch.1
Part 25 r.25.12, substituted: SI 2012/3061 Sch.1
Part 25 r.25.13, substituted: SI 2012/3061 Sch.1
Part 25 r.25.14, substituted: SI 2012/3061 Sch.1
Part 25 r.25.15, substituted: SI 2012/3061 Sch.1
Part 25 r.25.16, substituted: SI 2012/3061 Sch.1
Part 25 r.25.17, substituted: SI 2012/3061 Sch.1
Part 25 r.25.18, substituted: SI 2012/3061 Sch.1
Part 25 r.25.19, substituted: SI 2012/3061 Sch.1
Part 25 r.25.20, substituted: SI 2012/3061 Sch.1
Part 29 r.29.2, amended: SI 2012/2007 Sch.1 para.125
Part 29 r.29.12, substituted: SI 2012/679 r.25
Part 31 r.31.17, amended: SI 2012/1462 r.3
Part 32 r.32.1, amended: SI 2012/679 r.26
Part 34, amended: SI 2012/2806 r.20
Part 34, amended: SI 2012/2806 r.22
Part 34 r.34.1, amended: SI 2012/2806 r.18

2010–cont.

2955. Family Procedure Rules 2010–*cont.*
Part 34 r.34.3, amended: SI 2012/679 r.27, SI 2012/2806 r.19
Part 34 r.34.28A, amended: SI 2012/679 r.28, SI 2012/2806 r.21
Part 34 r.34.29A, amended: SI 2012/2806 r.23
Part 34 r.34.30, amended: SI 2012/2806 r.24
Part 34 r.34.31, amended: SI 2012/2806 r.25
Part 34 r.34.32, amended: SI 2012/2806 r.26
Part 34 r.34.34, amended: SI 2012/2806 r.27
Part 34 r.34.35, amended: SI 2012/2806 r.28
Part 34 r.34.36A, amended: SI 2012/2806 r.29
Part 34 r.34.36B, added: SI 2012/2806 r.30
Part 34 r.34.38, amended: SI 2012/2806 r.31
Part 34 r.34.39, amended: SI 2012/679 r.29, SI 2012/2806 r.32
Part 34 r.34.40, substituted: SI 2012/2806 r.33
Pt 30, see *NLW v ARC* [2012] EWHC 55 (Fam), [2012] 2 F.L.R. 129 (Fam Div), Mostyn, J.
r.4.1, see *Guidance Note to Family Proceedings Courts* [2012] 1 F.L.R. 432 (Fam Div)
r.12.73, see *B (A Child: Disclosure of Evidence in Care Proceedings), Re* [2012] 1 F.L.R. 142 (Fam Div), Bodey, J.
r.16.2, see *Guidance Note to Family Proceedings Courts* [2012] 1 F.L.R. 432 (Fam Div)
r.16.4, see *Guidance Note to Family Proceedings Courts* [2012] 1 F.L.R. 432 (Fam Div)
r.25.1, see *A Local Authority v DS* [2012] EWHC 1442 (Fam), [2012] 1 W.L.R. 3098 (Fam Div), Sir Nicholas Wall (President, Fam)
r.30.3, see *AV v RM (Appeal)* [2012] EWHC 1173 (Fam), [2012] 2 F.L.R. 709 (Fam Div), Moor, J.; see *NLW v ARC* [2012] EWHC 55 (Fam), [2012] 2 F.L.R. 129 (Fam Div), Mostyn, J.
r.30.8, see *NB v Haringey LBC* [2011] EWHC 3544 (Fam), [2012] 2 F.L.R. 125 (Fam Div), Mostyn, J.

2969. National Assembly for Wales (Disqualification) Order 2010
Sch.1 Part 1, amended: SI 2012/2672 Art.2

2984. Merchant Shipping and Fishing Vessels (Health and Safety at Work) (Asbestos) Regulations 2010
Reg.4, amended: SI 2012/632 Sch.3

2999. Scottish Parliament (Elections etc.) Order 2010
varied: 2012 c.11 s.3
Sch.3 para.5, amended: SI 2012/1479 Sch.1 para.65

3018. Private Security Industry Act 2001 (Exemption) (Aviation Security) Regulations 2010
Reg.4, amended: SI 2012/1567 Reg.2
Reg.4, revoked (in part): SI 2012/1567 Reg.2

3020. Higher Education (Higher Amount) (England) Regulations 2010
see *R. (on the application of Hurley) v Secretary of State for Business, Innovation and Skills* [2012] EWHC 201 (Admin), [2012] H.R.L.R. 13 (DC), Elias, L.J.
Reg.3, amended: SI 2012/433 Reg.5
Reg.3, substituted: SI 2012/433 Reg.5
Reg.4, amended: SI 2012/433 Reg.5
Reg.5A, added: SI 2012/433 Reg.5

3021. Higher Education (Basic Amount) (England) Regulations 2010
see *R. (on the application of Hurley) v Secretary of State for Business, Innovation and Skills* [2012] EWHC 201 (Admin), [2012] H.R.L.R. 13 (DC), Elias, L.J.
Reg.3, amended: SI 2012/433 Reg.4

2010–cont.

3021. Higher Education (Basic Amount) (England) Regulations 2010–cont.
Reg.3, substituted: SI 2012/433 Reg.4
Reg.4, amended: SI 2012/433 Reg.4
Reg.5A, added: SI 2012/433 Reg.4

3024. Wireless Telegraphy Act 2006 (Directions to OFCOM) Order 2010
Art.8, applied: SI 2012/2817
Art.9, applied: SI 2012/2817

3025. Tax Treatment of Financing Costs and Income (Correction of Mismatches) Regulations 2010
Reg.16A, added: SI 2012/3111 Reg.3
Reg.16B, added: SI 2012/3111 Reg.3

3031. Designation of Schools Having a Religious Character (Independent Schools) (England) (No.4) Order 2010
Sch.1, amended: SI 2012/3174 Sch.2

2011

22. Dormant Bank and Building Society Accounts (Tax) Regulations 2011
Reg.3, revoked: SI 2012/756 Reg.3
Reg.4, revoked: SI 2012/756 Reg.3

38. Smoke Control Areas (Exempted Fireplaces) (Wales) Order 2011
revoked: SI 2012/244 Art.3

99. Electronic Money Regulations 2011
Sch.2 Part 2 para.25, amended: SI 2012/1741 Sch.1 para.12, SI 2012/1791 Reg.4

169. Occupational Pension Schemes (Levy Ceiling Earnings Percentage Increase) Order 2011
revoked: SI 2012/528 Sch.1

170. Inheritance Tax Avoidance Schemes (Prescribed Descriptions of Arrangements) Regulations 2011
referred to: SI 2012/1836 Reg.4

171. Tax Avoidance Schemes (Information) (Amendment) Regulations 2011
revoked: SI 2012/1836 Sch.1

191. Integrated Family Support Teams (Family Support Functions) (Wales) (Amendment) Regulations 2011
revoked: SI 2012/204 Reg.3

209. Criminal Procedure and Investigations Act 1996 (Defence Disclosure Time Limits) Regulations 2011
applied: SI 2012/1726 r.22.9, r.3.11
referred to: SI 2012/1726 r.2.3

231. Plastic Materials and Articles in Contact with Food (England) (Amendment) Regulations 2011
revoked: SI 2012/2619 Reg.31

233. Plastic Materials and Articles in Contact with Food (Wales) (Amendment) Regulations 2011
revoked: SI 2012/2705 Reg.30

309. Registrar of Companies (Fees) (Companies, Overseas Companies and Limited Liability Partnerships) (Amendment) Regulations 2011
revoked: SI 2012/1907 Reg.8

324. Registrar of Companies (Fees) (European Economic Interest Grouping) (Amendment) Regulations 2011
revoked: SI 2012/1908 Reg.6

371. School Finance (England) Regulations 2011
applied: SI 2012/335 Reg.25
revoked: SI 2012/2991 Reg.2
Reg.15, applied: SI 2012/335 Sch.4 para.5

2011–cont.

371. School Finance (England) Regulations 2011–cont.
Reg.20, disapplied: SI 2012/335 Sch.4 para.1
Reg.23, applied: SI 2012/335 Sch.4 para.5
Reg.23, disapplied: SI 2012/335 Sch.4 para.1
Reg.24, disapplied: SI 2012/335 Sch.4 para.1
Reg.25, applied: SI 2012/335 Sch.4 para.1
Sch.2 para.37, applied: SI 2012/335 Sch.2 para.36
Sch.3 Part 1 para.8, disapplied: SI 2012/335 Sch.4 para.1
Sch.3 Part 1 para.14, disapplied: SI 2012/335 Sch.4 para.1
Sch.3 Part 1 para.28, disapplied: SI 2012/335 Sch.4 para.1
Sch.3 Part 1 para.33, disapplied: SI 2012/335 Sch.4 para.1

439. Wireless Telegraphy (Register) (Amendment) Regulations 2011
revoked: SI 2012/2186 Sch.1

445. Immigration and Nationality (Fees) Order 2011
applied: SI 2012/813, SI 2012/813 Reg.7, SI 2012/971, SI 2012/971 Reg.7, SI 2012/2276
Art.3, applied: SI 2012/813 Reg.3, Reg.4, SI 2012/971 Reg.3, Reg.4, Reg.6
Art.4, applied: SI 2012/813 Reg.4, SI 2012/971 Reg.3, Reg.6
Art.5, applied: SI 2012/813 Reg.3, SI 2012/971 Reg.3
Art.6, applied: SI 2012/813 Reg.5, Reg.6, SI 2012/971 Reg.5

452. Poultrymeat (England) Regulations 2011
Reg.9, amended: SI 2012/2897 Art.39
Reg.11, amended: SI 2012/2897 Art.39
Reg.11, revoked (in part): SI 2012/2897 Art.39

463. Seed Marketing Regulations 2011
Reg.3, amended: SI 2012/3035 Reg.3
Reg.21A, added: SI 2012/3035 Reg.4
Sch.2 Part 3 para.24, amended: SI 2012/3035 Reg.5
Sch.3 Part 2 para.9, amended: SI 2012/3035 Reg.6

517. Armed Forces and Reserve Forces (Compensation Scheme) Order 2011
Art.11, amended: SI 2012/1573 Art.3
Art.28, revoked (in part): SI 2012/1573 Art.4
Art.39, applied: SI 2012/2885 Sch.5 para.1, SI 2012/2886 Sch.1, SSI 2012/303 Sch.4 para.19, SSI 2012/319 Sch.3 para.1
Art.53, amended: SI 2012/1573 Art.5
Art.53, revoked (in part): SI 2012/1573 Art.5
Art.66, amended: SI 2012/1573 Art.6
Sch.3 Part 1, amended: SI 2012/1573 Art.7

549. London Thames Gateway Development Corporation (Planning Functions) (Amendment) Order 2011
revoked: SI 2012/2167 Art.8

560. West Northamptonshire Development Corporation (Planning Functions) (Amendment) Order 2011
revoked: SI 2012/535 Art.2

565. Protection of Vulnerable Groups (Scotland) Act 2007 (Consequential Modifications) Order 2011
Art.2, amended: SI 2012/3006 Art.34

581. Fostering Services (England) Regulations 2011
applied: SI 2012/2885 Sch.1 para.25, SI 2012/2886 Sch.1, SI 2012/3144 Sch.1 para.19, SI 2012/3145 Sch.1, SSI 2012/303 Reg.28, SSI 2012/319 Reg.29
Reg.2, amended: SI 2012/3006 Art.32
Reg.23, amended: SI 2012/1479 Sch.1 para.91

2011– cont.

581. **Fostering Services (England) Regulations 2011**– *cont.*
Sch.7, amended: SI 2012/ 3006 Art.33

582. **Arrangements for Placement of Children by Voluntary Organisations and Others (England) Regulations 2011**
Reg.18, amended: SI 2012/ 1479 Sch.1 para.92

602. **Education (Head Teachers Qualifications) (England) (Amendment) Regulations 2011**
revoked: SI 2012/ 18 Sch.1

605. **Libya (Asset-Freezing) Regulations 2011**
Reg.3, revoked (in part): SI 2012/ 56 Reg.2

631. **Terrorism Act 2000 (Remedial) Order 2011**
revoked: 2012 c.9 Sch.9 para.34, Sch.10 Part 4

632. **National Assembly for Wales (Returning Officers Charges) Order 2011**
Art.4, amended: SI 2012/ 2478 Art.3
Art.5, amended: SI 2012/ 2478 Art.3
Art.6, amended: SI 2012/ 2478 Art.3
Art.7, amended: SI 2012/ 2478 Art.3
Art.8, amended: SI 2012/ 2478 Art.3
Art.9, amended: SI 2012/ 2478 Art.3
Sch.1, substituted: SI 2012/ 2478 Art.3
Sch.2, amended: SI 2012/ 2478 Art.3

643. **A303 Trunk Road (Hayes End Roundabout, South Petherton) (40mph Speed Limit and Derestriction) Order 2011**
Art.2, amended: SI 2012/ 1378 Art.2
Art.3a, added: SI 2012/ 1378 Art.2

674. **Social Security (Miscellaneous Amendments) Regulations 2011**
applied: SI 2012/ 3144 Sch.1 para.10

688. **Jobseeker's Allowance (Mandatory Work Activity Scheme) Regulations 2011**
Reg.7, revoked: SI 2012/ 2568 Reg.8
Reg.8, revoked: SI 2012/ 2568 Reg.8

691. **Student Fees (Qualifying Courses and Persons) (Wales) Regulations 2011**
Reg.3, amended: SI 2012/ 1630 Reg.2

693. **Badger (Control Area) (Wales) Order 2011**
referred to: SI 2012/ 1387
revoked: SI 2012/ 1387 Art.2

696. **Environment Agency (Levies) (England and Wales) Regulations 2011**
Reg.7, amended: SI 2012/ 2914 Reg.12
Reg.11, amended: SI 2012/ 460 Sch.1 para.18

708. **National Assistance (Assessment of Resources and Sums for Personal Requirements) (Amendment) (Wales) Regulations 2011**
Reg.2, revoked: SI 2012/ 842 Reg.3

712. **Qualifying Care Relief (Specified Social Care Schemes) Order 2011**
Art.2, amended: SI 2012/ 794 Art.2
Art.3, substituted: SI 2012/ 794 Art.2
Art.6, substituted: SI 2012/ 794 Art.2
Art.7, added: SI 2012/ 794 Art.2

715. **Smoke Control Areas (Authorised Fuels) (England) (Amendment) Regulations 2011**
revoked: SI 2012/ 814 Sch.2

723. **Government Resources and Accounts Act 2000 (Estimates and Accounts) Order 2011**
varied: SI 2012/ 147 Art.7

738. **Consular Fees Order 2011**
revoked: SI 2012/ 798 Sch.2

748. **Tunisia (Restrictive Measures) (Overseas Territories) Order 2011**
Sch.1, amended: SI 2012/ 362 Sch.3

751. **Parliamentary Commissioner Order 2011**
varied: SI 2012/ 147 Art.7

2011– cont.

765. **Aviation Greenhouse Gas Emissions Trading Scheme (Amendment) Regulations 2011**
revoked: SI 2012/ 3038 Reg.85

778. **School Finance (England) (Amendment) Regulations 2011**
revoked: SI 2012/ 2991 Reg.2

790. **Immigration and Nationality (Cost Recovery Fees) Regulations 2011**
revoked: SI 2012/ 813 Reg.8

817. **Accounts and Audit (England) Regulations 2011**
Reg.2, amended: SI 2012/ 854 Art.4
Reg.7, disapplied: SI 2012/ 2892 Art.3
Reg.8, disapplied: SI 2012/ 2892 Art.3

821. **Social Security Benefits Up-rating Order 2011**
revoked: SI 2012/ 780 Art.29

827. **Pensions Increase (Review) Order 2011**
applied: SI 2012/ 782 Art.3, Art.4

830. **Social Security Benefits Up-rating Regulations 2011**
revoked: SI 2012/ 819 Reg.6

840. **Pension Protection Fund (Pension Compensation Cap) Order 2011**
revoked: SI 2012/ 528 Sch.1

841. **Occupational Pension Schemes (Levy Ceiling) Order 2011**
revoked: SI 2012/ 528 Sch.1

881. **Animal By-Products (Enforcement) (England) Regulations 2011**
Reg.21, amended: SI 2012/ 2897 Art.40
Sch.2 para.2, revoked: SI 2012/ 811 Sch.2 para.6

886. **Assembly Learning Grants and Loans (Higher Education) (Wales) (No.2) Regulations 2011**
applied: SI 2012/ 1904 Art.3
Part 6, amended: SI 2012/ 14 Reg.15
Reg.2, amended: SI 2012/ 14 Reg.3, SI 2012/ 1156 Reg.3
Reg.4, amended: SI 2012/ 14 Reg.4, SI 2012/ 1156 Reg.4
Reg.5, amended: SI 2012/ 1156 Reg.5
Reg.6, amended: SI 2012/ 14 Reg.5, SI 2012/ 1156 Reg.6
Reg.7, amended: SI 2012/ 14 Reg.6
Reg.10, amended: SI 2012/ 14 Reg.7
Reg.13, amended: SI 2012/ 1156 Reg.7
Reg.19, amended: SI 2012/ 14 Reg.8
Reg.20, amended: SI 2012/ 14 Reg.9
Reg.21, amended: SI 2012/ 14 Reg.10
Reg.23, amended: SI 2012/ 14 Reg.11
Reg.24A, added: SI 2012/ 14 Reg.12
Reg.24B, added: SI 2012/ 14 Reg.12
Reg.25, amended: SI 2012/ 14 Reg.13, SI 2012/ 1156 Reg.8
Reg.25, applied: SSI 2012/ 303 Reg.20
Reg.26, amended: SI 2012/ 1156 Reg.9
Reg.46, amended: SI 2012/ 1156 Reg.10
Reg.47, amended: SI 2012/ 14 Reg.14
Reg.51, amended: SI 2012/ 14 Reg.15
Reg.65, substituted: SI 2012/ 14 Reg.16
Reg.65A, added: SI 2012/ 14 Reg.17
Reg.65A, applied: SI 2012/ 1904 Art.3
Reg.70, applied: SI 2012/ 1904 Art.3
Reg.74, amended: SI 2012/ 1156 Reg.11
Reg.86, amended: SI 2012/ 14 Reg.18
Reg.89, amended: SI 2012/ 1156 Reg.12
Reg.89, revoked (in part): SI 2012/ 1156 Reg.12
Reg.105, amended: SI 2012/ 1156 Reg.13
Sch.1 Part 1 para.1, amended: SI 2012/ 1156 Reg.14

2011– cont.

886. Assembly Learning Grants and Loans (Higher Education) (Wales) (No.2) Regulations 2011– *cont.*

Sch.1 Part 2 para.9, amended: SI 2012/14 Reg.19

Sch.3, applied: SI 2012/1904 Art.3

889. British Waterways Board (Kennet and Avon Canal) (Reclassification) Order 2011

varied: SI 2012/1659 Art.2

Art.1, varied: SI 2012/1659 Art.2

917. Jobseeker's Allowance (Employment, Skills and Enterprise Scheme) Regulations 2011

Reg.5A, amended: SI 2012/397 Reg.3

Reg.7, revoked: SI 2012/2568 Reg.7

Reg.8, revoked: SI 2012/2568 Reg.7

Reg.9, revoked: SI 2012/2568 Reg.7

Reg.10, revoked: SI 2012/2568 Reg.7

Reg.17, revoked: SI 2012/2568 Reg.7

Reg.18, revoked (in part): SI 2012/2568 Reg.7

935. Road Traffic Exemptions (Special Forces) (Variation and Amendment) Regulations 2011

Reg.3, applied: SI 2012/16 Art.6, SI 2012/27 Art.6, SI 2012/29 Art.6, SI 2012/30 Art.6, SI 2012/31 Art.7, SI 2012/32 Art.6, SI 2012/37 Art.4, SI 2012/39 Art.6, SI 2012/41 Art.8, SI 2012/43 Art.10, SI 2012/44 Art.4, SI 2012/54 Art.10, SI 2012/70 Art.5, SI 2012/77 Art.10, SI 2012/81 Art.6, SI 2012/87 Art.6, SI 2012/88 Art.11, SI 2012/91 Art.7, SI 2012/94 Art.4, SI 2012/95 Art.6, SI 2012/100 Art.6, SI 2012/101 Art.7, SI 2012/112 Art.8, SI 2012/117 Art.8, SI 2012/120 Art.12, SI 2012/128 Art.9, SI 2012/130 Art.10, SI 2012/132 Art.8, SI 2012/133 Art.4, SI 2012/135 Art.6, SI 2012/137 Art.6, SI 2012/142 Art.6, SI 2012/164 Art.4, SI 2012/173 Art.8, SI 2012/174 Art.8, SI 2012/175 Art.8, SI 2012/176 Art.7, SI 2012/182 Art.6, SI 2012/184 Art.5, SI 2012/186 Art.6, SI 2012/200 Art.6, SI 2012/201 Art.4, SI 2012/208 Art.6, SI 2012/211 Art.7, SI 2012/214 Art.6, SI 2012/226 Art.8, SI 2012/227 Art.8, SI 2012/240 Art.7, SI 2012/257 Art.4, SI 2012/258 Art.8, SI 2012/259 Art.7, SI 2012/262 Art.7, SI 2012/270 Art.6, SI 2012/271 Art.6, SI 2012/280 Art.4, SI 2012/281 Art.6, SI 2012/289 Art.6, SI 2012/294 Art.6, SI 2012/298 Art.7, SI 2012/299 Art.5, SI 2012/300 Art.8, SI 2012/301 Art.6, SI 2012/302 Art.8, SI 2012/303 Art.7, SI 2012/313 Art.6, SI 2012/314 Art.6, SI 2012/315 Art.4, SI 2012/316, SI 2012/341 Art.6, SI 2012/348 Art.6, SI 2012/350 Art.6, SI 2012/354 Art.7, SI 2012/355 Art.7, SI 2012/383 Art.9, SI 2012/404 Art.6, SI 2012/406 Art.7, SI 2012/407 Art.11, SI 2012/409 Art.6, SI 2012/410 Art.7, SI 2012/413 Art.6, SI 2012/418 Art.7, SI 2012/420 Art.6, SI 2012/424 Art.7, SI 2012/434 Art.6, SI 2012/436 Art.8, SI 2012/437 Art.7, SI 2012/438 Art.7, SI 2012/439 Art.5, SI 2012/440 Art.6, SI 2012/447 Art.6, SI 2012/451 Art.6, SI 2012/452 Art.6, SI 2012/454 Art.8, SI 2012/455 Art.6, SI 2012/457 Art.4, SI 2012/474 Art.6, SI 2012/475 Art.6, SI 2012/477 Art.5, SI 2012/482 Art.6, SI 2012/483 Art.4, SI 2012/484 Art.7, SI 2012/493 Art.6, SI 2012/495 Art.6, SI 2012/496 Art.6, SI 2012/498 Art.6, SI 2012/499 Art.5, SI 2012/507 Art.6, SI 2012/509 Art.6, SI 2012/510 Art.6, SI 2012/512 Art.6, SI 2012/527 Art.7, SI 2012/529 Art.8, SI 2012/530 Art.8, SI 2012/540 Art.6, SI 2012/541 Art.9, SI 2012/543 Art.8, SI 2012/545 Art.7, SI 2012/549 Art.6, SI 2012/551 Art.7, SI 2012/552 Art.5, SI 2012/554 Art.7, SI 2012/556 Art.7, SI 2012/563 Art.5, SI 2012/564 Art.6, SI 2012/567 Art.7, SI

2011– cont.

935. Road Traffic Exemptions (Special Forces) (Variation and Amendment) Regulations 2011– *cont.*

Reg.3, applied:– *cont.*

2012/596 Art.6, SI 2012/598 Art.6, SI 2012/600 Art.4, SI 2012/602 Art.6, SI 2012/604 Art.6, SI 2012/620 Art.6, SI 2012/650 Art.8, SI 2012/656 Art.6, SI 2012/657 Art.6, SI 2012/658 Art.7, SI 2012/661 Art.6, SI 2012/665 Art.6, SI 2012/719 Art.6, SI 2012/721 Art.8, SI 2012/722 Art.6, SI 2012/723 Art.4, SI 2012/770 Art.6, SI 2012/772 Art.6, SI 2012/776 Art.6, SI 2012/778 Art.6, SI 2012/850 Art.6, SI 2012/855 Art.6, SI 2012/902, SI 2012/902 Art.6, SI 2012/905 Art.5, SI 2012/912 Art.6, SI 2012/926 Art.7, SI 2012/928 Art.7, SI 2012/932 Art.8, SI 2012/968 Art.6, SI 2012/996 Art.7, SI 2012/997 Art.7, SI 2012/1000 Art.6, SI 2012/1001 Art.7, SI 2012/1010 Art.7, SI 2012/1040 Art.4, SI 2012/1041 Art.7, SI 2012/1045 Art.6, SI 2012/1048 Art.8, SI 2012/1049 Art.5, SI 2012/1056 Art.6, SI 2012/1057 Art.6, SI 2012/1068 Art.6, SI 2012/1072 Art.4, SI 2012/1076 Art.7, SI 2012/1078 Art.4, SI 2012/1091 Art.6, SI 2012/1092 Art.11, SI 2012/1112 Art.7, SI 2012/1114 Art.6, SI 2012/1117 Art.7, SI 2012/1119 Art.9, SI 2012/1149 Art.8, SI 2012/1152 Art.6, SI 2012/1160 Art.5, SI 2012/1162 Art.9, SI 2012/1163 Art.7, SI 2012/1178 Art.7, SI 2012/1180 Art.6, SI 2012/1183 Art.7, SI 2012/1214 Art.7, SI 2012/1216 Art.7, SI 2012/1217 Art.7, SI 2012/1220 Art.13, SI 2012/1222 Art.5, SI 2012/1226 Art.6, SI 2012/1236 Art.8, SI 2012/1237 Art.6, SI 2012/1239 Art.7, SI 2012/1240 Art.6, SI 2012/1242 Art.7, SI 2012/1247 Art.6, SI 2012/1250 Art.6, SI 2012/1255 Art.6, SI 2012/1279 Art.6, SI 2012/1306 Art.7, SI 2012/1308 Art.9, SI 2012/1361 Art.6, SI 2012/1364 Art.6, SI 2012/1365 Art.5, SI 2012/1370 Art.7, SI 2012/1371 Art.5, SI 2012/1381 Art.5, SI 2012/1383 Art.9, SI 2012/1409 Art.6, SI 2012/1411 Art.4, SI 2012/1413 Art.6, SI 2012/1414 Art.8, SI 2012/1416 Art.7, SI 2012/1447 Art.10, SI 2012/1448 Art.13, SI 2012/1451 Art.11, SI 2012/1452 Art.7, SI 2012/1453 Art.6, SI 2012/1459 Art.6, SI 2012/1461 Art.6, SI 2012/1472 Art.8, SI 2012/1473 Art.6, SI 2012/1476 Art.6, SI 2012/1481 Art.13, SI 2012/1527 Art.4, SI 2012/1533 Art.6, SI 2012/1535 Art.4, SI 2012/1539 Art.6, SI 2012/1541 Art.6, SI 2012/1542 Art.8, SI 2012/1543 Art.6, SI 2012/1546 Art.6, SI 2012/1550 Art.6, SI 2012/1558 Art.6, SI 2012/1561 Art.7, SI 2012/1564 Art.4, SI 2012/1572 Art.5, SI 2012/1589 Art.6, SI 2012/1596 Art.6, SI 2012/1601 Art.7, SI 2012/1608 Art.6, SI 2012/1609 Art.7, SI 2012/1611 Art.6, SI 2012/1612 Art.7, SI 2012/1626 Art.6, SI 2012/1627 Art.6, SI 2012/1707 Art.6, SI 2012/1708 Art.12, SI 2012/1717 Art.8, SI 2012/1722 Art.8, SI 2012/1727 Art.9, SI 2012/1729 Art.7, SI 2012/1730 Art.13, SI 2012/1733 Art.6, SI 2012/1735 Art.6, SI 2012/1737 Art.6, SI 2012/1780 Art.6, SI 2012/1785 Art.7, SI 2012/1786 Art.4, SI 2012/1787 Art.9, SI 2012/1788 Art.5, SI 2012/1789 Art.6, SI 2012/1800 Art.6, SI 2012/1801 Art.7, SI 2012/1822 Art.6, SI 2012/1830 Art.7, SI 2012/1854 Art.6, SI 2012/1855 Art.7, SI 2012/1862 Art.8, SI 2012/1873 Art.6, SI 2012/1939 Art.7, SI 2012/1947 Art.8, SI 2012/1948 Art.6, SI 2012/1949 Art.8, SI 2012/1951 Art.6, SI 2012/1952 Art.6, SI 2012/1962 Art.8, SI 2012/1973 Art.9, SI 2012/1991 Art.13, SI 2012/1992 Art.7, SI 2012/2013 Art.7, SI 2012/2014 Art.7, SI 2012/2019

Art.7, SI 2012/2020 Art.8, SI 2012/2021 Art.7, SI 2012/2022 Art.23, SI 2012/2035 Art.9, SI 2012/2037 Art.6, SI 2012/2039 Art.6, SI 2012/2041 Art.6, SI 2012/2042 Art.6, SI 2012/2060 Art.8, SI 2012/2064 Art.7, SI 2012/2065 Art.6, SI 2012/2070 Art.4, SI 2012/2071 Art.6, SI 2012/2074 Art.6, SI 2012/2076 Art.6, SI 2012/2077 Art.6, SI 2012/2078 Art.6, SI 2012/2083 Art.12, SI 2012/2098 Art.6, SI 2012/2101 Art.6, SI 2012/2116 Art.9, SI 2012/2120 Art.9, SI 2012/2130 Art.5, SI 2012/2131 Art.7, SI 2012/2133 Art.8, SI 2012/2135 Art.4, SI 2012/2136 Art.6, SI 2012/2137 Art.6, SI 2012/2138 Art.4, SI 2012/2139 Art.6, SI 2012/2141 Art.6, SI 2012/2145 Art.6, SI 2012/2149 Art.5, SI 2012/2151 Art.9, SI 2012/2153 Art.10, SI 2012/2161 Art.7, SI 2012/2163 Art.6, SI 2012/2169 Art.6, SI 2012/2170 Art.6, SI 2012/2174 Art.6, SI 2012/2176 Art.6, SI 2012/2198 Art.7, SI 2012/2199 Art.6, SI 2012/2200 Art.5, SI 2012/2205 Art.6, SI 2012/2206 Art.12, SI 2012/2207 Art.8, SI 2012/2212 Art.6, SI 2012/2214 Art.7, SI 2012/2220 Art.14, SI 2012/2223 Art.7, SI 2012/2227 Art.6, SI 2012/2228 Art.6, SI 2012/2232 Art.7, SI 2012/2237 Art.9, SI 2012/2239 Art.6, SI 2012/2241 Art.6, SI 2012/2243 Art.8, SI 2012/2246 Art.7, SI 2012/2247 Art.6, SI 2012/2248 Art.8, SI 2012/2250 Art.7, SI 2012/2253 Art.7, SI 2012/2256 Art.6, SI 2012/2259 Art.7, SI 2012/2286 Art.9, SI 2012/2288 Art.6, SI 2012/2296 Art.8, SI 2012/2308 Art.6, SI 2012/2310 Art.4, SI 2012/2321 Art.6, SI 2012/2323 Art.6, SI 2012/2325 Art.6, SI 2012/2327 Art.6, SI 2012/2328 Art.6, SI 2012/2329 Art.4, SI 2012/2331 Art.6, SI 2012/2339 Art.12, SI 2012/2340 Art.6, SI 2012/2341 Art.4, SI 2012/2342 Art.8, SI 2012/2343 Art.7, SI 2012/2344 Art.8, SI 2012/2345 Art.5, SI 2012/2346 Art.6, SI 2012/2347 Art.11, SI 2012/2348 Art.9, SI 2012/2351 Art.7, SI 2012/2352 Art.6, SI 2012/2355 Art.6, SI 2012/2357 Art.6, SI 2012/2359 Art.11, SI 2012/2362 Art.4, SI 2012/2363 Art.6, SI 2012/2364 Art.6, SI 2012/2368 Art.6, SI 2012/2426 Art.9, SI 2012/2427 Art.5, SI 2012/2428 Art.8, SI 2012/2429 Art.5, SI 2012/2430 Art.7, SI 2012/2431 Art.5, SI 2012/2432 Art.9, SI 2012/2435 Art.7, SI 2012/2436 Art.13, SI 2012/2437 Art.8, SI 2012/2438 Art.4, SI 2012/2441 Art.6, SI 2012/2442 Art.6, SI 2012/2443 Art.6, SI 2012/2449 Art.8, SI 2012/2450 Art.10, SI 2012/2452 Art.5, SI 2012/2454 Art.6, SI 2012/2455 Art.8, SI 2012/2459 Art.7, SI 2012/2460 Art.6, SI 2012/2462 Art.8, SI 2012/2464 Art.4, SI 2012/2467 Art.6, SI 2012/2468 Art.8, SI 2012/2470 Art.6, SI 2012/2471 Art.6, SI 2012/2472 Art.6, SI 2012/2475 Art.6, SI 2012/2482 Art.5, SI 2012/2483 Art.7, SI 2012/2484 Art.6, SI 2012/2486 Art.9, SI 2012/2490 Art.7, SI 2012/2493 Art.8, SI 2012/2496 Art.7, SI 2012/2501 Art.6, SI 2012/2508 Art.4, SI 2012/2509 Art.6, SI 2012/2511 Art.6, SI 2012/2513 Art.5, SI 2012/2515 Art.6, SI 2012/2517 Art.6, SI 2012/2518 Art.6, SI 2012/2520 Art.6, SI 2012/2526 Art.6, SI 2012/2527 Art.4, SI 2012/2528 Art.9, SI 2012/2564 Art.6, SI 2012/2577 Art.7, SI 2012/2578 Art.7, SI 2012/2580 Art.10, SI 2012/2581 Art.7, SI 2012/2585 Art.6, SI 2012/2586 Art.6, SI 2012/2615 Art.6, SI 2012/2616 Art.6, SI 2012/2618 Art.6, SI 2012/2620 Art.11, SI 2012/2622 Art.10, SI 2012/2628 Art.7, SI 2012/2637 Art.6, SI 2012/2639 Art.6, SI 2012/2641 Art.6, SI 2012/2645 Art.7, SI 2012/2646 Art.4, SI 2012/2653 Art.8, SI 2012/2662 Art.6, SI 2012/2663 Art.6, SI 2012/2671 Art.8, SI 2012/2673 Art.9, SI 2012/

2011– cont.

935. Road Traffic Exemptions (Special Forces) (Variation and Amendment) Regulations 2011– cont.

Reg.3, applied:– cont.

2692 Art.4, SI 2012/2693 Art.6, SI 2012/2694 Art.6, SI 2012/2695 Art.7, SI 2012/2697 Art.7, SI 2012/2738 Art.4, SI 2012/2739 Art.6, SI 2012/2744 Art.6, SI 2012/2759 Art.7, SI 2012/2760 Art.8, SI 2012/2766 Art.4, SI 2012/2772 Art.5, SI 2012/2774 Art.6, SI 2012/2779 Art.6, SI 2012/2780 Art.6, SI 2012/2783 Art.6, SI 2012/2784 Art.6, SI 2012/2792 Art.6, SI 2012/2809 Art.6, SI 2012/2815 Art.7, SI 2012/2816 Art.7, SI 2012/2823 Art.8, SI 2012/2826 Art.6, SI 2012/2827 Art.6, SI 2012/2835 Art.6, SI 2012/2836 Art.9, SI 2012/2847 Art.6, SI 2012/2848 Art.10, SI 2012/2849 Art.4, SI 2012/2850 Art.3, SI 2012/2851 Art.6, SI 2012/2857 Art.4, SI 2012/2858 Art.4, SI 2012/2859 Art.7, SI 2012/2860 Art.4, SI 2012/2861 Art.4, SI 2012/2863 Art.5, SI 2012/2864 Art.6, SI 2012/2866 Art.7, SI 2012/2868 Art.6, SI 2012/2869 Art.6, SI 2012/2871 Art.6, SI 2012/2872 Art.7, SI 2012/2873 Art.7, SI 2012/2908 Art.6, SI 2012/2924 Art.6, SI 2012/2925 Art.6, SI 2012/2927 Art.4, SI 2012/2928 Art.7, SI 2012/2936 Art.6, SI 2012/2955 Art.7, SI 2012/2958 Art.6, SI 2012/2959 Art.7, SI 2012/2960 Art.6, SI 2012/2961 Art.6, SI 2012/2979 Art.5, SI 2012/2981 Art.6, SI 2012/2983 Art.9, SI 2012/2997 Art.5, SI 2012/2998 Art.8, SI 2012/3000 Art.6, SI 2012/3108 Art.8, SI 2012/3114 Art.6, SI 2012/3115 Art.6, SI 2012/3116 Art.6, SI 2012/3140 Art.9, SI 2012/3155 Art.7, SI 2012/3157 Art.6, SI 2012/3190 Art.6, SI 2012/3191 Art.4, SI 2012/3211 Art.6, SI 2012/3213 Art.4, SI 2012/3214 Art.5, SSI 2012/12 Art.7, SSI 2012/13 Art.7, SSI 2012/14 Art.7, SSI 2012/15 Art.7, SSI 2012/17 Art.3, SSI 2012/46 Art.3, SSI 2012/47 Art.8, SSI 2012/56 Art.7, SSI 2012/57 Art.7, SSI 2012/58 Art.7, SSI 2012/59 Art.7, SSI 2012/62 Reg.5, SSI 2012/97 Art.7, SSI 2012/98 Art.7, SSI 2012/103 Art.3, SSI 2012/112 Art.4, SSI 2012/115 Art.3, SSI 2012/120 Art.7, SSI 2012/121 Art.7, SSI 2012/122 Art.7, SSI 2012/123 Art.7, SSI 2012/134 Art.8, SSI 2012/156 Art.7, SSI 2012/157 Art.7, SSI 2012/158 Art.7, SSI 2012/159 Art.7, SSI 2012/200 Art.4, SSI 2012/203 Art.7, SSI 2012/204 Art.7, SSI 2012/207 Art.3, SSI 2012/222 Art.3, SSI 2012/224 Art.7, SSI 2012/225 Art.7, SSI 2012/226 Art.7, SSI 2012/227 Art.7, SSI 2012/231 Art.3, SSI 2012/234 Art.7, SSI 2012/235 Art.7, SSI 2012/254 Art.7, SSI 2012/255 Art.7, SSI 2012/256 Art.7, SSI 2012/257 Art.7, SSI 2012/268 Art.6, SSI 2012/277 Art.7, SSI 2012/278 Art.7, SSI 2012/279 Art.7, SSI 2012/280 Art.7, SSI 2012/309 Art.7, SSI 2012/310 Art.7, SSI 2012/311 Art.7, SSI 2012/312 Art.7, SSI 2012/313 Art.3, SSI 2012/320 Reg.4, SSI 2012/343 Reg.4, SSI 2012/344 Reg.4

Reg.3, referred to: SI 2012/182 Art.6, SI 2012/200 Art.6, SI 2012/301 Art.6, SI 2012/302 Art.8, SI 2012/303 Art.7, SI 2012/313 Art.6, SI 2012/314 Art.6, SI 2012/316, SI 2012/2459 Art.7, SI 2012/2460 Art.6, SI 2012/2470 Art.6, SI 2012/2471 Art.6, SI 2012/2472 Art.6, SSI 2012/244 Art.3

965. Higher Education Funding Council for Wales (Supplementary Functions) Order 2011

revoked: SI 2012/1904 Art.2

988. Waste (England and Wales) Regulations 2011

applied: SI 2012/767 Reg.10

Reg.13, substituted: SI 2012/1889 Reg.2

2011– cont.

988. Waste (England and Wales) Regulations 2011– cont.
Reg.14, amended: SI 2012/1889 Reg.2
Reg.38, amended: SI 2012/1889 Reg.2
Reg.39, amended: SI 2012/1889 Reg.2
Reg.42, amended: SI 2012/1889 Reg.2
Reg.49, added: SI 2012/1889 Reg.2
Sch.4 Part 2 para.17, revoked: SI 2012/767 Reg.37

994. Vegetable Seed (Wales) (Amendment) Regulations 2011
revoked: SI 2012/245 Reg.34

1017. Landfill Tax (Qualifying Material) Order 2011
Sch.1, amended: SI 2012/940 Art.2

1035. Tax Credits Up-rating Regulations 2011
applied: SI 2012/849 Reg.5
Reg.2, applied: SI 2012/849 Reg.5
Reg.3, applied: SI 2012/849 Reg.5
Reg.4, applied: SI 2012/849 Reg.5

1055. Immigration and Nationality (Fees) Regulations 2011
revoked: SI 2012/971 Reg.8
Reg.37, see *Basnet (Validity of Application: Respondent: Nepal)* [2012] UKUT 113 (IAC), [2012] Imm. A.R. 673 (UT (IAC)), Blake, J. (President)

1080. Libya (Restrictive Measures) (Overseas Territories) Order 2011
Art.2, amended: SI 2012/356 Art.4
Sch.1, applied: SI 2012/356 Art.3

1127. Export Control (Amendment) (No.3) Order 2011
revoked: SI 2012/929 Art.2

1128. Wireless Telegraphy (Licence Charges) Regulations 2011
applied: SI 2012/2187 Reg.8
Reg.2, amended: SI 2012/1075 Reg.3
Reg.4, amended: SI 2012/1075 Reg.4
Reg.4, applied: SI 2012/2187 Reg.8
Sch.2, amended: SI 2012/1075 Reg.5
Sch.4 Part 3 para.5, amended: SI 2012/1075 Reg.6
Sch.5, amended: SI 2012/1075 Reg.7
Sch.9, amended: SI 2012/1075 Reg.8
Sch.13, amended: SI 2012/1075 Reg.9
Sch.15 Part 1 para.1, added: SI 2012/1075 Reg.10
Sch.15 Part 1 para.2, added: SI 2012/1075 Reg.10
Sch.15 Part 2 para.3, added: SI 2012/1075 Reg.10
Sch.15 Part 2 para.4, added: SI 2012/1075 Reg.10
Sch.15 Part 2 para.5, added: SI 2012/1075 Reg.10
Sch.15 Part 3 para.6, added: SI 2012/1075 Reg.10
Sch.15 Part 3 para.7, added: SI 2012/1075 Reg.10

1157. Skipton Fund Limited (Application of Sections 731, 733 and 734 of the Income Tax (Trading and Other Income) Act 2005) Order 2011
Art.2, amended: SI 2012/1188 Art.2

1181. Feed-in Tariffs (Specified Maximum Capacity and Functions) (Amendment) Order 2011
revoked: SI 2012/2782 Sch.3

1197. Trade in Animals and Related Products Regulations 2011
Reg.11, applied: SI 2012/2629 Reg.4
Reg.32, amended: SI 2012/2897 Art.41

1244. Syria (Asset-Freezing) Regulations 2011
revoked: SI 2012/129 Reg.24
Reg.9, applied: SI 2012/129 Reg.25

1267. Pensions Act 2007 (Commencement No 4) Order 2011
Art.2, amended: SI 2012/911 Art.2

2011– cont.

1267. Pensions Act 2007 (Commencement No 4) Order 2011– cont.
Art.3, amended: SI 2012/911 Art.2

1268. Whole of Government Accounts (Designation of Bodies) Order 2011
varied: SI 2012/147 Art.7

1297. Export Control (Iran) Order 2011
revoked: SI 2012/1243 Art.1

1304. Export Control (Syria and Miscellaneous Amendments) Order 2011
Art.1, revoked: SI 2012/810 Sch.1
Art.2, revoked: SI 2012/810 Sch.1
Art.3, revoked: SI 2012/810 Sch.1
Art.4, revoked: SI 2012/810 Sch.1
Art.5, revoked: SI 2012/810 Sch.1
Art.6, revoked: SI 2012/810 Sch.1
Art.7, revoked: SI 2012/810 Sch.1
Art.10, revoked: SI 2012/810 Sch.1

1327. Medicines (Miscellaneous Amendments) Order 2011
revoked: SI 2012/1916 Sch.35

1349. Employment and Support Allowance (Work-Related Activity) Regulations 2011
Reg.8, revoked (in part): SI 2012/2756 Reg.7
Reg.9, amended: SI 2012/2756 Reg.7

1454. Air Navigation (Dangerous Goods) (Amendment) (No.2) Regulations 2011
revoked: SI 2012/3054 Reg.3

1466. Electoral Registration Data Schemes Order 2011
revoked: SI 2012/1944 Art.6

1484. Civil Jurisdiction and Judgments (Maintenance) Regulations 2011
see *Practice Direction 34C (Fam Div: Applications for Recognition and Enforcement to or from European Union Member States)* [2012] 1 F.L.R. 1075 (Fam Div), Sir Nicholas Wall (President, Fam)
Sch.1 Part 2 para.4, amended: SI 2012/2814 Sch.5 para.8
Sch.1 Part 2 para.4, revoked (in part): SI 2012/2814 Sch.5 para.8
Sch.1 Part 5 para.11, added: SI 2012/2814 Sch.5 para.8
Sch.2 para.1, amended: SI 2012/2814 Sch.5 para.8
Sch.2 para.1, revoked (in part): SI 2012/2814 Sch.5 para.8
Sch.2 para.3, amended: SI 2012/2814 Sch.5 para.8
Sch.2 para.4, amended: SI 2012/2814 Sch.5 para.8
Sch.2 para.6, added: SI 2012/2814 Sch.5 para.8
Sch.6, applied: SI 2012/2814 Sch.1 para.7
Sch.6 para.16, amended: SI 2012/2814 Sch.5 para.8

1506. Greenhouse Gas Emissions Trading Scheme (Nitrous Oxide) Regulations 2011
Reg.3, revoked: SI 2012/3038 Reg.85
Reg.4, revoked: SI 2012/3038 Reg.85

1508. Wireless Telegraphy (Register) (Amendment) (No.2) Regulations 2011
revoked: SI 2012/2186 Sch.1

1515. Building (Amendment) Regulations 2011
Reg.2, revoked: SI 2012/3118 Sch.3

1519. Shropshire Community Health National Health Service Trust (Establishment) Order 2011
Art.4, amended: SI 2012/2317 Art.2

1524. Energy Information Regulations 2011
Reg.4, amended: SI 2012/2897 Art.42
Sch.1 para.1, amended: SI 2012/3005 Reg.3

2011–cont.

1534. A3 Trunk Road (Hindhead) (Derestriction and Variable Speed Limit) Order 2011
revoked: SI 2012/2138 Art.5

1543. Environmental Protection (Controls on Ozone-Depleting Substances) Regulations 2011
Reg.2, amended: SI 2012/2897 Art.43
Reg.7, amended: SI 2012/2897 Art.43
Reg.8, amended: SI 2012/2897 Art.43

1551. Care Quality Commission (Additional Functions) Regulations 2011
Reg.4, amended: SI 2012/921 Reg.10

1556. National Health Service (Charges to Overseas Visitors) Regulations 2011
Reg.2, amended: SI 2012/1586 Reg.2
Reg.6, amended: SI 2012/1586 Reg.2
Reg.8, amended: SI 2012/1586 Reg.2
Reg.23, revoked (in part): SI 2012/1586 Reg.2
Reg.24, substituted: SI 2012/1586 Reg.2
Sch.3, revoked: SI 2012/1586 Reg.2

1568. Contracting Out (Local Authorities Social Services Functions) (England) Order 2011
Art.2, amended: SI 2012/3003 Art.2
Art.4, amended: SI 2012/3003 Art.2

1588. Disabled Persons (Badges for Motor Vehicles) (Wales) (Amendment) Regulations 2011
Reg.5, varied: 2012 c.11 s.12

1613. Undertakings for Collective Investment in Transferable Securities Regulations 2011
Reg.8, amended: SI 2012/2015 Reg.5

1627. Education (Non-Maintained Special Schools) (England) Regulations 2011
Sch.1 Part 1 para.4, amended: SI 2012/979 Sch.1 para.32
Sch.1 Part 1 para.5, amended: SI 2012/979 Sch.1 para.32

1654. Cancellation of Student Loans for Living Costs Liability (Wales) Regulations 2011
applied: SI 2012/1518 Reg.5

1655. Feed-in Tariffs (Specified Maximum Capacity and Functions) (Amendment No.2) Order 2011
revoked: SI 2012/2782 Sch.3

1668. Prospectus Regulations 2011
applied: SI 2012/1538 Reg.10

1678. Syria (Restrictive Measures) (Overseas Territories) Order 2011
revoked: SI 2012/1755 Art.48
Sch.1, amended: SI 2012/362 Sch.3

1679. Egypt (Restrictive Measures) (Overseas Territories) Order 2011
Sch.1, amended: SI 2012/362 Sch.3

1691. Consular Fees (Amendment) Order 2011
revoked: SI 2012/798 Sch.2

1709. Criminal Procedure Rules 2011
applied: SI 2012/1726, SI 2012/1726 r.2.1
see *Practice Direction (Sen Cts: Criminal Proceedings: Forms)* [2012] 1 W.L.R. 778 (Sen Cts), Lord Judge, L.C.J.; see *R. v Newell (Alan)* [2012] EWCA Crim 650, [2012] 1 W.L.R. 3142 (CA (Crim Div)), Sir John Thomas (President)
r.4.4, see *Whiteside v DPP* [2011] EWHC 3471 (Admin), (2012) 176 J.P. 103 (QBD (Admin)), Elias, L.J.
r.5.8, see *R. (on the application of Guardian News and Media Ltd) v City of Westminster Magistrates' Court* [2012] EWCA Civ 420, [2012] 3 W.L.R. 1343 (CA (Civ Div)), Lord Neuberger (M.R.)

2011–cont.

1709. Criminal Procedure Rules 2011–*cont.*
r.14.2, see *R. v F* [2012] EWCA Crim 720, [2012] 1 W.L.R. 3133 (CA (Crim Div)), Jackson, L.J.
r.29.3, see *Practice Direction (Sen Cts: Criminal Proceedings: Forms)* [2012] 1 W.L.R. 778 (Sen Cts), Lord Judge, L.C.J.
r.29.24, see *Practice Direction (Sen Cts: Criminal Proceedings: Forms)* [2012] 1 W.L.R. 778 (Sen Cts), Lord Judge, L.C.J.
r.34.3, see *R. v SVS Solicitors* [2012] EWCA Crim 319, [2012] 3 Costs L.R. 502 (CA (Crim Div)), Hughes, L.J. (Vice President)

1716. Legal Services Act 2007 (The Law Society and The Council for Licensed Conveyancers) (Modification of Functions) Order 2011
Art.5, amended: SI 2012/2987 Art.4
Sch.1 para.1, amended: SI 2012/2987 Art.5
Sch.1 para.2, amended: SI 2012/2987 Art.5
Sch.1 para.3, amended: SI 2012/2987 Art.5
Sch.1 para.4, amended: SI 2012/2987 Art.5

1718. Humber Bridge (Debts) Order 2011
revoked: SI 2012/716 Art.3

1730. Pensions Act 2008 (Abolition of Protected Rights) (Consequential Amendments) (No.2) Order 2011
Art.3, substituted: SI 2012/709 Art.2
Art.5, amended: SI 2012/709 Art.2
Art.6, amended: SI 2012/709 Art.2

1731. Ecclesiastical Judges, Legal Officers and Others (Fees) Order 2011
revoked: SI 2012/1846 Art.3

1735. Legal Officers (Annual Fees) Order 2011
revoked: SI 2012/1847 Art.4

1753. Betting and Gaming Duties Act 1981 (Amendment) Order 2011
revoked: 2012 c.14 Sch.24 para.53

1824. Town and Country Planning (Environmental Impact Assessment) Regulations 2011
applied: SI 2012/637 Reg.23
Reg.2, amended: SI 2012/637 Sch.3 para.4
Reg.25, amended: SI 2012/637 Sch.3 para.5
Reg.29A, added: SI 2012/637 Sch.3 para.6
Reg.29A, applied: SI 2012/637 Reg.23, Reg.24
Reg.36, amended: SI 2012/637 Sch.3 para.7
Reg.38, amended: SI 2012/637 Sch.3 para.8
Reg.43, amended: SI 2012/637 Sch.3 para.9
Reg.47, amended: SI 2012/637 Sch.3 para.10
Reg.49, amended: SI 2012/637 Sch.3 para.11
Reg.64, amended: SI 2012/637 Sch.3 para.12
Sch.3 para.2, amended: SI 2012/637 Sch.3 para.13

1848. Defence and Security Public Contracts Regulations 2011
applied: SSI 2012/88 Reg.6, SSI 2012/89 Reg.6
Reg.3, amended: SSI 2012/88 Sch.7 Part B
Reg.4, amended: SSI 2012/88 Sch.7 Part B, SSI 2012/89 Sch.5 Part B
Reg.6, amended: SSI 2012/88 Sch.7 Part B, SSI 2012/89 Sch.5 Part B
Reg.7, disapplied: SSI 2012/89 Reg.6
Reg.9, disapplied: SSI 2012/89 Reg.6
Reg.16, amended: SSI 2012/88 Sch.7 Part B
Reg.31, amended: SSI 2012/88 Sch.7 Part B
Reg.33, amended: SSI 2012/88 Sch.7 Part B
Reg.46, amended: SSI 2012/88 Sch.7 Part B

1916. A38 Trunk Road (Smithaleigh Junction, Plympton Bypass) (Temporary Prohibition of Traffic) Order 2011
revoked: SI 2012/110 Art.6

2011– cont.

1917. School Teachers Pay and Conditions Order 2011
revoked: SI 2012/2051 Art.3

1947. National Curriculum (Assessment Arrangements on Entry to the Foundation Phase) (Wales) Order 2011
revoked: SI 2012/935 Art.2

1986. Education (Student Support) Regulations 2011
Reg.2, amended: SI 2012/1653 Reg.9
Reg.13, amended: SI 2012/1653 Reg.10
Reg.22, amended: SI 2012/1653 Reg.11
Reg.22, revoked (in part): SI 2012/1653 Reg.11
Reg.23, amended: SI 2012/1653 Reg.12
Reg.38, amended: SI 2012/1653 Reg.13
Reg.38, applied: SSI 2012/303 Reg.20
Reg.41, amended: SI 2012/1653 Reg.14
Reg.42, amended: SI 2012/1653 Reg.15
Reg.44, amended: SI 2012/1653 Reg.16
Reg.45, amended: SI 2012/1653 Reg.17, Reg.18
Reg.47, amended: SI 2012/1653 Reg.19
Reg.49A, added: SI 2012/1653 Reg.20
Reg.56, amended: SI 2012/1653 Reg.21
Reg.57, amended: SI 2012/1653 Sch.1
Reg.58, amended: SI 2012/1653 Sch.1
Reg.59, amended: SI 2012/1653 Sch.1
Reg.60, amended: SI 2012/1653 Reg.22, Sch.1
Reg.61, amended: SI 2012/1653 Reg.23
Reg.62, amended: SI 2012/1653 Reg.24, Sch.1
Reg.63, amended: SI 2012/1653 Sch.1
Reg.64, amended: SI 2012/1653 Reg.25, Sch.1
Reg.65, amended: SI 2012/1653 Sch.1
Reg.68, amended: SI 2012/1653 Sch.1
Reg.72, amended: SI 2012/1653 Sch.1
Reg.73, amended: SI 2012/1653 Sch.1
Reg.74, amended: SI 2012/1653 Sch.1
Reg.75, amended: SI 2012/1653 Reg.26, Sch.1
Reg.76, amended: SI 2012/1653 Sch.1
Reg.80, amended: SI 2012/1653 Sch.1
Reg.124, amended: SI 2012/1653 Reg.27, Sch.1
Reg.125, amended: SI 2012/1653 Sch.1
Reg.127, amended: SI 2012/1653 Reg.28
Reg.141, amended: SI 2012/1653 Reg.29, Sch.1
Reg.142, amended: SI 2012/1653 Sch.1
Reg.144, amended: SI 2012/1653 Reg.30
Reg.147, amended: SI 2012/1653 Reg.31
Reg.149, amended: SI 2012/1653 Reg.32
Reg.157, amended: SI 2012/1653 Reg.33
Reg.159, amended: SI 2012/1653 Reg.34
Reg.166, amended: SI 2012/1653 Reg.35
Sch.1 Part 1 para.1, amended: SI 2012/1653 Reg.36
Sch.1 Part 2 para.10, amended: SI 2012/1653 Reg.37
Sch.4 para.3, amended: SI 2012/1653 Reg.38

2010. Export Control (Belarus) and (Syria Amendment) Order 2011
Art.10, revoked: SI 2012/810 Sch.1

2019. Access to the Countryside (Appeals against Works Notices) (England) Regulations 2011
Reg.4, revoked (in part): SI 2012/67 Reg.2
Reg.6, substituted: SI 2012/67 Reg.2
Reg.12A, added: SI 2012/67 Reg.2
Reg.15, amended: SI 2012/67 Reg.2

2023. M1 and M6 Motorways (M1 Junction 19) (Temporary Restriction and Prohibition of Traffic) Order 2011
revoked: SI 2012/253 Art.11

2011– cont.

2055. Infrastructure Planning (Changes to, and Revocation of, Development Consent Orders) Regulations 2011
varied: SI 2012/147 Art.7
Reg.2, amended: SI 2012/635 Reg.11, SI 2012/2732 Reg.7
Reg.4, amended: SI 2012/635 Reg.11
Reg.5, amended: SI 2012/635 Reg.11
Reg.6, amended: SI 2012/635 Reg.11
Reg.7, amended: SI 2012/635 Reg.11
Reg.8, amended: SI 2012/635 Reg.11
Reg.9, amended: SI 2012/635 Reg.11
Reg.10, amended: SI 2012/635 Reg.11
Reg.12, amended: SI 2012/635 Reg.11
Reg.13, amended: SI 2012/635 Reg.11
Reg.14, amended: SI 2012/635 Reg.11
Reg.16, amended: SI 2012/635 Reg.11
Reg.17, amended: SI 2012/635 Reg.11
Reg.18, amended: SI 2012/635 Reg.11
Reg.19, amended: SI 2012/635 Reg.11
Reg.19, revoked (in part): SI 2012/635 Reg.11
Reg.20, amended: SI 2012/635 Reg.11
Reg.21, amended: SI 2012/635 Reg.11
Reg.22, amended: SI 2012/635 Reg.11
Reg.22, revoked (in part): SI 2012/635 Reg.11
Reg.23, amended: SI 2012/635 Reg.11
Reg.24, amended: SI 2012/635 Reg.11
Reg.25, revoked: SI 2012/635 Reg.11
Reg.26, amended: SI 2012/635 Reg.11
Reg.26, revoked (in part): SI 2012/635 Reg.11
Reg.28, amended: SI 2012/635 Reg.11
Reg.32, amended: SI 2012/635 Reg.11
Reg.34, amended: SI 2012/635 Reg.11
Reg.35, amended: SI 2012/635 Reg.11
Reg.40, amended: SI 2012/635 Reg.11
Reg.42, amended: SI 2012/635 Reg.11
Reg.43, amended: SI 2012/635 Reg.11
Reg.43, revoked (in part): SI 2012/635 Reg.11
Reg.47, amended: SI 2012/635 Reg.11
Reg.47, revoked (in part): SI 2012/635 Reg.11
Reg.48, revoked: SI 2012/635 Reg.11
Reg.49, amended: SI 2012/635 Reg.11
Reg.49, revoked (in part): SI 2012/635 Reg.11
Reg.50, amended: SI 2012/635 Reg.11
Reg.51, amended: SI 2012/635 Reg.11
Reg.51, revoked (in part): SI 2012/635 Reg.11
Reg.52, amended: SI 2012/635 Reg.11
Reg.52, revoked (in part): SI 2012/635 Reg.11
Reg.53, amended: SI 2012/635 Reg.11
Reg.54, amended: SI 2012/635 Reg.11
Reg.55, amended: SI 2012/635 Reg.11
Reg.55, revoked (in part): SI 2012/635 Reg.11
Reg.56, amended: SI 2012/635 Reg.11
Reg.57, amended: SI 2012/635 Reg.11
Reg.58, amended: SI 2012/635 Reg.11
Reg.58, revoked (in part): SI 2012/635 Reg.11
Reg.59, amended: SI 2012/635 Reg.11
Reg.60, amended: SI 2012/635 Reg.11
Reg.61, amended: SI 2012/635 Reg.11
Reg.63, amended: SI 2012/635 Reg.11
Reg.64, amended: SI 2012/635 Reg.11
Reg.67, amended: SI 2012/635 Reg.11
Reg.69, amended: SI 2012/635 Reg.11
Sch.1, amended: SI 2012/1659 Art.2, SI 2012/2654 Sch.1, SI 2012/2732 Reg.7
Sch.1, varied: 2012 c.11 s.12
Sch.2 para.1, amended: SI 2012/635 Reg.11
Sch.2 para.2, amended: SI 2012/635 Reg.11

2011– cont.

2055. Infrastructure Planning (Changes to, and Revocation of, Development Consent Orders) Regulations 2011– cont.
Sch.2 para.3, amended: SI 2012/635 Reg.11
Sch.2 para.4, amended: SI 2012/635 Reg.11
Sch.2 para.5, amended: SI 2012/635 Reg.11
Sch.2 para.6, amended: SI 2012/635 Reg.11
Sch.2 para.7, amended: SI 2012/635 Reg.11

2058. Town and Country Planning (Compensation) (England) Regulations 2011
revoked: SI 2012/749 Reg.7

2065. Criminal Defence Service (Funding) (Amendment) Order 2011
Art.25, see *R. (on the application of Law Society of England and Wales) v Lord Chancellor* [2012] EWHC 794 (Admin), [2012] 3 Costs L.R. 558 (DC), Stanley Burnton, L.J.

2105. Smoke Control Areas (Authorised Fuels) (England) (Amendment) (No.2) Regulations 2011
revoked: SI 2012/814 Sch.2

2106. Smoke Control Areas (Exempted Fireplaces) (England) (No.2) Order 2011
revoked: SI 2012/815 Art.3

2131. Plant Protection Products Regulations 2011
applied: SI 2012/1657 Reg.5, Sch.2 para.9
Reg.2, amended: SI 2012/1657 Sch.5
Reg.6, substituted: SI 2012/1657 Sch.5
Sch.1 para.1, amended: SI 2012/1657 Sch.5
Sch.1 para.2, amended: SI 2012/1657 Sch.5
Sch.1 para.3, amended: SI 2012/1657 Sch.5
Sch.1 para.4, amended: SI 2012/1657 Sch.5
Sch.1 para.5, revoked: SI 2012/1657 Sch.5
Sch.1 para.8, amended: SI 2012/1657 Sch.5

2132. Plant Protection Products (Fees and Charges) Regulations 2011
Reg.6, applied: SI 2012/1657 Reg.29

2136. National Health Service (Pharmaceutical Services) Amendment Regulations 2011
revoked: SI 2012/1909 Sch.8 para.9

2154. Pigs (Records, Identification and Movement) Order 2011
Art.25, amended: SI 2012/2897 Art.44

2159. Veterinary Medicines Regulations 2011
Sch.5 para.7, substituted: SI 2012/2711 Reg.2
Sch.5 para.17, amended: SI 2012/2711 Reg.3
Sch.5 para.22, amended: SI 2012/2711 Reg.4

2237. NHS Commissioning Board Authority (Establishment and Constitution) Order 2011
revoked: SI 2012/1641 Sch.2 para.3

2238. M27 Motorway (Junctions 11 12) (Temporary Restriction and Prohibition of Traffic) Order 2011
revoked: SI 2012/16 Art.7

2250. NHS Commissioning Board Authority Regulations 2011
revoked: SI 2012/1641 Sch.2 para.4
Reg.14, applied: SI 2012/1641 Art.6

2251. A38 Trunk Road (Chudleigh, Near Newton Abbot) (Temporary Prohibition of Traffic) Order 2011
revoked: SI 2012/113 Art.5

2260. Equality Act 2010 (Specific Duties) Regulations 2011
Sch.1, amended: SI 2012/641 Art.2, SI 2012/1641 Sch.4 para.20
Sch.1, varied: SI 2012/725 Art.2

2011– cont.

2296. Police Act 1997 (Criminal Records and Registration) (Isle of Man) Regulations 2011
Reg.8, amended: SI 2012/2667 Reg.2
Reg.9, revoked: SI 2012/2109 Reg.2

2323. Health Research Authority (Establishment and Constitution) Order 2011
Art.1, amended: SI 2012/1109 Art.2
Art.3, amended: SI 2012/1109 Art.2
Art.4, substituted: SI 2012/1109 Art.2

2330. A55 Trunk Road (Glan Conwy Conwy Morfa, Conwy County Borough) (Temporary 70 mph Speed Limit) Order 2011
disapplied: SI 2012/6 Art.11, SI 2012/141 Art.15, SI 2012/163 Art.15, SI 2012/275 Art.11

2341. Health Research Authority Regulations 2011
Reg.1, amended: SI 2012/1108 Reg.2, SI 2012/1641 Sch.3 para.15, Sch.4 para.21
Reg.2, substituted: SI 2012/1108 Reg.2
Reg.2A, added: SI 2012/1108 Reg.2
Reg.2A, amended: SI 2012/1641 Sch.3 para.15
Reg.2B, added: SI 2012/1108 Reg.2
Reg.2C, added: SI 2012/1108 Reg.2
Reg.2D, added: SI 2012/1108 Reg.2
Reg.2E, added: SI 2012/1108 Reg.2
Reg.2F, added: SI 2012/1108 Reg.2
Reg.2G, added: SI 2012/1108 Reg.2
Reg.3, amended: SI 2012/1108 Reg.2
Reg.8, amended: SI 2012/1108 Reg.2
Sch.1 para.1, substituted: SI 2012/1108 Reg.2
Sch.1 para.2, substituted: SI 2012/1108 Reg.2
Sch.1 para.3, substituted: SI 2012/1108 Reg.2
Sch.1 para.4, substituted: SI 2012/1108 Reg.2
Sch.1 para.5, substituted: SI 2012/1108 Reg.2
Sch.1 para.6, substituted: SI 2012/1108 Reg.2

2364. Feed-in Tariffs (Specified Maximum Capacity and Functions) (Amendment No.3) Order 2011
revoked: SI 2012/2782 Sch.3

2368. M5 and M6 Motorways (M5 Junction 2 to M6 Junction 9) (Temporary Restriction and Prohibition of Traffic) Order 2011
revoked: SI 2012/224 Art.10

2432. Air Navigation (Amendment) Order 2011
applied: 2012 c.19 Sch.6 para.4

2440. Belarus (Restrictive Measures) (Overseas Territories) Order 2011
Sch.1, amended: SI 2012/362 Sch.3

2441. Double Taxation Relief and International Tax Enforcement (South Africa) Order 2011
see *Revenue and Customs Commissioners v Ben Nevis (Holdings) Ltd* [2012] EWHC 1807 (Ch), [2012] S.T.C. 2157 (Ch D), Judge Pelling Q.C.

2451. Agricultural Holdings (Units of Production) (England) Order 2011
revoked: SI 2012/2573 Art.3

2452. Energy Performance of Buildings (Certificates and Inspections) (England and Wales) (Amendment) Regulations 2011
revoked: SI 2012/3118 Sch.3
Reg.2, revoked (in part): SI 2012/809 Reg.12
Reg.3, revoked (in part): SI 2012/809 Reg.12
Reg.5, varied: SI 2012/809 Reg.13

2479. Syria (Asset-Freezing) (Amendment) Regulations 2011
revoked: SI 2012/129 Reg.24

2482. M5 Motorway (Junctions 14-13, Michael Wood Services) (Temporary Prohibition of Traffic) Order 2011
revoked: SI 2012/53 Art.5

2011– cont.

2489. Immigration (Designation of Travel Bans) (Amendment No.6) Order 2011
revoked: SI 2012/ 1663 Sch.2

2555. Landfill Allowances Scheme (Wales) (Amendment) Regulations 2011
revoked: SI 2012/ 65 Reg.2

2654. M25 Motorway (Junctions 29 30) (Temporary Prohibition of Traffic) Order 2011
revoked: SI 2012/ 1190 Art.5

2699. Recognised Auction Platforms Regulations 2011
Reg.5, amended: SI 2012/ 1906 Art.8
Reg.5A, added: SI 2012/ 1906 Art.8
Reg.5B, added: SI 2012/ 1906 Art.8

2756. Wireless Telegraphy (Register) (Amendment) (No.3) Regulations 2011
revoked: SI 2012/ 2186 Sch.1

2759. Food Protection (Emergency Prohibitions) (Radioactivity in Sheep) (Wales) (Partial Revocation) Order 2011
revoked: SI 2012/ 2978 Sch.1

2771. A27 Trunk Road (Selmeston Firle) (Temporary Restriction and Prohibition of Traffic) Order 2011
Art.2, amended: SI 2012/ 26 Art.2
Art.3, substituted: SI 2012/ 26 Art.2

2785. General Teaching Council for England (Disciplinary Functions) (Amendment) Regulations 2011
revoked: SI 2012/ 1153 Sch.1

2831. Agricultural Holdings (Units of Production) (Wales) Order 2011
revoked: SI 2012/ 3022 Art.3

2859. Regulated Covered Bonds (Amendment) Regulations 2011
Reg.2, amended: SI 2012/ 2977 Reg.2

2860. Renewable Heat Incentive Scheme Regulations 2011
Reg.2, amended: SI 2012/ 1999 Reg.3
Reg.22, amended: SI 2012/ 1999 Reg.4
Reg.23, amended: SI 2012/ 1999 Reg.5
Reg.25, amended: SI 2012/ 1999 Reg.6
Reg.26, amended: SI 2012/ 1999 Reg.7
Reg.43, amended: SI 2012/ 1999 Reg.8
Reg.51A, added: SI 2012/ 1999 Reg.9
Reg.51B, added: SI 2012/ 1999 Reg.9
Sch.1 para.1, amended: SI 2012/ 1999 Reg.10, SSI 2012/ 360 Sch.11 para.26

2883. Non-Commercial Movement of Pet Animals Order 2011
Art.13, amended: SI 2012/ 2897 Art.45

2911. Greenhouse Gas Emissions Trading Scheme (Amendment) (Registries and Fees etc.) Regulations 2011
Sch.1 para.1, revoked: SI 2012/ 3038 Reg.85
Sch.1 para.2, revoked: SI 2012/ 3038 Reg.85
Sch.1 para.3, revoked: SI 2012/ 3038 Reg.85
Sch.1 para.4, revoked: SI 2012/ 3038 Reg.85
Sch.1 para.5, revoked: SI 2012/ 3038 Reg.85
Sch.1 para.6, revoked: SI 2012/ 3038 Reg.85
Sch.1 para.7, revoked: SI 2012/ 3038 Reg.85
Sch.1 para.8, revoked: SI 2012/ 3038 Reg.85
Sch.1 para.9, revoked: SI 2012/ 3038 Reg.85
Sch.1 para.10, revoked: SI 2012/ 3038 Reg.85
Sch.1 para.11, revoked: SI 2012/ 3038 Reg.85
Sch.1 para.12, revoked: SI 2012/ 3038 Reg.85
Sch.1 para.13, revoked: SI 2012/ 3038 Reg.85
Sch.1 para.14, revoked: SI 2012/ 3038 Reg.85
Sch.1 para.15, revoked: SI 2012/ 3038 Reg.85

2011– cont.

2911. Greenhouse Gas Emissions Trading Scheme (Amendment) (Registries and Fees etc.) Regulations 2011–*cont.*
Sch.1 para.16, revoked: SI 2012/ 3038 Reg.85
Sch.1 para.17, revoked: SI 2012/ 3038 Reg.85
Sch.1 para.18, revoked: SI 2012/ 3038 Reg.85
Sch.1 para.19, revoked: SI 2012/ 3038 Reg.85
Sch.1 para.20, revoked: SI 2012/ 3038 Reg.85
Sch.1 para.22, revoked (in part): SI 2012/ 2788 Reg.17
Sch.1 para.23, revoked (in part): SI 2012/ 2788 Reg.17
Sch.1 para.28, revoked (in part): SI 2012/ 2788 Reg.17

2914. Local Authorities (Referendums)(Petitions)(England) Regulations 2011
Reg.17, applied: SI 2012/ 323 Reg.4, Reg.14
Reg.18, applied: SI 2012/ 323 Reg.14
Reg.19, applied: SI 2012/ 323 Reg.14

2922. River Tyne (Tunnels) (Revision of Tolls) Order 2011
revoked: SI 2012/ 3053 Art.3

2930. Immigration (Designation of Travel Bans) (Amendment No 7) Order 2011
revoked: SI 2012/ 1663 Sch.2

2936. Wine Regulations 2011
Reg.3, amended: SI 2012/ 2897 Art.46
Reg.9, amended: SI 2012/ 2897 Art.46

2939. Carers Strategies (Wales) Regulations 2011
Reg.9, revoked (in part): SI 2012/ 282 Reg.3
Sch.1, amended: SI 2012/ 282 Reg.2

2942. Mental Health (Care Co-ordination and Care and Treatment Planning) (Wales) Regulations 2011
Sch.1 para.1, amended: SI 2012/ 1479 Sch.1 para.66, Sch.1 para.93

2955. Health Service Branded Medicines (Control of Prices and Supply of Information) Amendment Regulations 2011
revoked: SI 2012/ 2791 Reg.3

2973. Occupational Pension Schemes (Employer Debt and Miscellaneous Amendments) Regulations 2011
Reg.5, see *BESTrustees Plc v Kaupthing Singer & Friedlander Ltd (In Administration)* [2012] EWHC 629 (Ch), [2012] 3 All E.R. 874 (Ch D), Sales, J.

2986. Parliamentary Commissioner (No.2) Order 2011
varied: SI 2012/ 147 Art.7

2989. Iran (Restrictive Measures) (Overseas Territories) Order 2011
Art.1, amended: SI 2012/ 1389 Art.3
Art.2, amended: SI 2012/ 1389 Art.4
Art.3, substituted: SI 2012/ 1389 Art.5
Art.3A, added: SI 2012/ 1389 Art.6
Art.3B, added: SI 2012/ 1389 Art.6
Art.3C, added: SI 2012/ 1389 Art.6
Art.3D, added: SI 2012/ 1389 Art.6
Art.3E, added: SI 2012/ 1389 Art.6
Art.3F, added: SI 2012/ 1389 Art.6
Art.3G, added: SI 2012/ 1389 Art.6
Art.3H, added: SI 2012/ 1389 Art.6
Art.3I, added: SI 2012/ 1389 Art.6
Art.3J, added: SI 2012/ 1389 Art.6
Art.3K, added: SI 2012/ 1389 Art.6
Art.3L, added: SI 2012/ 1389 Art.6
Art.3M, added: SI 2012/ 1389 Art.6
Art.3N, added: SI 2012/ 1389 Art.6

2011– cont.

2989. Iran (Restrictive Measures) (Overseas Territories) Order 2011– *cont.*
Art.3O, added: SI 2012/ 1389 Art.6
Art.13, amended: SI 2012/ 1389 Art.7
Sch.2 paraA.1, added: SI 2012/ 1389 Art.8
Sch.2 para.1, amended: SI 2012/ 1389 Art.8
Sch.2 para.2, amended: SI 2012/ 1389 Art.8
Sch.2 para.2A, added: SI 2012/ 1389 Art.8
Sch.4 paraA.1, added: SI 2012/ 1389 Art.9
Sch.4 para.1, amended: SI 2012/ 1389 Art.9
Sch.4 para.2, amended: SI 2012/ 1389 Art.9
Sch.4 para.3, amended: SI 2012/ 1389 Art.9
Sch.4 para.3A, added: SI 2012/ 1389 Art.9

3006. Employment Rights (Increase of Limits) Order 2011
revoked: SI 2012/ 3007 Art.2

3019. Police Reform and Social Responsibility Act 2011 (Commencement No 3 and Transitional Provisions) Order 2011
Art.7, amended: SI 2012/ 2892 Art.8
Art.8, amended: SI 2012/ 2892 Art.8
Sch.1, amended: SI 2012/ 75 Art.2

3027. Police (Performance and Conduct) (Amendment Metropolitan Police) Regulations 2011
revoked: SI 2012/ 2631 Reg.3

3028. Police (Complaints and Misconduct) (Amendment Metropolitan Police) Regulations 2011
revoked: SI 2012/ 1204 Reg.2

3029. Police Appeals Tribunals (Amendment Metropolitan Police) Rules 2011
revoked: SI 2012/ 2630 r.2

3038. Council Tax (Demand Notices) (England) Regulations 2011
applied: SI 2012/ 444 Reg.10
Sch.1 Part 2, substituted: SI 2012/ 3087 Reg.2
Sch.1 Part 2 para.18, amended: SI 2012/ 3087 Reg.2
Sch.1 Part 2 para.19, amended: SI 2012/ 3087 Reg.2
Sch.1 Part 2 para.19A, added: SI 2012/ 3087 Reg.2
Sch.1 Part 2 para.19B, added: SI 2012/ 3087 Reg.2
Sch.1 Part 2 para.27, amended: SI 2012/ 3087 Reg.2

3042. Landfill Allowances Scheme (Wales) (Amendment) (No.2) Regulations 2011
revoked: SI 2012/ 65 Reg.3

3050. Elected Local Policing Bodies (Specified Information) Order 2011
Sch.1 Part 1 para.2A, added: SI 2012/ 2479 Art.3
Sch.1 Part 1 para.3, amended: SI 2012/ 2479 Art.4
Sch.1 Part 1 para.4, amended: SI 2012/ 2479 Art.5
Sch.1 Part 1 para.8, substituted: SI 2012/ 2479 Art.6
Sch.1 Part 2 para.9, amended: SI 2012/ 2479 Art.7
Sch.1 Part 2 para.12, amended: SI 2012/ 2479 Art.8
Sch.1 Part 2 para.13, substituted: SI 2012/ 2479 Art.9

3058. Local Policing Bodies (Consequential Amendments) Regulations 2011
Reg.20, revoked: SI 2012/ 767 Reg.37

3060. Severn Bridges Tolls Order 2011
revoked: SI 2012/ 3136 Art.3

3087. A38 Trunk Road (Drybridge Junction to Marley Head Junction, Near South Brent) (Temporary Prohibition and Restriction of Traffic) (Number 2) Order 2011
Art.3, amended: SI 2012/ 242 Art.2

2012

10. School Admissions (Infant Class Sizes) (England) Regulations 2012
applied: SI 2012/ 2991 Sch.2 para.10

2012– cont.

83. Air Navigation (Restriction of Flying) (Southend-on-Sea) Regulations 2012
Reg.3, amended: SI 2012/ 1208 Reg.3

103. Plant Health (Import Inspection Fees) (England) (Amendment) Regulations 2012
revoked: SI 2012/ 745 Reg.7

114. Uplands Transitional Payment Regulations 2012
Reg.2, referred to: SI 2012/ 2573 Sch.1
Reg.3, applied: SI 2012/ 2573 Sch.1
Reg.5, applied: SI 2012/ 2573 Sch.1

115. Education (School Teachers Appraisal) (England) Regulations 2012
applied: SI 2012/ 1115 Sch.1 para.24
Reg.1, amended: SI 2012/ 2055 Reg.2
Reg.6, amended: SI 2012/ 431 Reg.9

129. Syria (European Union Financial Sanctions) Regulations 2012
Reg.3, amended: SI 2012/ 639 Reg.3, SI 2012/ 2524 Reg.2
Reg.4, amended: SI 2012/ 639 Reg.4, SI 2012/ 2524 Reg.2
Reg.5, amended: SI 2012/ 639 Reg.4, SI 2012/ 2524 Reg.2
Reg.6, amended: SI 2012/ 639 Reg.5, SI 2012/ 2524 Reg.2
Reg.7, amended: SI 2012/ 639 Reg.5, SI 2012/ 2524 Reg.2
Reg.8A, added: SI 2012/ 639 Reg.6
Reg.8A, revoked: SI 2012/ 2524 Reg.2

150. Air Navigation (Restriction of Flying) (Duxford) Regulations 2012
Reg.3, amended: SI 2012/ 1348 Reg.3

190. Iran (European Union Financial Sanctions) (Amendment) Regulations 2012
revoked: SI 2012/ 925 Reg.28

194. Air Navigation (Restriction of Flying) (Farnborough Air Show) Regulations 2012
Reg.3, amended: SI 2012/ 1946 Reg.2, SI 2012/ 1958 Reg.2

202. Integrated Family Support Teams (Composition of Teams and Board Functions) (Wales) Regulations 2012
Reg.1, amended: SI 2012/ 1479 Sch.1 para.94

215. Automatic Enrolment (Miscellaneous Amendments) Regulations 2012
referred to: SI 2012/ 1257 Reg.1

276. Misuse of Drugs (Designation) (Amendment) (England, Wales and Scotland) Order 2012
revoked: SI 2012/ 384 Art.2

277. Misuse of Drugs (Amendment) (England, Wales and Scotland) Regulations 2012
revoked: SI 2012/ 385 Reg.2

285. Plant Health (Import Inspection Fees) (Wales) (Amendment) Regulations 2012
revoked: SI 2012/ 1493 Reg.7

292. Local Digital Television Programme Services Order 2012
referred to: SI 2012/ 1842
Sch.1 Part 1 para.10, amended: SI 2012/ 1842 Art.3
Sch.1 Part 2 para.13A, added: SI 2012/ 1842 Art.4

322. Special Educational Needs Tribunal for Wales Regulations 2012
Reg.66, amended: SI 2012/ 3006 Art.96, Art.97

323. Local Authorities (Conduct of Referendums)(England) Regulations 2012
applied: SI 2012/ 2031 Sch.4 para.8
Reg.2, varied: SI 2012/ 444 Sch.4 para.1, SI 2012/ 2031 Sch.4 para.32

2012– cont.

323. Local Authorities (Conduct of Referendums)(England) Regulations 2012– *cont.*
Reg.10, varied: SI 2012/444 Sch.4 para.1, SI 2012/2031 Sch.4 para.33
Reg.11, varied: SI 2012/444 Sch.4 para.1, SI 2012/2031 Sch.4 para.34
Reg.15, referred to: SI 2012/336 Reg.3, Reg.5
Sch.5 Part 6 para.38, applied: SI 2012/1918 Reg.4

335. School Finance (England) Regulations 2012
Reg.9, applied: SI 2012/2991 Reg.9, Sch.4 para.1
Reg.16, applied: SI 2012/2991 Reg.19
Reg.23, amended: SI 2012/1033 Sch.2 para.9
Reg.23, varied: SI 2012/1107 Art.4, Art.13
Sch.2, referred to: SI 2012/2991 Sch.4 para.1
Sch.2 para.13, applied: SI 2012/2991 Sch.2 para.5
Sch.2 para.31, applied: SI 2012/2991 Sch.2 para.5
Sch.2 para.33, applied: SI 2012/2991 Sch.2 para.5
Sch.2 para.34, applied: SI 2012/2991 Sch.2 para.5
Sch.2 para.36, applied: SI 2012/2991 Reg.6, Sch.2 para.5
Sch.3, applied: SI 2012/2991 Sch.4 para.1
Sch.3 Part 1 para.8, applied: SI 2012/2991 Sch.4 para.1

425. Street Works (Charges for Occupation of the Highway) (England) Regulations 2012
applied: SI 2012/1322 Art.2

432. Double Taxation Relief (Bank Levy) (Federal Republic of Germany) Order 2012
Sch.1 Part 1, referred to: SI 2012/2933 Art.2
Sch.1 Part 2, referred to: SI 2012/2933 Art.2

444. Local Authorities (Conduct of Referendums) (Council Tax Increases) (England) Regulations 2012
applied: SI 2012/2031 Sch.4 para.8
Reg.17, varied: SI 2012/2031 Sch.4 para.36
Sch.5, applied: SI 2012/1918 Reg.4

487. Air Navigation (Restriction of Flying) (Jet Formation Display Teams) (No.2) Regulations 2012
Sch.1, amended: SI 2012/1231 Reg.2

490. Air Navigation (Restriction of Flying) (Trooping the Colour) Regulations 2012
Reg.3, amended: SI 2012/1061 Reg.3

504. Medicines (Products for Human Use) (Fees) Regulations 2012
Reg.20, amended: SI 2012/2546 Reg.2
Reg.33, amended: SI 2012/2546 Reg.2

509. A14 Trunk Road (Junction 40 Higham Interchange to Junction 41 Risby Interchange, Suffolk) (Temporary Restriction and Prohibition of Traffic) Order 2012
revoked: SI 2012/1459 Art.7

605. Town and Country Planning (Tree Preservation)(England) Regulations 2012
Part 6, applied: SI 2012/2167 Sch.2 para.5
Reg.24, applied: SI 2012/2167 Sch.1 para.4

607. A34 Trunk Road and the M3 Motorway (M3 Junction 9) (Temporary Prohibition of Traffic) Order 2012
revoked: SI 2012/2350 Art.5

628. Localism Act 2011 (Commencement No 4 and Transitional, Transitory and Saving Provisions) Order 2012
Art.12, revoked: SI 2012/2029 Art.4

632. Control of Asbestos Regulations 2012
applied: SI 2012/1652 Reg.5, Reg.6, Sch.5

639. Syria (European Union Financial Sanctions) (Amendment) Regulations 2012
revoked: SI 2012/2524 Reg.3

2012– cont.

671. Feed-in Tariffs (Specified Maximum Capacity and Functions) (Amendment) Order 2012
revoked: SI 2012/2782 Sch.3

717. Government Resources and Accounts Act 2000 (Estimates and Accounts) Order 2012
Sch.1, amended: SI 2012/3135 Art.2, Sch.1, Sch.2

747. Further Education Teachers Qualifications, Continuing Professional Development and Registration (England) (Amendment) Regulations 2012
Reg.3, revoked: SI 2012/2165 Reg.2

762. Education (Specified Work) (England) Regulations 2012
Sch.1 para.2, revoked (in part): SI 2012/1736 Reg.3

767. Town and Country Planning (Local Planning) (England) Regulations 2012
Reg.4, amended: SI 2012/2613 Reg.2

780. Social Security Benefits Up-rating Order 2012
applied: SI 2012/819 Reg.2, Reg.3

789. Town and Country Planning (Compensation) (Wales) Regulations 2012
revoked: SI 2012/2319 Reg.7

798. Consular Fees Order 2012
Sch.1 Part 2, amended: SI 2012/1752 Art.2

799. Copyright and Performances (Application to Other Countries) Order 2012
Sch.1, amended: SI 2012/1754 Art.2

801. Town and Country Planning (Development Management Procedure) (Wales) Order 2012
Art.5, applied: SI 2012/2319 Reg.6
Art.6, applied: SI 2012/2319 Reg.6
Art.27, applied: SI 2012/789 Reg.5
Art.27, referred to: SI 2012/2319 Reg.5
Sch.4, amended: SI 2012/1659 Art.2

809. Energy Performance of Buildings (Certificates and Inspections)(England and Wales)(Amendment) Regulations 2012
revoked: SI 2012/3118 Sch.3
Reg.3, varied: 2012 c.11 s.12

810. Export Control (Syria Sanctions) and (Miscellaneous Amendments) Order 2012
Art.3, amended: SI 2012/2125 Art.3
Art.4, substituted: SI 2012/2125 Art.3
Art.10A, added: SI 2012/2125 Art.3
Art.13, amended: SI 2012/2125 Art.3
Art.14, amended: SI 2012/2125 Art.3

811. Controlled Waste (England and Wales) Regulations 2012
Reg.4, added: SI 2012/2320 Reg.2
Reg.4A, added: SI 2012/2320 Reg.2
Sch.1 para.4, amended: SI 2012/2320 Reg.2
Sch.1 para.4, revoked (in part): SI 2012/2320 Reg.2

813. Immigration and Nationality (Cost Recovery Fees) Regulations 2012
Sch.1 Part 2 para.3A, added: SI 2012/2276 Reg.2
Sch.1 Part 3 para.4, amended: SI 2012/2276 Reg.2
Sch.1 Part 5 para.8, amended: SI 2012/2276 Reg.2
Sch.1 Part 5 para.10, amended: SI 2012/2276 Reg.2

814. Smoke Control Areas (Authorised Fuels) (England) Regulations 2012
revoked: SI 2012/2281 Reg.3

815. Smoke Control Areas (Exempted Fireplaces) (England) Order 2012
revoked: SI 2012/2282 Art.3

822. Income Tax (Pay As You Earn) (Amendment) Regulations 2012
Reg.54, varied: SI 2012/821 Reg.15
Reg.56, varied: SI 2012/821 Reg.16

2012– cont.

834. **Guardian's Allowance Up-rating Order 2012**
applied: SI 2012/845 Reg.2, Reg.3

835. **Guardian's Allowance Up-rating (Northern Ireland) Order 2012**
applied: SI 2012/845 Reg.2, Reg.3

871. **Air Navigation (Restriction of Flying) (Shoreham-by-Sea) Regulations 2012**
Reg.3, amended: SI 2012/1347 Reg.3

892. **Air Navigation (Restriction of Flying) (Saltburn-by-the-Sea, Durham) Regulations 2012**
revoked: SI 2012/895 Reg.2

922. **National Health Service Trust Development Authority Regulations 2012**
Reg.1, amended: SI 2012/1641 Sch.3 para.16, Sch.4 para.22
Reg.3, amended: SI 2012/1641 Sch.3 para.16, Sch.4 para.22

925. **Iran (European Union Financial Sanctions) Regulations 2012**
Reg.3, amended: SI 2012/2909 Reg.3
Reg.4, amended: SI 2012/2909 Reg.4
Reg.5, amended: SI 2012/2909 Reg.4
Reg.6, amended: SI 2012/2909 Reg.3
Reg.7, amended: SI 2012/2909 Reg.3
Reg.8A, added: SI 2012/2909 Reg.5

978. **Air Navigation (Restriction of Flying) (Jet Formation Display Teams) (No.3) Regulations 2012**
revoked: SI 2012/1230 Reg.1

982. **Air Navigation (Restriction of Flying) (Elgin offshore installation) Regulations 2012**
revoked: SI 2012/1402 Reg.2
Reg.2, amended: SI 2012/1018 Reg.2
Reg.3, amended: SI 2012/983 Reg.2, SI 2012/1016 Reg.2
Sch.1, amended: SI 2012/1018 Reg.2
Sch.1, referred to: SI 2012/1016

1017. **Civil Aviation (Air Travel Organisers Licensing) Regulations 2012**
Reg.4, amended: SI 2012/1134 Reg.2
Reg.18, amended: SI 2012/1134 Reg.2
Reg.18, revoked (in part): SI 2012/1134 Reg.2
Reg.18, substituted: SI 2012/1134 Reg.2
Reg.20, amended: SI 2012/1134 Reg.2
Reg.22, amended: SI 2012/1134 Reg.2
Reg.50, amended: SI 2012/1134 Reg.2
Reg.72, amended: SI 2012/1134 Reg.2
Reg.74, amended: SI 2012/1134 Reg.2

1034. **School Governance (Constitution) (England) Regulations 2012**
Part 5, applied: SI 2012/1035 Reg.31, Reg.35, Reg.41
Reg.16, applied: SI 2012/1035 Reg.23
Reg.17, applied: SI 2012/1035 Reg.23
Reg.18, amended: SI 2012/1035 Sch.5 para.1
Reg.18, applied: SI 2012/1035 Reg.23
Reg.19, applied: SI 2012/1035 Reg.21, Reg.23, Reg.46, Sch.1 para.2
Reg.20, applied: SI 2012/1035 Reg.23
Reg.21, applied: SI 2012/1035 Reg.23
Reg.22, applied: SI 2012/1035 Reg.23
Reg.23, applied: SI 2012/1035 Reg.23
Reg.24, amended: SI 2012/1035 Sch.5 para.2
Reg.24, applied: SI 2012/1035 Reg.23
Reg.25, applied: SI 2012/1035 Reg.23
Reg.26, amended: SI 2012/1035 Sch.5 para.3
Reg.26, applied: SI 2012/1035 Reg.23
Reg.27, applied: SI 2012/1035 Reg.23
Reg.28, applied: SI 2012/1035 Reg.23

2012– cont.

1034. **School Governance (Constitution) (England) Regulations 2012**– *cont.*
Reg.28, varied: SI 2012/1035 Sch.5 para.4
Reg.29, applied: SI 2012/1035 Reg.23
Reg.29, varied: SI 2012/1035 Sch.5 para.5
Reg.30, applied: SI 2012/1035 Reg.4, Reg.23, Reg.44
Reg.30, varied: SI 2012/1035 Sch.5 para.6
Reg.31, applied: SI 2012/1035 Reg.23
Reg.31, varied: SI 2012/1035 Sch.5 para.7
Sch.4, applied: SI 2012/1035 Reg.23
Sch.4 para.1, amended: SI 2012/1035 Sch.5 para.8

1080. **A31 Trunk Road (Cadnam Interchange West Moors Interchange) (Temporary Prohibition of Traffic) Order 2012**
revoked: SI 2012/3197 Art.5

1115. **Education (Induction Arrangements for School Teachers) (England) Regulations 2012**
applied: SI 2012/115 Reg.1

1153. **Education Act 2011 (Abolition of the GTCE Consequential Amendments and Revocations) Order 2012**
Art.2, amended: SI 2012/3006 Art.34

1204. **Police (Complaints and Misconduct) Regulations 2012**
referred to: SI 2012/2630 r.4, r.5

1209. **Air Navigation (Restriction of Flying) (Tottenham Court Road, London) Regulations 2012**
revoked: SI 2012/1210 Reg.2

1230. **Air Navigation (Restriction of Flying) (Jet Formation Display Teams) (No.4) Regulations 2012**
Sch.1, amended: SI 2012/1959 Reg.2

1232. **Air Navigation (Restriction of Flying) (Royal International Air Tattoo RAF Fairford) (No.2) Regulations 2012**
Reg.3, amended: SI 2012/1403 Reg.2, SI 2012/1971 Reg.2

1236. **A38 Trunk Road (Marsh Mills to Forder Valley, Plymouth) (Temporary Restriction and Prohibition of Traffic) Order 2012**
revoked: SI 2012/1862 Art.9

1246. **Welfare Reform Act 2012 (Commencement No 2) Order 2012**
Art.2, amended: SI 2012/1440 Art.2
Art.2, revoked (in part): SI 2012/2530 Art.2

1290. **Health Education England Regulations 2012**
Reg.1, amended: SI 2012/1641 Sch.3 para.17, Sch.4 para.23
Reg.3, amended: SI 2012/1641 Sch.3 para.17

1305. **Mental Health (Primary Care Referrals and Eligibility to Conduct Primary Mental Health Assessments) (Wales) Regulations 2012**
Sch.1 para.1, amended: SI 2012/1479 Sch.1 para.69, Sch.1 para.95

1318. **A40 Trunk Road (Whitchurch to Ross-on-Wye, Herefordshire) (Temporary Restriction and Prohibition of Traffic) Order 2012**
revoked: SI 2012/2049 Art.13

1338. **Air Navigation (Restriction of Flying) (London 2012 Olympic and Paralympic Games, Road Cycle Event, Leatherhead, Surrey) Regulations 2012**
Reg.3, amended: SI 2012/1972 Reg.2

1339. **Air Navigation (Restriction of Flying) (London 2012 Olympic and Paralympic Games, Lee Valley White Water Centre, Broxbourne, Hertfordshire) Regulations 2012**
Reg.3, amended: SI 2012/1940 Reg.2

3051. Air Navigation (Restriction of Flying) (Shivering Sands) Regulations 2012–*cont.*
Sch.2 Part 1 para.2, amended: SI 2012/3085 Reg.4
Sch.2 Part 4, amended: SI 2012/3085 Reg.4
Sch.3 para.1, amended: SI 2012/3085 Reg.5
Sch.5 para.19, amended: SI 2012/3085 Reg.6
2886. Council Tax Reduction Schemes (Default Scheme) (England) Regulations 2012
Sch.1, amended: SI 2012/3085 Reg.8, Reg.9, Reg.10, Reg.11
Sch.1, applied: SI 2012/2885 Sch.1 para.7, Sch.1 para.8, Sch.3 para.1, Sch.5 para.19

2891. NHS Foundation Trusts (Trust Funds Appointment of Trustees) Amendment Order 2012
revoked: SI 2012/2950 Art.3
2991. School and Early Years Finance (England) Regulations 2012
Reg.12, applied: SI 2012/2261 Reg.8
3051. Air Navigation (Restriction of Flying) (Shivering Sands) Regulations 2012
revoked: SI 2012/3052 Reg.2